W9-CRE-321

Rating system

★★★★★ Excellent
★★★★ Very Good
★★★ Good
★★ Fair
★ Poor
🦃 Turkey

VIDEO MOVIE GUIDE 1987

Mick Martin
& Marsha Porter

Consulting Editor:
Ed Remitz

BALLANTINE BOOKS • NEW YORK

Library of Congress Catalog Card Number: 86-91310

ISBN 0-345-33872-3

Manufactured in the United States of America

First Edition: January 1987

Cover Photo of Sly Stallone by Globe Photos; photo of Ingrid Bergman by Wide World Photos, Inc.
Spine Photo of Humphrey Bogart by Wide World Photos, Inc.

CONTENTS

Acknowledgments   vii
Introduction   ix
Foreword   xi
Action/Mystery/Adventure   1
Children's Viewing   169
Comedy   214
Drama   387
Horror/Suspense   643
Musicals   768
Science-Fiction/Fantasy   815
Westerns   878
Cast Index   947
Director Index   1090
Family Viewing Index   1123
Alphabetical Listing of Movies   1131
About the Authors   1169

CHIEF CONTRIBUTORS

Ethan Aronson, Derrick Bang, Rich Garrison, Phil Hoover, Jack Keaton, Richard Leathers, Bill McLeod, Linda Rajotte, Dennis Rood, Bob Shaw, Tom Tolley, Wendy Welker, and Robert Young Jr.

ACKNOWLEDGMENTS

Video Movie Guide came into being as the result of a phone call. Cary Nosler, better known as the multimedia health adviser Captain Carrot to thousands of Northern Californians, called film critic Mick Martin at the *Sacramento Union* newspaper.

"Why don't you write a book on videos?" he asked. "I'm sick and tired of getting stuck with bad movies."

It sounded like a great idea, so Martin went to the powers that be at the *Sacramento Union* and secured their cooperation in the development of the book. His reviews from ten years of writing for the paper formed its basis.

In addition, the writings on the subject by past and present staff and free-lance writers of the *Sacramento Union* also were made available. We would like to thank Twila J. Walker, Peter Anderson, Jim Carnes, Richard Simon, Cathy Cassinos, Alison ApRoberts, Ana Sandoval, Lou Thelen, Steve Connell, Mark Halverson, Kevin Valine, and Tom Miner for permission to use their past writings.

To create a comprehensive guide, Martin joined forces with co-author Marsha Porter and writer/publisher Ed Remitz to form Static Studios. It was through their company that the various activities involved were coordinated.

Although Porter and Martin wrote most of the material,

other writers helped in covering the field. Rich Garrison and Robert Young Jr. wrote about Hollywood classics, Derrick Bang, Phil Hoover, Jack Keaton, Dick Leathers, Bill McLeod, Bob Shaw, Tom Tolley and Wendy Welker covered a wide variety of films, Ethan Aronson specialized in the action-adventure category, and Dennis Rood split his time between horror and comedy. All are ongoing contributors to *Video Movie Guide*.

In addition, Roy Engoran, Don Norris, Gary Zilaff, Tim Eldred, David Linck, Linda Rajotte, Del Forsythe, Paul Freeman, Gerry D. Watt, Paul C. Plain, Ross Woodbury, J. Douglas Halford, Bill Smith, Jack Schwab, Mitchell Cohen, Mike Antonaros, Sherry Kramer, Matias Bombal, Mark Steensland, Fritz Rodrigues, Vicki and Marc Sazaki, and Mary Scott wrote reviews on movies in their particular fields of interest and expertise.

Video Movie Guide began as a Sacramento-released pamphlet called "The Video Rental Guide." It was printed by U.S. Mailist, which is operated by Lyle, Marty, and Linda Hintz. Thanks also go to typists Nancy Nealis, Sam Damiani, Dennis Rood and the Sazaki family for research.

Others who made this book possible include: Bob Badgley, Marilyn Abraham, Sheila Curry, Joe Blades, Stan Goman, Russ Solomon, Rob Heidt, Walter and Pat Rice, Paul Hodgkins, Jerry Pompei, Mike Farrace, Linda Phillips, Eric Sakach, Steve Johnson, Ron and Steve Pacheco, Mark Brown, Carol Johnson, Linda Forsythe, Greg Guertin, Phyllis Donovan, Hope Svrcek, Diane, Hada and Francesca Martin, Matt and Norma Condo, Heidi Keller, Duncan Mandrill, John Sudman, Jim Dixon, Cynthia Wright, Catherine Coulter, Robert J. Kantor and Shannon Bryony.

INTRODUCTION

In creating THE VIDEO MOVIE GUIDE we have attempted to give you the most up-to-the-minute book, with a clear rating system and easy access to the titles covered. Only movies that had been scheduled for release as videos at the time of publication are included in this edition. You will find movies listed in alphabetical order at the beginning of the book and then discussed in depth in their respective genres:

- Action/Mystery/Adventure
- Children's
- Comedy
- Drama
- Horror-Suspense
- Musicals
- Science-Fiction/Fantasy
- Westerns

In addition, you will find indexes on page 000–000, organized by directors and performers, as well as a list of films recommended for family viewing.

The rating system runs from five stars to a turkey. We feel a five-star film is a must; a four-star rating means it's well worth watching. The desirability of a film with a lesser rating depends on your liking for a particular type of film or a movie star. A turkey by any other name is still a bad movie. If a film is particularly offensive, even though it has a big-name star, we want you to know why. Likewise, if a little-known gem has special attributes, we've done our best to call your attention to them.

Certain kinds of movies have been purposely ignored.

Sex-and-violence films, such as *99 Women* and *Terminal Island*, are similar to porno movies; a tear-off-their-tops-and-whip-the-women genre that we don't feel is appropriate for review here.

We've included kung fu movies featuring well-known stars such as Bruce Lee and Chuck Norris. However, the all-the-same Chinese imports with lots of bang-pow fist-and-foot action but no plot don't vary much above mediocre in quality. So we've left them out.

We have, however, been more lenient about the inclusion of horror films. Since there is a huge audience for them and they are readily available, we've attempted to include even the lowest of the low to help prevent you from getting stuck with a turkey.

Overall, we feel this is the most practical guide to what's available on video. We hope you agree.

FOREWORD

Welcome to the second annual edition of *Video Movie Guide*. In our never-ending search for movies on videocassette, we've managed to swell the number of entries in this volume from last year's 2,500-plus titles to just under 4,500. How's that for bigger and better?

All of this was accomplished without resorting to padding out the book with triple-X adult movies, sex-and-violence flicks, and kung-fu imports. We still see no point in reviewing trash.

For the 1987 edition we have gone deeper into the B-western and foreign-film categories. Not only are these types of movies becoming more readily available to renters, they are also even easier to buy from the ever-growing number of video mail-order houses.

Since the shoot-'em-ups of Gene Autry, Hopalong Cassidy (William Boyd), and Roy Rogers are starting to show up on the shelves of some video stores, we elected to give them in-depth coverage while also spotlighting those B westerns on better-known labels. Yet there are many hundreds more available by mail order.

Both Discount Video (3711 Clark Avenue, Suite B, Burbank, CA 91505) and Cumberland Video (Suite 104, 3917 W. Riverside Drive, Burbank, CA 91505) have extensive lists of cowboy movies that go far beyond the titles starring Buck Jones, Tim McCoy, Bob Steele, Tom

Tyler, Johnny Mack Brown, John Wayne, and the others listed herein.

With respect to foreign films (which are listed under genres like Comedy and Drama), we've included classics as well as recent hits. Many of the former, as well as the latter, are available from Facets Multimedia, Inc. (1517 Fullerton Avenue, Chicago, IL 60614). Its catalogue (which costs $2) has the most complete list of foreign-language films on video we've ever seen. Some of the titles from the 1920s, '30s, and '40s seem to be available only through this company. These are public domain titles that are not carried by any other distributor.

In a similar sense, Kartes Video Communications (7225 Woodland Drive, Indianapolis, IN 46278) has the market cornered on other titles. Its inventory of American movies from the 1930s, '40s, and '50s is seldom available for rental but can be bought at bookstores and from the company itself through your local video store owner or from its catalogue.

All of the aforementioned outlets offer a wide variety of titles outside their area of specialization. Other mail-order houses include:

Blackhawk Films, 1 Old Eagle Brewery, P.O. Box 3990, Davenport, ID 52808.

Budget Video, 1534 N. Highland, Los Angeles, CA 90028.

Instant Replay Video Cassettes, 3414 Folsom Boulevard, Sacramento, CA 95816.

Movies Unlimited, 6736 Castor Avenue, Philadelphia, PA 19149.

Video Images (Video Yesteryear), Box C, Sandy Hook, CT 06482.

Any one of these companies should be able to fill your movie needs, including those specialties mentioned earlier. Since individuals cannot order directly from video manufacturers, these outlets offer an alternative should your local video shop be unable to order a title direct.

In finding any cassette, we do recommend that you talk to your local video dealer first. These folks have access to most everything and can usually get it quicker and cheaper.

Should you use any of the mail-order houses listed

here, please let us know how you were treated. Their track record of completeness, courtesy, and promptness will determine whether or not they are listed in future editions.

In fact, we welcome your comments on any matter concerning movies on video and especially suggestions on how best to serve you with this book. Please send all comments to *Video Movie Guide 1987*, Ballantine Books, 201 E. 50th Street, New York, N.Y. 10022. We'd love to hear from you.

say, please let us know how you were treated. Their very courtesy and promptness will determine whether or not they are held in high esteem.

In fact, we welcome your comments on any matter pertaining to this book, especially suggestions on how best to serve you with this book. Please send all comments to: Ballantine Books, 201 E. 50th Street, New York, N.Y. 10022. We'd love to hear from you.

ACTION/MYSTERY/ ADVENTURE

ACROSS 110TH STREET
★★★½

DIRECTOR: Barry Shear
CAST: Anthony Quinn, Yaphet Kotto, Anthony Franciosa, Richard Ward

This one is a real sleeper! An action-packed, extremely violent film concerning gang warfare between the Mafia and their black counterparts. Entire cast is very good, as are the action scenes. Rated R for violence, language.

1972   102 minutes

ADVENTURES OF CAPTAIN MARVEL, THE
★★★★

DIRECTOR: William Witney, John English
CAST: Tom Tyler, Frank Coghlan Jr., William Benedict, Louise Currie

Fawcett Comics Captain Marvel is splendidly brought to life by Republic Studios in what is generally regarded as the best serial of all time, certainly the best superhero chapter play ever produced. An expedition seeking relics and information on the lost Scorpion cult is trapped in a tomb in remote Siam. The members are eventually rescued by assistant radio operator Billy Batson in the guise of Captain Marvel, champion of truth and justice, who can be summoned by the magic word 'Shazam.' The expedition discovers a golden scorpion with five powerful lenses which become a lethal weapon when properly arranged. They divide the lenses among the expedition members and return to America. There a mysterious villain who calls himself Scorpion steals the lenses back one by one. Captain Marvel, perfectly portrayed by Tom Tyler as a no-nonsense hero, eventually overcomes and unmasks the Scorpion and destroys the golden idol that threatens the world. Sincerely acted by all involved, this serial set the standards for flying stunts for years to come and still contains some of the best flying scenes ever recorded on film. If you've never seen a serial, watch this one.

1941   B & W   12 chapters

ADVENTURES OF CAPTAIN FABIAN

DIRECTOR: William Marshall
CAST: Errol Flynn, Vincent Price, Agnes Moorehead

The career of Errol Flynn was a roller-coaster ride to be sure, but seldom did it get as low as this turkey. Flynn doesn't have the heart needed to rise above this lackluster swashbuckler. A sad sight for fans of the genre and Errol Flynn alike.

1951   100 minutes

ADVENTURES OF ROBIN HOOD, THE
★★★★★

DIRECTOR: Michael Curtiz
CAST: Errol Flynn, Basil Rathbone, Ian Hunter, Olivia De Havilland, Claude Rains, Alan Hale, Eugene Pallette, Montagu Love

This classic presents Errol Flynn at his swashbuckling best, backed up by a perfect cast of supporting actors. Olivia De Havilland is Maid Marian. Alan Hale and Eugene Pallette are Little John and Friar Tuck. The bad guys are also at their evil best, as played by Basil Rathbone and Claude Rains. Even the smallest roles are colorfully represented. Lavish sets and a stirring musical score help place *Robin Hood* among the very best adventure films.

1938   106 minutes

ADVENTURES OF SHERLOCK HOLMES, THE
★★★★½

DIRECTOR: Alfred Werker

CAST: Basil Rathbone, Nigel Bruce, Ida Lupino, George Zucco

The best of all the Basil Rathbone–Nigel Bruce Sherlock Holmes movies, this pits the Great Detective against his arch-nemesis, Dr. Moriarty (played by George Zucco). The period setting, atmospheric photography, and the spirited performances of the cast (which includes a young Ida Lupino as Holmes's client) make this a must-see for mystery fans.

1939   B & W   85 minutes

ADVENTURES OF SHERLOCK HOLMES: A SCANDAL IN BOHEMIA
★★★★½

DIRECTOR: Paul Annett
CAST: Jeremy Brett, David Burke, Gayle Hunnicutt, Wolf Kahler, Michael Carter, Max Faulkner, Tim Pearce, Rosalie Williams

The supremely independent Sherlock Holmes falters in this episode of the popular series and almost succumbs to the charms of a female temptress, one Irene Adler, who also happens to be a clever crook. Holmes and Watson come to the aid of the King of Bohemia (who is being blackmailed) and encounter the delightfully unscrupulous Miss Adler, who turns out to be directly involved in the crime. Finely played by all involved, this is one of the best of the series and offers a rare chance to see Sherlock Holmes emotionally involved in a case. Terrific show.

1984   52 minutes

ADVENTURES OF SHERLOCK HOLMES: THE BLUE CARBUNCLE
★★★★

DIRECTOR: David Carson

CAST: Jeremy Brett, David Burke, Rosalind Knight, Ros Simmons, Ken Campbell, Desmond McNamara, Amelda Brown, Brian Miller, Rosalie Williams, Frank Mills

Sherlock Holmes delves into the darkest corners of London's slums in order to solve the mystery of a fabulous gem and save a man's life. Aided by his friend and colleague, Dr. John Watson, the seemingly supernatural Holmes braves danger from all sides and tenaciously follows the clues until he has solved the problem. Splendidly done (as are all of the stories in this series), this episode captures the flavor of Victorian London and gives the viewer the sense of being involved in the dark doings. Jeremy Brett and David Burke as Holmes and Watson are perhaps the finest team to essay the roles, and the adaptations are the most authentic versions of the original stories ever filmed.

1984   52 minutes

ADVENTURES OF SHERLOCK HOLMES: THE COPPER BEECHES
★★★★

DIRECTOR: Paul Annett
CAST: Jeremy Brett, David Burke, Joss Ackland, Natasha Richardson, Lottie Ward, Patience Collier, Angela Browne, Peter Jonfield

In this exquisitely crafted BBC series of adaptations of Sir Arthur Conan Doyle's celebrated detective stories, Jeremy Brett, as Sherlock Holmes, and David Burke, as his faithful biographer John H. Watson, M.D., transcend all who have gone before. While Basil Rathbone and Nigel Bruce may be the quintessential Holmes and Watson to many movie buffs, Brett and Burke get much closer to the original characters. The result is an authenticity that should please even the most discriminating Sherlockian. In this one, the world's most famous consulting detective comes to the aid of a young governess (Natasha Richardson) who suspects her employer (Joss Ackland) is up to something sinister.

1985   54 minutes

ADVENTURES OF SHERLOCK HOLMES: THE CROOKED MAN
★★★★

DIRECTOR: Alan Grint
CAST: Jeremy Brett, David Burke, Norman Jones, Lisa Daniely, Denys Hawthorne, Fiona Shaw, Paul Chapman

Jeremy Brett stars in another entry in the British television series. This time, he and Dr. Watson (David Burke) must solve an apparent murder/suicide, which (naturally) turns out to have hidden complexities—most notably the muddy, oddly shaped footprints left at the scene of the crime. Although this case does not suitably tax the master sleuth's investigative mind, Brett is—as always—a thrill to watch.

1983   52 minutes

ADVENTURES OF SHERLOCK HOLMES: THE DANCING MEN
★★★★

DIRECTOR: John Bruce
CAST: Jeremy Brett, David Burke, Tenniel Evans, Betsy Brantley, David Ross, Eugene Lupinski, Lorraine Peters, Wendy Jane Walker

An innocent-looking group of stick-figure drawings puzzles Sherlock Holmes and Scotland Yard until the great sleuth uncovers nefarious underworld goings on and plunges himself and his companion in adventure, Dr. Watson, into deadly danger. Carefully crafted after the original short story by Conan Doyle, this ingenious episode is one of six complete tales of the Baker Street detective currently available on video. There are no weak entries in this popular series, and Holmes and his chronicler Dr. Watson are perfectly portrayed by Jeremy Brett and David Burke.

1984   52 minutes

ADVENTURES OF SHERLOCK HOLMES: THE FINAL PROBLEM
★★★★

DIRECTOR: Alan Grint
CAST: Jeremy Brett, David Burke, Eric Porter, Rosalie Williams, Olivier-Pierre, Claude Le Sache, Michael Goldie, Robert Henderson

Sherlock Holmes is pursued by murderers after he exposes a gang of art forgers led by his rival, Professor Moriarty. After thwarting Moriarty's plans to sell perfect duplicates of the *Mona Lisa*, Holmes meets him face to face, and the two engage in a deadly game that traps Moriarty's gang behind bars, but leaves the evil genius loose to pursue his persecutor. The thrilling climax to this fast-moving story takes place in the picturesque Alps, where the two foes square off and fight to the death. Imaginative, exciting, and blessed with a surprise ending, this entry into the popular series first broadcast on public television is perhaps the finest of them all.

1985   52 minutes

ADVENTURES OF SHERLOCK HOLMES: THE GREEK INTERPRETER
★★★★

DIRECTOR: Derek Marlowe

CAST: Jeremy Brett, David Burke, Charles Gray, Alkis Kritikos, George Costigan, Nick Field, Anton Alexander, Victoria Harwood

This complex, tragic story pits Sherlock Holmes, Dr. Watson, and Holmes's brother Mycroft against vicious killers who have kidnapped a Greek national and tortured him into signing some important documents against his will. The interpreter who the criminals engage is the man who brings the story to the sleuth, and he very nearly loses his life to a diabolical fiend before justice is done. A fickle woman, a chuckling murderer, and an exciting climax aboard a speeding train highlight this dark story, but it's Charles Gray as Sherlock's brother Mycroft who steals the show and finally traps the murderer with his quick mind and deft actions.

1985   52 minutes

ADVENTURES OF SHERLOCK HOLMES: THE NAVAL TREATY
★★★★

DIRECTOR: Alan Grint
CAST: Jeremy Brett, David Burke, David Gwillim, Gareth Thomas, Alison Skilbeck, Ronald Russell, Nicholas Geake, Pamela Pitchford, John Malcolm

An old friend of Dr. Watson's is on the verge of being implicated in a treasonous case of espionage, and Sherlock Holmes comes to the aid of friend and country. Cleverly constructed and steeped in the atmosphere of Conan Doyle's London, this episode of the original six-part series was first telecast in this country on PBS's *Mystery* in 1984 and has taken its place with the others as perhaps the best translation of Holmes to the screen. Jeremy Brett seems the personification of the constantly alert Holmes, while David Burke's humorous, dependable Watson is yet another welcome step away from the bumbling image that Nigel Bruce left after so many films with Basil Rathbone.

1984   52 minutes

ADVENTURES OF SHERLOCK HOLMES: THE NORWOOD BUILDER
★★★½

DIRECTOR: Ken Grieve
CAST: Jeremy Brett, David Burke, Rosalie Crutchley, Colin Jeavons, Helen Ryan, Jonathan Adams, Matthew Solon, Anthony Langdon

Holmes and Watson become involved in murder when a young solicitor seeks their help after being accused of doing away with a wealthy recluse. Holmes concentrates on his own powers of deduction and re-creates the crime after disguising himself as a vagrant and uncovering a damning piece of evidence. With enough plot twists to hold the attention of even the most jaded viewer, this episode is highly entertaining and supplies the necessary thrills as Holmes literally smokes the killer out of hiding.

1985   52 minutes

ADVENTURES OF SHERLOCK HOLMES: THE RED-HEADED LEAGUE
★★★½

DIRECTOR: John Bruce
CAST: Jeremy Brett, David Burke, Roger Hammond, Richard Wilson, Tim McInnerty, Bruce Dukov, John Woodnutt, John Labonowski, Eric Porter, Rog Stuart

Holmes is given a three-pipe problem as he endeavors to unravel an intricate plot that involves a red-headed man, an underpaid employee, a bogus organization, and a bank full of gold. Holmes's malevolent nemesis Professor Moriarty is at the bottom of it all and learns a new respect (and hatred) for his clever antagonist. Jeremy Brett and David Burke make a fine Holmes and Watson. These episodes crackle with excitement and suspense as well as humor and irony.

1985   52 minutes

ADVENTURES OF SHERLOCK HOLMES: THE RESIDENT PATIENT
★★★½

DIRECTOR: David Carson
CAST: Jeremy Brett, David Burke, Nicholas Clay, Patrick Newell, Tim Barlow, Brett Forrest, Charles Cork, John Ringham, David Squire

This grim murder mystery begins as Holmes and Watson are recruited by a young medical man to come to the aid of his benefactor, a secretive man who has reinforced his home with steel bars and lives in constant fear of intruders. After refusing to level with the famous detective and his chronicler, the patron (Mr. Blessington) is found hanged, and the police are prepared to write off his death as suicide until Holmes comes up with a deadly scenario of premeditated, brutal murder. Clever storytelling, engrossing and highly enjoyable.

1985   52 minutes

ADVENTURES OF SHERLOCK HOLMES: THE SOLITARY CYCLIST
★★★★

DIRECTOR: Paul Annett

CAST: Jeremy Brett, David Burke, Barbara Wilshere, John Castle, Michael Siberry, Ellis Dale, Sarah Aitchinson, Simon Bleackley

Intricately woven plot finds Holmes and Watson coming to the aid of a woman who is being mysteriously followed by a man on a bicycle! But, of course, there's more going on than meets the eye, and the world's foremost consulting detective is just the chap to discover it. Atmospheric and exciting.

1984   52 minutes

ADVENTURES OF SHERLOCK HOLMES: THE SPECKLED BAND

★★★★½

DIRECTOR: John Bruce
CAST: Jeremy Brett, David Burke, Jeremy Kemp, Rosalyn Landor, Denise Armon, John Gill, Rosalie Williams

This addition to the Sherlock Holmes saga is one of the most remarkable of Conan Doyle's marvelous stories. Holmes is engaged by a woman who fears for her life after her sister dies mysteriously and horribly in a room that no one has entered. Holmes and Watson uncover the motive and the party responsible, but it's up to Sherlock to offer himself as bait and discover the method of murder. Grim yet fascinating, this is one of the best remembered of these tales and perhaps the finest crafted of them all. Topnotch.

1984   52 minutes

AFRICA—TEXAS STYLE!

★★

DIRECTOR: Andrew Marton
CAST: Hugh O'Brian, John Mills, Tom Nardini

The idea of a movie about cowboys rounding up animals in Af-rica must have sounded good in theory. But in practice, it's pretty dull going. Even the location photography doesn't help. Give us *Hatari!* any day.

1966   106 minutes

AFTER THE THIN MAN

★★★★

DIRECTOR: W. S. Van Dyke II
CAST: William Powell, Myrna Loy, James Stewart, Elissa Landi, Joseph Calleia, Sam Levene

Second of the six wonderful *Thin Man* films made with William Powell and Myrna Loy, following on the heels of 1934's *The Thin Man*. Powell, Loy, and Asta, the incorrigible terrier, trade quips and drinks in this decent murder mystery. Rising star James Stewart merely adds to the fun. The dialogue is fast-paced and quite droll, and Powell and Loy demonstrate a chemistry that explains the dozen hits they had together. Not to be missed. Followed, in 1939, by *Another Thin Man*.

1936   B & W 113 minutes

AGUIRRE: WRATH OF GOD

★★★★

DIRECTOR: Werner Herzog
CAST: Klaus Kinski, Ruy Guerra, Del Negro, Helena Rojo, Cecilia Rivera, Peter Berling, Danny Ades

Klaus Kinski gives one of his finest screen performances in the title role as the mad, traitorous Spanish conquistador who leads an expedition through the South American wilds in a quest for the lost golden city of El Dorado. That real-life madman, German director Werner Herzog, took his cameras, cast, and crew into the jungles of the Amazon for this spectacular adventure story. In German with English subtitles. Unrated, the film has violence.

1972   90 minutes

AIR FORCE
★★★★
DIRECTOR: Howard Hawks
CAST: John Garfield, John Ridgely, Gig Young, Charles Drake

This is essentially wartime propaganda about a flying fortress and its crew taking on the enemy at Pearl Harbor, Manila, and the Coral Sea. However, the direction by Howard Hawks puts the film head and shoulders above similar motion pictures. It has an impressive supporting cast, including Harry Carey, Arthur Kennedy, George Tobias, and Edward Brophy. Essentially a character study, it gives each of the players time to bring his role alive.

1943   B & W 124 minutes

AIRPORT
★★★★
DIRECTOR: George Seaton
CAST: Burt Lancaster, Dean Martin, Helen Hayes, Jacqueline Bisset, Van Heflin, Jean Seberg

The daddy of them all, this *Grand Hotel* in the air is slick, enjoyable entertainment. Taking place on a fateful winter night, it miraculously rises above some stiff performances and an often hackneyed plot. Rated G.

1970   137 minutes

ALL QUIET ON THE WESTERN FRONT
★★★★★
DIRECTOR: Lewis Milestone
CAST: Lew Ayres, Louis Wolheim

Despite some dated moments and an "old movie" look, this film still stands as a powerful statement against war and man's inhumanity to man. Lew Ayres and Louis Wolheim star in this story, set during World War I, which follows several young men into battle, examining their disillusionment and eventual death.

1930   B & W 155 minutes

ALOHA, BOBBY AND ROSE
★★
DIRECTOR: Floyd Mutrux
CAST: Paul LeMat, Diane Hull, Tim McIntire

B-movie treatment of two kids on the lam for a murder they didn't mean to commit. Paul LeMat's first starring role after *American Graffiti*. He is interesting, but the film is downbeat and uninspired. Rated R.

1975   88 minutes

AMERICAN NINJA
★
DIRECTOR: Sam Firstenberg
CAST: Michael Dudikoff, Guich Koock, Judie Aronson, Steve James, John Fujioka

Dumb, dumb comic book–style adventure film about an American soldier (Michael Dudikoff) who single-handedly takes on an army of martial-arts mercenaries in the Philippines. Chuck Norris does it better. Rated R for profanity and violence.

1985   95 minutes

AMSTERDAM KILL, THE
★
DIRECTOR: Robert Clouse
CAST: Robert Mitchum, Bradford Dillman, Richard Egan, Leslie Nielsen, Keye Luke

Fresh from his successes in *Farewell My Lovely* and *The Yakuza*,

Robert Mitchum dived into this dud about an international drug conspiracy. He's a retired narcotics agent who comes to the aid of an old buddy accused of smuggling. It sounds exciting, but it's terribly dull, and just more proof that director Robert Clouse must have had a rare, rare good day when he made *Enter the Dragon*. Rated R.

1977   90 minutes

ANDERSON TAPES, THE
★★★★

DIRECTOR: Sidney Lumet
CAST: Martin Balsam, Sean Connery, Dyan Cannon, Ralph Meeker, Margaret Hamilton

Sean Connery is perfectly cast in this exciting film about an ex-con under surveillance who wants to pull off the Big Heist. Slickly done, with tight editing and direction to keep the viewer totally involved, it holds up extremely well on video. Rated PG.

1972   98 minutes

ANGEL
★

DIRECTOR: Robert Vincent O'Neil
CAST: Cliff Gorman, Susan Tyrrell, Dick Shawn, Donna Wilkes

Bad, low-budget flick about a 15-year-old who moonlights as a Hollywood Boulevard hooker and is menaced by a psychotic killer. Rated R for nudity, violence, suggested sex and profanity.

1983   94 minutes

ANGEL OF H.E.A.T.
★

DIRECTOR: Myrl A. Schreibman
CAST: Marilyn Chambers, Dan Jesse, Mary Woronov, Stephen Johnson

Marilyn Chambers should stick with what she knows best . . . and this isn't it. Porn queen Chambers appears as Angel Harmony, head of Harmony's Elite Attack Team . . . which should be renamed Hardly Ever Any Talent. Not enough sex and skin for the hardcore crowd, and not enough plot, good acting, or production values for the spy flick lovers. Projects like this which attempt to cross genres usually fail in both; *Angel of H.e.a.t.* is no exception. Very anticlimactic. Rated R—considerable nudity and sexual situations.

1982   93 minutes

ANGELS DIE HARD
★★

DIRECTOR: Richard Compton
CAST: William Smith, Tom Baker, R. G. Armstrong, Dan Haggerty

The bikers turn out to help a community during a mining disaster. Less ridiculous than most of its predecessors and contemporaries. Look for Dan Haggerty in an early role. Violence; adult situations. Rated R.

1970   86 minutes

ANGELS WITH DIRTY FACES
★★★★½

DIRECTOR: Michael Curtiz
CAST: James Cagney, Pat O'Brien, Humphrey Bogart, Ann Sheridan, George Bancroft, Bobby Jordan

This is thoroughly enjoyable entertainment—thanks primarily to its stars and director. Certainly, the tale is anything but new and wasn't even new when the movie was released. The plot is that old Hollywood standby about two childhood friends, the one who goes bad (James Cagney) and the other who follows the right path (Pat O'Brien, as the priest), and the conflict between them. Yet, as directed by Warner Bros.' stalwart Michael Curtiz (*Casablanca*; *Captain Blood*), it often seems surprisingly fresh. There's not a wasted moment on the screen. Everything works, making it one of Cagney's best starring vehicles.

1938   B & W   97 minutes

APOCALYPSE NOW
★★★★½

DIRECTOR: Francis Ford Coppola
CAST: Marlon Brando, Martin Sheen, Robert Duvall, Harrison Ford

An exceptional war film in every sense, this work pulsates with artistic ambition. It reaches for truth, struggles for greatness—and almost succeeds. The central character, Captain Willard (Martin Sheen), tells the story of his slow progress toward a fateful meeting with a man named Kurtz, a highly decorated officer who the army contends has gone mad. To reach Kurtz, Willard must endure a danger-filled journey through the jungle on a Navy patrol boat. During this time, Willard reads the file on Kurtz and begins to doubt the logic of his superiors. Kurtz is doing what they apparently cannot. He's winning. Rated R.

1979   153 minutes

APPOINTMENT IN HONDURAS
★★½

DIRECTOR: Jacques Tourneur
CAST: Glenn Ford, Ann Sheridan, Zachary Scott, Jack Elam

Good cast helps this far-fetched story of an idealistic American (Glenn Ford) helping local misfits free their country from political tyranny. Actors do their level best, but rather silly material gets in their

way. Plot and dialogue are somewhat laughable. Ann Sheridan is highly watchable, as usual.

1953   79 minutes

ARABESQUE
★★★

DIRECTOR: Stanley Donen
CAST: Gregory Peck, Sophia Loren, Kieron Moore, Alan Badel, Carl Duering, George Coulouris

Fast-paced espionage adventure about college professor Gregory Peck and his nightmarish involvement with death-dealing secret agents is an entertaining "chase" film and a conscious effort to capture the "now" look of the 1960s. Beautiful Sophia Loren keeps Peck company as they alternate chasing and being pursued by tough-looking men in trench coats across picturesque parts of the world. Entertaining and clever at times, but basically a hollow and calculated attempt to cash in on the Continental spy trend of the time, this film is vague enough to relax the viewers and run its course without causing undue concern about the consequences of all this violence to the characters on the screen. Worth the cost of the rental just for the close-up of Loren's lips.

1966   118 minutes

ARK OF THE SUN GOD... TEMPLE OF HELL, THE

DIRECTOR: Anthony M. Dawson
CAST: David Warbeck, John Steiner, Susie Sudlow, Alan Collins, Riccardo Palacio

Gosh, where did they get the name from? Some people have no shame. A big-time thief is commissioned to steal an ancient artifact from an ark buried thousands of years ago.

Not only are the title and story ripoff of *Raiders of the Lost Ark*, we are also subject to anti-Arabic sentiment and a hero who mutters pseudocool 007-style wisecracks. On top of all this, the video box is a lie, promising Nazis and an all-out war that never materialize in the flick. The film takes place in Turkey. How appropriate. Not rated; violence.

1986   92 minutes

AROUND THE WORLD UNDER THE SEA
★★

DIRECTOR: Andrew Marton
CAST: Lloyd Bridges, Shirley Eaton, David McCallum, Brian Kelly, Keenan Wynn, Marshall Thompson

Volcanoes, a giant eel, a submarine, scuba gear, and a quarrel over who's in charge make this lackluster, harmless viewing. Shirley Eaton was in *Goldfinger*, in case you're a James Bond fan.

1966   117 minutes

ASSAULT ON PRECINCT 13
★★★★½

DIRECTOR: John Carpenter
CAST: 102tin Stoker, Laurie Zimmer, Tony Burton, Nancy Loomis, Darwin Joston

Here's director John Carpenter's (*Halloween*) riveting movie about a nearly deserted L.A. police station that finds itself under siege by a youth gang. It's a modern-day version of Howard Hawks's *Rio Bravo*, with exceptional performances by its entire cast. Rated R.

1976   90 minutes

AT SWORD'S POINT
★★½

DIRECTOR: Lewis Allen

CAST: Cornel Wilde, Maureen O'-Hara, Alan Hale Jr., Dan O'-Herlihy, Blanche Yurka, Robert Douglas

Colorful story of the offspring of the Three Musketeers joining forces to rid the country of villainy is familiar but harmless. Cornel Wilde displays his Olympic-caliber skill with the sword and Maureen O'Hara is as beautiful and feisty as ever, but this time she backs it up with swordplay. Typical of the mindless sort of historical and costume epics that Hollywood kept churning out in the late 1940s and into the middle 1950s—pleasant but not really memorable.

1952   81 minutes

ATTACK FORCE Z
★★

DIRECTOR: Tim Burstall
CAST: John Phillip Law, Sam Neill, Mel Gibson, Chris Haywood, John Waters

Okay Australian film concerning a group of commandos on a secret mission against the Japanese in World War II. Most notable is a young Mel Gibson as the leader of the commandos. Unrated.

1981   84 minutes

AVALANCHE
🐢

DIRECTOR: Corey Allen
CAST: Rock Hudson, Mia Farrow, Robert Forster, Jeanette Nolan

It's movies like this bomb that gave disaster pictures a bad name. Rock Hudson, Mia Farrow, Robert Forster, and Jeanette Nolan are among those fooling around and fighting before the catastrophe of the title. Their performances are so bad, you're glad to see them go. Rated PG.

1978   91 minutes

AVENGING ANGEL
🐾

DIRECTOR: Robert Vincent O'Neil
CAST: Betsy Russell, Rory Calhoun, Susan Tyrrell, Ossie Davis

Remember *Angel*, the high-school student who doubled as a Hollywood hooker? Well, she's back. Only this time our heroine is out to avenge the murder of the cop who acted as her mentor. Dumb. Rated R for nudity, profanity, and violence.

1985   96 minutes

AWAY ALL BOATS
★½

DIRECTOR: Joseph Pevney
CAST: Jeff Chandler, George Nader, Julie Adams, Lex Barker, Keith Andes, Richard Boone, Jock Mahoney, William Reynolds, Charles McGraw, John McIntire

In this war film, Jeff Chandler plays Captain Hanks, commander of an attack transport unit in the South Pacific during World War II. We follow Chandler and his men as they train for heavy combat awaiting them. Julie Adams is thrown in for love interest. As the film progresses, we see Japanese kamikaze attacks, huge assaults on Japanese strongholds, and submarine attacks. But the film never really adds up too much. Too many preposterous acts of heroism and routine performances combine with a lackluster script and direction, to make it a throwaway.

1956   B & W 114 minutes

BACK TO BATAAN
★★★★

DIRECTOR: Edward Dmytryk
CAST: John Wayne, Anthony Quinn, Richard Loo, Beulah Bondi

A fun World War II action film with John Wayne at his two-fisted best. Good script, photography, acting, and battle action make this film well worth your time. Video quality is quite good. If you like good war films, you'll love this.

1945   B & W   95 minutes

BAD GUYS
★★

DIRECTOR: Joel Silberg
CAST: Adam Baldwin, Mike Jolly, Michelle Nicastro, Ruth Buzzi, Sgt. Slaughter

A somewhat contrived story about two police officers who are suspended indefinitely, without pay. After having no luck with interim jobs, they decide to become professional wrestlers. They achieve moderate success, then decide to become "bad guys" to further their popularity. They soon find themselves opposing the world tag team champs. That leads to a no-holds-barred, slug-fest finish. Although sophomoric, this film should be great fun for youngsters and wrestling fans. Rated PG.

1985   87 minutes

BADGE 373
★½

DIRECTOR: Howard W. Koch
CAST: Robert Duvall, Verna Bloom, Eddie Egan, Henry Darrow

This very low-rent police drama casts Robert Duvall as a cop out to nab his partner's killer and break the mob in New York City. Pretty routine stuff is thrown together in a even more routine fashion. For hard-core fans of the genre only. Rated R.

1973   116 minutes

BAND OF THE HAND
★★½

DIRECTOR: Paul Michael Glaser
CAST: Stephen Lang, Michael Carmine, Lauren Holly, John Cameron Mitchell, Daniele Quinn, Leon Robinson, James Remar

Executive produced by Michael "Miami Vice" Mann, this is like an episode of the popular television series without Don Johnson or Edward James Olmos. It has the car chases, shootouts, and drug scenes from the TV show combined with an even more lightweight plot than usual. This concerns a Vietnam vet (Stephen Lang) who takes a group of incorrigible Florida teens and turns them into an anti-drug squad. That's right, it's "Mod Squad" for the 1980s and just as silly as it sounds. Rated R for profanity, brief nudity, cocaine use, and violence.

1986   109 minutes

BATAAN
★★★★½

DIRECTOR: Tay Garnett
CAST: Robert Taylor, George Murphy, Thomas Mitchell, Lloyd Nolan, Robert Walker, Desi Arnaz, Barry Nelson

One of the best films about World War II chronicles the exploits of an army patrol attempting to stall the Japanese onslaught in the Philippines. Good sets, a fine cast, and exciting battle scenes add to the overall effect. It's a must for fans of the genre. No rating; has violence.

1943   B & W 114 minutes

BATTLE BENEATH THE EARTH
★★½

DIRECTOR: Montgomery Tully
CAST: Kerwin Mathews, Robert Ayres, Martin Benson, Viviane Ventura

Stalwart Kerwin Mathews leads the fight against the Chinese hordes who intend to invade the United States via underground tunnels. Pretty good adventure fantasy in the comic book/pulp magazine tradition. Silent star Bessie Love, who starred in 1925's *The Lost World*, has a small role.

1967   91 minutes

BATTLE CRY
★★★

DIRECTOR: Raoul Walsh
CAST: Van Heflin, Tab Hunter, Dorothy Malone, Anne Francis

A platoon of Marines is followed into battle during World War II. The conflicts they face on the islands of the Pacific are contrasted to the emotional conflicts faced by their girlfriends at home. All in all, it is a successful piece of wartime fluff.

1955   149 minutes

BATTLE FORCE
★★

DIRECTOR: Humphrey Longon
CAST: Henry Fonda, John Huston, Stacy Keach, Helmut Berger, Samantha Eggar

The effect of war on the lives and destinies of two families, one American, the other German, is chronicled in this passable World War II adventure.

1976   92 minutes

BATTLE OF EL ALAMEIN, THE
★★★

DIRECTOR: Calvin Jackson Padget

CAST: Michael Rennie, Robert Hossein, Frederick Stafford, Ettore Manni, George Hilton

A re-creation of the famous twelve-day 1942 turning point clash between the artillery, tanks, and infantry of the British Eighth Army under General Montgomery and the German army's fabled Afrika Korps commanded by Field Marshal Rommel in the windswept Libyan Desert southwest of Alexandria. We know the outcome, but getting there makes for exciting watching. Rated PG.

1968   96 minutes

BATTLE OF THE BULGE
★★

DIRECTOR: Ken Annakin
CAST: Henry Fonda, Robert Shaw, Robert Ryan, Dana Andrews

This fairly good war film on the cinema screen suffers on video for two reasons: the small screen hurts the epic scale and 23 minutes are cut from the original print, with some good footage missing. It has good acting and good battle actions but a poor script and historical inaccuracies. Worth a look if you like war films.

1965   140 minutes

BATTLE OF THE COMMANDOS
★

DIRECTOR: Umberto Lenzi
CAST: Jack Palance, Curt Jurgens, Tomas Hunter, Diana Largo, Wolfgang Preirs

Jack Palance stars in this boring World War II adventure of commandos attacking the Germans on the eve of D-Day. Lots of phony battle scenes, bad acting, and poor script all add up to a big bomb.

1969   94 minutes

BEHIND THE RISING SUN
★★½

DIRECTOR: Edward Dmytryk
CAST: Margo, Tom Neal, J. Carrol Naish, Robert Ryan

The versatile J. Carrol Naish plays a Japanese publisher whose political views bring him into conflict with his son, educated in the U.S. It all takes place when Japan was fighting China, not long before World War II.

1943   B & W   89 minutes

BELARUS FILE, THE
★★½

DIRECTOR: Robert Markowitz
CAST: Telly Savalas, Suzanne Pleshette, Max von Sydow, Herbert Berghof, George Savalas

Telly Savalas returns as the lollipop-sucking police detective Kojak in this made-for-television movie about a maniac murdering Russian survivors of a Nazi concentration camp. Our hero's investigation into the killings turns up some damaging information on an old friend (Max von Sydow) who may be one of the murderer's targets. For fans of the series only.

1986   95 minutes

BENEATH THE 12-MILE REEF
★★★

DIRECTOR: Ted Post
CAST: Robert Wagner, Gilbert Roland, Terry Moore, Richard Boone

Here is some good old-fashioned Hollywood entertainment that requires nothing more from the viewer than to sit back, relax, and enjoy. Film deals with sponge divers off the Florida coast. Beautiful scenery keeps viewers' attention away from the lack of plot. Light, enjoyable fluff.

1953　　　　　　　　　102 minutes

BEN-HUR
★★★★★

DIRECTOR: William Wyler
CAST: Charlton Heston, Jack Hawkins, Sam Jaffe

In this film, which won eleven Oscars, a wealthy Jewish nobleman during the time of Christ incurs the hostility of the Roman military governor, who was his childhood friend. He is reduced to manning an oar on a slave galley, and his family is sent to prison. Years later he returns to seek vengeance upon his Roman tormentor. This culminates in a spectacular chariot race. Charlton Heston won an Oscar for his first-rate performance in the title role.

1959　　　　　　　　　211 minutes

BEST REVENGE
★★½

DIRECTOR: John Trent
CAST: John Heard, Levon Helm, Alberta Watson, John Rhys-Davies

Granger (John Heard), masquerading as an American tourist, has come to Spain to team up with Bo (Levon Helm), who has promised him the contacts for a $4 million hashish deal. Granger will make money on the deal, but his real reason for participating is that his best friend is being tortured by the gangster who set up the deal. This fast-moving action adventure has some good acting, but fails to rise above its pedestrian plot.

1984　　　　　　　　　92 minutes

BEYOND ATLANTIS
★★

DIRECTOR: Eddie Romero
CAST: Patrick Wayne, John Ashley, Leigh Christian, Sid Haig

Unexciting movie about a motley bunch of adventurers looking for a fabulous treasure on an uncharted isle. They get more than they bargained for from the ancient race of amphibious humans there who don't exactly welcome the intrusion. Nice location photography, but good scenery can't overcome the wooden acting, inane dialogue, and repetitious music, which'll have you climbing the walls. Rated PG for mild violence.

1973　　　　　　　　　89 minutes

BEYOND THE POSEIDON ADVENTURE
★

DIRECTOR: Irwin Allen
CAST: Michael Caine, Sally Field, Telly Savalas, Jack Warden, Peter Boyle

Probably one of the weakest ideas yet for a sequel. Michael Caine heads one of two salvage crews (his being the good one, of course) that race each other and time to probe the upside-down wreck of the *Poseidon*. Naturally, our heroes get stuck in the old tub, and disaster-flick king Irwin Allen knocks 'em off, one by one. An incredible waste of a talented cast, most notably Sally Field, who got trapped in this mess the same year she won an Oscar for *Norma Rae*! Rated PG for mild violence and language.

1979　　　　　　　　　114 minutes

BIG BAD MAMA
★★

DIRECTOR: Steve Carver
CAST: Angie Dickinson, Tom Skerritt, William Shatner, Joan Prather

Here's an okay film concerning a mother (Angie Dickinson), sort of a second-rate Ma Barker, leading her daughters on a robbery spree during the Depression. It's not a classic by any means, but the action keeps things moving along. Rated R for violence, nudity, and sex.

1974   83 minutes

BIG BRAWL, THE
★★★

DIRECTOR: Robert Clouse
CAST: Jackie Chan, José Ferrer, Kristine DeBell, Mako

Director Robert Clouse again fails to reach the heights attained with his *Enter the Dragon*. Nevertheless, this kung-fu comedy has its moments—most provided by its agile star, Jackie Chan. Still, one wonders what a martial arts hero is doing in the 1930s taking on snarling gangsters. If you like fist-and-foot action, however, it's fun. Rated R.

1980   95 minutes

BIG CAT, THE
★★★

DIRECTOR: Phil Karlson
CAST: Lon McCallister, Preston Foster, Forrest Tucker

A marauding mountain lion complicates feuding between high country ranchers in this enjoyable adventure film.

1949   75 minutes

BIG COMBO, THE
★★★

DIRECTOR: Joseph H. Lewis
CAST: Cornel Wilde, Jean Wallace, Richard Conte

A classic American gangster film done in the *film noir* style. Cornel Wilde has the starring role as a half-crazed policeman who is after gangsters and will do whatever is necessary to get them. Quite vi-

olent for its time and very well photographed, with an exciting climax.

1955   B & W   89 minutes

BIG FIX, THE
★★★½

DIRECTOR: Jeremy Paul Kagan
CAST: Richard Dreyfuss, Susan Anspach, Bonnie Bedelia

Novelist Roger Simon's laid-back detective, Moses Wine, comes to the screen in this flawed thriller. Richard Dreyfuss sleepwalks as the private dick, forcing the picture to survive in spite of his lethargic performance. The setting—which harkens back to the revolutionary 1960s—has become dated, but a murder mystery of any stripe is still suspenseful. And Wine *really* knows how to have fun with the board game *Clue*. Rated PG.

1978   108 minutes

BIG HEAT, THE
★★★★

DIRECTOR: Fritz Lang
CAST: Glenn Ford, Lee Marvin, Gloria Grahame, Carolyn Jones

If you are looking for a first-rate cop film, look no further than this one. Film deals with a cop's vengeance against the criminals who murdered his wife. Extremely well made. Scene of Lee Marvin throwing coffee into the face of Gloria Grahame is a classic. Glenn Ford has never been better.

1953   B & W   90 minutes

BIG RED ONE, THE
★★★★½

DIRECTOR: Samuel Fuller
CAST: Lee Marvin, Mark Hamill, Robert Carradine, Bobby DiCicco

This release gave Lee Marvin his best role in years. As a grizzled sergeant leading a platoon of "wet-noses" into the dangers of battle, he's excellent. In fact, he's better than excellent. He's perfect. Marvin is to the war film what John Wayne was to the western and James Cagney was to the gangster picture. *The Big Red One* is based on writer-director Sam Fuller's personal reminiscences of World War II. It's a terrific war movie. Rated PG.

1980   113 minutes

BIG SCORE, THE
★★½

DIRECTOR: Fred Williamson
CAST: Fred Williamson, John Saxon, Richard Roundtree, Nancy Wilson, Ed Lauter, Joe Spinell, Michael Dante

Dirty Harry (Fred Williamson) breaks all the rules in going after drug king Joe Spinell. Wait a minute, you say? Williamson doesn't play Dirty Harry? Well, in this screenplay, originally written for the San Francisco—set detective series—but rejected by Clint Eastwood—Williamson, the actor, does everything but squint his eyes like you-know-who. Unfortunately, Williamson, the director, doesn't make the story move fast enough. We guess you could call this doing yourself in. Rated R for violence and profanity.

1983   85 minutes

BIG SLEEP, THE (ORIGINAL)
★★★★

DIRECTOR: Howard Hawks
CAST: Humphrey Bogart, Lauren Bacall, John Ridgely, Martha Vickers, Dorothy Malone, Regis Toomey, Elisha Cooke, Jr., Bob Steele

A Humphrey Bogart–Lauren Bacall film means sharp verbal re-

partee, heightened sensuality lurking just below the surface, and performances one feels are natural and instinctive. *The Big Sleep* certainly fits that mold. It is sheer joy to watch the pair match wits. The plot, adapted by William Faulkner and director Howard Hawks, is complicated at best. Bogart, as Raymond Chandler's cynical private eye, Philip Marlowe, is hired to track down a blackmailer. Soon he is involved in a web of murder, deception, and wanton violence. The story has so many twists that audiences have at times been left confused. The actors themselves complained they didn't know what the whole thing was about, either. Try not to rationalize all the irrational events. The confusion is, in fact, essential to the general mood of the film. Just sit back and watch the sparring between Bacall and Bogart that has lifted this movie to its classic status.

1946   B & W 114 minutes

BIG SLEEP, THE
🐾

DIRECTOR: Michael Winner
CAST: Robert Mitchum, James Stewart, Sarah Miles, Oliver Reed, Candy Clark, Edward Fox

Director Michael Winner came up with a loser in this remake of the classic screen detective yarn. Even the considerable talents of Robert Mitchum (repeating the interpretation of the Philip Marlowe created in *Farewell My Lovely*), James Stewart, and Oliver Reed can't raise this travesty above the threshold of pain. Rated R for violence, profanity, and nudity.

1978   100 minutes

BIG TREES, THE
★★½

DIRECTOR: Felix Feist

CAST: Kirk Douglas, Eve Miller, Patrice Wymore, Edgar Buchanan, John Archer, Alan Hale

Lumberman Kirk Douglas wants the redwoods on homesteaders' land in this colorful adventure set in northwest California in 1900. Eve Miller is the passive Quaker-like girl who wins his heart; Patrice Wymore is the obligatory saloon singer who, as usual, gets jilted. A remake of 1938's *Valley of the Giants*.

1952   89 minutes

BIG TROUBLE IN LITTLE CHINA
★★★½

DIRECTOR: John Carpenter
CAST: Kurt Russell, Kim Catrall, Dennis Dun, James Hong, Victor Wong, Kate Burton, Donald Li, Carter Wong

An adventure fantasy with Kurt Russell as a pig trucker unwittingly swept into a mystical world underneath San Francisco's Chinatown. It's an empire ruled by a sinister 2,000-year-old ghost who must marry a green-eyed woman to restore his youth. The movie is a lighthearted special-effects showcase designed to look a bit silly, in the style of old serials, thriller comics, and Saturday morning cartoon shows. The characters' motivations are superficial, the mushy stuff is kept to a minimum, and the plot is explained in rapid-fire run-on sentences to avoid slowing down the action. Russell's hero has all the bravado of John Wayne and all the intelligence of a rainbow trout. The film's intentionally clumsy style helps to excuse its many flaws. Inconsequential, but fast-moving, self-deprecating, and a lot of fun. Rated PG-13.

1986   99 minutes

BILLY JACK
★★½

DIRECTOR: Tom Laughlin
CAST: Tom Laughlin, Delores Taylor, Clark Howat, Bert Freed, Julie Webb

A film that seems to suggest that a good kick in the groin will bring "peace and love," *Billy Jack* was a box-office sensation. The star, Tom Laughlin, and his wife, Delores Taylor (who plays the schoolteacher), produced and directed both this film and its prequel, *Born Losers*. They saturated television with advertising, rented local theaters outright, and made a bundle. Neither film can be called art. Laughlin is superb, but the rest can be called mediocre at best. Rated PG.

1971   114 minutes

BIRD OF PARADISE
★★½

DIRECTOR: King Vidor
CAST: Joel McCrea, Dolores Del Rio, John Halliday, Skeets Gallagher, Lon Chaney Jr.

Even the reliable Joel McCrea can't save this bit of South Sea island silliness. Amid sacrifices and angry volcano gods, the sea faring McCrea attempts to woo native princess Dolores Del Rio. This kind of thing was fairly typical (and popular) in the 1930s, but it looks awfully dumb today.

1932   B & W   80 minutes

BIRDS OF PREY
★★★★

DIRECTOR: William Graham
CAST: David Janssen, Ralph Meeker, Elayne Heilveil

Ex–World War II fighter pilot turned peacetime Salt Lake City traffic helicopter jockey (David

Janssen) hears the siren song of war anew when he witnesses a bank heist in progress and chases the robbers, who make their getaway in their own 'copter. An aerial battle of wits follows. Terrific flying sequences. There is an atmosphere and quality about this made-for-TV film that makes it one to savor and think about.

1973   81 minutes

BIRGIT HAAS MUST BE KILLED
★★★★★
DIRECTOR: Laurent Heynemann
CAST: Phillippe Noiret, Jean Rochefort, Lisa Kreuzer, Bernard Le Coq

It is hard to imagine a more perfect film than this spellbinding, French thriller-drama. Though its plot revolves around the assassination of a German terrorist (Birgit Haas) by a French counterspy organization, this film says as much about human relationships as it does espionage. And that's what makes it such a thoroughly fulfilling movie experience. Unrated, the film contains well-handled violence and nudity. In French with English subtitles.

1981   105 minutes

BLACK ARROW, THE
★★★½
DIRECTOR: Gordon Douglas
CAST: Louis Hayward, George Macready, Janet Blair, Edgar Buchanan

Hero Louis Hayward is in fine form as he fights the evil George Macready in this highly enjoyable entry into the swashbuckler genre. Some fine action scenes, with a slam-bang finale.

1948   B & W   76 minutes

BLACK BELT JONES
★★★
DIRECTOR: Robert Clouse
CAST: Jim Kelly, Scatman Crothers, Gloria Hendry

A likable kung-fu action film about a self-defense school in Watts combatting a "mafioso"-type group. Not a classic film, but an easy pace and good humor make this a good action movie. Rated PG for violence.

1974   87 minutes

BLACK JACK
★★★
DIRECTOR: Julien Duvivier
CAST: George Sanders, Herbert Marshall, Agnes Moorehead, Patricia Roc, Marcel Dalio

George Sanders is soldier of fortune Michael Alexander who has a drug-smuggling scheme in Tangiers aboard his yacht, the *Black Jack*. Patricia Roc plays his less-than-passionate love interest, Ingrid Decker. More interesting than the principal couple may be Agnes Moorehead as the rich widow, Mrs. Burke, and Herbert Marshall as Michael Alexander's war buddy in their supporting roles. Despite the initial feeling that this is a dated film, the twists in plot will hold viewers' attention.

1949   B & W 103 minutes

BLACK MOON RISING
★★
DIRECTOR: Harley Cokliss
CAST: Tommy Lee Jones, Linda Hamilton, Robert Vaughn, Richard Jaeckel, Lee Ving, Bubba Smith

The only redeeming point of this little car theft number is its occasional accent on humor. Unfortunately, the lighter moments are few and far between. The cast is topnotch, but the material is mostly pedestrian. Rated R for language, nudity, sex, and some rather gruesome scenes of violence.

1986   93 minutes

BLACK SUNDAY
★★★

DIRECTOR: John Frankenheimer
CAST: Robert Shaw, Bruce Dern, Marthe Keller, Fritz Weaver

This film is about an Arab terrorist group attempting to blow up the president. It features an exciting chase involving the Goodyear blimp and police helicopters over the skies of a Superbowl in Miami's Orange Bowl. Tension is maintained throughout. Rated R.

1977   143 minutes

BLACKOUT
★★★

DIRECTOR: Eddy Matalon
CAST: Jim Mitchum, Robert Carradine, Belinda Montgomery, June Allyson, Jean-Pierre Aumont, Ray Milland

At times, this movie, about a New York City apartment building attacked by a gang of escaped criminals during a blackout reeks of a disaster film. There's the establishing of cardboard characters, the setup for the unfolding drama, and some pretty wooden acting. Still, there are good action scenes and enough drama to make you almost forget the shortcomings. Rated R for violence.

1978   86 minutes

BLOOD IN THE STREETS
★★

DIRECTOR: Sergio Sollima
CAST: Oliver Reed, Fabio Testi, Agostine Belli

In this French-Italian film, a prison warden (Oliver Reed) is forced to release a prisoner as ransom for his kidnapped wife. When he realizes that the prisoner will be killed when he's turned over to these underworld figures, he has second thoughts about making the trade. There are some exciting chase scenes in this overall so-so film. Rated R for sex, nudity, language, and violence.

1974   111 minutes

BLOOD ON THE SUN
★★★½

DIRECTOR: Frank Lloyd
CAST: James Cagney, Robert Armstrong, Wallace Ford, Sylvia Sidney

This hard-hitting action drama finds James Cagney fighting Japanese military and government men in Japan during World War II. An unusual plot and good pace make this worth watching.

1945   B & W   98 minutes

BLOOD SIMPLE
★★★★½

DIRECTOR: Joel Coen
CAST: John Getz, Frances McDormand, Don Hedaya, M. Emmet Walsh, Samm-Art Williams

"In Russia, they've got it mapped out," intones the narrator (a sleazy private eye played to perfection by character actor M. Emmet Walsh). "Everyone pulls for everyone else. That's the theory, anyway. What I know is Texas. Down here, you're on your own." What follows is a slyly suspenseful, exciting (and sometimes agonizing) edge-of-your-seat story of how a bar owner named Julian Marty (Don Hedaya) hires the private eye to follow his wife, Abby (Frances McDormand), to find out if she's cheating on him. She is—with bartender Ray (John Getz), who works at Marty's club, the Neon Boot. So Marty hires the detective (who remains nameless) to kill them both. Thus begins a series of inventive twists and turns based on the title, *Blood Simple*, which is defined as a "state of confusion that follows the commission of a murder, i.e., 'He's gone blood simple.'" This state of mind, first described by hardboiled detective fiction great Dashiell Hammett (*The Maltese Falcon*; *Red Harvest*), makes the perfect murder impossible. Yet all of the major characters in this terrific film think they have done so at least once during its running time. Rated R for suggested sex, violence, and profanity.

1984   96 minutes

BLOODY MAMA
★★½

DIRECTOR: Roger Corman
CAST: Shelley Winters, Don Stroud, Pat Hingle, Robert Walden, Bruce Dern

Shelley Winters plays Ma Barker in this gangster flick. Her four sons share her notoriety as Depression-era bandits. Rated R.

1970   90 minutes

BLUE CITY

DIRECTOR: Michelle Manning
CAST: Judd Nelson, Ally Sheedy, David Caruso, Paul Winfield, Scott Wilson, Anita Morris

Probably one of the worst adaptations of a solid thriller ever made. Ross Macdonald must be rolling over in his grave. Estranged son Judd Nelson returns to his hometown and learns that his father, previously the mayor, has been killed. Determined to avenge this murder, Nelson goes on a ludicrous destructive spree against the local crime lord. All characters act like puppets on strings, with no motivation for their actions. The script makes no sense, and first-time director Michelle Manning shouldn't be let out without a leash. The biggest mistake was in updating the story from its 1946 setting to the 1980s; World War II–era tough-guy tales simply don't play outside that setting. Rated R for language and violence.

1986   83 minutes

BLUE MAX, THE
★★★

DIRECTOR: John Guillermin
CAST: George Peppard, James Mason, Ursula Andress, Jeremy Kemp, Carl Schell

George Peppard ("The A-Team") stars in this passable treatment of World War I flying aces.

1966   156 minutes

BLUE SUNSHINE
★★½

DIRECTOR: Jeff Lieberman
CAST: Zalman King, Deborah Winters, Mark Goddard, Robert Walden, Charles Siebert

Oddball mystery-thriller dealing with a series of random killings committed by former college students suffering the side-effects of a drug taken ten years previously. Low-budget film is both ridiculous and terrifying at the same time. Not for all tastes, but worth a look. Rated PG for mild language and violence.

1976   97 minutes

BLUE THUNDER
★★★★½

DIRECTOR: John Badham
CAST: Roy Scheider, Malcolm McDowell, Candy Clark, Warren Oates

A state-of-the-art helicopter is the centerpiece of this action-paced police melodrama. Piloted by Roy Scheider, the craft—a.k.a. "Blue Thunder"—battles combat jets commanded by villain Malcolm McDowell high above the crowded streets of downtown Los Angeles. The result is a gripping and immensely entertaining—if somewhat implausible—adventure thriller. Rated R for violence, nudity, and profanity.

1983   109 minutes

BOB LE FLAMBEUR
★★★★★

DIRECTOR: Jean-Pierre Melville
CAST: Roger Duchesne, Isabel Corey, Daniel Cauchy, Howard Vernon

This is an exquisite example of early French *film noir* (which translates as "dark film" and was a style of movie made predominantly by European directors in Hollywood during the 1940s). Moreover, it is an exquisite example of filmmaking—period. In it are all the trappings of the classic gangster movie—a flamboyant main character, tough cops, tougher gangsters, and the seedy joints where criminal plots are hatched. But there is more to it. The most fascinating element of this import is the title character, Bob Montagne (Roger Duchesne). A one-time bank robber and gang member, he has spent the last twenty years of his life without venturing into crime. All he does is gamble. He hasn't been lucky in a long time, however, and plans

to rob a casino of $800 million. But pulling it off isn't as easy as it seems.

1955   B & W 102 minutes

BOBBIE JO AND THE OUTLAW
★½

DIRECTOR: Mark L. Lester
CAST: Marjoe Gortner, Lynda Carter, Jesse Vint, Merrie Lynn Ross, Belinda Belaski, Gerrit Graham

This one is criminal, indeed. Lynda Carter, hungry for excitement, tags along with Marjoe Gortner and his gang. An orgy of murders and robberies ensues. Lots of violence, little credibility. Unless you're burning to see Wonder Woman semi nude for a few seconds, skip it. Rated R for nudity, violence, and profanity.

1976   89 minutes

BOMBARDIER
★★★½

DIRECTOR: Richard Wallace
CAST: Pat O'Brien, Randolph Scott, Eddie Albert, Robert Ryan, Anne Shirley, Barton MacLane

This is a solid action film dealing with the training of fliers during World War II. There is nothing new in the familiar formula of this film, but a good cast and fast pace make it enjoyable.

1943   B & W 99 minutes

BONNIE AND CLYDE
★★★★★

DIRECTOR: Arthur Penn
CAST: Warren Beatty, Faye Dunaway, Gene Hackman, Estelle Parsons, Michael J. Pollard, Gene Wilder

This still-fresh and innovative gangster film was one of the first to depict graphic violence, turning the genre inside-out, combining comedy, bloodshed, pathos, and social commentary with fascinating results.

1967   111 minutes

BONNIE'S KIDS
★★½
DIRECTOR: Arthur Marks
CAST: Tiffany Bolling, Steve Sandor, Robin Mattson, Scott Brady

Although this film has no redeeming social value, you can't really call it boring. In it, two amoral girls molested by their stepfather kill him and move in with their criminal uncle. They plan to rob their uncle but are pursued by thugs. Lots of action, but it's all rather pointless. Rated R for simulated sex, nudity, adult themes, and violence.

1982   105 minutes

BORDER, THE
★★★½
DIRECTOR: Tony Richardson
CAST: Jack Nicholson, Harvey Keitel, Valerie Perrine, Warren Oates, Elpidia Carrillo

Jack Nicholson stars in this often effective drama about a border patrol officer who rebels against the corruption in his department and the rampant greed of his wife, Valerie Perrine. This film features what was Nicholson's best major role in years (we're not counting his supporting bits in *Reds* or *Terms of Endearment* here). In addition, Harvey Keitel, Perrine, and Warren Oates give outstanding support. Rated R.

1982   107 minutes

BORDERLINE
★★★½
DIRECTOR: Jerrold Freedman

CAST: Charles Bronson, Bruno Kirby, Bert Remsen, Ed Harris

Old Stone Face Charles Bronson gives one of his better, more committed recent screen portrayals in this release, which got the jump on the similar *The Border*, with Jack Nicholson, by nearly two years (because of the latter's story problems). As in the latter film, the central character—a border guard—becomes involved with the problems of an illegal alien and her child. The result is a watchable action film. Rated R.

1980   105 minutes

BORN LOSERS
★★★
DIRECTOR: T. C. Frank
CAST: Tom Laughlin, Elizabeth James, Jeremy Slate, William Wellman Jr., Robert Tessier

This biker exploitation movie is better than the celebrated *Billy Jack*, which also starred Tom Laughlin. Granted, we still have to sit through scenes with terrible amateur actors, both kids and adults, but at least there is no girl singing off-key about her brother being dead.

1967   112 minutes

BOTANY BAY
★★★
DIRECTOR: John Farrow
CAST: Alan Ladd, James Mason, Sir Cedric Hardwicke, Patricia Medina, Murray Matheson

It is the 1790s, England still rules the waves, maritime officers are still sadistic, and the innocent are still punished. At least, until the last reel. In this picturesque action tale, Alan Ladd is a wrongly convicted student being transported to penal Australia. James Mason is the captain of the outward-bound convict ship, keelhauling and flogging his cargo of human flotsam with heinous delight. He has eyes for beauteous Patricia Medina, but she's interested in another Ladd. The color is nice.

1953   94 minutes

BOUNTY, THE
★★★★

DIRECTOR: Roger Donaldson
CAST: Mel Gibson, Anthony Hopkins, Laurence Olivier, Edward Fox

Mel Gibson (*Road Warrior*) is Fletcher Christian, and Anthony Hopkins is Captain William Bligh in this, the fourth and most satisfying screen version of *The Mutiny on the Bounty*. The 1935 original, with Clark Gable and Charles Laughton, is undeniably one of the screen's finest adventure films, just as the 1962 remake with Marlon Brando and Trevor Howard was a multimillion-dollar mistake. This sweeping sea faring epic from the director of *Smash Palace* is the first movie to present the historic events accurately—and to do so fascinatingly. Rated PG for nudity and violence.

1984   132 minutes

BOXCAR BERTHA
★★½

DIRECTOR: Martin Scorsese
CAST: David Carradine, Barbara Hershey, Barry Primus, Bernie Casey, John Carradine

Small-town girl (Barbara Hershey) hooks up with gang of train robbers (led by David Carradine) in this *Bonnie and Clyde* coattailer. Martin Scorsese buffs will be disappointed. Rated R.

1972   97 minutes

BOYS IN COMPANY C, THE
★★★

DIRECTOR: Sidney J. Furie
CAST: Stan Shaw, Andrew Stevens, James Canning, James Whitmore Jr.

The film opens with the arrival of various draftees in the Marine Corps induction center and comes close, at times, to being the powerful film the subject of the Vietnam War suggests. The combat scenes are particularly effective, and the deaths of soldiers are gory without being overdone. Rated R for violence.

1978   127 minutes

BRADY'S ESCAPE
★★★

DIRECTOR: Pal Gabor
CAST: John Savage, Kelly Reno

A minor HBO-produced film concerning an American attempting to escape the Nazis in Europe during WWII. Nothing original is added to the familiar plot.

1984   96 minutes

BRANNIGAN
★★½

DIRECTOR: Douglas Hickox
CAST: John Wayne, Richard Attenborough, Judy Geeson, Mel Ferrer, Ralph Meeker, John Vernon

An aging John Wayne travels to London to bring back a fugitive in this cops-and-robbers chase film that is long on just about everything but plot and credibility. It's kind of fun to see the Duke in jolly old England and the cast is outstanding, but the film is flat and slow and doesn't deliver the excitement or impact one expects from one of the world's greatest stars. Rated PG.

1975   111 minutes

BRASS TARGET
★★

DIRECTOR: John Hough
CAST: Sophia Loren, George Kennedy, John Cassavetes, Robert Vaughn, Max von Sydow, Bruce Davison

Pure Hollywood hokum at its most ridiculous would ask us to believe that Gen. George Patton (George Kennedy) was murdered after World War II because of a large gold robbery committed by his staff. Not much to recommend this boring film. Rated PG for moderate language and violence.

1978   111 minutes

BREAKER! BREAKER!
★

DIRECTOR: Don Hulette
CAST: Chuck Norris, George Murdock, Terry O'Connor, Don Gentry

A quickie thrown together to cash in on the CB craze, this Chuck Norris flick promises, but does not deliver, a slam-bang ending. Rated PG.

1977   86 minutes

BREAKER MORANT
★★★★★

DIRECTOR: Bruce Beresford
CAST: Edward Woodward, Jack Thompson, John Waters, Bryan Brown

This is one motion picture you won't want to miss. Imagine the high adventure of the original *Gunga Din*, the wisecracking humor of *To Have and Have Not*, and the character drama of *The Caine Mutiny* all rolled into one super movie and you'll have an idea of just how good *Breaker Morant* is. Edward Woodward (*The Wicker Man*) stars in this film about the court-martial of three soldiers during the Boer War. Rated PG.

1979   107 minutes

BREAKOUT
★★★

DIRECTOR: Tom Gries
CAST: Charles Bronson, Robert Duvall, Jill Ireland, John Huston, Sheree North, Randy Quaid

While not exactly Charles Bronson at his best, this action-adventure film does have its moments as the star, playing a devil-may-care helicopter pilot, rescues Robert Duvall, an American businessman framed for murder and held captive in a Mexican jail. Director-turned-actor John Huston also adds some class to this production, which suffers equally from a featured role played by the untalented Jill Ireland (Mrs. Bronson). In all, *Breakout* is a basically entertaining time-passer. Rated PG.

1975   96 minutes

BREAKTHROUGH
★

DIRECTOR: Andrew V. McLaglen
CAST: Richard Burton, Robert Mitchum, Rod Steiger, Curt Jurgens

This dull war film— a sequel to Sam Peckinpah's *Cross of Iron*— stars Richard Burton as Sergeant Steiner, a heroic German officer who saves the life of an American colonel (Robert Mitchum) after the Nazis thwart an attempt on Hitler's life. The Allies are placed in danger by their agreement to a discussion of surrender by the conspirators. Rated PG.

1978   115 minutes

BRIDGE ON THE RIVER KWAI, THE

★★★★★

DIRECTOR: David Lean
CAST: William Holden, Alec Guinness, Jack Hawkins, Sessue Hayakawa, James Donald

Considered by many to be David Lean's greatest work, this war epic brought the British director his first Oscar. The powerful, dramatic story centers around the construction of a bridge by British and American prisoners of war under the command of Japanese colonel Sessue Hayakawa. Alec Guinness, a Lean semiregular since *Great Expectations*, is the stiff-upper-lipped British commander who uses the task as a way of proving British superiority. William Holden is the American soldier escapee who must return to the camp and, with the aid of British commando Jack Hawkins, blow the bridge up.

1957   161 minutes

BRIDGE TOO FAR, A

★★★½

DIRECTOR: Richard Attenborough
CAST: Dirk Bogarde, James Caan, Michael Caine, Sean Connery, Laurence Olivier, Robert Redford

Here's another story of a famous battle with the traditional all-star cast. In this case it's World War II's "Operation Market Garden," a disastrous Allied push to get troops behind German lines and capture an early bridgehead on the Rhine. Rated PG.

1977   175 minutes

BUCCANEER, THE

★★

DIRECTOR: Anthony Quinn
CAST: Yul Brynner, Charlton Heston, Claire Bloom, Charles Boyer, Douglass Dumbrille, Lorne Greene, Ted de Corsia

Studio-bound remake of C. B. deMille's 1938 romance of pirate Jean Lafitte and his involvement in the War of 1812 boasts a cast capable of hamming *and* acting, but that's not enough to make this stiff color creaker come alive. Veteran deMille actor Henry Wilcoxen and son-in-law Anthony Quinn produced and directed this film in his florid and fact-bending style but lacked C.B.'s schoolboy enthusiasm and infectious idealism. Some memorable sequences (including the dawn battle between the red-coated British and the Americans and pirates led by Charlton Heston and Yul Brynner), but this overlong historical hokum was a dinosaur when released in 1958 and hasn't acquired any real charm or reputation in the ensuing years. C. B. deMille's last public appearance was in December of 1958 while promoting this film in New York; he died January 21, 1959.

1958   121 minutes

BULLDOG DRUMMOND

★★★

DIRECTOR: F. Richard Jones
CAST: Ronald Colman, Joan Bennett, Lilyan Tashman, Montagu Love, Lawrence Grant, Claud Allister, Tetsu Komai

Ronald Colman smoothly segued from silent to sound films playing the title's ex–British army officer adventurer in this exciting, witty, definitive first stanza of what became of popular series.

1929   B & W   89 minutes

BULLFIGHTER AND THE LADY, THE
★★★★
DIRECTOR: Budd Boetticher
CAST: Robert Stack, Joy Page, Gilbert Roland, Katy Jurado

Many of the themes explored in the superb series of low-budget westerns director Budd Boetticher later made with Randolph Scott (*Decision at Sundown, The Tall T*) are evident in this first-rate drama. A skeet-shooting champ (Robert Stack) decides to become a bullfighter and enlists the aid of a top professional (Gilbert Roland). This is the finest film on the subject.
1951　　　　B & W　　87 minutes

BULLITT
★★★★
DIRECTOR: Peter Yates
CAST: Steve McQueen, Robert Vaughn, Jacqueline Bisset, Norman Fell

Although a bit dated now, this police drama directed by Peter Yates (*Breaking Away*) still features one of star Steve McQueen's best screen performances. Co-starring Robert Vaughn and Jacqueline Bisset, it features McQueen as a "Dirty Harry"–type renegade cop who smells a rat when his efforts to guard government witnesses are suspiciously thwarted. The San Francisco car-chase sequence is still a corker.
1968　　　　113 minutes

BUNCO
★★½
DIRECTOR: Alexander Singer
CAST: Robert Urich, Tom Selleck, Donna Mills, Michael Sacks, Will Geer, Arte Johnson, James Hampton, Bobby Van

Passable made-for-television crime thriller has Robert Urich and Tom Selleck, sans mustache, as a pair of police detectives out to bust a confidence ring. They enlist the aid of a female undercover cop (Donna Mills), who soon finds herself paired with a psycho (Michael Sacks) and her life in danger. Typical TV fare.
1985　　　　90 minutes

BUSHIDO BLADE
🦴
DIRECTOR: Tom Kotani
CAST: Richard Boone, Frank Converse, James Earl Jones, Toshiro Mifune, Mako, Sonny Chiba, Laura Gemser

Top-billed Richard Boone gives an outrageously hammy performance in this Japanese-made answer to *Shogun* as Commander Matthew Perry, whose mission is to find a valuable sword. Gesturing with no regard to believable movement or character, Boone is embarrasingly bad in his last film. The all-star cast of Frank Converse (in the action-hero role), James Earl Jones, Toshiro Mifune (as, what else, a shogun), and Mako (from the *Conan* series and *The Sand Pebbles*) fare little better in this poorly directed adventure. Rated R for violence.
1979　　　　104 minutes

CABO BLANCO
★
DIRECTOR: J. Lee Thompson
CAST: Charles Bronson, Dominique Sanda, Jason Robards Jr.

When will they ever learn? This is a miserable suspense-thriller remake of *Casablanca*. As good as he can be when he wants to, Charles Bronson is no Humphrey Bogart. And we shouldn't expect him to be. So why is he playing a nightclub owner saving a damsel in distress (Dominique Sanda) from a modern-day Nazi (Jason Robards Jr.)? We don't know—and neither will you. Rated R.

1982   87 minutes

CALL OF THE WILD
★★★½
DIRECTOR: Ken Annakin
CAST: Charlton Heston, Michele Mercier, Maria Rohm, Rik Battaglia

Charlton Heston stars in this adaptation of Jack London's famous novel. This one is a real tear-jerker. A domesticated dog is stolen and forced to pull a snow sled in Alaska as John (Charlton Heston) searches for gold. Some profanity and violence. Rated PG.

1972   100 minutes

CAME A HOT FRIDAY
★★
DIRECTOR: Ian Mune
CAST: Peter Bland, Philip Gordon, Billy T. James, Michael Lawrence, Marshall Napier, Erna Larsen, Patricia Philips, Don Selwyn

Mildly amusing film set in 1949 New Zealand, where two conmen make their fortune cheating bookmakers all across the country. Their luck runs out when they reach a small town—the locals turn the tables on them and take the money. So our two "heroes," with the help of the local nut-case, go all out to get the money back. Rated PG for language and adult situations.

1985   101 minutes

CANNONBALL
★½
DIRECTOR: Paul Bartel

CAST: David Carradine, Veronica Hamel, Gerrit Graham, Sylvester Stallone, Robert Carradine, Carl Gottlieb, Belinda Balaski

Before writer/director Paul Bartel got involved with original notions, such as *Eating Raoul*, he was busily copying other successful concepts. This plays like a poor man's *Cannonball Run* or *Gumball Rally*, executed by somebody having neither the skill nor understanding of complex vehicular stunts. As usual, David Carradine plays an unpleasant antihero out to beat the rest of the cast in an exotic race. Look for cameos by directors Roger Corman, Joe Dante, and Martin Scorsese. Rated R for violence.

1976   93 minutes

CAPTAIN BLOOD
★★★★½
DIRECTOR: Michael Curtiz
CAST: Errol Flynn, Olivia De Havilland, Basil Rathbone, Lionel Atwill

This classic film made Errol Flynn a star and typecast him as a swashbuckler. Flynn plays Peter Blood, a physician, humanist, and buccaneer par excellence. It's a rousing adventure!

1935   B & W   95 minutes

CAPTAIN KIDD
★★
DIRECTOR: Rowland V. Lee
CAST: Charles Laughton, Randolph Scott, Reginald Owen, John Carradine, Sheldon Leonard, Barbara Britton, Gilbert Roland

Not even Charles Laughton's mugging and posturing can redeem this swashbuckling yarn about the pirate whose treasure is still being sought. Great cast, from whom more should have been expected.

1945   89 minutes

CAPTAINS COURAGEOUS
★★★★

DIRECTOR: Victor Fleming
CAST: Spencer Tracy, Freddie Bartholomew, Lionel Barrymore, Mickey Rooney

Spoiled rich boy (Freddie Bartholomew) falls off a luxury liner. Rescued by a Portuguese fisherman (Spencer Tracy), he comes of age aboard a fishing trawler (captained by Lionel Barrymore), learning there is much more to life than the comforts and privileges of wealth. Topnotch. Tracy won an Oscar.

1937   B & W 116 minutes

CAST A GIANT SHADOW
★★

DIRECTOR: Melville Shavelson
CAST: Kirk Douglas, Senta Berger, Angie Dickinson

The early history of Israel is told through the fictionalized biography of American Col. Mickie Marcus (Kirk Douglas). Marcus, an expatriate army officer, is cajoled into aiding Israel in its impending war to wrest independence from its hostile Arab neighbors. It is a highly romanticized piece of historical fluff. Frank Sinatra, John Wayne, and Yul Brynner make cameo appearances.

1966   142 minutes

CAT AND MOUSE
★★★★½

DIRECTOR: Claude Lelouch
CAST: Michèle Morgan, Jean-Pierre Aumont, Serge Reggiani, Valerie LaGrangg

Written, produced, and directed by Claude Lelouch, *Cat and Mouse* is a deliciously urban and witty whodunit guaranteed to charm and deceive while keeping you marvelously entertained. The plot has more twists and turns than a country road, and the characters are . . . well . . . just slightly corrupt and totally fascinating. Rated PG.

1975   107 minutes

CATCH ME A SPY
★★★

DIRECTOR: Dick Clement
CAST: Kirk Douglas, Marlene Jobert, Trevor Howard

This is a good suspense thriller with, surprisingly, a few laughs. The story is built around an East-West espionage theme in which both sides trade for their captured spies. Unfortunately, the West loses its hostage in an accident and is forced to scramble to find new barterable material. This yarn is interesting, suspenseful, and humorous. Rated PG.

1971   93 minutes

C.C. & COMPANY
★★½

DIRECTOR: Seymour Robbie
CAST: Joe Namath, Ann-Margret, William Smith, Sid Haig, Jennifer Billingsley, Greg Mullavey

Basically idiotic action film has Broadway Joe Namath (in his first feature) cast as C.C. Ryder, misfit member of a rowdy biker gang, attempting to "split" when he falls for top fashion photographer Ann-Margret. It's not that easy. Joe's acting is stiff and unnatural, William Smith is good as the gang leader, and cronies Sid Haig and Greg Mullavey handle the comic relief with a certain zeal. Rated R for mild language and nudity.

1970   90 minutes

CERTAIN FURY
🐱

DIRECTOR: Stephen Gullenhaal
CAST: Tatum O'Neal, Irene Cara, Nicholas Campbell, George Murdock, Moses Gunn, Peter Fonda

Somebody certainly should be furious about this tasteless, stupid movie. It's a vicious, gratuitously violent film with lots of guns and blood and fire and action—with no purpose. Tatum O'Neal is Scarlet ("Scar")—a dumb white street woman; Irene Cara is Tracy—a dumb pampered black woman. They're thrown together in an opening-scene bloodbath and through the rest of the movie run for their lives from police and drug dealers. Rated R for violence.

1985　　　　　　　87 minutes

CHAIN REACTION
★★★

DIRECTOR: Ian Barry, George Miller
CAST: Steve Bisley, Anna-Maria Winchester, Ross Thompson, Ralph Cotterill, Patrick Ward

This slick and stylish Australian political thriller, co-directed by George Miller before he hit it big with the "Mad Max" films, is a brilliantly photographed, generally engrossing drama following a nuclear power plant employee (Ross Thompson) accidentally exposed to a lethal dose of radiation during a near meltdown. Determined to let the public know of the disaster (which the utility company wants to keep under wraps), he makes a mad dash for the nearest city, while the authorities in hot pursuit. The first half is a scathing political exposé (à la *The China Syndrome*), while the second half regresses to a series of high-powered chase scenes (à la *Mad Max*),

but the whole film is involving and visually enticing. Don't blink or you'll miss Mel Gibson in an unbilled cameo. Rated R. Some explicit sex, nudity, and violence.

1980　　　　　　　87 minutes

CHAINED HEAT
★

DIRECTOR: Paul Nicolas
CAST: Linda Blair, John Vernon, Nita Talbot, Stella Stevens, Sybil Danning, Tamara Dobson

The story of women in prison, this cheapo offers few surprises. It's just another visit to the snake pit, with a few lines of phenomenally bad—therefore funny—dialogue. Only those who like cheap laughs, nudity, sex, violence, profanity, and bad acting will enjoy this exploitation flick. Rated R.

1983　　　　　　　95 minutes

CHALLENGE, THE
★★★½

DIRECTOR: John Frankenheimer
CAST: Scott Glenn, Toshiro Mifune, Calvin Young

An American (Scott Glenn, the charismatic bad guy of *Urban Cowboy*) gets caught in the middle of a decades-old private war between two brothers in modern-day Japan. This movie has ample rewards for both samurai film aficionados and regular moviegoers. Sharing top billing and right in the thick of the action is Toshiro Mifune (*The Seven Samurai*; *Shogun*), the greatest Japanese screen actor of them all. Rated R for profanity and violence.

1982　　　　　　　112 minutes

CHARADE
★★★★½

DIRECTOR: Stanley Donen

CAST: Cary Grant, Audrey Hepburn, Walter Matthau, James Coburn, George Kennedy

A comedy/mystery directed in the Alfred Hitchcock suspense style by Stanley Donen (*Singin' in the Rain*; *Blame It on Rio*), this features the ever-suave Cary Grant helping widow Audrey Hepburn find the fortune stashed by her late husband. Walter Matthau, George Kennedy, and James Coburn are the baddies attempting to get to the loot first.

1963   114 minutes

CHARGE OF THE LIGHT BRIGADE, THE
★★★★

DIRECTOR: Michael Curtiz
CAST: Errol Flynn, Olivia De Havilland, Patric Knowles, Donald Crisp, David Niven, Henry Stephenson

October 25, 1854: Balaclava, the Crimea; military minds blunder, and six hundred gallant Britishers, sabers flashing, ride to their deaths. The film, which climaxes with one of the most dramatic cavalry charges in history, is based on Tennyson's famous poem. Errol Flynn and Olivia De Havilland are star-crossed lovers. Donald Crisp and Henry Stephenson are superbly English, as always. Good show!

1936   B & W 116 minutes

CHARLEY VARRICK
★★★★

DIRECTOR: Don Siegel
CAST: Walter Matthau, Joe Don Baker, Felicia Farr, Andy Robinson, John Vernon

Still on a roll after *Dirty Harry*, director Don Siegel turns into a classic this story about a bank robber (Walter Matthau) who acci-

dentally steals money from the mob (he hits a bank where its ill-gotten gains are laundered). Matthau is superb as Varrick, the "last of the independents," and Joe Don Baker sends chills up the spine as the hit man relentlessly pursuing him. Rated PG.

1973   111 minutes

CHINA SEAS
★★★½

DIRECTOR: Tay Garnett
CAST: Clark Gable, Jean Harlow, Wallace Beery, Lewis Stone

MGM boasted that it once had all the stars that were in the heavens. *China Seas* brings an element of truth to the boast. The all-star adventure drama reteams Clark Gable and Jean Harlow in roles very similar to those in their popular *Red Dust*. Gable is the captain of a Chinese river steamer in pirate-infested waters. Harlow is once again the lady with a spotted past, who we all know is the perfect mate for Gable if he'd only realize it himself. Wallace Beery, Rosalind Russell, and Lewis Stone are also along on what becomes an enjoyable screen romp.

1935   B & W   90 minutes

CHINATOWN
★★★★½

DIRECTOR: Roman Polanski
CAST: Jack Nicholson, Faye Dunaway, John Huston, Perry Lopez, Diane Ladd

One of the great detective films, this stars Jack Nicholson as a 1940s Los Angeles private eye who stumbles onto a crooked land deal as well as a murder. Faye Dunaway, John Huston, and Perry Lopez offer standout support. Director Roman Polanski has a cameo as a knife-wielding hood.

Rated R for language, violence, nudity.

1974   131 minutes

CHINESE CONNECTION, THE
★★★

DIRECTOR: Lo Wei
CAST: Bruce Lee, Miao Ker Hsio

This action-packed import, in which Bruce Lee plays a martial arts expert out to avenge the death of his mentor, is good, watchable fare. But be forewarned: It's dubbed, and not all that expertly. Rated R.

1979   107 minutes

CHRISTINA
★★

DIRECTOR: Paul Krasny
CAST: Barbara Parkins, Peter Haskell, James McEachin, Marlyn Mason

Unbelievable mystery film about a wealthy foreigner (Barbara Parkins) who pays an unemployed aircraft engineer (Peter Haskell) twenty-five thousand dollars to marry her so she can acquire a U.S. passport... or so we think. The story begins to unfold as the man falls in love with the millionaire. Mildly interesting, but still a bit too contrived to recommend.

1974   95 minutes

CINCINNATI KID, THE
★★★★

DIRECTOR: Norman Jewison
CAST: Steve McQueen, Ann-Margret, Edward G. Robinson, Karl Malden

Steve McQueen had one of his earliest acting challenges in this study of a determined young poker player on his way to the big time. He lets nothing stand in his way, especially not the reigning king of the card tables, Edward G. Ro-

binson. The film is made more interesting by some delicious performances in supporting roles. Most notable are Karl Malden as McQueen's teacher and Joan Blondell as a has-been whose nerves and pocketbook can't stand the strain of the "big games" anymore. Tuesday Weld and Ann-Margret try to provide McQueen with a little feminine distraction from his relentless quest, but it's not in the cards.

1965   113 minutes

CIRCLE OF IRON
★★★

DIRECTOR: Richard Moore
CAST: David Carradine, Jeff Cooper, Christopher Lee, Roddy McDowall, Eli Wallach, Erica Creer

Bruce Lee was preparing the screenplay for this film shortly before he died as the follow-up to his tremendously successful first American film *Enter the Dragon*. Ironically, the lead role fell to David Carradine, who had also been chosen over Lee for the lead in the television series "Kung Fu." This is a highly satisfying adventure movie about a seeker (Jeff Cooper) who encounters four mysterious martial arts masters (all played by Carradine). Fans of the genre will love it. Rated R for violence.

1979   102 minutes

CLEOPATRA JONES

DIRECTOR: Jack Starrett
CAST: Tamara Dobson, Shelley Winters, Bernie Casey, Brenda Sykes

Secret agent Cleopatra Jones returns from an overseas assignment to save her old neighborhood, including a halfway house run by her ex-boyfriend, from an evil drug queen gang leader (Shelley Winters) known as "Mommy." Rated PG for violence.

1973   80 minutes

CLOAK AND DAGGER
★★★★

DIRECTOR: Richard Franklin
CAST: Henry Thomas, Dabney Coleman, Michael Murphy, John McIntire

A highly imaginative boy (Henry Thomas, of *E.T.*) who often plays pretend games of espionage with his fantasy friend, Jack Flack (Dabney Coleman, who also plays Thomas's father), finds himself involved in a real life-and-death situation when he stumbles onto the evil doings of a group of spies (led by Michael Murphy). Directed by Richard Franklin (*Psycho II*), this movie offers the best of all possible worlds for young and old viewers alike. It's suspenseful and fast-paced enough to keep adults interested and entertained, but not so scary and violent as to upset the kiddies. Rated PG.

1984   101 minutes

CLOUD DANCER
★★★½

DIRECTOR: Barry Brown
CAST: David Carradine, Jennifer O'-Neill, Joseph Bottoms, Colleen Camp

A story about competing stunt flyers, this film features one of David Carradine's best performances (right up there with those he gave in *Bound for Glory* and *The Long Riders*). As the king of daredevil pilots, he struggles to keep ahead of his ambitious protégé (Joseph Bottoms) as well as fighting his love for Jennifer O'-

Neill (in one of her few effective portrayals). His brother (brilliantly played by Albert Salmi) is simple-minded, so Carradine refuses to marry and have children. Yet, unbeknownst to him, he is the father of a perfectly normal child—an element of just one of the films highly effective subplots. It's a touching and exciting sleeper. Rated PG.

1980   108 minutes

COBRA
★★

DIRECTOR: George Cosmatos
CAST: Sylvester Stallone, Brigitte Nielsen, Reni Santoni, Andrew Robinson, Art Le Fleur, Val Avery, Bert Williams

Sylvester Stallone comes back for more *Rambo*-like action as a tough city cop on the trail of a serial killer in this unrelentingly grim and gruesome thriller. It is packed with action and violence, but there is so much of it that the effect is numbing rather than exhilarating. In fact, it is more like a slasher flick or a *Death Wish* sequel than the *Dirty Harry* detective movies it seeks to emulate. Rated R for violence, gore, and profanity.

1986   95 minutes

COCKFIGHTER
★★

DIRECTOR: Monte Hellman
CAST: Warren Oates, Harry Dean Stanton, Richard B. Schull, Troy Donahue, Millie Perkins

Title says it all. Warren Oates and Harry Dean Stanton can't breathe life into this simplistic look at the illegal sport of cockfighting. For Oates fans only. Rated R.

1974   83 minutes

CODE NAME: EMERALD
★★★★
DIRECTOR: Jonathan Sanger
CAST: Ed Harris, Max von Sydow, Horst Buchholz, Helmut Berger, Cyrielle Claire, Eric Stoltz

Better-than-average World War II espionage film about a double agent (Ed Harris) who attempts to rescue a U.S. Army officer (Eric Stoltz) held for interrogation in a French prison because he knows the details of the planned Allied invasion at Normandy. Like the best spy thrillers, the plot moves along at a good clip despite the lack of action—and when the action does pick up in the last ten minutes, it proves to be worth the wait. Harris's performance is inconsistent, however; his subtle machismo occasionally hampers his ability to evoke a mood. Still, most of the time he is believable, and Max von Sydow's performance is up to his usual high standard. Rated PG for violence and sex.

1985   95 minutes

CODE OF SILENCE
★★★★
DIRECTOR: Andy Davis
CAST: Chuck Norris, Henry Silva, Bert Remsen, Mike Genovese, Ralph Foody, Nathan Davis

With this film, Chuck Norris proved himself the heir to Charles Bronson as the king of the no-nonsense action movie. In *Code of Silence*, the star gives a right-on-target performance as tough cop Sgt. Eddie Cusack, who takes on warring mob families and corrupt police officers. This one's a treat for Norris fans and nonfans alike.

Rated R for violence and profanity.

1985   102 minutes

COMMANDO
★★★★
DIRECTOR: Mark L. Lester
CAST: Arnold Schwarzenegger, Rae Dawn Chong, Dan Hedaya, James Olson, Alyssa Milano

"Commando" John Matrix makes Rambo look like a wimp. As played by big, beefy Arnold Schwarzenegger, he "eats Green Berets for breakfast." When we first see him, Big John is making like Paul Bunyan, carrying a tree he has chopped down near his mountain home. This, we know immediately, is one tough guy (and a very silly movie). He soon goes on the warpath when his 11-year-old daughter is kidnapped by a South American dictator (Dan Hedaya) he once helped depose. Matrix is supposed to put the evil guy back in power, but opts instead to put him out of commission. The result is the most outrageously action-packed (and therefore funniest) comic-book-style adventure film of the 1980s. Rated R for violence and profanity.

1986   90 minutes

COMMANDOS
★½
DIRECTOR: Armando Crispino
CAST: Lee Van Cleef, Jack Kelly, Marino Mase, Giampiero Albertini

Italian World War II film with dubbed English and not enough action to make it worth looking in on. Jack Kelly and Lee Van Cleef lead a small special force into North Africa to spy on the German army. Rated PG for violence and sex.

1968   89 minutes

CONFIDENTIALLY YOURS
★★

DIRECTOR: Francois Truffaut
CAST: Fanny Arandt, Jean-Louis Trintignant, Jean-Pierre Kalfon, Philippe Laudenbach, Philippe Morier-Genoud

Francois Truffaut's last film is a stylized murder mystery in the tradition of Hitchcock (whom Truffaut so fervently admired). Truffaut might have had a jolly time making this homage, but it's only a lighthearted soufflé of a film that is too thin to hold its air. The movie tips its hat to good old suspense films without becoming one itself. Jean-Louis Trintignant plays a real estate agent framed for murder. His secretary (Fanny Ardant) helps him solve the case. Rated PG.

1983   B & W 110 minutes

CONQUEROR, THE
🐾

DIRECTOR: Dick Powell
CAST: John Wayne, Susan Hayward, Pedro Armendariz, Agnes Moorehead

John Wayne plays Genghis Khan, and the results are unintentionally hilarious as the Duke spouts stilted, clichéd barbarian dialogue in his familiar drawling fashion. *The Conqueror* was perhaps the most tragic motion picture ever made. Unbeknownst to the cast and crew of this period adventure, eleven atomic bombs had been exploded at the U.S. government's testing ground in Yucca Flat, Nevada—just 137 miles from the location. The largest of these was four times the size of the one dropped on Hiroshima. As a possible result, all of the principal actors (Wayne, Susan Hayward, Pedro Armendariz, and Agnes Moorehead), director Dick Powell, and nearly forty crew members died of cancer.

1956   111 minutes

CONVOY
★½

DIRECTOR: Sam Peckinpah
CAST: Kris Kristofferson, Ali MacGraw, Ernest Borgnine, Madge Sinclair, Burt Young

This Sam Peckinpah action film will not be remembered as one of the director's best. Yet the film does possess the crisp editing, accent on action, and exciting photography that we associate with all of Peckinpah's movies. The story concerns some truckers, led by Kris Kristofferson, who go on a tri-state protest over police brutality, high gas prices, and other complaints. An uneven script and just fair acting certainly mar this picture. Rated PG.

1978   110 minutes

COOGAN'S BLUFF
★★★★

DIRECTOR: Don Siegel
CAST: Clint Eastwood, Lee J. Cobb, Susan Clark, Tisha Sterling, Don Stroud, Betty Field, Tom Tully

This modern-day-cowboy-in-the-big-city adventure provided the basis for the "McCloud" TV series, starring Dennis Weaver. Film star Clint Eastwood and director Don Siegel, in their first collaboration, proved they could handle the theme much better with the squinty-eyed star hunting down a murderous fugitive (Don Stroud) in the asphalt jungle. Lee J. Cobb is also memorable as a hard-bitten New York detective. Rated PG.

1968   100 minutes

COOL HAND LUKE
★★★★★

DIRECTOR: Stuart Rosenberg
CAST: Paul Newman, George Kennedy, J. D. Cannon, Lou Antonio, Robert Drivas, Strother Martin

One of Paul Newman's greatest creations is the irrepressible Luke. Luke is a prisoner on a southern chain gang and not even the deprivations of these subhuman conditions will break his spirit. He even manages to win the admiration of his rival on the chain gang, George Kennedy. Kennedy's performance was equally memorable and won him a supporting Oscar.

1967　　　　126 minutes

COP IN BLUE JEANS, THE
★

DIRECTOR: Bruno Corbucci
CAST: Thomas Milian, Jack Palance, Maria Rosaria Omaggio, Guido Mannari, Jack La Cayennie, Raf Luca, Benito Stefanelli

This film about an undercover cop (Thomas Milian) trying to take out an underworld boss (Jack Palance) has plenty of action scenes. But after enduring the shoddy voice dubbing and the poorly developed characters, the viewer is all too relieved to push the rewind button. Not rated; contains violence.

1978　　　　92 minutes

CORNERED
★★★

DIRECTOR: Edward Dmytryk
CAST: Dick Powell, Walter Slezak, Micheline Cheirel, Luther Adler, Morris Carnovsky, Edgar Barrier, Steven Geray

Fresh from his success as hard-boiled sleuth Philip Marlowe in *Murder, My Sweet,* former song-and-dance man Dick Powell continued to score as a dramatic actor in this thriller about a discharged Canadian airman on the trail of Nazi collaborators who murdered his French wife. The hunt takes him from France to Switzerland to Argentina and a rendezvous within a nest of corrupt Europeans.

1946　　　B & W 102 minutes

CORRUPT ONES, THE
★★★

DIRECTOR: James Hill
CAST: Robert Stack, Nancy Kwan, Elke Sommer, Werner Peters

Robert Stack plays a photographer who receives the key to a Chinese treasure. Not surprisingly, he soon finds that he's not alone in his search for the goodies. This is a good—but not great—adventure film.

1966　　　　92 minutes

CORSICAN BROTHERS, THE
★★★½

DIRECTOR: Gregory Ratoff
CAST: Douglas Fairbanks Jr., Ruth Warrick, J. Carrol Naish, Akim Tamiroff, H. B. Warner, Henry Wilcoxon

Alexandre Dumas's classic story of twins who remain spiritually tied, though separated, crackles in this lavish old Hollywood production. Intrigue and swordplay abound. Douglas Fairbanks Jr. is fine, backed by two of the best supporting players ever: J. Carrol Naish and Akim Tamiroff.

1941　　　B & W 112 minutes

CORVETTE SUMMER
★

DIRECTOR: Matthew Roberts
CAST: Mark Hamill, Kim Melford, Annie Potts

This mindless car-chase film finds Mark Hamill in Las Vegas hunting car thieves who have ripped off his Corvette. This film is not even up to par with *Cannonball Run*. Rated PG.

1978   105 minutes

COTTON CLUB, THE
★★★★½

DIRECTOR: Francis Ford Coppola
CAST: Richard Gere, Diane Lane, James Remar, Gregory Hines, Lonette McKee

Despite all the scandal, an inflated budget of more than $50 million, and some ragged last-minute trimming, *The Cotton Club* is a thing of wonder. With this exciting gangster movie and its fabulous musical numbers, director Francis Coppola recovered from his three-movie slump (*One from the Heart*; *The Outsiders*; and *Rumble Fish*), and Richard Gere gives his best performance ever. The story about two pairs of brothers, one black and one white, is set at Harlem's most famous nightclub. Cornet player Gere and moll Diane Lane make love while gangster James Remar (as Dutch Schultz) fumes, and Gregory Hines dances his way into the heart of songbird Lonette McKee in this flawed but brilliant film. Rated R for violence, nudity, profanity, and suggested sex.

1984   128 minutes

COUNT OF MONTE CRISTO, THE (REMAKE)
★★★½

DIRECTOR: David Greene
CAST: Richard Chamberlain, Tony Curtis, Louis Jourdan, Donald Pleasence, Taryn Power

Superlative TV adaptation of the Alexandre Dumas classic. Richard Chamberlain cuts a dashing figure as the persecuted Edmond Dantes. The casting of Tony Curtis as the evil Mondego works surprisingly well.

1975   100 minutes

COUNT OF MONTE CRISTO, THE (ORIGINAL)
★★★★

DIRECTOR: Rowland V. Lee
CAST: Robert Donat, Elissa Landi, Irene Hervey, Louis Calhern, Sidney Blackmer, Raymond Walburn, O. P. Heggie

In the title role, Robert Donat heads a superb, fine-tuned cast in this now classic film of Dumas's great story. Innocent sailor Edmund Dantes, falsely accused of aiding the exiled Napoleon and infamously imprisoned for fifteen years, escapes to levy revenge on those who framed him. A secret cache of treasure makes it all very sweet.

1934   B & W 119 minutes

CRAZY MAMA
★★★

DIRECTOR: Jonathan Demme
CAST: Stuart Whitman, Cloris Leachman, Ann Sothern, Jim Backus

Vibrant film blends crime, comedy, and finely drawn characterizations in this story of three women on a crime spree from California to Arkansas and their experiences with the various men they pick up along the way. Successful mixture of music and atmosphere of the 1950s, coupled with a 1970s attitude, makes this an enjoyable film. Rated PG.

1975   82 minutes

CROSS OF IRON
★★★

DIRECTOR: Sam Peckinpah
CAST: James Coburn, Maximilian Schell, James Mason, David Warner

With this action-packed war film, director Sam Peckinpah proved that he hadn't lost the touch that made *Ride the High Country* and *The Wild Bunch* such memorable movies. Still, *Cross of Iron* did not receive much acclaim when released. Perhaps it was the theme: the heroics and humanism of weary German soldiers in World War II. A precursor of *Das Boot*, this film couldn't be called great, but it is certainly an interesting work done by one of Hollywood's more original directors. Rated R.

1977   119 minutes

CRY OF BATTLE
★½

DIRECTOR: Irving Lerner
CAST: James MacArthur, Van Heflin, Rita Moreno, Leopoldo Salcedo, Sidney Clute

The son (James MacArthur) of a wealthy businessman gets caught in the Philippines during the Japanese occupation and has to resort to guerrilla warfare. Poorly directed, but does address the ethical questions of racism and the conduct of war. Not rated; with violence.

1957   B & W   99 minutes

CRY OF THE INNOCENT
★★★½

DIRECTOR: Michael O'Herlihy
CAST: Rod Taylor, Joanna Pettet, Nigel Davenport, Cyril Cusack, Jim Norton, Alexander Knox

This made-for-TV suspense thriller has Rod Taylor playing the grieving husband and father who loses his wife and children when a plane crashes into their summer home in Ireland. When a Dublin detective tells Taylor the crash was no accident, Taylor is determined to find out who planted the bomb in the plane. Joanna Pettet has two parts, first as Taylor's sweet Irish wife and then as a writer who has a theory about corporate espionage that may have led to the crash. This film lacks no excitement as the corporate plot unfolds.

1980   93 minutes

CUBA
★★★

DIRECTOR: Richard Lester
CAST: Sean Connery, Brooke Adams, Jack Weston, Hector Elizondo, Denholm Elliott, Chris Sarandon, Lonette McKee

A thinly veiled remake of *Casablanca*, this Richard Lester film is nonetheless far superior to J. Lee Thompson's similar *Cabo Blanco* (which starred Charles Bronson). Sean Connery and Brooke Adams play one-time lovers renewing their passion amid the dangerous doings during the fall of Batista in 1959. As usual, Lester invests his tale with memorable bits. Rated R.

1979   121 minutes

DAIN CURSE, THE
★

DIRECTOR: E. W. Swackhamer
CAST: James Coburn, Hector Elizondo, Jason Miller, Jean Simmons

A poor, two-hour version of a just passable TV miniseries based on the Dashiell Hammett mystery classic. James Coburn is fine as the dapper detective hero but is thwarted by a muddled screenplay. Unrated.

1978   123 minutes

DAM BUSTERS, THE
★★★★½

DIRECTOR: Michael Anderson
CAST: Richard Todd, Michael Redgrave, Ursula Jeans, Basil Sydney

Richard Todd and Michael Redgrave star in this British film about the development and use of a specially designed bomb to destroy a dam in Germany during World War II. An outstanding cast and great script make this one of the finer World War II films.

1954   102 minutes

DAREDEVILS OF THE RED CIRCLE
★★★

DIRECTOR: William Witney, John English
CAST: Charles Quigley, Herman Brix, David Sharpe, Carole Landis

One of the most action-packed serials of all time pits three college athletes (including former Tarzan Herman Brix and ace stunt man David Sharpe) against the evil #39013, a former convict who disguises himself in order to gain power and exact vengeance on the society that imprisoned him. Malevolently brought to life by Charles Middleton (Ming the Merciless from *Flash Gordon*), convict #39013 and his gang use every dirty trick in the book to destroy the three friends and their damsel in distress, lovely Carole Landis. But they are always outwitted by the quick thinking and athletic prowess of the trio. Fast-paced and well acted, this is one of the sat-

isfying and fondly remembered of the pre—World War II serials.

1939   B & W   12 chapters

DARING DOBERMANS, THE
★★½

DIRECTOR: Byron Chudnow
CAST: Charles Knox Robinson, Tim Considine, David Moses, Joan Caulfield

Fun sequel to *The Doberman Gang* is a little more kiddy-oriented, but it's still okay, featuring another well-planned caper for the canine stars. Rated PG for very light violence and language.

1973   90 minutes

DARK PASSAGE
★★★

DIRECTOR: Delmar Daves
CAST: Humphrey Bogart, Lauren Bacall, Bruce Bennett, Agnes Moorehead

This is an okay Humphrey Bogart vehicle in which the star plays an escaped convict who hides out at Lauren Bacall's apartment while undergoing a face change. The stars are watchable, but the uninspired direction (including some disconcerting subjective camera scenes) and the outlandish plot keep the movie from being a real winner.

1947   B & W   106 minutes

DAS BOOT (THE BOAT)
★★★★★

DIRECTOR: Wolfgang Petersen
CAST: Jurgen Prochnow, Herbert Grongmeyer, Klaus Wennemann

During World War II, forty thousand young Germans served aboard Nazi submarines. Only ten thousand survived. This magnificent $13 million West German film masterpiece recreates the tension and claustrophobic conditions of forty-three men assigned to a U-boat in 1941. This is the English-dubbed version. Rated R for tense situations, violence, and profanity.

1981   150 minutes

DAWN PATROL, THE
★★★★

DIRECTOR: Edmund Goulding
CAST: Errol Flynn, Basil Rathbone, David Niven, Melville Cooper, Barry Fitzgerald, Donald Crisp

This film is what is meant when someone says, "They don't make 'em like that anymore." It has a taut story, a superb cast, and emotionally charged action. Basil Rathbone is excellent as a commanding officer of a frontline British squadron during World War I who has no choice but to order raw replacements into the air against veteran Germans. Errol Flynn and David Niven shine as gentlemen at war. As always, Donald Crisp, one of old Hollywood's best, is superb. Aged it may be, but this is a fine film.

1938   B & W 103 minutes

DAY OF THE JACKAL, THE
★★★★

DIRECTOR: Fred Zinnemann
CAST: Edward Fox, Alan Badel, Tony Britton, Cyril Cusack

Edward Fox is a cunning assassin roaming Europe in hopes of a crack at General Charles de Gaulle. High suspense and a marvelous performance by Fox underscore a strong storyline. Rated PG.

1973   141 minutes

DEADLY FORCE
★★★

DIRECTOR: Paul Aaron
CAST: Wings Hauser, Joyce Ingalls, Paul Shenar, Al Ruscio

The best way to describe this release is *Dirty Harry* meets *Death Wish*. Wings Hauser (*Vice Squad*) plays "Stony" Jackson Cooper, an ex-cop who returns to his old Los Angeles stomping grounds to stomp people until he finds the maniac who stomped a buddy's daughter to death. Unlike *Sudden Impact*, it won't make your day. But you won't be bored. Rated R for violence, nudity, and profanity.

1983   95 minutes

DEATH HUNT
★★★½

DIRECTOR: Peter R. Hunt
CAST: Charles Bronson, Lee Marvin, Andrew Stevens, Angie Dickinson, Carl Weathers, Ed Lauter

Based on the true story of a hazardous manhunt in the Canadian Rockies, *Death Hunt* pits trapper Charles Bronson against Mountie Lee Marvin. This gritty adventure film, directed by Peter Hunt, also features vicious dogfights and bloody shootouts set against the spectacular scenery of the Yukon Territory. Rated R.

1981   97 minutes

DEATH KISS, THE
★★★

DIRECTOR: Edwin L. Marin
CAST: Bela Lugosi, David Manners, Adrienne Ames, John Wray, Vince Barnett, Edward Van Sloan

Entertaining movie-within-a-movie whodunit is a treat for fans of early

1930s films and a pretty well-paced mystery to boot as Bela Lugosi (in fine, hammy form) is embroiled in the investigation of a murder that took place during filming. Familiar faces from the past pop in and out of this little thriller, and Lugosi is reunited with Edward Van Sloan (Dr. Van Helsing to his Dracula), a man who distinguished many classic horror films of that golden age.

1933   B & W   75 minutes

DEATH ON THE NILE
★★★½

DIRECTOR: John Guillermin
CAST: Peter Ustinov, Bette Davis, David Niven, Mia Farrow, Angela Lansbury, George Kennedy, Jack Warden

The second in the series of films based on the Hercule Poirot mysteries, written by Agatha Christie, is good, but nothing special. Peter Ustinov stars as the fussy Belgian detective adrift in Africa with a set of murder suspects well-played by Bette Davis, Angela Lansbury, Jack Warden, Maggie Smith, David Niven, Mia Farrow, and George Kennedy. Even though it features an all-star cast, lavish sets and settings, and a better-than-average Christie plot, this film, directed by John Guillermin (*The Towering Inferno*) tends to sag here and there. While it never becomes boring, it's never really riveting, either. Rated PG.

1978   140 minutes

DEATH SQUAD, THE
★★

DIRECTOR: Harry Falk
CAST: Robert Forster, Michelle Phillips, Claude Akins, Melvyn Douglas

A self-appointed coterie of cops is rubbing out criminals beating the rap on legal technicalities. A former officer is given the job of finding out who's doing it and cleaning house. Clint Eastwood did it all infinitely better in *Magnum Force*. Made for television.

1974   78 minutes

DEATH WISH
★★★★

DIRECTOR: Michael Winner
CAST: Charles Bronson, Hope Lange, Vincent Gardenia, Jeff Goldblum

Charles Bronson gives an excellent performance as Paul Kersey, a mild-mannered New Yorker moved to violence when his daughter is raped and his wife killed by sleazy muggers. It's a gripping story of one man's revenge. Rated R because of nudity and violence (includes a graphic rape scene).

1974   93 minutes

DEATH WISH II
★★

DIRECTOR: Michael Winner
CAST: Charles Bronson, Jill Ireland, Vincent Gardenia, J. D. Cannon, Anthony Franciosa, Ben Frank

This carbon-copy sequel to the successful *Death Wish* is best described as a revolting, violent crime chiller. Picking up where the first left off, Paul Kersey (Charles Bronson) now lives in Los Angeles, where his daughter and his housekeeper (instead of his wife, as in the first *Death Wish*) are murdered. Once again Kersey metes out his own justice. Rated R because of nudity and violence.

1982   93 minutes

DEATH WISH III

DIRECTOR: Michael Winner

CAST: Charles Bronson, Deborah Raffin, Ed Lauter, Martin Balsam

Winner is one of those filmmakers who packs his works with the most revolting scenes imaginable and cloaks them in a phony perspective of righteousness. The *Death Wish* films are the best examples of this. Winner has a hero, Paul Kersey (Charles Bronson), who becomes a bloodthirsty maniac in reaction to the scum around him. We are supposed to cheer him on, but he's as big a puke as the villains he dispatches by the truckload. The formula, now growing very tired, is always the same: Kersey loses a loved one and then goes on a rampage. Someone should go on a rampage and destroy all the copies of this piece of trash. Rated R for violence, profanity, drug use, nudity, and sex.

1985　　　　　　　　99 minutes

DEEP, THE
★★

DIRECTOR: Peter Yates
CAST: Robert Shaw, Jacqueline Bisset, Nick Nolte, Louis Gossett Jr., Eli Wallach, Robert Tessier

The success of *Jaws* prompted this screen adaptation of another Benchley novel, but the results weren't nearly as satisfying. A good cast flounders in this water logged tale of treasure-hunting. Rated PG.

1977　　　　　　　　123 minutes

DEFIANCE
★★★

DIRECTOR: John Flynn
CAST: Jan-Michael Vincent, Art Carney, Theresa Saldona, Danny Aiello, Fernando Lopez

Potent story depicts savage New York street gang terrorizing help-less neighborhood. Outsider Jan-Michael Vincent reluctantly gets involved. This well-directed film packs quite a wallop. Rated R for violence and profanity.

1980　　　　　　　　102 minutes

DELIVERANCE
★★★★★

DIRECTOR: John Boorman
CAST: Jon Voight, Burt Reynolds, Ned Beatty, Ronny Cox, James Dickey

Jon Voight, Burt Reynolds, and Ned Beatty are superb in this first-rate film about a canoe trip down a dangerous river that begins as a holiday but soon turns into a weekend of sheer horror. Based on the novel by James Dickey. Rated R for profanity, sex, and violence.

1972　　　　　　　　109 minutes

DELTA FORCE, THE
★★

DIRECTOR: Menahem Golan
CAST: Chuck Norris, Lee Marvin, Martin Balsam, Joey Bishop, Robert Forster, Lainie Kazan, George Kennedy, Hanna Schygulla, Susan Strasberg, Bo Svenson, Robert Vaughn, Shelley Winters

In this disappointing action film, which is perhaps best described as "The Dirty Dozen at the Airport," Chuck Norris and Lee Marvin are leaders of an anti-terrorist group charged with saving the passengers on a hijacked airliner. Director Menahem Golan makes some events in this re-creation of the 1985 hijacking of TWA flight 847 in Athens a bit too realistic and thus works against the comic-book-style heroism of the bulk of the movie. Rated R for profanity and violence.

1986　　　　　　　　126 minutes

DESERT FOX, THE
★★★★
DIRECTOR: Henry Hathaway
CAST: James Mason, Jessica Tandy, Sir Cedric Hardwicke, Luther Adler, Desmond Young

A tour-de-force performance by James Mason marks this film biography of German Field Marshal Rommel. Rommel is treated with great sympathy in this historically accurate depiction of America's one-time enemy. His military exploits are glossed over in favor of the human story of the disillusionment and eventual involvement in the plot to assassinate Hitler.

1951   B & W   88 minutes

DIAMONDS ARE FOREVER
★★★★
DIRECTOR: Guy Hamilton
CAST: Sean Connery, Jill St. John, Charles Gray, Bruce Cabot

This release was supposed to be Sean Connery's last appearance as James Bond before he decided to *Never Say Never Again*. It's good fun for 007 fans and far superior to the Roger Moore films that followed it. Rated PG.

1971   119 minutes

DICK TRACY
★½
DIRECTOR: William Berke
CAST: Morgan Conway, Anne Jeffreys, Mike Mazurki, Jane Greer

Standard second-feature fare with Morgan Conway as an unconvincing Dick Tracy tangling with the denizens of the underworld. Mike Mazurki, fresh from his role as Moose Malloy in Raymond Chandler's *Murder My Sweet*, provides all the color as the man Dick Tracy has to deal with. Ralph Byrd, who created the role of Dick Tracy in the serials and continued on into feature films and television, is sorely needed to make this one work.

1945   B & W   62 minutes

DICK TRACY MEETS GRUESOME
★★½
DIRECTOR: John Rawlins
CAST: Ralph Byrd, Boris Karloff, Anne Gwynne, Edward Ashley, June Clayworth

Everybody's favorite Dick Tracy, Ralph Byrd, returns to the role he originated in serials for Republic Studios just in time to do battle with Gruesome, played with his usual style by the great Boris Karloff. Although ten years older than when he started the series, Byrd, like Buster Crabbe in the Flash Gordon serials, brings a conviction to his character that redeems the slim storyline and often meager production values and effects. As usual, Boris Karloff is eminently watchable and makes a fine addition to Chester Gould's gallery of bizarre villains.

1947   B & W   65 minutes

DILLINGER
★★★
DIRECTOR: Max Nosseck
CAST: Edmund Lowe, Anne Jeffreys, Lawrence Tierney, Eduardo Ciannelli, Marc Lawrence, Elisha Cook Jr.

A genre film, this look at the life and style of archetypal American gangster/antihero John Dillinger bids fair to be rated a *film noir*. Tough guy off-screen Lawrence Tierney is perfect in the title role. Baddy lovers will be delighted by old pros Eduardo Ciannelli, Marc Lawrence, and Elisha Cook, Gutman's boy Wilmer in *The Maltese Falcon*. Remade in color in 1973.

1945   B & W   89 minutes

DINNER AT THE RITZ
★★½

DIRECTOR: Harold Schuster
CAST: David Niven, Paul Lukas, Annabella, Romney Brent

Good cast makes British whodunit about Annabella seeking her father's murderer an enjoyable diversion. Well-produced, with just a light enough touch to balance out all the familiar elements of crime melodrama. Early David Niven effort displays his unique qualities at comedy and light drama.

1937   B & W   77 minutes

DIRTY DOZEN, THE
★★★★½

DIRECTOR: Robert Aldrich
CAST: Lee Marvin, Ernest Borgnine, Charles Bronson, Jim Brown, John Cassavetes, Donald Sutherland, Clint Walker

Lee Marvin is assigned to take a group of military prisoners behind German lines and strike a blow for the Allies. It's a terrific entertainment—funny, star-studded, suspenseful, and even touching. In short, a real winner.

1967   145 minutes

DIRTY HARRY
★★★★½

DIRECTOR: Don Siegel
CAST: Clint Eastwood, Harry Guardino, John Mitchum, Reni Santoni, Andy Robinson

This is the original and still the best screen adventure of Clint Eastwood's maverick San Francisco detective. Outfoxed by a maniacal killer (Andy Robinson), "Dirty Harry" Callahan finally decides to deal out justice in his own inimitable and controversial fashion for an exciting, edge-of-your-seat climax. Rated R.

1971   102 minutes

DISAPPEARANCE, THE
★★★★

DIRECTOR: Stuart Cooper
CAST: Donald Sutherland, Francine Racete, David Hemmings, John Hurt, Christopher Plummer

This exciting film has Donald Sutherland portraying a professional hit man who can't do his job properly after his wife disappears. He pursues a top man in the organization (Christopher Plummer) because he believes that he is responsible for his wife's disappearance. The ironic ending only adds to the many twists and turns throughout this very watchable film. Rated R for sex and violence.

1977   80 minutes

DOBERMAN GANG, THE
★★½

DIRECTOR: Byron Chudnow
CAST: Byron Mabe, Julie Parrish, Simmy Bow, Hal Reed

A vicious pack of Doberman pinschers are trained as bank robbers in this implausible but well-made action tale. Rated PG for language, mild violence.

1972   87 minutes

DR. KILDARE'S STRANGE CASE
★★★

DIRECTOR: Harold S. Bucquet
CAST: Lew Ayres, Lionel Barrymore, Laraine Day, Nat Pendleton, Samuel S. Hinds, Emma Dunn

Friendly old Dr. Gillespie and his medical whiz junior, Dr. Kildare, are featured in this tale of the deranged. Lew Ayres deals with a cuckoo. Nurse Laraine Day provides love interest; Lionel Barrymore is at the ready to counsel as Dr. Gillespie. This is one of the best of the Kildare series.

1940   B & W   76 minutes

DR. NO
★★★★

DIRECTOR: Terence Young
CAST: Sean Connery, Ursula Andress, Jack Lord, Bernard Lee

The first of the James Bond movie sensations, it was in this film that Sean Connery began his ascent to stardom as the indomitable British secret agent 007. Bond is sent to Jamaica to confront the evil Dr. No, a villain bent on world domination. Ursula Andress was the first of the (now traditional) sensual Bond heroines. As with most of the series's films, there is a blend of nonstop action and tongue-in-cheek humor.

1963   111 minutes

DOGS OF WAR, THE
★★

DIRECTOR: John Irvin
CAST: Christopher Walken, Tom Berenger, Colin Blakely, Hugh Millais

A graphic account of the coup d'etat of a West African dictatorship (starring Christopher Walken as the leader of a band of mercenaries), this film depicts a senseless act of violence totally motivated by the lust for wealth and power. Unfortunately, this movie doesn't quite hold together. With a more carefully drawn script and more skillful direction, Dogs of War could have been a very powerful film. Instead, we are presented with a sometimes fascinating and sometimes dull entertainment, which is worth watching only if you have nothing better to do. Rated R for violence.

1980   102 minutes

$ (DOLLARS)
★★★★★

DIRECTOR: Richard Brooks
CAST: Warren Beatty, Goldie Hawn, Gert Fröbe, Robert Webber

Simply one of the best heist capers ever filmed. Warren Beatty, bank employee, teams with Goldie Hawn, hooker, to duplicate critical safe deposit keys for a cool $1.5 million. Intriguing concept, deftly directed in a fashion that reveals continuous unexpected plot twists. Gert Fröbe is a great villain, in his best part since Goldfinger. The picture concludes with a harrowing chase that lasts nearly half an hour. Don't miss this one. Rated R for violence and sexual situations.

1972   119 minutes

DON IS DEAD, THE
★★★½

DIRECTOR: Richard Fleischer
CAST: Anthony Quinn, Frederic Forrest, Robert Forster, Al Lettieri, Angel Tompkins, Charles Cioffi

Director Richard Fleisher (Boston Strangler, Mr. Majestyk) gives us yet another story of a Mafia family struggling for control of Las Vegas interest (à la The Godfather). Well-acted performances make for better-than-average viewing in this movie about the code of honor among thieves. Rated R for violence.

1973   115 minutes

DONOVAN'S REEF
★★★

DIRECTOR: John Ford
CAST: John Wayne, Lee Marvin, Elizabeth Allen, Jack Warden, Dorothy Lamour

Director John Ford's low, knock-about style of comedy prevails in this tale of two old drinking, sea-faring buddies—John Wayne and Lee Marvin—forced to set aside their playful head-knocking to aid another pal, Jack Warden, in putting on an air of respectability to impress the latter's visiting daughter (Elizabeth Allen).

1963   109 minutes

DR. SYN
★★½

DIRECTOR: Roy William Neill
CAST: George Arliss, Margaret Lockwood, John Loder, Roy Emerton, Graham Moffatt

Master character actor George Arliss's final film has him playing a traditional English vicar who blossoms into a pirate when the sun goes down. Nothing earthshaking here, but direction and rich atmosphere make it all palatable.

1937   B & W   80 minutes

DRAGNET
★★★★

DIRECTOR: Jack Webb
CAST: Jack Webb, Ben Alexander, Richard Boone, Ann Robinson, Dennis Weaver

Dragnet is the feature-length (color!) version of the popular detective series with director-star Jack Webb as the no-nonsense Sgt. Joe Friday, and Ben Alexander as his original partner, Frank Smith. In the story, based as always on a true case, Friday and Smith are assigned to solve the murder of a mobster. All clues seem to lead to his former associates.

1954   89 minutes

DRESSED TO KILL
★★★

DIRECTOR: Roy William Neill

CAST: Basil Rathbone, Nigel Bruce, Patricia Morrison, Edmund Breon, Frederic Worlock, Harry Cording

Final entry in Universal's popular Rathbone/Bruce Sherlock Holmes series. This one involves counterfeiting, specifically a Bank of England plate hidden in one of three music boxes. Even in this, his fourteenth outing as the master sleuth, Basil Rathbone retains all the dramatic integrity for which his portrayal is known. After filming was completed, Rathbone—fearing typecasting—had had enough; his concerns clearly were genuine, as he did not work again for nearly nine years. Unrated—suitable for family viewing.

1946   B & W   72 minutes

DRIVER, THE
★★★★

DIRECTOR: Walter Hill
CAST: Ryan O'Neal, Bruce Dern, Isabelle Adjani, Ronee Blakley, Matt Clark

High-energy crime drama focuses on a professional getaway driver (Ryan O'Neal) and his police pursuer (Bruce Dern). Walter Hill's break-neck pacing and spectacular chase scenes make up for the lack of plot or character development. It's an action movie pure and simple. Rated R for violence and profanity.

1978   90 minutes

DROWNING POOL, THE
★★½

DIRECTOR: Stuart Rosenberg
CAST: Paul Newman, Joanne Woodward, Anthony Franciosa, Richard Jaeckel, Murray Hamilton, Melanie Griffith, Gail Strickland, Linda Haynes

Poor followup to *Harper*, with Paul Newman re-creating the title role.

Director Stuart Rosenberg (*Brubaker*) doesn't come up with anything fresh in this stale entry into the detective genre. Rated PG—violence.

1976   108 minutes

DRUMS
★★★½

DIRECTOR: Zoltan Korda
CAST: Sabu, Raymond Massey, Valerie Hobson, Roger Livesey, David Tree

Stiff-upper-lip British Empire epic starts slow but builds to an exciting climax as soldiers of the queen aid young Prince Sabu in his struggle against usurping uncle Raymond Massey. Early Technicolor adds to the overall tone of this action drama, one of nearly a dozen pro-British war spectacles made in the magic era between 1935 and 1940. Massey as the crazed pretender to the throne is a standout and young Sabu is at his beguiling best, while Valerie Hobson (better known as Henry Frankenstein's wife in *Bride of Frankenstein*) is a beautiful addition to any film.

1938   99 minutes

DUELLISTS, THE
★★★★

DIRECTOR: Ridley Scott
CAST: Keith Carradine, Harvey Keitel, Albert Finney, Edward Fox, Cristina Raines, Robert Stephens, Tom Conti

The Duellists traces a long and seemingly meaningless feud between two soldiers in the Napoleonic Wars. This fascinating study of honor among men is full of irony and heroism. Keith Carradine plays Armand D'Hubert, a young Hussar who is sent by his general to arrest a hotheaded officer, Gabriel Feraud (Harvey Keitel), for dueling. In the process, D'Hubert finds himself challenged by Feraud to a swordfight. Reluctantly, he obliges and wounds his opponent. But that is not the end of it. Rated R.

1977   101 minutes

EAGLE HAS LANDED, THE
★★★

DIRECTOR: John Sturges
CAST: Michael Caine, Donald Sutherland, Robert Duvall

Michael Caine is a Nazi agent who is given orders to plan and carry out the kidnapping or murder of Prime Minister Churchill. This movie gets started on a promising note, but it is sabotaged by a weak, contrived ending. Rated PG.

1977   123 minutes

EARTHLING, THE
★★★½

DIRECTOR: Peter Collinson
CAST: William Holden, Ricky Schroder, Jack Thompson, Olivia Hamnett, Alwyn Kurts

A dying man (William Holden) and an orphaned boy (Ricky Schroder) meet in the Australian wilderness in this surprisingly absorbing family film. Despite some glaring flaws, this is an extremely enjoyable piece of entertainment for young and old, thanks primarily to the direction of Peter Collinson and the magnificent photography of Don McAlpine. A warning to parents: There is a minor amount of profanity, and a scene in which the boy's mother and father are killed may be too shocking for small children. Rated PG.

1980   102 minutes

EARTHQUAKE
★

DIRECTOR: Mark Robson

CAST: Charlton Heston, Genevieve Bujold, Lorne Greene, Ava Gardner, Walter Matthau, George Kennedy

Once you get past the special-effects mastery of seeing Los Angeles destroyed, you've got a pretty weak film on your hands. The old classic *San Francisco* did it better. Acting honors go to Walter Matthau, who plays a drunk. Everyone else looks as though they really are in the middle of a week-long bender. If they weren't, they should have been, especially Lorne Greene and Ava Gardner. Rated PG.

1974   129 minutes

EAT MY DUST
★

DIRECTOR: Charles Griffith

CAST: Ron Howard, Christopher Norris, Dave Madden, Warren Kemmerling

A low-budget 1976 race yarn notable only for the fact that it gave Ron Howard the power to direct his next starring vehicle, *Grand Theft Auto*, which, in turn, led to such treats as *Night Shift* and *Splash*. Rated PG.

1976   90 minutes

EDDIE MACON'S RUN
★★½

DIRECTOR: Jeff Kanew

CAST: John Schneider, Kirk Douglas, Lee Purcell, Leah Ayres

John Schneider, of television's "Dukes of Hazard," makes his silver screen debut as a prison escapee who manages to stay one step ahead of the law. Kirk Douglas co-stars as the hard-nosed policeman on his trail. It's a predictable, lightweight movie obviously tailored for "Dukes" watchers. The results are nothing to write home about, yet it is rarely boring. Rated PG for vulgar language and violence.

1983   95 minutes

EIGER SANCTION, THE
★★½

DIRECTOR: Clint Eastwood

CAST: Clint Eastwood, George Kennedy, Jack Cassidy, Thayer David, Vonette McGee

Laughable but entertaining adaptation of Trevanian's equally laughable but entertaining novel. Clint Eastwood is a college professor by day (named Hemlock, no less) and supersecret agent by night sent to expose a killer during a dangerous mountain climb. Outrageously overblown characters with silly names—a woman called "Buns," for example—and plenty of opportunities for Eastwood to strut his macho stuff, but it's all in good fun. A good soundtrack by John Williams, which helps relieve the picture's length. Hardly a classic, but who cares? Rated R for violence and sex.

1975   128 minutes

8 MILLION WAYS TO DIE
★★★

DIRECTOR: Hal Ashby

CAST: Jeff Bridges, Rosanna Arquette, Alexandra Paul, Andy Garcia

An alcoholic ex-cop, Jeff Bridges, attempts to help a high-priced L.A. prostitute get away from her boss and crazed Colombian coke dealer boyfriend, Andy Garcia. This only leads to her death and sends him into the nether world of cocaine dealers and expensive hookers. Considering the talent involved, this one should have been a real killer, but there are too many holes in the script and several dead spots throughout. Bridges and Garcia walk off with the acting honors while director Hal Ashby fails to capture the fire of his earlier works—such as *Shampoo* and *Harold and Maude*. Rated R for violence, nudity, and language.

1986   115 minutes

EL CID
★★★

DIRECTOR: Anthony Mann
CAST: Charlton Heston, Sophia Loren, Raf Vallone, Hurd Hatfield

Some of the best battle action scenes ever filmed are included in this 1961 spectacle about the medieval Spanish hero El Cid. Unfortunately, on smaller home screens much of the splendor will be lost. You will be left with the wooden Charlton Heston and the beautiful Sophia Loren in a love story that was underdeveloped due to the movie's emphasis on spectacle.

1961   184 minutes

ELEPHANT BOY
★★★

DIRECTOR: Robert Flaherty, Zoltan Korda
CAST: Sabu, W. E. Holloway, Walter Hudd, Bruce Gordon

Sabu, in later years the butt of many cheap jokes, made his film debut and became a star in this drama about a boy who claims to know where elephants go to die. Robert Flaherty's direction gives the film a travelogue quality, but it interests and delights just the same. The Indian atmosphere and backgrounds are true and authentic. A Rudyard Kipling story provided the plot.

1937   B & W   80 minutes

11 HARROWHOUSE
★★½

DIRECTOR: Aram Avakian
CAST: Charles Grodin, Candice Bergen, James Mason, John Gielgud

Confused heist caper which vacillates too wildly between straight drama and dark comedy. Diamond salesman Charles Grodin is talked into stealing valuable gems. Too farfetched to be taken seriously, yet that seems to be the intent. An excellent cast goes to waste. Rated PG—mild sexual overtones.

1974   95 minutes

EMERALD FOREST, THE
★★★★

DIRECTOR: John Boorman
CAST: Powers Boothe, Meg Foster, Charley Boorman

In this riveting adventure film based on a true story, Powers Boothe stars as Bill Markham, an American engineer who, with his family, goes to the Amazon jungle to build a dam. There, his 5-year-old son is stolen by a native tribe known as the Invisible People. Markham spends the next ten years trying to find his son. Rated R for nudity, suggested sex, profanity, and violence.

1985   110 minutes

ENDLESS SUMMER, THE
★★★★

DIRECTOR: Bruce Brown
CAST: Mike Hynson, Robert August

The only surfing documentary ever to gain an audience outside the "Beach Boy" set, this is an imaginatively photographed travelogue that captures the joy, danger, and humor of two youths searching worldwide for the perfect wave.

Much of the success is attributable to the whimsical narration. You don't have to be a surfer to enjoy this picture.

1966   95 minutes

ENFORCER, THE
★★★★

DIRECTOR: James Fargo
CAST: Clint Eastwood, Tyne Daly, Harry Guardino, Bradford Dillman, John Mitchum

A step up from the muddled *Magnum Force* and a nice companion piece to *Dirty Harry*, this third entry in the popular series has detective Harry Callahan grudgingly team with a female cop (Tyne Daly) during his pursuit of a band of terrorists. John Mitchum gives a standout performance in his final series bow as tough cop Frank DiGeorgio. It'll make your day. Rated R.

1976   96 minutes

ENIGMA
★★

DIRECTOR: Jeannot Szwarc
CAST: Martin Sheen, Brigitte Fossey, Sam Neill, Derek Jacobi, Michael Lonsdale, Frank Finlay

Espionage yarn succumbs to lethargy. The KGB sics an elite group of assassins on five Soviet dissidents. A CIA agent (Martin Sheen) attempts to thwart the insidious scheme by entangling his former lover with the top Russian agent. Uninteresting intrigue. Rated PG.

1982   101 minutes

ENTER THE DRAGON
★★★★

DIRECTOR: Robert Clouse

CAST: Bruce Lee, John Saxon, Jim Kelly, Ahna Capri, Yang Tse, Angela Mao

Bruce Lee soared to international superstardom with this fast-paced, tongue-in-cheek kung-fu film. A big-budget American version of the popular Chinese genre, it has a good plot and strong performances—from Lee, John Saxon, and Jim Kelly. In short, it's highly enjoyable and highly recommended. Rated R, due to violence.

1973   97 minutes

ENTER THE NINJA
★★

DIRECTOR: Menahem Golan
CAST: Franco Nero, Susan George, Sho Kosugi, Alex Courtney

A passable martial arts adventure about practitioners of an ancient Oriental art of killing. Rated R.

1981   94 minutes

ESCAPE FROM ALCATRAZ
★★★★

DIRECTOR: Don Siegel
CAST: Clint Eastwood, Patrick McGoohan, Roberts Blossom, Jack Thibeau

Any movie that combines the talents of star Clint Eastwood and director Don Siegel is more than watchable. This is a gripping and believable film about the 1962 breakout from the supposedly perfect prison. Patrick McGoohan is also excellent as the neurotic warden. Rated PG.

1979   112 minutes

ESCAPE FROM NEW YORK
★★★½

DIRECTOR: John Carpenter

CAST: Kurt Russell, Lee Van Cleef, Ernest Borgnine, Donald Pleasence, Adrienne Barbeau

The year is 1997. Air Force One—with the president (Donald Pleasence) on board—is hijacked by a group of revolutionaries and sent crashing into the middle of Manhattan, which has been turned into a top-security prison. It's up to Snake Plassken (Kurt Russell), a former war hero gone renegade, to get him out in twenty-four hours. That's the premise of this science-fiction–adventure film by director John Carpenter. Like *Halloween* and *The Fog*, Carpenter's previous films, it's fun, surprised-filled entertainment from beginning to end. Rated R.

1981   99 minutes

ESCAPE TO ATHENA
★★★
DIRECTOR: George Pan Cosmatos
CAST: Roger Moore, Telly Savalas, David Niven, Claudia Cardinale, Stephanie Powers, Richard Roundtree, Elliott Gould, Sonny Bono

Roger Moore as a Nazi officer? Sonny Bono as a member of the Italian Resistance? Elliott Gould as a hippie in a World War II concentration camp? Sound ridiculous? It is. *Escape to Athena* is a silly, improbable movie. It's a "Hogan's Heroes" for the big screen but, in a dumb sort of way, entertaining. Rated PG.

1979   101 minutes

EVEL KNIEVEL
★★½
DIRECTOR: Marvin C. Homsky
CAST: George Hamilton, Sue Lyon, Rod Cameron

Autobiography of motorcycle stunt man Evel Knievel. George Hamilton is surprisingly good as Knievel. Some nice stunts. Rated PG.

1972   90 minutes

EVIL THAT MEN DO, THE
★★★½
DIRECTOR: J. Lee Thompson
CAST: Charles Bronson, Theresa Saldana, José Ferrer, Joseph Maher

Believe it or not, Charles Bronson has made a watchable film for a change. This revenge film à la *Death Wish* is not classic, mind you. But it is definitely much better than the sort of junk Bronson has been associated with in the last few years. In it, Bronson plays a professional killer who comes out of retirement to avenge the brutal murder of an old friend. Rated R for violence and profanity.

1984   90 minutes

EVIL UNDER THE SUN
★★★★
DIRECTOR: Guy Hamilton
CAST: Peter Ustinov, Jane Birkin, Colin Blakely, James Mason, Roddy McDowall, Diana Rigg, Maggie Smith, Nicholas Clay

This highly entertaining mystery, starring Peter Ustinov as Agatha Christie's Belgian detective Hercule Poirot, is set on a remote island in the Adriatic Sea where a privileged group gathers at a luxury hotel. Of course, someone is murdered and Poirot cracks the case. Rated PG because of a scene involving a dead rabbit.

1982   102 minutes

EXTERMINATOR, THE
★★
DIRECTOR: James Glickenhaus

CAST: Christopher George, Samantha Eggar, Robert Ginty, Steve James, Tony DiBenedetto

The Exterminator is a low-budget, extraordinarily violent film. It's the story of a vigilante who takes the law into his own hands when the law refuses to punish the gang members who make a cripple of his best friend during a mugging. The hero runs down the guilty gang and wipes them out, thereby doing the community a favor. He becomes a media hero, and the cops look the other way as he wages his one-man war on crime. Rated R.

1980   101 minutes

EXTERMINATOR 2, THE
🦃

DIRECTOR: Mark Buntzman
CAST: Robert Ginty, Deborah Gefner, Frankie Faison, Mario Van Peeples

In this disgusting cheapo, Robert Ginty returns as the one-man vigilante force set on cleaning up New York City à la *Death Wish*. He's just another Vietnam vet who's sick and tired of all the funny-looking people who rule the midnight streets of the Big Apple and make life miserable for law-abiding taxpayers. This time, though, our "hero" has graduated from using a gun to using a blowtorch. Rated R for violence, nudity, and profanity.

1984   104 minutes

EYE FOR AN EYE
★★½

DIRECTOR: Steve Carver
CAST: Chuck Norris, Christopher Lee, Richard Roundtree, Matt Clark

This surprisingly entertaining kung-fu movie features Chuck Norris as a human weapon battling a variety of bullies. Shawn Kane (Norris) is an ex-cop trying to crack a narcotics-smuggling ring. With the help of a lovely news editor (Maggie Cooper) and a martial arts master (Matt Clark) who doubles as a walking fortune cookie, Kane confronts a sinister Christopher Lee and, finally, a human tank called The Professor. This fist-and-foot opera features some passable acting, good action sequences, and even some intended laughs. Rated R.

1981   106 minutes

EYE OF THE NEEDLE
★★★½

DIRECTOR: Richard Marquand
CAST: Donald Sutherland, Ian Bannen, Kate Nelligan, Christopher Cazenove

Never read the book before you see the movie. That way, there's less chance of being disappointed—as we were with this screen version of Ken Follett's enthralling suspense novel. Donald Sutherland stars as the deadly Nazi agent who discovers a ruse by the Allies during World War II and attempts to get the information to his superiors. Sutherland is excellent. The rest of the film, however, suffers because the novel's hero (played by Ian Bannen) has been all but eliminated. That throws the screen version of *Eye of the Needle* a bit off balance. Nevertheless, it does have plenty of suspense and thrills for those new to the story. Rated R because of nudity, sex, and violence.

1981   112 minutes

F/X
★★★½

DIRECTOR: Robert Mandel

CAST: Bryan Brown, Brian Dennehy, Diane Venora, Cliff De Young, Mason Adams, Jerry Orbach

In this fast-paced, well-acted suspense thriller, Bryan Brown (*Breaker Morant*) plays special effects wizard Rollie Tyler, who accepts thirty thousand dollars from the Justice Department's Witness Relocation Program to stage the fake assassination of a mob figure who has agreed to name names. After he successfully fulfills his assignment, Tyler is double-crossed and must use his wits and movie magic to survive. Rated R for profanity, suggested sex, and violence.

1986   110 minutes

FALCON TAKES OVER, THE
★★★

DIRECTOR: Irving Reis
CAST: George Sanders, James Gleason, Ward Bond, Hans Conried, Lynn Bari

Early entry in the popular *Falcon* mystery film series sets star George Sanders in a search for a missing woman. During the course of this search he encounters a good many of Hollywood's favorite character actors and actresses as well as much of the plot from Raymond Chandler's *Farewell My Lovely*, of which this is the first filmed version. Well-acted, entertaining, and a gem for lovers of mystery fiction.

1942   B & W 63 minutes

FAMILY, THE
★★★

DIRECTOR: Sergio Sollima
CAST: Charles Bronson, Jill Ireland, Telly Savalas, Michael Constantine, George Savalas

Charles Bronson is mad. Some creep framed him and, what's worse, stole his girl! Bronson is out for revenge. This film has plenty of action, but nothing new to offer. Rated R.

1970   100 minutes

FAREWELL MY LOVELY
★★★★½

DIRECTOR: Dick Richards
CAST: Robert Mitchum, Charlotte Rampling, John Ireland, Sylvia Miles, Harry Dean Stanton, Jack O'Halloran

This superb film adaptation of Raymond Chandler's celebrated mystery novel stands as a tribute to the talents of actor Robert Mitchum. In director Dick Richards's brooding classic of *film noir*, Mitchum makes a perfect, world-weary Philip Marlowe, private eye. The detective's search for the long-lost love of gangster Moose Malloy (Jack O'Halloran) takes us into the nether world of post–World War II Los Angeles for a fast-paced, fascinating period piece. Rated R.

1975   97 minutes

FASTER PUSSYCAT! KILL! KILL!
★★★½

DIRECTOR: Russ Meyer
CAST: Tura Satana, Haji, Jori Williams, Juan Bernard

This movie has everything you could want from a Russ Meyer film. Beautiful girls, fast-paced action, and lots of wild and wacky humor. In its day it was considered fairly hard-core, yet today it could even be shown on late-night television. For fans of the unusual and the bizarre.

1962   B & W 83 minutes

FEAR CITY
★★

DIRECTOR: Abel Ferrara

CAST: Tom Berenger, Billy Dee Williams, Rae Dawn Chong, Melanie Griffith, Rossano Brazzi, Jack Scalia

After a promising directorial debut with *Ms. 45*, Abel Ferrara backslid with this all-too-familiar tale about a psychopath killing prostitutes in New York City. Some good performances and action sequences still can't save this one. Rated R for violence, nudity, and profanity.

1985   93 minutes

FFOLKES
★★½

DIRECTOR: Andrew V. McLaglen
CAST: Roger Moore, James Mason, Anthony Perkins, Michael Parks, David Hedison

Of course, no movie with Roger Moore is a classic, but this tongue-in-cheek spy thriller with the actor playing against his James Bond stereotype provides some good, campy entertainment. This film features Moore as a woman-hating, but cat-loving, gun for hire who takes on a band of terrorists. Rated PG.

1980   99 minutes

FIFTH MUSKETEER, THE
★★

DIRECTOR: Ken Annakin
CAST: Beau Bridges, Sylvia Kristel, Ursula Andress, Cornel Wilde, Olivia De Havilland, José Ferrer, Rex Harrison, Lloyd Bridges, Alan Hale

You really can't blame filmmakers for taking advantage of the popularity of Richard Lester's two superb swashbucklers, *The Three Musketeers* and *The Four Musketeers*, can you? You can if it's as bad as this uninspired retelling of *The Man in the Iron Mask*. Beau

Bridges is watchable enough as King Louis XIV and his twin brother, Philipe, who was raised as a peasant by D'Artagnan (Cornel Wilde) and the three musketeers (Lloyd Bridges, José Ferrer, and Alan Hale). It sounds promising. However, the film never springs to life. Rated PG.

1979   103 minutes

FIGHTING BACK
★★★

DIRECTOR: Robert Leiberman
CAST: Robert Urich, Art Carney, Bonnie Bedelia, Richard Herd, Howard Cosell, Simone Griffeth

It may not be totally realistic, but this film is so action-packed that you'll be captivated throughout. A deli owner decides to organize a neighborhood committee against crime after his wife and mother are victims of violence. Unfortunately, his emotionalism gets in the way of his professionalism, but he still makes his mark—and you can't help but cheer him on. A rapid succession of violent acts, lots of profanity, and occasional nudity make this R-rated film questionable for young audiences.

1980   100 minutes

FIGHTING SEABEES, THE
★★★

DIRECTOR: Edward Ludwig
CAST: John Wayne, Dennis O'Keefe, Susan Hayward, William Frawley, Duncan Renaldo

John Wayne and Dennis O'Keefe are construction workers fighting the Japanese in their own way while each attempts to woo Susan Hayward away from the other. This 1944 war film, which co-stars William Frawley, is actually better than it sounds.

1944   B & W 100 minutes

FINAL CHAPTER—WALKING TALL
★

DIRECTOR: Jack Starrett
CAST: Bo Svenson, Margaret Blye, Forrest Tucker, Lurene Tuttle, Morgan Woodward, Libby Boone

The original *Walking Tall* surprised everyone by becoming a big box-office success. It was a cheaply made, often amateurish film with only graphic violence, a basis in truth, and a powerful performance by Joe Don Baker. Apparently that was enough. The film spawned many imitators, some starring Baker, and two sequels, that oddly enough, did not. The last one is titled *Final Chapter*. While it is not as bad technically as the first, which included an outdoor scene with a boom microphone in plain view, it is flawed just the same, because the script has nothing new to tell us about the life of the protagonist, Buford T. Pusser (Bo Svenson). Rated R for violence.

1977   112 minutes

FINAL JUSTICE

DIRECTOR: Greydon Clark
CAST: Joe Don Baker, Venantino Venantini, Helena Abella, Bill McKinney

In this incoherent ripoff of the Clint Eastwood cops-and-robbers film *Coogan's Bluff*, Joe Don Baker plays a rural sheriff who travels to Italy to take on the Mafia and halt criminal activities. Poor dubbing and mindless violence make this a repelling movie. Rated R for nudity, violence, and language.

1984   90 minutes

FINAL OPTION, THE
★★★★

DIRECTOR: Ian Sharp
CAST: Judy Davis, Lewis Collins, Richard Widmark, Robert Webber

Judy Davis stars in this first-rate British-made suspense thriller as the leader of a fanatical anti-nuclear group that takes a group of U.S. and British officials hostage and demands that a nuclear missile be launched at a U.S. base in Scotland. If not, the hostages—who include the American secretary of state (Richard Widmark) and chief of the U.S. Strategic Air Command (Robert Webber)—will die. And it's up to Special Air Services undercover agent Peter Skellen (Lewis Collins) to save their lives. The result is a terrific movie with a hold-your-breath, thrill-a-minute conclusion. Rated R for violence and profanity.

1982   125 minutes

FIREFOX
★★★½

DIRECTOR: Clint Eastwood
CAST: Clint Eastwood, Freddie Longs, David Huffmann, Warren Clarke, Ronald Lacey, Stephan Schnabel

Clint Eastwood doffs his contemporary cowboy garb to direct, produce, and star in this action-adventure film about an American fighter pilot assigned to steal a sophisticated Russian aircraft. The film takes a while to take off, but when it does, it's good, action-packed fun. Rated PG for violence.

1982   124 minutes

FIRE OVER ENGLAND
★★★

DIRECTOR: Alexander Korda

CAST: Laurence Olivier, Vivien Leigh, Flora Robson

A swashbuckling adventure of Elizabethan England's outnumbered stand against the Spanish Armada. Made in the mid 1930s, it wasn't released in this country until 1941, in order to evoke American support and sympathy for Britain's plight against the Nazi Juggernaut during its darkest days. This is only one of the two films that united husband and wife, Laurence Olivier and Vivien Leigh, as co-stars. They play lovers and courtiers to the queen who fight Spanish treachery within the English court.

1936   B & W   92 minutes

FIREPOWER
★★

DIRECTOR: Michael Winner
CAST: Sophia Loren, James Coburn, O. J. Simpson, Eli Wallach, Vincent Gardenia, Anthony Franciosa

Chalk up another loser for director Michael Winner. *Firepower* is a muddled, mindless mess. The film opens with typical Winner violence. A research chemist is blown up by a letter bomb while his wife, Adele Tasca (Sophia Loren), watches helplessly. The chemist was about to prove to the world that a company owned by the third-richest man in the world, Carl Stegner (George Touliatos), has been distributing contaminated drugs responsible for causing the cancerous deaths of a great many people. The widow joins Justice Department agent James Coburn in trying to bring Stegner out of seclusion to face, among other things, charges of tax evasion. Rated R.

1979   104 minutes

FIRST BLOOD
★★★½

DIRECTOR: Ted Kotcheff
CAST: Sylvester Stallone, Richard Crenna, Brian Dennehy, David Caruso, Jack Starrett

Sylvester Stallone is top-notch as a former Green Beret who is forced to defend himself from a redneck cop (Brian Dennehy) in the Oregon Mountains. The action never lets up. A winner for fans. Rated R for violence and profanity.

1982   97 minutes

FIRST DEADLY SIN, THE
★★

DIRECTOR: Brian Hutton
CAST: Frank Sinatra, Faye Dunaway, James Whitmore, David Dukes, Brenda Vaccaro, Martin Gabel, Anthony Zerbe

Lawrence Sanders's excellent mystery is turned into a so-so cop flick with Frank Sinatra looking bored as aging Detective Edward X. Delaney, who is on the trail of a murdering maniac (David Dukes). He, however, fares much better than co-star Faye Dunaway, who spends the entire picture flat on her back in a hospital bed. It's pretty dreary stuff. Rated R.

1980   112 minutes

FIRST YANK INTO TOKYO
★½

DIRECTOR: Gordon Douglas
CAST: Tom Neal, Barbara Hale, Richard Loo, Keye Luke, Benson Fong

Tom Neal has plastic surgery so he can pose as a Japanese soldier and help an American POW escape. As usual, Hollywood casts some fine Asian actors as sinister types. This low-budget melodrama is not worth the time.

1945   B & W   82 minutes

FISTS OF FURY
★★★

DIRECTOR: Lo Wei
CAST: Bruce Lee, Maria Yi, James Tien, Nora Miao

Bruce Lee's first chop-socky movie (made in Hong Kong) is corny, action-filled, and violent. It's no *Enter the Dragon*, but his fans—who have so few films to choose from—undoubtedly will want to see it again. Rated R.

1972   102 minutes

FIVE FOR HELL

DIRECTOR: Frank Kramer
CAST: Klaus Kinski, John Garko, Margaret Lee, Nick Jordan, Sal Borgese, Luciano Rosi, Sam Burke

In this Italian-made World War II bomb, a special unit of American soldiers goes behind enemy lines to copy the plans of an all-out German offensive. The gimmick in this film is that every soldier has an expertise in one thing or another—none of them having anything to do with combat. One guy is an acrobat who takes a trampoline with him so he can do flips over electrified fences. Another soldier is a baseball player who keeps a hardball with him so he can knock out the guards with his pinpoint pitchs. If this sounds ridiculous, that's because it is. Not rated; has sex and violence.

1985   88 minutes

FIVE WEEKS IN A BALLOON
★★★

DIRECTOR: Irwin Allen

CAST: Red Buttons, Barbara Eden, Fabian, Cedric Hardwicke, Peter Lorre, Herbert Marshall, Billy Gilbert, Reginald Owen, Henry Daniell, Barbara Luna, Richard Haydn

Up, up, and away on a balloon expedition to Africa, or, Kenya here we come! Author Jules Verne wrote the story. Nothing heavy here, just good, clean fun and adventure in the mold of *Around the World in Eighty Days*.

1962   101 minutes

FLAME OF THE BARBARY COAST
★★½

DIRECTOR: Joseph Kayne
CAST: John Wayne, Ann Dvorak, William Frawley, Joseph Schildkraut

John Wayne plays a Montana rancher who fights with a saloon owner (Joseph Schildkraut) over the affections of a dance hall girl (Ann Dvorak). This romantic triangle takes place against the backdrop of the San Francisco earthquake. It's watchable, nothing more.

1945   B & W   91 minutes

FLASH AND THE FIRECAT
★

DIRECTOR: Ferd Sebastian
CAST: Richard Kiel, Roger Davis, Tricia Sembera

Flash (Roger Davis) and Firecat (Tricia Sembera) blaze across the California beaches, stealing cars and robbing banks and doing other dumb things. Nevertheless, surprisingly, they outwit the authorities and eventually get away with their crime spree, proving once again that crime pays—but only in trashy movies like this one. Made for television.

1975   94 minutes

FLASHPOINT
★★★½

DIRECTOR: William Tannen
CAST: Kris Kristofferson, Treat Williams, Rip Torn, Kevin Conway, Tess Harper

Kris Kristofferson and Treat Williams star in this taut, suspenseful, and action-filled thriller as two Texas border officers who accidentally uncover an abandoned jeep containing a skeleton, a rifle, and $800,000 in cash—a discovery that puts their lives in danger. Rated PG-13 for profanity and violence.

1984   95 minutes

FLAT TOP
★★

DIRECTOR: Lesley Selander
CAST: Richard Carlson, Sterling Hayden, Keith Larsen, Bill Phillips

A mediocre World War II action film following the exploits of an aircraft carrier battling the Japanese forces in the Pacific. Most of the battle scenes are taken from actual combat footage.

1952   B & W   83 minutes

FLESH AND BLOOD
★★★½

DIRECTOR: Paul Verhoeven
CAST: Rutger Hauer, Jennifer Jason Leigh, Tom Burlinson, Susan Tyrell, Ronald Lacey, Jack Thompson

Set in medieval Europe, *Flesh and Blood* follows the lives of two men—mercenary soldier Rutger Hauer and the son of a feudal lord (Tom Burlinson)—and their love for the same woman (Jennifer Jason Leigh). Like most films by Paul Verhoeven (*Soldier of Orange*, *Spetters*, *The Fourth Man*), the dialogue is awkward, but this weak point is more than made up for by the Dutch director's keen eye for the visceral and erotic. The cast is stellar, the sets are lavish, and the plot turns will keep the viewer guessing, but not in the dark. Rated R for violence, sex, nudity, profanity.

1985   126 minutes

FLETCH
★★★★

DIRECTOR: Michael Ritchie
CAST: Chevy Chase, Joe Don Baker, Tim Matheson, Dana Wheeler-Nicholson, Richard Libertini, M. Emmet Walsh

After seven years and seven disappointing movie performances, Chevy Chase proved that he could be a big-screen presence with this *Beverly Hills Cop*–style cops-and-comedy caper. Chase plays Gregory Mcdonald's wisecracking reporter, I. M. "Fletch" Fletcher, who starts out doing what seems to be a fairly simple expose of drug dealing in Los Angeles and ends up taking on a corrupt cop (Joe Don Baker), a tough managing editor (Richard Libertini), and a powerful millionaire (Tim Matheson) who wants Fletch to kill him. The laughs are plenty and the action almost nonstop in director Michael Ritchie's best film since *The Bad News Bears*. Rated PG for violence and profanity.

1985   96 minutes

FLIGHT OF THE EAGLE
★★★½

DIRECTOR: Jan Troell

CAST: Max von Sydow, Eva Von Hanno

This Swedish production presents the true adventure of three foolhardy 1897 polar explorers (including Max von Sydow) who tried to conquer the Arctic in a balloon. Unrated, the film has some gore. In Swedish with English subtitles.

1982   139 minutes

FLIGHT OF THE PHOENIX, THE
★★★★

DIRECTOR: Robert Aldrich

CAST: James Stewart, Richard Attenborough, Peter Finch, Ernest Borgnine, Hardy Kruger, Ronald Fraser, Christian Marquand, Richard Jaeckel, Ian Bannen, George Kennedy, Dan Duryea

An all-star international cast shines in this gripping adventure about the desert crash of a small plane and the grueling efforts of the meager band of passengers to rebuild and repair it against impossible odds, not the least of which are starvation and/or heat prostration. Tension mounts as the determined bunch begin to realize the futility of their task under the blazing Arabian sun . . . and their own well-fueled tempers. Directed with style by veteran Robert Aldrich in the rugged area near Yuma, Arizona, with stalwart performances by all. Watch this movie by all means, but keep a water cooler handy!

1965   147 minutes

FLYING LEATHERNECKS, THE
★★★½

DIRECTOR: Nicholas Ray

CAST: John Wayne, Robert Ryan, Jay C. Flippen

John Wayne is the apparently heartless commander of an airborne fighting squad, and Robert Ryan is the caring officer who questions his decisions in this well-acted war film from 1951. The stars play off each other surprisingly well, and it's a shame they didn't do more films together.

1951   102 minutes

FLYING TIGERS, THE
★★½

DIRECTOR: David Miller

CAST: John Wayne, Mae Clarke, Gordon Jones

Exciting dogfight action scenes make this low-budget John Wayne World War II vehicle watchable, but the story sags a bit.

1942   B & W 102 minutes

FOLLOW THAT CAR
★

DIRECTOR: Daniel Haller

CAST: Dirk Benedict, Tanya Tucker, Teri Nunn

Typical good-ol'-boy action-adventure with our three stars, Dirk Benedict, Tanya Tucker, and Teri Nunn, joining forces with uncle Sam to get bad guys who are running booze and tobacco without paying any taxes. Lots of singing for Tucker fans and car chases and corny dialogue for the *Cannonball Run* crowd. Nothing new here. Rated PG for language and violence.

1980   96 minutes

FOR YOUR EYES ONLY
★★★★

DIRECTOR: John Glen

CAST: Roger Moore, Carol Bouquet, Lynn-Holly Johnson, Topol

For the first time since Roger Moore took over the role of 007 from Sean Connery, we have a film in the style that made the best Bond films—*From Russia with Love* and *Goldfinger*—so enjoyable. Gone are the outrageous gadgets and campy humor; instead, *For Your Eyes Only* is genuine spy adventure, closer in spirit to the novels by Ian Fleming. Rated PG.

1981   127 minutes

FORCE FIVE
★★

DIRECTOR: Walter Grauman
CAST: Gerald Gordon, Nick Pryor, Bradford Dillman

In this action-packed but predictable martial arts film, a soldier of fortune and his four buddies rescue a woman held against her will by an evil cult leader on a remote island. Rated R for violence, nudity, and profanity.

1975   78 minutes

FORCE OF ONE
★★★

DIRECTOR: Paul Aaron
CAST: Chuck Norris, Jennifer O'Neill, James Whitmore, Pepe Serna

This is the sequel to *Good Guys Wear Black*. In this karate film, Chuck Norris cleans up a California town that has drug problems. As always, it only takes one (Norris) to kick and/or punch some sense into the bad guys. Rated PG.

1979   90 minutes

FORCE TEN FROM NAVARONE
★

DIRECTOR: Guy Hamilton
CAST: Robert Shaw, Harrison Ford, Edward Fox, Franco Nero, Barbara Bach, Carl Weathers, Richard Kiel

This is a really bad film and poor sequel to the classic *Guns of Navarone*. Decent acting is the only good thing you can say about this World War II film of a commando group out to destroy a bridge.

1978   118 minutes

FORCED VENGEANCE
★★½

DIRECTOR: James Fargo
CAST: Chuck Norris, Mary Louise Weller, Camilla Griggs, Michael Cavanaugh, David Opatoshu, Seiji Sakaguchi

Even pacing and a somewhat suspenseful plot are not enough to make this film a must-see—unless you're a die-hard Chuck Norris fan, that is. This time, our martial arts master plays an ex–Vietnam vet turned casino security chief living in the Far East who gets vengeance on an underworld crime syndicate. Rated R for violence, nudity, and profanity.

1982   90 minutes

FOUR DEUCES, THE
★★

DIRECTOR: William H. Bushnell Jr.
CAST: Jack Palance, Carol Lynley, Warren Berlinger, Adam Roarke, Gianni Russo, H. B. Haggerty, John Haymer, Martin Kove, E. J. Peaker

Jack Palance (*Shane*, the *Ripley's Believe It or Not* TV show) is a gang leader during Prohibition times in this high-camp action film about gangsters. Adam Roarke (*The Stunt Man*) plays a reporter who is allowed to follow the boss around and get exclusives on gangland activities. Palance's performance is excellent, but the movie is poorly conceived, with an odd mixture of blood and spoof. Not a black comedy; not a serious drama, either. *The Four Deuces* does not have an MPAA rating, but it contains sex, nudity, violence, and profanity.

1975   87 minutes

FOUR FEATHERS, THE
★★★★

DIRECTOR: Zoltán Korda
CAST: Ralph Richardson, John Clements, June Duprez, C. Aubrey Smith

A young man (John Clements) from a military background is branded a coward when he forsakes military duty for a home and family during time of war. Rejected by his family, friends, and fiancée, he sets out to prove his manhood. This motion picture was one of the few English productions of its era to gain wide acceptance. It still holds up well today.

1939   115 minutes

FOUR HORSEMEN OF THE APOCALYPSE
★★

DIRECTOR: Vincente Minnelli
CAST: Glenn Ford, Ingrid Thulin, Charles Boyer, Lee J. Cobb, Paul Henreid, Paul Lukas

The 1921 silent version of this complex anti-war tale of two brothers who fight on opposite sides during World War I is still the best. When Rudolph Valentino played Julio, you cared. This one, updated to World War II, falls flat, despite a fine cast.

1961   153 minutes

FOUR MUSKETEERS, THE
★★★★★

DIRECTOR: Richard Lester
CAST: Oliver Reed, Raquel Welch, Richard Chamberlain, Frank Finlay, Michael York, Christopher Lee, Faye Dunaway, Charlton Heston

In this superb sequel to Richard Lester's The Three Musketeers, the all-star cast is remarkably good, and the director is at the peak of his form. The final duel between Michael York and Christopher Lee is a stunner. Watched together, the two splendid swashbucklers make a memorable evening of entertainment. If only they made movies this well more often. Rated PG.

1975   108 minutes

FRAMED
★

DIRECTOR: Phil Karlson
CAST: Joe Don Baker, Conny Van Dyke, Gabriel Dell, Brock Peters, John Marley

Thoroughly nauseating and graphically violent story of a man (John Don Baker) framed for a crime he did not commit, and the outrageous lengths to which he resorts in order to clear his name. This is little more than an attempt to capitalize on the success of Walking Tall and deserves to stay buried. Rated R for gory violence and language.

1975   106 minutes

FRENCH CONNECTION, THE
★★★★★

DIRECTOR: William Friedkin
CAST: Gene Hackman, Fernando Rey, Roy Scheider, Eddie Egan, Sonny Gross

Gene Hackman is an unorthodox New York narcotics cop in this Oscar-winning performance. He and his partner (Roy Scheider) are investigating the flow of heroin coming into the city from France. The climactic chase is the best in movie history. Hackman's pursuit of the bad guy in a subway train, his car, and finally by foot is as exciting a scene as Hollywood has ever turned out. Rated R.

1971   104 minutes

FROM RUSSIA WITH LOVE
★★★★½
DIRECTOR: Terence Young
CAST: Sean Connery, Lotte Lenya, Robert Shaw, Daniela Bianchi

The definitive James Bond movie. Sean Connery's second portrayal of Agent 007 is right on target. Lots of action, beautiful women, and great villains. Connery's fight aboard a passenger train with baddy Robert Shaw is as good as they come.

1963   118 minutes

FUNERAL IN BERLIN
★★★½
DIRECTOR: Guy Hamilton
CAST: Michael Caine, Oscar Homolka, Eva Renzi, Paul Hubschmid, Guy Doleman

Second in Michael Caine's series of three "Harry Palmer" films, following *The Ipcress File* and preceding *The Billion-Dollar Brain*. This time, working-class spy Palmer assists in the possible defection of a top Russian security chief (Oscar Homolka). Director Guy Hamilton abandons his usually light touch for this more somber examination of cold war relationships. As usual, Caine can do no wrong; his brittle performance and the authentic footage of the Berlin Wall add considerably to the film's bleak tone. The other, more intriguing, side of James Bond–type secret agents. Unrated; suitable for family viewing.

1967   102 minutes

GAME OF DEATH
★
DIRECTOR: Robert Clouse
CAST: Bruce Lee, Kareem Abdul-Jabbar, Danny Inosanto, Gig Young, Hugh O'Brian, Colleen Camp, Dean Jagger, Chuck Norris

The climactic twenty minutes of Bruce Lee in action fighting Kareem Abdul-Jabbar and Danny Inosanto are thrilling. It's too bad the rest of the film is not. Though top-billed, Lee only appears in those few scenes. He died shortly after their completion. It was left to film producer Raymond Chow and his associates to build a film around them to capitalize on Lee's popularity. The story, designed by Jan Spears to fit the final scenes, is schlocky and inept. Plus, the phony Bruce Lees look nothing like him. Rated R.

1979   102 minutes

GANGSTER WARS
★★½
DIRECTOR: Richard C. Sarafian
CAST: Michael Nouri, Brian Benben, Joe Penny

This TV movie traces the lives of mobsters "Lucky" Luciano, "Bugsy" Siegel, and Meyer Lansky from their childhood friendship on to becoming the most powerful leaders in organized crime during the 1920s. This is an action-packed gangster movie, which at times is difficult to follow and tends to lead the viewer down some deadends. Rated PG for violence.

1981   121 minutes

GATOR
★★
DIRECTOR: Burt Reynolds
CAST: Burt Reynolds, Jack Weston, Lauren Hutton, Jerry Reed, Alice Ghostley, Mike Douglas, Dub Taylor

Burt Reynolds directed this mildly entertaining sequel to *White Lightning*. In it, Burt plays an ex-con out to get revenge—with the help of undercover agent Jack Weston—on some nasty southern politicians. Rated PG.

1976   116 minutes

GAUNTLET, THE
★½

DIRECTOR: Clint Eastwood
CAST: Clint Eastwood, Sondra Locke, Pat Hingle, William Prince

One of actor-director Clint Eastwood's few failures, this release features the squinty-eyed star as an alcoholic, barely capable cop assigned to bring a prostitute (Sondra Locke) to trial. Corrupt officials do everything they can to stop him, which leads to a completely preposterous and violent showdown. Rated R.

1977   109 minutes

GETAWAY, THE
★★★★

DIRECTOR: Sam Peckinpah
CAST: Steve McQueen, Ali MacGraw, Ben Johnson, Sally Struthers

Top-notch adventure and excitement occur when convict Steve McQueen has his wife seduce the Texas Parole Board chairman (Ben Johnson) in exchange for his early freedom. McQueen becomes jealous and resentful after the deal is consummated and kills the chairman, setting off a shotgun-charged chase. High-quality acting and exciting gunfire exchanges orchestrated by master director Sam Peckinpah make this film. Rated PG.

1972   122 minutes

GLITTER DOME, THE
★★½

DIRECTOR: Stuart Margolin
CAST: James Garner, Margot Kidder, John Lithgow, Colleen Dewhurst, John Marley

Made-for-HBO cable television version of Joseph Wambaugh's depressingly downbeat story concerning two police detectives in Los Angeles, James Garner and John Lithgow, out to solve a murder. Both cops appear on the edge of losing control. This one will not go down as one of the better Wambaugh adaptations. Check out *The Onion Field* or *The Black Marble* for the author at his best.

1985   90 minutes

GLORIA
★★★½

DIRECTOR: John Cassavetes
CAST: Gena Rowlands, Buck Henry, John Adames, Julie Carmen, Lupe Buarnica

After his family is executed by the Mafia, a little boy hides out with a female neighbor. Together they must flee or be killed. Gena Rowlands is very good in the title role as the streetwise Gloria, whose savvy and brains keep the two alive. Rated R—language, violence.

1980   121 minutes

GO FOR IT
★★

DIRECTOR: Paul Rapp
CAST: Documentary

Go For It is just like those documentary shorts that sometimes precede a first-run film in order to fill out the program. The only difference is that this is ninety minutes long and repetitive. We see all sorts of leisure sports. Included are snow skiing, surfing, mountain climbing, rafting, hang gliding, and skateboarding. Director Paul Rapp attempts to break the monotony by switching from one sport to another. The result is that the audience keeps expecting the film to end. Rated PG for nudity.

1978   90 minutes

GO TELL THE SPARTANS
★★★★

DIRECTOR: Ted Post
CAST: Burt Lancaster, Craig Wasson, Marc Singer

In one of the best Vietnam war films, Burt Lancaster is as a commander who begins to wonder "what we're doing over there." It's a very honest portrayal of America's early days in Vietnam, with Lancaster giving an excellent performance. Ted Post's direction has never been better. Rated R.

1978   114 minutes

GOLDFINGER
★★★★

DIRECTOR: Guy Hamilton
CAST: Sean Connery, Gert Fröbe, Honor Blackman

This ranks just below *From Russia with Love* as the best of the Bonds. Sean Connery, who recently returned to the role in the big hit *Never Say Never Again*, is at his athletic and sophisticated best as 007, and Gert Fröbe makes a formidable foe in the title role.

1964   108 minutes

GOLIATH AND THE BARBARIANS
★★

DIRECTOR: Carlo Campogalliani
CAST: Steve Reeves, Bruce Cabot, Giulia Rubini, Chelo Alonso

Steve Reeves plays Goliath in this so-so Italian action film. In this episode, he saves Italy from invading barbaric tribes. As in many of Reeves's films, the only object of interest is the flexing of his muscles.

1960   86 minutes

GONE IN 60 SECONDS
★

DIRECTOR: H. B. Halicki
CAST: H. B. Halicki, Marion Busia, George Cole, James McIntyre, Jerry Daugirda

Stuntman-turned-film-auteur H. B. Halicki can wreck a bunch of cars faster than you can say Hal Needham, but when it comes to making a watchable action film, George Miller he ain't. This movie, about a ring of car thieves working under the front of an insurance adjustment firm, is bone dull except for the forty-minute car chase finale, which is twenty minutes too long. Rated PG for violence.

1974   97 minutes

GOOD GUYS WEAR BLACK
★★

DIRECTOR: Ted Post
CAST: Chuck Norris, Anne Archer, James Franciscus, Lloyd Haynes, Jim Backus, Dana Andrews

This Chuck Norris action film starts out well but quickly dissolves into a routine political action-thriller that really goes nowhere. Lightweight entertainment. Rated PG.

1979   96 minutes

GOONIES, THE
★★★

DIRECTOR: Richard Donner
CAST: Sean Astin, Josh Brolin, Jeff Cohen, Corey Feldman, Kerri Green, Martha Plimpton, Ke Huy-Quan

This "Steven Spielberg production" is a mess. But it's sometimes an entertaining mess. Directed in jerky style by Richard Donner (*Superman—The Movie*) from a quirky screenplay by Chris Columbus, it's a grab bag of good and bad. One minute it's frustratingly weird and inane; the next minute something utterly delightful happens. The screenplay, taken from a story by Spielberg, concerns a feisty group of underprivileged kids—whose housing project is about to be destroyed—spending one last adventure-filled Saturday afternoon together. This happens after they find a treasure map, which could be the solution to all their problems. Rated PG for profanity.

1985   111 minutes

GORKY PARK
★★½

DIRECTOR: Michael Apted
CAST: William Hurt, Lee Marvin, Joanna Pacula, Brian Dennehy, Ian Bannen, Alexander Knox

In this maddeningly uninvolving screen version of Martin Cruz Smith's best-selling mystery novel, three mutilated bodies are found in the Moscow park, and it's up to Russian policeman Arkady Renko (a miscast William Hurt) to find the maniacal killer. Lee Marvin is quite good as a suave bad guy, as are Joanna Pacula and Brian Dennehy in their supporting roles. Still, there's something missing in this release, directed by Michael Apted (*Coal Miner's Daughter*). It's a thriller that isn't all that thrilling. Rated R for nudity, sex, violence, and profanity.

1983   128 minutes

GOTCHA!
★★★★

DIRECTOR: Jeff Kanew
CAST: Anthony Edwards, Linda Fiorentino, Alex Rocco, Nick Corri, Marla Adams, Klaus Loewitsch

In this wonderfully entertaining mixture of the coming-of-age comedy and the suspense thriller, a college boy (Anthony Edwards from *Revenge of the Nerds*) goes to Paris in search of romance and adventure. He gets both when he meets a beautiful, mysterious woman (Linda Fiorentino, of *Vision Quest*) who puts both of their lives in danger. When you're not laughing, you're on the edge of your seat. That's what entertainment is all about. Rated PG-13 for slight nudity, suggested sex, profanity, and violence.

1985   97 minutes

GRAND THEFT AUTO
★★½

DIRECTOR: Ron Howard
CAST: Ron Howard, Nancy Morgan

The basic plot of *It's a Mad, Mad, Mad, Mad, World* is given a retread by first-time director—and star—Ron Howard in this frantic 1977 car-chase comedy. Sadly, little of the style that made *Night Shift* and *Splash* such treats is evident here. Rated PG.

1977   89 minutes

GREASED LIGHTNING
★★★

DIRECTOR: Michael Schultz
CAST: Richard Pryor, Pam Grier, Beau Bridges, Cleavon Little, Richie Havens

Greased Lightning is a funny and exciting film. Richard Pryor is a knockout in the lead role, and the film is a real audience pleaser. Because the story is true, it carries a punch even *Rocky* couldn't match. Comparisons of the two films are inevitable, as both center on the ambitions of sports hopefuls and feature slam-bang endings that bring the audience to its feet rooting for the hero. While Rocky Balboa remains a stirring character of fiction, Wendell Scott's story is the more dramatic of the two. Scott was the first black man to break into the lily-white field of car racing. Rated PG.

1977 96 minutes

GREAT RIVIERA BANK ROBBERY, THE
★★★½

DIRECTOR: Francis Megahy
CAST: Ian McShane, Warren Clarke, Stephen Greif, Christopher Malcolm

In 1976, a group of French right-wing terrorists called "The Chain," with the assistance of a gang of thieves, pulled off one of the largest heists in history. The step-by-step illustration of this bold operation proves to be interesting, and the fact that this incident really happened makes this film all the more enjoyable.

1979 98 minutes

GREAT CHASE, THE
★★★★

DIRECTOR: Narrated by Frank Gallop
CAST: Buster Keaton, Douglas Fairbanks Sr., Lillian Gish, Pearl White

Silent film chases from several classics comprise the bulk of this compilation, including the running acrobatics of Douglas Fairbanks in *The Mark of Zorro*, the escape of Lillian Gish over the ice floes in *Way Down East*, and car chases and stunts of all descriptions from silent comedies. A large part of the film is devoted to Buster Keaton's locomotive chase from *The General*.

1963 B & W 79 minutes

GREAT ESCAPE, THE
★★★★★

DIRECTOR: John Sturges
CAST: Steve McQueen, James Garner, Charles Bronson, Richard Attenborough, James Coburn

If ever there was a movie that could be called pure forget-your-troubles entertainment, it's *The Great Escape*. The plot centers around a German prison camp in World War II. The commandant has received the assignment of housing all the escape-minded Allied prisoners, or, as he puts it, "putting all the rotten eggs in one basket." The Germans are obviously playing with fire with this all-star group, and, sure enough, all hell breaks loose with excitement galore.

1963 168 minutes

GREAT SMOKEY ROADBLOCK, THE
★★½

DIRECTOR: John Leone
CAST: Henry Fonda, Eileen Brennan, John Byner, Dub Taylor, Susan Sarandon, Austin Pendleton

Entertaining if somewhat hokey comedy-drama casts Henry Fonda as a trucker on the verge of losing his rig, when along comes a homeless entourage of prostitutes (led by Eileen Brennan), who persuade Henry to take them for a ride. Good-natured film is a good time-passer. Rated PG for language.

1976 84 minutes

GREAT TEXAS DYNAMITE CHASE, THE

★½

DIRECTOR: Michael Pressman

CAST: Claudia Jennings, Jocelyn Jones, Johnny Crawford, Chris Pennock

Bullets and bodies fly in this low-budget cult film about two female bank robbers who blast their way across the countryside. Former Playmate Claudia Jennings adds the extra zest to this otherwise routine drive-in feature. Look for Johnny Crawford, of "The Rifleman" fame, in featured role. Violence, some nudity, suggestive scenes. Rated R.

1977   90 minutes

GREAT TRAIN ROBBERY, THE

★★★★

DIRECTOR: Michael Crichton

CAST: Sean Connery, Lesley-Anne Down, Donald Sutherland, Alan Webb

Michael Crichton's film version of *The Great Train Robbery* is just as entertaining as his novel of the same name. Based on a true incident, this suspense-filled caper has plenty of hooks to keep you interested. But the title may be misleading; it is not a remake of the famous silent western. In fact, the story takes place in Victorian England. The cast is superb. Sean Connery is dashing and convincing as mastermind Edward Pierce. Lesley-Anne Down is stunning as his mistress, accomplice, and disguise expert. Add a pinch of Donald Sutherland as a boastful pickpocket and cracksman and you have a trio of crooks that can steal your heart. Rated PG.

1979   111 minutes

GREAT WALDO PEPPER, THE

★★★

DIRECTOR: George Roy Hill

CAST: Robert Redford, Bo Svenson, Susan Sarandon, Bo Brudin

The daredevil barnstorming pilots of the era between the world wars are sent a pleasant valentine by director George Roy Hill in this flying film. Robert Redford, in a satisfying low-key performance, is Waldo Pepper, a barnstormer who yearns for the action of the World War I dogfights. The flight scenes are top-notch. Only the script leaves the audience wanting more. It just isn't meaty enough to hold the interest of those who aren't flying buffs. Rated PG.

1975   196 minutes

GREEN BERETS, THE

★★★½

DIRECTOR: John Wayne, Ray Kellogg

CAST: John Wayne, David Janssen, Jim Hutton, Aldo Ray, Raymond St. Jacques, Bruce Cabot, Jack Soo, George Takei, Patrick Wayne

John Wayne's Vietnam war movie is much better than its reputation would suggest. We were fully prepared to hate the film after having avoided it when originally released. However, it turned out to be an exciting and enjoyable (albeit typical) Wayne vehicle. Although somewhat simplistic politically, it fits in well with such contemporary releases as *Uncommon Valor* and *Missing in Action*. Rated G.

1968   141 minutes

GREEN ICE

★½

DIRECTOR: Ernest Day

CAST: Ryan O'Neal, Anne Archer, Omar Sharif

Unconvincing tale of an emerald theft in Colombia. Ryan O'Neal engineers the robbery. Rated PG.

1981　　　　　　115 minutes

GREYSTOKE: THE LEGEND OF TARZAN, LORD OF THE APES
★★★½

DIRECTOR: Hugh Hudson
CAST: Christopher Lambert, Andie McDowell, Ian Holm, Ralph Richardson, James Fox, Cheryl Campbell

Director Hugh Hudson, whose uplifting *Chariots of Fire* swept the Oscars in 1982, has made the first Tarzan movie to remain faithful to the books and original character created by Edgar Rice Burroughs. For those unacquainted with the ape man made famous—or infamous, depending on whether you're a Burroughs purist or not— by the barely verbal Johnny Weissmuller, Tarzan is a half-savage survivor of the jungle. Here, in one dramatic leap, he goes from the dank, dangerous rain forests of West Africa to claim his rightful heritage—a baronial mansion in Scotland and a title as the Seventh Earl of Greystoke. Rated PG for nudity and violence.

1984　　　　　　129 minutes

GUMBALL RALLY, THE
★★½

DIRECTOR: Chuck Bail
CAST: Michael Sarrazin, Gary Busey, Tim McIntyre, Raul Julia, Normann Burton

First film based on an anything-goes cross-country road race. Featuring some excellent stunt driving, with occasional laughs, it's much better than *Cannonball Run*. Rated PG for language.

1976　　　　　　107 minutes

GUNG HO
★★½

DIRECTOR: Ray Enright
CAST: Randolph Scott, Grace McDonald, Alan Curtis, Noah Beery Jr., J. Carrol Naish, David Bruce, Robert Mitchum, Sam Levene

Although not meant to be funny, this ultrapatriotic war film has its truly outrageous moments. It must have been a real booster for wartime film-goers in America. Today it's almost embarrassing—particularly during the scene in which a recruit is accepted into a special team of commandos simply because he "hates Japs."

1943　　　B & W　88 minutes

GUNGA DIN
★★★★★

DIRECTOR: George Stevens
CAST: Cary Grant, Victor McLaglen, Douglas Fairbanks Jr., Joan Fontaine, Sam Jaffe, Eduardo Ciannelli

An acknowledged classic, this release has it all: laughs, thrills, and chills. Howard Hawks was originally set to direct it and played a large part in its creation. That explains why it is so unlike the rest of director George (*Shane*; *Giant*) Stevens's other films. For sheer entertainment, regardless of who directed it, *Gunga Din* is tops. Plot: Three soldiers in nineteenth-century India put down a native uprising with the help of an Indian water carrier.

1939　　　B & W　117 minutes

GUNS OF NAVARONE, THE
★★★★

DIRECTOR: J. Lee Thompson
CAST: Gregory Peck, David Niven, Anthony Quinn, Stanley Baker, Anthony Quayle, James Darren

Along with *The Great Escape*, this film is one of the best World War II adventure yarns. Gregory Peck, David Niven, and Anthony Quinn are part of a multinational task force that is sent to Greece with a mission to destroy two huge German batteries that threaten a fleet of Allied troop transports. Their attempt to land undetected and blow up the guns from under the Nazis' noses keeps you on the edge of your seat from start to finish.

1961   157 minutes

GYMKATA
★

DIRECTOR: Robert Clouse
CAST: Kurt Thomas, Tetchie Agbayani, Richard Norton, Edward Bell, John Barrett

Gold medal–winning World Champion gymnast Kurt Thomas stars in this disappointing fist-and-foot actioner as a secret agent who must compete in a deadly athletics competition to retrieve U.S. secrets. If the plot sounds suspiciously familiar to *Enter the Dragon*, it should. Director Robert Clouse and producer Fred Weintraub scored their biggest commercial and artistic success with that classic adventure film starring Bruce Lee. *Gymkata* not only doesn't come close to the latter; it's an insult to its star. Rated R for violence.

1985   90 minutes

HAMMETT
★

DIRECTOR: Wim Wenders
CAST: Frederic Forrest, Peter Boyle, Marilu Henner, Elisha Cook Jr., R. G. Armstrong

A disappointing homage to mystery writer Dashiell Hammett, this Wim Wenders–directed and Francis Ford Coppola–meddled production was two years in the making and hardly seems worth it. The plot is nearly incomprehensible, something that could never be said of the real-life Hammett's works (*The Maltese Falcon*; *The Thin Man*; etc.). Rated PG.

1982   97 minutes

HAPPY NEW YEAR (LA BONNE ANNEE)
★★★★

DIRECTOR: Claude Lelouch
CAST: Lino Ventura, Francoise Fabian, Charles Gerard

Delightful French crime caper mixed with romance and comedy. As two thieves plot a jewel heist, one (Lino Ventura) also plans a meeting with the lovely antique dealer (Francoise Fabian) who runs the shop next-door to their target. Director Claude Lelouch's film blends suspense with engaging wit. Rated PG for profanity and sex. Available in French version or dubbed.

1974   114 minutes

HARD COUNTRY
★★★½

DIRECTOR: David Greene
CAST: Jan-Michael Vincent, Michael Parks, Kim Basinger, Gailard Sartain, Tanya Tucker, Ted Neeley

Though it tries to make a statement about the contemporary

cowboy lost in the modern world and feminism in the boondocks, this is really just light-hearted entertainment. It's full of barroom brawls, beer-chugging contests, and hillbilly jokes. It's a lot like a Clint Eastwood comedy; a rockabilly love story of the macho man (Jan-Michael Vincent) versus the liberated woman (Kim Basinger). The foot-stomping soundtrack is by Tanya Tucker and Michael Martin Murphey, with his Great American Honky Tonk Band. Rated PG.

1981   104 minutes

HARD TIMES
★★★★½

DIRECTOR: Walter Hill
CAST: Charles Bronson, James Coburn, Jill Ireland, Strother Martin

This release is far and away one of Charles Bronson's best starring vehicles. In it he plays a bareknuckles fighter who teams up with a couple of hustlers, James Coburn and Strother Martin, to "sting" some local hoods. Bronson's wife, Jill Ireland, is surprisingly good as the love interest. Rated PG.

1975   97 minutes

HARD WAY, THE
★★

DIRECTOR: Michael Dryhurst
CAST: Patrick McGoohan, Lee Van Cleef, Donal McCann, Edna O'Brien, Michael Muldoon

Patrick McGoohan is an international terrorist who wants out of the business. His wife has taken the children, so he decides to quit before he loses his freedom or his life. Unfortunately for him, a former associate (Lee Van Cleef) wants him to do one more job and

will have him killed if he doesn't.

1979   88 minutes

HARPER
★★★★½

DIRECTOR: Jack Smight
CAST: Paul Newman, Lauren Bacall, Shelley Winters, Arthur Hill, Julie Harris, Janet Leigh, Robert Wagner

Ross MacDonald's detective, Lew Archer, undergoes a name change but still survives as a memorable screen character in the capable hands of Paul Newman. This one ranks right up there with *The Maltese Falcon*, *The Big Sleep* (the Humphrey Bogart version), *Farewell My Lovely*, and *The Long Goodbye* as one of the best of its type. The story, in which Harper is hired to find a missing husband, has its dated moments, but the impressive all-star cast more than pulls it through.

1966   121 minutes

HATARI!
★★★

DIRECTOR: Howard Hawks
CAST: John Wayne, Elsa Martinelli, Red Buttons, Hardy Krüger

If only Howard Hawks had been able to do as he wanted and cast Clark Gable along with John Wayne in this story of zoo-supplying animal hunters in Africa, this could have been a great film. As it is, it's still enjoyable, with a near-perfect blend of action, romance, and comedy.

1962   159 minutes

HAWK THE SLAYER
★★★

DIRECTOR: Terry Marcel
CAST: Jack Palance, John Terry

In this sword-and-sorcery adventure, John Terry plays the good Hawk, who, with his band of warriors—a dwarf and an elf among them—fights Jack Palance, his evil older brother. Palance's performance saves the film from mediocrity. Not rated; has violence.

1980   90 minutes

HEART LIKE A WHEEL
★★★★

DIRECTOR: Jonathan Kaplan
CAST: Bonnie Bedelia, Beau Bridges, Leo Rossi, Hoyt Axton, Bill McKinney, Dean Paul Martin, Dick Miller

A first-rate film biography of hot-rod champion Shirley "Cha Cha" Muldowney, this features a marvelous performance by Bonnie Bedelia as the first woman to crack the National Hot Rod Association's embargo against female competitors. When the NHRA won't let her race, veteran drivers "Big Daddy" Garlitts (Bill McKinney) and Connie Kalitta (Beau Bridges) take the lead in trying to get her on the track. It's an emotionally involving, thrilling tale of success and heartache. Rated PG for language.

1983   113 minutes

HEARTS AND ARMOUR
★★½

DIRECTOR: Giacomo Battiato
CAST: Zenda Araya, Barbara de Rossi, Rick Edwards, Ron Moss, Maurizio Nichetti, Tanya Roberts, Giovanni Vesentin, Tony Vogel

Warrior Orlando (Rick Edwards) seeks victory over the Moors and the rescue of his love (Tanya Roberts), while his female comrade-in-arms, Bradamante (Barbara de Rossi), falls in love with Ruggero (Ron Moss), the Moor whom Orlando is fated to kill. This film is loosely based on the legend of Orlando Furioso, and attempts to do for that story what *Excalibur* did for the Arthurian legends. Unfortunately, the script is not strong enough to do justice to the complex plot. Entertaining, but not extraordinary. Not rated; has violence and nudity.

1983   101 minutes

HELL ON FRISCO BAY
★★★

DIRECTOR: Frank Tuttle
CAST: Alan Ladd, Joanne Dru, Edward G. Robinson, William Demarest, Fay Wray

A 1930s-type hardboiled crime story of a framed cop who does his time, is released from prison, and goes after the bigwig gangster who set him up. Lots of action on San Francisco's streets and its famous bay.

1955   98 minutes

HELLCATS OF THE NAVY
★★★

DIRECTOR: Nathan Juran
CAST: Ronald Reagan, Nancy Davis, Arthur Franz, Harry Lauter

This none-too-exciting 1957 drama has one thing to attract viewers. President Ronald Reagan and First Lady Nancy co-star.

1957   B & W   82 minutes

HELLFIGHTERS
★★

DIRECTOR: Andrew V. McLaglen
CAST: John Wayne, Katharine Ross, Vera Miles, Jim Hutton, Bruce Cabot

Once again the talents of John Wayne have been squandered. The Duke is cast as a high-priced fireman sent around the world to put out dangerous oil rig fires. Even hard-core Wayne fans will wince at this one. Rated PG.

1969   121 minutes

HELL'S ANGELS ON WHEELS
★★½

DIRECTOR: Richard Rush

CAST: Adam Roarke, Jack Nicholson, Sabrina Scharf, John Garwood, Jana Taylor

This film is one of the better 1960s biker films, most notably because Jack Nicholson has a big role in it. Not a great film by any means, but if you like biker films . . .

1967   95 minutes

HELL'S BRIGADE
★

DIRECTOR: Henry Mankiewirk

CAST: Jack Palance, John Douglas

Fairly rotten film concerning a commando raid on Hitler's Germany during World War II. Low-budget, poorly acted.

1980   99 minutes

HELL'S HOUSE
★★

DIRECTOR: Howard Higgin

CAST: Junior Durkin, Bette Davis, Pat O'Brien, Junior Coghlan, Charley Grapewin, Emma Dunn

Gangster and prison films in the 1930s had their junior counterparts. In this barely so-so example, an innocent boy does time in a harsh reformatory because he won't rat on an adult crook friend. Junior Durkin is the poor kid, Pat O'Brien is the crook—a bootlegger—and Bette Davis is his girl. All hot stuff in Big Al's time.

1932 B & W 72 minutes

HERCULES
★★½

DIRECTOR: Pietro Fancisci

CAST: Steve Reeves, Sylva Koscina, Ivo Garrani

The first and still the best of the Italian-made epics based on the mythical superhero. Steve Reeves looks perfect in the part as Hercules out to win over his true love, the ravishing Sylva Koscina. Some nice action scenes.

1959   107 minutes

HIDDEN FORTRESS, THE
★★★★★

DIRECTOR: Akira Kurosawa

CAST: Toshiro Mifune, Misa Uehara, Minoru Chiaki, Kamatari Fujiwara

Toshiro Mifune stars in this recently reconstructed, uncut, and immensely entertaining 1958 Japanese period epic directed by Akira Kurosawa (*The Seven Samurai*, *Kagemusha*, *Ran*). George Lucas has openly admitted the film's influence on his *Star Wars* trilogy. *Hidden Fortress* deals with the adventures of a strong-willed princess (à la Carrie Fisher in the space fantasy) and her wise, sword-wielding protector (Mifune in the role adapted for Alec Guinness). There are even a couple of comic characters whose misadventures act as the thread that holds the story together (the same role fulfilled by the robots C3PO and R2D2 in Lucas's work). In Japanese with English subtitles. Unrated, the film has violence.

1958 B & W 126 minutes

HIGH-BALLIN'
★★

DIRECTOR: Peter Carter

CAST: Peter Fonda, Jerry Reed, Helen Shaver, Chris Wiggins, David Ferry

Peter Fonda and Jerry Reed are good old boys squaring off against the bad boss of a rival trucking company. The film has enough action and humor to make it a passable entertainment. Helen Shaver is its most provocative element. Rated PG.

1978　　　　　100 minutes

HIGH CRIME
★★

DIRECTOR: Enzo G. Castellari
CAST: Franco Nero, James Whitmore, Fernando Rey

Narcotics cop vs. Mafia kingpin in the picturesque Italian seaport of Genoa. Full of action, but no surprises. Rated PG.

1973　　　　　100 minutes

HIGH RISK
★★½

DIRECTOR: Stewart Raffill
CAST: James Brolin, Cleavon Little, Bruce Davison, Chick Vennera, Anthony Quinn, James Coburn, Ernest Borgnine, Lindsay Wagner

While snatching $5 million from a South American drug smuggler (James Coburn), four amateur conspirators (James Brolin, Cleavon Little, Bruce Davison, and Chick Vennera) blaze their way through numerous shootouts, crossing paths with a sleazy bandit leader (Anthony Quinn), hordes of Colombian soldiers, and plenty of riotous trouble. Alternately hysterically funny, exciting, hokey, crass, and tacky, this preposterous comic-strip adventure offers diversion, but a lot of it is just plain awful. Rated R.

1981　　　　　94 minutes

HIGH ROAD TO CHINA
★★★★

DIRECTOR: Brian G. Hutton
CAST: Tom Selleck, Bess Armstrong, Jack Weston, Wilford Brimley, Robert Morley, Brian Blessed

Old-fashioned movie fun is yours in this adventure film. Tom Selleck (of television's "Magnum P.I.") stars as a World War I flying ace who, with the aid of his sidekick/mechanic, Jack Weston, helps a spoiled heiress (Bess Armstrong) track down her missing father (Wilford Brimley). Directed by Brian Hutton (*Kelly's Heroes*), it's just like the B movies of yesteryear: predictable, silly, and fun. Rated PG for violence.

1983　　　　　120 minutes

HIGH ROLLING

DIRECTOR: Igor Auzins
CAST: Joseph Bottoms, Grigor Taylor, Sandy Hughs, Judy Davis, John Clayton

Two out-of-work carnival workers hitchhike through Australia until they are picked up by a drug runner. They end up stealing the runner's dope, money, and his car— a hot Corvette. They soon find a young girl who joins them in their outrageous criminal adventures. One such adventure is the hijacking of a bus. Rated PG for profanity and brief nudity, this feature is a big disappointment.

1977　　　　　88 minutes

HIGH SIERRA
★★★★½

DIRECTOR: Raoul Walsh
CAST: Humphrey Bogart, Ida Lupino, Alan Curtis, Arthur Kennedy, Joan Leslie, Henry Hull

Humphrey Bogart is at his best as a bad guy with a heart of gold in this 1941 gangster film. Bogart pays for the operation that corrects pretty Joan Leslie's crippled foot, but he finds his love is misplaced. The film's mountain top finale—as well as several scenes involving co-stars Ida Lupino, Arthur Kennedy, and Henry Hull—make it one of the finest of the Warner Bros. genre entries.

1941   B & W 100 minutes

HIGHEST HONOR, THE
★★★★★

DIRECTOR: Peter Maxwell
CAST: John Howard, Atsuo Nakamura, Stuart Wilson

A story of a unique friendship between two enemies: Captain Robert Page, a young World War II U.S. Army officer, and Winoyu Tamiya, a security officer in the Japanese army. After being captured for attempting to raid Japanese ships, Page is imprisoned in Singapore and befriends Tamiya as he waits for his trial for spying. This great war film, packed with high adventure and warm human drama, is also a true story. Rated R.

1984   99 minutes

HIS KIND OF WOMAN
★★★½

DIRECTOR: John Farrow
CAST: Robert Mitchum, Jane Russell, Vincent Price, Tim Holt, Charles McGraw, Raymond Burr, Jim Backus, Marjorie Reynolds

Entertaining chase film is an adventure to watch and figure out as two-fisted gambler Robert Mitchum breezes down to South America to pick up fifty thousand dollars only to find out he's being set up for the kill. Jane Russell is in fine shape as the worldly-looking gal with a good heart, and Vincent Price steals the show as a hammy Hollywood actor who is thrilled to be involved in *real* danger and intrigue. A *Who's Who* of character actors amd B-movie leads, this film is a successful blend of comedy, romance, and excitement, and in style and attitude is still superior to current color productions cut from the same cloth.

1951   B & W 120 minutes

HIT, THE
★★★★

DIRECTOR: Stephen Frears
CAST: John Hurt, Terence Stamp, Tim Roth, Fernando Rey, Laura Del Sol, Bill Hunter

The British seem to have latched on to the gangster film with a vengeance. First, they made the superb film *The Long Good Friday*, and now they've scored again with this gripping character study. John Hurt gives an unusually restrained (and highly effective) performance as a hit man assigned to take care of a squealer (Terence Stamp) who has been hiding in Spain after testifying against the mob. Hurt finds his prey full of surprises and his contract more difficult to fulfill than he might have imagined. Rated R for violence.

1984   97 minutes

HITLER'S CHILDREN
★★★★

DIRECTOR: Edward Dmytryk, Irving Reis
CAST: Tim Holt, Bonita Granville, Kent Smith, Otto Kruger

A great love story is created with the horror of Nazi Germany as a background. This film shows a young German boy who falls in love with an American girl. The boy gets caught up in Hitler's enticing web of propaganda, while his girlfriend resists all of Hitler's ideas. When the government decides to severely punish her for her resistance, her boyfriend comes to her aid.

1942   B & W   83 minutes

HOLCROFT COVENANT, THE
★★

DIRECTOR: John Frankenheimer
CAST: Michael Caine, Anthony Andrews, Victoria Tennant, Mario Adorf, Lilli Palmer

In the closing days of World War II, three infamous Nazi officers deposit a large sum of money into a Swiss bank account to be withdrawn years later by their children. The three then kill themselves to hide their secret from all but their heirs. Years later the offspring must sign a covenant before withdrawing the fortune, then use it for reparations to those who suffered during the war. But people begin to be eliminated and Caine unravels a plot to use the money to establish an international terrorist network that would send the world crashing into anarchy and out of which will arise a "Fourth Reich." This slow, but intriguing film, based on the novel by Robert Ludlum, will undoubtedly please spy film enthusiasts, although others may find it tedious and contrived. Rated R for adult situations.

1985   105 minutes

HOLLYWOOD VICE SQUAD
★

DIRECTOR: Penelope Spheeris
CAST: Ronny Cox, Frank Gorshin, Leon Issack Kennedy, Tris Van Devere, Carrie Fisher

Despite a name cast and a director—Penelope Spheeris (Suburbia)—who once showed promise, this semisequel to Vice Squad lacks even the raw energy of its predecessor. Instead, it's a tepid affair about a woman (Trish Van Devere) who goes searching for her runaway daughter in the sleazoid areas of Hollywood. Her fear is that the teenager may have becomed involved in porno or prostitution—just like George C. Scott's daughter in Hardcore. This similarity brings the movie's only point of interest: Van Devere and Scott are married. Big deal that they made essentially the same film, right? Right. Rated R for nudity, profanity, and violence.

1986   93 minutes

HONOR AMONG THIEVES
★★½

DIRECTOR: Jean Herman
CAST: Charles Bronson, Alain Delon, Brigitte Fossey

Charles Bronson plays a mercenary who is locked in a French bank over the weekend with Alain Delon, a doctor. Bronson is there to rob the bank of its 200 million francs, while Delon is there to replace some misappropriated securities. The two men are in constant conflict but find that they must work together. In the end, they discover they have been betrayed in a web of murder and intrigue. This is a little different type of picture for Bronson—a bit more subtle, a little slower-paced, and with more dialogue than action. Rated R.

1983   93 minutes

HOPSCOTCH
★★★★

DIRECTOR: Ronald Neame

CAST: Walter Matthau, Ned Beatty, Glenda Jackson

Walter Matthau is wonderful in this fast-paced and funny film as a spy who decides to extract a little revenge on the pompous supervisor (Ned Beatty) who demoted him. Glenda Jackson has a nice bit as Matthau's romantic interest. Rated R.

1980   104 minutes

HOT ROCK, THE
★★★★

DIRECTOR: Peter Yates
CAST: Robert Redford, George Segal, Ron Leibman, Paul Sand, Zero Mostel, Moses Gunn, William Redfield, Charlotte Rae

A neatly planned jewelry heist goes awry and the fun begins. Peter Yates's direction is razor sharp. The cast is absolutely perfect. This movie is a crowd-pleasing blend of action, humor, and suspense. It's the best caper film imaginable. Rated PG.

1972   105 minutes

HOUND OF THE BASKERVILLES, THE (ORIGINAL)
★★★★½

DIRECTOR: Sidney Lanfield
CAST: Basil Rathbone, Nigel Bruce, John Carradine, Lionel Atwill, Mary Gordon, E. E. Clive, Richard Greene

The second best of the Basil Rathbone/Nigel Bruce Sherlock Holmes movies, this 1939 release marked the stars' debut in the roles for which they would forever be known. While *The Adventures of Sherlock Holmes*, which was made the same year, featured the on-screen detective team at its peak, this 20th Century-Fox–produced adaptation of Sir Arthur Conan

Doyle's most famous mystery novel still can be called a classic. For those unfamiliar with the story, Holmes and Watson are called upon by Henry Baskerville (Richard Greene) to save him from a curse—in the form of a hound from hell—that has plagued his family for centuries.

1939   B & W   84 minutes

HOUND OF THE BASKERVILLES, THE (REMAKE)
★★★★

DIRECTOR: Terence Fisher
CAST: Peter Cushing, Christopher Lee, André Morell, Marla Landi, Miles Malleson

One of the better adaptations of A. Conan Doyle's moody novel, and particularly fascinating for its presentation of Peter Cushing (as Sherlock Holmes) and Christopher Lee together early in their careers. This British entry (from the Hammer House of Horror) caught more of the murky atmosphere than any other version of any other Holmes tale. Intelligent scripting, compelling acting, and spooky cinematography. Doyle would have been pleased.

1959   84 minutes

HUNTER
★★½

DIRECTOR: Leonard Horn
CAST: John Vernon, Steve Ihnat, Fritz Weaver, Edward Binns

A brainwashed agent is programmed to release a deadly virus. The scheme is discovered, and a good guy takes his place to catch the bad guys. Made for television.

1971   73 minutes

HUNTER, THE
★★

DIRECTOR: Buzz Kulik

CAST: Steve McQueen, Eli Wallach, LeVar Burton, Ben Johnson, Kathryn Harrold

The Hunter, an uneven action film, focuses on a modern-day bounty hunter. Steve McQueen plays real-life troubleshooter Ralph "Papa" Thorson. Though old and a bit awkward, Thorson leads—at least on screen—a dangerous, action-filled life. Traveling from one state to another in pursuit of fugitives, he is constantly putting his life on the line. Rated PG.

1980   97 minutes

HURRICANE

DIRECTOR: Jan Troell
CAST: Jason Robards, Mia Farrow, Dayton Ka'ne, Max von Sydow, Trevor Howard

Another Dino de Laurentiis misfire, this remake of the John Ford classic details a love affair between Charlotte Bruckner (Mia Farrow), daughter of the governor (Jason Robards) of Pago Pago, and the young native chief, Matangi (Dayton Ka'ne). Charlotte, recently returned to the lush tropic isle, is at first courted by Ensign Jack Sanford (Timothy Bottoms, in absolutely awful portrayal), but she is ultimately drawn to the intelligent and willful young leader. Though Matangi is betrothed to a young native girl, he falls in love with Charlotte and the groans build like the storm of the title. Rated PG.

1979   119 minutes

HURRICANE EXPRESS
★★

DIRECTOR: Armand Schaefer, J. P. McGowan
CAST: John Wayne, Tully Marshall, Conway Tearle, Shirley Gray

Big John Wayne stars in his second serial for Mascot Pictures and plays an aviator on the trail of the mysterious "Wrecker," who has been wreaking havoc with the local trains and is responsible for the death of his father. This feature, edited down from a twelve-chapter serial, features many famous western character actors and stunt men as the villains' sidekicks and henchmen. Even in this somewhat confused state it is fun and displays a high level of energy and excitement, a great deal of it as a direct result of young Wayne's wholehearted involvement in this basically simple chase film. Although the production values are missing, this vigorous outing has as much to offer as any of the famed serials from Universal and Republic.

1932   B & W   80 minutes

HUSTLE
★★½

DIRECTOR: Robert Aldrich
CAST: Burt Reynolds, Eddie Albert, Ernest Borgnine, Jack Carter, Ben Johnson

The Hustle reteams director Robert Aldrich and actor Burt Reynolds after their box-office success with *The Longest Yard*. Fine character performances from Eddie Albert, Ernest Borgnine, and Jack Carter help to elevate the macho/action yarn, but it is Academy Award–winner Ben Johnson who provides the real show. Rated R.

1975   120 minutes

I COVER THE WATERFRONT
★★★

DIRECTOR: James Cruze
CAST: Claudette Colbert, Ernest Torrence, Ben Lyon, Winifred Lucas, George Humbert

One, and one of the better, of a spate of newspaper stories that vied with gangster films on 1930s screens. In this one, a ruthless fisherman who smuggles Chinese into the United States doesn't think twice about pushing them overboard when approached by the Coast Guard. Claudette Colbert is his innocent daughter. Ace reporter Ben Lyon courts her in an effort to get at the truth. A great moment takes place when the daughter chats with a cathouse madam while waiting to take home her drunken father.

1933   B & W   70 minutes

I, THE JURY
★

DIRECTOR: Richard T. Heffron
CAST: Armand Assante, Barbara Carrera, Alan King

In the mid-1940s, Mickey Spillane wrote *I, the Jury*, introducing Mike Hammer, his no-nonsense private eye. For this updated version, Spillane's basic plot—Hammer out to find the killer of his old army buddy—has been kept intact. However, the film is a disappointing and sleazy hybrid of James Bond and *Death Wish II*, in which there is one man against a mean, globally involved system. Rated R.

1982   111 minutes

ICE STATION ZEBRA
★★★

DIRECTOR: John Sturges
CAST: Rock Hudson, Ernest Borgnine, Patrick McGoohan, Jim Brown, Tony Bill, Lloyd Nolan

This long cold war cliff-hanger about a submarine skipper awaiting orders while cruising to the North Pole under the ice was ec-centric billionaire Howard Hughes's favorite film. The suspense comes with a British agent's hunt for the usual Russian spy. Rated G.

1968   148 minutes

INSIDE OUT
★★★

DIRECTOR: Peter Duffell
CAST: Telly Savalas, Robert Culp, James Mason, Aldo Ray

An unlikely trio (Telly Savalas, Robert Culp, and James Mason) band together to recover $6 million in gold that Hitler had hidden. Only one man knows where the gold is, so the trio must get this ex-Nazi out of a maximum-security prison so that he can lead them to it. The action and suspense in this film should hold most viewers' attention. Rated PG.

1975   98 minutes

INVASION U.S.A.
★★★½

DIRECTOR: Joseph Zito
CAST: Chuck Norris, Richard Lynch, Melissa Prophet

There is no question that Chuck Norris is the new king of the action movie. As star and co-screenwriter of this preposterous but enjoyable film about America being invaded by terrorists, he's sculpted a story around his ever-growing talents. His fans will have to content themselves with silly B-style movies like this, in which Norris plays a one-man army (as always) who comes to the rescue of the old U.S. of A. and pummels the minions of psychotic spy Richard Lynch. Rated R for violence, gore, and profanity.

1985   107 minutes

IRON EAGLE
★★

DIRECTOR: Sidney J. Furie
CAST: Louis Gossett Jr., Jason Gedrick, Tim Thomerson, David Suchet

A better name for this modern war movie might have been *Ramboy*, so shamelessly does it attempt to be a *Rambo* for the teen-age set. Jason Gedrick stars as an 18-year-old would-be pilot who steals an F-16 fighter plane to rescue his father (Tim Thomerson), a prisoner of war in the Middle East. Louis Gossett plays a retired colonel who aids the young man on his dangerous, improbable mission. Comparing *Iron Eagle* with *Rambo* may be unfair in a way. Love him or hate him, Sylvester Stallone knows how to make a movie move. *Iron Eagle*, on the other hand, can only make one crawl. His film, therefore, is a terminally dull fantasy of bloodlust. Furie intended for viewers to cheer on his hero, but all one can muster during this movie's nearly two hours of painful predictability is an occasional groan. Rated PG-13 for violence and profanity.

1986   115 minutes

ISLAND TRADER
★★

DIRECTOR: Howard Rubie
CAST: John Ewart, Ruth Cracknell, Eric Oldfield

A young boy on an island finds a wrecked airplane laden with gold bullion. He is then pursued by a dangerous criminal and a tugboat skipper, both of whom want the treasure. All three are soon involved in a chase through shark-infested waters and dense jungle. This potentially exciting adventure film is marred by amateurish direction, a low budget, and uninspired acting.

1970   95 minutes

IVANHOE
★★★★

DIRECTOR: Richard Thorpe
CAST: Robert Taylor, Elizabeth Taylor, Joan Fontaine, George Sanders, Sebastian Cabot

Robert Taylor stars as Sir Walter Scott's dashing knight Ivanhoe. His mission is to secure the ransom for King Richard the Lionhearted, who has been captured while returning from the Crusades. Action and swordplay abound as Ivanhoe strives for Richard's release and protects two very fair maidens (Elizabeth Taylor and Joan Fontaine) from the lecherous grasp of arch villain George Sanders.

1952   106 minutes

JACKSON COUNTY JAIL
★★★½

DIRECTOR: Michael Miller
CAST: Yvette Mimieux, Tommy Lee Jones

This chase film is pretty good. Yvette Mimieux escapes from jail with fellow inmate Tommy Lee Jones. Audiences can't help but sympathize with Mimieux, because she was unfairly arrested and then raped by her jailer. Rated R.

1976   89 minutes

JAKE SPEED
★★★½

DIRECTOR: Andrew Lane
CAST: Wayne Crawford, Dennis Christopher, Karen Kopins, John Hurt, Leon Ames, Donna Pescow, Roy London, Barry Primus, Monte Markham

This quirky little adventure thriller, from the folks involved with the equally deft *Night of the Comet*, postulates that the book adventures of a pulp hero named Jake Speed actually are biographical chapters in the life of a real person. When Karen Kopins's younger sister is kidnapped and threatened with white slavery by John Hurt's delightfully oily villain, Speed (Wayne Crawford) and his associate Remo (Dennis Christopher) materialize and offer to help. What follows is paced a bit too slowly and demonstrates questionable taste by using an African civil war as a backdrop, but the droll premise remains quite intriguing. Things pick up when Hurt appears; it's a shame he couldn't have arrived sooner. The dialogue occasionally is inspired, as when Kopins sarcastically asks if other pulp heroes will show up to assist, and Remo calmly replies that they "work for another publisher." Rated PG for mild violence.

1986   100 minutes

JEWEL OF THE NILE, THE
★★★½
DIRECTOR: Lewis Teague
CAST: Michael Douglas, Kathleen Turner, Danny DeVito, Spiros Focas, Avner Eisenberg, and the Flying Karamazov Brothers

This sequel to *Romancing the Stone* details the further adventures of novelist Joan Wilder (Kathleen Turner) and soldier of fortune Jack Colton (Michael Douglas) in the deserts of North Africa. Joan is asked by an Arab leader, Omar (Spiros Focas), to write his life story. She accepts and then discovers too late that Omar is a rather nasty fellow. So it's up to Jack—with the jewel-crazy Ralph (Danny DeVito) watching

his every move—to save the day. The story seems to come to a logical conclusion three-quarters of the way through, and the viewer must endure a rather protracted build-up to the exciting climax. That said, *Jewel of the Nile* will not displease those seeking fun video fare. Turner and Douglas make appealing protagonists, and delightful comedy bits by the wisecracking DeVito (who wrote many of his lines) and Avner Eisenbert (as an impossibly cheerful guru) come at just the right times. Therefore, those who loved the original will find much to like in this sequel. Rated PG.

1985   106 minutes

JOHNNY ANGEL
★★★
DIRECTOR: Edwin L. Marin
CAST: George Raft, Claire Trevor, Signe Hasso, Hoagy Carmichael

Above-average gangster film provides some nice moments. George Raft seeks the killer of his father while busting up the mob. Nothing special, but fun to watch.

1945   B & W   79 minutes

JUDEX
★★★½
DIRECTOR: Georges Franju
CAST: Channing Pollock, Jacques Jouanneau, Edith Scob, Michel Vitold, Francine Berge

This funny look at an old serial from the early days of cinema will make you laugh out loud one moment and become misty-eyed with nostalgia the next. Based on an old potboiler serial by Feuillade and Bernede, *Judex* ("the judge") is an enjoyable adventure of a superhero who is lovable, human, and fallible. In French with English subtitles.

1963   B & W 103 minutes

JUGGERNAUT
★★★★½

DIRECTOR: Richard Lester
CAST: Richard Harris, Omar Sharif, David Hemmings, Anthony Hopkins, Shirley Knight, Ian Holm, Roy Kinnear

Here's a first-rate, suspenseful thriller about demolitions expert Richard Harris attempting to deactivate a bomb aboard a luxury liner. Richard Lester elevates the familiar plot line with inspired direction, and Lester regular Roy Kinnear is on hand to add some deft bits of comedy. Rated PG.

1974   109 minutes

JUNGLE HEAT
★½

DIRECTOR: Gus Trikonis
CAST: Peter Fonda, Deborah Raffin, John Amos, Carlos Palomino

Although this film is considered to be an adventure tale, it tries to please everyone with a little horror and romance thrown in. Unfortunately, it fails to use any of these elements effectively. Dr. Evelyn Howard (Deborah Raffin), an anthropologist from L.A., hires an alcoholic ex–Viet Nam vet (Peter Fonda) to fly her into the jungles of South America. There she looks for an ancient tribe of pygmies but finds instead monsters that greatly resemble the Creature from the Black Lagoon. Rated PG for language and gore.

1984   93 minutes

JUNGLE MASTER, THE
★

DIRECTOR: Miles Deem
CAST: Johnny Kissmuller, Simone Blondell, Edward Mann, Jerry Ross

An expedition journeys to Africa in search of the legendary ape-man, Karzan, no not Tarzan—Karzan. Somebody must have been sued for this movie, if not for copyright infringment, then bad film-making. Obviously foreign, the dubbing is exceptionally bad. Parents who watch any of their children's cartoons may hear some familiar voices. If you've sharp eyes, watch the wildlife scenes. You'll catch some of the footage used in the credits of Wild Kingdom. This movie is not a total loss, though; there is quite a bit of unintentional humor. In fact, this film would have been a turkey if it weren't so funny. A gem for bad film buffs.

1985   90 minutes

JUNKMAN, THE
★

DIRECTOR: H. B. Halecki
CAST: Christopher Stone, Susan Shaw, Lang Jeffries, Lynda Day George

From the makers of Gone in 60 Seconds, this sequel is tagged as the "chase film for the '80s." What this story lacks in plot and acting, it makes up for in action. More than 150 cars, trucks, and airplanes were destroyed in this "wall-to-wall" chase movie. There are so many crash scenes that it actually becomes boring. The story is about a junk dealer–turned—millionaire–turned–filmmaker being chased by a gang of thugs hired by his advertising agent to kill him. The ad agent seeks to reap the publicity benefits from his boss's death in order to promote the film our star is making. Thin. Rated PG.

1982   99 minutes

KAGEMUSHA
★★★★★

DIRECTOR: Akira Kurosawa
CAST: Tatsuya Nakadai, Tsutomo Yamazaki

The 70-year-old Japanese director Akira Kurosawa outdoes himself in this epic masterpiece about honor and illusion. Kurosawa popularized the samurai genre—which has been described as the Japanese equivalent of the western—in America with his breathtaking, action-packed films. *Seven Samurai* (which was adapted by Western filmmakers as *The Magnificent Seven* and *Battle beyond the Stars*), *Yojimbo* (remade by Italian director Sergio Leone as *A Fistful of Dollars*, with Clint Eastwood), *Rashomon*, and *Sanjuro* are perhaps his best-known classics. *Kagemusha* is yet another feast for the eyes, heart, and mind. Rated PG.

1980   159 minutes

KARATE KID, PART 2, THE
★★★½

DIRECTOR: John G. Avildsen
CAST: Ralph Macchio, Noriyuki "Pat" Morita, Danny Kamekona, Nobu McCarthy, Tamlyn Tomita, Yuji Okumoto, Martin Kove, William Zabka

This second in the *Karate Kid* series begins moments after the conclusion of the first film. Mr. Miyagi (Noriyuki "Pat" Morita) receives word that his father, residing in Okinawa, is dying, so he drops everything and heads for home, with young Daniel (Ralph Macchio) along for the ride. Once in Okinawa, Miyagi encounters an old rival and an old love, while Daniel makes a new enemy and a new love; the latter is quite well played by newcomer Tamlyn Tomita. The film runs a bit long, and Miyagi's little philosophies aren't quite as well integrated as they were in the first film, but this new installment still is quite pleasant for all ages. As was true in the first film, the show belongs to Morita. Rated PG for mild violence.

1986   113 minutes

KASHMIRI RUN, THE
🐢

DIRECTOR: John Peyser
CAST: Pernell Roberts, Alexandra Gasteda, Julian Mateos, Gloria Camara

Pernell Roberts is an American adventurer in the Far East who is commissioned to take two scientists to India and bring back a load of yak skins. On the way he faces communist Chinese soldiers, bandits, and wild animals. If you can watch further than this either you have the world's strongest stomach our you're brain-dead. Roberts must have nightmares about this film, it's so bad. The only redeeming quality is some beautiful scenery.

1969   93 minutes

KELLY'S HEROES
★★★

DIRECTOR: Brian G. Hutton
CAST: Clint Eastwood, Telly Savalas, Donald Sutherland, Don Rickles, Gavin McLeod, Carroll O'Connor

An amiable rip-off of *The Dirty Dozen*, this 1970 war comedy was funnier at the time of its original release. Stoic Clint Eastwood is stuck with a bunch of goof-offs (Telly Savalas, Donald Sutherland, Don Rickles, and Gavin McLeod) as he searches for Nazi treasure. Sutherland's World War II hippie ("Give me those positive waves, man") is a little tough to take these days, but this caper picture still has its moments. Rated PG.

1970   145 minutes

KENNEL MURDER CASE, THE
★★★★

DIRECTOR: Michael Curtiz

CAST: William Powell, Mary Astor, Eugene Pallette, Ralph Morgan, Jack LaRue

A classic detective thriller, this features William Powell as the dapper Philo Vance solving a locked-door murder. The supporting players complement his suave characterization perfectly. Dated, but good.

1933   B & W   73 minutes

KEY LARGO
★★★★

DIRECTOR: John Huston

CAST: Humphrey Bogart, Lauren Bacall, Edward G. Robinson, Claire Trevor, Lionel Barrymore

Humphrey Bogart is one of a group of dissimilar individuals held in a run-down Florida Keys hotel by a band of hoodlums on the lam. Lauren Bacall looks to him as her white knight, but as a disillusioned war vet he has had enough violence. That is, until a crime kingpin (Edward G. Robinson) pushes things a little too far.

1948   B & W 101 minutes

KIDNAPPED
★★★

DIRECTOR: Robert Stevenson

CAST: James MacArthur, Peter Finch

Walt Disney takes a shot at filming this Robert Louis Stevenson eighteenth-century adventure. A young man (James MacArthur) is spirited away to sea just as he is about to inherit his family's estate. Plenty of swashbuckling sword play for children of all ages.

1960   94 minutes

KILL AND KILL AGAIN
★★

DIRECTOR: Ivan Hall

CAST: James Ryan, Anneline Kriel

Kung fu champ James Ryan repeats his starring role from *Kill or Be Killed* in this sequel to that box-office winner. This time, martial arts master Steve Chase (Ryan) has been hired to rescue a Nobel Prize-winning chemist from the clutches of a demented billionaire who wants his victim's formula for synthetic fuel. Rated R.

1981   100 minutes

KILL CASTRO
🦃

DIRECTOR: Peter Barton

CAST: Stuart Whitman, Caren Kaye, Robert Vaughn, Woody Strode, Albert Salmi, Michael Gazzo, Sybil Danning, Raymond St. Jacques

Espionage and murder are the formulas for this implausible adventure yarn. Captain Tony (Stuart Whitman) is a Key West boat skipper who is "blackmailed" into helping a C.I.A. agent named Hud (Robert Vaughn) carry out an assassination plot against Fidel Castro. The C.I.A. is helping the Mafia bring drugs into Cuba in return for help in carrying out its murder plot. If Castro were to see this turkey, he would probably die—laughing.

Rated R for violence, profanity, and incompetence.

1978 90 minutes

KILL OR BE KILLED
★½

DIRECTOR: Ivan Hall
CAST: James Ryan, Norman Combes, Charlotte Michelle, Danie DuPlessis

A former Nazi pits himself against the Japanese master who defeated him in an important tournament during World War II. Run-of-the-mill martial-arts nonsense. James Ryan shows a glimmer of personality to go with his physical prowess. Rated PG.

1980 90 minutes

KILL POINT
★

DIRECTOR: Frank Harris
CAST: Leo Fong, Richard Roundtree, Cameron Mitchell, Stark Pierce, Hope Holiday

Incredibly bloody tale of gang warfare, revenge, and justice in L.A. Leo Fong plays a police detective whose brother is murdered by a gang of hoods. Fong is out to get the killers, who have also robbed a National Guard armory and are passing out weapons to all the scum in L.A. Weak performances and gratuitous violence mar this low-budget thriller. Rated R for violence and language.

1984 89 minutes

KILLER ELITE, THE
★★½

DIRECTOR: Sam Peckinpah
CAST: James Caan, Robert Duvall, Arthur Hill, Bo Hopkins, Mako, Burt Young, Gig Young

Secret service agent James Caan is double-crossed by his partner (Robert Duvall) while guarding a witness. Disabled by a bullet wound, he has to begin a long process of recovery. He wants revenge. The story seems to have a lot of promise, but this is never realized. There are some good action scenes. However, considering all the top-flight talent involved, it is a major disappointment. Rated PG.

1975 120 minutes

KILLERS, THE
★★★★

DIRECTOR: Robert Siodmak
CAST: Burt Lancaster, Ava Gardner, Edmond O'Brien, Albert Dekker, Sam Levene

Burt Lancaster made an impressive film debut in this *film noir* masterwork directed by Robert Siodmak. *Film noir*, for those who aren't movie buffs, is a particular style of film story-telling bathed in light and shadow and dealing with the darker doings of mankind. Based on an Ernest Hemingway story, the plot concerns the murder of an ex-fighter (Lancaster) and the subsequent investigation into the circumstances that led to his death.

1946 B & W 105 minutes

KIM
★★★½

DIRECTOR: Victor Saville
CAST: Errol Flynn, Dean Stockwell, Paul Lukas, Thomas Gomez, Cecil Kellaway

Rudyard Kipling's India comes to life in this colorful story of the young son of a soldier and his adventures with a dashing secret operative in defense of Queen and country. Dean Stockwell is one of the finest and most believable of child stars, and the great Errol Flynn is still capable of personifying the spirit of adventure and romance in this one-dimensional but entertaining story. Good supporting cast, beautiful photography, and exotic settings help to make this film fun for the whole family.

1951 113 minutes

KING ARTHUR, THE YOUNG WARLORD
★½

DIRECTOR: Sidney Hayers, Patrick Jackson, Peter Sasdy

CAST: Oliver Tobias, Michael Gothard, Jack Watson, Brian Blessed, Peter Firth

King Arthur, the Young Warlord follows the English legend in his early years through subplots that lead nowhere. Some of these vignettes promise some kind of conclusion and build upon opening narration (which sets the stage for the unification of the English tribes into a nation lead by Arthur), but in the end none of the stories deliver the goods. The acting is second-rate, and while some of the action scenes are good, it must be noted that the violence displayed may not be some people's idea of good ol' G-rated fun despite the MPAA approval.

1975 96 minutes

KING SOLOMON'S MINES (1950)
★★★★★

DIRECTOR: Compton Bennett, Andrew Marton

CAST: Stewart Granger, Deborah Kerr, Hugo Haas

The "great white hunter" genre of adventure films has been a movie staple for ages, yet only one rates as a cinema classic. That picture is the rousing adventure *King Solomon's Mines*. Stewart Granger guides a party through darkest Af-

rica in search of a lady's husband. Don't let this surprise you, but on the way, the hunter and the lady (Deborah Kerr) become fast friends. Sounds like a pretty basic plot, doesn't it? Why, then, has it stood the test of time where other jungle safari pics have faded? The seemingly routine script is actually an exceptional blend of action and suspense. The brilliant location photography has never been excelled, and the acting is first-rate.

1950 102 minutes

KING SOLOMON'S MINES (1985)
🦃

DIRECTOR: J. Lee Thompson

CAST: Richard Chamberlain, Sharon Stone, John Rhys-Davies, Herbert Lom, Ken Gampu

A bad movie may not be a crime against nature, but this film is definitely a crime against H. Rider Haggard's classic adventure novel. The previous film versions in 1937 and 1950 were rousing entertainment, whereas this one is nothing more than a blatant rip-off of *Raiders of the Lost Ark*. Starring Richard Chamberlain as Allan Quartermain, the film is an embarrassment—a compendium of cornball clichés and stupid slapstick. Rated PG for violence.

1985 100 minutes

KNIGHTRIDERS
★★★

DIRECTOR: George A. Romero

CAST: Ed Harris, Tom Savini, Amy Ingersoll

What was supposed to be a modern-day look at the lost Code of Honor comes across on screen as a bunch of weirdos dressed in armor riding motorcycles in a traveling circus. At a length of almost two-and-a-half hours, there isn't enough to hold the viewer's interest. A novel idea, but it wears thin in a very short while. Rated PG.

1981   145 minutes

KNIGHTS OF THE ROUND TABLE
★★½

DIRECTOR: Richard Thorpe
CAST: Robert Taylor, Ava Gardner, Mel Ferrer, Stanley Baker, Felix Aylmer, Robert Urquhart

Colorful wide-screen epic of King Arthur's court is long on pageantry but lacks the spirit required to make this type of film work well. MGM mainstay Robert Taylor plays another of his one-dimensional storybook heroes against a backdrop of real English hills, meadow, and castles. Able-bodied assistance is offered in the form of Stanley Baker and Mel Ferrer, and Ava Gardner is as lovely as ever, but this tale of Camelot is not as fondly remembered as other films of its ilk.

1953   115 minutes

KOJIRO
★★★★

DIRECTOR: Hiroshi Inagaki
CAST: Kikunosuke Onoe, Yuriko Hoshi, Yoko Tsukasa, Tatsuya Nakadai

This first-rate semisequel to director Hiroshi Inagaki's superb *Samurai Trilogy* casts Tatsuya Nakadai as the fabled master swordsman, Musashi Miyamoto, whose exploits made up the three previous films. But he is not the main character here. Instead, the focus is on Kojiro (Kikunosuke Onoe), whose goal is to become the greatest swordsman in all Japan and thus follow the trail blazed by Miyamoto, who was the first

to become a respected masterless samurai. This goal puts the younger man on a path that leads to the final, death-dealing duel with his hero. Unrated, the film contains violence. In Japanese with English subtitles.

1967   152 minutes

KUNG FU
★★★

DIRECTOR: Jerry Thorpe
CAST: David Carradine, Keye Luke, Philip Ahn, Keith Carradine, Barry Sullivan

The pilot of the 1970s television series starring David Carradine has its moments for those who fondly remember the show. Carradine plays a Buddhist monk roaming the Old West. When his wisdom fails to mollify the bad guys, he is forced to use martial arts to see justice done.

1971   75 minutes

LA BALANCE
★★★★

DIRECTOR: Bob Swaim
CAST: Nathalie Baye, Philippe Léotard, Richard Berry, Maurice Ronet, Christophe Malavoy, Jean-Paul Connart

Early on in this French import directed by American filmmaker Bob Swaim, we see posters of *The Enforcer*, starring Clint Eastwood as "Dirty Harry" Callahan, and *Bullitt*, with Steve McQueen in the title role. Swaim is making it clear that *La Balance* is an homage of sorts to the American cop thriller. He turns the genre inside out, however, by not focusing on the problems of the detective (Richard Berry). Instead, he concentrates on the plights of two unfortunates—a prostitute (Nathalie Baye) and a petty criminal

(Philippe Léotard)—who get caught in a vise between the cops and a gangland chief. The result is a first-rate crime story. In French with English subtitles. Rated R for nudity, profanity, and violence.

1982   102 minutes

LADY FROM SHANGHAI
★★★½

DIRECTOR: Orson Welles
CAST: Rita Hayworth, Orson Welles, Everett Sloane, Glenn Anders, Erskine Sanford, Ted De Corsia, Gus Schilling

Orson Welles and Rita Hayworth were husband and wife when they made this taut, surprising thriller about a beautiful, amoral woman, her crippled, repulsive lawyer husband, his partner, and a somewhat naive Irish sailor made cat's-paw in a murder scheme. Under Welles's inventive direction, Everett Sloane and the camera steal the show with a climactic scene in the hall of mirrors at San Francisco's old oceanfront Playland.

1948   B & W   87 minutes

LADY OF BURLESQUE
★★★

DIRECTOR: William Wellman
CAST: Barbara Stanwyck, Michael O'Shea, J. Edward Bromberg, Iris Adrian, Pinky Lee

Slick and amusing adaptation of Gypsy Rose Lee's clever mystery novel of top bananas, blackouts, and strippers, *The G-String Murder*. Interesting look into an aspect of show business that now exists only in fading memories. "Slowly I turned . . ."

1943   B & W   91 minutes

LADYHAWKE
★★★½

DIRECTOR: Richard Donner

CAST: Matthew Broderick, Rutger Hauer, Michelle Pfeiffer, Leo McKern, John Wood

In this seven-hundred-year-old legend of love and honor, Rutger Hauer and Michelle Pfeiffer are lovers separated by an evil curse. Hauer, a valiant knight, is aided by a wisecracking thief, Matthew Broderick, in his quest to break the spell by destroying its creator. This is a lush and lavish fantasy that will please the young and the young at heart. Rated PG-13 for violence.

1985   121 minutes

LASSITER
★★★

DIRECTOR: Roger Young
CAST: Tom Selleck, Jane Seymour, Lauren Hutton, Bob Hoskins

Tom Selleck (of television's "Magnum P.I." and *High Road to China*) stars in yet another period adventure film as a jewel thief in the 1930s who attempts to steal a cache of uncut diamonds from the Nazis. This could be called good-but-not-great entertainment. Rated R for nudity, suggested sex, violence, and profanity.

1984   100 minutes

LAST AMERICAN HERO, THE
★★★★

DIRECTOR: Lamont Johnson
CAST: Jeff Bridges, Valerie Perrine, Geraldine Fitzgerald, Ned Beatty, Gary Busey, Art Lund, Ed Lauter, William Smith II

Hollywood took a lot of the bite out of the Tom Wolfe article this movie was based on, but *The Last American Hero* holds up as an entertaining action film about the famous whiskey runner from North Carolina who becomes a legend when he proves himself a great stock-car driver. Jeff Bridges's portrait of the rebel Johnson is engaging, but Art Lund steals the show as Johnson's bootlegger father. Rated PG for profanity and sex.

1973   95 minutes

LAST DRAGON, THE
★★★½

DIRECTOR: Michael Schultz
CAST: Taimak, Vanity, Chris Murney

Produced by Motown Records man Berry Gordy, this is lively, unpretentious nonsense about a shy karate champ (Taimak) fending off villains threatening a disc jockey (Vanity). A combined music video and comic strip, it's good, silly fun. Rated PG-13 for violence.

1985   109 minutes

LAST EMBRACE, THE
★★★½

DIRECTOR: Jonathan Demme
CAST: Roy Scheider, Janet Margolin, Sam Levene, Marcia Rodd, Christopher Walken, John Glover, Charles Napier

A CIA agent must track down an obsessed, methodical killer. A complex, intelligent thriller in the Hitchcock style with skilled performances, a lush music score, and a cliff-hanging climax at Niagara Falls. Rated R for nudity and violence.

1979   102 minutes

LAST OF SHEILA, THE
★★★★

DIRECTOR: Herbert Ross
CAST: James Coburn, Dyan Cannon, James Mason, Raquel Welch, Richard Benjamin

A cleverly planned, very watchable whodunit. Because of some unusual camera angles and subtle dialogue, the audience is drawn into active participation in the mystery. A sundry collection of Hollywood types are invited on a yachting cruise by James Coburn. It seems one of them has been involved in the murder of Coburn's wife. Rated PG.

1973   120 minutes

LAST PLANE OUT
🦃

DIRECTOR: David Nelson
CAST: Jan-Michael Vincent, Lloyd Batista, Julie Carmen

Poor rip-off of *Under Fire*, with Jan-Michael Vincent playing a news reporter in Nicaragua during the final days of the Somoza regime in 1979. Bad acting, a poor script, and historical inaccuracies all add up to a big bomb. Not hard to understand why this film was not released in the cinema. Unrated.

1983   98 minutes

LATE SHOW, THE
★★★★½

DIRECTOR: Robert Benton
CAST: Art Carney, Howard Duff, Lily Tomlin, Bill Macy, John Considine

Just prior to directing *Kramer vs. Kramer*, Robert Benton created this little gem. It stars Art Carney as an aging private eye out to avenge the death of his partner (Howard Duff) with the unwanted help of wacky Lily Tomlin. Loosely lifted from Sam Peckinpah's *Ride the High Country* and John Huston's *The Maltese Falcon*, this detective story is a bittersweet, sometimes tragic, takeoff on the genre. That it works so well is a credit to all involved. Rated PG.

1977   94 minutes

LAUGHING POLICEMAN, THE
★★★½
DIRECTOR: Stuart Rosenberg
CAST: Walter Matthau, Bruce Dern, Louis Gossett, Albert Paulsen, Cathy Lee Crosby, Anthony Zerbe

Little-known police thriller that deserved far better than it got at the box office. Walter Matthau and Bruce Dern are a pair of cops seeking a mass murderer who preys on bus passengers. Taut drama, taken from the superb thriller by Maj Sjowall and Per Wahloo...although characterization suffers a bit in the transition from book to screen. Rated R for violence.
1974   111 minutes

LAURA
★★★★★
DIRECTOR: Otto Preminger
CAST: Gene Tierney, Dana Andrews, Vincent Price, Judith Anderson, Clifton Webb

A lovely socialite (Gene Tierney) is apparently murdered, and the police detective (Dana Andrews) assigned to the case is up to his neck in likely suspects. To compound matters, he has developed a strange attraction for the deceased woman through her portrait. So starts one of the most original mysteries ever to come from Hollywood. Vincent Price and Judith Anderson highlight an excellent supporting cast, but the role still remembered today belongs to Clifton Webb. In his first screen performance as the acid-tongued columnist, he stole the show from this talented cast. A haunting music score also contributes to this fast-paced classic,

which has always delighted audiences.
1944   B & W   88 minutes

LAWRENCE OF ARABIA
★★★★★
DIRECTOR: David Lean
CAST: Peter O'Toole, Alec Guinness, Anthony Quinn, Arthur Kennedy, Omar Sharif

Director David Lean brings us an expansive screen biography of T. E. Lawrence, the complex English leader of the Arab revolt against Turkey in World War I. This is a tremendous accomplishment in every respect. Peter O'Toole is stunning in his motion picture debut as Lawrence. The supporting cast is superb. The cinematography captures the beauty of the desert as never before. Maurice Jarré has added a stirring musical score. A definite thinking person's spectacle.
1962   222 minutes

LEFT HAND OF GOD, THE
★★★½
DIRECTOR: Edward Dmytryk
CAST: Humphrey Bogart, Lee J. Cobb, Gene Tierney, Agnes Moorehead

This 1955 release features Humphrey Bogart as an American forced to pose as a priest while on the run from a renegade Chinese warlord (Lee J. Cobb). It's not the fastest-moving adventure story, but Bogart and Cobb are quite good, and Gene Tierney is an effective heroine. The result is worthy entertainment.
1955   87 minutes

LEGAL EAGLES
★★★½
DIRECTOR: Ivan Reitman

CAST: Robert Redford, Debra Winger, Daryl Hannah, Brian Dennehy, Terence Stamp, Steven Hill, Jennie Dundas, Roscoe Lee Browne

This droll courtroom comedy succeeds due to the engaging presence of Robert Redford as assistant district attorney and Debra Winger as defense attorney. The two become uneasy partners in a complex case involving art theft and a loopy performance artist, played by Daryl Hannah. A charming subplot involves Redford's daughter (nicely played by Jennie Dundas) who visits when his ex-wife permits. The story doesn't bear close examination, but Redford and Winger keep things moving with energy and charisma. Rated PG for mild adult situations.

1986   114 minutes

LEGEND OF BILLY JEAN, THE
★

DIRECTOR: Matthew Robbins
CAST: Helen Slater, Keith Gordon, Christian Slater, Peter Coyote

Another one of those teen rebel flicks. This one is about a girl from Texas (*Supergirl*'s Helen Slater) who becomes an outlaw and ends up with all the youths in Corpus Christi backing her up. There are few subtleties here and the obvious is exploited for the dim of wit. Rated PG-13 for language and (only a little) violence.

1985   92 minutes

LEGEND OF THE EIGHT SAMURAI
★★

DIRECTOR: Haruki Kaduwara
CAST: Hiroku Yokoshimaru, Sonny Chiba, Sue Shihomi, Henry Sanada

Shizu (Sue Shihomi) is the warrior princess who, aided by eight loyal samurai, attempts to lift a curse from her clan. She leads her warriors into battle against a giant centipede, ghosts, and the nearly immortal witch who cursed the clan a hundred years ago. This Japanese fantasy features an interesting storyline, but is derivative, slow in spots, badly dubbed, and disappointing. Unrated, has moderate violence.

1984   130 minutes

LEPKE
★★★

DIRECTOR: Menahem Golan
CAST: Tony Curtis, Anjanette Comer, Michael Callan, Warren Berlinger, Milton Berle, Vic Tayback

Tony Curtis gives an effective performance in the lead role of this gangster drama. He's the head of Murder Inc. The story sticks close to the facts. It's no classic, but watchable. Rated R.

1975   110 minutes

LION AND THE HAWK, THE
★★★

DIRECTOR: Peter Ustinov
CAST: Peter Ustinov, Herbert Lom, Simon Dutton, Leonie Mellinger, Denis Quilley, Michael Elphick

Turkey in 1923, with its social, religious, and economic revolution picking up steam, is the backdrop for this film about a young rebel (Simon Dutton) who defies cultural tradition and runs off with a woman betrothed to a powerful regional governor's nephew. Peter Ustinov is excellent as the governor, who seeks revenge on the young Turk. *The Lion and the*

Hawk is entertaining but lacks definition: the viewer may watch the film from start to finish and never really get the point. Not rated; has sex, nudity, and violence.

1983   105 minutes

LION OF THE DESERT
★★★½

DIRECTOR: Moustapha Akkad
CAST: Anthony Quinn, Oliver Reed, Rod Steiger

This epic motion picture gives an absorbing portrait of the 1929–31 war in the North African deserts of Libya when Bedouin troops on horseback faced the tanks and mechanized armies of Mussolini. Anthony Quinn is Omar Mukhtar, the desert lion who became a nationalist and a warrior at the age of 52 and fought the Italians until they captured and hanged him twenty years later. Rated PG.

1981   162 minutes

LIST OF ADRIAN MESSENGER, THE
★★★★½

DIRECTOR: John Huston
CAST: George C. Scott, Dana Wynter, Clive Brook, Herbert Marshall

Excellent suspenser has a mysterious stranger visiting an English estate and the puzzling series of murders that coincide with his arrival. Crisp acting, coupled with John Huston's taut direction, makes this crackerjack entertainment. Superb finale involving a fox hunt is not to be missed. With cameo appearances by Kirk Douglas, Tony Curtis, Burt Lancaster, Robert Mitchum, Frank Sinatra. Rated PG.

1963   B & W 98 minutes

LITTLE CAESAR
★★★

DIRECTOR: Mervyn LeRoy
CAST: Edward G. Robinson, Douglas Fairbanks Jr.

Historically, this is an important film. Made in 1930, it started the whole genre of gangster films. As entertainment, this veiled biography of Al Capone is terribly dated. Edward G. Robinson's performance is like a Warner Bros. cartoon in places, but one has to remember this is the original; the rest are imitators.

1930   B & W 80 minutes

LITTLE DRUMMER GIRL, THE
★★½

DIRECTOR: George Roy Hill
CAST: Diane Keaton, Yorgo Voyagis, Klaus Kinski

Director George Roy Hill (*Butch Cassidy and the Sundance Kid*) did everything he could to make this adaptation of John Le Carré's bestseller a fast-paced, involving political thriller. However, his work is thwarted by an unconvincing lead performance by Diane Keaton, who plays an actress recruited by an Israeli general (Klaus Kinski) to help trap a Palestinian terrorist. Even though the movie has its moments, Keaton's poor acting eventually does it in. Rated R for violence, profanity, suggested sex, and nudity.

1984   130 minutes

LITTLE LAURA AND BIG JOHN
🐾

DIRECTOR: Luke Moberly, Bob Woodburn
CAST: Karen Black, Fabian Forte, Ivy Thayer, Ken Miller, Paul Gleason, Jerry Albert, Lee Warren, Ben Rossi

A very cheap response to the popular outlaw films of the late 1960s (*Bonnie and Clyde*, *Butch Cassidy and the Sundance Kid*, etc.) *Little Laura and Big John* is about the Ashley Gang, a bunch of losers who can put you to sleep by just saying "Stick 'em up." The acting is bad enough, but what really stands out here is the canned dialogue, or at least the poorly handled on-the-set-audio—everyone sounds like they're in a wind tunnel. If you dare to rent this, you'll be amazed how boring the Roaring Twenties seemed to this team of directors. Rated R for violence, nudity, and profanity.

1972   82 minutes

LITTLE TREASURE
★★★
DIRECTOR: Alan Sharp
CAST: Margot Kidder, Ted Danson, Burt Lancaster

While the synopsis on the back of the box may give one the impression this release is a ripoff of *Romancing the Stone*, only the rough outline of the story is lifted from the 1984 hit. The Margot Kidder/Ted Danson team is not a copy of the Kathleen Turner/Michael Douglas couple; these characters are more down-home. And the concentration on domestic drama almost fills the gap left by the absence of action. Plodding at times, but generally satisfying. Rated R for nudity and language.

1985   95 minutes

LIVE AND LET DIE
★★
DIRECTOR: Guy Hamilton
CAST: Roger Moore, Jane Seymour, Yaphet Kotto, Geoffrey Holder

The first Roger Moore (as James Bond) adventure is a hodgepodge of the surrealistic and the slick that doesn't quite live up to its Sean Connery–powered predecessors. The chase-and-suspense formula wears thin in this series entry. Rated PG.

1973   121 minutes

LIVES OF A BENGAL LANCER, THE
★★★★½
DIRECTOR: Henry Hathaway
CAST: Gary Cooper, Franchot Tone, Richard Cromwell, Sir Guy Standing, C. Aubrey Smith, Monte Blue, Kathleen Burke

One of the great adventure films, this action-packed epic stars Gary Cooper and Franchot Tone as fearless friends in the famed British regiment. Their lives become complicated when they take the commander's son (Richard Cromwell) under their wings and he turns out to be less than a model soldier.

1935   B & W 109 minutes

LOADED GUNS
🐢
DIRECTOR: Fernando Di Leo
CAST: Ursula Andress, Woody Strode, Isabella Biagin, Lino Banfi, Aldo Giuffre, Maurizio Arena

Thoroughly stupid espionage flick from Italy that tries to be comical when it's not and is a laugh riot when it's supposed to be serious. Ursula Andress (*Dr. No, What's New Pussycat?*) is a spy who tries to bust up a cocaine-smuggling ring. For those who couldn't care less about the story or the dubbed dialogue, Ursula does walk around naked a lot. Not rated, but would be an R by MPAA standards due to sex, nudity, violence, and profanity.

1975   90 minutes

LONE WOLF MCQUADE
★★★½

DIRECTOR: Steve Carver
CAST: Chuck Norris, L. Q. Jones, R. G. Armstrong, David Carradine, Barbara Carrera

Chuck Norris plays a maverick Texas ranger who forgets the rules in his zeal to punish the bad guys. He still isn't a great actor, but director Steve Carver compensates by surrounding Norris with a quality supporting cast and by meticulously setting up and pacing the film. As McQuade, Norris meets his match in David Carradine (who starred in TV's "Kung Fu"), the ruthless leader of a gun-smuggling ring. The worth-waiting-for climax is a martial arts battle between the two. Rated PG for violence and profanity.

1983   107 minutes

LONG GOOD FRIDAY, THE
★★★★★

DIRECTOR: John MacKenzie
CAST: Bob Hoskins, Helen Mirren, Pierce Brosnan

This superb British film depicts the struggle of an underworld boss (Bob Hoskins, in a brilliant performance) to hold on to his territory. It's a classic in the genre on a par with The Godfather, The Public Enemy, and High Sierra. Rated R for nudity, profanity, and violence.

1980   114 minutes

LONG JOHN SILVER
★★★

DIRECTOR: Byron Haskin
CAST: Robert Newton, Connie Gilchrist, Kit Taylor, Grant Taylor

Avast me hearties, Robert Newton is at this scene-chewing best in this otherwise unexceptional (and unofficial) sequel to Disney's Treasure Island.

1954   109 minutes

LONGEST DAY, THE
★★★★★

DIRECTOR: Ken Annakin, Andrew Marton, Bernhard Wicki
CAST: John Wayne, Robert Mitchum, Henry Fonda, Richard Burton, Rod Steiger, Sean Connery, Robert Wagner

A magnificent recreation of the Allied invasion of Normandy in June of 1944 with an all-star cast, this epic war film succeeds where others may fail—Midway and Tora! Tora! Tora!, for example. A big-budget film that shows you where the money was spent, it's first-rate in all respects.

1963   B & W 180 minutes

LONGEST YARD, THE
★★★★½

DIRECTOR: Robert Aldrich
CAST: Burt Reynolds, Eddie Albert, Michael Conrad, Bernadette Peters, Ed Lauter

An ex-professional football quarterback (Burt Reynolds) is sent to a Florida prison for stealing his girlfriend's car. The warden (Eddie Albert) forces Reynolds to put together a prisoner team to play his semi-pro team made up of guards. Great audience participation film with the last third dedicated to the game. Very funny, with some truly touching moments. Rated R for language and violence.

1974   123 minutes

LORD JIM
★★★★

DIRECTOR: Richard Brooks
CAST: Peter O'Toole, James Mason, Eli Wallach

Joseph Conrad's complex novel of human weakness has been simplified for easier appreciation and brought to the screen in a lavish visual style. Peter O'Toole is Jim, a sailor in Southeast Asia who is adopted by a suppressed village as its leader in spite of a past clouded by allegations of cowardice. The belief shown in him by the native villagers is put to the test by a group of European thugs.

1965   154 minutes

LOST PATROL, THE
★★★★

DIRECTOR: John Ford
CAST: Victor McLaglen, Boris Karloff, Wallace Ford, Reginald Denny, Alan Hale, J. M. Kerrigan, Billy Beven

An intrepid band of British cavalrymen lost in the Mesopotamian desert are picked off by the Arabs, one by one. Brisk direction and topnotch characterizations make this a winner—though it is grim. Stout heart, forever England, and all that.

1934   B & W   65 minutes

LOVE AND BULLETS
★½

DIRECTOR: Stuart Rosenberg
CAST: Charles Bronson, Rod Steiger, Strother Martin, Bradford Dillman, Henry Silva, Jill Ireland

Incredibly dull Charles Bronson thriller marred by Jill Ireland. Bronson is hired to snatch Ireland from crime lord Rod Steiger. An absolute waste of a good cast and completely lacking the savage bite

that powered earlier Bronson vehicles, such as *The Mechanic*. Don't bother. Rated PG for violence.

1979   103 minutes

LOVE SPELL
★

DIRECTOR: Tom Donavan
CAST: Richard Burton, Kate Mulgrew, Nicholas Clay, Cyril Cusack, Kathryn Dowlin

In this film based on the legend of Tristan and Isolde and their doomed love, Richard Burton portrays Mark, King of Cornwall, who sends his nephew, Tristan, to fetch Isolde, Mark's intended bride. Unfortunately, the two fall in love, creating the most difficult of triangles. The chase and battle scenes are unimaginatively filmed, and most of the acting mediocre. Burton, however, does his best with the material at hand. Hopeless romantics may find some entertainment here, but others will find this grand-legend-turned-soap-opera a bore.

1979   90 minutes

LUCKY LUCIANO
★★

DIRECTOR: Francesco Rosi
CAST: Gian Maria Volonte, Rod Steiger, Edmond O'Brien, Vincent Gardenia, Charles Cioffi

This U.S.-Franco-Italian production, deals with the last years of one of crimeland's most "influential" bosses. The film started out to be an important one for Francesco Roszi, but the distributors of the English edition went in for the sensationalism with too graphic subtitles and/or dubbing, depending on the version. Not a bad film if you know Italian. If you don't, stick with *The Godfather*. Rated R for profanity and violence.

1974 110 minutes

MACKINTOSH MAN, THE
★★★

DIRECTOR: John Huston
CAST: Paul Newman, James Mason, Dominique Sanda, Ian Bannen, Nigel Patrick

A cold war spy thriller with all the edge-of-seat trimmings: car chases, beatings, escapes, and captures. Trouble is, it has been done before, before, and before. Paul Newman is the agent; wily and wonderful James Mason is the Communist spy he must catch. Rated PG.

1973 98 minutes

MACON COUNTY LINE
★★★

DIRECTOR: Richard Compton
CAST: Alan Vint, Max Baer Jr., Geoffrey Lewis

A very effective little thriller based on a true incident. Set in Georgia in the 1950s, the story concerns three youths hunted by the law for a murder they did not commit. Producer Max Baer Jr. has a good eye for detail and the flavor of the times. Rated R.

1974 89 minutes

MAD DOG MORGAN
★★½

DIRECTOR: Philippe Mora
CAST: Dennis Hopper, Jack Thompson, David Gulpilil, Michael Pate

Dennis Hopper plays an Australian bush ranger in this familiar tale of a man forced into a life of crime. Good support from aborigine David Gulpilil and Australian actor Jack Thompson help this visually stimulating film, but Hopper's excesses and a muddled ending weigh against it. Early prison sequences and scattered scenes are brutal. Violence, brutality, and offensive scenes. Rated R.

1976 102 minutes

MADIGAN
★★★½

DIRECTOR: Don Siegel
CAST: Richard Widmark, Henry Fonda, Harry Guardino, James Whitmore, Inger Stevens, Michael Dunn, Steve Ihnat, Sheree North

Well-acted, atmospheric police adventure-drama pits tough Brooklyn cop Richard Widmark and New York's finest against a crazed escaped murderer. Veteran Henry Fonda and a fine cast of character actors and actresses breathe life into this taut pre–*Dirty Harry* outing by director Don Siegel, and location shooting adds to the authentic, gritty tone of this film. Realistic and exciting, this is still one of the best of the "behind-the-scenes" police films and topflight entertainment. Tame by today's standards, this is still not ideal fare for young children.

1968 101 minutes

MAGNUM FORCE
★★★

DIRECTOR: Ted Post
CAST: Clint Eastwood, Hal Holbrook, David Soul, Tim Matheson, Robert Urich

This is the second and least enjoyable of the four Dirty Harry films. Harry (Clint Eastwood) must deal with vigilante cops as well as the usual big-city scum. Body count is way up there, Clint is iron-jawed and athletic, but the film still lacks something. Rated R for lan-

guage, violence, nudity, and gore.
1973   124 minutes

MALTESE FALCON, THE
★★★★★

DIRECTOR: John Huston
CAST: Humphrey Bogart, Mary Astor, Sydney Greenstreet, Peter Lorre, Elisha Cook Jr., Ward Bond

One of the all-time great movies, John Huston's first effort as a director is the definitive screen version of Dashiell Hammett's crime story. In a maze of double-crosses and back-stabbing, Humphrey Bogart, as Sam Spade, fights to get hold of a black bird, "the stuff that dreams are made of." One of the greatest casts of supporting heavies fits perfectly into the Hammett characterizations. Sydney Greenstreet, in his first movie, is especially memorable as Kasper Gutman, the "Fat Man" behind the search for the falcon. Mary Astor, Peter Lorre, and Elisha Cook Jr. complete this perfect rogues gallery.
1941   B & W 100 minutes

MAN, A WOMAN AND A BANK, A
★★

DIRECTOR: Noel Black
CAST: Donald Sutherland, Brooke Adams, Paul Mazursky

An odd little caper flick which never quite gets off the ground. A couple of guys decide to rob a bank via computer, and—of course—things don't work out as planned. Donald Sutherland and Paul Mazursky (usually on the other side of the camera) are quite charming, and Brooke Adams delightfully appealing, but these characters can't rise above the weak plot. Could

(and should) have been much better. Rated PG.
1979   100 minutes

MAN FROM SNOWY RIVER
★★★★

DIRECTOR: George Miller
CAST: Tom Burlinson, Kirk Douglas, Jack Thompson, Bruce Kerr

If you've been looking for an adventure film for the whole family, this Australian western about the coming of age of a mountain man (Tom Burlinson) is it. Like a first-rate Disney movie from the 1950s, sometimes it's corny and a little too cutesy. But it's just right for folks who are tired of all the cussing, nudity, and gore that seem to pervade most modern so-called family films. Rated PG, the film has no objectionable material.
1982   115 minutes

MAN IN THE IRON MASK, THE
★★★

DIRECTOR: Mike Newell
CAST: Richard Chamberlain, Patrick McGoohan, Louis Jourdan, Jenny Agutter, Ralph Richardson

This the Alexandre Dumas tale of twin brothers, separated at birth. One becomes the wicked King of France, the other, a heroic peasant. The story receives a top-drawer treatment in this classy TV movie. Richard Chamberlain proves he's the most appealing swashbuckler since Errol Flynn retired his sword.
1977   100 minutes

MAN INSIDE, THE
★★½

DIRECTOR: Gerald Mayer

CAST: James Franciscus, Stefanie Powers, Jacques Godin, Len Birman, Donald Davis, Allan Royale

In this so-so film, James Franciscus is a Canadian vice squad agent who works his way into the organization of a major heroin dealer. In the course of his assignment he has the opportunity to split with $2 million, and is tempted to do so. This would provide the means for a new way of life, which his girlfriend (Stefanie Powers) is demanding. It would also put a heroin dealer out of business for good. This Canadian film is unrated.

1984   96 minutes

MAN WHO WOULD BE KING, THE
★★★★½

DIRECTOR: John Huston
CAST: Sean Connery, Michael Caine, Christopher Plummer

A superb screen adventure, this is loosely based on Rudyard Kipling's story and was made at the same time Sean Connery and John Huston starred in the other sand-and-camel flick, the excellent *The Wind and the Lion*. Both are classics in the adventure genre. Rated PG.

1975   129 minutes

MAN WITH BOGART'S FACE, THE
★★½

DIRECTOR: Robert Day
CAST: Robert Sacci, Michelle Phillips, Olivia Hussey, Franco Nero, Misty Rowe, Victor Buono, Herbert Lom, Sybil Danning, George Raft, Mike Mazurki

A modern-day Humphrey Bogart-type mystery. Film has fun with the genre while avoiding outright parody. A warm-hearted

homage. Enjoyable, but of no great importance. Rated PG.

1980   106 minutes

MAN WITH THE GOLDEN GUN, THE
★½

DIRECTOR: Guy Hamilton
CAST: Roger Moore, Christopher Lee, Britt Ekland, Maud Adams, Herve Villechaize, Bernard Lee, Lois Maxwell

In spite of the potentially sinister presence of Christopher Lee as the head baddie, this is the weakest and most poorly constructed of all the Bond films. Roger Moore sleepwalks through the entire picture, and the plot tosses in every cliché, including the (then) obligatory nod to kung-fu. Even John Barry's score is less spirited than usual, and Britt Ekland represents a low in leading ladies . . . even in *this series*. Sorry 'bout that, James. Rated PG—some violence.

1974   125 minutes

MANHUNT IN THE AFRICAN JUNGLE (SECRET SERVICE IN DARKEST AFRICA)
★★

DIRECTOR: Spencer Bennet
CAST: Rod Cameron, Joan Marsh, Duncan Renaldo, Lionel Royce

American undercover agent Rod Cameron, posing as a Nazi, joins forces with United Nations agent Joan Marsh, posing as a journalist, to defeat the Axis in North Africa, which is headed by Lionel Royce, who in turn is disguised as an Arab leader. Duncan Renaldo (*The Cisco Kid*) as a French officer comes along to help and takes his turn in being pummeled, conked on the head, and tied up in true serial fashion. The good guys naturally win in the end, although they make a pretty bland bunch compared with Nazis Kurt Kreuger and Kurt Katch. Not the most thrill-laden of serials.

1943   B & W 15 chapters

MANHUNTER
★★★★½

DIRECTOR: Michael Mann
CAST: William Petersen, Kim Greist, Brian Cox, Dennis Farina, Joan Allen, Chris Elliot

Thoroughly engrossing tale of an FBI man (William Petersen of *To Live and Die in L.A.*) following a trail of blood through the Southeast left by a ruthless, calculating psychopath known only as "The Tooth Fairy," for reasons made shockingly clear. This genuine edge-of-your-seat nail-biter from *Miami Vice* creator and producer Michael Mann must be viewed very attentively if one is to catch all the details and motives in the intricate plot. Produced with the utmost care and skill, *Manhunter* also features tight performances and some beautiful imagery in the best *Vice* tradition, with Iron Butterfly's classic "In-a-gadda-da-vida" used to create maximum impact at the jarring climax. A certified winner, intense and compelling from beginning to end. Rated R for violence and various adult contents.

1986   118 minutes

MARATHON MAN
★★★★

DIRECTOR: John Schlesinger
CAST: Dustin Hoffman, Laurence Olivier, Roy Scheider, William Devane, Marthe Keller

A young student (Dustin Hoffman) unwittingly becomes involved in the pursuit of an ex–Nazi war criminal (Laurence Olivier) in this chase-thriller. The action holds your interest throughout. Most chilling is the scene where Olivier makes use of his ex-profession of dentistry to persuade Hoffman to share some information. A few of the more violent moments may be too excessive for some viewers' tastes. Rated R.

1976   125 minutes

MARK OF ZORRO
★★★★

DIRECTOR: Rouben Mamoulian
CAST: Tyrone Power, Linda Darnell, Basil Rathbone

A superb swashbuckler, this is the finest screen adventure of the masked man from south of the border. Tyrone Power (Zorro) and Basil Rathbone are well-matched adversaries in this excellent entertainment.

1940   B & W 93 minutes

MASKED MARVEL, THE
★★½

DIRECTOR: Spencer Bennet
CAST: William Forrest, Louise Currie, Johnny Arthur, David Bacon

The mysterious Masked Marvel comes to the aid of the World-Wide Insurance Company to battle the evil Sakima, a former Japanese envoy, and his gang of saboteurs, who are threatening the security of America. The Masked Marvel finally triumphs after dodging bombs, bullets, falls, and runaway vehicles of all kinds. He keeps his identity a secret, too, ready to emerge again when America needs a champion. Practically nonstop action and top stunt work highlight this wartime Republic serial, which is about as patriotic as a serial can be.

1943   B & W 12 chapters

MCQ
★★★½

DIRECTOR: John Sturges
CAST: John Wayne, Al Lettieri, Eddie Albert, Diana Muldaur, Clu Gulager, Colleen Dewhurst

The success of *Dirty Harry* and slow death of the western prompted John Wayne to shed his Stetson and six guns for cop clothes. While this John Sturges film doesn't quite match the Clint Eastwood–Don Siegel production that inspired it, there are some good scenes and suspense. The best moment comes when Big John bangs around bad guy Al Lettieri in a men's room. Recommended for fans of the Duke only. Rated PG.

1974   116 minutes

MEAN JOHNNY BARROWS
🦃

DIRECTOR: Fred Williamson
CAST: Fred Williamson, Roddy McDowall, Stuart Whitman, Elliott Gould, Jenny Sherman

Fred Williamson plays Jonny Barrows, a Vietnam war hero, dishonorably discharged for striking an officer. Trying to make it as a civilian, he becomes involved in a gang war, bad acting, and horrible music. This is one of the *Shaft*-inspired black black exploitation films, and like too many of them, it's a waste of time. Rated R.

1976   80 minutes

MEAN SEASON, THE
★★★½

DIRECTOR: Phillip Borsos
CAST: Kurt Russell, Richard Jordan, Mariel Hemingway, Richard Masur

Miami crime reporter Kurt Russell finds himself the unwilling confidant of a maniacal killer in this exciting thriller. The film occasionally relies on stock shocks. Still, it is fast-paced and inventive enough to overcome the clichés. Mariel Hemingway is featured as the journalist's imperiled girlfriend, with Richard Jordan effective in a change-of-pace role as the villain. Rated R for violence.

1985   109 minutes

MECHANIC, THE
★★½

DIRECTOR: Michael Winner
CAST: Charles Bronson, Jan-Michael Vincent, Jill Ireland, Keenan Wynn

A professional hit man (Charles Bronson) teaches his craft to a young student (Jan-Michael Vincent). Slow-moving for the most part, with a few good action scenes. The ending has a nice twist to it, but the film is generally much ado about nothing. Rated R for violence and language.

1972   100 minutes

MEN IN WAR
★★★★

DIRECTOR: Anthony Mann
CAST: Robert Ryan, Aldo Ray, Vic Morrow

This outstanding Korean War action film with Robert Ryan and Aldo Ray fighting the Chinese and each other is one of the very best "war is hell" films. Battle scenes are first-rate, thanks to Anthony Mann's crisp and uncompromising direction.

1957   B & W 104 minutes

MIAMI VICE
★★★★

DIRECTOR: Thomas Carter

CAST: Don Johnson, Philip Michael Thomas, Saundra Santiago, Michael Talbott, John Diehl, Gregory Sierra, Bill Smitrovich, Belinda Montgomery, Martin Ferrero, Mykel T. Williamson, Olivia Brown, Miguel Pinero

This pilot for the popular NBC series is slam-bang entertainment. A New York City cop (Philip Michael Thomas) on the trail of the powerful drug kingpin who killed his brother traces him to Miami, running into a vice cop (Don Johnson) who's after the same guy. All the trademarks of the series are here: great music, rapid-fire editing, gritty low-key performances, and bursts of sporadic violence. Combine these elements with a superb video transfer (far better than network TV), and you have a dynamite action show outdone only by its sequel episode, "The Return of Calderone." The only real flaw in this tape is the sound quality, which, even in hi-fi stereo, is muffled.

1984   97 minutes

MIAMI VICE: "THE PRODIGAL SON"
★★★

DIRECTOR: Paul Michael Glaser
CAST: Don Johnson, Philip Michael Thomas, Edward James Olmos, Olivia Brown, Penn Jilette, Pam Grier

The pastel duo, Crockett (Don Johnson) and Tubbs (Philip Michael Thomas), trek up to New York in search of the bad guys in this second-season opener. Out of Miami and into the Big Apple's glitz, Crockett falls in love with a criminal's girlfriend and almost gets killed. The bad guys turn out to be good guys, and everyone is running through the crowded streets of the city with Uzis, pistols, and shotguns blaring, without ever once seeing a uniformed cop.

1985   99 minutes

MIDWAY
★★★

DIRECTOR: Jack Smight
CAST: Henry Fonda, Charlton Heston, Robert Mitchum, Hal Holbrook, Edward Albert, Cliff Robertson

An all-star cast was assembled to bring to the screen this famous sea battle of World War II. Midway became famous as the site of the overwhelming victory of American carrier forces, which shifted the balance of power in the Pacific. As a historical drama, this film is accurate and maintains interest. However, a subplot involving Charlton Heston's son (Edward Albert) and his romance with a Japanese girl is totally out of place. Rated PG.

1976   132 minutes

MIRROR CRACK'D, THE
★½

DIRECTOR: Guy Hamilton
CAST: Elizabeth Taylor, Kim Novak, Tony Curtis, Angela Lansbury, Edward Fox, Rock Hudson

Elizabeth Taylor, Kim Novak, and Tony Curtis seem to be vying to see who can turn in the worst performance in this tepid adaptation of the Agatha Christie murder mystery. Angela Lansbury makes an excellent Miss Marple, and Edward Fox is topnotch as her Scotland Yard inspector nephew. But overall this film—awkwardly directed by James Bond specialist Guy Hamilton (*Goldfinger*; *The Man with the Golden Gun*)—is a definite step down from the other Christie films, such as *Murder on the Orient Express* and *Death on the Nile*. Rated PG.

1980   105 minutes

MISSING IN ACTION
★★★½

DIRECTOR: Joseph Zito

CAST: Chuck Norris, M. Emmet Walsh, Lenore Kasdorf, James Hong

Chuck Norris is a one-man army in this Vietnam-based action film. Anyone else might be laughable in such a role. But the former karate star makes it work, resulting in the best film he'd made to date. The story focuses on an attempt by Col. James Braddock (Norris), a former Vietnam prisoner of war, to free the other Americans he believes are still there. Rated R for profanity, violence, and brief nudity.

1984   101 minutes

MISSING IN ACTION 2: THE BEGINNING
★★½

DIRECTOR: Lance Hool

CAST: Chuck Norris, Cosie Costa, Soon-Teck Oh, Steven Williams, Bennett Ohta

Following on the heels of the previous year's surprise hit, this "prequel" is really the same movie, only it tells the story of how Colonel Braddock (Chuck Norris) and his men escaped their Vietnam prison camp after ten years of torture. The acting is nonexistent, the action predictable and violent. Soon-Teck Oh (from television's *East of Eden*) stars as the sadistic camp commandant and prime enemy in this martial arts/action drama. Rated R for violence.

1985   95 minutes

MR. ACE
★½

DIRECTOR: Edwin L. Marin

CAST: George Raft, Sylvia Sidney, Stanley Ridges, Sara Haden, Jerome Cowan

Studio potboiler about spoiled society woman (Sylvia Sidney) who uses gangster (George Raft) to win congressional election goes through the motions but very little else. Raft, an interesting nonactor at best, seems to be in this film simply because he fills the part; he never brings the kind of excitement or character that a Lloyd Nolan could have breathed into it. The acting is okay, but the story is too familiar and the ending too trite to be taken seriously. Basically a programmer and a vehicle for the two aging stars, this film never really takes off and offers a pretty low-priority rental choice when compared with the better films in which these actors and actresses appeared.

1946   B & W   84 minutes

MR. BILLION
★★★½

DIRECTOR: Jonathan Kaplan

CAST: Terence Hill, Valerie Perrine, Jackie Gleason, Slim Pickens, William Redfield, Chill Wills, Dick Miller

Sappy but seductive story about a humble Italian mechanic (Terence Hill) who will inherit a financial empire if he can get to the signing over of his uncle's will before a gang of kidnappers or the corporation's chairman (Jackie Gleason) gets to him first. Valerie Perrine plays a call girl who is hired to seduce the benefactor and get him to sign over his inheritance. While this all sounds like heavy drama, there are enough car chases and fist fights to earn this one a place in the action category. Rated PG for violence and sex.

1977   89 minutes

MR. LUCKY
★★★

DIRECTOR: H. C. Potter
CAST: Cary Grant, Laraine Day

Cary Grant is a gambler attempting to bilk money from a charity relief program. He changes his tune when he falls for a wealthy society girl, Laraine Day. This is a slick piece of wartime fluff. The plot has nothing you haven't seen before, but the charm of Grant makes it watchable.

1943   B & W 100 minutes

MR. MAJESTYK
★★★½

DIRECTOR: Richard Fleischer
CAST: Charles Bronson, Al Lettieri, Linda Cristal, Lee Purcell, Paul Koslo

In this better-than-average Charles Bronson vehicle, he's a watermelon grower (!) coming up against gangster Al Lettieri (in a first-rate performance). If you like Chuck, you'll love this one. Rated R.

1974   103 minutes

MR. MOTO'S LAST WARNING
★★★

DIRECTOR: Norman Foster
CAST: Peter Lorre, Ricardo Cortez, Virginia Field, John Carradine, George Sanders

One of the last in the low-budget series that produced eight films in less than three years. This time out, the detective gets involved with terrorist spies intent on blowing up the French fleet in the Suez Canal. Enjoyable, quaint entertainment with a good supporting cast.

1939   B & W 71 minutes

MR. ROBINSON CRUSOE
★★★

DIRECTOR: Edward Sutherland
CAST: Douglas Fairbanks Sr., William Farnum, Maria Alba

Dashing Douglas Fairbanks Sr. bets he can survive like Crusoe on a South Sea island. Just how he does it makes for great fun. Fairbanks was just short of 50 when he made this film, but he was still the agile, athletic swashbuckler whose wholesome charm made him the idol of millions.

1932   B & W 76 minutes

MR. WONG, DETECTIVE
★★★

DIRECTOR: William Nigh
CAST: Boris Karloff, Grant Withers, Evelyn Brent, Maxinne Jennings, Lucien Prival

First of five Mr. Wong films starring Boris Karloff as Hugh Wiley's black-suited sleuth is a notch above most of Mascot Pictures' programmers. Mr. Wong (with the dubious assistance of Captain Street of Homicide) attempts to solve the deaths of three industrialists, which have baffled the authorities and have the government and media in an uproar. The great Karloff is always a treat to watch and this series marked his only continuing character that wasn't a monster or villain of some sort. Fun for mystery and detective fans and a nice complement to the other Oriental sleuths of the 1930s, Charlie Chan and Mr. Moto.

1938   B & W 69 minutes

MIXED BLOOD
★★★½

DIRECTOR: Paul Morrissey
CAST: Marilia Pera, Richard Ulacia, Linda Kerridge, Geraldine Smith, Angel David, Ulrich Berr, Rodney Harvey

Paul Morrissey, the same man who brought you Andy Warhol's versions of *Frankenstein* and *Dracula*, has made a serious film about the Alphabet City drug subculture and its inherent violent nature. *Mixed Blood* is actually a mixed bag. Morrissey's choice of actors has changed; they all read their lines devoid of emotion. While this detracts from the story most of the time, there are moments when this makes complete sense. The film is similar to Penelope Spheeris' *Suburbia*. The lack of emotion in the characters shifts the focus from the actor to the landscape to which he is reacting. Here the surroundings are brutal and unforgiving, and the cheap film stock gives the movie a newsreel feeling. Not rated but contains an abundance of violence and profanity

1985   98 minutes

MOBY DICK
★★★★½

DIRECTOR: John Huston

CAST: Gregory Peck, Richard Basehart, Leo Genn, Orson Welles

Director John Huston's brilliant adaptation of Herman Melville's classic novel features Gregory Peck in one of his best performances as the driven Captain Ahab. Richard Basehart, Leo Genn, and Orson Welles lend fine support. The final action scenes are pure Hollywood magic. No rating, with some violence, but all right for the family.

1956   116 minutes

MOGAMBO
★★★

DIRECTOR: John Ford

CAST: Clark Gable, Grace Kelly, Ava Gardner

This remake of the film classic *Red Dust* stars Clark Gable as the great white hunter who dallies with a sophisticated married woman (Grace Kelly), only to return to the arms of a jaded lady (Ava Gardner, who is quite good in the role of the woman with a past). It's not great John Ford, but it'll do.

1953   115 minutes

MOONLIGHTING
★★★★

DIRECTOR: Robert Butler

CAST: Cybill Shepherd, Bruce Willis, Allyce Beasley

This is the pilot film for the delightfully offbeat ABC series. Maddie, a super-successful model, suddenly finds herself facing poverty, thanks to an embezzler. She decides to sell off all her assets, including a money-losing detective agency. David, a fast-talking, irresistible eccentric, tries to talk her into making a career of sleuthing instead. Bruce Willis is dazzling as David. And the chemistry beween Willis and Cybill Shepherd heats up to just the right temperature. The pilot displays a degree of wit and style rarely seen in a TV movie.

1985   97 minutes

MOONRAKER
★

DIRECTOR: Lewis Gilbert

CAST: Roger Moore, Lois Chiles, Michael Lonsdale

The James Bond series hit absolute rock bottom in 1979 with this outer-space adventure featuring Roger Moore as the famed secret agent. It's a groaner for 007 fans and nonfans alike. Rated PG.

1979   126 minutes

MOONSHINE COUNTY EXPRESS
★★

DIRECTOR: Gus Trikonis
CAST: John Saxon, Susan Howard, William Conrad, Dub Taylor

In this bogus action flick, William Conrad has his hands full with the three vengeful daughters of a man he just murdered. Rated PG for mild language and violence.

1977   95 minutes

MORGAN THE PIRATE
★★★

DIRECTOR: André de Toth, Primo Zeglio
CAST: Steve Reeves, Valerie Lagrange, Ivo Garbani, Lidia Alfonsi, Giulio Bosetti, Angelo Zanolli

This fictionalized account of the adventures of the historical Henry Morgan (with muscleman Steve Reeves in the title role) is perhaps the most entertaining of that actor's many Italian-made features. Even by current standards, there is plenty of action and romance.

1961   93 minutes

MOTHER LODE
★★

DIRECTOR: Charlton Heston
CAST: Charlton Heston, John Marley, Nick Mancuso, Kim Basinger

Although this modern-day adventure yarn about a search for gold boasts a feasible plot and fine acting by Charlton Heston (who also directed) and John Marley, its liabilities far outweigh its assets. It is uneven, lacks character development, and the performances of Nick Mancuso and Kim Basinger leave much to be desired. Despite a good deal of suspense in the second half, it remains a mediocre piece of escapism. Rated PG, the film contains occasional obscenities and violence.

1982   101 minutes

MS. .45
★★★★

DIRECTOR: Abel Ferrara
CAST: Zoe Tamerlis

An attractive mute woman is raped and beaten twice in the same evening. She slips into madness and seeks revenge with a .45 pistol. A female version of *Death Wish* with an ending at a Halloween costume party that will knock your socks off. Not for all tastes. Rated R for violence, nudity, rape, language, and gore.

1981   90 minutes

MURDER BY DECREE
★★★½

DIRECTOR: Bob Clark
CAST: Christopher Plummer, James Mason, Donald Sutherland, Genevieve Bujold, Susan Clark, David Hemmings, John Gielgud, Anthony Quayle

Excellent cast stylishly serves up this Sherlock Holmes mystery. Christopher Plummer and James Mason are well suited to the roles of Holmes and Dr. Watson. The murky story deals with Jack the Ripper. Rated R for violence and gore.

1979   121 minutes

MURDER MY SWEET
★★★★

DIRECTOR: Edward Dmytryk
CAST: Dick Powell, Claire Trevor, Anne Shirley

In the mid-1940s, Dick Powell decided to change his clean-cut crooner image by playing Raymond Chandler's hard-boiled detective, Philip Marlowe. It worked marvelously, with Powell making a fine white knight in tarnished armor on the trail of killers and blackmailers.

1944　　　B & W　　95 minutes

MURDER ON THE ORIENT EXPRESS
★★★★½

DIRECTOR: Sidney Lumet
CAST: Albert Finney, Ingrid Bergman, Lauren Bacall, Sean Connery, Vanessa Redgrave, Michael York, Jacqueline Bisset

Belgian detective Hercule Poirot solves a murder on a train in this stylish prestige picture based on the Agatha Christie mystery. Albert Finney stars as the detective and is supported by an all-star cast. Rated PG.

1974　　　127 minutes

MURDERERS' ROW
★★½

DIRECTOR: Henry Levin
CAST: Dean Martin, Ann-Margret, Karl Malden, James Gregory

This entry into the Matt Helm secret-agent series is pretty dismal. Dean Martin has been much better in other films. The Matt Helm series was an attempt to grab the Bond and Flint audience, but Martin just couldn't cut it as a superspy.

1966　　　108 minutes

MURPH THE SURF
★★½

DIRECTOR: Marvin Chomsky
CAST: Robert Conrad, Don Stroud, Donna Mills, Luther Adler

In this based-on-real-life thriller, two Florida beachniks connive to do the impossible: steal the fabled 564-carat Star of India sapphire out of New York's American Museum of Natural History. Recreation of the 1964 crime induces sweat, along with a good speedboat chase, but the picture never really catches a wave.

1975　　　101 minutes

MURPHY'S LAW
★★

DIRECTOR: J. Lee Thompson
CAST: Charles Bronson, Carrie Snodgress, Kathleen Wilhoite

Guess what! Charles Bronson plays a tough guy! He's a cop framed for the murder of his ex-wife, who escapes from jail handcuffed to the teenage girl who stole his car. It's a plot line used before in The Defiant Ones, The Gauntlet, and 48 Hrs, all of which are better films. The movie suffers from a complete lack of subtlety. The bad guys are snarling Neanderthals, the good guys are honest to a fault, and Bronson's young cohort (Kathleen Wilhoite) is so relentlessly spunky, she makes you want to retch. The only thing Murphy's Law does well is prove Murphy's Law. Rated R.

1986　　　101 minutes

MURPHY'S WAR
★★★

DIRECTOR: Peter Yates
CAST: Peter O'Toole, Sian Phillips, Horst Janson, Philippe Noiret, John Hallam

World War II sea drama follows British seaman, sole survivor of a brutal massacre of his ship's crew by a German U-boat, as he seeks revenge. Peter O'Toole gives a hard-hitting, no-holds-barred performance as the outraged, bloodthirsty Murphy. This film is something of a psychological study. Action sequences are great, but talky scenes tend to slow things to a bore. Well done nonetheless. Rated PG.

1971   108 minutes

MUTINY ON THE BOUNTY (ORIGINAL)
★★★★

DIRECTOR: Frank Lloyd
CAST: Charles Laughton, Clark Gable, Franchot Tone, Dudley Digges, Eddie Quillan, Donald Crisp, Henry Stephenson, Spring Byington, Herbert Mundin, Douglas Walton, Ian Wolfe

The first and best known of three versions of the now classic account of mutiny against the tyranny of Captain William Bligh during a worldwide British naval expedition in 1789. Charles Laughton is superb as the merciless Bligh, Clark Gable unquestionably fine as the leader of the mutiny, Fletcher Christian. The film won an Oscar for best picture and still entertains today.

1935   B & W 132 minutes

MUTINY ON THE BOUNTY (REMAKE)
★★

DIRECTOR: Lewis Milestone
CAST: Marlon Brando, Trevor Howard, Richard Harris, Hugh Griffith, Richard Haydn, Gordon Jackson

This years-later remake hits the South Seas with a gigantic belly flop. The color is beautiful, Trevor Howard is commanding as the tyrannical Captain Bligh, but Marlon Brando as mutiny leader Fletcher Christian? Yucko!

1962   179 minutes

NAKED AND THE DEAD, THE
★★★

DIRECTOR: Raoul Walsh

CAST: Aldo Ray, Joey Bishop, Cliff Robertson, Raymond Massey

This action-packed World War II film is based on Norman Mailer's famous book. Not nearly as good as the book, nevertheless the film is still quite powerful and exciting. Worth a watch. Bernard Herrmann did the film score.

1958   131 minutes

NAKED PREY, THE
★★★½

DIRECTOR: Cornel Wilde
CAST: Cornel Wilde, Gert Van Den Bergh, Ken Gampu

An African safari takes a disastrous turn and Cornel Wilde winds up running naked and unarmed through the searing jungle as a large band of native warriors keeps on his heels, determined to finish him off. This is an amazingly intense adventure of man versus man and man verus nature. Wilde does a remarkable job, both as star and director.

1966   94 minutes

NATE AND HAYES
★★★

DIRECTOR: Ferdinand Fairfax
CAST: Tommy Lee Jones, Michael O'Keefe, Max Phipps

Tommy Lee Jones as a good pirate, Michael O'Keefe as his missionary accomplice, and Max Phipps as their cutthroat nemesis make this a jolly movie. Set in the South Seas of the late nineteenth century, it's unpretentious, old-fashioned movie fun. Rated PG for violence.

1983   100 minutes

NEVER CRY WOLF
★★★★★

DIRECTOR: Carroll Ballard
CAST: Charles Martin Smith, Brian Dennehy

Carroll Ballard (*The Black Stallion*) made this breathtakingly beautiful, richly rewarding Disney feature about a lone biologist (Charles Martin Smith, of *American Grafitti*) learning firsthand about the white wolves of the Yukon by living with them. It's an extraordinary motion picture in every sense of the word. Not only is it the kind of movie the whole family can enjoy, but it's also a state-of-the-art cinematic creation. Rated PG for brief nudity.

1983   105 minutes

NEVER SAY NEVER AGAIN
★★★★½

DIRECTOR: Irvin Kershner
CAST: Sean Connery, Klaus Maria Brandauer, Barbara Carrera, Max von Sydow, Kim Basinger, Bernie Casey

In the battle of the Bonds, Sean Connery wins over Roger Moore by a hair—or is that hairpiece? (Sorry, Sean.) All kidding aside, it's great to see Connery back in the role he made—and that made him—famous. Although *Never Say Never Again* is essentially a remake of *Thunderball*, it is a far superior film; much funnier, sexier, and more action-filled than its predecessor. Rated PG for violence, suggested sex, and nudity.

1983   137 minutes

NEVER TOO YOUNG TO DIE
★

DIRECTOR: Gil Bettman
CAST: John Stamos, Vanity, Gene Simmons, George Lazenby

A really rotten film that steals everything it can from the James Bond and *Road Warrior* series. John Stamos plays the son of George Lazenby, an American secret agent who is murdered by a gang of crazies, led by Gene Simmons. The gang's plan is to poison the water supply of Los Angeles if $50 million ransom isn't paid to them. Unbelievably bad dialogue, and boring action scenes make this a real bomb, with only Vanity's good looks and charm left for enjoyment. Rated R for language, sex, and violence.

1986   90 minutes

NEWMAN'S LAW
★

DIRECTOR: Richard Heffron
CAST: George Peppard, Roger Robinson, Abe Vigoda, Eugene Roche

George Peppard plays a good cop accused of corruption and suspended from the force, who privately pursues the case he is on. Sound familiar? It is, with all the clichés intact. Rated PG for violence.

1974   98 minutes

NIGHT CROSSING
★★★½

DIRECTOR: Delbert Mann
CAST: John Hurt, Jane Alexander, Beau Bridges, Ian Bannen

This Disney film is about a real-life escape from East Germany by two families in a gas-filled balloon. The performances by John Hurt, Jane Alexander, Beau Bridges, and Ian Bannen are excellent, and director Delbert Mann makes the most of the possibilities for suspense. Unfortunately, minor flaws, such as mismatched accents and Americanized situations, prevent it from being a total success. Rated PG for violence.

1981   106 minutes

NIGHT MOVES
★★★★

DIRECTOR: Arthur Penn

CAST: Gene Hackman, Susan Clark, Melanie Griffith

A dark and disturbing detective study with Gene Hackman superb as the private eye trying to solve a baffling mystery. This release was unfairly overlooked when in theaters—but you don't have to miss it now. Rated R.

1975   95 minutes

NIGHT OF THE GENERALS
★

DIRECTOR: Anatole Litvak
CAST: Peter O'Toole, Omar Sharif, Tom Courtenay, Donald Pleasence, Joanna Pettet, Christopher Plummer

This lurid WWII murder mystery, revolving around a group of Nazi generals, has very little to offer. It will leave you bored, confused, and slightly repulsed.

1967   148 minutes

NIGHT OF THE JUGGLER
★★

DIRECTOR: Robert Butler
CAST: James Brolin, Cliff Gorman, Richard Castellano, Abby Bluestone, Linda G. Miller, Mandy Patinkin

Psychopath kidnaps little girl for ransom. It's the wrong little girl. Her daddy's an ex-cop with no money and lots of rage. The movie, buoyed by James Brolin's potent performance, initially grabs viewers' attention. Eventually, a cruel streak undermines the drama as it wheezes to a predictable conclusion. Rated R.

1980   101 minutes

NIGHTHAWKS
★★★★½

DIRECTOR: Bruce Malmuth
CAST: Sylvester Stallone, Billy Dee Williams, Rutger Hauer, Lindsay Wagner

From its explosive first scene to the breathtakingly suspenseful denouement, *Nighthawks*, about a police detective hunting a wily terrorist, is a thoroughly enjoyable, supercharged action film. Rated R for violence, nudity, and profanity.

1981   99 minutes

NIGHTKILL
★★★

DIRECTOR: Ted Post
CAST: Jaclyn Smith, Robert Mitchum, James Franciscus

Largely unreleased in theaters, this is a tidy little cat-and-mouse thriller with former Charlie's Angel Jaclyn Smith as a conniving widow and Mitchum as the world-weary investigator who gets caught up in her scheme. Smith and Mitchum are very good. Despite some inept direction, the last half-hour is a nail-biter, particularly scenes in a bathroom shower. Financed by a German company and filmed with a German crew by director Post. Rated R for violence, nudity, and profanity.

1983   97 minutes

NINE DEATHS OF THE NINJA
🐾

DIRECTOR: Emmet Alston
CAST: Sho Kosugi, Brent Huff, Emilia Lesniak, Blackie Dammett

Sho Kosugi (*Enter the Ninja*) stars in yet another grunt-and-groan, low-budget martial-arts mess. This time, he attempts to rescue a congressman who has been kidnapped by terrorists. You'll need chopsticks to keep your eyes open, and a good kick in the head to find it enjoyable. Rated R.

1985   94 minutes

99 AND 44/100 PERCENT DEAD
★★

DIRECTOR: John Frankenheimer
CAST: Richard Harris, Chuck Connors, Edmond O'Brien, Bradford Dillman, Ann Turkel

A hit man is hired to rub out a gangland boss. The first five minutes are stylish, and Bradford Dillman's impersonation of Elmer Fudd is sort of fun, but the rest of the film is a bore. If you are forced to watch it, try to entertain yourself by counting how many times the cast says "Hello, Harry." (Or in Dillman's case, "Hewwo, Hawwy.") Rated PG for violence.

1974   98 minutes

NINJA III: THE DOMINATION
🔪

DIRECTOR: Sam Firstenberg
CAST: Lucinda Dickey, Sho Kosugi

Now that *Ghostbusters* has spoofed the whole demonic-possession genre out of existence, it's only natural that the quick-buck moviemakers of the Cannon Group would come up with a completely idiotic film of that kind. Best described as *The Exorcist* meets *Enter the Dragon*, this turkey stars Lucinda Dickey (*Breakin'*) as a young woman possessed by the spirit of an evil revenge-seeking Ninja. And only Sho Kosugi (*Enter the Ninja* and *Revenge of the Ninja*) can bring her bloody rampage to an end. Even its many moments of unintentional humor don't make this pathetic picture worth watching. Avoid it at all costs. Rated R for violence and profanity.

1984   95 minutes

NORSEMAN, THE
🔪

DIRECTOR: Charles B. Pierce
CAST: Lee Majors, Charles B. Pierce Jr., Cornel Wilde, Mel Ferrer

This low-budget story of the Vikings landing in America in A.D. 1022 is so full of stupid historical errors and unbelievable elements that it should never have been released. Star Lee Majors, in addition to a performance so wooden it is almost petrified, speaks with a Southern accent. Who ever heard of a Viking with a Southern accent? Unbelievable. Writer-producer-director Charles B. Pierce committed the worst kind of nepotism by casting his untalented son, Charles B. Pierce Jr., as one of the Vikings. Rated PG.

1978   90 minutes

NORTH STAR, THE
★★★★

DIRECTOR: Lewis Milestone
CAST: Ruth Gordon, Walter Huston, Anne Baxter, Dana Andrews

This is a well-done World War II film about Russian peasants battling Nazi invaders during the early days of the German invasion of Russia in 1941. This film was reedited in the early 1950s, during the McCarthy witch-hunt days, and released as *Armored Attack*. The reedited version became an anti-Soviet, incoherent mess. Thanks to home video, we can now see the original. It's a bit corny and sentimental in places, but the battle scenes have the usual Milestone high-quality excitement. The cast does an excellent job.

1943   B & W 105 minutes

NORTHERN PURSUIT
★★★

DIRECTOR: Raoul Walsh

CAST: Errol Flynn, Julie Bishop, Tom Tully

This was the first picture made by Errol Flynn for Warner Bros. following his rape trial. Its uninspired plot and low budget seem to bespeak a certain lack of confidence in the star on the part of the studio. Despite Raoul Walsh's capable direction, this film, about a German heritage Canadian Mountie (Flynn) who feigns defection and guides a party of Nazi saboteurs to their secret base, is pure claptrap. It marked the beginning of Flynn's slow descent into obscurity and, eventually, illness.

1943   B & W   94 minutes

NYOKA AND THE TIGER MEN (PERILS OF NYOKA)
★★½

DIRECTOR: William Witney
CAST: Kay Alridge, Clayton Moore, William Benedict, Lorna Gray

Nyoka, the Jungle Girl, aids archeologist Clayton Moore ("The Lone Ranger") in saving and deciphering the long-lost Tablets of Hippocrates, which contain the medical knowledge of the ancient Greeks. The evil Vultura, ruler of a band of ruthless desert no-goods who hand out in a temple with a giant gorilla named Satan, covets the same tablets, and does everything possible to obtain them and do away with her competitors. It's one chase after another as the players scramble all over one another to secure the tablets, which only Nyoka can read. Plenty of stunts and familiar heavies Charles Middleton and Tristram Coffin make this an enjoyable afternoon diversion.

1942   B & W   15 chapters

OCEAN'S ELEVEN
★★★

DIRECTOR: Lewis Milestone
CAST: Frank Sinatra, Dean Martin, Sammy Davis Jr., Peter Lawford, Angie Dickinson, Cesar Romero

A twist ending, several stars, and good production values save this tale of an attempted robbery in Las Vegas. Frank Sinatra is the leader of the gang, and his now-famous "rat pack" are the gang members. Lightweight but pleasant.

1960   127 minutes

OCTAGON, THE
★★★

DIRECTOR: Eric Karson
CAST: Chuck Norris, Karen Carlson, Lee Van Cleef, Jack Carter

This "kung-fu" flick stars Chuck Norris as a bodyguard for Karen Carlson. Norris naturally takes on multiple opponents and beats them easily. Rated R.

1980   103 minutes

OCTOPUSSY
★★★★

DIRECTOR: John Glen
CAST: Roger Moore, Maud Adams, Louis Jourdan

Roger Moore returns as James Bond in the thirteenth screen adventure of Ian Fleming's superspy. It's like an adult-oriented *Raiders of the Lost Ark*: light, fast-paced, funny, and almost over before you know it—almost, because the film tends to overstay its welcome just a bit. The ending, though full of the usual thrills and chills, could have been shorter. Rated PG for violence and suggested sex.

1983   130 minutes

ODESSA FILE, THE
★½
DIRECTOR: Ronald Neame
CAST: Jon Voight, Maximilian Schell, Derek Jacobi, Maria Schell

Frederick Forsyth wrote the best-selling novel, but little of the zip remains in this weary film adaptation. German journalist Jon Voight learns of a secret file that may expose some former Nazis. That's about all there is to tell. Rated PG for violence.

1974   128 minutes

ON HER MAJESTY'S SECRET SERVICE
★★★★
DIRECTOR: Peter Hunt
CAST: George Lazenby, Diana Rigg, Telly Savalas

With Sean Connery temporarily out of the James Bond series, Australian actor George Lazenby stepped into the 007 part for this entry—and did remarkably well. While not as charismatic as Connery, he carries himself well and fights convincingly. Director Peter Hunt keeps this moving at an incredibly fast pace, and this story about everyone's favorite superspy falling in love with an heiress (Diana Rigg) is one of author Ian Fleming's best. Rated PG.

1969   140 minutes

ONCE UPON A TIME IN AMERICA (LONG VERSION)
★★★★
DIRECTOR: Sergio Leone
CAST: Robert DeNiro, James Woods, Elizabeth McGovern, Tuesday Weld, Treat Williams, Burt Young

Italian director Sergio Leone's richly rewarding gangster epic; a $30 million production starring Robert DeNiro in a forty-five-year saga of Jewish gangsters in New York City. Leone is best known for his spaghetti westerns *A Fistful of Dollars*, *The Good, the Bad and the Ugly*, and *Once upon a Time in the West*. This release culminates ten years of planning and false starts by the filmmaker. It was well worth the wait. Rated R for profanity, nudity, suggested sex, and violence.

1984   225 minutes

ONE DOWN, TWO TO GO
★★
DIRECTOR: Fred Williamson
CAST: Fred Williamson, Jim Brown, Jim Kelly, Richard Roundtree

Kung-fu fighter (Jim Kelly) suspects a tournament is fixed and calls on his buddies (Jim Brown and director Fred Williamson) for help in this low-budget, theatrically unreleased sequel to *Three the Hard Way*. This time, Richard Roundtree (*Shaft*) joins in the action. Some actors are hopelessly amateurish, and the story is a mere sketch. Considering all the talent involved, it's a major disappointment. Unrated, the film has violence.

1983   84 minutes

OPERATION C.I.A.
★★½
DIRECTOR: Christian Nyby
CAST: Burt Reynolds, Kieu Chinh, Danielle Aubry, John Hoyt, Cyril Collack

Political intrigue in Vietnam before the United States' full involvement finds a youthful Burt Reynolds at his physical peak as an agent assigned to derail an assassination attempt. Good location photography and Reynolds's enthusiasm and believability mark this film and the first few films he starred in as minor action classics and the best chase films of the mid-1960s. Look for a U.S. world in the Far East that doesn't exist anymore and was on its way out then.

1965   B & W   90 minutes

OPERATION THUNDERBOLT
★½

DIRECTOR: Menahem Golan

CAST: Yehoram Gaon, Klaus Kinski, Assaf Dayan

Another film, like *The Raid on Entebbe*, dealing with the Israeli commando raid in Uganda in 1976 to free 104 hijacked airline passengers. Overly sentimental, with poor performances and rather routine action sequences. No MPAA rating.

1977   125 minutes

ORDEAL BY INNOCENCE
★★

DIRECTOR: Desmond Davis

CAST: Donald Sutherland, Sarah Miles, Christopher Plummer, Ian McShane, Diana Quick, Faye Dunaway

In this production of but another Agatha Christie novel, the cast may be stellar, but the performances are almost all phoned in. Donald Sutherland plays a man who is certain that justice has been ill served in a small British community. Half of the film is disjointed flashbacks and echoed voices of conversations long over. Dave Brubeck provides the mood music. And while his groove is good on record, it's hardly the proper soundtrack for a murder mystery set in Great Britain. Rated PG-13 for language and nudity.

1984   91 minutes

ORGANIZATION, THE
★★★

DIRECTOR: Don Medford

CAST: Sidney Poitier, Barbara McNair, Raul Julia, Sheree North

This is the third and last installment of the Virgil Tibbs series based on the character Sidney Poitier originated in *In the Heat of the Night*. Tibbs is out to break up a ring of dope smugglers. A pretty good cop film, with some exciting action scenes. Rated PG, some strong stuff for the kids.

1971   107 minutes

OSTERMAN WEEKEND, THE
★★★

DIRECTOR: Sam Peckinpah

CAST: Rutger Hauer, John Hurt, Burt Lancaster, Dennis Hopper, Chris Sarandon, Meg Foster

When a brilliant but erratic director makes his first film after a five-year absence, the first question is: Is it a classic? In the case of *The Osterman Weekend*, Sam Peckinpah's last, the answer is no. That, however, does not make it a bad picture. *The Osterman Weekend* is, in fact, a good action movie, with many viewing rewards for the filmmaker's fans. But you have to pay attention. Based on Robert Ludlum's novel, it tells a complicated and convoluted story of espionage, revenge, and duplicity. Rated R for profanity, nudity, sex, and violence.

1983   102 minutes

OUT OF BOUNDS
★½

DIRECTOR: Richard Tuggle

CAST: Anthony Michael Hall, Jenny Wright, Jeff Kober, Glynn Turman, Raymond J. Barry

Teen star Anthony Michael Hall, seeking a more mature role, took a wrong turn and wound up in this incomprehensible thriller. He plays a naïve Iowa boy who journeys to Los Angeles and accidentally switches luggage with a nasty heroin smuggler. Tony Kayden's script assumes lunatic proportions: the story progresses only because every character behaves like a total idiot at all times. It remains barely watchable thanks to Richard Tuggle's dark and moody direction, a style he use with Clint Eastwood in *Tightrope*. *Out of Bounds*, however, is out of control. Rated R for extreme violence.

1986   93 minutes

OUT OF THE PAST
★★★★½

DIRECTOR: Jacques Tourneur
CAST: Robert Mitchum, Jane Greer, Kirk Douglas, Richard Webb, Rhonda Fleming, Dickie Moore, Steve Brodie

This film, which stars Robert Mitchum, is perhaps the quintessential example of *film noir*. Film noir, which translates roughly as "dark film," is a phrase the French coined to describe a popular style of European-influenced filmmaking in Hollywood in the 1940s. Bathed in darkness and shadow, the characters in these movies are inevitably doomed as they cross, double-cross, and triple-cross each other. In *Out of the Past*, a private eye (Mitchum in a role intended for Bogart) allows himself to be duped by the beautiful but two-faced mistress (Jane Greer) of a big-time gangster (Kirk Douglas). It's a forgotten masterwork.

1947   B & W 97 minutes

P.O.W.: THE ESCAPE
★★½

DIRECTOR: Gideon Amir
CAST: David Carradine, Mako, Charles R. Floyd, Steve James

David Carradine's considerable acting talents are wasted once again in this *Rambo* ripoff that is missing everything but action. Carradine plays battle-hardened vet Col. Jim Cooper, who leads a group of POWs through enemy lines to freedom during the closing days of the Vietnam war. For Carradine at his best, try *Bound for Glory*, *The Long Riders*, or his self-directed *Americana*. Rated R for profanity and violence.

1986   90 minutes

PAPER TIGER
★★

DIRECTOR: Ken Annakin
CAST: David Niven, Toshiro Mifune, Ando, Hardy Krüger

Stiffly British David Niven is tutor to the son (Ando) of a Japanese ambassador (Toshiro Mifune). He and his young charge are kidnapped by terrorists for political reasons. Derring-do follows, but it's all lukewarm and paplike. Rated PG.

1976   99 minutes

PAPILLON
★★★★½

DIRECTOR: Frank Schaffner
CAST: Steve McQueen, Dustin Hoffman, Victor Jory, Don Gordon

Unfairly criticized, this is a truly exceptional film biography of the man who escaped from Devil's Island. Steve McQueen gives an excellent performance, and Dustin Hoffman is once again a chameleon. Director Frank Schaffner invests the same gusto here as he did in *Patton*. Rated PG.

1973   150 minutes

PARADISE
★½

DIRECTOR: Stuart Gillard

CAST: Willie Aames, Phoebe Cates, Tuvia Tavi

Willie Aames (of television's "Eight Is Enough") and Phoebe Cates star as two teenagers who, as members of a caravan traveling from Bagdad to Damascus in the nineteenth century, escape a surprise attack by a sheik intent on adding Cates to his harem. While fleeing the villain and looking for help, they have time to diddle à la Brooke Shields and Christopher Atkins in *Blue Lagoon*. It's just as dumb and unoriginal as it sounds. Rated R for frontal male and female nudity and graphic sexual treatment.

1982   100 minutes

PARTNERS IN CRIME—THE SECRET ADVERSARY
★★★

DIRECTOR: Tony Wharmby

CAST: James Warwick, Francesca Annis, George Baker, Peter Barkworth, Honor Blackman, John Fraser, Toria Fuller, Donald Houston, Alec McCowen, Gavan O'Herlihy

Originally broadcast on PBS, this film serves to introduce the *Partners in Crime* series, based on Agatha Christie's mysteries. Tommy Beresford (James Warwick), recently discharged from World War I, meets Tuppence Cowley, the girl who nursed him when he was wounded. Together they look for work and are offered a job that leads them in a race to find a secret treaty which, in the wrong hands, could overthrow the British government. Set in the 1920s, the film maintains high production values, and the characters are charming if at times too whimsically British.

1983   120 minutes

PASSAGE TO MARSEILLES
★★★

DIRECTOR: Michael Curtiz

CAST: Humphrey Bogart, Claude Rains, Sydney Greenstreet, Peter Lorre

The performances of Humphrey Bogart, Claude Rains, Sydney Greenstreet, and Peter Lorre are all that's good about this muddled film about an escape from Devil's Island during World War II. Directed by Michael Curtiz, its Flashback-within-flashback scenes all but totally confuse the viewer.

1944   B & W 110 minutes

PENDULUM
★★

DIRECTOR: George Schaefer

CAST: George Peppard, Richard Kiley, Jean Seberg, Charles McGraw

In this rather confusing mystery, police captain George Peppard must acquit himself of a murder charge and catch the real culprit. One of the most oft-used plots in detective films doesn't get any special treatment here. A good cast perks things up some, but the story is too full of holes to be taken seriously. Some violence, adult situations. Rated PG.

1969   106 minutes

PENITENTIARY I AND II
★★

DIRECTOR: Jamaa Fanaka

CAST: Leon Isaac Kennedy

Leon Isaac Kennedy dons boxing gloves as the black Rocky to

triumph over pure evil in these lurid, but entertaining, movies. Rated R.

1979   202 minutes

PERILS OF GWENDOLINE, THE
★

DIRECTOR: Just Jaeckin
CAST: Tawny Kitaen, Brent Huff

Adapting this film from the 1940s comic strip "The Adventures of Sweet Gwendoline," Just Jaeckin, who is also responsible for *Emmanuelle* and *The Story of O*, claims to have made a sexy comedy adventure. What he's made instead is a poorly acted escapade that tries to titillate through glorification of sadomasochistic forays into sex. This partly dubbed fiasco will probably develop a cult following. Stars Tawny Kitaen (*Bachelor Party*) in the role of the young heroine searching for her explorer father in the land of Yik-Yak. Yuck! Rated R for violence, profanity, and sexual content.

1985   96 minutes

PERMISSION TO KILL
★★

DIRECTOR: Cyril Frankel
CAST: Dirk Bogarde, Ava Gardner, Bekim Fehmiu, Timothy Dalton, Nicole Calfan, Frederic Forrest

An exiled politician (Bekim Fehmiu) from an Eastern Bloc natian living in Austria decides to return to his native country. A Western intelligence agent (Dirk Bogarde) must stop him. He uses extortion to persuade four people with personal or professional connections to the politician to try to prevent him from returning. Ava Gardner is the ex-lover who trys to speak to his heart, Frederic Forrest is the reporter and buddy giving friendly advice, Timothy Dalton is the financial secretary giving him money to call off the trip. And if all else fails, the politician is to be assassinated by another blackmail victim (Nicole Calfan). With a lineup like this, it's shocking to find that only Bogarde and Dalton are believable. *Permission to Kill* has some interesting things to say about international politics vis-à-vis personal freedom, but the screenplay and the acting make the film hard to take seriously. Rated PG for violence, profanity, and nudity.

1975   96 minutes

PHANTOM EMPIRE
★★★

DIRECTOR: Otto Brewer, B. Reeves "Breezy" Eason
CAST: Gene Autry, Franie Darro, Betsy King Ross, "Smiley" Burnette

Gene Autry, with the aid of Frankie Darro, champion rider Betsy King Ross, and the Junior Thunder Riders, overcomes threats from above ground (greedy crooks who want his radium-riddled Radio Ranch and do their best to interrupt his frequent radio broadcasts) and the deadly threat of Murania, the futuristic city twenty thousand feet beneath the ground. Ruled by the statuesque Queen Tika (played to the hilt by Dorothy Christy), Murania is on the verge of a revolt when Gene and the other "surface dwellers" enter and throw a monkey wrench into their plan of surface domination. Plenty of action, the wonders of the "city of the future," and good special effects (including a death ray) make this one of Mascot Films' best serials before they merged the next year to form Republic Pictures, producers of the best chapter-plays of the 1930s and '40s.

1935   B & W   12 chapters

POSEIDON ADVENTURE, THE
★★★

DIRECTOR: Ronald Neame
CAST: Gene Hackman, Ernest Borgnine, Shelley Winters, Roddy McDowall, Red Buttons, Stella Stevens

It's New Year's Eve on the passenger liner *Poseidon*. A tidal wave overturns the ship, and from here on out the all-star cast, special effects, and imaginative sets take over. It's a fairly watchable disaster flick, nothing more. Rated PG.

1972   117 minutes

PRIME CUT
★★

DIRECTOR: Michael Ritchie
CAST: Lee Marvin, Gene Hackman, Angel Tompkins, Gregory Walcott, Sissy Spacek

Sissy Spacek made her film debut in this sleazy but energetic crime thriller about big-time gangsters and the slaughterhouse they use to convert their enemies into sausage. The talents of Lee Marvin and Gene Hackman elevate this essentially tasteless offering. Rated R for nudity, gore, and violence.

1972   86 minutes

PRIME RISK
★★★½

DIRECTOR: Michael Frakas
CAST: Lee Montgomery, Samuel Bottoms, Toni Hudson, Keenan Wynn, Clu Gulager, John Lykes, Roy Stuart

Two frustrated young people (Lee Montgomery and Samuel Bottoms) devise a scheme to rip off automatic-teller machines. Trouble arises when they stumble onto a greater conspiracy involving foreign agents planning to sabotage the Federal Reserve System. There is nonstop action in this entertaining thriller, with Keenan Wynn as a suitable villain. Rated PG-13 for mature situations and language.

1984   98 minutes

PRISONER OF ZENDA, THE
★★★

DIRECTOR: Richard Thorpe
CAST: Stewart Granger, Deborah Kerr, Jane Greer, Louis Calhern, James Mason, Lewis Stone

An innocent traveler in a small European country is the exact double of its king and gets involved in a murder plot. This is a flashy Technicolor remake of the famous 1937 Ronald Colman version.

1952   101 minutes

PRIVATE LIFE OF SHERLOCK HOLMES, THE
★★★★½

DIRECTOR: Billy Wilder
CAST: Robert Stephens, Colin Blakely, Genevieve Page, Christopher Lee, Irene Handl, Clive Revill, Stanley Holloway

Director Billy Wilder's affectionately satirical pastiche of the Conan Doyle stories reveals the "secrets" allegedly shared by Sherlock Holmes (Robert Stephens) and Dr. John H. Watson (Colin Blakely). It does so with wit, humor, taste, and even suspense. Originally made as a 3½-hour roadshow production, *The Private Life of Sherlock Holmes* was trimmed nearly by half before its release. While what remains is eminently satisfying and memorable, after seeing it, one can only hope Wilder's unique and highly personal film will one day be available in its entirety. For now, we can enjoy the performances of Stephens (as a wonderfully droll and sometimes sad Holmes), Blakely (as his too earnest helpmate), Genevieve Page (as a client with a special appeal), and Christopher Lee (as Mycroft Holmes); the funny and quotable screenplay by Wilder and I.A.L. Diamond; and two adventures (including an encounter with the Loch Ness Monster) that are more than worthy of the Great Detective. Rated PG.

1970   125 minutes

PROFESSIONALS, THE
★★★★½

DIRECTOR: Richard Brooks

CAST: Lee Marvin, Burt Lancaster, Robert Ryan, Woody Strode, Claudia Cardinale, Ralph Bellamy

A rip-snorting adventure film with Lee Marvin, Burt Lancaster, Robert Ryan, and Woody Strode as the title characters out to rescue the wife (Claudia Cardinale) of a wealthy industrialist (Ralph Bellamy) from the clutches of a Mexican bandit (Jack Palance) who allegedly kidnapped her. Directed with a fine eye for character and action by Richard Brooks.

1966   117 minutes

PROTECTOR, THE
★★½

DIRECTOR: James Glickenhaus

CAST: Jackie Chan, Danny Aiello, Roy Chiao, Victor Arnold, Kim Bass, Richard Clark

Standard kung-fu film distinguished by nicely photographed action sequences and a sense of humor. Story has Jackie Chan as an undercover New York cop traveling to Hong Kong to break up a big heoin ring that is shipping its goods to New York City. Rated R for violence, nudity, and language.

1985   94 minutes

PUBLIC ENEMY, THE
★★★★½

DIRECTOR: William A. Wellman

CAST: James Cagney, Jean Harlow, Mae Clarke, Eddie Woods, Beryl Mercer

Public Enemy, with a snarling, unredeemable James Cagney in the title role, is still a highly watchable gangster film. William A. Wellman directed this fast-paced and unpretentious portrait of the rise and fall of a vicious hoodlum. Jean Harlow and Mae Clarke play the women in Cagney's life. Audiences will always remember Miss Clarke as the target of Cagney's grapefruit in one of the truly classic scenes in movie history.

1931   B & W   84 minutes

PURSUIT OF D. B. COOPER
★★½

DIRECTOR: Roger Spottiswoode

CAST: Treat Williams, Robert Duvall, Kathryn Harrold, Ed Flanders, Paul Gleason, R. G. Armstrong

The famous skyjacker is turned into a fun-loving good old boy in this hit-and-miss comedy starring Treat Williams, Robert Duvall, and Kathryn Harrold. If you liked *Smokey and the Bandit*, you'll probably enjoy this. Otherwise, avoid it. Rated PG because of minimal violence and sexuality.

1981 100 minutes

PURSUIT TO ALGIERS
★★★

DIRECTOR: Roy William Neill

CAST: Basil Rathbone, Nigel Bruce, John Abbott, Marjorie Riordan, Martin Kosleck, Gerald Hamer, Rosalind Ivy, Rex Evans

Basil Rathbone's Holmes and Nigel Bruce's Watson become bodyguards accompanying the young heir to a royal throne on a hazardous sea voyage. Their client disguises himself as Watson's nephew, which makes for some droll dialogue. One of the few Rathbone/Bruce films that borrows nothing from the book canon. Unrated—suitable for family viewing.

1945 B & W 65 minutes

QUIET MAN, THE
★★★★★

DIRECTOR: John Ford

CAST: John Wayne, Maureen O'-Hara, Victor McLaglen, Barry Fitzgerald, Mildred Natwick, Arthur Shields, Ward Bond, Jack MacGowran

As with many Irish-Americans, John Ford held a very romanticized love of his ancestral home. The Quiet Man is Ford's easygoing and marvelously entertaining tribute to the people and the land of Ireland. He was to win a best-director Oscar for his efforts. The story centers around an American ex-boxer (John Wayne) who returns to his native land, his efforts to understand the culture and people of a rural village, and especially his interest in taming a

spirited colleen (Maureen O'Hara) in spite of the disapproval of her brother (Victor McLaglen). Nearly every Irish character actor makes an appearance in this wonderful film.

1952 129 minutes

RAD
★★½

DIRECTOR: Hal Needham

CAST: Bill Allen, Lori Laughlin, Talia Shire, Ray Walston, Jack Weston, Bart Connor

Staunch character players Talia Shire, Ray Walston, and Jack Weston support a cast of youthful actors in this film about a daredevil bicyclist (Bill Allen) who competes to win a thousand dollars at Hell Track, "the most dangerous bicycle race in the world." Although the direction is unimpressive and the story predictable, Rad turns out to be fairly entertaining, thanks to the exciting race sequences. Rated PG.

1986 95 minutes

RADAR MEN FROM THE MOON
★★

DIRECTOR: Fred Brannon

CAST: George Wallace, Aline Towne, Roy Barcroft, William Blakewell

Commando Cody, Sky Marshal of the Universe and inventor of a flying suit and a rocket ship, uses all the means at his disposal to aid America in combating Retik, the ruler of the moon, who is bent on (what else?) invading the Earth. The bullet-headed hero chases villains on land, in the air, and all the way to the moon and back and gets his fair share of abuse along the way. Shrinking serial budgets are evident from sparse sets and unimaginative props and special effects. Clayton Moore moonlights from "The Lone Ranger" to play Graber, one of the heavies. Lots of fisticuffs and stock footage.

1952   B & W   12 chapters

RAID ON ROMMEL
★

DIRECTOR: Henry Hathaway
CAST: Richard Burton, John Colicos, Cliton Greyn, Wolfgang Preiss, Danielle Demetz

Veteran director Henry Hathaway must have had his mind somewhere else when he was making this substandard war film. Richard Burton plays a British Intelligence officer who leads a small group of Allied POWs behind enemy lines in North Africa. His mission: destroy the big guns at Tobruk before the British invasion fleet lands. During the course of this mission, Burton must match wits with General Erwin Rommel (poorly played by Wolfgang Preiss). Of course, our hero outsmarts Rommel at every turn. Rated PG for violence.

1971   98 minutes

RAISE THE TITANIC
★

DIRECTOR: Jerry Jameson
CAST: Jason Robards, David Selby, Richard Jordan, Anne Archer, Alec Guinness, J. D. Cannon

In this disastrously dull disaster flick, a marine research foundation headed by Jason Robards has developed a laser protective screen that could be installed around the perimeter of the United States to make it impregnable to missile attack. But to power the screen, the government needs byzanium, a precious radioactive metal whose only known world supply reportedly went down as contraband aboard the *Titanic*. The bulk of this boring movie surrounds plans to locate and raise the big ship and recover the metal. Rated PG.

1980   112 minutes

RAMBO: FIRST BLOOD II
★★★

DIRECTOR: George P. Cosmatos
CAST: Sylvester Stallone, Richard Crenna, Charles Napier, Steven Berkoff, Julia Nickson, Martin Kove

Rambo is an old-fashioned war movie. Its hero is larger than life, and the villains are pure mulemean. In other words, it's an action fan's delight. Sylvester Stallone returns as Johnny Rambo, the disillusioned but not-to-be-messed-with ex–Green Beret who all but wiped out an unfriendly Oregon town singlehandedly in *First Blood*. This time, he follows in the footsteps of Gene Hackman (in *Uncommon Valor*) and Chuck Norris (in *Missing in Action*) by going back to Vietnam to rescue American prisoners of war. Hold on to your seat—this is an exciting, involving, and explosive entertainment. Rated R.

1985   94 minutes

RANSOM
★★½

DIRECTOR: Richard Compton
CAST: Oliver Reed, Stuart Whitman, Deborah Raffin, John Ireland, Jim Mitchum, Paul Koslo

When a psycho begins killing people in a small town and refuses to stop until he receives a $4 million ransom, Stuart Whitman (the richest man in town) hires a mercenary (Oliver Reed) to kill the extortionist. Reed manages to find time for a pretty reporter (Deborah Raffin), while the chief of police (John Ireland) frowns at his tactics. There are some slow moments, but worse than these are the unanswered questions about why the murderer dresses like an American Indian and what his motive really is. Rated PG for violence.

1977   90 minutes

RAW COURAGE
★★★★

DIRECTOR: Robert L. Rosen

CAST: Ronny Cox, Tim Maier, Art Hindle, M. Emmet Walsh, William Russ, Lisa Sutton, Lois Chiles

Three cross-country runners must fend for themselves when they run into a group of weekend warriors in the Colorado desert lands. Ronny Cox is excellent as one of the runners. His performance here is equal to his fine job in *Deliverance*. However, Cox, who wrote the screenplay, has taken a few too many pages from James Dickey's survival-horror story. Still, *Raw Courage* has enough white-knuckle moments to make you forget about the lack of originality. Rated R for violence and profanity.

1983   -   90 minutes

RAW DEAL
★★★½

DIRECTOR: John Irvin

CAST: Arnold Schwarzenegger, Kathryn Harrold, Darren McGavin, Sam Wanamaker, Paul Shenar, Steven Hill, Joe Regalbuto, Ed Lauter, Robert Davi

Big Arnold Schwarzenegger stars in this fast-paced action film as a former FBI agent who is recruited by his former boss (Darren McGavin) to infiltrate the Chicago mob as an act of revenge. It's predictable, even formula. But the formula works because we like Schwarzenegger's character and hate the bad guys—well played by Sam Wanamaker, Paul Shenar, Robert Davi, and Joe Regalbuto. Director John Irvin (*Turtle Diary*) keeps things moving so fast the viewer forgets about everything except what is happening at the moment on-screen. That's entertainment. Rated R for profanity and violence.

1986   97 minutes

RED DAWN
★★★★

DIRECTOR: John Milius

CAST: Patrick Swayze, C. Thomas Howell, Ron O'Neal, Lea Thompson, Ben Johnson, Harry Dean Stanton, William Smith, Powers Boothe

Some viewers undoubtedly will feel that right-wing writer-director John Milius (*The Wind and the Lion* and *Conan the Barbarian*) has gone too far with this tale of the Russians invading a small American town. But we took this film as a simple "what if?" entertainment and, perhaps because we happen to like war movies anyway, really enjoyed it. Rated PG for violence and profanity.

1984   '   114 minutes

RED DUST
★★★★

DIRECTOR: Victor Fleming

CAST: Clark Gable, Jean Harlow, Mary Astor, Donald Crisp, Gene Raymond, Tully Marshall, Willie Fung

Red Dust is one of those remarkable films in which the performances of the stars propel a movie to classic status in spite of rather uninspired stories. The erotic chemistry between Clark Gable and Jean Harlow generates much more magic than the hackneyed story of a rubber plantation boss (Gable) who dallies with another man's wife only to return to the arms of a shady lady (Harlow) with the proverbial heart of gold.

1932   B & W   83 minutes

RED SONJA
🖤

DIRECTOR: Richard Fleischer
CAST: Arnold Schwarzenegger, Brigitte Nielsen, Sandahl Bergman, Paul Smith, Ernie Reyes Jr.

Agony, agoneee...this dreadful sword-and-sorcery film introduces us to Red Sonja (Brigitte Nielsen), pulp author Robert E. Howard's female counterpart to Conan. With the help of superswordsman Kalifor (Arnold Schwarzenegger), our heroine takes on the evil minions of cruel Queen Gedren (Sandahl Bergman). It's all to save the world from a powerful green light bulb. Although there are some unintended laughs, the groans in this movie greatly outnumber them. Unlike *Conan the Destroyer*, which also was directed by Richard Fleischer, it is not a good bad movie...it's just plain bad. Rated PG-13 for violence.

1985   89 minutes

REHEARSAL FOR MURDER
★★★½

DIRECTOR: David Greene
CAST: Robert Preston, Lynn Redgrave, Jeff Goldblum, Patrick MacNee, William Daniels, Lawrence Pressman

Richard Levinson and William Link, those clever fellows behind the creation of "Columbo," occasionally stray into the realm of made-for-television movies; this is one of the best. Robert Preston leads his stage friends through the reading of a "play" designed to ferret out the killer of star Lynn Redgrave. "The play's the thing," as Shakespeare would have said; this technique for trapping the guilty party goes all the way back to Alfred Hitchcock's *Murder*, made in 1930. The excellent cast does a fine job with the witty material, and Levinson and Link deliver another of their surprise conclusions.

1982   100 minutes

REMO WILLIAMS: THE ADVENTURE BEGINS
★★★

DIRECTOR: Guy Hamilton
CAST: Fred Ward, Joel Grey, Wilford Brimley, J. A. Preston, George Coe, Charles Cioffi, Kate Mulgrew

Directed by Guy Hamilton (*Goldfinger*) and scripted by Christopher Wood (*The Spy Who Loved Me*), this adaptation of the *Destroyer* novels is like a second-rate James Bond adventure. It offers pleasant diversion and nothing more. Fred Ward is fine as the hero of the title and Joel Grey is a kick as his Asian martial arts mentor, but the film takes too much time establishing the characters and too little giving us the adventure promised in the title. Rated PG-13 for violence and profanity.

1985   121 minutes

RETURN OF THE DRAGON
★★★½

DIRECTOR: Bruce Lee
CAST: Bruce Lee, Chuck Norris, Nora Miao

After seeing *Return of the Dragon*, we have no doubt that Bruce Lee, not Robert Clouse, directed *Enter the Dragon.* Lee was credited with staging the fight scenes, but our guess is that he was well aware of the latter film's possible impact and exercised control over the creative nonacting facets of the film whenever he could. *Return of the Dragon* was made before *Enter*, and it shows Lee's considerable directorial talent, although he did not think it would be popular with western audiences. On the contrary, it is a delightful film, brimfull of comedy, action, and the superb physical (including facial) acrobatics of the unmatchable Bruce Lee. Even the fight scenes have comedy interwoven, and it works marvelously. Rated R.

1973   91 minutes

RETURN OF THE MAN FROM U.N.C.L.E., THE
★★★
DIRECTOR: Ray Austin
CAST: Robert Vaughn, David McCallum, Patrick MacNee, Tom Mason, Gayle Hunnicutt, Geoffrey Lewis, Anthony Zerbe, Keenan Wynn, George Lazenby

Secret agents Napoleon Solo (Robert Vaugh) and Illya Kuryakin (David McCallum) are called out of a fifteen-year retirement by U.N.C.L.E. to battle their nemesis Justin Sepheran (Anthony Zerbe) and the evil organization T.H.R.U.S.H. Half the fun of this TV reunion is seeing so many actors known for their secret-agent roles from film and television. Patrick MacNee, star of the smash series *The Avengers*, portrays Mother, leader of U.N.C.L.E. (a role originally played by Leo G. Carroll), and in a hilarious chase scene, former James Bond, George Lazenby (*On Her Majesty's Secret Service*) drives a specially equipped Aston Martin. Fans of the original series will find this light-hearted spy adventure especially entertaining. Not rated, but suitable for all family members.

1983   109 minutes

RETURN TO MACON COUNTY
★
DIRECTOR: Richard Compton
CAST: Don Johnson, Nick Nolte, Robin Mattson

Two fun-loving boneheads run afoul of the law in the rural south. No style or substance. A lame sequel to the surprisingly good thriller *Macon County Line*. Interesting only to see Nick Nolte in his first film and Don Johnson before *A Boy and His Dog* and "Miami Vice." Rated PG.

1975   104 minutes

REVENGE OF THE NINJA
🎬
DIRECTOR: Sam Firstenberg
CAST: Sho Kosugi, Keith Vitali, Arthur Roberts, Mario Gallo

Japanese karate experts take on the Mob in this kung-fu flick, which is a cut or so above most of the Hong Kong–made martial arts junk. Rated R for violence and nudity.

1983   88 minutes

RIDDLE OF THE SANDS
★★★★
DIRECTOR: Tony Maylam
CAST: Michael York, Jenny Agutter, Simon MacCorkindale

Based on the spy novel by Erskine Childers, this is the story of two young Englishmen (Michael York, Simon MacCorkindale) who set sail on a holiday just prior to World War I and stumble upon political intrigue and adventure in the North Sea. The result is an absorbing adventure film. Rated PG for slight violence and profanity.

1984   102 minutes

RIDER ON THE RAIN
★★★★

DIRECTOR: Rene Clement
CAST: Charles Bronson, Marlene Jobert, Jill Ireland

Charles Bronson gives one of his finest screen performances in this gripping, Hitchcock-style thriller made in France. The story deals with the plight of a woman (Marlene Jobert) who kills an unhinged rapist and dumps his body into the sea. She is soon pursued by a mysterious American (Bronson). Thus begins a fascinating game of cat and mouse. Rated R for violence.

1970   115 minutes

RIFIFI
★★★★

DIRECTOR: Jules Dassin
CAST: Jean Servais, Carl Mohner, Perlo Vita, Robert Manuel, Magali Noel

A milestone that begat a continuing breed of films hinging on the big, carefully planned robbery that falls apart—usually just as the criminals and the audience are convinced of success. This one is sure to have you pumping adrenaline from start to finish, especially during the brilliant twenty-minutes silent robbery sequence that is its selling point, and the falling out of thieves which follows.

1955   B & W 115 minutes

RIOT IN CELL BLOCK ELEVEN
★★★

DIRECTOR: Don Siegel
CAST: Neville Brand, Leo Gordon, Emile Meyer, Frank Faylen

This taut prison drama with a message depicts an aborted prison escape that ends with the convicts barricaded and demanding to be heard. Made at the height of the "exposé" and true-crime wave in the mid-fifties, this film avoids the sensational and documentary style of its contemporaries and focuses on the action and the characterizations of the convicts, the prison staff, and the media. The message gets a bit heavy, but a good cast and quick pacing make this one of the best of its kind.

1954   B & W   80 minutes

ROADHOUSE 66
★★★½

DIRECTOR: John Mark Robinson
CAST: William Dafoe, Judge Reinhold, Kaaren Lee, Kate Vernon, Stephen Elliott, Alan Autry, Kevyn Major Howard, Peter Van Norden, Erica Yohn

As teen exploitation films go, this one is pretty good. Judge Reinhold plays a yuppie stuck in a small New Mexico town with car trouble. Willem Dafoe is an ex-rock-and-roller and all-around tough guy who helps the young executive in dealing with the existential crisis. The film drags a bit and Dafoe overplays his role, but there are some good moments to be had. Rated R for sex, nudity, violence, and profanity.

1984   94 minutes

ROARING TWENTIES, THE
★★★★½

DIRECTOR: Raoul Walsh
CAST: James Cagney, Humphrey Bogart, Priscilla Lane, Gladys George, Jeffrey Lynn, Frank McHugh, Joe Sawyer

James Cagney and Humphrey Bogart star in this superb Warner Bros. gangster entry. Produced by Mark Hellinger and directed by Raoul Walsh (*White Heat*), it's one of the best of its kind, with Cagney featured as a World War I veteran who comes back to no job and no future after fighting for his country. Embittered by all this, he turns to crime.

1939   B & W 104 minutes

ROBBERS OF THE SACRED MOUNTAIN
★★★

DIRECTOR: Bob Schulz

CAST: John Marley, Simon Mac-Corkindale, Louise Vallance, George Touliatos, Blanca Guerra

This action-adventure film could have been another *Raiders of the Lost Ark*. Unfortunately, poor acting and choppy editing leave it in the mediocre range. Simon MacCorkindale does, however, stand out as a determined British reporter who wants to interview a famous anthropologist (John Marley). MacCorkindale becomes part of an expedition seeking lost Indian treasure after he's kidnapped with Marley's granddaughter (Louise Vallance). George Touliatos plays Murdock, a ruthless millionaire, who is determined to use the treasure to rule the world. Rated R for sex, nudity, and violence.

1982   90 minutes

ROBIN AND MARIAN
★★★★½

DIRECTOR: Richard Lester

CAST: Sean Connery, Audrey Hepburn, Richard Harris, Ian Holm, Robert Shaw, Nicol Williamson, Denholm Elliott, Kenneth Haigh

Take the best director of swashbucklers, Richard Lester; add the foremost adventure film actor, Sean Connery; mix well with a fine actress with haunting presence,

Audrey Hepburn; and finish off with some of the choicest character actors: You get *Robin and Marian*, a triumph for everyone involved. Rated PG.

1976   112 minutes

ROBIN HOOD AND THE SORCERER
★★★★½

DIRECTOR: Ian Sharp

CAST: Michael Praed, Anthony Valentine, Nickolas Grace, Clive Mantle, Peter Williams, Phil Rose, Judi Trott, Phillip Jackson

While the telling of the Robin Hood legend in this film may be less straightforward than most, the added element of the mysticism enhances the all-too-familiar story and gives the dusty old characters new life. Michael Praed (best known for his work on the TV series *Dynasty*) plays the legendary English outlaw with conviction. Great performances are given by Anthony Valentine as the evil Simon De Belleme and Nickolas Grace as the scheming Sheriff of Nottingham. The story has a natural drama to it that will entertain adults as well as youngsters. *Robin Hood and the Sorcerer* is the first episode in a video series called *Robin Hood ... The Legend*, released by Playhouse Video. Not rated. Contains violence.

1983   115 minutes

ROLLING THUNDER
★★★★

DIRECTOR: John Flynn

CAST: William Devane, Tommy Lee Jones, Linda Haynes, James Best, Dabney Coleman, Lisa Richards, Luke Askew

William Devane delivers a fine performance as a Vietnam POW

returned home to a small town in Texas. For his courage and endurance under torture, he is honored with two thousand silver dollars by the local merchants. (A dollar for every day served as a POW.) A gang of vicious killers attempts to rob him, but his conditioning to pain under the Vietnamese will not let him tell them where the silver is, even when they begin to torture him. They then threaten to kill his family. He reveals the whereabouts of the money; they kill his family anyway. After some hospitalization, Devane recruits his Vietnam buddy (played superbly by Tommy Lee Jones) and the hunt is violently and realistically played out. Rated R.

1977   99 minutes

ROMANCING THE STONE
★★★★½

DIRECTOR: Robert Zemeckis
CAST: Kathleen Turner, Michael Douglas, Danny DeVito, Alfonso Arau, Zack Norman

A rip-snorting adventure film that combines action, a love story, suspense, and plenty of laughs, this movie stars Kathleen Turner (*Body Heat*) as a timid romance novelist who becomes involved in a situation more dangerous, exciting, and romantic than anything she could ever dream up. Michael Douglas plays the shotgun-wielding soldier of fortune who comes to her aid while Danny DeVito ("Taxi"), Alfonso Arau (*The Wild Bunch*), and Zack Norman add delightful bits of comedy. Director Robert Zemeckis keeps the film interesting. Whenever the romantic angle becomes a little too much, he throws in some humor or an action sequence, helping to make this movie a feast of fun. Rated PG for violence, nudity, and profanity.

1984   105 minutes

ROUGH CUT
★★★

DIRECTOR: Don Siegel
CAST: Burt Reynolds, Lesley-Anne Down, David Niven, Patrick Magee

The screenplay, by Francis Burns, is a welcome return to the stylish romantic comedies of the 1930s and '40s with the accent on witty dialogue, action, and suspense. Burt Reynolds and Lesley-Anne Down are a perfect screen combination. As two sophisticated jewel thieves who plot to steal $30 million in uncut diamonds, they exchange quips, become romantically entwined, and are delightful. Rated R.

1980   112 minutes

RUCKUS
★★★½

DIRECTOR: Max Kleven
CAST: Dirk Benedict, Linda Blair, Ben Johnson, Richard Farnsworth, Matt Clark

This light-hearted adventure film is like *Rambo* without the killing. There's lots of action, chases, explosions, and outright destruction, but nobody dies. That's one of the appealing things about this tale of a Vietnam soldier, Dirk Benedict (of TV's *A-Team*), who escapes from an army psycho ward in Mobile and ends up in a little Southern town where he is harassed by the locals—but not for long. An impressive supporting cast features Richard Farnsworth as the sheriff, Ben Johnson as the town's kingpin, and Linda Blair as the hero's helper. Comic relief is provided by a cowardly country bumpkin played by veteran character actor Matt Clark. Willie Nelson, Hank Cochran, and Janie Fricke provide the music for some surprisingly good fun. A PG for violence and language.

1984   91 minutes

RUMOR OF WAR, A
★★★

DIRECTOR: Richard T. Heffron

CAST: Brad Davis, Keith Carradine, Stacy Keach, Michael O'-Keefe

A well-made television movie about a Marine combat unit in Vietnam. Brad Davis plays a young officer who bravely leads his men into combat. He eventually gets charged with murder. The video version is about an hour and a half shorter than the original television print. Too bad.

1980   105 minutes

RUN SILENT, RUN DEEP
★★★★

DIRECTOR: Robert Wise

CAST: Clark Gable, Burt Lancaster, Jack Warden, Don Rickles

Clark Gable becomes the captain of a submarine that Burt Lancaster had been commanding. Although he resents his new boss, Lancaster stays on. Tensions rise among Lancaster, Gable, and the crew as they set out from Pearl Harbor to destroy a Japanese cruiser. This film is noted as one of the finest World War II submarine movies.

1958   B & W   93 minutes

RUNAWAY TRAIN
★★★★

DIRECTOR: Andrei Konchalovsky

CAST: Jon Voight, Eric Roberts, Rebecca DeMornay, John P. Ryan, Kenneth McMillan, Kyle T. Heffner, T. K. Carter

In this riveting, pulse-pounding adventure movie, based on a screenplay by Akira Kurosawa, two convicts escape from prison and, accompanied by a hostage (Rebecca DeMornay), make the mistake of hopping a train speeding straight for disaster. While the story gets a bit too allegorical and philosophical for its own good on occasion, the film's unrelenting intensity more than makes up for it. In addition, Roberts is hilarious as the young, terminally dumb prisoner who tags along with wild man Voight (in a performance that just skirts parody) and lives long enough to whine about it. Rated R for violence, gore, and profanity.

1986   112 minutes

RUNNING SCARED (1986)
★★★★

DIRECTOR: Peter Hyams

CAST: Gregory Hines, Billy Crystal, Steven Bauer, Darlanne Fluegel, Joe Pantoliano, Dan Hedaya, Jimmy Smits, Jonathan Gries, Tracy Reed

Fast, funny, and exciting, this *Beverly Hills Cop*–style comedy–cop thriller features inspired on-screen teamwork from Gregory Hines and Billy Crystal as a pair of wisecracking detectives on the trail of a devious drug dealer. For his film-making debut in 1973, director Peter Hyams made an underrated action-comedy called *Busting*, which starred the perfect team of Elliott Gould and Robert Blake. *Running Scared* is just a tad better than its predecessor, which makes it one of the best films of its kind. Rated R for violence, nudity, and profanity.

1986   107 minutes

RUNNING SCARED (1980)
★★★

DIRECTOR: Paul Glicker
CAST: Ken Wahl, Judge Reinhold, Bradford Dillman, Pat Hingle, Lonny Chapman, John Saxon

Ken Wahl and Judge Reinhold are servicemen returning home after two years in the Panama Canal Zone. Reinhold has appropriated some military property, including cameras and guns. He takes an aerial photo to check out the camera. Unknowingly, he has filmed a secret base that is to be used in the Bay of Pigs operation. When their plane lands, authorities find negatives and the case is on. Lonny Chapman picks up the hitchhiking Wahl and becomes an unsuspecting accomplice. Pursuit in the Florida Everglades adds to the adventure. Unrated.

1980   82 minutes

SAHARA
★★★½

DIRECTOR: Zoltán Korda
CAST: Humphrey Bogart, Bruce Bennett, Lloyd Bridges, Dan Duryea, J. Carrol Naish

One of the better war films, this production contains plenty of action, suspense, and characterization. Humphrey Bogart plays the head of a British-American unit stranded in the desert. The soldiers must keep the ever-present Nazi forces at bay while searching for the precious water they need to stay alive. It's a down-to-the-bone, exciting World War II drama.

1943   B & W   97 minutes

SAHARA

DIRECTOR: Andrew V. McLaglen
CAST: Brooke Shields, Lambert Wilson, Horst Buchholz, John Rhys-Davies, John Mills

Brooke Shields (*Blue Lagoon* and *Endless Love*) stars in this turkey of an adventure picture as a young heiress who, in order to fulfill a promise to her dying father, enters "the world's most treacherous auto race" (across the Sahara Desert), gets kidnapped by an Arab sheik (Lambert Wilson), and eventually falls in love with him. Sound awful? It is! Rated PG for violence and profanity.

1984   104 minutes

ST. IVES
★★★½

DIRECTOR: J. Lee Thompson
CAST: Charles Bronson, Jacqueline Bisset, John Houseman, Maximilian Schell, Harry Guardino, Dana Elcar, Dick O'Neill, Elisha Cook Jr.

This is a good Charles Bronson film about a former police reporter who becomes involved in a murder. Director J. Lee Thompson pulls an understated and believable performance out of the star and the added treat of excellent support from John Houseman, Jacqueline Bisset, Maximilian Schell, Harry Guardino, Dana Elcar, Dick O'Neill, and Elisha Cook make this actioner one of Bronson's memorable films. Rated PG.

1976   93 minutes

ST. VALENTINE'S DAY MASSACRE, THE
★★

DIRECTOR: Roger Corman

CAST: Jason Robards Jr., George Segal, Ralph Meeker, Jean Hale, Frank Silvera, Joseph Campanella, Bruce Dern

Watching the leads ham it up provides sporadic fun, but this gaudy gangster picture is long on violence and short on dramatic impact. The massacre itself has been depicted in more exciting style in other films. Where's Eliot Ness when you need him?

1967   100 minutes

SAMURAI TRILOGY, THE
★★★★★

DIRECTOR: Hiroshi Inagaki
CAST: Toshiro Mifune, Koji Tsuruta, Rentaro Mikuni, Kaoru Yachigusa, Kuroemon Onoe, Sachio Sakai, Akihiko Hirata, Mariko Okada, Yu Fujiki, Daisuke Kato

This brilliant and cinematically beautiful three-deck epic by director Hiroshi Inagaki tells the story of the legendary Japanese hero Musashi Miyamoto, a sixteenth-century samurai who righted wrongs in the fashion of Robin Hood and Zorro. Toshiro Mifune is impeccable as Miyamoto, whom we follow from his wild youth through spiritual discovery to the final battle with his archenemy, Sasaki Kojiro (Koji Tsuruta). The samurai film, for the uninitiated, is the Japanese equivalent of the American western. It has all of the action, code-of-honor mythic quality, and entertainment value of its counterpart. Hiroshi and Akira Kurosawa (*The Seven Samurai*) have raised the samurai film to the level of high art. The thrills are matched scene for scene with inspired visual moments and riveting characterizations. *The Samurai Trilogy* is one of the best films in the genre; a perfect introduction to some of the most gratifying experiences in film viewing. In Japanese with English subtitles.

1954   B & W 303 minutes

SAND PEBBLES, THE
★★★½

DIRECTOR: Robert Wise
CAST: Steve McQueen, Richard Crenna, Richard Attenborough, Candice Bergen, Mako, Simon Oakland, Gavin MacLeod

In Robert Wise's thoughtful film *The Sand Pebbles*, Steve McQueen gives his most compelling performance as Hollman, an ordinary seaman, is on an American warship stationed off China in the early 1930s. He prefers to remain below deck with his only love, the ship's engines. That way he avoids involvement or decisions, and as long as he obeys orders his life will flow smoothly, yet uneventfully, along. In many ways, China in 1930 was just like Hollman. It was sleeping quietly after years of foreign domination, but events were happening that would bring about revolution. Hollman is forced by these changes in China to become involved with the world outside his engine room. The result is an enjoyable, sweeping epic with unforgettable characters.

1966   179 minutes

SANDERS OF THE RIVER
★★½

DIRECTOR: Zoltan Korda
CAST: Paul Robeson, Leslie Banks, Nina Mae McKinney, Robert Cochran

"Sandy the lawgiver" is the heavy right hand of the British Empire in this action drama of colonialism in darkest Africa. Famed actor and singer Paul Robeson rises above demeaning circumstances and fills the screen with his commanding presence. Great footage of the people and terrain of Africa add to the mood of this adventure and give it an aura lacking in many jungle films. The theme music as sung by Robeson is reprised throughout the film and stays with you, but his other songs tend to pad and interrupt the flow of the film. Leslie Banks as the unyielding, godlike Sanders is condescending and aloof, a man who has learned the language of the Congo and knows its history and secrets, yet remains the classic embodiment of British imperialism. Overall a pretty enjoyable film, but the racial overtones of another age might disturb today's audiences.

1935   B & W   98 minutes

SANDS OF IWO JIMA
★★★★½

DIRECTOR: Allan Dwan
CAST: John Wayne, John Agar, Forrest Tucker, Richard Jaeckel, Arthur Franz

Every time some misguided soul opines that John Wayne can't act, after letting out a hearty derisive laugh, we instruct him or her to watch one of three movies: *The Quiet Man*, *She Wore a Yellow Ribbon*, and this superb war film. The Duke was never better than as the haunted Sergeant Stryker, a man hated by his men (with a few exceptions) for his unyielding toughness, but it is by that attitude that he hopes to keep them alive in combat. Watch it and see how good the Duke really was.

1949   B & W   110 minutes

SANJURO
★★★★½

DIRECTOR: Akira Kurosawa
CAST: Toshiro Mifune, Tatsuya Nakadai, Takashi Shimura, Yuzo Kayama, Reiko Dan

First-rate sequel to *Yojimbo* has the original Man With No Name (Toshiro Mifune) again stirring up trouble in feudal Japan. He is recruited by several young wouldbe samurai as their teacher and leader in exposing corruption in their clan. In his usual gentle manner, Mifune wreaks all sorts of havoc while occasionally warning, "Watch it, I'm in a bad mood." In Japanese, with English subtitles.

1962   B & W   96 minutes

SATAN'S SATELLITES
★½

DIRECTOR: Fred C. Brannon
CAST: Judd Holdren, Aline Towne, Wilson Wood, Lane Bradford, John Crawford, Graig Kelly, Leonard Nimoy, Ray Boyle

Heroic Judd Holdren of the Inter-Planetary Patrol, aided by his two assistants and his flying suit, battles otherwordly villains Lans Bradford and Leonard Nimoy, who want to blow the Earth out of its orbit. Originally released by Republic Studios as a twelve-episode serial entitled *Zombies of the Stratosphere*, this sequel to *Radar Men from the Moon* is a cheaply done paste-up job that uses stock footage from previous serials and forgotten feature films of the 1930s and 1940s. Condensed from over three hours into its present length, this hodgepodge of absurdities has only Leonard Nimoy's presence as an alien with a change of heart to recommend it.

1958   B & W   70 minutes

SAVAGE STREETS
🚫

DIRECTOR: Danny Steinmann

CAST: Linda Blair, Robert Dryer, Sal Landi, John Vernon, Johnny Venocur, Scott Mayer

That *Exorcist* kid, Linda Blair, is at it again. Only instead of throwing up because she's possessed by the devil, she's making us sick to our stomachs with another violent exploitation film. This time, she's the tough leader of a street gang that stops terrorizing tourists and senior citizens when her sister is raped by a rival gang. Poor sis is a deaf-mute, which makes it all the more disgusting a scene, and Blair decides "this means war." But it really means bore. Rated R for everything imaginable.

1985   90 minutes

SCARFACE (ORIGINAL)
★★★★½

DIRECTOR: Howard Hawks

CAST: Paul Muni, Ann Dvorak, George Raft, Boris Karloff, Osgood Perkins

Subtitled "Shame of the Nation" when released in the 1930s, this thinly veiled account of the rise and fall (the latter being fictional) of Al Capone easily ranks as one of the very best films in the gangster genre right up there with *The Public Enemy*, *The Roaring Twenties*, *High Sierra*, and *White Heat*. Paul Muni is first-rate as the Chicago gangster and receives excellent support from Ann Dvorak, George Raft, and, outstanding as a rival gangster, Boris Karloff. See it.

1932   B & W   93 minutes

SCARFACE (REMAKE)
★★★★½

DIRECTOR: Brian De Palma

CAST: Al Pacino, Steven Bauer, Robert Loggia, Paul Shenar

One-time "Godfather" Al Pacino returns to his screen beginnings with a bravura performance in the title role of this updating of Howard Hawks's 1932 gangster classic. Rather than bootleg gin as Paul Muni did in the original, Pacino imports and sells cocaine. Directed by Brian De Palma (*Carrie* and *Dressed to Kill*), it's the most violent, thrilling, revolting, surprising, and gruesome gangster movie ever made. Although it runs nearly three hours, you hardly notice the time. What's more, you can't take your eyes off the screen. Rated R for nudity, violence, sex, and profanity.

1983   170 minutes

SCARLET PIMPERNEL, THE
★★★

DIRECTOR: Harold Young

CAST: Leslie Howard, Raymond Massey, Merle Oberon, Nigel Bruce

Leslie Howard plays Sir Percy, an English aristocrat engaged in the underground effort to snatch out from under the blade of the guillotine Frenchmen caught in the Reign of Terror. In the tradition of many swashbucklers, he hides his activities under the guise of a fop. His ruse may throw off the French authorities, as ably represented by a sinister Raymond Massey, but he is also turning off his beautiful wife, Merle Oberon.

1934   B & W   95 minutes

SEA DEVILS
★★

DIRECTOR: Ben Stoloff

CAST: Victor McLaglen, Preston Foster, Ida Lupino, Donald Woods

Victor McLaglen and Ida Lupino play father and daughter in this soggy tale of Coast Guard trial and tribulation. McLaglen and Preston Foster are service rivals given to settling problems with their fists. Unfortunately, the audience can't fight back.

1937   B & W   88 minutes

SEA HAWK, THE
★★★★

DIRECTOR: Michael Curtiz
CAST: Errol Flynn, Flora Robson, Claude Rains, Donald Crisp, Alan Hale, Henry Daniell, Gilbert Roland

Errol Flynn was the best of the screen's costumed adventurers. *The Sea Hawk* shows him at his swashbuckling peak. He plays a buccaneer sea captain who is given tacit approval by Queen Elizabeth I (Flora Robson) to wreak havoc on the Spanish fleet and their cities in the New World. It is a fun-packed adventure for the whole family.

1940   B & W   109 minutes

SEA SHALL NOT HAVE THEM, THE
★★½

DIRECTOR: Lewis Gilbert
CAST: Michael Redgrave, Dirk Bogarde, John Mitchell

Nicely done World War II film about British air rescue operations. Main story follows an RAF bomber crew shot down over the North Sea and their rescue from the ocean. This film could have used more action scenes and a faster pace, but it is worth watching if you like war films.

1955   B & W   92 minutes

SEA WOLVES, THE
★★★

DIRECTOR: Andrew V. McLaglen

CAST: Gregory Peck, Roger Moore, David Niven, Trevor Howard, Barbara Kellerman, Patrick MacNee, Kenneth Griffith

A World War II version of *The Over the Hill Gang*. Gregory Peck and Roger Moore play two British officers who recruit a bunch of Boer War veterans now in their autumn years to do some espionage against the Germans along the coast of India. While the film relies too heavily on comedy that doesn't work, the last twenty minutes has enough spirit to redeem it. The film is based on a true story. Rated PG for violence and sex.

1980   120 minutes

SEARCH AND DESTROY
★½

DIRECTOR: William Fruet
CAST: Perry King, Don Stroud, Tisa Farrow, George Kennedy, Park Jong Soo

Though *Search and Destroy* is a pain to watch—the continuity problems are so serious that the viewer may get a headache by watching the camera's subject jump from one side of the screen to the other—the film illuminates a curious phenomenon evident in American cinema since the Tet offensive in Vietnam. With the rise of the *Dirty Harry* films as well as Charles Bronson's antihero flicks, one can see the people's lack of confidence in law enforcement and the judicial system and a swing to a more anarchistic form of crime deterrence. Perry King is an American Vietnam veteran who is being chased by a Vietnamese seeking revenge. Of course, the cops are ineffectual and even a little hostile to the ex-soldier, so he has to face the bad guy alone. Not rated, the film has violence and profanity.

1981 93 minutes

SECRET AGENT, THE
★★★

DIRECTOR: Alfred Hitchcock

CAST: John Gielgud, Madeleine Carroll, Robert Young, Peter Lorre, Percy Marmont, Lilli Palmer

Off-beat espionage film by the master of suspense contains many typical Alfred Hitchcock touches, but lacks the pacing and characterizations that set his best efforts apart from those of his contemporaries. Great collection of fine performers and familiar faces still comes short of making this one of the master's better-known classics, although Peter Lorre's portrayal of the murderous spy is one of his most memorable. Alternately grim and humorous, this uneven film (based on a novel by Joseph Conrad) is still watchable and comparable with many of the best films in the genre.

1936 B & W 93 minutes

SERGEANT YORK
★★★

DIRECTOR: Howard Hawks

CAST: Gary Cooper, Walter Brennan, George Tobias, Ward Bond, Noah Beery Jr., June Lockhart

A World War II morale booster that succeeded beyond mere propaganda and is still good entertainment today. Gary Cooper got an Academy Award as the deeply religious young farmer from backwoods Tennessee who tries to avoid service in World War I because of his religious convictions only to become the war's most decorated American war hero!

1941 B & W 134 minutes

SEVEN-PER-CENT SOLUTION, THE
★★★★

DIRECTOR: Herbert Ross

CAST: Nicol Williamson, Alan Arkin, Robert Duvall, Laurence Olivier, Vanessa Redgrave, Joel Grey

Sherlock Holmes (Nicol Williamson) attempts to get rid of his cocaine addiction by getting treatment from Sigmund Freud (Alan Arkin). This is a fast-paced adventure with touches of humor. Robert Duvall's portrayal of Dr. Watson nearly steals the show. Great fun. Rated PG; okay for everyone.

1976 113 minutes

SEVEN SAMURAI, THE
★★★★★

DIRECTOR: Akira Kurosawa

CAST: Toshiro Mifune, Takoshi Shimura, Yoshio Inaba

This Japanese release—about seven swordsmen coming to the aid of a besieged peasant village—is one of those rare screen wonders that seem to end much too soon. That's because its timeless and appealing story, which served as the basis for *The Magnificent Seven* and other American films, moves so fast it carries the viewer along. How many movies can you say that about? Unrated, the film has violence. In Japanese, with English subtitles.

1954 B & W 141 minutes

SEVEN-UPS, THE
★★½

DIRECTOR: Philip D'Antoni

CAST: Roy Scheider, Tony LoBianco, Richard Lynch

Hoping to cash in on the popularity of *The French Connection*, the producer of that film directs this slam-bang action flick in an intellectual vacuum. All that's missing are William Friedkin, Gene Hackman, and an intelligent story . . . but what the hey, we've got a better car chase! Roy Scheider is, as always, quite appealing, but he can't make something out of this nothing. Only for those who prefer form over content. Rated PG for violence.

1973　　　　　　　　103 minutes

SHADOW OF THE THIN MAN
★★★★
DIRECTOR: W. S. Van Dyke II
CAST: William Powell, Myrna Loy, Sam Levene, Donna Reed, Barry Nelson

Fourth in the series, with sleuths Nick and Nora Charles (William Powell and Myrna Loy) dividing their time between mysteries, Asta the wonder dog, and a stroller-bound Nick Jr. (who arrived in the previous film). Barry Nelson and Donna Reed are among the innocents this time around, and the story concerns dire deeds at the local race track. Another sumptuous serving of sophisticated fun.

1941　　　B & W　97 minutes

SHAFT
★★★
DIRECTOR: Gordon Parks
CAST: Richard Roundtree, Charles Cioffi, Moses Gunn

One of the best black films from the late 1960s and early 1970s. There is plenty of action and raw energy as private eye Shaft (Richard Roundtree) battles the bad guys in order to rescue a kidnapped woman. Great musical score by Isaac Hayes. Rated PG for violence.

1971　　　　　　　　100 minutes

SHAKER RUN
★½
DIRECTOR: Bruce Morrison
CAST: Cliff Robertson, Leif Garrett, Lisa Harrow, Shane Briant, Ian Mune, Peter Rowell, Peter Hayden, Bruce Phillips

A New Zealand laboratory accidentally creates a deadly virus that the military wants as a weapon. But the culture is lifted by a conscientious doctor (Lisa Harrow) who commissions a daredevil driver and his mechanic (Cliff Robertson and Leif Garrett, respectively) to transport it across the country. Yes, folks, another car flick, and like most of its kind, it lacks credibiltiy: on more than one occasion, a wall of secret service men with automatic weapons can't seem to shoot out the tires of the hot rod; the bad guys are reduced to pure evil icons so they are easy to identify; and our hero is an ex—if that really matters here—but ex-teen idol Garrett is just awful. Not rated, but the equivalent of a PG for violence and profanity.

1985　　　　　　　　91 minutes

SHAMUS
★★½
DIRECTOR: Buzz Kulik
CAST: Burt Reynolds, Dyan Cannon, John Ryan, Joe Santos

An okay detective thriller, with Burt playing Burt. Nothing new to add to the genre, but lots of action keeps things moving along in this story of a private eye investigating a weapons-smuggling ring. Rated PG.

1973　　　　　　　　106 minutes

SHAOLIN TEMPLE
★★★★
DIRECTOR: Chang Hsin Yen

CAST: Li Lin Jei, Yue Chen Wei, Yue Hai, Din Nan

The best kung-fu film since *Enter the Dragon*, this period piece, set in seventh-century China, traces the history of the Shaolin Temple. It stars the country's top martial-arts experts, yet characterization and plot are not slighted. The hokey camera tricks and dumb sound effects so common to the kung-fu genre are absent in this Hong Kong production, which was filmed on location. As always in films of this kind, the accent is on nonstop action. Unrated, the film has violence. In Chinese, with English subtitles.

1982   111 minutes

SHARK! (AKA MANEATERS!)
★

DIRECTOR: Samuel Fuller
CAST: Burt Reynolds, Barry Sullivan, Arthur Kennedy, Sylvia Pinal, Enrique Lucero

Waterlogged undersea adventure about Burt Reynolds and the boys braving man (and ham)-eating sharks to retrieve sunken loot is nothing new and loaded with scenic and stock footage to pad out the tired storyline. Not as good as the adventure films Reynolds was making prior to this weak entry. Director Samuel Fuller disavowed his association with his joint Mexico-U.S. production. Rated PG.

1969   92 minutes

SHARK HUNTER, THE

DIRECTOR: Enzo G. Castellari
CAST: Franco Nero, Jorge Luke, Mike Forrest, Eduardo Fajardo

Franco Nero (*Force Ten from Navarone*, *Enter the Ninja*) stars as a Caribbean island recluse who beats up sharks and searches for buried treasure. Good for a laugh, thanks to the lame voice dubbing. Otherwise, feed this one to the you-know-what. Not rated, but the equivalent of a PG for violence and brief nudity.

1984   92 minutes

SHARK'S TREASURE
🦈

DIRECTOR: Cornel Wilde
CAST: Cornel Wilde, Yaphet Kotto, John Nellson, Cliff Osmond

Good guys and bad guys search for sunken treasure while Cornel Wilde and tiger sharks mete out justice. This was the first film to cash in on the success of *Jaws*, though these sharks look downright anemic. Silly and pompous, with jarring homosexual overtones. A complete embarrassment. Rated PG for violence.

1975   95 minutes

SHARKY'S MACHINE
★★★★½

DIRECTOR: Burt Reynolds
CAST: Burt Reynolds, Rachel Ward, Brian Keith, Bernie Casey, Vitorio Gassman, Charles Durning

This is one of the best cop thrillers ever made. It's exciting, suspenseful, funny, and intelligent, so good it joins *48 Hrs*, *Dirty Harry*, and *Tightrope* as the best of the genre. Burt Reynolds stars under his own direction as an undercover cop who has a compulsion to crack down on a new wave of crime in his city. He does so by turning a crew of vice cops into a personal police machine. Rated R because of violence and profanity.

1981   119 minutes

S.H.E.
★★★

DIRECTOR: Robert Lewis
CAST: Omar Sharif, Cornelia Sharpe, Robert Lansing, Anita Ekberg

This average made-for-TV spy/action thriller has one twist . . . a female James Bond. Beautiful Cornelia Sharpe is S.H.E. (Security Hazards Expert). She pursues Robert Lansing, the U.S. syndicate boss, throughout Europe. Omar Sharif makes an appearance as a wine baron. The beautiful sights (both Sharpe and Europe) make the film more than watchable.

1979   105 minutes

SHEENA
★

DIRECTOR: John Guillermin
CAST: Tanya Roberts, Ted Wass, Donovan Scott

Tanya Roberts (of *Beastmaster* and TV's "Charlie's Angels") stars as the comic book heroine Sheena, Queen of the Jungle. In this adventure film, an evil African prince tries to take over his brother's kingdom while our heroine, with the help of reporters Ted Wass and Donovan Scott, attempts to stop him. Rated PG.

1984   117 minutes

SHERLOCK HOLMES AND THE SECRET WEAPON
★★★

DIRECTOR: Roy William Neill
CAST: Basil Rathbone, Nigel Bruce, Lionel Atwill, Karen Verne, Dennis Hoey, Mary Gordon

Although the contemporary (1940s) setting makes the Baker Street sleuth seem oddly out of place, Basil Rathbone remains one of the definitive Holmeses. In this case, he once again faces the ruthless Professor Moriarty (Lionel Atwill), who tries to torture a scientist into revealing the plans of a revolutionary bombsight. A code that appears in this film is borrowed from *The Adventure of the Dancing Man*. This also is the first Rathbone Holmes to be rereleased in color, a dubious distinction that won't improve it a bit; these films were made for the shadowy world of black and white.

1942   68 minutes

SHOGUN (SHORT VERSION)
★★★

DIRECTOR: Jerry London
CAST: Richard Chamberlain, Toshiro Mifune, John Rhys-Davies

This is a two-hour condensation of writer James Clavell's epic twelve-hour TV miniseries starring Richard Chamberlain and Toshiro Mifune. If you haven't seen the spectacular TV version of the story of an English seaman's experiences in feudal Japan, it is definitely worth the effort to see it in this shortened form. If you have seen it, you may find this version a disappointment.

1980   125 minutes

SHOGUN (FULL-LENGTH VERSION)
★★★★

DIRECTOR: Jerry London
CAST: Richard Chamberlain, Toshiro Mifune, Yoko Shimada, Damien Thomas

Forget about the shortened version that is also out on video; this ten-hour original is the only one that does justice to James Clavell's sweeping novel. Richard Chamberlain began his reign as king of the mini-series with his portrayal of Blackthorne, the English sailor shipwrecked among the feudal Japanese. Rarely has television been the original home for a program of this epic scope, and it all works, from the breath-taking cinematography to the superb acting by the entire cast. The stranger-in-a-strange-land feeling is heightened by the on-screen use of Japanese dialogue; if you recall being confused the first time around, though, don't fret, because subtitles are now added.

1980   600 minutes

SHOGUN ASSASSIN
★★★

DIRECTOR: (Japan) Kenji Masuni; (United States) David Weisman and Robert Hous

CAST: Tomisaburo Wakayama, Masahiro Tomikawa

This film will rate a zero for the squeamish and close to five for fans of the nineteen-film "Baby Cart" series, so popular in Japan in the 1970s. The color red predominates in this meticulously reedited, rescripted, rescored (by Mark Lindsay), and English-dubbed version of the original *Baby-Cart at the River Styx*: swords enter bodies at the most imaginative angles; a body-count is impossible; all records are broken for bloodletting. But there is no time to cry over spilled blood for Lone Wolf—a disillusioned samurai (an "official decapitator" for a deranged shogun)—and his 6-year-old son as they wander the back roads of feudal Japan on an odyssey of vengeance. Rated R for the violence, which really is fairly aesthetic.

1980   90 minutes

SHOOT
★★★½

DIRECTOR: Harvey Hart

CAST: Cliff Robertson, Ernest Borgnine, Henry Silva

A group of buddies spending a weekend hunting are attacked by another group of hunters who are after game more interesting than deer. when one of their party is wounded, the attacked hunters, led by Cliff Robertson and Ernest Borgnine, want revenge and mount a military-style campaign to get it. Robertson and Borgnine give us fine portrayals as the hunters go from frightened to angry and vengeful in this better-than-average action adventure. Rated R for violence and profanity.

1976   98 minutes

SHOUT AT THE DEVIL
★★

DIRECTOR: Peter Hunt

CAST: Lee Marvin, Roger Moore, Barbara Parkins, Ian Holm

Good action scenes elevate this otherwise distasteful and overly complicated film about a hard-drinking American adventurer (Lee Marvin) and an upper-crust Englishman (Roger Moore) who join forces to blow up a German battleship before the breakout of World War I. Rated PG.

1976   119 minutes

SIDEWINDER 1
★★

DIRECTOR: Earl Bellamy

CAST: Marjoe Gortner, Michael Parks, Susan Howard, Alex Cord

Michael Parks (*The Bible*) is a quiet, reclusive motocross racer who becomes a partner in developing a new dirt bike. *Sidewinder 1* has good racing scenes—motocross fans will love them—but the story is studded with sexist remarks and attitudes about women as sex objects and professional women as frigid and misguided. Rated PG.

1977   97 minutes

SILENT RAGE
★

DIRECTOR: Michael Miller
CAST: Chuck Norris, Ron Silver, Stephen Furst

A Texas sheriff is pitted against a psychotic killer who has become virtually indestructible through genetic engineering in this karate-horror-thriller-western. Rated R for nudity, profanity, sex, and violence.

1982   105 minutes

SILVER BLAZE
★★★

DIRECTOR: Thomas Bentley
CAST: Arthur Wontner, Ian Fleming, Lyn Harding, John Turnbull, Robert Horton, Lawrence Grossmith, Judy Gunn, Arthur Goulet

In the '30s, noted Sherlockian Vincent Starrett proclaimed, "No better Sherlock Holmes than Arthur Wontner is likely to be seen and heard in pictures in our time. His detective is the veritable fathomer of Baker Street in person." This tall, gaunt British actor was the living image of the Sidney Paget illustrations that graced Conan Doyle's mystery stories in *Strand* magazine. Beginning with *Sherlock Holmes' Fatal Hour*, in 1931, Wontner starred as Holmes in five handsome but low-budget films, of which *Silver Blaze* was the last. Ironically, the latter movie was not released in America until after the 1939 *Hound of the Baskervilles* introduced Basil Rathbone as the screen's most famous detective. So impressive was Rath-

bone's debut as Holmes, the American distributor retitled *Silver Blaze* as *Murder at the Baskervilles*. Indeed, Sir Henry Baskerville himself pops up in this loose adaptation of the original story about the disappearance of a prized racehorse. In a further variation, Professor Moriarty (Lyn Harding) and Colonel Moran (Arthur Goulet) are behind the nefarious goings-on. It may not be faithful, but *Silver Blaze* is fun for mystery fans even though it shows its age. Most of all, it is a treat to have Arthur Wontner's seldom-seen interpretation of Sherlock Holmes on video.

1937   B & W   60 minutes

SINBAD THE SAILOR
★★★

DIRECTOR: Richard Wallace
CAST: Douglas Fairbanks Jr., Walter Slezak, Maureen O'Hara, Jane Greer, Anthony Quinn, Sheldon Leonard

Ho for the Bounding Main and strange doings in exotic lands! Aping his father, Douglas Fairbanks Jr., as Sinbad, sails forth in search of Alexander the Great's fabled treasure and hits a variety of reefs. Unfortunately, the plot not only thickens but gets murky, to boot. Some say it's all tongue-in-cheek, but it's really more foot-in-mouth. Pictorially lavish and impressive, but definitely not steak. Nonetheless, it is fun.

1947   117 minutes

SLAVE OF THE CANNIBAL GOD
🐾

DIRECTOR: Sergio Martino
CAST: Stacy Keach, Ursula Andress

A woman (Ursula Andress) encounters a cult of flesh-eaters while attempting to find her missing husband in New Guinea. Her resourceful guide (Stacy Keach) helps her through one close call after another as they are pursued by a helicopter full of bad guys. The low, low budget and inept production team—look for the occasional intrusion of a boom mike in the dialogue scenes—offer a few laughs, but the groans greatly outnumber them. Rated R for violence and nudity.

1979   87 minutes

SLEEPING DOGS
★★½
DIRECTOR: Roger Donaldson
CAST: Sam Neill, Warren Oates, Nevan Rowe, Ian Mune

Here's a "what if?" film set in New Zealand during a time of economic crisis. Sam Neill plays a husband and father who discovers his wife is having an affair, so he goes off to live by himself for a while. Meanwhile, a group of government agents manufacture a revolution by killing innocent bystanders during demonstrations and making it look like the work of the protesters. Neill's wife and her boyfriend accidentally get caught up in an encounter between police and revolutionaries and are pegged as conspirators. Soon he, too, is a wanted man, the so-called mastermind behind the phony revolt. No MPAA rating.

1977   107 minutes

SMALL TOWN IN TEXAS, A
★★
DIRECTOR: Jack Starrett
CAST: Timothy Bottoms, Susan George, Bo Hopkins, Art Hindle, Morgan Woodward

Fairly effective B picture pits a revenge-lusting Timothy Bottoms against the crooked sheriff (Bo Hopkins) who framed him in a drug bust and stole his wife (Susan George). Car crashes, fights, and even a little suspense. Rated R.

1976   95 minutes

SOLDIER, THE

DIRECTOR: James Glickenhaus
CAST: Ken Wahl, Klaus Kinski, William Prince

In this boring, stupid, and disgusting "thriller" by writer-director James Glickenhaus (*The Exterminator*), Russian agents pretending to be a terrorist group steal enough plutonium for a large nuclear explosion, and it is up to the soldier (Ken Wahl, of *The Wanderers*) to sabotage their plan without the official sanction or support of the United States government. It's all about as thrilling as a traffic jam. Rated R for blood, gore, violence, and profanity.

1982   96 minutes

SOLDIER OF ORANGE
★★★★★
DIRECTOR: Paul Verhoeven
CAST: Rutger Hauer, Peter Faber, Jeroen Krabbe

Rutger Hauer became an international star thanks to his remarkable performance in this 1979 Dutch release, in which he plays one of four college buddies galvanized into action when the Nazis invade the Netherlands. This is an exceptional work; an exciting, suspenseful, and intelligent war-adventure film that is a rich in character and performance as it is in story and direction. Rated R for nudity, profanity, implied sex, and violence.

1979   165 minutes

SOLDIER'S STORY, A
★★★★★

DIRECTOR: Norman Jewison
CAST: Howard E. Rollins Jr., Adolph Caesar

A murder mystery, a character study, and a deeply affecting drama rolled into one, *A Soldier's Story*, based on Charles Fuller's 1981 Pulitzer Prize–winning play, is an unforgettable viewing experience. This riveting movie examines man's inhumanity to man in one of its most venal forms: racial hatred. Rated PG for violence and profanity.

1984   102 minutes

SOMETHING OF VALUE
★★★

DIRECTOR: Richard Brooks
CAST: Rock Hudson, Dana Wynter, Sidney Poitier, Wendy Hiller, Frederick O'Neal, Juano Hernandez, William Marshall, Michael Pate

White settlers in Kenya are preyed upon by bloodthirsty Mau Mau tribesmen sick of oppression in this often too-graphic drama, which opens with a specially filmed foreword from Winston Churchill.

1957   B & W 113 minutes

SONG OF THE THIN MAN
★★★½

DIRECTOR: Edward Buzzell
CAST: William Powell, Myrna Loy, Keenan Wynn, Dean Stockwell, Gloria Grahame, Patricia Morrison

Sixth and final entry in the series, a cut above the previous few because of its involvment in jazz music circles. Nick and Nora Charles (William Powell and Myrna Lay) match wits with a murderer this time out, and the setting helps their dialogue regain its crisp sparkle.

Nick Jr. isn't around as much; his absence also keeps things moving. All in all, a worthy effort with which to conclude things.

1947   B & W 86 minutes

SOUTH OF PAGO PAGO
★★

DIRECTOR: Alfred E. Green
CAST: Victor McLaglen, Jon Hall, Frances Farmer, Olympe Bradna, Gene Lockhart

A good title is wasted on this so-so action tale of pirates heisting native-harvested pearls and being pursued and engaged by the locals. Typical South Sea fare.

1940   B & W 98 minutes

SOUTHERN COMFORT
★★★★

DIRECTOR: Walter Hill
CAST: Keith Carradine, Powers Boothe, Fred Ward, Byron James

Director Walter (*48 HRS*) Hill's 1981 "war" film focuses on the plight of a National Guard unit lost in Cajun country while on routine training maneuvers. Armed only with M-16 rifles loaded with blanks, the soldiers (who include Keith Carradine and Powers Boothe) find themselves ill-equipped to deal with the hostile locals—and an edge-of-your-seat entertainment is the result. Rated R for violence.

1981   106 minutes

SPARTACUS
★★★★½

DIRECTOR: Stanley Kubrick
CAST: Kirk Douglas, Jean Simmons, Laurence Olivier, Peter Ustinov, Charles Laughton, Tony Curtis

One of the more rewarding big-budget epics that marked the late

1950s and '60s. Even though this fictional story of an actual slave revolt against the Roman Empire is large-scale in every detail, it never lets the human drama get lost in favor of spectacle. Except for an inept effort by Tony Curtis, the large cast of movie luminaries excel in their many fine roles.

1960   196 minutes

SPY SMASHER
★★★

DIRECTOR: William Witney

CAST: Kane Richmond, Sam Flint, Marguerite Chapman, Hans Schumm, Tristram Coffin

The costumed radio hero (Kane Richmond) takes on the Nazis in this fun-for-fans cliff-hanger serial.

1942   B & W   12 chapter

SPY WHO LOVED ME, THE
★★★★

DIRECTOR: Lewis Gilbert

CAST: Roger Moore, Barbara Bach, Curt Jurgens, Richard Kiel, Bernard Lee, Lois Maxwell, Desmond Llewellyn, Caroline Munro

This, the tenth James Bond epic, is Roger Moore's third, and he finally hits his stride. Directed with a blend of excitement and tongue-in-cheek humor, the film teams Bond with Russian agent XXX (Barbara Bach) in an effort to stop an industrialist (Curt Jurgens) from destroying the surface world so he can rule an undersea kingdom. This marked the first appearance by Richard Kiel's "Jaws," and he's menacing indeed. Bach has an equally good part, a strong female lead in a series famous for its lack thereof. The music, by Marvin Hamlisch, lacks the bite of series regular John Barry, but Carly Simon's rendition of the title theme is excellent. Rated PG for violence, sexual situations.

1977   125 minutes

SQUIZZY TAYLOR
★★½

DIRECTOR: Kevin Dobson

CAST: David Atkins, Jacki Weaver, Alan Cassell, Michael Long, Robert Hughes

Fairly interesting film about the notorious Australian gangster of the 1920s who rose to fame in Melbourne because of his keen wit and flamboyant style. David Atkins gives a convincing performance. But the story begins to lose its edge after a while. Not rated. Has sex, nudity, and violence.

1983   103 minutes

STALAG 17
★★★★★

DIRECTOR: Billy Wilder

CAST: William Holden, Robert Strauss, Peter Graves, Otto Preminger

Many critics felt William Holden's Academy Award for Stalag 17 was a gift for failing to give him proper recognition in Sunset Boulevard. Those critics should view this prison camp comedy-drama again. This film still holds up brilliantly today. Billy Wilder successfully alternated between suspense and comedy in this story of a World War II prison camp. It seems all the prisoners' activities are being reported to their German commandant. Holden plays an opportunistic and cynical sergeant whose actions make him a natural suspect as the spy in the POWs' midst.

1953   B & W   120 minutes

STAR OF MIDNIGHT
★★½

DIRECTOR: Stephen Roberts

CAST: William Powell, Ginger Rogers, Paul Kelly, Gene Lockhart, Ralph Morgan

William Powell, in a role cloned from his *Thin Man* series, is a debonair, urbane lawyer accused of murder. Abetted by Ginger Rogers, he sallies forth, repartee in mouth, to catch the real culprit. The police and gangsters alike make it difficult. Not bad.

1935   B & W   90 minutes

STICK
★★★

DIRECTOR: Burt Reynolds
CAST: Burt Reynolds, Charles Durning, George Segal, Candice Bergen, Castulo Guerra

Directed by and starring Burt Reynolds, *Stick* is an odd mixture of comedy and violence that more than once strains the viewer's suspension of disbelief. Fans of the original novel, by Elmore Leonard, will be shocked at how far Reynolds's film strays from its source. Leonard's hardened criminal—who in the story gets out of prison only to find himself right back on the wrong side of the law and on the bad side of some ruthless gangsters—is turned by Reynolds into a variation of his *Smokey and the Bandit* good ol' boy. What should have been a tough, lean, and mean movie contains a surprising amount of clowning by its stars. Despite all this, it has enough action and genuine laughs to please Reynolds's fans. It's no critic's movie, but you could do worse. Rated R for profanity and violence.

1985   109 minutes

STILETTO
★½

DIRECTOR: Bernard Kowalski

CAST: Alex Cord, Britt Ekland, Patrick O'Neal, Barbara McNair

Alex Cord has the starring role in this weak picture about a rich jetsetter who also happens to be a professional killer who decides to quit his job. The Mafia doesn't like that idea, so they decide to kill him. Lots of violent action and sexy situations, but it all adds up to a disappointment. Harold Robbins wrote the story. Rated R.

1969   98 minutes

STING, THE
★★★★½

DIRECTOR: George Roy Hill
CAST: Paul Newman, Robert Redford, Robert Shaw, Charles Durning, Ray Walston, Eileen Brennan, Harold Gould, Dana Elcar

Those *Butch Cassidy and the Sundance Kid* stars, Paul Newman and Robert Redford, were reunited for this fast-paced entertainment as two con men who out-con a con. Winner of seven Academy Awards—including best picture—this film, directed by George Roy Hill (*A Little Romance* and *Butch Cassidy*) revived Scott Joplin's music. For that, and the more obvious reasons, it is not to be missed. Rated PG.

1973   129 minutes

STING II, THE
★★★

DIRECTOR: Jeremy Paul Kagan
CAST: Jackie Gleason, Mac Davis, Teri Garr, Karl Malden, Oliver Reed, Bert Remsen

You could hardly expect a sequel to such a joyously entertaining film as *The Sting* to measure up. True to those expectations, this film, starring Jackie Gleason, Mac Davis, Teri Garr, and Karl Malden doesn't come close. What it lacks, of course, is Paul Newman and Robert Redford. But then, comparisons are odious and, in this case especially, perhaps unfair. There is much to enjoy in this comedy if taken on its own terms ...so enjoy. Rated PG for violence.

1983 102 minutes

STONE COLD DEAD
★★

DIRECTOR: George Mendeluk
CAST: Richard Crenna, Belinda J. Montgomery, Paul Williams, Linda Sorenson

This fair film, based on the novel *Sin Sniper*, by Hugh Garner, centers on the investigation by Sergeant Boyd (Richard Crenna) into a bizarre series of prostitute killings. The murderer photographs his victims at the moment of death with a camera mounted on a high-powered rifle. Sandy McCauley (Belinda Montgomery), an undercover agent, is also assigned to the case. In addition to posing as a prostitute and acting as bait for the murderer, Boyd wants her to help him get incriminating evidence on Julius Kurtz (Paul Williams), the city's biggest dope trafficker and an occasional pimp. Rated R.

1980 97 minutes

STONE KILLER, THE
★★★½

DIRECTOR: Michael Winner
CAST: Charles Bronson, Martin Balsam, David Sheiner, Norman Fell, Ralph Waite

A *Dirty Harry*–style cop thriller, this casts Charles Bronson as a no-nonsense New York cop who gets transferred to Los Angeles because of his direct way of dealing with gun-toting criminals ... he shoots them. Called even more violent than the Eastwood original by critics of the time, *The Stone Killer* looks pretty mild today— even in the uncut video version (which is far superior to the TV print). It still packs enough of a wallop to make it a good bet for action fans. Rated R.

1973 95 minutes

STOPOVER TOKYO
★★

DIRECTOR: Richard L. Breen
CAST: Robert Wagner, Edmond O'Brien, Joan Collins, Ken Scott

Based on a story by John P. Marquand, this ho-hum espionage tale has an American spy (Robert Wagner) chasing a communist undercover agent all over Tokyo, making this a combination spy/travelogue movie. Wagner is earnest, as usual, but even the cast's enthusiasm can't put life into this one. Joan Collins is worth watching, as always.

1957 100 minutes

STRANGER ON THE THIRD FLOOR
★★★★

DIRECTOR: Boris Ingster
CAST: Peter Lorre, John McGuire, Elisha Cook Jr., Margaret Tallichet, Charles Waldron

This intriguing film from RKO is a gem that transcends its potboiler storyline (innocent man accused of murder) and predates the later more highly acclaimed *film noir* favorites of the mid to late 1940s. Peter Lorre gives yet another singular performance as a disinterested murderer, a character truly alien yet strangely sympathetic. A great hallucination sequence and good performances all the way around make this a compelling treat.

1940 B & W 64 minutes

STREETHAWK

★

DIRECTOR: Virgil W. Vogel

CAST: Rex Smith, Jayne Modean, Christopher Lloyd, Richard Venture, Joe Regalbuto, Lawrence Pressman, Robert Beltran

Only kiddies—and fans of the short-lived television series, if there are any—will find much to enjoy in this story of a police officer (Rex Smith) left for dead by drug dealers. He is "resurrected" by the FBI to become a black-costumed, undercover crime fighter who rides a souped-up motorcycle. This two-wheeled retread of TV's *Knight Rider* could have been worse, but its only real asset is a score by Tangerine Dream.

1986   60 minutes

STREETS OF FIRE

★★★

DIRECTOR: Walter Hill

CAST: Diane Lane, Michael Pare, Rick Moranis, Amy Madigan, Willem DaFoe

Directed by Walter Hill (*48 HRS*), this is a self-proclaimed "rock 'n' roll fable" that takes place in "another time, another place." Those expecting any more than that will undoubtedly be disappointed. Yet taken on its own terms, this comic book-style movie is a diverting compendium of nonstop action and stylized storytelling set to a rocking backbeat. In it a famous rock singer (played by Diane Lane, of *The Outsiders* and *A Little Romance*) is captured by a motorcycle gang in Hill's mythic world, which combines 1950s attitudes and styles with a futuristic feel. It's up to her two-fisted former boyfriend, Tom Cady (Michael Pare, of *Eddie and the Cruisers*),

to save her. Rated R for profanity and violence.

1984   93 minutes

SUBWAY

★★

DIRECTOR: Luc Besson

CAST: Isabelle Adjani, Christopher Lambert, Richard Bohringer, Jean-Pierre Bacri, Jean Reno, Michel Galabru, Jean Bouise

The stunning Isabelle Adjani (*The Story of Adele H*, *The Driver*) plays a young wife who becomes involved with a streetwise rogue played by Christopher Lambert (*Greystoke*). The plot is not very clear and the bad jokes don't help. Fast-paced action scenes keep the film interesting, but they all lead to nowhere. Rated R for language and violence.

1985   110 minutes

SUDDEN IMPACT

★★★★

DIRECTOR: Clint Eastwood

CAST: Clint Eastwood, Sondra Locke, Pat Hingle, Bradford Dillman

"Dirty Harry" Callahan (Clint Eastwood) is back, and he's meaner, nastier, and—surprise!—funnier than ever in this, his fourth screen adventure. In the story, a killer (Sondra Locke in a rare, effective performance) is methodically extracting bloody revenge on the sickos who raped her and a younger sister. It becomes Harry's job to track her down, but not until he's done away with a half-dozen villains and delivered twice as many quips including, "Go ahead, make my day." Rated R for violence and profanity.

1983   117 minutes

SUMMER CITY
★★

DIRECTOR: Christopher Fraser
CAST: Mel Gibson, Phil Avalon, Steve Bisley, John Jarrat, Debbie Forman, James Elliot

Mel Gibson (the *Mad Max* films) stars in this Australian teen rebel flick that lacks a fresh approach to one of the oldest stories in film: four wild and crazy teens go on a surfing weekend at a sleepy little seaside community only to find trouble when one of the delinquents messes around with a local's daughter. A few intense moments, and the acting is not bad, but even some of the dialogue is indistinguishable in the muddy audio, and the Aussie vulgate only aggravates the problem. Not rated, but the equivalent of PG for some sex, partial nudity, and violence.

1976   83 minutes

SUMMERTIME KILLER, THE
★★½

DIRECTOR: Antonio Isasi
CAST: Christopher Mitchum, Karl Malden, Olivia Hussey, Raf Vallone, Claudine Auger, Gerard Tichy

A 6-year-old boy witnesses the beating and drowning of his father by a gang of hoods. Twenty years pass, and we follow the grown-up son (Christopher Mitchum) as he systematically pursues and kills these men in New York, Rome, and Portugal. While a police detective (Karl Malden) is investigating one of the murders, a Mafia boss hires him to privately track down the killer. There are some exciting motorcycle pursuits along the way before the ending takes a slight twist. Rated R for violence and language.

1972   100 minutes

SUNBURN
★

DIRECTOR: Richard C. Sarafian
CAST: Farrah Fawcett-Majors, Charles Grodin, Art Carney, William Daniels, Joan Collins

Farrah Fawcett-Majors's second feature film is worse than her first, (*Somebody Killed Her Husband*). This time she pretends to be the wife of insurance investigator Charles Grodin to get the real scoop on a suicide case in Acapulco. Breathy acting and hamhanded scripting do not help the paper-thin plot. Rated PG.

1979   94 minutes

SUPERFLY
★★★

DIRECTOR: Gordon Parks Jr.
CAST: Ron O'Neal, Carl Lee, Sheila Frazier, Julius W. Harris, Charles McGregor

This exciting film follows a Harlem drug dealer's last big sale before he attempts to leave the drug world for a normal life. Rated R.

1972   96 minutes

SURFACING
★

DIRECTOR: Claude Jutra
CAST: Joseph Bottoms, Kathleen Beller, R. H. Thompson

This adventure film is essentially *Deliverance* stirred with pyschological mumbo jumbo and kinky sex. The result is unsavory and illogical. Kathleen Beller and friends search for traces of her father and an ancient Indian civilization in a beautiful but brutal wilderness. You'll root for Mother Nature. Rated R.

1984   90 minutes

SWASHBUCKLER, THE

DIRECTOR: Jean-Paul Rappeneau
CAST: Jean-Paul Belmond, Marlene Jobert, Laura Antonelli, Michel Auclair, Julien Guiomar

Stupid story about a naturalized American who gets caught up in the French Revolution while delivering grain and seeking a divorce from his wife. This is not the Robert Shaw movie of the same name, but a French export that has been dubbed in English. Beware!

1984   100 minutes

SWEET SIXTEEN
★½

DIRECTOR:
CAST: Aliesa Shirley, Bo Hopkins, Patrick Macnee, Susan Strasberg, Don Stroud

In this static mystery, which is surprisingly "clean" by today's mad-slasher movie standards, a young woman (Aliesa Shirley) from the big city reluctantly spends her summer—and her sixteenth birthday—in a small Texas town and becomes the chief suspect in a series of murders. Rated R for profanity and partial nudity.

1984   96 minutes

SWEET SWEETBACK'S BAADASSSSS SONG
★★★½

DIRECTOR: Melvin Van Peebles
CAST: Melvin Van Peebles, Rhetta Hughes, Simon Chuckster, John Amos

Minor cult black film about a man running from racist white police forces. Melvin Van Peebles plays the title character, who will do anything to stay free. Very controversial when released in 1971. Lots of sex and violence gave this an X rating at the time. Probably the best of the black-produced and -directed films of the early 1970s. Rated R.

1971   97 minutes

SWORD OF LANCELOT
★★★

DIRECTOR: Cornel Wilde
CAST: Cornel Wilde, Jean Wallace, Brian Aherne, George Baker

Colorful production and location photography highlight this pre-*Camelot* version of life at the court of King Arthur and the forbidden love between Lancelot and Queen Guinevere (Mr. and Mrs. Cornel Wilde in real life). Long on pageantry, action, and chivalrous acts of derring-do, this is a "fun" film in the same vein as *Ivanhoe* and *The Vikings*, and glosses over the serious overtones that made the better-known version a popular tragedy. Over a period of twenty-five years Cornel Wilde was one of the industry's most successful actor/producer/directors, and his films range from underwater adventures and science fiction to starkly primitive survival stories. These carefully constructed films always benefit from the integrity and realism Wilde brings to his work as well as his commanding presence and insistence on personally supervised stunts and location shooting. Young and old both will enjoy this high-spirited romp through the distant past.

1963   116 minutes

TAKING OF PELHAM ONE TWO THREE, THE
★★★★

DIRECTOR: Joseph Sargent
CAST: Walter Matthau, Robert Shaw, Martin Balsam, Tony Roberts

Walter Matthau is at his growling, grumbling, gum-chewing best in this film. He plays the chief detective of security on the New York subway who must deal with the unthinkable: the hijacking of a commuter train by four men (with a fine Robert Shaw as their leader) and a demand by them for a $1 million ransom to prevent their killing the passengers one by one. It was at this time that Matthau made two similar films, *Charley Varrick* and *The Laughing Policeman*, and the three pictures stand out as prime examples of the actor at his dramatic (as opposed to comedic) best. The story and direction in this motion picture are also topnotch, making for a fine edge-of-your-seat entertainment. Rated PG.

1974   104 minutes

TAMARIND SEED, THE
★★★

DIRECTOR: Blake Edwards

CAST: Omar Sharif, Julie Andrews, Anthony Quayle

A sudsy melodrama in the old tradition, but still a lot of fun. Julie Andrews falls in love with a foreign emissary played by Omar Sharif, only to be told (by her own State Department) to stay away from him. The cold war intrigue seems pretty absurd these days, but Andrews and Sharif generate a playful chemistry that overlooks many sins. A trifle overlong, but worth more than the obscurity granted it by most critics. Rated PG.

1974   123 minutes

TANK
★★½

DIRECTOR: Marvin J. Chomsky

CAST: James Garner, Shirley Jones, C. Thomas Howell, G. D. Spradlin

The always likable James Garner plays Sgt. Maj. Zack Carey, an army career soldier who has to use his privately owned Sherman tank to rescue his family (Shirley Jones and C. Thomas Howell) from the clutches of a mean country sheriff (G. D. Spradlin). It's all a bunch of hokum, but a sure audience pleaser. Rated PG.

1984   113 minutes

TARGET
★★★

DIRECTOR: Arthur Penn

CAST: Gene Hackman, Matt Dillon, Gayle Hunnicutt, Josef Sommer, Victoria Fyodora, Herbert Berghof

In this fast-paced, entertaining suspense-thriller directed by Arthur Penn (*Bonnie and Clyde*), a father (Gene Hackman) and son (Matt Dillon) put aside their differences when they become the targets of an international spy ring. *Target* is a tad predictable, but it is the kind of predictability that adds to the viewer's enjoyment rather than detracting from it. Rated R for violence, profanity, and nudity.

1985   117 minutes

TARZAN OF THE APES
★★★½

DIRECTOR: Scott Sidney

CAST: Elmo Lincoln, Enid Markey, George French, Colin Kenny, Thomas Jefferson, True Boardman, Kathleen Kirkham, Gordon Griffith (as young Tarzan)

The first filmed version of Edgar Rice Burroughs's classic jungle story adheres closely to the original book-length novel first published in a pulp magazine in 1912. It's one of the first silent feature-length films to earn over $1 million. Heavily advertised and widely seen upon initial release, this blockbuster tells the story of Lord and Lady Greystoke, their shipwreck and abandonment on the African coast, and the fate of their boy child, John. Raised by Kala the she-ape, infant John becomes Tarzan of the Apes. The upbringing and education of the young man-ape are creatively filmed (even though gymnasts in monkey suits play all the apes in the film), and the major changes in plot don't really affect the movie itself. Barrel-chested Elmo Lincoln (who changed his name from Otto Linkenhelt) portrayed Tarzan as an adult and actually killed the lion he fights in one of the film's more exciting moments. Rather than end the film with Tarzan's realization that he is actually Lord Clayton, the crafty producer left Tarzan and Jane in Africa awaiting to depart to America, thus saving the second half of the book for a sequel, *The Romance of Tarzan*, released in 1919. Shot on the East Coast and parts of the southern United States, this landmark film spawned the jungle film as surefire audience bait and was the first of dozens of Tarzan films, most of which treated the Lord of the Jungle as a monosyllabic bug eater who grudgingly helped safaris, smashed guns, and hung around with a chimpanzee. Enhanced with a synchronized musical score, this silent extravaganza is well worth the watch.

1918   B & W   130 minutes

TARZAN THE APE MAN (ORIGINAL)
★★★½

DIRECTOR: W. S. Van Dyke
CAST: Johnny Weissmuller, Maureen O'Sullivan, Neil Hamilton

Tarzan the Ape Man is the film that made Johnny Weissmuller a star and Tarzan an idiot. That classic "Me Tarzan, you Jane" blasphemy is here in its original splendor. Maureen O'Sullivan seduces the dumb beast, and it's all great fun. Hollywood at its peak . . . but no relation to Edgar Rice Burroughs's hero.

1932   B & W   99 minutes

TARZAN THE APE MAN (REMAKE)
🐾

DIRECTOR: John Derek
CAST: Bo Derek, Richard Harris, Miles O'Keeffe, John Phillip Law

One suggestion for anyone planning to watch this movie: grab a book. That way, you'll have something interesting to do while it's on the screen. Even counting the lowest of the low-budget Tarzan flicks, this one, with Bo Derek, Richard Harris, and Miles O'Keeffe (in the title role), is the absolute worst. Rated R because of profanity, sex, and nudity.

1981   112 minutes

TARZAN THE FEARLESS
★

DIRECTOR: Robert Hill
CAST: Buster Crabbe, Jacqueline Wells, E. Alyn Warren, Edward Woods

Buster Crabbe stars as the Lord of the Jungle in this low, low-budget feature. Johnny Weissmuller he ain't. Crabbe fared much better in the now campy "Flash Gordon" and "Buck Rogers" serials. Leave this one on the vine.

1933   B & W   85 minutes

TARZAN'S REVENGE
★

DIRECTOR: Ross Lederman

CAST: Glenn Morris, Eleanor Holm, George Barbier, C. Henry Gordon, Hedda Hopper, George Meeker

Back-lot nonsense with Olympic champions Glenn Morris as the Lord of the Jungle and Eleanor Holm as his Jane gives the hammy supporting actors (including gossip queen Hedda Hopper and slimy villain C. Henry Gordon) plenty of opportunity to chew on the scenery. The 1930s saw four screen Tarzans, but Sol Lesser's choice of Morris as the fourth wasn't exactly inspired. He made much less of an impression (and money) than did his illustrious predecessors, Johnny Weissmuller, Buster Crabbe, and Herman Brix.

1938   B & W   70 minutes

TELEFON
★★★½

DIRECTOR: Don Siegel
CAST: Charles Bronson, Lee Remick, Donald Pleasence, John Mitchum, Patrick Magee

Charles Bronson is a KGB agent who, with the help of the CIA's Lee Remick, is out to stop some preprogrammed Soviet spies from blowing up the United States. Donald Pleasence (*Halloween*) shines as an unhinged maniac, and John Mitchum (*The Enforcer*) has a nice bit as a car mechanic who starts the show off with a bang. Rated PG.

1977   102 minutes

TEN LITTLE INDIANS

DIRECTOR: Peter Collinson
CAST: Oliver Reed, Richard Attenborough, Elke Sommer, Herbert Lom, Gert Frobe

Absolutely dismal third version of the Agatha Christie classic. This one completely mucks up the plot, switching from an isolated island mansion to a hotel deep in the Iranian desert(!). The entire cast overacts abysmally, and the script must have been written with a purple pen. The plot concerns an unseen killer who sequentially knocks off the visitors. Avoid at all costs and stick with the original, 1945's *And Then There Were None*. Rated PG—mild violence.

1975   98 minutes

TEN TO MIDNIGHT
★

DIRECTOR: J. Lee Thompson
CAST: Charles Bronson, Andrew Stevens, Lisa Eilbacher, Cosie Costa

They might as well have titled this one *Charles Bronson Meets the Slasher*. Old "Death Wish" himself goes up against a *Friday the 13th*–type killer in this disappointing action film. It's all rather disgusting, and Bronson looks bored. Rated R for sex, nudity, profanity, and violence.

1983   101 minutes

TENNESSEE STALLION
★★★

DIRECTOR: Don Hulette
CAST: Audrey Landers, Judy Landers, Jimmy Van Patten, Reid Smith, Frederick Cole

Interesting background, beautiful photography, and more than competent acting save this otherwise ordinary action-adventure film set in the world of the Tennessee walking horse show circuit. Jimmy Van Patten is excellent as a man from the wrong circles of society who makes it to the big time with his outstanding horse and the help of the woman who loves him.

1978   87 minutes

TERROR BY NIGHT
★★★

DIRECTOR: Roy William Neill
CAST: Basil Rathbone, Nigel Bruce, Alan Mowbray, Renee Godfrey, Billy Bevan, Dennis Hoey

Penultimate entry in the Rathbone/Bruce Sherlock Holmes series, with the master sleuth and his loyal companion up against a series of murders on a train bound from London to Edinburgh. The culprit ultimately turns out to be Col. Sebastian Moran, but you'll have to watch the film to discover which of the passengers he impersonates!

1946　　B & W　69 minutes

THEY CALL ME *MISTER* TIBBS
★★★

DIRECTOR: Gordon Douglas
CAST: Sidney Poitier, Barbara McNair, Martin Landau

An inferior follow-up, this contains the further adventures of the character Sidney Poitier created for the film *In the Heat of the Night*. Detective Virgil Tibbs is again investigating a murder and trying to clear his friend, as well. Rated PG—contains strong language and some violence.

1970　　108 minutes

THEY DRIVE BY NIGHT
★★★★

DIRECTOR: Raoul Walsh
CAST: Geroge Raft, Humphrey Bogart, Ann Sheridan, Ida Lupino

Here's a Warner Bros. gem! George Raft and Humphrey Bogart star as truck-driving brothers who cope with crooked bosses while wooing Ann Sheridan and Ida Lupino. The dialogue is terrific, and the direction by Raoul Walsh is crisp.

1940　　B & W　93 minutes

THEY WERE EXPENDABLE
★★★★½

DIRECTOR: John Ford
CAST: John Wayne, Robert Montgomery, Donna Reed, Jack Holt, Ward Bond, Marshall Thompson, Louis Jean Heydt

First-rate action drama about American PT boat crews fighting a losing battle against advancing Japanese forces in the Philippines. Director John Ford based this film, his most personal, on his war experiences and the people he knew in the conflict. No phony heroics or glory here, but a realistic, bleak, and ultimately inspiring picture of men in war. John Wayne gives an uncharacteristically restrained performance as Rusty Ryan, second in command to John Brickly (Robert Montgomery), who reluctantly leads his men on a suicide mission. Donna Reed plays Sandy Davis, a navy nurse who falls in love with Wayne.

1945　　B & W　136 minutes

THIEF
★★★★

DIRECTOR: Michael Mann
CAST: James Caan, Tuesday Weld, Jim Belushi, Willie Nelson

James Caan stars in this superb study of a jewel thief. Caan's character tries desperately to create the life he visualized while in prison—one complete with a car, money, house, wife, and kids. But as soon as he manages to acquire these things, they start slipping away. It's an interesting plot, and Michael Mann's direction gives it a sense of realism. Visually stunning, with a great score by Tangerine Dream. Rated R for violence, language, and brief nudity.

1981　　122 minutes

THIN MAN, THE
★★★★½
DIRECTOR: W. S. Van Dyke
CAST: William Powell, Myrna Loy, Edward S. Brophy, Porter Hall, Maureen O'Sullivan, Asta

Viewers and critics alike were captivated by William Powell and Myrna Loy in this first (and best) of a series based on Dashiell Hammett's mystery novel about his "other" detective and wife, Nick and Nora Charles. The thin man is a murder victim. But never mind. The delight of this fun film is the banter between its stars. You'll like their little dog, too.

1934   B & W   89 minutes

THIN MAN GOES HOME, THE
★★½
DIRECTOR: Richard Thorpe
CAST: William Powell, Myrna Loy, Lucile Watson, Gloria De-Haven, Anne Revere, Helen Vinson, Henry Davenport, Leon Ames, Donald Meek, Edward Brophy

Fifth and weakest entry in the series. Nick Charles (William Powell) returns to his old hometown, accompanied by Nora (Myrna Loy) and young Nick Jr. The mystery this time around just doesn't have the same spark, and the witty dialogue sounds a bit wilted. Part of the problem may be young Nick; the casual consumption of alcohol—one of this series' trademarks—just doesn't feel right with a small child in the wings. Still entertaining, but a lesser effort.

1944   B & W   101 minutes

13 RUE MADELEINE
★★★
DIRECTOR: Henry Hathaway
CAST: James Cagney, Annabella, Watler Abel, Frank Lattimore, Melville Cooper, E. G. Marshall, Red Buttons, Karl Malden, Sam Jaffe, Richard Conte

Espionage thriller, inspired by *March of Time* series, shot in semidocumentary style. James Cagney is OSS chief who goes to France to complete a mission when one of his men is killed.

1946   B & W   95 minutes

THIRTY SECONDS OVER TOKYO
★★★★
DIRECTOR: Mervyn LeRoy
CAST: Spencer Tracy, Van Johnson, Robert Walker, Phyllis Thaxter, Scott McKay, Robert Mitchum, Stephen McNally, Louis Jean Heydt, Paul Langton, Leon Ames

Spencer Tracy is in top form as General Doolittle, who led the first bombing attack on Tokyo during World War II. Robert Mitchum and Van Johnson give effective supporting performances as air crew chiefs. We follow Doolittle and his men as they train for the big mission, bomb Tokyo, and make their way home on foot through China. A true-life adventure that, despite its length, never bogs down.

1944   B & W   138 minutes

THIRTY-NINE STEPS, THE (SECOND REMAKE)
★★★½
DIRECTOR: Don Sharp
CAST: Robert Powell, David Warner, Eric Porter, Karen Dotrice, John Mills

An innocent man stumbles onto a spy plot in pre-WWI London. Hunted by enemy agents who think he has intercepted an important communiqué, and civil authorities who believe he is a murderer, the man has nowhere to turn. The best of several Hitchcock remakes in the 1970s. It can't compete with the original, of course, but the cast is good. The script is witty, and the climax atop Big Ben is exciting. Rated PG.

1978   102 minutes

THIS GUN FOR HIRE
★★★★

DIRECTOR: Frank Tuttle
CAST: Alan Ladd, Robert Preston, Veronica Lake

Alan Ladd made his first big impression in this 1942 gangster film as a bad guy who turns good guy in the end. Robert Preston and Veronica Lake co-star in this still enjoyable revenge film.

1942   B & W   80 minutes

THOMAS CROWN AFFAIR, THE
★★★★

DIRECTOR: Norman Jewison
CAST: Steve McQueen, Faye Dunaway, Paul Burke

Combine an engrossing bank-heist caper with an offbeat romance and you have the ingredients for a fun-filled movie. Steve McQueen and Faye Dunaway are at their best as the sophisticated bank robber and unscrupulous insurance investigator who happens to be tracking him. The emotional tricks and verbal sparring between these two are a joy. This is one of the few films where the split-screen technique really moves the story along.

1968   102 minutes

THREE DAYS OF THE CONDOR
★★★★

DIRECTOR: Sydney Pollack
CAST: Robert Redford, Cliff Robertson, Max von Sydow, Faye Dunaway, John Houseman

Robert Redford is a C.I.A. information researcher who is forced to flee for his life when his New York cover operation is blown and all his co-workers brutally murdered. What seems at first to be a standard man-on-the-run drama gradually deepens into an engrossing mystery as to who is chasing him and why. Faye Dunaway expertly handles a vignette as the stranger Redford uses to avoid capture. Rated R.

1975   117 minutes

THREE MUSKETEERS, THE (1973)
★★★★★

DIRECTOR: Richard Lester
CAST: Michael York, Oliver Reed, Raquel Welch, Richard Chamberlain, Faye Dunaway, Charlton Heston

Alexandre Dumas's oft-filmed swashbuckler classic—there may have been as many as ten previous versions—finally came to full life with this 1973 release, directed by Richard Lester (Superman II). It is a superb adventure romp with scrumptious moments of comedy, character, and action. There's never a dull moment. Throughout, Lester injects throwaway bits of slapstick and wordplay—you have to pay careful attention to catch them, and it's well worth it. Rated PG.

1973   105 minutes

THREE MUSKETEERS, THE (1948)
★★

DIRECTOR: George Sidney
CAST: Gene Kelly, Lana Turner, June Allyson, Van Heflin, Vincent Price, Gig Young, Angela Lansbury, Keenan Wynn

MGM's all-star version of the classic swashbuckler by Alexandre Dumas gets its swords crossed up. This is primarily due to some blatant miscasting. Gene Kelly as D'Artagnan and his co-star June Allyson playing the queen's seamstress are never convincing as French citizens during the reign of Louis XIII. The production has lots of energy, but little substance. Fans of Lana Turner may find the movie worthwhile, because hidden in this fluff is one of her finest performances as the villainous Lady DeWinter.

1948   B & W 128 minutes

THREE THE HARD WAY
★★★

DIRECTOR: Gordon Parks Jr.

CAST: Fred Williamson, Jim Brown, Jim Kelly, Sheila Frazier, Jay Robinson

A white supremacist (Jay Robinson) attempts to wipe out the black race by putting a deadly serum in the country's water supply. Fred Williamson, Jim Brown (*The Dirty Dozen*), and Jim Kelly (*Enter the Dragon*) team up to stop him in this action-packed movie. Rated PG for violence.

1974   93 minutes

THUNDER AND LIGHTNING
★★

DIRECTOR: Corey Allen

CAST: David Carradine, Kate Jackson, Roger C. Carmel, Sterling Holloway, Ed Barth

Weak "action film" about moonshiners and their misadventures. Stars David Carradine and Kate Jackson are watchable enough, but a few touches of originality wouldn't have hurt. Rated PG for profanity and violence.

1977   95 minutes

THUNDER BAY
★★★½

DIRECTOR: Anthony Mann

CAST: James Stewart, Dan Duryea, Joanne Dru, Jay C. Flippen, Gilbert Roland

Star James Stewart and director Anthony Mann teamed up for a series of memorable westerns in the 1950s, *The Man from Laramie*, *The Far Country*, and *Bend of the River* among them. But they also made some nonwesterns together, arguably the best of which was this release. In it, Stewart plays an oil driller forced to take on a nasty group of Louisiana shrimp fishermen. The story is full of action and fine characterizations from a talented cast.

1953   102 minutes

THUNDER RUN

DIRECTOR: Gary Hudson

CAST: Forrest Tucker, John Ireland, John Shepherd, Jill Whitlow, Wally Ward, Cheryl M. Lynn, Marilyn O'Connor

Forrest Tucker stars in this grade Z action flick as a truck driver who is persuaded by an old army pal (John Ireland) to act as bait in a scheme to catch terrorists. He is to haul plutonium so they can be caught trying to steal it. Therefore, this movie is a bomb in more ways than one. Rated R for nudity, profanity, suggested sex, and violence.

1986   89 minutes

THUNDERBALL
★★★

DIRECTOR: Terence Young

CAST: Sean Connery, Claudine Auger, Adolfo Celi

When originally released in 1965, this fourth entry in the James Bond series suffered from comparison to its two admittedly superior predecessors, *From Russia with Love* and *Goldfinger*. However, time has proved it to be one of the more watchable movies based on the books by Ian Fleming, with Sean Connery in top form as 007 and assured direction by Terence Young.

1965   129 minutes

THUNDERBOLT AND LIGHTFOOT
★★★★

DIRECTOR: Michael Cimino
CAST: Clint Eastwood, Jeff Bridges, George Kennedy, Geoffrey Lewis, Gary Busey

Clint Eastwood's right-on-target performance is equaled by those of co-stars Jeff Bridges, George Kennedy, and Geoffrey Lewis in this decidedly offbeat caper picture. The stoic top-lined actor plays an ex-con who hooks up with petty thief Bridges to hunt down the hidden spoils of a heist committed several years before. The only problem is that his ex-partners in the crime, Kennedy and Lewis, have the same idea, but no intention of sharing the loot. *Thunderbolt and Lightfoot* is a little-known action gem that proved a little too offbeat for Clint's fans when originally released in 1974. However, movie buffs have since proclaimed it a cinematic gem, a reputation it deserves. Look for Gary Busey (*The Buddy Holly Story* and *Barbarosa*) in a brief supporting role. Rated R.

1974   114 minutes

TIMERIDER

DIRECTOR: William Dear
CAST: Fred Ward, Belinda Bauer, Peter Coyote, L. Q. Jones, Ed Lauter

There are the films that just sort of sit there, never achieving anything. This is one of those films. A motorcycle rider and his motorcycle break the time barrier and end up being chased by cowboys in the Old West. It sounds far more interesting than it is. If you're having difficulty sleeping, this is the cure. Rated PG.

1983   94 minutes

TO HAVE AND HAVE NOT
★★★½

DIRECTOR: Howard Hawks
CAST: Humphrey Bogart, Lauren Bacall, Walter Brennan

Director Howard Hawks once bet Ernest Hemingway he could make a good film from one of the author's worst books. Needless to say, he won the bet with this exquisite entertainment, which teamed Humphrey Bogart and Lauren Bacall for the first time. The story takes place before the events of the book and concerns the decision of an apathetic soldier of fortune (Bogart) to fight the Nazis.

1944   B & W 100 minutes

TO HELL AND BACK
★★½

DIRECTOR: Jesse Hibbs
CAST: Audie Murphy, Marshall Thompson, Charles Drake, Gregg Palmer, Jack Kelly, Paul Picerni, Susan Kohner, David Janssen

Real-life war hero Audie Murphy plays himself in this sprawling World War II action film. We follow Audie Murphy and his buddies (Marshall Thompson, Jack Kelly, and David Janssen) from North Africa to Berlin. Murphy received twenty-four medals, including the Congressional Medal of Honor, which made him the most decorated soldier in World War II. But the price of war is high, as most of Murphy's friends were killed, along with countless Germans and other Americans. Good performances and true-life drama make up for a static script and rather routine battle sequences.

1955 106 minutes

TO LIVE AND DIE IN L.A.
🐢

DIRECTOR: William Friedkin

CAST: William L. Petersen, Willem Dafoe, John Pankow, Dean Stockwell, Debra Feuer, John Turturro, Darlanne Fluegel

This vile and violent exercise in bloody self-indulgence is one of the bleakest cinema statements mankind ever produced. There is no way to distinguish bad from good; every character is equally insensitive, manipulative, and emotionally bankrupt. Director William Friedkin clearly wanted a hit thriller to re-create his success with *The French Connection*. What he made, with co-scripter and ex–Secret Service agent Gerald Petievich (on whose book the film is based), is an overly violent account of lone wolf William L. Petersen's attempt to shut down counterfeiter Willem Dafoe. This film goes so far overboard that it's only for the *Friday the 13th* gore crowd. Rated R for sex, nudity, and excessive violence.

1985 114 minutes

TOBRUK
★★★

DIRECTOR: Arthur Hiller

CAST: Rock Hudson, George Peppard, Guy Stockwell, Nigel Green

Rock Hudson, Nigel Green, and George Peppard lead a ragtag group of British soldiers and homeless Jews against the Nazi and Italian armies in the North African desert during World War II. To do so, they must sneak through Axis lines disguised as German soldiers escorting Allied prisoners through the desert. Their mission is to blow up the big guns at Tobruk before the British invasion fleet lands. Along the way our heroes encounter hostile Arabs, spies, beautiful women, and much more. An exciting climax, beautiful photography, and good performances help offset a farfetched script.

1966 110 minutes

TOMBOY
★

DIRECTOR: Herb Freed

CAST: Betsy Russell, Kristi Somers, Jerry Dinome

Mindless nonsense (with plenty of skin) about a female race car driver named Tommy (Betsy Russell) who takes on the man of her dreams (Jerry Dinome) on and off the track. Rated R.

1985 91 minutes

TOP GUN
★★★½

DIRECTOR: Tony Scott

CAST: Tom Cruise, Kelly McGillis, Val Kilmer, Anthony Edwards, Tom Skerritt, Michael Ironside, John Stockwell, Rick Rossovich, Barry Tubb, Whip Hubley

Tom Cruise stars as a student at the navy's Fighter Weapons School, where flyers are turned into crack fighter pilots. While competing for the title of Top Gun there, he falls in love with an instructor (Kelly McGillis of *Witness*). Because the film moves like a supersonic bullet for most of its running time, one is inclined to forgive most of its eyebrow-raising "commercial elements" and the fact that its story is merely a thinly veiled rewrite of *An Officer and a Gentleman*. Rated PG for light profanity, suggested sex, and violence.

1986   118 minutes

TOPKAPI
★★★★★

DIRECTOR: Jules Dassin
CAST: Peter Ustinov, Melina Mercouri, Maximilian Schell

This is one of the finest and funniest of the "big heist" genre. Director Jules Dassin assembled a highly talented international cast. They are members of a charming group of jewel thieves whose target is a priceless jeweled dagger in a Turkish museum. The execution of their clever plan is both humorous and exciting.

1964   120 minutes

TORA! TORA! TORA!
★★★★

DIRECTOR: Richard Fleischer, Toshio Masuda, Kinji Fakasaku
CAST: Jason Robards, Martin Balsam, James Whitmore, Joseph Cotten, So Yamamura

An American-Japanese cooperative venture reenacts the events up to and including the December 7 attack on Pearl Harbor. Although many well-known actors contribute their skills, they are overshadowed by the technical brilliance of the realistic recreation of the climactic attack. Rated G.

1970   143 minutes

TOUGH ENOUGH
★★½

DIRECTOR: Richard Fleischer
CAST: Dennis Quaid, Warren Oates, Stan Shaw, Pam Grier, Wilford Brimley

Dennis Quaid plays the "Country-and-Western Warrior," a singer-fighter who slugs his way through taxing "Toughman" contests from Fort Worth to Detroit in a quest for fame and fortune. It's *Rocky* meets *Honeysuckle Rose*, yet still mildly enjoyable. The main reason for that is the watchability of stars Quaid, the late Warrren Oates, Stan Shaw, Pam Grier, and Wilford Brimley, with screenwriter John Leone's nice touches of humor coming in a close second. Rated PG for profanity and violence.

1983   106 minutes

TOWERING INFERNO, THE
★★★★

DIRECTOR: John Guillermin, Irwin Allen
CAST: Steve McQueen, Paul Newman, William Holden, Faye Dunaway, Fred Astaire, Richard Chamberlain

This is the undisputed king of the disaster movies of the 1970s. An all-star cast came together for this big-budget thriller about a newly constructed San Francisco high-rise hotel and office building that is set ablaze due to substandard materials. The action is nonstop as fire chief Steve McQueen and architect Paul Newman combine their efforts to free a score of big-name stars who become trapped in its penthouse restaurant. Rated PG.

1974   165 minutes

TOY SOLDIERS
★

DIRECTOR: David Fisher
CAST: Jason Miller, Cleavon Little, Rodolfo DeAnda

This is an inept and poorly acted film about a group of vacationing college students in Latin America. As the unconvincing story unfolds, we find our young heroes attempting to rescue a captured friend. Rated R.

1983   85 minutes

TRAIN, THE
★★★★

DIRECTOR: John Frankenheimer
CAST: Burt Lancaster, Paul Scofield, Michel Simon, Jeanne Moreau

A suspenseful World War II adventure about the French Resistance's attempt to stop a train loaded with fine art, seized from French museums, from reaching its destination in Nazi Germany. Burt Lancaster is fine as the head of the French railway system, but he is far outclassed by the performance of Paul Scofield as the unrelenting German commander.

1965   B & W 113 minutes

TREASURE OF THE FOUR CROWNS
🐾

DIRECTOR: Ferdinando Baldi
CAST: Tony Anthony, Ana Obregon, Gene Quintano

In this rip-off of Raiders of the Lost Ark by the folks who created the dreadful Comin' at Ya, a group of adventurers attempt to steal invaluable Visigoth treasures from a crazed cult leader. The story is boring. The acting is pitiful. Rated PG for violence and gore.

1983   97 minutes

TREASURE OF THE SIERRA MADRE, THE
★★★★★

DIRECTOR: John Huston
CAST: Humphrey Bogart, Tim Holt, Walter Huston, Bruce Bennett

Humphrey Bogart gives a brilliant performance in this study of greed. The setting is rugged mountains in Mexico where Bogart, with Tim Holt and a grizzled prospector, played marvelously by Walter Huston, set out to make a fortune in gold prospecting. They do, with their troubles getting worse. Seamless script and magnificent performances add up to a classic. Witness Bogart's amazing portrayal of creeping dementia, and listen for one of moviedom's most famous lines, "Badges . . . ."

1948   B & W 126 minutes

TWELVE O'CLOCK HIGH
★★★★

DIRECTOR: Henry King
CAST: Gregory Peck, Dean Jagger, Gary Merrill, Hugh Marlowe

Gregory Peck is the flight commander who takes over an England-based bomber squadron during World War II. He begins to feel the strain of leadership and becomes too involved with the men in his command. This is a well-produced and well-acted film. The compassion Peck shows in his role is superb, and it helped assure him a place in Hollywood immortality. Dean Jagger won an Oscar for supporting actor for his fine performance.

1950   B & W 132 minutes

20,000 LEAGUES UNDER THE SEA
★★★★

DIRECTOR: Richard Fleischer
CAST: Kirk Douglas, James Mason, Paul Lukas, Peter Lorre

In this Disney version of the famous Jules Verne adventure/fantasy, a sailor (Kirk Douglas) and a scientist (Paul Lukas) get thoroughly involved with Captain Nemo, played by James Mason, and his fascinating submarine of the future. The cast is great, the action sequences ditto. Good popcorn pic.

1954   127 minutes

TWILIGHT'S LAST GLEAMING
★★★

DIRECTOR: Robert Aldrich
CAST: Burt Lancaster, Paul Winfield, Burt Young, William Smith, Charles Durning, Richard Widmark, Melvyn Douglas, Joseph Cotten

Although this is another maniac-at-the-button Doomsday chronicle, it is so convincing that it makes the well-worn premise seem new. From the moment a group of ex-cons (Burt Lancaster, Paul Winfield, Burt Young, and William Smith) seize control of an Air Force pickup truck, it becomes obvious the audience is in the front seat of a non-stop roller coaster. Lancaster and his henchmen take over an atomic missile station and exploit his knowledge as a former general and designer of the Titan base to force the President (Charles Durning) to become their hostage in order to compel him to reveal the "truth" about Vietnam. Rated R for violence and profanity.

1977   146 minutes

TYCOON
★

DIRECTOR: Richard Wallace
CAST: John Wayne, Laraine Day, Cedric Hardwicke, Judith Anderson, Anthony Quinn, James Gleason

Planned and budgeted as a titanic epic of the building of a railroad through the Andes. John Wayne stinks as the headstrong and reckless engineer who feuds with tycoon Cedric Hardwicke while listlessly romancing his daughter,

Laraine Day. It's all overblown, ridiculous, and unconvincing.

1947   128 minutes

UNCOMMON VALOR
★★★★

DIRECTOR: Ted Kotcheff
CAST: Gene Hackman, Fred Ward, Reb Brown, Randall "Tex" Cobb, Harold Sylvester, Robert Stack

In this action-packed adventure film, directed by Ted Kotcheff (*First Blood*), retired Marine Gene Hackman learns that his son may still be alive in a Vietnamese prison camp ten years after being listed as missing in action. He decides to go in after him. Rated R for profanity and violence.

1983   105 minutes

UNDER FIRE
★★½

DIRECTOR: Roger Spottiswoode
CAST: Nick Nolte, Gene Hackman, Joanna Cassidy, Ed Harris, Jean-Louis Trintignant

Take a little *Missing*, mix it with a generous portion of *The Year of Living Dangerously*, and add a dash of *Reds* and you have this release. Sound awful? Actually, passable is a more accurate appraisal of this movie, starring Nick Nolte, Gene Hackman, and Joanna Cassidy as journalists covering political upheaval in Central America circa 1979. While *Under Fire* has its moments (found primarily in the superb supporting performances of Ed Harris and French actor Jean-Louis Trintignant), you have to wade through a bit of sludge to get to them. Rated R for profanity, violence, and gore.

1983   128 minutes

UNTOUCHABLES: ALCATRAZ EXPRESS, THE
★★½

DIRECTOR: John Peyser

CAST: Robert Stack, Neville Brand, Bruce Gordon, Paul Picerni, Nicholas Georgiade, Abel Fernandez

Originally aired as a two-part episode on the popular television series, this feature-length film chronicles gang leader Al Capone's train trip to prison and the efforts by Frank Nitti and "the boys" to break him out. Robert Stack as federal agent Elliot Ness is the larger-than-life, fanatically devoted public servant who thwarts the escape efforts with his devoted assistants Rico, Lee, and Youngblood, and sees to it that Scarface makes it safely to the penitentiary to serve his sentence from income-tax evasion. Well acted and produced, this film was theatrically released in Europe before it made it to the drive-ins of America.

1960   B & W   96 minutes

UNTOUCHABLES: SCARFACE MOB, THE
★★★

DIRECTOR: Phil Karlson

CAST: Robert Stack, Keenan Wynn, Barbara Nichols, Pat Crowley, Neville Brand, Bruce Gordon, Jerry Paris, Anthony George, Abel Fernandez, Nick Giorgiade

This violence-ridden film was released theatrically in 1962 but was actually the original two-part pilot for this popular series, first telecast in 1959. Steely-eyed Robert Stack as Elliot Ness gets the government's go-ahead to form his own special team of uncorruptible agents and leads them in forays against the enemy; bootleggers, racketeers, and especially the minions of kingpin Al "Scarface" Capone and his enforcer, Frank Nitti, played to perfection by Neville Brand and the incomparable Bruce Gordon. Veteran actor Keenan Wynn is the bad apple in the Ness organization, and the bullets, booze, and blood flow freely in this hard-hitting, enormously popular effort by Phil Karlson, one of the gritty, realistic directors who made their mark in American films of the 1950s. This is a tough movie, full of heroics and retribution. This still seems like strong fare, even for today's gore-saturated audiences. Narrated by often caricatured Walter Winchell.

1962   B & W   90 minutes

UTU
★★★★★

DIRECTOR: Geoff Murphy

CAST: Anzac Wallace, Bruno Lawrence, Kelly Johnson, Tim Elliot

This stunner from New Zealand contains all the action of the great American westerns, but with a moral message that leaves most of that genre's best in the dust. Anzac Wallace plays Te Wheke, a Maori corporal in the nineteenth-century British army who finds his family slaughtered by his own army. It is there at his burning village that he vows "utu" (Maori for revenge) and goes on a march with fellow Maori rebels to rid his land of white people. This moral tale is not as simple as retribution, however. The story masterfully introduces and develops many characters along the way; Bruno Lawrence is brilliant as a white settler who seeks his own revenge on Wheke, and Kelly Johnson is convincing as an aspiring soldier in the British army who develops personal reasons for wanting

Wheke's capture. Rated R for violence.

1985　　　　　　　　100 minutes

VANISHING POINT
★★½

DIRECTOR: Richard C. Sarafian

CAST: Cleavon Little, Barry Newman, Dean Jagger

Interesting story of a marathon car chase through Colorado and California. Cleavon Little gives a stand-out performance as the disc jockey who helps a driver (Barry Newman) elude the police. Richard Sarafian's direction is competent, but the story eventually runs out of gas before the film ends. Rated PG.

1971　　　　　　　　107 minutes

VEGA$
★★½

DIRECTOR: Richard Lang

CAST: Robert Urich, Judy Landers, Tony Curtis, Will Sampson, Greg Morris

A few days in the life of a high-flying, T-Bird–driving private eye whose beat is highways, byways, and gambling casinos of Las Vegas. Robert Urich, an ex-cop, is hired to find a runaway teen-age girl who's gotten in too deep with the sleazy side of Fortune Town.

1978　　　　　　　　104 minutes

VICE SQUAD
★★★½

DIRECTOR: Gary A. Sherman

CAST: Season Hubley, Wings Hauser, Gary Swanson, Beverly Todd

Slick, fast-paced thriller set in the seamy world of pimps and prostitutes. Season Hubley is an adorable mom by day and a smart-mouthed hooker by night forced to help cop Gary Swanson capture a sicko killer, played with frightening intensity by Wings Hauser. The police get their man, but he breaks away—after learning that Hubley set him up—and then the fun *really* begins. A total fairy tale, but it moves quickly enough to mask improbabilities. Hauser's one of the best psycho nutcases since *Dirty Harry*'s Andy Robinson. Not for the squeamish. Rated R.

1982　　　　　　　　97 minutes

VICTORY
★★★

DIRECTOR: John Huston

CAST: Sylvester Stallone, Michael Caine, Pelé, Max von Sydow

Sylvester Stallone and Michael Caine star in this entertaining but predictable World War II drama about a soccer game between Allied prisoners of war and the Nazis. Germany intends to cheat. But our boys want to strike a blow for democracy. With a title like *Victory*, guess who wins. A hokey ending—in which the prisoners forgo certain escape to win the game—destroys the film's credibility. Rated PG.

1981　　　　　　　　110 minutes

VIEW TO A KILL, A
★★★

DIRECTOR: John Glen

CAST: Roger Moore, Tanya Roberts, Christopher Walken, Grace Jones

Despite a spectacular opening sequence and some dandy little moments along the way, the James Bond series is starting to look a little old and tired—just like its star, Roger Moore. Christopher Walken co-stars as the maniacal villain who plans to corner the world's microchip market by flooding the San Andreas Fault. Good for fans only. Rated PG for violence and suggested sex.

1985   131 minutes

VIKINGS, THE
★★★½

DIRECTOR: Richard Fleischer
CAST: Kirk Douglas, Tony Curtis, Ernest Borgnine, Janet Leigh

Well-done action film following the exploits of a group of Vikings (led by Tony Curtis and Kirk Douglas). Many good battle scenes and beautiful photography and locations make the picture a standout. Ernest Borgnine gives a great performance as Curtis's comrade. Don't miss it.

1958   114 minutes

VILLAIN STILL PURSUED HER, THE
★

DIRECTOR: Edward F. Cline
CAST: Anita Louise, Richard Cromwell, Hugh Herbert, Alan Mowbray, Buster Keaton, Billy Gilbert, Margaret Hamilton

Dull, old-fashioned melodrama is pretty thick sledding even with a veteran crew of character actors and actresses to break the monotony. Buster Keaton adds a little pep to this otherwise tired production, but the overall tone of this movie is that of tedium.

1940   B & W   66 minutes

VIVA KNIEVEL
★

DIRECTOR: Gordon Douglas
CAST: Evel Knievel, Marjoe Gortner, Leslie Nielsen, Gene Kelly, Lauren Hutton

Despite a healthy budget, this film is highly reminiscent of the old Republic Studio cheapie cliff-hangers complete with goody good guys, nasty bad guys, stereotyped supporting characters, and lots of action. The film is too corny for adults, but still too complex for the kiddies, which leaves it in a state of limbo as far as audience appeal is concerned. The story has Evel Knievel (playing himself) being duped by a former buddy, Jessie (Marjoe Gortner), into doing a stunt tour of Mexico. What Evel doesn't know is that Jessie's boss, Stanley Millard (Leslie Nielsen), plans to murder him during the climax of one of his feats of daring. Rated PG, the film has no profanity, sex, or nudity, and very little violence.

1977   106 minutes

VON RYAN'S EXPRESS
★★★★

DIRECTOR: Mark Robson
CAST: Frank Sinatra, Trevor Howard, Edward Mulhare, James Brolin, Luther Adler

This is a World War II tale of escape from a prisoner-of-war camp aboard a German train to neutral Switzerland. Trevor Howard is the officer in charge until a feisty Frank Sinatra takes over the escape plan. This is a great action story, with Sinatra playing the hero's role perfectly. The antagonism between Howard, as the "safety of the men first" commander, and Sinatra, as the "escape at any cost" colonel, is well acted and believable.

1965   117 minutes

WAKE ISLAND
★★★★

DIRECTOR: John Farrow
CAST: Brian Donlevy, Macdonald Carey, Robert Preston, Albert Dekker, William Bendix, Walter Abel

Hard-hitting tale of a small gallant detachment of U.S. marines holding out against attack after attack by the Japanese army, navy, and air force. A true story from the early dark days of World War II when there had been no American victories. These marines held out for sixteen days while all of America held its breath. Brian Donlevy commands the troops, and William Bendix and Robert Preston fight each other as much as they fight the Japanese. *Wake Island* received four Academy Award nominations and was the first realistic American film made about World War II.

1942　　　B & W　88 minutes

WAKE OF THE RED WITCH
★★★★

DIRECTOR: Edward Ludwig

CAST: John Wayne, Gail Russell, Gig Young, Luther Adler

Good, sea faring adventure tale with John Wayne outstanding as a wronged ship's captain seeking justice and battling an octopus for sunken treasure.

1948　　　B & W　106 minutes

WALKING TALL
★★½

DIRECTOR: Phil Karlson

CAST: Joe Don Baker, Elizabeth Hartman, Noah Beery, Rosemary Murphy

Poor Joe Don Baker never outran his one-note performance as Buford Pusser, the baseball bat—toting southern sheriff who decided to take the law into his own hands in his fight against the cancerous scum of society. Unpleasantly brutal and difficult to enjoy for any reason; good guy Baker is almost worse than the outrageously stereotyped baddies he reduces to pulp. Talented Elizabeth Hartman

is completely wasted. Not a family picture. Rated R.

1973　　　125 minutes

WALKING TALL PART II
★½

DIRECTOR: Earl Bellamy

CAST: Bo Svenson, Luke Askew, Richard Jaeckel, Noel Berry Jr.

In this sequel, there is more baseball than justice from Sheriff Buford T. Pusser (Bo Svenson). This follow-up to the successful *Walking Tall* proves that sequels are better off not being made at all. This storyline gives Svenson a chance to flex his muscles and look mean, but that's about it. Rated R for violence and language.

1975　　　109 minutes

WARNING, THE
🦃

DIRECTOR: Damiano Damiani

CAST: Martin Balsam, Giuliano Gemma, Giancarlo Zanetti, Guido Leontini, Marcello Mando

Convoluted dirty-cop flick from Italy. The folks who dubbed this thing must not have been up on the really emotionally loaded colloquialisms of modern English— to be really insulted in this flick is to be called a "turd." Martin Balsam's performance is pure paycheck and everyone else takes the whole affair far too seriously. Not rated, but probably equal to an R for violence, profanity, and nudity.

1985　　　101 minutes

WARRIORS, THE
★★★★

DIRECTOR: Walter Hill

CAST: Michael Beck, James Remar, Thomas Waites

Comic book–style violence and sensibilities made this Walter Hill film an unworthy target for those worried about its prompting real-life gang wars. It's just meant for fun, and mostly it is, as a group of kids try to make their way home through the territories of other, less-understanding gangs in a surrealistic New York. Rated R.

1979   94 minutes

WE OF THE NEVER NEVER
★★★★½

DIRECTOR: Igor Auzins

CAST: Angela Punch McGregor, Arthur Dignam, Tony Barry

The compelling story of a woman's year in the Australian Outback, where she learns about aborigines and they learn about her, is based on a true-life account written by Jeannie Gunn and published in 1908. Angela Punch McGregor stars in this first-rate import from Down Under. Rated G.

1983   132 minutes

WHEELS OF FIRE
🐾

DIRECTOR: Cirio Santiago

CAST: Gary Watkins, Laura Banks, Lynda Wiesmeiser, Linda Grovenor

Shameless ripoff of *The Road Warrior*, lacks the taste of most of the films that have come in the wake of George Miller's action masterpiece. Nudity, violence, and rape dominate this story about a gang of nomadic bad guys with a leader named Scourge. If you can handle the misogyny, this one might be good for the mistaken humor: the cast members talk like high-school teenagers—*Frankie and Annette Meet Mad Max*?

Rated R for sex, nudity, violence, and profanity.

1984   81 minutes

WHERE EAGLES DARE
★★★

DIRECTOR: Brian G. Hutton

CAST: Richard Burton, Clint Eastwood, Mary Ure, Michael Hordern, Patrick Wymark, Anton Diffring, Robert Beatty, Donald Houston, Ingrid Pitt

Clint Eastwood and Richard Burton portray Allied commandos in this World War II adventure film which is short on realism. Instead we have far-fetched but exciting shootouts, explosions, and mass slaughter. Our heroes must break out an American general being held captive in a heavily fortified German castle before the Nazis can get highly secret information out of him. Basically a spaghetti western set during World War II, this movie should please most action-adventure buffs.

1969   158 minutes

WHITE DAWN, THE
★★★★

DIRECTOR: Phil Kaufman

CAST: Warren Oates, Louis Gossett Jr., Timothy Bottoms, Simonie Kopapik, Joanasie Salomonie

This is a gripping and thought-provoking adventure film. Three whalers (Warren Oates, Louis Gossett Jr., and Timothy Bottoms) get lost in the Arctic and are rescued by Eskimos, whom they end up exploiting. Rated PG.

1974   109 minutes

WHITE HEAT
★★★★½

DIRECTOR: Raoul Walsh

CAST: James Cagney, Margaret Wycherly, Virginia Mayo, Edmond O'Brien, Steve Cochran

James Cagney gives one of his greatest screen performances as a totally insane mama's boy and gangster, Cody Jarrett, in this film. Margaret Wycherly is chillingly effective as the evil mom, and Virginia Mayo is uncommonly outstanding as the badman's moll. But it is Cagney's picture pure and simple as he ironically makes it to "the top of the world, Ma!"

1949   B & W 114 minutes

WHITE LIGHTNING
★★

DIRECTOR: Joseph Sargent
CAST: Burt Reynolds, Jennifer Billingsley, Ned Beatty, Bob Hopkins, Matt Clark, Louise Latham, Diane Ladd

Good old boy Burt Reynolds as a speed-loving moonshiner fights the inevitable mean and inept cops and revenue agents in this comic-book chase and retribution film. A good cast of character actors make this stock drive-in movie entertaining, and there's plenty of mindless action to keep your eyes on the screen, but this throwback to Robert Mitchum's *Thunder Road* is just like the majority of Burt Reynolds's car films—gimmicky and predictable. Not bad if you consider a VCR as something to keep you company rather than to enlighten and inform, but basically a longer episode of *The Dukes of Hazzard*. Rated PG.

1973   101 minutes

WHITE LINE FEVER
★★★

DIRECTOR: Jonathan Kaplan

CAST: Jan-Michael Vincent, Kay Lenz, Slim Pickens, L. Q. Jones, Leigh French, Don Porter

Jan-Michael Vincent plays an incorruptible young trucker in this film. He is angered when forced to smuggle goods in his truck. He fights back after he and his pregnant wife (Kay Lenz) are attacked. Rated PG.

1975   92 minutes

WHITEWATER SAM
★★½

DIRECTOR: Keith Larsen
CAST: Keith Larsen

Keith Larsen wrote, directed, coproduced, and stars in this family film of a wilderness adventure. He plays the legendary Whitewater Sam, the first white man to survive the harsh Rocky Mountain winters. The real star, however, seems to be his darling, intelligent dog, Sybar. The beautiful scenery makes this film more than watchable. Rated PG for violence.

1978   85 minutes

WHO'LL STOP THE RAIN
★★★★½

DIRECTOR: Karel Reisz
CAST: Nick Nolte, Michael Moriarty, Tuesday Weld, Anthony Zerbe, Richard Masur, Ray Sharkey, David Opatoshu, Gail Strickland

In this brilliant film, Nick Nolte gives one of his finest performances as a hardened vet who agrees to smuggle drugs for a buddy (the always effective Michael Moriarty). What neither of them knows is that it's a setup, so Nolte and Moriarty's neurotic wife, played to perfection by Tuesday Weld, have to hide out from the baddies (Anthony Zerbe, Richard Masur, and Ray Sharkey) who want to steal their stash and then kill them. Directed by Karel Riesz, this gripping and suspenseful film builds to a powerful climax that's reminiscent of Raoul Walsh's classic *High Sierra*. Rated R.

1978 126 minutes

WICKED LADY, THE

DIRECTOR: Michael Winner

CAST: Faye Dunaway, Alan Bates, John Gielgud, Denholm Elliott, Prunella Scales, Oliver Tobias, Glynis Barber

An absolutely awful swashbuckler directed by Michael Winner (*Death Wish*), this wastes the talents of stars Faye Dunaway and Alan Bates. Despite the presence of two such high-powered acting talents, this period adventure film about an aristocrat who gets her kicks robbing travelers is a real groaner, and it's easy to see why the production company (Cannon Films) decided not to release it to the theaters. Rated R.

1983 98 minutes

WILD ANGELS, THE
★★

DIRECTOR: Roger Corman

CAST: Peter Fonda, Nancy Sinatra, Bruce Dern, Michael J. Pollard, Diane Ladd, Gayle Hunnicutt

It's 1960s hip, low-budget Hollywood style. If they gave Oscars for cool, Peter Fonda—in shades, three-day growth of beard, and leather—would win for sure. This cool motorcycle gang leader needs a hot mama. Unfortunately, he has to make do with Nancy ("These Boots Are Made for Walkin") Sinatra. It's always fun to watch Bruce Dern doing his psychotic biker routine. But the movie's greatest asset is "Blue's Theme," which

revs up the proceedings with wonderfully tacky fuzz-tone guitar.

1966 93 minutes

WILD GEESE, THE
★★★

DIRECTOR: Andrew V. McLaglen

CAST: Richard Burton, Roger Moore, Richard Harris, Stewart Granger, Hardy Kruger, Jack Watson, Frank Finley, Jeff Wrey, Winston Ntshona

The Wild Geese features the unlikely combination of Richard Burton, Roger Moore, and Richard Harris as three mercenaries hired by a rich British industrialist (Stewart Granger) to go into Rhodesia and free a captured humanist leader so the millionaire's company can again have the copper rights to the country. Burton is first-rate. His usual overblown, theatrical approach is subdued, making this one of the most effective film performances he ever achieved. He is perfect as the cool-headed leader. Moore is acceptable as the roguish part-time crook. Harris adds humanity as the brilliant strategist and loving father who reluctantly joins the mission because of his political beliefs. The battle scenes are some of the best ever. Rated R.

1978 134 minutes

WILD GEESE II
★

DIRECTOR: Peter Hunt

CAST: Scott Glenn, Barbara Carrera, Edward Fox, Laurence Olivier, Stratford Johns

In this contrived and vastly inferior sequel to the adventure film that starred Richard Burton, Richard Harris and Roger Moore, a new group of mercenaries attempt to break into a Berlin prison to free Nazi war criminal Rudolf Hesse.

Even more ludicrous, this operation is backed by an American television network. Gone from this film are the earlier film's believable situations and three-dimensional characters. Here the characters, dialogue, and violence are straight out of a comic book. The actors do their best, but even Olivier can't turn in a decent performance with this script. Rated R for violence and language.

1985   118 minutes

WILD ONE, THE
★★★½

DIRECTOR: Laslo Benedek
CAST: Marlon Brando, Mary Murphy, Robert Keith, Lee Marvin, Jay C. Flippen, Jerry Paris, Alvy Moore, Gil Stratton

This classic film (based loosely on a real event in Hollister, California) about rival motorcycle gangs taking over a small town is pretty tame stuff these days and provides more laughs than thrills. Producer Stanley Kramer's heavy-handed moralizing and the incredible dialogue mark this as one of the first of the "phony" teen films, where young people were played by actors in their twenties and thirties, and the slang and "hip-talk" were made up on the spot. Marlon Brando and his brooding Johnny are at the heart of this film's popularity; that coupled with the theme of motorcycle nomads have assured the film a cult following, but it is Lee Marvin's Chino who stands out as a real character. Naïve yet exploitative, this was Marlon Brando's first popular film. The image of him in blue jeans, leathers jacket and cap, and motorcycle boots emblazoned itself on the 1950s and was echoed in all the media of that decade.

1953   B & W   79 minutes

WIND AND THE LION, THE
★★★★

DIRECTOR: John Milius
CAST: Sean Connery, Brian Keith, Candice Bergen, John Huston, Geoffrey Lewis, Steve Kanaly, Vladek Sheybal

In the 1970s, Sean Connery made a trio of memorable adventure movies, one being this release, directed by John Milius (*Conan the Barbarian*). As in the other two films—*The Man Who Would Be King* and *Robin and Marian*—*The Wind and the Lion*, in which Connery plays a dashing Arab chieftain, is a thoroughly satisfying motion picture. Rated PG.

1975   119 minutes

WINGS
★★★★

DIRECTOR: William Wellman
CAST: Clara Bow, Charles Rogers, Richard Arlen, Jobyna Ralston, Gary Cooper, Arlette Marchal, El Brendel

The first recipient of the Academy Award for best picture, this is a silent film with organ music in the background. The story concerns two buddies who join the Air Corps in World War I and go to France to battle the Germans. War scenes are excellent, even by today's standards. Anti-war message is well done, although the love story tends to bog the film down a bit. Look for a young Gary Cooper. Much of the story rings true.

1927   B & W 139 minutes

WINNING
★★★½

DIRECTOR: James Goldstone
CAST: Paul Newman, Joanne Woodward, Robert Wagner, Richard Thomas

Paul Newman is very good as a race car driver who puts winning above all else, including his family. Some very good racing sequences and fine support from Joanne .Woodward and Richard Thomas. Rated PG.

1969   123 minutes

WITNESS
★★★★½

DIRECTOR: Peter Weir

CAST: Harrison Ford, Kelly McGillis, Josef Summer, Lukas Haas, Alexander Godunov, Danny Glover

This is three terrific movies in one: an exciting cop thriller, a touching romance, and a fascinating screen study of a modern-day clash of cultures. Harrison Ford is superb in the starring role as a police captain who must protect an 8-year-old boy, the only witness to a drug-related murder. The policeman's attentions are welcomed (in more than one way) by the boy's mother (Kelly McGillis). However, both are thwarted by her friends and family—being Amish, they shun the devices and denizens of the modern world. Nevertheless, everyone is endangered when the murderer turns out to be a corrupt cop. Rated R for violence, profanity, and nudity.

1985   112 minutes

WOMAN IN GREEN, THE
★★★

DIRECTOR: Roy William Neill

CAST: Basil Rathbone, Nigel Bruce, Hillary Brooke, Henry Daniell, Paul Cavanagh, Matthew Boulton

This is a grisly little entry in the Rathbone/Bruce Sherlock Holmes series, with the master sleuth investigating a series of severed fingers sent to Scotland Yard. The culprit is, once again, Professor Moriarty (Henry Daniell), this time

masterminding a hypnosis-blackmail-murder scheme. Careful viewers will detect moments from *The Adventure of the Empty House*.

1945   B & W   68 minutes

YAKUZA, THE
★★★★★

DIRECTOR: Sydney Pollack

CAST: Robert Mitchum, Brian Keith, Ken Takakura, Herb Edelman, Richard Jordan, Kishi Keiko

This superb blending of the American gangster and Japanese samurai genres was directed by Sydney Pollack (*Tootsie*). In the screenplay, by Paul Schrader (*Taxi Driver*), Robert Mitchum plays Harry Kilmer, an ex-G.I. who returns to Japan to do a dangerous favor for a friend, George Tanner (Brian Keith). The latter's daughter has been kidnapped by a Japanese gangster—a Yakuza—who is holding her for ransom. This forces Kilmer to call on Tanaka (Ken Takakura), a one-time enemy who owes him a debt. Thus begins a clash of cultures and a web of intrigue that keep the viewers on the edge of their seats. Rated R.

1975   112 minutes

YEAR OF LIVING DANGEROUSLY, THE
★★★★½

DIRECTOR: Peter Weir

CAST: Mel Gibson, Sigourney Weaver, Linda Hunt, Michael Murphy, Bill Kerr, Noel Ferrier

The Year of Living Dangerously is set in 1965 Indonesia when the Sukarno regime was toppling from pressures left and right. As in his previous efforts, Weir creates so much atmosphere that it seems to fill your nostrils at times. Mel Gibson and Sigourney Weaver star as an Australian journalist and a British diplomatic attaché, respectively. The film, however, belongs to Linda Hunt, in her Academy Award–winning role as free-lance photographer Billy Kwan. Rated R for profanity, nudity, and violence.

1983   115 minutes

YEAR OF THE DRAGON
★

DIRECTOR: Michael Cimino
CAST: Mickey Rourke, John Lone, Ariane, Leonard Termo, Ray Barry

This film about the attempts of a New York police officer (Mickey Rourke) to stop the violence caused by youth gangs in Chinatown has some exciting and effectively dramatic moments. Overall, however, it's racist, sexist, foulmouthed, overly violent, and just plain disgusting, another study in excess from director Michael Cimino. As with the overly praised *The Deer Hunter* and the overly criticized *Heaven's Gate*, *Year of the Dragon* sometimes fascinates and thrills. Its better moments come wrapped in a decidedly distasteful package. Rated R for violence, profanity, gore, simulated sex, and nudity.

1985   136 minutes

YOJIMBO
★★★★½

DIRECTOR: Akira Kurosawa
CAST: Toshiro Mifune, Eijiro Tono

Viewed from different perspectives, *Yojimbo* ("bodyguard") is: the most devastating comedy ever made; Kurosawa's parody of the American western; or his satire on the United States and Soviet Union's achieving peace through nuclear proliferation. Toshiro Mifune, an unemployed samurai in nineteenth-century Japan, sells his services to two rival merchants, each with killer gangs that are tearing the town apart. Both groups of thugs are efficiently and systematically eliminated. The film is boisterous—*lots* of bones crunching and samurai swords flashing and slashing—and exuberant. It is a rare Japanese film that is accessible to a broad spectrum of Americans. (Remade by Sergio Leone as *A Fistful of Dollars*.) No rating, but very violent.

1961   B & W 110 minutes

YOU ONLY LIVE TWICE
★★★

DIRECTOR: Lewis Gilbert
CAST: Sean Connery, Akiko Wakabayashi, Tetsuro Tamba, Mie Hama, Karin Dor, Bernard Lee, Lois Maxwell, Desmond Llewellyn, Donald Pleasence

Sean Connery as James Bond—who could expect more, especially in these days of cheap imitations? Well, a better plot and more believable cliff-hanger situations come to mind. Still, this entry isn't a bad 007, and it does star the best Bond.

1967   116 minutes

YOUNG AND INNOCENT
★★★

DIRECTOR: Alfred Hitchcock
CAST: Derick de Marney, Nova Pilbeam, Percy Marmont, Edward Rigby, Mary Clare, Basil Radford

Reputedly director Alfred Hitchcock's favorite of the films he made in Great Britain, this chase-within-a-chase film employs one of his favorite devices, that of an innocent man avoiding the police while attempting to catch the real criminal and prove his innocence. Convincingly played against a series of different backdrops and settings by a cast of players all but unknown to contemporary American audiences, this neat little thriller (based on Josephine Tey's first mystery novel) is a skillful blend of comedy and suspense and boasts one of Hitchcock's best touches, an elaborate soundstage-length moving close-up that reveals the real murderer to the audience as a member of a performing band. Not as well known as many of his other films, this seldom-seen movie is vintage Hitchcock and on a par with much of his best work.

1937   B & W   80 minutes

YOUNG SHERLOCK HOLMES
★★½

DIRECTOR: Barry Levinson

CAST: Nicholas Rowe, Alan Cox, Sophie Ward, Anthony Higgins, Freddie Jones

This disappointingly derivative Steven Spielberg production speculates on what might have happened if Sherlock Holmes (Nicholas Rowe) and Dr. John H. Watson (Alan Cox) had met during their student days in 1870 England. A better name for it might be *Sherlock Holmes and the Temple of Doom*. While youngsters are likely to enjoy it, most adults—especially frequent filmgoers or video viewers—are cautioned to avoid it. It is yet another example of the sure-fire commercial package, which means we have seen nearly everything in it at least once before in one of Spielberg's other productions. As in *E.T.* and *The Goonies*, a group of kids take on a gang of nasty adults. In addition, a supporting character creates Rube Goldberg–type inventions similar to those in *The Goonies*, *Back to the Future*, and, (in effect, anyway) *The Money Pit*. And finally a deadly drug used by the villains produces hallucinations, which include re-animated corpses à la *Poltergeist* and gruesome little beasties like those in *Gremlins*. The result is a kind of high-class assembly-line product, which is hardly what we expect from Spielberg and his collaborators. Rated PG-13 for violence and scary stuff.

1985   115 minutes

ZOMBIES OF THE STRATOSPHERE (SATAN'S SATELLITES)
★★

DIRECTOR: Fred Brannon

CAST: Judd Holdren, Aline Towne, Wilson Wood, Lane Bradford

Judd Holdren, representing the Inter-Planetary Patrol, dons a flying suit and tracks down part-human zombies who have enlisted the aid of a renegade scientist to construct a hydrogen bomb that will blow Earth off its orbit and enable them to conquer what's left of the world. Balsa wood rocket ships and stock footage from the other "Rocket Man" serials make this one of the more ludicrous entries from Republic Studios in the last years of the movie serial. Enjoy the stunts in this one and skip the story.

1952   B & W   12 chapters

ZULU
★★★★½

DIRECTOR: Cy Endfield

CAST: Stanley Baker, Michael Caine, Jack Hawkins, Nigel Green

Several films have been made about the British army and its exploits in Africa during the nineteenth century, *Zulu* ranks with the finest. A stellar cast headed by Stanley Baker and Michael Caine (in his film debut) charged through this story of an outmanned British garrison laid to siege by several thousand Zulu warriors. Based on fact, this one delivers the goods for action and tension.

1964   138 minutes

ZULU DAWN
★★★

DIRECTOR: Douglas Hickox
CAST: Burt Lancaster, Peter O'-Toole, Simon Ward, John Mills, Nigel Davenport

This prequel to the film *Zulu*, which was made fifteen years earlier, seems quite pale when compared with the first. Based on the crushing defeat to the British army at the hands of the Zulu warriors, *Zulu Dawn* depicts the events leading up to the confrontation portrayed in *Zulu*. Considering all involved, this a disappointment. Rated PG for vioence.

1979   121 minutes

CHILDREN'S VIEWING

ABSENT-MINDED PROFESSOR, THE
★★★★

DIRECTOR: Robert Stevenson
CAST: Fred MacMurray, Nancy Olson, Tommy Kirk, Ed Wynn, Keenan Wynn

One of Disney's best live-action comedies, this stars Fred MacMurray in the title role of a scientist who discovers "flubber" (flying rubber). Only trouble is, no one will believe him—except Keenan Wynn, who tries to steal his invention.

1961   B & W 104 minutes

ACROSS THE GREAT DIVIDE
★★

DIRECTOR: Stewart Raffill
CAST: Robert Logan, George Flower, Heather Rattray, Mark Edward Hall

Across the Great Divide is family entertainment at its most unchallenging. Two kids (Heather Rattray and Mark Hall) meet up with a shifty gambler (Robert Logan), and the three eventually unite for safety on their monotonous trek

through valleys, mountains, and rivers. There are some bright spots. The dog, Chastity, humorously romps with a playful beaver. An attack by mountain lions and another by wolves are both suspenseful. The Indians are well played and sensitively presented. Rated G.

1976   89 minutes

ADVENTURES OF AN AMERICAN RABBIT, THE
★★★

DIRECTOR: Steward Moskowitz
CAST: Animated

In this enjoyable-for-kids feature-length cartoon, mild-mannered and sweet-natured Rob Rabbit becomes the heir to the Legacy, which magically transforms him into the star-spangled protector of all animalkind, the American Rabbit. Rated G.

1986   85 minutes

ADVENTURES OF HUCKLEBERRY FINN, THE
★★

DIRECTOR: Jack B. Hively

CAST: Forrest Tucker, Larry Storch, Brock Peters

This drawn-out version of Mark Twain's classic has its moments but lacks continuous action. In it, young Huck fakes his own drowning to avoid attendance of a proper eastern school for boys. When his friend, the slave Jim (Brock Peters), is accused of his murder, he must devise a plan to free him. Huck and Jim find themselves rafting down the Mississippi with two likable con artists (Larry Storch and Forrest Tucker).

1978   97 minutes

ADVENTURES OF THE WILDERNESS FAMILY

★★★½

DIRECTOR: Stuart Raffill

CAST: Robert Logan, Susan D. Shaw, Ham Larsen, Heather Rattray, George (Buck) Flower, Hollye Holmes, William Cornford

This is a variation on the Swiss Family Robinson story. A family (oddly enough named Robinson) moves to the Rocky Mountains to escape the frustrations and congestion of life in Los Angeles. They're sick of smog, hassles, and crime. And, more important, the daughter, Jenny (Heather Rattray), has a serious respiratory problem that only fresh, clean air can rectify. They build a cabin and brave the dangers of the wild. Rated G.

1975   100 minutes

ADVENTURES OF TOM SAWYER, THE

★★★★

DIRECTOR: Norman Taurog

CAST: Tommy Kelly, Jackie Moran, Victor Jory, May Robson, Walter Brennan, Ann Gillis

One of the better screen adaptations of Mark Twain's works.

Tommy Kelly is a perfect Tom Sawyer, but it's Victor Jory as the villainous Indian Joe who steals the show. Good sets and beautiful cinematography make this one work. Fine family entertainment for the young and old.

1938   B & W   93 minutes

ALADDIN AND HIS WONDERFUL LAMP

★★★½

DIRECTOR: Tim Burtin

CAST: Valerie Bertinelli, Robert Carradine, James Earl Jones, and Leonard Nimoy

This *Faerie Tale Theatre* interpretation of the classic Arabian Nights tale adds a few twists. One is the offer of the genie (James Earl Jones) to rearrange Aladdin's (Robert Carradine) face when Aladdin makes demands on him. The second surprise is the TV the genie produces to satisfy the sultan and win the princess (Valerie Bertinelli) for Aladdin. Leonard Nimoy is good as the manipulative wizard who entices Aladdin into retrieving the magic lamp from a dangerous and spooky cave. The whole family can enjoy this one.

1985   60 minutes

ALICE IN WONDERLAND

★★★½

DIRECTOR: Clyde Geronimi, Hamilton Luske, Wilfred Jackson

CAST: Animated

The magic of the Walt Disney Studio animators is applied to Lewis Carroll's classic in this feature-length cartoon with mostly entertaining results. As with the book, the film is episodic and lacking the customary Disney warmth. But a few absolutely wonderful sequences—like the Mad Hatter's tea party and the appearances of the Cheshire cat—make it worth seeing. Rated G.

1951   75 minutes

ALICE'S ADVENTURES IN WONDERLAND
★★

DIRECTOR: William Sterling
CAST: Fiona Fullerton, Dudley Moore, Peter Sellers, Sir Ralph Richardson, Spike Milligan

This British live-action version of Lewis Carroll's classic tale is too long and boring. It is a musical that employs an endless array of silly songs, dances, and riddles. Although it sticks closely to the book, it's not as entertaining as Disney's fast-paced animated version of 1951. Fiona Fullerton stars as Alice. Dudley Moore is featured as the Dormouse, Peter Sellers plays the March Hare, and Sir Ralph Richardson is the caterpillar. Children between 5 and 10 may enjoy this, but parents will undoubtedly fall asleep. Rated G.

1973   97 minutes

ALMOST ANGELS
★★½

DIRECTOR: Steve Previn
CAST: Peter Weck, Hans Holt, Fritz Eckhardt, Bruni Lobel, Sean Scully

Schmaltzy film focusing on the Vienna Boys' Choir and the problems one boy encounters when his voice cracks and he can no longer sing in the choir. Rated G.

1962   93 minutes

AMAZING DOBERMANS
★★

DIRECTOR: David and Byron Chudnow
CAST: James Franciscus, Barbara Eden, Fred Astaire, Jack Carter

Third in a series of films about do-gooder dogs pits a treasury agent (James Franciscus) against inept crooks who can dodge the long arm of the law but can't compete with the dogged determination of the Dobermans. This odd film not only features Fred Astaire as the colorful top-dog of the canine corps but throws in everyone's favorite midget, Billy Barty, as a special bonus. Harmless but hardly inspired. Rated G.

1976   94 minutes

APPLE DUMPLING GANG, THE
★★

DIRECTOR: Norman Tokar
CAST: Bill Bixby, Tim Conway, Don Knotts, Susan Clark, David Wayne, Slim Pickens, Harry Morgan

A gambler (Bill Bixby) inherits three children who find a huge gold nugget in a supposedly played-out mine in 1870. Tim Conway and Don Knotts trip and foul up as left-footed bad guys. The best word for this is "innocuous." Good, clean, unoriginal, predictable fare from Disney. The kids will love it. Rated G.

1975   100 minutes

APPLE DUMPLING GANG RIDES AGAIN, THE
★½

DIRECTOR: Vincent McEveety
CAST: Tim Conway, Don Knotts, Harry Morgan, Jack Elam, Kenneth Mars, Ruth Buzzi, Robert Pine

A cast composed of comic actors, each of whom is topnotch in solo spots, is no guarantee of hilarious ensemble playing. In this sequel to the 1975 original, Tim Conway and Don Knotts again play bumbling, inept outlaws in the Old West. Not quite a turkey, but close! Even so, the kids will enjoy it—once. Rated G.

1979   88 minutes

BAREFOOT EXECUTIVE, THE
★★

DIRECTOR: Robert Butler
CAST: Kurt Russell, Joe Flynn, Harry Morgan, Wally Cox, Heather North, Alan Hewitt, John Ritter

Mild Disney comedy about an individual (Kurt Russell) who finds a chimpanzee that can select top television shows. Based on the chimp's selections, a network moves to the top of the ratings charts, and Russell becomes a vice president in charge of programming. The usual confusions come about as Russell tries to explain that the monkey did the selecting. Rated G.

1971   92 minutes

BATMAN
★★★

DIRECTOR: Leslie Martinson
CAST: Adam West, Burt Ward, Frank Gorshin, Burgess Meredith, Lee Meriwether, Cesar Romero

Holy success story! The caped crusader and his youthful sidekick jump from their popular mid-1960s television series into a full-length feature film. Adam West and Burt Ward keep quip in cheek as they battle the Fearsome Foursome: the Riddler (Frank Gorshin), the Penguin (Burgess Meredith), the Catwoman (Lee Meriwether), and the Joker (Cesar Romero). Even summer isn't this camp. The plot, a thin excuse for a series of exciting bat-chases and clever bat-traps, concerns a plot to transform United Nations delegates into small piles of dust. Very silly material played with ludicrous seriousness, resulting in a lot of fun. Pretty bat-ty.

1966   105 minutes

BEAUTY AND THE BEAST
★★★★

DIRECTOR: Roger Vadim
CAST: Klaus Kinski, Susan Sarandon

A merchant's daughter takes her father's place as the prisoner of a melancholy beast and finds that love can change all things. Klaus Kinski is marvelous as the Beast and Susan Sarandon a fine Beauty in this Faerie Tale Theatre production.

1983   52 minutes

BEDKNOBS AND BROOMSTICKS
★★★½

DIRECTOR: Robert Stevenson
CAST: Angela Lansbury, David Tomlinson, Roddy McDowall

Angela Lansbury is a witch who uses her powers to aid the Allies against the Nazis during World War II. She transports two children to faraway and strange locales during which they meet and play soccer with talking animals, among other things. This Disney film is an effective combination of special effects, animation, and live actions. While some may consider it a weaker version of *Mary Poppins*, it has plenty of what it takes to stand on its own. Rated G.

1971   117 minutes

BENJI
★★★★

DIRECTOR: Joe Camp
CAST: Peter Breck, Deborah Walley, Edgar Buchanan, Frances Bavier, Patsy Garrett

Benji parallels *Lassie* and *Rin Tin Tin* by intuitively doing the right thing at the right time. In this film, a dog saves two children who get kidnapped. Unlike Lassie or Rin Tin Tin, Benji is a small, unassuming mutt, which makes him all the more endearing. Deborah Walley and Edgar Buchanan co-star with Benji (who played Higgins on television's "Petticoat Junction"), but the lovable mutt is the real star in this one. Rated G.

1974   86 minutes

BIG RED
★★★

DIRECTOR: Norman Tokar
CAST: Walter Pidgeon, Gilles Payant, Emile Genest, Janette Bertrand

This pleasant family film drawn from the beloved children's book of the same title features Walter Pidgeon as the owner of a sleek Irish setter named Big Red, which spends its formative years in loving companionship with young Gilles Payant. When the dog grows older and is groomed for professional shows, it escapes and tries to find its youthful friend.

1962   89 minutes

BLACKBEARD'S GHOST
★★★½

DIRECTOR: Robert Stevenson
CAST: Peter Ustinov, Dean Jones, Suzanne Pleshette, Elsa Lanchester

This fun Disney comedy has Peter Ustinov playing a ghost who must prevent his ancestors' home from becoming a gambling casino.

1968   107 minutes

BLACK STALLION, THE
★★★★★

DIRECTOR: Carroll Ballard
CAST: Kelly Reno, Mickey Rooney, Teri Garr, Hoyt Axton, Clarence Muse

Before taking our breath away with the superb *Never Cry Wolf*, director Carroll Ballard made an impressive directorial debut with this gorgeous screen version of the well-known children's story. Kelly Reno plays the young boy stranded on a deserted island with "The Black," a wild, but very intelligent, horse who comes to be his best friend. The scenes in the first half of the film are absolutely hypnotic. Even small children are transfixed by the story, told only via director of photography Caleb Deschanel's images and composer Carmine Coppola's music. It's a treat the whole family can enjoy. Rated G.

1979   118 minutes

BLACK STALLION RETURNS, THE
★★★★

DIRECTOR: Robert Dalva
CAST: Kelly Reno, Vincent Spano, Teri Garr, Allen Goorwitz, Woody Strode

A sequel to the 1979 film *The Black Stallion*, this is first-rate fare for the young and the young at heart. The story, based on the novel by Walter Farley, picks up where the first film left off. Alec Ramsey (Kelly Reno) is a little older and a little taller, but he still loves his horse, The Black. And this time, Alec must journey halfway around the world to find the stallion, which has been stolen by an Arab chieftain. Rated PG for slight violence.

1983   93 minutes

BLUE YONDER, THE
★★★½

DIRECTOR: Mark Rosman
CAST: Peter Coyote, Huckleberry Fox, Art Carney, Dennis Lipscomb, Joe Flood, Mittie Smith, Frank Simons

Heartfelt tale of a boy (Huckleberry Fox) who goes back in time in a time machine to warn his late grandfather (Peter Coyote) of his unsuccessful attempt at a nonstop transatlantic flight. Good performances keep the creaky plot airborne.

1985   89 minutes

BOATNIKS, THE
★★½

DIRECTOR: Norman Tokar
CAST: Stephanie Powers, Phil Silvers, Norman Fell, Robert Morse, Mickey Shaughnessy

Disney comedy in which Robert Morse plays a heroic Coast Guard officer who manages a romantic relationship with Stephanie Powers while pursuing bumbling thieves (Phil Silvers, Norman Fell, and Mickey Shaughnessy). Rated G.

1970   99 minutes

BON VOYAGE, CHARLIE BROWN
★★★

DIRECTOR: Bill Melendez
CAST: Animated

An animated film starring the "Peanuts" gang, this is well suited for the viewing of the younger generation. It's basically a "Peanuts" guide to world travel. *Bon Voyage* ... begins as Charlie Brown, Linus, Marcie, and Peppermint Patty discover themselves headed toward France as part of a student-exchange program. Of course, Snoopy and Woodstock must come along for the ride. Although much of the film chronicles their travels through England and France, the emphasis is on their stay in a small French village where Charlie and Linus find themselves invited to a dark,

scary castle in which no one seems to live. Rated G.

1980   75 minutes

BORN FREE
★★★★★

DIRECTOR: James Hill
CAST: Virginia McKenna, Bill Travers, Geoffrey Keen, Peter Lukoye

An established family classic, this is the tale of Elsa the lioness and her relationship with an African game warden and his wife. Not since *The Yearling* and *National Velvet* has such compassion been given to the interaction between people and the animals they love and eventually lose. A brilliant film.

1966   96 minutes

BOY NAMED CHARLIE BROWN, A
★★★★

DIRECTOR: Bill Melendez
CAST: Animated

Charles Schulz's "Peanuts" gang jumps to the big screen in this delightful, wistful tale of Charlie Brown's shot at fame in a national spelling bee. Great jazzy piano score by the incomparable Vince Guaraldi brings life to great sequences, such as Snoopy's ice skating debut. Lucy and her girl gang are a bit hard on ol' Chuck at times, and things definitely pick up when Charlie Brown, Linus, and Snoopy are off on their own. Good songs, including a poignant title tune by Rod McKuen. Rated G.

1969   85 minutes

BOY WHO LEFT HOME TO FIND OUT ABOUT THE SHIVERS, THE
★★★½

DIRECTOR: Graeme Clifford

CAST: Peter MacNicol, Dana Hill, Christopher Lee, David Warner, Frank Zappa, Jeff Corey

In this Faerie Tale Theatre production narrated by Vincent Price, a boy (Peter MacNicol, of *Sophie's Choice*) goes off to a Transylvanian castle (operated by Christopher Lee, no less) to find out about fear. Good moments overcome a rather protracted midsection where our hero does a bit too much goofing around with ghosts. Not for children.

1985   54 minutes

BROTHERS LIONHEART, THE
★★½

DIRECTOR: Olle Hellbom
CAST: Staffan Gotestam, Lars Soderdahl, Allan Edwall, Gunn Wallgren

This slow-moving children's fantasy was filmed in Sweden, Denmark, and Finland. Two brothers are reunited after death in a medieval world where they fight dragons and villains in an attempt to free their war leader, Ulva, who will rid the country of tyrants. If you don't fall asleep within the first forty-five minutes, you will be rewarded with a fine fairy tale. Rated G.

1977   108 minutes

BUGS BUNNY/ROAD RUNNER MOVIE, THE
★★★★

DIRECTOR: Chuck Jones, Phil Monroe
CAST: Animated

Classic cartoons made by Chuck Jones for Warner Bros. are interwoven into this laugh fest; the first and best of the 1970s and '80s feature-length compilations. Includes such winners as "Duck Amuck" and "What's Opera, Doc?" Rated G.

1979   92 minutes

BUGSY MALONE
★★★½

DIRECTOR: Alan Parker
CAST: Scott Baio, Florrie Augger, Jodie Foster, John Cassisi, Martin Lev

The 1920s gangsters weren't really as cute as these children, who run around shooting whipping cream out of their pistols. But if you can forget that, this British musical provides light diversion. Rated G.

1976   93 minutes

CANDLESHOE
★★½

DIRECTOR: Norman Tokar
CAST: David Niven, Helen Hayes, Jodie Foster, Leo McKern, Vivian Pickles

Confused Disney comedy about a street kid (Jodie Foster) duped by shady Leo McKern into posing as an heir to Helen Hayes. All the better to swipe your estate, my dear. David Niven is an identity-laden butler whose smugness, for once, becomes tiresome. Marred by typically excessive Disney physical "humor" (read: slapstick). Average for younger folks. Rated G.

1977   101 minutes

CARE BEARS MOVIE, THE
★★★

DIRECTOR: Aran Selznick
CAST: (voice) Mickey Rooney, (voice) Georgia Engel

Poor animation mars this children's movie about bears who cheer up a pair of kids. However, the music of John Sebastian keeps things hopping along, and adults don't have to worry about letting the kiddies watch it (unless they can't afford to buy the stuffed versions of the title characters). Rated G, no objectionable material.

1985   80 minutes

CASEY'S SHADOW
★★½

DIRECTOR: Martin Ritt
CAST: Walter Matthau, Alexis Smith, Robert Webber, Murray Hamilton

Only the droll playing of star Walter Matthau makes this family film watchable. Matthau is a horse trainer deserted by his wife and left to raise three sons. It lopes along at a slow pace, and only the star's fans will want to ride it out. Rated PG.

1978   116 minutes

CASTAWAY COWBOY, THE
★★★½

DIRECTOR: Vincent McEveety
CAST: James Garner, Vera Miles, Robert Culp, Eric Shea

James Garner plays a Texas cowboy in Hawaii during the 1850s. There he helps a lovely widow (Vera Miles) start a cattle ranch despite problems created by a land-grabbing enemy (played by Robert Culp). Good family entertainment. Rated G.

1974   91 minutes

CAT FROM OUTER SPACE, THE
★★½

DIRECTOR: Norman Tokar
CAST: Ken Berry, Sandy Duncan, Harry Morgan, Roddy McDowall

Disney comedy/sci-fi about a cat from outer space with a magical collar. The cat needs United States help to return to its planet. Rated G.

1978   103 minutes

CHARLIE AND THE ANGEL
★★

DIRECTOR: Vincent McEveety
CAST: Fred MacMurray, Cloris Leachman, Harry Morgan, Kurt Russell, Vincent Van Patten, Kathleen Cody

Time-worn plot about a guardian angel who teaches an exacting man (Fred MacMurray) a few lessons in kindness and humility before his time on Earth is up is reminiscent of many better, more sincere films. Harry Morgan is okay as the angel, and the rest of the cast is competent enough, but one gets the impression that everyone is just going through the motions in this lesser effort from Walt Disney Productions. The kids won't mind, but chances are you've seen a better version already.

1973   93 minutes

CHARLIE, THE LONESOME COUGAR
★★★

DIRECTOR: Not Credited
CAST: Ron Brown, Brian Russell, Linda Wallace, Jim Wilson, Rex Allen (narrator)

A misunderstood cougar comes into a lumber camp in search of food and companionship. After adopting the animal, the men are not certain whether it will adapt back to its wild habitat, or even if they want it to. This entertaining Disney animal film is more believable than the storyline would suggest. Rated G.

1968   75 minutes

CHARLOTTE'S WEB
★★

DIRECTOR: Charles A. Nichols, Iwao Takamoto
CAST: (voices only): Debbie Reynolds, Paul Lynde, Henry Gibson

Absolutely wretched adaptation of E. B. White's beloved children's book. Charlotte the spider, Wilbur the pig, and Templeton the rat lose all their charm and turn into simpering participants in a vacuous musical. Blocky animation, typical of Hanna-Barbera's Saturday-morning drivel, and insipid songs. Only for those less than age four. Rated G.

1973   85 minutes

CHITTY CHITTY BANG BANG
★★½

DIRECTOR: Ken Hughes
CAST: Dick Van Dyke, Sally Ann Howes, Anna Quayle, Lionel Jeffries, Benny Hill

This musical extravaganza, based on a book by Ian Fleming, is aimed at a children's audience. In it, a car flies, but the flat jokes and songs leave adult viewers a bit seasick as they hope for a quick finale. However, the kiddies will like it. Rated G.

1968   142 minutes

CHRISTMAS CAROL, A
★★★★★

DIRECTOR: Brian Desmond Hurst
CAST: Alastair Sim, Kathleen Harrison, Jack Warner, Michael Hordern

Starring Alastair Sim as Ebenezer Scrooge, the meanest miser in all of London, this is a wondrously uplifting story—as only Charles Dickens could craft one. Recommended for the whole family, *A Christmas Carol* is sure to bring a tear to your eye and joy to your heart.

1951   B & W   86 minutes

CHRISTMAS STORY, A
★★★★

DIRECTOR: Bob Clark

CAST: Peter Billingsley, Darren McGavin, Melinda Dillon, Ian Petrella

Both heartwarming and hilarious, this is humorist Jean Shepherd's wacky recollections of being a kid in the 1940s and the monumental Christmas that brought the ultimate longing—for a regulation Red Ryder air rifle. Problem is, his parents don't think it's such a good idea. But our hero isn't about to give up. Peter Billingsley is marvelous as the kid. Melinda Dillon (*Close Encounters of the Third Kind*) and Darren McGavin also shine as the put-upon parents. A delight for young and old.

1983   98 minutes

CINDERELLA
★★★★

DIRECTOR: Mark Cullingham
CAST: Jennifer Beals, Matthew Broderick, Jean Stapleton, Eve Arden, Jane Alden, Edie McClurg

One of the most entertaining of producer Shelley Duvall's FaerieTale Theatre entries. Jennifer Beals is a shy, considerate, and absolutely gorgeous Cinderella; Matthew Broderick does his aw-shucks best as the smitten Prince Henry. The dialogue is wonderful: "It's hard to be anonymous when your face is on all the money," Henry confesses. Nicely wacky Fairy Godmother by Jean Stapleton, and delightfully shrewish stepmother and stepdaughters by Eve Arden, Jane Alden, and Edie McClurg. Sweetly romantic, a treat for all. Unrated—family fare.

1985   60 minutes

COLD RIVER
★★★★

DIRECTOR: Fred G. Sullivan

CAST: Suzanna Weber, Pete Teterson, Richard Jaeckel

In the autumn of 1932, an experienced guide takes his 14-year-old daughter and his 12-year-old stepson on an extended camping trip. Far out in the wilderness, the father dies of a heart attack, and the children must survive a blizzard, starvation, and an encounter with a wild mountain man. This wonderful family movie is rated PG but should be seen by all.

1981   94 minutes

THE COMPUTER WORE TENNIS SHOES, THE
★★

DIRECTOR: Robert Butler
CAST: Kurt Russell, Cesar Romero, Joe Flynn, William Schallert

In the late 1960s and early 1970s, it was the practice of the Disney Studios to produce and distribute low-budget comedies at the beginning of each year. Medfield College was often the locale. This was the first production to star Kurt Russell in the college comedies, after Fred MacMurray (*The Absent-Minded Professor* and *Son of Flubber*) and Tommy Kirk left the fold. The flimsy premise is that a student accidentally becomes a genius after being short-circuited with a computer. The movie is weak, with the "excitement" provided by a group of mobsters and gamblers which attempts to use the student for its nefarious purposes. Not rated.

1969   87 minutes

CONDORMAN
★½

DIRECTOR: Charles Jarrot
CAST: Michael Crawford, Oliver Reed, James Hampton, Barbara Carrera

This Disney film has everything you've ever seen in a spy film—but it was better the first time. A comic book writer (Michael Crawford) gets his chance to become a spy when he goes after a beautiful Russian defector (Barbara Carrera). Despite all the ridiculous gadgetry and car wrecks, there's very little excitement to the action, and even less humor. The best thing that can be said is that it's a watchable film that you can show your kids. Rated PG.

1981   90 minutes

DAFFY DUCK'S MOVIE: FANTASTIC ISLAND
★★

DIRECTOR: Friz Freleng
CAST: Animated

This pedestrian compilation is for Warner Brothers cartoon fanatics and toddlers only. Chunks of fairly funny shorts are strung together with a weak, dated parody of TV's "Fantasy Island." Daffy deserved better. Rated G.

1983   78 minutes

DANCING PRINCESSES, THE
★★★★

DIRECTOR: Peter Medak
CAST: Lesley Ann Warren, Peter Weller, Roy Dotrice

This enchanting *Faerie Tale Theatre* production features Roy Dotrice as an overprotective king who locks his daughters in their room each night. When the shoe cobbler insists the princesses are wearing out a pair of dancing slippers each day, he offers one of his daughters to any man who can discover where the girls go each night. Lesley Ann Warren plays the eldest and cleverest princess, Janetta. Peter Weller is the dashing soldier who discovers their secret. There is a wonderful absence of violence in this charming tale, which is suitable for the entire family.

1984   50 minutes

DARBY O'GILL AND THE LITTLE PEOPLE

★★★½

DIRECTOR: Robert Stevenson
CAST: Albert Sharpe, Janet Munro, Sean Connery, Jimmy O'Dea

Darby O'Gill is an Irish storyteller who becomes involved with some of the very things he talks about, namely leprechauns, the banshee, and other Irish folk characters. Darby tricks the leprechaun king into granting him three wishes but soon regrets his trickery. This wonderful tale is one of Disney's best films and a delightful fantasy film in its own right. It features a young and relatively unknown Sean Connery as Darby's future son-in-law.

1959   93 minutes

DAVY CROCKETT AND THE RIVER PIRATES

★★★

DIRECTOR: Norman Foster
CAST: Fess Parker, Buddy Ebsen, Kenneth Tobey, Jeff York

Fess Parker, as idealized Davy Crockett, takes on Big Mike Fink (Jeff York) in a keelboat race and tangles with Indians in the second Walt Disney–produced Davy Crockett feature composed of two television episodes. Thoroughly enjoyable and full of the kind of boyhood images that Disney productions evoked so successfully in the late 1940s and '50s. Fun for the whole family.

1956   81 minutes

DAVY CROCKETT (KING OF THE WILD FRONTIER)

★★★½

DIRECTOR: Norman Foster

CAST: Fess Parker, Buddy Ebsen, Hans Conried, Kenneth Tobey

One of Walt Disney's most unexpected surprises of the 1950s was this colorful, history-bending saga of frontier hero Davy Crockett and his irascible but capable sidekick, Georgie Russell, and their adventures in the early part of the nineteenth century. Finely played by all involved, this is actually a compilation of three episodes that appeared originally on television and were then released theatrically. Davy's journeys take him to the swamps of the South, where he fights Indians and helps restore peace; to the halls of Congress, where he fights politicians and tries to restore peace. His last and most famous journey is, of course, to Texas and the Alamo mission where he and the other gallant defenders laid down their lives for their land and their beliefs, joined by that other frontier legend, Jim Bowie (ruggedly played by Kenneth Tobey). Fine family fare.

1955   88 minutes

DAYDREAMER, THE

★★★

DIRECTOR: Jules Bass
CAST: Paul O'Keefe, Burl Ives, Tallulah Bankhead, Terry-Thomas, Victor Borge, Ed Wynn, Patty Duke, Boris Karloff, Ray Bolger, Hayley Mills, Jack Gilford, Margaret Hamilton

This "Children's Treasure" presentation combines live action with puppetry to bring a young Hans Christian Andersen and his tales to life. Paul O'Keefe plays the young Andersen and Jack Gilford plays his shoemaker father. Young Andersen prefers daydreaming to his studies as he takes us with him into his fantasy world. In "The

Little Mermaid," Hayley Mills provides the voice for the generous mermaid who saves his life. Burl Ives is her Father. Next, young Chris Andersen becomes an apprentice to two shady tailors in "The Emperor's New Clothes." Finally, Patty Duke gives voice to Thumbelina and Boris Karloff speaks for the evil Rat who captures Chris and Thumbelina. The characters occasionally burst into song to convey their feelings but not so much as to intrude on the story.

1966   80 minutes

DOCTOR DOLITTLE
★★½

DIRECTOR: Richard Fleischer
CAST: Rex Harrison, Samantha Eggar, Anthony Newley, Richard Attenborough

Rex Harrison plays the title role in this children's tale, about a man who finds more satisfaction being around animals than people. Children may find this film amusing, but for the most part, the acting is weak, and any real script is nonexistent. This film almost broke Fox Studios, even though it did gain an Oscar nomination for best picture.

1967   152 minutes

DOG OF FLANDERS, A
★★★★

DIRECTOR: James B. Clark
CAST: David Ladd, Donald Crisp, Theodore Bikel

Ouida's world-famous 1872 tear-jerking novel about a boy and his dog and their devotion to each other tastefully filmed in its European locale. Nello (David Ladd) delivers milk from a cart pulled by the dog Patrasche. Donald Crisp and Theodore Bikel shine in character roles, but the picture belongs to Ladd and the scene-stealing mutt fans will recall from *Old Yeller*. Have Kleenex handy.

1960   96 minutes

DUMBO
★★★★

DIRECTOR: Ben Sharpsteen
CAST: Animated

Disney's cartoon favorite about the outcast circus elephant with the big ears is a family classic. It has everything: personable animals, a poignant story, and a happy ending. It is good fun and can still invoke a tear or two in the right places.

1941   64 minutes

ENCHANTED FOREST, THE
★★★

DIRECTOR: Lew Landers
CAST: Edmund Lowe, Harry Davenport, Brenda Joyce, Billy Severn, John Litel

Pleasant fantasy about an old hermit who teaches a young boy to love the forest and its creatures is one of the best films to come out of bargain-basement PRC Films as well as being the best surviving example of the Cinecolor process. Veteran actors Edmund Lowe and Harry Davenport provide the solid support this simple story needs, and Billy Severn as the lost boy is engaging. This long-neglected little gem lacks a big-studio budget but is fine family fare.

1945   77 minutes

ESCAPADE IN FLORENCE
★½

DIRECTOR: Steve Previn
CAST: Ivan Desny, Tommy Kirk, Annette Alliotto, Nino Castelnuovo

Uninspired story about two young men and their misadventures in picturesque Italy contains the obligatory chases and seemingly perilous situations that seem to be a prerequisite for movies about art theft and forgery. Walt Disney star Tommy Kirk is pleasant enough, but this film is routine. Too bad Tommy Kirk didn't have Annette Funicello along on this one.

1962   80 minutes

ESCAPE ARTIST, THE
★★

DIRECTOR: Caleb Deschanel
CAST: Griffin O'Neal, Raul Julia, Teri Garr, Joan Hackett, Desi Arnaz Sr.

Annoying little adventure film from producer Francis Ford Coppola which feels like it was reedited and dumped on the market. Confusing, rambling account of a boy (Griffin O'Neal, who might be appealing with better material) who uses a love of magic and escape artistry to frame the city politicos responsible for killing his father. What's left makes little sense, although it is composed beautifully by Caleb Deschanel, better known for *The Black Stallion*. Don't expect much. Rated PG—mild violence and profanity.

1982   96 minutes

ESCAPE TO WITCH MOUNTAIN
★★★½

DIRECTOR: John Hough
CAST: Eddie Albert, Ray Milland, Kim Richards, Ike Eisenmann

In this engaging Disney mystery/fantasy, two children with strange powers are pursued by men who want to use them for evil purposes. It's good! Rated G.

1975   97 minutes

FATTY FINN
★★★

DIRECTOR: Maurice Murphy
CAST: Ben Oxenbould, Bert Newton, Noni Haglehurst

This film seems to borrow from the Little Rascals comedy series. In it, young Fatty Finn is desperately trying to earn money to buy a radio. But every time he tries, the neighborhood bully and his gang sabotage Fatty's efforts. The happy ending makes up for all the hardships 10-year-old Fatty has endured along the way.

1984   91 minutes

FIGHTING PRINCE OF DONEGAL, THE
★★½

DIRECTOR: Michael O'Herlihy
CAST: Peter McEnery, Susan Hampshire, Tom Adams, Gordon Jackson

A rousing adventure-action film set in sixteenth-century Ireland. When Peter McEnery succeeds to the title of Prince of Donegal, the Irish clans are ready to fight English troops to make Ireland free. McEnery convinces them to let him try and negotiate a treaty first. He is captured, imprisoned, and tortured, but finally escapes to lead the Irish clans in defeating the English and rescuing his castle, lady love, and country's freedom. This is a Disney British endeavor that is often overlooked but definitely worth watching.

1966   110 minutes

FOLLOW ME BOYS!
★★★½

DIRECTOR: Norman Tokar
CAST: Vera Miles, Fred MacMurray, Lillian Gish, Kurt Russell

Heart-warming Disney film in which Fred MacMurray plays the

new Boy Scout leader in a small 1930s town.

1966   131 minutes

FREAKY FRIDAY
★★★½

DIRECTOR: Gary Nelson
CAST: Jodie Foster, Barbara Harris, John Astin, Ruth Buzzi, Kaye Ballard

One of Disney's better comedies from the 1970s, this perceptive fantasy allows mom Barbara Harris and daughter Jodie Foster to share a role-reversing out-of-body experience. Harris, due to her experience, does better mixing with school traumas than Foster does figuring out how to wash clothes and cook dinners. Husband/father John Astin has a lot of fun trying to make sense of the situation. Adapted with wit by Mary Rodgers from her own book. This is a good family conversation-starter, although such lofty intentions are nearly sabotaged by the slapstick conclusion. Rated G.

1977   95 minutes

GNOME-MOBILE, THE
★★½

DIRECTOR: Robert Stevenson
CAST: Walter Brennan, Ed Wynn, Mathew Garber, Karen Dotrice

This one is kid city. From Disney, of course. Walter Brennan doubles as a wealthy businessman and a gnome who must find a wife for his grandson-gnome. The Gnome-Mobile is one fancy Rolls-Royce.

1967   104 minutes

GOLDEN SEAL, THE
★★★½

DIRECTOR: Frank Zuniga
CAST: Torquil Campbell, Steven Railsback, Penelope Milford

A young boy (Torquil Campbell) living with his parents (Steven Railsback and Penelope Milford) on the Aleutian Islands makes friends with a rare golden seal and her pup, and tries to protect them from fur hunters. It's a good story, predictably told. Rated PG.

1983   95 minutes

GOLDILOCKS AND THE THREE BEARS
★

DIRECTOR: Gilbert Cates
CAST: Tatum O'Neal, Hoyt Axton, Alex Karras, John Lithgow, Brandis Kemp, Carole King, Donovan Scott

Although it features a well-known and talented cast, this Faerie Tale Theatre production is a lifeless adaptation of the story about a little girl who trespasses into the home of three bears and creates havoc. Its attempts at humor fall flat. In addition, the characters are hardly memorable, with the bears being too nerdish and Goldilocks far from lovable. Read the story to your child instead.

1982   51 minutes

GREAT LOCOMOTIVE CHASE, THE
★★★

DIRECTOR: Francis D. Lyon
CAST: Fess Parker, Jeffrey Hunter, Jeff York, Kenneth Tobey

Walt Disney Civil War film based on an actual event features Fess Parker as a Union spy and the leader of a group of soldiers who capture a Confederate train and race it back to Union territory. Good color and action sequences, memorable characters.

1956   85 minutes

GREAT MUPPET CAPER, THE
★★★★
DIRECTOR: Jim Henson
CAST: Muppets, Diana Rigg, Charles Grodin, Peter Falk, Peter Ustinov, Jack Warden, Robert Morley

Miss Piggy, Kermit the Frog, Fozzie Bear, and the Great Gonzo attempt to solve the mysterious theft of the fabulous baseball diamond in this, the second feature-length motion picture Muppet outing. From the disarmingly funny opening credits to its gangbusters conclusion, this film, directed by Muppet creator Jim Henson, is a significant improvement over *The Muppet Movie*, which was pretty darn good to begin with. Rated G.

1981   95 minutes

GREYFRIARS BOBBY
★★★
DIRECTOR: Don Chaffey
CAST: Donald Crisp, Laurence Naismith, Alex Mackenzie, Kay Walsh

Somewhat lethargic tale of a dog that is befriended by an entire town after his owner dies. The plot drags, but the cast and the atmosphere of the settings make it worth watching. A Disney British import.

1961   91 minutes

GULLIVER'S TRAVELS
★★½
DIRECTOR: Dave Fleischer
CAST: Singing voices of Lanny Ross and Jessica Dragonette

Made and issued as an answer to Disney's *Snow White and the Seven Dwarfs*, this full-length cartoon of the famous Jonathan Swift satire about an English sailor who falls among tiny people in a land called Lilliput is just so-so. Strictly for kids.

1939   74 minutes

GUS
★★★½
DIRECTOR: Vincent McEveety
CAST: Edward Asner, Don Knotts, Gary Grimes, Dick Van Patten

This Disney comedy has a mule named Gus delivering the winning kicks for a losing football team. Naturally, the rival team kidnaps the mule before the big game, and the search is on. Lots of slapstick comedy for the kids to enjoy in this one. Rated G.

1976   96 minutes

HANS BRINKER
★★★
DIRECTOR: Robert Scheerer
CAST: Robin Askwith, Eleanor Parker, Richard Basehart, Roberta Torey, John Gregson, Cyril Ritchard

This is the well-known tale of Hans Brinker and his silver skates. Made this time as a musical, it stars Robin Askwith as Hans with Eleanor Parker and Richard Basehart as his mother and invalid father. Cyril Ritchard has a cameo musical number, and there are some pleasant skating sequences. This film would make particularly good family viewing for the holidays. It is unrated, but if so would be considered G.

1979   103 minutes

HANSEL AND GRETEL
★★★
DIRECTOR: James Frawley
CAST: Joan Collins, Ricky Schroder, Paul Dooley, Bridgette Anderson

Joan Collins is a perfectly wicked stepmother-cum-witch in this Faerie Tale Theatre production of the classic tale of two children (Ricky Schroder, Bridgette Anderson) who learn a valuable lesson when they take candy from a stranger.

1982   51 minutes

HAPPIEST MILLIONAIRE, THE
★★★

DIRECTOR: Norman Tokar
CAST: Fred MacMurray, Tommy Steele, Greer Garson, Geraldine Page, Gladys Cooper

The Disney version of a factual memoir of life in the Philadelphia household of eccentric millionaire Anthony J. Drexel Biddle. Lively light entertainment that hops along between musical numbers.

1967   118 minutes

HEARTBEEPS
★★★

DIRECTOR: Alan Arkush
CAST: Andy Kaufman, Bernadette Peters

Andy Kaufman and Bernadette Peters play robots who fall in love, leave a factory, and decide to explore the world around them. It's a good family film by director Alan Arkush, and the kids will probably love it. Rated PG.

1981   79 minutes

HEATHCLIFF—THE MOVIE
★

DIRECTOR: Bruno Bianchi
CAST: Animated

An example of everything that is wrong with cartoons today, this release is sloppily drawn, poorly scripted, and generally pointless. What's worse, its main character (whose voice is provided by Mel Blanc) is a mean-spirited cat who likes nothing better than to cause trouble—and this is a children's movie! Rated G.

1986   89 minutes

HEIDI
★★★★

DIRECTOR: Allan Dwan
CAST: Shirley Temple, Jean Hersholt, Arthur Treacher

This classic stars a spunky Shirley Temple as the girl who is taken away from her kind and loving grandfather's home in the Swiss Alps and forced to live with her cruel aunt. Love triumphs when Heidi finds a way to return to her grandfather. Lots of touching scenes, so have plenty of Kleenex on hand. Children will especially love this one.

1937   B & W   88 minutes

HEIDI'S SONG
★½

DIRECTOR: Robert Taylor
CAST: Animated

Only those 5 years old and younger will enjoy this feature-length cartoon adaptation of Johanna Spyri's classic children's tale. The producers, William Hanna and Joseph Barbera, made what many aficionados consider to be the best "Tom and Jerry" shorts for MGM. But they are best known as the creators of "Yogi Bear" and "The Flintstones," TV shows that ushered in the age of limited (as in cheap and unconvincing) animation. It is the latter style that pervades and—along with a mediocre screenplay and musical score—ultimately ruins *Heidi's Song.* Rated G.

1982   94 minutes

HERBIE GOES BANANAS
★★½

DIRECTOR: Vincent McEveety

CAST: Cloris Leachman, Charles Martin Smith, John Vernon, Stephan W. Burns, Harvey Korman

This is the corniest and least funny of Disney's "Love Bug" series. This time Herbie is headed for Brazil to compete in the Grand Primio. He is waylaid in Panama after a small Mexican boy named Paco is found stowed away in Herbie's trunk. Cloris Leachman plays an eccentric aunt who is willing to bail Herbie out if Herbie's owner will woo her homely, intellectual niece. Rated G.

1980   93 minutes

HERBIE GOES TO MONTE CARLO
★★★½
DIRECTOR: Vincent McEveety
CAST: Dean Jones, Don Knotts, Julie Sommars, Eric Braeden, Roy Kinnear, Jacque Marin

Herbie the VW stars in this Walt Disney comedy. This time he falls in love with a sports car as they compete in a race from Paris to Monte Carlo. Don Knotts plays Herbie's mechanic, and Dean Jones is his owner. Complications arise when jewel thieves hide a $6 million diamond in Herbie's gas tank. Julie Sommars co-stars as Jones's love interest, while Eric Braeden plays his racetrack rival. There are lots of laughs in this one. Rated G.

1977   104 minutes

HERBIE RIDES AGAIN
★★★½
DIRECTOR: Robert Stevenson
CAST: Helen Hayes, Ken Berry, Stephanie Powers, Keenan Wynn

This Disney comedy/adventure is a sequel to *The Love Bug*. This time, Helen Hayes, Ken Berry, and Stephanie Powers depend on Herbie, the magical Volkswagen, to save them from an evil Keenan Wynn. Rated G.

1974   88 minutes

HEY THERE, IT'S YOGI BEAR
★★★
DIRECTOR: William Hanna, Joseph Barbera
CAST: Animated

With this movie, Hanna-Barbera Studios made the jump from TV to feature-length cartoon. The result is consistently pleasant. The animation is limited, the songs are forgettable, and the humor is mild, but the characters are likable, and kids under nine should find the movie quite entertaining. Voices of Mel Blanc, J. Pat O'Malley, Julie Bennett, Daws Butler, and Don Messick. Rated G.

1964   89 minutes

HORSEMASTERS
★★
DIRECTOR: Bill Fairchild
CAST: Annette Funicello, Janet Munro, Tommy Kirk, Donald Pleasence, Tony Britton

Annette and Tommy team up once again in this average story about young Americans pursuing their careers in horse training among the great riding academies of Europe. Shot on location for *Walt Disney Presents*, this two-part episode was released later as a feature. Lots of beautiful horses on display for all the horse fanciers in the audience. Fine character actor Donald Pleasence makes an early film appearance in this one.

1961   77 minutes

IN SEARCH OF THE CASTAWAYS
★★★★
DIRECTOR: Robert Stevenson

CAST: Hayley Mills, Maurice Chevalier, George Sanders, Wilfrid Hyde-White, Michael Anderson, Jr.

Director Robert Stevenson gives a Disney interpretation of this Jules Verne adventure tale. A young Hayley Mills plays the kidnapped daughter of a sea captain (Maurice Chevalier). There are lots of great special effects depicting natural disasters for them to overcome.

1962   100 minutes

INCREDIBLE JOURNEY, THE
★★★★½
DIRECTOR: Fletcher Markle
CAST: Emile Genest, John Drainie

This live-action Walt Disney film, narrated by Rex Allen, is the story of two dogs and a cat that make a treacherous journey across Canada to find their home and family. The distinct personalities given to the Labrador retriever, the bull terrier, and the Siamese cat carry the film, making it a delight for viewers. It's impossible to dislike this heart-warming tale.

1963   80 minutes

INTERNATIONAL VELVET
★★
DIRECTOR: Bryan Forbes
CAST: Tatum O'Neal, Christopher Plummer, Anthony Hopkins

A disappointing sequel to *National Velvet* (1944), with Tatum O'Neal only passable as the young horsewoman who rides to victory. Fine supporting performances by Anthony Hopkins and Christopher Plummer help raise this family film to the level of watchability. Rated PG.

1978   127 minutes

IT'S AN ADVENTURE, CHARLIE BROWN
★★★★
DIRECTOR: Bill Melendez
CAST: Animated

This made-for-television program was the first "Peanuts" special to present short sketches and blackouts taken directly from the material in Charles Schulz's newspaper strip. With no central theme, each segment runs only as long as it needs to. By far the best—and one of the most poignant tales ever constructed within the strip—is "Sack," wherein Charlie Brown goes to summer camp with a bag over his head and becomes a hero. A masterful and entertaining package, in a style that later was used for the Saturday-morning "Charlie Brown and Snoopy Show." Unrated, family fare.

1983   50 minutes

JACK AND THE BEANSTALK
★★★
DIRECTOR: Lamont Johnson
CAST: Dennis Christopher, Elliott Gould, Jean Stapleton, Mark Blankfield, Katherine Helmond

This *Faerie Tale Theatre* production sticks more to the original story than most. Katherine Helmond plays Jack's complaining mom. Jean Stapleton plays a kind giantess, while Elliott Gould is a very dumb giant. Jack sells the family cow (named Spot) for five magic beans and manages to acquire great wealth while learning about his past.

1982   60 minutes

JIMMY THE KID
★★
DIRECTOR: Gary Nelson

CAST: Paul Le Mat, Gary Coleman, Cleavon Little, Fay Hauser, Dee Wallace

Paul Le Mat (of *American Graffiti*) leads a band of bungling criminals in an attempt to kidnap the precocious son (Gary Coleman) of some extremely wealthy country-western singers (Cleavon Little and Fay Hauser). To everyone's surprise, Jimmy doesn't mind being kidnapped; in fact, he sort of likes it. Yawn. This is the kind of silly film the Walt Disney studios stopped making. Rated PG.

1983   85 minutes

JOHNNY TREMAIN
★★★½

DIRECTOR: Robert Stevenson
CAST: Hal Stalmaster, Luanna Patten, Sebastian Cabot, Richard Beymer

Colorful Walt Disney Revolutionary War entry is a perfect blend of schoolboy heroics and Hollywood history, with young Johnny Tremain an apprentice silversmith caught up in the brewing American Revolution. Heavy on the patriotism, with picture-book tableaus of the Boston Tea Party, Paul Revere's ride, and the battles at Concord. Infectious score throughout.

1957   80 minutes

JOURNEY BACK TO OZ
★★½

DIRECTOR: Hal Sutherland
CAST: Animated

This cartoon version sequel to *The Wizard of Oz* leaves the Wizard out. The voices of famous stars help maintain adult interest. Ironically, Liza Minnelli plays Dorothy (as her mother did in the original *Oz*). Milton Berle, Paul Lynde, Ethel Merman, Mickey Rooney, and Danny Thomas provide other voices. Rated G.

1974   90 minutes

JOURNEY OF NATTY GANN, THE
★★★★★

DIRECTOR: Jeremy Paul Kagan
CAST: Meredith Salenger, Ray Wise, John Cusack, Lainie Kazan, Scatman Crothers

With this superb film, the Disney Studios returned triumphantly to the genre of family films. It is a wonderful movie for all ages. Not since *E.T.—The Extraterrestrial* has there been such a touching and involving wide-audience movie. Meredith Salenger stars as Natty, a 14-year-old street urchin who must ride the rails from Chicago to Seattle during the Depression to find her father (Ray Wise). Do not miss this one. Rated PG for light violence.

1985   101 minutes

JUNGLE BOOK
★★★★

DIRECTOR: Zoltán Korda
CAST: Sabu, Joseph Calleia, John Qualen

This one's for fantasy fans of all ages. Sabu stars in Rudyard Kipling's tale of a boy raised by wolves in the jungle of India. Beautiful color presentation holds the viewer from start to finish. Rated G.

1942   109 minutes

KID FROM LEFT FIELD, THE
★★★

DIRECTOR: Adell Aldrich
CAST: Gary Coleman, Tab Hunter, Gary Collins, Ed McMahon

Gary Coleman plays a batboy who leads the San Diego Padres to victory through the advice of his father (a former baseball great). Ed

McMahon co-stars in this remake of the 1953 Dan Dailey version. Made for TV.

1979   100 minutes

KID WITH THE 200 I.Q., THE
★★

DIRECTOR: Leslie Martinson
CAST: Gary Coleman, Robert Guillaume, Dean Butler, Kari Michaelson, Harriet Nelson

In this predictable TV movie, Gary Coleman plays a 13-year-old genius who enters college. Academics present no problem. Social life does. It's mildly amusing at best.

1983   96 minutes

KING OF THE GRIZZLIES
★★½

DIRECTOR: Ron Kelly
CAST: Wahb, John Yesno, Chris Wiggins, Hug Webster, Jack Van Evera

Wahb, a grizzly cub, loses his mother and sister to cattlemen protecting their herd. He quickly gets into trouble but is rescued by John Yesno, a Cree Indian. Descended from the Indian Clan of the Bear, Yesno feels a mystical attachment to Wahb and risks his job with the cattlemen to take Wahb to safety. Wahb grows up to be the largest grizzly and eventually returns to wreak havoc on the cattlemen's ranch. Yesno is the only person who can stop him, and he must rely upon that mystical attachment he felt. Average animal adventure film in the Disney mold. Rated G.

1969   93 minutes

LAST FLIGHT OF NOAH'S ARK
★★★

DIRECTOR: Charles Jarrott
CAST: Elliott Gould, Genevieve Bujold, Ricky Schroder, Vincent Gardenia

This is the story of an unemployed pilot (Elliott Gould) who, against his better judgment, agrees to fly a plane full of farm animals to a Pacific island for a young missionary (Genevieve Bujold). The plane, a converted B-29, is forced down by a storm on an out-of-the-way island and Gould, Bujold, and Ricky Shroder are put upon to rescue themselves from the island. This film, while not one of Disney's best, does offer clean, wholesome fun for the younger (and young-at-heart) audience. Rated G.

1980   21397 minutes

LEGEND OF SLEEPY HOLLOW, THE
★★★★

DIRECTOR: Jack Kinney, Clyde Geronimi, James Algar
CAST: Animated

One of the finest of the Disney "novelette" cartoons, this adaptation of the spooky Washington Irving tale is given a properly sepulchral tone by narrator Bing Crosby. Reasonably scary, particularly for small fry, who might get pretty nervous during poor Ichabod Crane's final, fateful ride. The tape includes two cartoon shorts, "Lonesome Ghosts" (1937) and "Trick or Treat" (1952); the former is a classic haunted house story starring Mickey Mouse, Donald Duck, and Goofy, the latter a weak entry featuring Donald and his three nephews. Unrated—family fare.

1949   49 minutes

LT. ROBIN CRUSOE, U.S.N.
★

DIRECTOR: Byron Paul
CAST: Dick Van Dyke, Nancy Kwan, Akim Tamiroff

Modern-day story of Robinson Crusoe, poorly done and with few laughs. Dick Van Dyke is stranded on a tropical island and gets involved with a female revolt against the island's male chauvinist ruler. Van Dyke's talents are totally wasted in a film that started with the idea by Walt Disney and ended without a decent script. Rated G.

1966   113 minutes

LIFE AND TIMES OF GRIZZLY ADAMS, THE
★½

DIRECTOR: Richard Friedenberg

CAST: Dan Haggerty, Don Shanks, Lisa Jones, Marjory Harper, Bozo

The big question is: Which one is Bozo? It seems that everyone connected with this sloppy, syrupy movie must have been a bozo. Fur trapper Dan Haggerty heads for the hills when he's unjustly accused of a crime. There he befriends an oversize bear and they live happily ever after. This film inspired (?) the TV series. Rated G.

1976   93 minutes

LIGHT IN THE FOREST, THE
★★½

DIRECTOR: Herschel Daugherty

CAST: James MacArthur, Fess Parker, Wendell Corey, Joanne Dru, Carol Lynley

James MacArthur stars as a young man who had been captured and raised by the Delaware Indians. When a treaty forces the Indians to release all of their white captives, he is returned to the family he doesn't know. He considers himself to be an Indian and rebels at having to conform to white ways. Generally a good story with

adequate acting, the ending is much too contrived and trite.

1958   92 minutes

LITTLE MATCH GIRL, THE
★★

DIRECTOR: Mark Hoeger, Wally Broadbent

CAST: Monica McSwain, Nancy Duncan, Matt McKim, Dan Hays

This "Children's Treasures" production was originally a stage play. Unfortunately, the pageantry and emotion of the live-action production are lost in the video translation. The song-and-dance routines throughout the film grow tiresome. The topic of this play seems much too somber and mature for children to handle. In it, a poor girl's grandmother, about to die, reveals a magic in the matches that they sell. After the grandmother's death, the girl (Monica McSwain) gets so caught up in the magic that she neglects to sell her wares. The story takes place in Russia just before the revolution and she is able to befriend the young, sickly prince before his family is killed. *Not* advised for children under 10.

1983   54 minutes

LITTLE MERMAID, THE
★★★½

DIRECTOR: Robert Iscove

CAST: Pam Dawber, Karen Black, Treat Williams, Brian Dennehy, Helen Mirren

In this segment of Shelley Duvall's Faerie Tale Theatre, Pam Dawber plays Pearl, a mermaid daughter of King Neptune. She falls hopelessly in love with a human and sacrifices all to win his love. Although this is a low-budget production, it still manages to keep its viewers entertained.

1984   50 minutes

LITTLE MISS MARKER
★★★★
DIRECTOR: Alexander Hall
CAST: Adolphe Menjou, Shirley Temple, Dorothy Dell, Charles Bickford, Lynne Overman

Delightful Shirley Temple vehicle has our little heroine left as an I.O.U. on a gambling debt and charming hard-hearted racetrack denizens into becoming better people. This is the best of the screen adaptations of Damon Runyon's story.

1934   B & W   88 minutes

LITTLE MISS MARKER
★★
DIRECTOR: Walter Bernstein
CAST: Walter Matthau, Julie Andrews, Tony Curtis, Bob Newhart, Sara Stimson, Lee Grant

Even the star power of Walter Matthau, Julie Andrews, and Bob Newhart can't save this turgid remake of the 1934 Shirley Temple classic. Sara Stimson is cute, and the stars try hard, but this one never leaves the gate. Rated PG.

1980   103 minutes

LITTLE PRINCESS, THE
★★★½
DIRECTOR: Walter Lang
CAST: Shirley Temple, Richard Greene, Anita Louise, Ian Hunter, Cesar Romero, Arthur Treacher

The 1930s supertyke Shirley Temple had one of her very best vehicles in this Victorian era tearjerker. In it, she's a sweet-natured child who is mistreated at a strict boarding school when her father disappears during the Boer War. Get out your handkerchiefs.

1939   B & W   93 minutes

LITTLE RED RIDING HOOD
★★★★
DIRECTOR: Graeme Clifford
CAST: Mary Steenburgen, Malcolm McDowell, Frances Bay, Darrell Larson

Malcolm McDowell plays a brazenly wicked wolf to a perky Red Riding Hood (Mary Steenburgen). Frances Bay makes for a rather zany grandmother. Although this production is highly entertaining, don't expect it to stick to the tale as most would remember it.

1983   51 minutes

LITTLEST HORSE THIEVES, THE
★★★
DIRECTOR: Charles Jarrott
CAST: Alastair Sim, Peter Barkworth, Maurice Colbourne, Susan Tebbs, Andrew Harrison, Chloe Franks

At the turn of the century, some children become alarmed when they learn that the pit ponies working in the coal mines are to be destoryed. To prevent the deaths, the children decide to steal the ponies. Rather predictable but with good characterizations and a solid period atmosphere. Rated G.

1976   104 minutes

LOVE BUG, THE
★★★½
DIRECTOR: Robert Stevenson
CAST: Michele Lee, Dean Jones, Buddy Hackett, Joe Flynn

This is a delightful Disney comedy. A family film about a Volkswagen with a mind of its own and some special talents as well, it was the first of the four "Herbie" films. Rated G.

1969   107 minutes

MAD MONSTER PARTY
★★½

DIRECTOR: Jules Bass
CAST: Voices of Boris Karloff, Phyllis Diller, Ethel Ennis, Gale Garnett

An amusing little puppet film; a lot more fun for genre buffs who will understand all the references made to classic horror films. All the beloved monsters (led by a Dr. Frankenstein given voice by Boris Karloff) gather for a great bash . . . sort of a *Thank God It's Friday* for the Transylvania set. Wry little script, co-written by Harvey Kurtzman of *Mad Magazine* fame. Worth seeing once, as a novelty.
1967   94 minutes

MAGIC OF LASSIE, THE
★★½

DIRECTOR: Don Chaffey
CAST: James Stewart, Mickey Rooney, Pernel Roberts, Stephanie Zimbalist, Michael Sharrett, Alice Faye, Gene Evans, Lane Davies, Mike Mazurki, Lassie

Like the Disney live-action films of yore, *The Magic of Lassie* tries to incorporate a little of everything: heartwarming drama, suspense, comedy and even music (by the Mike Curb Congregation). But here the formula is bland. There's Grandpa (James Stewart) and the cute little boy (Michael Sharrett), the villain (Pernell Roberts) who tries to take Lassie away, and the kind people (Mickey Rooney, Mike Mazurki) who help Lassie on her way home while providing comedy relief. Stewart can make just about anything palatable—and this syrupy concoction definitely benefits from his measured delivery and mastery of pathos. The story is okay, as far as cute kids pining for their dogs go, but it is all too long. To make things worse, screenwriters Robert B. Sherman and Richard M. Sherman also added a bunch of awful songs. Rated G.
1978   100 minutes

MAGIC SWORD, THE
★★

DIRECTOR: Bert I. Gordon
CAST: Gary Lockwood, Anne Helm, Basil Rathbone, Estelle Winwood, Liam Sullivan

Fanciful juvenile adventure from low-budget film czar Bert I. Gordon is long on imagination but short on the props and effects necessary to pull a film like this off. Young Gary Lockwood is on a quest to free an imprisoned princess and fights his way through an ogre, dragon, and other uninspired monsters with the help of the witch in the family, Estelle Winwood. It's Basil Rathbone who makes the show work, and he makes a fine old evil sorcerer, relishing his foul deeds and eagerly planning new transgressions. The kids might like it, but compared with Ray Harryhausen's efforts of that period and the phenomenal special effects of the past decade, it's laughable.
1962   80 minutes

MARY POPPINS
★★★★★

DIRECTOR: Robert Stevenson
CAST: Julie Andrews, Dick Van Dyke, David Tomlinson, Glynis Johns, Karen Dotrice, Matthew Garber, Jane Darwell, Ed Wynn, Arthur Treacher, Hermione Baddeley

Here's Julie Andrews in her screen debut. She plays a nanny who believes that "a spoonful of sugar makes the medicine go down." Andrews is great in the role and sings ever so sweetly. The song and dance numbers are attractively laid on, with Dick Van Dyke, as Mary's Cockney beau, giving an amusing performance. Rated G.

1964   140 minutes

MICKEY'S CHRISTMAS CAROL
★★★★

DIRECTOR: Burney Matinson
CAST: Animated

Mickey Mouse plays Bob Cratchit in this adaptation of the Dickens classic. A pleasant animated feature with cameos by Donald Duck, Jimminy Cricket, Goofy, and other Disney characters. Rated G.

1984   26 minutes

MILLION DOLLAR DUCK, THE
★★

DIRECTOR: Vincent McEveety
CAST: Dean Jones, Sandy Duncan, Joe Flynn, Tony Roberts

A duck is accidentally given a dose of radiation that makes it produce eggs with solid gold yolks. Dean Jones and Sandy Duncan, as the owners of the duck, use the yolks to pay off bills until the Treasury Department gets wise. Mildly entertaining comedy in the Disney tradition. Rated G.

1971   92 minutes

MINOR MIRACLE, A
★★½

DIRECTOR: Raoul Lomas
CAST: John Huston, Pele, Peter Fox

A heartwarming story about a group of orphaned children and their devoted guardian (John Huston), who band together to save the St. Francis School for Boys. If you liked *Going My Way* and *Oh God!* you'll like this G-rated movie.

1983   100 minutes

MIRACLE ON 34TH STREET
★★★★★

DIRECTOR: George Seaton
CAST: Natalie Wood, Edmund Gwenn, Maureen O'Hara

In this, one of Hollywood's most delightful fantasies, the spirit of Christmas is rekindled in a young girl (Natalie Wood) by a department store Santa. Edmund Gwenn is perfect as the endearing Macy's employee who causes a furor when he claims to be the real Kris Kringle. Is he or isn't he? That is for you to decide in this heartwarming family classic.

1947   B & W 96 minutes

MISADVENTURES OF MERLIN JONES, THE
★★½

DIRECTOR: Robert Stevenson
CAST: Tommy Kirk, Annette Funicello, Leon Ames, Stuart Erwin, Alan Hewitt

Tommy Kirk stars in this Disney family programmer as a boy genius whose talents for mind reading and hypnotism land him into all sorts of trouble. Annette Funicello is on hand for some overly wholesome romantic fun. Entertaining for the young or indiscriminate; pretty bland for everybody else.

1964   88 minutes

MONKEY'S UNCLE, THE
★★

DIRECTOR: Robert Stevenson
CAST: Tommy Kirk, Annette Funicello, Leon Ames, Arthur O'Connell, Frank Faylen

This sequel to *The Misadventures of Merlin Jones* finds whiz kid Tommy Kirk up to no good with a flying machine and a sleep-learning technique employed on a monkey. More of the same from Disney, really: bumbling scientific highjinks, mild slapstick, and G-rated romance with Annette Funicello. For young minds only.

1965   87 minutes

MOON PILOT
★★★½

DIRECTOR: James Neilson
CAST: Tom Tryon, Brian Keith, Edmond O'Brien, Dany Saval

Tom Tryon gets volunteered to become the first astronaut to circle the moon. A mysterious woman appears and seemingly breaches the confidentiality surrounding the mission. The FBI is called in, and the launch takes place on schedule. The woman appears in the capsule, however, and love blooms between her and the astronaut. Good script, with satire and laughs in ample quantities. Rated G.

1962   98 minutes

MOONCUSSERS
★★½

DIRECTOR: James Neilson
CAST: Oscar Homolka, Kevin Corcoran, Robert Emhardt, Rian Garrick, Joan Freeman

Kevin Corcoran stars as a boy who discovers the secrets of the Mooncussers—pirates who work on moonless nights to draw ships to their doom by means of false signal lamps on shore. After the ships are wrecked, the Mooncussers plunder the cargo and kill the crew. The ship owners try to investigate the cause of the wreck but are unsuccessful until Corcoran helps them with his knowledge and daring.

1962   85 minutes

MOONSPINNERS, THE
★★★

DIRECTOR: James Neilson
CAST: Hayley Mills, Eli Wallach, Pola Negri, Peter McEnery, Joan Greenwood

A young girl (Hayley Mills) becomes involved in a jewel theft in Crete. A young man is accused of the theft and has to work with the girl to prove his innocence. The best features of this film are the appearance of a "grown-up" Hayley Mills and the return to the screen of Pola Negri. The film is essentially a lightweight melodrama in the Hitchcock mold.

1964   118 minutes

MOUNTAIN FAMILY ROBINSON
★★½

DIRECTOR: John Cotter
CAST: Robert Logan, Susan D. Shaw, Heather Rattray, Ham Larsen

Though it could just as easily have been titled *Wilderness Family, Part 3*, the sum of this Pacific International Enterprises, Inc., film is that its simplicity is its merit. *Mountain Family Robinson* delivers exactly what it set out to achieve. It does not purport to have any other message than that of the value of familial love, understanding, and togetherness. Predictable and a bit corny. Robert Logan, Susan Shaw, Heather Rattray, and Ham Larsen display an affability that should charm the children and make this film a relaxing, easy time for parents as well. Rated G.

1979   100 minutes

MUPPET MOVIE, THE
★★★½

DIRECTOR: James Frawley

CAST: Muppets, Edgar Bergen, Charlie McCarthy, Milton Berle, Mel Brooks, James Coburn, Dom De Luise, Elliott Gould, Bob Hope, Madeline Kahn, Carol Kane, Cloris Leachman, Steve Martin, Richard Pryor, Telly Savalas, Orson Welles, Paul Williams

Though there is a huge all-star guest cast, the Muppets are the real stars of this superior family film in which the characters trek to Hollywood in search of stardom. Rated G.

1979   94 minutes

MUPPETS TAKE MANHATTAN, THE
★★★

DIRECTOR: Frank Oz
CAST: Muppets, Art Carney, Dabney Coleman, Joan Rivers, Elliott Gould, Liza Minnelli, Brooke Shields

Jim Henson's popular puppets take a bite of the Big Apple in their third and least effective screen romp. The screenplay, by director Frank Oz, Tom Patchett, and Jay Tarses, is of the old "let's put on a show" genre, with playwright Kermit and his pals trying to get their musical on the Broadway stage. It's hackneyed and unnecessarily padded, but occasionally fun even for adults—thanks to a number of plot digressions. Surprisingly, the best of these have nothing to do with the cameo appearances. So what are we to make of *The Muppets Take Manhattan*? An excellent show for the kiddies, that's what. And there's nothing wrong with that. Rated G.

1984   94 minutes

MY LITTLE PONY: THE MOVIE
★★★

DIRECTOR: Michael Joens

CAST: Animated voices provided by Danny DeVito, Madeline Kahn, Cloris Leachman, Rhea Perlman, Tony Randall

Darling ponies are threatened by the evil witch family (Cloris Leachman, Madeline Kahn, and Rhea Perlman) who live in the Volcano of Gloom. When the witches release the purple, lavalike "smooze," it destroys the contryside as well as the ponies' Dream Castle. Before this catastrophe, one proud baby pony, Licketysplit, runs away from home, followed by the dragon baby, Spike. Trapped by smooze, they meet the troll-like Grundles. Danny DeVito, the Grundle King, helps them escape. It takes the magic of the flutter ponies to reverse the damage caused by the witches and their smooze. The brilliant colors soften most of the potentially frightening scenes. All subplots reaffirm that everybody needs a friend. Children under 7 should enjoy this, but older children and adults may feel it's too long. Rated G.

1986   85 minutes

MYSTERY ISLAND
★★★

DIRECTOR: Gene Scott
CAST: Jayson Duncan, Niklas Juhlin

When four children whose boat has run out of gas discover what appears to be a deserted island, they promptly name it Mystery Island. There is actually an old pirate who lives there. The children find a case of counterfeit money which belongs to villains, who later return to the island for it. The old pirate's timely intervention saves the kids. The best part about this children's film is the beautiful underwater photography.

1981   75 minutes

NATIONAL VELVET
★★★½

DIRECTOR: Clarence Brown
CAST: Mickey Rooney, Elizabeth Taylor, Donald Crisp, Anne Revere, Angela Lansbury, Reginald Owen

This heartwarming tale of two youngsters determined to train a beloved horse to win the famed Grand National Race is good for the whole family, and especially good for little girls who love horses and sentimentalists who fondly recall Elizabeth Taylor when she was young, innocent, and adorable. Have Kleenex on hand.

1944   125 minutes

NEVER A DULL MOMENT
½

DIRECTOR: Jerry Paris
CAST: Dick Van Dyke, Edward G. Robinson, Dorothy Provine, Henry Silva

Undoubtedly one of the weakest of all Disney feature films, this dismal effort has all the finesse one would expect from Dick Van Dyke doing his sophisticated version of Jerry Lewis at his worst. Hackneyed, boring, and inane are the adjectives that come to mind in discussing this film. Not even Edward G. Robinson and the character actors can save this one. Rated G.

1968   100 minutes

NIGHTINGALE, THE
★★★½

DIRECTOR: Ivan Passer
CAST: Mick Jagger, Bud Cort, Barbara Hershey, Edward James Olmos

An emperor (Mick Jagger) survives court intrigue to discover true friendship from a lowly maid (Barbara Hershey) with the help of a nightingale in this *Faerie Tale Theatre* production. Some of the best-designed sets in the series provide lovely backdrops for the acting—most of it serene and heartfelt. Jagger makes a superb emperor (although Rolling Stones fans may be disappointed with his passiveness), and the corny humor found in other films in the series is happily absent. This one is made especially for children under 10, so older viewers may find it slow moving. One concession made to the younger viewers is that the traditional imperial command "Off with your head" is converted to "A punch in your stomach."

1983   51 minutes

NO DEPOSIT, NO RETURN
★★

DIRECTOR: Norman Tokar
CAST: David Niven, Don Knotts, Darren McGavin, Herschel Bernardi, Barbara Feldon

Two kids decide to escape from their multimillionaire grandfather (David Niven) and visit their mother in Hong Kong. On their way to the airport, they end up in a getaway car with two incompetent safe-crackers with (surprise!) a soft spot in their hearts for kids. The kids end up taking over the hideout and engineer their own "kidnapping"—demanding ransom from their grandfather for the fare to Hong Kong. The attempt backfires, and the movie degenerates into a cops-and-robbers chase scene. It is typical of the Disney movie products of the mid-1970s with Ron Miller as producer: unrealistic and not very believable, with occasional bits of real entertainment. Rated G.

1976   115 minutes

NORTH AVENUE IRREGULARS, THE
★★★

DIRECTOR: Bruce Bilson
CAST: Edward Herrmann, Barbara Harris, Cloris Leachman, Susan Clark, Karen Valentine, Michael Constantine, Patsy Kelly, Virginia Capers

Average Disney film about a young priest (Edward Herrmann) who wants to do something about crime. He enlists a group of churchgoing, do-good women to work with him. Quality cast is wasted on marginal script. Rated G.

1979   100 minutes

NOW YOU SEE HIM, NOW YOU DON'T
★★

DIRECTOR: Robert Butler
CAST: Kurt Russell, Joe Flynn, Jim Backus, Cesar Romero, William Windom

Medfield College, the campus of Fred MacMurray in *The Absent-Minded Professor* and *Son of Flubber*, is once again host to college high-jinks. This is the second of the Kurt Russell films which followed the tradition of the MacMurray and Tommy Kirk college films. In this one, Russell discovers a formula that will make a person or item invisible. Bad guy Cesar Romero attempts to hijack the discovery for nefarious purposes, which leads to disastrous results. Rated G.

1972   85 minutes

OH, HEAVENLY DOG!
★

DIRECTOR: Joe Camp
CAST: Benji, Chevy Chase, Jane Seymour, Omar Sharif, Robert Morley

Chevy Chase should have known better. This movie is an overly silly cutesy about a private eye (Chase) who is murdered and then comes back as a dog (Benji) to trap his killers. Kids, however, should enjoy it. Rated PG.

1980   103 minutes

OLD YELLER
★★★★

DIRECTOR: Robert Stevenson
CAST: Dorothy McGuire, Fess Parker, Tommy Kirk, Chuck Connors

Here's a live-action Walt Disney favorite. A big yellow mongrel is taken in by a Southwestern family. The warm attachment and numerous adventures of the dog and the two boys of the family are sure to endear this old mutt to your heart. A few tears are guaranteed to fall at the conclusion, so you'd best bring a hankie.

1957   83 minutes

ONE OF OUR DINOSAURS IS MISSING
★★½

DIRECTOR: Robert Stevenson
CAST: Peter Ustinov, Helen Hayes, Derek Nimmo, Clive Revill

In this moderately entertaining comedy spy film, Peter Ustinov plays a Chinese intelligence agent attempting to recover some stolen microfilm. Helen Hayes plays a nanny who becomes involved in trying to get the film to the British authorities. The film is in a dinosaur skeleton that Hayes and other nannies take to the streets of London. Rated G.

1975   101 minutes

1001 RABBIT TALES
★★★★

DIRECTOR: Friz Freleng, Chuck Jones

CAST: Animated

Fourteen classic cartoons are interwoven with new footage to make another feature-length film out of the well-known Warner Brothers characters. This time the theme is fairy tales. Bugs and the gang spoof "Goldilocks and the Three Bears," "Jack and the Bean Stalk,"and "Little Red Riding Hood," among others. This one also contains Chuck Jones's "One Froggy Evening," one of the greatest cartoons ever! Rated G.

1982   76 minutes

ON THE RIGHT TRACK
★★

DIRECTOR: Lee Philips
CAST: Gary Coleman, Maureen Stapleton, Michael Lembeck, Norman Fell

Gary Coleman (of television's "Diff'rent Strokes") plays a tyke who sets up residence in a railroad station to escape the hustle and bustle of the city. Once the word gets around that he has a talent for picking the winners in horse races, his life becomes complicated all over again. Without Coleman, this would be an awful movie. Even with him, it is nothing to shout about. At best it has a kind of cornball charm—like an old-style Disney movie with a little extra zing—but other times it lulls you to sleep. Rated PG.

1981   98 minutes

PARENT TRAP, THE
★★★★

DIRECTOR: David Swift
CAST: Hayley Mills, Brian Keith, Maureen O'Hara, Joanna Barnes

Walt Disney doubled the fun in this comedy when he had Hayley Mills play twins. Mills plays twin daughters who meet for the first time at summer camp and decide to reunite their divorced parents (Brian Keith and Maureen O'-Hara).

1961   124 minutes

PETE'S DRAGON
★★½

DIRECTOR: Don Chaffey
CAST: Mickey Rooney, Jim Dale, Helen Reddy, Red Buttons, Jim Backus, Sean Marshall

Only the kiddies will get a kick out of this Disney feature, which combines live action featuring stars such as Mickey Rooney, Jim Dale, Helen Reddy, Red Buttons, and Jim (Mr. Magoo) Backus, with animation. The story takes place in Maine circa 1908 when a 9-year-old boy (Sean Marshall) escapes with his overbearing foster parents with the aid of the pet dragon that only he can see. Sort of a children's version of *Harvey*, it's generally lackluster and uninspired. But, again, most children will probably enjoy it. Parents, on the other hand, may want to read a book while the film is running. Rated G.

1977   134 minutes

PETRONELLA
★★★★

DIRECTOR: Rick Locke
CAST: S Sylvia, Mayf Nutter, James Arrington, Jerry Maren, David Jensen, David E. Morgan

This live-action production of "Enchanted Muscial Playhouse" stars the lovely country-pop singer Sylvia as a liberated princess who sets out to rescue an imprisoned prince. When her two elder brothers set out to seek their fortunes, she insists that she will do the same rather than wait for a prince to find her. When she encounters Albion the Enchantor, superbly played by Mayf Nutter, she agrees to spend three nights with some vicious animals—a dog, a horse, and a falcon—in order to free an imprisoned prince. After successfully performing her three tasks, she rides off with the reluctant prince only to find out he hadn't been a prisoner at all. Happiness reigns in the surprise ending when the spunky princess finds her true love. The whole family can enjoy this delightful tale with its cheerful songs and humorous moments.

1985   30 minutes

PIED PIPER OF HAMELIN, THE
★★★★★

DIRECTOR: Nicholas Meyer
CAST: Eric Idle, Tony Van Bridge, Keram Malicki-Sanchez, Peter Blaise

Nicholas Meyer, who also directed *The Day After* and *Star Trek III*, does a terrific job of adapting Robert Browning's eerie poem for this *Faerie Tale Theatre* episode. Eric Idle does remarkably well with his two major parts: as poet Robert Browning and the medieval piper. As the piper, he agrees to rid Hamelin of its rats if the mayor will pay him his fee. When the mayor refuses, the piper spirits the town's children away, as well. Because the dialogue is totally done in rhyming couplets (sticking closely to Browning's original style), it may be difficult for children under 8 to follow. Also, the close-ups of huge, ugly rats should be considered before showing this to the wee ones. Otherwise, the cast, costumes, sets, and production are outstanding and should entertain the whole family.

1985   60 minutes

PINOCCHIO
★★★★★

DIRECTOR: Walt Disney
CAST: Animated

In this timeless Walt Disney animated classic, a puppet made by a lonely old man gets the chance to become a real boy. *Pinocchio* is one of those rare motion pictures that can be enjoyed over and over again by adults as well as children. If you remember it as a "kid's show," watch it again. You'll be surprised at what a wonderfully entertaining viewing experience it is. Rated G.

1940   87 minutes

PINOCCHIO
★★★★

DIRECTOR: Peter Medak
CAST: James Coburn, Carl Reiner, Paul Reubens, Jim Belushi, Lainie Kazan, Don Novello (narrating as Father Guido Sarducci)

An excellent adaptation of the classic tale about the adventures of a wooden puppet who turns into a real boy. This Faerie Tale Theatre production, as with most of the others, will be best appreciated—and understood—by adults. It's blessed with just the right touch of humor, and Lainie Kazan is wonderful as the "Italian" fairy godmother.

1983   51 minutes

POLLYANNA
★★★½

DIRECTOR: David Swift
CAST: Hayley Mills, Jane Wyman, Agnes Moorehead, Adolphe Menjou, Karl Malden, Nancy Olson

Walt Disney's version of this classic childhood book is good entertainment for the whole family. Hayley Mills is the energetic and optimistic young girl who improves the lives of everyone she meets. Jane Wyman, Agnes Moorehead, and Adolphe Menjou head an exceptional supporting cast for this film.

1960   134 minutes

POPEYE
★★★

DIRECTOR: Robert Altman

CAST: Robin Williams, Shelley Duvall, Ray Walston, Paul Smith, Paul Dooley, Richard Libertini, Wesley Ivan Hurt

This adaptation of the famous comic strip by director Robert Altman (*A Wedding*) is the cinematic equivalent of the old "good news, bad news" routine. The good news is that the casting, dialogue, and sets are superb. Robin Williams makes a terrific Popeye, and Shelley Duvall was born to play Olive Oyl. The bad news is it's often boring. And the songs (by Harry Nilsson) seem to go on forever. Still, it's hard to really dislike *Popeye*—it's so wonderfully weird to look at and so much fun at times. Rated PG.

1980   114 minutes

PRINCE AND THE PAUPER, THE (ORIGINAL)
★★★★½

DIRECTOR: William Keighley

CAST: Errol Flynn, Claude Rains, Barton MacLane, Alan Hale, Billy and Bobby Mauch

Exciting story of the young Prince of England trading places with his identical look-alike, a street beggar. One of Errol Flynn's lesser-known films but still one of his best. This film captures the flavor of the times. Erich Wolfgang Korngold wrote the music.

1937   B & W 120 minutes

PRINCE AND THE PAUPER, THE (REMAKE)
★★★½

DIRECTOR: Richard Fleischer

CAST: Charlton Heston, Oliver Reed, George C. Scott, Rex Harrison, Mark Lester

An all-star cast brings Mark Twain's novel of mistaken identity in not-so-jolly old England to life. Edward, the only son of King Henry VIII (Charlton Heston), trades places with his double, a child from the London slums. The young prince has trouble reclaiming his crown even with the aid of a swashbuckling soldier-of-fortune (Oliver Reed). Nothing pretentious here, just a costumed adventure that should satisfy young and old. Rated PG.

1978   113 minutes

PRINCESS AND THE PEA, THE
★★★½

DIRECTOR: Tony Bill

CAST: Liza Minnelli, Tom Conti, Beatrice Straight, Tim Kazurinsky

One of the most interesting Faerie Tale Theatre productions, this film features fine performances from Liza Minnelli and Tom Conti. In a way, it's sort of a takeoff on *Arthur*, in which Minnelli starred with Dudley Moore. The actress delivers some rather familiar lines of dialogue as she plays a princess tested for her royal qualities, which include a special kind of sensitivity.

1983   53 minutes

PRINCESS WHO HAD NEVER LAUGHED, THE
★★★★

DIRECTOR: Mark Cullingham

CAST: Howie Mandel, Ellen Barkin, Howard Hesseman

In this funny Grimm's fairy tale, laughter does prove to be the best medicine for the forlorn princess (Ellen Barkin). Growing up with her father (Howard Hesseman), who prefers to be called "Your Seriousness," she has never had a happy or amusing moment. When she locks herself in her room, her father decrees a Royal Laugh-off to make his daughter happy. At this point Howie Mandel appears as Weinerhead Waldo and the fun begins.

1984   51 minutes

PRIZEFIGHTER, THE
★★½

DIRECTOR: Michael Preece
CAST: Tim Conway, Don Knotts, David Wayne

In addition to starring in this goofy comedy, Tim Conway wrote the story. In it, we get a glimpse of 1930s boxing, with Conway playing a stupid boxer who has Don Knotts for his manager. Children may find the corny gags amusing, but most adults will be disappointed. Rated PG.

1979   99 minutes

PUSS IN BOOTS
★★★★

DIRECTOR: Robert Iscove
CAST: Ben Vereen, Gregory Hines, George Kirby, Brock Peters, Alfre Woodard

To ensure himself an easy life, a wily feline carries out a plan to turn his impoverished master into a rich marquis by winning him an ogre's castle and the hand of the king's daughter in marriage. Ben Vereen is purringly convincing as the cat and Brock Peters a standout as the ogre in this Faerie Tale Theatre production.

1984   53 minutes

RACE FOR YOUR LIFE, CHARLIE BROWN
★★★

DIRECTOR: Bill Melendez
CAST: Animated

Third entry in the "Peanuts" film series has moved further away from the poignant sophistication of A Boy Named Charlie Brown and closer to the mindless pap of Saturday-morning cartoon fare. The gang travels to summer camp and gets involved in a river-rafting race, which gives the film its title. The story lies dead in the water most of the time, with the tedium relieved only by the far better—and quite recognizable—echoes from Charles Schulz's newspaper strip. Rated G.

1977   75 minutes

RAINBOW BRITE AND THE STAR STEALER
★★★

DIRECTOR: Bernard Deyries, Kimio Yabuki
CAST: Animated

When the Dark Princess tries to steal Spectra (the world's light source), Rainbow Brite teams up with a chauvinistic, but admittedly brave, little boy named Krys to prevent the theft. Rainbow Brite teaches Krys that girls are as smart and brave as boys, and their bond helps them overcome the evil of the princess. This is Rainbow Brite's first feature-length film, and should continue to thrill the little girls who tend to be her most avid fans.

1985   85 minutes

RAPUNZEL
★★★½

DIRECTOR: Gilbert Cates
CAST: Jeff Bridges, Shelley Duvall, Gena Rowlands

A pregnant woman's desire for radishes results in her having to give her baby daughter to the witch who owns the radish garden. Shelley Duvall is amusing as both the mother and a grown Rapunzel. Jeff Bridges makes a fine, put-upon husband and a handsome prince who must rescue Rapunzel from the man-hating witch, delightfully played by Gena Rowlands. Another *Faerie Tale Theatre* production.

1982   51 minutes

RED BALLOON, THE
★★★★★

DIRECTOR: Albert Lamorisse
CAST: Pascal Lamorisse, Georges Sellier, Wladimir Popof, Renee Marion

This fanciful, endearing tale of a giant balloon that befriends a small boy in Paris is a delight for children and adults alike. Outside of a catchable word or two here and there, the film is without dialogue. The story is crystal clear in the visual telling, punctuated by an engaging musical score. A unique film, in 1956 it won a Golden Palm at the Cannes Film Festival, the Gold Medal of the French Cinema, and, in Hollywood, an Oscar for best original screenplay.

1956   34 minutes

RED PONY, THE
★★

DIRECTOR: Lewis Milestone
CAST: Myrna Loy, Robert Mitchum, Peter Miles, Louis Calhern, Shepperd Strudwick, Margaret Hamilton

It is very hard to make a dull movie from a John Steinbeck novel. This rendition manages to accomplish that. Myrna Loy and Robert Mitchum are wasted in this story of a young Northern California boy who is given a colt, which runs away.

1948   89 minutes

RETURN FROM WITCH MOUNTAIN
★★

DIRECTOR: John Hough
CAST: Bette Davis, Christopher Lee, Kim Richards, Ike Eisenmann

Christopher Lee and Bette Davis capture Ike Eisenmann to use his supernatural powers to accomplish their own purposes. Sequel to *Escape to Witch Mountain*, in which Eisenmann and Kim Richards discover their powers and the effect they can have on humans. Lee wants to conquer the world, while Davis just wants to get rich. A good children's film, but weak Disney. Rated G.

1978   93 minutes

RETURN TO OZ
★★★★½

DIRECTOR: Walter Murch
CAST: Fairuza Balk, Nicol Williamson, Jean Marsh, Piper Laurie, Matt Clark

In this semi-sequel to *The Wizard of Oz*, viewers will hear no songs nor see any Munchkins. It is a very different, but equally enjoyable, trip down the Yellow Brick Road, with young star Fairuza Balk outstanding as Dorothy. It gets pretty scary at times and isn't all fluff and wonder like the Oz of yore. However, this is nevertheless a magical film for the child in everyone. Rated PG for scary stuff. 1986 release.

1985   110 minutes

ROB ROY, THE HIGHLAND ROGUE
★★

DIRECTOR: Harold French

CAST: Richard Todd, Glynis Johns, James Robertson Justice, Michael Gough, Finlay Currie, Jean Taylor-Smith

Slow-moving historical saga is not up to the usual Walt Disney adventure film and is perhaps the weakest of the three films made in England with sturdy Richard Todd as the heroic lead. The few battle scenes are enjoyable enough and the scenery is lovely, but the pace is erratic and there is just too much dead time. This one is for Richard Todd fans only.

1954   85 minutes

ROBIN HOOD
★★★

DIRECTOR: Wolfgang Reitherman
CAST: Animated

A feature-length cartoon featuring the adventures of Robin Hood and his gang, this is one of the lesser animated works from the Walt Disney Studios, but still good entertainment for the kiddies. Rated G.

1973   83 minutes

RUMPELSTILTSKIN
★★★½

DIRECTOR: Emile Andolino
CAST: Herve Villechaize, Shelley Duvall, Ned Beatty, Jack Fletcher, Bud Cort

In this *Faerie Tale Theatre* production, a poor miller's daughter (Shelley Duvall, the series' executive producer) becomes a queen by outwitting a dwarf (Herve Villechaize) and fulfilling her boastful father's promise that she can spin straw into gold. Villechaize is great as a rather unsavory Rumpelstiltskin, and Ned Beatty is convincing as the selfish king who learns to think about others as well as

himself. The sets are especially beautiful.

1982   53 minutes

RUN, REBECCA, RUN
★★★★

DIRECTOR: Peter Maxwell
CAST: Henri Szeps, Simone Buchanan, John Stanton

This action-filled adventure finds a brave young girl captured by an illegal alien on an Australian island. Her fear of him soon dissolves as she helps him face the Australian authorities in order to be legally admitted to their country.

1983   81 minutes

SANTA CLAUS—THE MOVIE
★★★★

DIRECTOR: Jeannot Szwarc
CAST: Dudley Moore, John Lithgow, David Huddleston, Burgess Meredith, Judy Cornwell, Christian Fitzpatrick, Carrie Kei Heim

In this enjoyable family film, one of Santa's helpers, an elf named Patch (Dudley Moore), visits Earth and innocently joins forces with an evil toy manufacturer (delightfully played by John Lithgow). It is up to Santa (David Huddleston) to save him—and the spirit of Christmas in children everywhere. Rated PG for light profanity.

1985   105 minutes

SAVAGE SAM
★★½

DIRECTOR: Norman Tokar
CAST: Brian Keith, Tommy Kirk, Kevin Corcoran, Dewey Martin, Jeff York, Marta Kristen

Officially a sequel to *Old Yeller*, the film has little in common with its predecessor, except for some of the character names. Captured by Indians, the only hope of rescue for three children lies with Savage Sam, Old Yeller's son. This is an entertaining action film, albeit without the characterizations and depth of its predecessor. Not rated.

1963   103 minutes

SAVANNAH SMILES
★★★½

DIRECTOR: Pierre DeMoro
CAST: Bridgette Anderson, Mark Miller, Donovan Scott, Peter Graves, Chris Robinson, Michael Parks

In this surprisingly good, independently made family film, a 6-year-old runaway named Savannah (Bridgette Anderson) accidentally hides in the backseat of a car operated by two small-time crooks, Alvie (Mark Miller) and Boots (Donovan Scott). It's love at first sight for the trio, who decide to try to be a real family. The authorities, however, have other ideas. Rated G.

1982   107 minutes

SAVE THE LADY
★★★

DIRECTOR: Leon Thau
CAST: Matthew Excell, Robert Clarkson, Miranda Cartledge, Kim Clifford

Four kids set out to fight City Hall after a bureaucrat orders the historic *Lady Hope* steam ferry to be destroyed. The kids rescue *Lady Hope's* former skipper from a retirement home. Together with an expert engineer, the team valiantly repairs and repaints the boat. The action picks up when the ferry must elude a fleet of police boats.

1981   76 minutes

SCANDALOUS JOHN
★★★

DIRECTOR: Robert Butler
CAST: Brian Keith, Alfonso Arau, Michele Carey, Rick Lenz, Harry Morgan, Simon Oakland

Brian Keith stars as an eccentric ranch owner fighting to maintain his way of life. In his world, a cattle drive consists of one steer, and gunfights are practiced in the house with live ammunition. He must battle with the law, the world in general, and reality to keep his ranch and the life he loves. Laughs and poignancy are combined in this movie. Rated G.

1971   113 minutes

SECRET OF NIMH, THE
★★★★★

DIRECTOR: Don Bluth
CAST: Voices of, Dom De Luise, Peter Strauss, John Carradine

Lovers of classic screen animation, rejoice! Don Bluth's *The Secret of Nimh* is the best feature-length cartoon to be released since the golden age of Walt Disney. This movie, about the adventures of a widow mouse, is more than just a children's tale. Adults will enjoy it, too. Indeed, it deserves to be considered a classic. Don't miss it. Rated G.

1982   82 minutes

SECRET OF THE SWORD, THE
★

DIRECTOR: Bill Reed, Gwen Wetzler, Ed Friedman, Lou Kachivas, Marsh Lamore
CAST: Animated

Characters from the television series "He-Man and the Masters of the Universe" are featured in this poorly animated, ineptly written feature-length cartoon. Rated G.

1985   90 minutes

(SESAME STREET PRESENTS) FOLLOW THAT BIRD
★★★★

DIRECTOR: Ken Kwapis
CAST: Sandra Bernhard, Chevy Chase, John Candy, Dave Thomas, Joe Flaherty, Waylon Jennings

Although this kiddie film has an impressive "guest cast," the real stars are "Sesame Street" TV show regulars Big Bird, the Cookie Monster, Oscar the Grouch, Count von Count, the Telly Monster, etc. Children will love this story about Big Bird being evicted from Sesame Street. Rated G.

1985   88 minutes

SHAGGY D.A., THE
★

DIRECTOR: Robert Stevenson
CAST: Dean Jones, Tim Conway, Suzanne Pleshette

Feeble sequel to Disney's far superior *The Shaggy Dog*, this retread stars Dean Jones as the victim of an ancient curse that turns him into a canine at the worst of moments. This entry is a pointless example of Disney slapstick at its worst, with no attention to the character interaction that made the original so charming. A real dog. Rated G.

1976   91 minutes

SHAGGY DOG, THE
★★★½

DIRECTOR: Charles Barton
CAST: Fred MacMurray, Jean Hagen, Tommy Kirk, Annette Funicello

An ancient spell turns a boy into a sheepdog, and the fur flies in this slapstick Disney fantasy. Many of the gags are good, but the film sometimes drags.

1959   104 minutes

SHERLOCK HOLMES AND THE BASKERVILLE CURSE
★★

DIRECTOR: Eddy Graham
CAST: Animated

We weren't very impressed by this feature-length cartoon version of Sir Arthur Conan Doyle's oft-filmed "The Hound of the Baskervilles." The animation is way below par, and the story trifled with a bit too much for our tastes. It may be an effective introduction for youngsters to the joys of the canon. Rated G.

1984   60 minutes

SIGN OF ZORRO, THE
★★½

DIRECTOR: Norman Foster, Lewis R. Foster
CAST: Guy Williams, Henry Calvin, Gene Sheldon, Britt Lomond, George J. Lewis, Lisa Gaye

Baby boomers, beware. If you have fond memories of this swashbuckling Disney television series about the Z-slashing Robin Hood of Old Mexico, you might want to skip this uneven feature compilation of original episodes. It's still fine for the kiddies, however.

1960   B & W   91 minutes

SLEEPING BEAUTY
★★★★½

DIRECTOR: Clyde Geronimi
CAST: Animated

This Disney adaptation of Charles Perrault's seventeenth-century version of the famous fairy tale features distinctive animation that may surprise those accustomed to the softer style of the studio's other feature-length cartoons. Nevertheless, it is the last genre classic to be supervised by Walt Disney himself and belongs in any list of the best children's films (while having the added asset of being enjoyable for adults, as well). Rated G.

1959   75 minutes

SLEEPING BEAUTY
★★★★

DIRECTOR: Jeremy Kagan
CAST: Beverly D'Angelo, Bernadette Peters, Christopher Reeve, Sally Kellerman

This is one of the funniest *Faerie Tale Theatre* episodes. The sets may not be as spectacular as most in the series, but the cast makes up for it. Viewers should not expect to see much of the original tale because a lot of time is spent on the prince's past and his quest for the perfect woman. Christopher Reeve is excellent as the handsome prince, and Bernadette Peters makes a sweet and pretty princess. Sally Kellerman is wonderful as the queen.

1983   60 minutes

SMURFS AND THE MAGIC FLUTE, THE
★

DIRECTOR: John Rust
CAST: Animated

Those little blue people from the popular Saturday-morning television cartoon show are featured in their first movie. Oily McCreep steals the musical instrument of the title—which causes anyone who hears it to dance until they collapse from exhaustion—and uses it to steal all the wealth from an ancient kingdom until the Smurfs intervene. The kiddies will probably love it, but parents should read a book. Rated G.

1983   80 minutes

SNOOPY, COME HOME
★★★½

DIRECTOR: Bill Melendez
CAST: Animated

Charming second entry in the "Peanuts" film series doesn't contain the childhood *angst* of the first but maintains the irreverent view of life found in the best of Charles Schulz's comic strips. Snoopy decides life at home ain't all it's cracked up to be, so he and Woodstock set off to find America. Needless to say, there's no place like home. Rated G.

1972   70 minutes

SNOW QUEEN
★★

DIRECTOR: Peter Medak
CAST: Melissa Gilbert, Lance Kerwin, Lee Remick, Lauren Hutton, Linda Manz, David Hemmings

This film is an exceedingly dull Faerie Tale Theatre tale of the Snow Queen (played by Lee Remick), who teaches an unruly boy a valuable lesson. The sets and special effects are second only to the actors' lines for their banality.

1983   48 minutes

SNOW WHITE AND THE SEVEN DWARFS
★★★★

DIRECTOR: Peter Medak
CAST: Elizabeth McGovern, Vanessa Redgrave, Vincent Price, Rex Smith

Both Vincent Price and Vanessa Redgrave are wickedly wonderful in this splendid adaptation of this Grimm's tale. Price plays the evil queen's (Redgrave) advising mirror. Lovely Elizabeth McGovern plays a sweet Snow White.

1983   51 minutes

SNOW WHITE AND THE THREE STOOGES
🐾

DIRECTOR: Walter Lang
CAST: The Three Stooges, Patricia Medina, Carol Heiss, Guy Rolfe, Buddy Baer, Edgar Barrier

Just about as bad as a film can be, this sad entry from what was left of the Three Stooges just lumbers on like a bad grammar-school play done on movie sets. Former temptress Patricia Medina as the wicked queen has every right to succeed in her efforts to eradicate ice-skating nonactress Carol Heiss as Snow White, but those darn Stooges keep upsetting her plans. This one is for Three Stooges completists *only*—the kids will hold it against you if you rent them this one.

1961   107 minutes

SO DEAR TO MY HEART
★★★★

DIRECTOR: Harold Schuster
CAST: Burl Ives, Beulah Bondi, Harry Carey, Luana Patten, Bobby Driscoll, Raymond Bond, Walter Soderling, Matt Willis, Spelman B. Collins

One of the finest of all feature-length Walt Disney films, this loving re-creation of small-town life in the early years of this century is wonderful entertainment for the whole family and a pure piece of Americana that mirrors simpler and much more pleasant times. Young Bobby Driscoll (one of the finest of all child actors) has taken a notion to enter his black lamb Danny in the county fair. A singing blacksmith (Burl Ives in his film debut) encourages him in his dreams. Sprinkled with lovely animated lead-ins and filmed in Sequoia National Park and Visalia, California, this gentle film presents a beautiful evocation of a time that has passed, and is loaded with love, goodwill, and sentiment. "Lavender Blue (Dilly Dilly)" was one of six new songs that debuted in this film.

1949   84 minutes

SOMEWHERE, TOMORROW
★★★

DIRECTOR: Robert Weimer
CAST: Sarah Jessica Parker, Nancy Addison, Tom Shea, Rick Weber

The Ghost and Mrs. Muir for a teen audience, this film is about a girl, played by Sarah Jessica Parker, who learns how to deal with her father's death by falling in love with the ghost of a teenage boy. The result is good family entertainment. Parker brings her usual solid competence to the role, and Tom Shea, as the ghost, is fine. Only a rather contrived happy ending dims the charm.

1986   91 minutes

SON OF FLUBBER
★★★½

DIRECTOR: Robert Stevenson
CAST: Fred MacMurray, Nancy Olson, Keenan Wynn, Tommy Kirk, William Demarest, Paul Lynde

This Disney sequel to *The Absent-Minded Professor* once again stars Fred MacMurray as the inventor of Flubber. Two new discoveries are featured: "dry rain" and "flubbergas." A multitude of character actors, including Keenan Wynn, William Demarest, and Paul Lynde, star in the supporting roles. While not as good as the original

"Flubber" film, it does have some moments reminiscent of the original.

1963   B & W 100 minutes

SWISS FAMILY ROBINSON, THE
★★★★½

DIRECTOR: Ken Annakin
CAST: John Mills, Dorothy McGuire, James MacArthur, Tommy Kirk, Sessue Hayakawa

Walt Disney's classic comedy-adventure film, adapted from the classic children's story by Johann Wyss about a family shipwrecked on a desert island.

1960   128 minutes

SWORD AND THE ROSE, THE
★★½

DIRECTOR: Ken Annakin
CAST: Richard Todd, Glynis Johns, James Robertson Justice, Michael Gough

Romance, intrigue, and heroic acts of derring-do are the order of the day in this colorful Walt Disney adaptation of *When Knighthood Was in Flower*, filmed in England as one of a series of historical adventures that Disney would continue making in America during the fifties. Richard Todd is adept with both the lance and the ladies and makes an ideal lead (as he does in Disney's *Rob Roy* and *Robin Hood*), and Michael Gough is a truly malevolent heavy. The rest of the cast is on the mark and makes this film fun for everyone. The England of Henry VIII never looked so good.

1953   93 minutes

SWORD IN THE STONE
★★★½

DIRECTOR: Wolfgang Reitherman
CAST: Animated

The legend of King Arthur provided the storyline for this animated feature film from the Walt Disney studios. Although not up to the film company's highest standards, it still provides fine entertainment for the young and the young at heart. Rated G.

1963   80 minutes

SWORD OF THE VALIANT
★★★½

DIRECTOR: Stephen Weeks
CAST: Miles O'Keeffe, Sean Connery, Trevor Howard

The Old English tale of Sir Gawain and the Green Knight is brought to the screen with an appealing blend of action-adventure and tongue-in-cheek humor. Miles O'Keeffe (Bo Derek's "Tarzan the Ape Man") plays Sir Gawain, a rookie knight in the court of King Arthur. He is sent out on a quest brought on by a challenge issued by the magical Green Knight (Sean Connery). His knightly concept of medieval chivalry is often in contrast to the modernistic collection of bad guys and alluring ladies Gawain meets on his quest. Rated PG.

1984   162 minutes

TALE OF THE FROG PRINCE
★★★★

DIRECTOR: Eric Idle
CAST: Robin Williams, Teri Garr, Rene Auberjonois, Candy Clark

Perhaps the best of the Faerie Tale Theatre presentations, this story about a slighted fairy godmother who exacts revenge by turning a prince (Robin Williams) into a frog was inventively written and directed by Eric Idle, of Monty Python fame. It's witty and well-acted.

1982   51 minutes

TEN WHO DARED
★

DIRECTOR: William Beaudine
CAST: Brian Keith, John Beal, James Drury, David Stollery

In 1869, Major John Wesley Powell and nine other explorers set out to explore the wild Colorado River. This movie is based on Major Powell's journal of that trip, but reading the journal would be more worthwhile and entertaining. An unbelievable and poorly crafted script, one-dimensional characters, and obvious studio and matte shots make this a movie to be missed by the entire family.

1960   92 minutes

THAT DARN CAT
★★½

DIRECTOR: Robert Stevenson
CAST: Dean Jones, Hayley Mills, Dorothy Provine, Roddy McDowall, Elsa Lanchester, Neville Brand, William Demarest, Ed Wynn, Frank Gorshin

Trust Disney to take a great book— *Undercover Cat*, by Gordon and Mildred Gordon—and turn it into a moronic slapstick farce. Hayley Mills and Dorothy Provine are a bit long in the tooth as the youthful (?) owners of a fulsome feline christened "DC" (for Darn Cat). One evening DC returns from his nightly rounds with an unusual collar: a watch belonging to a woman taken hostage in a recent bank robbery. Enter Dean Jones as an aelurophobic FBI agent who, with the stumble-footed assistance of his men, attempts to tail DC. The great supporting cast includes Roddy McDowall as a duck-hunting neighbor, Elsa Lanchester as the local snoop, and a pre-Rid-

dler Frank Gorshin as one of the hoods.

1965   116 minutes

THEY WENT THAT-A-WAY AND THAT-A-WAY
★★

DIRECTOR: Edward Montagne, Stuart E. McGowan
CAST: Tim Conway, Chuck McCann, Reni Santoni, Richard Kiel, Lenny Montana, Dub Taylor

Tim Conway wrote and stars in this prison-escape comedy. He plays a small-town deputy who follows the governor's orders by being secretly placed in a maximum-security prison as an undercover agent posing as a hardened criminal. Fellow deputy (Chuck McCann) is his partner on the mission. When the governor suddenly dies, the two must escape from the prison. There are some silly gags, but this film does provide fair entertainment if you are looking for a few laughs and no deep plots. Rated PG.

1978   106 minutes

THIRD MAN ON THE MOUNTAIN
★★★

DIRECTOR: Ken Annakin
CAST: Michael Rennie, James MacArthur, Janet Munro, Herbert Lom

James MacArthur stars as a young man whose father was killed in a climbing accident. He wants badly to get into climbing, but his mother forbids it. He still sneaks practice and develops his skills. The Citadel (actually the Matterhorn) has never been scaled, and the boy's father died in an attempt. Several groups decide to try the climb independently, and MacArthur is among them. Miraculously, he finds the secret passage his father had been seeking. Breath-taking scenery and an excellent script make this film an excellent adventure story for the family. Not rated.

1959   106 minutes

THOSE CALLOWAYS
★★★★

DIRECTOR: Norman Tokar
CAST: Brian Keith, Vera Miles, Brandon de Wilde, Linda Evans

Sensitive, sentimental film about a family in New England. Man battles townspeople and nature to preserve a safe haven for geese. Marvelous scenes of life in a small town and the love between individuals. Rated G.

1965   131 minutes

THREE CABALLEROS, THE
★★★

DIRECTOR: Walt Disney
CAST: Animated

In Walt Disney's first attempt at combining animation and live action, Donald Duck is joined by two Latin feathered friends for a trip down to Rio. Originally, this cartoon travelogue was designed as a World War II propaganda piece promoting inter-American unity. It still holds up well today and remains a timeless learning experience for the kids.

1942   72 minutes

THREE LITTLE PIGS, THE
★★★★

DIRECTOR: Howard Storm
CAST: Billy Crystal, Jeff Goldblum, Valerie Perrine

Billy Crystal plays the industrious little pig who proves that "haste makes waste" when he takes his time building a sturdy house to keep the big, bad wolf away. The twist in this Faerie Tale Theatre

version is that they've added a female companion (Valerie Perrine) who flees from the wolf with Crystal. Jeff Goldblum makes a hilarious, cigar-chomping wolf.

1984   51 minutes

THUMBELINA
★★★★

DIRECTOR: Michael Lindsay-Hogg
CAST: Carrie Fisher, William Katt, Burgess Meredith, narration by David Hemmings

This is an *Alice in Wonderland*–type tale of a thumb-size girl (Carrie Fisher) and her adventures as she tries to find her way home. The creatures she meets along the way are well characterized. This is one of the more rewarding Faerie Tale Theatre productions.

1983   48 minutes

THREE LIVES OF THOMASINA, THE
★★★★

DIRECTOR: Don Chaffey
CAST: Patrick McGoohan, Susan Hampshire, Karen Dotrice, Vincent Winter

An excellent cast and innovative ways of telling the story highlight this tale of love and caring. A young girl's cat is brought back to life by a woman who also teaches the girl's father to let others into his life. The cat's trip to cat heaven is outstandingly executed.

1964   97 minutes

TIGER TOWN
★★½

DIRECTOR: Alan Shapiro
CAST: Roy Scheider, Justin Henry

In this passable movie, made for the Disney Channel, Roy Scheider stars as a legendary baseball player whose final year with the Detroit Tigers looks dismal until a young boy (Justin Henry) "wishes" him to success. At least, that's what the boy believes. Both Scheider and Henry give good performances, but the overall effect is not as impressive as it could have been. Rated G.

1984   76 minutes

TOBY TYLER
★★★½

DIRECTOR: Charles Barton
CAST: Kevin Corcoran, Henry Calvin, Gene Sheldon, Bob Sweeney, Mr. Stubbs, James Drury

Disney version of the popular juvenile book about a young runaway and his adventures with the circus is breezy entertainment and a showcase for young Kevin Corcoran (Moochie of many Disney television shows and the *Mickey Mouse Club*). The animals are charming, Mr. Stubbs the chimpanzee provides laughs and tears, young Corcoran is effective, and the recreated small towns of early twentieth-century America are reminiscent of old photographs and book illustrations of the period. Good entertainment for the family but certainly not the best of Disney's period films. Originally made as a silent film starring Jackie Coogan.

1960   96 minutes

TOM EDISON—THE BOY WHO LIT UP THE WORLD
★★★★

DIRECTOR: Henning Schellerup
CAST: David Huffman, Adam Arkin, Michael Callan, Rosemary DeCamp, James Griffith

A fine cast makes this film enjoyable. Tom Edison (David Huffman) and Cole Bogardis (Adam Arkin) begin working for the telegraph company at the same time. In Tom's spare time, he works on an assortment of inventions, including a cockroach electrocutor and a direct telegraph machine. Mr. Craner (Michael Callan) is threatened by Edison's inventiveness and tries to sabotage his efforts.

1983   49 minutes

TOM SAWYER
★★

DIRECTOR: James Nielson
CAST: Josh Albee, Jeff Tyler, Jane Wyatt, Buddy Ebsen, Vic Morrow, John McGiver

Mark Twain's classic story loses its satirical edge in this homogenized made-for-television production about the adventures of Tom Sawyer (Josh Albee) and Huckleberry Finn (Jeff Tyler). The kids may enjoy it, but adults will want to reread the book. Better yet, read the book to your kids. Rated G.

1973   78 minutes

TOM THUMB
★★★½

DIRECTOR: George Pal
CAST: Russ Tamblyn, June Thorburn, Peter Sellers, Terry-Thomas, Alan Young, Jessie Matthews, Bernard Miles

This underrated George Pal fantasy is a treat for young and old viewers. Good effects, pleasant tunes, and a distinguished cast of veteran British performers combine with Russ Tamblyn's infectious lead to make this a surefire choice for the VCR when the kids demand colorful entertainment and the adults don't want to watch another minute of "Rainbow Bright" or "The Care Bears." Worth a try.

1958   98 minutes

TONKA
★★★

DIRECTOR: Lewis R. Foster

CAST: Sal Mineo, Philip Carey, Jerome Courtland

Sal Mineo is White Bull, a Sioux Indian who captures and tames a wild stallion and names it Tonka Wakan—The Great One. Tribal law requires him to give the horse to his older Indian cousin, a bully who would mistreat the animal. Rather than do so, Mineo frees the horse. The horse is captured again and sold to the U.S. cavalry. Mineo tracks down the horse and finds it being gently handled by a captain. The cavalry is ordered to join Custer at the Little Big Horn, and Tonka, White Bull, and the captain face each other on the battlefield.

1958   97 minutes

TRANSFORMERS, THE MOVIE
🐾

DIRECTOR: Nelson Shin

CAST: Animated

In this animated vehicle for violence and destruction, the "good" autobots (who convert or transform into cars) and the dinobots (who change into dinosaurs) must battle the evil forces of Unicrom (Orson Welles) and Megatron (who later becomes Galvatron). There are endless shootouts and bombings between the two groups but in case that's not enough, other villains (such as the savage Octogons) wreak havoc as well. Throughtout the film the heavy metal music proves to be distracting. The animation is sketchy and for non-Transformer fans it's impossible to keep track of who's good and who's bad. Rated PG for violence and occasional obsceni-

ties, and we do not recommend it for children under 12.

1986   80 minutes

TREASURE ISLAND
★★★★

DIRECTOR: Victor Fleming

CAST: Wallace Beery, Lionel Barrymore, Jackie Cooper, Lewis Stone

This is an MGM all-star presentation of Robert Louis Stevenson's children's classic of a young boy's adventure with pirates, buried treasure, and that delightful rogue of fiction Long John Silver. It seems all the great character actors of the 1930s put in an appearance, including Wallace Beery, as Silver, and Lionel Barrymore, as Billy Bones.

1934   B & W 105 minutes

TREASURE ISLAND
★★★★

DIRECTOR: Byron Haskin

CAST: Robert Newton, Bobby Driscoll, Basil Sydney

Disney remake of the Robert Louis Stevenson pirate adventure is powered by a memorable Robert Newton as Long John Silver.

1950   87 minutes

UGLY DACHSHUND, THE
★★

DIRECTOR: Norman Tokar

CAST: Dean Jones, Suzanne Pleshette, Charlie Ruggles, Parley Baer, Kelly Thordsen

In this Disney movie, Dean Jones and Suzanne Pleshette are husband and wife; she loves dachshunds and owns a number of puppies. Charlie Ruggles convinces Jones to take a Great Dane puppy to raise. Since all of its peers are dachshunds, the Great Dane assumes it is one, too, and tries to act like them. The disparity in size causes various misfortunes and calamities. Finally, the Dane gets recognized on his own merits after winning a dog show. Somewhat entertaining along the lines of a made-for-TV-movie. Not rated.

1966   93 minutes

UNIDENTIFIED FLYING ODDBALL
★★½

DIRECTOR: Russ Mayberry
CAST: Dennis Dugan, Jim Dale, Ron Moody, Kenneth More

Inept astronaut is transported to the court of King Arthur in his spacecraft. Once there, he discovers that Merlin and a knight are plotting against the king and sets out to expose them with his modern technology. Uneven script with situations not fully developed or explored hampers this Disney trifle. Rated G.

1979   92 minutes

WESTWARD HO THE WAGONS
★★½

DIRECTOR: William Beaudine
CAST: Fess Parker, Kathleen Crowley, Jeff York, David Stollery, Sebastian Cabot, George Reeves

Episodic film about a wagon train traveling west. Vignettes inlcude children being captured by Indians, an Indian attack on the wagon train, and an Indian boy being medically saved by a combination of Indian and white man's medicine. The basic appeal is seeing Fess Parker in another Davy Crockett–type role and four of the Mouseketeers as children in the train. Devoid of a real beginning or end, this movie just rambles along for its entire running time. Not rated.

1956   90 minutes

WHERE THE RED FERN GROWS
★★★★

DIRECTOR: Norman Tokar
CAST: James Whitmore, Beverly Garland, Jack Ging, Lonnie Chapman, Stewart Peterson

Fine family fare about a boy's love for two hunting dogs and his coming of age in Oklahoma in the 1930s. Rated G.

1974   90 minutes

WILBUR AND ORVILLE: THE FIRST TO FLY
★★★★

DIRECTOR: Henning Schellerup
CAST: James Carroll Jordon, Chris Beaumont, John Randolph, Louise Latham, Edward Andrews

This entertaining biography of the Wright brothers shows their determination in the face of ridicule and harassment. In their early years, their experiments with flying machines cause some damage to their hometown and earn them the scorn of the townspeople. In an attempt to lead respectable lives, they begin working at a bicycle repair shop. Not surprisingly, they decide to use a bike for the next flying machine. The moral of this delightlful film lies in sticking to something when you know you're right.

1973   47 minutes

WILDERNESS FAMILY, PART 2, THE
★★★

DIRECTOR: Frank Zuniga
CAST: Robert Logan, Susan D. Shaw, Heather Rattray, Ham Larsen, George (Buck) Flower, Brian Cutler

Taken on its own terms, *The Wilderness Family, Part 2* isn't a bad motion picture. It's certainly one of the best of its kind. Film fans who want thrills and chills or something challenging to the mind should skip it; however, for pleasant family entertainment that will entrance the kiddies and mildly divert the adults, you could do a whole lot worse. Rated G.

1978   105 minutes

WILLY WONKA AND THE CHOCOLATE FACTORY
★★★
DIRECTOR: Mel Stuart
CAST: Gene Wilder, Jack Albertson, Peter Ostrum, Roy Kinnear, Aubrey Woods, Michael Bollner, Ursula Reit

Gene Wilder plays a candy company owner who allows some lucky kids to tour the facility. However, a few of his guests get sticky fingers (pun intended) and suffer the consequences. This essentially entertaining movie has its memorable moments—as well as bad. Its biggest problem is the Oompa Loompas, not-so-cuddly dwarfs who were supposed to delight kids but, instead, scared most of them. Rated G.

1971   98 minutes

WIND IN THE WILLOWS, THE
★★★★★
DIRECTOR: Wolfgang Reitherman
CAST: Animated

One of Disney's finest. This adaptation of Kenneth Grahame's classic deals with the adventures of J. Thaddeus Toad and his friends Cyril, Mole, Rat, and Mac Badger. Basil Rathbone narrates this classic short (which was originally released with *The Legend of Sleepy Hollow*). Disney artists on this project included Olile Johnston, Frank Thomas, Ward Kimball, and Wolfgang Reitherman.

1949   75 minutes

WORLD'S GREATEST ATHLETE, THE
★★★
DIRECTOR: Robert Scheerer
CAST: Jan-Michael Vincent, John Amos, Tim Conway, Roscoe Lee Browne

John Amos is the athletics instructor at Merrivale College and has the misfortune to coach a large group of bumblers and incompetents. He and his assistant, Tim Conway, travel to Africa to get away from their toubles and come across Nanu (Jan-Michael Vincent), the greatest natural athelete in the world. To save their careers and give the college a winning team, they trick Nanu into coming to the United States and enroll him at the college. Some laughs take place as they introduce him to the various sports and develop a love interest for him. The big finale is the NCAA track-and-field championship, where Nanu singlehandedly takes on the other teams. The final sequence is improved by a young Howard Cosell as the announcer. One of the better Disney college films. Rated G.

1973   89 minutes

YEARLING, THE
★★★★½
DIRECTOR: Clarence Brown
CAST: Gregory Peck, Jane Wyman, Claude Jarman Jr., Chill Wills

A beautiful film version of Marjorie Kinnan Rawlings's sensitive story of a young boy's love for a pet fawn that his father must destroy. Simply told, this emotionally charged drama has been rated one of the finest films ever made.

1946   134 minutes

COMEDY

ABBOTT AND COSTELLO IN HOLLYWOOD

★★

DIRECTOR: S. Sylvan Simon
CAST: Bud Abbott, Lou Costello, Frances Rafferty, Robert Stanton

Lesser Abbott and Costello effort has Bud and Lou trying to make it big as movie stars. Best scenes occur early in the film, with Lou playing a barber.

1945　　B & W　83 minutes

ABBOTT AND COSTELLO MEET CAPTAIN KIDD

★½

DIRECTOR: Charles Lamont
CAST: Bud Abbott, Lou Costello, Charles Laughton, Hillary Brooke, Leif Erickson

One of Abbott and Costello's few color films, this is strictly preschooler fare. As the title suggests, the boys play a pair of jerks who get chased around uncharted islands, pirate ships, etc., by the infamous Captain Kidd, as portrayed by Charles Laughton, who makes every effort to retain his dignity. Only worthwhile aspect of the film is the rare opportunity to see the comedy team in living color.

1952　　　70 minutes

ABBOTT AND COSTELLO MEET DR. JEKYLL AND MR. HYDE

★★★½

DIRECTOR: Charles Lamont
CAST: Bud Abbott, Lou Costello, Boris Karloff

Fun mixture of comedy and horror has the team up against the smooth Dr. Jekyll and the maniacal Mr. Hyde. The laughs come fast and furious in this, one of the boys' better films of the 1950s. Boris Karloff is in top form in the dual role, and don't miss the hilarious scene in which Lou is turned into a mouse!

1953　　B & W　77 minutes

ABBOTT AND COSTELLO MEET FRANKENSTEIN

★★★★

DIRECTOR: Charles Barton
CAST: Bud Abbott, Lou Costello, Lon Chaney Jr., Bela Lugosi

Whenever someone writes about the Universal horror classics, they always cite this film as evidence of how the series fell into decline. Likewise, screen historians call it the beginning of the end for the comedy team. It deserves neither rap. For Bud Abbott and Lou Costello, it meant a resurgence of popularity after a slow fall from favor as the 1940s box-office champs. Yet it never compromises the characters of Dracula (Bela Lugosi), the Wolfman (Lon Chaney), or the Frankenstein monster (Glenn Strange). Director Charles Barton mixes fright and fun without sacrificing either.

1948   B & W   83 minutes

ADAM'S RIB
★★★★½

DIRECTOR: George Cukor
CAST: Spencer Tracy, Katharine Hepburn, Judy Holliday, Tom Ewell, David Wayne

The screen team of Spencer Tracy and Katharine Hepburn was always watchable, but never more so than in this comedy, directed by George Cukor. As husband-and-wife lawyers on opposing sides of the same case, they remind us of what movie magic is really all about. The supporting performances by Judy Holliday, Tom Ewell, David Wayne, and Jean Hagen greatly add to the fun.

1949   B & W 101 minutes

ADVENTURES OF SHERLOCK HOLMES' SMARTER BROTHER, THE
★★½

DIRECTOR: Gene Wilder
CAST: Gene Wilder, Madeline Kahn, Marty Feldman, Dom De Luise

Even discounting the effrontery of writer-director-star Gene Wilder's creating a smarter sibling, Sigerson Holmes (Gene Wilder), one is still left with a less-than-hilarious, highly uneven romp. There are a few laughs, but you have to wait patiently for them. In the story, Sigerson falls in love with a dance hall damsel in distress (Madeline Kahn) and finds himself pursued by the baddies (Leo McKern and Roy Kinnear). Though the principals—who also include Marty Feldman and Dom De Luise—try hard, the film's soggy structure (and Wilder's poor research into the canon) plunge the whole thing into mediocrity. Rated PG.

1975   91 minutes

AFRICA SCREAMS
★★

DIRECTOR: Charles Barton
CAST: Bud Abbott, Lou Costello, Frank Buck, Shemp Howard

Just passable Abbott and Costello hijinks.

1949   B & W   87 minutes

AFTER HOURS
★★★★

DIRECTOR: Martin Scorsese
CAST: Griffin Dunne, Rosanna Arquette, Teri Garr, John Heard, Linda Fiorentino, Richard "Cheech" Marin, Tommy Chong, Catherine O'Hara, Verna Bloom

Watching *After Hours* is not unlike listening to someone tell very funny jokes while scraping his fingers across a blackboard. If you can survive the agony, the laughs are well worth it. It is the most brutal and bizarre black (as in dark) comedy we are ever likely to see—a mixture of guffaws and goose pimples. Griffin Dunne, who was so ghoulishly hilarious as the decaying friend of wolfman David

Naughton in *An American Werewolf in London*, stars as a computer operator who unwillingly spends a night in the SoHo area of downtown Manhattan. A trio of strange women (played by Rosanna Arquette, Teri Garr, and Linda Fiorentino) mystify, seduce, and horrify our hapless hero, and his life soon becomes a total nightmare. Director Martin Scorsese has never been better, and a topflight cast (which also includes John Heard, Cheech & Chong, and Catherine O'Hara) is wonderful to watch. Rated R for profanity, nudity, violence, and general weirdness.

1985   94 minutes

AFTER THE FOX
★

DIRECTOR: Vittorio De Sica
CAST: Peter Sellers, Victor Mature, Britt Ekland, Martin Balsam

Peter Sellers is at his worst, playing an Italian movie director in this flat farce. Victor Mature gives an amusing portrayal of a leading man whose ego remains mammoth, though his screen popularity is declining rapidly. The script for this fiasco was written by none other than Neil Simon.

1966   103 minutes

AIRPLANE!
★★★★

DIRECTOR: Jim Abrahams, David and Jerry Zucker
CAST: Robert Hays, Julie Hagerty, Leslie Nielsen, Kareem Abdul-Jabbar, Lloyd Bridges, Peter Graves, Robert Stack

This is a hilarious spoof of the *Airport* series—and movies in general. While the jokes don't always work, there are so many of them that this comedy ends up with enough laughs for three movies. Rated PG.

1980   88 minutes

AIRPLANE II: THE SEQUEL
★★★½

DIRECTOR: Ken Finkleman
CAST: Robert Hays, Julie Hagerty, Peter Graves, William Shatner

Viewers who laughed uncontrollably through *Airplane!* will find much to like about this sequel. The stars of the original are back, with silly jokes and sight gags galore. However, those who thought the original was more stupid than funny undoubtedly will mutter the same about the sequel. Rated PG for occasional adult content.

1982   85 minutes

ALFIE
★★★★

DIRECTOR: Lewis Gilbert
CAST: Michael Caine, Shelley Winters, Millicent Martin, Julia Foster, Shirley Anne Field

Wild and ribald comedy about a Cockney playboy (Michael Caine) who finds "birds" irresistible. Full of sex and delightful charm, this quick-moving film also tells the poignant tragedy of a man uncertain about his lifestyle. Nominated for five Oscars, including best picture and best actor.

1966   113 minutes

ALLEGRO NON TROPPO
★★★★

DIRECTOR: Bruno Bozzetto
CAST: Animated

An animated spoof of Disney's *Fantasia* by Italian filmmaker Bruno Bozzetto, this release entertainingly weds stylish slapstick with the music of Debussy, Ravel,

Vivaldi, Stravinsky, Dvorak, and Sibelius. Rated PG.

1976   75 minutes

ALL OF ME
★★★★½

DIRECTOR: Carl Reiner
CAST: Steve Martin, Lily Tomlin, Victoria Tennant, Richard Libertini

Steve Martin finds himself haunted from within by the soul of a recently deceased Lily Tomlin when an attempt to put her spirit in another woman's body backfires. This delightful comedy is directed by Carl Reiner (*Where's Poppa?*; *The Man with Two Brains*) and gives its two stars the best showcase for their talents to date. Rated PG for suggested sex, violence, and profanity.

1984   93 minutes

ALL THE MARBLES

DIRECTOR: Robert Aldrich
CAST: Peter Falk, Vicki Frederick, Laurene Landon, Burt Young, Tracy Reed, Ursalin Bryant-King

Peter Falk stars as the unscrupulous manager of two female wrestlers in this dreadful movie, directed by Robert Aldrich (*The Dirty Dozen*). Bad taste . . . total waste. Rated R because of nudity, violence, and profanity.

1981   113 minutes

ALMOST YOU
★★★★

DIRECTOR: Adam Books
CAST: Brooke Adams, Griffin Dunne, Karen Young, Marty Watt

Brooke Adams and Griffin Dunne give excellent performances in this film about a restless husband and his down-to-earth wife. Dunne,

who displayed similar characteristics in Martin Scorsese's *After Hours*, perfectly emulates the frustrated over-30 businessman and husband with comic results. Adams plays his wife, who is recovering from a car accident that gives her a new perspective on life. Rated R for language, sex, and nudity.

1985   91 minutes

AMAZING ADVENTURE
★★★

DIRECTOR: Alfred Zeisler
CAST: Cary Grant, Mary Brian, Peter Gawthorne, Henry Kendall, Leon M. Lion

Feeling guilty after inheriting a fortune, Cary Grant sets out to earn his living in this comedy of stout hearts among the poor-but-honest in England during the Depression.

1936   B & W   70 minutes

AMERICAN DREAMER
★★★½

DIRECTOR: Rick Rosenthal
CAST: JoBeth Williams, Tom Conti, Giancarlo Giannini

JoBeth Williams (*The Big Chill*) plays Cathy Palmer, a would-be novelist who, in a short story contest, successfully captures the style of a series of adventure stories that feature a superspy named Rebecca Ryan and thereby wins a trip to London. But once there, Palmer is hit by a car and wakes up believing she is the fictional character. That's when she starts causing all sorts of trouble for a hapless fellow she thinks is her sidekick (Tom Conti, of *Reuben, Reuben*) and a French diplomat (Giancarlo Giannini) whose life she fears is in danger. The picture is sort of a *Romancing the Stone II*, but never quite shines as brightly as one expects. Rated PG for violence.

1984   105 minutes

AMERICAN GRAFFITI
★★★★½

DIRECTOR: George Lucas
CAST: Richard Dreyfuss, Ron Howard, Paul LeMat, Cindy Williams, Candy Clark, Mackenzie Phillips, Wolfman Jack, Harrison Ford, Bo Hopkins, Suzanne Somers, Charles Martin Smith

Star Wars creator George Lucas discovered his talent for creating light-hearted, likable entertainment with this film about the coming of age of a group of high-school students in Northern California. Blessed with a superb rock 'n' roll score and fine performances by Richard Dreyfuss, Ron Howard, Paul LeMat, Cindy Williams, Charles Martin Smith, and Candy Clark, it's the best of its kind and inspired the long-running television series "Happy Days." Rated PG.

1973   110 minutes

AMERICATHON
🎭

DIRECTOR: Neal Israel
CAST: John Ritter, Harvey Korman, Nancy Morgan, Peter Riegert, Zane Buzby, Fred Willard, Chief Dan George

Before managing to entertain audiences with such questionable movies as *Bachelor Party* and *Moving Violations*, director Neal Israel made this absolutely abysmal comedy about a bankrupt American government staging a telethon to save itself. Rated R for profanity and sleaze.

1979   86 minutes

AND NOW FOR SOMETHING COMPLETELY DIFFERENT
★★★½

DIRECTOR: Ian McNaughton
CAST: John Cleese, Eric Idle, Terry Jones, Michael Palin, Graham Chapman, Terry Gilliam

Fitfully funny but still a treat for their fans, this was the first screen outing of the Monty Python comedy troupe. It's a collection of the best bits from the team's television series. With delightful ditties, such as "The Lumberjack Song," how can you go wrong? Rated PG.

1972   89 minutes

ANIMAL CRACKERS
★★★★

DIRECTOR: Victor Heerman
CAST: The Marx Brothers, Margaret Dumont, Lillian Roth, Robert Greig, Hal Thompson, Louis Sorin

Animal Crackers is pure Marx Brothers, a total farce loosely based on a hit play by George S. Kaufman. Highlights include Groucho's African lecture—"One morning I shot an elephant in my pajamas. How he got into my pajamas, I'll never know"—and the uproariously funny card game with Harpo, Chico, and the ever-put-upon Margaret Dumont.

1930   B & W   98 minutes

ANIMAL HOUSE
★★★★½

DIRECTOR: John Landis
CAST: John Belushi, Tim Matheson, Karen Allen, Peter Riegert, John Vernon

Although it has spawned a seemingly relentless onslaught of inferior carbon copies, this comedy is still one of the funniest movies ever made. If you're into rock 'n' roll, partying, and general craziness, this picture—directed by John Landis (*The Blues Brothers*)—is for you. We gave it a 95, because it has a good beat and you can dance to it. The late John Belushi, Tim Matheson, Karen Allen (*Raiders of the Lost Ark*), Peter Riegert (*Local Hero*), and John Vernon all are terrific in this story of a wild college fraternity that gets put on "double secret probation" and, of course, blows it. But guess who gets the last laugh. Rated R.

1978 109 minutes

ANNIE HALL
★★★★★

DIRECTOR: Woody Allen

CAST: Woody Allen, Diane Keaton, Tony Roberts, Paul Simon, Shelley Duvall, Carol Kane

Woody Allen's exquisite romantic comedy won the 1977 Academy Awards for best picture, actress (Diane Keaton), director (Allen), and screenplay (Allen and Marshall Brickman)—and deserved every one of them. This delightful semiautobiographical romp features Allen as Alvy Singer, a more assured version of Alan Felix, from *Play It Again Sam*, who falls in love (again) with Keaton (in the title role), proving that a kiss is still just a kiss—and wonderfully entertaining when in a classic motion picture. Rated PG for profanity and bedroom scenes.

1977 94 minutes

A NOUS LA LIBERTE
★★½

DIRECTOR: Rene Claire

CAST: Raymond Cordy, Henri Marchand

Louis and Emile are two prisoners who plan an escape. Only Louis gets away and, surprisingly, he becomes a rich, successful businessman. When Emile gets released, he seeks romantic advice from his friend, but trouble arises when other ex-cons threaten to expose Louis. There are some slapstick segments, and many believe that this film was the inspiration for Charlie Chaplin's *Modern Times*. In French, with English subtitles.

1931 B & W 87 minutes

ANY WHICH WAY YOU CAN
★

DIRECTOR: Buddy Van Horn

CAST: Clint Eastwood, Sondra Locke, Geoffrey Lewis, William Smith, Ruth Gordon

Another comedy clinker from Clint Eastwood and company, this features the same cast and story (about the adventures of a streetfighter and his pet orangutan) from *Every Which Way But Loose*, a movie that wasn't very good to begin with. Aside from a few funny moments provided by Clyde (the orangutan), it's a waste. Rated PG.

1980 116 minutes

APARTMENT, THE
★★★★★

DIRECTOR: Billy Wilder

CAST: Jack Lemmon, Shirley MacLaine, Fred MacMurray, Ray Walston, Jack Kruschen, Edie Adams

Rarely have comedy and drama been satisfyingly blended into a cohesive whole. Director Billy Wilder does it masterfully in this film. With career advancement in mind, Jack Lemmon permits his boss (Fred MacMurray) to use his apartment for illicit love affairs. Then he gets involved with the boss's emotionally distraught girlfriend (Shirley MacLaine). Lemmon sparkles. MacLaine is irresistible. And MacMurray, playing a heel, is a revelation.

Beautifully balancing wit and pathos, the film bears repeated viewing.

1960   B & W 125 minutes

ARMED AND DANGEROUS
★★

DIRECTOR: Mark L. Lester
CAST: John Candy, Eugene Levy, Robert Loggia, Kenneth McMillan, Meg Ryan, Jonathan Banks, Brion James

Comedy fizzle from two talented SCTV graduates whose theatrical films have consistently fallen short of their usually hilarious TV sketches and bits. The story concerns fired cop Frank Dooley (John Candy) and former lawyer Norman Kane (Eugene Levy), who meet and become partners at their new jobs as private security guards for a firm known as Guard Dog. When Dooley uncovers an embezzling plot by the owner of the company (Robert Loggia), the pair find themselves in a real mess. There are a few comedic gems, to be sure, but most of the gags are just rehashed from countless other films of this sort, and the obligatory slapstick chase finale in which numerous perfectly good cars are demolished is simply too much. Rated PG-13 for language.

1986   89 minutes

AROUND THE WORLD IN 80 DAYS
★★★

DIRECTOR: Michael Anderson
CAST: David Niven, Cantinflas, Shirley MacLaine, Marlene Dietrich, Robert Newton

An all-star spectacular with David Niven, Cantinflas, and Shirley MacLaine in the pivotal roles, this inflated travelogue was a spectacular success when originally released. However, it seems hopelessly dated today and loses all too much on the small screen. Even picking out the dozens of stars in cameo roles doesn't yield as much joy under the plodding direction of Michael Anderson as it could have. It's a curiosity at best.

1956   167 minutes

ARSENIC AND OLD LACE
★★★★½

DIRECTOR: Frank Capra
CAST: Cary Grant, Priscilla Lane, Jack Carson, James Gleason, Peter Lorre, Raymond Massey, Jean Adair, Josephine Hull

Two sweet old ladies have found a solution for the loneliness of elderly men with no family or friends—they poison them! Then they give them a proper Christian burial in their basement. Their nephew, Mortimer (Cary Grant), an obvious party pooper, finds out and wants them to stop. This delightful comedy is crammed with sparkling performances. Jean Adair and Josephine Hull re-create their Broadway roles as the daffy sisters. Peter Lorre, Raymond Massey, and Jack Carson also add some memorable characterizations to this screen version of the Joseph Kesselring play.

1944   B & W 118 minutes

ARTHUR
★★★★

DIRECTOR: Steve Gordon
CAST: Dudley Moore, Liza Minnelli, Stephen Elliott, John Gielgud

Dudley Moore is Arthur, the world's richest (and obviously happiest) alcoholic. But all is not well in his pickled paradise. Arthur will lose access to the family's great wealth if he doesn't marry the uptight debutante picked out for him by his parents. He doesn't love her...in fact, he doesn't even like her. And what's worse, he's in love with a wacky shoplifter (Liza Minnelli). Most of the time, it's hilarious, with John Gielgud as a sharp-tongued butler providing the majority of the laughs. Rated PG because of profanity.

1981   97 minutes

ATOLL K (UTOPIA)
👎

DIRECTOR: Léo Joannon
CAST: Stan Laurel, Oliver Hardy

The final screen outing of the great comedy team of Stan Laurel and Oliver Hardy is a keen disappointment. Laurel became ill during its making and looks just awful (making his crying scenes more sad than funny). It's a regrettable final bow for two of the screen's greatest clowns.

1950   B & W   80 minutes

ATTACK OF THE KILLER TOMATOES
👎

DIRECTOR: John De Bello
CAST: David Miller, Sharon Taylor, George Wilson, Jack Riley

In this campy cult film, the tomatoes are funnier than the actors, most of whom are rank amateurs. Jack Riley, of the first "Bob Newhart" television show, supplies the few moments of subtle comic timing as an agriculture department official. Unfortunately for him and the viewers, he is killed by thousands of squished tomatoes. George Wilson, as presidential aide Jim Richardson, is not bad either. There is little that they can do to soften the bludgeoning sophomoric comedy of the screenplay. The plot? Killer tomatoes begin terrorizing the western United

States while the military plans inept strategies. Rated PG.

1980   87 minutes

AT THE CIRCUS
★★★½

DIRECTOR: Edward Buzzell
CAST: The Marx Brothers, Margaret Dumont, Kenny Baker, Eve Arden

The Marx Brothers were running out of steam as a comedy team by the time of this film. Still, any film with Groucho, Harpo, and Chico is worth watching, although you'll probably feel like punching the comedy's "hero" (or is that a zero?), Kenny Baker, when he sings that highly forgettable ditty "Step Up, Take a Bow."

1939   B & W   87 minutes

AT WAR WITH THE ARMY
★★★★

DIRECTOR: Hal Walker
CAST: Dean Martin, Jerry Lewis, Polly Bergen, Angela Greene, Mike Kellin

Dean Martin and Jerry Lewis were still fresh and funny at the time of this comedy release, but a classic it isn't (though some scenes are gems).

1950   B & W   93 minutes

AUDIENCE WITH MEL BROOKS, AN
★★★½

DIRECTOR: Mel Brooks
CAST: Mel Brooks

This is a reserved, delightfully anecdotal evening with the comic genius. Filmed in England, it features Brooks answering questions from the audience about his career, life, and famous collaborators. There are a few clips from his version of To Be or Not to Be, which smacks a little too much of self-promotion. However, it's one of the better comedy videos, primarily because it features the master of the ad-lib at his funniest. Unrated.

1984   55 minutes

AUNTIE MAME
★★★½

DIRECTOR: Morton Da Costa
CAST: Rosalind Russell, Forrest Tucker, Coral Brown, Fred Clark

Rosalind Russell, in the title role, plays a free-thinking eccentric woman whose young nephew is placed in her care. Russell created the role on the stage; it was a once-in-a-lifetime showcase that she made uniquely her own.

1958   143 minutes

AUTHOR! AUTHOR!
★★★

DIRECTOR: Arthur Hiller
CAST: Al Pacino, Dyan Cannon, Alan King, Tuesday Weld

Al Pacino stars as a playwright whose wife (Tuesday Weld) leaves him with five kids (not all his) to raise in this nicely done bittersweet comedy. Dyan Cannon plays the actress with whom he falls in love. Rated PG for brief profanity.

1982   110 minutes

AVIATOR'S WIFE, THE
★★★½

DIRECTOR: Eric Rohmer
CAST: Philippe Marlaud, Marie Riviere, Anne-Laure Marie, Matthieu Carrière

Not much happens in a film by French director Eric Rohmer, at least not in the traditional sense. Mostly, there's just talk. Yet if you pay close attention, a few special things do happen—and they are quite enough. In the story, a young law student named Francois (Philippe Marlaud) is crushed when he discovers his lover, Anne (Marie Riviere), in the company of another man and decides to spy on them. In French with English subtitles. Unrated, the film has no objectionable material.

1981   104 minutes

BACHELOR AND THE BOBBY-SOXER
★★½

DIRECTOR: Irving Reis
CAST: Cary Grant, Myrna Loy, Shirley Temple, Rudy Vallee

Lady judge Myrna Loy cleverly sentences playboy Cary Grant to baby-sit Shirley Temple, her sister, a panting nubile teenager with a crush on him. There are some hilarious moments, but the comedy gets thin as Loy's lesson begins to cloy. Best bit is the play on words about the Man with the Power, Voodoo and Youdo.

1947   B & W   95 minutes

BACHELOR PARTY
★★

DIRECTOR: Neil Israel
CAST: Tom Hanks, Tawny Kitaen, Adrian Zmed, George Grizzard, Robert Prescott

Even Tom Hanks (of *Splash*) can't save this "wild" escapade into degradation when a carefree bus driver who has decided to get married is given an all-out bachelor party by his friends. Rated R for profanity and nudity.

1984   106 minutes

BACK TO SCHOOL
★★★½

DIRECTOR: Alan Metter

CAST: Rodney Dangerfield, Sally Kellerman, Burt Young, Keith Gordon, Robert Downey Jr., Ned Betty, M. Emmet Walsh, Adrienne Barbeau, William Zabka, Severn Darden

A true surprise from the usually acerbic Rodney Dangerfield, who sheds his lewd-'n-crude image in favor of one more sympathetic and controlled. He stars as the self-made owner of a chain of "Tall and Fat" stores who decides to return to college for a never-achieved diploma. He selects the college attended by his son in order to spend more time with the boy (well played, with eyes that frequently roll heavenward, by Keith Gordon). The story then focuses on their differing approaches to life: Gordon wants his own victories or failures, but Dangerfield prefers to buy his way through life.... He even hires Kurt Vonnegut (who appears as himself) to write an English report, which is rejected for being an obvious crib job by "somebody who knows nothing about the author." Rated PG-13 for occasionally vulgar humor.

1986   96 minutes

BAD MEDICINE
★★★½
DIRECTOR: Harvey Miller
CAST: Steve Guttenberg, Julie Hagerty, Alan Arkin, Bill Macy, Curtis Armstrong, Julie Kavner, Joe Grifasi, Robert Romanus, Taylor Negron

Steve Guttenberg (*Cocoon, Diner*) and Julie Hagerty (*Lost in America*, the *Airplane* movies) play students attending a "Mickey Mouse" med school in Central America. When they find the health conditions in a nearby village unacceptable, they set up a medical clinic, stealing the needed drugs from the school's pharmacy. The all-star cast does not disappoint. Alan Arkin's role as the owner of the school is especially fine. Rated PG-13 for profanity, sex, and adult situations.

1985   97 minutes

BAD NEWS BEARS, THE
★★★★★
DIRECTOR: Michael Ritchie
CAST: Walter Matthau, Tatum O'-Neal, Vic Morrow, Alfred Lutter

An utterly hilarious comedy directed by Michael Ritchie, this film focuses on the antics of some foul-mouthed Little Leaguers, their beer-guzzling coach (Walter Matthau), and girl pitcher (Tatum O'-Neal). But be forewarned, the sequels, *Breaking Training* and *The Bad News Bears Go to Japan*, are strictly no-hitters. Rated PG.

1976   102 minutes

BAD NEWS BEARS GO TO JAPAN, THE
★★
DIRECTOR: John Berry
CAST: Tony Curtis, Jackie Earle Haley, Tomisaburo Wakayama, George Wyner, Lonnie Chapman

Worst of the *Bad News Bears* trio of films, this features Tony Curtis as a small-time promoter with big ideas, which involve taking the unpredictable (but now sanitized) pint-size ball team to Japan. Unfunny and too cutesy, it was their last screen romp. Rated PG.

1978   91 minutes

BAD NEWS BEARS IN BREAKING TRAINING, THE
★★
DIRECTOR: Michael Pressman
CAST: William Devane, Jackie Earle Haley, Clifton James

Without Walter Matthau, Tatum O'Neal, and director Michael Ritchie, this sequel to *The Bad News Bears* truly is bad news...and rather idiotic. How many kids do *you* know who'd be allowed to hop into a minibus and drive to Houston *sans* adult supervision? Jackie Earle Haley returns as the team star, and William Devane has a reasonable part as Haley's footloose father. Don't expect much. Rated PG for mild language.

1977   100 minutes

BAKER'S WIFE, THE
★★★★

DIRECTOR: Marcel Pagnol

CAST: Raimu, Ginette Leclerc, Charles Moulin, Robert Battier, Robert Brassac, Charpin

The new baker is coming to a town that has been without fresh-baked goods for too long. With great fanfare, the baker and his new wife arrive, but she has a roving eye for another. Caught in an upheaval of emotions, the baker begins to function badly in his kitchen after his wife leaves. This comedy is a gem of French film-making. In French with English subtitles.

1938   B & W 124 minutes

BALL OF FIRE
★★★½

DIRECTOR: Howard Hawks

CAST: Gary Cooper, Barbara Stanwyck, Dana Andrews, Oscar Homolka, S. Z. Sakall, Richard Haydn, Henry Travers, Tully Marshall, Leonid Kinskey, Allen Jenkins, Aubrey Mather

Stuffy linguistics professor Gary Cooper meets hotch-cha dancer Barbara Stanwyck. He and seven lovable colleagues are putting together an encyclopedia. She's recruited to fill them in on slanguage. She does this, and more! Gangster Dana Andrews and motor-mouthed garbage man Allen Jenkins add to the madcap antics in what has been dubbed the last of the prewar screwball comedies. Good show!

1941   B & W 111 minutes

BANANAS
★★★★

DIRECTOR: Woody Allen

CAST: Woody Allen, Louise Lasser, Carlos Montalban, Howard Cosell

Before he started making classic comedies, such as *Annie Hall*, *Zelig*, and *Broadway Danny Rose*, writer-director-star Woody Allen made some pretty wild—though generally uneven—wacky movies. This 1971 comedy, with Woody's hapless hero becoming involved in a South American revolution, does have its share of hilarious moments. It is, in fact, one of the better examples of Allen's early experiments in laugh-getting and film-making. Rated PG.

1971   82 minutes

BANK DICK, THE
★★★★★

DIRECTOR: Eddie Cline

CAST: W. C. Fields, Cora Witherspoon, Una Merkel, Shemp Howard

W. C. Fields is at his best in this laugh-filled comedy. In it, Fields plays a drunkard who becomes a hero. But the story is just an excuse for the moments of hilarity—of which there are many.

1940   B & W 74 minutes

BAREFOOT IN THE PARK
★★★★½

DIRECTOR: Gene Saks

CAST: Robert Redford, Jane Fonda, Charles Boyer, Mildred Natwick, Herb Edelman

A young Robert Redford and Jane Fonda team up as newlyweds in this adaptation of Neil Simon's Broadway play. The comedy focuses on the adjustments of married life. Ethel Banks and Mildred Natwick play the mothers-in-law, and Charles Boyer is a daffy, unconventional neighbor.

1967   105 minutes

BEACH GIRLS, THE
★½
DIRECTOR: Pat Townsend
CAST: Debra Blee, Val Kline, Jeana Tomasina

Dumb sex comedy about a couple of teen-age girls who throw a big party at Uncle's Malibu beach house while he's away. Typical unrealistic nonsense. Rated R for nudity.

1982   91 minutes

BEAT THE DEVIL
★★★★
DIRECTOR: John Huston
CAST: Humphrey Bogart, Robert Morley, Peter Lorre, Jennifer Jones, Gina Lollobrigida, Edward Underdown, Ivor Bernard, Marco Tulli

Because it's all played straight, critics and audiences alike didn't know what to make of this delightful though at times baffling satire of films in the vein of *The Maltese Falcon* and *Key Largo* when it first hit screens. Sadly, some still do not. Nonetheless, this droll comedy, cobbled on location in Italy by John Huston and Truman Capote, is a twenty-four-carat gem. It has everything: a once rich, now broke fortune hunter; four disparate and desperate international crooks; a paranoiac hit man; a chronic liar; an airheaded fake British peer; and assorted accented characters. Steadily mounting appreciation has made this a solidly statured cult film. Humphrey Bogart said "only the phonies" liked it, but cynicism isn't criticism. In a unique context, "Try posting" is one of filmdom's all-time hilarious great lines.

1954   B & W   93 minutes

BEAU PERE
★★★★
DIRECTOR: Bernard Blier
CAST: Patrick Dewaere, Ariel Besse, Maurice Ronet, Nicole Garcia

Patrick Dewaere stars again for French director Bernard Blier (*Get Out Your Handkerchiefs*) in this film, about a stepfather who falls in love with his adopted pubescent daughter. It could have been shocking—or just plain perverse. But *Beau Pere* is nothing of the sort. Rather, it is a bittersweet, thoroughly charming motion picture. Blier handles the subject with such wit, humor, and inventiveness that it never descends into the realms of exploitation or bad taste. In French, with English subtitles. Unrated, the film has nudity, profanity, and adult themes.

1982   120 minutes

BEDAZZLED
★★★★
DIRECTOR: Stanley Donen
CAST: Peter Cook, Dudley Moore, Raquel Welch, Eleanor Bron

A cult favorite, this British comedy stars Dudley Moore as a fry cook tempted by the devil (played by his one-time comedy partner, Peter Cook). Co-starring Raquel Welch, it's an often-hilarious updating of the Faust legend.

1967   107 minutes

BEDTIME FOR BONZO
★★★

DIRECTOR: Frederick De Cordova
CAST: Ronald Reagan, Diana Lynn, Walter Slezak, Jesse White, Lucille Barkley

This film is worth watching just to look at Ronald Reagan before his political career began. He plays a young college professor who uses a chimpanzee to prove that environment, not heredity, determines a person's moral fiber. He hires a young woman (Diana Lynn) to pose as the chimp's mom while he plays father to it. Not surprisingly, Mom and Dad fall in love. Walter Slezak adds some funny moments with his mispronunciations and comic expressions.

1951   B & W   83 minutes

BEER
★★★★

DIRECTOR: Patrick Kelly
CAST: Loretta Swit, Rip Torn, Kenneth Mars, David Alan Grier, William Russ, Saul Stein, Peter Michael Goetz, Dick Shawn

Hilarious comedy that examines the seamy side of the advertising industry. Loretta Swit plays a cold-blooded advertising agent who tries to turn three ordinary guys (David Alan Grier, William Russ, and Saul Stein) into beer-drinking American heroes. The plan works, and soon they are the talk of the country. If you think the beer commercials on television are sexist and macho, wait until you see this. The controversy over the regressive attitudes in these ads is central to the film's theme. Rip Torn is excellent as the alcoholic director of the commercials. Dick Shawn's impression of Phil Donahue must be seen to be believed.

Rated R for profanity, sex, and adult subject matter.

1985   83 minutes

BEING THERE
★★★★½

DIRECTOR: Hal Ashby
CAST: Peter Sellers, Shirley MacLaine, Melvyn Douglas, Jack Warden

This sublimely funny and bitingly satiric comedy features Peter Sellers's last great screen performance. It's too bad that it, rather than the abysmal *Fiendish Plot of Dr. Fu Manchu*, will not be remembered as his final bow. His portrayal of a simple-minded gardener—who knows only what he sees on television yet rises to great political heights—is a classic. Shirley MacLaine and Melvyn Douglas are also excellent in this memorable film, directed by Hal Ashby (*Harold and Maude*). Rated PG.

1979   130 minutes

BELL, BOOK AND CANDLE
★★★½

DIRECTOR: Richard Quine
CAST: James Stewart, Kim Novak, Jack Lemmon, Ernie Kovacs

A modestly entertaining bit of whimsy about a beautiful witch (Kim Novak) who works her magic on an unsuspecting publisher (James Stewart). Although the performances (including those in support by Jack Lemmon, Ernie Kovacs, and Hermione Gingold) are fine, this comedy is only mildly diverting.

1958   103 minutes

BELLBOY, THE
★★

DIRECTOR: Jerry Lewis

CAST: Jerry Lewis, Alex Gerry, Sonny Sands

A typical hour-plus of Jerry Lewis mugging and antics so dear to those who find him funny. This time around, Jerry is a bellboy at a swank Miami Beach hotel. Years ago, "Fatty" Arbuckle made a film of the same name that was funny. This, unfortunately, is plotless drivel seasoned with guest appearances by Milton Berle and Walter Winchell. Rated G when rereleased in 1972.

1960   B & W   72 minutes

BELLES OF ST. TRINIAN'S, THE
★★★½

DIRECTOR: Frank Launder
CAST: Alastair Sim, Joyce Grenfell, Hermione Baddeley, George Cole

Alastair Sim doubles as the dotty headmistress of a bonkers school for girls and her crafty bookie brother, who wants to use the place as a cover for his nefarious operations. Joyce Grenfell adds to the hilarity in this British comedy based on English cartoonist Ronald Searle's schoolgirls with a genius for mischief.

1955   B & W   90 minutes

BELLISSIMA
★★★

DIRECTOR: Luchino Visconti
CAST: Anna Magnani, Walter Chiari, Tina Apicella

Luchino Visconti is known for such pioneering works as *Ossessione*, *La Terra Trema*, *Rocco and His Brothers*, *The Damned* and *Death in Venice*. As for *Bellissima*, if you are programming an Anna Magnani festival, you might be interested in this oddly and determinedly lightweight comedy. Otherwise, there is not much going for this offbeat trifle. The story is set in the Cinecitta Studios, where a search is on for the prettiest child in Rome. Magnani seems a bit out of place as an earnest neo-realist mother who enters her daughter, only to get trapped in a stampede of hysterical stage mothers and contestants. In Italian with English subtitles.

1951   B & W   95 minutes

BEST DEFENSE
★★★

DIRECTOR: Willard Huyck
CAST: Dudley Moore, Eddie Murphy, Kate Capshaw, George Dzundza, Helen Sharler

Any movie that features the combined talents of Dudley Moore and Eddie Murphy has to be funny. Sometimes, however, laughs aren't enough. It's very easy to get confused, as the story jumps back and forth between the 1982 segments, featuring Moore as the inept inventor of a malfunctioning piece of defense equipment, and the 1984 footage, with Murphy as the hapless soldier forced to cope with it. Another minus is that the stars never have a scene together. Still, *Best Defense* works fairly often, although the liberal use of profanity and several sex scenes make this R-rated romp unfit for youngsters.

1984   94 minutes

BEST FRIENDS
★★

DIRECTOR: Norman Jewison
CAST: Burt Reynolds, Goldie Hawn, Ron Silver, Jessica Tandy

Burt Reynolds and Goldie Hawn star in this disappointingly tepid romantic comedy as a pair of successful screenwriters who decide to marry—thus destroying their profitable working relationship.

Rated PG for profanity and adult situations.

1982　　　　　　　　116 minutes

BEST OF TIMES, THE
★★★

DIRECTOR: Roger Spottiswoode
CAST: Robin Williams, Kurt Russell, Pamela Reed, Holly Palance, Donald Moffat, Margaret Whitton, M. Emmet Walsh, R. G. Armstrong, Dub Taylor

This comedy starts off well, then continues to lose momentum right up to the *Rocky*-style ending. That said, it is an amiable enough little movie which benefits from likable performances by its lead players. Robin Williams and Kurt Russell star as two former football players who dropped the ball when their moment for hometown glory came and went. But they get a second chance to win one for the folks in Taft (formerly Moron), California. Rated PG-13 for profanity and suggested sex.

1986　　　　　　　　100 minutes

BETTER LATE THAN NEVER
★★½

DIRECTOR: Richard Crenna
CAST: Harold Gould, Larry Storch, Strother Martin, Tyne Daly, Harry Morgan, Victor Buono, George Gobel, Donald Pleasence, Lou Jacobi

Your average made-for-television comedy about a motley mixture of nursing home inhabitants who revolt against house rules that limit their freedom. The premise is good, the execution so-so. Theft of a train is a nice touch. Rated PG.

1979　　　　　　　　100 minutes

BETTER OFF DEAD
★★

DIRECTOR: Savage Steve Holland
CAST: John Cusack, David Ogden Stiers, Diane Franklin, Kim Darby, Amanda Wyss

A mixture of clever ideas and awfully silly ones, this comedy focuses on the plight of teen-age Everyman, Lance Meyer (John Cusack), who finds his world shattered when the love of his life, Beth (Amanda Wyss), takes up with a conceited jock. Lance figures he is "Better Off Dead" than Bethless. The film is at its best when writer-director Savage Steve Holland throws in little sketches that stand out from the familiar plot. For some of these, he uses animation in highly original ways. *Better Off Dead* is sometimes gross and predictable, but there are some little gems of hilarity scattered throughout. Rated PG for profanity.

1985　　　　　　　　97 minutes

BEVERLY HILLS COP
★★★★

DIRECTOR: Martin Brest
CAST: Eddie Murphy, Lisa Eilbacher, Judge Reinhold, John Ashton

In this highly entertaining cops-and-comedy caper, Eddie Murphy plays a street-wise policeman from the East Coast who takes a leave of absence to track down the men who killed his best friend. This quest takes him to the unfamiliar hills of ritzy Southern California, where he's greeted as anything but a hero. Rated R for violence and profanity.

1984　　　　　　　　105 minutes

BIG TROUBLE
★★

DIRECTOR: John Cassavetes

CAST: Peter Falk, Alan Arkin, Beverly D'Angelo, Charles Durning, Robert Stack, Paul Dooley, Valerie Curtin, Richard Libertint

While this movie may be a major disappointment, this is so only because we expect more of the outstanding cast. *Big Trouble* has its moments, but alas, they are few and far between. Alan Arkin is an honest insurance salesman trying to put his three talented sons through Yale. When he meets up with a rich married woman (Beverly D'Angelo), the two plot against her husband (Peter Falk). Crazy plots twists abound, but none of them are all that funny. Director John Cassavetes tries to create a comic mood similar to director Arthur Hiller's *The In-Laws*, in which Falk and Arkin also starred. But he never comes close. Rated R for profanity and adult subject matter.

1985   93 minutes

BIG BUS, THE
★★★

DIRECTOR: James Frawley
CAST: Joseph Bologna, Stockard Channing, John Beck, Lynn Redgrave, José Ferrer, Ruth Gordon, Richard B. Shull, Sally Kellerman, Ned Beatty, Richard Mulligan, Larry Hagman, Howard Hesseman, Harold Gould

A super-luxurious nuclear-powered bus runs into trouble while carrying a group of misfits from New York to Denver. This spoof of disaster movies appeared four years before *Airplane!*. It's not as funny or as tightly paced, but it does have a silly and sarcastic playfulness that grows on you. One of those few films that work better on the small screen. Rated PG.

1976   88 minutes

BILL COSBY—HIMSELF
★★★★

DIRECTOR: William H. Cosby Jr.
CAST: Bill Cosby

The wit and wisdom of Bill Cosby on the subjects of childbirth, raising a family (and being raised), going to the dentist, taking drugs and drinking, and life in general provide laughs and food for thought in this excellent comedy video. One can see how the hugely successful television series "The Cosby Show" evolved from his family and observations of their behavior. Rated G.

1985   104 minutes

BINGO LONG TRAVELING ALL-STARS AND MOTOR KINGS, THE
★★★

DIRECTOR: John Badham
CAST: Billy Dee Williams, James Earl Jones, Richard Pryor, Ted Ross

This is a comedy-adventure of a barnstorming group of black baseball players as they tour rural America in the late 1930s. Billy Dee Williams, Richard Pryor, and James Earl Jones are three of the team's players and must resort to conniving, clowning, and conning to ensure their team's survival. Only the lack of a cohesive script keeps this from receiving a few more stars. Rated PG.

1976   110 minutes

BISHOP'S WIFE, THE
★★★

DIRECTOR: Henry Koster
CAST: Cary Grant, Loretta Young, David Niven, James Gleason

Harmless story of debonair angel (Cary Grant) sent to Earth to aid a bishop (David Niven) in his quest for a new church. The kind of film they just don't make anymore. No rating, but okay for the whole family.

1947   B & W   108 minutes

BLACK BIRD, THE
★★★

DIRECTOR: David Giler
CAST: George Segal, Stéphane Audran, Lionel Stander, Lee Patrick

Surprisingly enjoyable comedy produced by and starring George Segal as Sam Spade Jr. The visual gags abound, and an air of authenticity is added by the performances of 1940s detective film regulars Lionel Stander, Elisha Cook, and Lee Patrick. The latter two co-starred with Humphrey Bogart in *The Maltese Falcon*, on which the film is based. It's funny, with a strong performance from Segal. This film continues the pursuit of the multi-jeweled prize bird. Rated PG.

1975   98 minutes

BLAME IT ON RIO
★★½

DIRECTOR: Stanley Donen
CAST: Michael Caine, Joseph Bologna, Valerie Harper, Michelle Johnson

A middle-aged male sex fantasy directed by Stanley Donen (*Lucky Lady*; *Charade*), this film—which equally combines both good and bad elements—features Michael Caine as a befuddled fellow who finds himself involved in an affair with the teen-age daughter (Michelle Johnson) of his best friend (Joseph Bologna). Although essentially in bad taste, *Blame It on Rio* does have a number of very funny moments. Rated R for nudity, profanity, and suggested sex.

1984   110 minutes

BLAZING SADDLES
★★★½

DIRECTOR: Mel Brooks
CAST: Cleavon Little, Gene Wilder, Harvey Korman, Madeline Kahn, Mel Brooks, Slim Pickens

Mel Brooks directed this sometimes hilarious, mostly crude spoof of westerns. The jokes come with machine-gun rapidity, and the stars race around like maniacs. If it weren't in such bad taste, it would be perfect for the kiddies. Rated R.

1974   93 minutes

BLOCK-HEADS
★★★★

DIRECTOR: John G. Blystone
CAST: Stan Laurel, Oliver Hardy, Patricia Ellis, Minna Gombell, Billy Gilbert, James Finlayson

Twenty years after the end of World War I, Stan Laurel is discovered still guarding a bunker. He returns to a veterans' home, where Oliver Hardy comes to visit and take him to dinner. A well-crafted script provides the perfect setting for the boys' escapades. Their characters have seldom been used as well in feature films.

1938   B & W   55 minutes

BLOODBATH AT THE HOUSE OF DEATH
★★

DIRECTOR: Ray Cameron
CAST: Vincent Price, Kenny Everett, Pamela Stephenson, Gareth Hunt, Don Warrington, John Fortune, Sheila Steafel

Although advertised as one, this British movie is not all that much of a spoof on horror films. There is realistic gore (especially in the opening scene, where the film lives up to its not-so-ironic title), and near the film's end the camp antics turn serious. In the story, a team of paranormal specialists investigates a house that was the scene of a mysterious massacre. Vincent Price plays a nutty devil worshiper who plots to get rid of the snoopy scientists who are inhabiting this house of Satan. As in most good parodies, the film draws liberally from the genre it's poking fun at. (Scenes from *Carrie*, *Poltergeist*, and *Alien* are used.) Science fiction is also spoofed (*Star Wars*). But borrowing shticks from Mel Brooks and the *Airplane* films is no fair. Not rated, but equivalent to an R for violence, gore, sex, nudity, and profanity.

1985   92 minutes

BLUE MONEY
★★★

DIRECTOR: Colin Bucksey
CAST: Tim Curry, Debby Bishop, Billy Connolly, Dermot Crowley, Frances Tomelty, George Irving, John Bind

Larry Gormley (Tim Curry) discovers a suitcase with half a million dollars in his cab. The money turns out to belong to the mob, and they want it back. Not a very original idea, but well written, acted, and directed, this comedy provides plenty of fast-moving fun. Made for British television.

1984   82 minutes

BLUES BROTHERS, THE
★★★★½

DIRECTOR: John Landis
CAST: John Belushi, Dan Aykroyd, John Candy, Carrie Fisher

Director John Landis attempted to film an epic comedy and came pretty darn close. In it, the musicians of the title, John Belushi and Dan Aykroyd, attempt to save an orphanage. The movie's excesses—too many car crashes and chases—are offset by Belushi and Aykroyd as the Laurel and Hardy of backbeat; the musical turns of Aretha Franklin, James Brown, and Ray Charles; and Landis's flair for comic timing. Rated R.

1980   132 minutes

BOB & CAROL & TED & ALICE
★★★★½

DIRECTOR: Paul Mazursky
CAST: Natalie Wood, Robert Culp, Elliott Gould, Dyan Cannon

In this comedy, Natalie Wood and Robert Culp (Carol and Bob) play a modern couple who believe in open marriage, pot-smoking, etc. Their friends, conservative Elliott Gould and Dyan Cannon (Ted and Alice), are shocked by Bob and Carol's behavior. Meanwhile, Bob and Carol try to liven up Ted and Alice's marriage by introducing them to their way of life. Lots of funny moments. Rated R.

1969   104 minutes

BOBO, THE
★

DIRECTOR: Robert Parrish
CAST: Peter Sellers, Britt Ekland, Rossano Brazzi

A bumbling matador (Peter Sellers) has to seduce a high-priced courtesan (Britt Ekland) in order to get employment as a singer. If this plot sounds stupid, then you have reached the core of this hopeless movie.

1967   105 minutes

BOCCACCIO 70
★★★★

DIRECTOR: Federico Fellini, Luchino Visconti, Vittorio De Sica

CAST: Anita Ekberg, Sophia Loren, Romy Schneider, Peppino De Filippo, Dante Maggio, Tomas Milian

As with its Renaissance namesake, this film tells stories—three of them, in fact, by three of Italy's greatest directors. Each has a trademark on his entry. Federico Fellini's entry, "The Temptation of Dr. Antonio," showcases Peppino De Filippo as the puritanical bluenose who becomes obsessed with a billboard that comes to life in the voluptuous form of a young Anita Ekberg. The second playlete, by Luchino Visconti, is "The Bet," which features Romy Schneider as a not-so-typical housewife who takes over the position (excuse the expression) of her husband's mistress. A funnier chain of events could not be imagined. The third entry, "The Raffle," by Vittorio De Sica, is pure farce and has wisely been left for last. The treatment of this story is reminiscent of a dirty joke told badly, and it tends to cheapen the panache of the first two. However, any film with Sophia Loren is worth watching, and this one is no exception. In Italian with English subtitles.

1962   165 minutes

BOHEMIAN GIRL, THE
★★★

DIRECTOR: James W. Horne, Charles R. Rogers
CAST: Stan Laurel, Oliver Hardy, Thelma Todd, Antonio Moreno

Laurel and Hardy portray gypsies in this typical tale of the gypsy band versus the country officials. A variety of misadventures occur, and the film is entertaining, especially with the hilarious scene of Stan attempting to fill wine bottles and

becoming more and more inebriated.

1936   B & W   70 minutes

BORN YESTERDAY
★★★★½

DIRECTOR: George Cukor
CAST: Judy Holliday, William Holden, Broderick Crawford, Howard St. John

Judy Holliday is simply delightful as a dizzy dame who isn't as dizzy as everyone thinks she is, in this comedy directed by George Cukor. William Holden is the professor hired by a junk-dealer-made-good (Broderick Crawford) to give Holliday lessons in how to be "high-toned." The results are highly entertaining—and very funny.

1950   B & W   103 minutes

BOUDU SAVED FROM DROWNING
★★★★★

DIRECTOR: Jean Renoir
CAST: Michel Simon, Charles Granval, Max Dalban, Jean Daste

This is the original *Down and Out in Beverly Hills*, except that the tramp (the beloved Michel Simon) is saved by an antiquarian bookseller after a suicide attempt in the Seine—down and out in Paris. As in the 1985 version, Boudu is taken into the rescuer's house and seduces the wife and maid. But here he marries the maid, then accidentally falls in the river after the ceremony and rediscovers his own brand of freedom. Unlike the play on which it was based and unlike the Hollywood version—both of which have the bum accept his responsibilities—*Boudu Saved from Drowning* is a celebration of joyful anarchy, and Simon's interpretation of his role is enchanting. A masterpiece. In French, with English subtitles.

1932   B & W   88 minutes

BOY, DID I GET A WRONG NUMBER!
🦃

DIRECTOR: George Marshall
CAST: Bob Hope, Elke Sommer, Phyllis Diller

When you get a wrong number, hang up and dial again. Too bad the cast and director didn't. This one is a bomb!

1966   99 minutes

BRAZIL
★★★★

DIRECTOR: Terry Gilliam
CAST: Jonathan Pryce, Robert De-Niro, Katherine Helmond, Ian Holm, Bob Hoskins, Michael Palin, Ian Richardson

A savage blend of *1984* and *The Time Bandits* from Monty Python director Terry Gilliam. Jonathan Pryce stars as a bemused paper shuffler in a red tape–choked future society at the brink of collapsing under its own bureaucracy. Content to remain anonymous until he glimpses the woman of his dreams, he enters a bizarre world of renegade service technicians and bomb-toting terrorists bent on overthrowing the government. Definitely not for all tastes, but a treat for those with an appreciation for social satire. Were it not for a chaotic conclusion and slightly overlong running time, this would be a perfect picture. Rated R for language and adult situations.

1985   131 minutes

BREAKFAST CLUB, THE
★★★★

DIRECTOR: John Hughes
CAST: Emilio Estevez, Molly Ringwald, Paul Gleason, Anthony Michael Hall, Ally Sheedy

A group of assorted high-school misfits get to be friends while serving weekend detention, in this comedy, directed by John Hughes (*Sixteen Candles*). Molly Ringwald, Anthony Michael Hall (both from *Sixteen Candles*), Emilio Estevez (*Repo Man*), Ally Sheedy (*War Games*), and Judd Nelson (*St. Elmos's Fire*) portray the teens. Rated R.

1985   100 minutes

BREAKING AWAY
★★★★★

DIRECTOR: Peter Yates
CAST: Dennis Christopher, Dennis Quaid, Daniel Stern, Jackie Earle Haley

There comes a time in every young man's life when he must loose the ties of home, family, and friends and test his mettle. Dennis Christopher is the young man who retains an innocence we too often mistake for naivete; Paul Dooley and Barbara Barrie are the often humorously confused parents who offer subtle, sure guidance. This is a warm portrayal of family life and love, of friendships, of growing up and growing away. Rated PG for brief profanity.

1979   100 minutes

BREATH OF SCANDAL, A
★★

DIRECTOR: Michael Curtiz
CAST: Sophia Loren, John Gavin, Maurice Chevalier, Angela Lansbury

This intended high-style romantic comedy set in Austria in the gossip-rife court of Franz Joseph has little going for it. Beautiful princess scorns mama's wish she marry a prince. Instead, encouraged by papa, she conveniently opts for a visiting American mining engineer. The script, taken from the Molnar play that poor John Gilbert adapted for his disastrous first talkie, is uninspired. The casting is uninspired. The directing is uninspired. But the scenery and costumes are nice.

1960   98 minutes

BREWSTER MCCLOUD
★★★

DIRECTOR: Robert Altman
CAST: Bud Cort, Sally Kellerman

If you liked Robert Altman's *M*A*S*H* (the movie) and *Harold and Maude*, and your humor lies a few degrees off-center, you'll enjoy this "flight of fantasy" about a boy (Bud Cort) who wants to make like a bird. Rated R.

1970   104 minutes

BREWSTER'S MILLIONS (1945)
★★½

DIRECTOR: Allan Dwan
CAST: Dennis O'Keefe, Helen Walker, June Havoc, Mischa Auer, Eddie "Rochester" Anderson, Gail Patrick

This is the fifth of seven film versions of the 1902 novel and stage success about a young man who will inherit millions if he is able to spend $1 million quickly and quietly within a set period of time. Dennis O'Keefe and company perform this Tinsel-town stalwart in fine fashion, making for a bright, entertaining comic romp. As always, Mischa Auer does one of his delightful noble idiot characterizations without flaw. Fun to watch. Curiously, this version is not listed in the recent history of Paramount Studios' 2,805 films.

1945   B & W   79 minutes

BREWSTER'S MILLIONS (1985)
★★★

DIRECTOR: Walter Hill
CAST: Richard Pryor, John Candy, Lonette McKee, Stephen Collins, Pat Hingle, Tovah Feldshuh, Hume Cronyn

It took director Walter Hill to bring Richard Pryor out of his movie slump with this unspectacular, but still entertaining, comedy about a minor-league baseball player who stands to inherit $300 million if he can fulfill the provisions of a rather daffy will. As Hill did with Eddie Murphy in *48 HRS.*, the filmmaker brings out the best in Pryor and gives him some fine supporting actors (with John Candy as the standout). It's no classic, but still much, much better than *The Toy* or *Superman III*. Rated PG for profanity.

1985   97 minutes

BRINGING UP BABY
★★★★★

DIRECTOR: Howard Hawks
CAST: Cary Grant, Katharine Hepburn, Charlie Ruggles, May Robson

Howard Hawks's *Bringing Up Baby* is a must-see. Starring Cary Grant and Katharine Hepburn, this screwball comedy has lost none of its punch. Hepburn plays a daffy rich girl who gets an absent-minded professor (Grant), who also happens to be engaged, into all sorts of trouble. It doesn't sound like much, but *Bringing Up Baby* is guaranteed to have you falling out of your seat in helpless laughter.

1938   B & W   102 minutes

BRINKS JOB, THE
★★★½

DIRECTOR: William Friedkin

CAST: Peter Falk, Peter Boyle, Allen Goorwitz, Warren Oates, Paul Sorvino, Gena Rowlands

Peter Falk stars in this enjoyable release in which a gang of klutzy crooks pulls off "the crime of the century." It's a breezy caper film reminiscent of George Roy Hill's *Butch Cassidy and the Sundance Kid* and *The Sting*. The cast is superb. Falk, who plays the wacky ringleader, gets strong support from Allen Goorwitz, Paul Sorvino, Gena Rowlands, and Peter Boyle. But the film's best performance comes from the late Warren Oates as the gang member who turns stool pigeon. He should have won an Oscar for it. Rated PG.

1978   103 minutes

BRITANNIA HOSPITAL
★★★

DIRECTOR: Lindsay Anderson
CAST: Leonard Rositer, Graham Crowden, Malcolm McDowell, Joan Plowright

A wildly inadequate hospital serves as a metaphor for a sick society in this okay black comedy by British director Lindsay Anderson (*If; O Lucky Man*). Rated R.

1982   115 minutes

BROADWAY DANNY ROSE
★★★★½

DIRECTOR: Woody Allen
CAST: Woody Allen, Mia Farrow, Milton Berle, Sandy Baron

The legendary talent agent Broadway Danny Rose (Woody Allen) takes on an alcoholic crooner (Nick Apollo Forte) and carefully nurtures him to the brink of stardom, in this hilarious comedy, also written and directed by Allen. Mia Farrow is delightful as a blond gangster's moll who inadvertently gets Rose in big trouble. Rated PG for brief violence.

1984   B & W   86 minutes

BUCK PRIVATES
★★★★

DIRECTOR: Arthur Lubin
CAST: Bud Abbott, Lou Costello, Lee Bowman, Alan Curtis, Jane Frazee

Abbott and Costello are at their best in their first starring film, but it's still no classic.

1941   B & W   82 minutes

BUDDY, BUDDY
★★

DIRECTOR: Billy Wilder
CAST: Jack Lemmon, Walter Matthau, Paula Prentiss, Klaus Kinski

Jack Lemmon is a clumsy would-be suicide who decides to end it all in a hotel. Walter Matthau is a hit man who rents the room next door and finds the filling of his contract difficult. The results are less than hilarious but do provoke a few smiles. Rated R because of profanity and brief nudity.

1981   96 minutes

BULLFIGHTERS, THE
★★★

DIRECTOR: Malcolm St. Clair
CAST: Stan Laurel, Oliver Hardy, Margo Woode, Richard Lane, Carol Andrews

While not a classic, this latter-day Laurel and Hardy film is surprisingly good—especially when you consider that the boys had lost all control over the making of their pictures by this time. The story has Laurel resembling a famous bullfighter, and, of course, this leads to chaos in the ring.

1945   B & W   61 minutes

BULLSHOT
★★½

DIRECTOR: Dick Clement
CAST: Alan Shearman, Diz White, Ron House, Frances Tomelty, Michael Aldridge

Sometimes a movie can be fun for a while, then overstay its welcome. Such is the case with this spoof of Herman Cyril "Scapper" McNiele's *Bulldog Drummond* mystery/spy adventures. Written by stars Alan Shearman, Diz White, and Ron House, the screenplay has Capt. Hugh "Bullshot Crummo..d" (Shearman), a former RAF pilot, once again confronting his wartime nemesis, Count Otto von Bruno (House), who recalls Snoopy's foe, the Red Baron. The film presents a kind of British comedy rarely seen in this country. As opposed to the dry, droll humor of the Monty Python troupe and the classic Ealing comedies starring Alec Guinness, for example, it is a very broad form of slapstick not unlike that perpetrated by Jerry Lewis. The stars mug shamelessly. Everything is played to the hilt, and the characters go beyond stereotypes to become caricatures. Although this is occasionally irritating, the star-screenwriters do create some funny moments. But you have to wade through an enormous amount of sludge to get to them. Rated PG for profanity, sex, and violence.

1985　　　　95 minutes

BUS STOP
★★★★½

DIRECTOR: Joshua Logan
CAST: Marilyn Monroe, Don Murray, Arthur O'Connell, Betty Field, Casey Adams

Marilyn Monroe plays a distraught showgirl who is endlessly pursued by an oaf of a cowboy named Bo (Don Murray). He even kidnaps her when she refuses to marry him. Lots of laughs as Bo mistreats his newly found "angel." Arthur O'Connell is excellent as Verg, Bo's older and wiser friend who advises Bo on the way to treat women.

1956　　　　96 minutes

BUSTIN' LOOSE
★★½

DIRECTOR: Oz Scott
CAST: Richard Pryor, Cicely Tyson, Robert Christian, Alphonso Alexander, Janet Wong

You take super-bad ex-con Richard Pryor, stick him on a school bus with goody-two-shoes teacher Cicely Tyson and eight ornery schoolchildren, and what have you got? A nonstop, cross-country, comic odyssey called *Bustin' Loose*. It's a hilarious comedy as long as the bus is rolling and Pryor is up to his madcap antics. But *Bustin' Loose* bogs down in its last half-hour. Rated R for profanity and violence.

1981　　　　94 minutes

CADDYSHACK
★★

DIRECTOR: Harold Ramis
CAST: Chevy Chase, Rodney Dangerfield, Ted Knight, Michael O'Keefe, Bill Murray

Only Rodney Dangerfield, as an obnoxious refugee from a leisure-suit collectors' convention, offers anything of value in this rip-off of the *Animal House* formula. Chevy Chase and Bill Murray sleepwalk through their poorly written roles, and Ted Knight looks a little weary of imitating his Ted Baxter routine from "The Mary Tyler Moore Show." The few laughs in this golf comedy are all but obliterated by the yawns. Rated R for nudity and sex.

1980 99 minutes

CALIFORNIA SUITE

★★★½

DIRECTOR: Herbert Ross

CAST: Jane Fonda, Alan Alda, Maggie Smith, Richard Pryor, Bill Cosby

This adaptation of the Neil Simon play features multiple stars, including Jane Fonda, Alan Alda, Maggie Smith, Michael Caine, Walter Matthau, Richard Pryor, and Bill Cosby. The action revolves around the various inhabitants of a Beverly Hills hotel room. We are allowed to enter and observe the private lives of the various guests in the room, in the four short stories within this watchable film. Rated PG.

1978 103 minutes

CAN I DO IT 'TIL I NEED GLASSES?

DIRECTOR: I. Robert Levy

CAST: Robin Williams, Roger Behr, Debra Klose, Moose Carlson, Walter Olkewicz

A follow-up to If You Don't Stop, You'll Go Blind. A trash-heap of prehistoric naughty jokes acted out by hopped-up extras in need of a buck. Robin Williams appears for all of a minute, enough for the filmmakers to cash in on his success. Williams sued to keep his name as small as possible in the credits. May this serve as a lesson to all struggling actors. Rated R for nudity and profanity.

1980 72 minutes

CANNERY ROW

★★★½

DIRECTOR: Davis S. Ward

CAST: Nick Nolte, Debra Winger, Audra Lindley, M. Emmet Walsh, Frank McRae

It's hard to really dislike this film, starring Nick Nolte and Debra Winger, even though it has so many problems. Despite its artificiality, halting pace, and general unevenness, there are so many marvelous moments—most provided by character actor Frank McRae as the lovable simpleton Hazel—that you don't regret having seen it. Rated PG for slight nudity, profanity, and violence.

1982 120 minutes

CANNONBALL RUN

★

DIRECTOR: Hal Needham

CAST: Burt Reynolds, Roger Moore, Farrah Fawcett, Dom De Luise, Dean Martin, Sammy Davis Jr.

This star-studded bore is the story of an unsanctioned, totally illegal cross-country car race in which there are no rules and few survivors. Director Hal Needham (Smokey and the Bandit; Smokey and the Bandit II) and writer Brock Yates team up once again with Burt Reynolds to make another action-comedy, but laughs have never been so rare nor stunts so unspectacular. Rated PG for profanity.

1981 95 minutes

CANNONBALL RUN II

DIRECTOR: Hal Needham

CAST: Burt Reynolds, Dom De Luise, Shirley MacLaine, Marilu Henner, Telly Savalas, Dean Martin, Sammy Davis Jr., Frank Sinatra

Take an Arab fortune, a pair of bogus nuns, inept underworld warfare, and a bunch of crazies willing to risk their necks in a mad cross-country race with no rules or regulations, and you have the starting line up for this typically awful Hal Needham rehash of *Cannonball Run*. What a waste of talent. Rated PG for simulated violence and profanity.

1984   108 minutes

CAN SHE BAKE A CHERRY PIE?
★★★

DIRECTOR: Henry Jaglom
CAST: Karen Black, Michael Emil

One critic, in admiring this film, by Henry Jaglom, observed that as it unfolds we "become keenly aware" that Jaglom is an independent filmmaker. This is true, but the first impression is not one of any great thematic freedom inherent in that unfolding but one of a movie that looks as if it had been made at N.Y.U. by sophomores. This, alas, all too often is the great independent-filmmaker tip-off: independent means cheap. It does not mean bad, however, and *Can She Bake a Cherry Pie?*, while often quite crude in its "unfolding," has its revelations. One of those is the performance of Karen Black. She plays a woman whose first name apparently is Zee and whose husband leaves her before she has fully awakened one morning. She meets Eli, played by Michael Emil, a balding character actor whose body is slowly sliding into his knees. They're both a little neurotic, and pretty dippy in the bargain. Thus begins a nearly plotless amble through the lives of Zee and Eli as they parry and thrust and decide to be in love with each other. This is a small film, and its appeal is quiet. It also is an example of what can be right with American movie-making, even when the money isn't there. No

rating, but considerable vulgar language, sexual situations.

1984   90 minutes

CARBON COPY
★★★½

DIRECTOR: Michael Schultz
CAST: George Segal, Susan Saint James, Jack Warden, Dick Martin

This amiable, lightweight comedy of racial manners stars George Segal as a white corporation executive who suddenly discovers he has a teen-age black son just itching to be adopted in lily-white San Marino, California. Rated PG.

1981   92 minutes

CARLIN AT CARNEGIE
★★★½

DIRECTOR: Steven J. Santos
CAST: George Carlin

This Home Box Office–backed video may not be as consistently funny as other comedy videos, but it has that special quality of having come from the heart—as well as hard-earned experience and deep thought. It's funny and sad at the same time. Carlin has found that you can't always have a nice day and does a very funny, brilliant routine on how being told to have one can be irritating. And, as always, Carlin uses the English language—and our taboos on certain parts of it—against itself in several bits. No one else can reduce us to tears of laughter by simply reading a list of words. Unrated, the film has profanity.

1983   60 minutes

CARRY ON COWBOY
★★½

DIRECTOR: Gerald Thomas

CAST: Sidney James, Kenneth Williams, Joan Sims, Angela Douglas, Jim Dale

Another in a very long, and weakening, line of British farces—*Carry on Doctor*, *Carry On Nurse*,—many of them spoofs of highly popular films. Replete with the usual double-entendre jokes and sight gags, this one sends up *High Noon*.

1966   91 minutes

CARRY ON NURSE
★★★

DIRECTOR: Gerald Thomas
CAST: Kenneth Connor, Kenneth Williams, Charles Hawtrey, Terence Longden

Daffy struggle between patients and hospital staff. It's one of the most consistently amusing entries in this distinctive British comedy series.

1960   90 minutes

CAR WASH
★★★½

DIRECTOR: Michael Schultz
CAST: Richard Pryor, Franklin Ajaye, Sully Boyar, Ivan Dixon

With *D.C. Cab*, writer-director Joel Schumacher attempted to recreate the success he achieved with his screenplay for this effective comedy-drama. This is an ensemble film that features memorable bits from Richard Pryor, George Carlin, Franklin Ajaye, Ivan Dixon, and the Pointer Sisters. There are plenty of laughs, music, and even a moral in this fine low-budget production. Rated PG.

1976   97 minutes

CASINO ROYALE
★★

DIRECTOR: John Huston, Ken Hughes, Robert Parrish, Joe McGrath, Val Guest
CAST: Peter Sellers, Ursula Andress, David Niven, Orson Welles, Joanna Pettet, Woody Allen, Deborah Kerr, William Holden, Charles Boyer, John Huston, George Raft, Jean-Paul Belmondo

What do you get when you combine the talents of this all-star ensemble? Not much. This is the black sheep of the James Bond family of films. The rights to *Casino Royale* weren't part of the Ian Fleming package. Not wanting to compete with the Sean Connery vehicles, this film was intended to be a stylish spoof. It's only sporadically amusing. For the most part, it's an overblown bore.

1967   130 minutes

CATCH-22
★★★

DIRECTOR: Mike Nichols
CAST: Alan Arkin, Martin Balsam, Richard Benjamin, Anthony Perkins, Art Garfunkel

This release stars Alan Arkin as a soldier in World War II most interested in avoiding the insanity of combat. Its sarcasm alone is enough to sustain interest. Rated R.

1970   121 minutes

CAVEMAN
★

DIRECTOR: Carl Gottlieb
CAST: Ringo Starr, Barbara Bach, John Matuszak, Shelley Long

Ex-Beatle Ringo Starr plays the prehistoric hero in this silly, vulgar, and sometimes outright stupid spoof of *One Million Years B.C.* Because of the amount of sexual innuendo, it is definitely not recommended for kids, although they are perhaps the only people who would really think it was funny. Rated PG.

1981   92 minutes

CHAMPAGNE FOR CAESAR
★★★★

DIRECTOR: Richard Whorf
CAST: Ronald Colman, Celeste Holm, Vincent Price, Barbara Britton, Art Linkletter

Satire of early television and the concept of game shows is funnier now than when it was originally released. A treasure trove of trivia and great one-liners, this intelligent spoof features classic actor Ronald Colman as Beauregarde Bottomley, self-proclaimed genius and scholar who exacts his revenge on soap tycoon Vincent Price by appearing on his quiz show and attempting to bankrupt his company by winning all their assets. Art Linkletter is great as the inane game show host, Colman is in top comedic form as a man of humor and integrity, and Vincent Price gives the comedy performance of his career. Bogged down with the love story between Colman and Celeste Holm (as Flame O'Neill!) and some needless physical humor, this gem is still solid entertainment and will please anyone who questions the mindless direction commercial television has taken since its inception.

1950   B & W 99 minutes

CHANGE OF SEASONS, A
🐢

DIRECTOR: Richard Lang

CAST: Shirley MacLaine, Anthony Hopkins, Bo Derek, Michael Brandon

Poor Shirley MacLaine. She seems destined to make the same movie over and over again. The only difference between this film and *Loving Couples*, which closely followed it into release, is that Anthony Hopkins and Bo Derek costar as the ultramodern mate-swappers who discover the real meaning of love just in the nick of time, instead of James Coburn and Susan Sarandon. It's pure corn, with a little nudity thrown in; another example of the "commercial" package at its worst. Miss it. Rated R.

1980   102 minutes

CHARLIE CHAN AND THE CURSE OF THE DRAGON QUEEN
★★

DIRECTOR: Clive Donner

CAST: Peter Ustinov, Lee Grant, Angie Dickinson, Richard Hatch

Although there are moments in this tongue-in-cheek send-up of the 1930s Charlie Chan mystery series that recapture the fun of yesteryear, overall it's just not a very good movie. The only thing that saves this film is that the stars— Peter Ustinov (who plays Chan), Lee Grant, Angie Dickinson, Brian Keith, Roddy McDowall, Rachel Roberts, and Richard Hatch— seem to be having so much fun it's hard not to get caught up in it, even though afterward you sometimes regret laughing. Besides, the Oriental sleuth belongs to another, less-aware age, which is perhaps where he should remain. Rated PG.

1981   97 minutes

CHARLIE CHAPLIN—THE EARLY YEARS, VOL. 1
★★★★★

DIRECTOR: Charlie Chaplin
CAST: Charlie Chaplin, Edna Purviance, Eric Campbell, Albert Austin

In this collection of early Charlie Chaplin shorts, we get three outstanding stories. "The Immigrant" finds Charlie, who meets Edna Purviance on the boat to America, in love and broke. The story is how they survive in the land of dreams. "The Count" has Charlie trying to lead the high life with no money. "Easy Street" finds Charlie "saved" by missionary Purviance and out to save everyone else. All three episodes are quite funny and heartwarming. If you like old silent comedies, you'll love these.

1916-17   B & W   62 minutes

CHARLIE CHAPLIN—THE EARLY YEARS, VOL. 2
★★★★★

DIRECTOR: Charlie Chaplin
CAST: Charlie Chaplin, Edna Purviance, Eric Campbell, Albert Austin

Volume Two of the Charlie Chaplin series presents three more classic shorts. The first is "The Pawnbroker," with Charlie running a pawnshop. As you might expect, nothing is quite normal in this pawnshop. The second feature is called "The Adventure," as Charlie plays an escaped con who gets mistaken for a high-society man and finds himself in the middle of wealthy society. And "One A.M." ends the collection as Charlie tries desperately to get some sleep after a long night of boozing it up. Everything in his room keeps moving. A must for Chaplin fans.

1916-17   B & W   61 minutes

CHARLIE CHAPLIN, THE EARLY YEARS, VOL. 3
★★★★★

DIRECTOR: Charlie Chaplin
CAST: Charlie Chaplin, Edna Purviance, Eric Campbell, Henry Bergman

In Volume 3 of this great series, we get three more classic Chaplin shorts. First off is "The Cure," where Charlie plays a drunk who goes to a health spa to dry out. He also happens to bring a trunkload of booze with him; the result is a spa full of smashed people. Next Charlie shows up as "The Floorwalker" in a large department store who catches his boss trying to make off with the store money. Last Charlie is "The Vagabond", a wandering violinist who saves a young girl's life and also falls in love with her. Unfortunately for Charlie, her mother takes her away from him. Don't miss these wonderful treasures from the past.

1916-17   B & W   64 minutes

CHARLIE CHAPLIN—THE EARLY YEARS, VOL. 4
★★★★★

DIRECTOR: Charlie Chaplin
CAST: Charlie Chaplin, Edna Purviance, Eric Campbell, Albert Austin, Lloyd Bacon, Charlotte Mineau, James T. Kelly, Leo White

In Volume Four of the Charlie Chaplin series, we start out with "Behind The Screen," as Charlie plays a movie studio stagehand who goes crazy from being overworked. The final pie-throwing clash is a classic. Next is "The Fireman," with Charlie a brave firefighter who must rescue Edna Purviance, his girlfriend, from a fire. The final story is "The Ring", with Charlie playing a bumbling waiter in a high-class restaurant.

All three stories are in the great Chaplin tradition.

1916   B & W   63 minutes

CHATTANOOGA CHOO CHOO
★★★

DIRECTOR: Bruce Bilson
CAST: George Kennedy, Barbara Eden, Joe Namath, Melissa Sue Anderson

A sillier and cornier movie you'll probably never see, yet *Chattanooga Choo Choo* fills a long-time void in screen entertainment. It's a family-oriented picture that's just a little naughtier than the live-action releases the Disney Studios used to make in the 1950s and '60s and most likely will appeal to those filmgoers who enjoyed *Smokey and the Bandit* and *Every Which Way but Loose*. The story deals with a bet to make a New York–to–Chattanooga train trip within a deadline. George Kennedy plays the comedy villain and owner of a football team on which Joe Namath is the coach. Barbara Eden starts out as Kennedy's girlfriend but soon falls in love with the "good guy"—Namath. Rated PG for mild profanity.

1984   102 minutes

CHEAPER TO KEEP HER
★

DIRECTOR: Ken Annakin
CAST: Mac Davis, Tovah Feldshuh, Art Metrano, Ian McShane

Mac Davis (*North Dallas Forty*) plays a sexist private detective whose investigations are confined to tracking down ex-husbands who haven't paid their alimony. Despite an advertising claim that it's about women's rights, this film cares as little about women as it does about good comedy. This in-sult to one's intelligence is simply a waste of time. Rated R.

1980   92 minutes

CHECK AND DOUBLE CHECK
★

DIRECTOR: Melville Brown
CAST: Freeman Gosden, Charles Correll, Sue Carol, Charles Norton, Ralf Harolde, Irene Rich, Duke Ellington and His Orchestra

This sad comedy starring radio's Amos 'n Andy in black face was RKO's biggest hit for the 1930 season and made Freeman Gosden and Charles Correll the top stars for that year—but by that time they weren't even with the studio anymore and never made another film. Very popular in the Midwest and the South when it was first released, this clinker looks its age and then some. Early footage of Duke Ellington and His Orchestra and the chance to see early radio at work on the screen are the main incentives for sitting through this one.

1930   B & W   80 minutes

CHEECH AND CHONG'S NEXT MOVIE
★★

DIRECTOR: Thomas Chong
CAST: Cheech and Chong, Evelyn Guerrero, Betty Kennedy

This is Cheech and Chong's (Richard Marin and Thomas Chong) in-between movie—in between *Up in Smoke*, their first, and *Nice Dreams*, number three. If you liked either of the other two, you'll like *Next Movie*. But if you didn't care for the duo's brand of humor there, you won't in this one either. Rated R for nudity and profanity.

1980   99 minutes

CHICKEN CHRONICLES, THE
★

DIRECTOR: Francis Simon
CAST: Steven Guttenberg, Ed Lauter, Lisa Reeves, Meredith Baer, Phil Silvers

This witless comedy centers on the carnal pursuits of Steve (*Police Academy*) Guttenberg, a charmless high school senior. Even Phil Silvers can't scare up many laughs in this one. Rated PG.

1977   95 minutes

CHU CHU AND THE PHILLY FLASH
★★

DIRECTOR: David Lowell Rich
CAST: Alan Arkin, Carol Burnett, Jack Warden, Ruth Buzzi

This is another bittersweet comedy about a couple of losers. It's supposed to be funny. It isn't. The stars, Alan Arkin and Carol Burnett, do manage to invest it with a certain wacky charm, but that isn't enough to make up for its shortcomings. Rated PG.

1981   100 minutes

CHUMP AT OXFORD, A
★★★

DIRECTOR: Alfred Goulding
CAST: Stan Laurel, Oliver Hardy, Wilfred Lucas, Forrester Harvey, James Finlayson, Anita Garvin

Stan Laurel receives a scholarship to Oxford, and Oliver Hardy accompanies him. Not accepted by the other students, they are the butt of pranks and jokes until Stan receives a blow on the head and becomes a reincarnation of a college hero. A fair script, but the Stan and Ollie characters never seem to fit well into it.

1940   B & W 63 minutes

CITY HEAT
★★★

DIRECTOR: Richard Benjamin
CAST: Clint Eastwood, Burt Reynolds, Jane Alexander, Madeline Kahn, Irene Cara, Richard Roundtree, Rip Torn, Tony Lo Bianco

Clint Eastwood and Burt Reynolds portray a cop and a private eye, respectively, in this enjoyable action comedy, directed by Richard Benjamin (*My Favorite Year*). Despite a few clashes while pursuing gangsters, the two have a "grudging mutual respect," according to the filmmakers. It's fun for fans of the stars. Rated PG for violence.

1984   94 minutes

CITY LIGHTS
★★★★★

DIRECTOR: Charles Chaplin
CAST: Charlie Chaplin, Virginia Cherrill, Harry Myers, Hank Mann

In his finest film, Charlie Chaplin's little tramp befriends a blind flower-seller, providing her with every kindness he can afford. Charlie develops a friendship with a drunken millionaire and takes advantage of it to help the girl even more. Taking money from the millionaire so the girl can have an eye operation, he is arrested and sent to jail. His release from jail and the subsequent reunion with the girl may well be the most poignant ending of all his films.

1931   B & W 81 minutes

CLAIRE'S KNEE
★★★★★

DIRECTOR: Eric Rohmer

CAST: Jean-Claude Brialy, Aurora Cornu, Beatrice Romand, Laurence De Monaghan, Michele Montel, Geral Falconetti, Fabrice Luchini

For anyone who thought that an adult comedy about sex and love must be x-rated, *Claire's Knee* is a must. There is no substitute for class, and director Eric Rohmer exhibits a great deal of it in this fifth film in a series entitled *Six Moral Tales*. The plot is simplicity itself. Jerome (Jean-Claude Brialy) is engaged. He awaits his fiancée at Annecy, where he has spent many happy times. He renews his friendship with a writer (Aurora Cornu) who has two daughters; one is Claire. Jerome is intrigued by Claire but is obsessed with her knee—her right knee, to be specific. Rohmer's work is economical but poignant. The denouement is so delicious, it would be folly to recount it here. In French with English subtitles. PG rating.

1971   103 minutes

CLASS

DIRECTOR: Lewis John Carlino
CAST: Rob Lowe, Jacqueline Bisset, Andrew McCarthy, Stuart Margolin

This is a generally unfunny and offensive comedy about two preppies, one of whom unwittingly falls in love with the other's alcoholic mother (Jacqueline Bisset). Rated R for nudity, profanity, sex, and violence.

1983   98 minutes

CLASS REUNION

DIRECTOR: Michael Miller
CAST: Gerrit Graham, Stephen Furst, Zane Buzby, Michael Lerner

The graduating class of 1972 returns to wreak havoc on its alma mater, Lizzie Borden High School, in this awful *Animal House*–style comedy. Gerrit Graham (who played Beef in *Phantom of the Paradise*), Stephen Furst (Flounder from *Animal House*), and Zane Buzby (the pill freak from *Up in Smoke*) are bound to have nightmares about appearing in this moronic mess. Avoid it. Rated R for nudity, leering sexual references, profanity, and drug-taking.

1982   84 minutes

CLEAN STATE (COUP DE TORCHON)
★★★★

DIRECTOR: Bertrand Tavernier
CAST: Philippe Noiret, Isabelle Huppert, Stéphane Audran, Irene Skobline

Set during 1938 in a French West African colonial town, this savage and sardonic black comedy (the title of which translates as "Clean Slate") is a study of the circumstances under which racism and fascism flourish. Philippe Noiret stars as a simple-minded sheriff who, though he loves eating, drinking, and taking bribes, decides that it's time to wipe out the corruption that runs rampant in his village. The way he does it is shocking—and often hilarious. In French, with English subtitles. Unrated, the film has nudity, implied sex, violence, profanity, and racial epithets.

1981   128 minutes

CLOWNS, THE
★★★★½

DIRECTOR: Federico Fellini
CAST: Mayo Morin, Lima Alberti, Alvaro Vitali, Gasparmo

Psychoautobiographical revelations . . . life as art and art as life

... transcending the documentary format ... expressing the spirit and the passing of the Commedia dell'Arte ... the tragicomic clown as the central metaphor for an existential century. Yes, yes—but good grief! Federico Fellini's television documentary is a three-ring spectacle of fun and silliness, too. Here, style is substance, and the only substance worth noting is the water thrown onto the journalist who asks the cast of circus crazies, "What does it all mean?" It only means that we are all in the predicament of survival, and we had better not take it too seriously. In Italian with English subtitles.

1971   90 minutes

CLUB PARADISE
👣

DIRECTOR: Harold Ramis
CAST: Robin Williams, Peter O'-Toole, Jimmy Cliff, Twiggy, Rick Moranis, Adolph Caesar, Eugene Levy, Joanna Cassidy

Lame, witless, boring, and offensive attempt to use adult stars in a concept overdone by moronic teen comedies. Robin Williams and Jimmy Cliff start their own little Club Med-style resort; other cast members play tourists who arrive for a vacation. This is film-making at the top of its lungs, everybody shouts and screams. The tasteless and sexist humor includes pot-shots at women, and drugs. A civil war is thrown in for good measure. Rarely have so many labored so long and delivered so little. Rated PG-13 for language and drug humor.

1986   104 minutes

CLUE
★★½

DIRECTOR: Jonathan Lynn

CAST: Eileen Brennan, Tim Curry, Madeline Kahn, Christopher Lloyd, Michael McKean, Martin Mull, Lesley Ann Warren

Inspired by the popular board game, the movie is a pleasant spoof of whodunits. The delightful ensemble establishes a suitably breezy style. Silliness eventually overwhelms the proceedings. As a gimmick, the film was originally shown in theatres with three different endings. All versions are included on the videocassette. Rated PG-13.

1985   100 minutes

COAST TO COAST
★★

DIRECTOR: Joseph Sargent
CAST: Dyan Cannon, Robert Blake, Quinn Redeker, Michael Lerner, Maxine Stuart, Bill Ucking

Dyan Cannon stars as a wacko blonde who's been railroaded into a mental hospital by her husband. He has had her declared insane so he can avoid an expensive divorce. Cannon escapes by bopping her psychiatrist over the head with a bust of Freud, and the chase is on. Trucker Charlie Calahan (Robert Blake) gives Cannon a lift, and they romp from Pennsylvania to California with a couple of private detectives and a thug who's trying to repossess Calahan's truck shadowing their journey. The abundance of their expletives may discourage some parents from making *Coast to Coast* a family outing, but Blake fans will find him as loose and energetic as always, and scrappy enough to be amusing. Rated PG.

1980   95 minutes

COCA COLA KID, THE
★★★

DIRECTOR: Dusan Makavejev
CAST: Eric Roberts, Greta Scacchi, Bill Kerr

A nude scene between Eric Roberts and Greta Scacchi in a bed covered with feathers is enough to make anyone's temperature rise, but as a whole this little film doesn't have enough bite to it. Roberts plays a gung-ho troubleshooter from the popular beverage company who comes to Australia to sell the drink to a hard-nosed businessman (Bill Kerr) who has a monopoly on a stretch of land with his own soft drink. Worth a look. Rated R for nudity.

1985   90 minutes

COLLEGE
★★★½

DIRECTOR: James W. Horne
CAST: Buster Keaton, Anne Cornwall, Flora Bramley, Harold Goodwin, Grant Winters, Snitz Edwards

An anti-athletics bookworm, Buster Keaton, goes to college with a scholarship. His girl falls for a jock, and Keaton decides to prove he can succeed in athletics to win her back. He fails hilariously in every attempt, but finally rescues her from the evil-intentioned jock by unwittingly using every athletic skill. Lack of a solid, complete script keeps the film from attaining the excellence of *Steamboat Bill, Jr*.

1927   B & W   65 minutes

COLONEL EFFINGHAM'S RAID
★★½

DIRECTOR: Irving Pichel
CAST: Charles Coburn, Joan Bennett, William Eythe, Allyn Joslyn, Elizabeth Patterson, Donald Meek

Slight small-town story about Charles Coburn's efforts to preserve a local monument and save the community's pride is pleasant enough and has marvelous characters like Donald Meek populating it. Similar in tone and story to several American productions of the same vintage, this entertaining little film, while espousing the values of wartime movies, shifts the emphasis from overseas to hometown America and pits a new and increasingly insidious enemy facing postwar America, the creeping rise of indifferent government bureaucracy. Not a great film, but harmless fun and at times thought-provoking.

1945   B & W   70 minutes

COMFORT AND JOY
★★★★½

DIRECTOR: Bill Forsyth
CAST: Bill Paterson, Eleanor David, C. P. Grogan, Alex North

Scottish filmmaker Bill Forsyth (*Local Hero*; *Gregory's Girl*) scores again with this delightful tale of a disc jockey (Bill Paterson) whose life is falling apart. His girlfriend walks out on him, taking nearly everything he owns. Birds seem to like decorating his pride and joy: a red BMW. And what's worse, he gets involved in a gangland war over—are you ready for this?—the control of ice cream manufacturing and sales. It's one you'll want to see. Rated PG.

1984   90 minutes

COMMIES ARE COMING, THE COMMIES ARE COMING, THE
★★

DIRECTOR: George Waggner
CAST: Jack Kelly, Jean Cooper, Peter Brown, Patricia Woodell, Andrew Duggan, Robert Conrad

Jack Webb narrates this 1950s anti-communist pseudodocumentary about what would happen if the Russians captured the United States. It's easy to laugh at this silly film. Unrated.

1984   B & W   60 minutes

COMPROMISING POSITIONS
★★

DIRECTOR: Frank Perry
CAST: Susan Sarandon, Raul Julia, Edward Herrmann, Judith Ivey, Mary Beth Hurt, Anne DeSalvo, Josh Mostel

In the first half-hour, this is a hilarious and innovative takeoff on murder mysteries and a devastatingly witty send-up of suburban life. However, it soon descends into the clichés of the mystery genre. That's too bad, because the plot, about an overly amorous dentist who is murdered, has great possibilities. Old Doc was given to taking pictures of his many sexual conquests . . . all female patients, many of whom are married. This brings many delightfully bitchy encounters as the women bemoan their respective fates. But it eventually collapses into a not-very-suspenseful whodunit. Rated R for nudity, profanity, and violence.

1985   98 minutes

CONTEMPT
★★★½

DIRECTOR: Jean-Luc Godard
CAST: Brigitte Bardot, Jack Palance, Fritz Lang, Jean-Luc Godard, Michel Piccoli

A cult film to be, if it isn't already, this one takes a tongue-in-cheek, raised-eyebrow look at European moviemaking. Jack Palance is a vulgar producer; Fritz Lang, playing himself, is his director; Jean-Luc Godard plays Lang's assistant, and in directing this film turned it into an inside joke—in real (not reel) life, he held the film's producer Joseph E. Levine in contempt.

1963   103 minutes

CONTINENTAL DIVIDE
★★★½

DIRECTOR: Michael Apted
CAST: John Belushi, Blair Brown, Allen Goorwitz, Carlin Glynn

As light-hearted romantic comedies go, this one is tops. John Belushi stars as Ernie Souchak, a Chicago newspaper columnist unexpectedly sent into the Rockies to write a story about an ornithologist (Blair Brown). Just as unexpectedly, they fall in love. Rated PG because of slight amounts of nudity.

1981   103 minutes

COPACABANA
★

DIRECTOR: Alfred E. Green
CAST: Groucho Marx, Carmen Miranda, Andy Russell, Steve Cochran, Abel Green

Not even Groucho Marx can save this slight comedy about the problems caused by a woman applying for two jobs at the same nightclub. Carmen Miranda does her "banana hat bit" and the viewer eventually falls asleep.

1947   B & W   92 minutes

CORSICAN BROTHERS, THE

DIRECTOR: Thomas Chong
CAST: Cheech and Chong, Roy Dotrice

The comedy team of Cheech and Chong apparently enjoyed working on the Monty Python–powered period pirate comedy *Yellowbeard* so much they decided to do a silly swashbuckler of their own. Loosely based on the book by Alexandre Dumas, this forgettable film features Tommy Chong and Richard "Cheech" Marin as twins dueling to the death with dastardly villains. Rated R.

1984   90 minutes

COURT JESTER, THE
★★★

DIRECTOR: Norman Panama, Melvin Frank

CAST: Danny Kaye, Glynis Johns, Basil Rathbone, Angela Lansbury, Mildred Natwick, Robert Middleton

Romance, court intrigue, a joust, and in the middle of it all the one and only Danny Kaye as a phony court jester full of double-takes and double-talk. This is one funny film of clever and complicated comic situations superbly brought off.

1956   101 minutes

COUSIN, COUSINE
★★★½

DIRECTOR: Jean-Charles Tacchella

CAST: Marie-Christine Barrault, Victor Lanoux, Marie-France Pisier, Guy Marchand, Ginette Garcin, Sybil Maas

Marie-Christine Barrault and Victor Lanoux star in this ever-popular French comedy. Both married to others, they become cousins by marriage. Once the kissing starts, their relationship expands beyond the boundaries of convention.

1975   95 minutes

CRACKERS
★½

DIRECTOR: Louis Malle

CAST: Donald Sutherland, Jack Warden, Sean Penn, Wallace Shawn

Crackers is a nearly unwatchable film directed by Louis Malle (*At-lantic City*; *My Dinner with Andre*). It isn't often Malle comes up with a turkey, but when he does, it comes complete with all the trimmings. Even the high-powered talents of stars Donald Sutherland, Sean Penn (*Bad Boys*; *The Falcon and the Snowman*), and Jack Warden can't lift this caper "comedy" above mediocrity. It's about a bunch of down-and-out San Franciscans who decide to turn to crime in order to survive. Rated PG.

1984   92 minutes

CRACKING UP
🐕

DIRECTOR: Jerry Lewis

CAST: Jerry Lewis, Herb Edelman, Zane Buzby, Dick Butkus, Milton Berle

A relatively new Jerry Lewis comedy. Translation: No laughs here. Rated R.

1983   83 minutes

CURSE OF THE PINK PANTHER, THE
★★★

DIRECTOR: Blake Edwards

CAST: Ted Wass, David Niven, Robert Wagner, Harvey Korman, Herbert Lom

No, this isn't another trashy compilation of outtakes featuring the late Peter Sellers. Instead, series producer-writer-director Blake Edwards has hired Ted Wass (of TV's "Soap") to play a bumbling American detective searching for the still-missing Jacques Clouseau, and he's a delight. The movie isn't always good. However, when Wass is featured, *Curse* is fresh and diverting—and, on a couple of memorable occasions, it's hilarious. Rated PG for nudity, profanity, violence, and scatological humor.

1983   109 minutes

DAY AT THE RACES, A
★★★½

DIRECTOR: Sam Wood

CAST: The Marx Brothers, Allan Jones, Maureen O'Sullivan, Margaret Dumont

The Marx Brothers—Groucho, Harpo, and Chico, that is—were still at the peak of their fame in this MGM musical-comedy. Though not as unrelenting hilarious and outrageous as the films they made at Paramount with Zeppo, it is nonetheless an enjoyable film. The first to follow *A Night at the Opera*, their biggest hit, and use a variation on its formula, it works very well—which, sadly, did not prove to be the case with most of the Marx Brothers movies that followed.

1937   B & W 111 minutes

D.C. CAB
🦃

DIRECTOR: Joel Schumacher

CAST: Gary Busey, Mr. T, Adam Baldwin, Charlie Barnett, Max Gail

A mindless "madcap" comedy with Gary Busey and Mr. T. Don't pay the fare. Rated R.

1983   99 minutes

DEAD MEN DON'T WEAR PLAID
★★★★

DIRECTOR: Carl Reiner

CAST: Steve Martin, Rachel Ward, Reni Santoni, Carl Reiner, George Gaynes, Frank McCarthy

In this often hilarious and always entertaining comedy, Steve Martin plays a private eye who confronts the suspicious likes of Humphrey Bogart, Burt Lancaster, Alan Ladd, Bette Davis, and other stars of Hollywood's golden age, with the help of tricky editing and writer-director Carl Reiner.

Rachel Ward co-stars as Martin's sexy client. Rated PG for adult themes.

1982   B & W 89 minutes

DEAL OF THE CENTURY
★★

DIRECTOR: William Friedkin

CAST: Chevy Chase, Sigourney Weaver, Gregory Hines, Vince Edwards

A two-bit arms hustler (Chevy Chase) peddles an ultrasophisticated superweapon to a Central American dictator. This black comedy has its good moments. Unfortunately, it also has its bad moments and, as a result, ends up in that nether world of the near misses. Rated PG for violence and profanity.

1983   99 minutes

DEAR WIFE
★★½

DIRECTOR: Richard Haydn

CAST: Joan Caulfield, William Holden, Mona Freeman, Edward Arnold, Billy DeWolfe

The second of three amusing films involving the same cast of characters, and mostly the same players. This sequel to *Dear Ruth* has fresh-faced younger sister (to Joan Caulfield) Mona Freeman conniving to elect heartthrob William Holden to the state senate seat sought by her politician father Edward Arnold. Billy DeWolfe fills it all out with his peculiar brand of haughty humor. William Holden had yet to break the boy-next-door mold when this was made. *Stalag 17* and *Picnic* were years in the future; *The Wild Bunch* and *Network* not even motes in the eyes of Destiny.

1949   B & W 88 minutes

DESPERATE LIVING

🎭

DIRECTOR: John Waters
CAST: Mink Stole, Edith Massey, Jean Hill, Liz Renay, Susan Lowe

A "monstrous fairy tale," director John Waters calls it. And that may be an understatement. This story about a murderess (played by Mink Stole) and her escapades through a village of criminals who are ruled by a demented queen (Edith Massey) is a bit redundant. But various scenes provide enough humor and wit for anyone with a taste for the perverse and a yen for some good old-fashioned misanthropy. This is unrated, but it is the equivalent of an X, due to violence, nudity, and unbridled gore.

1977   95 minutes

DESPERATELY SEEKING SUSAN

★★★★½

DIRECTOR: Susan Siedelman
CAST: Rosanna Arquette, Madonna, Robert Joy, Mark Blum, Laurie Metcalf

Even the clichés in this film seem fresh. It's a delightfully daffy, smart, and intriguing comedy made from a feminine perspective. Rosanna Arquette stars as a bored housewife who adds spice to her life by following the personal column love adventures of the mysterious Susan (Madonna). One day, Susan is to meet someone close by, so our heroine decides to catch a glimpse of her idol and, through a set of unlikely but easy-to-take plot convolutions, ends up switching places with her. After this, it's nothing but amusing and watchable. Rated PG-13 for violence.

1985   104 minutes

DEVIL AND MAX DEVLIN, THE

★★

DIRECTOR: Steven Hillard Stern
CAST: Elliott Gould, Bill Cosby, Susan Anspach, Adam Rich

This is visible proof that it takes more than just a few talented people to create quality entertainment. Despite Elliott Gould, Bill Cosby, and Susan Anspach, this Disney production—another take-off on the Faustian theme of a pact made with the devil—offers little more than mediocre fare. It's basically a waste of fine talent. Rated PG.

1981   96 minutes

DEVIL AND MISS JONES, THE

★★★★

DIRECTOR: Sam Wood
CAST: Jean Arthur, Robert Cummings, Charles Coburn, Spring Byington, S. Z. Sakall, William Demarest

One of those wonderful comedies Hollywood used to make. Witty, sophisticated, poignant, and breezy, this one has millionaire Charles Coburn going undercover as a clerk in his own department store in order to probe employee complaints and unrest. Delightful doings.

1941   B & W   92 minutes

DEVIL'S EYE, THE

★★

DIRECTOR: Ingmar Bergman
CAST: Jarl Kulle, Bibi Andersson, Gunnar Bjornstrand, Nib Poppe

Disappointing comedy based on the Danish radio play Don Juan Returns. In order to cure the stye in his eye, the devil sends Don Juan (Jarl Kulle) from hell to breach a woman's chastity. Bibi Andersson plays Britt-Marie, the pastor's virgin daughter. The film is without spark or significance.

1960 90 minutes

DIE LAUGHING

DIRECTOR: Jeff Werner
CAST: Robby Benson, Linda Grovernor, Charles Durning, Bud Cort

Robby Benson stars as Pinsky, a young cabbie with aspirations of becoming a rock recording star. He gets mixed up in a conspiracy that involves the changing of nuclear waste into weapons-grade plutonium. It's neither very funny nor exciting. Rated PG.

1980 108 minutes

DINER
★★★★½

DIRECTOR: Barry Levinson
CAST: Steven Guttenberg, Daniel Stern, Mickey Rourke, Kevin Bacon

Writer-director Barry Levinson's much-acclaimed bittersweet tale of growing up in the late 1950s, unlike *American Graffiti*, is never cute or idealized. Instead, it combines insight, sensitive drama, and low-key humor. Rated R for profanity and adult themes.

1982 110 minutes

DINNER AT EIGHT
★★★★★

DIRECTOR: George Cukor
CAST: John Barrymore, Jean Harlow, Marie Dressler, Billie Burke

A sparkling, sophisticated, and witty comedy of character written by George S. Kaufman and Edna Ferber for the Broadway stage, this motion picture has a terrific all-star cast and lots of laughs. It's an all-time movie classic.

1933 B & W 113 minutes

DIRTY TRICKS

DIRECTOR: Alvin Rakoff
CAST: Elliott Gould, Kate Jackson, Rich Little, Arthur Hill, Nick Campbell

The makers of this film couldn't have picked a more appropriate title. People who pay to see it will undoubtedly feel that they've been the victims of a dirty trick. This Canadian-made movie brings the comedy-thriller genre to an all-time low. The story is ridiculous, the dialogue insipid, and the characters unappealing. Worse than that, this movie is incredibly dull. Rated PG.

1980 91 minutes

DISCREET CHARM OF THE BOURGEOISIE, THE
★★★★

DIRECTOR: Luis Buñuel
CAST: Fernando Rey, Delphine Seyrig, Stephane Audran, Bulle Ogier, Jean-Pierre Cassel, Michel Piccoli

Dinner is being served in this Louis Buñuel masterpiece, but the food never gets a chance to arrive at the table. Every time the hosts and guests try to begin the meal, some outside problem rises. Typically French, typically Buñuel, topically hilarious. Winner of the best foreign film Oscar for 1972.

1972 100 minutes

DIVORCE OF LADY X, THE
★★★★

DIRECTOR: Tim Whelan
CAST: Merle Oberon, Laurence Olivier, Binnie Barnes, Ralph Richardson

In this British comedy, Laurence Olivier plays a lawyer who allows Merle Oberon to spend the night at his place. Although nothing actually happened that night, Olivier finds himself branded "the other man" in her divorce. A series of hilarious misunderstandings are the result.

1938   90 minutes

DOCTOR AT LARGE
★★★

DIRECTOR: Ralph Thomas
CAST: Dirk Bogarde, James Robertson Justice, Shirley Eaton

Young Dr. Simon Sparrow wants to join the hospital staff, but the grumpy superintendent isn't buying. Comic conniving ensues as Sparrow seeks a place. Third in a series of six films featuring Dr. Sparrow.

1957   98 minutes

DOCTOR AT SEA
★★★

DIRECTOR: Ralph Thomas
CAST: Dirk Bogarde, Brigitte Bardot, Brenda de Banzie, James Robertson Justice

Fed up with the myriad complications of London life and romance, young, handsome Dr. Simon Sparrow seeks a rugged man's world by signing on a passenger-carrying freighter as ship's doctor. He goes from the frying pan into the fire when he meets Brigitte Bardot on the high seas! Second in the highly successful British comedy series.

1955   92 minutes

DOCTOR DETROIT
★★½

DIRECTOR: Michael Pressman
CAST: Dan Aykroyd, Howard Hesseman, Nan Martin, T. K. Carter

Dan Aykroyd (*Trading Places*; *The Blues Brothers*) stars in this comedy as a soft-spoken Chicago English professor who becomes a comic book–style pimp and takes on the local mob. Aykroyd has some genuinely funny moments, but the movie is uneven overall. Rated R for profanity, nudity, and violence.

1983   89 minutes

DOCTOR IN DISTRESS
★★★

DIRECTOR: Ralph Thomas
CAST: Dirk Bogarde, Samantha Eggar, James Robertson Justice

In this high jinks–jammed British comedy of medical student and young physician trials and tribulations, head of hospital Sir Lancelot Spratt reveals he is human when he falls in love. Hero Dr. Simon Sparrow has trouble romancing a beautiful model. It's all fast-pace and very funny. Fourth in a series of six that began with *Doctor in the House*.

1963   B & W   103 minutes

DR. STRANGELOVE OR HOW I LEARNED TO STOP WORRYING AND LOVE THE BOMB
★★★★★

DIRECTOR: Stanley Kubrick
CAST: Peter Sellers, Sterling Hayden, George C. Scott, Slim Pickens, Keenan Wynn

Stanley Kubrick's black comedy masterpiece about the dropping of the "bomb." Great performances from an all-star cast, including Peter Sellers in three hilarious roles. Don't miss it.

1964   B & W   93 minutes

DOGPOUND SHUFFLE
★

DIRECTOR: Jeffery Bloom
CAST: Ron Moody, David Soul, Raymond Sutton, Pamela McMyler, Ray Sticklyn

Movies don't get much worse than this piece of sentimental slop.

Story has Ron Moody and David Soul as two drifters who rescue a dog from the pound and spend the rest of the movie working up a song-and-dance team with their four-legged friend. Even kids will be bored with this mess. Rated PG for language.

1974   98 minutes

DOIN' TIME
★

DIRECTOR: George Mendeluk
CAST: Jeff Altman, Dey Young, Richard Mulligan, John Vernon, Judy Landers, Colleen Camp, Melanie Chartoff, Graham Jarvis, Pat McCormick, Eddie Velez, Jimmie Walker

Doin' Time is a bum rap: It resorts to the worst toilet humor and uses physical comedy that was rendered trite years ago. A pie fight within the first 15 minutes of this film should be an effective "we told you so" if you decide to ignore this review. We must admit, however, that there are some funny moments—like flotsam in a swamp of bad taste. Rated R for profanity and sex.

1984   84 minutes

DONA FLOR AND HER TWO HUSBANDS
★★★★

DIRECTOR: Bruno Barreto
CAST: Sonia Braga, José Wilker, Maura Mendonca, Denorah Billanti

A ribald Brazilian comedy about a woman (Sonia Braga) haunted by the sexy ghost of her first husband (José Wilker), who's anything but happy about her impending remarriage, this film inspired the Sally Field vehicle *Kiss Me Goodbye*. The original is more adult and better all around. In Portuguese, with English subtitles.

Unrated, the film has sex and nudity.

1978   106 minutes

DON'S PARTY
★★★½

DIRECTOR: Bruce Beresford
CAST: John Hargreaves, Pat Bishop, Graham Kennedy, Veronica Lang

Directed by Australian Bruce Beresford (*Breaker Morant*), *Don's Party* is a hilarious, and at times vulgar, adult comedy. Like the characters in *Who's Afraid of Virginia Woolf?*, the eleven revelers at Don's party lose all control, and the evening climaxes in bitter hostilities and humiliating confessions. With no MPAA rating, the film has nudity and profanity.

1976   91 minutes

DON'T RAISE THE BRIDGE, LOWER THE RIVER
★

DIRECTOR: Jerry Paris
CAST: Jerry Lewis, Terry-Thomas, Jacqueline Pearce, Bernard Cribbins

Weak vehicle for Jerry Lewis concerns the once-outstanding comedian's efforts to keep his marriage alive, even as everything seems to be going against him. This just isn't funny. Rated G.

1968   99 minutes

DOWN AMONG THE "Z" MEN
★

DIRECTOR: Maclean Rogers
CAST: Peter Sellers, Harry Secombe, Michael Bentine, Spike Milligan, Carol Carr

Before there was a Monty Python there were the Goons, a British comedy team that featured Peter Sellers, among others (see cast). This comedy troupe was not all that funny, as this film so vividly illustrates. An absent minded professor misplaces his formula for a special combat gas. What follows is a madcap and tired race between the professor, the military, and a couple of crooks to find the secret formula.

1961   B & W   82 minutes

DOWN AND OUT IN BEVERLY HILLS
★★★½

DIRECTOR: Paul Mazursky
CAST: Nick Nolte, Bette Midler, Richard Dreyfuss, Little Richard, Tracy Nelson, Elizabeth Peno, Evan Richards

When a Los Angeles bum (Nick Nolte) loses his dog to a happy home, he decides to commit suicide in a Beverly Hills swimming pool. The pool's owner (Richard Dreyfuss) saves the seedy-looking character's life and thereby sets in motion a chain of events that threaten to destroy his family's rarefied existence. The result is an uneven but often funny and always outrageous adult sex comedy. Based on Jean Renoir's 1932 film, *Boudu Saved From Drowning*, this is not a film for everyone. Some people love it and others hate. Rated R for profanity, violence, nudity, and simulated sex.

1986   102 minutes

DUCK SOUP
★★★★★

DIRECTOR: Leo McCarey
CAST: The Marx Brothers, Margaret Dumont, Louis Calhern, Raquel Torres, Edgar Kennedy

Groucho, Harpo, Chico, and Zeppo in their best film: an anti-establishment comedy that failed miserably at the box office at the time of its release. Today, this Leo McCarey–directed romp has

achieved its proper reputation as the quintessential Marx Brothers classic.

1933   B & W   70 minutes

EASY MONEY
★½

DIRECTOR: James Signorelli
CAST: Rodney Dangerfield, Joe Pesci, Geraldine Fitzgerald, Candy Azzara

Nothing is worse than an unfunny comedy—except maybe an unfunny comedy with someone who is ordinarily hilarious. So it is with this film, starring Rodney Dangerfield as a high-living, good-time guy who has to give up all his vices or forfeit a $10 million inheritance. After seeing it, you understand how the comic put-upon stage character feels; in the case of *Easy Money*, it's viewers who get no respect. Rated R for profanity and suggested sex.

1983   95 minutes

EATING RAOUL
★★★★

DIRECTOR: Paul Bartel
CAST: Paul Bartel, Mary Woronov, Robert Beltran, Susan Saiger

A hilarious black comedy co-written and directed by Paul Bartel (*Death Race 2000*), this low-budget film presents an inventive but rather bizarre solution to the recession. When Mary Bland (Mary Woronov) is saved by her frying-pan-wielding husband, Paul (Bartel), from a would-be rapist, the happily married couple happily discover that the now-deceased attacker was rolling in dough—so they roll him and hit on a way to end their economic woes. Rated R for nudity, profanity, sexual situations, and violence.

1982   83 minutes

EDDIE MURPHY—DELIRIOUS
★★★

DIRECTOR: Bruce Gowers
CAST: Eddie Murphy, The Bus Boys

Stand-up comedy performance by the superstar at Constitution Hall, Washington, D.C., runs more hot than cold, as Eddie hurls barbs at gays, Michael Jackson, Ralph Kramden and Ed Norton of "The Honeymooners," his parents, Mr. T, etc. Most of the gags are obscene and often hilarious, but there are also occasional stretches of boredom as the show progresses. Very entertaining overall, though, with Eddie showing flashes of true inspiration every now and then. Be forewarned: contains strong language.

1983   70 minutes

EDUCATING RITA
★★★★½

DIRECTOR: Lewis Gilbert
CAST: Michael Caine, Julie Walters, Michael Williams

A boozing, depressed English professor (Michael Caine) takes on a sharp-witted, eager-to-learn hairdresser (Julie Walters) for Open University tutorials and each educates the other, in this delightful romantic comedy based on a London hit play. Rated PG for profanity.

1983   110 minutes

ELECTRIC DREAMS
★★★

DIRECTOR: Steve Barron
CAST: Lenny Von Dohlen, Virginia Madsen, Bud Cort (voice)

An ingenious blending of the motion picture with the rock music video, this release deals with the complications that arise when an absent-minded architect, Miles (Lenny Von Dohlen), buys his first home computer. It's a wonderful convenience—at least at first. But it isn't long before the computer (the voice for which is supplied by Bud Cort, of *Harold and Maude* fame) begins to develop a rather feisty personality and even starts wooing Miles's cellist girlfriend, Madeline (Virginia Madsen). Rated PG for profanity.

1984   96 minutes

END, THE
★★★

DIRECTOR: Burt Reynolds
CAST: Burt Reynolds, Sally Field, Dom De Luise, Joanne Woodward, David Steinberg, Pat O'Brien, Myrna Loy, Kristy McNichol, Robby Benson

The blackest of black comedies, this stars Burt Reynolds (who also directed) as an unfortunate fellow who is informed he's dying of a rare disease. Poor Burt can hardly believe it. What's worse, his friends and family don't seem to care. So he decides to end it all. In the process, he meets a maniac (Dom De Luise) who is more than willing to lend a hand. This is when Burt realizes he'd prefer to enjoy whatever time he has left. But De Luise doesn't believe him. It's surprisingly funny. Rated R.

1978   100 minutes

ENSIGN PULVER
★★★

DIRECTOR: Joshua Logan
CAST: Robert Walker Jr., Burl Ives, Walter Matthau, Tommy Sands, Millie Perkins, Kay Medford, Larry Hagman, Jack Nicholson

This sequel to *Mr. Roberts* doesn't quite measure up. The comedy, which takes place aboard a World War II cargo ship, can't stay afloat despite the large and impressive cast. Robert Walker Jr. is no match for Jack Lemmon, who played the original Ensign Pulver in 1955.

1964   104 minutes

ENTER LAUGHING
★★½

DIRECTOR: Carl Reiner
CAST: Reni Santoni, José Ferrer, Shelley Winters, Elaine May, Jack Gilford, Janet Margolin, Michael J. Pollard, Don Rickles, Rob Reiner, Nancy Kovack

Carl Reiner's semiautobiographical comedy, about a young man who shucks his training and ambitions as a pharmacist to become a comedian, is studded with familiar faces and peopled by engaging personalities—but doesn't really leave a lasting memory. There are more than a few genuinely funny scenes, but overall the film is bland. Much of this material might have worked better on television, where gags don't have to extend too long and commercials save scenes from becoming stale.

1967   112 minutes

ERRAND BOY, THE
★★★

DIRECTOR: Jerry Lewis
CAST: Jerry Lewis, Brian Donlevy, Sig Ruman

One of Jerry Lewis's better solo efforts, as he proceeds (in his own inimitable style) to make a shambles of the Hollywood movie studio where he is employed as the local gofer. Very funny. Watch for Howard McNear, best remembered as Floyd, the barber on "The Andy Griffith Show."

1961   B & W   92 minutes

EUROPEAN VACATION
🦃

DIRECTOR: Amy Heckerling
CAST: Chevy Chase, Beverly D'Angelo, Dana Hill, Jason Lively, Eric Idle, Victor Lanoux, John Astin

The sappy sequel to *Vacation*, this moronic mess has three laughs. Two of them are provided by Eric Idle as a veddy, veddy polite British bicyclist mangled by the vacationing Griswalds (Chevy Chase, Beverly D'Angelo, Dana Hill, and Jason Lively). They win an all-expense (but decidedly low-budget) European vacation grand prize on the television game show "Pig in a Poke." It was —surprisingly— written by John Hughes (*Weird Science*; *The Breakfast Club*) and directed—not surprisingly—by Amy Heckerling (*Johnny Dangerously*; *Fast Times at Ridgemont High*). Rated PG-13 for nudity, violence, and profanity.

1985   95 minutes

EVENING WITH ROBIN WILLIAMS, AN
★★★★

DIRECTOR: Don Mischer
CAST: Robin Williams

Here's a remarkably good comedy video with Robin Williams going back to his stand-up comedy roots. He's totally unpredictable when improvising on stage, and this adds to his charm. Filmed at San Francisco's Great American Music Hall, it provides ample proof why Williams was considered one of the finest live comedians of his era before scoring on television (with "Mork and Mindy") and the movies. Unrated, it has profanity.

1983   60 minutes

EVERY GIRL SHOULD BE MARRIED
★★½

DIRECTOR: Don Hartman

CAST: Cary Grant, Betsy Drake, Franchot Tone, Diana Lynn, Alan Mowbray

A bit of light comedy froth balanced mostly on Cary Grant's charm and polish. He plays a baby doctor. Betsy Drake, who later got him off-screen, plays a salesgirl bent on leading him to the altar. The title is irksome, but the picture's diverting, innocent fun.

1948   B & W   85 minutes

EVERY WHICH WAY BUT LOOSE
★★★

DIRECTOR: James Fargo
CAST: Clint Eastwood, Sondra Locke, Geoffrey Lewis, Clyde (the ape), Ruth Gordon

After Smokey and the Bandit cleaned up at the box office, Clint Eastwood decided to make his own modern-day cowboy movie. This 1978 release proved to be one of the squinty-eyed star's biggest moneymakers. The film is far superior to its sequel, Any Which Way You Can. Rated R.

1978   114 minutes

EVERYTHING YOU ALWAYS WANTED TO KNOW ABOUT SEX BUT WERE AFRAID TO ASK
★★★★

DIRECTOR: Woody Allen
CAST: John Carradine, Woody Allen, Lou Jacobi, Louise Lasser, Anthony Quayle, Lynn Redgrave, Tony Randall, Burt Reynolds, Gene Wilder

Everything You Always Wanted to Know about Sex But Were Afraid to Ask gave Woody Allen, scriptwriter, star, and director, an opportunity to stretch out without having to supply all the talent himself. Several sequences do not feature Woody at all. As the film is broken up into vignettes supposedly relating to questions asked,

it was possible for him to direct and concentrate on the strengths of his stars without the obvious strain of having to turn in a strong performance himself. Rated R.

1972   87 minutes

EXPERIENCE PREFERRED ... BUT NOT ESSENTIAL
★★★★★

DIRECTOR: Peter Duffell
CAST: Elizabeth Edmonds, Sue Wallace, Geraldine Griffith, Karen Meagher, Ron Bain, Alun Lewis, Robert Blythe

This delightful British import, which is somewhat reminiscent of Scottish director Bill Forsyth's Gregory's Girl and Local Hero, follows the awkward and amusing adventures of a young woman during her first summer job at a Welsh coastal resort in 1962. She comes to town insecure and frumpy and leaves at the end of the summer pretty, sexy, and confident. Can you guess why? Right! Rated PG for language.

1983   80 minutes

EXTERMINATING ANGEL, THE
★★★★★

DIRECTOR: Luis Buñuel
CAST: Silvia Pinal, Enrique Rambal, Jacqueline Andere, Jose Baviera, Augusto Benedico

Luis Buñuel always did love a good dinner party. In The Discreet Charm of the Bourgeoisie, the dinner party never could get under way, and here the elite après-opéra diners find they cannot escape the host's sumptuous music room. This is a very funny film—in a very black key. The Exterminating Angel was made in Mexico, and a Mexican proverb may be one key to Buñuel's intent: "After twenty-four hours, corpses and guests smell bad." That is the satiric surreal side. The more serious allegorical side is Buñuel's reflecting upon the spectre of bourgeois vacuity. A seminal work from the director's middle period. In Spanish with English subtitles.

1962   B & W   95 minutes

FALLING IN LOVE AGAIN
★★½

DIRECTOR: Steven Paul
CAST: Elliott Gould, Susannah York, Michelle Pfeiffer, Stuart Paul

Elliott Gould stars as a middle-aged dreamer who is obsessed with his younger days in the Bronx. Gould and wife (Susannah York) are on vacation and headed east to recapture the past. The film suffers from countless long flashbacks of his youth and romance with WASP princess (Michelle Pfeiffer) and is a poor attempt at romantic comedy. Rated R.

1980   103 minutes

FANDANGO
★★

DIRECTOR: Kevin Reynolds
CAST: Kevin Costner, Judd Nelson, Sam Robards, Chuck Bush, Brian Cesak

This is an unfunny comedy about a group of college chums (led by Kevin Costner of *Silverado* and Judd Nelson of *St. Elmo's Fire*) going on one last romp together before being inducted into the army—or running away from the draft—in 1971. Slow-going and a bit too angst-ridden, *Fandango* seems as if it's going to get better any minute, but it doesn't. Rated PG for profanity.

1984   91 minutes

FARMER'S DAUGHTER, THE
★★★

DIRECTOR: H. C. Potter

CAST: Loretta Young, Joseph Cotten, Ethel Barrymore, Charles Bickford, Lex Barker, Keith Andes, James Arness

Loretta Young won the best actress Oscar for her delightful performance in this charming comedy about a Swedish woman who clashes with the man she loves over a congressional election.

1947   B & W   97 minutes

FASTBREAK
★★½

DIRECTOR: Jack Smight
CAST: Gabriel Kaplan, Harold Sylvester, Mike Warren, Bernard King, Reb Brown

As a basketball coach, Gabe Kaplan resurrects some of the laughs he got with his sweathogs on "Welcome Back, Kotter." Kaplan plays a New York deli worker who quits to coach a college basketball team in Nevada. He brings four blacks from his New York ghetto to help the team, and one turns out to be a girl. Kaplan must beat a tough rival team in order to get a $30,000-a-year contract at the university, so he whips the unpromising team into shape. Rated PG.

1979   107 minutes

FAST TIMES AT RIDGEMONT HIGH
★★½

DIRECTOR: Amy Heckerling
CAST: Sean Penn, Jennifer Jason Leigh, Judge Reinhold, Brian Backer, Phoebe Cates, Ray Walston

In 1979, Cameron Crow went back to high school to discover what today's teens are up to and wrote about his experiences. From his excellent book, they've made a kind of *Animal House* of the teenage set. Youngsters will love it, but adults will probably want to skip the movie and read the book. Rated R for nudity, profanity, and simulated sex.

1982 92 minutes

FATHER GOOSE
★★★

DIRECTOR: Ralph Nelson
CAST: Cary Grant, Leslie Caron

A bedraggled, unshaven, and unsophisticated Cary Grant is worth watching even in a mediocre comedy. Grant plays a hard-drinking Australian coast watcher during the height of World War II. His reclusive lifestyle on a remote Pacific island is interrupted when he is forced to play nursemaid to a group of adolescent schoolgirls and their prudish teacher (Leslie Caron).

1964 115 minutes

FATHER'S LITTLE DIVIDEND
★★★

DIRECTOR: Vincente Minnelli
CAST: Spencer Tracy, Elizabeth Taylor, Joan Bennett, Don Taylor, Billie Burke

In *Father of the Bride*, the marriage of daughter Elizabeth Taylor to Don Taylor made a wreck out of Spencer Tracy. Now, in the sequel, she's expecting, and Tracy is not exactly overjoyed at the prospect of being a grandfather. This play off a winner doesn't measure up to the original, but it's entertaining fare anyway. Spencer Tracy could bluster and be flustered with the best.

1951 82 minutes

FEMALE TROUBLE

DIRECTOR: John Waters
CAST: Divine, Edith Massey, Cookie Mueller, David Lochary, Mink Stole, Michael Potter

The story of Dawn Davenport (Divine) from her days as a teen-age belligerent through her rise to fame as a criminal and then to her death as a convicted murderer. As in other films by Waters, the theme here is the Jean Genet–like credo "crime equals beauty." Also, as in other films by the enfant terrible from Baltimore, *Female Trouble* will offend just about anyone who takes the bourgeois life, with its voyeurlike view on fame, too seriously. He sees the status quo as something far sicker than his films. Though it is unrated, this film is the equivalent of an X, due to sex, nudity, and violence.

1973 90 minutes

FERNANDEL THE DRESSMAKER
★★

DIRECTOR: Jean Boyer
CAST: Fernandel, Suzy Delair, Françoise Fabian, Georges Chamarat

Using Fernandel as the hub, the film is a bit of whimsy about a gentleman's tailor who desires to become a world-famous couturier. Even with a lightweight plot, watching this famous comedian is certainly worth the time and effort to wade through the nonsense. A bit of Red Skelton, a dash of Danny Kaye, and soupçon of Jerry Lewis. No pretense here—just good fun. In French with English subtitles.

1957 B & W 84 minutes

FERRIS BUELLER'S DAY OFF
★★★★

DIRECTOR: John Hughes
CAST: Matthew Broderick, Alan Ruck, Mia Sara, Jeffrey Jones, Jennifer Grey, Charlie Sheen, Cindy Pickett, Lyman Ward

Writer-director John Hughes strikes again, this time with a

charming tale of a high-school legend in his own time (Matthew Broderick, playing the title character) who pretends to be ill in order to have a day away from school. After Ferris springs his girlfriend (sloe-eyed Mia Sara) and best friend (Alan Ruck, who makes a good nebbish), the trio heads into the Big City for eight hours of excitement. The dangerous thrill of breaking the rules transforms each event into an exciting challenge. The expressive Broderick owns the film, although he receives heavy competition from Jeffrey Jones, whose broadly played dean of students has been trying to nail Ferris Bueller for months. One subplot, involving an expensive car owned by Ferris' friend's father, is too uncomfortable to be funny, but the rest of the film succeeds on all accounts. Rated PG-13 for mild profanity.

1986   104 minutes

FIENDISH PLOT OF DR. FU MANCHU, THE
🥴

DIRECTOR: Pier Haggard
CAST: Peter Sellers, Helen Mirren, Sid Caesar, David Tomlinson

Peter Sellers plays a dual role of "insidious Oriental villain" Fu Manchu, who is out to rule the world, and his arch-enemy, the Holmes-like Nayland Smith of Scotland Yard. It's unfunny, racist, and just plain awful. Sellers's last movie. Rated PG.

1980   108 minutes

FINDERS KEEPERS
★★½
DIRECTOR: Richard Lester
CAST: Louis Gossett Jr., Michael O'-Keefe, Beverly D'Angelo

Director Richard Lester (A Hard Day's Night; Superman II) went back to his comedy roots with this disappointingly uneven slapstick chase film, which stars Louis Gossett Jr. (An Officer and a Gentleman), Michael O'Keefe (The Great Santini), and Beverly D'Angelo (Vacation) as a trio of wacky characters. The story deals with a missing $5 million and a wild train ride at the end of which the winner takes all. Rated PG for profanity and violence.

1983   96 minutes

FINE MADNESS, A
★★★
DIRECTOR: Irvin Kershner
CAST: Sean Connery, Joanne Woodward, Jean Seberg

Whimsical story of a daffy, radical poet, well portrayed by Sean Connery (proving that, even in the 1960s, he could stretch further than James Bond). Many of the laughs come from his well-developed relationship with wife Joanne Woodward, although the film occasionally lapses into lurid slapstick. A late-era screwball comedy, similar in tone to those made in the 1930s and 1940s. Unrated; adult themes.

1966   104 minutes

FINE MESS, A
(1987 Release)
★
DIRECTOR: Blake Edwards
CAST: Ted Danson, Howie Mandel, Richard Mulligan, Stuart Margolin, Maria Conchita Alonso, Jennifer Edwards, Paul Sorvino

Blake Edwards deserves a heavy fine for inflicting this mess on an unsuspecting public. Supposedly inspired by the Laurel and Hardy classic, The Music Box, this movie is totally lacking in originality. The illogical plot has Ted Danson and

Howie Mandel winning a bundle on a fixed horse race and spending the rest of the picture running from gangster Paul Sorvino's henchmen. The pace is that of an old gray mare on Quaaludes. Gag after gag falls embarrassingly flat. The cast works hard to no avail. Rated PG.

1986 100 minutes

FIRST FAMILY

DIRECTOR: Buck Henry
CAST: Bob Newhart, Gilda Radner, Madeline Kahn, Richard Benjamin, Harvey Korman, Bob Dishy, Rip Torn

The superior comic talents of Bob Newhart, Madeline Kahn, Gilda Radner, Richard Benjamin, and Harvey Korman are totally wasted in this unfunny farce about an inept president, his family, and his aides, written and directed by Buck Henry. Watching it, you get the impression that Henry had a vague idea of what he wanted to do but was never quite able to make up his mind. It's a mess. Rated R.

1980 104 minutes

FISH THAT SAVED PITTSBURGH, THE
★★½

DIRECTOR: Gilbert Moses
CAST: Stockard Channing, Flip Wilson, Jonathan Winters, Julius Irving

Curious mixture of disco, astrology, and comedy. A failing basketball team turns to a rather eccentric medium for help, and the resulting confusion makes for a few amusing moments. Features a veritable smorgasbord of second-rate actors, from Jonathan Winters to basketball great Julius Irving (Dr.

J.). Proceed at your own risk. Rated PG for profanity.

1979 102 minutes

FLAMINGO KID, THE
★★★½

DIRECTOR: Garry Marshall
CAST: Matt Dillon, Richard Crenna, Jessica Walter, Janet Jones, Hector Elizondo

A teen comedy-drama with more on its mind than stale sex jokes. Matt Dillon stars as Jeffrey Willis, a Brooklyn kid who discovers how the other half lives when he takes a summer job at a beach resort. A good story which explores the things (and people) that shape our values as we reach adulthood. Dillon's clashes with his poor-but-proud-of-it parents are a bit difficult to swallow, but the rest of the film rings quite clearly, particularly Richard Crenna's smooth-talking wheeler-dealer. A genuine pleasure, and you'll be glad you tried it. Rated PG-13 for frank sexual situations.

1984 100 minutes

FLYING DEUCES
★★★

DIRECTOR: Edward Sutherland
CAST: Stan Laurel, Oliver Hardy, Jean Parker

Stan Laurel and Oliver Hardy join the Foreign Legion to help Ollie forget his troubled romantic past. Their attempts at adjusting to Legion life provide many laugh-filled situations, although the script has weak areas and the movie occasionally drags.

1939 B & W 65 minutes

FOOLIN' AROUND
★★★

DIRECTOR: Richard T. Heffron

CAST: ~~Gary Busey, Annette O'Toole,~~ John Calvin, Eddie Albert, Cloris Leachman, Tony Randall

Gary Busey went from his acclaimed title performance in *The Buddy Holly Story* to starring in this amiable rip-off of *The Graduate* and *The Heartbreak Kid*. Still, Busey, as a working-class boy who falls in love with rich girl Annette O'Toole, is always watchable. He and O'Toole make an appealing screen team, and this makes the movie's lack of originality easier to take. Rated PG.

1980   111 minutes

FOR PETE'S SAKE
★★★

DIRECTOR: Peter Yates
CAST: Barbra Streisand, Michael Sarrazin, Estelle Parsons, Molly Picon

Lightweight comedy vehicle tailor-made to fit the talents of Barbra Streisand. In this one she plays the wife of cab driver Michael Sarrazin, trying to raise money for him while becoming involved with underworld thugs. Strictly for Streisand fans. Rated PG.

1974   90 minutes

FORTUNE COOKIE, THE
★★★★½

DIRECTOR: Billy Wilder
CAST: Jack Lemmon, Walter Matthau, Ron Rich, Cliff Osmond

Jack Lemmon is accidently injured by a player while filming a football game from the sidelines. His brother-in-law, Walter Matthau, sees this as an ideal attempt to make some lawsuit money. So starts the first of the usually delightful Lemmon-Matthau comedies. Matthau is at his scene-

stealing best in this Oscar-winning role.

1966   B & W 125 minutes

FORTY CARATS
★★★½

DIRECTOR: Milton Katselas
CAST: Liv Ullmann, Edward Albert, Gene Kelly, Nancy Walker, Deborah Raffin

This comedy has Liv Ullmann playing a 40-year-old divorcée being pursued by a rich 22-year-old, Edward Albert. Laughs come in as Ullmann's grown daughter (Deborah Raffin) and ex-husband (Gene Kelly) react to her latest suitor. Rated PG.

1973   110 minutes

48 HRS.
★★★★½

DIRECTOR: Walter Hill
CAST: Eddie Murphy, Nick Nolte, Annette O'Toole, Frank McRae, James Remar, David Patrick Kelly

Add *48 Hrs.* to the list of the best cops-and-robbers movies ever made. It's so action-packed, it'll keep you on the edge of your seat from beginning to end. There's more good news: It's funny too. In the story, a cop (Nick Nolte) goes looking for a psychotic prison escapee (James Remar) with the help of a fast-talking con man (Eddie Murphy). It's a dangerous mission, and there's never a dull moment. Rated R for violence, profanity, and nudity.

1982   96 minutes

FOUL PLAY
★★★

DIRECTOR: Colin Higgins
CAST: Goldie Hawn, Chevy Chase, Dudley Moore, Burgess Meredith, Marilyn Sokol

Gloria Mundy (Goldie Hawn) accidentally becomes involved in a plot to assassinate the Pope. Detective Tony Carlson (Chevy Chase) tries to protect and seduce her. Hawn is good as the damsel in distress, but Chase is not quite the Cary Grant type. Still it's fun. Rated PG.

1978   116 minutes

FRANCIS, THE TALKING MULE
★★★½

DIRECTOR: Arthur Lubin
CAST: Donald O'Connor, Patricia Medina, Zasu Pitts, Tony Curtis, Ray Collins, voice of Chill Wills

First in a series from Universal, this well-known comedy tells the story of how a dimwitted student at West Point (Donald O'Connor) first met up with the famous talking mule of the title. The gags really fly as Francis proceeds to get O'Connor in all sorts of outrageous predicaments, consistently pulling him out just in the nick of time. Some screamingly funny scenes. Followed by six sequels.

1950   B & W   91 minutes

FRATERNITY VACATION
🦃

DIRECTOR: James Frawley
CAST: Stephen Geoffreys, Sheree Wilson, Cameron Dye, Leigh McCloskey

A teen-lust comedy with no laughs, no imagination, and no point in existing, Fraternity Vacation stars Stephen Geoffreys as a world-class nerd who somehow scores during vacation time in Palm Springs. He scores and the viewer snores. Rated R for profanity and nudity.

1985   95 minutes

FREEBIE AND THE BEAN
★★★

DIRECTOR: Richard Rush
CAST: Alan Arkin, James Caan, Valerie Harper, Loretta Swit

Before astounding filmgoers with the outrageous black comedy The Stunt Man, director Richard Rush twisted the cop genre around with this watchable (but not spectacular) release. James Caan and Alan Arkin play San Francisco detectives who wreak havoc while on the trail of gangster Jack Kruschen. Rated R.

1974   113 minutes

FRENCH POSTCARDS
★★★½

DIRECTOR: Willard Huyck
CAST: David Marshall Grant, Blanche Baker, Miles Chapin, Debra Winger

Written, produced, and directed by the couple who gave us American Graffiti, Gloria Katz and Willard Huyck, this film benefits greatly from the skillful supporting performances by two noted French film stars, Marie-France Pisier (Love on the Run) and Jean Rochefort (Till Marriage Do Us Part). The younger set of characters are well played by David Marshall Grant, Miles Chapin, Valerie Quennessen, and Blanche Baker. French Postcards is an enjoyable way to spend a couple of hours. Rated PG.

1979   92 minutes

FRITZ THE CAT
★★★

DIRECTOR: Ralph Bakshi
CAST: Animated

This is an X-rated rendition of Robert Crumb's revolutionary feline and the most outrageous cartoon ever produced. Fritz the Cat has appeared in Zap Comix and Head Comix, as well as in other underground mags. It's sometimes funny and sometimes gross, but mostly just so-so.

1972   77 minutes

FRONT PAGE, THE
★★★★

DIRECTOR: Lewis Milestone
CAST: Pat O'Brien, Adolphe Menjou, Mary Brian, Edward Everett Horton

A newspaper editor and his ace reporter do battle with civic corruption and each other in the first version of this oft-filmed hit comedy. The fast-paced, sparkling dialogue and the performances of the Warner Bros. stable of character actors have not aged after more than fifty years. This classic movie retains a great deal of charm.

1931   B & W   99 minutes

FULL MOON IN PARIS
★★

DIRECTOR: Eric Rohmer
CAST: Pascale Ogier, Fabrice Luchini, Tcheky Karyo

This French film from Eric Rohmer, the director of the delightful *My Night at Maud's* and *Pauline at the Beach*, does not sustain his momentum with this tale of a young girl's disillusionment with her live-in lover. Perhaps the problem is her self-absorption and lack of commitment, but you just don't seem to care about what happens. Whatever the reason, it lacks the fun of his earlier films. In French with English subtitles.

1984   102 minutes

FULLER BRUSH GIRL, THE
★★★

DIRECTOR: Lloyd Bacon

CAST: Lucille Ball, Eddie Albert, Jerome Cowan, Lee Patrick

Lucy's in typical form as a dizzy cosmetics salesgirl up to her mascara in murder and hoodlums. Wisecracking dialogue and familiar character faces help this one out. Harmless fun.

1950   B & W   85 minutes

FULLER BRUSH MAN, THE
★★★

DIRECTOR: S. Sylvan Simon
CAST: Red Skelton, Janet Blair, Don McGuire, Adele Jergens, Buster Keaton

Red Skelton slapsticks along his route as a door-to-door salesman and gets involved with murder. Sadly, unsung master gagster Buster Keaton deserves a lot of credit for the humor he adds to many other Skelton films.

1948   B & W   93 minutes

FUNNY DIRTY LITTLE WAR (NO HABRA MAS PENSAS NI OLVIDO)
★★★

DIRECTOR: Hector Olivera
CAST: Federico Luppi, Hector Bidonde, Victor Laplace Commissar, Rodolfo Ranni, Miquel Angel Sola, Julio de Grazia

This allegorical, comedic piece begins in the small town of Colonia Vela. The comedy centers around the struggle between the Marxists and the Peronistas in 1974, shortly before the death of Juan Peron. The action quickly builds from a series of foolish misunderstandings to a very funny confrontation. The confrontation then leads to real bullets, the torture of prisoners, and the arrival of newsmen from Buenos Aires to cover the war. The photography, acting, and writing are all above average, but the viewer who is not aware of the history of Juan, Evita, and Isabel Peron may have difficulty following the allegorical line. Not rated. Spanish with English subtitles.

1985   80 minutes

FUNNY THING HAPPENED ON THE WAY TO THE FORUM, A
★★★★

DIRECTOR: Richard Lester
CAST: Zero Mostel, Phil Silvers, Jack Gilford, Michael Crawford, Buster Keaton

Ancient Rome is the setting for this fast-paced musical comedy. Zero Mostel is a never-ending source of zany plots to gain his freedom and line his toga with loot as a cunning slave. He is ably assisted by Phil Silvers and Jack Gilford in this bawdy romp through classic times. Look for Buster Keaton in a nice cameo.

1966   99 minutes

FUN WITH DICK AND JANE
★★★★

DIRECTOR: Ted Kotcheff
CAST: Jane Fonda, George Segal, Ed McMahon

How does one maintain one's lifestyle after a sacking from a highly paid aerospace position? George Segal and Jane Fonda have a unique solution. They steal. This comedy caper is well named, because once they begin their career in crime, some quality fun is in store for the audience. Rated PG.

1977   95 minutes

FUZZ
★★★

DIRECTOR: Richard A. Colla
CAST: Raquel Welch, Burt Reynolds, Yul Brynner, Tom Skerritt

Raquel Welch and Burt Reynolds star as police in this comedy-drama. Yul Brynner plays a bomb-happy villain. It has a few good moments, but you'd have to be a member of the Burt Reynolds fan club to really love it. Rated PG.

1972   92 minutes

GABRIELA
★★★

DIRECTOR: Bruno Barreto
CAST: Sonia Braga, Marcello Mastroianni, Antonio Cantafora, Ricardo Petraglia

Sexy Sonia Braga is both cook and mistress for bar owner Marcello Mastroianni in this excellent adaptation of Brazilian novelist Jorge Amado's comic romp *Gabriela, Clove and Cinnamon*. In Portuguese, with English subtitles. Rated R.

1983   102 minutes

GARBO TALKS
★★★★

DIRECTOR: Sidney Lumet
CAST: Anne Bancroft, Ron Silver, Carrie Fisher, Howard Da Silva, Dorothy Loudon, Hermione Gingold

In this often funny and touching contemporary comedy, Anne Bancroft is delightful as an outspoken crusader against the small injustices in the world. But she has her fantasies, too, and enlists the aid of her son (Ron Silver) in finding Greta Garbo, who at age 79 can occasionally be spotted walking around New York. Rated PG for profanity.

1984   103 minutes

GAS
🐢

DIRECTOR: Les Rose

CAST: Sterling Hayden, Peter Aykroyd, Susan Anspach, Donald Sutherland, Howie Mandel, Sanee Currie, Helen Shaver

America's past petroleum shortages (whether real or conspiratorial) have not been laughing matters, and neither is this tasteless, tedious comedy about an artificial gas-crisis in a Midwest city. More frenetic than funny and overstuffed with offensive ethnic stereotyping, car chases, and stale humor, it's generally a moronic mess. Rated R because of sex and rough language.

1981   94 minutes

GENERAL, THE
★★★★★
DIRECTOR: Buster Keaton
CAST: Buster Keaton, Marion Mack, Glen Cavender, Jim Farley, Joseph Keaton

The General is a film based on an incident in the Civil War. Buster Keaton is an engineer determined to recapture his stolen locomotive. Magnificent battle scenes are mere backdrops for Keaton's inspired acrobatics and comedy. Solid scripting, meticulous attention to detail, and ingenious stunt work make this picture excellent.

1927   B & W   74 minutes

GENTLEMEN PREFER BLONDES
★★
DIRECTOR: Howard Hawks
CAST: Jane Russell, Marilyn Monroe, Charles Coburn, Tony Noonan, Elliott Reid, George Winslow

Howard Hawks gets surprisingly good performances from his stars, Jane Russell and Marilyn Monroe, in this 1953 musical comedy. As usual, Hawks does his best to make good scenes, but this time the silly plot—about two women searching for husbands—thwarts his esteemable talents.

1953   91 minutes

GET CRAZY
★★★½
DIRECTOR: Allan Arkush
CAST: Malcolm McDowell, Allen Goorwitz, Daniel Stern, Ed Begley Jr., Miles Chapin, Lou Reed, Stacey Nelkin, Bill Henderson, Franklin Ajaye, Bobby Sherman, Fabian Forte

Here's the wildest, weirdest, and most outrageous rock 'n' roll comedy any of us is likely to see. It's a story about a rock concert on New Year's Eve, during which everything that can go wrong does. It is basically a jumping-off point for sight gags, low humor, high humor, and general nuttiness. You're never bored. Malcolm McDowell plays a Mick Jagger–style rock singer, Allen Goorwitz is a Bill Graham–ish promoter, and Daniel Stern is his lovesick stage manager. Rated R for nudity, profanity, violence, and suggested sex.

1983   92 minutes

GET OUT YOUR HANDKERCHIEFS
★★★½
DIRECTOR: Bertrand Blier
CAST: Gerard Depardieu, Patrick Dewaere, Carol Laure

Winner of the 1978 Academy Award for best foreign film, this stars Gerard Depardieu as a clumsy husband so desperate to make his melancholic wife happy and pregnant that he provides her with a lover (Patrick Dewaere). A mostly improbable existential drama, what comedy there was in the original version was sacrificed for lip-synchronization in the dubbed version. Nevertheless, this film has a few surprises in store not only for the two male leads but also for the viewer, when young Christian Beloeil (Riton) appears on the scene. Unrated, contains nudity.

1978   108 minutes

GHOSTBUSTERS
★★★★

DIRECTOR: Ivan Reitman
CAST: Bill Murray, Dan Aykroyd, Sigourney Weaver, Harold Ramis, Annie Potts, Ernie Hudson, William Atherton, Rick Moranis

Bill Murray, Dan Aykroyd, Sigourney Weaver, and Harold Ramis (*Stripes*) are terrific in this very funny and often frightening comedy-horror film about a special organization that fights evil spirits. Is it *The Exorcist* meets "Saturday Night Live"? That's pretty close—but it's better. This big-budget horror-comedy delivers a bellyful of laughs as well as lots of unexpected shocks and excitement. Even little kids might enjoy it. There are some really scary scenes, but because the whole thing is done in a comedic vein, children just might be able to see it without having nightmares. Rated PG for profanity and scary scenes.

1984   107 minutes

GHOST GOES WEST, THE
★★★★

DIRECTOR: René Clair
CAST: Robert Donat, Jean Parker

A millionaire buys a Scottish castle and transports it stone by stone to America only to discover that it comes complete with a ghost. Robert Donat gives a memorable performance in this bit of whimsy.

1935   B & W 100 minutes

GHOSTS ON THE LOOSE
★½

DIRECTOR: William Beaudine
CAST: The East Side Kids, Bela Lugosi, Ava Gardner, Rick Valine

Silly movie pits Monogram's moronic East Side Kids against a bored Bela Lugosi and his German henchmen in this pallid variation on the "old haunted house" theme. No real thrills, no real laughs in this tired creaker. Even a youthful Ava Gardner can't perk this pooch up, and one wonders why on Earth it was even packaged for the video market. This is the kind of movie you turn off when it's on TV, so why would you go out and spend money just so you can do the same thing?

1943   B & W 65 minutes

GIDGET
★★½

DIRECTOR: Paul Wendkos
CAST: Sandra Dee, James Darren, Arthur O'Connell, Cliff Robertson, Doug McClure

The eternal beach bunny, Gidget (Sandra Dee), becomes involved with Cliff Robertson in order to make the man she's infatuated with (James Darren) notice her. This is the first and the best of a sub-par surfer series.

1959   95 minutes

GIDGET GOES HAWAIIAN
★★

DIRECTOR: Paul Wendkos
CAST: Deborah Walley, James Darren, Michael Callan, Carl Reiner, Peggy Cass, Eddie Foy Jr.

Everyone's favorite "girl-midget" (played here by Deborah Walley, taking over from Sandra Dee) returns to the screen in this inoffensive, brainless sequel to the 1959 box-office hit. This time around, she's off to Waikiki with her family for another series of romantic mis-adventures amid songs, surfing, and other adolescent fluff that movie producers in the early 1960s apparently thought teenagers were obsessed with. Some picturesque Hawaiian locations (all of which you've already seen in other, better movies) and a bright supporting cast are the main assets.

1961   102 minutes

GIFT, THE
★★★

DIRECTOR: Michael Lang
CAST: Clio Goldsmith, Pierre Mondy, Claudia Cardinale

A 55-year-old bank worker (Pierre Mondy) decides to take early retirement because he fears stress will kill him. So his co-workers give him an unusual retirement gift, an expensive hooker (Clio Goldsmith), who is asked to seduce him without his knowing her profession. The chuckles in this import do not come fast and furious. Yet it is an amiable sex comedy that most adult viewers will find quite charming and diverting. In French with English subtitles. Rated R for partial nudity and profanity.

1982   105 minutes

GILDA LIVE
★★

DIRECTOR: Mike Nichols
CAST: Gilda Radner, Don Novello, Paul Shaffer, Candy Slice

We've always loved Gilda Radner's characters from "Saturday Night Live," and they're all represented in *Gilda Live*. But something is missing in her live show. The result is very few laughs. Rated R.

1980   96 minutes

GIRL IN EVERY PORT, A
★½

DIRECTOR: Chester Erskine
CAST: Groucho Marx, William Bendix, Marie Wilson, Don DeFore, Gene Lockhart

Silly film about sailors involved in horse-racing scheme milks the old hide-the-horse-on-the-ship gag for all that it's worth (which isn't much) and then some. Only the presence of Groucho Marx makes this tired story worthy of note, and he, like the other fine character players stuck in this vacuum, can't do a thing with laughs that just aren't there. The kids might like it, but don't plan it for the evening's entertainment.

1952   B & W   86 minutes

GIRLS JUST WANT TO HAVE FUN

DIRECTOR: Alan Metter
CAST: Sarah Jessica Parker, Lee Montgomery, Morgan Woodward, Jonathan Silverman

Sarah Jessica Parker (*Footloose*) stars as a young woman whose family moves to Chicago, where the popular television show "Dance TV" is filmed. She just lovvves to dance, and it just so happens the show is holding auditions for new dancers. She's going to give it a try, but will she be picked? This is a predictable, boring, and dumb movie. Rated PG for profanity.

1985   90 minutes

GIZMO!
★★★★½

DIRECTOR: Howard Smith
CAST: Documentary

A collection of short films from the 1920s and 1930s featuring early daredevils, flying machines, and enthusiastic inventors demonstrating their questionable benefits to mankind. It's up to the audience to decide whether these people were complete morons or just ahead of their time. A delightful, often hysterical celebration of the American spirit. Rated G.

1977 B & W 77 minutes

GO WEST
★★★½

DIRECTOR: Edward Buzzell
CAST: The Marx Brothers, John Carroll, Diana Lewis, Walter Woolf King

Far from prime-screen Marx Brothers, this is still one of their best MGM movies and a treat for their fans. Good comedy bits combine with a rip-roaring climax (stolen by screenwriter Buster Keaton from *The General*) for a highly watchable star comedy.

1940 B & W 81 minutes

GODS MUST BE CRAZY, THE
★★★★★

DIRECTOR: Jamie Uys
CAST: Marius Meyers, Sandra Prinsloo

This work, by South African filmmaker Jamie Uys, is a hilarious, poignant, exciting, thought-provoking, violent, and slapstick concoction that involves three separate stories. One is about a Bushman whose tribe selects him to get rid of an evil thing sent by the gods: a Coke bottle. The second features the awkward love affair of a teacher and a klutzy scientist. The last involves a band of terrorists fleeing for their lives. These all come together for a surprising and satisfying climax. Unrated, the film has violence.

1980 109 minutes

GOING APE!
★

DIRECTOR: Jeremy Kronsberg

CAST: Tony Danza, Jessica Walter, Stacey Nelkins, Danny DeVito, Art Metrano, Joseph Maher

If one orangutan can help Clint Eastwood rack up millions at the box office, then three should make motion picture history, right? Wrong. There's nothing very original here. Tony Danza plays the heir to a million-dollar fortune-with-a-catch: In order to get the money, he has to care for three unpredictable simians. Because the film is padded with all-too-familiar material, very little fun shines through. Rated PG.

1981 87 minutes

GOING BERSERK
★

DIRECTOR: David Steinberg
CAST: John Candy, Joe Flaherty, Eugene Levy, Alley Mills, Pat Hingle, Richard Libertini

This is an unfunny comedy starring former SCTV regulars John Candy, Joe Flaherty, and Eugene Levy. Written and directed by David Steinberg (a former stand-up comedian who made his filmmaking debut with *Paternity*, starring Burt Reynolds), it never really goes anywhere, and its collection of supposedly "zany" bits just isn't funny. Rated R.

1983 85 minutes

GOING IN STYLE
★★★★

DIRECTOR: Martin Brest
CAST: George Burns, Art Carney, Lee Strasberg, Charles Hallahan, Pamela Payton-Wright

Three retirees who gather daily on a park bench need to add some spice to their empty existence. One of their sons needs help in paying his bills, so they decide to pitch in by robbing a bank. This crime caper has some unexpected plot twists mixed with a perfect sprinkling of humor. It is a delight throughout. Rated PG.

1979   96 minutes

GOING PLACES
★★

DIRECTOR: Bertrand Blier
CAST: Gerard Depardieu, Patrick Dewaere, Miou-Miou, Jeanne Moreau, Isabelle Huppert, Brigitte Fossey

Memorable only as one of Gerard Depardieu's first screen appearances. He and Patrick Dewaere play a couple of amiable lowlifes who dabble in petty thievery and have their way with all the local women. Contains one of filmdom's most acutely uncomfortable scenes, when one of the young lads gets shot in the testicles. Too unpleasant and chauvinistic for a sex farce, but too unbelievable as straight drama. Don't blink, or you'll miss Jeanne Moreau's brief cameo. Rated R for sex.

1974   117 minutes

GOLDEN AGE OF COMEDY, THE
★★★★

DIRECTOR: COMPILER: Robert Youngson
CAST: Laurel and Hardy, Will Rogers, Harry Langdon, Ben Turpin, Carole Lombard, Snub Pollard

First and most popular of Robert Youngson's tributes to silent film comedy, this compilation of highlights introduced new generations of moviegoers to the great years of silent comedy and continues to do so. Many of the shorts with Laurel and Hardy (including the classics "Two Tars") will be familiar to viewers due to their popularity and availability, but the segments with Will Rogers spoofing silent film greats Douglas Fairbanks and Tom Mix, and the footage with Harry Langdon (who was at one time considered a comedic equal to Charlie Chaplin, Buster Keaton, and Harold Lloyd) are seldom seen and worth the wait. Future star Carole Lombard shows her form rather than her famous screwball style in a Mack Sennett short, and the Keystone Kops go through their paces. Fun for everyone, but it's a shame all these films aren't available in their entirety on video.

1957   B & W   78 minutes

GOLD RUSH, THE
★★★★★

DIRECTOR: Charles Chaplin
CAST: Charlie Chaplin, Mack Swain, Tom Murray, Georgia Hale

Charlie Chaplin's classic comedy is immortal for the scrumptious supper of a boiled boot, the teetering Klondike cabin, and the dance of the dinner rolls. Some parts are very sentimental, but these give the viewer time to catch his or her breath after laughing so much.

1925   B & W   100 minutes

GOOD NEIGHBOR SAM
★★★

DIRECTOR: David Swift
CAST: Jack Lemmon, Romy Schneider, Dorothy Provine, Edward G. Robinson

This comedy is similar to many of the lightweight pot-boilers given to Jack Lemmon in the 1960s. He is a likable average American forced by circumstances beyond his control to bumble his way out of misadventures. Good Neighbor Sam makes only marginal use of Lemmon's comic gifts. It is an overlong farce about a married advertising designer who pretends marriage to his foreign neighbor next door so she can secure an inheritance. He must continue the charade to avoid offending his firm's puritanical client who chanced to see them together.

1964   130 minutes

GOOD SAM
★★

DIRECTOR: Leo McCarey
CAST: Gary Cooper, Ann Sheridan, Edmund Lowe

Gary Cooper plays a guy who can't say no in this barely watchable "comedy." He's Mr. Nice-Guy to everyone but his own family and feels he has to help everyone. So he lends all his money to "friends" and the "needy." Unfortunately, when it comes to buying things for his family (such as a house) he has no money left.

1948   B & W 114 minutes

GOODBYE COLUMBUS
★★★★

DIRECTOR: Larry Peerce
CAST: Richard Benjamin, Ali MacGraw, Jack Klugman

This drama marked the start of Ali McGraw's and Richard Benjamin's movie careers. Ali plays a rich, spoiled Jewish-American princess who meets college dropout (Benjamin) at her country club. They have an affair, and we get to see her flaws through his "average guy" eyes. Rated R.

1969   105 minutes

GOODBYE GIRL, THE
★★★★½

DIRECTOR: Herbert Ross
CAST: Richard Dreyfuss, Marsha Mason, Quinn Cummings

Neil Simon's sparkling screenplay and the acting of Marsha Mason and Richard Dreyfuss combine to produce one of the best pure comedies since Hollywood's golden '30s. Mason and Dreyfuss are a mismatched pair of New Yorkers forced into becoming roommates. Rated PG.

1977   110 minutes

GOODBYE NEW YORK
★★★★

DIRECTOR: Amos Kollek
CAST: Julie Hagerty, Amos Kollek, David Topaz, Shmuel Shiloh, Christopher Goutman

An insurance salesperson (Julie Hagerty) becomes fed up with her job and husband and leaves for Paris. After falling asleep on the plane, she wakes up in Israel with no money and no luggage. This is similar to Lost in America, a comedy about survival in which she also starred, only this one is more like Lost in the Middle East. The film showcases Hagerty's talents without treating the film as merely a vehicle for the star. Rated R for language and very brief nudity.

1984   90 minutes

GORILLA, THE
★★

DIRECTOR: Allan Dwan
CAST: The Ritz Brothers, Bela Lugosi, Lionel Atwill

This is another one of those horror comedies that takes place in an old mansion and again wastes poor Bela Lugosi's acting talents. The Ritz Brothers were an acquired taste, to be sure, and this is not their best vehicle by any stretch of the imagination.

1939   B & W 66 minutes

GRACE QUIGLEY
★★½

DIRECTOR: Anthony Harvey

CAST: Katharine Hepburn, Nick Nolte, Elizabeth Wilson, Chip Zien, Christopher Murney, Kitle Fever

After witnessing the murder of her landlord, spinster Katharine Hepburn enlists the aid of freelance hit man Nick Nolte. Hepburn wants Nolte to end her life, but not before he puts to rest some of her elderly friends who feel it is time for them to die. Extremely black comedy doesn't have enough humor and warmth to rise above its gruesome subject matter. Not for all tastes, to be sure, although Nolte and Hepburn work well together. Rated R.

1985   87 minutes

GRASS IS ALWAYS GREENER OVER THE SEPTIC TANK, THE
★★★½

DIRECTOR: Robert Day
CAST: Carol Burnett, Charles Grodin, Alex Rocco, Linda Gray

Carol Burnett and Charles Grodin shine in this tale of the domestic horrors of suburban life taken from Erma Bombeck's bestseller. The comedy doesn't always work, but when it does it rivals Grodin's *The Heartbreak Kid* and some of the best moments of Burnett's TV show. No rating, but the equivalent of a PG for language.

1978   98 minutes

GRASS IS GREENER, THE
★★★½

DIRECTOR: Stanley Donen
CAST: Cary Grant, Deborah Kerr, Jean Simmons, Robert Mitchum

Cary Grant and Deborah Kerr star as a married couple experimenting with extramarital affairs in this comedy. Jean Simmons plays Grant's girlfriend, while Robert Mitchum courts Kerr. Some funny moments, but it's not hilarious.

1960   105 minutes

GREAT BANK HOAX, THE
★★½

DIRECTOR: Joseph Jacoby
CAST: Richard Basehart, Burgess Meredith, Paul Sand, Ned Beatty, Michael Murphy, Arthur Godfrey

It is doubtful that viewers today will think of Watergate when watching this comedy caper, but it was originally intended as a parable. When the pillars of the community find out that the bank has been embezzled they decide to rob it. Great characterizations by all-star cast. Rated PG.

1977   89 minutes

GREAT DICTATOR, THE
★★★★★

DIRECTOR: Charles Chaplin
CAST: Charlie Chaplin, Jack Oakie, Paulette Goddard

Charlie Chaplin stars in and directed this devastating lampoon of the Third Reich. The celebrated clown's first all-talking picture, it casts him in two roles—as his famous Little Tramp and as Adenoid Hynkel, the Hitler-like ruler of Tomania. As with the similarly themed *Duck Soup*, starring the Marx Brothers, the comedy was a little too whimsical for wartime audiences. But it has to be regarded as a classic.

1940   B & W 128 minutes

GREAT GUNS
★★

DIRECTOR: Monty Banks
CAST: Stan Laurel, Oliver Hardy, Sheila Ryan, Dick Nelson

Although it's a cut below their classics, Sons of the Desert will love it, and so will most—especially the young. Stan and Ollie have jobs guarding a rich man's playboy son, Dick Nelson. He gets drafted; the fellows join up to continue their work. The playboy gets along just fine in khaki. The boys get up to their ears in trouble with an archetypical sergeant.

1941   B & W   74 minutes

GREAT RACE, THE
★★★½

DIRECTOR: Blake Edwards
CAST: Tony Curtis, Natalie Wood, Jack Lemmon, Peter Falk, Keenan Wynn, Larry Storch, Arthur O'Connell, Vivian Vance

Set in the early 1900s, this film comically traces the daily events of the first New York–to–Paris car race. Unfortunately, two-and-a-half hours of silly spoofs will have even the most avid film fan yawning.

1965   150 minutes

GREGORY'S GIRL
★★★★½

DIRECTOR: Bill Forsyth
CAST: Gordon John Sinclair, Dee Hepburn, Chic Murray, Jake D'Arcy, Alex Norton, John Bett, Clare Grogan

In this utterly delightful movie from Scotland, a gangly, good-natured kid named Gregory—who has just gone through a five-inch growth spurt that has left him with the physical grace of a drunken stilt walker and made him a problem player on the school's winless soccer team—falls in love with the team's newest and best player: a girl named Dorothy. Unrated, the film has no objectionable content.

1981   91 minutes

GROOVE TUBE, THE
★★½

DIRECTOR: Ken Shapiro
CAST: Ken Shapiro, Lane Sarasohn, Chevy Chase, Richard Belzer, Mary Mendham, Bill Kemmill

A sometimes funny and most times just silly—or gross—1974 takeoff on television by writer-director Ken Shapiro. The V.D. commercial is a classic, however. Look for Chevy Chase in his first, brief screen appearance. Rated R.

1974   75 minutes

GUESS WHO'S COMING TO DINNER
★★★½

DIRECTOR: Stanley Kramer
CAST: Spencer Tracy, Katharine Hepburn, Sidney Poitier, Katharine Houghton, Cecil Kellaway, Beah Richards, Roy E. Glenn Sr., Virginia Christine

The final film pairing of Spencer Tracy and Katharine Hepburn, this was also one of the first to deal with interracial marriage. Though quite daring at the time of its original release, this movie, directed by the heavy-handed Stanley Kramer, seems rather quaint today. Still, Tracy and Hepburn are fun to watch, and Sidney Poitier and Katharine Houghton (Hepburn's niece) make an appealing young couple.

1967   108 minutes

GUIDE FOR THE MARRIED MAN, A
★★★½

DIRECTOR: Gene Kelly
CAST: Walter Matthau, Inger Stevens, Robert Morse, Sue Ane Langdon, Lucille Ball, Jack Benny, Joey Bishop, Art Carney, Jayne Mansfield, Carl Reiner, Sid Caesar, Phil Silvers, Jeffrey Hunter, Sam Jaffe

Worldly Robert Morse tries to teach reluctant Walter Matthau the fundamentals of adultery. His lessons are acted out by a dazzling roster of top comedy stars. This episodic film provides a steady stream of laughs. The bit in which Joey Bishop is caught red-handed and practices the "deny, deny, deny" technique is a classic.

1967　　　　　　　89 minutes

GUMSHOE
★★★½

DIRECTOR: Stephen Frears

CAST: Albert Finney, Billie Whitelaw, Frank Finlay, Janice Rule, Caroline Seymour

Every hard-bitten private-eye film and film noir is saluted in this crime-edged comedy. Liverpool bingo caller Albert Finney finds himself in deep, murky water when he tries to live his fantasy of being a Humphrey Bogart–type shamus. Raymond Chandler and Dashiell Hammett fans will love every frame. Rated PG.

1972　　　　　　　88 minutes

GUNG HO
★★★★

DIRECTOR: Ron Howard

CAST: Michael Keaton, Gedde Watanabe, George Wendt, Mimi Rogers, John Turturro, Sab Shimono, Clint Howard

Another winner from director Ron Howard and writers Lowell Ganz and Babaloo Mandel, who previously teamed on *Night Shift* and *Splash*. This is a pointed and relevant study of the cultural chaos that occurs when small-town Hadleyville's automobile plant is rescued from closure by imported Japanese management. Michael Keaton holds things together as the fast-talking liaison between employees and management; he squares off against baby-faced Gedde Watanabe, as the exec who must look good to the big bosses back in Japan. Extremely unflattering in its portrait of the "Ugly American," the script bravely suggests that we could learn a thing or two from other cultures. Rated PG-13 for language.

1985　　　　　　111 minutes

HAMBURGER—THE MOTION PICTURE
🐷

DIRECTOR: Mike Marvin

CAST: Leigh McCloskey, Sandy Hackett, Randi Brooks, Charles Tyner, Chuck McCann, Dick Butkus

A very funny comedy could be made about the fast-food industry, but this isn't it. From the beginning of this insipid and achingly predictable movie, it is obvious the viewer is in trouble. In short order, we are introduced to a dopey nun (whose job, it seems, is to be bashed about whenever the filmmakers need a cheap laugh), a fat man (who jolts himself with electricity to stay on his diet), and a slobbering nerd (who prefers radio commercials to real music). The story involves a promiscuous fellow (Leigh McCloskey) who has to clean up his act or lose a $250,000 inheritance. We are supposed to care about this, but McCloskey's character is so one-dimensional we can hardly stand him. In fact, all the characters in *Hamburger* are lifeless jokes. Put this one on the back burner. Rated R for profanity, nudity, suggested sex, and violence.

1986　　　　　　90 minutes

HANKY PANKY
★

DIRECTOR: Sidney Poitier

CAST: Gene Wilder, Gilda Radner, Richard Widmark, Kathleen Quinlan, Robert Prosky

In an obvious takeoff on the Hitchcock suspense formula, this seldom funny comedy features Gene Wilder as an innocent man caught up in international intrigue and murder. Gilda Radner is Wilder's confused helpmate, and Richard Widmark leads the baddies in this ultimately disappointing and, in the last half, boring film, directed by Sidney Poitier (*Stir Crazy*). Rated PG for violence and gore.

1982   110 minutes

HANNAH AND HER SISTERS
★★★★★

DIRECTOR: Woody Allen

CAST: Woody Allen, Michael Caine, Mia Farrow, Carrie Fisher, Barbara Hershey, Maureen O'Sullivan, Diane Wiest, Max Von Sydow, Daniel Stern, Lloyd Nolan, Sam Waterston

One of Woody Allen's very best, a two-year study of a family held together by house-mother Mia Farrow. Hannah is best friend, trusted confidante, and sympathetic peacemaker for sisters Barbara Hershey and Diane Wiest, husband Michael Caine, and parents Maureen O'Sullivan and Lloyd Nolan. Woody's along for a glib part as a hypochondriac who may get his fondest wish: a fatal disease. Farrow is superb as the woman in control of everything and everybody, until she snaps upon realizing the others may not *want* her ever-vigilant assistance. A change for Woody, because the film—and, most important, its conclusion—remains optimistic. Rated PG-13 for sexual situations.

1986   106 minutes

HAPPY HOOKER, THE
★★★

DIRECTOR: Nicholas Sgarro

CAST: Lynn Redgrave, Jean-Pierre Aumont, Elizabeth Wilson, Tom Poston, Lovelady Powell, Nicholas Pryor

After Xaviera Hollander's novel became a bestseller, Lynn Redgrave was cast as Hollander in this offbeat comedy. Redgrave adds a wry touch as she recounts Hollander's rise from free-lance prostitute to one of New York's most infamous madams. Additionally, viewers get a peek at the kinky scenes one gets into when they play the sex-for-hire game. Rated R for nudity and sex.

1975   96 minutes

HAPPY HOOKER GOES TO WASHINGTON, THE

DIRECTOR: William A. Levey

CAST: Joey Heatherton, George Hamilton, Ray Walston, Jack Carter

Xaviera Hollander (Joey Heatherton) is innocently pursuing her career as a madam when she is surprised by a process server and called to Washington. Once there, she is forced to give testimony to a Senate committee sworn to uphold the morals of America. Naturally, she finds that all the senators use call girls and are unfit to judge her. But not before this soft-core sex film features plenty of nudity and profanity. Rated R for profanity, nudity, and sex.

1977   89 minutes

HARDBODIES

DIRECTOR: Mark Griffith

CAST: Grant Cramer, Teal Roberts, Gary Wood, Michael Rappaport, Roberta Collins

In this disgusting, insulting, and degrading-to-women sexploitation flick, three middle-aged, successful, but far-from-sexy men rent a summer beach house in hopes of seducing teen-age girls. They have no luck until Scotty Palmer (Grant Cramer), "the hottest guy on the beach," according to the press kit, decides to help them score. A few years ago, this piece of trash would have been considered hard-core pornography. The "target audience" (in film industry jargon) of this release is teenagers. We find that depressing. Rated R for nudity, simulated sex, and profanity.

1984   90 minutes

HARDLY WORKING
★

DIRECTOR: Jerry Lewis
CAST: Jerry Lewis, Susan Oliver, Roger C. Carmel, Deanna Lund, Harold J. Stone, Steve Franken

Jerry Lewis's 1980s screen comeback is passable family fare. As a middle-aged, out-of-work clown, he tries his hand at a number of jobs and flubs them all. As a gas station attendant, he nearly blows a service station sky-high. As a bartender in a strip joint, he gets bounced for handling the help. As a teriyaki chef, he fends off disgruntled customers with verbal karate: "I have a black and blue belt." His fans will love it; others need not apply. Rated PG.

1981   91 minutes

HAROLD AND MAUDE
★★★★★

DIRECTOR: Hal Ashby
CAST: Bud Cort, Vivian Pickles, Ruth Gordon, Cyril Cusack, Charles Tyner, Ellen Geer

Hal Ashby (*Coming Home*; *Shampoo*) directed this delightful black comedy about an odd young man named Harold (Bud Cort) who devises some rather elaborate fake deaths to jar his snooty, manipulative mother (Vivian Pickles). Soon his attention turns to an octogenarian named Maude (Ruth Gordon), with whom he falls in love. Featuring a superb soundtrack of songs by Cat Stevens, this is one of the original cult classics—and deservedly so. Rated PG.

1972   90 minutes

HARPER VALLEY P.T.A.
★

DIRECTOR: Richard Bennett
CAST: Barbara Eden, Ronny Cox, Nanette Fabray, Susan Swift, Ron Masak

Based on the popular country song, this silly piece of fluff features Barbara Eden as the sexy woman who gives her gossiping neighbors their proper comeuppance. Rated PG.

1978   102 minutes

HARRY AND WALTER GO TO NEW YORK
★★½

DIRECTOR: Mark Rydell
CAST: James Caan, Elliott Gould, Michael Caine, Diane Keaton, Charles Durning

Harry and Walter Go to New York looks as if it were fun for the principals to make. James Caan and Elliott Gould appear to be having the time of their lives portraying two inept con men. Michael Caine and Diane Keaton are, as always, excellent. Mark Rydell directs this unusually light film with an invisible touch. *Harry and Walter* is sort of like Chinese food—an hour later, you feel as if you haven't had anything. Rated PG.

1976   123 minutes

HAUNTED HONEYMOON
★

DIRECTOR: Gene Wilder
CAST: Gene Wilder, Gilda Radner, Dom De Luise, Jonathan Pryce, Paul L. Smith, Peter Vaughan, Bryan Pringle, Jim Carter, Eve Ferret

Writer-director-star Gene Wilder fails to scare up a single solid laugh in this sadly limp chiller spoof. He once again squanders the talents of his wife, Gilda Radner. They play 40s radio stars who plan to wed at an ominous family estate, which is populated by loonies, werewolves, and transvestites. Even Dom De Luise, improbably cast as Wilder's elderly aunt, fails to amuse. The movie drags on interminably. Rated PG.

1986   90 minutes

HAWMPS!
🐾

DIRECTOR: Joe Camp
CAST: James Hampton, Christopher Connelly, Slim Pickens, Denver Pyle, Jack Elam

An extremely unfunny movie from the director of *Benji*, centering on an Old West cavalry unit that uses camels instead of horses. The cast is made up of familiar faces who appear uninspired. A very dumb film. Rated G.

1976   120 minutes

HEARTBREAK KID, THE
★★★★

DIRECTOR: Elaine May
CAST: Charles Grodin, Cybill Shepherd, Jeannie Berlin, Eddie Albert, Audra Lindley

The lack of care or commitment in the modern marriage is satirized in this comedy. Charles Grodin plays a young man who's grown tired of his wife while driving to their honeymoon in Florida. By the time he sees beautiful Cybill Shepherd on the beach, his marriage has totally disintegrated. Jeannie Berlin, director Elaine May's daughter, is the big scene stealer as Grodin's whining bride. Rated PG.

1972   104 minutes

HEARTBURN
★★★

DIRECTOR: Mike Nichols
CAST: Meryl Streep, Jack Nicholson, Jeff Daniels, Maureen Stapleton, Stockard Channing, Richard Masur, Catherine O'Hara, Milos Forman

Uneven adaptation of Nora Ephron's novel (she also wrote the screenplay) and a thinly disguised account of her own separation from Watergate journalist Carl Bernstein. Jack Nicholson and Meryl Streep, both veterans of previous relationships, meet, fall in love, get married, and drift apart. Little explanation is given for this eventual drift, which is the film's weakness; its strength, on the other hand, comes from the superb performances by the stars and an incredible supporting cast. At times quite funny, such as during the wedding itself, or later, when Streep's character announces her pregnancy. Needlessly rated R for language.

1986   108 minutes

HEAT OF DESIRE
★★½

DIRECTOR: Luc Beraud
CAST: Patrick Dewaere, Clio Goldsmith, Jeanne Moreau, Guy Marchand

So many sex comedies are about married men who discover adultery brings new vitality, this plot has become a cinematic cliché. But this didn't stop director Luc Beraud from using it again in this disappointing film about a writer (Patrick Dewaere) who dallies with an unpredictable flirt (Clio Goldsmith). This one's only for fans of typical Gallic movies. In French, with English subtitles. Unrated, the film has nudity and suggested sex.

1984   91 minutes

HEAVEN CAN WAIT
★★★★½

DIRECTOR: Warren Beatty, Buck Henry

CAST: Warren Beatty, Julie Christie, Jack Warden, Dyan Cannon, Charles Grodin, James Mason, Buck Henry, Vincent Gardenia

In this charming, thoroughly entertaining remake of *Here Comes Mr. Jordan* (1941), Warren Beatty stars as quarterback Joe Pendleton, who meets a premature demise when an overzealous angel (Buck Henry) takes the athlete's spirit out of his body after an accident. As it turns out, it wasn't Joe's time to die. However, in the interim, his body is cremated. Thus begins a quest by Joe, the angel, and his superior (James Mason) to find a proper earthly replacement. This, of course, brings a number of humorous and touching complications. Rated PG.

1978   100 minutes

HEAVEN HELP US
★

DIRECTOR: Michael Dinner

CAST: Andrew McCarthy, Kevin Dillon, Malcolm Dunarie, Stephen Geoffreys, Donald Sutherland, John Heard, Wallace Shawn, Kate Reid

Donald Sutherland, John Heard, Wallace Shawn, and Kate Reid support the youthful cast of this generally unfunny and often repulsive comedy about a group of schoolboys (played by Andrew McCarthy, Kevin Dillon, Malcolm Danarie, and Stephen Geoffreys) discovering the opposite sex and other adolescent pursuits. Rated R.

1985   90 minutes

HEAVENLY BODIES
★½

DIRECTOR: Lawrence Dane

CAST: Cynthia Dale, Richard Rebiere, Laura Henry, Walter George Alton

More sweaty dancing bodies à la *Flashdance* are featured in this low-budget release about a secretary who is tired of her nine-to-five existence and opens her own aerobics exercise club in a warehouse. With at least five credited production companies mentioned—one of them being Playboy Enterprises—before they even get to the title, you'd figure this film would have something going for it. Unfortunately, the only thing going here is the audience moving for the exits. Rated R for nudity, profanity, and sexual innuendo.

1985   90 minutes

HEAVENLY KID, THE
★★

DIRECTOR: Cary Medoway

CAST: Lewis Smith, Jason Gedrick, Jane Kaczmarek, Richard Mulligan, Nancy Valen, Anne Sawyer

Despite a wee bit of physical humor, marginally amusing dope jokes, and an unobstructed shot of teen-throb Jason Gedrick's well-muscled backside, *The Heavenly Kid* is earthbound with lead in its black engineer boots. Cocky Bobby Fontana (Lewis Smith) bit the big one in a chicken race seventeen years ago: which would make it 1968, but the soundtrack and the wardrobe are definitely 1955—a basic problem rendering this otherwise simply stupid film completely unintelligible. To get out of limbo (a subway train to nowhere, no less) and into heaven, angel Bobby needs a special project. Spazzola Lenny Barnes (Gedrick) is the lucky guy. And if you hadn't guessed by now, Bobby left behind a pregnant girlfriend, making him you-know-who's daddy-o. Richard Mulligan has a thankless role as a grizzled, motorcycle-riding archangel. Rated PG-13 for language, situations, and bare body parts.

1985   90 minutes

HEAVENS ABOVE
★★★

DIRECTOR: John Boulting, Roy Boulting
CAST: Peter Sellers, Cecil Parker, Isabel Jeans, Eric Sykes

Another low-key gem from the late Peter Sellers, this irreverent story of a clergyman with the common touch spoofs just about everything within reach, some of it brilliantly. Sellers shows his congregation the error of their selfish ways and engages them in some odd charities, often with hilarious results. Not as successful as other British comedies of this period, this slightly overblown romp is still intelligently crafted and has the laughs and witty dialogue to hold the viewer's attention.

1963   B & W 105 minutes

HERE COMES MR. JORDAN
★★★★★

DIRECTOR: Alexander Hall

CAST: Robert Montgomery, Evelyn Keyes, Claude Rains, Rita Johnson, Edward Everett Horton, James Gleason, John Emery

We all know that bureaucracy can botch up almost anything. Well, the bureaucrats of heaven can really throw a lulu at boxer Joe Pendleton (Robert Montgomery). The heavenly administrators have called Joe up before his time, and they've got to set things straight. That's the basis for the delightful fantasy *Here Comes Mr. Jordan*. A sequel was made with Rita Hayworth in 1947, and Warren Beatty recycled the whole thing in 1978's *Heaven Can Wait*. Excellent supporting performances are given by Claude Rains and Edward Everett Horton in the air and Evelyn Keyes and James Gleason on the ground in this comedy classic.

1941   B & W   93 minutes

HERO AT LARGE
★★★½

DIRECTOR: Martin Davidson
CAST: John Ritter, Anne Archer, Bert Convy, Kevin McCarthy

In this enjoyably lightweight film, John Ritter plays Steve Nichols, an out-of-work actor who takes a part-time job to promote a movie about a crusading superhero, "Captain Avenger." Along with thirty or so other young men, he dresses up like the film's title character and signs autographs for youngsters who see the movie. Unlike the other impersonators, who grumble about how degrading the job is, Nichols finds pleasure in representing, if only in the minds of children, the powers of justice. Shortly, he saves an old couple and becomes a real hero. Rated PG.

1980   98 minutes

HIGH ANXIETY

DIRECTOR: Mel Brooks
CAST: Mel Brooks, Madeline Kahn, Cloris Leachman, Harvey Korman, Dick Van Patten, Ron Carey

Mel Brooks successfully spoofed the horror film with *Young Frankenstein* and the western with *Blazing Saddles*. However, this takeoff of the Alfred Hitchcock suspense movies falls miserably flat. Rated PG.

1977   94 minutes

HIGH HEELS
★★

DIRECTOR: Claude Chabrol
CAST: Laura Antonelli, Jean-Paul Belmondo, Mia Farrow, Daniel Lecourtois

A French comedy to make you chuckle more often than not. The story involves a medical student who marries the homely daughter of a hospital president to ensure himself of a job after graduation. He soon falls in love with his beautiful sister-in-law and, in some of the film's funniest moments, begins eliminating her suitors. Director Chabrol borrows from Monty Python in a unique dream sequence, which is guaranteed to make you smile. Not rated, but recommended for viewers over 18 years of age. In French with English subtitles.

1980   90 minutes

HIGH POINT
★★

DIRECTOR: Peter Carter
CAST: Christopher Plummer, Richard Harris

The only high point in this movie is the ending. Christopher Plummer and Richard Harris co-star in this would-be comedy. The C.I.A. pays to eliminate a king, but when the king flees on his own, they want their money back. Rated PG for violence.

1984   91 minutes

HIGH SCHOOL, USA
★★

DIRECTOR: Rod Amateau
CAST: Michael J. Fox, Dwayne Hickman, Angela Cartwright

The fact that the dancing robot is the best actor in this film should tell you something. This made-for-TV feature is your typical teen flick, which is exceptional only because it doesn't rely on nudity and foul language to hold its audience's attention. Michael J. Fox and his pals fight back against the rich preppies who run the school. Fox races his car against Beau's (the preppy leader) and wins both the race and Beau's girlfriend. Subplots include a romance between Dwayne Hickman and Angela Cartwright, who play teachers; the school genius's creation of a robot; and the contest for teacher of the year. The thing that makes this film fun to watch is that almost everyone in it is a recognizable star from a TV sitcom. Most viewers will forget about the lack of plot as they identify the shows these people come from. Trivial pursuit fans should find this "name-that-show" game the film's one redeeming aspect.

1983   96 minutes

HILLBILLYS IN A HAUNTED HOUSE

DIRECTOR: Jean Yarbrough
CAST: Ferlin Husky, Joi Lansing, Don Bowman, John Carradine, Lon Chaney Jr., Basil Rathbone, Molly Bee, Merle Haggard, Sonny James

Unbelievably bad mishmash of country corn and horror humor is an insult to both genres and deserves its star only because of the appearance of great horror film veterans (including Basil Rathbone's last film role). The acting, story, and songs are inane and make director Jean Yarbrough's earlier efforts *King Of The Zombies* and *Devil Bat* look like classics. Except for the cameos by the stars, and the thrill of seeing country and western stars acting like morons, there is little excuse for watching this film and one questions the advisability of even making it available on video. Rent at your own risk.

1967   88 minutes

HIS DOUBLE LIFE
★★★

DIRECTOR: Arthur Hopkins, Wm. C. de Mille

CAST: Lillian Gish, Roland Young

Edwardian novelist Arnold Bennett's comedy about a wealthy recluse who finds a better life by becoming a valet when his valet dies and is buried under his name. Remade with Monty Woolley and Gracie Fields as *Holy Matrimony* in 1943.

1933   B & W 67 minutes

HIS GIRL FRIDAY
★★★★

DIRECTOR: Howard Hawks

CAST: Cary Grant, Rosalind Russell, Ralph Bellamy, Gene Lockhart, Helen Mack, Ernest Truex

Based on Ben Hecht and Charles MacArthur's *The Front Page*, which was filmed on two other occasions, this is undoubtedly the best of Howard Hawks's comedies. Originally with two male leads, Hawks converted this gentle spoof of newspapers and reporters into a hilarious battle of the sexes. Rosalind Russell is the reporter bent on retirement, and Cary Grant is the editor bent on maneuvering her out of it—and winning her heart in the process. The dialogue comes fast, funny, and furious, and there's never a dull moment.

1940   B & W 92 minutes

HOBSON'S CHOICE
★★★★★

DIRECTOR: David Lean

CAST: Charles Laughton, John Mills, Brenda de Banzie, Daphne Anderson

Charles Laughton gives one of his most brilliant performances as a turn-of-the-century London shoemaker whose love for the status quo and his whiskey is shattered by the determination of his daughter to wed. This is the original 1954 movie version of the British comedy. Laughton is expertly supported by John Mills and Brenda de Banzie as the two who wish to marry.

1954   B & W 107 minutes

HOLD THAT GHOST
★★★½

DIRECTOR: Arthur Lubin

CAST: Bud Abbott, Lou Costello, Richard Carlson, Joan Davis

Abbott and Costello score in this super comedy about two goofs (guess who) inheriting a haunted house where all kinds of bizarre events occur. You may have to watch this one a few times to catch all the gags.

1941   B & W 86 minutes

HOLIDAY HOTEL
★★★

DIRECTOR: Michel Lang

CAST: Sophie Barjac, Myrian Bager, Daniel Ceccaldi, Michel Grellier, Bruno Guillain, Francis Lemoire, Robert Lombard, Guy Marchand

It's August, and all of France is going on vacation for the entire month. The cast of this fast-paced comedy is heading toward the Brittany coast. Birds do it, bees do it, and everyone from oldsters to the younsters are doing it (or trying) in this film. Michel Lang keeps the tempo moving with clever farcical bits and dialogue. Paradoxically, that is one of the weak points. The subtitles come fast and furiously and sometimes prove difficult to read. But the cast has just the right touch to keep the viewer interested. Partially in English, the movie has an R rating due to nudity and profanity.

1978   109 minutes

HOLLYWOOD BOULEVARD
★★★

DIRECTOR: Joe Dante, Allan Arkush
CAST: Candice Rialson, Mary Woronov, Rita George, Jeffrey Kramer, Dick Miller, Paul Bartel

A would-be actress goes to work for inept movie-makers in this comedy. This is the first film that Joe Dante (Gremlins) directed. Rated R.

1976   83 minutes

HOLLYWOOD HOT TUBS
🎭

DIRECTOR: Chuck Vincent
CAST: Paul Gunning, Donna McDaniel, Michael Andrew

In this ludicrous video a young man wangles a job at a local hot tub firm in L.A. Lots of imbecilic jokes, naked girls, and a frenetic climax all help *not* to distinguish this quickie from the rest of the crowd. Somebody pull the drain plug, please. Rated R for nudity.

1984   103 minutes

HOLLYWOOD OUTTAKES
★★½

DIRECTOR: Bruce Goldstein
CAST: Humphrey Bogart, Bette Davis, Errol Flynn, George Raft, James Cagney, Judy Garland, Mickey Rooney

This is a sometimes terrific, most times passable, collection of blooper and newsreel footage from the 1930s, '40s, and '50s. No MPAA rating.

1984   90 minutes

HOME MOVIES
★★

DIRECTOR: Brian De Palma
CAST: Nancy Allen, Keith Gordon, Kirk Douglas, Gerrit Graham, Vincent Gardenia

A little film produced with the help of Brian De Palma's film-making students at Sarah Lawrence College. A director, played by Kirk Douglas, gives "star therapy" to a young man who feels he is a mere exra in his own life. The film is quirky and fun at times, but more often it's simply pointless. Interesting as an experiment by an established talent, but as entertainment, it's quite tedious. Rated PG.

1980   90 minutes

HONKY TONK FREEWAY
★★★

DIRECTOR: John Schlesinger
CAST: William Devane, Beverly D'Angelo, Beau Bridges, Geraldine Page, Teri Garr

Director John Schlesinger captures the comedy of modern American life in a small Florida town. The stars keep you laughing. Rated R.

1981 107 minutes

HOOPER
★★★★

DIRECTOR: Hal Needham

CAST: Burt Reynolds, Sally Field, Jan-Michael Vincent, Brian Keith

Fresh from their success with *Smokey and the Bandit*, director Hal Needham and stars Burt Reynolds and Sally Field are reunited for this humorous, knockabout comedy about Hollywood stuntmen. Jan-Michael Vincent adds to the film's impact as an up-and-coming fall guy out to best top-of-the-heap Reynolds. Good fun. Rated PG.

1978 99 minutes

HOSPITAL, THE
★★★★½

DIRECTOR: Arthur Hiller

CAST: George C. Scott, Diana Rigg, Barnard Hughes

You definitely don't want to check in. But if you like to laugh, you'll want to check it out. This 1971 black comedy did for the medical profession what . . . *And Justice for All* did for our court system and *Network* did for television. Paddy Cheyefsky's Oscar-winning screenplay casts George C. Scott as an embittered doctor battling against the outrageous goings-on at the institution of the title. Rated PG.

1971 103 minutes

HOT DOG...THE MOVIE
★★

DIRECTOR: Peter Markle

CAST: David Naughton, Shannon Tweed

He may no longer be a Pepper, but David Naughton (*An American Werewolf in London*) co-stars with one-time Playboy Playmate of the Year Shannon Tweed in this comedy about high jinks on the ski slopes that will no doubt delight its youthful target audience. *Hot Dog* is another one of those made-to-order teen flicks and is a first-rate example of its genre. Rated R for nudity, profanity, and suggested sex.

1984 96 minutes

HOT MOVES
🦃

DIRECTOR: Jim Sotos

CAST: Michael Zorek, Adam Blair, Jeff Fishman, Johnny Timko

Here's another rip-off of *Animal House*; a teen lust comedy with little lust and less laughs. Rated R.

1985 80 minutes

HOT STUFF
★★★½

DIRECTOR: Dom De Luise

CAST: Dom De Luise, Jerry Reed, Suzanne Pleshette, Ossie Davis

Movie fans who love to laugh will appreciate *Hot Stuff*. It's an entertaining, old-fashioned comedy that whips right along. Director/star Dom De Luise makes the most of his dual role. His is a good-natured kind of comedy. You like all of the characters, even the bad guys. The story concerns a government fencing operation for capturing crooks. And the results are humorous. Rated PG.

1979 87 minutes

HOUSE CALLS
★★★★½

DIRECTOR: Howard Zieff

CAST: Walter Matthau, Glenda Jackson, Richard Benjamin, Art Carney

Here's a romantic comedy reminiscent of films Spencer Tracy and Katharine Hepburn made together in the 1940s and '50s, mostly because of the teaming of Walter Matthau and Glenda Jackson. A recently widowed doctor (Matthau) finds his bachelor spree cut short by a romantic encounter with a nurse (Jackson) who refuses to be just another conquest. It is a bit more risqué than the ones from that earlier period, but it still is a delightful battle of the sexes with two equally matched opponents. Rated PG.

1978   96 minutes

HOW I WON THE WAR
★★★½

DIRECTOR: Richard Lester
CAST: Michael Crawford, John Lennon, Michael Hordern, Jack MacGowran

John Lennon had his only solo screen turn (away from the Beatles) in this often hilarious war spoof. Directed by Richard Lester (*A Hard Day's Night*; *Superman II*), it features Michael Crawford as a military man who has a wacky way of distorting the truth as he reminisces about his adventures in battle.

1967   109 minutes

HOW TO BEAT THE HIGH CO$T OF LIVING
★★

DIRECTOR: Robert Scheerer
CAST: Jessica Lange, Susan Saint James, Jane Curtin, Richard Benjamin, Fred Willard, Dabney Coleman

A great cast all dressed up with no place to go . . . except Jane Curtin, whose shopping-mall strip-tease is a marginal high point in a caper comedy not even up to the substandards of an average made-for-television movie. Curtin, Jessica Lange, and Susan Saint James are a trio of housewives who decide to heist a large display of cash in order to meet the grocery payments. Tiresome and taxing; rarely have so many labored to produce so little. Rated PG.

1980   110 minutes

HOW TO BREAK UP A HAPPY DIVORCE
★★★

DIRECTOR: Jerry Paris
CAST: Hal Linden, Barbara Eden, Harold Gould

Ex-wife Barbara Eden wants ex-husband Hal Linden back. To make him jealous, she dates a well-known playboy. Comic mayhem follows. Lots of sight gags. This is an unrated TV movie.

1976   78 minutes

HOW TO MARRY A MILLIONAIRE
★★★

DIRECTOR: Jean Negulesco
CAST: Lauren Bacall, Marilyn Monroe, Betty Grable, William Powell, Cameron Mitchell, David Wayne, Rory Calhoun

The stars, Marilyn Monroe, Lauren Bacall, and Betty Grable, are fun to watch in this comedy. However, director Jean Negulesco doesn't do much to keep our interest. The story in this slight romp is all in the title—with William Powell giving the girls a run for his money.

1953   96 minutes

HYSTERICAL
★½

DIRECTOR: Chris Bearde

CAST: William, Mark, and Brett Hudson, Cindy Pickett, Richard Kiel, Julie Newmar, Bud Cort, Robert Donner, Murray Hamilton, Clint Walker, Franklin Ajaye, Charlie Callas, Keenan Wynn, Gary Owens

Zany horror spoof generates only a sprinkling of laughs as the bulk of its off-the-wall humor thuds embarrassingly. This movie was supposed to make the Hudson Brothers the Marx Brothers of the 1980s. The Hudsons have an undeniable charm, but their film debut is more like chicken poop than *Duck Soup*. Rated PG.

1983   87 minutes

I LOVE MY WIFE

★½

DIRECTOR: Mel Stuart
CAST: Elliott Gould, Brenda Vaccaro, Angel Tompkins, Dabney Coleman, Joan Tompkins

Barely laughable sex comedy dealing with the problems of an upper-class couple (Elliott Gould, Brenda Vaccaro) and their ridiculous attempts to solve them. Rather daring for the time and far too tame for today's audiences, this film would have been silly no matter when it was released. This a classic example of the way Elliott Gould was overexposed into near oblivion by a host of stupid exploitative films after his great success with *M*A*S*H*. This pointless film seems to go on and on. Rated PG.

1970   95 minutes

I LOVE YOU ALICE B. TOKLAS!

★★★

DIRECTOR: Hy Averback
CAST: Peter Sellers, Leigh Taylor-Young, Jo Van Fleet

Peter Sellers plays a lawyer-cum-hippie in this far-out comedy about middle-age crisis. Rated PG.

1968   93 minutes

I WILL, I WILL...FOR NOW

½

DIRECTOR: Norman Panama
CAST: Elliott Gould, Diane Keaton, Paul Sorvino, Victoria Principal, Robert Alda, Warren Berlinger

This is one of those mid-1970s trashers complete with mistaken-identity plot and a Santa Barbara sex clinic where "nothing is unnatural." Diane Keaton is the only one who comes out of this mess without looking ridiculous. Half a star for her ability to float above the wreckage. Rated R.

1976   96 minutes

IF...

★★★★

DIRECTOR: Lindsay Anderson
CAST: Malcolm McDowell, David Wood, Richard Warwick

This is British director Lindsay Anderson's black comedy about English private schools and the revolt against its strict code of behavior taken to the farthest limits of the imagination. Malcolm McDowell's movie debut. Rated R.

1969   111 minutes

I'M ALL RIGHT JACK

★★★½

DIRECTOR: John Boulting
CAST: Peter Sellers, Terry-Thomas, Ian Carmichael

British comedies can be marvelously entertaining, especially when they star Peter Sellers, as in this witty spoof of the absurdities of the labor movement carried to its ultimate extreme. This is humor at its best.

1960   B & W 101 minutes

IMPROPER CHANNELS
★

DIRECTOR: Eric Till
CAST: Alan Arkin, Mariette Hartley, Sarah Stevens, Monica Parker

Is this comedy ... or bureaucratic nightmare? The two should mix, but unfortunately don't, in this story of an overeager social worker who accuses a father (Alan Arkin) of child abuse. Only the child (Sarah Stevens) is more than passably likable. The cheap cliché treatment of the doctors, nurses, policemen, lawyers, social workers, etc., is deplorable; and ethnic slurs abound. Rated PG for language.

1981   92 minutes

INCREDIBLE SHRINKING WOMAN, THE
★★

DIRECTOR: Joel Schumacher
CAST: Lily Tomlin, Ned Beatty, Henry Gibson, Elizabeth Wilson, Charles Grodin, Pamela Bellwood, Mike Douglas, Mark Blankfield

The great temptation in reviewing this comedy, starring Lily Tomlin, is to say that it falls prey to the law of diminishing returns—because it, like that assessment, all too often relies on bad puns and clichés. But to simply dismiss it as a failure would be inaccurate and unfair. This comic adaptation of Richard Matheson's classic science-fiction novel (*The Shrinking Man*) is not a bad movie. It's more like ... well ... the perfect old-fashioned Disney movie—a little

corny and strained at times but not a total loss. Rated PG.

1981   88 minutes

INDISCREET
★

DIRECTOR: Leo McCarey
CAST: Gloria Swanson, Ben Lyon, Arthur Lake

Near-boring comedy drama in which Gloria Swanson spends most of her time trying to conceal her questionable past from Ben Lyon. That she sings three songs does not help things a bit. Not to be confused with 1958's fine film of same title starring Ingrid Bergman and Cary Grant.

1931   B & W 92 minutes

IN-LAWS, THE
★★★★

DIRECTOR: Arthur Hiller
CAST: Peter Falk, Alan Arkin, Penny Peyser, Michael Lembeck

This delightful caper comedy mixes mystery and action with the fun. Vince Ricardo (Peter Falk) is the mastermind behind a bold theft of engravings of U.S. currency from a Treasury Department armored car. The caper is finished just in time for him to attend a dinner. His son, Tommy (Michael Lembeck), is to be married on Saturday, and Vince is to meet the parents of the bride (Penny Peyser). Her father, Sheldon Kornpett (Alan Arkin), is a slightly neurotic dentist. After just a few minutes with Vince, he is convinced the man is completely out of his mind, and soon they're off on a perilous mission. Falk and Arkin make a great team, playing off each other brilliantly. Rated PG.

1979   103 minutes

INSPECTOR GENERAL, THE
★★★★

DIRECTOR: Henry Koster
CAST: Danny Kaye, Walter Slezak, Elsa Lanchester

In this classic comedy set in Russia of the 1800s, Danny Kaye is the town fool who is mistaken for a confidant of Napoleon. The laughs come when Danny is caught up in court intrigue and really has no idea what is going on. Kaye's talents are showcased in this film.

1949   102 minutes

I OUGHT TO BE IN PICTURES
★★★★

DIRECTOR: Herbert Ross
CAST: Walter Matthau, Ann-Margret, Dinah Manoff

Neil Simon's best work since *The Goodbye Girl*, this heartwarming story stars Walter Matthau as a father who deserts his Brooklyn family. Dinah Manoff is the daughter who wants to be a movie star, and Ann-Margret is the woman who brings the two together. Rated PG for mild profanity and brief nudity.

1982   107 minutes

IRMA LA DOUCE
★★★

DIRECTOR: Billy Wilder
CAST: Shirley MacLaine, Jack Lemmon, Lou Jacobi, Herschel Bernardi

Gendarme Jack Lemmon gets involved with prostitute Shirley MacLaine in what director Billy Wilder hoped would be another MacLaine/Lemmon hit like *The Apartment*. It isn't. It's raw humor in glorious color. Send the "Silver Spoons" set off to bed before you screen this one.

1963   142 minutes

IT CAME FROM HOLLYWOOD
★★★

DIRECTOR: Malcolm Leo, Andrew Solt
CAST: Dan Aykroyd, John Candy, Cheech and Chong, Gilda Radner

Dan Aykroyd, John Candy, Cheech and Chong, and Gilda Radner appear in comedy vignettes as the hosts of this watchable "That's Entertainment"–style compilation of the worst all-time (but hilarious) losers as "Plan 9 from Outer Space," "Robot Monster," "Batmen of Africa," and "Untamed Women." The *Star Wars* generation may not understand what's so funny about all this, but those who grew up in the 1950s and '60s, when flying saucers were often hubcaps tossed into the air and monsters were guys in gorilla suits, are sure to get a kick out of it. Rated PG for sexual references and scatological humor.

1982   80 minutes

IT HAPPENED ONE NIGHT
★★★★★

DIRECTOR: Frank Capra
CAST: Clark Gable, Claudette Colbert, Ward Bond

Prior to *One Flew over the Cuckoo's Nest*, this 1934 comedy was the only film to capture all the major Academy Awards. Clark Gable stars as a cynical reporter on the trail of a runaway heiress, Claudette Colbert. They fall in love, of course, and the result is vintage movie magic.

1934   B & W 105 minutes

IT SHOULD HAPPEN TO YOU
★★½

DIRECTOR: George Cukor
CAST: Judy Holliday, Peter Lawford, Jack Lemmon, Milo O'Shea, Vaughn Taylor

Judy Holliday plays an actress who's desperate to garner publicity and hopes splashing her name across billboards all over New York City will ignite her career. The movie provides a steady stream of chuckles. Jack Lemmon makes an amusing screen debut. Holliday is hard to resist.

1954   B & W 81 minutes

IT'S A GIFT
★★★★

DIRECTOR: Norman Z. McLeod
CAST: W. C. Fileds, Kathleen Howard, Baby LeRoy, Julian Madison, Jean Rouverol, Tommy Bupp, Tammany Young, T. Roy Barnes (looking for Carl LaFong), Charles Sellon (Mr. Muckle, the blind man)

It's a treat for everyone to have the great W. C. Fields's best Paramount film available on videotape. In a class with the best of the comedies of the 1930's (including *Duck Soup*, *I'm No Angel*, *My Man Godfrey*), this classic was produced during the peak of Fields' association with Paramount Studios and is his archetypal vehicle, peopled with characters whose sole purpose in life seems to be to annoy the long-suffering Harold Bissonette. Originally titled *The Back Porch* and assembled from some of his vaudeville sketches as well as parts of his silent film *It's the Old Army Game*, this gem combines many of the elements Fields used in his short subjects and subsequent feature films (including *The Pharmacist* and *The Bank Dick*) and blends them into a side-splitting series of visual delights punctuated by the great comedian's verbal observations and dark mutterings. The film falters toward the end and the final scenes are anticlimactic, but the scenes of fields attempting to nap on the second-level porch of the building he lives in can only compare in hilarity to the action that takes place in his mercantile as he attempts to conduct business and defend his premises against a cane-wielding blind man, Mr. Muckle. Spiced with a family that would give gray hairs to a bald man, and an ice pick-dropping Baby LeRoy, this is Fields at his best and the purest example of his unique brand of humor. Once viewed, this movie will give new dimensions to the word "kumquat," and the simple mention of the name "Carl LaFong" will evoke gales of laughter as well as the inevitable rejoinder "capital L, small a, capital F, small o, small n, small g; LaFong! Don't miss this one.

1934   B & W 73 minutes

IT'S A MAD MAD MAD MAD WORLD
★★★★

DIRECTOR: Stanley Kramer
CAST: Spencer Tracy, Milton Berle, Jonathan Winters, Buddy Hackett, Sid Caesar, Phil Silvers, Mickey Rooney, Peter Falk, Dick Shawn, Ethel Merman, Buster Keaton, Jimmy Durante, Edie Adams, Dorothy Provine, Terry-Thomas, William Demarest, Andy Devine

Spencer Tracy and a cast made up of "Who's Who of American comedy" are combined in this wacky chase movie to end all chase movies. Tracy is the crafty police captain who is following the progress of various money-mad citizens out to beat one another in discovering the buried hiding place of 350,000 stolen dollars.

1963   154 minutes

IT'S IN THE BAG
★★★

DIRECTOR: Richard Wallace
CAST: Fred Allen, Jack Benny, Binnie Barnes, Robert Benchley, Victor Moore, Sidney Toler, Rudy Vallee, William Bendix, Don Ameche

The plot (if there ever was one) derives from the Russian fable about an impoverished nobleman on a treasure hunt. Continuity soon goes out the window, however, when the cast starts winging it in one hilarious episode after another. This is Fred Allen, acerbic and nasal as always, in his best screen comedy. Those who yearn for the return of vaudeville and radio as it once was will love this wacky romp. A high point is an encounter between Fred and Jack that's bound to stir a lot of memories.

1945   B & W   87 minutes

JABBERWOCKY
★★½

DIRECTOR: Terry Gilliam
CAST: Michael Palin, Max Wall, Deborah Fallender, Annette Badland

Monty Python fans will be disappointed to see only one group member, Michael Palin, in this British film. Palin plays a dim-witted peasant during the Dark Ages. A monster called Jabberwocky is destroying villages all over the countryside, so Palin tries to destroy the monster. There are some funny moments but nothing in comparison with true Python films. No MPAA rating.

1977   100 minutes

JEKYLL & HYDE—TOGETHER AGAIN
★★★

DIRECTOR: Jerry Belson

CAST: Mark Blankfield, Bess Armstrong, Krista Erickson

If you like offbeat, crude, and timely humor, you'll enjoy this 1980s-style version of Robert Louis Stevenson's horror classic. Though the film needs some editing, Mark Blankfield is a riot as the mad scientist who can't snort enough of the powdery white stuff he's invented. Rated R for heavy doses of vulgarity and sexual innuendo.

1982   87 minutes

JERK, THE
★★★★

DIRECTOR: Carl Reiner
CAST: Steve Martin, Bernadette Peters, Bill Macy, Jackie Mason

Steve Martin made a very funny film debut in this wacky comedy. Nonfans probably won't like it, but then Martin has always had limited appeal. For those who think he's hilarious, the laughs just keep on coming. Rated R.

1979   94 minutes

JINXED
★★★

DIRECTOR: Don Siegel
CAST: Bette Midler, Ken Wahl, Rip Torn, Benson Fong

Bette Midler is in peak form as a would-be cabaret singer who enlists the aid of a blackjack dealer (Ken Wahl) in a plot to murder her gambler boyfriend (Rip Torn) in this often funny black comedy, directed by Don Siegel (*Dirty Harry*; *Invasion of the Body Snatchers*). It it weren't for Midler, you'd notice how silly and unbelievable it all is. However, she's so watchable you don't mind suspending your disbelief. Rated R for profanity and sexual situations.

1982   103 minutes

JOHNNY DANGEROUSLY
★

DIRECTOR: Amy Heckerling
CAST: Michael Keaton, Joe Piscopo, Marilu Henner, Maureen Stapleton

In this fitfully funny spoof of 1930s gangster movies, Michael Keaton (*Mr. Mom*) and Joe Piscopo ("Saturday Night Live") play rival crime lords. Directed by Amy Heckerling (*Fast Times at Ridgemont High*), it leaves the viewer with genuinely mixed feelings. That's because many of its gags rely on shock laughs (such as when Maureen Stapleton confesses to Marilu Henner that she "goes both ways"—sick!) and others never seem to make it to the punchline. Rated PG-13 for violence and profanity.

1984   90 minutes

JOKE OF DESTINY
★★

DIRECTOR: Lina Wertmuller
CAST: Ugo Tognazzi, Piera Degli Esposti, Gastone Moschin

Italian audiences may have laughed uproariously at this new film by director Lina Wertmuller (*Swept Away, Seven Beauties*). However, American viewers are unlikely to get the joke. It shows what happens to a government official (Ugo Tognazzi of *La Cage aux Folles*) when a computerized car carrying his country's highest official breaks down in front of his house. The problem is, its elements of social satire are unfathomable for those unfamiliar with political events in Italy. Rated PG for profanity. In Italian with English subtitles.

1984   105 minutes

JOSEPH ANDREWS
★★

DIRECTOR: Tony Richardson
CAST: Ann-Margret, Peter Firth, Beryl Reid, Michael Hordern, Jim Dale, John Gielgud, Hugh Griffith, Wendy Craig, Peggy Ashcroft

Follows the adventures of Joseph Andrews (Peter Firth) as he rises from lowly servant to personal footman and becomes the fancy of Lady Boaby (Ann-Margret). This is director Tony Richardson's second attempt to transform a Henry Fielding novel to film. Unfortunately, the first-rate cast cannot save this ill-fated attempt to restage *Tom Jones*. Rated R for sex and profanity.

1977   99 minutes

JOSHUA THEN AND NOW
★★★★½

DIRECTOR: Ted Kotcheff
CAST: James Woods, Alan Arkin, Gabrielle Lazure, Michael Sarrazin, Linda Sorensen

Based by screenwriter Mordecai Richler (*The Apprenticeship of Duddy Kravitz*) on his autobiographical novel of the same name, this little-known gem is blessed with humor, poignancy, and insight. James Woods, better known for villainous roles in films like *Once Upon a Time in America* and *Against All Odds*, is wonderful as Jewish writer Joshua Shapiro, whose life seems to be in shambles at the beginning of the picture. But, as we see in flashbacks, he is a hard guy to keep down. Surviving an embarrassing upbringing by a gangster father (Alan Arkin in his funniest performance ever) and a would-be entertainer mother (Linda Sorensen), who as a special treat strips at his bar mitzvah, Joshua nearly meets his match in the snobbish high society of his WASP wife (Gabrielle Lazure). Although *Joshua Then and Now* may occasionally be a bit too raw for some viewers, its unerring sense of humanity and humor should put aside all objections. It is worth seeing for Arkin's performance alone and will more than please those looking for wit, warmth and originality. Rated R for profanity, nudity, suggested sex, and adult themes.

1985 118 minutes

JOY OF SEX, THE
★★

DIRECTOR: Martha Coolidge
CAST: Michelle Meyrink, Cameron Dye, Lisa Langois

You have to give credit to director Martha Coolidge (*Valley Girl*) for trying to do something different with *The Joy of Sex*. With a title like that, you'd expect it to be another teen lust movie with lots of topless young women, boys leering and drooling after girls, and gross humor. This comedy, about the plight of two virgins, male and female, unhappy with their status in a sex-crazy age, has very few such offensive elements. But there is one problem: It isn't funny. Rated R for profanity, suggested sex, and scatological humor.

1984 93 minutes

JOY STICKS
🦃

DIRECTOR: Greydon Clark
CAST: Joe Don Baker, Leif Green, Logan Ramsey

The alleged story in *Joy Sticks* is that a wealthy businessman (Joe Don Baker) wants to shut down the local video gameroom frequented by his teen-age daughter. Little of interest happens. Rated R.

1983 88 minutes

JULIET OF THE SPIRITS
★★★★★

DIRECTOR: Federico Fellini
CAST: Giulietta Masina, Sandra Milo, Mario Pisu, Valentina Cortese, Lou Gilbert, Sylva Koscina

"Are your eyes in good condition, able to encompass and abide some of the liveliest, most rococo resplendence ever fashioned in a fairyland on film . . . and enjoy a game of armchair psychoanalyzing in a spirit of good bawdy fun?" Such was the way Bosley Crowther began his review of *Juliet of the Spirits*. The convoluted plot centers around a wealthy wife suspicious of her cheating husband. Giulietta Masina (in real life, Mrs. Fellini) has never been so tantalizingly innocent with her Bambi eyes. This is Fellini's first attempt with color. It seems obvious that he wants his audience to have as much fun in this surreal world as he had creating it. The results are a feast for the eye, the ear, and the brain. Not too heavy, not too light—just right.

1965 148 minutes

JUPITER'S THIGH
★★★★½

DIRECTOR: Philippe de Broca
CAST: Annie Girardot, Philippe Noiret

The delightful *Dear Inspector* duo is back in this delicious sequel directed by Philippe de Broca (*King of Hearts*). This time, the lady detective (Annie Girardot) and her Greek archeologist lover (Philippe Noiret) get married and honeymoon—where else?—in Greece. But they aren't there long before they find themselves caught up in murder, madness, and mayhem. It's great fun, served up with sophistication.

1983 90 minutes

JUST ONE OF THE GUYS
★★★

DIRECTOR: Lisa Gottlieb
CAST: Joyce Hyser, Clayton Rohner, Billy Jacoby, Toni Hudson

A sort of reverse *Tootsie*, this surprisingly restrained and humanistic teen-lust comedy stars Joyce Hyser as Terry Griffith, an attractive young woman who switches high schools and sexes to overcome an imagined prejudice against her writing and win a journalism prize. The premise is flimsy and forced, but director Lisa Gottlieb and her cast do a wonderful job of keeping the viewer interested and entertained. Rated PG-13 for nudity, violence, and profanity.

1985　　　　　　　88 minutes

JUST TELL ME WHAT YOU WANT
★½

DIRECTOR: Sidney Lumet
CAST: Alan King, Ali MacGraw, Peter Weller, Myrna Loy, Keenan Wynn, Tony Roberts, Dina Merrill

Alan King gives a fine performance in this otherwise forgettable film as an executive who attempts to get his mistress (Ali MacGraw) back. She's in love with a younger man (Peter Weller), and King will do anything to get her back. She's not interested, and the viewer is soon fast asleep. Rated R.

1980　　　　　　112 minutes

KENTUCKY FRIED MOVIE
★★★

DIRECTOR: John Landis
CAST: Evan Kim, Master Bong SooHan, Bill Bixby, Donald Sutherland

The first film outing of the creators of *Airplane!* is an on-again, off-again collection of comedy skits. Directed by John Landis, the best bits involve a Bruce Lee takeoff and a surprise appearance by Wally and the Beaver. Rated R.

1977　　　　　　　78 minutes

KEYSTONE COMEDIES, VOL. 1
★★★

DIRECTOR: Roscoe Arbuckle
CAST: Roscoe Arbuckle, Minta Durfee, Al St. John, Louise Fazenda, Edgar Kennedy, Joe Bordeaux

"Fatty's Faithful Fido," "Fatty's Tintype Tangle," and "Fatty's New Role"—three fast-moving bop-and-bash comedies in the celebrated Fatty series produced by Mack Sennett at Keystone Studios in 1915—compose this first of five volumes devoted to the famed silent comedian's artistry. "Fatty's Faithful Fido" is a comedy action gem. The dog comes close to stealing the show. Slapstick humor in the classic mold.

1915　　　B & W　46 minutes

KEYSTONE COMEDIES, VOL. 2
★★★

DIRECTOR: Roscoe Arbuckle
CAST: Roscoe Arbuckle, Mabel Normand, Minta Durfee, Al St. John, Alice Davenport, Joe Bordeaux

Mack Sennett hit real reel paydirt when he teamed rotund comic Roscoe Arbuckle and elfin comedienne Mabel Normand in a film series. These three examples—'Fatty and Mabel at the San Diego Exposition," "Fatty and Mabel's Simple Life," and "Mabel's Washday"—amply show why. Classic double-take slapstick silent comedy.

1915　　　B & W　42 minutes

KEYSTONE COMEDIES, VOL. 3
★★★

DIRECTOR: Roscoe Arbuckle

CAST: Roscoe Arbuckle, Mabel Normand, Minta Durfee, Dora Rogers, Alice Davenport, Al St. John, Owen Moore

Four more stanzas in the screen lives of two of silent film's great comedic performers: Roscoe Arbuckle and Mabel Normand. They're all "watch springs and elastic" as they create marvelous mayhem in "Mabel Lost and Won" 'Wished on Mabel," "Mabel, Fatty and the Law" and "Fatty's Plucky Pup." This quartet from Mack Sennett's legendary film fun factory can't help but raise laughter.

1915 B & W 58 minutes

KEYSTONE COMEDIES: VOL. 4
★★★

DIRECTOR: Roscoe Arbuckle
CAST: Roscoe Arbuckle, Mabel Normand, Edgar Kennedy, Glenn Cavender, Ford Sterling, Mae Busch, Al St. John, Alice Davenport

Three stanzas in the sidesplitting Fatty-and-Mabel slapstick series Mack Sennett connived and contrived between 1912 and 1916: "Mabel's Willful Way," "That Little Band of Gold," and "Mabel and Fatty's Married Life." Mayhem and mirth only past masters of the double take and pratfall can muster. Roscoe Arbuckle and Mabel Normand are marvelous in these comedy capers from days long gone.

1915 B & W 44 minutes

KEYSTONE COMEDIES: VO. 5
★★★

DIRECTOR: Roscoe Arbuckle
CAST: Roscoe Arbuckle, Bill Bennett, Walter Reed, Edgar Kennedy, Harold Lloyd, Joe Bordeaux, Minta Durfee, Ford Sterling, Charles Arling, Joe Swickard, Dora Rogers, Nick Cogley, Charles Chase, W. C. Hauber

Fabled Mack Sennett's madcap mob of laugh-catchers dish up three more hilarious happy helpings of classic silent comedy: "Miss Fatty's Seaside Lovers," "Court House Crooks," and "Love Loot and Crash." Keystone Studio's pride, roly-poly Roscoe Arbuckle, is a tubby terror in drag. Here's slapstick comedy in the sea and off the wall in days of yore.

1915 B & W 45 minutes

KID FROM BROOKLYN, THE
★★★

DIRECTOR: Norman Z. McLeod
CAST: Danny Kaye, Virginia Mayo, Vera-Ellen, Steve Cochran, Eve Arden

Danny Kaye is fine as the comedy lead in this remake of Harold Lloyd's *The Milky Way*. He plays the milkman who becomes a prizefighter. Good family entertainment.

1946 104 minutes

KIND HEARTS AND CORONETS
★★★★

DIRECTOR: Robert Hamer
CAST: Dennis Price, Alec Guinness, Valerie Hobson

A young man (Dennis Price) thinks up a novel way to speed up his inheritance—by killing off all the other heirs. This is the central premise of this arresting black comedy, which manages to poke fun at mass murder and get away with it. Alec Guinness plays all eight of his victims.

1949 104 minutes

KING IN NEW YORK, A
★★½

DIRECTOR: Charles Chaplin
CAST: Charlie Chaplin, Dawn Addams, Michael Chaplin

Supposedly anti-American, this 1957 film by Charles Chaplin, not seen in the United States until 1973, was a big let-down to his fans, who had built their worship on *Easy Street*, *City Lights*, *Modern Times*, and *The Great Dictator*. It pokes fun at the 1950s, with its witch hunts and burgeoning postwar technology. It is not the Chaplin of old, but just old Chaplin, and too much of him.

1957   B & W   105 minutes

KING OF HEARTS
★★★★½
DIRECTOR: Philippe de Broca
CAST: Alan Bates, Genevieve Bujold

Philippe de Broca's wartime fantasy provides delightful insights into human behavior. A World War I Scottish infantryman (Alan Bates) searching for a hidden enemy bunker enters a small town that, after being deserted by its citizens, has been taken over by inmates of an insane asylum. In assuming the characters of the village people and affecting normalcy, the "crazies" emphasize the senselessness of war. In French, with English subtitles. No MPAA rating.

1966   102 minutes

KISS ME GOODBYE
★★★
DIRECTOR: Robert Mulligan
CAST: Sally Field, James Caan, Jeff Bridges, Claire Trevor

Sally Field plays a widow of three years who has just fallen in love again. Her first husband was an electrifying Broadway choreographer named Jolly (James Caan). Her husband-to-be is a slightly stuffy Egyptologist (Jeff Bridges). Before her wedding day she receives a visit from Jolly's ghost,

who is apparently upset about the approaching wedding. Rated PG for profanity and sexual situations.

1982   101 minutes

KOTCH
★★★★
DIRECTOR: Jack Lemmon
CAST: Walter Matthau, Deborah Winters, Felicia Farr

Walter Matthau gives an affecting performance in this heartwarming film. He plays a senior citizen who has a lot more smarts than anyone gives him credit for and a lot more heart than anyone around him deserves. It's a splendid motion picture the whole family will love. Rated PG.

1971   113 minutes

LA CAGE AUX FOLLES
★★★★½
DIRECTOR: Edouard Molinaro
CAST: Ugo Tognazzi, Michel Serrault

A screamingly funny French comedy and the biggest-grossing foreign-language film ever released in America, this stars Ugo Tognazzi and Michel Serrault as two male lovers who must masquerade as husband and wife so as not to obstruct the marriage of Tognazzi's son to the daughter of a stuffy bureaucrat. In French, with English subtitles. Rated PG for mature situations.

1978   110 minutes

LA CAGE AUX FOLLES II
★★
DIRECTOR: Eduard Molinaro
CAST: Ugo Tognazzi, Michel Serrault

This follow-up to the superb French comedy is just more proof sequels aren't equals. Though it reunites Ugo Tognazzi and Michel Serrault as those crazy "Birds of a Feather," it has little of the original's special charm and unbridled hilarity. Rated PG for mature situations.

1981   101 minutes

LA CAGE AUX FOLLES III, THE WEDDING
🐦

DIRECTOR: Georges Lautner
CAST: Michel Serrault, Ugo Tognazzi, Stephane Audran, Michel Galabru

Another pathetic and dreadful sequel to *La Cage Aux Folles (Birds of a Feather)*. The two gay entrepreneurs are back, and in an effort to save their financially failing night club, Renato (Ugo Tognazzi) sends Albin (Michel Serrault) to the reading of a distant relative's will in which he stands to inherit a fortune. One of the stipulations Albin must comply with before he receives the inheritance is that he must get legally married to a woman and have a child by her. Simply put, this movie is preposterous, and an offense to both gay and straight audiences alike. In French with English subtitles. Rated PG-13.

1986   88 minutes

LA RONDE
★★★

DIRECTOR: Max Ophuls
CAST: Anton Walbrook, Serge Reggiani, Simone Simon, Simone Signoret, Daniel Gelin, Danielle Darrieux, Fernand Gravet, Odette Joyeux, Jean-Louis Barrault, Isa Miranda, Gerard Philippe

It would be hard to imagine any film more like a French farce than *La Ronde*, in spite of its Austrian origins from the play by Arthur Schnitzler. This fast-paced, witty, and sometimes wicked look at amours and indiscretions begins with the soldier (Serge Reggiani) and lady of easy virtue (Simone Signoret). Their assignation starts a chain of events that is charmingly risqué. Unfortunately, the film's release occurred at a time when the world was infested with "commie hunters" and neo-Victorians—and it was heavily criticized. Ultimately, though, *La Ronde* was approved by the Supreme Court of the United States of America and the House of Representatives Committee on Un-American Activities. In French with English subtitles.

1950   B & W   97 minutes

LADY EVE, THE
★★★★

DIRECTOR: Preston Sturges
CAST: Barbara Stanwyck, Henry Fonda, Charles Coburn, William Demarest

Barbara Stanwyck, Henry Fonda, and Charles Coburn are first-rate in this romantic comedy, which was brilliantly written and directed by Preston Sturges. Fonda is a rather simple-minded millionaire, and Stanwyck is the conniving woman who seeks to snare him. The results are hilarious.

1941   B & W   94 minutes

LADYKILLERS, THE
★★★★½

DIRECTOR: Alexander Mackendrick
CAST: Alec Guinness, Peter Sellers, Cecil Parker

England had a golden decade of great comedies during the 1950s. *The Ladykillers* is one of the best. Alec Guinness and Peter Sellers are teamed as a couple of small-time criminals who have devised what they believe to be the perfect crime. Unfortunately, their plans are thwarted by the sweetest, most innocent little old landlady you'd ever want to meet. Great fun!

1955   87 minutes

LADY ON THE BUS
★★

DIRECTOR: Neville D'Almeida
CAST: Sonia Braga

Story of a shy bride who is frigid on her wedding night. She first turns to her husband's friends and then goes on to sample strangers she meets on buses. Her psychiatrist thinks she is normal, although she is driving her husband mad. Marginal comedy. Rated R for sex.

1978   102 minutes

LAST AMERICAN VIRGIN, THE
★

DIRECTOR: Boaz Davidson
CAST: Lawrence Monoson, Diane Franklin, Steve Antin, Joe Rubbo, Louisa Moritz

Tawdry teen-sex flick with one of the worst morals ever captured on film: don't bother to help a friend, 'cause he (or she) will burn you every time. Writer/director Boaz Davidson must have led one miserable childhood. Lawrence Monoson, Steve Antin, and Joe Rubbo are three buddies in search of the usual sexual thrills; the lame comedy of the premise is offset by the graphic cruelty of the encounters. Most ludicrous is a scene where two of our heroes start getting hot with a couple of curvaceous cuties, only to discover distinctly male genitals on their "women." Diane Franklin, a charming young actress, has what must be the meanest part ever written. Only for masochists. Rated R for sex.

1982   92 minutes

LAST MARRIED COUPLE IN AMERICA, THE
★★

DIRECTOR: Gilbert Cates
CAST: Natalie Wood, George Segal, Arlene Golonka, Bob Dishy, Priscilla Barnes, Dom De Luise, Valerie Harper

Lame-brained little sex farce about one perfect couple's struggle to hold their own marriage together amid the divorces and separations around them. The cast includes Dom De Luise as a plumber-turned-porn star and Valerie Harper as a seductress in a blond wig. Tries desperately to be hip but ends up as nothing more than a smutty little dirty joke with a lot of very annoying characters. Redeemed only by the incandescent Natalie Wood. Rated R for profanity and nudity.

1980   103 minutes

LAST OF THE RED HOT LOVERS
★½

DIRECTOR: Gene Saks
CAST: Alan Arkin, Paula Prentiss, Sally Kellerman

Alan Arkin plays a married man trying to sneak around, in this 1972 comedy. He uses his mother's apartment for his rendezvous and cracks us up with his unsuave manner. Rated PG.

1972   98 minutes

LAST POLKA, THE
★★★★

DIRECTOR: John Blanchard
CAST: John Candy, Eugene Levy, Catherine O'Hara, Rick Moranis

This made-for-HBO special features the unique Second City comedy of Yosh (John Candy) and Stan (Eugene Levy) Schmenge, a delightful pair of polka bandleaders, as they reminisce about their checkered musical careers. Fellow SCTV troupe members Catherine O'Hara and Rick Moranis add to the hilarity in this adept send-up of *The Last Waltz*, Martin Scorsese's documentary chronicling the final concert of real-life rock legends The Band.

1984   60 minutes

LAST REMAKE OF BEAU GESTE, THE
★

DIRECTOR: Marty Feldman
CAST: Marty Feldman, Michael York, Ann-Margret, Trevor Howard

We have Marty Feldman's success in *Young Frankenstein* to thank for this vapid Foreign Legion comedy, Feldman's first (and last) attempt at the triple crown of writing, directing, and starring. Most of the desert hijinks play like television outtakes, and the good supporting cast is given little to do. If you try for the long haul, watch for Feldman's sequence with "co-star" Gary Cooper in footage intercut from the 1939 classic. Overall, this is pretty dry stuff. Rated PG—sexual situations.

1977   84 minutes

LAVENDER HILL MOB, THE
★★★★★

DIRECTOR: Charles Crichton
CAST: Alec Guinness, Stanley Holloway, Sidney James, Alfie Bass

Fun, fun, and more fun from this 1951 most celebrated British comedy. Alec Guinness is a mousy bank clerk. He has a plan for intercepting the bank's armored-car shipment. With the aid of a few friends he forms an amateur robbery squad. Lo and behold, they escape with the loot. After all, the plan was foolproof. Or was it? Be sure to see the outcome for yourself.

1951   B & W   82 minutes

LE BEAU MARIAGE
★★★★

DIRECTOR: Eric Rohmer
CAST: Beatrice Romand, Arielle Dombasle, André Dussollier

A young woman decides it is high time she got married. She chooses the man she wants, a busy lawyer, and tells her friends of their coming wedding. He knows nothing of this, but she is confident. After all, is she not beautiful, intelligent, and impossible to resist? That is the premise in this film by French director Eric Rohmer, whose works have always been more concerned with human nature than plot. As a result, we have a character-rich import that will please those with a taste for something different. In French with English subtitles. Rated R.

1982   100 minutes

LE CAVALEUR
★★★★

DIRECTOR: Philippe de Broca
CAST: Jean Rochefort, Annie Girardot

A poignantly philosophical, yet witty and often hilarious, farce about the perils of the middle-aged heartbreak kid. Our cad about town is unerringly portrayed by Jean Rochefort (*French Postcards*; *Till Marriage Do Us Part*) as a classical pianist trying to juggle his art and the many past, present, and possible future women in his life. He does so well he almost loses them all. Annie Girardot warmly plays his ex-wife, and Catherine Le Prince the almost girl of his dreams. Written and directed by Philippe de Broca (*King of Hearts*), this film will be a delight for those who usually eschew foreign films. Nudity but generally innocent adult situations.

1980   106 minutes

LE CHEVRE (THE GOAT)
★★½
DIRECTOR: Francis Veber
CAST: Pierre Richard, Gerard Depardieu, Corynne Charbit, Michel Robin, Andre Valardy, Pedro Armendariz Jr

The stars of *Les Comperes*, Pierre Richard and Gerard Depardieu, romp again in this French comedy as two investigators searching for a missing girl in Mexico. While this import may please staunch fans of the stars, it is far from being a laugh riot. Unrated, the film has profanity and violence. In French with English subtitles.

1981   91 minutes

LE MILLION
★★★★
DIRECTOR: René Clair
CAST: Annabella, Rene Lefevre, Louis Allibert, Wanda Greville, Paul Olivier

Made more than fifty years ago, this delightful comedy about the efforts of a group of people to retrieve an elusive lottery ticket is more applicable to American audiences of today than it was when originally released. René Clair's classic fantasy-adventure is freewheeling and fun. The plot is secondary to the form in this movie, and the clever camera work and ingenious situations carry the audience along at a dizzying pace. A memorable experience and lots of fun for everyone. Subtitled in English.

1931   B & W   85 minutes

LES COMPERES
★★★★
DIRECTOR: Bernard Bher
CAST: Pierre Richard, Gerard Depardieu

Pierre Richard and Gerard Depardieu star in this madcap French comedy as two strangers who find themselves on the trail of a runaway teenager. Both think they're the father—it was the only way the boy's mother could think of to enlist their aid. In French with English subtitles. Rated PG for profanity and brief violence.

1984   90 minutes

LET'S DO IT AGAIN
★★★½
DIRECTOR: Sidney Poitier
CAST: Sidney Poitier, Bill Cosby, Jimmie Walker, Calvin Lockhart, John Amos

After scoring with *Uptown Saturday Night*, Sidney Poiter and Bill Cosby decided to reteam for another enjoyable comedy in 1975. Jimmie Walker, Calvin Lockhart, and John Amos are also on hand to add to the fun in this tale of a couple of lodge brothers taking on the gangsters. Rated PG.

1975   112 minutes

LIBELED LADY
★★★★★
DIRECTOR: Jack Conway
CAST: William Powell, Myrna Loy, Spencer Tracy, Jean Harlow

Their fame as Nick and Nora Charles in the *Thin Man* series notwithstanding, this is the finest film to have paired William Powell and Myrna Loy. They take part in a deliciously funny tale of a newspaper that, when faced with a libel suit from an angered woman, attempts to turn the libel into irrefutable fact. Spencer Tracy and

Jean Harlow lend their considerable support, and the result is a delight from start to finish. In spite of its age, the story remains fresh; if anything, it takes on even more meaning during these times of litigation run amok.

1936   B & W   98 minutes

LIFE OF BRIAN
★★★★

DIRECTOR: Terry Jones
CAST: Terry Jones, John Cleese, Eric Idle, Michael Palin, Terry Gilliam, Graham Chapman

Religious fanaticism gets a real drubbing in this irreverent and often sidesplitting comedy, which features and was created by those Monty Python crazies. Graham Chapman plays the title role of a reluctant "savior" born in a manger just down the street from Jesus Christ's. Rated R for nudity and profanity.

1979   93 minutes

LIFE WITH FATHER
★★★★

DIRECTOR: Michael Curtiz
CAST: William Powell, Irene Dunne, Edmund Gwenn, ZaSu Pitts, Jimmy Lydon, Elizabeth Taylor, Martin Milner

A warm, witty, charming, nostalgic memoir of life and the coming of age of author Clarence Day in turn-of-the-century New York City. Centering on his staid, eccentric father (William Powell), the film is a 100 percent delight. Based on the long-running Broadway play.

1947   118 minutes

LILY IN LOVE
★★★★

DIRECTOR: Karoly Makk

CAST: Christopher Plummer, Maggie Smith, Elke Sommer, Adolph Green

Christopher Plummer is superb as an aging, egocentric actor who disguises himself as a younger man in an attempt to snag a plum role in a film written by his wife (Maggie Smith), and succeeds all too well. *Lily in Love* is a marvelously warm and witty adult comedy. That's adult as in appealing to mature audiences rather than steeped in sex and nudity. There are no teenagers, special effects, sex scenes, or acts of violence. It is simply a very fine motion picture that dares to do something different, and does it extremely well. Unrated, the film has some profanity.

1985   105 minutes

LIMELIGHT
★★★½

DIRECTOR: Charles Chaplin
CAST: Charlie Chaplin, Claire Bloom, Buster Keaton, Sydney Chaplin, Nigel Bruce

Too long and too much Charlie Chaplin (who trimmed Buster Keaton's part when it became obvious he was stealing the film), this is nevertheless a poignant excursion. Chaplin is an aging music hall comic on the skids who saves a ballerina (Claire Bloom) from suicide and, while bolstering her hopes, regains his confidence. The comedy skit with Chaplin and Keaton is a "keeper." The score, by Chaplin, is haunting.

1952   B & W 145 minutes

LITTLE DARLINGS
★★★

DIRECTOR: Ronald F. Maxwell
CAST: Tatum O'Neal, Kristy McNichol, Matt Dillon

A story of the trials and tribulations of teen-age virginity, this film too often lapses into chronic cuteness, with characters more darling than realistic. *Little Darlings* follows the antics of two 15-year-old outcasts—rich, sophisticated Ferris Whitney (Tatum O'Neal) and poor, belligerent Angel Bright (Kristy McNichol)—as they spend their summer at Camp Little Wolf and compete to "score" with a boy first. Rated R.

1980   95 minutes

LITTLE ROMANCE, A
★★★★½

DIRECTOR: George Roy Hill
CAST: Thelonious Bernard, Diane Lane, Laurence Olivier, Sally Kellerman, Broderick Crawford

Everyone needs *A Little Romance* in their life. This absolutely enchanting film by director George Roy Hill (*Butch Cassidy and the Sun-dance Kid; The Sting*) has something for everyone. Its story of two appealing youngsters (Thelonious Bernard and Diane Lane) who fall in love in Paris is full of surprises, laughs, and uplifting moments. Supporting cast adds to the fun. Rated PG.

1979   108 minutes

LITTLE SEX, A
★½

DIRECTOR: Bruce Paltrow
CAST: Tim Matheson, Kate Capshaw

A New York director of television commercials can't keep his hands off his actresses, even though he's married to a beautiful, intelligent woman. This is a tepid romantic comedy. Rated R.

1982   95 minutes

LOCAL HERO
★★★★½

DIRECTOR: Bill Forsyth
CAST: Burt Lancaster, Peter Riegert, Fulton MacKay

A wonderfully offbeat comedy by Bill Forsyth (*Gregory's Girl*). Burt Lancaster plays a Houston oil baron who sends Peter Riegert (*Animal House*) to the west coast of Scotland to negotiate with the natives for North Sea oil rights. As with *Gregory's Girl*, which was about a gangly, good-natured boy's first crush, this film is blessed with sparkling little moments of humor, unforgettable characters, and a warmly human story. Rated PG for language.

1983   111 minutes

LONELY GUY, THE
★★★½

DIRECTOR: Arthur Hiller
CAST: Steve Martin, Robyn Douglass, Charles Grodin, Merv Griffin, Dr. Joyce Brothers

Steve Martin stars in this okay comedy as a struggling young writer who makes his living working for a greeting card company. One day he comes home to find his live-in mate (Robyn Douglass) in bed with another man and becomes the "Lonely Guy" of the title. Only recommended for Steve Martin fans. Rated R for brief nudity and profanity.

1984   90 minutes

LOOKIN' TO GET OUT
★★★

DIRECTOR: Hal Ashby
CAST: Jon Voight, Burt Young, Ann-Margret

This off-beat comedy stars Jon Voight and Burt Young as a couple of compulsive gamblers out to hit the fabled "big score" in Las Vegas. It'll keep you interested for most of its running time, although it does drag a bit in the middle. However, the first hour zips by before you know it, and the ending is a humdinger. Rated R for violence and profanity.

1982 104 minutes

LOOSE SHOES
★

DIRECTOR: Ira Miller
CAST: Buddy Hackett, Howard Hesseman, Bill Murray, Susan Tyrell, Avery Shreiber

Failed attempt to spoof B movies. The successful gags are very few and the whole outing reeks of a *Kentucky Fried Movie* ripoff. At least with that film the sex, nudity, and profanity were used to poke fun at sexploitation flicks. Here, these qualities are exposed simply for the drive-in audience's satisfaction. Rated R.

1977 73 minutes

LOSIN' IT
★★★

DIRECTOR: Curtis Hanson
CAST: Tom Cruise, Shelley Long, Jackie Earle Haley, John Stockwell

Better-than-average teen exploitation flick, this one has four boys off to Tijuana for a good time. Shelley Long ("Cheers") adds interest as a runaway wife who joins them on their journey. Rated R.

1982 104 minutes

LOST AND FOUND
★

DIRECTOR: Melvin Frank
CAST: Glenda Jackson, George Segal, Maureen Stapleton

After teaming up successfully for *A Touch of Class*, writer-director Melvin Frank and his stars, Glenda

Jackson and George Segal, tried again. But the result was an unfunny comedy about two bickering, cardboard characters. Rated PG.

1979 112 minutes

LOST IN AMERICA
★★★★½

DIRECTOR: Albert Brooks
CAST: Albert Brooks, Julie Hagerty, Garry Marshall

Writer-director-star Albert Brooks is one of America's great natural comedic resources. *Lost in America* is his funniest film to date. Some viewers may be driven to distraction by Brooks's all-too-true study of what happens when a "successful" and "responsible" married couple chucks it all and goes out on an *Easy Rider*–style trip across the country. Brooks makes movies about the things most adults would consider their worst nightmare. He cuts close to the bone and makes us laugh at ourselves in a very original way. If you can stand the pain, the pleasure is well worth it. Rated R for profanity and adult situations.

1985 92 minutes

LOVE AND ANARCHY
★★★★★

DIRECTOR: Lina Wertmuller
CAST: Giancarlo Giannini, Mariangela Melato, Eros Pagni, Lina Polito

Giancarlo Giannini gets to eat up the screen with this role. Comic, tragic, and intellectually stimulating, this is Wertmuller's best film. Giannini is bent on assassinating Mussolini right after the rise of Fascism but somehow gets waylaid. Imagine the possibilities and they're probably in the film. A classic. Rated R for sexual situations, language, and some nudity.

1973   117 minutes

LOVE AND DEATH
★★★★

DIRECTOR: Woody Allen
CAST: Woody Allen, Diane Keaton, Harold Gould, Alfred Lutter, Zvee Scooler

This comedy set in 1812 Russia is one of Woody Allen's funniest films. Diane Keaton is the high-minded Russian with assassination (of Napoleon) in mind. Allen is her cowardly accomplice with sex on the brain. The movie satirizes not only love and death, but politics, classic Russian literature (Tolstoy's *War and Peace*), and foreign films, as well. Use of Prokofiev music enhances the piece. Rated PG.

1975   82 minutes

LOVE AT FIRST BITE
★★★★

DIRECTOR: Stan Dragoti
CAST: George Hamilton, Susan Saint James, Richard Benjamin, Dick Shawn, Arte Johnson

The Dracula legend is given the comedy treatment in this amusing parody of horror films. George Hamilton plays the campy Count, who has an unorthodox way with the ladies. (In this case, it's Susan Saint James, much to the chagrin of her boyfriend, Richard Benjamin.) Even though the humor is heavy-handed in parts, you find yourself chuckling continually in spite of yourself. Rated PG.

1979   96 minutes

LOVE HAPPY
★★

DIRECTOR: David Miller
CAST: The Marx Brothers, Marilyn Monroe, Raymond Burr

The last Marx Brothers movie, this 1949 production was originally set to star only Harpo, but Chico and, later, Groucho were brought in to beef up its box-office potential. They should've known better. This "Let's put on a show" retread doesn't even come close to their lesser works at MGM. Only Groucho's ogling of then-screen-newcomer Marilyn Monroe makes it interesting for movie buffs.

1949   B & W   91 minutes

LOVE LAUGHS AT ANDY HARDY
★★

DIRECTOR: Willis Goldbeck
CAST: Mickey Rooney, Lewis Stone, Fay Holden, Sara Haden, Bonita Granville

America's all-American, lovable, irritating, well-meaning wimp comes home from World War II and plunges back into the same adolescent rut of agonizing young love. The change of times has made this cookie-cutter film very predictable. But it's fun anyway.

1946   B & W   93 minutes

LOVELINES

DIRECTOR: Rod Amateau
CAST: Michael Winslow, Greg Bradford, Mary Beth Evans

Michael Winslow, the sound-effects cop in *Police Academy*, is the only recognizable face in this dreadful teen comedy. The film is supposed to be about a teen telephone service and an all-girl rock band attempting to break into the big time. But there are so many plot digressions, it ends up being about how not to make a movie. The point seems to be sex and laughs at any cost. Yet the sex is just a tease, and the humor is all but nonexistent. Rated R for nudity, suggested sex, violence, and profanity.

1984   93 minutes

LOVER COME BACK
★★★★

DIRECTOR: Delbert Mann
CAST: Rock Hudson, Doris Day, Tony Randall, Edie Adams, Jack Oakie, Jack Kruschen, Ann B. Davis, Joe Flynn, Jack Albertson

Rock Hudson and Doris Day are rival advertising executives battling professionally, psychologically, and sexually. A bright comedy that builds nicely. One of their best. Silly, innocent fun with a great supporting cast.

1961   107 minutes

LOVERS AND LIARS
★★½

DIRECTOR: Mario Monicelli
CAST: Goldie Hawn, Giancarlo Giannini, Laura Betti

The first thing that occurs to you while watching this film is a question: What's Goldie Hawn doing in a dubbed Italian sex comedy? It was obviously released to take advantage of her box-office success at the time with films like *Private Benjamin* and *Seems like Old Times*. But we doubt it will prove very popular on video—especially when people discover it is anything but a typical Goldie Hawn comedy. Co-starring Giancarlo Giannini (*Swept Away*), it is a modestly entertaining piece of fluff tailored primarily for European tastes and, therefore, will probably disappoint most of Hawn's fans. Rated R.

1979   96 minutes

LOVESICK
★★★½

DIRECTOR: Marshall Brickman

CAST: Dudley Moore, Elizabeth McGovern, Alec Guinness, John Huston

This is a sweet romantic comedy that tugs at your heart as it tickles your funnybone. You won't fall out of your seat laughing or grab a tissue to dab away the tears. But this movie, about a psychiatrist's (Dudley Moore) obsession with his patient (Elizabeth McGovern), does have its moments. Rated PG.

1983   95 minutes

LOVING COUPLES
★★★

DIRECTOR: Jack Smight
CAST: Shirley MacLaine, James Coburn, Susan Sarandon, Stephen Collins

Can a film be both entertaining and boring? If the film is *Loving Couples*, the answer is yes. This romantic comedy can have you roaring with laughter one minute and yawning the next. The good moments outnumber the bad. But after it's over, you can't decide whether it was worth seeing or not. The plot is that old and tired one, about two couples who swap partners for a temporary fling only to reunite by film's end happier and wiser for the experience. It's a premise that's been worn thin by filmmakers and especially television since the swinging '60s and badly in need of retirement. Rated PG.

1980   97 minutes

LUST IN THE DUST
★★★

DIRECTOR: Paul Bartel
CAST: Tab Hunter, Divine, Lainie Kazan, Geoffrey Lewis, Henry Silva, Cesar Romero

Tab Hunter and female impersonator Divine (who's anything but), who first teamed in *Polyester*, star in this so-so spoof of spaghetti westerns, directed by Paul Bartel (*Eating Raoul*). The ad blurb tells all: "He rode the West. The girls rode the rest. Together they ravaged the land." Rated R for nudity, suggested sex, and violence.

1985   86 minutes

LUV
★★

DIRECTOR: Clive Donner
CAST: Jack Lemmon, Elaine May, Peter Falk, Severn Darden

When talent the caliber of Jack Lemmon, Peter Falk, and Elaine May cannot breathe life into a film, then nothing can. The plot concerns three New York intellectuals and their tribulations through life. Who cares?

1967   95 minutes

MACARONI
★★★★½

DIRECTOR: Ettore Scola
CAST: Jack Lemmon, Marcello Mastroianni, Daria Nicolodi, Isa Danieli, Maria Luisa Santella, Patrizia Sacchi

Wonderful Italian comedy-drama from the director of *A Special Day* and *Le Bal*. This one concerns an American executive (Jack Lemmon) who returns to Naples for a business meeting forty years after his stay there with the army. He is visited by an old friend (Marcello Mastroianni). *Macaroni* addresses the ideals of friendship with a fresh approach that defies clichés and gives sentimentality a more intelligent definition. Both Lemmon and Mastroianni deliver brilliant performances. Rated PG for profanity.

1985   104 minutes

MAD MISS MANTON, THE
★★★

DIRECTOR: Leigh Jason
CAST: Barbara Stanwyck, Henry Fonda, Sam Levene, Frances Mercer, Stanley Ridges, Whitney Bourne, Leona Maricle, James Burke, Penny Singleton

A group of high-society ladies led by Miss Manton (Barbara Stanwyck) help solve a murder mystery with comic results—sometimes. The humor is pretty outdated, and the brand of romanticism, while being in step with the 1930s, comes off rather silly in the latter part of the twentieth century. Henry Fonda plays a newspaper editor who falls in love with the mad Miss Manton.

1938   B & W   80 minutes

MADE FOR EACH OTHER
★★★★

DIRECTOR: John Cromwell
CAST: Carole Lombard, James Stewart, Charles Coburn, Lucile Watson, Harry Davenport

This is a highly appealing comedy/drama centering on the rocky first years of a marriage. The young couple (Carole Lombard and James Stewart) must do battle with interfering in-laws, inept servants, and the consequences of childbirth. The real strength of this film lies in the screenplay, by Jo Swerling. It gives viewers a thoughtful and tasteful picture of events that we can all relate to.

1939   B & W   100 minutes

MAGIC CHRISTIAN, THE
★★★

DIRECTOR: Joseph McGrath

CAST: Peter Sellers, Ringo Starr, Christopher Lee, Raquel Welch, Richard Attenborough, Yul Brynner

A now-dated comedy about the world's wealthiest man (Peter Sellers) and his adopted son (Ringo Starr) testing the depths of degradation to which people will plunge themselves for money still has some funny scenes and outrageous cameos by Christopher Lee (as Dracula), Raquel Welch, and Richard Attenborough. Rated PG.

1970   93 minutes

MAIN EVENT, THE
★

DIRECTOR: Howard Zieff
CAST: Barbra Streisand, Ryan O'Neal, Paul Sand

A limp boxing comedy that tried unsuccessfully to reunite the stars of *What's Up Doc?*, Barbra Streisand and Ryan O'Neal. This movie will put you to sleep the hard way. Rated PG.

1979   112 minutes

MAKE MINE MINK
★★★★

DIRECTOR: Robert Asher
CAST: Terry-Thomas, Athene Seyler, Billie Whitelaw

Bright dialogue and clever situations make this crazy comedy from Britain highly enjoyable. An ex-officer, a dowager, and a motley crew of fur thieves team to commit larceny for charity. Gap-toothed Terry-Thomas is in top form in this one.

1960   100 minutes

MAKING THE GRADE
★★½

DIRECTOR: Dorian Walker

CAST: Judd Nelson, Jonna Lee, Carey Scott

A rich kid pays a surrogate to attend prep school for him. Typical teen-exploitation fare. Rated R.

1984   105 minutes

MALICIOUS
★★★½

DIRECTOR: Salvatore Samperi
CAST: Laura Antonelli, Turi Ferro, Alessandro Momo, Tina Aumont

Italian beauty Laura Antonelli (*Wifemistress, The Innocent*) is hired as a housekeeper for a widower and his three sons. Not surprisingly, she becomes the object of affection for all four men—particularly 14-year-old Nino. While Papa makes proper and methodical plans to court and marry, Nino ensnares the somewhat willing lady in a compelling game of sexual power. Antonelli is tantalizing, and director Samperi easily traverses moods from amusement with the boy's awakening sexual awareness to sequences of disturbing, slightly dangerous, eroticism. Rated R.

1974   98 minutes

MANHATTAN
★★★★★

DIRECTOR: Woody Allen
CAST: Diane Keaton, Woody Allen, Michael Murphy, Mariel Hemingway, Meryl Streep

Reworking the same themes he explored in *Play It Again Sam* and *Annie Hall*, Woody Allen again comes up with a masterpiece in this film—perhaps his greatest. Diane Keaton returns as the object of his awkward but well-meaning affections. It's heartwarming, insightful, screamingly funny, and a feast for the eyes. The black-and-white cinematography of long-time Allen collaborator Gordon Willis recalls the great visuals of *Citizen Kane* and *The Third Man*. In short, it's wonderful. Rated R.

1979   B & W   96 minutes

MAN IN THE WHITE SUIT, THE
★★★★★

DIRECTOR: Alexander Mackendrick

CAST: Alec Guinness, Joan Greenwood, Cecil Parker

In *The Man in the White Suit*, Alec Guinness is the perfect choice to play an unassuming scientist who invents a fabric that can't be torn, frayed, or stained! Can you imagine the furor this causes in the textile industry? This uniquely original script pokes fun at big business and big labor as they try to suppress his discovery. Joan Greenwood is a treasure in a supporting role.

1952   B & W   84 minutes

MAN OF FLOWERS
★★★★★

DIRECTOR: Paul Cox

CAST: Norman Kaye, Alyson Best, Chris Haywood, Werner Herzog

Kinky, humorous, and touching, this winner from Australia affirms Paul Cox (of *Lonely Hearts* fame) as one of the wittiest and most sensitive directors from Down Under. Norman Kaye is terrific as an eccentric old man who collects art and flowers and watches pretty women undress. To him these are things of beauty that he can observe but either can't touch or can't participate in, thanks to an oppressive upbringing. The story moves slyly from the funny to the erotic to the macabre without warning. Rated R for nudity.

1984   90 minutes

MAN WHO LOVED WOMEN, THE
★★★

DIRECTOR: Blake Edwards

CAST: Burt Reynolds, Julie Andrews, Marilu Henner, Kim Basinger, Barry Corkin

The first screen collaboration of Burt Reynolds, Julie Andrews, and her director hubby, Blake Edwards (*The Pink Panther; S.O.B.*), didn't sound like the kind of thing that would make screen history. And it isn't. But, surprise of surprises, it is a pleasantly entertaining—and sometimes uproariously funny—adult sex comedy. The always likable Reynolds plays a guy who just can't say no to the opposite sex, and Andrews is the psychiatrist who wants him to try. Rated R for nudity and profanity.

1983   110 minutes

MAN WHO WASN'T THERE, THE
🦃

DIRECTOR: Bruce Malmuth

CAST: Steve Guttenberg, Jeffrey Tambor, Lisa Langlois, Art Hindle, Vincent Baggetta

Clumsy comedy involves Steve Guttenberg in espionage and invisibility. This was originally released in 3-D, but the characters are barely one-dimensional. The film disappeared quickly from movie theaters, making it *The Movie That Wasn't There*. Rated R for nudity, language.

1983   111 minutes

MAN WITH ONE RED SHOE, THE
★★★½

DIRECTOR: Stan Dragoti

CAST: Tom Hanks, Dabney Coleman, Charles Durning, Lori Singer, Jim Belushi, Carrie Fisher, Edward Herrmann

An American remake of the French comedy *The Tall Blond Man with*

One Black Shoe, this casts Tom Hanks (*Splash*) as a concert violinist who becomes pursued by a group of spies led by Dabney Coleman. It's all because Edward Herrmann, assistant to head of the C.I.A. Charles Durning, picked Hanks as a decoy to confuse the power-hungry Coleman. Sound complicated? It is—but fun, too. Hanks is nearly the whole show. However, Jim Belushi (as his practical-joke-loving buddy) and Carrie Fisher (as an overly amorous flute player) also provide some hearty laughs. And Lori Singer (*Footloose*) makes a very sexy spy. Rated PG for profanity and violence.

1985   96 minutes

MAN WITH TWO BRAINS, THE
★★★★

DIRECTOR: Carl Reiner
CAST: Steve Martin, Kathleen Turner, David Warner, Paul Benedict

Steve Martin stars in this generally amusing takeoff of 1950s horror/sci-fi flicks as a scientist involved with two women: a nasty wife (Kathleen Turner, of *Body Heat*) and a sweet patient (the voice of Sissy Spacek). There's only one problem in his relationship with the latter: All that's left of her is her brain. While those who aren't partial to Martin's silly brand of humor are likely to remain so, fans of the wild and crazy guy will no doubt think this is his funniest film yet. Rated R for nudity, profanity, and violence.

1983   93 minutes

MARCH OF THE WOODEN SOLDIERS
★★★★

DIRECTOR: Gus Meins
CAST: Stan Laurel, Oliver Hardy, Charlotte Henry

Originally titled *Babes in Toyland* this film features Stan Laurel and Oliver Hardy as the toymaker's assistants in the land of Old King Cole. Utterly forgettable songs slow down an otherwise enjoyable fantasy film. Stan and Ollie are integrated well into the storyline, finally saving the town from the attack of the boogeymen.

1934   B & W   73 minutes

M*A*S*H
★★★★½

DIRECTOR: Robert Altman
CAST: Elliott Gould, Donald Sutherland, Sally Kellerman, Tom Skerritt, Robert Duvall, JoAnn Pflug, Bud Cort

Fans of the television series of the same name and "Trapper John, M.D." may have a bit of trouble recognizing their favorite characters, but this is the original. One of eccentric film director Robert Altman's few true artistic successes, this release is outrageous good fun. Rated PG.

1970   116 minutes

M*A*S*H: GOODBYE, FAREWELL, AMEN
★★★★

DIRECTOR: Alan Alda
CAST: Alan Alda, Henry Morgan, Loretta Swit, Jamie Farr

A beautiful send-off to one of the great television series. Alan Alda and company have finally seen the end of the Korean War and are headed home. This last episode is handled with the usual excellence that one has come to associate with the series. A must for "M*A*S*H" fans and those who think there is nothing worth watching on television.

1983   120 minutes

MASTER OF THE HOUSE (DU SKAL AERE DIN HUSTRU)
★★★★

DIRECTOR: Carl Dreyer
CAST: Johannes Meyer, Astrid Holm, Karin Nellmose, Mathilde Nielsen

In this funny satire of middle-class life, a wife (played with charm by Karin Nellmose) runs away from her husband (Johannes Meyer), a male chauvinist who treats her brutally. Later, the wife is reunited with her husband after an old nurse has taught him a lesson. These may seem like light themes for the director who later went on to make films like *The Passion of Joan of Arc* and *Vampyr*. However, it is very enjoyable.
1925   B & W   81 minutes

MATILDA
★★★½

DIRECTOR: Daniel Mann
CAST: Elliott Gould, Clive Revill, Harry Guardino, Roy Clark, Lionel Stander, Art Metrano, Karen Carlson, Robert Mitchum

A cute comedy about a boxing kangaroo who becomes a legend in the sport. Elliott Gould plays a small-time booking agent who becomes the manager of the heavyweight marsupial. Despite some problems in the directing, the film is watchable and humorous. Sentimental at times and a bit corny, too, but worth the time. Recommended for family viewing. Rated G.
1978   105 minutes

MAXIE
★★

DIRECTOR: Paul Aaron
CAST: Glenn Close, Mandy Patinkin, Ruth Gordon, Barnard Hughes, Valerie Curtin

Cute but not particularly impressive fantasy about a conservative secretary (Glenn Close) who becomes possessed by the spirit of a flamboyant flapper (Close, too). The star is wonderful, but the predictable plot and the uninspired direction let her—and the viewer—down. Few laughs and no surprises. Rated PG for suggested sex.
1985   98 minutes

MEATBALLS
★★★½

DIRECTOR: Ivan Reitman
CAST: Bill Murray, Harvey Atkin, Kate Lynch, Chris Makepeace

Somehow, this *Animal House*-style comedy's disjointedness is easier to swallow than it should be. Elmer Bernstein's music gets sentimental in the right places, and star Bill Murray is fun to watch. Rated PG.
1979   92 minutes

MEATBALLS PART II

DIRECTOR: Ken Weiderhorn
CAST: Richard Mulligan, Kim Richards, John Mengatti, Misty Rowe

This lame sequel to *Meatballs* should never have been made. Pitifully unfunny high jinx at summer camp, with an alien getting in on the action this time. In fact, he has all three of the good lines. Rated PG for sexual references.
1984   87 minutes

MEL BROOKS' HISTORY OF THE WORLD, PART I
★★

DIRECTOR: Mel Brooks
CAST: Mel Brooks, Dom De Luise, Madeline Kahn, Harvey Korman

Sometimes funny, always in poor taste, Brooks's history lesson will appeal to junior highschoolers of all ages. The film is full of toilet and racial jokes, and funny scenes are few and far between. When it works, it works well—as in the Busby Berkeley takeoff on the the Spanish Inquisition—but when it doesn't work, it really doesn't work. Rated R.

1981   92 minutes

MELVIN AND HOWARD
★★★★★
DIRECTOR: Jonathan Demme
CAST: Paul LeMat, Jason Robards, Mary Steenburgen

This brilliantly directed slice-of-life film works marvelously well . . . on two levels. On the surface, it's the entertaining tale of how Melvin Dummar (Paul LeMat) met Howard Hughes, (Jason Robards)—or did he? Underneath, it's a hilarious spoof of our society. Mary Steenburgen co-stars in this triumph of American filmmaking, a rare gem that deserves to be seen and talked about. Rated R.

1980   95 minutes

MICKI & MAUDE
★★★★½
DIRECTOR: Blake Edwards
CAST: Dudley Moore, Amy Irving, Ann Reinking, George Gaynes, Wallace Shawn

In this hysterically funny comedy Dudley Moore stars as a television personality who tries to juggle marriages to two women, Amy Irving and Ann Reinking. Directed by Blake Edwards (10), it's a triumph for filmmaker and cast alike: One of the funniest films of its year. Rated PG-13 for profanity and suggested sex.

1984   96 minutes

MIDNIGHT MADNESS

DIRECTOR: David Wechter, Michael Nankin
CAST: David Naughton, Debra Clinger, Eddie Deezen, Stephen Furst

Absolutely awful post–*Animal House* Disney production about a bunch of teen-age idiots going on a midnight scavenger hunt. Rated PG.

1980   110 minutes

MIDSUMMER NIGHT'S SEX COMEDY, A
★★½
DIRECTOR: Woody Allen
CAST: Woody Allen, Mia Farrow, José Ferrer, Julie Hagerty, Tony Roberts, Mary Steenburgen

Woody Allen's sometimes dull cinematic treatise—albeit sweet-natured, and beautifully photographed by Gordon Willis—on the star-writer-director's favorite subjects: sex and death. That's not to say *A Midsummer Night's Sex Comedy* doesn't have its humorous moments. Allen's fans will undoubtedly enjoy it. But, like *Stardust Memories*, it isn't really a comedy, and viewers expecting one will be disappointed. Rated PG for adult themes.

1982   88 minutes

MIKEY AND NICKY
★★★
DIRECTOR: Elaine May
CAST: Peter Falk, John Cassavetes, Ned Beatty, Joyce Van Patten, Rose Arrick, Carol Grace

The story of a fateful day and the relationship of two small-time crooks who have considered each other best friends since childhood. This hauntingly funny film slowly builds to its climax in the Elaine May tradition. Great acting from

Peter Falk and John Cassavetes. Rated R for profanity.

1976   119 minutes

MILKY WAY, THE
★★★★

DIRECTOR: Leo McCarey

CAST: Harold Lloyd, Adolphe Menjou, Helen Mack

In this superb compendium of gags flowing from his character of a milkman who innocently decks the champion during a brawl, the great Harold Lloyd amply proves why he was such a success. It's all carefully thought out and planned (a switch from his old silent days when off the cuff was good enough), but highly entertaining just the same. Harold Lloyd was a master comic craftsman. This is the finest of his few talking films.

1936   B & W 83 minutes

MISCHIEF
★★★

DIRECTOR: Mel Damski

CAST: Doug McKeon, Catherine Mary Stewart, Chris Nash, Kelly Preston, D. W. Brown

In this disarming coming-of-age comedy, Doug McKeon (*On Golden Pond*) plays Jonathan, whose hopes of romance are thwarted until Gene (Chris Nash, in an impressive debut), a kid from the big city, shows him how. Rated R for violence, profanity, nudity, and simulated sex.

1985   93 minutes

MISSIONARY, THE
★★★½

DIRECTOR: Richard Loncraine

CAST: Michael Palin, Maggie Smith, Denholm Elliott, Trevor Howard, Michael Hordern

Monty Python's Michael Palin, who also wrote the script, plays a well-meaning American minister assigned the task of saving the souls of London's fallen women. Those familiar with its British-style comedy, and even those who are not, will probably get most of the jokes. It is not a nonstop, gag-filled descent into absurdity like the Monty Python movies. It is, instead, a warm-hearted spoof with the accent on character and very sparing but effective in its humor. Rated R.

1982   90 minutes

MR. AND MRS. SMITH
★★★★

DIRECTOR: Alfred Hitchcock

CAST: Carole Lombard, Robert Montgomery, Gene Raymond, Jack Carson

This film deals with the love-hate-love relationship of Carole Lombard and Robert Montgomery, who play a couple who discover their marriage isn't legal. The bouncy dialogue by Norman Krasna is justly famous and includes some of the most classic comedy scenes ever to come out of this screwball gender of films. Directing this enjoyable farce, in his only pure comedy, is Alfred Hitchcock.

1941   B & W 95 minutes

MR. BLANDINGS BUILDS HIS DREAM HOUSE
★★★★

DIRECTOR: H. C. Potter

CAST: Cary Grant, Myrna Loy, Melvyn Douglas

In this screwball comedy, Cary Grant plays a man tired of the hustle and bustle of city life. He decides to move to the country, construct his private Shangri-La, and settle back into what he feels will be a serene rural lifestyle. His fantasy and reality come into comic conflict. Myrna Loy is cast as his ever-patient wife in this very fine film.

1948   B & W   94 minutes

MR. HULOT'S HOLIDAY
★★★½

DIRECTOR: Jacques Tati
CAST: Jacques Tati, Nathale Pascaud

A delightfully light-hearted film about the natural comedy to be found in vacationing. Jacques Tati plays the famous Monsieur Hulot, who has some silly adventures at a seaside resort. Although partially dubbed in English, this film has a mime quality that is magical.

1953   B & W   86 minutes

MR. MOM
★★★★

DIRECTOR: Stan Dragoti
CAST: Michael Keaton, Teri Garr, Ann Jillian, Martin Mull

Michael Keaton is hilarious as an engineer who loses his job at an automobile manufacturing plant and, when wife Teri Garr gets a high-paying job at an advertising agency, becomes a hopelessly inept househusband. The story is familiar and the events somewhat predictable, but Keaton's off-the-wall antics and boyish charm make it all seem fresh and lively. In addition, Garr is perfect as the wife, and there's fine support from Ann Jillian and Martin Mull. Rated PG for light profanity.

1983   91 minutes

MR. PEABODY AND THE MERMAID
★★

DIRECTOR: Irving Pichel
CAST: William Powell, Ann Blyth, Irene Hervey

This is *Splash*, 1940s-style. A married New Englander (William Powell) snags an amorous mermaid while fishing and transfers her to his swimming pool, with the expected results.

1948   B & W   89 minutes

MR. ROBERTS
★★★★½

DIRECTOR: John Ford, Mervyn LeRoy
CAST: Henry Fonda, James Cagney, Jack Lemmon, William Powell, Ward Bond

A Navy cargo ship well outside the World War II battle zone is the setting for this hit comedy-drama. Henry Fonda is Lieutenant Roberts, the first officer who helps the crew battle their ceaseless boredom and tyrannical captain (James Cagney). Jack Lemmon began his road to stardom with his sparkling performance as the irrepressible con-man Ensign Pulver.

1955   123 minutes

MR. WINKLE GOES TO WAR
★★★

DIRECTOR: Alfred E. Green
CAST: Edward G. Robinson, Ruth Warrick, Richard Lane, Robert Armstrong, Richard Gaines

Edward G. Robinson is a henpecked bookkeeper who gets drafted into the army during World War II. As the saying goes, the army makes a man out of him. Like so many films of its time, *Mr. Winkle Goes to War* was part of the war effort and as such hasn't worn very well; what was considered heartfelt or patriotic back in the 1940s is now rendered maudlin or just corny. Still, the acting is excellent.

1944   B & W   80 minutes

MODERN PROBLEMS
★★

DIRECTOR: Ken Shapiro

CAST: Chevy Chase, Patti D'Arbanville, Mary Kay Place

In this passable comedy, directed
by Ken (*The Groove Tube*) Shapiro, Chevy Chase plays an air
traffic controller who may be permanently out to lunch. His girlfriend has left him, and a freak
nuclear accident has endowed him
with telekinetic powers. Rated PG
because of its brief nudity and sexual theme.

1981   91 minutes

MODERN ROMANCE
★★★★

DIRECTOR: Albert Brooks
CAST: Albert Brooks, Kathryn Harrold, Bruno Kirby

Love may be a many-splendored
thing for some people, but it's sheer
torture for Robert Cole (Albert
Brooks) in this contemporary
comedy. Brooks wrote, directed,
and stars in this very entertaining,
often hilarious story about a self-
indulgent, narcissistic Hollywood
film editor whose love life has the
stability of Mount St. Helens. Offbeat lunacy, wit, and insight give
this rethrashing of the old "you
can't live with 'em and you can't
live without 'em" axiom a full sail
of wind. Kathryn Harrold co-stars
as the intelligent and beautiful recipient of Cole's compulsively
jealous affections. Rated R.

1981   93 minutes

MODERN TIMES
★★★★

DIRECTOR: Charles Chaplin
CAST: Charlie Chaplin, Paulette
Goddard

Charlie Chaplin must have had a
crystal ball when he created *Modern Times*. His satire of life in an
industrial society has more relevance today than when it was
made. Primarily it is still pure

Chaplin, with his perfectly timed
and edited sight gags. The story
finds the Little Tramp confronting
all the dehumanizing inventions of
a futuristic manufacturing plant.
Especially delightful is the sequence in which Chaplin is used
as a guinea pig for an automatic
feeding machine that goes berserk. Paulette Goddard plays the
beautiful waif the tramp befriends
during his adventures.

1936   B & W   89 minutes

MONDO TRASHO
👎

DIRECTOR: John Waters
CAST: Divine, Mary Vivian Pearce,
Mink Stole, David Lochary

Director John Waters's longest
film—and you can feel every minute of it. This is not a sync-sound
movie, and the 1950s rock 'n' roll,
along with the occasional wild
dubbed-over dialogue, gets tiresome after twenty minutes. The
images do not reveal anything visionary or even vaguely humorous. Waters put it best—this is a
"gutter film." Unrated, but this is
equivalent to an X for violence,
gore, and sex.

1971   130 minutes

MONKEY BUSINESS
★★★★½

DIRECTOR: Norman Z. McLeod
CAST: The Marx Brothers, Thelma
Todd, Ruth Hall

The Marx Brothers are stowa-
ways on a cruise ship, deflating
pomposity and confusing authority. This movie dispenses with
needless subplots and stagy musical numbers. It's undiluted Marx
zaniness, and one of the team's
best films.

1931   B & W   77 minutes

MONSIEUR VERDOUX
★★★★

DIRECTOR: Charles Chaplin
CAST: Charlie Chaplin, Martha Raye, Isobel Elsom, Marilyn Nash, William Frawley

A trend-setting black comedy in which a dandified Parisian Bluebeard murders wives for their money. Charlie Chaplin is superb in the title role. But it's Martha Raye who steals the film—most decidedly in the rowboat scene. The genius that made Charles Spencer Chaplin famous the world over shows throughout.

1947   B & W 123 minutes

MONTENEGRO
★★★★

DIRECTOR: Dusan Makavejev
CAST: Susan Anspach, John Zacharias

Susan Anspach stars as a discontented housewife who wanders into a Yugoslavian nightclub, finds herself surrounded by sex and violence, and discovers she rather likes it, in this outlandish, outrageous, and sometimes shocking black comedy. The laughs come with the realization that everyone in this movie is totally bonkers. Rated R because of profanity, nudity, sex, and violence.

1981   98 minutes

MONTY PYTHON AND THE HOLY GRAIL
★★★½

DIRECTOR: Terry Gilliam
CAST: Terry Jones, Graham Chapman, John Cleese, Terry Gilliam, Terry Jones, Michael Palin

The Monty Python gang assault the legend of King Arthur and his knights in this often uproariously funny, sometimes tedious, movie. Rated PG.

1974   90 minutes

MONTY PYTHON LIVE AT THE HOLLYWOOD BOWL
★★★★

DIRECTOR: Terry Hughes
CAST: John Cleese, Eric Idle, Graham Chapman, Terry Jones, Michael Palin, Terry Gilliam

Hold on to your sides! Those Monty Python crazies are back with more unbridled hilarity. The first thirty minutes of this 73-minute concert film nearly had us on the floor. After that, we either had most of the laughs out of our systems or the material was not as funny. Either way, we were never bored—which is a lot more than you can say for most comedies these days. Rated R for profanity, nudity, and the best in bad taste.

1982   73 minutes

MONTY PYTHON'S THE MEANING OF LIFE
★★★★

DIRECTOR: Terry Jones
CAST: John Cleese, Eric Idle, Graham Chapman, Terry Jones, Terry Gilliam

Those Monty Python goons perform a series of sketches on the important issues of life. According to Michael Palin, the film "ranges from philosophy to history to medicine to halibut—especially halibut." It's the English troupe's finest feature film to date—a heady mixture of satiric and surreal bits about the life cycle from birth to death. It may prove offensive to some and a sheer delight to others. Rated R for all manner of offensive goings-on.

1983   103 minutes

MOON IS BLUE, THE
★★

DIRECTOR: Otto Preminger
CAST: William Holden, David Niven, Maggie McNamara, Tom Tully, Dawn Addams

It's hard to believe this comedy, based on a stage hit, was once considered highly controversial. We doubt that even your grandmother would be offended by the sexual innuendos in this very moral film. The thin plot concerns a young woman who fends off two slightly aging playboys by repeatedly vowing to remain a virgin until married. The laughs are few in this stagnant piece. It's fun to watch such smooth performers as William Holden and David Niven, but the material betrays them. Today, racier dialogue can be found on any TV sitcom.

1953   B & W   95 minutes

MORGAN
★★★★

DIRECTOR: Karel Reisz
CAST: Vanessa Redgrave, David Warner, Robert Stephens, Irene Handl

In this cult favorite, Vanessa Redgrave decides to leave her wacky husband (David Warner). He's a wild man who has a thing for gorillas (this brings scenes from *King Kong*). Nevertheless, he tries to win her back in an increasingly unorthodox manner. Deeply imbedded in the 1960s, this film still brings quite a few laughs.

1966   B & W   97 minutes

MORONS FROM OUTER SPACE
★★½

DIRECTOR: Mike Hodges
CAST: Griff Rhys Jones, Mel Smith, James B. Sikking, Dindsdale Landen, Jimmy Nail, Joanne Pearce, Paul Brown

Four aliens from a distant planet crash-land on Earth, but unlike most of the recent films dealing with this idea, their arrival is not a secret and they soon become international celebrities. The comedy comes from the fact that they're idiots and act accordingly. Unfortunately, the morons are not as funny as the viewer would hope. Some good gags and a cohesive plot that hits the corporate world's exploitation of popular culture heroes where it hurts, but on the whole, not enough laughs to deem it a good comedy. Rated PG for language.

1985   78 minutes

MOSCOW ON THE HUDSON
★★★★½

DIRECTOR: Paul Mazursky
CAST: Robin Williams, Maria Conchita Alonso, Cleavant Derricks

Robin Williams stars in this sweet, funny, sad, and sexy comedy as a Russian circus performer who, while on tour in the United States, decides to defect after experiencing the wonders of Bloomingdale's department store in New York. Paul Mazursky (*An Unmarried Woman*; *Blume in Love*) co-wrote and directed this touching character study, which features William's best screen performance and impressive American screen bows by Maria Conchita Alonso and Cleavant Derricks. Rated R for profanity, nudity, suggested sex, and violence.

1984   115 minutes

MOUSE THAT ROARED, THE
★★★★

DIRECTOR: Jack Arnold
CAST: Peter Sellers, Jean Seberg, Leo McKern

Any film that combines the comic talents of Peter Sellers at his peak can't help but be funny. In this British movie, a tiny European nation devises a foolproof method of filling its depleted treasury. It declares war on the United States, then loses and collects war reparations from the generous Americans. Even foolproof plans don't always go as expected . . . in this case with hilarious results.

1958   83 minutes

MOVERS AND SHAKERS
★★★

DIRECTOR: William Asher
CAST: Walter Matthau, Charles Grodin, Vincent Gardenia, Tyne Daly, Bill Macy, Gilda Radner, Steve Martin, Penny Marshall

This star-studded film starts off well but quickly falls apart. Walter Matthau plays a Hollywood producer who, through loyalty to an old friend and business associate, begins work on a movie project with only the title, *Love in Sex*, to start with. Charles Grodin plays the screenwriter who is commissioned to write the script, which is intended as a tribute to love. But with serious marital problems, Grodin is hardly the proper candidate. Bill Macy is the hack director who is looking for the inspiration to pull off the project. All performances are good, which makes the weak plot more bearable. Rated PG for profanity.

1985   80 minutes

MOVIE MOVIE
★★★½

DIRECTOR: Stanley Donen

CAST: George C. Scott, Trish Van Devere, Eli Wallach, Red Buttons, Barry Bostwick, Harry Hamlin, Barbara Harris, Art Carney, Ann Reinking, Kathleen Beller

Clever, affectionate spoof of 1930s pictures presents a double feature: *Dynamite Hands* is a black-and-white boxing story; *Baxter's Beauties of 1933* is a lavish, Busby Berkeley–type extravaganza. The nostalgic package even includes a preview of coming attractions. Rated PG.

1978   107 minutes

MOVING VIOLATIONS
★★★

DIRECTOR: Neal Israel
CAST: John Murray, Jennifer Tilly, James Keach, Wendy Jo Sperber, Sally Kellerman, Fred Willard

Neal Israel and Pat Proft, who brought us *Police Academy* and *Bachelor Party*, writhe again with another "subject" comedy—this time about traffic school. The team has come up with more laughs than usual, and star John Murray does a reasonable job of imitating his older brother, Bill. Definitely a beer-and-popcorn time-passer. Rated R for profanity and suggested sex.

1985   90 minutes

MURDER BY DEATH
★★★★

DIRECTOR: Robert Moore
CAST: Peter Sellers, Peter Falk, David Niven, Maggie Smith, James Coco, Alec Guinness

Mystery buffs will get a big kick out of this spoof of the genre, penned by Neil Simon. Peter Sellers, Peter Falk, David Niven, Maggie Smith, and James Coco play thinly disguised send-ups of famed fiction detectives who are invited to the home of Truman Capote to solve a baffling murder. Rated PG.

1976   94 minutes

MY CHAUFFEUR
★★½

DIRECTOR: David Beaird

CAST: Deborah Foreman, Sam Jones, Howard Hesseman, E. G. Marshall, Sean McClory, John O'Leary

In this better-than-average (for the genre) softcore sex comedy, an aggressive, slightly kooky young woman (Deborah Foreman of *Valley Girl*) upsets things at an all-male limousine company. Rated R for oodles of nudity, leering dirty old men by the truckload, suggested sex, and profanity. Don't let the kids rent this while you're out playing poker.

1986   97 minutes

MY FAVORITE BRUNETTE
★★★★½

DIRECTOR: Elliott Nugent

CAST: Bob Hope, Dorothy Lamour, Peter Lorre, Lon Chaney, John Hoyt, Elisha Cook Jr.

Classic Bob Hope comedy with Bob as a photographer who, thanks to a case of mistaken identity, makes No. 1 on the death list of a gang of thugs, played beautifully by Peter Lorre, Lon Chaney, John Hoyt, and Elisha Cook Jr. The gags fly one after another as Bob tries every trick in the book to save his neck, as well as Dorothy Lamour's. A scream!

1947   B & W   87 minutes

MY FAVORITE WIFE
★★★★★

DIRECTOR: Garson Kanin

CAST: Cary Grant, Irene Dunne, Randolph Scott

Cary Grant and Irene Dunne teamed up for many hilarious films but the best is this often-copied comedy. Grant is a widower about to be remarried when his long-lost and presumed-dead wife (Dunne) is rescued after years on an island with a handsome young scientist (Randolph Scott). The delightful complications that result make this one of the 1940s' best comedies.

1940   B & W   88 minutes

MY FAVORITE YEAR
★★★★½

DIRECTOR: Richard Benjamin

CAST: Peter O'Toole, Joseph Bologna, Lainie Kazan, Bill Macy

This warm-hearted, hilarious comedy is an affectionate tribute to the frenzied Golden Age of television, that period when uninhibited comics like Sid Caesar faced the added pressure of performing live. With superb performances all around and on-the-money direction by Richard Benjamin, it's a real treasure. Rated PG for slight profanity and sexual situations.

1982   92 minutes

MY LITTLE CHICKADEE
★★★★★

DIRECTOR: Edward Kline

CAST: W. C. Fields, Mae West, Dick Foran, Joseph Calleia

W. C. Fields and Mae West enter a marriage of convenience in the Old West. It seems the card sharp (Fields) and the tainted lady (West) need to create an aura of respectability before they descend upon an ususpecting town. That indicates trouble ahead for the town, and lots of fun for viewers.

1940   B & W   83 minutes

MY MAN GODFREY
★★★★★

DIRECTOR: Gregory La Cava
CAST: Carole Lombard, William Powell

My Man Godfrey is one of the great screwball comedies of the 1930s. The standard formula for a screwball comedy is quite simple. You take a wacky family, preferably rich, and add one relatively sane individual loosely sprinkled in their midst. Then mix thoroughly until all the craziness boils to the surface. In My Man Godfrey, Carole Lombard plays the most eccentric member of an eccentric family. William Powell is the relatively sane portion of the formula. Carole finds him when she is sent to find a "lost man." Powell seems to fit the bill, since he's living a hobo's life on the wrong side of the tracks. She brings him home to act as the umpteenth butler the family has employed. Most seem to last only a few days in this nut house, but Powell has some surprises in store for the family.

1936   B & W   95 minutes

MY TUTOR
★

DIRECTOR: George Bowers
CAST: Matt Lattanzi, Caren Kaye, Kevin McCarthy

It looks like a dumb exploitation movie. It sounds like a ripoff of Private Lessons. It's advertised like a sleazoid trash. Put it all together and that's exactly what this film—in which a young man (Matt Lattanzi) gets an education in more than just reading, writing, and 'rithmetic from his warm and willing tutor, Caren Kaye—is. Beware. Rated R for nudity and implied sex.

1983   97 minutes

MY UNCLE (MON ONCLE)
★★★★

DIRECTOR: Jacques Tati
CAST: Jacques Tati, Jean-Pierre Zola, Adrienne Servantie, Alain Bercourt

The second of Jacques Tati's cinematic romps as Mr. Hulot (the first was the famous Mr. Hulot's Holiday), this delightful comedy continues Tati's recurrent theme of the common man confronted with an increasingly mechanized and depersonalized society. (It's also the only Tati film to win the Academy Award for best foreign film.) This time around, the bumbling but lovable Mr. Hulot is taken under the wing of his oh-so-chic Parisian in-laws who live in a sterile, futuristic suburban house dominated by every conceivable form of ridiculous electronic gadget. Needless to say, Hulot's old-world mentality can't easily adapt to this bizarre new environment, and the results are, to put it mildly, catastrophic. Though overlong and occasionally uncentered, this remains one of Tati's most rewarding films, a universally appealing blend of satire, sentiment, and slapstick. (As with all Tati films, there are no subtitles needed, as the minimal dialogue consists of little more than mumbled gibberish.)

1958   116 minutes

NASTY HABITS
★★

DIRECTOR: Michael Lindsay-Hogg
CAST: Glenda Jackson, Sandy Dennis, Susan Penhaligon, Edith Evans, Melina Mercouri

Nasty Habits promises much more than it delivers. As a satire of the Watergate conspiracy placed in a convent, it relies too heavily on the true incident for its punch.

Philadelphia is the setting for the confrontation between Alexandra (Glenda Jackson) and Felicity (Susan Penhaligon), who are vying for the position of abbess after the sudden death of the incumbent, Hildgarde (Edith Evans). Because the script only superficially exploits the potential of the theme, it falls to the performers to supply the film's high points, which they do admirably. In the end, however, the film surpasses neither *Network* as a biting satire of the American culture nor *All the President's Men* as an indictment of our country's political practices. Rated PG with some profanity.

1977   96 minutes

NEIGHBORS
★★★½

DIRECTOR: John G. Avildsen
CAST: John Belushi, Dan Aykroyd, Cathy Moriarty, Kathryn Walker

This is a strange movie. John Belushi plays a suburban homeowner whose peaceful existence is threatened when his new neighbors (played by Dan Aykroyd and Cathy Moriarty of *Raging Bull*) turn out to be complete wackos. It isn't a laugh-a-minute farce, but there are numerous chuckles and a few guffaws along the way. It's never boring.... You're always wondering what outrageous thing will happen next. Rated R because of profanity and sexual content.

1981   94 minutes

NEVER GIVE A SUCKER AN EVEN BREAK
★★★★

DIRECTOR: Edward Cline
CAST: W. C. Fields, Gloria Jean, Leon Errol

This is a wild and wooly pastiche of hilarious gags and bizarre comedy routines revolving around W. C. Fields's attempt to sell an outlandish script to a movie studio. Some of the jokes misfire, but the absurdity of the situations makes up for the weak spots.

1941   B & W   71 minutes

NICE DREAMS
★★★

DIRECTOR: Thomas Chong
CAST: Cheech and Chong, Evelyn Guerrero, Paul Reubens, Stacy Keach

Cheech and Chong, the counterculture kings of drug-oriented comedy, haven't run out of steam yet. Their third feature film doesn't have quite as many classic comic gems as its predecessors, but it's more consistently entertaining. Rated R for nudity and profanity.

1981   87 minutes

NIGHT AT THE OPERA, A
★★★★★

DIRECTOR: Sam Wood
CAST: The Marx Brothers, Margaret Dumont, Kitty Carlisle, Allen Jones, Sigfried Ruman

Despite the songs and sappy love story, the Marx Brothers (minus Zeppo) are in peak form in this classical musical comedy, which co-stars the legendary Margaret Dumont.

1935   B & W   92 minutes

NIGHT PATROL
★

DIRECTOR: Jackie Kong
CAST: Linda Blair, Pat Paulson, Jaye P. Morgan, Jack Riley, Billy Barty

In this dumb variation on *Police Academy*, screenwriter Murray Langston plays a bumbling rookie policeman who doubles at night as "The Unknown Comic," cracking jokes in Los Angeles comedy clubs while wearing a paper bag over his head. The jokes often are offensive and the plot even worse. Even the few laughs it contains don't make this cheapo release worth sitting through. Miss it. Rated R for the usual garbage.

1985   84 minutes

NIGHT SHIFT
★★★★

DIRECTOR: Ron Howard
CAST: Henry Winkler, Shelley Long, Michael Keaton

When a nerdish morgue attendant (Henry Winkler) gets talked into becoming a pimp by a sweet hooker (Shelley Long) and his crazed co-worker (Michael Keaton), the result is uproarious comedy. While the concept is a little weird, director Ron Howard (Winkler's co-star in the old "Happy Days" television series) packs it with so many laughs and such appealing characters that you can't help but like it. Rated R for nudity, profanity, sex, and violence.

1982   105 minutes

NIGHT THEY RAIDED MINSKY'S, THE
★★★½

DIRECTOR: William Friedkin
CAST: Britt Ekland, Jason Robards, Elliott Gould

Director William Friedkin's (*The French Connection*) tale of a religious girl's (Britt Ekland) involvement, much to her father's dismay, with a burlesque comic (Jason Robards). It's a nice look at what early burlesque was like, with good performances by all. Rated PG.

1968   99 minutes

1941

DIRECTOR: Steven Spielberg
CAST: John Belushi, Dan Aykroyd, Toshiro Mifune, Christopher Lee, Slim Pickens, Ned Beatty, John Candy, Nancy Allen, Tim Matheson, Murray Hamilton, Treat Williams

Steven Spielberg laid his first and (so far) only multimillion-dollar egg with this unfunny what-if comedy about the Japanese attacking Los Angeles during World War II. An all-star cast is all but completely wasted in this—pardon the pun—bomb. Rated PG.

1979   118 minutes

NINE TO FIVE
★★★★

DIRECTOR: Colin Higgins
CAST: Jane Fonda, Lily Tomlin, Dolly Parton, Dabney Coleman

In this delightful comedy, Jane Fonda almost ends up playing third fiddle to two marvelous comediennes, Lily Tomlin and Dolly Parton. (That's right, Dolly Parton!) The gifted singer/songwriter makes one of the brightest acting debuts ever in this hilarious farce about three secretaries who decide to get revenge on their sexist, egomaniacal boss (Dabney Coleman). Rated PG.

1980   110 minutes

NINOTCHKA
★★★★★

DIRECTOR: Ernst Lubitsch
CAST: Greta Garbo, Melvyn Douglas, Bela Lugosi

"Garbo laughs," proclaimed the ads of its day; and so will you in this classic screen comedy. Greta Garbo is a soviet commissar sent to Paris to check on the lack of progress of three bumbling trade envoys who have been seduced by the decadent trappings of capitalism. Melvyn Douglas, as a Parisian playboy, meets Garbo at the Eiffel Tower and plans a seduction of his own, in this most joyous of Hollywood comedies.

1939   B & W 110 minutes

NO MAN OF HER OWN
★★★★

DIRECTOR: Wesley Ruggles
CAST: Clark Gable, Carole Lombard

A big-time gambler marries a local girl on a bet and tries to keep her innocent of his activities. This vintage film has everything the average film fan looks for—drama, romance, and comedy.

1932   B & W 85 minutes

NO SMALL AFFAIR
★★½

DIRECTOR: Jerry Schatzberg
CAST: Jon Cryer, Demi Moore

A 16-year-old amateur photographer named Charles Cummings (Jon Cryer) falls in love with an up-and-coming 23-year-old rock singer, Laura Victor (Demi Moore), and his passion for her eventually leads to the performer's big break. A mixture of delightfully clever and unabashedly stupid elements, *No Small Affair* ultimately fails as a screen entertainment. That's really too bad. In the first half-hour, it seems to be adding up to a little comic gem. Yet it goes on to prompt extreme disbelief and disappointment. Rated R for nudity, violence, and profanity.

1984   102 minutes

NO TIME FOR SERGEANTS
★★★★

DIRECTOR: Mervyn LeRoy

CAST: Andy Griffith, Nick Adams, Myron McCormick, Murray Hamilton, Don Knotts

In this hilarious film version of the Broadway play by Ira Levin, young Andy Griffith is superb as a country boy drafted into the service. You'll scream with laughter as good-natured Will Stockdale (as portrayed by Andy on stage as well as here) proceeds to make a complete shambles of the U.S. Air Force through nothing more than sheer ignorance. This is film comedy at its best. One criticism: Don Knotts's only scene is way too short, though it alone is worth the price of a rental.

1957   B & W 119 minutes

NORMAN LOVES ROSE
★★★½

DIRECTOR: Henry Safran
CAST: Carol Kane, Tony Owen, Warren Mitchell, Myra deGroot, David Downer

In this Australian-made comedy, Tony Owen plays a love-struck teenager who is enamored of his sister-in-law, Carol Kane. When she gets pregnant, the question of paternity arises. Lots of laughs in this one! Rated R.

1982   98 minutes

NOT FOR PUBLICATION
★★½

DIRECTOR: Paul Bartel
CAST: Nancy Allen, David Naughton

A writer and a photographer attempt to break out of sleazy tabloid journalism by doing an investigative piece about high-level corruption. Amusing story starts off well but loses momentum. Playful, but not as distinctive as Paul Bartel's other works, such as

Eating Raoul and *Lust in the Dust*. Rated PG for profanity.

1984 87 minutes

NOTHING PERSONAL
★

DIRECTOR: George Bloomfield
CAST: Donald Sutherland, Suzanne Somers, Lawrence Dane, Roscoe Lee Browne, Dabney Coleman, Saul Rubinek, John Dehner

A romantic comedy about the fight to stop the slaughter of baby seals? This is how Suzanne Somers decided to launch her motion picture career? Sure, Donald Sutherland is a dependable leading man, but even he looks silly in this mishmash of message and entertainment. It should have been called *Nothing Playing*. Rated PG.

1980 97 minutes

NOTHING SACRED
★★★★

DIRECTOR: William Wellman
CAST: Carole Lombard, Frederic March, Walter Connolly, Charles Winninger, Frank Fay

Ace scriptwriter Ben Hecht's cynical mixture of slapstick and bitterness perfectly performed by Frederic March and Carole Lombard makes this satirical comedy a real winner. Vermont innocent Lombard is mistakenly thought to be dying of a rare disease. Goaded by his editor, Walter Connolly, a crack New York reporter (March) pulls out all the stops in exploiting her to near national sainthood. The boy-bites-man scene is priceless.

1937 75 minutes

NUDO DI DONNA (PORTRAIT OF A WOMAN, NUDE)
★★★

DIRECTOR: Nino Manfredi

CAST: Nino Manfredi, Eleonora Giorgi

Nino Manfredi stars in this Italian comedy as a husband shocked to discover his wife (Eleonora Giorgi) may have posed nude for a painting. Told the model was a hooker, the skeptical Manfredi attempts to discover the truth, in this madcap import. In Italian, with English subtitles. Unrated.

1982 112 minutes

NUTCASE
🦃

DIRECTOR: Roger Donaldson
CAST: Nevan Rowe, Ian Watkin, Michael Wilson, Ian Mune, Melissa Donaldson, Peter Shand, Aaron Donaldson

The kids are the only ones who aren't complete idiots in this silly movie. The plot, which is extremely far-fetched, has a group of wacky villains threatening to blow up New Zealand's volcanoes if they don't receive $5 million. The bumbling police department gets even worse when their coffee is laced with laughing powder. Only the children can stop the villains by using the anti-gravity device that young Jamie has invented. The show is both bizarre and low budget. The villains, the police, and even the garbage men sing weird tunes at strange times. This show is not recommended for anyone, but 8- to 12-year-olds—and anyone who enjoys the Keystone Kops—may find it mildly amusing.

1983 49 minutes

NUTTY PROFESSOR, THE
★★★★

DIRECTOR: Jerry Lewis
CAST: Jerry Lewis, Stella Stevens, Kathleen Freeman

Jerry Lewis's funniest self-directed comedy, this release—a takeoff on Robert Louis Stevenson's *Dr. Jekyll and Mr. Hyde*—about a klutz who becomes a smoothy when he drinks a magic formula. Reportedly, this was Lewis's put-down of former partner Dean Martin.

1963   107 minutes

ODD COUPLE, THE
★★★★

DIRECTOR: Gene Saks
CAST: Walter Matthau, Jack Lemmon, John Fiedler, Herb Edelman

Walter Matthau as Oscar Madison and Jack Lemmon as Felix Unger bring Neil Simon's delightful stage play to life in this comedy. They play two divorced men who try living together. Felix has just split up with his wife of twelve years and is going through an emotional crisis. The biggest laughs come from the fact that Felix is "Mr. Clean" and Oscar is a total slob—they're constantly getting on each other's nerves. Rated G.

1968   105 minutes

OFF BEAT
★★★

DIRECTOR: Michael Dinner
CAST: Meg Tilly, Judge Reinhold, Cleavant Derricks, Harvey Keitel

This attempt at an old-fashioned romantic comedy succeeds as a romance, but as a comedy, it elicits only an occasional chuckle. One gains instant sympathy for captivating Meg Tilly's vulnerable big-city police officer. She finds herself falling for her partner, Judge Reinhold, while trying out for a mixed precinct police dance program. The humor was intended to be generated from the fact that Reinhold is only masquerading as a cop; he's actually a shy, fumbling librarian. As much as we like the Tilly-Reinhold pairing, the script leaves them with nothing unpredictable or interesting to do. Rated PG.

1986   100 minutes

OFF LIMITS
★½

DIRECTOR: George Marshall
CAST: Bob Hope, Mickey Rooney, Marilyn Maxwell, Marvin Miller

Marilyn Maxwell adds a little "oomph" to this otherwise silly story of two army buddies and their inane and seldom hilarious antics. Yet another of those limp comedies about an ineffectual loser who winds up a boxing contender; the concept was stale years before this dud was filmed, having been done by most of the comedy greats and not-so-greats as well as comedy teams. Only the presence of Bob Hope and Mickey Rooney makes this film worth watching, and both are represented on video in much better films. Basically lightweight filler and a source of much-needed revenue for Mickey Rooney in those lean years following his departure from the protection of the MGM fold.

1953   B & W   89 minutes

OH DAD, POOR DAD—MAMA'S HUNG YOU IN THE CLOSET AND I'M FEELING SO SAD
★★★½

DIRECTOR: Richard Quine
CAST: Rosalind Russell, Robert Morse, Barbara Harris, Jonathan Winters, Lionel Jeffries

A cult favorite, and deservedly so. The plot has something to do with an odd young man (Robert Morse) whose mother (Rosalind Russell) drags him off on a vacation in the tropics with the boy's dead father. Morse excels in this unique, well-written, often hilarious film.

1967   86 minutes

OH GOD!
★★★★

DIRECTOR: Carl Reiner
CAST: George Burns, John Denver, Teri Garr, Ralph Bellamy

God is made visible to a supermarket manager in this modern-day fantasy. The complications that result make for some predictable humor, but the story is kept flowing by some inspired casting. Ageless George Burns is a perfect vision of a God for Everyman in his tennis shoes and golf hat. John Denver exudes the right degree of naivete as the put-upon grocer. Rated PG.

1977   104 minutes

OH, GOD! BOOK II
★★

DIRECTOR: Gilbert Cates
CAST: George Burns, Suzanne Pleshette, David Birney, Louanne, Howard Duff

George Burns, as God, returns in this fair sequel and enters a little girl's life, assigning her the task of coming up with a slogan that will revive interest in him. So she comes up with "Think God" and begins her campaign. It's passable family fare. Rated PG.

1980   94 minutes

OH GOD, YOU DEVIL!
★★★★½

DIRECTOR: Paul Bogart
CAST: George Burns, Ted Wass, Roxanne Hart, Ron Silver, Eugene Roche

George Burns is back as the wisecracking, cigar-smoking deity. Only this time he plays a dual role—appearing as the devil. Ted Wass (Curse of the Pink Panther) is the songwriter who strikes a Faustian bargain with Burns's bad side. This delightful comedy-with-a-moral is guaranteed to lift your spirits and make the whole world seem brighter. It's as emotionally moving as Frank Capra's It's a Wonderful Life and as funny as anything ever made by Hollywood's greatest clowns—the Marx Brothers, W. C. Fields, Laurel and Hardy, Mae West . . . you name it. Rated PG for suggested sex and profanity.

1984   96 minutes

ONCE BITTEN
★★★

DIRECTOR: Howard Storm
CAST: Lauren Hutton, Jim Carrey, Karen Kopins, Cleavon Little

Sly little vampire film about an ancient bloodsucker (Lauren Hutton) who can remain young and beautiful only by periodically supping on youthful male virgins. Likable Jim Carrey is her latest target, and their first few encounters (three's the magic number) leave him with an appetite for raw hamburgers and a tendency to sleep during the day so as to avoid sunlight. Girlfriend Karen Kopins enters the picture and faces a climactic decision: Is her virtue more important than Carrey's life? Cleavon Little has a droll supporting part as Hutton's prim and proper personal servant. A tasty little treat. Rated PG-13 for sexual situations.

1985   92 minutes

ONCE UPON A HONEYMOON
★★½

DIRECTOR: Leo McCarey
CAST: Ginger Rogers, Cary Grant, Walter Slezak, Albert Dekker, Albert Bassermann, Ferike Boros, Harry Shannon, Natasha Lytess, John Banner

In this travesty, one Cary Grant prefers to forget, he plays a newspaperman trying to get innocent stripteaser Ginger Rogers out of Europe as the German army advances. Complicating matters is her marriage to Nazi officer Walter Slezak. This amusing adventure comedy is a bit dated, but Grant fans won't mind.

1942   B & W 117 minutes

ONE CRAZY SUMMER
★★½

DIRECTOR: Savage Steve Holland
CAST: John Cusack, Demi Moore, Curtis Armstrong, Bobcat Goldthwait, Joel Murray, Joe Flaherty, Tom Villard, Kimberly Foster

Star John Cusack and writer-director Savage Steve Holland of Better Off Dead are reunited in this weird, slightly sick, and sometimes stupidly funny comedy about a college hopeful (Cusack) who must learn about love to gain entrance to an institute of higher learning. Say What? If you accept that silly premise, then you may get a few laughs out of One Crazy Summer. But we make no guarantee. Rated PG.

1986   94 minutes

ONE MORE SATURDAY NIGHT
★★★½

DIRECTOR: Dennis Klein
CAST: Al Franken, Tom Davis, Moira Harris, Frank Howard, Bess Meyer, Dave Reynolds, Chelcie Ross, Nan Woods, Eric Saiet, Jessica Schwartz

Al Franken and Tom Davis, who were writers and semiregulars on the original Saturday Night Live TV show, star in this enjoyable comedy, which they also wrote, about the problems encountered by adults and teenagers when trying to get a date on the most important night of the week. In its humane and decidely offbeat way, One More Saturday Night is about the human condition in all its funny/sad complexity. Rated R for profanity and simulated sex.

1986   95 minutes

ONE, TWO, THREE
★★★½

DIRECTOR: Billy Wilder
CAST: James Cagney, Arlene Francis, Horst Buchholz, Pamela Tiffin, Lilo Pulver, Howard St. John, Hanns Lothar, Leon Askin, Red Buttons

James Cagney's "retirement" film (and his only movie with famed director Billy Wilder) is a nonstop, madcap assault on the audience. Dialogue and one-liners are thrown and caught by the principals with the timing of a professional sports team, but whether this is amusing or annoying is an individual choice. A throwback to the mayhem and wacky antics of the silent comedians coupled with the clever situations and biting repartee of the great screwball comedies of the mid to late 1930s, this is Cagney's movie and could only have succeeded with him in the lead. Wilder's questionable humor and odd plot about the clash between capitalism and communism and its effect on a young couple could have spelled catastrophe for any other leading man, but veteran Cagney pulls it off with style and leaves the audience wishing that he'd never stopped making films for twenty years when he was so desperately needed.

1961　　　　B & W　108 minutes

ONE TOUCH OF VENUS
★★

DIRECTOR: William Seifer
CAST: Robert Walker, Ava Gardner

The Pygmalion myth gets the Hollywood treatment, long before *My Fair Lady*, although this is a wee bit diluted. Robert Walker plays a department store window decorator who becomes smitten, predictably, when a display statue of Venus comes to life in the form of Ava Gardner. The potentially entertaining premise is left flat by a script that lacks originality and wit.

1948　　　　B & W　90 minutes

OPERATION PETTICOAT
★★★★

DIRECTOR: Blake Edwards
CAST: Cary Grant, Tony Curtis, Dina Merrill, Gene Evans, Arthur O'Connell, Richard Sargent

The ageless Cary Grant stars with Tony Curtis in this wacky service comedy. They are captain and first officer of a submarine that undergoes a madcap series of misadventures during World War II. Their voyage across the Pacific is further complicated when a group of Navy women is forced to join the crew.

1959　　　　　　124 minutes

OUR RELATIONS
★★★½

DIRECTOR: Harry Lachman
CAST: Stan Laurel, Oliver Hardy, James Finlayson, Alan Hale, Sidney Toler

Stan Laurel and Oliver Hardy play two sets of twins. One set are sailors; the other are happily married civilians. When the boys' ship docks in the same city, a hilarious case of mistaken identity occurs. Highly enjoyable, the film doesn't lag at all. It features excellent performances by James Finlayson, Alan Hale, and Sidney Toler.

1936　　　　B & W　74 minutes

OUT OF THE BLUE
★★★

DIRECTOR: Leigh Jason
CAST: George Brent, Virginia Mayo, Ann Dvorak, Turhan Bey, Carole Landis, Hadda Brooks

A not very innocent young woman passes out in a naive married man's apartment, making all sorts of trouble in this entertaining romantic comedy of errors and such.

1947　　　　B & W　84 minutes

OUTLAW BLUES
★★½

DIRECTOR: Richard Heffron
CAST: Peter Fonda, Susan Saint James, James Callahan, Michael Lerner

Yet another of Peter Fonda's harmless but rather bland light comedies. He's an ex-con with a talent for song-writing but little in the way of industry smarts; he naively allows established country-western star James Callahan to make off with a few hits. Aided by backup singer Susan Saint James, in a charming little part, Fonda figures out how to outfox the Establishment and succeed on his own. Would have made a good television film, but it's too understated for the big screen. Rated PG for light violence and brief nudity.

1977　　　　　　100 minutes

OUT OF TOWNERS, THE
★★★

DIRECTOR: Arthur Hiller

CAST: Jack Lemmon, Sandy Dennis, Sandy Baron, Anne Meara, Billy Dee Williams

Jack Lemmon and Sandy Dennis star in this Neil Simon comedy of a New York City vacation gone awry. It's a good idea that doesn't come off as well as one would have hoped. Rated PG for language.

1970   97 minutes

OUTRAGEOUS
★★★★

DIRECTOR: Richard Benner
CAST: Craig Russell, Hollis McLaren, Richard Easely

A very offbeat and original comedy drama concerning a gay nightclub performer's relationship with a pregnant mental patient. A different kind of love story, told with taste and compassion. Female impersonator Craig Russell steals the show. Take a chance on this one. Rated R.

1977   100 minutes

OVER THE BROOKLYN BRIDGE
★★½

DIRECTOR: Menahem Golan
CAST: Elliott Gould, Shelley Winters, Sid Caesar, Carol Kane, Burt Young, Margaux Hemingway

Elliott Gould stars in this occasionally interesting but mostly uneven slice-of-life story about a slovenly, diabetic Jewish luncheonette owner who dreams of getting out by buying a restaurant in downtown Manhattan. Standing in the way are his strict but loony relatives and his chic fashion-model girlfriend, who isn't Jewish. Full of eccentric characters, including Sid Caesar as Gould's uncle and Shelley Winters in her umpteenth Jewish-mother turn. Marred by poor direction and some extremely crude and unnecessary scenes. Rated R for nudity and profanity.

1983   108 minutes

OWL AND THE PUSSYCAT, THE
★★★★

DIRECTOR: Herbert Ross
CAST: Barbra Streisand, George Segal, Robert Klein

Barbra Streisand plays a streetsmart but undereducated prostitute who teams up with intellectual snob and bookstore clerk George Segal. The laughs abound as the two express themselves, with numerous debates, in this comedy. Rated R.

1970   95 minutes

PACK UP YOUR TROUBLES
★★★

DIRECTOR: George Marshall
CAST: Stan Laurel, Oliver Hardy

Stan Laurel and Oliver Hardy join the army in World War I, with the usual disastrous results. After being discharged, they assume responsibility for a fallen comrade's young daughter and search for her grandparents. The plot line and scripting aren't as solid as other films, but the boys squeeze out every laugh possible.

1932   B & W   68 minutes

PADDY
★★½

DIRECTOR: Daniel Haller
CAST: Des Cave, Milo O'Shea, Dearbha Molloy, Peggy Cass

Excellent performances by all the actors, especially Des Cave in the title role, cannot save this rather confused coming-of-age comedy. Despite moments of true hilarity, the film remains at best mildly amusing.

1969   97 minutes

PAIN IN THE A———, A
★★

DIRECTOR: Edouard Molinaro
CAST: Lino Ventura, Jacques Brel, Xavier Depraz

A professional hit man (Lino Ventura) arrives in Montpellier, Italy, to fulfill a contract by killing a government witness (Xavier Depraz) who is set to testify against the mob. While waiting in the squealer's hotel room, the hit man notices something strange through a window. In the next room, a man (Jacques Brel) tries to hang himself but fails. The hit man decides to save the would-be suicide, much to his regret; he has gained an unwanted companion who consistently interferes in the carrying-out of his contract. This unfunny slapstick comedy was adapted by director Billy Wilder for the equally disappointing *Buddy, Buddy* with Jack Lemmon and Walter Matthau. In Italian, with English subtitles. Rated PG for light violence.

1973   90 minutes

PALEFACE, THE
★★★★½

DIRECTOR: Norman McLeod
CAST: Bob Hope, Jane Russell, Robert Armstrong

When most people think of Bob Hope comedies, they tend to remember his perfectly putrid pictures from the 1960s and '70s. But there was a time—in the 1930s, '40s, and early '50s—that the name Hope on a theater marquee meant marvelous movie merriment. Take this delightful 1948 western spoof, for example. Hope stars as a cowardly dentist who marries Calamity Jane (Jane Russell in rare form) and becomes, thanks to her quick draw, a celebrated gunslinger. It inspired a sequel, *Son of Paleface*, and a remake, *The Shakiest Gun*

in the West, with Don Knotts, but the original is still tops.

1948   91 minutes

PAPER MOON
★★★★★

DIRECTOR: Peter Bogdanovich
CAST: Ryan O'Neal, Tatum O'Neal, Madeline Kahn, John Hillerman

Critic-turned-director Peter Bogdanovich ended his four-film winning streak—which included *Targets*, *The Last Picture Show*, and *What's Up Doc?*—with this comedy, starring Ryan O'Neal and Tatum O'Neal as a con man and a kid in the 1930s who get involved in some pretty wild predicaments and meet up with a variety of wacky characters. It's a delightful entertainment from beginning to end. Rated PG.

1973   B & W 102 minutes

PARDON MON AFFAIRE
★★★★

DIRECTOR: Yves Robert
CAST: Jean Rochefort, Claude Brasseur, Anny Duperey, Guy Bedos, Victor Lanoux

Enjoyable romantic comedy about a middle-class, happily married man (Jean Rochefort) who pursues his fantasy of meeting a beautiful model (Anny Duperey) and having an affair. Later remade in America as *The Woman in Red*. Rated PG.

1976   105 minutes

PARDON US
★★★★

DIRECTOR: James Parrott
CAST: Stan Laurel, Oliver Hardy, Wilfred Lucas

Stan Laurel and Oliver Hardy are sent to prison for selling home-brewed beer. They encounter all the usual prison stereotypical characters and play off them to delightful comedy effect. During an escape, they put on black faces and pick cotton along with blacks and Ollie sings "Lazy Moon." Always amusing, this film has few slow or weak spots.

1931   B & W   55 minutes

PARTNERS
★★★
DIRECTOR: James Burrows
CAST: Ryan O'Neal, John Hurt

Ryan O'Neal and John Hurt are two undercover detectives assigned to pose as lovers in order to track down the murderer of a gay in this warm, funny, and suspenseful comedy-drama written by Francis Veber (*La Cage aux Folles*). Rated R for nudity, profanity, violence, and adult themes.

1982   98 minutes

PARTY ANIMAL

DIRECTOR: Havey Hart
CAST: Mathew Causey, Robin Harlan, Tim Carhart, Jerry Jones, Luci Roucis

Not even a great rock soundtrack can save this despicable piece of sludge. Another one of those sex-crazed frat boy films—a genre that could use a moratorium. Rated R for sex, nudity, and profanity.

1983   78 minutes

PATERNITY
★★★½
DIRECTOR: David Steinberg
CAST: Burt Reynolds, Beverly D'Angelo, Norman Fell, Elizabeth Ashley, Lauren Hutton

Buddy Evans (Burt Reynolds) decides to have a son—without the commitment of marriage—and recruits a music student working as a waitress (Beverly D'Angelo) to bear his child in this adult comedy. The first two-thirds provide belly laughs and chuckles. The problem comes with the unoriginal and predictable romantic ending. But it's still mostly fun. Rated PG because of dialogue involving sex and childbirth.

1981   94 minutes

PATSY, THE
★★½
DIRECTOR: Jerry Lewis
CAST: Jerry Lewis, Everett Sloane, Ina Balin, Keenan Wynn, Peter Lorre, John Carradine

A very minor Jerry Lewis comedy, though the stellar supporting cast is fun to watch. This one is for Lewis fans only; new viewers to Jerry's type of comedy should take in *The Errand Boy* or *The Nutty Professor* first.

1964   101 minutes

PEE-WEE'S BIG ADVENTURE
★★★½
DIRECTOR: Tim Burton
CAST: Pee-Wee Herman, Elizabeth Daily, Mark Holton, Diane Salinger, Judd Omen

You want weird? Here it is. Pee-Wee Herman, best known for his appearances on "Late Night with David Letterman," makes the jump from television to feature films with this totally bizarre movie about a man-size petulant 12-year-old goofball (Herman) going on a big adventure after his most prized possession—a bicycle—is stolen by some nasties. The film has some terrific sequences—don't miss the appearance of Large Marge—but overall, it seems more likely to please Herman's fans and his fans alone. Rated PG for a scary scene and some daffy violence.

1985   90 minutes

PERFECT FURLOUGH
★★

DIRECTOR: Blake Edwards
CAST: Tony Curtis, Janet Leigh, Keenan Wynn, Linda Cristal, Elain Stritch, Troy Donahue

Perfectly forgettable fluff about soldier Tony Curtis (who is taking the leave for his entire unit, which is stationed in the Arctic) and his "perfect" vacation in Paris. The usual setbacks and misunderstandings plague poor Tony's furlough, but at least he gets to meet and eventually win Janet Leigh (Mrs. Tony Curtis at that time) two years before her fatal rendezvous with Norman Bates's mother in a shower stall. An early Blake Edwards film, this harmless escapism typifies American film farces of the late 1950s.

1958   93 minutes

PERILS OF PAULINE, THE
★★★

DIRECTOR: George Marshall
CAST: Betty Hutton, John Lund, Billy de Wolfe, William Demarest, Constance Collier, Frank Faylen

Betty Hutton plays Pearl White, the queen of the silent serials, in this agreeable little movie. The old-style chase scenes and cliff-hanger situations make up for the overdose of sentimentality.

1947   96 minutes

PETIT CON
★

DIRECTOR: Gerard Lauzier
CAST: Guy Marchand, Caroline Cellier, Bernard Brieux, Souad Amidou

France's equivalent of our American teen-age-boy-in-heat flicks, with a few differences. The film tries for a serious side involving the trauma that Michel (Bernard Brieux) is causing his family. This movie doesn't glorify Michel, as one of our films might. It shows him to be a pain in the neck. The film doesn't get the one-star rating for the failed attempt to bring something more substantial to the storyline. The girls in *Petit Con* are smart and savvy and create situations that are cause for some very funny sexual dialogue that keeps this movie away from the turkey farm—though not by much. Rated R. In French with English subtitles.

1986   90 minutes

PHILADELPHIA STORY, THE
★★★★★

DIRECTOR: George Cukor
CAST: Katharine Hepburn, Cary Grant, Jimmy Stewart, Ruth Hussey

This is one of the best comedies to come out of Hollywood. From the first scene, where Tracy Lord (Katharine Hepburn) deposits her ex-husband's (Cary Grant) golf clubs in a heap at her front door and in return Grant deposits Hepburn in a heap right next to the clubs, the 1940s version of *The Taming of the Shrew* proceeds at a blistering pace. The scene shifts to the Lord estate, where all is in readiness for Hepburn's second marriage to a stuffy businessman. Some uninvited guests arrive, namely her "ex" and two reporters from a gossip magazine (Ruth Hussey and Jimmy Stewart). Needless to say, this wedding is headed for chaos for Hepburn and grand entertainment for you.

1940   B & W 112 minutes

PIECE OF THE ACTION, A
★★★

DIRECTOR: Sidney Poitier

CAST: Sidney Poitier, Bill Cosby, Denise Nicholas, James Earl Jones, Hope Clark

Third entry in the Bill Cosby–Sidney Poitier partnership (after *Uptown Saturday Night* and *Let's Do It Again*), this one showing Poitier's greater comfort on both sides of the camera. The story concerns a pair of rascals given one of Life's Awful Choices: prison, or a team-up with some social workers to help a group of ghetto kids. It's all been done before, but the material is handled adequately, and Bill Cosby gets his usual chances to mug. A heavy-handed moral, but what else can one expect from such stories? Rated PG.

1977   135 minutes

PILLOW TALK
★★★★

DIRECTOR: Michael Gordon
CAST: Doris Day, Rock Hudson, Tony Randall, Thelma Ritter

If you like the fluffy light comedy of Doris Day and Rock Hudson, this is their best effort. The ever-virginal Miss Day is keeping the wolves at bay. In the tradition of Ralph Bellamy and Gig Young, Tony Randall is excellent as the suitor who never wins the girl.

1959   105 minutes

PINK FLAMINGOS
🐷

DIRECTOR: John Waters
CAST: Divine, Mink Stole, David Lochary, Mary Vivian Pearce, Edith Massey, Danny Mills, Channing Wilroy

One of the most infamous films of all times is also an acute study of the seamy underbelly of the bourgeois. *Pink Flamingos* is the story of Babs Johnson (Divine), the "filthiest person alive," and Connie and Raymond Marble (Mink Stole and David Lochary), two challengers who are jealous of Babs's notoriety. The film is shot in cheap 16mm cheesy color, which adds to the sleaziness. As in all of Waters's films, don't look for brilliant acting or sophisticated plot turns—the point here is to shock. If this doesn't, nothing will. Not for the faint at heart. Due to violence, nudity, and very poor taste, we'd rate this one an X.

1972   95 minutes

PINK PANTHER, THE
★★★½

DIRECTOR: Blake Edwards
CAST: Peter Sellers, David Niven, Capucine, Claudia Cardinale, Robert Wagner

Peter Sellers is featured in his first bow as Inspector Jacques Clouseau, the inept French detective, on the trail of a jewel thief known as the Phantom in this, the original *Pink Panther*. This release has some good—and even hilarious—moments. But the sequel, *A Shot in the Dark*, is better.

1964   113 minutes

PINK PANTHER STRIKES AGAIN, THE
★★★½

DIRECTOR: Blake Edwards
CAST: Peter Sellers, Herbert Lom, Lesley-Anne Down, Burt Kwouk, Colin Blakely

Peter Sellers's fourth time out as the clumsy Inspector Clouseau. Clouseau's former supervisor, Herbert Lom, cracks up and tries to destroy the world with a superlaser. Meanwhile, he's hired a team of international killers to do away with Clouseau. One turns out to be Lesley-Anne Down, who falls in love with the diminutive Frenchman . . . the result of which is a surprisingly erotic bedroom scene. Henry Mancini recycles his famous theme yet again; the opening credits, by the Richard Williams Studios, are the best in the series. Rated PG.

1976   103 minutes

PIRATES
🦃

DIRECTOR: Roman Polanski
CAST: Walter Matthau, Cris Campion, Charlotte Lewis, Roy Kinnear

A turgid, overblown mess which doesn't even succeed as the pirate comedy it's intended to be. Walter Matthau is horribly miscast as Captain Red, a luckless scoundrel. He sets his eyes on a golden throne and spends most of this interminable picture trying to steal it. Nothing much happens, because the camera's too busy making love with the re-created Spanish galleon (costing eight of the picture's thirty million bucks). Director and co-scripter Roman Polanski has no business even attempting this genre, and the performers should strike it from their résumés. Rated PG-13 for vulgarity.

1986   117 minutes

PLAY IT AGAIN SAM
★★★★½

DIRECTOR: Herbert Ross
CAST: Woody Allen, Diane Keaton, Tony Roberts, Jerry Lacy, Susan Anspach

Woody Allen plays a movie columnist and feature writer who lives his life watching movies. Humphrey Bogart is his idol, and the film commences with the final scenes from Casablanca. Allen's wife leaves him for a life of adventure, and the film revolves around some unsuccessful attempts by his friends (Diane Keaton and Tony Roberts) to set him up with a girl. What evolves from that synopsis is a procession of pointed, sometimes ironic, and generally humorous stabs at stereotypes and "manufactured" images. In an age when funny movies may make you smile at best, this is an oasis of sidesplitting humor. Rated PG.

1972   87 minutes

PLAYTIME
★★★½

DIRECTOR: Jacques Tati
CAST: Jacques Tati, Barbara Denneck, Jacqueline Lecomte, Valerie Camille

Mr. Hulot is back again in this slapstick comedy as he attempts to keep an appointment in the big city. Paris and all of its buildings, automobiles, and population seem to conspire to thwart Mr. Hulot at every turn, and there are plenty of visual gags and situations worthy of the great silent comedians. The subtitled American release version is over thirty minutes shorter than the original French release and it shows in the continuity, but what's left for our viewing is more than enough to provide the laughs.

1967   108 minutes

PLAZA SUITE
★★★★½

DIRECTOR: Arthur Hiller
CAST: Walter Matthau, Maureen Stapleton, Barbara Harris, Lee Grant

Walter Matthau is at his comic best as he recreates three separate roles from Neil Simon's stage comedy. The movie is actually three tales of what goes on in a particular suite. Rated PG.

1971   115 minutes

POLICE ACADEMY
★★

DIRECTOR: Hugh Wilson
CAST: Steve Guttenberg, George Gaynes, Kim Cattrall, Bubba Smith, Michael Winslow, Andrew Rubin

Here's another *Animal House*–style comedy that tries very hard to be funny. Sometimes it is, and sometimes it isn't. But overall, it's highly forgettable. Director Hugh Wilson created, wrote, produced, and directed the television situation comedy "WKRP in Cincinnati." And whether he realizes it or not, Wilson is still doing TV comedy—all that's missing in *Police Academy* is the laugh track. Or is it just the laughs? Steve Guttenberg (*The Man Who Wasn't There*) and George Gaynes (*Tootsie*) star. Rated R for nudity, violence, and profanity.

1984   95 minutes

POLICE ACADEMY II: THEIR FIRST ASSIGNMENT
★

DIRECTOR: Jerry Paris
CAST: Steve Guttenberg, Bubba Smith, David Graf, Michael Winslow, Bruce Mahler, Colleen Camp, Martin Ramsey, Howard Hesseman, George Gaynes

Those inept would-be police officers from Hugh Wilson's *Police Academy* (which was written by Neal Israel and Pat Proft, of *Bachelor Party*) return in this less funny, but still box office–potent production. Episodic and silly, it has no story to speak of, just more mindless high jinks with the boys in blue. Rated PG-13 for profanity.

1985   90 minutes

POLICE ACADEMY III: BACK IN TRAINING

DIRECTOR: Jerry Paris
CAST: Steve Guttenberg, Bubba Smith, David Graf, Mechael Winslow, Marion Ramsey, Leslie Easterbrook, Art Metrano, Tim Kazurinsky, Bobcat Goldthwait, George Gaynes

The graduates from the original *Police Academy* return to their alma mater to aid their muddle headed mentor (George Gaynes), who is engaged in a pitched battle with his rival (Art Metrano). The governor has decided to close one of the state's two police academies, and which one survives depends on results. So Steve Guttenberg, Bubba Smith, Michael Winslow, and others come back to take on the training of a new gang of nerds. This, of course, brings one moronic joke after another in a nearly plotless and poorly edited series of set pieces. Rated PG for silly violence and references to body parts.

1986   90 minutes

POLICE SQUAD!
★★★★

DIRECTOR: Jim Abrahams, David Zucker, Jerry Zucker, Joe Dante, Reza S. Badiyi
CAST: Leslie Nielsen, Alan North

Originally a 1982 summer TV show, with only six episodes aired, this is now a minor cult classic. The folks who made *Airplane!* went all out on this. Each one of the episodes is hilarious, much funnier than the popular film *Police Academy*.

1982   150 minutes

POLYESTER

🐢

DIRECTOR: John Waters

CAST: Divine, Tab Hunter, Edith Massey, Mary Garlington, Ken King

Anyone for bad taste? Female impersonator Divine and 1950s heartthrob Tab Hunter play lovers in this film by writer-producer-director John Waters (*Pink Flamingos*). A special gimmick called "Odorama" allows viewers to experience the story's various smells via a scratch-and-sniff card. That's just one reason why *Polyester* really stinks, and it's all intentional. Rated R because of bad taste.

1981   86 minutes

PORKY'S

★½

DIRECTOR: Bob Clark

CAST: Dan Monahan, Mark Herrier, Wyatt Knight, Roger Wilson, Kim Cattrall, Scott Colomby

The ads lied when they called this the "funniest movie about growing up ever made." Dumbest is a better description. Bob Clark (*Tribute*) wrote and directed this "comedy" about teenagers in the 1950s whose hormones and hot tempers lead them into all kinds of strange situations, including a fateful trip to a redneck dive called Porky's. Rated R for vulgarity, nudity, and adult themes.

1981   94 minutes

PORKY'S II: THE NEXT DAY

DIRECTOR: Bob Clark

CAST: Dan Monahan, Wyatt Knight, Mark Herrier, Roger Wilson, Kaki Hunter, Scott Colomby, Nancy Parsons, Edward Winter

Bob Clark (*Tribute*) wrote and directed this sequel to his hit comedy. This time, the lustful kids of Angel Beach High battle with the Ku Klux Klan, which is trying to prevent (of all things) a Shakespeare festival. Dumb. Rated R for the usual garbage.

1983   95 minutes

PORKY'S REVENGE

🐢

DIRECTOR: James Komack

CAST: Don Monahan, Wyatt Knight, Tony Ganios, Mark Herrier, Kaki Hunter, Scott Colomby

James Komack (creator of TV's "Chico and the Man") took over the directorial reins from creator Bob Clark for the third installment in this teen-lust comedy series. You'd think this switch would bring an improvement, but no-o-o! It's just more of the same stupidity. This time, the owner of the redneck dive that gave the series its name attempts to get even with the goons from Angel Beach High. This turkey gives new meaning to the word "sleeper." Rated R for profanity, suggested sex, and nudity.

1985   90 minutes

PREPPIES

🐢

DIRECTOR: Chuck Vincent

CAST: Nitchie Barrett, Dennis Drake, Steven Holt, Jo-Ann Marshall, Peter Brady Reardon, Katt Shea

Adult movie king Chuck Vincent, with the assistance of Playboy Enterprises, attempted to make the minor leap from porno to R-rated sexploitation flicks with this teen sex comedy. He didn't make it. The performances he elicits from his cast are embarrassingly amateurish. The screenplay he co-authored with Rick Marx about three women of easy virtue who are hired to prevent a trio of college students from passing an important final exam (thus making it possible for a cousin of one of the victims to inherit the family fortune) is just as insipid as those normally found in the substandard explicit sex films with which Vincent made his reputation. Rated R for nudity, simulated sex, and profanity.

1984   90 minutes

PRINCE AND THE SHOWGIRL, THE
★★½

DIRECTOR: Laurence Olivier
CAST: Laurence Olivier, Marilyn Monroe, Sybil Thorndike, Jeremy Spencer

In a romantic comedy about the attraction of a nobleman for an American showgirl, you'd want to stress the attraction of opposites. Marilyn Monroe and Laurence Olivier's acting talents are in full flower, and they are fun to watch; however, they are so dissimilar that they never click.

1957   117 minutes

PRINCESS AND THE PIRATE, THE
★★★

DIRECTOR: David Butler
CAST: Bob Hope, Virginia Mayo, Victor McLaglen, Walter Brennan, Walter Selzak

A happy, hilarious Bob Hope howler. He and the beautiful Virginia Mayo are pursued by pirates and trapped by potentate Walter Slezak. Victor McLaglen is properly menacing as a buccaneer bent on their destruction. Walter Brennan is something else—a pirate? This one's lots of fun for all!

1944   94 minutes

PRISONER OF SECOND AVENUE, THE
★★★★

DIRECTOR: Melvin Frank
CAST: Neil Simon, Jack Lemmon, Anne Bancroft, Gene Saks, Elizabeth Wilson, Florence Stanley

Neil Simon blends laughter with tears in this film about an executive (Jack Lemmon) who loses his job and has a nervous breakdown. Anne Bancroft plays Lemmon's wife. Rated PG.

1975   105 minutes

PRISONER OF ZENDA, THE
★★★½

DIRECTOR: Richard Quine
CAST: Peter Sellers, Lionel Jeffries, Elke Sommer, Lynne Frederick

Zany rendition of the classic tale of a look-alike commoner who stands in for the endangered King of Ruritania. A warm and hilarious film despite the lack of critical acclaim. Rated PG for language.

1979   108 minutes

PRIVATE BENJAMIN
★★★★

DIRECTOR: Howard Zeiff
CAST: Goldie Hawn, Eileen Brennan, Armand Assante, Robert Webber, Sam Wanamaker

Here's an upbeat, delightful comedy with a gentle message. The movie is at its best in the first half, when Goldie Hawn, as a spoiled Jewish princess, joins the army after the surprise termination of her second marriage. Thanks to the sales pitch of a double-crossing army recruiter, she expects her hitch to be like a vacation in the Bahamas. Of course, it isn't—and that's where most of the fun comes in. The last part of the movie gets a little heavy on the message end, but Hawn's buoyant personality makes it easy to take. Rated R for profanity, nudity, and implicit sex.

1980   110 minutes

PRIVATE EYES, THE
★

DIRECTOR: Lang Elliott
CAST: Tim Conway, Don Knotts, Trisha Noble, Bernard Fox, John Fujioka

If Tim Conway and Don Knotts had depended on movies like this to make it in show business, they could easily have wound up on unemployment rather than television. This Holmes and Watson send-up, directed by Lang Elliott (*The Prize Fighter*), is neither consistently funny nor engaging. In short, a waste of time. Rated PG.

1980   91 minutes

PRIVATE FUNCTION, A
★★★★

DIRECTOR: Malcolm Mowbray
CAST: Michael Palin, Maggie Smith, Denholm Elliott, Richard Griffiths, Tony Haygarth, Bill Paterson, John Normington, Liz Smith, Alison Steadman

The Michael Palin/Maggie Smith team repeat the success of *The Missionary* with this hilarious film about a meek foot doctor and his socially aspiring wife who become involved with the black market during the food rationing days of post–World War II England when they acquire an unlicensed pig. The humor is open to those who like Monty Python, but is also accessible to audiences who do not find that brand of humor funny. Rated R.

1985   96 minutes

PRIVATE LESSONS
★

DIRECTOR: Alan Myerson
CAST: Sylvia Kristel, Howard Hesseman, Eric Brown, Pamela Bryant

This soft-porn comedy, about a wealthy, virginal teen-age boy being seduced by his sexy, conniving 30-year-old housekeeper, is a seedy movie, run through with amateurish acting, cheap production values, and silly dialogue. Rated R because of nudity and sexual content.

1981   87 minutes

PRIVATE POPSICLE
★

DIRECTOR: Boaz Davidson
CAST: Yftach Katzur, Zachi Noy, Jonathan Segall, Bea Fiedler, Dietmar Siegert

In this fourth film featuring the Lemon Popsicle gang, a popular comedy team in Europe, we find the trio joining the Israeli army. But all three of the lads are more interested in the opposite sex than they are in military training or discipline. The attempts at comedy fall flat throughout, from the characters' attempts at sneaking into the female barracks to the impersonation of women officers. The inept dubbing just makes it all the worse. The picture is unrated, but there is much nudity and sex in it.

1982   100 minutes

PRIVATE SCHOOL

DIRECTOR: Noel Black
CAST: Phoebe Cates, Martin Mull, Sylvia Kristel, Ray Walston, Julie Payne, Fran Ryan, Michael Zorek

If *Porky's*, *Porky's II*, *Bachelor Party*, *Class*, etc., haven't sated your appetite for slobbering sexploitation comedies geared to adolescents, this awful film with Phoebe Cates, Martin Mull (uncredited), Sylvia Kristel (*Emmanuelle*), and Ray Walston offers more of the same: skin, stupidity, and more skin. Enroll at your own risk. Rated R for nudity and profanity.

1983   97 minutes

PRIVATES ON PARADE
★★★½

DIRECTOR: Michael Blakemore
CAST: John Cleese, Denis Quilley, Michael Elphick, Simon Jones, Joe Melia, John Standing, Nicola Pagett

While this story of a gay USO-type unit in the British army is a comedy, it has its serious moments. These come when the unit accidentally runs into a gang of gunrunners. John Cleese is hilarious as the pathetic army major who's ignorant of the foul play that goes on under his nose. Those who dislike Monty Python need not worry—most of the comedy in this film is universal. Rated PG-13 for adult situations and profanity.

1983   107 minutes

PRODUCERS, THE
★★★★

DIRECTOR: Mel Brooks
CAST: Zero Mostel, Gene Wilder, Kenneth Mars, Dick Shawn, Lee Meredith, Christopher Hewett

Mel Brooks's first film as a director remains a laugh-filled winner. Zero Mostel stars as a sleazy Broadway promoter who, with the help of a neurotic accountant (Gene Wilder), comes up with a scheme to produce an intentional flop titled *Springtime for Hitler* and bilk its backers. The plan backfires, and the disappointed duo ends up with a hit and more troubles than before. Rated PG.

1968   88 minutes

PROJECTIONIST, THE
★★

DIRECTOR: Harry Hurwitz
CAST: Chuck McCann, Ina Balin, Rodney Dangerfield

A projectionist in a New York movie palace escapes his drab life by creating fantasies, casting himself as the hero in various films. The movie intercuts new footage into old classics, a technique used later by Steve Martin in *Dead Men Don't Wear Plaid*. While interesting as a low-budget experiment, the film has surprisingly little entertainment value. Rodney Dangerfield plays the gruff theatre manager, but don't expect the Rodney we know today. Rated R for profanity and partial nudity.

1970   85 minutes

PROTOCOL
★★★½

DIRECTOR: Herbert Ross
CAST: Goldie Hawn, Chris Sarandon, Richard Romanos, Cliff DeYoung, Gail Strickland

In this film, directed by Herbert Ross, Goldie Hawn is a lovable airhead who goes through a startling metamorphosis to become a true individual. Sound a little like *Private Benjamin*? You bet your blonde movie actress. As unoriginal as it is, this comedy-with-a-message works surprisingly well. It's no classic. However, viewers could do a lot worse. Rated PG for violence, partial nudity, and adult situations.

1984   96 minutes

PURPLE ROSE OF CAIRO, THE
★★★★
DIRECTOR: Woody Allen
CAST: Mia Farrow, Jeff Daniels, Danny Aiello, Edward Herrmann, John Wood

Woody Allen's clever screen creation recalls his story for *Play It Again Sam*. The latter had Allen's character interacting with the specter of Humphrey Bogart, who sagely advised him on his love life. In *The Purple Rose of Cairo*, Mia Farrow is a Depression-era housewife who finds her dreary day-to-day existence enlivened when a dashing, romantic hero walks off the screen and sweeps her off her feet. The film becomes even more outlandish and delightful by the minute. It's not a laugh-a-minute farce. Like Allen's other recent films, *Zelig* and *Broadway Danny Rose*, it mixes humor with very human situations. The result, as in the two previous cases, is a very satisfying work of celluloid. Rated PG for violence.

1985   85 minutes

PUTNEY SWOPE
★★★★
DIRECTOR: Robert Downey
CAST: Alan Abel, Mel Brooks, Allen Garfield, Arnold Johnson, Pepi Hermine, Ruth Hermine, Antonio Fargas

This wildly funny film concerns a black man who takes over a Madison Avenue advertising firm. Alan Abel, Mel Brooks, and Allen Garfield appear in this zany parody of American lifestyles. Rated R.

1969   88 minutes

RABBIT TEST

DIRECTOR: Joan Rivers
CAST: Billy Crystal, Roddy McDowall, Joan Prather

Horrible comedy about the world's first pregnant man. Joan Rivers borrows her leaden stage persona for her directing debut, and even the occasionally talented Billy Crystal can't do anything with this wretched material. Too awful, even, to be viewed as camp. A miscarriage of cinema. Rated R—profanity.

1978   84 minutes

RAFFERTY AND THE GOLD DUST TWINS
★★½
DIRECTOR: Dick Richards
CAST: Sally Kellerman, Mackenzie Phillips, Alan Arkin, Alex Rocco, Charlie Martin Smith, Harry Dean Stanton

Amusing and entertaining little film with Sally Kellerman and Mackenzie Phillips kidnapping a hapless Alan Arkin and forcing him to drive them to New Orleans from California. Good cast and pacing make up for simple plot. Rated PG for profanity.

1975   92 minutes

RAVISHING IDIOT, THE

DIRECTOR: Edouard Molinaro
CAST: Anthony Perkins, Brigitte Bardot

A big bomb of a comedy that can be recommended only for insomniacs. Thin plot concerns a spy out to steal NATO plans of ship movements. Skip it.

1965   B & W 110 minutes

REACHING FOR THE MOON
★★★
DIRECTOR: Edmund Goulding
CAST: Douglas Fairbanks, Bebe Daniels, Edward Everett Horton

Robust and energetic Douglas Fairbanks plays a financier on whom liquor has an interesting effect. Edward Everett Horton is his valet and Bebe Daniels is the girl.

1931   B & W   62 minutes

REAL GENIUS
★★★

DIRECTOR: Martha Coolidge

CAST: Val Kilmer, Gabe Jarret, Michelle Meyrink, William Atherton, Ed Lauter

This is a mildly amusing but predictable comedy about a group of science prodigies (led by Val Kilmer, of *Top Secret!*) who decide to thwart the plans of their egomaniacal mentor (William Atherton) who is secretly using their research to build a rather nasty little laser weapon for the C.I.A. Screenwriters Neal Israel and Pat Proft throw in a few witty lines and silly—but effective—slapstick situations here and there, yet overall the film comes off rather flat. Director Martha Coolidge does her best to keep things interesting, but she can't overcome the predictability of the climax. Rated PG for profanity.

1985   105 minutes

REAL LIFE
★★★

DIRECTOR: Albert Brooks

CAST: Albert Brooks, Charles Grodin, Frances Lee McCain, J. A. Preston, Matthew Tobin

Albert Brooks's fans will eat up this tasty satire parodying an unrelenting PBS series that put the day-to-day life of an American family under the microscope. In Brooks's film the typical family comes hilariously unglued under the omnipresent eye of the camera. The script (written by Brooks) eventually falters, but not before

a healthy number of intelligent laughs are produced. Rated PG.

1979   99 minutes

REEFER MADNESS
★★½

DIRECTOR: Louis J. Gasnier

CAST: Dave O'Brien, Dorothy Short, Warren McCollum, Lilian Miles, Carleton Young, Thelma White

This 1930s anti-marijuana film is very silly, and sometimes funny. It's a cult film that really isn't as good as its reputation suggests.

1936   B & W   67 minutes

REIVERS, THE
★★★★

DIRECTOR: Mark Rydell

CAST: Steve McQueen, Rupert Crosse, Will Geer, Sharon Farrell, Mitch Vogel, Michael Constantine

Grand adaptation of the William Faulkner tale concerning a young boy (Mitch Vogel) who, with the help of his mischievous older friends (Steve McQueen and Rupert Crosse), "borrows" an automobile and heads for fun and excitement in 1905 Mississippi. The charming vignettes include a stopover in a brothel and a climactic horse race that could spell doom for the adventurers. Good period soundtrack by John Williams. Lots of fun for everybody; don't miss it. Rated PG.

1969   107 minutes

REPO MAN
★★★½

DIRECTOR: Alex Cox

CAST: Emilio Estevez, Harry Dean Stanton, Vonetta McGee, Olivia Barash, Sy Richardson, Tracy Walter

Wild, weird, and upredictable, this film stars Emilio Estevez as a young man who gets into the repossession racket. Under the tutelage of Harry Dean Stanton (in a typically terrific performance), Estevez learns how to steal cars from people who haven't kept up their payments. Meanwhile, a succession of increasingly bizarre events lead them to an encounter with what may be beings from space. Sound weird? You bet. *Repo Man* is not for every taste. However, those who occasionally like to watch something different will enjoy it. Rated R.

1984   92 minutes

RETURN OF THE PINK PANTHER, THE
★★★★

DIRECTOR: Blake Edwards

CAST: Peter Sellers, Christopher Plummer, Herbert Lom, Catherine Schell, Burt Kwouk, Peter Arne, Gregoire Aslan, Andre Maranne, Victor Spinetti

Writer-director Blake Edwards and star Peter Sellers revived their Inspector Clouseau character for a new series of comic adventures beginning with this slapstick classic. There are many funny scenes as Sellers attempts to track down the Phantom (Christopher Plummer) while making life intolerable for the chief inspector (Herbert Lom). Rated PG.

1975   113 minutes

RETURN OF THE SECAUCUS 7
★★★★½

DIRECTOR: John Sayles

CAST: Mark Arnott, Gordon Clapp, Maggie Cousineau, Adam Lefevre, Bruce MacDonald, Jean Passanante, Maggie Renzl

Here's an absolute gem of a movie. Written, produced, and directed by John Sayles, it's a story about the reunion of seven friends ten years after they were wrongfully busted in Secaucus, New Jersey, while on their way to the last demonstration against the Vietnam War in Washington, D.C. It is a delicious blend of characterization, humor, and insight. No MPAA rating, but *Secaucus 7* has nudity, profanity, and implicit sex.

1980   100 minutes

RETURN OF THE TALL BLOND MAN WITH ONE BLACK SHOE, THE
★★★½

DIRECTOR: Yves Robert

CAST: Pierre Richard, Mireille Darc, Jean Rochefort

This sequel to the original *Tall Blond Man . . .* is, unfortunately, inferior. But it's still a delight to watch Pierre Richard go through his comic paces. The plot is, once again, really not important, except that in this case it takes away from the fun instead of adding to it. Once again our hero is caught up in intrigue and derring-do, and his reactions to what he's faced with are the reason to see this or the original. If you haven't seen the original, do. If you have, we might even go so far as to recommend you have a second laugh with it rather than watching this. No MPAA rating.

1974   84 minutes

REUBEN, REUBEN
★★★★½

DIRECTOR: Robert Ellis Miller

CAST: Tom Conti, Kelly McGillis, Roberts Blossom, Cynthia Harris, E. Katherine Kerr, Joel Fabiani, Kara Wilson, Lois Smith

A funny, touching, and memorable character study about an irascible Scottish poet, this film, directed by Robert Ellis Miller (*The Heart Is a Lonely Hunter*) and written by Julius J. Epstein (*Casablanca*), ranges from romantic to ribald, and from low-key believability to blistering black comedy. In short, it's a rare cinematic treat. First and foremost among the picture's assets is a superb leading performance by Tom Conti. Rated R for profanity and suggested sex.

1983   101 minutes

REVENGE OF THE NERDS
★★★½

DIRECTOR: Jeff Kanew
CAST: Robert Carradine, Anthony Edwards, Julie Montgomery, Curtis Armstrong, Ted McGinley, Michelle Meyrink, James Cromwell, Bernie Casey

The title characters, Lewis (Robert Carradine) and Gilbert (Anthony Edwards), strike back at the jocks who torment them in this watchable, fitfully funny comedy. Rated R.

1984   90 minutes

REVENGE OF THE PINK PANTHER, THE
★★★★½

DIRECTOR: Blake Edwards
CAST: Peter Sellers, Dyan Cannon, Robert Webber, Marc Lawrence, Herbert Lom, Burt Kwouk, Robert Loggia, Paul Stewart, Andre Maranne, Graham Stark, Ferdy Mayne

This is arguably the best of the slapstick series about an inept French police inspector. It contains inspired bits penned by director Blake Edwards and played to perfection by Peter Sellers. Rated PG.

1978   99 minutes

RHINESTONE
★½

DIRECTOR: Bob Clark
CAST: Sylvester Stallone, Dolly Parton

It was hard enough to believe Clint Eastwood as a country singer in *Honkytonk Man*. But Sylvester Stallone? Forget it. In the screenplay, by Phil Alden Robinson and Stallone, Dolly Parton plays Jake (Jacqueline) Ferris, a country singer who bets her lascivious manager she can take an average guy off the street and turn him into a country star in two weeks. What she gets stuck with is a New York cabbie named Nick Martinelli (Stallone), who, when she first meets him, can't carry a tune in a bag. While the film does have its moments of laugh-getting comedy and deft characterization, the hokey premise eventually does it in. If judged on its overall effectiveness, *Rhinestone* goes out with a whimper instead of the intended bang. Rated PG for profanity, sexual innuendo, and violence.

1984   111 minutes

RICHARD PRYOR—HERE AND NOW
★★★★½

DIRECTOR: Richard Pryor
CAST: Richard Pryor

The popular comedian doing what he does best, stand-up comedy. Rated R for profanity.

1983   83 minutes

RICHARD PRYOR—LIVE AND SMOKIN'

★★½

DIRECTOR: Michael Blum

CAST: Richard Pryor

The title of this never-before-released, disappointing comedy concert film featuring Richard Pryor must refer to the star's frequent smoking of cigarettes. Certainly, there's nothing smokin' in this film. It's not boring, but Pryor is clearly unnerved by the presence of the film crew. He refers to the fact that he's nervous often and can't seem to get his routines moving with any kind of comedic rhythm. While there are some nice bits, the laughs are few. Pryor's recreations of ghetto life are poignant. However, those looking for hilarity will want to try his other tapes. Unrated, the film has profanity.

1985   45 minutes

RICHARD PRYOR—LIVE IN CONCERT

★★★★★

DIRECTOR: Jeff Margolis

CAST: Richard Pryor

Comedian/movie star Richard Pryor's first live comedy performance film is still the best. Life has never been so sad and funny at the same time. You'll be exhausted from laughter by its end and be left with a lot to think about. Rated R for profanity.

1979   78 minutes

RICHARD PRYOR LIVE ON THE SUNSET STRIP

★★★

DIRECTOR: Joe Layton

CAST: Richard Pryor

Richard Pryor's second concert film (and first film after his accidental burning) is highly watchable. *Richard Pryor—Live in Concert* and *Richard Pryor—Here and Now*, however, are superior. Rated R for nonstop profanity and vulgarity.

1982   82 minutes

RIDING ON AIR

★★★

DIRECTOR: Edward Sedgwick

CAST: Joe E. Brown, Florence Rice, Vinton Haworth, Guy Kibbee, Clem Bevans

Lots of thrills and laughs in this topically dated comedy adventure about two small-town newspaper corresondents vying for the same girl and the scoop on a story involving aerial smugglers and a device for flying airplanes by a remote control radio beam—a reality today, but not when the film was made. Joe E. Brown is, as always, warm, winning, and wholesome. Guy Kibbee plays a stinker.

1937   B & W 58 minutes

RISKY BUSINESS

★★★★

DIRECTOR: Paul Brickman

CAST: Tom Cruise, Rebecca De Mornay, Curtis Armstrong, Bronson Pinchot, Raphael Sbarge, Joe Pantoliano, Nicholas Pryor, Janet Carroll, Richard Masur

An ordinarily well-behaved boy (Tom Cruise) goes wild when his parents are on vacation. His troubles begin when a gorgeous hooker (Rebecca De Mornay) who doesn't exactly have a heart of gold makes a house call at his request and he doesn't have enough in his piggy bank to cover the cost of her services. It's stylish, funny, and sexy—everything, in fact, that most movies of this kind generally are not. Rated R for nudity, profanity, and suggested sex.

1983   99 minutes

RITZ, THE
★★★★

DIRECTOR: Richard Lester
CAST: Jack Weston, Rita Moreno, Jerry Stiller, Kaye Ballard, F. Murray Abraham, Treat Williams, Paul Price, George Coulouris, Bessie Love

This film is brim-full of belly laughs that will leave you exhausted. Richard Lester is at his best directing comedy, and this film tops his celebrated success with the Beatles in *A Hard Day's Night* and 1974's popular *Three Musketeers*. One reason is the story. After the death of this father-in-law, Jack Weston (as Geatano Proclo) flees Cleveland. His brother-in-law has put out a contract on him to prevent his inheriting any part of the family garbage business. His escape takes him to New York City and, by accident, a gay hotel called The Ritz. The confusion that results will have you gasping for air. Rated R for profanity.

1976   91 minutes

ROAD TO BALI
★★★½

DIRECTOR: Hal Walker
CAST: Bob Hope, Bing Crosby, Dorothy Lamour, Murvyn Vye

Excellent entry in the Bob Hope/Bing Crosby *Road* series is the only one to make it to video as yet. In this one the boys play a pair of vaudeville performers in competition for Dorothy Lamour, pursuing her to the South Seas island of Bali, where they must contend with all sorts of jungle dangers, from cannibalistic natives to various Hollywood stars who appear in hilarious (though very brief) ca-

meos. The Humphrey Bogart scene is a classic.

1952   90 minutes

ROCK 'N ROLL WRESTLING WOMEN VS. THE AZTEC MUMMY

DIRECTOR: René Cardona, Manuel San Fernando
CAST: Lorena Velazquez, Armand Silvestre, Elizabeth Campbell, Eugenia Saint Martin, Chucho Salinas, Raymond Bugarini, Victor Velazques

Some folks found this old Mexican horror flick and attempted to turn it into a comedy by redubbing the dialogue, giving it a comical rock-'n'-roll soundtrack, and retitling it. Two female wrestlers assist an archeologist in foiling a madman's plans of ruling the world by possessing the secrets of an ancient mummy's tomb. What these revisers didn't realize is that this film would have been more entertaining if left alone. It could have been another *Plan 9 From Outer Space*. Not rated; has violence.

1986   B & W   88 minutes

ROCK 'N' ROLL HIGH SCHOOL
★★★½

DIRECTOR: Allan Arkush
CAST: P. J. Soles, Vincent Van Patten, Clint Howard, Dey Young, The Ramones

The stern new principal tries to turn a school into a concentration camp. The popular Riff (P. J. Soles) goes against the principal by playing loud Ramones music all the time. Meanwhile, boring Tom (Vincent Van Patten) has a crush on Riff. The film includes lots of laughs and good rock 'n' roll music—a cult favorite. Rated PG.

1979   93 minutes

ROMANCE WITH A DOUBLE BASS
★★★½
DIRECTOR: Robert Young
CAST: John Cleese, Connie Booth, Graham Crowden, Desmond Jones, Freddie Jones, Johnathan Lynn, Andrew Sachs, Denis Ramsden

Monty Python madman John Cleese stars in this delightfully silly vignette about a double-bass player and a princess who are caught naked in a pond when a thief makes off with their clothes. The ensuing romance will tickle and charm most adult viewers with its refreshing subtlety; but a word of caution for parents: this short will not win any awards for costume design.
1974   40 minutes

ROMANTIC COMEDY
★★★
DIRECTOR: Arthur Hiller
CAST: Dudley Moore, Mary Steenburgen, Frances Sternhagen, Janet Eilber, Robyn Douglass, Ron Liebman

In this enjoyable comedy, based on the 1979 Broadway play, Dudley Moore and Mary Steenburgen star as two collaborating playwrights who, during their long association, suffer from "unsynchronized passion." Rated PG for profanity and suggested sex.
1983   103 minutes

ROOM SERVICE
★★★
DIRECTOR: William A. Seiter
CAST: The Marx Brothers, Lucille Ball, Ann Miller

After leaving his brothers (Groucho, Harpo, and Chico) to try movie producing, Zeppo Marx came up with this Broadway play about a foundering stage production and attempted to have it re-written to suit his siblings' talents. He wasn't completely successful, but this romp does have its moments. Look for Lucille Ball and Ann Miller in early supporting roles.
1938   B & W   78 minutes

ROSEBUD BEACH HOTEL, THE
🐢
DIRECTOR: Harry Hurwitz
CAST: Colleen Camp, Peter Scolari, Christopher Lee, Hamilton Camp, Eddie Deezen, Chuck McCann, Hank Garrett

An absolutely awful attempt to combine comedy with softcore porn. Colleen Camp and Peter Scolari take over her father's failing hotel and hire prostitutes as bellgirls to improve business. Scolari rips off Chevy Chase at every turn. Poor Christopher Lee, as Camp's father, looks as though he wishes he were back making Dracula movies for Hammer Films. Stay away from this mess. Rated R.
1985   82 minutes

RSVP
★★★
DIRECTOR: John Almo, Lem Almo
CAST: Ray Colbert, Veronica Hart, Carey Hayes, Lola Mason, Adam Mills, Steve Nave, Robert Pinkerton, Harry Reems, Katt Shea, Allene Simmons, Arlene Steger, Dustin Stevens, Lynda Weismeier

This is an out-and-out sex comedy with lots of nudity and sexual situations. The plot concerns an author who has written a novel that turns out to be based on fact. The people who inspired the "characters" have been invited to a Hollywood party to celebrate the making of a movie from the book and discover the truth. The writing is lively, and the puns and gags are funny. For those who enjoy a sex comedy, this one has beautiful bodies and funny lines. Rated R for sexual situations and language that will be offensive to some.

1984   87 minutes

RULES OF THE GAME, THE
★★★★★

DIRECTOR: Jean Renoir
CAST: Marcel Dalio, Nora Gregor, Mila Parely

This is Jean Renoir's comedy/farce that deftly exposes the moral bankruptcy of the French upper classes. A French manor house is the location for a high livers' party as the shallowness of each party-goer is brilliantly exposed. Some scenes may be a trifle too "French" for American comprehension, but it's a visual feast for the eye and no less than intriguing.

1939   B & W 110 minutes

RULING CLASS, THE
★★★★

DIRECTOR: Peter Medak
CAST: Peter O'Toole, Alastair Sim, Arthur Lowe, Harry Andrews, Coral Browne

Superbly irreverent satire about upper-crust British eccentricities. Peter O'Toole plays the heir to a peerage who proves problematic because of his insane belief that he is Jesus Christ. Rated PG.

1972   154 minutes

RUSSIANS ARE COMING, THE RUSSIANS ARE COMING, THE
★★★½

DIRECTOR: Norman Jewison
CAST: Alan Arkin, Carl Reiner, Paul Ford, Theodore Bikel, Brian Keith, Jonathan Winters, Eva Marie Saint

A Russian submarine runs aground off Nantucket Island, and the townspeople go gaga, not knowing what to do first, get guns or pour vodka. Cued by Alan Arkin's engaging portrayal of an out-of-his-depth Russian sailor, the cast delivers a solid comedy as cultures clash. With Jonathan Winters aboard, think wacky.

1966   120 minutes

RUSTLER'S RHAPSODY
★★★

DIRECTOR: Hugh Wilson
CAST: Tom Berenger, G. W. Bailey, Marilu Henner, Andy Griffith, Fernando Rey, Patrick Wayne

In this fun spoof of the singing cowboy movies of the 1930s, '40s, and '50s, Tom Berenger plays the "greatest" horseback crooner of them all, Rex O'Herlihan, who must face his greatest challenge. Thanks to a rather unkind narrator (G. W. Bailey, who also plays Rex's sidekick), our hero finds himself in a modern western, with nastier villains than he's ever encountered before, women who won't take no for an answer, and a character who questions his confidence as a heterosexual. (Rex, like most of his ilk, wears rather bright, fringy clothes and seems to prefer his horse to the fairer sex.) It's all quite tastefully done by writer-director Hugh Wilson (*Police Academy*). There's only one problem: Viewers need to be familiar with the old B westerns to get the jokes. If you are, it's a hoot. Rated PG for mild violence and slight profanity.

1985   88 minutes

RUTHLESS PEOPLE
★★★★½

DIRECTOR: Jim Abrahams, David Zucker, Jerry Zucker

CAST: Danny DeVito, Bette Midler, Judge Reinhold, Helen Slater, Anita Morris

Hollywood's only three-man directing team comes up with another comedy classic. Danny DeVito portrays a man who decides to murder his obnoxious but rich wife, played by Bette Midler. But when he arrives home to carry out the deed, he discovers she has been abducted. The kidnappers demand fifty thousand dollars "or else." *Or else* is exactly what DeVito has in mind, so he refuses to pay a cent. As the ransom drops, tempers flare, and DeVito does all he can to ensure his wife's demise. Everyone in the film is selfish and evil except the kidnappers, who haven't the heart to carry out their threat and are hopelessly victimized by their victim. A hilarious black comedy from the makers of *Airplane!* An excellent example of ensamble acting, comic timing, and snowballing confusion, with a brilliantly intricate script by first-time screenwriter Dale Launer. Rated R for nudity and profanity.

1986   90 minutes

SAME TIME NEXT YEAR
★★★★

DIRECTOR: Robert Mulligan
CAST: Ellen Burstyn, Alan Alda

Funny, touching film begins with an accidental meeting in 1951 between two married strangers at a rural California inn. Doris (Ellen Burstyn) is a young housewife from California, and George (Alan Alda) an accountant from New Jersey. At first, as they begin their romance, it's awkward and very funny. But later, they realize they truly care for each other. Their meetings become an annual event. And through them, we see the changes in America and its people as we return to the same cottage every five years until 1977. Rated PG.

1978   117 minutes

SAPS AT SEA
★★★

DIRECTOR: Gordon Douglas
CAST: Oliver Hardy, Stan Laurel, Ben Turpin

Oliver Hardy contracts "hornophobia," and the only cure is rest and sea air. The boys rent a houseboat, but an escaped killer strands them all at sea to avoid the police. Comedy timing is off and some of the jokes misfire, but enough of them work to make the movie enjoyable.

1940   B & W   57 minutes

SCANDALOUS
★★

DIRECTOR: Rob Byrum
CAST: Robert Hays, Pamela Stephenson, John Gielgud, Jim Dale, M. Emmet Walsh, Bow Wow Wow

The star of *Airplane* takes a nosedive in this inept attempt at a spy thriller. Robert Hays plays an investigative reporter who gets mixed up with spies, con men, and murder in London. The cast, who seem to be working at feverish pitch to keep things interesting, includes Pamela Stephenson (from "Saturday Night Live") and John Gielgud, as a pair of con artists, and a casual concert appearance by Bow Wow Wow. Gielgud seems to be having a grand old time playing everything from an old Chinese man to the world's oldest punk rocker, while Jim Dale is embarrassing as an eccentric detective chasing Hays. Rated PG for profanity, nudity, and brief violence.

1983   93 minutes

SCAVENGER HUNT

DIRECTOR: Michael Schultz
CAST: Richard Benjamin, James Coco, Scatman Crothers, Ruth Gordon, Cloris Leachman, Roddy McDowall, Cleavon Little, Robert Morley, Richard Mulligan, Tony Randall, Vincent Price

It's a Mad Mad Mad Mad World writhes again as a bunch of wackos run hither, thither, and yawn to reap a dead man's inheritance in this "comedy." Rated PG.

1979   117 minutes

SCHLOCK

★★★

DIRECTOR: John Landis
CAST: John Landis, Saul Kahan, Joseph Piantadosi

Directed by and starring John Landis (*Thriller*; *An American Werewolf in London*; et al.), this film is a spoof of not only "missing link" monster movies but other types of horror and science-fiction films. It involves the discovery of a prehistoric man (still alive) and his "rampages" in the world of modern man. This is Landis's first film, and while it doesn't have the laughs of his later effort *Animal House*, it does include some chuckles of its own. Rated PG.

1971   80 minutes

SCHOOL SPIRIT

DIRECTOR: Alan Holleb
CAST: Tom Nolan, Elizabeth Foxx, Larry Linville, Roberta Collins, Daniele Arnaud, Nick Segal, Toni Hudson, Frank Mugavero, John Finnegan

Stupid high-school flick about an obnoxious libido case (Tom Nolan) who dies in an auto accident and returns as a ghost. Now he can see all the naked girls he wants, and director Alan Holleb doesn't pull the punches in that department. Come back, *Heavenly Kid*, all is forgiven! Not rated, but an easy R for sex, nudity, and profanity.

1985   90 minutes

SCREEN TEST

DIRECTOR: Sam Auster
CAST: Michael Allan Bloom, Robert Bundy, Paul Leuken, David Simpatico, Cynthia Kahn, Mari Laskarin

Unfunny "naughty" comedy about a group of teenage boys who pose as film producers in order to audition beautiful women nude for a bogus sex comedy. When one of their "stars" turns out to be the daughter of a big-time gangster, they have to come up with a real movie or else. It's stupid and tasteless as it sounds. Rated R.

1986   84 minutes

SCREWBALLS

DIRECTOR: Rafal Zielinski
CAST: Peter Keleghan, Lynda Speciale, Linda Shayne

Set in 1965, this dreadful teen-lust comedy takes place at Taft and Adams Educational Center, otherwise know as "T&A High." (Get it?) The ads say it features "the nuts who always score" in the game of getting girls. It should have been rained out. Rated R for nudity, sex, and profanity.

1983   80 minutes

SECRET ADMIRER

★★½

DIRECTOR: David Greenwalt

CAST: C. Thomas Howell, Lori Laughlin, Kelly Preston, Dee Wallace Stone, Cliff De-Young, Fred Ward, Leigh Taylor-Young

A sweet-natured sex comedy that suffers from predictability, this stars teen heartthrob C. Thomas Howell as a 16-year-old who, on the last day of school before summer vacation, receives an anonymous letter from a female who swears undying love. He hopes it's from the girl of his dreams (Kelly Preston) and decides to find out. Meanwhile, the letter falls into a number of other hands, the owners of which each interpret the letter differently. This causes all sorts of problems. Rated R for nudity, light violence, and profanity.

1985   100 minutes

SECRET LIFE OF AN AMERICAN WIFE, THE
★★

DIRECTOR: George Axelrod

CAST: Walter Matthau, Anne Jackson, Patrick O'Neal, Edy Williams, Richard Bull, Paul Napier, Gary Brown

To see if she still has sex appeal, bored wife Anne Jackson decides to moonlight as a call girl. Her first client is her husband's employer. Husband walks in on wife and employer, etc. Director and writer George Axelrod had a cute idea, but it really doesn't jell.

1968   93 minutes

SECRET LIFE OF WALTER MITTY, THE
★★★★

DIRECTOR: Norman Z. McLeod

CAST: Danny Kaye, Virginia Mayo, Boris Karloff, Reginald Denny, Florence Bates, Ann Rutherford, Thurston Hall

This is a comedy fit for the whole family. Based on James Thurber's story, this film presents Danny Kaye as a timid man who dreams of being a brave, glory-bound hero. This film provides plenty of laughs and enjoyable moments.

1947   105 minutes

SECRET POLICEMAN'S PRIVATE PARTS, THE
★★★

DIRECTOR: Roger Graef, Julian Temple

CAST: John Cleese, Michael Palin, Terry Jones, Graham Chapman, Peter Cook, Terry Gilliam, Pete Townshend, Phil Collins, Donovan, Bob Geldof

Monty Python fans will find some of their favorite sketches in this Amnesty International production, but they have been executed elsewhere in better form. The whole film seems lackluster, with so-so performances by the musical guests. If you are a fan, you probably will enjoy it, but if you're less of an enthusiast, you might check out *Monty Python Live at the Hollywood Bowl* first. *Bowl* has the team in fine form and is technically superior as well. The chuckles, guffaws, and quirky surprises are here, too, though, so you could do worse. Rated R.

1984   77 minutes

SECRET POLICEMEN'S OTHER BALL, THE
★★★★

DIRECTOR: Julian Temple, Roger Graef

CAST: John Cleese, Graham Chapman, Michael Palin, Terry Jones, Eric Clapton, Jeff Beck, Pete Townshend, Peter Cook

British comedians John Cleese, Graham Chapman, Michael Palin, and Terry Jones (of Monty Python) join with rock performers Sting (of the Police), Eric Clapton, Jeff Beck, and Peter Townshend (of the Who) in a live performance to benefit Amnesty International. The comedy bits—which also feature Dudley Moore's former partner, Peter Cook—go from funny to hilarious, and the music is surprisingly effective. *Ball* jumps from comedy to rock and back again somewhat erratically, but the material included makes it well worth watching. Rated R for profanity and adult themes.

1982   91 minutes

SECRET WAR OF HARRY FRIGG, THE
★★

DIRECTOR: Jack Smight
CAST: Paul Newman, Sylva Koscina, Andrew Duggan, James Gregory

A group of Allied generals has been captured by the Italians. Strangely, they make no attempt to escape. In their vast wisdom, the high command chooses a disgruntled private (Paul Newman) to go behind the lines and free them if possible. This is a very basic comedy, with few original laughs. Sylva Koscina is on hand to provide Newman with some female diversion. Rated PG.

1968   110 minutes

SECRETS OF WOMEN (OR WAITING WOMEN)
★★★½

DIRECTOR: Ingmar Bergman
CAST: Anita Bjork, Jarl Kulle, Eva Dahlbeck, Gunnar Bjornstrand, Maj-Britt Nilsson, Birger Malmsten, Gerd Anderson

Infidelity is the theme of this early Ingmar Bergman film. Three wives (Anita Bjork, Maj-Britt Nilsson, and Eva Dahlbeck) who are staying at a summer house recount adventures from their marriages while they are waiting for their husbands' return. Bergman staged the film in three segments, and although it is often referred to as a comedy, the film is grave. There are amusing moments in the first two segments, but the third is by far the best. Karin (Dahlbeck) and Fredrik (Gunnar Bjornstrand) portray a married couple who are trapped in an elevator. They are forced to talk to each other for the first time in years. Clearly illustrates Bergman's talent for comedy and was his first commercial success.

1952   B & W 107 minutes

SEDUCED AND ABANDONED
★★★

DIRECTOR: Pietro Germi
CAST: Saro Urzi, Stefania Sandrelli, Aldo Puglisi

This raucous Italian film takes wonderfully funny pot shots at Italian life and codes of honor. It centers on a statute of Italian law that absolves a man for the crime of seducing and abandoning a girl if he marries her. This is one of the funniest movies exposing the strategems of saving face. In Italian with English subtitles.

1964   B & W 118 minutes

SEDUCTION OF MIMI, THE
★★★★

DIRECTOR: Lina Wertmuller
CAST: Giancarlo Giannini, Mariangela Melato, Agostina Belli, Elena Fiore

Giancarlo Giannini gives an unforgettable performances as the sad-eyed Mimi, a Sicilian who migrates to the big city as a member of the working class. He soon gets into trouble because of his obstinate character and his simple mind. Like all Wertmuller's films, sex and politics are at the heart of her dark humor. Includes one of the funniest love scenes ever filmed. Rated R for language and sex.

1974   89 minutes

SEEMS LIKE OLD TIMES
★★★

DIRECTOR: Jay Sandrich
CAST: Goldie Hawn, Chevy Chase, Charles Grodin, Robert Guillaume, Harold Gould

This slick, commercial package is much better than it deserves to be. It's another predictable Neil Simon sit-com packed with one-liners. But at least it's funny most of the time, which is more than you can say for some of his films. Rated PG.

1980   121 minutes

SEMI-TOUGH
★★★

DIRECTOR: Michael Ritchie
CAST: Burt Reynolds, Jill Clayburgh, Kris Kristofferson, Robert Preston, Bert Convy, Lotte Lenya

Semi-humorous love triangle set in a professional football background is just not as funny as it should be. Some inspired moments and very funny scenes make it a highly watchable film (especially Lotte Lenya's guest bit as an untemptable masseuse), and the character actors are fine, but the film is mean-spirited at times and much of the humor relies on profanity and cruel situations the female pawns in the story are subjected to. About as much fun as watching a guy eat glass can be. Burt Reynolds hams it up as usual, Kris Kristofferson doesn't say much, and Jill Clayburgh is the rather unbelievable object of their

passions and eventual competition. Rated R.

1977   108 minutes

SENATOR WAS INDISCREET, THE
★★★

DIRECTOR: George S. Kaufman
CAST: William Powell, Ella Raines, Peter Lind Hayes, Arleen Whelan, Hans Conried

A staid and unreproachable U.S. senator's diary disclosures cause considerable embarrassment in this satire. Urbane and suave as always, William Powell is perfect in the title role.

1947   B & W   81 minutes

SERIAL
★★★½

DIRECTOR: Bill Persky
CAST: Martin Mull, Tuesday Weld, Jennifer McAlister, Bill Macy, Tom Smothers, Christopher Lee

Perhaps the best-known California joke is Cyra McFadden's best-selling novel *The Serial*, which mercilessly pokes fun at the laid-back, trendy lifestyle of a group of "average" affluent Marin County residents. At the center of this farce is the Holroyd family. Harvey Holroyd (Martin Mull) finds it difficult to go with the flow, especially when he finds out his wife, Kate (Tuesday Weld), is having an affair with a Cuban poodle-groomer while his daughter, Joan (Jennifer McAlister), has joined a religious cult. That's when the problems really begin. Rated R.

1980   86 minutes

SEVEN BEAUTIES
★★★★★

DIRECTOR: Lina Wertmuller
CAST: Giancarlo Giannini, Fernando Rey, Shirley Stoler

Winner of many international awards, this Italian film classic is not what the title might suggest. *Seven Beauties* is actually the street name for a small-time gangster, played by Giancarlo Giannini. We watch him struggle and survive on the streets and in a World War II German prisoner-of-war camp. Excellent! Rated R.

1976   115 minutes

SEVEN MINUTES IN HEAVEN
★★½

DIRECTOR: Linda Feferman
CAST: Jennifer Connelly, Byron Thames, Maddie Corman, Michael Zaslow, Polly Draper, Alan Boyce, Billy Wirth

When her only parent leaves town on business, 15-year-old Natalie (Jennifer Connelly) allows classmate Jeff (Byron Thames) to move into her home. Their relationship is purely platonic, but no one will believe them. Average but well-meant teen comedy. Rated PG for tastefully suggested sex.

1986   95 minutes

SEVEN YEAR ITCH, THE
★★★★

DIRECTOR: Billy Wilder
CAST: Tom Ewell, Marilyn Monroe, Oscar Homolka, Carolyn Jones

This movie is Marilyn Monroe's most enjoyable comedy—she plays the innocent "dumb blonde" to perfection. Marilyn lives upstairs from average American Tom Ewell. It seems his wife has escaped the heat of their New York home by going on vacation. This leaves Tom alone and unprotected, and one visit from luscious neighbor Marilyn leads him on a Walter Mitty–style adventure that is a joy to behold.

1957   105 minutes

SEX SHOP, LE
★★★½

DIRECTOR: Claude Berri
CAST: Claude Berri, Juliet Berto, Jean-Pierre Marielle

This French sex comedy stars and was directed by Claude Berri. He plays a bookstore owner struggling to make a living. Unable to make ends meet, he converts his store into a sex shop specializing in pornography and sex gadgets. The laughs begin when he, acting clumsy and nerdlike, tries to get in on the action that his customers are a part of. His wife allows him to realize he's no Romeo. Rated R for nudity and sexual reference.

1974   93 minutes

SEX WITH A SMILE
★½

DIRECTOR: Sergio Martino
CAST: Marty Feldman, Edwise Fenech, Sydne Rome, Barbara Bouchet, Dayle Haddon

Silly, badly dubbed Italian film featuring five short stories on sexual misunderstandings. Marty Feldman's section produces some laughs, but the film is too broad and too dependent on sexism Italian-style. Rated R for nudity and sex.

1976   100 minutes

SEXTETTE
★

DIRECTOR: Ken Hughes, Irving Rapper
CAST: Mae West, Timothy Dalton, Dom DeLuise, Tony Curtis, Ringo Starr, George Hamilton

A dreadful movie only *barely* worth a viewing on fast-forward to witness the vulgar campiness of the nearly 80-year-old Mae West barely able to move through a bevy of barely clad beefcake—and certainly unable to shock or amuse. Her famous way with innuendo, her sexy purr, her let's-see-if-whatcha-got-measures-up and come-hither-with-it look—the whole package is decades past its expiration date. This is the vanity production that really led people to suspect that Mae West was a drag queen with one helluva secret. Rated R.

1978 91 minutes

SHOCK TREATMENT
DIRECTOR: Jim Sharman
CAST: Jessica Harper, Cliff De-Young, Richard O'Brien, Ruby Wax

Forgettable sequel to *The Rocky Horror Picture Show* that bombed out even with the rabid *Rocky Horror* crowd. Plot concerns two heroes, Janet and Brad, going on a TV game show and ending up trying to escape from it. Avoid this one at all costs. Rated PG.

1981 94 minutes

SHOT IN THE DARK, A
★★★★
DIRECTOR: Blake Edwards
CAST: Peter Sellers, Elke Sommer, George Sanders, Burt Kwouk, Herbert Lom, Graham Stark

A Shot in the Dark is a one-man show, with Peter Sellers outdoing himself as the character he later reprised in *The Return of the Pink Panther*, *The Pink Panther Strikes Back*, and *The Revenge of the Pink Panther*. In this slapstick delight, Clouseau attempts to discover whether or not a woman (Elke Sommer) is guilty of murdering her lover.

1964 101 minutes

SILENT MOVIE
★★★½
DIRECTOR: Mel Brooks
CAST: Mel Brooks, Marty Feldman, Dom De Luise, Bernadette Peters, Sid Caesar, James Caan, Burt Reynolds, Paul Newman, Liza Minnelli, Anne Bancroft, Marcel Marceau, Harry Ritz, Ron Carey

Mel Brooks's *Silent Movie* is another kitchen-sink affair, with Brooks going from the ridiculous to the sublime with a beautiful idea that bears more exploring. Silent films were the best for comedy, and Brooks, along with co-stars Marty Feldman, Dom De Luise, and Sid Caesar, supply numerous funny moments. The biggest surprises are the guest stars, who make the film thrilling, each in his own talented way. *Silent Movie* is well worth seeing for the laughs among the clutter. Rated PG.

1976 86 minutes

SILVER BEARS
★★
DIRECTOR: Ivan Passer
CAST: Michael Caine, Cybill Shepherd, Louis Jourdan, Martin Balsam, Stéphane Audran, Tommy Smothers, David Warner

If *Silver Bears* was meant to be a comedy, it isn't funny. If it was meant to be a drama, it isn't gripping. It's boring. Michael Caine stars as a Mafia henchman sent to Switzerland to buy a bank for a Las Vegas gambler (Martin Balsam). He's swindled and ends up buying two rooms over a pizza parlor. It's all he can do to evade the gangsters on his trail. It's all the viewer can do to stay awake. Rated PG.

1978 113 minutes

SILVER STREAK
★★★★½

DIRECTOR: Arthur Hiller
CAST: Gene Wilder, Jill Clayburgh, Richard Pryor, Patrick Mc-Goohan, Ray Walston, Ned Beatty, Richard Kiel

Films with a slam-bang finish have long had one problem: What do you do to fill up the time it takes to get to that half-hour thrill? All you need is a fast-paced, action story laced with comedy and stars like Gene Wilder, Jill Clayburgh, and Richard Pryor. It will have you cheering, laughing, gasping, and jumping. *Streak* pits neurotic Wilder, sexy Clayburgh, and shifty Pryor against cool millionaire villain Patrick McGoohan and his evil henchman, Ray Walston, in a wild high-speed chase that brings back the train as a modern-day source for good thrillers. Rated PG.

1976   113 minutes

SIMON
★★

DIRECTOR: Marshall Brickman
CAST: Alan Arkin, Madeline Kahn, Austin Pendleton, William Finneu, Fred Gwynne

Weird, weird comedy about an average guy (Alan Arkin) who is brainwashed into thinking he's a visitor from outer space. The film has some funny moments, as well as a few interesting things to say, but it just doesn't work as a whole. Rated PG.

1980   97 minutes

SIMON OF THE DESERT
★★★★½

DIRECTOR: Luis Buñuel
CAST: Claudio Brook, Silvia Pinal, Hortensia Santovena

Even though it won the Special Jury Prize at the 1965 Venice Film Festival and is hailed by some critics (not generally prone to hyperbole) as "the best short film ever made," one still has the feeling that *Simon of the Desert* is a short film because Luis Buñuel simply ran out of money (and tacked on a fairly unsatisfactory ending). It is, however, impossible to deny the sly pleasure we have with St. Simon Stylites, the desert anchorite who spent thirty-seven years atop a sixty-foot column (circa A.D. 400) preaching to Christian flocks and avoiding temptation—particularly with blond knockout Silvia Pinal, as the devil, who comes along to tempt him. (She/he travels in a self-propelled casket!) Good nasty fun for aficionados and novices alike. In Spanish with English subtitles.

1965   B & W   40 minutes

SIN OF HAROLD DIDDLEBOCK (AKA MAD WEDNESDAY)
★★★½

DIRECTOR: Preston Sturges
CAST: Harold Lloyd, Frances Ramsden, Jimmy Conlin, Raymond Walburn, Edgar Kennedy, Arline Judge, Lionel Stander, Margaret Hamilton, Rudy Vallee

The result of a disastrous joint effort of director Preston Sturges, silent-screen great Harold Lloyd, and backer Howard Hughes is a much better film than popular Hollywood legend implies and is a bonus addition to anyone's library or viewing experience. This story about a middle-aged man fired from his job and set adrift with nothing but unfulfilled potential doesn't sound like a scream. However, Lloyd's bizarre antics when under-the-influence redeem the character, who has let life slip by and makes a positive statement about dealing with life's futilities.

A great roster of veteran character actors and actresses and some outstanding gags make this one of the most enjoyable "comeback" comedies of all time and on a par with any of the comedies made by the still-active comedy greats or teams of the 1940s. All the principals disagreed about the film upon its completion and distribution was spotty. Hughes rereleased it in 1950 as *Mad Wednesday* and edited it down to seventy-nine minutes. Lloyd wears the best zoot suit in films.

1947   B & W   90 minutes

SIX PACK

DIRECTOR: Daniel Petrie
CAST: Kenny Rogers, Diane Lane, Erin Gray

In this unimaginative retread of *Rocky*, *Smokey and the Bandit*, and every bachelor-father comedy ever made, country crossover king Kenny Rogers plays a footloose stock-car racer who is latched on to by six homeless, sticky-fingered kids ranging in age from 7 to 16. In his feature-film debut, Rogers is wooden and unconvincing, but then so is the whole movie. Rated PG for profanity.

1982   110 minutes

SIXTEEN CANDLES
★★★★

DIRECTOR: John Hughes
CAST: Molly Ringwald, Paul Dooley, Blanche Baker, Edward Andrews, Anthony Michael Hall, Billie Bird

Molly Ringwald stars in this fast and funny teen comedy as a high-school student who is crushed when the whole family forgets her sixteenth birthday. Things, it seems to her, go downhill from there— that is, until the boy of her dreams suddenly starts showing some interest. Sort of the female flip side of *Risky Business*, this work was written and directed by John Hughes (screenwriter of *Mr. Mom* and *Vacation*). Rated PG for profanity.

1984   93 minutes

SKYLINE
★★★

DIRECTOR: Fernando Colombo
CAST: Antonio Resines, Susana Ocana

Although there are a few laughs in this film, it—while billed as one— could hardly be called a comedy. Antonio Resines plays a Spanish photographer named Gustavo who comes to New York seeking international fame. Once there, he struggles to learn English, find work, and pursue friendship and romance. In Spanish and English, with subtitles it would be excellent for bilingual viewers. The twist ending really gives one a jolt. We'd rate it PG for slight profanity and because most children would not appreciate or understand it.

1984   84 minutes

SLAP SHOT
★★★★

DIRECTOR: George Roy Hill
CAST: Paul Newman, Strother Martin, Jennifer Warren, Lindsay Crouse, Melinda Dillon

When released in 1977, this comedy about a down-and-out hockey team was criticized for its liberal use of profanity. The controversy tended to obscure the fact that *Slap Shot* is a very funny, marvelously acted movie. Paul Newman, as an aging player-coach who's a loser in love and on the ice until he instructs the members of his team to behave like animals during their matches, has never been better.

The marvelous Strother Martin still manages to steal half the film from him. Rated R.

1977   122 minutes

SLAPSTICK OF ANOTHER KIND
🐨

DIRECTOR: Steven Paul

CAST: Jerry Lewis, Madeline Kahn, Marty Feldman

Jerry Lewis hasn't made a funny film in years, and this sci-fi spoof is no exception. The gags are old, predictable, and forced. It seems the harder Jerry tries, the fewer laughs he generates. All of the elaborate costumes and props and the help of the usually funny Marty Feldman and Madeline Kahn cannot save this turkey, based on a Kurt Vonnegut story. Rated PG.

                             minutes

SLEEPER
★★★★

DIRECTOR: Woody Allen

CAST: Woody Allen, Diane Keaton, John McLiam, John Beck

Writer-star-director Woody Allen finally exhibited some true film-making talent with this 1973 sci-fi spoof. The frenetic gag-a-minute comedy style of Allen's earlier films (*Take the Money and Run*; *Bananas*; and *Everything You Always Wanted to Know About Sex*) was replaced by some nice bits of character comedy. This makes *Sleeper* the most enjoyable of Allen's pre–*Annie Hall* creations. Rated PG.

1973   88 minutes

SLUGGER'S WIFE, THE
★★

DIRECTOR: Hal Ashby

CAST: Michael O'Keefe, Rebecca De Mornay, Martin Ritt, Randy Quaid, Cleavant Derricks

The most shallow of Neil Simon's works to date, this is bad television situation comedy blown up to big-screen size. Darryl Palmer (Michael O'Keefe, the son in *The Great Santini*) is a self-centered baseball player who bullies his way into the affections of Debby Palmer (Rebecca De Mornay, from *Risky Business*), a would-be rock star. O'Keefe's Darryl is essentially a jerk, and Debby winds up with guilt by association, because we can't believe she could fall in love with such an egotist. Rated PG-13 for nudity and profanity.

1985   105 minutes

SMOKEY AND THE BANDIT
★★★½

DIRECTOR: Hal Needham

CAST: Burt Reynolds, Pat McCormick, Jerry Reed, Sally Field, Mike Henry, Jackie Gleason, Paul Williams

Smokey and the Bandit may strain credibility, but it never stops being fun. The Bandit (Burt Reynolds) is an infamous independent trucker who is hired by Big Enos Burdette (Pat McCormick) to transport four hundred cases of Coors beer from Texarkana, Texas, where it is legal, to Atlanta, Georgia, where it is not, for the reward of eighty-thousand dollars. There is also a twenty-eight-hour time limit. What the Bandit doesn't know is that Burdette has made this offer to other truckers, who were all arrested for bootlegging, and that he delights in putting them out of business. With his buddy, the Snowman (Jerry Reed), the Bandit picks up the beer and something he didn't expect, a girl in a wedding gown (Sally Field). What she doesn't tell him is that she is jilting the son (Mike Henry) of Texarkana's sheriff, Buford T. Justice (Jackie Gleason), who is in hot pursuit. Hold on to your hat. Rated PG for profanity.

1977   97 minutes

SMOKEY AND THE BANDIT II
★★

DIRECTOR: Hal Needham
CAST: Burt Reynolds, Jerry Reed, Pat McCormick, Paul Williams, Mike Henry, Jackie Gleason, Dom De Luise

Smokey II is just more proof that "sequels aren't equal." But it isn't a total loss. If you find yourself sitting through this pale imitation, don't turn it off until the credits roll (although you may want to fast-forward). Outtakes featuring the stars flubbing their lines are spliced together at the end, and they're hilarious. If only the movie had been that good . . . Rated PG.

1980   101 minutes

SMOKEY AND THE BANDIT III
🐾

DIRECTOR: Dick Lowry
CAST: Jerry Reed, Jackie Gleason, Paul Williams, Pat Mc-Cormick

The Bandit may be back, but it ain't Burt. Instead, Jerry Reed, who played Reynolds's buddy Cletus in the first two films, takes over that half of the title roles, with Jackie Gleason returning for the other as Sheriff Buford T. Justice. You can easily see why Reynolds decided to pass—it's an embarrassing waste of celluloid and money. Avoid it. Rated PG for nudity, profanity, and scatological humor.

1983   86 minutes

S.O.B.
★★★

DIRECTOR: Blake Edwards

CAST: Julie Andrews, William Holden, Robert Preston, Richard Mulligan, Robert Vaughn, Loretta Swit, Larry Hagman, Craig Stevens, Shelley Winters, Rosanna Arquette

Director Blake Edwards vents his resentment over Hollywood's treatment of him in the early 1970s in this potent satire. Self-indulgent, but frequently on target. Rated R.

1981   121 minutes

SO FINE
★

DIRECTOR: Andrew Bergman
CAST: Ryan O'Neal, Jack Warden, Richard Kiel, Fred Gwynne, Mike Kellin, David Round

This so-called sex comedy—about a fashion house (run by Ryan O'-Neal and Jack Warden) that introduces a new line of designer jeans with see-through plastic inserts in the seat—is little more than a television situation comedy with leers, skin, and foul language. It's amazing that it's even watchable. But it is. Just barely. Rated R because of nudity and brief profanity.

1981   91 minutes

SOME KIND OF HERO
★½

DIRECTOR: Michael Pressman
CAST: Richard Pryor, Margot Kidder, Ronny Cox, Olivia Cole

This Richard Pryor movie can't decide whether it should tell the story of a Vietnam prisoner of war and his problems returning to American society or be another comedy caper film. As a result, it's neither very funny nor worth thinking about. Rated R for profanity, nudity, and violence.

1982   97 minutes

SOME LIKE IT HOT
★★★★★
DIRECTOR: Billy Wilder
CAST: Marilyn Monroe, Jack Lemmon, Tony Curtis, Joe E. Brown, George Raft, Pat O'Brien, Nehemiah Persoff, Mike Mazurki

Billy Wilder's *Some Like It Hot* is the outlandish story of two men (Jack Lemmon and Tony Curtis) who accidentally witness a gangland slaying. They pose as members of an all-girl band in order to avoid the gangsters, who are now trying to silence them permanently. Marilyn Monroe is at her sensual best as the band's singer. Joe E. Brown is also hilarious as a wealthy playboy who develops an attraction for an obviously bewildered Lemmon.

1959   B & W 119 minutes

SONS OF THE DESERT
★★★★★
DIRECTOR: William A. Seiter
CAST: Stan Laurel, Oliver Hardy, Charley Chase

In *Sons of the Desert*, Stan Laurel and Oliver Hardy scheme to get away from their wives and attend a lodge convention in Chicago. After persuading the wives that Ollie needs to sail to Honolulu for his health, they go off to Chicago. The boat sinks on the way back from Hawaii, and the boys end up having to explain how they got home a day earlier than the other survivors (they ship-hiked). This film has no flaws.

1933   B & W   69 minutes

SOUP FOR ONE
★★★
DIRECTOR: Jonathon Kaufer
CAST: Saul Rubinek, Marcia Strassman, Teddy Pendergrass

Marcia Strassman (formerly the wife on "Welcome Back Kotter") stars as the dream girl to an often disappointed lover. When he finds her, he tries to persuade her to marry him. Although there are a few slow-moving parts, it is a generally enjoyable comedy. Rated R for sexual themes.

1982   87 minutes

SPACESHIP
🐢
DIRECTOR: Bruce Kimmel
CAST: Cindy Williams, Bruce Kimmel, Leslie Nielsen, Gerrit Graham

This "comedy" is all about an unwanted alien tagging along on a rocket full of idiots. Tries to be another *Airplane!*, even going as far as to steal that film's co-star (Leslie Nielsen), but there's not one funny moment in this dud. A complete failure. Original title: *The Creature Wasn't Nice*. Rated PG.

1981   88 minutes

SPIES LIKE US
★★★
DIRECTOR: John Landis
CAST: Chevy Chase, Dan Aykroyd, Bruce Davison, William Prince, Steve Forrest, Bernie Casey, Donna Dixon

Chevy Chase and Dan Aykroyd, who were co-stars on the original "Saturday Night Live" television show, appeared together on the big screen for the first time in this generally enjoyable comedy about two inept recruits in a U.S. intelligence organization counterespionage mission. The stars are fun to watch even though the movie only occasionally elicits laughter. Rated PG for violence and profanity.

1985   104 minutes

SPLASH
★★★★★

DIRECTOR: Ron Howard
CAST: Tom Hanks, Daryl Hannah, John Candy, Eugene Levy, Dody Goodman, Richard B. Shull

If you split your sides laughing at actor-turned-director Ron Howard's *Night Shift*, get ready for another achingly funny screen treat. Howard, co-star of *The Shootist* and one-time regular on TV's "The Andy Griffith Show" and "Happy Days," helmed this uproarious comedy about a young man (Tom Hanks) who unknowingly falls in love with a mermaid (Daryl Hannah, of *Reckless* and *Blade Runner*). Former SCTV regulars John Candy and Eugene Levy add some marvelous bits of comedy. Rated PG for profanity and brief nudity.

1984   111 minutes

SPOOKS RUN WILD
★½

DIRECTOR: Phil Rosen
CAST: Bela Lugosi, East Side Kids, Dave O'Brien, Dennis Moore

Bottom-of-the-barrel "entertainment" from Poverty Row filmgrinders Monogram Studios wastes a rapidly deteriorating Bela Lugosi in another silly role that gives the aging East Side Kids a chance to humiliate him on-screen. Inane, laughless, and overlong at sixty-nine minutes, this film fails on all levels, and only the presence of Lugosi and energetic Dave O'-Brien lend it any value at all. Made before the equally dreadful *Ghosts On the Loose*, this film joins the growing list of video releases that should always be on the "bargain" table at any sales or rental outlet. The kids might like it, but don't count on it as a baby-sitter substitute.

1941   B & W   69 minutes

SPRING BREAK
★

DIRECTOR: Sean S. Cunningham
CAST: David Knell, Steve Basset, Perry Lang, Paul Land

Here's a numbingly stupid movie about four guys on the make in Fort Lauderdale. It's reminiscent of the old "Beach Party" films, with one major exception—Annette Funicello never took off her top. Parents of the teenagers it's directed at may be shocked by the nudity, implied sex, and profanity that rightfully earned *Spring Break* its R rating.

1983   101 minutes

SPRING FEVER
★

DIRECTOR: Joseph L. Scanlan
CAST: Jessica Walter, Susan Anton, Frank Converse, Carling Bassett, Stephen Young

In spite of an advertising come-on that promised another beach romp in the tradition of *Where the Boys Are*, this limp Canadian production is an unbelievably dull story about a rising young tennis star (Carling Bassett). Susan Anton has neither the screen time nor the skill to be a successful vamp. Even the tennis sequences are boring, making the film seem to run an hour too long. Rated PG.

1983   100 minutes

STAGE DOOR
★★★★

DIRECTOR: Gregory La Cava
CAST: Katharine Hepburn, Ginger Rogers, Eve Arden, Lucille Ball, Ann Miller

A funny and tender taste of New York theatrical life. Katharine Hepburn and Ginger Rogers are two aspiring actresses who undergo the stifling yet stimulating life of a lodging house that caters to a vast array of prospective actresses trying any avenue to break into the big time. Eve Arden, Lucille Ball, and Ann Miller also take residence in this overcrowded and active boardinghouse.

1937   B & W   92 minutes

STAND-IN
★★★

DIRECTOR: Tay Garnett
CAST: Leslie Howard, Humphrey Bogart, Joan Blondell, Jack Carson, Alan Mowbray

This send-up of Hollywood rubbed more than one Tinsel Town mogul the wrong way by satirizing Front Office studio manipulators. Eastern financial genius (Leslie Howard) is sent west to "stand in" for stockholders and find why Colossal Pictures is heading for skidsville. Ignorant of film-making, he gets a lot of smoke until star stand-in (Joan Blondell) takes him in hand, and he links with lush producer (Humphrey Bogart) to salvage a turkey. The relish with which Howard and Bogart play their parts strongly suggests they thoroughly enjoyed biting the hands that fed them. Alan Mowbray's performance is a fine burlesque of the stripe of foreign-born director that inhabited sound stages in the 1920s and '30s.

1937   B & W   91 minutes

STARDUST MEMORIES
★

DIRECTOR: Woody Allen

CAST: Woody Allen, Charlotte Rampling, Jessica Harper, Marie-Christine Barrault

Absolutely unwatchable Woody Allen film, his most chaotic and Bergmanesque attempt to claim that he can't stand his fans. Boring, self-indulgent, and completely lacking the charm and perception of Allen's other films. And if this all was intended, as he has claimed, then he should be smacked for maiming the hand that feeds him. Rated PG—profanity.

1980   88 minutes

STARTING OVER
★★★★

DIRECTOR: Alan Pakula
CAST: Burt Reynolds, Jill Clayburgh, Candice Bergen, Charles Durning, Frances Sternhagen

Burt Reynolds and Jill Clayburgh are delightful in this Alan Pakula film about two lonely hearts trying to find romance in a cynical world. Candice Bergen is superb as Reynolds's off-key singer/ex-wife, whom he has trouble trying to forget in this winner. Rated R.

1979   106 minutes

START THE REVOLUTION WITHOUT ME
★★★★

DIRECTOR: Bud Yorkin
CAST: Gene Wilder, Donald Sutherland, Hugh Griffith, Jack MacGowran

Gene Wilder and Donald Sutherland star in this hilarious comedy as two sets of twins who meet just before the French Revolution. Cheech and Chong's *The Corsican Brothers* covered pretty much the same ground. Only trouble was it wasn't funny. If you want to see the story done right, check this one out. Rated PG.

1970   98 minutes

STEAGLE, THE
★★★

DIRECTOR: Paul Sylbert

CAST: Richard Benjamin, Cloris Leachman, Chill Wills, Susan Tyrrell, Jean Allison, Suzanne Charny, Ivor Francis, Jack Bernard, Susan Kussman, Peter Hobbs

Black comedy about how a day-dreaming college professor (Richard Benjamin) deals with his mortality during the Cuban missile crisis. The week-long living spree he goes on over the fear that it might be his last has some hilarious consequences, but the screenplay is not handled very well despite the excellent cast. Rated PG for profanity and sex.

1971   94 minutes

STEAMBOAT BILL JR.
★★★★½

DIRECTOR: Charles F. Reisner

CAST: Buster Keaton, Ernest Torrence, Marion Byron, Tom Lewis, Tom McGuire

Buster Keaton is at his comedic-genius best in this delightful silent film as an accident-prone college student who is forced to take over his father's old Mississippi steamboat. The climax features spectacular stunts by Keaton. It is truly something to behold—and laugh with.

1928   B & W   71 minutes

STEELYARD BLUES
★★★½

DIRECTOR: Alan Meyerson

CAST: Jane Fonda, Donald Sutherland, Peter Boyle, Alan Myerson, Gary Goodrow

This is a quirky little film about a group of social misfits who band together to help one of their own against his government-employed brother. Jane Fonda, Donald Sutherland, and Peter Boyle seem to have fun playing the misfits. This movie has its ups and downs, with Boyle's imitation of Marlon Brando a highlight. Rated PG for language.

1973   93 minutes

STILL SMOKIN

DIRECTOR: Thomas Chong

CAST: Cheech and Chong, Hansman In't Veld, Carol Van Herwijnen

Richard "Cheech" Marin and Thomas Chong, who also directed, hit rock bottom with this humorless shambles about a film festival in Amsterdam, Holland. It seems to indicate Cheech and Chong's disrespect for their audience. Rated R for nudity and scatological humor.

1983   91 minutes

STIR CRAZY
★★★½

DIRECTOR: Sidney Poitier

CAST: Richard Pryor, Gene Wilder, Georg Stanford Brown, JoBeth Williams

Richard Pryor and Gene Wilder work something close to a miracle in this comedy, making something out of nothing or, at least, close to nothing. It's a simple-minded spoof of crime and prison movies with, of all things, a little *Urban Cowboy* thrown in. You've seen it all before, but you have so much fun watching the stars, you don't mind. You're too busy laughing. Rated R.

1980   111 minutes

STOLEN KISSES
★★★★★

DIRECTOR: François Truffaut
CAST: Jean-Pierre Leaud, Delphine Seyrig, Michel Lonsdale, Claude Jade, Harry Max, Daniel Ceccaldi

This is François Truffaut's third film in the continuing story about Antoine Doinel (Jean-Pierre Leaud) which began with *400 Blows*. Like the other films in the series, this work resembles Truffaut's autobiography as he romantically captures the awkwardness of Doinel and his encounters with women. This delightful comedy is often considered one of Truffaut's best movies.

1968   90 minutes

STORM IN A TEACUP
★★★

DIRECTOR: Victor Saville, Ian Dalrymple
CAST: Vivien Leigh, Rex Harrison, Cecil Parker, Sara Allgood

The refusal of an old lady to pay for a dog license touches off this amusing farrago on love, politics, and life. Rex Harrison is, of course, smashing. The dialogue is the thing.

1937   B & W   87 minutes

STRANGE BREW
★★★½

DIRECTOR: Dave Thomas, Rick Moranis
CAST: Rick Moranis, Dave Thomas, Max von Sydow, Paul Dooley, Lynne Griffin

Okay, all you hosers and hoseheads, here come those SCTV superstars from the Great White North, Bob and Doug McKenzie (Rick Moranis and Dave Thomas) in their first feature film. Beauty, eh? A mad scientist employed by a brewery controls a group of mental patients by feeding them beer laced with a mind-controlling drug. Rated PG.

1983   90 minutes

STRANGER THAN PARADISE
★★★★½

DIRECTOR: Jim Jarmusch
CAST: John Lurie, Richard Edson, Eszter Balint

In this superb independently made comedy, three oddball characters go on a spontaneous road trip through the United States, where they encounter boredom, routine problems, bad luck, and outrageous good fortune. The film, which won acclaim at the Cannes and New York film festivals, plays a lot like a Woody Allen comedy. It's a silly film for smart people—and marvelously entertaining because of it. Rated R for profanity.

1985   B & W   90 minutes

STRIKE UP THE BAND
★★★

DIRECTOR: Busby Berkeley
CAST: Mickey Rooney, Judy Garland, June Preisser, Paul Whiteman

This encore to *Babes in Arms* has ever-exuberant Mickey Rooney leading a high-school band that would shade Glenn Miller's going for the gold in a nation wide radio contest hosted by Paul Whiteman. Second banana Judy Garland sings, "Come on, kids, let's put on a show" in a different setting.

1940   B & W 120 minutes

STRIPES
★★★★

DIRECTOR: Ivan Reitman
CAST: Bill Murray, Harold Ramis, John Candy, Warren Oates, P. J. Soles, Sean Young, John Larroquette

It's laughs aplenty when "Saturday Night Live" graduate Bill Murray enlists in the army. But hey, as Murray might say, after a guy loses his job, his car, and his girl all in the same day, what else is he supposed to do? Thanks to Murray, Harold Ramis, and John Candy, the U.S. Army may never be the same—or at least our perception of it. The late Warren Oates also is in top form as the boys' no-nonsense sergeant. Rated R.

1981   105 minutes

STROKER ACE
★★★

DIRECTOR: Hal Needham
CAST: Burt Reynolds, Ned Beatty, Jim Nabors, Loni Anderson, Parker Stevenson

Film critics all over the country jumped on this Burt Reynolds's latest car-crash-and-cornpone comedy with both feet. That doesn't seem quite fair, so we'll only use one foot. Besides, it's not all that bad. About an egotistical, woman-chasing race-car driver (Reynolds, of course) who gets himself tangled up with a nasty fast-food chain owner (Ned Beatty), it's the same old predictable nonsense. Yet it's certain to please the audience it was intended for, and, after all, isn't that what movies are all about? Rated PG for sexual innuendo and violence.

1983   96 minutes

SUMMER RENTAL
★★½

DIRECTOR: Carl Reiner
CAST: John Candy, Richard Crenna, Karen Austin, Rip Torn, Kerri Green, Joey Lawrence, Aubrey Jene

John Candy is watchable in his first film as star. Unfortunately, the film itself does not live up to his talents. It starts off well enough—with air traffic controller Candy exhibiting the kind of stress that causes his superiors to suggest a vacation—but after a fairly funny first hour, it sinks into the mire of plot resolution as our hero decides to take up sailing and take on snobbish Richard Crenna. After Candy nooks up with sailing expert Rip Torn, the film rarely provides a chuckle. Rated PG for profanity.

1985   88 minutes

SUNSHINE BOYS, THE
★★★★

DIRECTOR: Herbert Ross
CAST: Walter Matthau, Richard Benjamin, George Burns, Lee Meredith, Carol Arthur, Howard Hesseman, Ron Rifkin

The Sunshine Boys tells the story of two feuding ex–vaudeville stars who make a TV special. Walter Matthau, Richard Benjamin, and (especially) George Burns give memorable performances. Director Herbert Ross (*Play It Again Sam*) turns this adaptation of the successful Broadway play by Neil Simon into a celluloid winner. Rated PG.

1975   111 minutes

SURE THING, THE
★★★½

DIRECTOR: Rob Reiner
CAST: John Cusack, Daphne Zuniga, Anthony Edwards, Boyd Gaines, Lisa Jane Persky

This enjoyable romantic comedy, about two college freshmen who discover themselves and each other through a series of misadventures on the road, is more or less director Rob Reiner's updating of Frank Capra's *It Happened*

One Night. John Cusack and Daphne Zuniga star as the unlikely protagonists. Rated PG-13 for profanity and suggested sex.

1985   100 minutes

SURVIVORS, THE
★★★½

DIRECTOR: Michael Ritchie
CAST: Robin Williams, Walter Matthau, Jerry Reed, James Wainright, Kristen Vigard

This is an often funny movie about a goofy "survivalist" (Robin Williams), who is "adopted" by a service station owner (Walter Matthau) and pursued by a friendly but determined hit man (Jerry Reed). Generally a black comedy, this movie features a variety of comedic styles, and they all work. Rated R for vulgar language and violence.

1983   102 minutes

SWEATER GIRLS
★

DIRECTOR: Don Jones
CAST: Harry Moses, Meegan King, Noelle North, Kate Sarchet, Michael Goodron, Charlene Tilton

One of the silliest of the teen sexcapade movies, this concerns a club called "Sweater Girls' that Meegan King and Noelle North decide to form because they are fed up with their drinking, pawing boyfriends. Charlene Tilton, who is featured on the box, does appear in a sweater in the final five minutes of the film. We give it a D, but not for cup size. Rated R for sex and language.

1984   84 minutes

SWEET LIBERTY
★★★★

DIRECTOR: Alan Alda
CAST: Alan Alda, Michael Caine, Michelle Pfeiffer, Bob Hoskins, Lise Hilboldt, Lillian Gish, Saul Rubinek, Lois Chiles, Linda Thorson

Writer-director-star Alan Alda strikes again, this time with the story of a small-town historian (Alda) whose prize-winning saga of the Revolutionary War is optioned by Hollywood and turned into a movie. When the film crew descends on Alda's hometown for location shooting, predictable chaos erupts. Star Elliot James (Michael Caine, in a droll portrayal) struggles to have his way with all the local women, including the historian's girlfriend, played by Lise Hilboldt. Alda, meanwhile, is concerned that his scholarly tome has been turned into mass-market junk food by a young turk director (Saul Rubinek) with three ingredients for movie success: characters must 1. defy authority, 2. destroy property, and 3. remove their clothes. Alda's attempts, with screenwriter Stanley Gould (the always excellent Bob Hoskins), to retain some of his book's substance makes up the bulk of this quite entertaining picture. Rated PG for mild sexual situations.

1986   107 minutes

SWINGIN' SUMMER, A
★

DIRECTOR: Robert Sparr
CAST: Raquel Welch, James Stacy, William A. Wellman Jr., Quinn O'Hara, Martin West

This is one of those swingin' sixties flicks where three swingin' teens move to a swingin' summer resort for a swingin' vacation. They start up their own swingin' dance concert schedule and book big-names act like Gary and the Playboys, the Rip Tides, and the Righteous Brothers. Raquel Welch debuts here and also sings. It's good for a few laughs.

1965 82 minutes

SWISS MISS
★★★

DIRECTOR: John Blystone

CAST: Stan Laurel, Oliver Hardy, Della Lind, Walter Woolf King, Eric Blore, Adia Kuznetzof

Here we have Stan Laurel and Oliver Hardy in the Swiss Alps. A weak and uneven script is overcome by the stars, who seize several opportunities for brilliant comedy. For the most part, however, the film is mediocre.

1938 B & W 72 minutes

TAKE DOWN
★★½

DIRECTOR: Keith Merrill

CAST: Edward Herrmann, Kathleen Lloyd, Lorenzo Lamas, Maureen McCormick, Kevin Hooks, Stephen Furst

Earnest comedy-drama set in the arena of high school wrestling. It centers on two initially reluctant participants: an intellectual teacher-turned-coach and a fiery student. The movie has enough heart to carry it to victory. Rated PG.

1978 107 minutes

TAKE THE MONEY AND RUN
★★★★

DIRECTOR: Woody Allen

CAST: Woody Allen, Janet Margolin, Marcel Hillaire

Woody Allen's first original feature is still a laugh-filled delight as the star-director plays an inept criminal in a story told in pseudo-documentary-style (à la *Zelig*). It's hilarious. Rated PG.

1969 85 minutes

TAKE THIS JOB AND SHOVE IT
★★★½

DIRECTOR: Gus Trikonis

CAST: Robert Hays, Art Carney, Barbara Hershey, Martin Mull, Eddie Albert

Robert Hays (*Airplane!*) stars as a rising corporate executive who returns, after a ten-year absence, to his hometown to take charge of a brewery where he once worked, and winds up organizing a revolt among his fellow employees. The serious side of this contemporary comedy-drama is shallow, but it isn't meant to be a landmark statement concerning labor strife or moral dilemmas. It's out to raise one's spirits, and it does just that. Rated PG.

1981 100 minutes

TALL BLOND MAN WITH ONE BLACK SHOE, THE
★★★★

DIRECTOR: Yves Robert

CAST: Pierre Richard, Bernard Blier, Mireille Darc

If you're looking for an entertaining, easy-to-watch comedy, this is one of the best. Pierre Richard plays the bumbling blond man with hilarious perfection, especially when it comes to physical comedy. The story involves spies, murder, a mysterious sexy woman, and plenty of action. The real fun comes in watching Richard's reactions to it all. Highly recommended, but try to see the original version, with subtitles, not the dubbed version. Rated PG.

1972 90 minutes

TAMING OF THE SHREW, THE
★★★★½
DIRECTOR: Franco Zeffirelli
CAST: Richard Burton, Elizabeth Taylor, Cyril Cusack, Michael York

As in his *Romeo and Juliet* (1968), director Franco Zeffirelli shows his unique knack for bringing Shakespeare vividly to life. This is a beautifully mounted comedy of the battle of the sexes. Petruchio (Richard Burton), a spirited minor nobleman of the Italian Renaissance, pits his wits against the man-hating Kate (Elizabeth Taylor) in order to win her hand. The zest with which this famous play is transferred to the screen can be enjoyed even by those who feel intimidated by Shakespeare.

1966   126 minutes

TEACHER'S PET
★★★
DIRECTOR: George Seaton
CAST: Clark Gable, Doris Day, Gig Young, Mamie Van Doren, Nick Adams, Jack Albertson, Marion Ross

Winsome journalism instructor Doris Day fascinates and charms hardboiled city editor Clark Gable in this near plotless but most diverting comedy of incidents. The two are terrific, but Gig Young, as the teacher's erudite but liquor-logged boyfriend, is the one to watch. His near picture-stealing performance earned him an Academy Award nomination. Slug this: Clever, cute, coy film fun.

1958   B & W 120 minutes

TEACHERS
★★
DIRECTOR: Arthur Hiller
CAST: Nick Nolte, JoBeth Williams, Judd Hirsch, Richard Mulligan, Ralph Macchio

This satirical look at a contemporary urban high-school flunks as a film. Students will hate it because it's not serious enough; teachers will hate it because it's just terrible. It promised to "do for high school what *Network* did for television." Actually, it's no more interesting than a dull day in high school. Rated R for sexual innuendo, violence, and profanity.

1984   106 minutes

10
★★★½
DIRECTOR: Blake Edwards
CAST: Bo Derek, Dudley Moore, Julie Andrews, Robert Webber, Dee Wallace

Ravel's "Bolero" enjoyed a renewed popularity, and Bo Derek rocketed to stardom because of this uneven but generally entertaining sex comedy, directed by Blake Edwards (*The Pink Panther*). Most of the film's funny moments come from the deftly timed physical antics of Dudley Moore, who plays a just-turned-40 songwriter who at long last meets the girl (Bo Derek) of his dreams—on her wedding day. Rated R.

1979   122 minutes

10 FROM YOUR SHOW OF SHOWS
★★★★
DIRECTOR: Max Liebman
CAST: Sid Caesar, Imogene Coca, Carl Reiner, Howard Morris, Louis Nye

Ten skits from the early 1950s television program that set the pace for all variety shows. Granted, the style is dated and far from subtle, but as a joyful look at television's formative years, it can't be beat. Unrated.

1973   B & W 92 minutes

TENDRES COUSINES
★★

DIRECTOR: David Hamilton
CAST: Thierry Tevini, Anja Shute

Okay soft-core sex comedy about the amorous adventures of two pubescent cousins. Directed by David Hamilton (*Bilitis*), this film has the problems innate in most movies of this type: It lacks the purpose and power of serious films and the explicit scenes of their hard-core cousins. In French, with English subtitles. Rated R.

1980   90 minutes

THAT SINKING FEELING
★★★★

DIRECTOR: Bill Forsyth
CAST: Robert Buchanan, Billy Greenlees, John Hughes

This is the first film by Scottish filmmaker Bill Forsyth (*Local Hero*; *Gregory's Girl*), and with it you can easily see the promise the young talent has proved in his later works. Shot on a shoestring budget, utilizing many of the Glasgow youths seen in *Gregory's Girl*, it's a delightful tale of a group of young men who decide to take their unemployment situation in hand in a most unusual way. Suffice it to say it has something to do with stainless-steel sinks. No MPAA rating, no objectionable material.

1979   82 minutes

THAT TOUCH OF MINK
★★★½

DIRECTOR: Delbert Mann
CAST: Doris Day, Cary Grant, Gig Young, Audrey Meadows, John Astin

This 1962 romantic comedy is enjoyable, but only as escapist fare. Doris Day stars as an unemployed girl pursued by a wealthy businessman (Cary Grant).

1962   99 minutes

THERE'S A GIRL IN MY SOUP
★★½

DIRECTOR: Roy Boulting
CAST: Peter Sellers, Goldie Hawn, Diana Dors, Tony Britton

Goldie Hawn hadn't completely shed her "Laugh-In" image when this British sex farce came out, and it didn't do her career any good. Quite a letdown, after her Oscar-winning performance in *Cactus Flower*. Peter Sellers is a middle-aged boob who falls in lust with flower-child Hawn. Very few laughs; would have been far better if made in France . . . they understand the genre much better. A low point for all concerned. Rated R.

1970   95 minutes

THEY ALL LAUGHED
★★★★

DIRECTOR: Peter Bogdanovich
CAST: Audrey Hepburn, Ben Gazzara, John Ritter, Dorothy Stratten

This is director Peter Bogdanovich at his best. A very offbeat comedy that looks at four New York private eyes' adventures and love lives. Final film of ex–Playboy bunny Dorothy Stratten. Worth a look. Rated PG.

1981   115 minutes

THEY CALL ME BRUCE?
★★

DIRECTOR: Elliot Hong
CAST: Johnny Yune, Ralph Mauro, Margaux Hemingway, Pam Huntington

In this unsophisticated kung-fu comedy, Johnny Yune portrays an Asian immigrant who, because of his "resemblance" to Bruce Lee and an accidental exhibition of craziness (misinterpreted as martial arts expertise), gets a reputation as a mean man with fists and feet. But it is Ralph Mauro, playing Bruce's chauffeur, who steals the show. Margaux Hemingway appears in a supporting role. Rated PG.

1982   88 minutes

THEY GOT ME COVERED
★★½

DIRECTOR: David Butler
CAST: Bob Hope, Dorothy Lamour, Lenore Aubert, Otto Preminger, Eduardo Ciannelli, Marion Martin, Donald MacBride, Walter Catlett, Donald Meek, Philip Ahn

Typical Bob Hope vehicle of the 1940s is full of gals, gags, goofy situations, snappy dialogue, and one-line zingers, and boasts an incredible supporting cast of great character actors and actresses. Thin story about spy nonsense in Washington, D.C., is secondary to the zany antics of Paramount's ski-nosed comedian before he became an American institution by sheer longevity if nothing else. Not a comedy classic, but harmless fun and clever to boot. This is basically *the* Bob Hope movie, which he continued to make, with varying degrees of success, for the next twenty-five years.

1943   B & W   95 minutes

THIEF WHO CAME TO DINNER, THE
★★★

DIRECTOR: Bud Yorkin
CAST: Ryan O'Neal, Jacqueline Bisset, Warren Oates, Jill Clayburgh, Charles Cioffi, Ned Beatty

Silly stuff about Ryan O'Neal leading a double life: as a bookish computer programmer by day and a jewel thief by night. Jacqueline Bisset is, as always, highly watchable—as is the great character actor Warren Oates. The film's most

interesting performance comes from Jill Clayburgh in an early screen role. It's mindless fluff and inoffensive. Rated PG.

1973   102 minutes

THINGS ARE TOUGH ALL OVER
★

DIRECTOR: Tom Avildsen
CAST: Cheech and Chong, Rikki Marin, Rip Taylor

If cheap laughs are worthless, then so is this romp starring Cheech and Chong. Not that it isn't amusing— it has a number of funny moments—unfortunately, they're mostly from the toilet. This time around, Richard "Cheech" Marin and Tommy Chong play dual roles: as their usual spaced-out characters, plus two Arab brothers up to no good. But you've seen most of the comedy bits before, in the team's previous pictures. Rated R for profanity and scatological humor.

1982   92 minutes

30 FOOT BRIDE OF CANDY ROCK, THE
★★

DIRECTOR: Sidney Miller
CAST: Lou Costello, Dorothy Provine, Gale Gordon, Charles Lane, Doodles Weaver

A nebbish inventor turns his girlfriend into a giant. A mild comedy with a certain amount of charm, this was the last film made by Columbia's B-picture unit, and Lou Costello's only feature film after breaking up with Bud Abbott. Although he proved to be an effective dramatic actor in television work during his later years, here he plays his usual bumbling character. But it's difficult to laugh at the movie due to a lame script and

Costello's ill health. He died before the film was released.

1959   B & W   75 minutes

THIS IS SPINAL TAP
★★★★½

DIRECTOR: Rob Reiner
CAST: Michael McKean, Christopher Guest, Harry Shearer, Rob Reiner

This is one of the funniest movies ever made about rock 'n' roll. Not since Monty Python member Eric Idle's spoof of the Beatles (*The Rutles*) has there been such an irreverently humorous look at the world of pop music. Directed by Rob Reiner, son of Carl and a one-time regular (Meathead) on "All in the Family," this is a satire of rock documentaries that tells the story of Spinal Tap, an over-the-hill British heavy-metal rock group that's fast rocketing to the bottom of the charts. *This Is Spinal Tap* isn't consistently funny, but does it ever have its moments. Some of the song lyrics are hysterical, and the performances are perfect. In fact, the actors are so good some younger film-goers in San Francisco reportedly took them for the real thing. Rated R for profanity.

1984   82 minutes

THOSE MAGNIFICENT MEN IN THEIR FLYING MACHINES
★★★★

DIRECTOR: Ken Annakin
CAST: Terry-Thomas, Stuart Whitman, Sarah Miles, Gert Frobe

Here is some fun, just plain fun, for the family. An air race between London and Paris in the early days of flight is this comedy's centerpiece. Around it hang an enjoyable number of rib-tickling vignettes. A large international cast each get their chance to shine as the contest's zany participants. Terry-Thomas stands out as the hapless villain. He reminds one of the coyote in the Road Runner cartoons. His ingenious evil schemes continually go wrong, with hilarious results.

1965   132 minutes

THOUSAND CLOWNS, A
★★★★

DIRECTOR: Fred Coe
CAST: Jason Robards, Barry Gordon, Barbara Harris, Martin Balsam, Gene Saks, William Daniels

Famous Broadway play comes to the screen with memorable performaces by all the principals and standout jobs by Jason Robards as a talented nonconformist and Barry Gordon as his precocious ward, who struggle against welfare bureaucracy in order to stay together. Very funny in spots and equally poignant at others, this well-written story about the loss of innocence and coming of age of the main characters has something to say to everyone about losing sight of early goals and conforming to an uncaring world. Gene Saks as the neurotic Chuckles the Chipmunk is just great, as are Martin Balsam as Robards's successful brother and William Daniels as the unyielding welfare investigator who realizes he is not "one of the warm ones." Barbara Harris (in the role Sandy Dennis originated on-stage) is the weakest of the characters, but her role is central to the success of the story, so it's a necessary evil. Good on many levels.

1965   B & W   118 minutes

THREE MEN AND A CRADLE
★★★★

DIRECTOR: Coline Serreau

CAST: Roland Giraud, Michel Boujenah, André Dussolier, Philipe Leroy Beulieu, Gwen-
doline Mourlet

In this sweet-natured character
study from France, three high-living bachelors become the guardi-
ans of a baby girl through a series
of misunderstandings. In addition
to turning their lifestyles inside out,
she forces them to confront their
values—with heartwarming results. Meanwhile, a favor for a
friend puts the trio at madcap odds
with crooks and cops. Rated PG
for profanity and nudity. In French
with English subtitles.

1985   105 minutes

THREE STOOGES, THE (VOLUMES 1–10)
★★★★

DIRECTOR: Various Directors
CAST: Moe Howard, Curly (Jerry)
Howard, Larry Fine

The Three Stooges made 190 two-
reel short subjects between 1934
and 1959, making them the most
prolific comedy team of all time.
For over fifty years, people have
either loved them or hated them.
Those in the latter category should,
of course, avoid these tapes. But
if you are a fan, you'll find these
collections the answer to a knuck-
lehead's dream. Each cassette features three shorts of impeccable
quality, transferred from brand-
new, complete 35-mm prints. After
years of scratchy, poorly edited
television prints, it's like seeing
them for the first time. All of the
films are from the classic "Curly"
period, when the team was at the
peak of its energy and originality.
One note of caution: These shorts
have been completely restored.
Since they were made in less en-
lightened times, they occasionally

display some unfortunate examples of racist comedy.

1934-45   B & W   60 minutes

TILL MARRIAGE DO US PART
★★★

DIRECTOR: Luigi Comencini
CAST: Laura Antonelli

Although a slight Italian sex comedy, its star, Laura Antonelli, is as
delicious as ever. It's a treat for
her fans only. Rated R.

1974   97 minutes

TILT
🐢

DIRECTOR: Rudy Durand
CAST: Brooke Shields, Ken Mar-
shall, Charles Durning,
Geoffrey Lewis

Brooke Shields's third movie (after
Alice Sweet Alice and Pretty Baby)
is a mess. Co-starring Ken Marshall (Krull), Charles Durning, and
Geoffrey Lewis, this film (written
and directed by Rudy Durand) is
pitiful at best and unbearable at
worst. The dialogue is laughable,
and the performances are generally putrid. Rated PG.

1978   104 minutes

TO BE OR NOT TO BE (ORIGINAL)
★★★★½

DIRECTOR: Ernst Lubitsch
CAST: Carole Lombard, Jack Benny,
Robert Stack

After gaining early stardom in
Twentieth Century, Carole Lombard returned to another black
comedy and another role as an
oddball theater performer, for the
last film of her life. One of Hollywood's premiere comedy directors, Ernst Lubitsch, coached
excellent performances from Carole Lombard and co-star Jack
Benny, in this hilarious farce about

a theater couple who outwit the Nazis.

1942   B & W   99 minutes

TO BE OR NOT TO BE (REMAKE)
★★★★

DIRECTOR: Alan Johnson
CAST: Mel Brooks, Anne Bancroft, Charles Durning, Tim Matheson

In this hilarious remake of the Jack Benny–Carole Lombard classic from 1942, Mel Brooks and Anne Bancroft are Polish actors who foil the Nazis at the outbreak of World War II. Charles Durning's Gestapo officer alone is worth the price of the rental of this delightful comedy-melodrama. It's producer-star Brooks's best film since *Young Frankenstein* and was directed by Alan Johnson, who choreographed *Springtime for Hitler* for Brooks's first film, *The Producers*. Rated PG, the film has no objectionable material.

1983   108 minutes

TOM JONES
★★★★★

DIRECTOR: Tony Richardson
CAST: Albert Finney, Susannah York, Hugh Griffith, Edith Evans

Rarely has a movie captured the spirit and flavor of its times or the novel on which it was based. This is a rambunctious, witty, and often bawdy tale of a youth's misadventures in eighteenth-century England. Albert Finney is a perfect rascal as Tom. We joyously follow him through all levels of British society as he tries to make his fortune and win the lovely Sophie (Susannah York). The entire cast is brilliant.

1963   129 minutes

TOOTSIE
★★★★★

DIRECTOR: Sydney Pollack
CAST: Dustin Hoffman, Bill Murray, Jessica Lange, Teri Garr, Dabney Coleman, Sydney Pollack

Dustin Hoffman is Michael Dorsey, an out-of-work actor who disguises himself as a woman—Dorothy Michaels—to get a job and becomes a big star on a popular television soap opera. An absolute delight, *Tootsie* is hilarious, touching, and marvelously acted. Rated PG for adult content.

1982   119 minutes

TO PARIS WITH LOVE
★★½

DIRECTOR: Robert Hamer
CAST: Alec Guinness, Odile Versois, Austin Trevor, Vernon Gray

Alec Guinness stands out like a pumpkin in a pea patch in this average comedy about a rich and indulgent father who takes his son to gay Paree to learn the facts of life. It's fun.

1955   78 minutes

TOP SECRET
★★½

DIRECTOR: Jim Abrahams, David Zucker, Jerry Zucker
CAST: Omar Sharif, Peter Cushing, Val Kilmer

By the makers of *Airplane!*, this film makes up for its flimsy plot with one gag after another. Nick Rivers (Val Kilmer) is the main character who, as a rock 'n' roll star, visits East Germany. There he falls in love with Hilary and becomes involved in the plot to free her scientist father. The soundtrack features lots of lively old Beach Boys and Elvis Presley tunes. Omar Sharif makes a cameo appearance as a much-abused spy. Rated PG for some profanity and sexually oriented gags.

1984   90 minutes

TOPPER
★★★★
DIRECTOR: Norman Z. McLeod
CAST: Cary Grant, Constance Bennett, Roland Young, Billie Burke

This is the original feature of what became a delightful fantasy movie series and television series. Cary Grant and Constance Bennett are the Kirbys, a duo of social high livers who, due to an unfortunate auto accident, become ghosts. They now want to transfer their spirit of living the good life to a rather stodgy banker, the fellow they are now haunting, one Cosmo Topper (Roland Young). Good fun all around.

1937   B & W   97 minutes

TOPPER RETURNS
★★★
DIRECTOR: Roy Del Ruth
CAST: Roland Young, Joan Blondell, Eddie Anderson, Carole Landis, Dennis O'Keefe, H. B. Warner

Cary Grant and Constance Bennett have gone on to their heavenly rewards, but Roland Young, as Cosmo Topper, is still seeing ghosts. This time the spooky personage is that of Joan Blondell, who helps our hero solve a murder, in this entertaining comedy.

1941   B & W   87 minutes

TOPPER TAKES A TRIP
★★½
DIRECTOR: Norman Z. McLeod

CAST: Constance Bennett, Roland Young, Billie Burke, Alan Mowbray, Franklin Pangborn, Cary Grant (in flashback)

Third and last film in the original series finds Cosmo and Henrietta Topper on the French Riviera accompanied by their ghostly friend Marion Kirby, portrayed by the star of the original film, Constance Bennett. Topper and Marion pool forces to stop Mrs. Topper from being victimized by a smooth-talking confidence man (Alan Mowbray), and overcome all obstacles with the special effects and sleight of hand that highlight the series. Marion's new companion is a pet dog, but Cary Grant makes a brief appearance in a flashback sequence. Harmless fun.

1939   B & W   85 minutes

TOPSY TURVY
★★
DIRECTOR: Edward Fleming
CAST: Lisbet Dahl, Ebbe Rode, Axel Strobye, Elin Reimer, Lars Bom, Nonny Sand, Thomas Alling

A conservative young man finds his world turned topsy-turvy when a swinging neighbor girl takes him on vacation in this European sex comedy, dubbed into English. The dubbing is fair to good. The humor tends to the European, and some may not find it to their liking. The main subject of the humor is sex. and at times it is very funny. the locations are beautiful, but the acting is uneven. Those who enjoy sex comedies will probably like this film.

1984   90 minutes

TOUCH OF CLASS, A
★★★★★
DIRECTOR: Melvin Frank

CAST: George Segal, Glenda Jackson, Paul Sorvino, Hildegard Neil

In one of the best romantic comedies of recent years, George Segal and Glenda Jackson are marvelously paired as a sometimes loving—sometimes bickering—couple who struggle through an extramarital affair. They begin their oddball romance when he runs over one of her children while chasing a fly ball in a baseball game. Fine acting and witty dialogue carry this film from this auspicious beginning. Rated PG.

1972   105 minutes

TOY, THE
★★

DIRECTOR: Richard Donner
CAST: Richard Pryor, Jackie Gleason, Scott Schwartz, Ned Beatty

You would think any comedy that combines the talents of Richard Pryor and Jackie Gleason would have to be exceptionally good, to say nothing of funny. But that's simply not true of this movie, about a spoiled rich kid (Scott Schwartz) whose father (Gleason) allows him to buy the ultimate toy (Pryor). Not that it isn't watchable. How could any picture with Pryor be otherwise? Rated PG for profanity and adult themes.

1982   99 minutes

TRADING PLACES
★★★★

DIRECTOR: John Landis
CAST: Dan Aykroyd, Eddie Murphy, Ralph Bellamy, Don Ameche, Jamie Lee Curtis

Here's an uproarious comedy about what happens when uptight Philadelphia broker (Dan Aykroyd) and dynamic black street hustler (Eddie Murphy) change places. *Trading Places* was directed by John Landis (*Animal House*; *The Blues Brothers*), who is undoubtedly the best director of comedies today. His sense of timing is exquisite—he knows how to milk every bit of mirth out of any situation. The stars share his expertise, and the result is a treat for those who love to laugh. Rated R for nudity and profanity.

1983   117 minutes

TRAIL OF THE PINK PANTHER, THE
★★½

DIRECTOR: Blake Edwards
CAST: Peter Sellers, David Niven, Herbert Lom, Capucine, Robert Wagner

Through the magic of editing, the late Peter Sellers "stars" as the bumbling Inspector Clouseau, in this late entry in the comedy series. Writer-director Blake Edwards uses outtakes of Sellers from previous films and combines them with new footage featuring David Niven, Herbert Lom, and Capucine. The results are disappointing. After Edwards runs out of never-before-seen Sellers scenes, the movie goes decidedly downhill. He should have left well enough alone. Rated PG for nudity and scatological humor.

1982   97 minutes

TRANSYLVANIA 6-5000
★★

DIRECTOR: Rudy DeLuca
CAST: Jeff Goldblum, Ed Begley Jr., Joseph Bologna, Carol Kane, Jeffrey Jones, John Byner, Michael Richards, Geena Davis, Teresa Ganzel, Norman Fell

Sometimes amusing but ultimately silly horror spoof focusing on an inept pair of tabloid reporters (Jeff Goldblum and Ed Begley Jr.) sent to Transylvania to investigate the possible resurgence of the Frankenstein Monster, and soon finding themselves up to their idiotic necks in trouble. The large cast does its best with what may generously be referred to as weak material, which the director hoped to compensate for by having everyone scream their lines and run around frantically throughout most of the film. Still, there are a few bright spots, most notably Michael Richards (of TV's *Fridays*) as a loosely wound butler, and a video transfer that ranks with the best. Rated PG for mild profanity.

1985   93 minutes

TRENCHCOAT
★½

DIRECTOR: Michael Tuchner
CAST: Margot Kidder, Robert Hays, Daniel Faraldo

No one is what he appears to be in this inept spoof of the detective genre. Margot Kidder plays Mickey Raymond, a would-be writer of hard-boiled detective fiction who is ensnared in a scheme that involves drugs (perhaps), stolen plutonium (most likely), and murder (definitely). While there are moments that will evoke some chuckles, *Trenchcoat* rarely hits the mark as being the spontaneous, unpredictable madcap chase film it was meant to be. Rated PG.

1983   91 minutes

TROUBLE IN THE GLEN
★★

DIRECTOR: Herbert Wilcox
CAST: Orson Welles, Margaret Lockwood, Victor McLaglen, Forrest Tucker

A white-haired, cigar-chomping Orson Welles in Scots kilts is far-fetched, to say the least. The film turns on a feud over a closed road. What was projected as a Highland comedy is thoroughly scotched by poor pacing and a script that misses the mark. Deep-dyed Welles fans will like it.

1953   91 minutes

TROUBLE WITH ANGELS, THE
★★★

DIRECTOR: Ida Lupino
CAST: Rosalind Russell, Hayley Mills, June Harding

Rosalind Russell stars as the Mother Superior at the St. Francis Academy for Girls. Her serenity and the educational pursuits of the institution are coming apart at the seams due to the pranks of two rambunctious teenagers, Hayley Mills and June Harding. This comedy's humor is uninspired, but the warmth and humanity of the entire production make it worthwhile family viewing.

1966   112 minutes

TROUBLE WITH HARRY, THE
★★★★

DIRECTOR: Alfred Hitchcock
CAST: John Forsythe, Edmund Gwenn, Shirley MacLaine, Mildred Natwick, Jerry Mathers

Shirley MacLaine made her film debut in this wickedly funny black comedy, directed by Alfred Hitchcock. This is the last of long-unseen screen works by the master of suspense to be re-released, and the most unusual, because the accent is on humor instead of tension-filled drama. In it, a murdered man causes no end of problems for his neighbors in a peaceful New England community. Rated PG when it was rereleased.

1955   100 minutes

TUNNELVISION
★★½

DIRECTOR: Neal Israel, Brad Swirnoff

CAST: Chevy Chase, Howard Hesseman, Betty Thomas, Laraine Newman

Here is a lightweight spoof of television. Sometimes it is funny, and other times it is just gross. The "stars," like Chevy Chase, have small bits, and it is not at all what one would expect from the billing. Still, there are some funny moments. *Tunnelvision* is like *The Groove Tube* in most respects, the good equally in proportion to the bad. Rated R.

1976 67 minutes

TURTLE DIARY
★★★★½

DIRECTOR: John Irvin

CAST: Glenda Jackson, Ben Kingsley, Richard Johnson, Michael Gambon, Rosemary Leach, Eleanor Bron, Harriet Walker, Jeroen Krabbe

Glenda Jackson and Ben Kingsley are absolutely delightful in this deliciously offbeat bit of British whimsy about urban life—of people living side by side but rarely touching. Jackson is Neaera Duncan, and author of children's books, while Kingsley is William Snow, a bookstore assistant. Both share an obsession for turtles and devise a plan to kidnap the shelled creatures, who are imprisoned in a nearby zoo, and release them into their natural habitat. The result is a thinking person's comedy that should please all but the *Porky's* and *Police Academy* crowd. Rated PG for nudity.

1986 97 minutes

TUTTLES OF TAHITI, THE
★★★

DIRECTOR: Charles Vidor

CAST: Charles Laughton, Jon Hall, Peggy Drake, Mala, Florence Bates, Alma Ross, Victor Francen, Curt Bois, Gene Reynolds

Captain Bligh goes native in this comedy of arch indolence and planned sloth in beautiful, bountiful Tahiti. Impoverished Charles Laughton and florence Bates are rivals whose son Jon Hall and Daughter Peggy Drake fall in love. A good-natured, congenial film of leisure life in which worries and woes include cockfights and a lack of gasoline.

1942 B & W 91 minutes

TWELVE CHAIRS, THE
★★★

DIRECTOR: Mel Brooks

CAST: Mel Brooks, Dom De Luise, Frank Langella, Ron Moody

Based on a Russian comedy-fable about an impoverished nobleman seeking jewels secreted in one of a dozen fancy dining room chairs. Ron Moody is the anguished Russian, Dom De Luise his chief rival in the hunt. Mel Brooks's direction keeps things moving with laughs. Rated G.

1970 94 minutes

TWO OF A KIND
★★

DIRECTOR: John Herzfeld

CAST: John Travolta, Olivia Newton-John, Charles Durning

John Travolta and Olivia Newton-John, who first teamed on screen in the box-office smash *Grease*, are reunited in this 1980s-style screwball comedy, which mixes clever ideas with incredibly stupid ones. The result is a movie the young viewers it was made for probably won't rave about, but neither will they be too disappointed. Others, however, should stay away. Rated PG for profanity and violence.

1983   87 minutes

UFORIA
★★★★

DIRECTOR: John Binder

CAST: Cindy Williams, Harry Dean Stanton, Fred Ward, Harry Carey Jr., Beverly Hope Atkinson, Robert Gray, Darrel Larson

Like *Repo Man* and *Stranger Than Paradise*, this low-budget American film deserved better treatment than the limited theatrical release it was given. Cindy Williams (TV's *Laverne and Shirley*) is hilarious as a born-again Christian who believes that salvation will come to the earth in the form of a flying saucer. Fred Ward (*The Right Stuff*, *Remo Williams*) is equally humorous as a truckdriving Waylon Jennings look-alike. Harry Dean Staton plays a crooked evangelist who exploits the Jesus-in-a-spaceship concept for every penny he can get. Rated PG for profanity.

1984   100 minutes

UNDER THE RAINBOW
★★½

DIRECTOR: Steve Rash

CAST: Chevy Chase, Carrie Fisher, Eve Arden, Joseph Maher

While this comedy is not quite jam-packed with laughs, it certainly keeps your interest. Set in 1938, the improbable story centers around the making of *The Wizard of Oz*, assassination attempts on a duke and duchess, the nefarious doings of Nazi and Japanese spies prior to World War II, and the li-

fespan of a dog named Streudel. *Rainbow* is fun—though not always in the best of taste (some of the jokes border on crude). Director Steve Rash (*The Buddy Holly Story*) keeps things popping at a good rate. Rated PG because of slight nudity and suggestive dialogue.

1981   98 minutes

UNDERGROUND ACES

DIRECTOR: Robert Butler

CAST: Dirk Benedict. Melanie Griffith, Rick Podell, Kario Salem, Robert Hegyes, Audrey Landers, Mimi Maynard, Frank Gorshin

In this stupid comedy à la *Car Wash*, a bunch of obnoxious big-city hotel parking attendants run amok. They don't spend much time parking cars, because that would be boring. So they do a lot of wild and crazy things like wreck the customers' vehicles, have sex, and poke fun at the hotel management. Rated PG for profanity and nudity.

1980   93 minutes

UNFAITHFULLY YOURS (ORIGINAL)
★★★

DIRECTOR: Preston Sturges

CAST: Rex Harrison, Linda Darnell, Kurt Kreuger, Barbara Lawrence, Rudy Vallee, Lionel Stander

Symphony conductor Rex Harrison suspects his wife of infidelity and contemplates several solutions to his "problem." This film follows all the prerequisites of screwball comedies—mistaken identities, misinterpreted remarks—but the humor seems forced and dated. Particularly tiresome are Harrison's endless fantasies, which seem to drag on forever. (The 1984 remake, whatever its other faults, used only one fantasy.) Harrison has fun as a sort of manic Henry Higgins, but his energy cannot sustain a film that runs about fifteen minutes too long. Unrated—family fare.

1948   B & W 105 minutes

UNFAITHFULLY YOURS (REMAKE)
★★★

DIRECTOR: Howard Zieff
CAST: Dudley Moore, Nastassja Kinski, Armand Assante, Albert Brooks

In this highly entertaining and often hilarious remake of Preston Sturges's 1948 comedy, Dudley Moore plays a symphony orchestra conductor who suspects his wife (Nastassja Kinski) of fooling around with a violinist (Armand Assante) and decides to get revenge. Rated PG for nudity and profanity.

1984   96 minutes

UP IN SMOKE
★★★★

DIRECTOR: Lou Adler
CAST: Cheech and Chong, Strother Martin, Stacy Keach, Edie Adams

This is Cheech and Chong's first, and best, film. Forget about any plot as Cheech and Chong go on the hunt for good weed, rock 'n' roll, and good times. Several truly hysterical moments, with Stacy Keach's spaced-out cop almost stealing the show. Rated R for language, nudity, and general rauchiness.

1978   87 minutes

UP THE ACADEMY
★½

DIRECTOR: Robert Downey

CAST: Ron Liebman, Wendell Brown, Ralph Macchio, Tom Citera, Tom Poston, Stacey Nelkin, Barbara Bach

This was *MAD* magazine's first and only attempt to emulate *National Lampoon*'s film success. Set in a strict military academy, the movie holds promise but is quickly done in by tasteless gags and gross overacting. Ron Liebman is the best thing in it. The film originally ran 96 minutes, but various people have been hacking it up over the years. Even *MAD* has disowned it. The only worthwhile element is the music score. Rated R for profanity and general disgustingness.

1980   88 minutes

UP THE CREEK
★★★

DIRECTOR: Robert Butler
CAST: Tim Matheson, Stephen Furst, Dan Monahan, John Hillerman, James B. Sikking

Two stars from *Animal House*, Tim Matheson ("Otter") and Stephen Furst ("Flounder"), are reunited in this mostly entertaining raft-race comedy. It doesn't beg you to laugh at it the way *Police Academy* does. Matheson is charismatic enough—in his own audacious way—to carry the film. Dan Monahan (*Porky's*), John Hillerman (of television's "Magnum, P.I."), and James Sikking ("Hill Street Blues") co-star. Rated R for nudity, profanity, suggested sex, scatological humor, and violence.

1984   95 minutes

UP THE SANDBOX
★

DIRECTOR: Irvin Kershner
CAST: Barbra Streisand, David Selby, Jane Hoffman

A weird, uneven comedy about a neglected housewife (Barbra

Streisand). Its fantasy sequences are among the strangest ever put on film. Rated R.

1972   97 minutes

UPTOWN SATURDAY NIGHT
★★★½

DIRECTOR: Sidney Poitier
CAST: Sidney Poitier, Bill Cosby, Harry Belafonte, Richard Pryor, Flip Wilson

Sidney Poitier (who also directed), Bill Cosby, Harry Belafonte, Richard Pryor, and Flip Wilson head an all-star cast in this enjoyable comedy about a couple of buddies (Poitier and Cosby) who get into all sorts of trouble during a night on the town. Rated PG.

1974   104 minutes

USED CARS
★★★★

DIRECTOR: Robert Zemeckis
CAST: Jack Warden, Kurt Russell, Frank McRae, Gerritt Graham, Deborah Harmon

This is a riotous account of two feuding used-car businesses. Jack Warden and Kurt Russell are both excellent in this overlooked comedy. Fine support is offered by Frank McRae, Gerritt Graham, and Deborah Harmon. Rated R for language, nudity, and some violence.

1980   111 minutes

UTILITIES
★★★½

DIRECTOR: Harvey Hart
CAST: Robert Hays, Brooke Adams, John Marley, James Blendick, Helen Burns, Benjamin Gordon

Despite some rather crude humor once in a while, this modest comedy has a lot of charm and the heart of a Frank Capra film. Robert Hays (the *Airplane* films) plays a fed-up social worker who turns vigilante against the public utility companies. Brooke Adams (*Days of Heaven, Almost You*) is a cop who is torn between her job as a peace officer and her feelings for Hays. Rated PG for profanity and sex.

1983   94 minutes

VACATION
🦃

DIRECTOR: Harold Ramis
CAST: Chevy Chase, Beverly D'Angelo, Anthony Michael Hall, Dana Barron, Christie Brinkley, John Candy

One of the unfunniest comedies ever made, *Vacation* contains one laugh. Count 'em...one. That's when Clark Griswold (Chevy Chase), who goes on a disastrous vacation with his wife, Ellen (Beverly D'Angelo), and kids, Rusty (Anthony Michael Hall) and Audrey (Dana Barron), falls asleep at the wheel and the family station wagon careens hilariously out of control. Otherwise, no laughs—only yawns. Rated R for nudity and profanity.

1983   98 minutes

VALLEY GIRL
★★★½

DIRECTOR: Martha Coolidge
CAST: Nicolas Cage, Deborah Foreman, Colleen Camp

The story of a romance between a San Francisco Valley girl and a Hollywood punker, *Valley Girl* claims the distinction of being one of the few teen movies directed by a woman: Martha Coolidge. And, perhaps for that reason, it's a little treasure; a funny, sexy, appealing story that makes fun of no one but contains something for nearly everyone. Rated R.

1983   95 minutes

VICTOR/VICTORIA
★★★★

DIRECTOR: Blake Edwards
CAST: Julie Andrews, James Garner, Robert Preston, Lesley Ann Warren

Director Blake Edwards takes us on a funny, off-the-wall romp through 1930s Paris. Julie Andrews plays a down-on-her-luck singer who poses as a gay Polish count to make ends meet. Rated PG because of adult situations.

1982   133 minutes

VIVA MAX!
★★★

DIRECTOR: Jerry Paris
CAST: Peter Ustinov, Jonathan Winters, Keenan Wynn, Pamela Tiffin

Skip credibility and enjoy. Peter Ustinov is a contemporary Mexican general who leads his men across the border to reclaim the Alamo as a tourist attraction. Jonathan Winters all but steals this romp, playing a bumbling, confused National Guard officer in the face of an audacious "enemy." Rated G.

1969   92 minutes

VOLUNTEERS
★★

DIRECTOR: Nicholas Meyer
CAST: Tom Hanks, John Candy, Rita Wilson, Tim Thomerson, Gedde Watanabe

At first glance, this comedy seems to have everything going for it: It reunites Tom Hanks and John Candy, who were so marvelously funny together in Ron Howard's *Splash*, and was directed by Nicholas Meyer, who made the first good "Star Trek" movie (*Star Trek II: The Wrath of Khan*). In truth, however, this film about high jinks in the Peace Corps in Thailand circa 1962 has very little going for it. Hanks and Candy do their best, but the laughs are far and few between. Rated R for profanity, violence, and sexual innuendo.

1985   105 minutes

WACKIEST SHIP IN THE ARMY, THE
★★★

DIRECTOR: Richard Murphy
CAST: Jack Lemmon, Ricky Nelson, John Lund, Chips Rafferty, Tom Tully, Joby Baker, Warren Berlinger

A battered ship becomes an unlikely implement for World War II heroism. The situation is played mostly for laughs, but dramatic moments are smoothly included. Jack Lemmon sets his performance at just the right pitch. Ricky Nelson is amiable and amusing. He even gets to sing "Do You Know What It Means to Miss New Orleans?"

1960   99 minutes

WALTZ OF THE TOREADORS
★★★★

DIRECTOR: John Guillermin
CAST: Peter Sellers, Margaret Leighton, Dany Robin

The unique Peter Sellers is superb as a retired military officer who can't subdue his roving eye. Margaret Leighton is fine, as always. Dany Robin is adorable. It's saucy and sex-shot, but intellectually stimulating nonetheless. A charming film, and not just for Sellers's fans.

1962   105 minutes

WATER
★★★

DIRECTOR: Dick Clement

CAST: Michael Caine, Brenda Vaccaro, Valerie Perrine, Billy Connelly, Fred Gwynne, George Harrison, Ringo Starr, Eric Clapton, Eddy Grant

In this delightful British comedy, Michael Caine is the governor of the small English colony located on the island of Cascara. The governor's wife (Brenda Vaccaro) is bored with life on Cascara (the Spanish word for rind!) until an oil company headed by Fred Gwynne sends out a famous actor to film a commercial. No one seems to notice that the oil company is using the commercial as a cover-up for actual oil drilling. The madness begins when instead of hitting oil, they hit Perrier! The oil company wants the rights to the water, as do the governments of several nations, a group of island rebels (headed by Billy Connelly), and a conservationist (Valerie Perrine), who turns out to be the daughter of the head of the oil company. What ensues is pleasant craziness accompanied by a great soundtrack featuring the music of Eddy Grant, and a jam session with Ringo Starr, George Harrison, and Eric Clapton. Rated PG-13.

1986　　　　　　　　91 minutes

WATERMELON MAN
★★★

DIRECTOR: Melvin Van Peebles
CAST: Godfrey Cambridge, Estelle Parsons

The life of a bigoted white man is turned inside-out when he wakes up one morning and finds himself black. Using the late, great black comedian Godfrey Cambridge in the title role shows that someone in production had his head on right. The film makes a statement. Trouble is, it makes it over and over and over again. Rated R.

1970　　　　　　　　97 minutes

WAY OUT WEST
★★★★★

DIRECTOR: James W. Horne
CAST: Stan Laurel, Oliver Hardy, Sharon Lynn

Stan Laurel and Oliver Hardy travel west to deliver a gold mine map to the daughter of a friend. The map is given to an imposter, and the boys have to retrieve it and ensure correct delivery. A delightful, marvelous film that demonstrates the team's mastery of timing and characterization.

1937　　　　B & W　　65 minutes

WEDDING, A
★★★

DIRECTOR: Robert Altman
CAST: Carol Burnett, Desi Arnaz Jr., Geraldine Chaplin, Amy Stryker, Vittorio Gassman, Lillian Gish, Lauren Hutton, Paul Dooley, Howard Duff, Pam Dawber, Dina Merrill, John Considine

This is one of those *almost* movies—one that has enough good things about it to recommend, but that could have been so much better. During the late 1970s, director Robert Altman's films had begun to lose their focus, and any kind of coherence had largely disappeared, as this film demonstrates. The story deals with a wedding between two relatively wealthy families and the comic implications that follow. Fine acting keeps things afloat, but this one is a disappointment. Rated PG.

1978　　　　　　　125 minutes

WEEKEND PASS
★

DIRECTOR: Lawrence Bassoff
CAST: D. W. Brown, Peter Ellenstein, Patrick Hauser, Chip McAllister

A quartet of stupid sailors on shore leave cavorts uncomically in Los Angeles, in this tired and lewd low-budget sex comedy. Rated R.

1984   92 minutes

WEIRD SCIENCE
★★

DIRECTOR: John Hughes

CAST: Anthony Michael Hall, Kelly LeBrock, Ilan Mitchell-Smith

In this wacky comedy by writer-director John Hughes (*16 Candles*; *The Breakfast Club*), two put-upon nerds (Anthony Michael Hall and Ilan Mitchell-Smith), desperate for a date, cop an idea from James Whale's *Frankenstein* (which is playing on television) and create a sexy woman via computer. Once brought to life (after the boys have fed *Penthouse* and *Playboy* centerfolds and a picture of Albert Einstein into the machine), she says, "Well, what do you little maniacs want to do first?" Thus begins a roller coaster ride of hit-and-miss humor laughs as the nerds get class fast. Rated PG-13 for slight violence, partial nudity, and profanity.

1985   94 minutes

WE'RE NO ANGELS
★★½

DIRECTOR: Michael Curtiz

CAST: Humphrey Bogart, Peter Ustinov, Aldo Ray, Basil Rathbone, Joan Bennett, Leo G. Carroll

The *New York Times* dubbed this "A slow, talky reprise of the delightful stage comedy" and was right. Three Devil's Island convicts "adopt" an inland family and protect it against an uncle it can do without. There is a roguishness about the trio that almost makes

them endearing, and there is humor, but the film does drag.

1955   106 minutes

WHAT PRICE GLORY
★★★

DIRECTOR: John Ford

CAST: James Cagney, Dan Dailey, Corinne Calvet, William Demarest, Robert Wagner, Marisa Pavan, James Gleason, Wally Vernon

James Cagney is Captain Flagg, Dan Dailey is Sergeant Quirt in this rough-and-tumble tale of rivalry in romance set against the sobering background of World War I in France. The feisty pair of Marines vies for the affections of adorable Charmaine (Corinne Calvet). Between quarrels, they fight in the trenches. John Ford's direction stresses the comedy aspects of the hard-drinking, brawling duo's conflict. The film is based upon the Broadway stage hit by Laurence Stallings and Maxwell Anderson. From it, the line "Hey, wait for baby!" passed permanently into the language.

1952   109 minutes

WHAT DO YOU SAY TO A NAKED LADY?
★

DIRECTOR: Allen Funt

CAST: Allen Funt, Richard Roundtree

Allen Funt's R-rated version of "Candid Camera" is a bust from the start. Imagine the same candid camera gags only with naked women and you've pretty well figured this dud out. Pass on this one. Rated R for nudity.

1970   90 minutes

WHAT'S NEW PUSSYCAT?
★★★

DIRECTOR: Clive Donner

CAST: Peter Sellers, Peter O'Toole, Woody Allen, Ursula Andress, Romy Schneider, Capucine, Paula Prentiss

Peter O'Toole is a fashion editor who can't stop becoming romantically involved with his models. In spite of a strong supporting cast, this dated 1960s "hip" comedy has few genuine laughs. Mostly, it's just silly.

1965   108 minutes

WHAT'S UP DOC?
★★★★

DIRECTOR: Peter Bogdanovich
CAST: Ryan O'Neal, Barbra Streisand, Kenneth Mars, Austin Pendleton

A virtual remake of Howard Hawks's classic Bringing Up Baby, with Ryan O'Neal and Barbra Streisand representing the Cary Grant and Katharine Hepburn roles, this manages to recapture much of the madcap charm and nonstop action of the original story. O'Neal is the studious scientist delightfully led astray by a dizzy Streisand, who keeps forcing herself into his life. The zany final chase through the streets of San Francisco is one of filmdom's best. Rated G.

1972   94 minutes

WHAT'S UP TIGER LILY?
★★★

DIRECTOR: Woody Allen
CAST: Tatsuya Mihashi Miyattana, Woody Allen

A dreadful Japanese spy movie has been given a zany English-language soundtrack by Woody Allen in one of his earliest movie productions. You are left with an offbeat spoof of the whole genre of spy films. The results are often

amusing, but its one-joke premise gets rather tedious before it's over.

1966   80 minutes

WHEN THINGS WERE ROTTEN
★★★

DIRECTOR: Coby Ruskin, Marty Peldman, Peter Bonerz
CAST: Dick Gautier, Dick Van Patten, Bernie Kopell, Richard Dimitri, Henry Polic II, Misty Rowe, David Sabin

This compilation of three episodes from the short-lived television series of the same name is sure to please fans of Blazing Saddles–style humor. Dick Gautier's nearly serious portrayal of Robin Hood is a perfect foil for the slapstick antics of the rest of the cast.

1975   78 minutes

WHERE THE BOYS ARE
★★★

DIRECTOR: Henry Levin
CAST: Dolores Hart, George Hamilton, Yvette Mimieux, Jim Hutton, Barbara Nichols, Connie Francis

Connie Francis warbles the title tune and made her movie debut in this frothy, mildly entertaining film about teenagers doing what's natural during Easter vacation in Fort Lauderdale. It's miles ahead of the idiotic remake.

1960   99 minutes

WHERE THE BOYS ARE '84
🦃

DIRECTOR: Hy Averback
CAST: Lisa Hartman, Russell Todd, Lorna Luft, Lynn-Holly Johnson, Wendy Schaal, Howard McGillin, Louise Sorel, Alana Stewart

No, this isn't a re-release of the 1960 film about teens tearin' it up in Fort Lauderdale, which Connie

Francis immortalized in the song of the same name. It's a poorly made remake by Mr. "Can't Stop the Music" himself: producer Allan Carr. Rated R.

1984 96 minutes

WHERE THE BUFFALO ROAM

🐾

DIRECTOR: Art Linson

CAST: Bill Murray, Peter Boyle, Bruno Kirby, Rene Auberjonois, R. G. Armstrong, Rafael Campos, Leonard Frey

Director Art Linson's horrendous film about the exploits of gonzo journalist Hunter S. Thompson. Bill Murray turns in one of his few bad performances as the consistently stoned-out writer. Thompson has reportedly sworn "to rip Murray's throat out" if they ever meet. It's our feeling it would have been better if this movie had never been released on video. Rated R.

1980 96 minutes

WHERE'S POPPA?

★★★★

DIRECTOR: Carl Reiner

CAST: George Segal, Ruth Gordon, Trish Van Devere, Ron Liebman, Rae Allen, Vincent Gardenia, Barnard Hughes, Rob Reiner, Garrett Morris

One of George Segal's best comic performances is found in this cult favorite. Ruth Gordon co-stars as the senile mother whom Segal tries to scare into having a cardiac arrest. Director Carl Reiner's son, Rob, makes a short appearance as a fervent draft resister. Rated R.

1970 82 minutes

WHICH WAY IS UP?

★★★★

DIRECTOR: Michael Shultz

CAST: Richard Pryor, Lonette McKee, Margaret Avery, Dolph Sweet, Morgan Woodward

This irreverent, ribald farce reunites the talented comedy team of director Michael Shultz and star Richard Pryor (*Greased Lightning*) for one of the funnier movies of the 1970s. Pryor plays three major roles. His ability to create totally separate and distinctive characters contributes greatly to the success of this oft-tried but rarely believable gimmick. The language and subject matter of this film are not suited for the young, but adults will convulse with laughter at the unexpected and hilarious comedy of *Which Way Is Up?* Rated R.

1977 94 minutes

WHOLLY MOSES!

★★½

DIRECTOR: Gary Weis

CAST: Dudley Moore, Richard Pryor, Laraine Newman, James Coco, Paul Sand, Jack Gilford, Dom De Luise, John Houseman, Madeline Kahn, David L. Lander, John Ritter

Wholly Moses! pokes fun at Hollywood biblical epics in a rapid-fire fashion. While the film is sometimes very funny, it is also loaded with a fair share of predictable, flat, and corny moments. It's so-so viewing fare. Rated R.

1980 109 minutes

WHO'S MINDING THE MINT?

★★★½

DIRECTOR: Howard Morris

CAST: Milton Berle, Jim Hutton, Dorothy Provine, Joey Bishop, Walter Brennan, Jamie Farr, Victor Buono

When a U.S. Mint employee (Jim Hutton) accidentally destroys thousands of newly printed bills, a group of misfits bands together to help him out. This film is often hilarious and always enjoyable.

1967   97 minutes

WILDCATS
★★★

DIRECTOR: Michael Ritchie
CAST: Goldie Hawn, Swoosie Kurtz, James Keach, Nipsy Russell, Woody Harrelson, M. Emmet Walsh

Standard Goldie Hawn vehicle, with her playing high-school football coach to a rowdy group of inner-city kids who need to prove their worth as much as she needs to prove her self-esteem and skill to chauvinistic athletic directors. Director Michael Ritchie shows little of the tension he brought to *The Bad News Bears*. Awkward subplot involves Hawn in a custody battle with wimpish James Keach over their two daughters. Another low point is an embarrassingly gratuitous nude shot of Hawn in a bathtub. On the other hand, the film ends on its best note: a spirited rendition of the "Football Rap" by Hawn and her fellas. Rated R for nudity and language.

1986   107 minutes

WILD LIFE, THE
★★

DIRECTOR: Art Linson
CAST: Christopher Penn, Lea Thompson, Ilan Mitchell-Smith, Jenny Wright, Eric Stoltz, Randy Quaid

A semi-sequel to *Fast Times at Ridgemont High*, this dull, stupid teen-lust comedy stars Christopher Penn (*Footloose*) as a dippy wrestler who wants to party. Viewers will probably want to party, too. Anything's better than watching this insulting film. Rated R.

1984   96 minutes

WISE GUYS
★★★½

DIRECTOR: Brian De Palma
CAST: Danny DeVito, Joe Piscopo, Harvey Keitel, Ray Sharkey, Captain Lou Albano, Dan Hedaya

Director Brian De Palma, apparently tired of derivative Hitchcockian thrillers, returned to his roots with this send-up of gangster movies. Danny DeVito and Joe Piscopo play Harry and Moe, a couple of goofball syndicate gofers trusted with little above the boss's laundry. The reason for this becomes obvious when they muck up a bet on the ponies; as punishment, the boss secretly instructs each to kill the other. To make sure everything works out properly, both are watchdogged by "The Fixer," a man-mountain played by pro-wrestler Captain Lou Albano. DeVito's and Piscopo's comedic talents notwithstanding, Albano owns this film; his growling delivery (his bark *and* bite are equally bad) is wonderful. Inexplicably rated R for language.

1986   91 minutes

WITHOUT RESERVATIONS
★★★

DIRECTOR: Mervyn LeRoy
CAST: John Wayne, Claudette Colbert, Don DeFore, Frank Puglia, Anee Triol, Phil Brown, Thurston Hall, Louella Parsons

Wartime comedy about authoress Claudette Colbert and her plan to turn soldier John Wayne into the leading man of her filmed novel is light and enjoyable and sprinkled with guest appearances by Hollywood celebrities. This is hardly the kind of war film in which one would expect to find John Wayne, but the Duke makes the best of a chance to act under top director Mervyn LeRoy (who was in a slump during this period). No telling what the executives at RKO had in mind when they came up with this idea, but after forty years, the idea of John Wayne teaming with Claudette Colbert in a comedy (or any other kind of film) still sounds ridiculous. However, this unlikely combination came out surprisingly well.

1946   B & W 107 minutes

WITH SIX YOU GET EGGROLL
★★

DIRECTOR: Howard Morris
CAST: Doris Day, Brian Keith, Barbara Hershey

Widow Doris Day has three kids; widower Brian Keith has a daughter. They get together. Awwwww! "Bachelor Father" meets "Mother Knows Best." The two stars refer to Doris and Brian, neither of whom helped their cause with this turkey. Strictly a picture for the 1960s. Unrated.

1968   99 minutes

WOMAN IN RED, THE
★★★★

DIRECTOR: Gene Wilder
CAST: Gene Wilder, Charles Grodin, Joseph Bologna, Gilda Radner, Judith Ivey, Michael Huddleston, Kelly Lebrock

Gene Wilder's funniest film in years, this is best described as a bittersweet romantic comedy. Wilder, who also adapted the screenplay and directed, plays an advertising executive and heretofore happily married man who becomes obsessed with a beautiful woman he happens to see one day in a parking garage. The results are hilarious. Rated PG-13 for partial nudity, brief violence, and profanity.

1984   87 minutes

WOMAN OF THE YEAR
★★★★★

DIRECTOR: George Stevens
CAST: Spencer Tracy, Katharine Hepburn, Fay Bainter, Reginald Owen, William Bendix

Ah, you knew it from the very first moments; these two had something. This is the film that first teamed Spencer Tracy and Katharine Hepburn, and it's impossible to imagine anybody else doing a better job. He's a sports reporter; she's a famed political journalist who needs to be reminded of life's simple pleasures. Like baseball . . . and her attempts to learn the game are priceless. The witty script garnered an Oscar for Ring Lardner Jr. and Michael Kanin. A classic in every respect; watch it several times. Unrated—family fare.

1942   B & W 112 minutes

WOMEN, THE
★★★★½

DIRECTOR: George Cukor
CAST: Norma Shearer, Joan Crawford, Rosalind Russell, Joan Fontaine, Paulette Goddard

Director George Cukor and some of Hollywood's finest female stars combine for a winning screen version of Claire Booth's stage hit. This look at the state of matrimony is great entertainment. The script is full of witty, stinging dialogue.

1939   B & W 132 minutes

WORLD OF ABBOTT AND COSTELLO, THE
★★★

DIRECTOR: Narrated by Jack E. Leonard

CAST: Bud Abbott, Lou Costello, various guest stars

Compilation of Abbott and Costello's best film footage is well handled, with many of their classic scenes intact: the frog in the soup, Lou in the wrestling ring, Lou meeting Dracula, and of course "Who's on First?" Would've been better without the narration, but the film never fails to entertain. Add one star if you're a fan.

1965　　　　B & W　79 minutes

WORLD OF HENRY ORIENT, THE
★★★★

DIRECTOR: George Roy Hill
CAST: Peter Sellers, Paula Prentiss, Angela Lansbury, Phyllis Thaxter

A quirky comedy for the whole family. Peter Sellers is a woman-crazy New York pianist who finds himself being followed by two teenage girls who have come to idolize him. Loads of fun, with a great performance by Angela Lansbury.

1964　　　　　106 minutes

WORLD'S GREATEST LOVER, THE
★★½

DIRECTOR: Gene Wilder
CAST: Gene Wilder, Carol Kane, Dom De Luise, Fritz Feld, Carl Ballantine, Michael Huddleston, Matt Collins, Ronny Graham

Gene Wilder plays a would-be silent-movie star who tests for the part of the "new Valentino" while his wife (Carol Kane) runs off with the real Rudolph. Dom De Luise is around to brighten things up, but writer-director Wilder's ideas

of what's funny and well-timed aren't quite right. Rated PG.

1977　　　　　89 minutes

WRONG BOX, THE
★★★★

DIRECTOR: Bryan Forbes
CAST: John Mills, Ralph Richardson, Dudley Moore, Peter Sellers, Peter Cook, Michael Caine, Nanette Newman, Wilfred Lawson, Tony Hancock

Some of Britain's best-known comics appear in this screwball farce about two zany families who battle over an inheritance in Victorian England. The film borders on black humor as the corpse of a wealthy brother is shuffled all over London by the contending parties—headed by John Mills and Ralph Richardson. Dudley Moore, Peter Sellers, and Peter Cook are just a few of the funnymen who give cameo performances in the delightful comedy.

1966　　　　　105 minutes

WRONG IS RIGHT
★★★★

DIRECTOR: Richard Brooks
CAST: Sean Connery, Robert Conrad, George Grizzard, Katherine Ross, G. D. Spradlin, John Saxon, Henry Silva, Leslie Nielsen, Robert Webber, Rosalind Cash, Hardy Krüger, Dean Stockwell, Ron Moody

Sean Connery, as a globe-trotting television reporter, gives what may be the best performance of his career, in this outrageous, thoroughly entertaining end-of-the-world black comedy, written, produced, and directed by Richard Brooks (*The Professionals* and *Bite the Bullet*). It's an updated combination of *Network* and *Dr. Strangelove*, and wickedly funny.

Rated R because of profanity and violence.

1982   117 minutes

YELLOWBEARD
★★½

DIRECTOR: Mel Damski
CAST: Graham Chapman, Eric Idle, John Cleese, Peter Cook, Cheech and Chong, Peter Boyle, Madeline Kahn, Marty Feldman, Kenneth Mars

This pirate comedy has a shipload of comedians; unfortunately, it barely contains a boatload of laughs under the directorship of first-timer Mel Damski. Rated PG for profanity, nudity, violence, gore, and scatological humor.

1983   101 minutes

YOUNG DOCTORS IN LOVE
★★★

DIRECTOR: Garry Marshall
CAST: Michael McKean, Sean Young, Harry Dean Stanton, Patrick Macnee, Hector Elizondo, Dabney Coleman, Pamela Reed, Michael Richards, Taylor Negron, Saul Rubinek, Titos Vandis

This comedy attempts to do for medical soap operas what *Airplane!* did for disaster movies— and doesn't quite make it. That said, director Garry Marshall (of television's "Laverne and Shirley") has nevertheless created an enjoyable movie for open-minded adults. The R-rated film is a bit too raunchy and suggestive for the younger set.

1982   95 minutes

YOUNG FRANKENSTEIN
★★★★½

DIRECTOR: Mel Brooks

CAST: Gene Wilder, Marty Feldman, Peter Boyle, Teri Garr, Madeline Kahn, Cloris Leachman, Kenneth Mars, Richard Haydn

This is one of Mel Brooks's best. *Young Frankenstein* is the story of Dr. Frankenstein's college professor descendant who abhors his family history. This spoof of the old Universal horror films is hilarious from start to finish. Rated PG.

1974   B & W 105 minutes

YOU'RE A BIG BOY NOW
★★★★½

DIRECTOR: Francis Ford Coppola
CAST: Peter Kastner, Elizabeth Hartman, Geraldine Page, Julie Harris, Rip Torn, Michael Dunn, Tony Bill, Karen Black

Francis Ford Coppola not only directed this (his first) film but also wrote the screenplay. Peter Kastner, the product of overprotective parents, learns about life from street-wise go-go dancer Elizabeth Hartman. Fast-paced and very entertaining.

1966   96 minutes

ZAPPED!
★★

DIRECTOR: Robert J. Rosenthal
CAST: Scott Baio, Willie Aames, Felice Schacter, Heather Thomas, Scatman Crothers, Robert Mandan, Greg Bradford

A campy takeoff on high-school movies that doesn't work. *Zapped* is a bore. Rated R for nudity and sexual situations.

1982   96 minutes

ZELIG
★★★★★

DIRECTOR: Woody Allen

CAST: Woody Allen, Mia Farrow

This is Woody Allen's masterpiece. He plays Leonard Zelig, a remarkable man who can fit anywhere in society because he can change his appearance at will. The laughs come fast and furious in this account of his adventures in the 1920s, when he became all the rage and hung out with the likes of F. Scott Fitzgerald, Jack Dempsey, and Babe Ruth. Mia Farrow plays the psychiatrist who tries in vain to figure out the funny little man. Allen seamlessly weds black-and-white newsreel footage with his humorous tale, allowing Zelig to be right in the thick of history. Rated PG.

1984　　　　B & W　79 minutes

ZORRO, THE GAY BLADE
★★★★
DIRECTOR: Peter Medak
CAST: George Hamilton, Lauren Hutton, Brenda Vaccaro, Ron Leibman

Here's another delight from (and starring) actor-producer George Hamilton. As with *Love at First Bite*, in which Hamilton played a slightly bent and bewildered Count Dracula, to great effect, the accent in *Zorro, the Gay Blade* is on belly-wrenching laughs . . . and there are plenty of them. Director Peter Medak (*The Ruling Class*) blends these elements—along with the supporting performances by Lauren Hutton, Brenda Vaccaro, Ron Liebman, and Donavan Scott—into the most consistently entertaining spoof of a classic movie since Mel Brooks's *Young Frankenstein*. Rated PG because of sexual innuendo.

1981　　　　　　93 minutes

ZOTZ!
★★★½
DIRECTOR: William Castle
CAST: Tom Poston, Jim Backus, Julia Meade

Charming, underrated little fantasy about a college professor (Tom Poston) who finds a magical coin blessed with three bizarre powers: sudden pain, slow motion, and explosive destruction. Good adaptation of the novel by Walter Karig, and an excellent opportunity for Poston to control a film in one of his rare leading parts. One of the last of William Castle's gimmick films—patrons at the original release were given plastic replicas of the coin. Give this a try; you won't be disappointed.

1962　　　　B & W　87 minutes

DRAMA

A NOS AMOURS
★★★

DIRECTOR: Maurice Pialat

CAST: Sandrine Bonnaire, Dominique Besnehard, Maurice Pialat

Winner of the Cesar (French Oscar) for best film of 1983, *A Nos Amours* examines the life of a working-class girl of 15 (Sandrine Bonnaire) who engages in one sexual relationship after another because, as she says, "I'm only happy when I'm with a guy." Her characters could be easy targets for snap judgments, but she has the ability to make us stave them off and just observe. Rated R for nudity.

1983   110 minutes

ABDUCTION
★★

DIRECTOR: Joseph Zito

CAST: Gregory Rozakis, Leif Erickson, Dorothy Malone, Lawrence Tierney

This film comes across as a cheap exploitation of the Patty Hearst kidnapping. It includes theories and conclusions that may or may not be true. The wealthy but distraught parents of Patty Prescott (Hearst, to us) are played by Dorothy Malone and Leif Erickson. As in the real incident, Patty is kidnapped from the house she shares with her boyfriend, Michael. Rated R for profanity, violence, nudity, and sex.

1975   100 minutes

ABE LINCOLN IN ILLINOIS
★★★★

DIRECTOR: John Cromwell

CAST: Raymond Massey, Ruth Gordon, Gene Lockhart, Mary Howard

Based on Sherwood Anderson's Broadway play, this is a reverent look at the early career and loves of the sixteenth president. As contrasted to John Ford's *Young Mr. Lincoln*, this is a more somber, historically accurate, and better-acted version.

1934   B & W   110 minutes

ABOUT LAST NIGHT
★★★★

DIRECTOR: Edward Zwick
CAST: Rob Lowe, Demi Moore, Jim Belushi, Elizabeth Perkins, George DiCenzo, Michael Alldredge

A slick adaptation of David Mamet's play, *Sexual Perversity in Chicago*, which focuses on the difficulties involved in "making a commitment." Demi Moore and Rob Lowe, as the central couple, meet for a one-night stand and then realize they *like* each other. The painful, hesitant steps toward a stable relationship—a shared drawer, living together first as friends, then as lovers—are detailed with excruciating familiarity by director Edward Zwick and screenwriters Tim Kazurinsky and Denise DeClue. If you haven't known people like this, you've probably *been* people like this. Jim Belushi and Elizabeth Perkins turn in solid performances as respective friends, but the film belongs to Moore, who finally has found a role worthy of her talent. Rated R for nudity and explicit adult situations.

1986   113 minutes

ABRAHAM LINCOLN
★★★★

DIRECTOR: D. W. Griffith
CAST: Walter Huston, Una Merkel, Kay Hammond, Ian Keith, Hobart Bosworth, Jason Robards, Henry B. Walthall

A milestone in many ways, this episodic film is legendary director Griffith's first "talkie," Hollywood's first sound biography of an American, the first attempt to cover Lincoln's life from cradle to grave, and the first about the martyred president to include the Civil War. Walter Huston's peerless performance in the title role dominates throughout. Ian Keith is properly hotheaded and flamboyant as murderer John Wilkes Booth. Una Merkel, later to be typecast as comic support, plays Lincoln's great love, Ann Rutledge; Kay Hammond portrays Mary Todd. The film shows its age, but is well worth the watching, nonetheless. Huston fans will treasure it.

1930   B & W   91 minutes

ABSENCE OF MALICE
★★★★

DIRECTOR: Sydney Pollack
CAST: Paul Newman, Sally Field, Bob Balaban, Melinda Dillon

Sally Field is a Miami reporter who writes a story implicating an innocent man (Paul Newman) in the mysterious disappearance—and possible murder—of a union leader in this taut, thoughtful drama about the ethics of journalism. It's sort of *All the President's Men* turned inside out. Rated PG because of minor violence.

1982   116 minutes

ACCIDENT
★★★★

DIRECTOR: Joseph Losey
CAST: Dirk Bogarde, Stanley Baker, Jacqueline Sassard, Michael York

Harold Pinter's complicated play retains its subtleties in this sometimes baffling film. Dirk Bogarde is excellent as a married professor pursuing an attractive student. There are enough twists and turns in the characters' actual desires to maintain your complete attention.

Fascinating character studies abound in this British film.

1967   105 minutes

ACT OF PASSION
★★

DIRECTOR: Simon Langton

CAST: Marlo Thomas, Kris Kristofferson, Jon De Vries, David Rasche, Linda Thorson, Edward Winter, Randy Rocca, George Dzundza

In this made-for-television movie, Marlo Thomas plays a single woman who picks up a stranger (Kris Kristofferson) at a party. She is subsequently subjected to harassments by the police and the press when the man turns out to be a suspected terrorist. The filmmakers attempt to examine the potential for mistreatment of the innocent by law enforcement agencies and the press. While there is good reason to sound such an alarm, the siren here is harsh and blatantly exaggerated. In this movie, the press and the police are too one-dimensional in their ruthlessness. Unrated.

1984   95 minutes

ADAM HAD FOUR SONS
★★★★

DIRECTOR: Gregory Ratoff

CAST: Ingrid Bergman, Warner Baxter, Susan Hayward

This classic has it all: good acting, romance, seduction, betrayal, tears, and laughter. Ingrid Bergman plays the good governess, and Susan Hayward plays the seductive hussy who tries to turn brother against brother. Warner Baxter offers a fine performance as Adam, the father.

1941   B & W 81 minutes

ADULTRESS, THE

DIRECTOR: Norbert Meisel

CAST: Tyne Daly, Eric Braeden, Greg Morton, Lynn Roth

Gobble, gobble, gobble ... this is an abysmal film about an impotent husband (Greg Morton) who hires a gigolo (Eric Braeden) to service his physically deprived wife (Tyne Daly). The only thing more painful to watch than the story in this turkey is the attempt at profundity and art by director Norbert Meisel.

1973   85 minutes

AFFAIR, THE
★★★

DIRECTOR: Gilbert Cates

CAST: Natalie Wood, Robert Wagner, Bruce Davison, Kent Smith, Pat Harrington

Touching, honest story of a crippled songwriter (Natalie Wood) tentatively entering into her first love affair—with an attorney (Robert Wagner). This is an unusually well-acted, sensitively told TV movie.

1973   74 minutes

AFRICAN QUEEN, THE
★★★★★

DIRECTOR: John Huston

CAST: Humphrey Bogart, Katharine Hepburn, Peter Bull

Humphrey Bogart and Katharine Hepburn star in this exciting World War I adventure film. Bogart's a drunkard, and Hepburn's the spinster sister of a murdered missionary. Together they take on the Germans and, in doing so, are surprised to find themselves falling in love.

1951   106 minutes

AFTER THE REHEARSAL
★★★½
DIRECTOR: Ingmar Bergman
CAST: Erland Josephson

This Ingmar Bergman movie—which was originally made for Swedish television—is about a director (Erland Josephson) who is approached by a young actress with a proposition: she wants to have an affair with him. The approach takes place at the end of their rehearsal of his presentation of Strindberg's *Dream Play*, and the director has a rather atypical response to her advances. Unrated.

1984   72 minutes

AGAINST ALL ODDS
★★★½
DIRECTOR: Taylor Hackford
CAST: Jeff Bridges, Rachel Ward, Alex Karras, James Woods

A respectable remake of *Out of the Past*, a 1947 *film noir* classic, this release stars Jeff Bridges as a man hired by a wealthy gangster (James Woods) to track down his girlfriend (Rachel Ward), who allegedly tried to kill him and made off with forty thousand dollars. Bridges finds her, they fall in love, and that's when the plot's twists really begin. Car chase fans will love the hair-raising race at the beginning of the film. Romance fans will find Bridges and Ward convincing as the star-crossed lovers. Thriller buffs will be kept on their seats by the tension-filled ending. Rated R for nudity, suggested sex, violence, and profanity.

1984   128 minutes

AGATHA
★★½
DIRECTOR: Michael Apted

CAST: Dustin Hoffman, Vanessa Redgrave, Cecelia Gregory, Paul Brooks

Supposedly based on a true event in the life of mystery author Agatha Christie (during which she disappeared for eleven days in 1926), this is a moderately effective thriller. Vanessa Redgrave is excellent in the title role, but co-star Dustin Hoffman is miscast as the American detective on her trail. Rated PG.

1979   98 minutes

AGENCY
★★
DIRECTOR: George Kaczender
CAST: Robert Mitchum, Lee Majors, Saul Rubinek, Valerie Perrine

Despite the presence of Robert Mitchum, this Canadian feature about a power struggle in the world of advertising doesn't convince. Nor do the supporting performances by wooden Lee Majors and lovely, but wasted, Valerie Perrine. Rated PG.

1981   94 minutes

AGNES OF GOD
★★★
DIRECTOR: Norman Jewison
CAST: Jane Fonda, Anne Bancroft, Meg Tilly, Anne Pitoniak, Winston Rekert, Gratien Gelinas

This fascinating drama features tour-de-force performances by Jane Fonda, Anne Bancroft, and Meg Tilly. Tilly's character, the childlike novice of an extremely sheltered convent, is discovered one night with the bloodied body of a baby she claims not to recognize. Psychiatrist Fonda is sent to determine Tilly's sanity in anticipation of a court hearing; Bancroft, as the Mother Superior, struggles to prevent the young girl's loss of innocence. John Pielmeier's screenplay, adapted from his stage play, sweeps through Catholic guilt, distrust of contemporary society, and old-fashioned whodunit trappings, all of which allow Fonda and Bancroft to jab each other with sharp verbal barbs. The film is ultimately sabotaged, though, by its own lack of conviction. An intriguing near-miss. Rated PG-13 for subject matter.

1985   101 minutes

AIRPORT 1975
★½

DIRECTOR: Jack Smight
CAST: Charlton Heston, George Kennedy, Karen Black, Sid Caesar, Helen Reddy

Universal waited four years after the release of the original *Airport* but could resist the temptation no longer. Released at the height of the disaster film craze, this second entry in the series profits from a strong performance by Charlton Heston and very little else. Characters get the most trifling introductions in an attempt to create drama, and the trend in supporting casts already was leaning toward a Love Boat–ish opportunity to empty the closets of B and C players. And Helen Reddy, as a (spare us) singing nun? Rated PG—moderate tension.

1974   - 106 minutes

AIRPORT 77
★

DIRECTOR: Jerry Jameson
CAST: Jack Lemmon, Lee Grant, George Kennedy, Christopher Lee

This movie is, at best, inoffensive diversion and, at worst, a regurgitation of all the clichéd situations and stereotyped characters we have come to expect from a disaster flick. If you've seen one *Airport*, you've seen them all. For those who haven't heard, this film is about a luxury 747 that is skyjacked and crashes in the sea at the Bermuda Triangle. Rated PG for violence.

1977   113 minutes

AIRPORT '79: THE CONCORDE
★

DIRECTOR: David Lowell Rich
CAST: Alain Delon, Robert Wagner, Susan Blakely, George Kennedy, Eddie Albert, Cicely Tyson

This is another in the seemingly endless *Airport* series. Robert Wagner is a ruthless tycoon with a scheme to destroy the aircaft to cover up for some of his dirty business affairs soon to be revealed by another affair, one with his mistress, Susan Blakely, a top newscaster with a hot story. Bring your own air sickness bag. Rated PG.

1979   113 minutes

ALAMO BAY
★★★★

DIRECTOR: Louis Malle
CAST: Ed Harris, Amy Madigan, Ho Nquyen, Donald Moffat

French director Louis Malle (*Atlantic City*) once again looks at the underbelly of the American dream. This time, he takes us to the Gulf Coast of Texas in the late 1970s where Vietnamese refugees arrived, expecting the land of opportunity and came face to face, instead, with the Ku Klux Klan. The immigrants joined the locals in fishing for shrimp and proved to be much better at it. This, in tough economic times, brought resentment—brilliantly brought to the screen by Ed Harris as a once-admirable man turned into a monster by resentment and frustration. Amy Madigan (also superb) is the woman who loves him but cannot condone his twisted attitude and actions. Rated R for nudity, violence, and profanity.

1985   105 minutes

ALEXANDER NEVSKY
★★★★

DIRECTOR: Sergei Eisenstein
CAST: Nikolai Cherkassov, Dmitri Orlov, Vassily Novikov

Another classic from the inimitable Russian director Sergei Eisenstein (*Ivan the Terrible*; *Battleship Potemkin*), this film is a Soviet attempt to prepare Russia for the coming conflict with Hitlerian Germany via portrayal of Alexander Nevsky, a thirteenth-century Russian prince, and his victories over the Teutonic knights of that era. As with all state-commissioned art, the situations can be corny, but the direction is superb, and there is the added bonus of an original musical score by Sergei Prokofieff.

1938   B & W 105 minutes

ALEXANDER THE GREAT
★★★½

DIRECTOR: Robert Rossen
CAST: Richard Burton, Fredric March, Claire Bloom, Danielle Darrieux

The strange, enigmatic, self-possessed Macedonian conqueror of Greece and most of the civilized world of his time rides again. Richard Burton, with his enthralling voice and uniquely hypnotic eyes, dominates an outstanding cast in this lavish epic of life and love among the upper crust in 356 to 323 B.C.

1956   141 minutes

ALGIERS
★★★½

DIRECTOR: John Cromwell
CAST: Charles Boyer, Hedy Lamarr, Sigrid Gurie

"Come with me to the Casbah." Charles Boyer set female hearts aflutter in the 1930s with his portrayal of Pepe Le Moko, a gentleman thief on the run from the authorities. It's still fun to watch.

1938   B & W 100 minutes

ALICE ADAMS
★★★★

DIRECTOR: George Stevens
CAST: Katharine Hepburn, Fred MacMurray, Evelyn Venable, Fred Stone, Frank Albertson, Hattie McDaniel, Charley Grapewin, Hedda Hopper

Life and love in a typical mid-American small town when there were still such things as concerts in the park and ice cream socials. Hepburn is a social-climbing girl wistfully seeking love while trying to overcome the stigma of her father's lack of money and ambition. High point of the film is the dinner scene, at once a comic gem and painful insight into character.

1935   B & W 99 minutes

ALICE DOESN'T LIVE HERE ANYMORE
★★★★½

DIRECTOR: Martin Scorsese
CAST: Ellen Burstyn, Kris Kristofferson, Harvey Keitel, Billy Green Bush, Alfred Lutter, Jodie Foster, Vic Tayback

The feature film that spawned the television series "Alice" is a memorable character study about a woman (Ellen Burstyn, who won an Oscar for her performance) attempting to survive after her husband's death has left her penniless and with a young son to support. The hard-edged direction by Martin Scorsese (*Taxi Driver*) adds grit to what might have been a lightweight yarn, and the supporting portrayals add greatly to the film's effectiveness. Rated PG for profanity and violence.

1975   113 minutes

ALICE'S RESTAURANT
★★★½

DIRECTOR: Arthur Penn
CAST: Arlo Guthrie, Pat Quinn, James Broderick, Michael McClanathan, Geoff Outlaw, Tina Chen

This film was based on Arlo Guthrie's hit record of the same name. Some insights into the 1960s counterculture can be found in this story of Guthrie's attempt to stay out of the draft. There is some fine acting by a basically unknown cast. Rated PG for language and some nudity.

1969   111 minutes

ALL ABOUT EVE
★★★★★

DIRECTOR: Joseph L. Mankiewicz
CAST: Bette Davis, Anne Baxter, Marilyn Monroe, George Sanders, Celeste Holm, Gary Merrill

The behind-the-scenes world of the New York theater is the subject of this classic. The picture won several Academy Awards, including best picture, but it is Bette Davis as Margo Channing that most remember. Her characterization is softer and more vulnerable than had been seen in her long stay at Warner Bros. It was also miles away from the assortment of hags she played in her later career. Margo Channing is a woman apparently at the apex of her career, but she's beginning to slide. A conniving Eve (Anne Baxter) is

there to give her a push downward as she attempts to take Margo's place. The dialogue sparkles, and the performances are of high caliber.

1950   B & W 138 minutes

ALL GOD'S CHILDREN
★★

DIRECTOR: Jerry Thorpe
CAST: Richard Widmark, Ned Beatty, Ossie Davis, Ruby Dee

Forced busing to achieve educational integration is the crux of this story of two families, one white and one black, whose sons are friends. The cast is excellent, but a wandering script makes comprehension difficult. Rated PG for violence.

1980   107 minutes

ALL NIGHT LONG
★★★

DIRECTOR: Jean-Claude Tramount
CAST: Gene Hackman, Barbra Streisand

Praised by some for its offbeat style and story, this comedy, starring the odd couple of Gene Hackman and Barbra Streisand, is only occasionally convincing. Hackman stars as an executive demoted to the position of managing a twenty-four-hour grocery store. There, he meets a daffy housewife (played by a miscast Streisand) and love blooms. This picture has its partisans (including several top-name critics), but it is still unlikely to satisfy most viewers.

1981   95 minutes

ALL QUIET ON THE WESTERN FRONT
★★★½

DIRECTOR: Delbert Mann
CAST: Richard Thomas, Ernest Borgnine, Donald Pleasence, Ian Holm, Patricia Neal

This is a television remake of the 1930 film, which was taken from Erich Maria Remarque's classic anti-war novel. It attempts to bring back all the horrors of World War I, but even the great detail issued to this film can't hide its TV mentality and melodramatic characters. The characters are exaggerated to promote the difference between good and bad, and while this dichotomy is one of the main points of the material, the viewer may feel a bit patronized. Despite this major flaw, the film is watchable for its rich look and compelling story.

1979　　　　126 minutes

ALL THE KING'S MEN
★★★★

DIRECTOR: Robert Rossen
CAST: Broderick Crawford, Joanne Dru, John Ireland, Mercedes McCambridge, John Derek

Broderick Crawford and Mercedes McCambridge won Academy Awards for their work in this adaptation of Robert Penn Warren's Pulitzer Prize–winning novel about a corrupt politician's ascension to power. Seen today, the film retains its relevance and potency.

1949　　　B & W 109 minutes

ALL THE PRESIDENT'S MEN
★★★★★

DIRECTOR: Alan J. Pakula
CAST: Dustin Hoffman, Robert Redford, Jason Robards Jr., Jane Alexander, Jack Warden, Martin Balsam

Robert Redford, who also produced, and Dustin Hoffman star in this gripping reenactment of the exposure of the Watergate conspiracy by reporters Bob Woodward and Carl Bernstein. What's so remarkable about this docudrama is, although we know how

it eventually comes out, we're on the edge of our seats from beginning to end. That's inspired moviemaking. Rated PG.

1976　　　　136 minutes

ALL THE RIGHT MOVES
★★★½

DIRECTOR: Michael Chapman
CAST: Tom Cruise, Craig T. Nelson, Christopher Penn

Tom Cruise (*Risky Business*) stars in this entertaining coming-of-age picture as a blue-collar high-school senior trying to get out of a Pennsylvania mill town by way of a football scholarship. Rated R for profanity, sex, and nudity.

1983　　　　91 minutes

ALLIGATOR SHOES
★★

DIRECTOR: Clay Borris
CAST: Gary Borris, Clay Borris, Ronalda Jones, Rose Mallais-Borris, Len Perry, Simone Champagne

As can be surmised from the cast, this is pretty much a home movie by two brothers, Gary and Clay Borris. Although grownup, they still live at home. When their mentally disturbed aunt (Ronalda Jones) moves in, trouble arises. How each deals with this problem forms the basis for this drama, which becomes strained before its fatal conclusion. This Canadian film is unrated.

1982　　　　98 minutes

ALPHABET CITY
★½

DIRECTOR: Amos Poe
CAST: Vincent Spano, Kate Vernon, Michael Winslow, Zohra Lampert, Raymond Serra

Talented Vincent Spano (*Baby It's You*; *The Black Stallion Returns*) plays a "sympathetic" drug dealer in this pretentious movie set in Manhattan's Lower East Side. Rated R for profanity, sex, nudity, and violence.

1984   98 minutes

AMARCORD
★★★½

DIRECTOR: Federico Fellini

CAST: Magali Noel, Bruno Zanin, Pupella Maggio, Armando Branciia

Another Federico Fellini film that is good if you like Fellini. A Fellini history of the Italy he remembers, with lots of color, humor, and sex . . . in other words, what it's like to be an Italian. Rated R.

1973   127 minutes

AMATEUR, THE
★★★½

DIRECTOR: Charles Jarrott

CAST: John Savage, Christopher Plummer, Marthe Keller, John Marley

A C.I.A. computer technologist (John Savage) blackmails The Company into helping him avenge the terrorist murder of his girl-friend, only to find himself abandoned—and hunted—by the CIA. Rated R because of violence.

1982   111 minutes

AMAZING HOWARD HUGHES, THE
★½

DIRECTOR: William A. Graham

CAST: Tommy Lee Jones, Ed Flanders, Tovah Feldshuh, Sorrell Booke, Lee Purcell, Arthur Franz

Howard Hughes was amazing, but little in this lackluster account of his life and career would so indicate. Best portrayal is Ed Flanders as longtime, finally turned-upon associate Noah Dietrich. An ambitious TV production that falls short of the mark.

1977   215 minutes

AMBASSADOR, THE
★★★½

DIRECTOR: J. Lee Thompson

CAST: Robert Mitchum, Rock Hudson, Ellen Burstyn, Fabio Testi, Donald Pleasence

Even if it simplifies a complex situation, The Ambassador confronts the Arab-Israeli conflict with a clear head and an optimistic viewpoint. Robert Mitchum plays the controversial U.S. ambassador to Israel, who tries to solve the Palestinian question while being criticized by all factions. Rock Hudson (in his last big-screen role) is the security officer who works around the clock saving the ambassador's life from KGB assassins and radicals from various camps. Ellen Burstyn plays the ambassador's wife, who complicates the situation when she is caught in an affair with a PLO leader. Rated R for violence, profanity, sex, and nudity.

1984   97 minutes

AMERICAN ANTHEM
★

DIRECTOR: Albert Magnoli

CAST: Mitch Gaylord, Janet Jones, Michelle Phillips

Starring 1984 Olympic gold medal gymnast Mitch Gaylord, and directed by Albert Magnoli (Purple Rain), this film features superb gymnastics. Otherwise, it is hard to find anything likable. The screenplay is amateurish, and the acting, except for a few brief moments by Gaylord, is even worse. Poorly executed technical effects simply exacerbate the problems. Rated PG.

1986   100 minutes

AMERICAN FLYERS
★★★½

DIRECTOR: John Badham
CAST: Kevin Costner, David Grant, Rae Dawn Chong, Alexandra Paul, Janice Rule, John Amos

Another bicycle-racing tale from writer Steve Tesich (*Breaking Away*), who correctly decided he could milk that theme at least one more time. Kevin Costner and David Grant star as estranged brothers who get to know and like each other again during their participation in a grueling three-day overland race. The script is best when it concentrates on that major premise, and worst when it lapses into a subplot concerning one brother's impending death from one of those Dread Hollywood Diseases That Always Prove Fatal. Rae Dawn Chong, as Costner's live-in lover, has *never* looked more appealing or seemed more credible. Her presence alone makes the film worthwhile; the excitement of the race is mere icing on the cake. Rated PG-13 for brief nudity and language.

1985   113 minutes

AMERICAN FRIEND, THE
★★★★½

DIRECTOR: Wim Wenders
CAST: Dennis Hopper, Bruno Ganz, Lisa Kreuzer, Gerard Blain, Jean Eustache

Tense story of an American criminal (Dennis Hopper) in Germany talking a picture framer into murdering a gangster. Extremely well done, with lots of surprises. Cameo appearances by American film directors Sam Fuller and Nicholas Ray. Rated R—language, violence.

1977   127 minutes

AMERICAN GIGOLO
★★

DIRECTOR: Paul Schrader
CAST: Richard Gere, Lauren Hutton, Hector Elizondo, Nina Van Pallandt

This story of a male hooker, Julian Kay (Richard Gere), who attends to the physical needs of bored, rich, middle-aged women in Beverly Hills, may be something different. But who needs it? This is sensationalism in the guise of social comment. It has some incidental humor (supplied by Hector Elizondo as a disheveled Columbo-like cop who learns about fashion from Kay) that is quite welcome. The performances of Richard Gere in the title role and Lauren Hutton as a non-client lover are impressive. However, it is steeped in sleaze. Rated R for explicit depictions of a low lifestyle.

1980   117 minutes

AMERICANA
★★½

DIRECTOR: David Carradine
CAST: David Carradine, Barbara Hershey, Michael Greene, Bruce Carradine, John Barrymore III, Fran Ryan

Strange, offbeat film about a Vietnam veteran (director David Carradine) who attempts to rebuild a merry-go-round in a rural Kansas town and meets with hostility from the locals. Carradine attempts to make a statement about rebuilding America and reinstating its simple, honest values, but this gets lost in the impressionistic haze of his film. A noble effort, competently directed and acted (by professionals and nonprofessionals alike), but ultimately unsatisfying. Rated PG for violence and profanity.

1981   90 minutes

AMIN: THE RISE AND FALL

DIRECTOR: Richard Fleischer
CAST: Joseph Olita

Putrid garbage isn't strong enough to describe adequately this awful movie about the atrocities committed by Idi Amin during his reign of terror in Uganda. But it'll have to do. It's exploitation in the worst sense—and boring, to boot. In the title role, Joseph Olita shows all the acting talent of a diseased goat. Rated R for violence, nudity, sex, and profanity.

1981   101 minutes

AMONG THE CINDERS
★★½

DIRECTOR: Rolf Haedrick
CAST: Paul O'Shea, Derek Hardwick, Amanda Jones, Rebecca Gigney, Yvonne Yawley

A teenager (Paul O'Shea) holds himself responsible for the accidental death of a friend, and it takes a trip to the wilds with his grandfather (Derek Hardwick) to pull him out of it. This coming-of-age drama from New Zealand has its good moments, but these are outnumbered by the unremarkable ones. Rated R for nudity, profanity, suggested sex, and brief gore.

1985   105 minutes

ANATOMY OF A MURDER
★★★★

DIRECTOR: Otto Preminger

CAST: James Stewart, Arthur O'Connell, Lee Remick, Ben Gazzara, Eve Arden, Kathryn Grant, George C. Scott, Joseph Welch, Orson Bean, Murray Hamilton

A clever plot, realistic atmosphere, smooth direction, and sterling performances from a topflight case make this frank and exciting small-town courtroom drama first-rate fare. For the defense, it's James Stewart at his best vs. prosecuting attorney George C. Scott. Ben Gazzara plays a moody young army officer charged with killing the man who raped his wife, Lee Remick. Real-life lawyer Joseph Welch, of McCarthy hearings fame, plays the judge. Honest realism saturates throughout.

1959   B & W 160 minutes

AND GOD CREATED WOMAN
★★½

DIRECTOR: Roger Vadim
CAST: Brigitte Bardot, Curt Jurgens, Jean-Louis Trintignant, Christian Marquand

Brigitte Bardot rose to international fame as the loose-moraled coquette who finds it hard to say no to an attractive male, especially a well-heeled one. Shot on location at the beach with as much of Bardot exposed as the law then allowed, this rather slight story works well and is peopled with interesting characters. In French, with English subtitles.

1957   92 minutes

AND JUSTICE FOR ALL
★★★½

DIRECTOR: Norman Jewison
CAST: Al Pacino, Jack Warden, John Forsythe, Craig T. Nelson

This is a bristling black comedy starring Al Pacino as a lawyer who becomes fed up with the red tape of our country's legal system. It's both heartrending and darkly hilarious—but not for all tastes. Rated R.

1979   117 minutes

AND NOW, MY LOVE
★★★½

DIRECTOR: Claude Lelouch
CAST: Marthe Keller, André Dussolier, Charles Denner, Gilbert Becaud, Carla Gravina, Gabriele Tinti, Charles Giraud

In biography-documentary style, director Claude Lelouch juxtaposes three generations of a family while depicting the moral, political, and artistic events that shaped the members' lives. All this is wonderfully designed to show how inevitable it is for two young people (played by André Dussolier and Marthe Keller) from different backgrounds to fall in love. This approach telescopes the generations in novel fashion to underscore the historical continuity that reduces the eventual meeting to a simple matter of fate. Yet it is at this crucial juncture that an otherwise scintillating film falls apart. Lelouch wallows around in modern irrelevances so that one begins to wonder if there is indeed any point to his work. However, the first part of the film is so good and original that the drawbacks of the rest are not all that bothersome. Dubbed.

1974   121 minutes

AND THE SHIP SAILS ON
★★

DIRECTOR: Federico Fellini
CAST: Freddie Jones, Barbara Jefford, Victor Poletti

Italian director Federico Fellini's heavily symbolic parable about a luxury liner filled with eccentric beautiful people sailing the Adriatic on the eve of World War I was called by one critic "a spellbinding, often magical tribute to the illusions and delusions of art." That's one way of looking at it. We found it boring. However, Fellini fans and lovers of foreign films may find it rewarding. No MPAA rating.

1984   138 minutes

AND THEN THERE WERE NONE
★★★★★

DIRECTOR: René Clair
CAST: Barry Fitzgerald, Walter Huston, Richard Haydn, Roland Young, Judith Anderson, Louis Hayward, June Duprez, Aubrey Smith

One of the best screen adaptations of an Agatha Christie mystery. A select group of people is invited to a lonely island and murdered one by one. René Clair's inspired visual style gives this release just the right atmosphere and tension.

1945   B & W   98 minutes

ANDY WARHOL'S BAD
★★★½

DIRECTOR: Jed Johnson
CAST: Carroll Baker, Perry King, Susan Tyrrell

Carroll Baker stars in this nasty and very sick outing from producer Andy Warhol. She plays a tough mama who runs a squad of female hit men out of her cheery suburban home while disguising it as an electrolysis operation. Into this strange company comes Perry King as a mysterious stranger who boards there until he completes his "mission." Full of sick scenes, including a baby being thrown out a window and splatting on the pavement below, and a dog stabbing. Everybody speaks very nasty to everyone else, just like in a John

Waters film, which this seems to be emulating. Not for weak stomachs, it includes one of the great actresses of trash cinema, Susan Tyrrell, as a sickly mother with a whining baby. Sick, but you may not be able to take your eyes off it. The film has gore, violence, and nudity.

1977 107 minutes

ANGEL ON MY SHOULDER
★★★★

DIRECTOR: Archie Mayo
CAST: Paul Muni, Anne Baxter, Claude Rains, George Cleveland, Onslow Stevens

In a break from his big-budget prestige screen biographies of the period, Paul Muni stars in this entertaining fantasy as a murdered gangster who makes a deal with the devil. He wants to return to his human form. He gets his wish and spends his time on Earth—as a judge—trying to outwit Satan.

1946 B & W 101 minutes

ANGELO MY LOVE
★★★★

DIRECTOR: Robert Duvall
CAST: Angelo and Michael Evans, Steve and Millie Tsigonoff, Cathy Kitchen

Robert Duvall wrote and directed this loosely scripted, wonderfully different movie about a street-wise 11-year-old gypsy boy. Duvall reportedly conceived the project when he spotted the fast-talking, charismatic Angelo Evans on a New York street and decided he ought to be in pictures. Rated R for profanity. Rated R.

1983 115 minutes

ANIMAL FARM
★★½

DIRECTOR: John Halas, Joy Batchelor

CAST: Animated

Serious, sincere animated adaptation of George Orwell's ingenious satire concerning the follies of government. The treatment would have benefited from greater intensity. The attempt at creating an optimistic ending was ill-advised. Keep in mind the film isn't children's fare.

1954 72 minutes

ANN VICKERS
★★★★

DIRECTOR: John Cromwell
CAST: Irene Dunne, Bruce Cabot, Walter Huston, Conrad Nagel, Edna May Oliver, J. Carrol Naish

Rebuffed by Bruce Cabot, noble and self-sacrificing Irene Dunne scorns all men and turns to social service. Against all odds she seeks penal reform. After writing a book exposing disgraceful prison conditions, she is appointed superintendent of a model women's detention home. Later she learns Walter Huston, a liberal judge, had quietly backed her career. When he is accused of graft, she comes to his aid, but he is convicted anyway. She waits while he serves eight years, and they are finally united. A somewhat unique women's prison film in that the heroine is not a victimized inmate.

1933 B & W 72 minutes

ANNA CHRISTIE
★★★★

DIRECTOR: Clarence Brown
CAST: Greta Garbo, Charles Bickford, Marie Dressler, Lee Phelps, George Marion

Greta Garbo is mesmerizing and Marie Dressler hilariously memorable in this early sound classic adapted from Eugene O'Neill's play. The tag line for it in 1930 was "Garbo speaks!" And speak she does, uttering the famous line "Gif me a viskey, ginger ale on the side, and don't be stingy, baby" while portraying a woman with a shady past.

1930　　B & W　90 minutes

ANNA KARENINA
★★★★

DIRECTOR: Clarence Brown
CAST: Greta Garbo, Fredric March, Basil Rathbone, Maureen O'-Sullivan, May Robson, Freddie Bartholomew

There's something still quite magical about watching the incomparable Greta Garbo in her few sound films—even though most of these are now badly dated. In this still-watchable release, Garbo plays a Russian aristocrat's wife who falls in love with a dashing cavalry officer, Fredric March.

1935　　B & W　95 minutes

ANNE OF THE THOUSAND DAYS
★★★

DIRECTOR: Charles Jarrott
CAST: Genevieve Bujold, Richard Burton, Anthony Quayle

The story of Anne Boleyn, Henry VIII's second wife and mother of Queen Elizabeth I, is given the big-budget treatment. Luckily, the tragic tale of a woman who is at first pressured into an unwanted union with England's lusty king, only to fall in love with him and eventually lose her head to court intrigue, is not lost beneath the spectacle. Genevieve Bujold's well-balanced performance of Anne carries the entire production. Richard Burton, however, offers only a hammy Henry. Rated PG.

1969　　146 minutes

ANOTHER COUNTRY
★★★½

DIRECTOR: Mark Kanievska
CAST: Rupert Everett, Colin Firth

For this film, directed by Mark Kanievska, Julian Mitchell adapted his stage play about Guy Burgess, an Englishman who became a spy for Russia in the 1930s. Little in this story reportedly was based on fact. Still, Mitchell's postulations provide interesting viewing, and Rupert Everett's lead performance—as Guy "Bennett"—is stunning. Rated PG for suggested sex and profanity.

1984　　90 minutes

ANOTHER TIME, ANOTHER PLACE
★★★

DIRECTOR: Michael Radford
CAST: Phyllis Logan, Paul Young

In this British import set in 1944, a woman named Janie (Phyllis Logan) lives on a small farm in Scotland with her husband, Dongal (Paul Young), fifteen years her senior. As part of a war rehabilitation program, the couple welcomes three Italian POW's onto their place, and Janie, infatuated with their accents and cultural differences, falls in love. Rated PG.

1984　　118 minutes

ANOTHER TIME, ANOTHER PLACE
★

DIRECTOR: Lewis Allen
CAST: Lana Turner, Barry Sullivan, Glynis Johns, Sean Connery, Sidney James

Ho-hum melodrama about American newspaperwoman whose brief affair with British journalist ends in tragedy when he dies during World War II. Flat and unconvincing, this indifferent weeper is notable mainly for the appearance of a young and sturdy-looking Sean Connery and an older, worldly-wise Lana Turner, who would soon face her greatest role as a mother during the trial of her daughter Cheryl, charged with murdering Turner's live-in lover, Johnny Stompanato. Connery gained some distinction and the admiration of the film crew when he flattened the overbearing Stompanato during production, but none of the behind-the-scenes excitement is evident in this dreary love story.

1958 B & W 98 minutes

ANTONY AND CLEOPATRA
★★
DIRECTOR: Charlton Heston
CAST: Charlton Heston, Hildegarde Neil, Eric Porter, Fernando Rey, John Castle

Marginal film interpretation of Shakespeare's play. Obviously a tremendous amount of work on Charlton Heston's part, casting himself as Antony, but the film is lacking in energy. Rated PG.

1973 160 minutes

APPRENTICESHIP OF DUDDY KRAVITZ, THE
★★★
DIRECTOR: Ted Kotcheff
CAST: Richard Dreyfuss, Jack Warden, Micheline Lanctot, Denholm Elliott, Randy Quaid

Richard Dreyfuss, in an early starring role, is the main attraction in this quirky little comedy about the rise of a poor Jewish lad from a Montreal ghetto. The story is full of cruel and smartassed humor, a trait that haunts Dreyfuss to this day. One of the brighter moments is a film-within-the-film, an avant-garde interpretation of a bar mitzvah (one of Duddy's attempts to get rich quick). Another involves the buoyancy of various parts of

the anatomy. Ultimately, the film is too long and too shrill. Rated PG for sexual content.

1974 121 minutes

ARCH OF TRIUMPH
★★★
DIRECTOR: Lewis Milestone
CAST: Ingrid Bergman, Charles Boyer, Charles Laughton, Louis Calhern

In Paris before the Nazis arrive, a refugee doctor meets and falls in love with a woman with a past in this long, slow-paced, emotionless drama. It's sad, frustrating, tedious, and sometimes murky, but fans of the principal players will forgive and enjoy.

1948 B & W 120 minutes

ARRANGEMENT, THE
★
DIRECTOR: Elia Kazan
CAST: Kirk Douglas, Deborah Kerr, Faye Dunaway, Richard Boone

The cast is the only real reason for watching this tedious talkfest between Kirk Douglas and whoever will listen after he botches a suicide attempt and reevaluates his life. Very nicely produced, but sets and style contribute only so much to a film. A hook that involves the audience is sadly lacking here. The principal performers deserve better. Rated R for adult themes, language.

1969 127 minutes

ARROWSMITH
★★★★
DIRECTOR: John Ford
CAST: Ronald Colman, Helen Hayes, Richard Bennett, DeWitt Jennings, Beulah Bondi, Myrna Loy

Mellifluous-voiced Ronald Colman is a young, career-dedicated research doctor tempted by the profits of commercialism in this faithful rendering of Sinclair Lewis's noted novel of medicine. Helen Hayes is his first wife—doomed to die before he sees the light. This is the first film to center seriously on a doctor's career and raise the question of professional integrity and morality versus quick money and social status.

1931   B & W 101 minutes

ASSASSIN OF YOUTH (AKA MARIJUANA)
★
DIRECTOR: Elmer Clifton
CAST: Luana Walter, Arthur Gardner, Earl Dwire, Fern Emmet

This silly, low-budget exploitation film tells the story of a courageous young reporter who goes undercover to infiltrate the marijuana cult that has been wreaking havoc with a local town. Cornball humor in the form of "Pop" Brady and the scooter-riding Henrietta Frisbie, the town snoop, gives this an extra edge on most films of this nature, but not much of an edge. Veteran silent film director Elmer Clifton and producer Leo J. McCarthy co-wrote this epic and appear to be responsible for the dialogue and the newspaper headlines which appear like title cards (MARIJUANA CRAZED YOUTH, MARIJUANA DEALS DEATH). Some hardboiled stuff, but not too dynamic.

1936   B & W 67 minutes

ATLANTIC CITY
★★★★★
DIRECTOR: Louis Malle
CAST: Burt Lancaster, Susan Sarandon, Kate Reid

This superb motion picture has all of the elements that made the films of Hollywood's golden age great—with a few appropriately modern twists tossed in. The screenplay, by John Guare—about a struggling casino worker (Susan Sarandon) who becomes involved in a drug deal—gives us powerful drama, wonderful characters, memorable dialogue, and delightfully funny situations. And the performances by Burt Lancaster, Sarandon, and Kate Reid, in particular, are topnotch. As a result, every moment is worth savoring. Rated R because of brief nudity and violence.

1981   104 minutes

ATOMIC CAFE, THE
★★
DIRECTOR: Kevin Rafferty, Jayne Loader, Pierce Rafferty
CAST: Documentary

Beyond being an interesting cultural document, this feature-length compilation of post–World War II propaganda, documentary, and newsreel footage on official and unofficial American attitudes toward the atomic bomb has little to offer, especially as entertainment. Advance word was that it was both funny and frightening. Well, it is funny in a very dark, unrelenting sort of way. Overall, however, it's just plain depressing. No MPAA rating. The film has no objectionable material, though some of the footage featuring casualties of atomic bomb explosions is quite graphic.

1982   B & W 88 minutes

AUTOBIOGRAPHY OF MISS JANE PITTMAN, THE
★★★★★
DIRECTOR: John Korty

CAST: Cicely Tyson, Richard Dysart, Odetta, Michael Murphy, Barbara Chuney, Thalmus Rasculala

This terrific television movie traces black history in America from the Civil War years to the turbulent civil rights movement of the 1960s. All this is seen through the eyes of 110-year-old ex-slave Jane Pittman (Cicely Tyson). The entire cast is superb, but Tyson still manages to tower above the others in the title role. This is a real must-see film. There is no rating, but it should be noted that there are some violent scenes.

1974   110 minutes

AUTUMN SONATA
★★★★★

DIRECTOR: Ingmar Bergman
CAST: Ingrid Bergman, Liv Ullmann, Lena Nyman

Ingmar Bergman directed this superb Swedish release about the first meeting in seven years of a daughter (Liv Ullmann) with her difficult concert pianist mother (Ingrid Bergman). A great film, without a doubt. Rated PG.

1978   97 minutes

AVIATOR, THE
★★

DIRECTOR: George Miller
CAST: Christopher Reeve, Rosanna Arquette, Jack Warden, Scott Wilson, Tyne Daly, Sam Wanamaker

This film, about a grumpy flyer (Christopher Reeve) during the 1920s who is forced to take a feisty passenger (Rosanna Arquette) on his mail route, is too similar to *High Road to China*. It has neither the high adventure nor the humor of the latter. What we're left with is a predictable boy-meets-girl drama that takes a left turn into a danger-in-the-wilderness cliché. To the credit of director George Miller, the second half works fairly well. But by that time most viewers will have given up on the movie, something the film company did as well (they put it on the shelf after a brief theatrical release). Rated PG.

1984   102 minutes

AVIATOR'S WIFE, THE
★★★½

DIRECTOR: Eric Rohmer
CAST: Philippe Marlaud, Marie Riviere, Anne-Laure Marie, Matthieu Carriere

Not much happens in a film by French director Eric Rohmer, at least not in the traditional sense. Mostly, there's just talk. Yet, if you pay close attention, a few special things do happen—and they are quite enough. In the story, a young law student named François (Philippe Marlaud) is crushed when he discovers his lover, Anne (Marie Riviere), in the company of another man and decides to spy on them. In French, with English subtitles. Unrated, the film has no objectionable material.

1981   104 minutes

BABY DOLL
★★★★

DIRECTOR: Elia Kazan
CAST: Carroll Baker, Eli Wallach, Karl Malden, Mildred Dunnock, Lonnie Chapman, Rip Torn

Set in hot, humid, sleazy Mississippi, this is the story of a child bride (Carroll Baker) who sleeps in a crib, her lusting, short-on-brains husband (Karl Malden), and a scheming business rival (Eli Wallach) determined to use and abuse them both. What else but a Tennessee Williams story? Tepid stuff today, but when first released, the film was condemned by the Legion of Decency. The cast, all of whom are identified with the playwright, is excellent. Baker's portrayal gave her a lifetime nickname. Her skimpy pajamas became fashionable.

1956   B & W   114 minutes

BABY THE RAIN MUST FALL
★★½

DIRECTOR: Robert Mulligan
CAST: Steve McQueen, Lee Remick, Don Murray

This confusing character study of a convict who is paroled and reunited with his family raises a lot of questions but answers none of them.

1965   B & W   100 minutes

BACK ROADS
★★★

DIRECTOR: Martin Ritt
CAST: Sally Field, Tommy Lee Jones, David Keith

Pug (Tommy Lee Jones) and prostitute (Sally Field) hitch and brawl down the back roads of the South in this sometimes raunchy, often hilarious romance-fantasy. Though it drags a bit, the performances by the two stars and an earthy, down-home charm make it worthwhile. Rated R.

1981   94 minutes

BACK STREET
★★★

DIRECTOR: David Miller
CAST: Susan Hayward, John Gavin, Vera Miles

Third version of novelist Fannie Hurst's romantic tearjerker about clandestine love, with Susan Hayward as the noble mistress who sacrifices all and stands by her lover even when he stupidly marries another woman.

1961   107 minutes

BAD BOYS
★★★★½

DIRECTOR: Rick Rosenthal
CAST: Sean Penn, Esai Morales, Reni Santoni, Ally Sheedy, Jim Moody, Eric Gurry

This is a grimly riveting vision of troubled youth. Sean Penn and Esai Morales are featured as Chicago street hoods sworn to kill each other in prison. It's exciting, thought-provoking, and violent, but the violence, for once, is justified and not merely exploitive. Rated R for language, violence, and nudity.

1983   123 minutes

BADLANDS
★★★★

DIRECTOR: Terence Malick
CAST: Martin Sheen, Sissy Spacek, Warren Oates, Ramon Bieri, Alan Vint

Featuring fine performances by Sissy Spacek, Martin Sheen, and Warren Oates, this is a disturbing recreation of the Starkweather-Fugate killing spree of the 1950s. It is undeniably a work of intelligence and fine craftsmanship. However, as with Martin Scorsese's *Taxi Driver* and Bob Fosse's *Star 80*, *Badlands* is not an easy film to watch. Rated PG.

1973   95 minutes

BALLAD OF A SOLDIER
★★★½

DIRECTOR: Grigori Chukhrai
CAST: Vladimir Ivashov, Shanna Prokhorenko, Antonina Maximova, Nikolai Kruchkov

A soldier finds love and adventure on a ten-day pass to see his mother.

This import features excellent cinematography and acting, and despite the always obvious Soviet propaganda, some piercing insights into the Russian soul. In Russian with English subtitles.

1959   B & W   89 minutes

BANG THE DRUM SLOWLY
★★★★

DIRECTOR: John Hancock
CAST: Robert De Niro, Michael Moriarty, Vincent Gardenia

Robert De Niro and Michael Moriarty are given a perfect showcase for their acting talents in this poignant film, and they don't disappoint. The friendship of two baseball players comes alive as the team's star pitcher (Moriarty) tries to assist journeyman catcher (De Niro) in completing one last season before succumbing to Hodgkin's disease. The story may lead to death, but it is filled with life, hope, and compassion. Rated PG.

1973   98 minutes

BARABBAS
★★½

DIRECTOR: Richard Fleischer
CAST: Anthony Quinn, Jack Palance, Ernest Borgnine, Katy Jurado

Early Dino De Laurentiis opus is long on production, short on credibility. Standard gory religious spectacle follows the life of the thief Barabbas, whom Pilate freed when Jesus was condemned to die. Good cast of veteran character actors attempts to move this epic along, but fails.

1962   144 minutes

BARRY LYNDON
★★★

DIRECTOR: Stanley Kubrick

CAST: Ryan O'Neal, Marisa Berenson, Patrick Magee, Hardy Krüger, Steven Berkoff, Gay Hamilton

This period epic directed by Stanley Kubrick will please only the filmmaker's most fervent admirers and get yawns from most other viewers. Although exquisitely photographed and meticulously designed, this three-hour motion picture adaptation of William Makepeace Thackeray's novel about an eighteenth-century rogue is a flawed masterpiece at best and is far too drawn out. In addition, Ryan O'Neal is a real zero in the title role. However, it is worth watching for the lush cinematography by John Alcott and its memorable moments, of which there are admittedly quite a few. Rated PG for brief nudity and violence.

1975   183 minutes

BATTLE OF ALGIERS
★★★★

DIRECTOR: Gillo Pontecorvo
CAST: Yacef Saadi, Jean Martin, Brahim Haggiag, Tomasso Neri, Samia Kerbash

This gut-wrenching Italian-Algerian pseudodocumentary about the war between Algerian citizens and their French "protectors" was released when America's involvement in Vietnam was still to reach its peak, but the parallels between the two stories are obvious. Covering the years from 1954 to 1962, this film is an emotional experience—it is not recommended for the casual viewer and is too strong (and depressing) for children, but if you want to take a look into a world without security and learn some history along the way, *Battle of Algiers* is a good choice.

1965   B & W   123 minutes

BATTLESHIP POTEMKIN, THE
★★★★★

DIRECTOR: Sergei Eisenstein
CAST: Alexander Antonov, Vladimir Barsky, Grigori Alexandrov, Mikhail Goronorov

One of a handful of landmark motion pictures. This silent classic, directed by the legendary Sergei Eisenstein, depicts the mutiny of the crew of a Russian battleship and its aftermath. It was primarily released by the infant Soviet government as propaganda to glorify those who first revolted against the Czar. Its impact far exceeded such narrow boundaries. The photography, editing, and directorial technique expanded the threshhold of what was then standard cinema story-telling. The massacre of civilians on the steppes of Odessa remains one of the most powerful scenes in film history.

1925   B & W   65 minutes

BAY BOY, THE
★★★★½

DIRECTOR: Daniel Petrie
CAST: Liv Ullmann, Keifer Sutherland, Robert Taylor, Joe MacPherson, Kevin McKenzie, Iris Currie, Francis MacNeil, Michael Egyes, Mary Mackinnon

The story of a brief period in an adolescent boy's life while growing up in a small mining town on the Nova Scotia coast during the mid-1930s, this film develops the character, including the sexual awakening, guilt, and terror, of Donald Campbell (Keifer Sutherland). Liv Ullmann is well cast as Donald's mother. Young Donald, an extremely fine student, is encouraged by his mother to enter the priesthood. Donald is much too interested in exploring his growing (yet still quite naive) interest in young ladies. Donald becomes the sole witness to a tragic murder and is forced to endure in silence the knowledge that the murderer is behind virtually every step he takes.

1985   104 minutes

BEACHCOMBER, THE
★★★

DIRECTOR: Erich Pommer
CAST: Charles Laughton, Elsa Lanchester, Tyrone Guthrie, Robert Newton

This Somerset Maugham story of a dissolute South Seas beachcomber and the lady missionary who reforms him is sculptor's clay in the expert dramatic hands of Charles Laughton and Elsa Lanchester. He is delightful as the shiftless, conniving bum; she is clever and captivating as his Bible-toting nemesis. There's a scene at a bar that is Charles Laughton at his wily, eye-rolling, blustering best.

1938   B & W   80 minutes

BECKET
★★★★

DIRECTOR: Peter Glenville
CAST: Richard Burton, Peter O'Toole, Martha Hunt, Pamela Brown

Magnificently acted spectacle of the stormy relationship between England's King Henry II (Peter O'Toole) and his friend and nemesis Archbishop Thomas Becket (Richard Burton). This visually stimulating historical pageant, set in twelfth-century England, garnered Oscar nominations for both its protagonists.

1964   148 minutes

BECKY SHARP
★★½

DIRECTOR: Rouben Mamoulian
CAST: Miriam Hopkins, Frances Dee, Cedric Hardwicke, Billie Burke, Alison Skipworth, Nigel Bruce

Well-mounted historical drama of a callous young woman who lives for social success is lovely to look at in its original three-strip Technicolor. Fine performances by a veteran cast bolster this first sound screen adaptation of Thackeray's *Vanity Fair*, and director Rouben Mamoulian shows his famous style and fluidity with the new color cameras. Title player Miriam Hopkins was at this point in her career at the top of the industry and considered by many (especially herself) to be a serious rival to Bette Davis, Katharine Hepburn, etc.

1935   83 minutes

BEDFORD INCIDENT, THE
★★★

DIRECTOR: James B. Harris
CAST: Richard Widmark, Sidney Poitier, Martin Balsam, Wally Cox, Eric Portman

A battle of wits aboard a U.S. destroyer tracking Soviet submarines off Greenland during the Cold War. Richard Widmark is a skipper with an obsession to hunt and hound a particular sub. A conflict develops between the captain and Sidney Poitier, a cocky magazine reporter along for the ride.

1965   B & W 102 minutes

BEGUILED, THE
★★★★

DIRECTOR: Don Siegel
CAST: Clint Eastwood, Geraldine Page, Jo Ann Harris

An atmospheric, daring change of pace for director Don Siegel (*Dirty Harry*) and star Clint Eastwood, this production features the squinty-eyed actor as a wounded Confederate soldier taken in by the head (Geraldine Page) of a girls' school. He becomes the catalyst for incidents of jealousy and hatred among its inhabitants, and this leads to a startling, unpredictable conclusion. Rated R.

1971   109 minutes

BEHOLD A PALE HORSE
★

DIRECTOR: Fred Zinnemann
CAST: Gregory Peck, Anthony Quinn, Omar Sharif

Gregory Peck is miscast in this slow, talky, vague drama of a Loyalist holdout in post–Civil War Spain who continues to harass the Franco regime. Everyone tries hard, but the film steadily sinks.

1963   118 minutes

BELFAST ASSASSIN
★★½

DIRECTOR: Lawrence Gordon Clark
CAST: Derek Thompson, Ray Lonnen, Margaret Shevlin, Gil Brailey, Benjamin Whitrow

This film, about an IRA hit man and a British antiterrorist who is ordered to track down the Irish assassin on his own turf, could have used a clipper-happy editor; the same statement could have been said in much less than two hours plus. The film takes a pro-IRA stand, yet is open-minded enough to see the other side of the story without resorting to self-righteousness. Not rated, but the equivalent of a PG for sex, violence, and profanity.

1982   130 minutes

BELL JAR, THE
★★★

DIRECTOR: Larry Peerce
CAST: Marilyn Hassett, Julie Harris, Anne Jackson, Barbara Barrie, Robert Klein, Donna Mitchell

Based on the novel by Sylvia Plath about the mental breakdown of an overachiever in the world of big business in the 1950s, this film has a strong lead performance by Marilyn Hassett and thoughtful direction by her husband, Larry Peerce. But the overriding melancholy of the subject matter makes it difficult to watch. Barbara Barrie is also memorable in a key supporting role. Rated R.

1979   107 minutes

BELLS OF ST. MARY'S, THE
★★★★½

DIRECTOR: Leo McCarey
CAST: Bing Crosby, Ingrid Bergman, Ruth Donnelly

An effective sequel to *Going My Way*, also directed by Leo McCarey, this film has Bing Crosby returning as the modern-minded priest once again up against a headstrong opponent, Mother Superior (played by Ingrid Bergman). While not as memorable as his encounter with hard-headed older priest Barry Fitzgerald in the first film, this relationship—and the movie as a whole—does have its viewing rewards.

1945   B & W 126 minutes

BERLIN ALEXANDERPLATZ
★★★½

DIRECTOR: Rainer Werner Fassbinder
CAST: Gunter Lamprecht, Hanna Schygulla, Barbara Sukowa, Gottfried John, Elisabeth Trissenaar

Remember the scene in Stanley Kubrick's *A Clockwork Orange* in which Malcolm MacDowell's eyes are wired open and he is forced to watch agonizing hour after agonizing hour of movies? That's how we often felt when wading through the fifteen-and-a-half hours of Rainer Werner Fassbinder's *magnum opus*, *Berlin Alexanderplatz*. Not that this much-praised German television production doesn't have its moments of interest, fascination, and yes, even genius. But as with all of Fassbinder's other films (*Lili Marleen*; *Veronika Voss*; *The Marriage of Maria Braun*; etc.), *Berlin Alexanderplatz* also has its excesses and false notes (only there are many more of them than usual, thanks to its length). Unrated.

1983   930 minutes

BEST LITTLE GIRL IN THE WORLD, THE
★★★★½

DIRECTOR: Sam O'Steen
CAST: Jennifer Jason Leigh, Charles Durning, Eva Marie Saint, Jason Miller

This gut-wrenching teleplay about a girl, portrayed by Jennifer Jason Leigh (*Fast Times at Ridgemont High*, *Eyes of a Stranger*, *Grandview U.S.A.*), who suffers from anorexia nervosa pulls no punches; some of the drama is hard to take, but if you can make it through the film's end, you'll feel rewarded. This was originally an after-school special. The entire cast turn in great performances, especially Leigh, who proves she is better than the teen exploitation films that are (hopefully) behind her. Not rated, but the equivalent of a PG for intense drama.

1986   90 minutes

BEST YEARS OF OUR LIVES, THE
★★★★★

DIRECTOR: William Wyler

CAST: Myrna Loy, Fredric March, Teresa Wright, Dana Andrews, Virginia Mayo, Harold Russell, Cathy O'Donnell

What happens when the fighting ends and warriors return home is the basis of this eloquent, compassionate film. Old master William Wyler takes his time and guides a superb group of players through a tangle of postwar emotional conflicts. Harold Russell's first scene has lost none of its impact. Keep in mind World War II had just ended when this film debuted.

1946   B & W 170 minutes

BETRAYAL
★★★★★

DIRECTOR: David Jones

CAST: Jeremy Irons, Ben Kingsley, Patricia Hodge

Harold Pinter's play about the slow death of a marriage has been turned into an intelligent and innovative film that begins with the affair breaking apart and follows it backward to the beginning. Stars Ben Kingsley (*Gandhi*), Jeremy Irons (*Moonlighting*), and Patricia Hodge are superb. Rated R for profanity.

1983   95 minutes

BETSY, THE
★★

DIRECTOR: Daniel Petrie

CAST: Laurence Olivier, Tommy Lee Jones, Robert Duvall, Katharine Ross, Lesley-Anne Down, Jane Alexander

Here is a classic example of how to waste loads of talent and money. The Harold Robbins novel about a wealthy family in the auto manufacturing business was trashy to start with, but after Hollywood gets done with it, not even the likes of Laurence Olivier can save this debacle. The cast is hopelessly lost in this mess. Rated R.

1978   125 minutes

BETWEEN FRIENDS
★★½

DIRECTOR: Lou Antonio

CAST: Elizabeth Taylor, Carol Burnett, Barbara Rush, Stephen Young, Henry Ramer

Two middle-aged divorcées meet and gradually form a life-sustaining friendship. This made-for-cable feature occasionally gets mired in melodramatic tendencies, but the dynamic performances of its two charismatic stars make it well worth watching. Unrated.

1983   100 minutes

BEYOND A REASONABLE DOUBT
★★★

DIRECTOR: Fritz Lang

CAST: Dana Andrews, Joan Fontaine, Sidney Blackmer, Philip Bourneuf, Shepperd Strudwick, Dan Seymour

To reveal the faults of the justice system, novelist Dana Andrews allows himself to be incriminated in a murder. The plan is to reveal his innocence and discredit capital punishment at the last minute. But the one man who can exonerate him is killed. As this plot develops, a variety of submerged elements slowly surfaces to make this film far more than just one of suspense. Don't expect surprise, but shock!

1956   B & W 80 minutes

BEYOND FEAR
★★★

DIRECTOR: Yannick Andrei

CAST: Michel Bouquet, Michel Constantin, Marilu Tolo, Moustache, Paul Crauchet, Gerard Borman

While dubbing foreign-language films with English is a major irritant in so many of the foreign films that come out on video these days, this movie is almost compelling enough to make the viewer forget this problem. The plot is not a new one: an innocent man is mistaken for a gangster and is informed of a robbery. Ultimately, his wife and child are taken hostage by the band of outlaws and he must work with the police to ensure the safety of his family. Rated R by mid-1970s standards due to violence and profanity (very little of both, actually).

1975   92 minutes

BEYOND THE LIMIT
★★½
DIRECTOR: John MacKenzie
CAST: Michael Caine, Richard Gere

A dull, unconvincing adaptation of *The Honorary Consul*, Graham Greene's novel about love and betrayal in an Argentinian town, stars Michael Caine as a kidnapped diplomat and Richard Gere as the doctor in love with his wife. It'll take you beyond your limit. Rated R.

1983   103 minutes

BEYOND THE VALLEY OF THE DOLLS
🐛
DIRECTOR: Russ Meyer
CAST: Dolly Reed, Cynthia Myers, Marcia McBroom

Like all other films by Russ Meyer, *Dolls* dabbles in petty political ideas and contains enough 1960s hip talk to make you lose your lunch. The folks down at Fox must have been on mushrooms to back

this one; it's like a bad acid trip, man. This was rated X when it came out, but by today's standards it's an R for gratuitous nudity and profanity.

1970   109 minutes

BIBLE, THE
★★★
DIRECTOR: John Huston
CAST: Michael Parks, Ulla Bergryd, Richard Harris, John Huston, Ava Gardner

An overblown all-star treatment of five of the early stories in the Old Testament. Director John Huston gives this movie the feel of a Cecil B. De Mille spectacle, but there is little human touch to any of the stories. This expensively mounted production forgets that in the Bible, individual accomplishments are equally relevant to grandeur.

1966   174 minutes

BICYCLE THIEF, THE
★★★★
DIRECTOR: Vittorio De Sica
CAST: Lamberto Maggiorani, Lianella Carell, Enzo Staiola, Elena Altieri

Considered by critics an all-time classic, this touching, honest, beautifully human film speaks realistically to the heart with simple cinematic eloquence. A bill poster's bicycle, on which his job depends, is stolen. Ignored by the police, who see nothing special in the loss, and by the Church, to which material things are of small consequence, the anguished worker and his young son search Rome for the thief. One of a number of superb films to come out of post war Italy, this one captured 1949 Oscar for best foreign film. In Italian with English subtitles.

1949   B & W   90 minutes

BIG CHILL, THE
★★★½

DIRECTOR: Lawrence Kasdan

CAST: Tom Berenger, William Hurt, Glenn Close, Jeff Goldblum, Meg Tilly

As with John Sayles's superb *Return of the Secaucus 7*, this equally impressive and thoroughly enjoyable film by writer-director Lawrence Kasdan (*Body Heat*) concerns a weekend reunion of old friends, all of whom have gone on to varied lifestyles after once being united in the hip, committed 1960s. It features a who's-who of today's hot young stars as the friends who find they must face the maxim "Never trust anyone over thirty" and reassess its validity, especially since they are now in that age bracket. Rated R for nudity and profanity.

1983   103 minutes

BIG WEDNESDAY
★★

DIRECTOR: John Milius

CAST: Jan-Michael Vincent, Gary Busey, William Katt, Lee Purcell, Patti D'Arbanville

Only nostalgic surfers with more than a little patience will enjoy this ode to the beach set and that perfect wave by writer-director John Milius (*Conan the Barbarian*). Rated PG.

1978   120 minutes

BILITIS
★★★★

DIRECTOR: David Hamilton

CAST: Patti D'Arbanville, Bernard Giraudeau, Gillis Kohler, Mona Kristensen, Mathieu Carriere

A surprisingly tasteful and sensitive soft-core sex film, this details the sexual awakening of the title character, a 16-year-old French girl (Mona Kristensen) while she spends the summer with a family friend (Patti D'Arbanville). The two briefly become lovers, but this ends when Bilitis encounters a young man (Bernard Giraudeau) and engages in a sweet summer romance. Rated R for nudity and simulated sex.

1982   93 minutes

BILL
★★★★½

DIRECTOR: Anthony Page

CAST: Mickey Rooney, Dennis Quaid, Largo Woodruff

Extremely moving drama based on the real-life experiences of Bill Sackter, a retarded adult forced to leave the mental institution that has been his home for the past forty-five years. Mickey Rooney won an Emmy for his excellent portrayal of Bill. Dennis Quaid plays a filmmaker who offers kindness and employment to Bill as he tries to cope with life on the "outside." Unrated.

1981   100 minutes

BILLY BUDD
★★★½

DIRECTOR: Peter Ustinov

CAST: Terence Stamp, Robert Ryan, Peter Ustinov

Herman Melville's brooding, allegorical novel of the overpowering of the innocent is set against a backdrop of life on an eighteenth-century British warship. The plight of a young sailor subjected to the treacherous whims of his ship's tyrannical first mate is well-acted throughout. It is powerful filmmaking and succeeds in leaving its audience unsettled and questioning.

1962   B & W 112 minutes

BILLY LIAR
★★★★

DIRECTOR: John Schlesinger
CAST: Tom Courtenay, Julie Christie, Finlay Currie, Ethel Griffies, Mona Washbourne

Poignant slices of English middle-class life are served expertly in this finely played story of a lazy young man who escapes dulling routine by retreating into fantasy. The eleven minutes Julie Christie is on-screen are electric and worth the whole picture.

1963   B & W 96 minutes

BIRDMAN OF ALCATRAZ
★★★★

DIRECTOR: John Frankenheimer
CAST: Burt Lancaster, Karl Malden, Thelma Ritter, Telly Savalas

In one of his best screen performances, Burt Lancaster plays Robert Stroud, the prisoner who became a world-renowned authority on birds.

1962   B & W 143 minutes

BIRDY
★★★★½

DIRECTOR: Alan Parker
CAST: Matthew Modine, Nicolas Cage, John Harkins, Sandy Baron, Karen Young, Bruno Kirby

Matthew Modine and Nicolas Cage give unforgettable performances in this dark, disturbing, yet somehow uplifting study of an odd young man named Birdy (Modine) from South Philadelphia who wants to be a bird. That way he can fly away from all his troubles—which worsen manifold after a traumatic tour of duty in Vietnam. Based on the novel by William Wharton, this is a multilevel and rewarding work directed with uncommon restraint and insight by Alan Parker. Rated R for violence, nudity, and profanity.

1985   120 minutes

BIRTH OF A NATION, THE
★★★★

DIRECTOR: D. W. Griffith
CAST: Lillian Gish, Mae Marsh, Henry B. Walthall, Miriam Cooper

Videotape will probably be the only medium in which you will ever see this landmark silent classic. D. W. Griffith's epic saga of the American Civil War and its aftermath is today considered too racist in its glorification of the Ku Klux Klan ever to be touched by television or revival theaters. This is filmdom's most important milestone (the first to tell a cohesive story) but should only be seen by those emotionally prepared for its disturbing point of view.

1915   B & W 158 minutes

BITCH, THE
★★

DIRECTOR: Gerry O'Hara
CAST: Joan Collins, Kenneth Haigh, Michael Coby

Joan Collins has the title role in this fiasco, an adaptation of sister Jackie Collins's book. Unfortunately, much was lost when transferred to the screen. It's about two "users," Fontaine (Collins) and Niko (Michael Coby), who find each other when she's in need of money because her disco almost goes under and he's fencing stolen jewels for the mob. This film spends too much time showing Joan Collins (and her lady friends) jumping into bed with younger men and then rejecting them. Only worth watching if you want to see Collins in the buff before her "Dynasty" days. Heavy British accents make the dialogue hard to follow. Rated R.

1979 93 minutes

BITTER HARVEST
★★★★

DIRECTOR: Roger Young
CAST: Ron Howard, Art Carney, Richard Dysart

In this made-for-television film based on a true incident, Ron Howard gives an excellent performance as an at-first panicky and then take-charge farmer whose dairy farm herd becomes sick and begins dying. His battle against bureaucracy, as he earnestly tries to find out the cause of the illness (chemicals in the feed), provides for scary, close-to-home drama. Good supporting cast.

1981 104 minutes

BLACK LIKE ME
★★★

DIRECTOR: Carl Lerner
CAST: James Whitmore, Roscoe Lee Browne, Will Geer, Sorrell Booke

Based on the book by John Griffin, this film poses the question: What happens when a white journalist takes a drug that turns his skin black? The interesting premise almost works. James Whitmore plays the reporter, who wishes to experience racism firsthand. Somewhat provocative at its initial release, but by today's standards, a lot of the punch is missing.

1964 B & W 107 minutes

BLACK MAGIC
★★½

DIRECTOR: Gregory Ratoff

CAST: Orson Welles, Akim Tamiroff, Nancy Guild, Raymond Burr, Frank Latimore

Orson Welles revels in the role of famous eighteenth-century charlatan Count Cagliostro—born Joseph Balsamo, a peasant with imagination and a flair for magic, hypnosis, and the power of superstition. The story is of his tempestuous life and career, and Cagliostro's attempt to gain influence and clout in Italy using his strange and sinister talents. The star co-directed (without credit) and enjoyed a busman's holiday performing legerdemain and other magic, an off-screen hobby for which he had considerable ability. Raymond Burr is a long way from Perry Mason in this one. Though a handsome film, under analysis it shakes down to a rather amateurish effort.

1949 B & W 105 minutes

BLACK MARBLE, THE
★★★

DIRECTOR: Harold Becker
CAST: Paula Prentiss, Harry Dean Stanton, Robert Foxworth

A Los Angeles cop (Robert Foxworth) and his new partner (Paula Prentiss) attempt to capture a dog snatcher (Harry Dean Stanton) who is demanding a high ransom from a wealthy dog lover. Along the way, they fall in love. Based on Joseph Wambaugh's novel. Directed by Harold Becker (The Onion Field). Overlooked at the time of its release, but well worth the viewer's time. Rated PG—language, some violence.

1980 110 minutes

BLACK NARCISSUS
★★★½

DIRECTOR: Michael Powell

CAST: Deborah Kerr, Jean Simmons, David Farrar, Flora Robson, Sabu

Worldly temptations, including those of the flesh, create many difficulties for a group of nuns starting a mission in the Himalayas. Superb photography makes this early postwar British effort a visual delight. Unfortunately, key plot elements in this unusual drama were cut from the American prints by censors.

1947   99 minutes

BLACK ORPHEUS
★★★★★

DIRECTOR: Marcel Camus
CAST: Breno Mello, Marpessa Dawn, Lea Garcia, Lourdes de Oliveira

The Greek myth of Orpheus, the unrivaled musician, and his ill-fated love for Eurydice has been updated and set in Rio de Janeiro during carnival in this superb film. A Portuguese-French co-production, it has all the qualities of a genuine classic. Its stunning photography captures both the magical spirit of the original legend and the tawdry yet effervescent spirit of Brazil. Fine acting and a haunting musical round out this splendid viewing treat.

1952   B & W   98 minutes

BLACKMAIL
★★★

DIRECTOR: Alfred Hitchcock
CAST: Anny Ondra, Sara Allgood, John Longden, Charles Paton, Donald Calthrop, Cyril Ritchard

Hitchock's first sound film stands up well when viewed today and was responsible for pushing Great Britain into the world film market. Many bits of film business that were to become Hitchcock trademarks are evident in this film, including the first of his cameo appearances. Story of a woman who faces the legal system as well as a blackmailer for murdering an attacker in self-defense was originally shot as a silent film but partially reshot and converted into England's first sound release in an effort to compete with American imports. Future Captain Hook Cyril Ritchard essays an early role in this film along with respected stage actress Sara Allgood, still years away from her contract with Twentieth Century Fox and classic films like *How Green Was My Valley* and *The Lodger*.

1929   B & W   86 minutes

BLESS THE BEASTS AND THE CHILDREN
★

DIRECTOR: Stanley Kramer
CAST: Billy Mumy, Barry Robins, Miles Chapin, Ken Swofford, Jesse White, Vanessa Brown

Stanley Kramer's heavy-handed allegory is about as subtle as a brick through a plate-glass window. A group of misfit teenagers (led by Billy Mumy, of "Lost in Space" fame) at a western ranch-resort rebel against their moronic counselors to save a nearby herd of buffalo from being slaughtered. This knee-jerk liberal treatise is a virtual textbook on excess: the kids are all sensitive and thoughtful, the adults all bigoted and brutal, and the storyline consistently overwrought. A major waste of a good cast and an intriguing premise. Rated R for explicit violence.

1972   109 minutes

BLOOD AND SAND
★★★

DIRECTOR: Rouben Mamoulian

CAST: Tyrone Power, Rita Hayworth, Anthony Quinn, Linda Darnell, Nazimova, John Carradine

The "Moment of Truth" is not always just before the matador places his sword, as Tyrone Power learns in this classic story of a poor boy who rises to fame in the bullring. Linda Darnell loves him, Rita Hayworth leads him on, in this colorful remake of a 1922 Valentino starrer.

1941   B & W 123 minutes

BLOODBROTHERS
★★★½
DIRECTOR: Robert Mulligan
CAST: Richard Gere, Paul Sorvino, Tony LoBianco, Marilu Henner

Richard Gere and Marilu Henner star in this drama. Plot revolves around a family of construction workers and the son (Gere) who wants to do something else with his life. Rated R.

1978   116 minutes

BLOODLINE
🦃
DIRECTOR: Terence Young
CAST: Audrey Hepburn, Ben Gazzara, James Mason, Omar Sharif

This is an inexcusably repulsive montage of bad taste, predictability, and incoherence. Fans of Audrey Hepburn will be sickened to see her in such a travesty. Rated R for graphic sex scenes.

1979   116 minutes

BLUE ANGEL, THE
★★★★★
DIRECTOR: Joseph von Sternberg
CAST: Emil Jannings, Marlene Dietrich, Kurt Gerron, Hans Albers

This stunning tale about a strait-laced schoolteacher's obsession with a strip-tease dancer in Germany is the subject of many film classes. The photography, set design, and script are all topnotch, and there are spectacular performances by all. Not just to be enjoyed by film students, this classic should sit well with anybody looking for an intelligent evening of entertainment. In German, with English subtitles.

1930   B & W 98 minutes

BLUE COLLAR
★★★★½
DIRECTOR: Paul Schrader
CAST: Richard Pryor, Harvey Keitel, Yaphet Kotto

This film delves into the underbelly of the auto industry by focusing on the fears, frustrations, and suppressed anger of three factory workers, superbly played by Richard Pryor, Harvey Keitel, and Yaphet Kotto. It is the social comment and intense drama that make this a highly effective and memorable film. Good music, too. Rated R for violence, sex, nudity, and profanity.

1978   114 minutes

BLUE LAGOON, THE
★★½
DIRECTOR: Randal Kleiser
CAST: Brooke Shields, Christopher Atkins, Leo McKern, William Daniels

Two things save The Blue Lagoon from being a complete waste: Nestor Almendros's beautiful cinematography and the hilarious dialogue. Unfortunately, the laughs are unintentional. The screenplay is a combination of Swiss Family Robinson and the story of Adam and Eve, focusing on the growing love and sexuality of two children stranded on a South Sea island. Rated R for nudity and suggested sex.

1980   101 minutes

BLUE SKIES AGAIN
★★

DIRECTOR: Richard Michaels
CAST: Harry Hamlin, Robyn Barto, Mimi Rogers, Kenneth McMillan, Dana Elcar

A sure-fielding, solid-hitting prospect tries to break into the lineup of a minor league team. There's just one problem: The determined ballplayer is a female. This "triumph of the underdog" story, set on a baseball diamond, aims at the skies but is nothing more than a routine grounder. Rated PG.

1983   96 minutes

BLUME IN LOVE
★★★★

DIRECTOR: Paul Mazursky
CAST: George Segal, Susan Anspach, Kris Kristofferson, Marsha Mason, Shelley Winters

Sort of the male version of *An Unmarried Woman*, this Paul Mazursky film is the heartrending, sometimes shocking tale of a lawyer (George Segal) who can't believe his wife (Susan Anspach) doesn't love him anymore. He tries everything to win her back (including rape), and the result is a drama the viewer won't soon forget. Superb performances by Segal, Anspach, and Kris Kristofferson (as the wife's new beau) help immensely. Strong stuff, but memorable. Rated R for suggested sex, profanity, and violence.

1973   117 minutes

BOAT IS FULL, THE
★★★

DIRECTOR: Markus Imhoof

CAST: Tina Engel, Marin Walz

Markus Imhoof's film about refugees from the Nazis trying to obtain refuge in Switzerland is tragic and extraordinarily effective. It could have been a better movie, but it could hardly have been more heartbreaking. No MPAA rating.

1983   100 minutes

BOBBY DEERFIELD
★★★½

DIRECTOR: Sydney Pollack
CAST: Al Pacino, Marthe Keller, Romolo Valli

In this film, a racing driver (Al Pacino) becomes obsessed with the cause of how a competitor was seriously injured in an accident on the track. In a visit to the hospitalized driver, he meets a strange lady (Marthe Keller) and has an affair. Adapted by Oscar winner Alvin Sargent from Erich Remarque's novel *Heaven Has No Favorites*. Rated PG.

1977   124 minutes

BODY AND SOUL (ORIGINAL)
★★★★★

DIRECTOR: Robert Rossen
CAST: John Garfield, Lilli Palmer, Hazel Brooks, Anne Revere, William Conrad

The best boxing film ever, this is an allegorical work that covers everything from the importance of personal honor to corruption in politics. It details the story of a fighter (John Garfield) who'll do anything to get to the top—and does, with tragic results. Great performances, gripping drama, and stark realism make this a must-see.

1947   B & W 104 minutes

BODY AND SOUL (REMAKE)
★★★

DIRECTOR: George Bowers

CAST: Leon Isaac Kennedy, Jayne Kennedy, Perry Lang

Okay remake of the 1947 boxing classic. It's not original, deep, or profound, but entertaining, and for a movie like this, that's enough. However, the original, with John Garfield, is better. Rated R for violence and profanity.

1981   100 minutes

BODY HEAT
★★★★½

DIRECTOR: Lawrence Kasdan
CAST: William Hurt, Kathleen Turner, Richard Crenna, Mickey Rourke

This is a classic piece of *film noir*; full of suspense, characterization, atmosphere, and sexuality. Lawrence Kasdan (*Raiders of the Lost Ark* screenwriter) makes his directorial debut with this top-flight 1940s-style entertainment about a lustful romance between an attorney (William Hurt) and a married woman (Kathleen Turner) that leads to murder. Rated R because of nudity, sex, and murder.

1981   113 minutes

BOGIE
★★½

DIRECTOR: Vincent Sherman
CAST: Kevin O'Connor, Kathryn Harrold, Ann Wedgeworth, Patricia Barry

Boring biography of Humphrey Bogart unconvincingly enacted by Bogie and Bacall look-alikes. Too much time is spent on the drinking and temper problems of Bogie's third wife, Mayo Methot, and not enough time is spent on Lauren Bacall. Kathryn Harrold, as Bacall, is so bad, however, that it's probably a blessing her part is small.

1980   100 minutes

BOLERO

DIRECTOR: John Derek
CAST: Bo Derek, George Kennedy, Andrea Occhipinti, Ana Obregon, Olivia D'Abo, Greg Benson

Bo Derek stars in this simply awful soft-core porno flick as an American heiress in the 1920s who goes to Morocco in search of a real-life version of the passionate sheiks played by Rudolph Valentino in order to lose her virginity. She finds one, but he turns out to be a little lacking in the passion department. Next stop, Spain, and the bed of a sensitive bullfighter. What follows is indeed a lot of bull—it's stupid, boring, and amateurish. Unrated, the film has explicit sex, profanity, and nudity.

1984   106 minutes

BORN INNOCENT
★★★

DIRECTOR: Donald Wyre
CAST: Linda Blair, Kim Hunter, Joanna Miles

Rape with a broomstick marked this made-for-television film a shocker when first aired. The scene has been toned down, but the picture still penetrates with its searing story of cruelty in a juvenile detention home. Linda Blair does well as the runaway teenager. Joanna Miles is excellent as a compassionate teacher whose heart lies with her charges. It's strong stuff.

1974   100 minutes

BOSTONIANS, THE
★★★

DIRECTOR: James Ivory

CAST: Christopher Reeve, Vanessa Redgrave, Jessica Tandy, Madeleine Potter, Nancy Marchand, Wesley Addy, Barbara Bryne, Linda Hunt, Charles McCaughan, Nancy New, John Van Ness Philip, Wallace Shawn

Another visually striking but dry production from Merchant Ivory Productions. Most of the sparks of conflict come not from the tortured love affair between Christopher Reeve and Madeleine Potter or the main theme of women's fight for equality, but from the few scenes of direct confrontation between Reeve and Vanessa Redgrave. Redgrave delivers another fascinating character study that draws you to the screen. Costumes and settings are, as always in these productions, lavish and rich. The setting is Boston during the Centennial. A good "quiet-evening-at-home-by-the-fire"–type movie.

1984   120 minutes

BOUND FOR GLORY
★★★★
DIRECTOR: Hal Ashby
CAST: David Carradine, Ronny Cox, Melinda Dillon, Randy Quaid, Gail Strickland, Ji-Tu Cumbuka, John Lehne

David Carradine had one of the best roles of his career as singer-composer Woody Guthrie. Film focuses on the depression years when Guthrie rode the rails across America. Director Hal Ashby explores the lives of those hit hardest during those times. Haskell Wexler won the Oscar for his beautiful cinematography. Rated PG.

1976   147 minutes

BOY IN BLUE, THE
★★★
DIRECTOR: Charles Jarrott
CAST: Nicolas Cage, Christopher Plummer, Cynthia Dale, David Naughton

Nice little screen biography of Ned Hanlan (Nicolas Cage), the famed Canadian lad who owned the sport of international sculling (rowing) for ten years during the end of the nineteenth century. Although the picture plays like a thin retread of *Rocky*—particularly with respect to its music—the result is no less inspirational. Cage makes Hanlan larger than life, which is appropriate for legends, and Cynthia Dale is quite appealing as his upper-class lover. Christopher Plummer, who has made a career of oily villains, makes a suitably sinister foil. Inexplicably rated R for very brief nudity and coarse language.

1986   97 minutes

BOY IN THE PLASTIC BUBBLE, THE
★
DIRECTOR: Randal Kleiser
CAST: John Travolta, Glynnis O'Connor, Ralph Bellamy, Robert Reed, Diana Hyland, Buzz Aldrin

John Travolta has his hands full in this significantly altered television adaptation of the boy who, because of an immunity deficiency, must spend every breathing moment in a sealed environment. Vapid stuff needlessly mired with sci-fi jargon and an embarrassing romance with Glynnis O'Connor. Considering the heroic struggles of the true David (who was much younger), this film is a grotesque insult. Unrated.

1976   100 minutes

BOY WHO COULD FLY, THE
★★★★

DIRECTOR: Nick Castle
CAST: Lucy Deakins, Jay Underwood, Bonnie Bedelia, Fred Savage, Colleen Dewhurst, Fred Gwynne, Mindy Cohn

Writer-director Nick Castle has created a marvelous motion picture which speaks to the dreamer in all of us. His heroine, Milly (Lucy Deakins), is a newcomer to a small town where her neighbor, Eric (Jay Underwood), neither speaks nor responds to other people. All he does is sit on his roof and pretend to fly. The authorities want to put him away, but Milly has other ideas. How these two outsiders overcome all odds is a story the entire family can enjoy. The performances are wonderful and the film leaves one feeling lighter than air—just like the title character. Rated PG for dramatic intensity.

1986   114 minutes

BOY WITH GREEN HAIR, THE
★★★

DIRECTOR: Joseph Losey
CAST: Dean Stockwell, Robert Ryan, Barbara Hale, Pat O'Brien

A young war orphan's hair changes color, makes him a social outcast, and brings a variety of bigots and narrow minds out of the woodwork in this food-for-thought fable. The medium is the message in this one.

1948   82 minutes

BOYS IN THE BAND, THE
★★★

DIRECTOR: William Friedkin
CAST: Kenneth Nelson, Peter White, Leonard Frey, Cliff Gorman

Widely acclaimed film about nine men who attend a birthday party and end up exposing their lives and feelings to one another in the course of the night. Eight of the men are gay; one is straight. One of the first American films to deal honestly with the subject of homosexuality. Sort of a large-scale *My Dinner with André* with the whole film shot on one set. Rated R.

1970   119 minutes

BREAKFAST AT TIFFANY'S
★★★★

DIRECTOR: Blake Edwards
CAST: Audrey Hepburn, George Peppard, Patricia Neal, Buddy Ebsen, Mickey Rooney, Martin Balsam

An offbeat yet tender love story of a New York writer and a fey party girl. Strong performances are turned in by George Peppard and Audrey Hepburn. Hepburn's Holly Golightly is a masterful creation that blends the sophistication of her job as a Manhattan "escort" with the childish country girl of her roots. Henry Mancini's score is justly famous, as it creates much of the mood for this wistful story.

1961   115 minutes

BREATHLESS (ORIGINAL)
★★★★★

DIRECTOR: Jean-Luc Godard
CAST: Jean-Paul Belmondo, Jean Seberg

Richard Gere or Jean-Paul Belmondo? The choice should be easy after you see the Godard version of this story of a carefree crook and his "along for the ride" girlfriend. Jean Seberg is the perfect "American in Paris," and Paris never looked more exotic or beckoning. In case you don't already know, the original screenplay was written by François Truffaut. See it for Belmondo's performance as the continent's most charming crook, but while you're along for the ride, note just how well-made a film can be.

1959　　　B & W　　89 minutes

BREATHLESS (REMAKE)
🦃

DIRECTOR: Jim McBride
CAST: Richard Gere, Valerie Kaprisky, Art Metrano, John P. Ryan

In this rambling, repulsive remake of Jean-Luc Godard's 1961 French film classic, Richard Gere plays a car thief hunted by police, and Valerie Kaprisky is the college student who is both attracted and repelled by the danger he represents. Watching these two aimless, amoral jerks fooling around for nearly two hours is not the proverbial good time at the movies. It's boring. Rated R for sex, nudity, profanity, and violence.

1983　　　　　　100 minutes

BRIAN'S SONG
★★★★★

DIRECTOR: Buzz Kulik
CAST: James Caan, Billy Dee Williams, Jack Warden, Judy Pace, Shelley Fabares

This is no doubt one of the best movies ever made originally for television. James Caan is Brian Piccolo, a running back for football's Chicago Bears. His friendship for superstar Gale Sayers (Billy Dee Williams) becomes a mutually stimulating rivalry on the field and inspirational strength when Brian is felled by cancer. As with any quality film that deals with death, this movie is buoyant with life and warmth. Rated G.

1970　　　　　　73 minutes

BRIDGE OF SAN LUIS REY, THE
★★½

DIRECTOR: Rowland V. Lee
CAST: Lynn Bari, Nazimova, Louis Calhern, Akim Tamiroff, Francis Lederer, Blanche Yurka, Donald Woods

Five people meet death when an old Peruvian rope bridge collapses. This snail's-pace, moody version of Thornton Wilder's fatalistic 1920s novel traces their lives. Not too hot, and neither was the 1929 version.

1944　　　B & W　　85 minutes

BROTHER SUN, SISTER MOON
★★★★

DIRECTOR: Franco Zeffirelli
CAST: Graham Faulkner, Judi Bowker, Alec Guinness

Alec Guinness stars as the Pope in this movie about religious reformation. This film shows a young Francis of Assisi starting his own church. He confronts the Pope and rejects the extravagant and pompous ceremonies of the Catholic Church, preferring simple religious practices. Rated PG.

1973　　　　　　121 minutes

BROTHERS KARAMAZOV, THE
★★★

DIRECTOR: Richard Brooks
CAST: Yul Brynner, Claire Bloom, Lee J. Cobb, Maria Schell, Richard Basehart, William Shatner, Albert Salmi

Director Richard Brooks, who also scripted, and a fine cast work hard to give life to Russian novelist Fyodor Dostoyevsky's turgid account of the effect of the death of a domineering father on his disparate sons: a fun lover, a scholar, a religious zealot, and an epileptic. Studio promotion called it absorbing and exciting. It is, but only in flashes. In the long haul, it's like a train trip across Kansas at night.

1957   146 minutes

BRUBAKER
★★★½
DIRECTOR: Stuart Rosenberg
CAST: Robert Redford, Yaphet Kotto, Jane Alexander, Murray Hamilton

Robert Redford stars as Henry Brubaker, a reform-minded penologist who takes over a decrepit Ohio prison, only to discover the state prison system is even more rotten than its facilities. The film begins dramatically enough, with Redford arriving undercover at the prison, masquerading as one of the convicts. He witnesses cruel and unusual punishments, the wholesale theft of prison food, and the rape of a new inmate. After that, its dramatic impact lessens. Rated R.

1980   132 minutes

BUDDY SYSTEM, THE
★★
DIRECTOR: Glenn Jordan
CAST: Richard Dreyfuss, Susan Sarandon, Nancy Allen

In the middle of this movie, the would-be novelist (Richard Dreyfuss) takes his unbound manuscripts to the edge of the sea and lets the wind blow the pages away. He should have done the same thing with the screenplay for this mediocre romantic comedy. Dreyfuss is too good for this kind of slush. Perhaps because he won the best actor Oscar in 1977 for a similar kind of role (a would-be actor) in Neil Simon's The Goodbye Girl, the star thought he could repeat his success. Doesn't the poor guy know lightning rarely strikes twice in the same place? The plot is that

old chestnut about a fatherless little kid (Whil Wheaton) who helps his mom (Susan Sarandon) and an eligible man (Dreyfuss) get together. Are you yawning yet? Rated PG for profanity.

1984   110 minutes

BURN!
★★★★
DIRECTOR: Gillo Pontecorvo
CAST: Marlon Brando, Evaristo Marquez, Renato Salvatori, Tom Lyons, Norman Hill

Marlon Brando's performance alone makes Burn! worth watching. Seldom has a star so vividly and memorably lived up to his promise as an acting great, and that's what makes this film, directed by Gillo Pontecarvo (The Battle of Algiers), a must-see. Brando plays Sir William Walker, an egotistical mercenary sent by the British to instigate a slave revolt on a Portuguese-controlled sugar-producing island. He succeeds all too well by turning José Dolores (Evaristo Marquez) into a powerful leader and soon finds himself back on the island, plotting the downfall of his Frankenstein monster. Rated PG.

1969   112 minutes

BURNING BED, THE
★★★★
DIRECTOR: Robert Greenwald
CAST: Farrah Fawcett, Paul LeMat, Richard Masur, Grace Zabriskie

Farrah Fawcett is remarkably good in this made-for-TV film based on a true story. She plays a woman reaching the breaking point with her abusive and brutish husband, well played by Paul LeMat. Fawcett not only proves she can act, but that she has the capacity to pull off a multilayered role. Believable from start to finish, this is a superior television film.

1985   105 minutes

BUS IS COMING, THE
★★★

DIRECTOR: Wendell J. Franklin
CAST: Mike Sims, Stephanie Faulkner, Burl Bullock, Sandra Reed

The message of this production is: racism (both black and white) is wrong. In this film, Billy Mitchell (Mike Sims) is a young black soldier who returns to his hometown after his brother is murdered. Billy's white friend encourages him to nonviolently investigate the death of his brother, while his black friends want to use the death as an excuse to tear the town down. The bigoted white sheriff is the counterpart to the black radicals. The acting is not the greatest, but the film does succeed in making its point. Rated PG for violence.

1971   102 minutes

BUSTER AND BILLIE
★★

DIRECTOR: Daniel Petrie
CAST: Jan-Michael Vincent, Joan Goodfellow, Pamela Sue Martin, Clifton James

A handsome high-school boy falls in love with a homely but loving girl in rural South. Set in the 1940s, the film has an innocent, sweet quality until it abruptly shifts tone and turns into a mean-spirited revenge picture. Rated R for violence and nudity.

1974   100 minutes

BUTTERFLIES ARE FREE
★★★★

DIRECTOR: Milton Katselas
CAST: Goldie Hawn, Edward Albert, Eileen Heckart, Mike Warren

Edward Albert is a blind youth determined to be self-sufficient in spite of his overbearing mother and the distraction of his will-o'-the-wisp next-door neighbor (Goldie Hawn). This fast-paced comedy benefits from some outstanding performances. None is better than that by Eileen Heckart. Her concerned, protective, and sometimes overloving mother is a treasure to behold. Rated PG.

1972   109 minutes

BUTTERFLY
★★

DIRECTOR: Matt Climber
CAST: Pia Zadora, Stacy Keach, Orson Welles, Lois Nettleton

Sex symbol Pia Zadora starts an incestuous relationship with her father (played by Stacy Keach). Orson Welles, as a judge, is the best thing about this film. Rated R.

1982   107 minutes

BYE BYE BRAZIL
★★★½

DIRECTOR: Carlos Diegues
CAST: Joe Wilker, Betty Faria, Fabio Junior, Zaira Zambelli

This is a bawdy, bizarre, satiric, and sometimes even touching film that follows a ramshackle traveling tent show—the Caravana Rolidei—through the cities, jungle, and villages of Brazil. On the dramatic level, it lifts the sparkling veil of illusion that surrounds the "glamorous" world of show business to reveal the threadbare strings of reality. Visually, it gives the audience a fascinating tour of the South American country and a taste of its culture. Rated R.

1980   110 minutes

CABIN IN THE SKY
★★★

DIRECTOR: Vincente Minnelli
CAST: Eddie Anderson, Lena Horne,
    Ethel Waters, Rex Ingram,
    Louis Armstrong

One of Hollywood's first general-release black films and Vincente Minnelli's first feature. Eddie Anderson shows acting skill that was sadly and too long diluted by his playing foil for Jack Benny. Ethel Waters, as always, is superb. The film is a shade racist, but bear in mind that it was made in 1943, when Tinsel Town still thought blacks did nothing but sing, dance, and love watermelon.

1943   B & W 100 minutes

CADDIE
★★★★

DIRECTOR: Donald Crombie
CAST: Helen Morse, Takis Emmanuel, Jack Thompson, Jacki Weaver, Melissa Jaffer

This is an absorbing character study of a woman (Helen Morse, of *A Town like Alice*) who struggles to support herself and her children in Australia in the 1920s. Thanks greatly to the star's performance, it is yet another winner from Down Under. MPAA unrated, but contains mild sexual situations.

1976   107 minutes

CAESAR AND CLEOPATRA
★½

DIRECTOR: Gabriel Pascal
CAST: Claude Rains, Vivien Leigh,
    Stewart Granger, Francis L.
    Sullivan, Flora Robson

George Bernard Shaw's wordy play about Rome's titanic leader and Egypt's young queen. Claude Rains and Vivien Leigh are brilliant, but talk alone does not save the film from slowly sinking into the sands surrounding the Sphinx.

1946   127 minutes

CAINE MUTINY, THE
★★★★

DIRECTOR: Edward Dmytryk
CAST: Humphrey Bogart, José Ferrer, Van Johnson, Robert Francis, Fred MacMurray

Superb performances by Humphrey Bogart, Van Johnson, José Ferrer, and Fred MacMurray, among others, make this adaptation of Herman Wouk's classic novel an absolute must-see. This brilliant film concerns the hard-nosed Captain Queeg (Bogart), who may or may not be slightly unhinged, and the subsequent mutiny by his first officer and crew, who are certain he is. Beautifully done, a terrific movie.

1954   125 minutes

CAL
★★★★

DIRECTOR: Pat O'Connor
CAST: Helen Mirren, John Lynch,
    Danal McCann, Kitty Gibson

This superb Irish film, which focuses on "the troubles" in Northern Ireland, stars newcomer John Lynch as Cal, a teenaged boy who wants to sever his ties with the IRA. This turns out to be anything but easy, as the leader of the group tells him, "Not to act is to act." In other words, if he isn't for them, he's against them. Cal hides out at the home of local librarian Marcella (Helen Mirren, in a knockout of a performance). She's the widow of a policeman he helped murder. Nevertheless, Cal falls in love with her, and she, eventually, with him. But their idyllic love affair is ill-fated. Not only does she not know of Cal's involvement in her husband's death, but the IRA has no intention of letting him slip out of their grasp. Rated R for sex, nudity, profanity, and violence.

1984   102 minutes

CALIFORNIA DREAMING
★★

DIRECTOR: John Hancock
CAST: Glynnis O'Connor, Seymore Cassel, Dennis Christopher, Tanya Roberts

Wimpy film about a dork from Chicago trying to fit into the California lifestyle. The cast is good, but the story is maudlin and slow-moving. Rated R for partial nudity.

1979   93 minutes

CALIGULA

DIRECTOR: Tinto Brass
CAST: Malcolm McDowell, Peter O'-Toole, Teresa Ann Savoy, Helen Mirren

A $15 million porno flick with big stars, this is a disgusting historical piece that follows the ruthless Roman ruler through an endless series of decapitations and disembowelments. Not satisfied with the amount of nudity and sex put into the film by director Tinto Brass, *Penthouse* magazine publisher and film producer Bob Guccione inserted scenes of homosexuality and other sex acts. This release is a waste of celluloid and filmgoers' time. Rated X for every excess imaginable.

1980   156 minutes

CALL IT MURDER
★★★

DIRECTOR: Chester Erskine
CAST: Sidney Fox, Humphrey Bogart, Lynn Overman, Henry Hull, O. P. Heggie, Margaret Wycherly, Henry O'Neill, Richard Whorf

An inflexible jury foreman casts the vote that sends a young girl to her death in the electric chair. Hounded by the press, he nevertheless says he would do it again—even if a loved one were involved. Then he learns his daughter has committed murder under the same circumstances. As was usual in his early films, Bogie gets blasted in this one, originally released under the title *Midnight*.

1934   B & W   73 minutes

CALL TO GLORY
★★★½

DIRECTOR: Thomas Carter
CAST: Craig T. Nelson, Cindy Pickett, Keenan Wynn, Elisabeth Shue, David Hollander

Engrossing pilot episode for what was to be a short-lived TV series. Set in the early 1960s, it follows an Air Force officer's family through the events of the Kennedy presidency. The taut script ably balances the story of their struggle to deal with military life and still retains the flavor of a historical chronicle of the times. This uniformly well-acted and -directed opening show promised much quality that was unfortunately unfulfilled in later episodes.

1984   97 minutes

CAMILA
★★★½

DIRECTOR: Maria Luisa Bemberg
CAST: Susu Pecoraro, Imanol Arias, Hector Alterio, Mona Maris, Elena Tasisto, Carlos Munoz

A romantic and true story of forbidden love in the classic tradition, as well as a nominee for best foreign film at the 1985 Academy Awards. Susu Pecoraro is Camila O'Gorman, the daughter of a wealthy aristocrat in Buenos Aires in the mid-1800s. Imanol Arias plays Ladislao Gutierrez, a Jesuit priest who falls in love with Camila. The film says nothing that hasn't been said hundreds of times in the past, but the cinematography is superb, and the love scenes are red-hot. Not rated, but with sex, nudity, and violence. In Spanish with English subtitles.

1984   105 minutes

CAMILLE
★★★★
DIRECTOR: George Cukor
CAST: Greta Garbo, Robert Taylor, Lionel Barrymore, Henry Daniell, Laura Hope Crews, Elizabeth Allan, Lenore Ulric, Jessie Ralph

Metro-Goldwyn-Mayer's lavish production of the Dumas classic provided screen goddess Greta Garbo with one of her last unqualified successes and remains the consummate adaptation of this popular weeper. The combined magic of the studio and Garbo's presence legitimized this archaic creaker about a dying woman and her love affair with a younger man (Robert Taylor, soon to be one of MGM's biggest stars). This is still a classic of its kind as well as being a thoughtful and beautifully produced movie graced with the distant, vulnerable quality that only Garbo could bring to a role. This is a richly textured film made as only MGM could, transforming accepted masterpieces into celluloid facsimiles that audiences could understand and appreciate without having to read. If you've never seen Garbo, watch this or *Ninotchka*.

1936   B & W 108 minutes

CAN YOU HEAR THE LAUGHTER? THE STORY OF FREDDIE PRINZE
★★½
DIRECTOR: Burt Brinckerhoff

CAST: Ira Angustain, Kevin Hooks, Randee Heller, Devon Ericson, Julie Carmen

Freddie Prinze was a Puerto Rican comedian who rose from the barrio to television superstardom in a relatively brief time. His premiere achievement was a starring role in *Chico and The Man*, with Jack Albertson. This is a sympathetic handling of his story, but no punches are pulled on the facts surrounding his death.

1979   106 minutes

CANDIDATE, THE
★★★½
DIRECTOR: Michael Ritchie
CAST: Robert Redford, Peter Boyle, Don Porter, Allen Garfield

Michael Ritchie (*The Bad News Bears*) directed this release, an incisive look at a political hopeful (Robert Redford) and the obstacles and truths he must confront on the campaign trail. Rated PG.

1972   109 minutes

CAPTAINS COURAGEOUS
★★★★★
DIRECTOR: Victor Fleming
CAST: Spencer Tracy, Freddie Bartholomew, Lionel Barrymore, Melvyn Douglas, Mickey Rooney

This is an exquisite adaptation of Rudyard Kipling's story about a spoiled rich kid who falls from an ocean liner and is rescued by fishermen. Through them, the lad learns about the rewards of hard work and genuine friendship. Spencer Tracy won a well-deserved best-actor Oscar for his performance as the fatherly fisherman.

1937   B & W 116 minutes

CAREFUL HE MIGHT HEAR YOU
★★★★½

DIRECTOR: Carl Schultz
CAST: Robyn Nevin, Nicholas Gledhill, Wendy Hughes, John Hargreaves, Geraldine Turner

A child's-eye view of the harsh realities of life, this Australian import is a poignant, heartwarming, sad, and sometimes frightening motion picture. A young boy named P.S. (played by 7-year-old Nicholas Gledhill) gets caught up in a bitter custody fight between his two aunts. While the movie does tend to become a tearjerker on occasion, it does so without putting off the viewer. The situations are always invested with an edge of realism. Rated PG for suggested sex and violence.

1983　　　　　　116 minutes

CARNAL KNOWLEDGE
★★★★

DIRECTOR: Mike Nichols
CAST: Jack Nicholson, Candice Bergen, Art Garfunkel, Ann-Margret

The sexual dilemmas of the modern American are analyzed and come up short in this thoughtful film. Jack Nicholson and singer Art Garfunkel are college roommates whose lives are followed through varied relationships with the opposite sex. Nicholson is somewhat of a stinker, and one finds oneself more in sympathy with the women in the cast. Rated R.

1971　　　　　　96 minutes

CARNIVAL IN FLANDERS
★★★★

DIRECTOR: Jacques Feyder
CAST: Françoise Rosay, Andre Alerme, Jean Murat, Louis Jouret, Micheline Cheirel, Bernard Lancret, Lynne Clevers

This sly drama about a village that postpones its destruction by collaborating with their conquerors and freely offering them their goods during carnival season was reputed to be one of Joseph Goebbels' favorite films and was considered a poor statement to make to the rest of the world in light of what Nazi Germany and Italy were attempting to do to their neighbors. A clever, subtle work and one of Jacques Feyder's finest achievements, this classic is a conscious effort to re-create on celluloid the great paintings of the masters depicting village life during carnival time. Interesting on many levels, this film poses some intriguing questions, not the least of which is: "To exactly what length did the women of the village collaborate in order to alleviate the threat of destruction?" In French with English subtitles.

1936　　　B & W　92 minutes

CARNIVAL STORY
★½

DIRECTOR: Kurt Neumann
CAST: Anne Baxter, Steve Cochran, Jay C. Flippen, George Nader

Familiar story of rivalry between circus performers over the affections of the girl they both love. No real surprises in this production, which was filmed in Germany on a limited budget, with the cast simply going through the motions. Star Anne Baxter gives it a try, but it's pretty tough sledding for her.

1954　　　　　　95 minutes

CARNY
★★★★

DIRECTOR: Robert Kaylor
CAST: Gary Busey, Jodie Foster, Robbie Robertson, Meg Foster, Bert Remsen

This film takes us behind the bright lights, shouting barkers, and games of chance into the netherworld of the "carnies," people who spend their lives cheating, lying, and stealing from others yet consider themselves superior to their victims. Gary Busey (*The Buddy Holly Story*), Jodie Foster, Robbie Robertson (former singer/songwriter/guitarist from the Band in his acting debut), and veteran character actor Elisha Cook are all outstanding. The accent in *Carny* is on realism. The characters aren't the typical motion-picture heroes and heroines. Instead, they're disenchanted losers who live only from day to day. Rated R.

1980   107 minutes

CARRINGTON, V. C.
★★★
DIRECTOR: Anthony Asquith
CAST: David Niven, Margaret Leighton, Noelle Middleton, Laurence Naismith, Victor Maddern, Maurice Denham

Everybody's Englishman David Niven gives one of the finest performances of his long film career in this story of a stalwart British army officer, accused of stealing military funds, who undertakes to conduct his own defense at court-martial proceedings. This is a solid, engrossing drama, but suffers from sticking too close to its confining stage origin. Filmed in England and released heavily cut in the United States under the title *Court Martial*.

1955   B & W 105 minutes

CASABLANCA
★★★★★
DIRECTOR: Michael Curtiz
CAST: Humphrey Bogart, Ingrid Bergman, Claude Rains, Paul Henreid, Peter Lorre, Sydney Greenstreet

A kiss may be just a kiss and a sigh just a sigh, but there is only one *Casablanca*. Some misguided souls tried to remake this classic in 1980 as *Caboblanco*, with Charles Bronson, Jason Robards, and Dominique Sanda, but film lovers are well advised to accept no substitutes. The original feast of romance and pre–World War II intrigue is still the best. Superb performances by Humphrey Bogart and Ingrid Bergman, Paul Henreid, Claude Rains, Peter Lorre, and Sydney Greenstreet, and the fluid direction of Michael Curtiz combined to make it an all-time classic.

1942   B & W 102 minutes

CASE OF LIBEL, A
★★★★★
DIRECTOR: Eric Till
CAST: Edward Asner, Daniel J. Travanti, Gordon Pinsent, Lawrence Dane

Slick, superb made-for-cable adaptation of Henry Denker's famed Broadway play, which itself is taken from the first portion of Louis Nizer's excellent biography, *My Life in Court*. The story closely follows the legendary Westbrook Pegler–Quentin Reynolds libel suit, wherein columnist Pegler had attempted to smear Reynolds's reputation with a series of vicious lies. Ed Asner plays the lawyer and Daniel Travanti the columnist, and the verbal give-and-take ranks with the finest courtroom dramas on film. Travanti is perfect for the part: stiff, unyielding, and charming. Asner, in contrast, is languid, flexible, and deadly. The final outcome proves once again that truth is always stranger than fiction. Unrated.

1984   92 minutes

CASSANDRA CROSSING, THE
🐾

DIRECTOR: George Pan Cosmatos
CAST: Richard Harris, Sophia Loren, Burt Lancaster, Ava Gardner, Martin Sheen

One of the worst all-star disaster pictures, this involves a plague-infested train heading for a weakened bridge. The star power of Burt Lancaster, Sophia Loren, Richard Harris, Martin Sheen, and Ava Gardner, among others, does little to relieve its boredom. Rated PG.

1977   127 minutes

CAT ON A HOT TIN ROOF (ORIGINAL)
★★★★

DIRECTOR: Richard Brooks
CAST: Elizabeth Taylor, Paul Newman, Burl Ives, Jack Carson

This heavy drama stars Elizabeth Taylor as the frustrated Maggie and Paul Newman as her alcoholic, ex-athlete husband. They've returned to his father's (Big Daddy, played by Burl Ives) home upon hearing he's dying. They are joined by Newman's brother, Gooper, and his wife, May, and their many obnoxious children. Maggie struggles against May and Gooper to get a larger share in Big Daddy's will.

1958   108 minutes

CAT ON A HOT TIN ROOF (REMAKE)
★★★½

DIRECTOR: Jack Hofsiss
CAST: Jessica Lange, Tommy Lee Jones, Rip Torn, Kim Stanley, David Dukes, Penny Fuller

Updated rendition of the famed Tennessee Williams play strikes to the core in most scenes but remains oddly distanced in others. The story itself is just as powerful as it must have been in 1955, with its acute examination of a family under stress and the things that bother us all: mendacity and "little no-neck monsters" (certainly one of the best ways yet to describe bratty children). Jessica Lange is far too melodramatic as Maggie the Cat; it's impossible to forget that she's acting. Things really come alive, though, when Big Daddy (Rip Torn) and Brick (Tommy Lee Jones) square off. The play ends on what is for Williams an uncharacteristically optimistic note. A near miss. Unrated—sexual situations.

1985   140 minutes

CATHERINE THE GREAT
★★

DIRECTOR: Paul Czinner
CAST: Elisabeth Bergner, Douglas Fairbanks Jr., Flora Robson, Joan Gardner, Gerald Du Maurier

Stodgy spectacle from Great Britain is sumptuously mounted but takes its own time in telling the story of the famed czarina of Russia and her (toned-down) love life. Elisabeth Bergner in the title role lacks a real star personality, and dashing Douglas Fairbanks Jr. and sage Flora Robson provide the only screen charisma evident. Pretty fair for a historical romance of this period, but it won't keep you on the edge of your seat.

1934   B & W   92 minutes

CATHOLICS
★★★★½

DIRECTOR: Jack Gold

CAST: Trevor Howard, Martin Sheen, Raf Vallone, Andrew Keir

This film has Martin Sheen playing the representative of the Father General (the Pope). He comes to Ireland to persuade the Catholic priests there to conform to the "new" teachings of the Catholic Church. The Irish priests and monks refuse to discard traditional ways and beliefs. Trevor Howard is excellent as the rebellious Irish abbot.

1973   78 minutes

CAUGHT
★★★

DIRECTOR: Max Ophuls
CAST: Robert Ryan, Barbara Bel Geddes, James Mason, Natalie Schafer, Ruth Brady, Curt Bois, Frank Ferguson

Starry-eyed model Barbara Bel Geddes marries neurotic millionaire Robert Ryan, who proceeds to make her life miserable. His treatment drives her away and into the arms of young doctor James Mason. Upon learning she is pregnant, she returns to her husband, who refuses to give her a divorce unless she gives him the child.

1949   B & W   88 minutes

CEASE FIRE
★★★½

DIRECTOR: David Nutter
CAST: Don Johnson, Lisa Blount, Robert F. Lyons, Richard Chaves, Rick Richards, Chris Noel, Jorge Gil

An answer to the comic book–style heroism of *Rambo* and the *Missing in Action* movies, *Cease Fire* is a heartfelt, well-acted, and touching drama about the aftereffects of Vietnam and the battle still being fought by some veterans. Don Johnson ("Miami Vice") stars as Tim Murphy, a veteran

whose life begins to crumble after fifteen years of valiant effort at fitting back into society. It is the story of one man's personal hell and how he triumphs over it. While director David Nutter has problems with pace, he does well with actors. Johnson, Lisa Blount (*An Officer and a Gentleman*) as his wife, and Robert F. Lyons as his even-more-troubled buddy give outstanding performances. And because the film is a tribute to those men and women who fought for their country overseas only to come home and fight an equally tough battle, we cannot help but cheer them (and the film) on. Rated R for profanity and violence.

1985   97 minutes

CERTAIN SACRIFICE, A

DIRECTOR: Stephen Jon Lewicki
CAST: Jeremy Pattnosh, Madonna

Avoid this one at all costs. A thoroughly inept film about two drifters who fall in love, are assaulted by a bigot, and then get revenge on him. The camera work is terrible, and while director Stephen Jon Lewicki attempts the avant-garde, he ends up making us all nauseous. The dialogue follows suit; favorite nonironic line by Madonna: "Do you think any lover of mine could be tamed?" Rated R for language, sex, nudity, violence.

1985   58 minutes

CHAMP, THE (ORIGINAL)
★★★★

DIRECTOR: King Vidor
CAST: Wallace Beery, Jackie Cooper, Irene Rich

Wallace Beery is at his absolute best in the Oscar-winning title role of this tearjerker, about a washed-up fighter and his adoring son

(Jackie Cooper) who are separated against their will. King Vidor manages to make even the hokiest bits of hokum work in this four-hankie feast of sentimentality.

1931   B & W   87 minutes

CHAMP, THE (REMAKE)
★★★½
DIRECTOR: Franco Zeffirelli
CAST: Jon Voight, Faye Dunaway, Ricky Schroder, Jack Warden

This remake is a first-class tearjerker. The main reason for this is Ricky Schroder. This little actor projects joy, fear, and innocence equally well. Schroder and Jon Voight, as son and father, may do more for family relations in America than all the counseling agencies put together. Billy Flynn (Voight), a former boxing champion, works in the back-stretch at Hialeah when not drinking or gambling away his money. His son, T.J. (Schroder), calls him "Champ" and tells all his friends about his father's comeback, which never seems to happen. Flynn was badly injured in his last bout, his only loss, and fear prevents him from going back into the ring. Rated PG.

1979   121 minutes

CHAMPION
★★★★
DIRECTOR: Stanley Kramer
CAST: Kirk Douglas, Arthur Kennedy, Ruth Roman

One of Hollywood's better efforts about the fight game. Kirk Douglas is a young boxer whose climb to the top is accomplished while forsaking his friends and family. He gives one of his best performances in an unsympathetic role.

1949   B & W 100 minutes

CHAMPIONS
★★★★
DIRECTOR: John Irvin
CAST: John Hurt, Edward Woodward, Jan Francis, Ben Johnson

The touching true story of English steeplechase jockey Bob Champion (John Hurt), who fought a desperate battle against cancer through chemotherapy to win the 1981 Grand National. Rated PG.

1984   113 minutes

CHANEL SOLITAIRE
★★
DIRECTOR: George Kaczender
CAST: Marie-France Pisier, Timothy Dalton, Rutger Hauer, Karen Black, Brigitte Fossey

This half-hearted rendering of the rise to prominence of French designer Coco Chanel (played by fragile Marie-France Pisier) is long on sap and short on plot. Timothy Dalton and Rutger Hauer, as two of Coco's well-heeled suitors, fare best; Miss Pisier wears a sour pout throughout. For the terminally romantic only. Rated R.

1981   120 minutes

CHANGE OF HABIT
★★
DIRECTOR: William Graham
CAST: Elvis Presley, Mary Tyler Moore, Barbara McNair, Jane Elliot, Edward Asner

In direct contrast to the many comedy/musicals that Elvis Presley starred in, this drama offers a more substantial plot. Elvis plays a doctor helping the poor in his clinic. Mary Tyler Moore plays a nun who is tempted to leave the order to be with Elvis. Rated G.

1970   93 minutes

CHANT OF JIMMIE BLACKSMITH, THE
★★★★

DIRECTOR: Fred Schepisi

CAST: Tommy Lewis, Freddy Reynolds, Ray Barrett, Jack Thompson

This superb film—based on true events—concerns the plight of a half-caste aborigine, Jimmie Blacksmith (Tommy Lewis), in racist turn-of-the century Australia. Educated by a local missionary (Jack Thompson, from *Breaker Morant*), the optimistic, eager Blacksmith sets out one day to make it on his own. He wants to be a man of property so he can find a wife (preferably white, as his guardian has instructed) and settle down. But, after making several unsuccessful attempts at fitting into society, he declares war on the white race. Written and directed by Fred Schepisi, it is a major work that combines the realism of a documentary with the emotional impact of high drama. MPAA-unrated.

1978   124 minutes

CHAPTER TWO
★★★½

DIRECTOR: Robert Moore

CAST: James Caan, Marsha Mason, Valerie Harper, Joseph Bologna

In *Chapter Two*, writer Neil Simon examines the problems that arise when a recently widowed author courts and marries a recently divorced actress. George Schneider (James Caan) is recovering from the death of his wife when he strikes up a whirlwind courtship with actress Jennie MacLaine (Marsha Mason). They get married, but George is tormented by the memory of his first, beloved wife. An idyllic honeymoon shifts from newlywed bliss to emotional misery for George, and his mental distress threatens to destroy his marriage to Jennie just as it's getting started. Rated PG.

1979   124 minutes

CHARIOTS OF FIRE
★★★★★

DIRECTOR: Hugh Hudson

CAST: Ben Cross, Ian Charleson, Nigel Havers, Nick Farrell, Alice Krige

Made in England, this is the beautifully told and inspiring story of two runners (Ian Charleson and Ben Cross) who competed for England in the 1924 Olympics. An all-star supporting cast—Ian Holm, John Gielgud, Dennis Christopher (*Breaking Away*), Brad Davis (*Midnight Express*), and Nigel Davenport—and taut direction by Hugh Hudson help make this a must-see motion picture. Rated PG, the film has no objectionable content.

1981   123 minutes

CHASE, THE
★★½

DIRECTOR: Arthur Penn

CAST: Robert Redford, Jane Fonda, Marlon Brando, Angie Dickinson, Janice Rule, James Fox, Robert Duvall, E. G. Marshall, Miriam Hopkins, Martha Hyer

Convoluted tale of prison escapee (Robert Redford) who returns to the turmoil of his Texas hometown. The exceptional cast provides flashes of brilliance, but overall, the film is rather dull. Redford definitely showed signs of his superstar potential here.

1966   135 minutes

CHEERS FOR MISS BISHOP
★★★

DIRECTOR: Tay Garnett
CAST: Martha Scott, William Gargan, Edmund Gwenn, Sterling Holloway, Mary Anderson, Sidney Blackmer

Nostalgic, poignant story of a schoolteacher in a midwestern town who devotes her life to teaching. A warm reassuring film in the tradition of *Miss Dove* and *Mr. Chips.*

1941   B & W   95 minutes

CHIEFS
★★★★

DIRECTOR: Jerry London
CAST: Charlton Heston, Wayne Rogers, Billy Dee Williams, Brad Davis, Keith Carradine, Stephen Collins, Tess Harper, Paul Sorvino, Victoria Tennant

An impressive cast turns in some excellent performances in this, one of the better TV miniseries. A string of unsolved murders in 1920 in a small southern town is at the base of this engrossing suspense drama. The story follows the various police chiefs from the time of the murders to 1962 when Billy Dee Williams, the town's first black police chief, is intrigued by the case and the spell it casts over the town and its political boss (Charlton Heston). Despite threats, he continues to delve into the mystery until its climactic conclusion. Some material not suitable for children.

1985   200 minutes

CHILDREN OF PARADISE
★★★★½

DIRECTOR: Marcel Carné
CAST: Jean-Louis Barrault, Arletty, Pierre Brasseur

This classic French film, directed by Marcel Carné, follows the career of a nineteenth-century mime (Jean-Louis Barrault) and his love affair with a beautiful courtesan (Arletty).

1944   B & W   188 minutes

CHILDREN OF SANCHEZ, THE
★★★

DIRECTOR: Hall Bartlett
CAST: Anthony Quinn, Dolores Del Rio

Anthony Quinn stars as a poor Mexican worker who tries to keep his large family together. This well-intentioned film is slightly boring. Rated PG.

1978   126 minutes

CHILLY SCENES OF WINTER
★★★★

DIRECTOR: Joan Micklin Silver
CAST: John Heard, Mary Beth Hurt, Peter Riegert, Kenneth McMillan, Gloria Grahame

You'll probably find this excellent little film in the comedy section of your local video store, but don't be fooled; it's funny all right, but it has some scenes that evoke the true pain of love. John Heard plays a man in love with a married woman (Mary Beth Hurt). She also loves him, but is still attached to her husband. Rated PG for language and sex.

1979   96 minutes

CHINA SYNDROME, THE
★★★★★

DIRECTOR: James Bridges
CAST: Jane Fonda, Jack Lemmon, Michael Douglas, Scott Brady

This taut thriller, about an accident at a nuclear power plant, has no real competition. It's superb entertainment with a timely message. Rated PG.

1979 123 minutes

CHOOSE ME
★★★★

DIRECTOR: Alan Rudolph

CAST: Lesley Ann Warren, Keith Carradine, Genevieve Bujold

A feast of fine acting and deliciously different situations, this stylish independent film works on every level and proves that inventive, non-mainstream entertainment is still a viable form. Written and directed by Alan Rudolph (*Welcome to L.A.*; *Remember My Name*), *Choose Me* is a funny, quirky, suspenseful, and surprising essay on love, sex, and the wacky state of male-female relationships in the 1980s. Rated R for violence and profanity.

1984 110 minutes

CHOSEN, THE
★★★★★

DIRECTOR: Jeremy Paul Kagen

CAST: Robby Benson, Rod Steiger, Maximilian Schell

The Chosen is a flawless, arresting drama illustrating the conflict between friendship and family loyalty. Based on the novel of the same name by Chaim Potok, the story, centering on Jewish issues, transcends its setting to attain universal impact. Rated G.

1978 105 minutes

CHRISTIANE F.
★½

DIRECTOR: Ulrich Edel

CAST: Natja Brunkhorst, Thomas Haustein, Jens Kuphal, Reiner Wolk

Although quite interesting in places, this West German film

dealing with young heroin addicts ultimately becomes a bore. Too many repetitive scenes of kids shooting dope, and bad acting, make this a yawn. No MPAA rating.

1981 124 minutes

CHRISTOPHER STRONG
★★½

DIRECTOR: Dorothy Arzner

CAST: Katharine Hepburn, Colin Clive,. Billie Burke, Helen Chandler, Jack LaRue, Ralph Forbes

Katharine Hepburn's second film, this one gave her her first starring role. She is a record-breaking flyer who falls passionately in love with a married man she cannot have. Pregnancy complicates things further. High-plane soap opera. Kate's legions of fans will love it, however.

1933 B & W 77 minutes

CIAO! MANHATTAN

DIRECTOR: John Palmer, David Weisman

CAST: Edie Sedgwick, Isabel Jewell, Baby Jane Holzer, Roger Vadim, Viva, Paul America

Far more pornographic than any skin flick, this sleazy, low-budget release features Edie Sedgwick, a one-time Andy Warhol "superstar," in a grotesque parody of her life. Sedgwick, who, at the age of 28, died shortly after the film's completion, is most often topless and slurs her way through this near-documentary of the last days of an aimless self-indulgent young woman. While watching *Ciao! Manhattan*, the viewer can't help but feel a morbid fascination. But afterward, you feel like you need a bath and reassurance that there is some hope in life. No MPAA rating, but rife with objectionable material.

1983   84 minutes

CIRCLE OF TWO
★½

DIRECTOR: Jules Dassin
CAST: Richard Burton, Tatum O'-Neal, Kate Reid, Robin Gammell

Thoroughly ludicrous tale of an eccentric artist (Richard Burton) who develops a romantic—but somehow platonic—relationship with a teen-age girl (Tatum O'-Neal). Laughable dialogue throughout, punctuated by heavy sighs and fluttering eyelashes. O'-Neal has a painfully embarrassing nude scene that is out of place in this story with its gentle tone. Rated PG for nudity.

1980   105 minutes

CITIZEN KANE
★★★★★

DIRECTOR: Orson Welles
CAST: Orson Welles, Joseph Cotten, Everett Sloane, Agnes Moorehead, Ray Collins, George Colouris, Ruth Chatterton

What can you say about the film considered by many to be the finest picture ever made in America? The story of a reporter's quest to find the "truth" about the life of a dead newspaper tycoon closely parallels the life of William Randolph Hearst. To 1940s audiences, the plot may have seemed obscured by flashbacks, unusual camera angles, and lens distortion. After forty years, however, most of these film tricks are now commonplace, but the story, the acting of the Mercury Company cast, Gregg Toland's camera work, and Bernard Herrmann's score haven't aged a bit. This picture is still a very enjoyable experience for first-time viewers, as well as for those who have seen it ten times.

1941   B & W 119 minutes

CLASH BY NIGHT
★★★½

DIRECTOR: Fritz Lang
CAST: Barbara Stanwyck, Paul Douglas, Robert Ryan, Marilyn Monroe, Keith Andes, J. Carrol Naish

Intense, adult story is a dramatist's dream but not entertainment for the masses. Barbara Stanwyck gives another of her strong characterizations as a woman with a past who marries amiable Paul Douglas only to find herself gravitating toward tough but sensual Robert Ryan. Gritty realism of fishing village locale adds to the strong mood of this somber love triangle, and outstanding performances by all the principals (including a young Marilyn Monroe and master character actor J. Carrol Naish) make this a slice-of-life tragedy that lingers in the memory. This film is justly remembered as one of the highlights of Hollywood's efforts of the early 1950s.

1952   B & W 105 minutes

CLASS OF '44
★★★

DIRECTOR: Paul Bogart
CAST: Gary Grimes, Jerry Houser, William Atherton, Deborah Winters

Sequel to the very popular *Summer of '42* proves once again it's tough to top the original. Gary Grimes and Jerry Houser are back again. This time we follow the two through college romances. No new ground broken, but Grimes is very watchable. Rated PG.

1973   95 minutes

CLASS OF MISS MACMICHAEL, THE
★★

DIRECTOR: Silvio Narizzano

CAST: Glenda Jackson, Oliver Reed, Michael Murphy

British film about obnoxious students battling obnoxious teachers. Mixes *The Blackboard Jungle*, *To Sir with Love*, and *Teachers* without expanding on them. Loud and angry, but doesn't say much. Rated R for profanity.

1978   91 minutes

CLEOPATRA
★★★★

DIRECTOR: Joseph L. Mankiewicz

CAST: Elizabeth Taylor, Richard Burton, Rex Harrison, Roddy McDowall, Pamela Brown

This multimillion-dollar, four-hour-long extravaganza created quite a sensation when released. Its all-star cast includes Elizabeth Taylor (as Cleopatra), Richard Burton (as Marc Antony), Rex Harrison (as Julius Caesar), Martin Landau (as Rufio), Roddy McDowall (as Octavian), and Carroll O'Connor (as Casca). The story begins when Caesar meets Cleopatra in her native Egypt and she has his son. Later she comes to Rome to join Caesar when he becomes the lifetime dictator of Rome. Marc Antony gets into the act as Cleopatra's Roman lover. It created quite a stir in 1963, but there is actually minimal sex and nudity by today's standards.

1963   243 minutes

CLOSELY WATCHED TRAINS
★★★★½

DIRECTOR: Jiří Menzel

CAST: Vaclau Neckar, Jitka Bendava

A bittersweet coming-of-age comedy-drama against a backdrop of the Nazi occupation of Czechoslovakia. A naive young train dispatcher is forced to grow up quickly when asked to help the Czech underground. This gentle film is one of the more artistic efforts to come from behind the Iron Curtain. Its release coincided with the brief period of relaxed government control before the Soviet crackdown in 1967. This production is unusual because it stresses the development of interpersonal relations among its characters, rather than the traditional heroic aspects of communist war films.

1966   B & W   91 minutes

COCAINE: ONE MAN'S SEDUCTION
★★★½

DIRECTOR: Paul Wendkos

CAST: Dennis Weaver, Karen Grassle, Pamela Bellwood, James Spader, David Ackroyd, Jeffrey Tambor, Richard Venture

Though this is not another *Reefer Madness*, the subject could have been handled a little more subtly. Still, the melodrama is not obtrusive enough to take away from Dennis Weaver's brilliant performance as a real estate salesman who gets hooked on the expensive habit to help cope with the pressure of his work. Not rated, but the equivalent of a PG for adult subject matter.

1983   97 minutes

COLONEL REDL
★★★½

DIRECTOR: Istvan Szabo

CAST: Klaus Maria Brandauer, Armin Mueller-Stahl, Gudrun Landgrebe, Jan Niklas, Hans Christian Blech

Director Istvan Szabo and star Klaus Maria Brandauer collaborated for the first time on the superb *Mephisto*. Their second teaming, on *Colonel Redl*, despite its Academy Award nomination, brings less felicitous results. Not that it's a bad film. No movie featuring Brandauer could be. However, the ponderous and delibrate nature of *Colonel Redl*, which tells the story of how the title character became a pawn in a struggle for power in the Austro-Hungarian Empire just prior to World War I, keeps it from becoming a fully satisfying film. Rated R for profanity, nudity, simulated sex, and violence. In German with English subtitles.

1985   144 minutes

COLOR PURPLE, THE
★★★★★

DIRECTOR: Steven Spielberg

CAST: Whoopi Goldberg, Danny Glover, Adolph Caesar, Margaret Avery, Oprah Winfrey, Rae Dawn Chong, Akousa Busia, Willard Pugh

Steven Spielberg's adaptation of Alice Walker's Pulitzer Prize—winning novel about the growth to maturity and independence of a mistreated black woman is one of those rare and wonderful movies that can bring a tear to the eye, a lift to the soul, and joy to the heart. Walker's story, set between 1909 and 1947 in a small town in Georgia, celebrates the qualities of kindness, compassion, and love. Her lead character, Celie (played marvelously by Whoopi Goldberg), is a gentle soul who endures hardship and humiliation, but never loses her humanity. In attempting to cover nearly forty years, *The Color Purple* becomes episodic, which is only bothersome in the beginning when other factors tend to distance the viewer from the story. Because Celie is a victimized, unassertive character, the film—although it is never less

than interesting—seems to ramble. In this respect, it is somewhat reminiscent of *Ragtime*, a fine film which told several loosely connected stories and required more commitment from the viewers than do most films. While *The Color Purple* also rewards those willing to expend extra effort, it shifts gears halfway through to become a forceful, unforgettable, exhilarating story of individualism and hope. Rated PG-13 for violence, profanity, and suggested sex.

1985   130 minutes

COME BACK TO THE FIVE AND DIME, JIMMY DEAN, JIMMY DEAN
★★★½

DIRECTOR: Robert Altman

CAST: Sandy Dennis, Cher, Karen Black, Sudie Bond, Kathy Bates, Marta Heflin

Directed by Robert Altman (*Popeye*; *Nashville*), this film adaptation of Ed Graczyk's failed Broadway play concerns the twenty-year reunion of the Disciples of James Dean, a group formed by high-school friends from a small Texas town after *Giant* was filmed on location nearby. Their get-together ends up being a catalyst that forces the members to confront the lies they have been living since those innocent days. Though a surreal work that deals with broken dreams and crippling illusions, *Jimmy Dean* is highlighted by some excellent comedy and dramatic moments as well as a terrific performance by Cher. Karen Black and Sandy Dennis are also memorable in this true American art film. Unrated, the film contains profanity and mature subject matter.

1982   110 minutes

COMIC, THE
★★★★
DIRECTOR: Carl Reiner
CAST: Dick Van Dyke, Mickey Rooney, Michele Lee, Cornel Wilde, Nina Wayne, Pert Kelton, Jeannine Riley

There's a bit of every famous silent film funny man—Chaplin, Keaton, Arbuckle, Langdon, and Lloyd—in this engrossing account of a beloved reel comedian who's an egocentric heel in real life. Dick Van Dyke is peerless in the title character. Well planned and executed, this is a gem of its genre. Beautiflly handled, the closing minutes alone are worth the entire film. Rated PG

1969   96 minutes

COMING HOME
★★★★½
DIRECTOR: Hal Ashby
CAST: Jane Fonda, Jon Voight, Bruce Dern, Robert Carradine, Robert Ginty, Penelope Milford

Jane Fonda, Jon Voight, and Bruce Dern give superb performances in this thought-provoking drama about the effect the Vietnam War has on three people. Directed by Hal Ashby (*Harold and Maude*; *The Last Detail*), it features a romantic triangle with a twist: Fonda, the wife of a gung-ho officer, Dern, finds real love when she becomes an aide at a veteran's hospital and meets a bitter but sensitive paraplegic, Voight. This release does have a few false moments, but overall, it's a movie with a message that still manages to entertain. What more could you ask? Rated R.

1978   127 minutes

COMPETITION, THE
★★★★½
DIRECTOR: Joel Oliansky

CAST: Richard Dreyfuss, Amy Irving, Lee Remick, Sam Wanamaker

Richard Dreyfuss and Amy Irving star in this exquisitely crafted and completely enjoyable romance about two classical pianists who, while competing for top honors in a recital program, fall in love. Lee Remick and Sam Wanamaker add excellent support. Watch it with someone you love. Rated PG.

1980   129 minutes

CONCRETE JUNGLE, THE (AKA THE CRIMINAL)
★★★
DIRECTOR: Joseph Losey
CAST: Stanley Baker, Margit Saad, Sam Wanamaker, Gregoire Aslan, Jill Bennett, Laurence Naismith, Edward Judd

Grim, claustrophobic prison drama is tightly directed and well acted (especially by the underrated Stanley Baker), and remains one of the best films of its kind as well as one of director Joseph Losey's most satisfying works. Often referred to in filmographies as *The Criminal*, this uncompromising look at life inside the concrete walls of confinement boasts gutsy, believable performances by a fine crew of veteran British character actors and convincingly conveys the hopelessness and despair of forced isolation.

1962   B & W   86 minutes

CONFESSIONS OF A POLICE CAPTAIN
★½
DIRECTOR: Damiano Damiani
CAST: Martin Balsam, Franco Nero, Marilu Tolo

Heavy-handed melodrama wastes a fine performance by Martin Balsam as a good cop trying to close a tough case amid an avalanche of bureaucratic corruption. This Italian-made film is given to excess, and the confusing story fails to sustain interest. Rated PG.

1971   102 minutes

CONFESSIONS OF A VICE BARON
★

DIRECTOR: Harvey Thew
CAST: Willy Castello

Fly-by-night film chronicling the rise and fall of vice baron Lombardo isn't quite as bad as it could have been. The shoddy production values of this basement opus don't get in the way of the sleazy story of Lombardo's world of flesh peddling and illegal operations (not to mention dope!) that fell apart when he went sappy and fell in love. In classic exploitation style, Lombardo wants to bare his soul and "tell all" in order to save future victims of the vice rackets before he walks "the last mile." Some nudity thrown in, but overall pretty tame. Last part of tape features previews of other exploitation titles.

1942   B & W   70 minutes

CONFORMIST, THE
★★★★

DIRECTOR: Bernardo Bertolucci
CAST: Jean-Louis Trintignant, Stefania Sandrelli, Dominique Sanda, Pierre Clementi

Fascinating character study of Marcello Clerici (Jean-Louis Trintignant), a young, driven follower of Mussolini. He becomes increasingly obsessed with conformity as he tries to suppress a traumatic homosexual experience suffered as a youth. After a strange series of events, he is forced to prove his loyalty to the fascist state by murdering a former professor who lives in exile. Interesting his-

torical study of a highly decadent society. Rated R for language and subject matter.

1971   107 minutes

CONRACK
★★★★

DIRECTOR: Martin Ritt
CAST: Jon Voight, Paul Winfield, Hume Cronyn, Madge Sinclair

In this sleeper, based on a true story, Jon Voight plays a dedicated white teacher determined to bring the joys of education to deprived blacks inhabiting an island off the coast of South Carolina. Rated PG.

1974   107 minutes

CONVERSATION, THE
★★★★★

DIRECTOR: Francis Ford Coppola
CAST: Gene Hackman, John Cazale, Allen Garfield, Cindy Williams, Harrison Ford

Following his box-office and artistic triumph with *The Godfather*, director Francis Ford Coppola made this absorbing character study about a bugging-device expert (Gene Hackman) who lives only for his work but finds himself developing a conscience. Although not a box-office hit when originally released, this is a fine little film. Rated PG.

1974   113 minutes

CONVERSATION PIECE
★

DIRECTOR: Luchino Visconti
CAST: Burt Lancaster, Silvana Mangano, Helmut Berger, Claudia Marsani, Claudia Cardinale

All the talent collected to produce this film can't save it from being mundane, wordy, and phlegmatic. Burt Lancaster portrays a bewildered, reclusive professor whose life changes direction when he encounters a countess and her children who live life for its pleasures rather than its meaning. The countess's lover (Helmut Berger) serves only to complicate and confuse the already ponderous story. In Italian with English subtitles.

1974   122 minutes

CORN IS GREEN, THE
★★★½

DIRECTOR: George Cukor
CAST: Katharine Hepburn, Ian Saynor, Bill Fraser, Patricia Hayes, Anna Massey

Based on Emlyn Williams's play and directed by George Cukor (*The Philadelphia Story*), this telefilm stars Katharine Hepburn. She gives a tour-de-force performance as the eccentric spinster-teacher who helps a gifted young man discover the joys of learning.

1979   100 minutes

COUNTDOWN
★★★

DIRECTOR: Robert Altman
CAST: James Caan, Robert Duvall, Charles Aidman

This lesser-known Robert Altman film finds James Caan and Robert Duvall as American astronauts preparing for a moonshot. The realistic scenes and great acting raise this film high above most films of this kind—well worth watching. Unrated.

1968   101 minutes

COUNTRY
★★★★

DIRECTOR: Richard Pearce
CAST: Jessica Lange, Sam Shepard, Wilford Brimley, Matt Clark

A quietly powerful movie about the plight of farmers struggling to hold on while the government and financial institutions seem intent on fostering their failure. Directed by Richard Pearce (*Heartland*), *Country* teams Jessica Lange and Sam Shepard on screen for the first time since the Oscar-nominated *Frances* in a film as topical as today's headlines. Rated PG.

1984   109 minutes

COUNTRY GIRL, THE
★★★★½

DIRECTOR: George Seaton
CAST: Bing Crosby, Grace Kelly, William Holden, Anthony Ross

Bing Crosby and Grace Kelly give terrific performances in this little-seen production. Crosby plays an alcoholic singer who wallows in self-pity until he seizes a chance to make a comeback. Kelly won an Oscar for her sensitive portrayal of his wife.

1954   B & W 104 minutes

CRAIG'S WIFE
★★★

DIRECTOR: Dorothy Arzner
CAST: Rosalind Russell, John Boles, Billie Burke, Jane Darwell, Thomas Mitchell, Alma Kruger, Dorothy Wilson

In her first film success, Rosalind Russell is brilliant as Harriet Craig, the wife of the title, a heartless domestic tyrant whose neurotic preference for material concerns over human feelings alienates all around her. John Boles is her long-suffering, slow-to-see-the-light husband. Note: In what hindsight pegs as plus-perfect typecasting, Joan Crawford plays the title role in *Harriet Craig*, the 1948 remake.

1936   B & W   75 minutes

CREATOR (1986 RELEASE)
★★

DIRECTOR: Ivan Passer
CAST: Peter O'Toole, Mariel Hemingway, Vincent Spano, Virginia Madsen, David Ogden Stiers, John Dehner

This film, about a scientist (Peter O'Toole) who is attempting to bring back to life the wife who died thirty years before during childbirth, is, at first, a very witty and occasionally heart-tugging comedy. However, in its last third, it turns into a sort of second-rate *Terms of Endearment*. As a result, the movie—to say nothing of the viewer—suffers. Rated R for nudity, profanity, and simulated sex.

1985   108 minutes

CRIES AND WHISPERS
★★★★★

DIRECTOR: Ingmar Bergman
CAST: Harriet Andersson, Liv Ullmann, Ingrid Thulin, Karl Sylwan

Directed and written by Ingmar Bergman and hauntingly photographed by cinematographer Sven Nykvist, this film tells a story of a dying woman, her two sisters, and a servant girl. Faultless performances by Liv Ullmann, Ingrid Thulin, and Harriet Andersson make this an unforgettable film experience. Rated R.

1972   106 minutes

CRIMES OF PASSION
🦃

DIRECTOR: Ken Russell
CAST: Kathleen Turner, Anthony Perkins, John Laughlin

Kathleen Turner (*Romancing the Stone*) stars in director Ken Russell's disgusting and perverse sex film as Joanna Crane, a woman who leads a double life. By day she's a highly paid fashion designer; by night, a kinky high-priced hooker called China Blue. Anthony Perkins (in a role reminiscent of his famous *Psycho* turn) is a sleazy street-corner preacher who becomes obsessed with her. His plans are complicated when an investigator (John Laughlin) discovers her secret and, because of a sexless marriage, finds himself drawn to Joanna's erotic alter ego. That's when things really get ugly. You'd have to dig pretty deep to find a more disgusting, pretentious, and ludicrous motion picture. Rated R for nudity, suggested sex, profanity, and violence.

1984   107 minutes

CRIMINAL CODE, THE
★★★★

DIRECTOR: Howard Hawks
CAST: Boris Karloff, Walter Huston, Phillips Holmes

A powerful performance by Boris Karloff as a revenge-minded convict elevates this Howard Hawks release from interesting to memorable. It's a lost classic that deserves its release on video. The story involves a district attorney (impressively played by Walter Huston) who overzealously pursues his job, with the result that an innocent man (Phillips Holmes) is sent to prison. When the ex-D.A. becomes warden at the institution where the young man is incarcerated, he has the chance to right this wrong.

1931   B & W   83 minutes

CROSS COUNTRY
★★

DIRECTOR: Paul Lynch
CAST: Richard Beymer, Nina Axelrod, Michael Ironside, Brent Carver

Michael Ironside plays Detective Ed Roersch, who pursues Richard

Beymer following the murder of an expensive call girl. Although this movie involves prostitution, blackmail, murder, and deceit, it still manages to bore. Rated R for nudity, sex, profanity, and violence.

1983   95 minutes

CROSS CREEK
★★★½

DIRECTOR: Martin Ritt
CAST: Mary Steenburgen, Rip Torn, Peter Coyote, Dana Hill

About the life of 1930s author Marjorie Kinnan Rawlings (Mary Steenburgen), this watchable release illustrates how Rawlings's relationships with backwoods folks inspired her novels, particularly *The Yearling* and *Jacob's Ladder*. Rated PG for brief violence.

1983   122 minutes

CRUISING
★★

DIRECTOR: William Friedkin
CAST: Al Pacino, Paul Sorvino, Karen Allen, Richard Cox, Don Scardino

Writer-director William Friedkin went on to make a movie more horrifying than his big blockbuster, *The Exorcist*, but *Cruising*, which was based on a series of brutal murders in New York City between 1962 and 1979, is horror in the real sense of the word. It is repulsive, sickening, and almost unbearable to watch. Friedkin throws in everything you can think of to make it a grisly ordeal for the viewer: dismembered body parts, graphic stabbing scenes, and the like. Scenes of men pawing, clawing, and gnawing at each other are interspersed throughout. The film begins when the skipper of a tugboat finds a rotted, bloated forearm floating in the East River. The

police captain, Edelson (Paul Sorvino), believes it's part of a series of brutal killings that have taken place in the homosexual community. Because all the known victims have had a general similarity, he offers the chance to become a detective to a patrolman, Steve Burns (Al Pacino), who bears a resemblance to the killer's targets. All Burns has to do is act as bait. Rated R.

1980   106 minutes

CUTTER'S WAY
★★★★

DIRECTOR: Ivan Passer
CAST: Jeff Bridges, John Heard, Lisa Eichhorn, Ann Dusenberry

Director Ivan Passer must be praised for attempting to create more than just mindless movie mush. *Cutter's Way* comes very close to being a masterpiece. It's hokey sometimes and some of its elements are clichéd, but, surprisingly, Passer manages to turn this to his advantage. The screenplay, by Jeffrey Alan Fiskin, adapted from the novel *Cutter and Bone*, by Newton Thornburg, is a murder mystery. The three lead performances (John Heard, Jeff Bridges, and Lisa Eichhorn) are first-rate. *Cutter's Way* is certainly not what anyone would call a commercial film—it's too tough and uncompromising for that—but there is still an audience for it, one composed of viewers who prefer pictures that aspire to greatness. Rated R because of violence, nudity, and profanity.

1981   105 minutes

CYRANO DE BERGERAC
★★★★

DIRECTOR: Michael Gordon
CAST: José Ferrer, Mala Powers, William Prince

Charming, touching story of steadfast devotion and unrequited love done with brilliance and panache. As the fearless soldier of the large nose, José Ferrer superbly dominates this fine film. Mala Powers is beautiful as his beloved Roxanne. William Prince, who now often plays heavies, makes Christian a proper handsome, unimaginative nerd.

1950　　　　B & W 112 minutes

D-DAY THE SIXTH OF JUNE
★½
DIRECTOR: Henry Koster
CAST: Robert Taylor, Richard Todd, Dana Wynter, Edmond O'Brien

Slow-moving account of the Normandy invasion in World War II. Story concentrates on Allied officers Robert Taylor's and Richard Todd's romantic and professional problems. The actual invasion scenes are good, but come way too late to save this poor excuse for a war film.

1956　　　　　　　106 minutes

D.O.A.
★★★½
DIRECTOR: Rudolph Maté
CAST: Edmond O'Brien, Pamela Britton, Luther Adler, Lynne Baggett, Neville Brand

CPA Edmond O'Brien, slowly dying from radiation poisoning, seeks those responsible in this fast-paced, stylized *film noir* thriller. Most unusual is the device of having the victim play detective and hunt his killers as time runs out. Neville Brand takes honors as a psychopath who tries to turn the tables on the victim before he can inform the police.

1949　　　　B & W　83 minutes

DAISY MILLER
★
DIRECTOR: Peter Bogdanovich
CAST: Cybill Shepherd, Barry Brown, Cloris Leachman, Mildred Natwick, Eileen Brennan, Duilio Del Prete

Even a world-class director has a bad outing now and then. Peter Bogdanovich, who has made such great films as *Targets*, *The Last Picture Show*, and *Mask*, seemed to have lost his edge on this effort. This limp screen adaptation of a story by the great novelist Henry James is more a study on rambling dialogue than on the clashing of two cultures. Cybill Shepherd (of *The Last Picture Show* and TV's "Moonlighting") plays a young American visiting Europe in the 1880s who sets the Victorian high society on its ear with her gauche behavior. She babbles her way through the film without really saying anything. Cloris Leachman and Eileen Brennan's talents are wasted in this exercise in vapid verbosity. Rated G.

1974　　　　　　　93 minutes

DAMNED, THE
★★★½
DIRECTOR: Luchino Visconti
CAST: Dirk Bogarde, Ingrid Thulin, Helmut Griem, Helmut Berger

Deep, heavy drama about a German industrialist family that is destroyed under Nazi power. This film is difficult to watch, as the images are as bleak as the story itself. In German, with English subtitles. Rated R for sex.

1969　　　　　　　155 minutes

DANCE HALL RACKET
★½
DIRECTOR: Phil Tucker
CAST: Lenny Bruce

Inane dance scenes, cheap sets, and ham acting take up a lot of this film, and screenplay writer Lenny Bruce takes up the rest of the scenes. Bruce plays creepy killer Vincent, bodyguard to a vice lord who enjoys hurting women and saying things like "Big deal, I killed a guy. That makes me a criminal?" The comedy relief is too bad to believe and most of the cast look like they'd rather be doing something else, but this is a genuine sleazy exploitation film from the 1950s underground and it has a nasty feeling all its own, aided by the score by Charles Ruddy. Bruce gives an uneven performance but goes out in glory at the end. Last part of the tape features trailers for *Racket Girls* and a women's wrestling film featuring the fabulous Peaches Page!

1953   B & W   60 minutes

DANCE WITH A STRANGER
★★★★½

DIRECTOR: Mike Newell

CAST: Miranda Richardson, Rupert Everett, Ian Holm, Matthew Carroll, Tom Chadbon, Jane Bertish

A superbly acted, solidly directed import, this British drama is a completely convincing tale of tragic love. It is not unlike a British version of *The Postman Always Rings Twice*, but it has none of the heavy breathing and melodramatic style found in the two screen versions of James M. Cain's celebrated novel of murder and unbridled lust. Newcomer Miranda Richardson makes a stunning film debut as the platinum-blonde hostess in a working-class night club who falls in love with a self-indulgent, upperclass snob (Rupert Everett). The screenplay was based on the true story of Ruth Ellis, who, on July 13, 1955, was hanged at London's Holloway prison for shooting her lover outside a pub. She was the last woman to be so executed in Britain, and her story provides gripping screen fare. Rated R for profanity, nudity, sex, and violence.

1985   102 minutes

DANGER LIGHTS
★★★

DIRECTOR: George B. Seitz

CAST: Louis Wolheim, Jean Arthur, Robert Armstrong, Hugh Herbert

Louis Wolheim plays a tough-as-nails rail-yard boss who befriends hobo Robert Armstrong and jeopardizes his chances with a young Jean Arthur, who is "almost" a fiancée. This story, done many times before and since, works well against the backdrop of a railroad world that is now largely gone. Wolheim was a standout in an era when ugly men and women (notably Wallace Beery and Marie Dressler) were among the top box-office draws, but he died within a year after completing this film and deprived the rest of the 1930s of a fine character star.

1930   B & W   73 minutes

DANGEROUS MOVES
★★★★½

DIRECTOR: Richard Dembo

CAST: Michel Piccoli, Leslie Caron, Alexandre Arbatt, Liv Ullman

Worthy of its Oscar for best foreign film of 1984, this French film about a chess match between two grand masters in Geneva is not just for fans of the game. Indeed, the real intensity that is created here comes from the sidelines: the two masters' camps, the psych-out attempts, the political stakes, and the personal dramas. Rated PG for adult situations and language.

1984   95 minutes

DANGEROUS SUMMER, A
★★

DIRECTOR: Quentin Masters
CAST: James Mason, Tom Skerritt, Ian Gilmour, Wendy Hughes

Set in Australia, this film deals with a posh resort—owned in part by American Howard Anderson (Tom Skerritt)—damaged by fire and the subsequent investigation by insurance troubleshooter George Engels (James Mason), sent by Lloyds of London to discover whether the incident was an accident or arson. The film was cheaply made, unimaginatively photographed, and poorly directed. Only the actors seem to know what they're doing, but, unfortunately, they aren't encouraged to do anything near their best. Even Mason's staunchest fans will be disappointed. Unrated, the film has violence and profanity.

1984   100 minutes

DANIEL
★★½

DIRECTOR: Sidney Lumet
CAST: Timothy Hutton, Mandy Patinkin, Lindsay Crouse, Edward Asner, Amanda Plummer

Sidney Lumet (*The Verdict*) directed this disappointing and ultimately depressing screen version of E. L. Doctorow's thinly veiled account of the Rosenberg case of thirty years ago, in which the parents of two young children were electrocuted as spies. If it weren't for Timothy Hutton's superb performance in the title role (as one of the children), *Daniel* would be much less effective. As it is, the film is powerful but frustrat-

ing, posing questions about the guilt of the Rosenbergs and then dodging them by dealing with a fictional family called the Isaacsons (with Mandy Patinkin and Lindsay Crouse excellent as the accused traitors) and then refusing to draw any conclusions. Rated R for profanity and violence.

1983   130 minutes

DANNY BOY
★★★★

DIRECTOR: Neil Jordan
CAST: Stephen Rea, Marie Kean, Ray McAnally, Donal McCann, Honor Heffernan

A young saxophone player witnesses the brutal murder of two people and becomes obsessed with understanding the act. Set in Ireland, this movie is enhanced by haunting musical interludes that highlight the drama of the people caught up in the Irish "troubles." The combination of the music, scenery, characters, and atmosphere creates an undeniably powerful experience. There are flaws, most notably in some of the coincidences, but the overall effect is mesmerizing. Rated R.

1982   92 minutes

DANTON
★★★½

DIRECTOR: Andrzej Wajda
CAST: Gerard Depardieu, Wojciech Pszoniak, Patrice Chereau

Polish director Andrzej Wajda (*Man of Iron*) takes the French revolutionary figure (well played by Gerard Depardieu) and the events surrounding his execution by one-time comrades and turns it into a parable of modern life. The struggle between the title character and Robespierre is not unlike that of America versus the Soviet Union. It may not be good history but the film does provide interesting viewing and food for thought. This French film has one more thing going for it: It has been subtitled in English rather than dubbed, a factor that undermined the video version of another Depardieu picture, *The Return of Martin Guerre*. Rated PG.

1982 136 minutes

DARK JOURNEY
★★★

DIRECTOR: Victor Saville
CAST: Vivien Leigh, Conrad Veidt, Joan Gardner, Anthony Bushell

Espionage with a twist. A British and a German spy fall in love in Stockholm during World War I.

1937 B & W 82 minutes

DARK VICTORY
★★★★

DIRECTOR: Edmund Goulding
CAST: Bette Davis, George Brent, Humphrey Bogart, Ronald Reagan, Geraldine Fitzgerald

This Warner Bros. release gave Bette Davis one of her best roles, as a headstrong heiress who discovers she has a brain tumor. A successful operation leads to a love affair with her doctor (George Brent). In the midst of all this bliss, Davis learns the tragic truth: surgery was only a halfway measure, and she will die in a year. Sure it's corny. But director Edmund Goulding, Davis, and her co-stars make it work. The only sour note comes from the miscasting of Humphrey Bogart as a Mexican (!) stablehand.

1939 B & W 106 minutes

DARK WATERS
★★½

DIRECTOR: André de Toth
CAST: Merle Oberon, Franchot Tone, Thomas Mitchell, Fay Bainter, Rex Ingram, John Qualen, Elisha Cook Jr.

Muddled story of orphaned girl(?) Merle Oberon and her strange and terrifying experiences with her aunt and uncle in the bayou backwaters of Louisiana is atmospheric and properly chilling at times, but fails to deliver enough of a story to justify its moody build-up. This has the potential to be a first-rated thriller à la Hitchcock or Val Lewton and boasts one of the finest character casts of any film of the 1940s (including the powerful Rex Ingram and the wonderfully odd Elisha Cook Jr.), but never quite succeeds on any level. The leads are all right, but the supporting players (along with the misty bogs) really carry the ball in this film.

1944 B & W 90 minutes

DARLING
★★★★

DIRECTOR: John Schlesinger
CAST: Julie Christie, Dirk Bogarde, Laurence Harvey, Jose Luis de Villalonga

John Schlesinger's direction is first-rate, and Julie Christie gives an Oscar-winning portrayal of a ruthless model who bullies, bluffs, and claws her way to social success, only to find life at the top depressing and meaningless.

1965 B & W 122 minutes

DAVID COPPERFIELD
★★★★½

DIRECTOR: George Cukor
CAST: Freddie Bartholomew, Frank Lawton, Lionel Barrymore, W. C. Fields, Edna May Oliver, Basil Rathbone

A first-rate production of Charles Dickens's rambling novel about a young man's adventures in nineteenth-century England. W. C. Fields and Edna May Oliver are standouts in an all-star cast.

1935   B & W 100 minutes

DAY FOR NIGHT
★★★★★

DIRECTOR: Francois Truffaut
CAST: Jacqueline Bisset, Jean-Pierre Léaud, Francois Truffaut

One of the best of the film-within-a-film movies ever made, this work by the late Francois Truffaut captures the poetry and energy of the creative artist at his peak. Rated PG.

1973   120 minutes

DAY OF THE LOCUST, THE
★★★★½

DIRECTOR: John Schlesinger
CAST: Donald Sutherland, Karen Black, Burgess Meredith, Bo Hopkins

This drama is both extremely depressing and spellbinding. It shows the unglamorous side of Hollywood in the 1930s. The people who don't succeed in the entertainment capital are the focus of the film. Rated R.

1975   144 minutes

DAY OF WRATH
★★★½

DIRECTOR: Carl Dreyer
CAST: Lisbeth Movin, Thorkild Roose, Sigrid Neiiendam, Preben Lerdorff, Olaf Ussing, Anna Svierkier

Slow-moving, intriguing story of a young woman who marries an elderly preacher but falls in love with his son is an allegorical indictment on the appearances of evil. It is reminiscent of Arthur Miller's *The Crucible* in that they both deal with the witch hunts of the Middle Ages, and they present the "pious" folk as being the real blight. Visually effective and well acted by all the principals, this film relies too much on symbolism and implied action but is still worthy as a study in hysteria and the motivations behind the fear. This is one of the last feature films made by internationally renowned director Carl Dreyer, perhaps best known for his *Passion of Joan of Arc*.

1944   B & W 98 minutes

DAYS OF HEAVEN
★★★★½

DIRECTOR: Terence Malick
CAST: Richard Gere, Brooke Adams, Sam Shepard, Linda Manz

Each frame of *Days of Heaven* looks like a page torn from an exquisitely beautiful picture book. The film begins in the slums of Chicago, where Bill (Richard Gere) works in a steel mill. He's hot-tempered, and a fight with the superintendent at the mill leaves him jobless. He decides to take Abby (Brooke Adams), his girl, and Linda (Linda Manz), his young sister, to the Texas Panhandle to work in the wheat fields at harvest time. "Bill and Abby told everybody they was brother and sister," explains narrator Manz in a heavy New York accent. "You know how people are. You tell 'em something and pretty soon they start talking." The owner of the farm (Sam Shepard) falls in love with Abby. Bill accidentally overhears a doctor tell the farmer he has a short time to live. Tired of seeing Abby work herself to exhaustion every day in the fields, Bill encourages her to respond to the farmer's attentions. That's the beginning of an idyllic year that ends in tragedy. Rated PG.

1978   95 minutes

DAYS OF WINE AND ROSES
★★★½

DIRECTOR: Blake Edwards
CAST: Jack Lemmon, Lee Remick, Charles Bickford, Jack Klugman

In this saddening film, Jack Lemmon and Lee Remick shatter the misconceptions about middle-class alcoholism.

1962   B & W 117 minutes

DEAD EASY
★★½

DIRECTOR: Bert Diling
CAST: Scott Burgess, Rosemary Paul, Tim McKenzie

George, Alexa, and Armstrong are three friends who try to break into the big-city night life. In doing so they anger a crime boss whose overreaction sets off a chain of events that results in every small-time hood and paid killer chasing them. Well-done contemporary crime thriller. Rated R for nudity, violence, language.

1978   90 minutes

DEAD END
★★★

DIRECTOR: William Wyler
CAST: Humphrey Bogart, Sylvia Sidney, Joel McCrea, Claire Trevor

Many famous names combined to film this story of people trying to escape their oppressive slum environment. Humphrey Bogart is cast in one of his many gangster roles from the 1930s. Joel McCrea conforms to his Hollywood stereotype by playing the "nice guy" architect, who dreams of rebuilding New York's waterfront.

1937   B & W 93 minutes

DEADLINE USA
★★★★

DIRECTOR: Richard Brooks
CAST: Humphrey Bogart, Kim Hunter, Ethel Barrymore

In this hard-hitting newspaper drama, Humphrey Bogart plays an editor who has to fight the city's underworld while keeping the publisher (superbly portrayed by Ethel Barrymore) from giving in to pressure and closing the paper down. While Kim Hunter is wasted in the small role as Bogart's ex-wife, the picture has much to recommend it. The scenes featuring Bogart and Barrymore together are absolutely electric.

1952   B & W 87 minutes

DEATH IN VENICE
★★★

DIRECTOR: Luchino Visconti
CAST: Dirk Bogarde, Marisa Berenson, Mark Burns, Silvana Mangano

This slow, studied film based on Thomas Mann's classic novel is about an artist's life and quest for beauty and perfection. The good cast seems to move through this movie without communicating with one another or the audience. Visually absorbing, but lifeless; seems longer than its 130-minute running time. Adult language, adult situations throughout. Rated PG.

1971   130 minutes

DEATH OF A CENTERFOLD
★★

DIRECTOR: Gabrielle Beaumont
CAST: Jamie Lee Curtis, Robert Reed, Bruce Weitz

This made-for-TV film chronicles the brutal murder of Playboy playmate Dorothy Stratten. Bob Fosse's *Star 80* does a much better job of getting inside the characters of Stratten and her power-crazy husband. Unrated.

1981 100 minutes

DEATHTRAP
★★★

DIRECTOR: Sidney Lumet

CAST: Michael Caine, Christopher Reeve, Dyan Cannon, Irene Worth, Henry Jones

An enjoyable mystery-comedy based on the long-running Broadway play, this Sidney Lumet film stars Michael Caine, Christopher Reeve, and Dyan Cannon. Caine plays a once-successful playwright who decides to steal a brilliant murder mystery just written by one of his drama students (Reeve), claim it as his own, murder the student, and collect the royalties. Rated PG for violence and adult themes.

1982 116 minutes

DEER HUNTER, THE
★★★★★

DIRECTOR: Michael Cimino

CAST: Robert De Niro, John Cazale, John Savage, Meryl Streep, Christopher Walken

Five friends—Michael (Robert De Niro), Stan (John Cazale), Nick (Christopher Walken), Steven (John Savage), and Axel (Chuck Aspergen)—work at the dangerous blast furnace in a steel mill of a dingy Midwestern industrial town in 1968. At quitting time, they make their way to their favorite local bar to drink away the pressures of the day. For Michael, Nick, and Steven it is the last participation in the ritual. In a few days, they leave for Vietnam, where they find horror and death. What follows is a gripping study of heroism and the meaning of friendship. Rated R for profanity and violence.

1978 183 minutes

DEFIANT ONES, THE
★★★★

DIRECTOR: Stanley Kramer

CAST: Tony Curtis, Sidney Poitier, Theodore Bikel, Charles McGraw, Lon Chaney Jr.

Director Stanley Kramer (*Inherit the Wind*) scored one of his few artistic successes with this compelling story about two escaped convicts (Tony Curtis and Sidney Poitier) shackled together—and coping with mutual hatred—as they run from the authorities in the South.

1958 B & W 97 minutes

DEJA VU
★

DIRECTOR: Anthony Richmond

CAST: Jaclyn Smith, Shelley Winters, Claire Bloom, Nigel Terry, Richard Kay, Frank Gatliff

Jaclyn Smith (of TV *Charlie's Angels* fame) and Nigel Terry (*Excalibur*) put in equally lame performances in this stupid story about reincarnation. Shelley Winters's portrayal of a stereotypical Russian gypsy is so bad it's laughable. The film's one and only good point is Claire Bloom, whose performance is so convincing that one wonders whether her scenes were not meant for this lamentable affair. Rated R for some sex, nudity, and violence.

1984 91 minutes

DERSU UZALA
★★★★½

DIRECTOR: Akira Kurosawa

CAST: Maxim Munzuk, Yuri Solomin

This epic about the charting of the Siberian wilderness (circa 1900) is surprisingly as intimate in relationships and details as it is grand in vistas and scope. A Japanese-Russian co-production, the second half of this Oscar winner, directed by Akira Kurosawa, is much better than the first. Still, as only a great film can do, it transports viewers to a time and place unknown to any of us, and we emerge exhilarated. The gorgeous photography (wide-screen in the theaters) and Maxim Munzuk's performance as Dersu Uzala, an old native hunter and guide, always carry the film through its occasional sluggish moments. In Russian and Japanese with English subtitles.

1974   140 minutes

DESERT BLOOM
★★★

DIRECTOR: Eugene Corr
CAST: Jon Voight, JoBeth Williams, Ellen Barkin, Allen Garfield, Annabeth Gish

This poignant study of awakening adolescence and family turmoil is effectively set against a backdrop of 1950 Las Vegas, as the atomic age dawns. The story unfolds slowly but sensitively. The cast is superb. Thirteen-year-old Annabeth Gish gives a remarkably complex performance as a brilliant girl who must cope with an abusive stepfather, an ineffectual mother, and a sexpot aunt. Rated PG.

1986   106 minutes

DESERT HEARTS
★★★½

DIRECTOR: Donna Deitch
CAST: Helen Shaver, Patricia Charbonneau, Audra Lindley, Andra Akers, Gwen Welles, Dean Butler, James Stanley

A sensitive portrayal of the evolving relationship between a young, openly lesbian woman and a quiet university professor ten years her senior. Set on a Reno "divorce ranch" in 1959. The excellent acting by Patricia Charbonneau and Helen Shaver superbly sets off the development of their individual and joint characters. Audra Lindley adds a welcome touch as the grumbling stepmother. Some may find the explicit love scenes upsetting, but the humor and characterization entirely overrule any objection on this basis, and the bonus of 1950s props and sets is a treat. Rated R for profanity and sex.

1986   90 minutes

DESIRE UNDER THE ELMS
★★

DIRECTOR: Delbert Mann
CAST: Sophia Loren, Anthony Perkins, Burl Ives, Anne Seymour, Frank Overton

If there is one thing that Hollywood can do well, it's butcher great material. Here a writer of musicals (Don Hartman), an ultramodern novelist (Irwin Shaw), and a TV-grown director (Delbert Mann) combine to carve, cut, and splice brooding playwright Eugene O'Neill's dark tragedy of family hatred, greed, and illicit love on a puritan New England farm into a tepid, turgid triangle tale. Sophia Loren, making her Tinsel Town debut, is perfectly miscast as the young and desirable wife of aged Burl Ives, and who cheats with his son, Anthony Perkins, with predictable, disastrous results.

1958   B & W 114 minutes

DESPAIR
★★★★

DIRECTOR: Rainer Werner Fassbinder
CAST: Dirk Bogarde, Klaus Lowitsch

Karlovich (Dirk Bogarde), a Russian living in Germany in 1930, runs an unsuccessful chocolate factory.

The stock market crash in America pushes his business into even deeper trouble, and he begins to lose touch with himself in a major way. Enjoying *Despair* requires a taste for black comedy at its blackest and an appreciation of ingenious film-making. Rated R.

1979   119 minutes

DETOUR
★★★

DIRECTOR: Edgar G. Ulmer

CAST: Tom Neal, Ann Savage, Claudia Drake, Edmund MacDonald, Tim Ryan, Esther Howard

This routine story about a drifter enticed into crime is skillfully constructed, economically produced, and competently acted; it has long been considered one of the best (if not *the* best) low-budget film ever made. German director Edgar G. Ulmer took the best that PRC (Producer's Releasing Corporation) had to offer him in the way of budget and resources and made the most acclaimed film PRC ever released. Ann Savage as the beguiling, destructive enchantress playing off Tom Neal's infatuation rings just as true in this bargain-basement production as it does in the highly acclaimed adult crime dramas produced by the major studios.

1945   B & W   69 minutes

DEVIL AT 4 O'CLOCK, THE
★★★

DIRECTOR: Mervyn LeRoy

CAST: Spencer Tracy, Frank Sinatra, Kerwin Mathews, Jean-Pierre Aumont

This script may be weak and predictable, but the acting of Spencer Tracy and Frank Sinatra make this a watchable motion picture. Tracy is a priest who is in charge of an orphanage. When their island home is endangered by an impending volcanic eruption, he seeks the aid of a group of convicts headed by Sinatra.

1961   126 minutes

DEVILS, THE
★★★★

DIRECTOR: Ken Russell

CAST: Oliver Reed, Vanessa Redgrave, Dudley Sutton, Max Adrian, Gemma Jones

Next to *Women in Love*, this is director Ken Russell's best film. Exploring witchcraft and politics in France during the seventeenth century, it's a mad mixture of drama, horror, camp, and comedy. Ugly for the most part (with several truly unsettling scenes), it is still fascinating. Rated R.

1971   109 minutes

DIARY OF A COUNTRY PRIEST
★★★★

DIRECTOR: Robert Bresson

CAST: Claude Laydu, Nicole Ladmiral, Jean Riveyre, Nicole Maurey, André Guibert, Martine Lemaire

The slow pace at the beginning of this tale about a priest trying to minister to his parish might tend to put some viewers off. However, with Bresson's poetic style and camera work, the wait is well worth it. The film flows like a stream rather than roaring like a river, but this only lends to its charm and beauty. In French with English subtitles.

1950   B & W 120 minutes

DIARY OF A MAD HOUSEWIFE
★★★

DIRECTOR: Frank Perry

CAST: Richard Benjamin, Carrie Snodgress, Frank Langella

Most women will detest Jonathan (Richard Benjamin), the self-centered, social climber husband of Tina (Carrie Snodgress). He has had an affair and also lost all their savings in a bad investment. Tina, a college graduate, has been unhappily stuck at home for years with their two children. She finally finds happiness in an affair with George (Frank Langella). Profanity, sex, and nudity are included in this film.

1970   94 minutes

DIARY OF ANNE FRANK, THE
★★★★½

DIRECTOR: George Stevens
CAST: Millie Perkins, Joseph Schildkraut, Shelley Winters

Excellent adaptation of the Broadway play dealing with the terror Jews felt during the Nazi raids of World War II. Two families are forced to hide in a Jewish sympathizer's attic to avoid capture by the Nazis. Anne (Millie Perkins) is the teen-age girl who doesn't stop dreaming of a better future. Shelley Winters won an Oscar for her role as the hysterical Mrs. Van Daan, who shares sparse food and space with the Frank family.

1959   B & W 170 minutes

DIFFERENT STORY, A
★★★½

DIRECTOR: Paul Aaron
CAST: Perry King, Meg Foster, Valerie Curtin, Peter Donat

Perry King and Meg Foster play homosexuals who realize their romances are just not clicking. They fall in love with each other, marry, grow rich, and, eventually, dissatisfied. To be fair, this is not a boring film. King and Foster are genuinely funny and appealing as the most modern of young adult couples. The screenplay, how-

ever, lets them down on more than one occasion, and whoever came up with the King character's voice and movement should be given a manual on why caricatures of humans sometimes fail to win an audience. Taken strictly as an entertainment, it works. Rated PG.

1979   107 minutes

DIM SUM: A LITTLE BIT OF HEART
★★★½

DIRECTOR: Wayne Wang
CAST: Laureen Chew, Kim Chew, Victor Wong, Ida F. O. Chung, Cora Miao

Dim Sum is an independent American movie about the tensions and affections between a Chinese mother and daughter living in San Francisco's Chinatown. The film moves along quietly, creeping up on you gently, winning you over with humor and subtlety. The restraint of the mother, who wants her daughter to marry, and the frustration of the daughter, who wants freedom of decision, are beautifully conveyed by real-life mother and daughter Laureen and Kim Chew. Victor Wong as a rambunctious uncle is a gas. Rated PG.

1985   88 minutes

DINO
★★½

DIRECTOR: Thomas Carr
CAST: Sal Mineo, Brian Keith, Susan Kohner, Joe De Santis

In this okay story of a wayward young man who comes to grips with his life and environment as a result of assistance from social worker Brian Keith and girlfriend Susan Kohner, Sal Mineo takes his place along with James Dean, James MacArthur, Paul Newman, and Steve McQueen as rebellious, troubled youths of the 1950s. Nothing new, but interestingly done.

1957   B & W   94 minutes

DIVINE NYMPH, THE
★★½

DIRECTOR: Giuseppe Patroni Griffi
CAST: Laura Antonelli, Terence Stamp, Marcello Mastroianni

This story of love and passion resembles an Italian soap opera at best. Laura Antonelli is the young beauty who is unfaithful to her fiancé. She has an affair with Terence Stamp, who coerces her into having another affair with Marcello Mastroianni. In Italian, with English subtitles. Rated R for nudity.

1977   89 minutes

DR. ZHIVAGO
★★★★

DIRECTOR: David Lean
CAST: Omar Sharif, Julie Christie, Geraldine Chaplin, Rod Steiger, Alec Guinness

An epic treatment was given to Boris Pasternak's novel of romance and revolution in this film. Omar Sharif is Zhivago, a Russian doctor and poet whose personal life is ripped apart by the upheaval of the Russian Revolution. The screenplay is choppy and overlong and is often sacrificed to the spectacle of vast panoramas, detailed sets, and impressive costumes. These artistic elements, along with a beautiful musical score, make for cinema on a grand scale, and it remains a most watchable movie.

1965   197 minutes

DODES 'KA-DEN
★★★★

DIRECTOR: Akira Kurosawa

CAST: Yoshitaka Zushi, Tomako Yamazaki, Hishashi Akutagawa, Noburu Mitsutahi

Akira Kurosawa's first color film is a spellbinding blend of fantasy and reality. The film chronicles the lives of a group of Tokyo slum dwellers that includes children, alcoholics, and the disabled. Illusion and imagination are their weapons as they fight for survival. This masterpiece is best known for its stellar photography and superb editing.

1970   140 minutes

DODSWORTH
★★★★

DIRECTOR: William Wyler
CAST: Walter Huston, Ruth Chatterton, Mary Astor, David Niven, Spring Byington, Paul Lukas, John Payne, Maria Ouspenskaya

Walter Huston, in the title role, heads an all-star cast in this outstanding adaptation of the Sinclair Lewis novel. Auto tycoon Samuel Dodsworth is the epitome of the classic American self-made man. His wife is an appearance-conscious *nouveau riche* snob who goes European during a vacation trip over the water. Suddenly Dodsworth's values are rustic, and he is a bumpkin. But for an idyllic affair in Italy, he comes close to losing the peace and contentment he believes he has achieved through hard work and adherence to basic ideals. An intelligent, mature script, excellent characterizations, and sensitive cinematography make this film a modern classic.

1936   B & W 101 minutes

DOG DAY AFTERNOON
★★★★½

DIRECTOR: Sidney Lumet

CAST: Al Pacino, John Cazale, Charles Durning, Carol Kane

Dog Day Afternoon is a masterpiece of contemporary commentary. Al Pacino once again proves himself to be in the front rank of America's finest actors. Director Sidney Lumet (*Murder on the Orient Express*; *Serpico*; etc.) scores high with masterful pacing and real suspense. This is an offbeat drama about a gay man who's involved in bank-robbing. Highly recommended. Rated R.

1975   130 minutes

DOLL'S HOUSE, A
★★★

DIRECTOR: Joseph Losey
CAST: Jane Fonda, David Warner, Trevor Howard

Jane Fonda is quite good in this screen version of Henrik Ibsen's play about a liberated woman in the nineteenth century, and her struggles to maintain her freedom. Pacing is a problem at times, but first-class acting and beautiful sets keep the viewer interested.

1973   103 minutes

DOMINO PRINCIPLE, THE
★

DIRECTOR: Stanley Kramer
CAST: Gene Hackman, Richard Widmark, Candice Bergen, Eli Wallach, Mickey Rooney

Never have so many been wasted on so little. The only true victims in this assassination/double-cross/conspiracy thriller are the viewers tricked into watching it. Even Gene Hackman can't do anything as a confused convict busted out of prison with the intent to kill somebody. Nothing makes sense in this mess, and the book from which it is taken is no better. Rated R—violence.

1977   100 minutes

DON'T CRY, IT'S ONLY THUNDER
★★★★

DIRECTOR: Peter Werner
CAST: Dennis Christopher, Susan Saint James

Here is one of those "little" movies that slipped by without much notice yet are so satisfying when discovered by adventurous video renters. A black market wheeler-dealer (Dennis Christopher, from *Breaking Away*) lining his pockets behind the lines during the Vietnam War is forced to aid some Asian nuns and their ever-increasing group of Saigon street orphans. The results are predictably heartwarming and occasionally heartbreaking, but the film never drifts off into sentimental melodrama. Rated PG.

1982   108 minutes

DOOMSDAY FLIGHT, THE
★★★

DIRECTOR: William Graham
CAST: Jack Lord, Edmond O'Brien, Van Johnson, John Saxon, Michael Sarrazin

Rod Serling wrote the script for this made-for-television movie, the first to depict the hijacking of an airliner. A distraught Edmond O'Brien blackmails an airline company by planting a bomb aboard a passenger plane. *The Doomsday Flight* offered good suspense at the time, but may not be as provocative today. Still, good acting is on hand as the search for the bomb is carried out.

1966   100 minutes

DOUBLE LIFE, A
★★★★

DIRECTOR: George Cukor
CAST: Ronald Colman, Edmond O'Brien, Shelley Winters, Ray Collins

Ronald Colman gives an Oscar-winning performance as a famous actor whose stage life begins to take over his personality and private life, forcing him to revert to stage characters, including Othello, to cope with everyday situations. Clever, brilliantly written by Garson Kanin and Ruth Gordon, and impressively acted by a stand-out cast of top character actors and actresses. Top treatment of a fine story.

1947   B & W 104 minutes

DOWNHILL RACER
★★★½
DIRECTOR: Michael Ritchie
CAST: Robert Redford, Gene Hackman, Camilla Sparv

Robert Redford struggles with an unappealing character, in this study of an Olympic skier. But Gene Hackman is excellent as the coach who tries to turn him around, and the exciting scenes of this snow sport hold the film together. Rated PG.

1969   101 minutes

DRAGON SEED
★★½
DIRECTOR: Jack Conway, Harold S. Bucquet
CAST: Katharine Hepburn, Walter Huston, Turhan Bey, Hurd Hatfield

This study of a Chinese town torn asunder by Japanese occupation is taken from the novel by Nobel Prize winner Pearl S. Buck. It's occasionally gripping but in general too long.

1944   B & W 145 minutes

DRESSER, THE
★★★★★
DIRECTOR: Peter Yates

CAST: Albert Finney, Tom Courtenay, Edward Fox, Zena Walker

Peter Yates (*Breaking Away*; *Bullitt*) directed this superb screen treatment of Ronald Harwood's play about an eccentric stage actor (Albert Finney) in wartime England and the loyal valet (Tom Courtenay) who cares for him, sharing his triumphs and tragedies. Rated PG for language.

1983   118 minutes

EAST OF EDEN (ORIGINAL)
★★★★★
DIRECTOR: Elia Kazan
CAST: James Dean, Jo Van Fleet, Julie Harris, Raymond Massey, Burl Ives

The final portion of John Steinbeck's renowned novel of miscommunication and conflict between a father and son was transformed into a powerful, emotional movie. James Dean burst onto the screen as the rebellious son in his first starring role. Jo Van Fleet received an Oscar for her role as Kate, a bordello madam and Dean's long-forgotten mother.

1955   115 minutes

EAST OF EDEN (REMAKE)
★★★½
DIRECTOR: Harvey Hart
CAST: Jane Seymour, Timothy Bottoms, Bruce Boxleitner, Warren Oates, Anne Baxter, Lloyd Bridges, Howard Duff

This above-average television miniseries maintains the integrity of the source material by John Steinbeck without dipping too far into bathos. One major change: the focus shifts from the two sons—Timothy Bottoms and Bruce Boxleitner—who crave Papa's affection, to the deliciously evil woman—Jane Seymour—who twists them all around her little finger. Excellent supporting cast tries to follow the script while Seymour chews up the scenery. Ponderous and overlong; although the tone is conserved with no commercial interruptions, it's a bit much for one sitting. Stick with the 1955 film version. Unrated.

1982   240 minutes

EASY RIDER
★★★½

DIRECTOR: Dennis Hopper
CAST: Peter Fonda, Dennis Hopper, Jack Nicholson, Karen Black, Luana Anders

Time has not been kind to this 1969 release, about two drifters (Peter Fonda and Dennis Hopper) motorcycling their way across the country only to be confronted with violence and bigotry. Jack Nicholson's keystone performance, however, still makes it worth watching. Rated R.

1969   94 minutes

ECHO PARK
★★★

DIRECTOR: Robert Dornhelm
CAST: Susan Dey, Thomas Hulce, Michael Bowen, Christopher Walker, Shirley Jo Feeney, Heinrich Schweiger, John Paragon, Richard "Cheech" Marin, Cassandra Peterson

Tom Hulce (*Amadeus*, *Animal House*), Susan Dey (formerly of TV's *The Partridge Family*), and Michael Bowen, half-brother of David Carradine, star as three young show-biz hopefuls living in one of Los Angeles's seedier neighborhoods and waiting for stardom to strike. Director Robert Dornhelm and screenwriter Michael Ventura have some interesting things to say about the quest

for fame, and the stars provide some memorable moments. But these are wrapped up in a meandering, espisodic, and sometimes off-putting package. Overall, it is a watchable "little" film that should please those with a taste for something different. Rated R for nudity, profanity, and violence.

1986   93 minutes

ECSTASY
★★½

DIRECTOR: Gustav Machaty
CAST: Hedy Kiesler (Lamarr), Aribert Mog, Jaromir Rogoz, Leopold Kramer

Completely overshadowed in the years since its release by the notoriety of Kiesler-Lamarr's nude scenes, this new packaging in video should shift the emphasis back to the film itself, which is basically a romance of illicit love between a married woman and a stranger to whom she is attracted. The justly famous seduction scene has probably received more frame-by-frame exposure in movie books than any other film in history, and the worldwide scandal wrought by young Hedy Lamarr's husband's efforts to destroy all copies of this movie has made it a cinema curio for over 50 years, a reputation today's jaded audiences will find hard to fathom. Filmed in pre-Hitler Czechoslovakia, this version is subtitled in English.

1933   B & W   88 minutes

8½
★★★

DIRECTOR: Federico Fellini
CAST: Marcello Mastroianni, Claudia Cardinale, Sandra Milo

Federico Fellini is at his most bizarre in telling this story about a filmmaker trying to make a movie and all the strange and weird things that take place within his reality. If you like Fellini, you'll love this; if you don't, forget it.

1963   B & W   135 minutes

EL NORTE
★★★★★

DIRECTOR: Gregory Nava
CAST: Aide Silvia Gutierrez, David Villalpando, Ernesto Cruz, Alicia Del Lago

This work, by the husband-wife film-making team of Gregory Nava and Anna Thomas is the kind of movie that will have viewers recommending it to their friends. It is essentially an American-made foreign film. Most of the dialogue is in Spanish. Sound odd? Well, it isn't really. In fact, it may be one of the most memorable movie experiences you'll ever have. A story about two Guatemalans, a young brother and sister, whose American dream takes them on a long trek through Mexico to El Norte—the United States. They end up in Los Angeles in a cheap motel for day laborers and a series of jobs in the illegal job market. This screen work is funny, frightening, poignant, and sobering—a movie that stays with you. Rated R for profanity and violence.

1983   139 minutes

ELECTRIC HORSEMAN, THE
★★★

DIRECTOR: Sydney Pollack
CAST: Robert Redford, Jane Fonda, Valerie Perrine, Willie Nelson, John Saxon, Nicolas Coster

Directed by Sydney Pollack (*Tootsie*), *The Electric Horseman* brought the third teaming of Jane Fonda and Robert Redford on the screen. The result is a winsome piece of light entertainment. *The Electric Horseman* explores themes like the importance of individual integrity and the dangers of manipulation by the rich. Redford plays Sonny Steele, a former rodeo star who has become the unhappy spokesman for Ranch Breakfast, a brand of cereal. He's always in trouble and in danger of blowing the job—until he decides to rebel. Fonda is the TV reporter who covers his story. Rated PG.

1979   120 minutes

ELENI
★★★

DIRECTOR: Peter Yates
CAST: Kate Nelligan, John Malkovich, Linda Hunt

Interesting film adaptation of Nicholas Gage's factual book *Eleni*. In 1948, during the civil war in Greece, a small mountain village is terrorized by a group of communist guerrillas. Eleni Gatzoyiannis (Kate Nelligan) defies the communists and their attempts to abduct her children to send them to prison camps behind the iron curtain, and is subsequently held captive, tortured, and eventually executed in cold blood. Eleni's son Nicholas Gage (John Malkovich) returns to Greece after many years as a reporter for the *New York Times*, devoting his life there to discovering the facts surrounding his mother's death while trying to unmask her killers. Rated PG for language and violence.

1985   116 minutes

ELEPHANT MAN, THE
★★★★

DIRECTOR: David Lynch
CAST: Anthony Hopkins, John Hurt, Anne Bancroft, Wendy Hiller, Freddie Jones

Though it has its flaws, this film is a fascinating and heartbreaking study of the life of John Merrick, a hopelessly deformed but kind and intelligent man who struggles for dignity. John Hurt is magnificent in the title role. Rated PG.

1980 B & W 125 minutes

ELMER GANTRY
★★★★

DIRECTOR: Richard Brooks
CAST: Burt Lancaster, Jean Simmons, Dean Jagger, Arthur Kennedy, Shirley Jones

Burt Lancaster gives one of his most memorable performances in this release as a phony evangelist who, along with Jean Simmons, exploits the faithful with his fire-and-brimstone sermons. Arthur Kennedy is the reporter out to expose their operation in this screen version of Sinclair Lewis's story set in the Midwest of the 1920s.

1960 145 minutes

ELUSIVE CORPORAL, THE
★★★★½

DIRECTOR: Jean Renoir
CAST: Jean-Pierre Cassel, Claude Brasseur, Claude Rich

Twenty-five years after he made his greatest masterpiece. *La Grande Illusion*, Renoir reexamines men in war with almost equally satisfying results. This time the soldiers are Frenchmen in a World War II prison camp. *The Elusive Corporal* is a delicate drama infused with considerable wit—mostly derived from fake heroics made all the more sadly comic when juxtaposed with genuine heroism. Good performances and well worth discovering.

1962 108 minutes

ELVIRA MADIGAN
★★★★

DIRECTOR: Bo Widerberg
CAST: Pia Degermark, Thommy Gerggren, Lennart Malmen, Cleo Jensen

This is a simple and tragic story of a young Swedish officer who falls in love with a beautiful circus performer. Outstanding photography makes this film. Try to see the subtitled version.

1967 89 minutes

EMILY
★★

DIRECTOR: Henry Herbert
CAST: Koo Stark

This British film was Koo Stark's premiere in soft-core porn. She plays a teenager returning home from boarding school who finds out that her mother is a well-paid prostitute. This bit of news upsets Emily momentarily, but she manages to create her own sexual world with a female painter, the painter's husband, and her boyfriend, James. Lots of nudity and sex, but it still manages to be boring. Rated R.

1982 87 minutes

EMMANUELLE
★★★

DIRECTOR: Just Jaeckin
CAST: Sylvia Kristel, Marika Green, Daniel Sarky, Alain Cuny

Sylvia Kristel (*Private Lessons*) became an international star as a result of this French screen adaptation of Emmanuelle Aran's controversial book about the initiation of a diplomat's young wife into the world of sensuality. In the soft-core sex film genre, this stands out as one of the best. That's not exactly high praise, but it is a movie that open-minded members of both sexes can enjoy. Rated R for nudity and sex.

1974 92 minutes

END OF THE ROAD
★★

DIRECTOR: Aram Avakian
CAST: Stacy Keach, Harris Yulin, Dorothy Tristan, James Earl Jones

As daring as this film is, it remains almost unwatchable as a general form of entertainment and at times a bit boring as an experiment. Stacy Keach plays a college graduate who falls out of society, receives help from an unorthodox psychotherapist named Doctor D (James Earl Jones), then becomes intimately involved with a married couple. The imagery can be compelling at times, but the finale is too graphic for the eyes. Graded leniently for sheer nerve. Rated X (by 1960s standards) but more like a hard R for sex, nudity, and adult themes.

1969   110 minutes

ENDLESS LOVE
★★

DIRECTOR: Franco Zeffirelli
CAST: Brooke Shields, Martin Hewitt, Shirley Knight, Don Murray

Though this story of a teen-age love affair has all the elements of a great romance, it is marred by implausibility and inconsistency. The film improves as it progresses and even offers some compelling moments, but not enough to compensate for its flaws. It's unfortunate that director Franco Zeffirelli didn't do more with this modern-day *Romeo and Juliet*. Rated R because of sex and nudity.

1981   115 minutes

ENOLA GAY: THE MEN, THE MISSION, THE ATOMIC BOMB
★★★

DIRECTOR: David Lowell Rich
CAST: Billy Crystal, Kim Darby, Patrick Duffy, Gary Frank, Gregory Harrison

In this made-for-TV drama, Patrick Duffy plays Paul Tibbets, the man in charge of the plane that dropped the atomic bomb over Hiroshima. The film delves into the lives and reactions of the crew members in a fairly effective manner.

1980   150 minutes

ENTRE NOUS (BETWEEN US)
★★★★★

DIRECTOR: Diane Kurys
CAST: Miou-Miou, Isabelle Huppert, Guy Marchand, Jean-Pierre Bacri

This down-to-earth, highly human story by director Diane Kurys concentrates on the friendship between two women, Madeline (Miou-Miou) and Lena (Isabelle Huppert), who find they have more in common with each other than with their husbands. Most of Kurys's works (*Peppermint Soda* and *Cocktail Molotov*, for example) have been autobiographical. *Entre Nous* is the story of her parents and her mother's dearest friend. It is an affecting remembrance the viewer won't soon forget. Rated PG for nudity, suggested sex, and violence.

1983   110 minutes

EQUUS
★★★★

DIRECTOR: Sidney Lumet
CAST: Richard Burton, Peter Firth, Colin Blakely, Joan Plowright, Harry Andrews, Eileen Atkins, Jenny Agutter

Peter Firth plays a stableboy whose mysterious fascination with horses results in an act of meaningless cruelty and violence. Richard Burton plays the psychiatrist brought in to uncover Firth's hidden hostilities. The expanding of Peter Shaffer's play leaves the film somewhat unfocused but the scenes between Burton and Firth are intense, riveting, and beautifully acted. This was Burton's last quality film role; he was nominated for best actor. Rated R for profanity and nudity.

1977 137 minutes

ERENDIRA
★★½

DIRECTOR: Ruy Guerra

CAST: Irene Papas, Claudia Ohana, Michael Lonsdale, Oliver Wehe

In this disturbing and distasteful black comedy, Irene Papas stars as a wealthy old woman who loses everything in a fire accidentally set by her sleepwalking granddaughter, Erendira (Claudia Ohana). To regain her lost riches, the grandmother turns her charge into a prostitute and insists that she earn back over $1 million by taking on all comers in modern-day Mexico. In Spanish, with English subtitles. Unrated, the film has nudity, profanity, simulated sex, simulated rape, gore, and violence.

1983 103 minutes

ESCAPE TO BURMA
★

DIRECTOR: Allan Dwan

CAST: Barbara Stanwyck, Robert Ryan, David Farr, Murvyn Vye

This features a tea plantation, wild animals, and a hunted man seeking refuge. Every great star makes a turkey, and this is Barbara Stanwyck's. But some films are so bad they are good. This may be one.

1955 B & W 87 minutes

ESCAPE TO THE SUN
★★★

DIRECTOR: Menahem Golan

CAST: Laurence Harvey, Josephine Chaplin, John Ireland, Jack Hawkins

Two young university students try to escape from the oppressive Soviet Union under the watchful eyes of the KGB. They try first for an exit visa; only one visa is issued, and one of the students is taken into custody. The two are forced to make a heroic escape to the West. Rated PG for violence.

1984 94 minutes

EUREKA
★★★★½

DIRECTOR: Nicolas Roeg

CAST: Gene Hackman, Theresa Russell, Rutger Hauer, Jane Lapotaire, Mickey Rourke, Ed Lauter, Joe Pesci

Another stunner from one of the greatest living directors, Nicolas Roeg (Don't Look Now, Insignificance). Eureka is about an ambitious gold miner (Gene Hackman) who makes his fortune in the snowbound Canadian wilderness, then retires to his very own Caribbean island. It is some twenty years after he struck it rich that he finds himself up against some prospectors of a different type: a fortune-hunting gigolo (Rutger Hauer) who wants to marry his daughter (Theresa Russell), and the mob, who want to purchase his island and build a casino. All of this expressed by Roeg's visionary cinematic eye with attention to irony and biting wit. Rated R for sex, nudity, violence, and profanity.

1983 130 minutes

EVERY MAN FOR HIMSELF AND GOD AGAINST ALL
★★★★
DIRECTOR: Werner Herzog
CAST: Bruno S., Walter Ladengast, Brigitte Mira

Based on a real incident, the story of Kasper Hauser (Bruno S.) tells of a man who had been kept in confinement since birth. Hauser's appearance in Nuremberg in the 1920s was a mystery. He was a man who tried to adjust to a new society while maintaining his own vision. One of Herzog's best. Also released as *The Mystery of Kasper Hauser*. In German, with English subtitles. No MPAA rating.
1975　　　　　　　　　110 minutes

EXECUTIONER'S SONG, THE
★★★½
DIRECTOR: Lawrence Schiller
CAST: Tommy Lee Jones, Rosanna Arquette, Christine Lahti, Eli Wallach

Pulitzer Prize novelist Norman Mailer's made-for-television adaptation of his engrossing account of convicted killer Gary Gilmore's fight to get Utah to carry out his death sentence. The performances of Tommy Lee Jones and Rosanna Arquette are electrifying. Unrated.
1982　　　　　　　　　200 minutes

EXECUTIVE ACTION
★★★★
DIRECTOR: David Miller
CAST: Burt Lancaster, Robert Ryan, Will Geer, Gilbert Green, John Anderson

This forceful film, based on Mark Lane's book *Rush to Judgment*, features a fascinating look at possible reasons for the assassination of John F. Kennedy. Rated PG.
1973　　　　　　　　　91 minutes

EXODUS
★★½
DIRECTOR: Otto Preminger
CAST: Paul Newman, Eva Marie Saint, Ralph Richardson, Peter Lawford, Lee J. Cobb, Sal Mineo

The early days of Israel are seen through the eyes of various characters, in this epic, adapted from the novel by Leon Uris. Directed by the heavy-handed Otto Preminger, its length and plodding pace caused comic Mort Sahl to quip, "Otto, let my people go," at a preview. Paul Newman simply called it "chilly."
1960　　　　　　　　　213 minutes

EXTREMITIES
★★½
DIRECTOR: Robert M. Young
CAST: Farrah Fawcett, James Russo, Diana Scarwid, Alfre Woodard

This well-meant but difficult-to-watch thriller casts Farrah Fawcett (in a first-rate performance) as a single woman who is brutalized and terrorized in her own home by a homicidal maniac (James Russo). When she manages to outwit her attacker and render him helpless, she must decide between bloody revenge and human compassion. Robert M. Young directs this adaptation by William Mastrosimone of his play with authority and realism, which makes it almost unendurable during the first hour. Nevertheless, the second part contains some fine moments of drama. Rated R for violence.
1986　　　　　　　　　100 minutes

EYES, THE MOUTH, THE
★
DIRECTOR: Marco Bellocchio
CAST: Lou Castel, Angela Molina, Emanuelle Riva

This movie presumes to tell the story of a man (Lou Castel) who liberates his soul from the past and embraces life after his twin brother commits suicide. It founders so much that your mind soon drifts from the plot to the face and mannerisms of Castel, who not only looks like Jack Nicholson but mugs like him through the entire film. He even does Nicholson-like things, such as standing upright in a fireplace removing his clothes. Somehow none of this jives. The movie feels like an impostor. In Italian with English subtitles. Rated R for language and nudity.

1983   100 minutes

F.I.S.T.
★★★
DIRECTOR: Norman Jewison
CAST: Sylvester Stallone, Rod Steiger, Peter Boyle, Melinda Dillon, David Huffman, Tony LoBianco

It's too bad that *F.I.S.T.* is so predictable and cliché-ridden, because Sylvester Stallone gives a fine performance. As Johnny Kovak, organizer and later leader of the Federation of Interstate Truckers, he creates an even more human and poignant character than his Rocky Balboa. It is ironic that Stallone, after being favorably compared with Marlon Brando, should end up in a film so similar to *On the Waterfront* . . . and with Rod Steiger yet! The story is a composite of *Waterfront*, *The Godfather*, and the Warner Bros. melodramas of the 1930s and '40s. Rated PG.

1978   145 minutes

FACE IN THE CROWD, A
★★★★
DIRECTOR: Elia Kazan

CAST: Andy Griffith, Patricia Neal, Lee Remick, Anthony Franciosa, Walter Matthau, Kay Medford

A sow's ear is turned into a silk purse in this Budd Shulberg story, scripted by the author, of a television executive who discovers gold in a winsome hobo she molds into a tube star. But all that glitters is not gold. A fine cast makes this a winning film, which brought Andy Griffith and Lee Remick to the screen for the first time.

1957   B & W 125 minutes

FAILSAFE
★★★★
DIRECTOR: Sidney Lumet
CAST: Henry Fonda, Walter Matthau, Fritz Weaver, Larry Hagman, Dom De Luise, Frank Overton

In this gripping film, a United States aircraft is mistakenly assigned to drop the big one on Russia, and the leaders of the two countries grapple for some kind of solution as time runs out.

1964   B & W 111 minutes

FALCON AND THE SNOWMAN, THE
★★★★★
DIRECTOR: John Schlesinger
CAST: Timothy Hutton, Sean Penn, Pat Hingle, Lori Singer, Richard Dysart

In this powerful motion picture, directed by John Schlesinger (*Midnight Cowboy*), Timothy Hutton and Sean Penn give stunning performances as two childhood friends who decide to sell United States secrets to the Russians. Based on a true incident, this release—to its credit—makes no judgments. The viewer is left to decide what's right and wrong, and whether Boyce met with justice. It is not an easy decision to make. We suspect most viewers will feel sorry for the two misguided youths and stunned and riveted by their story. Rated R for violence and profanity.

1985   131 minutes

FALL OF THE ROMAN EMPIRE, THE
★★★★

DIRECTOR: Anthony Mann
CAST: Sophia Loren, James Mason, Stephen Boyd, Alec Guinness, Christopher Plummer, John Ireland, Mel Ferrer

During the early and mid-1960s, Hollywood looked to the history books for many of its films. Director Anthony Mann was involved with two of the best within the genre, *El Cid* and *The Fall of the Roman Empire*. Having the advantage of a brilliant cast and an intelligent script, Mann has fashioned an epic that is a feast for the eyes and does not insult the viewers' intelligence. Like Stanley Kubrick's earlier film *Spartacus*, *The Fall of the Roman Empire* has thrilling moments of action and characters the viewer cares about. Though running over two and a half hours, this one is well worth it.

1964   149 minutes

FALLEN ANGEL
★★★½

DIRECTOR: Robert Lewis
CAST: Dana Hill, Richard Masur, Melinda Dillon, Ronny Cox, David Hayward

This drama deals with the controversial topic of child pornography. A young girl, Jennifer (played by Dana Hill), is pushed into pornography by a so-called adult friend, Howard (played by Richard Masur). Jennifer sees no hope of getting out of her predicament, because she can't communicate with her mother (played by Melinda Dillon). Very timely topic!

1981   100 minutes

FALLEN IDOL, THE
★★★★

DIRECTOR: Carol Reed
CAST: Ralph Richardson, Michelle Morgan, Bobby Henrey, Jack Hawkins, Bernard Lee

A small boy hero-worships a household servant suspected of murdering his wife in this quiet Graham Greene thriller. Largely told from the child's point of view, this one is pulse-raising. As always, the late Ralph Richardson is great. Bernard Lee later became "M" in the Bond films.

1948   B & W 94 minutes

FALLING IN LOVE
★★★

DIRECTOR: Ulu Grosbard
CAST: Robert De Niro, Meryl Streep, Harvey Keitel

Robert De Niro and Meryl Streep are fine as star-crossed lovers who risk their marriages for a moment of passion. Thanks to the uneven direction of Ulu Grosbard and an unbelievable story by Michael Cristofer, the stars' performances are the only outstanding features in this watchable love story. Rated PG for profanity and adult situations.

1984   107 minutes

FAMILY UPSIDE DOWN, A
★★★

DIRECTOR: David Lowell Rich
CAST: Helen Hayes, Fred Astaire, Efrem Zimbalist Jr., Patty Duke Astin

A touching, all too real drama about a previously self-sufficient couple whose age makes them dependent on their grown children. Hayes, Astin, and Zimbalist were nominated, and Astaire won an Emmy for this affecting made-for-television film.

1978　　　　　　　100 minutes

FANNY
★★★★

DIRECTOR: Joshua Logan
CAST: Leslie Caron, Maurice Chevalier, Charles Boyer, Horst Buchholz, Baccaloni, Lionel Jeffries

Leslie Caron is a beautiful and lively Fanny in this 1961 film. She plays a young girl seeking romance with the boy she grew up with. Unfortunately, he leaves her pregnant as he pursues a life at sea.

1961　　　　　　　133 minutes

FANNY AND ALEXANDER
★★★★★

DIRECTOR: Ingmar Bergman
CAST: Pernilla Allwin, Bertil Guve, Gunn Wallgren, Allan Edwall, Ewa Froling, Jan Malmsjo

Set in Sweden around the turn of the century, this movie follows the adventures of two children. Some have called this Ingmar Bergman's first truly accessible work. We wouldn't go quite that far. Viewers still have to work a little to reap its rewards. Still, it is undeniably his most optimistic—and thus most enjoyable—motion picture. In Swedish, with English subtitles. Rated R for profanity and violence.

1983　　　　　　　197 minutes

FANTASIES

DIRECTOR: John Derek
CAST: Bo Derek, Peter Hotten, Anna Alexiaous, Nicos Paschalidis

Bo Derek stars in this ridiculous story of the adopted sister of a well-to-do orphan in Greece. Derek lives her life like a female Walter Mitty, always lost in a fantasy world. This has to be one of the worst films ever made, though it does have one merit: director John Derek's gorgeous cinematography. Rated R for brief nudity and adult situations.

1984　　　　　　　81 minutes

FAR PAVILIONS, THE
★★★

DIRECTOR: Peter Duffell
CAST: Ben Cross, Amy Irving, Omar Sharif, Christopher Lee, Benedict Taylor, Rossano Brazzi

In this romantic adventure, based on a novel by M. M. Kaye, Ben Cross plays Ash, a young British officer in Imperial India. Oddly enough, he had been raised as an Indian until he was eleven. As an adult, he is reunited with his childhood friend the Princess Anjuli (played by Amy Irving). Despite her impending marriage to the elderly Rajaha (Rossano Brazzi), Ash and Anjuli fall in love. Although this is a watchable film, there is an overabundance of meaningful glances, which fail to take the place of dialogue and action. Rated PG for sex and violence.

1983　　　　　　　108 minutes

FAREWELL TO ARMS, A
★★★★

DIRECTOR: Frank Borzage
CAST: Helen Hayes, Gary Cooper, Adolphe Menjou, Mary Philips, Jack LaRue

Macho author Ernest Hemingway's well-crafted story of doomed love between a wounded ambulance driver and a nurse in Italy during World War I. Adolphe

Menjou is peerless as the Italian army officer, Helen Hayes dies touchingly, and Gary Cooper strides away in the rain.

1932   B & W   78 minutes

FAST-WALKING
★★★½

DIRECTOR: James B. Harris

CAST: James Woods, Kay Lenz, Tim McIntire, Robert Hooks, Susan Tyrrell

This one is definitely not for everyone, but if you are adventurous, it may surprise you. James Woods plays a prison guard whose yearning for the good life leads him into a jail-break scheme. Film plays for black comedy and generally succeeds. Some very good acting and nice plot twists make this one worth your time. Rated R for violence, language, nudity.

1983   116 minutes

55 DAYS AT PEKING
★★

DIRECTOR: Nicholas Ray

CAST: Charlton Heston, Ava Gardner, David Niven, John Ireland

A lackluster big-screen adventure about the Boxer Revolt in 1900. The story about a group of multinational embassy officials who become besieged within the Peking embassy compound takes no time to develop any rounded characterizations. Charlton Heston, David Niven, and the rest of the large cast seem made of wood.

1963   150 minutes

FINGERS
★★★★

DIRECTOR: James Toback

CAST: Harvey Keitel, Jim Brown, Tisa Farrow, Michael V. Gazzo

Harvey Keitel gives an electric performance as a would-be concert pianist who is also a death-dealing collector for his loan-sharking dad. Film is extremely violent and not for all tastes, but there is an undeniable fascination one feels toward the Keitel character and his tortured life. Rated R.

1978   91 minutes

FIRE DOWN BELOW
★★★

DIRECTOR: Robert Parrish

CAST: Rita Hayworth, Robert Mitchum, Jack Lemmon, Herbert Lom, Anthony Newley

Rita Hayworth is a lady of dubious background and virtue on a voyage between islands aboard a tramp steamer owned by adventurers Robert Mitchum and Jack Lemmon, both of whom chase her. A below-decks explosion traps one of the partners. The other comes to his rescue while Rita and the audience hold their breaths. The plot is familiar, contrived, but entertaining just the same.

1957   116 minutes

FIRE WITH FIRE
★★

DIRECTOR: Duncan Gibbins

CAST: Craig Sheffer, Virginia Madsen, Jon Polito, Jeffrey Jay Cohen, Kate Reid, Jean Smart

What hath Shakespeare wrought? The true story of a girl's Catholic school that invited the residents of a neighboring boy's reform school to a dance has been turned into another of those good girl/bad boy melodramas wherein misunderstood teens triumph against all odds. Craig Sheffer and Virginia Madsen are very appealing newcomers whose shared scenes generate pleasant chemistry, but the plot is laughable. Jon Polito has a thankless part as a gun-crazy reform boss, and a book could be filled with the dangling questions left unresolved at film's end. It even swipes that great plunge into the river made by Paul Newman and Robert Redford in *Butch Cassidy and the Sundance Kid*. Rated PG-13 for mild sex and language.

1986   103 minutes

FIRST BORN
★★★★

DIRECTOR: Michael Apted
CAST: Teri Garr, Peter Weller

An emotionally charged screen drama that deftly examines some topical, thought-provoking themes, this stars Teri Garr (*Mr. Mom*) as a divorced woman who gets involved with the wrong man (Peter Weller) to the horror of her two sons. "It's about the world of adults seen through the eyes of a kid," says screenwriter Ron Koslow. And it works. Rated PG for profanity and violence.

1984   100 minutes

FIRST MONDAY IN OCTOBER
★★★

DIRECTOR: Ronald Neame
CAST: Walter Matthau, Jill Clayburgh, Barnard Hughes, Jan Sterling

This enjoyable, old-fashioned entertainment is reminiscent of the days when people went to see "a Humphrey Bogart picture" or "a Clark Gable picture." It's a Walter Matthau picture, with all the joys that implies. As he did in *Hopscotch*, director Ronald Neame allows Matthau, who plays a crusty Supreme Court justice, to make the most of every screen moment. *The First Monday in October* also had the advantage of perfect timing: Jill Clayburgh plays the first woman appointed to the Supreme Court (mirrored in real life the same year by the appointment of Sandra Day O'Connor). Rated R because of nudity and profanity.

1981   98 minutes

FITZCARRALDO
★★★½

DIRECTOR: Werner Herzog
CAST: Klaus Kinski, Claudia Cardinale, Paul Hittscher

For German film director Werner Herzog, the making of this film was reportedly quite an ordeal. Watching it may be an ordeal for some viewers as well. In order to bring Caruso, the greatest voice in the world, to the backwater town of Iquitos, the title character (Klaus Kinski) decides to become a rubber baron. A virgin forest that's just waiting to make a man rich is inaccessible by water because of raging rapids. He decides to haul a large boat over a mountain from a good river to a navigable portion of the bad one. The real Fitzcarraldo used a 28-ton boat that was dismantled for the task, but Herzog decided to drag a complete 328-ton steamboat inch-by-inch. As a result, probably only film buffs will enjoy this quirky triumph of a real-life madman. Unrated, this film has profanity. In German, with English subtitles.

1982   157 minutes

FIVE CAME BACK
★★★

DIRECTOR: John Farrow
CAST: Chester Morris, Wendy Barrie, John Carradine, Allen Jenkins, Joseph Calleia, C. Aubrey Smith, Patric Knowles, Lucille Ball

A plane carrying the usual mixed bag of passengers goes down in the jungle. Only five of the group will survive. The cast, fine character players all, makes this melodrama worthwhile, though it shows its age.

1939　　B & W　75 minutes

FIVE DAYS ONE SUMMER
★★★

DIRECTOR: Fred Zinnemann
CAST: Sean Connery, Anna Massey, Betsy Brantley, Lambert Wilson

This is an old-fashioned romance, with Sean Connery as a mountain climber caught in a triangle involving his lovely niece and a handsome young guide. Two handkerchiefs and a liking for soap opera are suggested. Rated PG for adult situations.

1983　　　　　108 minutes

FLASH OF GREEN, A
★★★½

DIRECTOR: Victor Nunez
CAST: Ed Harris, Blair Brown, Richard Jordan, George Coe, Isa Thomas, William Mooney, Joan Goodfellow, Helen Stenborg, John Glover

This is a compelling adaptation of John D. MacDonald's novel about a small-town Florida reporter (Ed Harris) whose boredom, lust, and curiosity lead him into helping an ambitious, amoral county official (Richard Jordan) win approval for a controversial housing project. Their tactics of deceit, blackmail, and coercion soon grow uglier than they expected. The acting is superb. The story is disturbing and thought-provoking.

1984　　　　　118 minutes

FLIM-FLAM MAN, THE
★★★

DIRECTOR: Irvin Kershner

CAST: George C. Scott, Michael Sarrazin, Sue Lyon, Harry Morgan, Jack Albertson

A con man (George C. Scott) teaches an army deserter (Michael Sarrazin) the art of fleecing yokels. Scott is an altogether charming, wry, winning rascal in this improbable, clever film, which is highlighted by a spectacular car-chase scene.

1967　　　　　104 minutes

FOOL FOR LOVE
★★★½

DIRECTOR: Robert Altman
CAST: Sam Shepard, Kim Basinger, Harry Dean Stanton, Randy Quaid

Writer-star Sam Shepard's disturbing, thought-provoking screenplay is about people who, as one of his characters comments, "can't help themselves." Shepard plays a cowboy-stuntman who is continuing his romantic pursuit of Kim Basinger in spite of her objections. A dark secret they share with a mysterious observer (Harry Dean Stanton) keeps them from finding contentment in each other's arms. Fool for Love deals with the anger, lies, and hurtful words that come from people who go on believing they are good or right or honest—like most of us. It does not depict any of these things graphically. Instead, it insinuates and teases until it makes the viewers feel a little dirty and a little sad. For open-minded adults who appreciate daring, original works. Rated R for profanity and violence.

1986　　　　　107 minutes

FORBIDDEN
★★★

DIRECTOR: Anthony Page

CAST: Jacqueline Bisset, Jurgen Prochnow, Irene Worth, Peter Vaughan

Made-for-cable film about a gentile woman who falls in love with a Jewish man during World War II: a crime in Hitler Germany. Enough suspense here to keep the viewer attentive, but not enough atmosphere to make it as intense as the melodramatic soundtrack assumes it to be. Not rated, but the equivalent of a PG for some violence and light sex.

1984   114 minutes

FORBIDDEN GAMES
★★★★★

DIRECTOR: René Clement
CAST: Brigitte Fossey, Georges Poujouly, Louis Herbert

It has been said that *Forbidden Games* is to World War II what *Grand Illusion* is to World War I. The horror of war has never been more real than as portrayed here against the bucolic surroundings of the French countryside. At the nucleus of the plot is Paulette, played by five-year-old Brigitte Fossey. Witnessing German troops kill her parents and pet dog twists the girl, who acquires an attraction for the symbols of death (much like Emily Dickinson). She and her friend (Georges Poujouly) wander about killing animals so they can give them ceremonial burials next to the dog. The fact that sentimentality is virtually nonexistent makes for a powerful, gut-wrenching film about the tragic follies, foibles, and frailties of mankind. The film is palatable only because of the tasteful artistry of Rene Clement. A truly tragic, must-see work. In French with English subtitles.

1951   B & W   87 minutes

FORCE OF EVIL
★★★

DIRECTOR: Abraham Polonsky
CAST: John Garfield, Thomas Gomez, Roy Roberts, Marie Windsor

A lawyer (John Garfield) abandons his principles and goes to work for a racketeer in this somber, downbeat story of corruption and loss of values. Compelling story and acting compensate for some of the heavy-handedness of the approach. A good study of ambition and the different paths it leads the characters on.

1948   B & W   78 minutes

FORMULA, THE
★★

DIRECTOR: John G. Avildsen
CAST: George C. Scott, Marlon Brando, Marthe Keller, John Gielgud, G. D. Spradlin

Take a plot to conceal a method producing enough synthetic fuel to take care of the current oil shortage and add two superstars like George C. Scott and Marlon Brando. Sounds like the formula for a real blockbuster, doesn't it? Unfortunately, it turns out to be the formula for a major disappointment. Rated R.

1980   117 minutes

FORT APACHE—THE BRONX
★★★½

DIRECTOR: Daniel Petrie
CAST: Paul Newman, Edward Asner, Kathleen Beller, Rachel Ticotin

Jarring violence surfaces throughout this story about New York's crime-besieged South Bronx, but absorbing dramatic elements give this routine cops-and-criminals format gutsy substance. Paul Newman, as an idealistic police veteran, proves his screen magnetism hasn't withered with time. The supporting cast is topnotch. Rated R for violence, profanity, and sexual references.

1981   125 minutes

49TH PARALLEL, THE
★★★★

DIRECTOR: Michael Powell
CAST: Laurence Olivier, Anton Wallbrook, Eric Portman, Leslie Howard, Raymond Massey, Finlay Currie, Glynis Johns

Rich suspense drama about a World War II German U-boat sunk off the coast of Canada whose crew makes it to shore and tries to reach safety in neutral territory. The cast is first-rate, the characterizations outstanding. Original story won an Oscar.

1941   B & W 105 minutes

FOUNTAINHEAD, THE
★★★½

DIRECTOR: King Vidor
CAST: Gary Cooper, Patricia Neal, Raymond Massey, Kent Smith, Robert Douglas

Gary Cooper tries his best in this Ayn Rand novel, brought to the screen without any of the book's vitality or character development. "Coop" is cast as Howard Roark, a Frank Lloyd Wright-type architect whose creations are ahead of their time and therefore go unappreciated. Patricia Neal is the love interest.

1949   B & W 114 minutes

FOUR FRIENDS
★★

DIRECTOR: Arthur Penn
CAST: Craig Wasson, James Leo Herlihy, Jodi Thelen

Arthur Penn (*Bonnie and Clyde*) directed and Steve Tesich (*Breaking Away*) wrote this interesting but ultimately disappointing film about America as seen through the eyes of a young immigrant (Craig Wasson) and the love he shares with two friends for a free-thinking young woman (Jodi Thelen). What could have been an arresting story of growing up in the 1960s and '70s is ruined by excessive, implausible sequences. Rated R because of violence, nudity, and profanity.

1981   114 minutes

400 BLOWS, THE
★★★★★

DIRECTOR: François Truffaut
CAST: Jean-Pierre Léaud, Patrick Auffay, Claire Maurier, Albert Remy

Poignant story of a boy and the life that seems to be at odds with him is true and touching as few films have ever been. Director François Truffaut's feature film debut is one of those marvelous rarities that on occasion can produce a new creative force as well as an instant screen classic. Jean-Pierre Léaud's disintegrating hold on the events that shape his fate, and his inability to gain the affection of the people he loves are vital struggles easily recognized. The boy's vain efforts and disguised pain echo all those secret hurts and rejections we try so hard to suppress. Filmed in a casual and disarming fashion, this film appears at times to be a documentary, and the audience is treated to what seem to be completely candid comments from a young boy about subjects that previously were considered to be adult topics. Powerful, tender, and at times overwhelmingly sad, this great film touches all the right buttons without being exploitative and losing its integrity. If you've never seen a classic foreign subtitled film, start yourself off right and see this one. In French with English subtitles.

1959   B & W   99 minutes

FOUR SEASONS, THE
★★★½

DIRECTOR: Alan Alda
CAST: Alan Alda, Carol Burnett, Len Cariou, Sandy Dennis, Rita Moreno, Jack Weston

Written and directed by Alan Alda, this film focuses on the pains and joys of friendship shared by three couples who are vacationing together. Despite a flawed and uneven script, the characters have been skillfully drawn by Alda and convincingly played by an excellent cast. *Four Seasons* is by no means a perfect film, yet it is an appealing, uplifting piece of entertainment. Rated PG.

1981   117 minutes

FOXES
★★★

DIRECTOR: Adrian Lyne
CAST: Jodie Foster, Sally Kellerman, Cherie Currie, Randy Quaid, Scott Baio

Adrian Lyne (*Flashdance*) directed this fitfully interesting film, about four young women who share an apartment in Los Angeles. The cast is good and the film has some interesting things to say about young society, but somehow it all falls flat. Rated R.

1980   106 minutes

FRANCES
★★★★½

DIRECTOR: Graeme Clifford
CAST: Jessica Lange, Kim Stanley, Sam Shepard, Jeffrey De-Munn, Jordan Charney

Director Howard Hawks called Frances Farmer "the best actress I ever worked with." However, the Seattle-born free-thinker was never allowed to reign as a star in Hollywood. This chilling, poignant motion picture explains why. Jessica Lange is superb as the starlet who snubs the power structure at every turn and pays a horrifying price for it. Kim Stanley is also impressive as Frances's mother, a money- and fame-hungry hag who uses her daughter. Sam Shepard is the one person who loves Frances for who and what she really is. An unforgettable film. Rated R.

1982   139 minutes

FRENCH CONNECTION II, THE
★★

DIRECTOR: John Frankenheimer
CAST: Gene Hackman, Fernando Rey, Bernard Fresson, Jean-Pierre Castaldi, Charles Milot

Disappointing sequel to the 1971 winner for best picture has none of the thrills, chills, and action of the original. Instead, New York detective Popeye Doyle (Gene Hackman), who has journeyed to Paris to track the drug trafficker who eluded him in the States, finds himself addicted to heroin and suffering withdrawal. He isn't the only one who suffers.... There's the viewer, too. Rated R.

1975   119 minutes

FRENCH LIEUTENANT'S WOMAN, THE
★★★★★

DIRECTOR: Karel Reisz
CAST: Meryl Streep, Jeremy Irons, Leo McKern, Hilton McRae, Emily Morgan

A brilliant adaptation of John Fowles's bestseller, starring Meryl Streep as the enigmatic title heroine and Jeremy Irons as her obsessed lover. Victorian and modern attitudes on love are contrasted in this intellectually and emotionally engrossing film. Rated R because of sexual references and sex scenes.

1981　　　　　　　123 minutes

FROM THE LIVES OF THE MARIONETTES
★★★★

DIRECTOR: Ingmar Bergman

CAST: Robert Atzorn, Christine Buchegger, Martin Benrath, Rita Russek, Lola Muethel, Heinz Bennent, Walter Schmidinger

This Ingmar Bergman film, which details the vicious sex murder of a prostitute by an outwardly compassionate and intelligent man, is a puzzle that never really resolves itself. Viewers expecting to be entertained will be disappointed. Bergman does not make movies that are intended to help us forget our cares. Instead, he challenges the viewer to think and feel. Because it is told in flashbacks which are not in chronological order, *From the Lives of the Marionettes* is somewhat difficult to follow. Nevertheless, fans of the acclaimed Swedish director's works will no doubt consider it another triumphant essay on the complexities of the human condition, containing the stunning visual imagery and dramatic power for which he's become famous. Rated R.

1980　　　·　B & W 104 minutes

FRONT, THE
★★★★

DIRECTOR: Martin Ritt

CAST: Woody Allen, Zero Mostel, Andrea Marcovicci, Joshua Shelley, Georgann Johnson

Focusing on the horrendous blacklist of entertainers in the 1950s, this film manages to drive its point home with wit and poignance. Joseph McCarthy started finding communists under every bush right after World War II and, by manipulating media, was able to destroy careers. Instead of defending their friends, people were frightened into silence. This film is about writers who find a man to submit their scripts to after they have been blacklisted. Woody Allen plays the title role. Rated PG.

1976　　　　　　　94 minutes

GALLIPOLI
★★★★½

DIRECTOR: Peter Weir

CAST: Mark Lee, Mel Gibson, Robert Grubb, Tim McKenzie, David Argue

Add this to the list of outstanding motion pictures from Australia and the very best films about war. Directed by Peter Weir (*The Last Wave*), this appealing character study, which is set during World War I, manages to say more about life on the battlefront than many of the more straightforward pictures in the genre. Rated PG because of violence.

1981　　　　　　　110 minutes

GAMBLER, THE
★★★½

DIRECTOR: Karel Reisz

CAST: James Caan, Paul Sorvino, Lauren Hutton, Jacqueline Brooks, Morris Carnovsky

This gritty film features James Caan in one of his best screen portrayals as a compulsive, self-destructive gambler. Director Karel Reisz (*The French Lieutenant's Woman*) keeps the atmosphere thick with tension. Always thinking he's on the edge of a big score, Caan's otherwise intelligent college professor character gets himself deeper and deeper into trouble.

It's a downer, but still worth watching. Rated R.

1974   111 minutes

GANDHI
★★★★★

DIRECTOR: Richard Attenborough
CAST: Ben Kingsley, Candice Bergen, Edward Fox, John Gielgud, Martin Sheen, John Mills, Trevor Howard

One of the finest screen biographies in the history of motion pictures, this film, by Richard Attenborough, chronicles the life of the deceased Indian leader (Ben Kingsley). Running three hours, it is an old-style "big" picture, with spectacle, great drama, superb performances, and, as they used to say, a cast of thousands. Yet for all its hugeness, Gandhi achieves a remarkable intimacy. Afterward, viewers feel as if they have actually known—and, more important, been touched by—the man Indians called the "Great Soul." Rated PG for violence.

1982   188 minutes

GARDEN OF THE FINZI-CONTINIS, THE
★★★★

DIRECTOR: Vittorio De Sica
CAST: Dominique Sanda, Helmut Berger, Lino Capolicchio, Fabio Testi

Vittorio De Sica's adaptation of a Giorgio Bassani novel views the life of an aristocratic Jewish family's misfortune in fascist Italy. Flawless acting by Dominique Sanda and Helmut Berger. One of De Sica's best. Rated R.

1971   95 minutes

GATHERING STORM
★

DIRECTOR: Herbert Wise

CAST: Richard Burton, Virginia McKenna, Robert Hardy, Ian Bannen

Richard Burton tries his best to bring some life to this dull movie, which covers Winston Churchill's life from 1937 to the start of World War II. Filmed almost entirely on a few indoor stages, this film plays more like an episode of Masterpiece Theater than a motion picture. Only for Churchill buffs.

1974   72 minutes

GENTLEMAN JIM
★★★★½

DIRECTOR: Raoul Walsh
CAST: Errol Flynn, Jack Carson, Alan Hale, Alexis Smith

Errol Flynn has a field day in this beautifully filmed biography of heavyweight champion Jim Corbett. Always cocky and light on his feet, Flynn is a joy to behold and will make those who considered him a star instead of a actor think twice. Ward Bond is equally fine as John L. Sullivan. Said to have been Flynn's favorite role.

1942   B & W 104 minutes

GETTING OF WISDOM, THE
★★★★

DIRECTOR: Bruce Beresford
CAST: Susannah Fowle, Sheila Helpmann, Patricia Kennedy, Hilary Ryan

Out of Australia, this better-than-average rites-of-passage story of an unrefined country girl (Susannah Fowle) who gets sent off to school in the city displays all the qualities of topnotch directing. (Beresford also did Breaker Morant and Don's Party.) Being from a remote area of the country, the girl is easy prey for her more sophisticated, yet equally immature classmates. Hilary Ryan is excellent as an older student who befriends her. The story takes place in the mid-1800s and is taken from the classic Australian novel by Henry Handel Richardson. Not rated but the equivalent of a G.

1980　　　　100 minutes

GETTING STRAIGHT
★★½

DIRECTOR: Richard Rush
CAST: Elliott Gould, Candice Bergen, Max Julien, Jeff Corey, Robert F. Lyons

During the campus riots of the 1960s, Hollywood jumped on the bandwagon with such forgettable films as *The Strawberry Statement* and *R.P.M.* Add *Getting Straight* to the list. Elliott Gould plays a "hip" graduate student caught up in campus unrest. Somewhat effective during its initial release, it now seems like an odd curio. Rated PG.

1970　　　　124 minutes

GIANT
★★★½

DIRECTOR: George Stevens
CAST: James Dean, Rock Hudson, Elizabeth Taylor, Carroll Baker, Dennis Hopper

The third part of director George Stevens's American Trilogy, which also included *Shane* and *A Place in the Sun*, this 1956 release traces the life of a cattle rancher through two generations. Although the lead performances by Elizabeth Taylor, Rock Hudson, and James Dean are unconvincing when the stars are poorly "aged" with make-up, *Giant* is still a stylish, if overlong movie that lives up to its title.

1956　　　　198 minutes

GILDA
★★★★

DIRECTOR: Charles Vidor

CAST: Glenn Ford, Rita Hayworth, George Macready, Joseph Calleia, Steven Geray

Glenn Ford plays a small-time gambler, who goes to work for a South American casino owner and his beautiful wife, Gilda (Rita Hayworth). When the casino owner disappears and is presumed dead, Ford marries Hayworth and they run the casino together. All goes well until the husband returns, seeking revenge against them. There is some violence in this film.

1946　　　B & W 110 minutes

GINGER IN THE MORNING
★★½

DIRECTOR: Gordon Wiles
CAST: Sissy Spacek, Monte Markham, Slim Pickens, Susan Oliver, Mark Miller.

A lonely salesman, Monte Markham, picks up a hitchhiker, Sissy Spacek, and romance blossoms in this okay romantic comedy. No great revelations about human nature will be found in this one, just harmless fluff that will be forgotten soon after it's been viewed.

1973　　　　89 minutes

GIRLFRIENDS
★★★★

DIRECTOR: Claudia Weill
CAST: Melanie Mayron, Anita Skinner, Eli Wallach, Christopher Guest, Viveca Lindfors

Realistic film about a young Jewish woman who learns to make it on her own after her best friend/roommate leaves to get married. Melanie Mayron's performance is the highlight of this touching and offbeat comic-drama. Rated PG.

1978　　　　88 minutes

GIVE 'EM HELL HARRY!
★★★★

DIRECTOR: Steve Binder
CAST: James Whitmore

This is the film version of James Whitmore's wonderful portrayal of President Harry S. Truman. Taken from the stage production, the film is a magnificent tribute and entertainment. Rated PG.

1975   102 minutes

GLASS HOUSE, THE
★★★★

DIRECTOR: Tom Gries
CAST: Vic Morrow, Clu Gulager, Billy Dee Williams, Dean Jagger, Alan Alda

This powerful prison drama is based on a story by Truman Capote. An idealistic new prison guard (Clu Gulager) is overwhelmed by the gang violence within the prison. Alan Alda plays a new prisoner who becomes the target of a violent gang leader (Vic Morrow). Dean Jagger plays the burnt-out warden who can offer no solutions for his prison's problems. This film is a powerful protest against our current prison system. Rated R for sex and violence.

1972   89 minutes

GLEN OR GLENDA
🦇

DIRECTOR: Edward D. Wood Jr.
CAST: Bela Lugosi, Dolores Fuller, Daniel Davis (director Ed Wood Jr.), Lyle Talbot, Timothy Farrell, George Weiss

Incredible film by the incomparably *inept* Edward D. Wood Jr., tells the powerful story of a young man who finally summons up the courage to come out of the closet and ask his fiancée if he can wear her sweater. Aided by some bizarre footage with Bela Lugosi as some sort of a mumbo jumbo artist and a pseudoscientific documentary approach, our hero/heroine (played by director Wood) takes us through the transvestite's world and gives us a soul-searching look at the problems they face daily. Sincere but cheaply done and hopelessly inept. Wood's films (including *Plan 9 from Outer Space* and *Bride of the Monster*) are all cult classics and have an outré charm of their own.

1953   B & W   67 minutes

GOD'S LITTLE ACRE
★★★★

DIRECTOR: Anthony Mann
CAST: Robert Ryan, Aldo Ray, Tina Louise, Jack Lord, Fay Spain, Buddy Hackett

This is a terrific little film focusing on poor Georgia farmers. Robert Ryan gives one of his best performances as an itinerant farmer. Aldo Ray, Jack Lord, and Buddy Hackett lend good support.

1958   B & W   110 minutes

GODFATHER, THE
★★★★

DIRECTOR: Francis Ford Coppola
CAST: Marlon Brando, Al Pacino, James Caan, Richard Costellano, John Cazale, Diane Keaton, Talia Shire, Robert Duvall, Sterling Hayden, John Marley, Richard Conte, Al Lettieri, Al Martino

Mario Puzo's incredibly popular novel comes to life in artful fashion. Filmed in foreboding tones, the movie takes us into the lurid world of the Mafia. Jarring scenes of violence don't overshadow the fascinating relationships among Don Corleone and his family. Marlon Brando, with stuffed cheeks, won an Oscar for his performance, but it's Al Pacino who grabs your attention with an unnerving intensity. Rated R.

1972   175 minutes

GODFATHER, THE, PART II
★★★★½

DIRECTOR: Francis Ford Coppola
CAST: Al Pacino, Robert Duvall, Diane Keaton, Robert DeNiro, John Cazale, Talia Shire, Lee Strasberg, Michael V. Gazzo

This is a sequel that equals the quality of the original, an almost unheard-of circumstance in Hollywood. Director Francis Ford Coppola skillfully meshes past and present, intercutting the story of young Don Corleone (Robert DeNiro), an ambitious, immoral immigrant, and his son Michael (Al Pacino), who lives up to his father's expectations, turning the family's crime organization into a sleek, cold, modern operation. This gripping film won seven Academy Awards. Rated R.

1974   200 minutes

GODFATHER EPIC, THE
★★★★★

DIRECTOR: Francis Ford Coppola
CAST: Marlon Brando, Talia Shire, James Caan, Robert Duvall, John Cazale, Al Pacino, Diane Keaton, Robert De Niro

Few screen creations qualify as first-class entertainment and cinematic art. Francis Ford Coppola's *The Godfather* series unquestionably belongs in that category. Yet as good as *The Godfather* and *The Godfather*, *Part II* are, they are no match for *The Godfather Epic*. A compilation of the two films with extra scenes added, it is nothing less than a masterwork. To refresh your memory, the 1972 original begins in 1945, with Don Vito Corleone

(Marlon Brando) at the height of his power as head of one of the five great Mafia families in America. We first see him at the wedding of his daughter (Talia Shire). Even at such a seemingly private family occasion, Corleone takes time for the business. We also meet the other members of the Corleone family: the hot-tempered Sonny (James Caan); the loyal adopted son and family lawyer, Tom (Robert Duvall); the weak-minded Fredo (John Cazale); and the Don's hope for the family's future, Michael (Al Pacino), who is accompanied by his fiancée (Diane Keaton). It is the elder Corleone's dream that Michael be the one son who does not become involved in the world of crime. But a nearly successful attempt on the old man's life forces Michael to take over. Picking up where the original left off, the 1974 sequel finds Michael at the height of his power and just barely surviving an attempt on his life. Entwined with his quest to track down whoever was behind the attack are scenes chronicling the early life of Vito Corleone (Robert De Niro) in New York and the circumstances that led him to crime. By editing the two films together in chronological order, for the videotape release of *The Godfather Epic*, Coppola has created a work greater than the sum of its parts. See it! Rated R.

1977   450 minutes

GOING MY WAY
★★★★½

DIRECTOR: Leo McCarey
CAST: Bing Crosby, Barry Fitzgerald, Rise Stevens, Gene Lockhart, Frank McHugh

Bing Crosby won the best-actor Oscar in 1944 for his delightful portrayal of the easygoing priest who finally wins over his strict superior (Barry Fitzgerald, who also won an Oscar for his supporting role). Leo McCarey (*Duck Soup*) wrote and directed this funny, heartwarming character study and netted two Academy Awards for his efforts, as well as crafting the year's Oscar-winning best picture.

1944   B & W 130 minutes

GOLDEN BOY
★★★★

DIRECTOR: Rouben Mamoulian
CAST: William Holden, Barbara Stanwyck, Adolphe Menjou, Lee J. Cobb

William Holden made a strong starring debut in this screen adaptation of Clifford Odets' play about a musician who becomes a boxer. Though a bit dated today, Holden and co-star Barbara Stanwyck still shine.

1939   B & W 100 minutes

GONE WITH THE WIND
★★★★★

DIRECTOR: Victor Fleming
CAST: Clark Gable, Vivien Leigh, Leslie Howard, Olivia De Havilland

The all-time movie classic with Clark Gable and Vivien Leigh as Margaret Mitchell's star-crossed lovers in the final days of the Old South. Need we say more?

1939   222 minutes

GOOD EARTH, THE
★★★★

DIRECTOR: Sidney Franklin
CAST: Paul Muni, Luise Rainer, Keye Luke, Walter Connolly, Jessie Ralph

Nobel Prize novelist Pearl Buck's engrossing, richly detailed story of a simple Chinese farm couple whose lives are ruined by greed is impressively brought to life in this milestone film. Luise Rainer won the second of her back-to-back best-actress Oscars for her portrayal of the ever-patient wife. The photography and special effects are outstanding.

1937   B & W 138 minutes

GOODBYE, MR. CHIPS
★★★★½

DIRECTOR: Sam Wood
CAST: Robert Donat, Greer Garson, John Mills

Robert Donat creates one of filmdom's most heartwarming roles as Chips, the Latin teacher of an English boys' school. The poignant movie follows Chips from his first bumbling, early teaching days until he becomes a beloved school institution. Greer Garson was introduced to American audiences in the rewarding role of Chips's loving wife.

1939   B & W 114 minutes

GOODBYE PEOPLE, THE
★★★★

DIRECTOR: Herb Gardner
CAST: Jud Hirsch, Martin Balsam, Pamela Reed, Ron Silver, Michael Tucker, Gene Saks

This unashamedly sentimental film is a delight. Martin Balsam is memorable as a man attempting to realize the dream of many years by rebuilding his Coney Island hot-dog stand. Pamela Reed and Judd Hirsch, as the young people who help him, turn in outstanding performances, and the hot-dog stand itself is a fantastic structure.

1984   104 minutes

GRADUATE, THE
★★★★½

DIRECTOR: Mike Nichols

CAST: Dustin Hoffman, Anne Ban-
     croft, Katharine Ross

Director Mike Nichols won an
Academy Award for his direction
of this touching, funny, unsettling,
and unforgettable release about a
young man (Dustin Hoffman, in
his first major role) attempting to
chart his future and develop his
own set of values (as opposed to
those of the swimming-pool-and-
sun set). He falls in love with Katharine Ross, but finds himself seduced by her wily, sexy mother,
Anne Bancroft (as Mrs. Robinson). Don't forget the superb
soundtrack of songs by Paul Simon and Art Garfunkel. A superb
coming-of-age film.

1967   105 minutes

GRAND HOTEL
★★★★
DIRECTOR: Edmund Goulding
CAST: John Barrymore, Greta Garbo,
     Wallace Beery, Joan Craw-
     ford, Lionel Barrymore, Lewis
     Stone

World War I is over. Life in the
fast lane has returned to Berlin's
Grand Hotel, crossroads of a
thousand lives, backdrop to as
many stories. This anthology of life
at various levels won an Oscar for
best picture. John Barrymore is a
suave jewel thief, Greta Garbo is
a world-weary ballerina, Lionel
Barrymore is dying but making the
most of living it up under the eye
of boss Wallace Beery, a jaded industrialist bent on making it with
stenographer Joan Crawford. A
sage selection of others people the
suites and salons.

1932   B & W 113 minutes

GRAND ILLUSION
★★★★★
DIRECTOR: Jean Renoir
CAST: Jean Gabin, Pierre Presnay,
     Erich von Stroheim, Marcel
     Dalio, Julien Carette, Dita
     Parlo, Gaston Modot

Shortly before Hitler plunged Europe into World War II, this monumental French film tried to
examine why men submit to warfare's "grand illusions." It brilliantly exposes the romantic
notions applied to war: the noble-
cause mentality, glorified chivalry,
needless nationalism. We are taken
to a German prison camp in World
War I, where it becomes quite easy
to see the hypocrisy of war while
watching the day-to-day mini-
world of camp life. This classic,
by Jean Renoir, has the universal
appeal and technical brilliance that
makes it one of the world's finest
films and a must-see for anyone
who appreciates great entertainment.

1937   B & W 74 minutes

GRANDE BOURGEOISE, LA
★½
DIRECTOR: Mauro Bolognini
CAST: Catherine Deneuve, Gian-
     carlo Giannini, Fernando Rey

This should be an impassioned,
suspenseful film about a brother
who murders his sister's lackluster husband because he believes
her true nature is suffocating in
marriage. However, the movie's
primary concern is with costume
and soft-focus lenses so that even
the lukewarm emotions are overshadowed. Giancarlo Giannini as
the brother tries hard to fire things
up, but when Catherine Deneuve
is on hand in one of her ice queen
performances, sympathizing becomes a difficult thing. She extin-
guishes all the sparks he sets.
Every time she gazes through a
veiled hat, her stony perfection

deadens the movie a little bit more. In Italian with English subtitles.

1974 115 minutes

GRANDVIEW, U.S.A
★

DIRECTOR: Randal Kleiser
CAST: Jamie Lee Curtis, C. Thomas Howell, Patrick Swayze, Jennifer Jason Leigh, Ramon Bieri, Carole Cook, Tony Donahue, William Windom

Jamie Lee Curtis is one of the finest actresses in movies today. Therefore, to see her talents wasted in *Grandview, U.S.A.*, another of director Randal Kleiser's (*Blue Lagoon*; *Summer Lovers*) blatantly commercial, light-headed entertainments, made our blood boil. *Grandview, U.S.A.* is a coming-of-age study totally lacking in depth and characterization. Rated R for nudity, violence, and profanity.

1984 97 minutes

GRAPES OF WRATH, THE
★★★★★

DIRECTOR: John Ford
CAST: Henry Fonda, John Carradine, Jane Darwell, Russell Simpson, Charley Grapewin, John Qualen

Henry Fonda stars in this superb screen adaptation of the John Steinbeck novel about farmers from Oklahoma fleeing the Dust Bowl and poverty of their home state only to be confronted by prejudice and violence in California. Directed by John Ford (*Young Mr. Lincoln* and *The Searchers*), it's a compelling drama beautifully acted by the director's stock company.

1940 B & W 129 minutes

GREAT DAN PATCH, THE
★★★

DIRECTOR: Joseph M. Newman
CAST: Dennis O'Keefe, Gail Russell, Ruth Warrick, Charlotte Greenwood

The story of the greatest trotting horse of them all. Good racing scenes. An opera for horse lovers.

1949 B & W 94 minutes

GREAT GABBO, THE
★★★½

DIRECTOR: James Cruze
CAST: Erich Von Stroheim, Betty Compson, Don Douglas, Margie Kane

Cinema giant Erich Von Stroheim gives a tour de force performance as a brilliant but cold ventriloquist whose disregard for the feelings of others comes back to haunt him when he realizes that he has lost the affection of a girl he has come to love. Von Stroheim and his little wooden pal are a compelling couple—this is a film that lingers in the memory and rates with other fine films about ventriloquism like *Dead Of Night* and *Magic*. Silent film director James Cruze seems to have pulled this effective drama out of a hat, but the sound seems smooth and realistic for a film of this vintage.

1929 B & W 89 minutes

GREAT GATSBY, THE
★★★★

DIRECTOR: Jack Clayton
CAST: Robert Redford, Mia Farrow, Karen Black, Sam Waterston, Bruce Dern

This is a well-mounted, well-acted film that is, perhaps, a bit overlong. However, Robert Redford, the mysterious title character, is marvelous as Gatsby. Bruce Dern is equally memorable as the man who always has been rich and selfish. He emits an animal brutality that acts as a perfect contrast to Mia Farrow's fragility as Daisy (Gatsby's love) and to Redford's grace and poise. Rated PG.

1974   144 minutes

GREAT GUY
★★

DIRECTOR: John G. Blystone
CAST: James Cagney, Mae Clarke, Edward Brophy

Depression film about a feisty inspector crusading against corruption in the meat-packing business. Not vintage James Cagney . . . but okay.

1936   B & W   75 minutes

GREAT SANTINI, THE
★★★★

DIRECTOR: Lewis J. Carlino
CAST: Robert Duvall, Blythe Danner, Michael O'Keefe

Robert Duvall's superb performance in the title role is the most outstanding feature of this fine "little" film. The story of a troubled family and its unpredictable patriarch (Duvall), it was released briefly in early 1980 as The Ace and then disappeared. But thanks to the efforts of the New York film critics, it was re-released with appropriate hoopla and did well at the box office. Rated PG for profanity and violence.

1979   116 minutes

GREAT WALLENDAS, THE
★★★

DIRECTOR: Larry Elikann
CAST: Lloyd Bridges, Britt Ekland, Taina Elg, John van Dreelen, Cathy Rigby, Michael McGuire

In this made-for-television movie, Lloyd Bridges stars as the head of the Wallenda family of high-wire artists. Bridges gives one of his most convincing performances as he keeps the spirit and determination of the family alive through their many tragedies. The viewer shares the excitement of their hard-won achievement in the creation of the legendary seven-person pyramid. A good family film.

1978   104 minutes

GREATEST SHOW ON EARTH, THE
★★★★

DIRECTOR: Cecil B. De Mille
CAST: Betty Hutton, James Stewart, Charlton Heston, Cornel Wilde, Dorothy Lamour, Gloria Grahame

The 1952 Oscar winner for best picture succeeds in the same manner as its subject, the circus; it's enjoyable family entertainment. Three major stories of backstage circus life all work well and blend in well in this film.

1952   153 minutes

GREATEST STORY EVER TOLD, THE
★★★

DIRECTOR: George Stevens
CAST: Max von Sydow, Charlton Heston, Carroll Baker, Angela Lansbury, Sidney Poitier, Telly Savalas, José Ferrer, Van Heflin, Dorothy McGuire, John Wayne, Ed Wynn, Shelley Winters

Although this well-meant movie is accurate to the story of Jesus, the viewer tends to be distracted by its long-running time and the appearance of Hollywood stars in unexpected roles.

1965   141 minutes

GREATEST, THE
★★

DIRECTOR: Tom Gries
CAST: Muhammad Ali, Ernest Borgnine, John Marley, Robert Duvall, James Earl Jones, Roger E. Mosley

Muhammad Ali plays himself in this disjointed screen biography, which is poorly directed by Tom Gries. Even the supporting performances of Robert Duvall, Ernest Borgnine, Ben Johnson, James Earl Jones, and John Marley don't help much. Only "Magnum, P.I." regular Roger E. Mosley shines, as Sonny Liston—and steals the movie from its star. Rated PG.

1977   101 minutes

GREEK TYCOON, THE
★★½

DIRECTOR: J. Lee Thompson
CAST: Anthony Quinn, Jacqueline Bisset, Raf Vallone, Edward Albert, Charles Durning, Camilla Sparv, James Franciscus

When this film was first shown, it stimulated much controversy and interest, because it promised to tell all about the Aristotle Onassis and Jackie Kennedy romance. Anthony Quinn borrows from his *Zorba the Greek* role to be a convincingly macho and callous Greek shipping tycoon. Jacqueline Bisset makes a beautiful Jackie O. Unfortunately, the plot was neglected and the story comes across as grade-B soap. Rated R.

1978   106 minutes

GREEN PASTURES, THE
★★★★

DIRECTOR: William Keighley, Marc Connelly
CAST: Rex Ingram, Oscar Polk, Eddie Anderson, Frank Wilson, George Reed

Now recognized as a classic, this was Hollywood's first all-black film given general release, and only the second made between 1929 and 1942. Based on Marc Connelly's play and true to the source, it retells stories from the Old Testament as they might be told in a black Sunday-school class in the Deep South. Rex Ingram is superb as "de Lawd," who is depicted as a dignified gray-haired patient and kind minister.

1936   B & W   90 minutes

GREEN PROMISE, THE
★★★

DIRECTOR: William D. Russell
CAST: Marguerite Chapman, Walter Brennan, Robert Paige, Natalie Wood

The hard life of farmers and their families is explored in this surprisingly involving and well-acted film. Walter Brennan gives his usual first-rate performance as the patriarch who toils over and tills the land.

1949   B & W   93 minutes

GREEN ROOM, THE
★★★

DIRECTOR: Francois Truffaut
CAST: Francois Truffaut, Nathalie Baye, Jean Daste, Jean-Paul Moulin

Based on the writings of Henry James, this is a lifeless and disappointing film by Francois Truffaut about a writer obsessed with death who turns a dilapidated chapel into a memorial for World War I soldiers. Not the French filmmaker at his best. In French, with English subtitles. Rated PG.

1978   93 minutes

GROUP, THE
★★★

DIRECTOR: Sidney Lumet
CAST: Joan Hackett, Elizabeth Hartman, Shirley Knight, Joanna Pettet, Jessica Walter, James Broderick, Larry Hagman, Richard Mulligan, Hal Holbrook

Based on the book by Mary McCarthy about the lives and loves of eight female college friends. Overlong, convoluted semi-sleazy fun. The impressive cast almost makes you forget it's just a catty soap opera. So watch it anyway.

1966　　　　　　　　　150 minutes

GUARDIAN, THE
★★★½

DIRECTOR: David Green
CAST: Martin Sheen, Louis Gossett Jr., Arthur Hill

When the tenants of an upper-class New York City apartment house become fed up with the violence of the streets intruding on their building, they hire a live-in guard (Louis Gossett Jr.). While he does manage to rid the building of lawbreakers, some begin to question his methods. This HBO made-for-cable film is notches above most cable fare. Language and violence.

1984　　　　　　　　　102 minutes

GUESS WHO'S COMING TO DINNER
★★★½

DIRECTOR: Stanley Kramer
CAST: Spencer Tracy, Katharine Hepburn, Sidney Poitier, Katharine Houghton, Cecil Kellaway, Beah Richards, Roy E. Glenn Sr., Virginia Christine

This final film pairing of Spencer Tracy and Katharine Hepburn was also one of the first to deal with interracial marriage. Though quite daring at the time of its original release, this movie, directed by the heavy-handed Stanley Kramer, seems rather quaint today. Still, Tracy and Hepburn are fun to watch, and Sidney Poitier and Katharine Houghton (Hepburn's niece) make an appealing young couple.

1967　　　　　　　　　108 minutes

GULAG
★★½

DIRECTOR: Roger Young
CAST: David Keith, Malcolm McDowell

This engrossing tale of an American athlete shipped to a Soviet prison camp works at odd moments in spite of a preposterous script. No viewer will swallow the notion of a multi–Olympic gold winner being carted off without so much as a by-your-leave. On the other hand, the escape sequence is clever and quite exciting. Needlessly violent, it also contains a laughably gratuitous skin shot of a minor actress. David Keith's final line of dialogue is a good reflection of viewer sentiment by the time it's all over.

1985　　　　　　　　　120 minutes

HAIL MARY
★★★★

DIRECTOR: Jean-Luc Godard
CAST: Myriem Roussel, Thierry Lacoste, Philippe Lacoste, Manon Anderson, Juliette Binoche, Johann Leysen, Anne Gauthier

This story of the coming of Christ in modern times will offend only the most dogmatic Christians, or narrow-minded religious zealots who have only heard a sketchy outline of the plot. Godard's eye for the aesthetic gives this film a compassionate feel, more so than a lot of the sandal epics that are about the Savior himself. Like many other French films, *Hail Mary* is sensuous yet nonexploitative. *The Book of Mary*, a film by Anne-Marie Mieville, is the prologue and is equally beautiful. Not rated; the equivalent of an R for nudity.

1985   107 minutes

HAMLET
★★★★★
DIRECTOR: Laurence Olivier
CAST: Laurence Olivier, Basil Sydney, Eileen Herlie, Jean Simmons, Felix Aylmer, Terence Morgan, Norman Wooland, Peter Cushing, Esmond Knight, Stanley Holloway

In every way a brilliant presentation of Shakespeare's best-known play masterminded by England's foremost player. Superb in the title role, Laurence Olivier won the 1948 Oscar for best actor, and (as producer) for best picture. Then an 18-year-old newcomer, Jean Simmons was nominated for best supporting actress. A high point among many is Stanley Holloway's droll performance as the First Gravedigger.

1948   B & W 150 minutes

HANNA K.
★½
DIRECTOR: Constantin Costa-Gavras
CAST: Jill Clayburgh, Jean Yanne, Gabriel Byrne, Muhamad Bakri, David Clennon, Oded Kotler

An intriguing premise that fails to live up to its promise. Jill Clayburgh is an Israeli lawyer appointed to defend a man who entered the country illegally in an attempt to reclaim the land where he grew up. Alas, the man is an Arab, which complicates matters between Clayburgh and her Israeli lover ... not to mention her French Catholic husband. The very talky story never explores the religious dichotomies and degenerates, instead, into a soap opera, all leading to a thoroughly annoying conclusion. Something good must have been in the story by Franco Solinas, but it didn't appear on the screen. Rated R for coarse language.

1984   110 minutes

HANOVER STREET

DIRECTOR: Peter Hyams
CAST: Harrison Ford, Lesley-Anne Down, Christopher Plummer, Alec McCowen

This inept story of a romance during World War II features Harrison Ford as an American soldier and Lesley-Anne Down as a British nurse who meet by accident and fall in love. There're complications. She won't tell him her name. Later we find that she's married to a British intelligence officer (Christopher Plummer) and has a little girl (Patsy Kensit). Naturally, Plummer and Ford end up on a secret mission behind German lines, becoming friends while they fend off bullets and tanks. Dumb. Rated PG.

1979   109 minutes

HARDCORE
★★
DIRECTOR: Paul Schrader
CAST: George C. Scott, Ilah Davis, Peter Boyle, Season Hubley, Dick Sargent, Leonard Gaines, David Nichols

This film stars George C. Scott as Jake Van Dorn, whose family leads a church-oriented life in their home in Grand Rapids, Michigan. When the church sponsors a youth trip to California, Van Dorn's daughter Kristen (Ilah Davis) is allowed to go. She disappears, so Van Dorn goes to Los Angeles to find her. Once there, he sees a cheaply made skin flick that features a girl seduced by two men. It's Kristen. *Hardcore* is rated R but is closer to an X. Even though it's cloaked in righteous respectability, it makes the most of its subject matter. It is rather reminiscent of those old porn films that were advertised as sex-education films. Who's kidding whom?

1979　　　　　　　108 minutes

HARDER THEY FALL, THE
★★★½

DIRECTOR: Mark Robson

CAST: Humphrey Bogart, Rod Steiger, Jan Sterling, Mike Lane, Max Baer, Jersey Joe Walcott

This boxing drama is as mean and brutal as they come. A gentle giant is built up, set up, and brought down by a collection of human vultures while sports writer Humphrey Bogart flip-flops on the moral issues. The ring photography is spectacular. Don't expect anything like *Rocky*.

1956　　　B & W 109 minutes

HARDHAT AND LEGS
★★★

DIRECTOR: Lee Philips

CAST: Kevin Dobson, Sharon Gless

The scene is New York City. Kevin Dobson is a horse-playing Italian construction worker who whistles at nice gams. Sharon Gless is democratic upper-class. The twain meet, and sparks fly as he tries to make it work despite educational and cultural differences. It's all cheerful and upbeat and works because of first-rate acting. Made for television.

1980　　　　　　　104 minutes

HARLAN COUNTY, U.S.A.
★★★★½

DIRECTOR: Barbara Kopple

CAST: Documentary

This Oscar-winning documentary concerning Kentucky coal miners is both tragic and riveting. Its grippping scenes draw the audience into the world of miners and their families. Superior from start to finish. Rated PG.

1977　　　　　　　103 minutes

HARLOW
★★

DIRECTOR: Gordon Douglas

CAST: Carroll Baker, Peter Lawford, Red Buttons, Michael Connors, Raf Vallone, Angela Lansbury, Martin Balsam, Leslie Nielsen

One of two films made in 1965 that dealt with the life of the late film star and sex goddess Jean Harlow. Carroll Baker simply is not the actress to play Harlow, and the whole thing is a trashy mess, with the emphasis on Harlow's sexual encounters. A cheap shot all around.

1965　　　　　　　125 minutes

HARRAD EXPERIMENT, THE
★★

DIRECTOR: Ted Post

CAST: Don Johnson, James Whitmore, Tippi Hedren, B. Kirby Jr., Laurie Walters

Uninvolving adaptation of Robert Rimmer's well-intentioned bestseller about an experimental college that makes exploration of sexual freedom the primary hands-on curriculum of the student body. The film is attractive as a novelty item today because of its erotic scenes between Don Johnson of TV's *Miami Vice* and Laurie Walters of *Eight Is Enough*. Rated R.

1973   88 minutes

HARRY AND SON
★★★★

DIRECTOR: Paul Newman
CAST: Paul Newman, Robby Benson, Joanne Woodward, Ellen Barkin, Ossie Davis, Wilford Brimley

A widower (Paul Newman) can land a wrecking ball on a dime but can't seem to make contact with his artistically inclined son, Howard (Robby Benson), in this superb character study. Directed, co-produced, and co-written by Newman, it's sort of a male *Terms of Endearment*. Rated PG for nudity and profanity.

1984   117 minutes

HARRY AND TONTO
★★★★

DIRECTOR: Paul Mazursky
CAST: Art Carney, Ellen Burstyn, Chief Dan George, Geraldine Fitzgerald, Larry Hagman, Arthur Hunnicut, Tonto the Cat

Art Carney won an Oscar for his tour-de-force performance in this character study, directed by Paul Mazursky (*Moscow on the Hudson*). In a role that's a far cry from his Ed Norton on Jackie Gleason's "The Honeymooners," the star plays an older gentleman who, with his cat, takes a cross-country trip and lives life to the fullest. Rated R.

1974   115 minutes

HAWAII
★★★★

DIRECTOR: George Roy Hill

CAST: Julie Andrews, Max von Sydow, Richard Harris, Gene Hackman, Carroll O'Connor

All-star epic presentation of Part III of James Michener's six-part novel of the same title. Excellent performances by Max von Sydow and Julie Andrews as the early 1800s missionaries to Hawaii, as well as by Richard Harris as the sea captain who tries to woo Andrews away.

1966   171 minutes

HEART BEAT
★★★★

DIRECTOR: John Byrum
CAST: Nick Nolte, Sissy Spacek, John Heard, Ray Sharkey, Ann Dusenberry

Heart Beat is a perfect title for this warm, bittersweet visual poem on the beat generation by writer-director John Byrum. It pulses with life and emotion, intoxicating the viewer with a rhythmic flow of stunning images and superb performances by Nick Nolte, Sissy Spacek, and John Heard. Over the opening montage, Carolyn Cassady (Spacek), wife of Neal (Nolte), reminisces, "After World War II, we all thought we knew who we were and where we were going . . . what each one of us wanted most in the world was a house in the suburbs, two cars and exactly 3.2 children." The story begins with the cross-country adventure that inspired Jack Kerouac's (Heard) *On the Road* and began a time of re-evaluation, introspection, and experimentation. Rated R.

1980   109 minutes

HEART IS A LONELY HUNTER, THE
★★★★

DIRECTOR: Robert Ellis Miller

CAST: Alan Arkin, Sondra Locke, Laurinda Barrett, Stacy Keach, Chuck McCann, Cicely Tyson

This release features Alan Arkin in a superb performance, which won him an Academy Award nomination. In it, he plays a sensitive and compassionate man who is also a deaf-mute. Rated G.

1968   125 minutes

HEART OF THE STAG
★★★★

DIRECTOR: Michael Firth
CAST: Bruno Lawrence, Terence Cooper, Mary Regan, Anne Flannery

The shocking subject matter of *Heart of the Stag*—forced incest—could have resulted in an uncomfortable film to watch. However, New Zealander Michael Firth, who directed the movie and conceived the story, handles it expertly, and the result is a riveting viewing experience. A drifter Peter Daly (powerfully played by Bruno Lawrence, of *Smash Palace*) becomes involved in the lives of a sheep rancher (Terence Cooper) who has made his daughter, Kathy (Mary Regan), into a sexual slave. The mother (Anne Flannery) has had a stroke and, as a result, can only sit in her wheelchair and whimper as her child suffers nightly abuse. The story in *Heart of the Stag* is handled in a thrillerlike fashion. This alleviates some of the natural distress the viewer feels in regard to the subject matter and provides for an exciting and satisfying conclusion. Rated R for violence, profanity, sexual situations.

1983   94 minutes

HEARTACHES
★★★

DIRECTOR: Donald Shebib
CAST: Robert Carradine, Margot Kidder, Annie Potts, Winston Rekert, George Touliatos, Guy Sanvido

A touching, yet light-hearted, film about love, friendship, and survival, *Heartaches* follows the trials and tribulations of a young pregnant woman (Annie Potts), who is separated from her husband (Robert Carradine), and the kooky girl-friend she meets on the bus (Margot Kidder). Although the two women are total opposites, they wind up rooming together and share a variety of experiences. The Canadian film is rated R for a minimal amount of sex, which is handled discreetly.

1981   93 minutes

HEARTBREAKERS
★★★½

DIRECTOR: Bobby Roth
CAST: Peter Coyote, Nick Mancuso, Max Gail, Kathryn Harrold

Two men in their thirties, Arthur Blue (Peter Coyote) and Eli Kahn (Nick Mancuso), friends since childhood, find their relationship severely tested when each is suddenly caught up in his own fervent drive for success. Rated R for simulated sex and profanity.

1984   106 minutes

HEARTS AND MINDS
★★★★½

DIRECTOR: Peter Davis
CAST: Documentary

The Vietnam War and its effects on America at home are vividly examined in this beautifully done documentary. Much of it is still high-voltage material. Not to be missed. Rated PG for language, riot scenes.

1974   110 minutes

HEAT AND DUST
★★★★

DIRECTOR: James Ivory
CAST: Julie Christie, Greta Scacchi, Shashi Kapoor, Christopher Cazenove, Julian Glover, Susan Fleetwood

Two love stories—one from the 1920s and one from today—are entwined in this classy, thoroughly enjoyable soap opera about two British women who go to India and become involved in its seductive mysteries. Julie Christie stars as a modern woman retracing the steps of her great-aunt (Greta Scacchi), who fell in love with an Indian ruler (played by the celebrated Indian star Shashi Kapoor). Rated R for nudity and brief violence.

1983   130 minutes

HEATWAVE
★★★

DIRECTOR: Phillip Noyce
CAST: Judy Davis, Richard Moir, Chris Haywood, Bill Hunter, John Gregg, Anna Jemison

Judy Davis (The Final Option; My Brilliant Career) plays an idealistic liberal opposed to proposed real estate developments that will leave some people homeless. In this political thriller, Davis's crusade leads to her involvement in a possible kidnap/murder and a love affair with the young architect of the housing project she's protesting. Unrated.

1983   99 minutes

HEAVY TRAFFIC
★★★

DIRECTOR: Ralph Bakshi

CAST: Animated

Ralph Bakshi's follow-up to Fritz the Cat is a mixture of live action and animation. Technically outstanding, but its downbeat look at urban life is rather unpleasant to watch. Rated R for profanity, nudity, and violence.

1973   76 minutes

HEIRESS, THE
★★★★½

DIRECTOR: William Wyler
CAST: Olivia De Havilland, Montgomery Clift, Ralph Richardson, Miriam Hopkins, Vanessa Brown, Mona Freeman, Ray Collins

This moving drama takes place in New York City around 1900. Olivia De Havilland is excellent (she won an Oscar for this performance) as a plain but extraordinarily rich woman who is pursued by a wily gold digger (played by Montgomery Clift). Ralph Richardson is great as her straitlaced father.

1949   B & W 115 minutes

HELL TO ETERNITY
★★★

DIRECTOR: Phil Karlson
CAST: Jeffrey Hunter, David Janssen, Vic Damone, Patricia Owens, Sessue Hayakawa

A trimly told and performed anti-prejudice, anti-war drama based on the life of World War II hero Guy Gabaldon, a Californian raised by Japanese-American parents. Jeffrey Hunter and Sessue Hayakawa share acting honors as the hero and the strong-minded Japanese commander who confronts him in the South Pacific. Lots of battle scenes.

1960   B & W 132 minutes

HELL'S ANGELS FOREVER
★★½

DIRECTOR: Richard Chase
CAST: The Hell's Angels, Bo Diddley, Willie Nelson

Most of this documentary, produced by and featuring the infamous outlaw motorcycle gang, focuses on the "runs" made by the Angels, trips where the bikers turn out in force to party. During these get-togethers, the Angels talk to the camera, telling their stories and talking about their beliefs. It's when their way of life is explored that the film is at its best. The last third of the movie attempts to prove that the government and law-enforcement agencies tried to destroy the organization by unfair means. At that point, it drags, and the viewer's interest wanes. Rated R for violence, nudity, sex, and profanity.
1983   92 minutes

HELTER SKELTER
★★★★

DIRECTOR: Tom Gries
CAST: George Dicenzo, Steve Railsback, Nancy Wolfe, Marilyn Burns

The story of Charles Manson's 1969 murder spree is vividly retold in this excellent TV movie. Steve Railsback (*The Stunt Man*) is superb as the crazed Manson. Based on prosecutor Vincent Bugliosi's novel, this is high-voltage stuff. Unrated and too intense for the kids.
1976   114 minutes

HENRY V
★★★★★

DIRECTOR: Laurence Olivier
CAST: Laurence Olivier, Robert Newton, Leslie Banks, Felix Aylmer, Renée Asherson, Leo Genn

The first of Laurence Olivier's three major film forays into Shakespeare (the others are *Hamlet* and *Richard III*), this 1946 best picture nominee blazed across screens like a meteor. This is a stirring, colorful film, full of sound and fury, and all the pageantry one expects from English history brought to vivid life. In the title role, Olivier is the heroic king personified. A success in England, the film was a triumph in the United States. Time has not dulled its eye- and ear-dazzling brilliance. Olivier won an honorary Oscar for acting, directing, and producing.
1944   137 minutes

HEROES
★★★½

DIRECTOR: Jeremy Paul Kagan
CAST: Henry Winkler, Sally Field, Harrison Ford, Val Avery

Henry Winkler is excellent in this compelling story of a confused Vietnam vet traveling cross-country to meet a few of his old war buddies who are planning to start a worm farm in California. Some hilarious scenes are mixed with some strong statements about the war in this first theatrical film for Henry, who's given solid support by Sally Field as his sort-of girl-friend, and a pre-stardom Harrison Ford as his best pal. One important note: MCA Home Video has elected to alter the film's closing theme for this release. Removing the emotionally charged "Carry on Wayward Son" by Kansas in favor of a teary generic tune somewhat diminishes the overall impact of the movie. Rated PG for mild language and violence.
1977   113 minutes

HESTER STREET
★★★★

DIRECTOR: Joan Micklin Silver
CAST: Carol Kane, Steven Keats, Mel Howard

Beautifully filmed look at the Jewish community in nineteenth-century New York City. Film focuses on the relationship of a young couple, he turning his back on the old Jewish ways while she fights to hold on to them. Fine performances and great attention to period detail make this very enjoyable. Rated PG.

1975　　　B & W　92 minutes

HEY GOOD LOOKIN'
★

DIRECTOR: Ralph Bakshi
CAST: Animated

This boring animated film from the director of *Wizards* follows the street gangs of New York City during the 1950s. It tends to put the viewer to sleep with its poor storyline and lousy animation. Skip it. Rated R.

1983　　　　　　　86 minutes

HIDE IN PLAIN SIGHT
★★★½

DIRECTOR: James Caan
CAST: James Caan, Jill Elkenberry, Robert Viharo, Joe Gripasi, Barbara Rae

James Caan is a tire factory laborer whose former wife marries a two-bit hoodlum who pulls a robbery and gets busted. The hood turns informant and, under the government's Witness Relocation Program, is given a secret identity. Caan's former wife and their two children are spirited off to points unknown. Caan's subsequent quest for his kids becomes a one-man-

against-the-system crusade in this watchable movie. Rated PG.

1980　　　　　　　98 minutes

HIGH SCHOOL CONFIDENTIAL!
★★½

DIRECTOR: Jack Arnold
CAST: Russ Tamblyn, Jan Sterling, John Drew Barrymore, Mamie Van Doren

A narcotics officer sneaks into a tough high school to bust hopheads. Incredibly naive treatment of drug scene is bad enough, but it's the actors' desperate attempts to look "hip" that make the film an unintentional laugh riot. Unrated.

1958　　　B & W　85 minutes

HIMATSURI
★★★★½

DIRECTOR: Mitsuo Yanaglmachi
CAST: Kinya Kitaoji, Kiwako Taichi, Norihei Miki

Metaphysical story about man's lustful and often destructive relationship with nature. Kinya Kitaoji plays a Hemingway-like lumberjack in a beautiful seaboard wilderness which is about to be marred by the building of a marine park. His struggle to deal with this reality results in dramatic consequences. Director Mitsuo Yanaglimachi has the flair of an Asian Peter Weir. Rated R for sex, nudity, and violence.

1985　　　　　　　120 minutes

HINDENBURG, THE
★

DIRECTOR: Robert Wise
CAST: George C. Scott, Anne Bancroft, William Atherton, Roy Thinnes, Burgess Meredith, Charles Durning

Another disaster movie whose major disaster is its own script. It is a fictionalized account of the German airship *Hindenburg*, which exploded over New Jersey in 1937. George C. Scott portrays a German official who suspects sabotage and races against time to prevent a catastrophe. The story drags so much you wish the dirigible never had gotten off the ground. This movie certainly doesn't. Rated PG.

1975   125 minutes

HIROSHIMA, MON AMOUR
★★★★

DIRECTOR: Alain Resnais
CAST: Emmanuelle Riva, Bernard Fresson, Eiji Okada

A mind-boggling tale about two people: one, a French woman, the other, a male survivor of the blast at Hiroshima. They meet and become lovers. Together they live their pasts, present, and futures in a complex series of dreams, fantasies, and nightmares that always puzzles the viewer. In French, with English subtitles.

1959   B & W   88 minutes

HISTORY IS MADE AT NIGHT
★★★

DIRECTOR: Frank Borzage
CAST: Charles Boyer, Jean Arthur, Colin Clive, Leo Carrillo

A preposterous film, but . . . Colin Clive is a sadistic jealous husband whose wife, Jean Arthur, falls for Parisian headwaiter Charles Boyer. He tries to frame the headwaiter for a murder he himself committed. He fails. Insanely determined to destroy the lovers, he arranges for his superliner to hit an iceberg! The film, once defined as a mixture of farce, melodrama, comedy, and tragedy, made from half a dozen scripts shuffled together, ends with a *Titanic*-like climax.

Talk about ways to get rid of the other man!

1937   B & W   97 minutes

HITLER
★★

DIRECTOR: Stuart Heisler
CAST: Richard Basehart, Cordula Trantow, Maria Emo, John Banner

Richard Basehart plays Adolf Hitler in this rather slow-moving, shallow account of *der Führer*'s last years. You're better off watching a good documentary on the subject.

1962   107 minutes

HITLER, THE LAST TEN DAYS
★★

DIRECTOR: Ennio Deconcini
CAST: Alec Guinness, Simon Ward, Adolfo Celi, Diane Cilento

This film should hold interest only for history buffs. It is a rather dry and tedious account of the desperate closing days of the Third Reich. Alec Guinness gives a capable, yet sometimes overwrought, performance as the Nazi leader from the time he enters his underground bunker in Berlin until his eventual suicide. Rated PG.

1973   108 minutes

HOME OF THE BRAVE
★★★

DIRECTOR: Mark Robson
CAST: James Edwards, Steve Brodie, Jeff Corey, Douglas Dick

This is one of the first films dealing with blacks serving in the military during World War II. The story finds James Edwards on a mission in the Pacific and deals with the racial abuse that he encounters from his own men. The good plot of this film could use some more "blood and guts"–type action, yet it is still worth watching.

1949   B & W   85 minutes

HOMEWORK

DIRECTOR: James Beshears
CAST: Joan Collins, Shell Kepler, Wings Hauser, Betty Thomas

Terrible film, about a high-school teacher who seduces one of her students, does its best to cash in on the Joan Collins craze, but it's a total ripoff. Since a double was used in Joan's nude scene, the poor sucker watching this trash is left with nothing but horrendous acting by all. Rated R for nudity.

1982   90 minutes

HONKYTONK MAN
★★★★

DIRECTOR: Clint Eastwood
CAST: Clint Eastwood, Kyle Eastwood, John McIntire

Clint Eastwood stars as an alcoholic, tubercular country singer headed for an audition at the Grand Ole Opry during the depths of the Depression. A bittersweet character study, it works remarkably well. You even begin to believe Eastwood in the role. The star's son, Kyle Eastwood, makes an impressive film debut. Rated PG for strong language and sexual content.

1982   122 minutes

HOT SPELL
★★★

DIRECTOR: Daniel Mann
CAST: Shirley Booth, Anthony Quinn, Shirley MacLaine, Earl Holliman, Eileen Heckart

Entertaining thoughts of leaving her for a younger woman, macho husband Anthony Quinn has anguishing housewife Shirley Booth sweating out this and younger-generation problems in this near remake of *Come Back, Little Sheba*. The impact of that film is lost here, however. Booth invokes empathy, Quinn again proves his depth of talent, Shirley MacLaine shows why stardom soon was hers; but a soap opera is a soap opera.

1958   B & W   86 minutes

HOTEL NEW HAMPSHIRE, THE
★

DIRECTOR: Tony Richardson
CAST: Beau Bridges, Jodie Foster, Rob Lowe, Nastassja Kinski, Amanda Plummer

Based on John (*The World According to Garp*) Irving's novel, this muddled motion picture has its moments, but very few of them. Unlike George Roy Hill's *The World According to Garp*, which had a touching quality about its zaniness, *Hotel* features all of Irving's quirks without any polish. As a result, the story seems to jump from one incident to another in a totally illogical manner. Beau Bridges stars as the head of a family (which includes Jodie Foster and Rob Lowe) that weathers all sorts of disasters—including rape, incest, and death—and keeps going in spite of it all. Rated R for profanity, violence, and sex.

1984   110 minutes

HOUSE ACROSS THE BAY, THE
★★½

DIRECTOR: Archie Mayo
CAST: George Raft, Joan Bennett, Lloyd Nolan, Gladys George, Walter Pidgeon

An airplane designer (Walter Pidgeon) swipes the waiting wife (Joan Bennett) of a gangster (George Raft) while Raft is paying his dues in the joint. Then he gets out. . . .

Classic Raft film. Tense, exciting, but familiar. Lloyd Nolan plays a shyster very well.

1940   B & W   86 minutes

HUD
★★★★★

DIRECTOR: Martin Ritt
CAST: Paul Newman, Patricia Neal, Melvyn Douglas, Brandon De Wilde

In one of his most memorable performances, Paul Newman stars as the arrogant ne'er-do-well son of a Texas rancher (Melvyn Douglas) who has fallen on hard times. Instead of helping his father, Hud drunkenly pursues the family's housekeeper (Patricia Neal), who wants nothing to do with him. When asked, Newman dubbed this one "pretty good." An understatement.

1963   B & W   112 minutes

HURRICANE, THE
★★★

DIRECTOR: John Ford
CAST: Jon Hall, Dorothy Lamour, Raymond Massey, Mary Astor

One of early Hollywood's disaster films. The lives and loves of a group of stereotyped characters on a Pacific island are interrupted by the big wind of the title. The sequences involving people are labored, but the special effects of the hurricane make this picture worth watching.

1937   B & W   120 minutes

HUSTLER, THE
★★★★★

DIRECTOR: Robert Rossen
CAST: Paul Newman, Jackie Gleason, Piper Laurie, George C. Scott, Myron McCormick, Murray Hamilton

This film may well contain Paul Newman's best screen performance. As pool shark Eddie Felson, he's magnificent. A two-bit hustler who travels from pool room to pool room taking suckers—whom he allows to win until the stakes get high enough, then wipes them out—Felson decides to take a shot at the big time. He challenges Minnesota Fats (nicely played by Jackie Gleason) to a big money match and almost wins—until overconfidence and booze do him in. The climax, of course, is a rematch—and writer-director Robert Rossen artfully milks it for all it's worth.

1961   B & W   135 minutes

HUSTLING
★★★★

DIRECTOR: Joseph Sargent
CAST: Lee Remick, Jill Clayburgh, Alex Rocco, Monte Markham

An investigative report delves into the world of big city prostitution in this adult TV movie. Fine performances and a good script place this above the average TV film.

1975   100 minutes

I AM A FUGITIVE FROM A CHAIN GANG
★★★★

DIRECTOR: Mervyn LeRoy
CAST: Paul Muni, Glenda Farrell, Helen Vinson, Preston Foster

Dark, disturbing, and effective Paul Muni vehicle. The star plays an innocent man who finds himself convicted of a crime and brutalized by a corrupt court system. An unforgettable film.

1932   B & W   90 minutes

I AM CURIOUS YELLOW
★½ .

DIRECTOR: Vilgot Sjoman
CAST: Lena Nyman, Borje Ahlstedt, Peter Lindgren

This Swedish import caused quite an uproar when it was released in the mid-1960s, because of its frontal nudity and sexual content. It seems pretty tame today. There isn't much of a plot built around the escapades of a young Swedish sociologist whose goal in life appears to be having sex in as many weird places as she can. If you want erotica, pass this one by. It was intended to present a good-natured and healthy sexual outlook, but after two hours of viewing, dull is the only word that comes to mind.

1967   B & W 121 minutes

I HEARD THE OWL CALL MY NAME
★★★½

DIRECTOR: Daryl Duke
CAST: Tom Courtenay, Dean Jagger, Paul Stanley, Marianna Jones

In this mystical tale of love and courage, Tom Courtenay beautifully portrays Father Mark Brian, a young Anglican priest whose bishop, played by Dean Jagger, sends him to make his mark and finds himself among the proud Indians of the Northwest. Rated G.

1973   79 minutes

I LOVE YOU (EU TE AMO)
★★★

DIRECTOR: Arnaldo Jabor
CAST: Sonia Braga, Paulo Cesar Pereio

This release, starring Brazilian sexpot Sonia Braga (*Dona Flor and Her Two Husbands*), is a high-class hard-core—though not close-up—sex film with pretensions of being a work of art. And if that turns you on, go for it. Unrated, the film has nudity, profanity, and explicit sex.

1982   104 minutes

I NEVER PROMISED YOU A ROSE GARDEN
★★★½

DIRECTOR: Anthony Page
CAST: Bibi Andersson, Kathleen Quinlan, Diane Varsi

Kathleen Quinlan plays a schizophrenic teenager seeking treatment from a dedicated psychiatrist in this well-acted but depressing drama. Rated R.

1977   96 minutes

I REMEMBER MAMA
★★★½

DIRECTOR: George Stevens
CAST: Irene Dunne, Barbara Bel Geddes, Oscar Homolka, Philip Dorn, Ellen Corby

Irene Dunne is Mama in this sentimental drama about an engaging Norwegian family in San Francisco. Definitely a feel-good film for the nostalgic-minded. Hearts of gold all the way!

1948   B & W 148 minutes

I SENT A LETTER TO MY LOVE
★★★

DIRECTOR: Moshe Mizrahi
CAST: Simone Signoret, Jean Rochefort, Delphine Seyrig

Simone Signoret and Jean Rochefort star as sister and brother in this absorbing—often painful—study of love, devotion, loneliness, and frustration. After Signoret places a personal ad (requesting male companionship) in the local paper, Rochefort responds—and they begin a correspondence, via mail, that brings passion and hope to their otherwise empty lives. The plot is twisty and interesting, but does drag a bit at times. It's an intelligent, thought-provoking film, but some may find it maudlin and melancholy. MPAA-unrated.

1981   96 minutes

I STAND CONDEMNED
★★★

DIRECTOR: Anthony Asquith
CAST: Harry Baur, Laurence Olivier, Penelope Dudley Ward, Robert Cochran

A jealous suitor frames a rival in order to have a clear field for the affections of the woman both love. Not much here, except a young and dashing Laurence Olivier in one of his first films.

1935   B & W   75 minutes

I'M DANCING AS FAST AS I CAN
★

DIRECTOR: Jack Hofsiss
CAST: Jill Clayburgh, Nicol Williamson, Geraldine Page

When a major motion picture with a top star is quickly stuck on a shelf shortly after a limited run, there's usually a good reason for it. The reason often turns out to be that it just doesn't work. Such is the case with this release, starring Jill Clayburgh. Based on documentary filmmaker Barbara Gordon's best-selling autobiography, which dealt with her valiant—and sometimes horrifying—struggle with Valium addiction, this film seems more like a "Saturday Night Live" parody of the subject than a serious examination of it. It's one movie that belongs on a shelf—permanently. Rated PG for profanity and violence.

1981   107 minutes

ICE CASTLES
★★½

DIRECTOR: Donald Wrye
CAST: Robby Benson, Lynn-Holly Johnson, Colleen Dewhurst, Tom Skerritt

Alexis Wintson (Lynn-Holly Johnson) is a girl from a small Midwestern town who dreams of skating in the Olympics. No matter how fetching and believable Johnson may be, or how accomplished her fellow cast members, nothing can surmount the soggy sentimentality and predictability of this cliché-ridden work. Rated PG.

1979   109 minutes

IDIOT'S DELIGHT
★★★½

DIRECTOR: Clarence Brown
CAST: Clark Gable, Norma Shearer, Edward Arnold, Charles Coburn, Burgess Meredith, Laura Hope Crews, Joseph Schildkraut, Virginia Grey

An all-star cast makes memorable movie history in this, the last anti-war film produced before World War II erupted. Norma Shearer is at her best as a Garbo-like fake-Russian-accented mistress companion of munitions tycoon Edward Arnold. Clark Gable is her ex, a wise-cracking vaudeville hoofer who's slipped while she's climbed. With other types, they are stranded in a European luxury hotel as war looms. It's all a bit dated, but nonetheless well worth the while.

1938   B & W   105 minutes

IF YOU COULD SEE WHAT I HEAR
★

DIRECTOR: Eric Till
CAST: Marc Singer, R. H. Thomson, Sarah Torgov, Shari Belafonte Harper, Douglas Campbell

The film is supposedly the biography of blind singer/composer Tom Sullivan. You'd have to be not only blind but deaf and, most of all, dumb to appreciate this one. Acting, directing, and script are lamentable. The serious moments are sappy. The attempts at humor are insulting . . . to Sullivan and the audience. Rated PG.

1982   103 minutes

IKIRU
★★★★½

DIRECTOR: Akira Kurosawa
CAST: Takashi Shimura, Nabuo Kaneko

Ikiru is the Japanese infinitive *to live*. The film opens with a shot of an X-ray; a narrator tells us the man—an Everyman—is dying of cancer. The narrator says the man has actually been "dead" for years, a spiritual victim of bureaucracy and of his job as a petty bureaucrat, of dreams rendered infeasible by the war and by postwar red tape. The man must now face death; he must find what it means to live. His family is cold, his coworkers unavailable; nights of carousing and debauchery just leave him hungover. But a dream flickers to life, and his last years are fulfilled by a lasting accomplishment. *Ikiru* packs a genuine emotional wallop. No rating.

1952   B & W 143 minutes

ILL MET BY MOONLIGHT
★★★

DIRECTOR: Michael Powell
CAST: Dirk Bogarde, Marise Goring, David Oxley, Cyril Cusack

In 1944 on the island of Crete, the British hatch a plot to kidnap a German general and smuggle him to Cairo. This sets off a manhunt with twenty thousand German troops and airplanes pursuing the partisans through Crete's mountainous terrain.

1957   B & W 105 minutes

IN COLD BLOOD
★★★★★

DIRECTOR: Richard Brooks
CAST: Robert Blake, Scott Wilson, John Forsythe, Jeff Corey

A chilling documentarylike recreation of the senseless murder of a Kansas farm family. This stark black-and-white drama follows two ex-convicts (Robert Blake and Scott Wilson) from the point at which they hatch their plan until their eventual capture and execution. This is an emotionally powerful film that is not for the faint of heart.

1967   B & W 134 minutes

IN NAME ONLY
★★★½

DIRECTOR: John Cromwell
CAST: Carole Lombard, Cary Grant, Kay Francis, Charles Coburn, Helen Vinson, Peggy Ann Garner

This is a classic soap opera. Cary Grant is desperately in love with sweet and lovely Carole Lombard. Unfortunately, he's married to venomous Kay Francis, who sadistically refuses to give him a divorce. You can't help but get completely wrapped up in the skillfully executed story. The performances are all topnotch.

1939   B & W 102 minutes

IN PRAISE OF OLDER WOMEN
🦃

DIRECTOR: George Kaczender
CAST: Tom Berenger, Karen Black, Susan Strasberg, Alexandra Stewart

This dull film about a man's reflections on the past two decades and his various affairs along the way goes nowhere fast with uninteresting characterizations and plot line. Rated R.

1978   108 minutes

IN THE HEAT OF THE NIGHT
★★★★

DIRECTOR: Norman Jewison
CAST: Sidney Poitier, Rod Steiger, Warren Oates, Lee Grant

This film is a rousing murder mystery elevated by the excellent acting of Rod Steiger and Sidney Poitier. Racial tension is created when a rural Southern sheriff (Steiger) and a black Northern detective reluctantly join forces to solve the crime. The picture received Oscars for best picture and Steiger's performance.

1967   109 minutes

IN WHICH WE SERVE
★★★★★

DIRECTOR: Noel Coward, David Lean
CAST: Noel Coward, John Mills, Michael Wilding

Noel Coward wrote, produced, directed, and acted in this, one of the most moving wartime portrayals of men at sea. It is not the stirring battle sequences that make this film stand out but the intimate human story of the crew, their families, and the ship they love. A great film in all respects.

1942   B & W 115 minutes

INCREDIBLE JOURNEY OF DR. MEG LAUREL, THE
★★★½

DIRECTOR: Guy Green
CAST: Lindsay Wagner, Jane Wyman, Dorothy McGuire, James Woods, Gary Lockwood, Charles Tyner, Andrew Duggan, Brook Peters, John Reilly

In this made-for-television film, Lindsay Wagner gives her usual solid performance as Meg Laurel. From humble beginnings as an orphan from the Appalachian Mountains, she becomes a doctor through the aid of the head of the orphanage (Dorothy McGuire). After graduating from Harvard Medical School, she sets up practice in 1930s Boston. Wagner is disturbed by repeated nightmares of a childhood illness and the attendance of a healer, which has left her scarred. She decides to return to the mountain people and administer the latest in medical procedures. She meets bitter opposition from the people who are unprepared to give up their antiquated ways and from Granny Arrowroot (Jane Wyman), a third-generation local healer.

1978   150 minutes

INDEPENDENCE DAY
★★★★

DIRECTOR: Robert Mandel
CAST: David Keith, Kathleen Quinlan, Richard Farnsworth, Frances Sternhagen, Cliff De Young, Dianne Wiest

Excellent little story about a young woman (Kathleen Quinlan) who wants to leave the stifling environment of her home town to become a big-city photographer. She's helped and hindered by a growing attachment to David Keith, a garage mechanic with his own problems. His sister, Dianne Wiest, is the uncomplaining victim of her wife-beating husband, played with unsavory menace by Cliff DeYoung. Both women are fabulous in their respective parts, and the story concludes with pleasant sincerity. A real treat. Rated R for violence and sex.

1983   110 minutes

INDISCRETION OF AN AMERICAN WIFE
★★½

DIRECTOR: Vittorio De Sica
CAST: Jennifer Jones, Montgomery Clift, Gino Cervi, Richard Beymer

One hour and three minutes of emotional turmoil played out against the background of Rome's railway station as adultress Jennifer Jones meets her lover, Montgomery Clift, for the last time. Yuck!

1954   B & W   63 minutes

INFORMER, THE
★★★★

DIRECTOR: John Ford
CAST: Victor McLaglen, Heather Angel, Preston Foster

John Ford's classic about a slow-witted Irish pug (Victor McLaglen) who turns his friend in for money to impress his ladylove and gets his comeuppance from the IRA has lost none of its atmospheric punch over the years. McLaglen is superb, and the movie lingers in your memory long after the credits roll.

1935   B & W   91 minutes

INHERIT THE WIND
★★★★★

DIRECTOR: Stanley Kramer
CAST: Spencer Tracy, Fredric March, Gene Kelly, Dick York, Claude Akins

In this superb film based on the stage play of the notorious Scopes monkey trial, a biology teacher is put on trial for teaching the theory of evolution. The courtroom battle that actually took place between Clarence Darrow and William Jennings Bryan could not have been more powerful or stimulating than the acting battle put on by two of America's most re-spected actors—Spencer Tracy and Fredric March.

1960   B & W   127 minutes

INHERITORS, THE
🦃

DIRECTOR: Walter Bannert
CAST: Nicholas Vogel, Rolef Schauer, Wolfgang Casser, Ottwald John, Helmut Kahn

A teen-age boy with a troubled family life stumbles into a Neo-Nazi group, which trains him in the use of weapons and how and who to hate. What could have been a work of some social significance is instead a muddled mess. A German film, the translations seem mismatched with the actions of the performers. The dubbed voices are so bad, one can't help but wince. Overall, this production didn't survive its trip overseas.

1984   90 minutes

INN OF THE SIXTH HAPPINESS, THE
★★★★

DIRECTOR: Mark Robson
CAST: Ingrid Bergman, Curt Jurgens, Robert Donat

Supurb acting marks this heart-warming biography of China missionary Gladys Aylward (Ingrid Bergman). The movie opens with her determined attempt to enter the missionary sevice and follows her to strife-torn China. The highlight is her cross-country adventure as she leads a group of orphans away from the war zone. Robert Donat is especially moving as a Mandarin lord.

1958   158 minutes

INNOCENT, THE
★★★★

DIRECTOR: Luchino Visconti
CAST: Laura Antonelli, Giancarlo Giannini

Some rate this as the most beautiful of all Luchino Visconti's films. Considering his meticulous attention to detail in bringing a time period to life, this should come as no surprise. Set in a nineteenth-century baronial manor, the main characters at first exhibit all the idealism one would expect of youth before their marriage. This is in sharp contrast to the later situation in which responsibilities of the relationship bring about the central conflict. It's the old tale of the real versus the ideal, but beautifully done. This film should not be confused with the 1961 British film *The Innocents*. Rated R due to some explicit scenes. In Italian with English subtitles.

1976   115 minutes

INSERTS
🦃

DIRECTOR: John Burum
CAST: Richard Dreyfuss, Jessica Harper, Bob Hoskins, Veronica Cartwright

Even Richard Dreyfuss can't save this dreary film about a once-great 1930s film director now making porno movies. Rated R.

1976   99 minutes

INSIDE MOVES
★★★★

DIRECTOR: Richard Donner
CAST: John Savage, David Morse, Amy Wright, Tony Burton

This is a film that grows on you as the heartwarming story unfolds. With a unique blend of humor and insight, director Richard Donner (*Superman*) and screenwriters Valerie Curtin and Barry Levinson (*And Justice for All*) provide a captivating look into a very special friendship. John Savage (*The Deer Hunter*) plays a man who, after failing at suicide, succeeds at

life with the help of some disabled friends. Rated PG.

1980   113 minutes

INTERIORS
★★★★

DIRECTOR: Woody Allen
CAST: Diane Keaton, E. G. Marshall, Geraldine Page, Richard Jordan, Sam Waterston

Woody Allen tips his hat to Swedish director Ingmar Bergman with this very downbeat drama about a family tearing itself apart. Extremely serious stuff, with fine performances by all. Allen shows he can direct more than comedy. Rated R for language.

1978   99 minutes

INTERMEZZO
★★★★

DIRECTOR: Gregory Ratoff
CAST: Leslie Howard, Ingrid Bergman, Cecil Kellaway

A love affair between a married concert violinist and a young woman doesn't stray very far from the standard eternal love triangle. This classic weeper has more renown as the English-language debut of Ingrid Bergman.

1939   B & W   70 minutes

INTO THE NIGHT
★★½

DIRECTOR: John Landis
CAST: Jeff Goldblum, Michelle Pfeiffer, Paul Mazursky, Kathryn Harrold, Richard Farnsworth, Irene Papas, David Bowie, Dan Aykroyd

Packed with cinematic in-jokes and guest appearances by more than a dozen film directors, this is a film fan's dream. Unfortunately, it might also be a casual viewer's nightmare. You need to know quite a bit about motion pictures (to say nothing of filmmakers) to appreciate it. Directed by John Landis, of *Animal House* and *Trading Places* fame, it still has much to offer. In the story two strangers (Jeff Goldblum and Michelle Pfeiffer) stumble into international intrigue and share a bizarre and deadly adventure in the night world of contemporary Los Angeles. Rated R for violence and profanity.

1985   115 minutes

INTOLERANCE
★★★★

DIRECTOR: D. W. Griffith
CAST: Lillian Gish, Bessie Love, Mae Marsh, Elmo Lincoln, Tully Marshall, Eugene Pallette, Todd Browning, Monte Blue, Robert Harron, Miriam Cooper, Constance Talmadge, Erich Von Stroheim

This milestone silent epic tells and blends four stories of injustice, modern and ancient. Gigantic, lavish, spectacular, and monumental are only a few of the adjectives that describe the film's scale, scope, and impact. The sets for the Babylonian sequence were the largest ever built for a film. One scene alone involved 15,000 people and 250 chariots. The acting is dated, but the picture presents a powerful viewing experience. A true classic and must-have for collectors.

1916   B & W 123 minutes

INVITATION AU VOYAGE
★★★½

DIRECTOR: Peter Del Monte
CAST: Laurent Malet, Aurore Clement, Mario Adorf, Nina Scott, Raymond Bussieres

Here is a strange but watchable French import with plenty of suspense and surprises for those willing to give it a chance to work its unusual magic. Peter Del Monte's film is a sometimes demanding and unpredictable work that plays little tricks on the audience. It allows the viewer to make assumptions and then shatters those conceptions with a succession of inventive twists and revelations. In French, with English subtitles. Rated R for adult content.

1982   100 minutes

IPHIGENIA
★★★★★

DIRECTOR: Michael Cacoyannis
CAST: Irene Papas, Tatiana Papamoskou, Costa Kazakos

A stunning film interpretation of the Greek classic *Iphigenia in Aulis*, by Euripedes. Irene Papas (*Electra*; *The Trojan Women*) is brilliant as Clytemnestra, the caring and outraged mother. Tatiana Papamoskou (Iphigenia) gives an intelligent and sensitive performance as the young girl who is sacrificed for man's greed and ambition. Intense score by Mikos Theodorakis. In Greek, with English subtitles. No MPAA rating.

1978   127 minutes

IREZUMI (SPIRIT OF TATTOO)
★★★★½

DIRECTOR: Yoichi Takabayashi
CAST: Masayo Utsunomiya, Tomisaburo Wakayama, Yuhsuke Takita, Masaki Kyomoto

An erotic tale of obsession that calls forth the rebirth of a near-dead art. A woman defies cultural taboos and gets her back elaborately tattooed to fulfill her mate's obsession. The subcult of this form of tattooing is all but dead when this woman approaches an old expert in the art. While the film gives the viewer an idea of how this ancient art applies to the culture and where its place in history belongs, it also shows the tattooing process as an erotic act. Rated R for nudity.

1983　　　　　　　　88 minutes

IRON DUKE, THE
★★★★

DIRECTOR: Victor Saville
CAST: George Arliss, A. E. Matthews, Allan Aynesworth, Edmund Willard, Farren Soutar, Emlyn Williams, Felix Aylmer, Gladys Cooper, Ellaline Terris

A thoroughly English stage actor, George Arliss did not make this, his first British film, until late in the decade he spent in the Hollywood studios. His Duke of Wellington, victor over Napoleon at Waterloo, is picture perfect—not the historical public conception of the duke, but real, eloquent, and as fascinating as the real man is said to have been. Buffs will particularly enjoy a younger Felix Aylmer, later Polonius in Laurence Olivier's 1948 *Hamlet*, and Gladys Cooper, David Niven's haughty, heartless scourge in *Separate Tables* in 1958. Of course, Emlyn Williams is, as almost always, matchless.

1936　　　B & W　88 minutes

IRRECONCILABLE DIFFERENCES
★★½

DIRECTOR: Charles Shyer
CAST: Drew Barrymore, Ryan O'Neal, Shelley Long

Drew Barrymore (*Firestarter*; *E.T.*) plays a little girl who sues her self-centered, career-conscious parents—Ryan O'Neal and Shelley Long (of television's "Cheers")—for divorce. This uneven comedy-drama was written by the creators of *Private Benjamin*, Nancy Meyers and Charles Shyer, who also directed. The laughs are few, but there are some effective scenes of character development. If ever a movie was just so-so, this is it. Rated PG for profanity and nudity.

1984　　　　　　　101 minutes

ISLANDS IN THE STREAM
★★★½

DIRECTOR: Franklin J. Schaffner
CAST: George C. Scott, Julius W. Harris, David Hemmings, Brad Savage, Hart Bochner, Claire Bloom

Islands in the Stream is really two movies in one. The first part is an affecting and effective look at a broken family. The second is a cheap action adventure. Thomas Hudson (George C. Scott), a famous painter and sculptor, lives the life of a recluse in the Bahamas. His only companions are his seagoing crew of Joseph (Julius Harris) and Eddy (David Hemmings). One summer, his three sons Tom (Hart Bochner), Andy (Brad Savage), and Davy (Michael-James Wixted) arrive by plane to see him for the first time in four years. The brooding character of Hudson fits Scott and the slow regeneration of his love for his sons is handled without the maudlin touches one would expect from a self-proclaimed "family picture." Too bad it goes downhill in the final third. Rated PG for violence and profanity.

1977　　　　　　　105 minutes

IT RAINED ALL NIGHT THE DAY I LEFT
★★½

DIRECTOR: Nicolas Gessner
CAST: Louis Gossett Jr., Sally Kellerman, Tony Curtis

Tony Curtis and Louis Gossett Jr. play two small-time weapons salesmen who are ambushed in Africa. They go to work for a recently widowed woman (Sally Kellerman) who controls all the water in this extremely hot and dry region. Because she blames the natives for her husband's death, she rations their water. That leads to trouble. The slow-moving parts to this movie make it just watchable and nothing out of the ordinary. Rated R for sex and violence.

1978   100 minutes

IT'S A WONDERFUL LIFE
★★★★½
DIRECTOR: Frank Capra
CAST: James Stewart, Donna Reed, Lionel Barrymore, Thomas Mitchell, Ward Bond

Have you ever wished you'd never been born? What if that wish were granted? That's the premise of Frank Capra's heartbreaking, humorous, and ultimately heartwarming *It's a Wonderful Life*. James Stewart was tapped for the lead role right after he left the service at the end of World War II. The story is about a good ambitious man so busy helping others that life seems to pass him by.

1946   B & W 129 minutes

IT'S MY TURN
★★
DIRECTOR: Claudia Weill
CAST: Jill Clayburgh, Michael Douglas, Beverly Garland, Charles Grodin

Jill Clayburgh is a college professor confused about her relationship with live-in lover Charles Grodin, a Chicago real-estate salesman. Then she meets baseball player Michael Douglas. They

fall in love. The viewer yawns. Rated R.

1980   91 minutes

IVAN THE TERRIBLE—PART I & PART II
★★★★★
DIRECTOR: Sergei Mikhailovich Eisenstein
CAST: Nikolai Cherkassov, Ludmila Tselikovskaya

Considered among the classics of world cinema, this certainly is the most impressive film to come out of the Soviet Union. This epic biography of Russia's first tsar was commissioned personally by Joseph Stalin to encourage acceptance of his harsh and historically similar policies. World-renowned director Sergei Eisenstein, instead, transformed what was designed as party propaganda into a panoramic saga of how power corrupts those seeking it. Eisenstein ended up in Stalin's doghouse and was little heard from again, but the world received a sweeping masterpiece.

1945   B & W 188 minutes

JACK LONDON
★★
DIRECTOR: Alfred Santell
CAST: Michael O'Shea, Susan Hayward, Osa Massen, Harry Davenport, Frank Craven, Virginia Mayo

Episodic, fictionalized account of the life of one of America's most popular authors is entertaining enough, but one wishes that a more accurate, detailed biography of this fabulous man were available on film. Bound by traditional studio restraints and seldom straying from the conventions of bio-pics of the time, this movie fails to capture the larger-than-life London who was almost as well-known as an adventurer and vagabond as he was a writer of young adult fiction, which is what he is best remembered for today. Heavily influenced by the anti-Japanese sentiment rampant at the time of its release, the colorful and tragic tale of the poor boy from Oakland who gained and alienated the love of America and the world cries out to be remade in today's more permissive and investigative atmosphere.

1943　　　B & W　94 minutes

JAGGED EDGE (1986 release)
★★★

DIRECTOR: Richard Marquand
CAST: Glenn Close, Jeff Bridges, Peter Coyote, Robert Loggia, Leigh Taylor-Young

A grand roller coaster of a film, pleasing to the eyes and fun to watch, that (alas) falls to pieces when the story is closely scrutinized. The characters behave according to the whims of writer Joe Eszterhas, rather than following the dictates of logic and intelligence. A publishing magnate (Jeff Bridges) is accused of the ritualistic slaying of his wife, who, it turns out, owned him lock, stock, and barrel; an attorney (Glenn Close) is hired to defend him. They fall in love, conduct an affair during the course of the trial(!), which is not noticed by the ambitious prosecutor (Peter Coyote) (!), and generally behave like total fools; during this, we and Close ponder the burning question: Did Bridges do the dirty deed? Excellent cinematography by Matthew F. Leonetti, superb score by John Barry; too bad the story doesn't match up. Rated R for violence and sexual vulgarity.

1985　　　　　108 minutes

JAMAICA INN
★★★

DIRECTOR: Alfred Hitchcock
CAST: Charles Laughton, Maureen O'Hara, Leslie Banks, Emlyn Williams, Robert Newton, Mervyn Johns

"Chadwick! Saddle the mares!" is this film's most memorable line, but the film in general is not one of Alfred Hitchcock's best directorial efforts. But the cast makes it, just the same. Charles Laughton is Squire Pengallon, the evil chief of a band of cutthroats who lure ships onto the rocks of the Cornish Coast in Victorian England. Maureen O'Hara is a beautiful damsel in distress who must contend with his madness. The opening of the film sets the tone: a sign half in gloom buffeted by wind and rain.

1939　　　B & W　98 minutes

JAMES JOYCE'S WOMEN
★★★★½

DIRECTOR: Michael Pearce
CAST: Fionnuala Flanagan, Timothy E. O'Grady, Chris O'Neill

James Joyce's Women is a delicious, verbally erotic movie. With Joyce as the writer and Fionnuala Flanagan (writer and producer) as interpreter, things are bound to be intense. The film is virtually a one-woman show, with Flanagan portraying seven different characters from Joyce's life and works. Flanagan's delivery of word and image feels right every step of the way. When her Molly Bloom rolls over in bed accompanied by a lion's roar on the soundtrack, you know you're in the hands of one who knows Joyce. The humor and sensuality will thrill Joyce fans. Rated R for nudity and sexual situations.

1985　　　　　89 minutes

JAYNE MANSFIELD STORY, THE
★½
DIRECTOR: Dick Lowry
CAST: Loni Anderson, Arnold Schwarzenegger, Kathleen Lloyd

Loni Anderson gives only an average performance as 1950s blond sex bomb Mansfield. She portrays Mansfield as a ruthless starlet who puts publicity stunts and fame ahead of all other life goals. Arnold Schwarzenegger is more convincing as her body-building mate, Mickey Hargitay. Unrated.

1980   100 minutes

JE VOUS AIME (I LOVE YOU ALL)
★★★
DIRECTOR: Claude Berri
CAST: Catherine Deneuve, Jean-Louis Trintignant, Serge Gainsbourg

Some films are so complicated and convoluted you feel you need a viewer's guide while watching them. So it is with this flashback-ridden French import directed by Claude Berri. About a 35-year-old woman, Alice (Catherine Deneuve), who finds it impossible to keep a love relationship alive, it hops, skips, and jumps back and forth through her life so confusingly you feel as if you need to stop the show occasionally to figure out what you've just seen. Therefore, even though the performances by Deneuve, Jean-Louis Trintignant, and Serge Gainsbourg are excellent, they get lost in the continual sequential shuffle. No MPAA rating; the film has sexual situations and nudity.

1981   105 minutes

JERICHO MILE, THE
★★★★
DIRECTOR: Michael Mann
CAST: Peter Strauss, Roger E. Mosley, Brian Dennehy, Billy Green Bush, Ed Lauter, Beverly Todd

This tough, inspiring TV movie tells the story of a man, serving a life sentence at Folsom Prison, who dedicates himself to becoming an Olympic-caliber runner. Director Michael Mann (of *Miami Vice* fame) makes sure the film is riveting and realistic at all times. Peter Strauss, in a powerful performance, gives the character an edge, never letting him appear too noble or sympathetic.

1979   100 minutes

JESSIE OWENS STORY, THE
★★★
DIRECTOR: Richard Irving
CAST: Dorian Harewood, Debbi Morgan, George Kennedy, Georg Stanford Brown, Tom Bosley, LeVar Burton

This made-for-TV movie of the Olympic hero provides a provocative insight into the many behind-the-scenes events that plague people who are thrust into public attention and admiration. Dorian Harewood is perfect in his performance of the not-always-admirable hero, a victim both of his own inabilities and of the uncontrollable events surrounding him. This film holds up a mirror to our society's many embarrassing racial actions.

1984   180 minutes

JEZEBEL
★★★★
DIRECTOR: William Wyler
CAST: Bette Davis, Henry Fonda, George Brent, Spring Byington

Bette Davis gives one of her finest performances as a spoiled Southern belle in this release. Devised by Warner Bros. as a consolation prize for their star, who was turned down when she tried for the role of Scarlett O'Hara, it's not as good a film as *Gone with the Wind*. But then, how many are? Directed by William Wyler, it brought Davis her second Best Actress Oscar—and a well-deserved one at that. She's superb as the self-centered "Jezebel" who takes too long in deciding between a banker (Henry Fonda) and a dandy (George Brent) and loses all.

1938   B & W   103 minutes

JO JO DANCER, YOUR LIFE IS CALLING
★★★★½

DIRECTOR: Richard Pryor

CAST: Richard Pryor, Debbie Allen, Art Evans, Fay Hauser, Barbara Williams, Carmen McRae, Paula Kelly, Diahnne Abbott, Scoey Mitchell, Billy Eckstine, Wings Hauser, Michael Ironside.

In this brilliant show-biz biography, Richard Pryor plays Jo Jo Dancer, a well-known entertainer at the peak of his popularity and the depths of self-understanding and love. A drug-related accident puts Jo Jo in the hospital and forces him to reexamine his life. Producer/co-writer/director/star Pryor has denied that this alternately hilarious, harrowing, and poignant movie is the story of his life. Perhaps it is not true in every detail, but it definitely draws on the life experiences leading to the near-fatal accident on June 9, 1980, which put the comedian in a Los Angeles hospital's burn ward. Pryor's best work has always come from his hard-edged, often bitterly honest observations of real life. Even while laughing at his comedy routines, one is always conscious of their sobering truths. *Jo Jo* takes

this approach to its zenith. Seldom has an artist reached so deep and ruthlessly into himself as Pryor has for this screen work. Like his comedy bits, it relies heavily on profanity, sex, drug use, and other adult themes. But these elements are never used gratuitously . . . always to make a point. At the very least, *Jo Jo Dancer, Your Life Is Calling* makes up for all the disappointing films Pryor has made of late. But more than that, it is a fulfillment of the promise he has always held as an entertainer/visionary, a masterpiece of heartfelt cinema. Rated R for profanity, nudity, suggested sex, drug use, violence, and unflinching honesty.

1986   100 minutes

JOAN OF ARC
★★★

DIRECTOR: Victor Fleming

CAST: Ingrid Bergman, Jose Ferrer, Francis L. Sullivan, J. Carrol Naish, Ward Bond

Ingrid Bergman is touching and devout in this by-the-book rendering of Maxwell Anderson's noted play, but too much talk and too little action strain patience and buttocks.

1948   100 minutes

JOE
★★★

DIRECTOR: John G. Avildsen

CAST: Peter Boyle, Dennis Patrick, Susan Sarandon

Peter Boyle stars in this violent film about a bigot who ends up associating much more closely with the people he hates. Falling short in the storytelling, *Joe* is nevertheless helped along by topnotch acting. Rated R.

1970   107 minutes

JOHNNY BELINDA
★★★★

DIRECTOR: Jean Negulesco
CAST: Jane Wyman, Lew Ayres, Charles Bickford, Agnes Moorehead

Jane Wyman won an Oscar for her remarkable performance as a deaf-mute farm girl. Her multidimensional characterization lifts this movie over mere melodrama. The many disasters that befall its put-upon heroine, including rape and trying to raise the resulting offspring in the face of community pressure, would be scoffed at in a lesser actress. Wyman brings off a heartwarming, convincing portrayal.

1948   B & W 103 minutes

JOHNNY GOT HIS GUN
★★½

DIRECTOR: Dalton Trumbo
CAST: Timothy Bottoms, Marsha Hunt, Jason Robards, Donald Sutherland, Diane Varsi, David Soul, Tony Geary

Featuring Timothy Bottoms (*The Last Picture Show*) as an American World War I soldier who loses his legs, eyes, ears, mouth, and nose after a German artillery shell explodes, this is a morbid, depressing anti-war film with flashes of brilliance. The beginning, when we meet Joe Bonham (Bottoms) and experience the tragedy that puts him all but dead in a military hospital, is very powerful. Likewise, the climax, wherein the haunted soldier, whom we see in the hospital hidden by bandages, begs doctors in Morse code to kill him by banging his head, will, indeed, long remain in the memories of those who see it. However, what comes in between is all too often pretentious, boring, and amateurish. Rated PG.

1971   111 minutes

JOHNNY TIGER
★★½

DIRECTOR: Paul Wendkos
CAST: Robert Taylor, Geraldine Brooks, Chad Everett

Chad Everett is a half-breed Seminole, Robert Taylor is a sympathetic teacher, and Geraldine Brooks is a sympathetic doctor, all trying to reach some valid conclusion about the American Indians' role in the modern world. It's nothing to get excited about.

1966   102 minutes

JONATHAN LIVINGSTON SEAGULL
★★

DIRECTOR: Hall Bartlett
CAST: Seagulls

You may have been convinced that a man can fly, but you'll never believe that a bird can talk. This misfired adaptation of Richard Bach's bestseller used real locations and actual seagulls, rather than infinitely more expressive animated counterparts. Needless to say, seagulls aren't the world's best method actors. Listen carefully for George Takei (Sulu in "Star Trek") as a supporting fowl. Overblown and laughable, in complete contrast to Bach's gentle fable. Catch this only for Neil Diamond's soundtrack; better yet, buy the album and skip the film. Rated G.

1973   120 minutes

JOURNEY INTO FEAR
★★

DIRECTOR: Daniel Mann
CAST: Sam Waterston, Zero Mostel, Yvette Mimieux, Scott Marlowe, Ian McShane, Joseph Wiseman, Shelley Winters, Stanley Holloway, Donald Pleasence, Vincent Price

This Canadian remake of Orson Welles' 1942 spy drama is occasionally intriguing but ultimately ambiguous and lacking in dramatic punch. Sam Waterston's portrayal of a research geologist, and wide-ranging European locations help sustain interest. Rated PG.

1975　　　　　　　　　103 minutes

JOY HOUSE
★★½

DIRECTOR: Rene Clement
CAST: Jane Fonda, Alain Delon, Lola Albright, Sorrell Booke

Spooky and interesting, but ultimately only mildly rewarding, this film features Jane Fonda in one of her sexy French roles as a free-spirited waif attempting to seduce her cousin's chauffeur (Alain Delon). Meanwhile, said cousin (Lola Albright) tries to help her criminal lover hide from the authorities. You could do worse.

1964　　　　　　　　　98 minutes

JOYRIDE
★★½

DIRECTOR: Joseph Ruben
CAST: Desi Arnaz Jr., Robert Carradine, Melanie Griffith, Anne Lockhart, Tom Ligon, Cliff Lenz

Four second-generation actors acquit themselves fairly well in this loosely directed drama about a quartet of youngsters who start off in search of adventure and find themselves turning to crime. Rated R.

1977　　　　　　　　　92 minutes

JUAREZ
★★★★

DIRECTOR: William Dieterle
CAST: Paul Muni, Bette Davis, Brian Aherne, Claude Rains, John Garfield

Warner Bros. in the 1930s and '40s seemed to trot out veteran actor Paul Muni every time they attempted to film a screen biography. This recreation of the life of Mexico's famous peasant leader was no exception. Surrounded by an all-star cast, including Bette Davis and Brian Aherne, this big budget bio is well-mounted and well-intentioned.

1939　　　B & W　132 minutes

JUDGE PRIEST
★★★½

DIRECTOR: John Ford
CAST: Will Rogers, Anita Louise, Stepin Fetchit, Henry B. Walthall, Tom Brown, Hattie McDaniel

A slice of Americana, and a good one. Life and drama in an old southern town, with all the clichés painted brilliantly. Will Rogers is fine. Stepin Fetchit is properly Uncle Tom. John Ford's sensitive direction makes this film one for the books. A touching, poignant portrait of community life lost and gone forever.

1934　　　B & W　71 minutes

JUDGMENT AT NUREMBERG
★★★★

DIRECTOR: Stanley Kramer
CAST: Spencer Tracy, Burt Lancaster, Maximilian Schell, Richard Widmark, Marlene Dietrich, Montgomery Clift, Judy Garland

An all-star cast shines in this thoughtful social drama. During the late stages of the Nazi war crimes trial, an American judge (Spencer Tracy) must ponder the issue of how extensive is the responsibility of citizens for carrying out the criminal orders of their governments. Maximilian Schell was to win an Oscar for his role as an impassioned defense attorney.

1961   B & W 178 minutes

JULES AND JIM
★★★★★

DIRECTOR: Francois Truffaut
CAST: Oskar Werner, Jeanne Moreau, Henri Serre

Superb character study, which revolves around a bizarre ménage à trois. It is really a film about wanting what you can't have and not wanting what you think you desire once you have it.

1961   B & W 104 minutes

JULIA
★★★★½

DIRECTOR: Fred Zinnemann
CAST: Jane Fonda, Vanessa Redgrave, Jason Robards, Maximilian Schell

Alvin Sargent won an Oscar for his taut screen adaptation of the late Lillian Hellman's best-selling memoir *Pentimento*. It's a harrowing tale of Hellman's journey into Germany to locate her childhood friend who has joined in the resistance against the Nazis. Great performances by all cast members. Rated PG.

1977   118 minutes

JUST BETWEEN FRIENDS
★★½

DIRECTOR: Allan Burns
CAST: Mary Tyler Moore, Christine Lahti, Sam Waterston, Ted Danson, Susan Rinell, Timothy Gibbs, Mark Blum

Mary Tyler Moore stars in this big-screen soap opera as a homemaker happily married to Ted Danson (of television's *Cheers*). One day at an aerobics class, she meets TV news reporter Christine Lahti and they become friends.

They have a lot in common—including being in love with the same man. The screenplay by director Allan Burns relies a bit too much on coincidence, and one particular plot twist is hopelessly contrived. Yet Lahti is a terrific actress and Moore nearly matches her scene for scene. Sam Waterston is also memorable as a well-meaning bystander. *Just Between Friends* is one of those films that ends up being less than the sum of its parts, yet those parts are enough to make it enjoyable for most of its running time. Rated PG-13 for profanity and suggested sex.

1986   115 minutes

JUST THE WAY YOU ARE
★★½

DIRECTOR: Edouard Molinaro
CAST: Kristy McNichol, Michael Ontkean, Kaki Hunter

In her first "grown-up" role, Kristy McNichol gives a good performance as a pretty flautist who cleverly overcomes the need to wear a leg brace—she had something akin to polio as a child—and fulfills her wish to "be like other people." But this deception brings an unexpected moment of truth. Even the plodding direction of Edouard Molinaro (*La Cage aux Folles I* and *II*) can't prevent this well-written work (by Allan Burns, of *A Little Romance*) from occasionally being witty, touching, and memorable. Rated PG.

1984   95 minutes

KARATE KID, THE
★★★★½

DIRECTOR: John G. Avildsen
CAST: Ralph Macchio, Noriyuki "Pat" Morita, Elizabeth Shue

A heartwarming, sure-fire crowd pleaser, this believable and touching work about the hazards of high-school days and adolescence will have you cheering during its climax and leave you with a smile on your face. You'll find yourself rooting for the put-upon hero, Daniel (Ralph Macchio), and booing the bad guys just as writer Robert Mark Kamen and director John G. Avildsen (*Rocky*) intended. Rated PG for violence and profanity.

1984   126 minutes

KEROUAC
★★★★

DIRECTOR: John Antonelli
CAST: Allen Ginsberg, Lawrence Ferlinghetti, Michael McClure, William Burroughs, Carolyn Cassady, Jack Coulter, Peter Coyote (N Narrator)

This is an unusually affecting and enlightening documentary on the major voice of the Beat Generation, author Jack Kerouac (*On the Road*). In examining the glory and tragedy of genius, director John Antonelli uses reenactments of events in the author's life (with Jack Coulter as Kerouac) played over passages read from his books, rare television footage, and interviews with the author's friends and contemporaries. The result is a surprisingly intimate portrait of a driven man, illustrating, as Michael McClure quotes, that "poetry is the language of crisis." Unrated, the film has no objectionable material.

1985   73 minutes

KEY EXCHANGE
★★★

DIRECTOR: Barnet Kellman
CAST: Brooke Adams, Ben Masters, Daniel Stern, Danny Aiello, Tony Roberts

This movie, taken from the Kevin Wade play, is a good study of modern-day relationships. Brooke Adams and Ben Masters play a couple who confront the idea of making a firm commitment in their relationship. Daniel Stern is hilarious as a friend of the couple who is going through his own domestic crisis. Masters plays the difficult-to-watch role. Rated R for language, sex, and nudity.

1985   96 minutes

KILLING 'EM SOFTLY
★★

DIRECTOR: Max Fischer
CAST: George Segal, Irene Cara, Joyce Gordon, Andrew Martin Thompson, Barbara Cook, Clark Johnson

George Segal is a down-and-out musician who kills the friend of a young singer (Irene Cara) in an argument over the death of his dog. While attempting to prove that Segal is not the killer, Cara falls in love with him. An interesting and well-acted story bogs down in the attempt to turn this film—billed as a "drama-musical"—into a music video. The music is good, but it overpowers the story and causes the whole to lose focus. Filmed in Canada.

1985   90 minutes

KILLING FIELDS, THE
★★★★★

DIRECTOR: Roland Joffe
CAST: Sam Waterston, Haing S. Ngor, John Malkovich, Julian Sands, Craig T. Nelson

Here's an unforgettable motion picture. Based on the experiences of *New York Times* correspondent Sidney Schanberg during the war in Cambodia and his friendship with Cambodian guide and self-proclaimed journalist Dith Pran (whom Schanberg fights to save from imprisonment), it is a tale of love, loyalty, political intrigue, and horror. The viewer cannot help but be jarred and emotionally moved by it. Rated R for violence.

1984 142 minutes

KILLING HEAT
★★½

DIRECTOR: Michael Raeburn

CAST: Karen Black, John Thaw, John Kani, Patrick Mynhardt

Uneven acting and a general lack of atmosphere hinder the screen adaptation of Doris Lessing's novel *The Grass is Singing*. Karen Black plays a city woman who marries a small-time farmer and slowly goes insane while trying to adapt herself to the rural lifestyle. Black's performance is sometimes unconvincing while at other times riveting. And by film's end there are still questions left unanswered. Set in South Africa in the early 1960s, *Killing Heat* may be interesting for those acutely aware of the civil rights movement in that country. Not rated but contains nudity and violence.

1984 104 minutes

KING
★★★★

DIRECTOR: Abby Mann

CAST: Paul Winfield, Cicely Tyson, Ossie Davis, Roscoe Lee Browne, Howard Rollins, Cliff De Young, Dolph Sweet, Lonny Chapman

Paul Winfield and Cicely Tyson star as the Rev. Martin Luther King Jr. and Coretta Scott King in this outstanding docudrama of the martyred civil rights leader's murder-capped battle against segregation and for black human dignity. Director Abby Mann, who also scripted, interpolated actual newsreel footage with restaged confrontation incidents for maxi-

mum dramatic impact. Friends and foes alike will learn much from this powerful slice of carefully re-created American history.

1978 272 minutes

KING DAVID
★★★★

DIRECTOR: Bruce Beresford

CAST: Richard Gere, Edward Woodward, Alice Krige, Denis Quilley

Only biblical scholars will be able to say whether the makers of *King David* remained faithful to the Old Testament. As a big-screen production, however, it is impressive. Directed by Australian filmmaker Bruce Beresford (*Tender Mercies*), it is one of the few responsible attempts at filming the Bible. Telling the story of David—who slew Goliath, ruled Israel, stole Bathsheba from her husband, and sired Solomon—in a serious and thoughtful manner, *King David* is a remarkable achievement. Rated PG-13 for nudity and violence.

1985 115 minutes

KING OF COMEDY, THE
★★★★

DIRECTOR: Martin Scorsese

CAST: Robert De Niro, Jerry Lewis, Sandra Bernhard

Director Brian De Palma called this the best film of 1983 in a *Playboy* interview. It's certainly one of the most unusual movies of all time; a sort of black-comedy variation on creator Martin Scorsese's *Taxi Driver*. The star of that film, Robert De Niro, stars as aspiring comic Rupert Pupkin. In order to get his big break on television, Pupkin kidnaps a talk-show host (Jerry Lewis). It's a bizarre look at the price of fame and what some misguided souls are willing to pay for it. Rated PG.

1983　　　　　　　109 minutes

KING OF KINGS, THE
★★★

DIRECTOR: Cecil B. De Mille

CAST: H. B. Warner, Ernest Torrence, Jacqueline Logan, Robert Edeson, William Boyd, Joseph Schildkraut

Cecil B. De Mille was more than ready when he made this one. It's silent, but Hollywood's greatest showman displays his gift for telling a story with required reverence. Naturally, since it's by De Mille, the production is a lavish one.

1927　　　　B & W　115 minutes

KING OF THE GYPSIES
★★★

DIRECTOR: Frank Pierson

CAST: Eric Roberts, Sterling Hayden, Susan Sarandon, Annette O'Toole, Brooke Shields, Shelley Winters

Dave Stepanowicz (Eric Roberts) is the grandson of King Zharko Stepanowicz (Sterling Hayden), the patriarch of a gypsy tribe who is both intelligent and violent. Though Dave renounces his gypsy heritage, he is unable to escape it. The performances are uniformly excellent. Director Frank Pierson is the only one who can be held responsible for the film's lack of power. As with his tragic remake of A Star Is Born, the finished product is hackneyed and disjointed. Rated R.

1978　　　　　　　112 minutes

KING OF THE MOUNTAIN
★½

DIRECTOR: Noel Nossack

CAST: Harry Hamlin, Richard Cox, Joseph Bottoms, Dennis Hopper

The quest for success and peer group immortality by a trio of buddies—Harry Hamlin, Richard Cox, and Joseph Bottoms—leads mostly to unexciting night races on Hollywood's winding Mulholland Drive and cliché back-stabbing in the music business. Dennis Hopper provides the film with a few good moments as a spaced-out 1960s has-been trying for a comeback but overall, King of the Mountain goes nowhere at low throttle. Rated PG.

1981　　　　　　　90 minutes

KING RAT
★★★★

DIRECTOR: Bryan Forbes

CAST: George Segal, Tom Courtenay, James Fox, John Mills

A Japanese prison camp in World War II is the setting for this stark drama of survival of the fittest, the fittest in this case being "King Rat" (George Segal), the opportunistic head of black market operations within the compound. In this camp the prisoners fight one another for the meager necessities of existence. This is not the traditional "prisoners against the enemy guards" prison camp movie.

1965　　　　B & W　133 minutes

KING'S ROW
★★★★★

DIRECTOR: Sam Wood

CAST: Ann Sheridan, Robert Cummings, Ronald Reagan, Claude Rains, Charles Coburn, Betty Field, Judith Anderson

A small American town at the turn of the century is the setting where two men (Ronald Reagan and Robert Cummings) grow up to experience the corruption and moral decay behind the facade of a peaceful, serene community. This brilliantly photographed drama is close to being a masterpiece, thanks to exceptional performances by many of Hollywood's best character actors.

1941 B & W 127 minutes

KISS OF THE SPIDER WOMAN (1986 Release)
★★★★

DIRECTOR: Hector Babenco
CAST: William Hurt, Raul Julia

This first English-language film by Hector Babenco (*Pixote*) is a somber, brilliantly acted tale about a gay window dresser, Molina (William Hurt), and a revolutionary, Valentin (Raul Julia), who slowly begin to care for each other and understand each other's viewpoint while imprisoned together in a South American prison. It is stark, violent, and daring. But its stars are magnificent to watch. Rated R for profanity, violence, and suggested sex.

1985 119 minutes

KITTY FOYLE
★★★★½

DIRECTOR: Sam Wood
CAST: Ginger Rogers, Dennis Morgan, James Craig, Eduardo Ciannelli

Ginger Rogers won an Oscar for her outstanding performance in this drama. She plays a poor girl who falls in love with a wealthy socialite.

1940 B & W 107 minutes

KLUTE
★★★★

DIRECTOR: Alan J. Pakula
CAST: Jane Fonda, Donald Sutherland, Roy Scheider

Jane Fonda dominates every frame in this study of a worldly call girl. Her Oscar-winning performance looks into the hidden sides of a prostitute's lifestyle; the dreams, fears, shame, and loneliness of Klute's world are graphically illustrated. Donald Sutherland co-stars as an out-of-town cop looking for a missing friend. He feels Fonda holds the key to his whereabouts. Rated R.

1971 114 minutes

KNIFE IN THE WATER
★★★★

DIRECTOR: Roman Polanski
CAST: Leon Niemczyk, Jolanta Umecka, Zygmunt Malanowicz

Absolutely fascinating feature-film debut for director Roman Polanski, who immediately demonstrated his strength with character studies. A couple off for a sailing holiday encounters a young hitchhiker and invite him along. The resulting sexual tension is riveting, the outcome impossible to anticipate. In many ways, this remains one of Polanski's finest pictures. In Polish, with English subtitles. Unrated, the film has sexual situations.

1962 B & W 94 minutes

KNOCK ON ANY DOOR
★★★½

DIRECTOR: Nicholas Ray
CAST: John Derek, Humphrey Bogart, Susan Perry, Allene Roberts

Before John Derek became a Svengali for Ursula Andress, Linda Evans, and Bo Derek, he was an actor—and a pretty good one, too, as he proves in this courtroom drama directed by Nicholas Ray. He's a kid who can't help having gotten into trouble, and Humphrey Bogart is the attorney who attempts to explain his plight to the jury.

1949   B & W 100 minutes

KNUTE ROCKNE—ALL AMERICAN
★★★

DIRECTOR: Lloyd Bacon
CAST: Ronald Reagan, Pat O'Brien, Donald Crisp

This is an overly sentimental biography of the famous Notre Dame football coach. But if you like football or you want to see Ronald Reagan show off his moves, it could hold your interest. Pat O'Brien has the cental role, and he plays it with real gusto.

1940   B & W 84 minutes

KRAMER VS. KRAMER
★★★★

DIRECTOR: Robert Benton
CAST: Dustin Hoffman, Meryl Streep, Jane Alexander, Howard Duff, JoBeth Williams

Dustin Hoffman and Meryl Streep star in the Academy Award–winning drama about a couple who separate, leaving their only son in the custody of the father, who is a stranger to his child. Just when the father and son have learned to live with each other, the mother fights for custody of the child. *Kramer vs. Kramer* jerks you from tears to laughs and back again—and all the while you're begging for more. Rated PG.

1979   104 minutes

L'ADDITION
★

DIRECTOR: Denis Amar
CAST: Richard Berry, Richard Bohringer, Victoria Abril, Fadril Chopel, Daniel Sarky, Fabrice Eberhard

L'Addition is a formula prison movie about a man accused of a crime he did not commit. This is not even an entertaining routine suspense flick. Richard Berry as the tough but stylish condemned man is like an Al Pacino sucked dry of emotion. Asking us to worry over Berry's fate is asking too much. This movie is a merciless question beggar. We know Berry's character is an actor because we're told he's one. We see nothing of his actor's life. Worse yet is the romantic relationship between Berry and a shoplifter (Victoria Abril). We are even deprived of Richard Bohringer's voice, which would have given the movie some power; unfortunately, *L'Addition* is dubbed. For a terrific, sexy thriller with good jokes and a magnificent Bohringer performance (complete with original voice), rent Michel Deville's *Peril. L'Addition* is rated R for language and violence.

1985   85 minutes

LA BETE HUMAINE
★★★★½

DIRECTOR: Jean Renoir
CAST: Jean Gabin, Julien Carette, Fernand Ledoux, Jean Renoir, Simone Simon

Remarkable performances by Jean Gabin, Fernand Ledoux, and Simone Simon, along with Jean Renoir's masterful editing and perfectly simple visuals, elevate a middling Emile Zola novel to fine cinema. The story—with a screenplay by Renoir—is a rather grim reworking of the even grimmer Atreus myth: A railway mechanic and hereditary alcoholic (Gabin) is pushed into crime; he becomes a lover to Simon, who wants him to kill her husband (Ledoux), himself a criminal; but he ends by strangling her. The artistry of *La Bête Humaine* more than transcends what, in other hands, could have been a seedy little tale—and becomes an absorbing unity of story and style. In French with English subtitles.

1938   B & W   99 minutes

LA BOUM
★★★

DIRECTOR: Claude Pinoteau
CAST: Sophie Marceau, Brigette Fossey, Claude Brasseur

A young teenager (Sophie Marceau) discovers a whole new world open to her when her parents move to Paris. Her new set of friends delight in giving "boums"—French slang for big parties. Although this film seems overly long for the subject matter and strains to hang together, many of its scenes are nevertheless tender and lovingly directed by Claude Pinoteau. No MPAA rating.

1980   100 minutes

LA DOLCE VITA
★★★½

DIRECTOR: Federico Fellini
CAST: Marcello Mastroianni, Anita Ekberg, Anouk Aimee, Nadia Gray

Mastroianni stars as a journalist who is caught up in the high society of Rome. He is both enchanted and repulsed by his life and the world around him. Entertaining, a trendsetter for the time. Not as complicated as most Fellini films. In Italian, with English subtitles.

1960   B & W   173 minutes

LA MARSEILLAISE
★★★★

DIRECTOR: Jean Renoir
CAST: Pierre Renoir, Louis Jouvet, Julien Carette

Though its plot is somewhat uneven, *La Marseillaise* contains many beautiful sequences, and it is still noted for its appropriate lack of idealizaton and dramatization. This documentarylike story (and Jean Renoir's call to his countrymen to stand fast against the growing threat of Hitler) parallels the rise of the French Revolution with the spread of the new rallying song as 150 revolutionary volunteers from Marseilles march to Paris and join with others to storm the Bastille. Since it was financed by the French trade unions, it is interesting that Louis XVI (played by Renoir's brother) is portrayed as an intelligent and sensible man (albeit a bit distrait) who is overwhelmed by the march of history. In French with English subtitles.

1937   B & W   130 minutes

LA NUIT DE VARENNES
★★½

DIRECTOR: Ettore De Scola
CAST: Marcello Mastroianni, Jean-Louis Barrault, Harvey Keitel

An ambitious and imaginative, but ultimately disappointing, film of King Louis XVI's flight from revolutionary Paris in 1791 as seen through the ideologically opposed sensibilities of Casanova (Marcello Mastroianni), Restif de la Bretonne (Jean-Louis Barrault), and Tom Paine (Harvey Keitel). This French import is a lot like Steve Allen's PBS series "Meeting of the Minds," with costumes and scenery. All these folks do is talk, talk, talk. Talk about the rights of the individual. Talk about the elegant ways of the aristocracy. Talk about boring! In French, with English subtitles. Rated R for nudity, sex, and profanity.

1983   133 minutes

LA STRADA
★★★★★

DIRECTOR: Federico Fellini
CAST: Giulietta Masina, Anthony Quinn, Richard Basehart

This is Fellini's first internationally acclaimed film. Gelsomina (Giulietta Masina), a simple-minded peasant girl, is sold to a circus strongman (Anthony Quinn), and as she follows him on his tour through the countryside, she falls desperately in love with him. She becomes the victim of his constant abuse and brutality until their meeting with an acrobat (Richard Basehart) dramatically changes the course of their lives. Masina's performance is unforgettable. This poetic masterpiece won the Academy Award for best foreign-language film.

1954   B & W   94 minutes

LA TRUITE (THE TROUT)
★★★½

DIRECTOR: Joseph Losey
CAST: Lissette Malidor, Isabelle Huppert, Jacques Spiesser, Roland Bertin, Daniel Ollrychski

Sometimes disjointed story of a young girl who leaves her rural background and arranged marriage to climb the rocky path to success in both love and business. Although director Joseph Losey generally has the right idea, La Truite, in the end, lacks warmth and a sense of cohesion. Many viewers may find it disappointingly dull and dreary. In French, with English subtitles. Rated R.

1982   100 minutes

LADY CHATTERLEY'S LOVER
★

DIRECTOR: Just Jaeckin
CAST: Sylvia Kristel, Nicholas Clay

A beautifully staged, but banal, version of the D. H. Lawrence classic. The sometimes compelling score is the only force to help this creep along. Viewers should compare other, always difficult attempts to portray Lawrence (Sons and Lovers, 1963; Women in Love, 1970). Rated R.

1981   105 minutes

LADY FOR A NIGHT
★½

DIRECTOR: Leigh Jason
CAST: John Wayne, Joan Blondell, Ray Middleton

John Wayne plays second fiddle to Joan Blondell. She's a saloon singer fighting for a measure of respectability in this release. If you plan to watch it, have some coffee brewed—you'll need it to help you stay awake.

1941   B & W   87 minutes

LADY OF THE HOUSE
🦃

DIRECTORS: Ralph Nelson and Vincent Sherman
CAST: Dyan Cannon, Armand Assante, Zohra Lampert, Susan Tyrrell

Dyan Cannon stars in this TV dramatization of the life of Sally Stanford, Mayor of Sausalito, California. Cannon gives a better performance than usual, and Armand Assante is even better. Quite a bit of footage was cut from the original TV broadcast, leaving the audience lost between scenes.

1978   90 minutes

LAND WITHOUT BREAD
★★★★½

DIRECTOR: Luis Buñuel
CAST: Documentary

Critics who had been unsympathetic to Luis Buñuel's first two films, the brilliant surrealist manifestos *Un Chien Andalou* and *L'Age d'Or*, were slapped flat by this documentary of the monstrous conditions of life in the poorest district of northern Spain. This "morbid fantasy" dramatizes the harshness of nature and the benign neglect of Christian tradition. Nearly every scene of poverty, disease, and death—as well as marriage and valiant struggle—is indelible. The ironic travelogue-style narration only serves to intensify the image of human degradation. *Land Without Bread* was financed by the twenty thousand pesetas given to Buñuel by an anarchist friend who had won the money in a lottery. It was his last film project without the aggravation of commerical strings attached. No rating, but not for the youngsters. In Spanish with English subtitles.

1932   B & W   27 minutes

LAST DAYS OF POMPEII, THE
★★★

DIRECTOR: Ernest B. Schoedsack
CAST: Preston Foster, Basil Rathbone, Dorothy Wilson, David Holt, Alan Hale, Louis Calhern

Roman blacksmith Preston Foster becomes a gladiator after tragedy takes his wife and baby. En route to fortune, he adopts the young son of one of his victims. In Judea, he sees but refuses to help Christ, who cures the boy following serious injury. Like Richard Blaine and Fred C. Dobbs, he sticks his neck out for nobody. Touched by Jesus, the boy grows up to help runaway slaves, a practice that undercuts his fathers's business. Things come to a head when the boy is arrested, faces death, and

Vesuvius lets go. Tremendous special effects.

1935   B & W   96 minutes

LAST DETAIL, THE
★★★★

DIRECTOR: Hal Ashby
CAST: Jack Nicholson, Otis Young, Randy Quaid, Michael Moriarty, Nancy Allen

Two veteran Navy men (Jack Nicholson and Otis Young) are assigned to transport a young sailor to the brig for theft. They take pity on the naive loser (Randy Quaid) and decide to show him one last good time. By opening the youngster's eyes to the previously unknown world around him, their kindness is in danger of backfiring in this drama. Rated R.

1973   105 minutes

LAST GAME, THE
★★

DIRECTOR: Martin Beck
CAST: Howard Segal, Ed L. Grady, Terry Alden, Jerry Rushing, Mike Allen, Toby Wallace, Julian Morton, Joan Hotchkis, Bob Supan

Maudlin tale of an attractive and responsible clean-cut college kid who works two jobs, goes to school, and takes care of his blind father while his father dreams that one day his boy will play pro football. In an attempt to spice up the plot, the filmmakers have added a few extra conflicts and miles of football footage, but this only contributes to the film's lack of focus. Video shoppers could do a lot worse, but this movie is just too banal for recommendation. No MPAA rating, but equal to a PG for sex and profanity.

1980   107 minutes

LAST LAUGH, THE
★★★★

DIRECTOR: F. W. Murnau
CAST: Emil Jannings, Mary Delshaft, Kurt Hiller

Historically recognized as the first film to exploit the moving camera, this titleless silent classic tells the story of a lordly luxury hotel doorman who is abruptly and callously demoted to the menial status of a washroom attendant. Deprived of his job and uniform, his life slowly disintegrates. Emil Jannings, one of the screen's early character stars in the mold of George Arliss and Paul Muni, gives a brilliant performance as the once-proud majordomo on whom the sin of pride visits cruel retribution. In a questionable effect-destroying epilogue, the old man inherits a fortune, and has *The Last Laugh*.

1924　　　B & W　74 minutes

LAST METRO, THE
★★★½

DIRECTOR: Francois Truffaut
CAST: Catherine Deneuve, Gerard Depardieu, Jean Poiret

Catherine Deneuve and Gerard Depardieu star in this drama about a Parisian theatrical company that believes "the show must go on" despite the restrictions and terrors of the Nazis during their World War II occupation of France. This film has several nice moments and surprises that make up for its occasional dull spots and extended running time. Rated PG.

1980　　　　　　133 minutes

LAST MILE, THE
★★★

DIRECTOR: Sam Bischoff
CAST: Preston Foster, Howard Phillips, George E. Stone, Noel Madison, Alan Roscoe, Paul Fix

No-win prison film (based on a then-current stage play) is a claustrophobic foray into death row, where cons talk tough and the audience better listen. Full of hardboiled sentiment, off-screen machine-gun bursts, and even a squealer or two, this archetypal prison-break melodrama has a quiet dignity that elevates the dialogue between the inmates to high drama. Preston Foster as Killer Miles plays the toughest con in the block and the leader of the break attempt, a role Clark Gable played on the stage in Los Angeles in 1930, but no longer needed by 1932.

1932　　　B & W　70 minutes

LAST PICTURE SHOW, THE
★★★★★

DIRECTOR: Peter Bogdanovich
CAST: Timothy Bottoms, Ben Johnson, Jeff Bridges, Cloris Leachman, Cybill Shepherd, Randy Quaid

Outstanding adaptation of Larry McMurtry's novel about a boy's rites of passage in a small Texas town during the 1950s. Virtually all the performances are excellent due to the deft direction of Peter Bogdanovich, who assured his fame with this picture. Ben Johnson, as a pool hall owner, and Cloris Leachman, as a lonely wife, deservedly won Oscars for their supporting performances. Filmed in black and white, which makes the gritty story even more stark, this will leave lasting impressions. An absolute must. Rated R for brief nudity and adult situations.

1971　　　B & W　118 minutes

LAST SUMMER
★★½

DIRECTOR: Frank Perry

CAST: Richard Thomas, Barbara Hershey, Bruce Davison, Cathy Burns, Ralph Waite, Conrad Bain

Engrossing tale of teen desires, frustrations, and fears, played out in disturbingly dark fashion. Bruce Davison and Cathy Burns are especially memorable in unusual roles. Rated R.

1969   97 minutes

LAST TANGO IN PARIS
★★★
DIRECTOR: Bernardo Bertolucci
CAST: Marlon Brando, Maria Schneider, Jean-Pierre Léaud

A middle-aged man (Marlon Brando) and a young French girl (Maria Schneider) have a doomed love affair. This pretentious sex melodrama was mainly notable for being banned when it first came out. Rated R for sex.

1972   129 minutes

LAST TYCOON, THE
★★★
DIRECTOR: Elia Kazan
CAST: Robert DeNiro, Robert Mitchum, Tony Curtis, Jeanne Moreau, Jack Nicholson, Donald Pleasence, Peter Strauss, Ray Milland, Ingrid Boulting, Dana Andrews, John Carradine

Tantalizing yet frustrating, this slow-moving attempt to film F. Scott Fitzgerald's last (and unfinished) book is a blockbuster conglomeration of talent at all levels, but fails to really capture the imagination of the average film-goer and appears to be a somewhat confusing collection of scenes and confrontations. Robert DeNiro as Monroe Starr, the sickly motion picture magnate and the "last tycoon" of the story, gives another fine, understated performance, but

the film just lacks the form and punch to entertain or inveigle the casual video renter, who knows little about the studio system (and especially MGM, Irving Thalberg, or Louis B. Mayer) and cares less. A satisfying treat for film history buffs and a unique chance to see an incredible collection of great actors and actresses from the old studio days (Ray Milland, Dana Andrews, John Carradine, Robert Mitchum) as well as some of today's finest talent (Jeanne Moreau, Jack Nicholson, Robert DeNiro).

1976   125 minutes

LAST WINTER, THE
★
DIRECTOR: Riki Shelach
CAST: Kathleen Quinlan, Yona Elian, Stephen Macht, Zipora Peled, Michael Schneider, Brian Aaron

Kathleen Quinlan (*Independence Day, Twilight Zone—The Movie*) and Yona Elian are wives of Israeli soldiers missing in action during the Yom Kippur War of 1973. Over the prospect of both women becoming widows, their friendship grows intense, with hints of homosexuality. This outing had potential, but it was bound for trouble with dialogue like "My body aches for him" and "I want to have his child," and a slow-motion sequence that tries to develop character when the screenwriter has run out of all other types of clichés to use. The entire film has a harsh tone about it that makes it difficult for the viewer to feel any sympathy for the two women. Rated R for sex, nudity, language, and adult situations.

1984   92 minutes

LAST YEAR AT MARIENBAD
★★★

DIRECTOR: Alain Resnais

CAST: Delphine Seyrig, Giorgio Albertazzi, Sacha Pitoeff, Françoise Bertin, Luce Garcia-Ville

This film provides no middle ground—you either love it or you hate it. The confusing story is about a young man (Giorgio Albertazzi) finding himself in a monstrous, baroque hotel trying to renew his love affair with a woman who seems to have forgotten that there is an affair to renew. The past, present, and future all seem to run parallel, cross over, and converge. Even the hotel loses its baroqueness at times. This has been called a landmark film by some. If that is the case, then it exists in that state for the most esoteric students, directors, and cinematographers. In French with English subtitles.

1962   B & W   93 minutes

LE JOUR SE LEVE (DAYBREAK)
★★★

DIRECTOR: Marcel Carne

CAST: Jean Gabin, Jules Berry, Arletty, Jacqueline Laurent

An affecting, atmospheric French melodrama by the director of the classic *Les Enfants du Paradis (Children of Paradise)*. Jean Gabin plays a man provoked to murder his lover's seducer, who then barricades himself in his room through the night. There is some brilliant, sensuous moviemaking here. The poetic realism of this 1939 film puts to shame all the ridiculously prudish American movies of the time. Written by Jacques Prevert. The existing print lacks sufficient subtitling but is still worth viewing.

1939   B & W   85 minutes

LENNY
★★★★★

DIRECTOR: Bob Fosse

CAST: Dustin Hoffman, Valerie Perrine, Jan Miner

Bob Fosse brilliantly directed this stark biography of self-destructive, controversial persecuted comic talent Lenny Bruce. Dustin Hoffman captures all those contrary emotions in his portrayal of the late 1950s and '60s stand-up comedian. Valerie Perrine is a treasure in her low-key role as Bruce's stripper wife. Rated R.

1974   B & W   112 minutes

LETTER OF INTRODUCTION
★★★★

DIRECTOR: John M. Stall

CAST: Adolphe Menjou, Andrea Leeds, Edgar Bergen and Charlie McCarthy, George Murphy, Eve Arden, Rita Johnson, Ernest Cossart, Ann Sheridan

An essentially enjoyable melodrama, *Letter of Introduction* is the story of a young actress (Andrea Leeds) who seeks out the advice of an old actor (Adolphe Menjou). The aging star encourages her in her various endeavors. The relationship between the two lead characters is so real, so warm that it carries the film. Look for Ann Sheridan in one of her early roles, along with the antics of Edgar Bergen and Charlie McCarthy.

1938   B & W   100 minutes

LETTER, THE
★★★★

DIRECTOR: William Wyler

CAST: Bette Davis, Herbert Marshall, James Stephenson

Bette Davis stars in this screen adaptation of Somerset Maugham's play as the coldly calculating wife of a rubber plantation owner (Herbert Marshall) in Malaya. In a fit of pique, she shoots her lover and concocts an elaborate tissue of lies to protect herself. With tension mounting all the way, we wonder if her evil ways will eventually lead to her downfall.

1940 B & W 95 minutes

LIANNA
★★★★

DIRECTOR: John Sayles
CAST: Linda Griffiths, Jane Halloren, Jon DeVries, Jo Henderson

The problem with most motion pictures about gays is they always seem to be more concerned with sex than love. In comparison, this film, written and directed by John Sayles (*Baby, It's You*; *Return of the Secaucus Seven*) stands as a remarkable achievement. About a married housewife named Lianna (Linda Griffiths) who decides to have an affair with, and eventually move in with, another woman (Jane Halloren), it is a sensitive study of one woman's life and loves. Rated R for nudity, sex, and profanity.

1983 110 minutes

LIAR'S MOON
★★★½

DIRECTOR: David Fisher
CAST: Matt Dillon, Cindy Fisher, Christopher Connelly, Hoyt Axton, Yvonne DeCarlo, Susan Tyrrell

Two young lovers encounter unusually hostile resistance from their parents. Their elopement produces many of the expected problems faced by youths just starting out: limited finances, inexperience, incompatibility. They also must come to grips with a major problem that is totally unexpected. The plight of the couple remains interesting throughout, mostly due to the leads' believable performances. Rated PG for language.

1983 106 minutes

LIBERATION OF L. B. JONES, THE
★★

DIRECTOR: William Wyler
CAST: Lola Falana, Roscoe Lee Browne, Lee J. Cobb, Lee Majors, Barbara Hershey

Famed director William Wyler really laid an egg in this uninteresting "message" movie. In what starts as a movie effort to portray race relations gone asunder, all we are given is cardboard cutout stereotypes and a confusing plot. This story, of a wealthy black man who is deluded into divorcing his wife (Lola Falana) because of her believed infidelity with a white cop, never gains our sympathy or interest. Rated R.

1970 102 minutes

LIFE AND DEATH OF COLONEL BLIMP, THE
★★★★★

DIRECTOR: Michael Powell, Emeric Pressburger
CAST: Roger Livesey, Deborah Kerr, Anton Walbrook

A truly superb film chronicling the life and times of a staunch for-king-and-country British soldier. Sentimentally celebrating the human spirit, it opens during World War II and unfolds through a series of flashbacks that reach as far back as the Boer War. Roger Livesey is excellent in the title role. Deborah Kerr portrays the four women in his life across four decades with charm and insight. Definitely a keeper.

1943 163 minutes

LIFE OF EMILE ZOLA, THE
★★★★

DIRECTOR: William Dieterle

CAST: Paul Muni, Joseph Schild-kraut, Gale Sondergaard, Gloria Holden, Donald Crisp, Louis Calhern

Paul Muni is excellent in the title role of the nineteenth-century novelist who championed the cause of the wrongly accused Captain Dreyfus (Joseph Schildkraut). A lavish production!

1937   B & W   93 minutes

LIFEBOAT
★★★½

DIRECTOR: Alfred Hitchcock

CAST: Tallulah Bankhead, John Hodiak, William Bendix, Walter Slezak, Henry Hull, Canada Lee, Hume Cronyn, Heather Angel, Mary Anderson

A microcosm of American society, survivors of a World War II torpedoing, adrift in a lifeboat, nearly come a cropper when they take a Nazi aboard. Dumbly dismissed as an artistic failure by most critics, it has some ridiculous flaws, but is nonetheless an interesting and engrossing film. Said one critic: "John Steinbeck wrote the allegorical story, screenwriter MacKinley Kantor heightened the allegory, screenwriter Jo Swerling provided Hollywood gloss, and Alfred Hitchcock created a thriller." Tunnel-voiced Tallulah Bankhead is tops in this sea-going *Grand Hotel*. Look for Hitchcock's pictorial trademark in a newspaper.

1944   B & W   96 minutes

LIFEGUARD
★★½

DIRECTOR: Daniel Petrie

CAST: Sam Elliott, Anne Archer, Kathleen Quinlan, Parker Stevenson, Stephen Young

Is happiness enough? Don't we have to do something with our lives? After his fifteen-year high-school reunion, Sam Elliott begins to feel twinges of fear and guilt. How long can he go on being a lifeguard? Shouldn't he be making the move into a career with a future? Shouldn't he be chasing the almighty dollar like everyone else? The film is likable and easygoing, like its star. If your interest starts to drift, Elliott's charisma will pull you back. Rated PG.

1976   96 minutes

LILIES OF THE FIELD
★★★★

DIRECTOR: Ralph Nelson

CAST: Sidney Poitier, Lilia Skala

Sidney Poitier won an Academy Award for his portrayal of a handyman who happens upon a group of nuns who have fled from East Germany and finds himself building a chapel for them. With little or no build-up, the movie went on to become a big hit.

1963   B & W   93 minutes

LILITH
★★

DIRECTOR: Robert Rossen

CAST: Warren Beatty, Jean Seberg, Peter Fonda, Kim Hunter, Anne Meacham, Jessica Walter, Gene Hackman

Producer-director Robert Rossen's adaptation of J. R. Salamanca's cult novel is an intriguing, somber, frequently indecipherable journey into the darker depths of the human psyche. Warren Beatty is a young psychiatric therapist at a mental institute who falls in love with a beautiful schizophrenic patient (Jean Seberg), with tragic results. Visually impressive, with its poetic, dreamlike imagery, it remains dramatically frustrating due to its ambiguous blending of sanity and madness, reality and fantasy. More of a feature-length experiment in mood than a traditional "movie," it's a fascinating film, though not an especially likable one.

1964   B & W   114 minutes

LION IN WINTER, THE
★★★★½

DIRECTOR: Anthony Harvey

CAST: Katharine Hepburn, Peter O'-Toole, Anthony Hopkins, John Castle, Timothy Dalton

Acerbic retelling of the clash of wits between England's King Henry II (Peter O'Toole) and Eleanor of Aquitaine (Katharine Hepburn), adapted by James Goldman from his Broadway play. Hepburn won an Oscar for her part, and it's quite well played. The story's extended power struggle rages back and forth, with Henry and Eleanor striking sparks throughout. Snappy dialogue, flawlessly delivered. O'Toole hasn't had a part this good since *Lawrence of Arabia*. Not at all boring, in spite of its length. Excellent score by John Barry. Rated PG.

1968   135 minutes

LITTLE LORD FAUNTLEROY
★★★★

DIRECTOR: John Cromwell

CAST: Freddie Bartholomew, C. Aubrey Smith, Dolores Costello, Jessie Ralph, Mickey Rooney, Guy Kibbee

Far from a syrupy-sweet child movie, this is the affecting tale of a long-lost American heir (Freddie Bartholomew) brought to live with a hard-hearted British lord (C. Au-

brey Smith) whose icy manner is warmed by the cheerful child.

1936   B & W   98 minutes

LITTLE MEN
★½

DIRECTOR: Norman Z. McLeod

CAST: Jack Oakie, Kay Francis, George Bancroft, Jimmy Lydon, Ann Gillis, Charles Esmond, William Demarest, Sterling Holloway, Isabel Jewell, Elsie the Cow

Louisa May Alcott's classic of childhood turned into a travesty. Poor writing and second-rate histrionic endeavors by mediocre cast stifled the charm and sentiment of the novel, making the production one of cheap jokes and dialogue from the ice age. Film was a box-officer loser.

1940   B & W   84 minutes

LITTLE MINISTER, THE
★★★½

DIRECTOR: Richard Wallace

CAST: Katharine Hepburn, Donald Crisp, John Beal, Andy Clyde

An early effort in the career of Katharine Hepburn. This charming story, of a proper Scottish minister who falls in love with what he believes is a gypsy girl, is not only of merit to just Hepburn fans.

1934   B & W   110 minutes

LITTLE WOMEN
★★★★½

DIRECTOR: George Cukor

CAST: Katharine Hepburn, Spring Byington, Joan Bennett, Frances Dee, Jean Parker

George Cukor's *Little Women* is far and away the best of the four film versions of Louisa May Alcott's timeless story of the March family. Katharine Hepburn is excellent as the tomboyish Jo. The remainder of the New England family, which endures the Civil War and grows to maturity, is wonderfully played by Spring Byington, Joan Bennett, Frances Dee, and Jean Parker.

1933   B & W 115 minutes

LOLITA
★★★

DIRECTOR: Stanley Kubrick
CAST: James Mason, Sue Lyon, Shelley Winters, Peter Sellers

A man's unconventional obsession for a "nymphet" is the basis for this bizarre satire. James Mason and Sue Lyon are the naughty pair in this film, which caused quite a stir in the 1960s but seems fairly tame today.

1962   B & W 152 minutes

LONELY HEARTS
★★★★½

DIRECTOR: Paul Cox
CAST: Norman Kaye, Wendy Hughes, Julia Blake

A funny, touching Australian romantic comedy about two offbeat characters who fall in love. Peter (Norman Kaye) is a 50-year-old mama's boy who doesn't know what to do with his life when his mother dies. Then he meets Patricia (Wendy Hughes), a woman who has never had a life of her own. It's a warmly human delight. Rated R.

1981   95 minutes

LONELY LADY, THE

DIRECTOR: Peter Sasdy
CAST: Pia Zadora, Lloyd Bochner, Bibi Besch

Adapted from the novel by Harold Robbins, this film stars Pia Zadora as Jerilee Randall, an aspiring writer who is used and abused by every man she meets. You never believe it for a moment. As a result, it's often a real hoot; a hilarious mixture of bad dialogue, campy performances, and outrageous situations. Rated R for sex, violence, nudity, and profanity.

1983   92 minutes

LONG DAY'S JOURNEY INTO NIGHT
★★★★★

DIRECTOR: Sidney Lumet
CAST: Katharine Hepburn, Ralph Richardson, Jason Robards Jr., Dean Stockwell

This superb film was based on Eugene O'Neill's play about a troubled turn-of-the-century New England family. Katharine Hepburn is brilliant as the drug-addict wife. Ralph Richardson is equally good as her husband, a self-centered actor. One of their sons is an alcoholic, while the other is dying of tuberculosis. Although depressing, it is an unforgettable viewing experience.

1962   B & W 136 minutes

LONG VOYAGE HOME, THE
★★★★½

DIRECTOR: John Ford
CAST: John Wayne, Barry Fitzgerald, Thomas Mitchell, Mildred Natwick

Life in the merchant marine as experienced and recalled by Nobel Prize–winning playwright Eugene O'Neill. The hopes and dreams and comradeship of a group of seamen beautifully blended in a gripping, moving account of men, a ship, and the ever-enigmatic sea. The major characters are superbly drawn by those playing them. Definitely a must-see, and see-again, film. Classic.

1940   B & W 105 minutes

LOOK BACK IN ANGER
★★★★½

DIRECTOR: Tony Richardson
CAST: Richard Burton, Claire Bloom

Based on the John Osborne play of the same name, this riveting look into one of the "angry young men" of the 1950s has Richard Burton and Claire Bloom at their best. Burton exposes the torment and frustration these men felt toward their country and private life with more vividness than you may want to deal with, but if you're looking for a realistic recreation of the period, look no further. Ultimately depressing but revealing, it leaves you thoughtful and haunted.

1958   B & W   99 minutes

LOOKING FOR MR. GOODBAR
★

DIRECTOR: Richard Brooks
CAST: Diane Keaton, Tuesday Weld, Richard Gere, LeVar Burton, Richard Kiley

A strong performance by star Diane Keaton can't save this dismal character study about a woman drawn to sleazy sex and lowlifes. Tuesday Weld and Richard Gere also are memorable in support, but director Richard Brooks obviously intended to revolt the audience through the main character's aimless immorality and untimely end—and did so to the detriment of his picture. Rated R.

1977   135 minutes

LOOKING GLASS WAR, THE
★★

DIRECTOR: Frank R. Pierson
CAST: Christopher Jones, Pia Degermark, Ralph Richardson, Anthony Hopkins

This plodding adaptation of John Le Carré's espionage novel about a Pole sent to get the scam on a rocket in East Berlin is replete with spy slang and the usual covert and clandestine operations. But it never gets off the ground. Having actor's actor Ralph Richardson in the cast should have, but did not, help. Most of the acting is as wooden as bleacher seating. Where's Smiley when we need him? Rated PG.

1970   106 minutes

LORD OF THE FLIES
★★★★

DIRECTOR: Peter Brook
CAST: James Aubrey, Hugh Edwards, Tom Chapin

William Golding's grim allegory comes to the screen in a near-perfect adaptation helmed by British stage director Peter Brook. English schoolboys, stranded on an island and left to their own devices, gradually revert to the savage cruelty of wild animals. Visually hypnotic and powerful, something you just can't tear your eyes away from. The cast is outstanding, and what the film fails to take from Golding's novel—much of the symbolism, for example—it compensates for with raw energy. It'll make you think twice about the little boys who live down the street.

1963   B&WB & W91 minutes

LORDS OF DISCIPLINE, THE
★★★½

DIRECTOR: Franc Roddam
CAST: David Keith, Robert Prosky, G. D. Spradlin, Rick Rossovich

A thought provoking film in every sense, *Lords* contains many emotionally charged well-written, well-directed, and well-played scenes. David Keith (*An Officer and a Gentleman*; *Brubaker*) stars as a student at a military academy who puts his life in danger by helping a black cadet being hazed by The Ten, a secret group of white students dedicated to the "purification" of the campus. Rated R for profanity, nudity, and violence.

1983   102 minutes

LORDS OF FLATBUSH, THE
★★½

DIRECTOR: Stephen F. Verona, Martin Davidson

CAST: Perry King, Sylvester Stallone, Henry Winkler, Paul Mace, Susan Blakely

Of all the leads, only Paul Mace didn't go on to bigger things. A stocky Sylvester Stallone shows promise as a character actor. Perry King is dashing. Susan Blakely is lovely. And Henry Winkler is particularly winning, playing an unexaggerated Fonzie-type character. The film provides a fairly satisfying blend of toughness and sentimentality, humor and pathos, as it tells a story of coming of age in 1950s New York. Rated PG.

1974   88 minutes

LOS OLVIDADOS
★★★★★

DIRECTOR: Luis Buñuel

CAST: Alfonso Mejia, Roberto Cobo, Estela Ina, Miguel Inclan

Although its basic plot was taken from police records, this film, which was released in England and the United States as *The Young and the Damned*, is a far cry from the soap opera its title might indicate. Luis Buñuel marks the beginning of his mature style with this film. Hyperpersonal, shocking, erotic, hallucinogenic, and surrealistic images are integrated into naturalistic action: two youths of the Mexican slums venture deeper and deeper into the criminal world until they are beyond redemption. Buñuel's focus is pit-

iless; his hardened eye and pained soul do not hold with the liberal sociologist's view of violence. His characters alone are responsible for their actions—and their deaths. In Spanish with English subtitles.

1950   B & W   88 minutes

LOST HONOR OF KATHARINA BLUM, THE
★★★

DIRECTOR: Volker Schlondorff

CAST: Angela Winkler

Angela Winkler's performance as Katharina Blum is the central force behind Schlondorff's interpretation of Heinrich Boll's novel. Katharina Blum is a poor, young housekeeper who spends one night with a suspected political terrorist. Her life is thereby ruined by the police and the media. This film dramatizes political statements and is without surprises. In German, with English subtitles. Rated R.

1977   97 minutes

LOST MOMENT, THE
★★★½

DIRECTOR: Martin Gable

CAST: Robert Cummings, Susan Hayward, Agnes Moorehead, Eduardo Ciannelli

A low-key, dark, offbeat drama based on Henry James's novel *The Aspern Papers*, which was based on the true story of Claire Clairmont, friend of the poet Percy Bysshe Shelley and mother of a love child by George Gordon, Lord Byron. A publisher (Robert Cummings), seeking love letters written by a long-dead great poet, goes to Italy to interview a very old lady and her niece. The old lady is spooky, the niece neurotic, the film fascinating. Those who know Cummings only from his TV series will be pleasantly surprised with his serious acting.

1947   B & W   88 minutes

LOST WEEKEND, THE
★★★★★

DIRECTOR: Billy Wilder
CAST: Ray Milland, Jane Wyman, Philip Terry, Howard Da-Silva, Frank Faylen

Gripping, powerful study of alcoholism and its destructive effect on one man's life. Arguably Ray Milland's best performance (he won an Oscar) and undeniably one of the most potent films of all time. Forty years after its release, the movie has lost none of its importance or effectiveness. Additional Oscars for best picture, director, and screenplay. A real gem.

1945   B & W   101 minutes

LOVE CHILD
★★★★

DIRECTOR: Larry Peerce
CAST: Amy Madigan, Beau Bridges, Mackenzie Phillips

Although its ads gave *Love Child* the appearance of a cheapo exploitation flick, this superb prison drama is anything but. Directed by Larry Peerce (*The Other Side of the Mountain*), it is the gripping story of a young woman, Terry Jean Moore (Amy Madigan), who became pregnant by a guard in a women's prison in Florida and fought for the right to keep her baby. Madigan gives a stirring performance. Rated R for profanity, nudity, sex, and violence.

1982   96 minutes

LOVE IN GERMANY, A
★★

DIRECTOR: Andrzej Wajda

CAST: Hanna Schygulla, Marie-Christine Barrault, Armin Mueller-Stahl, Elisabeth Trissenaar, Bernhard Wicki

During World War II, the Germans bring in Polish POWs to do menial labor. While Frau Kopp's (Hanna Schygulla) husband is off fighting, she is finding it increasingly difficult to run the family grocery store alone, so she hires a young Polish POW to handle the crates. Eventually the POW's visits to the store bring about an illicit affair. The first half of the film effectively creates the sense of danger and the political consequences of the clandestine affair but the second half receives an excessively sensationalistic treatment, ultimately diminishing the flavor and appeal. Rated R for violence, nudity.

1984   107 minutes

LOVE IS A MANY-SPLENDORED THING
★★★

DIRECTOR: Henry King
CAST: Jennifer Jones, William Holden, Isobel Elsom, Richard Loo

Clichéd story of ill-starred lovers from two different worlds who don't make it. Jennifer Jones is a Eurasian doctor who falls in love with war correspondent William Holden during the Korean conflict. Love does not win out, but the effort is superbly made. The title song was a hit.

1955   102 minutes

LOVE LETTERS
★★★★

DIRECTOR: Amy Jones
CAST: Jamie Lee Curtis, Amy Madigan, Bud Cort, James Keach

At one time or another, we've all wondered what our lives would have been like had we taken a radical step in another direction. In this impressive character study, the heroine, played by Jamie Lee Curtis, wonders aloud to her friend (Amy Madigan): "Sometimes it's right to do the wrong thing, isn't it?" But is it? Probing the emotions that lead to infidelity, *Love Letters* is a true adult motion picture. It deals explicitly with themes and ideas from which most movies shy away. This concept is intelligently explored by writer-director Amy Jones in this, her second film. Curtis's remarkable portrayal adds greatly to the believability. The result is resounding screen work that stays with the viewer long after the ending credits have rolled. Rated R for graphic sex.

1983   98 minutes

LOVE ON THE RUN
★★★½

DIRECTOR: Francois Truffaut
CAST: Jean-Pierre Léaud, Claude Jade, Marie-France Pisier

Francois Truffaut's tribute to himself. *Love on the Run* is the fifth film (*400 Blows*; *Love at Twenty*; *Stolen Kisses*; *Bed & Board*) in the series for character Antoine Doinel (Jean-Pierre Léaud). Now in his thirties and on the eve of divorce, Doinel rediscovers women. Light romantic work filled with humor and compassion. In French, with English subtitles. Rated PG.

1979   93 minutes

LOVE STORY
★★★★

DIRECTOR: Arthur Hiller
CAST: Ryan O'Neal, Ali MacGraw, Ray Milland, John Marley

Unabashedly sentimental and manipulative, this film was a box-office smash. Directed by Arthur Hiller (*Silver Streak*; *Making Love*) and adapted by Erich Segal from his best-selling novel, it features Ryan O'Neal and Ali MacGraw as star-crossed lovers who meet, marry, make it, and then discover she is dying. Liking this kind of soap opera means never having to say you're sorry. Rated PG.

1970   99 minutes

LOVE STREAMS
★★

DIRECTOR: John Cassavetes
CAST: John Cassavetes, Gena Rowlands, Diahnne Abbott, Seymour Cassel, Margaret Abbott

A rather depressing story of a writer who involves himself in the lives of lonely women for inspiration, and his emotionally unstable sister, whom he takes in after a difficult divorce has left her without possession of her child. There are some funny moments and some heartfelt scenes, as well, but John Cassavetes's direction, though suggesting more than what Ted Allan's play implies, is awkward. Rated PG-13 for language and adult situations.

1984   122 minutes

LUCAS
★★★★

DIRECTOR: David Seltzer
CAST: Corey Haim, Kerri Green, Charlie Sheen, Courtney Thorne-Smith, Winona Ryder

Charming tale of young love, leagues above the usual teen-oriented fare due to an intelligent and compassionate script by writer/director David Seltzer. Corey Haim stars as a 14-year-old whiz kid "accelerated" into high school who falls in love, during the summer between terms, with 16-year-old Kerri Green. They form a budding relationship destined to wilt upon the return to school, when Green shows interest in boys closer to her own age, notably football star Charlie Sheen (another talented son of Martin Sheen). Poignant, powerful, and quite perceptive in its examinatiion of high-school life. Rated PG-13 for language.

1986   100 minutes

MACARTHUR
★★★

DIRECTOR: Joseph Sargent
CAST: Gregory Peck, Dan O'Herlihy, Ed Flanders

Gregory Peck is cast as the famous general during the latter years of his long military career. It begins with his assumption of command of the Philippine garrison in World War II and continues through his sacking by President Truman during the Korean Conflict. The film takes a middle ground in its depiction of this complex man and the controversy that surrounded him. Peck's performance is creditable, but the film remains uneven and flat. Rated PG.

1977   130 minutes

MACARTHUR'S CHILDREN
★★

DIRECTOR: Masahiro Shinoda
CAST: Takaya Yamauchi, Yoshiyuki Omori, Shiori Shakura, Masaka Natsume, Shuji Otaki, Haruko Kato, Ken Watanabe

This import deals with effects of Japan's defeat during World War II, and its subsequent occupation by America, on a group of youngsters and adults living on a tiny Japanese island. While there are some brilliant touches by director Masahiro Shinoda, the film as a whole fails to live up to them. It is essentially a collection of vignettes that never quite come together. It results in frustration for the viewer and the feeling of having watched an overlong yet incomplete motion picture. Rated PG for profanity and suggested sex. In English with Japanese subtitles.

1984   120 minutes

MACBETH
★★★½

DIRECTOR: Roman Polanski
CAST: Jon Finch, Francesca Annis, Martin Shaw, Nicholas Selby, John Stride, Stephan Chase

The violent retelling of this classic story was commissioned and underwritten by publisher Hugh Hefner. Shakespeare's tragedy about a man driven to self-destruction by the forces of evil is vividly brought to life by director Roman Polanski, no stranger to violence and adversity himself. Grim yet compelling, this version of one of our great plays is not for everyone and contains scenes that make it objectionable for children (or sequeamish adults). The star is Jon Finch, perhaps best known as the star of Alfred Hitchcock's black comedy Frenzy.

1971   140 minutes

MACBETH
★★★

DIRECTOR: Orson Welles
CAST: Orson Welles, Roddy McDowall, Jeanette Nolan, Edgar Barrier, Dan O'Herlihy

Shakespeare's noted tragedy, filmed according to a script by Orson Welles. Interesting moviemaking on a low budget of $700,000 within a time frame of three weeks. Welles is an intriguing MacBeth, but Jeanette Nolan as his lady is out of her element. Edgar Barrier and Dan O'Herlihy are fine as Banquo and MacDuff. Wear your Kilt. Everybody speaks with a Scottish accent.

1948   B & W 105 minutes

MADAME BOVARY
★★★

DIRECTOR: Vincente Minnelli
CAST: Jennifer Jones, Louis Jourdan, Van Heflin, James Mason

Emma Bovary is an incurable romantic whose affairs of the heart ultimately lead to her destruction. Jennifer Jones is superb as Emma. Louis Jourdan plays her most engaging lover. Van Heflin portrays her betrayed husband. James Mason portrays Gustave Flaubert, on whose classic French novel the film is based.

1949　　B & W　115 minutes

MADAME ROSA
★★★★★

DIRECTOR: Moshe Mizrahi
CAST: Simone Signoret, Sammy Den Youb, Claude Dauphin

This superbly moving motion picture features Simone Signoret in one of her greatest roles. It is a simple, human story that takes place six flights up in a dilapidated building where a once-beautiful prostitute and survivor of Nazi concentration camps cares for the children of hookers. No MPAA rating.

1977　　105 minutes

MADAME X
★★★

DIRECTOR: David Lowell Rich
CAST: Lana Turner, John Forsythe, Constance Bennett, Ricardo Montalban, Burgess Meredith

In this sentimental old chestnut, filmed six times since 1909, a woman is defended against murder charges by an attorney who is not aware he is her son. Lana Turner is good and is backed by a fine cast, but Technicolor and a big budget make this one of producer Ross Hunter's mistakes. Constance Bennett's last film.

1966　　100 minutes

MAGIC TOWN
★★

DIRECTOR: William Wellman
CAST: James Stewart, Jane Wyman, Ned Sparks

After successfully collaborating with Frank Capra on some of his finest films, writer Robert Riskin teamed with director William Wellman for this mildly entertaining but preachy tale. An advertising executive (James Stewart) finds the perfect American community, which is turned topsy-turvy when the secret gets out.

1947　　B & W　103 minutes

MAGICIAN, THE
★★★

DIRECTOR: Ingmar Bergman
CAST: Max von Sydow, Ingrid Thulin, Gunnar Bjorstrand, Bibi Andersson

Dark and somber parable deals with the quest for an afterlife by focusing on confrontation between a mesmerist and a magician and their attempts to show their power over life and death. This shadowy allegory may not be everyone's idea of entertainment, but the richness of ideas and the excellent acting of director Ingmar Bergman's fine stable of dependable actors and actresses make this a compelling film with rewards on all levels. Subtitled in English.

1959　　B & W　102 minutes

MAGNIFICENT AMBERSONS, THE
★★★★★

DIRECTOR: Orson Welles
CAST: Joseph Cotten, Tim Holt, Agnes Moorehead

Orson Welles's legendary depiction of the decline of a wealthy Midwestern family and the comeuppance of its youngest member is a definite must-see motion picture. Much has been made about the callous editing of the final print by studio henchmen, but that doesn't change the total impact. It's still a classic. The stars can take bows for their acting. Special notice must be given to Welles and cameraman Stanley Cortez for the artistic, almost portraitlike, look of the film.

1942   B & W   88 minutes

MAGNIFICENT OBSESSION
★★★

DIRECTOR: Douglas Sirk
CAST: Jane Wyman, Rock Hudson, Agnes Moorehead, Otto Kruger

Rock Hudson, a drunken playboy, blinds Jane Wyman in an auto accident. Stricken, he reforms and becomes a doctor in order to restore her sight in this melodramatic tearjerker from the well-known Lloyd C. Douglas novel. First filmed in 1935, with Irene Dunne and Robert Taylor.

1954   108 minutes

MAHLER
★★½

DIRECTOR: Ken Russell
CAST: Robert Powell, Georgina Hale, Richard Morant

Ken Russell's fantasy film about the biography of composer Gustav Mahler. Robert Powell's portrayal of Mahler as a man consumed with passion and ambition is a brilliant one. Georgina Hale as Alma, Mahler's wife, is also well played. Unfortunately, the cast cannot give coherence to the script.

1974   115 minutes

MAHOGANY
★★½

DIRECTOR: Berry Gordy
CAST: Diana Ross, Anthony Perkins, Billy Dee Williams

The highlight of this unimpressive melodrama is Diana Ross's lovely wardrobe. She plays a poor girl who makes it big as a famous model and, later, dress designer after Anthony Perkins discovers her. That's when she leaves boyfriend Billy Dee Williams behind to pursue a world of glamour and success. This one jerks more yawns than tears. Rated PG.

1975   109 minutes

MAKING LOVE
★

DIRECTOR: Arthur Hiller
CAST: Kate Jackson, Michael Ontkean, Harry Hamlin

A wife (Kate Jackson) discovers that her husband (Michael Ontkean) is in love with another ... man (Harry Hamlin) in this contrived soap opera, directed by Arthur Hiller (Love Story; The In-Laws). Rated R because of adult subject matter, profanity, and implicit sexual activity.

1982   113 minutes

MALTA STORY, THE
★★★

DIRECTOR: Brian Desmond Hurst
CAST: Alec Guinness, Jack Hawkins, Anthony Steel, Muriel Pavlow

Set in 1942, this is about British pluck on the island of Malta while the British were under siege from the Axis forces and the effect the war has on private lives. Flight Lieutenant Ross's (Alec Guinness) love for a native girl (Muriel Pavlow) goes unrequited when his commanding officer (Anthony

Steel) sends him on a dangerous mission.

1953   B & W 103 minutes

MAN FOR ALL SEASONS, A
★★★★★

DIRECTOR: Fred Zinnemann

CAST: Paul Scofield, Wendy Hiller, Robert Shaw, Orson Welles, Susannah York

This splendid film, about Sir Thomas More's heartfelt refusal to help King Henry VIII break with the Catholic Church and form the Church of England, won the best-picture Oscar in 1966. Paul Scofield, who is magnificent in the title role, also won best actor. Directed by Fred Zinnemann and written by Robert Bolt, the picture also benefits from memorable supporting performances by an all-star cast.

1966   120 minutes

MAN IN GREY, THE
★★★

DIRECTOR: Leslie Arliss

CAST: Margaret Lockwood, James Mason, Phyllis Calvert, Stewart Granger, Martita Hunt

A tale of attempted husband-stealing that worked well to make the prey, James Mason, a star. Margaret Lockwood is the love thief who proves to intended victim Phyllis Calvert that with her for a friend she needs no enemies. Mason is a stand-out as the coveted husband.

1943   B & W 116 minutes

MAN, WOMAN AND CHILD
★★★½

DIRECTOR: Dick Richards

CAST: Martin Sheen, Blythe Danner, Sebastian Dungan

Here's a surprisingly tasteful and well-acted tearjerker directed by Dick Richards (Farewell My Lovely) and written by Erich Segal (Love Story). Martin Sheen stars as a married college professor who finds out he has a son in France, the result of an affair that took place there ten years before. The boy's mother, who kept their son's existence a secret, is dead—the victim of a car accident. So, with the grudging approval of his wife, Blythe Danner, Sheen decides to bring his son to America, which causes complications for the boy, the couple, and their two daughters. Rated PG for language and adult situations.

1983   99 minutes

MANDINGO
★

DIRECTOR: Richard Fleischer

CAST: James Mason, Susan George, Perry King, Richard Ward, Brenda Sykes

Sick film concerning the southern plantations before the Civil War and the treatment of the black slaves. The top-name cast should have known better. Rated R.

1975   127 minutes

MARIA'S LOVERS
★

DIRECTOR: Andrei Konchalovsky

CAST: Nastassja Kinski, John Savage, Keith Carradine, Robert Mitchum, Vincent Spano, Bud Cort

The story details the unhappy marriage of a former World War II prisoner of war (John Savage) and his loving wife (Nastassja Kinski). Only problem is there isn't too much loving going on. While Savage was in the Japanese P.O.W. camps he fantasized about being married to Kinski and imagined enduring the tortures for her. Once he comes home and actually weds her, all he can think about when they're together are the horrors of imprisonment. Finally, he seeks sexual relief with the town trollop and is caught by Kinski, so she takes up with a traveling troubadour (Keith Carradine). Can their marriage survive this? Who cares? This film, despite all its artistic pretentions, is just another dumb soap opera. Even a fine, understated performance by Robert Mitchum as Savage's father can't save it. Rated R for profanity, nudity, suggested sex, and violence.

1985   105 minutes

MARIE
★★★

DIRECTOR: Roger Donaldson
CAST: Sissy Spacek, Jeff Daniels, Keith Szarabajka, Don Hood, Fred Thompson, Rob Benson, Dawn Carmen, Shane Wexel

Sissy Spacek plays real-life heroine Marie Ragghianti, whose courage and honesty brought about the fall of a corrupt administration in Tennessee. At the beginning of the film, Marie is a battered housewife who leaves her cruel husband. Struggling to raise her three children and get an education at the same time, she works in a bar at night to make ends meet. Upon graduating, she gets a government job and works her way up to becoming the state's first female parole board head, and this is where she discovers some ugly truths. Spacek is typically fine as the title character, and Jeff Daniels does well as her shady mentor. But somehow the movie lacks punch. Rated PG-13 for violence and profanity.

1986   100 minutes

MARIUS
★★★

DIRECTOR: Alexander Korda
CAST: Raimu, Pierre Fresnay, Charpin, Alida Rouffe, Orane Demazis

This French movie is a marvelous view of the working class in Marseilles between the wars. The story revolves around Marius (Pierre Fresnay) and his love for Fanny (Orane Demazis), the daughter of a fish store proprietess. The poetic essence of the film is captured with style as Marius ships out to sea, unknowingly leaving Fanny with child. The film is based on the play by Marcel Pagnol, which in turn is the basis for the Broadway muscial *Fanny* (later filmed as a semimusical). The excess exposition may make this version turgid to Americans, but the story and peformances (especially Raimu as Marius's father) are worthwhile. In French with English subtitles.

1931   B & W 125 minutes

MARJOE
★★★½

DIRECTOR: Howard Smith, Sarah Kernochan
CAST: Marjoe Gortner

The life of evangelist-turned-actor Marjoe Gortner is traced in this entertaining documentary. Film offers the viewer a peek into the world of the traveling evangelist. When Marjoe gets his act going, the movie is at its best. At times a little stagy, but always interesting. Rated PG for language.

1972   88 minutes

MARTY
★★★★★

DIRECTOR: Delbert Mann
CAST: Ernest Borgnine, Betsy Blair, Joe De Santis

This heartwarming "little" movie about a New York butcher captured the Academy Award for best picture and another for Ernest Borgnine's poignant portrayal. In it, two lonely people manage to stumble into romance in spite of their own insecurities and the pressures of others. Based on a television production by author Paddy Chayefsky, this love story of everyday people is much more moving than the perfect "Barbie and Ken" romances of the "beautiful people" we are accustomed to watching.

1955　　　　B & W　91 minutes

MARVIN AND TIGE
★★★★

DIRECTOR: Eric Weston
CAST: John Cassavetes, Gibran Brown, Billy Dee Williams, Denise Nicholas-Hill, Fay Hauser

Touching story of a runaway (Gibran Brown) who finds a friend in a poor and lonely man (John Cassavetes). Cassavetes' beautiful loser character works so well with Brown's street-wise pomp that the tension created by the clash of personalities makes their eventual deep relationship that much more rewarding for the viewer. Rated PG for a few profane words.

1982　　　　　　104 minutes

MARY OF SCOTLAND
★★★★

DIRECTOR: John Ford
CAST: Katharine Hepburn, Fredric March, John Carradine

Katharine Hepburn plays one of history's tragic figures in director John Ford's biography of the sixteenth-century queen of Scotland. Fredric March is Bothwell, her supporter (and eventual lover) in her battle for power. The last scene, where Mary confronts her English accusers in court, is so well acted and photographed, it alone is worth the price of the rental.

1936　　　　B & W 123 minutes

MASADA
★★★★

DIRECTOR: Boris Sagal
CAST: Peter O'Toole, Peter Strauss, Barbara Carrera

A spectacular TV movie based on the famous battle of Masada during the Roman domination of the known world. Fine acting, especially by Peter O'Toole, and excellent production values elevate this one far above the average small-screen movie. Unrated.

1984　　　　　　131 minutes

MASK (1986 Release)
★★★★★

DIRECTOR: Peter Bogdanovich
CAST: Cher, Sam Elliott, Eric Stoltz, Laura Dern

They used to call them moving pictures, and few films fit this phrase as well as this one, starring Cher, Sam Elliott, and Eric Stoltz. The story of a teen-age boy coping with a disfiguring disease, it touches the viewer's heart as few movies have ever done. The only releases of recent memory in its class in this respect are *Terms of Endearment* and *E.T.* But even those two mega-hits provide poor comparison. *E.T.* is a lovely fantasy, and *Terms* is essentially a situation comedy with emotional resonance. *Mask*, on the other hand, rises above simple entertainment with its uplifting true-life tale. Rated PG13.

1985　　　　　　120 minutes

MASS APPEAL
★★★★½

DIRECTOR: Glenn Jordan
CAST: Jack Lemmon, Zeljko Ivanek, Charles Durning, Louise Latham, James Ray

A first-rate discussion of the dichotomy between private conscience and mass appeal, this film finds a mediocre and worldly priest, Father Tim Farley (Jack Lemmon), walking a political tightrope between the young seminarian (Zeljko Ivanek) he has befriended and his superior, Monsignor Burke (Charles Durning). Based on the stage play of the same title and funded as a memorial to Ray Kroc (of MacDonald's hamburger fame) by his widow, there is hardly a false note throughout. Witty, powerful, and at times both comic and tragic, it is not only a fine memorial but also a splendid motion picture. Rated PG.

1984   99 minutes

MASTER RACE, THE
★★★

DIRECTOR: Herbert J. Biberman
CAST: George Coulouris, Stanley Ridges, Osa Massen, Lloyd Bridges

Hitler's Third Reich collapses. A dedicated Nazi officer escapes. His refusal to accept defeat becomes an engrossing study of blind obedience to immorality.

1944   B & W   96 minutes

MATTER OF TIME, A
★

DIRECTOR: Vincente Minnelli
CAST: Liza Minnelli, Ingrid Bergman, Charles Boyer, Spiro Andros, Isabella Rossellini

A penniless countess takes a country-bumpkin-come-to-the-big-city hotel chambermaid in hand and feeds her dreams of becoming a famous movie star. Skipping between present and past, this is a film of small consequence made palatable by adroit editing. Director Vincente Minnelli should have and could have done far better by daughter Liza in this first collaboration. Ingrid Bergman and Charles Boyer, fading shadows of themselves, are misused. Rated PG.

1976   99 minutes

MAX DUGAN RETURNS
★★½

DIRECTOR: Herbert Ross
CAST: Jason Robards, Marsha Mason, Donald Sutherland

After spending many years in jail and gambling to big winnings, Max Dugan (Jason Robards) seeks his widowed daughter (Marsha Mason) to bestow gifts upon her and her son. Though grateful for her new-found wealth, she finds it difficult to explain to her policeman-boyfriend, Donald Sutherland. The charm of this Neil Simon fable wears thin through repetition. Rated PG.

1983   98 minutes

MAYERLING
★★★

DIRECTOR: Anatole Litvak
CAST: Charles Boyer, Danielle Darrieux, Suzy Prim, Jean Dax, Vladimir Sokoloff

Fine-tuned, convincing performances mark this French-made romantic tragedy based upon one of history's most dramatic personal incidents: Austrian Crown Prince Rudolph's ill-starred clandestine love for court lady-in-waiting Countess Marie Vetsera, in 1889. Mayerling is the royal hunting lodge where it all comes together—and falls apart. Despite a topnotch cast, a 1969 British remake stinks by comparison. In French with English subtitles.

1936   B & W   91 minutes

MCVICAR
★★★

DIRECTOR: Tom Clegg

CAST: Roger Daltrey, Adam Faith, Jeremy Blake

In this interesting British film, Roger Daltrey (lead singer for the Who) portrays John McVicar, whose real-life escape from the high-security wing of a British prison led to him being named "public enemy No. 1." Rated R.

1980   111 minutes

MEAN STREETS
★★★★½

DIRECTOR: Martin Scorsese

CAST: Robert De Niro, Harvey Keitel, Amy Robinson, Robert Carradine, David Carradine

This impressive first film by director Martin Scorsese has criminal realism and explosive violence. Robet De Niro gives a high-energy performance as a ghetto psycho in New York's Little Italy who insults a Mafia loan shark by avoiding payment. He then rips off the friend who tries to save him. This study of street life at its most savage is a cult favorite. Rated R.

1973   110 minutes

MEDIUM COOL
★★★★½

DIRECTOR: Haskell Wexler

CAST: Robert Forster, Verna Bloom, Peter Bonerz

Robert Forster stars as a television news cameraman in Chicago during the 1968 Democratic convention. All the political themes of the 1960s are here—many scenes were filmed during the riots. Cinematographer Haskell Wexler's first try at directing is a winner. Highly recommended. Rated R for nudity and language.

1969   110 minutes

MEET JOHN DOE
★★★★

DIRECTOR: Frank Capra

CAST: Gary Cooper, Barbara Stanwyck, Walter Brennan, Spring Byington

A penniless drifter (Gary Cooper) gets caught up in a newspaper publicity stunt. He is groomed and presented as the spokesman of the common man by powerful men who manipulate his every action for their own purposes. When he finally resists, he is exposed as a fraud. His fellow common men turn against him, or do they? Barbara Stanwyck is the newspaperwoman who first uses him and with whom she predictably falls in love.

1941   B & W   132 minutes

MEN, THE
★★★★

DIRECTOR: Fred Zinnemann

CAST: Marlon Brando, Jack Webb, Teresa Wright

Marlon Brando's first film, this is about a paralyzed World War II vet trying to deal with his injury. A sensitive script and good acting make this film a classic. Better than *Coming Home* in depicting vets' feelings and attitudes about readjusting to society.

1950   B & W   85 minutes

MEPHISTO
★★★★★

DIRECTOR: Istvan Szabo

CAST: Klaus Maria Brandauer, Krystyna Janda, Karin Boyd

Winner of the 1981 Academy Award for best foreign-language film, this brilliant movie, by Hungarian writer-director Istvan Szabo, examines the conceits of artists with devastating honesty and insight. Klaus Maria Brandauer, in a stunning performance, plays an actor whose overwhelming desire for artistic success leads to his becoming a puppet of the Nazi government. *Mephisto* is so powerful, so full of truth, it not only merited its Oscar, but should be considered a cinematic work of art. No MPAA rating. The film has nudity and violence. In German, with English subtitles.

1981   135 minutes

MERRY CHRISTMAS, MR. LAWRENCE
★★★½

DIRECTOR: Nagisa Oshima
CAST: David Bowie, Ryuichi Sakomoto, Tom Conti

Set in a prisoner-of-war camp in Java in 1942, this film, by Nagisa Oshima (*In the Realm of the Senses*), focuses on a clash of cultures—and wills. Oshima's camera looks on relentlessly as a British officer (David Bowie), who refuses to cooperate or knuckle under, is beaten and tortured by camp commander Ryuichi Sakomoto. Rated R for violence, strong language, and adult situations.

1983   122 minutes

MESSAGE, THE (MOHAMMAD, MESSENGER OF GOD)
★★½

DIRECTOR: Moustapha Akkad
CAST: Anthony Quinn, Irene Papas, Michael Ansara, Johnny Sekka, Michael Forest, Neville Jason

Viewers expecting to see Mohammad in this three-hour epic will be disappointed.... He never appears on the screen. Instead, we see Anthony Quinn, as Mohammad's uncle, struggling to win religious freedom for Mohammad. The film tends to drag a bit and is definitely overlong. Only those who are truly interested in following the last twenty years of Mohammad's life will be able to sit still to the end of this film. Rated PG.

1977   180 minutes

MIDNIGHT COWBOY
★★★★★

DIRECTOR: John Schlesinger
CAST: Jon Voight, Dustin Hoffman, Sylvia Miles, Barnard Hughes, Brenda Vaccaro

In this tremendous film, about the struggle for existence in the urban nightmare of New York's Forty-second Street area, Jon Voight and Dustin Hoffman deliver brilliant performances. The film won Oscars for best picture, best director (John Schlesinger), and best screenplay. Voight plays handsome Joe Buck, who arrives from Texas to make his mark as a hustler, only to be out-hustled by everyone else, including the crafty, sleazy "Ratso," superbly played by Hoffman. One of the best films of the 1960s, this has a sad but stunning twist ending. Rated R.

1969   113 minutes

MIDNIGHT EXPRESS
★★★★½

DIRECTOR: Alan Parker
CAST: Brad Davis, John Hurt, Randy Quaid

This is the true story of Billy Hayes, who was busted for trying to smuggle hashish out of Turkey and spent five years in the squalor and terror of a Turkish prison. It was brought to the screen with exquisite skill by director Alan Parker and screenwriter Oliver Stone. *Midnight Express* is not an experience easily shaken. After you see this work, the events during Hayes's imprisonment come back to haunt you long afterward. Yet it is a film for our times that teaches a powerful and important lesson. Rated R.

1978   121 minutes

MIKE'S MURDER
★★★

DIRECTOR: James Bridges
CAST: Debra Winger, Mark Keyloun

This could have been an interesting tale of a small-time Los Angeles drug dealer and part-time tennis pro who becomes involved in a drug ripoff. But the confusing plot device of having his one-night stand with Debra Winger lead to her subsequent search into why he was killed doesn't work. A much better film is buried in this unfortunate misfire. Rated R for violence, language, and nudity.

1984   97 minutes

MILDRED PIERCE
★★★★

DIRECTOR: Michael Curtiz
CAST: Joan Crawford, Jack Carson, Zachary Scott, Eve Arden, Ann Blyth, Bruce Bennett, George Tobias, Lee Patrick, Moroni Olson, Jo Ann Marlowe, Barbara Brown

A hardboiled melodrama of the strictly American *film noir* genre. Bored housewife Joan Crawford parlays waiting tables into a restaurant chain and an infatuation with Zachary Scott. Her spoiled daughter, Ann Blyth, hits on him. Emotions run high and taut as everything unravels in this A-one adaptation of James M. Cain's novel of murder and cheap love.

Her performance in the title role won Joan Crawford an Oscar for best actress.

1945   B & W 109 minutes

MILL ON THE FLOSS, THE
★★★½

DIRECTOR: Tim Whelan
CAST: Geraldine Fitzgerald, James Mason

Geraldine Fitzgerald is Maggie and James Mason is Tom Tolliver in this careful and faithful adaptation of novelist George Eliot's story of ill-starred romance in a tradition-bound English village.

1939   B & W 77 minutes

MIN AND BILL
★★★

DIRECTOR: George Hill
CAST: Marie Dressler, Wallace Beery, Dorothy Jordan, Marjorie Rambeau, Frank McGlynn

Their first picture together as a team puts Marie Dressler and Wallace Beery to the test when the future of the waif she has reared on the rough-and-tumble waterfront (Dorothy Jordan) is threatened by the girl's disreputable mother, Marjorie Rambeau. Her emotional portarayal won Marie Dressler an Oscar for best actress and helped make the film the box-office hit of its year.

1931   B & W 70 minutes

MIRACLE OF THE BELLS, THE
★★★

DIRECTOR: Irving Pichel
CAST: Fred MacMurray, Valli, Frank Sinatra, Lee J. Cobb

A miracle takes place when a movie star is buried in her coal-mining hometown. Hard-bitten press agent Fred MacMurray turns mushy to see "the kid" gets the right send-off. The story is trite and its telling too long, but the cast is earnest and the film has a way of clicking.

1948   B & W 120 minutes

MIRACLE WORKER, THE
★★★★½

DIRECTOR: Arthur Penn
CAST: Anne Bancroft, Patty Duke (Astin), Andrew Prine

Anne Bancroft and Patty Duke are superb when creating their acclaimed Broadway performances in this production. Patty Duke is the untamed and blind deaf-mute Helen Keller and Bancroft is her equally strong-willed, but compassionate, teacher. Their harrowing fight for power and the ultimately touching first communication make up one of the screen's great sequences.

1962   B & W 107 minutes

MISFITS, THE
★★★

DIRECTOR: John Huston
CAST: Marilyn Monroe, Clark Gable, Montgomery Clift, Thelma Ritter, Eli Wallach, James Barton, Estelle Winwood

Arthur Miller's parable of a hope-stripped divorcee and a gaggle of her boot-shod cowpoke boyfriends shagging wild horses in the Nevada desert, this film was the last hurrah for Marilyn Monroe and Clark Gable. The acting is good, but the storyline is mean.

1961   B & W 124 minutes

MISHIMA: A LIFE IN FOUR CHAPTERS
★★★★

DIRECTOR: Paul Schrader
CAST: Ken Ogata, Ken Swada, Yasusuka Brando, Toshiyuku Nagashimaj

By depicting this enigmatic writer's life through his art, filmmaker Paul Schrader has come close to illustrating the true heart of an artist. This is not a standard narrative biography but a bold attempt to meld an artist's life with his life's work. The movie is, as suggested in the title, divided into four parts: "Beauty," "Art," "Action," and the climactic "A Harmony of Pen and Sword." This film is not for everyone, but literary enthusiasts should appreciate its innovative approach. Rated R for sex, nudity, and adult situations.

1985   121 minutes

MISS SADIE THOMPSON
★★½

DIRECTOR: Curtis Bernhardt
CAST: Rita Hayworth, José Ferrer, Aldo Ray

A remake of *Rain*, the 1932 adaptation of Somerset Maugham's novel with Joan Crawford and Walter Huston, this production (with music) is notable only for the outstanding performance by Rita Hayworth in the title role.

1953   91 minutes

MISSING
★★★★★

DIRECTOR: Constantin Costa-Gavras
CAST: Jack Lemmon, Sissy Spacek, John Shea, Melanie Mayron, Janice Rule, David Clennon

A superb political thriller directed by Costa-Gavras (*Z; State of Siege*), this stars Jack Lemmon and Sissy Spacek as the father and wife of a young American journalist who disappears during a bloody South American coup. Rated R for violence, nudity, and profanity.

1982   122 minutes

MISSION TO GLORY
★

DIRECTOR: Ken Kennedy
CAST: Ricardo Montalban, Cesar Romero, Rory Calhoun, Michael Ansara, Keenan Wynn, Richard Egan

The true story of Father Francisco Kin, the Spanish padre who helped develop California in the late seventeenth century. This film has all the dullness of one of those elementary-school movies you were forced to suffer through, complete with narrator, soundtrack, and acting that all stoop to the occasion. You'd almost expect a pop quiz after the closing credits. As for Ricardo Montalban, Cesar Romero, and Keenan Wynn, their performances are very brief. For California historians only. Rated PG for violence.

1979   97 minutes

MR. HALPERN AND MR. JOHNSON
★★★

DIRECTOR: Alvin Rakoff
CAST: Laurence Olivier, Jackie Gleason

This one-hour show could be called My Dinner with Andre (After He Romanced My Wife). Laurence Olivier plays a recently widowed Jewish manufacturer who, to his surprise, is asked to join a seemingly well-off stranger named Johnson (Jackie Gleason) for a drink after the funeral. It seems that Johnson was once in love with the late Mrs. Halpern. What's more, they carried on a friendship (and monthly platonic get-togethers) for a number of years right up to just before her death. Mr. Halpern is, of course, shocked. And therein lies the drama of this slight tale.

1983   57 minutes

MR. KLEIN
★★★½

DIRECTOR: Joseph Losey
CAST: Alain Delon, Jeanne Moreau, Juliet Berto, Michel Lonsdale, Jean Bouise, Francine Berge

Dark-sided charcter study of a Parisian antique dealer who buys artwork and personal treasures from Jews trying to escape Paris in 1942. He (Alain Delon) finds himself mistaken for a missing Jew of the same name. This thriller builds around the search to reveal the identity of the second Mr. Klein. Rated PG. Available in French version.

1976   123 minutes

MR. SMITH GOES TO WASHINGTON
★★★★★

DIRECTOR: Frank Capra
CAST: James Stewart, Jean Arthur, Claude Rains

This Frank Capra classic is the story of a naive senator's fight against political corruption. James Stewart stars as Jefferson Smith, the idealistic scoutmaster who is appointed to fill out the term of a dead senator. Upon arriving in the capitol, he begins to get a hint of the corruption in his home state. His passionate filibuster against this corruption remains one of the most emotionally powerful scenes in film history.

1939   B & W 129 minutes

MRS. SOFFEL
★★★

DIRECTOR: Gillian Armstrong
CAST: Diane Keaton, Mel Gibson, Matthew Modine, Edward Herrmann, Trini Alvarado

We assume Australian director Gillian Armstrong's intent was to make more than a simple entertainment of this story about a warden's wife (Diane Keaton) who helps two prisoners (Mel Gibson and Matthew Modine) escape. But in aiming for this, she expands what sounded like promising material into a kind of shapeless "statement" about the plight of women at the turn of the century. Even the stars' excellent performances can't save it. Rated PG-13 for violence, suggested sex, and profanity.

1984 •   112 minutes

MISUNDERSTOOD
★

DIRECTOR: Jerry Schatzberg
CAST: Gene Hackman, Henry Thomas, Huckleberry Fox

A rich businessman (Gene Hackman) has to cope with the problem of raising two young sons (Henry Thomas, of *E.T.*, and Huckleberry Fox, of *Terms of Endearment*) who are traumatized by the sudden death of their mother. This is a dull, almost unbearable, tearjerker. Rated PG for profanity.

1984   91 minutes

MOLLY MAGUIRES, THE
★★★

DIRECTOR: Martin Ritt
CAST: Sean Connery, Richard Harris, Samantha Eggar, Frank Finlay, Art Lund

The Molly Maguires were a group of terrorists in the 1870s who fought for better conditions for the Pennsylvania coal miners. In this dramatization, Sean Connery is their leader and Richard Harris is a Pinkerton detective who infiltrates the group. The film gives a vivid portrayal of the period and the miners' dreadful existence. Performances are first-rate. Unfortunately, more people heard the theme music by Henry Mancini

than saw the movie. A little long, but worth checking out.

1970   123 minutes

MOMMIE DEAREST
★★★½

DIRECTOR: Frank Perry
CAST: Faye Dunaway, Diana Scarwid, Steve Forrest

At times this trashy screen version of Christine Crawford's controversial autobiography—which stars Faye Dunaway in an astounding performance as Joan Crawford—is so harrowing and grotesque you're tempted to stop the tape. But it's so morbidly fascinating you can't take your eyes off the screen. Rated PG.

1981   129 minutes

MONA LISA
★★★★½

DIRECTOR: Neil Jordan
CAST: Bob Hoskins, Cathy Tyson, Michael Caine, Robbie Coltrane, Clark Peters, Kate Hardie, Sammi Davies

Bob Hoskins is Britain's answer to Humphrey Bogart and James Cagney. In this crime thriller, which was crafted specifically for its star by director Neil Jordan, Hoskins plays a simple but moral man whose less than honest endeavors have landed him in prison. Upon his release, he goes to his former boss (Michael Caine) in search of a job. He gets one—driving a prostitute (Cathy Tyson) on her nightly rounds. He doesn't like the job, but he likes her. And the more he likes her, the less he can understand why she does what she does. Eventually, his quest for the truth—which comes in the form of a search for her friend, who has been enslaved by a black pimp—leads to a *Taxi Driver*-style conclusion. Hoskins equals his outstanding performance in *The Long Good Friday*. Unrated, the film has profanity, suggested sex, and violence.

1986   100 minutes

MONSIGNOR
★½

DIRECTOR: Frank Perry
CAST: Christopher Reeve, Genevieve Bujold, Fernando Rey, Jason Miller

Christopher Reeve stars in the highly implausible story of a Vatican priest who sleeps with a student nun and makes deals with the Mafia to help the Church's finances. It's an outrageous melodrama that will have you groaning in no time at all. Rated R for profanity, nudity, sex, and violence.

1982   122 minutes

MOON IN THE GUTTER, THE
★

DIRECTOR: Jean-Jacques Beineix
CAST: Gerard Depardieu, Nastassja Kinski, Victoria Abril

A pretentious, self-consciously artistic bore that seems to defy any viewer to sit through it. Gerard Depardieu, who co-stars in this piece of directorial meandering with Nastassja Kinski, was openly critical of co-scriptwriter-director Jean-Jacques Beineix, who scored such a critical and commercial success with his first film, *Diva*. Shortly after the film was completed, the prolific French film actor complained the movie didn't make any sense and had serious problems in pacing. He was absolutely right. Rated R for profanity, nudity, and violence.

1983   126 minutes

MOONLIGHTING
★★★★½

DIRECTOR: Jerzy Skolimowski
CAST: Jeremy Irons, Eugene Lipinski, Jiri Stanislav, Eugeniusz Haczkiewicz

This film, a political parable criticizing the Soviet Union's suppression of Solidarity in Poland, may sound rather heavy, gloomy, and dull. It isn't. Written and directed by Jerzy Skolimowski, it is a thoroughly entertaining film; funny, suspenseful, thought-provoking, and even exciting. It essentially focuses on four Polish construction workers remodeling a flat in London. Give it a look. In Polish, with English subtitles. Rated PG for very brief nudity.

1983   97 minutes

MOSCOW DOES NOT BELIEVE IN TEARS
★★★★

DIRECTOR: Vladimir Menshov
CAST: Vera Alentova, Irina Muravyova

You wouldn't think it possible. A sensitive, richly rewarding movie from the Soviet Union? But it's true. *Moscow Does Not Believe in Tears*, the 1981 Academy Award winner for best foreign film, is that—and then some. Few movies allow you to know their characters so well and care so much about them. Director Vladimir Menshov achieves this without resorting to the clichés and devices of soap opera. That makes it a very special experience. But for all its rewards, *Moscow Does Not Believe in Tears* requires a bit of patience on the part of the viewer. The first hour of this tragic comedy is almost excruciatingly slow. You're tempted to give up on it and walk out. But once it gets deeper into the story, you're very glad you toughed it out. MPAA unrated, but contains brief nudity and brief violence.

1980 152 minutes

MOSES
★★★

DIRECTOR: Gianfranco De Bosio
CAST: Burt Lancaster, Anthony Quayle, Irene Papas, Ingrid Thulin, William Lancaster

This biblical screen story of the Hebrew lawgiver is fairly standard as such films go. Burt Lancaster is well-suited to play the stoic Moses. However, in trimming down this six-hour miniseries for theatrical release, its makers lost most of the character development in the supporting roles. Unrated.

1975 141 minutes

MURPHY'S ROMANCE
★★★★

DIRECTOR: Martin Ritt
CAST: James Garner, Sally Field, Brian Kerwin, Corey Haim

Director Martin Ritt and star Sally Field get together again for this sweet little love story which also marks the finest performance given on film by James Garner. He's a crusty small-town pharmacist, a widower with no shortage of home-cooked meals but little interest in anything more permanent; she's a recently arrived divorcee, complete with son Corey Haim, determined to make a living by boarding and training horses. To complicate matters a little further, her ex (Brian Kerwin) shows up and tries to rekindle the flame. The story's complete inevitability isn't the point here; getting there is all the fun. Garner and Field are great together, and the result is a complete charmer. Rated PG-13.

1985 107 minutes

MURROW
★★★★

DIRECTOR: Jack Gold
CAST: Daniel J. Travanti, Dabney Coleman, Edward Herrmann, John McMartin, David Suchet, Kathryn Leigh Scott

Compassionate film about the famous radio and television journalist Edward R. Murrow, played brilliantly by Daniel Travanti (from *Hill Street Blues*). Travanti expresses Murrow's ambivalence and caution in confronting Joseph McCarthy with a subtlety worthy of an Oscar. The film devotes most of its running time to the journalist's struggle against McCarthyism. While Murrow's battle with McCarthy was, in reality, not as heroic as the filmmakers would have you believe, the drama is seductive enough to make the story very watchable. Perhaps the most fascinating issue that *Murrow* confronts is the conflict between the media's responsibility to the public and the media corporations' profit incentive. The film starts out disjointed and difficult to watch. (The cheap special effects don't help the matter, either.) Still, this is a hard one to pass up.

1985 114 minutes

MUSSOLINI AND I
★★★

DIRECTOR: Alberto Negrin
CAST: Anthony Hopkins, Susan Sarandon, Bob Hoskins, Annie Girardot, Barbara De Rossi, Dietlinde Turban, Vittorio Mezzogiorno, Fabio Testi, Kurt Raab

A weak and confusing narrative hinders this HBO film about the

Fascist leader and his family's struggle with power. Bob Hoskins (*The Long Good Friday*) plays the Italian premier with a British accent; ditto for Anthony Hopkins (*The Elephant Man*, *The Bounty*), who portrays Galeazzo Ciano, Italy's minister of foreign affairs and the dictator's brother-in-law. Still, the story is kept interesting despite its length. Not rated, but the equivalent of a PG for violence.

1985   130 minutes

MY BEAUTIFUL LAUNDERETTE
★★★★½

DIRECTOR: Stephen Frears
CAST: Saeed Jaffrey, Roshan Seth, Daniel Day Lewis, Gordon Warnecke, Shirley Anne Field

In modern-day England, a young Pakistani immigrant (Gordon Warnecke) is given a launderette by his rich uncle (Saeed Jaffrey) and, with the help of his punk-rocker boyfriend (Daniel Day Lewis), turns it into a showplace. Everything goes along reasonably well until a racist gang decides to close them down. British director Stephen Frears (*The Hit*) keeps things from becoming too heavy by adding deft touches of comedy in just the right places. The result is an uncommonly satisfying and original film on the subject of human relations. Rated R for profanity, suggested and simulated sex, and violence.

1985   103 minutes

MY BODYGUARD
★★★★★

DIRECTOR: Tony Bill
CAST: Chris Makepeace, Matt Dillon, Martin Mull, Ruth Gordon

This is a wonderfully funny and touching movie. This story (by Alan Ormsby) deals with a situation that all ages can identify with. Fifteen-year-old Clifford Peache (Chris Makepeace) must face the challenges of public high school (in Chicago, no less) after nine years of private education. His classes are easy. It's his schoolmates who cause problems. Specifically, there's Moody (Matt Dillon), a good-looking but nasty young thug who extorts money from the other students. He and his gang terrorize the younger, less aggressive kids unmercifully—until Clifford comes along. Unaccustomed to dealing with hoodlums like Moody, Clifford refuses to pay the protection money demanded by the gang. This attitude threatens Moody's little empire, and Clifford's days at school turn into a continuing nightmare. Rated PG.

1980   96 minutes

MY BRILLIANT CAREER
★★★★½

DIRECTOR: Gillian Armstrong
CAST: Judy Davis, Sam Neill, Wendy Hughes

A superb Australian import, *My Brilliant Career* is about a young woman clearly born before her time. It is the waning years of the nineteenth century, when the only respectable status for a woman is to be married. Sybylla Melvyn (Judy Davis), who lives with her family in the Australian bush, does not want to marry. She has "immortal longings," and—when pressed by her conventional and rather perplexed mother—she reveals, "I want to be a concert pianist." Rated G.

1979   101 minutes

MY DINNER WITH ANDRE
★★★★★

DIRECTOR: Louis Malle

CAST: Andre Gregory, Wallace Shawn

One of the most daring films ever made, this fascinating work consists almost entirely of a dinner conversation between two men. It's a terrific little movie. You'll be surprised how entertaining it is. No MPAA rating. The film has no objectionable material.

1981   110 minutes

MY FIRST WIFE
★★★½
DIRECTOR: Paul Cox
CAST: John Hargreaves, Wendy Hughes

In the tradition of *Ordinary People*, *Kramer vs Kramer*, *Shoot the Moon*, and *Smash Palace* comes another film about the dissolution of a marriage. This film contains scenes that rival some of the best and worst of those movies. The story deals with a classical music programmer/composer who finds that his wife doesn't love him anymore. Unlike some of the other films, this one ends on a positive, albeit somber note. Rated PG for adult situations and language.

1985   95 minutes

MY NIGHT AT MAUD'S
★★★★
DIRECTOR: Eric Rohmer
CAST: Jean-Louis Trintignant, Françoise Fabian, Marie-Christine Barrault, Antoine Vitez

My Night At Maud's was the first feature by Eric Rohmer to be shown in the United States. It is the third film of the cycle he called *Six Moral Tales*. The premise of the morality is quite simple: A man is in love with a woman, but his eyes wander to another. However, the transgression is only brief, for, according to Rohmer, the only true love is the love ordained by God. Beautifully photographed in black and white, the camera looks the actors straight in the eye and captures every nuance. The acting is sedate and dignified (that is *not* a euphemism for boring), especially the portrayal of Jean-Louis by Jean-Louis Trintignant. This is French cinema at its best. No pretenses, just honest story-telling. In French with English subtitles.

1970   B & W 105 minutes

MY OLD MAN
★★★★
DIRECTOR: John Erman
CAST: Warren Oates, Kristy McNichol, Eileen Brennan

Excellent made-for-television adaptation of a short story by Ernest Hemingway about a down-on-his-luck horse trainer (Warren Oates) and the daughter (Kristy McNichol) who loves him even more than horses. Oates gives a fabulous performance; certainly one of the best of his too-brief career. Eileen Brennan lends support as a sympathetic waitress. Made once before for the big screen, in 1950, and called *Under My Skin*. A good, solid drama, though filled with Hemingway's characteristically depressing scenarios. Unrated; suitable for family viewing.

1979   104 minutes

MY OTHER HUSBAND
★★★★
DIRECTOR: Georges Lautner
CAST: Miou-Miou, Roger Hanin, Eddie Mitchell, Charlotte de Tuckheim, Dominique Lavanant, Rachid Ferrache

At first, this French import starring the marvelous Miou-Miou seems rather like a scatterbrained, faintly funny retread of the old person-with-two-spouses comedy

plot (à la *Micki & Maude*, etc.).
But it goes on to become an affecting, sweetly sad little treasure.
In French with English subtitles.
Rated PG-13 for profanity.

1981   110 minutes

NAPOLEON
★

DIRECTOR: Sacha Guitry
CAST: Orson Welles, Maria Schell,
Yves Montand, Erich von
Stroheim

It seems inconceivable that Napoleon, who towered historically over Patton, MacArthur, and Rommel and is equaled only by Attila the Hun and Alexander the Great, could be the subject of such an insignificant little film. This offering mumbles its way from nowhere to nowhere with little along the way. It's boring.

1955   115 minutes

NAPOLEON (1986 Release)
★★★★★

DIRECTOR: Abel Gance
CAST: Albert Dieudonné, Antonin
Artaud

The first film to use the three-screen process, director Abel Gance's 1927 silent epic may be the greatest cinematic event of the century. Over a half century after its debut, *Napoleon* remains a visual wonder, encompassing a number of film-making techniques, some of which still seem revolutionary. The complete film—as pieced together by British film historian Kevin Brownlow over a period of twenty years—is one motion picture event no lover of the art form will want to miss even on the small screen without the full effect of its spectacular three-screen climax.

1927   B & W 235 minutes

NASHVILLE
★★★★★

DIRECTOR: Robert Altman
CAST: Keith Carradine, Lily Tomlin,
Ned Beatty, Henry Gibson,
Karen Black, Ronee Blakley

Robert Altman's classic study of American culture is, on the surface, a look into the country-western music business. But underneath, Altman has many things to say about all of us. Great ensemble acting by Keith Carradine, Lily Tomlin, Ned Beatty, and Henry Gibson, to name just a few, makes this one of the great films of the 1970s. Rated R for language and violence.

1975   159 minutes

NATURAL, THE
★★★★

DIRECTOR: Barry Levinson
CAST: Robert Redford, Robert Duvall, Glenn Close, Kim Basinger, Wilford Brimley,
Richard Farnsworth

A thoroughly rewarding, old-fashioned screen entertainment, this adaptation of Bernard Malamud's novel about an unusually gifted baseball player is a must-see. With its brilliant all-star cast, superb story, unforgettable characters, sumptuous cinematography, and sure-handed direction, this two-and-a-half–hour feast of film-watching recalls the Golden Age of Hollywood at its best. Rated PG for brief violence.

1984   134 minutes

NEA (A YOUNG EMMANUELLE)
★★★

DIRECTOR: Nelly Kaplan
CAST: Sammy Frey, Ann Zacharias,
Micheline Presle, Francoise
Brion, Heinz Bennent

In this French sex comedy, a young girl, Sybille Ashby (Ann Zacharias), stifled by the wealth of her parents turns to anonymously writing erotic literature via first-hand experience. Her anonymity betrayed, she perfects her novel, *Nea*, by the sweetest revenge she can devise. A relatively successful and entertaining film of its kind, this has sex and adult themes. In French, with English subtitles. Rated R.

1978　103 minutes

NETWORK
★★★★★
DIRECTOR: Sidney Lumet
CAST: Peter Finch, William Holden, Faye Dunaway, Robert Duvall, Ned Beatty

"I'm mad as hell and I'm not going to take it anymore!" Peter Finch (who won a posthumous Academy Award for best actor), William Holden, Faye Dunaway, Robert Duvall, and Ned Beatty give superb performances in this black comedy about the world of television as penned by Paddy Chayefsky. It's a biting satire on the inner workings of this century's most powerful medium. Rated R.

1976　121 minutes

NEVER LET GO
★★
DIRECTOR: John Guillermin
CAST: Peter Sellers, Richard Todd, Elizabeth Sellars, Carol White, Mervyn Johns

Peter Sellers bombs out in his first dramatic role as a ruthless criminal in this thin story about car stealing. The sure acting of Mervyn Johns, longtime dependable supporting player, helps things but cannot begin to save the film. Nor can Richard Todd's efforts.

1960　B & W　90 minutes

NEVER ON SUNDAY
★★★★
DIRECTOR: Jules Dassin
CAST: Melina Mercouri, Jules Dassin

A wimpy egghead tries to make a lady out of an earthy, fun-loving prostitute. The setting is Greece; the dialogue and situations are delightful. Melina Mercouri is terrific.

1960　91 minutes

NEW CENTURIONS, THE
★★★★
DIRECTOR: Richard Fleischer
CAST: George C. Scott, Stacy Keach, Jane Alexander, Erik Estrada

The New Centurions is a blend of harsh reality and soap opera. The moral seems to be "It is no fun being a cop." Watching George C. Scott and Stacy Keach get their lumps, we have to agree. Rated R.

1972　103 minutes

NEWSFRONT
★★★★
DIRECTOR: Phillip Noyce
CAST: Bill Hunter, Wendy Hughes, Gerald Kennedy

A story of a newsreel company from 1948 until technology brought its existence to an end, this is a warm and wonderful film about real people. It's an insightful glimpse at the early days of the news business, with good character development. Rated PG.

1978　110 minutes

NICHOLAS AND ALEXANDRA
★★
DIRECTOR: Franklin Schaffner
CAST: Michael Jayston, Janet Suzman, Tom Baker, Laurence Olivier, Michael Redgrave

This is an overlong, overdetailed depiction of the events preceding the Russian Revolution until the deaths of Czar Nicholas (Michael Jayston), his wife (Janet Suzman) and family. Some of the performances are outstanding, particularly Suzman's, and the sets and costumes are topnotch. However, the film gets mired in trying to encompass too much historical detail. Rated PG.

1971   183 minutes

NICHOLAS NICKLEBY
★★★½
DIRECTOR: Alberto Cavalcanti
CAST: Derek Bond, Cedric Hardwicke, Sally Ann Howes, Cathleen Nesbitt, Alfred Drayton

Proud but penniless young Nicholas Nickleby struggles to forge a life for himself and his family while contending with a money-mad scheming uncle and lesser villains. Good acting and authentic Victorian settings bring this classic Dickens novel to vivid screen life. Not quite in the mold of *Great Expectations*, but well above average.

1947   B & W 108 minutes

NIGHT AND DAY
★★
DIRECTOR: Michael Curtiz
CAST: Cary Grant, Alexis Smith, Jane Wyman, Monty Woolley, Eve Arden

The life of composer Cole Porter, told with cloying pretension. The story vaguely resembles truth and is mostly song-stuffed baloney. The film is too long, too smug, and too deceiving. Cary Grant sings, Alexis Smith tries, and Monty Woolley is funny now and then.

1946   128 minutes

NIGHT GAMES
★★★
DIRECTOR: Don Taylor
CAST: Barry Newman, Susan Howard, Albert Salmi, Luke Askew, Ralph Meeker, Stephanie Powers

This film, which was originally made for television, led to the "Petrocelli" TV series for Barry Newman. He plays a lawyer who defends Stephanie Powers when she's accused of her husband's murder. There's enough intrigue and suspense in this film to capture most viewers' attention. Rated R.

1974   78 minutes

NIGHT IN HEAVEN, A

DIRECTOR: John G. Avildsen
CAST: Lesley Ann Warren, Christopher Atkins, Robert Logan, Carrie Snodgress

As incredible as it may seem, this movie is just as bad and tasteless as it appears to be. Lesley Ann Warren (*Choose Me*) plays a respectable college teacher who falls in lust with student/male stripper Christopher Atkins (*Blue Lagoon*). All in all, it's a movie to forget. Rated R for nudity, slight profanity, and simulated sex.

1983   80 minutes

NIGHT OF THE IGUANA, THE
★★★
DIRECTOR: John Huston
CAST: Richard Burton, Ava Gardner, Deborah Kerr, Sue Lyon

Mexico sets the scene for Richard Burton (as Reverend Shannon), Ava Gardner (as Maxine, who runs the hotel), and Deborah Kerr (the unhappy old maid). In this film, based on Tennessee Williams's play, Burton is a former minister trying to be reinstated in his church. Meanwhile, he takes a menial job as a tour guide, from which he gets fired. His attempted suicide is foiled and confusing. Finally, he finds other reasons to continue living. Sound dull? If not for the stars, it would be.

1964 B & W 118 minutes

NIGHT OF THE SHOOTING STARS
★★½

DIRECTORS: Paolo and Vittorio Taviani
CAST: Omero Antonutti, Margarita Lozano

Made by Paolo and Vittorio Taviani (*Padre Padrone*), this Italian import is about the flight of peasants from their mined village in pastoral Tuscany during the waning days of World War II. Despite its subject matter, the horrors of war, it is a strangely unaffecting—and ineffective—motion picture. It has no central character or strong dramatic thrust. Instead, it is a series of vignettes. Consequently, though it runs only 104 minutes, the film seems much longer. In Italian, with English subtitles. Unrated, the film has violence.

1982 104 minutes

NIGHT PORTER, THE
★★

DIRECTOR: Liliana Cavani
CAST: Dirk Bogarde, Charlotte Rampling, Philippe Leroy, Gabriele Ferzetti, Isa Miranda

Sordid little outing about a sadomasochistic relationship between an ex-Nazi and the woman he used to abuse sexually in a concentration camp. With the darkly sensual Charlotte Rampling, and the irritating Dirk Bogarde. Lots of kinky scenes, including love-

making on broken glass. Rated R for violence, nudity, and profanity.

1974 115 minutes

NIGHT THE LIGHTS WENT OUT IN GEORGIA, THE
★★★½

DIRECTOR: Rowald F. Maxwell
CAST: Kristy McNichol, Mark Hamill, Dennis Quaid, Sunny Johnson, Don Stroud

Gutsy, lusty, and satisfying film about a country singer (Dennis Quaid) with wayward appetites and his level-headed sister-manager (Kristy McNichol) who run into big trouble while working their way to Nashville. The gritty deep-South settings, fine action, a cast of credible extras, some memorable musical moments, and a dramatic script with comic overtones add up to above-average entertainment. Rated PG.

1981 120 minutes

9 1/2 WEEKS
★★

DIRECTOR: Adrian Lyne
CAST: Mickey Rourke, Kim Basinger, Margaret Whitton, David Margulies, David Branski, Karen Young

Adrian Lyne (*Flashdance*) creates some exceptional music video-type sequences in adapting the Elizabeth McNeil book. Somewhere between toning down the bondage and liberating the heroine in this adaptation, the story definitely loses out to the imagery. Mickey Rourke is quite believable in the lead role of the masochistic seducer, but Kim Basinger does little more than look pretty. However, together this couple makes steamy work of simple things like dressing and eating. Rated R for sex and violence.

1986   116 minutes

NINTH CONFIGURATION, THE
★★★★½

DIRECTOR: William Peter Blatty

CAST: Stacy Keach, Scott Wilson, Jason Miller, Ed Flanders, Neville Brand, George Di Dicenzo, Moses Gunn, Robert Loggia, Joe Spinell, Alejandro Rey, Tom Atkins

This terse, intense film is not for everyone; a barroom brawl near the film's close is one of the most uncomfortable scenes in all of flickdom, but the plot, screenplay, and acting are topnotch. Stacy Keach plays a psychiatrist caring for Vietnam War veterans who suffer from acute emotional disorders. The drama is at first light and focuses on the patients but soon shifts to Keach taking on a more serious tone. Any more and we'd be spilling the beans. Rated R for profanity and violence.

1979   115 minutes

NO WAY TO TREAT A LADY
★★★★

DIRECTOR: Jack Smight

CAST: Rod Steiger, George Segal, Lee Remick, Eileen Heckart, Michael Dunn, Murray Hamilton

Excellent thriller with a tour-de-force performance by Rod Steiger, who dons various disguises and personas to strangle women and imprint them with red lipstick lips. Superb script, adapted from William Goldman's novel, and a skilled supporting cast: George Segal as a mothered cop, Eileen Heckart as his delightfully pick-pick-picking mother, and Lee Remick as the attractive love interest. Segal and company get all the good lines, but the show belongs to Steiger; not since Alec Guinness in *Kind Hearts and Coronets* has an actor so successfully taken so many roles in a single picture. Don't miss this. Rated PG for violence.

1968   108 minutes

NONE BUT THE LONELY HEART
★★★

DIRECTOR: Clifford Odets

CAST: Cary Grant, Ethel Barrymore, Barry Fitzgerald, Jane Wyatt, June Duprez, Dan Duryea

Old pro Ethel Barrymore won an Oscar for her sympathetic portrayal of moody, whining Cockney Cary Grant's mother Ma Mott in this murky drama of broken dreams, thwarted hopes, and petty crime in the slums of London in the late 1930s. Director Clifford Odets and star Grant never get together, yet the film has a certain appeal. Nothing else like it in the Grant filmography.

1944   B & W 113 minutes

NORMA RAE
★★★★

DIRECTOR: Martin Ritt

CAST: Sally Field, Ron Leibman, Pat Hingle, Beau Bridges

Sally Field won her first Oscar for her outstanding performance as a southern textile worker attempting to unionize the mill with the aid of organizer Ron Leibman. Film is based on a true story and has good eyes and ears for authenticity. Entire cast is first-rate. Rated PG, some language, minor violence.

1979   113 minutes

NORTH DALLAS FORTY
★★★★½

DIRECTOR: Ted Kotcheff

CAST: Nick Nolte, Bo Svenson, G. D. Spradlin, Dayle Haddon, Mac Davis

Remarkably enough, *North Dallas Forty* isn't just another numbingly predictable sports film. It's an offbeat, sometimes brutal, examination of the business of football. Not that it isn't entertaining. Director Ted Kotcheff has a fine feel for the outrageous and genuinely funny and makes the most of it in this picture. Yet the overriding theme is one of exploitation for profit and self-realization. Kotcheff turns it all into a compelling mixture. A first-rate Nick Nolte stars, and the film has other superb performances. Bo Svenson is a knockout as a not-too-bright-but-lethal star player. G. D. Spradlin oozes calculated menace as the coach. Dayle Haddon gives depth to her role as Nolte's concerned lover, and even singer/songwriter Mac Davis is convincing as a laconic, aging quarterback. Rated R.

1979   119 minutes

NOTHING IN COMMON
★★★

DIRECTOR: Garry Marshall
CAST: Tom Hanks, Jackie Gleason, Eva Marie Saint, Hector Elizondo, Barry Corbin, Bess Armstrong, Sela Ward

In his most impressive performance to date, Tom Hanks plays a hotshot advertising executive who must deal with his increasingly demanding parents, who are divorcing after thirty-four years of marriage. Jackie Gleason gives a subtle, touching portrayal of the father. The film succeeds at making the difficult shift from zany humor to pathos. Rated PG for profanity and suggested sex.

1986   120 minutes

NOW AND FOREVER
★

DIRECTOR: Adrian Carr
CAST: Cheryl Ladd, Robert Coleby, Carmen Duncan

In this sappy romance flick, Cheryl Ladd (formerly of television's "Charlie's Angels") is a boutique owner who comes back from a clothes-buying trip to New York to find that her husband (Robert Coleby) has been accused of rape. This Australian production has a good first half, with fine acting and strong suspense, and a perfectly awful second half, where drama and logic are abandoned in favor of sequences that look like outtakes from perfume commercials. In other words, it's a mess. Rated R for violence, profanity, and sex.

1983   93 minutes

NOW, VOYAGER
★★★½

DIRECTOR: Irving Rapper
CAST: Bette Davis, Claude Rains, Paul Henreid

"As far as I'm concerned, it's the greatest one of all!" said Bette Davis of this tearjerker. Davis plays a neurotic, unattractive spinster named Charlotte Vail; an ugly duckling, who, of course, blossoms into a beautiful swan. And it's all thanks to the expert counsel of her psychiatrist (Claude Rains) and a shipboard romance with a married man (Paul Henreid). Directed by Irving Rapper, it features the famous cigarette-lighting ritual that set a trend in the 1940s. Davis considers it one of her favorites—primarily because it was one of the few films that came out right during her contract years at Warner Bros. Once again, she had to fight for the role.

Originally, Irene Dunne was supposed to star in the film.

1942   B & W 117 minutes

NURSE EDITH CAVELL
★★★

DIRECTOR: Herbert Wilcox
CAST: Anna Neagle, Edna May Oliver, George Sanders, ZaSu Pitts, H. B. Warner, May Robson, Robert Coote, Martin Kosleck, Fritz Leiber, Mary Howard

The story of England's second most famous nurse, who helped transport refugee soldiers out of German-held Belgium during World War I. The film delivered a dramatically satisfying antiwar message just as World War II got under way.

1939   B & W 95 minutes

O LUCKY MAN!
★★★★

DIRECTOR: Lindsay Anderson
CAST: Malcolm McDowell, Rachel Roberts, Ralph Richardson, Alan Price, Lindsay Anderson

Offbeat, often stunning story of a young salesman (Malcolm McDowell) and his efforts and obstacles in reaching the top rung of the success ladder. Allegorical and surrealistic at times, this film takes its own course like a fine piece of music. Great acting by a great cast (many of the principals play multiple roles) makes this a real viewing pleasure. Although it is very long, this film is at once a full course in film-making and a rewarding study of corporate power and control. Some adult situations and language. Rated R.

1973   173 minutes

OCCURRENCE AT OWL CREEK BRIDGE, AN
★★★½

DIRECTOR: La Riviere du Hibou
CAST: Roger Jacquet, Anne Cornaly

This fascinating French film looks at the last fleeting moments of the life of a man being hanged from the bridge of the title during the American Civil War. This memorable short film works on all levels.

1962   B & W 22 minutes

ODD ANGRY SHOT, THE
★★★

DIRECTOR: Tom Jeffrey
CAST: Bryan Brown, John Hargreaves, Graham Kennedy, John Jarratt

This low-key film about Australian soldiers stationed in Vietnam during the undeclared war is a good attempt to make sense out of a senseless situation as Bryan Brown and his comrades attempt to come to grips with the reality and morality of their involvement in a fight they have no heart for. Odd, sometimes highly effective blend of comedy and drama characterize this offbeat war entry. Some violence; adult situations and language.

1979   89 minutes

ODE TO BILLY JOE
★★★

DIRECTOR: Max Baer
CAST: Robby Benson, Glynnis O'Connor, Joan Hotchkis

For those who listened to Bobbie Gentry's hit song and wondered why Billy Joe jumped off the Talahachi Bridge, this movie tries to provide one hypothesis. Robby Benson plays Billy Joe with just the right amount of innocence and confusion to be convincing as a youth who doubts his sexual orientation. Rated PG.

1976   108 minutes

OF HUMAN BONDAGE (ORIGINAL)
★★★★½

DIRECTOR: John Cromwell
CAST: Bette Davis, Leslie Howard, Alan Hale, Frances Dee

A young doctor (Leslie Howard) becomes obsessed with a sluttish waitress (Bette Davis), almost causing his downfall. Fine acting by all, with Davis an absolute knockout. No rating, but still a little adult for the kiddies.

1934   B & W   83 minutes

OF HUMAN BONDAGE (REMAKE)
★★★★½

DIRECTOR: Kenneth Hughes
CAST: Kim Novak, Laurence Harvey, Robert Morley, Siobhan McKenna, Roger Livesey, Jack Hedley, Nanette Newman, Ronald Lacey

Excellent remake of the 1934 film with Bette Davis. This time Kim Novak plays Mildred Rogers, the promiscuous free spirit who becomes the obsession of Philip Carey (Laurence Harvey). Harvey's performance is wonderfully understated, and Novak plays the slut to the hilt without overdoing it. With the attention going to the two main characters, something must be said about Siobhan McKenna, who plays the soft-spoken Nora Nesbitt, who takes in the lovestruck Carey for a short period. Her matronlike appearance and disposition give the part she plays the pathos that adds to the complexity of emotions that spill out from W. Somerset Maugham's story of obsession.

1964   B & W 100 minutes

OF MICE AND MEN
★★★½

DIRECTOR: Reza Badiyi
CAST: Robert Blake, Randy Quaid, Lew Ayres, Pat Hingle, Cassie Yates

Robert Blake is George, Randy Quaid is big, dimwitted Lenny in this Blake-produced TV remake of the classic 1939 Burgess Meredith/Lon Chaney Jr. rendition of John Steinbeck's morality tale of migrant-working life on a California ranch during the Depression. While not as sensitive as the original, this version merits attention and appreciation.

1981   125 minutes

OFFICER AND A GENTLEMAN, AN
★★★★½

DIRECTOR: Taylor Hackford
CAST: Richard Gere, Debra Winger, Louis Gossett Jr., David Keith, Harold Sylvester

Soap opera has never been art. However, this funny, touching, corny, and predictable movie, starring Richard Gere and Debra Winger, takes the genre as close to it as any of the old three-hand-kerchief classics—i.e., Now Voyager; Waterloo Bridge; Gone with the Wind—ever did. Director Taylor Hackford keeps just the right balance between the ridiculous and the sublime, making An Officer and a Gentleman one of the best of its kind. Rated R for nudity, profanity, and simulated sex.

1982   125 minutes

OH, ALFIE
★

DIRECTOR: Ken Hughes
CAST: Alan Price, Jill Townsend, Joan Collins, Annie Ross, Sheila White, Rula Lenska, Paul Copley, Hannah Gordon

Alan Price is an uncaring ladies' man who beds every woman he comes in contact with and then goes on to the next conquest. But there's always one who resists, isn't there? This time it's Jill Townsend, a successful business-woman who seems most unsuited to our trucker Lothario. About the only interest in this cheap sequel to the classic *Alfie* is a nude Joan Collins. Rated R for nudity, language, and sex.

1975   99 minutes

OLD BOYFRIENDS
★½

DIRECTOR: Joan Tewkesbury
CAST: Talia Shire, Richard Jordan, Keith Carradine, John Belushi, John Houseman, Buck Henry

Fresh from her successes in *The Godfather* and *Rocky* series, Talia Shire plunged into this muddled morass about a woman who decides to exact some revenge on those men who made her past miserable. The viewer is miserable, too, within a very few minutes of this picture, which can't be saved even by John Belushi. Rated R for profanity and violence.

1979   103 minutes

OLD ENOUGH
★

DIRECTOR: Marisa Silver
CAST: Sarah Boyd, Rainbow Harvest, Neill Barry, Danny Aiello

A pre-pubescent "coming of age" movie. The two principal characters live on opposite sides of the tracks. It is their curiosity about each other and their radically different lifestyles that spark their friendship, or so we are led to believe. This film, while showing great promise and potential from both the character portrayals and

the story, fails to deliver. The picture is plagued with a major problem from start to finish. Sarah Boyd's character, the rich kid, is always trying to please her street-wise friend, while the tough girl (Rainbow Harvest) never really tries to meet her nice friend halfway. There is a vain attempt to pad the script with a little diversion from Danny Aiello, who portrays the rough kid's father, but this also ends up feeling very narrow and shallow. Rated PG.

1984   91 minutes

OLIVER TWIST
★★★★

DIRECTOR: David Lean
CAST: Alec Guinness, Robert Newton, John Howard Davies

Alec Guinness and Robert Newton give superb performances as the villains in this David Lean adaptation of the Charles Dickens story about a young boy who is forced into a life of thievery until he's rescued by a kindly old gentleman.

1948   B & W 105 minutes

OLIVER TWIST
★★

DIRECTOR: William Cowen
CAST: Dickie Moore, Irving Pichel, William Boyd, Doris Lloyd

This early talkie version of the Charles Dickens tale about a London youngster who falls among thieves is no match for the classic 1948 British version, directed by David Lean. What the latter has in atmosphere, great performances, and riveting drama this low-budget release completely lacks.

1933   B & W   77 minutes

OLIVER'S STORY
★

DIRECTOR: John Korty
CAST: Ryan O'Neal, Candice Bergen, Nicola Pagett, Edward Binns, Ray Milland

Even if you loved *Love Story* you'll find it difficult to like this lame sequel. O'Neal's character apparently decides money's not so bad after all and courts an heiress. Movies like this mean always having to say you're sorry. Rated PG.

1978   92 minutes

ON GOLDEN POND
★★★★★

DIRECTOR: Mark Rydell
CAST: Henry Fonda, Katharine Hepburn, Jane Fonda, Doug McKeon

Henry Fonda, Katharine Hepburn, and Jane Fonda are terrific in this warm, funny, and often quite moving film, written by Ernest Thompson, about the conflicts and reconciliations among the members of a family that take place during a fateful summer. Rated PG because of brief profanity.

1981   109 minutes

ON THE WATERFRONT
★★★★★

DIRECTOR: Elia Kazan
CAST: Marlon Brando, Eva Marie Saint, Karl Malden, Lee J. Cobb, Rod Steiger

Tough, uncompromising look at corruption on the New York waterfront. Marlon Brando is brilliant as Terry Malloy, a one-time fight contender who is now a longshoreman. Led into crime by his older brother (Rod Steiger), Terry is disgusted by the violent tactics of boss Lee J. Cobb. Yet if he should turn against the crooks, it could mean his life. A classic American film with uniformly superb performances.

1954   B & W   108 minutes

ONE AND ONLY, THE
★★★

DIRECTOR: Carl Reiner
CAST: Henry Winkler, Kim Darby, Herve Villechaize, Harold Gould, Gene Saks, William Daniels

Writer Steve Gordon (*Arthur*) got started with this tale of an obnoxious college show-off who eventually finds fame as a wrestling showboater. Henry Winkler was still struggling to find a big-screen personality, but his occasional character flaws often are overshadowed by Gordon's deft little script. The material has become more timely, considering the current fascination with big-time wrestling. Rated PG.

1978   98 minutes

ONE FLEW OVER THE CUCKOO'S NEST
★★★★★

DIRECTOR: Milos Forman
CAST: Jack Nicholson, Louise Fletcher, Will Sampson, Danny DeVito, Christopher Lloyd, Scatman Crothers

Not since Capra's *It Happened One Night* had a motion picture swept all the major Academy Awards. This stunning film deserved to become the second picture to receive that honor. Jack Nicholson sparkles as Randall P. McMurphy, a convict who is committed to a northwestern mental institution for examination. While there, he stimulates in each of his ward inmates an awakening spirit of self-worth and frees them from their passive acceptance of the hospital authorities' domination. Louise Fletcher is brilliant as the insensitive head nurse. This film is one of those rarities that get better with each viewing. Rated R.

1975   133 minutes

ONE MAGIC CHRISTMAS
★★★★½

DIRECTOR: Phillip Borsos
CAST: Mary Steenburgen, Harry Dean Stanton, Gary Basaraba, Arthur Hill, Elizabeth Harnois, Robbie Magwood, Ken Pogue

Mary Steenburgen stars in this touching, feel-good movie as a young mother who has lost the spirit of Christmas. She regains it with the help of her 6-year-old daughter (Elizabeth Harnois) and a Christmas angel (played by that terrific character actor Harry Dean Stanton). The story is somewhat reminiscent of Frank Capra's *It's a Wonderful Life*, in which a good man (James Stewart) is so busy helping others that he finds life passing him by. He wishes he had never been born and gets his wish, an experience that reveals to him the true joys of living. In *One Magic Christmas*, Steenburgen loses something more important than her life. So heartrending is her plight that we sat watching the movie with lumps in our throats. Be not deceived, however. Although this movie has quite a bit of dramatic power, its ultimate purpose is to uplift, and this it does marvelously and memorably. Rated G.

1985   95 minutes

ONE ON ONE
★★★★

DIRECTOR: Lamont Johnson
CAST: Robby Benson, Annette O'-Toole, G. D. Spradlin

The harsh world of big-time college athletics is brought into clearer focus by this unheralded "little film." Robby Benson is a naive small-town basketball star who has his eyes opened when he wins a scholarship to a large western university. He doesn't play up to his coach's expectations, and the pressure is put on to take away his scholarship. Annette O'Toole turns in a winning performance as Benson's helpmate. Rated R.

1980   98 minutes

ONE SINGS, THE OTHER DOESN'T
★★½

DIRECTOR: Agnes Varda
CAST: Valerie Mairesse, Thérèse Liotard

Labeled early on as a feminist film, this story is about a friendship between two different types of women spanning 1962 to 1976. When they meet again at a women's rally after ten years, they renew their friendship by discussing events in their lives.

1977   105 minutes

ONE WILD MOMENT
★★★★

DIRECTOR: Claude Berri
CAST: Jean-Pierre Marielle, Victor Lanoux, Agnes Soral, Christine Dejoux, Martine Sarcey

In French director Claude Berri's warm and very sensitive film, a middle-aged man (Jean-Pierre Marielle) is told by his best friend's daughter (Agnes Soral) that she's in love with him. Not knowing whether to tell his friend (Victor Lanoux) about it or not, our hero lets things go a bit too far one night and she seduces him. Enjoy the story (which was adapted by director Stanley Donen for *Blame it on Rio* as it should be told, as delicately and thoughtfully handled by Berri. Unrated, the film has sex, nudity, and profanity.

1980 90 minutes

ONION FIELD, THE
★★★½

DIRECTOR: Harold Becker
CAST: John Savage, James Woods, Franklyn Seales, Ted Danson, Ronny Cox

Based on Joseph Wambaugh's book, this is a tough, uncompromising crime drama. John Savage, James Woods, and Franklyn Seales star in this true story of a cop killing that suffers a bit from trying to stay too true to the events and thus loses a fair amount of dramatic punch. It's still interesting for what it attempts to do. Rated R for violence and profanity.

1979 122 minutes

ONLY WHEN I LAUGH
★★★

DIRECTOR: Glenn Jordan
CAST: Marsha Mason, Kristy McNichol, James Coco, Joan Hackett

A brilliant but self-destructive actress (Marsha Mason) and her daughter (Kristy McNichol) reach toward understanding in this sometimes funny, sometimes tearful, but always entertaining adaptation by Neil Simon of his play *The Gingerbread Lady.* Rated R for profanity.

1981 121 minutes

OPEN CITY
★★★★½

DIRECTOR: Robert Rossellini
CAST: Aldo Fabrizi, Anna Magnani, Marcello Pagliero, Harry Feist, Vito Annicchiarico, Nando Bruno, Giovanna Galletti

Stunning study of resistance and survival in World War II Italy was the first important film to come out of postwar Europe and has been considered a classic in realism. Co-scripted by a young Federico Fellini, this powerful story traces the threads of people's lives as they interact and eventually entangle and doom themselves in the shadow of their Gestapo-controlled "open city." Anna Magnani became the first of a new breed of international stars as a result of her portrayal of Pina, the young widow whose fiancé is snatched away by the Gestapo, but all the performers are superlative. *Open City* drags the viewer down into the horror of a world controlled by a vengeful enemy. Not the most pleasant of films, but an experience to linger long after more amiable images have faded. In Italian with English subtitles.

1946 B & W 105 minutes

ORDEAL OF DR. MUDD, THE
★★★½

DIRECTOR: Paul Wendkos
CAST: Dennis Weaver, Susan Sullivan, Richard Dysart, Arthur Hill

The true story of Dr. Samuel Mudd, who innocently aided the injured, fleeing John Wilkes Booth following Lincoln's assassination and was sent to prison for alleged participation in the conspiracy. Dennis Weaver's fine portrayal of the ill-fated doctor makes this film well worthwhile. More than a century passed before Mudd was cleared, thanks to the efforts of a descendant, newscaster Roger Mudd. Rated PG.

1980 143 minutes

ORDINARY PEOPLE
★★★★½

DIRECTOR: Robert Redford
CAST: Mary Tyler Moore, Donald Sutherland, Timothy Hutton, Judd Hirsch, Elizabeth McGovern, Dinah Manoff, James B. Sikking

This moving human drama, which won the Academy Award for best picture of 1980, marked the directorial debut of Robert Redford . . . and an auspicious one it is, too. Redford elicits memorable performances from Mary Tyler Moore, Donald Sutherland, Timothy Hutton, and Judd Hirsch and makes the intelligent, powerful script by Alvin Sargent seem even better. Rated R for adult situations.

1980   123 minutes

OSCAR, THE
🦃

DIRECTOR: Russell Rouse
CAST: Stephen Boyd, Elke Sommer, Tony Bennett, Eleanor Parker, Ernest Borgnine, Joseph Cotten

Take a trite story of an unscrupulous actor trying to advance his career at the expense of others. Add some acting by the entire cast that is so embarrassing it makes you slump in your seat. Give it a form of anarchy attempting to pass as direction. What you get is a real stinker. And that's what you have here. Avoid this turkey at all costs.

1966   119 minutes

OTHER SIDE OF MIDNIGHT, THE
★½

DIRECTOR: Charles Jarrot
CAST: Marie-France Pisier, John Beck, Susan Sarandon, Raf Vallone, Clu Gulager

Glossy, tasteless soap opera derived from schlockmaster Sidney Sheldon's best-selling novel. The story runs from 1939 to 1947 and the movie seems to last that long. This picture definitely needs an injection of panache. Stick to *Dynasty*. Rated R.

1977   165 minutes

OTHER SIDE OF THE MOUNTAIN, THE
★★★

DIRECTOR: Larry Peerce
CAST: Marilyn Hassett, Beau Bridges

Absolutely heart-wrenching account of Jill Kinmont, an Olympic-bound skier whose career was cut short by a fall that left her paralyzed. Marilyn Hassett, in her film debut, makes Kinmont a fighter whose determination initially backfires and prompts some to have unreasonable expectations of her limited recovery. The accident itself looks horrifyingly authentic, the subsequent therapy grim and uncompromising. Sudsy at times (particularly at the end), but generally a reasonable story about a fighter trying to make the most of her new life. Far superior to its sequel. Rated PG.

1975   103 minutes

OTHER SIDE OF THE MOUNTAIN, PART II, THE
★★

DIRECTOR: Larry Peerce
CAST: Marilyn Hassett, Timothy Bottoms, Nan Martin, Belinda J. Montgomery, Gretchen Corbett

A sequel to the modest 1975 hit, the film continues the story of Jill Kinmont, a promising young skier who was paralyzed from the shoulders down in an accident. The tender romance, well played by Hassett and Bottoms, provides some fine moments. Rated PG.

1978   100 minutes

OUR DAILY BREAD
★★½

DIRECTOR: King Vidor
CAST: Tom Keene, Karen Morley, John Qualen, Addison Richards

This vintage Depression social drama about an idealistic man organizing community farms and socialistic society is pretty creaky despite sincere effort by director Vidor. Lead actor Tom Keene did better in cowboy films, and his appearances detract from the rest of the cast, which is pretty good. Look for John Qualen in a role that's a precursor to his "Muley Jones" from *The Grapes of Wrath*.

1934　　B & W　74 minutes

OUR TOWN
★★★★

DIRECTOR: Sam Wood
CAST: Frank Craven, William Holden, Martha Scott, Thomas Mitchell, Fay Bainter

Superb performances from a top-flight cast add zest to this well-done adaptation of Thornton Wilder's play about life in a small town.

1940　　B & W　90 minutes

OUT OF AFRICA
★★★★½

DIRECTOR: Sydney Pollack
CAST: Robert Redford, Meryl Streep, Klaus Maria Brandauer, Michael Kitchen, Malick Bowens, Michael Gough, Suzanna Hamilton

Robert Redford and Meryl Streep are at the peaks of their considerable talents in this 1985 Oscar winner for best picture, a grand-scale motion picture also blessed with inspired direction (by Sydney Pollack), gorgeous cinematography, and a haunting score (by John Barry). An epic romance, it was based by Kurt Luedtke (*Absence of Malice*) on the life and works of Isak Dinesen and concerns the love of two staunch individualists for each other and the land in which they live. There are so many levels of meaning and so many stunning sequences in *Out of Africa* that it begs to be seen more than once. Rated PG for a discreet sex scene and some moments of suspense.

1985　　　　160 minutes

OUTSIDERS, THE
★½

DIRECTOR: Francis Ford Coppola
CAST: C. Thomas Howell, Matt Dillon, Ralph Macchio, Emilio Estevez, Tom Cruise, Leif Garrett

Based on S. E. Hinton's popular novel, which has sold some four million copies, this is a fairly simple—and simplistic—movie about kids from the wrong side of the tracks. The pace is slow, and staying interested while watching it soon becomes a trial—even though it was directed by Francis Ford Coppola. In fact, if it weren't for Coppola's sometimes stunning visuals and some scenes of gang violence, *The Outsiders* would be more suitable as an after-school TV special than as a feature film. Rated PG for profanity and violence.

1983　　　　91 minutes

OVER THE EDGE
★★★★

DIRECTOR: Jonathan Kaplan
CAST: Matt Dillon, Michael Kramer, Pamela Ludwig

An explosive commentary on the restlessness of today's youth, this film also serves as an indictment against America's hypocritically permissive society. The violence that was supposedly caused by the release of gang films like *The Warriors*, *Boulevard Nights*, and *The Wanderers* caused the movie's makers to shelve it. However, Matt Dillon, who made his film debut herein, is now a hot property, and that's why this deserving movie is out on video. Rated R.

1979　　　　　　　　95 minutes

OXFORD BLUES
★★

DIRECTOR: Robert Boris
CAST: Rob Lowe, Amanda Pays

Rob Lowe plays a brash American who attempts to woo the beautiful Lady Victoria (Amanda Pays) while attending England's Oxford University. Writer-director Robert Boris has even worked in the sports angle, by making Lowe a rowing champ who has to prove himself. This, in short, is a formula picture. However, Boris makes it watchable by inserting a few well-placed surprises, nice bits of comedy, and an underlying theme of the importance of personal honor. Rated PG-13.

1984　　　　　　　　93 minutes

PAISAN
★★★½

DIRECTOR: Roberto Rossellini
CAST: Carmela Sazio, Robert Van Loon, Dots Johnson, Alfonsino, Gar Moore, Maria Michi, Harriet White, Renzo Avanzo, Bill Tubbs, Dale Edmonds

Six separate stories of survival are hauntingly presented by writer Federico Fellini and director Roberto Rossellini in this early postwar Italian film. Released the year after the landmark *Open City*, this movie solidified Rossellini's position as the leader in the school of Neo-Realism and reestablished Italy's place in world cinema. Shot on the streets and often improvised, this strong drama exposes the raw nerves brought on by living in a battleground and drags the audience into the lives of these victims. This is compelling adult drama, still powerful today.

1946　　　　B & W　90 minutes

PALOOKA
★★½

DIRECTOR: Bejamin Stoloff
CAST: Jimmy Durante, Stu Erwin, Lupe Velez, Majorie Rambeau, Robert Armstrong, William Cagney, Thelma Todd, Mary Carlisle

First filmed version of Ham Fisher's popular *Joe Palooka* is an okay little film about country bumpkin Stu Erwin's rise to the top in the fight game. Jimmy Durante as Palooka's manager is overwhelming (as usual), but he's got some top competition in the forms of spitfire Lupe Velez, boisterous Robert Armstrong, luscious Thelma Todd (the "ice cream blonde"), and tough William Cagney, even tougher James Cagney's brother. This film shares a niche with the other seldom-seen comic-strip film adaptations of the 1930s, including *Little Orphan Annie* and *L'il Abner*, and its availability on video is a pleasant gift to the fan who loves those tough and slightly goofy movies of the early 1930s.

1934　　　　B & W　86 minutes

PANDORA'S BOX
★★★★½

DIRECTOR: G. W. Pabst
CAST: Louise Brooks, Fritz Kortner, Franz Lederer, Carl Gotz

Here is a gem from the heyday of German silent screen expressionism. The film follows a winning yet amoral temptress, Lulu (a sparkling performance by largely ignored American actress Louise Brooks). Without concerns or inhibitions, Lulu blissfully ensnares a variety of weak men, only to contribute to their eventual downfall. Brooks plays Lulu, not as the traditional silent screen vamp, but as a freespirited victim of her own sexuality. This movie is primarily a showcase for the beautiful Miss Brooks, but credit must be given to director Pabst's technical innovations, and the originality of its story.

1929　　　B & W 131 minutes

PAPA'S DELICATE CONDITION
★★½

DIRECTOR: George Marshall
CAST: Jackie Gleason, Glynis Johns, Charlie Ruggles, Laurel Goodwin, Charles Lane, Elisha Cook Jr., Juanita Moore, Murray Hamilton

Somewhat stolid but pleasant enough story of family life in a small Texas town and the sometimes unpleasant notoriety brought to a family by their alcoholic patriarch, Jackie Gleason. Gleason, an audience favorite for years and highly visible on television in the 1950's and early 1960's, opted for drama in this film and imbues his character with a poignant sensitivity reminiscent of Chaplin and Keaton, but the result is uneven and at times saccharine although well-intentioned. Not as good a film as it was considered when released, this is still an enjoyable movie and a good chance to watch "the great one" tackle some serious acting, something he is very good at. Based on the reminiscences of silent film star Corinne Griffith and patterned largely after her father and her own small-town upbringing.

1963　　　98 minutes

PAPER CHASE, THE
★★★★

DIRECTOR: James Bridges
CAST: Timothy Bottoms, John Houseman, Lindsay Wagner

John Houseman won the Oscar for best actor in a supporting role in 1973 with his first-rate performance in this excellent film. Timothy Bottoms stars as a law student attempting to earn his law degree in spite of a stuffy professor (Houseman). Rated PG.

1973　　　111 minutes

PARADISE ALLEY
🦃

DIRECTOR: Sylvester Stallone
CAST: Sylvester Stallone, Armand Assante, Lee Canalito

Sylvester Stallone wrote, directed (his debut), and starred in this turgid mess about three brothers hoping for a quick ride out of the slums and into high society. The dialogue is infantile, the delivery mawkish, the direction completely inept. Even when on familiar ground—Stallone's character hopes to turn his brother into a champion wrestler—Stallone's guiding hand feels more like a punch in the mouth. Avoid at all costs. Rated PG for violence.

1978　　　107 minutes

PARALLAX VIEW, THE
★★★★

DIRECTOR: Alan J. Pakula
CAST: Warren Beatty, Paula Prentiss, William Daniels

This fine film offers a fascinating study of a reporter, played by Warren Beatty, trying to penetrate the cover-up of an assassination in which the hunter becomes the hunted. Rated R.

1974　　　102 minutes

PARIS BLUES
★★★★

DIRECTOR: Martin Ritt
CAST: Paul Newman, Sidney Poitier, Joanne Woodward, Diahann Carroll

Overlooked and underrated best describe this story of two jazz musicians, Paul Newman and Sidney Poitier, plying their trade in Paris, France. A summer romance with two American tourists, Joanne Woodward and Diahann Carroll, makes up the basis for the plot. Good performances by all, coupled with a great jazz score, make this one worthwhile.

1961   B & W   98 minutes

PARIS, TEXAS
★★★★½

DIRECTOR: Wim Wenders
CAST: Harry Dean Stanton, Nastassja Kinski, Dean Stockwell, Aurore Clement, Hunter Carson

This is a film about disillusionment, isolation, lost love, and the American dream gone bad. Adapted from the story by playwright Sam Shepard by L. M. Kit Carson. *Paris, Texas* is a haunting vision of personal pain and universal suffering, with Harry Dean Stanton impeccable as the weary wanderer who returns after four years to reclaim his son (Hunter Carson) and search for his wife (Nastassja Kinski). It is the kind of motion picture we rarely see, one that attempts to say something about our country and its people—and succeeds. (This is all the more impressive/ironic when you consider that it was directed by German filmmaker Wim Wenders.) For those who want something different and with substance. A thinking person's movie. Rated R for profanity and adult content.

1984   144 minutes

PARK IS MINE, THE
★★½

DIRECTOR: Steven Hilliard Stern
CAST: Tommy Lee Jones, Helen Slater, Yaphet Kotto

After his friend is killed, unstable Vietnam vet (Tommy Lee Jones) invades New York's Central Park and proclaims it to be his. Using combat tactics, Jones holds off the authorities until the predictable ending. Pretty far-fetched stuff. An HBO Film.

1985   102 minutes

PASSAGE TO INDIA, A
★★★★★

DIRECTOR: David Lean
CAST: Judy Davis, Victor Banerjee, Alec Guinness, Peggy Ashcroft

After an absence from the screen of fourteen years, British director David Lean has returned triumphantly, with the brilliant *A Passage to India*. Based on the 1924 novel by E. M. Forster, it is a work that compares favorably with the 76-year-old filmmaker's finest: *Great Expectations*; *Oliver Twist*; *The Bridge on the River Kwai*; and *Lawrence of Arabia*. Ostensibly about the romantic adventures of a young Englishwoman in "the mysterious East" that culminate in a court trial (for attempted rape), it is also a multi-layered, symbolic work about, in the words of Forster, "the difficulty of living in the universe." Rated PG.

1984   163 minutes

PASSENGER, THE
★★

DIRECTOR: Michelangelo Antonioni
CAST: Jack Nicholson, Maria Schneider, Jenny Runacre, Ian Hendry, Stephen Berkoff

Billed as a suspense drama, *The Passenger* is a very slow-moving tale about a disillusioned TV reporter (Jack Nicholson) working in Africa. He exchanges identities with a dead Englishman and thereby becomes involved with underworld international arms smugglers. Rated R.

1975   119 minutes

PASSION OF JOAN OF ARC, THE
★★★★★
DIRECTOR: Carl Dreyer
CAST: Maria Falconetti, Silvain, Antonin Artaud

This is simply one of the greatest films ever made. Its emotional intensity is unsurpassed. Faces tell the tale of this movie. Maria Falconetti's Joan is unforgettable. *The Passion of Joan of Arc* will break your heart and leave you speechless.

1928   B & W 114 minutes

PASSION OF LOVE
★★★★
DIRECTOR: Ettore Scola
CAST: Valeria D'Obici, Bernard Giraudeau, Laura Antonelli, Bernard Blier, Jean-Louis Trintignant, Massimo Girotti

In 1862 Italy just after the war, a decorated captain (Bernard Giraudeau) has a passionate affair with a beautiful married woman (Laura Antonelli). Giraudeau is transferred to a faraway outpost, where he becomes the love object of his commander's cousin (Valeria D'Obici). What follows is a fascinating study of torment and anguish as the incredibly ugly and illness-plagued D'Obici relentlessly pursues Giraudeau. There are outstanding performances by all. Awards went to D'Obici and the film at the Cannes Film Festival. Dubbed in English and unrated.

1982   117 minutes

PATHS OF GLORY
★★★★★
DIRECTOR: Stanley Kubrick
CAST: Kirk Douglas, Adolphe Menjou, George Macready, Timothy Carey, Ralph Meeker

A great anti-war movie! Stanley Kubrick gives us a scathing indictment against the staff-officer mentality that cares about promotions more than the men who make those promotions possible. Kirk Douglas plays the compassionate French officer in World War I who must lead his men against insurmountable enemy positions, and then must defend three of them against charges of cowardice when the battle is lost. Adolphe Menjou and George Macready perfectly portray Douglas's monstrous senior officers.

1957   B & W   86 minutes

PATTON
★★★★★
DIRECTOR: Franklin Schaffner
CAST: George C. Scott, Karl Malden, Stephen Young, Tim Considine

Flamboyant, controversial General George S. Patton is the subject of this Oscar-winning picture. George C. Scott is spellbinding in the title role. Scott's brilliant performance manages to bring alive this military hero, who strode a fine line between effective battlefield commander and demigod. Rated PG.

1970   169 minutes

PAULINE AT THE BEACH
★★★★
DIRECTOR: Eric Rohmer

CAST: Amanda Langlet, Arielle Dombasle, Pascal Gregory, Feodor Atkine

The screen works of French writer-director Eric Rohmer are decidedly unconventional. Nothing particularly monumental happens in them. All the characters really do is talk, talk, talk. Yet Rohmer's movies still manage to keep the viewer interested, because their creator cares deeply about people and all the underlying quirks and complications that make them who and what they are. In this, the latest in what he calls his "Comedies and Proverbs," the 14-year-old title character (Amanda Langlet) shows herself to have a better sense of self and reality than the adults around her. In French, with English subtitles. Rated R for nudity.

1983   94 minutes

PAWNBROKER, THE
★★★★★
DIRECTOR: Sidney Lumet
CAST: Rod Steiger, Geraldine Fitzgerald, Brock Peters

This is a somber and powerfully acted portrayal of a Jewish man who survived the Nazi holocaust, only to find his spirit still as bleak as the Harlem ghetto in which he operates a pawnshop. Rod Steiger gives a tour-de-force performance as a man with dead emotions who is shocked out of his zombielike existence by confronting the realities of modern urban life.

1965   B & W 116 minutes

PAYDAY
★★★★
DIRECTOR: Daryl Duke
CAST: Rip Torn, Ahna Capri, Elayne Heilveil, Cliff Emmich, Michael C. Gwynne

Bravura performance by Rip Torn as a hard-drinking, ruthless country singer who's bent on destroying himself and everyone around him. Gripping, emotionally draining drama. Rarely seen in theaters, this one is definitely worth viewing on tape. Rated R for language, nudity, sexual situations.

1973   103 minutes

PEARL OF THE SOUTH PACIFIC
★½
DIRECTOR: Allan Dwan
CAST: Virginia Mayo, Dennis Morgan, David Farrar, Murvyn Vye

Allan Dwan guides another one down the tubes. A dull film about murder in the tropics that tries to be intriguing and exotic but fails on both counts.

1955   86 minutes

PENNY SERENADE
★★★★
DIRECTOR: George Stevens
CAST: Cary Grant, Irene Dunne, Edgar Buchanan

Cary Grant and Irene Dunne are one of the most fondly remembered comedy teams in films such as *The Awful Truth* and *My Favorite Wife*. This 1941 film is a radical change of pace, for it is a ten-hankie tearjerker about a couple's attempt to have children. They are excellent in this drama far removed from their standard comic fare.

1941   B & W 125 minutes

PEPE LE MOKO
★★★½
DIRECTOR: Julien Duvivier
CAST: Jean Gabin, Mireille Balin, Gabriel Gario, Lucas Gridoux, Marcel Dalio

Algiers criminal Pepe Le Moko (Jean Gabin) is safe just as long as he remains in the city's picturesque, squalid native quarter, the Casbah, a sanctuary for fugitives where the police have no power. His passionate infatuation with a beautiful visitor from his beloved Paris, however, spells his doom. His superb performance in this film, *La Grande Illusion,* and *Port of Shadows*—all milestones of French cinema—made Jean Gabin's reputation as a strong, silent, deeply human hero and, often, antihero. *Algiers,* the U.S. remake with suave Charles Boyer and Hedy Lamarr, in her American film debut, is as good, but not better. Knock offs rarely are. In French with English subtitles.

1937   B & W   93 minutes

PERFECT
★★½

DIRECTOR: James Bridges
CAST: John Travolta, Jamie Lee Curtis, Jann Wenner, Marilu Henner, Laraine Newman

In this irritatingly uneven and unfocused film, John Travolta stars as a *Rolling Stone* reporter out to do an exposé on the current health-club boom. Jamie Lee Curtis is the uncooperative aerobics instructor he attempts to spotlight in his story. What could have been the *Saturday Night Fever* of the Perrier and pumping iron set turns out to be just another moralizing mess about journalistic ethics. Rated R for profanity, suggested sex, and violence. 1986 release.

1985   120 minutes

PERFORMANCE
★★★★

DIRECTOR: Nicolas Roeg, Donald Cammell
CAST: Mick Jagger, James Fox, Anita Pallenberg

Mick Jagger, the leader of the Rolling Stones rock group, stars in this bizarre film as Turner, a rock singer who decides to switch identities with a hunted hit man (James Fox). Co-directed by Nicolas Roeg (*Don't Look Now*; *The Man Who Fell to Earth*) and Donald Cammell, *Performance* is a chilling, profoundly disturbing cinematic nightmare about the dark side of man's consciousness. Rated R for profanity, nudity, violence, and all manner of perversity and evil.

1970   105 minutes

PERIL
★★

DIRECTOR: Michel Deville
CAST: Christophe Malavoy, Nicole Garcia, Richard Bohringer, Anemone, Michel Piccoli, Anais Jeanneret

Despite some guitar transcriptions of Brahms and Schubert, the absence of a soundtrack gives this film a harsh and stagnant tone that makes the story difficult to experience. And while there may be some justification for the cold feel, it does nothing for the viewer's patience. Nicole Garcia plays the wife of a wealthy businessman who is having an affair with their daughter's guitar instructor (Christophe Malavoy). From there the story becomes very complex, with possible hidden agendas revealed every twenty minutes or so. Filmmaker Michel Deville aims too high in his direction with French New Wave–like scene cuts; they come off more amateurish than artistic. French cinema enthusiasts will welcome the appearance of Richard Bohringer, the lovable rogue hero from *Diva*, who plays a lovable hit man here. Rated R for sex, nudity, violence, profanity, and adult subject matter. In French with English subtitles.

1985   100 minutes

PERSONAL BEST
★★★★

DIRECTOR: Robert Towne

CAST: Mariel Hemingway, Patrice Donnelly, Scott Glenn

Oscar-winning screenwriter Robert Towne (*Chinatown*) wrote, directed, and produced this tough, honest, and nonexploitive story about two women who are friends, teammates, and sometimes lovers (Mariel Hemingway, Patrice Donnelly) preparing for the 1980 Olympics. Hemingway's and Donnelly's stunning performances make the film an impressive achievement. Rated R for male and female frontal nudity, strong language, and drug use.

1982   124 minutes

PETRIFIED FOREST, THE
★★★★½

DIRECTOR: Archie Mayo

CAST: Humphrey Bogart, Leslie Howard, Bette Davis, Dick Foran

This adaptation of the Robert Sherwood play seems a bit dated at first. It's about a gangster (Humphrey Bogart, in one of his first important screen roles) who holds a writer (Leslie Howard), a waitress (Bette Davis), and others hostage in a diner. The first-rate story, exquisite ensemble acting by the stars, and taut direction by Archie Mayo soon mesmerize the viewer. The result is a memorable movie-watching experience.

1936   B & W 83 minutes

PHAR LAP
★★★★

DIRECTOR: Simon Wincer

CAST: Tom Burlinson, Ron Leibman, Martin Vaughn

Absolutely chilling (and true) account of the superb Australian racehorse that chewed up the track in the 1920s and early 1930s. Tom Burlinson, remembered as *The Man from Snowy River*, stars as the stableboy who first believed in, and then followed to fame, the indefatigable Phar Lap. This film's indictment of early horse-racing practices will make you shudder; when an animal (such as Phar Lap) did too well, it was weighted down in an attempt to prevent its being able to move at all. Such measures won't stop heroes, though . . . not even the four-legged variety. Keep the Kleenex handy. Rated PG—very intense for younger children.

1984   106 minutes

PIANO FOR MRS. CIMINO, A
★★★★

DIRECTOR: George Schaefer

CAST: Bette Davis, Keenan Wynn, Alexa Kenin, Penny Fuller, Christopher Guest, George Hearn

Blessed with great humor and a terrific performance by Bette Davis, this made-for-television film about growing old with dignity is manipulative at times. In light of all the wonderful moments, however, the contrivances don't seem so bad. Davis plays a widow who is institutionalized for senility. The film follows her through her recovery and her rebirth as a single, self-sufficient woman. Keenan Wynn also puts in a good peformance as an old musician friend.

1982   96 minutes

PILOT, THE
★★½

DIRECTOR: Cliff Robertson
CAST: Cliff Robertson, Frank Converse, Diane Baker, Gordon MacRae, Dana Andrews, Milo O'Shea, Ed Binns

Cliff Robertson directed and starred in this film about an airline pilot's struggle with alcohol. A lot of heart went into this film, and we are glad to announce that despite the all-star cast and the subject matter, this is not a disaster flick. Just the same, Robertson's directing is not as convincing as his acting, and the screenplay is sometimes sickeningly sweet. Rated PG for profanity.

1979   98 minutes

PIPE DREAMS
★

DIRECTOR: Stephen F. Verona
CAST: Gladys Knight, Barry L. Hankerson, Bruce French, Wayne Tippitt, Sherry Bain, Barbara Shaw

While writer/director/producer Stephen F. Verona may have had good intentions, the story is trite, and the poor acting and weak direction only aggravate the problem. Gladys Knight (of Pip fame) plays a wife who moves to Alaska to win back her estranged man who is working on the pipe line. The title pun is a good example of the wit involved here. Rated PG for sex, violence, profanity, and adult subject matter.

1976   89 minutes

PIXOTE
★★★★

DIRECTOR: Hector Babenco
CAST: Fernando Ramos Da Silla, Marilia Pera, Jorge Juliano, Gilberto Moura

In Rio, Brazil, half the population is younger than 18. Kids, only 10- or 12-year-olds, become thieves, beggars, and prostitutes. *Pixote* is the story of one of these unfortunates. For some viewers it may be too powerful and disturbing, yet it is not the least bit exploitative or exaggerated. Though fictional, it is based on fact, and that makes *Pixote* all the more unsettling. Rated R for violence, explicit sex, and nudity.

1981   127 minutes

PLACE IN THE SUN, A
★★★★

DIRECTOR: George Stevens
CAST: Elizabeth Taylor, Montgomery Clift, Shelley Winters, Keefe Brasselle, Raymond Burr, Anne Revere

Elizabeth Taylor, Montgomery Clift, and Shelley Winters are caught in a tragic love triangle in this picture, based on Theodore Dreiser's *An American Tragedy*. All three artists give first-rate performances. The story of a working-class man who falls for a wealthy girl is a traditional one, yet the eroticism conveyed in the scenes between Taylor and Clift keeps this production well above a standard story of doomed lovers.

1951   B & W 122 minutes

PLACES IN THE HEART
★★★★★

DIRECTOR: Robert Benton
CAST: Sally Field, Ed Harris, Lindsay Crouse, John Malkovich, Danny Glover

Writer-director Robert Benton's *Places in the Heart* is a great film. Based on Benton's childhood memories in Waxahachie, Texas, the film stars Sally Field, Ed Harris, Lindsay Crouse, with special performances by John Malkovich and Danny Glover. Field plays Edna Spalding, a mother of two who is suddenly widowed. Almost immediately, she is pressured by the bank to sell her home and the surrounding property. But Edna vows, despite all supposed "logic," to make it on her own. The result is a movie celebrating the human spirit. Rated PG for suggested sex, violence, and profanity.

1984   110 minutes

PLAYERS
🐾

DIRECTOR: Anthony Harvey
CAST: Ali MacGraw, Dean-Paul Martin, Maximilian Schell

It boggles the mind to consider that the man responsible for this un-relenting bomb also directed *The Lion in Winter*. Ali MacGraw is the bored mistress of Maximilian Schell; she falls for tennis pro Dean-Paul Martin. Ludicrous dialogue, banal acting, lethargic directing . . . even the tennis scenes are terrible. Rated PG—sexual situations.

1979   120 minutes

PLEASURE PALACE
★★

DIRECTOR: Walter Grauman
CAST: Omar Sharif, Victoria Principal, Walter Grauman, J. D. Cannon, Gerald S. O'Loughlin, José Ferrer, Hope Lange

No, this is not a porno flick—in fact, the characters in this made-for-TV movie are more like old-fashioned melodrama icons. Hope Lange plays an honest widowed casino owner (yay!) who is afraid she will loose her casino to an influential oil baron (boo!). Omar Sharif portrays a high-rolling international gambler (a similar role to the one he played in *Funny Girl*) who comes to the rescue—gam-

bler's style. Despite the lack of subtlety in characters, some of the gambling scenes have real tension in them. And screenwriter Blanche Hanalis should watch her anti-Arab insults. Not rated, but the equivalent of a PG for violence.

1980   92 minutes

PLENTY
★★★★

DIRECTOR: Fred Schepisi
CAST: Meryl Streep, Charles Dance, Sam Neill, Tracey Ullman, John Gielgud, Sting, Ian McKellen

In this difficult but rewarding film, which is like a superb stage production played out with high movie style on screen, Meryl Streep is superb as a former member of the French Resistance who finds life in her native England increasingly maddening during the postwar reconstruction period. Rated R for profanity, suggested sex, and violence.

1985   120 minutes

POCKETFUL OF MIRACLES
★★★

DIRECTOR: Frank Capra
CAST: Bette Davis, Glenn Ford, Ann-Margret, Thomas Mitchell

Frank Capra's last film; Ann-Margret's first. A not-as-good remake of Capra's *Lady for a Day*, with Bette Davis playing Apple Annie, a Damon Runyon Broadway character, whom producer Glenn Ford turns into a lady. It's sentimental hokum worth watching, but not well worth watching, and it's too long.

1961   136 minutes

POPE OF GREENWICH VILLAGE, THE
★★★★½

DIRECTOR: Stuart Rosenberg

CAST: Eric Roberts, Mickey Rourke, Daryl Hannah, Geraldine Page

This highly watchable film focuses on the hard-edged misadventures of two Italian cousins, Paulie (Eric Roberts) and Charlie (Mickey Rourke). Paulie is a not-so-bright dreamer who's obviously headed for trouble, and Charlie, who is smart enough to know better, always seems to get caught up in the middle of his cousin's half-baked and dangerous ripoff schemes. Rated R for profanity and violence.

1984   120 minutes

PORT OF CALL
★★★
DIRECTOR: Ingmar Bergman
CAST: Nine Christine Jonsson, Bengt Eklund

When a seaman begins working on the docks, he falls in love with a suicidal young woman. The woman has had an unhappy childhood and a wild past, which has given her a bad reputation. Their relationship falters when he has trouble loving and accepting her in spite of her past indiscretions. This drama seems dated today.

1948   B & W 100 minutes

PORTNOY'S COMPLAINT
★
DIRECTOR: Ernest Lehman
CAST: Richard Benjamin, Karen Black, Lee Grant, Jack Somack, Jeannie Berlin, Jill Clayburgh

It's worth viewing only as a curiosity. Amazing that anyone had the nerve to attempt to translate Philip Roth's infamous novel to the screen. The neurotic Jewish boy, who has a strange relationship with his mother and an obsession with sex, should be neutered. Richard Benjamin is at his most annoying in the role. Karen Black's poignant portrayal of "Monkey" provides the only worthwhile moments. Rated R for profanity and sex.

1972   101 minutes

PORTRAIT OF A STRIPPER
★★
DIRECTOR: John A. Alonzo
CAST: Lesley Ann Warren, Edward Herrmann, Vic Tayback, Sheree North

A dancer is forced to strip in order to support her fatherless son, causing the authorities to label her an unfit mother. Since this was originally made for TV, its timid presentation will, no doubt, disappoint many drooling video renters.

1979   100 minutes

POSSESSED
★★★
DIRECTOR: Curtis Bernhardt
CAST: Van Heflin, Joan Crawford, Raymond Massey, Geraldine Brooks, Stanley Ridges

A cold and clinical account of loveless marriage, mysterious suicide, frustrated love for a scoundrel, murder, and schizophrenia. The much-maligned Joan Crawford heads a fine, mature cast and gives one of her finer performances as a mentally troubled nurse whose head and heart problems destroy her life. Extremely watchable. The opening scene is a real grabber.

1947   B & W 108 minutes

POSTMAN ALWAYS RINGS TWICE, THE (ORIGINAL)
★★★★
DIRECTOR: Tay Garnett

CAST: John Garfield, Lana Turner, Cecil Kellaway, Hume Cronyn

If you wondered what went wrong in the sometimes steamily sexy and all too often soggy 1981 screen version of James M. Cain's celebrated novel, you need only watch this 1946 adaptation. John Garfield and Lana Turner play the lovers who murder the husband who stands in the way of their lust and suffer the consequences. While not as good as Billy Widler's film of Cain's equally famous *Double Indemnity*, this picture is still superior to the remake.

1946   B & W 113 minutes

POSTMAN ALWAYS RINGS TWICE, THE (REMAKE)
★★★½

DIRECTOR: Bob Rafelson
CAST: Jessica Lange, Jack Nicholson, John Colicos, Michael Lerner, John P. Ryan, Anjelica Huston

Jack Nicholson plays the drifter whose lust for a married woman (Jessica Lange) leads to murder in this disappointing remake based on James M. Cain's hard-boiled novel of sex and violence. After an electric first hour, it begins to ramble and ends abruptly, leaving the viewer dissatisfied. Rated R for graphic sex and violence.

1981   123 minutes

POT O' GOLD
★★

DIRECTOR: George Marshall
CAST: James Stewart, Paulette Goddard, Horace Heidt, Charles Winninger, Mary Gordon

An amusing time-passer based on a one-time popular radio show. Obviously a studio effort to use contract talent. The plot concerns an enthusiastic young man's effort to get Horace Heidt and his orchestra on his uncle's radio program. Gee!

1941   B & W   86 minutes

POWER
★★★★½

DIRECTOR: Sidney Lumet
CAST: Richard Gere, Julie Christie, Gene Hackman, Kate Capshaw, Denzel Washington, E. G. Marshall, Beatrice Straight

Sidney Lumet, who directed the much-praised black comedy about television, *Network*, once again takes viewers into the bowels of an American institution with this hard-edged study of the manipulation of the political process by market research and advertizing. Richard Gere gives one of his best performances as a ruthless hustler who is given pause when the one politician he believes in (E. G. Marshall) becomes a pawn in the political power trade. Julie Christie is the ex-wife/journalist who helps Gere discover the truth, and Gene Hackman is his former mentor and chief critic. Rated R for profanity, violence, and suggested sex.

1986   111 minutes

PRETTY BABY
★★★½

DIRECTOR: Louis Malle
CAST: Brooke Shields, Susan Sarandon, Keith Carradine, Frances Faye, Antonio Fargas, Matthew Anton

Forcing the audience to reexamine many accepted concepts is just one of the effects of this brilliant work by Louis Malle. He is clearly fascinated by Violet (Brooke Shields), the young girl we see growing up in a whorehouse in New Orleans. For Violet, all that goes on around her is normal and quite unshocking. The first scene in the film shows Violet watching as her mother (Susan Sarandon) is gasping and groaning on the bed. We naturally assume that she is with one of her many clients. But as the camera pulls back, we see that she is giving birth, and the first of Malle's searching questions is instilled in the viewer. It is not Violet or her mother who has the dirty mind, but we, the audience. Rated R.

1978   109 minutes

PRETTY IN PINK
★★★★

DIRECTOR: Howard Deutch
CAST: Molly Ringwald, Harry Dean Stanton, Jon Cryer, Andrew McCarthy, Annie Potts, James Spader

Molly Ringwald is wonderful to watch as a young woman "from the poor side of town" who falls in love with rich kid Andrew McCarthy (*St. Elmo's Fire*). The feeling is mutual, but their peers do everything they can to keep them apart. Harry Dean Stanton gives a typically terrific performance as Molly's understanding troubled dad, and Jon Cryer (*No Small Affair*) is a delight as her secret lover. Written by John Hughes (*Sixteen Candles*, *The Breakfast Club*), it is that rare teenage-oriented release that can be enjoyed by all ages. Rated PG-13 for profanity and violence.

1986   96 minutes

PRIDE AND PREJUDICE
★★★★

DIRECTOR: Robert Z. Leonard
CAST: Greer Garson, Laurence Olivier, Maureen O'Sullivan, Marsha Hunt

This film is an accurate adaptation of Jane Austen's famous novel. The comic action takes place in nineteenth-century England with five sisters looking for suitable husbands.

1940   B & W 116 minutes

PRIDE AND THE PASSION, THE
★★

DIRECTOR: Stanley Kramer
CAST: Frank Sinatra, Cary Grant, Sophia Loren, Theodore Bikel, John Wengray

Here is a supreme example of how miscasting can ruin a movie's potential. Frank Sinatra is horrible as the Spanish peasant leader of a guerrilla army during the Napoleonic era. He secures the services of a gigantic cannon and a British Navy officer (Cary Grant) to fire it. Sophia Loren is also in the cast, primarily as window dressing. Sinatra treks the cannon and his ragtag army across Spain in order to capture a walled city from the supporters of Napoleon. The idea sounds exciting, but Sinatra's performance makes you want to look away from the screen.

1957   132 minutes

PRIDE OF THE BOWERY
★

DIRECTOR: Joseph H. Lewis
CAST: Leo Gorcey, Bobby Jordan, Donald Haines, Carleton Young, Kenneth Howell, David Gorcey

This offshoot of the famous Dead-End Kids features Leo Gorcey and Bobby Jordan, two of the original "kids," along with Gorcey's brother David, who continued on and off for the rest of the series. Not quite as bad as their later efforts, this film still needs a dyed-in-the-wool East Side Kids fan to really enjoy it. No surprises in this routine programmer, which is basically the same film these perennial juveniles will make for the next seventeen years.

1940   B & W   63 minutes

PRIDE OF THE YANKEES, THE
★★★★★

DIRECTOR: Sam Wood
CAST: Gary Cooper, Teresa Wright, Babe Ruth, Walter Brennan, Dan Duryea, Ludwig Stossel

Gary Cooper gives one of his finest performances as he captures the courageous spirit of New York Yankee immortal Lou Gehrig. This 1942 drama is a perfect blend of an exciting sports biography and a touching melodrama as we follow Gehrig's baseball career from its earliest playground beginnings until an illness strikes him down in his prime. Teresa Wright is just right in the difficult role of his loving wife.

1942   B & W   127 minutes

PRIEST OF LOVE
★★★★½

DIRECTOR: Christopher Miles
CAST: Ian McKellen, Janet Suzman, Ava Gardner, Penelope Keith, Joe Rivero

An unerringly accurate, dramatically engrossing, and ravishingly beautiful biography of D. H. Lawrence, with Ian McKellen as the tormented novelist, Janet Suzman as his tempestuous wife, Frieda, and Ava Gardner as one of his more predatory lady admirers. Rated R for profanity.

1981   125 minutes

PRINCE OF THE CITY
★★★★½

DIRECTOR: Sidney Lumet
CAST: Treat Williams, Jerry Orbach, Richard Foronjy, Don Billet, Kenny Marino

Director Sidney Lumet (*Serpico*; *Dog Day Afternoon*) has created one of the screen's most intense character studies out of the true story of a corrupt New York narcotics cop, played wonderfully by Treat Williams. In becoming a government agent, the cop destroys the lives of his closest friends. Rated R because of violence and strong profanity.

1981   167 minutes

PRIVATE LIFE OF DON JUAN, THE
★★

DIRECTOR: Alexander Korda
CAST: Douglas Fairbanks, Merle Oberon, Binnie Barnes, Benita Hume, Joan Gardner, Melville Cooper, Owen Naves

A vehicle for the aging Douglas Fairbanks, his last picture is set in seventeenth-century Spain. A famous lover (Fairbanks) fakes a suicide in order to make a comeback in disguise. To quote Oscar Wilde, "Life imitates art"; this is the case here. It is somewhat tragic that the first great hero of the screen should have ended up in this disappointment. It is better to remember him as *Robin Hood* or *The Black Pirate*. The supporting cast seems idle, as if the whole picture is just a party to humor Fairbanks.

1934   B & W   90 minutes

PRIVATE LIFE OF HENRY THE EIGHTH, THE
★★★★

DIRECTOR: Alexander Korda
CAST: Charles Laughton, Robert Donat, Merle Oberon, Elsa Lanchester, Binnie Barnes

This well-paced historical chronicle of England's bluebeard monarch and his six wives was to be Britain's first successful entry into worldwide movie-making. Charles

Laughton's tour-de-force as the notorious king remains one of filmdom's greatest portrayals. The segment dealing with his relationship with Anne of Cleves is the funniest and most rewarding portion of the film. Laughton's real-life spouse, Elsa Lanchester, plays Anne, the fourth wife. She manages to keep her head off the chopping block by humoring the volatile king during a memorable game of cards.

1933   B & W   87 minutes

PRIVATE LIVES OF ELIZABETH AND ESSEX, THE
★★★½

DIRECTOR: Michael Curtiz
CAST: Bette Davis, Errol Flynn, James Cagney, Humphrey Bogart, Olivia De Havilland

Bette Davis is Queen Elizabeth and Errol Flynn is her dashing suitor in this enjoyable costume drama directed by Michael Curtiz (*Casablanca*).

1939   106 minutes

PRIZZI'S HONOR
(1986 Release)
★★★★★

DIRECTOR: John Huston
CAST: Jack Nicholson, Kathleen Turner, Robert Loggia, John Randolph, William Hickey, Anjelica Huston

This totally bent black comedy is perhaps best described as *The Godfather* gone stark, raving mad. It is not a film for every taste. Jack Nicholson plays a Mafia hit man who falls in love with a mystery woman (Kathleen Turner), who turns out to be full of surprises. Perhaps the blackest black comedy ever made, *Prizzi's Honor* makes *Being There*, *Harold and Maude*, and even *Dr. Strangelove* seem tame in comparison. In other

words, it's a real find for fans of the genre. Rated R for nudity, suggested sex, profanity, and violence.

1985   130 minutes

PROMISES IN THE DARK
★★★½

DIRECTOR: Jerome Hellman
CAST: Marsha Mason, Ned Beatty, Susan Clark, Michael Brandon, Kathleen Beller, Paul Clemens, Donald Moffat

This film is about a young girl dying of cancer. Marsha Mason co-stars as her sympathetic doctor. Good movie, but very depressing! Rated PG.

1979   115 minutes

PROVIDENCE
★★★★

DIRECTOR: Alain Resnais
CAST: Dirk Bogarde, John Gielgud, Ellen Burstyn, David Warner, Elaine Stritch

Director Alain Resnais's first English-language film includes the great cast of Dirk Bogarde, John Gielgud, Ellen Burstyn, and David Warner. An old and dying writer (Gielgud) completing his last novel invites his family up for the weekend. The film's fast cutting between the writer's imagined thoughts and real life makes this film difficult to follow for some. Rated R.

1977   104 minutes

PT 109
★★½

DIRECTOR: Leslie Martinson
CAST: Cliff Robertson, Robert Culp, Ty Hardin, James Gregory, Robert Blake, Grant Williams

Cliff Robertson is John F. Kennedy in this monument to the former President's war adventures on a World War II PT boat. Robertson is credible, but the story is only interesting because of the famous people and events it represents.

1963   140 minutes

PUBERTY BLUES
★★★½

DIRECTOR: Bruce Beresford
CAST: Nell Schofield, Jad Capelja

This film takes a frank look at the coming of age of two teenagers as they grow up on the beaches of Australia. The two girls become temporary victims of peer group pressure that involves drugs, alcohol, and sex. Unlike many other teen-age films, *Puberty Blues* offers interesting insights into the rite of passage as seen from a female point of view. Rated R.

1981   86 minutes

PUMPING IRON
★★★★

DIRECTOR: George Butler, Robert Fiore
CAST: Arnold Schwarzenegger, Lou Ferrigno, Matty and Victoria Ferrigno, Mike Katz

Very good documentary concerning professional body building. Arnold Schwarzenegger and Lou Ferrigno ("The Hulk") are at the forefront as they prepare for the Mr. Universe contest. Always interesting and at times fascinating. Rated PG for language.

1977   85 minutes

PUMPING IRON II: THE WOMEN
★★★★½

DIRECTOR: George Butler
CAST: Lori Bowen, Carla Dunlap, Bev Francis, Rachel McLish

This documentary on the 1983 Women's World Cup held at Caesar's Palace is more than just beauty and brawn. While it does seem to side with one contestant (and when you see Bev Francis's massive body, you'll know why), the film has all the passion and wit of a first-rate narrative. The movie follows four competitors for the prize from their arrival in Las Vegas, through their workouts, to the moment they've all been waiting for. This picture also gives the viewer an in depth view of these bodybuilders through illuminating interviews. Not rated, but an equivalent of a PG.

1985   107 minutes

PURPLE HEART, THE
★★★★

DIRECTOR: Lewis Milestone
CAST: Dana Andrews, Richard Conte, Farley Granger, Sam Levene, Tala Birell, Nestor Paiva

Dana Andrews and Richard Conte are leaders of a group of American fliers who are captured by the Japanese after they bomb Tokyo and put on trial for war crimes. This fascinating film is a minor classic.

1944   B & W   99 minutes

PURPLE HEARTS
★

DIRECTOR: Sidney J. Furie
CAST: Ken Wahl, Cheryl Ladd

Anyone who can sit all the way through this Vietnam war-film romance deserves a medal. Ken Wahl (*The Wanderers*; *Fort Apache— The Bronx*) stars as a surgeon in the United States Navy Medical Corps who falls in love with a nurse (Cheryl Ladd, formerly of television's "Charlie's Angels"). Halfway through this film, directed by Sidney J. Furie (*The Boys in Company C*; *The Entity*), there's a natural and satisfying ending. But does it end there? Noooo. There's an additional forty minutes of unnecessary and unoriginal story tacked on. What Furie is going for is a ripoff of *An Officer and a Gentleman*, complete with a teary-eyed ending—and he gets it. But the tears are more from eyestrain than emotional involvement or release. Rated R for nudity, profanity, violence, and gore.

1984   115 minutes

PURPLE TAXI, THE
★★★

DIRECTOR: Yves Boisset

CAST: Fred Astaire, Edward Albert, Philippe Noiret, Peter Ustinov, Charlotte Rampling, Agostine Belli

Fred Astaire, Edward Albert, and Philippe Noiret star in this exploration of angst, love, and friendship in Ireland, where a collection of expatriate characters impaled on memories and self-destructive compulsions work out their kinks before returning to various homelands. Capably supporting are Peter Ustinov, as a tortured and despicable con man, and Charlotte Rampling, as the spoiled and distraught sister of troubled Jerry (Edward Albert). Fine backdrops in Ireland's "curtain of rain" and impressive acting. Rated R.

1977   107 minutes

QB VII
★★★★

DIRECTOR: Tom Gries

CAST: Anthony Hopkins, Ben Gazzara, Leslie Caron, Lee Remick, Anthony Quayle

Leon Uris's hefty bestseller is vividly brought to life in this five-hours-plus made-for-television drama about a Polish expatriate doctor living in England who sues an American writer for libel when the writer accuses him of carrying out criminal medical activities for the Nazis during World War II. Anthony Hopkins is brilliant as the physician, Ben Gazzara outraged and tenacious as the writer. Expect a powerful, engrossing ending.

1974   312 minutes

QUACKSER FORTUNE HAS A COUSIN IN THE BRONX
★★★★

DIRECTOR: Waris Hussein

CAST: Gene Wilder, Margot Kidder, Eileen Colga, Seamus Ford, David Kelly

This movie falls into the category of sleeper. Gene Wilder is delightful as an Irishman who marches to the beat of a different drummer. Margot Kidder is a rich American going to univeristy in Dublin who meets and falls in love with him. Humor and sadness abound in this insightful comedy-drama. Don't be put off by the strange title; it becomes very meaningful. Filmed in Ireland and rated R for nudity and language.

1970   88 minutes

QUARTET
★★

DIRECTOR: James Ivory

CAST: Isabelle Adjani, Alan Bates, Anthony Higgins, Maggie Smith

In terms of acting, this is a first-rate film. If movies are a ninety-percent visual medium, then the scenes of Paris in the 1920s would make this well worthwhile. Unfortunately, the pathetic characters that mope around in this period piece drag down any positive points to the film. Isabelle Adjani plays the wife of a convicted criminal who ends up in a *ménage à trois* with a married couple, played by Alan Bates and Maggie Smith. Rated R for nudity.

1981   101 minutes

QUEEN OF THE STARDUST BALLROOM
★★★★

DIRECTOR: Sam O'Steen
CAST: Maureen Stapleton, Charles Durning, Michael Brandon, Michael Strong

Touching love story about a lonely widow (Maureen Stapleton) who finally finds Mr. Right (Charles Durning). Stapleton is outstanding.

1975   100 minutes

QUERELLE
★★½

DIRECTOR: Rainer Werner Fassbinder
CAST: Rainer Werner Fassbinder, Brad Davis, Franco Nero, Jeanne Moreau, Gunther Kaufmann, Hanna Poschl

In what turned out to be his last film, the late German film director Rainer Werner Fassbinder uses Jean Genet's *Querelle de Bres* as a way of confronting his own homosexuality. In this murky, unhappy rendering of Genet's story, Brad Davis (*Midnight Express*) stars in the title role as a young sailor whose good looks set off a chain reaction. As filmed by an obviously enfeebled Fassbinder, who died a drug-related death at 36, this is a disturbing and depressing portrait of terminally unhappy people doomed to destroy either themselves, one another, or both. Rated R for homosexual sex and obscenity.

1982   120 minutes

QUESTION OF SILENCE, A
★★★★½

DIRECTOR: Marleen Gorris
CAST: Cox Habbema, Nelly Frijda, Henriette Tol, Edda Barends

After an unusual murder is committed, three women, all strangers to one another, stand trial for the same crime. A woman psychiatrist is appointed to the case after the three openly display their hostilities toward male-dominated society. The psychiatrist is forced to examine her own nature as her understanding and sympathy for the women evolve. Rated R for profanity. Available in original Dutch or dubbed.

1983   92 minutes

QUICKSILVER
★

DIRECTOR: Tom Donnelly
CAST: Kevin Bacon, Jami Gertz, Paul Rodriguez, Rudy Ramos, Andrew Smith

Wretched mess of a film, which moves in too many directions and succeeds with none. Kevin Bacon stars as a Wall Street wizard who blows it all one day—including his parents' savings account—and then puts his natural talents to work by becoming...a bicycle messenger. Nice bicycle-level camera work and a decent performance by Jami Gertz, but the rest is a mess of rock video sequences and weak plot elements: the nasty drug dealer, the independent young girl who gets in over her head, the lad whose idea of American success is opening his own hot dog stand. Puh-*leaze*. Bacon displays none of the talent he's shown in the past. Rated PG for mild violence.

1986   101 minutes

R.P.M. (REVOLUTIONS PER MINUTE)
★★

DIRECTOR: Stanley Kramer

CAST: Anthony Quinn, Ann-Margret, Gary Lockwood

In this story set on a small-town college campus in the late 1960s, a liberal professor (Anthony Quinn) and his coed mistress (Ann-Margret) become involved in the efforts of a liberal student (Gary Lockwood) to have the professor made president of the university. Good intentions turn into campus unrest and violence. This movie starts out interesting, but as with many of director Stanley Kramer's efforts, it falls short. Rated R for violence.

1970   92 minutes

RABBIT RUN
★★

DIRECTOR: Jack Smight
CAST: James Caan, Carrie Snodgress, Jack Albertson, Henry Jones, Anjanette Comer

John Updike's novel concerning an ex–high school athlete's trouble adjusting to life off the playing field is brought to the screen in a very dull fashion. James Caan has the title role as the lost ex-jock who can't find out why life is so hard. Supporting cast is good, but the script sinks everyone involved.

1970   74 minutes

RACHEL, RACHEL
★★★½

DIRECTOR: Paul Newman
CAST: Joanne Woodward, James Olson, Kate Harrington, Estelle Parsons

Paul Newman's directorial debut focuses on a spinsterish schoolteacher (Joanne Woodward) and her awakening to a world beyond her job and her elderly mother's influence. One of the first and still one of the best modern "women's" films made in America, this bittersweet story is perfectly acted by Woodward, with strong support by James Olson as her short-term lover and Estelle Parsons as her friend. Rewarding on all levels and one of the best "first efforts" by any director. Rated R.

1968   101 minutes

RACING WITH THE MOON
★★★★½

DIRECTOR: Richard Benjamin
CAST: Sean Penn, Elizabeth McGovern, Nicolas Cage, John Karlen, Rutianya Alda, Carol Kane

Sean Penn and Elizabeth McGovern star in this thoroughly entertaining and touching comedy-romance set during World War II. He's just a regular town boy who discovers he's fallen in love with a "Gatsby," one of the area's rich girls. But that doesn't stop him from trying to win her heart. Richard Benjamin does a fabulous job of directing, perfectly balancing moments of romance, comedy, excitement, and suspense. The stars are attractive, believable, and likable. Rated R for nudity, profanity, suggested sex, and brief violence.

1984   108 minutes

RAGE
★★★

DIRECTOR: George C. Scott
CAST: George C. Scott, Martin Sheen, Richard Basehart, Barnard Hughes

This pits a lone man against the impersonal Establishment (in this instance the U.S. Army). This is not a happy film by any means, but it is an interesting one. Making his directorial debut, George C. Scott plays a peaceful sheep rancher whose son is the victim of military chemical testing. Seeking revenge, he sets out to nail those responsible. Rated PG.

1972   104 minutes

RAGING BULL
★★★★½

DIRECTOR: Martin Scorsese
CAST: Robert De Niro, Cathy Moriarty, Joe Pesci, Frank Vincent, Nicholas Colasanto, Theresa Saldana

This is a tough, compelling film . . . in fact, a great one. Directed by Martin Scorsese (*Alice Doesn't Live Here Anymore* and *Taxi Driver*) and starring the incredible Robert De Niro, it's one movie you won't want to miss. In playing prize fighter Jake La Motta from his twenties through to middle age, De Niro undergoes a transformation that takes him from his normal weight of 150 to 212 pounds. That is startling in itself, but the performance he gives is even more startling—see it. Rated R.

1980   B & W 128 minutes

RAGTIME
★★★★½

DIRECTOR: Milos Forman
CAST: James Cagney, Brad Dourif, Pat O'Brien, Donald O'Connor, Elizabeth McGovern, Mary Steenburgen

James Cagney returned to the screen after an absence of twenty years in this brilliant screen adaptation of E. L. Doctorow's best-selling novel about New York City at the turn of the century. It's a bountifully rewarding motion picture. Rated PG because of violence.

1981   155 minutes

RAIN
★★★★

DIRECTOR: Lewis Milestone

CAST: Joan Crawford, Walter Huston, William Gargan, Guy Kibbee, Walter Catlett, Beulah Bondi

Joan Crawford plays island hussy Sadie Thompson in this depressing drama. Walter Huston is the preacher who wants to "save" her—for himself.

1932   B & W 93 minutes

RAIN PEOPLE, THE
★★★★

DIRECTOR: Francis Ford Coppola
CAST: James Caan, Shirley Knight, Robert Duvall, Marya Zimmet, Tom Aldredge, Lloyd Crews

James Caan plays a retired football star who is picked up by a bored pregnant woman (played by Shirley Knight). She felt trapped as a housewife and ran away from her husband to be free. Directed by Francis Ford Coppola, this is an interesting, well-acted character study. Rated R.

1969   102 minutes

RAINTREE COUNTY
★★★

DIRECTOR: Edward Dmytryk
CAST: Elizabeth Taylor, Montgomery Clift, Eva Marie Saint, Nigel Patrick, Lee Marvin, Rod Taylor, Agnes Moorehead, Walter Abel, Rhys Williams

Civil War melodrama with Elizabeth Taylor as a southern belle is two and one-half hours of showy tedium that wastes a fine cast and miles of film. Best-selling novel comes to the screen as an extended soap opera with little promise and less results. Beautiful Elizabeth Taylor fiddle-de-dees her way around spectacular settings guided by impressive music, but the whole production is hollow and has no purpose or substance. Montgomery Clift's near-fatal car crash forced production to slow down on this ponderous epic, but even the extra time couldn't produce enough of a story to spark this overblown effort. Clift plays a wary second lead in this film, and his insecurities and physical pain as a result of the accident and subsequent plastic surgery are evident in his lack of success in imbuing this MGM entry with some of his charm and acting skill.

1957   168 minutes

RAISIN IN THE SUN, A
★★★★
DIRECTOR: Daniel Petrie
CAST: Sidney Poitier, Claudia McNeil, Ruby Dee, Diana Sands, Ivan Dixon, John Fiedler, Louis Gossett Jr.

A black family tries to escape from their crowded apartment life by moving to a house in an all-white neighborhood. Sidney Poitier delivers his usual outstanding performance in this film with a message about the limited opportunities open to blacks in the 1950s.

1961   B & W 128 minutes

RAMPARTS OF CLAY
★★★★
DIRECTOR: Jean-Louis Bertucelli
CAST: Leila Schenna and the villagers of Tehouda, Algeria

Terse but hauntingly beautiful documentary-style film set against the harsh background of a poor North African village. A young woman (Leila Schenna) struggles to free herself from the second-class role imposed on her by the village culture, much as the village tries to liberate itself from subservience to the corporate powers that control its salt mines, the citizens' only means of survival and live-lihood. In Arabic, with English subtitles. Rated PG.

1970   87 minutes

RAN
★★★★★
DIRECTOR: Akira Kurosawa
CAST: Tatsuya Nakadai, Akira Terao, Jinpachi Nezu, Daisuke Ryu, Mieko Harada, Peter

This superb Japanese historical epic tells the story of a sixteenth-century warlord's time of tragedy. Based on Shakespeare's *King Lear*, this is yet another masterwork from director Akira Kurosawa, a film on a par with D. W. Griffith's *Birth of a Nation*, Abel Gance's *Napoleon*, and Orson Welles' *Citizen Kane* as a triumph of personal artistic vision. It is stunningly photographed and acted, and blessed with touches of great drama, glorious humor, and hair-raising battle sequences. In other words, it is what motion pictures were meant to be but so seldom are. In Japanese with English subtitles. Rated R for violence and suggested sex.

1985   160 minutes

RASHOMON
★★★★★
DIRECTOR: Akira Kurosawa
CAST: Toshiro Mifune, Machiko Kyo, Masayuki Mori, Takashi

After a violent murder and rape is committed by a bandit, four people tell their own different versions of what happened. Set in medieval Japan, this examination of truth and guilt is charged with action. The combination of brilliant photography, stellar acting, direction, and script won this film the Oscar for best foreign film.

1951   B & W 83 minutes

RAZOR'S EDGE, THE (ORIGINAL)
★★★★½

DIRECTOR: Edmund Goulding
CAST: Tyrone Power, Gene Tierney, Clifton Webb, Herbert Marshall, Anne Baxter, John Payne, Elsa Lanchester

A long but engrossing presentation of Somerset Maugham's philosophical novel about a young man seeking the goodness in life. Full of memorable characterizations and scenes. Herbert Marshall steers the plot, playing the author. Clifton Webb is brilliant as arch-snob Elliot Templeton; Gene Tierney is beautiful and selfish, Tyrone Power fine as Larry, who sees more to life than money and social position. Standing out are Anne Baxter as Sophie, whose tragic personal losses drive her to dipsomania, and Elsa Lanchester as a prim social secretary with a soft center.

1946   B & W   146 minutes

RAZOR'S EDGE, THE (REMAKE)
★★★½

DIRECTOR: John Byrum
CAST: Bill Murray, Theresa Russell, Catharine Hicks, James Keach, Brian Doyle-Murray

Bill Murray gives a finely balanced comic and dramatic portrayal as Larry Darrell, a man searching for meaning after World War I in this adaptation of W. Somerset Maugham's novel. The result is a richly rewarding film, which survives the unevenness of John Byrum's direction. Rated PG-13 for suggested sex, violence, and profanity.

1984   128 minutes

REBECCA
★★★★★

DIRECTOR: Alfred Hitchcock
CAST: Laurence Olivier, Joan Fontaine, George Sanders, Nigel Bruce, Reginald Denny, Judith Anderson

Alfred Hitchcock made a very auspicious debut in American films with *Rebecca*, which won an Oscar for best picture and nominations for its stars, Laurence Olivier and Joan Fontaine. The popular Daphne du Maurier novel was transferred to the screen by cameraman George Barnes without losing any of its gothic blend of romance and mystery. In it, a shy American (Fontaine) is acting as a conceited woman's traveling companion in Europe. After a whirlwind courtship, she marries the brooding Max de Winter (Olivier). Her chances for happiness with this secretive man hinge on her ability to break through the shroud that envelops his past. Somehow the key to unlocking the mystery lies with his dead first wife, Rebecca. Judith Anderson as the sinister housekeeper is one of the most compelling figures in film history.

1940   B & W   130 minutes

REBEL WITHOUT A CAUSE
★★★★★

DIRECTOR: Nicholas Ray
CAST: James Dean, Natalie Wood, Sal Mineo, Jim Backus, Ann Doran, Corey Allen, Edward Platt, Dennis Hopper, Nick Adams

This is the film that made James Dean a legend. Directed by Nicholas Ray, it is undoubtedly the classic film about juvenile delinquency. Featuring fine performances by Dean (in one of only three screen appearances, the others being *East of Eden* and *Giant*), Natalie Wood, and Sal Mineo as the teens in trouble, it has stood up surprisingly well over the years.

It and *The Wild One* are the only 1950s "bad youth" movies that still pack a punch today.

1955   111 minutes

RECKLESS
★★

DIRECTOR: James Foley
CAST: Aidan Quinn, Daryl Hannah, Kenneth McMillan, Cliff DeYoung, Lois Smith, Adam Baldwin, Dan Hedaya

A 1980s version of the standard 1950s "angry young man" movie, this features Aidan Quinn as a motorcycle-riding, mumbling (à la James Dean and Marlon Brando) outcast and Daryl Hannah (*Summer Lovers*) as the "good girl." She is the A-student cheerleader both attracted and repelled by the danger he represents. Wait a minute . . . wasn't that the synopsis of *Breathless*? It was, and that should give you an idea of how original this movie is—about as original as the cliché "a stitch in time saves nine." You can save some money if you skip this uninspired release. Rated R for nudity, profanity, violence, and suggested sex.

1984   90 minutes

RED BEARD
★★★★½

DIRECTOR: Akira Kurosawa
CAST: Toshiro Mifune, Yuzo Kayama, Yoshio Tsuchiya

In the early nineteenth-century, a newly graduated doctor, Yasumoto (Yuzo Kayama), hopes to become a society doctor. Instead, he is posted at an impoverished clinic run by Dr. Niide (Toshiro Mifune), whose destitute patients affectionately call him "Red Beard." We are never once fidgety during the three hours. At first we are caught up in the story's soap opera web, and then won by the wisdom of Red Beard's words and ways. Won over, too, of course, is Yasumoto. Mifune is at his most brilliant. Akira Kurosawa, at one of his many directorial pinnacles, describes his film as a "monument to the goodness in man." In Japanese with English subtitles.

1965   B & W 185 minutes

RED DUST
★★★★

DIRECTOR: Victor Fleming
CAST: Clark Gable, Jean Harlow, Mary Astor, Donald Crisp, Gene Raymond, Tully Marshall, Willie Fung

Red Dust is one of those remarkable films where the performances of its stars propel a movie to classic status despite a rather uninspired story. The erotic chemistry between Clark Gable and Jean Harlow generates much more magic than the hackneyed story of a rubber plantation boss (Gable) who dallies with another man's wife only to return to the arms of a shady lady (Harlow) with the proverbial heart of gold.

1932   B & W 83 minutes

RED LIGHT STING, THE
★★

DIRECTOR: Rod Holcomb
CAST: Farrah Fawcett, Beau Bridges, Harold Gould, Paul Burke, Alex Henteloff, Conrad Janis, Sunny Johnson, James Luisi, Philip Charles MacKenzie

Pale TV film about a young district attorney (Beau Bridges) who is assigned to buy a whorehouse to bring out an elusive big-time crook (Harold Gould). Farrah Fawcett plays a hooker whom Bridges confides in. Very few surprises and the screenplay is pedestrian, but entertaining enough to engage the attention. Not rated, but the equivalent of a PG for adult subject matter.

1984   96 minutes

REDS
★★★★★

DIRECTOR: Warren Beatty
CAST: Warren Beatty, Diane Keaton, Jack Nicholson, Gene Hackman, Edward Herrmann, Maureen Stapleton, Jerzy Kosinski

Warren Beatty produced, directed, co-wrote, and starred in this $33 million American film masterpiece. This three-hour-plus film biography of left-wing American journalist John Reed (Beatty) and Louise Bryant (Diane Keaton) also features brilliant bits from Jack Nicholson, Gene Hackman, Edward Herrmann, Maureen Stapleton, and Jerzy Kosinski (author of *Being There*). Rated PG because of profanity, silhouetted sex scenes, and war scenes.

1981   200 minutes

REFLECTIONS IN A GOLDEN EYE
★★½

DIRECTOR: John Huston
CAST: Marlon Brando, Elizabeth Taylor, Brian Keith, Julie Harris, Robert Forster, Zorro David

Very bizarre film concerning a homosexual army officer (Marlon Brando) stationed in the South. This very strange film very rarely works—despite a high-powered cast.

1967   108 minutes

REMBRANDT
★★★★

DIRECTOR: Alexander Korda
CAST: Charles Laughton, Gertrude Lawrence, Elsa Lanchester

This is one of the few satisfying movie biographies of an artist. The depiction of the famous Dutch painter and his struggle to maintain his artistic integrity is related with respectful restraint and attention to factual detail. Charles Laughton, as Rembrandt, is brilliant in what was for him an atypically low-key performance. More than any of his screen characterizations, this role shows how completely Laughton was a master of his craft. The sets deserve special praise. They capture the feel of Dutch life in the seventeenth century.

1936   B & W   90 minutes

REQUIEM FOR A HEAVYWEIGHT
★★★½

DIRECTOR: Ralph Nelson
CAST: Anthony Quinn, Julie Harris, Jackie Gleason, Mickey Rooney, Muhammad Ali

Anthony Quinn, Julie Harris, Jackie Gleason, Mickey Rooney, and Muhammad Ali (at that time Cassius Clay) give fine performances in this watchable film about boxing corruption. An over-the-hill boxer (Quinn) receives career counseling from a social worker (Harris).

1962   B & W   100 minutes

RETURN OF MARTIN GUERRE, THE
★★★★½

DIRECTOR: Daniel Vigne
CAST: Gerard Depardieu, Nathalie Baye, Roger Planchon, Maurice Jaquemont, Bernard Pierre, Donna Dieu

Brilliantly absorbing account of an actual sixteenth-century court case in which a man returns to his family and village after years away at the wars, only to have his identity questioned. Gerard Depardieu and

Nathalie Baye give outstanding, carefully restrained performances in this haunting historical drama. No MPAA rating.

1982 111 minutes

RETURN OF THE SOLDIER, THE
★★★★★

DIRECTOR: Alan Bridges

CAST: Glenda Jackson, Julie Christie, Ann-Margret, Alan Bates, Ian Holm, Frank Finlay, Jeremy Kemp

During World War I, a soldier (Alan Bates) suffers shell shock and forgets the last twenty years of his life. His doctors must decide whether he should be allowed to enjoy what has resulted in a carefree second youth, or be brought back to real life and the responsibilities—to say nothing of horrifying battle experience memories—that go with it. Glenda Jackson is the childhood sweetheart he longs to hold once again. Julie Christie is the selfish wife who wants him "normal" (and unhappy) again. Ann-Margret is the loving sister who only wishes him happiness. Everyone in the cast is superb. Not rated, the film contains adult situations.

1985 105 minutes

REVOLT OF JOB, THE
★★★★

DIRECTOR: Imre Gyongyossy

CAST: Fereno Zenthe, Hedi Tenessy, Gabor Feher, Peter Rudolph, Leticia Caro

In this moving account of the Holocaust in rural Hungary, an old Jewish couple awaiting the inevitable Nazi takeover adopt a gentile orphan boy to survive them. Nominated for best foreign-language film in 1983's Academy Awards. In Hungarian, with English subtitles. No rating.

1983 97 minutes

REVOLUTION
★★

DIRECTOR: Hugh Hudson

CAST: Al Pacino, Nastassja Kinski, Donald Sutherland

Director Hugh Hudson must have had good intentions going into this project, examining what it might have been like to be involved in the American Revolution. The sets, costumes, battle scenes, and cinematography are some of the best to be put on film. Unfortunately, his actors are so miscast and the script so ragged that Hudson's project stalls almost before it gets started. Al Pacino and his son become caught up in the frenzy of the early days of the Revolution and soon find themselves facing the British, led by Donald Sutherland. We follow them through several years and historical events for the next two grueling hours. Nastassja Kinski plays a wealthy daughter of a pro-English family who goes to the side of the revolutionists and becomes Pacino's love interest, as well. Filmed on a budget that would bail most Third-World countries out of debt, *Revolution* is beautiful but has no substance to sustain its worthy topic. Rated R.

1986 125 minutes

RICH AND FAMOUS
★★★★

DIRECTOR: George Cukor

CAST: Jacqueline Bisset, Candice Bergen, David Selby, Hart Bochner, Steven Hill, Meg Ryan, Matt Latanzi, Michael Brandon

Jacqueline Bisset and Candice Bergen star in this warm, witty, and involving chronicle of the ups, downs, joys, and heartbreak experienced by two friends during a twenty-year relationship. Hollywood great George Cukor (*The Philadelphia Story*) directed in his inimitable style. Rated R because of profanity and sex.

1981   117 minutes

RICH KIDS
★★

DIRECTOR: Robert M. Young
CAST: Trini Alvarado, Jeremy Levy, John Lithgow, Kathryn Walker, Terry Kiser, Paul Dooley

A poor screenplay (which includes some incredibly bad jokes) plagues this movie about two kids going through puberty at the same time they are experiencing the dissolution of their parents' marriages. A great cast helps. Also, there is an unforgettable heartfelt moment between mother and daughter (Kathryn Walker and Trini Alvarado). Rated PG for language.

1979   97 minutes

RICHARD III
★★★★

DIRECTOR: Laurence Olivier
CAST: Laurence Olivier, Ralph Richardson, John Gielgud, Claire Bloom

Once again, as in *Henry V* and *Hamlet*, England's foremost player displays his near-matchless acting and directing skills in bringing Shakespeare to life on film. His royal crookback usurper is beautifully malevolent, a completely intriguing, smiling villain. The film fascinates from first to last.

1955   161 minutes

RIGHT OF WAY
★★★★

DIRECTOR: George Shaefer
CAST: James Stewart, Bette Davis, Melinda Dillon, Priscilla Morrill, John Harkins

This made-for-cable work deals with a rather unusual decision made by an old married couple, Mini and Teddy Dwyer (Bette Davis and James Stewart, respectively), who have decided to commit suicide. Mini has a terminal blood disease and doesn't want to go through the agony of a slow death. And Teddy, who is completely devoted to his lifelong mate, has no desire to go on without her. Thus begins a battle between daughter (Melinda Dillon) and parents: one that grows from a personal dispute to a newspaper scandal. The result is a surprisingly gripping character study. Davis is excellent as the strong-willed, sharp-tongued matriarch. Stewart, of course, is as watchable as always. But it is Dillon who nearly steals the picture, with her affecting portrayal of the confused but concerned daughter.

1983   106 minutes

RIGHT STUFF, THE
★★★★★

DIRECTOR: Phil Kaufman
CAST: Sam Shepard, Scott Glenn, Ed Harris, Dennis Quaid, Barbara Hershey, Fred Ward, Kim Stanley, Veronica Cartwright, Pamela Reed, Donald Moffat, Levon Helm, Scott Wilson, Jeff Goldblum, Harry Shearer

The most impressive American screen drama since *The Godfather*. From Tom Wolfe's bestseller about the early years of the American space program, writer-director Phil Kaufman has created an epic screen tribute to, and examination of, the men (both test pilots and astronauts) who "pushed the outside of the envelope," and the women who watched and waited while the world watched them. Rated PG for profanity.

1983   193 minutes

RIOT IN CELL BLOCK 11
★★★★

DIRECTOR: Don Siegel
CAST: Neville Brand, Emile Meyer, Frank Faylen, Leo Gordon, Robert Osterloh

The taste and tension with which he would make memorable movies such as *Dirty Harry*, *Charley Varrick*, and *The Shootist* is evident in this hard-edged prison drama by director Don Siegel. Neville Brand, Emile Meyer, and Leo Gordon give outstanding performances.

1954   B & W   80 minutes

RITA HAYWORTH: THE LOVE GODDESS
★★½

DIRECTOR: James Goldstone
CAST: Lynda Carter, Michael Lerner, John Considine, Alejandro Rey

This lifeless attempt to recreate pinup queen Rita Hayworth's exciting life falls short of its goal. Beautiful Lynda Carter ("Wonder Woman") as Hayworth, however, keeps the viewer's attention. Unrated.

1983   100 minutes

RIVER, THE
★★★½

DIRECTOR: Mark Rydell
CAST: Mel Gibson, Sissy Spacek, Scott Glenn

Had it been the first of its kind, this film, starring Mel Gibson, Sissy Spacek, and Scott Glenn, could very well have been heralded as a powerful drama, if not a great motion picture. But following as it does on the heels of two other first-rate farmer films, this work by director Mark Rydell (*On Golden Pond*) often seems hopelessly unoriginal and, as a result, boring. As with *Country*, it deals with a farming family—the Garveys—who must battle a severe storm and foreclosure proceedings. Like Sally Field's character in *Places in the Heart*, the Garveys must resort to extreme methods to survive. *The River* is not a bad film. It is, in fact, a very good one. It simply has little new to say. Rated PG for nudity, violence, and profanity.

1984   122 minutes

RIVER RAT, THE
★★★½

DIRECTOR: Tom Rickman
CAST: Tommy Lee Jones, Martha Plimpton, Brian Dennehy

Although essentially the story of the growing love between a long-separated father (Tommy Lee Jones), who has been in prison for thirteen years, and daughter (newcomer Martha Plimpton), this release is much more than a simple tearjerker. Writer-director Tom Rickman has invested his story with a grit and realism that set it apart from similar works. As a result, he's created a powerful, thought-provoking motion picture. Rated R for profanity and violence.

1984   109 minutes

ROBE, THE
★★★★

DIRECTOR: Henry Koster

CAST: Richard Burton, Victor Mature, Jean Simmons, Michael Rennie, Richard Boone, Dean Jagger, Dawn Addams, Jan Robinson

Richard Burton is the Roman tribune charged with overseeing the execution of Christ in this story of his involvement with the followers of Christ and the effect the robe of Jesus has on all involved. It is a well-made film, and although it revolves around a religious subject, it is not heavy-handed in its approach. Well-acted performances are turned in by Burton, the tribune who must make a choice, and Victor Mature, as the follower of Christ who loses his faith.

1953   135 minutes

ROBERT ET ROBERT
★★★★½

DIRECTOR: Claude Lelouch
CAST: Charles Denner, Jacques Villeret, Jean-Claude Brialy, Macha Meril, Germaine Montero, Regine

A brilliant film about two lonely but very different men (Charles Denner and Jacques Villeret) who strike up a tenuous friendship while waiting for their respective computer dates. It is a bittersweet tale of loneliness and compassion, of the painful differences that separate people, and of the dream of discovering full human potential. No MPAA rating.

1978   105 minutes

ROCKY
★★★★½

DIRECTOR: John G. Avildsen
CAST: Sylvester Stallone, Talia Shire, Burt Young, Burgess Meredith, Carl Weathers, Thayer David

Despite the spectacular success of *Rocky III*, this initial adventure of Sylvester Stallone's boxing Everyman is still the best. It is a moving portrait of a man's fight to regain his dignity. Rated PG.

1976   119 minutes

ROCKY II
★★

DIRECTOR: Sylvester Stallone
CAST: Sylvester Stallone, Carl Weathers, Talia Shire, Burgess Meredith, Burt Young

The weakest entry in Sylvester Stallone's boxing trilogy, about a down-and-out fighter attempting to prove himself through a rematch with the champ (Carl Weathers). Talia Shire, Burgess Meredith, and Burt Young reprise their series roles in this soaper in the ring. Rated PG.

1979   119 minutes

ROCKY III
★★★

DIRECTOR: Sylvester Stallone
CAST: Sylvester Stallone, Talia Shire, Burgess Meredith, Mr. T, Carl Weathers

Writer-director-star Sylvester Stallone's third entry in the Rocky Balboa series is surprisingly entertaining. Though we've seen it all before, Stallone manages to make it work one more time—and even better than in *Rocky II*. That's no small feat. Rated PG for violence and mild profanity.

1982   99 minutes

ROCKY IV
★★★

DIRECTOR: Sylvester Stallone
CAST: Sylvester Stallone, Talia Shire, Burt Young, Carl Weathers, Brigette Nielsen, Tony Burton, Michael Pataki, Dolph Lundgren

Sylvester Stallone's Everyman boxing hero returns to take on a massive Russian fighter (Dolph Lundgren) trained via computer and programmed to kill. The result is deliciously corny, enjoyably predictable entertainment. *Rocky IV* is not unlike an old-fashioned chapter serial with its cliffhanger situations, goody good guys, and dastardly villains. Even though we know the *Rocky* formula—an early failure by the good guys, a bit of soul searching by the hero, the training sequence, and the final confrontation—the movie works. Rated PG for violence.

1985   90 minutes

RODEO GIRL
★★★★
DIRECTOR: Jackie Cooper
CAST: Katherine Ross, Bo Hopkins, Candy Clark, Jacqueline Brookes, Wilford Brimley

Katharine Ross (*The Graduate*, *Butch Cassidy and the Sundance Kid*) is Sammy, the wife of rodeo champ Will Garrett (Bo Hopkins). When she decides to try her hand at roping and bronco riding, she finds that she has the potential to be a rodeo champ. But complications arise when she discovers she is pregnant. Of course, Will wants Sammy to forget the rodeo circuit, and with Sammy's refusal, the conflict begins. *Rodeo Girl* offers a fresh resolution to an old conflict. Still, the film has its drawbacks: Ross's performance is inconsistent, and Candy Clark (*American Grafitti, Blue Thunder*), who plays Sammy's roping teammate, misses the "good ol' cowgirl" mark by overdoing a southern twang. Based on a true story.

1980   92 minutes

ROLLOVER
★★★½
DIRECTOR: Alan J. Pakula
CAST: Jane Fonda, Kris Kristofferson, Hume Cronyn, Josef Sommer, Bob Gunton

Jane Fonda plays an ex–film star who inherits a multimillion-dollar empire when her husband is mysteriously murdered in this gripping, but not great, film. Kris Kristofferson is the financial troubleshooter who joins forces with her to save the company. Soon both their lives are in danger. Rated R because of profanity.

1981   118 minutes

ROMAN HOLIDAY
★★★★★
DIRECTOR: William Wyler
CAST: Gregory Peck, Audrey Hepburn, Eddie Albert

Amid the beauty and mystique of Rome, an American newspaperman (Gregory Peck) is handed a news scoop on the proverbial silver platter. A princess (Audrey Hepburn) has slipped away from her stifling royal lifestyle. In her efforts to hide as one of Rome's common people, she encounters Peck. Their amiable adventures provide the basis for a charming fantasy-romance.

1953   B & W 119 minutes

ROMAN SPRING OF MRS. STONE, THE
★★½
DIRECTOR: Jose Quintero
CAST: Vivien Leigh, Warren Beatty, Lotte Lenya, Jill St. John

A sensitive, elegant middle-aged actress (Vivien Leigh) has retreated to Rome to get a new focus. Warren Beatty plays a sleek, surly, wet-lipped Italian gigolo out for what he can get with the help of a crass, waspish procuress

(Lotte Lenya). It's all banal. Based on a Tennessee Williams novel.

1961　　　　　　　　104 minutes

ROMANTIC ENGLISHWOMAN, THE
★★★★

DIRECTOR: Joseph Losey
CAST: Glenda Jackson, Michael Caine, Helmut Berger

Though not a completely successful adaptation of Thomas Wiseman's novel (by Wiseman and playwright Tom Stoppard), this is likely to be vastly more engaging than anything on television on any given night. Casual infidelity among the wealthy intelligentsia is always at least voyeuristically satisfying. And here pulp novel writer Michael Caine actually impels his discontented, but presumably faithful, wife Glenda Jackson into an affair with gigolo Helmut Berger. This tragicomedy of manners is scarcely explicit: it is as superficially refined as are its characters—but there is real Continental sleaze lurking beneath the snappy dialogue, the lush scenery, and the impeccably tailored clothes. All the principals are in top form, however Helmut Berger's role fits him like a fine glove. Rated R for language, adult situations.

1975　　　　　　　　115 minutes

ROMEO AND JULIET
★★★★½

DIRECTOR: Franco Zeffirelli
CAST: Olivia Hussey, Leonard Whiting, John McEnery, Michael York, Milo O'Shea

Franco Zeffirelli directed this excellent version of *Romeo and Juliet*. When it was filmed, Olivia Hussey was only 15 and Leonard Whiting was only 17, keeping their characters in tune with Shakespeare's hero and heroine. Rated PG.

1968　　　　　　　　138 minutes

ROOM WITH A VIEW, A (1987 RELEASE)
★★★★★

DIRECTOR: James Ivory
CAST: Maggie Smith, Helena Bonham Carter, Denholm Elliot, Julian Sands, Daniel Day Lewis, Simon Callow, Judi Dench, Rosemary Leach

Adapted from the novel by E. M. Forster, this is a triumph of tasteful, intelligent filmmaking. Director James Ivory (*The Bostonians*) painstakingly re-creates the mood, manners, and milieu of 1908 Edwardian England as he explores the consequence of a tour of Florence, Italy, taken by an innocently curious young woman (Helena Bonham Carter) and her persnickety, meddling aunt (Maggie Smith, in top form). The characters, even down to the smallest supporting bit, are skillfully drawn by screenwriter Ruth Prawer Jhabvala, and the acting is exquisite. *A Room With a View* will especially please those with a fondness for the best in literature, music, and art. Even those with less cultivated tastes may find watching it a rare and wonderful experience. Unrated, the film has one brief scene of violence and some male frontal nudity.

1986　　　　　　　　115 minutes

ROSELAND
★★★½

DIRECTOR: James Ivory
CAST: Christopher Walken, Geraldine Chaplin, Teresa Wright, Lou Jacobi, Don DeNatale, Lilia Skala

Protean—and gentleman—filmmaker James Ivory (*Shakespeare*

Wallah, The Guru, and the quasi-documentary on David Hockney *A Bigger Splash*) and his collaborators (Ruth Prawer Jhabvala, screenplay, Ismail Merchant, producer) have fashioned a somewhat overly respectful triptych set in the famous, now-tattered, New York dance palace. The three stories about aging people seeking a haven of nostalgia are quietly compelling, but only Christopher Walken (certainly a good enough dancer and showing here a preview of his talents in *Pennies from Heaven*) and Don DeNatale (who was an emcee at Roseland) give the film any vim. It did receive a seven-minute standing ovation at the New York Film Festival; we don't ask that you do the same.

1977   103 minutes

RUBY GENTRY
★★★
DIRECTOR: King Vidor
CAST: Jennifer Jones, Charlton Heston, Karl Malden, Tom Tully

An excellent cast and sensitive direction make this drama of a Carolina swamp girl's social progress better than might be expected. Its focus is the caste system and prejudice in a picturesque region of the great melting pot.

1952   B & W   82 minutes

RUMBLE FISH
★★
DIRECTOR: Francis Ford Coppola
CAST: Christopher Penn, Tom Waites, Matt Dillon, Dennis Hopper, Vincent Spano

Francis Ford Coppola's black-and-white screen portrait of S. E. Hinton's second-rate novel about a teen-age boy (Matt Dillon) seeking to escape his hellish life is a disappointing misfire. Rated R.

1983   B & W   94 minutes

RUNNER STUMBLES, THE
★★★
DIRECTOR: Stanley Kramer
CAST: Dick Van Dyke, Kathleen Quinlan, Maureen Stapleton, Beau Bridges

A good adaptation of Milan Stitt's play, which certainly did not deserve the scorching hatred generated during its brief box-office appearance. Dick Van Dyke plays a priest who falls in love with Kathleen Quinlan's appealing nun. Subsequent thoughts and counterthoughts are talked to death, which betrays the story's origin on-stage, but both leads contribute sensitive performances. The subject may make viewers uneasy, but the film is by no means tacky or exploitative. A near miss, but still worth catching. Rated PG for adult subject matter.

1979   99 minutes

RUNNING BRAVE
★★★★
DIRECTOR: Don Shebib
CAST: Robby Benson, Pat Hingle, Jeff McCracken

Robby Benson stars as Billy Mills, whose winning the ten-thousand meter race in the 1964 Olympics was one of the biggest upsets in sports history. The direction, credited to "D. S. Everett" (a pseudonym for Don Shebib, who demanded his name be taken off the credits after the film was re-edited), is pedestrian at best. But Benson's fine performance and the true-life drama of Mills's determination to set a positive example of achievement for his people—the Sioux and all Native Americans—are affecting enough to carry the film. Rated PG for profanity.

1983   105 minutes

RUNNING HOT
★★★

DIRECTOR: Mark Griffiths
CAST: Eric Stoltz, Stuart Margolin, Monica Carrico, Virgil Frye

Eric Stoltz gives a very good performance as a 17-year-old convicted of killing his father and sentenced to death row. The publicity of his case arouses the interest of 30-year-old Monica Carrico, who sends him love letters in prison. His escape and bizarre affair with her have serious consequences in this fast-paced drama. Through flashbacks we are shown the surprising facts to the crime. Rated R for sex, violence, language, and nudity.

1983   88 minutes

RYAN'S DAUGHTER
★★½

DIRECTOR: David Lean
CAST: Sarah Miles, Christopher Jones, Robert Mitchum, Trevor Howard, John Mills, Leo McKern

Director David Lean, who had been acclaimed for such films as *The Bridge on the River Kwai*, *Lawrence of Arabia*, and *Dr. Zhivago*, took a critical beating with this release, about a spoiled woman (Sarah Miles) who shamelessly lusts after an officer (Christopher Jones). Robert Mitchum, as Miles's long-suffering husband, is the best thing about this watchable misfire. Rated R.

1970   176 minutes

S.O.S. TITANIC
★★★

DIRECTOR: William Hale
CAST: David Janssen, Cloris Leachman, Susan Saint James, David Warner

The "unsinkable" pride of the Ismay Line once again goes to her watery grave deep beneath the cold Atlantic in this made-for-television docudrama compounded of fiction and fact.

1979   105 minutes

SAILOR WHO FELL FROM GRACE WITH THE SEA, THE
★★

DIRECTOR: Lewis John Carlino
CAST: Sarah Miles, Kris Kristofferson, Margo Cunningham, Earl Rhodes

Much of Japanese culture remains misunderstood, and this inept adaptation of Yukio Mishima's novel is a perfect example. Kris Kristofferson doesn't have to stretch his limited abilities as an amiable sailor who falls in love with Sarah Miles. Her son, unfortunately, views the relationship with less than delight . . . although he views it a lot, through an unseen peephole. Story attempts to turn its audience into voyeurs, like the boy, but the celebrated love scenes are too stiff and artificial. The boy then meets up with a friend who likes to dissect cats; things go downhill from there. Quite dull. Rated R for violence and sex.

1976   104 minutes

ST. ELMO'S FIRE
★★★

DIRECTOR: Joel Schumacher
CAST: Emilio Estevez, Rob Lowe, Andrew McCarthy, Demi Moore, Judd Nelson, Ally Sheedy, Mare Winningham, Martin Balsam, Andie MacDowell, Joyce Van Patten

Written and directed by Joel Schumacher, this film would have us believe a group of college graduates are, at the age of 22, all suffering from mid-life crises. It's a little hard to believe. However, the fine acting by some of the screen's hottest young stars helps us forgive this off-kilter premise. In addition, Schumacher adds some nice touches of humanity and humor. The result is a good, though not great, movie that succeeds almost in spite of itself. Rated R for suggested sex, violence, nudity, and profanity.

1985   110 minutes

ST. HELENS
★★½

DIRECTOR: Ernest Pintoff
CAST: Art Carney, David Huffman, Cassie Yates, Albert Salmi, Ron O'Neal

Very shallow look at the Mount St. Helens volcanic eruption and the following disasters. Art Carney plays Harry, the old man who refuses to move from his home as the upcoming fiasco is about to take place. Pretty bland stuff. Rated PG for no particular reason.

1981   90 minutes

SAINT JACK
★★★½

DIRECTOR: Peter Bogdanovich
CAST: Ben Gazzara, Denholm Elliott, James Villiers, Joss Ackland, Peter Bogdanovich, George Lazenby

Although an interesting film, *Saint Jack* lacks power and a sense of wholeness. The story has all the right elements, but the treatment by director Peter Bogdanovich is rambling and lacking a specific point of view. Ben Gazzara plays an oddly likable pimp plying his trade in Singapore in the 1970s who wants to become rich and powerful by running the classiest whorehouse in the Far East. Even with its problems, this offbeat character study has its share of memorable moments. Gazzara and

Denholm Elliott are first-rate. Rated R.

1979   112 minutes

SAKHAROV
★★★★

DIRECTOR: Jack Gold
CAST: Jason Robards Jr., Glenda Jackson, Michael Bryant, Paul Freeman, Anna Massey, Joe Melia, Lee Montague, Jim Norton

Compassionate story of the nuclear physicist and designer of the H-bomb, Andrei Sakharov (Jason Robards), who won the Nobel Peace Prize after waking up to the global terror of the nuclear gambit and contributing to the budding human rights movement in the Soviet Union during the late 1960s. The story bogs down at times, and while the predominantly British cast puts in fine performances (including Glenda Jackson, who plays Elena Bonner Sakharov, Andrei's brave and headstrong wife and political comrade), the accents do become a bit obtrusive at times.

1984   118 minutes

SALVADOR
★★★★

DIRECTOR: Oliver Stone
CAST: James Woods, John Savage, Jim Belushi, Michael Murphy, Elpedia Carrillo, Tony Plana, Cynthia Gibb

James Woods (*Joshua Then and Now*) plays screenwriter/photojournalist Richard Boyle in the latter's semiautobiographical account of the events that occurred in El Salvador circa 1980–81. It is a fascinating movie despite its flaws and outrageousness. Overt audience manipulation cannot dull its impact as a gripping thriller or thwart the outstanding performances by Woods, John Savage, Jim Belushi, and Michael Murphy. Oliver Stone directs with uncommon skill. Rated R for profanity, nudity, suggested sex, drug use, and violence.

1986   120 minutes

SAM'S SON
★★★½

DIRECTOR: Michael Landon
CAST: Timothy Patrick Murphy, Eli Wallach, Anne Jackson

Written and directed by Michael Landon, this sweetly nostalgic, semiautobiographical family film features Timothy Patrick Murphy as the young Eugene Orowitz (Landon's real name), whose parents, Sam (Eli Wallach) and Harriet (Anne Jackson), seem destined never to realize their fondest dreams until their son takes a hand. Rated PG for brief violence.

1984   104 minutes

SAMSON AND DELILAH
★★★★

DIRECTOR: Cecil B. De Mille
CAST: Hedy Lamarr, Victor Mature, George Sanders, Angela Lansbury

This Cecil B. De Mille extravaganza still looks good today. Hedy Lamarr plays the beautiful vixen Delilah, who robs Samson (Victor Mature) of his incredible strength. Dumb but fun.

1949   128 minutes

SAN FRANCISCO
★★★★

DIRECTOR: W. S. Van Dyke
CAST: Clark Gable, Jeanette MacDonald, Spencer Tracy

In its heyday, MGM boasted it had more stars than were in the heavens, and it made some terrific star-studded movies as a result. Take this 1936 production, starring Clark Gable, Jeanette MacDonald, and Spencer Tracy, for example. It's entertainment of the first order, with special effects—of the San Francisco earthquake—that still stand up today.

1936   B & W 115 minutes

SANDPIPER, THE
★½

DIRECTOR: Vincente Minnelli
CAST: Richard Burton, Elizabeth Taylor, Eva Marie Saint, Charles Bronson

Corny love triangle involves barefoot Elizabeth Taylor, who loves Richard Burton, who is married to Eva Marie Saint. Lots of surf and birds in this so-what star vehicle, which capitalizes on its location shooting off the California coast. Watch for Charles Bronson in his pre-star days.

1965   116 minutes

SAVAGE IS LOOSE, THE

DIRECTOR: George C. Scott
CAST: George C. Scott, Trish Van Devere, John David Carson, Lee H. Montgomery

Kill it before it multiplies. In addition to acting and directing, George C. Scott also produced and distributed this pretentious disaster. The tedious tale strands a young man and his parents on an island for many years. They explore a recreational activity the Swiss Family Robinson never considered: incest. Rated R.

1974   114 minutes

SAVE THE TIGER
★★★

DIRECTOR: John G. Avildsen
CAST: Jack Lemmon, Jack Gilford, Thayer David

Jack Lemmon won the Academy Award for best actor for his portrayal in this 1973 film as a garment manufacturer who is at the end of his professional and emotional rope. His excellent performance helps offset the fact that the picture is essentially a downer. Rated R.

1973   101 minutes

SAWDUST AND TINSEL
★★★½

DIRECTOR: Ingmar Bergman
CAST: Harriet Andersson, Ake Grönberg, Anders Ek, Gudrun Brost

A traveling circus is the background for this study of love relationships between a circus manager, the woman he loves, and her lover. Director Ingmar Bergman scores some emotional bull's-eyes in this early effort with many haunting scenes. Love triangles lead to powerful climax, somewhat reminiscent of *The Blue Angel*.

1953   B & W   95 minutes

SAYONARA
★★★★

DIRECTOR: Joshua Logan
CAST: Marlon Brando, Red Buttons, Miyoshi Umeki, Ricardo Montalban, James Garner

Marlon Brando is an American airman who engages in a romance with a Japanese actress while stationed in Japan after World War II. His love is put to the test by each culture's misconceptions and prejudices. James A. Michener's thought-provoking tragedy-romance still holds up well. Red Buttons and Miyoshi Umeki deservedly won Oscars for their roles as star-crossed lovers "American Occupation"–style.

1957   147 minutes

SCARECROW
★★★

DIRECTOR: Jerry Schatzberg
CAST: Al Pacino, Gene Hackman, Eileen Brennan, Richard Lynch

A real downer about two losers (Al Pacino and Gene Hackman) trying to make something of themselves, this drama is made watchable by the performances. Rated R.

1973   115 minutes

SCARLET STREET
★★★½

DIRECTOR: Fritz Lang
CAST: Edward G. Robinson, Joan Bennett, Dan Duryea, Margaret Lindsay, Rosalind Ivan

The director (Fritz Lang) and stars (Edward G. Robinson, Joan Bennett, and Dan Duryea) of the excellent *Woman in the Window* reteamed with less spectacular results for this film about a mild-mannered fellow (Robinson) seduced into a life of crime by a temptress (Bennett).

1945   B & W   103 minutes

SCENES FROM A MARRIAGE
★★★★★

DIRECTOR: Ingmar Bergman
CAST: Liv Ullmann, Erland Josephson, Bibi Andersson

Director Ingmar Bergman successfully captures the pain and emotions of a marriage that is disintegrating. Several scenes are extremely hard to watch because there is so much truth to what is being said. Originally a six-part film for Swedish television, the theatrical version was edited by Bergman. Believable throughout, this one packs a real punch. No rating (contains some strong language).

1973   168 minutes

SECRETS
★★

DIRECTOR: Philip Saville
CAST: Jacqueline Bisset, Per Oscarsson, Shirley Knight Hopkins, Robert Powell

Jacqueline Bisset's torrid sex scene is about the only interesting thing in this turgid soap opera about the romantic "secrets" of a husband, wife, and daughter. Rated R for nudity, suggested sex, and profanity.

1971   86 minutes

SEDUCTION OF JOE TYNAN, THE
★★★

DIRECTOR: Jerry Schatzberg
CAST: Alan Alda, Barbara Harris, Meryl Streep, Rip Torn, Charles Kimbrough, Melvyn Douglas

Alan Alda plays Senator Joe Tynan in this story of behind-the-scenes romance and political maneuvering in Washington, D.C. Tynan must face moral questions about himself and his job. It's familiar ground for Alda but still entertaining. Rated PG for language, brief nudity.

1979   107 minutes

SEPARATE TABLES
★★★★★

DIRECTOR: John Schlesinger
CAST: Julie Christie, Alan Bates, Claire Bloom

Adapted from Terence Rattigan's play and directed by veteran John Schlesinger, this is a cable-television remake of the 1958 film with Burt Lancaster and Wendy Hiller. This time the work achieves a remarkable intimacy on tape with a topnotch British cast. Divided into two segments, this is a sort of British *Grand Hotel* room with Alan Bates as a philandering husband and retired colonel with a questionable background and the radiant Julie Christie as his mistress in the first section and a wallflower in the second half. Richly engrossing adult entertainment. Rated PG for adult subject matter.

1983   108 minutes

SERPENT'S EGG, THE
★½

DIRECTOR: Ingmar Bergman
CAST: Liv Ullmann, David Carradine, Gert Frobe, James Whitmore

Two trapeze artists are trapped in Berlin during pre-Nazi Germany. They find work in a strange clinic, where they discover a satanic plot. Director Ingmar Bergman's nightmare vision is disappointing at best. David Carradine gives a poor performance. Sven Nykvist's cinematography is the one redeeming element of this film.

1977   120 minutes

SERPICO
★★★★

DIRECTOR: Sidney Lumet
CAST: Al Pacino, Tony Roberts, John Randolph

Al Pacino is magnificent in this poignant story of an honest man who happens to be a cop. The fact that this is a true story of one man's fight against corruption adds even more punch. Rated R.

1973   130 minutes

SERVANT, THE
★★★★

DIRECTOR: Joseph Losey
CAST: Dirk Bogarde, Sarah Miles, James Fox

A conniving manservant (Dirk Bogarde) gradually dominates the life of his spoiled master in this psychological horror story. By preying on his sexual weaknesses, he is able to easily maneuver him to his will. The taut, well-acted adult drama holds your interest throughout, mainly because the shock value is heightened for the audience because of its plausibility.

1963   B & W 115 minutes

SET-UP, THE
★★★★

DIRECTOR: Robert Wise
CAST: Robert Ryan, Audrey Totter, George Tobias, Alan Baxter, James Edwards, Wallace Ford

Taut *film noir* boxing flick takes the simple story of an over-the-hill boxer who refuses to disregard his principles and throw the big fight and elevates it to true tragedy. Robert Ryan as the has-been fighter gives another of the finely drawn and fiercely independent portrayals that marked his illustrious career as one of Hollywood's finest character actors/ stars. This claustrophobic but deeply moving picture combines fine acting and personal integrity, which results in one of the best boxing films of all time, right up there with *Body and Soul* and *Raging Bull*. An early coup for famed director Robert Wise.

1949   B & W 72 minutes

SEVEN DAYS IN MAY
★★★★

DIRECTOR: John Frankenheimer
CAST: Burt Lancaster, Fredric March, Kirk Douglas, Ava Gardner, Edmond O'Brien, Martin Balsam

A highly suspenseful account of an attempted military takeover of the U.S. government. After a slow buildup, the movie's tension snowballs toward a thrilling conclusion. This is one of those rare films that treat their audiences with respect. A working knowledge of the political process is helpful for optimum appreciation. Fredric March, as a president under pressure, heads an all-star cast, all of whom give admirable performances.

1964   B & W 120 minutes

SEVENTH SEAL, THE
★★★★

DIRECTOR: Ingmar Bergman
CAST: Max von Sydow, Bibi Andersson, Gunnar Bjornstrand

This is considered by many to be director Ingmar Bergman's masterpiece. It tells the story of a knight coming back from the Crusades. He meets Death, who challenges him to a chess match, the stakes being his life. The knight is brilliantly played by Max von Sydow.

1956   B & W 96 minutes

SHAMPOO
★★★★

DIRECTOR: Hal Ashby
CAST: Warren Beatty, Julie Christie, Lee Grant, Jack Warden, Goldie Hawn, Carrie Fisher

Star Warren Beatty and Robert Towne co-wrote this perceptive comedy of morals, most of them bad, which focuses on a hedonistic Beverly Hills hairdresser played by Beatty. Although portions come perilously close to slapstick, the balance is an insightful study of the pain caused by people who try for no-strings-attached relationships. Watch for a brief, but potent, appearance by (pre–Princess Leia) Carrie Fisher, as well as cameos by several Hollywood directors. Rated R—sexuality and adult themes.

1975   112 minutes

SHIP OF FOOLS
★★★★★

DIRECTOR: Stanley Kramer
CAST: Vivien Leigh, Oskar Werner, Simone Signoret, José Ferrer, Lee Marvin, Jose Greco, George Segal, Michael Dunn, Elizabeth Ashley, Lilia Skala, Charles Korvin

In 1933, a vast and varied group of characters take passage on a German liner sailing from Mexico to Germany amidst impending doom. The all-star cast features most memorable performances by Vivien Leigh (her last film) as the neurotic divorcee, Oskar Werner as the ship's doctor, who has an affair with the despairing Simone Signoret, Lee Marvin as the forceful American baseball player, and Michael Dunn as the wise dwarf. Superb screen adaptation of the Katherine Anne Porter novel of the same name. Ernest Laszlo received an Academy Award for cinematography in this film.

1965   B & W 150 minutes

SHOAH
★★★★★

DIRECTOR: Claude Lanzmann
CAST: Documentary

In this magnificent document, director Claude Lanzmann depicts the horrors of the Holocaust through the eyes of the survivors. Rather than use stock or newsreel footage of concentration camp casualties, Lanzmann opts for capturing the memories and emotions of those who lived through the Nazis' reign of terror. He re-creates the past through the voices and scenes from the present. The result is an unforgettable viewing experience.

1985   570 minutes

SHOOT THE MOON
★★

DIRECTOR: Alan Parker
CAST: Albert Finney, Diane Keaton, Karen Allen, Dana Hill, Tracey Gold, Tina Yothers

Why didn't they just call it Ordinary People Go West? If we knew it was a sequel, perhaps Shoot the Moon wouldn't be such a disappointment. Of course, this film isn't really a sequel to the 1980 Oscar winner for best picture. It's closer to a ripoff; another somber movie about the disintegration of a marriage and a family. Yet it has none of the style, believability, or consistency of its predecessor. A few really good moments are provided by stars Albert Finney and Diane Keaton, but the far-fetched conclusion nearly negates them all. Rated R because of profanity, violence, and adult themes.

1982   123 minutes

SHOOTING PARTY, THE
★★★★

DIRECTOR: Alan Bridges
CAST: James Mason, Edward Fox, Dorthy Tutin, John Gielgud, Gordon Jackson, Cheryl Campbell, Robert Hardy

This meditation on the fading English aristocracy is an acting showcase. All main characters are played with verve, or at least the verve one would expect from English nobility in the years preceding World War I. While nothing much happens here, the rich texture of the characters, the highly stylized sets, and the incidental affairs in the plot are enough to sustain the viewer. Not rated, but equivalent to a PG for partial nudity and sex.

1985   97 minutes

SHOP ON MAIN STREET, THE
★★★★

DIRECTOR: Ján Kadár
CAST: Elmar Klos, Josef Kroner, Ida Kaminska, Han Slivkova

This World War II film finds a Jewish woman removed from her small business and portrays her growing relationship with the man who has been put in charge of her shop. Set among the turbulent and depressing days of the Nazi occupation of Czechoslovakia, this tender film depicts the instincts of survival among the innocent pawns of a brutal war and the innate decency that is able to survive in even such a bleak atmosphere. A moving film.

1964   B & W   128 minutes

SHORT EYES
★★★★

DIRECTOR: Robert M. Young
CAST: Bruce Davison, Jose Perez

Film version of Miguel Pinero's hard-hitting play about a convicted child molester at the mercy of other prisoners. A brutal and frightening film. Excellent, but difficult to watch. Rated R for violence and profanity.

1977   104 minutes

SIDEWALKS OF LONDON
★★★★

DIRECTOR: Tim Whelan
CAST: Vivien Leigh, Charles Laughton, Rex Harrison, Larry Alder, Tyrone Guthrie, Gus McNaughton

Street entertainer Charles Laughton puts pretty petty thief Vivien Leigh in his song-and-dance act, then falls in love with her. Befriended by successful songwriter Rex Harrison, she puts the streets and old friends behind her and rises to stage stardom while her rejected and dejected mentor hits the skids and winds up masquerading as a blind beggar. Vivien Leigh is entrancing, and Charles Laughton is compelling and touching, in this dramatic sojourn in London byways. A British production, originally released as *St. Martin's Lane*.

1940   B & W   85 minutes

SILENCE OF THE NORTH
★★

DIRECTOR: Allan Winton King
CAST: Ellen Burstyn, Tom Skerritt, Gordon Pinsent

There are some of us here at the *Video Movie Guide* who would follow Ellen Burstyn anywhere. Imagine our surprise when *Silence of the North* turned out to be like a movie from the *Wonderful World of Disney* series, minus the mischievous racoon wreaking havoc in the cabin. Now, we've got nothing against Disney productions—indeed, a little of Walt's humor here would've helped—but Burstyn's naration is pure melodrama, and ninety minutes of one catastrophe after the next is more tiring than entertaining. Burstyn portrays a woman who falls in love with a fur trapper, played by Tom Skerritt (*Alien*), and moves into the Canadian wilderness. Rated PG for violence.

1981   94 minutes

SILKWOOD
★★★★

DIRECTOR: Mike Nichols
CAST: Meryl Streep, Kurt Russell, Cher, Craig T. Nelson, Fred Ward, Sudie Bond

At more than two hours, *Silkwood* is a shift-and-squirm movie that's worth shifting and squirming through. While it seems slow and drawn-out at times, the fine portrayals by Meryl Streep, Kurt Russell, and Cher keep the viewer's interest. Based on real events, the story focuses on 28-year-old nuclear worker and union activist Karen Silkwood, who died in a mysterious car crash while she was attempting to expose the alleged dangers in the Oklahoma plutonium plant where she was employed. Director Mike Nichols could have made better use of the suspense elements inherent in the story, but chose instead to make a character study. As a result, he's given us a very good—but not great—motion picture. Rated R for nudity, sex, and profanity.

1984   128 minutes

SIMPLE STORY, A
★★★½
DIRECTOR: Claude Sautet
CAST: Romy Schneider, Bruno Cremer, Claude Brasseur, Roger Pigaut

Marie (Romy Schneider) is pregnant and decides to have an abortion. At forty, she is forced to reevaluate her life and her relationships with men. Film is paced very slowly and plot is interwoven with subplots of other characters in distress. One of Romy Schneider's best performances. In French, with English subtitles. No MPAA rating.

1978   110 minutes

SIX WEEKS
★★★½
DIRECTOR: Tony Bill
CAST: Dudley Moore, Mary Tyler Moore, Katherine Healy, Joe Regalbuto

Dudley Moore and Mary Tyler Moore star as two adults trying to make the dreams of a young girl (Katherine Healy)—who has a very short time to live—come true

in this tearjerker. Directed by Tony Bill (*My Bodyguard*), it's enjoyable for viewers who like a good cry. Rated PG for strong content.

1982   107 minutes

16 DAYS OF GLORY
★★★★
DIRECTOR: Bud Greenspan
CAST: Documentary

Dramatic retelling of the 1984 Summer Olympics held in Los Angeles. This presentation of the games comes with interesting historical notes, in-depth background information on the athletes (not all of them winners), and no commercials! Particularly exciting are the pieces on swimmer Rowdy Gaines and gymnast Mary Lou Retton. Terrific cinematography. Rated G.

1985   145 minutes

SKAG
★★★½
DIRECTOR: Frank Perry
CAST: Karl Malden, Piper Laurie, Craig Wasson, Peter Gallagher, George Voskovec

Home-ridden to recuperate after being felled by a stroke, veteran steelworker Pete Skagska must deal with family problems, his own poor health, and the chance his illness may leave him impotent. In the title role, Karl Malden gives a towering, hard-driving performance as a man determined to prevail, no matter what the emotional cost. TV movie.

1980   152 minutes

SLAVE OF LOVE, A
★★★★½
DIRECTOR: Nikita Mikhalkov
CAST: Elena Solovei, Rodion Nakhapetov, Alexandar Kalyagin

Shortly after the Bolshevik revolution, a crew of silent filmmakers attempt to complete a melodrama while fighting the forces of the changing world around them. This examines the role of the Bourgeois as Olga (Elena Solovei) changes from matinee idol to revolutionary. Politically and emotionally charged. In Russian, with English subtitles. Unrated.

1978   94 minutes

SLEUTH
★★★★★
DIRECTOR: Joseph L. Mankiewicz
CAST: Michael Caine, Laurence Olivier

Michael Caine and Laurence Olivier engage in a heavyweight acting *bataille royal* in this stimulating mystery. Both actors are brilliant as the characters engage in the struggle of one-upmanship and social game-playing. Without giving away the movie's twists and turns, we can let on that the ultimate game is being played on its audience. It is great fun. Rated PG.

1972   138 minutes

SLIGHTLY SCARLET
★½
DIRECTOR: Allan Dwan
CAST: John Payne, Arlene Dahl, Rhonda Fleming, Kent Taylor

Confused blend of romance, crime, and political corruption focuses on good girl falling for gang leader. The fact that she's the mayor's secretary mucks the plot of this one up even further. Based on a book by James Cain and about as muddled as they come. Forget the story. Just watch the character actors and actresses interplay.

1956   99 minutes

SMALL CHANGE
★★★★★
DIRECTOR: Francois Truffaut
CAST: Geary Desmouceaux, Philippe Goldman, Claudia Deluca

One of Francois Truffaut's best pictures, this is a charming and perceptive film viewing the joys and sorrows of young children's lives in a small French town. Wonderfully and naturally acted by a cast of young children.

1976   104 minutes

SMASH PALACE
★★★★
DIRECTOR: Roger Donaldson
CAST: Bruno Lawrence, Anna Jemison, Greer Robson, Desmond Kelly

A scrap yard of crumpled and rusting automobiles serves as a backdrop to the story of a marriage in an equally deteriorated condition in this well-made, exceptionally acted film from New Zealand. Explicit sex and nude scenes may shock some viewers, yet they are intrinsic to the thrust of the storyline. It's a *Kramer vs. Kramer*, *Ordinary People*–style of movie that builds to a scary, nail-chewing climax. No MPAA rating; this has sex, violence, nudity, and profanity.

1981   100 minutes

SMASH-UP: THE STORY OF A WOMAN
★★★
DIRECTOR: Stuart Heisler
CAST: Susan Hayward, Lee Bowman, Marsha Hunt, Eddie Albert, Carleton Young, Carl Esmond

Night-club songbird Susan Hayward puts her songwriter husband's (Lee Bowman) career first. As he succeeds, she slips. His subsequent neglect and indifference make her a scenery-shedding bottle baby until near tragedy restores her sobriety and his attention. Skoal!

1947   B & W 103 minutes

SMITHEREENS
★★★

DIRECTOR: Susan Siedelman
CAST: Susan Berman, Brad Rinn, Richard Hell, Roger Jett

An independently made feature (its budget was only $100,000), this work by producer-director Susan Siedelman examines the life of an amoral and aimless young woman (Susan Berman) living in New York. Rated R.

1982   90 minutes

SMOOTH TALK
★★★★

DIRECTOR: Joyce Chopra
CAST: Laura Dern, Treat Williams, Mary Kay Place, Elizabeth Berridge, Levon Helm

Coltish Laura Dern owns this film, an uncompromising adaptation of the Joyce Carol Oates short story "Where Are You Going, Where Have You Been?" Dern hits every note as a sultry woman-child poised on the brink of adulthood and sexual maturity. Mary Kay Place does well as an exasperated mom, and Elizabeth Berridge is a sympathetic older sister. The picture takes an unexpected turn when Dern attracts the attention of Treat Williams, a sinister, sunglassed stranger anxious to cut through the coyness...and who may exist only in the girl's mind. Rarely has a film better captured this awkward time of life. Rated PG-13 for language and sexual situations.

1985   92 minutes

SOFT SKIN, THE
★★★½

DIRECTOR: François Truffaut
CAST: Jean Desailly, Nelly Benedetti, Françoise Dorleac

Up to this point, Truffaut was batting a perfect 1.000: *The 400 Blows*, *Shoot the Piano Player*, *Jules and Jim*. For some critics, *The Soft Skin* ranks as one of the New Wave master's worst; for some it remains one of his best. As usual, the truth lies in between. What keeps this from being at least a minor classic is the less-than-fresh plot (eminent literary journalist meets and keeps a lovely, decent stewardess half his age and is murdered by his wife when she learns of the affair) and the fact that by the conclusion of the film, we know scarcely more about the trio than at the beginning. Still, Truffaut suffuses the film with his trademark effortless style, with amusing detail and sensuality. In French with English subtitles.

1964   118 minutes

SOLDIER IN THE RAIN
★★★

DIRECTOR: Ralph Nelson
CAST: Steve McQueen, Tony Bill, Jackie Gleason, Tuesday Weld, Tom Poston

My Bodyguard director Tony Bill is among the featured performers in this fine combination of sweet drama and rollicking comedy starring Steve McQueen, Jackie Gleason, and Tuesday Weld. The Great One (Gleason) is, well, great as a high-living, worldly master sergeant, and McQueen is equally good as his protégé.

1963   B & W 88 minutes

SOLO
★

DIRECTOR: Tony Williams

CAST: Vincent Gil, Lisa Peer, Perry Armstrong

An uninteresting love story with three forgettable characters. This movie will cure the most serious case of insomnia. Rated PG.

1977   90 minutes

SOLOMON AND SHEBA
★★★

DIRECTOR: King Vidor
CAST: Yul Brynner, Gina Lollobrigida, George Sanders

High times in biblical times as Sheba vamps Solomon. Don't look for too much of a script, because the emphasis is on lavish spectacle. Eyewash, not brain food.

1959   139 minutes

SOME CALL IT LOVING
★

DIRECTOR: James B. Harris
CAST: Zalman King, Carol White, Tisa Farrow, Richard Pryor, Logan Ramsey, Brandy Herrod

Herein lies the bizarre tale of a rich jazz musician, Zalman King, who buys a "Sleeping Beauty" (Carol White) from a circus side show for his own perverse enjoyment. Don't let the Richard Pryor billing draw you in. His performance does nothing for him or the film, which is a rambling, incoherent mess. Rated R for nudity, sex, and language.

1974   103 minutes

SOMETIMES A GREAT NOTION
★★★

DIRECTOR: Paul Newman
CAST: Paul Newman, Henry Fonda, Lee Remick, Michael Sarrazin, Richard Jaeckel

In the story, adapted from the novel by Ken Kesey (One Flew over the Cuckoo's Nest), Paul Newman plays the elder son of an Oregon logging family that refuses to go on strike with the other lumberjacks in the area. The family pays dearly for its unwillingness to go along. One scene in particular, which features Newman aiding Richard Jaeckel, who has been pinned in the water by a fallen tree, is unforgettable. Rated PG.

1971   114 minutes

SOPHIE'S CHOICE
★★★★★

DIRECTOR: Alan J. Pakula
CAST: Meryl Streep, Kevin Kline, Peter MacNicol

A young, inexperienced southern writer named Stingo (Peter MacNichol) learns about love, life, and death in this absorbing, wonderfully acted, and heartbreaking movie. One summer, while observing the affair between Sophie (Meryl Streep), a victim of a concentration camp, and Nathan (Kevin Kline), a charming, but sometimes explosive biologist, Stingo falls in love with Sophie, a woman with deep, dark secrets. Rated R.

1982   157 minutes

SORROW AND THE PITY, THE
★★★★½

DIRECTOR: Marcel Ophüls
CAST: Documentary

This four-and-a-half-hour documentary about France during the Occupation is more than just cinema. It is a penetrating examination of the human condition. Director Marcel Ophüls edited fifty hours of interviews with people from all walks of life and newsreel footage from Germany, England, and France into a devastating masterpiece. Ophüls does not take a stance in this study of racial prejudice and political ambiguities in war-torn France; rather, he allows his subjects to paint a picture of confusion, commitment, fear, and courage. Instead of presenting a clear political statement, Ophüls makes the viewer painfully aware of the consequences of war by presenting it from all sides. Rated PG.

1970   B & W   260 minutes

SOUNDER
★★★★★

DIRECTOR: Martin Ritt
CAST: Cicely Tyson, Paul Winfield, Kevin Hooks, Carmen Mathews, Taj Mahal, James Best, Janet Maccachlan

Beautifully made film detailing the struggle of a black sharecropper and his family. Director Martin Ritt (*Norma Rae*; *Cross Creek*) gets outstanding performances from Cicely Tyson and Paul Winfield. When her husband is sent to jail, Tyson must raise her family and run the farm by herself while trying to get the eldest son an education. A truly moving and thought-provoking film. Don't miss this one. Rated G.

1972   105 minutes

SOUTHERNER, THE
★★★★

DIRECTOR: Jean Renoir
CAST: Zachary Scott, Betty Field, J. Carrol Naish

Stark life in the rural South before civil rights. Dirt-poor tenant farmer (Zachary Scott) struggles against insurmountable odds to provide for his family while maintaining his dignity. Visually a beautiful film, but uneven in dramatic continuity. Nonetheless, its high rating is deserved.

1945   B & W   91 minutes

SPARROWS
★★★

DIRECTOR: William Beaudine
CAST: Mary Pickford, Gustav von Seyffertitz, Roy Stewart, Mary Louise Miller

The now legendary Mary Pickford—"Our Mary" to millions during her reign as Queen of Hollywood when this film was made—plays the resolute, intrepid champion of a group of younger orphans besieged by an evil captor. Silent melodrama at its best, folks.

1926   B & W   84 minutes

SPECIAL DAY, A
★★★★

DIRECTOR: Ettore Scola
CAST: Sophia Loren, Marcello Mastroianni

Antonietta (Sophia Loren), a slovenly housewife, and Gabriele (Marcello Mastroianni), a depressed homosexual, meet in the spring of 1938—the same day Hitler arrives in Rome. Their experience together enriches but does not change the course of their lives. Escapes usual dramatics and contrivance of woman-meets-homosexual plots. In Italian, with English subtitles. No MPAA rating.

1977   106 minutes

SPETTERS
★★★★½

DIRECTOR: Paul Verhoeven
CAST: Hans Van Tongeren, Toon Agterberg, Renee Soutenduk, Marteen Boyer

A study of the dreams, loves, discoveries, and tragedies of six young people in modern-day Holland, this is yet another tough, uncompromising motion picture from Dutch director Paul Verhoeven (*Soldier of Orange*). Though the sex scenes are more graphic than anything we've ever had in a major American movie, *Spetters* is never exploitative. Instead, it captures the attitude of the young toward all aspects of life, resulting in a credible and rewarding film experience for open-minded adults. MPAA-unrated, it contains violence, profanity, nudity, and sex.

1980   115 minutes

SPIRIT OF ST. LOUIS, THE
★★★★

DIRECTOR: Billy Wilder
CAST: James Stewart, Patricia Smith, Murray Hamilton, Marc Connelly

Jimmy Stewart always wanted to portray Charles Lindbergh in a recreation of his historic solo flight across the Atlantic. When he finally got his chance, at age 48, many critics felt he was too old to be believable. Stewart did just fine. Within his performance, the actor ensures the quiet courage of one of America's greatest heroes comes through. The action does drag at times, but this remains a quality picture for the whole family.

1957   138 minutes

SPITFIRE
★★★½

DIRECTOR: John Cromwell
CAST: Katharine Hepburn, Robert Young, Ralph Bellamy, Martha Sleeper, Sara Haden, Sidney Toler

A girl (Katharine Hepburn) believes herself to have healing powers and is cast out from her Ozark Mountain home as a result. It's an interesting premise, and well-acted.

1934   B & W   88 minutes

SPLENDOR IN THE GRASS
★★★★

DIRECTOR: Elia Kazan
CAST: Warren Beatty, Natalie Wood, Pat Hingle, Audrey Christie

Warren Beatty made his film debut in this 1961 film, as a popular, rich high-school boy. Natalie Wood plays his less prosperous girlfriend who has a nervous breakdown when he dumps her. A few tears shed by the viewer make this romantic drama all the more intriguing.

1961   124 minutes

SPLIT IMAGE
★★★★

DIRECTOR: Ted Kotcheff
CAST: Peter Fonda, James Woods, Karen Allen, Michael O'Keefe

This is a very interesting, thought-provoking film about religious cults and those who become caught up in them. Michael O'Keefe plays a young man who is drawn into a pseudo-religious organization run by Peter Fonda. The entire cast is good, but Fonda stands out in one of his best roles. Rated R for language and nudity.

1982   113 minutes

STAGE DOOR CANTEEN
★★

DIRECTOR: Frank Borzage
CAST: William Terry, Cheryl Walkers, Katharine Hepburn, Harpo Marx, Helen Hayes, Count Basie, Edgar Bergen

An all-star cast play themselves in this mildly amusing romance about the behind-the-scenes world of Broadway. Unless you enjoy looking at the many stage luminaries during their early years, you will find this entire film to be ordinary, predictable, and uninspired.

1943   B & W   85 minutes

STAND BY ME
★★★★½

DIRECTOR: Rob Reiner
CAST: Wil Wheaton, River Phoenix, Corey Feldman, Jerry O'Connell, Keifer Sutherland, John Cusack, Richard Dreyfuss

Finally, someone has proven that a Stephen King story can be adapted successfully to the screen. Based on King's novella, *The Body*, the story involves four young boys in the last days of summer and their search for the missing body of a young boy believed hit by a train. Morbid as it may sound, this is not a horror movie. Rather, it is a story of leaving boyhood behind and ascending to manhood. Sometimes sad and often funny, this film, with its rich acting and marvelous direction, is guaranteed to leave you with a feeling that could keep you warm through the coldest winter. Rated R.

1986   90 minutes

STANLEY AND LIVINGSTONE
★★★

DIRECTOR: Henry King
CAST: Spencer Tracy, Cedric Hardwicke, Richard Greene, Nancy Kelly

When Spencer Tracy delivers the historic line, "Doctor Livingstone, I presume," to Cedric Hardwicke in this production, you know why he was such a great screen actor. It is primarily his performance, as a reporter who journeys to Africa in order to find a lost Victorian explorer, that injects life and interest into what could have been just another stodgy prestige picture from the 1930s.

1939   B & W 101 minutes

STAR 80
★★★★

DIRECTOR: Bob Fosse
CAST: Mariel Hemingway, Eric Roberts, Cliff Robertson, Carroll Baker

A depressing, uncompromising, but brilliantly filmed and acted portrait of a tragedy. Mariel Hemingway stars as Dorothy Stratten, the Playboy playmate of the year who was murdered in 1980 by the husband (an equally impressive portrayal by Eric Roberts) she had outgrown. The movie paints a bleak portrait of her life, times, and death. Rated R for nudity, violence, profanity, and sex.

1983   102 minutes

STAR CHAMBER, THE
★★★★

DIRECTOR: Peter Hyams
CAST: Michael Douglas, Hal Holbrook, Yaphet Kotto, Sharon Gless, Jack Kehoe

A model group of Superior Court judges lose faith in the constitutional bylaws that they have sworn to uphold and decide to take the law into their own hands. Michael Douglas (*The China Syndrome*) plays the idealistic young judge who uncovers the organization. Rated PG for profanity and violence.

1983   109 minutes

STAR IS BORN, A (ORIGINAL)
★★★★

DIRECTOR: William Wellman
CAST: Fredric March, Janet Gaynor, Adolphe Menjou, May Robson

The first version of this trice-filmed in-house Hollywood weeper, this is the story of an aging actor (Fredric March) whose career is beginning to go on the skids while his youthful bride's (Janet Gaynor) career is starting to blossom. Great acting and a tight script keep this poignant movie from falling into melodrama.

1937　　　　　　　111 minutes

STAR IS BORN, A (REMAKE)
★★★★½

DIRECTOR: George Cukor

CAST: Judy Garland, James Mason, Charles Bickford, Jack Carson, Tom Noonan

Judy Garland's acting triumph is the highlight of this movie, which is considered to be the best version of this classic romantic tragedy. Newly restored to its original length via long-lost footage, stills, and a complete soundtrack, this one is well worth watching. James Mason is also memorable in the role originated by Fredric March. Be sure to get the full restored version.

1954　　　　　　　154 minutes

STAR IS BORN, A (REMAKE)
★★

DIRECTOR: Frank Pierson

CAST: Barbra Streisand, Kris Kristofferson, Gary Busey, Oliver Clark

The third and by far least watchable version of this venerable Hollywood warhorse has been sloppily crafted into a vehicle for star Barbra Streisand. The rocky romance between a declining star (Kris Kristofferson) and an up-and-coming new talent (Streisand) has been switched from the world of the stage to that of rock 'n' roll. A weak script and uneven direction leaves the viewer with no feeling for the central characters. Even Streisand's fans may find it difficult to watch. Rated R.

1976　　　　　　　140 minutes

STARDUST MEMORIES
★★★

DIRECTOR: Woody Allen

CAST: Woody Allen, Charlotte Rampling, Marie-Christine Barrault, Jessica Harper

Director Sandy Bates (a filmmaker much like star Woody Allen himself) takes time out from editing his latest film to attend a weekend retrospective of his work at an Upstate New York resort. There he sees his whole life pass before him. At the resort (patterned after the Judith Crist seminars at Tarrytown, New York), Bates is mobbed by people who keep telling him, "I love your work." Bates would rather chase women than sign autographs. He spends a good chunk of time with three—a manic-depressive actress (Charlotte Rampling), a lovely French divorcée (Marie-Christine Barrault), and a lesbian violinist (Jessica Harper). It's far from prime Allen and not a comedy. Rated PG.

1980　　　B & W　91 minutes

STARS LOOK DOWN, THE
★★★★

DIRECTOR: Carol Reed

CAST: Michael Redgrave, Margaret Lockwood, Edward Rigby, Emlyn Williams, Nancy Price, Cecil Parker, Linden Travers

Classic film about Welsh coal miner and his struggle to rise above his station and maintain his identity and the respect of his community is every bit as good today as it was when released. While lacking the sentimentality of John Ford's *How Green Was My Valley*, this film boasts the same high caliber of acting talent and remains a vital and highly personal look at a conflict that still exists in today's society. A coup for director Carol

Reed and another great performance by Michael Redgrave as a man of quiet dignity and determination. Well worth the watching.

1939   B & W 110 minutes

STATE OF SEIGE
★★★½

DIRECTOR: Constantin Costa-Gavras

CAST: Yves Montand, O. E. Hasse, Renato Salvatori

This is a highly controversial but brilliant film about the kidnapping of an American A.I.D. official by left-wing guerrillas in Uruguay. The film follows step-by-step how U.S. aid is sent to fascist countries through the pretext of helping the economy and strengthening democracy. Strong action and flashback scenes make this film a winner. No MPAA rating.

1973   120 minutes

STATE OF THE UNION
★★★

DIRECTOR: Frank Capra

CAST: Spencer Tracy, Katharine Hepburn, Adolphe Menjou, Van Johnson, Angela Lansbury

Combine the acting talents of Spencer Tracy and Katharine Hepburn with the direction of Frank Capra, and you can be guaranteed something of interest will result. In this case, it's a political fable about an American businessman who is encouraged by opportunities to run for the presidency, and leave his integrity behind in the process. Tracy and Hepburn are a joy to watch, as usual. This film loses much of its impact due to the overuse of obvious political stereotypes in its supporting players.

1948   B & W 124 minutes

STAY AS YOU ARE
★★★★

DIRECTOR: Alberto Lattuada

CAST: Nastassja Kinski, Marcello Mastroianni, Francisco Rabal, Monica Randal, Giuliana Cazandra

This film begins conventionally but charmingly as the story of a romance between a 20-year-old girl, Francesca (Nastassja Kinski), and Giulio (Marcello Mastroianni), a man old enough to be her father. It remains charming, but the charm becomes mingled with a controlled anguish when it becomes evident that Giulio may indeed be her father. No MPAA rating.

1978   95 minutes

STAY HUNGRY
★★★★½

DIRECTOR: Bob Rafelson

CAST: Jeff Bridges, Sally Field, R. G. Armstrong, Arnold Schwarzenegger

An underrated film dealing with a young southern aristocrat's (Jeff Bridges) attempt to complete a real estate deal by purchasing a bodybuilding gym. Bridges begins to appreciate those who work and train at the gym as well as getting some insights into his own life. A wonderful film; highly recommended. Rated R for violence, brief nudity, and language.

1976   103 minutes

STELLA DALLAS
★★★★

DIRECTOR: King Vidor

CAST: Barbara Stanwyck, Anne Shirley, John Boles, Alan Hale, Tim Holt, Marjorie Main

Barbara Stanwyck's title-role performance as the small-town vulgar innocent who sacrifices everything for her daughter got her a well-deserved Oscar nomination and set the standard for this type of screen character. John Boles is the elegant wealthy heel who does her wrong. Anne Shirley is Laurel, the object of her mother's completely self-effacing conduct. In its time a winner, and still well worth the viewing.

1937   B & W 111 minutes

STERILE CUCKOO, THE
★★★★

DIRECTOR: Alan J. Pakula
CAST: Liza Minnelli, Wendell Burton, Tim McIntire

Painfully poignant story about a dedicated young college lad (Wendell Burton) and the loopy young woman (Liza Minnelli) who, unable to handle people on their own terms, demands too much of those with whom she becomes involved. Minnelli's Pookie Adams won the actress a well-deserved Academy Award nomination. Her character is an uncomfortable blend of free spirits and frightening instability. An excellent directorial debut from Alan J. Pakula. Don't watch this film if you're in the middle of an unpleasant love affair. Rated PG for sexual situations.

1969   107 minutes

STEVIE
★★★★

DIRECTOR: Robert Enders
CAST: Glenda Jackson, Mona Washbourne, Trevor Howard, Alec McCowen

Glenda Jackson gives a brilliant performance (which won her best-actress honors at the Montreal Film Festival in 1978) as reclusive poet Stevie Smith in this stagey, but still interesting, film. Mona Washbourne ("stuff and nonsense") is the film's true delight as Smith's doting—and slightly dotty—aunt. Trevor Howard nar-

rates and co-stars in this British release. Rated PG for brief profanity.

1978   102 minutes

STONE BOY, THE
★★★★★

DIRECTOR: Christopher Cain
CAST: Robert Duvall, Frederic Forrest, Glenn Close, Wilford Brimley

A superb ensemble cast elevates this rural *Ordinary People*–style film about a boy who accidentally shoots the older brother he adores and begins losing touch with reality. It's a tough subject, exquisitely handled. For some reason, this fine film was never theatrically released on a wide scale. Thanks to video, it can be seen and appreciated. Rated PG for brief violence and some profanity.

1984   93 minutes

STORY OF ADELE H, THE
★★★

DIRECTOR: Francois Truffaut
CAST: Isabelle Adjani, Bruce Robinson, Sylvia Marriott, Joseph Blatchley

This basically simple story of author Victor Hugo's daughter, who loves a soldier in vain, is surprisingly textured and intriguing. Slow, exquisite unfolding of many-layered love story is arresting and pictorially beautiful. Nicely done. Some adult situations. Rated PG.

1975   97 minutes

STRAIGHT TIME
★★★★

DIRECTOR: Ulu Gosbard
CAST: Dustin Hoffman, Harry Dean Stanton, Gary Busey, Theresa Russell, M. Emmet Walsh

Well-told story of an ex-convict (Dustin Hoffman) attempting to make good on the outside only to return to crime after a run-in with his parole officer (M. Emmet Walsh). Hoffman's performance is truly chilling, exposing a side of him rarely seen on the screen. Harry Dean Stanton is equally fine as Hoffman's partner in crime. A very grim and powerful film that was sadly overlooked on its initial release. Rated R for violence, nudity, and language.

1978   114 minutes

STRANGE LOVE OF MARTHA IVERS, THE
★★★

DIRECTOR: Lewis Milestone

CAST: Barbara Stanwyck, Van Heflin, Kirk Douglas, Lizabeth Scott, Judith Anderson, Darryl Hickman

Terrible title doesn't do this well-acted drama justice. Woman-with-a-past Barbara Stanwyck excels in this story of a secret that comes back to threaten her now-stable life and the lengths she must go to in order to ensure her securtiy. Full of deep emotions and seething passions this class production boasts a haunting score by great Hollywood composer Miklos Rozsa and a tight story by Robert Rossen. Young Kirk Douglas in his film debut already charges the screen with the electricity that he will continue to discharge for generations to come. A little long, but worth the time.

1946   B & W 117 minutes

STRAWBERRY BLONDE, THE
★★★

DIRECTOR: Raoul Walsh

CAST: James Cagney, Olivia De Havilland, Rita Hayworth, Alan Hale, Jack Carson, George Tobias, Una O'Conner, George Reeves.

Sentimental flashback story of young man's unrequited love for *The Strawbery Blonde* (Rita Hayworth) is a change of pace for dynamic James Cagney and one of the most evocative period pieces produced in America about the innocent "Gay Nineties." Winsome Olivia De Havilland and a great cast of characters (including Alan Hale as Cagney's father) breathe life into this tragicomic tale of the rise and fall and subsequent regeneration of a street-wise man who endures disgrace and imprisonment only to find the real happiness he's been seeking has been at hand all along. Clever, gentle, and at times emotionally charged, this is very comfortable, low-key fare and not necessarily the sort of film one would expect from action director Raoul Walsh. Full of sentimental touches and scored with barbershop quartet tunes, this is a nice, leisurely paean to a world that may or may not have existed but is pleasant to visit now and then. Originally made in 1933 with Gary Cooper and subsequently remade as a musical featuring Dennis Morgan in 1948.

1941   B & W 97 minutes

STRAWBERRY STATEMENT, THE
★½

DIRECTOR: Stuart Hagman

CAST: Kim Darby, Bruce Davison, Bob Balaban, James Kunen

Inane "message" film attempts to make some sense (and money) out of student dissidents and rebellion, focusing on the Columbia University riots of the late 1960s. Some good performances in this hodgepodge of comedy, drama, and youth-authority confrontations and clichés. Halfway serious attempt to study student activists ends up as a safe, establishment movie. Rated R.

1970 103 minutes

STREAMERS
★★★½

DIRECTOR: Robert Altman
CAST: Matthew Modine, Michael Wright

This tense film is about four recruits and two veterans awaiting orders that will send them to Vietnam. The six men are a microcosm of American life in the late 1960s and early 1970s. A powerful, violent drama, this film is not suitable for everyone. Rated R.

1984 118 minutes

STREET SCENE
★★★½

DIRECTOR: King Vidor
CAST: Sylvia Sidney, William Collier Jr., Beulah Bondi, David Landau, Estelle Taylor, Walter Miller

Playwright Elmer Rice wrote the screenplay for this fine film version of his Pulitzer Prize–winning drama of life in the New York tenements and the yearning and anguish of the young and hopeful who are desperate to get out and rise above the mean streets. The cast is excellent, the score classic Alfred Newman, the camera work outstanding. Still under the arcs today, Sylvia Sidney is old big-time Hollywood beside which talentless newcomers pale to oblivion.

1931 B & W 80 minutes

STREETCAR NAMED DESIRE, A
★★★★★

DIRECTOR: Elia Kazan
CAST: Vivien Leigh, Marlon Brando, Kim Hunter, Karl Malden

Virtuoso acting highlights this powerful and disturbing drama based on the Tennessee Williams play. Vivien Leigh once again is the southern belle. Unlike Scarlett O'Hara, however, her Blanche DuBois is no longer young. She is a sexually disturbed woman who lives in a world of illusion. Her world begins to crumble when she moves in with her sister and brutish brother-in-law (Marlon Brando). Well-deserved Academy Awards were garnered by Leigh, and by Kim Hunter and Karl Malden in supporting roles.

1951 B & W 122 minutes

STREETWALKIN'
★

DIRECTOR: Joan Freeman
CAST: Julie Newmar, Melissa Leo, Dale Midkiff, Leon Robinson, Antonio Fargas

As a lesson on why not to become a prostitute, this film has a lot to say. As entertainment, it is unsuccessful. Good acting cannot save an incoherent and pointless script. Too little character development and a heavy reliance on profanity and brutality blunt Melissa Leo's portrayal of Cookie, the runaway-turned-prostitute, and reduce Julie Newmar's soft-hearted madam character to a stereotype. Rated R for simulated sex, profanity, and violence.

1985 84 minutes

STRIKE
★★★★

DIRECTOR: Sergei Eisenstein
CAST: Grigori Alexandrov, Maxim Strauch, Mikhail Gomarov, Alexander Antonov

Shot in a documentarylike style, this drama about a labor dispute during the czarist era was Russian director Sergei Eisenstein's first feature film. Advanced for its time and using techniques Eisenstein would perfect in his later masterpieces, *Strike* remains a remarkable achievement and still holds one's interest today. Silent.

1924   B & W   82 minutes

STROMBOLI
★★

DIRECTOR: Roberto Rossellini
CAST: Ingrid Bergman, Mario Vitale, Renzo Cesana, Mario Spanza

This potboiler from the director of *Open City* is a brooding, sometimes boring movie about an attractive woman who marries a fisherman and attempts to adjust to the isolation and tedium of the life. Even screen beauty Ingrid Bergman (by this time married to Rossellini) couldn't salvage this film. Watch for the volcanic action at the end if you're still awake. Subtitled.

1950   B & W   81 minutes

STUD, THE
🐛

DIRECTOR: Quentin Masters
CAST: Joan Collins, Oliver Tobias

Joan Collins reaches new lows in the boring, sordid soft-core porn film concerning a young man's rise to fortune through his various affairs. This one will be tough to get through, even for hardcore Collins fans. Rated R.

1978   95 minutes

STUNT MAN, THE
★★★★½

DIRECTOR: Richard Rush
CAST: Peter O'Toole, Steven Railsback, Barbara Hershey, Chuck Bail, Allen Goorwitz, Adam Roarke, Alex Rocco

Nothing is ever quite what it seems in this fast-paced, superbly crafted film. It's a Chinese puzzle of a movie and, therefore, may not please all viewers. Nevertheless, this directorial tour de force by Richard Rush has ample thrills, chills, suspense, and surprises for those with a taste for something different. Rated R.

1980   129 minutes

SUBURBIA
★★★

DIRECTOR: Penelope Spheeris
CAST: Chris Pederson, Bill Coyne, Jennifer Clay, Timothy Eric O'Brien

Penelope Spheeris, who directed the punk-rock documentary *Decline of Western Civilization*, did this low-budget film of punk rockers versus local rednecks and townspeople in a small suburban area. Not for all tastes, but a good little film for people who are bored with releases like *Cannonball Run II*. Rated R.

1983   96 minutes

SUDDENLY
★★★★

DIRECTOR: Lewis Allen
CAST: Frank Sinatra, Sterling Hayden, James Gleason, Nancy Gates

Here's topnotch entertainment with Frank Sinatra perfectly cast as a leader of a gang of assassins out to kill the President of the United States. *Suddenly* has gone largely unnoticed over the last few years, but thanks to home video, we can all enjoy this gem of a picture. Reportedly, Sinatra has kept this film out of public circulation for fifteen years, most likely because he plays the role of a psychopath too well.

1954   B & W   77 minutes

SUDDENLY, LAST SUMMER
★★★

DIRECTOR: Joseph L. Mankiewicz
CAST: Elizabeth Taylor, Montgomery Clift, Katherine Hepburn

Another one of those unpleasant but totally intriguing forays of Tennessee Williams. Elizabeth Taylor is a neurotic girl being prodded into madness by the memory of her gay cousin's bizarre death, a memory that Katherine Hepburn, his adoring mother, wants to remain vague if not submerged. She prevails upon Montgomery Clift to make sure it does. Lots of talk in this one leading up to lots more.

1959   B & W 114 minutes

SUGAR CANE ALLEY
★★★★★

DIRECTOR: Euzhan Paloy
CAST: Garry Cadenat, Darling Legitimus, Douta Seck, Joby Bernabe, Fransico Charles

Set in Martinque of the 1930s, this superb French import examines the lives led by black sugar cane plantation workers. Specifically, it focuses on the hopes and dreams of Jose (Garry Cadenat), an 11-year-old orphan with a brilliant mind, which just may be the key to his breaking the bonds of slavery. Lest the reader think *Sugar Cane Alley* a depressing exposé of man's inhumanity to man, we should mention here that this motion picture, despite its setting, is a joyous celebration of life, love, and courage. In French with English subtitles. Unrated, the film has some scenes of slight violence.

1983   100 minutes

SUGARLAND EXPRESS, THE
★★★★

DIRECTOR: Steven Spielberg
CAST: Goldie Hawn, Ben Johnson, Michael Sauls, William Atherton

A rewarding film in many respects, this was Steven Spielberg's first feature effort. Based on an actual incident in Texas during the late 1960s, a couple released from prison tries to regain custody of their infant child. Their desperation results in a madcap chase across the state with the stolen child and a kidnapped state trooper. Rated PG.

1974   109 minutes

SUMMER HEAT
★

DIRECTOR: Jack Starrett
CAST: Bruce Davison, Susan George, Tony Franciosa

The cover may look sexy, but the film isn't. In fact, most of the time it's just plain silly. Bruce Davison stars as Dolin Pike, a young sheepherder who, upon being sentenced to prison, attempts to escape with his new love, Baby (Susan George). First, they must rob Baby's wealthy gangster ex-boyfriend, Charlie (Tony Franciosa). Although the acting is fine, as is director Jack Starrett's pacing, the film falls flat due to predictability, implausibility, and corniness. Rated R for violence, profanity, and implied sex.

1983   101 minutes

SUMMER LOVERS

DIRECTOR: Randal Kleiser
CAST: Peter Gallagher, Daryl Hannah, Valerie Quennessen, Barbara Rush, Carole Cook

The director of *Grease* and *Blue Lagoon*, Randal Kleiser, returns with more young lust in this self-penned study of a *ménage à trois* in Greece. *Summer Lovers* is really little more than a two-hour commercial for teen-age promiscuity. When stars Peter Gallagher, Daryl Hannah, and Valerie Quennessen finally end up in bed together, the soundtrack booms the rock song *I'm So Excited*, which is profoundly disturbing. Rated R for nudity, profanity, and implied sex.

1982   98 minutes

SUMMER OF '42
★★★★

DIRECTOR: Robert Mulligan

CAST: Gary Grimes, Jennifer O'Neill, Jerry Houser, Oliver Conant, Katherine Allentuck, Christopher Norris, Lou Frizell

This is one of the more acceptable depictions of the sexual rites of passage of a teen-age boy. Set against the backdrop of a vacationers' resort island off the New England coast during World War II, an inexperienced young man (Gary Grimes) has a crush on the 22-year-old bride (Jennifer O'Neill) of a serviceman. His stumbling attempts to acquire sexual knowledge are handled tenderly and thoughtfully. The climactic scene between the two becomes believable in spite of the audience's initial resistance to such a union. Rated PG.

1971   102 minutes

SUMMERTIME
★★★★

DIRECTOR: David Lean

CAST: Katharine Hepburn, Rossano Brazzi, Edward Andrews, Darren McGavin, Isa Miranda

Katharine Hepburn is a sensitive, vulnerable spinster on holiday in Venice. She falls in love with unhappily married shopkeeper Rossano Brazzi, and the romantic idyll is beautiful. David Lean's direction is superb, Jack Hildyard's cinematography excellent. The film has its light moments, but keep the Kleenex handy.

1955   99 minutes

SUNDAY TOO FAR AWAY
★★★½

DIRECTOR: Ken Hannam

CAST: Jack Thompson, Max Cullen, John Ewart, Reg Lye, Lisa Peers

An Australian film about the life and lot of a sheepshearer Down Under circa 1956. The title comes from a piece of verse titled "The Shearer's Wife's Lament" that states: "Friday night, he's too tired, Saturday night too drunk, Sunday too far away." This refers to the many miles traveled to sheep stations by the shearer and the brief weekends he has at home in the city. Jack Thompson stars as Foley, a champion shearer who finds his mantle challenged. Unrated, the film has profanity, nudity, and violence.

1983   100 minutes

SUNDAY, BLOODY SUNDAY
★★★

DIRECTOR: John Schlesinger

CAST: Peter Finch, Glenda Jackson, Murray Head, Peggy Ashcroft, Maurice Denham

Brilliant performances by Peter Finch and Glenda Jackson are the major reason to watch this very British three-sided love story; the sides are a bit different, though . . . both love Murray Head. His performance is the film's weak point; it's difficult to imagine anybody falling in love with such a bland, unpleasant person. The script, by Penelope Gilliat, takes a pleasantly intelligent approach to the complexities of the gay relationship. Difficult to watch at times, but intriguing from a historical standpoint. Rated R for sexual situations.

1971 110 minutes

SUNRISE AT CAMPOBELLO
★★★★★

DIRECTOR: Vincent J. Donehue
CAST: Ralph Bellamy, Greer Garson, Alan Bunce, Hume Cronyn

Producer/writer Dore Schary's inspiring and heartwarming drama of Franklin Delano Roosevelt's public political battles and private fight against polio. Ralph Bellamy is FDR; Greer Garson is Eleanor. Both are superb. The acting is tops, the entire production sincere. Taken from Schary's impressive stage play, with all the fine qualities intact.

1960 143 minutes

SUNSET BLVD.
★★★★★

DIRECTOR: Billy Wilder
CAST: William Holden, Gloria Swanson, Erich von Stroheim, Fred Clark, Jack Webb, Hedda Hopper, Buster Keaton

Sunset Boulevard is one of Hollywood's strongest indictments against its own excesses. It justly deserves its place among the best films ever made. William Holden plays an out-of-work gigolo-screenwriter who attaches himself to a faded screen star attempting a comeback. Gloria Swanson, in a stunning parody, is brilliant as the tragically deluded Norma Desmond.

1950 B & W 110 minutes

SWANN IN LOVE
★★★★

DIRECTOR: Volker Schlondorff
CAST: Jeremy Irons, Ornella Muti, Alain Delon, Fanny Ardant, Marie-Christine Barrault

Slow-moving but fascinating film portrait of a Jewish aristocrat (Jeremy Irons) totally consumed by his romantic and sexual obsession with an ambitious French courtesan (Ornella Muti). It's definitely not for all tastes. However, those who can remember the overwhelming ache of first love may find it worth watching. Based on the first two volumes of Marcel Proust's *Remembrance of Things Past*. Rated R for nudity and suggested sex.

1985 110 minutes

SWEPT AWAY
★★★

DIRECTOR: Lina Wertmuller
CAST: Giancarlo Giannini, Mariangela Melato

The full title is *Swept Away by an Unusual Destiny in the Blue Sea in August*, and what this Italian import addresses is a condescending, chic goddess who gets hers on a deserted island. Rated R.

1975 116 minutes

SWIMMER, THE
★★★★

DIRECTOR: Frank Perry
CAST: Burt Lancaster, Janet Landgard, Janice Rule, Joan Rivers, Tony Bickley, Marge Champion, Kim Hunter, Bill Fiore

A middle-aged man in a gray flannel suit who has never achieved his potential swims from neighbor's pool to neighbor's pool on his way home on a hot afternoon in social Connecticut. Each stop brings back memories of what was and what might have been. Burt Lancaster is excellent in the title role. Rated PG.

1968   94 minutes

SWING SHIFT
★

DIRECTOR: Jonathan Demme
CAST: Goldie Hawn, Kurt Russell, Ed Harris, Fred Ward, Christine Lahti, Sudie Bond

Goldie Hawn stars in this unbelievably dull and disappointing 1940s-era romance as Kay Walsh, the girl who's left behind when her husband, Jack (Ed Harris), goes off to fight in World War II. With America's work force depleted by the country's need for soldiers, women are needed to replace men on the assembly line. So Kay goes to work and, despite a few misgivings, finds she has all sorts of hidden talents—including an untapped potential for passion, fulfilled by co-worker Lucky Lockhart (Kurt Russell, of *Silkwood*). Rated PG for profanity and suggested sex.

1984   100 minutes

SYBIL
★★★★

DIRECTOR: Daniel Petrie
CAST: Joanne Woodward, Sally Field, William Prince

Sally Field is outstanding in this deeply disturbing but utterly fascinating made-for-TV drama of a young woman whose intense pyschological childhood trauma has given her seventeen distinct personalities. Joanne Woodward is the

patient, dedicated psychiatrist who sorts it all out.

1976   116 minutes

SYLVESTER
★★★★

DIRECTOR: Tim Hunter
CAST: Melissa Gilbert, Richard Farnsworth, Michael Schoeffling, Constance Towers, Yankton Hatten, Shane Sherwin

Director Tim Hunter (*Tex*) does an admirable job with this hard-edged *National Velvet*–style drama about a tomboy (Melissa Gilbert) who rides her horse, Sylvester (named after the Italian Stallion himself, Sylvester Stallone), to victory in the Olympics' Three-Day Event in Lexington, Kentucky. Gilbert is first-rate as the aspiring horsewoman, and Richard Farnsworth is his reliable, watchable self as her cantankerous mentor. It's a touching story with the grit and punch of reality. Rated PG-13 for profanity and violence.

1985   109 minutes

TABLE FOR FIVE
★★★

DIRECTOR: Robert Lieberman
CAST: Jon Voight, Richard Crenna, Millie Perkins

Had it up to here with *Kramer vs. Kramer* clones about single parents coping with their kids? If you have, you'll probably decide to skip this movie—and that would be a shame, because it's a good one. Jon Voight stars as J. P. Tannen, a divorcé who takes his three youngsters on a Mediterranean cruise in hopes of getting back into their lives full-time. But despite his good intentions, Tannen has never really grown up. If his dream is to come true, that is exactly what he has to do. Rated PG for mature situations.

1983   122 minutes

TALE OF TWO CITIES, A
★★★★★

DIRECTOR: Jack Conway

CAST: Ronald Coleman, Basil Rathbone, Edna May Oliver, Elizabeth Allan

A Tale of Two Cities is a satisfactory rendition of Charles Dickens's novel. It is richly acted, with true Dickens flavor. Ronald Coleman is ideally cast in the role of Sidney Carton, the English no-account who finds purpose in life amid the turmoil of the French Revolution. The photography in this film is one of its most outstanding features. The dark shadows are in keeping with the spirit of this somber Dickens story.

1935   B & W 121 minutes

TAMMY AND THE BACHELOR
★★★

DIRECTOR: Joseph Pevney

CAST: Debbie Reynolds, Leslie Nielsen, Walter Brennan, Mala Powers, Fay Wray, Sidney Blackmer, Mildred Natwick, Louise Beavers

Like Debbie Reynolds's number-one hit song *Tammy*, the movie is corny but irresistible. Ingenuous country girl Reynolds falls in love with injured pilot Leslie Nielsen and nurses him back to health. The romance and humor are sweet and charming, though predictable. Reynolds and Nielsen have never been more likable, and a crew of classic character actors contribute solid support. The movie's success led to sequels and a TV series.

1957   89 minutes

TAMMY AND THE DOCTOR
★

DIRECTOR: Harry Keller

CAST: Sandra Dee, Peter Fonda, Macdonald Carey, Beulah Bondi, Margaret Lindsay, Reginald Owen, Adam West

There's an audience for this kind of film somewhere, and thanks to the video revolution, closet Sandra Dee fans can enjoy this undemanding fare without the snickers and giggles that would certainly accompany a public screening. Cutesy romance between country gal Sandra Dee and young Peter Fonda is relatively harmless and studded with familiar character faces, but this is definitely an example of a youth film with a limited audience. No muss, no fuss, no rough stuff—in fact, not much of anything at all.

1963   88 minutes

TAPS
★★★½

DIRECTOR: Harold Becker

CAST: George C. Scott, Timothy Hutton, Ronny Cox, Tom Cruise

George C. Scott is an iron-jawed commander of a military academy and Timothy Hutton a gung-ho cadet who leads a student revolt in this often exciting but mostly unbelievable and unnecessarily violent drama. Rated R.

1981   118 minutes

TATTOO
👎

DIRECTOR: Bob Brooks

CAST: Bruce Dern, Maud Adams, Rikke Borge, John Getz

Simply the most vile, reprehensible, sexist, and misogynistic piece of tripe ever released under the guise of a mainstream film. Bruce

Dern is a demented tattoo artist who kidnaps Maud Adams to use as a "living tableau." The film concludes with her scarred for life, and we're supposed to believe it's an upbeat ending. Incredibly, this trash was written by a woman: Joyce Buñuel, daughter-in-law of Luis. Only for demented minds. Rated R for gross violence and kinky sex.

1981   103 minutes

TAXI DRIVER
★★★★★

DIRECTOR: Martin Scorsese
CAST: Robert De Niro, Harvey Keitel, Cybill Shepherd, Jodie Foster, Peter Boyle

Robert De Niro plays an alienated Vietnam-era vet thrust into the nighttime urban sprawl of New York City. In his despair after a romantic rejection by an attractive political campaign aide, he focuses on "freeing" a 12-year-old prostitute by unleashing violent retribution on her pimp. It's unnerving and realistic, with a great twist ending. Rated R for violence and profanity.

1976   113 minutes

TELL ME A RIDDLE
★★★★

DIRECTOR: Lee Grant
CAST: Melvyn Douglas, Lila Kedrova, Brooke Adams, Dolores Dorn, Bob Elross, Joan Harris, Zalman King

Actress Lee Grant directed this genuinely moving, marvelously acted film adaptation of Tillie Olsen's novella about an elderly immigrant couple (Melvyn Douglas and Lila Kedrova) who, after years of quarreling, rediscover the love that originally brought them together. Although it may require concentration and commitment,

Tell Me a Riddle gives much in return. It defies the traditionally acceptable—and overdone—formulas for movie-making to become a fresh and rewarding experience. Unrated, the film has profanity.

1980   90 minutes

TEMPEST
★

DIRECTOR: Paul Mazursky
CAST: John Cassavetes, Gena Rowlands, Vittorio Gassman, Molly Ringwald, Susan Sarandon

This isn't a movie; it's an endurance test. About an architect (John Cassavetes) who has prophetic dreams and is going through a mid-life crisis, nothing ever really happens. The only thing that saves it from being a complete bust is the acting. Unfortunately, the cast can't quite make up for the fact that this film, directed by Paul Mazursky (Willie and Phil; An Unmarried Woman), is just plain boring. Rated PG, the film has nudity and profanity.

1982   140 minutes

TEN COMMANDMENTS, THE
★★★

DIRECTOR: Cecil B. De Mille
CAST: Charlton Heston, Yul Brynner, John Carradine, Edward G. Robinson, Anne Baxter

The biblical story of the Jewish exodus is given a grand-scale Cecil B. De Mille going-over. Unfortunately, the visual splendor is given such priority that believable characterization is forsaken for hammy melodrama. A uniformly good cast and some creditable effects save it often enough to make it worth watching. Charlton Heston is Moses, and Yul Brynner is his adversary, the Pharaoh Ramses.

1956   228 minutes

TEN DAYS THAT SHOOK THE WORLD (OCTOBER)
★★★★

DIRECTOR: Sergei Eisenstein
CAST: Documentary

A loose depiction of the months between the February 1917 Russian Revolution against the Czar and the eventual triumph of the Bolsheviks in October of that year. This documentarylike film is considered one of the great silent classics by legendary director, Sergei Eisenstein. It lacks the emotional power of his *Strike* and *Battleship Potemkin*, because the narrative is often interrupted by political satire and symbolic imagery that can best be appreciated by those steeped in Russian history. If for no other reason, the stunning recreation of the storming of the Czar's Winter Palace makes this movie worth watching. Not rated.

1928   B & W   92 minutes

TENDER MERCIES
★★★★★

DIRECTOR: Bruce Beresford
CAST: Robert Duvall, Tess Harper, Ellen Barkin

Robert Duvall more than deserved his best-actor Oscar for this superb character study about a down-and-out country singer trying for a comeback. His Mac Sledge is a man who still has songs to sing, but barely the heart to sing them. That is, until he meets up with a sweet-natured widow (Tess Harper) who gives him back the will to live. Rated PG.

1983   89 minutes

TERMS OF ENDEARMENT
★★★★★

DIRECTOR: James L. Brooks
CAST: Shirley MacLaine, Debra Winger, Jack Nicholson, Danny DeVito

This stylish soap opera, written, produced, and directed by James L. Brooks, covers thirty years in the lives of a Houston matron, played by Shirley MacLaine, and her daughter, played by Debra Winger, who marries an English teacher with a wandering eye. Jack Nicholson is also on hand, to play MacLaine's neighbor, an astronaut with the wrong stuff. Funny, touching, and unforgettable, it's one of the best of its kind. Rated PG for profanity and suggested sex.

1983   132 minutes

TESS
★★★★½

DIRECTOR: Roman Polanski
CAST: Nastassja Kinski, Peter Firth, John Bett

A hypothetically beautiful adaptation of Thomas Hardy's late-nineteenth-century novel *Tess of the D'Urbervilles*, this is director Roman Polanski's finest artistic achievement. Nastassja Kinski is stunning as the country girl who is "wronged" by a suave aristocrat and the man she marries. The story unfolds at the pace of a lazy afternoon stroll, and the drama is sedated, but Polanski's technical skills and the cinematography are spellbinding. Rated PG.

1979   170 minutes

TEST OF LOVE, A
★★

DIRECTOR: Gil Brealey

CAST: Angela Punch McGregor, Drew Forsythe, Tina Arhondis, Wallas Eaton, Simon Chilvers, Monica Maughan, Mark Butler

This tearjerker, taken from the Australian best-selling novel *Annie's Coming Out*, vividly displays the love and determination a therapist (Angela Punch McGregor) has in fighting for the rights of Anne O'Farrell, a severely disabled teenager who was misdiagnosed as being retarded. In that sense the film is a winner. Yet the makers of this movie lack the finesse it takes to make the antagonists of this story more than one-dimensional. Indeed, with nasty nurses and hostile hospital officials against our heroes, the stacked deck is all too obvious, and the viewer can't help feeling manipulated. All performances are sound, including Tina Arhondis, a disabled 9-year-old who plays the role of Anne. Rated PG for profanity.

1984   93 minutes

TEX
★★★★½
DIRECTOR: Tim Hunter
CAST: Matt Dillon, Jim Metzler, Ben Johnson, Emilio Estevez

This adaptation of S. E. Hinton's novel is what Francis Ford Coppola's *The Outsiders*, which was based on another book by Hinton, should have been but wasn't. Matt Dillon, Jim Metzler, and Ben Johnson star in this superb coming-of-age adventure about the struggles and conflicts of two teenage brothers growing up in the Southwest without parental guidance. Rated PG for violence and mature situations.

1982   103 minutes

THAT CHAMPIONSHIP SEASON
★★★½
DIRECTOR: Jason Miller
CAST: Bruce Dern, Stacy Keach, Martin Sheen, Paul Sorvino, Robert Mitchum

Former high-school basketball stars (Bruce Dern, Stacy Keach, Martin Sheen, and Paul Sorvino) and their coach (Robert Mitchum) get together for the twenty-fourth annual celebration of their championship season. However, it turns out to be a fiasco as the longtime friendships begin disintegrating under the pressure of a mayoral election. While there's nothing wrong with a sobering look at broken dreams and the pain of midlife crisis, we've seen it all on screen before. And, more to the point, most of us have enough problems of our own without taking on those of a quintet of shallow, self-centered men. Rated R for profanity, racial epithets, violence, and adult content.

1982   110 minutes

THAT HAMILTON WOMAN
★★★½
DIRECTOR: Alexander Korda
CAST: Vivien Leigh; Laurence Olivier

The legendary acting duo of Mr. and Mrs. Laurence Olivier re-creates one of England's legendary romantic scandals: the love of naval hero Horatio Nelson for the alluring Lady Emma Hamilton. The affair between these two already married lovers caused quite a stir in early nineteenth-century Britain. This was Winston Churchill's favorite movie, no doubt because when it was released in mid World War II, it showed a man choosing duty to country over the attraction of a beautiful woman. With Vivien

Leigh looking more striking than in her famous portrayal of Scarlett O'Hara, one has trouble being convinced. The film drags in places, but remains quite watchable.

1941   B & W   128 minutes

THAT OBSCURE OBJECT OF DESIRE
★★★★½
DIRECTOR: Luis Buñuel
CAST: Fernando Rey, Carole Bouquet, Angela Molina, Pieral, Julien Bertheau

Luis Buñuel's last film cunningly combines erotic teasing, wit, and social comment. Mathieu (Fernando Rey) is a 50-year-old man who falls hopelessly in love with a young woman. Bunuel, a master of surrealism, tantalizes the viewer by casting two actresses to play the heroine and a third actress to do the voice of both. Conchita, who is part tramp (Carole Bouquet) and part virgin (Angela Molina) torments and humiliates Mathieu. The entire film is seen in flashbacks as he confesses his dilemma to a dwarf psychologist (Pieral). Rated R for language and nudity.

1977   100 minutes

THAT WAS THEN...THIS IS NOW
★★★★
DIRECTOR: Christopher Cain
CAST: Emilio Estevez, Craig Sheffer, Kim Delaney, Morgan Freeman, Frank Howard, Larry B. Scott, Barbara Babcock

The best film to be adapted from a novel by S. E. Hinton (The Outsiders, Rumble Fish), this work, directed by Christopher Cain, has a tough, raw edge and a resounding ring of truth. The cuteness and condescension that mar most coming-of-age films are laudably absent in its tale of two working-class teenagers (Emilio Estevez and Craig Sheffer) coming to grips with adulthood. Cain makes us feel as if we are watching a movie about real kids. Sharing the credit for this is Estevez, who also wrote the screenplay. They have created a work that teens and adults alike can appreciate. Rated R for violence and profanity.

1985   103 minutes

THESE THREE
★★★★
DIRECTOR: William Wyler
CAST: Miriam Hopkins, Merle Oberon, Joel McCrea, Bonita Granville, Marcia Mae Jones

A superb cast brings alive this story of two upright and decent schoolteachers victimized by the lies of a malicious student. Miriam Hopkins and Merle Oberon are the pair brutally slandered; Bonita Granville is the evil liar. Script by Lillian Hellman, loosely based on her play The Children's Hour, under which title the film was remade in 1961.

1936   B & W   93 minutes

THEY CAME TO CORDURA
★★
DIRECTOR: Robert Rossen
CAST: Gary Cooper, Rita Hayworth, Van Heflin, Tab Hunter, Richard Conte

This film, which examines the true character of the war hero, is not one of Gary Cooper's best. The story has Cooper in Mexico during World War I as one of six military men returning to base. The hardships they encounter on the way create the drama. The movie has a nice look, but just not enough action.

1959   123 minutes

THEY KNEW WHAT THEY WANTED
★★★

DIRECTOR: Garson Kanin
CAST: Charles Laughton, Carole Lombard, William Gargan, Harry Carey, Frank Fay

This film is a fine example of off-beat casting that somehow succeeds. Charles Laughton and Carole Lombard, two actors noted for their exuberant acting styles, were required to submerge their histrionics in order to bring off a low-key, little tragedy. The story is of the unrequited love of an Italian wine grower for the opportunistic hash house waitress that he marries. Lombard is excellent as the greedy wife, but Laughton's heavily accented performance does not always ring true.

1940   B & W   96 minutes

THEY MADE ME A CRIMINAL
★★★

DIRECTOR: Busby Berkeley
CAST: John Garfield, Claude Rains, Ann Sheridan, Gloria Dickson, The Dead-End Kids, Ward Bond

John Garfield's film persona is a direct result of this Warner Brothers story about the redemption of a loner on the lam from the law for a crime he didn't commit. A great cast (including a young Ann Sheridan, the great Claude Rains, and the Dead-End Kids in their fourth film) still doesn't change the fact that this remake of 1933's *The Life of Jimmy Dolan* is muddled and not too solidly constructed. This film was director Busby Berkeley's only venture outside the realm of the movie musicals he made for his home studio, but the image of the antihero as epitomized by a defiant John Garfield was the first of a series of young

rebels that still scowl out at us from the screen.

1939   B & W   92 minutes

THEY MIGHT BE GIANTS
★★★★

DIRECTOR: Anthony Harvey
CAST: George C. Scott, Joanne Woodward, Jack Gilford

George C. Scott stars in this charming film as a slightly kooky lawyer who thinks he is Sherlock Holmes. Joanne Woodward is the psychiatrist trying to cure him but not doing very well at it. You see, her name is Dr. Watson. This one's a delight. Rated PG.

1971   88 minutes

THEY SHOOT HORSES, DON'T THEY?
★★★★★

DIRECTOR: Sydney Pollack
CAST: Jane Fonda, Gig Young, Michael Sarrazin

The desperation and hopelessness of the Great Depression is graphically shown in this powerful drama, in a pitiful collection of marathon dancers. Some of the group will endure this physical and mental assault on their human spirit; some will not. Jane Fonda, as a cynical casualty of the Depression, and Gig Young, as the uncaring master of ceremonies, give stunning performances. Rated PG.

1969   121 minutes

THEY'RE PLAYING WITH FIRE
🦃

DIRECTOR: Howard Avedis
CAST: Sybil Danning, Eric Brown, Andrew Prine

A high-school student is seduced by his English teacher, who is hatching a plot that will enmesh the student in a plan to defraud an elderly relative of her estate. The scheme turns into murder, with the student suspected of the crime. The movie is punctuated with steamy seduction scenes involving the teacher and the student. In the end, the immoral woman rushes off with the money and the student. Everyone wins, except whoever watches this turkey. Rated R.

1983   96 minutes

THIEF OF HEARTS
★★★

DIRECTOR: Douglas Day Stewart
CAST: Steven Bauer, Barbara Williams

A young, upwardly mobile married woman loses her intimate diary of sexual fantasies to a thief who has broken into her home. In an interesting premise, the woman becomes a willing participant in the thief's sexual manipulations without knowing that he is the man who stole her secrets. Rated R.

1984   100 minutes

THIS LAND IS MINE
★★★

DIRECTOR: Jean Renoir
CAST: Charles Laughton, Maureen O'Hara, George Sanders, Walter Slezak

Charles Laughton in another fine characterization, this time as a timid French teacher who blossoms as a hero when he is incited to vigorous action by the Nazi occupation. Time has dulled the cutting edge of this obviously patriotic wartime film, but the artistry of the director and players remains sharp.

1943   B & W 103 minutes

THIS PROPERTY IS CONDEMNED
★★½

DIRECTOR: Sydney Pollack

CAST: Natalie Wood, Robert Redford, Charles Bronson, Kate Reid, Robert Blake

Marginal film interpretation of Tennessee Williams's play. Owen Legate (Robert Redford) is a stranger in town, there for the purpose of laying off local railroaders. Alva (Natalie Wood) is a flirtatious southern girl who casts her spell of romance on the stranger, who is staying at her mother's boardinghouse. Her vengeful mother is willing to sacrifice her daughter's happiness to soothe her own ego. Co-scripted by Francis Ford Coppola.

1966   109 minutes

THORN BIRDS, THE
★★★

DIRECTOR: Daryl Duke
CAST: Richard Chamberlain, Rachel Ward, Christopher Plummer, Bryan Brown, Barbara Stanwyck, Richard Kiley, Jean Simmons

In this made-for-television miniseries, a handsome and ambitious priest becomes a moral cropper when he falls in love with the nubile promise of an innocent, trusting child, whom he eventually betrays sexually while on his way up the apostolic ladder. It's all played out against shifting backgrounds of outback Australia, Vatican Rome, and idyllic Greece.

1983   500 minutes

THRONE OF BLOOD
★★★★★

DIRECTOR: Akira Kurosawa
CAST: Toshiro Mifune, Isuzu Yamada, Minoru Chiaki, Akira Kubo, Takamoru Sasaki, Yoichi Tachikoiwa, Takashi Shimura

Japanese director Akira Kurosawa's retelling of *Macbeth* may be the best film adaptation of Shakespeare ever made. Kurosawa uses the medium to present Shakespeare's themes in visual images. And what images they are! When Birnam Wood literally comes to Dunsinane, it is a truly great moment you would have believed could only happen in the limitless landscapes of a dream. In Japanese with English subtitles.

1957   B & W 105 minutes

THURSDAY'S GAME
★★★

DIRECTOR: Robert Moore

CAST: Gene Wilder, Bob Newhart, Ellen Burstyn, Cloris Leachman, Rob Reiner, Nancy Walker, Valerie Harper

Engaging made-for-television film about two ordinary guys (Gene Wilder and Bob Newhart) who continue to get together on Thursday nights after their weekly poker game collapses. Both have reasons for wanting to leave the house, and both make the most of this small rebellion. The supporting cast is excellent; this is one of those little films that attracted talented performers before they broke loose in their own careers. Newhart is the standout, as a prissy businessman who merely wants more control of his life. Unrated; adult themes.

1974   74 minutes

TICKET TO HEAVEN
★★★

DIRECTOR: Ralph L. Thomas

CAST: Nick Mancuso, Saul Rubinek, Meg Foster, Kim Cattrall, R. H. Thompson

This Canadian film presents a lacerating look at the frightening phenomenon of contemporary religious cults. Nick Mancuso is riveting as the brainwashed victim. Saul Rubinek and Meg Foster are splendid in support. And R. H. Thompson almost steals the show as a painfully pragmatic deprogrammer. Nice touches of humor give the movie balance. Rated PG.

1981   107 minutes

TILL THE END OF TIME
★★★

DIRECTOR: Edward Dmytryk

CAST: Dorothy McGuire, Guy Madison, Robert Mitchum, Jean Porter

Three veterans of World War II come home to find life, in general and how it was when they left, considerably changed. Readjustment is tough, and the love they left has soured. A good drama.

1946   B & W 105 minutes

TIM
★★★★½

DIRECTOR: Michael Pate

CAST: Mel Gibson, Piper Laurie, Alwyn Kurts, Pat Evison

An unforgettable character study from Down Under, this features Mel Gibson in his film debut as a simple-minded young adult and Piper Laurie as the older woman who finds herself falling in love with him. Superb supporting performances by the Australian cast—especially Alwyn Kurts and Pat Evison, as Tim's parents—help make this screen adaptation of the first novel by Colleen McCullough (*The Thorn Birds*) a heartwarming and profoundly moving viewing experience. Rated PG for suggested sex.

1979   108 minutes

TIME STANDS STILL
★★½
DIRECTOR: Peter Gothar
CAST: Ben Barenholtz, Albert Schwartz, Michael S. Landes, Istvan Znamenak, Henrik Pauer, Sandor Soth, Aniko Ivan, Agi Kakassy, Lajos Oze

This Hungarian export dwells so much on the "art for art's sake" credo that it nearly destroys some of the life the film tries to depict. The cinematography is stunning at first and really drives home what the filmmaker sees as Budapest in the early 1960s, but after a half-hour, the blue-and-red-tinted scenes grow tiresome. *Time Stands Still* is about restless youths in Hungary at the threshold of adulthood. The film is presented in the original language with subtitles. Not rated, but the equivalent of an R for sex, nudity, and language.
1982   99 minutes

TIMES OF HARVEY MILK, THE
★★★★
DIRECTOR: Robert Epstein
CAST: Documentary

This sensitive documentary uses television footage and personal observations from friends, fans, and fellows to follow the political life of slain politician Harvey Milk, from his acknowledgment of his homosexuality at age 14 through his murder at the hands of Dan White in San Francisco. No MPAA rating; no objectionable material.
1985   87 minutes

TIN DRUM, THE
★★★★½
DIRECTOR: Volker Schlondorff
CAST: David Bennent, Mario Adorf, Angela Winkler, Daniel Olbrychski

This is the film version of Günter Grass's bizarre tale of three-year-old Oskar, who stops growing as the Nazis rise to power in Germany. He expresses his outrage by banging on a tin drum. This unique German film has a disturbing dreamlike quality, while its visuals are alternately startling and haunting. It's fascinating. *The Tin Drum* won an Academy Award for Best Foreign Film. In German, with English subtitles. Rated R for nudity and gore.
1979   142 minutes

TO KILL A MOCKINGBIRD
★★★★★
DIRECTOR: Robert Mulligan
CAST: Gregory Peck, Mary Badham, Philip Alford, John Megna

To Kill a Mockingbird is a leisurely paced, flavorful filming of Harper Lee's best-selling novel. Gregory Peck earned an Oscar as a small-town southern lawyer who defends a black man accused of rape. Mary Badham, Philip Alford, and John Megna are superb as Peck's children and a visiting friend who are trying to understand life in a small town.
1962   B & W 129 minutes

TO SIR WITH LOVE
★★★★
DIRECTOR: James Clavell
CAST: Sidney Poitier, Judy Geeson, Christian Roberts, Suzy Kendall, Lulu

A moving, gentle portrait of the influence of a black teacher upon a classroom of poverty-ridden teenagers in London's East End, this stars Sidney Poitier, in one of his finer performances, as the teacher. He instills in his pupils a belief in themselves and respect for one another.
1967   105 minutes

TOM BROWN'S SCHOOL DAYS
★★½
DIRECTOR: Robert Stevenson
CAST: Cedric Hardwicke, Freddie Bartholomew, Gale Storm, Jimmy Lydon, Josephine Hutchinson, Polly Moran, Billy Halop

"Old school tie" story mixes top Hollywood production values and minor classic of British secondary schools into an enjoyable froth filled with all the clichés that have since been completely devalued by constant exposure in ludicrous movie and television treatments. Everybody's favorite English kid Freddie Bartholomew and veteran Cedric Hardwicke do their duty in the best tradition while blatantly American juveniles recruited from the "East Side Kids" and "Henry Aldrich" series perform surprisingly well in this structured effort. Better than one would think and not the creaky old groaner it could have been.

1940   B & W   86 minutes

TOMORROW
★★★★★
DIRECTOR: Joseph Anthony
CAST: Robert Duvall, Olga Bellin, Sudie Bond, Richard McConnell

Robert Duvall gives yet another sensitive, powerful, and completely convincing performance in this superb black-and-white character study about a caretaker who finds himself caring for—in both senses—a pregnant woman (Olga Bellin) who turns up one day at the lumber mill where he works. Viewers will never forget this simple tale of a brief but devastating episode in one man's life. Rated PG for violence.

1972   B & W 103 minutes

TONI
★★★★
DIRECTOR: Jean Renoir
CAST: Charles Blavette, Edouard Delmont, Max Dalban, Jenny Helia

Of the Italian neorealists, only Luchino Visconti is known to have been aware of this film before 1950, but in story, style, and mood, *Toni* anticipates the methods of the future master postwar directors. The film is direct, spare, simple, and touching. A love quadrangle, a murder, a trial, an execution, a confession—these are the everyday elements director Jean Renoir chose to show "without makeup," as objectively as possible. No studio sets were used, and many citizens of the town where *Toni* was shot filled out the cast. Renoir was proud of his film (something of an experiment), and it holds up well. In French with English subtitles.

1934   B & W   90 minutes

TORCHLIGHT
★½
DIRECTOR: Tom Wright
CAST: Pamela Sue Martin, Steve Railsback, Ian McShane, Al Corley, Rita Taggart

Pamela Sue Martin, of "Nancy Drew" and "Dynasty" TV fame, produced, co-wrote, and starred in this less-than-memorable film. In it, her successful but insecure husband, Jake (Steve Railsback), becomes hopelessly addicted to cocaine. Naturally their marriage suffers as a result of his addiction. Ian McShane plays Sidney, the pusher everyone loves to hate. Although the idea behind this film could have been captivating, nothing can make up for the poor dialogue and acting. If viewers do somehow manage to stay awake until the end of this film, they will be rewarded with Carly Simon's sweet voice as she sings the theme song. Rated R for explicit drug use and sadism.

1985   90 minutes

TOUCHED BY LOVE
★★★
DIRECTOR: Gus Trikonis
CAST: Deborah Raffin, Diane Lane, Michael Learned, Cristina Raines, Mary Vickes, Clu Gulager, John Amos

Strong performances make this affecting sentimental drama about a teen-age cerebral palsy victim given hope through correspondence with singer Elvis Presley. Deborah Raffin is excellent as the nurse who nurtures patient Diane Lane from cripple to functioning teenager. Originally titled *From Elvis with Love*. Rated PG.

1980   95 minutes

TRACKS

DIRECTOR: Henry Jaglom
CAST: Dennis Hopper, Taryn Power, Dean Stockwell, Topo Swope, Michael Emil

Dennis Hopper plays a Vietnam War veteran who escorts his dead buddy on a train across country and goes crazy in the process. Rated R.

1977   90 minutes

TRAIN KILLER, THE
★★
DIRECTOR: Sandor Simo
CAST: Michael Sarrazin, Towje Kleiner, Armin Mueller-Stahl, Ferenc Bacs

The true story of Sylvester Matushka, the Hungarian businessman who was responsible for a number of train wrecks in 1931. What is frustrating about this film is that it prepares the viewer for political intrigue that is never fully explained by the end of the film. Also, Michael Sarrazin *(The Flim-Flam Man, They Shoot Horses, Don't They?)* puts in a trying performance as Matushka. On the other hand, Towje Kleiner is superb as Dr. Epstein, the cool, Hitchcockian character who is the investigator in the train wrecks. *The Train Killer* is not rated, but contains sex, nudity, and violence.

1983   90 minutes

TRAPEZE
★★½
DIRECTOR: Carole Reed
CAST: Burt Lancaster, Tony Curtis, Gina Lollobrigida, Katy Jurado, Thomas Gomez, Johnny Puleo

Overly familiar tale of professional (Burt Lancaster) who takes young protégé (Tony Curtis) under his wing and teaches him all he knows about aerial acrobatics only to have scheming opportunist Gina Lollobrigida come between them is okay but nothing out of the ordinary. Solid performances and competent stunting highlight this international effort set in European circus circuit, but director Carol Reed and a good cast have been involved in better films.

1956   105 minutes

TRIBUTE
★★★½
DIRECTOR: Bob Clark
CAST: Jack Lemmon, Robby Benson, Lee Remick, Colleen Dewhurst, John Marley

A moving portrait of a man in crisis, *Tribute* bestows a unique gift to its audience: the feeling that they have come to know a very special man. Jack Lemmon stars as a

Broadway press agent who has contracted a terminal blood disease and is feted by his friends in show business. Though adjusted to his fate, Lemmon finds that he has some unfinished business: to make peace with his son, Robby Benson. Rated PG.

1980　　　　　　　　121 minutes

TRIP, THE
★★

DIRECTOR: Roger Corman
CAST: Peter Fonda, Susan Strasberg, Bruce Dern, Dennis Hopper, Dick Miller, Luana Anders, Peter Bogdanovich

Peter Fonda plays a director of TV commercials who discovers the kaleidoscopic pleasures of LSD. This curio of the psychedelic era features outdated special effects and sensibilities. Screenplay by Jack Nicholson.

1967　　　　　　　　85 minutes

TRIP TO BOUNTIFUL, THE
★★★★½

DIRECTOR: Peter Masterson
CAST: Geraldine Page, John Heard, Carlin Glynn, Richard Bradford, Rebecca DeMornay, Kevin Cooney

In 1947, an elderly widow (wonderfully played by Oscar-winner Geraldine Page) leaves the cramped apartment where she lives with her loving but weak son (John Heard) and his demanding wife (Carlin Glynn) to return to Bountiful, the small town where she had spent her happy youth . . . unaware that it no longer exists. Along the way, she meets a kindred spirit (Rebecca DeMornay) and the film becomes a joyous celebration of life. Rated PG.

1986　　　　　　　　105 minutes

TRIUMPH OF THE WILL
★★★★

DIRECTOR: Leni Riefenstahl
CAST: Documentary

World-renowned German documentary of the rise of Hitler's Third Reich is a masterpiece of propaganda and remains a chilling testament to the insanity that can lurk in great art. Director Leni Riefenstahl created a powerful and noble image of a German empire that was already threatening Europe and would eventually engulf the world in a devastating war. Riefenstahl's editing of this massive paean to the grandiose dreams of Adolph Hitler is a textbook lesson to future filmmakers, and the footage used is some of the most stunning political persuasion any power-seeking potentate ever had access to. Along with Riefenstahl's *Olympia*, this film qualifies as an unquestioned classic of its kind.

1935　　　　B & W 110 minutes

TROJAN WOMEN, THE
★½

DIRECTOR: Michael Cacoyannis
CAST: Katharine Hepburn, Vanessa Redgrave, Genevieve Bujold, Irene Papas

This Greek-American film is worth seeing only for the four female leads: Katharine Hepburn, Vanessa Redgrave, Genevieve Bujold, and Irene Papas. Unfortunately, the plot (revolving around the Trojan War and their defeat) is lost, and even the most ardent fans can't find it. Rated PG.

1972　　　　　　　　105 minutes

TROUBLE IN MIND
★★★★

DIRECTOR: Alan Rudolph

CAST: Kris Kristofferson, Keith Carradine, Genevieve Bujold, Lori Singer, Joe Morton, Divine

An ex-cop, Kris Kristofferson, is paroled from prison and returns to Rain City, hoping to rekindle his romance with café owner Genevieve Bujold. Once there, he falls in love with the wife (Lori Singer) of a thief (Keith Carradine). Director Alan Rudolph's ultrabizarre, semi-futuristic tale is a free-form character study, an unusual screen experience that almost defies description. Beautiful cinematography (the film was shot in Seattle) and fine acting make up for the lack of a strong plot. Like Rudolph's *Choose Me*, it is not for all tastes. Rated R.

1986   111 minutes

TRUE CONFESSIONS
★★★★½
DIRECTOR: Ulu Grosbard
CAST: Robert De Niro, Robert Duvall, Charles Durning, Burgess Meredith

This is the thoughtful, powerful story of two brothers (Robert De Niro and Robert Duvall)—one a priest, the other a jaded detective—caught in the sordid world of power politics in post–World War II Los Angeles. It's a brilliant and disturbing film. Rated R.

1981   108 minutes

TRUE HEART SUSIE
★★★
DIRECTOR: D. W. Griffith
CAST: Lillian Gish, Robert Herron, Wilbur Higby, Loyola O'Connor, George Fawcett, Clarine Seymour, Kate Bruce, Carol Dempster, Raymond Cannon

Lillian Gish and Robert Herron are sweethearts in a small, rural, bedrock-solid American town in this sentimental silent film account of a young girl's transition from scatterbrained, uninhibited adolescent to dignified, self-assured woman. Sensitive acting and directing make what could have been cloying mush a touching, charming excursion back to what are nostalgically recalled as "the good old days," whether they were or not.

1919   B & W   62 minutes

TUFF TURF
★★
DIRECTOR: Fritz Kiersch
CAST: James Spader, Kim Richards, Paul Mones

"He's always been a rebel—Now, he's about to become a hero." So reads the advertisements for this forgettable movie about young love as the new kid in town falls for a street-wise young woman with a dangerous lover. Featuring music by Southside Johnny, Lene Lovich, Marianne Faithfull, Jim Carroll, Jack Mack and the Heart Attack. Rated R for violence, profanity, and suggested sex.

1984   112 minutes

TULSA
★★½
DIRECTOR: Stuart Heisler
CAST: Susan Hayward, Robert Preston, Pedro Armendariz, Chill Wills, Ed Begley Sr.

Typical pot-boiler has feisty Susan Hayward as a strong-willed woman intent on drilling oil wells on her property no matter who tries to interfere. Standard stock situations made more palatable by fine cast of character actors typify this story of a hard-headed businesswoman humanized during the course of the action.

1949   90 minutes

TUNES OF GLORY
★★★★

DIRECTOR: Ronald Neame
CAST: Alec Guinness, John Mills, Susannah York, Dennis Price, Duncan Macrae, Kay Walsh, Gordon Jackson, John Fraser, Allan Cuthbertson

Gripping drama of rivalry between embittered Alec Guinness and his younger replacement John Mills is a classic study of cruelty as Guinness loses no opportunity to bully and belittle the competent but less aggressive Mills. Superb acting highlights this tragic story, and its universal message could be applied to similar situations in any walk of life. Guinness excels as the cold, calculating old soldier who choreographs the humiliation and downfall of the younger officer, and Mills is superb as the sensitive victim whose self-doubt and insecurities increase with each passing day. Certainly no light entertainment, this strong fare might not qualify as an evening's diversion, but it's an emotional, cathartic experience and one of the finest films of any period.

1960   107 minutes

TURK 182
★★

DIRECTOR: Bob Clark
CAST: Timothy Hutton, Robert Urich, Kim Cattrall, Robert Culp, Darren McGavin, Peter Boyle

Timothy Hutton stars as Jimmy Lynch, a young man who embarks on a personal crusade against injustice. His older brother, Terry (Robert Urich), a fireman, has been denied his pension after being injured while saving a child from a burning building when he was off-duty. So Jimmy decides to right this wrong. *Turk 182* is one of those hollow, manipulative movies obviously thought by their makers to be sure-fire crowd-pleasers. It's anything but. Rated PG-13 for violence, profanity, and suggested sex.

1985   102 minutes

12 ANGRY MEN
★★★★★

DIRECTOR: Sidney Lumet
CAST: Henry Fonda, Lee J. Cobb, Ed Begley Sr., E. G. Marshall, Jack Klugman, Jack Warden, Martin Balsam, John Fiedler, Robert Webber, George Voskovec, Edward Binns, Joseph Sweeney

A superb cast under inspired direction makes this film brilliant in every aspect. Henry Fonda is the holdout on a jury who desperately seeks to convince his eleven peers to reconsider their hasty conviction of a boy accused of murdering his father. The struggle behind closed doors is taut, charged, and fascinating.

1957   B & W   95 minutes

TWICE IN A LIFETIME
★★★★★

DIRECTOR: Bud Yorkin
CAST: Gene Hackman, Ann-Margret, Ellen Burstyn, Amy Madigan, Ally Sheedy, Brian Dennehy

Superior slice-of-life drama about a Washington mill worker (Gene Hackman) who reaches a mid-life crisis and decides that he and wife Ellen Burstyn can't sustain the magic anymore. That decision is helped by a sudden interest in local barmaid Ann-Margret, but the script isn't that simplistic. There aren't any "bad guys" and "good guys" . . . just several decent people forced to make painful choices. Oscar-nominated Amy Madigan plays the elder daughter as a fire-brand who, fearful of her *own* marriage, takes her anger out on Dad. The cast is uniformly fine, the story poignant without being sugary. Rated R for adult situations.

1985   111 minutes

TWO ENGLISH GIRLS
★★★★½

DIRECTOR: François Truffaut
CAST: Jean-Pierre Léaud, Kiki Markham, Stacey Tendeter

Twenty-two minutes were recently added to make this very civilized and rewarding film actually as long as it always had seemed. Thanks to the skills of a mellowed master director and the cinematography of Nestor Almendros, *Two English Girls* is quite worth the patience sometimes needed. Set in pre–World War I Europe and based on the Henri-Pierre Roché novel (his only other being *Jules et Jim*, the modern flip-side of the arrangement here), Truffaut's studied work has Frenchman Léaud the object of two English sisters' desire. Whereas the *Jules and Jim* ménage à trois explored the intolerable extremes of freedom, *Two English Girls* concentrates on the damage that Victorianism wreaked upon the European spirit, and on the consequences of trying to rid oneself of such stultifying repression. In French with English subtitles.

1972   130 minutes

UGETSU
★★★★½

DIRECTOR: Kenji Mizoguchi
CAST: Machiko Kyo, Masayuki Mori, Sakae Ozawa

Set in sixteenth-century Japan, this film follows the lives of two Japanese peasants as their quest for greed and ambition brings disaster upon their families. There is a fine blending of action and comedy in this ghostly tale. In Japanese, with English subtitles.

1953   94 minutes

UMBERTO D
★★★★★

DIRECTOR: Vittorio De Sica
CAST: Carlo Battisti, Maria Pia Casilio, Lina Gennari

With the constant threat of cuts in the Social Security System, *Umberto D* seems to be as poignant now as when it was initially released. Quite simply, the plot centers upon a retired civil servant trying to maintain some sort of dignity and life for himself and his dog on his meager government pension. The film is a sordid, unromanticized view of the human condition in modern Italy. It is agonizingly candid and almost unbearably heartbreaking. This is even more amazing considering the fact that Carlo Battisti (Umberto D) had never acted before. A Vittorio De Sica masterpiece that should be shown to every government employee and should not be missed by anyone. In Italian with English subtitles.

1955   B & W   89 minutes

UMBRELLAS OF CHERBOURG, THE
★★★★

DIRECTOR: Jacques Demy
CAST: Catherine Deneuve, Nino Castelmuovo, Marc Michel, Ellen Farnen

Simply the most romantic film to come from France in the 1960s. Catherine Deneuve made her first popular appearance, and we've been madly in love with her ever since. Simple story—boy meets girl—but played against a luxuriously photographed backdrop. Exquisite score from Michel Legrand. Watch this with somebody you love.

1964   91 minutes

UNDER CAPRICORN
★★★

DIRECTOR: Alfred Hitchcock

CAST: Michael Wilding, Ingrid Bergman, Joseph Cotten

This film is about a nineteenth-century Australian household that is hiding some dark secrets. Michael Wilding is drawn into solving the family's mystery because of his attraction to the lady of the house, Ingrid Bergman. This is not a typical Alfred Hitchcock movie. It lacks his customary suspense, and its pace could be called leisurely at best.

1949   117 minutes

UNDER THE CHERRY MOON
★★

DIRECTOR: Prince

CAST: Prince, Jerome Benton, Steve Berkoff, Alexandra Stewart, Kristin Scott Thomas, Francesca Annis, Emmanuelle Sallet

Although this film is slow moving, it will appeal to teenagers, especially Prince fans. Prince plays a gigolo-type singer who pursues a debutante, Mary (Kristin Scott Thomas), who's due to inherit a huge trust on her twenty-first birthday. Mary's greedy father (Steve Berkoff) has planned a marriage for Mary that will merge two large fortunes. When Mary realizes her dad is using her, she takes off with Prince and his friend Tricky (Jerome Benton). Benton provides the few humorous moments in an otherwise melodramatic film. Viewers will marvel at the bizarre variety of clothes that

Prince wears. Rated PG for language and mature theme.

1986   B & W 100 minutes

UNDER THE VOLCANO
★★★★

DIRECTOR: John Huston

CAST: Albert Finney, Jacqueline Bisset, Anthony Andrews

Director John Huston's brilliant, but disturbing, adaptation of the Malcolm Lowry novel about a suicidal, alcoholic British consul in Mexico on the eve of World War II. Albert Finney's performance is superb, as is that by co-star Jacqueline Bisset, who plays Finney's wife. Rated R for suggested sex, violence, and profanity.

1984   109 minutes

UNION CITY
★★★

DIRECTOR: Mark Reichert

CAST: Deborah Harry, Dennis Lipscomb, Irina Maleeva, Pat Benatar

Called the "punk rock *film noir*," *Union City* is a quietly disturbing tale of murder and paranoia circa 1953. Deborah Harry (of the rock group Blondie) stars as a bored housewife; Dennis Lipscomb is her high-strung, paranoid husband. Though the plot of the film isn't especially strong, Mark Reichert's direction is. The mood, tone, and feel of the film are spooky, though it may be too oblique for some. Rated PG for adult themes and violence.

1980   87 minutes

UNMARRIED WOMAN, AN
★★★★★

DIRECTOR: Paul Mazursky

CAST: Jill Clayburgh, Michael Murphy, Alan Bates, Pat Quinn

Jill Clayburgh's Erica starts out as a well-adjusted wife who doesn't mind her part-time job and loves her family. She has settled into a comfortable rut and barely notices it when things begin to go wrong. One day, after lunch with her husband, Martin (Michael Murphy), she is shocked by his sobbing admission that he is in love with another woman. Her world is shattered. This first-rate film concerns itself with her attempts to cope with the situation. Rated R for sex, nudity, and profanity.

1978   124 minutes

UNTIL SEPTEMBER
★½

DIRECTOR: Richard Marquand
CAST: Karen Allen, Thierry Lhermitte, Christopher Cazenove

A midwestern divorcée (Karen Allen, of *Raiders of the Lost Ark*) falls in love with a married Parisian banker (Thierry Lhermitte, of *My Best Friend's Girl*) during the summer vacation in this unabashed soap opera. Rated R.

1984   95 minutes

UPTOWN NEW YORK
★★

DIRECTOR: Victor Schertzinger
CAST: Jack Oakie, Shirley Grey

Sobby melodrama about a doctor whose family forces him to jilt the girl he loves and marry for money. She bounces into marriage with a bubble gum machine salesman who nobly offers her a divorce when he learns the truth.

1932   B & W   80 minutes

URBAN COWBOY
★★★

DIRECTOR: James Bridges
CAST: John Travolta, Debra Winger, Scott Glenn, Madolyn Smith, Charlie Daniels Band

The film is a slice-of-life *Saturday Night Fever*–like look at the after-hours life of blue-collar cowboys. Overall, the film works because of excellent directing by James Bridges and the fine acting of John Travolta, Debra Winger, and Scott Glenn. This film had a strong cultural impact, moving country music into the mainstream of American life. Rated PG.

1980   132 minutes

USERS, THE
★★

DIRECTOR: Joseph Hardy
CAST: Jaclyn Smith, Tony Curtis, Joan Fontaine, Red Buttons

Another overbloated TV movie boasts a fine cast and little else. Jaclyn Smith stars as a beautiful girl who plays a major role in the resurgence of a down-and-out movie star's career. Standard "television" production values and "television" dialogue do this one in.

1978   125 minutes

VAGABOND
★★★½

DIRECTOR: Agnes Varda
CAST: Sandrine Bonnaire, Macha Meril, Stephane Freiss, Marthe Jarnais

French New Wave writer-director Agnes Varda's dispassionate but beautifully photographed "investigation"—via flashbacks—of a young misfit's meandering trek through the French countryside features a superb performance by Sandrine Bonnaire. Her *Vagabond* is presented as rude, lazy, ungrateful, and therefore unsympathetic, which makes it difficult for the viewer to become completely involved. Yet in some subliminal way the film draws one into the alienation that fuels this outsider's journey into death. Although fictional, the film tends to resemble a documentary. In French with English subtitles. Rated R for profanity and suggested sex.

1986   105 minutes

VERDICT, THE
★★★★½

DIRECTOR: Sidney Lumet
CAST: Paul Newman, James Mason, Charlotte Rampling, Jack Warden

In this first-rate drama, Paul Newman brilliantly plays an alcoholic Boston lawyer who redeems himself by taking on slick James Mason in a medical malpractice suit. Rated R for profanity and adult situations.

1982   129 minutes

VIOLETS ARE BLUE
★★★½

DIRECTOR: Jack Fisk
CAST: Sissy Spacek, Kevin Kline, Bonnie Bedelia, John Kellogg, Jim Standiford, Augusta Dabney

In this watchable screen soap opera, former high-school sweethearts Sissy Spacek and Kevin Kline are reunited when she, a successful photojournalist, returns to her hometown after a particularly debilitating assignment in strife-torn Belfast. Their romance is rekindled although he is now married (to Bonnie Bedelia, who is terrific in her all-too-brief on-screen bits) and has a 13-year-old son. Without the occasionally inspired lines of dialogue by screenwriter Naomi Foner, *Violets Are Blue* would be a lightweight star vehicle. Even with them, this romance movie directed by Spacek's husband Jack Fisk falls a bit

short. Rated PG for suggested sex and light profanity.

1986   89 minutes

VIRIDIANA
★★★★★

DIRECTOR: Luis Buñuel
CAST: Silvia Pinal, Fernando Rey, Francisco Rabal, Margarita Lozano

Angelic Viridiana (Silvia Pinal) visits her uncle (Fernando Rey) prior to taking her religious vows. Uncle Jaime is overcome by her resemblance to his wife, who died on their wedding night, and has his niece drugged. Unable to rape her, he nevertheless tells her he has and then hangs himself with a jump rope. This is just the first reel! The film was an amazing cause célèbre at the time: the script for the first fictional film Buñuel had directed in his native Spain had been approved and the film "in the can" when the authorities got wind of its subversive nature. Despite the government's massive efforts to confiscate all copies of the film, one or two had made their way to France, as had Buñuel, and *Viridiana*—much to Spain's and the Catholic Church's consternation—won the Palme d'Or at Cannes. In Spanish with English subtitles.

1961   B & W   90 minutes

VISION QUEST
★★★½

DIRECTOR: Harold Becker
CAST: Matthew Modine, Linda Fiorentino, Michael Schoeffling, Ronny Cox, Harold Sylvester

Here's yet another movie in which a young athlete makes good against all odds. If you can get past the (over) familiarity of the plot, it isn't bad. It benefits particularly from a charismatic lead performance by

Matthew Modine (who played Mel Gibson's brother in *Mrs. Soffel*). He's likable and, as a result, so is the movie. Rated R for nudity, suggested sex, violence, and profanity.

1985   96 minutes

VIVA ZAPATA!
★★★★½

DIRECTOR: Elia Kazan
CAST: Marlon Brando, Anthony Quinn, Jean Peters, Joseph Wiseman

This film chronicles Mexican revolutionary leader Emiliano Zapata from his peasant upbringings until his death as a weary, disillusioned political liability. Marlon Brando was to win an Oscar nomination for his inciteful portrayal of Zapata. Anthony Quinn, as Zapata's brother, did manage to hold his own against the powerful Brando characterization and was rewarded with a supporting actor Oscar.

1952   B & W   113 minutes

VOLPONE
★★★★

DIRECTOR: Maurice Tourneur
CAST: Harry Baur, Louis Jouvet

Filmed in 1939, this superb screen version of Shakespeare contemporary Ben Jonson's classic play of greed was not released until after World War II, by which time star Harry Baur, a titan of French cinema, was mysteriously dead, having been, it is supposed, erased by the Nazis in 1941. Aided by his avaricious and parasitic servant, Mosca, Volpone, an old Venetian, pretends he is dying and convinces his greedy friends that each of them is his heir. To buy preference, the friends shower the conniving faker with rich gifts. Each expects to get his gift and

more back when the will is read. Not satisfied with their success, Volpone and Mosca spin a web of lies until they themselves are caught. In French with English subtitles.

1939   B & W   80 minutes

VOYAGE OF THE DAMNED
★★★★

DIRECTOR: Stuart Rosenberg
CAST: Oskar Werner, Faye Dunaway, Max von Sydow, Orson Welles, Malcolm McDowell, James Mason, Julie Harris, Lee Grant

This fine drama takes place in 1939 as a shipload of Jewish refugees are refused refuge in Havana and are forced to return to Germany for certain imprisonment and/or death. Rated PG.

1976   134 minutes

WANDERERS, THE
★★★★

DIRECTOR: Phil Kaufman
CAST: Ken Wahl, John Friedrich, Karen Allen, Tony Ganios

This enjoyable film is set in the early 1960s and focuses on the world of teenagers. Though it has ample amounts of comedy and excitement, because it deals with life on the streets of the Bronx, there is an atmosphere of ever-present danger and fear. It is the dark side of adolescence, with all the anguish, brutality, and painful reality that comes with survival and growing up. The Wanderers are a gang of Italian-American youths who have banded together for safety and good times. While they are not overt troublemakers, life in the asphalt jungle presents dangers both real and imagined. Rated R.

1979   113 minutes

WANTON CONTESSA, THE
★★★★½
DIRECTOR: Luchino Visconti
CAST: Alida Valli, Farley Granger, Massimo Girotti

Luchino Visconti—aristocrat by birth, Marxist by conviction—offers one of the lushest and most expressive Italian films ever made (known there as *Senso*). The large-budget spectacular is operatic in scope and look. The story, too, is an opera romance. Venice, 1866: Patriots are conspiring against the occupying Austrians; a countess (the alluring Alida Valli) finds herself passionately in love with a young Austrian officer (Farley Granger), forsaking family and patriotic allegiances; but, of course, the officer turns out to be a coward and a cad. Visconti seemed to have turned his back on neorealism, embracing neoromanticism, confounding critics and audiences. But this film's reputation has grown steadily, and it is now something of a classic. Dubbed in English (with dialogue by Tennessee Williams and Paul Bowles).

1954   120 minutes

WAR AND PEACE
★★½
DIRECTOR: King Vidor
CAST: Henry Fonda, Audrey Hepburn, Mel Ferrer, John Mills

Mammoth international effort to film this classic novel results in an overlong, unevenly constructed melodrama. The massive battle scenes and outdoor panoramas are truly impressive, as are the performers on occasion. But the whole production seems to swallow up the principals and the action, leaving a rather lifeless film. An early Dino De Laurentiis co-production (with Carlo Ponti), and the next-to-last effort of King Vidor, legendary American director.

1956   208 minutes

WAR LOVER, THE
★★½
DIRECTOR: Philip Leacock
CAST: Steve McQueen, Robert Wagner, Shirley Ann Field

This is a very slow-moving account of pilots (Steve McQueen and Robert Wagner) in England during World War II. Both pilots are seeking the affections of the same woman. Nothing in the film raises it above the level of mediocrity.

1962   B & W 105 minutes

WASHINGTON AFFAIR, THE
★★★★
DIRECTOR: Victor Stoloff
CAST: Tom Selleck, Barry Sullivan, Carol Lynley, Arlene Banas

Jim Hawley (Tom Selleck) is an incorruptible federal agent who must award a government contract. Walter Nicholson (Barry Sullivan) is a wheeler-dealer who tries to blackmail Hawley into giving him the contract. When Nicholson hires someone to film Hawley in his hotel bedroom, he's shocked to find out that his own wife, Barbara (Carol Lynley), is Hawley's lover. There's enough heavy breathing and surprises in this film to keep most viewers on the edge of their couch wondering what will happen next. Rated R for simulated sex.

1977   104 minutes

WATCH ON THE RHINE
★★★★
DIRECTOR: Herman Shumlin
CAST: Paul Lukas, Bette Davis, Geraldine Fitzgerald

Lillian Hellman's expose of Nazi terrorism was brought from Broadway to the screen in first-rate form. Paul Lukas won a best-actor Oscar for his role of an underground leader who fled Germany for the U.S., only to be hunted down by Nazi agents. Bette Davis is wonderful in what was one of her few small supporting roles.

1943   B & W 114 minutes

WATERLOO BRIDGE
★★★★
DIRECTOR: Mervyn LeRoy
CAST: Vivien Leigh, Robert Taylor, Lucile Watson

A five-hanky romance about the lives of two people caught up in the turmoil of World War II, this is a poignant tale of a beautiful ballerina (Vivien Leigh) who falls in love with a British officer (Robert Taylor) and how her life is altered when he leaves for the battlefields of Europe. This is one of Leigh's best performances, although she rarely gave a bad one.

1941   B & W 103 minutes

WAY DOWN EAST
★★★
DIRECTOR: D. W. Griffith
CAST: Lillian Gish, Richard Barthelmess, Lowell Sherman, Mary Hay

Classic story of young woman ostracized by her family and community for moral reasons was an audience favorite of the early part of this century but old hat even by 1920, when this melodrama was released. Justly famous for the exciting and dangerous flight of the beautiful Lillian Gish across the ice floes, pursued and eventually rescued by stalwart yet sensitive Richard Barthelmess, this was one of classic director D. W. Griffith's

best-remembered films, but was also one of his last solid critical and commercial blockbusters. Although he made films for another ten years with stars ranging from W. C. Fields to Walter Huston, "the Master" was never able to match his earlier successes and gradually made way for newer, less stage-bound film directors.

1920   B & W 119 minutes

WAY WE WERE, THE
★★★½
DIRECTOR: Sydney Pollack
CAST: Barbra Streisand, Robert Redford, Patrick O'Neal, Viveca Lindfors, Bradford Dillman, Lois Chiles

The popular theme song somewhat obscured the fact this is a rather slow-moving romance about a Jewish girl (Barbra Streisand) who marries a WASPish writer (Robert Redford). The film has its moments, but the portion dealing with the McCarthy communist witch hunt falls flat. Rated PG.

1973   118 minutes

WELCOME TO L.A.
★★★½
DIRECTOR: Alan Rudolph
CAST: Keith Carradine, Geraldine Chaplin, Harvey Keitel, Sally Kellerman, Sissy Spacek, Lauren Hutton

Extremely well made film concerning the disjointed love lives of several Los Angeles nouveaux riches. Film's focal point is songwriter Keith Carradine, whose romantic interludes set the wheels in motion. Entire cast is first-rate, with Richard Baskin's musical score the only drawback. Director Alan Rudolph's prelude to the cult favorite *Choose Me*. Rated R.

1977   106 minutes

WHEN FATHER WAS AWAY ON BUSINESS
★★★

DIRECTOR: Emir Kusturica
CAST: Moreno D'e Bartolli, Miki Manojlovic, Mirfana Karanovic

Seen through the eyes of a young boy, the film deals with the sudden disappearance of a father from a family because of a few minor yet commonly held opinions of the party in power and the party in disfavor. Tension mounts when it becomes clear that it is the father's brother-in-law who turned him in and had him sent to a work camp. The story is touchingly realistic and able to carry the audience step by step through this Yugoslavian drama. It is not surprising that the film received the Gold Palm at the 1985 Cannes Film Festival. Rated R for sex and nudity. In Slavic with English subtitles.

1985   144 minutes

WHEN WOLVES CRY
★

DIRECTOR: Terence Young
CAST: William Holden, Virna Lisi, Brook Fuller, Bourvil

Poorly directed melodrama about a 10-year-old boy, Pascal, who is diagnosed as being terminally ill. His father, Laurent (William Holden), dedicates himself to indulging his son's every whim—including stealing two wild wolves from the Paris zoo. Originally titled *The Christmas Tree*. Rated G.

1983   108 minutes

WHERE THE GREEN ANTS DREAM
★★★★

DIRECTOR: Werner Herzog

CAST: Bruce Spence, Wandjuk Marika, Roy Marika, Ray Barrett, Norman Kaye, Colleen Clifford, Nicolas Lathouris, Gary Williams, Trevor Orford

Another stark, yet captivating vision from perhaps the most popular director of current German cinema. The film is basically an ecological tug of war between progress and tradition, namely uranium mining interests against aborigines and their practices. The basic theme is nothing new, but Herzog's treatment, and in particular the film's quirky elements, is nothing short of fascinating.

1984   100 minutes

WHITE NIGHTS
★★★½

DIRECTOR: Taylor Hackford
CAST: Mikhail Baryshnikov, Gregory Hines, Geraldine Page, Jerzy Skolimowski, Isabella Rosellini

Russian defector and ballet star Mikhail Baryshnikov, finding himself back in the U.S.S.R., joins forces with American defector Gregory Hines to escape to freedom in this soap opera–styled thriller directed by Taylor Hackford (*An Officer and a Gentleman*). The plot is contrived, but the dance sequences featuring the two stars together and separately are spectacular. Rated PG-13 for violence and profanity.

1985   135 minutes

WHO ARE THE DEBOLTS AND WHERE DID THEY GET 19 KIDS?
★★★★★

DIRECTOR: John Korty
CAST: Documentary

This Academy Award–winning documentary features Dorothy and Bob Debolt and their nineteen children—some natural, most adopted. Their family is unique not only for its great size but for the multiple physical disabilities their adopted children have, the positive way these problems are dealt with, and the fantastic organizational system under which their daily lives are run. This film is an eyeopener for adults as well as children and helps us all see our problems in a new perspective. Although there are sad and touching moments, there are also hilarious ones. By the end of the film, you don't pity the disabled kids, you just wish that you could be as strong and "whole" as they are. This is an excellent and inspirational film. Rated G.

1978   73 minutes

WHO'S AFRAID OF VIRGINIA WOOLF?
★★★★★

DIRECTOR: Mike Nichols
CAST: Elizabeth Taylor, Richard Burton, Sandy Dennis, George Segal

Edward Albee's powerful play about the love-hate relationship of a college professor and his bitchy wife was brilliantly transferred to the screen by director Mike Nichols. Elizabeth Taylor gives her best acting performance as Martha, a screeching bitch caught in an unfulfilled marriage. Richard Burton is equally stunning as the quiet, authoritative professor who must decide between abandoning or salvaging their marriage after a night of bitter recriminations and painful revelations. Sandy Dennis and George Segal more than hold their own in support.

1966   B & W 129 minutes

WHOSE LIFE IS IT, ANYWAY?
★★★★

DIRECTOR: John Badham

CAST: Richard Dreyfuss, John Cassavetes, Christine Lahti, Bob Balaban, Kenneth McMillan, Kaki Hunter, Janet Eilber, Thomas Carter

Richard Dreyfuss is superb as a witty and intellectually dynamic sculptor who is paralyzed after an auto accident and fights for his right to be left alone to die. John Cassavetes and Christine Lahti co-star as doctors in this surprisingly upbeat movie. Rated R.

1981   118 minutes

WHY SHOOT THE TEACHER?
★★★

DIRECTOR: Silvio Narizzano
CAST: Bud Cort, Samantha Eggar, Chris Wiggins, Gary Reineke, John Friesen, Michael J. Reynolds

Bud Cort (Harold and Maude) stars in this intimate and simple film about a young instructor whose first teaching position lands him in the barren plains of Canada. Lean realism and bright dashes of humor give the picture some memorable moments, but this story of an outsider trying to adapt to the lifestyle of an isolated community develops with a disengaging slowness. This PG-rated project has a warm charm, but not enough grit.

1977   101 minutes

WIFEMISTRESS
★★★½

DIRECTOR: Marco Vicario
CAST: Marcello Mastroianni, Annie Belle, Laura Antonelli, Leonard Mann, Gaston Muschin, William Berger

Marcello Mastroianni stars as a husband in hiding, and Laura Antonelli as his repressed wife. When Mastroianni is falsely accused of murder, he hides out in a building across the street from his own home. His wife, not knowing where he is, begins to relive his sexual escapades. There are some comic moments as the former philandering husband must deal with his wife's new sexual freedom. Nudity and sex are included in this film.

1977   110 minutes

WILD DUCK, THE
★★½

DIRECTOR: Henri Safran
CAST: Liv Ullmann, Jeremy Irons, Lucinda Jones, Arthur Dignam, John Meillon, Michael Pate

Despite the cast, or maybe because of it, this poignant story of love and tragedy falls short of its ambitious mark. Jeremy Irons (Moonlighting, The French Lieutenant's Woman) and Liv Ullmann (Autumn Sonata, Cries and Whispers) are struggling parents whose child is slowly going blind. An idealistic friend (Arthur Dignam) complicates matters by unearthing truths that were better off buried. The touching story is botched up by an awkward screenplay. Both Ullmann's and Irons's performances are inconsistent, and while there may be some justification for their odd behavior, it is incongruous with the general mood of the plot. Rated PG for profanity.

1983   96 minutes

WILD IN THE COUNTRY
★★★

DIRECTOR: Philip Dunne
CAST: Elvis Presley, Hope Lange, Tuesday Weld, Millie Perkins, John Ireland

Elvis Presley is encouraged to pursue a literary career when counseled during his wayward youth. Most viewers will find it interesting to see Elvis in such a serious role. The supporting cast also has something to add to the okay script.

1961   114 minutes

WILD PARTY, THE
★★★½

DIRECTOR: James Ivory
CAST: James Coco, Raquel Welch, Perry King, David Dukes

This is a very grim look at how Hollywood treats its fading stars. James Coco plays a one-time comedy star trying to come back with a hit film. Raquel Welch plays Coco's longtime girlfriend who plans a party for Hollywood's elite in order to push his film. Things fall apart during the party. The film is based on the career of Fatty Arbuckle and provides some interesting insights into the Hollywood power structure, with good performances by Coco and Welch. Rated R.

1975   107 minutes

WILD ROSE
★★

DIRECTOR: John Hanson
CAST: Lisa Eichhorn, Tom Bower, James Cada, Cinda Jackson, Dan Nemanick, Lydia Olson

This low-budget film, shot in and around the Wisconsin coal mine fields, floats between being a love story (showing a woman's search for independence) and a social commentary on mining conditions. By trying to cover all the bases, writer-director John Hanson fails to cover even one satisfactorily. Far too many dead spots in the script and the extensive use of nonactors and sparse dialogue sink this one quickly.

1984   96 minutes

WILD STRAWBERRIES
★★★★

DIRECTOR: Ingmar Bergman
CAST: Victor Sjöström, Ingrid Thulin, Bibi Andersson, Gunner Bjorstrand, Folk Sundquist, Bjorn Bjelvenstam

This film is probably Ingmar Bergman's least ambiguous. Superbly photographed and acted, the film tells the story of an elderly professor facing old age and reviewing his life's disappointments. The use of flashbacks is very effective in this film.

1957   B & W   90 minutes

WILL, G. GORDON LIDDY
★★★½

DIRECTOR: Robert Leiberman
CAST: Robert Conrad, Katherine Cannon, Gary Bayer, Peter Rattray, James Rebhorn, Red West, Maurice Woods, Danny Lloyd

Robert Conrad ("The Wild Wild West") is transformed into the fanatic, strong-willed Watergate mastermind Liddy. The first half lacks excitement or revelation for most viewers who remember the Watergate scandal. Liddy's stay in prison, however, is a fascinating study of his personality.

1982   100 minutes

WILMA
★★½

DIRECTOR: Bud Greenspan
CAST: Cicely Tyson, Shirley Jo Finney, Joe Seneca, Jason Bernard

This made-for-TV film chronicles the early years of Olympic star Wilma Rudolph (Cicely Tyson) and follows her career up to her winning the gold. Film fails to do justice to its subject matter. Lackluster production.

1977   100 minutes

WINDY CITY
★★★

DIRECTOR: Armyan Bernstein
CAST: John Shea, Kate Capshaw, Josh Mostel, Jim Borrelli, Jeffrey DeMunn, Eric Pierpoint, Lewis J. Stadlen, James Sutorius

Very uneven, very frustrating attempt to chronicle the story of a group of young adults who have known one another since they were kids. Told through the eyes of one of their own, a writer (John Shea), it has the feel of being based on real-life experiences but is embarrassingly true to some of the more rude and off-putting behavior most people would rather have private memories of. It gets three stars for its honesty, the fun of watching Kate Capshaw (who is charming even when given silly things to say) and because we were touched by its idealistic and sentimental view of "friends forever." Rated R.

1984   103 minutes

WINSLOW BOY, THE
★★★★

DIRECTOR: Anthony Asquith
CAST: Robert Donat, Margaret Leighton, Cedric Hardwicke, Basil Radford, Francis X. Sullivan, Frank Lawton, Wilfrid Hyde-White, Neil North

Robert Donat is superb as the proper British barrister defending a young naval cadet, wrongly accused of theft, against the overbearing pomp and indifferent might of the Crown. At stake in this tense Edwardian courtroom melodrama is the long cherished and maintained democratic right to be regarded as innocent until proven guilty by a fair trial. Opposing the boy and his defender are the complacent lethargy of officialdom and the apparent blindness of justice. "Let right be done" is the key line.

Playwright Terence Rattigan scripted from his West End and Broadway stage hit, based on an actual 1912 case. The case is excellent, the cause just, the drama and suspense first-rate.

1950   B & W 118 minutes

WINTER KILLS
★★★★

DIRECTOR: William Richert
CAST: Jeff Bridges, John Huston, Belinda Bauer, Richard Boone, Anthony Perkins, Toshiro Mifune, Sterling Hayden, Eli Wallach, Ralph Meeker, Dorothy Malone, Tomas Milian, Elizabeth Taylor

An all-star cast is featured in this sometimes melodramatic, but often wry, account of a presidential assassination. Rated R.

1979   97 minutes

WINTER LIGHT
★★★

DIRECTOR: Ingmar Bergman
CAST: Ingrid Thulin, Gunnar Bjorstrand, Max von Sydow, Gunnel Lindblom

Second film in director Bergman's "faith" trilogy (it follows *Through a Glass Darkly* and precedes *The Silence*) centers on a disillusioned priest who attempts to come to grips with his religion and his position in the inner workings of the church. Not an easy film to watch. This honest effort to explore the psyche of a cleric and answer the questions that have troubled the "spiritual" side of man for centuries is a thoughtful, incisive drama with great performances that inveigles the audience into participating in this quest for truth and the answers of life.

1962   B & W   80 minutes

WINTER OF OUR DREAMS
★★

DIRECTOR: John Duigan
CAST: Judy Davis, Bryan Brown, Cathy Downes, Baz Luhrmann, Peter Mochrie, Mervyn Drake

An all-too-typical soaper, this downbeat film has good acting but less-than-adequate direction. Rated R.

1981   90 minutes

WINTERSET
★★½

DIRECTOR: Alfred Santell
CAST: Burgess Meredith, Margo, Eduardo Ciannelli, John Carradine, Paul Guilfoyle, Stanley Ridges, Mischa Auer

Heavy-duty drama of bitter young man's efforts to clear his father's name lacks the punch it must have possessed as a top stage play in the 1930s but boasts a great cast of distinguished character actors and marks the screen debut of the versatile Burgess Meredith. Talkfest is long on moralizing and short on action, but it's a class production and has impressive, if stagy, set of actors and circumstances.

1936   B & W   78 minutes

WISE BLOOD
★★★★

DIRECTOR: John Huston
CAST: Brad Dourif, Harry Dean Stanton, Ned Beatty, Amy Wright, Dan Shor

While there are many laughs in this fascinating black comedy about a slow-witted country boy (Brad Dourif) who decides to become a man of the world, they tend to stick in your throat. Underneath the wryly comic surface is the poignant, often disturbing story of a man's desperate search for something or someone to believe in. Flannery O'Connor wrote the novel on which Benedict Fitzgerald's screenplay was based. As brilliant as it is, this searing satire on southern do-it-yourself religion comes so close to the truth, it is almost painful to watch at times. But you can't take your eyes off the screen as it holds you in a grip of morbid fascination. Rated PG.

1979　　　　　　　108 minutes

WITCHCRAFT THROUGH THE AGES (HAXAN)
★★★½

DIRECTOR: Benjamin Christensen

CAST: Maren Pedersen, Clara Pontoppidan, Elith Pio, Oscar Stribolt, Benjamin Christensen, John Andersen, Astrid Holm, Poul Roumert, Alice O'Fredericks

After almost seventy years of notoriety, this controversial film is still unique as one of the most blasphemous and outrageous movies of all time. Envisioned by director Benjamin Christensen as a study of black magic, witchcraft, and demonology from the Middle Ages to the present, this silent Scandinavian epic fluctuates between lecture material and incredibly vivid footage that gave the censors ulcers back in the early 1920s. Benjamin Christensen (who also plays a demon in the film) was one of the European directors lured to Hollywood in the mid-1920s, where he directed Lon Chaney in *The Mockery* and transferred A. Merritt's classic fantasy *Seven Footprints to Satan* to the screen before returning to his native Denmark. This film might not be acceptable to all family members and is not recommended for impressionable children. There is a version available with William Burroughs reading the narration;

other prints are captioned and subtitled in English.

1921　　　　　B & W　82 minutes

WITHOUT A TRACE
★★★½

DIRECTOR: Stanley Jaffe

CAST: Kate Nelligan, Judd Hirsch, David Dukes, Stockard Channing, Jacqueline Brookes, Kathleen Widdoes

A drama about a boy who vanishes and his mother's unrelenting faith that he will return, this is yet another entry in the family-in-trouble movie genre. If you didn't get your fill of that from *Kramer vs. Kramer*, *Ordinary People*, *Shoot the Moon*, and the rest, you might enjoy this well-acted but sometimes overwrought and predictable film. Rated PG for mature content.

1983　　　　　　　120 minutes

WITNESS FOR THE PROSECUTION
★★★★★

DIRECTOR: Billy Wilder

CAST: Tyrone Power, Charles Laughton, Marlene Dietrich, Elsa Lanchester, John Williams, Henry Daniell, Una O'Connor

Superb performances from Tyrone Power, Charles Laughton, and Marlene Dietrich help make this gripping courtroom drama an enduring favorite of film buffs. The screenplay was adapted from a play by mystery novelist Agatha Christie and features Laughton as an aging lawyer called upon to defend an alleged murderer (Power). It is Dietrich, in what is perhaps her greatest screen performance, who nearly steals the show.

1957　　　　　B & W　114 minutes

WOMAN CALLED GOLDA, A
★★★½

DIRECTOR: Alan Gibson
CAST: Ingrid Bergman, Judy Davis, Leonard Nimoy

Ingrid Bergman won an Emmy for her outstanding performance as Israeli Prime Minister Golda Meir. Leonard Nimoy co-stars in this highly watchable film, which was originally made for TV.

1982   200 minutes

WOMAN IN FLAMES, A
★★★★

DIRECTOR: Robert Van Ackeren
CAST: Gudrun Landgrebe, Mathieu Carriere

A male and a female prostitute fall in love and decide to set up shop in the same household, insisting that their business trysts will not interfere with their personal relationship. They do. At times steamy, intense, and provocative. If erotic drama and bizarre twists are your fancy, this should be your film. Rated R for sexual situations and language.

1984   104 minutes

WOMAN NEXT DOOR, THE
★★★★½

DIRECTOR: Francois Truffaut
CAST: Gerard Depardieu, Fanny Ardant, Henri Garcin, Michele Baumgartner, Veronique Silver

Francois Truffaut is on record as one of the greatest admirers of Alfred Hitchcock, and the influence shows in his gripping, well-made film about guilt, passion, and the growing influence of a small sin that grows. MPAA unrated but contains nudity and violence.

1981   106 minutes

WOMAN OF PARIS, A
★★★★

DIRECTOR: Charles Chaplin
CAST: Edna Purviance, Adolphe Menjou, Carl Miller, Lydia Knott, Henry Bergman

In this now-classic silent, a simple country girl (Edna Purviance) goes to Paris and becomes the mistress of a wealthy philanderer (Adolphe Menjou). In her wake follow her artist sweetheart and his mother. Resulting complications trigger an engrossing study of human relationships. Director Charles Chaplin surprised everyone with this film by suddenly forsaking, if only momentarily, his Little Tramp comedy for serious caustic drama, auguring what was to ultimately come in *The Great Dictator*, *Monsieur Verdoux*, and *Limelight*.

1923   B & W 112 minutes

WOMEN IN LOVE
★★★★½

DIRECTOR: Ken Russell
CAST: Glenda Jackson, Oliver Reed, Alan Bates, Eleanor Bron, Jennie Linden, Alan Webb

Glenda Jackson won an Oscar for her performance in this British film. Two love affairs are followed simultaneously in this excellent adaptation of D. H. Lawrence's novel. Rated R.

1970   B & W 129 minutes

WORD, THE
★★★

DIRECTOR: Richard Lang
CAST: David Janssen, John Huston, James Whitmore

In a catacomb beneath Ostia, Italy, an archeologist discovers an ancient manuscript that could cause chaos in the Christian world. The manuscript is said to contain the writings of Christ's younger brother, James the Just. The writings contain heretofore unknown fragments of Jesus' life and death, which turns the religious world upside-down and confusion to conflict. A good story, with wonderful actors. Unrated.

1978   188 minutes

WORLD ACCORDING TO GARP, THE
★★★★½

DIRECTOR: George Roy Hill
CAST: Robin Williams, Glenn Close, John Lithgow, Mary Beth Hurt, Hume Cronyn, Jessica Tandy, Swoosie Kurtz, Amanda Plummer

Director George Roy Hill (*Butch Cassidy and the Sundance Kid* and *A Little Romance*) and screenwriter Steven Tesich (*Breaking Away*) have captured the quirky blend of humor and pathos of John Irving's bestseller. The acting is impressive, with first-rate turns by Robin Williams (in the title role), Glenn Close as his mother, Jenny Fields, and John Lithgow as a kindly transsexual. Rated R for nudity, profanity, sexual situations, and violence.

1982   136 minutes

WORLD AT WAR VOL. 1–26
★★★★★

DIRECTOR: John Pett
CAST: Laurence Olivier (Narrator)

These twenty-six volumes, approximately one hour each, comprise the best historical account of World War II ever assembled. Made by the Thames company for British and American television, it is topnotch in all respects. Each volume incorporates interviews with former soldiers, civilian accounts, and lots of actual newsreel footage from the war. Highly recommended for anyone interested in the subject. Unrated.

1980   60 minutes

WUTHERING HEIGHTS
★★★★

DIRECTOR: William Wyler
CAST: Merle Oberon, Laurence Olivier, Flora Robson, David Niven

Time and talk have made this film a classic. Taken from the Emily Brontë novel, this is a haunting, mesmerizing film. Set on the murky, isolated moors, it tells the tale of Heathcliff, a foundling Gypsy boy who loves Cathy, the spoiled daughter of the house. Their affair, born in childhood, is doomed. She dies; he is left to brood and despair. The moors abide in wind and rain and eerie gloom. As the star-crossed lovers, Olivier and Oberon are impressive.

1939   B & W 103 minutes

YOL
★★★½

DIRECTOR: Serif Goren
CAST: Tarik Akin, Serif Sezer, Halil Ergun, Heral Orhonsoy, Necmettin Cobanoglu

Winner of the Grand Prix at the Cannes Film Festival, this work, by Turkish filmmaker and political prisoner Yilmaz Gurney, follows several inmates of a minimum-security prison who are granted a few days' leave, telling their stories in parallel scenes. Although Gurney—who smuggled instructions out of prison to his trusted assistants, then escaped from prison and edited the film—was hailed at Cannes for creating an eloquent protest against suppression and totalitarian government, *Yol* is more of a study in slavery of the women they dominate, humiliate, torture, and even murder. Unrated, the film has violence and suggested sex.

1982   111 minutes

YOLANDA AND THE THIEF
★★

DIRECTOR: Vincente Minnelli
CAST: Fred Astaire, Lucille Bremer, Frank Morgan, Mildred Natwick, Mary Nash, Ludwig Stossel, Leon Ames; Gigi Perreau

An exotic fantasy, staged with near-cloying opulence, and now a cult favorite. Down on his luck con man Fred Astaire finds beautiful, rich, convent-bred Lucille Bremer praying to her guardian angel. His eye on her money, he claims to be the angel come to earth to protect her. While pursuing his swindle, he falls in love with his mark. This film begins with charm, then goes steadily downhill, thanks to a poor screenplay and inappropriate casting. Fred can't play a con man; Lucille is too cool to be sweet, too lofty to be trusting.

1945   108 minutes

YOU LIGHT UP MY LIFE
★★½

DIRECTOR: Joseph Brooks
CAST: Didi Conn, Michael Zaslow, Joe Silver

Pretty weak story concerning a young girl, Didi Conn, trying to make it in show business. Notable for the title song, which was Debbie Boone's only claim to fame. Film proves it's tough to make a hit song stretch into a feature film. Rated PG.

1977   90 minutes

YOU ONLY LIVE ONCE
★★★

DIRECTOR: Fritz Lang

CAST: Henry Fonda, Sylvia Sydney, William Gargan, Barton MacLane, Jean Dixon, Jerome Cowan, Margaret Hamilton, Ward Bond, Guinn Williams

About a three-time loser (Henry Fonda) who can't even be saved by the love of a good woman (Sylvia Sydney) because society won't allow him to go straight, this film is definitely not a light-hearted or even enjoyable entertainment. In fact, it's a real downer—recommended for Fonda fans only.

1937   B & W   86 minutes

YOUNG AND WILLING
★★½

DIRECTOR: Edward H. Griffith
CAST: William Holden, Susan Hayward, Eddie Bracken, Barbara Britton, Robert Benchley

Hope springs eternal in the hearts of a gaggle of show business neophytes living and loving in a New York theatrical boardinghouse. Cute and entertaining, but formula. Summer stock in Manhattan.

1943   B & W   82 minutes

YOUNG LOVE, FIRST LOVE
★★

DIRECTOR: Steven Hilliard Stern
CAST: Valerie Bertinelli, Timothy Hutton

Boy loves girl, girl loves boy. Does girl love boy enough to go all the way? Nothing better to do? Then watch and find out. Valerie Bertinelli is super-cute as the girl in the quandary of whether to or not. Timothy Hutton is wasted as the boy with the sweats. Unrated.

1979   100 minutes

YOUNG PHILADELPHIANS, THE
★★★★

DIRECTOR: Vincent Sherman

CAST: Robert Vaughn, Paul Newman, Barbara Rush, Alexis Smith, Brian Keith, Adam West, Diane Brewster, Billie Burke, John Williams, Otto Kruger

In this excellent film, Robert Vaughn stars as a rich young man framed for murder. Paul Newman, a young lawyer, defends Vaughn while pursuing society girl Barbara Rush.

1959　　　B & W 136 minutes

YOUNG WINSTON
★★★

DIRECTOR: Richard Attenborough
CAST: Simon Ward, Anne Bancroft, Robert Shaw, John Mills, Jack Hawkins, Robert Flemyng, Patrick Magee, Laurence Naismith

A first-rate cast peoples this rousing and thoroughly entertaining account of this century's man for all seasons, England's indomitable Winston Leonard Spencer Churchill: journalist, politician, historian, prime minister, bricklayer, peer, brandy and cigar expert. The film takes him from his often wretched school days to his beginnings as a journalist of resource and daring in South Africa during the Boer War, up to his first election to Parliament and the start of an incredible career of many turns and hues. Simon Ward is excellent in the title role. History fares quite well, despite ample opportunity and temptation to gilt truth. Rated PG.

1972　　　145 minutes

YOUNGBLOOD
★½

DIRECTOR: Peter Markle
CAST: Rob Lowe, Patrick Swayze, Cynthia Gibb, Ed Lauter, Jim Youngs, Fionnula Flanagan

Rob Lowe has stated that this *Rocky* ripoff will be the last of his movies "about teenage problems." Good for him. But he could have stopped before making this bit of silliness about a sensitive kid who tries to make it in the world of hockey. Lowe's character can race around anyone to score a goal. The problem is, he lacks the killer instinct this movie would have us believe is an integral part of the game. Some nice character moments help the story along, but writer/director Peter Markle drops the puck when it comes to comedy bits and credibility. Rated R for profanity, nudity, simulated sex, and violence.

1986　　　110 minutes

Z
★★★★

DIRECTOR: Constantin Costa-Gavras
CAST: Yves Montand, Irene Papas, Jean-Louis Trintignant, Charles Denner, Georges Geret, Jacques Perrin, François Périer, Marcel Bozzuffi

Director Costa-Gavras (*Missing*) first explored political corruption in this taut French thriller. Yves Montand plays a political leader who is assassinated. Based on a true story. Academy Award for best foreign film. Well worth a try. No rating, with some violence and coarse language.

1969　　　127 minutes

ZABRISKIE POINT
★★½

DIRECTOR: Michelangelo Antonioni
CAST: Mark Freshene, Daria Halprin, Rod Taylor

An interesting but confusing story of a young college radical who shoots a policeman during a campus demonstration in the late 1960s. This film examines subjects such as Vietnam, black power, and government repression but does not really say too much. The finale is quite exciting, but not worth waiting for. Rated R.

1970   112 minutes

ZERO FOR CONDUCT
★★★★½

DIRECTOR: Jean Vigo
CAST: Jean Daste, Robert le Flon, Louis Lefebvre, Constantin Kelber, Gerard De Bedarieux

This unique fantasy about the rebellion of a group of young boys in a French boarding school is told from the point of view of the students and provides perhaps the purest picture in the history of cinema of what authority appears to be to young minds. Shot from the angle that a youth would view things from and slowed down to present a dreamlike picture, this allegorical tale depicts the boys of the school as inmates and incisively illustrates their frustrations and suppression at the hands of the adult schoolmasters, who force them to obey rules and conventions that have no meaning to them. This all too short gem was sadly one of only four films made by terminally ill director Jean Vigo, who was to die the year following its release at the age of 29. Banned across the Continent when first released, this 50-year-old film provided much of the storyline for Lindsay Anderson's 1969 update *If....* starring Malcolm McDowell, and has continued to delight audiences at colleges and film societies. In French with English subtitles.

1933   B & W   44 minutes

ZORBA THE GREEK
★★★★

DIRECTOR: Michael Cacoyannis
CAST: Anthony Quinn, Alan Bates, Irene Papas, Lila Kedrova, George Foundas

A tiny Greek village in Crete is the home of Zorba, a zesty, uncomplicated man whose love of life is a joy to his friends and an eye-opener to a visiting stranger, Alan Bates. Anthony Quinn is a delight as Zorba, a role he has become identified with. Lila Kedrova was to win an Oscar for her poignant role as an aging courtesan in this 1963 drama.

1963   B & W 146 minutes

HORROR/SUSPENSE

ABOMINABLE DR. PHIBES, THE
★★★½

DIRECTOR: Robert Fuest
CAST: Vincent Price, Joseph Cotten, Hugh Griffith, Virginia North, Terry-Thomas

A stylish horror film directed by Robert Fuest, this features Vincent Price in one of his best latter-day roles as a man disfigured in a car wreck taking revenge on those he considers responsible for the death of his wife. Rated PG.

1971   93 minutes

AGAINST ALL ODDS (KISS AND KILL, BLOOD OF FU MANCHU)
★

DIRECTOR: Jess (Jesus) Franco
CAST: Christopher Lee, Richard Greene, Tsai Chin, Shirley Eaton

Next-to-last entry in the low-budget series that got worse with each outing. The evil Fu Manchu hatches another dastardly plan for world domination. This time he saturates ten beautiful slave girls with a deadly poison and sends them out to kiss his enemies to

death. The stars of the film disappear for long stretches, no doubt to keep their fees down. A complete bore. Believe it or not, three of these were filmed in one year. The dialogue was postdubbed, so everyone is a bit out of sync. The film print is dirty, scratchy, and fuzzy. Don't be misled by the picture of the topless girl on the cassette box. It was taken from the foreign version of the film, not this one. Rated PG.

1968   93 minutes

ALICE, SWEET ALICE (COMMUNION AND HOLY TERROR)
★★

DIRECTOR: Alfred Sole
CAST: Brooke Shields, Tom Signorelli, Louisa Horton, Paula E. Sheppard, Mildred Clinton, Lillian Roth

A 12-year-old girl goes on a chopping spree. No, it's not Brooke Shields. She only has a small role in this, her first film. But after the success of *Pretty Baby* the following year, the distributor changed the title, gave Brooke top billing, and rereleased this uninteresting thriller. Rated R for violence.

1977   96 minutes

ALIEN PREY

DIRECTOR: Norman J. Warren
CAST: Barry Stokes, Sally Faulkner, Glory Annan

This is not just another science-fiction/horror alien film. This savage alien is on a protein mission. Unfortunately the vegetarian dinner served up by his two lesbian hosts does not satisfy him. This film contains sexual and cannibalistic scenes, making it unsuitable for the squeamish. Unrated.

1984   85 minutes

ALISON'S BIRTHDAY
★★½

DIRECTOR: Ian Coughlan
CAST: Joanne Smuel, Lou Brown, Bunny Brooke, John Bluthal, Vincent Ball

A slow but interesting Australian horror story involving curses and possession. A young girl is told by her father's ghost to leave home before her nineteenth birthday, but as you may guess, she's summoned back days before the big day, and things get nasty. Not only is the acting tight, but if a Gothic setting can be transplanted to suburbia, then it happens here.

1984   99 minutes

ALLIGATOR
★★★½

DIRECTOR: Lewis Teague
CAST: Robert Forster, Michael Gazzo, Robin Riker, Perry Lang, Jack Carter, Bart Braverman, Henry Silva, Dean Jagger

The wild imagination of screenwriter John Sayles (writer-director of *Return of the Secaucus Seven* and *Brother From Another Planet*) invests this comedy-horror film with wit and style. It features Robert Forster as a cop tracking down a giant alligator. It's good, unpretentious fun, but you have to be on your toes to catch all the gags (be sure to read the hilarious graffiti). Rated R.

1980   94 minutes

ALONE IN THE DARK

DIRECTOR: Jack Sholder
CAST: Jack Palance, Donald Pleasence, Martin Landau, Dwight Schultz, Deborah Hedwall

The inmates of a New Jersey mental institution (played by Jack Palance, Martin Landau, and Erland Van Lidth) break out during a blackout (with a little help from psychiatrist Donald Pleasence) to terrorize a doctor and his family. No matter how quickly they're all killed, it isn't soon enough. Rated R.

1982   92 minutes

AMERICAN WEREWOLF IN LONDON, AN
★★★½

DIRECTOR: John Landis
CAST: David Naughton, Jenny Agutter, Griffin Dunne

This is one of the better horror films to come out in many a moon—pun intended. Director John Landis weaves humor, violence, and the classic horror elements of suspense in the tale of the two American travelers who find more than they bargained for on the English moors. A great soundtrack, featuring Van Morrison and Creedence Clearwater Revival, adds greatly to the total effect. Rated R for violence, nudity, and gore.

1981 97 minutes

AMITYVILLE HORROR, THE

DIRECTOR: Stuart Rosenberg
CAST: James Brolin, Margot Kidder, Rod Steiger

A better title for this turgid mishmash would be *The Amityville Bore*. Based on a supposedly true story, it's a hackneyed, unbelievable horror flick. Avoid it. Rated R.

1979 117 minutes

AMITYVILLE II: THE POSSESSION
★★½

DIRECTOR: Damiano Damiani
CAST: Burt Young, Rutanya Alda, James Olson, Moses Gunn

Okay, so it's not a horror classic. But thanks to tight pacing, skillful special effects, and fine acting, *Amityville II: The Possession* is a fairly suspenseful flick. And—thank goodness—this "prequel" is much better than *Amityville Horror*. Preceding the events in the latter film, a family of six moves into the eerie Long Island house, and the eldest son winds up being possessed. James Olson (the priest who tries to exorcise the house) and Burt Young (the boy's father) head the cast. Rated R for violence, implied sex, light profanity, and adult themes.

1982 104 minutes

AMITYVILLE III: THE DEMON
★

DIRECTOR: Richard Fleischer
CAST: Tony Roberts, Tess Harper, Lori Laughlin, Meg Ryan

In this soggy second sequel to *The Amityville Horror*, one of the worst movies of all time, Tony Roberts

(Woody Allen's pal in *Play It Again, Sam* and *Annie Hall*) plays a reporter who, along with photographer Candy Clark (*American Graffiti*), investigates the spooky goings-on at the infamous house in Amityville, New York, and ends up as one of its victims. It's hack horror. Rated PG for violence and gore.

1983 105 minutes

AND NOW THE SCREAMING STARTS
★★★

DIRECTOR: Roy Ward Baker
CAST: Peter Cushing, Stephanie Beacham, Herbert Lom, Patrick Magee, Ian Ogilvy

Frightening British horror film about a young newlywed couple moving into a house haunted by a centuries-old curse on the husband's family. Well done, with a great cast, but occasionally a bit too bloody. Rated R.

1973 87 minutes

ANDY WARHOL'S DRACULA
★

DIRECTOR: Paul Morrissey
CAST: Udo Kier, Joe Dallesandro, Vittorio DeSica, Roman Polanski, Arno Juerging

Companion piece to Andy Warhol's equally revolting version of *Frankenstein*. The "joke" this time is that Dracula (Udo Kier) can survive only on the blood of "were-gins" and vomits that which comes from more experienced ladies. Needless to say, considerable amounts of blood gush into various bathtubs and sinks. Plucky Joe Dallesandro, learning of the Count's weakness, engages in a madcap race to deflower the castle women before Dracula can empty them. The Count gets so upset that he literally goes to pieces. Rated

X for excessive violence and kinky sex.

1974   93 minutes

ANDY WARHOL'S FRANKENSTEIN

DIRECTOR: Paul Morrissey
CAST: Joe Dallesandro, Monique Van Vooren, Udo Kier, Srdjan Zelewovic

"Bore, bore, bore," says Kate Hepburn to Jane Fonda during a mother-daughter talk in *On Golden Pond*. She could easily have been critiquing this stupendously awful "horror film" by Warhol's New York Pop Art crowd. Third-rate Marlon Brando imitator Joe Dallesandro meanders around muttering inane dialogue. Blood and gore gush at every opportunity. This turkey should have been left on the shelf. Rated R for obvious reasons.

1974   94 minutes

APE MAN, THE
★★

DIRECTOR: William Beaudine
CAST: Bela Lugosi, Louise Currie, Wallace Ford, Minerva Urecal

In the 1930s, thanks to the success of *Dracula* at the beginning of the decade, Bela Lugosi was one of the great horror film stars. However, the monster-movie boom stopped short in 1935, leaving the Hungarian actor out of work. When shockers came back in vogue four years later, Lugosi took any and every role he was offered. The result was grade-Z pictures such as this one, about a scientist (Lugosi) attempting to harness the physical power of apes for humankind. Too bad.

1943   B & W   64 minutes

APRIL FOOL'S DAY
★★★

DIRECTOR: Fred Walton
CAST: Jay Baker, Deborah Foreman, Griffin O'Neal, Amy Steel

A group of college kids on spring break are invited to a mansion on a desolate island by a rich girl named Muffy St. John. They read Milton, quote Boswell, play practical jokes, and get killed off in a nice, orderly fashion. The surviors get anxious, Muffy turns squirrelly, and the party is a total bust. Not really a horror film; more of a mystery à la *Ten Little Indians*. It will probably disappoint fans of gore, naked starlets, and gratuitous stupidity, but it's a pleasant surprise that creates suspense without turning stomachs. Rate R for violence and profanity.

1986   90 minutes

ARNOLD
★½

DIRECTOR: Georg Fenady
CAST: Roddy McDowall, Elsa Lanchester, Stella Stevens, Farley Granger, Victor Buono, John McGiver, Shani Wallis

A delightful cast cannot save this rather muddled mess of murder and mirth. Stella Stevens, married to a corpse, suddenly discovers her co-stars meeting their maker in a variety of strange ways reminiscent of *The Abominable Dr. Phibes*. Unfortunately, director Georg Fenady doesn't display one-tenth of that film's style, and the characters are rather cheerless. Pretty ho-hum. Rated PG for violence.

1973   100 minutes

ASTRO-ZOMBIES

DIRECTOR: Ted V. Mikels

CAST: Wendell Corey, John Carradine, Tom Pace, Joan Patrick, Rafael Campos

A grade-Z horror film that wastes the talent of star John Carradine.

1967   83 minutes

ASYLUM
★★★★

DIRECTOR: Roy Ward Baker
CAST: Barbara Parkins, Sylvia Syms, Peter Cushing, Barry Morse, Richard Todd, Herbert Lom, Patrick Magee

A first-rate horror anthology from England featuring fine performances. Four seemingly unrelated stories of madness are interwoven, leading to a nail-biting climax. Rated PG.

1972   92 minutes

ATOM AGE VAMPIRE
🦔

DIRECTOR: Richard McNamara (aka Anton Giulio Masano)
CAST: Alberto Lupo, Susanne Loret

Badly dubbed Italian time waster with cheese-ball special effects and a tired premise. A mad professor restores the face of a scarred accident victim. To keep her beautiful, he must kill other women and swipe their glands. Every so often, just for fun, the doc transforms into something resembling that troll doll your sister used to have.

1961   B & W   87 minutes

ATTACK OF THE CRAB MONSTERS
★★★

DIRECTOR: Roger Corman
CAST: Richard Garland, Pamela Duncan, Mel Welles, Russell Johnson, Leslie Bradley, Ed Nelson

Neat Roger Corman low-budget movie, seemed scarier when you were a kid, but it's still a lot of fun. A remote Pacific atoll is besieged by a horde of giant land crabs that, upon devouring members of a scientific expedition, absorb their brains and acquire the ability to speak in their voices. Though the lack of available funds caused some scenes to be unintentionally funny, the movie has more than its share of chills, along with plenty of eerie atmosphere.

1957   B & W   64 minutes

ATTACK OF THE 50-FOOT WOMAN
★★★

DIRECTOR: Nathan Juran
CAST: Allison Hayes, William Hudson, Yvette Vickers, Roy Gordon

One of the best "schlock" films from the 1950s. Allison Hayes stars as a woman who's kidnapped by a tremendous bald alien and transformed into a giant herself. Duddy special effects only serve to heighten the enjoyment of this kitsch classic.

1958   B & W   66 minutes

ATTACK OF THE SWAMP CREATURE
🦔

DIRECTOR: Arnold Stevens
CAST: Frank Crowell, Patricia Robertson, Patrick Allison, Lee Kropiewnicki, David Robertson

In one of Elvira's "thriller Video" movies, we're treated to the story of a mad scientist who turns himself into a giant, man-eating, walking catfish. Need we go further? We'll say one thing for Elvira and her producers: they know how to pick the worst films in the horror genre. This one is so bad, it's not even funny—just boring.

1985   96 minutes

ATTIC, THE
★½

DIRECTOR: George Edwards
CAST: Carrie Snodgress, Ray Milland, Ruth Cox, Francis Bay

Rather slow-moving and routine story concerning a young woman (Carrie Snodgress) fighting to free herself from the clutches of her crippled, almost insane, father. Tries to be deep and psychological and falls flat on its face. Rated PG.

1979   97 minutes

AUDREY ROSE
★

DIRECTOR: Robert Wise
CAST: Marsha Mason, Anthony Hopkins, John Beck

Plodding melodrama about a man (Anthony Hopkins) who constantly annoys a couple by claiming that his dead daughter has been reincarnated as their live one. Bad script is only one problem in one of director Wise's few duds. Rated PG.

1977   113 minutes

AWAKENING, THE
★★½

DIRECTOR: Michael Newell
CAST: Charlton Heston, Susannah York, Jill Townsend, Patrick Drury, Stephanie Zimbalist

In this mediocre horror flick, Charlton Heston plays an Egyptologist who discovers the tomb of a wicked queen. The evil spirit escapes the tomb and is reincarnated in Heston's newborn daughter. Years later Heston's daughter (Stephanie Zimbalist) is possessed. A bit hard to follow the plot. Rated R for gore.

1980   102 minutes

BABY, THE
★★★

DIRECTOR: Ted Post
CAST: Ruth Roman, Mariana Hill, David Manzy

Extremely odd film by veteran director Ted Post about a teenager who has remained an infant all his life (yes, he still lives in his crib) and his insane, overprotective mother. Eerily effective chiller is highly entertaining, though many will undoubtedly find it repulsive and ridiculous. Rated PG.

1974   80 minutes

BASKET CASE
★★★★

DIRECTOR: Frank Henenlotter
CAST: Kevin Vanhentryck, Terri Susan Smith, Beverly Bonner, Robert Vogel, Diana Browne

Comedy and horror are mixed beautifully in this weird tale of a young man and his deformed Siamese twin out for revenge against the doctors who separated them. Extremely entertaining and highly recommended for shock buffs. Rated R.

1982   91 minutes

BEAR ISLAND
★

DIRECTOR: Don Sharp
CAST: Donald Sutherland, Richard Widmark, Vanessa Redgrave, Christopher Lee, Lloyd Bridges

Alistair MacLean writes some of the best thrillers around; why can't they be turned into better films? This is one of the worst, a pointlessly melodramatic tale mixing gold fever, murder, and other incidental intrigue. Beautiful snowbound setting just emphasizes the empty script. Without question, read the book. Rated PG for mild violence.

1980   118 minutes

BEAST IN THE CELLAR, THE
★½

DIRECTOR: James Kelly
CAST: Beryl Reid, Flora Robson, T. P. McKenna, John Hamill

Boring story about a pair of aging sisters (well played by veterans Beryl Reid and Flora Robson) with something to hide. Only, instead of a skeleton in the closet, they've got a beast in the cellar. More specifically, their deranged, deformed brother is down there, and he wants out! Intriguing idea is given a lackluster treatment here that not even the topflight cast can save. Weak. Rated R.

1971   87 minutes

BEAST MUST DIE, THE
★★

DIRECTOR: Paul Annett
CAST: Calvin Lockhart, Peter Cushing, Marlene Clark, Charles Gray, Anton Diffring

A millionaire hunter invites a group of guests to an isolated mansion. One of them is a werewolf he intends to destroy. This tame, talky reworking of Agatha Christie's *Ten Little Indians* featured a "werewolf break," ostensibly to provide the theatrical audience time to ponder clues and determine the identity of the hairy beast. In practice, however, the gimmick merely resulted in derisive laughter and scattered obscenities. Rated PG.

1974   98 minutes

BEAST WITHIN, THE
★

DIRECTOR: Phillippe Mora
CAST: Ronny Cox, Bibi Besch, Paul Clemens, Don Gordon

This unbelievably gory movie consists mainly of one grisly murder after another. Phillippe Mora, an Australian documentary filmmaker, tries his best to create an atmosphere of intelligent horror (as does top-billed Ronny Cox), but there's no competing with the excessive gore. Rated R for violence, gore, and nudity.

1982   90 minutes

BEDLAM
★★★

DIRECTOR: Mark Robson
CAST: Boris Karloff, Anna Lee, Ian Wolfe, Richard Fraser, Billy House, Jason Robards Jr.

One of the lesser entries in the Val Lewton-produced horror film series at RKO, this release still has its moments as the courageous Anna Lee tries to expose the cruelties and inadequacies of an insane asylum run by Boris Karloff, who is first-rate, as usual.

1946   B & W   79 minutes

BEES, THE
★½

DIRECTOR: Alfredo Zacharias
CAST: John Saxon, John Carradine, Alicia Encinias

Despite all temptation to label this a honey of a picture, it's a drone that will probably give viewers the hives. Rated PG.

1978   83 minutes

BEFORE I HANG
★★★

DIRECTOR: Nick Grindé
CAST: Boris Karloff, Evelyn Keyes, Bruce Bennett, Pedro de Cordoba, Edward Van Sloan

Neat little thriller has Boris Karloff as a good-hearted doctor who creates an age-retardant serum. Trouble begins when he tests it on himself, with horrible side effects. Nicely done, the film benefits from a good supporting performance by horror veteran Edward Van Sloan.

1940   B & W   71 minutes

BEING, THE

DIRECTOR: Jackie Kong

CAST: Martin Landau, José Ferrer, Dorothy Malone, Ruth Buzzi, Rexx Coltrane (Johnny Commander)

This inept little horror film must have taxed the funds or patience of its producers, since gaping hunks of plot are missing and replaced with laughable narration. Hard to choose between the picture's funniest moments: the *Alien*-esque creature so obviously pushed around on wheels, or Martin Landau saying, with a straight face, that water contaminated with nuclear waste is harmless. This particular batch of water spawned a beast that likes to shove itself *through* people . . . or maybe the monster is the deformed child of Dorothy Malone; the story's that confusing. Creature supposedly melts away in direct light, which allows for dim nighttime shooting that disguises the poor effects. Unwatchable. Rated R for gore and nudity.

1984   82 minutes

BEN

★

DIRECTOR: Phil Karlson

CAST: Arthur O'Connell, Lee Harcourt Montgomery, Rosemary Murphy

The only thing going for this silly sequel to *Willard* is an awkwardly charming title song performed by a young Michael Jackson (a love song for a rat, no less). Turgid entry in the beasts-get-even subgenre of horror films. Where's a better rattrap when you need one? Rated PG—violence.

1972   95 minutes

BEST OF SEX AND VIOLENCE

★★

DIRECTOR: Ken Dixon

CAST: Hosted by John Carradine

A quickie video production containing unrelated clips and preview trailers from low-budget exploitation films. John Carradine hosts with a wink, and his sons David and Keith drop by for some ad-lib kidding. A ripoff, to be sure, but not without laughs and a certain sleazy charm. Unrated, the film has profanity, nudity, and, of course, sex and violence.

1981   76 minutes

BEYOND EVIL

★

DIRECTOR: Herb Freed

CAST: John Saxon, Lynda Day George, Michael Dante, Mario Milano, Janice Lynde

Larry Andrews (John Saxon) and his wife, Barbara (Lynda Day George), travel to a tropical island to mix business with their honeymoon. Andrews is to supervise a construction project for Barbara's ex-spouse, and the former husband lodges the newlyweds in a luxurious mansion, which happens to be haunted. The ghost is Alma Martin, a well-to-do lady who was murdered by her husband, and she's out to possess poor Barbara. Rated R.

1980   94 minutes

BEYOND THE DOOR

★

DIRECTOR: Ovidio Assonitis (Oliver Hellman)

CAST: Juliet Mills, Richard Johnson, David Colin Jr.

Sick ripoff of *The Exorcist* has Juliet Mills as a woman possessed by guess what. Or should we say guess who? Disgusting production only serves to induce nausea. Made in Italy. Rated R.

1975 94 minutes

BEYOND THE DOOR 2
★★

DIRECTOR: Mario Bava
CAST: Daria Nicolodi, John Steiner, David Colin Jr.

Why, why, why? Actually, this semi-sequel is much better than the original mainly because its director was the famed Mario Bava (his final film). This time a young boy becomes possessed by the unseen power of Hell, and many die. Alternate title: *Shock*. Rated R.

1979 92 minutes

BIG FOOT

DIRECTOR: Robert Slatzer
CAST: John Carradine, Joi Lansing, John Mitchum, Chris Mitchum, Joy Wilkerson

Legendary monster comes down from the hills and beats the hell out of everybody. Laughable film is worthless, one of John Carradine's worst. Why does he keep makin' 'em? Rated R.

1971 94 minutes

BILLY THE KID VS. DRACULA
★½

DIRECTOR: William Beaudine
CAST: John Carradine, Chuck Courtney, Melinda Plowman, Virginia Christine, Harry Carey Jr.

Hokey horror film casts John Carradine as the famous vampire, on the loose in a small western town.

From the director of *Bela Lugosi Meets a Brooklyn Gorilla*, another so-bad-it's-funny film.

1966 95 minutes

BIRD WITH THE CRYSTAL PLUMAGE, THE
★★½

DIRECTOR: Dario Argento
CAST: Tony Musante, Suzy Kendall, Eva Renzi, Enrico Maria Salerno, Renato Romano, Umberto Rano

Stylish thriller weaves a complex story thread in adventure of an American writer who witnesses a murder and is drawn into the web of mystery and violence. Plenty of clues and red herrings, but the story is convoluted and hard to follow at times. Minor cult and detective genre favorite, well photographed and nicely acted by resilient Tony Musante and fashion plate Suzy Kendall. Rated PG.

1969 98 minutes

BIRDS, THE
★★★★

DIRECTOR: Alfred Hitchcock
CAST: Rod Taylor, Tippi Hedren, Suzanne Pleshette, Jessica Tandy

After scaring the socks off filmgoers with *Psycho* in 1960, director Alfred Hitchcock took one more successful slash at the horror genre with this suspenseful shocker.

1963 120 minutes

BLACK SABBATH
★★★½

DIRECTOR: Mario Bava
CAST: Boris Karloff, Mark Damon, Suzy Andersen

Above-average trio of horror tales given wonderful atmosphere by Italian director Mario Bava. Boris

Karloff plays host, echoing the function he performed on television's *Thriller*, and stars in the third story, a vampire opus entitled "The Wurdalak." One of the others, "A Drop of Water," is based on a story by Chekhov; the third, "The Telephone," involves disconnected calls of the worst sort. Great fun late at night, and Karloff's narration adds considerable dignity.

1964   99 minutes

BLACKENSTEIN

DIRECTOR: William A. Levy
CAST: John Hart, Joe DiSue, Ivory Stone

Tasteless and grotesque entry in the tiny subgenre of "blaxploitation" horror films. Mad doctor John Hart takes a maimed Vietnam veteran (Joe DiSue) and transforms him into a shambling nightmare. Perhaps one of the sickest excuses for a plot ever conceived. All the horror in this film comes from the notion that human beings actually put it together. Rated R for violence and nudity.

1973   92 minutes

BLACK ROOM, THE
★★★

DIRECTOR: Roy William Neill
CAST: Boris Karloff, Marian Marsh, Robert Allen, Katherine DeMille, Thurston Hall

Boris Karloff is excellent as usual in a dual role of twin brothers with an age-old family curse hanging over their heads and the strange way it affects their lives. Well-handled thriller never stops moving. Also worth noting is the video quality of this tape, which is superb, resulting in a film that looks as if it were shot yesterday. The

sound is also exceptionally good, the clearest we've heard from a film of this vintage.

1935   B & W   67 minutes

BLACULA
★★★½

DIRECTOR: William Crain
CAST: William Marshall, Denise Nicholas, Vonetta McGee, Thalmus Rasulala

An old victim (William Marshall) of Dracula's bite is loose in modern L.A. Surprisingly well-done shocker. Fierce and energetic, with a solid cast. Rated R for violence.

1972   92 minutes

BLOB, THE
★★★

DIRECTOR: Irvin S. Yeaworth Jr.
CAST: Steve McQueen, Aneta Corseaut, Earl Rowe, Olin Howlin

This was Steve McQueen's first starring role. He plays a teenager battling parents and a voracious hunk of protoplasm from outer space. Long surpassed by more sophisticated sci-fi, it's still fun to watch.

1958   86 minutes

BLOOD AND BLACK LACE
★★½

DIRECTOR: Mario Bava
CAST: Cameron Mitchell, Eva Bartok, Mary Arden

This sometimes frightening Italian horror film features a psychotic killer eliminating members of the modeling industry with gusto. Decent entry in the genre from specialist Mario Bava.

1964   88 minutes

BLOOD OF DRACULA'S CASTLE

DIRECTOR: Al Adamson, Jean Hewitt

CAST: John Carradine, Paula Raymond, Alex D'Arcy, Robert Dix

Quite possibly the worst Dracula movie ever made. The count and countess spend most of the film sitting around, rambling incoherently, sipping blood cocktails provided by their butler (John Carradine). The film has a werewolf, a hunchback, women in chains, human sacrifices, a laughable script, and a ten-dollar budget. Rated PG.

1967   84 minutes

BLOOD ON SATAN'S CLAW
★★★

DIRECTOR: Piers Haggard

CAST: Patrick Wymark, Barry Andrews, Linda Hayden, Simon Williams

Fun, frightening horror film set in seventeenth-century England. A small farming community is besieged by the devil himself, who succeeds in turning the local children into a coven of witches. Familiar story is presented in a unique manner by director Piers Haggard, helped by excellent period detail and clever effects. Not for the kids, though. Rated R.

1971   93 minutes

BLOOD BEACH
★

DIRECTOR: Jeffrey Bloom

CAST: John Saxon, Mariana Hill, Otis Young

Poor horror story of mysterious forces sucking people down into the sand isn't nearly as fun as it sounds. Bad acting, bad writing, and bad special effects. Rated R.

1981   89 minutes

BLOOD FEAST
★

DIRECTOR: Herschell Gordon Lewis

CAST: Connie Mason, Thomas Wood, Mal Arnold, Lyn Bolton

First and most infamous of the drive-in gore movies bolsters practically nonexistent plot of crazed murderer with gallons of director Herschell Gordon Lewis's patented stage blood as well as props like a sheep's tongue and a power saw. Crude, vulgar, and ineptly acted, this bargain-basement production was one of the low-budget bonanzas of the 1960s and set the tone for dozens of subsequent nauseating hack-and-slash films.

1963   75 minutes

BLOODBEAT
★

DIRECTOR: Fabrice A. Zaphiratos

CAST: Helen Benton, Terry Brown, Claudia Peyton, Dana Day, James Fitz Gibbons

If Prokofiev and Vivaldi knew that their music was being used in a death-fest like this film, the masters would be spinning in their crypts like drill bits. This cheap supernatural flick also tries to pass off the idea that a samurai ghost is haunting the backwoods of an American wilderness because of an old war debt—we think. The plot is not at all clear, and the bad acting and poor direction only aggravate the problem. May be of some interest to those fascinated with fifteenth-century Japanese war armor. No MPAA rating, but with sex, nudity, profanity, and a mean samurai ghost loose, it's a sure R rating.

1985   84 minutes

BLOODSUCKERS, THE
★★½

DIRECTOR: David Hewitt
CAST: Lon Chaney Jr., John Carradine

Lots of blood, gory special effects, and some good humor. Not bad for this type of film. Also known as *Return from the Past* and *Dr. Terror's Gallery of Horrors*. Not for the squeamish.

1967　　　　　　　　　84 minutes

BLOODTHIRSTY BUTCHERS
🐝

DIRECTOR: Andy Milligan
CAST: John Miranda, Annabella Wood, Berwick Kaler

As the title suggests, an extremely violent series of murders is committed in very gruesome fashion. A dreadful ripoff of *The Demon Barber of Fleet Street*, with Sweeney Todd and his baker friend selling human meat pies. Nothing new here. Rated R.

1970　　　　　　　　　80 minutes

BLOODTIDE
🐝

DIRECTOR: Richard Jeffries
CAST: James Earl Jones, José Ferrer, Lila Kedrova

Cheap horror film that isn't worthy of your time. A dud! Rated R.

1984　　　　　　　　　82 minutes

BLOW OUT
★★★★

DIRECTOR: Brian De Palma
CAST: John Travolta, Nancy Allen, John Lithgow, Dennis Franz, Peter Boyden

John Travolta and Nancy Allen are terrific in this thriller by director Brian De Palma (*Dressed to Kill*; *Carrie*). The story concerns a motion picture sound man (Travolta) who becomes involved in murder when he rescues a young woman (Allen) from a car that crashes into a river. It's suspenseful, thrill-packed, adult entertainment. Rated R because of sex, nudity, profanity, and violence.

1981　　　　　　　　107 minutes

BLOW-UP
★★★★★

DIRECTOR: Michelangelo Antonioni
CAST: Vanessa Redgrave, David Hemmings, Sarah Miles, Jill Kennington

Director Michelangelo Antonioni's first English-language film was this stimulating examination into what is or is not reality. On its surface, a photographer (David Hemmings) believes he has taken a snapshot of a murder taking place. Vanessa Redgrave arrives at his studio and tries to seduce him out of the photo. This sometimes baffling film challenges its audience to think.

1966　　　　　　　　108 minutes

BLUEBEARD
★★★

DIRECTOR: Edgar G. Ulmer
CAST: John Carradine, Jean Parker, Nils Asther, Ludwig Stossel, Iris Adrian, Emmett Lynn

Atmospheric low-budget thriller by resourceful German director Edgar G. Ulmer gives great character actor John Carradine one of his finest leading roles as a strangler who preys on women. Full of swirling mists, constricted sets, and familiar faces, this film, while initially considered a lesser entry, is on a par with the better known "mist-and-murder" films of the mid-1940s, including *The Lodger*, *Hangover Square*, and *The Picture of Dorian Gray*. Cadaverous

Carradine cuts a fine figure as the refined maniac who aims to make lovely Jean Parker his next victim. Make up some popcorn, grab a zombie movie for a second feature, and sit back and enjoy this low-key creeper.

1944   B & W   73 minutes

BLUEBEARD
★★½

DIRECTOR: Edward Dmytryk

CAST: Richard Burton, Raquel Welch, Karin Schubert, Joey Heatherton

Richard Burton stars in *Bluebeard*, a film with its tongue planted firmly in cheek. The legend of the multiple murderer is intermingled with Nazi lore to come out as a reasonably convincing foray into a combination of black comedy and classic horror films. Rated R.

1972   125 minutes

BODY DOUBLE
★★★½

DIRECTOR: Brian De Palma

CAST: Craig Wasson, Melanie Griffith

This Brian De Palma (*Carrie*; *Scarface*) thriller, which owes quite a bit to Alfred Hitchcock's *Rear Window* and *Vertigo*, is often gruesome, disgusting, and exploitative. But you can't take your eyes off the screen. Craig Wasson is first-rate as a young actor who witnesses a brutal murder, and Melanie Griffith is often hilarious as the porno star who holds the key to the crime. De Palma experiments with new ways—often tongue-in-cheek—of portraying violence on screen. Some may call it sick and tasteless; others will find it surprisingly entertaining.

Rated R for nudity, suggested sex, profanity, gore, and violence.

1984   110 minutes

BODY SNATCHER, THE
★★★★

DIRECTOR: Robert Wise

CAST: Henry Daniell, Boris Karloff, Bela Lugosi, Russell Wade

Boris Karloff gives one of his finest screen performances in the title role of this 1945 Val Lewton production, adapted from the novel by Robert Louis Stevenson. Karloff is a sinister grave robber who provides dead bodies for illegal medical research and then uses his activities as blackmail to form a bond of "friendship" with the doctor he services, Henry Daniell (in an equally impressive turn).

1945   B & W   77 minutes

BOG

DIRECTOR: Don Keeslar

CAST: Gloria Dehaven, Aldo Ray, Marshall Thompson

Extremely low-budget film is entertaining for just that reason. Unlucky group of people on an excursion into the wilderness run into the recently defrosted monster Bog. Needless to say, things go downhill from there. Rated PG.

1983   87 minutes

BOOGEYMAN, THE
★★★½

DIRECTOR: Ulli Lommel

CAST: Suzanna Love, Michael Love, John Carradine, Ron James

Despite the lame title, this is an inventive, atmospheric fright flick about pieces of a broken mirror causing horrifying deaths. Good special effects add to the creepiness. Rated R for violence and gore.

1980   86 minutes

BOOGEYMAN 2, THE
★

DIRECTOR: Bruce Star
CAST: Suzanna Love, Shana Hall, Ulli Lommel

Not nearly as good as *The Boogeyman*, this cheapo sequel uses footage from the original and a substandard plot to cash in on success of its predecessor. Don't be fooled. Rated R for violence and gore.

1983   79 minutes

BOSTON STRANGLER, THE
★★★

DIRECTOR: Richard Fleischer
CAST: Tony Curtis, Henry Fonda, Mike Kellin, Murray Hamilton, Sally Kellerman, Hurd Hatfield, George Kennedy, Jeff Corey

True account, told in semi-documentary-style, of Beantown's notorious deranged murderer, plumber Albert De Salvo. Tony Curtis gives a first-class performance as the woman-killer. Credibility abounds in the portrayals of Henry Fonda, Murray Hamilton, and the rest. Color softens the impact, which would have been far more arresting in black and white.

1968   120 minutes

BOYS FROM BRAZIL, THE
★★½

DIRECTOR: Franklin J. Schaffner
CAST: Gregory Peck, Laurence Olivier, James Mason, Lilli Palmer

In this thriller, Gregory Peck plays an evil Nazi war criminal with farfetched plans to resurrect the Third Reich. Laurence Olivier pursues him throughout as a Jewish Nazi-hunter. Rated R.

1978   123 minutes

BOYS FROM BROOKLYN, THE
🐵

DIRECTOR: William Beaudine
CAST: Bela Lugosi, Duke Mitchell, Sammy Petrillo, Ramona the Chimp

Absolutely hilarious bomb with Bela Lugosi as a mad scientist turning people into apes on a forgotten island. Standout performance by Sammy Petrillo as a Jerry Lewis clone will have you rolling in the aisles! Better known as *Bela Lugosi Meets a Brooklyn Gorilla*, a much more appropriate title.

1952   B & W   72 minutes

BRIDE, THE
★½

DIRECTOR: Franc Roddam
CAST: Sting, Jennifer Beals, Geraldine Page, Clancy Brown, Anthony Higgins, David Rappaport

This remake of James Whale's classic 1935 horror comedy of the macabre, *Bride of Frankenstein*, has some laughs. But these, unlike in the original, are unintentional. Rock singer Sting (of the Police) makes a rather stuffy, unsavory Dr. Charles (?!) Frankenstein, and Jennifer Beals (*Flashdance*) is terribly miscast as his second creation. In fact, the film's few good moments come in a subplot about the adventures of the Frankenstein monster (Clancy Brown) and a happy-go-lucky, positive-thinking midget (charismatically portrayed by David Rappaport, of *Time Bandits*). This movie gives new meaning to the word pretentious. Rated PG-13 for violence, suggested sex, and nudity.

1985   119 minutes

BRIDE OF THE MONSTER
★★

DIRECTOR: Edward D. Wood Jr.
CAST: Bela Lugosi, Tor Johnson, Tony McCoy, Loretta King

Another incredibly inept film from Ed Wood Jr., who brought us *Plan 9 From Outer Space* and *Glen or Glenda?*, this stinker uses most of the mad scientist clichés and uses them poorly as a cadaverous-looking Bela Lugosi tries to do fiendish things to an unconscious (even while alert) Loretta King. Grade Z favorite Tor (*Beast of Yucca Flats*) Johnson lumbers through his scenes and into most of the hokey sets, prompting a toothless Bela Lugosi to quip "Don't be afraid of Lobo—he's as harmless as a kitchen." This bottom-of-the-barrel independent monstrosity boasts possibly the worst special-effects monster of all time, a rubber octopus that any novelty store would be ashamed to stock. Right down there with *Mesa of the Lost Women*, but more fun and worth the two-star rating as a classic of its kind.

1955　　B & W　69 minutes

BRIDE OF FRANKENSTEIN
★★★★★

DIRECTOR: James Whale
CAST: Boris Karloff, Colin Clive, Valerie Hobson, Dwight Frye, Ernest Thesiger, Elsa Lanchester

This is a first-rate sequel to *Frankenstein*. Many of the cast members from the original—most importantly Boris Karloff, Colin Clive, and Dwight Frye—returned for one of the few follow-ups to outclass its predecessor. Their performances and Whale's bizarre sense of humor make *Bride* a real treat. This time, Henry Frankenstein (Clive) is coerced by the evil Dr. Praetorius (Ernest Thesiger in a delightfully weird and sinister performance) into creating a mate for the monster.

1935　　B & W　75 minutes

BRIGHTON STRANGLER, THE
★★½

DIRECTOR: Max Nosseck
CAST: John Loder, June Duprez, Miles Mander, Michael St. Angel, Rose Hobart, Gilbert Emery, Ian Wolfe

Actor John Loder runs amok after a Nazi bomb destroys the London theatre where he has been playing a murderer in a drama. Stunned in the explosion, he confuses his true identity with the character he has been playing. A chance remark by a stranger sends him off to the seaside resort of Brighton, where he performs his stage role for real!

1945　　B & W　67 minutes

BRIMSTONE AND TREACLE
★★★

DIRECTOR: Richard Loncraine
CAST: Denholm Elliott, Joan Plowright, Suzanne Hamilton, Sting

Sting, of the rock group the Police, plays an angelic-diabolic young drifter who insinuates himself into the home lives of respectable Denholm Elliott and Joan Plowright in this British-made shocker. Rated R.

1982　　　　85 minutes

BROOD, THE
★★

DIRECTOR: David Cronenberg
CAST: Oliver Reed, Samantha Eggar, Art Hindle, Cindy Hinds

Fans of director David Cronenberg (*Dead Zone*) will no doubt enjoy this offbeat, grisly horror tale about genetic experiments. Others need not apply. Rated R.

1979   90 minutes

BROTHERHOOD OF SATAN
★

DIRECTOR: Bernard McEveety
CAST: Strother Martin, L. Q. Jones, Charles Bateman, Ahna Capri

Strong cast is wasted in this ridiculous thriller about a small town taken over by witches and devil worshipers, led by maniacal Strother Martin. Boring. Rated PG.

1971   92 minutes

BRUTE MAN, THE
★½

DIRECTOR: Jean Yarbrough
CAST: Tom Neal, Rondo Hatton, Jane Adams

A homicidal maniac escapes from an asylum. Unmemorable, standard B-movie stuff, notable mainly as a showcase for actor Rondo Hatton. Hatton appeared in several low-budget thrillers in the 1940s, usually as a menacing thug. He needed no make-up; he suffered from acromegaly, a genetic disease that causes distortion of the facial features. *The Brute Man* was one of Hatton's last films. He died in the year of its release, at the age of 42.

1946   B & W   60 minutes

BUG
★★½

DIRECTOR: Jeannot Szwarc
CAST: Bradford Dillman, Joanna Miles, Richard Gilliland, Jamie Smith Jackson

Weird horror film with the world, led by Bradford Dillman, staving off masses of giant mutant beetles with the ability to commit arson, setting fire to every living thing they can find. Rated PG for violence.

1975   100 minutes

BURNING, THE

DIRECTOR: Tony Maylam
CAST: Brian Matthews, Leah Ayres, Brian Backer, Larry Joshua, Lou David

This tedious film is just one more stab at the horror genre that trades surprises and suspense for buckets of blood and severed limbs. Similar to many other blood feasts of late, it's the story of a summer camp custodian who, savagely burned as a result of a teenage prank, comes back years later for revenge. With an excessive amount of blood and absolutely no surprises, you're far more likely to be disgusted than frightened. Rated R.

1981   90 minutes

BURNT OFFERINGS
★½

DIRECTOR: Dan Curtis
CAST: Oliver Reed, Karen Black, Burgess Meredith, Bette Davis

Good acting by Bette Davis, Karen Black, and Oliver Reed cannot save this predictable horror film concerning a haunted house. More of a made-for-television type of film than a true motion picture. Barely watchable. Rated PG.

1976   115 minutes

C.H.U.D.
★

DIRECTOR: Douglas Cheek
CAST: John Heard, Daniel Stern, Christopher Curry

The performances by John Heard and Daniel Stern are all that make this cheapo horror film even barely watchable. *C.H.U.D.* (Cannibalistic Humanoid Underground Dwellers) are New York City bag people who have been exposed to large doses of radiation and start treating the other inhabitants of the city as lunch. Rated R for violence, profanity, and gore.

1984   88 minutes

CABINET OF DOCTOR CALIGARI, THE
★★★½

DIRECTOR: Robert Wiene
CAST: Werner Krauss, Conrad Veidt, Lil Dagover

A nightmarish story and surrealistic settings are the main ingredients of this early German classic of horror and fantasy. Cesare, a hollow-eyed sleepwalker (Conrad Veidt), commits murder while under the spell of the evil hypnotist Dr. Caligari (Werner Krauss). Ordered to kill Jane, a beautiful girl (Lil Dagover), Cesare defies Caligari, and instead abducts her. The chase that follows takes Cesare to his death. It's all very real and unreal, tricking until the very end. Veidt specialized in horror at the outset of his career following World War I. Nearly half a century later, he was last seen as the suave, ill-fated Nazi Major Strasser of *Casablanca*.

1919   B & W   51 minutes

CAPTAIN KRONOS: VAMPIRE HUNTER
★★★½

DIRECTOR: Brian Clemens
CAST: Horst Janson, John David Carson, Caroline Munro, Shane Briant

British film directed by the producer of "The Avengers" television show. It's an unconventional horror tale about a sword-wielding vampire killer. An interesting mix

of genres. Good adventure, with high production values. Rated PG for violence.

1974   91 minutes

CARNIVAL OF SOULS
★★★★

DIRECTOR: Herk Harvey
CAST: Candace Hilligoss, Sidney Berger, Francis Feist, Stan Levitt

Creepy film made on shoestring budget in Lawrence, Kansas, concerns a girl who, after a near-fatal car crash, is haunted by a ghoulish, zombielike character. Extremely eerie, with nightmarish black-and-white photography, this little-known gem has a way of getting to you and causing a feeling of uneasiness long after it's over. Better keep the lights on.

1962   B & W   80 minutes

CARPATHIAN EAGLE
★★

DIRECTOR: Francis Meahy
CAST: Anthony Valentine, Suzanne Danielle, Barry Stanton, Sian Phillips

Murdered men begin popping up with their hearts cut out. A police detective scours the town and racks his brain looking for the killer, not realizing how close he is. What all this has to do with the title is never resolved in this addition to Elvira's "Thriller Video." Also, Pierce Brosnan makes a brief cameo appearance.

1982   60 minutes

CARRIE
★★★★½

DIRECTOR: Brian De Palma
CAST: Sissy Spacek, Piper Laurie, John Travolta, Nancy Allen

Carrie is the ultimate revenge tale for the person who remembers high school as a time of rejection and ridicule. The story follows the strange life of Carrie White (Sissy Spacek), a student severely humiliated by her classmates and stifled by the Puritan beliefs of her mother (Piper Laurie), a religious fanatic who considers adolescence the first step for a woman into a life of sin and degradation. Many of us have wanted to see those cruel, self-important high-school big shots get their just deserts, and *Carrie* does it as completely and frighteningly as only Brian De Palma could envision it. Rated R for nudity, violence, and profanity.

1976   97 minutes

CARS THAT EAT PEOPLE (THE CARS THAT ATE PARIS)
★½

DIRECTOR: Peter Weir
CAST: John Meillen, Terry Camilleri, Kevin Miles

Peter Weir, director of *Witness* and *The Year of Living Dangerously*, had to start somewhere. He began with this fantastic and weird black comedy about an Outback Australian town where motorists and their cars are trapped each night. Rated PG.

1975   90 minutes

CAT AND THE CANARY, THE
★★★½

DIRECTOR: Radley Metzger
CAST: Honor Blackman, Michael Callan, Edward Fox, Wendy Hiller, Carol Lynley, Olivia Hussey

This is a surprisingly entertaining remake of the 1927 period thriller about a group of people trapped in a British mansion and murdered one by one. Rated PG.

1978   90 minutes

CAT PEOPLE (ORIGINAL)
★★★★

DIRECTOR: Jacques Tourneur
CAST: Simone Simon, Kent Smith, Tom Conway

Simone Simon, Kent Smith, and Tom Conway are excellent in this movie about a shy woman (Simon) who believes she carries the curse of the panther. Producer Lewton and director Jacques Tourneur knew the imagination was stronger and more impressive than anything filmmakers could show visually and played on it with impressive results.

1942   B & W   73 minutes

CAT PEOPLE (REMAKE)
★

DIRECTOR: Paul Schrader
CAST: Nastassja Kinski, Malcolm McDowell, John Heard, Scott Paulin

While technically a well-made film, *Cat People* spares the viewer nothing—incest, bondage, fellatio, cunnilingus, bestiality—for no worthy purpose. It makes one yearn for the films of yesteryear, which achieved horror through implication and the viewer's own imagination. Rated R for nudity, profanity, sex, and gore.

1982   118 minutes

CAT'S EYE
★★★½

DIRECTOR: Lewis Teague
CAST: James Woods, Robert Hays, Kenneth McMillan, Drew Barrymore, Candy Clark, Alan King

Writer Stephen King and director Lewis Teague, who brought us *Cujo*, reteam for this even better horror release: a trilogy of terror in the much-missed "Night Gallery" anthology style. In the first story, James Woods plays a poor fellow who wants to quit smoking and goes to a clinic that guarantees results (which he finds, to his horror, will be gotten through the torturing of his wife and child if necessary). It's funny and spooky—the best of the three. In number two, Robert Hays is a tennis bum who takes up with the wrong man's wife and finds himself involved in a deadly wager. The last has Drew Barrymore (*Firestarter*; *E.T.*) as a tyke plagued by a rather nasty troll. It's good, old-fashioned, tell-me-a-scarystory fun. Rated PG-13 for violence and gruesome scenes.

1985   98 minutes

CAULDRON OF BLOOD
★

DIRECTOR: Edward Mann
CAST: Boris Karloff, Viveca Lindfors, Jean-Pierre Aumont

One of several films Boris Karloff made outside the U.S. shortly before his death, this is far from one of his best. Boris plays a blind sculptor who uses the skeletons of women his wife has murdered as the foundations for his projects. Slow going. Unrated.

1968   95 minutes

CHAMBER OF HORRORS
★★½

DIRECTOR: Hy Averback
CAST: Patrick O'Neal, Cesare Danova, Wilfrid Hyde-White, Suzy Parker, Tun Tun, Tony Curtis, Jeanette Nolan

A mad killer stalks 1880s Baltimore. Two wax museum owners attempt to bring him to justice. Originally produced as a television pilot titled *House of Wax*, but it was considered too violent. So extra scenes were shot, and a gimmick was added for theatrical release. Before all of the "shocking" parts, the action freezes while the "fear flasher" and the "horror horn" go off so you can cover your eyes. Don't bother; it's tame stuff. But Patrick O'Neal is deliciously demented as the one-handed killer with a custom-made stump that accommodates an assortment of wild and wicked attachments.

1966   99 minutes

CHANGELING, THE
★★★★

DIRECTOR: Peter Medak
CAST: George C. Scott, Trish Van Devere, Melvyn Douglas, Jean Marsh, Barry Morse

The first film from Canada's production boom to be released in America, this is blessed with everything a good thriller needs: a suspenseful story, excellent performances by a top-name cast, and well-paced solid direction by Peter Medak. The story centers around John Russell (Scott), a composer whose wife and daughter are killed in a tragic auto accident not far from their home in New York City. He decides he must get away from the memories of happier times, which haunt him on every familiar street corner, so he accepts a teaching position in Seattle, where he hopes to build some kind of a life for himself and continue with the only thing he has left: music. But dreams of his family plague his sleep, and strange things begin to happen in the house. Rated R.

1979   109 minutes

CHARLIE BOY

DIRECTOR: Robert Young
CAST: Leigh Lawson, Angela Bruce

Charlie Boy is an African fetish, inherited by a young British couple, that will take care of all your problems—usually by killing them. Unfortunately, the couple curses themselves and races to try to destroy the fetish and break the curse. It sounds interesting enough, but poor acting and bad direction hamper what could have been a worthwhile film.

1982   60 minutes

CHILDREN OF THE FULL MOON

DIRECTOR: Tom Clegg
CAST: Christopher Cazenove, Celia Gregory, Diana Dors

Even the curvaceous horror hostess Elvira and her off brand of humor can't salvage this cross between *Rosemary's Baby* and *The Wolfman*. Fans of truly bad films won't want to waste their time on this one.

1982   60 minutes

CHILDREN, THE

DIRECTOR: Max Calmanowicz
CAST: Martin Shaker, Gil Rogers, Gale Garnett, Joy Glacum

This is really a terrible film about kids marked by a radioactive accident while they were on a school bus. The picture should be avoided. Rated R.

1980   89 minutes

CHILDREN OF THE CORN

DIRECTOR: Fritz Kiersch
CAST: Peter Horton, Linda Hamilton, R. G. Armstrong, John Franklin

Yet another adaptation of one of author Stephen (*Carrie*; *Christine*) King's horror novels comes to the screen. This time, it's a total mess.

Peter Horton and Linda Hamilton play a young couple who come to a Midwestern farming town where a young preacher with mesmerizing powers has instructed all the children to slaughter adults in order to appease a satanic demon. The scary and serious parts in this low-budget horror flick are often laughable, but it's not funny enough to rank with *Yor: The Hunter from the Future* or *Plan 9 from Outer Space* as a classic bad movie. In other words, it's just plain bad. Rated R for violence and profanity.

1984   93 minutes

CHILDREN SHOULDN'T PLAY WITH DEAD THINGS
★

DIRECTOR: Benjamin (Bob) Clark
CAST: Alan Ormsby, Anya Ormsby, Jeffrey Gillen, Valerie Mauches, Jane Daly

If the film were as good as its title, this might have amounted to something; instead, it's notable only as an example of Bob (*Porky's*) Clark's early career. Amazing he survived such beginnings. Typical "evil dead" entry; amateur filmmakers work in a spooky graveyard and make enough noise to, well, wake the dead. Poor, washed-out cinematography and an all-but-unintelligible soundtrack make this more trouble than it's worth. Pretty grave stuff. Rated PG for violence.

1972   85 minutes

CHRISTINE
★★★½

DIRECTOR: John Carpenter
CAST: Keith Gordon, John Stockwell, Alexandra Paul, Harry Dean Stanton, Robert Prosky, Christine Belford, Roberts Blossom

Novelist Stephen King (*Carrie*; *Dead Zone*) and director John Carpenter (*Halloween*; *The Thing*) team up for top-flight, tasteful terror with this movie about a 1958 Plymouth Fury with spooky powers. It's scary without being gory; a triumph of suspense and atmosphere. Rated R for profanity and violence.

1983   111 minutes

CHRISTMAS EVIL
★½

DIRECTOR: Lewis Jackson
CAST: Brandon Maggart, Jeffery De Munn

This film about a toy factory employee who goes slowly insane has some great black comedy moments, but not enough to save the rest of the boring narrative from putting the viewer to sleep. Brandon Maggart plays the toy maker who goes over the edge and becomes a sick Santa Claus just in time to reward the nice and do some terrible things to the naughty. A great idea handled poorly. Gore fans will be disappointed by the modest body count. Not rated, but the equivalent of an R rating for sex and violence.

1983   91 minutes

CIRCUS OF HORRORS
★★★

DIRECTOR: Sidney Hayers
CAST: Anton Diffring, Erika Remberg, Yvonne Romain, Donald Pleasence

Lurid British thriller about a renegade plastic surgeon using a circus as a front. After making female criminals gorgeous, he enslaves them in his Temple of Beauty. When they want out, he colorfully offs them. Well made with good

performances. This is the more violent European version.

1960   87 minutes

CLASS OF 1984
★★½

DIRECTOR: Mark Lester
CAST: Perry King, Merrie Lynn Ross, Roddy McDowall, Timothy Van Patten

Violent punkers run a school, forcing teachers to arm and security to be hired. A new teacher arrives and tries to change things, but he's beaten, and his pregnant wife is raped. He takes revenge by killing all the punkers. Rated R for violence.

1982   ·   93 minutes

COLLECTOR, THE
★★★★½

DIRECTOR: William Wyler
CAST: Terence Stamp, Samantha Eggar, Maurice Dallimore, Mona Washbourne

In this chiller, Terence Stamp plays a disturbed young man who, having no friends, collects things. Unfortunately, one of the things he collects is beautiful Samantha Eggar. He keeps her as his prisoner and waits for her to fall in love with him. Extremely interesting profile of a madman but most disturbing to sane viewers.

1965   119 minutes

COLOR ME BLOOD RED
🐣

DIRECTOR: Herschell Gordon Lewis
CAST: Don Joseph, Candi Conder

An artist discovers the perfect shade of red for his paintings. (Take a guess.) Another low-budget gore film from the people who brought you *Blood Feast*. Everything about this movie is absolutely awful. Neither as funny nor as sick as

Herschell Gordon Lewis's other works. Unrated, the film has violence.

1965   70 minutes

COMA
★★★½

DIRECTOR: Michael Crichton
CAST: Genevieve Bujold, Michael Douglas, Richard Widmark, Rip Torn

A woman doctor (Genevieve Bujold) becomes curious about several deaths at a hospital where patients have all lapsed into comas. Very original melodrama keeps the audience guessing. One of Michael Crichton's better film efforts. Rated PG for brief nudity and violence.

1978   113 minutes

CORPSE VANISHES, THE
★

DIRECTOR: Wallace Fox
CAST: Bela Lugosi, Luana Walters, Tristram Coffin, Minerva Urecal, George Eldredge, Elizabeth Russell

Hokey pseudoscientific thriller about crazed scientist Bela Lugosi and his efforts to keep his elderly wife young through transfusions from young girls. Another cheap quickie rushed through production and made primarily to capitalize on Bela Lugosi's waning popularity at the box office. Look for veteran character actor Tristram Coffin (*King of the Rocketmen*), but don't bother looking for Manton Moreland—he was busy making a zombie movie on Monogram's other soundstage.

1942   B & W   64 minutes

COSMIC MONSTERS, THE
★★

DIRECTOR: Gilbert Gunn
CAST: Forrest Tucker, Gaby André

Low-budget horror from Great Britain. Giant carnivorous insects invade our planet. (Sounds plausible.) No one on Earth can stop them. (I can believe that.) An alien in a flying saucer arrives to save the day. (It could happen.) Forrest Tucker plays a scientist. (Oh, come on! Now you're just getting silly.) The effects are so cheap that the monsters are transparent. But the English accents do give the picture a partial dignity.

1958   B & W   75 minutes

COUNT DRACULA
★★½

DIRECTOR: Jess Franco
CAST: Christopher Lee, Herbert Lom, Klaus Kinski

Christopher Lee dons the cape once again in this mediocre version of the famous tale about the undead fiend terrorizing the countryside. Lee makes a good Count, but the film's few strengths lie in its formidable supporting cast. Rated R.

1970   98 minutes

COUNT YORGA, VAMPIRE
★★★

DIRECTOR: Bob Kelljan
CAST: Robert Quarry, Roger Perry, Donna Anders, Michael Murphy

Contemporary vampire terrorizes Los Angeles. Somewhat dated, but a sharp and powerful thriller. Stars Robert Quarry, an intense, dignified actor who appeared in several horror films in the early 1970s, then abruptly left the genre. Rated R for violence.

1970   91 minutes

CRATER LAKE MONSTER, THE
★

DIRECTOR: William R. Stromberg
CAST: Richard Cardella, Glenn Roberts, Kacey Cobb

Inexpensive, unimpressive film about a prehistoric creature emerging from the usually quiet lake of the title and raising hell. Rated PG.

1977   89 minutes

CRAWLING EYE, THE
★★★

DIRECTOR: Quentin Lawrence
CAST: Forrest Tucker, Janet Munro

Acceptable horror thriller about an unseen menace hiding within the dense fog surrounding a mountaintop. A nice sense of doom builds throughout, and the monster remains unseen (always the best way) until the very end. That public appearance isn't a letdown, either; this is one vile beast. Forrest Tucker is an acceptable hero, but the real star is the picture itself ...it delivers a good case of the jitters.

1958   B & W   85 minutes

CRAWLING HAND, THE
½

DIRECTOR: Herbert L. Strock
CAST: Peter Breck, Rod Lauren, Kent Taylor

Low-budget tale of a dismembered hand at large in a small town, killing off the local residents in a psychotic "reign of terror." Goofy film really is as dumb as it sounds.

1963   B & W   89 minutes

CREATURE FROM BLACK LAKE
★★

DIRECTOR: Joy Houck Jr.
CAST: Jack Elam, Dub Taylor, Dennis Fimple, John David Carson

This is another forgettable, cliché-ridden horror film. The "stars," Jack Elam and Dub Taylor, actually play small supporting roles, while the leads were given to two novices. That's a shame, because Elam and Taylor provide the only relief from a routine and inconsistent script. Dennis Fimple and John David Carson play two college students from Chicago who go to the swamps of Louisiana in search of the missing link. Through the reluctant help of the locals, they come face to face with a man in an ape suit. Rated PG.

1979   97 minutes

CREATURE FROM THE BLACK LAGOON
★★★½

DIRECTOR: Jack Arnold
CAST: Richard Carlson, Julia Adams, Richard Denning, Nestor Paiva, Antonio Moreno, Whit Bissell

In the remote backwaters of the Amazon, members of a scientific expedition run afoul of a vicious prehistoric man-fish inhabiting the area and are forced to fight for their lives. Excellent film (first in a trilogy) features true-to-life performances, a bone-chilling score by Joseph Gershenson, and beautiful, lush photography that unfortunately turns to mud in this murky 3-D video print.

1954   79 minutes

CREEPERS
★★

DIRECTOR: Dario Argento
CAST: Jennifer Connelly, Donald Pleasence, Daria Nicolodi, Dalila Di Lazzaro

Plodding Italian production casts Jennifer Connelly as a young girl with the ability to communicate with, and control, insects (à la

Willard and his rats). This unique power comes into play when she must use her little friends to track down the maniac who's been murdering students at the Swiss girl's school she's attending, as bugs are attracted to rotting corpses. Yes, it's all as dumb as it sounds, with numerous close-ups of maggots to make the viewer cringe. Originally released overseas as *Phenomena*, one would hate to have to sit through that version, as it's at least thirty minutes longer. Rated R for gore and slime.

1985   82 minutes

CREEPING FLESH, THE
★★★

DIRECTOR: Freddie Francis
CAST: Peter Cushing, Christopher Lee, Lorna Heilbron, George Benson

Peter Cushing and Christopher Lee are, as always, topnotch, in this creepy tale about an evil entity accidentally brought back to life by an unsuspecting scientist. While not as good as the stars' Hammer Film collaborations (*Horror of Dracula*; *The Mummy*), this will still prove pleasing to their fans. Rated PG.

1972   91 minutes

CREEPSHOW
★★★★

DIRECTOR: George Romero
CAST: Hal Holbrook, Adrienne Barbeau, Fritz Weaver, Leslie Nielsen, Stephen King

Stephen King, the modern master of printed terror, and George Romero, the director who frightened unsuspecting moviegoers out of their wits with *Night of the Living Dead*, teamed for this funny and scary tribute to the E.C. horror comics of the 1950s. Like *Vault of Horror* and *Tales from the Crypt*,

two titles from that period, it's an anthology of ghoulish bedtime stories. Rated R for profanity and gore.

1982   120 minutes

CRITTERS
★★★

DIRECTOR: Stephen Hereck
CAST: Dee Wallace Stone, M. Emmet Walsh, Scott Gimes, Don Opper, Terrence Mann

This mild horror film with its hilarious spots could become a cult classic. In it, eight ravenous critters escape from a distant planet and head for earth. Two futuristic bounty hunters pursue them, and the fun begins. The creatures kill a sheriff, then invade a farm to terrorize that family. The comedy begins when the creatures talk and the audience enjoys the subtitles. The bounty hunters also provide some light moments as they drive in reverse all the way to the town and then exhibit their outstanding strength to a "prove-it-to-me" Kansas crowd. These humorous touches set this film apart from the other takeoffs of *E.T.* and *Gremlins* and make it well worth watching. Rated PG for gore and profanity.

1986   90 minutes

CRUCIBLE OF HORROR
★★★½

DIRECTOR: Viktors Ritelis
CAST: Michael Gough, Yvonne Mitchell, Sharon Gurney

Intense story of a violent, domineering man (Michael Gough in one of his better roles) who drives his passive wife (Yvonne Mitchell) and nubile daughter (Sharon Gurney) to murder in this English spine-chiller. The suspense and terror build unrelentingly as the two begin to suspect that their victim may not be as dead as they led themselves to believe, and is now quite possibly stalking *them*! Keep the lights on! Rated R.

1971   91 minutes

CRUISE INTO TERROR
★

DIRECTOR: Bruce Kessler

CAST: Dirk Benedict, John Forsythe, Lynda Day George, Christopher George, Stella Stevens, Ray Milland, Frank Converse, Lee Meriwether, Hugh O'Brian

Dreadful suspense flick made for the tube. When a band of TV actors, old-timers, and hacks assemble on one boat for a cruise, you know something dull is going to take place. This one is about an ancient Egyptian sarcophagus that is haunting the small ocean liner and the poor souls on board. Completely predictable. This made-for-TV movie is not rated, but would be a PG for adult subject matter.

1977   100 minutes

CUJO
★★★½

DIRECTOR: Lewis Teague

CAST: Dee Wallace, Danny Pintauro, Daniel Hugh-Kelly, Christopher Stone

Stephen King's story of a mother and son terrorized by a rabid Saint Bernard results in a movie that keeps viewers on the edge of their seats. Rated R for violence, language.

1983   91 minutes

CURSE OF THE DEMON
★★★★½

DIRECTOR: Jacques Tourneur

CAST: Dana Andrews, Peggy Cummins, Niall MacGinnis, Maurice Denham

Horrifying tale of an American occult expert, Dr. Holden (Dana Andrews), traveling to London to expose a supposed devil cult led by sinister Professor Karswell (Niall MacGinnis). Unfortunately for Holden, Karswell's cult proves to be all too real as a demon from hell is dispatched by the professor to put an end to the annoying investigation. Riveting, electric production is a true classic of the genre, with knockout effects and Clifton Parker's dynamite score adding to the fun. Based on the story "Casting the Runes," by M. R. James.

1958   B & W   96 minutes

CURSE OF FRANKENSTEIN, THE
★★★½

DIRECTOR: Terence Fisher

CAST: Peter Cushing, Christopher Lee, Robert Urquhart, Noel Hood

Hammer Films' version of the Frankenstein story about a scientist who creates a living man from the limbs and organs of corpses. Peter Cushing gives a strong performance as the doctor, with Christopher Lee his equal as the sympathetic creature. Some inspired moments are peppered throughout this well-handled horror tale.

1957   83 minutes

CURSE OF KING TUT'S TOMB, THE
★½

DIRECTOR: Philip Leacock

CAST: Eva Marie Saint, Robin Ellis, Raymond Burr, Harry Andrews, Tom Baker

Made-for-TV misfire concerning the mysterious events surrounding the opening of King Tut's tomb. Dumb film made even more ridiculous by Paul Scofield's uninspired narration. Close the lid and bury this one.

1980   100 minutes

CURSE OF THE CAT PEOPLE, THE
★★★

DIRECTOR: Gunther Von Fristch, Robert Wise

CAST: Simone Simon, Kent Smith, Jane Randolph, Elizabeth Russell

When Val Lewton was ordered by the studio to make a sequel to the successful *Cat People*, he came up with this gentle fantasy about a child who is haunted by spirits. Not to be confused with the 1980s version of *Cat People*.

1944   B & W   70 minutes

CURTAINS
★

DIRECTOR: Jonathan Stryker

CAST: John Vernon, Samantha Eggar, Linda Thorson, Anne Ditchburn

Samantha Eggar stars in this mediocre splatter flick as a movie actress who, with the help of her director (John Vernon, from *Animal House*), gets herself committed to a mental institution as preparation for an upcoming film. However, she is left in the funny farm while the director and the movie go on without her. She escapes, and, one by one, the actresses trying out for her role are murdered. Watching your clothes toss around in a machine at a coin laundry offers more excitement. Rated R for nudity, profanity, violence, and sex.

1983   89 minutes

CYCLOPS, THE
★★½

DIRECTOR: Bert I. Gordon

CAST: James Craig, Lon Chaney Jr., Gloria Talbott

Low-budget whiz Bert I. Gordon does it again with this cheaply made but effective film about a woman (Gloria Talbott) whose brother is transformed into a big, crazy monster by—what else?— radiation. Neat little movie.

1957   B & W   75 minutes

DAMIEN: OMEN II
★★★½

DIRECTOR: Don Taylor

CAST: William Holden, Lee Grant, Lew Ayres, Sylvia Sidney

In this first sequel to *The Omen*, William Holden plays the world's richest man, Richard Thorn. In the previous picture, Richard's brother Robert (Gregory Peck) is shot by police while attempting to kill his son, who he believed to be the Antichrist, son of Satan. *Damien: Omen II* picks up seven years later and shows Richard and his wife, Ann (Lee Grant), raising Damien (Jonathon Scott-Taylor) as their own son. He and their real son, Mark (Lucas Donat), get along well, and the family is the picture of happiness... until Damien reaches puberty. Rated R.

1978   107 minutes

DANGEROUSLY CLOSE
★★

DIRECTOR: Albert Pyun

CAST: John Stockwell, Carey Lowell, Bradford Bancroft, Madison Mason, J. Eddie Peck

In this disappointing modern-day vigilante film, a group of students, led by a Vietnam veteran teacher, tries to purge their school of "undesirable elements" by any means necessary—including murder. Film starts out promising enough but soon loses focus with its rambling script and stereotypical situations. Director Albert Pyun does well in building suspense and evolving characters, but spoils everything by opting for an unimaginative, trite ending. Rated R for profanity, violence, and brief nudity.

1986 95 minutes

DARK FORCES
★★★

DIRECTOR: Simon Wincer

CAST: Robert Powell, Broderick Crawford, David Hemmings, Carmen Duncan, Alyson Best

Robert Powell plays a modern-day conjurer who gains the confidence of a family by curing their terminally ill son; or does he? The evidence stacks up against Powell as we find he may be a foreign spy and stage magician *extraordinaire*. Twists and turns run rampant in this supernatural thriller. Powell is as intense and flamboyant as he was in any of his previous roles, while Broderick Crawford is two-dimensional and dull. While uneven in pacing at times, this film is decent entertainment. Rated PG for brief nudity and some violence.

1984 96 minutes

DARK PLACES
★★★½

DIRECTOR: Don Sharp

CAST: Christopher Lee, Joan Collins, Herbert Lom, Robert Hardy, Jane Birkin, Jean Marsh

Better-than-average British haunted house film complete with Mr. Dracula himself—Christopher Lee! The Count and Joan Collins play two fortune hunters trying to scare away the caretaker of a dead man's mansion (Robert Hardy) so they can get to the bundle of cash stashed in the old house. The film has a sophisticated psychological twist to it that is miss-

ing in most horror films of late, but the cardboard bats on clearly visible wires have got to go! Rated PG for gore, sex, and profanity.

1973 91 minutes

DARK SECRET OF HARVEST HOME, THE
★★½

DIRECTOR: Leo Penn

CAST: Bette Davis, Rosanna Arquette, David Ackroyd, Michael O'Keefe

Novelist-actor Tom Tryon's bewitching story of creeping horror gets fair treatment in this dark and foreboding film of Janus personalities and incantations in picturesque New England.

1978 118 minutes

DARK, THE
★½

DIRECTOR: John "Bud" Cardos

CAST: William Devane, Cathy Lee Crosby, Richard Jaeckel, Keenan Wynn, Vivian Blaine

If your parents told you there was nothing frightening about the dark, you should have listened to them. This unthrilling thriller pits writer William Devane and TV reporter Cathy Lee Crosby against a deadly alien. Little tension and few surprises. Rated R.

1979 92 minutes

DARK MIRROR, THE
★★★½

DIRECTOR: Robert Siodmak

CAST: Olivia De Havilland, Lew Ayres, Thomas Mitchell, Richard Long

Olivia De Havilland, who did this sort of thing extremely well, plays twin sisters—one good, one evil—enmeshed in murder. Lew Ayres is the shrink who must divine who is who as the evil sibling deftly connives to muddy the waters. Good suspense.

1946   B & W   85 minutes

DAUGHTER OF DR. JEKYLL
★★

DIRECTOR: Edgar G. Ulmer
CAST: Gloria Talbott, John Agar, Arthur Shields, John Dierkes

Okay horror film about a girl (Gloria Talbott) who thinks she's inherited the famous dual personality after several local citizens turn up dead.

1957   B & W   71 minutes

DAWN OF THE DEAD
★★★★

DIRECTOR: George A. Romero
CAST: David Emge, Ken Foree, Scott Reiniger, Gaylen Ross, Tom Savini

This movie can only be described as hard-core blood and gore. The central characters are three men and one woman who try to escape from man-eating corpses. This film is the sequel to *Night of the Living Dead*. As a horror movie, it's a masterpiece, but if you have a weak stomach, avoid this one. Rated R.

1979   126 minutes

DAY OF THE ANIMALS
🐾

DIRECTOR: William Girdler
CAST: Christopher George, Lynda Day George, Richard Jaeckel, Leslie Nielsen, Michael Ansara, Ruth Roman

Nature goes nuts after being exposed to the sun's radiation when the Earth's ozone layer is destroyed. Another solidly laughable piece of nonsense from the star of *Pieces* and *Grizzly*, Christopher George. Teaming up with his wife, Lynda Day, these two became the Tracy and Hepburn of junk films, and here's an example of their prime. Chock full of the kind of gory violence that action fans crave, *Animals* masquerades as an ecological horror story but is really nothing more than a sick, dull bloodbath. With Leslie Nielsen, who is getting harder to take seriously anyway, and a lot of very talented German shepherds, which do us all a favor by helping their furry friends finish off the cast. Rated R for violence, profanity, and gore.

1977   98 minutes

DEAD AND BURIED
★★

DIRECTOR: Gary A. Sherman
CAST: James Farentino, Melody Anderson, Jack Albertson, Dennis Redfield

Although this cinematic venture by the creators of *Alien* (Ronald Shusett and Dan O'Bannon) is a notch above many science-fiction/horror films, it falls short on intelligence and excitement. The story involves a series of gory murders, and the weird part is that the victims seem to be coming back to life. The puzzle is resolved during the suspenseful, eerie ending—definitely the high point of the movie. James Farentino stars as the sheriff investigating the murders. Jack Albertson, in his last film, is a sinister mortician. Rated R for sex and violence.

1981   92 minutes

DEAD MEN WALK
★★

DIRECTOR: Sam Newfield
CAST: George Zucco, Mary Carlisle, Nedrick Young, Dwight Frye

Master character actor George Zucco makes the most of one of his few leading roles, a dual one at that, in this grade-Z cheapie from Hollywood's infamous Poverty Row. Zucco is two brothers, one good, one evil, in this spooky tale about vampires and zombies. Dwight Frye adds to the fun in a supporting role that recalls those he played in *Dracula* and *Frankenstein*. For buffs only.

1943 B & W 67 minutes

DEAD OF NIGHT
★

DIRECTOR: Dan Curtis
CAST: Ed Begley Jr., John Hackett, Patrick MacNee

This trilogy of shockers written by Richard Matheson (*Incredible Shrinking Man*) and directed by Dan Curtis (*Dark Shadows*) has some suspense and interesting twists, but is far inferior to these gentlemen's other achievements. Elvira is host on this, another in her "Thriller Video" series, and offers some light comedy and nice scenery to round out the film.

1977 76 minutes

DEAD ZONE, THE
★★★★

DIRECTOR: David Cronenberg
CAST: Christopher Walken, Brooke Adams, Tom Skerritt, Herbert Lom, Martin Sheen

This is an exciting adaptation of the Stephen King suspense novel about a man who uses his psychic powers to solve multiple murders and perhaps prevent the end of the world. Rated R for violence and profanity.

1983 103 minutes

DEADLY BLESSING
★

DIRECTOR: Wes Craven

CAST: Maren Jensen, Susan Buckner, Sharon Strong, Lois Nettleton, Ernest Borgnine, Jeff East

If beautiful women were enough to make a horror film succeed, this one would rate a 10. Unfortunately, that's all this film—about a young woman (Maren Jensen) who marries a member of a strange religious sect and finds herself plagued by strange forces after he is murdered—has going for it. The tactics are, for the most part, obvious, and the story is predictable. Wes Craven (*The Last House on the Left*; *The Hills Have Eyes*) directed. Rated R because of nudity and bloody scenes.

1981 102 minutes

DEADLY EYES
★

DIRECTOR: Robert Clouse
CAST: Sam Groom, Sara Botsford, Scatman Crothers

Grain full of steroids creates rats the size of small dogs in this seemingly familiar horror tale adapted from British author James Herbert's novel *The Rats*. "Character development" is ridiculously slow, making us wait for another rat attack, but those are so silly that the whole film rapidly descends into the sewer. Cast turns in reasonable performances, but the script and direction are both by the numbers. Only for diehard Scatman Crothers fans. This is a B movie, all right—but the B stands for Boring. Rated R for gore, nudity, and simulated sex.

1982 87 minutes

DEADLY SANCTUARY
🦃

DIRECTOR: Jess Franco

CAST: Sylva Koscina, Mercedes McCambridge, Jack Palance, Klaus Kinski, Akim Tamiroff

Based on the writings of the Marquis de Sade, this poor excuse for a horror film follows the tragic lives of two newly orphaned sisters as they fall prey to prison, prostitution, murder, and a torturous hellfire club led by Jack Palance. All this is framed by sequences of de Sade (Klaus Kinski) wiping the perspiration from his brow, sitting at his writing table . . . and on and on. This film was supposedly banned in Europe because of its violent content, though any graphic violence is limited. Nudity is brief, and scenes of torture are only intimated.

1970   93 minutes

DEAR DEAD DELILAH
★

DIRECTOR: John Farris
CAST: Agnes Moorehead, Will Geer, Michael Ansara, Dennis Patrick

Delilah (Agnes Moorehead) is about to die, but there's a fortune buried somewhere on her property that her loony relatives will do anything to get a hold of. Idiotic from the outset, with many well-known stars wasted. Rated R for blood.

1972   90 minutes

DEATH AT LOVE HOUSE
★★

DIRECTOR: E. W. Swackhamer
CAST: Robert Wagner, Kate Jackson, Sylvia Sidney, Joan Blondell, Dorothy Lamour, John Carradine, Bill Macy, Marianna Hill

Much tamer than the lurid title would suggest. Robert Wagner plays a writer who becomes obsessed with a movie queen who died years earlier. He struggles to hang on to his personality and sanity as he investigates the link between her and his own past. This mildly suspenseful hokum is made more palatable by the engaging cast, particularly the veteran performers, who turn in juicy character bits. Unrated.

1976   78 minutes

DEATH VALLEY
★★

DIRECTOR: Dick Richards
CAST: Paul Le Mat, Catharine Hicks, Stephen McHattie, A. Wilford Brimley

Paul Le Mat (*American Graffiti*) and Catharine Hicks star in this okay horror film about a vacation that turns into a nightmare. Rated R for violence and gore.

1982   87 minutes

DEEP END
★★½

DIRECTOR: Jerzy Skolimowski
CAST: John Moulder-Brown, Jane Asher, Diana Dors

A young man working in a London bath house becomes obsessed with a beautiful female co-worker, which eventually leads to disaster. Offbeat drama with realistic performances by the cast. Rated R.

1970   88 minutes

DEEP RED
★★★

DIRECTOR: Dario Argento
CAST: David Hemmings, Daria Nicolodi, Gabrielle Lavia

Another stylish and brutal horror-mystery from Italian director Dario Argento. His other works include *The Bird with the Crystal Plummage* and *Suspiria*. Like those, this film is slim on plot and a bit too talky, but Argento builds tension beautifully with rich atmosphere and driving electronic music. Rated R for violence.

1975 98 minutes

DEMENTIA 13
★★½

DIRECTOR: Francis Coppola
CAST: William Campbell, Luana Anders, Mary Mitchel, Patrick Magee

Early Francis Ford Coppola film is a low-budget shocker centering on a family plagued by violent ax murders that are somehow connected with the death of the youngest daughter many years before. Acting is standard, but the dreary photography, creepy locations, and weird music are what make this movie click. Produced by Roger Corman.

1963 B & W 75 minutes

DEMON LOVER, THE
🙊

DIRECTOR: Donald B. Jackson
CAST: Christmas Robbins, Val Mayeric, Gunnar Hansen, Tom Hutton, Sonny Bell

A bunch of college kids and bikers get involved with a Satanist who raises a demon that tears almost everyone apart. Not only is the acting rotten, but half the incantations are stolen from Robert Howard's Conan stories. A point of interest is that the star, Val Mayeric, is the man who designed the comic-book character Howard the Duck. Only true horror and gore fans will find entertainment here. Rated R for nudity, profanity, and violence.

1976 87 minutes

DEMONS OF LUDLOW, THE
🙊

DIRECTOR: Bill Rebane
CAST: Paul Von Hausen, Shephanie Cushna, James Robinson, Carol Perry, C. Dave Davis, Debra Dulman

Regrettable little horror flick about an eastern seaboard community haunted by an old piano that is possessed. Terrible special effects and an ending that leaves a few questions unanswered. But by that time, will you really care? Not rated, but the equivalent of an R for sex, nudity, profanity, violence, and gore.

1983 83 minutes

DEVIL BAT, THE
★★

DIRECTOR: Jean Yarbrough
CAST: Bela Lugosi, Suzanne Kaaren, Dave O'Brien, Guy Usher, Yollande Mallot, Donald Kerr

Pretty fair thriller from PRC, chief competition to Monogram Studios for the title of Poverty Row King, gives us Bela Lugosi as yet another bloodthirsty mad scientist who trains oversize rubber bats to suck blood from selected victims by use of a scent. Lugosi is as hammy as ever, and popular B star Dave O'Brien (*Captain Midnight*) plays an enthusiastic and resilient hero with conviction. One of director Jean Yarbrough's better efforts, but typical of the kind of roles once-important actor Lugosi reprised for the rest of his career.

1941 B & W 69 minutes

DEVIL DOG: THE HOUND OF HELL
🙊

DIRECTOR: Curtis Harington
CAST: Richard Crenna, Yvette Mimieux, Victor Jory, Ken Kercheval

This made-for-television movie is even more ridiculous than the title implies. Richard Crenna tries to save the wife and kids from the family pooch, which is actually a demon in disguise. It gets worse as Crenna uses Indian magic to battle lousy acting and poor special effects.

1976　　　　　　　　95 minutes

DEVIL DOLL, THE
★★★½

DIRECTOR: Tod Browning
CAST: Lionel Barrymore, Maureen O'Sullivan, Frank Lawton, Henry B. Walthall

This imaginative fantasy thriller pits crazed Lionel Barrymore and his tiny "devil dolls" against those who have done him wrong. Although not as original an idea now as it was then, the acting, special effects, and director Tod Browning's odd sense of humor make this worth seeing.

1936　　　　B & W　79 minutes

DEVIL GIRL FROM MARS
½

DIRECTOR: David McDonald
CAST: Patricia Laffan, Hazel Court, Hugh McDermott, Peter Reynolds

This oddball British "horror" film must be the overseas answer to *Cat Women of the Moon*, except that it doesn't have the saving grace of Sonny Tufts' presence. This novel story of a lanky messenger (the Devil Girl) sent from her native planet to kidnap Earthmen for reproductive purposes is lacking in thrills, special effects, tension, and just about everything else a good horror film should have—but like its sister entry *Fire Maidens from Outer Space*, it has a certain audacity that earns its half star. If you want to be glued to your seat, pass this one by; if you just want a few laughs or a nondemanding film this might be for you.

1955　　　　B & W　76 minutes

DEVIL'S RAIN, THE
★★½

DIRECTOR: Robert Fuest
CAST: Ernest Borgnine, Ida Lupino, William Shatner, Eddie Albert, Tom Skerritt, Keenan Wynn

Great cast in a fair shocker about a band of devil worshipers at large in a small town. Terrific make-up, especially Ernest Borgnine's! Rated PG for language, violence.

1975　　　　　　　　85 minutes

DEVIL'S UNDEAD, THE
★★★½

DIRECTOR: Peter Sasdy
CAST: Christopher Lee, Peter Cushing, Georgia Brown, Diana Dors

A surprisingly entertaining and suspenseful release starring the two kings of British horror, Christopher Lee and Peter Cushing, as a sort of modern-day Holmes and Watson in a tale of demonic possession. Rated PG.

1979　　　　　　　　91 minutes

DEVONSVILLE TERROR, THE
★★★

DIRECTOR: Ulli Lommel
CAST: Paul Wilson, Suzanna Love, Donald Pleasence

Three witches are killed in Devonsville in 1683, and one of them places a curse on the townspeople. Flash forward to the present, when three women arrive in Devonsville. Are they, or are they not, the reincarnations of the witches? Although this may sound like pure exploitation, this film is actually a complex psychological text about the difficulties of being a woman. Good performances, high production values, and a competently scary script that is not based on special effects. Rated R for nudity, violence, mild gore.

1983   97 minutes

DIABOLIQUE
★★★★

DIRECTOR: Henri-Georges Clouzot
CAST: Simone Signoret, Vera Clouzot, Charles Vanel, Paul Meurisse

This classic thriller builds slowly but rapidly gathers momentum along the way. Both wife and mistress of a headmaster conspire to kill him. This twisted plot of murder has since been copied many times. In French, with English subtitles.

1955   B & W 107 minutes

DIAL M FOR MURDER
★★★★

DIRECTOR: Alfred Hitchcock
CAST: Grace Kelly, Robert Cummings, Ray Milland, John Williams

Alfred Hitchcock imbues this classic thriller with his well-known touches of sustained suspense and clever camera vantages. Ray Milland is a rather sympathetic villain whose desire to inherit his wife's fortune leads him to one conclusion: murder. His plan for pulling off the "perfect crime" is foiled temporarily. Undaunted, he quickly switches to Plan B, with even more entertaining results.

1954   105 minutes

DIE! DIE! MY DARLING!
★★½

DIRECTOR: Silvio Narizzano

CAST: Tallulah Bankhead, Stephanie Powers, Peter Vaughn, Donald Sutherland

This British thriller was Tallulah Bankhead's last movie. She plays a crazed woman who kidnaps her late son's fiancée for punishment and salvation. Grisly fun for Bankhead fans, but may be too heavy-handed for others. Unrated, the film has violence.

1965   97 minutes

DIE SCREAMING, MARIANNE
★

DIRECTOR: Pete Walker
CAST: Susan George, Barry Evans, Chris Sandford

Graphic horror film concerns a young girl (Susan George), pursued by numerous crazies who try their best to prevent her from reaching her twenty-first birthday. Why does trash like this have to made? Full of clichés and bad acting. Rated R.

1972   99 minutes

DINOSAURUS!
★★½

DIRECTOR: Irvin S. Yeaworth Jr.
CAST: Ward Ramsey, Paul Lukather, Kristina Hanson, Alan Roberts

Workers at a remote construction site accidentally stumble upon a prehistoric brontosaurus, tyrannosaurus rex, and a caveman (all quite alive) while excavating the area. Sure, the monsters look fake, and most of the humor is unintentional, but this film is entertaining nonetheless.

1960   85 minutes

DIVA
★★★★

DIRECTOR: Jean-Jacques Beineix

CAST: Frederic Andrei, Wilhemenia Wiggins Fernandez, Roland Berlin

In this stunningly stylish suspense film by first-time director Jean-Jacques Beineix, a young opera lover unknowingly becomes involved with the underworld. Unbeknownst to him, he's in possession of some very valuable tapes—and the delightful chase is on. In French, with English subtitles. Rated R for profanity, nudity, and violence.

1982   123 minutes

DOCTOR AND THE DEVILS, THE
★★★

DIRECTOR: Freddie Francis
CAST: Timothy Dalton, Jonathan Pryce, Twiggy, Julian Sands, Stephen Rea, Phyllis Logan, Beryl Reid, Sian Phillips

This film, based on a true story, with an original screenplay by Dylan Thomas, is set in England in the 1800s. Dr. Cook (Timothy Dalton) is a professor of anatomy, and his philosophy is, "Anatomy is vital to the progress of medicine, medicine is vital to the progress of mankind, and any end justifies the means to see that I fulfill this." His problem is not having enough corpses to use in class demonstrations. The law provides for only the use of bodies of hanged criminals. Since he has used up this resource, he pays grave robbers for his supply. Enter two of the most ruthless and unsavory murderers in recent film history, Fallon (Jonathan Pryce) and Broom (Stephen Rea). Dr. Murray (Julian Sands), Cook's assistant, who develops a love interest with a local prostitute (Twiggy), discovers and disapproves of Cook's methods. After several encounters, with scenes not for the squeamish, our

villains meet an ironic conclusion. Rated R for language, simulated sex, and violence.

1985   93 minutes

DR. JEKYLL AND MR. HYDE
★★★

DIRECTOR: Victor Fleming
CAST: Spencer Tracy, Ingrid Bergman, Lana Turner, Donald Crisp, C. Aubrey Smith, Sara Allgood

A well-done version of Robert Louis Stevenson's classic story about a good doctor who dares to venture into the unknown. The horror of his transformation is played down in favor of the emotional and psychological consequences. Spencer Tracy and Ingrid Bergman are excellent, the production lush.

1941   B & W 114 minutes

DR. PHIBES RISES AGAIN
★★★½

DIRECTOR: Robert Fuest
CAST: Vincent Price, Robert Quarry, Peter Jeffrey, Valli Kemp, Fiona Lewis, Peter Cushing, Hugh Griffith, Terry-Thomas, Beryl Reid

Good-natured terror abounds in this fun sequel to *The Abominable Dr. Phibes*, with Vincent Price reprising his role as a disfigured doctor desperately searching for a way to restore his dead wife, Victoria, to life. This time there appears to be a slight ray of hope in Egypt, but there's also competition from Robert Quarry's expedition to contend with. So begins Phibes's gradual elimination of his adversaries, with the help of his dedicated assistant, Vulnavia (Valli Kemp), in the ingenious fashion that makes these films so entertaining. Rated PG for mild violence.

1972　　　　　　　　89 minutes

DR. TERROR'S HOUSE OF HORRORS
★★★

DIRECTOR: Freddie Francis
CAST: Peter Cushing, Christopher Lee, Ray Castle, Donald Sutherland, Neil McCallum

Good anthology horror entertainment about a fortune-teller (Peter Cushing) who has some frightening revelations for his clients. A top-flight example of British genre movie-making.

1965　　　　　　　　98 minutes

DOMINIQUE IS DEAD
★★

DIRECTOR: Michael Anderson
CAST: Cliff Robertson, Jean Simmons, Jenny Agutter, Flora Robson, Judy Geeson

Weird film from England about a greedy man attempting to rid himself of his wife in order to get his hands on her money. Of course, things don't quite work out as planned. Mildly interesting movie has too many dull spots to make it worthwhile. Also known as *Dominique*. Rated PG.

1978　　　　　　　　98 minutes

DON'T ANSWER THE PHONE
★★

DIRECTOR: Robert Hammer
CAST: James Westmoreland, Flo Gerrish, Ben Frank, Nicholas Worth

Also known as *The Hollywood Strangler*, this unpleasantly brutal exploitation quickie might have been better in more competent hands. Nicholas Worth is a truly horrific killer in the *Hillside Strangler* mode, and the screenplay is far above average. All the other actors, though, are so wooden they warp. James Westmoreland seems determined to be a poor imitation of James Brolin, as one of the investigative cops, and Flo Gerrish is simply awful as a radio psychologist. The other few high points are marred by lurid and lengthy scenes of the killer as he strangles half-naked women; the first fifteen minutes are the work of a depraved mind. Music by Byron Allred, which is appropriate. Rated R for violence and nudity.

1981　　　　　　　　94 minutes

DON'T BE AFRAID OF THE DARK
★★★

DIRECTOR: John Newland
CAST: Kim Darby, Jim Hutton, Pedro Armendariz Jr., Barbara Anderson, William Demarest

Scary TV movie as newlyweds Kim Darby and Jim Hutton move into a weird old house inhabited by eerie little monsters who want Kim for one of their own. The human actors are okay, but the creatures steal the show.

1973　　　　　　　　74 minutes

DON'T LOOK NOW
★★★★

DIRECTOR: Nicolas Roeg
CAST: Julie Christie, Donald Sutherland

Excellent psychic thriller about a married couple who, just after the accidental drowning of their young daughter, start having strange occurrences in their lives. Beautifully photographed by director Nicolas Roeg. Strong performances by Julie Christie and Donald Sutherland make this film a must-see. Rated R.

1973　　　　　　　　110 minutes

DORIAN GRAY

DIRECTOR: Massimo Dallamano
CAST: Helmut Berger, Richard Todd, Herbert Lom

Horrid updating of the Oscar Wilde classic novel. Helmut Berger plays the title role this time as the man who remains eternally young while a painting of him grows increasingly decrepit. Fascinating story has never been more boring, with some actors wasted. Alternate title: *The Secret of Dorian Gray.* Rated R.

1970   93 minutes

DORM THAT DRIPPED BLOOD, THE

DIRECTOR: Jeffrey Osbrow, Stephen Carpenter
CAST: Pamela Holland, Stephen Sachs, Laurie Lapinski

The only good thing about this film is the title, and the producers got the idea for it from a memorable genre film starring Christopher Lee and Peter Cushing from the 1970s, *The House That Dripped Blood.* It turns out this mess was originally titled *Pranks.* Whatever they want to call it, this awful, low-budget flick is just another excuse to serve up gratuitous violence with college students—once again—being hacked up at every turn. Don't see it! Rated R for violence.

1981   84 minutes

DOUBLE EXPOSURE
★★★½

DIRECTOR: William Byron Hillman
CAST: Michael Callan, Joanna Pettet, James Stacy, Pamela Hensley, Cleavon Little, Seymour Cassel, Robert Tessier

This psychological thriller about a photographer (Michael Callan) who has nightmares of murders that come true has some pretty ghoulish scenes, but the tension created here comes more from the element of surprise rather than the fashion of violence displayed. The cast of lesser-known actors puts in solid performances. Not rated, the film contains violence, profanity, nudity, and adult subject matter.

1982   95 minutes

DRACULA (ORIGINAL)
★★★★

DIRECTOR: Tod Browning
CAST: Bela Lugosi, Dwight Frye, David Manners, Helen Chandler, Edward Van Sloan

Bela Lugosi found himself forever typecast after brilliantly bringing to life the bloodthirsty Transylvanian vampire of the title in this 1930 genre classic, directed by Tod Browning. His performance and that of Dwight Frye as the spider-eating Renfield still impress even though this early talkie seems somewhat dated today.

1931   B & W   75 minutes

DRACULA (REMAKE)
★★½

DIRECTOR: John Badham
CAST: Laurence Olivier, Frank Langella, Donald Pleasence, Tony Haygarth, Jan Francis

This *Dracula* is a film of missed opportunities. Not that it doesn't have something to offer—it does—but not enough to make it a fully satisfying experience. Frank Langella makes an excellent Count Dracula. He projects just the right combination of menace, animal appeal, and mystery. His reading of the classic lines, "I never drink . . . wine" and "The children of the night, what music they make," is refreshingly untheatrical and effective. It's a pity he has so little screen time. The story, for the uninitiated, revolves around the activities of a bloodthirsty vampire who leaves his castle in Transylvania for fresh hunting in London. There, he comes up against Professor Van Helsing (Laurence Olivier), whose daughter, Mina (Jan Francis), becomes the first to join his legion of the undead. Rated R.

1979   109 minutes

DRACULA VS. FRANKENSTEIN
½

DIRECTOR: Al Adamson
CAST: J. Carrol Naish, Lon Chaney Jr., Zandor Vorkov

This dud rates higher than a bomb simply for the presences of J. Carrol Naish and Lon Chaney, but even they can't save this piece of junk about Dracula's eternal search for blood, eventually leading to a showdown with a dumb-looking Frankenstein monster. Pretty bad. Rated R.

1971   90 minutes

DREAM LOVER
★½

DIRECTOR: Alan J. Pakula
CAST: Kristy McNichol, Ben Masters, Paul Shenar, Justin Deas, John McMartin, Gayle Hunnicutt, Joseph Culp

This dull and pretentious psychological thriller presents Kristy McNichol as a struggling musician living alone, in New York City no less, for the first time. After barely escaping from a knife-wielding maniac her first night in a new apartment, she suffers bloodcurdling nightmares. When she turns to a sleep researcher (Ben Masters) for help, the treatment backfires and the dream-created horrors begin taking over her life. Despite the promising premise, things seem to take forever to happen, and when they do, the viewer wishes they had not. As a result, *Dream Lover* is more of an endurance test than an entertainment. Rated R for violence.

1986   104 minutes

DRESSED TO KILL
★★★½

DIRECTOR: Brian De Palma
CAST: Michael Caine, Angie Dickinson, Nancy Allen, Keith Gordon

Director Brian De Palma again borrows heavily from Alfred Hitchcock in this story of sexual frustration, madness, and murder set in New York City. Angie Dickinson plays a sexually active housewife whose affairs lead to an unexpected conclusion. At times it is slow-moving, but De Palma's visual style will keep you interested. The elevator scene will send chills up your spine. Rated R for violence, strong language, nudity, and simulated sex.

1980   105 minutes

DUEL
★★★★★

DIRECTOR: Steven Spielberg
CAST: Dennis Weaver, Eddie Firestone, Tim Herbert

Duel, an early Spielberg film, was originally a 73-minute ABC made-for-TV movie, but this full-length version was released theatrically overseas. The story is a simple one: a mild-mannered businessman (Dennis Weaver) alone on a desolate stretch of highway suddenly finds himself the unwitting prey of the maniacal driver of a big, greasy, oil tanker. Blessed with a heart-pounding music score and some truly odd camera angles, this nonstop thriller never lets go. Based on a real-life situation encountered by author Richard Matheson, who wrote the screenplay, this film established Spielberg as a major new talent in Hollywood.

1971　　　　91 minutes

DUNWICH HORROR, THE
★

DIRECTOR: Daniel Haller
CAST: Sandra Dee, Dean Stockwell, Sam Jaffe, Ed Begley Sr., Talia Coppola

Torpid horror thriller made back in the good ol' days when folks didn't know that it's impossible to adapt H. P. Lovecraft. Dean Stockwell foreshadowed his hammy role in *Dune* with this laughable portrayal of a warlock whose talents run more toward hooded expressions than magical incantations. Watch for a quick part by Talia Shire, back when she still shared brother Francis's last name. Epitome of that type of video that, as it's being watched, makes you think, "It can't get worse"...and then the conclusion comes along, and it *does* get worse! Rated PG for violence.

1970　　　　90 minutes

EATEN ALIVE

DIRECTOR: Tobe Hooper
CAST: Mel Ferrer, Stuart Whitman, Carolyn Jones, Marilyn Burns

A monster stalks the swamps of Louisiana in this sickening low-budget horror flick. Rated R.

1976　　　　96 minutes

ENTITY, THE

DIRECTOR: Sidney J. Furie
CAST: Barbara Hershey, Ron Silver, Jacqueline Brooks, David Lablosa

Barbara Hershey (*The Stuntman*) stars in this reprehensible horror flick as a woman who is sexually molested by an invisible, sex-crazed demon. Director Sidney J. Furie (*Lady Sings the Blues*; *The Boys in Company C*) has created what amounts to a two-hour celebration of rape and the degradation of women. Rated R for nudity, profanity, violence, and rape.

1983　　　　115 minutes

EQUINOX (THE BEAST)
★★

DIRECTOR: Jack Woods
CAST: Edward Connell, Barbara Hewitt, Frank Boers Jr., Robin Christopher

Good special effects save this unprofessional movie about college students searching for their archeology professor. On their search, they must face monsters and the occult. Rated PG.

1971　　　　82 minutes

ERASERHEAD
★★★½

DIRECTOR: David Lynch
CAST: John Nance, Charlotte Stewart, Allen Joseph, Jeanne Bates

Weird, weird movie...director David Lynch (*Elephant Man*) created this nightmarish film about Henry Spencer (John Nance), who, we assume, lives in the far (possibly post-apocalyptic) future when everyone is given a free lobotomy at birth. Nothing else could explain the bizarre behavior of its characters. Be forewarned: This unrated film has no objectionable elements in the traditional sense, yet still leaves you nauseous.

1978　　　B & W　90 minutes

EVIL DEAD, THE
★

DIRECTOR: Sam Raimi

CAST: Bruce Campbell, Ellen Sandweiss, Betsy Baker, Hal Delrich, Sarah York

An amateurish horror movie about a handful of college kids trapped in a haunted house, this is all special effects, no plot, no acting, no point. Unrated, the film has violence and gore.

1983   85 minutes

EVILSPEAK

DIRECTOR: Eric Weston

CAST: Clint Howard, R. G. Armstrong, Joseph Cortese, Claude Earl Jones

The alleged script centers on a devil-worshiping medieval Spanish priest brought into modern times by a student (Clint Howard) on a computer. Everything goes downhill—three minutes into the story—when the reborn father lops off the head of a topless female. Ick! Rated R for nudity, violence, and a lot of cheap, pointless, and disgusting gore.

1982   89 minutes

EXORCIST, THE
★★★★½

DIRECTOR: William Friedkin

CAST: Ellen Burstyn, Max von Sydow, Linda Blair, Jason Miller, Lee J. Cobb

A sensation at the time of its release, this horror film—directed by William Friedkin (*The French Connection*)—has lost some of its punch because of the numerous imitations it spawned. An awful sequel, *Exorcist II: The Heretic*, didn't help much either. Rated R.

1973   121 minutes

EXORCIST II: THE HERETIC

DIRECTOR: John Boorman

CAST: Richard Burton, Linda Blair, Louise Fletcher, Kitty Winn, James Earl Jones, Max von Sydow

The script is bad, the acting poor, and the direction lacking in pace or conviction. The story concerns a priest, Father Lamount (Richard Burton), assigned by the Vatican to investigate the work of Father Merrin (Max von Sydow), who died freeing Regan MacNeil from possession by the devil. Rated R for violence and profanity.

1977   110 minutes

EXPERIMENT IN TERROR
★★★½

DIRECTOR: Blake Edwards

CAST: Glenn Ford, Lee Remick, Stefanie Powers, Ross Martin, Ned Glass

A sadistic killer (Ross Martin) kidnaps the teenage sister (Stephanie Powers) of a bank teller (Lee Remick). An FBI agent is hot on the trail, fighting the clock. The film crackles with suspense. The acting is uniformly excellent. Martin paints an unnerving portrait of evil.

1962   B & W 123 minutes

EXPOSED
★

DIRECTOR: James Toback

CAST: Nastassja Kinski, Rudolph Nureyev, Harvey Keitel, Ian McShane

Nastassja Kinski stars, in this mediocre and confusing film directed by James Toback (*Fingers*; *Love and Money*), as a high-priced fashion model whose constant exposure in magazines and on television have made her the target for the sometimes dangerous desires of two men. Former ballet star Rudolph Nureyev (*Valentino*) is also featured. Rated R.

1983　　　　　　　100 minutes

EYES OF A STRANGER
★★

DIRECTOR: Ken Weiderhorn
CAST: Lauren Tewes, Jennifer Jason Leigh, John DiSanti, Peter Dupre, Gwen Lewis

"The Love Boat's" Julie, Lauren Tewes, makes an unexpected appearance in this blood-and-guts horror film. She plays a reporter who decides to track down a psychopathic killer. Lots of blood and some sexual molestation. Rated R.

1981　　　　　　　85 minutes

EYES OF LAURA MARS, THE
★★★

DIRECTOR: Irvin Kershner
CAST: Faye Dunaway, Tommy Lee Jones, Brad Dourif, René Auberjonois

Laura Mars (Faye Dunaway) is a kinky commercial photographer who is haunted by psychic visions of murder. Her photographs, which are composed of violent scenes, somehow become the blueprints for a series of actual killings. Bodies are found positioned exactly like the models in Mars's simulations. That is, until the killer begins attacking Mars's associates. It soon becomes apparent the maniac is really after her. Although well-acted and suspenseful, *The Eyes of Laura Mars* is an unrelentingly cold and gruesome movie. It is part of a budding genre of films that seduce, coax, cajole, and even occasionally force the viewer to wallow in the twisted lives of its unsavory characters and, what's worse, participate in torture and murder. Therefore, we cannot in good conscience recommend it. Rated R for the aforementioned content.

1978　　　　　　　103 minutes

EYEWITNESS
★★★★

DIRECTOR: Peter Yates
CAST: William Hurt, Sigourney Weaver, Christopher Plummer, James Woods

Director Peter Yates and screenwriter Steve Tesich (the team that created *Breaking Away*) have done it again. *Eyewitness* has everything: suspense, romance, laughs, thrills, surprises...in short, it's a humdinger of a movie. The story is in the Hitchcock vein of mystery and terror. William Hurt (*Gorky Park* and *Altered States*) plays a janitor who, after discovering a murder victim, meets the glamorous television reporter (Sigourney Weaver, of *Alien*) he has admired from afar. In order to prolong their relationship, he pretends to know the killer's identity—and puts both their lives in danger. Rated R for sex, violence, and profanity.

1981　　　　　　　102 minutes

FADE TO BLACK
★★★½

DIRECTOR: Vernon Zimmerman
CAST: Dennis Christopher, Linda Kerridge, Tim Thomerson, Morgan Paull, Marya Small

Movie buffs and horror fans will especially love *Fade to Black*, a funny, suspenseful, and entertaining low-budget film that features Dennis Christopher (the pseudo-Italian bicyclist of *Breaking Away*) in a tour-de-force performance. Christopher plays Eric Binford, an odd young man who spends most of his time absorbing films. He can quote entire passages of dialogue and reel off cast lists for the most obscure B movies. But his talents aren't of much use to him in the real world. His all-night videotaping sessions and movie orgies only make him late for work and out of step with other people his age, and soon Eric goes over the edge. Rated R.

1980   100 minutes

FAMILY PLOT
★★★★

DIRECTOR: Alfred Hitchcock
CAST: Karen Black, Bruce Dern, Barbara Harris, William Devane, Ed Lauter, Cathleen Nesbitt, Katherine Helmond

Alfred Hitchcock's last film proved to be a winner. He interjects this story with more humor than in his later films, which emphasized suspense and terror. A seedy medium and her ne'er-do-well boyfriend (Barbara Harris and Bruce Dern) encounter a sinister couple (Karen Black and William Devane) while searching for a missing heir. They all become involved in diamond theft and attempted murder. Rated PG.

1976   120 minutes

FAN, THE
★★★½

DIRECTOR: Edward Bianchi
CAST: Lauren Bacall, James Garner, Maureen Stapleton, Michael Biehn

In this fast-moving suspense yarn, a young fan is obsessed with a famous actress (Lauren Bacall). When his love letters to her are ignored, he embarks on a murder spree. Bacall is superb as the sassy, chain-smoking celebrity; James Garner is her amiable ex-husband and confidant; and Maureen Stapleton almost steals the show as Bacall's all-suffering secretary. *The Fan* is an absorbing thriller. The acting is first-rate, the camera work breathtaking, and the script plausible. Rated R.

1981   95 minutes

FATAL GAMES

DIRECTOR: Michael Elliot
CAST: Sally Kirkland, Lynn Banashek, Sean Masterson, Teal Roberts

At first, it's difficult to determine whether or not this one is a comedy or a horror film. Then it becomes evident that this is just another slasher-type flick that is so stupid it's funny. In a school for young athletes, a murderer begins eliminating the students, using a javelin. The film is filled with bad acting and resembles a porno film rather than a slasher flick. Not rated, but contains explicit nudity, profanity, and violence.

1984   88 minutes

FEAR IN THE NIGHT (DYNASTY OF FEAR)
★★★½

DIRECTOR: Jimmy Sangster
CAST: Ralph Bates, Judy Geeson, Peter Cushing, Joan Collins

Effective British shocker about a teacher and his off-balance bride encountering lust, jealousy, and murder at a desolate boys' school. Another suspenseful, literate offering from Hammer Films. Following Joan Collins's television success, the film was rereleased on video under the title *Dynasty of Fear*, with altered credits to give her top billing. Rated PG.

1972   94 minutes

FEAR NO EVIL

DIRECTOR: Frank Laloggia

CAST: Stephan Arngrim, Elizabeth Hoffman, Kathleen Rong McAllen, Frank Birney, Daniel Eden

Advertised as an exercise in horrific thrills and special effects, this is no horror movie. It's just plain horrible. The story of the satanic high-school student hell-bent on destroying a senior class, this film tries to be a male *Carrie*, a punk rock *The Exorcist*, and a contemporary *Night of the Living Dead*, all in one. It just doesn't work. Rated R.

1981 96 minutes

FER-DE-LANCE
★★

DIRECTOR: Russ Mayberry
CAST: David Janssen, Hope Lange, Jason Evers, Ivan Dixon

Made-for-TV suspense film is mildly entertaining as a cargo of poisonous snakes escape aboard a crippled submarine at the bottom of the sea, making life unpleasant for all concerned.

1974 100 minutes

FIEND WITHOUT A FACE
★★★½

DIRECTOR: Arthur Crabtree
CAST: Marshall Thompson, Kim Parker, Gil Winfield, Terence Kilburn

Surprisingly effective little horror chiller with slight overtones of the "Id" creature from *Forbidden Planet*. Scientific thought experiment goes awry and creates nasty creatures that look like brains with coiled tails. Naturally, they eat people. Story builds to a great climax as our heroes hole up in a shack and try to fend off an army of the repulsive beasties. Lots of fun.

1958 B & W 74 minutes

FIFTH FLOOR, THE
½

DIRECTOR: Howard Avedis
CAST: Bo Hopkins, Dianne Hull, Patti D'Arbanville, Mel Ferrer, Sharon Farrell

Thoroughly contemptible and completely unbelievable tale of an attractive college lass who is mistakenly popped into an insane asylum. Weak script is a poor excuse for disgusting treatment of women. Even fans of the always intriguing Patti D'Arbanbville will have trouble sitting through this one. Bo Hopkins chews through the scenery in a mad attempt to escape into a better picture. Don't watch this with the woman you love. Rated R for violence and nudity.

1980 90 minutes

FINAL CONFLICT, THE
★★

DIRECTOR: Graham Baker
CAST: Sam Neill, Rossano Brazzi, Don Gordon, Lisa Harrow, Mason Adams

The third and last in the *Omen* trilogy, this disturbing but passionless film concerns the rise to power of the son of Satan, Damien Thorn (Sam Neill, of *My Brilliant Career*), and the second coming of the Saviour. It is a crassly commercialized version of the ultimate clash between good and evil that depends more on shocking spectacle than gripping tension for its impact. It takes more energy and endurance to sit through than it deserves. Rated R.

1981 108 minutes

FINAL EXAM

DIRECTOR: Jimmy Huston
CAST: Celice Bagdadi, Joel S. Rice, Ralph Brown

A mad slasher hacks his way through a college campus in this *Friday the 13th* ripoff; and a bad ripoff it is. Even gore fans will find this film a bore. Rated R.

1981   90 minutes

FINAL TERROR, THE
★½
DIRECTOR: Andrew Davis
CAST: Rachel Ward, Daryl Hannah, John Friedrich, Adrian Zmed

Rachel Ward (*Against All Odds*) and Daryl Hannah (*Splash*) weren't big stars when they made this mediocre low-budget slasher flick for one-time B-movie king Sam Arkoff (*Beach Party*; *The Raven*) and now probably wish they hadn't. Although it's a cut above most films in its genre, *The Final Terror* is nothing special. Rated R for brief nudity and violence.

1981   82 minutes

FIRE!
★★
DIRECTOR: Earl Bellamy
CAST: Ernest Borgnine, Vera Miles, Alex Cord, Donna Mills, Lloyd Nolan, Ty Hardin, Neville Brand, Gene Evans, Erik Estrada

Another of producer Irwin Allen's suspense spectaculars involving an all-star cast caught in a major calamity. This one concerns a mountain town in the path of a forest fire set by an escaped convict. Worth watching once.

1977   100 minutes

FIRESTARTER
★★★½
DIRECTOR: Mark L. Lester
CAST: David Keith, Drew Barrymore, George C. Scott, Martin Sheen, Heather Locklear

Stephen King writhes again. This time, Drew Barrymore (*E.T.*) stars as the gifted (or is that haunted) child of the title, who has the ability—sometimes uncontrollable—to ignite objects around her. David Keith is the father who tries to protect her from the baddies, played by George C. Scott and Martin Sheen. *Firestarter* is an old-fashioned terror movie. It's a suspenseful, poignant, and sometimes frightening entertainment that goes beyond its genre. Rated PG for violence.

1984   115 minutes

FLESHBURN
★★★½
DIRECTOR: George Gage
CAST: Sonny Landham, Steve Kanaly, Karen Carlson, Macon McCalman

An Indian who left five men in the desert to die breaks out of an insane asylum to hunt down and wreak his revenge against the psychiatrists who sentenced him. From the moment the opening credits roll, giving the background on the story, this film promises to be more than exploitation, and it does not let you down. The characters are neatly established before the action begins, and the dialogue has a certain snappiness to it. Sonny Landham's performance as the Indian is chillingly good. Rated R for profanity, violence.

1983   91 minutes

FLOOD!
★★★
DIRECTOR: Earl Bellamy
CAST: Robert Culp, Martin Milner, Barbara Hershey, Ricard Basehart, Carol Lynley, Roddy McDowall, Cameron Mitchell, Eric Olson, Teresa Wright

Bureaucratic peevishness is responsible for a small town being caught short when a dam bursts. The resulting flood threatens to wipe out everybody and everything. Slick and predictable, but interesting just the same. If you like this, you'll like its sister film, *Fire!*

1976   100 minutes

FLY, THE (ORIGINAL)
★★★★

DIRECTOR: Kurt Neumann
CAST: Al Hedison, Patricia Owens, Vincent Price, Herbert Marshall

Classic horror film builds slowly but really pays off. A scientist (Al Hedison, soon to become David) experimenting with unknown forces turns himself into the hideous title character. Impressive production with top-notch acting and real neat special effects.

1958   94 minutes

FLY, THE (REMAKE)
★★★

DIRECTOR: David Cronenberg
CAST: Jeff Goldblum, Geena Davis, John Getz, Joy Boushel, Les Carlson

Promising film from the director of the ever popular *Scanners* and *Videodrome*. It's the story of a brilliant research scientist, Seth Brundle (Jeff Goldblum in the role originated by David Hedison in the 1958 version), who has developed a way to transport matter from one point to another instantaneously by means of molecular breakdown/reconstruction. One night, thoroughly gassed, he decides to test the device on himself. Unfortunately, a pesky housefly finds its way into the chamber with the scientist, causing the confused machine to merge their genes at the

receiving end across the room. To say more would surely ruin the film, though it must be stated that this is one of the grossest, most brutally unnerving movies in history as far as the special effects are concerned. It must also be said that this otherwise entertaining update simply falls apart at the conclusion. Rated R for gore and slime.

1986   100 minutes

FOG, THE
★★★

DIRECTOR: John Carpenter
CAST: Adrienne Barbeau, Jamie Lee Curtis, John Houseman, Hal Holbrook

This is one of those almost movies. Director John Carpenter is on familiar ground with this story of eighteenth-century pirates back from the dead, terrorizing a modern-day fishing village. There's plenty of blood and gore, but the lack of any real chills or surprises makes this one a nice try but no cigar. Rated R.

1980   91 minutes

FORBIDDEN WORLD
★★

DIRECTOR: Allan Holzman
CAST: Jesse Vint, Dawn Dunlap, June Chadwick, Linden Chiles, Don Olivera, Fox Harris

Jesse Vint was rescued from the obscurity of his deep-space death in *Silent Running*, and his reward was a starring role in this ripoff of *Alien*. Vint is a troubleshooter sent to an isolated science colony where a medical experiment has gone awry; instead of synthesizing a protein foodstuff that would replicate itself at a grand rate, a team of Dedicated Scientists wound up with a monster after implanting a gene-spliced mutant into the womb of a rather dense volunteer. (Well, what did they expect?) Typical acts of lunacy—impassioned idealists who try to communicate with the thing, crew members who persist in wandering around alone, and women who undress in the wrong cubicle—quickly decimate the cast until a truly clever means is discovered to kill the beast. Where was that sort of thinking earlier in the story? Rated R for violence and sex.

1982   77 minutes

FOREIGN CORRESPONDENT
★★★★★

DIRECTOR: Alfred Hitchcock
CAST: Joel McCrea, Laraine Day, Herbert Marshall, George Sanders, Edmund Gwenn

Classic Alfred Hitchcock thriller still stands as one of his most complex and satisfying films. Joel McCrea stars as an American reporter in Europe during the war, caught up in all sorts of intrigue, romance, etc., in his dealings with Nazi spies, hired killers, and the like as he attempts to get the truth to the American public. This truly great movie features many standout scenes, including one where a suspect is lost in a desolate field of windmills, a daring escape along a narrow hotel ledge, and a pilot's-eye view of a plane crash. One of the best. Don't miss it.

1940   B & W 120 minutes

FOREST, THE
★

DIRECTOR: Don Jones
CAST: Dean Russell, Michael Brody, Elaine Warner

This is an extremely amateurish attempt at a horror film. A very low budget coupled with an unprofessional cast makes this film a boorish waste of time. Two of the campers are served in a cannibal feast and the other two campers are left to destroy the evil. Unrated.

1983   90 minutes

FOURTH MAN, THE
★★★½

DIRECTOR: Paul Verhoeven
CAST: Jeroen Krabbe, Renee Soutenduk, Thom Hoffman

Jeroen Krabbe plays Gerard Reve, a gay alcoholic writer prone to hallucinations. Invited to lecture at a literary society, he meets a mysterious woman (Renee Soutenduk, of *Spetters*), who he becomes convinced intends to kill him or his—and her—lover, Herman (Thom Hoffman). Some filmgoers will be shocked by the explicitness of many of the scenes in this import. Yet with all this, *The Fourth Man* emerges as an atmospheric, highly original chiller, albeit one only for broad-minded adults. In Dutch, with English subtitles. Unrated, the film has full frontal nudity, simulated sex, blood, gore, violence, and profanity.

1984   128 minutes

FRANKENSTEIN (ORIGINAL)
★★★★

DIRECTOR: James Whale
CAST: Colin Clive, Mae Clarke, Boris Karloff, John Boles

Despite all the padding, grease paint, and restrictive, awkward costuming, Boris Karloff gives a strong, sensitive performance in this 1931 horror classic—with only eyes and an occasional grunt to convey meaning. It still stands as one of the great screen performances.

1931   B & W 71 minutes

FRANKENSTEIN (RESTORED VERSION)
★★★★★

DIRECTOR: James Whale
CAST: Boris Karloff, Colin Clive, Mae Clarke, Edward Van Sloan, John Boles, Marilyn Harris

The classic adaptation of Mary Shelly's novel about a scientist (Colin Clive) who creates a living man (a then unknown Boris Karloff) from parts of old dead bodies can now be seen in its entirety for the first time in over fifty years, as Universal Pictures has finally unearthed the missing scene where the monster throws a little girl (Marilyn Harris) into a lake in the hope that she will float, just like the flowers they had been tossing together moments before. While the excised footage was very brief, it did change the complexity of the character considerably. In the regular cut version we've all seen a hundred times, the monster is shown to have apparently murdered the child and violently thrown her body into the lake, whereas the complete print tells it like it really was as we see his confusion and panic as the girl drowns before his terrified eyes. The scene was admittedly too strong for audiences of the day, but now at last on video, it serves to make a great film still better. Universal deserves congratulations.

1931   B & W   72 minutes

FRANKENSTEIN (REMAKE)
★★½

DIRECTOR: Glenn Jordan
CAST: Robert Foxworth, Susan Strasberg, Bo Svenson, Willie Aames

Bo Svenson's sympathetic portrayal of the monster is the one saving grace of this essentially made-for-TV average retelling of Mary Wollstonecraft Shelley's horror tale. Because of Svenson's outstanding performance, one is reminded of the original Universal film and Boris Karloff's history-making interpretation. This is not particularly good because this 1973 version, which was produced by Dan Curtis (*The Night Stalker*), has little of the atmosphere which makes director James Whale's 1931 creation worth watching again and again for fans of the horror genre.

1973   130 minutes

FRANKENSTEIN ISLAND
🐾

DIRECTOR: Jerry Warren
CAST: John Carradine, Robert Clarke, Steve Brodie, Cameron Mitchell, Andrew Duggan, Robert Christopher

A group of men stranded on a remote island stumble upon a colony of young women in leopard-skin bikinis. Sounds like fun until they run up against a relative of the famous doctor, who's creating a monster of his very own. Worse than you'd think. In fact, the best thing about this piece of junk is the cover of the video box, which shows the Frankenstein monster doing a jig. Rated PG.

1981   89 minutes

FRANKENSTEIN MEETS THE WOLF MAN
★★★½

DIRECTOR: Roy William Neill
CAST: Lon Chaney Jr. Patric Knowles, Bela Lugosi, Ilona Massey, Maria Ouspenskaya

As the title suggests, two of Universal's most famous monsters clash in this series horror film. Very atmospheric, with beautiful photography, music, set design, and special effects (especially the miniature work). Only drawback is

Bela Lugosi's overblown portrayal of the Frankenstein Monster. This is countered, though, by Lon Chaney Jr.'s excellent performance in the role that made him a horror movie legend: the Wolf Man.

1943   B & W   73 minutes

FRANKENSTEIN—1970
★

DIRECTOR: Howard W. Koch
CAST: Boris Karloff, Tom Duggan, Jana Lund, Donald Barry

This poor excuse for a movie wastes Boris Karloff as the great-grandson of the famous doctor, attempting to create a monster of his own. Unfortunately, the only ones who succeeded were the producers of this movie. Rates higher than a turkey solely because of Karloff's appearance.

1958   B & W   83 minutes

FREAKS
★★★★

DIRECTOR: Tod Browning
CAST: Wallace Ford, Leila Hyams, Olga Baclanova, Henry Victor, Roscoe Ates, Harry and Daisy Earles, Daisy and Violet Hilton, Rose Dione, Edward Brophy, Matt McHugh, Randion, Johnny Eck, Martha the Armless Wonder

This legendary "horror" film by fabled director Tod Browning (who was also responsible for Universal's *Dracula* and most of the Lon Chaney films for MGM) is perhaps the most unique film ever made and certainly one of the most unsettling. Unavailable for general release in America from the early 1930s to the mid-1960s, this uneven story of romance and revenge among side-show attractions has been a staple of midnight movies and underground cinemas since

it found its way back to America and is now available to mass audiences for the first time since 1932 (when it was reputed to have sent patrons screaming into the aisles). Based on Tod Robbin's *Spurs*, this is the story of a circus midget who falls in love with a statuesque trapeze artist and nearly becomes her victim as she attempts to poison him for his money. Incensed by her betrayal and near murder of their little friend, the armless, legless, pinheaded "freaks" exact their revenge on the cold-blooded woman and her strong-man lover in one of the most horrifying sequences ever filmed. Generally sympathetic in tone to the unfortunate circus folk, this film falters at times and attempts to milk some humor out of hypothetical situations. (Roscoe Ates falls in love with one-half of a pair of Siamese twins.) But it's the simple shots of the circus personnel conducting their daily business as well as the classic wedding feast and final chase that remain in the memory. This film might be objectionable to most audiences and could very well provide children with sleepless nights. Beware.

1932   B & W   64 minutes

FRENZY
★★★★½

DIRECTOR: Alfred Hitchcock
CAST: Jon Finch, Barry Foster, Barbara Leigh-Hunt, Anna Massey, Alec McCowen

Frenzy makes a return to one of Hitchcock's favorite themes: that of a man accused of a murder he did not commit and all but trapped by the circumstantial evidence. Alfred Hitchcock described a scene from his movie by saying: "There's a body of a murdered girl that has fallen off of a potato truck.

She falls out of a sack of potatoes in which the murderer stuffed her. This follows a scene in which the murderer has escaped, leaving the body hidden in the truck. Due to the braking of the truck, the body was shot out. The most significant thing about the whole scene is how it improved the taste of the potatoes." The master's wry sense of humor is evident in this description just as much as it is in his structuring of shock sequences in his films. Rated R.

1972   116 minutes

FRIDAY THE 13TH
★½

DIRECTOR: Sean S. Cunningham
CAST: Betsy Palmer, Harry Crosby, Adrienne King

In *Friday the 13th* the accent is on gore rather than entertainment. The victims are introduced only to be graphically mutilated. They are totally without personality, and therefore we feel no sympathy for them. What's worse, the grisly murders are experienced vicariously by the audience. Sean S. Cunningham, the producer-director, uses a subjective camera in the stabbing scenes, which, essentially, makes the viewer the killer. The camera moves in on the screaming, pleading victim, "looks down" at the knife, and then plunges it into chest, ear, or eyeball. Now that's sick. Rated R.

1980   95 minutes

FRIDAY THE 13TH, PART II
★

DIRECTOR: Steve Miner
CAST: Amy Steel, John Furey, Adrienne King, Betsy Palmer

This sequel to the box-office hit of the same name is essentially the *Psycho* shower scene repeated *ad nauseum* (literally!) but without any of the elements that made Hitchcock's film a horror classic. Because the murders are very gruesome, most viewers will be as disgusted as they are scared. Rated R.

1981   87 minutes

FRIDAY THE 13TH, PART III
★

DIRECTOR: Steve Miner
CAST: Dana Kimmel, Paul Kratka, Traice Savage, Jeffrey Rogers, Catherine Parks, Larry Zerner

More gruesome axe, knife, and meat cleaver murders occur at sunny Crystal Lake. For the theatrical release, the blood, gore, and guts were in excellent 3-D (the only reason this thoroughly disgusting film rated two stars). So instead of covering your eyes during a particularly horrific scene, all you had to do was remove the glasses. Not a bad idea. But the video isn't in 3-D, so we suggest you avoid this trash altogether. Rated R for obvious reasons.

1982   96 minutes

FRIDAY THE 13TH—THE FINAL CHAPTER
🦃

DIRECTOR: Joseph Zito
CAST: Kimberly Beck, Corey Feldman, Peter Barton, Joan Freeman, Alan Hayes

More gruesome and nauseating axe, knife, and meat cleaver murders occur at sunny Crystal Lake. The producers promise it will be "The Final Chapter" of this blood, gore, and guts series, which tends to disgust and revolt more often than shock and scare. That turns out to be a cheat. The story does bring, as advertised, "the end of Jason," but the ending still leaves room for a sequel. And what if it makes money? Will there be a *Friday the 13th—The Final Chapter Part II*? The mind boggles—and the stomach churns. Rated R for gore, violence, nudity, sex, profanity, and sheer tastelessness.

1984　　　　　　　90 minutes

FRIDAY THE 13TH, PART V—A NEW BEGINNING

DIRECTOR: Danny Steinmann
CAST: Jean Shepherd, Shavar Ross, Melanie Kinnaman, Richard Young

Well, they did it. The producers promised *Friday the 13th—The Final Chapter* would be the last of its kind. They lied. So we get more disgusting trash. Rated R for graphic violence and simulated sex.

1985　　　　　　　92 minutes

FRIDAY THE 13TH PART VI: JASON LIVES

★★

DIRECTOR: Tom McLoughlin
CAST: Thom Mathews, Jennifer Cooke, David Kagen

It may be hard to believe, but this fifth sequel to the unmemorable *Friday the 13th* is actually better than all those that preceded it. After all, what can you say about a film that features Arnold Horshack (Ron Palillo) of TV's *Welcome Back Kotter* as the first victim of the immortal, maniacal Jason Voorhees? Of course this thing is loaded with violence, but it is also nicely buffered by good comedy bits and one-liners. For instance, when Jason is stalking a group of young children, one turns to the other and says: "So, what *were* you going to be when you grew up?" Moments like this let us know that the people responsible for this stuff have their

tongues planted very firmly in cheek, thus making the movie a (sort-of) black comedy and, as such, quite palatable for those who are game. Rated R for language and violence.

1986　　　　　　　85 minutes

FRIGHT NIGHT

★★★★½

DIRECTOR: Tom Holland
CAST: Chris Sarandon, William Ragsdale, Roddy McDowall, Amanda Bearse, Stephen Geoffreys

Charley Brewster (William Ragsdale) is a fairly normal teenager save one thing: He's convinced his new next-door neighbor, Jerry Dandrige (Chris Sarandon), is a vampire—and he is! So Charley enlists the aid of former screen vampire hunter Peter Vincent (Roddy McDowall), and the result is a screamingly funny horror spoof. It's the most fun you've had being scared since *Ghostbusters*. Rated R for nudity, profanity, violence, blood, and gore.

1985　　　　　　　105 minutes

FROGS

★★

DIRECTOR: George McCowan
CAST: Ray Milland, Sam Elliott, Joan Van Ark

In this fair horror film, Ray Milland has killed frogs, so frogs come to kill his family. Milland accurately imitates Walter Brennan, and the whole cast dies convincingly. The film is no asset to the argument that horror flicks are good cinema. Rated PG.

1972　　　　　　　91 minutes

FUNHOUSE, THE

★★½

DIRECTOR: Tobe Hooper

CAST: Elizabeth Berridge, Cooper Huckabee, Miles Chapin, Largo Woodruff, Sylvia Miles

Looking for watchable modern horror film? Then welcome to *The Funhouse*. This film about a group of teens trapped in the carnival attraction of the title proves that buckets of blood and severed limbs aren't essential elements to movie terror. Rated R.

1981   96 minutes

FURY, THE
★★★★

DIRECTOR: Brian De Palma
CAST: Kirk Douglas, Andrew Stevens, Amy Irving, Fiona Lewis, John Cassavetes, Charles Durning, Gordon Jump

The Fury is a riveting and totally unpredictable film experience. It is a contemporary terror tale that avoids the archaic religion-versus-evil syndrome and utilizes instead the average-man-against-the-unknown approach that made Hitchcock's suspense films so effective. This time it is Peter (Kirk Douglas), battling against a supersecret government agency. They have attempted to kill him and have succeeded in kidnapping his son Robin (Andrew Stevens), who has unusual psychic powers. Peter once worked for the agency, so he knows their methods and uses them to avoid being captured or killed as he struggles to locate and free his son. In his search, he finds Gillian (Amy Irving), who has powers similar to those of Robin and is in danger of being abducted by the agency herself. She achieves a psychic connection with Robin and leads his father to him. That's only the beginning. Rated R.

1978   118 minutes

FUTURE-KILL
†

DIRECTOR: Ronald W. Moore
CAST: Edwin Neal, Marilyn Burns, Gabriel Folse, Wade Reese, Barton Faulks, Rob Rowley, Craig Kannet, Jeffrey Scott

Thoroughly rotten film about some obnoxious frat boys who get stuck on the wrong side of town and run into a gang of punks—one of whom has been exposed to radiation. This is as cheap as B movies get. Rated R for profanity, nudity, and gallons of gore.

1984   83 minutes

GASLIGHT
★★★★

DIRECTOR: George Cukor
CAST: Ingrid Bergman, Joseph Cotten, Charles Boyer

Ingrid Bergman won her first Academy Award as the innocent young bride who, unfortunately, marries Charles Boyer. Boyer is trying to persuade her she is going insane. He, you see, is trying to find some hidden jewelry, and the only way to do so is to make Bergman think she's crazy. Many consider this the definitive psychological thriller.

1944   B & W 114 minutes

GHIDRAH, THE THREE-HEADED MONSTER
★★★

DIRECTOR: Inoshiro Honda
CAST: Yosuke Natsuki, Yuriko Hoshi, Hiroshi Koizumi, Emi Ito

A giant egg from outer space crashes into Japan and hatches the colossal three-headed flying monster of the title. It takes the combined forces of Godzilla, Rodan, and Mothra to save Tokyo from Ghidrah's rampage of destruction. Good Japanese monster movie is marred only by dumb subplot of evil agent out to kidnap a Martian princess. Fast-forward these boring scenes, as they really slow the action.

1965   85 minutes

GHOST STORY
★

DIRECTOR: John Irvin
CAST: John Houseman, Douglas Fairbanks Jr., Melvyn Douglas, Fred Astaire, Alice Krige, Craig Wasson, Patricia Neal

Ghost stories are supposed to be scary, aren't they? Then what happened here? This film, based on the best-selling novel by Peter Straub, is about as frightening as an episode of "Sesame Street," and much less interesting. Indeed, the only horrifying thing about *Ghost Story* is the shameless waste of its distinguished cast. Rated R because of shock scenes involving rotting corpses and violence.

1981   110 minutes

GHOUL, THE
★★½

DIRECTOR: Freddie Francis
CAST: Peter Cushing, John Hurt, Gwen Watford

"Stay out of the garden, dear, there's a flesh-eating monster living there." One of Peter Cushing's many horror films. No gore, but not boring, either. Rated R.

1975   88 minutes

GHOULIES

DIRECTOR: Luca Bercovici
CAST: Peter Liapis, Lisa Pelikan, Keith Joe Dick, John Nance

The ad for this low-budget horror film featured a gruesome little reptilian creature—in a jumpsuit, no less—poking his head out of a toilet under the tag line, "They'll get you in the end." Could the movie be as tasteless as its promotion? Yes! Rated PG-13 for violence and sexual innuendo.

1985   87 minutes

GODZILLA, KING OF THE MONSTERS
★★★½

DIRECTOR: Inoshiro Honda (original version)—Terry Morse (U.S. version)
CAST: Raymond Burr, Takashi Shimura

First, and by far the best, film featuring the four-hundred-foot monstrosity that was later reduced to a superhero. Here he's all death and destruction, and this movie really works, thanks to some expert photographic effects and weird music. Ignore all subsequent efforts; this is the *real* Godzilla. Originally filmed in 1954 and in color, scenes of Raymond Burr looking up, reacting, etc., were added for American release two years later but were accidentally shot in black and white. So the entire U.S. version had to be released that way, though actually it does add to the atmosphere and serves to make the film that much more nightmarish.

1956   B & W   80 minutes

GODZILLA VS. MOTHRA
★★★

DIRECTOR: Inoshiro Honda
CAST: Akira Takarada, Yuriko Hiroshi Koisumi

Fine Godzilla movie pits the "king of the monsters" against arch-enemy Mothra for its first half, later has him taking on twin caterpillars recently hatched from the moth's giant egg that had been incubating on a nearby beach. Excellent battle scenes in this one, with Godzilla's first appearance a doozy. As is the case with another Paramount release, *Godzilla vs. Monster Zero*, the title of this film was altered for video also. Originally known as *Godzilla vs. the Thing*.

1964   90 minutes

GODZILLA VS. MONSTER ZERO
★★½

DIRECTOR: Inoshiro Honda
CAST: Nick Adams, Akira Takarada

Pretty good monster movie has an alien civilization "borrowing" Godzilla and Rodan to help defeat the hometown menace Monster Zero (known previously and since as Ghidrah). After massive destruction on their planet, the wily aliens decide to transport the three leviathans to Earth to continue the battle, at *our* expense. Great special effects, as usual, but poor dubbing hurts the scenes with human actors. Originally called simply *Monster Zero*, the title was apparently changed to help video rentals.

1966   90 minutes

GODZILLA 1985

DIRECTOR: Kohji Hashimoto, R. J. Kizer
CAST: Raymond Burr, Keiji Kobayashi, Ken Tanaka, Yasuka Sawaguchi

Once again, the giant Japanese lizard tramples cars and crushes tall buildings in his search for radioactive nutrition. Raymond Burr, who co-starred with the lizard in his 1956 debut film, *Godzilla*, returns to suffer even more on-screen embarrassment. What was okay in the 1950s and '60s in the giant-monster genre is totally out of place today, as a sci-fi flick even with

more sophisticated special effects. Rated PG for gore.

1985   91 minutes

GORGO
★★★½

DIRECTOR: Eugene Lourie
CAST: Bill Travers, William Sylvester, Vincent Winter, Martin Benson

Unpretentious thriller from England has a dinosaur-type monster captured and put on display in London's Piccadilly Circus, only to have its towering two-hundred-foot parent destroy half the city looking for it. Brisk pacing and well-executed effects propel this film into the must-see category. Sure-handed direction by Eugene Lourie.

1961   76 minutes

GORGON, THE
★★★

DIRECTOR: Terence Fisher
CAST: Peter Cushing, Christopher Lee

Peter Cushing and Christopher Lee take on a Medusa-headed monster in this British Hammer Films chiller. A good one for horror buffs.

1964   83 minutes

GRADUATION DAY
★

DIRECTOR: Herb Freed
CAST: Christopher George, Patch MacKenzie, E. Danny Murphy, Michael Pataki, E. J. Peaker

A high-school runner dies during a competition. Soon someone begins killing all her teammates. Christopher George, as the coach, becomes a suspect along with the principal and the victim's sister. The only plus in this blood-and-guts flick is the surprising twist at the end. Plenty of violence in this one. Rated R.

1981   96 minutes

GRAVE OF THE VAMPIRE
★½

DIRECTOR: John Hayes

CAST: William Smith, Michael Pataki

Although it's far from the classic it's reputed to be, this film was groundbreaking for its day. The story involves a vampire who interrupts a couple's first date, killing the boyfriend and raping the girl. She eventually gives birth to a baby bloodsucker who grows up to search for his father and discover his birthright.

1972   95 minutes

GRIZZLY
★★

DIRECTOR: William Girdler

CAST: Christopher George, Andrew Prine, Richard Jaeckel, Joan McCall

Another "nature runs amok" film with Christopher George going up against an eighteen-foot killer bear this time out. Some taut action, but the movie has no style or pizzazz. Rated PG for violence.

1976   92 minutes

GUARDIAN OF THE ABYSS
★½

DIRECTOR: Don Sharp

CAST: Ray Lonnen, Rosalyn Landor, John Carson, Paul Darrow

Uneventful devil-worship flick from England; the kind that winds up on the late late show. An antiques broker buys a mirror that is actually a window to hell. Few surprises and an anticlimactic ending. Not rated, but the equivalent of a soft PG for some sex.

1985   50 minutes

HALLOWEEN
★★★★½

DIRECTOR: John Carpenter

CAST: Jamie Lee Curtis, Donald Pleasence, Nancy Loomis, P. J. Soles, Charles Cyphers, Kyle Richards

Considered the most successful independently made film of all time (having grossed over $40 million at the box office), this is a surprisingly tasteful and enjoyable slasher film. Director John Carpenter puts the accent on suspense and atmosphere rather than blood, gore, and guts, as in other films of this kind. In addition, fine performances are given by the cast—with Jamie Lee Curtis (her debut) and Donald Pleasence, a veteran British character actor, the stand-outs. The story revolves around the escape of a soulless maniac who returns to the town where he murdered his sister to kill again. Rated R for violence, profanity, and nudity.

1978   93 minutes

HALLOWEEN II
★★★½

DIRECTOR: Rick Rosenthal

CAST: Jamie Lee Curtis, Donald Pleasence, Charles Cyphers, Jeffrey Kramer, Lance Guest, Pamela Susan Shoop

This respectable sequel picks up where the original left off: with the boogeyman on the prowl and Jamie Lee Curtis running for her life. Rated R because of violence and nudity.

1981   92 minutes

HALLOWEEN III: SEASON OF THE WITCH
★★½

DIRECTOR: Tommy Lee Wallace

CAST: Tom Atkins, Stacey Nelkin, Dan O'Herlihy, Ralph Strait, Michael Currie

A maniacal mask manufacturer in Northern California provides kiddies with devilishly designed pumpkin masks. Not a true sequel to the gruesome *Halloween* twosome, but still watchable. Rated R.

1983   96 minutes

HAND, THE
🐱

DIRECTOR: Oliver Stone
CAST: Michael Caine, Andrea Marcovicci, Annie McEnroe, Bruce McGill

Thumbs down on this dull film. It's the story of a successful cartoonist (Michael Caine) whose life is shattered when he loses his drawing hand in a car accident. Pretty soon he begins to think that the missing hand has a life of its own. Too bad this film doesn't have a life of its own. Rated R.

1981   104 minutes

HAPPY BIRTHDAY TO ME
★

DIRECTOR: J. Lee Thompson
CAST: Melissa Sue Anderson, Glenn Ford, Tracy Bergman, Jack Blum, Matt Craven

After surviving a tragic car accident that killed her mother, a young woman (Melissa Sue Anderson) suffers recurrent blackouts. During these lapses of consciousness, other—more popular and more intelligent—students at her exclusive prep school are murdered in bizarre and vicious ways. Does she or doesn't she? Only her psychiatrist (Glenn Ford) knows for sure. Despite a few fresh splashes of brutality packaged in a psychological mystery framework, it's more than evident that story coherence and credibility have taken a back seat to all the bloodletting. Rated R.

1981   108 minutes

HATCHET FOR THE HONEYMOON
🐱

DIRECTOR: Mario Bava
CAST: Stephen Forsythe, Dagmar Lassander, Laura Betti

The man who brought you such substandard chillers as *Beyond the Door 2*, *Blood and Black Lace*, and *The House of Exorcism* strikes again with another forgettable fright flick. This one is about a psychotic killer fashion mogul who hacks up brides with a . . . guess what. The dialogue comes close to being black comedy, but the tone of this wretched little number is too earnest. Too bad. It is good for a couple of laughs, thanks to the poorly dubbed voices. Rated PG for violence.

1974   90 minutes

HAUNTED STRANGLER, THE
★★★½

DIRECTOR: Robert Day
CAST: Boris Karloff, Anthony Dawson, Elizabeth Allan

Boris Karloff is well cast in this effective story of a writer who develops the homicidal tendencies of a long-dead killer he's been writing about. Gripping horror film.

1958   B & W   81 minutes

HE KNOWS YOU'RE ALONE
🐱

DIRECTOR: Armand Mastroianni
CAST: Don Scardino, Caitlin O'Henry, Elizabeth Kemp, Tom Rolfing, Tom Hanks, Patsy Pease, Joseph Leon, James Rebhorn

There's a killer (Tom Rolfing) on the loose, specializing in brides-to-be. His current target for dismemberment is pretty Amy (Caitlin O'Henry), who can't decide whether to marry her male-chauvinist fiancé, Phil (James Carroll), or return to her former admirer, Marvin (Don Scardino), a lively lad who works in the morgue and is given to playing practical jokes. While stalking his special prey, the killer keeps his knife sharp by decimating the population of Staten Island. Rated R.

1981   94 minutes

HE WALKED BY NIGHT
★★★★½

DIRECTOR: Alfred L. Werker
CAST: Richard Basehart, Scott Brady, Jack Webb, Roy Roberts, Whit Bissell

Richard Basehart is superb in this documentary-style drama as a killer stalked by methodical policemen. A little-known cinematic gem, it's first-rate in every department.

1948   B & W   79 minutes

HEARSE, THE
👣

DIRECTOR: George Bowers
CAST: Trish Van Devere, Joseph Cotten, David Gautreaux, Donald Hotton, Med Flory

This film is about a satanic pact between an old woman and her lover. When Jane (Trish Van Devere) discovers this pact in her aunt's diary, the house starts shaking . . . literally. She tells the story to her own mysterious suitor, Tom (but we know who he really is, don't we?), who has an unusually high interest in the matter. What does Satan want with Jane? This film fails to answer that question. In some scenes he tries to kill her

and in others he tries to possess her. This film is not only confusing; it's dull as well. Rated PG.

1980   100 minutes

HELL NIGHT
★

DIRECTOR: Tom Desimone
CAST: Linda Blair, Vincent Van Patten, Peter Barton, Jenny Neumann

Linda Blair (*The Exorcist*) returns to the genre that spawned her film career in this poor low-budget horror flick about fraternity and sorority pledges spending the night in a mansion "haunted" by a crazed killer. Rated R.

1981   101 minutes

HIDEOUS SUN DEMON, THE
★

DIRECTOR: Robert Clarke
CAST: Robert Clarke, Patricia Manning, Nan Peterson, Patrick Whyte, Fred La Porta, Bill Hampton

Everyone who saw this horror film as a kid when it was originally released probably remembers it as one of the scariest movies ever made. But look again—it's dreadful and just plain silly. Robert Clarke directed this and also stars as the scientist turned into a lizardlike monster by radiation.

1959   B & W   74 minutes

HILLS HAVE EYES, THE
👣

DIRECTOR: Wes Craven
CAST: Susan Lamer, Robert Houston, Virginia Vincent, Russ Grieve, Dee Wallace

The first scenes of this horror film reek of cheapness, and it gets worse. Foolish city folk have inherited a silver mine and are stopping on their way to California to check it out. The old-timer warns them to stay on the main road and head straight for California: "There ain't been no silver in them hills for years and you don't want to see what is out there." Naturally, they go out to find their fortune and the car breaks down. That's when a ghoulish family comes crawling out of the rocks. Rated R for violence and profanity.

1977   89 minutes

HITCHER, THE
★★★½

DIRECTOR: Robert Harmon

CAST: Rutger Hauer, C. Thomas Howell, Jeffrey Demunn, Jennifer Jason Leigh

C. Thomas Howell plays Jim Halsey, a young, squeamish California-bound motorist who picks up a hitchhiker, played by Rutger Hauer, somewhere in the barren Northwest. What transpires in the following ninety-six minutes is action that will leave you physically and emotionally drained. *The Hitcher* is about a hitchhiker who murders all those who give him a ride, except for Halsey, who narrowly excapes death. Halsey must toughen up and fend for himself: the cops suspect him of the roadside murders and the hitchhiker tests the innocent's mettle before he attempts to kill him—rites of passage à la Clint Eastwood. On this landscape of death, the filmmakers deliver the action with no moral strings attached—even the protagonist Halsey comes across as a bit of a psycho at the film's Sergio Leone showdown close. *The Hitcher* has all of the unflinching horror of a Wes Craven film and the kinetic power of a George Miller movie. If you thought *The Terminator* was too violent, this one will redefine the word for you.

The Hitcher has an uneasy ending—not one of hope, but one of tentative resolve, a condition of today. Not for the faint of heart. Rated R for profanity and extreme violence. Viewer discretion is strongly advised.

1986   96 minutes

HOLOCAUST 2000
★

DIRECTOR: Alberto De Martino

CAST: Kirk Douglas, Agnosta Belli, Simon Ward, Anthony Quayle

This is a shameless ripoff of *The Omen*. The Antichrist plans to destroy the world, using nuclear reactors. This movie stinks. Rated R.

1978   96 minutes

HOMEBODIES
★★★

DIRECTOR: Larry Yust

CAST: Douglas Fowley, Ruth McDevitt, Francis Fuller, Ian Wolfe, Bill Hansen, Paula Trueman

A cast of aging screen veterans liven up this offbeat thriller about a group of senior citizens who turn into a hit squad when faced with eviction. Director Larry Yust keeps things moving at a lively pace and even manages a few bizarre twists in the final scenes. Rated PG for violence, language.

1974   96 minutes

HORROR EXPRESS
★★★

DIRECTOR: Eugenio Martin

CAST: Peter Cushing, Christopher Lee, Telly Savalas

Director Eugenio Martin creates a neat shocker about a prehistoric manlike creature terrorizing a trans-Siberian train when he is awakened from his centuries-old tomb. Lively cast includes veterans Christopher Lee and Peter Cushing as well as a pre-Kojak Telly Savalas in the role of a crazed Prussian officer intent on killing the thing. Break out the Jiffy Pop and enjoy. The original title: *Panic on the Trans-Siberian Express.* Rated R.

1972   88 minutes

HORROR HOSPITAL
★★

DIRECTOR: Anthony Balch
CAST: Michael Gough, Robert Askwith, Dennis Price, Skip Martin

A crazy doctor (Michael Gough) performing gruesome brain experiments at a remote English hospital runs into trouble when a nosy young couple checks in and begins snooping around. Slow-moving gorefest features a hammy performance by Michael Gough in a typical lunatic role which became his trademark in the late 1960s and early 1970s. Watch it if you must. Rated R for violence and blood.

1973   84 minutes

HORROR OF DRACULA
★★★★½

DIRECTOR: Terence Fisher
CAST: Christopher Lee, Peter Cushing, Michael Gough, Melissa Stribling, Miles Malleson

This is the one that launched Hammer Films' popular "Dracula" series, featuring Christopher Lee in the first—and best—of his many appearances as the Count and Peter Cushing as his archnemesis Van Helsing. A stylish, exciting reworking of Bram Stoker's classic story of a bloodthirsty vampire on the prowl from Transylvania to London and back

again. Genuinely scary film, with a hell of an ending, too.

1958   82 minutes

HORROR OF FRANKENSTEIN
★★★★

DIRECTOR: Jimmy Sangster
CAST: Ralph Bates, Kate O'Mara, Graham Jones, Veronica Carlson, Dennis Price

Young medical student, fed up with school, decides to drop out and continue his studies alone. So what if his name just happens to be Frankenstein and he just happens to be making a monster? Good entry in the series has many ghoulish sequences, along with some welcome touches of humor. Recommended. Rated R.

1970   95 minutes

HOUSE
★★½

DIRECTOR: Steve Miner
CAST: William Katt, George Wendt, Kay Lenz, Richard Moll

A comedy-thriller about an author who moves into an old mansion left to him by an aunt who committed suicide. He's looking for solitude, but instead he finds an assortment of slimy monsters. The cast is good, but the creatures look phony, the shocks are predicatable, and the comedy is clumsy, crippling the suspense. In short, the structure of this house is rotten. Rated R for violence and profanity.

1986   93 minutes

HOUSE OF EXORCISM, THE

DIRECTOR: Mickey Lion, Mario Bava
CAST: Telly Savalas, Robert Alda, Elke Sommer

Early in this incomprehensible film, one of the characters prophetically proclaims, "It's awful." That it is. It looks as if the producers took a cheap horror film from Italy and added scenes of exorcism, including the now-standard cursing and vomiting, to update and commercialize it. They bear no apparent relationship to the rest of the film. Rated R for profanity, nudity, sex, gore, and violence.

1975   93 minutes

HOUSE OF SEVEN CORPSES, THE
★★½

DIRECTOR: Paul Harrison
CAST: John Ireland, Faith Domergue, John Carradine

Veteran cast almost saves this minor yarn about the grisly events that happen to the members of a film crew shooting a horror movie in a foreboding old mansion. Semientertaining nonsense. Rated PG.

1973   90 minutes

HOUSE OF THE DEAD

DIRECTOR: Knute Allmendinger
CAST: John Erickson, Charles Aidman, Bernard Fox, Ivor Francis

A young man stranded in a haunted house finds he is not alone. Don't ask why anyone would watch or enjoy this bomb. Rotten, rotten, rotten.

1980   90 minutes

HOUSE OF THE LONG SHADOWS
★★★

DIRECTOR: Pete Walker
CAST: Vincent Price, John Carradine, Christopher Lee, Desi Arnaz Jr., Peter Cushing

This is the good old-fashioned–type horror film that doesn't rely on blood and gore to give the viewer a scare. This gothic thriller is a great choice for horror fans who still like to use their imagination. Rated PG.

1984   102 minutes

HOUSE OF WAX
★★★½

DIRECTOR: André De Toth
CAST: Vincent Price, Phyllis Kirk, Carolyn Jones

Vincent Price stars as a demented sculptor who, after losing the use of his hands in a fire, turns to murder to continue his work in this above-average horror film. A remake of the 1933 *Mystery of the Wax Museum*, *House of Wax* was long thought to be inferior to the original, which until three years ago was considered a lost film. The discovery of a print of *Mystery* brought about a reevaluation of both and the general agreement of the superiority of the Price version, which was also the first film to be made in 3-D by a major studio.

1953   88 minutes

HOUSE ON HAUNTED HILL
★★★

DIRECTOR: William Castle
CAST: Vincent Price, Carol Ohmart, Richard Long, Elisha Cook Jr., Carolyn Craig, Alan Marshal

Vincent Price is at his most relaxed and confident in this fun fright flick about the wealthy owner of a creepy old fortress who offers a group a fortune if they can survive a night there. Humorous at times, deadly serious at others. Robb White's intriguing script is well acted by the ensemble cast, with Elisha Cook Jr. outstanding as the one who knows the old house's secrets.

1958   B & W   75 minutes

HOUSE ON SORORITY ROW
🐾

DIRECTOR: Mark Rosman
CAST: Eileen Davidson, Kathryn McNeil, Robin Meloy

In this low-budget horror film, a group of college girls take over their sorority and kills the house mother. While the house mother may be down, she's not out—at least not out of the picture—as she comes back from the dead to wreak havoc. Rated R.

1983   90 minutes

HOUSE THAT BLED TO DEATH, THE
★★

DIRECTOR: Tom Clegg
CAST: Nicolas Ball, Rachel Davies, Brian Crouchen, Bat Maynard

Marginally scary horror film about a house that is possessed. Possessed by what or who? Don't ask us—the film refuses to give up the reason for all the blood that keeps shooting out of the pipes, or the various bloody members that show up in the fridge now and then. Not rated, but would probably merit a PG for violence and gore.

1985   50 minutes

HOUSE THAT DRIPPED BLOOD, THE
★★★½

DIRECTOR: Peter John Duffell
CAST: John Bennett, Christopher Lee, Peter Cushing, Denholm Elliott, Jon Pertwee, Ingrid Pitt

All-star horror-anthology high jinks adapted from the stories of Robert Bloch. It's not quite on a par with the pioneering British release *Dead of Night*, but it'll do. Best segment: A horror star (Jon Pertwee) discovers a vampire's cape and finds himself becoming a little too convincing in the role of a bloodsucker. Rated PG.

1970   102 minutes

HOUSE WHERE EVIL DWELLS, THE
★★

DIRECTOR: Kevin O'Connor
CAST: Edward Albert, Susan George, Doug McClure

Depressing little horror romp with a Japanese background. In a savagely violent opening, a young samurai swordsman discovers the amorous activities of his less-than-faithful wife, and a gory fight ensues wherein everyone is either beheaded or commits hara-kiri. This traps some really angry spirits in the house, which Edward Albert and Susan George move into centuries later. Pretty soon things go a lot more than bump in the night. Occasionally a quite interesting little ghost story, but it is marred by too much gruesome violence and some really sad nude scenes with an overweight Doug McClure and the always ready-to-peel Susan George, and the sleepwalking Edward Albert. Rated R for nudity, violence, language.

1985   91 minutes

HOWLING, THE
★★★★

DIRECTOR: Joe Dante
CAST: Dee Wallace, Christopher Stone, Patrick Macnee, Dennis Dugan, Slim Pickens, John Carradine

The Howling has everything—every spooky scene you've ever seen, every horror movie cliché that's ever been overspoken, and every guaranteed-to-make-'em jump, out-of-the-dark surprise that Hollywood ever came up with for its scary movies. It also has the best special effects since *Alien* and some really off-the-wall humor, which makes this shocker truly bizarre. Rated R for gruesome adult horror.

1981   91 minutes

HOWLING II...YOUR SISTER IS A WEREWOLF
🐺

DIRECTOR: Philippe Mora
CAST: Christopher Lee, Reb Brown, Annie McEnroe, Sybil Danning, Marsha A. Hunt

Poor follow-up to *The Howling* concerns the plight of Ben White (Reb Brown, best remembered for the title role in *Yor; the Hunter from the Future*) to uncover and destroy the colony of werewolves that infected his sister. Fortunately, he has help in the person of Christopher Lee (who's great at keeping a straight face) as a professor who leads Ben to the wolves' sacred temple in Transylvania. An awful sequel; even Sybil Danning as the Leader of the Pack can't save it. Mediocre on all counts, with a video transfer that is so dark that the viewer is left mystified half the time as to what is going on. Skip this one—it doesn't even rate as a comedy. Rated R for nudity, blood, and gore.

1984   91 minutes

HUMAN MONSTER, THE (DARK EYES OF LONDON)
★★★

DIRECTOR: Walter Summers
CAST: Bela Lugosi, Hugh Williams, Greta Gynt, Edmon Ryan, Wilfred Walter

Creaky but sometimes clever suspense thriller about a humanitarian (Bela Lugosi) who may not be as philanthropic as he seems. Strange murders have been occurring in the vicinity of his char-itable facility. This preposterous Edgar Wallace story has its moments.

1939   B & W   73 minutes

HUMANOIDS FROM THE DEEP
★★★

DIRECTOR: Barbara Peters
CAST: Doug McClure, Ann Turkel, Vic Morrow

As in *Jaws*, beachgoers are terrified by water beasts in this science-fiction film. This time, it's underwater vegetable monsters who attack seaside frolickers. This is a never-a-dull-moment thriller. Rated R.

1980   80 minutes

HUMONGOUS
★

DIRECTOR: Paul Lynch
CAST: Janet Julian, David Wallace

The title is the best thing about this dumb thriller. Rated R.

1981   93 minutes

HUNCHBACK OF NOTRE DAME, THE (ORIGINAL)
★★★★½

DIRECTOR: Wallace Worsley
CAST: Lon Chaney, Patsy Ruth Miller, Ernest Torrence

This is the original silent classic. Although it has been remade, with varying degrees of success, in the sound era, nothing can touch the Lon Chaney version in screen spectacle or in the athletic excellence of moviedom's "man of a thousand faces." Chaney somehow conveys the tragic poignance of Victor Hugo's deformed bell ringer, from under layers of makeup. This film manages to hold up so well today, modern audiences don't even notice the lack of sound. A musical score has been added.

1923   B & W 108 minutes

HUNCHBACK OF NOTRE DAME, THE (REMAKE)

★★★★½

DIRECTOR: William Dieterle
CAST: Charles Laughton, Thomas Mitchell, Maureen O'Hara, Edmond O'Brien

In this horror classic, Charles Laughton gives a tour-de-force performance as the deformed bellringer who comes to the aid of a pretty gypsy (Maureen O'Hara). Cedric Hardwicke, as the hunchback's evil master, Thomas Mitchell, and Edmond O'Brien also give strong performances in this remake of the Lon Chaney silent film.

1939   B & W 117 minutes

HUNGER, THE

★

DIRECTOR: Tony Scott
CAST: Catherine Deneuve, David Bowie, Susan Sarandon, Cliff DeYoung

Arty and visually striking yet cold, this kinky sci-fi/horror film, directed by Tony Scott (brother of Alien director Ridley Scott), features French actress Catherine Deneuve as a seductive vampire. Her centuries-old boyfriend (David Bowie) is about to disintegrate, so she picks a new lover (Susan Sarandon). In the old-time vampire movies, you felt something for the victims—and maybe even the monster. As you watch this beautifully photographed but sluggish film, the only thing you feel is the urge to be somewhere else. Rated R for blood, gore, profanity, nudity, and sex.

1983   94 minutes

HUSH...HUSH, SWEET CHARLOTTE

★★★

DIRECTOR: Robert Aldrich
CAST: Bette Davis, Olivia De Havilland, Joseph Cotten, Agnes Moorehead, Cecil Kellaway, Mary Astor, Bruce Dern

Originally planned as a sequel to What Ever Happened to Baby Jane?, reuniting stars of that movie, Bette Davis and Joan Crawford, this effort was filmed with Bette opposite her old Warner Bros. cellmate—Olivia De Havilland. (Both walked out on what they felt were unfair contracts at the studio.) This time they're on opposite sides of the magnolia bush, with Olivia trying to drive poor Bette, who's not all there to begin with, mad.

1965   B & W 133 minutes

I CONFESS

★★★

DIRECTOR: Alfred Hitchcock
CAST: Montgomery Clift, Karl Malden, Anne Baxter, Brian Aherne, O. E. Haas, Dolly Haas

Alfred Hitchcock's method direction clashes with Montgomery Clift's method acting, and the result falls short of the Master of Suspense's best work. In spite of such shortcomings, this is the film that best reflects many of Hitch's puritanical ethics. Clift stars as a priest who takes confession from a man who—coincidentally—killed a blackmailer who knew of Clift's pre-vows relationship with Baxter. (Whew!) Karl Malden, as a police investigator, demonstrates where Peter Falk got a lot of his ideas for Columbo. Moody and atmospheric, but the notion of dual guilt never quite comes off.

1953   B & W 95 minutes

I DISMEMBER MAMA

★

DIRECTOR: Paul Leder

CAST: Zooey Hall, Geri Reischl, Greg Mullavey

Great title—horrible movie. Mama's boy escapes from institution and goes on a "purifying" spree. In a sick plot turn, he falls in love with an 11-year-old girl after carving up her mother. A low-budget bore. Too tame for gore fans, too silly for anyone else. Rated R for violence and nudity.

1972   86 minutes

I SPIT ON YOUR GRAVE

DIRECTOR: Meir Zarchi
CAST: Camille Keaton, Epon Tabor, Richard Pace, Anthony Nichols

After being brutally raped by a gang of thugs (one of whom is retarded), a young woman takes sadistic revenge. An utterly reprehensible motion picture with shockingly misplaced values. It seems to take more joy in presenting its heroine's degradation than her victory. She is repeatedly raped and tortured. When the tables finally turn, she proves to be just as vicious as her attackers. The scene where she robs a man of his offending "weapon" is one of the most appalling moments in cinema history. This is, beyond a doubt, one of the most tasteless, irresponsible, and disturbing movies ever made. Regardless of how much you may enjoy "bad" films, you will hate yourself for watching this one. The cassette box claims the movie is rated R; however, most videotapes of this title contain the longer X-rated version. Rated R or X.

1981   88 minutes

I WALKED WITH A ZOMBIE
★★★★½

DIRECTOR: Jacques Tourneur

CAST: Frances Dee, Tom Conway, James Ellison, Edith Barrett, James Bell

Director Jacques Tourneur made this classic horror film, involving voodoo and black magic, on an island in the Pacific. One of the best of its kind, this is a great Val Lewton production. Get the video and get ready to enjoy a great film.

1943   B & W   69 minutes

IMPULSE
★★

DIRECTOR: Graham Baker
CAST: Tim Matheson, Meg Tilly, Hume Cronyn

This mildly interesting thriller takes place in a town where the inhabitants find they have increasing difficulties in controlling their urges. Starring Meg Tilly (*The Big Chill*) and Tim Matheson (*Animal House*), the film attempts to tie up its plot in a hasty, unconvincing final ten minutes. Rated R for profanity and violence.

1984   91 minutes

IN THE SHADOW OF KILIMANJARO
★

DIRECTOR: Raju Patel
CAST: John Rhys-Davies, Timothy Bottoms, Irene Miracle, Michelle Carey, Leonard Trolley, Patty Foley

This is the gory but supposedly true story of what happened in Kenya when ninety thousand baboons went on a killing spree because of the 1984 drought. They were hungry, and people were the only readily available source of food. Rated R for violence and gore.

1986   97 minutes

INCUBUS, THE

DIRECTOR: John Hough
CAST: John Cassavetes, Kerrie Keane, Helen Hughes, John Ireland

About a spate of sex murders in a small town, this is a vile and mean-spirited film, a nightmare of bad taste and burdensome plotting, and a depressing example of movie-making at its most prurient. Rated R for all manner of gruesome goings-on.

1982   90 minutes

INDESTRUCTIBLE MAN
★★

DIRECTOR: Jack Pollexfen
CAST: Lon Chaney, Marian Carr, Ross Elliott, Casey Adams

Lon Chaney looks uncomfortable in the title role of an electrocuted man brought back to life who seeks revenge on the old gang who betrayed him. Nothing new has been added to the worn-out story, unless you want to count the awful narration, which makes this passable thriller seem utterly ridiculous at times.

1956   B & W   70 minutes

INITIATION OF SARAH, THE
★★

DIRECTOR: Robert Day
CAST: Kay Lenz, Shelley Winters, Kathryn Crosby, Morgan Brittany, Tony Bill

Adequate TV movie features Kay Lenz as a young college girl being victimized by other students during initiation, and her subsequent revenge upon acquiring supernatural powers. Hokey thriller should have been better, judging from the cast.

1978   100 minutes

INTERNECINE PROJECT, THE
★★★

DIRECTOR: Ken Hughes
CAST: James Coburn, Lee Grant, Harry Andrews, Ian Hendry, Michael Jayston, Christiane Kruger, Keenan Wynn

Ken Hughes, the director of *Chitty Chitty Bang Bang*, attempts a Hitchcock-style thriller. The results are mixed; the acting is good and the story is intriguing, but the screenplay drags and Hughes spends too much time tinkering with Hitchcock imagery and doesn't bother to pick up the pace. James Coburn plays an ambitious business tycoon who finds he has to kill four associates to meet a business agreement. The fashion in which he does this proves to be interesting. Worth a look for the trick ending. Rated PG for violence, partial nudity, and a little profanity.

1974   89 minutes

INVISIBLE GHOST
★

DIRECTOR: Joseph H. Lewis
CAST: Bela Lugosi, Polly Ann Young, John McGuire, Betty Compson, Jack Mulhall

This low-budget Monogram programmer features Bela Lugosi as an unwitting murderer, used by his supposedly dead wife to further her schemes—much the same as Lugosi himself was killed in films by overexposure in exploitative poverty row productions like this. Short on thrills, but look for silent cowboy hero Jack Mulhall in a supporting role as well as pretty Betty Compson, co-star of *Of Mice and Men* in 1940. If the choice is given, go for a zombie movie.

1941   B & W   64 minutes

ISLAND, THE

★½

DIRECTOR: Michael Ritchie
CAST: Michael Caine, David Warner, Angela Punch McGregor

Dreadful horror-adventure movie featuring Michael Caine as a reporter investigating the mysterious disappearances of pleasure crafts and their owners in an area of the Caribbean. At the beginning of the film, when author Peter "Jaws" Benchley's explanation for these documented disappearances is still a mystery, *The Island* is quite suspenseful and frightening. But when Caine discovers that the force behind the phenomenon is a band of pirates who have remained untouched by progress for three centuries, all impact is lost. In fact, if the movie wasn't so gruesome and gory, it would be funny. But it's just sick. Rated R.

1980   113 minutes

ISLAND CLAWS

★★

DIRECTOR: Hernan Cardenas
CAST: Robert Lansing, Barry Nelson, Steve Hanks, Nita Talbot

As science-fiction/horror thrillers go, this one is about average. *Attack of the Killer Crabs* would have been a more appropriate title, though. Dr. McNeal (Barry Nelson) is a scientist who is experimenting to make larger crabs as a food source. All goes well until a multitude of crabs (along with one giant crab) go berserk and begin attacking people in the nearby fishing village. Robert Lansing, as Moody the bar owner, delivers the best performance among many mediocre ones. The special effects were developed by Glen Robinson, who also did them for the 1976

version of *King Kong*. Rated PG for violence and gore.

1980   91 minutes

ISLE OF THE DEAD

★★★½

DIRECTOR: Mark Robson
CAST: Boris Karloff, Ellen Drew, Jason Robards

Atmospheric goings-on dominate this typically tasteful horror study from producer Val Lewton. A group of people are stranded on a Greek island during a quarantine. Star Boris Karloff is, as usual, outstanding.

1945   B & W   72 minutes

IT CAME FROM BENEATH THE SEA

★★★★

DIRECTOR: Robert Gordon
CAST: Kenneth Tobey, Faith Domergue, Donald Curtis, Ian Keith, Chuck Griffiths

Ray Harryhausen's powerhouse special effects light up the screen in this story of a giant octopus from the depths of the Pacific that causes massive destruction along the North American coast as it makes its way toward San Francisco. A little talky at times, but the brilliantly achieved effects make this a must-see movie even on the small screen; don't miss the now classic attack on the Golden Gate Bridge.

1955   B & W   80 minutes

IT LIVES AGAIN

★★★

DIRECTOR: Larry Cohen
CAST: Frederic Forrest, Kathleen Lloyd, John Ryan, John Marley, Andrew Duggan

In an effort to outdo the original *It's Alive!* this film has three mutated babies on the loose, and everybody in a panic. Doesn't quite measure up to its predecessor, but still successful due to another fine make-up job on the monsters by Rick Baker, and some nice directorial touches by Larry Cohen, who helmed both projects. Rated R.

1978   91 minutes

IT'S ALIVE!
★★★½

DIRECTOR: Larry Cohen
CAST: John Ryan, Sharon Farrell, Andrew Duggan, Guy Stockwell, Michael Ansara

This camp classic about a mutated baby with a thirst for human blood has to be seen to be believed. Convincing effects work by Rick Baker and a fantastic score by Bernard Herrmann make this film one to remember. Rated PG.

1974   91 minutes

JACK THE RIPPER
★★

DIRECTOR: Jess Franco
CAST: Klaus Kinski, Josephine Chaplin

Klaus Kinski plays Jack the Ripper, and Josephine Chaplin is Cynthia, the Scotland Yard inspector's girlfriend. Jack the Ripper is terrorizing London by killing women and disposing of their bodies in the Thames River. When Cynthia (Chaplin) tries to help her boyfriend capture Jack, she puts herself in danger. Rated R for violence and nudity.

1979   82 minutes

JAWS
★★★★★

DIRECTOR: Steven Spielberg
CAST: Roy Scheider, Robert Shaw, Richard Dreyfuss, Lorraine Gary

A young Steven Spielberg (27 at the time) directed this 1975 scare masterpiece based on the Peter Benchley novel. A large shark is terrorizing the tourists at the local beach. The eerie music by John Williams heightens the tension to underscore the shark's presence and scare the audience right out of their seats. Roy Scheider, Robert Shaw, and Richard Dreyfuss offer outstanding performances. Rated PG.

1975   124 minutes

JAWS 2
★★★

DIRECTOR: Jeannot Szwarc
CAST: Roy Scheider, Lorraine Gary, Murray Hamilton, Jeffrey Kramer

Even though it's a sequel, Jaws 2 delivers. It has all the thrills, chills, shocks, and screams that could be desired. The story can best be described as Close Encounters of the Third Kind meets Jaws. Police chief Martin Brody (Roy Scheider) believes there's a shark in the waters off Amity again, but his wife and employers think he's crazy. Rated PG.

1978   120 minutes

JAWS 3
★★½

DIRECTOR: Joe Alves
CAST: Louis Gossett Jr., Dennis Quaid, Bess Armstrong, Simon MacCorkindale

Just when you thought it was safe to watch a video movie, this second sequel to Steven Spielberg's megabucks box-office hit rears its ugly head. Among those marked for lunch in this soggy, unexciting sequel are Louis Gossett Jr., Dennis Quaid, and Bess Armstrong (High Road to China). They look bored. You'll be bored. Rated PG for profanity, gore, and violence.

1983   97 minutes

JESSE JAMES MEETS FRANKENSTEIN'S DAUGHTER
🦃

DIRECTOR: William Beaudine
CAST: John Lupton, Estelita, Cal Bolder, Jim Davis

At last! The one we've all been wating for! The one they said couldn't be made! Well, they were almost right. From the director of *Bela Lugosi Meets a Brooklyn Gorilla* comes a film that *shouldn't* have been made. The feeble plot pits hero Jesse James against the evil daughter of the infamous doctor of the title. Watch if you must.

1966   88 minutes

JIGSAW MAN, THE
★★★★

DIRECTOR: Freddie Francis
CAST: Michael Caine, Laurence Olivier, Susan George, Robert Powell, Charles Gray

In this suspense film, Michael Caine plays Sir Philip Kimberly, a British secret agent who has defected, under orders, to Russia. Before leaving, he discovered a list of Soviet spies operating in England and hid it. After forty years, he returns to England in order to get the list with spies from both countries hot on his trail. This is a wonderfully entertaining puzzle of a movie that keeps you guessing throughout. Caine is reunited with his *Sleuth* co-star, Laurence Olivier, who plays his chief nemesis. Rated PG for violence and profanity.

1984   90 minutes

JOURNEY INTO FEAR
★★★

DIRECTOR: Daniel Mann
CAST: Zero Mostel, Yvette Mimieux, Shelley Winters, Vincent Price

This Canadian remake of Orson Welles's 1942 film pales somewhat by comparison. The film deals with smuggling American arms between Turkey and the United States.

1975   103 minutes

KEEP, THE
★½

DIRECTOR: Michael Mann
CAST: Ian McKellen, Alberta Watson, Scott Glenn, Jurgen Prochnow

This is a visually impressive but otherwise flat and disappointing horror film set during World War II. Ian McKellen and Alberta Watson play Jewish prisoners freed by the Nazis when a centuries-old presence awakens in an old castle. After an impressive beginning with good special effects, this ends up being no more than an interesting curio. Rated R for nudity, sex, and violence.

1983   96 minutes

KEEPER, THE
🦃

DIRECTOR: T. Y. Drake
CAST: Christopher Lee, Tell Schreiber, Sally Gray

You'd probably be more entertained by watching commercials on TV. Bad, bad, bad. Christopher Lee plays the title role of the owner of an insane asylum who preys on the wealthy families of his charges. Rated R.

1984   96 minutes

KIDNAPPING OF THE PRESIDENT, THE
★★★★

DIRECTOR: George Mendeluk
CAST: William Shatner, Hal Holbrook, Van Johnson, Ava Gardner

As the title implies, terrorist kidnap the president and hold him hostage in this excellent action thriller. Hal Holbrook plays the feisty president, who is locked up in an armored truck and wired to explode at the slightest touch. William Shatner portrays a secret service agent who finds himself in charge of the crisis and unprepared for the situation. Van Johnson is the crooked vice president being asked by Holbrook to resign. As acting head of state, he ultimately holds the president's life in his hands, leading to a suspenseful twist in the hostage crisis. The acting is excellent, the suspense taut, and the direction tightly paced. You can't go wrong with this one.

1979   120 minutes

KILLING HOUR, THE
★½

DIRECTOR: Armand Mastroianni
CAST: Perry King, Elizabeth Kemp, Norman Parker, Kenneth McMillan

Elizabeth Kemp (*He Knows You're Alone*) plays a clairvoyant art student who, through her drawings, becomes involved in a series of murders. The story is a blatant ripoff of *The Eyes of Laura Mars*. With that said, suspense is achieved during the last fifteen minutes of the film. Unfortunately, the viewer must suffer through the first hour, which moves at a snail's pace, to make sense of the climax. Rated R for violence, nudity, and profanity.

1984   97 minutes

KING OF THE ZOMBIES
★

DIRECTOR: Jean Yarbrough
CAST: Dick Purcell, Joan Woodbury, Henry Victor, Manton Moreland, John Archer

Typical mad scientist–zombie movie with evil genius attempting to create an invulnerable army of mindless slaves to further the cause of evil. Thinly veiled Nazis in this limp entry are inevitably overcome by the forces of good, who adhere to the code of the bad zombie movie: it must take place on a phony tropical island, it must involve Nazis of some sort, it must look cheap, and it must have Manton Moreland in there somewhere. Jean Yarbrough has to join the ranks of the great low-budget directors for the steady stream of grade D clinkers that Monogram Studios loosed upon a monster-glutted public in the 1940s.

1941   B & W   67 minutes

KINGDOM OF THE SPIDERS
★★★

DIRECTOR: John (Bud) Cardos
CAST: William Shatner, Tiffany Bolling, Woody Strode

William Shatner stars in this unsuspenseful thriller with lurid special effects. The title tells it all. Rated PG.

1977   94 minutes

KING KONG (ORIGINAL)
★★★★★

DIRECTOR: Merian C. Cooper, Ernest B. Schoedsack
CAST: Robert Armstrong, Fay Wray, Bruce Cabot, Frank Reicher, Noble Johnson

This classic was one of early sound film's most spectacular successes. The movie, about the giant ape who is captured on a prehistoric island and proceeds to tear New York City apart until his final stand on the Empire State Building, is the stuff of which legends are made. It utilized every known form of special effect, some of which are still secret. Its marriage of sound, music, image, energy, pace, and excitement made *King Kong* stand as a landmark film and a testament to the genius of its creators.

1933   B & W 100 minutes

KING KONG (REMAKE)
★★

DIRECTOR: John Guillermin
CAST: Jeff Bridges, Jessica Lange, Charles Grodin

This remake, starring Jeff Bridges and Jessica Lange, is a pale imitation of the 1933 classic. For kids only. Rated PG for violence.

1976   135 minutes

KISS OF THE TARANTULA
★

DIRECTOR: Chris Munger
CAST: Suzanne Ling, Eric Mason, Herman Wallner, Patricia Landon

Boring, unpleasant story of an unhinged girl who obliterates her enemies with the help of some eight-legged friends. Rated PG for mild gore.

1972   85 minutes

LADY FRANKENSTEIN
½

DIRECTOR: Mel Welles
CAST: Joseph Cotten, Mickey Hargitay, Paul Whiteman, Sarah Bey

Bottom-rung horror film with Joseph Cotten ill-used as Baron Frankenstein attempting once again to create life in yet another silly-looking assemblage of spare parts. The twist to this one is that the Baron's daughter, Sarah Bey, takes over the duties and does her best to animate the lump on the operating table. Nothing new here—even the gore is listless. Violence. Rated R.

1971   84 minutes

LADY IN A CAGE
★★★★

DIRECTOR: Walter Grauman
CAST: Olivia De Havilland, James Caan, Ann Sothern

Superb shocker may finally get the recognition it deserves, thanks to home video. Olivia De Havilland is terrorized by a gang of punks when she becomes trapped in an elevator in her home. Good acting, especially by a young James Caan, and excellent photography help make this film really something special. Very violent at times.

1964   B & W 93 minutes

LADY VANISHES, THE (ORIGINAL)
★★★★★

DIRECTOR: Alfred Hitchcock
CAST: Margaret Lockwood, Michael Redgrave, May Whitty

Along with *The Thirty-nine Steps*, this is the most admired film from Alfred Hitchcock's early directorial career. The comedy-suspense thriller centers around a group of British "types" on a train trip from England to central Europe. A young woman (Margaret Lockwood) seeks the aid of a fellow passenger (Michael Redgrave) in an attempt to locate a charming old lady (May Whitty) she had met earlier on the train and now is apparently missing. Something is amiss. Not all the travelers are who they appear to be. Great fun in the Hitchcock tradition.

1938   B & W   97 minutes

LAST HORROR FILM, THE
🐢

DIRECTOR: David Winters
CAST: Caroline Munro, Joe Spinell, Judd Hamilton

Mama's boy obsessed with a horror movie actress goes on a killing spree at the Cannes Film Festival. This one is really sick. Even gore fans may find it overwhelming. It's unpleasant, unrelenting, and an embarrassment to everyone involved. Rated R for violence.

1984   87 minutes

LAST HOUSE ON THE LEFT
🐢

DIRECTOR: Wes Craven
CAST: David Hess, Lucy Grantham, Sandra Cassel, Marc Sheffler, Jeramie Rain

This is a sick slasher movie in which two teenage girls are tortured and killed by a sadistic trio. Later, one of the girls' parents take revenge. This movie will probably turn your stomach and keep you awake at night. Graphic torture and humiliation scenes rate this one an R at best.

1972   91 minutes

LAST WAVE, THE
★★★

DIRECTOR: Peter Weir
CAST: Richard Chamberlain, Olivia Hamnett

In this suspenseful, fascinating film, directed by Australia's Peter Weir (Gallipoli; Picnic at Hanging Rock), Richard Chamberlain plays a lawyer defending a group of aborigines on trial for murder. His investigation into the incident leads to a frightening series of apoca-

lyptic visions. It's not quite a horror film. However, it is often quite scary. Superbly made, it's a real treat for movie buffs. Rated PG.

1977   106 minutes

LEGACY, THE
★★

DIRECTOR: Richard Marquand
CAST: Katharine Ross, Sam Elliott, John Standing, Roger Daltrey

A young American couple (Katharine Ross and Sam Elliott) staying at a mysterious English mansion discover that the woman has been chosen as the mate for some sort of ugly, demonic creature upstairs. The bulk of the action surrounds their attempts to escape from this bizarre "legacy." Could be enjoyable if you're in the right mood. Rated R for violence and language.

1979   100 minutes

LEGEND OF BOGGY CREEK
★★

DIRECTOR: Charles B. Pierce
CAST: Willie E. Smith, John P. Nixon, John W. Gates, Jeff Crabtree, Buddy Crabtree

One of the better "mystery of" docudramas, which were the rage of the early 1970s, this supposedly true story focuses on a monster that lurks in the swamps of Arkansas. Included are interviews with people who have come in contact with the creature and reenactments of said encounters. Rated PG.

1972   95 minutes

LEGEND OF HELL HOUSE, THE
★★★½

DIRECTOR: John Hough
CAST: Roddy McDowall, Pamela Franklin, Gayle Hunnicutt, Clive Revill

Richard Matheson's riveting suspense tale of a group of researchers attempting to survive a week in a haunted house in order to try to solve the mystery of the many deaths that have occurred there. Jarring at times, with very inventive camera shots and a great cast headed by Roddy McDowall as the only survivor of a previous investigation. Rated PG for violence, tense situations.

1973   95 minutes

LEOPARD MAN, THE
★★★½

DIRECTOR: Jacques Tourneur
CAST: Dennis O'Keefe, Isabel Jewell

This Val Lewton–produced thriller depicts the havoc and killing that begin when a leopard (used for publicity) escapes and terrorizes a New Mexico village.

1943   B & W   59 minutes

LET'S SCARE JESSICA TO DEATH
★★

DIRECTOR: John Hancock
CAST: Zohra Lampert, Barton Heyman, Gretchen Corbett

A young woman staying with some odd people out in the country witnesses all sorts of strange things, like ghosts and blood-stained corpses. Is it real, or some kind of elaborate hoax? The title tells it all in this disjointed terror tale, though it does contain a few spooky scenes. Rated PG.

1971   89 minutes

LIFT, THE
★★★

DIRECTOR: Dick Maas
CAST: Huub Stapel, Willeke van Ammelrooy, Josie van Dalam

An inquisitive mechanic (Huub Stapel) discovers that an elevator is possessed by some dark power and is killing the people who ride in it. The authorities don't believe him, and he alone is left to battle the unholy force. Competent acting and good production values lend considerable suspense to this dubbed-to-English German production, despite an unusual premise. Definitely worth watching for horror film fans.

1985   95 minutes

LIPSTICK

DIRECTOR: Lamont Johnson
CAST: Margaux Hemingway, Mariel Hemingway, Anne Bancroft

This film proved that acting was not the career for model Margaux Hemingway. In it, both she and her little sister (Mariel Hemingway) are sexually molested by a composer. When Margaux gets no justice in court, she takes matters into her own hands. Rated R.

1976   89 minutes

LITTLE GIRL WHO LIVES DOWN THE LANE, THE
★★★½

DIRECTOR: Nicolas Gessner
CAST: Jodie Foster, Martin Sheen, Alexis Smith

The Little Girl Who Lives Down the Lane is a remarkably subdued film from a genre that has existed primarily on gore, violence, and audience manipulation. Whatever shocks and suspense *Little Girl* has—and there is an atmosphere throughout that rivals a good, scary book by the fireside—are achieved through genuine skill on the part of author/screenwriter Laird Koenig and director Nicolas Gessner. Jodie Foster gives an absorbingly realistic performance in the title role. Martin Sheen is the child molester who menaces her. It's a well-acted chiller. Rated PG.

1976   94 minutes

LITTLE SHOP OF HORRORS, THE
★★★★

DIRECTOR: Roger Corman
CAST: Jonathan Haze, Mel Welles, Jackie Joseph, Jack Nicholson, Dick Miller

Dynamite Roger Corman super-quickie about a meek florist shop employee (Jonathan Haze) who inadvertently creates a ferocious man-eating plant. This horror-comedy was filmed in two days and is one of the funniest ever made.

1960   B & W   72 minutes

LOVE FROM A STRANGER
★★★

DIRECTOR: Richard Whorf
CAST: Sylvia Sidney, John Hodiak, John Howard, Isobel Elsom, Ernest Cossart

Just-married woman suspects her new husband is a murderer and that she will be his next victim in this suspense thriller in the vein of *Suspicion*.

1947   B & W   81 minutes

LOVE BUTCHER
🐽

DIRECTOR: Mikel Angel, Don Jones
CAST: Erik Stern, Kay Neer, Robin Sherwood

A series of grisly murders of young women are committed by a deranged psycho. Pretty original, huh? Poorly conceived thriller doesn't even rate a turkey. Rated R.

1983   84 minutes

LUST FOR A VAMPIRE
★★★

DIRECTOR: Jimmy Sangster

CAST: Susanna Leigh, Michael Johnson, Yutte Stensgaard, Ralph Bates, Barbara Jefford

All-girls school turns out to be a haven for vampires, with a visiting writer (Michael Johnson) falling in love with one of the undead students (Yutte Stensgaard). Atmospheric blending of chills and fleshy eroticism combined with a terrific ending. American version was retitled *To Love a Vampire* and severely edited. This is the original English version, and not for kids or the squeamish. Rated R.

1970   95 minutes

M
★★★★★

DIRECTOR: Fritz Lang
CAST: Peter Lorre, Gustav Grundgens, Ellen Widman, Inge Landgut

A child-killer is chased by police, and by other criminals who would prefer to mete out their own justice. Peter Lorre, in his first film role, gives a striking portrayal of a man driven by uncontrollable forces. Detested by all elements of society, his character is both pitiful and frightening. A classic German film, understated, yet filled with haunting images. Beware of videocassettes containing edited versions of the movie, and badly translated, illegible subtitles. Unrated. In German, with English subtitles.

1931   B & W   99 minutes

MAGIC
★★★½

DIRECTOR: Richard Attenborough
CAST: Anthony Hopkins, Burgess Meredith, Ed Lauter, Ann-Margret

Magic will make your skin crawl. The slow descent into madness of the main character, Corky (Anthony Hopkins), a ventriloquist-magician, is the most disturbing study in terror to hit the screens since *Psycho*. Rated R.

1978   106 minutes

MANHATTAN PROJECT, THE
★★★

DIRECTOR: Marshall Brickman
CAST: John Lithgow, Christopher Collet, Cynthia Nixon, Jill Eikenberry

This contemporary comedy-adventure-thriller concerns a high-school youth (Christopher Collet) who, with the aid of his idealistic girlfriend (Cynthia Nixon), steals some plutonium and makes his own nuclear bomb. Though the film is sometimes far-fetched, there's a pleasing balance of humor and suspense. Director Marshall Brickman doesn't hit the audience over the head with his anti-nuke message. John Lithgow gives an endearing performance as the scientist who has tunnel vision when it comes to his work. Rated PG for violence.

1986   115 minutes

MANIAC
👹

DIRECTOR: William Lustig
CAST: Joe Spinell, Caroline Munro, Gail Lawrence, Kelly Piper, Rita Montone, Tom Savini

For maniacs only. A plethora of shootings, stabbings, decapitations, and scalpings sadistically depicted in graphic detail will send even those with strong stomachs rushing out for airsick bags. Rated R for every excess imaginable.

1980   87 minutes

MANIAC
★★★

DIRECTOR: Michael Carreras

CAST: Kerwin Mathews, Nadia Gray, Donald Houston, Justine Lord

Spooky mystery film about a mad-man on the loose in France, with Kerwin Mathews perfect as an American artist whose vacation there turns out to be anything but. Chilling atmosphere.

1962   B & W   86 minutes

MANITOU, THE

DIRECTOR: William Girdler
CAST: Tony Curtis, Susan Strasberg, Michael Ansara, Ann Sothern, Burgess Meredith, Stella Stevens

Hilariously hokey film about a woman (Susan Strasberg) who by some strange trick of chance, is growing an ancient Indian out of her neck! It's apparently supposed to be scary, but wait until you see the birth scene. You'll be rolling on the floor in a puddle of tears! Oh well, one can only hope the stars were well paid for their efforts. Rated PG for foul language.

1978   104 minutes

MAN THEY COULD NOT HANG, THE
★★★

DIRECTOR: Nick Grindé
CAST: Boris Karloff, Lorna Gray, Robert Wilcox, Roger Pryor

Boris Karloff's fine performance carries this fast-paced tale of a scientist executed for murder, brought back to life, and his bizarre plan of revenge on the judge and jury who convicted him. Guaranteed to hold the attention.

1939   B & W   72 minutes

MAN WHO HAUNTED HIMSELF, THE
★★★½

DIRECTOR: Basil Deardon

CAST: Roger Moore, Hildegard Neil, Alastair Mackenzie, Hugh Mackenzie

Freaky melodrama about a car crash with unexpected side effects. Recovering from the wreck, a man (Roger Moore) begins to question his sanity when it appears that his exact double has assumed his position in the world. Imaginative film keeps the viewer involved from start to finish as we follow Moore in his attempt to solve the puzzle. Rated PG.

1970   94 minutes

MAN WHO KNEW TOO MUCH, THE (ORIGINAL)
★★★★★
DIRECTOR: Alfred Hitchcock
CAST: Leslie Banks, Peter Lorre, Edna Best, Nova Pilbeam

The remake with James Stewart can't hold a candle (or even a shakily held flashlight) to this superb suspense film about a man (Leslie Banks) who stumbles onto a conspiracy and then is forced into action when his child is kidnapped to ensure his silence. This is Hitchcock at his best, with Peter Lorre in fine fettle as the sneering villain.

1934   B & W 83 minutes

MAN WHO KNEW TOO MUCH, THE (REMAKE)
★★★
DIRECTOR: Alfred Hitchcock
CAST: James Stewart, Doris Day, Carolyn Jones

James Stewart and Doris Day star in this fairly entertaining Alfred Hitchcock suspense thriller as a married couple who take a vacation trip to Africa and become involved in international intrigue when they happen on the scene of a murder. The dying victim whispers an important political secret into Stewart's ear. The villains then kidnap the couple's 10-year-old son to ensure the safekeeping of the secret, which involves an assassination. It's no match for the original, but the director's fans no doubt will enjoy it.

1955   120 minutes

MAN WITH TWO HEADS
🦃
DIRECTOR: Scott Williams

This semi-remake of *Dr. Jekyll & Mr. Hyde* is loaded with gore and guts. Another piece of slime that has nothing going for it. Rated R.

1982   80 minutes

MARNIE
★★★½
DIRECTOR: Alfred Hitchcock
CAST: Sean Connery, Tippi Hedren, Diane Baker, Martin Gabel, Bruce Dern

Unsung Alfred Hitchcock film about a strange young woman (Tippi Hedren) who isn't at all what she appears to be, and Sean Connery as the man determined to get under the surface and find out what makes her tick. Compelling if overlong, confusing as well, but in the best Hitchcock tradition, with striking compositions and matte paintings, as well as another great Bernard Herrmann score. Video transfer is superb, too.

1964   129 minutes

MARTIN
★★★
DIRECTOR: George A. Romero
CAST: John Amplas, Lincoln Maazel, Christine Forrest, Elyane Nadeau

Director George Romero (of *Dawn of the Dead* and *Night of the Living Dead*) creates a good chiller with a lot of bloodcurdling power about a young man who thinks he's a vampire. This is very well done. Rated R.

1978 95 minutes

MASQUE OF THE RED DEATH, THE

★★★

DIRECTOR: Roger Corman
CAST: Vincent Price, Hazel Court, Jane Asher, David Weston, Patrick Magee

The combination of Roger Corman, Edgar Allan Poe, and Vincent Price meant first-rate (though low-budget) horror films in the early 1960s. This was one of the best. Price is deliciously villainous. The period sets and costumes are more impressive than usual. The cinematography of Nicolas Roeg is a big plus. The film is stylish and eerie. The plague has never been so entertaining.

1964 86 minutes

MASSACRE AT CENTRAL HIGH

★★★

DIRECTOR: Renee Daalder
CAST: Andrew Stevens, Kimberly Beck, Derrel Maury, Robert Carradine

Low-budget production has a teenager exacting his own brand of revenge on a tough gang who are making things hard for the students at a local high school. This violent drama has a lot going for it, except for some goofy dialogue and wooden performances. Otherwise, nicely done. Rated R.

1976 85 minutes

MAUSOLEUM

★½

DIRECTOR: Jerry Zimmerman, Michael Franzese
CAST: Bobbie Bresee, Marjoe Gortner

Exorcist V, anyone? Actually, this is a reasonably spooky supernatural shocker about a rich, sexy housewife (Bobbie Bresee) who wreaks devastation on assorted victims because of a demonic possession dating back to 1682. Evangelist-turned-actor Marjoe Gortner (remember him?) plays her timid husband. Rated R.

1983 96 minutes

MAXIMUM OVERDRIVE

DIRECTOR: Stephen King
CAST: Emilio Estevez, Pat Hingle, Laura Harrington, Yeardley Smith, John Short, Ellen McElduff, J. C. Quinn

As "Dirty Harry" Callahan has said, "A man needs to know his own limitations," and author Stephen King should have realized that his were restricted to the written word. This boring, turgid, chaotic mess, loosely based on King's short story "Trucks," is a waste from start to finish. As a director, King hasn't the faintest idea how to elicit good performances from his cast, and the picture is paced abysmally. Violence and gore were toned down after the film was threatened with an X rating, but what remains is pretty vile. Do we really need to watch Little Leaguers get crushed? As if that weren't unpleasant enough, King fills in some of the many gaps with crude bathroom humor. Absolutely unwatchable. Rated R for violence.

1986 97 minutes

MICROWAVE MASSACRE

DIRECTOR: Wayne Betwick
CAST: Jackie Vernon

The title says it all. Lounge comedian Jackie Vernon makes his movie debut in this pile of sludge about a henpecked husband who does away with his wife and feeds her to his mysterious microwave. Once he starts, there is no stopping, and he gets hooked on murder as a form of sexual gratification. Sound hilarious? This film is basically an attempt at black comedy, and watching it is as much fun as being at a funeral. Rated R for violence, nudity, gore, and profanity.

1979   75 minutes

MIND SNATCHERS, THE
★★★

DIRECTOR: Bernard Girard
CAST: Christopher Walken, Ronny Cox, Joss Ackland, Ralph Meeker

Christopher Walken (*The Deer Hunter, The Dead Zone*) plays a nihilistic U.S. soldier in West Germany who is admitted to a mental institution. He finds out later the hospital is actually a laboratory where a German scientist is testing a new form of psychological control. Like *One Flew Over the Cukoo's Nest*, this film deals with the philosophical and moral issues of psychological treatment versus the freethinking human mind. Walken's performance is excellent and the idea is an interesting one, but the film moves a bit slowly. Rated PG for violence and profanity.

1972   94 minutes

MONSTER CLUB, THE
★★★½

DIRECTOR: Roy Ward Baker
CAST: Vincent Price, John Carradine, Donald Pleasence, Stuart Whitman, Britt Ekland, Simon Ward

Better-than-average series of horror tales by Ronald Chetwynd-Hayes linked by a sinister nightclub where the guys 'n' ghouls can hang out. All the stories keep tongue firmly in cheek and involve imaginary creatures of mixed parentage, such as a "shadmonk," borne of a vampire and werewolf. The best scenes take place inside the nightspot; particularly memorable is a stripper who peels off clothes—and then skin—to reveal the bare bones underneath. Now *that's* a striptease! Rated PG for violence.

1981   97 minutes

MONSTER DOG

DIRECTOR: Clyde Anderson
CAST: Alice Cooper, Victoria Vera

Alice Cooper's music video, shown in the first five minutes of the film, is the only part of this release worth watching. This incoherent attempt to make a werewolf film using a pack of tail-wagging, playful German shepherds with poorly dubbed growls hasn't enough gore to please slasher-flick fans and no plot with which to entertain fans of classical horror. The title is a perfect review. Unrated, the film has violence.

1986   88 minutes

MONSTER FROM GREEN HELL
★★

DIRECTOR: Kenneth Crane
CAST: Jim Davis, Robert E. Griffin, Barbara Turner, Eduardo Ciannelli

Giant rubber wasps on the rampage in Africa. Our heroes battle a lethargic script to the death. In an attempt to revive the audience, the last reel of the movie was filmed in color. Big deal.

1957 B & W and color 71 minutes

MOON OF THE WOLF
★★

DIRECTOR: Daniel Petrie
CAST: David Janssen, Barbara Rush, Bradford Dillman, John Beradino

Another ABC Movie of the Week makes it to video. Disappointing yarn of the search for a werewolf on the loose in Louisiana. Good acting by the leads, but there's not enough action or excitement to sustain interest.

1972   73 minutes

MORTUARY
👹

DIRECTOR: Howard Avedis
CAST: Christopher George, Lynda Day George

Christopher George and Lynda Day George are featured in this low-budget horror flick; one of the sickest entries in what has come to be called the knife-kill genre. All the standard "commercial" elements of profanity, gore, nudity, blood, and sex have been thrown together into a presentation that leaves one with little hope for the human race. Rated R for the aforementioned elements.

1984   91 minutes

MOST DANGEROUS GAME, THE
★★★½

DIRECTOR: Ernest B. Shoedsack, Irving Pichel
CAST: Joel McCrea, Fay Wray, Leslie Banks, Robert Armstrong

This sister production to *King Kong* utilizes the same sets, same technical staff, and most of the same cast to tell the story of Count Zaroff, the insane ruler of a secret island who spends his time hunting the victims of the ships that he wrecks. Filmed and acted in a grand fashion, this is the epitome of the classic pulp magazine story, although this story was originally published in a "slick" magazine and won an O. Henry award as best short story of the year. Filmed many times since and used as a theme for countless television plots, this original is still the standard to measure all the others by. Non-stop action for sixty-three tight minutes.

1932   B & W   63 minutes

MOTEL HELL
★★½

DIRECTOR: Kevin Connor
CAST: Rory Calhoun, Nancy Parsons, Paul Linke, Nina Axelrod, Elaine Joyce, Wolfman Jack

"It takes all kinds of critters to make Farmer Vincent Fritters!" Ahem! This above average horror-comedy stars Rory Calhoun (who overplays grandly) as a nice ol' farmer who has struck gold with his dried pork treats. What the public doesn't know—and, frankly, wouldn't *want* to know—is that his secret ingredient happens to be human flesh. A variety of attractive victims, male and female, wind up in his "fattening grounds" before the entire scheme collapses. Wait until half an hour after meals before viewing. Rated R for violence.

1980   102 minutes

MULTIPLE MANIACS
👹

DIRECTOR: John Waters
CAST: Divine, Mink Stole, Paul Swift, Cookie Mueller, David Lochary, Mary Vivian Pearce, Edith Massey

A homage to gore king Herschell Gordon Lewis's *Two Thousand Maniacs*, *Multiple Maniacs* is director John Waters's favorite film.

You can expect plenty of bad taste in this black-and-white movie, which trashes Christianity (Divine is seduced in a Catholic church) and just about any other established and respected institution that crosses Waters's viewfinder. In this film even the transvestite Divine seems harmless compared with the host of other deviants and degenerates who roam the landscapes looking for trouble. Unrated, but the equivalent of an X, due to sex, violence, and gore.

1971   B & W   70 minutes

MUMMY, THE (ORIGINAL)
★★★★★

DIRECTOR: Karl Freund
CAST: Boris Karloff, Zita Johann, David Manners, Edward Van Sloan

First-rate horror thriller about an Egyptian mummy returning to life after 3,700 years. Boris Karloff plays the title role in one of his very best performances. Superb makeup, dialogue, atmosphere, and direction make this one of the best horror films using technique (rather than blood and guts) to terrify its audience. Despite its age, this all-time classic has lost none of its power.

1932   B & W   73 minutes

MUMMY, THE (REMAKE)
★★★½

DIRECTOR: Terence Fisher
CAST: Peter Cushing, Christopher Lee, Yvonne Furneaux, Eddie Byrne

Excellent updating of the "mummy" legend from Hammer Films. Christopher Lee is terrifying as the ancient Egyptian awakened from his centuries-old sleep to take revenge on those who desecrated the tomb of his beloved princess. Well - photo-graphed, atmospheric production is high-quality entertainment.

1959   88 minutes

MURDER BY PHONE
★★★

DIRECTOR: Michael Anderson
CAST: Richard Chamberlain, John Houseman

In this okay shocker, Richard Chamberlain, the star of TV's *Shogun* and *The Thorn Birds*, is cast as an environmentalist whose lecture engagement in New York City turns out to be an opportunity to investigate the gruesome death of one of his students, who picked up a phone one day and was zapped by an extremely powerful charge of electricity. The circumstances of her death are being kept secret by "the phone company" and Chamberlain, a one-time 1960s radical, must resort to his old "rock-the-establishment" methods in order to solve the mystery. Rated R.

1980   79 minutes

MURDER IN TEXAS
★★★★

DIRECTOR: Billy Hale
CAST: Farrah Fawcett, Sam Elliott, Katharine Ross, Andy Griffith, Bill Dana

Absorbing TV docudrama based on a true story. *Mask* star Sam Elliott is Dr. John Hill, a prominent plastic surgeon accused of murdering his socialite wife. At times a gripping study of psychopathic behavior. Good performances all around, including Farrah Fawcett and Andy Griffith, who reaped an Emmy nomination.

1983   200 minutes

MURDERS IN THE RUE MORGUE
★★

DIRECTOR: Gordon Hessler
CAST: Jason Robards, Herbert Lom, Michael Dunn, Lilli Palmer, Christine Kaufmann, Adolfo Celi

Members of a horror theatre troupe in nineteenth-century Paris are dispatched systematically by a mysterious fiend. Good cast, nice atmosphere, but confusing and altogether too artsy for its own good. Rated PG.

1971   87 minutes

MUTANT
★★½

DIRECTOR: John "Bud" Cardos
CAST: Bo Hopkins, Wings Hauser, Jody Medford, Jennifer Warren, Cary Guffey, Lee Montgomery

An incredibly frustrating film that displays well-crafted mood and tension during the first half and then lapses into the idiocy of yet another *Night of the Living Dead* ripoff. Wings Hauser lands in a small southern town, meets up with cute schoolteacher/barmaid Jody Medford (it's a *very* small town), and encounters decent folk who mutate into flesh-eaters after exposure to toxic waste. Bo Hopkins does well as a sheriff who takes occasional refuge in a bottle, and the atmosphere in the near-empty town is quite eerie for the first hour. The payoff, however, fails to equal the delivery. Too bad; this could—and should—have been much better. Rated R for violence.

1983   100 minutes

MY BLOODY VALENTINE
★½

DIRECTOR: George Mihalka
CAST: Paul Kelman, Lori Hallier, Neil Affleck

Candy boxes stuffed with bloody human hearts signal the return of a legendary murderous coal miner to Valentine Bluffs. Another variation on the *Halloween* holiday horror formula, this film provides a few doses of excitement and a tidal wave of killings. Unfortunately, it relies more on manipulative shocks than suspense for its impact. Rated R.

1981   91 minutes

MY SISTER, MY LOVE
★★★

DIRECTOR: Karen Arthur
CAST: Carol Kane, Lee Grant, Will Geer, James Olson

Offbeat story concerns two loving, but unbalanced, sisters who eliminate anyone who tries to come between them. Good acting all around and a perverse sense of style are just two elements that make this movie click. Alternate title—*The Mafu Cage*. Rated R.

1979   99 minutes

NAKED FACE, THE
★★★½

DIRECTOR: Bryan Forbes
CAST: Roger Moore, Rod Steiger, Elliott Gould, Art Carney, Anne Archer

A psychiatrist (Roger Moore) finds himself the target of murder in this enjoyable suspense film. Only trouble is the police think he's the killer, as the first attempt on his life results in the death of a patient who had borrowed his raincoat. One of the investigators (Rod Steiger) is still mad about the psychiatrist's having testified in a case that involved the death of a policeman and helping the killer obtain an insanity plea. So the detective is unwilling to believe the psychiatrist is innocent and works overtime to get him. He's not the only one, and the other fellow is playing for keeps. Rated R for violence, gore, and profanity.

1984   98 minutes

NESTING, THE
★★

DIRECTOR: Armand Weston

CAST: Robin Groves, Christopher Loomis, Michael David Lally, John Carradine, Gloria Grahame

Tolerable haunted house film about a writer (Robin Groves) who rents a house in the country so as to get some peace and quiet. But guess what. You got it—the house is plagued with undead spirits who seek revenge for their untimely deaths many years ago. The final scene doesn't make a whole lot of sense, but then neither does the purely gratuitous nude scene. Rated R for nudity and violence.

1980   104 minutes

NEW KIDS, THE
🐓

DIRECTOR: Sean S. Cunningham

CAST: Shannon Presby, Lori Loughlin, James Spader

In this horror film, directed by gore specialist Sean S. Cunningham (*Friday the 13th*), two easygoing kids try to make friends at a new high school. Their attempt is thwarted by the town bully, who is angry because they refuse to bow to his superiority. This brings acts of violence from both sides. This theme was handled with greater intelligence, imagination, and taste in Tony Bill's *My Bodyguard*. In comparison, *The New Kids* is exploitative teen trash. Rated R for profanity, nudity, and violence.

1985   96 minutes

NIGHTCOMERS, THE
★★½

DIRECTOR: Michael Winner

CAST: Marlon Brando, Stephanie Beacham, Thora Hird, Harry Andrews, Verna Harvey, Christopher Ellis, Anna Palk

Strange prequel to *The Turn of the Screw*, this uneven effort contains some fine acting and boasts some truly eerie scenes, but is hampered by Michael Winner's loose direction and a nebulous storyline. Marlon Brando is in good form as the mysterious catalyst, and Harry Andrews is fine as usual, but this murky melodrama still lacks the solid story and cohesiveness that could have made it a true chiller. Interesting but flawed. Rated R.

1971   96 minutes

NIGHT GALLERY
★★★

DIRECTOR: Boris Sagal, Steven Spielberg, Barry Shear

CAST: Roddy McDowall, Joan Crawford, Richard Kiley

Pilot for the TV series. Three tales of terror by Rod Serling told with style and flair. Segment one is the best, with Roddy McDowall eager to get his hands on an inheritance. Segment two features Joan Crawford as a blind woman with a yearning to see. Segment three, involving a paranoid war fugitive, is the least of the three. All in all, though, very entertaining and way above par for a made-for-TV movie.

1969   98 minutes

NIGHTMARE IN WAX (CRIMES IN THE WAX MUSEUM)
★½

DIRECTOR: Bud Townsend

CAST: Cameron Mitchell, Anne Helm, Scott Brady

Cameron Mitchell plays a disfigured ex–makeup man running a wax museum in Hollywood. His idea of a good time is to inject movie stars with a formula that turns them into statues. Lowgrade, barely watchable mess with an unsatisfying ending. Rated PG.

1969   91 minutes

NIGHTMARE ON ELM STREET, A
★★★★

DIRECTOR: Wes Craven
CAST: John Saxon, Ronee Blakley, Heather Langenkamp

Wes Craven (*The Hills Have Eyes*; *Swamp Thing*) directed this clever shocker about a group of teenagers afflicted with the same bad dreams. Horror movie buffs, take note. Rated R for nudity, violence, and profanity.

1985   91 minutes

NIGHTMARE ON ELM STREET PART 2: FREDDY'S REVENGE, A
★

DIRECTOR: Jack Sholder
CAST: Mark Patton, Kim Myers, Clu Gulager, Hope Lange

The only thing this substandard horror film has in common with its far superior predecessor is the title and gruesome old Freddy Krueger. Outside of the obvious, it is dull and lacks the tension the first one had. Another teen exploitation film. Ugh! Rated R for nudity, language, and gore, gore, gore.

1985   83 minutes

NIGHTMARES
★★

DIRECTOR: Joseph Sargent
CAST: Cristina Raines, Emilio Estevez, Lance Henriksen, Timothy James

Four everyday situations are twisted into tales of terror in this mostly mediocre horror film in the style of *Twilight Zone—the Movie* and *Creepshow*. Number one features Cristina Raines as a nicotine addict who goes out for a carton of cigarettes even though there's a slasher stalking the neighborhood. It's just ho-hum. Two has a video game whiz-kid (Emilio Estevez) taking on a super-powered arcade attraction. This one's kinda dumb. In three, a retread of Steven Spielberg's *Duel*, a priest (Lance Henriksen) is pursued by a pickup from hell. Only number four, "Night of the Rats," features any real chills—and those are nearly nullified by the bargainbasement special effects. Rated R for violence and profanity.

1983   99 minutes

NIGHT OF THE DEMON
🐾

DIRECTOR: James C. Wasson
CAST: Michael Cutt, Jay Allen, Robert Collings, Jodi Lazarus

This is a boring little bomb of a movie with an intriguing title and nothing else. Not to be confused with the 1958 classic *Curse of the Demon*.

1983   97 minutes

NIGHT OF THE GHOULS
★

DIRECTOR: Edward Wood
CAST: Keene Duncan, Criswell

From the director of *Plan 9 from Outer Space* and *Glen or Glenda* comes a film so bad it was never released. Not nearly as enjoyably bad as Edward Woods's other work, but definitely worth a look, for movie buffs. For the record, two young innocents stumble upon a haunted house (filled with some very tiresome bad actors).

1958   B & W   75 minutes

NIGHT OF THE HOWLING BEAST

DIRECTOR: M. I. Bonns
CAST: Paul Naschy, Grace Mills, Gil Vidal, Silvia Solar

One of the all-time worst! Paul Naschy stars in this mess as a guy who has a slight problem whenever the full moon rises. Lon Chaney Jr. and Universal Pictures did it better—much better. Rated R.

1984   87 minutes

NIGHT OF THE LIVING DEAD
★★★★

DIRECTOR: George A. Romero
CAST: Duane Jones, Judith O'Dea, Keith Wayne

This gruesome low-budget horror film still packs a punch for those who like to be frightened out of their wits. It is an unrelenting shock fest laced with touches of black humor that deserves its cult status.

1968   B & W   96 minutes

NIGHT OF THE ZOMBIES

DIRECTOR: Vincent Dawn
CAST: Frank Garfield, Margit Newton

A low-budget horror film about the dead coming back to life à la George Romero's *Night of the Living Dead* and about feasting on the living, this is a thoroughly disgusting motion picture. It's just one long cannibal feast—who needs this kind of trash? Rated R for violence and gore.

1983   101 minutes

NIGHT STALKER, THE
★★★★

DIRECTOR: John Llewellyn Moxey
CAST: Darren McGavin, Carol Lynley, Claude Akins

A superb made-for-television chiller about a modern-day vampire stalking the streets of Las Vegas. Richard Matheson's teleplay is tight and suspenseful, with Darren McGavin fine as the intrepid reporter on the bloodsucker's trail.

1971   73 minutes

NIGHT VISITOR, THE
★

DIRECTOR: Laslo Benedek
CAST: Liv Ullmann, Trevor Howard, Andrew Keir, Max von Sydow

Director Laslo Benedek and Max von Sydow wasted their skills on this film about a mental patient out for revenge. It is slow-moving and confusing. Keep plenty of No-Doz on hand. Rated PG.

1970   106 minutes

NIGHT WARNING
★★

DIRECTOR: William Asher
CAST: Jimmy McNichol, Bo Svenson, Susan Tyrrell

As in many gory movies, the victims and near-victims have a convenient and unbelievable way of hanging around despite clear indications they are about to get it. Consequently, *Night Warning*, in spite of good performances by stars Jimmy McNichol, Bo Svenson, and Susan Tyrrell, is an unremarkable splatter film. Rated R for violence and gore.

1982   96 minutes

NIGHTWING

DIRECTOR: Arthur Hiller

CAST: David Warner, Kathryn Harrold, Nick Mancuso, Strother Martin

Absolutely laughable tale, derived from an abysmal Martin Cruz Smith novel, about a flock (herd? pack?) of vampire bats—the real ones, not the two-legged cousins that prey on nubile young women—terrorizing a small community. David Warner has never looked worse than as this deranged vampire-bat killer, and he spouts ludicrous lines that actually make him wince. Ambitious production values couldn't do a thing to save this turkey . . . er, this rabid bat. Rated PG.

1979   105 minutes

NOMADS
★★★

DIRECTOR: John McTiernan

CAST: Lesley-Anne Down, Pierce Brosnan, Anna-Maria Monticelli, Adam Ant, Jose Cotton, Mary Woronov

In this thought-provoking and chilling shocker, Pierce Brosnan (of television's "Remington Steele") is a French anthropologist who discovers a secret society of malevolent ghosts living in modern-day Los Angeles. In doing so, he incurs their wrath and endangers the life of a doctor (Lesley-Anne Down) fated to share his terrifying experiences. Those who appreciate original movie fare will want to give this one a look. Although its story poses a number of questions that are not answered in a typically neat movie ending, this makes it all the more powerful. If you don't mind thinking—and even better, discussing—what you see, *Nomads*, something different in video fare, is well worth

watching. Rated R for profanity, nudity, and violence.

1986   95 minutes

NORTH BY NORTHWEST
★★★★★

DIRECTOR: Alfred Hitchcock

CAST: Cary Grant, Eva Marie Saint, James Mason, Martin Landau

Cary Grant and Eva Marie Saint star in this classic thriller by the master himself, Alfred Hitchcock, who plays (or preys) on the senses and keeps the action at a feverish pitch. The story is typical Hitchcock fare—a matter of mistaken identity embroils a man in espionage and murder. Fans can rejoice at the chance to experience one of the most exciting scenes ever filmed—a manhunt scaling the heights of Mount Rushmore—by one of the most imitated directors of our time.

1959   136 minutes

NOSFERATU
★★★★

DIRECTOR: F. W. Murnau

CAST: Max Schreck, Gustav von Wagenheim, Greta Schroeder, Alexander Granach

A product of the German expressionist era, *Nosferatu* is a milestone in the history of world cinema. Each shot is a masterpiece of photography. Director F. W. Murnau seems to make the characters jump out at you. With his skeletal frame, rodent face, long nails, and long, pointed ears, Max Schreck is the most terrifying of all screen vampires. Fans of the Dracula myth may be disappointed when Nosferatu's image appears in a mirror, or that his demise is not by the stake. Nevertheless, this picture stands as a tribute to the power of the silent screen.

1922   B & W   63 minutes

NOTORIOUS
★★★★½

DIRECTOR: Alfred Hitchcock
CAST: Cary Grant, Ingrid Bergman, Claude Rains

Notorious is among the finest Alfred Hitchcock romantic thrillers. Cary Grant, as an American agent, and Ingrid Bergman, as the "notorious" daughter of a convicted traitor, join forces to seek out Nazis in postwar Rio. Claude Rains gives one of his greatest performances—at times touching as the mommy's boy who has been betrayed by the woman he adores and at other times chillingly dangerous as the head of Nazi activities in Argentina.

1946   B & W   101 minutes

OBLONG BOX, THE
★★½

DIRECTOR: Gordon Hessler
CAST: Vincent Price, Christopher Lee, Rubert Davies, Uta Levka, Sally Geeson, Alister Williamson

This little gothic horror is nothing to shiver about. Although it is taken from an Edgar Allan Poe short story, it can't escape the clichés of its genre: grave robbers, screaming women (with close-up shots of their widening eyes), lots of cleavage, and of course, the hero's bride-to-be, who is unaware of her betrothed's wrongdoings. Sound familiar? Rated R (but more like a PG by today's standards) for simulated sex and violence.

1969   91 minutes

OBSESSION
★★★★

DIRECTOR: Brian De Palma
CAST: Cliff Robertson, Genevieve Bujold, John Lithgow

This is director Brian De Palma's tour de force. Cliff Robertson, Genevieve Bujold, and John Lithgow transcend normal film acting. Bernard Herrmann scores again, his music as effective as that in *Taxi Driver*. In fact, the script, about a widower who meets his former wife's exact double, was written by Paul Schrader (in collaboration with De Palma), who also wrote the latter film. Critics enthusiastically compare this with prime Hitchcock, and it more than qualifies. Rated PG.

1976   98 minutes

OCTAMAN
★½

DIRECTOR: Harry Essex
CAST: Kerwin Matthews, Pier Angeli, Jeff Morrow, Norman Fields

Dull low-budget effort with a group of vacationers under attack by a funny-looking walking octopusman created by a very young Rick Baker, who has since gone on to much bigger and better things. Rated PG for mild violence.

1971   90 minutes

OF UNKNOWN ORIGIN
★★½

DIRECTOR: George Dan Cosmatos
CAST: Peter Weller, Jennifer Dale, Lawrence Dane

Flashes of unintentional humor enliven this shocker, about a suburban family terrorized in their home by a monstrous rat. Contains some inventive photography and effects, but mediocre acting and forgettable music keep this film well away from "classic" status. Bring on the exterminator! Rated R.

1983   88 minutes

OMEN, THE
★★★★

DIRECTOR: Richard Donner
CAST: Gregory Peck, Lee Remick, Billie Whitelaw, David Warner

This, first of a series of movies about the return to Earth of the devil, is a real chiller. In the form of a young boy, Damien, Satan sets about reestablishing his rule over man. A series of bizarre deaths point to the boy. His stepfather (Gregory Peck), the American ambassador to England, suspects something is amiss, and his attempts to delve into the boy's past set the stage for a startling climax. Rated R.

1976   111 minutes

ONE DARK NIGHT
★★½

DIRECTOR: Tom McLoughlin
CAST: Meg Tilly, Adam West, Robin Evans, Elizabeth Daily

Meg Tilly, from *Agnes of God*, and Adam "Batman" West star in this story of a young woman (Tilly) who is menaced by an energy-draining ghost. Rated R.

1983   89 minutes

ORCA
★★★½

DIRECTOR: Michael Anderson
CAST: Richard Harris, Keenan Wynn, Will Sampson, Bo Derek, Robert Carradine, Charlotte Rampling

It is not the summertime tourists we see slaughtered in this thought-provoking tale but rather a mammal of the sea with a brain larger than that of a human. Where *Jaws* was an exaggerated horror story, *Orca* is based on the tragic truth. Motivated by profit, Richard Harris and his crew go out with a huge net and find a family of whales. He misses the male and harpoons the female, who dies and aborts, leaving her huge mate to wreak havoc on the tiny seaport. Rated PG.

1977   92 minutes

PACK, THE
★★

DIRECTOR: Robert Clouse
CAST: Joe Don Baker, Hope Alexander Willis, Richard B. Shull, R. G. Armstrong

Slightly above average horror film about a pack of dogs that goes wild and tries to kill two families. Rated R.

1977   99 minutes

PARASITE
★★½

DIRECTOR: Charles Band
CAST: Robert Glaudini, Demi Moore, Luca Bercovici, Vivian Blaine

If director Charles Band intended a film that would sicken its audience, he succeeded with this futuristic monster movie. Memorable scenes include parasites bursting through the stomach of one victim and the face of another. The film's use of special effects makes it all the more gory. Luckily, the plot isn't as predictable as that of most horror films, so at least it's suspenseful. However, *Parasite* may be too much for kids. Rated R.

1982   85 minutes

PATRICK
★★½

DIRECTOR: Richard Franklin

CAST: Susan Penhaligon, Robert Helpmann

This film revolves around Patrick, who has been in a coma for four years. He is confined to a hospital, but after a new nurse comes to work on his floor he begins to exhibit psychic powers. He begins by sending her messages on a nearby typewriter but gets violent when he perceives certain people as his enemies. This Australian film is similar to many other films that use the highly developed psychic power as a theme. The dubbing of this film does more damage than it probably deserves. (The director, Richard Franklin, went on to direct *Psycho II*.) Some violence, but nothing extremely bloody. Rated PG.

1979   96 minutes

PEEPING TOM
★★★½
DIRECTOR: Michael Powell
CAST: Carl Boehm, Moira Shearer, Anna Massey

Carl Boehm gives a chilling performance as a lethal psychopath who photographs his victims as they are dying. This film outraged both critics and viewers alike when it was first released, and rarely has been revived since. Not for all tastes, to be sure, but if you're adventurous, give this one a try. Rated R.

1960   109 minutes

PHANTASM
★★½
DIRECTOR: Don Coscarelli
CAST: Michael Baldwin, Bill Thornbury, Reggie Bannister, Kathy Lester

This strange mixture of horror and science-fiction, while not an outstanding film by any account, does provide viewers with several thrills and unexpected twists. If you like to jump out of your seat, watch this alone with all the lights out. R-rated after scenes were cut from the original X-rated 1979 version.

1979   87 minutes

PHANTOM CREEPS, THE
★★½
DIRECTOR: Ford Beebe, Saul A. Goodkind
CAST: Bela Lugosi, Robet Kent, Regis Toomey, Dorothy Arnold

This Saturday-afternoon crowd-pleaser features a crazed scientist, a giant robot, an invisibility belt, and a meteorite fragment that can render an entire army immobile—just about anything a kid can ask for in a serial. There's a stalwart hero and a snoopy newspaper reporter thrown in for good measure, but it's the evil Dr. Alex Zorka (Bela Lugosi hamming it up) and his giant robot and wild inventions that rivet everyone's attention in this Universal chapter play. Lugosi is once again teamed with his nemesis from *Dracula*, Edward Van Sloan as Chief Jarvis, and they do their best for twelve episodes to do each other in. Not as slick as the Republic serials, but great fun.

1939   B & W   12 chapters

PHANTOM OF THE OPERA
★★★★★
DIRECTOR: Rupert Julian
CAST: Lon Chaney, Mary Philbin, Norman Kerry, Snitz Edwards

Classic silent horror with Lon Chaney in his most poignant and gruesome role combined with theater organ accompaniment. Sounds like a prescription for an old-fashioned good time, doesn't it? That's right. This 1925 sample of Chaney's brilliance—he was truly the "man of a thousand faces"—still has enough power to send chills up your spine and tug at your heart. But aren't these old-time melodramas pretty corny? Sure—and that's part of the fun. Enjoy.

1925   B & W   79 minutes

PICTURE OF DORIAN GRAY, THE
★★★★

DIRECTOR: Albert Lewin
CAST: George Sanders, Hurd Hatfield, Donna Reed, Angela Lansbury, Peter Lawford

The classic adaptation of Oscar Wilde's famous novel, this features Hurd Hatfield giving a nicely restrained performance in the title role of a young man whose portrait ages while he remains eternally youthful. Though talky and slow-moving, this film nevertheless keeps you glued to the screen for its nearly two-hour running time, generating a chilling atmosphere and a foreboding sense of horror. A few key scenes shot in Technicolor for effect.

1945   B & W   110 minutes

PIECES
🐣

DIRECTOR: Juan Piquer Simon
CAST: Christopher George, Lynda Day George, Edmund Purdom

Christopher George and Lynda Day George, who were fast becoming the Lunt and Fontane of sicko horror flicks, star in this movie, which promises, "You don't have to go to Texas for a chainsaw massacre!" Sounds lovely. While not rated by the MPAA, the picture would probably qualify for an X rating.

1983   85 minutes

PIRANHA
★★★

DIRECTOR: Joe Dante
CAST: Bradford Dillman, Kevin McCarthy, Heather Menzies, Keenan Wynn

Director Joe Dante (Gremlins) and writer John Sayles (Return of the Secaucus 7; Brother from Another Planet) sent up Jaws in this nifty, gag-filled 1978 horror film. Full of scares and chuckles, with stars Bradford Dillman, Kevin McCarthy, and Heather Menzies. Rated R.

1978   92 minutes

PIRANHA PART TWO: THE SPAWNING
★

DIRECTOR: James Cameron
CAST: Tricia O'Neil, Steve Marachuk, Lance Henriksen, Leslie Graves

Sorry sequel to Piranha by the man who would later grace us with The Terminator. A mutated strain of piranha (with the ability to fly, no less) launches an air and sea tirade of violence against a group of vacationers at a tropical resort. Interesting idea poorly executed. The action bogs down time and time again to make way for "character development," leading to extreme boredom. Best sequence is the opening credits, with bizarre visuals and ominous music that trick the viewer into thinking this is going to be a great movie. No such luck. Rated R for mild gore.

1981   88 minutes

PIT AND THE PENDULUM, THE
★★★

DIRECTOR: Roger Corman
CAST: Vincent Price, John Kerr, Barbara Steele, Luana Anders, Anthony Carbong

More stylish, low-budget Edgar Allan Poe–inspired terror with star Vincent Price and director Roger Corman reteaming for this release. This is for fans of the series only.

1961   80 minutes

PLAY MISTY FOR ME
★★★★

DIRECTOR: Clint Eastwood

CAST: Clint Eastwood, Jessica Walter, Donna Mills, John Larch, Irene Hervey

A suspenseful shocker in which director-star Clint Eastwood, playing a disc jockey, is stalked by a crazed "fan" (Jessica Walter). It puts goosebumps on your goosebumps and marked an auspicious directorial debut for the squinty-eyed star. Rated R.

1971   102 minutes

PLUMBER, THE
★★★½

DIRECTOR: Peter Weir

CAST: Ivar Kants, Judy Morris, Robert Coleby

A slightly unhinged plumber completely destroys a young couple's bathroom and begins to terrorize the woman of the house during his visits to make the repairs. A very black comedy-horror-film from the director of *Witness*. Originally made for Australian television, this one is worth your attention. No rating (contains some strong language).

1980   76 minutes

POLTERGEIST
★★★★★

DIRECTOR: Tobe Hopper

CAST: Craig T. Nelson, JoBeth Williams, Beatrice Straight, Dominique Dunne

The ultimate screen ghost story, *Poltergeist* is guaranteed to raise goosepimples while keeping viewers marvelously entertained. What *The Haunting* and *The Legend of Hell House* attempted, this Steven Spielberg production achieves— and then some. Though directed by Tobe Hooper (*Texas Chainsaw Massacre*), it definitely bears the Spielberg stamp. A sort of *Close Encounters* of the supernatural, it's a scary story about the plight of a suburban family whose home suddenly becomes a house of horrors. Rated PG for tense situations.

1982   114 minutes

POLTERGEIST II: THE OTHERSIDE
★★

DIRECTOR: Brian Gibson

CAST: JoBeth Williams, Craig T. Nelson, Heather O'Rourke, Oliver Robins, Zelda Rubinstein, Will Sampson, Julian Beck, Geraldine Fitzgerald

Mere months (screen time) after their last film adventure, the stalwart Freeling family is up to its eyeballs in spooks again—although the ghosts stay backstage while another collection of effects parades before the audience. Coherence and common sense aren't in much evidence, and—in the real world—the Freeling adults probably could be charged with child endangerment. Although Julian Beck is a uniquely ghoulish villain, and Will Sampson lends credibility to the notion of "good Native American magic," the whole project collapses under its own weight. Some truly fine design work by H. R. Giger is all but unnoticed, due to poor editing. Rated PG-13 for intensity and violence.

1986   90 minutes

POWER, THE
★½

DIRECTOR: Jeffrey Obrow, Stephen Carpenter
CAST: Susan Stokey, Warren Lincoln, Lisa Erickson

Although the creators of this low-budget horror flick deserve a certain amount of credit for trying to make more than just another stab-'em, slash-'em horror gore fest, this is nowhere near a classic. It has a nearly incomprehensible story in which a centuries-old Aztec idol that holds the culture's forces of evil is unearthed by some youngsters, who must face the consequences. Teenagers who like to be scared and don't care too much about plot, performance, and directorial execution might enjoy it. For the rest of us, however, The Power is just more of the same old thing. Rated R for profanity, violence, and gore.

1980   87 minutes

PREMATURE BURIAL, THE
★★★

DIRECTOR: Roger Corman
CAST: Ray Milland, Hazel Court, Richard Ney

A medical student's paranoia about being buried alive causes his worst fears to come true. Roger Corman's only Poe-derived film without Vincent Price. Although eventually released by A.I.P., the movie was originally produced for Pathè Distribution, which couldn't acquire Price, due to his contract with A.I.P. Film has the usual lush Corman atmosphere but is less ambitious and more stagey than his other Poe translations. Lacking Price's playful and hammy acting style, it all seems too serious.

1962   81 minutes

PREY, THE
★

DIRECTOR: Edwin Scott Brown
CAST: Debbie Thureson, Steve Bond, Lori Lethin, Robert Wald, Gayle Gannes, Philip Wenckus, Jackson Bostwick, Jackie Coogan

Run-of-the-mill horror flick complete with young, attractive adults having sex before they get slaughtered (Horror Film Cliché No. 398) and a lot of scenes shot form the monster's point of view as he closes in on his prey (Horror Film Cliché No. 279) accompanied by a loud heartbeat (Horror Film Cliché No. 194). Six young hikers go up into the woods, where they run into a ghoul who hunts them down and has them for dinner. Yum. Rated R for sex, nudity, and violence.

1980   80 minutes

PROM NIGHT
★★

DIRECTOR: Paul Lynch
CAST: Jamie Lee Curtis, Leslie Nielsen, Casey Stevens

This okay slasher flick has a group of high-school students being systematically slaughtered as payment for the accidental death of one of their friends when they were all children. Watchable enough, though Leslie Nielsen looks as if he's about to break up while delivering his rather absurd dialogue. Rated R.

1980   92 minutes

PROPHECY
★

DIRECTOR: John Frankenheimer
CAST: Talia Shire, Robert Foxworth, Armand Assante, Richard Dysart, Victoria Racimo

A dumb ecological-horror thriller with laughable special effects. Rated PG.

1979   95 minutes

PSYCHO
★★★★★

DIRECTOR: Alfred Hitchcock
CAST: Janet Leigh, Anthony Perkins, Vera Miles, John Gavin, John McIntire, Simon Oakland, John Anderson, Frank Albertson, Patricia Hitchcock

The quintessential shocker, which started a whole genre of films about psychotic killers enacting mayhem on innocent victims, still holds up well today. If all you can remember about this film is its famous murder of Janet Leigh in the shower, you might want to give it a second look. Anthony Perkins's performance and the ease with which Hitchcock maneuvers your emotions make *Psycho* far superior to the numerous films that tried to duplicate it.

1960   B & W 109 minutes

PSYCHO II
★★★

DIRECTOR: Richard Franklin
CAST: Anthony Perkins, Vera Miles, Meg Tilly, Robert Loggia, Dennis Franz, Hugh Gillin

Picking up where Alfred Hitchcock's original left off, this sequel begins with Norman Bates (Anthony Perkins) being declared sane after twenty-two years in an asylum. Old Normie goes right back to the Bates Motel, and strange things begin to happen. Directed with exquisite taste and respect for the old master by Richard Franklin. It's suspenseful, scary, and funny. Rated R for nudity, profanity, and violence.

1983   113 minutes

PSYCHO III
★★

DIRECTOR: Anthony Perkins
CAST: Anthony Perkins, Diana Scarwid, Jeff Fahey, Roberta Maxwell, Hugh Gillin, Lee Garlington, Robert Alan Browne

Second follow-up to *Psycho* works mainly because actor-director Anthony Perkins understands poor Norman Bates inside and out. Although lensed beautifully by Bruce Surtees and infused with a deliciously macabre wit, the film fails in the most critical area: creating suspense. There are no mysteries in Charles Edward Pogue's script, and grisly humor cannot mask that missing ingredient. Many of the camera angles, bits of dialogue, and plot points fondly echo Alfred Hitchcock's original, but it's impossible to create tension when everything is so straightforward. The film concludes with a chaotic plot summation that reduces the picture to the level of a mindless soap opera. Rated R for gory violence.

1986   93 minutes

PSYCHOMANIA
★★½

DIRECTOR: Don Sharp
CAST: George Sanders, Nicky Henson, Mary Larkin, Patrick Holt, Beryl Reid

This British-made film may better be called *Motorcycle-Mania*, because it's about a motorcycle gang. They call themselves the "Living Dead" gang, because they committed a group suicide and only came back to life through a pact with the devil. As the undead, they terrorize and murder people who are unfortunate enough to encounter them. The film moves slowly and is a little dull. Includes lots of violence. Rated R.

1971   95 minutes

PSYCHO SISTERS
★★★★

DIRECTOR: Reginald LeBorg
CAST: Susan Strasberg, Faith Domergue, Charles Knox Robinson

After her husband is killed, a woman goes to stay with her sister—her sister that has only recently emerged from an insane asylum and is still hearing their dead mother's voice. This film is a classic of the early 1970s horror/gore/exploitation cycle, and it reminds one of Hammer, A.I.P., and the best of Roger Corman. Do not expect too much, and make sure you break out plenty of popcorn and soda when sitting down to watch it. Rated PG for mild violence.

1972   76 minutes

PUMA MAN, THE
½

DIRECTOR: Alberto DeMartino
CAST: Donald Pleasence, Sydne Rome, Walter George Alton

Humorless Italian junk about a man given extraordinary powers to fight evil. Low-budget and lowbrow, with insulting special effects. Thankfully, the movie was never released in the U.S.

1980   80 minutes

Q
★★★★

DIRECTOR: Larry Cohen
CAST: Michael Moriarty, David Carradine, Candy Clark, Richard Roundtree, John Capordice, James Dixon, Malachy McCourt

This is an old-fashioned giant monster film. The stop-motion animation is excellent, the acting (done tongue-in-cheek) is perfect, and the moments of humor are well worth waiting for. The story revolves around the arrival of a giant flying lizard in New York City. A series of ritualistic murders follows and points to the monster being Quetzelcoatl (the flying serpent god of the Aztecs). An ex-junkie stumbles upon the nest and blackmails the city for millions for the nest's location. Rated R.

1982   93 minutes

RABID
★★

DIRECTOR: David Cronenberg
CAST: Marilyn Chambers, Frank Moore, Joe Silver, Patricia Gage, Susan Roman

This horror flick has become a cult favorite despite many repulsive scenes. In it, porn queen Marilyn Chambers lives on human blood after a motorcycle accident operation. For fans of director David Cronenberg only. Rated R.

1977   90 minutes

RACE WITH THE DEVIL
★★

DIRECTOR: Jack Starrett
CAST: Warren Oates, Peter Fonda, Loretta Swit, Lara Parker

Good cast and exciting chase sequences can't save this muddled yarn, about two couples who accidentally intrude on a witches' sacrificial ceremony while on a vacation that literally becomes "hell on Earth" when they're discovered observing the proceedings. Rated PG for violence.

1975   88 minutes

RAGGEDY MAN
★★★½

DIRECTOR: Jack Fisk
CAST: Sissy Spacek, Eric Roberts, William Sanderson, Tracy Walter, Sam Shepard, Henry Thomas, Carey Hollis Jr.

Sissy Spacek gives another outstanding performance as a World War II divorcée trying to raise two sons and improve their lives in a small Texas Gulf Coast town. *Raggedy Man* is a curious mixture of styles. It begins as a character study and ends like a horror film. But it works. Rated PG for nudity and violence.

1981 94 minutes

RATS ARE COMING!, THE WEREWOLVES ARE HERE!, THE
★

DIRECTOR: Andy Milligan
CAST: Hope Stansbury, Jackie Skarvellis

England is besieged by a pack of werewolves in the 1800s. Boring horror film was made on shoestring budget, and it shows. Also featured in this nonsense are the pets of one of the werewolves' daughters—killer rats! Good title, bad movie. Rated R.

1972 92 minutes

RAVEN, THE
★★★★

DIRECTOR: Roger Corman
CAST: Boris Karloff, Vincent Price, Peter Lorre, Jack Nicholson, Hazel Court, Olive Sturgess

The best of the Roger Corman–directed Edgar Allan Poe adaptations, this release benefits from a humorous screenplay by Richard Matheson and tongue-in-cheek portrayals by Boris Karloff, Vincent Price, and Peter Lorre. Look for Jack Nicholson in an early role as Lorre's mincing son.

1963 86 minutes

RAVEN AND THE BLACK CAT, THE
★★★★

DIRECTOR: Edgar G. Ulmer, Lew Landers
CAST: Boris Karloff, Bela Lugosi

A first-rate repacking of two 1930s Boris Karloff–Bela Lugosi shockers. The first is a straightforward thriller about a mad scientist (Lugosi) enamored of Edgar Allan Poe's murder devices who uses surgery to deform a fugitive (Karloff) and thus force him to do his evil will. The second is Edgar G. Ulmer's surrealistic, beautifully designed thriller about a neurotic doctor (Lugosi) out to get revenge on the satanist (Karloff) who stole his wife. Both are acknowledged, but slightly dated, classics.

1934/35 B & W 126 minutes

RAZORBACK
★★★½

DIRECTOR: Russell Mulcahy
CAST: Gregory Harrison

This Australian film, concerning a giant pig that is terrorizing a small Aussie village, surprises the viewer by turning into a great little film. The special effects, photography, editing, and acting are great. Rated R.

1983 95 minutes

RE-ANIMATOR
★★★★

DIRECTOR: Stuart Gordon
CAST: Bruce Abbott, Barbara Crampton, David Gale, Robert Sampson, Jeffrey Combs

Stylishly grotesque and gory filming of H. P. Lovecraft's "Herbert West, Reanimator" hits the mark where all previous efforts to put this master storyteller on celluloid have failed. From the opening credits (stolen from Bernard Herrmann's intensely riveting score from the original *Psycho*) this film moves in a rhythmic cadence toward its inevitable conclusion, uniting the principals and the audience in a grim blood bath that is horrifying yet so outrageous that it evokes as many nervous laughs and giggles as screams. This is Grand Guignol in the classic sense as we follow brilliant young medical student Herbert West in his deranged efforts to bring the dead back to life to prove that he's not just another crackpot. Some outrageous scenes highlight this terror entry and, although very well done, it's not for the squeamish.

1985   86 minutes

REAR WINDOW
★★★★★

DIRECTOR: Alfred Hitchcock
CAST: James Stewart, Raymond Burr, Grace Kelly, Wendell Corey, Thelma Ritter, Judith Evelyn

James Stewart plays a magazine photographer who, confined to a wheelchair because of a broken leg, seeks diversion in watching his neighbors, often with a telephoto lens. He soon becomes convinced that one neighbor (Raymond Burr) has murdered his spouse and dismembered the body. One of the director's best, *Rear Window* will keep you fascinated and laughing right up until the edge-of-your-seat climax.

1954   112 minutes

RED HOUSE, THE
★★★½

DIRECTOR: Delmer Daves

CAST: Edward G. Robinson, Lon McCallister, Allene Roberts, Julie London, Judith Anderson, Rory Calhoun, Ona Munson

A gripping suspense melodrama enhanced by a musical score by Miklos Rozsa. Edward G. Robinson employs Rory Calhoun to keep the curious away from the decaying old house of the title deep in the woods near his farm. But his niece and a young hired hand *must* learn the secret. Allene Roberts is endearing as the niece, with Lon McCallister just right as the "hand" who loves her. Robinson is excellent as the guilt-ridden uncle who harbors a secret too horrible to tell!

1947   B & W 100 minutes

REINCARNATION OF PETER PROUD, THE
★★

DIRECTOR: J. Lee Thompson
CAST: Michael Sarrazin, Jennifer O'Neill, Margot Kidder, Cornelia Sharpe

Laughably melodramatic tale of bewildered Michael Sarrazin, who—through dream research—recalls having been murdered in a previous life. Much to the dismay of girlfriend Cornelia Sharpe (bad, as always), he returns to the scene of the crime and falls in love with "his" daughter. Unfortunately, "his" former wife, Margot Kidder, isn't about to sit still for such rubbish. Turgid direction, contrived plot, adapted by Max Erlich from his not-much-better book. Rated R for considerable nudity.

1975   104 minutes

RETURN OF THE ALIEN'S DEADLY SPAWN, THE
★★

DIRECTOR: Douglas McKeown

CAST: Charles George Hildebrandt, Tom De Franco, Jean Tafler, Karen Tigue

Blood-filled horror film about alien creatures from outer space who kill and destroy anyone and everything that gets in their way. Lots of gore, ripped flesh, off-the-wall humor. For people who like sick movies. Rated R for violence, profanity, and gore.

1984   90 minutes

RETURN OF THE FLY, THE
★★★

DIRECTOR: Edward L. Bernds
CAST: Vincent Price, Brett Halsey, David Frankham

In this fine sequel to *The Fly*, the son of the original insect makes the same mistake as his father . . . with identical results. Effective film benefits from stark black-and-white photography and solid effects. Watch out for the guinea pig scene!

1959   B & W   80 minutes

RETURN OF THE LIVING DEAD, THE
★★★★

DIRECTOR: Dan O'Bannon
CAST: Clu Gulager, James Karen, Don Calfa, Thom Mathews

Extremely gory horror film produced with a great deal of style and ample amounts of comedy as well. The residents of a small New Orleans cemetery are brought back to life after accidental exposure to a strange chemical, and they're hungry . . . for human brains. It's up to the employees of the nearby Uneeda Medical Supply warehouse, along with a gang of punks, to discover a way of stopping the creatures before we're all turned into lunch. While it's all tongue-in-cheek for the most part, there are still many horrifying moments

as this clever movie manages to sustain a perfect balance between absolute hilarity and sheer terror throughout. The only drawback, as stated, is that it's as gruesome as can be. Viewers who are the least bit squeamish are advised to stay clear; all others—hang on! Rated R for violence, gore, nudity, and language.

1985   91 minutes

RETURN OF THE VAMPIRE, THE
★★★

DIRECTOR: Lew Lander, Kurt Neuman
CAST: Bela Lugosi, Frieda Inescort, Nina Foch, Miles Mander, Roland Varno, Matt Willis

Set during World War II, this surprisingly good vampire tale has the supposedly destroyed fiend, Armand Tesla (Bela Lugosi), unearthed by a German bombing raid on London to resume his reign of terror after twenty-three years of undead sleep. Exceptional production is marked by offbeat camera work, strong characters, and believable dialogue by screenwriter Griffin Jay. Also noteworthy is Columbia's use of a pristine print for this release, and the hi-fi sound is incredibly clean.

1943   B & W   69 minutes

REVENGE
★★

DIRECTOR: Jud Taylor
CAST: Shelley Winters, Stuart Whitman, Bradford Dillman, Roger Perry

Made for television, this has Shelley Winters out for—you guessed it—revenge for her daughter's rape. Not as bad as it could have been.

1971   78 minutes

REVENGE OF THE ZOMBIES
★★½

DIRECTOR: Steve Sekely
CAST: John Carradine, Robert Lowery, Gale Storm, Veda Ann Borg, Mantan Moreland, Mauritz Hugo, Bob Steele

As soon as the Hollywood backlot native walks across the foggy bog in baggy underwear and begins to wail "Whoooooo," you know this is going to be one of those films. And it sure is, with mad scientist John Carradine, his zombie wife Veda Ann Borg (in her best role), do-gooders Gale Storm and Robert Lowery, and "feets do yo' stuff" Mantan Moreland aiding/escaping zombies and Nazis in this low budget howler. Former cowboy and serial star Bob Steele plays a Nazi in this one, his performances in *The Big Sleep* and *The Enforcer* still before him. John Carradine is at his hammy best and Gale Storm displays the spunk that will make her name a household word in 1950s television. Mantan Moreland adds the finishing touch to this outrageous horror film with his usual low-key, subdued form of ethnic comedy. Lots of fun to watch.

1943   B & W   61 minutes

REVENGE OF THE DEAD

DIRECTOR: Pupi Avati
CAST: Gabriele Lavia, Anne Canovas

Talky Italian film with misleading title. It's not part of George Romero's series, or even a bad imitation. It's an incredibly dull movie. Impossible to tell what it's about or why it was made. Rated R for violence and profanity.

1984   98 minutes

RIPPER, THE

DIRECTOR: Christopher Lewis
CAST: Tom Schreier, Wade Tower, Mona VanPernis, Andrea Adams

In this poorly filmed modernization of the Jack the Ripper legend, a college professer finds a ring, originally belonging to the nineteenth-century killer, which when worn turns him into—yes, you guessed it—Jack the Ripper. Amateurish throughout, this film has nothing to recommend it, even to die-hard fans of the genre.

1985   104 minutes

ROAD GAMES
★★½

DIRECTOR: Richard Franklin
CAST: Stacy Keach, Jamie Lee Curtis, Marion Howard, Grant Page, Bill Stacey

An elusive latter-day Jack the Ripper is loose in Australia. He cruises desolate areas in a mysterious, customized van, picking up female hitchhikers and then raping, killing, and dismembering them. Even though director Richard Franklin (*Psycho II*) actually studied under Alfred Hitchcock at USC's renowned film school, he doesn't show any of his mentor's ability here. While it has its moments, *Road Games* is essentially a thriller without any thrills. Rated PG.

1981   100 minutes

ROBOT MONSTER

DIRECTOR: Phil Tucker
CAST: George Nader, Gregory Moffett, Claudia Barrett, Selena Royle, John Mylong

Take a desolate-looking canyon outside of Los Angeles, borrow

Lawrence Welk's bubble machine, and add a typical family on an outing and a man dressed in a gorilla suit wearing a diving helmet, and you have a serious competitor for the worst film of all time. This absurd drama of the last days of Earth and its conquest by robot gorillas has long been considered the most inept of all science-fiction films and shares the same closet space with *Plan 9 from Outer Space*, *Bride of the Monster*, and *Mesa of the Lost Women*. This film is a lot more fun to watch than many of its serious counterparts of the 1950s and puts the late Phil Tucker on a par with directors Edward D. Wood Jr. and William Beaudine as one of the true kings of hoke. Try and count how many times you can see the same scene reversed and the same location used over and over. This is a must-see for all fans of truly terrible films.

1953   B & W   63 minutes

ROLLERCOASTER
★★★★½

DIRECTOR: James Goldstone
CAST: George Segal, Richard Widmark, Timothy Bottoms, Susan Strasberg, Henry Fonda

Fast-paced suspense film about an extortionist (Timothy Bottoms) blowing up rides in some of the nation's most famous amusement parks, and the efforts of a county safety inspector (George Segal) and an FBI agent (Richard Widmark) to nab him. Very well done, this much-maligned film has great action, crisp dialogue, and a brilliant, nail-biting climax seamlessly combined to provide a first-class entertainment. Rated PG for language and violence.

1977   119 minutes

ROPE
★★★★½

DIRECTOR: Alfred Hitchcock
CAST: James Stewart, John Dall, Farley Granger, Cedric Hardwicke

This recently resurrected Alfred Hitchcock film is based in part on the famous Leopold-Loeb thrill-murder case in Chicago in the 1920s. In it, the two killers divulge clues to their horrific escapade at a dinner party, to the growing suspicion of the other guests. It's one of Hitchcock's best.

1948   80 minutes

ROSEMARY'S BABY
★★★★

DIRECTOR: Roman Polanski
CAST: Mia Farrow, John Cassavetes, Ruth Gordon, Ralph Bellamy, Elisha Cook Jr., Maurice Evans, Patsy Kelly

This is the first movie to open up the subject of the modern-day practice of the occult. Mia Farrow is a young woman forced by her husband (John Cassavetes) into an unholy arrangement with a group of devil-worshipers. The suspense is sustained as she is made aware that those friendly people around her are not what they seem. Ruth Gordon is priceless in her Oscar-winning role as one of the seemingly normal neighbors. Rated R.

1968   136 minutes

RUBY
★★

DIRECTOR: Curtis Harrington
CAST: Piper Laurie, Stuart Whitman, Roger Davis, Janit Baldwin

A sleazy drive-in movie theater is the setting for this unexciting horror film about a young girl possessed by the homicidal ghost of a dead gangster. Rated R for gore.

1977   84 minutes

RUDE AWAKENING
★★½

DIRECTOR: Peter Sasdy
CAST: Denholm Elliott, James Laurenson, Pat Heywood

In another of Elvira's "Thriller Video" series, and one of the best, a real estate broker finds himself sucked into dreams that seem like reality; or is it the other way around? It sounds standard, but it's better than you would think. Definitely worth a look.

1982   60 minutes

RUN STRANGER RUN
★★★½

DIRECTOR: Darren McGavin
CAST: Patricia Neal, Cloris Leachman, Ron Howard, Bobby Darren

Ron Howard (formerly of TV's "The Andy Griffith Show" and "Happy Days" and a top movie director these days) takes a detour from comedy in this horror film. He plays a teenager searching for his biological parents in a seaside town. Once there, he discovers that some of the town inhabitants have been disappearing. Unfortunately, the disappearances are closely linked to his past. Cloris Leachman plays Howard's real mother, and Bobby Darren is her boyfriend. Patricia Neal turns out to be Howard's aunt, and her family strongly resembles the Munsters. Overall, this film keeps viewer interest without dwelling on the slash-'em-up theme. Rated PG for gore.

1973   92 minutes

SABOTAGE
★★★

DIRECTOR: Alfred Hitchcock
CAST: Sylvia Sidney, Oscar Homolka, John Loder, Desmond Tester, Joyce Barbour

One of the first of Alfred Hitchcock's characteristic thrillers. London's being terrorized by an unknown bomber, and movie theater cashier Sylvia Sidney begins to fear that her husband (Oscar Homolka), who owns the theater, is behind it all. Hitch was still experimenting, and his use of shadows and sound effects betrays the influence of German silent films. The master director made one of his few artistic mistakes here: Sidney's young son, told to deliver a package—which, unknown to him, contains a bomb—by a certain hour, wastes time with youthful distractions and draws out the suspense to an unbelievable degree, until— BOOM!—he's killed when the bomb goes off. Audiences never forgave Hitch for that one.

1936   B & W   76 minutes

SABOTEUR
★★★★½

DIRECTOR: Alfred Hitchcock
CAST: Robert Cummings, Priscilla Lane, Norman Lloyd, Otto Kruger

Outstanding Alfred Hitchcock film about a World War II factory worker (Robert Cummings) turned fugitive after he's unjustly accused of sabotage. The briskly paced story follows his efforts to elude police while he tries to unmask the real culprit. Hitchcock is in top form in this first-rate thriller. A humdinger of a climax.

1942   B & W   108 minutes

SALEM'S LOT
★★★★

DIRECTOR: Tobe Hooper
CAST: David Soul, James Mason, Reggie Nalder, Lance Kerwin, Elisha Cook Jr., Ed Flanders

This story of vampires in modern-day New England is one of the better adaptations of Stephen King's novels on film. Some real chills go along with an intelligent script in what was originally a two-part TV movie. Be prepared for some frightening scenes.

1979   112 minutes

SATAN'S SCHOOL FOR GIRLS
★★½

DIRECTOR: David Lowell Rich
CAST: Pamela Franklin, Kate Jackson, Roy Thinnes, Cheryl Ladd

Originally made as an ABC Movie of the Week, this decent shocker concerns a series of apparent "suicides" at a prominent girls' school, but we all know better. Interesting story has good acting and some creepy atmosphere, but the typical TV ending falls flat.

1973   74 minutes

SATURDAY THE 14TH
★

DIRECTOR: Howard R. Cohen
CAST: Richard Benjamin, Paula Prentiss, Jeffrey Tambor, Rosemary DeCamp

Richard Benjamin and Paula Prentiss (who are husband and wife in real life) star in this low-budget horror comedy about a family that moves into a haunted house. Thanks to the curiosity of their son, Billy, they find themselves at the mercy of the Book of Evil and its onslaught of terrors. The jokes are tired, the monsters insipid, and the

plot weak. It's a good horror movie for kids who don't really want to be scared. Rated PG.

1981   75 minutes

SAVAGE ATTRACTION
★★★★

DIRECTOR: Frank Shields
CAST: Kerry Mack, Ralph Schicha, Judy Nunn, Clare Binney

A psychotic German, Walter, becomes sadistically obsessed with a lovely Australian girl, Christine, in this bizarre but true tale. He uses both mental and physical cruelty to keep her with him. The suspense is never lacking as viewers continually wonder, What will he do to her next? Rated R for sex, sadism, nudity, and violence.

1983   93 minutes

SAVAGES
★★★

DIRECTOR: Lee H. Katzin
CAST: Andy Griffith, Sam Bottoms, Noah Beery, James Best

Man hunts man! Sam Bottoms is guiding Andy Griffith on a hunt in the desert when Griffith goes bananas and begins a savage, relentless pursuit of Bottoms. A sandy rendition of the famous short story, "The Most Dangerous Game." Thrilling, suspenseful, intriguing to watch. Made for TV.

1974   78 minutes

SAVAGE WEEKEND
★

DIRECTOR: John Mason Kirby
CAST: Christopher Allport, James Doerr, Marilyn Hamlin, William Sanderson

Several couples head out from the big city into the backwoods to watch a boat being built, but they are killed off one by one. The only reason this movie earns any stars is for talented actor William Sanderson's performance as a demented lunatic who may or may not be the killer in this very drab, boring thriller. The sequences with him are interesting, but the rest of this film looks as if it were made by high-schoolers. Rated R for nudity, simulated sex, violence.

1979   88 minutes

SCALPEL
★

DIRECTOR: John Grissmer
CAST: Robert Lansing, Judith Chapman, Arlen Dean Snyder, David Scarroll, Sandy Martin

Robert Lansing is a cunning, unscrupulous plastic surgeon who transforms a young accident victim into the spitting image of his missing daughter to pull an inheritance swindle. A rather dull melodrama sinks to deplorable depths when it uses graphic, repulsive scenes of surgery. Rated R.

1976   96 minutes

SCANNERS
★★★½

DIRECTOR: David Cronenberg
CAST: Jennifer O'Neill, Patrick McGoohan, Stephen Lack, Lawrence Dane

From its first shocking scene—in which a character's head explodes, spewing blood, flesh, and bone all over—Scanners poses a challenge to its viewers: How much can you take? Shock specialist David Cronenberg (The Brood and Rabid) wrote and directed this potent film, about a bloody war among a group of people with formidable extrasensory powers. If feeling decidedly queasy after being shocked and nauseated by watching a movie is your idea of a good time, then don't miss it.

But remember: You have been warned. Rated R.

1981   102 minutes

SCARS OF DRACULA
★★★

DIRECTOR: Roy Ward Baker
CAST: Christopher Lee, Dennis Waterman, Jenny Hanley, Christopher Matthews

A young couple searching for the husband's brother follow the trail to Dracula's castle, and soon regret it. Compares well with other films in the series, thanks primarily to Christopher Lee's dynamite portrayal of the Count, and the first-rate direction of horror veteran Roy Ward Baker. Rated R.

1970   94 minutes

SCHIZOID
★½

DIRECTOR: David Paulsen
CAST: Klaus Kinski, Mariana Hill, Craig Wasson, Christopher Lloyd

This is an unimaginative slasher flick with typically gory special effects. Not for the squeamish. Rated R.

1980   91 minutes

SCREAM AND SCREAM AGAIN
★★★½

DIRECTOR: Gordon Hessler
CAST: Vincent Price, Peter Cushing, Christopher Lee, Alfred Marks, Judy Huxtable, Christopher Matthews, Michael Gothard, Marshall Jones

A top-notch cast propels in this chilling, suspenseful story of a crazed scientist (Vincent Price) attempting to create a race of superbeings while a baffled police force copes with a series of brutal murders that may or may not be related. Complex film benefits from polished performances by some horror greats, who look very comfortable in their respective roles. Based on the novel *The Disoriented Man*, by Peter Saxon. Rated PG for violence, language, brief nudity.

1970   95 minutes

SCREAM GREATS, VOL. 1
★★★

DIRECTOR: Damon Santostefano

The first in a projected series by *Starlog Magazine*. A documentary on horror effects master Tom Savini. Gory highlights are featured from many of his movies, including *Friday the 13th, Creepshow,* and *Dawn of the Dead.* Savini shows his secrets, explains his techniques, and tries to justify what he does for a living. Funny, disgusting, and fascinating, but too talky for repeat viewing. Unrated, contains massive but clinical gore.

1986   52 minutes

SCREAMERS
🐾

DIRECTOR: Sergio Martino, Dan T. Miller

CAST: Claudio Cassinelli, Richard Johnson, Joseph Cotten

Just what we needed, another low-budget horror film. Claudio Cassinelli, who is reportedly Italy's most popular male star, finds himself stranded on an uncharted island and at the mercy of a mad doctor (Richard Johnson), a crazy inventor (Joseph Cotten), and a bunch of underpaid extras in native costumes. Rated R.

1979   90 minutes

SEANCE ON A WET AFTERNOON
★★★★½

DIRECTOR: Bryan Forbes

CAST: Kim Stanley, Richard Attenborough, Patrick Magee, Nanette Newman

This is an absolutely fabulous movie. An unbalanced medium (Kim Stanley) involves her meek husband (Richard Attenborough) in a kidnapping scheme that brings about their downfall. Brilliant acting by all, working from a superb script. No rating, but some intense sequences.

1964   B & W 115 minutes

SEDUCTION, THE
★

DIRECTOR: David Schmoeller

CAST: Morgan Fairchild, Andrew Stevens, Vince Edwards, Michael Sarrazin

This is a silly suspense film about a lady newscaster (Morgan Fairchild) stalked by an unbalanced admirer (Andrew Stevens) patched together from *The Fan* and all those Brian De Palma movies combining implausible menace with soapy eroticism. Rated R for nudity, sex, and violence.

1982   104 minutes

SEE NO EVIL
★★★½

DIRECTOR: Richard Fleischer

CAST: Mia Farrow, Dorothy Alison, Robin Bailey

Chilling, suspenseful yarn follows a young blind woman (Mia Farrow) as she tries to escape the clutches of a ruthless killer who has done away with her entire family at their quiet country farm. Mia Farrow is very convincing as the maniac's next target, and there are enough shocks along the way to please the most hardened horror fan. Rated PG for tense moments.

1971   90 minutes

SENDER, THE
★★★

DIRECTOR: Roger Christian
CAST: Kathryn Harrold, Shirley Knight, Paul Freeman

Roger Christian, winner of Oscars for best set direction (*Star Wars*) and best short subject (*The Dollar Bottom*), makes his directorial debut with this horror film, which features bleeding mirrors and rats coming out of people's mouths. Rated R.

1982   91 minutes

SENTINEL, THE
★

DIRECTOR: Michael Winner
CAST: Chris Sarandon, Cristina Raines, Martin Balsam, John Carradine, José Ferrer, Ava Gardner, Arthur Kennedy, Burgess Meredith, Sylvia Miles, Deborah Raffin, Eli Wallach

Mr. Michael Winner once again causes the stomach to churn and the throat to gag. This is a dismal genre piece about a woman (Cristina Raines) who unknowingly moves into an apartment building over the gates of hell. *The Sentinel* doesn't have much suspense, nor does it deliver many shocks. Instead, it has a sort of nauseating relentlessness, which builds slowly to a nightmarish climax. Rated R for nudity, profanity, and violence.

1977   93 minutes

SEVERED ARM, THE
★★½

DIRECTOR:
CAST: Paul Carr, Deborah Walley, Marvin Kaplan

Before being rescued from a cave-in, a group of trapped mine explorers cut off the arm of one of the men as food for the others. Many years later, the survivors of the expedition find are systematically slaughtered by an unseen psychopath. This low-budget independent production is fairly suspenseful, though the acting is often listless and the gore a bit excessive. Rated R.

1973   86 minutes

SHINING, THE
★★½

DIRECTOR: Stanley Kubrick
CAST: Jack Nicholson, Shelley Duvall, Scatman Crothers

A struggling writer (Jack Nicholson) accepts a position as the caretaker of a large summer resort hotel during the winter season. The longer he and his family spend in the hotel, the more Nicholson becomes possessed by it. Considering the talent involved, this is a major disappointment. Director Stanley Kubrick keeps things at a snail's pace, and Nicholson's performance approaches high camp. Rated R for violence and language.

1980   146 minutes

SHOCK WAVES (DEATH CORPS)
★½

DIRECTOR: Ken Wiederhorn
CAST: Peter Cushing, Brooke Adams, John Carradine, Fred Buch

Vacationers stumble upon a crazed ex-Nazi controlling an army of underwater zombies. It's just as stupid as it sounds. The sopping-wet zombies wear full dress uniforms, perky little swimming goggles, and a stunning complement of seaweed accessories. They're a riot. Rated PG.

1977   86 minutes

SHOUT, THE
★★★

DIRECTOR: Jerzy Skolimowski
CAST: Alan Bates, Susannah York, John Hurt, Robert Stephens, Tim Curry

Enigmatic British chiller about a wanderer's chilling effect on an unsuspecting couple. He possesses the ancient power to kill people by screaming. Well made, with an excellent cast. The film may be too offbeat for some viewers. Rated R.

1979   87 minutes

SILENT NIGHT, DEADLY NIGHT
★

DIRECTOR: Charles E. Sellier Jr.
CAST: Lilyan Chauvin, Gilmer McCormick, Robert Brian Wilson, Toni Nero

This is the one that caused such a commotion among parents' groups for its depiction of Santa Claus as a homicidal killer. It was pulled from release just a week into its theatrical run, only to resurface on video. It will serve to satisfy the curiosity of those who want to see what all the fuss was about. What they'll find is no more than another routine slasher flick. A kid sees his parents slaughtered by a hitchhiker in a Santa Claus suit and is, understandably, haunted by the memory for years. Ten years later, while working as a stock boy at a toy store, he is asked to dress up as St. Nick for Christmas, which sends him off the deep end and out on a killing spree. Fortunately, this occurs late in the film, and the tormented youth (not to mention the poor viewer) is soon put out of his misery. No rating, but contains gobs of nudity and violent bloodshed.

1984   92 minutes

SILENT PARTNER, THE
★★★★

DIRECTOR: Daryl Duke
CAST: Elliott Gould, Christopher Plummer, Susannah York, John Candy

This suspense thriller is what they call a sleeper. It's an absolutely riveting tale about a bank teller (Elliott Gould) who, knowing of a robbery in advance, pulls a switch on a psychotic criminal (Christopher Plummer) and might not live to regret it. A Canadian production inventively directed by Daryl Duke, *Silent Partner* is a real find for movie buffs. But be forewarned; it has a couple of truly unsettling scenes of violence. Rated R.

1978   103 minutes

SILENT SCREAM
★★½

DIRECTOR: Denny Harris
CAST: Yvonne De Carlo, Barbara Steele, Avery Schreiber, Rebecca Balding

This is a well-done shock film with a semi-coherent plot and enough thrills to satisfy the teens. Rated R.

1980   87 minutes

SILVER BULLET
★★★★

DIRECTOR: Daniel Attias
CAST: Gary Busey, Everett McGill, Corey Haim, Megan Follows, James Gammon, Robin Groves, Leon Russom

A superior Stephen King horror film, this release moves like the projectile after which it was named. From the opening scene, in which a railroad worker (gloriously played by that underrated character actor James Gammon) meets his gruesome demise at the claws of a werewolf, to the final confrontation between our heroes (Gary Busey and Corey Haim) and the hairy beast, it's an edge-of-your-seat winner. King, who adapted the screenplay from his novelette *Cycle of the Werewolf*, balances the terror with nice touches of humor; as things get very grisly at times, this offers a much-appreciated respite. Although a bit too gory in parts, *Silver Bullet* remains good, old tell-me-a-scary-story fun. Rated R for violence and gore.

1985   90 minutes

SISTERS
★★★★½
DIRECTOR: Brian De Palma
CAST: Margot Kidder, Charles Durning, Jennifer Salt, Barnard Hughes

A terrifying tale of two twin sisters (Margot Kidder), this is arguably Brian De Palma's best film to date. One is normal; the other is a dangerous psychopath. It's an extremely effective thriller on all levels. Charles Durning and Jennifer Salt give the stand-out performances in this release, which is not for the faint-hearted. Rated R for violence, nudity, and language.

1973   93 minutes

SKULLDUGGERY
★
DIRECTOR: Ota Richter
CAST: Thom Haverstock, Wendy Crewson, David Calderisi, David Main, Clark Johnson, Geordie Johnson

Thom Haverstock plays a costume store employee who inherits a satanic curse that sends him on a killing rampage. The soundtrack hints at black comedy and the board game motifs suggest the whole story is like a game, but these messages are not handled with enough skill to give the embellishments meaning of any worth to the viewer. Too odd to be taken seriously as a horror flick and not odd enough to be interesting. Terrible attempts at humor, too. Leave this one on the shelf for the Dungeons and Dragons freaks and devil worshipers. Not rated, but would earn a PG for sex, violence, and profanity.

1983   95 minutes

SLITHIS
★★
DIRECTOR: Stephen Traxler
CAST: Alan Blanchard, Judy Motulsky, Mello Alexandria, Dennis Lee Falt

Okay horror tale of a gruesome monster, derived from garbage and radiation in Southern California, and his reign of terror in and around the L.A. area. While earnestly done, the film just can't overcome its budget restrictions. Actual on-screen title: *Spawn of the Slithis*. Rated PG.

1978   92 minutes

SOLE SURVIVOR
★★
DIRECTOR: Thom Eberhardt
CAST: Anita Skinner, Kurt Johnson, Robin Davidson, Caren Larkey

A gory remake of a fine English suspense thriller of the same title—about the lone survivor of an airplane crash, haunted by the ghosts of those who died in the tragedy. A psychic tries to help this haunted woman by keeping the ghosts from killing her. Although there are some chills, this version pales in comparison to its predecessor. Fans of the supernatural will undoubtedly find this film entertaining, but you'd be better off tracking down the original with Robert Powell and Jenny Agutter. Rated R for sexual situations and violence.

1985   85 minutes

SON OF BLOB (BEWARE! THE BLOB)
★★

DIRECTOR: Larry Hagman
CAST: Robert Walker, Richard Stahl, Godfrey Cambridge, Carol Lynley, Larry Hagman, Cindy Williams, Shelly Berman, Marlene Clark, Gerrit Graham, Dick Van Patten

Larry Hagman made this sequel to *The Blob* in his low period between "I Dream of Jeannie" and "Dallas." It looks like he just got some friends together and decided to have some fun. The result is rather lame, but so was the original. Check out the opening titles, though . . . very strange. Rated PG.

1972   88 minutes

SON OF GODZILLA
★★

DIRECTOR: Jun Fukuda
CAST: Tadao Takashima, Akira Kubo, Bibari Maeda, Kenji Sahara

Juvenile production has the cute offspring of one of Japan's biggest stars taking on all sorts of crazy-looking monsters, with a little help from Dad. Good special effects and miniature sets make this at least watchable, but the story is just too goofy for its own good. Recommended viewing age: 2 and under. Rated PG.

1969   86 minutes

SON OF KONG, THE
★★½

DIRECTOR: Ernest B. Schoedsack

CAST: Robert Armstrong, Helen Mack, Victor Wong, John Marston, Frank Reicher, Lee Kohlmar

To cash in on the phenomenal success of *King Kong*, the producers hastily rushed this sequel into production using virtually the same cast and crew. This time out, Carl Denham (Robert Armstrong) returns to Skull Island in search of a lost treasure only to find King Kong's easygoing son trapped in a pool of quicksand. Denham saves the twelve-foot albino gorilla, who becomes his protector, and they continue the search together. Considering the pace at which this kiddy-oriented film was produced, the results are quite good. The special effects of Willis O'Brien are first-rate, as always, the acting is good; but the script is weak and contains too much silliness.

1933   B & W   70 minutes

SORRY, WRONG NUMBER
★★★★

DIRECTOR: Anatole Litvak
CAST: Barbara Stanwyck, Burt Lancaster, Wendell Corey, Ed Begley Sr., Ann Richards

Slick cinema adaptation, by the author herself, of Lucille Fletcher's famed radio drama. Barbara Stanwyck is superb—and received an Oscar nomination—as an invalid who, due to those "crossed wires" so beloved in fiction, overhears two men plotting the murder of a woman. Gradually Stanwyck realizes that she is the target. Burt Lancaster is fine as her spineless husband. The bulk of the story takes place via imaginative flashbacks, so pay attention. Great finale.

1948   B & W   89 minutes

SPASMS

🐍

DIRECTOR: William Fruet
CAST: Peter Fonda, Oliver Reed, Kerrie Keane, Al Waxman, Marilyn Lightstone, George Bloomfield

An ancient snake monster transforms a number of people into mutants in this dud. How many of these lame, cheap, and trashy horror films are they gonna make? Forget it. Rated R.

1982   92 minutes

SPECIAL EFFECTS

★

DIRECTOR: Larry Cohen
CAST: Zoe Tamerlis, Eric Bogosian, Brad Rum, Kevin O'Connor

Low-budget, rather sick horror film about a film director (Eric Bogosian) who, in a fit of rage, murders a would-be actress (Zoe Tamerlis) and attempts to pin the rap on her holier-than-thou husband (Brad Rum). The director commits the act because his victim happens to mention his failure with a big special-effects picture. Writer-director Larry Cohen made a film called *Q*, which had special effects and did not get much box-office play (although it is entertaining). One can understand, therefore, where Cohen got the idea, but not why he made such an ugly, repulsive film. The acting—except by Kevin O'Connor as a starstruck cop—is poor, and the photography very grainy and dark. Only for Cohen fans. Unrated, the film has nudity and violence.

1984   90 minutes

SPELLBOUND

★★★★

DIRECTOR: Alfred Hitchcock
CAST: Ingrid Bergman, Gregory Peck, Leo G. Carroll, John Emery, Michael Chekhov, Wallace Ford, Rhonda Fleming, Bill Goodwin

There is little we can say about the plot of *Spellbound* without giving away any of the suspense in this Alfred Hitchcock thriller. Hitchcock said in his usual, understated manner that *Spellbound* "is just another manhunt story wrapped up in pseudo-psychoanalysis." The story is more than just another manhunt story; of that we can assure you. We can divulge that Ingrid Bergman plays the psychiatrist, Gregory Peck is the patient, and Salvador Dalí provides the nightmare sequences. The eerie musical score heightened the drama and won an Oscar for Miklos Rozsa.

1945   B & W 111 minutes

SPHINX

★★

DIRECTOR: Franklin J. Schaffner
CAST: Lesley-Anne Down, Frank Langella, Maurice Ronet, John Gielgud

This is a watchable film . . . but not a good one. Taken from the tedious novel by Robin Cook (*Coma*), it concerns the plight of an Egyptologist (Lesley-Anne Down) who inadvertently runs afoul of the underworld. Directed by Franklin J. Schaffner (*Patton*), this movie has a few suspenseful moments, but because of a ridiculously contrived plot, the best we can say about it is that it's better than the book. Rated PG.

1981   117 minutes

SPIRIT OF THE DEAD

★★★½

DIRECTOR: Peter Newbrook

CAST: Robert Stephens, Robert Powell, Jane Lapotaire

Originally titled *The Asphyx*, slightly edited for videocassette. Interesting tale of a scientist who discovers the spirit of death possessed by all creatures. If the spirit is trapped, its owner becomes immortal. Well-made British film with sincere performances. Rated PG for mild violence.

1972　　　　　82 minutes

SPLATTER UNIVERSITY

DIRECTOR: Richard W. Haris
CAST: Francine Forbes, Ric Randig, Dick Biel, Suzy Collins

Typical slasher film featuring students having sex and then getting hacked to pieces. The school halls run red enough to thrill any splatter fan. Those who don't care for exploitative violence, or have weak stomachs, will more than likely be offended. Rated R for profanity, brief nudity, and violence.

1985　　　　　78 minutes

SQUIRM
★½

DIRECTOR: Jeff Lieberman
CAST: Don Scardino, Patricia Pearcy

Ugly, disgusting horror film has hordes of killer worms attacking a small town. Only serves to nauseate. Rated PG.

1976　　　　　92 minutes

STAGE FRIGHT
★★★

DIRECTOR: Alfred Hitchcock
CAST: Marlene Dietrich, Jane Wyman, Michael Wilding, Alastair Sim, Richard Todd, Kay Walsh, Patricia Hitchcock

Master director Alfred Hitchcock cheats with this one, the only time he deliberately misleads his audi-ence. As a result, the drama loses most of its impact at the climax. Drama student Jane Wyman spies on actress Marlene Dietrich to prove she murdered her husband. Alastair Sim steals his moments as Wyman's protective parent, but most of the other moments go to the hypnotic Dietrich. Watch for Patricia Hitchcock (yes, the director's daughter) in a small, but very pleasant, part.

1950　　　B & W　110 minutes

STANLEY
★★

DIRECTOR: William Grefe
CAST: Chris Robinson, Alex Rocco, Susan Carroll, Steve Alaimo

A crazy Vietnam vet (Chris Robinson) uses an army of deadly snakes to destroy his enemies in this watchable, though rather grim, horror yarn. Rated PG for violence and unpleasant situations.

1972　　　　　106 minutes

STEPHEN KING'S NIGHT SHIFT COLLECTION
★

DIRECTOR: Frank Durabont, Jeffrey C. Schiro
CAST: Michael Cornelison, Dee Croxton, Brion Libby, Michael Reid, Bert Linder, Mindy Silverman

In this so-called collection, featuring two short-story adaptations from Stephen King's book, *Night Shift*, we see again how hard it is to bring King's writing to the screen. Not that these filmmakers don't try. In fact, they come close in the first story, "The Lady in the Room," about a son and his terminally ill mother coming to terms with her impending death. This story will surely choke you up, if not bring tears to your eyes. However, in the second feature, director Schiro ruins one of King's most frightening stories, "The Boogey Man." In this, the Boogey Man is blamed for the crib deaths and fatal accidents that happen to children. They've rewritten, rather than adapted, this once horrifying yarn. It has poor acting and poor direction. Although this film has its moments, do yourself a favor: check *Night Shift* out of the library and *read* the stories.

1986   61 minutes

STILL OF THE NIGHT
★★★½
DIRECTOR: Robert Benton
CAST: Roy Scheider, Meryl Streep, Jessica Tandy, Joe Grifasi, Sara Botsford

In this well-crafted thriller by writer-director Robert Benton (*Kramer vs. Kramer*), a psychiatrist (Roy Scheider) falls in love with an art curator (Meryl Streep) who may have killed one of his patients and may be after him next. If you like being scared out of your wits, you won't want to miss it. Rated PG for violence and adult themes.

1982   91 minutes

STRAIT-JACKET
★★★½
DIRECTOR: William Castle
CAST: Joan Crawford, Diane Baker, Leif Erickson

Chilling vehicle for Joan Crawford as a convicted axe murderess returning home after twenty years in an insane asylum, where it appears she was restored to sanity. But was she? Genuinely frightening film features one of Joan's most powerful, as well as restrained, performances. George Kennedy is almost as good in an early role as a farm hand.

1964   B & W 89 minutes

STRANGE BEHAVIOR
★★★½
DIRECTOR: Michael Laughlin
CAST: Michael Murphy, Marc McClure, Dan Shor, Fiona Lewis, Louise Fletcher, Arthur Dignam

Michael Murphy stars as the small-town police chief, John Brady, of Galesburg, Illinois, who suddenly finds himself inundated by unexplained knife murders. At least one of the murders was committed by the mild-mannered Oliver (Marc McClure), close friend of Brady's son (Dan Shor). But why? Perhaps it's the result of his participation in the experiments conducted by the Galesburg College Psychology Department, presided over by Professor Gwen Parkinson (Fiona Lewis). He's been getting a hundred dollars a day to participate in a series of secret experiments. To Pete, this sounds like a great way to raise money for his college tuition. And the terror builds. In all, this release is a true treat for horror movie fans and other viewers with a yen for something spooky. Rated R.

1981   98 minutes

STRANGENESS, THE
★
DIRECTOR: David Michael Hillman
CAST: Dan Lunham, Terri Berland

Extremely low-budget horror film shot mostly in the dark. The Gold Spike Mine is haunted by a creature from down deep inside the earth. Who of the wimpish cast will dare to challenge this "strangeness?" This film is not worth watching to find out. Unrated.

1985   90 minutes

STRANGER, THE
★★★★
DIRECTOR: Orson Welles

CAST: Orson Welles, Edward G. Robinson, Loretta Young, Richard Long, Martha Wentworth

Nazi war criminal (Orson Welles) assumes a new identity in a Midwestern town following World War II, unaware that a government agent (Edward G. Robinson) is tailing him. Extremely well done film, holds the viewer's interest from start to finish.

1946 B & W 95 minutes

STRANGER IS WATCHING, A
★

DIRECTOR: Sean S. Cunningham
CAST: Kate Mulgrew, Rip Torn, James Naughton, Shawn Von Schreiber

A psychotic killer kidnaps two young ladies and keeps them prisoner in the catacombs beneath Grand Central Station. This commuter's nightmare is directed by Sean S. Cunningham (*Friday the 13th*) and is an ugly, dimly lit suspenser for horror buffs only. Rated R.

1982 92 minutes

STRANGERS ON A TRAIN
★★★★★

DIRECTOR: Alfred Hitchcock
CAST: Farley Granger, Robert Walker, Ruth Roman, Leo G. Carroll, Patricia Hitchcock, Marion Lorne

Imagine yourself on a train, bus, or some other form of public transport. An eccentric stranger approaches you and proposes to commit a heinous crime for you, a crime you may have secretly been wishing for. In exchange you must commit a crime for him. This is the situation that confronts a tennis pro (Farley Granger) in what remains today one of the most discussed and analyzed of all of Alfred Hitchcock's films. *Strangers on a Train* was made during the height of Hitchcock's most creative period, the early 1950s. When you add a marvelous performance by Robert Walker as the stranger, you have one of the most satisfying Hitchcock thrillers ever.

1951 B & W 101 minutes

STRAW DOGS
★★★★

DIRECTOR: Sam Peckinpah
CAST: Dustin Hoffman, Susan George, Peter Vaughn, T. P. McKenna, Peter Arne, David Warner

With this release, director Sam Peckinpah established his credentials as a master of the contemporary drama. An American intellectual mathematician (played brilliantly by Dustin Hoffman) takes a wife (Susan George) and returns to her ancestral village on the coast of England. Her former boyfriends become jealous, resentful, and desirous of her. She taunts them with her wealth and power, and soon she is viciously raped. When Hoffman takes in the local village idiot who is suspected of killing and molesting a young girl, their house is put under siege by the incensed locals. He defends his house with a ferocity. The highly charged sequences of carnage in the conclusion make this a controversial film. Rated R.

1971 113 minutes

STUDENT BODIES
★★½

DIRECTOR: Mickey Rose
CAST: Kristin Ritter, Matthew Goldsby, Richard Brando, Joe Flood, Joe Talarowski

This comedy-horror release has something extra, because it is a parody of the blood-and-guts horror films. Rated R.

1981   86 minutes

STUFF, THE
🎃

DIRECTOR: Larry Cohen
CAST: Michael Moriarty, Andrea Marcovicci, Garrett Morris, Paul Sorvino, Danny Aiello

A scrumptious, creamy dessert devours from within all those who eat it in this not funny and not scary horror-comedy. It's as flat as month-old whipped cream and just as enjoyable. Rated R for gore and profanity.

1985   93 minutes

SUSPICION
★★★★

DIRECTOR: Alfred Hitchcock
CAST: Joan Fontaine, Cary Grant, Cedric Hardwicke, Nigel Bruce, May Whitty, Isabel Jeans

Alfred Hitchcock had a problem. He had an excellent script: A timid woman gradually unnerved by apprehension. Bits of evidence lead her to believe that her charming husband is a killer and that she is the intended victim. He had the perfect "timid woman," Joan Fontaine, who played a similar role in *Rebecca* and eventually won a Best Actress Oscar for her performance in *Suspicion*. He had the most charming of all Hollywood actors, Cary Grant. So what's the problem? Studio executives would not think of allowing their charming Cary to play a killer. How Hitchcock effectively managed to make Grant threatening, yet keep his "image" intact and still build up the subtle suspense for which he is famous, is here for you to see.

1941   B & W   99 minutes

SVENGALI
★★★★

DIRECTOR: Archie Mayo
CAST: John Barrymore, Marian Marsh, Donald Crisp, Carmel Myers, Bramwell Fletcher

In case you don't know, John Barrymore was Drew Barrymore's grandfather. This film is adapted from the George Du Maurier novel that put Svengali into the language as one who controls another. Barrymore, a fine stage actor and excellent in his early films, of which this is a notable example, plays Svengali, a demonic artist obsessed with Trilby, a young artist's model. Under his hynotic influence, she becomes a singer who obeys his every command. John Barrymore's make-up is grotesque, his voice magnificent. Bizarre sets and arresting visual effects make this a surrealistic delight.

1931   B & W   76 minutes

SWAMP THING
★½

DIRECTOR: Wes Craven
CAST: Louis Jourdan, Adrienne Barbeau, Ray Wise, David Hess, Nicholas Worth

Kids will love this movie, about a monster-hero—part plant, part scientist—who takes on a super-villain (Louis Jourdan) and saves heroine Adrienne Barbeau. But adults will no doubt find it too corny and sloppily made for their tastes. *Swamp Thing* was based on the popular 1972 comic book of the same name. Rated PG, it has some tomato-paste violence and brief nudity.

1982   91 minutes

SWARM, THE
🦟

DIRECTOR: Irwin Allen
CAST: Michael Caine, Katharine Ross, Richard Widmark, Henry Fonda, Olivia De Havilland, Richard Chamberlain, Fred MacMurray

"Irwin Allen is still 'Lost in Space,' " science-fiction author Ray Bradbury once said of the notorious television and film producer who also fathered *The Poseidon Adventure* and *The Towering Inferno*. And there is no better proof of Allen's ineptitude than this dreadful, self-directed killer-bee ripoff of Alfred Hitchcock's *The Birds*. It wastes the talents of a top-flight cast. Rated PG.

1978   116 minutes

TALES FROM THE CRYPT
★★★½

DIRECTOR: Freddie Francis
CAST: Peter Cushing, Joan Collins, Ralph Richardson

Excellent anthology has five people gathered in a mysterious cave where the keeper (Ralph Richardson) foretells their futures, one by one, in gruesome fashion. Director Freddie Francis keeps things moving at a brisk pace, and the performances are uniformly fine, most notably Peter Cushing's in one of the better segments—*Poetic Justice*. Don't miss it. Rated PG.

1972   92 minutes

TALES OF TERROR
★★★

DIRECTOR: Roger Corman
CAST: Vincent Price, Basil Rathbone, Peter Lorre, Debra Paget

An uneven anthology of horror stories adapted from the works of Edgar Allan Poe. Directed by cult favorite Roger Corman, it does have a few moments.

1962   90 minutes

TARGETS
★★★★★

DIRECTOR: Peter Bogdanovich
CAST: Tim O'Kelly, Boris Karloff, Nancy Hsueh, James Brown, Peter Bogdanovich

The stunning film-making debut of critic-turned-director Peter Bogdanovich juxtaposes real-life terror, in the form of an unhinged mass murderer (Tim O'Kelly), with its comparatively subdued and safe screen counterpart, as represented by the scare films of Byron Orlock (Boris Karloff in a brilliant final bow). This rarely seen release is nothing short of a masterpiece. Rated PG.

1968   90 minutes

TEEN WOLF
★

DIRECTOR: Rod Daniel
CAST: Michael J. Fox, James Hampton, Scott Paulin, Susan Ursitti, Jerry Levine

Pitifully bad film about a teenager (Michael J. Fox) who discovers he has the ability to change into a werewolf, making him a hit at high school when he carries their losing basketball team to the championships. It's the same old story, even considering the "wolf" angle, with the usual cliché-ridden plot and "be yourself" message at the end. Boring and tiresome. Rated PG for mild language.

1985   95 minutes

TENANT, THE
★★★

DIRECTOR: Roman Polanski
CAST: Roman Polanski, Melvyn Douglas, Shelley Winters

Roman Polanski is superb in this flawed cryptic thriller about a bumbling Polish expatriate in France who leases an apartment owned previously by a young woman who committed suicide. Increasingly, Polanski believes the apartment's tenants conspired demonically to destroy the woman and are attempting to do the same to him. Supporting are Melvyn Douglas as the building's owner and Shelley Winters as the irascible concierge. Rated R.

1976   125 minutes

TENTACLES

DIRECTOR: Ovidio Assonitis (Oliver Hellman)

CAST: John Huston, Shelley Winters, Henry Fonda, Bo Hopkins, Cesare Danova

Rotten monster movie from Italy about a phony-looking octopus attacking and devouring some famous Hollywood stars, who should all be ashamed of themselves for appearing in this sleaze. Unbelievably poor. You want an octopus movie? Try *It Came from Beneath the Sea.* Rated PG.

1977   90 minutes

TERMINAL CHOICE
★★

DIRECTOR: Sheldon Larry

CAST: Joe Spano, Diane Venora, David McCallum, Robert Joy, Don Francks, Nicholas Campbell, Ellen Barkin

If it's blood you want, you'll get your money's worth with this one—by the gallons! There's some real tension in this film about a hospital that has a staff that secretly bets on the mortality of its patients—not exactly family entertainment. And when the hero of the day is an alcoholic doctor who has a history of accidentally killing patients by performing unnecessary operations under the influence, well, you know the cast of characters aren't a bunch of Ben Caseys. Rated R for sex, nudity, language, and plenty o'gore.

1984   98 minutes

TERMINAL MAN, THE
★★

DIRECTOR: Mike Hodges

CAST: George Segal, Joan Hackett, Jill Clayburgh

A dreary adaptation of the crackling novel by Michael Crichton, although George Segal tries hard to improve the film's quality. He stars as a paranoid psychotic who undergoes experimental surgery designed to quell his violent impulses; unfortunately (and quite predictably), he becomes even worse. What's missing is the credibility that Crichton himself, in films he later directed, manages to inject into a story of this type. Most of the cast doesn't seem to believe in what's taking place; as a result, we don't, either. Rated R for violence.

1974   104 minutes

TERROR, THE

DIRECTOR: Roger Corman

CAST: Boris Karloff, Jack Nicholson, Sandra Knight

This is an incomprehensible sludge of mismatched horror scenes even Boris Karloff can't save, but he does better than a miscast Jack Nicholson in this forgettable Roger Corman loser, which was shot in three days and shows it.

1963   81 minutes

TERROR IN THE AISLES
★★★

DIRECTOR: Andrew Kuehn
CAST: Donald Pleasence, Nancy Allen

Donald Pleasence (*Halloween*) and Nancy Allen (*Carrie*) host this basically enjoyable compilation film of the most graphic scenes from seventy-five horror films. Rated R for violence, profanity, nudity, and suggested sex.

1984   82 minutes

TERROR IN THE WAX MUSEUM
★

DIRECTOR: Georg Fenady
CAST: Ray Milland, Broderick Crawford, Elsa Lanchester, Maurice Evans, Shani Wallis, John Carradine, Louis Hayward, Patric Knowles

The all-star cast from yesteryear looks like a sort of Hollywood wax museum. Their fans will suffer through this unsuspenseful murder mystery. It belongs in a museum—of missed opportunities. With a cast like this, it should have at least been fun. Rated PG.

1973   93 minutes

TERROR ON THE 40TH FLOOR
★★

DIRECTOR: Jerry Jameson
CAST: John Forsythe, Joseph Campanella, Don Meredith

A typical disaster film, this deals with a skyscraper fire that traps a group of office workers on the top floor. In the face of impending death, they recount their lives. Unrated.

1974   100 minutes

TEXAS CHAINSAW MASSACRE, THE
★★½

DIRECTOR: Tobe Hooper
CAST: Marilyn Burns, Gunnar Hansen, Ed Neal

This, the first film about a cannibalistic maniac by horror specialist Tobe Hooper (*Funhouse*), went pretty much unnoticed in its original release. That's probably because it sounds like the run-of-the-mill drive-in exploitation fare. While it was made on a very low budget, it nevertheless has been hailed as a ground-breaking genre work by critics and film buffs and became a cult classic. Be forewarned if you intend to see it: you need a strong stomach. Rated R for blood and gore.

1974   83 minutes

TEXAS CHAINSAW MASSACRE 2, THE
★★★

DIRECTOR: Tobe Hooper
CAST: Dennis Hopper, Caroline Williams, Jim Siedow, Bill Johnson, Phil Keller

Leatherface is back! In fact, so is most of the family in this maniacal sequel to *The Texas Chainsaw Massacre*. Dennis Hopper stars as a retired lawman out to avenge the gruesome murder of his nephew, and Caroline Williams plays the disc jockey who helps him locate the butchers. Once they do, this film becomes an unrelenting exercise in stark terror and very black comedy, and in scene after scene it asks: can you take it? What makes the horrifying mutilations palatable is the comic book style in which they are presented, along with some of the most uproarious dialogue in recent memory. Excellent (albeit hammy) performances by all, with superb makeup, lighting, and camerawork place this several cuts above the countless insipid slasher films on the market today. Unrated, but loaded with repulsive gore. Recommended for those with strong stomachs.

1986   112 minutes

THE GOLEM (HOW HE CAME INTO THE WORLD) (DER GOLEM, WIE ER IN DIE WELT KAM)
★★★★

DIRECTOR: Paul Wegener
CAST: Paul Wegener, Albert Steinrück, Lydia Salmonova, Ernst Deutch, Hannes Sturm, Max Kronert, Greta Schroder

Director Paul Wegener plays the lead role as the Golem, an ancient clay figure from Hebrew mythology that is brought to life by Rabbi Loew (Albert Steinrück) by means of an amulet activated by the magic word "Aemaet" (the Hebrew word for truth). The Golem becomes the rabbi's servant but later turns against him. In a story similar to *Frankenstein*, the man of clay roams through medieval Prague in a mystic atmosphere created by the brilliant cameraman Karl Freund. A superb rendition of a classic myth by the German film industry of the 1920s.

1920   B & W   70 minutes

THEATER OF BLOOD
★★★★

DIRECTOR: Douglas Hickox
CAST: Vincent Price, Diana Rigg, Robert Morley

Deliciously morbid horror-comedy about a Shakespearean actor (Vincent Price) who, angered by the thrashing he receives from a series of critics, decides to kill them in uniquely outlandish ways. He turns to the Bard for inspiration, and each perceived foe is eliminated in a manner drawn from one of Shakespeare's plays, such as losing a critical "pound of flesh." Although similar in tone to his two

Dr. Phibes films, Price benefits here from better production values. We hope he finds *this* review sufficiently kind, as several plays still remain unused . . . Rated R for violence.

1973   104 minutes

THEATRE OF DEATH
★★½

DIRECTOR: Samuel Gallu
CAST: Christopher Lee, Julian Glover, Lelia Goldoni, Jenny Till

Mildly interesting mystery succeeds mainly due to Christopher Lee's assured performance and some well-timed scares as a series of gruesome murders is committed in Paris with an apparent connection to the local theater company. Good title sequence deserves mention.

1967   90 minutes

THEY SAVED HITLER'S BRAIN
★½

DIRECTOR: David Bradley
CAST: Walter Stocker, Audrey Caire, Carlos Rivas, John Holland, Marshall Reed, Nestor Paiva, Dani Lynn

This bargain-basement bomb is actually a used movie since a major portion of it was lifted from an entirely different film made ten years earlier, edited together with new footage and given a snappy new title to attract the drive-in crowd. The story of a girl whose pursuit of her kidnapped scientist father leads her to an island teeming with Nazis is secondary to the question of *why* anybody would bother to save Hitler's brain and why anyone in their right mind would get involved in a mess like this. This film has a certain reputation among bad film aficionados, but if you are looking for a straight horror film or some sort of a war film, you're out of luck. Fun to watch if you know what you're getting into.

1963　　　B & W　74 minutes

THIRD MAN, THE
★★★★★

DIRECTOR: Carol Reed
CAST: Joseph Cotten, Orson Welles, Alida Valli, Trevor Howard

Considered by many to be the greatest suspense film of all time, this classic inevitably turns up on every best-film list. It rivals any Hitchcock thriller as being the ultimate masterpiece of film suspense. A writer (Joseph Cotten) discovers an old friend he thought dead to be the head of a vicious European black market organization. Unfortunately for him, that information makes him a marked man.

1949　　　B & W　104 minutes

13 GHOSTS
★★★

DIRECTOR: William Castle
CAST: Charles Herbert, Donald Woods, Martin Milner, Rosemary DeCamp, Jo Morrow, Margaret Hamilton

Light-hearted horror tale of an average family inheriting a haunted house complete with a creepy old housekeeper (Margaret Hamilton) who may also be a witch, and a secret fortune hidden somewhere in the place. William Castle directs with his customary style and flair. Pretty neat.

1960　　　B & W　88 minutes

THIRTY-NINE STEPS, THE
★★★★★

DIRECTOR: Alfred Hitchcock
CAST: Robert Donat, Madeleine Carroll, Lucie Mannheim

If one film could be held responsible for the career of Alfred Hitchcock, it's *The Thirty-nine Steps*. Hitchcock's early directing assignments were spent making B movies in England. He was assigned to direct what was intended to be another simple, low-budget spy-chase thriller, but to give Hitchcock a thriller was like giving Rembrandt a paintbrush. Using the style and technique that were to make him famous, he gained immediate audience sympathy for the plight of his central character, an innocent Canadian (Robert Donat) who while visiting England is implicated in the theft of national secrets and murder. The film gained instant popularity, and Hitchcock was never to look back on B movies again.

1935　　　B & W　87 minutes

TIGHTROPE
★★★★★

DIRECTOR: Richard Tuggle
CAST: Clint Eastwood, Genevieve Bujold, Dan Hedaya, Alison Eastwood, Jennifer Beck

A terrific, taut suspense thriller, this ranks with the best films in the genre. Written and directed by Richard Tuggle, *Tightrope* casts Clint Eastwood as Wes Block, homicide inspector for the New Orleans Police Department. His latest assignment is to track down a Jack the Ripper—style sex-murderer. This case hits disturbingly close to home in more ways than one. Rated R for violence, profanity, and sex.

1984　　　　　　115 minutes

TIME WALKER

DIRECTOR: Tom Kennedy
CAST: Ben Murphy, Nina Axelrod, Kevin Brophy, Shari Belafonte-Harper

Imagine sitting through a movie that isn't all that great to begin with and, as the story seems to be building up to a pretty good climax, the words "To Be Continued" flash on the screen. Outrageous, you say? Well, that's exactly what happens at the end of this sci-fihorror ripoff, which features Ben Murphy (*The Winds of War*) as an Egyptologist who accidentally brings an ancient mummy back to life. Avoid it. Rated PG for nudity, profanity, and violence.

1982   83 minutes

TO ALL A GOOD NIGHT
★★

DIRECTOR: David Hess
CAST: Jennifer Runyon, Forrest Swenson, Linda Gentille, William Lauer

In this typical slasher film, a group of young teen-age girls gets away from supervision, and the mad killer shows up with a sharp weapon. There is some build-up of terror and suspense. The camera work is good and the timing fair, adding up to a slightly above average film of its genre. Rated R; has nudity, violence, and profanity.

1983   90 minutes

TO CATCH A KING
★★

DIRECTOR: Clive Donner
CAST: Robert Wagner, Teri Garr, Horst Janson, Barbara Parkins

Made-for-cable spy thriller that fails to live up to its promising premise. In 1940, cunning Nazis plot to kidnap the Duke and Duchess of Windsor during the romantic couple's respite in Lisbon. Robert Wagner plays a café owner, a more debonair version of *Casablanca*'s Rick. Teri Garr is a nightclub singer. The film is neither convincing nor exciting.

1984   113 minutes

TO CATCH A THIEF
★★★★

DIRECTOR: Alfred Hitchcock
CAST: Cary Grant, Grace Kelly, John Williams, Jessie Royce Landis

John Robie (Cary Grant) is a retired cat burglar living in France in peaceful seclusion. When a sudden rash of jewel thefts hit the Riviera, he is naturally blamed. He sets out to clear himself, and the fun begins. This is certainly one of director Alfred Hitchcock's most amusing, if not one of his most gripping, films. The unbounded charm of Cary Grant and his co-star, Grace Kelly, coupled with Hitchcock's unique treatment of suspense, make the film consistently appealing.

1955   103 minutes

TO KILL A CLOWN
★

DIRECTOR: George Bloomfield
CAST: Alan Alda, Blythe Danner, Heath Lambert

A husband (Heath Lambert) and wife (Blythe Danner) move from the big city to a remote island in an effort to save their marriage. Their new landlord (Alan Alda) appears at first to be a pleasant sort of fellow, but as time goes on, he is revealed to be a maniac bent on their destruction. *To Kill a Clown* is an unnecessarily depressing and essentially uninvolving drama. Rated R for violence and profanity.

1983   82 minutes

TO THE DEVIL, A DAUGHTER
★★★½
DIRECTOR: Peter Sykes
CAST: Richard Widmark, Christopher Lee, Honor Blackman, Denholm Elliott, Michael Goodliffe, Eva Maria Meinke, Nastassja Kinski

Dennis Wheatley wrote a number of books on the occult. This film was based on one of them, and it is his influence that raises this above the average thriller. Director Peter Sykes has also left some of the horror to the imagination. This commendable practice has become a rarity in recent years as emphasis has been placed on gory, explicit death scenes. Another plus is in the acting. Richard Widmark gives an understated and effective performance as occult novelist John Verney, who finds himself pitted against real satanists. As the leader of the opposition, Christopher Lee is once again brilliantly menacing. Nastassja Kinski is appealingly waifish as the victim protégée of the cult. Rated R, the film contains nudity, profanity, and violence in small quantities.
1976   95 minutes

TOMB OF LIGEIA
★★★
DIRECTOR: Roger Corman
CAST: Vincent Price, Elizabeth Shepherd, John Westbrook, Oliver Johnson

A grieving widower is driven to madness by the curse of his dead wife. Filmed in England, this was Roger Corman's final Poe-inspired movie. The most subtle and atmospheric entry in the series, it was photographed by Nicholas Roeg on sets left over from *Becket*. The screenplay was by Robert Towne, who went on to write *Chinatown*.
1964   81 minutes

TOO SCARED TO SCREAM

DIRECTOR: Tony Lo Bianco
CAST: Mike Connors, Anne Archer, Leon Isaac Kennedy, Ian McShane

Pathetic "demented killer" movie features *Mannix*'s Mike Connors as a grizzled New York detective on the trail of a psychopath who's knocking off tenants at a posh Manhattan apartment building. No suspense, just tedium, in a film laced with bad acting, writing, photography, etc. Director Tony Lo Bianco should stick to acting. Rated R for nudity and gore.
1982   104 minutes

TOPAZ
★★★
DIRECTOR: Alfred Hitchcock
CAST: John Forsythe, Frederick Stafford, Dany Robin, John Vernon

Medium-to-rare Hitchcock suspense thriller about cloak-and-dagger intrigue concerning Russian involvement in Cuba and infiltration of the French government. Constant shift of scene keeps viewers on their toes. Rated PG.
1969   127 minutes

TORMENT
★★
DIRECTOR: Samson Aslanian, John Hopkins
CAST: Taylor Gilbert, William Witt, Eve Brenner

This low-budget slasher film starts off slow and, if it weren't for one interesting plot twist halfway through, would be an exercise in boredom. The story revolves around a middle-aged man who becomes a psychotic killer when he is rejected by a younger woman. The detective assigned to capture the psycho sends his fiancée, Jennifer, to meet his mother for the first time. Who should the killer then decide to stalk? You guessed it, Jennifer. She thinks that the invalid mother is crazy when she insists that there is a man in the house. Without giving away the single interesting point in the whole movie, we will only say that you end up rooting for Mom, hoping the killer gets Jennifer for being such an airhead, and being glad that the poorly acted part of the detective is kept to only ten minutes of screen time. One last point—watch for the dead body that continues to breathe near the end of this one. View this as a gory comedy, not as a suspenseful thriller. Rated R for violence and gore.

1986   90 minutes

TORN CURTAIN
★★★

DIRECTOR: Alfred Hitchcock
CAST: Paul Newman, Julie Andrews, Lila Kedrova, David Opatoshu

This just-okay film was directed by Alfred Hitchcock in 1966. Paul Newman plays an American scientist posing as a defector, with Julie Andrews as his secretary/lover. Somehow we aren't moved by the action or the characters.

1966   128 minutes

TORTURE CHAMBER OF BARON BLOOD, THE
★★

DIRECTOR: Mario Bava

CAST: Joseph Cotten, Elke Sommer, Massimo Girotti, Rada Rassimov

Boring Italian production is basically nonsense as a long-dead nobleman (Joseph Cotten) is inadvertently restored to life, only to (naturally) embark on a horrendous killing spree. Can he be stopped? Worth watching for Mario Bava's unique directorial style, but you can skip the rest. Originally titled *Baron Blood*. Rated R.

1972   90 minutes

TORTURE GARDEN
★★★

DIRECTOR: Freddie Francis
CAST: Burgess Meredith, Jack Palance, Beverly Adams, Peter Cushing, Maurice Denham, Robert Hutton, Barbara Ewing

A group of patrons at a carnival sideshow has their possible futures exposed to them by a screwball barker (Burgess Meredith) who exclaims, "I've promised you horror . . . and I intend to keep that promise." Which he more than does in this frightening film laced with plenty of shocks, plot twists, and intense situations. The video transfer features superb color as well, though the soundtrack is muted. Rated PG.

1968   93 minutes

TOUCH OF EVIL
★★★★½

DIRECTOR: Orson Welles
CAST: Orson Welles, Charlton Heston, Marlene Dietrich, Janet Leigh, Zsa Zsa Gabor

In 1958, director-actor Orson Welles proved that he was still a film-making genius, with this dark and disturbing masterpiece about crime and corruption in a border town.

1958   B & W   93 minutes

TOURIST TRAP
★

DIRECTOR: David Schmoeller
CAST: Chuck Connors, Joan Van Ness, Jocelyn Jones, Tanya Roberts

Another in the endless stream of psycho-hack films with a lot of stupid unpaid actors wondering where all these life-size dummies in Chuck Connors's basement museum have come from. Some scary moments, and Connors carries a lethal axe. With Tanya Roberts in her pre-*Sheena* days. Rated R for violence, gore, nudity, and profanity.

1979   83 minutes

TOWN THAT DREADED SUNDOWN, THE
★★★½

DIRECTOR: Charles B. Pierce
CAST: Ben Johnson, Andrew Prine, Jim Citty, Dawn Wells, Robert Aquino, Bud Davis

The fact that *The Town that Dreaded Sundown* is based on actual events makes this effective little film all the more chilling. The story takes place in the year 1946 in the small Texas–Arkansas border town of Texarkana. It begins in documentary style, with a narrator describing the post–World War II atmosphere, but soon gets to the unsettling business of the Phantom, a killer who terrorized the locals. Rated R for violence.

1977   90 minutes

TRAP, THE
★★★

DIRECTOR: Norman Panama

CAST: Richard Widmark, Lee J. Cobb, Earl Holliman, Tina Louise, Carl Benton Reid, Lorne Greene, Peter Baldwin

Fast pace and taut suspense mark this thriller about as fine a gaggle of fleeing gangsters as ever menaced the innocent inhabitants of a small California desert town. Don't expect any dull spots as the tension mounts and the safety valve lets go. This is edge-of-chair stuff. It was in films such as this that Richard Widmark made his name praisingly hissable. Lee J. Cobb is not exactly lovable, either.

1958   84 minutes

TRILOGY OF TERROR
★★½

DIRECTOR: Dan Curtis
CAST: Karen Black, Robert Burton, John Karlen

Karen Black stars in this trio of horror stories, the best of which is the final episode, about an ancient Indian doll coming to life and stalking Black. It's often very frightening, and well worth wading through the first two tales. This was originally made as an ABC Movie of the Week.

1974   78 minutes

TWILIGHT ZONE—THE MOVIE
★★★

DIRECTOR: Steven Spielberg, John Landis, Joe Dante, George Miller
CAST: Vic Morrow, Scatman Crothers, Kathleen Quinlan, John Lithgow

A generally enjoyable tribute to the 1960s television series created by Rod Serling, this film, directed by Steven Spielberg (*E.T.*), John Landis (*Trading Places*), Joe Dante (*The Howling*), and George Miller (*Road Warrior*), is broken into four parts. In Landis's segment, a bigot (Vic Morrow) walks out of a neighborhood bar to become the victim of Nazis, the Ku Klux Klan, and U.S. troops in Vietnam. Spielberg helmed the next story, about a stranger (Scatman Crothers) who transforms the elderly in a retirement home into the young at heart. In Dante's, a schoolteacher (Kathleen Quinlan) encounters a boy with strange, frightening powers. Miller, however, brings us the best: a tale about a white-knuckled air traveler (John Lithgow) who sees a gremlin doing strange things on the wing of a jet. Rated PG.

1983   102 minutes

TWINS OF EVIL
★★★
DIRECTOR: John Hough
CAST: Peter Cushing, Madeleine and Mary Collinson, Luan Peters, Dennis Price

Playboy magazine's first twin Playmates, Madeleine and Mary Collinson, were tapped for this British Hammer Films horror entry about a good girl and her evil, blood-sucking sister. Peter Cushing adds class to what should in theory have been a forgettable exploitation film but provides surprisingly enjoyable entertainment for genre buffs. Rated R for nudity, violence, and gore.

1972   85 minutes

UNCANNY, THE
★
DIRECTOR: Denis Heroux
CAST: Peter Cushing, Ray Milland, Susan Penhaligon, Joan Greenwood, Donald Pleasence, Samantha Eggar, John Vernon

A paranoid writer tells three tales of cat-related horror. He believes felines are trying to take over the world. Judging from this film, they're trying to bore us to death. Rated R.

1977   88 minutes

UNION STATION
★★★
DIRECTOR: Rudolph Mate
CAST: William Holden, Nancy Olson, Allene Roberts, Barry Fitzgerald, Lyle Bettger, Jan Sterling, Ralph Sanford, Herbert Heyes

A big, bustling railroad terminal is the backdrop of this suspense-thriller centering on the manhunt that ensues following the kidnapping of a blind girl for ransom. William Holden is the hero, Lyle Bettger is the villain, Allene Roberts is the victim. The plot's tired, but ace cinematographer-turned-director Rudolph Mate keeps everything moving fast and frantic to a climax guaranteed to make hearts pound and palms sweat.

1950   B & W   80 minutes

UNSEEN, THE
🦃
DIRECTOR: Peter Foleg
CAST: Barbara Bach, Sidney Lassick, Stephen Furst

This awful horror film should remain unseen. Rated R.

1981   89 minutes

VAMP
★★★
DIRECTOR: Richard Wenk
CAST: Chris Makepeace, Grace Jones, Robert Rusler, Sandy Baron, Gedde Watanabe, Dedee Pfeiffer

Effective comedy-shocker concerns a pair of college kids (Chris Makepeace and Robert Rusler) who, in order to make it into the best fraternity on campus, must find a stripper for a big party being thrown that night. With the help of the resident school oddball (Gedde Watanabe in an inspired portrayal), the guys head off on their sacred mission. Upon arriving at the After Dark Club, the trio quickly decide on the outrageous Katrina (Grace Jones) as their unanimous choice, little realizing that she is actually a vicious, bloodthirsty vampire in disguise. This visually impressive production features ghoulish special effects, realistic performances, and a dank atmosphere of certain doom as the boys soon discover there's no escape from this nightmare. Rated R for gore and brief nudity.

1986   93 minutes

VAMPYR
★★★★★

DIRECTOR: Carl Dreyer
CAST: Julian West, Sybille Schmitz, Maurice Schultz, Rena Mandel, Jan Hieronimko

Director Carl Dreyer believed that horror is best implied. By relying on the viewer's imagination, he created a classic film. A young man arrives at a very bizarre inn, where he discovers an unconscious woman who had been attacked by a vampire in the form of an old woman. The young man finds a book on vampire legends. By following the instructions in the book, he succeeds in destroying the old woman and her evil assistant. This outstanding film is one of the few serious films of the macabre.

1931   B & W   68 minutes

VARAN, THE UNBELIEVABLE
★★½

DIRECTOR: Inoshiro Honda
CAST: Jerry Baerwitz, Myron Healy, Tsuruko Kobayashi

Another Godzilla ripoff with better-than-average effects.

1962   B & W   70 minutes

VAULT OF HORROR
★★

DIRECTOR: Roy Ward Baker
CAST: Daniel Massey, Anna Massey, Terry-Thomas, Glynis Johns, Curt Jurgens, Dawn Addams, Tom Baker, Denholm Elliott, Michael Craig, Edward Judd

British sequel to Tales from the Crypt boasts a fine cast and five short stories borrowed from the classic EC comics line of the early 1950s but delivers very little in the way of true chills and atmosphere. Not nearly as effective as the earlier five-story thriller Dr. Terror's House of Horrors and not as much fun as the most recent homage to the EC horror story, Creepshow. Rated R.

1973   87 minutes

VENOM
★

DIRECTOR: Piers Haggard
CAST: Nicol Williamson, Klaus Kinski, Susan George, Oliver Reed, Sterling Hayden, Sarah Miles

This combination horror film and police thriller doesn't really work as either. The plot centers on the bungled kidnapping of a 10-year-old scion of a wealthy London family. Police trap the kidnappers in the boy's home, in which, unknown to either the police or criminals, a vicious black mamba snake stalks victims and slithers through the ventilation ducts. It wastes fine cast and the viewer's time. Rated R for nudity and violence.

1982   98 minutes

VERTIGO
★★★★

DIRECTOR: Alfred Hitchcock
CAST: James Stewart, Kim Novak, Barbara Bel Geddes

The first hour of this production is slow, gimmicky, and artificial. However, the rest of this suspense picture takes off at high speed. James Stewart stars as a San Francisco detective who has a fear of heights and is hired to shadow an old friend's wife (Kim Novak). He finds himself falling in love with her—then tragedy strikes.

1958   128 minutes

VIDEODROME
★★½

DIRECTOR: David Cronenberg
CAST: James Woods, Deborah Harry, Sonja Smits, Peter Dvorsky

Director David Cronenberg (*Scanners*; *Rabid*; and *The Brood*) strikes again with a clever, gory nightmare set in the world of television broadcasting. James Woods and Deborah Harry (of the rock group Blondie) star in this eerie, occasionally sickening horror film about the boss (Woods) of a cable TV station catering to the "subterranean market" who falls victim to his own TV set. Rated R for profanity, sex, nudity, violence, gore, and pure nausea.

1983   88 minutes

VILLAGE OF THE DAMNED
★★★★

DIRECTOR: Wolf Rilla
CAST: George Sanders, Barbara Shelley, Michael Gwynne

A science-fiction thriller about twelve strangely emotionless children all born at the same time in a small village in England. Sanders plays their teacher, who tries to stop their plans for conquest.

This excellent low-budget film provides chills for the viewer that many high-budgeted films fail to provide. The telepathic powers of the children are not overdone, and the horror comes from a well-written and well-acted script rather than blood and guts.

1960   B & W   78 minutes

VILLAGE OF THE GIANTS
★★

DIRECTOR: Bert I. Gordon
CAST: Tommy Kirk, Beau Bridges, Ron Howard, Johnny Crawford, Toni Basil

Utterly ridiculous story of a gang of teenage misfits taking over a small town after they ingest a bizarre substance created by a 12-year-old named "Genius" and grow to gigantic heights. What makes this worth watching, though, are the famous faces of the many young stars-to-be. Some cool songs by the Beau Brummels also help keep things moving along. Be warned that the special effects are a joke.

1965   80 minutes

VISITING HOURS
🐾

DIRECTOR: Jean Claude Lord
CAST: Lee Grant, William Shatner, Linda Purl, Michael Ironside

Here's a Canadian production that actually forces the viewer to wallow in the degradation, humiliation, and mutilation of women. What Lee Grant, William Shatner, and Linda Purl are doing in such an awful picture is anybody's guess. Rated R for blood, gore, violence, and general unrelenting ugliness.

1982   103 minutes

W
★★★½

DIRECTOR: Richard Quine
CAST: Twiggy, Michael Witney, Eugene Roche, John Vernon, Dirk Benedict

Someone is trying to kill the Lewises, Katy (Twiggy) and Ben (Michael Witney). Each gets into a car and finds too late that it has been tampered with and nearly is killed in a head-long, high-speed crash. On each vehicle, the letter W is scrawled in the dust. Who could be after them? Katy knows, but she's afraid to tell. This is a highly involving, Hitchcockian thriller that will keep mystery lovers captivated as they pick up clues bit by bit. Rated PG.

1974   95 minutes

WAGES OF FEAR, THE
★★★★

DIRECTOR: Henri-Georges Clouzot
CAST: Yves Montand, Charles Vanel, Peter Van Eyck, Vera Clouzot, Folco Lulli, William Tubbs

This masterpiece of suspense pits four seedy and destitute men against the challenge of driving two nitroglycerin-laden trucks over crude and treacherous Central American mountain roads to quell a monstrous oil well fire. Incredible risk and numbing fear ride along as the drivers, goaded by high wages, cope with dilemma after dilemma. Be ready to sweat. This one really is a cliff-hanger. In French with English subtitles.

1953   B & W 105 minutes

WAIT UNTIL DARK
★★★★

DIRECTOR: Terence Young
CAST: Audrey Hepburn, Alan Arkin, Richard Crenna, Efrem Zimbalist Jr.

Suspense abounds in this chiller about a blind housewife (Audrey Hepburn) who is being pursued by a gang of criminals. She has inadvertently gotten hold of a doll filled with heroin. Alan Arkin is especially frightening as the psychotic gang's mastermind who alternates between moments of deceptive charm and sudden violence in his attempt to separate Hepburn from the doll.

1967   108 minutes

WARNING SIGN
★★★

DIRECTOR: Hal Barwood
CAST: Sam Waterston, Kathleen Quinlan, Yaphet Kotto, Jeffrey De Munn, Richard Dysart, G. W. Bailey, Rick Rossovich

A sort of *The Andromeda Strain* meets *The Night of the Living Dead*, this is a passable science-fiction thriller about what happens when an accident occurs at a plant, producing a particularly virulent microbe for germ warfare. The screenplay, by director Hal Barwood and executive producer Matthew Robbins, occasionally strays into all-too-familiar territory, but the fine performances by Sam Waterston (best-actor nominee for *The Killing Fields*), Kathleen Quinlan (*I Never Promised You a Rose Garden*), Yaphet Kotto (*Alien*), and Jeffrey De Munn keep the viewer's interest. Rated R for violence and gore.

1985   99 minutes

WATCH ME WHEN I KILL
🐢

DIRECTOR: Anthony Bido
CAST: Richard Stewart, Sylvia Kramer

You've heard of the spaghetti western? Now here's the spaghetti slasher. Sylvia Kramer plays a woman who is witness to a murder and is now in danger of becoming one of the killer's next victims. Dubbed in English and stupid. Not rated; has violence and profanity.

1981					94 minutes

WATCHER IN THE WOODS, THE
★★

DIRECTOR: John Hough

CAST: Bette Davis, Lynn-Holly Johnson, Carroll Baker, David McCallum

This typical teenage gothic plot (family moves into old mansion and strange things begin to happen) is completely obscure and ends by defiantly refusing to explain itself. Rated PG because of minor violence.

1980					84 minutes

WHAT EVER HAPPENED TO BABY JANE?
★★★

DIRECTOR: Robert Aldrich

CAST: Bette Davis, Joan Crawford, Victor Buono

One of the last hurrahs of screen giants Bette Davis and Joan Crawford in a chillingly unpleasant tale of two aged sisters. Davis plays a former child movie star who spends her declining years dreaming of lost fame and tormenting her sister (Crawford). Victor Buono deserves special notice in a meaty supporting role.

1962			B & W 132 minutes

WHEN A STRANGER CALLS
★★★

DIRECTOR: Fred Walton

CAST: Carol Kane, Charles Durning, Colleen Dewhurst, Tony Beckley, Rachel Roberts, Ron O'Neal

A *Psycho II*–style atmosphere pervades this film when the murderer of two children returns after seven years to complete his crime.

1979					97 minutes

WHEN TIME RAN OUT!
★½

DIRECTOR: James Goldstone

CAST: Paul Newman, Jacqueline Bisset, William Holden, James Franciscus, Edward Albert, Red Buttons, Ernest Borgnine, Burgess Meredith, Valentine Cortese, Alex Karras, Barbara Carrera

This disastrous disaster film runs out of plot and characterization after the first few scenes. Time never seems to run out as we wait and wait for a volcano to erupt and put the all-star cast out of its misery. Producer Irwin Allen deserves to have a molten lava shampoo for inflicting this one on the public. Rated PG.

1980					121 minutes

WHITE ZOMBIE
★★★★

DIRECTOR: Victor Halperin

CAST: Bela Lugosi, Madge Bellamy, Robert Frazer, Brandon Hurst

This eerie little thriller is the consummate zombie film, with hordes of the walking dead doing the bidding of evil Bela Lugosi as their overseer and master. A damsel-in-distress story with a new twist, this independently produced gem features sets and production standards usually found in films by the major studios. A minor classic, with a stand-out role by Lugosi.

1932			B & W 73 minutes

WHO SLEW AUNTIE ROO?
★★

DIRECTOR: Curtis Harrington

CAST: Shelley Winters, Mark Lester, Chloe Franks, Ralph Richardson, Lionel Jeffries, Hugh Griffith

Ghoulish horror version of *Hansel and Gretel*, with Shelley Winters as the madwoman who lures two children (Mark Lester, Chloe Franks) into her evil clutches. Rated R for violence.

1971   89 minutes

WICKER MAN, THE
★★★★½
DIRECTOR: Robin Hardy
CAST: Edward Woodward, Christopher Lee, Britt Ekland, Diane Cilento, Ingrid Pitt, Lindsay Kemp

To call this simply one of the finest horror films ever made would be a grave disservice. It has plenty of suspense and terror, to be sure, but there is also ample mystery, comedy, and eroticism. An anonymous letter that implies a missing girl has been murdered brings Sergeant Howie (Edward Woodward), of Scotland Yard, to Summerisle, an island off the coast of England. The islanders are anything but cooperative. Lord Summerisle (Christopher Lee), the ruler and religious leader of the island, seems to take it all as a joke, so Howie swears to find the truth. Rated R.

1973   95 minutes

WILLARD
★★½
DIRECTOR: Daniel Mann
CAST: Bruce Davison, Ernest Borgnine, Sondra Locke

This worked far better as a novel, although the film accurately follows the elements of Stephen Gilbert's *Ratman's Notebooks*. Bruce Davison plays a put-upon wimp who identifies more with rodents than people. When nasty Ernest Borgnine becomes too unpleasant, Davison decides to make him the bait in a better rattrap. Pretty cheesy stuff . . . but it was destined to get worse in the sequel, entitled *Ben*. Rated PG—mild violence.

1971   95 minutes

WITCHING, THE (NECROMANCY)
★
DIRECTOR: Bert I. Gordon
CAST: Orson Welles, Pamela Franklin, Michael Ontkean, Lee Purcell, Harvey Jason, Sue Bernard

Whenever he was making a movie just for the money, Orson Welles would disguise himself. In this piece of trash from director Bert I. Gordon, he wears both a false nose and a beard. But there can be no doubt that *Citizen Kane* himself is playing Cato, the head of a community whose one enterprise is the manufacture of occult toys. Cato, as it turns out, takes his witchcraft seriously and attempts to use it to bring his dead son back to life. To do so, he needs a willing sacrifice: Pamela Franklin, still haunted by debuting in *The Innocents*. Rated PG.

1972   82 minutes

WITCHING TIME
★★
DIRECTOR: Don Leaver
CAST: Jon Finch, Patricia Quinn, Prunella Gee, Ian McCulloch

Another entry from "Thriller Video," hosted by TV's Elvira, "Mistress of the Dark." The owner of an English farmhouse is visited by a previous occupant, a seventeenth-century witch. Unfortunately for him, after three hundred years, the old gal is hot to trot. Nice production values, but it fails to conjure up the needed suspense. Originally filmed for the British television series *Hammer House of Horror*. Unrated; nudity edited out of the print used for this cassette.

1985   60 minutes

WIZARD OF GORE, THE
★½

DIRECTOR: Herschell Gordon Lewis
CAST: Ray Sager, Judy Clark, Wayne Raven

Herschell Gordon Lewis (*Blood Feast*) is at it again! Blood and guts galore as a sideshow magician takes the old "saw the girl in half" trick a bit too far. Disgusting. Rated R.

1982   80 minutes

WOLFEN
★★

DIRECTOR: Michael Wadleigh
CAST: Albert Finney, Diane Venora, Gregory Hines, Tom Noonan, Edward James Olmos, Dick O'Neill

The best features of this sluggish horror film are its innovative visual work and actors (Albert Finney, Diane Venora, and Gregory Hines), who make the most of an uneven script. Directed by Michael Wadleigh (*Woodstock*), *Wolfen* follows a sequence of mysterious murders that are sometimes disturbingly bloody. (This explains the "R" rating.)

1981   115 minutes

WRONG MAN, THE
★★★★

DIRECTOR: Alfred Hitchcock
CAST: Henry Fonda, Vera Miles, Anthony Quayle, Harold J. Stone, Nehemiah Persoff

In this frightening true-life tale, Henry Fonda plays a man falsely accused of robbery. Vera Miles is his wife, who can't handle the changes wrought in their lives by this gross injustice. Fonda is excellent.

1956   B & W 105 minutes

XTRO
½

DIRECTOR: Harry Davenport
CAST: Philip Sayer, Bernice Stegers, Maryam D'Abo, Danny Brainin, Simon Nash

Grotesquely slimy sci-fi/horror flick with an idiot plot—one that requires every character to behave like a jerk at all times—that revolves around a series of repulsive bladder effects. Average dad Philip Sayer is abducted by aliens; he returns three years later and, just to prove his love, infects his son, kills countless people, and turns the family *au pair* girl into an alien breeding chamber. Hard to decide which of the many "wet" effects is the worst; probable winner is Sayer's return as he bursts, full-grown, from the stomach of an "impregnated" woman. Sick, sick, sick. Rated R.

1982   84 minutes

ZOMBIE
½

DIRECTOR: Lucio Fulci
CAST: Tisa Farrow, Ian McCulloch, Richard Johnson

Gruesome, gory, and ghastly unauthorized entry in George Romero's zombie series. Richard Johnson is a mad scientist who reanimates the dead; the flesh-eating stiffs can be destroyed only by bullets in the brain . . . a chore that Johnson embraces lovingly and director Lucio Fulci's camera repeats *ad nauseum*. Tisa Farrow (yes, Mia's sister) joins an ever-dwindling group of adventurers who meet their fates on this un-named Caribbean island. Watch for the grand moment when a sliver of wood punctures the eyeball of one unlucky lass. She never blinks; bet you will! Rated X for gore and nudity.

1979   91 minutes

ZOMBIES OF MORA TAU
★

DIRECTOR: Edward Cahn
CAST: Gregg Palmer, Allison Hayes

Laughable, low-budget time-waster about zombies and sunken treasure. Shows how dull zombies were before *Night of the Living Dead*. Unrated, but timid enough for your aunt Sally.

1957   B & W   70 minutes

MUSICALS

ABSOLUTE BEGINNERS
★★★★

DIRECTOR: Julien Temple
CAST: Eddie O'Connell, Patsy Kensit, David Bowie, James Fox, Ray Davies, Anita Morris, Sade Adu, Mandy Rice Davies

Julien Temple has taken what he learned from rock videos (the Stones' "She Was Hot" and Bowie's "Jazzin' for Blue Jean"), TV movies (*It's All True*, with Orson Welles, Grace Jones, and Mel Brooks), and feature films (the Sex Pistols' *The Great Rock 'n' Roll Swindle*), and has rekineticized the movie musical for the 1980s. The likes of *Absolute Beginners* has not been seen in quite some time: daring, inventive, and original; riveting colors and vivid sounds. It is based on the cult novel by Colin MacInnes, who chronicled the musical and social scene in London during the pivotal summer of 1958. Occasionally the accents are too thick and the references too obscure for Americans, but the overall effect is an unequivocal high. Rated PG-13 for stylized, but rather intense, violence and some profanity.

1986   107 minutes

ALL THAT JAZZ
★★★★

DIRECTOR: Bob Fosse
CAST: Roy Scheider, Jessica Lange, Ann Reinking

While it may not be what viewers expect from a musical, this story of a gifted choreographer, Joe Gideon (Roy Scheider, in his finest performance), who relentlessly drives himself to exhaustion is daring, imaginative, shocking, and visually stunning. The screenplay, co-written by director Bob Fosse with producer Robert Alan Arthur, tells of Gideon's rise from an ambitious young dancer in sleazy strip joints (in flashback) to the most respected director-choreographer on Broadway. But while his success is unquestioned, Gideon's private life is a shambles. His health is hampered by overwork, amphetamines, and alcohol. And he gives so much of himself to his work, he has precious little left over for those who love him. Rated R.

1979   123 minutes

AMADEUS
★★★★★

DIRECTOR: Milos Forman

CAST: Tom Hulce, F. Murray Abraham, Elizabeth Berridge

Peter Shaffer adapted his acclaimed stage play into what is certain to be an enduring screen work. F. Murray Abraham, who won an Oscar for his performance, gives a haunting portrayal of Antonio Salieri, the court composer for Hapsburg Emperor Joseph II. A second-rate musician, Salieri felt jealousy and admiration for the young musical genius Wolfgang Amadeus Mozart (Tom Hulce), who died at the age of thirty-five—perhaps by Salieri's hand. It's a stunning film full of great music, drama, and wit. Rated PG for mild violence.

1984   158 minutes

AMERICAN IN PARIS, AN
★★★★★

DIRECTOR: Vincente Minnelli

CAST: Gene Kelly, Leslie Caron, Nina Foch, Oscar Levant

One of Gene Kelly's classic musicals, this release features the hoofer as the free-spirited author of the title. The picture is a heady mixture of light entertainment and the music of George Gershwin.

1951   113 minutes

ANNIE
★★★★

DIRECTOR: John Huston

CAST: Albert Finney, Carol Burnett, Bernadette Peters, Edward Herrmann, Aileen Quinn

A sparkling $40 million movie musical based on the Broadway production of the long-running comic strip "Little Orphan Annie." Ten-year-old Aileen Quinn is just fine in the title role. Rated PG for brief profanity.

1982   128 minutes

BABES IN ARMS
★★★

DIRECTOR: Busby Berkeley

CAST: Mickey Rooney, Judy Garland, June Preisser, Douglas McPhail, Guy Kibbee, Charles Winninger, Henry Hull, Margaret Hamilton

Richard Rodgers and Larry Hart wrote the Broadway musical from which this film was taken—although most of the songs they wrote are absent. But never mind; Mickey and Judy sing, dance, and prance up a storm as the kids in town put on a show! If the tune "Good Morning" seems familiar, it's because you know it from the later, classic *Singin' in the Rain*.

1939   B & W   96 minutes

BAND WAGON, THE
★★★★

DIRECTOR: Vincente Minnelli

CAST: Fred Astaire, Cyd Charisse, Jack Buchanan, Nanette Fabray, Oscar Levant

One of Vincente Minnelli's best grand-scale musicals and one of Fred Astaire's most endearing roles. He plays a Hollywood has-been who decides to try his luck on stage. The story has a behind-the-scenes approach that blossoms into another "Let's put on a show!" extravaganza. Watch for the slick dance sequence that lampoons Mickey Spillane. Best of all, this is the film that gave us *That's*

Entertainment. Lots of fun. Unrated—family fare.

1953   112 minutes

BEACH BLANKET BINGO
★★½

DIRECTOR: William Asher

CAST: Frankie Avalon, Annette Funicello, Paul Lynde, Harvey Lembeck, Don Rickles, Linda Evans, Jody McCrea, Marta Kristen, John Ashley, Deborah Walley, Buster Keaton

The fifth in the series, and the last true "Beach Party" film. Basically, it's the same old stuff: stars on their way up (Linda Evans) or on their way down (Buster Keaton) or at their peak (Frankie and Annette), spouting silly dialogue and singing through echo chambers. But it's one of the best of the series, whether you're laughing with it or at it. Enjoyable for those who lived through that era, but don't be surprised if your kids wonder what the attraction is. Unrated.

1965   98 minutes

BEACH BOYS: AN AMERICAN BAND, THE
★★★

DIRECTOR: Malcolm Leo

CAST: Brian, Carl, and Dennis Wilson, Al Jardine, Bruce Johnston, Mike Love

Even the most fervent fans of the country's number-one surf group are likely to be a bit disappointed by this "authorized biography," directed by Malcolm Leo (*This Is Elvis*). It skims the surface of the band's troubled but ultimately triumphant history and only occasionally catches a wave. The disturbing problems of the Beach Boys' "genius" songwriter, Brian Wilson, who spent three years in bed because, in his words, he "got

hold of all these drugs, and they messed me up," and his younger brother, drummer-singer-songwriter Dennis, who drowned in 1983 and was prevented from playing with the group in later years because of drinking and drug use, are glossed over. We are left wanting to know more and, more important, why. Still, there is much for Beach Boys fans to enjoy here, more than forty songs from their twenty-five-year career. Rated G.

1984   90 minutes

BEAT STREET
★½

DIRECTOR: Stan Lathan

CAST: Rae Dawn Chong, Guy Davis, Robert Taylor, Jon Chardiet

Even though it has better production values and a stronger storyline than *Breakin'*, the low-budget movie about break dancing that preceded it, *Breakin'* is the better film. That's only because the emphasis in *Breakin'* is placed squarely where it belongs: on the amazing abilities of today's break dancers. Not so in this release, where the hackneyed plot, about kids breaking into show biz, and just-okay acting by Rae Dawn Chong (*Quest For Fire*), Guy Davis (son of Ossie Davis and Ruby Dee), and Jon Chardiet overpower the dancing and undermine the picture's excitement. Rated PG for profanity and violence.

1984   106 minutes

BEST FOOT FORWARD
★★★

DIRECTOR: Edward Buzzell

CAST: Lucille Ball, William Gaxton, Virginia Weidler, Tommy Dix, June Allyson, Nancy Walker, Gloria DeHaven

Film star Lucille Ball accepts military cadet Tommy Dix's invitation to his school's annual dance. The film introduced June Allyson and Nancy Walker and gave numerous high schools a fight song by adapting its biggest hit, "Buckle Down, Winsocki." Wholesome family fun.

1943   95 minutes

BEST LITTLE WHOREHOUSE IN TEXAS, THE
★★★½

DIRECTOR: Colin Higgins
CAST: Burt Reynolds, Dolly Parton, Dom De Luise, Charles Durning

Dolly Parton and Burt Reynolds in a so-so version of the Broadway play, whose title explains all. Rated R for nudity, profanity, and sexual situations.

1982   114 minutes

BIKINI BEACH
★★

DIRECTOR: William Asher
CAST: Frankie Avalon, Annette Funicello, Keenan Wynn, Don Rickles

This silly film captures Frankie Avalon and Annette Funicello in their best swim attire. There are lots of girls in bikinis and some drag-racing for an added diversion. A group of kids who always hang out at the beach try to prevent a man from closing it. Ho-hum.

1964   100 minutes

BIZET'S CARMEN
★★★★★

DIRECTOR: Francesco Rosi
CAST: Placido Domingo, Julia Migenes-Johnson

Julia Migenes-Johnson and Placido Domingo star in this film adaptation of the opera by Georges Bizet based on the short story by Prosper Mérimée about a poor girl whose fierce independence maddens the men who become obsessed with her. Francesco Rosi directed this, the most satisfying treatment of an opera yet to be done in a big commercial film. In French, with English subtitles. Rated PG for mild violence.

1985   152 minutes

BLUE HAWAII
★★★½

DIRECTOR: Norman Taurog
CAST: Elvis Presley, John Blackman, Angela Lansbury, Iris Adrian

In this enjoyable Elvis Presley flick, the star plays a returning soldier who works with tourists against his mom's (Angela Lansbury) wishes.

1962   101 minutes

BODY ROCK
👤

DIRECTOR: Marcelo Epstein
CAST: Lorenzo Lamas, Vicki Frederick, Cameron Dye, Ray Sharkey

A boring pop musical, this features Lorenzo Lamas as a youngster from the South Bronx who sees the break-dancing subculture as his ticket to the big time. Rated PG-13.

1984   93 minutes

BREAKIN'
★½

DIRECTOR: Joel Silberg
CAST: Lucinda Dickey, Adolfo Quinones, Michael Chambers, Ben Lokey

It it weren't for the acting, direction, and plot, this would be a terrific little movie. The dancing scenes are wonderful. As a whole, *Breakin'* is pretty lame. Sort of

Flashdance meets street break-dancing, the film would have us believe that jazz dancer Kelly (Lucinda Dickey) could hook up with street dancers Ozone ("Shabba-Do") and Turbo ("Boogaloo Shrimp") to win dance contests and finally break (no pun intended) into big-time show biz. No way. She's no match for them. Anyone watching *Breakin'* would know director Joel Silberg was only fakin'. But my, oh, my, those crazy dancin' feet—they almost make this movie worth sitting through. Rated PG for profanity and violence.

1984   90 minutes

BREAKIN' 2 ELECTRIC BOOGALOO
★★½

DIRECTOR: Sam Firstenberg
CAST: Lucinda Dickey, Adolfo Quinones, Michael Chambers

This sometimes exhilarating break-dancing movie is a follow-up to *Breakin'*, which grossed $38 million, and it's better than the original. This time, instead of trying to break into show business, Kelly (Lucinda Dickey), Ozone (Adolfo "Shabba-Doo" Quinones), and Turbo (Michael "Boogaloo Shrimp" Chambers) have to "put on a show" to save a local arts center for children. The result is generally an entertaining contemporary musical. Rated PG for brief violence and suggested sex.

1984   90 minutes

BREAKING GLASS
★★½

DIRECTOR: Brian Gibson
CAST: Phil Daniels, Hazel O'Connor, Jon Finch, Jonathan Pryce

British film about a new wave singer's rise to the top, at the expense of personal relationships. Hazel O'Connor's heavy music

isn't for all tastes, and the plot line is as old as film itself, but the actors are sincere, and the film contains some striking visual imagery. Rated PG.

1980   104 minutes

BRIGADOON
★★★★

DIRECTOR: Vincente Minnelli
CAST: Gene Kelly, Van Johnson, Cyd Charisse, Elaine Stewart, Barry Jones, Hugh Laing

This enchanting musical stars Van Johnson and Gene Kelly as two Americans who discover Brigadoon, a Scottish village with a lifespan of only one day for every hundred years. In the village, Kelly meets Cyd Charisse, and they naturally dance up a storm.

1954   108 minutes

BRING ON THE NIGHT
★

DIRECTOR: Michael Apted
CAST: Sting, Omar Hakim, Darryl Jones, Kenny Kirkland, Branford Marsalis

Obnoxious, self-serving documentary about popular rock star Sting (formerly of The Police) and the formation of his new band. The first three-quarters of the film features nothing more than a few rehearsal sessions and far too much of Sting talking about Sting, followed by a live concert finale which is intercut with unnecessary scenes of his son being born. Strictly for die-hard fans, this movie earns its one star for the dynamic performances of the Police classic "Roxanne." Rated PG-13 for the birth scene.

1985   97 minutes

BROADWAY MELODY OF 1936
★★★

DIRECTOR: Roy Del Ruth

CAST: Jack Benny, Eleanor Powell, Robert Taylor, Una Merkel, Buddy Ebsen

Backstage musical comedy. Obnoxious gossip columnist Jack Benny tries to use dancer Eleanor Powell to harass producer Robert Taylor. Forget the plot and enjoy the singing and dancing—including Taylor's rendition of "I've Got a Feelin' You're Foolin'," the only time he sang on-screen in his own voice.

1935   B & W 110 minutes

BROADWAY MELODY OF 1938
★★½

DIRECTOR: Roy Del Ruth
CAST: Robert Taylor, Eleanor Powell, George Murphy, Binnie Barnes, Sophie Tucker, Judy Garland, Buddy Ebsen, Willie Howard, Billy Gilbert

Fifteen-year-old Judy Garland stops the show and steals it in this tuneful musical anthology when she sings the now legendary "Dear Mr. Gable" version of "You Made Me Love You." The finale stretches credibility until it snaps as Eleanor Powell, in top hat and tails, dances with a division of chorus boys before a neon sky-line. It's all sauce without substance, with a song to remember. The 1936 and 1940 editions are better by far.

1937   B & W 110 minutes

BYE BYE BIRDIE
★★★

DIRECTOR: George Sidney
CAST: Dick Van Dyke, Ann-Margret, Janet Leigh, Paul Lynde, Bobby Rydell

A rock star's approaching appearance in a small town turns several lives upside down in this pleasant musical comedy. Based on the successful Broadway play, this is pretty lightweight stuff, but a likable cast and good production numbers make it worthwhile. No rating; okay for the whole family.

1963   112 minutes

CABARET
★★★★½

DIRECTOR: Bob Fosse
CAST: Liza Minnelli, Michael York, Helmut Griem, Joel Grey

This classic musical-drama takes place in Germany in 1931. The Nazi party has not yet assumed complete control, and the local cabaret unfolds the story of two young lovers, the ensuing mood of the country, and the universal touch of humanity. Everything is handled with taste—bisexual encounters, the horrors of the Nazi regime, and the bawdy entertainment of the nightclub. "Host" Joel Grey is brilliant. Michael York and Liza Minnelli are first-rate. So is the movie. Rated PG.

1972   128 minutes

CAMELOT
★★★

DIRECTOR: Joshua Logan
CAST: Richard Harris, Vanessa Redgrave, Franco Nero, David Hemmings, Lionel Jeffries

The legend of King Arthur and the Round Table—from the first meeting of Arthur (Richard Harris) and Guinevere (Vanessa Redgrave) to the affair between Guinevere and Lancelot (Franco Nero), and finally the fall of Camelot—is brought to life in this enjoyable musical.

1967   178 minutes

CAN'T STOP THE MUSIC

DIRECTOR: Nancy Walker

CAST: The Village People, Valerie Perrine, Bruce Jenner, Steve Guttenberg, Paul Sand, Tammy Grimes, June Havoc, Jack Weston, Barbara Rush, Leigh Taylor-Young

Despite the positive-thinking title, the music of the Village People ("Macho Man," "YMCA") was stopped cold by this basically awful movie musical about the world of show biz. The only thing happy about this irrepressibly sunny groaner are the members of the featured musical group, which has completely slipped into obscurity. Rated PG.

1980   118 minutes

CAREFREE
★★★

DIRECTOR: Mark Sandrich
CAST: Fred Astaire, Ginger Rogers, Ralph Bellamy, Jack Carson

In this blend of music, slapstick situations, and romantic byplay, Ginger Rogers is a crazy, mixed-up girl-child who goes to psychiatrist Fred Astaire for counsel. His treatment results in her falling in love with him. While trying to stop this, he falls in love with her. Of course they dance! All along the way! Ralph Bellamy is the sap Ginger cannot decide about. "Change Partners" is the best-known of the Irving Berlin songs dotting the landscape. It's more a Rogers film than an Astaire film, and more screwball comedy than musical.

1938   B & W   80 minutes

CHORUS LINE, A
★★★★

DIRECTOR: Richard Attenborough

CAST: Michael Douglas, Alyson Reed, Terence Mann, Audrey Landers, Michael Belvins, Yamil Borges, Jan Gan Boyd, Sharon Brown, Gregg Burge, Janet Jones, Michelle Johnston, Pam Klinger, Cameron English, Tony Fields, Nicole Fosse, Vicki Frederick, Charles McGowan, Justin Ross, Matt West

The screen version of Michael Bennett's hit Broadway musical allows the viewer to experience the anxiety, struggle, and triumph of a group of dancers auditioning for a stage production. Director Richard Attenborough blends big production numbers with intimate moments as gracefully as he did the panorama and character development in *Gandhi*. The songs are not the kind one hums afterward. However, they do convey the feelings and personalities of the characters, a more important function in this film. In the story, a group of would-be Broadway hoofers strut their stuff for a demanding choreographer (Michael Douglas), who chooses from among them for his chorus line. Rated PG for profanity and sexual descriptions.

1985   120 minutes

CINDERFELLA
★

DIRECTOR: Frank Tashlin
CAST: Jerry Lewis, Anna Maria Alberghetti, Ed Wynn

This musical version of the oft-told fairy tale has little to recommend it. Adapted for the talents of star Jerry Lewis, it has no laughs to speak of and will only appeal to his fans.

1960   91 minutes

COAL MINER'S DAUGHTER
★★★★½

DIRECTOR: Michael Apted
CAST: Sissy Spacek, Tommy Lee Jones, Beverly D'Angelo, Levon Helm

Sissy Spacek gives a superb, totally believable performance in this film biography of country singer Loretta Lynn. The title role takes Spacek from Lynn's impoverished Appalachian childhood through marriage at thirteen up to her mid-thirties and reign as the "First Lady of Country Music." Directed with documentarylike credibility by Michael Apted. Rated PG.

1980   125 minutes

COMEBACK
★★★½

DIRECTOR: Christel Buschmann
CAST: Eric Burdon

Real-life rock singer Eric Burdon (lead singer of the Animals) stars in this rock 'n' roll drama. Burdon plays a part that mirrors his own life: that of a white blues singer trying to get back on top. He has several obstacles to overcome: a huge debt to record companies, a wacky wife who goes on binges, and a manager who keeps giving him drugs. At one point Burdon refuses some cocaine offered by the latter, saying, "You know, anyone who's ever been managed by you is either dead or dying." The businessman replies that Burdon would be worth more to him dead. "When you're dead, you're great," he says in a phrase that evokes the posthumous fame of Jimi Hendrix, Janis Joplin, and Jim Morrison. Unrated.

1982   96 minutes

COMPLEAT BEATLES, THE
★★★★

DIRECTOR: Patrick Montgomery
CAST: Malcolm McDowell, The Beatles

Even experts on the life and times of the Fab Four are likely to find something new and enlightening in *The Compleat Beatles*. Furthermore, while not a consistent work, this film provides something of interest for fans and non-fans. Narrated by Malcolm McDowell, it focuses not only on the careers of John Lennon, Paul McCartney, George Harrison, and Ringo Starr but also on the era that made and molded them. Unrated.

1982   119 minutes

CROSSOVER DREAMS
★★★★

DIRECTOR: Leon Ichaso
CAST: Reuben Blades, Shawn Elliot, Elizabeth Peña, Tom Signorelli, Frank Robles

Reuben Blades plays a popular Latino musician who tries his talents at the big time. The price he pays for his efforts is high. And while this may all sound like one big movie cliché, it's now time to add that the cast put in performances that redefine the story, giving this trite tale a bite that will surprise the viewer, who may expect nothing but music and laughs. *Crossover Dreams* does not have an MPAA rating, but would probably be a PG for sex and profanity.

1985   85 minutes

CROSSROADS
★★★½

DIRECTOR: Walter Hill
CAST: Ralph Macchio, Joe Seneca, Jami Gertz, Joe Morton, Robert Judd, Steve Vai, Dennis Lipscomb, Harry Carey Jr.

A superb blues score by guitarist Ry Cooder (featuring the inspired harmonica playing of Sonny Terry) highlights this enjoyable fantasy about an ambitious young bluesman (Ralph Macchio) who "goes down to the crossroads," in the words of Robert Johnson, to make a deal with the devil for fame and fortune. Joe Seneca co-stars as the veteran blues singer and harp player Willie Brown, who takes Macchio on his journey. In some ways, this is just a music-oriented version of *The Karate Kid*, but this will bother only some viewers. Most will enjoy the performances, the story, and the music in this all-too-rare big-screen celebration of the blues and its mythology. Rated R for profanity, suggested sex, and violence.

1986　　　　　　　　　　105 minutes

DAMES
★★★

DIRECTOR: Ray Enright
CAST: Joan Blondell, Dick Powell, Ruby Keeler, Zasu Pitts, Guy Kibbee, Hugh Herbert

Music, songs, dancing, great Busby Berkeley production numbers. Plot? Know the one about backing a Broadway musical? But, gee, it's fun to see and hear Joan Blondell, Dick Powell, Ruby Keeler, Zasu Pitts, Guy Kibbee, and Hugh "Woo-woo" Herbert again.

1934　　　B & W　90 minutes

DAMN YANKEES
★★★½

DIRECTOR: George Abbott, Stanley Donen
CAST: Gwen Verdon, Ray Walston, Tab Hunter

A torrid, wiggling vamp teams with a sly, hissing Devil to frame the Yankees by turning a middle-aged baseball fan into a wunderkind and planting him on the team. Gwen Verdon is sensational as the temptress Lola, who gets whatever she wants. Hollywood called on her to reprise her role in the original Broadway musical hit. Lots of pep and zing in this one.

1958　　　　　　　　　　110 minutes

DAMSEL IN DISTRESS, A
★★★

DIRECTOR: George Stevens
CAST: Fred Astaire, Joan Fontaine, Gracie Allen, George Burns, Constance Collier, Reginald Gardiner

By choice, Fred Astaire made this one without Ginger, who complemented him, but with Joan Fontaine—then a beginner—who did not, and who could not dance. Fred's an American popular composer in stuffy London. He mistakenly thinks heiress Joan is a chorus girl. The best sequence in this last Gershwin film musical has Fred, George, and Gracie romping through a fun house. It won choreographer Hermes Pan an Oscar, but falls far short of making the film a winner. Vintage Astaire, however.

1937　　　B & W　98 minutes

DANGEROUS WHEN WET
★★

DIRECTOR: Charles Walter
CAST: Esther Williams, Fernando Lamas, Jack Carson, Charlotte Greenwood, Denise Darcel

Fame and fortune await she who swims the English Channel. Esther Williams plays a cornfed wholesome who goes for it, Fernando Lamas cheers her on. Semisour Jack Carson and high-kicking Charlotte Greenwood clown. Good music and a novel underwater Tom and Jerry cartoon sequence.

1953　　　　　　　　　　95 minutes

DIVINE MADNESS
★★★½

DIRECTOR: Michael Ritchie
CAST: Bette Midler

Here's the sassy, unpredictable Bette Midler as captured in concert by director Michael Ritchie (*Bad News Bears*). Some of it is great; some of it is not. It helps if you're a Midler fan. Rated R for profanity.

1980   95 minutes

DON'T LOOK BACK
★★★

DIRECTOR: D. A. Pennebaker
CAST: Bob Dylan, Joan Baez, Donovan, Alan Price

A documentary account directed by D. A. Pennebaker of folk singer/poet ("guitarist," he calls himself) Bob Dylan on a 1965 tour of England. The tedium of travel and pressures of performing are eased by relaxing moments with fellow travelers Joan Baez, Alan Price, and (briefly) Donovan. Shot in striking black and white, with excellent sound quality, *Don't Look Back* has not been exhibited in about a decade. Unrated, it contains some vulgarity.

1967   B & W   96 minutes

DOUBLE TROUBLE
★½

DIRECTOR: Norman Taurog
CAST: Elvis Presley, Annette Day

Typical Elvis Presley musical. This time he plays a rock 'n' roll singer touring England. When a teenage heiress (whose life is constantly threatened) falls for him, he gets caught up in the action. Lots of Elvis songs, the most popular of which is "Long Legged Girls."

1967   92 minutes

DU BARRY WAS A LADY
★★½

DIRECTOR: Roy Del Ruth
CAST: Red Skelton, Lucille Ball, Gene Kelly, Zero Mostel, Virginia O'Brien, Donald Meek, Louis Beavers, Tommy Dorsey, George Givot

Despite the incredible collection of talent showcased in this film, the result is a slow-moving adaptation of a popular stage hit minus most of the music that made it popular in the first place. Set in the court of Louis XIV, this musical romp gives Red Skelton a chance to mug and Gene Kelly a chance to dance, while Lucille Ball and the other gals traipse about in a continuous change of costumes. Tommy Dorsey and the boys liven this one up to a point, but it's still a filmed stage play and forced to conform to stage conventions. Not a bad film, but not as good as the cast would indicate.

1943   101 minutes

EASTER PARADE
★★★★

DIRECTOR: Charles Walters
CAST: Judy Garland, Fred Astaire, Peter Lawford, Jules Munshin, Ann Miller

Judy Garland and Fred Astaire team up for this thoroughly enjoyable musical. Irving Berlin provided the songs for the story, about Astaire trying to forget ex-dance partner Ann Miller as he rises to the top with Garland. The result is an always watchable—and repeatable—treat. Gene Kelly was originally set to co-star, but he broke an ankle on the eve of production. To avert potential disaster, MGM talked Astaire out of a two-year retirement, and in addition to producing a classic picture, the company gave Astaire's career a new boost, adding thirty more illustrious years to its glow.

1948   103 minutes

EASY TO LOVE
★★½

DIRECTOR: Charles Walters
CAST: Esther Williams, Tony Martin, Van Johnson, Carroll Baker, John Bromfield

Tony Martin and Van Johnson vie for the love of mermaid Esther Williams in this most lavish of her numerous water spectacles. A toe-curling, high-speed sequence performed on water skis tops the Busby Berkeley numbers staged in lush Cypress Gardens at Winter Haven, Florida. It was Mae West who remarked: "Wet, Esther Williams can act; dry, she can't."

1953   96 minutes

EDDIE AND THE CRUISERS
★★★½

DIRECTOR: Martin Davidson
CAST: Tom Berenger, Michael Pare, Ellen Barkin

Long after his death, rock 'n' roll singer Eddie Wilson's (Michael Pare) songs become popular all over again. This revives interest in a long-shelved concept album. The tape for it has been stolen, and it's up to Wilson's one-time song writing collaborator (Tom Berenger) to find them. Only trouble is, other people want the tapes, too, and they may be willing to kill to get them. This isn't one of the great rock 'n' roll movies, but it's not terrible, either. The songs are great! Rated PG.

1983   92 minutes

EDITH AND MARCEL
★★★★

DIRECTOR: Claude Lelouch
CAST: Evelyn Bouix, Marcel Cerdan Jr., Jacques Villeret, Francis Huster

Based on the real life of famous torch singer Edith Piaf (Evelyn Bouix), this powerful musical-drama follows the passionate affair she had with champion boxer Marcel Cerdan (Marcel Cerdan Jr.). Director Claude Lelouch brings to life the stormy romance that at one time captured the attention of the world. Powerful acting combined with the wealth of Piaf's own recordings add up to quality fare.

1983   170 minutes

FABULOUS DORSEYS, THE
★★

DIRECTOR: Alfred E. Green
CAST: Tommy Dorsey, Jimmy Dorsey, Janet Blair, William Lundigan, Paul Whiteman

A mildly musical, plotless dual biography of the Dorsey brothers as they fight their way to the top while fighting with each other, trombone and clarinet at the ready. Janet Blair is cute, William Lundigan is personable, and Paul "Pops" Whiteman is along for the ride.

1947   B & W   88 minutes

FAME
★★★½

DIRECTOR: Alan Parker
CAST: Irene Cara, Lee Curreri, Eddie Barth, Laura Dean, Paul McCrane, Barry Miller, Gene Anthony Ray, Maureen Teefy

In generations past, the ambitions of the young generally ranged from growing up to be president to becoming a doctor or a nurse or perhaps even a lawyer or a fireman. But today nearly everybody wants to be a star. *Fame* addresses that contemporary dream in a most charming and lively fashion. By focusing on the aspirations, struggles, and personal lives of a group of talented and ambitious students at New York City's High School of the Performing Arts, it manages to say something about all of us and the age we live in. Rated R.

1980   130 minutes

FAST FORWARD
★★★
DIRECTOR: Sidney Poitier
CAST: John Scott Clough, Don Franklin, Tamara Mark, Gretchen Palmer

An obvious attempt to capitalize on the success of *Fame*, *Flashdance*, and *Footloose* (if only in name), this is an undisguised variation on the cliché of "let's put on a show so we can make it in show biz." In other words, it's *Breakin' 3*—only this time from the Midwest. In it, eight high-school kids from Sandusky, Ohio, journey to the big city of New York for a promised audition. *Fast Forward* is a bubbly bit of fluff that relies on sheer energy to patch up its plot and make up for the lack of an inspired score. In general, it works. Rated PG.

1985   100 minutes

FIDDLER ON THE ROOF
★★★★
DIRECTOR: Norman Jewison
CAST: Topol, Norman Crane, Leonard Frey, Molly Picon, Paul Mann, Rosalind Harris, Isaac Stern

A lavishly mounted musical, this 1979 screen adaptation of the long-running Broadway hit, based on the stories of Sholem Aleichem, works remarkably well. This is primarily thanks to Topol's immensely likable portrayal of Tevye, the proud but put-upon father clinging desperately to the old values in a changing world. The score of Sheldon Harnick and Jerry Bock (featuring such songs as "If I Were a Rich Man" and "Sunrise, Sunset") is a delight. Isaac Stern is the rooftop fiddler. Rated G.

1971   181 minutes

FINIAN'S RAINBOW
★★½
DIRECTOR: Francis Ford Coppola
CAST: Fred Astaire, Petula Clark, Tommy Steele, Keenan Wynn, Barbara Hancock, Don Francks

Those who believe Fred Astaire can do no wrong haven't seen this little oddity. Francis Ford Coppola's heavy direction is totally inappropriate for a musical—a genre with which he clearly was not comfortable—and the story's concerns about racial progress, which were outdated when the film first appeared, are positively embarrassing now. The mix of Irish leprechauns and the American deep South is an uneasy vehicle for demonstrating the injustices of bigotry. Rated G.

1968   145 minutes

FIRST NUDIE MUSICAL, THE
★★★
DIRECTOR: Mark Haggard
CAST: Bruce Kimmel, Stephen Nathan, Cindy Williams, Diana Canova

A struggling young director saves the studio by producing the world's first pornographic movie musical à la Busby Berkeley. Pleasant but extremely crude little romp. Bruce Kimmel and Cindy Williams make a cute couple who act as if it's all nothing more than just harmless fun. At times it is. The score includes such memorable ditties as "Four Dancing Dildos out on a

Spree!" and "Butch Dyke" (and that's a tango!). Not as bad as it sounds, but definitely for the very open-minded, and that's being generous. Rated R for nudity, profanity, and sex.

1979   100 minutes

FLASHDANCE
★★★
DIRECTOR: Adrian Lyne
CAST: Jennifer Beals, Michael Nouri, Lilia Skala

Director Adrian Lyne explodes images on the screen with eye-popping regularity while the spare screenplay centers on the ambitions of Alex Owens (Jennifer Beals), a welder who dreams of making the big time as a dancer. Alex finds this goal difficult to attain—until contractor Nick Hurley (Michael Nouri) decides to help. Rated R for nudity, profanity, and implied sex.

1983   96 minutes

FLOWER DRUM SONG
★★
DIRECTOR: Henry Koster
CAST: Jack Soo, Nancy Kwan, Benson Fong, Miyoshi Umeki, Juanita Hall, James Shigeta, Kam Tong, Reiko Sato

Set in San Francisco's colorful Chinatown, this Rogers and Hammerstein musical rings sour. It has its bright moments, but the score is largely second-rate. Whistled "Chop Suey" or hummed "I Enjoy Being A Girl" lately? The plot is conventional: a modern son's views versus those of an old-fashioned father. Ingredients include the usual Oriental cliché of an arranged marriage. Casting a pall over all is the obvious condescension displayed toward Chinese-Americans and the Bay City's Grant Avenue community. Moreover, the film is entirely too long.

1962   131 minutes

FLYING DOWN TO RIO
★★½
DIRECTOR: Thornton Freeland
CAST: Dolores Del Rio, Ginger Rogers, Fred Astaire

We're sure the joy of watching Fred Astaire and Ginger Rogers dance is the only thing that has prevented the negatives of this embarrassing movie from being burned. The ludicrous plot centers around an attempt to keep a Rio hotel afloat. The climactic dance number, in which chorus girls perform on airplane wings, is so corny it has now passed into the realm of camp humor.

1933   B & W   89 minutes

FOLLOW THE FLEET
★★★★
DIRECTOR: Mark Sandrich
CAST: Fred Astaire, Ginger Rogers, Randolph Scott, Harriet Hilliard, Betty Grable

In this musical Fred Astaire and Ginger Rogers are at their best, as a dance team separated by World War II. However, sailor Astaire still has time to romance Rogers while shipmate Randolph Scott gives the same treatment to her screen sister Harriet Hilliard (a.k.a. Harriet—Mrs. Ozzie—Nelson). Look for Lucille Ball in a small part.

1936   B & W   110 minutes

FOOTLIGHT PARADE
★★★½
DIRECTOR: Lloyd Bacon
CAST: James Cagney, Ruby Keeler, Joan Blondell, Dick Powell, Guy Kibbee, Hugh Herbert, Frank McHugh

Brash and cocksure James Cagney is a hustling stage director bent upon continually topping himself with Busby Berkeley–type musical numbers, which, not surprisingly, are directed by Busby Berkeley. Another grand-scale musical from the early days of sound films.

1933   B & W 100 minutes

FOOTLOOSE
★★★★

DIRECTOR: Herbert Ross

CAST: Kevin Bacon, Lori Singer, John Lithgow

A highly entertaining film that combines the rock beat exuberance of *Flashdance* and *Risky Business* with an entertaining—and even touching—story. This features Kevin Bacon (*Diner*) as a Chicago boy who finds himself transplanted to a small rural town where rock music and dancing are banned—until he decides to do something about it. Rated PG for slight profanity and brief violence.

1984   107 minutes

42ND STREET
★★★★

DIRECTOR: Lloyd Bacon

CAST: Dick Powell, Ruby Keeler, Ginger Rogers, Warner Baxter, Una Merkel

Every understudy's dream is to get a big chance and rise to stardom. Such is the premise of *42nd Street*. This Depression-era musical of 1933 is lifted above cliché by its vitality and sincerity. Ruby Keeler plays the youngster with a dream, and Dick Powell is the romantic interest. Busby Berkeley began his illustrious choreographic career by staging the elaborate dance numbers.

1933   B & W 98 minutes

FROM MAO TO MOZART
★★★★½

DIRECTOR: Murray Lerner

CAST: Isaac Stern, David Golub, Tan Shuzhen

Violinist Isaac Stern's concert tour of Red China is the subject of this warm and perceptive Academy Award–winning documentary. Stern is seen playing with mainland Chinese orchestras and working with students who are all but incapable of understanding Western music. Beautifully photographed, this is a must for those interested in Stern, violin music, teaching, or a glimpse of mainland China not otherwise available. Unrated.

1980   88 minutes

FUN IN ACAPULCO
★★½

DIRECTOR: Richard Thorpe

CAST: Elvis Presley, Ursula Andress, Paul Lukas, Alejandro Rey, Elsa Cardenas

Beautiful Acapulco sets the stage for this sun-filled Elvis Presley musical. This time he's a lifeguard by day and a singer by night at a fancy beachfront resort. Typical of Elvis's films, this one never lacks romance.

1963   97 minutes

FUNNY FACE
★★★½

DIRECTOR: Stanley Donen

CAST: Fred Astaire, Audrey Hepburn, Kay Thompson, Michel Auclair, Ruta Lee

One of the best of Fred Astaire's later pictures. This time he's a fashion photographer who discovers naive Audrey Hepburn and turns her into a sensation. Typical fairy-tale plot, enlivened by Astaire's usual charm and a good score based on the works of George Gershwin. Kay Thompson has a good supporting part as a feisty magazine editor. Good fun. Unrated family fare.

1957　　　　　　　103 minutes

FUNNY GIRL
★★★★

DIRECTOR: William Wyler

CAST: Barbra Streisand, Omar Sharif, Walter Pidgeon, Kay Medford

The early years of Ziegfeld Follies star Fanny Brice was the inspiration for a superb stage musical. Barbra Streisand recreated her Broadway triumph in as stunning a movie debut in 1968 as Hollywood ever witnessed. She sings, roller-skates, cracks jokes, and tugs at your heart in a tour-de-force performance. Even though Streisand alone is reason enough to watch this classic, the costumes and sets go a long way in capturing an authentic flavor of the 1920s. Omar Sharif's cool sexuality is in perfect contrast to the fluttery Brice/Streisand. Rated G.

1968　　　　　　　155 minutes

FUNNY LADY
★★★

DIRECTOR: Herbert Ross

CAST: Barbra Streisand, James Caan, Omar Sharif, Ben Vereen

The sequel to Barbra Streisand's *Funny Girl* is not quite up to the original, but still worth seeing. We follow comedienne Fanny Brice after she became a stage luminary only to continue her misfortunes in private life. James Caan plays her second husband, producer Billy Rose, and Omar Sharif returns in his role of Fanny's first love. But Streisand's performance

and a few of the musical numbers carry the day.

1975　　　　　　　149 minutes

GAY DIVORCEE, THE
★★★★

DIRECTOR: Mark Sandrich

CAST: Fred Astaire, Ginger Rogers, Edward Everett Horton, Alice Brady, Erik Rhodes, Eric Blore, Betty Grable

This delightful musical farce was the only Fred Astaire/Ginger Rogers film to be nominated for a best-picture Oscar. The outstanding score includes "Night and Day" and "The Continental." Edward Everett Horton heads the supporting cast, which, as usual, manages to add some comic touches to the wisp of a plot. After all, the fairy-tale nature of an Astaire/Rogers picture has only one essential, and that's a glistening dance floor.

1934　　　　B & W 107 minutes

G.I. BLUES
★★★½

DIRECTOR: Norman Taurog

CAST: Elvis Presley, Juliet Prowse

Juliet Prowse improves this otherwise average Elvis Presley film. The action takes place in Germany, where Elvis makes a bet with his G.I. buddies he can date the aloof Prowse, who plays a nightclub dancer.

1960　　　　　　　104 minutes

GIGI
★★★★

DIRECTOR: Vincente Minnelli

CAST: Leslie Caron, Maurice Chevalier, Louis Jourdan, Hermione Gingold, Jacques Bergerac, Eva Gabor

Maurice Chevalier plays guardian to lovely Leslie Caron, who is coming of age in France in the early 1900s. Louis Jourdan plays her romantic interest.

1959 116 minutes

GIMME SHELTER
★★★★

DIRECTOR: David Maysles, Albert Maysles, Charlotte Zwerin

CAST: Mick Jagger, Keith Richards, Mick Taylor, Bill Wyman, Charlie Watts, Melvin Belli

This documentary chronicles the events leading up to and including the now infamous free Rolling Stones concert in 1969 at the Altamont Speedway outside San Francisco. It's the dark side of Woodstock, with many unforgettable scenes, including the actual murder of a spectator by the Hell's Angels in front of the stage as the Stones are playing. Mick Jagger's facial expressions tell all. Thought by many to have brought the curtain down on the flower-powered 1960s, the event on file is a must-see. Rated R for violence, language, and scenes of drug use.

1970 91 minutes

GIRLS! GIRLS! GIRLS!
★★

DIRECTOR: Norman Taurog

CAST: Elvis Presley, Stella Stevens, Benson Fong, Laurel Goodwin, Jeremy Slate

In this musical comedy, Elvis Presley is chased by an endless array of beautiful girls. Sounds like the ideal situation? Not for poor Elvis as he tries to choose just one.

1962 105 minutes

GIVE MY REGARDS TO BROAD STREET
★★

DIRECTOR: Peter Webb

CAST: Paul McCartney, Ringo Starr, Barbara Bach, Linda McCartney

Paul McCartney has openly admitted he "wants to fill the world with silly love songs," which is fine, because he does them so well. However, now it seems he wants to do the same with silly movies. McCartney wrote and stars in the odd, but not really offensive, combination of great rock music and a truly insipid story as a rock singer who loses the master tapes for his album and finds his future seriously threatened. If the album isn't found by midnight, a sinister-looking fellow will then be able to take over his record company. Forget the story and enjoy the songs. Rated PG for mild violence.

1984 108 minutes

GLENN MILLER STORY, THE
★★★½

DIRECTOR: Anthony Mann

CAST: James Stewart, June Allyson, Charles Drake, Harry Morgan, Frances Langford, Gene Krupa, Louis Armstrong

Follows the life story of famous trombonist and bandleader Glenn Miller, who disappeared in a plane during World War II. Jimmy Stewart delivers a convincing portrayal of the popular bandleader whose music had all of America tapping its feet. Miller's music is the highlight of the film, with guest appearances by Louis Armstrong and Gene Krupa.

1954 116 minutes

GOLD DIGGERS OF 1933
★★★★

DIRECTOR: Mervyn LeRoy

CAST: Joan Blondell, Ruby Keeler, Dick Powell, Aline MacMahon, Ginger Rogers, Sterling Holloway

This typical 1930s song-and-dance musical revolves around a Broadway show. Notable tunes include: "We're in the Money," sung by Ginger Rogers; "Forgotten Man," sung by Joan Blondell; and "Shadow Waltz," by the chorus girls. Enjoyable fare if you like nostalgic musicals.

1933   B & W   96 minutes

GOLDWYN FOLLIES, THE
🐢

DIRECTOR: George Marshall
CAST: Adolphe Menjou, Andrea Leeds, Kenny Baker, The Ritz Brothers, Vera Zorina, Edgar Bergen and Charlie McCarthy

Goldwyn's folly is a better title for this turkey. The cast must have been standing around doing nothing on contract, and someone said, "Hey, let's make a movie! Adolphe, you be a producer. Andrea can be the wholesome ingenue. The Ritz Brothers can act zany, Zorina can dance, Edgar can do his thing, and Kenny can sing and sing and sing." And so they all did, darn it!

1938   120 minutes

GOOD NEWS
★★★

DIRECTOR: Charles Walters
CAST: June Allyson, Peter Lawford, Patricia Marshall, Joan McCracken, Mel Torme

Football hero Peter Lawford resists the class vamp and wins the big game and the campus cutie who loves him in this quintessential musical of college life. The plot's got a beard, the dialogue is painfully trite and trying, but energy and exuberance abound in the musical numbers. Set in the 1920s,

it's fun to watch, if only as a nostalgic curiosity.

1948   95 minutes

GOSPEL
★★★★

DIRECTOR: David Levick, Frederick A. Rizenberg
CAST: Mighty Clouds of Joy, Clark Sisters, Walter Hawkins and the Hawkins Family, Shirley Caesar, Rev. James Cleveland

Featuring many of the top stars of black gospel music, this is a joyous, spirit-lifting music documentary that contains the highlights of a five-and-a-half-hour concert filmed in June 1981 at Oakland Paramount Theater. The spirited performances might even make a believer out of you—that is, if you aren't already. Rated G.

1982   92 minutes

GRATEFUL DEAD MOVIE, THE
★★★½

DIRECTOR: Jerry Garcia, Leon Gast
CAST: Grateful Dead

Deadheads will undoubtedly love this combination of backstage, concert, and animated psychedelic scenes. Supervised by Dead lead guitarist/vocalist Jerry Garcia, it's a laughable look at the mechanics and magic of rock. But the uninitiated and unconverted may find it tedious after a while.

1976   131 minutes

GREASE
★★

DIRECTOR: Randal Kleiser
CAST: John Travolta, Olivia Newton-John, Stockard Channing, Jeff Conaway, Didi Conn, Eve Arden, Sid Caesar

After they meet and enjoy a tender summer romance, John Travolta and Olivia Newton-John tearfully part. Surprisingly, they are reunited when she becomes the new girl at his high school. Around his friends, he must play Mr. Tough-Guy, and her goody-two-shoes image doesn't quite fit in. Some laughs, but quite a few yawns. Rated PG.

1978 110 minutes

GREASE 2
★★★

DIRECTOR: Patricia Birch

CAST: Maxwell Caufield, Michelle Pfeiffer, Adrian Zmed, Lorna Luft, Didi Conn

A sequel to the most successful screen musical of all time, *Grease 2* takes us back to Rydell High for more 1950s adolescent angst. *Grease* stars John Travolta and Olivia Newton-John have apparently graduated, leaving it up to Maxwell Caufield and Michelle Pfeiffer to lead the rockin' and romancin' in and out of the classroom. Choreographer-director Patricia Birch obviously didn't take it too seriously and keeps things moving at a fast pace, throwing in comedy, action, and musical numbers whenever things threaten to become dull. The result is a fun little movie that seems to work almost in spite of itself. Rated PG for suggestive gestures and lyrics.

1982 115 minutes

GREAT CARUSO, THE
★★★★

DIRECTOR: Richard Thorpe

CAST: Mario Lanza, Ann Blyth, Dorothy Kirsten, Jarmila Novatna

A number of factual liberties are taken in this lavish screen biography of the great Italian tenor, but no matter. Mario Lanza's voice is magnificent; Ann Blyth and Dorothy Kirsten sing like birds. Devotees of music will love the arias.

1950 109 minutes

GUYS AND DOLLS
★★

DIRECTOR: Joseph L. Mankiewicz

CAST: Marlon Brando, Frank Sinatra, Jean Simmons, Vivian Blaine, Stubby Kaye, Veda Ann Borg

This passable musical stars Marlon Brando and Frank Sinatra as New York gamblers with a gangsterlike aura. Brando and Sinatra bet on whether or not a lovely Salvation Army soldier (Jean Simmons) is date bait.

1955 150 minutes

GYPSY
★★★

DIRECTOR: Mervyn LeRoy

CAST: Natalie Wood, Rosalind Russell, Karl Malden

The story of the backstage mother has been told so often it has become a stereotype. *Gypsy* tries to surpass this hackneyed situation with an energetic musical score and a story about real people. In this case, the characters are stripper Gypsy Rose Lee and her backstage mother supreme, Rose. The music is excellent, but the characters are weakly defined. They end up very little removed from caricature.

1962 149 minutes

HAIR
★★★★

DIRECTOR: Milos Forman

CAST: Treat Williams, John Savage, Beverly D'Angelo, Annie Golden, Cheryl Barnes, Charlotte Rae

Neglected adaptation of the hit Broadway play about 1960s unrest deserved far better than it received at the box office. John Savage is the uptight Midwesterner who pals up with a group of (shudder) hippies celebrating the Age of Aquarius. Grand musical moments, due to Twyla Tharp's impressive choreography; particularly droll is Treat Williams's rendition of the title song at an upper-crust dinner party. However dated some of the concepts, the final role-reversal retains considerable emotional impact. Rated PG for nudity.

1979   121 minutes

HAPPY GO LOVELY
★★★

DIRECTOR: Bruce Humberstone
CAST: David Niven, Vera-Ellen, Cesar Romero

Perky Vera-Ellen is a dancing darling in this lightweight musical with a very tired plot about a producer who hires a chorus girl with the idea her boyfriend has money to invest in his show. It's all cute, but nothing startling.

1951   87 minutes

HARD DAY'S NIGHT, A
★★★★★

DIRECTOR: Richard Lester
CAST: The Beatles, Wilfred Brambell, Victor Spinetti, Anna Quayle

Put simply, this is the greatest rock 'n' roll movie ever made. Scripted by Alan Owen as a sort of "day in the life of the Beatles," it's fast-paced, funny, and full of great Lennon-McCartney songs. Even more than twenty years after its release, it continues to delight several generations of viewers. That is in no small way due to the inspired direction of Richard Lester

(The Three Musketeers; Superman II)—and, of course, the charisma of John Lennon, Paul McCartney, George Harrison, and Ringo Starr.

1964   B & W   85 minutes

HARD TO HOLD
★½

DIRECTOR: Larry Peerce
CAST: Rick Springfield, Janet Eilber, Patti Hansen, Albert Salmi

In this highly forgettable, mostly mediocre film, directed by Larry Peerce (The Other Side of the Mountain), Rick Springfield— we'll pause for screams from his fans here—makes his screen debut as—what else?—a sexy rock star. The former regular on the TV soap "General Hospital" and singer of such hits as "Jessie's Girl" and "Love Somebody" plays James "Jamie" Roberts, a music superstar who has everything except the one thing he really wants: the woman (Janet Eilber) he loves. Poor baby. The first half-hour, which is light and funny, is quite good, but from there it goes decidedly downhill, into sappy soap opera, making Hard to Hold hard to watch. Rated PG for brief nudity and profanity.

1984   93 minutes

HARDER THEY COME, THE
★★★★

DIRECTOR: Perry Henzell
CAST: Jimmy Cliff, Janet Barkley, Carl Bradshaw, Ras Daniel Hartman, Bobby Charlton

Made in Jamaica by Jamaicans, this film has become an underground cult classic. In it, a rural boy comes to the big city to become a singer. There, he is forced into a life of crime. Rated R.

1973   98 minutes

HARUM SCARUM
★½

DIRECTOR: Gene Nelson
CAST: Elvis Presley, Mary Ann Mobley, Fran Jeffries, Michael Ansara

Unbelievable tale of a movie star (Elvis Presley) who is kidnapped during a promotional tour of the Middle East.

1965 86 minutes

HELLO, DOLLY!
★

DIRECTOR: Gene Kelly
CAST: Barbra Streisand, Walter Matthau, Michael Crawford, E. J. Peaker, Marianne MacAndrew

A multimillion-dollar disaster, this 1969 "spectacular" features a miscast Barbra Streisand as an intrepid matchmaker. Streisand's co-star, Walter Matthau, has commented she is one of the few performers with whom he never wants to work again—and that has nothing to do with the box-office failure of this awkward musical, directed by Gene Kelly. Rated G.

1969 146 minutes

HELP!
★★★★

DIRECTOR: Richard Lester
CAST: John Lennon, Paul McCartney, George Harrison, Ringo Starr, Leo McKern, Eleanor Bron, Victor Spinetti

Though neither as inventive nor as charming as *A Hard Day's Night*, this second collaboration between director Richard Lester and the Fab Four has enough energy, fun, and memorable songs to make it worth viewing again and again. The slim plot has a bizarre religious cult trying to retrieve a sacrificial ring from Ringo. From the reverberating opening chord of the title tune, the movie sweeps you up in its irresistibly zesty spirit.

1965 90 minutes

HIGH SOCIETY
★★★½

DIRECTOR: Charles Walters
CAST: Bing Crosby, Frank Sinatra, Grace Kelly, Louis Armstrong

The outstanding cast in this film is reason enough to watch this enjoyable musical remake of *The Philadelphia Story*. The film moves at a leisurely pace, helped by some nice songs by Cole Porter.

1956 107 minutes

HOLIDAY INN
★★★★

DIRECTOR: Mark Sandrich
CAST: Bing Crosby, Fred Astaire, Marjorie Reynolds, Virginia Dale, Rosemary Clooney

Irving Berlin's music and the delightful teaming of Bing Crosby and Fred Astaire are the high points of this wartime musical. The timeless renditions of "White Christmas" and "Easter Parade" more than make up for a script that at best could be called fluff.

1942 B & W 101 minutes

HOLLYWOOD HOTEL
★★

DIRECTOR: Busby Berkeley
CAST: Dick Powell, Rosemary Lane, Lola Lane, Ted Healy, Alan Mowbray, Frances Langford, Hugh Herbert, Louella Parsons, Glenda Farrell, Edgar Kennedy

Saxophonist Dick Powell wins a talent contest, gets a film contract, but gets the boot because he won't cozy up to bitchy star Lola Lane, preferring her sister instead. Hired to voice-double nonsinging Alan Mowbray, he finally works his way upward when Mowbray is kept off Louella Parsons's "Hollywood Hotel" radio program. Powell appears, sings, and the truth comes out. Songs by Johnny Mercer and Richard Whiting, including "Hooray for Hollywood," help bolster this otherwise average musical mishmash. Glenda Farrell wisecracks; Edgar Kennedy blusters. Louella Parsons simpers and fawns.

1937   B & W 109 minutes

HONEYSUCKLE ROSE
★★½

DIRECTOR: Jerry Schatzberg
CAST: Willie Nelson, Dyan Cannon, Amy Irving, Slim Pickens

For his first starring role, country singer Willie Nelson is saddled with a rather stodgy film that all but sinks in the mire of its unimaginative handling and sappy story. As a result, *Honeysuckle Rose* is something only his devoted fans will love, and even then with a bit of effort. Rated PG.

1980   119 minutes

HOW TO STUFF A WILD BIKINI
★★

DIRECTOR: William Asher
CAST: Frankie Avalon, Annette Funicello, Dwayne Hickman, Mickey Rooney, Buster Keaton

It's no surprise to see Frankie Avalon and Annette Funicello together in this beach party film. Dwayne Hickman (TV's Dobie Gillis) tries his hand at romancing Annette in this one. Not much plot, but lots of crazy (sometimes funny) things are going on (including a motorcycle race).

1965   90 minutes

IDOLMAKER, THE
★★★★

DIRECTOR: Taylor Hackford
CAST: Ray Sharkey, Tovah Feldshuh, Peter Gallagher, Maureen McCormick

This superior rock 'n' roll drama stands with a handful of pictures—*The Buddy Holly Story* and *American Hot Wax* among them—as one of the few to capture the excitement of rock music while still offering something in the way of a decent plot and characterization. Ray Sharkey is excellent as a songwriter-manager who pulls, pushes, punches, and plunders his way to the top of the music world. The score, by Jeff Barry, is topnotch. Rated PG.

1980   119 minutes

IN THE GOOD OLD SUMMERTIME
★★★

DIRECTOR: Robert Z. Leonard
CAST: Judy Garland, Van Johnson, S. Z. Sakall, Buster Keaton, Spring Byington

Despite its title, most of the action of this remake of the classic romantic comedy *The Shop Around the Corner* takes place in winter. Judy Garland and Van Johnson work in the same music store. They dislike each other, but are unknowingly secret pen pals who have much in common. Truth does out, but by the time it does, love has struck. Lovely setting, some fine old tunes, but cutsey-pie. Buster Keaton is wasted as comic relief.

1949   102 minutes

INVITATION TO THE DANCE
★★★

DIRECTOR: Gene Kelly

CAST: Gene Kelly, Igor Youskevitch, Claire Sombert, David Paltenghi, Claude Bessy, Tommy Rall, Carol Haney, Daphne Dale

Strictly for lovers of the dance, this film tells three stories entirely by the art. It sort of drags until Gene Kelly appears in a live action/cartoon sequence about "Sinbad" of Arabian Nights fame.

1957   93 minutes

IT HAPPPENED AT THE WORLD'S FAIR
★★½

DIRECTOR: Norman Taurog
CAST: Elvis Presley, Joan O' Brien, Gary Lockwood, Yvonne Craig

Adorable tyke plays matchmaker for Elvis Presley and Joan O'Brien at Seattle Worlds's Fair. It's a breezy romantic comedy with bouncy songs. Elvis hadn't yet reached the point where he was just going through the motions. He seems to be having fun and you will, too.

1963   105 minutes

IT'S ALWAYS FAIR WEATHER
★★★

DIRECTOR: Gene Kelly, Stanley Donen
CAST: Gene Kelly, Dan Dailey, Michael Kidd, Cyd Charisse, Dolores Gray, David Burns

WWII buddies Gene Kelly, Dan Dailey, and Michael Kidd meet a decade after discharge and find they no longer have anything in common and actively dislike one another. Enter romance, reconciliation ploys, and attempted exploitation of their reunion on televison. In between are exuberant, clever musical dance sequences involving ashcan lids, roller skates, and boxers in a gym.

Don't be surprised to realize it recalls *On the Town*.

1955   102 minutes

JAILHOUSE ROCK
★★★★

DIRECTOR: Richard Thorpe
CAST: Elvis Presley, Mickey Shaughnessy, Dean Jones, Judy Tyler

Quite possibly Elvis Presley's best as far as musical sequences go, this 1957 film is still burdened by a sappy plot. Good-hearted Presley gets stuck in the slammer, only to hook up with a conniving manager (Mickey Shaughnessy). Forget the plot and enjoy the great rock 'n' roll songs.

1957   B & W   96 minutes

JAZZ SINGER, THE
★

DIRECTOR: Richard Fleischer
CAST: Neil Diamond, Laurence Olivier, Lucie Arnaz

After completing this film, in which Neil Diamond plays the title role, Laurence Olivier called it "the worst piece of garbage" that he'd ever been associated with. We'll buy that. Diamond is a total nonactor, showing all the finesse of a comatose bill collector. Only Lucie Arnaz shines, as a sexy show business manager, in this film about a fifth-generation Jewish cantor who leaves his wife, father, and synagogue to become a big rock 'n' roll star. It's a mushy mishmash that only Diamond's most devoted fans will love. Rated PG.

1980   115 minutes

JESUS CHRIST SUPERSTAR
★★★½

DIRECTOR: Norman Jewison
CAST: Ted Neeley, Carl Anderson, Yvonne Elliman

Believe it or not, this could be the ancestor of such rock videos as Michael Jackson's "Thriller." The movie illustrates segments of Jesus Christ's later life by staging sets and drama to go along with the soundtrack. This will not offer any religious experiences in the traditional sense, but is interesting nonetheless. Rated G.
1973   103 minutes

KIDS ARE ALRIGHT, THE
★★★½
DIRECTOR: Jeff Stein
CAST: The Who, Ringo Starr, Steve Martin, Tom Smothers

More a documentary detailing the career of British rock group the Who than an entertainment, this film by Jeff Stein still manages to capture the essence of the trend-setting band and, in doing so, the spirit of rock 'n' roll. Rated PG.
1979   108 minutes

KING AND I, THE
★★★★½
DIRECTOR: Walter Lang
CAST: Yul Brynner, Deborah Kerr, Rita Moreno

Yul Brynner and Deborah Kerr star in this superb 1956 Rodgers and Hammerstein musicalization of *Anna and the King of Siam*. Kerr is the widowed teacher who first clashes, then falls in love with, the King (Brynner). The songs include "Hello, Young Lovers," "Getting to Know You," and "Shall We Dance?" (Kerr's singing was dubbed by Marni Nixon.)
1956   133 minutes

KING CREOLE
★★★★
DIRECTOR: Michael Curtiz
CAST: Elvis Presley, Carolyn Jones, Dolores Hart, Dean Jagger, Walter Matthau

A surprisingly strong Elvis Presley vehicle, this musical, set in New Orleans, benefits by strong direction from Michael Curtiz (*Casablanca*).
1958   116 minutes

KING OF JAZZ, THE
★★★
DIRECTOR: John Murray Anderson
CAST: Paul Whiteman and His Orchestra, John Boles, The Rhythm Boys (Bing Crosby, Al Rinker, Harry Barris)

Lavish big-budget musical revue chock-full of big production numbers and great songs. Shot in early two-color Technicolor. Imaginative settings and photography make this last of the all-star extravaganzas most impressive. Clever cartoon sequence opens the show.
1930   93 minutes

KISS ME KATE
★★★
DIRECTOR: George Sidney
CAST: Howard Keel, Katherine Grayson, Keenan Wynn, James Whitmore, Ann Miller, Tommy Rall, Bobby Van, Bob Fosee

That which is Shakespeare's *Taming of the Shrew* in the original is deftly rendered by Cole Porter scripter Dorothy Kingsley, and George Sidney's graceful direction, by way of some fine performances by Howard Keel and Katherine Grayson as a married pair whose on-stage and off-stage lives mingle. Keenan Wynn and James Whitmore play as engaging a duo of low comic gangster types as ever brushed up on their Shakespeare.
1953   109 minutes

KNICKERBOCKER HOLIDAY
★★

DIRECTOR: Harry Brown

CAST: Nelson Eddy, Charles Coburn, Shelley Winters, Chester Conklin, Constance Dowling, Percy Kilbride

A plodding, lackluster rendition of the Kurt Weill/Maxwell Anderson musical about Peter Stuyvesant and Dutch New York. The best song, "September Song," was originally sung by Walter Huston. Unfortunately, he's not in the film.

1944   B & W   85 minutes

KOYAANISQATSI
★★★★

DIRECTOR: Godfrey Reggio

The title is a Hopi Indian word meaning "crazy life, life in turmoil, life disintegrating, life out of balance, a state of life that calls for another way of living." In keeping with this, director Godfrey Reggio contrasts scenes of nature to the hectic life of the city. There is no plot or dialogue. Instead, the accent is on the artistic cinematography, by Ron Fricke, and the score, by Philip Glass. It's a feast for the eyes and ears. No MPAA rating.

1983   87 minutes

LA TRAVIATA
★★★★

DIRECTOR: Franco Zeffirelli

CAST: Teresa Stratas, Placido Domingo, Cornell McNeill

Director Franco Zeffirelli set out to make an opera film of Verdi's *La Traviata* that would appeal to a general audience as well as opera buffs, and he has handsomely succeeded. He has found the right visual terms for the pathetic romance of a courtesan compelled to give up her aristocratic lover. The score is beautifully sung by Teresa Stratas, as Violetta; Placido Domingo, as Alfredo; and Cornell McNeill, as his stern father, who feels obliged to bring the romance to an end. In Italian, with English subtitles. Rated G.

1982   112 minutes

LADY SINGS THE BLUES
★★★½

DIRECTOR: Sidney J. Furie

CAST: Diana Ross, Billy Dee Williams, Richard Pryor

Former Supremes lead singer Diana Ross made a dynamic screen debut in this screen biography of another singing great, Billie Holiday, whose career was thwarted by drug addiction. Rated R.

1972   144 minutes

LAST WALTZ, THE
★★★★

DIRECTOR: Martin Scorsese

CAST: The Band, Bob Dylan, Neil Young, Joni Mitchell, Van Morrison, Eric Clapton, Neil Diamond

Director Martin Scorsese's (*Taxi Driver*) superb documentary of the Band's final concert appearance. With guest stars such as Eric Clapton, Joni Mitchell, Neil Young, Van Morrison, Muddy Waters, Paul Butterfield, and more, it's an unforgettable celebration of American music. Rated PG.

1978   117 minutes

LE BAL
★★★★

DIRECTOR: Ettore Scola

European history of the last half-century is reduced to some fifty popular dance tunes—and a variety of very human dancers—in this innovative and entertaining film by Italian director Ettore Scola (*La Nuit de Varennes*). Nominated for the Academy Award for best foreign-language film (it lost to Ingmar Bergman's *Fanny and Alexander*), this unusual import eschews dialogue for tangos, fox trots, and jazz to make its points. Scola chronicles the dramatic changes in political power, social behavior, and fashion trends from the 1930s to the present without ever moving his cameras out of an art deco ballroom. No MPAA rating; the film has brief violence.

1983   109 minutes

LES GIRLS
★★★★

DIRECTOR: George Cukor
CAST: Gene Kelly, Kay Kendall, Taina Elg, Mitzi Gaynor, Jacques Bergerac

Gene Kelly is charming, Mitzi Gaynor is funny, Taina Elg is funnier, Kay Kendall is funniest in this tale of a libel suit over a published memoir. Three conflicting accounts of what was and wasn't emerge in flashback from the courtroom. A nifty, witty, wholly entertaining film with Cole Porter music and stylish direction by George Cukor. C'est magnifique!

1957   114 minutes

LET IT BE
★★★½

DIRECTOR: Michael Lindsay-Hogg
CAST: John Lennon, Paul McCartney, George Harrison, Ringo Starr

The last days of the Beatles are chronicled in this *cinéma vérité* production, which was originally meant to be just a documentary on the recording of an album. What emerges, however, is a portrait of four men who have outgrown their images and, sadly, one another.

There are moments of abandon, in which they recapture the old magic—especially in the rooftop concert climax—but overall, the movie makes it obvious that the Beatles would never "get back to where [they] once belonged." Rated G.

1970   80 minutes

LET'S SPEND THE NIGHT TOGETHER
★★★½

DIRECTOR: Hal Ashby
CAST: Mick Jagger, Keith Richard, Bill Wyman, Charlie Watts, Ron Wood, Ian Stewart

In this documentary, directed by Hal Ashby (*Being There*; *Harold and Maude*), the Rolling Stones—Mick Jagger, Keith Richard, Bill Wyman, Charlie Watts, Ron Wood, and Ian Stewart—are seen rockin' and rollin' in this footage, shot during the band's 1981 American tour. It's a little too long—but Stone fans and hard-core rockers should love it. Rated PG for suggestive lyrics and behavior.

1982   94 minutes

LISZTOMANIA
🐢

DIRECTOR: Ken Russell
CAST: Roger Daltrey, Sara Kestleman, Paul Nicholas, Fiona Lewis, Ringo Starr

Ken Russell lets his lurid imagination run sickeningly wild in this hokey "screen biography" on the life of composer Franz Liszt (played by Roger Daltrey, lead singer for the rock group the Who). The director's fans will revel in this onslaught of bad taste and outrageousness, but those not lobotomized will want to avoid it. Rated R.

1975   105 minutes

LITTLE NIGHT MUSIC, A
★★½

DIRECTOR: Harold Prince
CAST: Elizabeth Taylor, Diana Rigg, Lesley-Anne Down

Based on Ingmar Bergman's comedy about sexual liaisons at a country mansion, this musical version doesn't quite come to life. Rated PG.

1978   124 minutes

LOVING YOU
★★★

DIRECTOR: Hal Kanter
CAST: Elvis Presley, Lizabeth Scott, Wendell Corey, Dolores Hart

This better-than-average Elvis Presley vehicle features him as a small-town country boy who makes good when his singing ability is discovered. It has a bit of romance but the main attraction is Elvis singing his rock 'n' roll songs, including the title tune.

1957   101 minutes

MAME
★

DIRECTOR: Gene Saks
CAST: Lucille Ball, Robert Preston, Jane Connell, Beatrice Arthur

You won't love Lucy in this one. Or Robert Preston, either. It's Roz Russell's boffo *Auntie Mame* with music, and the notes are all sour. Rated PG.

1974   131 minutes

MAN OF LA MANCHA
🎦

DIRECTOR: Arthur Hiller
CAST: Peter O'Toole, Sophia Loren, James Coco, Harry Andrews

For those who loved the hit Broadway musical and those who heard about it and looked forward to this film, this is a shameful and outrageous letdown. This is what happens when Hollywood thinks it can do better than a hundred-percent successful stage original. Rated G.

1972   130 minutes

MAYTIME
★★★

DIRECTOR: Robert Z. Leonard
CAST: Jeanette MacDonald, Nelson Eddy, John Barrymore, Herman Bing, Sig Ruman

A curio of the past. A penniless tenor meets and falls in love with an opera star suffering in a loveless marriage to her adoring and jealous teacher and mentor. The hands Fate deals are not pat. See if you can tell that John Barrymore is reading his lines from idiot boards off camera. This film is one of the Eddy/MacDonald duo's best.

1937   B & W 132 minutes

MEET ME IN ST. LOUIS
★★★★

DIRECTOR: Vincente Minnelli
CAST: Judy Garland, Margaret O'-Brien, Tom Drake

Here's a fun-filled entertainment package made at the MGM studios during the heyday of their musicals. This nostalgic look at a family in St. Louis before the 1903 World's Fair dwells on the tension when the father announces an impending transfer to New York. Judy Garland's songs remain fresh and enjoyable today.

1944   112 minutes

METROPOLIS (MUSICAL VERSION)
★★★★★

DIRECTOR: Fritz Lang (and Giorgio Moroder)
CAST: Brigitte Helm, Alfred Abel, Gustav Froelich

Fritz Lang's 1926 silent science-fiction classic has been enhanced with special individual coloring and tints, recently recovered scenes, storyboards and stills. The rock score, supervised by Giorgio Moroder, features Pat Benatar, Bonnie Tyler, Loverboy, Billy Squier, Adam Ant, Freddie Mercury, Jon Anderson, and Cycle V. A modern screen triumph.

1984   120 minutes

MILLION DOLLAR MERMAID
★★

DIRECTOR: Mervyn LeRoy
CAST: Esther Williams, Victor Mature, Walter Pidgeon, David Brian, Jesse White

Esther William swims through her role as famous early distaff aquatic star Annette Kellerman, who pioneered one-piece suits and vaudeville tank acts. Victor Mature woos her in this highly fictionalized film biography. The Busby Berkeley production numbers are a highlight.

1952   115 minutes

MR. QUILP
★★★

DIRECTOR: Michael Tuchner
CAST: Anthony Newley, David Hemmings, David Warner, Michael Hordern, Jill Bennett, Sarah Jane Varley

This enjoyable British-made follow-up to *Scrooge*, the successful musical adaptation of Charles Dickens' *A Christmas Carol*, adds tunes to the author's *The Old Curiosity Shop* and casts songwriter-singer Anthony Newley as the title villain. Rated PG.

1975   118 minutes

MRS. BROWN YOU'VE GOT A LOVELY DAUGHTER
★★

DIRECTOR: Saul Swimmer
CAST: Herman's Hermits, Stanley Holloway

England's Herman's Hermits star in this film, named after one of their hit songs. The limited plot revolves around the group acquiring a greyhound and deciding to race it. Caution: Only for hard-core Herman's Hermits fans! Rated G.

1968   110 minutes

MUSIC MAN, THE
★★★★½

DIRECTOR: Morton Da Costa
CAST: Robert Preston, Shirley Jones, Buddy Hackett, Ronny Howard, Paul Ford, Hermione Gingold

They sure don't make musicals like this anymore, a smashing adaptation of Meredith Willson's Broadway hit. Robert Preston reprises the role of his life as a smooth-talkin' salesman who cajoles the parents of River City, Iowa, into purchasing band instruments and uniforms for their children. Rarely has a single musical produced so many recognizable, toe-tapping songs, including "Trouble" and—of course—"Seventy-six Trombones." A few new songs were added to this film version, but the spirit and excitement of the play remain intact.

1962   151 minutes

MY FAIR LADY
★★★★

DIRECTOR: George Cukor
CAST: Rex Harrison, Audrey Hepburn, Stanley Holloway

Pygmalion, the timeless George Bernard Shaw play, has been a smashing success in every form in which it has been presented. This Oscar-winning 1964 movie musical adaptation is no exception. Rex Harrison, as Professor Henry Higgins, is the perfect example of British class snobbishness. Higgins accepts a bet that he can't take a cockney guttersnipe and transform her into a socially acceptable lady. Audrey Hepburn gives a fine performance as his subject, Eliza Doolittle (with Marni Nixon supplying the singing).

1964   170 minutes

NEPTUNE'S DAUGHTER
★★½

DIRECTOR: Edward Buzzell

CAST: Esther Williams, Red Skelton, Keenan Wynn, Ricardo Montalban, Betty Garrett, Mel Blanc, Mike Mazurki, Ted de Corsica, Xavier Cugat

Big-budgeted aquatic musical from MGM studios has Esther Williams playing a (what else?) swimsuit designer on holiday in South America floating in and out of danger with Red Skelton. Esther takes a back seat to the incredible waterworks and never-ending parade of arresting character actors (and voices) like Mel Blanc, Mike Mazurki, Ted de Corsica, and young Ricardo Montalban. The plot isn't too important to this film as long as you can keep in time with Xavier Cugat's mamba beat and not lose your place in the conga line. Harmless, enjoyable nonsense.

1949   93 minutes

NEVER STEAL ANYTHING SMALL
★★½

DIRECTOR: Charles Lederer

CAST: James Cagney, Shirley Jones, Roger Smith, Cara Williams, Nehemiah Persoff, Royal Dano, Horace MacMahon

Unbelievable musical comedy-drama about a goodhearted union labor leader is saved by the dynamic James Cagney, who was always enough to make even the most hackneyed story worth watching. Supported by the lovely Shirley Jones and a fine cast of top charcter actors, Cagney manages to pull this movie off where a lesser talent would have foundered. Certainly not one of the great or near-great films, this tuneful comedy-drama is still entertaining enough to stand on its own merits and offers another look at the incomparable Cagney.

1959   94 minutes

NEW YORK, NEW YORK
★★★½

DIRECTOR: Martin Scorsese

CAST: Robert De Niro, Liza Minnelli, Lionel Stander, Georgie Auld, Mary Kay Place

This is a difficult film to warm to, but worth it. Robert De Niro gives a splendid performance as an egomaniacal saxophonist who woos sweet-natured singer Liza Minnelli. The songs (especially the title tune) are great, and those with a taste for something different in musicals will find it rewarding. Rated PG.

1977   163 minutes

NO NUKES
★★★½

DIRECTOR: Julian Schlossberg, Danny Goldberg, Anthony Potenza

CAST: Jackson Browne, Crosby, Stills, and Nash, The Doobie Brothers, John Hall, Gil Scott-Heron, Bonnie Raitt, Carly Simon, Bruce Springsteen, James Taylor, Jessie Colin Young

Entertaining record of the MUSE concerts presented for five nights at Madison Square Garden to benefit the anti-nuclear movement. Your enjoyment will depend greatly on appreciation of the artists involved, but the rare footage of Bruce Springsteen in concert is electrifying and shouldn't be missed. While the picture is grainy, the stereo soundtrack is excellent. Rated PG for profanity.

1980   103 minutes

OKLAHOMA!
★★★★

DIRECTOR: Fred Zinnemann

CAST: Shirley Jones, Gordon MacRae, Rod Steiger, Eddie Albert

This movie adaptation of Rodgers and Hammerstein's Broadway musical stars Shirley Jones as a country girl (Laurie) who is courted by Curly, a cowboy (Gordon MacRae). Rod Steiger plays a villainous Jud, who also pursues Laurie. A very entertaining musical, it features great tunes like "Oh, What a Beautiful Mornin'" and "Oklahoma!"

1956   145 minutes

OLIVER
★★★★★

DIRECTOR: Carol Reed

CAST: Ron Moody, Oliver Reed, Hugh Griffith, Shani Wallis, Mark Lester, Jack Wild

Charles Dickens never was such fun. *Oliver Twist* has become a luxurious musical and multiple Oscar-winner (including best picture). Lionel Bart's songs are not as instrusive as those found in average musicals. Mark Lester is the angelic Oliver, whose adventures begin one mealtime when he pleads, "Please, sir, I want some more." Jack Wild is an impish Artful Dodger, and Ron Moody steals the show as the scoundrel Fagin. Then there's Oliver Reed, whose narrow-eyed menace prevents the tale from becoming *too* sugarcoated. Lester is the perfect star; you'd rather die than watch him suffer . . . and Dickens always includes a lot of suffering. A must-see. Rated G—suitable for family viewing.

1968   153 minutes

ON A CLEAR DAY, YOU CAN SEE FOREVER
★

DIRECTOR: Vincente Minnelli

CAST: Barbra Streisand, Yves Montand, Bob Newhart, Larry Blyden, Jack Nicholson

Crashing, thudding bore of a musical about a psychiatrist (Yves Montand) who discovers that one of his patients (Barbra Streisand) has lived a former life and can recall it under hypnosis. The flashbacks to nineteenth-century England provide work for the costume and set designers, but neither century contains characters who matter a whit to the viewer. Pompous screenplay filled with its own importance interrupted by vacuous songs. A poor epitaph for the classic Hollywood musical. Rated PG for violence.

1970   129 minutes

ON THE TOWN
★★★★

DIRECTOR: Gene Kelly, Stanley Donen

CAST: Gene Kelly, Frank Sinatra, Ann Miller, Vera-Ellen

This is a classic boy-meets-girl, boy-loses-girl fable set to music. Three sailors are on a twenty-four-hour leave and find themselves (for the first time) in the big city of New York. They seek romance and adventure during their leave—and find it.

1949   98 minutes

ONE FROM THE HEART
★★

DIRECTOR: Francis Ford Coppola
CAST: Teri Garr, Frederic Forrest, Raul Julia, Nastassja Kinski, Harry Dean Stanton, Allen Goorwitz, Luana Anders

This Francis Ford Coppola film is a ballet of graceful and complex camera movements occupying magnificent sets—but the characters get lost in the process. Teri Garr and Frederic Forrest play a couple flirting with two strangers (Raul Julia and Nastassja Kinski), but they fade away in the flash and fizz. Rated R.

1982   100 minutes

ONE TRICK PONY
★★★½

DIRECTOR: Robert M. Young
CAST: Paul Simon, Lou Reed, Rip Torn, Blair Brown, Joan Hackett, Sam and Dave, The B-52's, Tiny Tim, The Lovin' Spoonful

This good little movie looks at life on the road with a has-been rock star. Paul Simon is surprisingly effective as the rock star who finds both his popularity slipping and his marriage falling apart. Rated R for nudity.

1980   98 minutes

PAGAN LOVE SONG
★½

DIRECTOR: Robert Alton
CAST: Esther Williams, Howard Keel, Minna Gombell, Rita Moreno

Watered-down love story about American schoolteacher Howard Keel who falls for native girl Esther Williams is just another excuse for singing, swimming, and studio-bound rehash of a tired old plot line. Basically an excuse to make an Esther Williams film with a time-tested script, this dull entry is for fans of soggy musicals and Esther Williams only.

1950   76 minutes

PAINT YOUR WAGON
★★

DIRECTOR: Joshua Logan
CAST: Clint Eastwood, Lee Marvin, Jean Seberg, Harve Presnell

Clint Eastwood and Lee Marvin play partners during the California gold rush era. They share everything, including a mail-order bride (Jean Seberg), in this hapless musical. Adapted from a hit Broadway play and given the big-budget treatment, this film never gets off the ground. The major blame should go to the script writers for not caring enough about the characterizations to put any effort into their development. Rated PG.

1969   166 minutes

PARADISE HAWAIIAN STYLE
★★½

DIRECTOR: Michael Moore
CAST: Elvis Presley, Suzanna Leigh

Elvis Presley returns to Hawaii after his 1962 film, *Blue Hawaii*. This time he plays a pilot who makes time for romance while setting up a charter plane service. Some laughs and lots of Elvis's songs add to the Hawaiian beauty to make this enjoyable to watch.

1966   91 minutes

PENNIES FROM HEAVEN
★★★½

DIRECTOR: Herbert Ross
CAST: Steve Martin, Bernadette Peters, Jessica Harper

Steve Martin and Bernadette Peters star in this depressingly downbeat musical (which still has its moments), directed by Herbert Ross (*The Turning Point* and *Play It Again, Sam*). The production numbers are fabulous, but the dreary storyline—with Martin as a down-and-out song-plugger in Depression-era Chicago—may disappoint fans of the genre. Rated R because of profanity and sexual situations.

1981   107 minutes

PHANTOM OF THE PARADISE
★★

DIRECTOR: Brian De Palma
CAST: Paul Williams, William Finley, Jessica Harper

Before he became obsessed with Hitchcock *hommages* and ultra-violent blood baths, director Brian De Palma did this odd little blend of Faust and *Phantom of the Opera*. William Finley sells his soul to Paul Williams and learns the dangers of achieving fame too quickly. Wildly erratic, with tedious dialogue alternating with droll visual bits (such as a poke at the shower scene in *Psycho*). Although the scathing attack on the music industry is occasionally interesting, the picture finally turns into a mess. Rated PG—mild violence.

1974   92 minutes

PINK FLOYD THE WALL
★½

DIRECTOR: Alan Parker
CAST: Bob Geldof, Christine Hargreaves, Bob Hoskins

For all its apparent intent, this visually impressive film, which has very little dialogue but, rather, uses garish visual images to the accompaniment of the British rock band's music, ends up being more of a celebration of insanity and inhumanity than an indictment of it as intended. Every conceivable kind of violence—even rape—is splashed on the screen to a pulsating rock beat. Seldom has a more bleak, negative, and just plain irresponsible work been foisted on the movie-going public. Written by Pink Floyd singer-songwriter Roger Waters and directed by Alan Parker (*Fame* and *Shoot the Moon*). Rated R for nudity, profanity, violence, and gore.

1982   99 minutes

PIRATE, THE
★★★

DIRECTOR: Vincente Minnelli
CAST: Gene Kelly, Judy Garland, Walter Slezak, Gladys Cooper, Reginald Owen

Technicolor musical winner with Gene Kelly and Judy Garland in top form.

1948   102 minutes

PIRATE MOVIE, THE
★★

DIRECTOR: Ken Annakin
CAST: Christopher Atkins, Kristy McNichol, Ted Hamilton, Bill Kerr

This rock 'n' roll adaptation of Gilbert and Sullivan's *The Pirates of Penzance* entertainment for the family. It's especially appropriate for teenagers, since the hero and heroine are Christopher Atkins (*The Blue Lagoon*) and Kristy McNichol. Expect a lot of music, a lot of swashbuckling, and a little sappy romance. Directed by Ken Annakin (*Swiss Family Robinson*), this film is rated PG for slight profanity and sexual innuendo (making it more fun for the parents).

1982   99 minutes

PIRATES OF PENZANCE, THE
★★★★

DIRECTOR: Wilford Leach
CAST: Angela Lansbury, Kevin Kline, Linda Ronstadt, Rex Smith, George Ross

In this film, directed by Wilford Leach, Angela Lansbury, Kevin Kline, rock superstar Linda Ronstadt, Rex Smith, and George Ross re-create the roles they originated in the Tony-winning Broadway adaptation of the Gilbert and Sullivan show. Stylized sets and takeoffs of Busby Berkeley camera setups give *Pirates* a true cinematic quality. Add to that outstanding work by the principals, some nice bits of slapstick comedy, and you have an enjoyable film for the entire family. Rated G.

1983   112 minutes

PRIVATE BUCKAROO
★★

DIRECTOR: Edward Cline
CAST: The Andrews Sisters, Joe E. Lewis, Dick Foran, Jennifer Holt, Donald O'Connor, Peggy Ryan, Harry James

Showcase vehicle for Patty, LaVerne, and Maxene, the Andrews Sisters, who decide to put on a show for soldiers. The Donald O'Connor/Peggy Ryan duo stands out.

1942   B & W   68 minutes

PURPLE RAIN
★★½

DIRECTOR: Albert Magnoli
CAST: Prince, Apollonia, Morris Day, Olga Karlatos, The Revolution

In his first movie, pop star Prince plays a struggling young musician searching for self-awareness and love while trying to break into the rock charts. The film unsuccessfully straddles the line between a concert release and a story-telling production. As it is, the music is great, but the plot leaves a lot to be desired. Rated R for nudity, suggested sex, and profanity.

1984   113 minutes

QUADROPHENIA
★★★½

DIRECTOR: Franc Roddam
CAST: Phil Daniels, Mark Wingett, Phillip Davis, Leslie Ash, Garry Cooper, Sting

Based on the Who's rock opera, this is the story of a teenager growing up in the early 1960s and the decisions he is forced to make on the path to adulthood. The backdrop for the tale is London, and the focus is on the conflict between two English youth cults, the Rockers, a typical "bike gang" outfit, and the Mods, who also ride bikes but are more "responsible" types, holding jobs that provide the money they spend on sharp clothes and drugs. The gangs hate each other, primarily because of their differences in style, and the movie's failure to establish the reason for this tension is its one major flaw. Rated R because the language is rough, the violence graphic, and both sex and masturbation are represented.

1979   115 minutes

RAPPIN'
★½

DIRECTOR: Joel Silberg
CAST: Mario van Peebles, Tasia Valenza, Charles Flohe, Melvin Plowden

Rap songs get the *Breakin'* treatment in this uninspired formula musical. Once again, a street performer (rap singer Mario van Peebles) takes on the baddies and still has time to make it in show biz.

Dumb stuff. Rated PG for profanity.

1985   92 minutes

RED SHOES, THE
★★★★
DIRECTOR: Michael Powell
CAST: Moira Shearer, Anton Walbrook

Fascinating backstage look at the world of ballet manages to overcome its unoriginal, often trite, plot. A ballerina (Moira Shearer) is urged by her forceful and single-minded impresario (Anton Walbrook) to give up a romantic involvement in favor of her career, with tragic consequences. Good acting and fine camera work save this film from its overlong standard story.

1948   133 minutes

ROCK, ROCK, ROCK
★★
DIRECTOR: Will Price
CAST: Tuesday Weld, Teddy Randazzo, Alan Freed, Frankie Lymon and the Teenagers, Chuck Berry, The Flamingos, The Johnny Burnette Trio

If you love Tuesday Weld, fifties rock, or entertainingly terrible movies, this nostalgic blast from the past is for you. The plot is so flimsy, "Dobie Gillis" would have rejected it. But watching a young Weld lip-synch to songs actually sung by Connie Francis is a wonderful treat.

1956   B & W   83 minutes

ROSE, THE
★★★★
DIRECTOR: Mark Rydell
CAST: Bette Midler, Alan Bates, Frederic Forrest, Harry Dean Stanton

Bette Midler stars as a Janis Joplin–like rock singer who falls prey to the loneliness and temptations of superstardom. Mark Rydell (*On Golden Pond*) directed this character study, which features memorable supporting performances by Alan Bates and Frederic Forrest, and a first-rate rock score. Rated R.

1979   134 minutes

ROSE MARIE
★★
DIRECTOR: W. S. Van Dyke
CAST: Nelson Eddy, Jeanette MacDonald, James Stewart, Alan Mowbray

If you enjoy MGM's perennial songbirds Nelson Eddy and Jeanette MacDonald, you might have fun with this musical romp into the Canadian Rockies. Unintentionally funny dialogue is created by the wooden way Eddy delivers it.

1936   B & W 110 minutes

ROUSTABOUT
★★½
DIRECTOR: John Rich
CAST: Barbara Stanwyck, Elvis Presley, Leif Erickson, Sue Anne Langdon

Barbara Stanwyck, as the carnival owner, upgrades this typical Elvis Presley picture. In this release, Presley is a young wanderer who finds a home in the carnival as a singer. Naturally, Elvis combines romance with hard work on the midway.

1964   101 minutes

ROYAL WEDDING
★★★
DIRECTOR: Stanley Donen
CAST: Fred Astaire, Jane Powell, Sarah Churchill, Peter Lawford, Keenan Wynn

Brother and sister Fred Astaire and Jane Powell are performing in London when Princess Elizabeth marries Philip, and manage to find their own true loves while royalty ties the knot.

1951   92 minutes

SATURDAY NIGHT FEVER
★★★★
DIRECTOR: John Badham
CAST: John Travolta, Donna Pescow, Karen Lynn Gorney

From the first notes of "Stayin' Alive" by the Bee Gees over the opening credits, it is obvious that *Saturday Night Fever* is more than just another youth exploitation film. It is *Rebel without a Cause* for the 1970s, an encapsulation of the era's moral and social attitudes combined with realistic dialogue and effective dramatic situations. The story revolves around Tony Manero (John Travolta), disco dancer supreme. He is the epitome of cool, and crowds part at the local nightclub when he and his friends make for the dance floor. With his styled hair, floral bodyshirt, skin-tight pants, and platform shoes, he redefined American masculinity in the 1970s. Rated R for profanity, violence, partial nudity, and simulated sex.

1977   119 minutes

SAY AMEN, SOMEBODY
★★★★
DIRECTOR: George T. Nierenberg
CAST: Thomas A. Dorsey, Willie Mae Ford Smith, Sallie Martin

This is a joyful documentary about gospel singers Thomas A. Dorsey and Willie Mae Ford Smith. Two dozen gospel songs make this modest film a treat for the ears as well as the eyes and soul. Rated G.

1982   100 minutes

SCROOGE
★★★
DIRECTOR: Ronald Neame
CAST: Albert Finney, Alec Guinness, Edith Evans, Kenneth Moore, Michael Medwin, Laurence Naismith, Kay Walsh

Tuneful retelling of Charles Dickens's classic *A Christmas Carol* may not be the best acted, but it's certainly the liveliest. Albert Finney paints old curmudgeon Ebeneezer Scrooge with a broad brush, but he makes his character come alive just as he embodied Daddy Warbucks in *Annie*. Decent attempt to translate a stage musical to the screen but nowhere near as popular as the earlier Dickens success, *Oliver*. This is a nice companion piece for the earlier (1935) version of *Scrooge* as well as the classic 1951 version of *A Christmas Carol*, both nonmusicals. Rated G.

1970   118 minutes

SECOND CHORUS
★★★
DIRECTOR: H. C. Potter
CAST: Paulette Goddard, Fred Astaire, Burgess Meredith, Charlie Butterworth, Artie Shaw and his orchestra

Rival trumpet players Fred Astaire and Burgess Meredith vie for the affections of Paulette Goddard, who works for Artie Shaw. The two want in to Shaw's orchestra and make a comic mess of Goddard's attempts to help them. Charlie Butterworth, in a typical more-money-than-brains role, brings order out of the chaos by backing a Shaw concert.

1940   B & W   83 minutes

SGT. PEPPER'S LONELY HEARTS CLUB BAND

DIRECTOR: Michael Schultz
CAST: The Bee Gees, Peter Frampton, Donald Pleasence, George Burns

Universally panned musical featuring the Bee Gees, Peter Frampton, etc., performing songs from the Beatles' famous album as they try to save the small town of Heartland from the rule of the evil Mr. Mustard. Rated PG.

1978   111 minutes

SEVEN BRIDES FOR SEVEN BROTHERS
★★★★

DIRECTOR: Stanley Donen
CAST: Howard Keel, Jane Powell, Russ Tamblyn, Julie Newmar

Delightful musical. Howard Keel takes Jane Powell as his wife. The fun begins when his six younger brothers decide they want to get married, too . . . immediately!

1954   108 minutes

1776
★★★★

DIRECTOR: Peter H. Hunt
CAST: William Daniels, Howard da Silva, Ken Howard, Blythe Danner

Broadway's hit musical about the founding of the nation is brought to the screen almost intact. Original cast members William Daniels, as John Adams, and Howard da Silva, as Benjamin Franklin, shine anew in this unique piece. Rated G.

1972   141 minutes

SHALL WE DANCE?
★★★★½

DIRECTOR: Mark Sandrich
CAST: Fred Astaire, Ginger Rogers, Eric Blore, Edward Everett Horton

Fred Astaire and Ginger Rogers team up (as usual) as dance partners in this musical comedy. The only twist is they must pretend to be married in order to get the job. Great songs include "Let's Call the Whole Thing Off."

1937   B & W 116 minutes

SHOW BOAT
★★★½

DIRECTOR: George Sidney
CAST: Kathryn Grayson, Howard Keel, Ava Gardner, Joe E. Brown, Agnes Moorehead, Marge and Gower Champion

This watchable musical depicts life and love on a Mississippi showboat during the early 1900s. Kathryn Grayson, Howard Keel, and Ava Gardner try but can't get any real sparks flying.

1951   107 minutes

SILK STOCKINGS
★★★

DIRECTOR: Rouben Mamoulian
CAST: Fred Astaire, Cyd Charisse, Janis Paige, Peter Lorre, Barrie Chase

In this remake, Greta Garbo's classic *Ninotchka* is given the Cole Porter musical treatment with a degree of success. Fred Astaire is a Hollywood producer who educates a Russian agent in the seductive allure of capitalism. Cyd Charisse plays the Garbo role.

1957   117 minutes

SINGIN' IN THE RAIN
★★★★★

DIRECTOR: Gene Kelly, Stanley Donen

CAST: Gene Kelly, Debbie Reynolds, Donald O'Connor, Jean Hagen, Cyd Charisse, Madge Blake, Rita Moreno

In the history of movie musicals, no single scene is more fondly remembered than Gene Kelly's song-and-dance routine to the title song of *Singin' in the Rain*. This picture has more to it than Kelly's well-choreographed splash through a wet city street. It has an interesting plot based on the panic that overran Hollywood during its conversion to sound. It has other show-stopping original tunes, such as "You Were Meant for Me" and "All I Do Is Dream about You." Last, it includes some excellent performances by Debbie Reynolds, Donald O'Connor, and Jean Hagen. So if you're expecting only to see Gene Kelly get his feet wet, be prepared for a whole lot more.

1952   102 minutes

SKY'S THE LIMIT, THE
★★★★

DIRECTOR: Edward H. Griffith
CAST: Fred Astaire, Joan Leslie, Robert Benchley, Elizabeth Patterson, Clarence Kolb, Robert Ryan, Richard Davis, Peter Lawford, Eric Blore

This rare blend of comedy and the dramatic uncertainty of human relationships under stress is more than just another Fred Astaire musical. He plays a Flying Tiger ace, on leave, who meets and falls in love with magazine photographer Joan Leslie, but nixes anything permanent. Both audiences and critics misjudged this film when it debuted, seeing it as light diversion rather than incisive comment on war and its effect on people.

1943   B & W   89 minutes

SMILIN' THROUGH
★★

DIRECTOR: Frank Borzage
CAST: Jeanette MacDonald, Gene Raymond, Brian Aherne, Ian Hunter

If you can believe it, an orphaned and brave Jeanette MacDonald falls in love with the son of a murderer. Directed and played for tear value. Best thing to come out of the picture was Jeannette's marriage to Gene Raymond.

1941   100 minutes

SOMETHING TO SING ABOUT
★★

DIRECTOR: Walter Schertzinger
CAST: James Cagney, William Frawley, Evelyn Daw, Gene Lockhart

Even the great talents of James Cagney can't lift this low-budget musical above the level of mediocrity. In it, he plays a New York bandleader who tests his mettle in Hollywood.

1937   B & W   93 minutes

SONG OF NORWAY
🦃

DIRECTOR: Andrew L. Stone
CAST: Florence Henderson, Torval Maurstad, Christina Schollin, Edward G. Robinson, Robert Morley

If he were not dead, Norwegian composer Edvard Grieg would expire upon seeing this insult to his life and career. Talk about butchering what was an engaging, tuneful stage musical! Pass the cranberry sauce. Rated G.

1970   142 minutes

SONG REMAINS THE SAME, THE
★★★

DIRECTOR: Peter Clifton, Joe Massot

CAST: Jimmy Page (electric guitar, bow, theramin), Robert Plant (vocals), John Paul Jones (bass, keyboards), John Bonham (drums), Peter Grant (manager, hysteria)

If any band is truly responsible for the genre of "heavy metal" music, it is Led Zeppelin. In *Song*, Zeppelin proves this claim by performing smashing versions of such hits as "Rock-n-Roll," "Whole Lotta Love," "Stairway to Heaven," and "Since I've Been Loving You." Although this movie is a must for Led Zeppelin fans, the untrained ear may find numbers such as the twenty-three-minute version of "Dazed and Confused" a bit tedious. Rated PG.

1976   136 minutes

SONG TO REMEMBER, A
★★★

DIRECTOR: Charles Vidor
CAST: Cornel Wilde, Merle Oberon, Paul Muni, George Coulouris, Nina Foch, Sig Arno, Stephen Bekassy

The music is superb, but the plot of this Chopin biography is as frail as the composer's health is purported to have been. Cornel Wilde received an Oscar nomination as the ill-fated tubercular Chopin, and Merle Oberon is resolute but vulnerable in the role of his lover, the emancipated trouser-wearing French female novelist George Sand. Paul Muni supports as Chopin's mentor; George Coulouris suffers genius as the piano baron Louis Playel in whose Paris concert hall the composer performs his greatest works as death steadily encroaches.

1945   113 minutes

SONGWRITER
★★★★

DIRECTOR: Alan Rudolph
CAST: Willie Nelson, Kris Kristofferson, Lesley Ann Warren, Melinda Dillon, Rip Torn

Wonderfully wacky and entertaining wish-fulfillment by top country stars Willie Nelson and Kris Kristofferson, who play—what else?—top country stars who take on the recording industry and win. Lesley Ann Warren, who also worked with director Alan Rudolph in the equally memorable *Choose Me*, is Nelson's protégée, and Melinda Dillon plays his loving but intolerant-of-his-lifestyle wife. Rip Torn is a sleazy yet somehow likable concert promoter. The actors are all excellent, and the film, despite its far-fetched premise, is a delight. Rated R for profanity, nudity, and brief violence.

1984   100 minutes

SOUND OF MUSIC, THE
★★★★½

DIRECTOR: Robert Wise
CAST: Julie Andrews, Christopher Plummer, Eleanor Parker

Winner of the Academy Award for best picture, this musical has it all: comedy, romance, suspense, and sadness. Julie Andrews plays the spunky Maria, who doesn't fit in at the convent. When she is sent to live with a large family as their governess, she falls in love with and marries her handsome boss, Baron Von Trapp (Christopher Plummer). Problems arise when the Nazi invasion of Austria forces the family to flee.

1965   174 minutes

OUTH PACIFIC
★★★

DIRECTOR: Joshua Logan
CAST: Mitzi Gaynor, Rossano Brazzi, Ray Walston, John Kerr

This extremely long film, adapted from the famous Broadway play about sailors during World War II, seems dated and is slow going for the most part. Fans of Rodgers and Hammerstein will no doubt appreciate this one more than others.

1958   171 minutes

SPARKLE
★★★

DIRECTOR: Sam O'Steen
CAST: Irene Cara, Dorian Harewood, Lonette McKee

Largely forgotten but immensely appealing study of a Supremes–like girl group's rise to fame in the 1960s Motown era. A chance to see some of today's more popular black stars at an earlier stage. Lots of good musical numbers from Curtis Mayfield and the luscious Lonette McKee (*The Cotton Club*). Affectionate at times but marred by some cloying sentimentality. Nevertheless, check this one out. Rated PG for profanity and nudity.

1976   100 minutes

SPEEDWAY
★★

DIRECTOR: Norman Taurog
CAST: Elvis Presley, Nancy Sinatra, Bill Bixby, Gale Gordon

Elvis Presley plays a generous stock-car driver who confronts a seemingly heartless IRS agent (Nancy Sinatra). Not surprisingly, she melts in this unremarkable musical. Rated G.

1968   94 minutes

STARSTRUCK
★★★½

DIRECTOR: Gillian Armstrong
CAST: Jo Kennedy, Ross O'Donovan, Pat Evison, Margo Lee, Max Cullen

For this movie, about a 17-year-old (Jo Kennedy) who wants to be a star and goes after it at top speed, director Gillian Armstrong (*My Brilliant Career*) has taken the "let's put on a show!" plot and turned it into an affable punk-rock movie. Rated PG for nudity and profanity.

1982   95 minutes

STAYING ALIVE
★

DIRECTOR: Sylvester Stallone
CAST: John Travolta, Cynthia Rhodes, Finola Hughes, Steve Inwood

This sequel to the gutsy, effective *Saturday Night Fever* is a slick, commercial near-ripoff. Six years have passed since Tony Manero (John Travolta) was king of the local disco, and he now attempts to break into the competitive life of Broadway dancing. For fans only. Rated PG for language and suggested sex.

1983   96 minutes

STOP MAKING SENSE
★★★★

DIRECTOR: Jonathan Demme
CAST: Talking Heads

Jonathan Demme's *Stop Making Sense* has been called a "star vehicle." Filmed over a three-night period in December 1983 at Hollywood's Pantages Theater, Demme (*Melvin and Howard*) and cinematographer Jordan Croneweth (*Blade Runner*) concentrate on the rock group Talking Heads. The movie is a straight recording of a

Talking Heads concert that offers the movie audience front-row-center seats. It offers great fun for the band's fans. Rated PG for suggestive lyrics.

1984   88 minutes

STORY OF VERNON AND IRENE CASTLE, THE
★★★★

DIRECTOR: H. C. Potter
CAST: Fred Astaire, Ginger Rogers, Edna May Oliver, Walter Brennan, Lew Fields

Another fine film with the flying footsies of Fred Astaire and the always lovely Ginger Rogers.

1939   B & W   93 minutes

SWEET DREAMS
★★★★½

DIRECTOR: Karel Reisz
CAST: Jessica Lange, Ed Harris, Ann Wedgeworth, David Clennon, Gary Basraba, John Goodman, Bruce Kirby, P. J. Soles, James Staley

Jessica Lange (*Frances*, *Tootsie*) is Patsy Cline, one of the greatest country-and-western singers of all time, in this film that is much more than a response to the popularity of *Coal Miner's Daughter*. Lange's performance is flawless right down to the singing, where she perfectly mouths Cline's voice. Ed Harris (*The Right Stuff*, *Under Fire*) is equally brilliant as Cline's "good ol' boy" husband. The film's only weak point is that it rarely confronts the singer's impact on the music world or how she dealt with her popularity. Rated PG for profanity and sex.

1985   115 minutes

SWING TIME
★★★★½

DIRECTOR: George Stevens

CAST: Ginger Rogers, Fred Astaire, Betty Furness, Victor Moore, Helen Broderick

Fred Astaire is a gambler trying to save up enough money to marry the girl he left behind (Betty Furness). By the time he's saved the money, he and Ginger Rogers are madly in love with each other.

1936   B & W   105 minutes

SYMPATHY FOR THE DEVIL
½

DIRECTOR: Jean-Luc Godard
CAST: Mick Jagger, Keith Richards, Brian Jones, Bill Wyman, Charlie Watts

Several uncompleted sessions on the title song and documentary style footage of black guerrillas with machine guns and white women in slips seem to be all that compose this boring film from internationally acclaimed director Jean-Luc Godard. Not recommended for the music fan who expects some concert footage, but an evening's diversion for anyone with enough patience to try and figure out what's going on and what it all means. Beware the longer version of this tedium, entitled *One Plus One*.

1970   92 minutes

THANK GOD IT'S FRIDAY
★★

DIRECTOR: Robert Klane
CAST: Donna Summer, The Commodores, Ray Vitte, Debra Winger, Jeff Goldblum

This film is episodic and light in mood and features a cast primarily of newcomers. The best-known performers on screen are Donna Summer and the Commodores. Summer plays an aspiring singer who pesters a club's master of ceremonies and disc jockey, Bobby

Speed (Ray Vitte), to let her sing. The Commodores have a brief dramatic appearance and spend the bulk of their screen time doing what they do best: performing their hits. Rated PG.

1978   90 minutes

THANK YOUR LUCKY STARS
★★★½

DIRECTOR: David Butler
CAST: Eddie Cantor, Dennis Morgan, Joan Leslie, Bette Davis, Olivia de Havilland, Ida Lupino, Ann Sheridan, Humphrey Bogart, Errol Flynn, John Garfield

Practically nonexistent plot involving banjo-eye Eddie Cantor as a cab driver and the organizer of this gala affair takes a back seat to the wonderful array of Warner Bros. talent gathered together for the first and only time in one film. Bette Davis and Errol Flynn perform musical numbers with Flynn disguised behind a handlebar moustache and Bette singing "They're Either Too Young or Too Old." John Garfield and Humphrey Bogart aren't spared a guest appearance, and they seem to be good sports about it. Basically a studio effort to display as many stars as possible in one film, this is an enjoyable collection of vignettes and skits and is one of the brightest of the all-star productions. Lots of fun for film fans and buffs and a perfect example of the type of control the studios exerted over those performers bound to them.

1943   B & W 127 minutes

THAT'S DANCING
★★★★

DIRECTOR: Jack Haley Jr.

CAST: Mikhail Baryshnikov, Ray Bolger, Sammy Davis Jr., Gene Kelly, Liza Minnelli

This is a glorious celebration of dance on film. From ballet to breakin', from Fred Astaire to Busby Berkeley, from James Cagney (in *Yankee Doodle Dandy*) to Marine Jahan (Jennifer Beals's stand-in in *Flashdance*), this one has it all. *That's Dancing* contains the best scenes from fifty years of musicals. All the dumb plot devices that are concocted to get the performers from one music segment to another are gone. That leaves all the high points. Mikhail Baryshnikov, Ray Bolger, Sammy Davis Jr., Gene Kelly, and Liza Minnelli host this superb compilation. Rated G.

1985   105 minutes

THAT'S ENTERTAINMENT
★★★★★

DIRECTOR: Jack Haley
CAST: Judy Garland, Fred Astaire, Frank Sinatra, Gene Kelly, Esther Williams

That's Entertainment is a feast of screen highlights. Culled from twenty-nine years of MGM classics, this release truly has something for everybody. Unlike films that rely on the continuity of story for their impact, it is an episodic collection of bits and pieces. Taken from Metro-Goldwyn-Mayer's glory days when it boasted "more stars than there are in heaven," nearly every sequence is a showstopper. Rated G.

1974   135 minutes

THAT'S ENTERTAINMENT PART II
★★★★

DIRECTOR: Gene Kelly
CAST: Gene Kelly, Fred Astaire

More wonderful scenes from the history of MGM highlight this compilation, hosted by director Gene Kelly and Fred Astaire. It's a real treat for film buffs. Rated G.

1976   132 minutes

THAT WAS ROCK
★★★★★

DIRECTOR: Steve Binder, Larry Peerce

CAST: The Rolling Stones, Chuck Berry, Tina Turner, Marvin Gaye, The Supremes, Smokey Robinson and the Miracles, James Brown, Ray Charles, Gerry and the Pacemakers, The Ronettes

Compilation of two previous films, *The T.A.M.I. Show* and *The Big T.N.T. Show*, which were originally shot on videotape in the mid-1960s. It's black and white, but color inserts have been added, featuring Chuck Berry giving cursory introductions to each act. The video is muddy, the simulated stereo is annoying, and the audience nearly drowns out the performers, but it's one of the best collections of rock 'n' roll and R&B talent you will ever see. Unrated.

1984   92 minutes

THERE'S NO BUSINESS LIKE SHOW BUSINESS
★★

DIRECTOR: Walter Lang

CAST: Ethel Merman, Dan Dailey, Marilyn Monroe, Donald O'Connor, Johnnie Ray, Mitzi Gaynor, Hugh O'Brian, Frank McHugh

Even the strength of the cast can't save this marginally entertaining musical-comedy about a show-biz family. Irving Berlin's tunes and Monroe's scenes are the only redeeming qualities in this one.

1954   117 minutes

THIS IS ELVIS
★★★★

DIRECTOR: Malcolm Leo, Andrew Solt

CAST: Elvis Presley, David Scott, Paul Boensh III

Even if you're not an Elvis Presley fan, this film may make you cry. At the very least, you will find it powerful as well as touching. *This Is Elvis* blends film footage of the "real" Elvis with other portions, played by convincing stand-ins. The result is a warm, nostalgic, funny, and tragic portrait of a man who touched the hearts and lives of young and old throughout the world. To many, he is still the King of rock 'n' roll—and this film explains why. Rated PG because of slight profanity.

1981   101 minutes

THIS IS THE ARMY
★★★

DIRECTOR: Michael Curtiz

CAST: George Murphy, Joan Leslie, Ronald Reagan, George Tobias, Alan Hale, Joe Louis, Kate Smith, Irving Berlin, Frances Langford, Charles Butterworth

Hoofer (later U.S. Senator) George Murphy portrays Ronald Reagan's father in this musical mélange penned by Irving Berlin to raise funds for Army Emergency Relief during World War II. It's a star-studded, rousing show of songs and skits from start to finish, but practically plotless.

1943   121 minutes

THOUSANDS CHEER
★★★

DIRECTOR: George Sidney

CAST: John Boles, Kathryn Grayson, Mickey Rooney, Judy Garland, Gene Kelly, Red Skelton, Lucille Ball, Ann Southern, Eleanor Powell, Frank Morgan, Lena Horne, Virginia O'Brien

The usual story about someone (in this case John Boles as an army officer) putting together a talent show for some good reason gets a major shot in the arm by the appearances of top MGM performers, including Mickey Rooney, Judy Garland, and Gene Kelly. Terrific cast in cameo performances make this musical worth the watch, and top comics Red Skelton, Lucille Ball, and Ann Southern do their best to keep things moving. Not as famous as many MGM musicals, but castwise the match for *any* studio extravaganza. Overlong, but catching Lena Horne is worth the wait.

1943   126 minutes

THREEPENNY OPERA, THE
★★★★

DIRECTOR: G. W. Pabst

CAST: Rudolph Forster, Lotte Lenya, Reinhold Schunzel, Carola Neher

Classic gangster musical features mob leader Rudolph Forster (alias Mack the Knife), his moll Lotte Lenya, and the hordes of the underworld as the king of the beggars joins forces with the gang chief to take control of their city and what may lie beyond. Their third partner? The police, of course. This Bertolt Brecht satire (with music by Kurt Weill), although not too popular with the Nazis or their predecessors, is always a favorite with the audience and has been filmed under its original title at least twice and in many subsequent guises.

1931   B & W 113 minutes

TICKLE ME
★★

DIRECTOR: Norman Taurog

CAST: Elvis Presley, Jocelyn Lane, Julie Adams, Jack Mullaney, Merry Anders

The plot falls below that found in a standard Elvis vehicle in this unfunny comedy/musical, which has Elvis working and singing at an all-female health ranch. Viewers seeking thought-provoking entertainment should avoid this mindless piece of fluff.

1965   90 minutes

TILL THE CLOUDS ROLL BY
★★½

DIRECTOR: Richard Whorf

CAST: Robert Walker, Van Heflin, Judy Garland, Lucille Bremer

Biography of songwriter Jerome Kern is a barrage of MGM talent that includes Judy Garland, Frank Sinatra, Lena Horne, Dinah Shore, Kathryn Grayson, and many more in short, tuneful vignettes that tie this all-out effort together. Not too bad as musical bio-pics go, but singing talent is definitely the star in this production—if you're following the story, the film seems too long; if you're just enjoying the segments, it's still about long enough. Typical top-quality job by postwar MGM studio.

1946   137 minutes

TIMES SQUARE
★½

DIRECTOR: Alan Moyle

CAST: Tim Curry, Robin Johnson, Trini Alvarado, Peter Coffield

A totally unbelievable story involving two New York teens who hang out in Times Square. Film generates no energy at all. Rated R for language, subject matter.

1980　　　　　　111 minutes

TOMMY
★★½

DIRECTOR: Ken Russell
CAST: Roger Daltrey, Ann-Margret, Jack Nicholson, Oliver Reed, Elton John, Tina Turner

In bringing the Who's groundbreaking rock opera to the screen, director Ken Russell (*Women in Love* and *Altered States*) let his penchant for bad taste and garishness run wild. The result is an outrageous movie about a deaf, dumb, and blind boy who rises to prominence as a "Pinball Wizard" and then becomes the new Messiah. The Who's lead singer, Roger Daltrey, plays the title role. Rated PG.

1975　　　　　　111 minutes

TOP HAT
★★★★★

DIRECTOR: Mark Sandrich
CAST: Fred Astaire, Ginger Rogers, Edward Everett Horton, Eric Blore, Helen Broderick

Top Hat is the most delightful and enduring of the Fred Astaire–Ginger Rogers musicals of the 1930s. This movie has an agreeable wisp of a plot and amusing, if dated, comedy dialogue. It is handled by an expert team of supporting comics: Edward Everett Horton, Eric Blore, and Helen Broderick. Irving Berlin's score includes: "Cheek to Cheek" and "Isn't It a Lovely Day?" as well as the title number. Astaire and Rogers were at the peak of their careers in this classic musical.

1935　　　B & W　99 minutes

200 MOTELS
★★

DIRECTOR: Frank Zappa
CAST: Tony Palmer, Frank Zappa and the Mothers of Invention, Theodore Bikel, Ringo Starr, Keith Moon

Indulgent full-length video is the kind of garish, free-association assault one would expect from the unconventional and downright bizarre Frank Zappa and the Mothers of Invention. Shot on videotape and edited to Zappa's specifications as a companion piece to the album of the same name, this episodic collage scores some laughs and has a few high points (including an X-rated animated sequence), but remains essentially an oddity and a staple for the midnight-movie crowd. Rated R.

1971　　　　　　98 minutes

UNSINKABLE MOLLY BROWN, THE
★★★

DIRECTOR: Charles Waters
CAST: Debbie Reynolds, Harve Presnell, Ed Begley, Hermione Baddeley, Jack Kruschen

Noisy, big-budget version of hit Broadway musical has Debbie Reynolds at her spunkiest as the tuneful gal from Colorado who survives the sinking of the *Titanic* and lives to sing about it. High-stepping dance numbers and the performances and songs by Reynolds and Harve Presnell as the object of her affections make this a favorite with musicals fans, but it does drag a bit for the casual viewer at 128 minutes. One of the last of the old-time, overblown studio musical entertainments.

1964　　　　　　128 minutes

VIDEO REWIND: THE ROLLING STONES GREAT VIDEO HITS
★★★★

DIRECTOR: Julian Temple
CAST: Mick Jagger, Bill Wyman, Keith Richards, Ron Wood, Charlie Watts

This is a real score for lovers of the Rolling Stones or lovers of rock video in general. Mick Jagger and Bill Wyman take us on a tour of a "rock" museum, using flashbacks as a showcase for the band's videos. Included along with the videos are vintage clips of the Stones in concert. Highlights feature the uncensored versions of "She Was Hot", and "Neighbors." Only gripe is the sound quality, which (though acceptable) could have been much cleaner and sharper. Unrated.

1984   60 minutes

VIVA LAS VEGAS
★★

DIRECTOR: George Sidney
CAST: Elvis Presley, Ann-Margret, Cesare Danova, William Demarest, Jack Carter

In this romantic musical, Elvis Presley plays a race car driver who also sings. Ann-Margret is a casino dancer who becomes jealous when her father becomes interested in Elvis's race car. Eventually Elvis and Ann-Margret get together, which comes as no surprise to any viewer who didn't fall asleep within the first ten minutes of the film.

1964   86 minutes

WAGNER
★★★

DIRECTOR: Tony Palmer

CAST: Richard Burton, Vanessa Redgrave, Gemma Craven, Laszlo Galff, Sir John Gielgud, Sir Ralph Richardson, Sir Laurence Olivier, Marthe Keller, Ekkehardt Schall, Ronald Pickup

There are some who believe the great composers of Western music have not been justly served in cinema: Ken Russell's *Lisztomania* and *Mahler* have been deemed too weird, even if their namesakes did lead interesting lives, and some feel the cackling of Tom Hulce in *Amadeus* undercut Mozart's genius. In the case of *Wagner*, the filmmakers have delivered a highly stylized epic drama without resorting to camp or vulgarity. Unfortunately, Richard Burton's Wagner comes off one-dimensional. This five-hour film gives you an idea of what the greatest opera composer may have been like, but it will not explain his behavior, and the legendary supporting cast, although credible, is not up to reputation. The first half of the movie centers on Wagner's efforts in the aborted German revolution of 1848–49 and artistic struggle during his subsequent exile. The second half focuses on the creation of his masterwork, *The Ring*, and hints at the composer's profound influence on a Germany entering the twentieth century. Not rated, but equal to an R for violence, profanity, sex, and nudity.

1982   300 minutes

WASN'T THAT A TIME!
★★★★★

DIRECTOR: Jim Brown
CAST: The Weavers: Pete Seeger, Lee Hays, Ronnie Gilbert, Fred Hellerman; with Arlo Guthrie, Don McLean, Holly Near, Mary Travers, Harry Reasoner, Studs Turkel

This is a folk music documentary about the Weavers' last reunion, as narrated wryly by group member Lee Hays. What really sets this apart from all the rest is the wealth of superb archival footage, all used in the proper proportion and sequence. The finale is the final reunion concert, and what a glorious and joyful event that was. Rated G.

1981   78 minutes

WEST SIDE STORY
★★★★★

DIRECTOR: Robert Wise, Jerome Robbins
CAST: Natalie Wood, Richard Beymer, Rita Moreno, George Chakiris

The Romeo-and-Juliet theme (with Richard Beymer and Natalie Wood in the lead roles) is updated to 1950s New York and given an endearing music score. The story of rival white and Puerto Rican youth gangs first appeared as a hit Broadway musical. None of the brilliance of the play was lost in its transformation to the screen. It received Oscars for best picture and its supporting players, Rita Moreno and George Chakiris. (Wood's vocals were dubbed by Marni Nixon.)

1961   151 minutes

WHOOPEE
★★½

DIRECTOR: Thornton Freeland
CAST: Eddie Cantor, Eleanor Hunt, Paul Gregory, Ethel Shutta

The first of six Eddie Cantor musical films of the 1930s, this one's a two-color draft of his 1928 Broadway hit of the same name. The banjo-eyed comic plays a superhypochondriac on an Arizona dude rance. Cowpokes and chorines abound. Busby Berkeley pro-

duction numbers make it palatable. Nostalgia note: look for a nubile 14-year-old Betty Grable singing and dancing as things get under way.

1930   B & W   93 minutes

WIZ, THE
★

DIRECTOR: Sidney Lumet
CAST: Diana Ross, Richard Pryor, Michael Jackson, Nipsey Russell, Ted Ross, Mabel King, Theresa Merritt, Thelma Carpenter, Lena Horne

Ineffective updating of The Wizard of Oz with an all-black cast, including Diana Ross (who is too old for the part), Richard Pryor, and Michael Jackson. Adapted from a successful Broadway play, this Sidney Lumet–directed picture should have been better. Rated G.

1978   133 minutes

WIZARD OF OZ, THE
★★★★★

DIRECTOR: Victor Fleming
CAST: Judy Garland, Ray Bolger, Bert Lahr, Jack Haley, Frank Morgan, Billie Burke, Margaret Hamilton, Charley Grapewin, Clara Blandick. The Singer Midgets

The all-time classic for children of all ages, this MGM release, directed by Victor Fleming (Gone with the Wind) and based on the story by L. Frank Baum, takes us "off to see the wizard . . . the wonderful wizard of Oz." Sometimes "there's no place like home" for watching great movies!

1939   101 minutes

WOODSTOCK
★★★½

DIRECTOR: Michael Wadleigh

CAST: Country Joe and the Fish, Jimi Hendrix, Jefferson Airplane, Ten Years After

Woodstock is probably, along with *Gimme Shelter*, the most important film documentation of the late 1960s counterculture in the United States. The bulk of the film consists of footage of the bands and various other performers who played at the festival. There are some great split-screen sequences and some imaginative interviews that make the film quite enjoyable today. Well worth viewing. Rated PG.

1970   184 minutes

XANADU
★★½

DIRECTOR: Robert Greenwald
CAST: Olivia Newton-John, Gene Kelly, Michael Beck, James Sloyan, Dimitri Arliss, Katie Hanley, Sandahl Bergman

This musical lacks inspiration and storyline. It is basically a full-length video that includes some good numbers by Olivia Newton-John and Gene Kelly. The rock groups the Tubes and the Electric Light Orchestra are also featured. See it for the musical entertainment, not for the story. Rated PG.

1980   88 minutes

YANKEE DOODLE DANDY
★★★★★

DIRECTOR: Michael Curtiz
CAST: James Cagney, Joan Leslie, Walter Huston, Irene Manning, Rosemary DeCamp, Richard Whorf, Jeanne Cagney

Magnetic James Cagney, stepping out of his gangster roles, gives a magnificent strutting performance in the life story of dancing vaudevillian George M. Cohan. An outstanding show-business story

with unassuming but effective production.

1942   B & W 126 minutes

YENTL
★★½

DIRECTOR: Barbra Streisand
CAST: Barbra Streisand, Mandy Patinkin, Amy Irving, Nehemiah Persoff, Steven Hill

Barbra Streisand, who also produced, co-scripted, and directed, stars as a woman who must disguise herself as a man in order to pursue an education among Orthodox Jews in turn-of-the-century eastern Europe. The story in this dramatic musical—based on Isaac Bashevis Singer's *Yentl, the Yeshiva Boy*—is well-handled, but the songs, by Michel Legrand and Alan and Marilyn Bergman, are uninspired. What's worse, they all sound the same. Still, *Yentl* is, overall, a watchable work. Rated PG for brief nudity.

1983   134 minutes

YES, GIORGIO
★★

DIRECTOR: Franklin J. Schaffner
CAST: Luciano Pavarotti, Kathryn Harrold, Eddie Albert, Paolo Barboni, James Hong, Beulah Quo

In this old-fashioned star vehicle, Luciano Pavarotti makes a less-than-memorable screen debut as Giorgio Fini, a macho Italian tenor who meets a pretty Boston throat specialist (Kathryn Harrold) when his voice suddenly fails him during a rehearsal. They fall in love and the viewer falls asleep. Rated PG for adult themes.

1982   110 minutes

YOU WERE NEVER LOVELIER
★★★★

DIRECTOR: William Seiter
CAST: Fred Astaire, Rita Hayworth, Adolphe Menjou, Leslie Brooks, Adele Mara

In this interesting story, Fred Astaire goes stepping about with the most glamorous of all the stars—Rita Hayworth. This film's worth seeing twice.

1942   B & W   97 minutes

YOU'LL NEVER GET RICH
★★★½

DIRECTOR: Sidney Lanfield
CAST: Fred Astaire, Rita Hayworth, John Hubbard, Robert Benchley, Osa Massen, Frieda Inescort, Guinn Williams

This musical-comedy has play producer Fred Astaire getting drafted right before his big show. Somehow he manages to serve his country and put the show on while romancing Rita Hayworth.

1941   B & W   88 minutes

ZIEGFELD FOLLIES
★★★

DIRECTOR: Vincent Minnelli
CAST: Fred Astaire, Lucille Ball, William Powell, Judy Garland, Fanny Brice, Lena Horne, Red Skelton, Victor Moore, Virginia O'Brien, Cyd Charisse, Gene Kelly, Edward Arnold, Esther Williams

MGM tries to imitate a Ziegfeld-style stage show. Don't get confused; this is not the Oscar-winning *The Great Ziegfeld* (with William Powell). The Ziegfeld name is merely a contrivance to provide some unified method of showcasing some of its stars.

1946   110 minutes

ZIGGY STARDUST AND THE SPIDERS FROM MARS
🎭

DIRECTOR: D. A. Pennebaker
CAST: David Bowie and band

Only the most devoted David Bowie fans will enjoy this documentary, filmed July 3, 1973, at London's Hammersmith Odeon Theatre during the English singer-songwriter's last live performance as an androgynous king (or queen, for that matter) with orange hair, black eyeshadow, and a spacesuit of glitter. Even they will probably be disappointed by this flat, uninspired, and overlong rock documentary by D. A. Pennebaker (*Monterey Pop*; *Don't Look Back*). Featured are such songs as "Space Oddity," "Suffragette City," "Cracked Actor," "Changes," "All the Young Dudes," and "Oh!" Rated PG for suggestive lyrics and stage movements.

1982   90 minutes

SCIENCE FICTION/ FANTASY

ADVENTURES OF BUCKAROO BANZAI, THE
★★★★
DIRECTOR: W. D. Richter
CAST: Peter Weller, John Lithgow, Ellen Barkin, Jeff Goldblum

Here's the wildest, wackiest science-fiction film ever to hit the screen. Peter Weller plays Buckaroo Banzai, a skilled neurosurgeon and physicist who becomes bored with his scientific and medical work and embarks on a career as a rock star and two-fisted defender of justice. This offbeat genre film is great fun for those who love highly original, laugh-filled, and action-packed entertainment; a silly movie for smart people. Rated PG.

1984   103 minutes

ADVENTURES OF HERCULES, THE
🎭
DIRECTOR: Lewis Coates
CAST: Lou Ferrigno, Milly Carlucci, Sonia Viviani, William Berger

This is the sequel to *Hercules*, the 1983 bomb with Lou "the Hulk" Ferrigno. But while you could argue that the first Ferrigno folly was a laughfest, one can only comment that this tiresome piece of junk would only benefit insomniacs. Rated PG for violence (yes, even *that* can be boring).

1984   89 minutes

AFTER THE FALL OF NEW YORK

DIRECTOR: Martin Dolman
CAST: Michael Sopkiw, Valentine Monnier, Anna Kanakis, Roman Geer, Vincent Scalondro

Dumb, dubbed, and dreadful Italian-made ripoff of the "Mad Max" series, with Michael Sopkiw as a two-fisted, post-apocalypse hero whose job is to save the human race by finding the last normal woman (she's been freeze-dried) and getting her pregnant. Not much to root for here. Rated R for violence, gore, and profanity.

1983   91 minutes

ALIEN
★★★★½
DIRECTOR: Ridley Scott

CAST: Tom Skerritt, Sigourney Weaver, John Hurt, Ian Holm, Harry Dean Stanton, Yaphet Kotto, Veronica Cartwright

A superb cinematic combination of science-fiction and horror, this is a heart-pounding, visually astounding shocker. The players are all excellent as the crew of a futuristic cargo ship that picks up an unwanted passenger: an alien that lives on human flesh and continually changes form. Rated R.

1979   116 minutes

ALIEN FACTOR, THE
★★★

DIRECTOR: Don Dohler
CAST: Don Leifert, Tom Griffith

As an amateur film, this is pretty decent. The cast and production crew are one and the same. There are four aliens on the planet Earth. Only one alien is good, and the Earthlings have a hard time figuring out which one is on their side. Rated PG.

1977   82 minutes

ALIEN WARRIOR
🐾

DIRECTOR: Edward Hunt
CAST: Brett Clark, Pamela Saunders, Reggie DeMorton, Nelson Anderson, Norman Bud

In this unwatchable film, a father on another planet sends his only remaining son (Brett Clark) to Earth to protect its people and confront the ultimate evil, who happens to be a pimp. If this story sounds at all familiar, it's because the only thing missing in this comic-book ripoff—besides an original idea—is Kryptonite. Although the hero isn't invulnerable, he may as well be. The only power he's lacking is the ability to act. In fact, the entire cast appears devoid of talent. If you decide to

watch this film, it's recommended that you view it in fast-forward. Rated R for nudity, violence, and profanity.

1985   100 minutes

ALIENS
★★★★½

DIRECTOR: James Cameron
CAST: Sigourney Weaver, Carrie Henn, Michael Biehn, Paul Reiser, Lance Henriksen, Jenette Goldstein

Ridley Scott's *Alien* may have been a tough act to follow, but writer-director James Cameron, who performed similar chores on the deft and exciting *Terminator*, is up to the job. Fifty-seven years have passed during Warrant Officer Ripley's (Sigourney Weaver) deep-space sleep; when she wakes, nobody believes her story, and the planet Acheron—where the crew of the ill-fated *Nostromo* first encountered the nasty extraterrestrial—has, meanwhile, been colonized. Then, to everybody's surprise except Ripley's, contact is lost with the colonists. Weaver breathes fire into Ripley, who's one of the best female leads created in years, and Cameron keeps everything bouncing at an absolutely frantic pace. Equal to, although different than, the original. Rated R for considerable violence and profanity.

1986   137 minutes

ALPHA INCIDENT, THE
★★

DIRECTOR: Bill Rebane
CAST: Ralph Meeker, Stafford Morgan, Carol Irene Newell

A deadly organism from Mars, an attempted government cover-up, a radiation leak, panic, and havoc.

Okay, if you like this sort of now-tired thing. Rated PG.

1977   84 minutes

ALTERED STATES
★★★½

DIRECTOR: Ken Russell

CAST: William Hurt, Blair Brown, Bob Balaban, Charles Haid, Drew Barrymore

At times in *Altered States*, you can't help but be swept along ... and almost overwhelmed. In those moments, it becomes more than just a movie—it's a mindblower. William Hurt, Blair Brown, Bob Balaban, and Charles Haid star in this suspenseful film as scientists involved in the potentially dangerous exploration of the mind. Rated R for nudity, profanity, violence, and sex.

1980   102 minutes

ANDROID
★★★★

DIRECTOR: Aaron Lipstadt

CAST: Klaus Kinski, Don Opper, Brie Howard, Kendra Kirchner

A highly enjoyable, exciting, and funny tongue-in-cheek sci-fi adventure, this takes place on a space station where a mad scientist, Dr. Daniel (played by a surprisingly subdued and effective Klaus Kinski), is trying to create the perfect android. As a group of criminal castaways arrives at the station, the doctor's current robot assistant, Max 404 (Dan Opper), learns it is about to be replaced by a buxom new female model and decides it is time to rebel. Rated PG for nudity, violence, and profanity.

1982   80 minutes

ANDROMEDA STRAIN, THE
★★★★

DIRECTOR: Robert Wise

CAST: Arthur Hill, David Wayne, James Olson, Kate Reid, Paula Kelly

A powerful, tense science-fiction thriller, this film focuses on a team of scientists attempting to isolate a deadly virus while racing against time and the possibility of nuclear war. Though not as flashy as other entries in the genre, it's highly effective. Rated G.

1971   130 minutes

ANGRY RED PLANET, THE
★★½

DIRECTOR: Ib Melchior

CAST: Gerald Mohr, Nora Hayden, Les Tremayne, Jack Kruschen

Entertaining (if unoriginal) science-fiction tale of an expedition to Mars running into all sorts of alien terrors, most notable of which is a terrifying kind of giant mouse/spider hybrid. A fun film, though it takes forever to get to the action, and the viewer might be tempted to hit the "scan" button more than once.

1959   83 minutes

ANNA TO THE INFINITE POWER
★★★★

DIRECTOR: Robert Wiemer

CAST: Martha Byrne, Dina Merrill, Mark Patton, Donna Mitchell, Jack Ryland, Loretta Devine, Jack Gilford

Is individuality determined purely by genetic code, or by some other factor beyond the control of science? This film explores the dimensions of that question via the struggles of a brilliant, troubled child—who is also the unwitting subject of a scientific experiment to establish her own identity. It also poses other questions, such as, What makes us who we are, and how much can we change? This kind of deep-think is not easy to explore on celluloid, but director Robert Weimer and his cast succeed in near brilliant fashion.

1982   107 minutes

AT THE EARTH'S CORE
★★½

DIRECTOR: Kevin Connor
CAST: Doug McClure, Peter Cushing, Caroline Munro, Cy Grant, Sean Lynch, Godfrey James

At the Earth's Core, an Edgar Rice Burroughs adaptation, benefits enormously from an inspired performance by British horror film stalwart Peter Cushing. He even manages to make Doug McClure look good occasionally. It's mostly for the kiddies, but we found ourselves clutching the arm of the chair a couple of times at the height of suspense. Rated PG.

1976   90 minutes

ATOMIC SUBMARINE, THE
★★★

DIRECTOR: Spencer Bennet
CAST: Arthur Franz, Dick Foran, Brett Halsey, Tom Conway, Bob Steele, Victor Varconi, Joi Lansing

Solid little thriller about U.S. atomic submarine and its encounter with an alien flying saucer in the Arctic suffers from budgetary limitations (and excess use of stock footage, a common ailment of 1950s science-fiction films), but benefits from a decent script, good direction, and an effective and thoroughly believable cast of fine character actors, including many former B-movie and series film stars. Even the smaller roles are taken by familiar faces with engaging personalities, like Sid Melton, and this adds to the believability of an otherwise threadbare and overused storyline. Veteran serial director Spencer Bennet did a good job on this one, and producer Alex Gordon (who at one time worked closely with the incredible Edward D. Wood Jr. and designed the "special effects" for *Bride of the Monster*) finally sunk his time and money into a project that most fans of low-budget monster films consider to be his best effort. Entertaining and effective without being too stupid or taking itself too seriously, this is decent fare for fantasy fans and one of the better "flying saucer" films to come out of the UFO-crazed 1950s.

1959   B & W   72 minutes

ATOR: THE FIGHTING EAGLE
🦃

DIRECTOR: David Hills
CAST: Miles O'Keeffe, Sabrina Siani, Warren Hillman

A low-budget stupid sword-and-sorcery flick with Miles O'Keeffe, from Bo Derek's *Tarzan, the Ape Man*. Rated PG for violence and nudity.

1983   98 minutes

BABY...SECRET OF THE LOST LEGEND
★★½

DIRECTOR: Bill Norton
CAST: William Katt, Sean Young, Patrick McGoohan, Julian Fellowes

Set on the Ivory Coast of West Africa, this Disney story offers more than a cute fable about the discovery of a family of brontosauri. Nudity, violence, and a hint of sex represent Disney's attempt to appeal to a wider audience. The special effects of the ancient critters make the show worth watching. Rated PG primarily for the violence.

1985   90 minutes

BACK TO THE FUTURE
★★★★½

DIRECTOR: Robert Zemeckis
CAST: Michael J. Fox, Christopher Lloyd, Lea Thompson, Crispin Glover, Thomas F. Wilson

This delightful Steven Spielberg production, directed by Robert Zemeckis (*Romancing the Stone*), features Michael J. Fox as a teenager who is zapped back in time courtesy of a souped-up Delorean modified by mad scientist Christopher Lloyd. Once there, Fox meets his parents as teenagers, an act that could result in disaster. The first fifteen minutes of this film are pretty bad (thus its less-than-five-star rating), but once Fox gets back to where he doesn't belong, it's a terrific entertainment. Rated PG for brief violence and profanity.

1985   116 minutes

BARBARELLA
★★½

DIRECTOR: Roger Vadim
CAST: Jane Fonda, John Phillip Law, Anita Pallenberg, Milo O'Shea

Futuristic fantasy has Jane Fonda in the title role of a space beauty being drooled over by various male creatures on a strange planet. Drags at times, but Jane's fans won't want to miss it. Rated PG for partial nudity, sexual content.

1968   98 minutes

BARBARIAN QUEEN

DIRECTOR: Hector Oliver

CAST: Lana Clarkson, Latta Shea, Frank Zagarino, Dawn Dunlap

Another one of those lame fantasy flicks à la *Yor*, the *Conan* films, and Lou Ferigno's *Hercules* films. Stupid and exploitative, this one is about a group of women who survive an attack on their village only to band together to defeat the raiders. Save your money. Although not rated, *Barbarian Queen* has lots of nudity, sex, and violence, and would qualify for an R rating under MPAA standards.

1985   75 minutes

BATTLE BEYOND THE STARS
★★★★

DIRECTOR: Jimmy T. Murakami
CAST: Richard Thomas, John Saxon, Robert Vaughn

Here's something different: a space fantasy-comedy. Richard Thomas stars in this funny and often exciting movie as an emissary from a peaceful planet desperately searching for champions to save it from destruction and domination by an evil warlord. It's *Star Wars* meets *The Magnificent Seven*, with fine tongue-in-cheek performances by George Peppard, Robert Vaughn (playing the same role he had in the western), and John Saxon. Rated PG.

1980   104 minutes

BATTLE FOR THE PLANET OF THE APES
★★

DIRECTOR: J. Lee Thompson
CAST: Roddy McDowall, Severn Darden, John Huston, Claude Akins, Paul Williams

Events come full circle in this final *Apes* film, with simian Roddy McDowall attempting peaceful coexistence with conquered humanity. Naturally, not everybody plays along with such a plan, and an impending nuclear threat adds little tension to a story whose outcome is known. Extensive use of stock footage from previous films must have helped this cheapie clean up at the box office. Although the series would have no further big-screen life, it next fell into the purgatory of a short-lived—and awful—network television series. Rated PG for violence.

1973　　　　　　　92 minutes

BATTLESTAR GALACTICA
★★

DIRECTOR: Richard A. Colla
CAST: Lorne Greene, Richard Hatch, Dirk Benedict, Lew Ayres, Jane Seymour

This film, adapted from the television series, opens with the preparation for a peace treaty by President Adar (Lew Ayres). He has arranged to end a thousand years of war between mankind and the subhuman Cylons. Events go downhill from there. It's seventh-rate *Star Wars*, as are the other "films" in this video series. Rated PG.

1978　　　　　　　125 minutes

BEASTMASTER, THE
★★★½

DIRECTOR: Don Coscarelli
CAST: Marc Singer, Tanya Roberts, Rip Torn, John Amos, Rod Loomis

A young medieval warrior (Marc Singer) who possesses the ability to communicate psychically with animals takes revenge—with the help of a slave (Tanya Roberts) and a master warrior (John Amos)—on the evil sorcerer (Rip Torn). It's fun for kids of all ages. Rated PG

for violence, gore, and brief nudity.

1982　　　　　　　118 minutes

BEAUTY AND THE BEAST
★★★★★

DIRECTOR: Jean Cocteau
CAST: Josette Day, Jean Marais

This French classic goes far beyond mere retelling of the well-known fairy tale. Its eerie visual beauty and surrealistic atmosphere mark it as a genuine original. The tragic love story between Beauty (Josette Day) and the all-too-human Beast (Jean Marais) resembles a moving painting. Every detail is presented with painstaking care by its innovative director, Jean Cocteau.

1946　　　B & W　　90 minutes

BENEATH THE PLANET OF THE APES
★★½

DIRECTOR: Ted Post
CAST: Charlton Heston, James Franciscus, Maurice Evans, Kim Hunter, Linda Harrison, James Gregory

Charlton Heston let himself get sucked into this sequel to *Planet of the Apes*. Astronaut James Franciscus—sent to find out what happened to the first team sent to the planet—has more than simians to contend with; he also discovers a race of u-g-l-y mutants that worships an atomic bomb, since it made them what they are. . . . Some of the original's energy remains, but this unpleasant sequel goes nowhere fast. Those who feel that nothing can happen after the world is destroyed need to check into the next entry, *Escape from the Planet of the Apes*. Rated PG for violence.

1970　　　　　　　95 minutes

BLACK HOLE, THE
★

DIRECTOR: Gary Nelson
CAST: Maximilian Schell, Anthony Perkins, Robert Forster, Joseph Bottoms, Yvette Mimieux, Ernest Borgnine

Let's hear it for *Herbie Goes to Outer Space*! Boooooo! Only the splendid special effects make this sappy science-fiction dud from the Disney Studios bearable. Complete with a cute little robot (á la *Star Wars*) and a colorful crew (like "Star Trek"), it's an uninspired collection of space movie clichés. Rated PG.

1979   97 minutes

BLADE RUNNER
★★★★½

DIRECTOR: Ridley Scott
CAST: Harrison Ford, Rutger Hauer, Sean Young, Daryl Hannah

A genuine science-fiction film, this Ridley Scott (*Alien*) production is daring, thought-provoking, and visually impressive. Harrison Ford stars as a futuristic Philip Marlowe trying to find and kill the world's remaining rebel androids in 2817 Los Angeles. *Blade Runner* may not be for everyone, but those who appreciate something of substance will find it worthwhile. Rated PG for brief nudity and violence.

1982   118 minutes

BOY AND HIS DOG, A
★★★★½

DIRECTOR: L. Q. Jones
CAST: Don Johnson, Suzanne Benton, Jason Robards

Looking for intelligence and biting humor in a science-fiction satire? Try this Hugo Award–winning screen adaptation of Harlan Ellison's novel, which focuses on the adventures of a young scavenger (Don Johnson, of television's "Miami Vice") and his telepathic dog as they roam the earth circa 2024 after a nuclear holocaust. It's funny, poignant, thought-provoking, and—especially at the conclusion—surprising. Rated R for violence, sexual references, and nudity.

1976   87 minutes

BRAIN FROM PLANET AROUS, THE
★★★

DIRECTOR: Nathan Juran
CAST: John Agar, Joyce Meadows, Robert Fuller

Great little film is much better than the plot or title would suggest. Giant brain from outer space takes over John Agar's body in an attempt to conquer the world. Not far behind is another brain that inhabits the body of Agar's dog and tries to prevent it. Good stuff.

1958   B & W   70 minutes

BRAIN THAT WOULDN'T DIE, THE
★★

DIRECTOR: Joseph Green
CAST: Herb Evers, Virginia Leith, Adele Lamont

Only the most dedicated science-fiction fans will enjoy this story, which revolves around a doctor who experiments with human limbs. When his fiancée is decapitated in a car accident, he saves her head and searches for the perfect body to go with it. There is some violence and plenty of blood.

1963   B & W   81 minutes

BRAINSTORM
★★★½

DIRECTOR: Douglas Trumbull
CAST: Christopher Walken, Natalie Wood, Louise Fletcher

Christopher Walken and Natalie Wood star in this sci-fi thriller about an invention that can read and record physical, emotional, and intellectual sensations as they are experienced by an individual and allow them to be re-experienced by another human being. The machine's potential for good—increasing communication and mutual understanding—is impressive. But what happens if it's used for evil? Rated PG for nudity and profanity.

1983   106 minutes

BROTHER FROM ANOTHER PLANET, THE
★★★★

DIRECTOR: John Sayles
CAST: Joe Morton, Darryl Edwards, Steve James

In this comic fantasy, directed by John Sayles (*Return of the Secaucus 7*), a dark-skinned extraterrestrial (Joe Morton) on the lam from alien cops crash-lands his spaceship in New York harbor, staggers ashore on Ellis Island, then makes his way to Harlem. As the Ellis Island opening suggests, this release is, like *Moscow on the Hudson*, about what it means to be an immigrant in America. Yet Sayles has more on his mind than "America the Beautiful," and that's what makes this alternately poignant, hilarious, and sobering study of our country so impressive. Unrated, the film has profanity and violence.

1984   110 minutes

BUCK ROGERS IN THE 25TH CENTURY
★★

DIRECTOR: Daniel Haller
CAST: Gil Gerard, Erin Gray, Pamela Hensley, Tim O'Connor, Henry Silva, Felix Silla

Updating of the Buck Rogers legend finds Buck (Gil Gerard), after years of suspended animation, awakened in a future society under attack by the power-mad Princess Ardala (Pamela Hensley). Of course, it's up to our hero to save the day, with the help of a female fighter pilot (Erin Gray) and a dopey robot named Twiki (Felix Silla, with the voice of Mel Blanc). Substandard space fare was originally made as a TV pilot for the recent series but was released theatrically instead. Rated PG for two off-color words.

1979   89 minutes

CAPRICORN ONE
★★★★

DIRECTOR: Peter Hyams
CAST: Elliott Gould, James Brolin, Hal Holbrook, Sam Waterston, Karen Black, O. J. Simpson, Telly Savalas

Peter Hyams, who also directed *2010*, made his first big impression at the box office with this exciting and suspenseful release. In this story, a space flight to Mars is aborted. However, to save face, the government stages a mock flight to the red planet in a television studio, with astronauts James Brolin, Sam Waterston, and O. J. Simpson pretending to be in outer space and landing on another planet. Everything goes well. It all looks convincing on the TV screen. Then the news is released by the Pentagon that the ship crashed upon re-entry and all aboard were killed, which puts the lives of the astronauts in danger. Elliott Gould co-stars as a newspaper reporter on the track of the truth in this highly recommended nail-biter. Rated PG.

1978   124 minutes

CAPTIVE PLANET

DIRECTOR: Al Bradley
CAST: Sharon Baker, Chris Avran, Anthony Newcastle, Yarti Somer

Earth is once again besieged by alien invaders in this very missable movie. There may have been an interesting idea at the heart of this film, but it was lost in wooden acting, poor script, and unimaginative, budget-priced special effects.

1986   105 minutes

CARS THAT ATE PARIS, THE (THE CARS THAT EAT PEOPLE)
★★★★

DIRECTOR: Peter Weir
CAST: John Meillon, Terry Camilleri, Kevin Miles

One of the first signs that Australian New Wave would bring a flood of brilliant films. This one, by perhaps the greatest director from Down Under, Peter Weir (*Witness*, *Picnic at Hanging Rock*, *The Last Wave*), is a black comedy about a small outback village plagued by driverless cars that come out by night. Weird, to be sure, but worth a look. Rated PG.

1975   90 minutes

CAT WOMEN OF THE MOON

DIRECTOR: Arthur Hilton
CAST: Sonny Tufts, Marie Windsor, Victor Jory

Another ludicrous entry in the travel-to-a-planet-of-barely-dressed-women subgenre which so fascinated makers of cheap, grade Z flicks in the 1950s. This one doesn't even qualify as camp entertainment; it's simply terrible. Avoid at all costs.

1954   64 minutes

CAVE GIRL

DIRECTOR: David Oliver
CAST: Daniel Roebuck, Cindy Ann Thompson

Yet another insult to the intelligence of the video-viewing public. This one is about a high-school student (who looks more like he is ready for his ten-year reunion) who gets lost in a cave during a field trip and pops up in prehistoric times. There he finds a beautiful woman with long blonde hair and pearly-white teeth. (It would seem that there were hairdressers and toothpaste back then.) Of course, he just has to have sex with her! And the first English words our hero teaches the Neanderthal nymphet are not suitable for this publication. Rated R for sex, nudity, and profanity.

1985   85 minutes

CHARLY
★★★★

DIRECTOR: Ralph Nelson
CAST: Cliff Robertson, Claire Bloom, Lilia Skala, Dick Van Patten, Leon Janney

Cliff Robertson won the best-actor Oscar for his role in this excellent science-fiction film as a retarded man turned into a genius through scientific experiments. Claire Bloom is also excellent as the caseworker who becomes his friend. Rated PG.

1968   103 minutes

CITY LIMITS

DIRECTOR: Aaron Lipstadt
CAST: Darrell Larson, John Stockwell, Kim Cattrall, Rae Dawn Chong, Robby Benson, James Earl Jones

Another in the endless parade of life-after-the-apocalypse, *Mad Max* ripoff films. In this dud, we have two rival youth gangs fighting it out for control of a big city. Most of the action involves gang members beating each other with chains and clubs while riding motorcycles in dark alleys. The acting talent of such stars as Rae Dawn Chong and James Earl Jones is thrown away, and the costumes all the characters wear are ridiculous beyond belief. Rated PG-13 for brief nudity, violence, and language.

1984   85 minutes

CLAN OF THE CAVE BEAR
★½

DIRECTOR: Michael Chapman
CAST: Daryl Hannah, Pamela Reed, Thomas G. Waites, John Doolittle

In this dreadfully dumb adaptation of Jean M. Auel's best-selling fantasy novel, Daryl Hannah plays a Cro-Magnon child who is grudgingly adopted by a tribe of Neanderthals, who, with a few exceptions, fear she is a dark spirit intent on destroying them. *Quest for Fire* did the cave man story best, and Hannah was better off in films like *Splash* and *Legal Eagles*. Even fans of the book will be disappointed. Rated R.

1986   100 minutes

CLASH OF THE TITANS
★★½

DIRECTOR: Desmond Davis
CAST: Laurence Olivier, Harry Hamlin, Judi Bowker, Burgess Meredith

Despite its spectacular special effects and great possibilities, *Clash of the Titans* is not the film it could have been. The story is the retelling of a Greek myth in which Perseus (Harry Hamlin), the son of Zeus (Laurence Olivier), mounts his flying horse, Pegasus, and fights for the hand of Andromeda (Judi Bowker) against an onslaught of mythological monsters. Plagued by corny situations and stilted dialogue, only the visual wonders by special-effects wizard Ray Harryhausen make this movie worth seeing. Rated PG for violence and gore.

1981   118 minutes

CLOCKWORK ORANGE, A
★★★★

DIRECTOR: Stanley Kubrick
CAST: Malcolm McDowell, Patrick Magee, Adrienne Corri, Aubrey Morris, James Marcus

Not for every taste, this stylized, "ultraviolent" black comedy by director Stanley Kubrick is as funny as it was prophetic. This film (which was adapted from the Anthony Burgess novel) chillingly presaged the British punk movement of the 1970s and the early '80s. Malcolm McDowell stars as the number-one "malchick," Alex, who leads his "droogs" through "a bit of the old ultraviolence" for a real "horror show." Rated R.

1971   137 minutes

CLONES, THE
★★½

DIRECTORS: Paul Hunt, Lamar Card
CAST: Michael Greene, Bruce Bennett, Gregory Sierra, John Barrymore Jr., Angelo Rossito.

In a sinister plot to control the weather, several government scientists are duplicated and placed in strategic meteorological stations. Of course, this scheme is discovered by one of the "good" scientists, who is marked for extermination from that point on.

Basically silly film is made watchable by the believable performances of Michael Greene and Gregory Sierra, and there's a terrific roller coaster-chase finale. Rated PG for language and violence.

1973   86 minutes

CLOSE ENCOUNTERS OF THE THIRD KIND
★★★★

DIRECTOR: Steven Spielberg
CAST: Richard Dreyfuss, Francois Truffaut, Teri Garr

This is director Steven Spielberg's enchanting, pre-*E.T.* vision of an extraterrestrial visit to Earth. The movie goes against many long-nurtured conceptions about space aliens. The humans, such as Richard Dreyfuss, act more bizarre than the non-threatening childlike visitors. Spielberg never surrenders his role as storyteller to the distractions of special effects. That is one reason why his films are better received than most films of the genre. Rated PG.

1977   132 minutes

COCOON
★★★★★

DIRECTOR: Ron Howard
CAST: Don Ameche, Wilford Brimley, Hume Cronyn, Jack Gilford, Steve Guttenberg, Barret Oliver, Maureen Stapleton, Jessica Tandy, Gwen Verdon, Tahnee Welch

Chalk up another winner for actor-turned-director Ron Howard. As with *Splash* and *Night Shift* before it, *Cocoon* is a splendid entertainment. The story in this science-fiction film revolves around a group of people in a retirement home who find what they believe is the fountain of youth. Only trouble is the

magic place belongs to a group of extraterrestrials, who may or may not be friendly. Rated PG-13 for suggested sex, brief nudity, and light profanity.

1985   118 minutes

COMPANY OF WOLVES, THE
★★★½

DIRECTOR: Neil Jordan
CAST: Angela Lansbury, David Warner, Sarah Patterson, Micha Bergese

Neither a horror film nor a fantasy for the kiddies, this dark, psychologically oriented rendering of the "Little Red Riding Hood" story is for thinking viewers only. Angela Lansbury stars as Grandmother, who turns the dreams of her granddaughter (Sarah Patterson) into tales of spooky terror. Artistically made by director Neil Jordan, this movie deserves to be seen. Rated R for violence and gore.

1985   95 minutes

CONAN THE BARBARIAN
★★½

DIRECTOR: John Milius
CAST: Arnold Schwarzenegger, Sandahl Bergman, James Earl Jones, Gerry Lopez

Featuring Arnold Schwarzenegger in the title role, this $19 million sword-and-sorcery epic is just as corny, raunchy, sexist, and unbelievably brutal as the original tales by Robert E. Howard. Therefore, it seems likely Conan fans will be delighted. Yes, it's often unintentionally hilarious and dumb. In other words, it's an old-fashioned B movie on a grand scale—and basically enjoyable because of it. Rated R for nudity, profanity, sex, and violence.

1982   129 minutes

CONAN THE DESTROYER
★★★

DIRECTOR: Richard Fleischer
CAST: Arnold Schwarzenegger, Grace Jones, Wilt Chamberlain, Tracy Walter

Thank goodness the creators of this sequel to *Conan the Barbarian* didn't take themselves as seriously as their predecessors, and the result is a lightweight, violent movie that works quite well. Once again, we're back in the Hyborean Age—a pre-history, mythical time created by Robert E. Howard—where we find Conan (Arnold Schwarzenegger) besting beasts and bloodthirsty battlers at every turn with the help of his sidekick (Tracy Walter), a wizard (Mako), a staff-wielding thief (androgynous Grace Jones), and a giant warrior (Wilt Chamberlain) as they take a virgin princess (Olivia D'Abo) on a perilous mission to find a sacred stone. Rated PG for violence.

1984   103 minutes

CONQUEST OF THE PLANET OF THE APES
★★

DIRECTOR: J. Lee Thompson
CAST: Roddy McDowall, Ricardo Montalban, Don Murray, Severn Darden

Having been rescued by Ricardo Montalban at the end of his previous film adventure, simian Roddy McDowall matures and leads his fellow apes—now domesticated—in a freedom revolt that sets the stage for the events in the very first film. Very melodramatic and formulaic, with few clichés left unused. Unfortunately, the well was to be emptied once more, with *Battle for the Planet of the Apes*. Rated PG for violence.

1972   87 minutes

CRAZY RAY, THE
★★★½

DIRECTOR: René Clair
CAST: Henri Rollan, Madeline Rodrigue, Albert Prejean

René Clair's classic fantasy about a scientist's paralyzing ray is basically an experimental film that utilizes camera tricks and location shooting to entertain and amuse the audience. A handful of people who have not been affected by the ray take advantage of the situation and help themselves to whatever they want but eventually begin to fight among themselves. After locating the scientist who has invented the ray, they persuade him to restore things to normal and meet with skepticism from the police when they attempt to explain things. This is more of an experience than a film, but however you want to approach it, it's very entertaining. Clair later edited prints of this film down to thirty-six minutes and declared those to be the film as it should be seen, but many copies run closer to sixty minutes, with many confusing subtitles included.

1923   B & W   60 minutes
   (also released at 36 minutes)

CREATURE

DIRECTOR: William Malone
CAST: Stan Ivar, Wendy Schaal, Klaus Kinski, Marie Laurin, Lyman Ward, Robert Jaffe

An insulting-to-the-intelligence ripoff of *Alien*, this film features the reawakening of human-devouring life on one of Jupiter's moons. Rated R for gore and violence.

1985   97 minutes

CYBORG: THE SIX MILLION DOLLAR MAN
★★★

DIRECTOR: Richard Irving
CAST: Lee Majors, Darren McGavin, Martin Balsam, Barbara Anderson

Pilot for the long-running ABC series is more serious and subdued than the episodes to follow. Col. Steve Austin (Lee Majors), flying an experimental jet that malfunctions, winds up in the hospital minus his left eye, right arm, and both legs. This gives the military the perfect opportunity to attempt a practical application of "cybornetics" they've been working with, turning the crippled pilot into a superman by giving him powerful robotic limbs capable of almost limitless strength. Unlike the subsequent series, this film is basically a human drama with dashes of sci-fi thrown in. Very good. High marks as well to MCA for the impeccable color and sound on this laserdisc.

1973   73 minutes

D.A.R.Y.L.
★★★★½

DIRECTOR: Simon Wince
CAST: Barret Oliver, Mary Beth Hurt, Michael McKean, Josef Sommer

In this delightful science-fiction film, Barret Oliver (from *The NeverEnding Story*) stars as a boy adopted by Mary Beth Hurt and Michael McKean (*This Is Spinal Tap*). He turns out to be a perfect little fellow... maybe a little too perfect. *D.A.R.Y.L.* is a film the whole family can enjoy: an entertaining cinematic gem that will have viewers recommending it to their friends. Rated PG for violence and light profanity.

1985   99 minutes

DAGORA, THE SPACE MONSTER
★½

DIRECTOR: Inoshiro Honda
CAST: Yosuke Natsuki

From the folks who brought you *Godzilla*. A cache of gems stolen by Japanese gangsters is ripped off by a giant, flying, diamond-eating jellyfish. Probably a true story.

1964   80 minutes

DAMNATION ALLEY
★★

DIRECTOR: Jack Smight
CAST: Jan-Michael Vincent, George Peppard, Dominique Sanda, Jackie Earle Haley, Paul Winfield

The nuclear holocaust movie, which disappeared after its heyday in the 1950s, was revived by *Damnation Alley*, complete with giant mutations and roaming survivors. While it's not a bad movie, it's not particularly good, either. The laser effects are awful. The film has its moments, and considering the outdated premise, that's quite an accomplishment. Rated PG, no violence, sex, or profanity.

1977   91 minutes

DARK CRYSTAL, THE
★★★★

DIRECTORS: Jim Henson, Frank Oz
CAST: Animation

Jim Henson of "The Muppets" fame created this lavish fantasy tale in the style of J.R.R. Tolkien (*The Lord of the Rings*), using the movie magic that brought E.T. and Yoda (*The Empire Strikes Back*) to life. It's a delight for children of all ages. Rated PG, the film has scenes that may be too strong for the younger set.

1983   93 minutes

DARK STAR
★★★½

DIRECTOR: John Carpenter
CAST: Dan O'Bannon, Brian Narelle, Dre Pahich

This is one of the strangest sci-fi films you are likely to run across. Four astronauts have been in space entirely too long as they seek and destroy unstable planets. Director John Carpenter's first film is very funny in spurts and always crazy enough to hold the viewer's attention. Rated PG because of language.

1974   83 minutes

DAY AFTER, THE
★★★★

DIRECTOR: Nicholas Meyer
CAST: Jason Robards, JoBeth Williams, Steve Guttenberg, John Cullum, John Lithgow

This excellent made-for-TV movie special received much advance publicity because of its timely topic: the effects of a nuclear war. Jason Robards plays a hospital doctor who treats many of the victims after the nuclear attack. Steve Guttenberg also stars, as a college student, and John Lithgow is a college professor.

1983   120 minutes

DAY OF THE DOLPHIN, THE
★★★

DIRECTOR: Mike Nichols
CAST: George C. Scott, Trish Van Devere, Paul Sorvino, Fritz Weaver

Fine film centering on a research scientist (George C. Scott) who teaches a pair of dolphins to speak, and how they're kidnapped and used in an assassination attempt. Rated PG for language.

1973   104 minutes

DAY OF THE TRIFFIDS, THE
★★★½

DIRECTOR: Steve Sekely
CAST: Howard Keel, Nicole Maurey, Janette Scott, Kieron Moore, Mervyn Johns

"Dallas" fans may be surprised to see Miss Ellie's husband, Clayton Farlow (Howard Keel), in a science-fiction flick. This British film has "triffids"—alien plants—arriving on Earth during a meteor shower. The shower blinds most of the Earth's people. Then the plants grow, begin walking, and eat humans. This one will grow on you.

1963   95 minutes

DAY THE EARTH CAUGHT FIRE, THE
★★★★

DIRECTOR: Val Guest
CAST: Edward Judd, Janet Munro, Leo McKern, Michael Goodliffe

Veteran director Val Guest helmed this near-classic film concerning the fate of the Earth following simultaneous nuclear explosions at both poles, sending the planet on a collision course with the sun. Incredibly realistic production is thought-provoking and more than a little unsettling, with Edward Judd perfectly cast as an Everyman caught up in the mass panic and hysteria as a frantic populace desperately searches for an answer.

1962   B & W   99 minutes

DAY THE EARTH STOOD STILL, THE
★★★★

DIRECTOR: Robert Wise
CAST: Michael Rennie, Patricia Neal, Hugh Marlowe, Sam Jaffe, Billy Gray

The Day the Earth Stood Still is one of the better science-fiction films. Even though some of the space gimmicks are campy and not up to today's standards of special effects, the film holds up well because of a good adult script and creditable performances by Michael Rennie and Patricia Neal. Rennie plays a man from another planet who visits Earth and does not receive what could be called a warm welcome.

1951   B & W   92 minutes

DEATH RACE 2000
★★★

DIRECTOR: Paul Bartel
CAST: David Carradine, Sylvester Stallone, Louisa Mortiz, Mary Woronov, Don Steele, Joyce Jameson, Fred Grandy

Futuristic look at what has become our national sport: road racing where points are accumulated for killing people with the race cars. David Carradine and Sylvester Stallone star in this tongue-in-cheek sci-fi action film. Does have plenty of gore but always has the audience smiling. Stallone is a howl as one of the competitors. Rated R—violence, nudity, language, sex.

1975   78 minutes

DEATHSPORT
★★

DIRECTOR: Henry Suso, Allan Arkush
CAST: David Carradine, Claudia Jennings, Richard Lynch

Not really a sequel to *Deathrace 2000*, but cut from the same cloth. Both are low-budget action films centered around futuristic no-holds-barred road races. The first film, though, was a lot more fun. Rated R for violence and nudity.

1978   82 minutes

DEATH WATCH
★★★★

DIRECTOR: Bertrand Tavernier
CAST: Romy Schneider, Harvey Keitel, Harry Dean Stanton, Max von Sydow

A thought-provoking look at the power and the misuse of the media in a future society. Harvey Keitel has a camera implanted in his brain. A television producer (Harry Dean Stanton) uses Keitel to film a documentary of a terminally ill woman (Romy Schneider) without her knowledge. Suspenseful science-fiction drama. Rated R for profanity and suggested sex.

1980   117 minutes

DEATHSTALKER

DIRECTOR: John Watson
CAST: Robert Hill, Barbi Benton, Lana Clarkson, Victor Bo

Mixing sex, sadism, and stupidity for a nearly unbearable movie experience, director John Watson (an obvious pseudonym) has created a thoroughly disgusting exploitation flick. A muscle-bound warrior (Robert Hill) attempts to save a beautiful princess (Barbi Benton) from an evil wizard. If the plot sounds familiar, it should. It's an unabashed ripoff of *Star Wars*. The only difference is that in George Lucas's far superior space fantasy, Carrie Fisher didn't have every stitch of her clothing torn off every fifteen minutes. However, for Benton, that's the extent of her "acting." Shame on her. Rated R for nudity, profanity, sex, simulated rape, and violence.

1984   80 minutes

DEFCON 4
★★½

DIRECTOR: Paul Donovan

CAST: Maury Chaykin, Kate Lynch, Tim Choate, Lenore Zann, Keven King, John Walsch

The first half of this film contains special effects the equal of any in modern science fiction, an intelligent script, and excellent acting by the three leads as astronauts in an orbiting space station that is part of an anti-nuclear war defense system. The tensions between the three (Maury Chaykin, Kate Lynch, and Tim Choate) are extremely well done. Global nuclear war breaks out, and lacking the signal to strike back, they wait and watch. In the second half of the film, they return to Earth, and the film becomes one more postholocaust yawn. The overall impression is that perhaps the filmmakers ran out of time or money or both. Had the film maintained the quality of the first half throughout, it would have been a four-star film. Rated R for language and violence.

1985   85 minutes

DEMON (GOD TOLD ME TO)
★★★½
DIRECTOR: Larry Cohen
CAST: Tony Lo Bianco, Sandy Dennis, Sylvia Sidney, Deborah Raffin, Sam Levene, Mike Kellin

A minor masterpiece, this horror and mystery opens with several mass murders. A sniper picks off pedestrians on the street below from a watertower, a grocer suddenly attacks his customers with a knife, and a policeman marching in a St. Patrick's Day parade begins firing at spectators and participants. The only thing that connects all these incidents is they are committed by pleasant, smiling people who explain their acts by saying, "God told me to." Rated R for nudity, profanity, and violence.

1977   95 minutes

DEMON SEED
★★★
DIRECTOR: Donald Cammell
CAST: Julie Christie, Fritz Weaver, Gerrit Graham, Lisa Lu

Good, but not great, science-fiction film about a super-intelligent computer designed by scientist Fritz Weaver to solve problems beyond the scope of man. The computer, however, has other ideas: It wants to study and experiment on the strange Earth species known as man. Weaver's wife (Julie Christie) becomes its unwilling guinea pig and, eventually, mate. Rated R.

1977   94 minutes

DESTINATION MOON
★★★½
DIRECTOR: Irving Pichel
CAST: Warner Anderson, John Archer, Tom Powers, Dick Wesson

This story involves the first American spaceship to land on the moon. Even though the sets are dated today, they were what scientists expected to find when people did land on the moon. This film boasts the classic pointed spaceship and bubble helmets on the space travelers, but it is still great fun for fans of the genre. The film has George Pal as producer and Robert Heinlein as one of its screenwriters.

1950   91 minutes

DOC SAVAGE...THE MAN OF BRONZE
★★★
DIRECTOR: Michael Anderson

CAST: Ron Ely, Pamela Hensley, Darrell Zwerling, Michael Miller, Paul Wexler, Paul Gleason

Perfectly acceptable—although campy—first appearance by the famed hero of pulp novels, Doc Savage. In these days of post–*Raiders of the Lost Ark* action epics, this seems a reasonable entry in the genre. Ron Ely makes a suitable Doc Savage, complete with torn shirt and deadpan delivery. One of the best straight lines occurs when Doc compliments co-star Pamela Hensley: "Mona... you're a brick." Paul Wexler is delightfully overbearing as the villain. Special effects and set design are minimal, a true shame since this is the last film produced by science-fiction pioneer George Pal. Rated PG—some violence.

1975   100 minutes

DR. WHO AND THE DALEKS
★★★½

DIRECTOR: Gordon Flemyng
CAST: Peter Cushing, Roy Castle, Roberta Tovey

An eccentric old scientist, Dr. Who (Peter Cushing) of the long-running BBC television series, takes his friends on a trip through space and time in this good sci-fi adventure for children.

1965   85 minutes

DRAGONSLAYER
★★½

DIRECTOR: Matthew Robbins
CAST: Peter MacNicol, Catlin Clarke, Ralph Richardson

Peter MacNicol plays a sorcerer's apprentice who, to save a damsel in distress, must face a fearsome fire-breathing dragon in this tale of romance and medieval magic. While the special effects are spec-tacular, the rest of the film doesn't quite live up to them. It's slow, and often too corny for older viewers. Rated PG for violence.

1981   110 minutes

DREAMCHILD
★★★★

DIRECTOR: Gavin Millar
CAST: Coral Browne, Peter Gallagher, Ian Holm, Jane Asher, Nicola Cowper, Caris Coffman, Amelia Shankey

Some of those familiar with *Alice's Adventures in Wonderland* may be surprised to learn that there was a real Alice. Author Lewis Carroll, whose real name was Rev. Charles Dodgson, first told his fanciful stories to 10-year-old Alice Liddel on a summer boat ride down the River Isis on July 1, 1862. In 1932, at the age of 80, Alice (then the widow Hargreaves) went to New York City to participate in a Columbia University tribute to Carroll on the one hundredth anniversary of his birth. From these facts, director Gavin Millar and writer Dennis Potter have fashioned this rich and thought-provoking film. Coral Browne is superb as the elderly Alice. Also impressive are Nicola Cowper as the young Alice, Ian Holm as Carroll, and Peter Gallagher (*The Idolmaker*) as a brash American reporter who helps Alice cash in on her celebrity. The film's PG rating comes not from any tangible or typical hard-edged movie elements, but rather as a result of the screenplay's suggestion that the terribly shy Carroll may have been in love with little Alice. While tiny tots may not be able to understand or endure it, older children and their parents should find *Dreamchild*, which also features Jim "Muppet" Henson creatures, to be very entertaining and provide much to talk about afterward.

1986   94 minutes

DREAMSCAPE
★★★★

DIRECTOR: Joseph Ruben
CAST: Dennis Quaid, Max von Sydow, Christopher Plummer, Eddie Albert, Kate Capshaw

If you can go along with its intriguing but far-fetched premise—that trained psychics can enter other people's nightmares and put an end to them—this film will reward you with top-flight special effects, thrills, chills, and surprises. But if you're one of those people who get hung up on realism, this is one release you probably should skip. Bizarre as it sounds, however, *Dreamscape* definitely has its moments of high tension and excitement. Rated PG-13 for suggested sex, violence, and profanity.

1984   99 minutes

DUNE
★½

DIRECTOR: David Lynch
CAST: Sting, Kyle MacLachlan, Max von Sydow, Jurgen Prochnow, Sean Young, Kenneth McMillan, Richard Jordan

The only good thing about the movie version of *Dune* is it makes one want to read (or reread) the book. Otherwise, it's a $47 million mess. Writer-director David Lynch (*The Elephant Man*) touches on most of the elements and events in Frank Herbert's celebrated five-hundred-page science-fiction novel and adequately explores none. The result is a study in viewer frustration. Rated PG-13 for gore, suggested sex, and violence.

1984   145 minutes

E.T.—THE EXTRA-TERRESTRIAL (1986 RELEASE)
★★★★★

DIRECTOR: Steven Spielberg
CAST: Dee Wallace (Stone), Henry Thomas, Peter Coyote, Robert MacNaughton, Drew Barrymore

The highest-grossing (and we think most entertaining) sci-fi film of all time, this is Steven Spielberg's gentle fairy tale about what happens when a boy (Henry Thomas) meets up with a very special fellow from outer space. Sheer wonder is joined with warmth and humor in this movie classic. Rated PG for one slightly vulgar remark.

1982   115 minutes

EARTH VS. THE FLYING SAUCERS
★★★★

DIRECTOR: Fred F. Sears
CAST: Hugh Marlowe, Joan Taylor, Donald Curtis, Morris Ankrum, Thomas B. Henry

Stunning special effects by Ray Harryhausen enhance this familiar 1950s plot about an invasion from outer space. After misinterpreting a message for peace from the initially easygoing aliens, the military opens fire—and then all hell breaks loose! While the film loses much of its visual power on the small screen, Fred F. Sears's smooth direction, as well as solid performances all around, elevate this to near classic status. Great finale, too.

1956   B & W   83 minutes

ELIMINATORS
★½

DIRECTOR: Peter Manoogian
CAST: Andrew Prine, Denise Crosby, Patrick Reynolds, Conan Lee, Roy Dotrice

Like a hokey comic-book story, this film about a mandroid (half human/half robot), a martial-arts expert, a modern-day pirate, and a concerned scientist trying to stop a mad genius from going back into the past in his time machine to rule the Roman Empire is pure camp. The film's humor provides a welcome safety valve for the viewer tired of the poor acting and dismal screenplay. Rated PG for violence and profanity.

1986   95 minutes

EMBRYO
★★½

DIRECTOR: Ralph Nelson
CAST: Rock Hudson, Barbara Carrera, Diane Ladd

Rock Hudson plays a scientist who succeeds in developing a fetus into a full-grown woman in record time. But something isn't quite right. Adequate thriller with a good ending. Rated PG.

1976   104 minutes

EMPEROR'S NEW CLOTHES, THE
★★

DIRECTOR: Peter Medak
CAST: Alan Arkin, Art Carney, Dick Shawn, Timothy Dalton (narrator)

Lavishly costumed (as one might expect from such a title), this *Faerie Tale Theatre* production presents a narcissistic king (Dick Shawn) whose vanity eventually makes him the laughingstock of his country. Alan Arkin and Art Carney have to deliver some painfully banal lines—in modern argot and out of sync with the story's time and setting.

1984   54 minutes

EMPIRE OF THE ANTS
★½

DIRECTOR: Bert I. Gordon
CAST: Joan Collins, Robert Lansing, Albert Salmi, Robert Pine

H. G. Wells must somersault in his grave every time somebody watches this insulting adaptation of one of his more intriguing sci-fi stories. Director Bert I. Gordon really hit bottom with this, a laughable blend of Joan Collins's terrible acting and giant hypnotic insects. This isn't good enough even to be considered camp. An embarrassment for all. Rated PG for violence.

1977   90 minutes

EMPIRE STRIKES BACK, THE
★★★★★

DIRECTOR: Irvin Kershner
CAST: Billy Dee Williams, Harrison Ford, Carrie Fisher, Mark Hamill, Anthony Daniels, Dave Prowse, James Earl Jones (voice)

In George Lucas's follow-up to *Star Wars*, Billy Dee Williams joins Mark Hamill (Luke Skywalker), Harrison Ford (Han Solo), Carrie Fisher (Princess Leia), and the gang in their fight against the forces of the Empire led by Darth Vader (Dave Prowse/James Earl Jones). It's more action-packed fun in that faraway galaxy a long time ago. It's also that rarity of rarities: a superior sequel. It has more plot, more characterization, more special effects—in fact, more of everything than the original. Don't miss it. Rated PG.

1980   124 minutes

ENCOUNTER WITH THE UNKNOWN
★★★½

DIRECTOR: Harry Thomason

CAST: Rod Serling, Rosie Holotik, Gene Ross

Rod Serling narrates a series of true events in psychic phenomena. The episodes are based on studies made by Dr. Jonathan Rankin between 1949 and 1970. Each deals with a person's encounter with the unknown or supernatural. Rated PG.

1973   90 minutes

END OF THE WORLD
🦃

DIRECTOR: John Hayes
CAST: Christopher Lee, Sue Lyon, Lew Ayres, Dean Jagger, MacDonald Carey

Impressive cast founders in this film about aliens plotting to destroy the Earth while disguised as religious figures. Laughably bad movie might be good for a few, if only it weren't so slowly paced. Rated PG.

1977   87 minutes

ENDANGERED SPECIES
★★★½

DIRECTOR: Alan Rudolph
CAST: Robert Urich, JoBeth Williams, Paul Dooley, Hoyt Axton

Everything about this science-fiction suspense thriller is very real—that's why it works so well. The story deals with bizarre incidents involving cattle mutilation and is based on fact. In it, a country sheriff (JoBeth Williams, of *Poltergeist*) and a hard-boiled New York detective (Robert Urich) join forces to find out who or what is responsible. Could it be a satanic cult? UFOs? Or something even more frightening? The answer puts both their lives in danger. Rated R for discreetly handled nudity, violence, gore, and profanity.

1982   97 minutes

ENDGAME

DIRECTOR: Steven Benson
CAST: Al Cliver, Moira Chen, George Eastman, Jack Davis, Al Yamanouchi, Gus Stone, Mario Pedone, Gordon Mitchell

Ho-hum, another *Road Warrior* ripoff—this one complete with mutants who communicate via telepathy. Well, at least they don't look as stupid as the rest of the cast, who suffer the dreaded postproduction humiliation of bad dubbing. Not rated, but the equivalent of a PG-13 for violence, gore, and partial nudity.

1985   98 minutes

ENEMY MINE
★½

DIRECTOR: Wolfgang Petersen
CAST: Dennis Quaid, Louis Gossett Jr., Brion James, Richard Marcus, Carolyn McCormick, Bumper Robinson, Jim Mapp, Lance Kerwin

A sort of science-fiction composite retelling of *The Defiant Ones* and *Hell in the Pacific*, this film by Wolfgang Petersen (*The NeverEnding Story, Das Boot*) is a good idea gone bad—a would-be outer-space epic that manages to disappoint on nearly every level. The story details what happens when two futuristic foes, an Earthman (Dennis Quaid) and a reptilian alien (Louis Gossett Jr.), are stranded on a hostile planet and forced to rely on each other for survival. The heart of the film is the supposed mutual understanding that grows between the two central characters. The actors do their best, but, apart from a few nice scenes, their relationship fails to convince because everything happens much too quickly. Perhaps Petersen wanted to get on with the more original elements in the story. This is commendable, but results in disaster. Later in the film there is a plot twist (which would be unfair to give away) by which the viewer is expected to be fascinated and touched, but the result is only mildly interesting. *Enemy Mine* should have been a terrific motion picture given the talent involved. As it is, this release will be best appreciated by youngsters and the most devout sci-fi buffs. Rated PG-13 for violence and profanity.

1985   108 minutes

ESCAPE FROM THE PLANET OF THE APES
★★★

DIRECTOR: Don Taylor

CAST: Roddy McDowall, Kim Hunter, Eric Braeden, Bradford Dillman, William Windom, Ricardo Montalban

Escaping the nuclear destruction of their own world and time, intelligent simians Roddy McDowall and Kim Hunter arrive on ours. This third *Apes* entry makes wonderful use of the *Strangers in a Strange Land* theme, which turns ugly all too quickly as humanity extends its own sort of warmth and decides to destroy the apes to prevent them from breeding. At this point, producer Arthur P. Jacobs knew he had something going, so the door is left open for subsequent films. Next would be *Conquest of the Planet of the Apes*. Rated PG for violence.

1971   98 minutes

ESCAPE 2000
🐽

DIRECTOR: Brian Trenchard-Smith

CAST: Steve Railsback, Olivia Hussey, Michael Craig, Carmen Duncan, Roger Ward

A nauseating science-fiction film from Britain, this consists of series of close-ups of people in the throes of death—garrotings, bludgeonings, gut-stabbings, shoulder-slashings, and assorted thrashings. Yuck! Rated R for—you guessed it—violence and gore.

1981   92 minutes

ESCAPES
★★★

DIRECTOR: David Steensland

CAST: Vincent Price, Michael Patton-Hall, John Mitchum, Todd Fulton, Jerry Grisham, Ken Thorley

Fast-paced anthology in the *Twilight Zone* vein, featuring six stories of the bizarre and done with great style by director David Steensland. Top honors go to "A Little Fishy," a grimly funny tale, and "Who's There?" a neat yarn about an escaped laboratory experiment and a Sunday jogger. While these two may be the best, the film never fails to entertain.

1985   71 minutes

EXCALIBUR
★★★★

DIRECTOR: John Boorman

CAST: Nicol Williamson, Nigel Terry, Helen Mirren, Nicholas Clay, Cherie Lunghi, Corin Redgrave, Paul Geoffrey

Swords cross and magic abounds in this spectacular, highly enjoyable version of the Arthurian legend. A gritty, realistic view of the rise to power of King Arthur, the forbidden love of Queen Guinevere and Sir Lancelot and the quest of the Knights of the Round Table for the holy grail. *Excalibur* is highlighted by lush photography and fine performances by the British cast—with Nicol Williamson especially memorable as Merlin the magician. Rated R.

1981   140 minutes

EXPLORERS
★★★½

DIRECTOR: Joe Dante
CAST: Ethan Hawke, River Phoenix, Jason Presson, Dick Miller, Robert Picardo

The young and the young at heart are certain to have a grand time watching *Explorers*. It's a just-for-fun fantasy about three kids (Ethan Hawke, River Phoenix, and Jason Presson) who literally share the same dream and soon find themselves taking off on the greatest adventure of all: a journey through outer space. Once there, they meet the most surprising—and entertaining—alien creatures ever to be in a movie. Directed by Joe Dante (*Gremlins*; *The Howling*), it's not a film for everyone. But if you love wacky, unpredictable humor, don't miss it. Rated PG for minor violence and light profanity.

1985   109 minutes

FAHRENHEIT 451
★★★★

DIRECTOR: Francois Truffaut
CAST: Oskar Werner, Julie Christie, Cyril Cusack, Anton Diffring, Alex Scott

Still the best adaptation of a Ray Bradbury book to hit the screen (big or small). Oskar Werner is properly troubled as a futuristic "fireman" responsible for the destruction of books, who begins to wonder about the necessity of his work. This is director Francois Truffaut's first English-language film, and he treats the subject of language and literature with a dignity not found in most Americans. Wonderfully moody and quite faithful to the tone of the book; the conclusion, Truffaut's own invention, is particularly poignant. Unrated—family fare.

1967   111 minutes

FANTASTIC PLANET
★★★

DIRECTOR: René Laloux
CAST: Animated

This French-Czechoslovakian production is an animated metaphor concerning the class struggles—and, eventually, war—between two races on an alien planet. Lovely animation and a non-preachy approach to the story combine to produce a fine little film that makes its points and sticks in the memory. Short, but sincere and effective. Voices of Barry Bostwick, Nora Heflin. Rated PG—intense subject matter, some violence.

1973   71 minutes

FANTASTIC VOYAGE
★★★

DIRECTOR: Richard Fleischer
CAST: Stephen Boyd, Raquel Welch, Edmond O'Brien, Donald Pleasence, Arthur O'Connell, William Redfield, Arthur Kennedy

Scientists Stephen Boyd, Raquel Welch, Edmond O'Brien, Donald Pleasence, and Arthur O'Connell journey into inner space—the human body—by being shrunk to microscopic size. They then are threatened by the system's natural defenses. This Richard Fleischer film still packs an unusually potent punch.

1966   100 minutes

FANTASY ISLAND
★★½

DIRECTOR: Richard Lang
CAST: Ricardo Montalban, Bill Bixby, Sandra Dee, Peter Lawford, Carol Lynley, Hugh O'Brian

Dreams and fantasies come true and then some on a mysterious millionaire's island paradise in this sub-average TV-er that spawned the hit series. Yawn.

1977   100 minutes

FINAL COUNTDOWN, THE
★★½

DIRECTOR: Don Taylor
CAST: Kirk Douglas, Martin Sheen, Katharine Ross

Far-fetched but passable story about an aircraft carrier traveling backward in time to just before the start of World War II. The crew must then decide whether or not to change the course of history. Some good special effects and performances by the leads manage to keep this one afloat. Rated PG.

1980   104 minutes

FIRE AND ICE
★★★★

DIRECTOR: Ralph Bakshi
CAST: Animated

This animated film is geared more to adults than children. Sword and sorcery fantasy keeps the action moving and the viewer interested to the point you may forget the characters aren't real. The plot begins with evil sorcerer Nekron planning world domination. It thickens when he kidnaps the princess, Teegra, to force her father to turn his kingdom over to him as his daughter's ransom. Rated PG.

1983   81 minutes

FIRST SPACESHIP ON VENUS
★

DIRECTOR: Kurt Maetzig
CAST: Yoko Tani, Oldrich Lukes, Ignacy Machowski

Low-budget, lackluster German science-fiction plants an international crew of astronauts on Venus with poor special effects and worse dialogue. There are some interesting questions raised in this "let's proceed with caution" story, but not enough to merit it a spot in the science fiction hall of fame.

1960   78 minutes

FLASH GORDON
★★★

DIRECTOR: Mike Hodges
CAST: Sam J. Jones, Topol, Max von Sydow, Melody Anderson

If you don't take it seriously, this campy film based on the classic Alex Raymond comic strip of the 1930s is a real hoot. Sam Jones, as Flash, and Melody Anderson, as Dale Arden, race through the intentionally hokey special effects to do battle with Max von Sydow, who makes an excellent Ming the Merciless. Rated PG.

1980   110 minutes

FLIGHT OF THE NAVIGATOR
★★★

DIRECTOR: Randal Kleiser
CAST: Joey Kramer, Veronica Cartwright, Cliff De Young, Sarah Jessica Parker, Howard Hessman, Matt Adler

This all-ages Disney delight concerns a youngster (Joey Kramer) who has the unique ability to communicate with machines and uses this to help a UFO find its way home. *Flight of the Navigator* has something for everyone. Kids will love its crazy creatures, special effects, and action-packed conclusion, while parents will appreciate its nice balance of sense and nonsense. Rated PG for mild cussing.

1986   90 minutes

FOOD OF THE GODS
🐷

DIRECTOR: Bert I. Gorden
CAST: Marjoe Gortner, Ida Lupino, Pamela Franklin, Ralph Meeker

H. G. Wells's story is thrashed in this typical Bert I. Gordon bomb. After ingesting an unknown substance, various animals become giant and threaten the occupants of a remote mountain cabin. Fakey special effects might have been acceptable in the 1950s, but they just don't cut it today. Rated PG for violence.

1976   88 minutes

FORBIDDEN PLANET
★★★★½

DIRECTOR: Fred McLeod Wilcox
CAST: Walter Pidgeon, Anne Francis, Leslie Nielsen, Jack Kelly

This is the most highly regarded sci-fi film of the 1950s. Its special-effects breakthroughs are rather tame today, but its story remains interesting. As a space mission from Earth lands on the Planet Altair-4 in the year 2200, they encounter a doctor (Walter Pidgeon) and his daughter (Anne Francis) who are all that remain from a previous colonization attempt. It soon becomes apparent that some unseen force on the planet does not bid them welcome.

1956   98 minutes

FORBIDDEN ZONE
🐷

DIRECTOR: Richard Elfman
CAST: Herve Villechaize, Susan Tyrrell, Marie-Pascale Elfman, Viva

Absurd "cult" film has Herve Villechaize as the ruler of a bizarre kingdom located in the "Sixth Dimension." A sort-of comedy, this should be avoided by all means. Rated R for nudity and adult content.

1980   B & W   76 minutes

4D MAN
★★★

DIRECTOR: Irvin S. Yeaworth Jr.
CAST: Robert Lansing, Lee Meriwether, James Congdon, Robert Strauss, Patty Duke

A scientist (Robert Lansing) learns of a method of moving through objects (walls, doors, bank vaults, etc.), without realizing the terrible consequences, which eventually lead to madness and murder. Eerie sci-fi film hampered only by an often brash music score by Ralph Carmichael. Still, quite spine-tingling. From the director of *The Blob*.

1959   85 minutes

FROM THE EARTH TO THE MOON
★★★

DIRECTOR: Byron Haskin
CAST: Joseph Cotten, George Sanders, Debra Paget, Don Dubbins

Entertaining tale based on Jules Verne's story of a turn-of-the-century trip to the Moon led by Joseph Cotten and sabotaged by George Sanders.

1958   100 minutes

FUTUREWORLD
★★★

DIRECTOR: Richard T. Heffron
CAST: Peter Fonda, Blythe Danner, Arthur Hill, Yul Brynner, Stuart Margolin, John Ryan

An amusement park of the future caters to any adult fantasy. Lifelike androids carry out your every whim. A fun place, right? Not so, as reporter Peter Fonda finds out in this sequel to "Westworld." Something is amiss. The androids are acting independent of how they were programmed. This is okay escapist fare. Rated PG.

1976　　　　　104 minutes

GALAXINA
★

DIRECTOR: William Sachs
CAST: Avery Schreiber, Dorothy R. Stratten, Stephen Macht, James David Hinton

See Captain Cornelius Butt (Avery Schreiber), of the spaceship *Infinity*, consume a raw egg and regurgitate a rubbery creature that later calls him "Mommy." Visit an inter-galactic saloon that serves humans (they're on the menu, not the guest list). And be amazed, then disgusted and bored by the general tackiness and idiocy of this low-budget space spoof. In this story, about a valuable space stone and a romance between a space cop and a robot, there are some funny moments, but not enough to make watching this movie worthwhile. Rated R.

1980　　　　　95 minutes

GALAXY OF TERROR
★★½

DIRECTOR: B. D. Clark
CAST: Erin Moran, Edward Albert, Ray Walston

The science-fiction film has certainly come a long way. Even the low-budget ones aren't as bad as they used to be. Take this movie, which was also known as *Planet of Horrors*, in which the crew of a spaceship sent to rescue a crash survivor finds itself facing one

horror after another on a barren planet. This chiller wastes no time in getting to the thrills. Rated R because of profanity, nudity, and violence.

1981　　　　　82 minutes

GAMMA PEOPLE, THE
★½

DIRECTOR: John Gilling
CAST: Paul Douglas, Eva Bartok, Leslie Phillips, Walter Rilla

Weak science-fiction tale about the children of the middle European country of Gudavia being transformed into homicidal monsters or geniuses by the all-powerful dictator Dr. Boronski (Walter Rilla). Even considering the year it was made, acting and effects just aren't up to snuff.

1956　　　B & W　79 minutes

GOLDEN VOYAGE OF SINBAD, THE
★★★★

DIRECTOR: Gordon Hessler
CAST: John Phillip Law, Tom Baker, Caroline Munro, Douglas Wilmer, Gregoire Aslan, John Garfield Jr.

This first-rate Arabian Nights adventure pits Captain Sinbad (John Phillip Law) against the evil Prince Koura (Tom Baker) for possession of a magical amulet with amazing powers. This is a superb fantasy, with some truly incredible effects by master animator Ray Harryhausen. Miklos Rozsa's excellent musical score greatly enhances the overall atmosphere of mystery present throughout the film. The battle scene with a six-armed sword-wielding bronze goddess is a knockout! Only drawback is RCA/Columbia's poor audio transfer to home video, resulting in an uninvolving "canned" sound quality. Nevertheless, this is a beautiful piece of film-making, and one not to be missed. Rated G.

1974   105 minutes

GOLDENGIRL

DIRECTOR: Joseph Sargent
CAST: Susan Anton, James Coburn, Curt Jurgens, Robert Culp, Leslie Caron, Jessica Walter

This modern retread of *Frankenstein* fails on all counts. Scientist Curt Jurgens turns Susan Anton into a super-athlete for Olympic glory. Acting, writing, and direction are terrible; the splicing between genuine Olympic footage and storyline fiction is equally lame. Anton—justifiably—must not have been too thrilled by this acting debut, because she's not been that noticeable since. Beware of a longer, television version: A boring film made even more interminable. Rated PG.

1979   104 minutes

GREMLINS
★★★★

DIRECTOR: Joe Dante
CAST: Zach Galligan, Phoebe Cates, Hoyt Axton, Frances Lee McCain, Polly Holliday, Glynn Turman, Dick Miller, Keye Luke, Scott Brady

This "Steven Spielberg Presentation" is a highly original, unpredictable, frantically paced, and just plain wacky movie. It's one part *E.T.—The Extra-Terrestrial*, one part scary/funny horror film (à la director Joe Dante's last picture, *The Howling*), one part Muppet movie, and one part Bugs Bunny/Warner Bros. cartoon. Sound strange? You got it. In the story, Billy Peltzer (Zach Galligan) gets a cute little pet from his inventor-father (Hoyt Axton) for Christmas. But there's a catch.

When Billy's father purchased the creature from a Chinese antique dealer, the latter told him, "Keep them away from water. Don't ever get them wet. Keep them out of light. They hate bright light. It will kill them. But the most important thing," he added ominously, "the thing you must never forget—no matter how much they cry, no matter how much they beg— never, never feed them after midnight." Rated PG for profanity and stylized violence.

1984   111 minutes

HANGAR 18

DIRECTOR: James L. Conway
CAST: Darren McGavin, Robert Vaughn, Gary Collins, Joseph Campanella, James Hampton

The story revolves around an alien spaceship that is accidentally disabled by a U.S. satellite. Two astronauts (Gary Collins and James Hampton) in a nearby rocket witness the accident—a fellow astronaut is decapitated during the event—and, when they return to Earth, are blamed for the death of their partner. Rated PG.

1980   93 minutes

HAUNTING PASSION, THE
★

DIRECTOR: John Korty
CAST: Jane Seymour, Gerald McRaney, Millie Perkins, Ruth Nelson, Paul Rossilli

An uneven made-for-TV supernatural romance in which a ghost seduces a housewife. Jane Seymour and the rest of the cast do the best they can with the bad romance novel dialogue they're given. There are a few chills, but more often than not, it falls short of the mark.

1983   98 minutes

HEAVENLY KID, THE

DIRECTOR: Cary Medoway
CAST: Lewis Smith, Jason Gedrick, Jane Kaczmarek, Richard Mulligan, Mark Metcalf

Hopelessly banal and derivative teen-exploitation flick has "angel" Bobby Fontana (Lewis Smith), who died in a *Rebel Without a Cause*-style chicken race, come to Earth to wise up a nerd named Lenny (Jason Gedrick). It's *Heaven Can Wait* (a.k.a. *Here Comes Mr. Jordan*) and *It's a Wonderful Life* brought to the level of asinine stupidity. Ugh! Rated PG-13.

1985   89 minutes

HELLSTROM CHRONICLE, THE
★★★★

DIRECTOR: Walon Green
CAST: Lawrence Pressman

This 1971 pseudo-documentary features fantastic close-up cinematography of insects and their ilk underpinning a storyline by Dr. Hellstrom (Lawrence Pressman), which contends the critters are taking over and we humans had better wise up before it's too late. Despite the dumb premise, *The Hellstrom Chronicle* remains a captivating film. Rated G.

1971   90 minutes

HERCULES

DIRECTOR: Lewis Coates
CAST: Lou Ferrigno, Sybil Danning, Brad Harris, Rosanna Podesta

Following the beefy footsteps of Conan, Ator, and Yor comes Lou Ferrigno (formerly TV's "The Incredible Hulk") as the most famous muscle man of them all, in this cheap and dreadful venture into Greek mythology. It was inevitable, but did it have to be so awful? Rated PG for violence.

1983   98 minutes

HERCULES UNCHAINED
★★

DIRECTOR: Pietro Francisci
CAST: Steve Reeves, Sylva Koscina, Primo Carnera, Sylvia Lopez

When the god of muscles sets his little mind on something, don't get in his way! In this one, he's out to rescue his lady fair. It's a silly but diverting adventure. Steve Reeves is still the best Hercules on film, dubbed voice and all.

1960   101 minutes

HIGHLANDER
★★

DIRECTOR: Russell Mulcahy
CAST: Christopher Lambert, Clancy Brown, Sean Connery

A sixteenth-century Scottish clansman discovers he is one of a small group of immortals destined to fight each other through the centuries. The last survivor will be rewarded with a valuable power. The movie climaxes in a fierce battle atop a skyscraper in modern-day Manhattan. Made by a pioneer music video director, the film is visually stunning, though sometimes distractingly so. If you're a style freak, you might enjoy it. If you prefer substance, watch out. The jumps in time are confusing, the film takes forty-five minutes to relay its basic plot, and the music by Queen is annoying and inappropriate. The movie is a treat for the eyes, but you'll owe your brain an apology. Rated R for violence.

1986   110 minutes

HOWARD THE DUCK
★

DIRECTOR: Willard Huyck
CAST: Lea Thompson, Jeffrey Jones, Tim Robbins, Ed Gale, Chip Zien, Tim Rose, Steve Sleap, Peter Baird

It requires truly monumental talent to botch the film debut of a character as clever as Steve Gerber's *Howard the Duck*, but writer-director Willard Huyck and writer-producer Gloria Katz—the same team that made a special-effects puppet of Indiana Jones in *The Temple of Doom*—managed to lay an extremely rotten egg. The potential for wry commentary expressed by a stranger in a strange land (handled so well by, say, Malcolm McDowell's H. G. Wells in *Time After Time*) is sacrificed on the megabudgetary altar: sensible plot and characterization are replaced with bigger and louder explosions, car wrecks, slimy monster makeup, more car wrecks, inane acting, and even more car wrecks. This is yet another (we needed one more?) perfect example of how an open wallet can ruin what might have been a perceptive little picture. Unwisely rated PG, considering some smarmy sex scenes and frightening monster makeup.

1986   111 minutes

I MARRIED A MONSTER FROM OUTER SPACE
★★★

DIRECTOR: Gene Fowler
CAST: Tom Tryon, Gloria Talbott, Ken Lynch, Maxie Rosenbloom

The story is about aliens who duplicate their bodies in the form of Earth men in hopes of repopulating their planet. One Earth woman who unknowingly marries one of the aliens discovers the secret, but can't get anyone to believe her. This film is different in that it doesn't have a bunch of rampaging monsters running amok destroying Earth cities or trying to conquer our planet. They just want to preserve their race. The film does have a certain flair.

1958   B & W   78 minutes

I MARRIED A WITCH
★★★½

DIRECTOR: René Clair
CAST: Veronica Lake, Fredric March, Cecil Kellaway, Robert Benchley

The whimsy of humorist Thorne Smith (the author of *Topper*) shows its age, but watching Veronica Lake and Fredric March perform together is a treat in this very, very pre-"Bewitched" farce. Look for Susan Hayward in a small role.

1942   B & W   76 minutes

ICE PIRATES
★★★½

DIRECTOR: Stewart Raffill
CAST: Robert Urich, Mary Crosby, John Matuszak, Anjelica Huston, John Carradine

Essentially a pirate movie set in outer space, this entertaining and often funny sci-fi film takes place countless years from now, when the universe has run out of water. The evil Templars control what few millions of gallons still remain and ship them between the outposts of their far-flung empire. Their only enemies are a race of pirates (led by Robert Urich) who prowl the space lanes in fast little ships and specialize in boarding the Templar vessels and stealing the water. Rated PG for violence, profanity, scatological humor, and suggested sex.

1984   91 minutes

ICEMAN
★★★½

DIRECTOR: Fred Schepisi
CAST: Timothy Hutton, Lindsay Crouse, John Lone, Josef Sommer

Timothy Hutton stars in this often gripping and always watchable movie as an anthropologist who is part of an arctic exploration team that discovers the body of a prehistoric man (John Lone), who has been frozen forty thousand years. To their surprise, the scientists (who include Lindsay Crouse) discover the man is still alive. The question of what to do with this piece of living human history comes up, and Hutton finds himself defending the creature from those who want to poke, prod, and even dissect their terrified subject. Rated PG for violence and profanity.

1984   99 minutes

INCREDIBLE HULK, THE
★★½

DIRECTOR: Kenneth Johnson
CAST: Bill Bixby, Susan Sullivan, Lou Ferrigno, Jack Colvin, Charles Siebert

Bill Bixby is sincere in the role of Dr. Bob Banner, a scientist whose experiments with gamma rays result in his being transformed into a huge green creature (Lou Ferrigno) whenever something angers him. Pilot for the series is a lot of fun, with better production values than most TV efforts. Based on the Marvel Comics character.

1977   100 minutes

INCREDIBLE MELTING MAN, THE
★★★

DIRECTOR: William Sachs
CAST: Alex Rebar, Burr DeBenning, Myron Healey, Ann Sweeney

Superb make-up by Rick Baker highlights this story of an astronaut (Alex Rebar) who contracts a strange ailment that results in his turning into a gooey, melting mess upon his return to Earth. Wild stuff. Rated R for terminal grossness.

1978   86 minutes

INCREDIBLE SHRINKING MAN, THE
★★★★

DIRECTOR: Jack Arnold
CAST: Grant Williams, Randy Stuart, Paul Langton, April Kent

Good special effects as a man (Grant Williams), exposed to a strange radioactive mist, finds himself becoming smaller...and smaller...and smaller. Well-mounted thriller from Universal with many memorable scenes, including the classic showdown with an ordinary house spider. Topflight entertainment.

1957   B & W   81 minutes

INDIANA JONES AND THE TEMPLE OF DOOM
★★★½

DIRECTOR: Steven Spielberg
CAST: Harrison Ford, Kate Capshaw, Ke Huy Quan, Amrish Puri

This sequel is almost as good as the original, *Raiders of the Lost Ark*. The story takes place before the events of *Raiders* with its two-fisted, whip-wielding hero, Dr. Indiana Jones (Harrison Ford) performing feats of derring-do in Singapore and India circa 1935. Parents may want to see this fast-paced and sometimes scary film before allowing their kids to watch it. Rated PG for profanity and violence.

1984   118 minutes

INFRA-MAN
★★½

DIRECTOR: Hua-Shan
CAST: Wang Hsieh, Lie Hsiu-Hsien

Mainly for kids, this *Ultraman* ripoff, about a giant superhero protecting the Earth from a bunch of crazy-looking monsters, still manages to succeed, despite the lame acting and hokey special effects. Ridiculous but enjoyable. Rated PG.

1976   92 minutes

INTRUDER WITHIN, THE
🌑

DIRECTOR: Peter Carter
CAST: Chad Everett, Joseph Bottoms, Jennifer Warren

Cheesy ripoff of Ridley Scott's classic *Alien*. Action takes place on an ocean oil-drilling rig instead of commercial spacecraft.

1981   100 minutes

INVADERS FROM MARS (ORIGINAL)
★★★★

DIRECTOR: William Cameron Menzies
CAST: Helena Carter, Jimmy Hunt, Leif Erickson, Arthur Franz

Everybody remembers this one. Kid sees a flying saucer land in a nearby field, only nobody will believe him. Some really weird visuals throughout this minor sci-fi classic.

1953   78 minutes

INVADERS FROM MARS (REMAKE)
★★★

DIRECTOR: Tobe Hooper
CAST: Karen Black, Hunter Carson, Timothy Bottoms, Laraine Newman, James Karen, Louise Fletcher, Bud Cort

Screenwriters Dan O'Bannon and Don Jakoby and director Tobe Hooper have done fairly well with their remake of William Cameron Menzies's 1953 science-fiction classic. This version retains the kid's-eye point of view, the kid in this case played by Hunter Carson, in his first role after *Paris, Texas*. He wakes one night in time to see a spaceship land in the sand pit behind his house; thereafter, everybody who visits the site comes back . . . changed. Soon the boy has the help of only his junior-high-school nurse, played a bit too broadly by Karen Black. Hooper maintains the tone of the original; this *Invaders from Mars* feels like a 1950s movie made with 1980s production values. Rated PG-13 for rather intense situations and ugly beasties.

1986   94 minutes

INVASION OF THE BEE GIRLS
★★★

DIRECTOR: Denis Sanders
CAST: Victoria Vetri, William Smith, Cliff Osmond, Anitra Ford

Enjoyable film about strange female invaders doing weird things to the male population of a small town in California. Plot is not too important in this wacky sci-fi spoof. Not for kids. Rated PG.

1973   85 minutes

INVASION OF THE BODY SNATCHERS (ORIGINAL)
★★★★★

DIRECTOR: Don Siegel
CAST: Kevin McCarthy, Dana Wynter, Carolyn Jones, King Donovan

Quite possibly the most frightening film ever made, this stars Kevin McCarthy as a small-town doctor who discovers his patients, family, and friends are being taken over by cold, emotionless human-duplicating pods from outer space. Not many films can be considered truly disturbing, but this one more than qualifies. Coming from the B-movie science-fiction boom of the 1950s, it has emerged as a cinema classic that can bring nightmares to the young and old.

1956　　B & W　80 minutes

INVASION OF THE BODY SNATCHERS (REMAKE)
★★★★

DIRECTOR: Phil Kaufman

CAST: Donald Sutherland, Brooke Adams, Leonard Nimoy, Jeff Goldblum, Veronica Cartwright

Excellent semi-sequel to Don Siegel's 1956 classic of the same name, with Donald Sutherland fine in the role originally created by Kevin McCarthy (who has a cameo here). This time the story takes place in San Francisco, with mysterious "seeds" from outer space duplicating—then destroying—San Francisco Bay Area residents at an alarming rate. Very suspenseful, with Philip Kaufman's sure direction and a truly bizarre musical score by Denny Zeitlin adding to the feeling of paranoia this film creates. It is well worth your time. Rated PG.

1978　　　　　115 minutes

INVASION UFO
★

DIRECTOR: Gerry Anderson, Dave Lane, David Tomblin

CAST: Ed Bishop, George Sewell, Michael Billington

Strictly for fans of the short-lived science-fiction TV series, whose title explains all. Others will find the story trite, the acting second-

rate, and the special effects primitive by today's standards.

1980　　　　　97 minutes

ISLAND AT THE TOP OF THE WORLD, THE
★★★

DIRECTOR: Robert Stevenson

CAST: David Hartman, Mako, Donald Sinden

David Hartman stars as a rich man who ventures into the Arctic in search of his son. Unbelievably, he finds a Viking kingdom. This is Disney director Robert Stevenson's second attempt (*In Search of the Castaways* was number one) to re-create a Jules Verne classic. Rated G.

1974　　　　　93 minutes

ISLAND OF DR. MOREAU, THE
★★

DIRECTOR: William Witney

CAST: Burt Lancaster, Michael York, Barbara Carrera, Richard Basehart

Remake of 1933's *Island of Lost Souls* isn't nearly as good. Burt Lancaster develops process of turning animals into half-humans on a desolate tropical island. Watchable only for Burt's sturdy performance and Richard Basehart's portrayal of one of the beasts. Rated PG.

1977　　　　　104 minutes

IT CAME FROM OUTER SPACE
★★★★

DIRECTOR: Jack Arnold

CAST: Richard Carlson, Barbara Rush, Charles Drake

Science-fiction author Ray Bradbury wrote the screenplay for this surprisingly effective 3-D chiller from the 1950s about creatures from outer space taking over the bodies of Earthlings. It was the first film to use this theme and still holds up today.

1953   B & W   81 minutes

JASON AND THE ARGONAUTS
★★★★

DIRECTOR: Don Chaffey
CAST: Todd Armstrong, Gary Raymond, Honor Blackman

The captivating special effects by master Ray Harryhausen are the actual stars of this movie. This is the telling of the famous myth of Jason (Todd Armstrong), his crew of derring-doers, and their search for the "Golden Fleece." We are treated to some spectacular creations, including the battle with the skeleton army and the conquest of the multi-headed Hydra. Good entertainment for all ages.

1963   104 minutes

JOURNEY TO THE CENTER OF THE EARTH
★★★½

DIRECTOR: Henry Levin
CAST: James Mason, Pat Boone, Arlene Dahl, Diane Baker

This Jules Verne story was impressive when first released, but it looks pretty silly these days. However, James Mason is always fascinating to watch, production values are high, and kids should enjoy its innocent fun.

1959   132 minutes

JOURNEY TO THE CENTER OF TIME
★★½

DIRECTOR: David L. Hewitt
CAST: Scott Brady, Gigi Perreau, Anthony Eisley, Abraham Sofaer, Lyle Waggoner

A group of scientists working on a time-travel device are accidentally propelled five thousand years into the future following an equipment malfunction. Once there, they discover an alien civilization (headed by a young Lyle Waggoner) attempting to take over the world. Low-budget film features passable special effects, but the dialogue and acting are subpar.

1967   82 minutes

KING OF THE ROCKETMEN
★★★

DIRECTOR: Fred Bannon
CAST: Tristram Coffin, Mae Clarke, Dale Van Sickel, Tom Steele

This chapter-play precursor to the "Commando Cody" television series has longtime baddie Tristram Coffin joining the good guys for a change. Strapping on his flying suit, he does battle with evil conspirators. Good fun for serial fans, with highly implausible last-minute escapes.

1949   B & W   12 chapters

KRONOS
★★★

DIRECTOR: Kurt Neumann
CAST: Jeff Morrow, Barbara Lawrence

Jeff Morrow stars in this alien invasion film. In it, a giant, featureless robot is sent to Earth to test Earth's potential for supplying energy to an alien civilization. The robot absorbs all forms of energy and grows as it feeds. The scientists must find a way to destroy the giant before it reaches the high-population areas of Southern California. Although this film's special effects are nothing by today's film-making standards, this picture is one of best from a decade dominated by giant monsters and alien invaders.

1957   B & W   78 minutes

KRULL
★½

DIRECTOR: Peter Yates
CAST: Ken Marshall, Freddie Jones, Lisette Anthony

In this poor sci-fi/sword-and-sorcery film, a young man (Ken Marshall of TV's "Marco Polo") is called upon by an old wizard (Freddie Jones) to take up an ancient weapon and do battle with a master of evil to save a beautiful princess (Lisette Anthony). Sound familiar? It should. It's an obvious and unimaginative ripoff of *Star Wars*. That said, the movie may not be a total loss. Younger kids might enjoy it. Most adults, however, will find *Krull* to be hopelessly dull. Rated PG for violence.

1983   117 minutes

LABYRINTH
★★★

DIRECTOR: Jim Henson
CAST: David Bowie, Jennifer Connelly, Toby Froud

A charming fantasy that combines live actors with another impressive collection of Jim Henson's Muppets. Jennifer Connelly stars as a young girl who wishes for the Goblin King (David Bowie) to kidnap her baby brother; when that idle desire is granted, she must journey to an enchanted land and solve a giant maze in order to rescue her little brother. The visuals and set design are quite impressive, particularly a chamber based on a famed drawing by M. C. Escher. The performers, alas, aren't up to that standard, although Bowie does reasonably well as the sly Goblin King. Rated PG for mild violence.

1986   101 minutes

LAND THAT TIME FORGOT, THE
★★

DIRECTOR: Kevin Connor
CAST: Doug McClure, Susan Penhaligon, John McEnery

Poor Edgar Rice Burroughs, his wonderful adventure books for kids rarely got the right screen treatment. This British production tries hard, but the cheesy special effects eventually do it in. A sequel, *The People That Time Forgot*, fared no better. Rated PG.

1975   90 minutes

LASERBLAST
★★

DIRECTOR: Michael Raye
CAST: Kim Milford, Cheryl Smith, Roddy McDowall, Keenan Wynn, Ron Masak

Dreadful low-budget film with some excellent special effects by David Allen. Story concerns a young man who accidentally lays his hands on an alien ray-gun and all sorts of bizarre things begin to happen. Plodding sci-fi only comes to life when the monsters are on screen, but they make it worth a look for buffs. Rated PG.

1978   90 minutes

LAST CHASE, THE
★★½

DIRECTOR: Martyn Burke
CAST: Lee Majors, Chris Makepeace, Burgess Meredith, Alexandra Stewart, Diane D'Aquila, George Touliatos, Ben Gordon, Harvey Atkins

Made at the end of the OPEC oil crisis, this film assumes the crisis only got worse until there was a civil war in America and the eastern states banned all cars and planes. Lee Majors (*The Six Million Dollar Man*) plays an aged race car driver who flees New York to

California with a runaway (Chris Makepeace). Burgess Meredith is an old fighter pilot who is ordered to kill the fleeing rebels. Confusing at times, and the Orwellian touches have been done so often that all the scare has left them. Not rated, but the equivalent of a PG for sex and profanity.

1980   106 minutes

LAST DAYS OF MAN ON EARTH, THE
★★★½

DIRECTOR: Robert Fuest
CAST: Jon Finch, Sterling Hayden, Patrick Magee, Jenny Runacre, Hugh Griffith

Kinetic adaptation of Michael Moorcock's weird little novel *The Final Programme*, the first of his adventures featuring Jerry Cornelius. Jon Finch plays Jerry as a smart-assed James Bond, and the prize he fights for is a microfilm containing the secret to self-replicating beings . . . highly useful in case of nuclear war. Finch encounters a variety of oddball characters, none stranger than Jenny Runacre, an enigmatic adversary who absorbs her lovers. Full of ideas and reasonably well executed, although the longer British version (89 minutes) is superior to the American release. Rated R for violence and sex.

1973   73 minutes

LAST MAN ON EARTH, THE
★★★

DIRECTOR: Sidney Salkow
CAST: Vincent Price, Franca Bettoia, Emma Danieli, Giacomo Rossi-Stuart

In this nightmarish tale, a scientist (Vincent Price) is a bit late in developing a serum to stem the tide of a plague epidemic. He becomes the last man on Earth and lives in fear of the walking dead, who crave his blood. This paranoid horror film (based on Richard Matheson's *I Am Legend*) is more chilling than its higher-budget remake, *The Omega Man*.

1964   B & W   86 minutes

LAST STARFIGHTER, THE
★★★★

DIRECTOR: Nick Castle
CAST: Lance Guest, Robert Preston, Don O'Herlihy, Catherine Mary Stewart, Barbara Bosson, Norman Snow

In this enjoyable comedy/science-fiction film, a young man (Lance Guest) beats a video game called the Starfighter and soon finds himself recruited by an alien (Robert Preston) to do battle in outer space. Thanks to its witty dialogue and hilarious situations, this hybrid is a viewing delight. Rated PG for violence and profanity.

1984   100 minutes

LAST UNICORN, THE
★★★½

DIRECTOR: Arthur Rankin Jr.
CAST: Animated

The voices of Alan Arkin, Jeff Bridges, Mia Farrow, Tammy Grimes, Angela Lansbury, and Christopher Lee are among those featured in this well-told feature-length cartoon from the Rankin-Bass company. As they proved with their television adaptation of J.R.R. Tolkien's *The Hobbit*, Arthur Rankin Jr. and Jules Bass know how to do a good story justice when telling it, but take too many shortcuts in their animation. Rated G.

1982   88 minutes

LEGEND

DIRECTOR: Ridley Scott
CAST: Tom Cruise, Tim Curry, Mia Sara, David Bennent, Billy Barty

Director Ridley Scott, always slick at creating the critical visual verisimilitude of otherworldly fantasies, strikes out completely with this one. *Legend* is a sad triumph of style over substance, a gorgeously-lensed but absolutely empty fantasy. Tom Cruise simply looks embarrassed as a forest-living lad who joins a quest to save a unicorn, keeper of his world's Light, from the evil entity who prefers to plunge the land into eternal Darkness. As that malevolent entity, Tim Curry looks properly scary; he's the only player even remotely comfortable with his character. The script is filled with witless and inane dialogue, attempts at juvenile humor which contrast horribly with Scott's darker tone. If you must watch this, turn the sound off. Rated PG for mild violence.

1986   89 minutes

LIFEFORCE
★

DIRECTOR: Tobe Hooper
CAST: Steven Railsback, Peter Firth, Mathilda May, Frank Finlay, Michael Gothard

In this disappointing and disjointed science-fiction/horror film by director Tobe Hooper (*Poltergeist*), ancient vampires from outer space return to Earth via Halley's Comet to feed on human souls. Rated R for violence, gore, nudity, profanity, and suggested sex.

1985   96 minutes

LIQUID SKY
★★★½

DIRECTOR: Slava Tsukerman
CAST: Anne Carlisle, Paula E. Sheppard

Here's a release that's the first of its kind: a punk-rock science-fiction movie. It's as much about alienation as aliens. An alien spaceship lands on Earth in search of chemicals produced in the body during sex. One of the aliens enters the life of a new-wave fashion model and feeds off her lovers, most of whom she's more than happy to see dead. *Liquid Sky* certainly can't be called boring. Producer-director-co-writer Slava Tsukerman, a Russian emigrée, alternately shocks and amuses us with this unusual, stark, and ugly—but somehow fitting—look at an American sub-culture. Still, we feel compelled to add: Watch at your own risk. Rated R for profanity, violence, rape, and suggested sex.

1983   112 minutes

LOGAN'S RUN
★★★

DIRECTOR: Michael Anderson
CAST: Michael York, Jenny Agutter, Peter Ustinov, Richard Jordan

Popular sci-fi film concerning a futuristic society where people are only allowed to live to the age of 30, and a policeman nearing the limit who searches desperately for a way to avoid mandatory extermination. Nice production is enhanced immeasurably by outlandish sets and beautiful, imaginative miniatures. Only real problem is the video's length. While only two hours, it somehow feels like three, causing the viewer to shift in his seat several times toward the climax. Rated PG.

1976   120 minutes

LOOKER
★★

DIRECTOR: Michael Crichton
CAST: Albert Finney, James Coburn, Susan Dey, Leigh Taylor-Young

Writer-director Michael Crichton describes this movie as "a thriller about television commercials," but it's really a fairly simple-minded suspense film. Plastic surgeon Albert Finney discovers a plot by evil mastermind James Coburn to clone models for television commercials. This is fiction? Rated PG because of nudity and violence.

1981   94 minutes

LORD OF THE RINGS, THE
★

DIRECTOR: Ralph Bakshi
CAST: Animated

J.R.R. Tolkien's beloved epic fantasy is all but trashed in this animated film, directed by Ralph Bakshi (*Fritz the Cat*). It deals with the first half of the trilogy, in which Frodo Baggins takes up the Ring of Power in order to save his fellow hobbits and all of Middle Earth from the forces of evil. The movie suffers from too much gore and cut-rate animation techniques, spoiling what should have been a cinematic event. Rated PG.

1978   133 minutes

LOST WORLD, THE
★★★★

DIRECTOR: Harry Hoyt
CAST: Bessie Love, Lewis Stone, Wallace Beery, Lloyd Hughes

Silent version of Arthur Conan Doyle's classic story of Professor Challenger and his expedition to a desolate plateau roaming with prehistoric beasts. The movie climaxes with a brontosaurus running amuck in London. An ambitious production, interesting as film history and quite entertaining, considering its age. The special effects by Willis O'Brien are actually superior to the 1960 remake. A few years later, the basic story and O'Brien's skills were used again in *King Kong*.

1925   60 minutes
B & W with color tints

MAD MAX
★★★½

DIRECTOR: George Miller
CAST: Mel Gibson, Joanne Samuel, Hugh Keays-Byrne, Tim Burns, Roger Ward

The most successful Australian film of all time ($100 million in worldwide rentals), this exciting sci-fi adventure features Mel Gibson (*The Bounty*) as a fast-driving cop who has to take on a gang of crazies in the dangerous world of the future. Rated R.

1979   93 minutes

MAD MAX BEYOND THUNDERDOME
★★★★½

DIRECTOR: George Miller, George Ogilvie
CAST: Mel Gibson, Tina Turner, Helen Buday, Frank Thring, Bruce Spence

Mad Max is back—and he's angrier than ever. Those who enjoyed *Road Warrior* will find more of the same—and then some—in director George Miller's third postapocalypse, action-packed adventure film. This time the resourceful futuristic warrior (Mel Gibson) begrudgingly confronts what is left of civilization (as run by evil ruler Tina Turner) and fulfills a prophecy by—again, begrudgingly—leading a group of children out of the death-dealing desert. Miller chose this time to concentrate solely on the action scenes and hired another director, George Ogilvie, to work with the actors. The result is the best film in the series. Rated PG-13 for violence and profanity.

1985   109 minutes

MAN WHO FELL TO EARTH, THE
★★★★

DIRECTOR: Nicolas Roeg

CAST: David Bowie, Rip Torn, Candy Clark, Buck Henry

Nicolas Roeg (*Performance*; *Don't Look Now*) directed this moody, cerebral science-fiction thriller about an alien (David Bowie) who becomes trapped on our planet. Its occasional ambiguities are overpowered by sheer mind-tugging bizarreness and directorial brilliance. Rated R.

1976   140 minutes

MAN WHO SAW TOMORROW, THE
★★★½

DIRECTOR: Robert Guenette

CAST: Orson Welles (narrator)

Orson Welles narrates and appears in this fascinating dramatization of the prophecies of sixteenth-century poet, physician, and psychic Michel de Nostradamus. Through a combination of clips from old movies, newsreels, and newly shot footage, it focuses on the man who, more than four hundred years ago, predicted the French Revolution, the rise and fall of Napoleon, the discoveries of Louis Pasteur, World War II, and Adolf Hitler's reign of terror, among many other startling things. It may be just a matter of interpretation in some cases, but the fact remains that Nostradamus was astonishingly accurate and, in some cases, actually cited names and dates. His prediction for the future is equally amazing—and, sometimes, terrifying. Rated PG.

1981   90 minutes

MAROONED
🐢🐢

DIRECTOR: John Sturges

CAST: Gregory Peck, Richard Crenna, David Janssen, Gene Hackman, James Franciscus, Lee Grant

The special effects are the only thing this bomb has going for it. Several dollars' worth of Hollywood acting talent is wasted in this tale of three astronauts unable to return to Earth and the ensuing rescue attempt. Rated PG.

1969   134 minutes

MASTER OF THE WORLD
★★★

DIRECTOR: William Witney

CAST: Vincent Price, Charles Bronson, Henry Hull, Mary Webster

Jules Verne's tale brought excitingly to the screen. Vincent Price plays a self-proclaimed god trying to end all war by flying around the world in a giant airship, armed to the teeth, blowing ships from the water, etc. Lots of fun.

1961   104 minutes

MEGAFORCE
🐢

DIRECTOR: Hal Needham

CAST: Barry Bostwick, Michael Beck, Persis Khambatta

Director Hal Needham (*Cannonball Run*; *The Villain*) makes us groan and gag with his biggest dud ever. This deadly dull sci-fi adventure is about a rapid-deployment defense unit that galvanizes into action whenever and wherever freedom is threatened. But rather than gasps, their exploits produce only yawns. PG for no discernible reason.

1982   99 minutes

METALSTORM: THE DESTRUCTION OF JARED-SYN
🦃

DIRECTOR: Charles Band
CAST: Jeffrey Byron, Mike Preston, Tim Thomerson, Kelly Preston

Charles Band, who was responsible for such forgettable turkeys as *Laserblast*, *End of the World*, and *Parasite*, directed this dud. In it, Jeffrey Byron plays an outer space ranger who, in order to save a barren planet, takes on the powerful villain of the title, Jared-Syn (Mike Preston). Even the title is a cheat. The bad guy gets away at the end—leaving it wide open for a sequel. The mind boggles. Rated PG for violence.

1983   84 minutes

METEOR
★★

DIRECTOR: Ronald Neame
CAST: Sean Connery, Natalie Wood, Karl Malden, Brian Keith, Henry Fonda

In this disaster film, which wastes an all-star cast, a comet strikes an asteroid, and sends a huge chunk of rock hurtling on a collision course with Earth. The United States and the U.S.S.R. must join forces to deflect the destructive mass, but the viewer wonders why they bother. Rated PG.

1979   103 minutes

METROPOLIS
★★★★★

DIRECTOR: Fritz Lang
CAST: Brigitte Helm, Alfred Abel, Gustav Froelich

Fritz Lang's 1926 creation embodies the fine difference between classic and masterpiece. Using some of the most innovative camerawork in film of any time, it's also an uncannily accurate projection of futuristic society. It is a silent screen triumph.

1926   B & W 120 minutes

MIDSUMMER NIGHT'S DREAM, A
★★★★

DIRECTOR: Max Reinhardt
CAST: James Cagney, Olivia De Havilland, Dick Powell, Mickey Rooney

Warner Bros. rolled out many of its big-name contract stars during the studio's heyday for this engrossing rendition of Shakespeare's classic comedy. Enchantment is the key element in this fairy-tale story of the misadventures of a group of mythical mischief-makers.

1935   B & W 117 minutes

MIGHTY JOE YOUNG
★★★½

DIRECTOR: Ernest B. Schoedsack
CAST: Terry Moore, Ben Johnson, Robert Armstrong, Frank McHugh

In this timeless fantasy from the creator of *King Kong* (Willis O'Brien with his young apprentice, Ray Harryhausen), the story follows the discovery of a twelve-foot gorilla in Africa by a fast-talking, money-hungry night-club owner (Robert Armstrong), who schemes to bring the animal back to Hollywood. Things go along reasonably well until a trio of drunks sneaks backstage and gets the star attraction drunk, which causes the big guy to go on a rampage through the club. *Mighty Joe Young* has been described as a *King Kong* for kids, and, in a way, it is; but the special effects are extremely well-done (which prompted an Oscar), and the story is paced so well that this movie is a pleasure.

1949   B & W   94 minutes

MOTHRA
★★★

DIRECTOR: Inoshiro Honda

CAST: Lee Kresel, Franky Sakai, Hiroshi Koizumi

Two six-inch-tall princesses are taken from their island home to perform in a Tokyo nightclub. A native tribe prays for the return of the princesses, and their prayers hatch a giant egg, releasing a giant caterpillar. The caterpillar goes to Tokyo searching for the princesses and turns into a giant moth while wrecking the city. Although the story may sound corny, this is one of the best of the giant-monster movies to come out of Japan. The special effects of the miniature girls and the giant insect are very good, and there are no people in costumes stomping miniature buildings. Even the tune the princesses sing when calling Mothra is catchy.

1962   100 minutes

MY SCIENCE PROJECT
★

DIRECTOR: Jonathan R. Betuel

CAST: John Stockwell, Danielle Von Zerneck, Fisher Stevens, Dennis Hopper, Raphael Sharge, Richard Masur

You could see it coming: First there was *Real Genius*, which brilliantly turned the military industrial complex into a popcorn machine; then came *Weird Science*, a weird but funny film. Now the fast-buck artists come out of the woodwork. This little piece of exploitation sports some of the most obnoxious characters ever to plague the video monitor. Rated PG for profanity.

1985   94 minutes

MYSTERIANS, THE
★★½

DIRECTOR: Inoshiro Honda

CAST: Kenji Sahara, Yumi Shirakawa

An alien civilization attempts takeover of Earth after its home planet is destroyed. Massive destruction from the director of *Godzilla*. Quaint Japanese-style special effects look pretty silly these days, but the film can be fun if seen in the right spirit.

1959   85 minutes

MYSTERIOUS ISLAND
★★★★

DIRECTOR: Cy Endfield

CAST: Michael Craig, Joan Greenwood, Michael Callan, Gary Merrill, Herbert Lom

Fantasy adventure based on Jules Verne's novel about a group of Civil War prisoners who escape by balloon and land on an uncharted island in the Pacific, where they must fight to stay alive against incredible odds, including a monster crab, colossal bees, and an unstable volcano on the verge of eruption. With fantastic effects work by Ray Harryhausen and a breathtaking Bernard Herrmann score. Topnotch entertainment.

1961   101 minutes

NEVERENDING STORY, THE
★★★★

DIRECTOR: Wolfgang Petersen

CAST: Barrett Oliver, Noah Hathaway, Tami Stronach

The imagination is truly a wondrous thing, and when it's sparked by a truly magical movie such as

The NeverEnding Story, it can leave the young and the young at heart with a warm glow. This is a superb fantasy about a sensitive 10-year-old boy named Bastian (Barrett Oliver) who takes refuge in the pages of a fairy tale. In reading it, he's swept off to a land of startlingly strange creatures and heroic adventure where a young warrior, Atreyu (Noah Hathaway), does battle with the Nothing, a force that threatens to obliterate the land of mankind's hope and dreams—and only he has the power to save the day. Rated PG for slight profanity.

1984　　　　　　　　92 minutes

NIGHT OF THE COMET
★★★½

DIRECTOR: Thom Eberhardt
CAST: Geoffrey Lewis, Mary Woronov, Catherine Mary Stewart

The passage of the comet, which last visited Earth 65 million years ago, when the dinosaurs disappeared, wipes out all but a few people on our planet. The survivors, mostly young adults, are hunted by a pair of baddies, played by Geoffrey Lewis and Mary Woronov (of *Eating Raoul*). The deadly duo, who were partially exposed to the comet's rays, drain the blood from those they capture in the hopes of coming up with a serum that will prevent them from becoming disfigured monsters. It all adds up to a zesty low-budget spoof of science-fiction movies. Rated PG-13.

1984　　　　　　　　94 minutes

1990: THE BRONX WARRIORS
🦃

DIRECTOR: Enzo G. Castellari
CAST: Vic Morrow, Christopher Connelly, Mark Gregory

Near the end of the 1980s, th Bronx is abandoned by law e forcement and becomes a kind no man's land ruled by motorcyc gangs. Vic Morrow plays a lor wolf cop who tries to clean up th town but instead delivers som horribly tasteless lines about h man decapitation. Obviously i spired by *Escape from New Yo* and *The Warriors*, it is a prime e ample of bad writing, acting, an direction. Rated R for violence an language.

1983　　　　　　　　89 minute

OMEGA MAN, THE
★★★½

DIRECTOR: Boris Sagal
CAST: Charlton Heston, Anthon Zerbe, Rosalind Cash

Charlton Heston does a last-man on-Earth number in this free ac aptation of Richard Matheson's *Am Legend*. The novel's vampi ism has been toned down, bu Chuck still is holed up in his high rise mansion by night, and killin robed (and sleeping) zombies b day. Although this is no mor faithful to Matheson's work tha 1964's *The Last Man on Earth*, *Th Omega Man* has enough throat grabbing suspense to keep it mov ing. It's also one of Rosalind Cash best roles. Rated PG—considera ble violence.

1971　　　　　　　　98 minute

ON THE BEACH
★★★★

DIRECTOR: Stanley Kramer
CAST: Gregory Peck, Ava Gardner Fred Astaire, Anthony Per kins

The effect of a nuclear holocaus on a group of people in Australi makes for engrossing drama in thi film. Gregory Peck is a submarin commander who ups anchor an goes looking for survivors as a radioactive cloud slowly descends upon this apparently last human enclave. Director Stanley Kramer is a bit heavy-handed in his moralizing and the romance between Peck and Ava Gardner is distracting, yet the film remains a powerful anti-war statement.

1959   B & W 133 minutes

ONE MILLION B.C.
★★

DIRECTORS: Hal Roach, Hal Roach Jr.

CAST: Victor Mature, Carole Landis, Lon Chaney Jr., Mano Clark

D. W. Griffith reportedly directed parts of this prehistoric-age picture before producer Hal Roach and his son took over. Victor Mature, Carole Landis, and Lon Chaney Jr. try hard—and there are some good moments—but the result is a pretty dumb fantasy film. A remake in 1966 with Raquel Welch had better special effects but was thwarted by the same silly story and no acting to speak of.

1940   B & W 80 minutes

OUTLAND
★★★★

DIRECTOR: Peter Hyams

CAST: Sean Connery, Peter Boyle, Frances Sternhagen

Sean Connery stars as the two-fisted marshal in this thoroughly enjoyable outer-space remake of *High Noon* directed by Peter Hyams (*Capricorn One*). Much of the credit for that goes to Connery. As he has proved in many pictures, he is one of the few actors today who can play a fully credible

adventure hero. And *Outland*, a movie that never takes itself too seriously, makes the most of this. Rated R.

1981   109 minutes

PEOPLE, THE
★★

DIRECTOR: John Korty

CAST: William Shatner, Dan O'Herlihy, Diane Varsi, Kim Darby

This TV movie is a fair interpretation of the science-fiction stories of Zenna Henderson about a group of psychically talented aliens whose home world has been destroyed and who must survive on Earth. Sheriff William Shatner and schoolteacher Kim Darby, both humans who come to know and interact with the aliens, are guilty of overacting, and Diane Varsi, one of "the People," is colorless. The script gives Henderson's subtle themes a heavy-handed and unbalanced treatment.

1971   74 minutes

PEOPLE THAT TIME FORGOT, THE
★

DIRECTOR: Kevin Conner

CAST: Doug McClure, Patrick Wayne, Sarah Douglas, Thorley Walters

Edgar Rice Burroughs probably would have been outraged by this and its companion piece, *The Land That Time Forgot*. Doug McClure gets rescued by friend Patrick Wayne from a fate worse than death on a strange island circa 1919. Laughable rubber-suited monsters mix it up with ludicrous wire-controlled beasties. Strictly for the under-five set. Rated PG.

1977   90 minutes

PHASE IV
★★★½

DIRECTOR: Saul Bass
CAST: Nigel Davenport, Michael Murphy, Lynne Frederick

An interesting sci-fi mood piece from 1973 about scientists (Nigel Davenport, Michael Murphy) attempting to outwit super-intelligent mutant ants. Good effects and fine acting. Rated PG.

1974   86 minutes

PHILADELPHIA EXPERIMENT, THE
★★★½

DIRECTOR: Stewart Raffill
CAST: Michael Pare, Nancy Allen, Bobby DiCicco, Eric Christmas

Reportedly based on a true incident during World War II involving an anti-radar experiment that caused a naval battleship to disappear in Virginia, this entertaining science-fiction film stars Michael Pare (*Streets of Fire*) as a sailor on that ship. But instead of ending up in Virginia, he finds himself in the modern world of 1984. Nancy Allen (*Dressed to Kill; Carrie*) co-stars as the woman who befriends Pare after his disorienting journey through time. The latter has its cataclysmic side-effects: a time warp that threatens to destroy the world. Rated PG for violence and profanity.

1984   102 minutes

PLAGUE DOGS, THE
★★★★½

DIRECTOR: Martin Rosen
CAST: Animated

This animated film is definitely *not* for children. It is a powerfully disturbing film which makes an unforgettable statement about animal rights. In it, two dogs escape from an experimental veterinary lab in which they had both been subjected to cruel and senseless operations and tests. Once free, the joy they feel is short-lived as they are hunted by both the "white coats" (lab doctors) and the nearby sheep owners. The animation team of *Watership Down*—Tony Guy and Colin White—does an excellent job while avoiding the darling Disney-type animation that would negate the torment that these animals undergo. Although this film is not rated, we do not recommend it for children under twelve.

1984   99 minutes

PLAN 9 FROM OUTER SPACE
★★★

DIRECTOR: Edward D. Wood Jr.
CAST: Bela Lugosi, Gregory Walcott, Tom Keene, Duke Moore, Mona McKinnon

Ever seen a movie that was so bad it was funny? Well, this low-budget 1950s program is considered to be the very worst picture ever made, and it's hilarious. Written and directed by Edward D. Wood, it's a ponderous science-fiction cheapie that attempts to deliver an anti-war message as well as thrills and chills. It does neither. The acting is atrocious, the sets are made of cardboard (and often bumped into by the stars), the dialogue incredibly moronic, and the filmmaking technique execrable. Even worse, Bela Lugosi is top-billed even though he died three months before the film was made. Undaunted, Wood used silent home-movie footage of the once great horror film star. Get the idea?

1959   B & W   79 minutes

PLANET OF THE APES
★★★★

DIRECTOR: Franklin J. Schaffner

CAST: Charlton Heston, Kim Hunter, Roddy McDowall, Maurice Evans

Here is the first and best of the "Planet of the Apes" sci-fi series. Four American astronauts crash on a far-off planet and discover a culture where evolution has gone awry. The dominant form of primates are apes and gorillas. Man is reduced to a beast of burden. Much of the social comment is cutesy and forced, but this remains an enjoyable fantasy. Rated PG for violence.

1968   112 minutes

PREHISTORIC WOMEN

DIRECTOR: Gregg Tallas
CAST: Laurette Luez, Allan Mixon, Joan Shawlee

One of the worst films ever made. A tribe of female bimbos runs into a tribe of male bimbos, and they bore each other to death. Among the astounding thrills: a stock-footage bird and a one-elephant stampede. The movie was shot silent with grunts and groans presumably dubbed by specialists in that sort of thing. A minimum-wage narrator babbles incessantly from beginning to end. If you can watch this one without hitting the scan button, you are a very troubled person.

1950   74 minutes

PRISONER, THE (TELEVISION SERIES)

★★ to ★★★★★

(Depending on episode)

DIRECTOR: Patrick McGoohan, David Tomblin, Don Chaffey, Pat Jackson
CAST: Patrick McGoohan, Angelo Muscat, Leo McKern, Peter Bowles, Nigel Stock, Peter Wyngarde

Probably the finest science-fiction series ever created for television, this summer-replacement show (it stood in for The Jackie Gleason Show) was the brainchild of star Patrick McGoohan, who intended it to be an oblique follow-up to his successful *Danger Man* and *Secret Agent* series. The main character (McGoohan), whose name never is given—although he is believed to be *Secret Agent's* John Drake—abruptly resigns from a sensitive Intelligence position without explanation. He is abducted and awakens one morning in a mysterious community known only as The Village (actually Portmerion, in North Wales). Now called "Number Six"—every resident is known only by a number, never by a name—this new prisoner tries to escape while matching wits with a series of Number Twos (each is replaced as he or she fails), who desire to know just why he resigned. McGoohan conceived the show as a limited series of seventeen episodes; it therefore was the *first* television miniseries. Superior episodes are "The Arrival," wherein the Prisoner is abducted and learns about his new surroundings; "The Chimes of Big Ben," which details his first complicated escape scheme; "Schizoid Man," wherein the Prisoner is brainwashed into a new identity and confronts another person claiming to be Number Six; "Many Happy Returns," wherein the Prisoner wakes one morning to find The Village completely deserted; "Living in Harmony," an episode never shown on American television, which finds the Prisoner replaying a weird parody of his life in a western setting; "The Girl Who Was Death," another parody, this time of supersecret agents; and "Once Upon a Time" and "Fallout," the two-parter that brings the story to a close. Once seen, this series never is forgotten; some of its ideas and visuals are absolutely hypnotic. Aside from McGoohan, the only continuing character is Angelo Muscat's enigmatic butler, who serves the ever-changing Number Twos. Do not miss.

1968   52 minutes each

QUEST FOR FIRE
★★★★½

DIRECTOR: Jean-Jacques Annaud
CAST: Jean-Jacques Annaud, Everett McGill, Rae Dawn Chong, Ron Perlman, Nameer Radi

In this movie, about the attempt to learn the secret of making fire by a tribe of primitive men, director Jean-Jacques Annaud (*Black and White in Color*) and screenwriter Gerard Brach (*Tess*) have achieved what once seemed to be impossible: a first-rate, compelling film about the dawn of man. Rated R for violence, gore, nudity, and semi-explicit sex.

1981   97 minutes

QUIET EARTH, THE
★★★★

DIRECTOR: Geoffrey Murphy
CAST: Bruno Lawrence, Alison Routledge, Peter Smith

First-rate science-fiction thriller from New Zealand. A scientific researcher (Bruno Lawrence) wakes one morning and discovers that all living beings—people and animals—have vanished. Fearful that the world-encircling energy grid on which he'd been working may have been responsible, he sets out to find other people. Intelligent and absorbing adaptation of the book by Craig Harrison. The film concludes with an apocalyptic image that rivals the final moments of *2001* for sheer power and

perverse ambiguity. Do not miss. Rated R for nudity and sexual situations.

1985   91 minutes

QUINTET
★★½

DIRECTOR: Robert Altman
CAST: Paul Newman, Fernando Rey, Bibi Andersson

This is about as pessimistic a view of the future as one is likely to see. Director Robert Altman has fashioned a very murky, hard-to-follow film, concerning the ultimate game of death, set against the background of a frozen postnuclear wasteland. An intriguing idea, but Altman doesn't pull this one off. Rated R.

1979   110 minutes

RAIDERS OF THE LOST ARK
★★★★★

DIRECTOR: Steven Spielberg
CAST: Harrison Ford, Karen Allen, Wolf Kahler, Paul Freeman, Ronald Lacey, John Rhys-Davies, Denholm Elliott

For sheer spirit-lifting entertainment, you can't do better than this film, by director Steven Spielberg (*E.T.*) and writer-producer George Lucas (*Star Wars*). Harrison Ford stars as Indiana Jones, the roughest, toughest, and most unpredictable hero to grace the silver screen, who risks life and limb against a set of the nastiest villains you've ever seen. It's all to save the world—what else? Rated PG for violence and gore.

1981   115 minutes

RESURRECTION
★★★★

DIRECTOR: Daniel Petrie

CAST: Ellen Burstyn, Sam Shepard, Richard Farnsworth, Robert Blossom, Clifford David, Pamela Payton-Wright, Eva Le Gallienne

Ellen Burstyn's superb performance is but one of the top-flight elements in this emotional powerhouse of a film written by Lewis John Carlino (*The Great Santini*) and directed by Daniel Petrie. After she loses her husband and the use of her legs in a freak automobile accident, Burstyn discovers she has the power to heal not only herself but anyone who is sick or crippled. Pulitzer Prize–winning playwright Sam Shepard is also memorable as the young hell-raiser who begins to believe she is Jesus reborn. It's strong stuff, intelligently handled. Rated PG.

1980   103 minutes

RESURRECTION OF ZACHARY WHEELER, THE
★★

DIRECTOR: Bob Wynn
CAST: Bradford Dillman, Angie Dickinson, Leslie Nielsen

Disappointing science-fiction/mystery has a well-known senator (Bradford Dillman) taken to a bizarre out-of-the-way treatment center in New Mexico after a serious car accident, and an investigation of the incident by an intrepid reporter (Leslie Nielsen). Confusing movie. Rated G.

1971   100 minutes

RETURN OF THE JEDI
★★★★★

DIRECTOR: Richard Marquand
CAST: Mark Hamill, Harrison Ford, Carrie Fisher, Billy Dee Williams, Dave Prowse, Peter Mayhew, Anthony Daniels, James Earl Jones

This third film in the "Star Wars" series more than fulfills the viewer's expectations. The story centers on the all-out attempt by the Rebel forces—led by Luke Skywalker (Mark Hamill), Han Solo (Harrison Ford), Princess Leia (Carrie Fisher), and Lando Calrissian (Billy Dee Williams)—to turn back the tidal wave of interplanetary domination by the evil Galactic Empire and its forces, led by Darth Vader (Dave Prowse—with the voice of James Earl Jones). A marvelous movie, this George Lucas production has thrills, chills, laughs, and eye-popping wonders galore. Rated PG.

1983   133 minutes

RIP VAN WINKLE
★★½

DIRECTOR: Francis Ford Coppola
CAST: Harry Dean Stanton, Talia Shire, Ed Begley Jr., Mark Blankfield, Tim Conway, Hunter Carson

This episode of *Faerie Tale Theatre* will probably not grab most viewers. Francis Ford Coppola does not seem suited to directing fantasies. The story remains basically unchanged as Rip falls asleep for twenty years in the Catskill Mountains only to awaken as an old man.

1985   60 minutes

ROAD WARRIOR, THE
★★★★

DIRECTOR: George Miller
CAST: Mel Gibson, Bruce Spence, Vernon Wells, Mike Preston, Virginia Hay, Emil Minty, Kjell Nilsson

A sequel to *Mad Max*, the most successful Australian film of all time ($100 million in worldwide rentals), this exciting science-fiction adventure features Mel Gibson (*Gallipoli*) as a fast-driving, cynical Robin Hood in the desolate, dangerous, post-apocalypse world of the future. Good fun! Rated R for violence, nudity, and profanity.

1981   94 minutes

ROCKETSHIP X-M
★★½

DIRECTOR: Kurt Neumann
CAST: Lloyd Bridges, Hugh O'Brian, Noah Beery Jr., Osa Massen, John Emery

A rocket heading for the moon is knocked off course by a meteor storm and is forced to land on Mars. The crewmen find Mars to be very inhospitable, as it has been devastated by atomic war and has mutated creatures inhabiting the planet. While the story is weak and the acting only passable, this is one of the first of the science-fiction films that dominated the 1950s.

1950   B & W 77 minutes

RODAN
★★½

DIRECTOR: Inoshiro Honda
CAST: Kenji Sawara, Yumi Shirakawa, Akihiko Hirato, Ako Kobori

Giant-monster silliness from Japan—a hit in 1957, when special effects were far less sophisticated ...as were we.

1957   72 minutes

ROLLERBALL
★★★★★

DIRECTOR: Norman Jewison
CAST: James Caan, John Houseman, Maud Adams, Ralph Richardson, John Beck

Vastly underappreciated science-fiction film makes a strong statement about the effects of violence on society. The futuristic setting envisions a world controlled by business corporations; with no wars or other aggressive activities, the public gets its release in rollerball, a violent combination of basketball, ice hockey, and roller derby. James Caan is a top rollerball champ who refuses to quit the game in spite of threats from industrialist John Houseman, who perceives that Caan may turn into a public folk hero. The moody, classical soundtrack includes Bach's eerie *Toccata in D minor*. Do not miss. Rated R for violence.

1975   128 minutes

RUNAWAY
★★★

DIRECTOR: Michael Crichton
CAST: Tom Selleck, Cynthia Rhodes, Gene Simmons, Kirstie Alley

Tom Selleck (of television's "Magnum, P.I.") is top-billed in this release as a futuristic cop trying to track down a bunch of killer robots controlled by the evil villain (Gene Simmons, from the rock band KISS). It's a cinematic comic book and, although meant to be a thriller, never really gets the viewer involved in the story except for fleeting moments. At best, it's just an enjoyable time-passer. Rated PG for violence and profanity.

1984   99 minutes

SANTA CLAUS CONQUERS THE MARTIANS

DIRECTOR: Nicholas Webster
CAST: John Call, Leonard Hicks

Sounds like a classic, doesn't it? Well, guess again. This film, about a bunch of aliens abducting St. Nick because they don't have one of their own, is actually pretty slow, and not much really happens, though Pia Zadora does show off her acting skills as one of the younger residents of the red planet.

1964   80 minutes

SATURN 3
★★★

DIRECTOR: Stanley Donen
CAST: Kirk Douglas, Farrah Fawcett, Harvey Keitel

Although this space shocker is endowed with a goodly amount of thrills, chills, and surprises, there's very little else to it. The premise is very basic, and the screenplay (by Martin Amis) supplies just the barest embellishments. The story takes place in the distant future on the Eden-like space station Titan, which is located deep beneath the surface of one of Saturn's moons. It is happily inhabited by two chemists (Kirk Douglas and Farrah Fawcett) who are working on developing new forms of food for a starving Earth. Their idyllic existence is thrown into turmoil when a strangely hostile newcomer (Harvey Keitel) arrives from Earth, bringing orders to speed up production. In doing his part toward achieving this goal, creating a superpowered, highly intelligent robot, Keitel unleashes a terror that threatens to destroy them all. Rated R.

1980   88 minutes

7 FACES OF DR. LAO
★★★★

DIRECTOR: George Pal
CAST: Tony Randall, Barbara Eden, Arthur O'Connell

A first-rate fantasy taken from Charles Finney's classic story, "The Circus of Dr. Lao." Tony Randall plays multiple roles as a mysterious Chinese gentleman and his many strange circus side show creatures. Magical doings bring good fortune to a deserving few and work against those with less than pure motives. Fabulous makeup and special effects, surrounded by a heartwarming story. Perfect for all ages, one of the few films to capture the wonder and sinister overtones of a traveling circus.

1964   100 minutes

7TH VOYAGE OF SINBAD, THE
★★★★

DIRECTOR: Nathan Juran
CAST: Kerwin Mathews, Kathryn Grant, Torin Thatcher

Kerwin Mathews is Sinbad in this fantasy. Kathryn Grant (who later married Bing Crosby) plays the beautiful Princess. Sinbad battles an evil magician who has reduced the Princess, who is also Sinbad's fiancée, to six inches in height. Our hero must battle a sword-wielding skeleton, a roc (giant bird), and other dangers to restore his bride-to-be to her normal size. This film contains some of the best stop-motion animation ever created by the master in that craft, Ray Harryhausen. His giant cyclops is fabulous and worth viewing alone.

1958   87 minutes

SHE

DIRECTOR: Avi Nesher
CAST: Sandahl Bergman, Quin Kessler, David Goss, Harrison Muller, Gordon Mitchell, David Brandon

Another one of those films that try to sell the viewer the idea of a woman warrior, a female Conan (*Barbarian Queen*, *Red Sonja*, etc.). All these films end up being are excuses for showing some skin. This one is no exception. Sandahl Bergman (*Conan the Barbarian*, *Red Sonja*) is She, the leader of a postapocalyptic nation that looks upon men as second-class citizens. Nevertheless, She defies her country's wishes by helping a man defeat a gang of mutants. Not rated, but would be an R for violence and nudity.

1983   90 minutes

SHORT CIRCUIT
★★★★

DIRECTOR: John Badham
CAST: Ally Sheedy, Steve Guttenberg, Fisher Stevens, Austin Pendleton, G. W. Bailey

In this enjoyable sci-fi comedy-adventure, a sophisticated robot, Number Five, is zapped by lightning during a storm and comes alive (à la Frankenstein's monster) to the shock of his creator (Steve Guttenberg). Created as the ultimate war weapon, the mechanical man learns the value of life from an animal lover (Ally Sheedy) and sets off on his own—with the military in hot pursuit. The young and the young at heart should delight in this entertaining movie with a gentle message. Rated PG for profanity and violence.

1986   95 minutes

SILENT RUNNING
★★★★

DIRECTOR: Douglas Trumbull
CAST: Bruce Dern, Cliff Potts, Ron Rifkin

True science-fiction is most entertaining when it is not just glittering special effects and is, instead, accompanied by a well-developed plot and worthwhile message. This is such a picture. Bruce Dern is in charge of a futuristic space station that is entrusted with the last living remnants of Earth's botanical heritage. His efforts to preserve those trees and plants in spite of an order to destroy them makes

for thoughtful movie-making. Rated G.

1971   89 minutes

SINBAD AND THE EYE OF THE TIGER
★★½

DIRECTOR: Sam Wanamaker
CAST: Patrick Wayne, Jane Seymour, Damian Thomas, Margaret Whiting, Patrick Troughton, Taryn Power

The story, what there is of it, has Sinbad (Patrick Wayne) sailing into a seaport, seeking the hand of Princess Farah (Jane Seymour) and permission from her brother, Prince Kassim (Damian Thomas), to wed. Kassim is next in line for Caliph but has been turned into a baboon by his wicked stepmother, Queen Zenobia (Margaret Whiting). In order to marry his princess, Sinbad must sail to a distant isle to find Melanthius (Patrick Troughton), the only wizard capable of breaking the spell. *Sinbad and the Eye of the Tiger* is not a terrible movie (children will love it), but it just provides more evidence that any film needs a good script and all the movie tricks in the world cannot disguise a bad one. Rated G.

1977   113 minutes

SLAUGHTERHOUSE FIVE
★★★★

DIRECTOR: George Roy Hill
CAST: Michael Sacks, Valerie Perrine, Eugene Roche, John Dehner, Holly Near

This film, based on Kurt Vonnegut's novel, centers around the activities of Billy Pilgrim, who has come unstuck in time. This enables, or forces, him to jump back and forth among different periods in his life and even experience two separate time/space incidents simultaneously. In portraying Billy Pilgrim, Michael Sacks is fascinatingly young and old. His face and physique seem to change with every switch. Even his motivations seem less adult when he is youthful in the wartime portions. Valerie Perrine, as an often topless starlet, has a body that is pleasant to see, as well as acting talent. Her portions are intended to be humorous, and they do succeed. With so few lines, she manages to add grace to a role that, in other hands, might simply be silly or even revolting. Rated R.

1972   104 minutes

SOMETHING WICKED THIS WAY COMES
★★★

DIRECTOR: Jack Clayton
CAST: Jason Robards, Jonathan Pryce, Pam Grier, Shawn Carson

Ray Bradbury's classic fantasy novel has been fashioned into a good, but not great, movie by the Walt Disney Studios. Jason Robards stars as the town librarian whose task it is to save his family and friends from the evil temptations of Mr. Dark (Jonathan Pryce) and his Pandemonium Carnival. It's an old-fashioned, even gentle, tale of the supernatural; a gothic *Wizard of Oz* that seems likely to be best appreciated by pre-teens. It is just strong enough to be scary, while not so brutal as to cause nightmares. Rated PG for scenes of suspense and slight gore.

1983   94 minutes

SOMEWHERE IN TIME
★★★

DIRECTOR: Jeannot Szwarc
CAST: Christopher Reeve, Jane Seymour, Christopher Plummer, Bill Erwin, Teresa Wright

This gentle, old-fashioned film directed by Jeannot Szwarc (*Jaws 2*) celebrates tender passions with great style and atmosphere. Szwarc takes the time to develop his characters and luxuriate in the moment. Today's desensitized and jaded viewer may have a little trouble adjusting to this movie's simple charms, but it's well worth the effort. The story does have a bit of a twist to it—instead of the lovers having to overcome such mundane obstacles as dissenting parents, terminal illness, or other "great tragedies," in the screenplay by Richard Matheson, they must overcome time itself. Rated PG.

1980   103 minutes

SORCERESS
★

DIRECTOR: Brian Stuart
CAST: Leigh and Lynette Harris

Even if you like swords, sorcery, demons, and dragons, you probably still won't like this film. Though the story—about twin girls who are bestowed with the power of sorcery and the fighting skills of the masters—is fairly entertaining, it winds up looking something like "Charlie's Angels Return to the Dark Ages." Leigh and Lynette Harris's dumb-blonde characterizations make the film too silly and cheap for most viewers' tastes. Rated R for nudity and simulated sex.

1982   83 minutes

SOYLENT GREEN
★★★

DIRECTOR: Richard Fleischer
CAST: Charlton Heston, Edward G. Robinson, Joseph Cotten, Chuck Connors

In this watchable science-fiction flick, the year is 2022, and New

York City is grossly overcrowded with a population of 40 million. Food is so scarce the government creates a product, Soylent Green, for people to eat. Heston plays the policeman who discovers what it's made of. There is some violence. Rated PG.

1973　　　　　　　97 minutes

SPACE RAIDERS
★★★½

DIRECTOR: Howard R. Cohen
CAST: Vince Edwards, David Mendenhall

In this low-budget sci-fi flick from B-movie king Roger Corman, a 10-year-old boy (David Mendenhall) is kidnapped by a group of space pirates led by Vince Edwards (once television's "Ben Casey"), who becomes his mentor. It's an entertaining adventure film which not-too-young-youngsters will enjoy. Rated PG for profanity and violence.

1983　　　　　　　82 minutes

SPACECAMP
★★★

DIRECTOR: Harry Winer
CAST: Kate Capshaw, Lea Thompson, Tom Skerritt, Kelly Preston, Tate Donovan, Leaf Phoenix

Kate Capshaw is a reluctant instructor at the U.S. Space Camp in Alabama. She and her independent charges—four teens and a younger child—board a real space shuttle and are accidentally launched on a perilous journey. With an attractive cast, impressive special effects, and a noble heart, the movie captures an adventurous pioneer spirit that should inspire the astronauts of the future. The cute robot and precocious Leaf Phoenix make this one especially entertaining for kids. Rated PG for suspense.

1986　　　　　　　104 minutes

SPACEHUNTER: ADVENTURES IN THE FORBIDDEN ZONE
🐢

DIRECTOR: Lamont Johnson
CAST: Peter Strauss, Molly Ringwald, Ernie Hudson, Andrea Marcovicci, Michael Ironside, Beeson Carroll

The grade-Z science-fiction flick is not dead; it just costs $12 million to make today. The kiddies undoubtedly will love this movie. Adults, however, will find it disappointing. The story is a compendium of cornball clichés and groan-worthy dialogue. Peter Strauss plays a futuristic hero who takes on an army of militant humanoids on a plague-infested planet in order to save a group of marooned women. Molly Ringwald co-stars as a babbling outer-space Valley Girl. Rated PG for violence.

1983　　　　　　　90 minutes

STAR CRASH
★

DIRECTOR: Lewis Coates
CAST: Caroline Munro, Christopher Plummer, Joe Spinell, Marjoe Gortner, David Hasselhoff

A vapid science-fiction space opera with but one redeeming quality: the scanty costumes worn by Caroline Munro as heroine Stella Star. An unbelievable waste of talent, most particularly Christopher Plummer, who seems embarrassed by the whole thing. Cheap special effects and a cheaper plot. Perfect for those with four-year-old mentalities. Rated PG—some violence.

1979　　　　　　　92 minutes

STAR TREK: THE MENAGERIE
★★★★

DIRECTOR: Marc Daniels
CAST: William Shatner, Leonard Nimoy, Jeffrey Hunter, Susan Oliver, DeForest Kelley, James Doohan, Nichelle Nichols, George Takei

Yes, we know. This wasn't originally a theatrical or even made-for-TV movie. However, it was, prior to the release of *Star Trek II: The Wrath of Khan*, the best thing the series, created by Gene Roddenberry, ever wrought. We also feel it constitutes a bona fide movie in its video form. Combining the original "Star Trek" pilot, which starred Jeffrey Hunter (*The Searchers*) as the space-adventuring captain, with new footage featuring the show's eventual stars (William Shatner, Leonard Nimoy, DeForest Kelley, etc.), it tells a fascinating story of how Spock (Nimoy) risks his reputation and career to bring comfort to his former commander on a planet capable of fulfilling any fantasy. It's science-fiction entertainment of the first order.

1967   100 minutes

STAR TREK—THE MOTION PICTURE
★★½

DIRECTOR: Robert Wise
CAST: William Shatner, Leonard Nimoy, DeForest Kelley, James Doohan, Nichelle Nichols, George Takei

Even though it reunites the cast (William Shatner, Leonard Nimoy, DeForest Kelley, James Doohan, Nichelle Nichols, George Takei, etc.) of the popular television series and was directed by Robert Wise, who made one of the best science-fiction films of all time (*The Day the Earth Stood Still*), this $35 million film is a real hit-and-miss affair. Fans of the series may find much to love, but others will be bewildered—and sometimes bored—by the overemphasis on special effects (especially in the needless protracted opening scenes of the starship *Enterprise*) and the underemphasis on characterization (one of the series's pluses). Rated G.

1979   132 minutes

STAR TREK II: THE WRATH OF KHAN
★★★★

DIRECTOR: Nicholas Meyer
CAST: William Shatner, Leonard Nimoy, DeForest Kelley, Ricardo Montalban, James Doohan

James T. Kirk (William Shatner), Mr. Spock (Leonard Nimoy), Doc "Bones" McCoy (DeForest Kelley) and the entire crew of the Starship *Enterprise* once more "boldly go where no man has gone before" in this "Star Trek" adventure. It's no *Gone with the Wind*—or even *Raiders of the Lost Ark*. But it is fun to watch, and Trekkies are sure to love it. Even nonfans will most likely find it enjoyable. As Khan, Ricardo Montalban reprises his supervillain role from the 1967 "Space Seed" episode of the television series. Rated PG for violence and gore.

1982   113 minutes

STAR TREK III: THE SEARCH FOR SPOCK
★★★★½

DIRECTOR: Leonard Nimoy
CAST: Leonard Nimoy, William Shatner, DeForest Kelley, James Doohan, George Takei, Nichelle Nichols, Walter Koenig

In this thrill-packed release, the crew of the U.S.S. *Enterprise* goes looking for their lost shipmate, Spock (Leonard Nimoy), who appeared to give his life to save his friends—at the end of *Star Trek II: The Wrath of Khan*. But is he dead? Finding out may be one of the most entertaining things you ever do in front of a TV set. Rated PG.

1984   105 minutes

STAR TREK (TELEVISION SERIES)
★★ to ★★★★★
(Depending on episode)

DIRECTORS: Marc Daniels, Joseph Pevney, James Goldstone, Gerd Oswald, Vincent McEveety, John Newland, Ralph Senensky, James Komack, John Meredyth Lucas, Jud Taylor

CAST: William Shatner, Leonard Nimoy, Deforrest Kelley, George Takei, Walter Koenig, Nichelle Nichols, Majel Barrett, Grace Lee Whitney, James Doohan

These are the voyages of the Starship *Enterprise*. Her original five-year mission was given short shrift by television executives who pulled the plug after a mere three years from late 1966 to mid-1969, and then watched in horror as fans turned it into the single most popular television series ever made. Beginning in 1979, it begat a successful film series, and the end is nowhere in sight. Paramount has reissued the original shows on tapes made from 35-mm masters, and the *Enterprise* and her crew never have looked lovelier. Superior episodes are "The City on the Edge of Forever," scripted by fantasist Harlan Ellison, wherein Captain Kirk (William Shatner),

Mr. Spock (Leonard Nimoy), and Dr. McCoy (DeForrest Kelley) travel back in time to the Depression-era United States; "The Trouble with Tribbles," which concerns a shipboard "invasion" by little fluff balls with voracious appetites; "Court Martial," which finds Kirk brought to trial for allegedly killing a crew member; "Shore Leave," scripted by science-fiction writer Theodore Sturgeon, which concerns a wacky planet that causes any person's secret fantasies to be brought to actual life; "A Piece of the Action," which sends the *Enterprise* to a planet that patterned its development on old Earth gangster stories; "Amok Time," also scripted by Sturgeon, which concerns Vulcan mating rituals and Mr. Spock's return to his home planet; "Menagerie," a two-parter that incorporates the program's original pilot, "The Cage," initially rejected for being "too cerebral for television"; "Balance of Terror," which introduces the Romulans and concerns what might turn into an interstellar war; "Space Seed," which introduces the evil Khan (Ricardo Montalban) and sets up the events later resolved in the second big-screen film; "Wolf in the Fold," scripted by horror writer Robert Bloch, which postulates that Jack the Ripper was a malevolent force that never died and has now invaded the *Enterprise*; and "Where No Man Has Gone Before," wherein two members of the *Enterprise* crew suddenly acquire incredible mental abilities at the expense of their humanity. Inferior episodes (those to be avoided at all costs) include "The Way to Eden," an embarrassment concerning space-faring hippies; "Spock's Brain," wherein the first officer's brain is kidnapped (!); "And the Children Shall Lead," a ludicrous mess featuring a cameo appearance by attorney Melvin Belli; "Plato's Stepchildren," wherein the *Enterprise* officers are turned into human puppets for the amusement of psychokinetic aliens; and "The Lights of Zetar," wherein Mr. Scott (James Doohan) has an embarrassing affair with a young woman whose mind is taken over by aliens.

1966-69   50 minutes each

STAR WARS
★★★★★

DIRECTOR: George Lucas
CAST: Mark Hamill, Harrison Ford, Carrie Fisher, Alec Guinness, Peter Cushing, Anthony Daniels, Kenny Baker

May the Force be with you! Writer-director George Lucas blended the best of vintage pulp science-fiction, old-fashioned cliff-hangers, comic books, and classic fantasy to come up with the ultimate adventure "a long time ago in a galaxy far, far away." Rated PG.

1977   121 minutes

STARFLIGHT ONE
★

DIRECTOR: Jerry Jameson
CAST: Lee Majors, Hal Linden, Lauren Hutton, Ray Milland, Gail Strickland, George Di Cenzo, Tess Harper, Terry Kiser, Robert Webber

Airport '82? A new supersonic jet experiences catastrophies, one after the other, and the action becomes split between the heroic people on board and the nervous ground crew looking at the little green bleeps on the radar screen. We get to know many of the characters and their troubled personal lives through a story as old as the

Spirit of St. Louis and as effective as a DC-10. All the actors in this all-star line-up phone in their performances in the grand tradition of disaster films.

1982   115 minutes

STARMAN
★★★★

DIRECTOR: John Carpenter
CAST: Jeff Bridges, Karen Allen, Charles Martin Smith, Richard Jaeckel

John Carpenter (*Halloween*; *The Thing*) directed this release, which is more of a romance than a space opera or a science-fiction thriller. Jeff Bridges stars as an alien who falls in love with Earthling, Karen Allen (of *Raiders of the Lost Ark* fame). *Starman* is best described as a fairy tale for adults, but the kiddies undoubtedly will enjoy it, too. Rated PG-13 for suggested sex, violence, and profanity.

1984   115 minutes

STRANGE INVADERS
★★★★

DIRECTOR: Michael Laughlin
CAST: Paul LeMat, Diana Scarwid, Nancy Allen, Louise Fletcher, Michael Lerner, Kenneth Tobey, June Lockhart

A splendid tribute/parody of 1950s science-fiction movies, this film begins in 1958, with buglike aliens taking over a farm town called Centerville, Illinois. The story then jumps to New York City, twenty-five years later, where a college professor (Paul LeMat) is suddenly running off to Illinois after his ex-wife (Diana Scarwid), who has disappeared during a visit to Centerville. She left their daughter with him in New York, but she hasn't returned, and the phone lines in Centerville are dead. *Strange Invaders* is everything you always hoped the sci-fi flicks of the 1950s would be and so often weren't. Rated PG for violence.

1983   94 minutes

STRYKER
★

DIRECTOR: Cirio Santiago
CAST: Steve Sandor, Andria Savio, William Osterander

A low-budget futuristic action thriller à la *Spacehunter* and *Road Warrior*, the story here deals with a soldier of fortune (Steve Sandor) attempting to wrest a group of warrior women from the clutches of an evil tribe. Rated R.

1983   86 minutes

SUPER FUZZ
★★½

DIRECTOR: Sergio Corbucci
CAST: Terence Hill, Ernest Borgnine, Joanne Dru, Marc Laurence, Julie Gordon, Lee Sandman

For adults, this is a silly, mindless film...but it's great fun for the kids. Terence Hill stars as Dave Speed, a police officer with supernatural powers that enable him to walk on water, intuitively sense when and where crimes are being committed, and the like. He and his ornery, befuddled partner (Ernest Borgnine) make an amusing team. Director Sergio Corbucci (*Odds and Evens*) maintains a lively pace. Rated PG apparently because of one scene involving provocatively dressed go-go dancers.

1981   94 minutes

SUPERGIRL
★★½

DIRECTOR: Jeannot Swarc

CAST: Faye Dunaway, Peter O'Toole, Helen Slater, Mia Farrow, Brenda Vaccaro, Simon Ward, Peter Cook, Hart Bochner

Helen Slater makes a respectable film debut as Superman's cousin in this screen comic book, which should delight the kiddies and occasionally tickle the adults. The stellar supporting cast doesn't seem to take it seriously, so why should we? Only the occasional lines of dialogue that border on blasphemy (although meant to be funny) might make this PG-rated release a questionable choice for some viewers, both young and old.

1984   105 minutes

SUPERMAN
★★★½

DIRECTOR: Richard Donner
CAST: Christopher Reeve, Margot Kidder, Jackie Cooper, Marc McClure, Marlon Brando, Glenn Ford

After a somewhat overblown introduction, which encompasses the end of Krypton and Clark Kent's adolescence in Smallville, this film takes off to provide some great moments as Superman swings into action. The *Daily Planet* scenes are blessed with fast-paced dialogue and wit, and the action scenes are thrilling. Christopher Reeve is the consummate Superman. The distinction between the personalities of Kent and the Man of Steel are created with laudable believability. Margot Kidder's Lois Lane and Jackie Cooper's Perry White transcend all that has gone before. The action is complemented by fine tongue-in-cheek comedy. Rated PG.

1978   143 minutes

SUPERMAN II
★★★★

DIRECTOR: Richard Lester

CAST: Margot Kidder, Christopher Reeve, Gene Hackman, Ned Beatty, Jackie Cooper

Slightly better than the original, this adventure of the Man of Steel includes a full-fledged—and beautifully handled—romance between Lois Lane (Margot Kidder) and Superman (Christopher Reeve) and a spectacular battle that pits our hero against three super-villains (during which the city of Metropolis is almost completely destroyed). Rated PG.

1980   127 minutes

SUPERMAN III
★★

DIRECTOR: Richard Lester

CAST: Christopher Reeve, Richard Pryor, Robert Vaughn, Annette O'Toole, Jackie Cooper, Marc McClure, Annie Ross, Pamela Stephenson

If it weren't for Christopher Reeve's excellent performance in the title role, *Superman III* would be a major disappointment. You would think the combination of Superman, Richard Pryor, and director Richard Lester (*A Hard Day's Night* and *The Three Musketeers*) would make for spectacular entertainment. It doesn't. The story features a subdued Pryor as a computer whiz who is hired by bad guy Robert Vaughn to do dastardly deeds with his magic programming. While it isn't awful, *Superman III* is definitely the least of the screen adventures of the Man of Steel. Rated PG.

1983   125 minutes

SWORD AND THE SORCERER, THE
★★

DIRECTOR: Albert Pyun

CAST: Lee Horsley, Kathleen Beller, Simon MacCorkindale, George Maharis, Richard Lynch, Richard Moll

But for the derring-do and bits of comedy provided by star Lee Horsley, this film would be a complete waste of time and talent. About a soldier of fortune (Horsley, star of television's "Matt Houston") who rescues a damsel in distress (Kathleen Beller) and her brother (Simon MacCorkindale) from an evil king and his powerful wizard, it was directed by Albert Pyun, who apprenticed under the great Japanese filmmaker Akira Kurosawa. Apparently, Pyun was able to pick up Kurosawa's visual sense, but not his gift for story-telling. Rated R because of nudity, violence, gore, and sexual references.

1982   100 minutes

TENTH VICTIM, THE
★★★½

DIRECTOR: Elio Petri

CAST: Marcello Mastroianni, Ursula Andress, Elsa Martinelli, Massimo Serato

A weird little science-fiction film that has achieved minor cult status, thanks to droll performances from Marcello Mastroianni and Ursula Andress and an intriguing plot taken from the novel by Robert Sheckley. The setting is the near future, and pop culture has embraced an assassination game that is played for keeps: ten participants start the hunt against one another, and the sequential elimination of opponents results in one winner. Unlike the paint pellets found in contemporary games, though, the ammo is live . . . and the losers aren't. Very imaginative; watch for a rather explosive bra. Unrated, contains sexual situations.

1965   92 minutes

TERMINATOR, THE
★★★½
DIRECTOR: James Cameron
CAST: Arnold Schwarzenegger, Linda Hamilton, Michael Biehn

In this science-fiction/time-travel adventure, Arnold Schwarzenegger (*Conan*) stars as a cyborg (part man, part machine) sent from the future to present-day Los Angeles to murder a woman (Linda Hamilton). Her offspring will play an important part in the world from which the killer came. Michael Biehn is the rebel soldier sent to thwart Schwarzenegger's plans. The film starts off like a shot out of a cannon. Fast-paced action fills the screen for the first twenty minutes. After that, it lurches along in fits and starts. Nevertheless, it is essentially an enjoyable, old-fashioned B movie. Rated R for nudity, simulated sex, violence, and profanity.

1984   108 minutes

TESTAMENT
★★★★★
DIRECTOR: Lynne Littman
CAST: Jane Alexander, William Devane, Ross Harris, Roxanna Zal, Lukas Haas, Lila Kedrova, Leon Ames, Mako

In its own quiet, unspectacular way, this film tells a simple story about what happens to one family when World War III begins and ends in a matter of minutes. Jane Alexander is superb as the mother attempting to cope with the unthinkable, and this fine movie is

one you won't soon forget. Rated PG.

1983   90 minutes

THEM!
★★★★
DIRECTOR: Gordon Douglas
CAST: Edmund Gwenn, James Arness, James Whitmore, Fess Parker

Classic 1950s sci-fi about colossal mutant ants, at large in a New Mexico desert, threatening to take over the world. Frightening special effects and lightning pace make this a supercharged entertainment, with Edmund Gwenn delivering a standout performance as the scientist who foretells the danger. Great.

1954   B & W   94 minutes

THIEF OF BAGHDAD, THE
★★★★★
DIRECTOR: Ludwig Berger, Tim Whelan, Michael Powell
CAST: Sabu, John Justin, June Duprez, Rex Ingram

Alexander Korda's 1940 version of *The Thief of Baghdad* is a thing of wonder, the screen embodiment of the charm and imagination of the Arabian Nights. With its flying carpets, giant genies, magic spells, and evil wizards, *Thief of Baghdad* ranks as one of the finest fantasy films of all time. John Justin plays a young king, Ahmad, who is duped by his Grand Vizier, Jaffar, and loses his throne. June Duprez is the beautiful princess for whom he yearns and, of course, Jaffer kidnaps. With the aid of a colossal genie (excellently played by Rex Ingram) and other magical devices, Ahmad must do battle with Jaffar in a rousing fairy tale of good versus evil.

1940   106 minutes

THIEF OF BAGHDAD, THE
★★★½

DIRECTOR: Raoul Walsh
CAST: Douglas Fairbanks, Julanne Johnson, Anna May Wong, Sojin

The first—and second best— of four spectacular versions of this classic Arabian Nights–ish fantasy adventure of derring-do with magically flying carpets, giant genies, and crafty evil sorcery. The now fabled Douglas Fairbanks is the thief, Julanne Johnson the beautiful princess he carries away on an airborne rug. Of all silent epics, this one is rated the most imaginative. Mr. Fairbanks is incredible, every flip proving him the superb athlete his legion of fans made King of Hollywood in the 1920s. The sets rival everything filmed before and since.

1924   B & W 140 minutes

THING, THE
★★★★

DIRECTOR: John Carpenter
CAST: Kurt Russell, A. Wilford Brimley, Richard Dysart

The modern master of fright, John Carpenter (*Halloween*), has created a movie so terrifying, it'll crawl right up your leg. Rather than a remake, this updated version of Howard Hawks's 1951 science-fiction horror classic is closer to a sequel, with Kurt Russell and his crew arriving at the Antarctic encampment after the chameleonlike creature from outer space has finished off its inhabitants. It's good ol' "tell me a scary story" fun. Rated R for profanity and gore.

1982   108 minutes

THING (FROM ANOTHER WORLD), THE
★★★★★

DIRECTOR: Christian Nyby (Howard Hawks)
CAST: Kenneth Tobey, Margaret Sheridan, James Arness

A highly entertaining film, this was based on John W. Campbell's story "Who Goes There?" about a hostile visitor from space at large at an army radar station in the Arctic. Considered by many to be a classic, this relies on the unseen rather than the seen for its power, and as such it is almost unbearably suspenseful. Tight direction, deliberate pacing—not to mention exceptional performances by the entire cast—make this viewing a must. James Arness, in an early role, plays the monster.

1951   B & W 87 minutes

THINGS TO COME
★★★★

DIRECTOR: William Cameron Menzies
CAST: Raymond Massey, Cedric Hardwicke, Ralph Richardson

The world of the future as viewed from the perspective of the 1930s, this is an interesting screen curio based on the book by H. G. Wells. Special effects have come a long way since then, but sci-fi fans will still enjoy the spectacular sets in this honorable, thoughtful production.

1936   B & W 92 minutes

THIS ISLAND EARTH
★★★

DIRECTOR: Joseph M. Newman
CAST: Jeff Morrow, Rex Reason, Faith Domergue

A fine 1950s sci-fi flick about scientists kidnapped by aliens to help them save their planet, this has good make-up and effects for the era.

1955   86 minutes

THRESHOLD
★★

DIRECTOR: Richard Pearce
CAST: Donald Sutherland, John Marley, Jeff Goldblum, Michael Lerner

Donald Sutherland stars in this film about the first artificial-heart transplant. Made before Barney Clark was the first recipient of such an organ, this Canadian film went from science-fiction to real-life drama during the period when it was being prepared for release. Rated PG.

1981   106 minutes

THX 1138
★★★½

DIRECTOR: George Lucas
CAST: Robert Duvall, Donald Pleasence, Maggie McOmie

Science-fiction and movie buffs may want to rent this moody, atmospheric picture, starring Robert Duvall and Donald Pleasence, to see an example of the type of work director George Lucas was doing pre–Star Wars. It was the fabulously successful filmmaker's first. Interesting. Rated PG.

1971   88 minutes

TIME AFTER TIME
★★★★

DIRECTOR: Nicholas Meyer
CAST: Malcolm McDowell, David Warner, Mary Steenburgen

Nicholas Meyer, who wrote The Seven-Per-Cent Solution and went on to helm Star Trek II: The Wrath of Khan, also adapted and directed this 1979 release. In it, H. G. Wells (Malcolm McDowell) pursues Jack the Ripper (David Warner) into modern-day San Francisco via a time machine. Co-starring Mary Steenburgen, it's an enjoyable pastiche that has quite a few nice moments. Rated PG.

1979   112 minutes

TIME BANDITS
★★★★

DIRECTOR: Terry Gilliam
CAST: Sean Connery, Shelley Duvall, Ralph Richardson, Ian Holm, David Warner, John Cleese, Michael Palin

Anyone with a sense of adventure will find a lot to like about this delightful tale of a boy and six dwarves—no, this isn't Snow White—who travel back in time via a map that charts a course through holes in the fabric of the universe. Rated PG for violence.

1981   110 minutes

TIME MACHINE, THE
★★★★

DIRECTOR: George Pal
CAST: Rod Taylor, Yvette Mimieux, Alan Young, Sebastian Cabot

Science-fiction need not always be thought-provoking to be entertaining; Star Wars proves that. The Time Machine won an Oscar for its special effects, but it is best remembered for its appealing story. Rod Taylor plays a scientist in the early 1900s who invents a device that can transport him within the dimensions of time. He goes forward past three world wars and into the year 802,701, where he encounters a world very different from the one he left. This movie has all the elements that make up a classic in science-fiction. It's adapted from a novel by H. G.

Wells, and it's directed by the king of 1950s and '60s sci-fi, George Pal.

1960   103 minutes

TRANCERS
★

DIRECTOR: Charles Band
CAST: Tim Thomerson, Helen Hunt, Michael Stefani, Art Le Fleur, Telma Hopkins, Richard Herd, Anne Seymour

Reprehensible ripoff of *Blade Runner* and *The Terminator* with none of the style or suspense of either. Tim Thomerson (*Fade to Black, Volunteers*) is Jack Death, a police officer in the 2280s who is sent into the past to bring back a violent cult leader who escaped into the twentieth century to cut off the bloodlines of his twenty-third-century leaders. Rated PG-13 for profanity and lots of violence.

1985   76 minutes

TROLL

DIRECTOR: John Buechler
CAST: Noah Hathaway, Michael Moriarty, Shelley Hack, Jenny Beck, June Lockhart, Anne Lockhart, Sonny Bono, Brad Hall, Phil Fondacaro

Michael Moriarty, who deserves better, plays the head of a family beseiged by evil little creatures in this horrendous horror film. If your children have been misbehaving lately, make them watch this piece of garbage. They'll be on their best behavior for months afterward for fear you might make them watch it again. But be sure to be out of the room when it's playing. This film, about a troll who lives in a laundry room and attempts to take over the world, is much harder for adults to watch than it is for kids.

Rated PG-13 for profanity, violence, and gore.

1986   95 minutes

TRON
★★★

DIRECTOR: Steven Lisberger
CAST: Jeff Bridges, David Warner, Bruce Boxleitner, Cindy Morgan, Barnard Hughes

An enjoyable, if somewhat lightheaded, piece of escapism, this science-fiction adventure concerns a computer genius (Jeff Bridges) who suspects evil doings by a corporate executive (David Warner). During his investigation, Bridges is zapped into another dimension and finds himself a player in a gladiatorial video game. Most of the action takes place inside the system, with dazzling computer-generated special effects dominating the screen. While the story direction and dialogue are weak, *Tron* has enough action and surprises to keep youngsters entertained. Rated PG for computer-simulated violence.

1982   96 minutes

2001: A SPACE ODYSSEY
★★★★★

DIRECTOR: Stanley Kubrick
CAST: Keir Dullea, William Sylvester, Gary Lockwood

There's no denying the visual magnificence of this highly overrated science-fiction epic. Ponderous, ambiguous, and arty, it's nevertheless considered a classic of the genre by many film buffs. The set design, costumes, cinematography, and Oscar-winning special effects combine to create unforgettable imagery. Rated G.

1968   139 minutes

2010
★★★★

DIRECTOR: Peter Hyams
CAST: Roy Scheider, John Lithgow, Helen Mirren, Bob Balaban, Keir Dullea

The exciting sequel to the epic 1968 version of Arthur C. Clarke's *2001: A Space Odyssey*, this stars Roy Scheider, John Lithgow, Helen Mirren, Bob Balaban, and Keir Dullea (reprising the role he played in the original) as participants in a joint American-Russian space mission. We finally find out what really happened to astronaut Dave Bowman (Dullea); the computer, HAL 9000; and the spaceship, *Discovery*, near the planet Jupiter. Rated PG.

1984   116 minutes

TWO WORLDS OF JENNIE LOGAN, THE
🐢

DIRECTOR: Frank DeFelitta
CAST: Lindsay Wagner, Marc Singer, Linda Gray, Alan Feinstein, Irene Tedrow, Henry Wilcoxon

A young woman in a troubled marriage finds an old dress in her new house. When she dons this aged garment, she is magically transported one hundred years into the past. There she meets and falls in love with a handsome young man with a horrible destiny she must try to prevent. Made for TV, this standard prime-time soap opera has some moments for romance fans, but the rest of us will be bored by bad acting and lack of suspense.

1979   99 minutes

ULTIMATE WARRIOR, THE
★★½

DIRECTOR: Robert Clouse
CAST: Yul Brynner, Max Von Sydow, Joanna Miles, William Smith, Stephen McHattie

The payoff doesn't match the promise of the premise in this less-than-thrilling science-fiction thriller. In the not-so-distant future, ragged residents of devastated New York City battle vicious gangs. Initially intriguing, the film stumbles to a ludicrous conclusion. Rated R.

1975   94 minutes

VOYAGE TO THE BOTTOM OF THE SEA
★★★

DIRECTOR: Irwin Allen
CAST: Walter Pidgeon, Joan Fontaine, Robert Sterling, Barbara Eden, Michael Ansara, Peter Lorre, Frankie Avalon, Henry Daniell

An atomic submarine rushes to save Earth from destruction by a burning radiation belt. Intrigue, adventure, and hokey fun, with a low-level all-star cast. Much better than the subsequent television show. Unrated, the film has mild violence.

1961   105 minutes

WAR OF THE WORLDS, THE
★★★★

DIRECTOR: Byron Haskin
CAST: Gene Barry, Les Tremayne, Ann Robinson

This science-fiction film stars Gene Barry as a scientist who is among the first Earthlings to witness the Martian invasion of Earth. The film is an updated version of H. G. Wells's classic story, with the action heightened by excellent special effects.

1953   85 minutes

WARGAMES
★★★★½

DIRECTOR: John Badham
CAST: Matthew Broderick, Dabney Coleman, Ally Sheedy, John Wood, Barry Corbin

Here's a terrific family movie that will have viewers on the edge of their seats from beginning to end. A young computer whiz (Matthew Broderick, from *Max Dugan Returns*) who thinks he's hooking into a game manufacturer's computer to get the scoop on its latest line accidentally starts World War III when he decides to "play" a selection titled "Global Thermonuclear Warfare." Though the movie contains almost no violence or any other sensationalistic content (apart from a wee bit of vulgar language), it still grips the viewer. This is the way movies should always be made. Rated PG.

1983   114 minutes

WARLORDS OF THE 21ST CENTURY
★★

DIRECTOR: Harley Cockliss
CAST: James Wainwright, Annie McEnroe, Michael Beck

If you've got time on your hands and want to see a movie that doesn't provoke, titillate, or stimulate, then *Warlords* is perfect. Set after the global apocalypse, a cold-blooded killer leads his band of roving outlaws in a siege against a peaceful community, only to face his comeuppance by an equally cold-blooded mystery man. James Wainwright as the villain, Annie McEnroe as the virtuous heroine, and Michael Beck (who achieved notoriety in that terrible musical *Xanadu*) give what they can to a predictable, uninspired script that has all the earmarks of a good old-fashioned shoot-'em-up without

the action to back it up. Rated R for violence.

1982   91 minutes

WARRIOR AND THE SORCERESS, THE
🦶

DIRECTOR: John Broderick
CAST: David Carradine, Luke Askew, Maria Socas

Why does David Carradine do films like this? In this sword-and-sorcery version of *A Fistful of Dollars*, two warring houses on opposite sides of a well in the middle of a desert both seek to control the well and destroy the other house. Carradine plays a "Dark Warrior" who arrives and pits the houses against each other while getting paid for it. Production values may seem high, and the photography has a certain comic-book flashiness, but poor David Carradine—he just can't make his Clint Eastwood imitation last—not even for eighty-one minutes. Rated R for gore, nudity.

1984   81 minutes

WARRIORS OF THE WIND
★★★★

DIRECTOR: Tokuma Shoten Pub. Co. Ltd.
CAST: Animated

This movie-length Japanese animated feature easily ranks with the best of American animated films. The characters are believable, the action is convincing, and the plot delivers the positive message that not everything good is beautiful and that ugliness, like true beauty, may take more than looking to be seen. Definitely not for the kiddies only.

1984   95 minutes

WATERSHIP DOWN
★★★★

DIRECTOR: Martin Rosen
CAST: Animated

Although it's a full-length cartoon about the adventures of a group of rabbits, you'll find no cutesy, Disney-styled Thumpers à la *Bambi*. The film has its lighter moments—and they are delightful—but the main thrust of the story is danger and courage. About the odyssey that a small group of rabbits undertakes after one of them has a vision of evil things coming to destroy their homes, this bears little resemblance to the melodramatic Disney children-oriented fare. However, their arduous journey is full of surprises and rewards. Rated PG.

1978   92 minutes

WAVELENGTH
★★★★

DIRECTOR: Mike Gray
CAST: Robert Carradine, Cherie Currie, Keenan Wynn

You've seen it all many times before in science-fiction movies of wide-ranging quality: the innocent visitors from outer space, the callous government officials who see them as guinea pigs instead of guests, the handful of compassionate Earthlings, even the race to the mother ship. But rarely has the plot been used so effectively. The film is both touching and exciting. Keenan Wynn gives a particularly affecting performance. Rated PG.

1983   87 minutes

WESTWORLD
★★★★

DIRECTOR: Michael Crichton
CAST: Yul Brynner, Richard Benjamin, James Brolin, Norman Bartold

This is another science-fiction yarn from the author (Michael Crichton) of *The Andromeda Strain*. The film concerns an expensive world for well-to-do vacationers. They can live out their fantasies in the Old West or King Arthur's Court with the aid of programmed robots repaired nightly by scientists so they can be "killed" the next day by tourists. Richard Benjamin and James Brolin are tourists who come up against a rebellious robot (Yul Brynner). Rated PG.

1973   88 minutes

WHEN WORLDS COLLIDE
★★

DIRECTOR: Rudolph Maté
CAST: Richard Derr, Barbara Rush, Peter Hanson, Larry Keating, John Hoyt

Interesting end-of-the-world sci-fi fable from George Pal has dated badly since its original release in 1951. Final scene of Earth pilgrims landing on the planet and walking into an obvious superimposed painting is laughable today, but many of the other Oscar-winning effects are still quite convincing.

1951   81 minutes

WITHOUT WARNING
🦃

DIRECTOR: Greydon Clark
CAST: Jack Palance, Martin Landau, Cameron Mitchell, Larry Storch, Sue Anne Langdon

A cast of Hollywood veterans battles with an intergalactic alien hunter (a rubber-faced leftover from the "Outer Limits" television series) and his hungry pets in this awful low-budget science-fiction effort. Guess who ends up as lunch. Moreover, who cares? You won't—after the first ten minutes. Rated R.

1980   89 minutes

X (THE MAN WITH THE X-RAY EYES)

★★★

DIRECTOR: Roger Corman
CAST: Ray Milland, Diana Van Der Vlis, Harold J. Stone, John Hoyt, Don Rickles

Intriguing, offbeat tale of a scientist (Ray Milland) who discovers a drug that gives him the power to see through objects. He has a great time at first, but soon becomes addicted and begins seeing more and more, until . . . Fine production is highly enjoyable, with a surprisingly effective role by comedian Don Rickles as a carnival barker. Not one penny of the low budget is wasted.

1963 80 minutes

YOR: THE HUNTER FROM THE FUTURE

DIRECTOR: Anthony M. Dawson
CAST: Reb Brown, Corinne Clery, John Steiner, Carole Andre, Alan Collins

In the glorious tradition of *Plan 9 from Outer Space* and *Robot Monster* comes *Yor, the Hunter from the Future*, a movie so incredibly awful that it's hilarious. In it, a mighty warrior (Reb Brown) attempts to discover his true identity on a planet trapped in a time warp where the past and the future collide. You'll howl at the pitiful "acting" of beefcake star Reb Brown. You'll guffaw at the unbelievable situations. You'll groan out loud at the insipid dialogue. In other words, it's a real hoot. Rated PG for violence and profanity.

1983 88 minutes

ZARDOZ

🦑

DIRECTOR: John Boorman
CAST: Sean Connery, Charlotte Rampling

Sorry sci-fi about a strange society of the future and Sean Connery's attempts to free the people from the evil rulers. Murky plot is hard to follow, and the viewer soon loses interest. Good photography is all but lost on the home screen, leaving nothing but Connery running around in a diaper for two hours. Rated R.

1974 105 minutes

WESTERNS

ABILENE TOWN
★★★
DIRECTOR: Edwin L. Marin
CAST: Randolph Scott, Ann Dvorak, Rhonda Fleming, Lloyd Bridges, Edgar Buchanan

Cattlemen and homesteaders are at loggerheads in the 1870s in this fast-paced shoot-'em-up.' Randolph Scott is the trusty tall man with the star who tries to sort it all out. Edgar Buchanan is sly, as always.

1946   B & W   89 minutes

AGAINST A CROOKED SKY
★★
DIRECTOR: Earl Bellamy
CAST: Richard Boone, Clint Ritchie, Henry Wilcoxon, Stewart Peterson

Nothing new in this familiar tale of a boy searching for his sister, who has been kidnapped by Indians. No more than just another inferior reworking of John Ford's classic western *The Searchers*. For fans who watch anything with a horse and a saddle. Rated PG for violence.

1975   89 minutes

ALAMO, THE
★★★½
DIRECTOR: John Wayne
CAST: John Wayne, Richard Widmark, Frankie Avalon, Richard Boone, Chill Wills, Laurence Harvey

This western, directed by and starring John Wayne, may have seemed overlong when originally released. But today it's the answer to a Duke-deprived fan's dream. Of course, there's the expected mushy flag-waving here and there. However, once Davy Crockett (Wayne), Jim Bowie (Richard Widmark), Will Travis (Laurence Harvey), and their respective followers team up to take on Santa Ana's forces, it's a humdinger of a period war movie.

1960   161 minutes

ALLEGHENY UPRISING
★★★
DIRECTOR: William A. Seiter
CAST: John Wayne, Claire Trevor, George Sanders, Moroni Olsen, Chill Wills, Brian Donlevy

John Wayne and Claire Trevor were reteamed the same year of

their co-starring triumph in 1939's *Stagecoach* for this potboiler set in the pre-Revolutionary American colonies, but the results were hardly as auspicious. Still, it's a decent time-passer and features Brian Donlevy in one of his better villain roles.

1939   B & W   81 minutes

ALONG CAME JONES
★★★★

DIRECTOR: Stuart Heisler
CAST: Gary Cooper, Loretta Young, Dan Duryea

Highly watchable comic western with Gary Cooper as an innocent cowboy who's mistaken for an infamous outlaw. Both lawmen and the real outlaw (Dan Duryea) pursue him.

1945   B & W   90 minutes

ALVAREZ KELLY
★★

DIRECTOR: Edward Dmytryk
CAST: William Holden, Richard Widmark, Janice Rule, Patrick O'Neal, Victoria Shaw

Edward Dymtryk unimaginatively directed this plodding western starring William Holden as a cattle driver supplying beef to the Yankees. He is kidnapped by Confederate officer Richard Widmark, who wants him to steal that much-needed food supply for the South. Dull.

1966   116 minutes

AMERICAN EMPIRE
★★★

DIRECTOR: William McGann
CAST: Richard Dix, Frances Gifford, Preston Foster, Leo Carrillo, Guinn Williams

A formula film featuring the now standard grand opening, dramatic problem-posing center, and slam-bang breathtaking climax, but a good, entertaining western nonetheless. Friends and Civil War veterans Richard Dix and Preston Foster team to found a cattle empire in Texas. Villain Leo Carrillo makes most of the trouble the pair encounter. Fans of the genre will love it.

1942   B & W   82 minutes

AMERICANO, THE
★★½

DIRECTOR: William Castle
CAST: Glenn Ford, Cesar Romero, Frank Lovejoy, Abbe Lane

Texas cowboy Glenn Ford gets embroiled with a bunch of Brazilian bad guys in this way-south-of-the-border western. A change of scenery is commendable, but a familiar plot makes this film all but pedestrian. As always, however, Frank Lovejoy is refreshing in his wry way. And Ford is Ford.

1954   85 minutes

ANGEL AND THE BADMAN
★★★★

DIRECTOR: James Edward Grant
CAST: John Wayne, Gail Russell, Harry Carey, Irene Rich, Bruce Cabot

A fine low-budget western with John Wayne as a gunman who sees the light through the love of Quaker girl Gail Russell. Harry Carey and Bruce Cabot also are memorable in this thoughtful action film directed by longtime Wayne screenwriter James Edward Grant.

1947   B & W   100 minutes

APACHE
★★

DIRECTOR: Robert Aldrich

CAST: Burt Lancaster, Jean Peters, Charles Bronson (Charinsky), John Dehner, Monte Blue

Moralistic message western features Burt Lancaster as an idealistic warrior who resents yet understands the encroachment of the whites and refuses to live on government reservations. Lancaster hams it up as the noble savage who eludes his pursuers while imparting bits of wisdom intended to make them (and the audience) feel guilty. Strangely typical of early-to-mid-1950s Hollywood westerns, this entry is long on conscience and short on action. Charles Bronson appears under his original screen name in one of his many ethnic American roles, this time as an Indian, joining the pantheon of immigrants-cum-natives that includes Anthony Caruso and Michael Ansara.

1954   91 minutes

BAD COMPANY
★★★★

DIRECTOR: Robert Benton
CAST: Jeff Bridges, Barry Brown, Jim Davis, David Huddleston, John Savage, Jerry Houser, Geoffrey Lewis

This is a much underrated Civil War–era western. The cultured Barry Brown and the street-wise Jeff Bridges team up as robbers. Charming performances by the leads and an intriguing, intelligent script by Robert Benton and David Newman make this well worth watching. Benton's vision of the West is a captivating blend of romance and realism. The late Jim Davis (of television's "Dallas") was given one of his rare opportunities to shine on the big screen in this offbeat gem, which was—along with *The Shootist*, *The Outlaw Josey Wales*, and *The Culpepper*

Cattle Company—one of the few important westerns made in the 1970s. Rated R.

1972   94 minutes

BAD MAN'S RIVER
★★★

DIRECTOR: Gene Martin
CAST: Lee Van Cleef, Gina Lollobrigida, James Mason

A humorous western about the "dreaded" King gang, which robbed banks along the Texas and Mexican borders. A Mexican revolutionary offers them a million dollars to blow up the arsenal used by the Mexican army, which the gang does, only to find that they have been double-crossed. A fun western in the old tradition.

1959   96 minutes

BADMAN'S TERRITORY
★★★

DIRECTOR: Tim Whelan
CAST: Randolph Scott, Ann Richards, George "Gabby" Hayes, Ray Collins, Chief Thundercloud

Staunch and true marshal combats saddle scum when they flee across the border into territory beyond the government's reach. Good watching.

1946   B & W   97 minutes

BALLAD OF CABLE HOGUE, THE
★★★★½

DIRECTOR: Sam Peckinpah
CAST: Jason Robards, Stella Stevens, Strother Martin, L. Q. Jones, David Warner

Many critics found it quite fashionable to refer continually to Sam Peckinpah's films as excercises in violence and mayhem. There was a tender side to his work, which can be found in *Junior Bonner*, *Ride the High Country*, and *The*

Ballad of Cable Hogue. Jason Robards has one of his finest roles as Hogue, a loner who discovers water in the desert and becomes a successful entrepreneur by opening a stagecoach stopover. Peckinpah's deft eye for period detail and outstanding acting by all involved make this one a winner. Rated R.

1970   121 minutes

BALLAD OF GREGORIO CORTEZ, THE
★★★★½

DIRECTOR: Robert M. Young
CAST: Edward James Olmos, James Gammon, Tom Bower, Alan Vint

This superb independent production tells the powerful story of one man's courage, pain, tragedy, and heartbreak—all of which come as the result of a simple misunderstanding. Edward James Olmos ("Miami Vice") gives a haunting portrayal of the title character, who becomes a fugitive through no fault of his own. Tom Bower and James Gammon lend solid support in this outstanding work solidly directed by Robert M. Young. Rated PG for violence.

1982   99 minutes

BANDOLERO!
★★★

DIRECTOR: Andrew V. McLaglen
CAST: James Stewart, Dean Martin, Raqauel Welch, Will Geer, George Kennedy, Andrew Prine

Escape south of the border with outlaw brothers James Stewart and Dean Martin (if you can buy this), who ride just a few furlongs ahead of the law (George Kennedy), taking Raquel Welch along as hostage.

1968   106 minutes

BARBAROSA
★★★★

DIRECTOR: Fred Schepisi
CAST: Willie Nelson, Gary Busey, Isela Vega, Gilbert Roland, Danny de la Paz, George Voskovec

This action-packed western stars Willie Nelson and Gary Busey as a pair of outcasts on the run. Australian director Fred Schepisi has created an exciting, funny movie that combines the scenic majesty of the great John Ford westerns (*Stagecoach*; *She Wore a Yellow Ribbon*; *The Searchers*; etc.) with the light touch of George Roy Hill's *Butch Cassidy and the Sundance Kid*. As a result, *Barbarosa* is everything devotees of the shoot-'em-up could ask for. If you've got a weakness for sagebrush, saddles, and shootouts, you won't want to miss it. Rated PG for violence.

1982   90 minutes

BELLS OF CORONADO
★★½

DIRECTOR: William Witney
CAST: Roy Rogers, Dale Evans, Pat Brady, Grant Withers, Leo Cleary, Clifton Young, Trigger

Former hero Grant Withers (*Jungle Jim* in the serial of the same name) takes time out from the character roles he played in John Ford films and heads an evil gang of foreign agents out to smuggle uranium to unfriendly powers. Roy Rogers plays a modern-day heroic insurance agent who, with the aid of Dale and Trigger and in spite of bumbling Pat Brady, is able to thwart the heavies and prevent them from flying the precious materials out of the country. Comic-book story is full of fast riding and action that carries it safely through any critical assaults (at least until the whole thing is over and you can catch your breath and say, "What?"). Color adds a lot to these later Rogers films.

1950   67 minutes

BEND OF THE RIVER
★★★★

DIRECTOR: Anthony Mann
CAST: James Stewart, Arthur Kennedy, Rock Hudson, Julia Adams

James Stewart and director Anthony Mann teamed up during the early 1950s to make a series of exceptional westerns that helped the genre return to popularity. This one deals with Stewart leading a wagon train across the country and his dealings with ex-friend Arthur Kennedy, who hijacks their supplies. Superior western fare in every sense.

1952   91 minutes

BETWEEN GOD, THE DEVIL AND A WINCHESTER
👹

DIRECTOR: Dario Silvester
CAST: Richard Harrison, Gilbert Roland, Dominique Boschero

Because of films like this one Spain now rivals Italy in making rotten westerns. A treasure is stolen from a church in Texas and a band of outlaws and a holy man go on the trail to find it. Guaranteed to net only horselaughs thanks to the dubbed dialogue. Not rated, but the equivalent of a PG for violence.

1972   98 minutes

BIG COUNTRY
★★★

DIRECTOR: William Wyler

CAST: Gregory Peck, Jean Simmons, Charlton Heston, Carroll Baker, Burl Ives, Charles Bickford

Big-budget western pits Gregory Peck and Charlton Heston as adversaries in an ongoing feud between rival cowmen Burl Ives and Charles Bickford. Basically low-key film presents Jean Simmons as a schoolmarm and Carroll Baker as Bickford's daughter. The two of them provide the love interest and get the boys' blood boiling enough to inspire a knockdown, drag-out fight between Peck and Heston. This would-be epic looks good but lacks the punch and plot of the best and most famous westerns. One of Charlton Heston's higher-grade roles, and one of his better performances. Sprawling and overlong.

1958   163 minutes

BIG JAKE
★★★

DIRECTOR: George Sherman
CAST: John Wayne, Richard Boone, Maureen O'Hara, Patrick Wayne, Chris Mitchum, Bobby Vinton, Bruce Cabot

Big John Wayne takes up the trail of a gang of no-goods who kidnapped his grandson and shot up Maureen O'Hara's homestead and hired hands. Aided by second-generation movie "stars" Patrick Wayne and Chris Mitchum (Robert Mitchum's son), the Duke pursues Richard Boone and his henchmen to their hideout and deals harshly with them when they continue to exclaim, "I heard you were dead." Richard Boone gives the Duke a strong and believable foe, Bruce Cabot and the regular character actors carry their weight, and the outdoor locations are fine, but the too-clever, resourceful, and obnoxious younger leads leave a bit to be desired. In the grim tradition that started with Montgomery Clift in *Red River* and continued downhill with Ricky Nelson and Fabian in the 1950s, John Wayne is saddled with some current teen-age or pop music idol, in this case Bobby Vinton. One wishes there had been more scenes with Wayne and Maureen O'Hara together in this film, their last together.

1971   110 minutes

BIG SKY, THE
★★★
DIRECTOR: Howard Hawks
CAST: Kirk Douglas, Arthur Hunnicutt, Dewey Martin

Even the normally reliable director Howard Hawks can't save this dreary tale of early-day fur trappers on an expedition up the Missouri River. Action was Hawks's forte, and there just isn't enough to sustain the viewer's interest. Plenty of beautiful scenery, but that's about it.

1952   B & W 122 minutes

BIG SOMBRERO, THE
★★½
DIRECTOR: Frank McDonald
CAST: Gene Autry, Elena Verdugo, Stephen Dunne, George J. Lewis, Vera Marshe, William Edmunds, Martin Garralaga, Gene Roth, Bob Cason

An impoverished Gene Autry comes to the aid of Elena Verdugo and saves her from land swindlers as well as a money-grubbing fiancé in this south-of-the-border tale. Filmed in Cinecolor with a largely Mexican cast, this is more of a musical than a horse opera and takes full advantage of the color process to inflict one garish production number after another

on what must have been a grumbling adolescent audience in the late 1940s. This was Autry's second and last color film and earns the extra half star for that reason as well as for *not* forcing the paying customers to watch usual sidekick Smiley Burnette.

1949   77 minutes

BIG TRAIL, THE
★★★★
DIRECTOR: Raoul Walsh
CAST: John Wayne, Marguerite Churchill, El Brendel, Ian Keith, Tyrone Power Sr.

Big John Wayne made his film debut in this exciting, but slightly dated, epic western directed by Raoul Walsh (*The Roaring Twenties*, *White Heat*). Although the Duke acquits himself well enough as the revenge-minded scout for a wagon train, the film was not a success because it was released in the experimental 55 mm instead of the standard 35 mm. As a result, Wayne found himself grinding out B westerns for the next nine years—until John Ford picked him to play the Ringo Kid in *Stagecoach*.

1930   B & W 110 minutes

BILLY THE KID RETURNS
★★½
DIRECTOR: Joseph Kane
CAST: Roy Rogers, Smiley Burnette, Lynne Roberts, Morgan Wallace, Fred Kohler, Trigger

Groomed to take over as Gene Autry's replacement in Republic's singing cowboy series, Roy Rogers made such an impact in his first starring role *Under Western Skies* that the studio decided to continue him in a series of his own. In this, his second featured lead, Rogers plays a look-alike to the dead Billy the Kid and restores the tranquillity of Lincoln County after subduing the criminal element. This well-produced oater has more action than its Gene Autry counterparts, but is also weighted down by hambone Smiley Burnette, whom Republic executives felt would strengthen Rogers's fast-rising popularity. Not the best in the series but already way ahead of the Autry films of this period.

1938   B & W   58 minutes

BITE THE BULLET
★★★★½

DIRECTOR: Richard Brooks
CAST: Gene Hackman, James Coburn, Candice Bergen, Ben Johnson, Jan-Michael Vincent, Dabney Coleman, Ian Bannen

A six-hundred-mile horse race is the subject of this magnificent adventure, an epic in every sense of the word. Made during Gene Hackman's busiest—and best—period, this intriguing character study allows equal understanding of the many contestants. The photography, by Harry Stradling Jr., is nothing short of magnificent. Particularly spectacular is a seamless shot when one horse passes another: the faltering animal moves only in slow motion, but the approaching horse thunders up at regular speed . . . then passes in slow motion . . . then roars off at full speed. A real sleeper, hardly noticed during its theatrical release. Do not miss. Rated PG.

1975   131 minutes

BLOOD ON THE MOON
★★★½

DIRECTOR: Robert Wise
CAST: Robert Mitchum, Barbara Bel Geddes, Robert Preston

Robert Mitchum is in top form in this western concerning cattle ranchers trying to terminate homesteaders on rangeland. This dark and disturbing film has much to offer.

1948   B & W   88 minutes

BLOODY TRAIL
🐾

DIRECTOR: Richard Robinson
CAST: Paul Harper, Rance Howard, John Mitchum, Ricki Richardson, Hagen Smith, Eve York

One of the worst movies you are likely to ever see—if you dare. This western has no plot, just an ex–Union soldier wandering through the recently defeated South meeting up with angry African tribesmen(?), stubborn Confederates, and women who are ready to show off some skin. The fillmmakers must have been deaf; you can clearly hear a bulldozer in the background of one scene. Rated R for sex, nudity, profanity, and violence.

1972   91 minutes

BLUE CANADIAN ROCKIES
★½

DIRECTOR: George Archainbaud
CAST: Gene Autry, Pat Buttram, Gail Davis, Carolina Cotton, Ross Ford, Tom London, John Merton, Don Beddoe, Gene Roth, Cass County Boys, David Garcia

Processed stock footage of Canada forms the backdrop for this weak story about a young girl's strong-willed ambitions and her father's efforts to save her and her dreams from tragedy. Gene Autry and his pal Pat Buttram help both parties and expose the inevitable villains, as well as helping preserve a wild-game preserve. Spunky Gail Davis (TV's Annie Oakley) brightens this one up.

1952   B & W   58 minutes

BLUE STEEL

DIRECTOR: Robert N. Bradbury
CAST: John Wayne, Eleanor Hunt, George "Gabby" Hayes, Ed Peil, Yakima Canutt, George Cleveland

Fun but undistinguished B western with a very young John Wayne as a cowpoke who saves a town from extinction when he reveals a secret known only to an outlaw gang: there's gold in them thar hills. *The Searchers* this isn't.

1934   B & W   60 minutes

BOOTS AND SADDLES

★★

DIRECTOR: Joseph Kane
CAST: Gene Autry, Smiley Burnette, Ra Hould, Judith Allen, Guy Usher, John Ward, Gordon (William) Elliott, Chris-Pin Martin, Frankie Marvin, Bud Osborne

An English tenderfoot learns his lessons in the "code of the West" from no-nonsense Gene Autry and his not-so-subtle sidekick Smiley Burnette in this standard story of a foreigner who inherits a working ranch. No real suprises in this one, but a good cast of character actors (including the future "Wild Bill" Elliott) make this worth watching. Gene provides the tunes, and Smiley is responsible for the intentional humor in this film.

1937   B & W   59 minutes

BORDER PHANTOM

★★½

DIRECTOR: S. Roy Luby
CAST: Bob Steele, Harley Wood, Don Barclay, Karl Hackett, Miki Morita, Perry Murdock

Most film buffs will know Bob Steele for his memorable performances as the jealous husband in the original *Of Mice and Men* and as Canino, the brutal killer, in Howard Hawk's *The Big Sleep*. But "Battling Bob," as he was known to juvenile audiences of the 1930s and '40s, was most prolific as a fast-draw star of numerous B westerns. While Steele was never a star outside of the western series, he became a familiar face in A films of the 1950s and '60s with some of his better supporting bits in *Rio Bravo*, *The Comancheros*, *Shenandoah*, *Hang 'Em High*, and *Rio Lobo*. Although *Border Phantom*, like all B westerns, looks pretty creaky today, it's entertaining, thanks to Steele's energetic performance and an intriguing premise, which involves mysterious murders and slavery.

1937   B & W   59 minutes

BORROWED TROUBLE

★★

DIRECTOR: George Archainbaud
CAST: William Boyd, Andy Clyde, Rand Brooks, Elaine Riley, John Kellogg, Helen Chapman, John Parrish, Cliff Clark, Herbert Rawlinson, Don Haggerty

Hopalong Cassidy and his pals get bogged down in this comedy-drama about a town gone to seed and the outspoken (and obnoxious) school-teacher who wants to run the bad element out and restore her idea of a real community. Cutesy at times and light on the action, this one is perked up occasionally by the dialogue. At one point the man in black introduces himself to the schoolmarm with the line, "Hello, ma'am, my name is Hopalong Cassidy." To which she replies, "Well, you can always change you name!" The end of the trail was almost in sight; this was the sixty-fourth of sixty-six films starring William Boyd as Hopalong Cassidy. Hoppy is one of the very few popular heroes of books and films that has never been revived or resurrected. William Boyd is a very tough act to follow.

1948   B & W   58 minutes

BREAKHEART PASS
★★★

DIRECTOR: Tom Gries
CAST: Charles Bronson, Ben Johnson, Ed Lauter, Richard Crenna, Charles Durning, Jill Ireland

Charles Bronson is a government agent on the trail of gun runners in the Old West. Most of the action of this modest western takes place aboard a train, so the excited pitch needed to sustain viewers' interest is never reached. Rated PG—some violence, rough language.

1976   95 minutes

BRONCO BILLY
★★★

DIRECTOR: Clint Eastwood
CAST: Clint Eastwood, Sondra Locke, Geoffrey Lewis, Scatman Crothers, Sam Bottoms, Bill McKinney, Dan Vadis

This okay character study centers around Clint Eastwood as the owner of a run-down Wild West show. Bronco Billy is an anachronism, a throwback to the values of the Old West. The crew (well played by Scatman Crothers, Sam Bottoms, Bill McKinney, and Dan Vadis) is loyal even though payday rarely comes. In the story, Antoinette Lily (Sondra Locke) is deserted on her honeymoon by her husband (Geoffrey Lewis). Desperate, Lily agrees to join the show as Billy's assistant until they reach the next town and she can phone for help, and that's when the lightweight tale takes a romantic turn. Rated PG.

1980   119 minutes

BUCK AND THE PREACHER
★★½

DIRECTOR: Sidney Poitier
CAST: Sidney Poitier, Harry Belafonte, Ruby Dee, Cameron Mitchell

Harry Belafonte and director Sidney Poitier play two escaped slaves heading west. On the way, they meet up with "bad guy" Cameron Mitchell and lovely Ruby Dee. So-so western. Rated PG.

1972   102 minutes

BUCKSKIN FRONTIER
★★★

DIRECTOR: Lesley Selander
CAST: Richard Dix, Jane Wyatt, Lee J. Cobb, Albert Dekker, Joe Sawyer, Victor Jory, Lola Lane

Railroad representative Richard Dix and freight line owner Lee J. Cobb fight over business and a crucial mountain pass in this big-budget, fast-action western. As usual, veteran heavies Joe Sawyer and Victor Jory make trouble.

1943   B & W   82 minutes

BUFFALO BILL AND THE INDIANS
★★★

DIRECTOR: Robert Altman
CAST: Paul Newman, Joel Grey, Kevin McCarthy, Burt Lancaster

In this offbeat western, Paul Newman, Burt Lancaster, Harvey Keitel, Geraldine Chaplin, Joel Grey, Kevin McCarthy, and Will Sampson all are fascinating as they interact like jazz musicians jamming on the theme of distorted history and the delusion of celebrity. The last fifteen minutes seem almost unnecessary, and some of the points are hammered home with a twenty-pound sledge, but the overall effect of this American period piece is that of ambling virtuosity and group dedication to the theme. Rated PG.

1976   120 minutes

BULLWHIP

★★½

DIRECTOR: Harmon Jones
CAST: Rhonda Fleming, Guy Madison, James Griffith, Don Beddoe

In this agreeable movie, Guy Madison avoids the hangin' tree by agreeing to marry a fiery halfbreed (Rhonda Fleming). If the plot sounds familiar, it should. Jack Nicholson used a similar one in *Goin' South*.

1958   80 minutes

BUTCH CASSIDY AND THE SUNDANCE KID

★★★★½

DIRECTOR: George Roy Hill
CAST: Paul Newman, Robert Redford, Katharine Ross

George Roy Hill (*A Little Romance*; *The Sting*) directed this gentle western spoof starring Paul Newman, Robert Redford, and Katharine Ross. A spectacular box-office success, and deservedly so, the release deftly combines action with comedy. Rated PG.

1969   112 minutes

BUTCH AND SUNDANCE: THE EARLY DAYS

★★

DIRECTOR: Richard Lester
CAST: William Katt, Tom Berenger, Brian Dennehy, John Schuck, Jeff Corey

Director Richard Lester has made better films (see *A Hard Day's Night* and *Superman II*), and because his usual film is a comedy, this outing is especially disappointing. Nearly all of the jokes fall flat despite a screenplay that hints at the original film with Paul Newman and Robert Redford. There are some action scenes that could have fit in with the original, but for the most part *Butch and Sundance: the Early Days* is a pale companion to the classic that inspired it. Rated PG for some mildly crude language and (very little) violence.

1979   111 minutes

CAHILL—US MARSHAL

★★½

DIRECTOR: Andrew V. McLaglen
CAST: John Wayne, George Kennedy, Gary Grimes, Neville Brand

John Wayne was still making B westerns in the 1970s—to the disappointment of those who (rightly) expected better. Although still enjoyable, this film about a lawman (Wayne) whose son (Gary Grimes) becomes a bank robber is routine at best. Still, the performances by the Duke and George Kennedy (as the chief baddie) do bring pleasure. Rated PG.

1973   103 minutes

CALL OF THE CANYON

★★

DIRECTOR: Joseph Santley
CAST: Gene Autry, Smiley Burnette, the Sons of the Pioneers, Ruth Terry, Thurston Hall, Marc Lawrence, Joseph Strauch Jr., Eddy Waller, Budd Buster

Confusing story about meat swindling (meat swindling?) puts Gene and his Radio Ranch right in the middle of a cattle stampede and local beef thieves as the boys try to help songstress Ruth Terry put her act across the airwaves from Mr. Autry's personal frontier. The Sons of the Pioneers provide some of the sounds, and hammy Thurston Hal and menacing Marc Lawrence perk things up. Smiley Burnette's embarrassing attempts at humor are evident in this and most of Autry's films.

1942   B & W   71 minutes

CAPTAIN APACHE
★½

DIRECTOR: Alexander Singer
CAST: Lee Van Cleef, Stuart Whitman, Carroll Baker, Percy Herbert

Muddled western has Lee Van Cleef in title role gunning down dozens of one-dimensional characters who cross his path or appear likely to. Clichés and stock situations and characters inhabit this low-level entry. Violent, gruesome in spots. Rated PG for violence.

1971   94 minutes

CAT BALLOU
★★★

DIRECTOR: Elliot Silverstein
CAST: Jane Fonda, Lee Marvin, Michael Callan, Jay C. Flippen

In this offbeat, uneven but fun comedy/western, Jane Fonda plays Cat, a former schoolteacher out to avenge her father's death. Michael Callan is her main romantic interest. Lee Marvin outshines all with his Oscar-winning performance in the dual roles of the drunken hired gun and his evil look-alike.

1965   96 minutes

CATTLE QUEEN OF MONTANA
★★

DIRECTOR: Allan Dwan
CAST: Barbara Stanwyck, Ronald Reagan, Gene Evans, Jack Elam

Barbara Stanwyck gives a strong performance in this otherwise routine western. Plot revolves around Stanwyck trying to protect her farm from land grabbers, who also murdered her father. Meanwhile, the Indians are out to wipe out everybody. Ronald Reagan is typically lackluster. For Stanwyck fans only.

1954   88 minutes

CHEYENNE AUTUMN
★★★½

DIRECTOR: John Ford
CAST: Richard Widmark, Karl Malden, Carroll Baker, James Stewart, Edward G. Robinson, Ricardo Montalban

John Ford strays away from his traditional glorification of western mythology to bring this story of the mistreatment of the American Indian. His standard heroes, the U.S. cavalry, are placed in the role of the villains as they try to stop a group of desperate Cheyenne Indians from migrating back to their Wyoming homeland from a barren reservation in Oklahoma. The Indians take on heroic proportions as they face numerous obstacles to their exodus. This movie is uniformly well acted, and as with any John Ford western, the scenery is breathtaking.

1964   160 minutes

CHINO
★★

DIRECTOR: John Sturges
CAST: Charles Bronson, Jill Ireland, Vincent Van Patten

A surprisingly low-key Charles Bronson western about a horse breeder who attempts to live a peaceful life. The film was trimmed of much of its violence, and all that's left is an above-average performance by Bronson and an adequate one by his wife, Jill Ireland, as Chino's love interest. Rated PG.

1973   98 minutes

CHISUM
★★★½

DIRECTOR: Andrew V. McLaglen

CAST: John Wayne, Forrest Tucker, Christopher George, Ben Johnson, Patric Knowles, Bruce Cabot, Glenn Corbett, Geoffrey Duel

The best of the John Wayne westerns directed by Andrew V. McLaglen, this sprawling epic centers around the revenge sought by Billy the Kid (Geoffrey Duel) after his mentor (Patric Knowles) is murdered by the corrupt, land-grabbing bad guys. Forrest Tucker, Bruce Cabot, Ben Johnson, Christopher George, and Glenn Corbett are also seen in nice character bits. Everyone is in top form. Rated G.

1970   111 minutes

CIRCUS WORLD
★

DIRECTOR: Henry Hathaway

CAST: John Wayne, Rita Hayworth, Claudia Cardinale, John Smith, Lloyd Nolan, Richard Conte

Even the presence of John Wayne can't help this sappy soap opera set under the big top. It's a Cinerama extravaganza that does not survive the transfer to videotape (less than a third of the three-screen picture survived). But that's okay—the story is dreadful.

1964   135 minutes

COLORADO
★★

DIRECTOR: Joseph Kane

CAST: Roy Rogers, George "Gabby" Hayes, Pauline Moore, Milburn Stone, Hal Taliaferro, Maude Eberene, Vester Pegg, Fred Burns, Jay Novello

Roy Rogers and "Gabby" Hayes settle comfortably into what became a profitable and highly successful series in this routine shoot-'em-up about the two riders who aid the embattled homesteaders and clean up the territory for decent folk. Not too imaginative, but enjoyable. Lots of familiar faces from other Roy Rogers films in this one. Look for a young Milburn Stone, later to become a household name as Doc on television's *Gunsmoke*.

1940   B & W   54 minutes

COMANCHEROS, THE
★★★★

DIRECTOR: Michael Curtiz

CAST: John Wayne, Stuart Whitman, Lee Marvin, Ina Balin, Bruce Cabot, Nehemiah Persoff

Big John Wayne is the laconic Texas Ranger assigned to bring in dandy gambler Stuart Whitman for murder. Along the way, Wayne bests bad guy Lee Marvin, and Whitman proves himself a hero by helping the big guy take on the ruthless gun- and liquor-running villains of the title, led by Nehemiah Persoff. Director Michael Curtiz (*Casablanca*) died during production, and Wayne completed the film. It's a fine western with lots of nice moments.

1961   107 minutes

COMES A HORSEMAN
★★★★

DIRECTOR: Alan J. Pakula

CAST: Jane Fonda, James Caan, Jason Robards Jr., George Grizzard, Richard Farnsworth, Jim Davis

Dark, somber, but haunting western set in the 1940s about the efforts of a would-be land baron (Jason Robards Jr.) to cheat his long-suffering neighbor (Jane Fonda) out of her land. She fights back with the help of a World War II veteran (James Caan) and a crusty old-timer (Richard Farnsworth, in the role that netted him a best-supporting-actor Oscar nomination after thirty years as a bit player and stunt man in the movies). When Robards and Fonda are facing each other down, *Comes a Horseman* is more of a psychological western. However, Caan's two-fisted cowhand adds some terrific moments of action, and Farnsworth—in a sort of updated Gabby Hayes part—adds some wry humor and heart. Rated PG for violence.

1978   118 minutes

COW TOWN
★★½

DIRECTOR: John English
CAST: Gene Autry, Gail Davis, Harry Shannon, Jock Mahoney, Harry Harvey, Steve Darrell, Sandy Sanders, Ralph Sanford, Bud Osborne, Ted Mapes

Later Gene Autry film about rustlers and range wars lacks Smiley Burnette but boasts Jock Mahoney (future Range Rider and Tarzan) as well as TV's Annie Oakley, Gail Davis. Action and stunts as well as a good crew of familiar faces make this, Gene's seventy-second film as himself, better than many of his earlier efforts. Grazing rights, stampedes, gunplay, and a song or two (or three) are packed into the film.

1950   B & W   70 minutes

COWBOYS, THE
★★★★½

DIRECTOR: Mark Rydell

CAST: John Wayne, Roscoe Lee Browne, Bruce Dern, Colleen Dewhurst, Slim Pickens

Along with Don Siegel's *The Shootist*, this is the best of John Wayne's latter-day westerns. The Duke plays a rancher whose wranglers get gold fever. He's forced to recruit a bunch of green kids in order to take his cattle to market. Bruce Dern is on hand as Longhair, the outlaw leader who fights our hero in one of the genre's most memorable (and violent) scenes. After the sequence was shot, Wayne remarked to Dern that he was going to be hated for his on-screen actions. "Yeah," said Dern, "but they'll love me in Berkeley." A classic. Rated PG.

1972   128 minutes

CROSSFIRE
🦃

DIRECTORS: Robert Conrad, Alfredo Zacarias
CAST: Robert Conrad, Jan-Michael Vincent, Manuel Lopez Ochoa, Roy Jenson

Insufferable western about three outlaws who are saved from execution by a gang of Mexican freedom fighters. The fugitives end up banding together with the rebels to fight the Spanish in the Mexican Revolution. Robert Conrad puts in a good performance. But as a director, he's better off selling flashlight batteries.

1986   82 minutes

DAKOTA
★★½

DIRECTOR: Joseph Kane
CAST: John Wayne, Vera Hruba Ralston, Walter Brennan, Ward Bond

Any western with John Wayne, Walter Brennan, and Ward Bond has to be a winner, right? Wrong.

This substandard film may be interesting to see for their performances, but you also have to put up with the incredibly untalented Vera Ralston (she was the wife of Republic Studio head Herbert Yates). It's almost worth it.

1945   B & W   82 minutes

DAKOTA INCIDENT
★★½

DIRECTOR: Lewis R. Foster
CAST: Dale Robertson, Linda Darnell, John Lund

It's a fight to the finish in this fairly good western as the Indians attack a stagecoach rolling through Dakota Territory in those thrilling days of yesteryear.

1956   88 minutes

DANGEROUS VENTURE
★★½

DIRECTOR: George Archainbaud
CAST: William Boyd, Andy Clyde, Rand Brooks, Fritz Leiber, Douglas Evans, Harry Cording, Betty Alexander, Francis McDonald, Patricia Tate, Ken Tobey

This better-than-average Hopalong Cassidy adventure finds our heroes searching for Aztec ruins in the Southwest and encountering hostile renegades and unscrupulous fortune hunters. Character greats Fritz Leiber, Harry Cording, and Richard Alexander (all veterans of serials and horror films) contribute to the quality of this film, and future monster fighter Kenneth Tobey (The Thing) makes an early appearance, as well. This movie was originally released in a fifty-nine-minute version.

1947   B & W   55 minutes

DANIEL BOONE
★★★

DIRECTOR: David Howard

CAST: George O'Brien, Heather Angel, John Carradine, Ralph Forbes, Clarence Muse, Harry Cording

Action-packed story of the early American frontier features rugged outdoor star George O'Brien in the title role and evil John Carradine as a renegade who aids the marauding Indians, a role similar to the one he reprised for John Ford in Drums Along the Mohawk. Not as well-known as cotemporaneous frontier films like Last of the Mohicans, Allegheny Uprising, and Northwest Passage, this rousing film is great schoolboy adventure stuff. The movies mentioned here are a unique grouping of films about the history of America before the Revolutionary War, and between them have provided the bulk of the action footage used in subsequent movies with the same theme.

1936   B & W   77 minutes

DARK COMMAND
★★★★½

DIRECTOR: Raoul Walsh
CAST: John Wayne, Claire Trevor, Walter Pidgeon, Roy Rogers, Gabby Hayes

Raoul Walsh, who directed John Wayne's first big western, The Big Trail, was reunited with the star after the latter's triumph in Stagecoach for this dynamic shoot-'em-up. Walter Pidgeon is Quantrill, a once-honest man who goes renegade and forms Quantrill's Raiders. It's up to the Duke, with help from his Stagecoach co-star Claire Trevor, Roy Rogers, and Gabby Hayes, to set things right.

1940   B & W   94 minutes

DAWN ON THE GREAT DIVIDE
★★★

DIRECTOR: Howard Bretherton

CAST: Buck Jones, Raymond Hatton, Rex Bell, Mona Barrie, Harry Woods, Robert Frazer, Robert Lowery, Christine MacIntyre, Betty Blythe, Tristram Coffin, Jan Wiley, Dennis Moore, Roy Barcroft, Silver

When Tim McCoy bid his final "So Long, Rough Riders" in 1942's *West of the Law*, it brought an end to the famous series. However, producer Scott Dunlap still had Buck Jones and Raymond Hatton under contract, so he reteamed them with former B-western series star Rex Bell in *Dawn on the Great Divide* that same year. With a bigger budget than usual and a story with more plot twists than the average B western, the result was a good shoot-'em'-up in the series vein. Jones, of course, dominates as the two-fisted leader of a wagon train who takes on Indians, bad guys, and corrupt officials with equal aplomb. (Bell, unfortunately, is not so lucky. In fact, one suspects that he made enemies of the director and producer, who use takes that show him stumbling over lines and missing the holster with his gun.) Nevertheless, this is an enjoyable film and an important one historically. It was the last movie made by Jones, who died heroically trying to save lives during a fire at Boston's Coconut Grove on November 28, 1942.

1942   B & W   63 minutes

DAWN RIDER
★★

DIRECTOR: Robert N. Bradbury
CAST: John Wayne, Marion Burns, Yakima Canutt, Reed Howes, Denny Meadows, Bert Dillard

John Wayne is out for revenge in this formula B western with no budget to speak of. His loving father is killed during a robbery, and it's up to a gangly, slightly stilted Wayne to get the bad guys.

1935   B & W   56 minutes

DEAD DON'T DREAM, THE
★★

DIRECTOR: George Archainbaud
CAST: William Boyd, Andy Clyde, Rand Brooks, John Parrish, Leonard Penn, Mary Tucker, Francis McDonald, Richard Alexander, Stanley Andrews, Don Haggerty

Hopalong Cassidy's partner Lucky finally decides to tie the knot, but his wedding plans are dashed when his fiancée's father is murdered before the ceremony. When Hoppy tries to get to the bottom of this mystery, he comes under suspicion and has to clear his own name as well as uncover the killers. Skulking desperadoes and mysterious goings on in an old mine add to the tension in this later entry in the Hopalong Cassidy series. Originally released at sixty-two minutes.

1948   B & W   55 minutes

DEATH RIDES A HORSE

DIRECTOR: Giulio Petroni
CAST: Lee Van Cleef, John Phillip Law, Mario Brega, Anthony Dawson, Luigi Pistilli

Needlessly tedious "spaghetti" western about a young boy who witnesses the butchery of his family and then grows up to be John Phillip Law so he can take his revenge. He and Lee Van Cleef spend most of the film saving and running from each other, all in the interests of those ludicrous gunfighters' codes. Wonderful dialogue, all badly dubbed: "This certainly is a surprise," says one victim as Van Cleef shows up. "Was it a good surprise," says the other, "or a bad surprise?" The picture's length results from weighty exchanges like that, triple takes, and pauses so pregnant they could give birth. Even Ennio Morricone's score is below par. Rated PG for violence.

1969   114 minutes

DEERSLAYER, THE
★★★

DIRECTOR: Dick Friedenberg
CAST: Steve Forrest, Ned Romero, John Anderson, Joan Prather

Made-for-television version of James Fenimore Cooper classic of a white man, Hawkeye, raised by Indians. So-so.

1978   100 minutes

DESERT TRAIL
★★

DIRECTOR: Robert N. Bradbury
CAST: John Wayne, Mary Kornman, Paul Fix, Edward Chandler, Lafe McKee, Henry Hull, Al Ferguson

Rodeo fans might like this standard B western about a big-time bronc rider (John Wayne) who fights on the side of justice, but others may want to ride in the opposite direction.

1935   B & W   54 minutes

DESPERATE WOMEN
★

DIRECTOR: Earl Bellamy
CAST: Dan Haggerty, Susan Saint James, Ronee Blakley, Ann Dusenberry, Susan Myers, Randy Powell

Three convicted women crossing a desert on their way to prison meet up with an ol' softy (Dan Haggerty) who takes them under his wing after the convicts' guards die of water poisoning. The comedy in this film is too sickly sweet to laugh over—the singing narrator should be strung up—and the action isn't fast enough to engage the John Wayne in us all. This film has no MPAA rating, and the little violence displayed would hardly be shocking to youngsters. Not a rotten film, but you might forget you even saw it when you're rewinding the thing.

1978   98 minutes

DEVIL'S PLAYGROUND
★★

DIRECTOR: George Archainbaud
CAST: William Boyd, Andy Clyde, Rand Brooks, Elaine Riley, Robert Elliot, Joseph J. Greene, Francis McDonald, Ned Young, Earle Hodgins, John George

This so-so entry in the long-running Hopalong Cassidy series was the first Hoppy movie in two years and the first to be produced by star William Boyd for his own company. Basically a mystery with supernatural overtones, the plot concerns crooked politicians, rumors of gold, and a forbidding, rugged area that holds the secrets to strange goings on in the adjoining valley. Rand Brooks as Lucky Jenkins joins saddle pals Hoppy and California for the first time in this film. The three of them will make an even dozen films for release by United Artists before the series finally runs its course in 1948. Boyd bought all rights to the series (including television rights) from former producer Harry Sherman and author Clarence Mulford. He had to sell practically everything he had to continue in his starring role. With the advent of television, he was able to deal directly with the medium and become a wealthy man, while making Hopalong Cassidy a household word and a symbol of manliness and square dealing to a generation of young Americans.

1946   B & W   65 minutes

DODGE CITY
★★★★

DIRECTOR: Michael Curtiz
CAST: Errol Flynn, Olivia De Havilland, Ann Sheridan, Bruce Cabot, Alan Hale, Ward Bond

Swashbuckler Errol Flynn sets aside his sword for a pair of six-guns to clean up the wild, untamed frontier city of the title. The best of Flynn's westerns, this release is beautifully photographed in color with an all-star supporting cast.

1939   105 minutes

DOWN DAKOTA WAY
★★½

DIRECTOR: William Witney
CAST: Roy Rogers, Dale Evans, Pat Brady, Monte Montana, Elizabeth Risdon, Roy Barcroft, Trigger

Roy Rogers takes a harder line with the bad guys in this film, tracking down the no-goods responsible for the death of his friend, a veterinarian who could finger the man responsible for flooding the market with diseased meat. Director William Witney rises above the confines of the ordinary Roy Rogers singing western and almost elevates it to the status of the "adult" westerns gaining popularity at that time. Dale is as perky as ever, and Pat Brady is the comic relief, which every studio felt was essential for audience acceptance.

1949   67 minutes

DRAW
★★½

DIRECTOR: Steven Hillard Stern
CAST: James Coburn, Kirk Douglas

This western should have been cause for celebration among the starving fans of the genre; unfortunately, such is not the case. Kirk Douglas and James Coburn play outlaw and lawman respectively. Both appear on a collision course for a gunfight but, alas, what we are treated to is a trick ending. Lots of missed chances in this one. Made for HBO cable television.

1984   98 minutes

DRUM BEAT
★★½

DIRECTOR: Delmer Daves
CAST: Alan Ladd, Audrey Dalton, Marisa Pavan, Robert Keith, Anthony Caruso, Warner Anderson, Elisha Cook Jr., Charles Bronson, Richard Gaines

Indian fighter Alan Ladd is detailed to ensure peace with marauding Modocs on the California-Oregon border in 1869. His chief adversary, in beads and buckskins, is Charles Bronson. Modoc maiden Marisa Pavan loves the hero, but the code dictates he settle for Audrey Dalton. As usual, white man speaks with forked tongue, but everything ends well.

1954   111 minutes

DUCHESS AND THE DIRTWATER FOX, THE
★

DIRECTOR: Melvin Frank
CAST: George Segal, Goldie Hawn, Conrad Janis, Thayer David

This western/comedy romp never clicks. George Segal and Goldie Hawn labor so hard to get a laugh it's almost painful to watch. There isn't much of a story behind them, just a frontier hooker and a saddle tramp trying to make a buck in the

Old West. It gets tedious real fast. Rated PG.

1976 103 minutes

EL DORADO
★★★★

DIRECTOR: Howard Hawks
CAST: John Wayne, Robert Mitchum, James Caan, Michele Carey, Johnny Crawford, Edward Asner, Arthur Hunnicut, Jim Davis

This film has a great cast. It is a western with a smooth blend of comedy and action. Robert Mitchum even gets to play a good guy. He teams with John Wayne in a fascinating takeoff on the fondly remembered Howard Hawks classic *Rio Bravo*. As in *Rio Bravo*, a hard-drinking sheriff (Mitchum) must collect a motley crew of deputies (Wayne, James Caan, and Arthur Hunnicut) to fight off a gang of land-grabbing "baddies" (Edward Asner, Jim Davis, and friends). The plot's not that important, because the real joy of *El Dorado* comes from the interplay among all these talented screen personalities.

1967 126 minutes

ELFEGO BACA: SIX GUN LAW
★★½

DIRECTOR: Christian Nyby
CAST: Robert Loggia, James Dunn, Lynn Bari, James Drury, Jay C. Flippen, Kenneth Tobey, Annette Funicello, Patric Knowles, Audrey Dalton

Two-fisted lawyer Elfego Baca is charismatically portrayed by top actor Robert Loggia in this compilation of episodes from "Walt Disney Presents" originally aired from 1958 to 1962. Defending justice in Tombstone, Arizona, Elfego Baca fights for the lives of an Englishman framed for murder and

a rancher charged with bank robbery. Wiry Robert Loggia later achieved minor cult status with his television show "T.H.E. CAT" and has been seen more recently in popular and critical successes *Jagged Edge*, *An Officer and a Gentleman*, and *Prizzi's Honor*. Great cast of co-stars, including Kenneth Tobey, Jay C. Flippen, and James Drury, as well as Disney ingenue Annette Funicello, help this drama click. This episodic series was originally broadcast on a rotating basis with *Texas John Slaughter*, *Swamp Fox*, and *Zorro*, and was known as *The Nine Lives of Elfego Baca*.

1962 77 minutes

FALSE COLORS
★★½

DIRECTOR: George Archainbaud
CAST: William Boyd, Andy Clyde, Jimmy Rogers, Tom Seidel, Claudia Drake, Douglas Dumbrille, Robert Mitchum, Glenn Strange, Roy Barcroft, Tom London

Typical entry in the Hopalong Cassidy series places Hoppy on the side of the innocent people who are being terrorized and murdered by ace heavy Douglas Dumbrille, who wants their property and water rights. Supported by a fine cast of character actors, including a young Robert Mitchum and future Frankenstein Glenn Strange, this film introduced Jimmy Rogers (son of the great Will Rogers) as Hoppy's hot-tempered young sidekick. Rogers was to appear in six films with William Boyd and Andy Clyde before being replaced by Rand Brooks. Look for veteran western actors Roy Barcroft and Tom London in supporting roles.

1943 B & W 65 minutes

FALSE PARADISE
★★

DIRECTOR: George Archainbaud
CAST: William Boyd, Andy Clyde, Rand Brooks, Joel Friedkin, Elaine Riley, Kenneth Mac-Donald, Don Haggerty, Cliff Clark, Richard Alexander

Straight-shooting Hopalong Cassidy comes to the aid of a girl in peril and finds himself inveigled in yet another situation involving crooked ranch owners and false mining claims. Sometimes it's oil, sometimes it's gold, this time it's silver that drives the local riffraff into a frenzy and gives Hoppy, California, and Lucky a chance to do their good deed for the week. Second-to-last film in the long-running series and the last in which William Boyd wore his traditional black outfit.

1948   B & W   59 minutes

FIGHTING CARAVANS
★★★½

DIRECTORS: Otto Brower and David Burton
CAST: Gary Cooper, Lily Damita, Ernest Torrence, Eugene Pallette, Charles Winninger, Tully Marshall, Frank Campeau

Despite the title, this is a Zane Grey western—and a good one, full of intrigue, action, and, for leavening, a smattering of comedy. Lanky, taciturn Gary Cooper, wanted by the law, avoids arrest by conning a wagon train girl to pose as his wife. Romance blooms as the train treks west, into the sights of hostile Indians. Circle the wagons!

1931   B & W   80 minutes

FIGHTING KENTUCKIAN, THE
★★★

DIRECTOR: George Waggner

CAST: John Wayne, Vera Hruba Ralston, Philip Dorn, Oliver Hardy, Mark Windsor

Worth seeing if only for the rare and wonderful on-screen combination of John Wayne and Oliver Hardy, this period adventure casts the duo as frontiersmen who come to the aid of the homesteading Napoleonic French, in danger of being tricked out of their lands by the bad guys. If only Vera Hruba Ralston weren't the Duke's love interest, this could have been a real winner.

1949   B & W   100 minutes

FISTFUL OF DOLLARS, A
★★★

DIRECTOR: Sergio Leone
CAST: Clint Eastwood, Mario Brega, Gian Maria Volonté

Clint Eastwood parlayed his multi-year stint on television's "Rawhide" into international fame with this film, a slick remake of Akira Kurosawa's *Yojimbo*. *Fistful* started the genre of spaghetti westerns. What most people don't realize is that both films are adaptations of Dashiell Hammett's *Red Harvest*. As in the book and samurai film, Eastwood's laconic "man with no name" blows into a town nearly blown apart by two feuding families; after considerable manipulation by all concerned, he moves on down the road. Poor dubbing doesn't hurt much, since ol' Clint doesn't have that many lines. Superlative soundtrack by Ennio Morricone adds greatly to the story tension.

1964   96 minutes

FLAMING STAR
★★★★

DIRECTOR: Don Siegel

CAST: Elvis Presley, Barbara Eden, Steve Forrest, Dolores Del Rio, John McIntire

A solid western directed by Don Siegel (*Dirty Harry*), this features Elvis Presley in a remarkably effective performance as a half-breed Indian who must choose sides when his mother's people go on the warpath.

1960   101 minutes

FOR A FEW DOLLARS MORE
★★½
DIRECTOR: Sergio Leone
CAST: Clint Eastwood, Lee Van Cleef, Gian Maria Volonte, Klaus Kinski, Mario Brega, Jose Egger

Plot-heavy and overlong sequel to *A Fistful of Dollars* finds Clint Eastwood's "man with no name" partnered with shifty Lee Van Cleef, with both in pursuit of badder guy Gian Maria Volonte. Sergio Leone's quick-cut back-and-forth direction began to seem pretentious this time around (an approach that proved more successful in the next entry, *The Good the Bad and the Ugly*). Ennio Morricone's superb soundtrack is, if anything, better than ever. Eastwood has his hands full, but the story contains few surprises. Fans will enjoy this, but everybody else will find it tedious.

1965   130 minutes

FORT APACHE
★★★★½
DIRECTOR: John Ford
CAST: John Wayne, Henry Fonda, Shirley Temple, Ward Bond, John Agar, George O'Brien

The first entry in director John Ford's celebrated cavalry trilogy (which also includes *She Wore a Yellow Ribbon* and *Rio Grande*), this western stars Henry Fonda as a post commandant who decides to make a name for himself by starting a war with the Apaches, against the advice of an experienced soldier (John Wayne). Great film.

1948   B & W 127 minutes

FOUR RODE OUT

DIRECTOR: John Peyser
CAST: Pernell Roberts, Sue Lyon, Julian Mateos, Leslie Nielsen, Maria Martin, Leonard Bell

Pernell Roberts plays a U.S. marshall in pursuit of a mexican bank robber. Accompanied by the bandit's girlfriend and a slimy and unlikable Pinkerton agent (Leslie Nielsen), Roberts and company set out across the desert toward Mexico, perhaps never to return. This film is bad with a capital *B*. No one turns in an even half-way decent performance, and to make matters worse, we have to listen to Janis Ian singing horrible folk songs every fifteen minutes. You may want to ride out rather than watch this waste of film.

1968   90 minutes

FRISCO KID, THE
★★★
DIRECTOR: Robert Aldrich
CAST: Gene Wilder, Harrison Ford, William Smith, Raymond Bieri, Penny Peyser

Gene Wilder and Harrison Ford make a surprisingly effective and funny team as a rabbi and outlaw, respectively, making their way to San Francisco. Originally started by director Dick Richards (*The Culpepper Cattle Company*), this release was completed by Robert Aldrich and features fine support by William Smith and Ramon Bieri

as a couple of nasty outlaws. Good
fun. Rated PG.

1979   122 minutes

FRONTIER PONY EXPRESS
★★½

DIRECTOR: Joseph Kane

CAST: Roy Rogers, Mary Hart (Lynne
Roberts), Raymond Hatton,
Edward Keane, Monte Blue,
Noble Johnson, George Letz
(Montgomery), Charles King,
Bud Osborne, Fred Burns, Er-
nie Adams, Jack O'Shea, Jack
Kirk

Good action-packed western finds
Roy Rogers (in one of his early
starring roles) coming to the aid of
Pony Express riders who have
been preyed on by robbers. Grizzled Raymond Hatton plays the
ornery old varmint, and former and
future cowboy stars Monte Blue,
Charles King, and George Montgomery (one of the rangers in the
original Lone Ranger serial) help
raise the dust and trample the cactus. The great black character actor Noble Johnson (*King Kong*,
The Most Dangerous Game, *Moby
Dick*) plays another of his numerous ethnic roles in this film as an
Indian, a role he played in serials
as well as John Ford classics.

1939   B & W   54 minutes

GENTLE SAVAGE
★★★½

DIRECTOR: Sean MacGregor

CAST: William Smith, Gene Evans,
Barbara Luna, Joe Flynn

In well-paced western, William
Smith portrays an American Indian framed for the rape and beating of a white girl in a small town.
The girl's stepfather, who actually
committed the crime, incites the
townsmen to go after the innocent
man. When the townsmen kill the
hapless fellow's brother, the

American Indian community re-
taliates. Rated R for violence.

1978   85 minutes

GIT ALONG, LITTLE DOGIES
★★

DIRECTOR: Joseph Kane

CAST: Gene Autry, Smiley Burnette,
Judith Allen, Weldon Hey-
burn, William Farnum, Wil-
lie Fung, Carleton Young,
Will Ahearn, Gladys Ahearn,
Frankie Marvin, Maple City
Four, The Cabin Kids, Lynton
Brent, Monte Montague

Typical of Gene Autry's prewar
films, this thin story of a spoiled,
willful girl who is eventually tamed
and socialized by the silver-voiced
cowboy is heavy on the music and
singing stars. It also has some of
the familiar faces that popped up
in films from all different studios
during the 1930s. Look for silent
film star William Farnum and rodeo rider Monte Montague in supporting roles.

1937   B & W   60 minutes

GOIN' SOUTH
★★★

DIRECTOR: Jack Nicholson

CAST: Jack Nicholson, Mary Steenburgen, John Belushi

Star Jack Nicholson also directed
this odd little western tale of an
outlaw (Nicholson) saved from the
gallows by a spinster (Mary Steenburgen). The catch is he must
marry her and work on her farm.
Lots of attempts at comedy, but
only a few work. Look for John
Belushi in a small role as a Mexican cowboy. Rated PG; some violence and language.

1978   109 minutes

GOLDEN STALLION, THE
★★½

DIRECTOR: William Witney

CAST: Roy Rogers, Dale Evans, Estelita Rodriguez, Pat Brady, Douglas Evans, Frank Fenton, Trigger, Trigger Jr.

This offbeat entry to the Roy Rogers series places the emphasis on Trigger and his efforts to save a cute Palomino mare from a life of crime. It seems this poor horse is innocently involved in diamond smuggling and is protected by Trigger, who kills one of the villains who has been mistreating her. Our human hero Roy takes the blame for the killing, but he in turn is aided by Trigger Jr., making it a family affair. Absolute hooey but fun to watch, and exciting for the kids and animal lovers in the audience.

1949   67 minutes

GOOD THE BAD AND THE UGLY, THE
★★★★

DIRECTOR: Sergio Leone
CAST: Clint Eastwood, Eli Wallach, Lee Van Cleef

The best of Italian director Sergio Leone's spaghetti westerns with Clint Eastwood, this release features the latter in the dubiously "good" role, with Lee Van Cleef as "the bad" and Eli Wallach as "the ugly." All three are after a cache of gold hidden in a Confederate army camp. For Leone fans, it's full of what made his movies so memorable. Others might find it a bit long, but no one can deny its sense of style.

1966   161 minutes

GRAND CANYON TRAIL
★★

DIRECTOR: William Witney
CAST: Roy Rogers, Jane Frazee, Andy Devine, Robert Livingston, Roy Barcroft, Charles Coleman, Trigger

Roy Rogers is saddled with what he thinks is a useless mine, and former serial hero Robert Livingston just about succeeds in swindling him out of what is actually a bonanza in silver. Fast-paced and almost tongue-in-cheek, this enjoyable entry benefits from a solid cast, including wheezing Andy Devine and perennial favorite Roy Barcroft. The Sons of the Pioneers are replaced by the Riders of the Purple Sage in the vocals department for this one.

1948   B & W   67 minutes

GREAT SCOUT AND CATHOUSE THURSDAY, THE
★★★

DIRECTOR: Don Taylor
CAST: Lee Marvin, Oliver Reed, Elizabeth Ashley, Robert Culp, Strother Martin, Kay Lenz

Eccentric western comedy involving a variety of get-rich-quick schemes concocted by an amusing band of rogues. Oliver Reed steals the show as a wacky American Indian whose double-crosses usually backfire. Not much plot and considerable silliness, but fun nonetheless. Rated PG for sexual situations.

1976   102 minutes

GREY FOX, THE
★★★★★

DIRECTOR: Phillip Borsos
CAST: Richard Farnsworth, Jackie Burroughs, Wayne Robson, Ken Pogue, Timothy Webber

Richard Farnsworth (*Comes a Horseman*) stars in this marvelously entertaining Canadian feature as the gentleman bandit Bill Miner who, as the movie poster proclaimed, "on June 17, 1901, after thirty-three years in San Quentin Prison for robbing stagecoaches, was released into the twentieth century." As directed by Phillip Borsos, it is highly reminiscent of the great westerns of John Ford. In other words, it's first-rate in every sense—a classic. Rated PG for brief violence.

1982   92 minutes

GUNFIGHT AT THE O.K. CORRAL
★★★★

DIRECTOR: John Sturges
CAST: Burt Lancaster, Kirk Douglas, Rhonda Fleming, Jo Van Fleet, John Ireland, Lee Van Cleef, Frank Faylen

The Wyatt Earp–Doc Holliday legend got another going-over in this rather good western. Burt Lancaster and Kirk Douglas portray these larger-than-life gunfighters, who shoot it out with the nefarious Clanton family in 1881 Tombstone. The movie effectively builds up its tension until the climactic gunfight.

1957   122 minutes

GUNMAN FROM BODIE
★★★½

DIRECTOR: Spencer G. Bennett
CAST: Buck Jones, Tim McCoy, Raymond Hatton, Christine MacIntyre, Dave O'Brien, Frank LaRue, Wilbur Mack, John Merton, Charles King, Silver

The best of the many trio series westerns of the 1930s and '40s, "The Rough Riders" teamed two of the genre's most charismatic stars, Buck Jones and Tim McCoy, with one of the best sidekicks in the business, Raymond Hatton. Jones and McCoy had each made a number of notable westerns since debuting in the 1920s—both having done their best work at Columbia in the 1930s—before joining forces for the first Rough Riders

film, *Arizona Bound*, in 1941. The second film in the series, *Gunman from Bodie*, is considered by most aficionados to be the best, and we agree. The plot, about a trio of marshals who set out to capture a gang of cattle thieves, may be old and worn-out, but the sheer star power and personality of Jones, McCoy, and Hatton make this formula B western a first-rate example of its kind.

1941   B & W   60 minutes

HANG 'EM HIGH
★★★

DIRECTOR: Ted Post
CAST: Clint Eastwood, Inger Stevens, Ed Begley Sr., Pat Hingle, Arlene Golonka, Ben Johnson

Clint Eastwood's first stateside spaghetti western is a good one, with the star out to get the vigilantes who tried to hang him for a murder he didn't commit. Pat Hingle is the hangin' judge who gives Clint his license to hunt, and Ben Johnson is the marshal who saves his life. Ed Begley Sr. is memorable as the leader of the vigilantes. Rated PG.

1968   114 minutes

HARLEM RIDES THE RANGE
★★½

DIRECTOR: Richard Kahn
CAST: Herbert Jeffrey (Jeffries), Lucius Brooks, Artie Young, F. E. Miller, Spencer Williams, Clarence Brooks

Uninspired oater is one of a handful of westerns made by black producers and directors for a black audience spread throughout the United States in the late 1930s and early 1940s. Not too different from its white counterparts, this low-budget horse opera from Hollywood Pictures has its own hero, evil heavy, saloon action, show-down, and inane comedy relief. Stale plot about stolen mine rights (to a radium mine this time) is secondary to the limited action and uniqueness of seeing an all-black cast in what has traditionally been the territory of white actors and actresses. Nothing special but worth a look. Spencer Williams of television's "Amos and Andy" show co-wrote the script for this film and plays a featured role.

1939   B & W   58 minutes

HARRY TRACY
★★★½

DIRECTOR: William A. Graham

CAST: Bruce Dern, Helen Shaver, Michael C. Gwynne, Gordon Lightfoot

Bruce Dern plays the title role in this surprisingly amiable little western, with the star as the last of a gentlemanly outlaw breed. Although he's a crafty character, Harry always seems to get caught. His mind is all too often on other things—in particular, a well-to-do woman (Helen Shaver, the chief engineer who seduces Dudley Moore in *Best Defense*). Dern gives his most likable portrayal in this Canadian-made film, and those who love shoot-'em-ups will find it to be an enjoyable time-passer. Rated PG.

1982   100 minutes

HATFIELDS AND THE MCCOYS, THE
★★½

DIRECTOR: Clyde Ware

CAST: Jack Palance, Steve Forrest, Richard Hatch, Joan Caulfield

The great American legend of backwoods feuding long celebrated in song and story. Jack Palance and Steve Forrest make the most of portraying the clan patriarchs. The feud was reason enough to leave the hills and head west in the 1880s. A guy could get killed for saying hello to the wrong face!

1975   74 minutes

HEART OF THE GOLDEN WEST
★★½

DIRECTOR: Joseph Kane

CAST: Roy Rogers, Smiley Burnette, George "Gabby" Hayes, Ruth Terry, Bob Nolan and the Sons of the Pioneers, Trigger

This modern-day adventure pits Roy Rogers and his fellow ranchers against cheating city slickers intent on defrauding the cowboys and putting them out of business. This film is a throwback to the earlier Gene Autry films in that the musical production numbers take precedence over the action; the increased budget granted this horse opera is evident in the singing segments rather than in more elaborate stunts and chases. Roy gets Smiley Burnett *and* Gabby Hayes in this one, and he's hard-pressed to make an impression when wedged between these two scene-stealers. Enjoyable western hokum.

1942   B & W   65 minutes

HEART OF THE RIO GRANDE
★★

DIRECTOR: William Morgan

CAST: Gene Autry, Smiley Burnette, Fay McKenzie, Edith Fellows, Pierre Watkins, Jimmy Wakely Trio, Gloria Gardner, Gladis Gardner, Budd Buster, Frankie Marvin

Gene Autry and the gang sing some sense into a snooty, spoiled rich girl and manage to bring her and her too busy father back together again. Standard story is given standard, simple-minded treatment, but it's the extras (like the Jimmy Wakely Trio) and the character parts that make this sort of programmer fun. After four more films like this, Gene would heed his country's call and join the air force, leaving the prairie wide open for Roy Rogers.

1942   B & W   70 minutes

HEARTLAND
★★★★

DIRECTOR: Richard Pearce
CAST: Conchata Ferrell, Rip Torn, Lilia Skala, Megan Folsom

This excellent and deceptively simple story, of a widow (Conchata Ferrell) who settled, with her daughter and a homesteader (Rip Torn), in turn-of-the-century Wyoming, deals with the complex problems of surviving in nature and society. It's well worth watching. Rated PG.

1979   96 minutes

HEAVEN'S GATE
★★★

DIRECTOR: Michael Cimino
CAST: Kris Kristofferson, John Hurt, Sam Waterston, Brad Dourif, Jeff Bridges, Joseph Cotten

Written and directed by Michael Cimino (*The Deer Hunter*), this $36 million epic western about the land wars in Wyoming, between the cattle barons and immigrant farmers, is awkward and overlong but at least makes sense in the complete video version. The beautiful cinematography and painstaking period recreation add much to its high quality. Too bad it's not the great film it should have been. Rated R for nudity, sex, and violence.

1980   219 minutes

HELLER IN PINK TIGHTS
★★½

DIRECTOR: George Cukor
CAST: Sophia Loren, Anthony Quinn, Margaret O'Brien, Edmund Lowe, Steve Forrest, Eileen Heckart, Ramon Navarro

The career of legendary nineteenth-century actress and love goddess Adah Issacs Menken inspired this odd film about a ragtag theatrical troupe wandering the West in the 1880s. Colorful but airfilled, it offers a busty blonde Sophia Loren with lusty Tony Quinn fending off belligerent townfolk, creditors, distrustful sheriffs, and ever-essential Indians while serving up a hash of gunslinging, backstage humor, burlesque, and rewritten dramatic history. Western novelist Louis L'Amour is blamed for the story.

1960   100 minutes

HELLFIRE
★★★½

DIRECTOR: R. G. Springsteen
CAST: William Elliott, Marie Windsor, Forrest Tucker, Jim Davis, Grant Withers, Paul Fix, Denver Pyle

Solid, offbeat western in which a ne'er-do-well gambler, William ("Wild Bill") Elliott, is shoved onto the path of righteousness when a preacher saves his life. Our hero, fast with his fists and his six-guns, devotes himself to the "peaceful" pursuit of raising funds to build a church, his rescuer's dying wish. To do so, he decides to talk a lady outlaw (Marie Windsor) into turning herself in so he can collect the reward money. Meanwhile, a lawman (Forrest Tucker) and a gang of cutthroats (led by Jim Davis) are on their trail. A bit preachy at times, *Hellfire* still packs a solid wallop of entertainment. Western buffs have favorably compared it with William S. Hart's classic silent shoot-'em-ups. It may not be a classic, but it is good fun.

1949   79 minutes

HIGH NOON
★★★★★

DIRECTOR: Fred Zinnemann
CAST: Gary Cooper, Grace Kelly, Lloyd Bridges, Thomas Mitchell, Katy Jurado, Otto Kruger, Lon Chaney

Gary Cooper won his second Oscar for his role of the abandoned lawman in this classic western. It's the sheriff's wedding day, and the head of an outlaw band, who has sworn vengeance against him, is due to arrive in town at high noon. When Cooper turns to his fellow townspeople for help, no one comes forward. The suspense of this movie keeps snowballing as the clock ticks ever closer to noon.

1952   B & W   85 minutes

HIGH NOON, PART TWO
🐓

DIRECTOR: Jerry Jameson
CAST: Lee Majors, David Carradine, J. A. Preston, Pernell Roberts, M. Emmet Walsh, Katherine Cannon, Michael Pataki

This is a poor attempt at a sequel. It begins in much the same way as the original, with a man standing against impossible odds. The difference is the actors and the director. Lee Majors is not believable as the hero, a strong man with a very human fear. The film also lacks the suspense of the original. Add to this a weak script, and you have a very forgettable film—despite an impressive supporting cast.

1980   100 minutes

HIGH PLAINS DRIFTER
★★★

DIRECTOR: Clint Eastwood
CAST: Clint Eastwood, Verna Bloom, Marianna Hill, Mitchell Ryan, Jack Ging, Geoffrey Lewis, Anthony James

Star-director Clint Eastwood tried to revive the soggy spaghetti-western genre one last time, with watchable results. The tale is almost horrific as Eastwood comes to a frontier town just in time to make sure its sleazy citizens are all but wiped out by a trio of revenge-seeking outlaws. Although atmospheric, it's also confusing and sometimes just downright nasty. Not great, but not bad either. Rated R for violence, profanity, and suggested sex.

1973   105 minutes

HILLS OF UTAH, THE
★★½

DIRECTOR: John English
CAST: Gene Autry, Pat Buttram, Elaine Riley, Onslow Stevens, Donna Martell, Harry Lauter, Tom London, Kenne Duncan, Denver Pyle, William Fawcett, Sandy Sanders, Teddy Infuhr, Lee Morgan, Billy Griffith, Tommy Ivo

Harking back to a classic theme, Gene returns to the town where his father was killed and manages to settle a local feud as well as uncover the truth about his father's murder. Even with Pat Buttram, this is somber for a Gene Autry film. Great character actors and second leads Tom London, Harry Lauter, and Denver Pyle enchance this film.

1951   B & W   70 minutes

HIS NAME WAS KING
★½

DIRECTOR: Don Reynolds

CAST: Richard Harrison, Klaus Kinski, Anne Pushin, John Silver, Lorenzo Finschi, Lucio Zarini

Spaghetti western about a bounty hunter named King (Richard Harrison) who tracks down a ring of gunrunners near the Mexican border. Plenty of action, but like most westerns from Italy, the bad guys are so bad that their psychotic behavior, coupled with stupid voice dubbing, comes off too close to comedy to be taken seriously. Klaus Kinski (*Fitzcarraldo*) plays a lawman and friend of King. Not rated, but equal to a PG for violence, sex, and profanity.

1983   90 minutes

HOMBRE
★★★★

DIRECTOR: Martin Ritt
CAST: Paul Newman, Fredric March, Richard Boone, Diane Cilento, Cameron Mitchell, Barbara Rush, Martin Balsam

Paul Newman gives a superb performance as a white man raised by Indians who is enticed into helping a stagecoach full of settlers make its way across treacherous country. Richard Boone is the baddie who makes this chore difficult, but the racism Newman encounters in this Martin Ritt film provides the real—and thought-provoking—thrust.

1967   111 minutes

HOPPY'S HOLIDAY
★★

DIRECTOR: George Archainbaud
CAST: William Boyd, Andy Clyde, Rand Brooks, Andrew Tombes, Jeff Corey, Mary Ware, Leonard Penn, Donald Kirke, Hollis Bane, Gil Patric, Frank Henry

A weak entry in the last of twelve Hopalong Cassidy films produced by William Boyd after he had purchased the rights to the character from former producer Harry "Pop" Sherman, this movie pits Hoppy and the Bar-20 cowboys against mechanized bank robbers. Programmers in the true sense of the term, these films did little more than keep Hopalong Cassidy's image alive and in front of America's children on Saturday afternoons. It worked out well because Boyd was able to insinuate himself into a wider audience than ever dreamed possible through the magic medium of early television.

1947   B & W   60 minutes

HORSE SOLDIERS, THE
★★★★

DIRECTOR: John Ford
CAST: John Wayne, William Holden, Constance Towers, Hoot Gibson

Based on a true incident during the Civil War, this is a minor, but enjoyable, John Ford cavalry outing. John Wayne and William Holden play well-matched adversaries in the Union Army.

1959   119 minutes

HOW THE WEST WAS WON
★★★½

DIRECTORS: John Ford, Henry Hathaway, George Marshall
CAST: Gregory Peck, Henry Fonda, James Stewart, John Wayne, Debbie Reynolds, Walter Brennan, Karl Malden, Richard Widmark, Robert Preston, George Peppard,

Any western that stars John Wayne, James Stewart, Henry Fonda, Gregory Peck, Walter Brennan, Richard Widmark, and Robert Preston is at least worth a glimpse. Sadly, this 1962 epic doesn't hold up that well on video because it was released on the three-screen Cinerama process. Much of the grandeur of the original version is lost. But shoot-'em-up fans won't want to miss a chance to see many of the genre's greats in one motion picture.

1962   155 minutes

IN OLD CALIFORNIA
★★★

DIRECTOR: William McGann

CAST: John Wayne, Helen Parrish, Patsy Kelly

John Wayne plays a mild-mannered dentist in the Old West. Good viewing for fans.

1942   B & W 88 minutes

INVITATION TO A GUNFIGHTER
★★

DIRECTOR: Richard Wilson

CAST: Yul Brynner, George Segal, Janice Rule, Pat Hingle

Studio-slick western is short on action and long on dialogue as a hired professional killer comes to town and changes the balance of power. Everybody gets a chance to emote in this gabfest—which helps, since the story is so slim. Typical of a Stanley Kramer message film but not quite as heavy-handed as most.

1964   92 minutes

JEREMIAH JOHNSON
★★★★

DIRECTOR: Sydney Pollack

CAST: Robert Redford, Will Geer, Charles Tyner

Robert Redford plays Johnson, a simple man who has no taste for cities. We see him as he grows from his first feeble attempts at survival to a hunter who has quickened his senses with wild meat and vegetation—a man who is a part of the wildlife of the mountains. *Jeremiah Johnson* gives a sense of humanness to a genre that had, up until its release, spent most of its history reworking the same myths. Here's an exciting new myth, and a slice of life to boot! Rated PG.

1972   107 minutes

JESSE JAMES
★★★½

DIRECTOR: Henry King

CAST: Tyrone Power, Henry Fonda, Nancy Kelly, Randolph Scott, Henry Hull, Jane Darwell, Brian Donlevy, Donald Meek, John Carradine, Slim Summerville, J. Edward Bromberg

Tyrone Power is Jesse and Henry Fonda is Frank in this legend-gilting account of the life and misdeeds of Missouri's most famous outlaw. Bending history, the film paints Jesse as a peaceful man driven to a life of crime by heartless big business in the form of a railroad, and a loving husband and father murdered for profit by a coward. Audiences ate it all up, and still do.

1939   105 minutes

JESSE JAMES AT BAY
★★½

DIRECTOR: Joseph Kane

CAST: Roy Rogers, George "Gabby" Hayes, Sally Payne, Pierre Watkin, Gale Storm, Roy Barcroft, Trigger

History-twistin' Republic Studios casts box-office smash Roy Rogers as a fictionalized Jesse James who rides not against the railroads, but against one evil bunch misrepresenting the railroad and stealing the land of poor, honest farmers. Just as entertaining as any of Rogers's pre-WWII films, but a top contender for *the* most far-fetched, fallacious frontier foolishness ever filmed. Hokum of the highest order, but fun to watch and full of familiar faces, including a perky young Gale Storm and the prolific Roy Barcroft.

1941   B & W   56 minutes

JOE KIDD
★★★½

DIRECTOR: John Sturges
CAST: Clint Eastwood, Robert Duvall, John Saxon, Don Stroud

While not exactly a thrill-a-minute movie, this western, has a number of memorable moments. Director John Sturges (*The Magnificent Seven*) has been better, but Clint Eastwood and Robert Duvall are at the peak of their respective forms in this story of a gunman (Eastwood) hired by a cattle baron (Duvall) to track down some Mexican-Americans who are fighting back because they've been cheated out of their land. Rated PG.

1972   88 minutes

JOHNNY GUITAR
★★★½

DIRECTOR: Nicholas Ray
CAST: Joan Crawford, Mercedes McCambridge, Sterling Hayden, Scott Brady, Ward Bond, Ernest Borgnine, John Carradine

A positively weird western, this Nicholas Ray film features the ultimate role reversal. Bar owner Joan Crawford and landowner Mercedes McCambridge shoot it out while their gun-toting boyfriends (Sterling Hayden and Scott Brady) look on.

1954   110 minutes

JUNIOR BONNER
★★★

DIRECTOR: Sam Peckinpah
CAST: Steve McQueen, Robert Preston, Ida Lupino, Joe Don Baker

A rodeo "has-been," Steve McQueen, returns home for one last rousing performance in front of the home folks. McQueen is quite good as the soft-spoken cowboy who tries to make peace with his family. Robert Preston is a real scene-stealer as his hard-drinking carouser of a father. Rated PG.

1972   103 minutes

KANSAN, THE
★★½

DIRECTOR: George Archainbaud
CAST: Richard Dix, Jane Wyatt, Victor Jory, Albert Dekker, Eugene Pallette, Robert Armstrong

Tough, two-fisted Richard Dix sets his jaw and routs the baddies in a wide-open prairie town but must then contend with a corrupt official in this routine western, the third to pair him with Jane Wyatt and heavies Victor Jory and Albert Dekker.

1943   B & W   79 minutes

KANSAS PACIFIC
★★½

DIRECTOR: Ray Nazarro
CAST: Sterling Hayden, Eve Miller, Barton MacLane, Douglas Fowley, Myron Healey, Clayton Moore, Reed Hadley

Railroad drama set in pre–Civil War days has rangy Sterling Hayden romancing Eve Miller and battling pro-Confederate saboteurs intent on hindering construction of the Kansas Pacific Railroad. Decent actioner features top heavy Barton Maclane, versatile Myron Healey, and moonlighting Lone Ranger, Clayton Moore.

1953   73 minutes

KENTUCKIAN, THE
★★★

DIRECTOR: Burt Lancaster

CAST: Burt Lancaster, Diana Lynn, Dianne Foster, Walter Matthau, John Carradine, Una Merkel

Pushing west in the 1820s, Burt Lancaster bucks all odds to reach Texas and begin a new life. A good mix of history, adventure, romance, and comedy make this one worth a family watching.

1955   104 minutes

KIT CARSON
★★★½

DIRECTOR: George B. Seitz
CAST: Jon Hall, Dana Andrews, Lynn Bari

This lively western about the two-fisted frontiersman gave Jon Hall one of his best roles. Good action scenes.

1940   B & W   97 minutes

LADY FROM LOUISIANA
★★

DIRECTOR: Bernard Vorhaus
CAST: John Wayne, Ray Middleton, Osa Massen

John Wayne is a crusading lawyer in this middling Republic period piece.

1941   B & W   82 minutes

LAST COMMAND, THE
★★★

DIRECTOR: Frank Lloyd
CAST: Sterling Hayden, Richard Carlson, Anna Maria Alberghetti, Ernest Borgnine, Arthur Hunnicutt, Jim Davis, J. Carrol Naish

This is a watchable western about the famed last stand at the Alamo during Texas's fight for independence from Mexico. Jim Bowie (Sterling Hayden), Davy Crockett (Arthur Hunnicutt), and Colonel Travis (Richard Carlson) are portrayed in a more realistic manner than they were in John Wayne's The Alamo, but the story is still mostly hokum. There are some exciting battle scenes and solid direction. This film is not rated, but note that it contains some violent scenes.

1955   110 minutes

LAST OF THE MOHICANS, THE
★★★★

DIRECTOR: George B. Seitz
CAST: Randolph Scott, Binnie Barnes, Heather Angel, Robert Barrat, Philip Reed, Henry Wilcoxon, Bruce Cabot

Blood, thunder, and interracial romance during the French and Indian War are brought to life from James Fenimore Cooper's novel. Randolph Scott is the intrepid Hawkeye; Robert Barrat is the noble Chingachgook; Binnie Barnes is Alice Monroe. The star-crossed lovers are Philip Reed, as Uncas, the title character, and Heather Angel, as Cora Monroe. Bruce Cabot plays the villainous Magua.

1936   B & W   100 minutes

LAST OF THE PONY RIDERS
★½

DIRECTOR: George Archainbaud
CAST: Gene Autry, Smiley Burnette, Buzz Henry, Harry Hines, Johnny Downs, Dick Jones, Gregg Barton, Arthur Space, Howard Wright, Harry Mackin

Gene Autry's last feature film is a limp addition to a genre—the series western—on its last legs. Reunited with his old sidekick Smiley Burnette for his last six films, Autry ended his nineteen-year film career with this lackluster mediocrity, his ninety-third film. Director George Archainbaud helmed Autry's last twelve movies; he's also the man who led the Hopalong Cassidy series off to pasture in 1948 after twelve films with William Boyd. Autry was to live the insulated life of a millionaire while his ex-partner Smiley Burnette continued to make personal appearances at shopping centers.

1953   B & W   80 minutes

LAST RIDE OF THE DALTON BOYS, THE
★★½

DIRECTOR: Dan Curtis
CAST: Jack Palance, Larry Wilcox, Dale Robertson, Bo Hopkins, Cliff Potts

When two former Dalton Gang train robbers are reunited in Hollywood in 1934, they relive the early days of the Dalton Gang as they share a bottle of whiskey. This western plays up the Daltons' poverty while steering clear of any bloodthirsty image of the boys. It is Jack Palance, as the detective hired by the railroad company, who comes out looking like the villain. Rated PG for violence.

1979   146 minutes

LAWLESS FRONTIER
★★½

DIRECTOR: Robert N. Bradbury
CAST: John Wayne, Sheila Terry, George "Gabby" Hayes, Earl Dwire, Yakima Canutt, Jack Rockwell

A Mexican bandit (Earl Dwire) manages to evade the blame for a series of crimes he's committed because the sheriff is sure that John Wayne is the culprit. The Duke, of course, traps the bad guy and clears his good name in this predictable B western notable for an early appearance of Gabby Hayes as the sidekick character he was to play in hundreds of subsequent shoot-'em-ups.

1935   B & W   59 minutes

LAWLESS RANGE
★★

DIRECTOR: Robert N. Bradbury
CAST: John Wayne, Sheila Manners, Earl Dwire, Frank McGlynn Jr., Jack Curtis, Yakima Canutt

In this low, low budget early John Wayne western, a banker attempts to drive out the local ranchers and get his hands on some rich gold mines. Wayne, sent by the governor, soon sets things aright.

1935   B & W   59 minutes

LAWMAN IS BORN, A
★★½

DIRECTOR: Sam Newfield
CAST: Johnny Mack Brown, Iris Meredith, Al St. John, Warner Richmond, Dick Curtis, Charles King

Former football star Johnny Mack Brown made his biggest impression by playing the title role in the 1930 version of *Billy the Kid* opposite Wallace Beery as Pat Garrett. This led to a series of B westerns, of which *A Lawman Is Born* is one of the better entries. As in so many of these films, Brown is a two-fisted good guy who foils the nefarious plans of an outlaw gang. This time, the baddies are after land (as opposed to the alternate formulas of cattle, money, gold, or horses). It's fun for fans, with former silent star (and nephew of Fatty Arbuckle) Al St. John doing the comedy sidekick honors.

1937   B & W   58 minutes

LEGEND OF THE LONE RANGER, THE
🐢

DIRECTOR: William A. Fraker
CAST: Klinton Spilsbury, Michael Horse, Jason Robards

Let your children watch *The Legend of the Lone Ranger*, but don't bother to watch it yourself. While kids will undoubtedly love what the advertising blurbs said was "the untold story of the man behind the mask and the legend behind the man," adults—after the first hour of this often corny, slow-paced western—will probably be falling asleep or, at least, daydreaming. Rated PG.

1981   98 minutes

LEGEND OF WALKS FAR WOMAN, THE
🌱

DIRECTOR: Mel Manski
CAST: Raquel Welch, Bradford Dillman, George Clutsei, Nick Mancuso, Elroy Phil Casados, Nick Ramos

Badly miscast Raquel Welch portrays an Indian heroine facing the perils of the Indian versus white man's culture clash. Her story leads to the climactic battle at Little Big Horn. Not even the scenery is enough to maintain interest.

1982   150 minutes

LIFE AND TIMES OF JUDGE ROY BEAN, THE
★★★

DIRECTOR: John Huston
CAST: Paul Newman, Stacy Keach, Victoria Principal, Jacqueline Bisset, Ava Gardner

Weird western with Paul Newman as the fabled hanging judge. It has some interesting set-pieces among the strangeness. Stacy Keach is outstanding as Bad Bob. Rated PG.

1972   120 minutes

LITTLE BIG MAN
★★★★

DIRECTOR: Arthur Penn

CAST: Dustin Hoffman, Chief Dan George, Faye Dunaway, Martin Balsam, Jeff Corey, Richard Mulligan

Dustin Hoffman gives a bravura performance as Jack Crabbe, a 121-year-old survivor of Custer's last stand. An offbeat western/comedy, this film chronicles, in flashback, Crabbe's numerous adventures in the Old West. It's a remarkable film in more ways than one, with special mention deserved by Dick Smith for the marvelous make-up he created for Hoffman as the elderly Crabbe. Rated PG.

1970   150 minutes

LONELY ARE THE BRAVE
★★★★

DIRECTOR: David Miller
CAST: Kirk Douglas, Walter Matthau, Gena Rowlands

A "little" Hollywood western set in modern times has a lot to offer those who can endure its heavy-handed message. Kirk Douglas is just right as the cowboy out of step with his times. His attempts to escape from jail on horseback in contrast to the mechanized attempts to catch him by a modern police force are handled well.

1962   B & W 107 minutes

LONELY MAN, THE
★★★

DIRECTOR: Henry Levin
CAST: Jack Palance, Anthony Perkins, Neville Brand, Robert Middleton, Elisha Cook Jr., Lee Van Cleef, Elaine Aiken

Interesting, but not exciting, this tautly directed oater is about a gunfighter, bent on reforming, who returns to his family after a seventeen-year hiatus. A brooding Jack Palance is the gunfighter. He is not warmly welcomed home by his deserted son, brooding Anthony Perkins. Two of a kind, the pair square off in a contest of wills and emotions. Hulking Robert Middleton, delightfully sleazy Elisha Cook Jr., veteran heavy Lee Van Cleef, and everybody's favorite saddle tramp Neville Brand add to the solid acting that makes this tired story worth the watching.

1957   B & W   87 minutes

LONE RANGER, THE
★★★½
DIRECTOR: Stuart Heisler
CAST: Clayton Moore, Jay Silverheels, Lyle Bettger, Bonita Granville

The first color feature film based on the legend of the Lone Ranger is a treat for the kids and not too tough for the adults to sit through. Clayton Moore and Jay Silverheels reprise their television roles and find themselves battling white settlers, led by an evil Lyle Bettger, and the much put-upon Indians, riled up by a surly Michael Ansara. Simple and straightforward, this film is a natural for a rainy afternoon and guaranteed to keep everyone's attention and is in no small way aided by the sincerity and credence lent it by Moore and Silverheels, the definitive Lone Ranger and Tonto.

1956   86 minutes

LONG RIDERS, THE
★★★½
DIRECTOR: Walter Hill
CAST: David, Keith, and Robert Carradine; Stacy and James Keach; Nicholas and Christopher Guest; Dennis and Randy Quaid

Fans of westerns will probably enjoy this release. However, this film about the James-Younger Gang has

a few deficiencies, which prevent it from being a completely satisfying shoot-'em-up. Director Walter Hill uses a sort of story-telling shorthand in which character development and plot complexity are ignored in favor of lots of action. This is partly offset by the casting of brothers—David, Keith, and Robert Carradine as the Youngers; Stacy and James Keach as the Jameses; Nicholas and Christopher Guest as the Fords; and Dennis and Randy Quaid as the Millers—in the roles. While it sounds like a gimmick, it actually works and adds a much-needed dimension of character to the picture. Rated R for violence.

1980   100 minutes

LOVE ME TENDER
★★★
DIRECTOR: Robert D. Webb
CAST: Elvis Presley, Debra Paget, Richard Egan

This western drama takes place in Texas after the Civil War, with Elvis and his brother fighting over Debra Paget. The most distinguishing characteristic of this movie is the fact that it was Elvis's first film. Elvis fans will, of course, enjoy his singing the ballad "Love Me Tender."

1956   B & W   89 minutes

LUCKY TEXAN
★★★
DIRECTOR: Robert N. Bradbury
CAST: John Wayne, Barbara Sheldon, George "Gabby" Hayes, Lloyd Whitlock, Yakima Canutt, Earl Dwire, Edward Parker

Gold miners John Wayne and Gabby Hayes strike it rich. But before they can cash in their claim, Hayes is falsely accused of robbery and murder. Of course, the

Duke rides to his aid. Creaky, but fun for fans.

1934   B & W 56 minutes

LUSTY MEN, THE
★★★☆

DIRECTOR: Nicholas Ray

CAST: Robert Mitchum, Susan Hayward, Arthur Kennedy

The world of rodeo cowboys is explored in this well-made film directed by cult favorite Nicholas Ray. Robert Mitchum has one of his best roles as a broken-down ex-rodeo star who gets a second chance at the big money by tutoring an egotistical newcomer on the circuit, well played by Arthur Kennedy.

1952   B & W 113 minutes

MACKENNA'S GOLD
★★

DIRECTOR: J. Lee Thompson

CAST: Gregory Peck, Omar Sharif, Telly Savalas, Julie Newman, Lee J. Cobb

Disappointing "big" western follows search for gold in a big canyon. Impressive cast cannot overcome poor script and uninspired direction.

1969   128 minutes

MAGNIFICENT SEVEN, THE
★★★★½

DIRECTOR: John Sturges

CAST: Yul Brynner, Steve McQueen, Charles Bronson, James Coburn, Eli Wallach, Robert Vaughn

Japanese director Akira Kurosawa's *The Seven Samurai* served as the inspiration for this enjoyable western, directed by John Sturges (*The Great Escape*). It's the rousing tale of how a group of American gunfighters come to the aid of a village of Mexican farmers

plagued by bandits. A classic shoot-'em-up.

1960   126 minutes

MAJOR DUNDEE
★★★

DIRECTOR: Sam Peckinpah

CAST: Charlton Heston, Richard Harris, James Coburn, Jim Hutton, Warren Oates

This is a flawed but watchable western directed with typical verve by master filmmaker Sam Peckinpah. The plot follows a group of Confederate prisoners who volunteer to go into Mexico and track down a band of rampaging Apache Indians. Charlton Heston plays the Union officer who must lead the sullen southern soldiers into battle. An outstanding cast, impressive action scenes, and beautiful photography give this film the usual Peckinpah trademark of excitement. Columbia's decision to edit the film resulted in incoherencies in the story.

1965   124 minutes

MAN ALONE, A
★★★

DIRECTOR: Ray Milland

CAST: Ray Milland, Mary Murphy, Ward Bond, Raymond Burr, Lee Van Cleef

Ray Milland's first directorial effort finds him hiding from a lynch mob in a small western town. And who is he hiding with? The sheriff's daughter! Not too bad, as westerns go.

1955   96 minutes

MAN CALLED HORSE, A
★★★

DIRECTOR: Elliot Silverstein

CAST: Richard Harris, Judith Anderson, Jean Gascon, Manu Tupou, Corinna Tsopei, Dub Taylor

Richard Harris (in one of his best roles) portrays an English aristocrat who's enslaved and treated like a pack animal by Sioux Indians in the Dakotas. He loses his veneer of sophistication and finds the core of his manhood. This strong film offers an unusually realistic depiction of American Indian life. Rated PG.

1970   114 minutes

MAN FROM MUSIC MOUNTAIN
★★

DIRECTOR: Joseph Kane
CAST: Gene Autry, Smiley Burnette, Carol Hughes, Sally Payne, Ivan Miller, Edward Cassidy, Polly Jenkins and her Plowboys, Frankie Marvin, Earl Dwire

Warbling Gene Autry and his simple-minded sidekick Smiley Burnette stymie the efforts of a swindler in this routine series film. Worthless mining stock and gullible townfolk are the ingredients in this warmed-over oater, twenty-sixth in the interminable ninety-three films in the Gene Autry series. More than enough tunes and good ol' country humor; a fair sampling of the majority of Autry's movies.

1938   B & W   54 minutes

MAN FROM UTAH, THE
★

DIRECTOR: Robert N. Bradbury
CAST: John Wayne, Polly Ann Young, George "Gabby" Hayes, Yakima Canutt, George Cleveland

Low, low budget western with a very young John Wayne as a lawman going undercover to catch some crooks using a rodeo to bilk unsuspecting cowboys. The rodeo footage was used over and over again by the film company, Monogram Pictures, in similar films. The best part is the dialogue, with such classic lines as "I'm gonna cloud up and rain all over you" and "Yeah? You and what army?"

1934   B & W   57 minutes

MAN OF THE FRONTIER, (RED RIVER VALLEY)
★★½

DIRECTOR: B. Reeves Eason
CAST: Gene Autry, Smiley Burnette, Frances Grant, Boothe Howard, Jack Kennedy, Champion, Sam Flint, George Chesebro, Charles King, Frank LaRue, Hank Bell

This early entry in the Gene Autry series features Gene as an undercover agent out to stop a gang bent on sabotaging construction of a much-needed dam. Disguised as a ditch digger, our hero teamed with his famous mount Champion for the first time. This is Autry's eighth film and his fifth at Republic Studios as the genial singing cowboy, and it contains enough action and good stunting to satisfy any western fan due in no small part to veteran serial and adventure director "Breezy" Eason and his fast-paced style. Very enjoyable, and a nice example of the kind of film Autry could make but didn't have to after a while.

1936   B & W   60 minutes

MAN WHO LOVED CAT DANCING, THE
★

DIRECTOR: Richard C. Sarafian
CAST: Burt Reynolds, Sarah Miles, George Hamilton, Lee J. Cobb, Jack Warden

Don't waste your time on this uninspired western. Burt Reynolds is wasted in this tale of a train robber who kidnaps a prim Sarah

Miles and falls in love with her. Rated PG.

1973   114 minutes

MAN WHO SHOT LIBERTY VALANCE, THE
★★★★★

DIRECTOR: John Ford

CAST: John Wayne, James Stewart, Vera Miles, Lee Marvin, Edmond O'Brien, Woody Strode, Andy Devine

This release was director John Ford's last great western. It's a bittersweet farewell to a genre he created and defined. The interplay of John Wayne, James Stewart, and Lee Marvin is inspired. Wayne replays his role of the western man of action, this time with a twist. Stewart's part could well be called *Mr Smith Goes to Shinbone* · it draws so much on his most famous image. Marvin has a field day as the meanest, nastiest, no-account outlaw that ever stalked the West. Combined with Ford's visual sense and belief in sparse dialogue, as well as fine ensemble playing in supporting roles, it adds up to a highly satisfying film.

1962   B & W 122 minutes

MAN WITHOUT A STAR
★★★

DIRECTOR: King Vidor

CAST: Kirk Douglas, Jeanne Crain, Claire Trevor, Richard Boone, Jack Elam, Mara Corday

With charm, fists, and guns, foreman Kirk Douglas swaggers through this stock story of rival ranchers. Jeanne Crain is his beautiful boss; Claire Trevor is, as usual, a big-hearted saloon hostess. Richard Boone and Jack Elam are in fine character.

1955   89 minutes

MANHATTAN MERRY-GO-ROUND
★★½

DIRECTOR: Charles F. Riesner

CAST: Gene Autry, Phil Regan, Leo Carrillo, Ann Dvorak, Tamara Geva, Ted Lewis, Cab Calloway and the Cotton Club Orchestra, Joe DiMaggio, Louis Prima, Henry Armetta, Max Terhune, Smiley Burnette, Jimmy Gleason

Incredible line-up of popular performers and celebrities is the main attraction of this catch-all production about a gangster who takes over a recording company. Basically a collection of performances strung together by a romantic thread, this oddity runs the gamut form Gene Autry's country crooning to the jivin' gyrations of legendary Cab Calloway. Even Joe DiMaggio makes a rare film appearance in a featured spot, and the comedy is handled by thick-accented Henry Armetta and ranch-house buffoons Smiley Burnette and Max Terhune. Definitely different and a showcase production typical of most studios that jammed as many names as possible into a film with the hope of garnering the widest possible audience.

1938   B & W 80 minutes

MARAUDERS
★★

DIRECTOR: George Archainbaud

CAST: William Boyd, Andy Clyde, Rand Brooks, Ian Wolfe, Dorinda Clifton, Mary Newton, Harry Cording, Earle Hodgins, Dick Bailey

Hopalong Cassidy and his two sidekicks take refuge in an abandoned church one rainy night and find themselves embroiled in a battle between a pious clegyman and mean-spirited Harry Cording, whose gang of thugs are intent on tearing the church down. This later effort by William Boyd still packs the good-natured humor and action of the earlier entries, but the story is routinely predictable. Fine character actor Ian Wolfe humbles it up as the man of the cloth.

1947   B & W   63 minutes

MASSACRE AT FORT HOLMAN (REASON TO LIVE...A REASON TO DIE, A)
★½

DIRECTOR: Tonino Valerii

CAST: James Coburn, Telly Savalas, Bud Spencer, Ralph Goodwin, Joseph Mitchell

Spaghetti western of marginal interest. Eight condemned men led by James Coburn, who plays a traitor to the Union Army in the Civil War, get a chance to redeem themselves by overtaking a rebel fort. Sound familar? *The Dirty Dozen, Kelly's Heroes*? Telly Savalas is the Confederate enemy he must defeat. Like most westerns of this sort, there is plenty of action, but that alone can't help the worn-out plot or western clichés. Rated PG for violence and profanity.

1984   90 minutes

MAVERICK QUEEN, THE
★★★

DIRECTOR: Joseph Kane

CAST: Barbara Stanwyck, Barry Sullivan, Scott Brady, Mary Murphy, Wallace Ford

Sparks erupt when a Pinkerton detective works undercover at a Wyoming gambling hotel that is a hangout for an outlaw gang. Barbara Stanwyck is cast aptly as the beauty who owns the hotel and is caught between her jealous lover and her love for the lawman.

1955   90 minutes

MCCABE AND MRS. MILLER
★★★★

DIRECTOR: Robert Altman

CAST: Warren Beatty, Julie Christie, Shelley Duvall, Keith Carradine

Life in the turn-of-the-century Northwest is given a first-class treatment in director Robert Altman's visually perfect comedy-drama. Sparkling performances are turned in by Warren Beatty, as a small-town wheeler-dealer, and Julie Christie, as a whore with a heart that beats to the jingle of gold and silver coins. Rated R.

1971   121 minutes

MELODY RANCH
★★½

DIRECTOR: Joseph Santley

CAST: Gene Autry, Jimmy Durante, Ann Miller, Barton MacLane, George "Gabby" Hayes, Vera Vague, Champion, Joe Sawyer, Bob Wills Orchestra, Tom London

It's hard to fathom what was going on in the minds of studio executives and the creative forces at Republic Studios in 1940, but somewhere along the line they decided to team Gene Autry with Jimmy Durante and Ann Miller and replace Smiley Burnette with Gabby Hayes and pretend nothing was different. One thing Gene Autry never needed was to be teamed with larger-than life actors. He was perhaps the blandest of top western stars and worked well enough within the confines of a programmer but definitely came in a poor second or third against a real trouper. Venerable heavy Barton MacLane provides the menace as a local gangster intent on running honorary sheriff Gene Autry out of town, but there isn't enough action to qualify this bigger-budgeted series entry as anything other than a curio and perhaps a failed effort to expand Autry's base of popularity.

1940   B & W   80 minutes

MELODY TRAIL
★★½

DIRECTOR: Joseph Kane

CAST: Gene Autry, Smiley Burnette, Ann Rutherford, Wade Boteler, Alan Bridge, Willy Castello, Marie Quillan, Fern Emmett, Gertrude Messinger, Ione Reed

The fifth Gene Autry–Smiley Burnette film is a pleasant story about a rodeo rider (Gene) who loses his winnings and is forced to work for a rancher with a romantic daughter. Needless to say, our hero manages to stop the omnipresent rustlers and save his boss's ranch as well as extricate himself from the clutches of the clinging female and escape to ever faithful and hopelessly inept Smiley Burnette.

1935   B & W   60 minutes

MISSOURI BREAKS, THE
★★

DIRECTOR: Arthur Penn

CAST: Marlon Brando, Jack Nicholson, Kathleen Lloyd, Harry Dean Stanton

For all its potential, this western really lets you down. The teaming of Marlon Brando and Jack Nicholson was looked upon with great anticipation when the film was announced. Nicholson is acceptable as the outlaw trying to make a clean start. Brando, on the other hand, is inconsistent as a relentless bounty hunter who's tracking Nicholson. The choppy script and the on-again, off-again, Brando performance subtract greatly from the impact of what

could have been a good film. Rated PG.

1976   126 minutes

MONTE WALSH
★★★½

DIRECTOR: William Fraker

CAST: Lee Marvin, Jack Palance, Jeanne Moreau, Mitchell Ryan, Jim Davis

Sad but satisfying western about a couple of saddle pals (Lee Marvin, Jack Palance) attempting to make the transition to a new age and century. Cinematographer William Fraker made an impressive directorial debut with this fine film. Rated R for violence.

1970   106 minutes

MOUNTAIN MEN, THE
★

DIRECTOR: Richard Lang

CAST: Charlton Heston, Brian Keith, Victoria Racimo, Stephen Macht

A buddy movie about two bickering fur trappers who get involved in Indian uprisings and so on, this dull and overly violent film wastes the talents of its stars, Charlton Heston and Brian Keith. The few moments of enjoyment provided by the leads do not make up for the tedium of sitting through this disappointment. Rated R.

1980   102 minutes

MR. HORN
★★★

DIRECTOR: Jack Starrett

CAST: David Carradine, Richard Widmark, Karen Black, Richard Masur, Jeremy Slate, Pat McCormick, Jack Starrett

William Goldman's version of the Tom Horn story lacks the screenwriter's usual light touch (as best evidenced in *Butch Cassidy and the Sundance Kid*). But this is perhaps because Goldman is more interested in debunking a western myth in this made-for-television product than promoting one. Whatever the reason, *Mr. Horn* is a bittersweet, near melancholy chronicle of the exploits of Horn (David Carradine), who is shown first as an idealistic young man helping an old-timer (Richard Widmark) track down Geronimo and later as a cynical gunman hired to eliminate some rustlers. His story ends, as did Steve McQueen's less successful *Tom Horn*, with the title character being framed and hanged for murder.

1979   200 minutes

MY DARLING CLEMENTINE
★★★★½

DIRECTOR: John Ford
CAST: Henry Fonda, Victor Mature, Walter Brennan, Linda Darnell, Ward Bond

The epic struggle between good and evil is wrapped up in this classic retelling of the shootout at the O.K. Corral, between the Earps and the lawless Clanton family. Henry Fonda gives his Wyatt Earp a feeling of believability, perfectly matched by Walter Brennan's riveting portrayal of villainy as the head of the Clanton gang. The best part of this movie remains the phenomenal black-and-white cinematography. When director John Ford trained his cameras on his beloved Monument Valley, he created some of the most beautiful visual images ever put on film.

1946   B & W 97 minutes

MY PAL TRIGGER
★★★½

DIRECTOR: Frank McDonald

CAST: Roy Rogers, George "Gabby" Hayes, Dale Evans, Jack Holt, LeRoy Mason, Roy Barcroft, Trigger

One of the most fondly remembered and perhaps the best of all the Roy Rogers movies, this gentle story centers on Roy's attempts to mate his mare with a superb golden stallion. Villain Jack Holt is responsible for the death of the mare, and Roy is blamed and incarcerated. The foal grows into the great horse Trigger and is able to clear Roy's name as well as save Gabby Hayes's ranch, and they all settle down to a happy life together. Charming and lovingly directed, this is a fine film for the whole family and one of the highlights of the long Roy Rogers series.

1946   B & W 79 minutes

MYSTERY MOUNTAIN
★★

DIRECTORS: Otto Brewer and B. Reeves "Breezy" Eason

CAST: Ken Maynard, Verna Hillie, Edmund Cobb, Sid Saylor, Gene Autry, Bob Kortman, Tom London, George Chesebro, Lafe McKee, Smiley Burnette, Wally Walse, Art Mix, Philo McCullough

Cowboy great Ken Maynard stars in his only serial, the story of the mysterious master of disguise known as the "Rattler," who lives to wreck trains. Mascot Studios retooled their earlier John Wayne serial *Hurricane Express* and made it into a western adventure to showcase Maynard's famous riding skills. Ironically, John Wayne once starred in a series of westerns that were sound remakes of some of Ken Maynard's best silent films. Gene Autry and his silly sidekick Smiley Burnette make their second screen appearance in this chapter play, and Gene would go on to star in the next vehicle planned for Maynard, the phenomenally successful *Phantom Empire*, released the following year.

1934　　B & W　12 chapters

NAKED IN THE SUN
★★½

DIRECTOR: R. John Hugh
CAST: James Craig, Barton MacLane, Lita Milan, Tony Hunter

Osceola (James Craig), war chief of the Seminole Indians, must battle unscrupulous whites, the United States Government, and his own tribe in order to live in dignity. One of many films of the 1950s that dealt with the American Indian as a noble, persecuted people. This is well-acted and effective in evoking audience sympathy, although it suffers from some script difficulties and slow pacing. Easily as enjoyable as some of the more famous "adult" westerns of the same vintage.

1957　　　　　79 minutes

'NEATH ARIZONA SKIES
★★½

DIRECTOR: Henry Frazer
CAST: John Wayne, Sheila Terry, Jay Wilsey, Yakima Canutt, Joan Rockwell, George "Gabby" Hayes

Formula B western has John Wayne as the protector of the heir to rich oil lands, a little Indian girl. Of course, the baddies try to kidnap her and the Duke rides to the rescue. Low-budget and predictable.

1934　　B & W　57 minutes

NEVADA SMITH
★★★

DIRECTOR: Henry Hathaway

CAST: Steve McQueen, Karl Malden, Brian Keith, Arthur Kennedy, Suzanne Pleshette, Raf Vallone, Pat Hingle, Howard da Silva, Martin Landau

Steve McQueen, in the title role, is butcher's-freezer-cold, calculating, and merciless in this hard-hitting, gripping western. The focus is on a senseless, vicious double murder and the revenge taken by the son of the innocent victims. Story and characters are excerpted from a section of Harold Robbins's sensational novel *The Carpetbaggers* not used in the 1964 film.

1966　　　　　135 minutes

NEW FRONTIER
★★½

DIRECTOR: Carl Pierson
CAST: John Wayne, Muriel Evans, Mary McLaren, Murdock McQuarrie, Warner Richmond, Sam Flint, Earl Dwire

In a familiar plot, John Wayne is the son of a murdered sheriff out to find the baddies who did the dirty deed. Creaky but fun for fans.

1935　　B & W　59 minutes

NIGHT STAGE TO GALVESTON
★★

DIRECTOR: George Archainbaud
CAST: Gene Autry, Pat Buttram, Virginia Huston, Robert Livingston, Frank Sully, Thurston Hall, Clayton Moore, Harry Cording, Dick Alexander

Old-fashioned actioner set in post–Civil War South finds Gene Autry and his buddy Pat Bottom working for a crusading newspaperman who intends to expose corruption in the ranks of the Texas Rangers. Brimming with character actors from serials, westerns, and films of all kinds (including former Lone Rangers Robert Livingston and

Clayton Moore), this otherwise routine story is easy to watch and not too hard to forget. Shorter than most Autry films.

1952   B & W   61 minutes

NIGHT OF THE GRIZZLY, THE
★★½

DIRECTOR: Joseph Pevney
CAST: Clint Walker, Martha Hyer, Ron Ely, Jack Elam

In order to maintain a peaceful standing in the rugged Old West, big Clint Walker must fight all the local bad guys (who should have known better) as well as a giant grizzly bear who moves in and out of camera range on a wheeled dolly. Nice outdoor sets and some good characterization help this no-frills family story, which culminates in the inevitable confrontation between Walker and the grizzly. Plenty of familiar faces among the character actors in this outdoor opus.

1966   102 minutes

NIGHT RIDERS, THE
★★½

DIRECTOR: George Sherman
CAST: John Wayne, Ray "Crash" Corrigan, Max Terhune, Doreen McKay, Ruth Rogers, Tom Tyler, Kermit Maynard

The Three Mesquiteers (John Wayne, Ray Corrigan, and Max Terhune) make like Zorro by donning cape and mask to foil a villain's attempt to enforce a phony Spanish land grant. Good formula western fun.

1939   B & W   58 minutes

NORTH OF THE GREAT DIVIDE
★½

DIRECTOR: William Witney

CAST: Roy Rogers, Penny Edwards, Gordon Jones, Roy Barcroft, the Riders of the Purple Sage, Trigger

No-good Roy Barcroft is at it again, this time as a greedy salmon cannery owner who overfishes the waters and forces the local Indians to go hungry or turn to a life of crime. Roy Rogers plays a variation on his government agent identity but lacks the familiar support of Dale Evans, Gabby Hayes, or even Pat Brady in this lesser entry to the popular series. Fewer thrills and more stock footage relegate this one to the also-ran category typical of the dying-hero horse operas of the early 1950s.

1950   67 minutes

NORTH TO ALASKA
★★★★

DIRECTOR: Henry Hathaway
CAST: John Wayne, Stewart Granger, Capucine, Fabian, Ernie Kovacs

Rather than a typical John Wayne western, this is a John Wayne northern. It's a rough-and-tumble romantic comedy directed by Henry Hathaway. Delightfully tongue-in-cheek, it presents the Duke at his two-fisted best.

1960   122 minutes

OKLAHOMA KID, THE
★★★

DIRECTOR: Lloyd Bacon
CAST: James Cagney, Humphrey Bogart, Rosemary Lane, Donald Crisp, Charles Middleton, Ward Bond, Harvey Stephens

This big-budget Warner Brothers western inevitably elicits the simple question, "Why?" Why did Warner's choose to pool some of their top talent and put them in a routine oater about a feared gunman's revenge against the lowdown snakes who hung his innocent father and eventually kill his brother? Why did the powers-that-be decide to take James Cagney and Humphrey Bogart out of the contemporary gangster and social dramas that they excelled at and saddle them with monikers like "The Oklahoma Kid" and "Whip McCord"? Whatever the reasons were, these two screen legends, like the professionals they were, made the best of a silly situation and contributed broad, near-comic performances to put this trite story in proper perspective. "Cagney looked like a mushroom under a huge western hat, " Bogart said later, and Bogart played the epitome of the saloon slime, dressed in black and oozing menace. Definitely one of the oddest of all major sagebrush sagas, this film boasts a great cast of familiar characters as well as a musical interlude with Cagney singing "I Don't Want to Play in Your Yard" to the accompaniment of a honky-tonk piano and pair of six-shooters. We still don't have a clue why this film was made, but it's a competent curio that's fun and worth the watch.

1939   B & W   85 minutes

OLD CORRAL, THE
★★★

DIRECTOR: Joseph Kane
CAST: Gene Autry, Smiley Burnette, Hope Manning, Roy Rogers, Sons of the Pioneers, Champion, Lon Chaney Jr., Buddy Roosevelt, Oscar and Elmer, Cornelius Keefe, John Bradford, Milburn Moranti, Abe Lufton, Lynton Brent

Early Gene Autry film finds the spud-shaped singer fighting East coast gangsters who have invaded the frontier in search of a girl who knows too much. Future cowboy great Roy Rogers appears with the Sons of the Pioneers to pick a few tunes, and former cowboy star Buddy Roosevelt makes an appearance in a supporting role. Young Lon Chaney Jr. takes a break from the serials he was appearing in at this stage of his career to lend support. Stardom as one of Universal Studio's masters of horror was still five years away for the former Creighton Chaney.

1936   B & W   56 minutes

ON TOP OF OLD SMOKY
★½

DIRECTOR: George Archainbaud
CAST: Gene Autry, Smiley Burnette, Gail Davis, Sheila Ryan, Kenne Duncan, Grandon Rhodes, Robert Bice, Cass County Boys, Jack Gargan

Gene Autry is reunited with old saddle pal Smiley Burnette in this familiar story of a singing cowpoke (Autry) who is mistaken for a Texas Ranger with a price on his head. Gene manages to dodge lead, inflict the audience with a few songs, and bring the bad guys to justice before the last reel ends. This is the eighty-ninth film in the long-running series and was originally released in an eighty-nine minute version.

1953   B & W   59 minutes

ONCE UPON A TIME IN THE WEST
★★★★★

DIRECTOR: Sergio Leone
CAST: Claudia Cardinale, Henry Fonda, Charles Bronson, Jason Robards, Jack Elam, Woody Strode, Lionel Stander

This superb film is the only spaghetti western that can be called a classic. A mythic tale about the coming of the railroad and the exacting of revenge with larger-than-life characters, it is a work on a par with the best by great American western film directors: John Ford, Howard Hawks, Sam Peckinpah, and Anthony Mann. Like Peckinpah's *The Wild Bunch*, it has a fervent—and well-deserved—cult following in America. Rated PG.

1969   165 minutes

ONE-EYED JACKS
★★★★

DIRECTOR: Marlon Brando

CAST: Marlon Brando, Karl Malden, Katy Jurado, Ben Johnson, Slim Pickens, Elisha Cook Jr.

Star Marlon Brando took over the reins of directing this western from Stanley Kubrick midway through production, and the result is a terrific entry in the genre. Superb supporting performances by Karl Malden, Katy Jurado, Ben Johnson, and Slim Pickens help this beautifully photographed film about an outlaw seeking revenge on a double-dealing former partner.

1961   141 minutes

100 RIFLES
★★

DIRECTOR: Tom Gries

CAST: Burt Reynolds, Raquel Welch, Jim Brown, Fernando Lamas, Dan O'Herlihy

The picture stirred controversy over guerrilla leader Raquel Welch's inter-racial love scene with deputy Jim Brown. But at this point, who cares? We're left with a so-so western yarn. Burt Reynolds, as a gun runner, has a rare opportunity to outact his co-stars. Rated R.

1969   110 minutes

OUTCAST, THE
★★

DIRECTOR: William Witney

CAST: John Derek, Joan Evans, Jim Davis

Before he became disenchanted with acting and turned to still photography, John Derek made a number of mostly mediocre films, this one among them. In this standard western, he fights to win his rightful inheritance. Justice prevails, of course, but you know that going in.

1954   90 minutes

OUTLAW, THE
★★

DIRECTORS: Howard Hughes, Howard Hawks

CAST: Jane Russell, Walter Huston, Thomas Mitchell, Jack Buetel

This once-notorious western now seems almost laughable. Jane Russell keeps her best attributes forward, but one wonders what Walter Huston and Thomas Mitchell are doing in this film. Only for those who want to know what all the fuss was about.

1943   103 minutes

OUTLAW JOSEY WALES, THE
★★★★½

DIRECTOR: Clint Eastwood

CAST: Clint Eastwood, Sondra Locke, Chief Dan George, William McKinney, John Vernon

This western, a masterpiece of characterization and action, is Clint Eastwood's best film as both an actor and director. With it, he took his place as one of the finest western film directors. Like the James Stewart/Anthony Mann collaborations of the 1950s, it focuses on a cowboy bent on bloody revenge. Josey Wales (Eastwood) is a farmer whose family is murdered by "Red Legs," a band of pillaging cutthroats who have allied themselves with the Union Army. Wales joins the Confederacy to avenge their deaths. After the war, everyone in his troop surrenders to the victorious Union except Wales. They are then murdered by Red Legs after being promised amnesty and he again becomes the hunter... and the hunted. Rated PG.

1976   135 minutes

OX-BOW INCIDENT, THE
★★★★½

DIRECTOR: William Wellman
CAST: Henry Fonda, Harry Morgan, Dana Andrews, Anthony Quinn, Francis Ford

Considered one of the finest westerns ever made, this film stars Henry Fonda and Harry Morgan as two drifters who try to stop the lynching of three men (Dana Andrews, Anthony Quinn, and Francis Ford). Never has the terror of mob rule been more effectively portrayed than in this thought-provoking and suspenseful production.

1943   B & W   75 minutes

PAINTED DESERT, THE
★★½

DIRECTOR: Howard Higgin
CAST: William Boyd, Helen Twelvetrees, William Farnum, J. Farrell MacDonald, Clark Gable

The future Hopalong Cassidy, William Boyd, plays a foundling who grows up on the other side of the range from his lady love and must decide between the family feud and the cattle or Helen Twelvetrees and the cattle. Silent greats, J. Farrell MacDonald and William Farnum play the rival parents locked in eternal conflict over

range rights, and Clark Gable plays the dark cloud that is menacing the future of these two nice kids. Not as brisk and action-packed as the programmer westerns of the same period, but enthusiastically acted and worth the viewing just to watch a young Clark Gable, who was already on his rapid way up at MGM and wouldn't play a cowboy again until he was a star.

1931   B & W   75 minutes

PALE RIDER
★★★½

DIRECTOR: Clint Eastwood
CAST: Clint Eastwood, Michael Moriarty, Carrie Snodgress, Christopher Penn, Richard Dysart, Richard Kiel, John Russell

Star-producer-director Clint Eastwood donned six-guns and a Stetson for the first time since the classic *The Outlaw Josie Wales* (1976) for this enjoyable western. The star is a mysterious avenger who comes to the aid of embattled gold prospectors in the Old West. *Pale Rider* is somewhat similar to Eastwood's 1973 *High Plains Drifter* in theme. Only this time he appears to have been sent from heaven rather than hell to right the usual wrongs. There is a welcome amount of humor in the newer film and the kind of action-oriented catharsis that prevented the 1973 release from being a first-rate entertainment. That said, *Pale Rider* is unlikely to be remembered as a milestone in the genre, even though it is well worth watching for fans. Rated R for violence and profanity.

1985   113 minutes

PALS OF THE SADDLE
★★½

DIRECTOR: George Sherman

CAST: John Wayne, Ray "Crash" Corrigan, Max Terhune, Doreen McKay, Frank Milan, Jack Kirk

The Three Mesquiteers (John Wayne, Ray Corrigan, and Max Terhune) help a woman government agent (Doreen McKay) trap a munitions ring in this enjoyable B western series entry.

1938   B & W   60 minutes

PANCHO VILLA
★★

DIRECTOR: Eugenio Martin
CAST: Telly Savalas, Clint Walker, Chuck Connors, Anne Francis

Telly Savalas plays the famous bandit to the hilt and beyond. Clint Walker runs guns for him. Chuck Connors postures as a stiff and stuffy military type. You'll soon see why the title role forever belongs to Wallace Beery. It all builds to a rousing head-on train wreck. Rated R.

1972   92 minutes

PARADISE CANYON
★★

DIRECTOR: Carl Pierson
CAST: John Wayne, Marion Burns, Yakima Canutt, Reed Howes, Peggy Murdock

A very young and sometimes awkward John Wayne stars in this low, low budget western as an undercover agent on the trail of counterfeiters (led by Yakima Canutt). For staunch Wayne and western fans only.

1935   B & W   59 minutes

PAT GARRETT AND BILLY THE KID
★★½

DIRECTOR: Sam Peckinpah
CAST: James Coburn, Kris Kristofferson, Bob Dylan, Jason Robards, Rita Coolidge

This is an interesting but flawed western. James Coburn, as Pat, and Kris Kristofferson, as Billy, are good as the title characters, and director Sam Peckinpah creates some fine action scenes. However, Bob Dylan is pitifully inept in an anachronistic supporting role as Alias, and the film simply fails to jell overall. Rated R.

1973   106 minutes

PONY EXPRESS
★★★

DIRECTOR: Jerry Hopper
CAST: Charlton Heston, Rhonda Fleming, Jan Sterling, Forrest Tucker

Bigger than they were in life, western legends Buffalo Bill Cody and Wild Bill Hickok battle stagecoach station owners and Sioux Indians to establish the short-lived but glamorous Pony Express mail route between St. Joseph, Missouri, and Sacramento, California, in the early 1860s. Rousing good action for the historical western fan who doesn't check every fact.

1953   101 minutes

PRAIRIE MOON
★★

DIRECTOR: Ralph Straub
CAST: Gene Autry, Smiley Burnette, Shirley Deane, Tommy Ryan, David Gorcey, Walter Tetley, Stanley Andrews, William Pawley, Tom London, Bud Osborne

Well-worn story about a promise to a dying man is shifted to Gene Autry's west and puts him in a position to care for a gangster's three children on his ranch. The kids are city-tough and cause no end of trouble, but by the end they have reformed (naturally) and help Gene and Smiley bring in a gang of rustlers. No real surprises, but familiar faces like David Gorcey and Stanley Andrews (the Old Ranger on *Death Valley Days*) make this tolerable viewing.

1938   B & W   58 minutes

PROUD REBEL, THE
★★★½

DIRECTOR: Michael Curtiz
CAST: Alan Ladd, Olivia De Havilland, David Ladd, Dean Jagger, Henry Hull

A post–Civil War sentimental drama about a Confederate veteran searching for a doctor who can cure his mute son, with father and son playing father and son. The principals in this one are excellent, the chemistry great. Well worth the watching, this was the ill-fated Alan Ladd's last "class" film.

1958   103 minutes

RACHEL AND THE STRANGER
★★★½

DIRECTOR: Norman Foster
CAST: William Holden, Loretta Young, Robert Mitchum

The leisurely-paced western is made easier to watch by a fine cast. William Holden's love for his wife Loretta Young finally comes to full blossom only after she is wooed by stranger Robert Mitchum. A nice story done with charm and class.

1948   B & W   93 minutes

RADIO RANCH (MEN WITH STEEL FACES, PHANTOM EMPIRE)
★★½

DIRECTORS: Otto Brewer and B. Reeves "Breezy" Eason

CAST: Gene Autry, Frankie Darro, Betsy King Ross, Dorothy Christy, Smiley Burnette, Wheeler Oakman

Condensed version of popular science-fiction serial *Phantom Empire*, this feature-length film sketchily tells the story of Gene Autry and his fight against scientists who want his Radio Ranch for the precious ore it contains, and his strange adventures in the underground city of Murania. This was Gene Autry's first leading role, and the success of the serial (also available on cassette) prompted the studio (Mascot recently merged to form Republic Studios) to rerelease it when Gene continued to be a success in a series of western movies. Running about one-third the length of the original serial, this version takes less time to view but doesn't make quite as much sense as the twelve-chapter serial.

1940   B & W   80 minutes

RANCHO NOTORIOUS
★★★½

DIRECTOR: Fritz Lang
CAST: Marlene Dietrich, Arthur Kennedy, Mel Ferrer, Lloyd Gough, William Frawley, Gloria Henry, Jack Elam, George Reeves

Brooding revenge western is a curio of the 1950s, one of those films that appears to mean something more than what the action implies. Carried out with style by a cast of capable second leads and bolstered by offbeat characters like Jack Elam and William Frawley, this film, while not a great western, is fun to watch and a treat for Marlene Dietrich fans. The great German director Fritz Lang, famous for foreign classics like *Metropolis* and *M* as well as the American films *Fury* and *Scarlet Street*, brings an interesting touch to this revered American art form, his second western. (*The Return of Frank James*, with Henry Fonda, was his first.) Not completely successful, but not too bad if you ignore the theme song.

1952   89 minutes

RANDY RIDES ALONE
★★★

DIRECTOR: Henry Frazer
CAST: John Wayne, Alberta Vaughan, George "Gabby" Hayes, Earl Dwire, Yakima Canutt

John Wayne stars in this enjoyable B western as a lawman who goes undercover to catch a gang that has been robbing an express office. The opening is particularly good.

1934   B & W   60 minutes

RARE BREED, THE
★★★

DIRECTOR: Andrew V. McLaglen
CAST: James Stewart, Maureen O'-Hara, Brian Keith, Juliet Mills, Jack Elam, Ben Johnson

This is a generally rewarding western. Jimmy Stewart is a Texas cattle rancher who grudgingly assists an Englishwoman's (Maureen O'-Hara) attempts to introduce a new line of short-horned cattle to the Texan range. The story is quite original and holds one's interest throughout.

1966   108 minutes

RED RIVER
★★★★★

DIRECTOR: Howard Hawks
CAST: John Wayne, Montgomery Clift, Walter Brennan, Noah Beery Jr., Harry Carey, Harry Carey Jr.

After seeing this western, directed by Howard Hawks, John Ford remarked, "I didn't know the big lug could act." The "big lug" he was referring to was the picture's star, John Wayne, whom Ford had brought to stardom in 1939's *Stagecoach*. This shoot-'em-up adaptation of *Mutiny on the Bounty* definitely features Wayne at his best in the role of a tough rancher making a historic cattle drive. The ending is a little unbelievable, but if you can accept it, the result is a classic cowboy picture.

1948   B & W   133 minutes

RED SUN
★★

DIRECTOR: Terence Young
CAST: Charles Bronson, Alain Delon, Toshiro Mifune, Ursula Andress, Capucine

Rambling pseudo–spaghetti western has an interesting premise but ultimately wastes the considerable talents of the great Japanese actor Toshiro Mifune and hands Charles Bronson another of those supporting-character roles that he underplays into a leading role just by staying away from the nonsense going on. Dashing Alain Delon has his hands full with beautiful Ursula Andress and steamy Capucine while stoic Mifune as a samurai warrior a long way from home calmly endures the humiliation required for him to collect his check and go back home. The action sequences in this overlong Italian/French/Spanish co-production are effective. Rated PG.

1972   112 minutes

RETURN OF A MAN CALLED HORSE, THE
★★★

DIRECTOR: Irvin Kershner
CAST: Richard Harris, Gale Sondergaard, Geoffrey Lewis, Bill Lucking, Jorge Luke, Enrique Lucero

The Return of a Man Called Horse is every bit as good as its predecessor, *A Man Called Horse*. Both films present an honest, and sometimes shocking, glimpse at the culture of the American Indian. The first film chronicled the events that change John Morgan (Richard Harris) from gentleman to warrior. To escape boredom, he arranges a hunt in the untamed wilderness of America. Everyone on the expedition is killed, except Morgan, who is taken as a slave by the Sioux Yellow Hand tribe and becomes a warrior. The new film picks up with a bored and unhappy Morgan deciding to return to America. Rated PG for violence.

1976   129 minutes

RETURN OF FRANK JAMES, THE
★★★

DIRECTOR: Fritz Lang

CAST: Henry Fonda, Gene Tierney, Donald Meek, John Carradine, Jackie Cooper, J. Edward Bromberg, Henry Hull

Gene Tierney made her film debut in this inevitable sequel to *Jesse James* (1939). Henry Fonda reprises his role as brother Frank and attempts to avenge Jesse's death at the hands of "dirty little coward" Bob Ford, played by John Carradine. Thanks to Fonda's fine acting and Fritz Lang's sensitive direction, what could have been a pale ripoff is an enjoyable western.

1940   92 minutes

RETURN OF THE BADMEN
★★★

DIRECTOR: Ray Enright

CAST: Randolph Scott, Ann Jeffreys, Robert Ryan, George "Gabby" Hayes, Lex Barker

Randolph Scott has his hands full in this routine western. No sooner does he settle down in Oklahoma than he must slap leather with Billy the Kid, the Dalton Gang, the Younger Brothers, and the Sundance Kid. As the latter, Robert Ryan shore ain't the appealing gunhand who rode with Butch Cassidy.

1948   B & W   90 minutes

RIDE IN THE WHIRLWIND
★½

DIRECTOR: Monte Hellman

CAST: Jack Nicholson, Cameron Mitchell, Millie Perkins, Harry Dean Stanton, Rupert Crosse, Tom Filer, Katherine Squire

Throwaway western with good cast of characters goes nowhere in the muddled story of three riders wrongfully pursued by an unrelenting posse. This sister production to *The Shooting* appears to have lost the toss on the editing and uses variations of the same camera shots over and over. A young Jack Nicholson also worked on the story and production end of this minor cult film.

1965   83 minutes

RIDE THE HIGH COUNTRY
★★★★½

DIRECTOR: Sam Peckinpah

CAST: Joel McCrea, Randolph Scott, Warren Oates, R. G. Armstrong, Mariette Hartley, John Anderson, James Drury, L. Q. Jones, Edgar Buchanan

Joel McCrea and Randolph Scott play two old-time gunslingers who team up to guard a gold shipment. McCrea just wants to do a good job so he can "enter (his) house justified." Scott, on the other hand, cares nothing for noble purpose and tries to steal the gold. From that point on, they are friends no longer. The result is a picture so good that McCrea and Scott decided to retire after making it—both wanted to go out with a winner and indeed did.

1962　　　　　　　94 minutes

RIDE THE MAN DOWN
★★

DIRECTOR: Joseph Kane
CAST: Brian Donlevy, Rod Cameron, Ella Raines, Chill Wills, Jack LaRue

A tradtional western shot in the traditional manner. Whilewatching for its new owners to arrive, a ranch manager fights to keep the property out of the greedy hands of land grabbers. Jack LaRue plays a stinker, as usual.

1952　　　　　　　90 minutes

RIDERS OF DESTINY
★★★

DIRECTOR: Robert N. Bradbury
CAST: John Wayne, Cecilia Parker, George "Gabby" Hayes, Forrest Taylor, Al St. John, Heinie Conklin, Earl Dwire

The earliest low, low-budget John Wayne B western available on tape, this casts an extremely young-looking Duke as Singin' Sandy, an undercover agent out to help ranchers regain their water rights. Fun for fans of the star.

1933　　　B & W　50 minutes

RIDERS OF THE DEADLINE
★★

DIRECTOR: Lesley Selander
CAST: William Boyd, Andy Clyde, Jimmy Rogers, Richard Crane, Frances Woodward, William Halligan, Robert Mitchum, Jim Bannon, Herbert Rawlinson, Montie Montana, Earl Hodgins, Bill Beckford, Pierce Lyden, Tony Warde

Hopalong Cassidy pretends to befriend a smuggler in order to smoke out the real boss of the bad guys, who turns out to be an unsuspected pillar of the community, the local banker. Silent star Herbert Rawlinson, Jim Bannon (future Red Ryder), and soon-to-be major star Robert Mitchum take a hand in this one. Routine stuff, but better than the later films in the series and superior to many programmers of the time.

1943　　　B & W　70 minutes

RIDIN' ON A RAINBOW
★½

DIRECTOR: Lew Landers
CAST: Gene Autry, Smiley Burnette, Mary Lee, Byron Foulger, Ed Cassidy, Forrest Taylor, Tom London, Ralf Harolde

Slow-moving, song-laden programmer spends too much time on a showboat focusing on Mary Lee (who also appeared opposite Roy Rogers) and ignores the sagebrush, cacti, and hoofbeats demanded by a largely adolescent audience. There's a pretty fair chase and roundup of bank robbers at the climax, but there are too many tunes in the middle for most action fans (even Autry fans!). Not one of the best of a generally mediocre bunch of westerns.

1941　　　B & W　79 minutes

RIO BRAVO
★★★★½

DIRECTOR: Howard Hawks
CAST: John Wayne, Walter Brennan, Ward Bond, Ricky Nelson, Dean Martin, John Russell, Claude Akins, Angie Dickinson, Bob Steele

A super-western, with John Wayne, Walter Brennan, Ward Bond, Ricky Nelson (aping Montgomery Clift's performance in *Red River*), and the scene-stealing Dean Martin taking on cattle baron John Russell, who's out to get his kill-crazy brother (Claude Akins) out of jail. Only Angie Dickinson is bothersome, as the Duke's too-talkative love interest, in this big-screen takeoff of the popular Warner Bros. TV series of the era ("Maverick," "Cheyenne," "Sugarfoot," "Lawman," "Wagon Train," etc.)

1959   141 minutes

RIO CONCHOS
★★★

DIRECTOR: Gordon Douglas
CAST: Richard Boone, Stuart Whitman, Tony Franciosa, Edmond O'Brien, Jim Brown

Rip-roaring western action ignites this briskly paced yarn set in post–Civil War Texas. Richard Boone and his macho buddies try to get rich with a shipment of stolen rifles. Boone gives a wry performance. Stuart Whitman is rugged. Jim Brown, making his film debut, fits in nicely. And that entertaining character actor Edmond O'Brien is a delight in a colorful role.

1964   107 minutes

RIO GRANDE
★★★★

DIRECTOR: John Ford
CAST: John Wayne, Maureen O'-Hara, Claude Jarman Jr., Ben Johnson, Harry Carey Jr., Victor McLaglen, Chill Wills, J. Carrol Naish

The last entry in director John Ford's celebrated cavalry trilogy (which also includes *Ford Apache* and *She Wore a Yellow Ribbon*), this stars John Wayne as a company commander coping with renegade Indians and a willful wife (Maureen O'Hara), who wants to take their soldier son (Claude Jarman Jr.) home.

1950   B & W 105 minutes

RIO LOBO
★★★

DIRECTOR: Howard Hawks
CAST: John Wayne, Jack Elam, Jorge Rivero, Jennifer O'Neill, Chris Mitchum, Mike Henry

Neither star John Wayne nor director Howard Hawks was exactly at the peak of his powers when this second reworking of *Rio Bravo* (the first being *El Dorado*) was released. If one adjusts the normally high expectations he or she would have for a western made by these two giants, *Rio Lobo* is a fun show. Jack Elam is terrific in a delightful supporting role. Rated G.

1970   114 minutes

ROBIN HOOD OF TEXAS
★★

DIRECTOR: Lesley Selander
CAST: Gene Autry, Lynne Roberts, Sterling Holloway, Adele Mara, James Cardwell, John Kellogg, James Flavin, Stanley Andrews, Edmund Cobb

More of a detective story than a formula western, Gene Autry's last film for Republic Studios finds him accused of bank robbery and keeping one step ahead of the law in order to clear his name. Better than many of his films and one of the best of his post-WWII movies, with a nicely turned story and more action and fisticuffs than most of Autry's product. Sterling Holloway fills the buffoon boots in this one, and he's infinitely more charming then the burlesque-quality antics of Smiley Burnette. Silent star Edmund Cobb has a small role.

1947   B & W 71 minutes

ROOSTER COGBURN
★★★½

DIRECTOR: Stuart Millar
CAST: John Wayne, Katharine Hepburn, Richard Jordan, Anthony Zerbe, Strother Martin, John McIntire

Okay, so this sequel to *True Grit* is only *The African Queen* reworked, with John Wayne playing the Humphrey Bogart part opposite the incomparable Katharine Hepburn, but we like—no, love—it. Watching these two professionals playing off each other is what movie-watching is all about. The plot? Well, it's not much, but the scenes with Wayne and Hepburn are, as indicated, priceless. Rated PG.

1975   107 minutes

ROOTIN' TOOTIN' RHYTHM
★½

DIRECTOR: Mack V. Wright
CAST: Gene Autry, Smiley Burnette, Armida, Monte Blue, Hal Taliaferro (Wally Wales), Al Clauser and his Oklahoma Outlaws, Ann Pendleton, Charles King

Gene Autry and his bumbling sidekick Smiley Burnette settle a range dispute and restore the peace to the prairie in this unimaginative programmer. The best thing about this one are the appearances by former cowboy greats Wally Wales and Monte Blue and veteran heavy Charles King. Too many songs and too much Smiley.

1938   B & W   55 minutes

ROUGH RIDERS' ROUNDUP
★★½

DIRECTOR: Joseph Kane
CAST: Roy Rogers, Mary Hart, Raymond Hatton, Eddie Acuff, William Pawley, George Meeker, Trigger

The accent is more on action than music in this early Roy Rogers western about the Rough Riders reuniting to rid the range of an outlaw gang. Raymond Hatton is along to add some first-rate sidekickery (and it is interesting to note that Hatton would team up with cowboy greats Buck Jones and Tim McCoy two years later for the Rough Riders series). In all, it's better than most of the Rogers vehicles that followed.

1939   B & W   58 minutes

RUTHLESS FOUR, THE
★

DIRECTOR: Giorgio Capitani
CAST: Van Heflin, Gilbert Roland, Klaus Kinski, George Hilton

This spaghetti western could have been a lot worse, but that's no reason to watch it. Van Heflin (*The Three Musketeers*, *Shane*) plays a prospector who strikes gold, only to have to split the fortune with three other men less honest than he. This movie has some good shoot'-em'-up scenes and a few surprises, but for the most part, it's quite dull.

1969   96 minutes

SACKETTS, THE
★★★★

DIRECTOR: Robert Totten
CAST: Sam Elliott, Tom Selleck, Glenn Ford, Ben Johnson, Ruth Roman, Gilbert Roland

Fine made-for-TV western adapted from two novels by Louis L'Amour, *The Daybreakers* and *The Sacketts*. Sam Elliott, Tom Selleck, Glenn Ford, and Ben Johnson are terrific in the lead roles, and there's plenty of action.

1979   200 minutes

SACRED GROUND
★★★½

DIRECTOR: Charles B. Pierce
CAST: Tim McIntire, Jack Elam, Serene Hedin

Inter-racial marriage between a white mountain man and an Apache woman is further complicated when they have their child on the ancient burial grounds of another Indian tribe. The couple's romance and the trials they endure should hold viewer interest. Rated PG.

1983   100 minutes

SAGA OF DEATH VALLEY
★★½

DIRECTOR: Joseph Kane
CAST: Roy Rogers, George "Gabby" Hayes, Donald Barry, Frank M. Thomas, Doris Day, Jack Ingram, Hal Taliaferro, Lew Kelly, Lane Chandler, Jimmy Wakely

Early Roy Rogers film finds him fighting a gang of outlaws led by a desperado who turns out to be his own brother! The hidden identity or look-a-like theme was a common one for Roy's films of the late 1930s, but this well-produced western isn't lacking in action and excitement. "Gabby" Hayes is always a treat to watch, and Don Barry (future Red Ryder) is fine as Roy's outlaw brother. Familiar westerners Hal Taliaferro and Lane Chandler texture this one, and future singing cowboy favorite Jimmy Wakely plays a role.

1939   B & W 56 minutes

SAGEBRUSH TRAIL
★★★

DIRECTOR: Armand Schaefer
CAST: John Wayne, Nancy Shubert, Lane Chandler, Yakima Canutt, Wally Wales, Art Mix, Robert Burns, Earl Dwire

Big John Wayne, almost before he was shaving, is sent to prison for a murder he didn't commit. Naturally, our hero breaks out of the big house to clear his name. In a nice twist, he becomes friends—unknowingly—with the killer, who dies bravely in a climactic shootout. Good B western.

1933   B & W 58 minutes

SANTA FE STAMPEDE
★★½

DIRECTOR: George Sherman
CAST: John Wayne, Ray "Crash" Corrigan, Max Terhune, June Martel, William Farnum, LeRoy Mason

The Three Mesquiteers (John Wayne, Ray Corrigan, and Max Terhune) ride to the rescue of an old friend (William Farnum) who strikes it rich with a gold mine. A villain (LeRoy Mason) is trying to steal his claim. Lightweight western with plenty of action.

1938   B & W 58 minutes

SANTA FE TRAIL
★★★½

DIRECTOR: Michael Curtiz
CAST: Errol Flynn, Alan Hale, Olivia De Havilland, Ronald Reagan, Raymond Massey, Ward Bond, Van Heflin

Errol Flynn, Alan Hale, and Olivia De Havilland save this muddled western, with Ronald Reagan as one of Flynn's soldier buddies who go after John Brown (Raymond Massey).

1940   B & W 110 minutes

SANTEE
★★½

DIRECTOR: Gary Nelson

CAST: Glenn Ford, Dana Wynter, Michael Burns, Robert Donner, Jay Silverheels, Harry Townes, John Larch, Robert Wilke

Bounty hunter with a heart (Glenn Ford) loses his son and adopts the son of an outlaw he kills. A fine variety of old western hands add zip to this otherwise average oater. As usual, Ford turns in a solid performance. PG.

1973   93 minutes

SEARCHERS, THE
★★★★★
DIRECTOR: John Ford
CAST: John Wayne, Natalie Wood, Jeffrey Hunter, Ward Bond, Vera Miles, Harry Carey Jr., Lana Wood

John Ford is without a doubt the most celebrated director of westerns, and *The Searchers* is considered by many to be his masterpiece. In it, he and his favorite actor, John Wayne, reached the peak of their long and successful screen collaboration. This thoughtful film follows Ethan Edwards (Wayne), an embittered Indian-hating, ex–Confederate soldier as he leads the search for his niece (Natalie Wood), who was kidnapped years earlier by Indians. As time goes on, we begin to wonder whether Edwards is out to save the girl or kill her.

1956   119 minutes

SHALAKO

DIRECTOR: Edward Dmytryk
CAST: Sean Connery, Brigitte Bardot, Stephen Boyd, Jack Hawkins, Honor Blackman, Woody Strode

Here's an awful British western about European immigrants Sean Connery, Brigitte Bardot, Stephen Boyd, Jack Hawkins, and Honor Blackman menaced by Apaches in the Old West. Ugh!

1968   113 minutes

SHANE
★★★★★
DIRECTOR: George Stevens
CAST: Alan Ladd, Jean Arthur, Jack Palance, Van Heflin, Ben Johnson, Elisha Cook Jr.

Shane is surely among the best westerns ever made. Alan Ladd plays the title role, the mysterious stranger who emerges to help a group of homesteaders in their struggle against the cattlemen.

1953   118 minutes

SHENANDOAH
★★★★
DIRECTOR: Andrew V. McLaglen
CAST: James Stewart, Doug McClure, Glenn Corbett, Patrick Wayne, Katharine Ross, George Kennedy, Strother Martin

James Stewart gives a superb performance in this, director Andrew V. McLaglen's best western. Stewart plays a patriarch determined to keep his family out of the Civil War. He ultimately fails and is forced into action to save his children from the ravages of war. It's an emotionally moving, powerful tale.

1965   105 minutes

SHE WORE A YELLOW RIBBON
★★★★★
DIRECTOR: John Ford
CAST: John Wayne, Ben Johnson, Victor McLaglen, Harry Carey Jr., Mildred Natwick

Lest we forget, John Wayne was one of the screen's greatest actors. The Duke gave what was arguably his greatest performance in this gorgeous color western made by John Ford. As the aging Captain Nathan Brittles, Wayne plays a man set to retire but unwilling to leave his command at a time of impending war with the Apaches. The Ford stock company was never better: Ben Johnson, Victor McLaglen, Harry Carey Jr., and Mildred Natwick are all excellent. As a result, this is one of the great westerns.

1949   103 minutes

SHINE ON HARVEST MOON
★★

DIRECTOR: Joseph Kane

CAST: Roy Rogers, Mary Hart (Lynne Roberts), Lulu Belle and Scotty, Stanley Andrews, William Farnum, Frank Jacquet, Pat Henning, David Sharpe

Roy Rogers rides to the rescue once again as he aids the forces of law and order and brings a gang of robbers to justice while clearing an old man's name. Early entry in the series boasts silent great William Farnum and character actor Stanley Andrews (The Old Ranger from *Death Valley Days*) as well as ace stunt man David Sharpe. Unfortunately, this film also showcases Lulu Bell and Scotty and gives us Mary Hart instead of Dale Evans, still years away from her fortunate teaming with the "King of the Cowboys."

1938   B & W   60 minutes

SHOOTING, THE
★★★

DIRECTOR: Monte Hellman

CAST: Warren Oates, Millie Perkins, Will Hutchins, Jack Nicholson

This early Jack Nicholson vehicle, directed by cult figure Monte Hellman, is a moody western about revenge and murder. An interest-

ing entry into the genre, it may not be everyone's cup of tea. No rating; has some violence.

1967   82 minutes

SHOOTIST, THE
★★★★½

DIRECTOR: Don Siegel

CAST: John Wayne, Lauren Bacall, James Stewart, Ron Howard, Richard Boone, Hugh O'-Brian, John Carradine, Harry Morgan, Scatman Crothers

The Shootist is a special film in many ways. Historically, it is John Wayne's final film. Cinematically, it stands on its own as an intelligent tribute to the passing of the era known as the "Wild West." Wayne's masterful performance is touching and bitterly ironic as well. He plays a famous gunfighter dying of cancer and seeking a place to die in peace, only to become a victim of his own reputation. Little did Wayne or the audience know he was, literally, dying of cancer. Rated PG.

1976   99 minutes

SILENT CONFLICT
★★

DIRECTOR: George Archainbaud

CAST: William Boyd, Andy Clyde, Rand Brooks, Virginia Belmont, Earl Hodgins, James Harrison, Forbes Murray, Herbert Rawlinson, Richard Alexander

A traveling charlatan hypnotizes and drugs Lucky into stealing money and trying to kill Hoppy and California. The same rocks, same shack, and same backgrounds found in all these later Hopalong Cassidy films get familiar to the viewer after a while, but what is different about this entry into the thirteen-year series is that Hoppy actually walks around in pajamas! Richard Alexander (Prince Baron of the *Flash Gordon* serials) makes one of his frequent appearances in the series in this film, the sixty-first made since 1935.

1948   B & W   61 minutes

SILVER QUEEN
★★

DIRECTOR: Lloyd Bacon

CAST: George Brent, Priscilla Lane, Bruce Cabot, Lynne Overman, Eugene Pallette, Quinn Williams

Young and devoted daughter Priscilla Lane is determined to uphold her family's honor and pay her father's debts. She does so by gambling in San Francisco, where she develops a reputation as a real sharpie.

1942   B & W   81 minutes

SILVERADO
★★★★

DIRECTOR: Lawrence Kasdan

CAST: Kevin Kline, Scott Glenn, Kevin Costner, Danny Glover, Rosanna Arquette, John Cleese, Brian Dennehy, Linda Hunt, Jeff Goldblum

Imagine a movie with the nonstop thrills of *Raiders of the Lost Ark*, the wisecracking humor of *Ghostbusters*, and the valiant heroes of the *Star Wars* series set in the Old West. This should give you a fairly good idea how entertaining this new-style western is. Directed by Lawrence Kasdan (*The Big Chill*; *Body Heat*), it tells the story of four strangers—Scott Glenn, Kevin Kline, Kevin Costner, and Danny Glover—who ride side by side to clean up the town of Silverado. Excitement, laughs, thrills, and chills abound in this marvelous movie. Even those who don't ordinarily like westerns are sure

to enjoy it. Rated PG-13 for violence and profanity.

1985   133 minutes

SINGING BUCKAROO
★★

DIRECTOR: Tom Gibson

CAST: Fred Scott, William Faversham, Victoria Vinton, Cliff Nazarro, Howard Hill, Dick Curtis

Lesser-known western hero Fred Scott yodels the range for fly-by-night Spectrum Studios in this hard-ridin' horse opera about a frontier knight who pounds the prairie to help an innocent girl pursued and eventually kidnapped by villains intent on relieving her of her money. Nothing special but full of action interrupted by a few tunes. Average low budget musical western; mercifully short at less than one hour long.

1937   B & W   50 minutes

SINISTER JOURNEY
★★

DIRECTOR: George Archainbaud

CAST: William Boyd, Andy Clyde, Rand Brooks, Elaine Riley, John Kellogg, Don Haggerty, Stanley Andrews, Harry Strang, John Butler, Herbert Rawlinson

Coming to the aid of an old friend, Hoppy and his saddle pals find themselves involved in a mystery on a west-bound railroad. Standard Hopalong Cassidy film; doesn't have the punch of the earlier ones but is still worth the watch even though Hoppy doesn't wear his world-famous black outfit. This is the sixty-third in a series that was to dominate television in the late 1940s and early 1950s.

1948   B & W   58 minutes

SIOUX CITY SUE
★★

DIRECTOR: Frank McDonald
CAST: Gene Autry, Lynne Roberts, Sterling Holloway, Richard Lane, Pierre Watkins, Minerva Urecal, Kenne Duncan, Tristram Coffin, Tex Terry

Gene Autry's first film after World War II finds him in Hollywood, where he tries his luck in the movie business. Originally intended as the voice of an animated donkey, Autry wins the leading role in the picture when the big shots hear him stretch his tonsils. Rampaging rustlers throw a monkey wrench into the proceedings and provide Gene with an opportunity to show his stuff on the ground and on horseback. The inimitable Sterling Holloway leads a great cast of veteran actors and actresses that includes Pierre Watkins, Minerva Urecal, Tristram Coffin, and Kenne Duncan.

1946   B & W   69 minutes

SKIN GAME
★★★★

DIRECTOR: Paul Bogart
CAST: James Garner, Louis Gossett Jr., Susan Clark, Edward Asner, Andrew Duggan

Perceptive social comedy/drama set during the slave era. James Garner and Louis Gossett Jr. are a pair of con artists; Garner "sells" Gossett to unsuspecting slave owners and later helps break him free. The fleecing continues until they meet up with evil Edward Asner, who catches on to the act . . . then the story takes a chilling turn toward realism. Susan Clark has a grand supporting part as another amiable bandit. Excellent on all levels. Rated PG for light violence.

1971   102 minutes

SOLDIER BLUE
★★½

DIRECTOR: Ralph Nelson
CAST: Candice Bergen, Peter Strauss, John Anderson, Donald Pleasence

An extremely violent film that looks at the mistreatment of Indians at the hands of the U.S. Cavalry. This familiar subject has fared much better in films such as *Little Big Man*. Final attack is an exercise in excessive gore and violence. Rated R.

1970   112 minutes

SONG OF NEVADA
★★½

DIRECTOR: Joseph Kane
CAST: Roy Rogers, Dale Evans, Mary Lee, Bob Nolan and the Sons of the Pioneers, Lloyd Corrigan, Thurston Hall, John Eldredge, Forrest Taylor, George Meeker, Emmett Vogan, LeRoy Mason, Kenne Duncan, Si Jenks, Jack O'Shea

Roy, Dale, and the boys at the ranch come to the aid of an innocent girl who has become prey of a crook and his henchmen. This tuneful, hard-riding horse opera is chock-full of former cowboys and familiar faces and was intended to get the blood tingling and the toes tapping. It's typical of Roy's mid-1940s movies.

1944   B & W   75 minutes

SONG OF TEXAS
★★½

DIRECTOR: Joseph Kane
CAST: Roy Rogers, Sheila Ryan, Barton MacLane, Pat Brady, Harry Shannon, Arline Judge, Bob Nolan and the Sons of the Pioneers, Hal Taliaferro, Yakima Canutt, Tom London, Forrest Taylor, Eve March, Trigger

Roy Rogers and his friendly cow-pokes help a former champion cowboy overcome his alcoholism and regain his self-esteem as well as corralling the bad guys and putting them in the pokey. Peopled with familiar faces like Tom London and Hal Taliaferro, this film also features great villain Barton MacLane and rodeo and stunt legend Yakim Canutt. Ignore Pat Brady and enjoy the action and even the songs in this entertaining western, one of the last of Roy's outings. Originally released at sixty-nine minutes.

1953   B & W   54 minutes

SONS OF KATIE ELDER, THE
★★★

DIRECTOR: Henry Hathaway
CAST: John Wayne, Dean Martin, Earl Holliman, Michael Anderson Jr., James Gregory, George Kennedy, Martha Hyer, Jeremy Slate, Paul Fix

John Wayne stars in this entertaining film. Although this western rarely goes beyond the predictable, it's better than no Duke at all. There's plenty of action and roughhouse comedy.

1965   112 minutes

SOUTH OF THE BORDER
★★½

DIRECTOR: George Sherman
CAST: Gene Autry, Smiley Burnette, Lupita Tovar, Duncan Renaldo, June Storey, Mary Lee, William Farnum, Frank Reicher, Alan Edwards, Rex Lease, Reed Howes, Charles King, Hal Price, Dick Botiller, Claire DuBrey

Gene and Smiley mosey on down to Mexico as government operatives in order to quell a rebellion engineered by foreign powers who wish to control that country's oil resources. This patriotic film contains some good action scenes and boasts a fine cast of former cowboy favorites (William Farnum, Rex Lease, Charles King), as well as Reed Howes (the Arrow Shirt Man and at one time "the Handsomest Man in the Movies") and future Cisco Kid, Duncan Renaldo. Veteran actor Frank Reicher (the skipper in *King Kong*) is along for the ride, and Lupita Tovar, June Storey, and Mary Lee provide the female companionship for these rugged hombres. Pretty good Gene Autry, directed by George Sherman of Hopalong Cassidy fame.

1939   B & W   71 minutes

SPOILERS, THE
★★★★

DIRECTOR: Ray Enright
CAST: Marlene Dietrich, Randolph Scott, John Wayne, Harry Carey, Russell Simpson, George Cleveland

John Wayne is a miner who strikes gold in Nome, Alaska. An unscrupulous gold commissioner (Randolph Scott) and his cronies plot to steal the rich claim. But the Duke, his partner (Harry Carey), and their backer (Marlene Dietrich) have other ideas. This was the fourth of five screen versions of Rex Beach's novel. The first, in 1914, created a sensation with its spectacular (for its time) climactic fistfight, and each remake attempted to outdo it. The Wayne-Scott battle royal still stands as the best and helps make this action-filled "northern" a real winner.

1942   87 minutes

STAGECOACH
★★★★★

DIRECTOR: John Ford

CAST: John Wayne, Claire Trevor, Thomas Mitchell, John Carradine, Donald Meek, Andy Devine

John Ford utilized the "*Grand Hotel* formula" of placing a group of unrelated characters together in some common setting or dangerous situation. A stagecoach trip across the Old West provides the common setting and plenty of shared danger. Riding together with the mysterious Ringo Kid (John Wayne) is a grand assortment of some of Hollywood's best character actors, including Claire Trevor, Thomas Mitchell, John Carradine, Donald Meek, and Andy Devine. *Stagecoach* was Wayne's first big starring vehicle.

1939   B & W   99 minutes

STAR PACKER, THE
★★½

DIRECTOR: Robert N. Bradbury
CAST: John Wayne, Verna Hillie, George "Gabby" Hayes, Yakima Canutt, Earl Dwire, George Cleveland

The Shadow and his band of outlaws have a group of ranchers cowed until John Wayne rides into town and turns the tables on the baddies. A good B western that will be best appreciated by Wayne fans.

1934   B & W   60 minutes

STRANGE GAMBLE
★★

DIRECTOR: George Archainbaud
CAST: William Boyd, Andy Clyde, Rand Brooks, Elaine Riley, Joan Barton, James Craven, Herbert Rawlinson, Alberto Morin, Lee Tung Foo, Joel Friedkin

The crooked "boss" of a small town steals valuable mining rights from a drunken customer and leaves his sick sister without any money or place to stay. Hoppy and his pals intervene and encounter gunplay and fast riding as they attempt to return to the victim her rightful fortune. Hopalong Cassidy eschews his usual somber black and dresses like a dude in this one—he resembles Sky King. The bad element in town can't figure Hoppy out, either, and reckons he's a rival gunman come to cut in on the easy pickings. This is the sixty-sixth and last film in the thirteen-year run of the Hopalong Cassidy series.

1948   B & W   61 minutes

STRANGER AND THE GUNFIGHTER, THE
★★½

DIRECTOR: Anthony Dawson
CAST: Lee Van Cleef, Lo Lieh, Patty Shepard

The world may never be ready for this improbable mix, a tongue-in-cheek spaghetti western by way of a standard kung-fu chop-chop flick. Lee Van Cleef, as another of his weary gunslingers, teams with martial arts master Lo Lieh to find a missing treasure. The only map is in sections, each of which is tattooed on the rather delicate backsides of various comely wenches. A classic this isn't, but the fast action and camp humor make it watchable. Rated PG for violence.

1976   107 minutes

SUNSET SERENADE
★★½

DIRECTOR: Joseph Kane
CAST: Roy Rogers, George "Gabby" Hayes, Helen Parrish, Onslow Stevens, Joan Woodbury, Frank M. Thomas, Bob Nolan and the Sons of the Pioneers, Roy Barcroft, Jack Kirk, Dick Wessell, Rex Lease, Jack Ingram, Budd Buster

Beady-eyed Roy Rogers and his ornery sidekick "Gabby" Hayes thwart the plans of a couple of no-goods who aim to murder the heir to a ranch and take it over for themselves. Bob Nolan and the boys sing up a storm and do some hard ridin' as well while character great Roy Barcroft and sagebrush veterans Rex Lease and Budd Buster give this oft-told story an element of class and authenticity. Enjoyable enough and not too demanding.

1942   B & W   58 minutes

SUPPORT YOUR LOCAL SHERIFF!
★★★★½

DIRECTOR: Burt Kennedy
CAST: James Garner, Joan Hackett, Walter Brennan, Harry Morgan, Jack Elam, Bruce Dern, Henry Jones

The time-honored backbone of the industry, the western, takes a real ribbing in this all-stops-out send-up. If it can be parodied, it is—in spades. James Garner is great as a gambler "just passing through" who gets roped into being sheriff and tames a lawless mining town against all odds, including an inept deputy, fem-lib mayor's daughter, and snide gunman. A very funny picture. Rated G.

1969   93 minutes

SUSANNA PASS
★½

DIRECTOR: William Witney
CAST: Roy Rogers, Dale Evans, Estelita Rogdriguez, Martin Garralaga, Robert Emmett Keane, Lucien Littlefield, Douglas Fowley, David Sharpe, Foy Willing and the Riders of the Purple Sage, Trigger

Another variation on the crooked newspaper publisher theme, this minor effort again teams Roy Rogers and Dale Evans, the "King and Queen of the Westerns," with "Cuban Fireball" Estelita Rodriguez. Too many tunes and production numbers, as well as Republic Studios' vain effort to promote their south-of-the-border discovery, detract from the action in this film. Famous stunt man David Sharpe has a role in this one as well as performing the leaps and fights he was famous for. Filmed in Trucolor.

1949   67 minutes

TALL IN THE SADDLE
★★★½

DIRECTOR: Edwin L. Marin
CAST: John Wayne, George "Gabby" Hayes, Ward Bond, Ella Raines

A first-rate B western that combines mystery with shoot-'em-up action. John Wayne is wrongly accused of murder and must find the real culprit. Helping him is Gabby Hayes, and hindering is Ward Bond.

1944   B & W   87 minutes

TELL THEM WILLIE BOY IS HERE
★★★

DIRECTOR: Abraham Polonsky
CAST: Robert Redford, Robert Blake, Katharine Ross

Robert Redford is a southwestern sheriff in the early days of this country. He is pursuing an Indian (Robert Blake) who is fleeing to avoid arrest. The story is elevated from a standard western chase by the dignity and concern shown to the Indian's viewpoint. Rated PG.

1969   96 minutes

TENNESSEE'S PARTNER
★★½

DIRECTOR: Allan Dwan
CAST: John Payne, Ronald Reagan, Rhonda Fleming, Colleen Gray

Allan Dwan directed this minor western featuring Ronald Reagan as a stranger who steps into the middle of a fight between gamblers and ends up befriending one (John Payne). This is one of Payne's better roles. He plays a bad guy who gets turned around by Reagan. Good little drama; better than the title suggests.

1955   87 minutes

TERROR OF TINY TOWN, THE
🐴

DIRECTOR: Sam Newfield
CAST: Billy Curtis, Yvonne Moray, Little Billy, John Bambury

The definitive all-midget western, with action, gunplay, romance, and a happy ending to boot. Just about as odd as they come, this turkey is an entertaining, if mysterious, bad movie. One keeps asking, "Why did they do this? Are they serious?" Well, they did it, and whether they were serious or not, this little film is one of a kind.

1938   B & W   63 minutes

TEXAS
★★★

DIRECTOR: George Marshall
CAST: William Holden, Glenn Ford, Claire Trevor, George Barcroft, Edgar Buchanan, Raymond Hatton

Friends William Holden and Glenn Ford are rivals for the affections of Claire Trevor in this lively, action-jammed western pitting cattleman against cattle rustler in the sprawling land of Sam Houston. It might have been an epic, but a cost-conscious producer kept a tight rein. Good, though! And no one could play a good-hearted, trail-wise-girl like Claire Trevor. Not even Dietrich or Stanwyck.

1941   B & W   93 minutes

TEXAS JOHN SLAUGHTER: GERONIMO'S REVENGE
★★½

DIRECTOR: James Neilson
CAST: Tom Tryon, Darryl Hickman, Betty Lynn, Brian Corcoran, Adeline Harris, Annette Gorman, Harry Carey Jr.

Peace-loving Texas John Slaughter is forced to take up arms against his Apache friends when renegade Geronimo goes on the warpath. Full of action and filmed in authentic-looking locations, this feature is composed of episodes originally broadcast on the popular television show *Walt Disney Presents*. Texas John Slaughter was a minor phenomenon, like the wildly popular Davy Crockett before him, and spawned a number of merchandising products, such as guns, hats, holsters, and comic books.

1960   77 minutes

TEXAS JOHN SLAUGHTER: STAMPEDE AT BITTER CREEK
★★½

DIRECTOR: Harry Keller
CAST: Tom Tryon, Harry Carey Jr., Adeline Harris, Annette Gorman, Betty Lynn, Stephen McNally, Grant Williams, Sidney Blackmer, Bill Williams

Former Texas Ranger John Slaughter is falsely accused of rustling as he attempts to drive his cattle into New Mexico despite threats from a rival rancher and his hired gun. Tom Tryon is ruggedly heroic as Texas John

Slaughter in this Disney adventure western culled from episodes originally featured on *Walt Disney Presents* from 1958 to 1962, rotating weekly with *The Nine Lives of Elfego Baca*, *Swamp Fox*, and *Zorro*. All of these shows were well produced and shot on picturesque outdoor locations. Director Harry Keller was a veteran western director at Republic Studios when they cranked out all those Roy Rogers, Gene Autry, and John Wayne shoot-'em-ups.

1962   52 minutes

TEXAS JOHN SLAUGHTER: WILD TIMES
★★½

DIRECTOR: Harry Keller
CAST: Tom Tryon, Harry Carey Jr., Adeline Harris, Annette Gorman, Betty Lynn, Brian Corcoran, Robert Middleton

This film is a compilation of episodes from the popular series starring future best-selling author Tom Tryon as the lawman-turned-rancher. Handsomely photographed and well acted, these shows were originally released theatrically in Europe and, thanks to the video revolution, are available once again. Western veteran Harry Carey Jr. plays a continuing role in this series, as he did for the earlier daytime serial *Spin and Marty*.

1962   77 minutes

TEXAS LADY
★★

DIRECTOR: Tim Whelan
CAST: Claudette Colbert, Barry Sullivan, John Litel

An out-of-her-element Claudette Colbert is a crusading newspaper editor in the Old West. If you're a western fan, you'll like it.

1955   86 minutes

THERE WAS A CROOKED MAN
★★★½

DIRECTOR: Joseph L. Mankiewicz
CAST: Kirk Douglas, Henry Fonda, Hume Cronyn, Warren Oates, Burgess Meredith, Arthur O'-Connell, Martin Gabel, Alan Hale, Lee Grant, John Randolph, Barbara Rhoades

Crooked-as-they-come Kirk Douglas bides and does his time harried by holier-than-thou Arizona prison warden Henry Fonda, who has more than redemption on his mind. A good plot and clever casting make this oater well worth the watching. And, yes, rattlesnakes do make good watchdogs. Rated R.

1970   123 minutes

THEY CALL ME TRINITY
★★½

DIRECTOR: E. B. Clucher
CAST: Terence Hill, Bud Spencer, Farley Granger

This western comedy can be best described as an Italian *Blazing Saddles*. Terence Hill and Bud Spencer team up as half-brothers trying to protect a colony from cattle rustlers and a shady sheriff. Rated G.

1971   109 minutes

THEY DIED WITH THEIR BOOTS ON
★★★★

DIRECTOR: Raoul Walsh
CAST: Errol Flynn, Olivia De Havilland, Arthur Kennedy, Gene Lockhart, Anthony Quinn, Sydney Greenstreet

Errol Flynn gives a first-rate performance as General George Custer in this Warner Bros. classic directed by Raoul Walsh. The superb supporting cast adds to this western epic.

1941   B & W 138 minutes

THREE FACES WEST
★★★

DIRECTOR: Bernard Vorhaus

CAST: John Wayne, Charles Coburn, Sigrid Gurie, Spencer Charters

John Wayne is the leader of a group of Dust Bowl farmers attempting to survive in this surprisingly watchable Republic release. Sigrid Gurie and Charles Coburn costar as the European immigrants who show them what courage means.

1940　　B & W　79 minutes

3:10 TO YUMA
★★★★

DIRECTOR: Delmer Daves

CAST: Glenn Ford, Van Heflin, Felicia Farr, Leora Dana, Henry Jones, Richard Jaeckel, Robert Emhardt

This first-rate adult western draws its riveting drama and power from the interaction of well-drawn characters rather than gun-blazing action. A farmer (Van Heflin) captures a notorious gunman (Glenn Ford) and, while waiting for the train to take them to Yuma prison, must hole up in a hotel and overcome the killer's numerous ploys to gain his freedom. This well-acted movie recalls the classic *High Noon*.

1957　　B & W　92 minutes

TOM HORN
★★½

DIRECTOR: William Wiard

CAST: Steve McQueen, Richard Farnsworth, Billy Green Bush, Slim Pickens, Elisha Cook Jr.

Steve McQueen doesn't give a great performance in his next-to-last motion picture, about the last days of a real-life Wyoming bounty hunter, nor does director William

Wiard craft a memorable western. But this 1980 release does have its moments—most of them provided by supporting players Richard Farnsworth (*The Grey Fox*), Billy Green Bush (*The Culpepper Cattle Company*), the late Slim Pickens, and the always reliable Elisha Cook. Rated R.

1980　　　　98 minutes

TRAIL BEYOND, THE
★★½

DIRECTOR: Robert N. Bradbury

CAST: John Wayne, Verna Hillie, Noah Beery Sr., Irish Lancaster, Noah Beery Jr., Robert Fraser, Earl Dwire

Once again, John Wayne rides to the rescue in a low-budget western from the 1930s. It's pretty typical stuff as the Duke fights outlaws who are attempting to steal a gold mine. But this B western has lots of action and a rare appearance of father and son actors Noah Beery Sr. and Noah Beery Jr.

1934　　B & W　55 minutes

TRAIL OF ROBIN HOOD
★★★

DIRECTOR: William Witney

CAST: Roy Rogers, Penny Edwards, Gordon Jones, Jack Holt, Emory Parnell, Clifton Young, Rex Allen, Allan "Rocky" Lane, Monte Hale, Kermit Maynard, Tom Keene, Ray "Crash" Corrigan, William Farnum, George Chesebro

This star-studded oddity finds Roy Rogers and a handful of contemporary western heroes aiding screen great Jack Holt (playing himself) in his effort to provide Christmas trees to needy families in time for the holidays. A pleasant yuletide gift to the children of America from Republic Studios, this warm-hearted film gives us nine sagebrush stars and former six-gun toters as well as reuniting near-legendary heavy George Chesebro with Jack Holt, one of the finest of all action stars and the father of 1950s hero Tim Holt. This ensemble film (like the previous *Bells of Rosarita*, etc.) gave the studio a chance to show off their contract stars. Enjoyable film for all ages and a special treat for fans of the genre. One of Roy's strangest films.

1950   67 minutes

TRAIN ROBBERS, THE
★★½

DIRECTOR: Burt Kennedy

CAST: John Wayne, Ben Johnson, Ann-Margret, Rod Taylor, Ricardo Montalban

This is a typical example of John Wayne's films during his last decade of work. A good cast and an interesting idea go to waste at the hands of a second-rate director. Burt Kennedy and fellow director Andrew V. McLaglen were at the helm during most of Wayne's westerns throughout the 1970s, and neither could do him justice. This is no exception. Wayne and Ben Johnson join Ann-Margret in a search for a lost train and gold. Some nice moments but generally unsatisfying. For hard-core Wayne fans only. Rated PG for violence, but nothing extreme.

1973   92 minutes

TRAITOR, THE
★★½

DIRECTOR: Sam Newfield

CAST: Tim McCoy, Frances Grant, Wally Wales, J. Frank Glendon, Karl Hackett, Jack Rockwell

Marshal Tim McCoy goes undercover to catch a gang of cutthroats. He succeeds in his plan of joining the outlaws, but his life is in constant danger. This routine western features a game performance by McCoy, but the story is too typical and the direction is plodding.

1936   B & W   56 minutes

TRAMPLERS, THE
★½

DIRECTOR: Albert Band

CAST: Gordon Scott, Joseph Cotten, James Mitchum, Ilaria Occhini, Franco Nero

Gordon Scott returns from the Civil War to find his father (Joseph Cotten) trying to preserve the prewar South by burning out settlers and starting mass lynchings. Scott and his younger brother (James Mitchum), unable to abide his fathers actions, leave and join up with their father's enemies. In typical spaghetti western fashion, the film ends with the big shootout. Hard-core western fans may enjoy this film, but all others will not find much entertainment.

1966   105 minutes

TREASURE OF PANCHO VILLA, THE
★

DIRECTOR: George Sherman

CAST: Rory Calhoun, Shelley Winters, Gilbert Roland, Joseph Calleia

The legendary Mexican bandit has long been a film subject. This slow account of his exploits does little for his reputation and appeal as a colorful character of history. Only a good cast keeps it from being dubbed a bomb.

1955   96 minutes

TRIGGER, JR.
★★★

DIRECTOR: William Witney

CAST: Roy Rogers, Dale Evans, Pat Brady, Gordon Jones, Grant Withers, Peter Miles, George Cleveland, Frank Fenton, I. Stanford Jolley, Stanley Andrews, Foy Willing and the Riders of the Purple Stage, The Raynor Lehr Circus

This Trucolor Roy Rogers film has everything going for it in the form of plot, songs, character actors, and hard ridin'. Roy, Dale, and the gang battle an unscrupulous gang of blackmailers as well as teaching a young boy to overcome his fear of horses, particularly Trigger and his son, Trigger Jr. There's even a circus to prompt some tunes from Roy and Dale and their backup ranch hands. Look for character actors Grant (Jungle Jim) Withers, Stanley (Old Ranger) Andrews, and George Cleveland, Gramps on television's "Lassie". Try to ignore lame-brained Pat Brady, a poor substitute for "Gabby" Hayes. Filmed in Trucolor, this is a good one for the kids and people who avoid old westerns because they don't like black and white.

1950   68 minutes

TRINITY IS STILL MY NAME
★★

DIRECTOR: E. B. Clucher
CAST: Bud Spencer, Terence Hill, Harry Carey Jr.

In this comedy sequel to *They Call Me Trinity*, Bud Spencer and Terence Hill again team up as the unlikely heroes of an Italian western. Rated G.

1972   117 minutes

TRIUMPHS OF A MAN CALLED HORSE
★½

DIRECTOR: John Hough
CAST: Richard Harris, Michel Beck, Ana De Sade

Richard Harris has his third go-round in the title role as John Morgan, an English nobleman who was captured by the Sioux in 1825 and eventually became their leader. Unlike its excellent predecessors, *A Man Called Horse* and *Return of a Man Called Horse*, *Triumphs* is cornball, cliché, and badly directed, by Englishman John Hough. In a real cheat, Harris is killed off in the first third of the film. That leaves the way clear for his gun-slinging son, Koda (Michael Beck), to take over the leadership of the tribe and battle the greedy gold prospectors invading their land. Yawn. Rated PG for violence and implied sex.

1983   86 minutes

TRUE GRIT
★★★★

DIRECTOR: Henry Hathaway
CAST: John Wayne, Kim Darby, Robert Duvall, Glen Campbell

John Wayne finally won his best-actor Oscar for his 1969 portrayal of a boozy marshal helping a tough-minded girl (Kim Darby) track down her father's killers. Well-directed by Henry Hathaway, it's still not one of the Duke's classics—although it does have many good scenes, the best of which is the final shootout between Wayne's Rooster Cogburn and chief baddie, Ned Pepper (Robert Duvall). Rated G.

1969   128 minutes

TWILIGHT IN THE SIERRAS
★★

DIRECTOR: William Witney
CAST: Roy Rogers, Dale Evans, Estelita Rodriguez, Pat Brady, Russ Vincent, George Meeker, Fred Kohler Jr., House Peters Jr., Edward Keane, Pierce Lyden, Bob Burns, Foy Willing and the Riders of the Purple Sage

Roy Rogers and his sweetheart Dale Evans are weighed down by Estelita Rodriguez and moronic comedy relief Pat Brady in this story about state parole officer Roy and his two-fisted battles with a group of counterfeiters. Not as good as most of the series, this one runs a long (for a Roy Rogers) sixty-seven minutes and was filmed in Trucolor. The offspring of silent star House Peters and hulking heavy Fred Kohler have parts in this later entry, and Foy Willing and the boys do the pickin' and the yodelin'.

1950   67 minutes

TWO MULES FOR SISTER SARA
★★★
DIRECTOR: Don Siegel
CAST: Clint Eastwood, Shirley MacLaine, Manolo Fabregas

Clint Eastwood returns in his role of the Man with No Name (originated in Sergio Leone's Italian spaghetti westerns: *A Fistful of Dollars; For a Few Dollars More*; etc.), and Shirley MacLaine is an unlikely nun in this entertaining comedy-western. Rated PG.

1970   105 minutes

UNDER CALIFORNIA STARS
★★½
DIRECTOR: William Witney
CAST: Roy Rogers, Jane Frazee, Andy Devine, Michael Chapin, Wade Crosby, House Peters Jr., Steve Clark, Bob Nolan and the Sons of the Pioneers

Trigger, the "Smartest Horse in the Movies," is the victim of a horse-napping plot in this Roy Rogers oater. A gang of no-goods decide to stop trapping and selling regular wild horses and set their sights on the golden stallion, much to Roy's dismay. With the help of wheezing Andy Devine and Bob Nolan and his singing cowpokes, Roy saves his prized palomino and brings the culprits to justice. Long for a Roy Rogers programmer at seventy-one minutes. Filmed in Trucolor.

1948   71 minutes

UNEXPECTED GUEST
★★
DIRECTOR: George Archainbaud
CAST: William Boyd, Andy Clyde, Rand Brooks, Una O'Connor, John Parrish, Earle Hodgins, Robert B. Williams, Patricia Tate, Ned Young, Joel Friedkin

Hopalong Cassidy comes to the aid of his saddle pal and comic relief California (Andy Clyde) after they discover that someone is trying to murder the cantankerous old cuss and all of his relatives. Hoppy gets to the bottom of things and uncovers a plot that revolves around an inheritance due the family. This is one of the last dozen titles that William Boyd produced himself, and everything about the series was threadbare by this, the fifty-seventh entry in a dozen years.

1947   B & W   59 minutes

VALLEY OF FIRE
★★
DIRECTOR: John English
CAST: Gene Autry, Pat Buttram Gail Davis, Russell Hayden, Riley Hall, Terry Frost, Gregg Barton, Harry Lauter, Margie Liszt, Victor Sen Yung

Gene Autry's bland personality, flashing fists, and spontaneous burst of song are more then enough to tame a wide-open town. After dispersing or recruiting the bad elements in town, Gene plays matchmaker and, along with comic relief Pat Buttram, delivers a flock of females just dying to marry up with smelly prospectors and settle down in greasy tents. Pretty good fun and peopled with cowboy (and cowgirl) favorites from films and television.

1951   B & W   63 minutes

VERA CRUZ
★★★

DIRECTOR: Robert Aldrich
CAST: Gary Cooper, Burt Lancaster, Denise Darcel, Ernest Borgnine

Two American soldiers of fortune find themselves in different camps during one of the many Mexican revolutions of the 1800s. Gary Cooper is the good guy, but Burt Lancaster steals every scene as the smiling, black-dressed baddie. The plot is pretty basic but holds your interest until the traditional climactic gunfight.

1954   94 minutes

VILLA RIDES
★★

DIRECTOR: Buzz Kulik
CAST: Yul Brynner, Robert Mitchum, Charles Bronson, Herbert Lom, Jill Ireland, Alexander Knox, Fernando Rey

Uneven rehash of the Pancho Villa legend ignores the wealth of the real story and becomes yet another comic-book adventure of the lethal yet patriotic bandit-hero and the gringo he comes to depend on and grudgingly respect. Yul Brynner puts on some hair and steps under the same sombrero worn on different occasions by Wallace Beery and Telly Savalas and brings about the same understanding to the role. Robert Mitchum reprises his character from Richard Fleischer's *Bandido* and is always interesting to watch even when he's laid back—the same goes for Charles Bronson, who plays an-

other of his enigmatic, dangerous characters. Good cast, but this ill-fated production doesn't deliver what it should, and film buffs will always chalk it up to the fact that Sam Peckinpah's screenplay was tampered with and his direct involvement with the project limited. There are still some good films to be made about the United States' "war" with Mexico and Villa in the second decade of this century, but unfortunately, this isn't one of them.

1968   125 minutes

WAGONMASTER
★★★★½

DIRECTOR: John Ford
CAST: Ben Johnson, Ward Bond, Harry Carey Jr., Joanne Dru, James Arness

John Ford was unquestionably the greatest director of westerns. This release ranks with the best of Ford's work. The only reason we can fathom for its being ignored is the absence of a big-name star. Yet Bond, who plays the elder in this story of a Mormon congregation migrating west, became a star, thanks to the popular television series it inspired: "Wagon Train." And Johnson, who won the best-supporting-actor Oscar in 1971 for *The Last Picture Show*, is excellent in his first starring role. Thanks to them and Ford's genius, *Wagonmaster* is a first-rate western.

1950   B & W   86 minutes

WAR OF THE WILDCATS
★★★

DIRECTOR: Albert S. Rogell
CAST: John Wayne, Martha Scott, Albert Dekker, George "Gabby" Hayes, Sidney Blackmer, Dale Evans

Big John Wayne takes on bad guy Albert Dekker in this story of oil drillers at the turn of the century. Gabby Hayes adds a vintage touch to this standard-formula Republic feature.

1943   B & W 102 minutes

WAR WAGON, THE
★★★½

DIRECTOR: Burt Kennedy
CAST: John Wayne, Kirk Douglas, Howard Keel, Keenan Wynn

While not John Wayne at his best, this western, co-starring Kirk Douglas and directed by Burt Kennedy, does have plenty of laughs and action. It's guaranteed to keep fans of the Duke and shoot-'em-ups pleasantly entertained.

1967   101 minutes

WARLOCK
★★★

DIRECTOR: Edward Dmytryk
CAST: Henry Fonda, Richard Widmark, Anthony Quinn, Dorothy Malone

Even a high-voltage cast cannot energize this slow-paced "adult" western. Lack of action hurts this film, which concentrates on psychological homosexual aspects of the relationship between gunfighter Henry Fonda and gambler Anthony Quinn. Richard Widmark is all but lost in the background as the town sheriff.

1959   121 minutes

WEST OF THE DIVIDE
★★★

DIRECTOR: Robert N. Bradbury
CAST: John Wayne, Virginia Brown Faire, George "Gabby" Hayes, Lloyd Whitlock, Yakima Canutt, Earl Dwire

John Wayne is on the trail of his father's murderer (again) in this standard B western, which has the slight twist of having the Duke also searching for his younger brother, who has been missing since dear old Dad took the fatal bullet. Looks as if it was made in a day—and probably was. Good stunt work, though.

1934   B & W   54 minutes

WESTERNER, THE
★★★★

DIRECTOR: William Wyler
CAST: Gary Cooper, Walter Brennan, Forrest Tucker, Chill Wills, Dana Andrews, Tom Tyler, Fred Stone, Doris Davenport

The plot revolves around earnest settlers being run off their land. But the heart of this classic yarn rests in the complex relationship that entwines Judge Roy Bean (Walter Brennan) and a lanky stranger (Gary Cooper). Bean is a fascinating character, burdened with a strange sense of morality and an obsession for actress Lily Langtree. Brennan won an Oscar for his portrayal. Cooper is at his laconic best. And director William Wyler gives the film a haunting, lyrical quality.

1940   B & W 100 minutes

WHEEL OF FORTUNE
★★½

DIRECTOR: John H. Auer
CAST: John Wayne, Frances Dee, Ward Bond

John Wayne in a screwball comedy? Yep. Also titled *A Man Betrayed*, the surprise is that this low-budget production is watchable.

1941   B & W   83 minutes

WHEN A MAN RIDES ALONE
★★

DIRECTOR: J. P. McGowan
CAST: Tom Tyler, Alan Bridge

Whenever John Wayne needed a formidable screen opponent, Tom Tyler was a good choice. John Ford used the deep-voiced, steely-eyed Tyler to portray Luke Plummer, the Ringo Kid's enemy, in *Stagecoach* (1939). Tyler also drew down on the Duke in Howard Hawk's *Red River* (1948) and played a heroic soldier who sang the title tune in Ford's *She Wore a Yellow Ribbon* (1949). But mostly, Tyler was a star of B westerns like this none too original entry about a Robin Hood–style good guy thwarting a crooked mine owner. Tyler became one of the Three Mesquiteers (with Bob Steele) toward the end of that popular series and is perhaps best known today as the star of the superhero serial *The Adventures of Captain Marvel* and as the title monster in *The Mummy's Hand*.

1933   B & W   60 minutes

WHEN THE LEGENDS DIE
★★★½

DIRECTOR: Stuart Millar
CAST: Richard Widmark, Frederic Forrest

A young Ute Indian is taken from his home in the Colorado Rockies after his parents die. In the modern white world he is taught the "new ways." His extraordinary riding abilities make him a target for exploitation as Red Dillon (Richard Widmark) trains him as a rodeo bronco rider, then proceeds to cash in on his protégé's success. A touching story that finds Widmark in one of his better roles and introduces a young Frederic Forrest. Rated PG for some mild profanity.

1972   105 minutes

WILD BUNCH, THE
★★★★½

DIRECTOR: Sam Peckinpah
CAST: William Holden, Ernest Borgnine, Robert Ryan, Ben Johnson, Edmond O'Brien, Warren Oates, Strother Martin, L. Q. Jones, Emilio Fernandez

The Wild Bunch, a classic western, was brilliantly directed by Sam Peckinpah. He created a whole new approach to violence in this landmark film about men making a last stand. It is without a doubt Peckinpah's greatest film and is bursting with action, vibrant characters, and memorable dialogue. Good acting, too, by a first-rate cast. Rated R.

1969   145 minutes

WILD TIMES
★★★

DIRECTOR: Richard Compton
CAST: Sam Elliott, Ben Johnson, Timothy Scott, Harry Carey Jr., Bruce Boxleitner, Penny Peyser, Dennis Hopper, Cameron Mitchell, Pat Hingle, Gene Evans, Leif Erickson, Trish Stewart

A two-cassette western originally made for television. Sam Elliott plays sharp-shooter High Cardiff, whose life is anything but easy as he makes his way across the Old West. This could have been helped by some trimming.

1980   200 minutes

WINDS OF THE WASTELAND
★★★

DIRECTOR: Mack V. Wright
CAST: John Wayne, Phyllis Fraser, Yakima Canutt, Lane Chandler, Sam Flint, Lew Kelly, Bob Kortman

Big John Wayne is the head of a stagecoach company that competes for a government mail contract in the days after the pony express. Better than most B westerns made by the Duke, because he was beginning to show more polish and confidence, but still no classic.

1936   B & W   57 minutes

WINDWALKER
★★★★

DIRECTOR: Keith Merril
CAST: Trevor Howard, Nick Ramus, James Remar, Serene Hedin, Dusty Iron, Wing McCrea

Trevor Howard plays the title role in this superb film which spans three generations of a Cheyenne Indian family. It refutes the unwritten rule that family entertainment has to be bland and predictable and is proof that films don't need to include sensationalism to hold the attention of modern filmgoers. *Windwalker* has all the joy, drama, and excitement you could ever ask for in a motion picture. Rated PG.

1980   108 minutes

WINNING OF THE WEST
★★

DIRECTOR: George Archainbaud
CAST: Gene Autry, Smiley Burnette, Gail Davis, Robert Livingston, Richard Crane, House Peters Jr., Gregg Barton, George Chesebro, Eddie Parker

Smiley Burnette was reunited with Gene Autry in this film. With the exception of one film in 1951, Gene and Smiley were not to be teamed for eleven years, and it's fitting that these two old-timers should ride off into the sunset in each other's company. The plot line? Same old stuff about a brave newspaper publisher who wants to stop corruption and lawlessness and enlists the aid of no-nonsense Gene and all-nonsense Smiley. Former stars Robert Livingston and House Peters Jr., as well as veteran stunt performers Gregg Barton and Eddie Parker, make this one interesting to watch. Perky Gail Davis reprises her role as somebody's daughter who has a yen for Gene but loses him to Smiley and Champion.

1953   B & W   57 minutes

YELLOW ROSE OF TEXAS
★★

DIRECTOR: Joseph Kane
CAST: Roy Rogers, Dale Evans, George Cleveland, Harry Shannon, Grant Withers, Bob Nolan and the Sons of the Pioneers, Hal Taliaferro, Tom London, Dick Botiller, Rex Lease, Jack O'Shea

Roy Rogers plays an undercover insurance agent out to clear the name of an old man who has been accused of aiding a stage robbery. Dale Evans and the Sons of the Pioneers give Roy a hand, and Grant Withers evils it up as the ruthless heavy. Former Cowboy stars Rex Lease and Hal Taliaferro join veteran character actors like Tom London to make this an enjoyable but standard Republic programmer. Originally released at sixty-nine minutes.

1944   B & W   55 minutes

CAST INDEX

Aames, Willie: Frankenstein (Remake), *688;* Paradise, *113;* Zapped!, *385*

Aaron, Brian: Last Winter, The, *515*

Abbott, Bruce: Re-animator, *733*

Abbott, Bud: Abbott and Costello in Hollywood, *214;* Abbott and Costello Meet Captain Kidd, *214;* Abbott and Costello Meet Dr. Jekyll and Mr. Hyde, *214;* Abbott and Costello Meet Frankenstein, *214;* Africa Screams, *215;* Buck Privates, *235;* Hold That Ghost, *281;* World of Abbott and Costello, The, *383*

Abbott, Diahnne: Jo Jo Dancer, Your Life Is Calling, *502;* Love Streams, *524*

Abbott, John: Pursuit to Algiers, *117*

Abbott, Margaret: Love Streams, *524*

Abdul-Jabbar, Kareem: Airplane!, *216;* Game of Death, *61*

Abella, Helena: Final Justice, *54*

Abel, Alan: Putney Swope, *337*

Abel, Alfred: Metropolis (musical version), *793;* Metropolis, *852*

Abel, Walter: Raintree County, *574;* 13 Rue Madeleine, *149*

Abraham, F. Murray: Amadeus, *769;* Ritz, The, *342*

Abril, Victoria: L'Addition, *510;* Moon in the Gutter, The, *538*

Ackland, Joss: Adventures of Sherlock Holmes: The Copper Beeches, *3;* Mind Snatchers, The, *717;* Saint Jack, *587*

Ackroyd, David: Cocaine: One Man's Seduction, *435;* Dark Secret of Harvest Home, The, *669*

Acuff, Eddie: Rough Riders' Roundup, *928*

Adair, Jean: Arsenic and Old Lace, *220*

Adames, John: Gloria, *62*

Adams, Andrea: Ripper, The, *736*

Adams, Beverly: Torture Garden, *758*

Adams, Brooke: Almost You, *217;* Cuba, *37;* Days of Heaven, *446;* Dead Zone, The, *671;* Invasion of the Body Snatchers (Remake), *845;* Key Exchange, *506;* Man, A Woman and a Bank, A, *95;* Shock Waves (Death Corps), *742;* Tell Me A Riddle, *612;* Utilities, *376*

Adams, Casey: Bus Stop, *236;* Indestructible Man, *705*

Adams, Edie: Apartment, The, *219;* It's a Mad Mad Mad Mad World, *288;* Lover Come Back, *303;* Up in Smoke, *375*

Adams, Ernie: Frontier Pony Express, *898*

Adams, Jane: Brute Man, The, *658*

Adams, Jonathan: Adventures of Sherlock Holmes: The Norwood Builder, *5*

Adams, Julie: Away All Boats, *11;* Tickle Me, *809;* Bend of the River, *882;* Creature from the Black Lagoon, *665*

Adams, Marla: Gotcha!, *64*

Adams, Mason: Final Conflict, The, *684;* F/X, *51*

Adams, Maud: Man With the Golden Gun, The, *96;* Octopussy, *109;* Rollerball, *860;* Tattoo, *611*

Adams, Nick: Godzilla vs. Monster Zero, *694;* No Time for Sergeants, *320;* Rebel without a Cause, *576;* Teacher's Pet, *364*

Adams, Tom: Fighting Prince of Donegal, The, *181*

Addams, Dawn: King in New York, A, *292;* Moon Is Blue, The, *314;* Robe, The, *581;* Vault of Horror, *761*

Addison, Nancy: Somewhere, Tomorrow, 206

Addy, Wesley: Bostonians, The, 417

Ades, Danny: Aguirre: Wrath of God, 6

Adjani, Isabelle: Driver, The, 45; Quartet, 571; Story of Adele H, The, 603; Subway, 142

Adler, Luther: Cornered, 35; Desert Fox, The, 42; D.O.A., 442; Murph the Surf, 104; Von Ryan's Express, 159; Wake of the Red Witch, 160

Adler, Matt: Flight of the Navigator, 837

Adorf, Mario: Holcroft Covenant, The, 74; Invitation au Voyage, 497; Tin Drum, The, 619

Adrian, Iris: Bluebeard, 654; Blue Hawaii, 771; Lady of Burlesque, 86

Adrian, Max: Devils, The, 450

Adu, Sade: Absolute Beginners, 768

Affleck, Neil: My Bloody Valentine, 720

Agar, John: Brain from Planet Arous, The, 821; Daughter of Dr. Jekyll, 670; Fort Apache, 897; Sands of Iwo Jima, 128

Agbayani, Tetchie: Gymkata, 68

Agterberg, Toon: Spetters, 598

Ahearn, Gladys: Git Along, Little Dogies, 898

Ahearn, Will: Git Along, Little Dogies, 898

Aherne, Brian: I Confess, 703; Juarez, 504; Smilin' Through, 803; Sword of Lancelot, 144

Ahlstedt, Borje: I Am Curious Yellow, 491

Ahn, Philip: Kung Fu, 85; They Got Me Covered, 366

Aidman, Charles: Countdown, 439; House of the Dead, 700

Aiello, Danny: Defiance, 41; Key Exchange, 506; Old Enough, 550; Protector, The, 116; Purple Rose of Cairo, The, 337; Stuff, The, 750

Aiken, Elaine: Lonely Man, The, 909

Aimee, Anouk: La Dolce Vita, 511

Airplane, Jefferson: Woodstock, 812

Aitchinson, Sarah: Adventures of Sherlock Holmes: The Solitary Cyclist, 5

Ajaye, Franklin: Car Wash, 239; Get Crazy, 266; Hysterical, 284

Akers, Andra: Desert Hearts, 449

Akins, Claude: Battle for the Planet of the Apes, 819; Death Squad, The, 40; Inherit the Wind, 495; Night Stalker, The, 723; Rio Bravo, 926

Akin, Tarik: Yol, 639

Akutagawa, Hishashi: Dodes 'Ka-Den, 452

Alaimo, Steve: Stanley, 747

Albano, Captain Lou: Wise Guys, 382

Alba, Maria: Mr. Robinson Crusoe, 101

Albee, Josh: Tom Sawyer, 210

Alberghetti, Anna Maria: Cinderfella, 774; Last Command, The, 907

Albers, Hans: Blue Angel, The, 415

Albertazzi, Giorgio: Last Year At Marienbad, 516

Albertini, Giampiero: Commandos, 33

Alberti, Lima: Clowns, The, 244

Albertson, Frank: Alice Adams, 392; Psycho, 731

Albertson, Jack: Dead and Buried, 670; Flim-Flam Man, The, 466; Lover Come Back, 303; Rabbit Run, 573; Teacher's Pet, 364; Willy Wonka and the Chocolate Factory, 213

Albert, Eddie: Airport '79: The Concorde, 391; Bombardier, 21; Devil's Rain, The, 674; Dreamscape, 832; Escape to Witch Mountain, 181; Foolin' Around, 261; Fuller Brush Girl, The, 264; Heartbreak Kid, The, 277; Hustle, The, 76; Longest Yard, The, 92; McQ, 98; Oklahoma!, 796; Roman Holiday, 583; Smash-up: The Story of a Woman, 595; Take This Job and Shove It, 363; Yes, Giorgio, 813

Albert, Edward: Butterflies Are Free, 422; Forty Carats, 262; Galaxy of Terror, 839; Greek Tycoon, The, 479; House Where Evil Dwells, The, 701; Midway, 99; Purple Taxi, The, 571; When Time Ran Out, 764

Albert, Jerry: Little Laura and Big John, 90

Albright, Lola: Joy House, 504

Alda, Alan: California Suite, 237; Four Seasons, The, 469; Glass House, The, 473; M*A*S*H: Goodbye Farewell, Amen, 307; Same Time Next Year, 345; Seduction of Joe Tynan, The, 590; Sweet Liberty, 362; To Kill a Clown, 756

Alda, Robert: House of Exorcism, The, 699; I Will, I Will... For Now, 285

Alda, Rutianya: Amityville II: The Possession, 645; Racing with the Moon, 573

Alden, Jane: Cinderella, 177

Alden, Terry: Last Game, The, 513

Alder, Larry: Sidewalks of London, 593

Aldredge, Tom: Rain People, The, 574

Aldridge, Michael: Bullshot, 236

Aldrin, Buzz: Boy in the Plastic Bubble, The, 418

Alentova, Vera: Moscow Does Not Believe in Tears, 538

Alerme, Andre: Carnival in Flanders, 426

Alexander, Alphonso: Bustin' Loose, 236

Alexander, Anton: Adventures of Sherlock Holmes: The Greek Interpreter, 4

Alexander, Ben: Dragnet, 45

Alexander, Betty: Dangerous Venture, 891

Alexander, Dick: Night Stage to Galveston, 917

Alexander, Jane: All the President's Men, 394; Betsy, The, 409; Brubaker, 421; City Heat, 243; Kramer vs. Kramer, 510; New Centurions, The, 543; Night Crossing, 106; Testament, 870

Alexander, Richard: Dead Don't Dream, The,

892; False Paradise, 896; Silent Conflict, 931

Alexandria, Mello: Slithis, 744

Alexandrov, Grigori: Battleship Potemkin, The, 406; Strike, 605

Alexiaous, Anna: Fantasies, 463

Alfonsino: Paisan, 556

Alfonsi, Lidia: Morgan the Pirate, 103

Alford, Philip: To Kill a Mockingbird, 619

Algeria: Ramparts of Clay, 575

Alison, Dorothy: See No Evil, 741

Ali, Muhammad: Greatest, The, 479; Requiem for a Heavyweight, 578

Allan, Elizabeth: Camille, 425; Haunted Strangler, The, 696; Tale of Two Cities, A, 611

Alldredge, Michael: About Last Night, 388

Allentuck, Katherine: Summer of '42, 608

Allen, Bill: Rad, 117

Allen, Corey: Rebel without a Cause, 576

Allen, Debbie: Jo Jo Dancer, Your Life Is Calling, 502

Allen, Elizabeth: Donovan's Reef, 44

Allen, Fred: It's in the Bag, 289

Allen, Gracie: Damsel in Distress, A, 776

Allen, Jay: Night of the Demon, 722

Allen, Joan: Manhunter, 97

Allen, Judith: Boots and Saddles, 885; Git Along, Little Dogies, 898

Allen, Karen: Animal House, 218; Cruising, 441; Raiders of the Lost Ark, 858; Shoot the Moon, 592; Split Image, 867; Starman, 867; Until September, 627; Wanderers, The, 629

Allen, Mike: Last Game, The, 513

Allen, Nancy: 1941, 319; Blow Out, 654; Buddy System, The, 421; Carrie, 659; Dressed to Kill, 679; Home Movies, 282; Last Detail, The, 513; Not for Publication, 320; Philadelphia Experiment, The, 856; Strange Invaders, 867; Terror in the Aisles, 753

Allen, Rae: Where's Poppa?, 381

Allen, Rex (narrator): Charlie, The Lonesome Cougar, 176; Trail of Robin Hood, 939

Allen, Robert: Black Room, The, 652

Allen, Woody: Annie Hall, 219; Bananas, 224; Broadway Danny Rose, 235; Casino Royale, 239; Everything You Always Wanted to Know about Sex But Were Afraid to Ask, 257; Front, The, 470; Hannah and Her Sisters, 275; Love and Death, 302; Manhattan, 305; Midsummer Night's Sex Comedy, A, 309; Play It Again Sam, 331; Sleeper, 354; Stardust Memories, 358; Stardust Memories, 601; Take the Money and Run, 363; What's New Pussycat?, 379; What's Up Tiger Lily?, 380; Zelig, 385

Alley, Kirstie: Runaway, 860

Allgood, Sara: Blackmail, 414; Dr. Jekyll and Mr. Hyde, 676

Allgood, Sara: Storm in a Teacup, 360

Allibert, Louis: Le Million, 298

Alling, Thomas: Topsy Turvy, 370

Alliotto, Annette: Escapade In Florence, 180

Allison, Jean: Steagle, The, 359

Allison, Patrick: Attack of the Swamp Creature, 647

Allister, Claud: Bulldog Drummond, 25

Allport, Christopher: Savage Weekend, 739

Allwin, Pernilla: Fanny and Alexander, 463

Allyson, June: Best Foot Forward, 770; Blackout, 19; Glenn Miller Story, The, 783; Good News, 784; Three Musketeers, The (1948), 150

Alonso, Chelo: Goliath and the Barbarians, 63

Alonso, Maria Conchita: Fine Mess, A, 260; Moscow on the Hudson, 314

Alridge, Kay: Nyoka and the Tiger Men (Perils of Nyoka), 109

Alterio, Hector: Camila, 424

Altieri, Elena: Bicycle Thief, The, 410

Altman, Jeff: Doin' Time, 253

Alton, Walter George: Heavenly Bodies, 278; Puma Man, The, 732

Alvarado, Trini: Mrs. Soffel, 536; Rich Kids, 580; Times Square, 809

Ameche, Don: Cocoon, 825; It's in the Bag, 289; Trading Places, 371

America, Paul: Ciao! Manhattan, 433

Ames, Adrienne: Death Kiss, The, 39

Ames, Leon: Jake Speed, 78; Misadventures of Merlin Jones, The, 192; Monkey's Uncle, The, 192; Testament, 870; Thin Man Goes Home, The, 149; Thirty Seconds Over Tokyo, 149; Yolanda and The Thief, 640

Amidou, Souad: Petit Con, 329

Amos, John: American Flyers, 396; Beastmaster, The, 820; Jungle Heat, 80; Let's Do It Again, 298; Sweet Sweetback's Baadasssss Song, 144; Touched by Love, 621; World's Greatest Athlete, The, 213

Amplas, John: Martin, 715

Andere, Jacqueline: Exterminating Angel, The, 257

Andersen, John: Witchcraft Through the Ages (HAXAN), 637

Andersen, Suzy: Black Sabbath, 651

Anderson, Barbara: Cyborg: The Six Million Dollar Man, 827; Don't Be Afraid of the Dark, 677

Anderson, Bridgette: Hansel and Gretel, 183; Savannah Smiles, 203

Anderson, Carl: Jesus Christ Superstar, 789

Anderson, Daphne: Hobson's Choice, 281

Anderson, Eddie "Rochester": Brewster's Millions (1945), 234; Cabin in the Sky, 423; Green Pastures, The, 479; Topper Returns, 370

Anderson, Gerd: Secrets of Women (or Waiting Women), 348

Anderson, John: Deerslayer, The, 893; Executive Action, 460; Psycho, 731; Ride the High Country, 925; Soldier Blue, 933

Anderson, Judith: And Then There Were None, 398; King's Row, 508; Laura, 88; Man

Called Horse, A, *911;* Rebecca, *576;* Red House, The, *734;* Strange Love of Martha Ivers, The, *604;* Tycoon, *156*

Anderson, Lindsay: O Lucky Man!, *548*

Anderson, Loni: Jayne Mansfield Story, The, *501;* Stroker Ace, *361*

Anderson, Manon: Hail Mary, *480*

Anderson, Mary: Cheers for Miss Bishop, *432;* Lifeboat, *518*

Anderson, Melissa Sue: Chattanooga Choo Choo, *242;* Happy Birthday to Me, *696*

Anderson, Melody: Dead and Buried, *670;* Flash Gordon, *837*

Anderson Jr., Michael: In Search of the Castaways, *185;* Sons of Katie Elder, The, *934*

Anderson, Nelson: Alien Warrior, *816*

Anderson, Warner: Destination Moon, *830;* Drum Beat, *894*

Andersson, Bibi: Devil's Eye, The, *250;* I Never Promised You a Rose Garden, *491;* Magician, The, *526;* Quintet, *858;* Scenes From A Marriage, *589;* Seventh Seal, The, *591;* Wild Strawberries, *635*

Andersson, Harriet: Cries and Whispers, *440;* Sawdust and Tinsel, *589*

Anders, Donna: Count Yorga, Vampire, *664*

Anders, Glenn: Lady from Shanghai, *86*

Anders, Luana: Dementia 13, *673;* Easy Rider, *455;* One from the Heart, *797;* Pit and the Pendulum, the, *728;* Trip, The, *622*

Anders, Merry: Tickle Me, *809*

Andes, Keith: Away All Boats, *11;* Clash by Night, *434;* Farmer's Daughter, The, *258*

Ando: Paper Tiger, *112*

Andrei, Frederic: Diva, *675*

Andress, Ursula: Blue Max, The, *20;* Casino Royale, *239;* Dr. No, *44;* Fifth Musketeer, The, *53;* Fun in Acapulco, *781;* Loaded Guns, *91;* Red Sun, *924;* Slave of the Cannibal God, *136;* Tenth Victim, The, *869;* What's New Pussycat?, *379*

Andrews, Anthony: Holcroft Covenant, The, *74;* Under the Volcano, *626*

Andrews, Barry: Blood on Satan's Claw, *653*

Andrews, Carol: Bullfighters, The, *235*

Andrews, Dana: Ball of Fire, *224;* Battle of the Bulge, *13;* Best Years of Our Lives, The, *409;* Beyond A Reasonable Doubt, *409;* Curse of the Demon, *667;* Good Guys Wear Black, *63;* Kit Carson, *907;* Last Tycoon, The, *515;* Laura, *88;* North Star, The, *108;* Ox-Bow Incident, The, *921;* Pilot, The, *563;* Purple Heart, The, *570;* Westerner, The, *944*

Andrews, Edward: Sixteen Candles, *353;* Summertime, *608;* Wilbur and Orville: The First To Fly, *212*

Andrews, Harry: Curse of King Tut's Tomb, The, *667;* Equus, *458;* Internecine Project, The, *705;* Man of La Mancha, *793;* Nightcomers, The, *721;* Ruling Class, The, *344*

Andrews, Julie: 10, *364;* Hawaii, *483;* Little

Miss Marker, *190;* Man Who Loved Women, The, *306;* Mary Poppins, *191;* Sound of Music, The, *804;* S.O.B., *355;* Tamarind Seed, The, *145;* Torn Curtain, *758;* Victor/Victoria, *377*

Andrews Sisters, The: Private Buckaroo, *799*

Andrews, Stanley: Dead Don't Dream, The, *892;* Prairie Moon, *922;* Robin Hood of Texas, *927;* Shine On Harvest Moon, *931;* Sinister Journey, *932;* Trigger, Jr., *940*

Andrew, Michael: Hollywood Hot Tubs, *282*

André, Gaby: Cosmic Monsters, The, *664*

Andre, Carole: Yor: The Hunter from the Future, *877*

Andros, Spiro: Matter of Time, A, *531*

Anemone: Peril, *561*

Angeli, Pier: Octaman, *725*

Angels, The Hell's: Hell's Angels Forever, *486*

Angel, Heather: Daniel Boone, *891;* Informer, The, *495;* Last of the Mohicans, The, *907;* Lifeboat, *518*

Angel, Michael St.: Brighton Strangler, The, *657*

Angustain, Ira: Can You Hear The Laughter? The Story of Freddie Prinze, *425*

Animated: Adventures of an American Rabbit, The, *169;* Alice in Wonderland, *170;* Allegro Non Troppo, *216;* Animal Farm, *399;* Bon Voyage, Charlie Brown, *174;* Boy Named Charlie Brown, A, *174;* Bugs Bunny/Road Runner Movie, the, *175;* Daffy Duck's Movie: Fantastic Island, *178;* Dumbo, *180;* Fantastic Planet, *836;* Fire and Ice, *837;* Fritz the Cat, *263;* Heathcliff—The Movie, *184;* Heavy Traffic, *485;* Heidi's Song, *184;* Hey Good Lookin', *487;* Hey There, It's Yogi Bear, *185;* It's an Adventure, Charlie Brown, *186;* Journey Back to Oz, *187;* Last Unicorn, The, *848;* Legend of Sleepy Hollow, The, *188;* Lord of the Rings, The, *850;* Mickey's Christmas Carol, *192;* 1001 Rabbit Tales, *196;* Pinocchio, *198;* Plague Dogs, The, *856;* Race for Your Life, Charlie Brown, *200;* Rainbow Brite and the Star Stealer, *200;* Robin Hood, *202;* Secret of the Sword, The, *203;* Sherlock Holmes and the Baskerville Curse, *204;* Sleeping Beauty, *204;* Smurfs and the Magic Flute, The, *205;* Snoopy, Come Home, *205;* Sword in the Stone, The, *207;* Three Caballeros, The, *209;* Transformers, The Movie, *211;* Warriors of the Wind, *875;* Watership Down, *876;* Wind in the Willows, The, *213;* Dark Crystal, The, *827*

Ankrum, Morris: Earth vs. the Flying Saucers, *832*

Annabella: 13 Rue Madeleine, *149;* Dinner at the Ritz, *43;* Le Million, *298*

Annan, Glory: Alien Prey, *644*

Annaud, Jean-Jacques: Quest for Fire, *858*

Annicchiarico, Vito: Open City, *553*

Annis, Francesca: Macbeth, *525;* Partners in Crime—The Secret Adversary, *113;* Under The Cherry Moon, *626*

Ann-Margret: Bye Bye Birdie, *773;* Carnal Knowledge, *426;* Cincinnati Kid, The, *31;* C.C. & Company, *28;* I Ought to Be in Pictures, *287;* Joseph Andrews, *290;* Last Remake of Beau Geste, The, *297;* Lookin' to Get Out, *300;* Magic, *713;* Murderers' Row, *104;* Pocketful of Miracles, *564;* Return of the Soldier, The, *579;* R.P.M. (Revolutions Per Minute), *572;* Tommy, *810;* Train Robbers, The, *940;* Twice in a Lifetime, *624;* Viva Las Vegas, *811*

Ansara, Michael: Day of the Animals, *670;* Dear Dead Delilah, *672;* Harum Scarum, *787;* It's Alive!, *707;* Manitou, The, *714;* Message, The (Mohammad, Messenger of God), *533;* Mission to Glory, *536;* Voyage to the Bottom of the Sea, *874*

Anspach, Susan: Big Fix, The, *15;* Blume in Love, *416;* Devil and Max Devlin, The, *250;* Gas, *265;* Montenegro, *313;* Play It Again Sam, *331*

Anthony, Lisette: Krull, *847*

Anthony, Tony: Treasure of the Four Crowns, *155*

Antin, Steve: Last American Virgin, The, *296*

Antonelli, Laura: Divine Nymph, The, *452;* High Heels, *280;* Innocent, The, *495;* Malicious, *305;* Passion of Love, *559;* Swashbuckler, The, *144;* Till Marriage Do Us Part, *368;* Wifemistress, *633*

Antonio, Lou: Cool Hand Luke, *35*

Antonov, Alexander: Battleship Potemkin, The, *406;* Strike, *605*

Antonutti, Omero: Night of the Shooting Stars, *545*

Anton, Matthew: Pretty Baby, *566*

Anton, Susan: Goldengirl, *840;* Spring Fever, *357*

Ant, Adam: Nomads, *724*

Apicella, Tina: Bellissima, *227*

Apollonia: Purple Rain, *799*

Aquino, Robert: Town That Dreaded Sundown, The, *759*

Arandt, Fanny: Confidentially Yours, *34*

Arau, Alfonso: Romancing the Stone, *124;* Scandalous John, *203*

Araya, Zenda: Hearts and Armour, *70*

Arbatt, Alexandre: Dangerous Moves, *443*

Arbuckle, Roscoe: Keystone Comedies, Vol. 1, *292;* Keystone Comedies, Vol. 2, *292;* Keystone Comedies, Vol. 3, *292;* Keystone Comedies, Vol. 4, *292;* Keystone Comedies: Vo. 5, *292*

Archer, Anne: Good Guys Wear Black, *63;* Green Ice, *66;* Hero at Large, *279;* Lifeguard, *518;* Naked Face, The, *720;* Raise the Titanic, *118;* Too Scared to Scream, *757*

Archer, John: Big Trees, The, *16;* Destination Moon, *830;* King of the Zombies, *709*

Ardant, Fanny: Swann In Love, *609;* Woman Next Door, The, *638*

Arden, Eve: Anatomy of a Murder, *397;* At the Circus, *221;* Cinderella, *177;* Grease, *784;* Kid from Brooklyn, The, *292;* Letter of Introduction, *516;* Mildred Pierce, *534;* Night and Day, *544;* Stage Door, *357;* Under the Rainbow, *374*

Arden, Mary: Blood and Black Lace, *652*

Arena, Maurizio: Loaded Guns, *91*

Argue, David: Gallipoli, *470*

Arhondis, Tina: Test of Love, A, *613*

Ariane: Year of the Dragon, *166*

Arias, Imanol: Camila, *424*

Arkin, Adam: Tom Edison—The Boy Who Lit Up The World, *210*

Arkin, Alan: Bad Medicine, *223;* Big Trouble, *228;* Catch-22, *239;* Chu Chu and the Philly Flash, *243;* Emperor's New Clothes, The, *833;* Freebie and the Bean, *263;* Heart Is a Lonely Hunter, The, *483;* Improper Channels, *286;* In-Laws, The, *286;* Joshua Then and Now, *290;* Last of the Red Hot Lovers, *296;* Rafferty and the Gold Dust Twins, *337;* Russians Are Coming, the Russians Are Coming, The, *344;* Seven-Per-Cent Solution, The, *131;* Simon, *352;* Wait until Dark, *763*

Arlen, Richard: Wings, *164*

Arletty: Children of Paradise, *432;* Le Jour Se Leve (DAYBREAK), *516*

Arling, Charles: Keystone Comedies: Vo. 5, *292*

Arliss, Dimitri: Xanadu, *813*

Arliss, George: Dr. Syn, *45;* Iron Duke, The, *498*

Armendariz Sr., Pedro: Conqueror, The, *34;* Tulsa, *623*

Armendariz Jr., Pedro: Le Chevre (The Goat), *298;* Don't Be Afraid of the Dark, *677*

Armetta, Henry: Manhattan Merry-Go-Round, *913*

Armida: Rootin' Tootin' Rhythm, *928*

Armon, Denise: Adventures of Sherlock Holmes: The Speckled Band, *6*

Armstrong, Bess: High Road to China, *72;* Jaws 3, *707;* Jekyll & Hyde—Together Again, *289;* Nothing In Common, *547*

Armstrong, Curtis: Bad Medicine, *223;* One Crazy Summer, *324;* Revenge of the Nerds, *340;* Risky Business, *341*

Armstrong, Louis: Cabin in the Sky, *423;* Glenn Miller Story, The, *783;* High Society, *787*

Armstrong, Perry: Solo, *596*

Armstrong, Robert: Blood on the Sun, *19;* Danger Lights, *443;* Kansan, The, *906;* King Kong (original), *709;* Mighty Joe Young, *852;* Most Dangerous Game, The, *718;* Mr. Winkle Goes to War, *311;* Paleface, The, *327;* Palooka, *556;* Son of Kong, The, *745*

Armstrong, R. G.: Angels Die Hard, *8;* Best of Times, The, *228;* Children of the Corn, *662;* Evilspeak, *681;* Hammett, *68;* Lone Wolf McQuade, *92;* Pack, The, *726;* Pursuit of D. B. Cooper, *116;* Ride the High Country, *925;* Stay Hungry, *602;* Where the Buffalo Roam, *381*

Armstrong, Todd: Jason and the Argonauts, *846*

Arnaud, Daniele: School Spirit, *346*

Arnaz Jr., Desi: House of the Long Shadows, *700;* Joyride, *504;* Wedding, A, *378*

Arnaz Sr., Desi: Escape Artist, The, *181;* Bataan, *12*

Arnaz, Lucie: Jazz Singer, The, *789*

Arness, James: Farmer's Daughter, The, *258;* Them!, *870;* Thing (From Another World), The, *871;* Wagonmaster, *943*

Arne, Peter: Return of the Pink Panther, The, *339;* Straw Dogs, *749*

Arngrim, Stephan: Fear No Evil, *683*

Arnold, Dorothy: Phantom Creeps, The, *727*

Arnold, Edward: Dear Wife, *249;* Idiot's Delight, *492;* Ziegfeld Follies, *814*

Arnold, Mal: Blood Feast, *653*

Arnold, Victor: Protector, The, *116*

Arnott, Mark: Return of the Secaucus 7, *339*

Arno, Sig: Song to Remember, A, *804*

Aronson, Judie: American Ninja, *7*

Arquette, Rosanna: 8 Million Ways to Die, *47;* After Hours, *215;* Aviator, The, *403;* Dark Secret of Harvest Home, The, *669;* Desperately Seeking Susan, *250;* Executioner's Song, The, *460;* Silverado, *932;* S.O.B., *355*

Arrick, Rose: Mikey and Nicky, *309*

Arrington, James: Petronella, *197*

Artaud, Antonin: Napoleon, *542;* Passion of Joan of Arc, The, *559*

Arthur, Beatrice: Mame, *793*

Arthur, Carol: Sunshine Boys, The, *361*

Arthur, Jean: Danger Lights, *443;* Devil and Miss Jones, The, *250;* History Is Made at Night, *488;* Mr. Smith Goes to Washington, *536;* Shane, *930;* Masked Marvel, The, *97*

Ashcroft, Peggy: Joseph Andrews, *290;* Passage to India, A, *558;* Sunday, Bloody Sunday, *608*

Asherson, Renée: Henry V, *486*

Asher, Jane: Deep End, *672;* Dreamchild, *831;* Masque of the Red Death, The, *716*

Ashley, Edward: Dick Tracy Meets Gruesome, *42*

Ashley, Elizabeth: Great Scout and Cathouse Thursday, The, *899;* Paternity, *328;* Ship of Fools, *592*

Ashley, John: Beach Blanket Bingo, *770;* Beyond Atlantis, *14;* Beverly Hills Cop, *228*

Ash, Leslie: Quadrophenia, *799*

Askew, Luke: Night Games, *544;* Rolling

Thunder, *123;* Walking Tall Part II, *160;* Warrior and the Sorceress, The, *875*

Askin, Leon: One, Two, Three, *324*

Askwith, Robert: Horror Hospital, *699*

Askwith, Robin: Hans Brinker, *183*

Aslan, Gregoire: Concrete Jungle, The (aka The Criminal), *437;* Golden Voyage of Sinbad, The, *839;* Return of the Pink Panther, The, *339*

Asner, Edward: Case of Libel, A, *427;* Change of Habit, *430;* Daniel, *444;* El Dorado, *895;* Fort Apache—The Bronx, *467;* Gus, *183;* Skin Game, *933*

Assante, Armand: I, the Jury, *77;* Lady of the House, *512;* Paradise Alley, *557;* Private Benjamin, *334;* Prophecy, *730;* Unfaithfully Yours (Remake), *375*

Astaire, Fred: Amazing Dobermans, *171;* Band Wagon, The, *769;* Carefree, *774;* Damsel in Distress, A, *776;* Easter Parade, *777;* Family Upside Down, A, *462;* Finian's Rainbow, *779;* Flying Down to Rio, *780;* Follow the Fleet, *780;* Funny Face, *781;* Gay Divorcee, The, *782;* Ghost Story, *693;* Holiday Inn, *787;* On the Beach, *854;* Purple Taxi, The, *571;* Royal Wedding, *800;* Second Chorus, *801;* Shall We Dance?, *802;* Silk Stockings, *802;* Sky's the Limit, The, *803;* Story of Vernon and Irene Castle, The, *806;* Swing Time, *806;* That's Entertainment Part II, *807;* That's Entertainment, *807;* Top Hat, *810;* Towering Inferno, The, *154;* Yolanda and The Thief, *640;* You Were Never Lovelier, *814;* You'll Never Get Rich, *814;* Ziegfeld Follies, *814*

Asta: Thin Man, The, *149*

Asther, Nils: Bluebeard, *654*

Astin, John: European Vacation, *256;* Freaky Friday, *182;* That Touch of Mink, *365*

Astin, Sean: Goonies, The, *63*

Astor, Mary: Dodsworth, *452;* Hurricane, The, *490;* Hush...Hush, Sweet Charlotte, *703;* Kennel Murder Case, The, *82;* Maltese Falcon, The, *95;* Red Dust, *119;* Red Dust, *577*

Ates, Roscoe: Freaks, *689*

Atherton, William: Class of '44, *434;* Ghostbusters, *267;* Hindenburg, The, *487;* Real Genius, *338;* Sugarland Express, The, *607*

Atkine, Feodor: Pauline at the Beach, *559*

Atkinson, Beverly Hope: Uforia, *374*

Atkins, Christopher: Blue Lagoon, The, *415;* Night in Heaven, A, *544;* Pirate Movie, The, *798*

Atkins, David: Squizzy Taylor, *139*

Atkins, Eileen: Equus, *458*

Atkins, Harvey: Last Chase, The, *847*

Atkins, Tom: Halloween III: Season of the Witch, *695;* Ninth Configuration, The, *546*

Atkin, Harvey: Meatballs, *308*

Attenborough, Richard: Brannigan, *23;*

Doctor Dolittle, *180;* Flight of the Phoenix, The, *58;* Great Escape, The, *65;* Magic Christian, The, *304;* Sand Pebbles, The, *127;* Seance on a Wet Afternoon, *741;* Ten Little Indians, *147*

Atwill, Lionel: Captain Blood, *27;* Gorilla, The, *271;* Hound of the Baskervilles, The (Original), *75;* Sherlock Holmes and the Secret Weapon, *134*

Atzorn, Robert: From the Lives of the Marionettes, *470*

Auberjoncis, René: Eyes of Laura Mars, The, *682;* Tale of the Frog Prince, *207;* Where the Buffalo Roam, *381*

Aubert, Lenore: They Got Me Covered, *366*

Aubrey, James: Lord of the Flies, *521*

Aubry, Danielle: Operation C.I.A., *110*

Auclair, Michel: Funny Face, *781;* Swashbuckler, The, *144*

Audran, Stéphane: Discreet Charm Of The Bourgeoisie, The, *251;* La Cage Aux Folles III, The Wedding, *295;* Black Bird, The, *230;* Clean State (Coup de Torchon), *244;* Silver Bears, *351*

Auer, Mischa: Brewster's Millions (1945), *234;* Winterset, *636*

Auffay, Patrick: 400 Blows, The, *468*

Auger, Claudine: Summertime Killer, The, *143;* Thunderball, *151*

Augger, Florrie: Bugsy Malone, *175*

August, Robert: Endless Summer, The, *48*

Auld, Georgie: New York, New York, *795*

Aumont, Jean-Pierre: Blackout, *19;* Cat and Mouse, *28;* Cauldron of Blood, *661;* Devil at 4 O'Clock, The, *450;* Happy Hooker, The, *275*

Aumont, Tina: Malicious, *305*

Austin, Albert: Charlie Chaplin—The Early Years, Vol.1, *241;* Charlie Chaplin—The Early Years, Vol.2, *241;* Charlie Chaplin—The Early Years, Vol.4, *241*

Austin, Karen: Summer Rental, *361*

Autry, Alan: Roadhouse 66, *122*

Autry, Gene: Big Sombrero, The, *883;* Blue Canadian Rockies, *884;* Boots and Saddles, *885;* Call of the Canyon, *887;* Cow Town, *890;* Git Along, Little Dogies, *898;* Heart of the Rio Grande, *901;* Hills of Utah, The, *903;* Last of the Pony Riders, *907;* Manhattan Merry-Go-Round, *913;* Man From Music Mountain, *912;* Man of the Frontier, (Red River Valley), *912;* Melody Ranch, *914;* Melody Trail, *915;* Mystery Mountain, *916;* Night Stage to Galveston, *917;* Old Corral, The, *919;* On Top of Old Smoky, *919;* Phantom Empire, *114;* Prairie Moon, *922;* Radio Ranch (Men With Steel Faces, Phantom Empire), *923;* Ridin' on a Rainbow, *926;* Robin Hood of Texas, *927;* Rootin' Tootin' Rhythm, *928;* Sioux City Sue, *933;* South of the Border,

934; Valley of Fire, *942;* Winning of the West, *946*

Avalon, Frankie: Alamo, The, *878;* Beach Blanket Bingo, *770;* Bikini Beach, *771;* How to Stuff a Wild Bikini, *788;* Voyage to the Bottom of the Sea, *874*

Avalon, Phil: Summer City, *143*

Avanzo, Renzo: Paisan, *556*

Avery, Margaret: Color Purple, The, *436;* Which Way Is Up?, *381*

Avery, Val: Cobra, *32;* Heroes, *486*

Avran, Chris: Captive Planet, *823*

Axelrod, Nina: Cross Country, *440;* Motel Hell, *718;* Time Walker, *755*

Axton, Hoyt: Black Stallion, The, *173;* Endangered Species, *834;* Goldilocks and the Three Bears, *182;* Gremlins, *840;* Heart Like a Wheel, *70;* Liar's Moon, *517*

Aykroyd, Dan: 1941, *319;* Blues Brothers, The, *231;* Doctor Detroit, *252;* Ghostbusters, *267;* Into the Night, *496;* It Came from Hollywood, *287;* Neighbors, *318;* Spies Like Us, *356;* Trading Places, *371*

Aykroyd, Peter: Gas, *265*

Aylmer, Felix: Hamlet, *481;* Henry V, *486;* Iron Duke, The, *498;* Knights of the Round Table, *85*

Aynesworth, Allan: Iron Duke, The, *498*

Ayres, Leah: Burning, The, *658;* Eddie Macon's Run, *47*

Ayres, Lew: All Quiet on the Western Front, *7;* Battlestar Galactica, *820;* Damien: Omen II, *668;* Dark Mirror, The, *669;* Dr. Kildare's Strange Case, *43;* End of the World, *834;* Johnny Belinda, *503;* Of Mice and Men, *549*

Ayres, Robert: Battle beneath the Earth, *12*

Azzara, Candy: Easy Money, *254*

Babcock, Barbara: That Was Then... This is Now, *615*

Bacall, Lauren: Big Sleep, The (Original), *16;* Dark Passage, *38;* Fan, The, *683;* Harper, *69;* How to Marry a Millionaire, *284;* Key Largo, *82;* Murder on the Orient Express, *104;* Shootist, The, *931;* To Have and Have Not, *152*

Baccaloni: Fanny, *463*

Bach, Barbara: Caveman, *240;* Force Ten from Navarone, *59;* Give My Regards to Broad Street, *783;* Spy Who Loved Me, The, *139;* Unseen, The, *760;* Up the Academy, *375*

Backer, Brian: Burning, The, *658;* Fast Times at Ridgemont High, *258*

Backus, Jim: Crazy Mama, *36;* Good Guys Wear Black, *63;* His Kind of Woman, *73;* Now You See Him, Now You Don't, *196;* Pete's Dragon, *197;* Rebel without a Cause, *576;* Zotzl, *386*

Baclanova, Olga: Freaks, *689*

Bacon, David: Masked Marvel, The, *97*

Bacon, Kevin: Diner, 251; Footloose, 781; Quicksilver, 572

Bacon, Lloyd: Charlie Chaplin—The Early Years, Vol.4, 241

Bacri, Jean-Pierre: Entre Nous (Between Us), 458; Entre Nous (Between Us), 458; Subway, 142

Bacs, Ferenc: Train Killer, The, 621

Baddeley, Hermione: Belles of St. Trinian's, The, 227; Mary Poppins, 191; Unsinkable Molly Brown, The, 810

Badel, Alan: Arabesque, 9; Day of the Jackal, The, 39

Badham, Mary: To Kill a Mockingbird, 619

Badland, Annette: Jabberwocky, 289

Baer, Buddy: Snow White and the Three Stooges, 205

Baer Jr., Max: Macon County Line, 94; Harder They Fall, The, 482

Baer, Meredith: Chicken Chronicles, The, 243

Baer, Parley: Ugly Dachshund, The, 211

Baerwitz, Jerry: Varan, the Unbelievable, 761

Baez, Joan: Don't Look Back, 777

Bagdadi, Celice: Final Exam, 684

Bager, Myrian: Holiday Hotel, 281

Baggetta, Vincent: Man Who Wasn't There, The, 306

Baggett, Lynne: D.O.A., 442

Bailey, Dick: Marauders, 913

Bailey, G. W.: Rustler's Rhapsody, 344; Short Circuit, 862; Warning Sign, 763

Bailey, Robin: See No Evil, 741

Bail, Chuck: Stunt Man, The, 606

Bainter, Fay: Dark Waters, 445; Our Town, 555; Woman of the Year, 383

Bain, Conrad: Last Summer, 514

Bain, Ron: Experience Preferred... But Not Essential, 257

Bain, Sherry: Pipe Dreams, 563

Baio, Scott: Bugsy Malone, 175; Foxes, 469; Zapped!, 385

Baird, Peter: Howard the Duck, 842

Baker, Betsy: Evil Dead, The, 681

Baker, Blanche: French Postcards, 263; Sixteen Candles, 353

Baker, Carroll: Andy Warhol's Bad, 398; Baby Doll, 403; Big Country, 882; Captain Apache, 888; Cheyenne Autumn, 888; Easy to Love, 778; Giant, 472; Greatest Story Ever Told, The, 478; Harlow, 482; Star 80, 600; Watcher in the Woods, The, 764

Baker, Diane: Journey to the Center of the Earth, 846; Marnie, 715; Pilot, The, 563; Strait-Jacket, 748

Baker, George: Partners in Crime—The Secret Adversary, 113; Sword of Lancelot, 144

Baker, Jay: April Fool's Day, 646

Baker, Joby: Wackiest Ship in the Army, The, 377

Baker, Joe Don: Charley Varrick, 30; Final Justice, 54; Fletch, 57; Framed, 60; Joy Sticks, 291; Junior Bonner, 906; Pack, The, 726; Walking Tall, 160

Baker, Kenny: At the Circus, 221; Goldwyn Follies, The, 784

Baker, Sharon: Captive Planet, 823

Baker, Stanley: Accident, 388; Concrete Jungle, The (aka The Criminal), 437; Guns of Navarone, The, 68; Knights of the Round Table, 85; Zulu, 167

Baker, Tom: Angels Die Hard, 8; Curse of King Tut's Tomb, The, 667; Golden Voyage of Sinbad, The, 839; Nicholas and Alexandra, 543; Vault of Horror, 761

Bakri, Muhamad: Hanna K., 481

Balaban, Bob: 2010, 874; Absence of Malice, 388; Altered States, 817; Strawberry Statement, The, 604; Whose Life Is It, Anyway?, 633

Balaski, Belinda: Cannonball, 27

Balding, Rebecca: Silent Scream, 743

Baldwin, Adam: Bad Guys, 11; D.C. Cab, 249; Reckless, 577

Baldwin, Janit: Ruby, 737

Baldwin, Michael: Phantasm, 727

Baldwin, Peter: Trap, The, 759

Balint, Eszter: Stranger than Paradise, 360

Balin, Ina: Comancheros, The, 889; Patsy, The, 328; Projectionist, The, 336

Balin, Mireille: Pepe Le Moko, 560

Balk, Fairuza: Return to Oz, 201

Ballantine, Carl: World's Greatest Lover, The, 384

Ballard, Kaye: Freaky Friday, 182; Ritz, The, 342

Ball, Lucille: Best Foot Forward, 770; Du Barry Was a Lady, 777; Five Came Back, 465; Fuller Brush Girl, The, 264; Guide For The Married Man, A, 273; Mame, 793; Room Service, 343; Stage Door, 357; Thousands Cheer, 808; Ziegfeld Follies, 384

Ball, Nicolas: House That Bled to Death, The, 701

Ball, Vincent: Alison's Birthday, 644

Balsam, Martin: 12 Angry Men, 624; After the Fox, 216; All the President's Men, 394; Anderson Tapes, The, 407; Breakfast at Tiffany's, 419; Catch-22, 239; Confessions of a Police Captain, 437; Cyborg: The Six Million Dollar Man, 827; Death Wish III, 40; Delta Force, The, 41; Goodbye People, The, 475; Harlow, 482; Hombre, 904; Little Big Man, 909; Sentinel, The, 742; Seven Days in May, 591; Silver Bears, 351; Stone Killer, The, 141; St. Elmo's Fire, 586; Taking of Pelham One Two Three, The, 144; Thousand Clowns, A, 367; Tora! Tora! Tora!, 154; Warning, The, 160

Bambury, John: Terror of Tiny Town, The, 937

Banashek, Lynn: Fatal Games, 683

Banas, Arlene: Washington Affair, The, 630

Bancroft, Anne: Agnes of God, 390; Elephant Man, The, 456; Garbo Talks, 265; Graduate, The, 475; Hindenburg, The, 487; Lipstick, 712; Miracle Worker, The, 535; Prisoner of Second Avenue, The, 334; Silent Movie, 351; To Be or Not to Be (Remake), 369; Young Winston, 641

Bancroft, Bradford: Dangerously Close, 668

Bancroft, George: Angels with Dirty Faces, 8; Little Men, 519

Band, Charlie Daniels: Urban Cowboy, 627

Band, David Bowie and: Ziggy Stardust and the Spiders from Mars, 814

Band, The: Last Waltz, The, 791

Banerjee, Victor: Passage to India, A, 558

Bane, Hollis: Hoppy's Holiday, 904

Banfi, Lino: Loaded Guns, 91

Bankhead, Tallulah: Daydreamer, The, 179; Die! Die! My Darling!, 675; Lifeboat, 518

Banks, Jonathan: Armed and Dangerous, 220

Banks, Laura: Wheels of Fire, 161

Banks, Leslie: Henry V, 486; Jamaica Inn, 500; Man Who Knew Too Much, The (original), 715; Most Dangerous Game, The, 718; Sanders of the River, 127

Bannen, Ian: Bite the Bullet, 884; Eye of the Needle, 51; Flight of the Phoenix, The, 58; Gathering Storm, 471; Gorky Park, 64; Mackintosh Man, The, 94; Night Crossing, 106

Banner, John: Hitler, 488; Once Upon a Honeymoon, 324

Bannister, Reggie: Phantasm, 727

Bannon, Jim: Riders of the Deadline, 926

Barash, Olivia: Repo Man, 338

Barbeau, Adrienne: Back To School, 222; Creepshow, 666; Escape from New York, 49; Fog, The, 686; Swamp Thing, 750

Barber, Glynis: Wicked Lady, The, 163

Barbier, George: Tarzan's Revenge, 146

Barboni, Paolo: Yes, Giorgio, 813

Barbour, Joyce: Sabotage, 738

Barclay, Don: Border Phantom, 885

Barcroft, Roy: Dawn on the Great Divide, 891; Down Dakota Way, 894; False Colors, 895; Grand Canyon Trail, 899; Jesse James at Bay, 905; My Pal Trigger, 916; North of the Great Divide, 918; Radar Men from the Moon, 117; Sunset Serenade, 935

Bardot, Brigitte: And God Created Woman, 397; Contempt, 247; Doctor at Sea, 252; Ravishing Idiot, The, 337; Shalako, 930

Barends, Edda: Question of Silence, A, 572

Barenholtz, Ben: Time Stands Still, 619

Bari, Lynn: Bridge of San Luis Rey, The, 420; Elfego Baca: Six Gun Law, 895; Falcon Takes Over, The, 52; Kit Carson, 907

Barjac, Sophie: Holiday Hotel, 281

Barker, Lex: Away All Boats, 11; Farmer's Daughter, The, 258; Return of the Badmen, 925

Barkin, Ellen: Adventures of Buckaroo Banzai, The, 815; Desert Bloom, 449; Eddie and the Cruisers, 778; Harry and Son, 483; Princess Who Had Never Laughed, The, 199; Tender Mercies, 613; Terminal Choice, 752

Barkley, Janet: Harder They Come, The, 786

Barkley, Lucille: Bedtime for Bonzo, 226

Barkworth, Peter: Littlest Horse Thieves, The, 190; Partners in Crime—The Secret Adversary, 113

Barlow, Tim: Adventures of Sherlock Holmes: The Resident Patient, 5

Barnes, Binnie: Broadway Melody of 1938, 773; Divorce of Lady X, The, 251; It's in the Bag, 289; Last of the Mohicans, The, 907; Private Life of Don Juan, The, 568; Private Life of Henry the Eighth, The, 568

Barnes, Cheryl: Hair, 785

Barnes, Joanna: Parent Trap, The, 197

Barnes, Priscilla: Last Married Couple in America, The, 296

Barnes, T. Roy: It's a Gift, 288

Barnett, Charlie: D.C. Cab, 249

Barnett, Vince: Death Kiss, The, 39

Baron, Sandy: Birdy, 412; Broadway Danny Rose, 235; Out of Towners, The, 325; Vamp, 760

Barrat, Robert: Last of the Mohicans, The, 907

Barrault, Jean-Louis: Children of Paradise, 432; La Nuit de Varennes, 511; La Ronde, 295

Barrault, Marie-Christine: Cousin, Cousine, 248; Love in Germany, A, 523; My Night At Maud's, 541; Stardust Memories, 358; Stardust Memories, 601; Swann In Love, 609

Barrett, Claudia: Robot Monster, 736

Barrett, Edith: I Walked with a Zombie, 704

Barrett, John: Gymkata, 68

Barrett, Laurinda: Heart Is a Lonely Hunter, The, 483

Barrett, Majel: Star Trek (television series), 866

Barrett, Nitchie: Preppies, 333

Barrett, Ray: Chant of Jimmie Blacksmith, The, 431; Where the Green Ants Dream, 632

Barrier, Edgar: Cornered, 35; Macbeth, 525; Snow White and the Three Stooges, 205

Barrie, Barbara: Bell Jar, The, 408

Barrie, Mona: Dawn on the Great Divide, 891

Barrie, Wendy: Five Came Back, 465

Barris, Harry: King of Jazz, The, 790

Barron, Dana: Vacation, 376

Barrymore, Drew: Altered States, *817;* Cat's Eye, *660;* E.T.—The Extra-terrestrial, *832;* Firestarter, *685;* Irreconcilable Differences, *498*

Barrymore, Ethel: Deadline USA, *447;* Farmer's Daughter, The, *258;* None But the Lonely Heart, *546*

Barrymore, John: Dinner at Eight, *251;* Grand Hotel, *476;* Maytime, *793;* Svengali, *750*

Barrymore, John Drew: Americana, *396;* High School Confidential!, *487;* Clones, The, *824*

Barrymore, Lionel: Camille, *425;* Captains Courageous, *28;* Captains Courageous, *425;* David Copperfield, *445;* Devil Doll, The, *674;* Dr. Kildare's Strange Case, *43;* Grand Hotel, *476;* It's a Wonderful Life, *499;* Key Largo, *82;* Treasure Island, *211*

Barry, Donald: Frankenstein—1970, *689;* Saga of Death Valley, *929*

Barry, Gene: War of the Worlds, The, *874*

Barry, Neill: Old Enough, *550*

Barry, Patricia: Bogie, *417*

Barry, Raymond J.: Out of Bounds, *111*

Barry, Ray: Year of the Dragon, *166*

Barry, Tony: We of the Never Never, *161*

Barsky, Vladimir: Battleship Potemkin, The, *406*

Bartel, Paul: Eating Raoul, *254;* Hollywood Boulevard, *282*

Barthelmess, Richard: Way Down East, *631*

Bartholomew, Freddie: Anna Karenina, *400;* Captains Courageous, *28;* Captains Courageous, *425;* David Copperfield, *445;* Little Lord Fauntleroy, *519;* Tom Brown's School Days, *620*

Barth, Eddie: Fame, *778;* Thunder and Lightning, *151*

Bartok, Eva: Blood and Black Lace, *652;* Gamma People, The, *839*

Bartold, Norman: Westworld, *876*

Barton, Gregg: Last of the Pony Riders, *907;* Valley of Fire, *942;* Winning of the West, *946*

Barton, James: Misfits, The, *535*

Barton, Joan: Strange Gamble, *935*

Barton, Peter: Friday the 13th—The Final Chapter, *690;* Hell Night, *697*

Barto, Robyn: Blue Skies Again, *416*

Barty, Billy: Legend, *849;* Night Patrol, *318*

Baryshnikov, Mikhail: That's Dancing, *807;* White Nights, *632*

Basaraba, Gary: One Magic Christmas, *552*

Basehart, Ricard: Flood!, *685;* Brothers Karamazov, The, *420;* Great Bank Hoax, The, *272;* Hans Brinker, *183;* He Walked by Night, *697;* Hitler, *488;* Island of Dr. Moreau, The, *845;* La Strada, *512;* Moby Dick, *102;* Rage, *573*

Basie, Count: Stage Door Canteen, *599*

Basil, Toni: Village of the Giants, *762*

Basinger, Kim: 91/2 Weeks, *545;* Fool For Love, *466;* Hard Country, *68;* Man Who Loved Women, The, *306;* Mother Lode, *103;* Natural, The, *542;* Never Say Never Again, *106*

Basraba, Gary: Sweet Dreams, *806*

Bassermann, Albert: Once Upon a Honeymoon, *324*

Bassett, Carling: Spring Fever, *357*

Basset, Steve: Spring Break, *357*

Bass, Alfie: Lavender Hill Mob, The, *297*

Bass, Kim: Protector, The, *116*

Bateman, Charles: Brotherhood of Satan, *658*

Bates, Alan: King of Hearts, *294;* Quartet, *571;* Return of the Soldier, The, *579;* Rose, The, *800;* Separate Tables, *590;* Shout, The, *743;* Unmarried Woman, An, *626;* Wicked Lady, The, *163;* Women in Love, *638;* Zorba the Greek, *642*

Bates, Florence: Secret Life of Walter Mitty, The, *347;* Tuttles of Tahiti, The, *373*

Bates, Jeanne: Eraserhead, *680*

Bates, Kathy: Come Back to the Five and Dime, Jimmy Dean, Jimmy Dean, *436*

Bates, Ralph: Fear in the Night (Dynasty of Fear), *683;* Horror of Frankenstein, *699;* Lust for a Vampire, *713*

Batista, Lloyd: Last Plane Out, *87*

Battaglia, Rik: Call of the Wild, *27*

Battier, Robert: Baker's Wife, The, *224*

Battisti, Carlo: Umberto D, *625*

Bauer, Belinda: Timerider, *152;* Winter Kills, *636*

Bauer, Steven: Running Scared (1986), *125;* Scarface (Remake), *129;* Thief of Hearts, *617*

Baumgartner, Michele: Woman Next Door, The, *638*

Baur, Harry: I Stand Condemned, *492;* Volpone, *629*

Baviera, Jose: Exterminating Angel, The, *257*

Bavier, Frances: Benji, *172*

Baxter, Alan: Set-Up, The, *591*

Baxter, Anne: All About Eve, *393;* Angel on My Shoulder, *399;* Carnival Story, *426;* East of Eden (Remake), *454;* I Confess, *703;* North Star, The, *108;* Razor's Edge, The (Original), *576;* Ten Commandments, The, *612*

Baxter, Warner: 42nd Street, *781;* Adam Had Four Sons, *389*

Bayer, Gary: Will, G. Gordon Liddy, *635*

Baye, Nathalie: Green Room, The, *479;* La Balance, *85;* Return of Martin Guerre, The, *578*

Bay, Frances: Little Red Riding Hood, *190;* Attic, The, *648*

Beacham, Stephanie: And Now the Screaming Starts, *645;* Nightcomers, The, *721*

Beals, Jennifer: Bride, The, *656;* Cinderella, *177;* Flashdance, *780*

Beal, John: Little Minister, The, *519;* Ten Who Dared, *208*

Bean, Orson: Anatomy of a Murder, *397*

Bearse, Amanda: Fright Night, *691*

Beasley, Allyce: Moonlighting, *102*

Beatles, The: Compleat Beatles, The, *775*; Hard Day's Night, A, *786*; Help!, *787*

Beatty, Ned: 1941, *319*; All God's Children, *393*; Big Bus, The, *229*; Deliverance, *41*; Great Bank Hoax, The, *272*; Hopscotch, *74*; Incredible Shrinking Woman, The, *286*; Last American Hero, The, *86*; Mikey and Nicky, *309*; Nashville, *542*; Network, *543*; Promises in the Dark, *569*; Rumpelstiltskin, *202*; Silver Streak, *352*; Stroker Ace, *361*; Superman II, *869*; Thief Who Came to Dinner, The, *366*; Toy, The, *371*; White Lightning, *162*; Wise Blood, *636*

Beatty, Robert: Where Eagles Dare, *161*

Beatty, Warren: Bonnie and Clyde, *21*; Heaven Can Wait, *278*; Lilith, *518*; McCabe and Mrs. Miller, *914*; Parallax View, The, *557*; Reds, *578*; Roman Spring of Mrs. Stone, The, *583*; Shampoo, *591*; Splendor in the Grass, *599*; $ (Dollars), *44*

Beaumont, Chris: Wilbur and Orville: The First To Fly, *212*

Beavers, Louise: Tammy and the Bachelor, *611*; Du Barry Was a Lady, *777*

Becaud, Gilbert: And Now, My Love, *398*

Beckford, Bill: Riders of the Deadline, *926*

Beckley, Tony: When a Stranger Calls, *764*

Beck, Jeff: Secret Policemen's Other Ball, The, *347*

Beck, Jennifer: Tightrope, *755*; Troll, *873*

Beck, John: Audrey Rose, *648*; Big Bus, The, *229*; Other Side of Midnight, The, *554*; Rollerball, *860*; Sleeper, *354*

Beck, Julian: Poltergeist II: The Otherside, *729*

Beck, Kimberly: Friday the 13th—The Final Chapter, *690*; Massacre at Central High, *716*

Beck, Michael: Megaforce, *851*; Warlords of the 21st Century, *875*; Warriors, The, *160*; Xanadu, *813*; Triumphs of a Man Called Horse, *941*

Beddoe, Don: Blue Canadian Rockies, *884*; Bullwhip, *887*

Bedelia, Bonnie: Big Fix, The, *15*; Boy Who Could Fly, The, *419*; Fighting Back, *53*; Heart Like a Wheel, *70*; Violets Are Blue, *628*

Bedos, Guy: Pardon Mon Affaire, *327*

Beery Jr., Noah: Gung Ho, *67*; Red River, *924*; Rocketship X-M, *860*; Sergeant York, *131*; Trail Beyond, The, *939*; Savages, *739*; Walking Tall, *160*

Beery Sr., Noah: Trail Beyond, The, *939*

Beery, Wallace: Champ, The (Original), *429*; China Seas, *30*; Grand Hotel, *476*; Lost World, The, *850*; Min and Bill, *534*; Treasure Island, *211*

Bee, Molly: Hillbillys in a Haunted House, *280*

Begley Jr., Ed: Dead of Night, *671*; Get Crazy, *266*; Rip Van Winkle, *859*; Transylvania 6-5000, *371*

Begley, Sr., Ed: 12 Angry Men, *624*; Dunwich Horror, The, *680*; Hang 'Em High, *900*; Sorry, Wrong Number, *745*; Tulsa, *623*; Unsinkable Molly Brown, The, *810*

Behr, Roger: Can I Do It 'Til I Need Glasses?, *237*

Bekassy, Stephen: Song to Remember, A, *804*

Belafonte-Harper, Shari: Time Walker, *755*

Belafonte, Harry: Buck and the Preacher, *886*; Uptown Saturday Night, *376*

Belaski, Belinda: Bobbie Jo and the Outlaw, *21*

Belford, Christine: Christine, *662*

Bel Geddes, Barbara: Caught, *429*

Bellamy, Madge: White Zombie, *764*

Bellamy, Ralph: Boy in the Plastic Bubble, The, *418*; Carefree, *774*; His Girl Friday, *281*; Oh God!, *323*; Professionals, The, *116*; Rosemary's Baby, *737*; Spitfire, *599*; Sunrise at Campobello, *609*; Trading Places, *371*

Beller, Kathleen: Fort Apache—The Bronx, *467*; Movie Movie, *315*; Promises in the Dark, *569*; Surfacing, *143*; Sword and the Sorcerer, The, *869*

Belle, Annie: Wifemistress, *633*

Bellin, Olga: Tomorrow, *620*

Belli, Agostina: Holocaust 2000, *698*; Seduction of Mimi, The, *348*; Blood in the Streets, *19*; Purple Taxi, The, *571*

Belli, Melvin: Gimme Shelter, *783*

Bellwood, Pamela: Cocaine: One Man's Seduction, *435*; Incredible Shrinking Woman, The, *286*

Bell, Edward: Gymkata, *68*

Bell, Hank: Man of the Frontier, (Red River Valley), *912*

Bell, James: I Walked with a Zombie, *704*

Bell, Leonard: Four Rode Out, *897*

Bell, Rex: Dawn on the Great Divide, *891*

Bell, Sonny: Demon Lover, The, *673*

Belmondo, Jean-Paul: Breathless (Original), *419*; Casino Royale, *239*; High Heels, *280*; Swashbuckler, The, *144*

Belmont, Virginia: Silent Conflict, *931*

Beltran, Robert: Eating Raoul, *254*; Streethawk, *142*

Belushi, Jim: About Last Night, *388*; Man With One Red Shoe, The, *306*; Pinocchio, *198*; Salvador, *587*; Thief, *148*

Belushi, John: 1941, *319*; Animal House, *218*; Blues Brothers, The, *231*; Continental Divide, *247*; Goin' South, *898*; Neighbors, *318*; Old Boyfriends, *550*

Belvins, Michael: Chorus Line, A, *774*

Belzer, Richard: Groove Tube, The, *273*

Benatar, Pat: Union City, *626*

Benben, Brian: Gangster Wars, *61*

Benchley, Robert: I Married a Witch, *842*; It's in the Bag, *289*; Sky's the Limit, The, *803*;

Young and Willing, 640; You'll Never Get Rich, 814

Bendava, Jitka: Closely Watched Trains, 435

Bendix, William: Girl in Every Port, A, 268; It's in the Bag, 289; Lifeboat, 518; Wake Island, 159; Woman of the Year, 383

Benedetti, Nelly: Soft Skin, The, 596

Benedico, Augusto: Exterminating Angel, The, 257

Benedict, Dirk: Battlestar Galactica, 820; Cruise into Terror, 667; Follow That Car, 58; Ruckus, 124; W, 763

Benedict, Paul: Man With Two Brains, The, 307

Benedict, William: Adventures of Captain Marvel, The, 1; Nyoka and the Tiger Men (Perils of Nyoka), 109

Benjamin, Richard: Catch-22, 239; Diary of a Mad Housewife, 450; First Family, 261; Goodbye Columbus, 271; House Calls, 283; How to Beat the High Co$t of Living, 284; Last of Sheila, The, 87; Love at First Bite, 302; Portnoy's Complaint, 565; Saturday the 14th, 739; Scavenger Hunt, 346; Steagle, The, 359; Sunshine Boys, The, 361; Westworld, 876

Benji: Oh, Heavenly Dog!, 196

Bennent, David: Legend, 849; Tin Drum, The, 619

Bennent, Heinz: From the Lives of the Marionettes, 470; Nea (A Young Emmanuelle), 542

Bennett, Bill: Keystone Comedies: Vo. 5, 292

Bennett, Bruce: Before I Hang, 649; Clones, The, 824; Dark Passage, 38; Mildred Pierce, 534; Sahara, 126; Treasure of the Sierra Madre, The, 155

Bennett, Constance: Madame X, 526; Topper Takes a Trip, 370; Topper, 369

Bennett, Jill: Concrete Jungle, The (aka The Criminal), 437; Mr. Quilp, 794

Bennett, Joan: Bulldog Drummond, 25; Colonel Effingham's Raid, 246; Father's Little Dividend, 259; House Across the Bay, The, 489; Little Women, 519; Scarlet Street, 589; We're No Angels, 379; House That Dripped Blood, The, 701

Bennett, Richard: Arrowsmith, 401

Bennett, Tony: Oscar, The, 554

Benny, Jack: Broadway Melody of 1936, 772; Guide For The Married Man, A, 273; It's in the Bag, 289; To Be or Not to Be (Original), 368

Benrath, Martin: From the Lives of the Marionettes, 470

Benson, George: Creeping Flesh, The, 666

Benson, Greg: Bolero, 417

Benson, Martin: Battle beneath the Earth, 12; Gorgo, 694

Benson, Robby: Chosen, The, 433; City Limits, 823; Die Laughing, 251; End, The, 255; End, The, 255; Harry and Son, 483; Ice

Castles, 492; Ode to Billy Joe, 548; One on One. 552; Running Brave, 585; Tribute, 621

Benson, Rob: Marie, 529

Bentine, Michael: Down Among the "Z" Men, 253

Benton, Barbi: Deathstalker, 829

Benton, Helen: Bloodbeat, 653

Benton, Jerome: Under The Cherry Moon, 626

Benton, Suzanne: Boy and His Dog, A, 821

Beradino, John: Moon of the Wolf, 718

Bercourt, Alain: My Uncle (Mon Oncle), 317

Bercovici, Luca: Parasite, 726

Berenger, Tom: Big Chill, The, 411; Butch and Sundance: The Early Days, 887; Dogs of War, The, 44; Eddie and the Cruisers, 778; Fear City, 52; In Praise of Older Women, 493; Rustler's Rhapsody, 344

Berenson, Marisa: Barry Lyndon, 405; Death in Venice, 447

Bergen, Candice: 11 Harrowhouse, 48; Bite the Bullet, 884; Carnal Knowledge, 426; Domino Principle, The, 453; Gandhi, 471; Getting Straight, 472; Oliver's Story, 551; Rich and Famous, 579; Sand Pebbles, The, 127; Soldier Blue, 933; Starting Over, 358; Stick, 140; Wind and the Lion, The, 164

Bergen, Edgar: Muppet Movie, The, 193; Stage Door Canteen, 599

Bergen, Polly: At War with the Army, 221

Bergerac, Jacques: Gigi, 782; Les Girls, 792

Berger, Helmut: Battle Force, 12; Code Name: Emerald, 33; Conversation Piece, 438; Damned, The, 442; Dorian Gray, 678; Garden of the Finzi-Continis, the, 471; Romantic Englishwoman, The, 584

Berger, Senta: Cast a Giant Shadow, 28

Berger, Sidney: Carnival of Souls, 659

Berger, William: Adventures of Hercules, The, 815; Wifemistress, 633

Bergese, Micha: Company of Wolves, The, 825

Berge, Francine: Judex, 79; Mr. Klein, 536

Berggren, Thommy: Elvira Madigan, 457

Berghof, Herbert: Belarus File, The, 13; Target, 145

Bergman, Henry: Charlie Chaplin, The Early Years, Vol.3, 241; Woman of Paris, A, 638

Bergman, Ingrid: Adam Had Four Sons, 389; Arch of Triumph, 401; Autumn Sonata, 403; Bells of St. Mary's, The, 408; Casablanca, 427; Dr. Jekyll and Mr. Hyde, 676; Gaslight, 692; Inn of the Sixth Happiness, The, 495; Intermezzo, 496; Joan of Arc, 502; Matter of Time, A, 531; Murder on the Orient Express, 104; Notorious, 725; Spellbound, 746; Stromboli, 606; Under Capricorn, 626; Woman Called Golda, A, 638

Bergman, Sandahl: Conan the Barbarian, 825; Red Sonja, 120; She, 861; Xanadu, 813

Bergman, Tracy: Happy Birthday to Me, 696

Bergner, Elisabeth: Catherine the Great, *428*

Bergryd, Ulla: Bible, The, *410*

Berkoff, Stephen: Passenger, The, *558*; Barry Lyndon, *405*; Rambo: First Blood II, *118*; Under The Cherry Moon, *626*

Berland, Terri: Strangeness, The, *748*

Berle, Milton: Broadway Danny Rose, *235*; Cracking Up, *248*; It's a Mad Mad Mad Mad World, *288*; Lepke, *89*; Muppet Movie, The, *193*; Who's Minding the Mint?, *381*

Berlinger, Warren: Four Deuces, The, *59*; I Will, I Will...For Now, *285*; Lepke, *89*; Wackiest Ship in the Army, The, *377*

Berling, Peter: Aguirre: Wrath of God, *6*

Berlin, Irving: This is the Army, *808*

Berlin, Jeannie: Heartbreak Kid, The, *277*; Portnoy's Complaint, *565*

Berlin, Roland: Diva, *675*

Berman, Shelly: Son of Blob (Beware! The Blob), *745*

Berman, Susan: Smithereens, *596*

Bernabe, Joby: Sugar Cane Alley, *607*

Bernardi, Herschel: Irma La Douce, *287*; No Deposit, No Return, *195*

Bernard, Ivor: Beat the Devil, *225*

Bernard, Jack: Steagle, The, *359*

Bernard, Jason: Wilma, *635*

Bernard, Juan: Faster Pussycat! Kill! Kill!, *52*

Bernard, Sue: Witching, The (Necromancy), *765*

Bernard, Thelonious: Little Romance, A, *300*

Bernhard, Sandra: King of Comedy, The, *507*; (Sesame Street Presents) Follow That Bird, *204*

Berridge, Elizabeth: Amadeus, *769*; Funhouse, The, *691*; Smooth Talk, *596*

Berri, Claude: Sex Shop, Le, *350*

Berry, Chuck: Rock, Rock, Rock, *800*; That Was Rock, *808*

Berry, Jules: Le Jour Se Leve (DAYBREAK), *516*

Berry, Ken: Cat from Outer Space, The, *176*; Herbie Rides Again, *185*

Berry, Richard: La Balance, *85*; L'Addition, *510*

Berr, Ulrich: Mixed Blood, *101*

Bertheau, Julien: That Obscure Object of Desire, *615*

Bertin, Françoise: Last Year At Marienbad, *516*

Bertin, Roland: La Truite (The Trout), *512*

Bertinelli, Valerie: Aladdin and His Wonderful Lamp, *170*; Young Love, First Love, *640*

Bertish, Jane: Dance With a Stranger, *443*

Berto, Juliet: Mr. Klein, *536*; Sex Shop, Le, *350*

Bertrand, Janette: Big Red, *173*

Besch, Bibi: Beast Within, The, *649*; Lonely Lady, The, *520*

Besnehard, Dominique: A Nos Amours, *387*

Besse, Ariel: Beau Pere, *225*

Bessy, Claude: Invitation to the Dance, *788*

Best, Alyson: Dark Forces, *669*; Man of Flowers, *306*

Best, Edna: Man Who Knew Too Much, The (original), *715*

Best, James: Rolling Thunder, *123*; Savages, *739*; Sounder, *598*

Bettger, Lyle: Lone Ranger, The, *910*; Union Station, *760*

Betti, Laura: Hatchet for the Honeymoon, *696*; Lovers and Liars, *303*

Bettoia, Franca: Last Man On Earth, The, *848*

Betty, Ned: Back To School, *222*

Bett, John: Gregory's Girl, *273*; Tess, *613*

Beulieu, Philipe Leroy: Three Men and a Cradle, *367*

Bevans, Clem: Riding on Air, *341*

Bevan, Billy: Terror By Night, *148*; Lost Patrol, The, *93*

Beymer, Richard: Cross Country, *440*; Indiscretion of an American Wife, *495*; Johnny Tremain, *187*; West Side Story, *812*

Bey, Sarah: Lady Frankenstein, *710*

Bey, Turhan: Dragon Seed, *454*; Out of the Blue, *325*

Biagin, Isabella: Loaded Guns, *91*

Bianchi, Daniela: From Russia with Love, *61*

Bianco, Tony Lo: City Heat, *243*

Bice, Robert: On Top of Old Smoky, *919*

Bickford, Charles: Anna Christie, *399*; Big Country, *882*; Days of Wine and Roses, *447*; Farmer's Daughter, The, *258*; Johnny Belinda, *503*; Little Miss Marker, *190*; Star Is Born, A (Remake), *601*

Bickley, Tony: Swimmer, The, *609*

Bidonde, Hector: Funny Dirty Little War (NO HABRA MAS PENSAS ni OLVIDO), *264*

Biehn, Michael: Aliens, *816*; Fan, The, *683*; Terminator, The, *870*

Biel, Dick: Splatter University, *747*

Bieri, Ramon: Badlands, *404*; Grandview, U.S.A., *477*; Frisco Kid, The, *897*

Bikel, Theodore: 200 Motels, *810*; Defiant Ones, The, *448*; Dog of Flanders, A, *180*; Pride and the Passion, The, *567*; Russians Are Coming, the Russians Are Coming, The, *344*

Billanti, Denorah: Dona Flor and Her Two Husbands, *253*

Billet, Don: Prince of the City, *568*

Billingsley, Jennifer: C.C. & Company, *28*; White Lightning, *162*

Billingsley, Peter: Christmas Story, A, *177*

Billington, Michael: Invasion UFO, *845*

Billy, Little: Terror of Tiny Town, The, *937*

Bill, Tony: Ice Station Zebra, *77*; Initiation of Sarah, The, *705*; Soldier in the Rain, *596*; You're a Big Boy Now, *385*

Bind, John: Blue Money, *231*

Bing, Herman: Maytime, *793*

Binney, Clare: Savage Attraction, 739

Binns, Edward: 12 Angry Men, 624; Hunter, 75; Oliver's Story, 551; Pilot, The, 563

Binoche, Juliette: Hail Mary, 480

Bird, Billie: Sixteen Candles, 353

Birell, Tala: Purple Heart, The, 570

Birkin, Jane: Dark Places, 669; Evil Under the Sun, 50

Birman, Len: Man Inside, The, 95

Birney, David: Oh, God! Book II, 323

Birney, Frank: Fear No Evil, 683

Bishop, Debby: Blue Money, 231

Bishop, Ed: Invasion UFO, 845

Bishop, Joey: Delta Force, The, 41; Guide For The Married Man, A, 273; Naked and the Dead, The, 105; Who's Minding the Mint?, 381

Bishop, Julie: Northern Pursuit, 108

Bishop, Pat: Don's Party, 253

Bisley, Steve: Chain Reaction, 29; Summer City, 143

Bissell, Whit: Creature from the Black Lagoon, 665; He Walked by Night, 697

Bisset, Jacqueline: Airport, 7; Bullitt, 26; Class, 244; Day for Night, 446; Deep, The, 41; Forbidden, 467; Greek Tycoon, The, 479; Life and Times of Judge Roy Bean, The, 909; Murder on the Orient Express, 104; Rich and Famous, 579; Secrets, 590; St. Ives, 126; Thief Who Came to Dinner, The, 366; Under the Volcano, 626; When Time Ran Out!, 764

Bixby, Bill: Apple Dumpling Gang, The, 171; Fantasy Island, 837; Incredible Hulk, The, 843; Kentucky Fried Movie, 292; Kentucky Fried Movie, 292; Speedway, 805

Bjelvenstam, Bjorn: Wild Strawberries, 635

Bjork, Anita: Secrets of Women (or Waiting Women), 348

Bjornstrand, Gunnar: Devil's Eye, The, 250; Secrets of Women (or Waiting Women), 348; Seventh Seal, The, 591; Magician, The, 526; Winter Light, 636; Wild Strawberries, 635

Blackman, Honor: Cat and The Canary, The, 660; Goldfinger, 63; Jason and the Argonauts, 846; Partners in Crime—The Secret Adversary, 113; Shalako, 930; To the Devil, a Daughter, 757

Blackman, John: Blue Hawaii, 771

Blackmer, Sidney: Beyond A Reasonable Doubt, 409; Cheers for Miss Bishop, 432; Count of Monte Cristo, The (Original), 36; Tammy and the Bachelor, 611; Texas John Slaughter: Stampede at Bitter Creek, 937; War of the Wildcats, 943

Black, Karen: Airport 1975, 391; Burnt Offerings, 658; Can She Bake a Cherry Pie?, 238; Capricorn One, 822; Chanel Solitaire, 430; Come Back to the Five and Dime, Jimmy Dean, Jimmy Dean, 436; Day of the Locust, The, 446; Easy Rider, 455; Family Plot, 683;

Great Gatsby, The, 477; In Praise of Older Women, 493; Invaders from Mars (Remake), 844; Killing Heat, 507; LIttle Laura and Big John, 90; Little Mermaid, The, 189; Mr. Horn, 915; Nashville, 542; Portnoy's Complaint, 565; Trilogy of Terror, 759; You're a Big Boy Now, 385

Blades, Reuben: Crossover Dreams, 775

Blaine, Vivian: Dark, The, 669; Guys and Dolls, 785; Parasite, 726

Blain, Gerard: American Friend, The, 396

Blair, Adam: Hot Moves, 283

Blair, Betsy: Marty, 529

Blair, Janet: Black Arrow, The, 18; Fabulous Dorseys, The, 778; Fuller Brush Man, The, 264

Blair, Linda: Born Innocent, 417; Chained Heat, 29; Exorcist II: The Heretic, 681; Exorcist, The, 681; Hell Night, 697; Night Patrol, 318; Ruckus, 124; Savage Streets, 128

Blaise, Peter: Pied Piper of Hamelin, The, 198

Blakely, Colin: Dogs of War, The, 44; Equus, 458; Evil Under the Sun, 50; Pink Panther Strikes Again, The, 330; Private Life of Sherlock Holmes, The, 115

Blakely, Susan: Airport '79: The Concorde, 391; Lords of Flatbush, The, 522

Blakewell, William: Radar Men from the Moon, 117

Blake, Jeremy: McVicar, 532

Blake, Julia: Lonely Hearts, 520

Blake, Madge: Singin' in the Rain, 802

Blake, Robert: Coast to Coast, 245; In Cold Blood, 493; Of Mice and Men, 549; PT 109, 569; Tell Them Willie Boy Is Here, 936; This Property is Condemned, 617

Blakley, Ronee: Desperate Women, 893; Driver, The, 45; Nashville, 542; Nightmare on Elm Street, A, 722

Blanchard, Alan: Slithis, 744

Blanc, Mel: Neptune's Daughter, 795

Blandick, Clara: Wizard of Oz, The, 812

Bland, Peter: Came a Hot Friday, 27

Blankfield, Mark: Incredible Shrinking Woman, The, 286; Jack and the Beanstalk, 186; Jekyll & Hyde—Together Again, 289; Rip Van Winkle, 859

Blatchley, Joseph: Story of Adele H, The, 603

Blavette, Charles: Toni, 620

Bleackley, Simon: Adventures of Sherlock Holmes: The Solitary Cyclist, 5

Blech, Hans Christian: Colonel Redl, 435

Blee, Debra: Beach Girls, The, 225

Blendick, James: Utilities, 376

Blessed, Brian: High Road to China, 72; King Arthur, The Young Warlord, 84

Blier, Bernard: Passion of Love, 559; Tall Blond Man With One Black Shoe, The, 363

Blondell, Joan: Dames, 776; Death at Love

House, 672; Footlight Parade, 780; Gold Diggers of 1933, 783; Lady for a Night, 512; Stand-In, 358; Topper Returns, 370

Blondell, Simone: Jungle Master, The, 80

Bloomfield, George: Spasms, 746

Bloom, Claire: Alexander the Great, 392; Brothers Karamazov, The, 420; Buccaneer, The, 25; Charly, 823; Deja Vu, 448; Islands in the Stream, 498; Limelight, 299; Look Back in Anger, 521; Richard III, 580; Separate Tables, 590

Bloom, Michael Allan: Screen Test, 346

Bloom, Verna: After Hours, 215; Badge 373, 11; High Plains Drifter, 903; Medium Cool, 532

Blore, Eric: Gay Divorcee, The, 782; Shall We Dance?, 802; Sky's the Limit, The, 803; Swiss Miss, 363; Top Hat, 810

Blossom, Roberts: Christine, 662; Escape from Alcatraz, 49; Reuben, Reuben, 339; Resurrection, 858

Blount, Lisa: Cease Fire, 429

Bluestone, Abby: Night of the Juggler, 107

Blue, Monte: Apache, 879; Frontier Pony Express, 898; Intolerance, 898; Lives of a Bengal Lancer, The, 91; Rootin' Tootin' Rhythm, 928

Blum, Jack: Happy Birthday to Me, 696

Blum, Mark: Desperately Seeking Susan, 250; Just Between Friends, 505

Bluthal, John: Alison's Birthday, 644

Blyden, Larry: On a Clear Day, You Can See Forever, 796

Blye, Margaret: Final Chapter—Walking Tall, 54

Blythe, Betty: Dawn on the Great Divide, 891

Blythe, Robert: Experience Preferred...But Not Essential, 257

Blyth, Ann: Great Caruso, The, 785; Mildred Pierce, 534; Mr. Peabody and the Mermaid, 311

Boardman, True: Tarzan of the Apes, 145

Bob Wills Orchestra: Melody Ranch, 914

Bochner, Hart: Islands in the Stream, 498; Rich and Famous, 579; Supergirl, 868

Bochner, Lloyd: Lonely Lady, The, 520

Boehm, Carl: Peeping Tom, 727

Boers Jr., Frank: Equinox (The Beast), 680; Equinox (The Beast), 680

Bogarde, Dirk: Accident, 388; Bridge Too Far, A, 25; Damned, The, 442; Darling, 445; Death in Venice, 447; Despair, 449; Doctor at Large, 252; Doctor at Sea, 252; Doctor in Distress, 252; Ill Met by Moonlight, 493; Night Porter, The, 545; Permission to Kill, 114; Providence, 569; Sea Shall Not Have Them, The, 130; Servant, The, 590

Bogart, Humphrey: African Queen, The, 389; Angels with Dirty Faces, 8; Beat the Devil, 225; Big Sleep, The (Original), 16; Caine

Mutiny, The, 423; Call It Murder, 424; Casablanca, 427; Dark Passage, 38; Dark Victory, 445; Dead End, 447; Deadline USA, 447; Harder They Fall, The, 482; High Sierra, 72; Hollywood Outtakes, 282; Key Largo, 82; Knock on Any Door, 509; Left Hand of God, The, 88; Maltese Falcon, The, 95; Oklahoma Kid, The, 918; Passage to Marseilles, 113; Petrified Forest, The, 562; Private Lives of Elizabeth and Essex, The, 569; Roaring Twenties, The, 122; Sahara, 126; Stand-In, 358; Thank Your Lucky Stars, 807; They Drive by Night, 148; To Have and Have Not, 152; Treasure of the Sierra Madre, The, 155; We're No Angels, 379

Bogdanovich, Peter: Saint Jack, 587; Targets, 751; Trip, The, 622

Bogosian, Eric: Special Effects, 746

Bohringer, Richard: L'Addition, 510; Peril, 561; Subway, 142

Bois, Curt: Caught, 429; Tuttles of Tahiti, The, 373

Bolder, Cal: Jesse James Meets Frankenstein's Daughter, 708

Boles, John: Craig's Wife, 439; Frankenstein (Original), 687; Frankenstein (Restored Version), 688; King of Jazz, The, 790; Stella Dallas, 602; Thousands Cheer, 808

Bolger, Ray: Daydreamer, The, 179; That's Dancing, 807; Wizard of Oz, The, 812

Bolling, Tiffany: Bonnie's Kids, 22; Kingdom of the Spiders, 709

Bollner, Michael: Willy Wonka and the Chocolate Factory, 213

Bologna, Joseph: Big Bus, The, 229; Blame It on Rio, 230; Chapter Two, 431; My Favorite Year, 316; Transylvania 6-5000, 371; Woman in Red, The, 383

Bolton, Lyn: Blood Feast, 653

Bom, Lars: Topsy Turvy, 370

Bondi, Beulah: Arrowsmith, 401; Back to Bataan, 11; Rain, 574; So Dear to My Heart, 206; Street Scene, 605; Tammy and the Doctor, 611

Bond, Derek: Nicholas Nickleby, 544

Bond, Raymond: So Dear to My Heart, 206

Bond, Steve: Prey, The, 730

Bond, Sudie: Come Back to the Five and Dime, Jimmy Dean, Jimmy Dean, 436; Silkwood, 593; Swing Shift, 610; Tomorrow, 620

Bond, Ward: Dakota, 890; Dodge City, 894; Falcon Takes Over, The, 52; Fort Apache, 897; It Happened One Night, 287; It's a Wonderful Life, 499; Joan of Arc, 502; Johnny Guitar, 906; Maltese Falcon, The, 95; Man Alone, A, 911; Mr. Roberts, 311; My Darling Clementine, 916; Oklahoma Kid, The, 918; Quiet Man, The, 117; Rio Bravo, 926; Santa Fe Trail, 929; Searchers, The, 930; Sergeant York, 131; Tall in the Saddle, 936; They Made Me a Criminal, 616; They Were Expendable, *148;* Wagonmaster, *943;* Wheel of Fortune, *944;* You Only Live Once, *640*

Bonerz, Peter: Medium Cool, *532*

Bonham, John: Song Remains the Same, The *803*

Bonnaire, Sandrine: A Nos Amours, *387;* Vagabond, *627*

Bonner, Beverly: Basket Case, *648*

Bono, Sonny: Escape to Athena, *50;* Troll, *873*

Booke, Sorrell: Amazing Howard Hughes, The, *395;* Black Like Me, *413;* Joy House, *504*

Boone, Libby: Final Chapter—Walking Tall, *54*

Boone, Pat: Journey to the Center of the Earth, *846*

Boone, Richard: Against a Crooked Sky, *878;* Alamo, The, *878;* Arrangement, The, *401;* Away All Boats, *11;* Beneath the 12-Mile Reef, *13;* Big Jake, *882;* Bushido Blade, *26;* Dragnet, *45;* Hombre, *904;* Man without a Star, *913;* Rio Conchos, *927;* Robe, The, *581;* Shootist, The, *931;* Winter Kills, *636*

Boorman, Charley: Emerald Forest, The, *48*

Boothe, Powers: Emerald Forest, The, *48;* Red Dawn, *119;* Southern Comfort, *138*

Booth, Connie: Romance With A Double Bass, *343*

Booth, Shirley: Hot Spell, *489*

Bordeaux, Joe: Keystone Comedies, Vol. 1, *292;* Keystone Comedies, Vol. 2, *292;* Keystone Comedies: Vo. 5, *292*

Borgese, Sal: Five for Hell, *56*

Borges, Yamil: Chorus Line, A, *774*

Borge, Rikke: Tattoo, *611*

Borge, Victor: Daydreamer, The, *179*

Borgnine, Ernest: All Quiet on the Western Front, *393;* Barabbas, *405;* Black Hole, The, *821;* Convoy, *34;* Deadly Blessing, *671;* Devil's Rain, The, *674;* Dirty Dozen, The, *43;* Escape from New York, *49;* Fire!, *685;* Flight of the Phoenix, The, *58;* Greatest, The, *479;* High Risk, *72;* Hustle, The, *76;* Ice Station Zebra, *77;* Johnny Guitar, *906;* Last Command, The, *907;* Marty, *529;* Oscar, The, *554;* Poseidon Adventure, The, *115;* Shoot, *135;* Super Fuzz, *868;* Vera Cruz, *943;* Vikings, The, *159;* When Time Ran Out!, *764;* Wild Bunch, The, *945;* Willard, *765*

Borg, Veda Ann: Guys and Dolls, *785;* Revenge of the Zombies, *736*

Borman, Gerard: Beyond Fear, *409*

Boros, Ferike: Once Upon a Honeymoon, *324*

Borrelli, Jim: Windy City, *635*

Borris, Clay: Alligator Shoes, *394*

Borris, Gary: Alligator Shoes, *394*

Boschero, Dominique: Between God, The Devil and a Winchester, *882*

Bosetti, Giulio: Morgan the Pirate, *103*

Bosley, Tom: Jessie Owens Story, The, *501*

Bosson, Barbara: Last Starfighter, The, *848*

Bostwick, Barry: Megaforce, *851;* Movie Movie, *315*

Bostwick, Jackson: Prey, The, *730*

Bosworth, Hobart: Abraham Lincoln, *388*

Boteler, Wade: Melody Trail, *915*

Botiller, Dick: South of the Border, *934;* Yellow Rose of Texas, *946*

Botsford, Sara: Deadly Eyes, *671;* Still of the Night, *748*

Bottoms, Joseph: Black Hole, The, *821;* Cloud Dancer, *32;* High Rolling, *72;* Intruder Within, The, *844;* King of the Mountain, *508;* Surfacing, *143*

Bottoms, Sam: Bronco Billy, *886;* Savages, *739;* Prime Risk, *115*

Bottoms, Timothy: East of Eden (Remake), *454;* In the Shadow of Kilimanjaro, *704;* Invaders from Mars (Remake), *844;* Johnny Got His Gun, *503;* Last Picture Show, The, *514;* Other Side of the Mountain, Part II, The, *554;* Paper Chase, The, *557;* Rollercoaster, *737;* Small Town in Texas, A, *137;* White Dawn, The, *161*

Bouchet, Barbara: Sex With a Smile, *350*

Bouise, Jean: Mr. Klein, *536;* Subway, *142*

Bouix, Evelyn: Edith and Marcel, *778*

Boujenah, Michel: Three Men and a Cradle, *367*

Boulting, Ingrid: Last Tycoon, The, *515*

Boulton, Matthew: Woman In Green, The, *165*

Bouquet, Carole: That Obscure Object of Desire, *615;* For Your Eyes Only, *58*

Bouquet, Michel: Beyond Fear, *409*

Bourneuf, Philip: Beyond A Reasonable Doubt, *409*

Bourne, Whitney: Mad Miss Manton, The, *304*

Bourvil: When Wolves Cry, *632*

Boushel, Joy: Fly, The (remake), *686*

Bowens, Malick: Out of Africa, *555*

Bowen, Lori: Pumping Iron II: The Women, *570*

Bowen, Michael: Echo Park, *455*

Bower, Tom: Ballad of Gregorio Cortez, The, *881;* Wild Rose, *634*

Bowie, David: Absolute Beginners, *768;* Hunger, The, *703;* Into the Night, *496;* Labyrinth, *847;* Man Who Fell to Earth, The, *851;* Merry Christmas, Mr. Lawrence, *533*

Bowker, Judi: Brother Sun Sister Moon, *420;* Clash of the Titans, *830*

Bowles, Peter: Prisoner, The (television series), *857*

Bowman, Don: Hillbillys in a Haunted House, *280*

Bowman, Lee: Buck Privates, *235;* Smashup: The Story of a Woman, *595*

Bow, Clara: Wings, *164*

Bow, Simmy: Doberman Gang, The, *43*

Bow Wow Wow: Scandalous, *345*

Boxleitner, Bruce: East of Eden (Remake), *454*; Tron, *873*; Wild Times, *945*

Boyar, Sully: Car Wash, *239*

Boyce, Alan: Seven Minutes In Heaven, *350*

Boyden, Peter: Blow Out, *654*

Boyd, Jan Gan: Chorus Line, A, *774*

Boyd, Karin: Mephisto, *532*

Boyd, Sarah: Old Enough, *550*

Boyd, Stephen: Fall of the Roman Empire, The, *462*; Fantastic Voyage, *836*; Oscar, The, *554*; Shalako, *930*

Boyd, William ("Stage"): Oliver Twist, *550*

Boyd, William: Borrowed Trouble, *885*; Dangerous Venture, *891*; Dead Don't Dream, The, *892*; Devil's Playground, *893*; False Colors, *895*; False Paradise, *896*; Hoppy's Holiday, *904*; King of Kings, *508*; Marauders, *913*; Painted Desert, The, *921*; Riders of the Deadline, *926*; Silent Conflict, *931*; Sinister Journey, *932*; Strange Gamble, *935*; Unexpected Guest, *942*

Boyer, Charles: Algiers, *392*; Arch of Triumph, *401*; Barefoot in the Park, *224*; Buccaneer, The, *25*; Casino Royale, *239*; Fanny, *463*; Four Horsemen of the Apocalypse, *60*; Gaslight, *692*; History Is Made at Night, *488*; Matter of Time, A, *531*; Mayerling, *531*

Boyer, Marteen: Spetters, *598*

Boyle, Peter: Beyond the Poseidon Adventure, *14*; Brinks Job, The, *234*; Candidate, The, *425*; F.I.S.T., *461*; Hammett, *68*; Hardcore, *481*; Joe, *502*; Outland, *855*; Steelyard Blues, *359*; Taxi Driver, *612*; Turk 182, *624*; Where the Buffalo Roam, *381*; Yellowbeard, *385*; Young Frankenstein, *385*

Boyle, Ray: Satan's Satellites, *128*

Bozo: Life and Times of Grizzly Adams, The, *189*

Bozzuffi, Marcel: Z, *641*

Bo, Victor: Deathstalker, *829*

Bracken, Eddie: Young and Willing, *640*

Bradford, Greg: Lovelines, *302*; Zapped!, *385*

Bradford, John: Old Corral, The, *919*

Bradford, Lane: Satan's Satellites, *128*; Zombies of the Stratosphere (Satan's Satellites), *167*

Bradford, Richard: Trip to Bountiful, The, *622*

Bradley, Leslie: Attack of the Crab Monsters, *647*

Bradna, Olympe: South of Pago Pago, *138*

Bradshaw, Carl: Harder They Come, The, *786*

Brady, Alice: Gay Divorcee, The, *782*

Brady, Pat: Bells of Coronado, *881*; Down Dakota Way, *894*; Golden Stallion, The, *898*; Song of Texas, *933*; T Trigger, Jr., *940*; Twilight in the Sierras, *941*

Brady, Ruth: Caught, *429*

Brady, Scott: Bonnie's Kids, *22*; China Syndrome, The, *432*; Gremlins, *840*; He Walked by Night, *697*; Johnny Guitar, *906*; Journey to the Center of Time, *846*; Maverick Queen, The, *914*; Nightmare In Wax (Crimes In The Wax Museum), *721*

Braeden, Eric: Adultress, The, *389*; Escape from the Planet of the Apes, *835*; Herbie Goes to Monte Carlo, *185*

Braga, Sonia: Dona Flor and Her Two Husbands, *253*; Gabriela, *265*; I Love You (Eu Te Amo), *491*; Lady on the Bus, *296*

Brailey, Gil: Belfast Assassin, *407*

Brainin, Danny: XTro, *766*

Brambell, Wilfred: Hard Day's Night, A, *786*

Bramley, Flora: College, *246*

Branciia, Armando: Amarcord, *395*

Brandauer, Klaus Maria: Colonel Redl, *435*; Mephisto, *532*; Never Say Never Again, *106*; Out of Africa, *555*

Brandon, David: She, *861*

Brandon, Michael: Change of Seasons, A, *240*; Promises in the Dark, *569*; Queen of the Stardust Ballroom, *572*; Rich and Famous, *579*

Brando, Marlon: Apocalypse Now, *9*; Burn!, *421*; Chase, The, *431*; Formula, The, *467*; Godfather, The, *473*; Godfather Epic, The, *474*; Guys and Dolls, *785*; Last Tango in Paris, *515*; Men, The, *532*; Missouri Breaks, The, *915*; Mutiny on the Bounty (Remake), *105*; Nightcomers, The, *721*; One-Eyed Jacks, *920*; On the Waterfront, *551*; Reflections in a Golden Eye, *578*; Sayonara, *589*; Streetcar Named Desire, A, *605*; Superman, *868*; Viva Zapata!, *629*; Wild One, The, *164*

Brando, Richard: Student Bodies, *749*

Brando, Yasusuka: Mishima: A Life in Four Chapters, *535*

Brand, Neville: Cahill—US Marshal, *887*; D.O.A., *442*; Fire!, *685*; Lonely Man, The, *909*; Ninth Configuration, The, *546*; Riot in Cell Block 11, *581*; That Darn Cat, *208*; Untouchables: Alcatraz Express, The, *157*; Untouchables: Scarface Mob, The, *157*

Branski, David: 9 1/2 Weeks, *545*

Brantley, Betsy: Adventures of Sherlock Holmes: The Dancing Men, *3*; Five Days One Summer, *466*

Brassac, Robert: Baker's Wife, The, *224*

Brasselle, Keefe: Place in the Sun, A, *563*

Brasseur, Claude: Elusive Corporal, The, *457*; La Boum, *511*; Pardon Mon Affaire, *327*; Simple Story, A, *594*

Brasseur, Pierre: Children of Paradise, *432*

Braverman, Bart: Alligator, *644*

Brazzi, Rossano: Bobo, The, *231*; Far Pavilions, The, *463*; Fear City, *52*; Final Conflict, The, *684*; South Pacific, *805*; Summertime, *608*

Breck, Peter: Benji, *172;* Crawling Hand, The, *665*

Brega, Mario: Death Rides a Horse, *892;* Fistful of Dollars, A, *896;* For a Few Dollars More, *897*

Brel, Jacques: Pain in the A———, A, *327*

Bremer, Lucille: Till the Clouds Roll By, *809;* Yolanda and The Thief, *640*

Brendel, El: Big Trail, The, *883;* Wings, *164*

Brennan, Eileen: Clue, *245;* Daisy Miller, *442;* Great Smokey Roadblock, The, *65;* My Old Man, *541;* Private Benjamin, *334;* Scarecrow, *589;* Sting, The, *144*

Brennan, Walter: Adventures of Tom Sawyer, The, *170;* Dakota, *890;* Gnome-Mobile, The, *182;* Green Promise, The, *479;* How the West Was Won, *904;* Meet John Doe, *532;* My Darling Clementine, *916;* Pride of the Yankees, The, *568;* Princess and the Pirate, The, *334;* Red River, *924;* Rio Bravo, *926;* Sergeant York, *131;* Story of Vernon and Irene Castle, The, *806;* Support Your Local Sheriff, *936;* Tammy and the Bachelor, *611;* To Have and Have Not, *152;* Westerner, The, *944;* Who's Minding the Mint?, *381*

Brenner, Eve: Torment, *757*

Brent, Evelyn: Mr. Wong, Detective, *101*

Brent, George: Dark Victory, *445;* Jezebel, *501;* Out of the Blue, *325;* Silver Queen, *932*

Brent, Lynton: Git Along, Little Dogies, *898;* Old Corral, The, *919*

Brent, Romney: Dinner at the Ritz, *43*

Breon, Edmund: Dressed to Kill, *45*

Bresee, Bobbie: Mausoleum, *716*

Brett, Jeremy: Adventures of Sherlock Holmes: A Scandal in Bohemia, *2;* Adventures of Sherlock Holmes: The Blue Carbuncle, *2;* Adventures of Sherlock Holmes: The Copper Beeches, *3;* Adventures of Sherlock Holmes: The Crooked Man, *3;* Adventures of Sherlock Holmes: The Dancing Men, *3;* Adventures of Sherlock Holmes: The Final Problem, *4;* Adventures of Sherlock Holmes: The Greek Interpreter, *4;* Adventures of Sherlock Holmes: The Naval Treaty, *4;* Adventures of Sherlock Holmes: The Norwood Builder, *5;* Adventures of Sherlock Holmes: The Red-Headed League, *5;* Adventures of Sherlock Holmes: The Resident Patient, *5;* Adventures of Sherlock Holmes: The Solitary Cyclist, *5;* Adventures of Sherlock Holmes: The Speckled Band, *6*

Brewster, Diane: Young Philadelphians, The, *640*

Brialy, Jean-Claude: Claire's Knee, *243;* Robert et Robert, *582*

Briant, Shane: Captain Kronos: Vampire Hunter, *659;* Shaker Run, *132*

Brian, David: Million Dollar Mermaid, *794*

Brian, Mary: Amazing Adventure, *217;* Front Page, The, *264*

Brice, Fanny: Ziegfeld Follies, *814*

Bridges, Alan: Melody Trail, *915;* When a Man Rides Alone, *944*

Bridges, Beau: Fifth Musketeer, The, *53;* Greased Lightning, *64;* Heart Like a Wheel, *70;* Honky Tonk Freeway, *282;* Hotel New Hampshire, The, *489;* Love Child, *523;* Night Crossing, *106;* Norma Rae, *546;* Other Side of the Mountain, The, *554;* Red Light Sting, The, *577;* Runner Stumbles, The, *585;* Village of the Giants, *636*

Bridges, Jeff: 8 Million Ways to Die, *47;* Against All Odds, *390;* Bad Company, *880;* Cutter's Way, *441;* Heaven's Gate, *902;* Jagged Edge, *500;* King Kong (remake), *710;* Kiss Me Goodbye, *294;* Last American Hero, The, *86;* Last Picture Show, The, *514;* Rapunzel, *200;* Starman, *867;* Stay Hungry, *602;* Thunderbolt and Lightfoot, *152;* Tron, *873;* Winter Kills, *636*

Bridges, Lloyd: Abilene Town, *878;* Airplane!, *216;* Around the World Under the Sea, *10;* Bear Island, *648;* East of Eden (Remake), *454;* Fifth Musketeer, The, *53;* Great Wallendas, The, *478;* High Noon, *903;* Master Race, The, *531;* Rocketship X-M, *860;* Sahara, *126*

Brien, Joan O': It Happpened at the World's Fair, *789*

Brieux, Bernard: Petit Con, *329*

Brimley, Wilford: Death Valley, *672;* Thing, The, *871;* Cocoon, *825;* Country, *439;* Harry and Son, *483;* High Road to China, *72;* Natural, The, *542;* Remo Williams: The Adventure Begins, *120;* Rodeo Girl, *583;* Stone Boy, The, *603;* Tough Enough, *154*

Brinkley, Christie: Vacation, *376*

Brion, Francoise: Nea (A Young Emmanuelle), *542*

Brittany, Morgan: Initiation of Sarah, The, *705*

Britton, Barbara: Captain Kidd, *27;* Champagne for Caesar, *240;* Young and Willing, *640*

Britton, Pamela: D.O.A., *442*

Britton, Tony: Day of the Jackal, The, *39;* Horsemasters, *185;* There's a Girl in my Soup, *365*

Brix, Herman: Daredevils of the Red Circle, *38*

Broderick, Helen: Swing Time, *806;* Top Hat, *810*

Broderick, James: Alice's Restaurant, *393;* Group, The, *480*

Broderick, Matthew: Cinderella, *177;* Ferris Bueller's Day Off, *259;* Ladyhawke, *86;* Wargames, *875*

Brodie, Steve: Frankenstein Island, *688;* Home of the Brave, *488;* Out of the Past, *112*

Brody, Michael: Forest, The, *687*

Brolin, James: Amityville Horror, The, *645;*

Capricorn One, 822; High Risk, 72; Night of the Juggler, 107; Von Ryan's Express, 159; Westworld, 876

Brolin, Josh: Goonies, The, 63

Bromberg, J. Edward: Jesse James, 905; Lady of Burlesque, 86; Return of Frank James, The, 925

Bromfield, John: Easy to Love, 778

Bronson, Charles: Apache, 879; Borderline, 22; Breakheart Pass, 886; Breakout, 24; Cabo Blanco, 26; Chino, 888; Death Hunt, 39; Death Wish, 40; Death Wish II, 40; Death Wish III, 40; Dirty Dozen, The, 43; Drum Beat, 894; Evil That Men Do, The, 50; Family, The, 52; Great Escape, The, 65; Hard Times, 69; Honor Among Thieves, 74; Love and Bullets, 93; Magnificent Seven, The, 911; Master of the World, 851; Mechanic, The, 98; Mr. Majestyk, 101; Murphy's Law, 104; Once Upon a Time in the West, 919; Red Sun, 924; Rider on the Rain, 122; Sandpiper, The, 588; Stone Killer, The, 141; St. Ives, 126; Telefon, 147; Ten to Midnight, 147; This Property is Condemned, 617; Villa Rides, 943

Bron, Eleanor: Bedazzled, 225; Help!, 787; Turtle Diary, 373; Women in Love, 638

Brookes, Jacqueline: Rodeo Girl, 583; Without a Trace, 637

Brooke, Bunny: Alison's Birthday, 644

Brooke, Hillary: Abbott and Costello Meet Captain Kidd, 214; Woman In Green, The, 165

Brook, Claudio: Simon of the Desert, 352

Brook, Clive: List of Adrian Messenger, The, 90

Brooks, Albert: Lost in America, 301; Modern Romance, 312; Real Life, 338; Unfaithfully Yours (Remake), 375

Brooks, Clarence: Harlem Rides the Range, 900

Brooks, Geraldine: Johnny Tiger, 503; Possessed, 565

Brooks, Hadda: Out of the Blue, 325

Brooks, Hazel: Body and Soul (Original), 416

Brooks, Jacqueline: Entity, The, 680; Gambler, The, 470

Brooks, Leslie: You Were Never Lovelier, 814

Brooks, Louise: Pandora's Box, 556

Brooks, Lucius: Harlem Rides the Range, 900

Brooks, Mel: Audience with Mel Brooks, An, 221; Blazing Saddles, 230; High Anxiety, 280; Mel Brooks' History of the World, Part I, 308; Muppet Movie, The, 193; Putney Swope, 337; Silent Movie, 351; To Be or Not to Be (Remake), 369; Twelve Chairs, The, 373

Brooks, Paul: 'Agatha, 390

Brooks, Randi: Hamburger—The Motion Picture, 274

Brooks, Rand: Borrowed Trouble, 885; Dangerous Venture, 891; Dead Don't Dream, The, 892; Devil's Playground, 893; False Paradise, 896; Hoppy's Holiday, 904; Marauders, 913; Silent Conflict, 931; Sinister Journey, 932; Strange Gamble, 935; Unexpected Guest, 942

Brook, Claudio: Simon of the Desert, 352

Brook, Clive: List of Adrian Messenger, The, 90

Brophy, Edward: Thin Man, The, 149; Freaks, 689; Great Guy, 478; Thin Man Goes Home, The, 149

Brophy, Kevin: Time Walker, 755

Brosnan, Pierce: Long Good Friday, The, 92; Nomads, 724

Brost, Gudrun: Sawdust and Tinsel, 589

Brothers, The Flying Karamazov: Jewel of the Nile, The, 79

Brothers, Dr. Joyce: Lonely Guy, The, 300

Brothers, The Doobie: No Nukes, 795

Brothers, The Marx: Animal Crackers, 218; At the Circus, 221; Day at the Races, A, 249; Duck Soup, 269; Go West, 269; Love Happy, 302; Monkey Business, 312; Night at the Opera, A, 318; Room Service, 343

Brothers, The Ritz: Goldwyn Follies, The, 784; Gorilla, The, 271

Browne, Angela: Adventures of Sherlock Holmes: The Copper Beeches, 3

Browne, Coral: Dreamchild, 831; Ruling Class, The, 344

Browne, Diana: Basket Case, 648

Browne, Jackson: No Nukes, 795

Browne, Robert Alan: Psycho III, 731

Browne, Roscoe Lee: Black Like Me, 413; Cowboys, The, 890; King, 507; Legal Eagles, 88; Liberation of L. B. Jones, The, 517; Nothing Personal, 321; World's Greatest Athlete, The, 213

Browning, Todd: Intolerance, 497

Brown, Amelda: Adventures of Sherlock Holmes: The Blue Carbuncle, 2

Brown, Barbara: Mildred Pierce, 534

Brown, Barry: Bad Company, 880; Daisy Miller, 442

Brown, Blair: Altered States, 817; Continental Divide, 247; Flash of Green, A, 466; One Trick Pony, 797

Brown, Bryan: Breaker Morant, 24; F/X, 51; Odd Angry Shot, The, 548; Thorn Birds, The, 617; Winter of our Dreams, 636

Brown, Clancy: Bride, The, 656; Highlander, 841

Brown, Coral: Auntie Mame, 222

Brown, D. W.: Mischief, 310; Weekend Pass, 378

Brown, Eric: Private Lessons, 335; They're Playing with Fire, 616

Brown, Gary: Secret Life of An American Wife, The, 347

Brown, Georgia: Devil's Undead, The, *674*

Brown, Georg Stanford: Jessie Owens Story, The, *501;* Stir Crazy, *359*

Brown, Gibran: Marvin and Tige, *530*

Brown, James: Targets, *751;* That Was Rock, *808*

Brown, Jim: 100 Rifles, *920;* Dirty Dozen, The, *43;* Fingers, *464;* Ice Station Zebra, *77;* One Down, Two to Go, *110;* Rio Conchos, *927;* Three the Hard Way, *151*

Brown, Joe E.: Riding on Air, *341;* Show Boat, *802;* Some Like It Hot, *356*

Brown, Johnny Mack: Lawman Is Born, A, *908*

Brown, Lou: Alison's Birthday, *644*

Brown, Olivia: Miami Vice, *98;* Miami Vice: "The Prodigal Son", *99*

Brown, Pamela: Becket, *406;* Cleopatra, *435*

Brown, Paul: Morons from Outer Space, *314*

Brown, Peter: Commies Are Coming, the Commies Are Coming, The, *246*

Brown, Phil: Without Reservations, *382*

Brown, Ralph: Final Exam, *684*

Brown, Reb: FastBreak, *258;* Howling II... Your Sister is a Werewolf, *702;* Uncommon Valor, *156;* Yor: The Hunter from the Future, *877*

Brown, Ron: Charlie, The Lonesome Cougar, *176*

Brown, Sharon: Chorus Line, A, *774*

Brown, Terry: Bloodbeat, *653*

Brown, Tom: Judge Priest, *504*

Brown, Vanessa: Bless the Beasts and the Children, *414;* Heiress, The, *485*

Brown, Wendell: Up the Academy, *375*

Bruce, Angela: Charlie Boy, *661*

Bruce, David: Gung Ho, *67*

Bruce, Kate: True Heart Susie, *623*

Bruce, Lenny: Dance Hall Racket, *442*

Bruce, Nigel: Adventures of Sherlock Holmes, The, *2;* Becky Sharp, *407;* Dressed to Kill, *45;* Hound of the Baskervilles, The (Original), *75;* Limelight, *299;* Pursuit to Algiers, *117;* Rebecca, *576;* Scarlet Pimpernel, The, *129;* Sherlock Holmes and the Secret Weapon, *134;* Suspicion, *750;* Terror By Night, *148;* Woman in Green, The, *165*

Brudin, Bo: Great Waldo Pepper, The, *66*

Brunkhorst, Natja: Christiane F., *433*

Bruno, Nando: Open City, *553*

Bryant, Michael: Sakharov, *587*

Bryant, Pamela: Private Lessons, *335*

Bryant-King, Ursalin: All the Marbles, *217*

Bryne, Barbara: Bostonians, The, *417*

Brynner, Yul: Brothers Karamazov, The, *420;* Buccaneer, The, *25;* Futureworld, *838;* Fuzz, *265;* Invitation to a Gunfighter, *905;* King and I, The, *790;* Magic Christian, The, *304;* Magnificent Seven, The, *911;* Solomon and Sheba, *597;* Ten Commandments, The, *612;* Ultimate Warrior, The, *874;* Villa Rides, *943;* Westworld, *876*

Buarnica, Lupe: Gloria, *62*

Buchanan, Edgar: Abilene Town, *878;* Benji, *172;* Big Trees, The, *16;* Black Arrow, The, *18;* Penny Serenade, *560;* Ride the High Country, *925;* Texas, *937*

Buchanan, Jack: Band Wagon, The, *769*

Buchanan, Robert: That Sinking Feeling, *365*

Buchanan, Simone: Run, Rebecca, Run, *202*

Buchegger, Christine: From the Lives of the Marionettes, *470*

Buchholz, Horst: Code Name: Emerald, *33;* Fanny, *463;* One, Two, Three, *324;* Sahara, *126*

Buch, Fred: Shock Waves (Death Corps), *742*

Buckner, Susan: Deadly Blessing, *671*

Buck, Frank: Africa Screams, *215*

Buday, Helen: Mad Max Beyond Thunderdome, *850*

Bud, Norman: Alien Warrior, *816*

Buetel, Jack: Outlaw, The, *920*

Bugarini, Raymond: Rock 'N Roll Wrestling Women Vs. The Aztec Mummy, *342*

Bujold, Genevieve: Anne of the Thousand Days, *400;* Choose Me, *433;* Coma, *664;* Earthquake, *46;* King of Hearts, *294;* Last Flight of Noah's Ark, *188;* Monsignor, *538;* Murder By Decree, *103;* Obsession, *725;* Tightrope, *755;* Trojan Women, The, *622;* Trouble in Mind, *622*

Bullock, Burl: Bus Is Coming, The, *422*

Bull, Peter: African Queen, The, *389*

Bull, Richard: Secret Life of An American Wife, The, *347*

Bunce, Alan: Sunrise at Campobello, *609*

Bundy, Robert: Screen Test, *346*

Buono, Victor: Arnold, *646;* Better Late than Never, *228;* Man with Bogart's Face, The, *96;* What Ever Happened to Baby Jane?, *764;* Who's Minding the Mint?, *381*

Bupp, Tommy: It's a Gift, *288*

Burdon, Eric: Comeback, *775*

Burgess, Scott: Dead Easy, *447*

Burge, Gregg: Chorus Line, A, *774*

Burke, Billie: Becky Sharp, *407;* Christopher Strong, *433;* Craig's Wife, *439;* Dinner at Eight, *251;* Father's Little Dividend, *259;* Topper Takes a Trip, *370;* Topper, *369;* Wizard of Oz, The, *812;* Young Philadelphians, The, *640*

Burke, David: Adventures of Sherlock Holmes: A Scandal in Bohemia, *2;* Adventures of Sherlock Holmes: The Blue Carbuncle, *2;* Adventures of Sherlock Holmes: The Copper Beeches, *3;* Adventures of Sherlock Holmes: The Crooked Man, *3;* Adventures of Sherlock Holmes: The Dancing Men, *3;* Adventures of Sherlock Holmes: The Final Problem, *4;* Adventures of Sherlock Holmes: The Greek Interpreter, *4;* Adventures of Sherlock Holmes: The Naval Treaty, *4;* Adventures of Sherlock Holmes:

The Norwood Builder, 5; Adventures of Sherlock Holmes: The Red-Headed League, 5; Adventures of Sherlock Holmes: The Resident Patient, 5; Adventures of Sherlock Holmes: The Solitary Cyclist, 5; Adventures of Sherlock Holmes: The Speckled Band, 6

Burke, James: Mad Miss Manton, The, 304

Burke, Kathleen: Lives of a Bengal Lancer, The, 91

Burke, Paul: Red Light Sting, The, 577; Thomas Crown Affair, The, 150

Burke, Sam: Five for Hell, 56

Burlinson, Tom: Flesh and Blood, 57; Man from Snowy River, 95; Phar Lap, 562

Burnette, Smiley: Billy The Kid Returns, 883; Boots and Saddles, 885; Call of the Canyon, 887; Git Along, Little Dogies, 898; Heart of the Golden West, 901; Heart of the Rio Grande, 901; Last of the Pony Riders, 907; Manhattan Merry-Go-Round, 913; Man From Music Mountain, 912; Man of the Frontier, (Red River Valley), 912; Melody Trail, 915; Mystery Mountain, 916; Old Corral, The, 919; On Top of Old Smoky, 919; Prairie Moon, 922; Radio Ranch (Men With Steel Faces, Phantom Empire), 923; Ridin' on a Rainbow, 926; Rootin' Tootin' Rhythm, 928; South of the Border, 934; Winning of the West, 946; Phantom Empire, 114

Burnett, Carol: Annie, 769; Between Friends, 409; Chu Chu and the Philly Flash, 243; Four Seasons, The, 469; Grass is Always Greener Over the Septic Tank, The, 272; Wedding, A, 378

Burns, Bob: Twilight in the Sierras, 941

Burns, Cathy: Last Summer, 514

Burns, David: It's Always Fair Weather, 789

Burns, Fred: Colorado, 889; Frontier Pony Express, 898

Burns, George: Damsel in Distress, A, 776; Going in Style, 269; Oh God!, 323; Oh, God! Book II, 323; Oh God, You Devil!, 323; Sgt. Pepper's Lonely Hearts Club Band, 802; Sunshine Boys, The, 361

Burns, Helen: Utilities, 376

Burns, Marilyn: Eaten Alive, 680; Future-Kill, 692; Helter Skelter, 486; Texas Chainsaw Massacre, The, 753

Burns, Marion: Dawn Rider, 892; Paradise Canyon, 920

Burns, Mark: Death in Venice, 447

Burns, Michael: Santee, 929

Burns, Robert: Sagebrush Trail, 929

Burns, Stephan W.: Herbie Goes Bananas, 184

Burns, Tim: Mad Max, 850

Burroughs, Jackie: Grey Fox, The, 899

Burroughs, William: Kerouac, 506;

Burr, Raymond: Black Magic, 413; Curse of King Tut's Tomb, The, 667; Godzilla 1985, 694; Godzilla, King of the Monsters, 693; His Kind of Woman, 73; Love Happy, 302; Man

Alone, A, 911; Place in the Sun, A, 563; Rear Window, 734

Burstyn, Ellen: Alice Doesn't Live Here Anymore, 392; Ambassador, The, 395; Exorcist, The, 681; Harry and Tonto, 483; Providence, 569; Resurrection, 858; Same Time Next Year, 345; Silence of the North, 593; Thursday's Game, 618; Twice in a Lifetime, 624

Burton, Kate: Big Trouble in Little China, 17

Burton, LeVar: Hunter, The, 75; Jessie Owens Story, The, 501; Looking for Mr. Goodbar, 521

Burton, Normann: Gumball Rally, The, 67

Burton, Richard: Alexander the Great, 392; Anne of the Thousand Days, 400; Becket, 406; Bluebeard, 655; Breakthrough, 24; Circle of Two, 434; Cleopatra, 435; Equus, 458; Exorcist II: The Heretic, 681; Gathering Storm, 471; Longest Day, The, 92; Look Back in Anger, 521; Love Spell, 93; Night of the Iguana, The, 544; Raid on Rommel, 118; Robe, The, 581; Sandpiper, The, 588; Taming of the Shrew, The, 364; Wagner, 811; Where Eagles Dare, 161; Who's Afraid of Virginia Woolf?, 633; Wild Geese, The, 163

Burton, Robert: Trilogy of Terror, 759

Burton, Tony: Assault on Precinct 13, 10; Inside Moves, 496; Rocky IV, 582

Burton, Wendell: Sterile Cuckoo, The, 603

Bus Boys, The: Eddie Murphy—Delirious, 255

Busch, Mae: Keystone Comedies: Vol. 4, 292

Busey, Gary: Barbarosa, 881; Big Wednesday, 411; Carny, 426; D.C. Cab, 249; Foolin' Around, 261; Gumball Rally, The, 67; Last American Hero, The, 86; Silver Bullet, 743; Star Is Born, A (Remake), 601; Straight Time, 603; Thunderbolt and Lightfoot, 152

Bushell, Anthony: Dark Journey, 445

Bush, Billy Green: Alice Doesn't Live Here Anymore, 392; Jericho Mile, The, 501; Tom Horn, 939

Bush, Chuck: Fandango, 258

Busia, Akousa: Color Purple, The, 436

Busia, Marion: Gone in 60 Seconds, 63

Bussieres, Raymond: Invitation au Voyage, 497

Buster, Budd: Call of the Canyon, 887; Heart of the Rio Grande, 901; Sunset Serenade, 935

Butkus, Dick: Cracking Up, 248; Hamburger—The Motion Picture, 274

Butler, Dean: Desert Hearts, 449; Kid With the 200 I.Q., The, 891

Butler, John: Sinister Journey, 932

Butler, Mark: Test of Love, A, 613

Butterworth, Charles: This is the Army, 808; Second Chorus, 801

Buttons, Red: 13 Rue Madeleline, 149; Five Weeks in a Balloon, 56; Harlow, 482; Hatari!,

69; Movie Movie, 315; One, Two, Three, 324; Pete's Dragon, 197; Poseidon Adventure, The, 115; Sayonara, 589; Users, The, 627; When Time Ran Out!, 764

Buttram, Pat: Blue Canadian Rockies, 884; Hills of Utah, The, 903; Night Stage to Galveston, 917

Buzby, Zane: Americathon, 218; Class Reunion, 244; Cracking Up, 248

Buzzi, Ruth: Apple Dumpling Gang Rides Again, The, 171; Bad Guys, 11; Being, The, 650; Chu Chu and the Philly Flash, 243; Freaky Friday, 182

Byington, Spring: Devil and Miss Jones, The, 250; Dodsworth, 452; In the Good Old Summertime, 788; Jezebel, 501; Little Women, 519; Meet John Doe, 532; Mutiny on the Bounty (Original), 105

Byner, John: Great Smokey Roadblock, The, 65; Transylvania 6-5000, 371

Byrd, Ralph: Dick Tracy Meets Gruesome, 42

Byrne, Eddie: Mummy, The (remake), 719

Byrne, Gabriel: Hanna K., 481

Byrne, Martha: Anna to the Infinite Power, 817

Byron, Jeffrey: Metalstorm: The Destruction of Jared-Syn, 852

Byron, Marion: Steamboat Bill Jr., 359

B-52's, The: One Trick Pony, 797

Caan, James: Brian's Song, 420; Bridge Too Far, A, 25; Chapter Two, 431; Comes a Horseman, 889; Countdown, 439; Harry and Walter Go to New York, 276; Hide in Plain Sight, 487

Cabot, Bruce: Angel and the Badman, 879; Ann Vickers, 399; Big Jake, 882; Chisum, 889; Comancheros, The, 889; Diamonds Are Forever, 42; Hellfighters, 70

Cabot, Sebastian: Ivanhoe, 78; Johnny Tremain, 187; Westward Ho The Wagons, 212

Cada, James: Wild Rose, 634

Caesar, Adolph: Club Paradise, 245; Color Purple, The, 436

Caesar, Sid: Airport 1975, 391; Guide For The Married Man, A, 273; It's a Mad Mad Mad Mad World, 288

Cage, Nicolas: Birdy, 412; Boy in Blue, The, 418

Cagney, James: Angels with Dirty Faces, 8; Blood on the Sun, 19; Hollywood Outtakes, 282; Midsummer Night's Dream, A, 952; What Price Glory, 379; White Heat, 161; Yankee Doodle Dandy, 813

Cagney, Jeanne: Yankee Doodle Dandy, 813

Caine, Michael: Alfie, 216; Beyond the Limit, 410; Beyond the Poseidon Adventure, 14; Blame It on Rio, 230; Bridge Too Far, A, 25; Deathtrap, 448; Hand, The, 696; Hannah and Her Sisters, 275; Harry and Walter Go to New York, 276; Holcroft Covenant, The, 74;

Island, The, 706; Jigsaw Man, The, 708; Man Who Would Be King, The, 96; Wrong Box, The, 384; Zulu, 167

Calhern, Louis: Bridge of San Luis Rey, The, 420; Arch of Triumph, 401; Count of Monte Cristo, The (Original), 36; Life of Emile Zola, The, 518; Red Pony, The, 201

Calhoun, Rory: Avenging Angel, 11; How to Marry a Millionaire, 284

Callan, Michael: Cat and The Canary, The, 660; Cat Ballou, 888; Lepke, 89

Callas, Charlie: Hysterical, 284

Calleia, Joseph: After the Thin Man, 6; Jungle Book, 187

Calloway, Cab, and the Cotton Club Orchestra: Manhattan Merry-Go-Round, 913

Calthrop, Donald: Blackmail, 414

Calvert, Phyllis: Man in Grey, The, 528

Calvet, Corinne: What Price Glory, 379

Calvin, Henry: Sign of Zorro, The, 204

Camara, Gloria: Kashmiri Run, The, 81

Cambridge, Godfrey: Son of Blob (Beware! The Blob), 745; Watermelon Man, 378

Cameron, Rod: Evel Knievel, 50; Manhunt in the African Jungle (Secret Service in Darkest Africa), 96; Ride the Man Down, 926

Camilleri, Terry: Cars That Ate Paris, The (The Cars That Eat People), 823; Cars That Eat People (The Cars That Ate Paris), 660

Campanella, Joseph: Hangar 18, 840; St. Valentine's Day Massacre, The, 126

Campbell, Bruce: Evil Dead, The, 681

Campbell, Cheryl: Shooting Party, The, 592

Campbell, Douglas: If You Could See What I Hear, 492

Campbell, Elizabeth: Rock 'N Roll Wrestling Women Vs. The Aztec Mummy, 342

Campbell, Eric: Charlie Chaplin, The Early Years, Vol.1, 241; Charlie Chaplin—The Early Years, Vol.2, 241; Charlie Chaplin—The Early Years, Vol.3, 241; Charlie Chaplin—The Early Years, Vol.4, 241

Campbell, Ken: Adventures of Sherlock Holmes: The Blue Carbuncle, 2

Campbell, Nicholas: Certain Fury, 29

Campbell, Nick: Dirty Tricks, 251

Campbell, William: Dementia 13, 673

Campos, Rafael: Astro-Zombies, 646; Where the Buffalo Roam, 381

Camp, Colleen: Cloud Dancer, 32; Rosebud Beach Hotel, The, 343

Camp, Hamilton: Rosebud Beach Hotel, The, 343

Candy, John: Armed and Dangerous, 220; Blues Brothers, The, 231; Brewster's Millions (1985), 235; It Came from Hollywood, 287; Last Polka, The, 296; Silent Partner, The, 743; Splash, 357; (Sesame Street Presents) Follow That Bird, 204

Canning, James: Boys in Company C, The, 23

Cannon, Dyan: Anderson Tapes, The, 8; Author! Author!, 222; Bob & Carol & Ted & Alice, 231; Coast to Coast, 245; Deathtrap, 448; Heaven Can Wait, 278; Honeysuckle Rose, 788; Lady of the House, 512; Last of Sheila, The, 87; Revenge of the Pink Panther, The, 340; Shamus, 132

Cannon, J. D.: Cool Hand Luke, 35; Death Wish II, 40

Cannon, Katherine: High Noon, Part Two, 903; Will, G. Gordon Liddy, 635

Canovas, Anne: Revenge of the Dead, 736

Cantinflas: Around the World in 80 Days, 220

Cantor, Eddie: Whoopee, 812

Canutt, Yakima: Blue Steel, 885; Dawn Rider, 892; Lawless Frontier, 908; Lawless Range, 908; Lucky Texan, 910; Man from Utah, The, 912; Sagebrush Trail, 929; Song of Texas, 933; Star Packer, The, 935; West of the Divide, 944; Winds of the Wasteland, 945

Capri, Ahna: Brotherhood of Satan, 658; Enter the Dragon, 49

Capshaw, Kate: Best Defense, 227; Indiana Jones and the Temple of Doom, 843; Little Sex, A, 300; SpaceCamp, 864; Windy City, 635

Capucine: Red Sun, 924; What's New Pussycat?, 379

Cara, Irene: Certain Fury, 29; City Heat, 243; Killing 'Em Softly, 506; Sparkle, 805

Cardella, Richard: Crater Lake Monster, The, 665

Cardinale, Claudia: Circus World, 889; Conversation Piece, 438; Escape to Athena, 50

Cardwell, James: Robin Hood of Texas, 927

Carell, Lianella: Bicycle Thief, The, 410

Carette, Julien: La Bete Humaine, 510; La Marseillaise, 511

Carey Jr., Harry: Billy The Kid Vs. Dracula, 651; Crossroads, 775; Red River, 924; Rio Grande, 927; Searchers, The, 930; She Wore a Yellow Ribbon, 930; Wild Times, 945

Carey Sr., Harry: Angel and the Badman, 879; Red River, 924; So Dear to My Heart, 206; Spoilers, The, 934

Carey, MacDonald: End of the World, 834

Carey, Michele: Scandalous John, 203; In the Shadow of Kilimanjaro, 704

Carey, Ron: High Anxiety, 280; Silent Movie, 351

Carlin, George: Carlin at Carnegie, 238

Carlisle, Anne: Liquid Sky, 849

Carlisle, Mary: Dead Men Walk, 670; Palooka, 556

Carlson, Karen: Matilda, 308; Octagon, The, 109

Carlson, Moose: Can I Do It 'Til I Need Glasses?, 237

Carlson, Richard: Creature from the Black Lagoon, 665; Hold That Ghost, 281; It Came from Outer Space, 845; Last Command, The, 907

Carlson, Veronica: Horror of Frankenstein, 699

Carlucci, Milly: Adventures of Hercules, The, 815

Carmel, Roger C.: Hardly Working, 276

Carmen, Dawn: Marie, 529

Carmen, Julie: Can You Hear The Laughter? The Story of Freddie Prinze, 425; Last Plane Out, 87

Carmichael, Hoagy: Johnny Angel, 79

Carmichael, Ian: I'm All Right Jack, 285

Carmine, Michael: Band of the Hand, 12

Carnera, Primo: Hercules Unchained, 841

Carney, Art: Bitter Harvest, 413; Blue Yonder, The, 173; Defiance, 41; Guide For The Married Man, A, 273; House Calls, 283; Late Show, The, 87; Movie Movie, 315; Muppets Take Manhattan, The, 194; Naked Face, The, 720; St. Helens, 587

Carnovsky, Morris: Cornered, 35

Carol, Sue: Check and Double Check, 242

Caron, Leslie: American in Paris, An, 769; Dangerous Moves, 443; QB VII, 571

Caro, Leticia: Revolt of Job, The, 579

Carpenter, Thelma: Wiz, The, 812

Carradine, Bruce: Americana, 396

Carradine, David: Americana, 396; Bound For Glory, 418; Boxcar Bertha, 23; Cannonball, 27; Circle of Iron, 31; Cloud Dancer, 32; Death Race 2000, 829; DeathSport, 829; High Noon, Part Two, 903; Kung Fu, 85; Lone Wolf McQuade, 92; Long Riders, The, 910; Mean Streets, 532; Mr. Horn, 915; P.O.W.: The Escape, 112; Q, 732; Serpent's Egg, The, 590; Long Riders, The, 910

Carradine, John: Best of Sex and Violence, 650; Astro-Zombies, 646; Bees, The, 649; Big Foot, 651; Billy The Kid Vs. Dracula, 651; Blood and Sand, 414; Blood of Dracula's Castle, 653; Bloodsuckers, The, 654; Bluebeard, 654; Boogeyman, The, 655; Boxcar Bertha, 23; Captain Kidd, 27; Daniel Boone, 891; Death at Love House, 672; Everything You Always Wanted to Know about Sex But Were Afraid to Ask, 257; Hillbillys in a Haunted House, 280; Hound of the Baskervilles, The (Original), 75; House of Seven Corpses, The, 700; House of the Long Shadows, 700; Howling, The, 701; Ice Pirates, 842; Jesse James, 905; Johnny Guitar, 906; Kentuckian, The, 906; Last Tycoon, The, 515; Mary of Scotland, 530; Monster Club, The, 717; Mr. Moto's Last Warning, 101; Nesting, The, 721; Patsy, The, 328; Return of Frank James, The, 925; Revenge of the Zombies, 736; Secret of Nimh, The, 203; Sentinel, The, 742; Shock Waves (Death Corps), 742; Shootist, The, 931; Stagecoach, 934; Winterset, 636

Carradine, Keith: Chiefs, 432; Choose Me,

433; Kung Fu, *85;* Long Riders, The *910;* Maria's Lovers, *528;* McCabe and Mrs. Miller, *914;* Nashville, *542;* Old Boyfriends, *550;* Pretty Baby, *566;* Rumor of War, A, *125;* Southern Comfort, *138;* Welcome to L.A., *631*

Carradine, Robert: Aladdin and His Wonderful Lamp, *170;* Big Red One, The, *15;* Blackout, *19;* Cannonball, *27;* Coming Home, *437;* Heartaches, *484;* Joyride, *504;* Long Riders, The, *910;* Massacre at Central High, *716;* Mean Streets, *532;* Orca, *736;* Revenge of the Nerds, *340;* Wavelength, *876*

Carrera, Barbara: Condorman, *178;* Island of Dr. Moreau, The, *845;* I, the Jury, *77;* Lone Wolf McQuade, *92;* Masada, *530;* Never Say Never Again, *106;* When Time Ran Out!, *764;* Wild Geese II, *163*

Carrey, Jim: Once Bitten, *323*

Carrico, Monica: Running Hot, *586*

Carrière, Mathieu: Bilitis, *411;* Woman in Flames, A, *638;* Aviator's Wife, The, *403;*

Carrillo, Elpedia: Salvador, *587;* Border, The, *22*

Carrillo, Leo: American Empire, *879;* History Is Made at Night, *488;* Manhattan Merry-Go-Round, *913*

Carroll, Beeson: Spacehunter: Adventures in the Forbidden Zone, *864*

Carroll, Diahann: Paris Blues, *558*

Carroll, Janet: Risky Business, *341*

Carroll, Leo G.: Spellbound, *746;* We're No Angels, *379*

Carroll, Madeleine: Secret Agent, The, *131*

Carroll, Matthew: Dance With a Stranger, *443*

Carroll, Susan: Stanley, *747*

Carr, Marian: Indestructible Man, *705*

Carr, Paul: Severed Arm, The, *742*

Carson, Hunter: Invaders from Mars (Remake), *844;* Paris, Texas, *558;* Rip Van Winkle, *859*

Carson, Jack: Arsenic and Old Lace, *220;* Carefree, *774;* Cat on a Hot Tin Roof (Original), *428;* Dangerous When Wet, *776;* Mildred Pierce, *534;* Mr. and Mrs. Smith, *310;* Stand-In, *358;* Star Is Born, A (Remake), *601*

Carson, John David: Captain Kronos: Vampire Hunter, *659;* Creature from Black Lake, *665;* Savage Is Loose, The, *588*

Carson, Shawn: Something Wicked This Way Comes, *863*

Carter, Helena Bonham: Room With a View, A (1987 Release), *584*

Carter, Helena: Invaders From Mars (Original), *844*

Carter, Jack: Alligator, *644;* Amazing Dobermans, *171;* Happy Hooker Goes to Washington, The, *275;* Hustle, The, *76;* Octagon, The, *109*

Carter, Jim: Haunted Honeymoon, *277*

Carter, Lynda: Bobbie Jo and the Outlaw, *21;* Rita Hayworth: The Love Goddess, *581*

Carter, Michael: Adventures of Sherlock Holmes: A Scandal in Bohemia, *2*

Carter, Thomas: Whose Life Is It Anyway?, *633*

Carter, T. K.: Runaway Train, *125*

Cartledge, Miranda: Save The Lady, *203*

Cartwright, Angela: High School, USA, *280*

Cartwright, Veronica: Alien, *815;* Inserts, *496;* Invasion of the Body Snatchers (Remake), *845;* Right Stuff, The, *580*

Caruso, David: Blue City, *20*

Carver, Brent: Cross Country, *440*

Casados, Elroy Phil: Legend of Walks Far Woman, The, *909*

Casey, Bernie: Boxcar Bertha, *23;* Cleopatra Jones, *31;* Never Say Never Again, *106;* Revenge of the Nerds, *340;* Sharky's Machine, *133;* Spies Like Us, *356*

Cash, Rosalind: Omega Man, The, *854;* Wrong Is Right, *384*

Cason, Bob: Big Sombrero, The, *883*

Cassady, Carolyn: Kerouac, *506*

Cassavetes, John: Brass Target, *24;* Dirty Dozen, The, *43;* Incubus, The, *705;* Love Streams, *524;* Marvin and Tige, *530;* Mikey and Nicky, *309;* Rosemary's Baby, *737;* Whose Life Is It, Anyway?, *633*

Cassell, Alan: Squizzy Taylor, *139*

Cassel, Jean-Pierre: Discreet Charm Of The Bourgeoisie, The, *251*

Cassel, Sandra: Last House on the Left, *711*

Cassel, Seymore: California Dreaming, *424;* Love Streams, *524*

Casser, Wolfgang: Inheritors, The, *495*

Cassidy, Edward: Man From Music Mountain, *912;* Ridin' on a Rainbow, *926*

Cassidy, Joanna: Club Paradise, *245*

Cassinelli, Claudio: Screamers, *741*

Cassisi, John: Bugsy Malone, *175*

Cass, Peggy: Paddy, *326*

Castellano, Richard: Night of the Juggler, *107*

Castello, Willy: Confessions of a Vice Baron, *438;* Melody Trail, *915*

Castelnuovo, Nino: Escapade In Florence, *180*

Castle, John: Adventures of Sherlock Holmes: The Solitary Cyclist, *5;* Antony and Cleopatra, *401;* Lion In Winter, The, *519*

Cates, Phoebe: Gremlins, Paradise, *113;* Private School, *335*

Catlett, Walter: Rain, *574*

Catrall, Kim: Big Trouble in Little China, *17;* City Limits, *823;* Police Academy, *332;* Porky's, *333*

Cauchy, Daniel: Bob le Flambeur, *21*

Caulfield, Maxwell: Grease 2, *785*

Caulfield, Joan: Daring Dobermans, The, *38;* Dear Wife, *249;* Hatfields and the McCoys, The, *901*

Causey, Mathew: Party Animal, 328

Cavanagh, Paul: Woman In Green, The, 165

Cavanaugh, Michael: Forced Vengeance, 59

Cavender, Glen: Keystone Comedies: Vol. 4, 392; General, The, 266

Cave, Des: Paddy, 326

Cazale, John: Conversation, The, 438; Deer Hunter, The, 448; Dog Day Afternoon, 452; Godfather, The, 473; Godfather Epic, The, 474; Godfather, The, Part II, 474

Cazenove, Christopher: Children Of The Full Moon, 662; Eye of the Needle, 51; Heat and Dust, 485

Ceccaldi, Daniel: Holiday Hotel, 281

Celi, Adolfo: Hitler, the Last Ten Days, 488; Murders In The Rue Morgue, 720

Cellier, Caroline: Petit Con, 329

Cerdan Jr., Marcel: Edith and Marcel, 778

Cervi, Gino: Indiscretion of an American Wife, 495

Cesak, Brian: Fandango, 258

Chadbon, Tom: Dance With a Stranger, 443

Chadwick, June: Forbidden World, 686

Chairi, Walter: Bellissima, 227

Chakiris, George: West Side Story, 812

Chamarat, Georges: Fernandel The Dressmaker, 259

Chamberlain, Richard: Count of Monte Cristo, The (Remake), 36; Four Musketeers, The, 60; King Solomon's Mines (1985), 84; Last Wave, The, 711; Man in the Iron Mask, The, 95; Murder by Phone, 719; Shogun (Full-Length Version), 134; Shogun (Short Version), 134

Chamberlain, Wilt: Conan the Destroyer, 826

Chambers, Marilyn: Angel of H.E.A.T., 8; Rabid, 732

Chambers, Michael: Breakin', 771; Breakin' 2 Electric Boogaloo, 772

Champagne, Simone: Alligator Shoes, 394

Champion: Man of the Frontier, (Red River Valley), 912; Melody Ranch, 914; Old Corral, The, 919

Champion, Gower: Show Boat, 802

Champion, Marge: Show Boat, 802

Chandler, Edward: Desert Trail, 893

Chandler, Helen: Christopher Strong, 433; Dracula (Original), 678

Chandler, Jeff: Away All Boats, 11

Chandler, Lane: Saga of Death Valley, 929; Sagebrush Trail, 929; Winds of the Wasteland, 945

Chaney Jr., Lon: Abbott and Costello Meet Frankenstein, 214; Bird of Paradise, 17; Bloodsuckers, The, 654; Cyclops, The, 668; Defiant Ones, The, 448; Dracula vs. Frankenstein, 679; Hillbillys in a Haunted House, 280; Old Corral, The, 919; One Million B.C., 855

Chaney, Lon: High Noon, 903; Indestructi-ble Man, 705; My Favorite Brunette, 316

Chaney, Sr., Lon: Hunchback of Notre Dame, The (original), 702; Phantom of the Opera, 727

Chan, Jackie: Big Brawl, The, 15; Protector, The, 116

Channing, Stockard: Big Bus, The, 229; Fish That Saved Pittsburgh, The, 261; Grease, 784; Heartburn, 277; Without a Trace, 637

Chapin, Michael: Under California Stars, 942

Chapin, Miles: Bless the Beasts and the Children, 414; French Postcards, 263; Funhouse, The, 691; Get Crazy, 266

Chapin, Tom: Lord of the Flies, 521

Chaplin, Charlie: Charlie Chaplin, The Early Years, Vol.1, 241; Charlie Chaplin—The Early Years, Vol.2, 241; Charlie Chaplin—The Early Years, Vol.3, 241; Charlie Chaplin—The Early Years, Vol.4, 241; City Lights, 243; Gold Rush, The, 272; King in New York, A, 292; Limelight, 299; Modern Times, 312; Monsieur Verdoux, 313

Chaplin, Geraldine: Dr. Zhivago, 452; Roseland, 584; Wedding, A, 378; Welcome to L.A., 631

Chaplin, Josephine: Escape to the Sun, 459; Jack the Ripper, 707

Chaplin, Michael: King in New York, A, 292

Chaplin, Sydney: Limelight, 299

Chapman, Graham: And Now for Something Completely Different, 218; Life of Brian, 299; Monty Python and the Holy Grail, 313; Monty Python Live at the Hollywood Bowl, 313; Monty Python's the Meaning of Life, 313; Secret Policeman's Private Parts, The, 347; Secret Policemen's Other Ball, The, 347; Yellowbeard, 385

Chapman, Helen: Borrowed Trouble, 885

Chapman, Judith: Scalpel, 740

Chapman, Lonny: Baby Doll, 403; Bad News Bears Go to Japan, The, 223; Where the Red Fern Grows, 212; King, 507; Running Scared (1980), 126

Chapman, Marguerite: Green Promise, The, 479; Spy Smasher, 139

Chapman, Paul: Adventures of Sherlock Holmes: The Crooked Man, 3

Charbit, Corynne: Le Chevre (The Goat), 298

Charbonneau, Patricia: Desert Hearts, 449

Chardiet, Jon: Beat Street, 770

Charisse, Cyd: Band Wagon, The, 769; Brigadoon, 772; It's Always Fair Weather, 789; Silk Stockings, 802; Singin' in the Rain, 802; Ziegfeld Follies, 814

Charleson, Ian: Chariots of Fire, 431

Charles, Fransico: Sugar Cane Alley, 607

Charles, Ray: That Was Rock, 808

Charlton, Bobby: Harder They Come, The, 786

Charney, Jordan: Frances, 469

Charny, Suzanne: Steagle, The, *359*

Charpin: Baker's Wife, The, *224*; Marius, *529*

Charters, Spencer: Three Faces West, *939*

Chartoff, Melanie: Doin' Time, *253*

Chase, Barrie: Silk Stockings, *802*

Chase, Charley: Keystone Comedies: Vo. 5, *292*; Sons of the Desert, *356*

Chase, Chevy: Caddyshack, *236*; Deal of the Century, *249*; European Vacation, *256*; Fletch, *57*; Foul Play, *262*; Groove Tube, The, *273*; Modern Problems, *311*; Oh, Heavenly Dog!, *196*; Seems Like Old Times, *349*; Spies Like Us, *356*; Tunnelvision, *373*; Under the Rainbow, *374*; Vacation, *376*; (Sesame Street Presents) Follow That Bird, *204*

Chase, Stephan: Macbeth, *525*

Chatterton, Ruth: Citizen Kane, *434*; Dodsworth, *452*

Chauvin, Lilyan: Silent Night, Deadly Night, *743*

Chaves, Richard: Cease Fire, *429*

Chaykin, Maury: Defcon 4, *829*

Cheirel, Micheline: Carnival in Flanders, *426*; Cornered, *35*

Chekhov, Michael: Spellbound, *746*

Chen, Moira: Endgame, *834*

Chen, Tina: Alice's Restaurant, *393*

Chereau, Patrice: Danton, *444*

Cherkassov, Nikolai: Alexander Nevsky, *392*; Ivan the Terrible—Part I & Part II, *499*

Cherrill, Virginia: City Lights, *243*

Cher: Come Back to the Five and Dime, Jimmy Dean, Jimmy Dean, *436*; Mask, *530*; Silkwood, *593*

Chesebro, George: Man of the Frontier, (Red River Valley), *912*; Mystery Mountain, *916*; Trail of Robin Hood, *939*; Winning of the West, *946*

Chevalier, Maurice: Breath of Scandal, A, *233*; Fanny, *463*; Gigi, *782*; In Search of the Castaways, *185*

Chew, Kim: Dim Sum: A Little Bit Of Heart, *451*

Chew, Laureen: Dim Sum: A Little Bit Of Heart, *451*

Chiaki, Minoru: Hidden Fortress, The, *71*; Throne of Blood, *617*

Chiao, Roy: Protector, The, *116*

Chiba, Sonny: Bushido Blade, *26*; Legend of the Eight Samurai, *89*

Chiles, Linden: Forbidden World, *686*

Chiles, Lois: Moonraker, *102*; Raw Courage, *119*; Sweet Liberty, *362*; Way We Were, The, *631*

Chilvers, Simon: Test of Love, A, *613*

Chimp, Ramona the: Boys from Brooklyn, The, *656*

Chinh, Kieu: Operation C.I.A., *110*

Chin, Tsai: Against All Odds (Kiss and Kill, Blood of Fu Manchu), *643*

Choate, Tim: Defcon 4, *829*

Chong, Cheech and: Cheech and Chong's Next Movie, *242*; Corsican Brothers, The, *247*; It Came from Hollywood, *287*; Nice Dreams, *318*; Still Smokin, *359*; Things Are Tough All Over, *366*; Up in Smoke, *375*; Yellowbeard, *385*

Chong, Rae Dawn: American Flyers, *396*; Beat Street, *770*; City Limits, *823*; Color Purple, The, *436*; Commando, *33*; Fear City, *52*; Quest for Fire, *858*

Chong, Tommy: After Hours, *215*

Chopel, Fadril: L'Addition, *510*

Christensen, Benjamin: Witchcraft Through the Ages (Haxan), *637*

Christian, Leigh: Beyond Atlantis, *14*

Christian, Robert: Bustin' Loose, *236*

Christie, Audrey: Splendor in the Grass, *599*

Christie, Julie: Billy Liar, *412*; Darling, *445*; Demon Seed, *830*; Don't Look Now, *677*; Dr. Zhivago, *452*; Fahrenheit 451, *836*; Heat and Dust, *485*; Heaven Can Wait, *278*; McCabe and Mrs. Miller, *914*; Power, *566*; Return of the Soldier, The, *579*; Separate Tables, *590*; Shampoo, *591*

Christine, Virginia: Billy The Kid Vs. Dracula, *651*; Guess Who's Coming to Dinner, *480*

Christmas, Eric: Philadelphia Experiment, The, *856*

Christopher, Dennis: Breaking Away, *233*; California Dreaming, *424*; Don't Cry, It's Only Thunder, *453*; Fade to Black, *682*; Jack and the Beanstalk, *186*; Jake Speed, *78*

Christopher, Robert: Frankenstein Island, *688*

Christopher, Robin: Equinox (The Beast), *680*

Christy, Dorothy: Radio Ranch (Men With Steel Faces, Phantom Empire), *923*

Chuckster, Simon: Sweet Sweetback's Baadasssss Song, *144*

Chuney, Barbara: Autobiography of Miss Jane Pittman, The, *402*

Chung, Ida F. O.: Dim Sum: A Little Bit Of Heart, *451*

Churchill, Marguerite: Big Trail, The, *883*

Churchill, Sarah: Royal Wedding, *800*

Ciannelli, Eduardo: Dillinger, *42*; Gunga Din, *67*; Kitty Foyle, *509*; Lost Moment, The, *522*; Monster From Green Hell, *717*; They Got Me Covered, *366*

Cilento, Diane: Hitler, the Last Ten Days, *488*; Hombre, *904*; Wicker Man, The, *765*; Winterset, *636*

Cioffi, Charles: Don is Dead, The, *44*; Lucky Luciano, *93*; Remo Williams: The Adventure Begins, *120*; Shaft, *132*; Thief Who Came to Dinner, The, *366*

Citera, Tom: Up the Academy, *375*

Citty, Jim: Town That Dreaded Sundown, The, *759*

Claire, Cyrielle: Code Name: Emerald, *33*

Clapp, Gordon: Return of the Secaucus 7, *339*

Clapton, Eric: Last Waltz, The, *791;* Secret Policemen's Other Ball, The, *347;* Water, *377*

Clare, Mary: Young and Innocent, *166*

Clarke, Catlin: Dragonslayer, *831*

Clarke, Mae: Flying Tigers, The, *58;* Frankenstein (Original), *687;* Frankenstein (Restored Version), *688;* Great Guy, *478;* King of the Rocketmen, *846;* Public Enemy, The, *116*

Clarke, Matt: Return to Oz, *201*

Clarke, Robert: Frankenstein Island, *688;* Hideous Sun Demon, The, *697*

Clarke, Warren: Firefox, *54;* Great Riviera Bank Robbery, The, *65*

Clarkson, Lana: Barbarian Queen, *819;* Deathstalker, *829*

Clarkson, Robert: Save The Lady, *203*

Clark, Brett: Alien Warrior, *816*

Clark, Candy: American Graffiti, *218;* Big Sleep, The, *16;* Blue Thunder, *21;* Cat's Eye, *660;* Man Who Fell to Earth, The, *851;* Q, *732;* Rodeo Girl, *583;* Tale of the Frog Prince, *207*

Clark, Cliff: Borrowed Trouble, *885;* False Paradise, *896*

Clark, Fred: Auntie Mame, *222;* Sunset Blvd., *609*

Clark, Hope: Piece of the Action, A, *329*

Clark, Judy: Wizard of Gore, The, *766*

Clark, Mano: One Million B.C., *855*

Clark, Marlene: Beast Must Die, The, *649;* Son of Blob (Beware! the Blob), *745*

Clark, Matt: Country, *439;* Driver, The, *45;* Eye for an Eye, *51;* Return to Oz, *201;* Ruckus, *124;* White Lightning, *162*

Clark, Oliver: Star Is Born, A (Remake), *601*

Clark, Petula: Finian's Rainbow, *779*

Clark, Richard: Protector, The, *116*

Clark, Roy: Matilda, *308*

Clark, Steve: Under California Stars, *942*

Clark, Susan: Apple Dumpling Gang, The, *171;* Coogan's Bluff, *34;* Murder By Decree, *103;* Night Moves, *106;* North Avenue Irregulars, The, *196;* Promises in the Dark, *569;* Skin Game, *933*

Clayburgh, Jill: First Monday in October, *465;* Hanna K., *481;* Hustling, *490;* It's My Turn, *499;* I'm Dancing As Fast As I Can, *492;* Portnoy's Complaint, *565;* Semi-Tough, *349;* Silver Streak, *352;* Starting Over, *358;* Terminal Man, The, *752;* Thief Who Came to Dinner, The, *366;* Unmarried Woman, An, *626*

Clayton, John: High Rolling, *72*

Clayworth, June: Dick Tracy Meets Gruesome, *42*

Clay, Jennifer: Suburbia, *606*

Clay, Nicholas: Adventures of Sherlock Holmes: The Resident Patient, *5;* Evil Under the Sun, *50;* Excalibur, *835;* Lady Chatterley's Lover, *512;* Love Spell, *93*

Cleary, Leo: Bells of Coronado, *881*

Cleese, John: And Now for Something Completely Different, *218;* Life of Brian, *299;* Monty Python and the Holy Grail, *313;* Monty Python Live at the Hollywood Bowl, *313;* Monty Python's the Meaning of Life, *313;* Privates on Parade, *336;* Romance With A Double Bass, *343;* Secret Policeman's Private Parts, The, *347;* Secret Policemen's Other Ball, The, *347;* Silverado, *932;* Time Bandits, *872;* Yellowbeard, *385*

Clemens, Paul: Beast Within, The, *649;* Promises in the Dark, *569*

Clementi, Pierre: Conformist, The, *438*

Clements, John: Four Feathers, The, *60*

Clement, Aurore: Invitation au Voyage, *497;* Paris, Texas, *558*

Clennon, David: Hanna K., *481;* Missing, *535;* Sweet Dreams, *806*

Clery, Corinne: Yor: The Hunter from the Future, *877*

Cleveland, George: Angel on My Shoulder, *399;* Blue Steel, *885;* Man from Utah, The, *912;* Spoilers, The, *934;* Star Packer, The, *935;* Trigger, Jr., *940;* Yellow Rose of Texas, *946*

Cleveland, Rev. James: Gospel, *784*

Clevers, Lynne: Carnival in Flanders, *426*

Clifford, Colleen: Where the Green Ants Dream, *632*

Clifford, Kim: Save The Lady, *203*

Cliff, Jimmy: Club Paradise, *245;* Harder They Come, The, *786*

Clifton, Dorinda: Marauders, *913*

Clift, Montgomery: Heiress, The, *485;* I Confess, *703;* Indiscretion of an American Wife, *495;* Judgment at Nuremberg, *504;* Misfits, The, *535;* Place in the Sun, A, *563;* Raintree County, *574;* Red River, *924;* Suddenly, Last Summer, *607*

Clinger, Debra: Midnight Madness, *309*

Clinton, Mildred: Alice, Sweet Alice (Communion and Holy Terror), *643*

Cliver, Al: Endgame, *834*

Clive, Colin: Bride of Frankenstein, *657;* Christopher Strong, *433;* Frankenstein (Original), *687;* Frankenstein (Restored Version), *688;* History Is Made at Night, *488*

Clive, E. E.: Hound of the Baskervilles, The (Original), *75*

Clooney, Rosemary: Holiday Inn, *787*

Close, Glenn: Big Chill, The, *411;* Jagged Edge, *500;* Maxie, *308;* Natural, The, *542;* Stone Boy, The, *603;* World According to Garp, The, *639*

Clough, John Scott: Fast Forward, *779*

Clouzot, Vera: Diabolique, *675;* Wages of Fear, The, *763*

Clute, Sidney: Cry of Battle, *37*

Clutsei, George: Legend of Walks Far Woman, The, *909*

Clyde (the ape): Every Which Way but Loose, *257*

Clyde, Andy: Borrowed Trouble, *885*; Dangerous Venture, *891*; Dead Don't Dream, The, *892*; Devil's Playground, *893*; False Colors, *895*; False Paradise, *896*; Hoppy's Holiday, *904*; Little Minister, The, *519*; Marauders, *913*; Riders of the Deadline, *926*; Silent Conflict, *931*; Sinister Journey, *932*; Strange Gamble, *935*; Unexpected Guest, *942*

Cobanoglu, Necmettin: Yol, *639*

Cobb, Edmund: Mystery Mountain, *916*; Robin Hood of Texas, *927*

Cobb, Kacey: Crater Lake Monster, The, *665*

Cobb, Lee J.: 12 Angry Men, *624*; Brothers Karamazov, The, *420*; Buckskin Frontier, *886*; Coogan's Bluff, *34*; Exodus, *460*; Exorcist, The, *681*; Four Horsemen of the Apocalypse, *60*; Golden Boy, *475*; Left Hand of God, The, *88*; Liberation of L. B. Jones, The, *517*; Mackenna's Gold, *911*; Man Who Loved Cat Dancing, The, *912*; Miracle of the Bells, The, *534*; On the Waterfront, *551*; Trap, The, *759*

Cobb, Randall "Tex": Uncommon Valor, *156*

Cobo, Roberto: Los Olvidados, *522*

Coburn, Charles: Colonel Effingham's Raid, *246*; Devil and Miss Jones, The, *250*; Gentlemen Prefer Blondes, *266*; Idiot's Delight, *492*; In Name Only, *493*; King's Row, *508*; Knickerbocker Holiday, *791*; Lady Eve, The, *295*; Made for Each Other, *304*; Three Faces West, *939*

Coburn, James: Bite the Bullet, *884*; Charade, *29*; Cross of Iron, *37*; Dain Curse, The, *37*; Draw, *894*; Firepower, *55*; Goldengirl, *840*; Great Escape, The, *65*; Hard Times, *69*; High Risk, *72*; Internecine Project, The, *705*; Last of Sheila, The, *87*; Looker, *850*; Loving Couples, *33*; Magnificent Seven, The, *911*; Major Dundee, *911*; Massacre At Fort Holman (Reason to Live ... A Reason to Die, A), *914*; Muppet Movie, The, *193*; Pat Garrett and Billy the Kid, *922*; Pinocchio, *198*

Coby, Michael: Bitch, The, *412*

Coca, Imogene: 10 from Your Show of Shows, *364*

Cochran, Robert: I Stand Condemned, *492*; Sanders of the River, *127*

Cochran, Steve: Carnival Story, *426*; Copacabana, *247*; Kid from Brooklyn, The, *292*; White Heat, *161*

Coco, James: Man of La Mancha, *793*; Murder by Death, *315*; Only When I Laugh, *553*; Scavenger Hunt, *346*; Wholly Moses!, *381*; Wild Party, The, *634*

Cody, Kathleen: Charlie and The Angel, *176*

Coe, George: Flash of Green, A, *466*; Remo Williams: The Adventure Begins, *120*

Coffield, Peter: Times Square, *809*

Coffin, Tristram: Corpse Vanishes, The, *664*; Dawn on the Great Divide, *891*; King of the Rocketmen, *846*; Sioux City Sue, *933*; Spy Smasher, *139*

Coffman, Caris: Dreamchild, *831*

Coghlan Jr., Frank: Adventures of Captain Marvel, The, *1*

Coghlan, Junior: Hell's House, *71*

Cogley, Nick: Keystone Comedies: Vo. 5, *292*

Cohen, Jeffrey Jay: Fire With Fire, *464*

Cohen, Jeff: Goonies, The, *63*

Cohn, Mindy: Boy Who Could Fly, The, *419*

Colasanto, Nicholas: Raging Bull, *574*

Colbert, Claudette: I Cover the Waterfront, *76*; It Happened One Night, *287*; Texas Lady, *938*; Without Reservations, *382*

Colbert, Ray: RSVP, *343*

Colbourne, Maurice: Littlest Horse Thieves, The, *190*

Coleby, Robert: Now and Forever, *547*; Plumber, The, *729*

Coleman, Charles: Grand Canyon Trail, *899*

Coleman, Dabney: Bite the Bullet, *884*; Cloak and Dagger, *32*; How to Beat the High Co$t of Living, *284*; I Love My Wife, *285*; Man With One Red Shoe, The, *306*; Muppets Take Manhattan, The, *194*; Murrow, *539*; Nine to Five, *319*; Nothing Personal, *321*; Rolling Thunder, *123*; Tootsie, *369*; Wargames, *875*; Young Doctors in Love, *385*

Coleman, Gary: Jimmy the Kid, *186*; Kid from Left Field, The, *187*; Kid With the 200 I.Q., The, *188*; On the Right Track, *197*

Cole, Frederick: Tennessee Stallion, *147*

Cole, George: Belles of St. Trinian's, The, *227*; Gone in 60 Seconds, *63*

Cole, Olivia: Some Kind of Hero, *355*

Colga, Eileen: Quackser Fortune Has a Cousin in the Bronx, *571*

Colicos, John: Postman Always Rings Twice, The (Remake), *566*; Raid on Rommel, *118*

Colin Jr., David: Beyond the Door, *650*; Beyond the Door 2, *651*

Collack, Cyril: Operation C.I.A., *110*

Collet, Christopher: Manhattan Project, The, *714*

Collier Jr., William: Street Scene, *605*

Collier, Constance: Damsel in Distress, A, *776*; Perils of Pauline, The, *329*

Collier, Patience: Adventures of Sherlock Holmes: The Copper Beeches, *3*

Collings, Robert: Night of the Demon, *722*

Collinson, Madeleine and Mary: Twins of Evil, *760*

Collins, Alan: Ark of the Sun God ... Temple of Hell, The, *9*; Yor: The Hunter from the Future, *877*

Collins, Gary: Hangar 18, *840*; Kid from Left

Field, The, 187

Collins, Joan: Bitch, The, 412; Dark Places, 669; Empire of the Ants, 833; Fear in The Night (Dynasty of Fear), 683; Hansel and Gretel, 183; Homework, 489; Oh, Alfie, 549; Stopover Tokyo, 141; Stud, The, 606; Sunburn, 143; Tales from the Crypt, 751

Collins, Lewis: Final Option, The, 54

Collins, Matt: World's Greatest Lover, The, 384

Collins, Phil: Secret Policeman's Private Parts, The, 347

Collins, Ray: Badman's Territory, 880; Citizen Kane, 434; Double Life, A, 453; Francis, the Talking Mule, 263; Heiress, The, 485

Collins, Roberta: Hardbodies, 275; School Spirit, 346

Collins, Spelman B.: So Dear to My Heart, 206

Collins, Stephen: Brewster's Millions (1985), 235; Chiefs, 432; Loving Couples, 33

Collins, Suzy: Splatter University, 747

Colman, Ronald: Arrowsmith, 401; Bulldog Drummond, 25; Champagne for Caesar, 240; Double Life, A, 453; Tale of Two Cities, 611

Colomby, Scott: Porky's, 333; Porky's Revenge, 333; Porky's, II 333

Colouris, George: Citizen Kane, 434

Coltrane, Rexx: Being, The, 650

Coltrane, Robbie: Mona Lisa, 537

Colvin, Jack: Incredible Hulk, The, 843

Combes, Norman: Kill or Be Killed, 83

Combs, Jeffrey: Re-animator, 733

Comer, Anjanette: Lepke, 89; Rabbit Run, 573

Commissar, Victor Laplace: Funny Dirty Little War (No Habra Mas Pensas ni Olvido), 264

Commodores, The: Thank God It's Friday, 806

Compson, Betty: Great Gabbo, The, 477; Invisible Ghost, 705

Conant, Oliver: Summer of '42, 608

Conaway, Jeff: Grease, 784

Conder, Candi: Color Me Blood Red, 663

Congdon, James: 4D Man, 838

Conklin, Chester: Knickerbocker Holiday, 791

Conklin, Heinie: Riders of Destiny, 926

Conlin, Jimmy: Sin of Harold Diddlebock (aka Mad Wednesday), 352

Connart, Jean-Paul: La Balance, 85

Connelly, Billy: Water, 377

Connelly, Christopher: 1990: The Bronx Warriors, 854; Hawmps!, 277; Liar's Moon, 517

Connelly, Jennifer: Creepers, 665; Labyrinth, 847; Seven Minutes In Heaven, 350

Connelly, Marc: Spirit of St. Louis, The, 599

Connell, Edward: Equinox (The Beast), 680

Connell, Jane: Mame, 793

Connery, Sean: Anderson Tapes, The, 8; Another Time, Another Place, 400; Bridge Too Far, A, 25; Cuba, 37; Darby O'Gill and the Little People, 179; Diamonds Are Forever, 42; Dr. No, 44; Fine Madness, A (1987 release), 260; Five Days One Summer, 466; From Russia with Love, 61; Goldfinger, 63; Great Train Robbery, The, 66; Highlander, 841; Longest Day, The, 92; Man Who Would Be King, The, 96; Marnie, 715; Meteor, 852; Molly Maguires, The, 537; Murder on the Orient Express, 104; Never Say Never Again, 106; Outland, 855; Robin and Marian, 123; Shalako, 930; Sword of the Valiant, 207; Thunderball, 151; Time Bandits, 872; Wind and the Lion, The, 164; Wrong Is Right, 384; You Only Live Twice, 166; Zardoz, 877

Connolly, Billy: Blue Money, 231

Connolly, Walter: Good Earth, The, 475; Nothing Sacred, 321

Connor, Bart: Rad, 117

Connor, Kenneth: Carry on Nurse, 239

Connors, Chuck: 99 and 44/100 Percent Dead, 108; Old Yeller, 196; Pancho Villa, 922; Soylent Green, 863; Tourist Trap, 759

Connors, Michael: Harlow, 482; Too Scared to Scream, 757

Conn, Didi: Grease 2, 785; Grease, 784; You Light Up My Life, 640

Conrad, Michael: Longest Yard, The, 92

Conrad, Robert: Commies Are Coming, the Commies Are Coming, 246; Crossfire, 890; Murph the Surf, 104; Will, G. Gordon Liddy, 635; Wrong Is Right, 384

Conrad, William: Body and Soul (Original), 416; Moonshine County Express, 103

Conried, Hans: Davy Crockett (King of the Wild Frontier), 179; Falcon Takes Over, The, 52; Senator Was Indiscreet, The, 349

Considine, John: Late Show, The, 87; Rita Hayworth: The Love Goddess, 581; Wedding, A, 378

Considine, Tim: Daring Dobermans, The, 38; Patton, 559

Constantine, Michael: Beyond Fear, 409; Family, The, 52; North Avenue Irregulars, The, 196; Reivers, The, 338

Conte, Richard: 13 Rue Madeleine, 149; Big Combo, The, 15; Circus World, 889; Godfather, The, 473; Purple Heart, The, 570; They Came to Cordura, 615

Conti, Tom: American Dreamer, 217; Duellists, The, 46; Merry Christmas, Mr. Lawrence, 533; Princess and the Pea, The, 199; Reuben, Reuben, 339

Converse, Frank: Bushido Blade, 26; Cruise into Terror, 667; Pilot, The, 563; Spring Fever, 357

Convy, Bert: Hero at Large, 279; Semi-Tough, 349

Conway, Kevin: Flashpoint, 57

Conway, Morgan: Dick Tracy, 42

Conway, Tim: Apple Dumpling Gang The,

171; Apple Dumpling Gang Rides Again, The, *171;* Private Eyes, The, *335;* Prizefighter, The, *200;* Rip Van Winkle, *859;* Shaggy D.A., The, *204;* They Went That-A-Way and That-A-Way, *208;* World's Greatest Athlete, The, *213*

Conway, Tom: Atomic Submarine, The, *818;* Cat People (Original), *660;* I Walked with a Zombie, *704*

Coogan, Jackie: Prey, The, *730*

Cook Jr., Elisha: Big Sleep, The (Original), *16;* Dark Waters, *445;* Dillinger, *42;* Drum Beat, *894;* Hammett, *68;* House on Haunted Hill, *700;* Lonely Man, The, *909;* Maltese Falcon, The, *95;* My Favorite Brunette, *316;* One-Eyed Jacks, *920;* Papa's Delicate Condition, *557;* Rosemary's Baby, *737;* Salem's Lot, *739;* Shane, *930;* St. Ives, *126;* Stranger on the Third Floor, *141;* Tom Horn, *939*

Cooke, Jennifer: Friday the 13th Part VI: Jason Lives, *691*

Cook, Barbara: Killing 'Em Softly, *506*

Cook, Carole: Grandview, U.S.A, *477;* Summer Lovers, *607*

Cook, Peter: Bedazzled, *225;* Secret Policeman's Private Parts, The, *347;* Secret Policemen's Other Ball, The, *347;* Supergirl, *868;* Wrong Box, The, *384;* Yellowbeard, *385;* Yellowbeard, *385*

Coolidge, Rita: Pat Garrett and Billy the Kid, *922*

Cooney, Kevin: Trip to Bountiful, The, *622*

Cooper, Alice: Monster Dog, *717*

Cooper, Garry: Quadrophenia, *799;* Along Came Jones, *879;* Ball of Fire, *224;* Farewell to Arms, A, *463;* Fighting Caravans, *896;* Fountainhead, The, *468;* Good Sam, *271;* High Noon, *903;* Lives of a Bengal Lancer, The, *91;* Meet John Doe, *532;* Pride of the Yankees, The, *568;* Sergeant York, *131;* They Came to Cordura, *615;* Vera Cruz, *943;* Westerner, The, *944;* Wings, *164*

Cooper, Gladys: Happiest Millionaire, The, *184;* Iron Duke, The, *498;* Pirate, The, *798*

Cooper, Jackie: Champ, The (Original), *429;* Return of Frank James, The, *925;* Superman, *869;* Superman II, *869;* Superman III, *868;* Treasure Island, *211*

Cooper, Jean: Commies Are Coming, the Commies Are Coming, The, *246*

Cooper, Jeff: Circle of Iron, *31*

Cooper, Melville: 13 Rue Madeleine, *149;* Dawn Patrol, The, *39;* Private Life of Don Juan, The, *568*

Cooper, Miriam: Birth of a Nation, The, *412;* Intolerance, *497*

Cooper, Terence: Heart of the Stag, *484*

Coote, Robert: Nurse Edith Cavell, *548*

Copley, Paul: Oh, Alfie, *549*

Coq, Bernard Le: Birgit Haas Must Be Killed, *18*

Corbett, Glenn: Chisum, *889;* Shenandoah, *930*

Corbett, Gretchen: Let's Scare Jessica to Death, *712;* Other Side of the Mountain, Part II, The, *554*

Corbin, Barry: Nothing In Common, *547;* Wargames, *875*

Corby, Ellen: I Remember Mama, *491*

Corcoran, Brian: Texas John Slaughter: Geronimo's Revenge, *937;* Texas John Slaughter: Wild Times, *938*

Corcoran, Kevin: Mooncussers, *193;* Savage Sam, *202;* Toby Tyler, *210*

Corday, Mara: Man without a Star, *913*

Cording, Harry: Dangerous Venture, *891;* Daniel Boone, *891;* Dressed to Kill, *45;* Marauders, *913;* Night Stage to Galveston, *917*

Cordy, Raymond: A Nous la Liberte, *219*

Cord, Alex: Fire!, *685;* Sidewinder 1, *135;* Stiletto, *140*

Corey, Isabel: Bob le Flambeur, *21*

Corey, Jeff: Boston Strangler, The, *656;* Boy Who Left Home to Find Out about the Shivers, The, *174;* Butch and Sundance: The Early Days, *887;* Getting Straight, *472;* Home of the Brave, *488;* Hoppy's Holiday, *904;* In Cold Blood, *493;* Little Big Man, *909*

Corey, Wendell: Astro-Zombies, *646;* Light In The Forest, The, *189;* Loving You, *793;* Rear Window, *734;* Sorry, Wrong Number, *745*

Corkin, Barry: Man Who Loved Women, The, *306*

Cork, Charles: Adventures of Sherlock Holmes: The Resident Patient, *5*

Corley, Al: Torchlight, *620*

Corman, Maddie: Seven Minutes In Heaven, *350*

Cornaly, Anne: Occurrence at Owl Creek Bridge, An, *548*

Cornelison, Michael: Stephen King's Night Shift Collection, *747*

Cornford, William: Adventures of the Wilderness Family, *170*

Cornu, Aurora: Claire's Knee, *243*

Cornwall, Anne: College, *246*

Cornwell, Judy: Santa Claus—The Movie, *202*

Correll, Charles: Check and Double Check, *242*

Corrigan, Lloyd: Song of Nevada, *933*

Corrigan, Ray "Crash": Night Riders, The, *918;* Pals of the Saddle, *921;* Santa Fe Stampede, *929;* Trail of Robin Hood, *939*

Corri, Adrienne: Clockwork Orange, A, *824*

Corseaut, Aneta: Blob, The, *652*

Cortese, Joseph: Evilspeak, *681*

Cortese, Valentina: Juliet of the Spirits, *291;* When Time Ran Out!, *764*

Cortez, Ricardo: Mr. Moto's Last Warning, *101*

Cort, Bud: Brewster McCloud, 234; Die Laughing, 251; Harold and Maude, 276; Hysterical, 284; Invaders from Mars (Remake), 844; Love Letters, 523; Maria's Lovers, 528; M*A*S*H, 307; Nightingale, The, 195; Rumpelstiltskin, 202; Why Shoot the Teacher?, 633

Cosby, Bill: Bill Cosby—Himself, 229; California Suite, 237; Devil and Max Devlin, The, 250; Let's Do It Again, 298; Piece of the Action, A, 329; Uptown Saturday Night, 376

Cosell, Howard: Bananas, 224; Fighting Back, 53

Cossart, Ernest: Letter of Introduction, 516; Love from a Stranger, 713

Costa, Cosie: Missing in Action 2: The Beginning, 100; Ten to Midnight, 147

Costellano, Richard: Godfather, The, 473

Costello, Dolores: Little Lord Fauntleroy, 519

Costello, Lou: 30 Foot Bride of Candy Rock, The, 366; Abbott and Costello in Hollywood, 214; Abbott and Costello Meet Captain Kidd, 214; Abbott and Costello Meet Dr. Jekyll and Mr. Hyde, 214; Abbott and Costello Meet Frankenstein, 214; Africa Screams, 215; Buck Privates, 235; Hold That Ghost, 281; World of Abbott and Costello, The, 383

Coster, Nicolas: Electric Horseman, The, 456

Costigan, George: Adventures of Sherlock Holmes: The Greek Interpreter, 4

Costner, Kevin: American Flyers, 396; Fandango, 258; Silverado, 932

Cotten, Joseph: Abominable Dr. Phibes, The, 643; Citizen Kane, 434; Farmer's Daughter, The, 258; From the Earth to the Moon, 838; Gaslight, 692; Hearse, The, 697; Heaven's Gate, 902; Hush...Hush, Sweet Charlotte, 703; Lady Frankenstein, 710; Magnificent Ambersons, The, 526; Oscar, The, 554; Screamers, 741; Soylent Green, 863; Third Man, The, 755; Tora! Tora! Tora!, 154; Torture Chamber Of Baron Blood, The, 758; Tramplers, The, 940; Twilight's Last Gleaming, 156; Under Capricorn, 626

Cotterill, Ralph: Chain Reaction, 29

Cotton, Carolina: Blue Canadian Rockies, 884

Cotton, Jose: Nomads, 724

Coulouris, George: Arabesque, 9; Master Race, The, 531; Ritz, The, 342; Song to Remember, A, 804

Coulter, Jack: Kerouac, 506; Kerouac, 506

Courtenay, Tom: Billy Liar, 412; Dresser, The, 454; I Heard the Owl Call My Name, 491; King Rat, 508; Night of the Generals, 107

Courtland, Jerome: Tonka, 211

Courtney, Alex: Enter the Ninja, 49

Courtney, Chuck: Billy The Kid Vs. Dracula, 651

Court, Hazel: Devil Girl from Mars, 674; Masque of the Red Death, The, 716; Premature Burial, The, 730; Raven, The, 733

Cousineau, Maggie: Return of the Secaucus 7, 339

Cowan, Jerome: Fuller Brush Girl, The, 264; Mr. Ace, 100; You Only Live Once, 640

Coward, Noel: In Which We Serve, 494

Cowau, Lester: High Sierra, 72

Cowper, Nicola: Dreamchild, 831

Cox, Alan: Young Sherlock Holmes, 167

Cox, Brian: Manhunter, 97

Cox, Richard: Cruising, 441; King of the Mountain, 508

Cox, Ronny: Beast Within, The, 649; Bound For Glory, 418; Deliverance, 41; Fallen Angel, 462; Harper Valley P.T.A., 276; Hollywood Vice Squad, 74; Mind Snatchers, The, 717; Onion Field, The, 553; Raw Courage, 119; Some Kind of Hero, 355; Taps, 611; Vision Quest, 628

Cox, Ruth: Attic, The, 648

Cox, Wally: Barefoot Executive, The, 172; Bedford Incident, The, 407

Coyne, Bill: Suburbia, 606

Coyote, Peter: Blue Yonder, The, 173; Cross Creek, 441; E.T.—The Extra-terrestrial, 832; Heartbreakers, 484; Jagged Edge, 500; Kerouac, 506; Legend of Billy Jean, The, 89; Timerider, 152

Crabbe, Buster: Tarzan the Fearless, 146

Crabtree, Buddy: Legend of Boggy Creek, 711

Crabtree, Jeff: Legend of Boggy Creek, 711

Cracknell, Ruth: Island Trader, 78

Craig, Carolyn: House on Haunted Hill, 700

Craig, James: Cyclops, The, 668; Kitty Foyle, 509; Naked in the Sun, 917

Craig, Michael: Escape 2000, 835; Mysterious Island, 853; Vault of Horror, 761

Craig, Wendy: Joseph Andrews, 290

Craig, Yvonne: It Happpened at the World's Fair, 789

Crain, Jeanne: Man without a Star, 913

Cramer, Grant: Hardbodies, 275

Crampton, Barbara: Re-animator, 733

Crane, Norman: Fiddler on the Roof, 779

Crane, Richard: Riders of the Deadline, 926; Winning of the West, 946

Crauchet, Paul: Beyond Fear, 409

Craven, Frank: Jack London, 499; Our Town, 555

Craven, Gemma: Wagner, 811

Craven, James: Strange Gamble, 935

Craven, Matt: Happy Birthday to Me, 696

Crawford, Broderick: All the King's Men, 394; Born Yesterday, 232; Dark Forces, 669; Little Romance, A, 300; Terror in the Wax Museum, 753

Crawford, Joan: Grand Hotel, 476; Johnny Guitar, 906; Mildred Pierce, 534; Night Gallery, 721; Possessed, 565; Rain, 574; Strait-Jacket, 748; What Ever Happened to Baby Jane?, 764; Women, The, 383

Crawford, Johnny: El Dorado, 895; Great Texas Dynamite Chase, The, 66; Village of the Giants, 762

Crawford, John: Satan's Satellites, 128

Crawford, Michael: Condorman, 178; Funny Thing Happened on the Way to the Forum, A, 265; Hello, Dolly!, 787; How I Won the War, 284

Crawford, Wayne: Jake Speed, 78

Creer, Erica: Circle of Iron, 31

Cremer, Bruno: Simple Story, A, 594

Crenna, Richard: Body Heat, 417; Breakheart Pass, 886; Devil Dog: The Hound Of Hell, 673; First Blood, 55; Flamingo Kid, The, 261; Marooned, 851; Rambo: First Blood II, 118; Sand Pebbles, The, 127; Stone Cold Dead, 141; Summer Rental, 361; Table for Five, 610; Wait until Dark, 763

Crews, Laura Hope: Camille, 425; Idiot's Delight, 492

Crews, Lloyd: Rain People, The, 574

Crewson, Wendy: Skullduggery, 744

Cribbins, Bernard: Don't Raise the Bridge, Lower the River, 253

Crisp, Donald: Charge of the Light Brigade, The, 30; Dawn Patrol, The, 39; Dog of Flanders, A, 180; Dr. Jekyll and Mr. Hyde, 676; Greyfriars Bobby, 183; Knute Rockne—All American, 510; Life of Emile Zola, The, 518; Little Minister, The, 519; Mutiny on the Bounty (Original), 105; National Velvet, 195; Oklahoma Kid, The, 918; Red Dust, 119; Red Dust, 577; Sea Hawk, The, 130; Svengali, 750

Cristal, Linda: Mr. Majestyk, 101; Perfect Furlough, 329

Criswell: Night of the Ghouls, 722

Cromwell, James: Revenge of the Nerds, 340

Cromwell, Richard: Lives of a Bengal Lancer, The, 91; Villain Still Pursued Her, The, 159

Cronyn, Hume: Brewster's Millions (1985), 235; Cocoon, 825; Conrack, 438; Impulse, 704; Lifeboat, 518; Postman Always Rings Twice, The (Original), 565; Rollover, 583; Sunrise at Campobello, 609; There Was a Crooked Man, 938; World According to Garp, The, 639

Crosby, Bing: Bells of St. Mary's, The, 408; Country Girl, The, 439; Going My Way, 474; High Society, 787; Holiday Inn, 787; Road to Bali, 342; King of Jazz, The, 790

Crosby, Cathy Lee: Dark, The, 669; Laughing Policeman, The, 88

Crosby, D: No Nukes, 795

Crosby, Denise: Eliminators, 832

Crosby, Harry: Friday the 13th, 691

Crosby, Kathryn: Initiation of Sarah, The, 705

Crosby, Mary: Ice Pirates, 842

Crosby, The Rhythm Boys (Bing: King of Jazz, The, 790

Crosby, Wade: Under California Stars, 942

Crosse, Rupert: Reivers, The, 338; Ride in the Whirlwind, 925

Cross, Ben: Chariots of Fire, 431; Far Pavilions, The, 463

Crothers, Scatman: Black Belt Jones, 18; Bronco Billy, 886; Deadly Eyes, 671; Journey of Natty Gann, The, 187; One Flew over the Cuckoo's Nest, 551; Scavenger Hunt, 346; Shining, The, 742; Shootist, The, 931; Twilight Zone—The Movie, 759; Zapped!, 385

Crouchen, Brian: House That Bled to Death, The, 701

Crouse, Lindsay: Daniel, 444; Iceman, 843; Places in the Heart, 563; Slap Shot, 353

Crowden, Graham: Britannia Hospital, 235; Romance With A Double Bass, 343

Crowell, Frank: Attack of the Swamp Creature, 647

Crowley, Dermot: Blue Money, 231

Crowley, Kathleen: Westward Go The Wagons, 212

Crowley, Pat: Untouchables: Scarface Mob, The, 157

Croxton, Dee: Stephen King's Night Shift Collection, 747

Cruise, Tom: All the Right Moves, 394; Legend, 849; Losin' It, 301; Outsiders, The, 555; Risky Business, 341; Taps, 611; Top Gun, 153

Crutchley, Rosalie: Adventures of Sherlock Holmes: The Norwood Builder, 5

Cruz, Ernesto: El Norte, 456

Cryer, Jon: No Small Affair, 320; Pretty in Pink, 567

Crystal, Billy: Enola Gay: The Men, the Mission, the Atomic Bomb, 458; Rabbit Test, 337; Running Scared (1986), 125; Three Little Pigs, The, 209

Cugat, Xavier: Neptune's Daughter, 795

Cullen, Max: Starstruck, 805; Sunday Too Far Away, 608

Cullum, John: Day After, The, 828

Culp, Joseph: Dream Lover, 679

Culp, Robert: Bob & Carol & Ted & Alice, 231; Castaway Cowboy, The, 176; Flood!, 685; Goldengirl, 840; Great Scout and Cathouse Thursday, The, 899; Inside Out, 77; PT 109, 569; Turk 182, 624

Cumbuka, Ji-Tu: Bound For Glory, 418

Cummings, Quinn: Goodbye Girl, The, 271

Cummings, Robert: Devil and Miss Jones, The, 250; Dial M for Murder, 675; King's Row, 508; Lost Moment, The, 522; Saboteur, 738

Cummins, Peggy: Curse of the Demon, 667

Cunningham, Margo: Sailor Who Fell from Grace with the Sea, The, *586*

Cuny, Alain: Emmanuelle, *457*

Curreri, Lee: Fame, *778*

Currie, Cherie: Foxes, *469;* Wavelength, *876*

Currie, Finlay: 49th Parallel, The, *468;* Billy Liar, *412;* Rob Roy, The Highland Rogue, *201*

Currie, Iris: Bay Boy, The, *406*

Currie, Louise: Adventures of Captain Marvel, The, *1;* Ape Man, The, *646;* Masked Marvel, The, *97*

Currie, Michael: Halloween III: Season of the Witch, *695*

Currie, Sanee: Gas, *265*

Curry, Christopher: C.H.U.D., *658*

Curry, Tim: Blue Money, *231;* Clue, *245;* Legend, *849;* Shout, The, *743;* Times Square, *809*

Curtin, Jane: How to Beat the High Co$t of Living, *284*

Curtin, Valerie: Big Trouble, *238;* Different Story, A, *451;* Maxie, *308*

Curtis, Alan: Buck Privates, *235;* Gung Ho, *67;* High Sierra, *72*

Curtis, Billy: Terror of Tiny Town, The, *937*

Curtis, Dick: Lawman Is Born, A, *908;* Singing Buckaroo, *932*

Curtis, Donald: Earth vs. the Flying Saucers, *832;* It Came from Beneath the Sea, *706*

Curtis, Jack: Lawless Range, *908*

Curtis, Jamie Lee: Death of a Centerfold, *447;* Fog, The, *686;* Grandview, U.S.A, *477;* Halloween, *695;* Halloween II, *695;* Love Letters, *523;* Perfect, *561;* Prom Night, *730;* Road Games, *736;* Trading Places, *371*

Curtis, Tony: Bad News Bears Go to Japan, The, *223;* Boston Strangler, The, *656;* Chamber of Horrors, *661;* Count of Monte Cristo, The (Remake), *36;* Defiant Ones, The, *448;* Francis, the Talking Mule, *263;* Great Race, The, *273;* It Rained All Night the Day I Left, *498;* Last Tycoon, The, *515;* Lepke, *89;* Little Miss Marker, *190;* Manitou, The, *714;* Mirror Crack'd, The, *99;* Operation Petticoat, *325;* Perfect Furlough, *329;* Sextette, *350;* Some Like It Hot, *356;* Spartacus, *138;* Trapeze, *621;* Users, The, *627;* Vega$, *158;* Vikings, The, *159*

Cusack, Cyril: Cry of the Innocent, *37;* Day of the Jackal, The, *39;* Fahrenheit 451, *836;* Harold and Maude, *276;* Ill Met by Moonlight, *493;* Love Spell, *93;* Taming of the Shrew, The, *364*

Cusack, John: Better Off Dead, *228;* Journey of Natty Gann, The, *187;* One Crazy Summer, *324;* Stand By Me, *600;* Sure Thing, The, *361*

Cushing, Peter: And Now the Screaming Starts, *645;* Asylum, *647;* At the Earth's Core, *818;* Beast Must Die, The, *649;* Creeping

Flesh, The, *666;* Curse of Frankenstein, The, *667;* Devil's Undead, The, *674;* Dr. Phibes Rises Again, *676;* Dr. Terror's House of Horrors, *677;* Dr. Who and the Daleks, *831;* Fear in The Night (Dynasty of Fear), *683;* Ghoul, The, *693;* Gorgon, The, *694;* Hamlet, *481;* Horror Express, *698;* Horror of Dracula, *699;* Hound of the Baskervilles, The (Remake), *75;* House of the Long Shadows, *700;* House That Dripped Blood, The, *701;* Mummy, The (remake), *719;* Scream and Scream Again, *740;* Shock Waves (Death Corps), *742;* Star Wars, *867;* Tales from the Crypt, *751;* Top Secret, *369;* Torture Garden, *758;* Twins of Evil, *760;* Uncanny, The, *760*

Cushna, Stephanie: Demons of Ludlow, The, *673*

Cuthbertson, Allan: Tunes of Glory, *624*

Cutler, Brian: Wilderness Family, Part 2, The, *212*

Cutt, Michael: Night of the Demon, *722*

Cyphers, Charles: Halloween, *695;* Halloween II, *695*

Dabney, Augusta: Violets Are Blue, *628*

DaFoe, Willem: Streets of Fire, *142;* To Live and Die in L.A., *153;* Roadhouse 66, *122*

Dagover, Lil: Cabinet of Doctor Caligari, The, *659*

Dahlbeck, Eva: Secrets of Women (or Waiting Women), *348*

Dahl, Arlene: Journey to the Center of the Earth, *846;* Slightly Scarlet, *595*

Dahl, Lisbet: Topsy Turvy, *370*

Dailey, Dan: It's Always Fair Weather, *789;* There's No Business Like Show Business, *808;* What Price Glory, *379*

Daily, Elizabeth: One Dark Night, *726;* Pee-Wee's Big Adventure, *328*

Dalban, Max: Boudu Saved From Drowning, *232;* Toni, *620*

Dale, Cynthia: Boy in Blue, The, *418;* Heavenly Bodies, *278*

Dale, Daphne: Invitation to the Dance, *788*

Dale, Ellis: Adventures of Sherlock Holmes: The Solitary Cyclist, *5*

Dale, Jennifer: Of Unknown Origin, *725*

Dale, Jim: Carry On Cowboy, *238;* Joseph Andrews, *290;* Pete's Dragon, *197;* Scandalous, *345;* Unidentified Flying Oddball, *212*

Dale, Virginia: Holiday Inn, *787*

Dalio, Marcel: Black Jack, *18;* Grand Illusion, *476;* Pepe Le Moko, *560;* Rules of the Game, The, *344*

Dall, John: Rope, *737*

Dallesandro, Joe: Andy Warhol's Dracula, *645;* Andy Warhol's Frankenstein, *646*

Dallimore, Maurice: Collector, The, *663*

Dalton, Audrey: Drum Beat, *894;* Elfego Baca: Six Gun Law, *895*

Dalton, Timothy: Chanel Solitaire, *430;* Doctor and the Devils, The, *676; (narrator)* Emperor's New Clothes, The, *833* Lion In Winter, The, *519;* Permission to Kill, *114;* Sextette, *350*

Daltrey, Roger: Legacy, The, *711;* Lisztomania, *792;* McVicar, *532;* Tommy, *810*

Daly, Jane: Children Shouldn't Play with Dead Things, *662*

Daly, Tyne: Adultress, The, *389;* Aviator, The, *403;* Better Late than Never, *228;* Enforcer, The, *49;* Movers and Shakers, *315*

Damita, Lily: Fighting Caravans, *896*

Dammett, Blackie: Nine Deaths of the Ninja, *107*

Damone, Vic: Hell to Eternity, *485*

Damon, Mark: Black Sabbath, *651*

Dana, Bill: Murder in Texas, *719*

Dana, Leora: 3:10 to Yuma, *939*

Dance, Charles: Plenty, *564*

Dane, Lawrence: Case of Libel, A, *427;* Nothing Personal, *321;* Of Unknown Origin, *725;* Scanners, *740*

Dangerfield, Rodney: Back To School, *222;* Caddyshack, *236;* Easy Money, *254;* Projectionist, The, *336*

Danieli, Emma: Last Man On Earth, The, *848*

Danieli, Isa: Macaroni, *304*

Danielle, Suzanne: Carpathian Eagle, *659*

Daniell, Henry: Body Snatcher, The, *655;* Camille, *425;* Five Weeks in a Balloon, *56;* Sea Hawk, The, *130;* Voyage to the Bottom of the Sea, *874;* Witness for the Prosecution, *637;* Woman In Green, The, *165*

Daniels, Anthony: Empire Strikes Back, The, *833;* Return of the Jedi, *859;* Star Wars, *867*

Daniels, Bebe: Reaching for the Moon, *337*

Daniels, Jeff: Heartburn, *277;* Marie, *529;* Purple Rose of Cairo, The, *337*

Daniels, Phil: Breaking Glass, *772;* Quadrophenia, *799*

Daniels, William: 1776, *802;* Blue Lagoon, The, *415;* One and Only, The, *551;* Parallax View, The, *557;* Rehearsal for Murder, *120;* Sunburn, *143;* Thousand Clowns, A, *367*

Daniely, Lisa: Adventures of Sherlock Holmes: The Crooked Man, *3*

Danner, Blythe: 1776, *802;* Futureworld, *838;* Great Santini, The, *478;* Man, Woman and Child, *528;* To Kill a Clown, *756*

Danning, Sybil: Chained Heat, *29;* Hercules, *841;* Howling II... Your Sister is a Werewolf, *702;* Kill Castro, *82;* Man with Bogart's Face, The, *96;* They're Playing with Fire, *616*

Danova, Cesare: Chamber of Horrors, *661;* Tentacles, *752;* Viva Las Vegas, *811*

Dano, Royal: Never Steal Anything Small, *795*

Danson, Ted: Fine Mess, A, *260;* Just Between Friends, *505;* Little Treasure, *91;* Onion Field, The, *553*

Dante, Michael: Beyond Evil, *650;* Big Score, The, *16*

Danza, Tony: Going Ape!, *269*

Dan, Reiko: Sanjuro, *128*

Darby, Kim: Better Off Dead, *228;* Don't Be Afraid of the Dark, *677;* Enola Gay: The Men, the Mission, the Atomic Bomb, *458;* One and Only, The, *551;* People, The, *855;* Strawberry Statement, The, *604;* True Grit, *941*

Darc, Mireille: Return of the Tall Blond Man with One Black Shoe, The, *339;* Tall Blond Man With One Black Shoe, The, *363*

Darcel, Denise: Dangerous When Wet, *776;* Vera Cruz, *943*

Darden, Severn: Back To School, *222;* Battle for the Planet of the Apes, *819;* Conquest of the Planet of the Apes, *826;* Luv, *304*

Darnell, Linda: Blood and Sand, *414;* Dakota Incident, *891;* Mark of Zorro, *97;* My Darling Clementine, *916;* Unfaithfully Yours (Original), *374*

Darrell, Steve: Cow Town, *890*

Darren, Bobby: Run Stranger Run, *738*

Darren, James: Gidget Goes Hawaiian, *267;* Gidget, *267;* Guns of Navarone, The, *68*

Darrieux, Danielle: Alexander the Great, *392;* La Ronde, *295;* Mayerling, *531*

Darro, Frankie: Phantom Empire, *114;* Radio Ranch (Men With Steel Faces, Phantom Empire), *923*

Darrow, Henry: Badge 373, *11*

Darwell, Jane: Craig's Wife, *439;* Grapes of Wrath, The, *477;* Jesse James, *905;* Mary Poppins, *191*

Da Silva, Fernando Ramos: Pixote, *563*

DaSilva, Howard: 1776, *802;* Garbo Talks, *265;* Nevada Smith, *917;* Lost Weekend, The, *523*

Dassin, Jules: Never on Sunday, *543*

Daste, Jean: Boudu Saved from Drowning, *232;* Green Room, The, *479;* Zero For Conduct, *642*

Daugirda, Jerry: Gone in 60 Seconds, *63*

Dauphin, Claude: Madame Rosa, *526*

Davenport, Alice: Keystone Comedies, Vol. 2, *292;* Keystone Comedies, Vol. 3, *292;* Keystone Comedies: Vol. 4, *292*

Davenport, Doris: Westerner, The, *944*

Davenport, Harry: Enchanted Forest, The, *180;* Jack London, *499;* Made for Each Other, *304;* Thin Man Goes Home, The, *149*

Davenport, Nigel: Cry of the Innocent, *37;* Phase IV, *114;* Zulu Dawn, *168*

Davidson, Eileen: House on Sorority Row, *701*

Davidson, Robin: Sole Survivor, *744*

David, Angel: Mixed Blood, *101*

David, Clifford: Resurrection, *858*

David, Eleanor: Comfort and Joy, *246*

David, Lou: Burning, The, *658*

David, Thayer: Duchess and the Dirtwater

Fox, The, 894; Eiger Sanction, The, 47; Rocky, 582; Save the Tiger, 588

David, Zorro: Reflections in a Golden Eye, 578

Davies, John Howard: Oliver Twist, 550

Davies, Lane: Magic of Lassie, The, 191

Davies, Mandy Rice: Absolute Beginners, 768

Davies, Rachel: House That Bled to Death, The, 701

Davies, Ray: Absolute Beginners, 768

Davies, Rubert: Oblong Box, The, 725

Davies, Sammi: Mona Lisa, 537

Davis Jr., Sammy: Cannonball Run, 237; Cannonball Run II, 237; Ocean's Eleven, 109; That's Dancing, 807

Davison, Bruce: Affair, The, 389; Brass Target, 24; High Risk, 72; Last Summer, 514; Short Eyes, 593; Spies Like Us, 356; Strawberry Statement, The, 604; Summer Heat, 607; Willard, 765

Davis, Ann B.: Lover Come Back, 303

Davis, Bette: All About Eve, 393; Burnt Offerings, 658; Dark Secret of Harvest Home, The, 669; Dark Victory, 445; Death on the Nile, 40; Hell's House, 71; Hollywood Outtakes, 282; Hush...Hush, Sweet Charlotte, 703; Jezebel, 501; Juarez, 504; Letter, The, 516; Now, Voyager, 547; Of Human Bondage (Original), 549; Petrified Forest, The, 562; Piano for Mrs. Cimino, A, 562; Pocketful of Miracles, 564; Private Lives of Elizabeth and Essex, The, 569; Return From Witch Mountain, 201; Right of Way, 580; Thank Your Lucky Stars, 807; Watcher in the Woods, The, 764; Watch on the Rhine, 630; What Ever Happened to Baby Jane?, 764

Davis, Brad: Chiefs, 432; Midnight Express, 533; Querelle, 572; Rumor of War, A, 125

Davis, Bud: Town That Dreaded Sundown, The, 759

Davis, C. Dave: Demons of Ludlow, The, 673

Davis, Daniel (director Ed Wood Jr.): Glen or Glenda, 473

Davis, Donald: Man Inside, The, 95

Davis, Gail: Blue Canadian Rockies, 884; Cow Town, 890; On Top of Old Smoky, 919; Valley of Fire, 942; Winning of the West, 946

Davis, Geena: Fly, The (remake), 686; Transylvania6-5000, 371

Davis, Guy: Beat Street, 770

Davis, Ilah: Hardcore, 481

Davis, Jack: Endgame, 834

Davis, Jim: Bad Company, 880; Comes a Horseman, 889; El Dorado, 895; Hellfire, 902; Jesse James Meets Frankenstein's Daughter, 708; Last Command, The, 907; Monster From Green Hell, 717; Monte Walsh, 915; Outcast, The, 920

Davis, Joan: Hold That Ghost, 281

Davis, Judy: Final Option, The, 54; Heatwave, 485; High Rolling, 73; My Brilliant Career, 540; Passage to India, A, 558; Winter of our Dreams, 636; Woman Called Golda, A, 638

Davis, Mac: Cheaper to Keep Her, 242; North Dallas Forty, 546; Sting II, The, 140

Davis, Nancy: Hellcats of the Navy, 70

Davis, Nathan: Code of Silence, 33

Davis, Ossie: All God's Children, 393; Avenging Angel, 11; Harry and Son, 483; Hot Stuff, 283; King, 507

Davis, Phillip: Quadrophenia, 799

Davis, Richard: Sky's the Limit, The, 803

Davis, Roger: Flash and the Firecat, 56; Ruby, 737

Davis, Tom: One More Saturday Night, 324

Davi, Robert: Raw Deal, 119

Dawber, Pam: Little Mermaid, The, 189; Wedding, A, 378

Dawn, Marpessa: Black Orpheus, 414

Dawson, Anthony: Death Rides a Horse, 892; Haunted Strangler, The, 696

Daw, Evelyn: Something to Sing About, 803

Dax, Jean: Mayerling, 531

Dayan, Assaf: Operation Thunderbolt, 111

Day, Annette: Double Trouble, 777

Day, Dana: Bloodbeat, 653

Day, Doris: Lover Come Back, 303; Man Who Knew Too Much, The (remake), 715; Pillow Talk, 330; Saga of Death Valley, 929; Teacher's Pet, 364; That Touch of Mink, 365; With Six You Get Eggroll, 383

Day, Josette: Beauty and the Beast, 820

Day, Laraine: Dr. Kildare's Strange Case, 43; Foreign Correspondent, 687; Mr. Lucky, 101; Tycoon, 156

Day, Morris: Purple Rain, 799

Deakins, Lucy: Boy Who Could Fly, The, 419

DeAnda, Rodolfo: Toy Soldiers, 154

Deane, Shirley: Prairie Moon, 922

Dean, James: East of Eden (Original), 454; Giant, 472; Rebel without a Cause, 576

Dean, Laura: Fame, 778

Deas, Justin: Dream Lover, 679

DeBell, Kristine: Big Brawl, The, 15

DeBenning, Burr: Incredible Melting Man, The, 843

DeCamp, Rosemary: 13 Ghosts, 755; Saturday the 14th, 739; Tom Edison—The Boy Who Lit Up The World, 210; Yankee Doodle Dandy, 813

DeCarlo, Yvonne: Liar's Moon, 517; Silent Scream, 743

Deezen, Eddie: Midnight Madness, 309; Rosebud Beach Hotel, The, 343

Dee, Frances: Becky Sharp, 407; I Walked with a Zombie, 704; Little Women, 519; Of Human Bondage (Original), 549; Wheel of Fortune, 944

Dee, Ruby: All God's Children, 393; Buck and the Preacher, 886; Raisin in the Sun, A, 575

Dee, Sandra: Dunwich Horror, The, 680; Fantasy Island, 837; Gidget, 267; Tammy and the Doctor, 611

DeFore, Don: Girl in Every Port, A, 268; Without Reservations, 382

Degermark, Pia: Elvira Madigan, 457; Looking Glass War, The, 521

deGroot, Myra: Norman Loves Rose, 320

DeHaven, Gloria: Best Foot Forward, 770; Bog, 655; Thin Man Goes Home, The, 149

Dehner, John: Apache, 879; Creator, 440; Nothing Personal, 321; Slaughterhouse Five, 862

de Banzie, Brenda: Doctor at Sea, 252; Hobson's Choice, 281

De Bedarieux, Gerard: Zero For Conduct, 642

de Cordoba, Pedro: Before I Hang, 649

de Corsia, Ted: Buccaneer, The, 25; Lady from Shanghai, 86; Neptune's Daughter, 795

De Filippo, Peppino: Boccaccio 70, 231

De Franco, Tom: Return of the Alien's Deadly Spawn, The, 734

de Grazia, Julio: Funny Dirty Little War (NO HABRA MAS PENSAS ni OLVIDO), 264

De Havilland, Olivia: Adventures of Robin Hood, The, 2; Captain Blood, 27; Charge of the Light Brigade, The, 30; Dark Mirror, The, 669; Dodge City, 894; Fifth Musketeer, The, 53; Gone with the Wind, 475; Heiress, The, 485; Hush...Hush, Sweet Charlotte, 703; Lady in a Cage, 710; Midsummer Night's Dream, A, 852; Private Lives of Elizabeth and Essex, The, 569; Proud Rebel, The, 923; Santa Fe Trail, 929; Strawberry Blonde, The, 604; Swarm, The, 751; Thank Your Lucky Stars, 807; They Died with their Boots On, 938

DeLuise, Dom: Adventures of Sherlock Holmes' Smarter Brother, The, 215; Best Little Whorehouse in Texas, The, 771; Cannonball Run, 237; Cannonball Run II, 237; End, The, 255; Failsafe, 461; Haunted Honeymoon, 277; Hot Stuff, 283; Last Married Couple in America, The, 296; Mel Brooks' History of the World, Part I, 308; Muppet Movie, The, 193; Secret of Nimh, The, 203; Sextette, 350; Silent Movie, 351; Smokey and the Bandit II, 355; Twelve Chairs, The, 373; Wholly Moses!, 381; World's Greatest Lover, The, 384; Sextette, 350

de Marney, Derick: Young and Innocent, 166

De Monaghan, Laurence: Claire's Knee, 243

De Mornay, Rebecca: Risky Business, 341; Slugger's Wife, The, 354; Runaway Train, 125; Trip to Bountiful, The, 622

De Munn, Jeffery: Christmas Evil, 663; Frances, 469; Hitcher, The, 698; Windy City,

635; Warning Sign, 763

De Niro, Robert: Bang the Drum Slowly, 405; Deer Hunter, The, 448; Falling in Love, 462; Godfather Epic, The, 474; King of Comedy, The, 507; Mean Streets, 532; New York, New York, 795; Raging Bull, 574; Taxi Driver, 612; True Confessions, 623; Brazil, 233; Godfather, The, Part II, 474; Last Tycoon, The, 515; Once upon a Time in America (Long Version), 110

de Rossi, Barbara: Hearts and Armour, 70; Mussolini and I, 539

De Sade, Ana: Triumphs of a Man Called Horse, 941

De Santis, Joe: Dino, 451; Marty, 529

de Tuckheim, Charlotte: My Other Husband, 541

de Villalonga, Jose Luis: Darling, 445

De Vries, Jon: Act of Passion, 389

De Wilde, Brandon: Hud, 490; Those Calloways, 209

De Young, Cliff: Flight of the Navigator, 837; F/X, 51; Hunger, The, 703; Protocol, 336; Reckless, 577; Secret Admirer, 346; Shock Treatment, 351; Independence Day, 494; King, 507

Dejoux, Christine: One Wild Moment, 552

Dekker, Albert: Buckskin Frontier, 886; Kansan, The, 906; Killers, The, 83; Once Upon a Honeymoon, 324; Wake Island, 159; War of the Wildcats, 943

Delair, Suzy: Fernandel The Dressmaker, 259

Delaney, Kim: That Was Then...This is Now, 615

Del Lago, Alicia: El Norte, 456

Del Prete, Duilio: Daisy Miller, 442

Del Rio, Dolores: Bird of Paradise, 17; Children of Sanchez, The, 432; Flaming Star, 896; Flying Down to Rio, 780

Del Sol, Laura: Hit, The, 73

Dell, Dorothy: Little Miss Marker, 190

Dell, Gabriel: Framed, 60

Delmont, Edouard: Toni, 620

Delon, Alain: Airport '79: The Concorde, 391; Honor among Thieves, 74; Joy House, 504; Mr. Klein, 536; Red Sun, 924; Swann In Love, 609

Delrich, Hal: Evil Dead, The, 681

Delshaft, Mary: Last Laugh, The, 514

Deluca, Claudia: Small Change, 595

Demarest, William: Devil and Miss Jones, The, 250; Don't Be Afraid of the Dark, 677; Hell on Frisco Bay, 70; It's a Mad Mad Mad Mad World, 288; Lady Eve, The, 295; Little Men, 519; Perils of Pauline, the, 329; Son of Flubber, 206; That Darn Cat, 208; Viva Las Vegas, 811; What Price Glory, 379

Demazis, Orane: Marius, 529

Demetz, Danielle: Raid on Rommel, 118

DeMille, Katherine: Black Room, The, 652

DeMorton, Reggie: Alien Warrior, 816

Dempster, Carol: True Heart Susie, 623

DeNatale, Don: Roseland, 584

Dench, Judi: Room With a View, A (1987 Release), 584

Deneuve, Catherine: Grande Bourgeoise, La, 476; Hunger, The, 703; Je Vous Aime (I Love You All), 501; Last Metro, The, 514; Umbrellas of Cherbourg, The, 625

Denham, Maurice: Carrington, V. C., 427; Curse of the Demon, 667; Sunday, Bloody Sunday, 608; Torture Garden, 758

Denneck, Barbara: Playtime, 331

Dennehy, Brian: Butch and Sundance: The Early Days, 887; Cocoon, 825; First Blood, 55; F/X, 51; Gorky Park, 64; Jericho Mile, The, 501; Legal Eagles, 88; Little Mermaid, The, 189; Never Cry Wolf, 105; River Rat, The, 581; Silverado, 932; Twice in a Lifetime, 624

Denner, Charles: And Now, My Love, 398; Robert et Robert, 582; Z, 641

Denning, Richard: Creature from the Black Lagoon, 665

Dennis, Sandy: Come Back to the Five and Dime, Jimmy Dean, Jimmy Dean, 436; Demon (God Told Me To), 800; Four Seasons, The, 469; Nasty Habits, 317; Out of Towners, The, 325; Who's Afraid of Virginia Woolf?, 633

Denny, Reginald: Lost Patrol, The, 93; Rebecca, 576; Secret Life of Walter Mitty, The, 347

Denver, John: Oh God!, 323

Depardieu, Gerard: Danton, 444; Get Out Your Handkerchiefs, 266; Going Places, 270; Last Metro, The, 514; Le Chevre (THE GOAT), 298; Les Comperes, 298; Moon in the Gutter, The, 538; Return of Martin Guerre, The, 578; Woman Next Door, The, 638

Depraz, Xavier: Pain in the A———, A, 327

Derek, Bo: 10, 364; Bolero, 417; Change of Seasons, A, 240; Fantasies, 463; Orca, 726; Tarzan the Ape Man (Remake), 146

Derek, John: All the King's Men, 394; Knock on Any Door, 509; Outcast, The, 920

Dern, Bruce: Black Sunday, 19; Bloody Mama, 20; Coming Home, 437; Cowboys, The, 890; Driver, The, 45; Family Plot, 683; Great Gatsby, The, 477; Harry Tracy, 901; Hush... Hush, Sweet Charlotte, 703; Laughing Policeman, The, 88; Marnie, 715; Silent Running, 862; St. Valentine's Day Massacre, The, 126; Support Your Local Sheriff, 936; Tattoo, 611; That Championship Season, 614; Trip, The, 622; Wild Angels, The, 163

Dern, Laura: Mask, 530; Smooth Talk, 596

Derricks, Cleavant: Moscow on the Hudson, 314; Off Beat, 322; Slugger's Wife, The, 354

Derr, Richard: When Worlds Collide, 876

Desailly, Jean: Soft Skin, The, 596

DeSalvo, Anne: Compromising Positions, 247

DeSica, Vittorio: Andy Warhol's Dracula, 645

Desmouceaux, Geary: Small Change, 595

Desny, Ivan: Escapade in Florence, 180

Deutch, Ernst: The Golem (How He Came Into The World) (DER GOLEM, Wie er in die Welt Kam), 754

Devane, William: Bad News Bears in Breaking Training, The, 223; Dark, The, 669; Family Plot, 683; Honky Tonk Freeway, 288; Marathon Man, 97; Rolling Thunder, 123; Testament, 870

Devine, Andy: Grand Canyon Trail, 899; It's a Mad Mad Mad Mad World, 288; Man Who Shot Liberty Valance, The, 913; Stagecoach, 934; Under California Stars, 942

Devine, Loretta D.: Anna to the Infinite Power, 817

DeVito, Danny: My Little Pony: The Movie (Animated voices), 194; Going Ape!, 269; Jewel of the Nile, The, 79; One Flew over the Cuckoo's Nest, 124; Romancing the Stone, 124; Ruthless People, 344; Terms of Endearment, 613; Wise Guys, 382

DeVries, Jon: Lianna, 517

Dewaere, Patrick: Beau Pere, 225; Get Out Your Handkerchiefs, 266; Going Places, 270; Heat of Desire, 277

Dewhurst, Colleen: Boy Who Could Fly, The, 419; Cowboys, The, 890; Glitter Dome, The, 62; Ice Castles, 492; McQ, 98; Tribute, 621; When a Stranger Calls, 764

DeWolfe, Billy: Dear Wife, 249; Perils of Pauline, The, 329

Dey, Susan: Echo Park, 455; Looker, 850

Diamond, Neil: Jazz Singer, The, 789; Last Waltz, The, 791

DiBenedetto, Tony: Exterminator, The, 50

DiCenzo, George: About Last Night, 388; Helter Skelter, 486

DiCicco, Bobby: Big Red One, The, 18; Philadelphia Experiment, The, 856

Dickey, James: Deliverance, 41

Dickey, Lucinda: Breakin' 2 Electric Boogaloo, 772; Breakin', 771; Ninja III: The Domination, 108

Dickinson, Angie: Big Bad Mama, 14; Cast a Giant Shadow, 28; Charlie Chan and the Curse of the Dragon Queen, 240; Chase, The, 431; Death Hunt, 39; Dressed to Kill, 679; Ocean's Eleven, 109; Resurrection of Zachary Wheeler, The, 859; Rio Bravo, 599

Dickson, Gloria: They Made Me a Criminal, 616

Dick, Douglas: Home of the Brave, 488

Dick, Keith Joe: Ghoulies, 693

Diddley, Bo: Hell's Angels Forever, 486

Diehl, John: Miami Vice, 98

Dierkes, John: Daughter of Dr. Jekyll, 670

Dietrich, Marlene: Around the World in 80 Days, 230; Blue Angel, The, 415; Judgment at Nuremberg, 504; Rancho Notorious, 923; Spoilers, The, 934; Stage Fright, 747; Touch of Evil, 758; Witness for the Prosecution, 637

Dieudonné, Albert: Napoleon, 542

Dieu, Donna: Return of Martin Guerre, The, 578

Diffring, Anton: Beast Must Die, The, 649; Circus Of Horrors, 663; Fahrenheit 451, 836; Where Eagles Dare, 161

Digges, Dudley: Mutiny on the Bounty (Original), 105

Dignam, Arthur: Strange Behavior, 748; We of the Never Never, 161; Wild Duck, The, 634

Di Cenzo, George: Starflight One, 867; Ninth Configuration, The, 546

Di Lazzaro, Dalila: Creepers, 665

Dillard, Bert: Dawn Rider, 892

Diller, Phyllis: Boy, Did I Get a Wrong Number!, 233; Mad Monster Party, 191

Dillman, Bradford: 99 and 44/100 Percent Dead, 108; Amsterdam Kill, The, 7; Bug, 658; Enforcer, The, 49; Escape from the Planet of the Apes, 835; Force Five, 59; Legend of Walks Far Woman, The, 909; Love and Bullets, 93; Moon of the Wolf, 718; Piranha, 728; Resurrection of Zachary Wheeler, The, 859; Revenge, 735; Running Scared (1980), 126; Sudden Impact, 142; Way We Were, The, 631

Dillon, Kevin: Heaven Help Us, 278

Dillon, Matt: Flamingo Kid, The, 261; Liar's Moon, 517; Little Darlings, 299; My Bodyguard, 540; Outsiders, The, 555; Over the Edge, 555; Rumble Fish, 585; Target, 145; Tex, 614

Dillon, Melinda: Absence of Malice, 388; Bound For Glory, 418; Christmas Story, A, 177; Fallen Angel, 462; F.I.S.T., 461; Right of Way, 580; Slap Shot, 353; Songwriter, 804

DiMaggio, Joe: Manhattan Merry-Go-Round, 913

Dimitri, Richard: When Things Were Rotten, 380

Dinome, Jerry: Tomboy, 153

Dione, Rose: Freaks, 689

DiSanti, John: Eyes of a Stranger, 682

Dishy, Bob: First Family, 261; Last Married Couple in America, The, 296

DiSue, Joe: Blackenstein, 652

Ditchburn, Anne: Curtains, 668

Divine: Female Trouble, 259; Lust in the Dust, 303; Mondo Trasho, 312; Multiple Maniacs, 718; Pink Flamingos, 330; Polyester, 333; Trouble in Mind, 622

Dixon, Donna: Spies Like Us, 356

Dixon, Ivan: Car Wash, 239; Fer-de-Lance, 684; Raisin in the Sun, A, 575

Dixon, James: Q, 732

Dixon, Jean: You Only Live Once, 640

Dix, Richard: American Empire, 879; Buckskin Frontier, 886; Kansan, The, 906

Dix, Robert: Blood of Dracula's Castle, 653

Dix, Tommy: Best Foot Forward, 770

Dobson, Kevin: Hardhat and Legs, 482

Dobson, Tamara: Chained Heat, 29; Cleopatra Jones, 31

Documentary: 16 Days of Glory, 594; Atomic Cafe, The, 402; Gizmo!, 268; Go for It, 62; Harlan County, U.S.A., 482; Land Without Bread, 512; Shoah, 592; Ten Days That Shook The World (October), 613; Times of Harvey Milk, The, 619; Triumph of the Will, 622; Who Are the Debolts and Where Did They Get 19 Kids?, 632

Doerr, James: Savage Weekend, 739

Doleman, Guy: Funeral In Berlin, 61

Dombasle, Arielle: Le Beau Mariage, 297; Pauline at the Beach, 559

Domergue, Faith: House of Seven Corpses, The, 700; It Came from Beneath the Sea, 706; Psycho Sisters, 732; This Island Earth, 871

Domingo, Placido: Bizet's Carmen, 771; La Traviata, 791

Donahue, Tony: Grandview, U.S.A. 477

Donahue, Troy: Cockfighter, 32; Perfect Furlough, 329

Donaldson, Aaron: Nutcase, 321

Donaldson, Melissa: Nutcase, 321

Donald, James: Bridge on the River Kwai, The, 25

Donat, Peter: Different Story, A, 451

Donat, Robert: Count of Monte Cristo, The (Original), 36; Ghost Goes West, The, 267; Goodbye, Mr. Chips, 475; Inn of the Sixth Happiness, The, 495; Private Life of Henry the Eighth, The, 568; Thirty-nine Steps, The, 755; Winslow Boy, The, 635

Donlevy, Brian: Allegheny Uprising, 878; Errand Boy, The, 256; Jesse James, 905; Ride the Man Down, 926; Wake Island, 159

Donnelly, Patrice: Personal Best, 562

Donnelly, Ruth: Bells of St. Mary's, The, 408

Donner, Robert: Hysterical, 284; Santee, 929

Donovan: Don't Look Back, 777; Secret Policeman's Private Parts, The, 347

Donovan, King: Invasion of the Body Snatchers (Original), 844

Donovan, Tate: SpaceCamp, 864

Doohan, James: Star Trek III: The Search for Spock, 865; Star Trek II: The Wrath of Khan, 865; Star Trek (television series), 866; Star Trek: The Menagerie, 865; Star Trek—The Motion Picture, 865

Dooley, Paul: Big Trouble, 228; Endangered Species, 834; Hansel and Gretel, 183; Popeye, 199; Rich Kids, 580; Sixteen Candles, 353; Strange Brew, 360; Wedding, A, 378

Doolittle, John: Clan of the Cave Bear, 824

Doran, Ann: Rebel without a Cause, 576

Dorleac, Françoise: Soft Skin, The, 596

Dorn, Dolores: Tell Me A Riddle, *612*

Dorn, Philip: Fighting Kentuckian, The, *896;* I Remember Mama, *491*

Dorsey, Jimmy: Fabulous Dorseys, The, *778*

Dorsey, Thomas A.: Say Amen, Somebody, *801*

Dorsey, Tommy: Du Barry Was a Lady, *777;* Fabulous Dorseys, The, *778*

Dors, Diana: Children Of The Full Moon, *662;* Deep End, *672;* Devil's Undead, The, *674;* There's a Girl in my Soup, *365*

Dor, Karin: You Only Live Twice, *168*

Dotrice, Karen: Gnome-Mobile, The, *182;* Mary Poppins, *191;* Thirty-Nine Steps, The (Second Remake), *149;* Three Lives Of Thomasina,The, *209*

Dotrice, Roy: Corsican Brothers, The, *247;* Dancing Princesses, The, *178;* Eliminators, *832*

Douglass, Robyn: Lonely Guy, The, *300;* Romantic Comedy, *343*

Douglas, Angela: Carry On Cowboy, *238*

Douglas, Don: Great Gabbo, The, *477*

Douglas, John: Hell's Brigade, *71*

Douglas, Kirk: 20,000 Leagues under the Sea, *155;* Arrangement, The, *401;* Big Sky, The, *883;* Big Trees, The, *16;* Cast a Giant Shadow, *28;* Catch Me a Spy, *28;* Champion, *430;* Draw, *894;* Eddie Macon's Run, *47;* Final Countdown, The, *837;* Fury, The, *692;* Gunfight at the O.K. Corral, *900;* Holocaust 2000, *698;* Home Movies, *882;* Lonely Are the Brave, *909;* Man from Snowy River, *95;* Man without a Star, *913;* Out of the Past, *112;* Paths of Glory, *559;* Saturn 3, *861;* Seven Days in May, *591;* Spartacus, *138;* Strange Love of Martha Ivers, The, *604;* There Was a Crooked Man, *938;* Vikings, The, *159;* War Wagon, The, *944*

Douglas, Melvyn: Being There, *226;* Captains Courageous, *425;* Changeling, The, *661;* Death Squad, The, *40;* Ghost Story, *693;* Hud, *490;* Mr. Blandings Builds His Dream House, *310;* Ninotchka, *319;* Seduction of Joe Tynan, The, *590;* Tell Me A Riddle, *612;* Tenant, The, *751;* Twilight's Last Gleaming, *156*

Douglas, Michael: China Syndrome, The, *432;* Chorus Line, A, *774;* Coma, *664;* It's My Turn, *499;* Jewel of the Nile, The, *79;* Romancing the Stone, *124;* Star Chamber, The, *600;* Gator, *61;* Incredible Shrinking Woman, The, *286*

Douglas, Paul: Clash by Night, *434;* Gamma People, The, *839*

Douglas, Robert: At Sword's Point, *10;* Fountainhead, The, *468*

Douglas, Sarah: People That Time Forgot, The, *855*

Dourif, Brad: Eyes of Laura Mars, The, *682;* Heaven's Gate, *902;* Ragtime, *574;* Wise Blood, *636*

Dowling, Constance: Knickerbocker Holiday, *791*

Dowlin, Kathryn: Love Spell, *93*

Downer, David: Norman Loves Rose, *320*

Downes, Cathy: Winter of our Dreams, *636*

Downey Jr., Robert: Back To School, *222*

Downs, Johnny: Last of the Pony Riders, *907*

Down, Lesley-Anne: Betsy, The, *409;* Great Train Robbery, The, *66;* Hanover Street, *481;* Little Night Music, A, *793;* Nomads, *724;* Pink Panther Strikes Again, The, *330;* Rough Cut, *124;* Sphinx, *746*

Doyle-Murray, Brian: Razor's Edge, The (Remake), *576*

Drainie, John: Incredible Journey, The, *186*

Drake, Betsy: Every Girl Should Be Married, *256*

Drake, Charles: Air Force, *7;* Glenn Miller Story, The, *783;* It Came from Outer Space, *845;* To Hell and Back, *152*

Drake, Claudia: Detour, *450;* False Colors, *895*

Drake, Dennis: Preppies, *333*

Drake, Mervyn: Winter of our Dreams, *636*

Drake, Peggy: Tuttles of Tahiti, The, *373*

Drake, Tom: Meet Me in St. Louis, *793*

Draper, Polly: Seven Minutes In Heaven, *350*

Drayton, Alfred: Nicholas Nickleby, *544*

Dressler, Marie: Anna Christie, *399;* Dinner at Eight, *251;* Min and Bill, *534*

Drew, Ellen: Isle of the Dead, *706*

Dreyfuss, Richard: American Graffiti, *218;* Apprenticeship of Duddy Kravitz, The, *401;* Big Fix, The, *15;* Buddy System, The, *421;* Close Encounters of the Third Kind, *825;* Competition, The, *437;* Down and Out in Beverly Hills, *254;* Goodbye Girl, The, *271;* Inserts, *496;* Jaws, *707;* Stand By Me, *600;* Whose Life Is It, Anyway?, *633*

Driscoll, Bobby: So Dear to My Heart, *206;* Treasure Island, *211*

Drivas, Robert: Cool Hand Luke, *35*

Drury, James: Elfego Baca: Six Gun Law, *895;* Ride the High Country, *925;* Ten Who Dared, *208;* Toby Tyler, *210*

Drury, Patrick: Awakening, The, *648*

Dru, Joanne: All the King's Men, *394;* Hell on Frisco Bay, *70;* Light In The Forest, The, *189;* Super Fuzz, *868;* Thunder Bay, *151;* Wagonmaster, *943*

Dryer, Robert: Savage Streets, *128*

Dubbins, Don: From the Earth to the Moon, *838*

DuBrey, Claire: South of the Border, *934*

Duchesne, Roger: Bob le Flambeur, *21*

Dudikoff, Michael: American Ninja, *7*

Duel, Geoffrey: Chisum, *889*

Duering, Carl: Arabesque, *9*

Duffy, Patrick: Enola Gay: The Men, the Mission, the Atomic Bomb, *458*

Duff, Howard: East of Eden (Remake), *454;*

Kramer vs. Kramer, 510; Late Show, The, 87; Oh, God! Book II, 323; Wedding, A, 378

Dugan, Dennis: Howling, The, 701; Unidentified Flying Oddball, 212

Duggan, Andrew: Commies Are Coming, the Commies Are Coming, The, 246; Frankenstein Island, 688; Incredible Journey of Dr. Meg Laurel, The, 494; It Lives Again, 706; It's Alive!, 707; Secret War of Harry Frigg, The, 348; Skin Game, 933

Duggan, Tom: Frankenstein— 1970, 689

Du Maurier, Gerald: Catherine the Great, 428

Dukes, David: Cat on a Hot Tin Roof (Remake), 428; First Deadly Sin, The, 55; Wild Party, The, 634; Without a Trace, 637

Duke, Patty: 4D Man, 838; Daydreamer, The, 179; Family Upside Down, A, 462; Miracle Worker, The, 535

Dukov, Bruce: Adventures of Sherlock Holmes: The Red-Headed League, 5

Dullea, Keir: 2001: A Space Odyssey, 873; 2010, 874

Dulman, Debra: Demons of Ludlow, The, 673

Dumbrille, Douglass: Buccaneer, The, 25; False Colors, 895

Dumont, Margaret: Animal Crackers, 218; At the Circus, 221; Day at the Races, A, 249; Duck Soup, 254; Night at the Opera, A, 318

Dunarie, Malcolm: Heaven Help Us, 278

Dunaway, Faye: Arrangement, The, 401; Bonnie and Clyde, 21; Champ, The (Remake), 430; Chinatown, 30; Eyes of Laura Mars, The, 682; First Deadly Sin, The, 55; Four Musketeers, The, 60; Little Big Man, 909; Mommie Dearest, 537; Network, 543; Ordeal By Innocence, 111; Supergirl, 868; Thomas Crown Affair, The, 150; Three Days of the Condor, 150; Three Musketeers, The (1973), 150; Towering Inferno, The, 154; Voyage of the Damned, 629; Wicked Lady, The, 163

Duncan, Carmen: Dark Forces, 669; Escape 2000, 835; Now and Forever, 547

Duncan, Jayson: Mystery Island, 194

Duncan, Kenne: Night of the Ghouls, 722; Hills of Utah, The, 903; On Top of Old Smoky, 919; Sioux City Sue, 933; Song of Nevada, 933

Duncan, Nancy: Little Match Girl, The, 189

Duncan, Pamela: Attack of the Crab Monsters, 647

Duncan, Sandy: Cat from Outer Space, The, 176; Million Dollar Duck, The, 192

Dundas, Jennie: Legal Eagles, 88

Dungan, Sebastian: Man, Woman and Child, 528

Dunlap, Carla: Pumping Iron II: The Women, 570

Dunlap, Dawn: Barbarian Queen, 819; Forbidden World, 686

Dunne, Dominique: Poltergeist, 729

Dunne, Griffin: After Hours, 215; Almost You, 217; American Werewolf in London, An, 644

Dunne, Irene: Ann Vickers, 399; I Remember Mama, 491; Life With Father, 299; My Favorite Wife, 316; Penny Serenade, 560

Dunne, Stephen: Big Sombrero, The, 883

Dunnock, Mildred: Baby Doll, 403

Dunn, Emma: Dr. Kildare's Strange Case, 43; Hell's House, 71

Dunn, James: Elfego Baca: Six Gun Law, 895

Dunn, Michael: Madigan, 94; Murders In The Rue Morgue, 720; No Way to Treat a Lady, 546; Ship of Fools, 592; You're a Big Boy Now, 385

Dun, Dennis: Big Trouble in Little China, 17

Duperey, Anny: Pardon Mon Affaire, 327

DuPlessis, Danie: Kill or Be Killed, 83

Duprez, June: And Then There Were None, 398; Brighton Strangler, The, 657; Four Feathers, The, 60; None But the Lonely Heart, 546; Thief of Baghdad, The, 870

Dupre, Peter: Eyes of a Stranger, 682

Durante, Jimmy: It's a Mad Mad Mad Mad World, 288; Melody Ranch, 914; Palooka, 556

Durfee, Minta: Keystone Comedies, Vol. 1, 292; Keystone Comedies, Vol. 2, 292; Keystone Comedies, Vol. 3, 292; Keystone Comedies: Vo. 5, 292

Durkin, Junior: Hell's House, 71

Durning, Charles: Best Little Girl in the World, The, 408; Best Little Whorehouse in Texas, The, 771; Big Trouble, 228; Breakheart Pass, 886; Die Laughing, 251; Dog Day Afternoon, 452; Fury, The, 692; Greek Tycoon, The, 479; Harry and Walter Go to New York, 276; Hindenburg, The, 487; Man With One Red Shoe, The, 306; Mass Appeal, 531; Queen of the Stardust Ballroom, 572; Sharky's Machine, 133; Sisters, 744; Starting Over, 358; Stick, 140; Sting, The, 144; Tilt, 368; To Be or Not to Be (Remake), 369; True Confessions, 623; Twilight's Last Gleaming, 156; Two of a Kind, 373; When a Stranger Calls, 764

Duryea, Dan: Along Came Jones, 879; Flight of the Phoenix, The, 58; None But the Lonely Heart, 546; Pride of the Yankees, The, 568; Sahara, 126; Scarlet Street, 589; Thunder Bay, 151

Dusenberry, Ann: Cutter's Way, 441; Desperate Women, 893; Heart Beat, 483; And Now, My Love, 398; Three Men and a Cradle, 367; Le Beau Mariage, 297

Dutton, Simon: Lion and the Hawk, The, 89

Duvall, Robert: Apocalypse Now, 9; Badge 373, 11; Betsy, The, 409; Breakout, 24; Chase, The, 431; Countdown, 439; Eagle Has Landed, The, 46; Godfather Epic, The, 474; Godfather, The, Part II, 474; Godfather, The,

473; Greatest, The, 479; Great Santini, The, 478; Joe Kidd, 906; Killer Elite, The, 83; M*A*S*H, 307; Natural, The, 542; Network, 543; Pursuit of D. B. Cooper, 116; Rain People, The, 574; Seven-Per-Cent Solution, The, 131; Stone Boy, The, 603; Tender Mercies, 613; THX 1138, 872; Tomorrow, 620; True Confessions, 623; True Grit, 941

Duvall, Shelley: Annie Hall, 219; McCabe and Mrs. Miller, 914; Popeye, 199; Rapunzel, 200; Rumpelstiltskin, 202; Shining, The, 742; Time Bandits, 872

Dvorak, Ann: Abilene Town, 878; Flame of the Barbary Coast, 56; Manhattan Merry-Go-Round, 913; Out of the Blue, 325; Scarface (original), 129.

Dvorsky, Peter: Videodrome, 762

Dwire, Earl: Assassin of Youth (aka Marijuana), 402; Lawless Frontier, 908; Lawless Range, 908; Lucky Texan, 910; Man From Music Mountain, 912; New Frontier, 917; Randy Rides Alone, 924; Riders of Destiny, 926; Sagebrush Trail, 929; Star Packer, The, 935; Trail Beyond, the, 939; West of the Divide, 944

Dye, Cameron: Body Rock, 771; Fraternity Vacation, 263; Joy of Sex, The, 291

Dylan, Bob: Don't Look Back, 777; Last Waltz, The, 791; Pat Garrett and Billy the Kid, 920

Dysart, Richard: Autobiography of Miss Jane Pittman, The, 402; Bitter Harvest, 413; Falcon and the Snowman, The, 461; Ordeal of Dr. Mudd, The, 553; Pale Rider, 921; Prophecy, 730; Thing, The, 871; Warning Sign, 763

Dzundza, George: Act of Passion, 389; Best Defense, 227

D'Abo, Maryam: XTro, 766

D'Abo, Olivia: Bolero, 417

D'Angelo, Beverly: Big Trouble, 228; Coal Miner's Daughter, 775; European Vacation, 256; Finders Keepers, 260; Hair, 785; Honky Tonk Freeway, 282; Paternity, 328; Sleeping Beauty, 205; Vacation, 376

D'Aquila, Diane: Last Chase, The, 847

D'Arbanville, Patti: Big Wednesday, 411; Bilitis, 411; Fifth Floor, The, 684; Modern Problems, 311

D'Arcy, Alex: Blood of Dracula's Castle, 653

D'Arcy, Jake: Gregory's Girl, 273

De Bartoli, Moreno: When Father Was Away On Business, 632

D'Obici, Valeria: Passion of Love, 559

Earles, Daisy: Freaks, 689

Earles, Harry: Freaks, 689

Easely, Richard: Outrageous, 326

Easterbrook, Leslie: Police Academy III: Back in Training, 332

Eastman, George: Endgame, 834

Eastwood, Alison: Tightrope, 755

Eastwood, Clint: Any Which Way You Can, 219; Beguiled, The, 407; Bronco Billy, 886;

City Heat, 243; Coogan's Bluff, 34; Dirty Harry, 43; Eiger Sanction, The, 47; Enforcer, The, 49; Escape from Alcatraz, 49; Every Which Way but Loose, 257; Firefox, 54; Fistful of Dollars, A, 896; For a Few Dollars More, 897; Gauntlet, The, 62; Good the Bad and the Ugly, The, 899; Hang 'Em High, 900; High Plains Drifter, 903; HonkyTonk Man, 489; Joe Kidd, 906; Kelly's Heroes, 81; Magnum Force, 94; Outlaw Josey Wales, The, 920; Paint Your Wagon, 797; Pale Rider, 921; Play Misty for Me, 729; Sudden Impact, 142; Thunderbolt and Lightfoot, 152; Tightrope, 755; Two Mules for Sister Sara, 942; Where Eagles Dare, 161

Eastwood, Kyle: HonkyTonk Man, 489

East, Jeff: Deadly Blessing, 671

Eaton, Shirley: Against All Odds (Kiss and Kill, Blood of Fu Manchu), 643; Around the World Under the Sea, 10; Doctor at Large, 252

Eaton, Wallas: Test of Love, A, 613

Eberene, Maude: Colorado, 889

Eberhard, Fabrice: L'Addition, 510

Ebsen, Buddy: Breakfast at Tiffany's, 419; Broadway Melody of 1936, 772; Broadway Melody of 1938, 773; Davy Crockett and the River Pirates, 179; Davy Crockett (King of the Wild Frontier), 179; Tom Sawyer, 210

Eckhardt, Fritz: Almost Angels, 171

Eckstine, Billy: Jo Jo Dancer, Your Life Is Calling, 502

Eck, Johnny: Freaks, 689

Eddy, Nelson: Knickerbocker Holiday, 791; Maytime, 793; Rose Marie, 800

Edelman, Herb: Barefoot in the Park, 224; Cracking Up, 248; Odd Couple, The, 322; Yakuza, The, 165

Eden, Barbara: 7 Faces of Dr. Lao, 861; Amazing Dobermans, 171; Chattanooga Choo Choo, 242; Five Weeks in a Balloon, 56; Flaming Star, 896; Harper Valley P.T.A., 276; How to Break Up a Happy Divorce, 284; Voyage to the Bottom of the Sea, 874

Eden, Daniel: Fear No Evil, 683

Edeson, Robert: King of Kings, The, 508

Edmonds, Dale: Paisan, 556

Edmonds, Elizabeth: Experience Preferred... But Not Essential, 257

Edmunds, William: Big Sombrero, The, 883

Edson, Richard: Stranger than Paradise, 360

Edwall, Allan: Brothers Lionheart, The, 175; Fanny and Alexander, 463

Edwards, Alan: South of the Border, 934

Edwards, Anthony: Gotcha!, 64; Revenge of the Nerds, 340; Sure Thing, The, 361; Top Gun, 153

Edwards, Darryl: Brother from Another Planet, The, 822

Edwards, Hugh: Lord of the Flies, 521

Edwards, James: Home of the Brave, 488; Set-Up, The, 591

Edwards, Jennifer: Fine Mess, A, *260*

Edwards, Penny: North of the Great Divide, *918;* Trail of Robin Hood, *939*

Edwards, Rick: Hearts and Armour, *70*

Edwards, Snitz: College, *246;* Phantom of the Opera, *727*

Edwards, Vince: Deal of the Century, *249;* Seduction, The, *741;* Space Raiders, *864*

Egan, Eddie: Badge 373, *11;* French Connection, The, *60*

Egan, Richard: Amsterdam Kill, The, *7;* Love Me Tender, *910;* Mission to Glory, *536*

Eggar, Samantha: Battle Force, *12;* Brood, The, *657;* Collector, The, *663;* Curtains, *668;* Doctor Dolittle, *180;* Doctor in Distress, *252;* Exterminator, The, *50;* Molly Maguires, The, *537;* Uncanny, The, *760;* Why Shoot the Teacher?, *633*

Egger, Jose: For a Few Dollars More, *897*

Egyves, Michael: Bay Boy, The, *406*

Eichhorn, Lisa: Cutter's Way, *441;* Wild Rose, *634*

Eikenberry, Jill: Manhattan Project, The, *714*

Eilbacher, Lisa: Beverly Hills Cop, *228;* Ten to Midnight, *147*

Eilber, Janet: Hard to Hold, *786;* Romantic Comedy, *343;* Whose Life Is It, Anyway?, *633*

Eisenberg, Avner: Jewel of the Nile, The, *79*

Eisenmann, Ike: Escape to Witch Mountain, *181;* Return From Witch Mountain, *201;* La Dolce Vita, *511;* S.H.E., *134*

Ekland, Britt: After the Fox, *216;* Bobo, The, *231;* Great Wallendas, The, *478;* Man With the Golden Gun, The, *96;* Monster Club, The, *717;* Night They Raided Minsky's, The, *319;* Stiletto, *140;* Wicker Man, The, *765*

Eklund, Bengt: Port of Call, *565*

Ek, Anders: Sawdust and Tinsel, *589*

Elam, Jack: Apple Dumpling Gang Rides Again, The, *171;* Appointment in Honduras, *9;* Cattle Queen of Montana, *888;* Creature from Black Lake, *665;* Hawmps!, *277;* Man without a Star, *913;* Night of the Grizzly, The, *918;* Once upon a Time in the West, *919;* Rancho Notorious, *923;* Rare Breed, The, *924;* Rio Lobo, *927;* Sacred Ground, *929;* Support Your Local Sheriff!, *936*

Elcar, Dana: Blue Skies Again, *416;* Sting, The, *144;* St. Ives, *126*

Eldredge, George: Corpse Vanishes, The, *664*

Eldredge, John: Song of Nevada, *933*

Elfman, Marie-Pascale: Forbidden Zone, *838*

Elg, Taina: Great Wallendas, The, *478;* Les Girls, *792*

Elian, Yona: Last Winter, The, *515*

Elizondo, Hector: American Gigolo, *396;* Cuba, *37;* Dain Curse, The, *37;* Flamingo Kid, The, *261;* Nothing In Common, *547;* Young Doctors in Love, *385*

Elkenberry, Jill: Hide in Plain Sight, *487*

Ellenstein, Peter: Weekend Pass, *378*

Elliman, Yvonne: Jesus Christ Superstar, *789*

Ellington, Duke and His Orchestra: Check and Double Check, *242*

Elliot, Chris: Manhunter, *97*

Elliot, Denholm: Room With a View, A (1987 Release), *584*

Elliot, James: Summer City, *143*

Elliot, Jane: Change of Habit, *430*

Elliot, Robert: Devil's Playground, *893*

Elliot, Shawn: Crossover Dreams, *775*

Elliot, Tim: UTU, *157*

Elliott, Denholm: Apprenticeship of Duddy Kravitz, The, *401;* Brimstone and Treacle, *657;* Cuba, *37;* House That Dripped Blood, The, *701;* Missionary, The, *310;* Private Function, A, *335;* Raiders of the Lost Ark, *858;* Robin and Marian, *123;* Rude Awakening, *738;* Saint Jack, *587;* To the Devil, a Daughter, *757;* Vault of Horror, *761;* Wicked Lady, The, *163*

Elliott, Ross: Indestructible Man, *705*

Elliott, Sam: Frogs, *691;* Legacy, The, *711;* Lifeguard, *518;* Mask, *530;* Murder in Texas, *719;* Sacketts, The, *928;* Wild Times, *945*

Elliott, Stephen: Arthur, *220;* Roadhouse 66, *122*

Elliott, William: Boots and Saddles, *885;* Hellfire, *902*

Ellison, James: I Walked with a Zombie, *704*

Ellis, Christopher: Nightcomers, The, *721*

Ellis, Patricia: Block-Heads, *230*

Ellis, Robin: Curse of King Tut's Tomb, The, *667*

Elphick, Michael: Lion and the Hawk, The, *89;* Privates on Parade, *336*

Elross, Bob: Tell Me A Riddle, *612*

Elsom, Isobel: Love from a Stranger, *713;* Love is a Many-Splendored Thing, *523;* Monsieur Verdoux, *313*

Ely, Ron: Doc Savage...The Man of Bronze, *830;* Night of the Grizzly, The, *918*

Emerton, Roy: Dr. Syn, *45*

Emery, Gilbert: Brighton Strangler, The, *657*

Emery, John: Here Comes Mr. Jordan, *279;* Rocketship X-M, *860;* Spellbound, *746*

Emge, David: Dawn of the Dead, *670*

Emhardt, Robert: 3:10 to Yuma, *939;* Mooncussers, *193*

Emil, Michael: Can She Bake a Cherry Pie?, *238;* Tracks, *621*

Emmanuel, Takis: Caddie, *423*

Emmett, Fern: Melody Trail, *915;* Assassin of Youth (aka Marijuana), *402*

Emmich, Cliff: Payday, *560*

Emo, Maria: Hitler, *488*

Encinias, Alicia: Bees, The, *649*

Engel, Tina: Boat Is Full, The, *416*

Engel, Georgia: Care Bears Movie, The, (voice) *175*

English, Cameron: Chorus Line, A, *774*

Ennis, Ethel: Mad Monster Party, *191*

Ergun, Halil: Yol, *639*

Erickson, John: House of the Dead, *700*

Erickson, Krista: Jekyll & Hyde—Together Again, *289*

Erickson, Leif: Abbott and Costello Meet Captain Kidd, *214;* Abduction, *387;* Invaders From Mars (Original), *844;* Roustabout, *800;* Strait-Jacket, *748;* Wild Times, *945*

Erickson, Lisa: Power, The, *730*

Ericson, Devon: Can You Hear The Laughter? The Story of Freddie Prinze, *425*

Errol, Leon: Never Give a Sucker an Even Break, *318*

Erwin, Bill: Somewhere in time, *863*

Erwin, Stuart: Misadventures of Merlin Jones, The, *192;* Palooka, *556*

Esmond, Carl: Smash-up: The Story of a Woman, *595*

Esmond, Charles: Little Men, *519*

Esposti, Piera Degli: Joke of Destiny, *290*

Estelita: Jesse James Meets Frankenstein's Daughter, *708*

Estevez, Emilio: Breakfast Club, The, *233;* Maximum Overdrive, *716;* Nightmares, *722;* Outsiders, The, *555;* Repo Man, *338;* St. Elmo's Fire, *586;* Tex, *614;* That Was Then... This is Now, *615*

Estrada, Erik: Fire!, *685;* New Centurions, The, *543*

Eustache, Jean: American Friend, The, *396*

Evans, Angelo: Angelo My Love, *399*

Evans, Art: Jo Jo Dancer, Your Life Is Calling, *502*

Evans, Barry: Die Screaming, Marianne, *675*

Evans, Dale: Bells of Coronado, *881;* Down Dakota Way, *894;* Golden Stallion, The, *898;* My Pal Trigger, *916;* Song of Nevada, *933;* Susanna Pass, *936;* T Trigger, Jr., *940;* Twilight in the Sierras, *941;* War of the Wildcats, *943;* Yellow Rose of Texas, *946*

Evans, Douglas: Dangerous Venture, *891;* Golden Stallion, The, *898*

Evans, Edith: Nasty Habits, *317;* Scrooge, *801;* Tom Jones, *369*

Evans, Gene: Cattle Queen of Montana, *888;* Fire!, *685;* Gentle Savage, *898;* Magic of Lassie, The, *191;* Operation Petticoat, *325;* Wild Times, *945*

Evans, Joan: Outcast, The, *920*

Evans, Linda: Beach Blanket Bingo, *770;* Those Calloways, *209*

Evans, Mary Beth: Lovelines, *302*

Evans, Maurice: Beneath the Planet of the Apes, *820;* Planet of the Apes, *856;* Rosemary's Baby, *737;* Terror in the Wax Museum, *753*

Evans, Michael: Angelo My Love, *399*

Evans, Muriel: New Frontier, *917*

Evans, Rex: Pursuit to Algiers, *117*

Evans, Robin: One Dark Night, *726*

Evans, Tenniel: Adventures of Sherlock Holmes: The Dancing Men, *3*

Evelyn, Judith: Rear Window, *734*

Everett, Chad: Intruder Within, The, *844;* Johnny Tiger, *503*

Everett, Kenny: Bloodbath at the House of Death, *230*

Everett, Rupert: Another Country, *400;* Dance With a Stranger, *443*

Evers, Herb: Brain That Wouldn't Die, The, *821*

Evers, Jason: Fer-de-Lance, *684*

Evison, Pat: Starstruck, *805;* Tim, *618*

Ewart, John: Island Trader, *78;* Sunday Too Far Away, *608*

Ewell, Tom: Adam's Rib, *215;* Seven Year Itch, The, *350*

Ewing, Barbara: Torture Garden, *758*

Excell, Matthew: Save The Lady, *203*

Eythe, William: Colonel Effingham's Raid, *246*

Fabares, Shelley: Brian's Song, *420*

Faber, Peter: Soldier of Orange, *137*

Fabiani, Joel: Reuben, Reuben, *339*

Fabian: Five Weeks in a Balloon, *56;* North to Alaska, *918*

Fabian, Françoise: Happy New Year (La Bonne Annee), *68;* Fernandel The Dressmaker, *259;* My Night At Maud's, *541*

Fabray, Nanette: Band Wagon, The, *769;* Harper Valley P.T.A., *276*

Fabregas, Manolo: Two Mules for Sister Sara, *942*

Fabrizi, Aldo: Open City, *553*

Fahey, Jeff: Psycho III, *731*

Fairbanks Jr., Douglas: Catherine the Great, *428;* Corsican Brothers, The, *35;* Ghost Story, *693;* Gunga Din, *67;* Little Caesar, *90;* Sinbad the Sailor, *136*

Fairbanks Sr., Douglas: Great Chase, The, *65;* Mr. Robinson Crusoe, *101;* Private Life of Don Juan, The, *568;* Reaching for the Moon, *337;* Thief of Baghdad, The, *871*

Fairchild, Morgan: Seduction, The, *741*

Faire, Virginia Brown: West of the Divide, *944*

Faison, Frankie: Exterminator 2, The, *51*

Faith, Adam: McVicar, *532*

Fajardo, Eduardo: Shark Hunter, The, *133*

Falana, Lola: Liberation of L. B. Jones, The, *517*

Falconetti, Geral: Claire's Knee, *243*

Falconetti, Maria: Passion of Joan of Arc, The, *559*

Falk, Peter: All the Marbles, *217;* Big Trouble, *228;* Brinks Job, The, *234;* Great Muppet Caper, The, *183;* Great Race, The, *273;* In-Laws, The, *286;* It's a Mad Mad Mad Mad World, *288;* Luv, *304;* Mikey and Nicky, *309;* Murder by Death, *315*

Fallender, Deborah: Jabberwocky, *289*

Falt, Dennis Lee: Slithis, *744*

Faraldo, Daniel: Trenchcoat, 372

Farentino, James: Dead and Buried, 670

Fargas, Antonio: Pretty Baby, 566; Putney Swope, 337; Streetwalkin', 605

Faria, Betty: Bye Bye Brazil, 422

Farina, Dennis: Manhunter, 97

Farley, Jim: General, The, 266

Farmer, Frances: South of Pago Pago, 138

Farnen, Ellen: Umbrellas of Cherbourg, The, 685

Farnsworth, Richard: Comes a Horseman, 889; Grey Fox, The, 899; Independence Day, 494; Into the Night, 496; Natural, The, 542; Resurrection, 858; Ruckus, 124; Sylvester, 610; Tom Horn, 939

Farnum, William: Git Along, Little Dogies, 898; Mr. Robinson Crusoe, 101; Painted Desert, The, 921; Santa Fe Stampede, 929; Shine On Harvest Moon, 931; South of the Border, 934; Trail of Robin Hood, 939

Farrar, David: Black Narcissus, 413; Pearl of the South Pacific, 560

Farrell, Glenda: Hollywood Hotel, 787; I Am a Fugitive from a Chain Gang, 490

Farrell, Nick: Chariots of Fire, 431

Farrell, Sharon: Fifth Floor, The, 684; It's Alive!, 707; Reivers, The, 338

Farrell, Timothy: Glen or Glenda, 473

Farrow, Mia: Avalanche, 10; Broadway Danny Rose, 235; Death on the Nile, 40; Great Gatsby, The, 477; Hannah and Her Sisters, 275; High Heels, 280; Hurricane, 76; Midsummer Night's Sex Comedy, A, 309; Purple Rose of Cairo, The, 337; Rosemary's Baby, 737; See No Evil, 741; Supergirl, 868; Zelig, 385

Farrow, Tisa: Fingers, 464; Search and Destroy, 130; Some Call It Loving, 597; Zombie, 766

Farr, David: Escape to Burma, 459

Farr, Felicia: 3:10 to Yuma, 939; Charley Varrick, 30; Kotch, 294

Farr, Jamie: M*A*S*H: Goodbye Farewell, Amen, 307; Who's Minding the Mint?, 381

Fassbinder, Rainer Werner: Querelle, 572

Faulkner, Graham: Brother Sun Sister Moon, 420

Faulkner, Max: Adventures of Sherlock Holmes: A Scandal in Bohemia, 2

Faulkner, Sally: Alien Prey, 644

Faulkner, Stephanie: Bus Is Coming, The, 422

Faulks, Barton: Future-Kill, 692

Faversham, William: Singing Buckaroo, 932

Fawcett, Farrah: Burning Bed, The, 421; Cannonball Run, 237; Extremities, 460; Murder in Texas, 719; Red Light Sting, The, Saturn 3, 861; Sunburn, 143

Fawcett, George: True Heart Susie, 623

Fawcett, William: Hills of Utah, The, 903

Faye, Alice: Magic of Lassie, The, 191

Faye, Frances: Pretty Baby, 566

Faylen, Frank: Gunfight at the O.K. Corral, 900; Lost Weekend, The, 523; Monkey's Uncle, The, 192; Perils of Pauline, the, 329; Riot in Cell Block 11, 581; Riot in Cell Block Eleven, 122

Fay, Frank: Nothing Sacred, 321; They Knew What They Wanted, 616

Fazenda, Louise: Keystone Comedies, Vol. 1, 292

Feeney, Shirley Jo: Echo Park, 455

Feher, Gabor: Revolt of Job, The, 579

Fehmiu, Bekim: Permission to Kill, 114

Feinstein, Alan: Two Worlds of Jennie Logan, The, 874

Feist, Francis: Carnival of Souls, 659

Feist, Harry: Open City, 553

Feldman, Corey: Friday the 13th—The Final Chapter, 690; Goonies, The, 63; Stand By Me, 600

Feldman, Marty: Adventures of Sherlock Holmes' Smarter Brother, The, 215; Last Remake of Beau Geste, The, 297; Sex With a Smile, 350; Silent Movie, 351; Slapstick of Another Kind, 354; Yellowbeard, 385; Young Frankenstein, 385

Feldon, Barbara: No Deposit, No Return, 195

Feldshuh, Tovah: Amazing Howard Hughes, The, 395; Brewster's Millions (1985), 235; Cheaper to Keep Her, 242; Idolmaker, The, 788

Feld, Fritz: World's Greatest Lover, The, 384

Fellowes, Julian: Baby . . . Secret of the Lost Legend, 818

Fellows, Edith: Heart of the Rio Grande, 901

Fell, Norman: Boatniks, The, 174; Bullitt, 26; On the Right Track, 197; Paternity, 328; Stone Killer, The, 141; Transylvania 6-5000, 371

Fenech, Edwise: Sex With a Smile, 350

Fenton, Frank: Golden Stallion, The, 898; T Trigger, Jr., 940

Ferguson, Al: Desert Trail, 893

Ferguson, Frank: Caught, 439

Ferlinghetti, Lawrence: Kerouac, 506; Kerouac, 506

Fernandez, Abel: Untouchables: Alcatraz Express, The, 157; Untouchables: Scarface Mob, The, 157

Fernandez, Emilio: Wild Bunch, The, 945

Fernandez, Wilhemenia Wiggins: Diva, 675

Ferrache, Rachid: My Other Husband, 541

Ferrell, Conchata: Heartland, 902

Ferrero, Martin: Miami Vice, 98

Ferrer, José: Being, The, 650; Big Brawl, The, 15; Big Bus, The, 229; Bloodtide, 654; Caine Mutiny, The, 423; Cyrano De Bergerac, 441; Enter Laughing, 256; Evil That Men Do, The, 50; Fifth Musketeer, The, 53; Greatest Story Ever Told, The, 478; Midsummer Night's Sex Comedy, A, 309; Miss

Sadie Thompson, 535; Pleasure Palace, 564; Sentinel, The, 742; Ship of Fools, 592; Joan of Arc, 502

Ferrer, Mel: Brannigan, 23; Eaten Alive, 680; Fall of the Roman Empire, The, 462; Fifth Floor, The, 684; Knights of the Round Table, 85; Norseman, The, 108; Rancho Notorious, 923; War and Peace, 630

Ferret, Eve: Haunted Honeymoon, 277

Ferrier, Noel: Year of Living Dangerously, The, 165

Ferrigno, Lou: Adventures of Hercules, The, 815; Hercules, 841; Incredible Hulk, The, 843; Pumping Iron, 570

Ferrigno, Matty: Pumping Iron, 570

Ferrigno, Victoria: Pumping Iron, 570

Ferro, Turi: Malicious, 305

Ferry, David: High-Ballin', 71

Ferzetti, Gabriele: Night Porter, The, 545

Fetchit, Stepin: Judge Priest, 504

Feuer, Debra: To Live and Die in L.A., 153

Fever, Kitie: Grace Quigley, 271

Fiedler, Bea: Private Popsicle, 335

Fiedler, John: 12 Angry Men, 624; Odd Couple, The, 322; Raisin in the Sun, A, 575

Fields, Lew: Story of Vernon and Irene Castle, The, 806

Fields, Norman: Octaman, 725

Fields, Tony: Chorus Line, A, 774

Fields, W. C.: Bank Dick, The, 224; David Copperfield, 445; My Little Chickadee, 316; Never Give a Sucker an Even Break, 318; It's a Gift, 288

Field, Betty: Bus Stop, 236; Coogan's Bluff, 34; King's Row, 508; Southerner, The, 598

Field, Nick: Adventures of Sherlock Holmes: The Greek Interpreter, 4

Field, Sally: Absence of Malice, 388; Back Roads, 404; Beyond the Poseidon Adventure, 14; End, The, 255; Heroes, 486; Hooper, 283; Kiss Me Goodbye, 294; Murphy's Romance, 539; Norma Rae, 546; Places in the Heart, 563; Smokey and the Bandit, 354; Stay Hungry, 602; Sybil, 610

Field, Shirley Anne: Alfie, 216; My Beautiful Laundrette, 540; War Lover, The, 630

Field, Virginia: Mr. Moto's Last Warning, 101

Filer, Tom: Ride in the Whirlwind, 925

Fimple, Dennis: Creature from Black Lake, 665

Finch, Jon: Breaking Glass, 772; Frenzy, 689; Last Days of Man on Earth, The, 848; Macbeth, 525; Witching Time, 765

Finch, Peter: Flight of the Phoenix, The, 58; Kidnapped, 82; Network, 543; Sunday, Bloody Sunday, 608

Fine, Larry: Three Stooges, The (Volumes1–10), 368

Finlayson, James: Block-Heads, 230; Chump at Oxford, A, 243; Our Relations, 325

Finlay, Frank: Enigma, 49; Four Musketeers, The, 60; Gumshoe, 274; Lifeforce, 849; Molly Maguires, The, 537; Return of the Soldier, The, 579; Wild Geese, The, 163

Finley, William: Phantom of the Paradise, 798

Finnegan, John: School Spirit, 346

Finneu, William: Simon, 352

Finney, Albert: Annie, 769; Dresser, The, 454; Duellists, The, 46; Gumshoe, 274; Looker, 850; Murder on the Orient Express, 104; Scrooge, 801; Shoot the Moon, 592; Tom Jones, 369; Under the Volcano, 626; Wolfen, 766

Finney, Shirley Jo: Wilma, 635

Finschi, Lorenzo: His Name Was King, 903

Fiorentino, Linda: After Hours, 215; Gotcha!, 64; Vision Quest, 628

Fiore, Bill: Swimmer, The, 609

Fiore, Elena: Seduction of Mimi, The, 348

Firestone, Eddie: Duel, 679

Firth, Colin: Another Country, 400

Firth, Peter: Equus, 458; Joseph Andrews, 290; King Arthur, The Young Warlord, 84; Lifeforce, 849; Tess, 613

Fisher, Carrie: Blues Brothers, The, 231; Empire Strikes Back, The, 833; Garbo Talks, 265; Hannah and Her Sisters, 275; Hollywood Vice Squad, 74; Man With One Red Shoe, The, 306; Return of the Jedi, 859; Shampoo, 591; Star Wars, 867; Thumbelina, 209; Under the Rainbow, 374

Fisher, Cindy: Liar's Moon, 517

Fishman, Jeff: Hot Moves, 283

Fitzgerald, Barry: And Then There Were None, 398; Dawn Patrol, The, 39; Going My Way, 474; Long Voyage Home, The, 520; None But the Lonely Heart, 546; Quiet Man, The, 117; Union Station, 760

Fitzgerald, Geraldine: Dark Victory, 445; Easy Money, 254; Harry and Tonto, 483; Last American Hero, The, 86; Mill On the Floss, The, 534; Pawnbroker, The, 560; Poltergeist II: The Otherside, 729; Watch on the Rhine, 630

Fitzpatrick, Christian: Santa Claus—The Movie, 202

Fix, Paul: Desert Trail, 893; Hellfire, 902; Last Mile, The, 514; Sons of Katie Elder, The, 934

Flaherty, Joe: Going Berserk, 269; One Crazy Summer, 324; (Sesame Street Presents) Follow That Bird, 204

Flamingos, The: Rock, Rock, Rock, 800

Flanagan, Fionnuala: James Joyce's Women, 500; Youngblood, 641

Flanders, Ed: Amazing Howard Hughes, The, 395; MacArthur, 525; Ninth Configuration, The, 546; Pursuit of D. B. Cooper, 116; Salem's Lot, 739

Flannery, Anne: Heart of the Stag, 484

Flavin, James: Robin Hood of Texas, *927*

Fleetwood, Susan: Heat and Dust, *485*

Fleming, Ian: Silver Blaze, *136*

Fleming, Rhonda: Abilene Town, *878;* Bullwhip, *887;* Gunfight at the O.K. Corral, *900;* Out of the Past, *112;* Pony Express, *922;* Slightly Scarlet, *595;* Spellbound, *746;* Tennessee's Partner, *937*

Flemyng, Robert: Young Winston, *641*

Fletcher, Bramwell: Svengali, *750*

Fletcher, Jack: Rumpelstiltskin, *202*

Fletcher, Louise: Brainstorm, *821;* Exorcist II: The Heretic, *681;* Invaders from Mars (Remake), *844;* One Flew over the Cuckoo's Nest, *551;* Strange Behavior, *748;* Strange Invaders, *867*

Flint, Sam: Man of the Frontier, (Red River Valley), *912;* New Frontier, *917;* Spy Smasher, *139;* Winds of the Wasteland, *945*

Flippen, Jay C.: Carnival Story, *426;* Cat Ballou, *888;* Elfego Baca: Six Gun Law, *895;* Flying Leathernecks, The, *58;* Thunder Bay, *151;* Wild One, The, *164*

Flohe, Charles: Rappin', *799*

Flood, Joe: Blue Yonder, The, *173;* Student Bodies, *749*

Flory, Med: Hearse, The, *697*

Flower, George (Buck): Adventures of the Wilderness Family, *170;* Wilderness Family, Part 2, The, *212;* Across the Great Divide, *169*

Floyd, Charles R.: P.O.W.: The Escape, *112*

Fluegel, Darlanne: Running Scared (1986), *125;* To Live and Die in L.A., *153*

Flynn, Errol: Adventures of Captain Fabian, *2;* Adventures of Robin Hood, The, *2;* Captain Blood, *27;* Charge of the Light Brigade, The, *30;* Dawn Patrol, The, *39;* Dodge City, *894;* Gentleman Jim, *471;* Hollywood Outtakes, *282;* Kim, *83;* Northern Pursuit, *108;* Prince and the Pauper, The (Original), *199;* Private Lives of Elizabeth and Essex, The, *569;* Santa Fe Trail, *929;* Sea Hawk, The, *130;* Thank Your Lucky Stars, *807;* They Died with their Boots On, *938*

Flynn, Joe: Barefoot Executive, The, *172;* Computer Wore Tennis Shoes, The, *178;* Gentle Savage, *898;* Love Bug, The, *190;* Lover Come Back, *303;* Million Dollar Duck, The, *192;* Now You See Him, Now You Don't, *196*

Focas, Spiros: Jewel of the Nile, The, *79*

Foch, Nina: American in Paris, An, *769;* Return of the Vampire, The, *735;* Song to Remember, A, *804*

Foley, Patty: In the Shadow of Kilimanjaro, *704*

Follows, Megan: Silver Bullet, *743*

Folse, Gabriel: Future-Kill, *692*

Folsom, Megan: Heartland, *902*

Fondacaro, Phil: Troll, *873*

Fonda, Henry: 12 Angry Men, *624;* Battle Force, *12;* Battle of the Bulge, *13;* Boston Strangler, The, *656;* Failsafe, *461;* Fort Apache, *897;* Grapes of Wrath, The, *477;* Great Smokey Roadblock, The, *65;* How the West Was Won, *904;* Jesse James, *905;* Jezebel, *501;* Lady Eve, The, *295;* Longest Day, The, *92;* Madigan, *94;* Mad Miss Manton, The, *304;* Meteor, *852;* Midway, *99;* Mr. Roberts, *311;* My Darling Clementine, *916;* Once upon a Time in the West, *919;* On Golden Pond, *551;* Ox-Bow Incident, The, *921;* Return of Frank James, The, *925;* Rollercoaster, *737;* Sometimes a Great Notion, *597;* Swarm, The, *751;* Tentacles, *753;* There Was a Crooked Man, *938;* War and Peace, *630;* Warlock, *944;* Wrong Man, The, *766;* You Only Live Once, *640*

Fonda, Jane: Agnes of God, *390;* Barbarella, *819;* Barefoot in the Park, *224;* California Suite, *237;* Cat Ballou, *888;* Chase, The, *431;* China Syndrome, The, *432;* Comes a Horseman, *889;* Coming Home, *437;* Doll's House, A, *453;* Electric Horseman, The, *456;* Fun with Dick and Jane, *265;* Joy House, *504;* Julia, *505;* Klute, *509;* Nine to Five, *319;* On Golden Pond, *551;* Rollover, *583;* Steelyard Blues, *359;* They Shoot Horses, Don't They?, *616*

Fonda, Peter: Certain Fury, *29;* Easy Rider, *455;* Futureworld, *838;* High-Ballin', *71;* Jungle Heat, *80;* Lilith, *518;* Outlaw Blues, *325;* Race with the Devil, *732;* Spasms, *746;* Split Image, *599;* Tammy and the Doctor, *611;* Trip, The, *622;* Wild Angels, The, *163*

Fong, Benson: First Yank into Tokyo, *55;* Flower Drum Song, *780;* Girls! Girls! Girls!, *783;* Jinxed, *289*

Fong, Leo: Kill Point, *83*

Fontaine, Joan: Beyond A Reasonable Doubt, *409;* Damsel in Distress, A, *776;* Gunga Din, *67;* Ivanhoe, *78;* Rebecca, *576;* Suspicion, *750;* Users, The, *627;* Voyage to the Bottom of the Sea, *874;* Women, The, *383*

Foody, Ralph: Code of Silence, *33*

Foo, Lee Tung: Strange Gamble, *935*

Foran, Dick: Atomic Submarine, The, *818;* My Little Chickadee, *316;* Petrified Forest, The, *562;* Private Buckaroo, *799*

Forbes, Francine: Splatter University, *747*

Forbes, Ralph: Christopher Strong, *433;* Daniel Boone, *891*

Ford, Anitra: Invasion of the Bee Girls, *844*

Ford, Francis: Ox-Bow Incident, The, *921*

Ford, Glenn: 3:10 to Yuma, *939;* Americano, The, *879;* Appointment in Honduras, *9;* Big Heat, The, *15;* Experiment in Terror, *681;* Four Horsemen of the Apocalypse, *60;* Gilda, *472;* Happy Birthday to Me, *696;* Pocketful of Miracles, *564;* Sacketts, The, *928;* Santee, *929;* Superman, *868;* Texas, *937*

Ford, Harrison: American Graffiti, 218; Apocalypse Now, 9; Blade Runner, 821; Conversation, The, 438; Empire Strikes Back, The, 833; Force Ten from Navarone, 59; Frisco Kid, The, 897; Hanover Street, 481; Heroes, 486; Indiana Jones and the Temple of Doom, 843; Raiders of the Lost Ark, 858; Return of the Jedi, 859; Star Wars, 867; Witness, 165

Ford, Paul: Music Man, The, 794; Russians Are Coming, the Russians Are Coming, The, 344

Ford, Ross: Blue Canadian Rockies, 884

Ford, Seamus: Quackser Fortune Has a Cousin in the Bronx, 571

Ford, Wallace: Ape Man, The, 646; Blood on the Sun, 19; Freaks, 689; Lost Patrol, The, 93; Maverick Queen, The, 914; Set-Up, The, 591; Spellbound, 746

Foree, Ken: Dawn of the Dead, 670

Foreman, Deborah: April Fool's Day, 646; My Chauffeur, 316; Valley Girl, 376

Forest, Michael: Message, The (Mohammad, Messenger of God), 533

Forman, Debbie: Summer City, 143

Forman, Milos: Heartburn, 277

Foronjy, Richard: Prince of the City, 568

Forrest, Brett: Adventures of Sherlock Holmes: The Resident Patient, 5

Forrest, Christine: Martin, 715

Forrest, Frederic: Don is Dead, The, 44; Hammett, 68; It Lives Again, 706; One from the Heart, 797; Permission to Kill, 114; Rose, The, 800; Stone Boy, The, 603; When the Legends Die, 945

Forrest, Mike: Shark Hunter, The, 133

Forrest, Steve: Deerslayer, The, 893; Flaming Star, 896; Hatfields and the McCoys, The, 901; Heller in Pink Tights, 902; Mommie Dearest, 537; Spies Like Us, 356

Forrest, William: Masked Marvel, The, 97

Forster, Robert: Alligator, 644; Avalanche, 10; Black Hole, The, 821; Death Squad, The, 40; Delta Force, The, 41; Don is Dead, The, 44; Medium Cool, 532; Reflections in a Golden Eye, 578

Forster, Rudolph: Threepenny Opera, The, 809

Forsythe, Drew: Test of Love, A, 613

Forsythe, John: And Justice for All, 397; Cruise into Terror, 667; In Cold Blood, 493; Madame X, 526; Terror on the 40th Floor, 753; Topaz, 757; Trouble With Harry, The, 372

Forsythe, Stephen: Hatchet for the Honeymoon, 696

Forte, Fabian: Get Crazy, 266; Little Laura and Big John, 90

Fortune, John: Bloodbath at the House of Death, 230

Fosse, Bob: Kiss Me Kate, 790

Fossey, Brigette: La Boum, 511; Chanel Solitaire, 430; Enigma, 49; Forbidden Games, 467; Going Places, 270; Honor Among Thieves, 74

Fosse, Nicole: Chorus Line, A, 774

Foster, Barry: Frenzy, 689

Foster, Dianne: Kentuckian, The, 906

Foster, Jodie: Alice Doesn't Live Here Anymore, 392; Bugsy Malone, 175; Candleshoe, 175; Carny, 426; Foxes, 469; Freaky Friday, 182; Hotel New Hampshire, The, 489; Little Girl Who Lives Down the Lane, The, 712; Taxi Driver, 612

Foster, Julia: Alfie, 216

Foster, Kimberly: One Crazy Summer, 324

Foster, Meg: Carny, 426; Different Story, A, 451; Emerald Forest, The, 48; Osterman Weekend, The, 111; Ticket to Heaven, 618

Foster, Preston: American Empire, 879; Big Cat, The, 15; I Am a Fugitive from a Chain Gang, 490; Informer, The, 495; Last Days of Pompeii, The, 513; Last Mile, The, 514; Sea Devils, 129

Foulger, Byron: Ridin' on a Rainbow, 926

Foundas, George: Zorba the Greek, 642

Four, Maple City: Git Along, Little Dogies, 898

Fowley, Douglas: Homebodies, 698; Kansas Pacific, 906; Susanna Pass, 936

Fowle, Susannah: Getting of Wisdom, The, 471

Foxworth, Robert: Black Marble, The, 413; Frankenstein (Remake), 688; Prophecy, 730

Foxx, Elizabeth: School Spirit, 346

Fox, Bernard: House of the Dead, 700; Private Eyes, The, 335

Fox, Edward: Big Sleep, The, 16; Bounty, The, 23; Cat and The Canary, The, 660; Day of the Jackal, The, 39; Dresser, The, 454; Duellists, The, 46; Force Ten from Navarone, 59; Gandhi, 471; Mirror Crack'd, The, 99; Shooting Party, The, 592; Wild Geese II, 163

Fox, Huckleberry: Blue Yonder, The, 173; Misunderstood, 537

Fox, James: Absolute Beginners, 768; Chase, The, 431; Greystoke: The Legend of Tarzan, Lord of the Apes, 67; King Rat, 508; Performance, 561; Servant, The, 590

Fox, Michael J.: Back to the Future, 819; High School, USA, 280; Teen Wolf, 751

Fox, Peter: Minor Miracle, A, 192

Fox, Sidney: Call It Murder, 424

Foy Jr., Eddie: Gidget Goes Hawaiian, 267

Frampton, Peter: Sgt. Pepper's Lonely Hearts Club Band, 802

Francen, Victor: Tuttles of Tahiti, The, 373

Franciosa, Anthony: Across 110th Street, 2; Death Wish II, 40; Drowning Pool, The, 45; Face in the Crowd, A, 461; Firepower, 55; Rio Conchos, 927; Summer Heat, 607

Franciscus, James: Amazing Dobermans, *171;* Beneath the Planet of the Apes, *820;* Good Guys Wear Black, *63;* Greek Tycoon, The, *479;* Man Inside, The, *95;* Marooned, *851;* Nightkill, *107;* When Time Ran Out!, *764*

Francis, Anne: Battle Cry, *12;* Forbidden Planet, *838;* Pancho Villa, *922*

Francis, Arlene: One, Two, Three, *324*

Francis, Bev: Pumping Iron II: The Women, *570*

Francis, Connie: Where the Boys Are, *380*

Francis, Ivor: House of the Dead, *700;* Steagle, The, *359*

Francis, Jan: Champions, *430;* Dracula (Remake), *678*

Francis, Kay: In 「 ～ e Only, *493;* Little Men, *519*

Francis, Robert: Caine Mutiny, The, *423*

Francks, Don: Finian's Rainbow, *779;* Terminal Choice, *752*

Franken, Al: One More Saturday Night, *324*

Franken, Steve: Hardly Working, *276*

Frankham, David: Return of the Fly, The, *735*

Franklin, Diane: Better Off Dead, *228;* Last American Virgin, The, *296*

Franklin, Don: Fast Forward, *779*

Franklin, John: Children of the Corn, *662*

Franklin, Pamela: Food of the Gods, *838;* Legend of Hell House, The, *711;* Satan's School for Girls, *739;* Witching, The (Necromancy), *765*

Franks, Chloe: Littlest Horse Thieves, The, *190;* Who Slew Auntie Roo?, *764*

Frank, Ben: Death Wish II, *40;* Don't Answer the Phone, *677*

Frank, Gary: Enola Gay: The Men, the Mission, the Atomic Bomb, *458*

Franz, Arthur: Amazing Howard Hughes, The, *395;* Atomic Submarine, The, *818;* Hellcats of the Navy, *70;* Invaders From Mars (Original), *844;* Sands of Iwo Jima, *128*

Franz, Dennis: Blow Out, *654;* Psycho II, *731*

Fraser, Bill: Corn Is Green, The, *439*

Fraser, John: Partners in Crime—The Secret Adversary, *113;* Tunes of Glory, *624*

Fraser, Phyllis: Winds of the Wasteland, *945*

Fraser, Richard: Bedlam, *649*

Fraser, Robert: Trail Beyond, The, *939*

Fraser, Ronald: Flight of the Phoenix, The, *58*

Frawley, William: Fighting Seabees, The, *53;* Flame of the Barbary Coast, *56;* Monsieur Verdoux, *313;* Rancho Notorious, *923;* Something to Sing About, *803*

Frazee, Jane: Buck Privates, *235;* Grand Canyon Trail, *899;* Under California Stars, *942*

Frazer, Robert: Dawn on the Great Divide, *891;* White Zombie, *764*

Frazier, Sheila: Superfly, *143;* Three the Hard Way, *151*

Frederick, Lynne: Phase IV, *856;* Prisoner of Zenda, The, *334*

Frederick, Vicki: All the Marbles, *217;* Body Rock, *771;* Chorus Line, A, *774*

Freed, Alan: Rock, Rock, Rock, *800*

Freed, Bert: Billy Jack, *17*

Freeman, Joan: Friday the 13th—The Final Chapter, *690;* Mooncussers, *193*

Freeman, Kathleen: Nutty Professor, The, *321*

Freeman, Mona: Dear Wife, *249;* Heiress, The, *485*

Freeman, Morgan: That Was Then...This is Now, *615*

Freeman, Paul: Raiders of the Lost Ark, *858;* Sakharov, *587;* Sender, The, *742*

Freiss, Stephane: Vagabond, *627*

French, Bruce: Pipe Dreams, *563*

French, George: Tarzan of the Apes, *145*

French, Leigh: White Line Fever, *162*

Freshene, Mark: Zabriskie Point, *641*

Fresnay, Pierre: Marius, *529*

Fresson, Bernard: French Connection II, The, *469;* Hiroshima, Mon Amour, *488*

Frey, Leonard: Boys in the Band, The, *419;* Fiddler on the Roof, *779;* Where the Buffalo Roam, *381*

Frey, Sammy: Nea (A Young Emmanuelle), *542*

Friedkin, Joel: False Paradise, *896;* Strange Gamble, *935;* Unexpected Guest, *942*

Friedrich, John: Final Terror, The, *685;* Wanderers, The, *629*

Friesen, John: Why Shoot the Teacher?, *633*

Frijda, Nelly: Question of Silence, A, *572*

Frizell, Lou: Summer of '42, *608*

Frobe, Gert: Serpent's Egg, The, *590;* Ten Little Indians, *147;* Those Magnificent Men in their Flying Machines, *367*

Froelich, Gustav: Metropolis (musical version), *793;* Metropolis, *852*

Froling, Ewa: Fanny and Alexander, *463*

Frost, Terry: Valley of Fire, *942*

Froud, Toby: Labyrinth, *847*

Fröbe, Gert: Goldfinger, *63;* $ (Dollars), *44*

Frye, Dwight: Bride of Frankenstein, *657;* Dead Men Walk, *670;* Dracula (Original), *678*

Frye, Virgil: Running Hot, *586*

Fujiki, Yu: Samurai Trilogy, The, *127*

Fujioka, John: American Ninja, *7;* Private Eyes, The, *335*

Fujiwara, Kamatari: Hidden Fortress, The, *71*

Fullerton, Fiona: Alice's Adventures in Wonderland, *171*

Fuller, Brook: When Wolves Cry, *632*

Fuller, Dolores: Glen or Glenda, *473*

Fuller, Francis: Homebodies, *698*

Fuller, Penny: Cat on a Hot Tin Roof (Remake), 428; Piano for Mrs. Cimino, A, 562

Fuller, Robert: Brain from Planet Arous, The, 821

Fuller, Toria: Partners in Crime—The Secret Adversary, 113

Fulton, Todd: Escapes, 835

Fung, Willie: Git Along, Little Dogies, 898; Red Dust, 119; Red Dust, 577

Funicello, Annette: Beach Blanket Bingo, 770; Bikini Beach, 771; Elfego Baca: Six Gun Law, 895; Horsemasters, 185; How to Stuff a Wild Bikini, 788; Misadventures of Merlin Jones, The, 192; Monkey's Uncle, The, 192; Shaggy Dog, The, 204

Funt, Allen: What Do You Say to a Naked Lady?, 379

Furey, John: Friday the 13th, Part II, 690

Furneaux, Yvonne: Mummy, The (remake), 719

Furness, Betty: Swing Time, 806

Furst, Stephen: Class Reunion, 244; Midnight Madness, 309; Silent Rage, 136; Take Down, 363; Unseen, The, 760; Up the Creek, 375

Fyodora, Victoria: Target, 145

Gabel, Martin: First Deadly Sin, The, 55; Marnie, 715; There Was a Crooked Man, 938

Gabin, Jean: Grand Illusion, 476; La Bete Humaine, 510; Le Jour Se Leve (DAYBREAK), 516; Pepe Le Moko, 560

Gable, Clark: China Seas, 30; Gone with the Wind, 475; Idiot's Delight, 492; It Happened One Night, 287; Misfits, The, 535; Mogambo, 102; Mutiny on the Bounty (Original), 105; No Man of Her Own, 320; Painted Desert, The, 921; Red Dust, 119; Red Dust, 577; Run Silent, Run Deep, 125; San Francisco, 588; Teacher's Pet, 364

Gabor, Eva: Gigi, 782

Gabor, Zsa Zsa: Touch of Evil, 758

Gage, Patricia: Rabid, 732

Gail, Max: D.C. Cab, 249; Heartbreakers, 484

Gaines, Boyd: Sure Thing, The, 361

Gaines, Leonard: Hardcore, 481

Gaines, Richard: Drum Beat, 894; Mr. Winkle Goes to War, 311

Gainsbourg, Serge: Je Vous Aime (I Love You All), 501

Galabru, Michel: La Cage Aux Folles III, The Wedding, 295; Subway, 142

Gale, David: Re-animator, 733

Gale, Ed: Howard the Duck, 842

Galff, Laszlo: Wagner, 811

Gallagher, Peter: Dreamchild, 831; Idolmaker, The, 788; Skag, 594; Summer Lovers, 607

Gallagher, Skeets: Bird of Paradise, 17

Galletti, Giovanna: Open City, 553

Galligan, Zach: Gremlins, 840

Gallo, Mario: Revenge of the Ninja, 121

Gambon, Michael: Turtle Diary, 373

Gammell, Robin: Circle of Two, 434

Gammon, James: Ballad of Gregorio Cortez, The, 881; Silver Bullet, 743

Gampu, Ken: King Solomon's Mines (1985), 84; Naked Prey, The, 105

Ganios, Tony: Porky's Revenge, 333; Wanderers, The, 629

Gannes, Gayle: Prey, The, 730

Ganzel, Teresa: Transylvania 6-5000, 371

Ganz, Bruno: American Friend, The, 396

Gaon, Yehoram: Operation Thunderbolt, 111

Garbani, Ivo: Morgan the Pirate, 103

Garber, Matthew: Gnome-Mobile, The, 182; Mary Poppins, 191

Garbo, Greta: Anna Christie, 399; Anna Karenina, 400; Camille, 425; Grand Hotel, 476; Ninotchka, 319

Garcia, Andy: 8 Million Ways to Die, 47

Garcia, David: Blue Canadian Rockies, 884

Garcia, Lea: Black Orpheus, 414

Garcia, Nicole: Beau Pere, 225; Peril, 561

Garcia-Ville, Luce: Last Year At Marienbad, 516

Garcin, Ginette: Cousin, Cousine, 248

Garcin, Henri: Woman Next Door, The, 638

Gardenia, Vincent: Bang the Drum Slowly, 405; Death Wish II, 40; Death Wish, 40; Firepower, 55; Heaven Can Wait, 278; Home Movies, 282; Last Flight of Noah's Ark, 188; Lucky Luciano, 93; Movers and Shakers, 315; Where's Poppa?, 381

Gardiner, Reginald: Damsel in Distress, A, 776

Gardner, Arthur: Assassin of Youth (aka Marijuana), 402

Gardner, Ava: 55 Days at Peking, 464; Bible, The, 410; Cassandra Crossing, The, 438; Earthquake, 46; Ghosts on the Loose, 267; Kidnapping of the President, The, 709; Killers, The, 83; Knights of the Round Table, 85; Life and Times of Judge Roy Bean, The, 909; Mogambo, 102; Night of the Iguana, The, 544; One Touch of Venus, 325; On the Beach, 854; Permission to Kill, 114; Priest of Love, 568; Sentinel, The, 742; Seven Days in May, 591; Show Boat, 802

Gardner, Gladis: Heart of the Rio Grande, 901

Gardner, Joan: Catherine the Great, 428; Dark Journey, 445; Private Life of Don Juan, The, 568

Garfield Jr., John: Golden Voyage of Sinbad, The, 839

Garfield, Allen: Black Stallion Returns, The, 173; Brinks Job, The, 234; Candidate, The, 425; Continental Divide, 247; Get Crazy, 266; One From the Heart, 797; Conversation, The,

438; Desert Bloom, *449;* Putney Swope, *337*
Stunt Man, The, *606*

Garfield, Frank: Night of the Zombies, *723*

Garfield, John: Air Force, *7;* Body and Soul (Original), *416;* Force of Evil, *467;* Juarez, *504;* Postman Always Rings Twice, The (Original), *565;* Thank Your Lucky Stars, *807;* They Made Me a Criminal, *616*

Garfunkel, Art: Carnal Knowledge, *426;* Catch-22, *239*

Gargan, Jack: On Top of Old Smoky, *919*

Gargan, William: Cheers for Miss Bishop, *432;* Rain, *574;* They Knew What They Wanted, *616;* You Only Live Once, *640*

Gario, Gabriel: Pepe Le Moko, *560*

Garko, John: Five for Hell, *56*

Garland, Beverly: It's My Turn, *499;* Where the Red Fern Grows, *212*

Garland, Judy: Babes in Arms, *769;* Broadway Melody of 1938, *773;* Easter Parade, *777;* Hollywood Outtakes, *282;* In the Good Old Summertime, *788;* Judgment at Nuremberg, *504;* Meet Me in St. Louis, *793;* Pirate, The, *798;* Star Is Born, A (Remake), *601;* Strike Up the Band, *360;* That's Entertainment, *807;* Thousands Cheer, *808;* Till the Clouds Roll By, *809;* Wizard of Oz, The, *812;* Ziegfeld Follies, *814*

Garland, Richard: Attack of the Crab Monsters, *647*

Garlington, Lee: Psycho III, *731*

Garlington, Mary: Polyester, *333*

Garner, James: Castaway Cowboy, The, *176;* Fan, The, *683;* Glitter Dome, The, *62;* Great Escape, The, *65;* Murphy's Romance, *539;* Sayonara, *589;* Skin Game, *933;* Support Your Local Sheriff, *936;* Tank, *145;* Victor/Victoria, *377*

Garner, Peggy Ann: In Name Only, *493*

Garnett, Gale: Children, The, *662;* Mad Monster Party, *191*

Garralaga, Martin: Big Sombrero, The, *883;* Susanna Pass, *936*

Garrani, Ivo: Hercules, *71*

Garrett, Betty: Neptune's Daughter, *795*

Garrett, Hank: Rosebud Beach Hotel, The, *343*

Garrett, Leif: Outsiders, The, *555;* Shaker Run, *132*

Garrett, Patsy: Benji, *172*

Garrick, Rian: Mooncussers, *193*

Garr, Teri: After Hours, *215;* Black Stallion Returns, The, *173;* Black Stallion, The, *173;* Close Encounters of the Third Kind, *825;* Escape Artist, The, *181;* First Born, *465;* Honky Tonk Freeway, *282;* Mr. Mom, *311;* Oh God!, *323;* One from the Heart, *797;* Sting II, The, *140;* Tale of the Frog Prince, *207;* To Catch a King, *756;* Tootsie, *369;* Young Frankenstein, *385*

Garson, Greer: Goodbye, Mr. Chips, *475;* Happiest Millionaire, The, *184;* Pride and Prejudice, *567;* Sunrise at Campobello, *609*

Garvin, Anita: Chump at Oxford, A, *243*

Garwood, John: Hell's Angels on Wheels, *71*

Gary, Lorraine: Jaws 2, *707;* Jaws, *707*

Gascon, Jean: Man Called Horse, A, *911*

Gasparmo : Clowns, The, *244*

Gassman, Vittorio: Sharky's Machine, *133;* Tempest, *612;* Wedding, A, *378*

Gasteda, Alexandra: Kashmiri Run, The, *81*

Gates, John W.: Legend of Boggy Creek, *711*

Gates, Nancy: Suddenly, *606*

Gatliff, Frank: Deja Vu, *448*

Gauthier, Anne: Hail Mary, *480*

Gautier, Dick: When Things Were Rotten, *380*

Gautreaux, David: Hearse, The, *697*

Gavin, John: Back Street, *404;* Breath of Scandal, A, *233;* Psycho, *731*

Gawthorne, Peter: Amazing Adventure, *217*

Gaxton, William: Best Foot Forward, *770*

Gaye, Lisa: Sign of Zorro, The, *204*

Gaye, Marvin: That Was Rock, *808*

Gaylord, Mitch: American Anthem, *395*

Gaynes, George: Dead Men Don't Wear Plaid, *249;* Micki & Maude, *309;* Police Academy III: Back in Training, *332;* Police Academy II: Their First Assignment, *332;* Police Academy, *332*

Gaynor, Janet: Star Is Born, A (Original), *600*

Gaynor, Mitzi: Les Girls, *792;* South Pacific, *805;* There's No Business Like Show Business, *808*

Gazzara, Ben: Anatomy of a Murder, *397;* Bloodline, *415;* QB VII, *571;* Saint Jack, *587;* They All Laughed, *365*

Gazzo, Michael V.: Fingers, *464;* Godfather, The, Part II, *474;* Alligator, *644;* Kill Castro, *82*

Geake, Nicholas: Adventures of Sherlock Holmes: The Naval Treaty, *4*

Geary, Tony: Johnny Got His Gun, *503*

Geddes, Barbara Bel: Blood on the Moon, *884;* I Remember Mama, *491;* Vertigo, *762*

Gedrick, Jason: Heavenly Kid, The, *278;* Heavenly Kid, The, *841;* Iron Eagle, *78*

Geer, Ellen: Harold and Maude, *276*

Geer, Roman: After the Fall of New York, *815*

Geer, Will: Bandolero!, *881;* Black Like Me, *413;* Bunco, *26;* Dear Dead Delilah, *672;* Executive Action, *460;* Jeremiah Johnson, *905;* My Sister, My Love, *720;* Reivers, The, *338*

Geeson, Judy: Brannigan, *23;* Dominique Is Dead, *677;* Fear in the Night (Dynasty of Fear), *683;* To Sir with Love, *619*

Geeson, Sally: Oblong Box, The, *725*

Gee, Prunella: Witching Time, *765*

Gefner, Deborah: Exterminator 2, The, *51*

Geldof, Bob: Pink Floyd the Wall, *798;* Secret Policeman's Private Parts, The, *347*

Belinas, Gratien: Agnes of God, 390

Belin, Daniel: La Ronde, 295

Gemma, Giuliano: Warning, The, 160

Gemser, Laura: Bushido Blade, 26

Genest, Emile: Big Red, 173; Incredible Journey, The, 186

Gennari, Lina: Umberto D, 625

Genn, Leo: Henry V, 486; Moby Dick, 102

Genovese, Mike: Code of Silence, 33

Gentille, Linda: To All a Good Night, 756

Gentry, Don: Breaker! Breaker!, 24

Geoffreys, Stephen: Fraternity Vacation, 263; Fright Night, 691; Heaven Help Us, 278

Geoffrey, Paul: Excalibur, 835

George, Anthony: Untouchables: Scarface Mob, The, 157

George, Chief Dan: Americathon, 218; Harry and Tonto, 483; Little Big Man, 909; Outlaw Josey Wales, The, 920

George, Christopher: Chisum, 889; Cruise into Terror, 667; Day of the Animals, 670; Exterminator, The, 50; Graduation Day, 694; Grizzly, 695; Mortuary, 718; Pieces, 728

George, Gladys: House Across the Bay, The, 489; Roaring Twenties, The, 122

George, John: Devil's Playground, 893

George, Lynda Day: Beyond Evil, 650; Cruise into Terror, 667; Day of the Animals, 670; Junkman, The, 80; Mortuary, 718; Pieces, 728

George, Rita: Hollywood Boulevard, 282

George, Susan: Die Screaming, Marianne, 675; Enter the Ninja, 49; House Where Evil Dwells, The, 701; Jigsaw Man, The, 708; Mandingo, 528; Small Town in Texas, A, 137; Straw Dogs, 749; Summer Heat, 607; Venom, 761

Georgiade, Nicholas: Untouchables: Alcatraz Express, The, 157

Gerard, Charles: Happy New Year (La Bonne Annee), 68

Gerard, Gil: Buck Rogers in the 25th Century, 822

Geray, Steven: Cornered, 35; Gilda, 472

Geret, Georges: Z, 641

Gere, Richard: American Gigolo, 396; Beyond the Limit, 410; Bloodbrothers, 415; Breathless (Remake), 420; Cotton Club, The, 36; Days of Heaven, 446; King David, 507; Looking for Mr. Goodbar, 521; Officer and a Gentleman, An, 549; Power, 566

Gerrish, Flo: Don't Answer the Phone, 677

Gerron, Kurt: Blue Angel, The, 415

Gerry, Alex: Bellboy, The, 226

Gertz, Jami: Crossroads, 775; Quicksilver, 572

Getz, John: Blood Simple, 19; Fly, The (remake), 686; Tattoo, 611

Geva, Tamara: Manhattan Merry-Go-Round, 913

Ghostley, Alice: Gator, 61

Giannini, Giancarlo: American Dreamer, 217;

Grande Bourgeoise, La, 476; Innocent, The, 495; Love and Anarchy, 301; Lovers and Liars, 303; Seduction of Mimi, The, 348; Seven Beauties, 349; Swept Away, 609

Gibbons, James Fitz: Bloodbeat, 653

Gibbs, Timothy: Just Between Friends, 505

Gibb, Cynthia: Salvador, 587; Youngblood, 641

Gibson, Henry: Charlotte's Web, 176; Incredible Shrinking Woman, The, 286; Nashville, 542

Gibson, Hoot: Horse Soldiers, The, 904

Gibson, Kitty: Cal, 423

Gibson, Mel: Attack Force Z, 10; Bounty, The, 23; Gallipoli, 470; Mad Max Beyond Thunderdome, 840; Mad Max, 850; Mrs. Soffel, 536; River, The, 581; Road Warrior, The, 859; Summer City, 143; Tim, 618; Year of Living Dangerously, The, 165

Gielgud, John: 11 Harrowhouse, 48; Arthur, 220; Formula, The, 467; Gandhi, 471; Joseph Andrews, 290; Murder By Decree, 103; Plenty, 564; Providence, 569; Richard III, 580; Scandalous, 345; Secret Agent, The, 131; Shooting Party, The, 592; Sphinx, 746; Wicked Lady, The, 163; Wagner, 811

Gifford, Frances: American Empire, 879

Gigney, Rebecca: Among the Cinders, 397

Gil, Jorge: Cease Fire, 429

Gil, Vincent: Solo, 596

Gilbert, Billy: Block-Heads, 230; Broadway Melody of 1938, 773; Five Weeks in a Balloon, 56; Villain Still Pursued Her, The, 159

Gilbert, Lou: Juliet of the Spirits, 291

Gilbert, Melissa: Snow Queen, 205; Sylvester, 610

Gilbert, Ronnie: Wasn't That a Time!, 811

Gilbert, Taylor: Torment, 757

Gilchrist, Connie: Long John Silver, 92

Gilford, Jack: Anna to the Infinite Power, 817; Cocoon, 825; Daydreamer, The, 179; Enter Laughing, 256; Funny Thing Happened on the Way to the Forum, A, 265; Save the Tiger, 588; They Might Be Giants, 616; Wholly Moses!, 381

Gill, John: Adventures of Sherlock Holmes: The Speckled Band, 6

Gillen, Jeffrey: Children Shouldn't Play with Dead Things, 662

Gilliam, Terry: And Now for Something Completely Different, 218; Life of Brian, 299; Monty Python and the Holy Grail, 313; Monty Python Live at the Hollywood Bowl, 313; Monty Python's the Meaning of Life, 313; Secret Policeman's Private Parts, The, 347

Gilliland, Richard: Bug, 658

Gillin, Hugh: Psycho III, 731; Psycho II, 731

Gillis, Ann: Adventures of Tom Sawyer, The, 170; Little Men, 519

Gilmour, Ian: Dangerous Summer, A, 444

Gimes, Scott: Critters, 666

Ging, Jack: High Plains Drifter, 903; Where

the Red Fern Grows, 212

Gingold, Hermione: Garbo Talks, 265; Gigi, 782; Music Man, The, 794

Ginsberg, Allen: Kerouac, 506; Kerouac, 506

Ginty, Robert: Coming Home, 437; Exterminator 2, The, 51; Exterminator, The, 50

Giorgiade, Nick: Untouchables: Scarface Mob, The, 157

Giorgi, Eleonora: Nudo di Donna (Portrait of a Woman, Nude), 321

Giradot, Annie: Le Cavaleur, 297; Jupiter's Thigh, 291; Mussolini and I, 539

Giraudeau, Bernard: Bilitis, 411; Passion of Love, 559

Giraud, Charles: And Now, My Love, 398

Giraud, Roland: Three Men and a Cradle, 367

Girotti, Massimo: Passion of Love, 559; Torture Chamber Of Baron Blood, The, 758; Wanton Contessa, The, 630

Gish, Annabeth: Desert Bloom, 449

Gish, Lillian: Birth of a Nation, The, 412; Follow Me Boys!, 181; Great Chase, The, 65; His Double Life, 281; Intolerance, 497; Sweet Liberty, 362; True Heart Susie, 623; Way Down East, 631; Wedding, A, 378

Giuffre, Aldo: Loaded Guns, 91

Givot, George: Du Barry Was a Lady, 777

Glacum, Joy: Children, The, 662

Glass, Ned: Experiment in Terror, 681

Glaudini, Robert: Parasite, 726

Gleason, Jackie: Hustler, The, 490; Mr. Billion, 100; Mr. Halpern and Mr. Johnson, 536; Nothing In Common, 547; Papa's Delicate Condition, 557; Requiem for a Heavyweight, 578; Smokey and the Bandit III, 355; Smokey and the Bandit II, 355; Smokey and the Bandit, 354; Soldier in the Rain, 596; Sting II, The, 140; Toy, The, 371

Gleason, James: Arsenic and Old Lace, 220; Bishop's Wife, The, 229; Falcon Takes Over, The, 52; Here Comes Mr. Jordan, 279; Suddenly, 606; Tycoon, 156; What Price Glory, 379; Manhattan Merry-Go-Round, 913

Gleason, Paul: Breakfast Club, The, 233; Doc Savage...The Man of Bronze, 830; Little Laura and Big John, 90; Pursuit of D. B. Cooper, 116

Gledhill, Nicholas: Careful He Might Hear You, 426

Glenn Sr., Roy E.: Guess Who's Coming to Dinner, 273; Guess Who's Coming to Dinner, 480

Glenn, Scott: Challenge, The, 29; Keep, The, 708; Personal Best, 562; Right Stuff, The, 580; River, The, 581; Silverado, 932; Urban Cowboy, 627; Wild Geese II, 163

Gless, Sharon: Hardhat and Legs, 482; Star Chamber, The, 600

Glover, Crispin: Back to the Future, 819

Glover, Danny: Color Purple, The, 436;

Places in the Heart, 563; Silverado, 93; Witness, 165

Glover, John: Flash of Green, A, 466; La Embrace, The, 87

Glover, Julian: Heat and Dust, 485; Theatr of Death, 754

Glynn, Carlin: Continental Divide, 247; Tri to Bountiful, The, 622

Gobel, George: Better Late than Never, 22

Godard, Jean-Luc: Contempt, 247

Goddard, Mark: Blue Sunshine, 20

Goddard, Paulette: Great Dictator, The, 27; Modern Times, 312; Pot O' Gold, 566; Second Chorus, 801; Women, The, 383

Godfrey, Arthur: Great Bank Hoax, The, 27

Godfrey, Renee: Terror By Night, 148

Godin, Jacques: Man Inside, The, 95

Godunov, Alexander: Witness, 165

Goetz, Peter Michael: Beer, 226

Goldberg, Whoopi: Color Purple, The, 43

Goldblum, Jeff: Adventures of Buckaro Banzai, The, 815; Big Chill, The, 411; Deat Wish, 40; Fly, The (remake), 686; Into th Night, 496; Invasion of the Body Snatcher (Remake), 845; Rehearsal for Murder, 126 Right Stuff, The, 580; Silverado, 932; Than God It's Friday, 806; Three Little Pigs, The 209; Threshold, 872; Transylvania6-5000, 37

Golden, Annie: Hair, 785

Goldie, Michael: Adventures of Sherloc Holmes: The Final Problem, 4

Goldman, Philippe: Small Change, 595

Goldoni, Lelia: Theatre of Death, 754

Goldsby, Matthew: Student Bodies, 749

Goldsmith, Clio: Gift, The, 268; Heat of De sire, 277

Goldstein, Jenette: Aliens, 816

Goldthwait, Bobcat: One Crazy Summer, 32 Police Academy III: Back in Training, 33

Gold, Tracey: Shoot the Moon, 592

Golonka, Arlene: Hang 'Em High, 900; La Married Couple in America, The, 296

Golub, David: From Mao to Mozart, 781

Gomarov, Mikhail: Strike, 605

Gombell, Minna: Block-Heads, 230; Paga Love Song, 797

Gomez, Thomas: Force of Evil, 467; Kin 83; Trapeze, 621

Goodfellow, Joan: Buster and Billie, 42 Flash of Green, A, 466

Goodliffe, Michael: Day the Earth Caugh Fire, The, 828; To the Devil, a Daughte 757

Goodman, Dody: Splash, 357

Goodman, John: Sweet Dreams, 806

Goodron, Michael: Sweater Girls, 362

Goodrow, Gary: Steelyard Blues, 359

Goodwin, Bill: Spellbound, 746

Goodwin, Harold: College, 246

Goodwin, Laurel: Girls! Girls! Girls!, 783; Pa pa's Delicate Condition, 557

Goodwin, Ralph: Massacre At Fort Holma

(Reason to Live… A Reason to Die, A), *914*

Gorcey, David: Prairie Moon, *922;* Pride of the Bowery, *567*

Gorcey, Leo: Pride of the Bowery, *587*

Gordon, Barry: Thousand Clowns, A, *367*

Gordon, Benjamin: Utilities, *376;* Last Chase, The, *847*

Gordon, Bruce: Elephant Boy, *48;* Untouchables: Alcatraz Express, The, *157;* Untouchables: Scarface Mob, The, *157*

Gordon, C. Henry: Tarzan's Revenge, *146*

Gordon, Don: Beast Within, The, *649;* Final Conflict, The, *684;* Papillon, *112*

Gordon, Gale: 30 Foot Bride of Candy Rock, The, *366;* Speedway, *805*

Gordon, Gerald: Force Five, *59*

Gordon, Hannah: Oh, Alfie, *549*

Gordon, Joyce: Killing 'Em Softly, *506*

Gordon, Julie: Super Fuzz, *868*

Gordon, Keith: Back To School, *223;* Christine, *662;* Dressed to Kill, *679;* Home Movies, *282;* Legend of Billy Jean, The, *89*

Gordon, Leo: Riot in Cell Block11, *581;* Riot in Cell Block Eleven, *122*

Gordon, Mary: Hound of the Baskervilles, The (Original), *75;* Pot O' Gold, *566;* Sherlock Holmes and the Secret Weapon, *134*

Gordon, Philip: Came a Hot Friday, *27*

Gordon, Roy: Attack of the 50-Foot Woman, *647*

Gordon, Ruth: Abe Lincoln in Illinois, *387;* Any Which Way You Can, *219;* Big Bus, The, *229;* Every Which Way but Loose, *257;* Harold and Maude, *276;* Maxie, *308;* My Bodyguard, *540;* North Star, The, *108;* Rosemary's Baby, *737;* Scavenger Hunt, *346;* Where's Poppa?, *381*

Goring, Marise: Ill Met by Moonlight, *493*

Gorman, Annette: Texas John Slaughter: Geronimo's Revenge, *937;* Texas John Slaughter: Stampede at Bitter Creek, *937;* Texas John Slaughter: Wild Times, *938*

Gorman, Cliff: Angel, *8;* Boys in the Band, The, *419;* Night of the Juggler, *107*

Gorney, Karen Lynn: Saturday Night Fever, *801*

Goronorov, Mikhail: Battleship Potemkin, The, *406*

Gorshin, Frank: Batman, *172;* Hollywood Vice Squad, *74;* That Darn Cat, *208;* Underground Aces, *374*

Gortner, Marjoe: Bobbie Jo and the Outlaw, *21;* Food of the Gods, *838;* Marjoe, *529;* Mausoleum, *716;* Sidewinder 1, *135;* Star Crash, *864;* Viva Knievel, *159*

Gosden, Freeman: Check and Double Check, *242*

Gossett Jr., Louis: Deep, The, *41;* Enemy Mine, *834;* Finders Keepers, *260;* Guardian, The, *480;* Iron Eagle, *78;* It Rained All Night the Day I Left, *498;* Jaws 3, *707;* Officer and a Gentleman, An, *549;* Raisin in the Sun, A,

575; Skin Game, *933;* White Dawn, The, *161;* Laughing Policeman, The, *88*

Goss, David: She, *861*

Gotestam, Staffan: Brothers Lionheart, The, *175*

Gothard, Michael: King Arthur, The Young Warlord, *84;* Lifeforce, *849;* Scream and Scream Again, *740*

Gottlieb, Carl: Cannonball, *27*

Gotz, Carl: Pandora's Box, *556*

Gough, Lloyd: Rancho Notorious, *923*

Gough, Michael: Crucible of Horror, *666;* Horror Hospital, *699;* Horror of Dracula, *699;* Out of Africa, *555;* Rob Roy, The Highland Rogue, *201;* Sword and the Rose, The, *307*

Gould, Elliott: Bob & Carol & Ted & Alice, *231;* Capricorn One, *822;* Devil and Max Devlin, The, *250;* Dirty Tricks, *251;* Escape to Athena, *50;* Falling in Love Again, *258;* Getting Straight, *473;* Harry and Walter Go to New York, *276;* I Love My Wife, *285;* I Will, I Will… For Now, *285;* Jack and the Beanstalk, *186;* Last Flight of Noah's Ark, *188;* Matilda, *308;* Mean Johnny Barrows, *98;* Muppet Movie, The, *193;* Muppets Take Manhattan, The, *194;* M*A*S*H, *307;* Naked Face, The, *720;* Night They Raided Minsky's, The, *319;* Over the Brooklyn Bridge, *326;* Silent Partner, The, *743*

Gould, Harold: Better Late than Never, *228;* Big Bus, The, *229;* How to Break Up a Happy Divorce, *284;* Love and Death, *302;* One and Only, The, *551;* Red Light Sting, The, *577;* Seems Like Old Times, *349;* Sting, The, *144*

Goulet, Arthur: Silver Blaze, *136*

Goutman, Christopher: Goodbye New York, *271*

Grable, Betty: Follow the Fleet, *780;* Gay Divorcee, The, *782;* How to Marry a Millionaire, *284*

Grace, Carol: Mikey and Nicky, *309*

Grace, Nickolas: Robin Hood and the Sorcerer, *123*

Grady, Ed L.: Last Game, The, *513*

Graf, David: Police Academy III: Back in Training, *332;* Police Academy II: Their First Assignment, *332*

Grahame, Gloria: Big Heat, The, *15;* Chilly Scenes of Winter, *432;* Greatest Show on Earth, The, *478;* Nesting, The, *721;* Song of the Thin Man, *138*

Graham, Gerrit: Used Cars, *376;* Bobbie Jo and the Outlaw, *21;* Cannonball, *27;* Class Reunion, *244;* Demon Seed, *830;* Home Movies, *282;* Son of Blob (Beware! The Blob), *745;* Spaceship, *356*

Graham, Ronny: World's Greatest Lover, The, *384*

Granach, Alexander: Nosferatu, *724*

Grandy, Fred: Death Race 2000, *839*

Granger, Farley: Arnold, *646;* Purple Heart, The, *570;* Rope, *737;* Strangers on a Train,

749; They Call Me Trinity, *938;* Wanton Contessa, The, *630*

Granger, Stewart: Caesar and Cleopatra, *423;* King Solomon's Mines, *84;* Man in Grey, The, *528;* North to Alaska, *918;* Prisoner of Zenda, The, *115;* Wild Geese, The, *163*

Grantham, Lucy: Last House on the Left, *711*

Grant, Cary: Amazing Adventure, *217;* Arsenic and Old Lace, *220;* Bachelor and the Bobby-soxer, The, *222;* Bishop's Wife, The, *229;* Bringing up Baby, *234;* Charade, *29;* Every Girl Should Be Married, *256;* Father Goose, *259;* Grass Is Greener, The, *272;* Gunga Din, *67;* His Girl Friday, *281;* In Name Only, *493;* Mr. Blandings Builds His Dream House, *310;* Mr. Lucky, *101;* My Favorite Wife, *316;* Night and Day, *544;* None But the Lonely Heart, *546;* North by Northwest, *724;* Notorious, *725;* Once Upon a Honeymoon, *324;* Operation Petticoat, *325;* Penny Serenade, *560;* Philadelphia Story, The, *329;* Pride and the Passion, The, *567;* Suspicion, *750;* That Touch of Mink, *365;* To Catch a Thief, *756;* Topper, *369*

Grant, Cy: At the Earth's Core, *818*

Grant, David Marshall: French Postcards, *263;* American Flyers, *396*

Grant, Eddy: Water, *377*

Grant, Frances: Man of the Frontier, (Red River Valley), *912;* Traitor, The, *940*

Grant, Kathryn: 7TH Voyage of Sinbad, The, *861;* Anatomy of a Murder, *397*

Grant, Lawrence: Bulldog Drummond, *25*

Grant, Lee: Airport 77, *391;* Charlie Chan and the Curse of the Dragon Queen, *240;* Damien: Omen II, *668;* In the Heat of the Night, *494;* Internecine Project, The, *705;* Little Miss Marker, *190;* Marooned, *851;* My Sister, My Love, *720;* Plaza Suite, *331;* Portnoy's Complaint, *565;* Shampoo, *591;* There Was a Crooked Man, *938;* Visiting Hours, *762;* Voyage of the Damned, *629*

Grant, Peter: Song Remains the Same, The, *803*

Granval, Charles: Boudu Saved From Drowning, *232*

Granville, Bonita: Hitler's Children, *73;* Lone Ranger, The, *910;* Love Laughs at Andy Hardy, *302;* These Three, *615*

Grapewin, Charley: Alice Adams, *392;* Grapes of Wrath, The, *477;* Hell's House, *71;* Wizard of Oz, The, *812*

Grassle, Karen: Cocaine: One Man's Seduction, *435*

Grauman, Walter: Pleasure Palace, *564*

Graves, Leslie: Piranha Part Two: The Spawning, *728*

Graves, Peter: Airplane II: The Sequel, *216;* Airplane!, *216;* Savannah Smiles, *203;* Stalag 17, *139*

Gravet, Fernand: La Ronde, *295*

Gravina, Carla: And Now, My Love, *398*

Grayson, Kathryn: Kiss Me Kate, *790;* Show Boat, *802;* Thousands Cheer, *808*

Gray, Billy: Day the Earth Stood Still, The, *828*

Gray, Charles: Adventures of Sherlock Holmes: The Greek Interpreter, *4;* Beast Must Die, The, *649;* Diamonds Are Forever, *42;* Jigsaw Man, The, *708*

Gray, Colleen: Tennessee's Partner, *937*

Gray, Dolores: It's Always Fair Weather, *789*

Gray, Erin: Buck Rogers in the 25th Century, *822;* Six Pack, *353*

Gray, Linda: Grass is Always Greener Over the Septic Tank, The, *272;* Two Worlds of Jennie Logan, The, *874*

Gray, Lorna: Man They Could Not Hang, The, *714;* Nyoka and the Tiger Men (Perils of Nyoka), *109*

Gray, Nadia: La Dolce Vita, *511;* Maniac, *714*

Gray, Robert: Uforia, *374*

Gray, Sally: Keeper, The, *708*

Gray, Shirley: Hurricane Express, *76*

Gray, Vernon: To Paris with Love, *369*

Greco, Jose: Ship of Fools, *592*

Greene, Angela: At War with the Army, *221*

Greene, Joseph J.: Devil's Playground, *893*

Greene, Lorne: Battlestar Galactica, *820;* Buccaneer, The, *25;* Earthquake, *46;* Trap, The, *759*

Greene, Michael: Americana, *396;* Clones, The, *824*

Greene, Richard: Against All Odds (Kiss and Kill, Blood of Fu Manchu), *643;* Hound of the Baskervilles, The, (The Original), *75;* Little Princess, The, *190;* Stanley and Livingstone, *600*

Greenlees, Billy: That Sinking Feeling, *365*

Greenstreet, Sydney: Casablanca, *427;* Maltese Falcon, The, *95;* Passage to Marseilles, *113;* They Died with their Boots On, *938*

Greenwood, Charlotte: Dangerous When Wet, *776;* Great Dan Patch, The, *477*

Greenwood, Joan: Man in the White Suit, The, *306;* Moonspinners, The, *193;* Mysterious Island, *853;* Uncanny, The, *760*

Green, Abel: Copacabana, *247*

Green, Adolph: Lily in Love, *299*

Green, Gilbert: Executive Action, *460*

Green, Kerri: Goonies, The, *63;* Lucas, *524;* Summer Rental, *361*

Green, Leif: Joy Sticks, *291*

Green, Marika: Emmanuelle, *457*

Green, Nigel: Tobruk, *153;* Zulu, *167*

Greer, Jane: Dick Tracy, *42;* Out of the Past, *112;* Prisoner of Zenda, The, *115;* Sinbad the Sailor, *136*

Gregg, John: Heatwave, *485*

Gregory, Andre: My Dinner with Andre, *540*

Gregory, Cecelia: Agatha, 390

Gregory, Celia: Children Of The Full Moon, 663

Gregory, James: Beneath the Planet of the Apes, 820; Murderers' Row, 104; PT 109, 569; Secret War of Harry Frigg, The, 348; Sons of Katie Elder, The, 934

Gregory, Mark: 1990: The Bronx Warriors, 854

Gregory, Pascal: Pauline at the Beach, 559

Gregory, Paul: Whoopee, 812

Gregor, Nora: Rules of the Game, The, 344

Gregson, John: Hans Brinker, 183

Greif, Stephen: Great Riviera Bank Robbery, The, 65

Greig, Robert: Animal Crackers, 218

Greist, Kim: Manhunter, 97

Grellier, Michel: Holiday Hotel, 281

Grenfell, Joyce: Belles of St. Trinian's, The, 227

Greville, Wanda: Le Million, 298

Greyn, Cliton: Raid on Rommel, 118

Grey, Jennifer: Ferris Bueller's Day Off, 259

Grey, Joel: Buffalo Bill and the Indians, 886; Cabaret, 773; Remo Williams: The Adventure Begins, 120; Seven-Per-Cent Solution, The, 131

Grey, Shirley: Uptown New York, 627

Grey, Virginia: Idiot's Delight, 492

Gridoux, Lucas: Pepe Le Moko, 560

Griem, Helmut: Cabaret, 773; Damned, The, 442

Grier, David Alan: Beer, 226

Grier, Pam: Greased Lightning, 64; Miami Vice: "The Prodigal Son", 99; Something Wicked This Way Comes, 863; Tough Enough, 154

Gries, Jonathan: Running Scared (1986), 125

Grieve, Russ: Hills Have Eyes, The, 697

Grifasi, Joe: Bad Medicine, 223; Still of the Night, 748

Griffeth, Simone: Fighting Back, 53

Griffies, Ethel: Billy Liar, 412

Griffin, Lynne: Strange Brew, 360

Griffin, Merv: Lonely Guy, The, 300

Griffin, Robert E.: Monster From Green Hell, 717

Griffith, Andy: Face in the Crowd, A, 461; Murder in Texas, 719; No Time for Sergeants, 320; Rustler's Rhapsody, 344; Savages, 739

Griffith, Billy: Hills of Utah, The, 903

Griffith, Geraldine: Experience Preferred ... But Not Essential, 257

Griffith, Hugh: Abominable Dr. Phibes, The, 643; Dr. Phibes Rises Again, 676; Joseph Andrews, 290; Last Days of Man on Earth, The, 848; Mutiny on the Bounty (Remake), 105; Oliver, 796; Start the Revolution Without Me, 358; Tom Jones, 369; Who Slew Auntie Roo?, 764

Griffith, James: Bullwhip, 887; Tom Edison—The Boy Who Lit Up The World, 210

Griffith, Kenneth: Sea Wolves, The, 130

Griffith, Melanie: Body Double, 655; Drowning Pool, The, 45; Fear City, 52; Joyride, 504; Night Moves, 106; Underground Aces, 374

Griffith, Tom: Alien Factor, The, 816

Griffiths, Gordon: Tarzan of the Apes, 145

Griffiths, Chuck: It Came from Beneath the Sea, 706

Griffiths, Linda: Lianna, 517

Griffiths, Richard: Private Function, A, 335

Griggs, Camilla: Forced Vengeance, 59

Grimes, Gary: Cahill—US Marshal, 887; Class of '44, 434; Gus, 183; Summer of '42, 608

Grimes, Tammy: Can't Stop the Music, 773

Gripasi, Joe: Hide in Plain Sight, 487

Grisham, Jerry: Escapes, 835

Grizzard, George: Bachelor Party, 222; Comes a Horseman, 889; Wrong Is Right, 384

Grodin, Charles: 11 Harrowhouse, 48; Grass is Always Greener Over the Septic Tank, The, 272; Great Muppet Caper, The, 183; Heartbreak Kid, The, 277; Heaven Can Wait, 278; Incredible Shrinking Woman, The, 286; It's My Turn, 499; King Kong (remake), 710; Lonely Guy, The, 300; Movers and Shakers, 315; Real Life, 338; Seems Like Old Times, 349; Sunburn, 143; Woman in Red, The, 383

Grogan, Clare: Gregory's Girl, 273

Grogan, C. P.: Comfort and Joy, 246

Grongmeyer, Herbert: Das Boot (The Boat), 38

Groom, Sam: Deadly Eyes, 671

Grossmith, Lawrence: Silver Blaze, 136

Gross, Sonny: French Connection, The, 60

Grovenor, Linda: Wheels of Fire, 161; Die Laughing, 251

Groves, Robin: Nesting, The, 721; Silver Bullet, 743

Grönberg, Ake: Sawdust and Tinsel, 589

Grubb, Robert: Gallipoli, 470

Grundgens, Gustav: M, 713

Guardino, Harry: Dirty Harry, 43; Enforcer, The, 49; Madigan, 94; Matilda, 308; St. Ives, 126

Guerra, Blanca: Robbers of the Sacred Mountain, 123

Guerra, Castulo: Stick, 140

Guerra, Ruy: Aguirre: Wrath of God, 6

Guerrero, Evelyn: Cheech and Chong's Next Movie, 242; Nice Dreams, 318

Guest, Christopher: Girlfriends, 472; Piano for Mrs. Cimino, A, 562; This Is Spinal Tap, 367

Guest, Lance: Halloween II, 695; Last Starfighter, The, 848

Guest, Nicholas and Christopher: Long Riders, The, 910

Guffey, Cary: Mutant, 720

Guibert, André: Diary Of A Country Priest, *450*

Guild, Nancy: Black Magic, *413*

Guilfoyle, Paul: Winterset, *636*

Guillain, Bruno: Holiday Hotel, *281*

Guillaume, Robert: Kid With the 200 I.Q., The, *188*; Seems Like Old Times, *349*

Guinness, Alec: Bridge on the River Kwai, The, *25*; Brother Sun Sister Moon, *420*; Dr. Zhivago, *452*; Fall of the Roman Empire, The, *462*; Hitler, the Last Ten Days, *488*; Kind Hearts and Coronets, *292*; Ladykillers, The, *295*; Lavender Hill Mob, The, *297*; Lawrence of Arabia, *88*; Lovesick, *303*; Malta Story, The, *527*; Man in the White Suit, The, *306*; Murder by Death, *315*; Oliver Twist, *550*; Passage to India, A, *558*; Raise the Titanic, *118*; Scrooge, *801*; Star Wars, *867*; To Paris with Love, *369*; Tunes of Glory, *624*

Guiomar, Julien: Swashbuckler, The, *144*

Gulager, Clu: Glass House, The, *473*; McQ, *98*; Nightmare on Elm Street Part 2: Freddy's Revenge, A, *722*; Other Side of Midnight, The, *554*; Prime Risk, *115*; Return of the Living Dead, The, *735*; Touched by Love, *621*

Gulpilil, David: Mad Dog Morgan, *94*

Gunning, Paul: Hollywood Hot Tubs, *282*

Gunn, Judy: Silver Blaze, *136*

Gunn, Moses: Amityville II: The Possession, *645*; Certain Fury, *29*; Hot Rock, The, *75*; Ninth Configuration, The, *546*; Shaft, *132*

Gunton, Bob: Rollover, *583*

Gurie, Sigrid: Algiers, *392*; Three Faces West, *939*

Gurney, Sharon: Crucible of Horror, *666*

Gurry, Eric: Bad Boys, *404*

Guthrie, Arlo: Alice's Restaurant, *393*; Wasn't That a Time!, *811*

Guthrie, Tyrone: Beachcomber, The, *406*; Sidewalks of London, *593*

Gutierrez, Aide Silvia: El Norte, *456*

Guttenberg, Steven: Chicken Chronicles, The, *243*; Diner, *251*; Bad Medicine, *223*; Can't Stop the Music, *773*; Cocoon, *825*; Day After, The, *828*; Man Who Wasn't There, The, *306*; Police Academy, *332*; Police Academy II: Their First Assignment, *332*; Police Academy III: Back in Training, *332*; Short Circuit, *862*

Guve, Bertil: Fanny and Alexander, *463*

Gwenn, Edmund: Cheers for Miss Bishop, *432*; Foreign Correspondent, *687*; Life With Father, *299*; Miracle on 34th Street, *192*; Them!, *870*; Trouble With Harry, The, *372*

Gwillim, David: Adventures of Sherlock Holmes: The Naval Treaty, *4*

Gwynne, Anne: Dick Tracy Meets Gruesome, *42*

Gwynne, Fred: Boy Who Could Fly, The, *419*; Simon, *352*; So Fine, *355*; Water, *377*

Gwynne, Michael C.: Harry Tracy, *901*; Payday, *560*; Village of the Damned, *762*

Gynt, Greta: Human Monster, The (Dark Eyes of London), *702*

Haas, Dolly: I Confess, *703*

Haas, Hugo: King Solomon's Mines, *84*

Haas, Lukas: Testament, *870*; Witness, *165*

Haas, O. E.: I Confess, *703*

Habbema, Cox: Question of Silence, A, *572*

Hackett, Buddy: God's Little Acre, *473*; It's a Mad Mad Mad Mad World, *288*; Loose Shoes, *301*; Love Bug, The, *190*; Music Man, The, *794*

Hackett, Joan: Escape Artist, The, *181*; Group, The, *480*; One Trick Pony, *797*; Only When I Laugh, *553*; Support Your Local Sheriff!, *936*; Terminal Man, The, *752*

Hackett, John: Dead of Night, *671*

Hackett, Karl: Border Phantom, *885*; Traitor, The, *940*

Hackett, Sandy: Hamburger—The Motion Picture, *274*

Hackman, Gene: All Night Long, *393*; Bite the Bullet, *884*; Bonnie and Clyde, *21*; Conversation, The, *438*; Domino Principle, The, *453*; Downhill Racer, *454*; Eureka, *459*; French Connection, The, *60*; French Connection II, The, *469*; Hawaii, *483*; Lilith, *518*; Marooned, *851*; Misunderstood, *537*; Night Moves, *106*; Poseidon Adventure, The, *115*; Power, *566*; Prime Cut, *115*; Reds, *578*; Scarecrow, *589*

Haczkiewicz, Eugeniusz: Moonlighting, *538*

Haddon, Dayle: North Dallas Forty, *546*; Sex With a Smile, *350*

Haden, Sara: Love Laughs at Andy Hardy, *302*; Mr. Ace, *100*; Spitfire, *599*

Hadley, Reed: Kansas Pacific, *906*

Hagen, Jean: Shaggy Dog, The, *204*; Singin' in the Rain, *802*

Hagerty, Julie: Airplane!, *216*; Airplane II, The Sequel, *216*; Bad Medicine, *223*; Goodbye New York, *271*; Lost in America, *301*; Midsummer Night's Sex Comedy, A, *309*

Haggard, Merle: Hillbillys in a Haunted House, *280*

Haggerty, Dan: Angels Die Hard, *8*; Borrowed Trouble, *885*; Dead Don't Dream, The, *892*; Desperate Women, *893*; False Paradise, *896*; Life and Times of Grizzly Adams, The, *189*; Sinister Journey, *932*

Haggerty, H. B.: Four Deuces, The, *59*

Haggiag, Brahim: Battle of Algiers, *405*

Haglehurst, Noni: Fatty Finn, *181*

Hagman, Larry: Big Bus, The, *229*; Ensign Pulver, *255*; Failsafe, *461*; Group, The, *480*; Harry and Tonto, *483*; S.O.B., *355*; Son of Blob (Beware! The Blob), *745*

Haid, Charles: Altered States, *817*

Haigh, Kenneth: Bitch, The, *412*; Robin and

Marian, *123*

Haig, Sid: Beyond Atlantis, *14;* C.C. & Company, *28*

Haim, Corey: Lucas, *524;* Murphy's Romance, *539;* Silver Bullet, *743*

Haines, Donald: Pride of the Bowery, *567*

Hai, Yue: Shaolin Temple, *132*

Haji: Faster Pussycat! Kill! Kill!, *52*

Hakim, Omar: Bring on the Night, *772*

Hale Jr., Alan: At Sword's Point, *10*

Hale, Alan: Adventures of Robin Hood, The, *2;* Big Trees, The, *16;* Dodge City, *894;* Fifth Musketeer, The, *53;* Gentleman Jim, *471;* Last Days of Pompeii, The, *513;* Lost Patrol, The, *93;* Of Human Bondage (Original), *549;* Our Relations, *325;* Prince and the Pauper, The (Original), *199;* Santa Fe Trail, *929;* Sea Hawk, The, *130*

Hale, Barbara: Boy With Green Hair, The, *419;* First Yank into Tokyo, *55*

Hale, Georgia: Gold Rush, The, *270*

Hale, Georgina: Mahler, *527*

Hale, Jean: St. Valentine's Day Massacre, The, *126*

Haley, Jackie Earle: Bad News Bears Go to Japan, The, *223;* Bad News Bears in Breaking Training, The, *223;* Breaking Away, *233;* Damnation Alley, *827;* Losin' It, *301*

Haley, Jack: Wizard of Oz The, *812*

Halicki, H. B.: Gone in 60 Seconds, *63*

Hallahan, Charles: Going in Style, *269*

Hallam, John: Murphy's War, *104*

Halliday, John: Bird of Paradise, *17*

Hallier, Lori: My Bloody Valentine, *720*

Halligan, William: Riders of the Deadline, *926*

Halloren, Jane: Lianna, *517*

Hall, Anthony Michael: Breakfast Club, The, *233;* Out of Bounds, *111;* Sixteen Candles, *353;* Weird Science, *379*

Hall, John: No Nukes, *795*

Hall, Jon: Hurricane, The, *490;* Kit Carson, *907;* South of Pago Pago, *138*

Hall, Juanita: Flower Drum Song, *780*

Hall, Mark Edward: Across the Great Divide, *169*

Hall, Ruth: Monkey Business, *312*

Hall, Shana: Boogeyman 2, The, *656*

Hall, Thurston: Black Room, The, *652;* Call of the Canyon, *887;* Night Stage to Galveston, *917;* Secret Life of Walter Mitty, The, *347;* Song of Nevada, *933;* Without Reservations, *382*

Hall, Zooey: I Dismember Mama, *703*

Halprin, Daria: Zabriskie Point, *641*

Halsey, Brett: Atomic Submarine, The, *818;* Return of the Fly, The, *735*

Hama, Mie: You Only Live Twice, *166*

Hamel, Veronica: Cannonball, *27*

Hamer, Gerald: Pursuit to Algiers, *117*

Hamill, John: Beast in The Cellar, The, *649*

Hamill, Mark: Big Red One, The, *15;* Corvette Summer, *35;* Empire Strikes Back, The, *833;* Night the Lights Went Out in Georgia, The, *545;* Return of the Jedi, *859;* Star Wars, *867*

Hamilton, Gay: Barry Lyndon, *405*

Hamilton, George: Evel Knievel, *50;* Happy Hooker Goes to Washington, The, *275;* Love at First Bite, *302;* Man Who Loved Cat Dancing, The, *912;* Sextette, *350;* Where the Boys Are, *380;* Zorro, the Gay Blade, *386*

Hamilton, Judd: Last Horror Film, The, *711*

Hamilton, Linda: Black Moon Rising, *18;* Children of the Corn, *662*

Hamilton, Margaret: Anderson Tapes, The, *8;* Babes in Arms, *769;* Daydreamer, The, *179;* Red Pony, The, *201;* Sin of Harold Diddlebock (aka Mad Wednesday), *352;* Wizard of Oz, The, *812;* You Only Live Once, *640*

Hamilton, Murray: 1941, *319;* Anatomy of a Murder, *397;* Boston Strangler, The, *656;* Brubaker, *421;* Casey's Shadow, *176;* Drowning Pool, The, *45;* Hustler, The, *490;* Hysterical, *284;* Jaws 2, *707;* No Time for Sergeants, *320;* No Way to Treat a Lady, *546;* Papa's Delicate Condition, *557;* Spirit of St. Louis, The, *599*

Hamilton, Suzanna: Brimstone and Treacle, *657;* Out of Africa, *555*

Hamilton, Ted: Pirate Movie, The, *798*

Hamlin, Harry: Blue Skies Again, *416;* Clash of the Titans, *824;* King of the Mountain, *508;* Making Love, *527;* Movie Movie, *315*

Hamlin, Marilyn: Savage Weekend, *739*

Hammond, Kay: Abraham Lincoln, *388*

Hammond, Roger: Adventures of Sherlock Holmes: The Red-Headed League, *5*

Hamnett, Olivia: Earthling, The, *46;* Last Wave, The, *711*

Hampshire, Susan: Fighting Prince of Donegal, The, *181*

Hampton, Bill: Hideous Sun Demon, The, *697*

Hampton, James: Bunco, *26;* Condorman, *178;* Hangar 18, *840;* Hawmps!, *277*

Hancock, Barbara: Finian's Rainbow, *779*

Hancock, Tony: Wrong Box, The, *384*

Handl, Irene: Morgan, *314;* Private Life of Sherlock Holmes, The, *115*

Haney, Carol: Invitation to the Dance, *788*

Hanin, Roger: My Other Husband, *541*

Hankerson, Barry L.: Pipe Dreams, *563*

Hanks, Steve: Island Claws, *706*

Hanks, Tom: Bachelor Party, *222;* He Knows You're Alone, *696;* Man With One Red Shoe, The, *306;* Nothing In Common, *547;* Splash, *357*

Hanley, Jenny: Scars of Dracula, *740*

Hanley, Katie: Xanadu, *813*

Hannah, Daryl: Blade Runner, *821;* Clan of

the Cave Bear, 824; Final Terror, The, 685; Legal Eagles, 88; Pope of Greenwich Village, The, 564; Reckless, 577; Splash, 357

Hanno, Eva Von: Flight of the Eagle, 57

Hansen, Bill: Homebodies, 698

Hansen, Gunnar: Demon Lover, The, 673

Hansen, Patti: Hard to Hold, 786

Hanson, Kristina: Dinosaurus!, 675

Hanson, Peter: When Worlds Collide, 876

Harada, Mieko: Ran, 575

Hardie, Kate: Mona Lisa, 537

Harding, Lyn: Silver Blaze, 136

Hardin, Ty: Fire!, 685; PT 109, 569

Hardwicke, Cedric: Becky Sharp, 407; Botany Bay, 22; Desert Fox, The, 42; Five Weeks in a Balloon, 56; Nicholas Nickleby, 544; Rope, 737; Stanley and Livingstone, 600; Winslow Boy, The, 635

Hardwick, Derek: Among the Cinders, 397

Hardy, Laurel and: Golden Age of Comedy, The, 270

Hardy, Oliver: Atoll K (Utopia), 221; Block-Heads, 230; Bohemian Girl, The, 232; Bullfighters, The, 235; Chump at Oxford, A, 243; Fighting Kentuckian, The, 896; Flying Deuces, 261; Great Guns, 272; March of the Wooden Soldiers, 307; Our Relations, 325; Pack Up Your Troubles, 326; Pardon Us, 327; Saps at Sea, 345; Sons of the Desert, 356; Way Out West, 378

Hardy, Robert: Dark Places, 669; Gathering Storm, 471; Shooting Party, The, 592

Harewood, Dorian: Jessie Owens Story, The, 501; Sparkle, 805

Hargitay, Mickey: Lady Frankenstein, 710

Hargreaves, Christine: Pink Floyd the Wall, 798

Hargreaves, John: Careful He Might Hear You, 426; Don's Party, 253; My First Wife, 541; Odd Angry Shot, The, 548

Harkins, John: Birdy, 412; Right of Way, 580

Harlan, Robin: Party Animal, 328

Harlow, Jean: China Seas, 30; Dinner at Eight, 251; Libeled Lady, 298; Public Enemy, The, 116; Red Dust, 577

Harnois, Elizabeth: One Magic Christmas, 552

Harolde, Ralf: Check and Double Check, 242; Ridin' on a Rainbow, 926

Harper, Jessica: Inserts, 496; Pennies from Heaven, 797; Phantom of the Paradise, 798; Shock Treatment, 351

Harper, Jessica: Stardust Memories, 601

Harper, Marjory: Life and Times of Grizzly Adams, The, 189

Harper, Paul: Bloody Trail, 884

Harper, Shari Belafonte: If You Could See What I Hear, 492

Harper, Tess: Amityville III: The Demon, 645; Chiefs, 432; Flashpoint, 57; Starflight One, 867

Harper, Valerie: Blame It on Rio, 230; Chap-
ter Two, 431; Freebie and the Bean, 263; Last Married Couple in America, The, 296

Harrelson, Woody: Wildcats, 382

Harrington, Kate: Rachel, Rachel, 573

Harrington, Laura: Maximum Overdrive, 716

Harrington, Pat: Affair, The, 389

Harris, Barbara: Family Plot, 683; Freaky Friday, 182; Movie Movie, 315; North Avenue Irregulars, The, 196; Oh Dad, Poor Dad—Mama's Hung You in the Closet and I'm Feeling So Sad, 322; Plaza Suite, 331; Seduction of Joe Tynan, The, 590

Harris, Brad: Hercules, 841

Harris, Cynthia: Reuben, Reuben, 339

Harris, Ed: Alamo Bay, 391; Borderline, 22; Code Name: Emerald, 33; Flash of Green, A, 466; Knightriders, 84; Places in the Heart, 563; Right Stuff, The, 580

Harris, Fox: Forbidden World, 686

Harris, Jo Ann: Beguiled, The, 407

Harris, Julie: Bell Jar, The, 408; East of Eden (Original), 454; Harper, 69; Reflections in a Golden Eye, 578; Requiem for a Heavyweight, 578; You're a Big Boy Now, 385

Harris, Julius W.: Islands in the Stream, 498

Harris, Leigh and Lynette: Sorceress, 863

Harris, Marilyn: Frankenstein (Restored Version), 688

Harris, Moira: One More Saturday Night, 324

Harris, Richard: 99 and 44/100 Percent Dead, 108; Bible, The, 410; Camelot, 773; Cassandra Crossing, The, 428; Return of a Man Called Horse, 924

Harrison, Andrew: Littlest Horse Thieves, The, 190

Harrison, George: Help!, 787; Let It Be, 792

Harrison, Gregory: Enola Gay: The Men, the Mission, the Atomic Bomb, 458; Razorback, 733

Harrison, James: Silent Conflict, 931

Harrison, Kathleen: Christmas Carol, A, 177

Harrison, Linda: Beneath the Planet of the Apes, 820

Harrison, Rex: Cleopatra, 435; Doctor Dolittle, 180; Fifth Musketeer, The, 53; My Fair Lady, 794; Prince and the Pauper, The (Remake), 198; Sidewalks of London, 925

Harris, Richard: Between God, The Devil and a Winchester, 882; Hawaii, 483; High Point, 280; His Name Was King, 903; Juggernaut, 80; Major Dundee, 911; Man Called Horse, A, 911; Molly Maguires, The, 537; Mutiny on the Bounty (Remake), 105; Orca, 726; Return of a Man Called Horse, The, 924; Robin and Marian, 123; Wild Geese, The, 163

Harris, Rosalind: Fiddler on the Roof, 779

Harrold, Kathryn: Bogie, 417; Heartbreakers, 484; Hunter, The, 75; Into the Night, 496; Modern Romance, 312; Nightwing, 723; Pursuit of D. B. Cooper, 116; Raw Deal, 119;

Sender, The, *742;* Yes, Giorgio, *813*

Harron, Robert: Intolerance, *497*

Harrow, Lisa: Final Conflict, The, *684;* Shaker Run, *132*

Hart, Dolores: King Creole, *790;* Loving You, *793;* Where the Boys Are, *380*

Hart, John: Blackenstein, *652*

Hart, Mary: Rough Riders' Roundup, *928*

Hart, Roxanne: Oh God, You Devil!, *323*

Hart, Veronica: RSVP, *343*

Hartley, Mariette: Improper Channels, *286;* Ride the High Country, *925*

Hartman, David: Island at the Top of the World, The, *845*

Hartman, Elizabeth: Group, The, *480;* You're a Big Boy Now, *385*

Hartman, Lisa: Where the Boys Are '84, *380*

Hartman, Ras Daniel: Harder They Come, The, *786*

Harvest, Rainbow: Old Enough, *550*

Harvey, Forrester: Chump at Oxford, A, *243*

Harvey, Harry: Cow Town, *890*

Harvey, Laurence: Alamo, The, *878;* Darling, *445;* Escape to the Sun, *459;* Of Human Bondage (Remake), *549*

Harvey, Rodney: Mixed Blood, *101*

Harvey, Verna: Nightcomers, The, *721*

Harwood, Victoria: Adventures of Sherlock Holmes: The Greek Interpreter, *4*

Haskell, Peter: Christina, *31*

Hasselhoff, David: Star Crash, *864*

Hassett, Marilyn: Bell Jar, The, *408;* Other Side of the Mountain, The, *554;* Other Side of the Mountain, Part II, The, *554*

Hasse, O. E.: State of Seige, *602*

Hasso, Signe: Johnny Angel, *79*

Hatch, Richard: Battlestar Galactica, *820;* Charlie Chan and the Curse of the Dragon Queen, *240;* Hatfields and the McCoys, The, *901*

Hatfield, Hurd: Boston Strangler, The, *656;* Dragon Seed, *454;* El Cid, *48;* Picture of Dorian Gray, The, *728*

Hathaway, Noah: NeverEnding Story, The, *853*

Hatton, Raymond: Dawn on the Great Divide, *891;* Frontier Pony Express, *898;* Gunman from Bodie, *900;* Rough Riders' Roundup, *928*

Hatton, Rondo: Brute Man, The, *658*

Hauber, W. C.: Keystone Comedies: Vo. 5, *292*

Hauer, Rutger: Blade Runner, *821;* Chanel Solitaire, *430;* Eureka, *459;* Flesh and Blood, *57;* Hitcher, The, *698;* Ladyhawke, *86;* Nighthawks, *107;* Osterman Weekend, The, *111;* Soldier of Orange, *137*

Hauser, Fay: Jimmy the Kid, *186;* Jo Jo Dancer, Your Life Is Calling, *502;* Marvin and Tige, *530*

Hauser, Patrick: Weekend Pass, *378*

Hauser, Wings: Deadly Force, *39;* Homework, *489;* Jo Jo Dancer, Your Life Is Calling, *502;* Mutant, *720*

Haustein, Thomas: Christiane F., *433*

Havens, Richie: Greased Lightning, *64*

Haverstock, Thom: Skullduggery, *744*

Havers, Nigel: Chariots of Fire, *431*

Havoc, June: Brewster's Millions (1945), *234;* Can't Stop the Music, *773*

Hawke, Ethan: Explorers, *836*

Hawkins, Jack: Ben-Hur, *14;* Bridge on the River Kwai, The, *25;* Escape to the Sun, *459;* Fallen Idol, The, *462;* Malta Story, The, *527;* Shalako, *930;* Young Winston, *641;* Zulu, *167*

Hawn, Goldie: Best Friends, *227;* Butterflies Are Free, *422;* $ (Dollars), *44;* Duchess and the Dirtwater Fox, The, *894;* Foul Play, *262;* Lovers and Liars, *303;* Private Benjamin, *334;* Protocol, *336;* Seems Like Old Times, *349;* Shampoo, *591;* Wildcats, *382*

Haworth, Vinton: Riding on Air, *341*

Hawthorne, Denys: Adventures of Sherlock Holmes: The Crooked Man, *3*

Hawtrey, Charles: Carry on Nurse, *239*

Hay, Mary: Way Down East, *631*

Hay, Virginia: Road Warrior, The, *859*

Hayakawa, Sessue: Bridge on the River Kwai, The, *25;* Hell to Eternity, *485*

Hayden, Linda: Blood on Satan's Claw, *653*

Hayden, Nora: Angry Red Planet, The, *817*

Hayden, Peter: Shaker Run, *132*

Hayden, Sterling: Dr. Strangelove or How I Learned to Stop Worrying and Love the Bomb, *252;* Flat Top, *57;* Gas, *265;* Godfather, The, *473;* Johnny Guitar, *906;* Kansas Pacific, *906;* King of the Gypsies, *508;* Last Command, The, *907;* Last Days of Man on Earth, The, *848;* Winter Kills, *636*

Haydn, Richard: And Then There Were None, *398;* Ball of Fire, *224;* Five Weeks in a Balloon, *56;* Mutiny on the Bounty (Remake), *105;* Young Frankenstein, *385*

Hayes, Alan: Friday the 13th—The Final Chapter, *690*

Hayes, Allison: Attack of the 50-Foot Woman, *647;* Zombies of Mora Tau, *767*

Hayes, Carey: RSVP, *343*

Hayes, Gabby: Dark Command, *891*

Hayes, George "Gabby": Badman's Territory, *880;* Blue Steel, *885;* Colorado, *889;* Heart of the Golden West, *901;* Jesse James at Bay, *905;* Lawless Frontier, *908;* Lucky Texan, *910;* Man from Utah, The, *912;* Melody Ranch, *914;* My Pal Trigger, *916;* 'Neath Arizona Skies, *917;* Randy Rides Alone, *924;* Return of the Badmen, *925;* Riders of Destiny, *926;* Saga of Death Valley, *929;* Star Packer, The, *935;* West of the Divide, *944*

Hayes, Helen: Airport, *7;* Arrowsmith, *401;* Candleshoe, *175;* Family Upside Down, A, *462;* Farewell to Arms, A, *463;* Herbie Rides Again, *185;* One Of Our Dinosaurs Is Missing, *196;* Stage Door Canteen, *599*

Hayes, Patricia: Corn Is Green, The, *439*

Hayes, Peter Lind: Senator Was Indiscreet, The, *349*

Haygarth, Tony: Dracula (Remake), *678*; Private Function, A, *335*

Haymer, John: Four Deuces, The, *59*

Haynes, Linda: Drowning Pool, The, *45*; Rolling Thunder, *123*; Good Guys Wear Black, *63*

Hays, Dan: Little Match Girl, The, *189*

Hays, Robert: Airplane!, *216*; Airplane II: The Sequel, *216*; Cat's Eye, *660*; Scandalous, *345*

Hayward, David: Fallen Angel, *462*

Hayward, Louis: And Then There Were None, *398*; Black Arrow, The, *18*

Hayward, Susan: Adam Had Four Sons, *389*; Back Street, *404*; Conqueror, The, *34*; Fighting Seabees, The, *53*; Jack London, *499*; Lost Moment, The, *522*; Lusty Men, The, *911*; Smash-up: The Story of a Woman, *595*; Young and Willing, *640*

Haywood, Chris: Attack Force Z, *10*; Heatwave, *485*; Man of Flowers, *306*

Hayworth, Rita: Blood and Sand, *414*; Circus World, *889*; Fire Down Below, *464*

Haze, Jonathan: Little Shop of Horrors, The, *713*

Healey, Myron: Incredible Melting Man, The, *843*; Kansas Pacific, *906*

Healy, Katherine: Six Weeks, *594*

Healy, Ted: Hollywood Hotel, *787*

Heard, John: After Hours, *815*; Best Revenge, *14*; Cat People (Remake), *660*; Chilly Scenes of Winter, *432*; C.H.U.D., *658*; Cutter's Way, *441*; Heart Beat, *483*; Heaven Help Us, *278*

Hearn, George: Piano for Mrs. Cimino, A, *562*

Heatherton, Joey: Bluebeard, *655*; Happy Hooker Goes to Washington, The, *275*

Heckart, Eileen: Butterflies Are Free, *423*; Heller in Pink Tights, *902*; Hot Spell, *489*; No Way to Treat a Lady, *546*

Hedaya, Dan: Blood Simple, *19*; Commando, *33*; Reckless, *577*; Running Scared (1986), *125*; Wise Guys, *382*

Hedin, Serene: Sacred Ground, *929*; Windwalker, *946*

Hedison, Al: Fly, The (original), *686*

Hedison, David: ffolkes, *53*

Hedley, Jack: Of Human Bondage (Remake), *549*

Hedren, Tippi: Birds, The, *651*; Harrad Experiment, The, *482*; Marnie, *715*

Hedwall, Deborah: Alone in the Dark, *644*

Heffernan, Honor: Danny Boy, *444*

Heffner, Kyle T.: Runaway Train, *125*

Heflin, Marta: Come Back to the Five and Dime, Jimmy Dean, Jimmy Dean, *436*

Heflin, Van: Airport, *7*; Battle Cry, *12*; Cry of Battle, *37*; Greatest Story Ever Told, The, *478*; Madame Bovary, *526*; Possessed, *565*; Ruthless Four, The, *928*; Santa Fe Trail, *929*; Shane, *930*

Heggie, O. P.: Call It Murder, *424*; Count of Monte Cristo, The (Original), *36*

Heidt, Horace: Pot O' Gold, *566*

Heilbron, Lorna: Creeping Flesh, The, *666*

Heilveil, Elayne: Birds of Prey, *17*; Payday, *560*

Heim, Carrie Kei: Santa Claus—The Movie, *202*

Heiss, Carol: Snow White and the Three Stooges, *205*

Hell, Richard: Smithereens, *596*

Heller, Randee: Can You Hear The Laughter? The Story of Freddie Prinze, *425*

Helmond, Katherine: Brazil, *233*; Family Plot, *683*; Jack and the Beanstalk, *186*

Helm, Anne: Magic Sword, The, *191*; Nightmare In Wax (Crimes In The Wax Museum), *721*

Helm, Brigitte: Metropolis (musical version), *793*; Metropolis, *858*

Helm, Levon: Best Revenge, *14*; Coal Miner's Daughter, *775*; Right Stuff, The, *580*; Smooth Talk, *596*

Helpmann, Robert: Patrick, *726*

Helpmann, Sheila: Getting of Wisdom, The, *471*

Hemingway, Margaux: Lipstick, *712*; Over the Brooklyn Bridge, *326*

Hemingway, Mariel: Creator, *440*; Lipstick, *712*; Manhattan, *305*; Mean Season, The, *98*; Personal Best, *562*; Star 80, *600*

Hemmings, David: Blow-Up, *654*; Camelot, *773*; Dark Forces, *669*; Deep Red, *672*; Disappearance, The, *43*; Islands in the Stream, *498*; Juggernaut, *80*; Mr. Quilp, *794*; Murder By Decree, *103*; Snow Queen, *205*

Henderson, Bill: Get Crazy, *266*

Henderson, Florence: Song of Norway, *803*

Henderson, Jo: Lianna, *517*

Henderson, Robert: Adventures of Sherlock Holmes: The Final Problem, *4*

Hendrix, Jimi: Woodstock, *812*

Hendry, Gloria: Black Belt Jones, *18*

Hendry, Ian: Internecine Project, The, *705*; Passenger, The, *558*

Henner, Marilu: Bloodbrothers, *415*; Cannonball Run II, *237*; Hammett, *68*; Johnny Dangerously, *290*; Man Who Loved Women, The, *306*; Perfect, *561*; Rustler's Rhapsody, *344*

Henning, Pat: Shine On Harvest Moon, *931*

Henn, Carrie: Aliens, *816*

Henreid, Paul: Casablanca, *427*; Four Horsemen of the Apocalypse, *60*; Now, Voyager, *547*

Henrey, Bobby: Fallen Idol, The, *462*

Henriksen, Lance: Aliens, *816*; Nightmares, *722*; Piranha Part Two: The Spawning, *728*

Henry, Buck: Gloria, *62*; Heaven Can Wait,

278; Man Who Fell to Earth, The, 851; Old Boyfriends, 550

Henry, Buzz: Last of the Pony Riders, 907

Henry, Charlotte: March of the Wooden Soldiers, 307

Henry, Frank: Hoppy's Holiday, 904

Henry, Gloria: Rancho Notorious, 923

Henry, Laura: Heavenly Bodies, 278

Henry, Mike: Rio Lobo, 927; Smokey and the Bandit II, 355; Smokey and the Bandit, 354

Henry, Thomas B.: Earth vs. the Flying Saucers, 832

Hensley, Pamela: Buck Rogers in the 25th Century, 822; Doc Savage... The Man of Bronze, 830; Double Exposure, 678

Henson, Nicky: Psychomania, 731

Henteloff, Alex: Red Light Sting, The, 577

Hepburn, Audrey: Bloodline, 415; Breakfast at Tiffany's, 419; Charade, 29; Funny Face, 781; My Fair Lady, 794; Robin and Marian, 123; Roman Holiday, 583

Hepburn, Dee: Gregory's Girl, 273

Hepburn, Katharine: Adam's Rib, 215; African Queen, The, 389; Alice Adams, 392; Bringing Up Baby, 234; Christopher Strong, 433; Corn Is Green, The, 439; Dragon Seed, 454; Grace Quigley, 271; Guess Who's Coming to Dinner, 460; Lion In Winter, The, 519; Little Minister, The, 519; Little Women, 519; Long Day's Journey into Night, 520; Mary of Scotland, 530; On Golden Pond, 551; Philadelphia Story, The, 329; Rooster Cogburn, 928; Spitfire, 599; Stage Door Canteen, 599; Stage Door, 357; State of the Union, 602; Woman of the Year, 383

Herbert, Hugh: Dames, 776; Danger Lights, 443; Footlight Parade, 780; Hollywood Hotel, 787

Herbert, Louis: Forbidden Games, 467

Herbert, Percy: Captain Apache, 888

Herbert, Tim: Duel, 679

Herd, Richard: Fighting Back, 53

Herlie, Eileen: Hamlet, 481

Herlihy, James Leo: Four Friends, 468

Herman, Pee-Wee: Pee-Wee's Big Adventure, 328

Hermine, Pepi: Putney Swope, 337

Hermine, Ruth: Putney Swope, 337

Hermits, Herman's: Mrs. Brown You've Got a Lovely Daughter, 794

Hernandez, Juano: Something of Value, 138

Herrier, Mark: Porky's, 333; Porky's Revenge, 333; Porky's II: The Next Day, 333

Herrmann, Edward: Annie, 769; Compromising Positions, 247; Man With One Red Shoe, The, 306; Mrs. Soffel, 536; Murrow, 539; North Avenue Irregulars, The, 196; Portrait of a Stripper, 565; Purple Rose of Cairo, The, 337; Reds, 578

Herrod, Brandy: Some Call It Loving, 597

Hershey, Barbara: Americana, 396; Boxcar

Bertha, 23; Entity, The, 680; Flood!, 685; Hannah and Her Sisters, 275; Last Summer, 514; Liberation of L. B. Jones, The, 517; Nightingale, The, 195; Right Stuff, The, 580; With Six You Get Eggroll, 383

Hersholt, Jean: Heidi, 184

Hervey, Irene: Count of Monte Cristo, The (Original), 36; Mr. Peabody and the Mermaid, 311; Play Misty for Me, 729

Herzog, Werner: Man of Flowers, 306

Hesseman, Howard: Big Bus, The, 229; Doctor Detroit, 252; Loose Shoes, 301; My Chauffeur, 316; Police Academy II: Their First Assignment, 332; Princess Who Had Never Laughed, The, 199; Private Lessons, 335; Flight of the Navigator, 837

Hess, David: Last House on the Left, 711

Heston, Charlton: 55 Days at Peking, 464; Airport 1975, 391; Antony and Cleopatra, 401; Awakening, The, 648; Beneath the Planet of the Apes, 820; Ben-Hur, 14; Big Country, 882; Buccaneer, The, 25; Call of the Wild, 27; Chiefs, 432; Earthquake, 46; El Cid, 48; Four Musketeers, The, 60; Greatest Show on Earth, The, 478; Greatest Story Ever Told, The, 478; Major Dundee, 911; Midway, 99; Mother Lode, 103; Mountain Men, The, 915; Omega Man, The, 854; Planet of the Apes, 856; Pony Express, 922; Prince and the Pauper, The (Remake), 198; Ruby Gentry, 585; Soylent Green, 863

Hewett, Christopher: Producers, The, 336

Hewitt, Alan: Barefoot Executive, The, 172; Misadventures of Merlin Jones, The, 192

Hewitt, Barbara: Equinox (The Beast), 680

Hewitt, Martin: Endless Love, 458

Heyburn, Weldon: Git Along, Little Dogies, 898

Heyman, Barton: Let's Scare Jessica to Death, 712

Heywood, Pat: Rude Awakening, 738

Hickey, William: Prizzi's Honor, 569

Hickman, Dwayne: High School, USA, 280; How to Stuff a Wild Bikini, 788

Hicks, Catharine: Death Valley, 672; Razor's Edge, The (Remake), 576

Hicks, Leonard: Santa Claus Conquers the Martians, 860

Higgins, Anthony: Bride, The, 656; Quartet, 571; Young Sherlock Holmes, 167

Hildebrandt, Charles George: Return of the Alien's Deadly Spawn, The, 734

Hill, Arthur: Andromeda Strain, The, 817; Dirty Tricks, 251; Futureworld, 838; Guardian, The, 480; Harper, 69; Killer Elite, The, 83; One Magic Christmas, 552; Ordeal of Dr. Mudd, The 553

Hill, Benny: Chitty Chitty Bang Bang, 177

Hill, Dana: Boy Who Left Home to Find Out about the Shivers, The, 174; Cross Creek, 441; European Vacation, 256; Fallen Angel, 462; Shoot the Moon, 592

Hill, Howard: Singing Buckaroo, 932

Hill, Jean: Desperate Living, 250

Hill, Mariana: Baby, The, 648; Blood Beach, 653; Death at Love House, 672; High Plains Drifter, 903; Schizoid, 704

Hill, Norman: Burn!, 421

Hill, Robert: Deathstalker, 829

Hill, Steven: Legal Eagles, 88; Raw Deal, 119; Rich and Famous, 579; Yentl, 813

Hill, Terence: Mr. Billion, 100

Hiller, Kurt: Last Laugh, The, 514

Hiller, Wendy: Cat and The Canary, The, 660; Elephant Man, The, 456; Man for All Seasons, A, 528; Something of Value, 138

Hillerman, John: Paper Moon, 327

Hilliard, Harriet: Follow the Fleet, 780

Hillie, Verna: Mystery Mountain, 916; Star Packer, The, 935

Hilligoss, Candace: Carnival of Souls, 659

Hillman, Warren: Ator: The Fighting Eagle, 818

Hilton, Daisy: Freaks, 689

Hilton, George: Battle of El Alamein, The, 12; Ruthless Four, The, 928

Hilton, Violet: Freaks, 689

Hindle, Art: Brood, The, 657; Man Who Wasn't There, The, 306; Raw Courage, 119; Small Town in Texas, A, 137

Hinds, Cindy: Brood, The, 657

Hinds, Samuel S.: Dr. Kildare's Strange Case, 43

Hines, Gregory: Cotton Club, The, 36; Deal of the Century, 249; Puss in Boots, 200; Running Scared (1986), 125; White Nights, 632; Wolfen, 766

Hines, Harry: Last of the Pony Riders, 907

Hingle, Pat: Bloody Mama, 20; Brewster's Millions (1985), 235; Falcon and the Snowman, The, 461; Gauntlet, The, 62; Going Berserk, 269; Hang 'Em High, 900; Invitation to a Gunfighter, 905; Maximum Overdrive, 716; Nevada Smith, 917; Norma Rae, 546; Of Mice and Men, 549; Running Brave, 585; Running Scared (1980), 126; Splendor in the Grass, 599; Wild Times, 945

Hinton, James David: Galaxina, 839

Hirato, Akihiko: Samurai Trilogy, The, 137; Rodan, 860

Hird, Thora: Nightcomers, The, 721

Hirsch, Judd: Ordinary People, 554; Without a Trace, 637; Goodbye People, The, 475

Hitchcock, Patricia: Psycho, 731; Stage Fright, 747

Hittscher, Paul: Fitzcarraldo, 465

Hobart, Rose: Brighton Strangler, The, 657

Hobson, Valerie: Bride of Frankenstein, 657; Drums, 46; Kind Hearts and Coronets, 292

Hodge, Patricia: Betrayal, 409

Hodgins, Earle: Devil's Playground, 893; Marauders, 913; Riders of the Deadline, 926; Silent Conflict, 931

Hodiak, John: Lifeboat, 518; Love from a Stranger, 713

Hoey, Dennis: Sherlock Holmes and the Secret Weapon, 134

Hoffman, Dustin: Agatha, 390; All the President's Men, 394; Graduate, The, 475; Kramer vs. Kramer, 510; Lenny, 516; Little Big Man, 909; Marathon Man, 97; Midnight Cowboy, 533; Papillon, 112

Hoffman, Elizabeth: Fear No Evil, 683

Hoffman, Thom: Fourth Man, The, 687

Holbrook, Hal: Capricorn One, 822; Creepshow, 666; Fog, The, 686; Group, The, 480; Kidnapping of the President, The, 709; Magnum Force, 94; Midway, 99; Star Chamber, The, 600

Holden, Fay: Love Laughs at Andy Hardy, 302

Holden, Gloria: Life of Emile Zola, The, 518

Holden, William: Alvarez Kelly, 879; Born Yesterday, 232; Bridge on the River Kwai, The, 25; Casino Royale, 239; Country Girl, The, 439; Damien: Omen II, 668; Dear Wife, 249; Earthling, The, 46; Golden Boy, 475; Horse Soldiers, The, 904; Love is a Many-Splendored Thing, 523; Moon Is Blue, The, 314; Network, 543; Our Town, 555; Rachel and the Stranger, 923; Stalag 17, 139; S.O.B., 355; When Time Ran Out, 764; When Wolves Cry, 632; Wild Bunch, The, 945; Young and Willing, 640

Holder, Geoffrey: Live and Let Die, 91

Holdren, Judd: Satan's Satellites, 128; Zombies of the Stratosphere (Satan's Satellites), 167

Holiday, Hope: Kill Point, 83

Hollander, David: Call to Glory, 424

Holland, Pamela: Dorm That Dripped Blood, The, 678

Holliday, Judy: Adam's Rib, 215; Born Yesterday, 232; It Should Happen to You, 287

Holliday, Polly: Gremlins, 840

Holliman, Earl: Hot Spell, 489; Sons of Katie Elder, The, 934

Hollis Jr., Carey: Raggedy Man, 733

Holloway, Stanley: Hamlet, 481; Journey Into Fear, 503; Lavender Hill Mob, The, 397; Mrs. Brown You've Got a Lovely Daughter, 794; My Fair Lady, 794; Private Life of Sherlock Holmes, The, 115

Holloway, Sterling: Cheers for Miss Bishop, 432; Gold Diggers of 1933, 783; Little Men, 519; Robin Hood of Texas, 927; Sioux City Sue, 933

Holloway, W. E.: Elephant Boy, 48

Holly, Lauren: Band of the Hand, 12

Holmes, Hollye: Adventures of the Wilderness Family, 170

Holmes, Phillips: Criminal Code, The, 440

Holm, Astrid: Master Of The House (Du Skal Aere Din Hustru), 308; Witchcraft Through the Ages (Haxan), 637

Holm, Celeste: All About Eve, 393; Champagne for Caesar, 240

Holm, Ian: Alien, 815; All Quiet on the Western Front, 393; Brazil, 233; Dance With a Stranger, 443; Dreamchild, 831; Greystoke: The Legend of Tarzan, Lord of the Apes, 67; Juggernaut, 80; Return of the Soldier, The, 579; Robin and Marian, 123; Shout at the Devil, 135

Holotik, Rosie: Encounter with the Unknown, 833

Holton, Mark: Pee-Wee's Big Adventure, 328

Holt, David: Last Days of Pompeii, The, 513

Holt, Hans: Almost Angels, 171

Holt, Jack: My Pal Trigger, 916

Holt, Jennifer: Private Buckaroo, 799

Holt, Patrick: Psychomania, 731

Holt, Steven: Preppies, 333

Holt, Tim: His Kind of Woman, 73; Hitler's Children, 73; Magnificent Ambersons, The, 526

Holzer, Baby Jane: Ciao! Manhattan, 433

Homolka, Oscar: Ball of Fire, 224; Funeral In Berlin, 61; I Remember Mama, 491; Mooncussers, 193; Sabotage, 738; Seven Year Itch, The, 350

Hong, James: Big Trouble in Little China, 17; Missing in Action, 100; Yes, Giorgio, 813

Hood, Don: Marie, 529

Hood, Noel: Curse of Frankenstein, The, 667

Hooks, Kevin: Can You Hear The Laughter? The Story of Freddie Prinze, 425; Sounder, 598

Hooks, Robert: Fast-Walking, 464

Hope, Bob: Boy, Did I Get a Wrong Number!, 233; Muppet Movie, The, 193; My Favorite Brunette, 316; Off Limits, 322; Paleface, The, 327; Princess and the Pirate, The, 334; Road to Bali, 342

Hopkins, Anthony: Audrey Rose, 648; Bounty, The, 23; Change of Seasons, A, 240; Elephant Man, The, 456; International Velvet, 186; Juggernaut, 80; Lion In Winter, The, 519; Looking Glass War, The, 521; Magic, 713; Mussolini and I, 539; QB VII, 571

Hopkins, Bo: American Graffiti, 218; Day of the Locust, The, 446; Fifth Floor, The, 684; Killer Elite, The, 83; Last Ride of the Dalton Boys, The, 908; Mutant, 720; Rodeo Girl, 583; Small Town in Texas, A, 137

Hopkins, Bob: White Lightning, 162

Hopkins, Miriam: Becky Sharp, 407; Chase, The, 431; Heiress, The, 485

Hopkins, Shirley Knight: Secrets, 590

Hopper, Dennis: American Friend, The, 396; Easy Rider, 455; Giant, 472; King of the Mountain, 508; Mad Dog Morgan, 94; My Science Project, 853; Osterman Weekend, The, 111; Rebel Without a Cause, 576; Rumble Fish, 585; Wild Times, 945

Hopper, Hedda: Alice Adams, 392

Hordern, Michael: Christmas Carol, A, 177; How I Won the War, 284; Joseph Andrews, 290; Missionary, The, 310; Mr. Quilp, 794; Where Eagles Dare, 161

Horne, Lena: Cabin in the Sky, 423; Wiz, The, 812; Ziegfeld Follies, 814

Horse, Michael: Legend of the Lone Ranger, The, 908

Horton, Edward Everett: Front Page, The, 264; Gay Divorcee, The, 782; Here Comes Mr. Jordan, 279; Reaching for the Moon, 337; Shall We Dance?, 802

Horton, Louisa: Alice, Sweet Alice (Communion and Holy Terror), 643

Horton, Peter: Children of the Corn, 662

Horton, Robert: Silver Blaze, 136

Hoshi, Yuriko: Ghidrah, the Three-Headed Monster, 692; Kojiro, 85

Hoskins, Bob: Brazil, 233; Inserts, 496; Lassiter, 86; Long Good Friday, The, 92; Mona Lisa, 537; Mussolini and I, 539; Pink Floyd the Wall, 798

Hossein, Robert: Battle of El Alamein, The, 12

Hotchkis, Joan: Last Game, The, 513; Ode to Billy Joe, 548

Hotten, Peter: Fantasies, 463

Hotton, Donald: Hearse, The, 697

Houghton, Katharine: Guess Who's Coming to Dinner, 480

Hould, Ra: Boots and Saddles, 885

Houseman, John: Fog, The, 686; Ghost Story, 693; Murder by Phone, 719; Old Boyfriends, 550; Paper Chase, The, 557; Rollerball, 860; St. Ives, 126; Wholly Moses!, 381

Houser, Jerry: Bad Company, 880; Class of '44, 434

House, Billy: Bedlam, 649

House, Ron: Bullshot, 236

Houston, Donald: Maniac, 714; Partners in Crime—The Secret Adversary, 113; Where Eagles Dare, 161

Houston, Robert: Hills Have Eyes, The, 697

Howard, Boothe: Man of the Frontier, (Red River Valley), 912

Howard, Brie: Android, 817

Howard, Clint: Evilspeak, 681; Gung Ho, 274; Rock 'n' Roll High School, 342

Howard, Esther: Detour, 450

Howard, Frank: One More Saturday Night, 324

Howard, John: Highest Honor, The, 73; Love from a Stranger, 713

Howard, Kathleen: It's a Gift, 288

Howard, Ken: 1776, 802

Howard, Kevyn Major: Roadhouse 66, 122

Howard, Leslie: 49th Parallel, The, 468; Gone with the Wind, 475; Intermezzo, 496; Of Human Bondage (Original), 549; Petrified Forest, The, 562; Scarlet Pimpernel, The, 129; Stand-In, 358

Howard, Marion: Road Games, 736

Howard, Mary: Abe Lincoln in Illinois, *387;* Nurse Edith Cavell, *548*

Howard, Mel: Hester Street, *487*

Howard, Rance: Bloody Trail, *884*

Howard, Ron: Music Man, The, *794;* American Graffiti, *218;* Bitter Harvest, *413;* Eat My Dust, *47;* Grand Theft Auto, *64;* Run Stranger Run, *738;* Shootist, The, *931*

Howard, Shemp: Africa Screams, *215;* Bank Dick, The, *324*

Howard, Susan: Moonshine County Express, *103;* Night Games, *544;* Sidewinder 1, *135*

Howard, Trevor: Catch Me a Spy, *28;* Catholics, *428;* Doll's House, A, *453;* Gandhi, *471;* Hurricane, *76;* Last Remake of Beau Geste, The, *297;* Missionary, The, *310;* Mutiny on the Bounty (Remake), *105;* Night Visitor, The, *723;* Ryan's Daughter, *586;* Sea Wolves, The, *130;* Windwalker, *946*

Howard, Willie: Broadway Melody of 1938, *773*

Howat, Clark: Billy Jack, *17*

Howell, C. Thomas: Grandview, U.S.A., *477;* Hitcher, The, *698;* Outsiders, The, *555;* Red Dawn, *119;* Secret Admirer, *346*

Howell, Kenneth: Pride of the Bowery, *567*

Howes, Reed: Dawn Rider, *892;* Paradise Canyon, *922;* South of the Border, *934*

Howes, Sally Ann: Chitty Chitty Bang Bang, *177;* Nicholas Nickleby, *544*

Howlin, Olin: Blob, The, *652*

Hoyt, John: My Favorite Brunette, *316;* Operation C.I.A., *110;* When Worlds Collide, *876;* X (The Man with the X-Ray Eyes), *877*

Hsieh, Wang: Infra-Man, *844*

Hsio, Miao Ker: Chinese Connection, The, *31*

Hsiu-Hsien, Lie: Infra-Man, *844*

Hubbard, John: You'll Never Get Rich, *814*

Hubley, Season: Hardcore, *481*

Hubschmid, Paul: Funeral In Berlin, *61*

Huckabee, Cooper: Funhouse, The, *691*

Huddleston, David: Bad Company, *880;* Santa Claus—The Movie, *202;* Woman in Red, The, *383;* World's Greatest Lover, The, *384*

Hudd, Walter: Elephant Boy, *48*

Hudson, Ernie: Ghostbusters, *267;* Spacehunter: Adventures in the Forbidden Zone, *864*

Hudson, Rock: Ambassador, The, *395;* Avalanche, *10;* Bend of the River, *882;* Embryo, *833;* Giant, *472;* Ice Station Zebra, *77;* Lover Come Back, *303;* Magnificent Obsession, *527;* Mirror Crack'd, The, *99;* Pillow Talk, *330;* Something of Value, *138*

Hudson, Toni: Just One of the Guys, *292;* Prime Risk, *115;* School Spirit, *346*

Hudson, William: Attack of the 50-Foot Woman, *647*

Huff, Brent: Nine Deaths of the Ninja, *107;* Perils of Gwendoline, The, *114*

Huffman, David: Firefox, *54;* F.I.S.T., *461;* St. Helens, *587*

Hughes, Barnard: First Monday in October, *465;* Hospital, The, *283;* Maxie, *308;* Midnight Cowboy, *533;* Rage, *573;* Sisters, *744;* Where's Poppa?, *381*

Hughes, Carol: Man From Music Mountain, *912*

Hughes, Helen: Incubus, The, *705*

Hughes, Lloyd: Lost World, The, *850*

Hughes, Robert: Squizzy Taylor, *139*

Hughes, Wendy: Careful He Might Hear You, *426;* Dangerous Summer, A, *444;* Lonely Hearts, *520;* My Brilliant Career, *540;* My First Wife, *541;* Newsfront, *543*

Hughs, Sandy: High Rolling, *72*

Hugh-Kelly, Daniel: Cujo, *667*

Hugo, Mauritz: Revenge of the Zombies, *736*

Hulce, Thomas: Echo Park, *455;* Amadeus, *769*

Hull, Dianne: Aloha, Bobby and Rose, *7;* Fifth Floor, The, *684*

Hull, Henry: Babes in Arms, *769;* Call It Murder, *424;* Desert Trail, *893;* High Sierra, *72;* Jesse James, *905;* Lifeboat, *518;* Master of the World, *911;* Proud Rebel, The, *923;* Return of Frank James, The, *925*

Hull, Josephine: Arsenic and Old Lace, *220*

Humbert, George: I Cover the Waterfront, *76*

Hume, Benita: Private Life of Don Juan, The, *568*

Hunnicutt, Arthur: Big Sky, The, *883;* Last Command, The, *907*

Hunnicutt, Gayle: Adventures of Sherlock Holmes: A Scandal in Bohemia, *2;* Dream Lover, *679;* Legend of Hell House, The, *711;* Return of the Man from U.N.C.L.E., The, *121;* Wild Angels, The, *163*

Hunnicutt, Arthur: El Dorado, *895;* Harry and Tonto, *483*

Hunt, Eleanor: Blue Steel, *885;* Whoopee, *812*

Hunt, Gareth: Bloodbath at the House of Death *230*

Hunt, Jimmy: Invaders From Mars (Original), *844*

Hunt, Linda: Bostonians, The, *417;* Eleni, *456;* Silverado, *932;* Year of Living Dangerously, The, *165*

Hunt, Marsha A: Howling II... Your Sister is a Werewolf, *702*

Hunt, Marsha: Johnny Got His Gune *503;* Pride and Prejudice, *567;* Smash-up: The Story of a Woman, *595;* Becket, *406*

Hunt, Martita: Man in Grey, The, *528*

Hunter, Bill: Heatwave, *485;* Hit, The, *73;* Newsfront, *543*

Hunter, Ian: Adventures of Robin Hood, The, *2;* Little Princess, The, *190;* Smilin' Through, *803*

Hunter, Jeffrey: Great Locomotive Chase, The, *182;* Guide For The Married Man, A, *273;* Hell to Eternity, *485;* Searchers, The, *930;* Star Trek: The Menagerie, *865*

Hunter, Kaki: Just the Way You Are, *505;* Proky's Revenge, *333;* Porky's II: The Next Day, *333;* Whose Life Is It, Anyway?, *633*

Hunter, Kim: Beneath the Planet of the Apes, *820;* Born Innocent, *417;* Deadline USA, *447;* Escape from the Planet of the Apes, *835;* Lilith, *518;* Planet of the Apes, *856*

Hunter, Tab: Battle Cry, *12;* Damn Yankees, *776;* Kid from Left Field, The, *187;* Lust in the Dust, *303;* Polyester, *333*

Hunter, Tomas: Battle of the Commandos, *13*

Hunter, Tony: Naked in the Sun, *917*

Huppert, Isabelle: Clean State (Coup de Torchon), *244;* Entre Nous (Between Us), *458;* Going Places, *270;* La Truite (The Trout), *512*

Hurst, Brandon: White Zombie, *764*

Hurt, John: Alien, *815;* Champions, *430;* Disappearance, The, *43;* Elephant Man, The, *456;* Ghoul, The, *693;* Heaven's Gate, *902;* Hit, The, *73;* Jake Speed, *78;* Midnight Express, *533;* Night Crossing, *106;* Osterman Weekend, The, *111;* Partners, *328;* Shout, The, *743*

Hurt, Mary Beth: Chilly Scenes of Winter, *432;* Compromising Positions, *247;* D.A.R.Y.L., *827;* World According to Garp, The, *639*

Hurt, Wesley Ivan: Popeye, *199*

Hurt, William: Altered States, *817;* Big Chill, The, *411;* Body Heat, *417;* Eyewitness, *682;* Gorky Park, *64;* Kiss of the Spider Woman, *509*

Husky, Ferlin: Hillbillys in a Haunted House, *280*

Hussey, Olivia: Cat and The Canary, The, *660;* Escape 2000, *835;* Man with Bogart's Face, The, *96;* Romeo and Juliet, *584*

Hussey, Ruth: Philadelphia Story, The, *329*

Huster, Francis: Edith and Marcel, *778*

Huston, Anjelica: Ice Pirates, *842;* Postman Always Rings Twice, The (Remake), *566;* Prizzi's Honor, *569*

Huston, John: Battle Force, *12;* Battle for the Planet of the Apes, *819;* Bible, The, *410;* Breakout, *24;* Casino Royale, *239;* Chinatown, *30;* Lovesick, *303;* Minor Miracle, A, *192;* Wind and the Lion, The, *164;* Winter Kills, *636;* Word, The, *638*

Huston, Virginia: Night Stage to Galveston, *917*

Huston, Walter: Abraham Lincoln, *388;* And Then There Were None, *398;* Ann Vickers, *399;* Criminal Code, The, *440;* Dodsworth, *452;* Dragon Seed, *454;* North Star, The, *108;* Outlaw, The, *920;* Rain, *574;* Yankee Doodle Dandy, *813*

Hutchins, Will: Shooting, The, *931*

Hutton, Betty: Greatest Show on Earth, The, *478;* Perils of Pauline, The, *329*

Hutton, Jim: Don't Be Afraid of the Dark, *677;* Green Berets, The, *66;* Hellfighters, *70;* Major Dundee, *911;* Where the Boys Are, *380;* Who's Minding the Mint?, *381*

Hutton, Lauren: American Gigolo, *396;* Gambler, The, *470;* Gator, *61;* Lassiter, *86;* Once Bitten, *323;* Paternity, *328;* Snow Queen, *205;* Starflight One, *867;* Wedding, A, *378;* Welcome to L.A., *631;* Zorro, the Gay Blade, *386*

Hutton, Timothy: Daniel, *444;* Falcon and the Snowman, The, *461;* Iceman, *843;* Ordinary People, *554;* Young Love, First Love, *640*

Hutton, Tom: Demon Lover, The, *673*

Huxtable, Judy: Scream and Scream Again, *740*

Huy-Quan, Ke: Goonies, The, *63*

Hyams, Leila: Freaks, *689*

Hyde-White, Wilfrid: Chamber of Horrors, *661;* In Search of the Castaways, *185;* Winslow Boy, The, *635*

Hyer, Martha: Chase, The, *431;* Night of the Grizzly, The, *918;* Sons of Katie Elder, The, *934*

Hyland, Diana: Boy in the Plastic Bubble, The, *418*

Hynson, Mike: Endless Summer, The, *48*

Hyser, Joyce: Just One of the Guys, *292*

Idle, Eric: And Now for Something Completely Different, *218;* European Vacation, *256;* Life of Brian, *299;* Monty Python Live at the Hollywood Bowl, *313;* Monty Python's the Meaning of Life, *313;* Pied Piper of Hamelin, The, *198;* Yellowbeard, *385*

Ihnat, Steve: Hunter, *75;* Madigan, *94*

Ina, Estela: Los Olvidados, *522*

Inaba, Yoshio: Seven Samurai, The, *131*

Inclan, Miguel: Los Olvidados, *522*

Inescort, Frieda: Return of the Vampire, The, *735;* You'll Never Get Rich, *814*

Infuhr, Teddy: Hills of Utah, The, *903*

Ingalls, Joyce: Deadly Force, *39*

Ingersoll, Amy: Knightriders, *84*

Ingram, Jack: Saga of Death Valley, *929*

Ingram, Rex: Cabin in the Sky, *423;* Dark Waters, *445;* Green Pastures, The, *479*

Inosanto, Danny: Game of Death, *61*

Ireland, Jill: Breakheart Pass, *886;* Breakout, *24;* Chino, *888;* Death Wish II, *40;* Family, The, *52;* Hard Times, *69;* Love and Bullets, *93;* Mechanic, The, *98;* Rider on the Rain, *122*

Ireland, John: 55 Days at Peking, *464;* All the King's Men, *394;* Escape to the Sun, *459;* Fall of the Roman Empire, The, *462;* Farewell My Lovely, *52;* Gunfight at the O.K. Corral, *900;* House of Seven Corpses, The, *700;* Incubus, The, *705;* Ransom, *118;* Wild

in the Country, 634
Iron, Dusty: Windwalker, 946
Irons, Jeremy: Betrayal, 409; French Lieutenant's Woman, The, 469; Moonlighting, 538; Wild Duck, The, 634
Ironside, Michael: Cross Country, 440; Jo Jo Dancer, Your Life Is Calling, 502; Spacehunter: Adventures in the Forbidden Zone, 864
Irving, Amy: Competition, The, 437; Far Pavilions, The, 463; Fury, The, 692; Honeysuckle Rose, 788; Micki & Maude, 309; Yentl, 813
Irving, George: Blue Money, 231
Irving, Julius: Fish That Saved Pittsburgh, The, 261
Ito, Emi: Ghidrah, the Three-Headed Monster, 692
Ivanek, Zeljko: Mass Appeal, 531
Ivan, Rosalind: Scarlet Street, 589
Ivar, Stan: Creature, 826
Ivashov, Vladimir: Ballad of a Soldier, 404
Ives, Burl: Big Country, 882; Cat on a Hot Tin Roof (Original), 428; Daydreamer, The, 179; Desire Under the Elms, 449; East of Eden (Original), 454; Ensign Pulver, 255; So Dear to My Heart, 206
Ivey, Judith: Compromising Positions, 247; Woman in Red, The, 383
Ivo, Tommy: Hills of Utah, The, 903
Ivy, Rosalind: Pursuit to Algiers, 117

Jackson, Anne: Bell Jar, The, 408; Sam's Son, 588; Secret Life of An American Wife, The, 347
Jackson, Cinda: Wild Rose, 634
Jackson, Glenda: Class of Miss MacMichael, The, 435; Hopscotch, 74; House Calls, 283; Lost and Found, 301; Nasty Habits, 317; Return of the Soldier, The, 579; Romantic Englishwoman, The, 584; Sakharov, 587; Women in Love, 638
Jackson, Gordon: Fighting Prince of Donegal, The, 181; Mutiny on the Bounty (Remake), 105; Shooting Party, The, 592
Jackson, Jamie Smith: Bug, 658
Jackson, Kate: Death at Love House, 672; Dirty Tricks, 251; Making Love, 527; Satan's School for Girls, 739; Wiz, The, 812
Jackson, Phillip: Robin Hood and the Sorcerer, 123
Jack, Wolfman: American Graffiti, 218; Motel Hell, 718
Jacobi, Derek: Enigma, 49; Odessa File, The, 110
Jacobi, Lou: Better Late than Never, 228; Everything You Always Wanted to Know about Sex But Were Afraid to Ask, 257; Irma La Douce, 287; Roseland, 584
Jacoby, Billy: Just One of the Guys, 292
Jacquet, Frank: Shine On Harvest Moon, 931

Jacquet, Roger: Occurrence at Owl Creek Bridge, An, 548
Jade, Claude: Love on the Run, 524
Jaeckel, Richard: Black Moon Rising, 18; Cold River, 177; Dark, The, 669; Day of the Animals, 670; Drowning Pool, The, 45; Flight of the Phoenix, The, 58; Grizzly, 695; Sands of Iwo Jima, 128; Sometimes a Great Notion, 597; Starman, 867
Jaffer, Melissa: Caddie, 423
Jaffe, Robert: Creature, 826
Jaffe, Sam: Ben-Hur, 14; Day the Earth Stood Still, The, 828; Dunwich Horror, The, 680; Guide For The Married Man, A, 273; Gunga Din, 67
Jaffrey, Saeed: My Beautiful Launderette, 540
Jagger, Dean: Alligator, 644; Elmer Gantry, 457; End of the World, 834; Game of Death, 61; Glass House, The, 473; I Heard the Owl Call My Name, 491; King Creole, 790; Proud Rebel, The, 923; Robe, The, 581
Jagger, Mick: Gimme Shelter, 783; Let's Spend the Night Together, 792; Nightingale, The, 195; Performance, 561
James, Byron: Southern Comfort, 138
James, Clifton: Bad News Bears in Breaking Training, The, 223; Buster and Billie, 422
James, Elizabeth: Born Losers, 22
James, Godfrey: At the Earth's Core, 818
James, Harry: Private Buckeroo, 799
James, Ron: Boogeyman, The, 655
James, Sidney: Another Time, Another Place, 400; Carry On Cowboy, 238; Lavender Hill Mob, The 297
James, Sonny: Hillbilly's in a Haunted House, 280
James, Steve: American Ninjak, 7 Brother from Another Planet, The, 822; Exterminator, The, 50; P.O.W.: The Escape, 112
James, Susan Saint: Carbon Copy, 238; Don't Cry, It's Only Thunder 453; How to Beat the High Co$t of Living, 284; Outlaw Blues, 325; S.O.S. Titanic, 586
James, Timothy: Nightmares, 722
James, Anthony: High Plains Drifter, 903
James, Billy T.: Came a Hot Friday, 27
James, Brion: Armed and Dangerous, 220; Enemy Mine, 834
Jameson, Joyce: Death Race 2000, 829
Janda, Krystyna: Mephisto, 532
Janis, Conrad: Duchess and the Dirtwater Fox, The, 894; Red Light Sting, The, 577
Janney, Leon: Charly, 823
Jannings, Emil: Blue Angel, The, 415; Last Laugh, The, 514
Janson, Horst: Captain Kronos: Vampire Hunter, 659; Murphy's War, 104
Janssen, David: Birds of Prey, 17; Fer-de-Lance, 684; Green Berets, The, 66; Hell to Eternity, 485; Marooned, 851; Moon of the Wolf, 718; S.O.S. Titanic, 586; To Hell and

Back, *152*; Word, The, *638*

Jaquemont, Maurice: Return of Martin Guerre, The, *578*

Jardine, Al: Beach Boys: An American Band, The, *770*

Jarman Jr., Claude: Rio Grande, *927*; Yearling, The, *213*

Jarnais, Marthe: Vagabond, *627*

Jarratt, John: Odd Angry Shot, The, *548*; Summer City, *143*

Jarret, Gabe: Real Genius, *338*

Jarvis, Graham: Doin' Time, *253*

Jason, Harvey: Witching, The (Necromancy), *765*

Jason, Neville: Message, The (Mohammad, Messenger of God), *533*

Jayston, Michael: Internecine Project, The, *705*; Nicholas and Alexandra, *543*

Jean, Gloria: Never Give a Sucker an Even Break, *318*

Jeanneret, Anaïs: Peril, *561*

Jeans, Isabel: Heavens Above, *279*; Suspicion, *750*

Jeans, Ursula: Dam Busters, The, *38*

Jeavons, Colin: Adventures of Sherlock Holmes: The Norwood Builder, *5*

Jefferson, Thomas: Tarzan of the Apes, *145*

Jefford, Barbara: And the Ship Sails On, *398*; Lust for a Vampire, *713*

Jeffrey, Herbert: Harlem Rides the Range, *900*

Jeffrey, Peter: Dr. Phibes Rises Again, *676*

Jeffreys, Anne: Dick Tracy, *42*; Dillinger, *42*; Return of the Badmen, *925*

Jeffries, Fran: Harum Scarum, *787*

Jeffries, Lang: Junkman, The, *80*

Jeffries, Lionel: Camelot, *773*; Chitty Chitty Bang Bang, *177*; Fanny, *463*; Oh Dad, Poor Dad—Mama's Hung You in the Closet and I'm Feeling So Sad, *322*; Prisoner of Zenda, The, *334*; Who Slew Auntie Roo?, *764*

Jei, Li Lin: Shaolin Temple, *132*

Jemison, Anna: Heatwave, *485*; Smash Palace, *595*

Jene, Aubrey: Summer Rental, *361*

Jenkins, Allen: Ball of Fire, *224*; Five Came Back, *465*

Jenks, Si: Song of Nevada, *933*

Jenner, Bruce: Can't Stop the Music, *773*

Jennings, Claudia: DeathSport, *829*; Great Texas Dynamite Chase, The, *66*

Jennings, DeWitt: Arrowsmith, *401*

Jennings, Maxinne: Mr. Wong, Detective, *101*

Jennings, Waylon: (Sesame Street Presents) Follow That Bird, *204*

Jensen, Cleo: Elvira Madigan, *457*

Jensen, David: Petronella, *197*

Jensen, Maren: Deadly Blessing, *671*

Jenson, Roy: Crossfire, *890*

Jergens, Adele: Fuller Brush Man, The, *264*

Jesse, Dan: Angel of H.E.A.T., *8*

Jett, Roger: Smithereens, *596*

Jewell, Isabel: Leopard Man, The, *712*; Little Men, *519*

Jilette, Penn: Miami Vice: "The Prodigal Son", *99*

Jillian, Ann: Mr. Mom, *311*

Jobert, Marlene: Catch Me a Spy, *28*; Rider on the Rain, *122*; Swashbuckler, The, *144*

Johann, Zita: Mummy, The (original), *719*

Johnny Burnette Trio, The: Rock, Rock, Rock, *800*

Johnson, Arnold: Putney Swope, *337*

Johnson, Arte: Bunco, *26*; Love at First Bite, *302*

Johnson, Ben: Bite the Bullet, *884*; Breakheart Pass, *886*; Champions, *430*; Chisum, *889*; Getaway, The, *62*; Hang 'Em High, *900*; Hunter, The, *75*; Hustle, The, *76*; Last Picture Show, The, *514*; Mighty Joe Young, *853*; One-Eyed Jacks, *920*; Rare Breed, The, *924*; Red Dawn, *119*; Rio Grande, *927*; Ruckus, *124*; Sacketts, The, *928*; Shane, *930*; She Wore a Yellow Ribbon, *930*; Sugarland Express, The, *607*; Tex, *614*; Town That Dreaded Sundown, The, *759*; Train Robbers, The, *940*; Wagonmaster, *943*; Wild Bunch, The, *945*; Wild Times, *945*

Johnson, Bill: Texas Chainsaw Massacre 2, The, *753*

Johnson, Clark: Killing 'Em Softly, *506*; Skullduggery, *744*

Johnson, Don: Boy and His Dog, A, *821*; Cease Fire, *429*; Harrad Experiment, The, *482*; Miami Vice, *98*; Miami Vice: "The Prodigal Son", *99*; Return to Macon County, *121*

Johnson, Dots: Paisan, *556*

Johnson, Geordie: Skullduggery, *744*

Johnson, Georgann: Front, The, *470*

Johnson, Julanne: Thief of Baghdad, The, *871*

Johnson, Kelly: UTU, *157*

Johnson, Kurt: Sole Survivor, *744*

Johnson, Lynn-Holly: For Your Eyes Only, *58*; Ice Castles, *492*; Watcher in the Woods, The, *764*; Where the Boys Are '84, *380*

Johnson, Michael: Lust for a Vampire, *713*

Johnson, Michelle: Blame It on Rio, *230*

Johnson, Noble: Frontier Pony Express, *898*; King Kong (original), *709*

Johnson, Oliver: Tomb of Ligeia, *757*

Johnson, Richard: Beyond the Door, *650*; Screamers, *741*; Turtle Diary, *373*; Zombie, *766*

Johnson, Rita: Here Comes Mr. Jordan, *279*; Letter of Introduction, *516*

Johnson, Robin: Times Square, *809*

Johnson, Russell: Attack of the Crab Monsters, *647*

Johnson, Stephen: Angel of H.E.A.T., *8*

Johnson, Sunny: Night the Lights Went Out in Georgia, The, *545*; Red Light Sting, The,

577; Caine Mutiny, The, 423; Doomsday Flight, The, 453; Easy to Love, 778; In the Good Old Summertime, 788; Kidnapping of the President, The, 709; State of the Union, 602; Thirty Seconds Over Tokyo, 149

Johnston, Bruce: Beach Boys: An American Band, The, 770

Johnston, Michelle: Chorus Line, A, 774

Johns, Glynis: 49th Parallel, The, 468; Another Time, Another Place, 400; Court Jester, The, 248; Mary Poppins, 191; Papa's Delicate Condition, 557; Rob Roy, The Highland Rogue, 201; Sword and the Rose, The, 207; Vault of Horror, 761

Johns, Mervyn: Day of the Triffids, The, 828; Jamaica Inn, 500; Never Let Go, 543

Johns, Stratford: Wild Geese II, 163

John, Al St.: Riders of Destiny, 926

John, Elton: Tommy, 810

John, Gottfried: Berlin Alexanderplatz, 408

John, Howard St.: Born Yesterday, 232; One, Two, Three, 324

John, Jill St.: Diamonds Are Forever, 42; Roman Spring of Mrs. Stone, The, 583

John, Ottwald: Inheritors, The, 495

Jolley, I. Stanford: Trigger, Jr., 940

Jolly, Mike: Bad Guys, 11

Jones, Allan: Day at the Races, A, 249; Night at the Opera, A, 318

Jones, Amanda: Among the Cinders, 397

Jones, Barry: Brigadoon, 772

Jones, Brian: Sympathy for the Devil, 806

Jones, Buck: Dawn on the Great Divide, 891; Gunman from Bodie, 900

Jones, Carolyn: Big Heat, The, 15; Eaten Alive, 680; House of Wax, 700; Invasion of the Body Snatchers (Original), 844; King Creole, 790; Man Who Knew Too Much, The (remake), 715; Seven Year Itch, The, 350

Jones, Christopher: Looking Glass War, The, 521; Ryan's Daughter, 586

Jones, Claude Earl: Evilspeak, 681

Jones, Darryl: Bring on the Night, 772

Jones, Dean: Blackbeard's Ghost, 173; Herbie Goes to Monte Carlo, 185; Jailhouse Rock, 789; Love Bug, The, 190; Million Dollar Duck, The, 192; Shaggy D.A., The, 204; That Darn Cat, 208; Ugly Dachshund, The, 211

Jones, Desmond: Romance With A Double Bass, 343

Jones, Dick: Last of the Pony Riders, 907

Jones, Duane: Night of the Living Dead, 723

Jones, Freddie: And the Ship Sails On, 408; Elephant Man, The, 456; Krull, 847; Romance With A Double Bass, 343; Young Sherlock Holmes, 167

Jones, Gemma: Devils, The, 450

Jones, Gordon: Flying Tigers, The, 58; North of the Great Divide, 918; Trigger, Jr., 940;

Trail of Robin Hood, 939; Conan the Destroyer, 826; Vamp, 760; View to a Kill, A, 158

Jones, Graham: Horror of Frankenstein, 699

Jones, Griff Rhys: Morons from Outer Space, 314

Jones, Henry: 3:10 to Yuma, 939; Deathtrap, 448; Rabbit Run, 573; Support Your Local Sheriff!, 936

Jones, James Earl: Aladdin and His Wonderful Lamp, 170; Bingo Long Traveling All-Stars and Motor Kings, The, 229; Bloodtide, 654; Bushido Blade, 26; City Limits, 823; Conan the Barbarian, 825; (voice) Empire Strikes Back, The, 833; End of the Road, 458; Exorcist II: The Heretic, 681; Greatest, The, 479; Piece of the Action, A, 329; (voice) Return of the Jedi, 859

Jones, Janet: American Anthem, 395; Chorus Line, A, 774; Flamingo Kid, The, 261

Jones, Jeffrey: Ferris Bueller's Day Off, 259; Howard the Duck, 842; Transylvania 6-5000, 371

Jones, Jennifer: Beat the Devil, 225; Indiscretion of an American Wife, 495; Love is a Many-Splendored Thing, 523; Madame Bovary, 526; Ruby Gentry, 585

Jones, Jerry: Party Animal, 328

Jones, Jocelyn: Great Texas Dynamite Chase, The, 66; Tourist Trap, 759

Jones, John Paul: Song Remains the Same, The, 803

Jones, Lisa: Life and Times of Grizzly Adams, The, 189

Jones, Lucinda: Wild Duck, The, 634

Jones, L. Q.: Ballad of Cable Hogue, The, 880; Brotherhood of Satan, 658; Lone Wolf McQuade, 92; Ride the High Country, 925; Timerider, 152; White Line Fever, 162; Wild Bunch, The, 945

Jones, Marcia Mae: These Three, 615

Jones, Marianna: I Heard the Owl Call My Name, 491

Jones, Marshall: Scream and Scream Again, 740

Jones, Norman: Adventures of Sherlock Holmes: The Crooked Man, 3

Jones, Ronalda: Alligator Shoes, 394

Jones, Sam J.: Flash Gordon, 837; My Chauffeur, 316

Jones, Shirley: Elmer Gantry, 457; Music Man, The, 794; Never Steal Anything Small, 795; Oklahoma!, 796; Tank, 145

Jones, Simon: Privates on Parade, 336

Jones, Terry: And Now for Something Completely Different, 218; Life of Brian, 299; Monty Python and the Holy Grail, 313; Monty Python Live at the Hollywood Bowl, 313; Monty Python's the Meaning of Life, 313; Secret Policeman's Private Parts, The, 347; Secret Policemen's Other Ball, The, 347

Jones, Tommy Lee: Amazing Howard

Hughes, The, 395; Back Roads, 404; Betsy, The, 409; Black Moon Rising, 18; Cat on a Hot Tin Roof (Remake), 428; Coal Miner's Daughter, 775; Executioner's Song, The, 460; Eyes of Laura Mars, The, 682; Jackson County Jail, 78; Nate and Hayes, 105; Park is Mine, The, 558; River Rat, The, 581; Rolling Thunder, 123

Jonfield, Peter: Adventures of Sherlock Holmes: The Copper Beeches, 3

Jonsson, Nine Christine: Port of Call, 585

Jordan, Bobby: Angels with Dirty Faces, 8; Pride of the Bowery, 567

Jordan, Dorothy: Min and Bill, 534

Jordan, Nick: Five for Hell, 56

Jordan, Richard: Dune, 832; Flash of Green, A, 466; Interiors, 496; Logan's Run, 849; Mean Season, The, 98; Old Boyfriends, 550; Raise the Titanic, 118; Rooster Cogburn, 928; Yakuza, The, 165

Jordon, James Carroll: Wilbur and Orville: The First To Fly, 212

Jory, Victor: Adventures of Tom Sawyer, The, 170; Buckskin Frontier, 886; Cat Women of the Moon, 823; Devil Dog: The Hound Of Hell, 673; Kansan, The, 906; Papillon, 112

Joseph, Allen: Eraserhead, 680

Joseph, Don: Color Me Blood Red, 663

Joseph, Jackie: Little Shop of Horrors, The, 713

Josephson, Erland: After the Rehearsal, 390; Scenes From A Marriage, 589

Joshua, Larry: Burning, The, 658

Joslyn, Allyn: Colonel Effingham's Raid, 246

Joston, Darwin: Assault on Precinct 13, 10

Jouanneau, Jacques: Judex, 79

Jourdan, Louis: Count of Monte Cristo, The (Remake), 36; Gigi, 782; Madame Bovary, 526; Man in the Iron Mask, The, 95; Octopussy, 109; Silver Bears, 351; Swamp Thing, 750

Jouvet, Louis: Carnival in Flanders, 426; La Marseillaise, 511; Volpone, 629

Joy, Mighty Clouds of: Gospel, 784

Joy, Robert: Desperately Seeking Susan, 250; Terminal Choice, 752

Joyce, Brenda: Enchanted Forest, The, 180

Joyce, Elaine: Motel Hell, 718

Joyeux, Odette: La Ronde, 295

Judd, Edward: Concrete Jungle, The (aka The Criminal), 437; Day the Earth Caught Fire, The, 828; Vault of Horror, 761

Judd, Robert: Crossroads, 775

Judge, Arline: Sin of Harold Diddlebock (aka Mad Wednesday), 352; Song of Texas, 933

Juerging, Arno: Andy Warhol's Dracula, 645

Juhlin, Niklas: Mystery Island, 194

Julian, Janet: Humongous, 702

Juliano, Jorge: Pixote, 563

Julia, Raul: Compromising Positions, 247; Escape Artist, The, 181; Gumball Rally, The, 67; Kiss of the Spider Woman, 509; One

from the Heart, 797; Organization, The, 111

Julien, Max: Getting Straight, 472

Jump, Gordon: Fury, The, 692

Jurado, Katy: Barabbas, 405; Bullfighter and the Lady, The, 36; High Noon, 903; One-Eyed Jacks, 920; Trapeze, 621

Jurgens, Curt: And God Created Woman, 397; Battle of the Commandos, 13; Breakthrough, 24; Goldengirl, 840; Inn of the Sixth Happiness, The, 495; Spy Who Loved Me, The, 139; Vault of Horror, 761

Justice, James Robertson: Doctor at Large, 252; Doctor at Sea, 252; Doctor in Distress, 252; Rob Roy, The Highland Rogue, 201; Sword and the Rose, The, 207

Justin, John: Thief of Baghdad, The, 870

Kaaren, Suzanne: Devil Bat, The, 673

Kaczmarek, Jane: Heavenly Kid, The, 278;

Kagen, David: Friday the 13th Part VI: Jason Lives, 691

Kahan, Saul: Schlock, 346

Kahler, Wolf: Adventures of Sherlock Holmes: A Scandal in Bohemia, 2; Raiders of the Lost Ark, 858

Kahn, Cynthia: Screen Test, 346

Kahn, Helmut: Inheritors, The, 495

Kahn, Madeline: Adventures of Sherlock Holmes' Smarter Brother, The, 215; Blazing Saddles, 230; City Heat, 243; Clue, 245; First Family, 261; High Anxiety, 280; Mel Brooks' History of the World, Part I, 308; Muppet Movie, The, 193; My Little Pony: The Movie, 194; Paper Moon, 327; Simon, 352; Slapstick of Another Kind, 354; Wholly Moses!, 381; Yellowbeard, 385; Young Frankenstein, 385

Kakassy, Agi: Time Stands Still, 619

Kaler, Berwick: Bloodthirsty Butchers, 654

Kalfon, Jean-Pierre: Confidentially Yours, 34

Kalyagin, Alexandar: Slave of Love, A, 594

Kamekona, Danny: Karate Kid, Part 2, The, 81

Kaminska, Ida: Shop on Main Street, The, 593

Kanakis, Anna: After the Fall of New York, 815

Kanaly, Steve: Fleshburn, 685; Wind and the Lion, The, 164

Kane, Carol: Annie Hall, 219; Dog Day Afternoon, 452; Hester Street, 487; Muppet Movie, The, 193; My Sister, My Love, 720; Norman Loves Rose, 330; Over the Brooklyn Bridge, 326; Racing with the Moon, 573; Transylvania 6-5000, 371; When a Stranger Calls, 764; World's Greatest Lover, The, 384

Kane, Margie: Great Gabbo, The, 477

Kaneko, Nabuo: Ikiru, 493

Kani, John: Killing Heat, 507

Kannet, Craig: Future-Kill, 692

Kanta, Ivar: Plumber, The, 729

Kaplan, Gabriel: FastBreak, 358

Kaplan, Marvin: Severed Arm, The, *742*

Kapoor, Shashi: Heat and Dust, *485*

Kaprisky, Valerie: Breathless (Remake), *420*

Karanovic, Mirfana: When Father Was Away On Business, *632*

Karen, James: Invaders from Mars (Remake), *844*; Return of the Living Dead, The, *735*

Karlatos, Olga: Purple Rain, *799*

Karlen, John: Racing with the Moon, *573*; Trilogy of Terror, *759*

Karloff, Boris: Abbott and Costello Meet Dr. Jekyll and Mr. Hyde, *214*; Bedlam, *649*; Before I Hang, *649*; Black Room, The, *652*; Black Sabbath, *651*; Body Snatcher, The, *655*; Bride of Frankenstein, *657*; Cauldron of Blood, *661*; Criminal Code, The, *440*; Daydreamer, The, *179*; Dick Tracy Meets Gruesome, *42*; Frankenstein (Original), *687*; Frankenstein (Restored Version), *688*; Frankenstein— 1970, *689*; Haunted Strangler, The, *696*; Isle of the Dead, *706*; Lost Patrol, The, *93*; Man They Could Not Hang, The, *714*; Mr. Wong, Detective, *101*; Mummy, The (original), *719*; Raven and the Black Cat, The, *733*; Raven, The, *733*; Scarface (original), *129*; Secret Life of Walter Mitty, The, *347*; Targets, *751*; Terror, The, *752*; Mad Monster Party, *191*

Karras, Alex: Against All Odds, *390*; Goldilocks and the Three Bears, *182*; When Time Ran Out, *764*

Karyo, Tcheky: Full Moon in Paris, *264*

Kasdorf, Lenore: Missing in Action, *100*

Kastner, Peter: You're a Big Boy Now, *385*

Kato, Daisuke: Samurai Trilogy, The, *127*

Kato, Haruko: MacArthur's Children, *525*

Katt, William: Baby... Secret of the Lost Legend, *818*; Big Wednesday, *411*; Butch and Sundance: The Early Days, *887*; House, *699*; Thumbelina, *209*

Katz, Mike: Pumping Iron, *570*

Katzur, Yftach: Private Popsicle, *335*

Kaufmann, Christine: Murders In The Rue Morgue, *720*

Kaufman, Andy: Heartbeeps, *184*

Kaufmann, Gunther: Querelle, *572*

Kavner, Julie: Bad Medicine, *223*

Kay, Richard: Deja Vu, *448*

Kayama, Yuzo: Red Beard, *577*; Sanjuro, *128*

Kaye, Caren: Kill Castro, *82*; My Tutor, *317*

Kaye, Danny: Court Jester, The, *248*; Inspector General, The, *287*; Kid from Brooklyn, The, *292*; Secret Life of Walter Mitty, The, *347*

Kaye, Norman: Lonely Hearts, *520*; Man of Flowers, *306*; Where the Green Ants Dream, *632*

Kaye, Stubby: Guys and Dolls, *785*

Kazakos, Costa: Iphigenia, *497*

Kazan, Lainie: Delta Force, The, *41*; Journey of Natty Gann, The, *187*; My Favorite Year,

Kazurinsky, Tim: Police Academy III: Back in Training, *332*; Princess and the Pea, The, *199*

Ka'ne, Dayton: Hurricane, *76*

Keach, James: Love Letters, *523*; Moving Violations, *315*; Razor's Edge, The (Remake), *576*; Wildcats, *382*; Long Riders, The, *910*

Keach, Stacy: Long Riders, The, *910*; Battle Force, *12*; Butterfly, *422*; End of the Road, *458*; Heart Is a Lonely Hunter, The, *483*; Life and Times of Judge Roy Bean, The, *909*; New Centurions, The, *543*; Nice Dreams, *318*; Ninth Configuration, The, *546*; Road Games, *736*; Rumor of War, A, *125*; Slave of the Cannibal God, *136*; That Championship Season, *614*; Up in Smoke, *375*

Kean, Marie: Danny Boy, *444*

Keane, Edward: Frontier Pony Express, *898*; Twilight in the Sierras, *941*

Keane, Kerrie: Incubus, The, *705*; Spasms, *746*

Keane, Robert Emmett: Susanna Pass, *936*

Keating, Larry: When Worlds Collide, *876*

Keaton, Buster: Beach Blanket Bingo, *770*; College, *246*; Fuller Brush Man, The, *264*; Funny Thing Happened on the Way to the Forum, A, *265*; General, The, *266*; Great Chase, The, *65*; How to Stuff a Wild Bikini, *788*; In the Good Old Summertime, *788*; It's a Mad Mad Mad Mad World, *288*; Limelight, *299*; Steamboat Bill Jr., *359*; Sunset Blvd., *609*; Villain Still Pursued Her, The, *159*

Keaton, Camille: I Spit On Your Grave, *704*

Keaton, Diane: Annie Hall, *219*; Godfather, The, *473*; Godfather Epic, The, *474*; Godfather, Part II, The *473*; Harry and Walter Go to New York, *276*; I Will, I Will... For Now, *285*; Interiors, *496*; Little Drummer Girl, The, *90*; Looking for Mr. Goodbar, *521*; Love and Death, *302*; Manhattan, *305*; Mrs. Soffel, *536*; Play It Again Sam, *331*; Reds, *578*; Shoot the Moon, *592*; Sleeper, *354*

Keaton, Joseph: General, The, *266*

Keaton, Michael: Gung Ho, *274*; Johnny Dangerously, *290*; Mr. Mom, *311*; Night Shift, *319*

Keats, Steven: Hester Street, *487*

Keays-Byrne, Hugh: Mad Max, *850*

Kedrova, Lila: Bloodtide, *654*; Tell Me A Riddle, *612*; Testament, *870*; Torn Curtain, *758*; Zorba the Greek, *642*

Keefe, Cornelius: Old Corral, The, *919*

Keeler, Ruby: Dames, *776*; Footlight Parade, *780*; 42nd Street, *781*; Gold Diggers of 1933, *783*

Keel, Howard: Day of the Triffids, The, *828*; Kiss Me Kate, *790*; Pagan Love Song, *797*; Seven Brides for Seven Brothers, *802*; Show Boat, *802*; War Wagon, The, *944*

Keene, Tom: Our Daily Bread, *555*; Plan 9

from Outer Space, 856; Trail of Robin Hood, 939

Keen, Geoffrey: Born Free, 174

Kehoe, Jack: Star Chamber, The, 600

Keiko, Kishi: Yakuza, The, 165

Keir, Andrew: Catholics, 428; Night Visitor, The, 723

Keitel, Harvey: Alice Doesn't Live Here Anymore, 392; Blue Collar, 415; Border, The, 22; Death Watch, 839; Duellists, The, 46; Exposed, 681; Falling in Love, 462; Fingers, 464; La Nuit de Varennes, 511; Mean Streets, 532; Off Beat, 322; Saturn 3, 861; Taxi Driver, 612; Welcome to L.A., 631; Wise Guys, 382

Keith, Brian: Dino, 451; Hooper, 283; Meteor, 852; Moon Pilot, 193; Mountain Men, The, 915; Nevada Smith, 917; Parent Trap, The, 197; Rare Breed, The, 924; Reflections in a Golden Eye, 578; Russians Are Coming, the Russians Are Coming, The, 344; Savage Sam, 202; Scandalous John, 203; Sharky's Machine, 133; Ten Who Dared, 208; Those Calloways, 209; Wind and the Lion, The, 164; With Six You Get Eggroll, 383; Yakuza, The, 165; Young Philadelphians, The, 640

Keith, David: Back Roads, 404; Firestarter, 685; Gulag, 480; Independence Day, 494; Lords of Discipline, The, 521; Officer and a Gentleman, An, 549

Keith, Ian: Abraham Lincoln, 388; Big Trail, The, 883; It Came from Beneath the Sea, 706

Keith, Penelope: Priest of Love, 568

Keith, Robert: Drum Beat, 894; Wild One, The, 164

Kelber, Constantin: Zero For Conduct, 642

Keleghan, Peter: Screwballs, 346

Kellaway, Cecil: Guess Who's Coming to Dinner, 480; Hush...Hush, Sweet Charlotte, 703; I Married a Witch, 842; Intermezzo, 496; Kim, 83; Postman Always Rings Twice, The (Original), 565

Kellerman, Barbara: Sea Wolves, The, 130

Kellerman, Sally: Back To School, 222; Big Bus, The, 229; Boston Strangler, The, 656; Brewster McCloud, 234; Foxes, 469; It Rained All Night the Day I Left, 498; Last of the Red Hot Lovers, 296; Little Romance, A, 300; Moving Violations, 315; M*A*S*H, 307; Rafferty and the Gold Dust Twins, 337; Sleeping Beauty, 205; Welcome to L.A., 631

Keller, Marthe: Amateur, The, 395; And Now My Love, 398; Black Sunday, 19; Bobby Deerfield, 416; Formula, The, 467; Marathon Man, 97; Wagner, 811

Keller, Phil: Texas Chainsaw Massacre 2, The, 753

Kelley, DeForest: Star Trek (television series) 866; Star Trek: The Menagerie, 865; Star Trek—The Motion Picture, 865; Star Trek II: The Wrath of Khan, 865; Star Trek III: The Search for Spock, 865

Kellin, Mike: At War with the Army, 221; Boston Strangler, The, 656; Demon (God Told Me To), 830; So Fine, 355

Kellogg, John: Borrowed Trouble, 885; Robin Hood of Texas, 927; Sinister Journey, 932; Violets Are Blue, 628

Kelly, Brian: Around the World Under the Sea, 10

Kelly, David Patrick: 48 Hrs., 262; Quackser Fortune Has a Cousin in the Bronx, 571

Kelly, Desmond: Smash Palace, 595

Kelly, Gene: American in Paris, An, 769; Brigadoon, 772; Du Barry Was a Lady, 777; Forty Carats, 262; Invitation to the Dance, 788; It's Always Fair Weather, 789; Les Girls, 792; On the Town, 796; Pirate, The, 798; Singin' in the Rain, 802; That's Dancing, 807; That's Entertainment, 807; That's Entertainment Part II, 807; Thousands Cheer, 808; Three Musketeers, The (1948), 150; Viva Knievel, 159; Xanadu, 813; Ziegfeld Follies, 814

Kelly, Grace: Country Girl, The, 439; Dial M for Murder, 675; High Noon, 903; High Society, 787; Mogambo, 102; Rear Window, 734; To Catch a Thief, 756

Kelly, Graig: Satan's Satellites, 128

Kelly, Jack: Commandos, 33; Commies Are Coming, the Commies Are Coming, The, 246; Forbidden Planet, 838; To Hell and Back, 152

Kelly, James T.: Charlie Chaplin—The Early Years, Vol.4, 241

Kelly, Jim: Black Belt Jones, 18; Enter the Dragon, 49; One Down, Two to Go, 110; Three the Hard Way, 151

Kelly, Lew: Saga of Death Valley, 929; Winds of the Wasteland, 945

Kelly, Nancy: Jesse James, 905; Stanley and Livingstone, 600

Kelly, Patsy: In Old California, 905; North Avenue Irregulars, The, 196; Rosemary's Baby, 737

Kelly, Paula: Andromeda Strain, The, 817; Jo Jo Dancer, Your Life Is Calling, 502

Kelly, Paul: Star of Midnight, 139

Kelly, Tommy: Adventures of Tom Sawyer, The, 170

Kelman, Paul: My Bloody Valentine, 720

Kelton, Pert: Comic, The, 437

Kemmerling, Warren: Eat My Dust, 47

Kemmill, Bill: Groove Tube, The, 273

Kemp, Brandis: Goldilocks and the Three Bears, 182

Kemp, Elizabeth: He Knows You're Alone, 696; Killing Hour, The, 709

Kemp, Jeremy: Adventures of Sherlock Holmes: The Speckled Band, 6; Blue Max, The, 20; Return of the Soldier, The, 579

Kemp, Lindsay: Wicker Man, The, 765

Kemp, Valli: Dr. Phibes Rises Again, 676

Kendall, Henry: Amazing Adventure, 217

Kendall, Kay: Les Girls, 792

Kendall, Suzy : To Sir with Love, 619; Bird with the Crystal Plumage, The, 651

Kenin, Alexa: Piano for Mrs. Cimino, A, 562

Kennedy, Arthur: Bend of the River, 882; Champion, 430; Elmer Gantry, 457; Fantastic Voyage, 836; High Sierra, 72; Lawrence of Arabia, 88; Lusty Men, The, 911; Nevada Smith, 917; Rancho Notorious, 923; Sentinel, The, 742; Shark! (aka Maneaters!), 133; They Died with their Boots On, 938

Kennedy, Betty: Cheech and Chong's Next Movie, 242

Kennedy, Edgar: Duck Soup, 254; Hollywood Hotel, 787; Keystone Comedies, Vol. 1, 292; Keystone Comedies: Vol. 4, 292; Keystone Comedies: Vo. 5, 292; Sin of Harold Diddlebock (aka Mad Wednesday), 352

Kennedy, George: Airport 77, 391; Airport 1975, 391; Airport '79: The Concorde, 391; Bandolero!, 881; Bolero, 417; Boston Strangler, The, 656; Brass Target, 24; Cahill—US Marshal, 887; Charade, 29; Chattanooga Choo Choo, 242; Cool Hand Luke, 35; Death on the Nile, 40; Delta Force, The, 41; Earthquake, 46; Eiger Sanction, The, 47; Flight of the Phoenix, The, 58; Jessie Owens Story, The, 501; Search and Destroy, 130; Shenandoah, 930; Sons of Katie Elder, The, 934; Thunderbolt and Lightfoot, 152

Kennedy, Gerald: Newsfront, 543

Kennedy, Graham: Don's Party, 253; Odd Angry Shot, The, 548

Kennedy, Jack: Man of the Frontier, (Red River Valley), 912

Kennedy, Jayne: Body and Soul (Remake), 416

Kennedy, Jo: Starstruck, 805

Kennedy, Leon Isaac: Body and Soul (Remake), 416; Penitentiary I and II, 113; Too Scared to Scream, 757; Hollywood Vice Squad, 74

Kennedy, Patricia: Getting of Wisdom, The, 471

Kennington, Jill: Blow-Up, 654

Kenny, Colin: Tarzan of the Apes, 145

Kensit, Patsy: Absolute Beginners, 768

Kent, April: Incredible Shrinking Man, The, 843

Kent, Robet: Phantom Creeps, The, 727

Kepler, Shell: Homework, 489

Kerbash, Samia: Battle of Algiers, 405

Kercheval, Ken: Devil Dog: The Hound Of Hell, 673

Kerridge, Linda: Fade to Black, 682; Mixed Blood, 101

Kerrigan, J. M.: Lost Patrol, The, 93

Kerry, Norman: Phantom of the Opera, 727

Kerr, Bill: Coca Cola Kid, The, 246; Pirate Movie, The, 798; Year of Living Dangerously, The, 165

Kerr, Bruce: Man from Snowy River, 95

Kerr, Deborah: Arrangement, The, 401;

Black Narcissus, 413; Casino Royale, 239; Grass Is Greener, The, 272; King and I, The, 790; King Solomon's Mines, 84; Life and Death of Colonel Blimp, The, 517; Night of the Iguana, The, 544; Prisoner of Zenda, The, 115

Kerr, Donald: Devil Bat, The, 673

Kerr, E. Katherine: Reuben, Reuben, 339

Kerr, John: Pit and the Pendulum, The, 728; South Pacific, 805

Kerwin, Brian: Murphy's Romance, 539

Kerwin, Lance: Enemy Mine, 834; Salem's Lot, 739; Snow Queen, 205

Kessler, Quin: She, 861

Kestleman, Sara: Lisztomania, 792

Keyes, Evelyn: Before I Hang, 649; Here Comes Mr. Jordan, 279

Keyloun, Mark: Mike's Murder, 534

Khambatta, Persis: Megaforce, 851

Kibbee, Guy: Babes in Arms, 769; Dames, 776; Footlight Parade, 780; Little Lord Fauntleroy, 519; Rain, 574; Riding on Air, 341

Kidder, Margot: Amityville Horror, The, 645; Glitter Dome, The, 62; Heartaches, 484; Little Treasure, 91; Quackser Fortune Has a Cousin in the Bronx, 579; Reincarnation of Peter Proud, The, 734; Sisters, 744; Some Kind of Hero, 355; Superman, 868; Superman II, 869; Trenchcoat, 372

Kidd, Michael: It's Always Fair Weather, 789

Kids, The Cabin: Git Along, Little Dogies, 898

Kids, The Dead-End: They Made Me a Criminal, 616

Kids, The East Side: Ghosts on the Loose, 267; Spooks Run Wild, 357

Kiel, Richard: Flash and the Firecat, 56; Force Ten from Navarone, 834; Hysterical, 284; Pale Rider, 921; Silver Streak, 352; So Fine, 355; Spy Who Loved Me, The, 139; They Went That-A-Way and That-A-Way, 208

Kier, Udo: Andy Warhol's Dracula, 645; Andy Warhol's Frankenstein, 646

Kiesler, Hedy (Lamarr): Ecstasy, 455

Kilbride, Percy: Knickerbocker Holiday, 791

Kilburn, Terence: Fiend without a Face, 684

Kiley, Richard: Looking for Mr. Goodbar, 521; Night Gallery, 721; Pendulum, 113; Thorn Birds, The, 617

Kilmer, Val: Real Genius, 338; Top Gun, 153; Top Secret, 369

Kimbrough, Charles: Seduction of Joe Tynan, The, 590

Kimmel, Bruce: First Nudie Musical, The, 779; Spaceship, 356

Kimmel, Dana: Friday the 13th, Part III, 690

Kim, Evan: Kentucky Fried Movie, 292; Kingsley, Ben: Betrayal, 409; Gandhi, 471; Turtle Diary, 373

King, Adrienne: Friday the 13th, 691; Friday the 13th, Part II, 690

King, Alan: Author! Author!, 222; Cat's Eye,

660; I, the Jury, *77;* Just Tell Me What You Want, *292*

King, Bernard: FastBreak, *258*

King, Carole: Goldilocks and the Three Bears, *182*

King, Charles: Frontier Pony Express, *898;* Gunman from Bodie, *900;* Lawman Is Born, A, *908;* Man of the Frontier, (Red River Valley), *912;* Rootin' Tootin' Rhythm, *928;* South of the Border, *934*

King, Ken: Polyester, *333*

King, Keven: Defcon 4, *829*

King, Loretta: Bride of the Monster, *657*

King, Mabel: Wiz, The, *812*

King, Meegan: Sweater Girls, *362*

King, Perry: Andy Warhol's Bad, *398;* Class of 1984, *663;* Different Story, A, *451;* Killing Hour, The, *709;* Lords of Flatbush, The, *523;* Mandingo, *528;* Search and Destroy, *130;* Wild Party, The, *634*

King, Stephen: Creepshow, *666*

King, Walter Woolf: Go West, *269;* Swiss Miss, *363*

King, Zalman: Blue Sunshine, *20;* Some Call It Loving, *597;* Tell Me A Riddle, *612*

Kinnaman, Melanie: Friday the 13th, Part V—A New Beginning, *690*

Kinnear, Roy: Herbie Goes to Monte Carlo, *185;* Juggernaut, *80;* Pirates, *331;* Willy Wonka and the Chocolate Factory, *213*

Kinskey, Leonid: Ball of Fire, *224*

Kinski, Klaus: Aguirre: Wrath of God, *6;* Android, *817;* Beauty and the Beast, *172;* Buddy, Buddy, *235;* Count Dracula, *664;* Creature, *826;* Deadly Sanctuary, *671;* Fitzcarraldo, *465;* Five for Hell, *56;* For a Few Dollars More, *897;* His Name Was King, *903;* Jack the Ripper, *707;* Little Drummer Girl, The, *90;* Operation Thunderbolt, *111;* Ruthless Four, The, *928;* Schizoid, *740;* Soldier, The, *137;* Venom, *761*

Kinski, Nastassja: Cat People (Remake), *660;* Exposed, *681;* Hotel New Hampshire, The, *489;* Maria's Lovers, *528;* Moon in the Gutter, The, *538;* One from the Heart, *797;* Paris, Texas, *558;* Revolution, *579;* Stay As You Are, *602;* Tess, *613;* To the Devil, a Daughter, *757;* Unfaithfully Yours (Remake), *375*

Kirby Jr., B.: Harrad Experiment, The, *482*

Kirby, Bruce: Sweet Dreams, *806*

Kirby, Bruno: Birdy, *412;* Borderline, *22;* Modern Romance, *312;* Where the Buffalo Roam, *381*

Kirby, George: Puss in Boots, *200*

Kirchner, Kendra: Android, *817*

Kirke, Donald: Hoppy's Holiday, *904*

Kirkham, Kathleen: Tarzan of the Apes, *145*

Kirkland, Kenny: Bring on the Night, *772*

Kirkland, Sally: Fatal Games, *683*

Kirk, Jack: Frontier Pony Express, *898;* Pals of the Saddle, *921;* Sunset Serenade, *935*

Kirk, Phyllis: House of Wax, *700*

Kirk, Tommy: Absent-Minded Professor,

The, *169;* Escapade In Florence, *180;* Horsemasters, *185;* Misadventures of Merlin Jones, The, *192;* Monkey's Uncle, The, *192;* Old Yeller, *196;* Savage Sam, *202;* Shaggy Dog, The, *204;* Son of Flubber, *206;* Swiss Family Robinson, The, *207;* Village of the Giants, *762*

Kirsten, Dorothy: Great Caruso, The, *785*

Kiser, Terry: Rich Kids, *580;* Starflight One, *867*

Kissmuller, Johnny: Jungle Master, The, *80*

Kitaen, Tawny: Bachelor Party, *222;* Perils of Gwendoline, The, *114*

Kitaoji, Kinya: Himatsuri, *487*

Kitchen, Cathy: Angelo My Love, *399*

Kitchen, Michael: Out of Africa, *555*

Kleiner, Towje: Train Killer, The, *621*

Klein, Robert: Bell Jar, The, *408;* Owl and the Pussycat, The, *326*

Kline, Kevin: Pirates of Penzance, The, *799;* Silverado, *932;* Sophie's Choice, *597;* Violets Are Blue, *628*

Kline, Val: Beach Girls, The, *225*

Klinger, Pam: Chorus Line, A, *774*

Klose, Debra: Can I Do It 'Til I Need Glasses?, *237*

Klos, Elmar: Shop on Main Street, The, *593*

Klugman, Jack: 12 Angry Men, *624;* Days of Wine and Roses, *447;* Goodbye Columbus, *271*

Knell, David: Spring Break, *357*

Knievel, Evel: Viva Knievel, *159*

Knight, Esmond: Hamlet, *481*

Knight, Gladys: Pipe Dreams, *563*

Knight, Rosalind: Adventures of Sherlock Holmes: The Blue Carbuncle, *2*

Knight, Sandra: Terror, The, *752*

Knight, Shirley: Endless Love, *458;* Group, The, *480;* Juggernaut, *80;* Rain People, The, *574;* Sender, The, *742*

Knight, Ted: Caddyshack, *236*

Knight, Wyatt: Porky's, *333;* Porky's Revenge, *333;* Porky's II: The Next Day, *333*

Knotts, Don: Apple Dumpling Gang, The, *171;* Apple Dumpling Gang Rides Again, The, *171;* Gus, *183;* Herbie Goes to Monte Carlo, *185;* No Deposit, No Return, *195;* No Time for Sergeants, *320;* Private Eyes, The, *335;* Prizefighter, The, *200*

Knott, Lydia: Woman of Paris, A, *638*

Knowles, Patric: Charge of the Light Brigade, The, *30;* Chisum, *889;* Elfego Baca: Six Gun Law, *895;* Five Came Back, *465;* Frankenstein Meets the Wolf Man, *688;* Terror in the Wax Museum, *753*

Knox, Alexander: Cry of the Innocent, *37;* Gorky Park, *64;* Villa Rides, *943*

Kobayashi, Keiji: Godzilla 1985, *694*

Kobayashi, Tsuruko: Varan, the Unbelievable, *761*

Kober, Jeff: Out of Bounds, *111*

Kobori, Ako: Rodan, *860*

Koenig, Walter: Star Trek (television series), 866; Star Trek III: The Search for Spock, 865

Kohler Jr., Fred: Twilight in the Sierras, 941

Kohler, Fred: Billy The Kid Returns, 883

Kohler, Gillis: Bilitis, 411

Kohlmar, Lee: Son of Kong, The, 745

Kohner, Susan: Dino, 451; To Hell and Back, 153

Koisumi, Yuriko Hiroshi: Godzilla vs. Mothra, 693

Koizumi, Hiroshi: Ghidrah, the Three-Headed Monster, 692; Mothra, 853

Kolb, Clarence: Sky's the Limit, The, 803

Kollek, Amos: Goodbye New York, 271

Komai, Tetsu: Bulldog Drummond, 25

Koock, Guich: American Ninja, 7

Kopapik, Simonie: White Dawn, The, 161

Kopell, Bernie: When Things Were Rotten, 380

Kopins, Karen: Jake Speed, 78; Once Bitten, 323

Korman, Harvey: Americathon, 218; Blazing Saddles, 230; Curse of the Pink Panther, The, 248; First Family, 261; Herbie Goes Bananas, 184; High Anxiety, 280; Mel Brooks' History of the World, Part I, 308

Kornman, Mary: Desert Trail, 893

Kortman, Bob: Mystery Mountain, 916; Winds of the Wasteland, 945

Kortner, Fritz: Pandora's Box, 556

Korvin, Charles: Ship of Fools, 592

Koscina, Sylva: Deadly Sanctuary, 671; Hercules, 71; Hercules Unchained, 841; Juliet of the Spirits, 391; Secret War of Harry Frigg, The, 348

Kosinski, Jerzy: Reds, 578

Kosleck, Martin: Nurse Edith Cavell, 548; Pursuit to Algiers, 171

Koslo, Paul: Mr. Majestyk, 101; Ransom, 118

Kosugi, Sho: Enter the Ninja, 49; Nine Deaths of the Ninja, 107; Ninja III: The Domination, 108; Revenge of the Ninja, 121

Kotler, Oded: Hanna K., 481

Kotto, Yaphet: Across 110th Street, 1; Alien, 815; Blue Collar, 415; Brubaker, 431; Live and Let Die, 91; Park is Mine, The, 558; Shark's Treasure, 133; Star Chamber, The, 600; Warning Sign, 763

Kovack, Nancy: Enter Laughing, 256

Kovacs, Ernie: Bell, Book and Candle, 226; North to Alaska, 918

Kove, Martin: Four Deuces, The, 59; Karate Kid, Part 2, The, 81; Rambo: First Blood II, 118

Krabbe, Jeroen: Fourth Man, The, 687; Soldier of Orange, 137; Turtle Diary, 373

Kramer, Jeffrey: Halloween II, 695; Hollywood Boulevard, 282; Jaws 2, 707

Kramer, Joey: Flight of the Navigator, 837

Kramer, Leopold: Ecstasy, 455

Kramer, Michael: Over the Edge, 555

Kramer, Sylvia: Watch Me When I Kill, 763

Kratka, Paul: Friday the 13th, Part III, 690

Krauss, Werner: Cabinet of Doctor Caligari, The, 659

Kresel, Lee: Mothra, 853

Kreuger, Kurt: Unfaithfully Yours (Original), 374

Kreuzer, Lisa: American Friend, The, 396; Birgit Haas Must Be Killed, 18

Kriel, Anneline: Kill and Kill Again, 82

Krige, Alice: Chariots of Fire, 431; Ghost Story, 693; King David, 507

Kristel, Sylvia: Emmanuelle, 457; Fifth Musketeer, The, 53; Lady Chatterley's Lover, 512; Private Lessons, 335; Private School, 335

Kristensen, Mona: Bilitis, 411

Kristen, Marta: Beach Blanket Bingo, 770; Savage Sam, 202

Kristofferson, Kris: Act of Passion, 389; Alice Doesn't Live Here Anymore, 392; Blume in Love, 416; Convoy, 34; Flashpoint, 57; Heaven's Gate, 902; Pat Garrett and Billy the Kid, 922; Rollover, 583; Sailor Who Fell from Grace with the Sea, The, 586; Semi-Tough, 349; Songwriter, 804; Star Is Born, A (Remake), 601; Trouble in Mind, 622

Kritikos, Alkis: Adventures of Sherlock Holmes: The Greek Interpreter, 4

Kronert, Max: The Golem (How He Came Into The World) (Der Golem, Wie er in die Welt Kam), 754

Kroner, Josef: Shop on Main Street, The, 593

Kropiewnicki, Lee: Attack of the Swamp Creature, 647

Kruchkov, Nikolai: Ballad of a Soldier, 404

Kruger, Alma: Craig's Wife, 439

Kruger, Christiane: Internecine Project, The, 705

Kruger, Hardy: Flight of the Phoenix, The, 58

Kruger, Otto: High Noon, 903; Hitler's Children, 73; Magnificent Obsession, 527; Saboteur, 738; Young Philadelphians, The, 640

Krupa, Gene: Glenn Miller Story, The, 783

Kruschen, Jack: Angry Red Planet, The, 817; Apartment, The, 219; Lover Come Back, 303; Unsinkable Molly Brown, The, 810

Krüger, Hardy: Barry Lyndon, 405; Hatari!, 69; Paper Tiger, 112; Wild Geese, The, 163; Wrong Is Right, 384

Kubo, Akira: Son of Godzilla, 745; Throne of Blood, 617

Kulle, Jarl: Devil's Eye, The, 250; Secrets of Women (or Waiting Women), 348

Kunen, James: Strawberry Statement, The, 604

Kuphal, Jens: Christiane F., 433

Kurts, Alwyn: Earthling, The, 46; Tim, 618

Kurtz, Swoosie: Wildcats, 382; World According to Garp, The, 639

Kussman, Susan: Steagle, The, 359

Kuznetzof, Adia: Swiss Miss, 363

Kwan, Nancy: Corrupt Ones, The, 35; Flower

Drum Song, 780; Lt. Robin Crusoe, U.S.N., 188

Kwouk, Burt: Pink Panther Strikes Again, The, 330; Return of the Pink Panther, The, 339; Revenge of the Pink Panther, The, 340; Shot in the Dark, A, 351

Kyomoto, Masaki: Irezumi (Spirit of Tattoo), 497

Kyo, Machiko: Rashomon, 575; Ugetsu, 625

Lablosa, David: Entity, The, 680

Labonowski, John: Adventures of Sherlock Holmes: The Red-Headed League, 5

Lacey, Ronald: Firefox, 54; Flesh and Blood, 57; Of Human Bondage (Remake), 549; Raiders of the Lost Ark, 858

Lack, Stephen: Scanners, 740

Lacoste, Philippe: Hail Mary, 480

Lacoste, Thierry: Hail Mary, 480

Lacy, Jerry: Play It Again Sam, 331

Ladd, Alan: Botany Bay, 22; Drum Beat, 894; Hell on Frisco Bay, 70; Proud Rebel, The, 923; Shane, 930; This Gun for Hire, 150

Ladd, Cheryl: Now and Forever, 547; Purple Hearts, 570; Satan's School for Girls, 739

Ladd, David: Dog of Flanders, A, 180; Proud Rebel, The, 923

Ladd, Diane: Chinatown, 30; Embryo, 833; White Lightning, 162; Wild Angels, The, 163

Ladengast, Walter: Every Man for Himself and God Against All, 460

Ladmiral, Nicole: Diary Of A Country Priest, 450

Laffan, Patricia: Devil Girl from Mars, 674

La grange, Valerie: Morgan the Pirate, 103; Cat and Mouse, 28

Lahr, Bert: Wizard of Oz, The, 812

Lahti, Christine: Executioner's Song, The, 460; Just Between Friends, 505; Swing Shift, 610; Whose Life Is It, Anyway?, 633

Laing, Hugh: Brigadoon, 772

La Cayennie, Jack: Cop in Blue Jeans, The, 35

Lake, Arthur: Indiscreet, 286

Lake, Veronica: I Married a Witch, 842; This Gun for Hire, 150

Lally, Michael David: Nesting, The, 721

Lamarr, Hedy: Algiers, 392; Samson and Delilah, 588

Lamas, Fernando: 100 Rifles, 920; Dangerous When Wet, 776

Lamas, Lorenzo: Body Rock, 771; Take Down, 363

Lambert, Christopher: Greystoke: The Legend of Tarzan, Lord of the Apes, 67; Highlander, 841; Subway, 142

Lambert, Heath: To Kill a Clown, 756

Lamer, Susan: Hills Have Eyes, The, 697

Lamont, Adele: Brain That Wouldn't Die, The, 821

Lamorisse, Pascal: Red Balloon, The, 201

Lamour, Dorothy: Death at Love House, 672;

Donovan's Reef, 44; Greatest Show on Earth, The, 478; Hurricane, The, 490; My Favorite Brunette, 316; Road to Bali, 342; They Got Me Covered, 366

Lampert, Zohra: Alphabet City, 394; Lady of the House, 512; Let's Scare Jessica to Death, 712

Lamprecht, Gunter: Berlin Alexanderplatz, 408

Lancaster, Burt: Airport, 7; Apache, 879; Atlantic City, 402; Birdman of Alcatraz, 412; Buffalo Bill and the Indians, 886; Cassandra Crossing, The, 428; Conversation Piece, 438; Elmer Gantry, 460; Executive Action, 460; Go Tell the Spartans, 63; Gunfight at the O.K. Corral, 900; Island of Dr. Moreau, The, 845; Judgment at Nuremberg, 504; Kentuckian, The, 906; Killers, The, 83; Little Treasure, 91; Local Hero, 300; Moses, 539; Osterman Weekend, The, 111; Professionals, The, 116; Run Silent, Run Deep, 125; Seven Days in May, 591; Sorry, Wrong Number, 745; Swimmer, The, 609; Train, The, 155; Trapeze, 621; Twilight's Last Gleaming, 156; Vera Cruz, 943; Zulu Dawn, 168

Lancaster, Irish: Trail Beyond, The, 939

Lancaster, William: Moses, 539

Lanchester, Elsa: Arnold, 646; Beachcomber, The, 406; Blackbeard's Ghost, 173; Bride of Frankenstein, 657; Inspector General, The, 287; Private Life of Henry the Eighth, The, 568; Razor's Edge, The (Original), 576; Rembrandt, 578; Terror in the Wax Museum, 753; That Darn Cat, 208; Witness for the Prosecution, 637

Lancret, Bernard: Carnival in Flanders, 426

Lanctot, Micheline: Apprenticeship of Duddy Kravitz, The, 401

Landau, David: Street Scene, 605

Landau, Martin: Alone in the Dark, 644; Being, The, 650; Nevada Smith, 917; North by Northwest, 724; They Call Me Mister Tibbs, 148; Without Warning, 876

Landen, Dindsdale: Morons from Outer Space, 314

Landers, Audrey: Chorus Line, A, 774; Tennessee Stallion, 147; Underground Aces, 374

Landers, Judy: Doin' Time, 253; Tennessee Stallion, 147; Vega$, 158

Lander, David L.: Wholly Moses!, 381

Landes, Michael S.: Time Stands Still, 619

Landgard, Janet: Swimmer, The, 609

Landgrebe, Gudrun: Colonel Redl, 435; Woman in Flames, A, 638

Landgut, Inge: M, 713

Landham, Sonny: Fleshburn, 685

Landis, Carole: Daredevils of the Red Circle, 38; One Million B.C., 855; Out of the Blue, 325; Topper Returns, 370

Landis, Jessie Royce: To Catch a Thief, 756

Landis, John: Schlock, 346

Landi, Elissa: After the Thin Man, 6; Count of Monte Cristo, The (Original), 36

Landi, Marla: Hound of the Baskervilles, The (Remake), 75

Landi, Sal: Savage Streets, 128

Landon, Laurene: All the Marbles, 217

Landon, Patricia: Kiss of the Tarantula, 710

Landor, Rosalyn: Adventures of Sherlock Holmes: The Speckled Band, 6; Guardian of the Abyss, 695

Land, Paul: Spring Break, 357

Lane, Abbe: Americano, The, 879

Lane, Allan "Rocky": Trail of Robin Hood, 939

Lane, Charles: 30 Foot Bride of Candy Rock, The, 366; Papa's Delicate Condition, 557

Lane, Diane: Cotton Club, The, 36; Little Romance, A, 300; Six Pack, 353; Streets of Fire, 142; Touched by Love, 621

Lane, Jocelyn: Tickle Me, 809

Lane, Lola: Buckskin Frontier, 886; Hollywood Hotel, 787

Lane, Mike: Harder They Fall, The, 482

Lane, Priscilla: Arsenic and Old Lace, 220; Roaring Twenties, The, 122; Saboteur, 738; Silver Queen, 932

Lane, Richard: Bullfighters, The, 235; Mr. Winkle Goes to War, 311; Sioux City Sue, 933;

Lane, Rosemary: Hollywood Hotel, 787; Oklahoma Kid, The, 918

Langdon, Anthony: Adventures of Sherlock Holmes: The Norwood Builder, 5

Langdon, Harry: Golden Age of Comedy, The, 270

Langdon, Sue Anne: Guide For The Married Man, A, 273; Roustabout, 800; Without Warning, 876

Langella, Frank: Diary of a Mad Housewife, 450; Dracula (Remake), 678; Sphinx, 746; Twelve Chairs, The, 373

Langenkamp, Heather: Nightmare on Elm Street, A, 722

Lange, Hope: Death Wish, 40; Fer-de-Lance, 684; Nightmare on Elm Street Part 2: Freddy's Revenge, A, 722; Pleasure Palace, 564; Wild in the Country, 634

Lange, Jessica: All That Jazz, 768; Cat on a Hot Tin Roof (Remake), 428; Country, 439; Frances, 469; How to Beat the High Co$t of Living, 284; King Kong (remake), 710; Postman Always Rings Twice, The (Remake), 866; Sweet Dreams, 806; Tootsie, 369

Langford, Frances: Glenn Miller Story, The, 783; Hollywood Hotel, 787; This is the Army, 808

Langlet, Amanda: Pauline at the Beach, 559

Langlois, Lisa: Man Who Wasn't There, The, 306; Joy of Sex, The, 291

Langton, Paul: Incredible Shrinking Man, The, 843; Thirty Seconds Over Tokyo, 149

Lang, Fritz: Contempt, 247

Lang, Perry: Alligator, 644; Body and Soul (Remake), 416; Spring Break, 357

Lang, Stephen: Band of the Hand, 18

Lang, Veronica: Don's Party, 253

Lanoux, Victor: Cousin, Cousine, 248; European Vacation, 256; One Wild Moment, 552; Pardon Mon Affaire, 327

Lansbury, Angela: Bedknobs and Broomsticks, 172; Blue Hawaii, 771; Breath of Scandal, A, 233; Company of Wolves, The, 825; Court Jester, The, 248; Death on the Nile, 40; Greatest Story Ever Told, The, 478; Harlow, 482; Mirror Crack'd, The, 99; National Velvet, 195; Picture of Dorian Gray, The, 728; Pirates of Penzance, The, 799; Samson and Delilah, 588; State of the Union, 602; Three Musketeers, The (1948), 150; World of Henry Orient, The, 384

Lansing, Joi: Atomic Submarine, The, 818; Big Foot, 651; Hillbillys in a Haunted House, 280

Lansing, Robert: 4D Man, 838; Empire of the Ants, 833; Island Claws, 706; Scalpel, 740; S.H.E., 134

Lanza, Mario: Great Caruso, The, 785

Lapinski, Laurie: Dorm That Dripped Blood, The, 678

Lapotaire, Jane: Eureka, 459; Spirit of the Dead, 746

Larch, John: Play Misty for Me, 739; Santee, 929

Largo, Diana: Battle of the Commandos, 13

Larkey, Caren: Sole Survivor, 744

Larkin, Mary: Psychomania, 731

Larroquette, John: Stripes, 360

Larsen, Erna: Came a Hot Friday, 27

Larsen, Ham: Adventures of the Wilderness Family, 170; Mountain Family Robinson, 193; Wilderness Family, Part 2, The, 213

Larsen, Keith: Flat Top, 57; Whitewater Sam, 162

Larson, Darrell: City Limits, 823; Little Red Riding Hood, 190; Uforia, 374

LaRue, Frank: Gunman from Bodie, 900; Man of the Frontier, (Red River Valley), 912

LaRue, Jack: Christopher Strong, 433; Farewell to Arms, A, 463; Kennel Murder Case, The, 82; Ride the Man Down, 926

Laskarin, Mari: Screen Test, 346

Lassander, Dagmar: Hatchet for the Honeymoon, 696

Lasser, Louise: Bananas, 224; Everything You Always Wanted to Know about Sex But Were Afraid to Ask, 257

Lassick, Sidney: Unseen, The, 760

Lassie: Magic of Lassie, The, 191

Latanzi, Matt: Rich and Famous, 579

Latham, Louise: Mass Appeal, 531; White Lightning, 162; Wilbur and Orville: The First To Fly, 212

Lathouris, Nicolas: Where the Green Ants Dream, 632

Lattanzi, Matt: My Tutor, 317

Lattimore, Frank: Black Magic, 413; 13 Rue Madeleline, 149

Laudenbach, Philippe: Confidentially Yours, *34*

Lauer, William: To All a Good Night, *756*

Laughlin, John: Crimes of Passion, *440*

Laughlin, Lori: Amityville III: The Demon, *645;* Rad, *117;* Secret Admirer, *346*

Laughlin, Tom: Billy Jack, *17;* Born Losers, *22*

Laughton, Charles: Abbott and Costello Meet Captain Kidd, *214;* Arch of Triumph, *401;* Beachcomber, The, *406;* Captain Kidd, *27;* Hobson's Choice, *281;* Hunchback of Notre Dame, The (remake), *703;* Jamaica Inn, *500;* Mutiny on the Bounty (Original), *105;* Private Life of Henry the Eighth, The, *568;* Rembrandt, *578;* Sidewalks of London, *593;* Spartacus, *138;* They Knew What They Wanted, *616;* This Land Is Mine, *617;* Tuttles of Tahiti, The, *373;* Witness for the Prosecution, *637*

Laurel, Stan: Atoll K (Utopia), *221;* Block-Heads, *230;* Bohemian Girl, The, *232;* Bullfighters, The, *235;* Chump at Oxford, A, *243;* Flying Deuces, *261;* Great Guns, *272;* March of the Wooden Soldiers, *307;* Our Relations, *325;* Pack Up Your Troubles, *326;* Pardon Us, *327;* Saps at Sea, *345;* Sons of the Desert, *356;* Swiss Miss, *363;* Way Out West, *378*

Laurence, Marc: Super Fuzz, *868*

Laurenson, James: Rude Awakening, *738*

Laurent, Jacqueline: Le Jour Se Leve (DayBreak), *516*

Lauren, Rod: Crawling Hand, The, *665*

Laure, Carol: Get Out Your Handkerchiefs, *266*

Laurie, Piper: Carrie, *659;* Hustler, The, *490;* Return to Oz, *201;* Ruby, *737;* Skag, *594;* Tim, *618*

Laurin, Marie: Creature, *826*

Lauter, Ed: Big Score, The, *16;* Breakheart Pass, *886;* Chicken Chronicles, The, *243;* Death Hunt, *39;* Death Wish III, *40;* Eureka, *459;* Family Plot, *683;* Jericho Mile, The, *501;* Last American Hero, The, *86;* Longest Yard, The, *92;* Magic, *713;* Raw Deal, *119;* Real Genius, *338;* Timerider, *152;* Youngblood, *641*

Lauter, Harry: Hellcats of the Navy, *70;* Hills of Utah, The, *903;* Valley of Fire, *942*

Lavanant, Dominique: My Other Husband, *541*

Lavia, Gabriele: Revenge of the Dead, *736;* Deep Red, *672*

Lawford, Peter: Easter Parade, *777;* Exodus, *460;* Fantasy Island, *837;* Good News, *784;* Harlow, *482;* It Should Happen to You, *287;* Ocean's Eleven, *109;* Picture of Dorian Gray, The, *728;* Royal Wedding, *800;* Sky's the Limit, The, *803*

Lawrence, Barbara: Kronos, *846;* Unfaithfully Yours (Original), *374*

Lawrence, Bruno: Heart of the Stag, *484;* Quiet Earth, The, *858;* Smash Palace, *595;*

Lawrence, Gail: Maniac, *714*

Lawrence, Gertrude: Rembrandt, *578*

Lawrence, Joey: Summer Rental, *361*

Lawrence, Marc: Call of the Canyon, *887;* Dillinger, *42;* Revenge of the Pink Panther, The, *340*

Lawrence, Michael: Came a Hot Friday, *27*

Lawson, Leigh: Charlie Boy, *661*

Lawson, Wilfred: Wrong Box, The, *384*

Lawton, Frank: David Copperfield, *445;* Devil Doll, The, *674;* Winslow Boy, The, *635*

Law, John Phillip: Attack Force Z, *10;* Barbarella, *819;* Death Rides a Horse, *892;* Golden Voyage of Sinbad, The, *839;* Tarzan the Ape Man (Remake), *146*

Laydu, Claude: Diary Of A Country Priest, *450*

Lazarus, Jodi: Night of the Demon, *722*

Lazenby, George: Never Too Young To Die, *106;* On Her Majesty's Secret Service, *110;* Return of the Man from U.N.C.L.E., The, *121;* Saint Jack, *587*

Lazure, Gabrielle: Joshua Then and Now, *290*

Leachman, Cloris: Charlie and The Angel, *176;* Crazy Mama, *36;* Daisy Miller, *442;* Foolin' Around, *261;* Herbie Goes Bananas, *184;* High Anxiety, *280;* Last Picture Show, The, *514;* Muppet Movie, The, *193;* My Little Pony: The Movie, *194;* North Avenue Irregulars, The, *196;* Run Stranger Run, *738;* Scavenger Hunt, *346;* Steagle, The, *359;* S.O.S. Titanic, *586;* Thursday's Game, *618;* Young Frankenstein, *385*

Leach, Rosemary: Room With a View, A (1987 Release), *584;* Turtle Diary, *373*

Learned, Michael: Touched by Love, *621*

Lease, Rex: South of the Border, *934;* Sunset Serenade, *935;* Yellow Rose of Texas, *946*

Leaud, Jean-Pierre: Stolen Kisses, *360*

LeBrock, Kelly: Weird Science, *379;* Woman in Red, The, *383*

Leclerc, Ginette: Baker's Wife, The, *224*

Lecomte, Jacqueline: Playtime, *331*

Lecourtois, Daniel: High Heels, *280*

Lederer, Francis: Bridge of San Luis Rey, The, *420*

Lederer, Franz: Pandora's Box, *556*

Ledoux, Fernand: La Bete Humaine, *510*

Leeds, Andrea: Goldwyn Follies, The, *784;* Letter of Introduction, *516*

Lee, Anna: Bedlam, *649*

Lee, Bernard: Dr. No, *44;* Fallen Idol, The, *462;* Man With the Golden Gun, The, *96;* Spy Who Loved Me, The, *139;* You Only Live Twice, *166*

Lee, Bruce: Chinese Connection, The, *31;* Enter the Dragon, *49;* Fists of Fury, *56;* Game of Death, *61;* Return of the Dragon, *120*

Lee, Canada: Lifeboat, *518*

Lee, Carl: Superfly, *143*

Lee, Christopher: 1941, *319;* Against All Odds

(Kiss and Kill, Blood of Fu Manchu), 643;
Airport 77, 391; Bear Island, 648; Boy Who
Left Home to Find Out about the Shivers,
The, 174; Circle of Iron, 31; Count Dracula,
664; Creeping Flesh, The, 666; Curse of
Frankenstein, The, 667; Dark Places, 669;
Devil's Undead, The, 674; Dr. Terror's House
of Horrors, 677; End of the World, 834; Eye
for an Eye, 51; Far Pavilions, The, 463; Four
Musketeers, The, 60; Gorgon, The, 694;
Horror Express, 698; Horror of Dracula, 699;
Hound of the Baskervilles, The (Remake),
75; House of the Long Shadows, 700; House
That Dripped Blood, The, 701; Howling II
... Your Sister is a Werewolf, 702; Keeper,
The, 708; Magic Christian, The, 304; Man
With the Golden Gun, The, 96; Mummy,
The (remake), 719; Oblong Box, The, 725;
Private Life of Sherlock Holmes, The, 115;
Return From Witch Mountain, 201; Rose-
bud Beach Hotel, The, 343; Scars of Dra-
cula, 740; Scream and Scream Again, 740;
Serial, 349; Theatre of Death, 754; To the
Devil, a Daughter, 757; Wicker Man, The,
765

Lee, Conan: Eliminators, 832
Lee, Jonna: Making the Grade, 305
Lee, Kaaren: Roadhouse 66, 122
Lee, Margaret: Five for hell, 56
Lee, Margo: Starstruck, 805
Lee, Mark: Gallipoli, 470
Lee, Mary: Ridin' on a Rainbow, 926; Song
of Nevada, 934; South of the Border, 934
Lee, Michele: Comic, The, 437; Love Bug,
The, 190
Lee, Pinky: Lady of Burlesque, 86
Lee, Ruta: Funny Face, 781
Lefevre, Louis: Zero For Conduct, 642
Lefevre, Adam: Return of the Secaucus 7,
339
Lefevre, Rene: Le Million, 298
Legitimus, Darling: Sugar Cane Alley, 607
Lehne, John: Bound For Glory, 418
Leiber, Fritz: Dangerous Venture, 891; Nurse
Edith Cavell, 548
Leibman, Ron: Hot Rock, The, 75; Norma
Rae, 546; Phar Lap, 562; Zorro, the Gay
Blade, 386
Leifert, Don: Alien Factor, The, 816
Leighton, Margaret: Carrington, V. C., 427;
Waltz of the Toreadors, 377; Winslow Boy,
The, 635
Leigh-Hunt, Barbara: Frenzy, 689
Leigh, Janet: Bye Bye Birdie, 773; Harper,
69; Perfect Furlough, 329; Psycho, 731; Touch
of Evil, 758; Vikings, The, 60
Leigh, Jennifer Jason: Best Little Girl in the
World, The, 408; Eyes of a Stranger, 682;
Fast Times at Ridgemont High, 258; Flesh
and Blood, 57; Grandview, U.S.A., 477;
Hitcher, The, 698
Leigh, Susanna: Lust for a Vampire, 713;
Paradise Hawaiian Style, 797

Leigh, Vivien: Caesar and Cleopatra, 423;
Dark Journey, 445; Fire over England, 54;
Gone with the Wind, 475; Roman Spring of
Mrs. Stone, The, 583; Ship of Fools, 592;
Sidewalks of London, 593; Storm in a Tea-
cup, 360; Streetcar Named Desire, A, 605;
That Hamilton Woman, 614; Waterloo Bridge,
631
Leith, Virginia: Brain That Wouldn't Die, The,
821
Le Fleur, Art: Cobra, 32; Trancers, 873
le Flon, Robert: Zero For Conduct, 642
Le Gallienne, Eva: Resurrection, 858
Le Sache, Claude: Adventures of Sherlock
Holmes: The Final Problem, 4
Lemaire, Martine: Diary Of A Country Priest,
450
LeMat, Paul: Jimmy the Kid, 186; Aloha,
Bobby and Rose, 7; American Graffiti, 218;
Burning Bed, The, 421; Death Valley, 672;
Melvin and Howard, 309; Strange Invaders,
867
Lembeck, Harvey: Beach Blanket Bingo, 770;
In-Laws, The, 286; On the Right Track, 197
Lemmon, Jack: Airport 77, 391; Apartment,
The, 219; Bell, Book and Candle, 226; Buddy,
Buddy, 235; China Syndrome, The, 432; Days
of Wine and Roses, 447; Fire Down Below,
464; Fortune Cookie, The, 262; Good
Neighbor Sam, 270; Great Race, The, 273;
Irma La Douce, 287; It Should Happen to
You, 287; Luv, 304; Macaroni, 304; Mass Ap-
peal, 531; Missing, 535; Mr. Roberts, 311;
Odd Couple, The, 322; Out of Towners, The,
325; Prisoner of Second Avenue, The, 334;
Save the Tiger, 588; Some Like It Hot, 356;
Tribute, 621; Wackiest Ship in the Army,
The, 377
Lemoire, Francis: Holiday Hotel, 281
Lennon, John: Help!, 787; How I Won the
War, 284; Let It Be, 792
Lenska, Rula: Oh, Alfie, 549
Lenya, Lotte: From Russia with Love, 61;
Roman Spring of Mrs. Stone, The, 583; Semi-
Tough, 349; Threepenny Opera, The, 809
Lenz, Cliff: Joyride, 504
Lenz, Kay: Fast-Walking, 464; Great Scout
and Cathouse Thursday, The, 899; House,
699; Initiation of Sarah, The, 705; White Line
Fever, 162
Lenz, Rick: Scandalous John, 203
Leonard, Sheldon: Captain Kidd, 27; Sinbad
the Sailor, 136
Leontini, Guido: Warning, The, 160
Leon, Joseph: He Knows You're Alone, 696
Leo, Melissa: Streetwalkin', 605
Lerdorff, Preben: Day of Wrath, 446
Lerner, Michael: Class Reunion, 244; Coast
to Coast, 245; Outlaw Blues, 325; Postman
Always Rings Twice, The (Remake), 566;
Rita Hayworth: The Love Goddess, 581;
Strange Invaders, 867; Threshold, 872
LeRoy, Baby: It's a Gift, 288

Leroy, Philippe: Night Porter, The, *545*

Leslie, Joan: High Sierra, *72;* Sky's the Limit, The, *803;* Thank Your Lucky Stars, *807;* This is the Army, *808;* Yankee Doodle Dandy, *813*

Lesniak, Emilia: Nine Deaths of the Ninja, *107*

Lester, Kathy: Phantasm, *727*

Lester, Mark: Oliver, *796;* Prince and the Pauper, The (Remake), *198;* Who Slew Auntie Roo?, *764*

Lethin, Lori: Prey, The, *730*

Lettieri, Al: Don is Dead, The, *44;* Godfather, The, *473;* McQ, *98;* Mr. Majestyk, *101*

Leuken, Paul: Screen Test, *346*

Levant, Oscar: American in Paris, An, *769;* Band Wagon, The, *769*

Levene, Sam: After the Thin Man, *6;* Demon (God Told Me To), *830;* Gung Ho, *67;* Killers, The, *83;* Last Embrace, The, *87;* Mad Miss Manton, The, *304;* Purple Heart, The, *570;* Shadow of the Thin Man, *132*

Levine, Jerry: Teen Wolf, *751*

Levitt, Stan: Carnival of Souls, *659*

Levka, Uta: Oblong Box, The, *725*

Levy, Eugene: Armed and Dangerous, *220;* Club Paradise, *245;* Going Berserk, *269;* Last Polka, The, *296;* Splash, *357*

Levy, Jeremy: Rich Kids, *580*

Lev, Martin: Bugsy Malone, *175*

Lewis, Ahn: Experience Preferred... But Not Essential, *257*

Lewis, Charlotte: Pirates, *331*

Lewis, Daniel Day: My Beautiful Launderette, *540;* Room With a View, A (1987 Release), *584*

Lewis, Diana: Go West, *269*

Lewis, Fiona: Dr. Phibes Rises Again, *676;* Fury, The, *692;* Lisztomania, *792;* Strange Behavior, *748*

Lewis, Geoffrey: Any Which Way You Can, *219;* Bad Company, *880;* Bronco Billy, *886;* Every Which Way but Loose, *257;* High Plains Drifter, *903;* Lust in the Dust, *303;* Macon County Line, *94;* Night of the Comet, *854;* Return of a Man Called Horse, The, *924;* Return of the Man from U.N.C.L.E., The, *121;* Thunderbolt and Lightfoot, *152;* Tilt, *368;* Wind and the Lion, The, *164*

Lewis, George J.: Big Sombrero, The, *883;* Sign of Zorro, The, *204*

Lewis, Gwen: Eyes of a Stranger, *682*

Lewis, Jerry: At War with the Army, *221;* Bellboy, The, *226;* Cinderfella, *774;* Cracking Up, *248;* Don't Raise the Bridge, Lower the River, *253;* Errand Boy, The, *256;* Hardly Working, *276;* King of Comedy, The, *507;* Nutty Professor, The, *321;* Patsy, The, *328;* Slapstick of Another Kind, *354*

Lewis, Joe E.: Private Buckaroo, *799*

Lewis, Ted: Manhattan Merry-Go-Round, *913*

Lewis, Tommy: Chant of Jimmie Blacksmith, The, *431*

Lewis, Tom: Steamboat Bill Jr., *359*

Leysen, Johann: Hail Mary, *480*

Léaud, Jean-Pierre: 400 Blows, The, *468;* Day for Night, *446;* Last Tango in Paris, *515;* Love on the Run, *524;* Two English Girls, *625*

Léotard, Philippe: La Balance, *85*

Lhermitte, Thierry: Until September, *627*

Liapis, Peter: Ghoulies, *693*

Libby, Brion: Stephen King's Night Shift Collection, *747*

Libertini, Richard: All of Me, *217;* Fletch, *57;* Going Berserk, *269;* Popeye, *199;* Big Trouble, *228*

Liebman, Ron: Romantic Comedy, *343;* Up the Academy, *375;* Where's Poppa?, *381*

Lieh, Lo: Stranger and the Gunfighter, The, *935*

Lightfoot, Gordon: Harry Tracy, *901*

Lightstone, Marilyn: Spasms, *746*

Ligon, Tom: Joyride, *504*

Lincoln, Elmo: Intolerance, *497;* Tarzan of the Apes, *145*

Lincoln, Warren: Power, The, *730*

Lindblom, Gunnel: Winter Light, *636*

Linden, Hal: How to Break Up a Happy Divorce, *284;* Starflight One, *867*

Linden, Jennie: Women in Love, *638*

Linder, Bert: Stephen King's Night Shift Collection, *747*

Lindfors, Viveca: Cauldron of Blood, *661;* Girlfriends, *472;* Way We Were, The, *631*

Lindgren, Peter: I Am Curious Yellow, *491*

Lindley, Audra: Cannery Row, *237;* Desert Hearts, *449;* Heartbreak Kid, The, *277*

Lindsay, Margaret: Scarlet Street, *589;* Tammy and the Doctor, *611*

Lind, Della: Swiss Miss, *363*

Ling, Suzanne: Kiss of the Tarantula, *710*

Linke, Paul: Motel Hell, *718*

Linkletter, Art: Champagne for Caesar, *240*

Linville, Larry: School Spirit, *346*

Lion, Leon M.: Amazing Adventure, *217*

Liotard, Thérèse: One Sings, The Other Doesn't, *552*

Lipinski, Eugene: Moonlighting, *538*

Lipscomb, Dennis: Blue Yonder, The, *173;* Crossroads, *775;* Union City, *626*

Lisi, Virna: When Wolves Cry, *632*

Liszt, Margie: Valley of Fire, *942*

Litel, John: Enchanted Forest, The, *180;* Texas Lady, *938*

Lithgow, John: 2010, *874;* Adventures of Buckaroo Banzai, The, *815;* Blow Out, *654;* Day After, The, *828;* Footloose, *781;* Glitter Dome, The, *62;* Goldilocks and the Three Bears, *182;* Manhattan Project, The, *714;* Obsession, *725;* Rich Kids, *580;* Santa Claus—The Movie, *202;* Twilight Zone—The Movie, *759;* World According to Garp, The, *639*

Littlefield, Lucien: Susanna Pass, *936*

Little, Cleavon: Blazing Saddles, *230;* Double Exposure, *678;* Greased Lightning, *64;* High Risk, *72;* Jimmy the Kid, *186;* Once Bitten, *323;* Scavenger Hunt, *346;* Toy Soldiers, *154;* Vanishing Point, *158*

Little, Rich: Dirty Tricks, *251*

Lively, Jason: European Vacation, *258*

Livesey, Roger: Drums, *46;* Life and Death of Colonel Blimp, The, *517;* Of Human Bondage (Remake), *549*

Livingston, Robert: Grand Canyon Trail, *899;* Night Stage to Galveston, *917;* Winning of the West, *946*

Li, Donald: Big Trouble in Little China, *17*

Llewellyn, Desmond: Spy Who Loved Me, The, *139;* You Only Live Twice, *166*

Lloyd, Christopher: Back to the Future, *819;* Clue, *245;* One Flew over the Cuckoo's Nest, *551;* Schizoid, *740;* Streethawk, *142*

Lloyd, Danny: Will, G. Gordon Liddy, *635*

Lloyd, Doris: Oliver Twist, *550*

Lloyd, Harold: Keystone Comedies: Vo. 5, *392;* Milky Way, The, *310;* Sin of Harold Diddlebock (aka Mad Wednesday), *352*

Lloyd, Kathleen: It Lives Again, *706;* Jayne Mansfield Story, The, *501;* Missouri Breaks, The, *915;* Take Down, *363*

Lloyd, Norman: Saboteur, *738*

Lobel, Bruni: Almost Angels, *171*

LoBianco, Tony: Bloodbrothers, *415;* F.I.S.T., *461;* Seven-Ups, The, *131*

Lochary, David: Female Trouble, *259;* Mondo Trasho, *312;* Multiple Maniacs, *718;* Pink Flamingos, *330*

Locke, Sondra: Any Which Way You Can, *219;* Bronco Billy, *886;* Gauntlet, The, *62;* Heart Is a Lonely Hunter, The, *483;* Outlaw Josey Wales, The, *920;* Sudden Impact, *142;* Willard, *765*

Lockhart, Anne: Joyride, *504;* Troll, *873*

Lockhart, Calvin: Beast Must Die, The, *649;* Let's Do It Again, *298*

Lockhart, Gene: Abe Lincoln in Illinois, *387;* Girl in Every Port, A, *268;* Going My Way, *474;* His Girl Friday, *281;* Something to Sing About, *803;* South of Pago Pago, *138;* Star of Midnight, *139;* They Died with their Boots On, *938*

Lockhart, June: Sergeant York, *131;* Strange Invaders, *867;* Troll, *873*

Locklear, Heather: Firestarter, *685*

Lockwood, Gary: 2001: A Space Odyssey, *873;* Incredible Journey of Dr. Meg Laurel, The, *494;* It Happpened at the World's Fair, *789;* Magic Sword, The, *191;* R.P.M. (Revolutions Per Minute), *572*

Lockwood, Margaret: Dr. Syn, *45;* Lady Vanishes, The (original), *710;* Man in Grey, The, *528;* Stars Look Down, The, *601;* Trouble in the Glen, *372*

Loder, John: Brighton Strangler, The, *657;* Dr. Syn, *45;* Sabotage, *738*

Loewitsch, Klaus: Gotchal, *64*

Logan, Jacqueline: King of Kings, The, *508*

Logan, Phyllis: Another Time, Another Place, *400;* Doctor and the Devils, The, *676*

Logan, Robert: Across the Great Divide, *169;* Adventures of the Wilderness Family, *170;* Mountain Family Robinson, *193;* Night in Heaven, A, *544;* Wilderness Family, Part 2, The, *212*

Loggia, Robert: Armed and Dangerous, *220;* Elfego Baca: Six Gun Law, *895;* Jagged Edge, *500;* Ninth Configuration, The, *546;* Prizzi's Honor, *569;* Psycho II, *731;* Revenge of the Pink Panther, The, *340;* Scarface (Remake), *129*

Lo Bianco, Tony: Demon (God Told Me To), *830*

Lokey, Ben: Breakin', *771*

Lollobrigida, Gina: Bad Man's River, *880;* Beat the Devil, *225;* Solomon and Sheba, *597;* Trapeze, *621*

Lombard, Carole: Golden Age of Comedy, The, *270;* In Name Only, *493;* Made for Each Other, *304;* Mr. and Mrs. Smith, *310;* My Man Godfrey, *317;* No Man of Her Own, *320;* Nothing Sacred, *321;* They Knew What They Wanted, *616;* To Be or Not to Be (Original), *368*

Lombard, Robert: Holiday Hotel, *281*

Lommel, Ulli: Boogeyman 2, The, *656*

Lomond, Britt: Sign of Zorro, The, *204*

Lom, Herbert: And Now the Screaming Starts, *645;* Asylum, *647;* Count Dracula, *664;* Curse of the Pink Panther, The, *248;* Dark Places, *669;* Dead Zone, The, *671;* Dorian Gray, *678;* Fire Down Below, *464;* King Solomon's Mines (1985), *84;* Lion and the Hawk, The, *89;* Man with Bogart's Face, The, *96;* Murders In The Rue Morgue, *720;* Mysterious Island, *853;* Pink Panther Strikes Again, The, *330;* Return of the Pink Panther, The, *339;* Revenge of the Pink Panther, The, *340;* Shot in the Dark, A, *351;* Ten Little Indians, *147;* Third Man On The Mountain, *208;* Trail of the Pink Panther, The, *371;* Villa Rides, *943*

London, Julie: Red House, The, *734*

London, Roy: Jake Speed, *78*

London, Tom: Blue Canadian Rockies, *884;* False Colors, *895;* Hills of Utah, The, *903;* Melody Ranch, *914;* Mystery Mountain, *916;* Prairie Moon, *922;* Ridin' on a Rainbow, *926;* Song of Texas, *933;* Yellow Rose of Texas, *946*

Lone, John: Iceman, *843;* Year of the Dragon, *166*

Longden, John: Blackmail, *414*

Longden, Terence: Carry on Nurse, *239*

Longs, Freddie: Firefox, *54*

Long, Michael: Squizzy Taylor, *139*

Long, Richard: Dark Mirror, The, *669;* House on Haunted Hill, *700;* Stranger, The, *748*

Long, Shelley: Caveman, *240;* Irreconcilable Differences, *498;* Losin' It, *301;* Night Shift, *319*

Lonnen, Ray: Belfast Assassin, *407;* Guardian of the Abyss, *695*

Lonsdale, Michael: Enigma, *49;* Erendira, *459;* Moonraker, *102*

Lonsdale, Michel: Mr. Klein, *536;* Stolen Kisses, *360*

Loomis, Christopher: Nesting, The, *721*

Loomis, Nancy: Assault on Precinct 13, *10;* Halloween, *695*

Loomis, Rod: Beastmaster, The, *820*

Loo, Richard: Back to Bataan, *11;* First Yank into Tokyo, *55;* Love is a Many-Splendored Thing, *523*

Lopez, Fernando: Defiance, *41*

Lopez, Gerry: Conan the Barbarian, *825*

Lopez, Perry: Chinatown, *30*

Lopez, Slyvia: Hercules Unchained, *841*

Lord, Jack: Doomsday Flight, The, *453;* Dr. No, *44;* God's Little Acre, *473*

Lord, Justine: Maniac, *714*

Loren, Sophia: Arabesque, *9;* Boccaccio 70, *231;* Brass Target, *24;* Breath of Scandal, A, *233;* Cassandra Crossing, The, *428;* Desire Under the Elms, *449;* El Cid, *48;* Fall of the Roman Empire, The, *462;* Firepower, *55;* Heller in Pink Tights, *902;* Man of La Mancha, *793;* Pride and the Passion, The, *567;* Special Day, A, *548*

Loret, Susanne: Atom Age Vampire, *647*

Lorne, Marion: Strangers on a Train, *749*

Lorre, Peter: 20,000 Leagues under the Sea, *155;* Arsenic and Old Lace, *220;* Beat the Devil, *225;* Casablanca, *427;* Five Weeks in a Balloon, *56;* Maltese Falcon, The, *95;* Man Who Knew Too Much, The (original), *715;* Mr. Moto's Last Warning, *101;* My Favorite Brunette, *316;* M, *713;* Passage to Marseilles, *113;* Patsy, The, *328;* Raven, The, *733;* Secret Agent, The, *131;* Silk Stockings, *802;* Stranger on the Third Floor, *141;* Tales of Terror, *751;* Voyage to the Bottom of the Sea, *874*

Lothar, Hanns: One, Two, Three, *324*

Louanne, L: Oh, God! Book II, *323*

Loudon, Dorothy: Garbo Talks, *265*

Loughlin, Lori: New Kids, The, *721*

Louise, Anita: Judge Priest, *504;* Little Princess, The, *190;* Villain Still Pursued Her, The, *159*

Louise, Tina: God's Little Acre, *473;* Trap, The, *759*

Louis, Joe: This is the Army, *808*

Lovejoy, Frank: Americano, The, *879*

Love, Bessie: Intolerance, *497;* Lost World, The, *850;* Ritz, The, *342*

Love, Mike: Boogeyman, The, *655;* Beach Boys: An American Band, The, *770*

Love, Montagu: Adventures of Robin Hood, The, *2;* Bulldog Drummond, *25*

Love, Suzanna: Boogeyman The, *655;* Boogeyman 2, The, *656;* Devonsville Terror, The, *674*

Lowell, Carey: Dangerously Close, *668*

Lowery, Robert: Dawn on the Great Divide, *891;* Revenge of the Zombies, *736*

Lowe, Arthur: Ruling Class, The, *344*

Lowe, Edmund: Dillinger, *42;* Enchanted Forest, The, *180;* Good Sam, *271;* Heller in Pink Tights, *902*

Lowe, Rob: About Last Night, *388;* Class, *244;* Hotel New Hampshire, The, *489;* Oxford Blues, *556;* St. Elmo's Fire, *586;* Youngblood, *641*

Lowe, Susan: Desperate Living, *250*

Lowitsch, Klaus: Despair, *449*

Loy, Myrna: After the Thin Man, *6;* Arrowsmith, *401;* Bachelor and the Bobbysoxer, The, *222;* Best Years of Our Lives, The, *409;* End, The, *255;* Just Tell Me What You Want, *292;* Libeled Lady, *298;* Mr. Blandings Builds His Dream House, *310;* Red Pony, The, *201;* Shadow of the Thin Man, *132;* Song of the Thin Man, *138;* Thin Man Goes Home, The, *149;* Thin Man, The, *149*

Lozano, Margarita: Night of the Shooting Stars, *545;* Viridiana, *628*

Lucas, Wilfred: Chump at Oxford, A, *243;* Pardon Us, *327;* I Cover the Waterfront, *76*

Luca, Raf: Cop in Blue Jeans, The, *35*

Lucero, Enrique: Return of a Man Called Horse, The, *924;* Shark! (aka Maneaters!), *133*

Luchini, Fabrica: Claire's Knee, *243;* Full Moon in Paris, *264*

Lucking, Bill: Return of a Man Called Horse, The, *924*

Ludwig, Pamela: Over the Edge, *555*

Luez, Laurette: Prehistoric Women, *857*

Lufton, Abe: Old Corral, The, *919*

Luft, Lorna: Grease 2, *785;* Where the Boys Are '84, *380*

Lugosi, Bela: Abbott and Costello Meet Frankenstein, *214;* Ape Man, The, *646;* Body Snatcher, The, *655;* Boys from Brooklyn, The, *656;* Bride of the Monster, *657;* Corpse Vanishes, The, *664;* Death Kiss, The, *39;* Devil Bat, The, *673;* Dracula (Original), *678;* Frankenstein Meets the Wolf Man, *688;* Ghosts on the Loose, *267;* Glen or Glenda, *473;* Gorilla, The, *271;* Human Monster, The (Dark Eyes of London), *702;* Invisible Ghost, *705;* Ninotchka, *319;* Phantom Creeps, The, *727;* Plan 9 from Outer Space, *856;* Raven and the Black Cat, The, *733;* Return of the Vampire, The, *735;* Spooks Run Wild, *357;* White Zombie, *764*

Luhrmann, Baz: Winter of our Dreams, *636*

Luisi, James: Red Light Sting, The, *577*

Lukas, Paul: 20,000 Leagues under the Sea, *155;* Dinner at the Ritz, *43;* Dodsworth, *452;* Four Horsemen of the Apocalypse, *60;* Fun in Acapulco, *781;* Kim, *83;* Watch on the Rhine, *630*

Lukather, Paul: Dinosaurus!, *675*

Lukes, Oldrich: First Spaceship on Venus, *837*

Luke, Jorge: Return of a Man Called Horse, The, *924;* Shark Hunter, The, *133*

Luke, Keye: Amsterdam Kill, The, *7;* First Yank into Tokyo, *55;* Good Earth, The, *475;* Gremlins, *840;* Kung Fu, *85*

Lukoye, Peter: Born Free, *174*

Lulli, Folco: Wages of Fear, The, *763*

Lulu, : To Sir with Love, *619*

Luna, Barbara: Five Weeks in a Balloon, *56;* Gentle Savage, *898*

Lundgren, Dolph: Rocky IV, *582*

Lundigan, William: Fabulous Dorseys, The, *778*

Lund, Art: Last American Hero, The, *86;* Molly Maguires, The, *537*

Lund, Deanna: Hardly Working, *276*

Lund, Jana: Frankenstein—1970, *689*

Lund, John: Dakota Incident, *891;* Perils of Pauline, the, *329;* Wackiest Ship in the Army, The, *377*

Lunghi, Cherie: Excalibur, *835*

Lunham, Dan: Strangeness, The, *748*

Lupino, Ida: Adventures of Sherlock Holmes, The, *2;* Devil's Rain, The, *674;* Food of the Gods, *838;* High Sierra, *72;* Junior Bonner, *906;* Sea Devils, *129;* Thank Your Lucky Stars, *807;* They Drive by Night, *148*

Lupinski, Eugene: Adventures of Sherlock Holmes: The Dancing Men, *3*

Lupo, Alberto: Atom Age Vampire, *647*

Luppi, Federico: Funny Dirty Little War (NO HABRA MAS PENSAS ni OLVIDO), *264*

Lupton, John: Jesse James Meets Frankenstein's Daughter, *708*

Lurie, John: Stranger than Paradise, *360*

Lutter, Alfred: Alice Doesn't Live Here Anymore, *392;* Bad News Bears, The, *223;* Love and Death, *302*

Lu, Lisa: Demon Seed, *830*

Lyden, Pierce: Riders of the Deadline, *926;* Twilight in the Sierras, *941*

Lydon, Jimmy: Life With Father, *299;* Little Men, *519;* Tom Brown's School Days, *620*

Lye, Reg: Sunday Too Far Away, *608*

Lykes, John: Prime Risk, *115;* Cal, *423*

Lynch, Kate: Defcon 4, *829;* Meatballs, *308*

Lynch, Ken: I Married a Monster from Outer Space, *842*

Lynch, Richard: DeathSport, *829;* Invasion U.S.A., *77;* Scarecrow, *589;* Seven-Ups, The, *131;* Sword and the Sorcerer, The, *869*

Lynch, Sean: At the Earth's Core, *818*

Lynde, Janice: Beyond Evil, *650*

Lynde, Paul: Beach Blanket Bingo, *770;* Bye Bye Birdie, *773;* Charlotte's Web, *176;* Son of Flubber, *206*

Lynley, Carol: Cat and The Canary, The, *660;* Fantasy Island, *837;* Flood!, *685;* Four Deuces, The, *59;* Light In The Forest, The, *189;* Night Stalker, The, *723;* Son of Blob (Beware! The Blob), *745;* Washington Affair, The, *630*

Lynn, Betty: Texas John Slaughter: Geron-imo's Revenge, *937;* Texas John Slaughter: Stampede at Bitter Creek, *937;* Texas John Slaughter: Wild Times, *938*

Lynn, Cheryl M.: Thunder Run, *151*

Lynn, Dani: They Saved Hitler's Brain, *754*

Lynn, Diana: Bedtime for Bonzo, *226;* Every Girl Should Be Married, *256;* Kentuckian, The, *906*

Lynn, Emmett: Bluebeard, *654*

Lynn, Jeffrey: Roaring Twenties, The, *122*

Lynn, Johnathan: Romance With A Double Bass, *343*

Lynn, Sharon: Way Out West, *378*

Lyons, Robert F.: Cease Fire, *429;* Getting Straight, *472*

Lyons, Tom: Burn!, *421*

Lyon, Ben: I Cover the Waterfront, *76;* Indiscreet, *286*

Lyon, Sue: End of the World, *834;* Evel Knievel, *50;* Flim-Flam Man, The, *466;* Four Rode Out, *897;* Lolita, *520;* Night of the Iguana, The, *544*

Lytess, Natasha: Once Upon a Honeymoon, *324*

Maas, Sybil: Cousin, Cousine, *248*

Maazel, Lincoln: Martin, *715*

Mabe, Byron: Doberman Gang, The, *43*

MacAndrew, Marianne: Hello, Dolly!, *787*

MacArthur, James: Cry of Battle, *37;* Kidnapped, *82;* Light In The Forest, The, *189;* Swiss Family Robinson, The, *207;* Third Man On The Mountain, *208*

MacBride, Donald: They Got Me Covered, *366*

Maccachlan, Janet: Sounder, *598*

Macchio, Ralph: Crossroads, *775;* Karate Kid The, *505;* Karate Kid, Part 2, The, *81;* Outsiders, The, *555;* Teachers, *364;* Up the Academy, *375*

MacCorkindale, Simon: Jaws 3, *707;* Riddle of the Sands, *121;* Robbers of the Sacred Mountain, *123;* Sword and the Sorcerer, The, *869*

MacDonald, Bruce: Return of the Secaucus 7, *339*

MacDonald, Edmund: Detour, *450*

MacDonald, Jeanette: Maytime, *793;* Rose Marie, *800;* San Francisco, *588;* Smilin' Through, *803*

MacDonald, J. Farrell: Painted Desert, The, *921*

MacDonald, Kenneth: False Paradise, *896*

MacDowell, Andie: St. Elmo's Fire, *586*

Mace, Paul: Lords of Flatbush, The, *522*

MacGinnis, Niall: Curse of the Demon, *667*

MacGowran, Jack: How I Won the War, *284;* Quiet Man, The, *117;* Start the Revolution Without Me, *358*

MacGraw, Ali: Convoy, *34;* Getaway, The, *62;* Goodbye Columbus, *271;* Just Tell Me What You Want, *292;* Love Story, *524;* Players, *564*

Machowski, Ignacy: First Spaceship on Venus, *837*

Macht, Stephen: Galaxina, *839;* Last Winter, The, *515;* Mountain Men, The, *915*

MacIntyre, Christine: Dawn on the Great Divide, *891;* Gunman from Bodie, *900*

Mack, Helen: His Girl Friday, *281;* Milky Way, The, *310;* Son of Kong, The, *745*

Mack, Kerry: Savage Attraction, *739*

Mack, Marion: General, The, *266*

Mack, Wilbur: Gunman from Bodie, *900*

MacKay, Fulton: Local Hero, *300*

Mackin, Harry: Last of the Pony Riders, *907*

Mackenzie, Alastair: Man Who Haunted Himself, The, *714*

Mackenzie, Alex: Greyfriars Bobby, *183*

Mackenzie, Hugh: Man Who Haunted Himself, The, *714*

MacKenzie, Patch: Graduation Day, *694*

MacKenzie, Philip Charles: Red Light Sting, The, *577*

Mackinnon, Mary: Bay Boy, The, *406*

MacLachlan, Kyle: Dune, *832*

MacLaine, Shirley: Apartment, The, *219;* Around the World in 80 Days, *220;* Being There, *226;* Cannonball Run II, *237;* Change of Seasons, A, *240;* Hot Spell, *489;* Irma La Douce, *287;* Loving Couples, *33;* Terms of Endearment, *613;* Trouble With Harry, The, *372;* Two Mules for Sister Sara, *942*

MacLane, Barton: Bombardier, *21;* Kansas Pacific, *906;* Melody Ranch, *914;* Naked in the Sun, *917;* Prince and the Pauper, The (Original), *199;* Song of Texas, *933;* You Only Live Once, *640*

MacLeod, Gavin: Sand Pebbles, The, *127*

MacMahon, Aline: Gold Diggers of 1933, *783*

MacMahon, Horace: Never Steal Anything Small, *795*

MacMurray, Fred: Absent-Minded Professor, The, *169;* Alice Adams, *392;* Apartment, The, *219;* Caine Mutiny, The, *423;* Charlie and The Angel, *176;* Follow Me Boys!, *181;* Happiest Millionaire, The, *184;* Miracle of the Bells, The, *534;* Shaggy Dog, The, *204;* Son of Flubber, *206;* Swarm, The, *751*

MacNaughton, Robert: E.T.—The Extraterrestrial, *832*

MacNee, Patrick: Dead of Night, *671;* Howling, The, *701;* Rehearsal for Murder, *120;* Return of the Man from U.N.C.L.E., The, *121;* Sea Wolves, The, *130;* Sweet Sixteen, *144;* Young Doctors in Love, *385*

MacNeil, Francis: Bay Boy, The, *406*

MacNicol, Peter: Boy Who Left Home to Find Out about the Shivers, The, *174;* Dragonslayer, *831;* Sophie's Choice, *597*

MacPherson, Joe: Bay Boy, The, *406*

Macrae, Duncan: Tunes of Glory, *624*

MacRae, Gordon: Oklahoma!, *796;* Pilot, The, *563*

Macready, George: Black Arrow, The, *18;*

Gilda, *472;* Paths of Glory, *559*

Macy, Bill: Bad Medicine, *223;* Death at Love House, *672;* Jerk, The, *289;* Late Show, The, *87;* Movers and Shakers, *315;* My Favorite Year, *316;* Serial, *349*

Madden, Dave: Eat My Dust, *47*

Maddern, Victor: Carrington, V. C., *427*

Madigan, Amy: Alamo Bay, *391;* Love Child, *523;* Love Letters, *523;* Streets of Fire, *142;* Twice in a Lifetime, *624*

Madison, Guy: Bullwhip, *887;* Till the End of Time, *618*

Madison, Julian: It's a Gift, *288*

Madison, Noel: Last Mile, The, *514*

Madonna: Certain Sacrifice, A, *429;* Desperately Seeking Susan, *280*

Madsen, Virginia: Creator, *440;* Electric Dreams, *255;* Fire With Fire, *464*

Maeda, Bibari: Son of Godzilla, *745*

Magee, Patrick: And Now the Screaming Starts, *645;* Asylum, *647;* Barry Lyndon, *405;* Clockwork Orange, A, *824;* Dementia 13, *673;* Last Days of Man on Earth, The, *848;* Masque of the Red Death, The, *716;* Rough Cut, *124;* Seance on a Wet Afternoon, *741;* Telefon, *147;* Young Winston, *641*

Maggart, Brandon: Christmas Evil, *663*

Maggiorani, Lamberto: Bicycle Thief, The, *410*

Maggio, Dante: Boccaccio 70, *231*

Maggio, Pupella: Amarcord, *395*

Magnani, Anna: Bellissima, *227;* Open City, *553*

Magwood, Robbie: One Magic Christmas, *552*

Mahal, Taj: Sounder, *598*

Maharis, George: Sword and the Sorcerer, The, *869*

Maher, Joseph: Evil That Men Do, The, *50;* Going Ape!, *269;* Under the Rainbow, *374*

Mahler, Bruce: Police Academy II: Their First Assignment, *332*

Mahoney, Jock: Away All Boats, *11;* Cow Town, *890*

Maier, Tim: Raw Courage, *119*

Main, David: Skullduggery, *744*

Main, Marjorie: Stella Dallas, *602*

Mairesse, Valerie: One Sings, The Other Doesn't, *552*

Majors, Lee: Agency, *390;* Cyborg: The Six Million Dollar Man, *827;* High Noon, Part Two, *903;* Last Chase, The, *847;* Liberation of L. B. Jones, The, *517;* Norseman, The, *108;* Starflight One, *867*

Makepeace, Chris: Last Chase, The, *847;* Meatballs, *308;* My Bodyguard, *540;* Vamp, *760*

Mako: Big Brawl, The, *15;* Bushido Blade, *26;* Island at the Top of the World, The, *845;* Killer Elite, The, *83;* P.O.W.: The Escape, *112;* Sand Pebbles, The, *127;* Testament, *870*

Malanowicz, Zygmunt: Knife in the Water,

509

Malavoy, Christophe: La Balance, 85; Peril, 561

Mala: Tuttles of Tahiti, The, 373

Malcolm, Christopher: Great Riviera Bank Robbery, The, 65

Malcolm, John: Adventures of Sherlock Holmes: The Naval Treaty, 4

Malden, Karl: 13 Rue Madeleine, 149; Baby Doll, 403; Birdman of Alcatraz, 412; Cheyenne Autumn, 888; Cincinnati Kid, The, 31; Gypsy, 785; How the West Was Won, 904; I Confess, 703; Meteor, 852; Murderers' Row, 104; Nevada Smith, 917; One-Eyed Jacks, 920; On the Waterfront, 551; Patton, 559; Pollyanna, 198; Ruby Gentry, 585; Skag, 594; Sting II, The, 140; Streetcar Named Desire, A, 605; Summertime Killer, The, 143

Maleeva, Irina: Union City, 626

Malet, Laurent: Invitation au Voyage, 497

Malicki-Sanchez, Keram: Pied Piper of Hamelin, The, 198

Malidor, Lissette: La Truite (The Trout), 512

Malkovich, John: Eleni, 456; Killing Fields, The, 506; Places in the Heart, 563

Mallais-Borris, Rose: Alligator Shoes, 394

Malleson, Miles: Horror of Dracula, 699; Hound of the Baskervilles, The (Remake), 75

Mallot, Yollande: Devil Bat, The, 673

Malmen, Lennart: Elvira Madigan, 457

Malmsjo, Jan: Fanny and Alexander, 463

Malmsten, Birger: Secrets of Women (or Waiting Women), 348

Malone, Dorothy: Abduction, 387; Battle Cry, 12; Being, The, 650; Big Sleep, The (Original), 16; Warlock, 944; Winter Kills, 636

Mancuso, Nick: Heartbreakers, 484; Legend of Walks Far Woman, The, 909; Mother Lode, 103; Nightwing, 723; Ticket to Heaven, 618

Mandan, Robert: Zapped!, 385

Mandel, Howie: Fine Mess, A, 260; Gas, 265; Princess Who Had Never Laughed, The, 199

Mandel, Rena: Vampyr, 761

Mander, Miles: Brighton Strangler, The, 657; Return of the Vampire, The, 735

Mando, Marcello: Warning, The, 160

Manfredi, Nino: Nudo di Donna (Portrait of a Woman, Nude), 321

Mangano, Silvana: Conversation Piece, 438; Death in Venice, 447

Mannari, Guido: Cop in Blue Jeans, The, 35

Manners, David: Death Kiss, The, 39; Dracula (Original), 678; Mummy, The (original), 719

Manners, Sheila: Lawless Range, 908

Mannheim, Lucie: Thirty-nine Steps, The, 755

Manning, Hope: Old Corral, The, 919

Manning, Irene: Yankee Doodle Dandy, 813

Manning, Patricia: Hideous Sun Demon, The,

697

Manni, Ettore: Battle of El Alamein, The, 12

Mann, Edward: Jungle Master, The, 80

Mann, Hank: City Lights, 243

Mann, Leonard: Wifemistress, 633

Mann, Paul: Fiddler on the Roof, 779

Mann, Terence: Chorus Line, A, 774; Critters, 666

Manoff, Dinah: I Ought to Be in Pictures, 287; Ordinary People, 554

Manojlovic, Miki: When Father Was Away On Business, 632

Mansfield, Jayne: Guide For The Married Man, A, 273

Mantle, Clive: Robin Hood and the Sorcerer, 123

Manuel, Robert: Rififi, 122

Manzy, David: Baby, The, 648

Manz, Linda: Days of Heaven, 446; Snow Queen, 205

Mao, Angela: Enter the Dragon, 49

Mapes, Ted: Cow Town, 890

Mapp, Jim: Enemy Mine, 834

Marachuk, Steve: Piranha Part Two: The Spawning, 728

Marais, Jean: Beauty and the Beast, 820

Maranne, Andre: Return of the Pink Panther, The, 339; Revenge of the Pink Panther, The, 340

Mara, Adele: Robin Hood of Texas, 927; You Were Never Lovelier, 814

Marceau, Marcel: Silent Movie, 351

Marceau, Sophie: La Boum, 511

March, Eve: Song of Texas, 933

March, Fredric: Alexander the Great, 392; Anna Karenina, 400; Best Years of Our Lives, The, 409; Hombre, 904; I Married a Witch, 842; Inherit the Wind, 495; Mary of Scotland, 530; Nothing Sacred, 321; Seven Days in May, 591; Star Is Born, A (Original), 600

Marchal, Arlette: Wings, 164

Marchand, Guy: Cousin, Cousine, 248; Entre Nous (Between Us), 458; Heat of Desire, 277; Holiday Hotel, 281; Petit Con, 329

Marchand, Henri: A Nous la Liberte, 219

Marchand, Nancy: Bostonians, The, 417

Marcovicci, Andrea: Front, The, 470; Hand, The, 696; Spacehunter: Adventures in the Forbidden Zone, 750; Stuff, The, 750

Marcus, James: Clockwork Orange, A, 824

Marcus, Richard: Enemy Mine, 834

Maren, Jerry: Petronella, 197

Margolin, Janet: Enter Laughing, 256; Last Embrace, The, 87; Take the Money and Run, 363

Margolin, Stuart: Class, 244; Fine Mess, A, 260; Futureworld, 838; Running Hot, 586

Margo, Ciannelli, Eduardo: Winterset, 636

Margulies, David: 9 1/2 Weeks, 545

Maricle, Leona: Mad Miss Manton, The, 304

Marielle, Jean-Pierre: One Wild Moment, 552; Sex Shop, Le, 350

Marie, Anne-Laure: Aviator's Wife, The, 222;

Aviator's Wife, The, *403*

Marika, Roy: Where the Green Ants Dream, *632*

Marika, Wandjuk: Where the Green Ants Dream, *632*

Marino, Kenny: Prince of the City, *568*

Marin, Jacque: Herbie Goes to Monte Carlo, *185*

Marin, Richard "Cheech": After Hours, *318*; Echo Park, *455*

Marin, Rikki: Things Are Tough All Over, *366*

Marion, George: Anna Christie, *399*

Marion, Renee: Red Balloon, The, *201*

Maris, Mona: Camila, *424*

Markey, Enid: Tarzan of the Apes, *145*

Markham, Kiki: Two English Girls, *625*

Markham, Monte: Ginger In The Morning, *472*; Hustling, *490*; Jake Speed, *78*

Marks, Alfred: Scream and Scream Again, *740*

Mark, Hudson, and Brett: Hysterical, *284*

Mark, Tamara: Fast Forward, *779*

Marlaud, Philippe: Aviator's Wife, The, *222*; Aviator's Wife, The, *403*

Marley, John: Amateur, The, *395*; Framed, *60*; Glitter Dome, The, *62*; Godfather, The, *473*; Greatest, The, *479*; It Lives Again, *706*; Love Story, *524*; Mother Lode, *103*; Robbers of the Sacred Mountain, *133*; Threshold, *872*; Tribute, *621*; Utilities, *376*

Marlowe, Hugh: Day the Earth Stood Still, The, *828*; Earth vs. the Flying Saucers, *833*; Twelve O'Clock High, *155*

Marlowe, Jo Ann: Mildred Pierce, *534*

Marlowe, Scott: Journey Into Fear, *503*

Marmont, Percy: Secret Agent, The, *131*; Young and Innocent, *166*

Marquand, Christian: And God Created Woman, *397*; Flight of the Phoenix, The, *58*

Marquez, Evaristo: Burn!, *421*

Marriott, Slyvia: Story of Adele H, The, *603*

Marsalis, Branford: Bring on the Night, *772*

Marsani, Claudia: Conversation Piece, *438*

Marsh, Jean: Changeling, The, *661*; Dark Places, *669*; Return to Oz, *201*

Marsh, Joan: Manhunt in the African Jungle (Secret Service in Darkest Africa), *96*

Marsh, Mae: Birth of a Nation, The, *412*; Intolerance, *497*

Marsh, Marian: Black Room, The, *652*; Svengali, *750*

Marshall, E. G.: 12 Angry Men, *624*; 13 Rue Madeleine, *149*; Chase, The, *431*; Interiors, *496*; My Chauffeur, *316*; Power, *566*

Marshall, Garry: Lost in America, *301*

Marshall, Herbert: Black Jack, *18*; Five Weeks in a Balloon, *56*; Fly, The (original), *686*; Foreign Correspondent, *687*; Letter, The, *516*; List of Adrian Messenger, The, *90*; Razor's Edge, The (Original), *576*

Marshall, Jo-Ann: Preppies, *333*

Marshall, Ken: Krull, *847*; Tilt, *368*

Marshall, Patricia: Good News, *784*

Marshall, Penny: Movers and Shakers, *315*

Marshall, Sean: Pete's Dragon, *197*

Marshall, Tully: Ball of Fire, *224*; Fighting Caravans, *896*; Hurricane Express, *76*; Intolerance, *497*; Red Dust, *119*; Red Dust, *577*

Marshall, William: Blacula, *652*; Something of Value, *138*

Marshal, Alan: House on Haunted Hill, *700*

Marshe, Vera: Big Sombrero, The, *883*

Marston, John: Son of Kong, The, *748*

Mars, Kenneth: Apple Dumpling Gang Rides Again, The, *171*; Beer, *226*; Producers, The, *336*; What's Up Doc?, *390*; Yellowbeard, *385*; Young Frankenstein, *385*

Martell, Donna: Hills of Utah, The, *903*

Martel, June: Santa Fe Stampede, *939*

Martinelli, Elsa: Hatari!, *69*; Tenth Victim, The, *869*

Martino, Al: Godfather, The, *473*

Martin, Chris-Pin: Boots and Saddles, *888*

Martin, Dean: Airport, *7*; At War with the Army, *221*; Bandolero!, *881*; Cannonball Run II, *237*; Cannonball Run, *237*; Murderers' Row, *104*; Ocean's Eleven, *109*; Rio Bravo, *926*; Sons of Katie Elder, The, *934*

Martin, DeanPaul: Heart Like a Wheel, *70*; Players, *564*

Martin, Dewey: Big Sky, The, *883*; Savage Sam, *202*

Martin, Dick: Carbon Copy, *238*

Martin, Eugenia Saint: Rock 'N Roll Wrestling Women Vs. The Aztec Mummy, *342*

Martin, Jean: Battle of Algiers, *405*

Martin, Maria: Four Rode Out, *897*

Martin, Marion: They Got Me Covered, *366*

Martin, Millicent: Alfie, *216*

Martin, Nan: Doctor Detroit, *252*; Other Side of the Mountain, Part II, The, *554*

Martin, Pamela Sue: Buster and Billie, *422*; Torchlight, *620*

Martin, Ross: Experiment in Terror, *681*

Martin, Sallie: Say Amen, Somebody, *801*

Martin, Sandy: Scalpel, *740*

Martin, Skip: Horror Hospital, *699*

Martin, Steve: All of Me, *217*; Dead Men Don't Wear Plaid, *249*; Jerk, The, *289*; Kids Are Alright, The, *790*; Lonely Guy, The, *300*; Man With Two Brains, The, *307*; Movers and Shakers, *315*; Muppet Movie, The, *193*; Pennies from Heaven, *797*

Martin, Strother: Ballad of Cable Hogue, The, *880*; Better Late than Never, *228*; Brotherhood of Satan, *658*; Cool Hand Luke, *35*; Great Scout and Cathouse Thursday, The, *899*; Hard Times, *69*; Love and Bullets, *93*; Nightwing, *723*; Rooster Cogburn, *928*; Shenandoah, *930*; Slap Shot, *353*; Up in Smoke, *375*; Wild Bunch, The, *945*

Martin, Tony: Easy to Love, *778*

Marvin, Frankie: Boots and Saddles, *885*; Git Along, Little Dogies, *898*; Heart of the Rio Grande, *901*; Man From Music Mountain, *912*

Marvin, Lee: Big Heat, The, *15;* Big Red One, The, *15;* Cat Ballou, *888;* Comancheros, The, *889;* Death Hunt, *39;* Delta Force, The, *41;* Dirty Dozen, The, *43;* Donovan's Reef, *44;* Gorky Park, *64;* Great Scout and Cathouse Thursday, The, *899;* Man Who Shot Liberty Valance, The, *913;* Monte Walsh, *915;* Paint Your Wagon, *797;* Prime Cut, *115;* Professionals, The, *116;* Raintree County, *574;* Ship of Fools, *592;* Shout at the Devil, *135;* Wild One, The, *164*

Marx Brother, The: Animal Crackers, *218;* At the Circus, *244;* Day at the Races, A, *249;* Duck Soup, *254;* Go West, *269;* Love Happy, *302;* Monkey Business, *312;* Night at the Opera, A, *318;* Room Service, *343*

Marx, Groucho: Copacabana, *247;* Girl in Every Port, A, *268*

Marx, Harpo: Stage Door Canteen, *599*

Masak, Ron: Harper Valley P.T.A., *276;* Laserblast, *847*

Mase, Marino: Commandos, *33*

Masina, Giulietta: Juliet of the Spirits, *291;* La Strada, *512*

Mason, Connie: Blood Feast, *653*

Mason, Eric: Kiss of the Tarantula, *710*

Mason, Jackie: Jerk, The, *289*

Mason, James: 11 Harrowhouse, *48;* 20,000 Leagues under the Sea, *155;* Bad Man's River, *880;* Bloodline, *415;* Blue Max, The, *20;* Botany Bay, *22;* Boys from Brazil, The, *656;* Caught, *429;* Cross of Iron, *37;* Dangerous Summer, A, *444;* Desert Fox, The, *42;* Evil Under the Sun, *50;* Fall of the Roman Empire, The, *462;* Ffolkes, *53;* Heaven Can Wait, *278;* Inside Out, *77;* Journey to the Center of the Earth, *87;* Lolita, *520;* Lord Jim, *93;* Mackintosh Man, The, *94;* Madame Bovary, *526;* Mandingo, *528;* Man in Grey, The, *528;* Mill On the Floss, The, *534;* Murder By Decree, *103;* North by Northwest, *724;* Prisoner of Zenda, The, *115;* Salem's Lot, *739;* Shooting Party, The, *592;* Star Is Born, A (Remake), *601;* Verdict, The, *628;* Voyage of the Damned, *629*

Mason, LeRoy: My Pal Trigger, *916;* Santa Fe Stampede, *929;* Song of Nevada, *933*

Mason, Lola: RSVP, *343*

Mason, Madison: Dangerously Close, *668*

Mason, Marlyn: Christina, *31*

Mason, Marsha: Audrey Rose, *648;* Blume in Love, *416;* Chapter Two, *431;* Goodbye Girl, The, *271;* Max Dugan Returns, *531;* Only When I Laugh, *553;* Promises in the Dark, *569*

Mason, Tom: Return of the Man from U.N.C.L.E., The, *121*

Massen, Osa: Jack London, *499;* Lady from Louisiana, *907;* Master Race, The, *531;* Rocketship X-M, *860;* You'll Never Get Rich, *814*

Massey, Anna: Corn Is Green, The, *439;* Five Days One Summer, *466;* Frenzy, *689;* Peeping Tom, *727;* Sakharov, *587;* Vault of Horror, *761*

Massey, Daniel: Vault of Horror, *761*

Massey, Edith: Desperate Living, *250;* Female Trouble, *259;* Multiple Maniacs, *718;* Pink Flamingos, *330;* Polyester, *333*

Massey, Ilona: Frankenstein Meets the Wolf Man, *688*

Massey, Raymond: 49th Parallel, The, *468;* Abe Lincoln in Illinois, *387;* Arsenic and Old Lace, *220;* Drums, *46;* East of Eden (Original), *454;* Fountainhead, The, *468;* Hurricane, The, *490;* Naked and the Dead, The, *105;* Possessed, *565;* Santa Fe Trail, *929;* Scarlet Pimpernel, The, *129;* Things to Come, *871*

Masterson, Sean: Fatal Games, *683*

Masters, Ben: Dream Lover, *679;* Key Exchange, *506*

Mastroianni, Marcello: 8½, *455;* Divine Nymph, The, *452;* Gabriela, *265;* La Dolce Vita, *511;* La Nuit de Varennes, *511;* Macaroni, *304;* Special Day, A, *598;* Stay As You Are, *602;* Tenth Victim, The, *869;* Wifemistress, *633*

Masur, Richard: Burning Bed, The, *421;* Fallen Angel, *462;* Heartburn, *277;* Mean Season, The, *98;* Mr. Horn, *915;* My Science Project, *853;* Risky Business, *341;* Who'll Stop the Rain, *162*

Mateos, Julian: Four Rode Out, *897;* Kashmiri Run, The, *81*

Mathers, Jerry: Trouble With Harry, The, *372*

Mather, Aubrey: Ball of Fire, *224*

Matheson, Murray: Botany Bay, *22*

Matheson, Tim: 1941, *319;* Animal House, *218;* Fletch, *57;* Impulse, *704;* Little Sex, A, *300;* Magnum Force, *94;* To Be or Not to Be (Remake), *369;* Up the Creek, *375*

Mathews, Carmen: Sounder, *598*

Mathews, Kerwin: 7TH Voyage of Sinbad, The, *861;* Battle beneath the Earth, *12;* Devil at 4 O'Clock, The, *450;* Maniac, *714;* Octaman, *725*

Mathews, Thom: Friday the 13th Part VI: Jason Lives, *691;* Return of the Living Dead, The, *735*

Matthau, Walter: Bad News Bears, The, *223;* Buddy, Buddy, *235;* Casey's Shadow, *176;* Charade, *29;* Charley Varrick, *30;* Earthquake, *46;* Ensign Pulver, *255;* Face in the Crowd, A, *461;* Failsafe, *461;* First Monday in October, *465;* Fortune Cookie, The, *262;* Guide For The Married Man, A, *273;* Hello, Dolly!, *787;* Hopscotch, *74;* House Calls, *283;* I Ought to Be in Pictures, *287;* Kentuckian, The, *906;* King Creole, *790;* Kotch, *294;* Laughing Policeman, The, *88;* Little Miss Marker, *190;* Lonely Are the Brave, *909;* Movers and Shakers, *315;* Odd Couple, The,

322; Pirates, 331; Plaza Suite, 331; Secret Life of An American Wife, The, 347; Sunshine Boys, The, 361; Survivors, The, 362; Taking of Pelham One Two Three, The, 144

Matthews, A. E.: Iron Duke, The, 498

Matthews, Brian: Burning, The, 658

Matthews, Christopher: Scars of Dracula, 740; Scream and Scream Again, 740

Matthews, Jessie: Tom Thumb, 210

Mattson, Robin: Bonnie's Kids, 22; Return to Macon County, 121

Mature, Victor: After the Fox, 216; Million Dollar Mermaid, 794; My Darling Clementine, 916; One Million B.C., 855; Robe, The, 581; Samson and Delilah, 588

Matuszak, John: Caveman, 240; Ice Pirates, 842

Mauches, Valerie: Children Shouldn't Play with Dead Things, 662

Mauch, Billy and Bobby: Prince and the Pauper, The (Original), 199

Maughan, Monica: Test of Love, A, 613

Maurey, Nicole: Day of the Triffids, The, 828; Diary Of A Country Priest, 450

Maurier, Claire: 400 Blows, The, 468

Mauro, Ralph: They Call Me Bruce?, 365

Maurstad, Torval: Song of Norway, 803

Maury, Derrel: Massacre at Central High, 716

Maximova, Antonina: Ballad of a Soldier, 404

Maxwell, Lois: Man With the Golden Gun, The, 96; Spy Who Loved Me, The, 139; You Only Live Twice, 166

Maxwell, Marilyn: Off Limits, 322

Maxwell, Roberta: Psycho III, 731

Max, Harry: Stolen Kisses, 360

Mayeric, Val: Demon Lover, The, 673

Mayer, Scott: Savage Streets, 128

Mayhew, Peter: Return of the Jedi, 859

Maynard, Bat: House That Bled to Death, The, 701

Maynard, Ken: Mystery Mountain, 916

Maynard, Kermit: Night Riders, The, 918; Trail of Robin Hood, 939

Maynard, Mimi: Underground Aces, 374

Mayne, Ferdy: Revenge of the Pink Panther, The, 340

Mayo, Virginia: Best Years of Our Lives, The, 409; Jack London, 499; Kid from Brooklyn, The, 292; Out of the Blue, 325; Pearl of the South Pacific, 560; Princess and the Pirate, The, 334; Secret Life of Walter Mitty, The, 347; White Heat, 161

Mayron, Melanie: Girlfriends, 472; Missing, 535

May, Elaine: Enter Laughing, 256; Luv, 304

May, Mathilda: Lifeforce, 849

Mazurki, Mike: Dick Tracy, 42; Magic of Lassie, The, 191; Man with Bogart's Face, The, 96; Neptune's Daughter, 795; Some Like It Hot, 356

Mazursky, Paul: Into the Night, 496; Man, A

Woman and a Bank, A, 95

McAlister, Jennifer: Serial, 349

McAllen, Kathleen Rong: Fear No Evil, 683

McAllister, Chip: Weekend Pass, 378

McAnally, Ray: Danny Boy, 444

McBroom, Marcia: Beyond the Valley of the Dolls, 410

McCain, Frances Lee: Gremlins, 840; Real Life, 338

McCallister, Lon: Big Cat, The, 15; Red House, The, 734

McCallum, David: Around the World Under the Sea, 10; Return of the Man from U.N.C.L.E., The, 131; Terminal Choice, 752; Watcher in the Woods, The, 764

McCallum, Neil: Dr. Terror's House of Horrors, 677

McCall, Joan: Grizzly, 695

McCalman, Macon: Fleshburn, 685

McCambridge, Mercedes: All the King's Men, 394; Deadly Sanctuary, 671; Johnny Guitar, 906

McCann, Chuck: Hamburger—The Motion Picture, 274; Heart Is a Lonely Hunter, The, 483; Projectionist, The, 336; Rosebud Beach Hotel, The, 343; They Went That-A-Way and That-A-Way, 208

McCann, Donal: Cal, 423; Danny Boy, 444; Hard Way, The, 69

McCarthy, Andrew: Class, 244; Heaven Help Us, 278; Pretty in Pink, 567; St. Elmo's Fire, 586

McCarthy, Charlie: Muppet Movie, The, 193

Bergen, Edgar: Goldwyn Follies, The, 784; Letter of Introduction, 516

McCarthy, Frank: Dead Men Don't Wear Plaid, 249

McCarthy, Kevin: Buffalo Bill and the Indians, 896; Hero at Large, 279; Invasion of the Body Snatchers (Original), 844; My Tutor, 317; Piranha, 728

McCarthy, Nobu: Karate Kid, Part 2, The, 81

McCartney, Linda: Give My Regards to Broad Street, 783

McCartney, Paul: Give My Regards to Broad Street, 783; Help!, 787; Let It Be, 792

McCaughan, Charles: Bostonians, The, 417

McClanathan, Michael: Alice's Restaurant, 393

McClory, Sean: My Chauffeur, 316

McCloskey, Leigh: Fraternity Vacation, 263; Hamburger—The Motion Picture, 274

McClure, Doug: At the Earth's Core, 818; Gidget, 267; House Where Evil Dwells, The, 701; Humanoids from the Deep, 702; Land That Time Forgot, The, 847; People That Time Forgot, The, 855; Shenandoah, 930

McClure, Marc: Strange Behavior, 748; Superman III, 869; Superman, 868

McClure, Michael: Kerouac, 506; Kerouac, 506

McClurg, Edie: Cinderella, 177

McCollum, Warren: Reefer Madness, *338;*

McConnell, Richard: Tomorrow, *620*

McCormick, Carolyn: Enemy Mine, *834*

McCormick, Gilmer: Silent Night, Deadly Night, *743*

McCormick, Maureen: Idolmaker, The, *788;* Take Down, *363*

McCormick, Myron: Hustler, The, *490;* No Time for Sergeants, *320*

McCormick, Pat: Doin' Time, *253;* Mr. Horn, *915;* Smokey and the Bandit III, *355;* Smokey and the Bandit II, *355;* Smokey and the Bandit, *354*

McCourt, Malachy: Q, *732*

McCowen, Alec: Frenzy, *689;* Hanover Street, *481;* Partners in Crime—The Secret Adversary, *113;* Stevie, *603*

McCoy, Tim: Gunman from Bodie, *900;* Traitor, The, *940*

McCoy, Tony: Bride of the Monster, *657*

McCracken, Jeff: Running Brave, *585*

McCracken, Joan: Good News, *784*

McCrane, Paul: Fame, *778*

McCrea, Jody: Beach Blanket Bingo, *770*

McCrea, Joel: Bird of Paradise, *17;* Dead End, *447;* Foreign Correspondent, *687;* Most Dangerous Game, The, *718;* Ride the High Country, *925;* These Three, *615*

McCrea, Wing: Windwalker, *946*

McCulloch, Ian: Witching Time, *765;* Zombie, *766*

McCullough, Philo: Mystery Mountain, *916*

McDaniel, Donna: Hollywood Hot Tubs, *282*

McDaniel, Hattie: Alice Adams, *392;* Judge Priest, *504*

McDermott, Hugh: Devil Girl from Mars, *674*

McDevitt, Ruth: Homebodies, *698*

McDonald, Francis: Dangerous Venture, *891;* Dead Don't Dream, The, *892;* Devil's Playground, *893*

McDonald, Grace: Gung Ho, *67*

McDormand, Frances: Blood Simple, *19*

McDowall, Roddy: Arnold, *646;* Battle for the Planet of the Apes, *819;* Bedknobs and Broomsticks, *172;* Cat from Outer Space, The, *176;* Circle of Iron, *31;* Class of 1984, *663;* Cleopatra, *435;* Conquest of the Planet of the Apes, *826;* Escape from the Planet of the Apes, *835;* Evil Under the Sun, *50;* Flood!, *685;* Fright Night, *691;* Laserblast, *847;* Legend of Hell House, The, *711;* Macbeth, *525;* Mean Johnny Barrows, *98;* Night Gallery, *721;* Planet of the Apes, *856;* Poseidon Adventure, The, *115;* Rabbit Test, *337;* Scavenger Hunt, *346;* That Darn Cat, *208*

McDowell, Andie: Greystoke: The Legend of Tarzan, Lord of the Apes, *67*

McDowell, Malcolm: Blue Thunder, *21;* Britannia Hospital, *235;* Caligula, *424;* Cat People (Remake), *660;* Clockwork Orange, A, *824;* Compleat Beatles, The, *775;* Get Crazy,

McEachin, James: Christina, *31*

McElduff, Ellen: Maximum Overdrive, *716*

McEnery, John: Land That Time Forgot, The, *847;* Romeo and Juliet, *584*

McEnery, Peter: Fighting Prince of Donegal, The, *181;* Moonspinners, The, *193*

McEnroe, Annie: Hand, The, *696;* Howling II...Your Sister is a Werewolf, *702;* Warlords of the 21st Century, *875*

McGavin, Darren: Christmas Story, A, *177;* Cyborg: The Six Million Dollar Man, *827;* Hangar 18, *840;* Night Stalker, The, *723;* No Deposit, No Return, *195;* Raw Deal, *119;* Summertime, *608;* Turk 182, *624*

McGee, Vonetta: Blacula, *652;* Repo Man, *338;* Eiger Sanction, The, *47*

McGillin, Howard: Where the Boys Are '84, *380*

McGillis, Kelly: Reuben, Reuben, *339;* Top Gun, *153;* Witness, *165*

McGill, Bruce: Hand, The, *696*

McGill, Everett: Quest for Fire, *858;* Silver Bullet, *743*

McGinley, Ted: Revenge of the Nerds, *340*

McGiver, John: Arnold, *646;* Tom Sawyer, *210*

McGlynn, Frank: Lawless Range, *908;* Min and Bill, *534*

McGoohan, Patrick: Baby...Secret of the Lost Legend, *818;* Escape from Alcatraz, *49;* Hard Way, The, *69;* Ice Station Zebra, *77;* Man in the Iron Mask, The, *95;* Prisoner, The (television series), *857;* Scanners, *740;* Silver Streak, *352;* Three Lives Of Thomasina, The, *209*

McGovern, Elizabeth: Lovesick, *303;* Once upon a Time in America (Long Version), *110;* Ordinary People, *554;* Racing with the Moon, *573;* Ragtime, *574;* Snow White and the Seven Dwarfs, *205*

McGowan,, Charles: Chorus Line, A, *774*

McGraw, Charles: Away All Boats, *11;* Defiant Ones, The, *448;* His Kind of Woman, *73;* Pendulum, *113*

McGregor, Angela Punch: Island, The, *706;* Test of Love, A, *613;* We of the Never Never, *161*

McGregor, Charles: Superfly, *143*

McGuire, Don: Fuller Brush Man, The, *264*

McGuire, Dorothy: Greatest Story Ever Told, The, *478;* Incredible Journey of Dr. Meg Laurel, The, *494;* Old Yeller, *196;* Swiss Family Robinson, The, *207;* Till the End of Time, *618*

McGuire, John: Invisible Ghost, *705;* Stranger on the Third Floor, *141*

McGuire, Michael: Great Wallendas, The, *478*

McGuire, Tom: Steamboat Bill Jr., *359*

McHattie, Stephen: Death Valley, *672;* Ultimate Warrior, The, *874*

McHugh, Frank: Footlight Parade, *780;* Going My Way, *474;* Mighty Joe Young, *852;* Roaring Twenties, The, *122;* There's No Business Like Show Business, *808*

McHugh, Matt: Freaks, *689*

McInnerty, Tim: Adventures of Sherlock Holmes: The Red-Headed League, *5*

McIntire, John: Away All Boats, *11;* Cloak and Dagger, *32;* Flaming Star, *896;* HonkyTonk Man, *489;* Psycho, *731;* Rooster Cogburn, *928*

McIntire, Tim: Aloha, Bobby and Rose, *7;* Fast-Walking, *464;* Sacred Ground, *929;* Sterile Cuckoo, The, *603;* Gumball Rally, The, *67*

McIntyre, James: Gone in 60 Seconds, *63*

McKay, Doreen: Night Riders, The, *918;* Pals of the Saddle, *921*

McKay, Scott: Thirty Seconds Over Tokyo, *149*

McKean, Michael: Clue, *245;* D.A.R.Y.L., *827;* This Is Spinal Tap, *367;* Young Doctors in Love, *385*

McKee, Lafe: Desert Trail, *893;* Mystery Mountain, *916*

McKee, Lonette: Brewster's Millions (1985), *235;* Cotton Club, The, *36;* Cuba, *37;* Sparkle, *805;* Which Way Is Up?, *381*

McKellen, Ian: Keep, The, *708;* Plenty, *564;* Priest of Love, *568*

McKenna, Siobhan: Of Human Bondage (Remake), *549*

McKenna, T. P.: Beast in The Cellar, The, *649;* Straw Dogs, *749*

McKenna, Virginia: Born Free, *174;* Gathering Storm, *471*

McKenzie, Fay: Heart of the Rio Grande, *901*

McKenzie, Kevin: Bay Boy, The, *406*

McKenzie, Tim: Dead Easy, *447;* Gallipoli, *470*

McKeon, Doug: Mischief, *310;* On Golden Pond, *551*

McKern, Leo: Blue Lagoon, The, *415;* Candleshoe, *175;* Day the Earth Caught Fire, The, *828;* French Lieutenant's Woman, The, *469;* Help!, *787;* Ladyhawke, *86;* Mouse That Roared, The, *314;* Prisoner, The (television series), *857;* Ryan's Daughter, *586*

McKim, Matt: Little Match Girl, The, *189*

McKinney, Bill: Bronco Billy, *886;* Final Justice, *54;* Heart Like a Wheel, *70*

McKinney, Nina Mae: Sanders of the River, *127*

McKinney, William: Outlaw Josey Wales, The, *920*

McKinnon, Mona: Plan 9 from Outer Space, *856*

McLaglen, Victor: Gunga Din, *67;* Informer, The, *495;* Lost Patrol, The, *93;* Princess and the Pirate, The, *334;* Quiet Man, The, *117;* Rio Grande, *927;* Sea Devils, *129;* She Wore

a Yellow Ribbon, *930;* South of Pago Pago, *138;* Trouble in the Glen, *372*

McLaren, Hollis: Outrageous, *326*

McLaren, Mary: New Frontier, *917*

McLean, Don: Wasn't That a Time!, *811*

McLeod, Gavin: Kelly's Heroes, *81*

McLiam, John: Sleeper, *354*

McLish, Rachel: Pumping Iron II: The Women, *570*

McMahon, Ed: Fun with Dick and Jane, *265;* Kid from Left Field, The, *187*

McMartin, John: Dream Lover, *679;* Murrow, *539*

McMillan, Kenneth: Armed and Dangerous, *220;* Blue Skies Again, *416;* Cat's Eye, *660;* Chilly Scenes of Winter, *432;* Dune, *832;* Killing Hour, The, *709;* Reckless, *557;* Runaway Train, *125;* Whose Life Is It, Anyway?, *633*

McMyler, Pamela: Dogpound Shuffle, *252*

McNair, Barbara: Change of Habit, *430;* Organization, The, *111;* Stiletto, *140;* They Call Me Mister Tibbs, *148*

McNally, Stephen: Texas John Slaughter: Stampede at Bitter Creek, *937;* Thirty Seconds Over Tokyo, *149*

McNamara, Desmond: Adventures of Sherlock Holmes: The Blue Carbuncle, *2*

McNamara, Maggie: Moon Is Blue, The, *314*

McNaughton, Gus: Sidewalks of London, *593*

McNeill, Cornell: La Traviata, *791*

McNeil, Claudia: Raisin in the Sun, A, *575*

McNeil, Kathryn: House on Sorority Row, *701*

McNichol, Jimmy: Night Warning, *723*

McNichol, Kristy: Dream Lover, *679;* End, The, *255;* Just the Way You Are, *505;* Little Darlings, *299;* My Old Man, *541;* Night the Lights Went Out in Georgia, The, *545;* Only When I Laugh, *553;* Pirate Movie, The, *798*

McOmie, Maggie: THX 1138, *872*

McPhail, Douglas: Babes in Arms, *769*

McQuarrie, Murdock: New Frontier, *917*

McQueen, Steve: Baby the Rain Must Fall, *404;* Blob, The, *652;* Bullitt, *26;* Cincinnati Kid, The, *31;* Getaway, The, *62;* Great Escape, The, *65;* Hunter, The, *75;* Junior Bonner, *906;* Magnificent Seven, The, *911;* Nevada Smith, *917;* Papillon, *112;* Reivers, The, *338;* Sand Pebbles, The, *127;* Soldier in the Rain, *596;* Thomas Crown Affair, The, *150;* Tom Horn, *939;* Towering Inferno, The, *154;* War Lover, The, *630*

McRae, Carmen: Jo Jo Dancer, Your Life Is Calling, *502*

McRae, Frank: 48 Hrs., *262;* Cannery Row, *237;* Used Cars, *376*

McRae, Hilton: French Lieutenant's Woman, The, *469*

McRaney, Gerald: Haunting Passion, The, *840*

McShane, Ian: Cheaper to Keep Her, *242;* Exposed, *681;* Great Riviera Bank Robbery,

The, 68; Journey Into Fear, 503; Ordeal By Innocence, 111; Too Scared to Scream, 757; Torchlight, 620

McSwain, Monica: Little Match Girl, The, 189

Meacham, Anne: Lilith, 518

Meade, Julia: Zotz!, 386

Meadows, Audrey: That Touch of Mink, 365

Meadows, Denny: Dawn Rider, 892

Meadows, Joyce: Brain from Planet Arous, The, 821

Meagher, Karen: Experience Preferred... But Not Essential, 257

Meara, Anne: Out of Towners, The, 325

Medford, Jody: Mutant, 720

Medford, Kay: Ensign Pulver, 255; Face in the Crowd, A, 461; Funny Girl, 782

Medina, Patricia: Botany Bay, 22; Francis, the Talking Mule, 263; Snow White and the Three Stooges

Medwin, Michael: Scrooge, 801

Meek, Donald: Colonel Effingham's Raid, 246; Du Barry Was a Lady, 777; Jesse James, 905; Return of Frank James, The, 925; Stagecoach, 934; They Got Me Covered, 366; Thin Man Goes Home, The, 149

Meeker, George: Rough Riders' Roundup, 928; Song of Nevada, 933; Tarzan's Revenge, 146; Twilight in the Sierras, 941

Meeker, Ralph: Alpha Incident, The, 816; Anderson Tapes, The, 8; Birds of Prey, 17; Brannigan, 23; Food of the Gods, 838; Mind Snatchers, The, 717; Night Games, 544; Paths of Glory, 559; St. Valentine's Day Massacre, The, 126; Winter Kills, 636

Megna, John: To Kill a Mockingbird, 619

Meillen, John: Cars That Eat People (The Cars That Ate Paris), 660; Cars That Ate Paris, The (The Cars That Eat People), 823; Wild Duck, The, 634

Meinke, Eva Maria: To the Devil, a Daughter, 757

Mejia, Alfonso: Los Olvidados, 522

Melato, Mariangela: Love and Anarchy, 301; Seduction of Mimi, The, 348; Swept Away, 609

Melford, Kim: Corvette Summer, 35

Melia, Joe: Privates on Parade, 336; Sakharov, 587

Mellinger, Leonie: Lion and the Hawk, The, 89

Mello, Breno: Black Orpheus, 414

Meloy, Robin: House on Sorority Row, 701

Mendenhall, David: Space Raiders, 864

Mendham, Mary: Groove Tube, The, 273

Mendonca, Maura: Dona Flor and Her Two Husbands, 253

Mengatti, John: Meatballs Part II, 308

Menjou, Adolphe: Farewell to Arms, A, 463; Front Page, The, 264; Golden Boy, 475; Goldwyn Follies, The, 784; Letter of Introduction, 516; Little Miss Marker, 190; Milky Way, The, 310; Paths of Glory, 559; Pol-

Iyanna, 198; Star Is Born, A (Original), 600; State of the Union, 602; Woman of Paris, A, 638; You Were Never Lovelier, 814

Menzies, Heather: Piranha, 728

Mercer, Beryl: Public Enemy, The, 116

Mercer, Frances: Mad Miss Manton, The, 304

Mercier, Michele: Call of the Wild, 27

Mercouri, Melina: Nasty Habits, 317; Never on Sunday, 543; Topkapi, 154

Meredith, Burgess: Batman, 172; Burnt Offerings, 658; Clash of the Titans, 834; Day of the Locust, The, 446; Foul Play, 262; Great Bank Hoax, The, 272; Hindenburg, The, 487; Idiot's Delight, 493; Last Chase, The, 847; Madame X, 526; Magic, 713; Manitou, The, 714; Rocky III, 582; Rocky II, 582; Rocky, 582; Santa Claus—The Movie, 203; Second Chorus, 801; Sentinel, The, 742; There Was a Crooked Man, 938; Thumbelina, 209; Torture Garden, 758; True Confessions, 623; When Time Ran Out!, 764; Winterset, 636

Meredith, Don: Terror on the 40th Floor, 753

Meredith, Iris: Lawman Is Born, A, 908

Meredith, Lee: Producers, The, 336; Sunshine Boys, The, 361

Meril, Macha: Robert et Robert, 582; Vagabond, 627

Meriwether, Lee: 4D Man, 838; Batman, 172; Cruise into Terror, 667

Merkel, Una: 42nd Street, 781; Abraham Lincoln, 388; Bank Dick, The, 224; Broadway Melody of 1936, 772; Kentuckian, The, 906

Merman, Ethel: It's a Mad Mad Mad Mad World, 288; There's No Business Like Show Business, 808

Merrill, Dina: Anna to the Infinite Power, 817; Just Tell Me What You Want, 292; Operation Petticoat, 325; Wedding, A, 378

Merrill, Gary: All About Eve, 393; Mysterious Island, 853; Twelve O'Clock High, 155

Merritt, Theresa: Wiz, The, 812

Merton, John: Blue Canadian Rockies, 884; Gunman from Bodie, 900

Messinger, Gertrude: Melody Trail, 915

Metcalf, Laurie: Desperately Seeking Susan, 250

Metcalf, Mark: Heavenly Kid, The, 841

Metrano, Art: Breathless (Remake), 420; Cheaper to Keep Her, 242; Going Ape!, 269; Matilda, 308; Police Academy III: Back in Training, 332

Metzler, Jim: Tex, 614

Meurisse, Paul: Diabolique, 675

Meyers, Marius: Gods Must Be Crazy, The, 269

Meyer, Bess: One More Saturday Night, 324

Meyer, Emile: Riot in Cell Block 11, 581; Riot in Cell Block Eleven, 122

Meyer, Johannes: Master Of The House (Du Skal Aere Din Hustru), 308

Meyrink, Michelle: Joy of Sex, The, *291;* Real Genius, *338;* Revenge of the Nerds, *340*

Mezzogiorno, Vittorio: Mussolini and I, *539*

Miao, Cora: Dim Sum: A Little Bit Of Heart, *451*

Miao, Nora: Fists of Fury, *56;* Return of the Dragon, *120*

Michaelson, Kari: Kid With the 200 I.Q., The, *188*

Michelle, Charlotte: Kill or Be Killed, *83*

Michel, Marc: Umbrellas of Cherbourg, The, *625*

Michi, Maria: Paisan, *556*

Middleton, Charles: Oklahoma Kid, The, *918*

Middleton, Noelle: Carrington, V. C., *427*

Middleton, Ray: Lady for a Night, *512;* Lady from Louisiana, *907*

Middleton, Robert: Court Jester, The, *248;* Lonely Man, The, *909;* Texas John Slaughter: Wild Times, *938*

Midgets, The Singer: Wizard of Oz, The, *812*

Midkiff, Dale: Streetwalkin', *605*

Midler, Bette: Divine Madness, *777;* Down and Out in Beverly Hills, *254;* Jinxed, *289;* Rose, The, *800;* Ruthless People, *344*

Mifune, Toshiro: 1941, *319;* Bushido Blade, *26;* Challenge, The, *29;* Hidden Fortress, The, *71;* Paper Tiger, *112;* Rashomon, *575;* Red Beard, *577;* Red Sun, *924;* Samurai Trilogy, The, *127;* Sanjuro, *128;* Seven Samurai, The, *131;* Shogun (Full-Length Version), *134;* Shogun (Short Version), *134;* Throne of Blood, *617;* Winter Kills, *636;* Yojimbo, *166*

Migenes-Johnson, Julia: Bizet's Carmen, *771*

Miki, Norihei: Himatsuri, *487*

Mikuni, Rentaro: Samurai Trilogy, The, *127*

Milano, Alyssa: Commando, *33*

Milano, Mario: Beyond Evil, *650*

Milan, Frank: Pals of the Saddle, *921*

Milan, Lita: Naked in the Sun, *917*

Miles, Bernard: Tom Thumb, *210*

Miles, Joanna: Born Innocent, *417;* Bug, *658;* Ultimate Warrior, The, *874*

Miles, Kevin: Cars That Eat Paris, The (The Cars That Eat People), *823;* Cars That Eat People (The Cars That Eat Paris), *660*

Miles, Lilian: Reefer Madness, *338*

Miles, Peter: Red Pony, The, *201;* Trigger, Jr., *940*

Miles, Sarah: Big Sleep, The, *16;* Blow-Up, *654;* Man Who Loved Cat Dancing, The, *912;* Ordeal By Innocence, *111;* Ryan's Daughter, *586;* Sailor Who Fell from Grace with the Sea, The, *586;* Servant, The, *590;* Those Magnificent Men in their Flying Machines, *367;* Venom, *761*

Miles, Sylvia: Funhouse, The, *691;* Farewell My Lovely, *52;* Midnight Cowboy, *533;* Sentinel, The, *742*

Miles, Vera: Back Street, *404;* Castaway Cowboy, The, *176;* Fire!, *685;* Follow Me Boys!, *181;* Hellfighters, *70;* Man Who Shot Liberty Valance, The, *913;* Psycho II, *731;* Psycho, *731;* Searchers, The, *930;* Those Calloways, *209;* Wrong Man, The, *766*

Milford, Kim: Laserblast, *847*

Milford, Penelope: Coming Home, *437;* Golden Seal, The, *182*

Milian, Tomas: Boccaccio 70, *231;* Cop in Blue Jeans, The, *35;* Winter Kills, *636*

Millais, Hugh: Dogs of War, The, *44*

Milland, Ray: Attic, The, *648;* Blackout, *19;* Cruise into Terror, *667;* Dial M for Murder, *675;* Escape to Witch Mountain, *181;* Frogs, *691;* Last Tycoon, The, *515;* Lost Weekend, The, *523;* Love Story, *524;* Man Alone, A, *911;* Oliver's Story, *551;* Premature Burial, The, *730;* Starflight One, *867;* Terror in the Wax Museum, *753;* Uncanny, The, *760;* X (The Man with the X-Ray Eyes), *877*

Miller, Ann: Easter Parade, *777;* Kiss Me Kate, *790;* Melody Ranch, *914;* On the Town, *796;* Room Service, *343;* Stage Door, *357*

Miller, Barry: Fame, *778*

Miller, Brian: Adventures of Sherlock Holmes: The Blue Carbuncle, *2*

Miller, Carl: Woman of Paris, A, *638*

Miller, David: Attack of the Killer Tomatoes, *221*

Miller, Dick: Explorers, *836;* Gremlins, *840;* Heart Like a Wheel, *70;* Hollywood Boulevard, *282;* Little Shop of Horrors, The, *713;* Mr. Billion, *100;* Trip, The, *622*

Miller, Eve: Big Trees, The, *16;* Kansas Pacific, *906*

Miller, F. E.: Harlem Rides the Range, *900*

Miller, Ivan: Man From Music Mountain, *912*

Miller, Jason: Best Little Girl in the World, The, *408;* Dain Curse, The, *37;* Exorcist, The, *681;* Monsignor, *538;* Ninth Configuration, The, *546;* Toy Soldiers, *154*

Miller, Ken: Little Laura and Big John, *90*

Miller, Linda G.: Night of the Juggler, *107*

Miller, Mark: Savannah Smiles, *203*

Miller, Marvin: Off Limits, *322*

Miller, Mary Louise: Sparrows, *598*

Miller, Michael: Doc Savage…The Man of Bronze, *830*

Miller, Patsy Ruth: Hunchback of Notre Dame, The (original), *702*

Miller, Walter: Street Scene, *605*

Miller, Mark: Ginger In The Morning, *472*

Milligan, Spike: Alice's Adventures in Wonderland, *171;* Down Among the "Z" Men, *253*

Mills, Adam: RSVP, *343*

Mills, Alley: Going Berserk, *269*

Mills, Danny: Pink Flamingos, *330*

Mills, Donna: Bunco, *26;* Fire!, *685;* Murph the Surf, *104;* Play Misty for Me, *729*

Mills, Frank: Adventures of Sherlock Holmes: The Blue Carbuncle, *2*

Mills, Grace: Night of the Howling Beast, *723*

Mills, Hayley: Daydreamer, The, *179;* In Search of the Castaways, *185;* Moonspinners, The, *193;* Parent Trap, The, *197;* Pollyanna, *198;* That Darn Cat, *208;* Trouble With Angels, The, *372*

Mills, John: Africa—Texas Style!, *6;* Gandhi, *471;* Goodbye, Mr. Chips, *475;* Hobson's Choice, *281;* In Which We Serve, *494;* King Rat, *508;* Ryan's Daughter, *586;* Sahara, *126;* Swiss Family Robinson, The, *207;* Thirty-Nine Steps, The (Second Remake), *149;* Tunes of Glory, *624;* War and Peace, *630;* Wrong Box, The, *384;* Young Winston, *641;* Zulu Dawn, *168*

Mills, Juliet: Beyond the Door, *680;* Rare Breed, The, *924*

Milner, Martin: 13 Ghosts, *755;* Flood!, *685;* Life With Father, *299*

Milot, Charles: French Connection II, The, *469*

Milo, Sandra: 8½, *455;* Juliet of the Spirits, *291*

Mimieux, Yvette: Black Hole, The, *821;* Devil Dog: The Hound Of Hell, *673;* Jackson County Jail, *78;* Journey Into Fear, *503;* Journey into Fear, *708;* Time Machine, The, *872;* Where the Boys Are, *380*

Mineau, Charlotte: Charlie Chaplin—The Early Years, Vol.4, *241*

Mineo, Sal: Dino, *451;* Exodus, *460;* Rebel without a Cause, *576;* Tonka, *211*

Miner, Jan: Lenny, *516*

Minnelli, Liza: Arthur, *220;* Cabaret, *773;* Matter of Time, A, *531;* Muppets Take Manhattan, The, *194;* New York, New York, *795;* Princess and the Pea, The, *199;* Silent Movie, *351;* Sterile Cuckoo, The, *603;* That's Dancing, *807*

Minty, Emil: Road Warrior, The, *859*

Miou-Miou: Entre Nous (Between Us), *458;* Going Places, *270;* My Other Husband, *541*

Miracles, Smokey Robinson and the: That Was Rock, *808*

Miracle, Irene: In the Shadow of Kilimanjaro, *704*

Miranda, Carmen: Copacabana, *247*

Miranda, Isa: La Ronde, *295;* Night Porter, The, *545;* Summertime, *608*

Miranda, John: Bloodthirsty Butchers, *654*

Mira, Brigitte: Every Man for Himself and God Against All, *460*

Mirren, Helen: 2010, *874;* Caligula, *424;* Cal, *423;* Excalibur, *835;* Fiendish Plot of Dr. Fu Manchu, The, *260;* Little Mermaid, The, *189;* Long Good Friday, The, *92*

Mitchell, Cameron: Blood and Black Lace, *652;* Buck and the Preacher, *886;* Flood!, *685;* Frankenstein Island, *688;* Hombre, *904;* How to Marry a Millionaire, *284;* Kill Point, *83;* Nightmare In Wax (Crimes In The Wax Museum), *721;* Ride in the Whirlwind, *925;* Wild Times, *945;* Without Warning, *876*

Mitchell, Donna: Anna to the Infinite Power,

Mitchell, Duke: Boys from Brooklyn, The, *656*

Mitchell, Eddy: My Other Husband, *541*

Mitchell, Gordon: Endgame, *834;* She, *861*

Mitchell, John Cameron: Band of the Hand, *12*

Mitchell, John: Sea Shall Not Have Them, The, *130*

Mitchell, Joni: Last Waltz, The, *791*

Mitchell, Joseph: Massacre At Fort Holman (Reason to Live . . . A Reason to Die, A), *914*

Mitchell, Scoey: Jo Jo Dancer, Your Life Is Calling, *502*

Mitchell, Thomas: Bataan, *12;* Craig's Wife, *439;* Dark Mirror, The, *669;* Dark Waters, *445;* High Noon, *903;* Hunchback of Notre Dame, The (remake), *703;* It's a Wonderful Life, *499;* Long Voyage Home, The, *520;* Our Town, *555;* Outlaw, The, *920;* Pocketful of Miracles, *564;* Stagecoach, *934*

Mitchell, Warren: Norman Loves Rose, *330*

Mitchell, Yvonne: Crucible of Horror, *666*

Mitchell-Smith, Ilan: Weird Science, *379;* Wild Life, The, *382*

Mitchel, Mary: Dementia 13, *673*

Mitchum, Christopher: Big Foot, *651;* Big Jake, *882;* Rio Lobo, *927;* Summertime Killer, The, *143*

Mitchum, James: Blackout, *19;* Ransom, *118;* Tramplers, The, *940*

Mitchum, John: Big Foot, *651;* Bloody Trail, *884;* Dirty Harry, *43;* Enforcer, The, *49;* Escapes, *835;* Telefon, *147*

Mitchum, Robert: Agency, *390;* Ambassador, The, *395;* Amsterdam Kill, The, *7;* Big Sleep, The, *16;* Blood on the Moon, *884;* Breakthrough, *24;* El Dorado, *895;* False Colors, *895;* Farewell My Lovely, *52;* Fire Down Below, *464;* Grass Is Greener, The, *272;* Gung Ho, *67;* His Kind of Woman, *73;* Last Tycoon, The, *515;* Longest Day, The, *92;* Lusty Men, The, *911;* Maria's Lovers, *528;* Matilda, *308;* Midway, *99;* Nightkill, *107;* Out of the Past, *112;* Rachel and the Stranger, *923;* Red Pony, The, *201;* Riders of the Deadline, *926;* Ryan's Daughter, *586;* That Championship Season, *614;* Thirty Seconds Over Tokyo, *149;* Till the End of Time, *618;* Villa Rides, *943;* Yakuza, The, *165*

Mitsutaki, Noburu: Dodes 'Ka-Den, *452*

Mixon, Allan: Prehistoric Women, *857*

Mix, Art: Mystery Mountain, *916;* Sagebrush Trail, *929*

Miyattana, Tatsuya Mihashi: What's Up Tiger Lily?, *380*

Mobley, Mary Ann: Harum Scarum, *787*

Mochrie, Peter: Winter of our Dreams, *636*

Modean, Jayne: Streethawk, *142*

Modine, Matthew: Birdy, *412;* Mrs. Soffel, *536;* Streamers, *605;* Vision Quest, *628*

Modot, Gaston: Grand Illusion, *476*

Moffatt, Graham: Dr. Syn, *45*

Moffat, Donald: Alamo Bay, *391;* Best of Times, The, *228;* Promises in the Dark, *569;* Right Stuff, The, *580*

Moffett, Gregory: Robot Monster, *736*

Mog, Aribert: Ecstasy, *455*

Mohner, Carl: Rififi, *122*

Mohr, Gerald: Angry Red Planet, The, *817*

Moir, Richard: Heatwave, *485*

Molina, Angela: Eyes, The Mouth, The, *460;* That Obscure Object of Desire, *615*

Molloy, Dearbha: Paddy, *326*

Moll, Richard: House, *699;* Sword and the Sorcerer, The, *869*

Momo, Alessandro: Malicious, *305*

Monahan, Dan: Porky's, *333;* Porky's, II: The Next Day, *333;* Up the Creek, *375;* Porky's Revenge, *333*

Mondy, Pierre: Gift, The, *268*

Mones, Paul: Tuff Turf, *623*

Monnier, Valentine: After the Fall of New York, *815*

Monoson, Lawrence: Last American Virgin, The, *296*

Monroe, Marilyn: All About Eve, *393;* Bus Stop, *236;* Clash by Night, *434;* Gentlemen Prefer Blondes, *266;* How to Marry a Millionaire, *284;* Love Happy, *302;* Misfits, The, *535;* Prince and the Showgirl, The, *334;* Seven Year Itch, The, *350;* Some Like It Hot, *356;* There's No Business Like Show Business, *808*

Montague, Lee: Sakharov, *587*

Montague, Monte: Git Along, Little Dogies, *898*

Montalban, Carlos: Bananas, *224*

Montalban, Ricardo: Cheyenne Autumn, *888;* Conquest of the Planet of the Apes, *826;* Escape from the Planet of the Apes, *835;* Fantasy Island, *837;* Madame X, *526;* Mission to Glory, *536;* Neptune's Daughter, *795;* Sayonara, *589;* Star Trek II: The Wrath of Khan, *865;* Train Robbers, The, *940*

Montana, Lenny: They Went That-A-Way and That-A-Way, *208*

Montana, Monte: Down Dakota Way, *894*

Montana, Montie: Riders of the Deadline, *926*

Montand, Yves: Napoleon, *542;* On a Clear Day, You Can See Forever, *796;* State of Seige, *602;* Wages of Fear, The, *763;* Z, *641*

Montel, Michele: Claire's Knee, *243*

Montero, Germaine: Robert et Robert, *582*

Montgomery, Belinda J.: Blackout, *19;* Miami Vice, *98;* Other Side of the Mountain, Part II, The, *554;* Stone Cold Dead, *141*

Montgomery, Julie: Revenge of the Nerds, *340*

Montgomery, Lee: Ben, *650;* Girls Just Want to Have Fun, *268;* Mutant, *720;* Prime Risk, *115*

Montgomery, Lee: Savage Is Loose, The, *588*

Montgomery, Robert: Here Comes Mr. Jordan, *279;* Mr. and Mrs. Smith, *310;* They Were Expendable, *148*

Monticelli, Anna-Maria: Nomads, *724*

Montone, Rita: Maniac, *714*

Moody, Jim: Bad Boys, *404*

Moody, Ron: Dogpound Shuffle, *252;* Oliver, *796;* Twelve Chairs, The, *373;* Unidentified Flying Oddball, *212;* Wrong Is Right, *384*

Mooney, William: Flash of Green, A, *466*

Moon, Keith: 200 Motels, *810*

Moore, Alvy: Wild One, The, *164*

Moore, Clayton: Kansas Pacific, *906;* Lone Ranger, The, *910;* Night Stage to Galveston, *917;* Nyoka and the Tiger Men (Perils of Nyoka), *109*

Moore, Demi: About Last Night, *388;* No Small Affair, *320;* One Crazy Summer, *324;* Parasite, *726;* St. Elmo's Fire, *586*

Moore, Dennis: Dawn on the Great Divide, *891;* Spooks Run Wild, *357*

Moore, Dickie: Oliver Twist, *550;* Out of the Past, *112*

Moore, Dudley: 10, *364;* Alice's Adventures in Wonderland, *171;* Arthur, *220;* Bedazzled, *225;* Best Defense, *227;* Foul Play, *262;* Lovesick, *303;* Micki & Maude, *309;* Romantic Comedy, *343;* Santa Claus—The Movie, *202;* Six Weeks, *594;* Unfaithfully Yours (Remake), *375;* Wholly Moses!, *381;* Wrong Box, The, *384*

Moore, Duke: Plan 9 from Outer Space, *856*

Moore, Frank: Rabid, *732*

Moore, Gar: Paisan, *556*

Moore, Juanita: Papa's Delicate Condition, *557*

Moore, Kenneth: Scrooge, *801*

Moore, Kieron: Arabesque, *9;* Day of the Triffids, The, *828*

Moore, Mary Tyler: Change of Habit, *430;* Just Between Friends, *505;* Ordinary People, *554;* Six Weeks, *594*

Moore, Owen: Keystone Comedies, Vol. 3, *292*

Moore, Pauline: Colorado, *889*

Moore, Roger: Cannonball Run, *237;* Escape to Athena, *50;* Ffolkes, *53;* For Your Eyes Only, *58;* Live and Let Die, *91;* Man Who Haunted Himself, The, *714;* Man With the Golden Gun, The, *96;* Moonraker, *102;* Naked Face, The, *720;* Octopussy, *109;* Sea Wolves, The, *130;* Shout at the Devil, *135;* Spy Who Loved Me, The, *139;* View to a Kill, A, *158*

Moore, Terry: Beneath the 12-Mile Reef, *13;* Mighty Joe Young, *852*

Moore, Victor: It's in the Bag, *289;* Swing Time, *806;* Ziegfeld Follies, *814*

Moorehead, Agnes: Adventures of Captain Fabian, *2;* Black Jack, *19;* Citizen Kane, *434;* Conqueror, The, *34;* Dark Passage, *38;* Dear Dead Delilah, *672;* Hush... Hush, Sweet Charlotte, *703;* Johnny Belinda, *503;* Left Hand of God, The, *88;* Lost Moment, The,

522; Magnificent Ambersons, The, *526;* Magnificent Obsession, *527;* Pollyanna, *198;* Raintree County, *574;* Show Boat, *802*

Morales, Esai: Bad Boys, *404*

Moranis, Rick: Club Paradise, *245;* Ghostbusters, *267;* Last Polka, The, *296;* Strange Brew, *360;* Streets of Fire, *142*

Moranti, Milburn: Old Corral, The, *919*

Morant, Richard: Mahler, *527*

Moran, Erin: Galaxy of Terror, *839*

Moran, Jackie: Adventures of Tom Sawyer, The, *170*

Moran, Polly: Tom Brown's School Days, *620*

Moray, Yvonne: Terror of Tiny Town, The, *937*

Moreau, Jeanne: Going Places, *270;* Heat of Desire, *277;* Jules and Jim, *505;* Last Tycoon, The, *515;* Monte Walsh, *915;* Mr. Klein, *536;* Querelle, *572;* Train, The, *155*

Moreland, Mantan: Revenge of the Zombies, *736;* King of the Zombies, *709*

Morell, André: Hound of the Baskervilles, The (Remake), *75*

Moreno, Antonio: Bohemian Girl, The, *232;* Creature from the Black Lagoon, *665*

Moreno, Rita: Cry of Battle, *37;* Four Seasons, The, *469;* King and I, The, *790;* Pagan Love Song, *797;* Ritz, The, *342;* Singin' in the Rain, *802;* West Side Story, *812*

More, Kenneth: Unidentified Flying Oddball, *212*

More, Roger: Wild Geese, The, *163*

Morgan, Cindy: Tron, *873*

Morgan, David E.: Petronella, *197*

Morgan, Debbi: Jessie Owens Story, The, *501*

Morgan, Dennis: Kitty Foyle, *509;* Pearl of the South Pacific, *560;* Thank Your Lucky Stars, *807*

Morgan, Emily: French Lieutenant's Woman, The, *469*

Morgan, Frank: Thousands Cheer, *808;* Wizard of Oz, The, *812;* Yolanda and The Thief, *640*

Morgan, Harry: Apple Dumpling Gang, The, *171;* Apple Dumpling Gang Rides Again, The, *171;* Barefoot Executive, The, *172;* Better Late than Never, *228;* Cat from Outer Space, The, *176;* Charlie and The Angel, *176;* Flim-Flam Man, The, *466;* Glenn Miller Story, The, *783;* M*A*S*H: Goodbye Farewell, Amen, *307;* Ox-Bow Incident, The, *921;* Scandalous John, *203;* Shootist, The, *931;* Support Your Local Sheriff!, *936*

Morgan, Jaye P.: Night Patrol, *318*

Morgan, Lee: Hills of Utah, The, *903*

Morgan, Michelle: Fallen Idol, The, *462*

Morgan, Michèle: Cat and Mouse, *28*

Morgan, Nancy: Americathon, *218;* Grand Theft Auto, *64;* Kennel Murder Case, The, *82*

Morgan, Ralph: Star of Midnight, *139*

Morgan, Stafford: Alpha Incident, The, *816*

Morgan, Terence: Hamlet, *481*

Moriarty, Cathy: Neighbors, *318;* Raging Bull, *574*

Moriarty, Michael: Bang the Drum Slowly, *405;* Last Detail, The, *513;* Pale Rider, *921;* Q, *732;* Stuff, The, *750;* Troll, *873;* Who'll Stop the Rain, *162*

Morier-Genoud, Philippe: Confidentially Yours, *34*

Morin, Alberto: Strange Gamble, *935*

Morin, Mayo: Clowns, The, *244*

Morita, Miki: Border Phantom, *885*

Morita, Noriyuki "Pat": Karate Kid, The, *505;* Karate Kid, Part 2, The, *81*

Moritz, Louisa: Last American Virgin, The, *296*

Mori, Masayuki: Rashomon, *575;* Ugetsu, *625*

Morley, Karen: Our Daily Bread, *555*

Morley, Robert: Beat the Devil, *225;* Great Muppet Caper, The, *183;* High Road to China, *72;* Of Human Bondage (Remake), *549;* Oh, Heavenly Dog!, *196;* Scavenger Hunt, *346;* Song of Norway, *803;* Theater of Blood, *754*

Morrill, Priscilla: Right of Way, *580*

Morrison, Patricia: Dressed to Kill, *45;* Song of the Thin Man, *138*

Morrison, Van: Last Waltz, The, *791*

Morris, Anita: Absolute Beginners, *768;* Blue City, *20;* Ruthless People, *344*

Morris, Aubrey: Clockwork Orange, A, *824*

Morris, Chester: Five Came Back, *465*

Morris, Garrett: Stuff, The, *750;* Where's Poppa?, *381*

Morris, Glenn: Tarzan's Revenge, *146*

Morris, Greg: Vega$, *158*

Morris, Howard: 10 from Your Show of Shows, *364*

Morris, Judy: Plumber, The, *729*

Morrow, Jeff: Kronos, *846;* Octaman, *725;* This Island Earth, *871*

Morrow, Jo: 13 Ghosts, *755*

Morrow, Vic: 1990: The Bronx Warriors, *854;* Bad News Bears, The, *223;* Glass House, The, *473;* Humanoids from the Deep, *702;* Men in War, *98;* Tom Sawyer, *210;* Twilight Zone—The Movie, *759*

Morse, Barry: Asylum, *647;* Changeling, The, *661*

Morse, David: Inside Moves, *496*

Morse, Helen: Caddie, *423*

Morse, Robert: Boatniks, The, *174;* Guide For The Married Man, A, *273;* Oh Dad, Poor Dad—Mama's Hung You in the Closet and I'm Feeling So Sad, *322*

Mortiz, Louisa: Death Race 2000, *829*

Morton, Greg: Adultress, The, *389*

Morton, Joe: Brother from Another Planet, The, *822;* Crossroads, *775;* Trouble in Mind, *622*

Morton, Julian: Last Game, The, *513*

Moschin, Gastone: Joke of Destiny, *290*

Moses, David: Daring Dobermans, The, *38*

Moses, Harry: Sweater Girls, *362*

Mosley, Roger E.: Greatest, The, *479;* Jericho Mile, The, *501*

Moss, Ron: Hearts and Armour, *70*

Mostel, Josh: Compromising Positions, *247;* Windy City, *635*

Mostel, Zero: Du Barry Was a Lady, *777;* Front, The, *470;* Funny Thing Happened on the Way to the Forum, A, *265;* Hot Rock, The, *75;* Journey Into Fear, *503;* Journey into Fear, *708;* Producers, The, *336*

Motulsky, Judy: Slithis, *744*

Moulder-Brown, John: Deep End, *672*

Moulin, Charles: Baker's Wife, The, *224*

Moulin, Jean-Paul: Green Room, The, *479*

Moura, Gilberto: Pixote, *563*

Mourlet, Gwendoline: Three Men and a Cradle, *367*

Moustache, Crauchet, Paul: Beyond Fear, *409*

Movin, Lisbeth: Day of Wrath, *446*

Mowbray, Alan: Every Girl Should Be Married, *256;* Hollywood Hotel, *787;* Rose Marie, *800;* Stand-In, *358;* Terror By Night, *148;* Topper Takes a Trip, *370;* Villain Still Pursued Her, The, *159*

Mueller, Cookie: Female Trouble, *259;* Multiple Maniacs, *718*

Mueller-Stahl, Armin: Colonel Redl, *435;* Love in Germany, A, *523;* Train Killer, The, *621*

Muethel, Lola: From the Lives of the Marionettes, *470*

Mugavero, Frank: School Spirit, *346*

Muldaur, Diana: McQ, *98*

Muldoon, Michael: Hard Way, The, *69*

Mulgrew, Kate: Love Spell, *93;* Remo Williams: The Adventure Begins, *120; 120;* Stranger Is Watching, A, *749*

Mulhall, Jack: Invisible Ghost, *705*

Mulhare, Edward: Von Ryan's Express, *159*

Mullaney, Jack: Tickle Me, *809*

Mullavey, Greg: C.C. & Company, *28;* I Dismember Mama, *703*

Muller, Harrison: She, *861*

Mulligan, Richard: Big Bus, The, *229;* Doin' Time, *253;* Fine Mess, A, *260;* Group, The, *480;* Heavenly Kid, The, *278;* Heavenly Kid, The, *841;* Little Big Man, *909;* Meatballs Part II, *308;* Scavenger Hunt, *346;* S.O.B., *355;* Teachers, *364*

Mull, Martin: Clue, *245;* Mr. Mom, *311;* My Bodyguard, *540;* Private School, *335;* Serial, *349;* Take This Job and Shove It, *363*

Mumy, Billy: Bless the Beasts and the Children, *414*

Mundin, Herbert: Mutiny on the Bounty (Original), *105*

Mune, Ian: Nutcase, *321;* Shaker Run, *132;* Sleeping Dogs, *137*

Muni, Paul: Angel on My Shoulder, *399;* Good Earth, The, *475;* I Am a Fugitive from a Chain Gang, *490;* Juarez, *504;* Life of Emile

Zola, The, *518;* Scarface (original), *129;* Song to Remember, A, *804*

Munoz, Carlos: Camila, *424*

Munro, Caroline: At the Earth's Core, *818;* Captain Kronos: Vampire Hunter, *659;* Golden Voyage of Sinbad, The, *839;* Last Horror Film, The, *711;* Maniac, *714;* Spy Who Loved Me, The, *139;* Star Crash, *864*

Munro, Janet: Crawling Eye, The, *665;* Darby O'Gill and the Little People, *179;* Day the Earth Caught Fire, The, *828;* Horsemasters, *185;* Third Man On The Mountain, *208*

Munshin, Jules: Easter Parade, *777*

Munson, Ona: Red House, The, *734*

Munzuk, Maxim: Dersu Uzala, *448*

Muppets: Great Muppet Caper, The, *183;* Muppet Movie, The, *193;* Muppets Take Manhattan, The, *194*

Murat, Jean: Carnival in Flanders, *426*

Muravyova, Irina: Moscow Does Not Believe in Tears, *538*

Murdock, George: Breaker! Breaker!, *24;* Certain Fury, *29*

Murdock, Peggy: Paradise Canyon, *922*

Murdock, Perry: Border Phantom, *885*

Murney, Christopher: Grace Quigley, *271*

Murphy, Audie: To Hell and Back, *152*

Murphy, Ben: Time Walker, *755*

Murphy, Eddie: 48 Hrs., *262;* Best Defense, *227;* Beverly Hills Cop, *228;* Eddie Murphy—Delirious, *255;* Trading Places, *371*

Murphy, E. Danny: Graduation Day, *694*

Murphy, George: Bataan, *12;* Broadway Melody of 1938, *773;* Letter of Introduction, *516;* This is the Army, *808*

Murphy, Mary: Man Alone, A, *911;* Maverick Queen, The, *914;* Wild One, The, *164*

Murphy, Michael: Autobiography of Miss Jane Pittman, The, *402;* Class of Miss MacMichael, The, *435;* Cloak and Dagger, *32;* Count Yorga, Vampire, *664;* Great Bank Hoax, The, *272;* Manhattan, *305;* Phase IV, *856;* Salvador, *587;* Strange Behavior, *748;* Unmarried Woman, An, *626;* Year of Living Dangerously, The, *165*

Murphy, Rosemary: Ben, *650;* Walking Tall, *160*

Murphy, Timothy Patrick: Sam's Son, *588*

Murray, Bill: Caddyshack, *236;* Ghostbusters, *267;* Loose Shoes, *301;* Meatballs, *308;* Razor's Edge, The (Remake), *576;* Stripes, *360;* Tootsie, *369;* Where the Buffalo Roam, *381*

Murray, Chic: Gregory's Girl, *273*

Murray, Don: Baby the Rain Must Fall, *404;* Bus Stop, *236;* Conquest of the Planet of the Apes, *826;* Endless Love, *458*

Murray, Forbes: Silent Conflict, *931*

Murray, Joel: One Crazy Summer, *324*

Murray, John: Moving Violations, *315*

Murray, Tom: Gold Rush, The, *270*

Musante, Tony: Bird with the Crystal Plumage, The, *651*

Muscat, Angelo: Prisoner, The (television series), 857

Muschin, Gaston: Wifemistress, 633

Muse, Clarence: Black Stallion, The, 173; Daniel Boone, 891

Muti, Ornella: Swann In Love, 609

Myerson, Alan: Steelyard Blues, 359

Myers, Carmel: Svengali, 750

Myers, Cynthia: Beyond the Valley of the Dolls, 410

Myers, Harry: City Lights, 243

Myers, Kim: Nightmare on Elm Street Part2: Freddy's Revenge, A, 722

Myers, Susan: Desperate Women, 893

Mylong, John: Robot Monster, 736

Mynhardt, Patrick: Killing Heat, 507

Nabors, Jim: Stroker Ace, 361

Nadeau, Elyane: Martin, 715

Nader, George: Away All Boats, 11; Carnival Story, 426; Robot Monster, 736

Nagashimaji, Toshiyuku: Mishima: A Life in Four Chapters, 535

Nagel, Conrad: Ann Vickers, 399

Nail, Jimmy: Morons from Outer Space, 314

Naish, J. Carrol: Ann Vickers, 399; Behind the Rising Sun, 13; Clash by Night, 434; Corsican Brothers, The, 35; Dracula vs. Frankenstein, 679; Gung Ho, 67; Joan of Arc, 502; Last Command, The, 907; Rio Grande, 927; Sahara, 126; Southerner, The, 598

Naismith, Laurence: Carrington, V. C., 427; Concrete Jungle, The (aka The Criminal), 437; Greyfriars Bobby, 183; Scrooge, 801; Young Winston, 641

Nakadai, Tatsuya: Kagemusha, 81; Kojiro, 85; Ran, 575; Sanjuro, 128

Nakamura, Atsuo: Highest Honor, The, 73

Nakhapetov, Rodion: Slave of Love, A, 594

Nalder, Reggie: Salem's Lot, 739

Namath, Joe: Chattanooga Choo Choo, 242; C.C. & Company, 28

Nance, John: Eraserhead, 680; Ghoulies, 693

Nan, Din: Shaolin Temple, 132

Napier, Charles: Last Embrace, The, 87; Rambo: First Blood II, 118; Came a Hot Friday, 27; Secret Life of An American Wife, The, 347

Nardini, Tom: Africa—Texas Style!, 6

Narelle, Brian: Dark Star, 828

Naschy, Paul: Night of the Howling Beast, 723

Nash, Graham: No Nukes, 795

Nash, Chris: Mischief, 310

Nash, Marilyn: Monsieur Verdoux, 313

Nash, Mary: Yolanda and The Thief, 640

Nash, Simon: XTro, 766

Nathan, Stephen: First Nudie Musical, The, 779

Natsuki, Yosuke: Dagora, the Space Monster, 837; Ghidrah, the Three-Headed Monster, 692

Natsume, Masaka: MacArthur's Children, 525

Natwick, Mildred: Barefoot in the Park, 224; Court Jester, The, 248; Daisy Miller, 442; Long Voyage Home, The, 520; Quiet Man, The, 117; She Wore a Yellow Ribbon, 930; Tammy and the Bachelor, 611; Trouble With Harry, The, 372; Yolanda and The Thief, 640

Naughton, David: American Werewolf in London, An, 644; Boy in Blue, The, 418; Hot Dog...The Movie, 283; Midnight Madness, 309; Not for Publication, 320; Stranger Is Watching, A, 749

Navarro, Ramon: Heller in Pink Tights, 902

Naves, Owen: Private Life of Don Juan, The, 568

Nave, Steve: RSVP, 343

Nazarro, Cliff: Singing Buckaroo, 932

Nazimova: Blood and Sand, 414; Bridge of San Luis Rey, The, 420

Neagle, Anna: Nurse Edith Cavell, 548

Neal, Edwin: Future-Kill, 692

Neal, Ed: Texas Chainsaw Massacre, The, 753

Neal, Patricia: All Quiet on the Western Front, 393; Breakfast at Tiffany's, 419; Day the Earth Stood Still, The, 828; Face in the Crowd, A, 461; Fountainhead, The, 468; Ghost Story, 693; Hud, 490; Run Stranger Run, 738

Neal, Tom: Behind the Rising Sun, 13; Brute Man, The, 658; Detour, 450; First Yank into Tokyo, 55

Near, Holly: Slaughterhouse Five, 862; Wasn't That a Time!, 811

Neckar, Vaclau: Closely Watched Trains, 435

Neeley, Ted: Hard Country, 68; Jesus Christ Superstar, 789

Neer, Kay: Love Butcher, 713

Negri, Pola: Moonspinners, The, 193

Negron, Taylor: Bad Medicine, 223; Young Doctors in Love, 385

Negro, Del: Aguirre: Wrath of God, 6

Neher, Carola: Threepenny Opera, The, 809

Neiiendam, Sigrid: Day of Wrath, 446

Neil, Hildegard: Antony and Cleopatra, 401; Man Who Haunted Himself, The, 714; Touch of Class, A, 370

Neill, Sam: Attack Force Z, 10; Enigma, 49; Final Conflict, The, 684; My Brilliant Career, 540; Plenty, 564; Sleeping Dogs, 137

Nelkin, Stacey: Going Crazy, 266; Going Ape!, 269; Halloween III: Season of the Witch, 695; Up the Academy, 375

Nelligan, Kate: Eleni, 456; Eye of the Needle, 51; Without a Trace, 637

Nellmose, Karin: Master Of The House (Du Skal Aere Din Hustru), 308

Nellson, John: Shark's Treasure, 133

Nelson, Barry: Bataan, 12; Island Claws, 706; Shadow of the Thin Man, 132

Nelson, Craig T.: All the Right Moves, 394;

And Justice for All, *397;* Call to Glory, *424;* Killing Fields, The, *506;* Poltergeist II: The Otherside, *729;* Poltergeist, *729;* Silkwood, *593*

Nelson, Dick: Great Guns, *272*

Nelson, Ed: Attack of the Crab Monsters, *647*

Nelson, Harriet: Kid With the 200 I.Q., The, *188*

Nelson, Judd: Blue City, *20;* Fandango, *258;* Making the Grade, *305;* St. Elmo's Fire, *586*

Nelson, Kenneth: Boys in the Band, The, *419*

Nelson, Ricky: Rio Bravo, *926;* Wackiest Ship in the Army, The, *377*

Nelson, Ruth: Haunting Passion, The, *840*

Nelson, Tracy: Down and Out in Beverly Hills, *254*

Nelson, Willie: Barbarosa, *881;* Electric Horseman, The, *456;* Hell's Angels Forever, *486;* Honeysuckle Rose, *788;* Songwriter, *804;* Thief, *148*

Nemanick, Dan: Wild Rose, *634*

Neri, Tomasso: Battle of Algiers, *405*

Nero, Franco: Camelot, *773;* Confessions of a Police Captain, *437;* Enter the Ninja, *49;* Force Ten from Navarone, *59;* High Crime, *72;* Man with Bogart's Face, The, *96;* Querelle, *572;* Shark Hunter, The, *133;* Tramplers, The, *940*

Nero, Toni: Silent Night, Deadly Night, *743*

Nesbitt, Cathleen: Family Plot, *683;* Nicholas Nickleby, *544*

Nettleton, Lois: Butterfly, *422;* Deadly Blessing, *671*

Neumann, Jenny: Hell Night, *697*

Nevin, Robyn: Careful He Might Hear You, *426*

New, Nancy: Bostonians, The, *417*

Newcastle, Anthony: Captive Planet, *823*

Newell, Carol Irene: Alpha Incident, The, *816*

Newell, Patrick: Adventures of Sherlock Holmes: The Resident Patient, *5*

Newhart, Bob: First Family, *261;* Little Miss Marker, *190;* On a Clear Day, You Can See Forever, *796;* Thursday's Game, *618*

Newley, Anthony: Doctor Dolittle, *180;* Fire Down Below, *464;* Mr. Quilp, *794*

Newman, Barry: Night Games, *544;* Vanishing Point, *158*

Newman, Julie: Mackenna's Gold, *911*

Newman, Laraine: Invaders from Mars (Re-make), *844;* Perfect, *561;* Tunnelvision, *373;* Wholly Moses!, *381*

Newman, Nanette: Of Human Bondage (Re-make), *549;* Seance on a Wet Afternoon, *741;* Wrong Box, The, *384*

Newman, Paul: Absence of Malice, *388;* Buffalo Bill and the Indians, *886;* Butch Cassidy and the Sundance Kid, *887;* Cat on a Hot Tin Roof (Original), *428;* Cool Hand Luke, *35;* Drowning Pool, The, *45;* Exodus, *460;*

Fort Apache—The Bronx, *467;* Harper, *69;* Harry and Son, *483;* Hombre, *904;* Hud, *490;* Hustler, The, *490;* Life and Times of Judge Roy Bean, The, *909;* Mackintosh Man, The, *94;* Paris Blues, *558;* Quintet, *858;* Secret War of Harry Frigg, The, *348;* Silent Movie, *351;* Slap Shot, *353;* Sometimes a Great Notion, *597;* Sting, The, *144;* Torn Curtain, *758;* Towering Inferno, The, *154;* Verdict, The, *628;* When Time Ran Out!, *764;* Winning, *164;* Young Philadelphians, The, *640*

Newmar, Julie: Hysterical, *284;* Seven Brides for Seven Brothers, *764;* Streetwalkin', *605*

Newton, Bert: Fatty Finn, *181*

Newton, Margit: Night of the Zombies, *723*

Newton, Mary: Marauders, *913*

Newton, Robert: Around the World in 80 Days, *220;* Beachcomber, The, *406;* Henry V, *486;* Jamaica Inn, *500;* Long John Silver, *92;* Oliver Twist, *550;* Treasure Island, *211*

Newton-John, Olivia: Grease, *784;* Two of a Kind, *373;* Xanadu, *813*

Ney, Richard: Premature Burial, The, *730*

Nezu, Jinpachi: Ran, *575*

Ngor, Haing S.: Killing Fields, The, *506*

Nicastro, Michelle: Bad Guys, *11*

Nichetti, Maurizio: Hearts and Armour, *70*

Nicholas-Hill, Denise: Marvin and Tige, *530*

Nicholas, Denise: Blacula, *652;* Piece of the Action, A, *329*

Nicholas, Paul: Lisztomania, *792*

Nichols, Anthony: I Spit On Your Grave, *704*

Nichols, Barbara: Untouchables: Scarface Mob, The, *157;* Where the Boys Are, *380*

Nichols, David: Hardcore, *481*

Nichols, Nichelle: Star Trek III: The Search for Spock, *865;* Star Trek (television series), *866;* Star Trek: The Menagerie, *865;* Star Trek—The Motion Picture, *865*

Nicholson, Jack: Border, The, *22;* Carnal Knowledge, *426;* Chinatown, *30;* Easy Rider, *455;* Ensign Pulver, *255;* Goin' South, *898;* Heartburn, *277;* Hell's Angels on Wheels, *71;* Last Detail, The, *513;* Last Tycoon, The, *515;* Little Shop of Horrors, The, *713;* Missouri Breaks, The, *915;* One Flew over the Cuckoo's Nest, *551;* On a Clear Day, You Can See Forever, *796;* Passenger, The, *558;* Postman Always Rings Twice, The (Re-make), *566;* Prizzi's Honor, *569;* Raven, The, *733;* Reds, *578;* Ride in the Whirlwind, *925;* Shining, The, *742;* Shooting, The, *931;* Terms of Endearment, *613;* Terror, The, *752;* Tommy, *810*

Nickson, Julia: Rambo: First Blood II, *118*

Nicolodi, Daria: Beyond the Door 2, *651;* Creepers, *665;* Deep Red, *672;* Macaroni, *304*

Nielsen, Brigette: Rocky IV, *582;* Cobra, *32;* Red Sonja, *120*

Nielsen, Leslie: Airplane!, *216;* Amsterdam Kill, The, *7;* Creepshow, *666;* Day of the Animals, *670;* Forbidden Planet, *838;* Four

Rode Out, 897; Harlow, 482; Police Squad!, 332; Prom Night, 730; Resurrection of Zachary Wheeler, The, 859; Spaceship, 356; Tammy and the Bachelor, 611; Viva Knievel, 159; Wrong Is Right, 384

Nielsen, Mathilde: Master Of The House (Du Skal Aere Din Hustru), 308

Niemczyk, Leon: Knife in the Water, 509

Niklas, Jan: Colonel Redl, 435

Nilsson, Kjell: Road Warrior, The, 859

Nilsson, Maj-Britt: Secrets of Women (or Waiting Women), 348

Nimmo, Derek: One Of Our Dinosaurs Is Missing, 196

Nimoy, Leonard: Aladdin and His Wonderful Lamp, 170; Invasion of the Body Snatchers (Remake), 845; Satan's Satellites, 128; Star Trek III: The Search for Spock, 865; Star Trek II: The Wrath of Khan, 865; Star Trek (television series), 866; Star Trek: The Menagerie, 865; Star Trek—The Motion Picture, 865; Woman Called Golda, A, 638

Niven, David: Around the World in 80 Days, 220; Bishop's Wife, The, 229; Candleshoe, 175; Carrington, V. C., 437; Casino Royale, 239; Charge of the Light Brigade, The, 30; Curse of the Pink Panther, The, 248; Dawn Patrol, The, 39; Death on the Nile, 40; Dinner at the Ritz, 43; Dodsworth, 452; Escape to Athena, 50; Guns of Navarone, The, 68; Happy Go Lovely, 786; Moon Is Blue, The, 314; Murder by Death, 315; No Deposit, No Return, 195; Paper Tiger, 112; Pink Panther, The, 330; Rough Cut, 124; Sea Wolves, The, 130; Trail of the Pink Panther, The, 371; Wuthering Heights, 639

Nixon, Cynthia: Manhattan Project, The, 714

Nixon, John P.: Legend of Boggy Creek, 711

Noble, Trisha: Private Eyes, The, 335

Noel, Chris: Cease Fire, 429

Noel, Magali: Amarcord, 395; Rififi, 122

Noiret, Philippe: Birgit Haas Must Be Killed, 18; Clean State (Coup de Torchon), 244; Jupiter's Thigh, 291; Murphy's War, 104; Purple Taxi, The, 571

Nolan, Bob, and the Sons of the Pioneers: Heart of the Golden West, 901; Song of Nevada, 933; Song of Texas, 933; Sunset Serenade, 935; Under California Stars, 942; Yellow Rose of Texas, 946

Nolan, Jeanette: Avalanche, 10; Chamber of Horrors, 661; Macbeth, 525

Nolan, Lloyd: Bataan, 12; Circus World, 889; Fire!, 685; Hannah and Her Sisters, 275; House Across the Bay, The, 489; Ice Station Zebra, 77

Nolan, Tom: School Spirit, 346

Nolte, Nick: 48 Hrs., 262; Cannery Row, 237; Deep, The, 41; Down and Out in Beverly Hills, 254; Grace Quigley, 271; Heart Beat, 483; North Dallas Forty, 546; Return to Macon County, 121; Teachers, 364; Under Fire, 156

Nolte, Nick: Who'll Stop the Rain, 162

Noonan, Tom: Star Is Born, A (Remake), 601; Wolfen, 766

Noonan, Tony: Gentlemen Prefer Blondes, 266

Normand, Mabel: Keystone Comedies, Vol. 2, 292; Keystone Comedies, Vol. 3, 292; Keystone Comedies: Vol. 4, 292

Norman, Zack: Romancing the Stone, 124

Normington, John: Private Function, A, 335

Norris, Christopher: Eat My Dust, 47; Summer of '42, 608

Norris, Chuck: Breaker! Breaker!, 24; Code of Silence, 33; Delta Force, The, 41; Eye for an Eye, 51; Forced Vengeance, 59; Force of One, 59; Game of Death, 61; Good Guys Wear Black, 63; Invasion U.S.A., 77; Lone Wolf McQuade, 92; Missing in Action 2: The Beginning, 100; Missing in Action, 100; Octagon, The, 109; Return of the Dragon, 120; Silent Rage, 136

North, Alan: Police Squad!, 332

North, Alex: Comfort and Joy, 246

North, Heather: Barefoot Executive, The, 172

North, Neil: Winslow Boy, The, 635

North, Noelle: Sweater Girls, 362

North, Sheree: Breakout, 24; Madigan, 94; Organization, The, 111; Portrait of a Stripper, 565

North, Virginia: Abominable Dr. Phibes, The, 643

Norton, Alex: Gregory's Girl, 273

Norton, Charles: Check and Double Check, 242

Norton, Jim: Cry of the Innocent, 37; Sakharov, 587

Norton, Richard: Gymkata, 68

Nouri, Michael: Flashdance, 780; Gangster Wars, 61

Novak, Kim: Bell, Book and Candle, 226; Mirror Crack'd, The, 99; Of Human Bondage (Remake), 549; Vertigo, 762

Novatna, Jarmila: Great Caruso, The, 785

Novello, Don: Gilda Live, 268; (narrating as Father Guido Sarducci) Pinocchio, 198

Novello, Jay: Colorado, 889

Novikov, Vassily: Alexander Nevsky, 392

Noy, Zachi: Private Popsicle, 335

Nquyen, Ho: Alamo Bay, 391

Ntshona, Winston: Wild Geese, The, 163

Nunn, Judy: Savage Attraction, 739

Nunn, Teri: Follow That Car, 58

Nureyev, Rudolph: Exposed, 681

Nutter, Mayf: Petronella, 197

Nye, Louis: 10 from Your Show of Shows, 364

Nyman, Lena: Autumn Sonata, 403; I Am Curious Yellow, 491

Oakie, Jack: Great Dictator, The, 272; Little Men, 519; Lover Come Back, 303; Uptown New York, 627

Oakland, Simon: Psycho, *731;* Sand Pebbles, The, *127;* Scandalous John, *203*

Oakman, Wheeler: Radio Ranch (Men With Steel Faces, Phantom Empire), *923*

Oates, Warren: Badlands, *404;* Blue Thunder, *21;* Border, The, *22;* Brinks Job, The, *234;* Cockfighter, *32;* East of Eden (Remake), *454;* In the Heat of the Night, *494;* Major Dundee, *911;* My Old Man, *541;* Race with the Devil, *732;* Ride the High Country, *925;* Shooting, The, *931;* Sleeping Dogs, *137;* Stripes, *360;* There Was a Crooked Man, *938;* Thief Who Came to Dinner, The, *366;* Tough Enough, *154;* White Dawn, The, *161;* Wild Bunch, The, *945*

O'Bannon, Dan: Dark Star, *828*

Oberon, Merle: Dark Waters, *445;* Divorce of Lady X, The, *251;* Private Life of Don Juan, The, *568;* Private Life of Henry the Eighth, The, *568;* Scarlet Pimpernel, The, *129;* Song to Remember, A, *804;* These Three, *615;* Wuthering Heights, *639*

Obregon, Ana: Bolero, *417;* Treasure of the Four Crowns, *155*

O'Brian, Hugh: Africa—Texas Style!, *6;* Cruise into Terror, *667;* Fantasy Island, *837;* Game of Death, *61;* Rocketship X-M, *860;* Shootist, The, *931;* There's No Business Like Show Business, *808*

O'Brien, Dave: Devil Bat, The, *673;* Gunman from Bodie, *900;* Reefer Madness, *338;* Spooks Run Wild, *357*

O'Brien, Edmond: 99 and 44/100 Percent Dead, *108;* Doomsday Flight, The, *453;* Double Life, A, *453;* D-Day the Sixth of June, *442;* D.O.A., *442;* Fantastic Voyage, *836;* Hunchback of Notre Dame, The (remake), *703;* Killers, The, *83;* Lucky Luciano, *93;* Man Who Shot Liberty Valance, The, *913;* Moon Pilot, *193;* Rio Conchos, *927;* Seven Days in May, *591;* Stopover Tokyo, *141;* White Heat, *161;* Wild Bunch, The, *945*

O'Brien, Edna: Hard Way, The, *69*

O'Brien, George: Daniel Boone, *891;* Fort Apache, *897*

O'Brien, Joan: It Happened at the World's Fair, *789*

O'Brien, Margaret: Heller in Pink Tights, *902;* Meet Me in St. Louis, *793*

O'Brien, Pat: Angels with Dirty Faces, *8;* Bombardier, *21;* Boy With Green Hair, The, *419;* End, The, *255;* Front Page, The, *264;* Hell's House, *71;* Knute Rockne—All American, *510;* Ragtime, *574;* Some Like It Hot, *356*

O'Brien, Richard: Shock Treatment, *351*

O'Brien, Timothy Eric: Suburbia, *606*

O'Brien, Virginia: Du Barry Was a Lady, *777;* Thousands Cheer, *808;* Ziegfeld Follies, *814*

Ocana, Susana: Skyline, *353*

Occhini, Ilaria: Tramplers, The, *940*

Occhipinti, Andrea: Bolero, *417*

Ochoa, Manuel Lopez: Crossfire, *890*

O'Connell, Arthur: 7 Faces of Dr. Lao, *861;* Anatomy of a Murder, *397;* Ben, *650;* Bus Stop, *236;* Fantastic Voyage, *836;* Gidget, *267;* Great Race, The, *273;* Monkey's Uncle, The, *192;* Operation Petticoat, *325;* There Was a Crooked Man, *938*

O'Connell, Eddie: Absolute Beginners, *768*

O'Connell, Jerry: Stand By Me, *600*

O'Conner, Una: Strawberry Blonde, The, *604*

O'Connor, Carroll: Hawaii, *483;* Kelly's Heroes, *81*

O'Connor, Donald: Francis, the Talking Mule, *363;* Private Buckaroo, *799;* Ragtime, *574;* Singin' in the Rain, *802;* There's No Business Like Show Business, *808*

O'Connor, Glynnis: Boy in the Plastic Bubble, The, *418;* California Dreaming, *424;* Ode to Billy Joe, *548*

O'Connor, Hazel: Breaking Glass, *772*

O'Connor, Kevin: Bogie, *417;* Special Effects, *746*

O'Connor, Loyola: True Heart Susie, *623*

O'Connor, Marilyn: Thunder Run, *151*

O'Connor, Terry: Breaker! Breaker!, *24*

O'Connor, Tim: Buck Rogers in the 25th Century, *822*

O'Connor, Una: Unexpected Guest, *942;* Witness for the Prosecution, *637*

O'Dea, Jimmy: Darby O'Gill and the Little People, *179*

O'Dea, Judith: Night of the Living Dead, *723*

O'Donnell, Cathy: Best Years of Our Lives, The, *409*

O'Fredericks, Alice: Witchcraft Through the Ages (HAXAN), *637*

Odetta: Autobiography of Miss Jane Pittman, The, *402*

Ogata, Ken: Mishima: A Life in Four Chapters, *535*

Ogier, Bulle: Discreet Charm Of The Bourgeoisie, The, *251*

Ogier, Pascale: Full Moon in Paris, *264*

Ogilvy, Ian: And Now the Screaming Starts, *645*

O'Grady, Timothy E.: James Joyce's Women, *500*

O'Halloran, Jack: Farewell My Lovely, *52*

Ohana, Claudia: Erendira, *459*

O'Hara, Catherine: After Hours, *215;* Heartburn, *277;* Last Polka, The, *296*

O'Hara, Maureen: At Sword's Point, *10;* Big Jake, *882;* Hunchback of Notre Dame, The (remake), *703;* Jamaica Inn, *500;* Miracle on 34th Street, *192;* Parent Trap, The, *197;* Quiet Man, The, *117;* Rare Breed, The, *924;* Rio Grande, *927;* Sinbad the Sailor, *136;* This Land Is Mine, *617*

O'Hara, Quinn: Swingin' Summer, A, *362*

O'Henry, Caitlin: He Knows You're Alone, *696*

O'Herlihy, Dan: 100 Rifles, *920;* At Sword's Point, *10;* Halloween III: Season of the Witch,*

695; MacArthur, 525; Macbeth, 525; People, The, 855

O'Herlihy, Don: Last Starfighter, The, 848
O'Herlihy, Gavan: Partners in Crime—The Secret Adversary, 113
Ohmart, Carol: House on Haunted Hill, 700
Ohta, Bennett: Missing in Action 2: The Beginning, 100
Oh, Soon-Teck: Missing in Action 2: The Beginning, 100
Okada, Eiji: Hiroshima, Mon Amour, 488
Okada, Mariko: Samurai Trilogy, The, 127
O'Keefe, Dennis: Brewster's Millions (1945), 234; Fighting Seabees, The, 53; Great Dan Patch, The, 477; Leopard Man, The, 712; Topper Returns, 370
O'Keefe, Michael: Caddyshack, 236; Dark Secret of Harvest Home, The, 669; Finders Keepers, 260; Great Santini, The, 478; Nate and Hayes, 105; Rumor of War, A, 125; Slugger's Wife, The, 354; Split Image, 599
O'Keefe, Paul: Daydreamer, The, 179
O'Keeffe, Miles: Ator: The Fighting Eagle, 818; Sword of the Valiant, 207; Tarzan the Ape Man (Remake), 146
O'Kelly, Tim: Targets, 751
Okumoto, Yuji: Karate Kid, Part 2, The, 81
Olbrychski, Daniel: Tin Drum, The, 619
Oldfield, Eric: Island Trader, 78
O'Leary, John: My Chauffeur, 316
Olita, Joseph: Amin: The Rise and Fall, 397
Oliveira, Lourdes de: Black Orpheus, 414
Olivera, Don: Forbidden World, 686
Oliver, Barret: Cocoon, 825; D.A.R.Y.L., 827; NeverEnding Story, The, 853
Oliver, Edna May: Ann Vickers, 399; David Copperfield, 445; Nurse Edith Cavell, 548; Story of Vernon and Irene Castle, The, 806; Tale of Two Cities, A, 611
Oliver, Susan: Ginger In The Morning, 472; Hardly Working, 276; Star Trek: The Menagerie, 865
Olivier, Laurence: 49th Parallel, The, 468; Betsy, The, 409; Bounty, The, 23; Boys from Brazil, The, 656; Bridge Too Far, A, 25; Clash of the Titans, 824; Divorce of Lady X, The, 251; Dracula (Remake), 678; Fire over England, 54; Hamlet, 481; Henry V, 486; I Stand Condemned, 492; Jazz Singer, The, 789; Jigsaw Man, The, 708; Little Romance, A, 300; Marathon Man, 97; Mr. Halpern and Mr. Johnson, 536; Nicholas and Alexandra, 543; Pride and Prejudice, 567; Prince and the Showgirl, The, 334; Rebecca, 576; Richard III, 580; Seven-Per-Cent Solution, The, 131; Sleuth, 595; Spartacus, 138; That Hamilton Woman, 614; Wagner, 811; Wild Geese II, 163; (Narrator) World at War Vol.1-26, 639; Wuthering Heights, 639
Olivier, Paul: Le Million, 298
Olivier-Pierre, O: Adventures of Sherlock Holmes: The Final Problem, 4
Olkewicz, Walter: Can I Do It 'Til I Need

Glasses?, 237
Ollrychski, Daniel: La Truite (The Trout), 512
Olmos, Edward James: Ballad of Gregorio Cortez, The, 881; Miami Vice: "The Prodigal Son", 99; Nightingale, The, 195; Wolfen, 766
O'Loughlin, Gerald S.: Pleasure Palace, 564
Olsen, Moroni: Allegheny Uprising, 878
Olson, Eric: Flood!, 685
Olson, James: Amityville II: The Possession, 645; Andromeda Strain, The, 817; Commando, 33; My Sister, My Love, 720; Rachel, Rachel, 573
Olson, Lydia: Wild Rose, 634
Olson, Moroni: Mildred Pierce, 534
Olson, Nancy: Absent-Minded Professor, The, 169; Pollyanna, 198; Son of Flubber, 206; Union Station, 760
Omaggio, Maria Rosaria: Cop in Blue Jeans, The, 35
O'Mara, Kate: Horror of Frankenstein, 699
Omen, Judd: Pee-Wee's Big Adventure, 328
Omori, Yoshiyuki: MacArthur's Children, 525
Ondra, Anny: Blackmail, 414
O'Neal, Frederick: Something of Value, 138
O'Neal, Griffin: April Fool's Day, 646; Escape Artist, The, 181
O'Neal, Patrick: Alvarez Kelly, 879; Chamber of Horrors, 661; Secret Life of An American Wife, The, 347; Stiletto, 140; Way We Were, The, 631
O'Neal, Ron: Red Dawn, 119; St. Helens, 587; Superfly, 143; When a Stranger Calls, 764
O'Neal, Ryan: Barry Lyndon, 405; Driver, The, 45; Green Ice, 66; Irreconcilable Differences, 498; Love Story, 524; Main Event, The, 305; Oliver's Story, 551; Paper Moon, 327; Partners, 328; So Fine, 355; Thief Who Came to Dinner, The, 366; What's Up Doc?, 380
O'Neal, Tatum: Bad News Bears, The, 223; Certain Fury, 29; Circle of Two, 434; Goldilocks and the Three Bears, 182; International Velvet, 186; Little Darlings, 299; Paper Moon, 327
O'Neill, Chris: James Joyce's Women, 500
O'Neill, Dick: St. Ives, 126; Wolfen, 766
O'Neill, Henry: Call It Murder, 424
O'Neill, Jennifer: Cloud Dancer, 32; Force of One, 59; Reincarnation of Peter Proud, The, 734; Rio Lobo, 927; Scanners, 740; Summer of '42, 608
O'Neil, Tricia: Piranha Part Two: The Spawning, 728
Onoe, Kikunosuke: Kojiro, 85
Onoe, Kuroemon: Samurai Trilogy, The, 127
Ontkean, Michael: Just the Way You Are, 505; Making Love, 527; Witching, The (Necromancy), 765
Opatoshu, David: Forced Vengeance, 59; Torn Curtain, 758; Who'll Stop the Rain, 162

Opper, Don: Android, *817;* Critters, *666*

Orbach, Jerry: F/X, *51;* Prince of the City, *568*

Orford, Trevor: Where the Green Ants Dream, *632*

Orhonsoy, Heral: Yol, *639*

Orlov, Dmitri: Alexander Nevsky, *392*

Ormsby, Alan: Children Shouldn't Play with Dead Things, *662*

Ormsby, Anya: Children Shouldn't Play with Dead Things, *662*

O'Rourke, Heather: Poltergeist II: The Otherside, *729*

Osborne, Bud: Boots and Saddles, *885;* Cow Town, *890;* Frontier Pony Express, *898;* Prairie Moon, *922*

Oscar and Elmer: Old Corral, The, *919*

Oscarsson, Per: Secrets, *590*

O'Shea, Jack: Frontier Pony Express, *898;* Song of Nevada, *933;* Yellow Rose of Texas, *946*

O'Shea, Michael: Jack London, *499;* Lady of Burlesque, *86*

O'Shea, Milo: Barbarella, *819;* It Should Happen to You, *287;* Paddy, *326;* Pilot, The, *563;* Romeo and Juliet, *584*

O'Shea, Paul: Among the Cinders, *397*

Osmond, Cliff: Fortune Cookie, The, *262;* Invasion of the Bee Girls, *844;* Shark's Treasure, *133*

Osterander, William: Stryker, *868*

Osterloh, Robert: Riot in Cell Block 11, *581*

Ostrum, Peter: Willy Wonka and the Chocolate Factory, *213*

O'Sullivan, Maureen : Thin Man, The, *149;* Anna Karenina, *400;* Day at the Races, A, *249;* Devil Doll, The, *674;* Hannah and Her Sisters, *275;* Pride and Prejudice, *567;* Tarzan the Ape Man (Original), *146*

Otaki, Shuji: MacArthur's Children, *525*

O'Toole, Annette: 48 Hrs., *262;* Foolin' Around, *261;* King of the Gypsies, *508;* One on One, *552;* Superman III, *869*

O'Toole, Peter: Becket, *406;* Caligula, *424;* Club Paradise, *245;* Creator, *440;* Lawrence of Arabia, *88;* Lion In Winter, The, *519;* Lord Jim, *93;* Man of La Mancha, *793;* Masada, *530;* Murphy's War, *104;* My Favorite Year, *316;* Night of the Generals, *107;* Ruling Class, The, *344;* Stunt Man, The, *606;* Supergirl, *868;* What's New Pussycat?, *379;* Zulu Dawn, *168*

Ouspenskaya, Maria: Dodsworth, *452;* Frankenstein Meets the Wolf Man, *688*

Outlaws, Al Clauser and his Oklahoma: Rootin' Tootin' Rhythm, *928*

Outlaw, Geoff: Alice's Restaurant, *393*

Overman, Lynne: Little Miss Marker, *190;* Silver Queen, *932;* Call It Murder, *424*

Overton, Frank: Desire Under the Elms, *449;* Failsafe, *461*

Owens, Gary: Hysterical, *284*

Owens, Patricia: Fly, The (original), *686;* Hell to Eternity, *485*

Owen, Reginald: Captain Kidd, *27;* Five Weeks in a Balloon, *56;* National Velvet, *195;* Pirate, The, *798;* Tammy and the Doctor, *611;* Woman of the Year, *383*

Owen, Tony: Norman Loves Rose, *320*

Oxenbould, Ben: Fatty Finn, *181*

Oxley, David: Ill Met by Moonlight, *493*

Ozawa, Sakae: Ugetsu, *625*

Oze, Lajos: Time Stands Still, *619*

Pacemakers, Gerry and the: That Was Rock, *808*

Pace, Judy: Brian's Song, *420*

Pace, Richard: I Spit On Your Grave, *704*

Pace, Tom: Astro-Zombies, *646*

Pacino, Al: And Justice for All, *397;* Author! Author!, *222;* Bobby Deerfield, *416;* Cruising, *441;* Dog Day Afternoon, *452;* Godfather Epic, The, *474;* Godfather, The, Part II, *474;* Godfather, The, *473;* Revolution, *579;* Scarecrow, *589;* Scarface (Remake), *139;* Serpico, *590*

Pacula, Joanna: Gorky Park, *64*

Pagett, Nicola: Oliver's Story, *551;* Privates on Parade, *336*

Paget, Debra: From the Earth to the Moon, *838;* Love Me Tender, *910;* Tales of Terror, *751*

Page, Genevieve: Private Life of Sherlock Holmes, The, *115;* Beguiled, The, *407;* Bride, The, *656;* Happiest Millionaire, The, *184;* Honky Tonk Freeway, *282;* Interiors, *496;* I'm Dancing As Fast As I Can, *492;* Pope of Greenwich Village, The, *564;* Trip to Bountiful, The, *622;* White Nights, *632;* You're a Big Boy Now, *385*

Page, Grant: Road Games, *736*

Page, Jimmy: Song Remains the Same, The, *803*

Page, Joy: Bullfighter and the Lady, The, *26*

Pagliero, Marcello: Open City, *553*

Pagni, Eros: Love and Anarchy, *301*

Pahich, Dre: Dark Star, *828*

Paige, Janis: Silk Stockings, *802*

Paige, Robert: Green Promise, The, *479*

Paiva, Nestor: Creature from the Black Lagoon, *665;* Purple Heart, The, *570;* They Saved Hitler's Brain, *754*

Palacio, Riccardo: Ark of the Sun God... Temple of Hell, The, *9*

Palance, Holly: Best of Times, The, *228*

Palance, Jack: Alone in the Dark, *644;* Barabbas, *405;* Battle of the Commandos, *13;* Contempt, *247;* Cop in Blue Jeans, The, *35;* Deadly Sanctuary, *671;* Four Deuces, The, *59;* Hatfields and the McCoys, The, *901;* Hawk the Slayer, *69;* Hell's Brigade, *71;* Last Ride of the Dalton Boys, The, *908;* Lonely Man, The, *909;* Monte Walsh, *915;* Shane, *930;* Torture Garden, *758;* Without Warning, *876*

Palin, Michael: And Now for Something

Completely Different, *218*; Brazil, *233*; Jabberwocky, *289*; Life of Brian, *299*; Missionary, The, *310*; Monty Python and the Holy Grail, *313*; Monty Python Live at the Hollywood Bowl, *313*; Private Function, A, *335*; Secret Policeman's Private Parts, The, *347*; Secret Policeman's Other Ball, The, *347*; Time Bandits, *872*

Palk, Anna: Nightcomers, The, *721*

Pallenberg, Anita: Barbarella, *819*; Performance, *561*

Pallette, Eugene: Adventures of Robin Hood, The, *2*; Fighting Caravans, *896*; Intolerance, *497*; Kansan, The, *906*; Kennel Murder Case, The, *82*; Silver Queen, *932*

Palmer, Betsy: Friday the 13th, Part II, *690*; Friday the 13th, *691*

Palmer, Gregg: To Hell and Back, *152*; Zombies of Mora Tau, *767*

Palmer, Gretchen: Fast Forward, *779*

Palmer, Lilli: Body and Soul (Original), *416*; Boys from Brazil, The, *656*; Holcroft Covenant, The, *74*; Murders In The Rue Morgue, *720*; Secret Agent, The, *131*

Palmer, Tony: 200 Motels, *810*

Palomino, Carlos: Jungle Heat, *80*

Paltenghi, David: Invitation to the Dance, *788*

Pangborn, Franklin: Topper Takes a Trip, *370*

Pankow, John: To Live and Die in L.A., *153*

Pantoliano, Joe: Risky Business, *341*; Running Scared (1986), *125*

Papamoskou, Tatiana: Iphigenia, *497*

Papas, Irene: Erendira, *459*; Into the Night, *496*; Iphigenia, *497*; Message, The (Mohammad, Messenger of God), *533*; Moses, *539*; Trojan Women, The, *622*; Zorba the Greek, *642*; Z, *641*

Paragon, John: Echo Park, *455*

Parely, Mila: Rules of the Game, The, *344*

Pare, Michael: Eddie and the Cruisers, *778*; Philadelphia Experiment, The, *856*; Streets of Fire, *142*

Paris, Jerry: Untouchables: Scarface Mob, The, *157*; Wild One, The, *164*

Parker, Cecilia: Riders of Destiny, *926*

Parker, Cecil: Heavens Above, *279*; Ladykillers, The, *295*; Man in the White Suit, The, *306*; Stars Look Down, The, *601*; Storm in a Teacup, *360*

Parker, Edward: Lucky Texan, *910*; Winning of the West, *946*

Parker, Eleanor: Hans Brinker, *183*; Oscar, The, *554*; Sound of Music, The, *804*

Parker, Fess: Davy Crockett and the River Pirates, *179*; Davy Crockett (King of the Wild Frontier), *179*; Great Locomotive Chase, The, *182*; Light In The Forest, The, *191*; Old Yeller, *196*; Them!, *870*; Westward Ho The Wagons, *212*

Parker, Jean: Bluebeard, *654*; Flying Deuces, *261*; Ghost Goes West, The, *267*; Little Women, *519*

Parker, Kim: Fiend without a Face, *684*

Parker, Lara: Race with the Devil, *732*

Parker, Monica: Improper Channels, *286*

Parker, Norman: Killing Hour, The, *709*

Parker, Sarah Jessica: Flight of the Navigator, *837*; Girls Just Want to Have Fun, *268*; Somewhere, Tomorrow, *206*

Parker, Suzy: Chamber of Horrors, *661*

Parkins, Barbara: Asylum, *647*; Christina, *31*; Shout at the Devil, *135*; To Catch a King, *756*

Parks, Catherine: Friday the 13th, Part III, *690*

Parks, Michael: Bible, The, *410*; ffolkes, *53*; Hard Country, *68*; Savannah Smiles, *203*; Sidewinder 1, *135*

Parlo, Dita: Grand Illusion, *476*

Parnell, Emory: Trail of Robin Hood, *939*

Parrish, Helen: In Old California, *905*; Sunset Serenade, *935*

Parrish, John: Borrowed Trouble, *885*; Dead Don't Dream, The, *892*; Unexpected Guest, *942*

Parrish, Julie: Doberman Gang, The, *43*

Parsons, Estelle: Bonnie and Clyde, *21*; For Pete's Sake, *262*; Rachel, Rachel, *573*; Watermelon Man, *378*

Parsons, Louella: Hollywood Hotel, *787*; Without Reservations, *382*

Parsons, Nancy: Motel Hell, *718*; Porky's II: The Next Day, *333*

Parton, Dolly: Best Little Whorehouse in Texas, The, *771*; Nine to Five, *319*; Rhinestone, *340*

Pascaud, Nathale: Mr. Hulot's Holiday, *311*

Paschalidis, Nicos: Fantasies, *463*

Passanante, Jean: Return of the Secaucus 7, *339*

Pataki, Michael: Graduation Day, *694*; Grave Of The Vampire, *695*; High Noon, Part Two, *903*; Rocky IV, *582*

Paterson, Bill: Comfort and Joy, *246*; Private Function, A, *335*

Pate, Michael: Mad Dog Morgan, *94*; Something of Value, *138*; Wild Duck, The, *634*

Patinkin, Mandy: Daniel, *444*; Maxie, *308*; Night of the Juggler, *107*; Yentl, *813*

Paton, Charles: Blackmail, *414*

Patrick, Dennis: Dear Dead Delilah, *672*; Joe, *502*

Patrick, Gail: Brewster's Millions (1945), *234*

Patrick, Joan: Astro-Zombies, *646*

Patrick, Lee: Black Bird, The, *230*; Fuller Brush Girl, The, *264*; Mildred Pierce, *534*

Patrick, Nigel: Mackintosh Man, The, *94*; Raintree County, *574*

Patric, Gil: Hoppy's Holiday, *904*

Patten, Joyce Van: Mikey and Nicky, *309*

Patten, Luana: Johnny Tremain, *187*; So Dear to My Heart, *206*

Patterson, Elizabeth: Colonel Effingham's Raid, *246*; Sky's the Limit, The, *803*

Patterson, Sarah: Company of Wolves, The, 825

Pattnosh, Jeremy: Certain Sacrifice, A, 429

Patton-Hall, Michael: Escapes, 835

Patton, Mark: Anna to the Infinite Power, 817; Nightmare on Elm Street Part 2: Freddy's Revenge, A, 722

Pauer, Henrik: Time Stands Still, 619

Paulin, Scott: Cat People (Remake), 660; Teen Wolf, 751

Paull, Morgan: Fade to Black, 682

Paulsen, Albert: Laughing Policeman, The, 88

Paulson, Pat: Night Patrol, 318

Paul, Alexandra: 8 Million Ways to Die, 47; American Flyers, 396; Christine, 662

Paul, Rosemary: Dead Easy, 447

Paul, Stuart: Falling in Love Again, 258

Pavan, Marisa: Drum Beat, 894; What Price Glory, 379

Pavarotti, Luciano: Yes, Giorgio, 813

Pavlow, Muriel: Malta Story, The, 527

Pawley, William: Prairie Moon, 922; Rough Riders' Roundup, 928

Payant, Gilles: Red Red, 173

Payne, John: Dodsworth, 452; Razor's Edge, The (Original), 576; Slightly Scarlet, 595; Tennessee's Partner, 937

Payne, Julie: Private School, 335

Payne, Sally: Jesse James at Bay, 905; Man From Music Mountain, 912

Pays, Amanda: Oxford Blues, 556

Payton-Wright, Pamela: Going in Style, 269; Resurrection, 858

Paz, Danny de la: Barbarosa, 881

Peaker, E. J.: Four Deuces, The, 59; Graduation Day, 694; Hello, Dolly!, 787

Pearce, Jacqueline: Don't Raise the Bridge, Lower the River, 253

Pearce, Joanne: Morons from Outer Space, 314

Pearce, Mary Vivian: Mondo Trasho, 312; Multiple Maniacs, 718; Pink Flamingos, 330

Pearce, Tim: Adventures of Sherlock Holmes: A Scandal in Bohemia, 2

Pearcy, Patricia: Squirm, 747

Pease, Patsy: He Knows You're Alone, 696

Peck, Gregory: Arabesque, 9; Behold a Pale Horse, 407; Big Country, 882; Boys from Brazil, The, 656; Guns of Navarone, The, 68; How the West Was Won, 904; MacArthur, 525; Mackenna's Gold, 911; Marooned, 851; Moby Dick, 102; Omen, The, 726; On the Beach, 854; Roman Holiday, 583; Sea Wolves, The, 130; Spellbound, 746; To Kill a Mockingbird, 619; Twelve O'Clock High, 155; Yearling, The, 213

Peck, J. Eddie: Dangerously Close, 668

Pecoraro, Susu: Camila, 424

Pedersen, Maren: Witchcraft Through the Ages (HAXAN), 637

Pederson, Chris: Suburbia, 606

Pedone, Mario: Endgame, 834

Peers, Lisa: Solo, 596; Sunday Too Far Away, 608

Pegg, Vester: Colorado, 889

Peil, Ed: Blue Steel, 885

Peled, Zipora: Last Winter, The, 515

Pelé, P: Minor Miracle, A, 192; Victory, 158

Pelikan, Lisa: Ghoulies, 693

Pendergrass, Teddy: Soup for One, 356

Pendleton, Ann: Rootin' Tootin' Rhythm, 928

Pendleton, Austin: Great Smokey Roadblock, The, 65; Short Circuit, 862; Simon, 352; What's Up Doc?, 380

Pendleton, Nat: Dr. Kildare's Strange Case, 43

Penhaligon, Susan: Land That Time Forgot, The, 847; Nasty Habits, 317; Patrick, 726; Uncanny, The, 760

Pennock, Chris: Great Texas Dynamite Chase, The, 66

Penny, Joe: Gangster Wars, 61

Penn, Christopher: All the Right Moves, 394; Pale Rider, 921; Rumble Fish, 585; Wild Life, The, 382

Penn, Leonard: Dead Don't Dream, The, 892; Hoppy's Holiday, 904

Penn, Sean: Bad Boys, 404; Crackers, 248; Falcon and the Snowman, The, 461; Fast Times at Ridgemont High, 258; Racing with the Moon, 573

Peno, Elizabeth: Down and Out in Beverly Hills, 254

Peña, Elizabeth: Crossover Dreams, 775

People, The Village: Can't Stop the Music, 773

Peppard, George: Blue Max, The, 20; Breakfast at Tiffany's, 419; Damnation Alley, 827; How the West Was Won, 904; Newman's Law, 106; Pendulum, 113; Tobruk, 153

Pera, Marília: Mixed Blood, 101; Pixote, 563

Pereau, Gigi: Yolanda and The Thief, 640

Pereio, Paulo Cesar: I Love You (Eu Te Amo), 491

Perez, Jose: Short Eyes, 593

Perkins, Anthony: Black Hole, The, 821; Catch-22, 239; Crimes of Passion, 440; Desire Under the Elms, 449; ffolkes, 53; Lonely Man, The, 909; Mahogany, 527; On the Beach, 854; Psycho III, 731; Psycho II, 731; Psycho, 731; Ravishing Idiot, The, 337; Winter Kills, 636

Perkins, Elizabeth: About Last Night, 388

Perkins, Millie: Cockfighter, 32; Diary of Anne Frank, The, 451; Ensign Pulver, 255; Haunting Passion, The, 840; Ride in the Whirlwind, 925; Shooting, The, 931; Table for Five, 610; Wild in the Country, 634

Perkins, Osgood: Scarface (original), 129

Perlman, Rhea: My Little Pony: The Movie, 194

Perlman, Ron: Quest for Fire, 858

Perreau, Gigi: Journey to the Center of Time, 846

Perrine, Valerie: Agency, 390; Border, The,

22; Can't Stop the Music, 773; Electric Horseman, The, 456; Last American Hero, The, 86; Lenny, 516; Mr. Billion, 100; Slaughterhouse Five, 862; Three Little Pigs, The, 209; Water, 377

Perrin, Jacques: Z, 641

Perry, Carol: Demons of Ludlow, The, 673

Perry, Len: Alligator Shoes, 394

Perry, Roger: Count Yorga, Vampire, 664; Revenge, 735

Perry, Susan: Knock on Any Door, 509

Persky, Lisa Jane: Sure Thing, The, 361

Persoff, Nehemiah: Comancheros, The, 889; Never Steal Anything Small, 795; Some Like It Hot, 356; Wrong Man, The, 766; Yentl, 813

Pertwee, Jon: House That Dripped Blood, The, 701

Pesci, Joe: Easy Money, 254; Eureka, 459; Raging Bull, 574

Pescow, Donna: Jake Speed, 78; Saturday Night Fever, 801

Peters, Bernadette: Annie, 769; Heartbeeps, 184; Jerk, The, 289; Longest Yard, The, 92; Pennies from Heaven, 797; Silent Movie, 351; Sleeping Beauty, 205

Peters, Brock: Adventures of Huckleberry Finn, The, 70; Framed, 60; Incredible Journey of Dr. Meg Laurel, The, 494; Pawnbroker, The, 560; Puss in Boots, 200;

Peters, Clark: Mona Lisa, 537

Peters Jr., House: Twilight in the Sierras, 941; Under California Stars, 942; Winning of the West, 946

Peters, Jean: Apache, 879; Viva Zapata!, 629

Peters, Lorraine: Adventures of Sherlock Holmes: The Dancing Men, 3

Peters, Luan: Twins of Evil, 760

Peters, Werner: Corrupt Ones, The, 35

Petersen, William: To Live and Die in L.A., 153; Manhunter, 97

Peterson, Cassandra: Echo Park, 455

Peterson, Nan: Hideous Sun Demon, The, 697

Peterson, Stewart: Against a Crooked Sky, 878; Where the Red Fern Grows, 212

Petraglia, Ricardo: Gabriela, 265

Petrella, Ian: Christmas Story, A, 177

Petrillo, Sammy: Boys from Brooklyn, The, 656

Pettet, Joanna: Casino Royale, 239; Cry of the Innocent, 37; Double Exposure, 678; Group, The, 480; Night of the Generals, 107

Peyser, Penny: Frisco Kid, The, 897; In-Laws, The, 286; Wild Times, 945

Peyton, Claudia: Bloodbeat, 653

Périer, François: Z, 641

Pfeiffer, Dedee: Vamp, 760

Pfeiffer, Michelle: Falling in Love Again, 258; Grease 2, 785; Into the Night, 496; Ladyhawke, 86; Sweet Liberty, 362

Pflug, JoAnn: M*A*S*H, 307

Phelps, Lee: Anna Christie, 399

Philbin, Mary: Phantom of the Opera, 727

Philippe, Gerard: La Ronde, 295

Philips, Mary: Farewell to Arms, A, 463

Philips, Patricia: Came a Hot Friday, 27

Philip, John Van Ness: Bostonians, The, 417

Phillips, Bill: Flat Top, 57

Phillips, Bruce: Shaker Run, 132

Phillips, Howard: Last Mile, The, 514

Phillips, Leslie: Gamma People, The, 839

Phillips, Mackenzie: American Graffiti, 218; Love Child, 523; Rafferty and the Gold Dust Twins, 337

Phillips, Michelle: American Anthem, 395; Death Squad, The, 40; Man with Bogart's Face, The, 96

Phillips, Sian: Carpathian Eagle, 659; Doctor and the Devils, The, 676; Murphy's War, 104

Phipps, Max: Nate and Hayes, 105

Phoenix, Leaf: SpaceCamp, 864

Phoenix, River: Explorers, 836; Stand By Me, 101

Pialat, Maurice: A Nos Amours, 387

Piantadosi, Joseph: Schlock, 346

Picardo, Robert: Explorers, 836

Piccoli, Michel: Contempt, 247; Dangerous Moves, 443; Discreet Charm Of The Bourgeoisie, The, 251; Peril, 561

Picerni, Paul: To Hell and Back, 152; Untouchables: Alcatraz Express, The, 157

Pichel, Irving: Oliver Twist, 550

Pickens, Slim: 1941, 319; Apple Dumpling Gang, The, 171; Blazing Saddles, 230; Cowboys, The, 890; Dr. Strangelove or How I Learned to Stop Worrying and Love the Bomb, 252; Ginger In The Morning, 472; Hawmps!, 277; Honeysuckle Rose, 788; Howling, The, 701; Mr. Billion, 100; One-Eyed Jacks, 920; Tom Horn, 939; White Line Fever, 162

Pickett, Cindy: Call to Glory, 424; Ferris Bueller's Day Off, 259; Hysterical, 284

Pickford, Mary: Sparrows, 598

Pickles, Vivian: Candleshoe, 175; Harold and Maude, 276

Pickup, Ronald: Wagner, 811

Picon, Molly: Fiddler on the Roof, 779; For Pete's Sake, 262

Pidgeon, Walter: Big Red, 173; Dark Command, 891; Forbidden Planet, 838; Funny Girl, 782; House Across the Bay, The, 489; Million Dollar Mermaid, 794; Voyage to the Bottom of the Sea, 874

Pieral, Bertheau, Julien: That Obscure Object of Desire, 615

Pierce Jr., Charles B.: Norseman, The, 108

Pierce, Stark: Kill Point, 83

Pierpoint, Eric: Windy City, 635

Pierre, Bernard: Return of Martin Guerre, The, 578

Pigaut, Roger: Simple Story, A, 594

Pilbeam, Nova: Man Who Knew Too Much, The (original), 715; Young and Innocent, 166

Pinal, Silvia: Exterminating Angel, The, 257;

Simon of the Desert, *352;* Viridiana, *628;* Shark! (aka Maneaters!), *133*

Pinchot, Bronson: Risky Business, *341*

Pinero, Miguel: Miami Vice, *98*

Pine, Robert: Apple Dumpling Gang Rides Again, The, *171;* Empire of the Ants, *833*

Pinkerton, Robert: RSVP, *343*

Pinsent, Gordon: Case of Libel, A, *427;* Silence of the North, *593*

Pintauro, Danny: Cujo, *667*

Pioneers, Bob Nolan and the Sons of the: Heart of the Golden West, *901;* Song of Nevada, *933;* Song of Texas, *933;* Sunset Serenade, *935;* Under California Stars, *942;* Yellow Rose of Texas, *946*

Pioneers, Sons of the: Call of the Canyon, *887;* Old Corral, The, *919*

Pio, Elith: Witchcraft Through the Ages (HAXAN), *637*

Piper, Kelly: Maniac, *714*

Piscopo, Joe: Johnny Dangerously, *290;* Wise Guys, *382*

Pisier, Marie-France: Chanel Solitaire, *430;* Cousine, Cousine, *248;* Love on the Run, *524;* Other Side of Midnight, The, *554*

Pistilli, Luigi: Death Rides a Horse, *892*

Pisu, Mario: Juliet of the Spirits, *291*

Pitchford, Pamela: Adventures of Sherlock Holmes: The Naval Treaty, *4*

Pitoeff, Sacha: Last Year At Marienbad, *516*

Pitoniak, Anne: Agnes of God, *390*

Pitts, ZaSu: Dames, *776;* Francis, the Talking Mule, *263;* Life With Father, *299;* Nurse Edith Cavell, *548*

Pitt, Ingrid: House That Dripped Blood, The, *701;* Where Eagles Dare, *161;* Wicker Man, The, *765*

Place, Mary Kay: Modern Problems, *311;* New York, New York, *795;* Smooth Talk, *596*

Plana, Tony: Salvador, *587*

Planchon, Roger: Return of Martin Guerre, The, *578*

Plant, Robert (vocals): Song Remains the Same, The, *803*

Platt, Edward: Rebel without a Cause, *576*

Pleasence, Donald: All Quiet on the Western Front, *393;* Alone in the Dark, *644;* Ambassador, The, *395;* Better Late than Never, *228;* Circus Of Horrors, *663;* Count of Monte Cristo, The (Remake), *36;* Creepers, *665;* Devonsville Terror, The, *674;* Dracula (Remake), *678;* Escape from New York, *49;* Fantastic Voyage, *836;* Halloween II, *695;* Halloween, *695;* Horsemasters, *185;* Journey Into Fear, *503;* Last Tycoon, The, *515;* Monster Club, The, *717;* Night of the Generals, *107;* Puma Man, The, *732;* Sgt. Pepper's Lonely Hearts Club Band, *802;* Soldier Blue, *933;* Telefon, *147;* Terror in the Aisles, *753;* THX 1138, *872;* Uncanny, The, *760;* You Only Live Twice, *166*

Pleshette, Suzanne: Belarus File, The, *13;* Birds, The, *651;* Blackbeard's Ghost, *173;*

Hot Stuff, *283;* Nevada Smith, *917;* Oh, God! Book II, *323;* Shaggy D.A., The, *204;* Ugly Dachshund, The, *211*

Plimpton, Martha: Goonies, The, *63;* River Rat, The, *581*

Plowboys, Polly Jenkins and her: Man From Music Mountain, *912*

Plowden, Melvin: Rappin', *799*

Plowden, Melinda: Billy The Kid Vs. Dracula, *651*

Plowright, Joan: Brimstone and Treacle, *657;* Britannia Hospital, *235;* Equus, *458*

Plummer, Amanda: Daniel, *444;* Hotel New Hampshire, The, *489;* World According to Garp, The, *639*

Plummer, Christopher: Amateur, The, *395;* Boy in Blue, The, *418;* Disappearance, The, *43;* Dreamscape, *832;* Eyewitness, *682;* Fall of the Roman Empire, The, *462;* Hanover Street, *481;* High Point, *280;* International Velvet, *186;* Lily in Love, *299;* Man Who Would Be King, The, *96;* Murder By Decree, *103;* Night of the Generals, *107;* Ordeal By Innocence, *111;* Return of the Pink Panther, The, *339;* Silent Partner, The, *743;* Somewhere in time, *863;* Sound of Music, The, *804;* Star Crash, *864;* Thorn Birds, The, *617*

Podell, Rick: Underground Aces, *374*

Podesta, Rosanna: Hercules, *841*

Pogue, Ken: Grey Fox, The, *899;* One Magic Christmas, *552*

Poiret, Jean: Last Metro, The, *514*

Poitier, Sidney: Bedford Incident, The, *407;* Buck and the Preacher, *886;* Defiant Ones, The, *448;* Greatest Story Ever Told, The, *478;* Guess Who's Coming to Dinner, *273;* Guess Who's Coming to Dinner, *480;* In the Heat of the Night, *494;* Let's Do It Again, *298;* Lilies of the Field, *518;* Organization, The, *111;* Paris Blues, *558;* Piece of the Action, A, *329;* Raisin in the Sun, A, *575;* Something of Value, *138;* They Call Me Mister Tibbs!, *148;* To Sir with Love, *619;* Uptown Saturday Night, *376*

Polanski, Roman: Andy Warhol's Dracula, *645;* Tenant, The, *751*

Poletti, Victor: And the Ship Sails On, *398*

Polic II, Henry: When Things Were Rotten, *380*

Polito, Jon: Fire With Fire, *464*

Polito, Lina: Love and Anarchy, *301*

Polk, Oscar: Green Pastures, The, *479*

Pollack, Sydney: Tootsie, *369*

Pollard, Michael J.: Bonnie and Clyde, *21;* Enter Laughing, *256;* Wild Angels, The, *163*

Pollard, Snub: Golden Age of Comedy, The, *270*

Pollock, Channing: Judex, *79*

Pontoppidan, Clara: Witchcraft Through the Ages (HAXAN), *637*

Popof, Wladimir: Red Balloon, The, *201*

Poppe, Nils: Devil's Eye, The, *250*

Porta, Fred La: Hideous Sun Demon, The, *697*

Porter, Don: Candidate, The, *425;* White Line Fever, *162*

Porter, Eric: Adventures of Sherlock Holmes: The Final Problem, *4;* Adventures of Sherlock Holmes: The Red-Headed League, *5;* Antony and Cleopatra, *401;* Thirty-Nine Steps, The (Second Remake), *149*

Porter, Jean: Till the End of Time, *618*

Portman, Eric: 49th Parallel, The, *468;* Bedford Incident, The, *407*

Poschl, Hanna: Querelle, *572*

Poston, Tom: Happy Hooker, The, *275;* Soldier in the Rain, *596;* Up the Academy, *375;* Zotz!, *386*

Potter, Madeleine: Bostonians, The, *417*

Potter, Michael: Female Trouble, *259*

Potts, Annie: Corvette Summer, *35;* Ghostbusters, *267;* Heartaches, *484;* Pretty in Pink, *567*

Potts, Cliff: Last Ride of the Dalton Boys, The, *908;* Silent Running, *862*

Poujouly, Georges: Forbidden Games, *467*

Powell, Dick: 42nd Street, *781;* Cornered, *35;* Dames, *776;* Footlight Parade, *780;* Gold Diggers of 1933, *783;* Hollywood Hotel, *787;* Midsummer Night's Dream, A, *852;* Murder My Sweet, *103*

Powell, Eleanor: Broadway Melody of 1936, *772;* Broadway Melody of 1938, *773;* Thousands Cheer, *808*

Powell, Jane: Royal Wedding, *800;* Seven Brides for Seven Brothers, *802*

Powell, Lovelady: Happy Hooker, The, *275*

Powell, Randy: Desperate Women, *893*

Powell, Robert: Dark Forces, *669;* Jigsaw Man, The, *708;* Mahler, *527;* Secrets, *590;* Spirit of the Dead, *746;* Thirty-Nine Steps, The (Second Remake) *149*

Powell, William: After the Thin Man, *6;* How to Marry a Millionaire, *284;* Kennel Murder Case, The, *82;* Libeled Lady, *298;* Life With Father, *299;* Mr. Peabody and the Mermaid, *311;* Mr. Roberts, *311;* My Man Godfrey, *317;* Senator Was Indiscreet, The, *349;* Shadow of the Thin Man, *132;* Song of the Thin Man, *138;* Star of Midnight, *139;* Thin Man Goes Home, The, *149;* Thin Man, The, *149;* Ziegfeld Follies, *814*

Powers, Mala: Cyrano De Bergerac, *441;* Tammy and the Bachelor, *611*

Powers, Stefanie: Experiment in Terror, *681;* Boatniks, The, *174;* Die! Die! My Darling!, *675;* Escape to Athena, *50;* Herbie Rides Again, *185;* Man Inside, The, *95;* Night Games, *544*

Powers, Tom: Destination Moon, *830*

Power, Taryn: Count of Monte Cristo, The (Remake), *36;* Sinbad and the Eye of the Tiger, *862;* Tracks, *621;* Big Trail, The, *883*

Power Sr., Tyrone Big Trail, The, *883*

Power, Tyrone: Blood and Sand, *414;* Jesse James, *905;* Mark of Zorro, *97;* Razor's Edge, The (Original), *576;* Witness for the Prosecution, *637*

Praed, Michael: Robin Hood and the Sorcerer, *123*

Prather, Joan: Big Bad Mama, *14;* Deerslayer, The, *893;* Rabbit Test, *337*

Preirs, Wolfgang: Battle of the Commandos, *13*

Preisser, June: Babes in Arms, *769;* Strike Up the Band, *360*

Preiss, Wolfgang: Raid on Rommel, *118*

Prejean, Albert: Crazy Ray, The, *826*

Preminger, Otto: Stalag 17, *139;* They Got Me Covered, *366*

Prentiss, Paula: Black Marble, The, *413;* Buddy, Buddy, *235;* Last of the Red Hot Lovers, *296;* Parallax View, The, *557;* Saturday the 14th, *739;* What's New Pussycat?, *379;* World of Henry Orient, The, *384*

Presby, Shannon: New Kids, The, *721*

Prescott, Robert: Bachelor Party, *222*

Presley, Elvis: Blue Hawaii, *771;* Change of Habit, *430;* Double Trouble, *777;* Flaming Star, *896;* Fun in Acapulco, *781;* Girls! Girls! Girls!, *783;* G.I. Blues, *782;* Harum Scarum, *787;* It Happpened at the World's Fair, *789;* Jailhouse Rock, *789;* King Creole, *790;* Love Me Tender, *910;* Loving You, *793;* Paradise Hawaiian Style, *797;* Roustabout, *800;* Speedway, *805;* This Is Elvis, *808;* Tickle Me, *809;* Viva Las Vegas, *811;* Wild in the Country, *634*

Presle, Micheline: Nea (A Young Emmanuelle), *542*

Presnay, Pierre: Grand Illusion, *476*

Presnell, Harve: Paint Your Wagon, *797;* Unsinkable Molly Brown, The, *810*

Pressman, Lawrence: Hellstrom Chronicle, The, *841;* Rehearsal for Murder, *120;* Streethawk, *142*

Presson, Jason: Explorers, *836*

Preston, J. A.: High Noon, Part Two, *903;* Real Life, *338;* Remo Williams: The Adventure Begins, *120*

Preston, Kelly: Metalstorm: The Destruction of Jared-Syn, *852;* Mischief, *310;* Secret Admirer, *346;* SpaceCamp, *864*

Preston, Mike: Metalstorm: The Destruction of Jared-Syn, *852;* Road Warrior, The, *859*

Preston, Robert: Blood on the Moon, *884;* How the West Was Won, *904;* Junior Bonner, *906;* Last Starfighter, The, *848;* Mame, *793;* Music Man, The, *794;* Rehearsal for Murder, *120;* Semi-Tough, *349;* S.O.B., *355;* This Gun for Hire, *150;* Tulsa, *623;* Victor/Victoria, *377;* Wake Island, *159*

Price, Alan: Don't Look Back, *777;* Oh, Alfie, *549;* O Lucky Man!, *548*

Price, Dennis: Horror Hospital, *699;* Horror of Frankenstein, *699;* Kind Hearts and Coronets, *292;* Tunes of Glory, *624;* Twins of

Evil, 760

Price, Hal: South of the Border, 934

Price, Nancy: Stars Look Down, The, 601

Price, Paul: Ritz, The, 342

Price, Vincent: Abominable Dr. Phibes, The, 643; Adventures of Captain Fabian, 2; Bloodbath at the House of Death, 230; Champagne for Caesar, 240; Dr. Phibes Rises Again, 676; Escapes, 835; Fly, The (original), 686; His Kind of Woman, 73; House of the Long Shadows, 700; House of Wax, 700; House on Haunted Hill, 700; Journey Into Fear, 503; Journey into Fear, 708; Last Man On Earth, The, 848; Laura, 88; Masque of the Red Death, The, 716; Master of the World, 851; Monster Club, The, 717; Oblong Box, The, 725; Pit and the Pendulum, The, 728; Raven, The, 733; Return of the Fly, The, 735; Scavenger Hunt, 346; Scream and Scream Again, 740; Snow White and the Seven Dwarfs, 205; Tales of Terror, 751; Theater of Blood, 754; Three Musketeers, The (1948), 150; Tomb of Ligeia, 757

Prima, Louis: Manhattan Merry-Go-Round, 913

Primus, Barry: Boxcar Bertha, 23; Jake Speed, 78

Prim, Suzy: Mayerling, 531

Prince: Purple Rain, 799; Under The Cherry Moon, 626

Prince, William: Cyrano De Bergerac, 441; Gauntlet, The, 62; Soldier, The, 137; Spies Like Us, 356; Sybil, 610

Principal, Victoria: I Will, I Will . . . For Now, 285; Life and Times of Judge Roy Bean, The, 909; Pleasure Palace, 564

Prine, Andrew: Bandolero!, 881; Eliminators, 832; Grizzly, 695; Miracle Worker, The, 535; They're Playing with Fire, 616; Town That Dreaded Sundown, The, 759

Pringle, Bryan: Haunted Honeymoon, 277

Prinsloo, Sandra: Gods Must Be Crazy, The, 269

Prival, Lucien: Mr. Wong, Detective, 101

Prochnow, Jurgen: Das Boot (The Boat), 38; Dune, 832; Forbidden, 467; Keep, The, 708

Prokhorenko, Shanna: Ballad of a Soldier, 404

Prophet, Melissa: Invasion U.S.A., 77

Prosky, Robert: Christine, 662; Hanky Panky, 274; Lords of Discipline, The, 521

Provine, Dorothy: 30 Foot Bride of Candy Rock, The, 366; Good Neighbor Sam, 270; It's a Mad Mad Mad Mad World, 288; Never a Dull Moment, 195; That Darn Cat, 208; Who's Minding the Mint?, 381

Prowse, Dave: Empire Strikes Back, The, 833; Return of the Jedi, 859

Prowse, Juliet: G.I. Blues, 782

Pryce, Jonathan: Brazil, 233; Breaking Glass, 772; Doctor and the Devils, The, 676; Haunted Honeymoon, 277; Something Wicked This Way Comes, 863

Pryor, Nicholas: Force Five, 59; Happy Hooker, The, 275; Risky Business, 341

Pryor, Richard: Bingo Long Traveling All-Stars and Motor Kings, The, 229; Blue Collar, 415; Brewster's Millions (1985), 235; Bustin' Loose, 236; California Suite, 237; Car Wash, 239; Greased Lightning, 64; Jo Jo Dancer, Your Life Is Calling, 502; Lady Sings the Blues, 791; Muppet Movie, The, 193; Richard Pryor Live on the Sunset Strip, 341; Richard Pryor—Here and Now, 340; Richard Pryor—Live and Smokin', 341; Richard Pryor—Live in Concert, 341; Silver Streak, 352; Some Call It Loving, 597; Some Kind of Hero, 355; Stir Crazy, 359; Superman III, 869; Toy, The, 371; Uptown Saturday Night, 376; Which Way Is Up?, 381; Wholly Moses!, 381; Wiz, The, 812; Man They Could Not Hang, The, 714

Pszoniak, Wojiech: Danton, 444

Pugh, Willard: Color Purple, The, 436

Puglia, Frank: Without Reservations, 382

Puglisi, Aldo: Seduced and Abandoned, 348

Puleo, Johnny: Trapeze, 621

Pulver, Lilo: One, Two, Three, 324

Purcell, Dick: King of the Zombies, 709

Purcell, Lee: Amazing Howard Hughes, The, 395; Big Wednesday, 411; Eddie Macon's Run, 47; Mr. Majestyk, 101; Witching, The (Necromancy), 765

Purdom, Edmund: Pieces, 728

Puri, Amrish: Indiana Jones and the Temple of Doom, 843

Purl, Linda: Visiting Hours, 762

Purviance, Edna: Charlie Chaplin—The Early Years, Vol.1, 241; Charlie Chaplin—The Early Years, Vol.2, 241; Charlie Chaplin—The Early Years, Vol.3, 241; Charlie Chaplin—The Early Years, Vol.4, 241; Woman of Paris, A, 638

Pushin, Anne: His Name Was King, 903

Pyle, Denver: Hawmps!, 277; Hellfire, 902; Hills of Utah, The, 903

Quaid, Dennis and Randy: Long Riders, The, 910

Quaid, Dennis: Bill, 411; Breaking Away, 233; Dreamscape, 832; Enemy Mine, 834; Jaws 3, 707; Night the Lights Went Out in Georgia, The, 545; Right Stuff, The, 580; Tough Enough, 154

Quaid, Randy: Apprenticeship of Duddy Kravitz, The, 401; Bound For Glory, 418; Breakout, 24; Fool For Love, 466; Foxes, 469; Last Detail, The, 513; Last Picture Show, The, 514; Midnight Express, 533; Of Mice and Men, 549; Slugger's Wife, The, 354; Wild Life, The, 382

Qualen, John: Dark Waters, 445; Grapes of Wrath, The, 477; Jungle Book, 187; Our Daily Bread, 555

Quan, Ke Huy: Indiana Jones and the Temple of Doom, 843

Quarry, Robert: Count Yorga, Vampire, *664;* Dr. Phibes Rises Again, *676*

Quayle, Anna: Chitty Chitty Bang Bang, *177;* Hard Day's Night, A, *786*

Quayle, Anthony: Anne of the Thousand Days, *400;* Everything You Always Wanted to Know about Sex But Were Afraid to Ask, *257;* Guns of Navarone, The, *68;* Holocaust2000, *698;* Moses, *539;* Murder By Decree, *103;* QB VII, *571;* Tamarind Seed, The, *145;* Wrong Man, The, *766*

Quennessen, Valerie: Summer Lovers, *607*

Quick, Diana: Ordeal By Innocence, *111*

Quigley, Charles: Daredevils of the Red Circle, *38*

Quillan, Eddie: Mutiny on the Bounty (Original), *105*

Quillan, Marie: Melody Trail, *915*

Quilley, Denis: King David, *507;* Lion and the Hawk, The, *89;* Privates on Parade, *336*

Quinlan, Kathleen: Hanky Panky, *274;* I Never Promised You a Rose Garden, *491;* Independence Day, *494;* Last Winter, The, *515;* Lifeguard, *518;* Runner Stumbles, The, *585;* Twilight Zone—The Movie, *759;* Warning Sign, *763*

Quinn, Aidan: Reckless, *577*

Quinn, Aileen: Annie, *769*

Quinn, Anthony: Across 110th Street, *1;* Back to Bataan, *11;* Barabbas, *405;* Behold a Pale Horse, *407;* Blood and Sand, *414;* Children of Sanchez, The, *432;* Don is Dead, The, *44;* Greek Tycoon, The, *479;* Guns of Navarone, The, *68;* Heller in Pink Tights, *902;* High Risk, *72;* Hot Spell, *489;* La Strada, *512;* Lawrence of Arabia, *88;* Lion of the Desert, *90;* Message, The (Mohammad, Messenger of God), *533;* Ox-Bow Incident, The, *921;* Requiem for a Heavyweight, *578;* R.P.M. (Revolutions Per Minute), *572;* Sinbad the Sailor, *136;* They Died with their Boots On, *938;* Tycoon, *158;* Viva Zapata!, *629;* Warlock, *944;* Zorba the Greek, *642*

Quinn, Daniele: Band of the Hand, *12*

Quinn, J. C.: Maximum Overdrive, *716*

Quinn, Patricia: Alice's Restaurant, *393;* Unmarried Woman, An, *626;* Witching Time, *765*

Quinones, Adolfo: Breakin' 2 Electric Boogaloo, *772;* Breakin', *771*

Quintano, Gene: Treasure of the Four Crowns, *155*

Quo, Beulah: Yes, Giorgio, *813*

Raab, Kurt: Mussolini and I, *539*

Rabal, Francisco: Stay As You Are, *602*

Rabal, Francisco: Viridiana, *628*

Racete, Francine: Disappearance, The, *43*

Racimo, Victoria: Mountain Men, The, *915;* Prophecy, *730*

Radford, Basil: Winslow Boy, The, *635;* Young and Innocent, *166*

Radi, Nameer: Quest for Fire, *858*

Radner, Gilda: First Family, *261;* Gilda Live, *268;* Hanky Panky, *274;* Haunted Honeymoon, *277;* It Came from Hollywood, *287;* Movers and Shakers, *315;* Woman in Red, The, *383*

Rae, Barbara: Hide in Plain Sight, *487*

Rae, Charlotte: Hair, *785;* Hot Rock, The, *75*

Rafferty, Chips: Wackiest Ship in the Army, The, *377*

Rafferty, Frances: Abbott and Costello in Hollywood, *214*

Raffin, Deborah: Death Wish III, *40;* Demon (God Told Me To), *830;* Forty Carats, *362;* Jungle Heat, *80;* Ransom, *118;* Sentinel, The, *742;* Touched by Love, *621*

Raft, George: Casino Royale, *239;* Hollywood Outtakes, *282;* House Across the Bay, The, *489;* Johnny Angel, *79;* Man with Bogart's Face, The, *96;* Mr. Ace, *100;* Scarface (original), *129;* Some Like It Hot, *356;* They Drive by Night, *148*

Ragsdale, William: Fright Night, *691*

Railsback, Steven: Golden Seal, The, *182;* Lifeforce, *849;* Stunt Man, The, *606;* Escape 2000, *835;* Helter Skelter, *486;* Torchlight, *620*

Raimu: Baker's Wife, The, *224;* Marius, *529*

Rain, Jeramie: Last House on the Left, *711*

Rainer, Luise: Good Earth, The, *475*

Raines, Cristina: Duellists, The, *46;* Nightmares, *722;* Sentinel, The, *742;* Touched by Love, *621*

Raines, Ella: Ride the Man Down, *926;* Senator Was Indiscreet, The, *349;* Tall in the Saddle, *936*

Rains, Claude: Adventures of Robin Hood, The, *2;* Angel on My Shoulder, *399;* Caesar and Cleopatra, *423;* Casablanca, *427;* Here Comes Mr. Jordan, *279;* Juarez, *504;* King's Row, *508;* Mr. Smith Goes to Washington, *536;* Notorious, *725;* Now, Voyager, *547;* Passage to Marseilles, *113;* Prince and the Pauper, The (Original), *199;* Sea Hawk, The, *130;* They Made Me a Criminal, *616*

Raitt, Bonnie: No Nukes, *795*

Rall, Tommy: Invitation to the Dance, *788;* Kiss Me Kate, *790*

Ralph, Jessie: Camille, *425;* Good Earth, The, *475;* Little Lord Fauntleroy, *519*

Ralston, Jobyna: Wings, *164*

Ralston, Vera Hruba: Dakota, *890;* Fighting Kentuckian, The, *896*

Rambal, Enrique: Exterminating Angel, The, *257*

Rambeau, Marjorie: Palooka, *556;* Min and Bill, *534*

Ramer, Henry: Between Friends, *409*

Ramis, Harold: Ghostbusters, *267;* Stripes, *360*

Ramones, The: Rock 'n' Roll High School, *342*

Ramos, Nick: Legend of Walks Far Woman, The, *909*

Ramos, Rudy: Quicksilver, 572

Rampling, Charlotte: Farewell My Lovely, 52; Night Porter, The, 545; Orca, 726; Purple Taxi, The, 571; Stardust Memories, 358; Stardust Memories, 601; Verdict, The, 628; Zardoz, 877

Ramsden, Denis: Romance With A Double Bass, 343

Ramsden, Frances: Sin of Harold Diddlebock (aka Mad Wednesday), 352

Ramsey, Logan: Joy Sticks, 291; Some Call It Loving, 597

Ramsey, Marion: Police Academy III: Back in Training, 332

Ramsey, Martin: Police Academy II: Their First Assignment, 332

Ramsey, Ward: Dinosaurus!, 675

Ramus, Nick: Windwalker, 946

Randall, Tony: 7 Faces of Dr. Lao, 861; Everything You Always Wanted to Know about Sex But Were Afraid to Ask, 257; Foolin' Around, 261; Lover Come Back, 303; My Little Pony: The Movie, 194; Pillow Talk, 330; Scavenger Hunt, 346

Randal, Monica: Stay As You Are, 602

Randazzo, Teddy: Rock, Rock, Rock, 800

Randig, Ric: Splatter University, 747

Randion: Freaks, 689

Randolph, Jane: Curse of the Cat People, The, 668

Randolph, John: Prizzi's Honor, 569; Serpico, 590; There Was a Crooked Man, 938; Wilbur and Orville: The First To Fly, 212

Ranni, Rodolfo: Funny Dirty Little War (NO HABRA MAS PENSAS ni OLVIDO), 264

Rano, Umberto: Bird with the Crystal Plumage, The, 651

Rappaport, David: Bride, The, 656

Rappaport, Michael: Hardbodies, 275

Rasche, David: Act of Passion, 389

Rasculala, Thalmus: Autobiography of Miss Jane Pittman, The, 402

Rassimov, Rada: Torture Chamber Of Baron Blood, The, 758

Rasulala, Thalmus: Blacula, 652

Rathbone, Basil: Adventures of Robin Hood, The, 2; Adventures of Sherlock Holmes, The, 2; Anna Karenina, 400; Captain Blood, 27; Court Jester, The, 248; David Copperfield, 445; Dawn Patrol, The, 39; Dressed to Kill, 45; Hillbillys in a Haunted House, 280; Hound of the Baskervilles, The (Original), 75; Last Days of Pompeii, The, 513; Magic Sword, The, 191; Mark of Zorro, 97; Pursuit to Algiers, 117; Sherlock Holmes and the Secret Weapon, 134; Tale of Two Cities, A, 611; Tales of Terror, 751; Terror By Night, 148; We're No Angels, 379

Rattray, Heather: Across the Great Divide, 169; Adventures of the Wilderness Family, 170; Mountain Family Robinson, 193; Wilderness Family, Part 2, The, 212

Rattray, Peter: Will, G. Gordon Liddy, 635

Raven, Wayne: Wizard of Gore, The, 766

Rawlinson, Herbert: Borrowed Trouble, 885; Riders of the Deadline, 926; Silent Conflict, 931; Sinister Journey, 932; Strange Gamble, 935

Raye, Martha: Monsieur Verdoux, 313

Raymond, Gary: Jason and the Argonauts, 846

Raymond, Gene: Mr. and Mrs. Smith, 310; Red Dust, 119; Red Dust, 577; Smilin' Through, 803

Raymond, Paula: Blood of Dracula's Castle, 653

Ray, Aldo: Bog, 655; God's Little Acre, 473; Green Berets, The, 66; Inside Out, 77; Men in War, 98; Miss Sadie Thompson, 535; Naked and the Dead, The, 105; We're No Angels, 379

Ray, Gene Anthony: Fame, 778

Ray, James: Mass Appeal, 531

Ray, Johnnie: There's No Business Like Show Business, 808

Reagan, Ronald: Bedtime for Bonzo, 226; Cattle Queen of Montana, 888; Dark Victory, 445; Hellcats of the Navy, 70; King's Row, 508; Knute Rockne—All American, 510; Santa Fe Trail, 929; Tennessee's Partner, 937; This is the Army, 808

Reardon, Peter Brady: Preppies, 333

Reasoner, Harry: Wasn't That a Time!, 811

Reason, Rex: This Island Earth, 871

Rea, Stephen: Danny Boy, 444; Doctor and the Devils, The, 676

Rebar, Alex: Incredible Melting Man, The, 843

Rebhorn, James: He Knows You're Alone, 696; Will, G. Gordon Liddy, 635

Rebiere, Richard: Heavenly Bodies, 278

Reddy, Helen: Airport 1975, 391; Pete's Dragon, 197

Redeker, Quinn: Coast to Coast, 245

Redfield, Dennis: Dead and Buried, 670

Redfield, William: Fantastic Voyage, 836; Hot Rock, The, 75; Mr. Billion, 100

Redford, Robert: All the President's Men, 394; Barefoot in the Park, 224; Bridge Too Far, A, 25; Brubaker, 421; Butch Cassidy and the Sundance Kid, 887; Candidate, The, 425; Chase, The, 431; Downhill Racer, 454; Electric Horseman, The, 456; Great Gatsby, The, 477; Great Waldo Pepper, The, 66; Hot Rock, The, 75; Jeremiah Johnson, 905; Legal Eagles, 88; Natural, The, 542; Out of Africa, 555; Sting, The, 144; Tell Them Willie Boy Is Here, 936; This Property is Condemned, 617; Three Days of the Condor, 150; Way We Were, The, 631

Redgrave, Corin: Excalibur, 835

Redgrave, Lynn: Big Bus, The, 229; Everything You Always Wanted to Know about Sex But Were Afraid to Ask, 257; Happy Hooker, The, 275; Rehearsal for Murder, 120

Redgrave, Michael: Dam Busters, The, *38;* Lady Vanishes, The (original), *710;* Nicholas and Alexandra, *543;* Sea Shall Not Have Them, The, *130;* Stars Look Down, The, *601*

Redgrave, Vanessa: Agatha, *390;* Bear Island, *648;* Blow-Up, *654;* Bostonians, The, *417;* Camelot, *773;* Devils, The, *450;* Julia, *505;* Morgan, *314;* Murder on the Orient Express, *104;* Seven-Per-Cent Solution, The, *131;* Snow White and the Seven Dwarfs, *205;* Trojan Women, The, *622;* Wagner, *811*

Reed, Alyson: Chorus Line, A, *774*

Reed, Dolly: Beyond the Valley of the Dolls, *410*

Reed, Donna: It's a Wonderful Life, *499;* Picture of Dorian Gray, The, *738;* Shadow of the Thin Man, *132;* They Were Expendable, *148*

Reed, George: Green Pastures, The, *479*

Reed, Hal: Doberman Gang, The, *43*

Reed, Ione: Melody Trail, *915*

Reed, Jerry: Gator, *61;* High-Ballin', *71;* Hot Stuff, *283;* Smokey and the Bandit III, *358;* Smokey and the Bandit II, *355;* Smokey and the Bandit, *354;* Survivors, The, *362*

Reed, Lou: Get Crazy, *266;* One Trick Pony, *797*

Reed, Marshall: They Saved Hitler's Brain, *754*

Reed, Oliver: Big Sleep, The, *16;* Blood in the Streets, *19;* Brood, The, *657;* Burnt Offerings, *658;* Class of Miss MacMichael, The, *435;* Condorman, *178;* Devils, The, *450;* Four Musketeers, The, *60;* Great Scout and Cathouse Thursday, The, *899;* Lion of the Desert, *90;* Oliver, *796;* Prince and the Pauper, The (Remake), *198;* Ransom, *118;* Spasms, *746;* Sting II, The, *140;* Ten Little Indians, *147;* Three Musketeers, The (1973), *150;* Tommy, *810;* Venom, *761;* Women in Love, *638*

Reed, Pamela: Best of Times, The, *228;* Clan of the Cave Bear, *824;* Goodbye People, The, *475;* Right Stuff, The, *580;* Young Doctors in Love, *385*

Reed, Philip: Last of the Mohicans, The, *907*

Reed, Robert: Boy in the Plastic Bubble, The, *418;* Death of a Centerfold, *447*

Reed, Sandra: Bus Is Coming, The, *422*

Reed, Tracy: All the Marbles, *217;* Running Scared (1986), *125*

Reed, Walter: Keystone Comedies: Vo. 8, *292*

Reems, Harry: RSVP, *343*

Reese, Wade: Future-Kill, *692*

Reeve, Christopher: Aviator, The, *403;* Bostonians, The, *417;* Deathtrap, *448;* Monsignor, *538;* Sleeping Beauty, *205;* Somewhere in time, *863;* Superman III, *869;* Superman II, *869;* Superman, *868*

Reeves, George: Rancho Notorious, *923;* Strawberry Blonde, The, *604;* Westward Ho The Wagons, *212;*

Reeves, Lisa: Chicken Chronicles, The, *243*

Reeves, Steve: Goliath and the Barbarians, *63;* Hercules Unchained, *841;* Hercules, *71;* Morgan the Pirate, *103*

Regalbuto, Joe: Raw Deal, *119;* Six Weeks, *594;* Streethawk, *142*

Regan, Mary: Heart of the Stag, *484*

Regan, Phil: Manhattan Merry-Go-Round, *913*

Reggiani, Serge: Cat and Mouse, *28;* La Ronde, *295*

Regine: Robert et Robert, *582*

Reicher, Frank: King Kong (original), *709;* Son of Kong, The, *745;* South of the Border, *934*

Reid, Beryl: Beast in The Cellar, The, *649;* Doctor and the Devils, The, *676;* Dr. Phibes Rises Again, *676;* Joseph Andrews, *290;* Psychomania, *731*

Reid, Carl Benton: Trap, The, *759*

Reid, Elliott: Gentlemen Prefer Blondes, *266*

Reid, Kate: Andromeda Strain, The, *817;* Atlantic City, *402;* Circle of Two, *434;* Fire With Fire, *464;* Heaven Help Us, *278;* This Property is Condemned, *617*

Reid, Michael: Stephen King's Night Shift Collection, *747*

Reilly, John: Incredible Journey of Dr. Meg Laurel, The, *494*

Reimer, Elin: Topsy Turvy, *370*

Reineke, Gary: Why Shoot the Teacher?, *633*

Reiner, Carl: 10 from Your Show of Shows, *364;* Dead Men Don't Wear Plaid, *249;* Gidget Goes Hawaiian, *267;* Guide For The Married Man, A, *273;* Pinocchio, *198;* Russians Are Coming, the Russians Are Coming, The, *344*

Reiner, Rob: Enter Laughing, *256;* This Is Spinal Tap, *367;* Thursday's Game, *618;* Where's Poppa?, *381*

Reinhold, Judge: Beverly Hills Cop, *228;* Fast Times at Ridgemont High, *258;* Off Beat, *322;* Roadhouse 66, *122;* Running Scared (1980), *126;* Ruthless People, *344*

Reiniger, Scott: Dawn of the Dead, *670*

Reinking, Ann: All That Jazz, *768;* Micki & Maude, *309;* Movie Movie, *315*

Reischl, Geri: I Dismember Mama, *703*

Reiser, Paul: Aliens, *816*

Reit, Ursula: Willy Wonka and the Chocolate Factory, *213*

Rekert, Winston: Agnes of God, *390;* Heartaches, *484*

Remar, James: 48 Hrs., *262;* Band of the Hand, *12;* Cotton Club, The, *36;* Warriors, The, *160;* Windwalker, *946*

Remberg, Erika: Circus Of Horrors, *663*

Remick, Lee: Anatomy of a Murder, *397;* Baby the Rain Must Fall, *404;* Competition, The, *437;* Days of Wine and Roses, *447;* Experiment in Terror, *681;* Face in the Crowd, A, *461;* Hustling, *490;* No Way to

Treat a Lady, 546; Omen, The, 726; QB VII, 571; Snow Queen, 205; Sometimes a Great Notion, 597; Telefon, 147; Tribute, 631

Remsen, Bert: Borderline, 22; Carny, 426; Code of Silence, 33; Sting II, The, 140

Remy, Albert: 400 Blows, The, 468

Renaldo, Duncan: Fighting Seabees, The, 53; Manhunt in the African Jungle (Secret Service in Darkest Africa), 96; South of the Border, 934

Renay, Liz: Desperate Living, 250

Rennie, Michael: Battle of El Alamein, The, 12; Day the Earth Stood Still, The, 838; Robe, The, 581; Third Man On The Mountain, 208

Renoir, Jean: La Bete Humaine, 510

Renoir, Pierre: La Marseillaise, 511

Reno, Jean: Subway, 142

Reno, Kelly: Black Stallion Returns, The, 173; Black Stallion, The, 173; Brady's Escape, 23

Renzi, Eva: Bird with the Crystal Plumage, The, 651; Funeral In Berlin, 61

Renzi, Maggie: Return of the Secaucus 7, 339

Resines, Antonio: Skyline, 353

Reubens, Paul: Nice Dreams, 318; Pinocchio, 198

Revere, Anne: Body and Soul (Original), 416; National Velvet, 195; Place in the Sun, A, 563; Thin Man Goes Home, The, 149

Revill, Clive: Legend of Hell House, The, 711; Matilda, 308; One Of Our Dinosaurs Is Missing, 196; Private Life of Sherlock Holmes, The, 115

Revolution, The: Purple Rain, 799

Reyes Jr., Ernie: Red Sonja, 120

Reynolds, Burt: 100 Rifles, 920; Best Friends, 227; Best Little Whorehouse in Texas, The, 771; Cannonball Run II, 237; Cannonball Run, 237; City Heat, 243; Deliverance, 41; End, The, 255; Everything You Always Wanted to Know about Sex But Were Afraid to Ask, 257; Fuzz, 265; Gator, 61; Hooper, 283; Hustle, The, 76; Longest Yard, The, 92; Man Who Loved Cat Dancing, The, 912; Man Who Loved Women, The, 306; Operation C.I.A., 110; Paternity, 328; Rough Cut, 124; Semi-Tough, 349; Shamus, 132; Sharky's Machine, 133; Shark! (aka Maneaters!), 133; Silent Movie, 351; Smokey and the Bandit II, 355; Smokey and the Bandit, 354; Starting Over, 358; Stick, 140; Stroker Ace, 361; White Lightning, 162

Reynolds, Dave: One More Saturday Night, 324

Reynolds, Debbie: How the West Was Won, 904; Singin' in the Rain, 802; Tammy and the Bachelor, 611; Unsinkable Molly Brown, The, 810

Reynolds, Debbie (voices only): Charlotte's Web, 176

Reynolds, Freddy: Chant of Jimmie Blacksmith, The, 431

Reynolds, Gene: Tuttles of Tahiti, The, 373

Reynolds, Marjorie: His Kind of Woman, 73; Holiday Inn, 787

Reynolds, Michael J.: Why Shoot the Teacher?, 633

Reynolds, Patrick: Eliminators, 832

Reynolds, Peter: Devil Girl from Mars, 674

Reynolds, William: Away All Boats, 11

Rey, Alejandro: Fun in Acapulco, 781; Ninth Configuration, The, 546; Rita Hayworth: The Love Goddess, 581

Rey, Fernando: Antony and Cleopatra, 401; Discreet Charm Of The Bourgeoisie, The, 251; French Connection II, The, 469; French Connection, The, 60; Grande Bourgeoise, La, 476; High Crime, 72; Hit, The, 73; Monsignor, 538; Quintet, 858; Rustler's Rhapsody, 344; Seven Beauties, 349; That Obscure Object of Desire, 615; Villa Rides, 943; Viridiana, 628

Rhoades, Barbara: There Was a Crooked Man, 938

Rhodes, Cynthia: Runaway, 860; Staying Alive, 805

Rhodes, Earl: Sailor Who Fell from Grace with the Sea, The, 586

Rhodes, Erik: Gay Divorcee, The, 782

Rhodes, Grandon: On Top of Old Smoky, 919

Rhys-Davies, John: Best Revenge, 14; In the Shadow of Kilimanjaro, 704; King Solomon's Mines (1985), 84; Raiders of the Lost Ark, 858; Sahara, 126; Shogun (Short Version), 134

Rialson, Candice: Hollywood Boulevard, 282

Rice, Florence: Riding on Air, 341

Rice, Joel S.: Final Exam, 684

Richard, Keith: Let's Spend the Night Together, 792

Richard, Little: Down and Out in Beverly Hills, 254

Richard, Pierre: Le Chevre (THE GOAT), 298; Les Comperes, 298; Return of the Tall Blond Man with One Black Shoe, The, 339; Tall Blond Man With One Black Shoe, The, 363

Richards, Addison: Our Daily Bread, 555

Richards, Ann: Badman's Territory, 880; Sorry, Wrong Number, 745

Richards, Beah: Guess Who's Coming to Dinner, 273; Guess Who's Coming to Dinner, 480

Richards, Evan: Down and Out in Beverly Hills, 254

Richards, Keith: Gimme Shelter, 783; Sympathy for the Devil, 806; Video Rewind: The Rolling Stones Great Video Hits, 811

Richards, Kim: Escape to Witch Mountain, 181; Meatballs Part II, 308; Return From Witch Mountain, 201; Tuff Turf, 623

Richards, Kyle: Halloween, 695

Richards, Lisa: Rolling Thunder, 123

Richards, Michael: Transylvania6-5000, 371; Young Doctors in Love, 385

Richards, Rick: Cease Fire, *429*

Richardson, Ian: Brazil, *233*

Richardson, Miranda: Dance With a Stranger, *443*

Richardson, Natasha: Adventures of Sherlock Holmes: The Copper Beeches, *3*

Richardson, Ralph: Divorce of Lady X, The, *251*; Dragonslayer, *831*; Exodus, *460*; Fallen Idol, The, *462*; Four Feathers, The, *60*; Greystoke: The Legend of Tarzan, Lord of the Apes, *67*; Heiress, The, *485*; Long Day's Journey into Night, *520*; Looking Glass War, The, *521*; Man in the Iron Mask, The, *95*; O Lucky Man!, *548*; Richard III, *580*; Rollerball, *860*; Tales from the Crypt, *751*; Things to Come, *871*; Time Bandits, *872*; Who Slew Auntie Roo?, *764*; Wrong Box, The, *384*

Richardson, Ricki: Bloody Trail, *884*

Richardson, Sir Ralph: Alice's Adventures in Wonderland, *171*; Wagner, *811*

Richardson, Sy: Repo Man, *338*

Richmond, Kane: Spy Smasher, *139*

Richmond, Warner: Lawman Is Born, A, *908*; New Frontier, *917*

Rich, Adam: Devil and Max Devlin, The, *250*

Rich, Claude: Elusive Corporal, The, *457*

Rich, Irene: Angel and the Badman, *879*; Champ, The (Original), *429*; Check and Double Check, *242*

Rich, Ron: Fortune Cookie, The, *262*

Rickles, Don: Beach Blanket Bingo, *770*; Bikini Beach, *771*; Enter Laughing, *256*; Kelly's Heroes, *81*; Run Silent, Run Deep, *125*; X (The Man with the X-Ray Eyes), *877*

Ridgely, John: Air Force, *7*; Big Sleep, The (Original), *16*

Ridges, Stanley: Mad Miss Manton, The, *304*; Master Race, The, *531*; Mr. Ace, *100*; Possessed, *565*; Winterset, *636*

Riegert, Peter: Americathon, *218*; Animal House, *218*; Chilly Scenes of Winter, *432*; Local Hero, *300*

Rifkin, Ron: Silent Running, *862*; Sunshine Boys, The, *361*

Rigby, Cathy: Great Wallendas, The, *478*

Rigby, Edward: Stars Look Down, The, *601*; Young and Innocent, *166*

Rigg, Diana: Evil Under the Sun, *50*; Great Muppet Caper, The, *183*; Hospital, The, *283*; Little Night Music, A, *793*; On Her Majesty's Secret Service, *110*; Theater of Blood, *754*

Riker, Robin: Alligator, *644*

Riley, Elaine: Borrowed Trouble, *885*; Devil's Playground, *893*; False Paradise, *896*; Hills of Utah, The, *903*; Sinister Journey, *932*; Strange Gamble, *935*

Riley, Jack: Attack of the Killer Tomatoes, *221*; Night Patrol, *318*

Riley, Jeannine: Comic, The, *437*

Rilla, Walter: Gamma People, The, *839*

Rinell, Susan: Just Between Friends, *505*

Ringham, John: Adventures of Sherlock Holmes: The Resident Patient, *5*

Ringwald, Molly: Breakfast Club, The, *233*; Pretty in Pink, *567*; Sixteen Candles, *353*; Spacehunter: Adventures in the Forbidden Zone, *864*; Tempest, *612*

Rinker, Al: King of Jazz, The, *790*

Rinn, Brad: Smithereens, *596*

Riordan, Marjorie: Pursuit to Algiers, *117*

Risdon, Elizabeth: Down Dakota Way, *894*

Ritchard, Cyril: Blackmail, *414*; Hans Brinker, *183*

Ritchie, Clint: Against a Crooked Sky, *878*

Ritter, John: Americathon, *218*; Barefoot Executive, The, *172*; Hero at Large, *279*; They All Laughed, *365*; Wholly Moses!, *381*

Ritter, Kristin: Student Bodies, *749*

Ritter, Thelma: Birdman of Alcatraz, *412*; Misfits, The, *535*; Pillow Talk, *330*; Rear Window, *734*

Ritt, Martin: Slugger's Wife, The, *354*

Ritz, Harry: Silent Movie, *351*

Rivas, Carlos: They Saved Hitler's Brain, *754*

Riva, Emanuelle: Eyes, The Mouth, The, *460*; Hiroshima, Mon Amour, *488*

Rivera, Cecilia: Aguirre: Wrath of God, *6*

Rivero, Joe: Priest of Love, *568*

Rivero, Jorge: Rio Lobo, *927*

Rivers, Joan: Muppets Take Manhattan, The, *194*; Swimmer, The, *609*

Riveyre, Jean: Diary Of A Country Priest, *450*

Riviere, Marie: Aviator's Wife, The, *222*; Aviator's Wife, The, *403*

Roarke, Adam: Four Deuces, The, *59*; Hell's Angels on Wheels, *71*; Stunt Man, The, *606*

Robards Jr., Jason: All the President's Men, *394*; Cabo Blanco, *26*; Comes a Horseman, *889*; Bedlam, *649*; Long Day's Journey into Night, *520*; Sakharov, *587*; St. Valentine's Day Massacre, The, *126*; Abraham Lincoln, *388*; Ballad of Cable Hogue, The, *880*; Boy and His Dog, A, *821*; Day After, The, *828*; Hurricane, *76*; Isle of Dead, *706*; Johnny Got His Gun, *503*; Julia, *505*; Legend of the Lone Ranger, The, *908*; Max Dugan Returns, *531*; Melvin and Howard, *309*; Murders In The Rue Morgue, *720*; Night They Raided Minsky's, The, *319*; Once upon a Time in the West, *919*; Pat Garrett and Billy the Kid, *922*; Raise the Titanic, *118*; Something Wicked This Way Comes, *863*; Thousand Clowns, A, *367*; Tora! Tora! Tora!, *154*

Robards, Sam: Fandango, *258*

Robbins, Christmas: Demon Lover, The, *673*

Robbins, Tim: Howard the Duck, *842*

Robertson, Cliff: Charly, *823*; Dominique Is Dead, *677*; Gidget, *267*; Midway, *99*; Naked and the Dead, The, *105*; Obsession, *725*; Pilot, The, *563*; PT 109, *569*; Shaker Run, *132*; Shoot, *135*; Star 80, *600*; Three Days of the Condor, *150*

Robertson, Dale: Dakota Incident, 891; Last Ride of the Dalton Boys, The, 908

Robertson, David: Attack of the Swamp Creature, 647

Robertson, Patricia: Attack of the Swamp Creature, 647

Robertson, Robbie: Carny, 426

Roberts, Alan: Dinosaurus!, 675

Roberts, Allene: Knock on Any Door, 509; Red House, The, 734; Union Station, 760

Roberts, Arthur: Revenge of the Ninja, 121

Roberts, Christian: To Sir with Love, 619

Roberts, Eric: Coca Cola Kid, The, 246; King of the Gypsies, 508; Pope of Greenwich Village, The, 564; Raggedy Man, 733; Runaway Train, 125; Star 80, 600

Roberts, Glenn: Crater Lake Monster, The, 665

Roberts, Lynne: Billy The Kid Returns, 883; Robin Hood of Texas, 927; Sioux City Sue, 933

Roberts, Pernell: Four Rode Out, 897; High Noon, Part Two, 903; Kashmiri Run, The, 81; Magic of Lassie, The, 191

Roberts, Rachel: O Lucky Man!, 548; When a Stranger Calls, 764

Roberts, Roy: Force of Evil, 467; He Walked by Night, 697

Roberts, Tanya: Beastmaster, The, 820; California Dreaming, 424; Hearts and Armour, 70; Sheena, 134; Tourist Trap, 759

Roberts, Tanya: View to a Kill, A, 158

Roberts, Teal: Fatal Games, 683; Hardbodies, 275

Roberts, Tony: Amityville III: The Demon, 645; Annie Hall, 219; Just Tell Me What You Want, 292; Key Exchange, 506; Midsummer Night's Sex Comedy, A, 309; Million Dollar Duck, The, 192; Play It Again Sam, 331; Serpico, 590; Taking of Pelham One Two Three, The, 144

Roberts, Lynne: Frontier Pony Express, 898; Shine On Harvest Moon, 931

Robeson, Paul: Sanders of the River, 127

Robins, Barry: Bless the Beasts and the Children, 414

Robins, Oliver: Poltergeist II: The Otherside, 729

Robin, Dany: Topaz, 757; Waltz of the Toreadors, 377

Robin, Michel: Le Chevre (THE GOAT), 298

Robinson, Amy: Mean Streets, 532

Robinson, Andrew: Charley Varrick, 30; Cobra, 32; Dirty Harry, 43

Robinson, Ann: Dragnet, 45; War of the Worlds, The, 874

Robinson, Bruce: Story of Adele H, The, 603

Robinson, Bumper: Enemy Mine, 834

Robinson, Charles Knox: Daring Dobermans, The, 38; Psycho Sisters, 732

Robinson, Chris: Savannah Smiles, 203; Stanley, 747

Robinson, Edward G.: Cheyenne Autumn,

888; Cincinnati Kid, The, 31; Good Neighbor Sam, 270; Hell on Frisco Bay, 70; Key Largo, 82; Little Caesar, 90; Mr. Winkle Goes to War, 311; Never a Dull Moment, 195; Red House, The, 734; Scarlet Street, 589; Song of Norway, 803; Soylent Green, 863; Stranger, The, 748; Ten Commandments, The, 612

Robinson, James: Demons of Ludlow, The, 673

Robinson, Jan: Robe, The, 581

Robinson, Jay: Three the Hard Way, 151

Robinson, Leon: Band of the Hand, 12; Streetwalkin', 605

Robinson, Roger: Newman's Law, 106

Robles, Frank: Crossover Dreams, 775

Robson, Flora: Beast in The Cellar, The, 649; Black Narcissus, 413; Caesar and Cleopatra, 423; Catherine the Great, 428; Dominique Is Dead, 677; Fire over England, 54; Sea Hawk, The, 130; Wuthering Heights, 639

Robson, Greer: Smash Palace, 595

Robson, May: Adventures of Tom Sawyer, The, 170; Anna Karenina, 400; Bringing up Baby, 234; Nurse Edith Cavell, 548; Star Is Born, A (Original), 600

Robson, Wayne: Grey Fox, The, 899

Rocca, Randy: Act of Passion, 389

Rocco, Alex: Gotcha!, 64; Grass is Always Greener Over the Septic Tank, The, 272; Hustling, 490; Rafferty and the Gold Dust Twins, 337; Stanley, 747; Stunt Man, The, 606

Rochefort, Jean: Birgit Haas Must Be Killed, 18; I Sent a Letter to My Love, 491; Le Cavaleur, 297; Pardon Mon Affaire, 327; Return of the Tall Blond Man with One Black Shoe, The, 339

Roche, Eugene: Newman's Law, 106; Oh God, You Devil!, 323; Slaughterhouse Five, 862; W, 763

Rockwell, Jack: Lawless Frontier, 908; Traitor, The, 940

Rockwell, Joan: 'Neath Arizona Skies, 917

Roc, Patricia: Black Jack, 18

Rodd, Marcia: Last Embrace, The, 87

Rode, Ebbe: Topsy Turvy, 370

Rodrigue, Madeline: Crazy Ray, The, 826

Rodriguez, Estelita: Golden Stallion, The, 898; Susanna Pass, 936; Twilight in the Sierras, 941

Rodriguez, Paul: Quicksilver, 572

Roebuck, Daniel: Cave Girl, 823

Rogers, Charles: Wings, 164

Rogers, Dora: Keystone Comedies, Vol. 3, 292; Keystone Comedies: Vo. 5, 292

Rogers, Gil: Children, The, 662

Rogers, Ginger: 42nd Street, 781; Carefree, 774; Flying Down to Rio, 780; Follow the Fleet, 780; Gay Divorcee, The, 782; Gold Diggers of 1933, 783; Kitty Foyle, 509; Once Upon a Honeymoon, 324; Shall We Dance?, 802; Stage Door, 357; Star of Midnight, 139;

Story of Vernon and Irene Castle, The, *806;* Swing Time, *806;* Top Hat, *810*

Rogers, Jeffrey: Friday the 13th, Part III, *690*

Rogers, Jimmy: False Colors, *895;* Riders of the Deadline, *926*

Rogers, Kenny: Six Pack, *353*

Rogers, Mimi: Blue Skies Again, *416;* Gung Ho, *274*

Rogers, Roy: Bells of Coronado, *881;* Billy The Kid Returns, *883;* Colorado, *889;* Dark Command, *891;* Down Dakota Way, *894;* Frontier Pony Express, *898;* Golden Stallion, The, *898;* Grand Canyon Trail, *899;* Heart of the Golden West, *901;* Jesse James at Bay, *905;* My Pal Trigger, *916;* North of the Great Divide, *918;* Old Corral, The, *919;* Rough Riders' Roundup, *928;* Saga of Death Valley, *929;* Shine On Harvest Moon, *931;* Song of Nevada, *933;* Song of Texas, *933;* Sunset Serenade, *935;* Susanna Pass, *936;* T Trigger, Jr., *940;* Trail of Robin Hood, *939;* Twilight in the Sierras, *941;* Under California Stars, *942;* Yellow Rose of Texas, *946*

Rogers, Ruth: Night Riders, The, *918*

Rogers, Wayne: Chiefs, *432*

Rogers, Will: Golden Age of Comedy, The, *270;* Judge Priest, *504*

Rogoz, Jaromir: Ecstasy, *455*

Rohm, Maria: Call of the Wild, *27*

Rohner, Clayton: Just One of the Guys, *292*

Rojo, Helena: Aguirre: Wrath of God, *6*

Roland, Gilbert: Barbarosa, *881;* Beneath the 12-Mile Reef, *13;* Between God, The Devil and a Winchester, *882;* Bullfighter and the Lady, The, *26;* Captain Kidd, *27;* Ruthless Four, The, *928;* Sacketts, The, *928;* Sea Hawk, The, *130;* Thunder Bay, *151;* Treasure of Pancho Villa, The, *940*

Rolfe, Guy: Snow White and the Three Stooges, *205*

Rolfing, Tom: He Knows You're Alone, *696*

Rollan, Henri: Crazy Ray, The, *826*

Rolling Stones, The: That Was Rock, *808*

Rollins Jr., Howard E.: Soldier's Story, A, *138;* King, *507*

Romain, Yvonne: Circus Of Horrors, *663*

Romand, Beatrice: Claire's Knee, *243;* Le Beau Mariage, *297*

Romanos, Richard: Protocol, *336*

Romano, Renato: Bird with the Crystal Plumage, The, *651*

Romanus, Robert: Bad Medicine, *223*

Roman, Ruth: Baby, The, *648;* Champion, *430;* Day of the Animals, *670;* Sacketts, The, *928;* Strangers on a Train, *749*

Roman, Susan: Rabid, *732*

Romero, Cesar: Americano, The, *879;* Batman, *172;* Computer Wore Tennis Shoes, The, *178;* Happy Go Lovely, *786;* Little Princess, The, *190;* Lust in the Dust, *303;* Mission to Glory, *536;* Now You See Him, Now You Don't, *196;* Ocean's Eleven, *109*

Romero, Ned: Deerslayer, The, *893*

Rome, Sydne: Puma Man, The, *732;* Sex With a Smile, *350*

Ronettes, The: That Was Rock, *808*

Ronet, Maurice: Beau Pere, *225;* La Balance, *85;* Sphinx, *746*

Ronstadt, Linda: Pirates of Penzance, The, *799*

Rooney, Mickey: Babes in Arms, *769;* Bill, *411;* Black Stallion, The, *173;* Breakfast at Tiffany's, *419;* Captains Courageous, *28;* Captains Courageous, *425;* Comic, The, *437;* Domino Principle, The, *453;* Hollywood Outtakes, *282;* How to Stuff a Wild Bikini, *788;* It's a Mad Mad Mad Mad World, *288;* Little Lord Fauntleroy, *519;* Love Laughs at Andy Hardy, *302;* Magic of Lassie, The, *191;* Midsummer Night's Dream, A, *852;* National Velvet, *195;* Off Limits, *322;* Pete's Dragon, *197;* Requiem for a Heavyweight, *578;* Strike Up the Band, *360;* Thousands Cheer, *808;* Care Bears Movie, The, (voice) *175*

Roosevelt, Buddy: Old Corral, The, *919*

Roose, Thorkild: Day of Wrath, *446*

Rosay, Françoise: Carnival in Flanders, *426*

Roscoe, Alan: Last Mile, The, *514*

Rosellini, Isabella: White Nights, *632*

Rosenbloom, Maxie: I Married a Monster from Outer Space, *842*

Rose, Phil: Robin Hood and the Sorcerer, *123*

Rose, Tim: Howard the Duck, *842*

Rositer, Leonard: Britannia Hospital, *235*

Rosi, Luciano: Five for Hell, *56*

Rossellini, Isabella: Matter of Time, A, *531*

Rossilli, Paul: Haunting Passion, The, *840*

Rossito., Angelo: Clones, The, *824*

Rossi, Ben: Little Laura and Big John, *90*

Rossi, Leo: Heart Like a Wheel, *70*

Rossi-Stuart, Giacomo: Last Man On Earth, The, *848*

Rossovich, Rick: Lords of Discipline, The, *521;* Top Gun, *153;* Warning Sign, *763*

Ross, Alma: Tuttles of Tahiti, The, *373*

Ross, Annie: Oh, Alfie, *549;* Superman III, *869*

Ross, Anthony: Country Girl, The, *439*

Ross, Betsy King: Phantom Empire, *114;* Radio Ranch (Men With Steel Faces, Phantom Empire), *923*

Ross, Chelcie: One More Saturday Night, *324*

Ross, David: Adventures of Sherlock Holmes: The Dancing Men, *3*

Ross, Diana: Lady Sings the Blues, *791;* Mahogany, *527;* Wiz, The, *812*

Ross, Gaylen: Dawn of the Dead, *670*

Ross, Gene: Encounter with the Unknown, *833*

Ross, George: Pirates of Penzance, The, *799*

Ross, Jerry: Jungle Master, The, *80*

Ross, Katharine: Betsy, The, *409;* Butch Cassidy and the Sundance Kid, *887;* Final

Countdown, The, 837; Graduate, The, 475; Hellfighters, 70; Legacy, The, 711; Murder in Texas, 719; Rodeo Girl, 583; Shenandoah, 930; Swarm, The, 751; Tell Them Willie Boy Is Here, 936; Wrong Is Right, 384

Ross, Marion: Teacher's Pet, 364

Ross, Merrie Lynn: Bobbie Jo and the Outlaw, 21; Class of 1984, 663

Ross, Shavar: Friday the 13th, Part V—A New Beginning, 690

Ross, Ted: Bingo Long Traveling All-Stars and Motor Kings, The, 229; Wiz, The, 812

Roth, Gene: Big Sombrero, The, 883; Blue Canadian Rockies, 884

Roth, Lillian: Alice, Sweet Alice (Communion and Holy Terror), 643; Animal Crackers, 218

Roth, Lynn: Adultress, The, 389

Roth, Tim: Hit, The, 73

Roucis, Luci: Party Animal, 328

Rouffe, Alida: Marius, 529

Roumert, Poul: Witchcraft Through the Ages (HAXAN), 637

Roundtree, Richard: Big Score, The, 16; City Heat, 243; Escape to Athena, 50; Eye for an Eye, 51; Kill Point, 83; One Down, Two to Go, 110; Q, 732; Shaft, 132; What Do You Say to a Naked Lady?, 379

Round, David: So Fine, 355

Rourke, Mickey: 9 1/2 Weeks, 545; Body Heat, 417; Diner, 251; Eureka, 459; Pope of Greenwich Village, The, 564; Year of the Dragon, 166

Roussel, Myriem: Hail Mary, 480

Routledge, Alison: Quiet Earth, The, 858

Rouverol, Jean: It's a Gift, 288

Rowell, Peter: Shaker Run, 132

Rowe, Earl: Blob, The, 652

Rowe, Misty: Man with Bogart's Face, The, 96; Meatballs Part II, 308; When Things Were Rotten, 380

Rowe, Nevan: Nutcase, 321; Sleeping Dogs, 137

Rowe, Nicholas: Young Sherlock Holmes, 167

Rowlands, Gena: Brinks Job, The, 234; Gloria, 62; Lonely Are the Brave, 909; Love Streams, 524; Rapunzel, 200; Tempest, 612

Rowley, Rob: Future-Kill, 692

Royale, Allan: Man Inside, The, 95

Royce, Lionel: Manhunt in the African Jungle (Secret Service in Darkest Africa), 96

Royle, Selena: Robot Monster, 736

Rozakis, Gregory: Abduction, 387

Rubbo, Joe: Last American Virgin, The, 296

Rubinek, Saul: Agency, 390; Nothing Personal, 321; Soup for One, 356; Sweet Liberty, 362; Ticket to Heaven, 618; Young Doctors in Love, 385

Rubini, Giulia: Goliath and the Barbarians, 63

Rubinstein, Zelda: Poltergeist II: The Otherside, 729

Rubin, Andrew: Police Academy, 332

Ruck, Alan: Ferris Bueller's Day Off, 259

Rudolph, Peter: Revolt of Job, The, 579

Ruggles, Charlie: Bringing up Baby, 234; Papa's Delicate Condition, 557; Ugly Dachshund, The, 211

Rule, Janice: Alvarez Kelly, 879; American Flyers, 396; Chase, The, 431; Gumshoe, 274; Invitation to a Gunfighter, 905; Missing, 535; Swimmer, The, 609

Ruman, Sig: Errand Boy, The, 256; Maytime, 793; Night at the Opera, A, 318

Rum, Brad: Special Effects, 746

Runacre, Jenny: Last Days of Man on Earth, The, 848; Passenger, The, 558

Runyon, Jennifer: To All a Good Night, 756

Ruscio, Al: Deadly Force, 39

Rushing, Jerry: Last Game, The, 513

Rush, Barbara: Between Friends, 409; Can't Stop the Music, 773; Hombre, 904; It Came from Outer Space, 845; Moon of the Wolf, 718; Summer Lovers, 607; When Worlds Collide, 876; Young Philadelphians, The, 640

Rusler, Robert: Vamp, 760

Russek, Rita: From the Lives of the Marionettes, 470

Russell, Andy: Copacabana, 247

Russell, Betsy: Avenging Angel, 11; Tomboy, 153

Russell, Brian: Charlie, The Lonesome Cougar, 176

Russell, Craig: Outrageous, 326

Russell, Dean: Forest, The, 687

Russell, Elizabeth: Corpse Vanishes, The, 664; Curse of the Cat People, The, 668

Russell, Gail: Angel and the Badman, 879; Great Dan Patch, The, 477; Wake of the Red Witch, 160

Russell, Harold: Best Years of Our Lives, The, 409

Russell, Jane: Gentlemen Prefer Blondes, 266; His Kind of Woman, 73; Outlaw, The, 920; Paleface, The, 327

Russell, John: Pale Rider, 921; Rio Bravo, 926

Russell, Kurt: Barefoot Executive, The, 172; Best of Times, The, 228; Big Trouble in Little China, 17; Charlie and The Angel, 176; Computer Wore Tennis Shoes, The, 178; Escape from New York, 49; Follow Me Boys!, 181; Mean Season, The, 98; Now You See Him, Now You Don't, 196; Silkwood, 593; Swing Shift, 610; Thing, The, 871; Used Cars, 376

Russell, Nipsey: Wiz, The, 812; Wildcats, 382

Russell, Ronald: Adventures of Sherlock Holmes: The Naval Treaty, 4

Russell, Rosalind: Auntie Mame, 222; Craig's Wife, 439; Gypsy, 785; His Girl Friday, 281; Oh Dad, Poor Dad—Mama's Hung You in the Closet and I'm Feeling So Sad, 323; Trouble With Angels, The, 372; Women, The,

383

Russell, Theresa: Eureka, *459;* Razor's Edge, The (the Remake), *576;* Straight Time, *603*

Russom, Leon: Silver Bullet, *743*

Russo, Gianni: Four Deuces, The, *59*

Russo, James: Extremities, *460*

Russ, William: Beer, *226;* Raw Courage, *119*

Rutherford, Ann: Melody Trail, *915;* Secret Life of Walter Mitty, The, *347*

Ruth, Babe: Pride of the Yankees, The, *568*

Ryan, Edmon: Human Monster, The (Dark Eyes of London), *702*

Ryan, Fran: Americana, *396;* Private School, *335*

Ryan, Helen: Adventures of Sherlock Holmes: The Norwood Builder, *5*

Ryan, Hilary: Getting of Wisdom, The, *471*

Ryan, James: Kill and Kill Again, *82;* Kill or Be Killed, *83*

Ryan, John P.: Breathless (Remake), *420;* Futureworld, *838;* It Lives Again, *706;* It's Alive!, *707;* Postman Always Rings Twice, The (Remake), *566;* Runaway Train, *125;* Shamus, *132*

Ryan, Meg: Amityville III: The Demon, *645;* Armed and Dangerous, *220;* Rich and Famous, *579*

Ryan, Mitchell: High Plains Drifter, *903;* Monte Walsh, *915*

Ryan, Peggy: Private Buckaroo, *799*

Ryan, Robert: Battle of the Bulge, *17;* Behind the Rising Sun, *13;* Billy Budd, *411;* Bombardier, *21;* Boy With Green Hair, The, *419;* Caught, *429;* Clash by Night, *434;* Escape to Burma, *459;* Executive Action, *460;* Flying Leathernecks, The, *58;* God's Little Acre, *473;* Men in War, *98;* Professionals, The, *116;* Return of the Badmen, *925;* Set-Up, The, *591;* Sky's the Limit, The, *803;* Wild Bunch, The, *945*

Ryan, Sheila: Great Guns, *272;* On Top of Old Smoky, *919;* Song of Texas, *933*

Ryan, Tim: Detour, *450*

Ryan, Tommy: Prairie Moon, *922*

Rydell, Bobby: Bye Bye Birdie, *773*

Ryder, Winona: Lucas, *524*

Ryland, Jack: Anna to the Infinite Power, *817*

Ryu, Daisuke: Ran, *575*

Saadi, Yacef: Battle of Algiers, *405*

Saad, Margit: Concrete Jungle, The (aka The Criminal), *437*

Sabin, David: When Things Were Rotten, *380;* Black Narcissus, *413*

Sabu: Drums, *46;* Elephant Boy, *48;* Jungle Book, *187;* Thief of Bagdad, The, *870*

Sacchi, Patrizia: Macaroni, *304*

Sacci, Robert: Man with Bogart's Face, The, *96*

Sachs, Andrew: Romance With A Double Bass, *343*

Sachs, Stephen: Dorm That Dripped Blood, The, *678*

Sacks, Michael: Bunco, *26;* Slaughterhouse Five, *862*

Sager, Ray: Wizard of Gore, The, *766*

Sahara, Kenji: Mysterians, The, *853;* Son of Godzilla, *745*

Saiet, Eric: One More Saturday Night, *324*

Saiger, Susan: Eating Raoul, *254*

Saint James, Susan: Desperate Women, *893;* Love at First Bite, *302*

Saint, Eva Marie: Best Little Girl in the World, The, *408;* Curse of King Tut's Tomb, The, *667;* Exodus, *460;* North by Northwest, *724;* Nothing In Common, *547;* On the Waterfront, *551;* Raintree County, *574;* Russians Are Coming, the Russians Are Coming, The, *344;* Sandpiper, The, *588*

St. Jacques, Raymond: Green Berets, The, *66;* Kill Castro, *82*

Sakaguchi, Seiji: Forced Vengeance, *59*

Sakai, Franky: Mothra, *853*

Sakai, Sachio: Samurai Trilogy, The, *127*

Sakall, S. Z.: Ball of Fire, *224;* Devil and Miss Jones, The, *250;* In the Good Old Summertime, *788*

Sakomoto, Ryuichi: Merry Christmas, Mr. Lawrence, *533*

Saks, Gene: Goodbye People, The, *475;* One and Only, The, *551;* Prisoner of Second Avenue, The, *334;* Thousand Clowns, A, *367*

Salcedo, Leopoldo: Cry of Battle, *37*

Saldana, Theresa: Evil That Men Do, The, *50;* Raging Bull, *574;* Defiance, *41*

Salem, Kario: Underground Aces, *374*

Salenger, Meredith: Journey of Natty Gann, The, *187*

Salerno, Enrico Maria: Bird with the Crystal Plumage, The, *651*

Salinas, Chucho: Rock 'N Roll Wrestling Women Vs. The Aztec Mummy, *342*

Salinger, Diane: Pee-Wee's Big Adventure, *328*

Sallet, Emmanuelle: Under The Cherry Moon, *626*

Salmi, Albert: Brothers Karamazov, The, *420;* Empire of the Ants, *833;* Hard to Hold, *786;* Kill Castro, *82;* Night Games, *544;* St. Helens, *587*

Sam and Dave: One Trick Pony, *797*

Sampson, Robert: Re-animator, *733*

Sampson, Will: One Flew over the Cuckoo's Nest, *551;* Orca, *726;* Poltergeist II: The Otherside, *729;* Vega$, *158*

Samuel, Joanne: Mad Max, *850*

Sanada, Henry: Legend of the Eight Samurai, *89*

Sand, Nonny: Topsy Turvy, *370*

Sand, Paul: Can't Stop the Music, 773; Great Bank Hoax, The, 272; Hot Rock, The, 75; Main Event, The, 305; Wholly Moses!, 381

Sands, Diana: Raisin in the Sun, A, 575

Sands, Julian: Doctor and the Devils, The, 676; Killing Fields, The, 506; Room With a View, A (1987 Release), 584

Sands, Sonny: Bellboy, The, 226

Sands, Tommy: Ensign Pulver, 255

Sanda, Dominique: Cabo Blanco, 26; Conformist, The, 438; Damnation Alley, 827; Garden of the Finzi-Continis, the, 471; Mackintosh Man, The, 94

Sanderson, William: Raggedy Man, 733; Savage Weekend, 739

Sanders, George: Allegheny Uprising, 878; All About Eve, 393; Black Jack, 18; Falcon Takes Over, the, 52; Foreign Correspondent, 687; From the Earth to the Moon, 838; In Search of the Castaways, 185; Ivanhoe, 78; Mr. Moto's Last Warning, 101; Nurse Edith Cavell, 548; Picture of Dorian Gray, The, 728; Psychomania, 731; Rebecca, 576; Samson and Delilah, 588; Shot in the Dark, A, 351; Solomon and Sheba, 597; This Land Is Mine, 617; Village of the Damned, 762

Sanders, Sandy: Cow Town, 890; Hills of Utah, The, 903

Sandford, Chris: Die Screaming, Marianne, 675

Sandman, Lee: Super Fuzz, 868

Sandor, Steve: Bonnie's Kids, 22; Stryker, 868

Sandrelli, Stefania: Conformist, The, 438; Seduced and Abandoned, 348

Sandweiss, Ellen: Evil Dead, The, 681

Sand, Nonny: Topsy Turvy, 370

Sand, Paul: Can't Stop the Music, 773; Great Bank Hoax, The, 272; Hot Rock, The, 75; Main Event, The, 305; Wholly Moses!, 381

Sanford, Erskine: Lady from Shanghai, 86

Sanford, Ralph: Cow Town, 890; Union Station, 760

Santella, Maria Luisa: Macaroni, 304

Santiago, Saundra: Miami Vice, 98

Santoni, Reni: Bad Boys, 404; Cobra, 32; Dead Men Don't Wear Plaid, 249; Dirty Harry, 43; Enter Laughing, 256; They Went That-A-Way and That-A-Way, 208

Santos, Joe: Shamus, 132

Santovena, Hortensia: Simon of the Desert, 352

Sanvido, Guy: Heartaches, 484

Sara, Mia: Ferris Bueller's Day Off, 259; Legend, 849

Sarandon, Chris: Cuba, 37; Fright Night, 691; Osterman Weekend, The, 111; Protocol, 336; Sentinel, The, 742

Sarandon, Susan: Atlantic City, 402; Beauty and the Beast, 172; Buddy System, The, 421; Compromising Positions, 247; Great Smokey Roadblock, The, 65; Great Waldo Pepper, The, 66; Hunger, The, 703; Joe, 502;

King of the Gypsies, 508; Loving Couples, 33; Mussolini and I, 539; Other Side of Midnight, The, 554; Pretty Baby, 566; Tempest, 612

Sarasohn, Lane: Groove Tube, The, 273

Sarcey, Martine: One Wild Moment, 552

Sarchet, Kate: Sweater Girls, 362

Sargent, Richard: Hardcore, 481; Operation Petticoat, 325

Sarky, Daniel: Emmanuelle, 457; L'Addition, 510

Sarrazin, Michael: Doomsday Flight, The, 453; Flim-Flam Man, The, 466; For Pete's Sake, 262; Gumball Rally, The, 67; Joshua Then and Now, 290; Reincarnation of Peter Proud, The, 734; Seduction, The, 741; Sometimes a Great Notion, 597; They Shoot Horses, Don't They?, 616; Train Killer, The, 621

Sartain, Gailard: Hard Country, 68

Sasaki, Takamoru: Throne of Blood, 617

Sassard, Jacqueline: Accident, 388

Satana, Tura: Faster Pussycat! Kill! Kill!, 52

Sato, Reiko: Flower Drum Song, 780

Sauls, Michael: Sugarland Express, The, 607

Saunders, Pamela: Alien Warrior, 816

Savage, Ann: Detour, 450

Savage, Brad: Islands in the Stream, 498

Savage, Fred: Boy Who Could Fly, The, 419

Savage, John: Amateur, The, 395; Bad Company, 880; Brady's Escape, 23; Deer Hunter, The, 448; Hair, 785; Inside Moves, 496; Maria's Lovers, 528; Onion Field, The, 553; Salvador, 587

Savage, Traice: Friday the 13th, Part III, 690

Savalas, George: Belarus File, The, 13; Family, The, 52

Savalas, Telly: Belarus File, The, 13; Beyond the Poseidon Adventure, 14; Birdman of Alcatraz, 412; Cannonball Run II, 237; Capricorn One, 822; Escape to Athena, 50; Family, The, 52; Greatest Story Ever Told, The, 478; Horror Express, 698; House of Exorcism, The, 699; Inside Out, 77; Kelly's Heroes, 81; Mackenna's Gold, 911; Massacre At Fort Holman (Reason to Live... A Reason to Die, A), 914; Muppet Movie, The, 193; On Her Majesty's Secret Service, 110; Pancho Villa, 922

Saval, Dany: Moon Pilot, 193

Savini, Tom: Dawn of the Dead, 670; Knightriders, 84; Maniac, 714

Savio, Andria: Stryker, 868

Savoy, Teresa Ann: Caligula, 424

Sawaguchi, Yasuka: Godzilla 1985, 694

Sawara, Kenji: Rodan, 860

Sawyer, Anne: Heavenly Kid, The, 278

Sawyer, Joe: Buckskin Frontier, 886; Melody Ranch, 914; Roaring Twenties, The, 122

Saxon, John: Battle beyond the Stars, 819; Bees, The, 649; Beyond Evil, 650; Big Score, The, 16; Blood Beach, 653; Doomsday Flight, The, 453; Electric Horseman, The, 456; Enter the Dragon, 49; Joe Kidd, 906; Moonshine County Express, 103; Nightmare on Elm Street, A, 722; Running Scared (1980), 126; Wrong Is Right, 384

Sayer, Philip: XTro, 766

Saylor, Sid: Mystery Mountain, 916

Saynor, Ian: Corn Is Green, The, 439

Sazio, Carmela: Paisan, 556

Sbarge, Raphael: Risky Business, 341

Scacchi, Greta: Coca Cola Kid, The, 246; Heat and Dust, 485

Scales, Prunella: Wicked Lady, The, 163

Scalia, Jack: Fear City, 52

Scalondro, Vincent: After the Fall of New York, 815

Scardino, Don: Cruising, 441; He Knows You're Alone, 696; Squirm, 747

Scarroll, David: Scalpel, 740

Scarwid, Diana: Extremities, 460; Mommie Dearest, 537; Psycho III, 731; Strange Invaders, 867

Schaal, Wendy: Creature, 826; Where the Boys Are '84, 380

Schacter, Felice: Zapped!, 385

Schafer, Natalie: Caught, 429

Schallert, William: Computer Wore Tennis Shoes, The, 178

Schall, Ekkehardt: Wagner, 811

Scharf, Sabrina: Hell's Angels on Wheels, 71

Schauer, Rolef: Inheritors, The, 495

Scheider, Roy: 2010, 874; All That Jazz, 768; Blue Thunder, 21; French Connection, The, 60; Jaws 2, 707; Jaws, 707; Klute, 509; Last Embrace, The, 87; Marathon Man, 97; Seven-Ups, The, 131; Still of the Night, 748; Tiger Town, 209

Schell, Carl: Blue Max, The, 20

Schell, Catherine: Return of the Pink Panther, The, 339

Schell, Maria: Brothers Karamazov, The, 420; Napoleon, 542; Odessa File, The, 110

Schell, Maximilian: Black Hole, The, 821; Chosen, The, 433; Cross of Iron, 37; Judgment at Nuremberg, 504; Julia, 505; Odessa File, The, 110; Players, 564; St. Ives, 126; Topkapi, 154

Schicha, Ralph: Savage Attraction, 739

Schildkraut, Joseph: Diary of Anne Frank, The, 451; Flame of the Barbary Coast, 56; Idiot's Delight, 492; King of Kings, The, 508; Life of Emile Zola, The, 518

Schilling, Gus: Lady from Shanghai, 86

Schmidinger, Walter: From the Lives of the Marionettes, 470

Schmitz, Sybille: Vampyr, 761

Schnabel, Stephan: Firefox, 54

Schneider, John: Eddie Macon's Run, 47

Schneider, Maria: Last Tango in Paris, 515; Passenger, The, 558

Schneider, Michael: Last Winter, The, 515

Schneider, Romy: Boccaccio 70, 231; Death Watch, 829; Good Neighbor Sam, 270; Simple Story, A, 594; What's New Pussycat?, 379

Schoeffling, Michael: Sylvester, 610; Vision Quest, 628

Schofield, Nell: Puberty Blues, 570

Schollin, Christina: Song of Norway, 803

Schreck, Max: Nosferatu, 724

Schreiber, Avery: Galaxina, 839; Silent Scream, 743

Schreiber, Tell: Keeper, The, 708

Schreier, Tom: Ripper, The, 736

Schroder, Greta: The Golem (How He Came Into The World) (DER GOLEM, Wie er in die Welt Kam), 754; Nosferatu, 724

Schroder, Ricky: Champ, The (Remake), 430; Earthling, The, 46; Hansel and Gretel, 183; Last Flight of Noah's Ark, 188

Schubert, Karin: Bluebeard, 655

Schuck, John: Butch and Sundance: The Early Days, 887

Schull, Richard B.: Cockfighter, 32

Schultz, Dwight: Alone in the Dark, 644; Vampyr, 761

Schumm, Hans: Spy Smasher, 139

Schunzel, Reinhold: Threepenny Opera, The, 809

Schwartz, Albert: Time Stands Still, 619

Schwartz, Jessica: One More Saturday Night, 324

Schwartz, Scott: Toy, The, 371

Schwarzenegger, Arnold: Commando, 33; Conan the Barbarian, 825; Conan the Destroyer, 826; Jayne Mansfield Story, The, 501; Pumping Iron, 570; Raw Deal, 119; Red Sonja, 120; Stay Hungry, 602; Terminator, The, 870

Schweiger, Heinrich: Echo Park, 455

Schygulla, Hanna: Berlin Alexanderplatz, 408; Delta Force, The, 41; Love in Germany, A, 523

Scob, Edith: Judex, 79

Scofield, Paul: Man for All Seasons, A, 528; Train, The, 155

Scolari, Peter: Rosebud Beach Hotel, The, 343

Scooler, Zvee: Love and Death, 302

Scott-Heron, Gil: No Nukes, 795

Scott, Alex: Fahrenheit 451, 836

Scott, Carey: Making the Grade, 305

Scott, David: This Is Elvis, 808

Scott, Donovan: Goldilocks and the Three Bears, 182; Savannah Smiles, 203; Sheena, 134

Scott, Fred: Singing Buckaroo, 932

Scott, George C.: Anatomy of a Murder, 397; Changeling, The, 661; Day of the Dolphin, The, 828; Dr. Strangelove or How I Learned to Stop Worrying and Love the Bomb, 252; Firestarter, 685; Flim-Flam Man, The, 466; Formula, The, 467; Hardcore, 481; Hindenburg, The, 487; Hospital, The, 283; Hustler, The, 490; Islands in the Stream, 498; List of Adrian Messenger, The, 90; Movie Movie, 315; New Centurions, The, 543; Patton, 559;

Prince and the Pauper, The (Remake), *198;* Rage, *573;* Savage Is Loose, The, *588;* Taps, *611;* They Might Be Giants, *616*

Scott, Gordon: Tramplers, The, *940*

Scott, Janette: Day of the Triffids, The, *828*

Scott, Jeffrey: Future-Kill, *692*

Scott, Kathryn Leigh: Murrow, *539*

Scott, Ken: Stopover Tokyo, *141*

Scott, Larry B.: That Was Then… This is Now, *615*

Scott, Lizabeth: Loving You, *793;* Strange Love of Martha Ivers, The, *604*

Scott, Martha: Cheers for Miss Bishop, *432;* Our Town, *555;* War of the Wildcats, *943*

Scott, Nina: Invitation au Voyage, *497*

Scott, Randolph: Abilene Town, *878;* Badman's Territory, *880;* Bombardier, *21;* Captain Kidd, *27;* Follow the Fleet, *780;* Gung Ho, *67;* Jesse James, *905;* Last of the Mohicans, The, *907;* My Favorite Wife, *316;* Return of the Badmen, *925;* Ride the High Country, *925;* Spoilers, The, *934*

Scott, Timothy: Wild Times, *945*

Scott, Zachary: Appointment in Honduras, *9;* Mildred Pierce, *534;* Southerner, The, *598*

Scully, Sean: Almost Angels, *171*

Seagulls: Jonathan Livingston Seagull, *503*

Seales, Franklyn: Onion Field, The, *553*

Seberg, Jean: Airport, *7;* Breathless (Original), *419;* Fine Madness, A (1987 release), *260;* Lilith, *518;* Mouse That Roared, The, *314;* Paint Your Wagon, *797;* Pendulum, *113*

Seck, Douta: Sugar Cane Alley, *607*

Secombe, Harry: Down Among the "Z" Men, *253*

Sedgwick, Edie: Ciao! Manhattan, *433*

Seeger, The Weavers: Pete: Wasn't That a Time!, *811*

Segall, Jonathan: Private Popsicle, *335*

Segal, George: Black Bird, The, *230;* Blume in Love, *416;* Carbon Copy, *238;* Duchess and the Dirtwater Fox, The, *894;* Fun with Dick and Jane, *265;* Hot Rock, The, *75;* Invitation to a Gunfighter, *905;* Killing 'Em Softly, *506;* King Rat, *508;* Last Married Couple in America, The, *296;* Lost and Found, *301;* No Way to Treat a Lady, *546;* Owl and the Pussycat, The, *326;* Rollercoaster, *737;* Ship of Fools, *592;* Stick, *140;* St. Valentine's Day Massacre, The, *126;* Terminal Man, The, *752;* Touch of Class, A, *370;* Where's Poppa?, *381;* Who's Afraid of Virginia Woolf?, *633*

Segal, Howard: Last Game, The, *513*

Segal, Nick: School Spirit, *346*

Seidel, Tom: False Colors, *895*

Sekka, Johnny: Message, The (Mohammad, Messenger of God), *533*

Selay, David: Rich and Famous, *579;* Raise the Titanic, *118*

Selby, David: Up the Sandbox, *375*

Selby, David: Macbeth, *525*

Sellars, Elizabeth: Never Let Go, *543*

Selleck, Tom: Bunco, *26;* High Road to China,

72; Lassiter, *86;* Runaway, *860;* Sacketts, The, *928;* Washington Affair, The, *630*

Sellers, Peter: After the Fox, *216;* Alice's Adventures in Wonderland, *171;* Being There, *226;* Bobo, The, *231;* Casino Royale, *239;* Down Among the "Z" Men, *253;* Dr. Strangelove or How I Learned to Stop Worrying and Love the Bomb, *252;* Fiendish Plot of Dr. Fu Manchu, The, *260;* Heavens Above, *279;* I Love You Alice B. Toklas!, *285;* I'm All Right Jack, *285;* Ladykillers, The, *295;* Lolita, *520;* Magic Christian, The, *304;* Mouse That Roared, The, *314;* Murder by Death, *315;* Never Let Go, *543;* Pink Panther Strikes Again, The, *330;* Pink Panther, The, *330;* Prisoner of Zenda, The, *334;* Return of the Pink Panther, The, *339;* Revenge of the Pink Panther, The, *340;* Shot in the Dark, A, *351;* There's a Girl in my Soup, *365;* Tom Thumb, *210;* Trail of the Pink Panther, The, *371;* Waltz of the Toreadors, *377;* What's New Pussycat?, *379;* World of Henry Orient, The, *384;* Wrong Box, The, *384*

Sellier, Georges: Red Balloon, The, *201*

Selwyn, Don: Came a Hot Friday, *27*

Selzak, Walter: Princess and the Pirate, The, *334*

Sembera, Tricia: Flash and the Firecat, *56*

Seneca, Joe: Crossroads, *775;* Wilma, *635*

Serato, Massimo: Tenth Victim, The, *869*

Serling, Rod: Encounter with the Unknown, *833*

Serna, Pepe: Force of One, *59*

Serrault, Michel: La Cage Aux Folles III, The Wedding, *295;* La Cage aux Folles II, *294;* La Cage aux Folles, *294*

Serra, Raymond: Alphabet City, *39*

Serre, Henri: Jules and Jim, *505*

Servais, Jean: Rififi, *122*

Servantie, Adrienne: My Uncle (Mon Oncle), *317*

Seth, Roshan: My Beautiful Launderette, *540*

Severn, Billy: Enchanted Forest, The, *180*

Sewell, George: Invasion UFO, *845*

Seyler, Athene: Make Mine Mink, *305*

Seymour, Anne: Desire Under the Elms, *449;* Trancers, *873*

Seymour, Caroline: Gumshoe, *274*

Seymour, Clarine: True Heart Susie, *623*

Seymour, Dan: Beyond A Reasonable Doubt, *409*

Seymour, Jane: Battlestar Galactica, *820;* East of Eden (Remake), *454;* Haunting Passion, The, *840;* Lassiter, *86;* Live and Let Die, *91;* Oh, Heavenly Dog!, *196;* Sinbad and the Eye of the Tiger, *862;* Somewhere in Time, *863*

Seyrig, Delphine: Discreet Charm Of The Bourgeoisie, The, *251;* I Sent a Letter to My Love, *491;* Last Year At Marienbad, *516;* Stolen Kisses, *360*

Sezer, Serif: Yol, *639*

Shaffer, Paul: Gilda Live, *268*

Shaker, Martin: Children, The, 662
Shakura, Shiori: MacArthur's Children, 525
Shand, Peter: Nutcase, 321
Shankey, Amelia: Dreamchild, 831
Shanks, Don: Life and Times of Grizzly Adams, The, 189
Shannon, Harry: Cow Town, 890; Once Upon a Honeymoon, 324; Song of Texas, 933; Yellow Rose of Texas, 946
Shapiro, Ken: Groove Tube, The, 273
Sharge, Raphael: My Science Project, 853
Sharif, Omar: Behold a Pale Horse, 407; Bloodline, 415; Dr. Zhivago, 452; Far Pavilions, The, 463; Funny Girl, 782; Funny Lady, 782; Green Ice, 66; Juggernaut, 80; Lawrence of Arabia, 88; Mackenna's Gold, 911; Night of the Generals, 107; Oh, Heavenly Dog!, 196; Pleasure Palace, 564; S.H.E., 134; Tamarind Seed, The, 145; Top Secret, 369
Sharkey, Ray: Body Rock, 771; Heart Beat, 483; Idolmaker, The, 788; Who'll Stop the Rain, 162; Wise Guys, 382
Sharler, Helen: Best Defense, 227
Sharpe, Albert: Darby O'Gill and the Little People, 179
Sharpe, Cornelia: Reincarnation of Peter Proud, The, 734; S.H.E., 134
Sharpe, David: Daredevils of the Red Circle, 38; Shine On Harvest Moon, 931; Susanna Pass, 936
Sharrett, Michael: Magic of Lassie, The, 191
Shatner, William: Airplane II: The Sequel, 216; Big Bad Mama, 14; Brothers Karamazov, The, 420; Devil's Rain, The, 674; Kidnapping of the President, The, 709; Kingdom of the Spiders, 709; People, The, 855; Star Trek III: The Search for Spock, 865; Star Trek II: The Wrath of Khan, 865; Star Trek (television series), 866; Star Trek: The Menagerie, 865; Star Trek—The Motion Picture, 865; Visiting Hours, 762
Shaughnessy, Mickey: Boatniks, The, 174; Jailhouse Rock, 789
Shaver, Helen: Desert Hearts, 449; Gas, 265; Harry Tracy, 901; High-Ballin', 71
Shaw, Artie, and his orchestra: Second Chorus, 801
Shawlee, Joan: Prehistoric Women, 857
Shawn, Dick: Angel, 8; Beer, 226; Emperor's New Clothes, The, 833; It's a Mad Mad Mad Mad World, 288; Love at First Bite, 302; Producers, The, 336
Shawn, Wallace: Bostonians, The, 417; Crackers, 248; Heaven Help Us, 278; Micki & Maude, 304; My Dinner with Andre, 540
Shaw, Barbara: Pipe Dreams, 563
Shaw, Fiona: Adventures of Sherlock Holmes: The Crooked Man, 3
Shaw, Martin: Macbeth, 525
Shaw, Robert: Battle of the Bulge, 13; Black Sunday, 19; Deep, The, 41; Force Ten from Navarone, 59; From Russia with Love, 61; Jaws, 707; Man for All Seasons, A, 528; Robin and Marian, 123; Sting, The, 144; Taking of Pelham One Two Three, The, 144; Young Winston, 641
Shaw, Stan: Boys in Company C, The, 23; Tough Enough, 154
Shaw, Susan D.: Adventures of the Wilderness Family, 170; Junkman, The, 80; Mountain Family Robinson, 193; Wilderness Family, Part 2, The, 212
Shaw, Victoria: Alvarez Kelly, 879
Shayne, Linda: Screwballs, 346
Shea, Eric: Castaway Cowboy, The, 176
Shea, John: Missing, 535; Windy City, 635
Shea, Katt: Preppies, 333; RSVP, 343
Shea, Latta: Barbarian Queen, 819
Shea, Tom: Somewhere, Tomorrow, 206
Shearer, Harry: Right Stuff, The, 580; This Is Spinal Tap, 367
Shearer, Moira: Peeping Tom, 727; Red Shoes, The, 800
Shearer, Norma: Idiot's Delight, 492; Women, The, 383
Shearman, Alan: Bullshot, 236
Sheedy, Ally: Bad Boys, 404; Blue City, 20; Breakfast Club, The, 233; Short Circuit, 862; St. Elmo's Fire, 586; Twice in a Lifetime, 624; Wargames, 875
Sheen, Charlie: Ferris Bueller's Day Off, 259; Lucas, 524
Sheen, Martin: Apocalypse Now, 9; Badlands, 404; Cassandra Crossing, The, 428; Catholics, 428; Dead Zone, The, 671; Enigma, 49; Final Countdown, The, 837; Firestarter, 685; Gandhi, 471; Guardian, The, 480; Little Girl Who Lives Down the Lane, The, 712; Man, Woman and Child, 528; Rage, 573; That Championship Season, 614
Sheffer, Craig: Fire With Fire, 464; That Was Then... This is Now, 615
Sheffler, Marc: Last House on the Left, 711
Sheiner, David: Stone Killer, The, 141
Sheldon, Barbara: Lucky Texan, 910
Sheldon, Gene: Sign of Zorro, The, 204; Toby Tyler, 210
Shelley, Barbara: Village of the Damned, 762
Shelley, Joshua: Front, The, 470
Shenar, Paul: Deadly Force, 39; Dream Lover, 679; Raw Deal, 119; Scarface (Remake), 129
Shepard, Patty: Stranger and the Gunfighter, The, 935
Shepard, Sam: Country, 439; Days of Heaven, 446; Fool For Love, 466; Frances, 469; Raggedy Man, 733; Resurrection, 858; Right Stuff, The, 580
Shepherd, Cybill: Daisy Miller, 442; Heartbreak Kid, The, 277; Last Picture Show, The, 514; Moonlighting, 102; Silver Bears, 351; Taxi Driver, 612
Shepherd, Elizabeth: Tomb of Ligeia, 757
Shepherd, Jean: Friday the 13th, Part V—A New Beginning, 690

Shepherd, John: Thunder Run, 151

Sheppard, Paula E.: Alice, Sweet Alice (Communion and Holy Terror), 643; Liquid Sky, 849

Sheridan, Ann: Angels with Dirty Faces, 8; Appointment in Honduras, 9; Dodge City, 494; Good Sam, 271; King's Row, 508; Letter of Introduction, 516; Thank Your Lucky Stars, 707; They Drive by Night, 148; They Made Me a Criminal, 616

Sheridan, Margaret: Thing (From Another World), The, 871

Sherman, Bobby: Get Crazy, 266

Sherman, Jenny: Mean Johnny Barrows, 98

Sherman, Lowell: Way Down East, 631

Sherwin, Shane: Sylvester, 610

Sherwood, Robin: Love Butcher, 713

Shevlin, Margaret: Belfast Assassin, 407

Sheybal, Vladek: Wind and the Lion, The, 164

Shields, Arthur: Daughter of Dr. Jekyll, 670; Quiet Man, The, 117

Shields, Brooke: Alice, Sweet Alice (Communion and Holy Terror), 643; Blue Lagoon, The, 415; Endless Love, 458; King of the Gypsies, 508; Muppets Take Manhattan, The, 194; Pretty Baby, 566; Sahara, 126; Tilt, 368

Shigeta, James: Flower Drum Song, 780

Shihomi, Sue: Legend of the Eight Samurai, 99

Shiloh, Shmuel: Goodbye New York, 271

Shimada, Yoko: Shogun (Full-Length Version), 134

Shimono, Sab: Gung Ho, 274

Shimura, Takashi: Godzilla, King of the Monsters, 693; Ikiru, 493; Sanjuro, 128; Throne of Blood, 617; Seven Samurai, The, 131

Shirakawa, Yumi: Mysterians, The, 853; Rodan, 860

Shire, Talia: Godfather Epic, The, 474; Godfather, The, Part II, 474; Godfather, The, 473; Old Boyfriends, 550; Prophecy, 730; Rad, 117; Rip Van Winkle, 859; Rocky III, 582; Rocky II, 582; Rocky IV, 582; Rocky, 582

Shirley, Aliesa: Sweet Sixteen, 144

Shirley, Anne: Bombardier, 21; Murder My Sweet, 103; Stella Dallas, 602

Shoop, Pamela Susan: Halloween II, 695

Short, Dorothy: Reefer Madness, 338

Short, John: Maximum Overdrive, 716

Shor, Dan: Strange Behavior, 748; Wise Blood, 636

Shreiber, Avery: Loose Shoes, 301

Shubert, Nancy: Sagebrush Trail, 929

Shue, Elisabeth: Call to Glory, 424; Karate Kid, The, 505

Shull, Richard B.: Big Bus, The, 229; Pack, The, 726; Splash, 357

Shute, Anja: Tendres Cousines, 365

Shutta, Ethel: Whoopee, 812

Shuzhen, Tan: From Mao to Mozart, 781

Siani, Sabrina: Ator: The Fighting Eagle, 818

Siberry, Michael: Adventures of Sherlock Holmes: The Solitary Cyclist, 5

Sidney, Sylvia: Blood on the Sun, 19; Damien: Omen II, 668; Dead End, 447; Death at Love House, 672; Demon (God Told Me To), 830; Love from a Stranger, 713; Mr. Ace, 100; Sabotage, 738; Street Scene, 605

Siebert, Charles: Blue Sunshine, 20; Incredible Hulk, The, 843

Siedow, Jim: Texas Chainsaw Massacre 2, The, 753

Siegert, Dietmar: Private Popsicle, 335

Sierra, Gregory: Clones, The, 824; Miami Vice, 98

Signorelli, Tom: Alice, Sweet Alice (Communion and Holy Terror), 643; Crossover Dreams, 775

Signoret, Simone: Diabolique, 675; I Sent a Letter to My Love, 491; La Ronde, 295; Madame Rosa, 526; Ship of Fools, 592

Sikking, James B.: Morons from Outer Space, 314; Ordinary People, 554; Up the Creek, 375

Silla, Felix: Buck Rogers in the 25th Century, 822

Silva, Henry: Alligator, 644; Buck Rogers in the 25th Century, 822; Code of Silence, 33; Love and Bullets, 93; Lust in the Dust, 303; Never a Dull Moment, 195; Shoot, 135; Wrong Is Right, 384

Silvain: Passion of Joan of Arc, The, 559

Silvera, Frank: St. Valentine's Day Massacre, The, 126

Silverheels, Jay: Lone Ranger, The, 910; Santee, 929

Silverman, Jonathan: Girls Just Want to Have Fun, 268

Silverman, Mindy: Stephen King's Night Shift Collection, 747

Silvers, Phil: Boatniks, The, 174; Chicken Chronicles, The, 243; Funny Thing Happened on the Way to the Forum, A, 265; Guide For The Married Man, A, 273; It's a Mad Mad Mad Mad World, 288

Silver, Joe: Rabid, 732; You Light Up My Life, 640

Silver, John: His Name Was King, 903

Silver, Ron: Best Friends, 227; Entity, The, 680; Garbo Talks, 265; Goodbye People, The, 475; Oh God, You Devil!, 323; Silent Rage, 136

Silver: Dawn on the Great Divide, 891; Gunman from Bodie, 900

Silver, Veronique: Woman Next Door, The, 638

Silvestre, Armand: Rock 'N Roll Wrestling Women Vs. The Aztec Mummy, 342

Simmons, Allene: RSVP, 343

Simmons, Gene: Never Too Young To Die, 106; Runaway, 860

Simmons, Jean: Big Country, 882; Black Narcissus, *413;* Dain Curse, The, *37;* Dominique Is Dead, *677;* Elmer Gantry, *457;* Grass Is Greener, The, *272;* Guys and Dolls, *785;* Hamlet, *481;* Robe, The, *581;* Spartacus, *138;* Thorn Birds, The, *617*

Simmons, Ros: Adventures of Sherlock Holmes: The Blue Carbuncle, *2*

Simons, Frank: Blue Yonder, The, *173*

Simon, Carly: No Nukes, *795*

Simon, Michel: Boudu Saved From Drowning, *232;* Train, The, *155*

Simon, Neil: Prisoner of Second Avenue, The, *334*

Simon, Paul: Annie Hall, *219;* One Trick Pony, *797*

Simon, Simone: Cat People (Original), *660;* Curse of the Cat People, The, *668;* La Bete Humaine, *510;* La Ronde, *295*

Simpatico, David: Screen Test, *346*

Simpson, O. J.: Capricorn One, *822;* Firepower, *55*

Simpson, Russell: Grapes of Wrath, The, *477;* Spoilers, The, *934*

Sims, Joan: Carry On Cowboy, *238*

Sims, Mike: Bus Is Coming, The, *422*

Sim, Alastair: Belles of St. Trinian's, The, *227;* Christmas Carol, A, *177;* Littlest Horse Thieves, The, *190;* Ruling Class, The, *344;* Stage Fright, *747*

Sinatra, Frank: Cannonball Run II, *237;* Devil at 4 O'Clock, The, *450;* First Deadly Sin, The, *55;* Guys and Dolls, *785;* High Society, *787;* Miracle of the Bells, The, *534;* Ocean's Eleven, *109;* On the Town, *796;* Pride and the Passion, The, *567;* Suddenly, *606;* That's Entertainment, *807;* Von Ryan's Express, *159*

Sinatra, Nancy: Speedway, *805;* Wild Angels, The, *163*

Sinclair, Gordon John: Gregory's Girl, *273*

Sinclair, Madge: Conrack, *438;* Convoy, *34*

Sinden, Donald: Island at the Top of the World, The, *845*

Singer, Lori: Falcon and the Snowman, The, *461;* Footloose, *781;* Man With One Red Shoe, The, *306;* Trouble in Mind, *622*

Singer, Marc: Beastmaster, The, *820;* Go Tell the Spartans, *63;* If You Could See What I Hear, *492;* Two Worlds of Jennie Logan, The, *874*

Singleton, Penny: Mad Miss Manton, The, *304*

Sisters, Clark: Gospel, *784*

Sjöström, Victor: Wild Strawberries, *635*

Skala, Lilia: Charly, *823;* Flashdance, *780;* Heartland, *902;* Lilies of the Field, *518;* Roseland, *584;* Ship of Fools, *592*

Skarvellis, Jackie: Rats Are Coming!, The Werewolves Are Here!, The, *733*

Skelton, Red: Du Barry Was a Lady, *777;* Fuller Brush Man, The, *264;* Neptune's Daughter, *795;* Thousands Cheer, *808;* Ziegfeld Follies, *814*

Skerritt, Tom: Alien, *815;* Big Bad Mama,

14; Dangerous Summer, A, *444;* Dead Zone, The, *671;* Devil's Rain, The, *674;* Fuzz, *265;* Ice Castles, *492;* M*A*S*H, *307;* Silence of the North, *593;* SpaceCamp, *864;* Top Gun, *153*

Skilbeck, Alison: Adventures of Sherlock Holmes: The Naval Treaty, *4*

Skinner, Anita: Girlfriends, *472;* Sole Survivor, *744*

Skipworth, Alison: Becky Sharp, *407*

Skobline, Irene: Clean State (Coup de Torchon), *244*

Skolimowski, Jerzy: White Nights, *632*

Slater, Christian: Legend of Billy Jean, The, *89*

Slater, Helen: Legend of Billy Jean, The, *89;* Park is Mine, The, *558;* Ruthless People, *344;* Supergirl, *868*

Slate, Jeremy: Born Losers, *22;* Girls! Girls! Girls!, *783;* Mr. Horn, *915;* Sons of Katie Elder, The, *934*

Slaughter, Sgt.: Bad Guys, *11*

Sleap, Steve: Howard the Duck, *842*

Sleeper, Martha: Spitfire, *599*

Slezak, Walter: Bedtime for Bonzo, *226;* Cornered, *35;* Inspector General, The, *287;* Lifeboat, *518;* Once Upon a Honeymoon, *324;* Pirate, The, *798;* Sinbad the Sailor, *136;* This Land Is Mine, *617*

Slivkova, Han: Shop on Main Street, The, *593*

Sloane, Everett: Citizen Kane, *434;* Lady from Shanghai, *86;* Patsy, The, *328*

Sloan, Edward Van: Frankenstein (Restored Version), *688*

Sloyan, James: Xanadu, *813*

Sylvia: Petronella, *197*

Small, Marya: Fade to Black, *682*

Smart, Jean: Fire With Fire, *464*

Smith II, William: Last American Hero, The, *86*

Smith, Alexis: Casey's Shadow, *176;* Gentleman Jim, *471;* Little Girl Who Lives Down the Lane, The, *712;* Night and Day, *544;* Young Philadelphians, The, *640*

Smith, Andrew: Quicksilver, *572*

Smith, Aubrey: And Then There Were None, *398*

Smith, Bubba: Black Moon Rising, *18;* Police Academy III: Back in Training, *332;* Police Academy II: Their First Assignment, *332;* Police Academy, *332*

Smith, Charles Martin: American Graffiti, *218;* Herbie Goes Bananas, *184;* Never Cry Wolf, *105;* Starman, *867;* Rafferty and the Gold Dust Twins, *337*

Smith, Cheryl: Laserblast, *847*

Smith, C. Aubrey: Dr. Jekyll and Mr. Hyde, *676;* Five Came Back, *465;* Four Feathers, The, *60;* Little Lord Fauntleroy, *519;* Lives of a Bengal Lancer, The, *91*

Smith, Geraldine: Mixed Blood, *101*

Smith, Hagen: Bloody Trail, *884*

Smith, Jaclyn: Deja Vu, *448;* Nightkill, *107;* Users, The, *627*

Smith, John: Circus World, *889*

Smith, Kate: This is the Army, *808*

Smith, Kent: Affair, The, *389;* Cat People (Original), *660;* Curse of the Cat People, The, *668;* Fountainhead, The, *468;* Hitler's Children, *73*

Smith, Lewis: Heavenly Kid, The, *278;* Heavenly Kid, The, *841*

Smith, Liz: Private Function, A, *335*

Smith, Lois: Reckless, *577;* Reuben, Reuben, *339*

Smith, Madolyn: Urban Cowboy, *627*

Smith, Maggie: California Suite, *237;* Evil Under the Sun, *50;* Lily in Love, *299;* Missionary, The, *310;* Murder by Death, *315;* Private Function, A, *335;* Quartet, *571;* Room With a View, A (1987 Release), *584*

Smith, Mel: Morons from Outer Space, *314*

Smith, Mittie: Blue Yonder, The, *173*

Smith, Patricia: Spirit of St. Louis, The, *599*

Smith, Paul L.: Haunted Honeymoon, *277;* Popeye, *199;* Red Sonja, *120*

Smith, Peter: Quiet Earth, The, *858*

Smith, Reid: Tennessee Stallion, *147*

Smith, Rex: Pirates of Penzance, The, *799;* Snow White and the Seven Dwarfs, *205;* Streethawk, *142*

Smith, Roger: Never Steal Anything Small, *795*

Smith, Terri Susan: Basket Case, *648*

Smith, William: Angels Die Hard, *8;* Any Which Way You Can, *219;* C.C. & Company, *28;* Frisco Kid, The, *897;* Gentle Savage, *898;* Grave Of The Vampire, *695;* Invasion of the Bee Girls, *844;* Red Dawn, *119;* Twilight's Last Gleaming, *156;* Ultimate Warrior, The, *874*

Smith, Willie E.: Legend of Boggy Creek, *711*

Smith, Willie Mae Ford: Say Amen, Somebody, *801*

Smith, Yeardley: Maximum Overdrive, *716*

Smitrovich, Bill: Miami Vice, *98*

Smits, Jimmy: Running Scared (1986), *125*

Smits, Sonja: Videodrome, *762*

Smothers, Tom: Silver Bears, *351;* Kids Are Alright, The, *790;* Serial, *349*

Smuel, Joanne: Alison's Birthday, *644*

Snodgrass, Carrie: Attic, The, *648;* Diary of a Mad Housewife, *450;* Murphy's Law, *104;* Night in Heaven, A, *544;* Pale Rider, *921;* Rabbit Run, *573*

Snow, Norman: Last Starfighter, The, *848*

Snyder, Arlen Dean: Scalpel, *740*

Socas, Maria: Warrior and the Sorceress, The, *875*

Soderdahl, Lars: Brothers Lionheart, The, *175*

Soderling, Walter: So Dear to My Heart, *206*

Sofaer, Abraham: Journey to the Center of Time, *846*

Sojin: Thief of Baghdad, The, *871*

Sokoloff, Vladimir: Mayerling, *531*

Sokol, Marilyn: Foul Play, *262*

Solar, Silvia: Night of the Howling Beast, *723*

Sola, Miquel Angel: Funny Dirty Little War (no habra mas pensas ni olvido), *264*

Soles, P. J.: Halloween, *695;* Rock 'n' Roll High School, *342;* Stripes, *360;* Sweet Dreams, *806*

Solomin, Yuri: Dersu Uzala, *448*

Solon, Matthew: Adventures of Sherlock Holmes: The Norwood Builder, *5*

Solovei, Elena: Slave of Love, A, *594*

Somack, Jack: Portnoy's Complaint, *565*

Sombert, Claire: Invitation to the Dance, *788*

Somer, Yarti: Captive Planet, *823*

Somers, Kristi: Tomboy, *153*

Somers, Suzanne: American Graffiti, *218;* Nothing Personal, *321*

Sommars, Julie: Herbie Goes to Monte Carlo, *185*

Sommer, Elke: Boy, Did I Get a Wrong Number!, *233;* Corrupt Ones, The, *35;* House of Exorcism, The, *699;* Lily in Love, *299;* Oscar, The, *554;* Prisoner of Zenda, The, *334;* Shot in the Dark, A, *351;* Ten Little Indians, *147;* Torture Chamber Of Baron Blood, The, *758*

Sommer, Josef: D.A.R.Y.L., *827;* Iceman, *843;* Rollover, *583;* Target, *145*

Sondergaard, Gale: Life of Emile Zola, The, *518;* Return of a Man Called Horse, The, *924*

SooHan, Master Bong: Kentucky Fried Movie, *292;* Kentucky Fried Movie, *292*

Soo, Jack: Flower Drum Song, *780;* Green Berets, The, *66*

Soo, Park Jong: Search and Destroy, *130*

Sopkiw, Michael: After the Fall of New York, *815*

Soral, Agnes: One Wild Moment, *552*

Sorel, Louise: Where the Boys Are '84, *380*

Sorensen, Linda: Joshua Then and Now, *290;* Stone Cold Dead, *141*

Sorin, Louis: Animal Crackers, *218*

Sorvino, Paul: Bloodbrothers, *415;* Brinks Job, The, *234;* Chiefs, *432;* Cruising, *441;* Day of the Dolphin, The, *828;* Fine Mess, A, *260;* Gambler, The, *470;* I Will, I Will... For Now, *285;* Stuff, The, *750;* That Championship Season, *614;* Touch of Class, A, *370*

Sothern, Ann: Crazy Mama, *36;* Lady in a Cage, *710;* Manitou, The, *714*

Soth, Sandor: Time Stands Still, *619*

Soul, David: Dogpound Shuffle, *252;* Johnny Got His Gun, *503;* Magnum Force, *94;* Salem's Lot, *739*

Soutar, Farren: Iron Duke, The, *498*

Soutenduk, Renee: Fourth Man, The, *687;* Spetters, *598*

Southern, Ann: Thousands Cheer, *808*

Spacek, Sissy: Badlands, *404;* Carrie, *659;*

Coal Miner's Daughter, *775;* Ginger In The Morning, *472;* Heart Beat, *483;* Marie, *529;* Missing, *535;* Prime Cut, *115;* Raggedy Man, *733;* River, The, *581;* Violets Are Blue, *628;* Welcome to L.A., *631*

Space, Arthur: Last of the Pony Riders, *907*

Spader, James: Cocaine: One Man's Seduction, *435;* New Kids, The, *721;* Pretty in Pink, *567;* Tuff Turf, *623*

Spain, Fay: God's Little Acre, *473*

Spano, Joe: Terminal Choice, *752*

Spano, Vincent: Alphabet City, *394;* Black Stallion Returns, The, *173;* Creator, *440;* Maria's Lovers, *528;* Rumble Fish, *585*

Spanza, Mario: Stromboli, *606*

Sparks, Ned: Magic Town, *526*

Sparv, Camilla: Downhill Racer, *454;* Greek Tycoon, The, *479*

Speciale, Lynda: Screwballs, *346*

Spencer, Bud: Massacre At Fort Holman (Reason to Live... A Reason to Die, A), *914;* They Call Me Trinity, *938;* Trinity Is Still My Name, *941*

Spencer, Jeremy: Prince and the Showgirl, The, *334*

Spence, Bruce: Mad Max Beyond Thunderdome, *850;* Road Warrior, The, *859;* Where the Green Ants Dream, *632*

Sperber, Wendy Jo: Moving Violations, *315*

Spiesser, Jacques: La Truite (The Trout), *512*

Spilsbury, Klinton: Legend of the Lone Ranger, The, *908*

Spinell, Joe: Big Score, The, *16;* Last Horror Film, The, *711;* Maniac, *714;* Ninth Configuration, The, *546;* Star Crash, *864*

Spinetti, Victor: Hard Day's Night, A, *786;* Help!, *787;* Return of the Pink Panther, The, *339*

Spradlin, G. D.: Formula, The, *467;* Lords of Discipline, The, *521;* North Dallas Forty, *546;* One on One, *552;* Tank, *145;* Wrong Is Right, *384*

Springfield, Rick: Hard to Hold, *786*

Springsteen, Bruce: No Nukes, *795*

Squire, David: Adventures of Sherlock Holmes: The Resident Patient, *5*

Squire, Katherine: Ride in the Whirlwind, *925*

Stacey, Bill: Road Games, *736*

Stack, Robert: Airplane!, *216;* Big Trouble, *228;* Bullfighter and the Lady, The, *26;* Corrupt Ones, The, *35;* To Be or Not to Be (Original), *368;* Uncommon Valor, *156;* Untouchables: Alcatraz Express, The, *157;* Untouchables: Scarface Mob, The, *157*

Stacy, James: Double Exposure, *678;* Swingin' Summer, A, *362*

Stadlen, Lewis J.: Windy City, *635*

Stafford, Frederick: Battle of El Alamein, The, *13;* Topaz, *757*

Stahl, Richard: Son of Blob (Beware! The Blob), *745*

Staiola, Enzo: Bicycle Thief, The, *410*

Staley, James: Sweet Dreams, *806*

Stallone, Sylvester: Cannonball, *27;* Cobra, *32;* Death Race 2000, *829;* First Blood, *55;* F.I.S.T., *461;* Lords of Flatbush, The, *522;* Nighthawks, *107;* Paradise Alley, *557;* Rambo: First Blood II, *118;* Rhinestone, *340;* Rocky III, *582;* Rocky II, *582;* Rocky IV, *582;* Rocky, *582;* Victory, *158*

Stalmaster, Hal: Johnny Tremain, *187*

Stamos, John: Never Too Young To Die, *106*

Stamp, Terence: Billy Budd, *411;* Collector, The, *663;* Divine Nymph, The, *452;* Hit, The, *73;* Legal Eagles, *88*

Stander, Lionel: Black Bird, The, *230;* Matilda, *308;* New York, New York, *795;* Once upon a Time in the West, *919;* Sin of Harold Diddlebock (aka Mad Wednesday), *352;* Unfaithfully Yours (Original), *374*

Standiford, Jim: Violets Are Blue, *628*

Standing, John: Legacy, The, *711;* Privates on Parade, *336*

Standing, Sir Guy: Lives of a Bengal Lancer, The, *91*

Stanislav, Jiri: Moonlighting, *538*

Stanley, Florence: Prisoner of Second Avenue, The, *334*

Stanley, James: Desert Hearts, *449*

Stanley, Kim: Cat on a Hot Tin Roof (Remake), *428;* Frances, *469;* Right Stuff, The, *580;* Seance on a Wet Afternoon, *741*

Stanley, Paul: I Heard the Owl Call My Name, *491*

Stansbury, Hope: Rats Are Coming!, The Werewolves Are Here!, The, *733*

Stanton, Barry: Carpathian Eagle, *659*

Stanton, Harry Dean: Alien, *815;* Black Marble, The, *413;* Christine, *662;* Cockfighter, *32;* Death Watch, *829;* Farewell My Lovely, *52;* Fool For Love, *466;* Missouri Breaks, The, *915;* One from the Heart, *797;* One Magic Christmas, *552;* Paris, Texas, *558;* Pretty in Pink, *567;* Rafferty and the Gold Dust Twins, *337;* Red Dawn, *119;* Repo Man, *338;* Ride in the Whirlwind, *925;* Rip Van Winkle, *859;* Rose, The, *800;* Straight Time, *603;* Uforia, *859;* Wise Blood, *636;* Young Doctors in Love, *385*

Stanton, John: Run, Rebecca, Run, *202*

Stanton, Robert: Abbott and Costello in Hollywood, *214*

Stanwyck, Barbara: Ball of Fire, *224;* Cattle Queen of Montana, *888;* Clash by Night, *434;* Escape to Burma, *459;* Golden Boy, *475;* Lady Eve, The, *295;* Lady of Burlesque, *86;* Mad Miss Manton, The, *304;* Maverick Queen, The, *914;* Meet John Doe, *532;* Roustabout, *800;* Sorry, Wrong Number, *745;* Stella Dallas, *602;* Strange Love of Martha Ivers, The, *604;* Thorn Birds, The, *617*

Stapel, Huub: Lift, The, *712*

Stapleton, Jean: Cinderella, *177;* Jack and the Beanstalk, *186*

Stapleton, Maureen: Cocoon, *825;* Fan, The, *683;* Heartburn, *277;* Johnny Dangerously, *290;* Lost and Found, *301;* On the Right Track, *197;* Plaza Suite, *331;* Queen of the Stardust Ballroom, *572;* Reds, *578;* Runner Stumbles, The, *585*

Stark, Graham: Revenge of the Pink Panther, The, *340;* Shot in the Dark, A, *351*

Stark, Koo: Emily, *457*

Starrett, Jack: First Blood, *55;* Mr. Horn, *915*

Starr, Ringo: 200 Motels, *810;* Caveman, *240;* Give My Regards to Broad Street, *783;* Help!, *787;* Kids Are Alright, The, *790;* Let It Be, *792;* Lisztomania, *792;* Magic Christian, The, *304;* Sextette, *350;* Water, *377*

Steadman, Alison: Private Function, A, *335*

Steafel, Sheila: Bloodbath at the House of Death, *230*

Steele, Barbara: Pit and the Pendulum, The, *728;* Silent Scream, *743*

Steele, Bob: Atomic Submarine, The, *818;* Big Sleep, The (Original), *16;* Border Phantom, *885;* Revenge of the Zombies, *736;* Rio Bravo, *926*

Steele, Don: Death Race 2000, *829*

Steele, Tommy: Finian's Rainbow, *779;* Happiest Millionaire, The, *184;* King of the Rocketmen, *846*

Steel, Amy: April Fool's Day, *646;* Friday the 13th, Part II, *690*

Steel, Anthony: Malta Story, The, *527*

Steenburgen, Mary: Cross Creek, *441;* Goin' South, *898;* Little Red Riding Hood, *190;* Melvin and Howard, *309;* Midsummer Night's Sex Comedy, A, *309;* One Magic Christmas, *552;* Ragtime, *574;* Romantic Comedy, *343;* Time after Time, *872*

Stefanelli, Benito: Cop in Blue Jeans, The, *35*

Stefani, Michael: Trancers, *873*

Stegers, Bernice: XTro, *766*

Steger, Arlene: RSVP, *343*

Steiger, Rod: Amityville Horror, The, *645;* Breakthrough, *24;* Chosen, The, *433;* Dr. Zhivago, *452;* F.I.S.T., *461;* Harder They Fall, The, *482;* In the Heat of the Night, *494;* Lion of the Desert, *90;* Longest Day, The, *92;* Love and Bullets, *93;* Lucky Luciano, *93;* Naked Face, The, *720;* No Way to Treat a Lady, *546;* Oklahoma!, *796;* On the Waterfront, *551;* Pawnbroker, The, *560*

Steinberg, David: End, The, *255*

Steiner, John: Ark of the Sun God ... Temple of Hell, The, *9;* Beyond the Door 2, *651;* Yor: The Hunter from the Future, *877*

Steinrück, Albert: The Golem (How He Came Into The World) (DER GOLEM, Wie er in die Welt Kam), *754*

Stein, Saul: Beer, *226*

Stenborg, Helen: Flash of Green, A, *466*

Stensgaard, Yutte: Lust for a Vampire, *713*

Stephenson, Henry: Charge of the Light Brigade, The, *30;* Mutiny on the Bounty (Original), *105*

Stephenson, James: Letter, The, *516*

Stephenson, Pamela: Bloodbath at the House of Death, *230;* Scandalous, *345;* Superman III, *869*

Stephens, Harvey: Oklahoma Kid, The, *918*

Stephens, Robert: Duellists, The, *46;* Morgan, *314;* Private Life of Sherlock Holmes, The, *115;* Shout, The, *743;* Spirit of the Dead, *746*

Sterling, Ford: Keystone Comedies: Vol. 4, *292;* Keystone Comedies: Vo. 5, *292*

Sterling, Jan: First Monday in October, *465;* Harder They Fall, The, *482;* High School Confidential!, *487;* Pony Express, *922;* Union Station, *760*

Sterling, Robert: Voyage to the Bottom of the Sea, *874*

Sterling, Tisha: Coogan's Bluff, *34*

Sternhagen, Frances: Independence Day, *494;* Outland, *855;* Romantic Comedy, *343;* Starting Over, *358*

Stern, Daniel: Breaking Away, *233;* C.H.U.D., *658;* Diner, *251;* Get Crazy, *266;* Hannah and Her Sisters, *275;* Key Exchange, *506*

Stern, Erik: Love Butcher, *713*

Stern, Isaac: Fiddler on the Roof, *779;* From Mao to Mozart, *781*

Stevenson, Parker: Lifeguard, *518;* Stroker Ace, *361*

Stevens, Andrew: Boys in Company C, The, *23;* Death Hunt, *39;* Fury, The, *692;* Massacre at Central High, *716;* Seduction, The, *741;* Ten to Midnight, *147*

Stevens, Casey: Prom Night, *730*

Stevens, Craig: S.O.B., *355*

Stevens, Dustin: RSVP, *343*

Stevens, Fisher: My Science Project, *853;* Short Circuit, *862*

Stevens, Inger: Guide For The Married Man, A, *273;* Hang 'Em High, *900;* Madigan, *94*

Stevens, Onslow: Angel on My Shoulder, *399;* Hills of Utah, The, *903;* Sunset Serenade, *935*

Stevens, Rise: Going My Way, *474*

Stevens, Sarah: Improper Channels, *286*

Stevens, Stella: Arnold, *646;* Ballad of Cable Hogue, The, *880;* Chained Heat, *29;* Cruise into Terror, *667;* Girls! Girls! Girls!, *783;* Manitou, The, *714;* Nutty Professor, The, *321;* Poseidon Adventure, The, *115*

Stewart, Alana: Where the Boys Are '84, *380*

Stewart, Alexandra: In Praise of Older Women, *493;* Last Chase, The, *847;* Under The Cherry Moon, *626*

Stewart, Catherine Mary: Last Starfighter, The, *848;* Mischief, *310;* Night of the Comet, *854*

Stewart, Charlotte: Eraserhead, *680*

Stewart, Elaine: Brigadoon, *772*

Stewart, Ian: Let's Spend the Night Together, *792*

Stewart, James: After the Thin Man, 6; Anatomy of a Murder, 397; Bandolero!, 881; Bell, Book and Candle, 226; Big Sleep, The, 16; Cheyenne Autumn, 888; Flight of the Phoenix, The, 58; Glenn Miller Story, The, 783; Greatest Show on Earth, The, 478; How the West Was Won, 904; It's a Wonderful Life, 499; Made for Each Other, 304; Magic of Lassie, The, 191; Magic Town, 526; Man Who Knew Too Much, The (remake), 715; Man Who Shot Liberty Valance, The, 515; Mr. Smith Goes to Washington, 536; Philadelphia Story, The, 329; Pot O' Gold, 566; Rare Breed, The, 924; Rear Window, 734; Right of Way, 580; Rope, 737; Rose Marie, 800; Shenandoah, 930; Shootist, The, 931; Spirit of St. Louis, The, 599; Thunder Bay, 151; Vertigo.

Stewart, Paul: Revenge of the Pink Panther, The, 340

Stewart, Richard: Watch Me When I Kill, 763

Stewart, Roy: Sparrows, 598

Stewart, Trish: Wild Times, 945

Sticklyn, Ray: Dogpound Shuffle, 252

Stiers, David Ogden: Better Off Dead, 228; Creator, 440

Stiller, Jerry: Ritz, The, 342

Stills, S: No Nukes, 795

Stimson, Sara: Little Miss Marker, 190

Sting: Bride, The, 656; Brimstone and Treacle, 657; Bring on the Night, 772; Dune, 832; Plenty, 564; Quadrophenia, 799

Stocker, Walter: They Saved Hitler's Brain, 754

Stockwell, Dean: Boy With Green Hair, The, 419; Dunwich Horror, The, 680; Kim, 83; Long Day's Journey into Night, 520; Paris, Texas, 558; Song of the Thin Man, 138; To Live and Die in L.A., 153; Tracks, 621; Wrong Is Right, 384

Stockwell, Guy: It's Alive!, 707; Tobruk, 153

Stockwell, John: Christine, 662; City Limits, 823; Dangerously Close, 668; Losin' It, 301; My Science Project, 853; Top Gun, 153

Stock, Nigel: Prisoner, The (television series), 857

Stoker, Austin: Assault on Precinct 13, 10

Stokes, Barry: Alien Prey, 644

Stokey, Susan: Power, The, 730

Stoler, Shirley: Seven Beauties, 349

Stole, Mink: Desperate Living, 250; Female Trouble, 259; Mondo Trasho, 312; Multiple Maniacs, 718; Pink Flamingos, 330

Stollery, David: Ten Who Dared, 208; Westward Ho The Wagons, 212

Stoltz, Eric: Code Name: Emerald, 33; Mask, 530; Running Hot, 586; Wild Life, The, 382

Stone, Christopher: Cujo, 667; Howling, The, 701; Junkman, The, 80

Stone, Dee Wallace: Critters, 666; Secret Admirer, 346

Stone, Fred: Alice Adams, 392; Westerner,

The, 944

Stone, George E.: Last Mile, The, 514

Stone, Gus: Endgame, 834

Stone, Harold J.: Hardly Working, 276; Wrong Man, The, 766; X (The Man with the X-Ray Eyes), 877

Stone, Ivory: Blackenstein, 652

Stone, Lewis: China Seas, 30; Grand Hotel, 476; Lost World, The, 850; Love Laughs at Andy Hardy, 302; Prisoner of Zenda, The, 115; Treasure Island, 211

Stone, Milburn: Colorado, 889

Stone, Sharon: King Solomon's Mines (1985), 84

Stooges, The Three: Snow White and the Three Stooges, 205

Storch, Larry: Adventures of Huckleberry Finn, The, 169; Better Late than Never, 228; Great Race, The, 273; Without Warning, 876

Storey, June: South of the Border, 934

Storm, Gale: Jesse James at Bay, 905; Revenge of the Zombies, 736; Tom Brown's School Days, 620

Stossel, Ludwig: Bluebeard, 654; Pride of the Yankees, The, 568; Yolanda and The Thief, 640

Straight, Beatrice: Poltergeist, 729; Power, 566; Princess and the Pea, The, 199

Strait, Ralph: Halloween III: Season of the Witch, 695

Strang, Harry: Sinister Journey, 932

Strange, Glenn: False Colors, 895

Strasberg, Lee: Godfather, The, Part II, 474; Going in Style, 269

Strasberg, Susan: Delta Force, The, 41; Frankenstein (Remake), 688; In Praise of Older Women, 493; Manitou, The, 714; Psycho Sisters, 732; Rollercoaster, 737; Sweet Sixteen, 144; Trip, The, 622

Strassman, Marcia: Soup for One, 356

Stratas, Teresa: La Traviata, 791

Stratten, Dorothy R.: Galaxina, 839; They All Laughed, 365

Stratton, Gil: Wild One, The, 164

Strauch Jr., Joseph: Call of the Canyon, 887

Strauch, Maxim: Strike, 605

Strauss, Peter: Jericho Mile, The, 501; Last Tycoon, The, 515; Masada, 530; Secret of Nimh, The, 203; Soldier Blue, 933; Spacehunter: Adventures in the Forbidden Zone, 864

Strauss, Robert: 4D Man, 838; Stalag 17, 139

Streep, Meryl: Deer Hunter, The, 448; Falling in Love, 462; French Lieutenant's Woman, The, 469; Heartburn, 277; Kramer vs. Kramer, 510; Manhattan, 305; Out of Africa, 555; Plenty, 564; Seduction of Joe Tynan, The, 590; Silkwood, 593; Sophie's Choice, 597; Still of the Night, 748

Streisand, Barbra: All Night Long, 393; For Pete's Sake, 262; Funny Girl, 782; Funny Lady, 782; Hello, Dolly!, 787; Main Event, The, 305; On a Clear Day, You Can See

Forever, 796; Owl and the Pussycat, The, 326; Star Is Born, A (Remake), 601; Up the Sandbox, 375; Way We Were, The, 631; What's Up Doc?, 380; Yentl, 813

Stribling, Melissa: Horror of Dracula, 699

Stribolt, Oscar: Witchcraft Through the Ages (HAXAN), 637

Strickland, Gail: Bound For Glory, 418; Drowning Pool, The, 45; Protocol, 336; Starflight One, 867; Who'll Stop the Rain, 162

Stride, John: Macbeth, 525

Stritch, Elaine: Providence, 569; Perfect Furlough, 329

Strobye, Axel: Topsy Turvy, 370

Strode, Woody: Black Stallion Returns, The, 173; Kill Castro, 82; Kingdom of the Spiders, 709; Loaded Guns, 91; Man Who Shot Liberty Valance, The, 913; Once upon a Time in the West, 919; Professionals, The, 116; Shalako, 930

Stronach, Tami: NeverEnding Story, The, 853

Strong, Michael: Queen of the Stardust Ballroom, 572

Strong, Sharon: Deadly Blessing, 671

Stroud, Don: Bloody Mama, 20; Coogan's Bluff, 34; Joe Kidd, 906; Murph the Surf, 104; Night the Lights Went Out in Georgia, The, 545; Search and Destroy, 130; Sweet Sixteen, 144

Strudwick, Shepperd: Beyond A Reasonable Doubt, 409; Red Pony, The, 201

Struthers, Sally: Getaway, The, 62

Stryker, Amy: Wedding, A, 378

Stuart, Maxine: Coast to Coast, 245

Stuart, Randy: Incredible Shrinking Man, The, 843

Stuart, Roy: Adventures of Sherlock Holmes: The Red-Headed League, 5; Prime Risk, 115

Stubbs, Mr.: Toby Tyler, 210

Sturgess, Olive: Raven, The, 733

Sturm, Hannes: The Golem (How He Came Into The World) (DER GOLEM, Wie er in die Welt Kam), 754

St. John, Al: Keystone Comedies, Vol. 1, 292; Keystone Comedies, Vol. 2, 292; Keystone Comedies, Vol. 3, 292; Keystone Comedies: Vol. 4, 292; Lawman Is Born, A, 908

Suchet, David: Iron Eagle, 78; Murrow, 539

Sudlow, Susie: Ark of the Sun God...Temple of Hell, The, 9

Sukowa, Barbara: Berlin Alexanderplatz, 408

Sullivan, Barry: Another Time, Another Place, 400; Kung Fu, 85; Maverick Queen, The, 914; Shark! (aka Maneaters!), 133; Texas Lady, 938; Washington Affair, The, 630

Sullivan, Francis: Caesar and Cleopatra, 423; Joan of Arc, 502; Winslow Boy, The, 635

Sullivan, Liam: Magic Sword, The, 191

Sullivan, Susan: Incredible Hulk, The, 843; Ordeal of Dr. Mudd, The, 553

Sully, Frank: Night Stage to Galveston, 917

Summerville, Slim: Jesse James, 905

Summer, Donna: Thank God It's Friday, 806

Summer, Josef: Witness, 165

Sundquist, Folk: Wild Strawberries, 635

Supan, Bob: Last Game, The, 513

Supremes, The: That Was Rock, 808

Sutherland, Donald: Bear Island, 648; Crackers, 248; Day of the Locust, The, 446; Die! Die! My Darling!, 675; Dirty Dozen, The, 43; Disappearance, The, 43; Don't Look Now, 677; Dr. Terror's House of Horrors, 677; Eagle Has Landed, The, 46; Eye of the Needle, 51; Gas, 265; Great Train Robbery, The, 66; Heaven Help Us, 278; Invasion of the Body Snatchers (Remake), 845; Johnny Got His Gun, 503; Kelly's Heroes, 81; Kentucky Fried Movie, 292; Klute, 509; Man, A Woman and a Bank, A, 95; Max Dugan Returns, 531; Murder By Decree, 103; M*A*S*H, 307; Nothing Personal, 321; Ordeal By Innocence, 111; Ordinary People, 554; Revolution, 579; Start the Revolution Without Me, 358; Steelyard Blues, 359; Threshold, 872

Sutherland, Keifer: Bay Boy, The, 406; Stand By Me, 600

Sutorius, James: Windy City, 635

Sutton, Dudley: Devils, The, 450

Sutton, Lisa: Raw Courage, 119

Sutton, Raymond: Dogpound Shuffle, 252

Suzman, Janet: Nicholas and Alexandra, 543; Priest of Love, 568

Svenson, Bo: Delta Force, The, 41; Final Chapter—Walking Tall, 54; Frankenstein (Remake), 688; Great Waldo Pepper, The, 66; Night Warning, 723; North Dallas Forty, 546; Walking Tall Part II, 160

Svierkier, Anna: Day of Wrath, 446

Swada, Ken: Mishima: A Life in Four Chapters, 535

Swain, Mack: Gold Rush, The, 270

Swanson, Gary: Vice Squad, 158

Swanson, Gloria: Indiscreet, 286; Sunset Blvd., 609

Swayze, Patrick: Grandview, U.S.A. 477; Red Dawn, 119; Youngblood, 641

Sweeney, Ann: Incredible Melting Man, The, 843

Sweeney, Bob: Toby Tyler, 210

Sweeney, Joseph: 12 Angry Men, 624

Sweet, Dolph: King, 507; Which Way Is Up?, 381

Swenson, Forrest: To All a Good Night, 756

Swickard, Joe: Keystone Comedies: Vo. 5, 292

Swift, Paul: Multiple Maniacs, 718

Swift, Susan: Harper Valley P.T.A., 276

Swit, Loretta: Beer, 226; Freebie and the Bean, 263; M*A*S*H: Goodbye Farewell, Amen, 307; Race with the Devil, 732; S.O.B., 355

Swofford, Ken: Bless the Beasts and the Children, 414

Swope, Topo: Tracks, *621*

Sydney, Basil: Dam Busters, The, *38*; Hamlet, *481*; Treasure Island, *211*

Sydney, Slyvia: You Only Live Once, *640*

Sydow, Max von: Seventh Seal, The, *591*

Sykes, Brenda: Cleopatra Jones, *31*; Mandingo, *528*

Sykes, Eric: Heavens Above, *279*

Sylvester, Harold: FastBreak, *258*; Officer and a Gentleman, An, *549*; Uncommon Valor, *156*; Vision Quest, *628*

Sylvester, William: 2001: A Space Odyssey, *873*; Gorgo, *694*

Sylwan, Karl: Cries and Whispers, *440*

Syms, Slyvia: Asylum, *647*

Szarabajka, Keith: Marie, *529*

Szeps, Henri: Run, Rebecca, Run, *202*

S., Bruno: Every Man for Himself and God Against All, *460*

Tabor, Epon: I Spit On Your Grave, *704*

Tachikoiwa, Yoichi: Throne of Blood, *617*

Tafler, Jean: Return of the Alien's Deadly Spawn, The, *734*

Taggart, Rita: Torchlight, *620*

Taichi, Kiwako: Himatsuri, *487*

Taimak: Last Dragon, The, *87*

Takakura, Ken: Yakuza, The, *165*

Takarada, Akira: Godzilla vs. Monster Zero, *694*; Godzilla vs. Mothra, *693*

Takashima, Tadao: Son of Godzilla, *745*

Takashi: Rashomon, *575*

Takei, George: Green Berets, The, *66*; Star Trek III: The Search for Spock, *865*; Star Trek (television series), *866*; Star Trek: The Menagerie, *865*; Star Trek—The Motion Picture, *865*

Takita, Yuhsuke: Irezumi (Spirit of Tattoo), *497*

Talarowski, Joe: Student Bodies, *749*

Talbott, Gloria: Cyclops, The, *668*; Daughter of Dr. Jekyll, *670*; I Married a Monster from Outer Space, *842*

Talbott, Michael: Miami Vice, *98*

Talbot, Lyle: Glen or Glenda, *473*

Talbot, Nita: Chained Heat, *39*; Island Claws, *706*

Taliaferro, Hal (Wally Wales): Colorado, *889*; Rootin' Tootin' Rhythm, *928*; Saga of Death Valley, *929*; Song of Texas, *933*; Yellow Rose of Texas, *946*

Tallichet, Margaret: Stranger on the Third Floor, *141*

Talmadge, Constance: Intolerance, *497*

Tamba, Tetsuro: You Only Live Twice, *166*

Tamblyn, Russ: High School Confidential!, *487*; Seven Brides for Seven Brothers, *802*; Tom Thumb, *210*

Tambor, Jeffrey: Cocaine: One Man's Seduction, *435*; Man Who Wasn't There, The, *306*; Saturday the 14th, *739*

Tamerlis, Zoe: Ms. .45, *103*; Special Effects, *746*

Tamiroff, Akim: Black Magic, *413*; Bridge of San Luis Rey, The, *420*; Corsican Brothers, The, *35*; Deadly Sanctuary, *671*; Lt. Robin Crusoe, U.S.N., *188*

Tanaka, Ken: Godzilla 1985, *694*

Tandy, Jessica: Best Friends, *227*; Birds, The, *651*; Bostonians, The, *417*; Cocoon, *825*; Desert Fox, The, *42*; Still of the Night, *748*; World According to Garp, The, *639*

Tani, Yoko: First Spaceship on Venus, *837*

Tashman, Lilyan: Bulldog Drummond, *25*

Tasisto, Elena: Camila, *424*

Tate, Patricia: Dangerous Venture, *891*; Unexpected Guest, *942*

Tati, Jacques: Mr. Hulot's Holiday, *311*; My Uncle (Mon Oncle), *317*; Playtime, *331*

Tavi, Tuvia: Paradise, *113*

Tayback, Vic: Alice Doesn't Live Here Anymore, *392*; Lepke, *89*; Portrait of a Stripper, *565*

Taylor, Benedict: Far Pavilions, The, *463*

Taylor, Delores: Billy Jack, *17*

Taylor, Don: Father's Little Dividend, *259*

Taylor, Dub: Best of Times, The, *228*; Creature from Black Lake, *665*; Gator, *61*; Great Smokey Roadblock, The, *65*; Man Called Horse, A, *911*; Moonshine County Express, *103*; They Went That-A-Way and That-A-Way, *208*

Taylor, Elizabeth: Between Friends, *409*; Cat on a Hot Tin Roof (Original), *428*; Cleopatra, *435*; Father's Little Dividend, *259*; Giant, *472*; Ivanhoe, *78*; Life With Father, *299*; Little Night Music, A, *793*; Mirror Crack'd, The, *99*; National Velvet, *195*; Place in the Sun, A, *563*; Raintree County, *574*; Reflections in a Golden Eye, *578*; Sandpiper, The, *588*; Suddenly, Last Summer, *607*; Taming of the Shrew, The, *364*; Who's Afraid of Virginia Woolf?, *633*; Winter Kills, *636*

Taylor, Estelle: Street Scene, *605*

Taylor, Forrest: Riders of Destiny, *926*; Ridin' on a Rainbow, *926*; Song of Nevada, *933*; Song of Texas, *933*

Taylor, Grant: Long John Silver, *92*

Taylor, Grigor: High Rolling, *72*

Taylor, James: No Nukes, *795*

Taylor, Jana: Hell's Angels on Wheels, *71*

Taylor, Joan: Earth vs. the Flying Saucers, *832*

Taylor, Kent: Crawling Hand, The, *665*; Slightly Scarlet, *595*

Taylor, Kit: Long John Silver, *92*

Taylor, Mick: Gimme Shelter, *783*

Taylor, Rip: Things Are Tough All Over, *366*

Taylor, Robert: Bataan, *12*; Bay Boy, The, *406*; Beat Street, *770*; Broadway Melody of 1936, *772*; Broadway Melody of 1938, *773*; Camille, *425*; D-Day the Sixth of June, *442*; Ivanhoe, *78*; Johnny Tiger, *503*; Knights of the Round Table, *85*; Waterloo Bridge, *631*

Taylor, Rod: Birds, The, *651*; Cry of the Innocent, *37*; Raintree County, *574*; Time Machine, The, 872; Train Robbers, The, 940; Zabriskie Point, 641

Taylor, Sharon: Attack of the Killer Tomatoes, 221

Taylor, Vaughn: It Should Happen to You, 287

Taylor-Smith, Jean: Rob Roy, The Highland Rogue, 201

Taylor-Young, Leigh: Can't Stop the Music, 773; I Love You Alice B. Toklas!, 285; Jagged Edge, 500; Looker, 850; Secret Admirer, 346

Ta: Last Dragon, The, 87

Tearle, Conway: Hurricane Express, 76

Tebbs, Susan: Littlest Horse Thieves, The, 190

Tedrow, Irene: Two Worlds of Jennie Logan, The, 874

Teefy, Maureen: Fame, 778

Teenagers, Frankie Lymon and the: Rock, Rock, Rock, 800

Tehouda, Leila Schenna and the villagers of : Ramparts of Clay, 575

Temple, Shirley: Bachelor and the Bobby-soxer, The, 222; Fort Apache, 897; Heidi, 184; Little Laura and Big John, 90; Little Miss Marker, 190; Little Princess, The, 190

Tendeter, Stacey: Two English Girls, 625

Tenessy, Hedi: Revolt of Job, The, 579

Tennant, Victoria: All of Me, 217; Chiefs, 432; Holcroft Covenant, The, 74

Terao, Akira: Ran, 575

Terhune, Max: Manhattan Merry-Go-Round, 913; Night Riders, The, 918; Pals of the Saddle, 921; Santa Fe Stampede, 929

Termo, Leonard: Year of the Dragon, 166

Terris, Ellaline: Iron Duke, The, 498

Terry, John: Hawk the Slayer, 69

Terry, Nigel: Deja Vu, 448; Excalibur, 835

Terry, Philip: Lost Weekend, The, 523

Terry, Ruth: Call of the Canyon, 887; Heart of the Golden West, 901

Terry, Sheila: Lawless Frontier, 908; 'Neath Arizona Skies, 917

Terry, Tex: Sioux City Sue, 933

Terry, William: Stage Door Canteen, 599

Terry-Thomas: Abominable Dr. Phibes, The, 643; Daydreamer, The, 179; Don't Raise the Bridge, Lower the River, 253; Dr. Phibes Rises Again, 676; It's a Mad Mad Mad Mad World, 288; I'm All Right Jack, 285; Make Mine Mink, 305; Those Magnificent Men in their Flying Machines, 367; Tom Thumb, 210; Vault of Horror, 761

Tessier, Robert: Born Losers, 22; Deep, The, 41; Double Exposure, 678

Tester, Desmond: Sabotage, 738

Testi, Fabio: Ambassador, The, 395; Blood in the Streets, 19; Garden of the Finzi-Continis, the, 471; Mussolini and I, 539

Teterson, Pete: Cold River, 177

Tetley, Walter: Prairie Moon, 922

Tevini, Thierry: Tendres Cousines, 365

Tewes, Lauren: Eyes of a Stranger, 682

Thames, Byron: Seven Minutes In Heaven, 350

Thatcher, Torin: 7TH Voyage of Sinbad, The, 861

Thaw, John: Killing Heat, 507

Thaxter, Phyllis: Thirty Seconds Over Tokyo, 149; World of Henry Orient, The, 384

Thayer, Ivy: Little Laura and Big John, 90

Thelen, Jodi: Four Friends, 468

Thesiger, Ernest: Bride of Frankenstein, 657

Thibeau, Jack: Escape from Alcatraz, 44

Thinnes, Roy: Hindenburg, The, 487; Satan's School for Girls, 739

Thomas, Betty: Homework, 489; Tunnelvision, 373

Thomas, Damian: Shogun (Full-Length Version), 134; Sinbad and the Eye of the Tiger, 862

Thomas, Dave: Strange Brew, 360; (Sesame Street Presents) Follow That Bird, 204

Thomas, Frank M.: Saga of Death Valley, 929; Sunset Serenade, 935

Thomas, Gareth: Adventures of Sherlock Holmes: The Naval Treaty, 4

Thomas, Heather: Zapped!, 385

Thomas, Henry: Cloak and Dagger, 32; E.T.—The Extra-terrestrial, 832; Misunderstood, 537; Raggedy Man, 733

Thomas, Isa: Flash of Green, A, 466

Thomas, Kristin Scott: Under The Cherry Moon, 626

Thomas, Kurt: Gymkata, 68

Thomas, Marlo: Act of Passion, 389

Thomas, Philip Michael: Miami Vice, 98; Miami Vice: "The Prodigal Son", 99

Thomas, Richard: All Quiet on the Western Front, 393; Battle beyond the Stars, 819; Last Summer, 514; Winning, 164

Thomerson, Tim: Fade to Black, 682; Iron Eagle, 78; Metalstorm: The Destruction of Jared-Syn, 852; Trancers, 873; Volunteers, 377

Thompson, Andrew Martin: Killing 'Em Softly, 506

Thompson, Cindy Ann: Cave Girl, 823

Thompson, Derek: Belfast Assassin, 407

Thompson, Fred: Marie, 529

Thompson, Hal: Animal Crackers, 218

Thompson, Jack: Breaker Morant, 24; Caddie, 423; Chant of Jimmie Blacksmith, The, 431; Earthling, The, 46; Flesh and Blood, 57; Mad Dog Morgan, 94; Man from Snowy River, 95; Sunday Too Far Away, 608

Thompson, Kay: Funny Face, 781

Thompson, Lea: Back to the Future, 819; Howard the Duck, 842; Red Dawn, 119; SpaceCamp, 864; Wild Life, The, 382

Thompson, Marshall: Around the World Under the Sea, 10; Bog, 655; Fiend without a Face, 684; They Were Expendable, 148; To Hell and Back, 152

Thompson, Ross: Chain Reaction, 29

Thompson, R. H.: If You Could See What I

Hear, *492*

Thompson, R. H.: Surfacing, *143;* Ticket to Heaven, *618;* Tom Thumb, *210*

Thordsen, Kelly: Ugly Dachshund, The, *211*

Thorley, Ken: Escapes, *835*

Thornbury, Bill: Phantasm, *727*

Thorndike, Sybil: Prince and the Showgirl, The, *334*

Thorne-Smith, Courtney: Lucas, *524*

Thorson, Linda: Act of Passion, *389;* Curtains, *668;* Sweet Liberty, *362*

Thring, Frank: Mad Max Beyond Thunderdome, *850*

Thulin, Ingrid: Cries and Whispers, *440;* Damned, The, *442;* Four Horsemen of the Apocalypse, *60;* Magician, The, *526;* Moses, *539;* Wild Strawberries, *635;* Winter Light, *636*

Thundercloud, Chief: Badman's Territory, *880*

Thurseon, Debbie: Prey, The, *730*

Tichy, Gerard: Summertime Killer, The, *143*

Ticotin, Rachel: Fort Apache—The Bronx, *467*

Tien, James: Fists of Fury, *56*

Tierney, Gene: Laura, *88;* Left Hand of God, The, *88;* Razor's Edge, The (Original), *576;* Return of Frank James, The, *925*

Tierney, Lawrence: Abduction, *387;* Dillinger, *42*

Tiffin, Pamela: One, Two, Three, *324;* Viva Max!, *377*

Tigue, Karen: Return of the Alien's Deadly Spawn, The, *734*

Tilly, Jennifer: Moving Violations, *315;* Theatre of Death, *754*

Tilly, Meg: Agnes of God, *390;* Big Chill, The, *411;* Impulse, *704;* Off Beat, *322;* One Dark Night, *726;* Psycho II, *731*

Tilton, Charlene: Sweater Girls, *362*

Timko, Johnny: Hot Moves, *283*

Tim, Tiny: One Trick Pony, *797*

Tinti, Gabriele: And Now, My Love, *398*

Tippitt, Wayne: Pipe Dreams, *563*

Tobey, Kenneth: Dangerous Venture, *891;* Davy Crockett and the River Pirates, *179;* Davy Crockett (King of the Wild Frontier), *179;* Elfego Baca: Six Gun Law, *895;* Great Locomotive Chase, The, *182;* It Came from Beneath the Sea, *706;* Strange Invaders, *867;* Thing (From Another World), The, *871*

Tobias, George: Mildred Pierce, *534;* Sergeant York, *131;* Set-Up, The, *591;* Strawberry Blonde, The, *604;* This is the Army, *808*

Tobias, Oliver: King Arthur, The Young Warlord, *84;* Stud, The, *606;* Wicked Lady, The, *163*

Tobin, Matthew: Real Life, *338*

Todd, Beverly: Jericho Mile, The, *501;* Vice Squad, *158*

Todd, Richard: Asylum, *647;* Dam Busters, The, *38;* Dorian Gray, *678;* D-Day the Sixth

of June, *442;* Never Let Go, *543;* Rob Roy, The Highland Rogue, *201;* Stage Fright, *747;* Sword and the Rose, The, *207*

Todd, Russell: Where the Boys Are '84, *380*

Todd, Thelma: Bohemian Girl, The, *232;* Monkey Business, *312;* Palooka, *556*

Tognazzi, Ugo: Joke of Destiny, *290;* La Cage Aux Folles III, The Wedding, *295;* La Cage aux Folles II, *294;* La Cage aux Folles, *294*

Toler, Sidney: It's in the Bag, *289;* Our Relations, *325;* Spitfire, *599*

Tolo, Marilu: Beyond Fear, *409;* Confessions of a Police Captain, *437*

Tol, Henriette: Question of Silence, A, *572*

Tomasina, Jeana: Beach Girls, The, *225*

Tombes, Andrew: Hoppy's Holiday, *904*

Tomelty, Frances: Blue Money, *231;* Bullshot, *236*

Tomikawa, Masahiro: Shogun Assassin, *135*

Tomita, Tamlyn: Karate Kid, Part 2, The, *81*

Tomlinson, David: Bedknobs and Broomsticks, *172;* Fiendish Plot of Dr. Fu Manchu, The, *260;* Mary Poppins, *191*

Tomlin, Lily: All of Me, *217;* Incredible Shrinking Woman, The, *286;* Late Show, The, *87;* Nashville, *542;* Nine to Five, *319*

Tompkins, Angel: Don is Dead, The, *44;* I Love My Wife, *285;* Prime Cut, *115*

Tompkins, Joan: I Love My Wife, *285*

Tone, Franchot: Dark Waters, *445;* Every Girl Should Be Married, *256;* Lives of a Bengal Lancer, The, *91;* Mutiny on the Bounty (Original), *105*

Tong, Kam: Flower Drum Song, *780*

Tono, Eijiro: Yojimbo, *166*

Toomey, Regis: Big Sleep, The (Original), *16;* Phantom Creeps, The, *727*

Topaz, David: Goodbye New York, *271*

Topol, David: Fiddler on the Roof, *779;* Flash Gordon, *837;* For Your Eyes Only, *58*

Torey, Roberta: Hans Brinker, *183*

Torgov, Sarah: If You Could See What I Hear, *492*

Torme, Mel: Good News, *784*

Torn, Rip: Baby Doll, *403;* Beastmaster, The, *820;* Beer, *226;* Cat on a Hot Tin Roof (Remake), *428;* City Heat, *243;* Coma, *664;* Cross Creek, *441;* First Family, *261;* Flashpoint, *57;* Heartland, *902;* Jinxed, *289;* Man Who Fell to Earth, The, *851;* One Trick Pony, *797;* Payday, *560;* Seduction of Joe Tynan, The, *590;* Songwriter, *804;* Stranger Is Watching, A, *749;* Summer Rental, *361;* You're a Big Boy Now, *385*

Torrence, Ernest: Fighting Caravans, *896;* Hunchback of Notre Dame, The (Origin. !), *702;* I Cover the Waterfront, *76;* King of Kings, The, *508;* Steamboat Bill Jr., *359*

Torres, Raquel: Duck Soup, *254*

Totter, Audrey: Set-Up, The, *591*

Touliatos, George: Heartaches, *484;* Last Chase, The, *847;* Robbers of the Sacred Mountain, *123*

Tovar, Lupita: South of the Border, *934*

Tovey, Roberta: Dr. Who and the Daleks, *831*

Towers, Constance: Horse Soldiers, The, *904*; Sylvester, *610*

Tower, Wade: Ripper, The, *736*

Townes, Harry: Santee, *929*

Towne, Aline: Radar Men from the Moon, *117*; Satan's Satellites, *128*; Zombies of the Stratosphere (Satan's Satellites), *167*

Townsend, Jill: Awakening, The, *648*; Oh, Alfie, *549*

Townshend, Pete: Secret Policeman's Private Parts, The, *347*; Secret Policemen's Other Ball, The, *347*

Tracy, Spencer: Adam's Rib, *215*; Captains Courageous, *28*; Captains Courageous, *425*; Devil at 4 O'Clock, The, *450*; Dr. Jekyll and Mr. Hyde, *676*; Father's Little Dividend, *259*; Guess Who's Coming to Dinner, *273*; Guess Who's Coming to Dinner, *480*; Inherit the Wind, *495*; It's a Mad Mad Mad Mad World, *288*; Judgment at Nuremberg, *504*; Libeled Lady, *298*; San Francisco, *588*; Stanley and Livingstone, *600*; State of the Union, *602*; Thirty Seconds Over Tokyo, *149*; Woman of the Year, *383*

Trantow, Cordula: Hitler, *488*

Travanti, Daniel J.: Case of Libel, A, *427*; Murrow, *539*

Travers, Bill: Born Free, *174*; Gorgo, *694*

Travers, Henry: Ball of Fire, *224*

Travers, Linden: Stars Look Down, The, *601*

Travers, Mary: Wasn't That a Time!, *811*

Travolta, John: Blow Out, *654*; Boy in the Plastic Bubble, The, *418*; Carrie, *659*; Grease, *784*; Perfect, *561*; Saturday Night Fever, *801*; Staying Alive, *805*; Two of a Kind, *373*; Urban Cowboy, *627*

Treacher, Arthur: Heidi, *184*; Little Princess, The, *190*; Mary Poppins, *191*

Tree, David: Drums, *46*

Tremayne, Les: Angry Red Planet, The, *817*; War of the Worlds, The, *874*

Trevor, Austin: To Paris with Love, *369*

Trevor, Claire: Allegheny Uprising, *878*; Dark Command, *891*; Dead End, *447*; Johnny Angel, *79*; Key Largo, *82*; Kiss Me Goodbye, *294*; Man without a Star, *913*; Murder My Sweet, *103*; Stagecoach, *934*; Texas, *937*

Trigger: Bells of Coronado, *881*; Billy The Kid Returns, *883*; Down Dakota Way, *894*; Golden Stallion, The, *898*; Grand Canyon Trail, *899*; Heart of the Golden West, *901*; Jesse James at Bay, *905*; My Pal Trigger, *916*; North of the Great Divide, *918*; Rough Riders' Roundup, *928*; Song of Texas, *933*; Susanna Pass, *936*

Trigger Jr.: Golden Stallion, The, *898*

Trintignant, Jean-Louis: And God Created Woman, *397*; Confidentially Yours, *34*; Conformist, The, *438*; Je Vous Aime (I Love You All), *501*; My Night At Maud's, *541*; Passion

of Love, *559*; Under Fire, *156*; Z, *641*

Triol, Anee: Without Reservations, *382*

Trio, Jimmy Wakely: Heart of the Rio Grande, *901*

Trissenaar, Elisabeth: Berlin Alexanderplatz, *408*; Love in Germany, A, *523*

Tristan, Dorothy: End of the Road, *458*

Trolley, Leonard: In the Shadow of Kilimanjaro, *704*

Trott, Judi: Robin Hood and the Sorcerer, *123*

Troughton, Patrick: Sinbad and the Eye of the Tiger, *862*

Trueman, Paula: Homebodies, *698*

Truex, Ernest: His Girl Friday, *281*

Truffaut, Francois: Close Encounters of the Third Kind, *825*; Day for Night, *446*; Green Room, The, *479*

Tryon, Tom: I Married a Monster from Outer Space, *842*; Moon Pilot, *193*; Texas John Slaughter: Geronimo's Revenge, *937*; Slaughter: Stampede at Bitter Creek, *937*; Texas John Slaughter: Wild Times, *938*; Texas John Tselikovskaya, Ludmila: Ivan the Terrible—Part I & Part II, *499*

Tse, Yang: Enter the Dragon, *49*

Tsigonoff, Steve and Millie: Angelo My Love, *399*

Tsopei, Corinna: Man Called Horse, A, *911*

Tsuchiya, Yoshio: Red Beard, *577*

Tsukasa, Yoko: Kojiro, *85*

Tsuruta, Koji: Samurai Trilogy, The, *127*

Tubb, Barry: Top Gun, *153*

Tubbs, William: Paisan, *556*; Wages of Fear, The, *763*

Tucker, Forrest: Adventures of Huckleberry Finn, The, *169*; Auntie Mame, *222*; Big Cat, The, *15*; Chisum, *889*; Cosmic Monsters, The, *664*; Crawling Eye, The, *665*; Final Chapter—Walking Tall, *54*; Hellfire, *902*; Pony Express, *922*; Sands of Iwo Jima, *128*; Thunder Run, *151*; Trouble in the Glen, *372*; Westerner, The, *944*

Tucker, Mary: Dead Don't Dream, The, *892*

Tucker, Michael: Goodbye People, The, *475*

Tucker, Sophie: Broadway Melody of 1938, *773*

Tucker, Tanya: Follow That Car, *58*; Hard Country, *68*

Tufts, Sonny: Cat Women of the Moon, *823*

Tulli, Marco: Beat the Devil, *225*

Tully, Tom: Coogan's Bluff, *34*; Moon Is Blue, The, *314*; Northern Pursuit, *108*; Ruby Gentry, *585*; Wackiest Ship in the Army, The, *377*

Tun, Tun: Chamber of Horrors, *661*

Tupou, Manu: Man Called Horse, A, *911*

Turban, Dietlinde: Mussolini and I, *539*

Turkel, Ann: 99 and 44/100 Percent Dead, *106*; Humanoids from the Deep, *702*

Turkel, Studs: Wasn't That a Time!, *811*

Turman, Glynn: Gremlins, *840*; Out of Bounds, *111*

Turnbull, John: Silver Blaze, *136*

Turner, Barbara: Monster From Green Hell, *717*

Turner, Geraldine: Careful He Might Hear You, *426*

Turner, Kathleen: Body Heat, *417;* Crimes of Passion, *440;* Jewel of the Nile, The, *79;* Man With Two Brains, The, *307;* Prizzi's Honor, *569;* Romancing the Stone, *124*

Turner, Lana: Another Time, Another Place, *400;* Dr. Jekyll and Mr. Hyde, *676;* Madame X, *526;* Postman Always Rings Twice, The (Original), *565;* Three Musketeers, The (1948), *150*

Turner, Tina: Mad Max Beyond Thunderdome, *850;* That Was Rock, *808;* Tommy, *810*

Turpin, Ben: Golden Age of Comedy, The, *270;* Saps at Sea, *345*

Turturro, John: Gung Ho, *274;* To Live and Die in L.A., *153*

Tutin, Dorthy: Shooting Party, The, *592*

Tuttle, Lurene: Final Chapter—Walking Tall, *54*

Tweed, Shannon: Hot Dog...The Movie, *283*

Twelvetrees, Helen: Painted Desert, The, *921*

Twiggy: Club Paradise, *245;* Doctor and the Devils, The, *676;* W, *763*

Tyler, Jeff: Tom Sawyer, *210*

Tyler, Judy: Jailhouse Rock, *789*

Tyler, Tom: Adventures of Captain Marvel, The, *1;* Night Riders, The, *918;* Westerner, The, *944;* When a Man Rides Alone, *944*

Tyner, Charles: Hamburger—The Motion Picture, *274;* Harold and Maude, *276;* Incredible Journey of Dr. Meg Laurel, The, *494;* Jeremiah Johnson, *905*

Tyrell, Susan: Flesh and Blood, *57;* Loose Shoes, *301*

Tyrrell, Susan: Andy Warhol's Bad, *398;* Angel, *8;* Avenging Angel, *11;* Fast-Walking, *464;* Forbidden Zone, *838;* Lady of the House, *512;* Liar's Moon, *517;* Night Warning, *723;* Steagle, The, *359*

Tyson, Cathy: Mona Lisa, *537*

Tyson, Cicely: Airport '79: The Concorde, *391;* Autobiography of Miss Jane Pittman, The, *402;* Bustin' Loose, *236;* Heart Is a Lonely Hunter, The, *483;* King, *507;* Sounder, *598;* Wilma, *635*

T, Mr.: D.C. Cab, *249;* Rocky III, *582*

Ucking, Bill: Coast to Coast, *245*

Uehara, Misa: Hidden Fortress, The, *71*

Ulacia, Richard: Mixed Blood, *101*

Ullmann, Liv: Autumn Sonata, *403;* Bay Boy, The, *406;* Cries and Whispers, *440;* Dangerous Moves, *443;* Forty Carats, *262;* Night Visitor, The, *723;* Scenes From A Marriage, *589;* Serpent's Egg, The, *590;* Wild Duck, The, *634*

Ullman, Tracey: Plenty, *564*

Ulric, Lenore: Camille, *425*

Umecka, Jolanta: Knife in the Water, *509*

Umeki, Miyoshi: Flower Drum Song, *780;* Sayonara, *589*

Underdown, Edward: Beat the Devil, *225*

Underwood, Jay: Boy Who Could Fly, The, *419*

Urecal, Minerva: Ape Man, The, *646;* Corpse Vanishes, The, *664;* Sioux City Sue, *933*

Ure, Mary: Where Eagles Dare, *161*

Urich, Robert: Bunco, *26;* Endangered Species, *834;* Fighting Back, *53;* Ice Pirates, *842;* Magnum Force, *94;* Turk182, *624;* Vega$, *158*

Urquhart, Robert: Curse of Frankenstein, The, *667;* Knights of the Round Table, *85*

Ursitti, Susan: Teen Wolf, *751*

Urzi, Saro: Seduced and Abandoned, *348*

Usher, Guy: Boots and Saddles, *885;* Devil Bat, The, *673*

Ussing, Olaf: Day of Wrath, *446*

Ustinov, Peter: Billy Budd, *411;* Blackbeard's Ghost, *173;* Charlie Chan and the Curse of the Dragon Queen, *240;* Death on the Nile, *40;* Evil Under the Sun, *50;* Great Muppet Caper, The, *183;* Lion and the Hawk, The, *89;* Logan's Run, *849;* One Of Our Dinosaurs Is Missing, *196;* Purple Taxi, The, *571;* Spartacus, *138;* Topkapi, *154;* Viva Max!, *377;* We're No Angels, *379*

Utsunomiya, Masayo: Irezumi (Spirit of Tattoo), *497*

Vaccaro, Brenda: First Deadly Sin, The, *55;* I Love My Wife, *285;* Midnight Cowboy, *533;* Supergirl, *868;* Water, *377;* Zorro, the Gay Blade, *386*

Vadim, Roger: Ciao! Manhattan, *433*

Vadis, Dan: Bronco Billy, *886*

Vague, Vera: Melody Ranch, *914*

Vai, Steve: Crossroads, *775*

Valardy, Andre: Le Chevre (THE GOAT), *298*

Valentine, Anthony: Carpathian Eagle, *659;* Robin Hood and the Sorcerer, *123*

Valentine, Karen: North Avenue Irregulars, The, *196*

Valenza, Tasia: Rappin', *799*

Valen, Nancy: Heavenly Kid, The, *278*

Valine, Rick: Ghosts on the Loose, *267*

Vallance, Louise: Robbers of the Sacred Mountain, *123*

Vallee, Rudy: Bachelor and the Bobby-soxer, The, *222;* It's in the Bag, *289;* Sin of Harold Diddlebock (aka Mad Wednesday), *352;* Unfaithfully Yours (Original), *374*

Valli, Alida: Third Man, The, *755;* Wanton Contessa, The, *630*

Valli, Romolo: Bobby Deerfield, *416*

Valli: Miracle of the Bells, The, *534*

Vallone, Raf: Catholics, *428;* El Cid, *48;* Greek Tycoon, The, *479;* Harlow, *482;* Nevada Smith, *917;* Other Side of Midnight, The, *554;* Summertime Killer, The, *143*

Vance, Vivian: Great Race, The, 273

Vandis, Titos: Young Doctors in Love, 385

Vanel, Charles: Diabolique, 675; Wages of Fear, The, 763

Vanhentryck, Kevin: Basket Case, 648

Vanity: Never Too Young To Die, 106

Vanity, Murney, Chris: Last Dragon, The, 87

Vanity, Simmons, Gene: Never Too Young To Die, 106

van Ammelrooy, Willeke: Lift, The, 712

Van Ark, Joan: Frogs, 691

Van Bridge, Tony: Pied Piper of Hamelin, The, 198

Van Cleef, Lee: Bad Man's River, 880; Captain Apache, 888; Commandos, 33; Death Rides a Horse, 892; Escape from New York, 49; For a Few Dollars More, 897; Good the Bad and the Ugly, The, 899; Gunfight at the O.K. Corral, 900; Hard Way, The, 69; Lonely Man, The, 909; Man Alone, A, 911; Octagon, The, 109; Stranger and the Gunfighter, The, 935

van Dalam, Josie: Lift, The, 712

Van Den Bergh, Gert: Naked Prey, The, 105

Van Der Vlis, Diana: X (The Man with the X-Ray Eyes), 877

Van Devere, Trish: Changeling, The, 661; Day of the Dolphin, The, 828; Hearse, The, 697; Hollywood Vice Squad, 74; Movie Movie, 315; Savage Is Loose, The, 588; Where's Poppa?, 381

Van Doren, Mamie: High School Confidential, 487; Teacher's Pet, 364

van Dreelen, John: Great Wallendas, The, 478

Van Dyke, Conny: Framed, 60

Van Dyke, Dick: Bye Bye Birdie, 773; Chitty Chitty Bang Bang, 177; Comic, The, 437; Lt. Robin Crusoe, U.S.N., 188; Mary Poppins, 191; Never a Dull Moment, 195; Runner Stumbles, The, 585

Van Evera, Jack: King of The Grizzlies, 188

Van Eyck, Peter: Wages of Fear, The, 763

Van Fleet, Jo: East of Eden (Original), 454; Gunfight at the O.K. Corral, 900; I Love You Alice B. Toklas!, 285

Van Herwijnen, Carol: Still Smokin, 359

Van Loon, Robert: Paisan, 556

Van Ness, Joan: Tourist Trap, 759

Van Norden, Peter: Roadhouse 66, 122

Van Pallandt, Nina: American Gigolo, 396

Van Patten, Dick: Charly, 823; Gus, 183; High Anxiety, 280; Son of Blob (Beware! The Blob), 745; When Things Were Rotten, 380

Van Patten, Jimmy: Tennessee Stallion, 147; St. Elmo's Fire, 586; Class of 1984, 663; Charlie and The Angel, 176; Chino, 888; Hell Night, 697; Rock 'n' Roll High School, 342; Rappin', 799; Sweet Sweetback's Baadasssss Song, 144; Exterminator 2, The, 51

Van Sickel, Dale: King of the Rocketmen, 846

Van Sloan, Edward: Death Kiss, The, 39;

Dracula (Original), 678; Mummy, The (original), 719

Van Tongeren, Hans: Spetters, 598

Van Vooren, Monique: Andy Warhol's Frankenstein, 646

VanPernis, Mona: Ripper, The, 736

Van, Bobby: Bunco, 26; Kiss Me Kate, 790

Van Sloan, Edward: Before I Hang, 649

Varconi, Victor: Atomic Submarine, The, 818

Varley, Sarah Jane: Mr. Quilp, 794

Varno, Roland: Return of the Vampire, The, 735

Varsi, Diane: I Never Promised You a Rose Garden, 491; Johnny Got His Gun, 503; People, The, 855

Vaughan, Alberta: Randy Rides Alone, 924

Vaughan, Peter: Die! Die! My Darling!, 675; Forbidden, 467; Haunted Honeymoon, 277; Straw Dogs, 749; Phar Lap, 562

Vaughn, Robert: Battle beyond the Stars, 819; Black Moon Rising, 18; Brass Target, 24; Bullitt, 26; Delta Force, The, 41; Hangar 18, 840; Kill Castro, 82; Magnificent Seven, The, 911; Return of the Man from U.N.C.L.E., The, 121; Superman III, 869; S.O.B., 355; Young Philadelphians, The, 640

Vega, Isela: Barbarosa, 881

Veidt, Conrad: Cabinet of Doctor Caligari, The, 659; Dark Journey, 445

Velazques, Victor: Rock 'N Roll Wrestling Women Vs. The Aztec Mummy, 342

Velazquez, Lorena: Rock 'N Roll Wrestling Women Vs. The Aztec Mummy, 342

Veld, Hansman In't: Still Smokin, 359

Velez, Eddie: Doin' Time, 253

Velez, Lupe: Palooka, 556

Venable, Evelyn: Alice Adams, 392

Venantini, Venantino: Final Justice, 54

Vennera, Chick: High Risk, 72

Venocur, Johnny: Savage Streets, 128

Venora, Diane: F/X, 51; Terminal Choice, 752; Wolfen, 766

Ventura, Lino: Happy New Year (La Bonne Annee), 68; Pain in the A———, A, 327

Ventura, Viviane: Battle beneath the Earth, 12

Venture, Richard: Cocaine: One Man's Seduction, 435; Streethawk, 142

Vera-Ellen: Happy Go Lovely, 786; Kid from Brooklyn, The, 292; On the Town, 796

Vera, Victoria: Monster Dog, 717

Verdon, Gwen: Cocoon, 825; Damn Yankees, 776

Verdugo, Elena: Big Sombrero, The, 883

Verson, Ben: Funny Lady, 782; Puss in Boots, 200

Verne, Karen: Sherlock Holmes and the Secret Weapon, 134

Vernon, Howard: Bob le Flambeur, 21

Vernon, Jackie: Microwave Massacre, 716

Vernon, John: Animal House, 218; Brannigan, 23; Chained Heat, 29; Charley Varrick,

30; Curtains, *668;* Doin' Time, *253;* Herbie Goes Bananas, *184;* Hunter, *75;* Outlaw Josey Wales, The, *920;* Savage Streets, *128;* Topaz, *757;* Uncanny, The, *760;* W, *763*

Vernon, Kate: Alphabet City, *394;* Roadhouse 66, *122*

Vernon, Wally: What Price Glory, *379*

Versois, Odile: To Paris with Love, *369*

Vesentin, Giovanni: Hearts and Armour, *70*

Vetri, Victoria: Invasion of the Bee Girls, *844*

Vickers, Martha: Big Sleep, The (Original), *16*

Vickers, Yvette: Attack of the 50-Foot Woman, *647*

Vickes, Mary: Touched by Love, *621*

Victor, Henry: Freaks, *689;* King of the Zombies, *709*

Vidal, Gil: Night of the Howling Beast, *723*

Vigard, Kristen: Survivors, The, *362*

Vigoda, Abe: Newman's Law, *106*

Viharo, Robert: Hide in Plain Sight, *487*

Villalpando, David: El Norte, *456*

Villard, Tom: One Crazy Summer, *324*

Villechaize, Herve: Forbidden Zone, *838;* Man With the Golden Gun, The, *96;* One and Only, The, *551;* Rumpelstiltskin, *202*

Villeret, Jacques: Edith and Marcel, *778;* Robert et Robert, *582*

Villiers, James: Saint Jack, *587*

Vincent, Frank: Raging Bull, *574*

Vincent, Jan-Michael: Big Wednesday, *411;* Bite the Bullet, *884;* Buster and Billie, *422;* Crossfire, *890;* Damnation Alley, *827;* Defiance, *41;* Hard Country, *68;* Hooper, *283;* Last Plane Out, *87;* Mechanic, The, *98;* White Line Fever, *162;* World's Greatest Athlete, The, *213*

Vincent, Russ: Twilight in the Sierras, *941*

Vincent, Virginia: Hills Have Eyes, The, *697*

Ving, Lee: Black Moon Rising, *18*

Vinson, Helen: I Am a Fugitive from a Chain Gang, *490;* In Name Only, *493;* Thin Man Goes Home, The, *149*

Vinton, Bobby: Big Jake, *882*

Vinton, Victoria: Singing Buckaroo, *932*

Vint, Alan: Badlands, *404;* Ballad of Gregorio Cortez, The, *881;* Macon County Line, *94*

Vint, Jesse: Bobbie Jo and the Outlaw, *21;* Forbidden World, *686*

Vitale, Mario: Stromboli, *606*

Vitali, Alvaro: Clowns, The, *244*

Vitali, Keith: Revenge of the Ninja, *131*

Vita, Perlo: Rififi, *122*

Vitez, Antoine: My Night At Maud's, *541*

Vitold, Michel: Judex, *774*

Vitte, Ray: Thank God It's Friday, *806*

Viva: Ciao! Manhattan, *433;* Forbidden Zone, *838*

Viviani, Sonia: Adventures of Hercules, The, *815*

Vogan, Emmett: Song of Nevada, *933*

Vogel, Mitch: Reivers, The, *338*

Vogel, Nicholas: Inheritors, The, *495*

Vogel, Robert: Basket Case, *648*

Vogel, Tony: Hearts and Armour, *70*

Voight, Jon: Champ, The (Remake), *430;* Coming Home, *437;* Conrack, *438;* Deliverance, *41;* Desert Bloom, *449;* Lookin' to Get Out, *300;* Midnight Cowboy, *533;* Odessa File, The, *110;* Runaway Train, *125;* Table for Five, *610*

Volonté, Gian Maria: Fistful of Dollars, A, *896;* For a Few Dollars More, *897;* Lucky Luciano, *93*

Von Dohlen, Lenny: Electric Dreams, *255*

Von Hausen, Paul: Demons of Ludlow, The, *673*

Von Schreiber, Shawn: Stranger Is Watching, A, *749*

von Seyffertitz, Gustav: Sparrows, *598*

von Stroheim, Erich: Grand Illusion, *476;* Great Gabbo, The, *477;* Intolerance, *497;* Napoleon, *542;* Sunset Blvd., *609*

von Sydow, Max: Belarus File, The, *13;* Brass Target, *24;* Code Name: Emerald, *33;* Death Watch, *829;* Dreamscape, *832;* Dune, *832;* Exorcist II: The Heretic, *681;* Exorcist, The, *681;* Flash Gordon, *837;* Flight of the Eagle, *57;* Greatest Story Ever Told, The, *478;* Hannah and Her Sisters, *275;* Hawaii, *483;* Hurricane, *76;* Magician, The, *526;* Never Say Never Again, *106;* Night Visitor, The, *723;* Strange Brew, *360;* Three Days of the Condor, *150;* Ultimate Warrior, The, *874;* Victory, *158;* Voyage of the Damned, *629;* Winter Light, *636*

von Wagenheim, Gustav: Nosferatu, *724*

Von Zerneck, Danielle: My Science Project, *853*

Vorkov, Zandor: Dracula vs. Frankenstein, *679*

Voskovec, George: 12 Angry Men, *624;* Barbarosa, *881;* Skag, *594*

Voyagis, Yorgo: Little Drummer Girl, The, *90*

Vye, Murvyn: Escape to Burma, *459;* Pearl of the South Pacific, *560;* Road to Bali, *342*

Wade, Russell: Body Snatcher, The, *655*

Waggoner, Lyle: Journey to the Center of Time, *846*

Wagner, Lindsay: High Risk, *72;* Incredible Journey of Dr. Meg Laurel, The, *494;* Nighthawks, *107;* Paper Chase, The, *557;* Two Worlds of Jennie Logan, The, *874*

Wagner, Robert: Affair, The, *389;* Airport '79: The Concorde, *391;* Beneath the 12-Mile Reef, *13;* Curse of the Pink Panther, The, *248;* Death at Love House, *672;* Harper, *69;* Longest Day, The, *92;* Pink Panther, The, *330;* Stopover Tokyo, *141;* To Catch a King, *756;* Trail of the Pink Panther, The, *371;* War Lover, The, *630;* What Price Glory, *379;* Winning, *164*

Wahb: King of The Grizzlies, *188*

Wahl, Ken: Jinxed, *289;* Purple Hearts, *570;* Running Scared (1980), *126;* Soldier, The, *137;* Wanderers, The, *629*

Wainwright, James: Survivors, The, *362;* Warlords of the21st Century, *875*

Waites, Thomas G.: Clan of the Cave Bear, *824;* Warriors, The, *160;* Rumble Fish, *585*

Waite, Ralph: Last Summer, *514;* Stone Killer, The, *141*

Wakabayashi, Akiko: You Only Live Twice, *166*

Wakayama, Tomisaburo: Bad News Bears Go to Japan, The, *223;* Irezumi (Spirit of Tattoo), *497;* Shogun Assassin, *135*

Wakely, Jimmy: Saga of Death Valley, *929*

Walbrook, Anton: La Ronde, *295;* Life and Death of Colonel Blimp, The, *517;* Red Shoes, The, *800*

Walburn, Raymond: Count of Monte Cristo, The (Original), *36;* Sin of Harold Diddlebock (aka Mad Wednesday), *352*

Walcott, Gregory: Plan 9 from Outer Space, *856;* Prime Cut, *115*

Walcott, Jersey Joe: Harder They Fall, The, *482*

Walden, Robert: Bloody Mama, *20;* Blue Sunshine, *20*

Waldron, Charles: Stranger on the Third Floor, *141*

Wald, Robert: Prey, The, *730*

Wales, Wally (Hal Taliaferro): Rootin' Tootin' Rhythm, *928;* Sagebrush Trail, *929;* Traitor, The, *940*

Walken, Christopher: Brainstorm, *821;* Dead Zone, The, *671;* Deer Hunter, The, *448;* Dogs of War, The, *44;* Last Embrace, The, *87;* Mind Snatchers, The, *717;* Roseland, *584;* View to a Kill, A, *158*

Walker Jr., Robert: Ensign Pulver, *255*

Walkers, Cheryl: Stage Door Canteen, *599*

Walker, Christopher: Echo Park, *455*

Walker, Clint: Dirty Dozen, The, *43;* Hysterical, *284;* Night of the Grizzly, The, *918;* Pancho Villa, *922*

Walker, Harriet: Turtle Diary, *373*

Walker, Helen: Brewster's Millions (1945), *234*

Walker, Jimmie: Doin' Time, *253;* Let's Do It Again, *298*

Walker, Kathryn: Neighbors, *318;* Rich Kids, *580*

Walker, Nancy: Best Foot Forward, *770;* Forty Carats, *262;* Thursday's Game, *618*

Walker, Robert: Bataan, *12;* One Touch of Venus, *325;* Strangers on a Train, *749;* Thirty Seconds Over Tokyo, *149;* Till the Clouds Roll By, *809*

Walker Jr., Robert: Son of Blob (Beware! The Blob), *745*

Walker, Wendy Jane: Adventures of Sherlock Holmes: The Dancing Men, *3*

Walker, Zena: Dresser, The, *454*

Wallace, Anzac: UTU, *157*

Wallace, David: Humongous, *702*

Wallace, Dee: 10, *364;* Cujo, *667;* E.T.—The Extra-terrestrial, *832;* Hills Have Eyes, The, *697;* Howling, The, *701;* Jimmy the Kid, *186*

Wallace, George: Radar Men from the Moon, *117*

Wallace, Jean: Big Combo, The, *15;* Sword of Lancelot, *144*

Wallace, Linda: Charlie, The Lonesome Cougar, *176*

Wallace, Morgan: Billy The Kid Returns, *883*

Wallace, Sue: Experience Preferred... But Not Essential, *257*

Wallace, Toby: Last Game, The, *513*

Wallach, Eli: Baby Doll, *403;* Circle of Iron, *31;* Deep, The, *41;* Domino Principle, The, *453;* Executioner's Song, The, *460;* Firepower, *55;* Girlfriends, *472;* Good the Bad and the Ugly, The, *899;* Hunter, The, *75;* Lord Jim, *93;* Magnificent Seven, The, *911;* Misfits, The, *535;* Moonspinners, The, *193;* Movie Movie, *315;* Sam's Son, *588;* Sentinel, The, *742;* Winter Kills, *636*

Wallbrook, Anton: 49th Parallel, The, *468*

Waller, Eddy: Call of the Canyon, *887*

Walley, Deborah: Beach Blanket Bingo, *770;* Benji, *172;* Gidget Goes Hawaiian, *267;* Severed Arm, The, *742*

Wallgren, Gunn: Brothers Lionheart, The, *175;* Fanny and Alexander, *463*

Wallis, Shani: Arnold, *646;* Oliver, *796* Terror in the Wax Museum, *753*

Wallner, Herman: Kiss of the Tarantula, *710*

Wall, Max: Jabberwocky, *289*

Walsch, John: Defcon 4, *829*

Walse, Wally: Mystery Mountain, *916*

Walsh, Kay: Greyfriars Bobby, *183;* Scrooge, *801;* Stage Fright, *747;* Tunes of Glory, *624*

Walsh, M. Emmet: Back To School, *222;* Best of Times, The, *228;* Blood Simple, *19;* Cannery Row, *237;* Critters, *666;* Fletch, *57;* High Noon, Part Two, *903;* Missing in Action, *100;* Raw Courage, *119;* Scandalous, *345;* Straight Time, *603;* Wildcats, *382*

Walston, Ray: Apartment, The, *219;* Damn Yankees, *776;* Fast Times at Ridgemont High, *258;* Galaxy of Terror, *839;* Happy Hooker Goes to Washington, The, *275;* Popeye, *199;* Private School, *335;* Rad, *117;* Silver Streak, *352;* South Pacific, *805;* Sting, The, *144*

Walters, Julie: Educating Rita, *255*

Walters, Laurie: Harrad Experiment, The, *482*

Walters, Luana: Assassin of Youth (aka Marijuana), *402;* Corpse Vanishes, The, *664*

Walters, Thorley: People That Time Forgot, The, *855*

Walter, Jessica: Flamingo Kid, The, *261;* Going Ape!, *269;* Goldengirl, *840;* Group, The, *480;* Lilith, *518;* Play Misty for Me, *729;* Spring Fever, *357*

Walter, Tracy: Conan the Destroyer, *826;* Raggedy Man, *733;* Repo Man, *338*

Walter, Wilfred: Human Monster, The (Dark Eyes of London), *702*

Walthall, Henry B.: Abraham Lincoln, *388;* Birth of a Nation, The, *412;* Devil Doll, The, *674;* Judge Priest, *504*

Walton, Douglas: Mutiny on the Bounty (Original), *105*

Walz, Marin: Boat Is Full, The, *416*

Wanamaker, Sam: Aviator, The, *403;* Competition, The, *437;* Concrete Jungle, The (aka The Criminal), *437;* Private Benjamin, *334;* Raw Deal, *119*

Warbeck, David: Ark of the Sun God... Temple of Hell, The, *9*

Warden, Jack: 12 Angry Men, *624;* All the President's Men, *394;* And Justice for All, *397;* Apprenticeship of Duddy Kravitz, The, *401;* Aviator, The, *403;* Being There, *226;* Beyond the Poseidon Adventure, *14;* Brian's Song, *420;* Carbon Copy, *238;* Champ, The (Remake), *430;* Chu Chu and the Philly Flash, *243;* Crackers, *248;* Death on the Nile, *40;* Donovan's Reef, *44;* Great Muppet Caper, The, *183;* Heaven Can Wait, *278;* Man Who Loved Cat Dancing, The, *912;* Run Silent, Run Deep, *125;* Shampoo, *591;* So Fine, *355;* Used Cars, *376;* Verdict, The, *628*

Warde, Tony: Riders of the Deadline, *926*

Ward, Burt: Batman, *172*

Ward, Fred: Remo Williams: The Adventure Begins, *120;* Right Stuff, The, *580;* Secret Admirer, *346;* Silkwood, *593;* Southern Comfort, *138;* Swing Shift, *610;* Timerider, *152;* Uforia, *374;* Uncommon Valor, *156*

Ward, John: Boots and Saddles, *885*

Ward, Lottie: Adventures of Sherlock Holmes: The Copper Beeches, *3*

Ward, Lyman: Creature, *826;* Ferris Bueller's Day Off, *259*

Ward, Patrick: Chain Reaction, *29*

Ward, Penelope Dudley: I Stand Condemned, *492*

Ward, Rachel: Against All Odds, *390;* Dead Men Don't Wear Plaid, *249;* Final Terror, The, *685;* Sharky's Machine, *133;* Thorn Birds, The, *617*

Ward, Richard: Across 110th Street, *1;* Mandingo, *528*

Ward, Roger: Escape 2000, *835;* Mad Max, *850*

Ward, Sela: Nothing In Common, *547*

Ward, Simon: Hitler, the Last Ten Days, *488;* Holocaust2000, *698;* Monster Club, The, *717;* Supergirl, *868;* Young Winston, *641;* Zulu Dawn, *168*

Ward, Sophie: Young Sherlock Holmes, *167*

Ward, Wally: Thunder Run, *151*

Ware, Mary: Hoppy's Holiday, *904*

Warnecke, Gordon: My Beautiful Launderette, *540*

Warner, David: Ballad of Cable Hogue, The,

880; Boy Who Left Home to Find Out about the Shivers, The, *174;* Company of Wolves, The, *825;* Cross of Iron, *37;* Doll's House, A, *453;* Island, The, *706;* Man With Two Brains, The, *307;* Morgan, *314;* Mr. Quilp, *794;* Nightwing, *723;* Omen, The, *726;* Providence, *569;* Silver Bears, *351;* Straw Dogs, *749;* S.O.S. Titanic, *586;* Thirty-Nine Steps, The (Second Remake), *149;* Time after Time, *872;* Time Bandits, *872;* Tron, *873*

Warner, Elaine: Forest, The, *687*

Warner, H. B.: Corsican Brothers, The, *35;* King of Kings, The, *508;* Nurse Edith Cavell, *548;* Topper Returns, *370*

Warner, Jack: Christmas Carol, A, *177*

Warren, E. Alyn: Tarzan the Fearless, *146*

Warren, Jennifer: Intruder Within, The, *844;* Mutant, *720;* Slap Shot, *353*

Warren, Lee: Little Laura and Big John, *90*

Warren, Lesley Ann: Choose Me, *433;* Clue, *245;* Dancing Princesses, The, *178;* Night in Heaven, A, *544;* Portrait of a Stripper, *565;* Songwriter, *804;* Victor/Victoria, *377*

Warren, Mike: Butterflies Are Free, *422;* FastBreak, *258*

Warrick, Ruth: Corsican Brothers, The, *35;* Great Dan Patch, The, *477;* Mr. Winkle Goes to War, *311*

Warrington, Don: Bloodbath at the House of Death, *230*

Warwick, James: Partners in Crime—The Secret Adversary, *113*

Warwick, Richard: If..., *285*

Washbourne, Mona: Billy Liar, *412;* Collector, The, *663;* Stevie, *603*

Washington, Denzel: Power, *566*

Wasson, Craig: Body Double, *655;* Four Friends, *468;* Ghost Story, *693;* Go Tell the Spartans, *63;* Schizoid, *740;* Skag, *594*

Wass, Ted: Curse of the Pink Panther, The, *248;* Oh God, You Devil!, *323;* Sheena, *134*

Watanabe, Gedde: Gung Ho, *274;* Vamp, *760;* Volunteers, *377*

Watanabe, Ken: MacArthur's Children, *525*

Waterman, Dennis: Scars of Dracula, *740*

Waterston, Sam: Capricorn One, *822;* Great Gatsby, The, *477;* Hannah and Her Sisters, *275;* Heaven's Gate, *902;* Interiors, *496;* Journey Into Fear, *503;* Just Between Friends, *505;* Killing Fields, The, *506;* Warning Sign, *763*

Waters, Ethel: Cabin in the Sky, *423*

Waters, John: Attack Force Z, *10;* Breaker Morant, *24*

Watford, Gwen: Ghoul, The, *693*

Watkins, Gary: Wheels of Fire, *161*

Watkins, Pierre: Heart of the Rio Grande, *901;* Sioux City Sue, *933*

Watkin, Ian: Nutcase, *168*

Watkin, Pierre: Jesse James at Bay, *905*

Watson, Alberta: Best Revenge, *14;* Keep, The, *708*

Watson, Jack: King Arthur, The Young Warlord, 84

Watson, Jack: Wild Geese, The, 163

Watson, Lucile: Made for Each Other, 304; Thin Man Goes Home, The, 149; Waterloo Bridge, 631

Watts, Charlie: Gimme Shelter, 783; Let's Spend the Night Together, 792; Sympathy for the Devil, 806; Video Rewind: The Rolling Stones Great Video Hits, 811

Watt, Marty: Almost You, 217

Waxman, Al: Spasms, 746

Wax, Ruby: Shock Treatment, 351

Wayne, David: Adam's Rib, 215; Andromeda Strain, The, 817; Apple Dumpling Gang, The, 171; How to Marry a Millionaire, 284; Prizefighter, The, 200

Wayne, John: Alamo, The, 878; Allegheny Uprising, 878; Angel and the Badman, 879; Back to Bataan, 11; Big Jake, 882; Big Trail, The, 883; Blue Steel, 885; Brannigan, 23; Cahill—US Marshal, 887; Chisum, 889; Circus World, 889; Comancheros, The, 889; Conqueror, The, 34; Cowboys, The, 890; Dakota, 890; Dark Command, 891; Dawn Rider, 892; Desert Trail, 893; Donovan's Reef, 44; El Dorado, 895; Fighting Kentuckian, The, 896; Fighting Seabees, The, 53; Flame of the Barbary Coast, 56; Flying Leathernecks, The, 58; Flying Tigers, The, 58; Fort Apache, 897; Greatest Story Ever Told, The, 478; Green Berets, The, 66; Hatari!, 69; Hellfighters, 70; Horse Soldiers, The, 904; How the West Was Won, 904; Hurricane Express, 76; In Old California, 905; Lady for a Night, 512; Lady from Louisiana, 907; Lawless Frontier, 908; Lawless Range, 908; Longest Day, The, 92; Long Voyage Home, The, 520; Lucky Texan, 910; Man from Utah, The, 912; Man Who Shot Liberty Valance, The, 913; McQ, 98; New Frontier, 917; Night Riders, The, 918; North to Alaska, 918; Pals of the Saddle, 921; Paradise Canyon, 922; Quiet Man, The, 117; Randy Rides Alone, 924; Red River, 924; Riders of Destiny, 926; Rio Bravo, 926; Rio Grande, 927; Rio Lobo, 927; Rooster Cogburn, 928; Sagebrush Trail, 929; Sands of Iwo Jima, 128; Santa Fe Stampede, 929; Searchers, The, 930; She Wore a Yellow Ribbon, 930; Shootist, The, 931; Sons of Katie Elder, The, 934; Spoilers, The, 934; Stagecoach, 934; Star Packer, The, 935; Tall in the Saddle, 936; They Were Expendable, 148; Three Faces West, 939; Trail Beyond, The, 939; Train Robbers, The, 940; True Grit, 941; Tycoon, 156; Wake of the Red Witch, 160; War of the Wildcats, 943; War Wagon, The, 944; West of the Divide, 944; Wheel of Fortune, 944; Winds of the Wasteland, 945; Without Reservations, 382; 'Neath Arizona Skies, 917

Wayne, Keith: Night of the Living Dead, 723

Wayne, Nina: Comic, The, 437

Wayne, Patrick: Beyond Atlantis, 14; Big

Jake, 882; Green Berets, The, 66; People That Time Forgot, The, 855; Rustler's Rhapsody, 344; Shenandoah, 930; Sinbad and the Eye of the Tiger, 862

Weathers, Carl: Death Hunt, 39; Force Ten from Navarone, 59; Rocky III, 582; Rocky II, 582; Rocky IV, 582; Rocky, 582

Weaver, Dennis: Cocaine: One Man's Seduction, 435; Dragnet, 45; Duel, 679; Ordeal of Dr. Mudd, The, 553

Weaver, Doodles: 30 Foot Bride of Candy Rock, The, 366

Weaver, Fritz: Black Sunday, 19; Creepshow, 666; Day of the Dolphin, The, 828; Demon Seed, 830; Failsafe, 461; Hunter, 75

Weaver, Jacki: Caddie, 423; Squizzy Taylor, 139

Weaver, Sigourney: Aliens, 816; Alien, 815; Deal of the Century, 249; Eyewitness, 682; Ghostbusters, 267; Year of Living Dangerously, The, 165

Webber, Robert: 10, 364; 12 Angry Men, 624; Casey's Shadow, 176; Final Option, The, 54; Private Benjamin, 334; Revenge of the Pink Panther, The, 340; Starflight One, 867; Wrong Is Right, 384; $ (Dollars), 44

Webber, Timothy: Grey Fox, The, 899

Webb, Alan: Great Train Robbery, The, 66; Women in Love, 638

Webb, Clifton: Laura, 88; Razor's Edge, The (Original), 576

Webb, Jack: Dragnet, 45; He Walked by Night, 697; Men, The, 532; Sunset Blvd., 609

Webb, Julie: Billy Jack, 17

Webb, Richard: Out of the Past, 112

Weber, Rick: Somewhere, Tomorrow, 206

Weber, Suzanna: Cold River, 177

Webster, Hug: King of The Grizzlies, 188

Webster, Mary: Master of the World, 851

Weck, Peter: Almost Angels, 171

Wedgeworth, Ann: Bogie, 417; Sweet Dreams, 806

Wegener, Paul: The Golem (How He Came Into The World) (DER GOLEM, Wie er in die Welt Kam), 754

Wehe, Oliver: Erendira, 459

Weidler, Virginia: Best Foot Forward, 770

Weismeier, Lynda: RSVP, 343

Weissmuller, Johnny: Tarzan the Ape Man (Original), 146

Weiss, George: Glen or Glenda, 473

Weitz, Bruce: Death of a Centerfold, 447

Wei, Yue Chen: Shaolin Temple, 132

Welch, Joseph: Anatomy of a Murder, 397

Welch, Raquel: 100 Rifles, 920; Bandolero!, 881; Bedazzled, 225; Bluebeard, 655; Fantastic Voyage, 836; Four Musketeers, The, 60; Fuzz, 265; Last of Sheila, The, 87; Legend of Walks Far Woman, The, 909; Magic Christian, The, 304; Swingin' Summer, A, 362; Three Musketeers, The (1973), 150; Wild Party, The, 634

Welch, Tahnee: Cocoon, 825

Weld, Tuesday: Author! Author!, *222*; Looking for Mr. Goodbar, *521*; Once upon a Time in America (Long Version), *110*; Rock, Rock, Rock, *800*; Serial, *349*; Soldier in the Rain, *596*; Thief, *148*; Who'll Stop the Rain, *162*; Wild in the Country, *634*

Weller, Mary Louise: Forced Vengeance, *59*

Weller, Peter: Adventures of Buckaroo Banzai, The, *815*; Dancing Princesses, The, *178*; First Born, *465*; Just Tell Me What You Want, *292*; Of Unknown Origin, *725*

Welles, Gwen: Desert Hearts, *449*

Welles, Mel: Attack of the Crab Monsters, *647*; Little Shop of Horrors, The, *713*

Welles, Orson: Black Magic, *413*; Butterfly, *422*; Casino Royale, *239*; Citizen Kane, *434*; Lady from Shanghai, *86*; Macbeth, *525*; Man for All Seasons, A, *528*; Moby Dick, *102*; Muppet Movie, The, *193*; Napoleon, *542*; Stranger, The, *748*; Third Man, The, *755*; Touch of Evil, *758*; Trouble in the Glen, *372*; Voyage of the Damned, *629*; Witching, The (Necromancy), *765*

Welles, Orson (narrator): Man Who Saw Tomorrow, The, *851*

Wellman Jr., William: Swingin' Summer, A, *362*; Born Losers, *22*

Wells, Dawn: Town That Dreaded Sundown, The, *759*

Wells, Jacqueline: Tarzan the Fearless, *146*

Wells, Vernon: Road Warrior, The, *859*

Wenckus, Philip: Prey, The, *730*

Wendt, George: Gung Ho, *274*; House, *699*

Wengray, John: Pride and the Passion, The, *567*

Wennemann, Klaus: Das Boot (The Boat), *38*

Wenner, Jann: Perfect, *561*

Wentworth, Martha: Stranger, The, *748*

Werner, Oskar: Fahrenheit 451, *836*; Jules and Jim, *505*; Ship of Fools, *592*; Voyage of the Damned, *629*

Wessell, Dick: Sunset Serenade, *935*

Wesson, Dick: Destination Moon, *830*

Westbrook, John: Tomb of Ligeia, *757*

Westmoreland, James: Don't Answer the Phone, *677*

Weston, David: Masque of the Red Death, The, *716*

Weston, Jack: Can't Stop the Music, *773*; Cuba, *37*; Four Seasons, The, *469*; Gator, *61*; High Road to China, *72*; Rad, *117*; Ritz, The, *342*

West, Adam: Batman, *172*; One Dark Night, *726*; Tammy and the Doctor, *611*; Young Philadelphians, The, *640*

West, Julian: Vampyr, *761*

West, Mae: My Little Chickadee, *316*; Sextette, *350*

West, Martin: Swingin' Summer, A, *362*

West, Red: Will, G. Gordon Liddy, *635*

Wexel, Shane: Marie, *529*

Wexler, Paul: Doc Savage...The Man of Bronze, *830*

Wheaton, Wil: Stand By Me, *600*

Wheeler-Nicholson, Dana: Fletch, *57*

Whelan, Arleen: Senator Was Indiscreet, The, *349*

White, Carol: Never Let Go, *543*; Some Call It Loving, *597*

White, Diz: Bullshot, *236*

White, Harriet: Paisan, *556*

White, Jesse: Bedtime for Bonzo, *226*; Bless the Beasts and the Children, *414*; Million Dollar Mermaid, *794*

White, Leo: Charlie Chaplin—The Early Years, Vol.4, *241*

White, Pearl: Great Chase, The, *65*

White, Peter: Boys in the Band, The, *419*

White, Sheila: Oh, Alfie, *549*

White, Thelma: Reefer Madness, *338*

Whitelaw, Billie: Gumshoe, *274*; Make Mine Mink, *305*; Omen, The, *766*

Whiteman, Paul: Fabulous Dorseys, The, *778*; Lady Frankenstein, *710*; Strike Up the Band, *360*

Whiteman, Paul, and His Orchestra: King of Jazz, The, *790*

Whiting, Leonard: Romeo and Juliet, *584*

Whiting, Margaret: Sinbad and the Eye of the Tiger, *862*

Whitlock, Lloyd: Lucky Texan, *910*; West of the Divide, *944*

Whitlow, Jill: Thunder Run, *151*

Whitman, Stuart: Captain Apache, *888*; Comancheros, The, *889*; Crazy Mama, *36*; Eaten Alive, *680*; Kill Castro, *82*; Mean Johnny Barrows, *98*; Monster Club, The, *717*; Ransom, *118*; Revenge, *735*; Rio Conchos, *927*; Ruby, *737*; Those Magnificent Men in their Flying Machines, *367*

Whitmore Jr., James: Boys in Company C, The, *23*

Whitmore, James: Black Like Me, *413*; First Deadly Sin, The, *55*; Force of One, *59*; Give 'Em Hell Harry!, *473*; Harrad Experiment, The, *482*; High Crime, *72*; Kiss Me Kate, *790*; Madigan, *94*; Serpent's Egg, The, *590*; Them!, *870*; Tora! Tora! Tora!, *154*; Where the Red Fern Grows, *212*; Word, The, *638*

Whitney, Grace Lee: Star Trek (television series), *866*

Whitrow, Benjamin: Belfast Assassin, *407*

Whitton, Margaret: 91/2 Weeks, *545*; Best of Times, The, *228*

Whitty, May: Lady Vanishes, The (original), *710*; Suspicion, *750*

Whorf, Richard: Call It Murder, *424*; Yankee Doodle Dandy, *813*

Who, The: Kids Are Alright, The, *790*

Whyte, Patrick: Hideous Sun Demon, The, *697*

Wicki, Bernhard: Love in Germany, A, *523*

Widdoes, Kathleen: Without a Trace, *637*

Widman, Ellen: M, *713*

Widmark, Richard: Alamo, The, *878;* All
God's Children, *393;* Alvarez Kelly, *879;* Bear
Island, *648;* Bedford Incident, The, *407;*
Cheyenne Autumn, *888;* Coma, *664;* Domino Principle, The, *453;* Final Option, The,
54; Hanky Panky, *274;* How the West Was
Won, *904;* Judgment at Nuremberg, *504;*
Madigan, *94;* Mr. Horn, *915;* Rollercoaster,
737; Swarm, The, *751;* To the Devil, a
Daughter, *757;* Trap, The, *759;* Twilight's Last
Gleaming, *156;* Warlock, *944;* When the
Legends Die, *945*

Wiesmeiser, Lynda: Wheels of Fire, *161*

Wiest, Dianne: Hannah and Her Sisters, *275;*
Independence Day, *494*

Wiggins, Chris: High-Ballin', *71;* King of The
Grizzlies, *188;* Why Shoot the Teacher?, *633*

Wilcoxon, Henry: Against a Crooked Sky,
878; Corsican Brothers, The, *35;* Last of the
Mohicans, The, *907;* Two Worlds of Jennie
Logan, The, *874*

Wilcox, Larry: Last Ride of the Dalton Boys,
The, *908*

Wilcox, Robert: Man They Could Not Hang,
The, *714*

Wild, Jack: Oliver, *796*

Wilde, Cornel: At Sword's Point, *10;* Big
Combo, The, *15;* Comic, The, *437;* Fifth
Musketeer, The, *478;* Greatest Show on Earth,
The, *478;* Naked Prey, The, *105;* Norseman,
The, *108;* Shark's Treasure, *133;* Song to Remember, A, *804;* Sword of Lancelot, *144*

Wilder, Gene: Adventures of Sherlock
Holmes' Smarter Brother, The, *215;* Blazing
Saddles, *230;* Bonnie and Clyde, *21;* Everything You Always Wanted to Know about
Sex But Were Afraid to Ask, *257;* Frisco Kid,
The, *897;* Hanky Panky, *274;* Haunted Honeymoon, *277;* Producers, The, *336;* Quackser Fortune Has a Cousin in the Bronx, *571;*
Silver Streak, *352;* Start the Revolution
Without Me, *358;* Stir Crazy, *359;* Thursday's
Game, *618;* Willy Wonka and the Chocolate
Factory, *213;* Woman in Red, The, *383;*
World's Greatest Lover, *384;* Young
Frankenstein, *385*

Wilding, Michael: In Which We Serve, *494;*
Stage Fright, *747;* Under Capricorn, *626*

Wiley, Jan: Dawn on the Great Divide, *891*

Wilhoite, Kathleen: Murphy's Law, *104*

Wilkerson, Joy: Big Foot, *651*

Wilker, José: Bye Bye Brazil, *422;* Dona Flor
and Her Two Husbands, *253*

Wilkes, Donna: Angel, *8*

Wilke, Robert: Santee, *929*

Willard, Edmund: Iron Duke, The, *498*

Willard, Fred: Americathon, *218;* How to
Beat the High Co$t of Living, *284;* Moving
Violations, *315*

Williamson, Alister: Oblong Box, The, *725*

Williamson, Fred: Big Score, The, *16;* Mean
Johnny Barrows, *98;* One Down, Two to Go,
110; Three the Hard Way, *151*

Williamson, Mykel T.: Miami Vice, *98*

Williamson, Nicol: Excalibur, *835;* I'm
Dancing As Fast As I Can, *492;* Robin and Marian, *123;* Seven-Per-Cent Solution, The, *131;* Venom, *761*

Williams, Barbara: Jo Jo Dancer, Your Life
Is Calling, *502;* Thief of Hearts, *617*

Williams, Bert: Cobra, *32*

Williams, Billy Dee: Bingo Long Traveling
All-Stars and Motor Kings, The, *229;* Brian's
Song, *420;* Chiefs, *432;* Empire Strikes Back,
The, *833;* Fear City, *52;* Glass House, The,
473; Lady Sings the Blues, *791;* Mahogany,
527; Marvin and Tige, *530;* Nighthawks, *107;*
Out of Towners, The, *325;* Return of the Jedi,
859

Williams, Bill: Texas John Slaughter:
Stampede at Bitter Creek, *937*

Williams, Cara: Never Steal Anything Small,
795

Williams, Caroline: Texas Chainsaw Massacre 2, The, *753*

Williams, Cindy: American Graffiti, *218;*
Conversation, The, *438;* First Nudie Musical, The, *779;* Son of Blob (Beware! The
Blob), *745;* Spaceship, *356;* Uforia, *374*

Williams, Edy: Secret Life of An American
Wife, The, *347*

Williams, Emlyn: Iron Duke, The, *498;* Jamaica Inn, *500;* Stars Look Down, The, *601*

Williams, Esther: Dangerous When Wet, *776;*
Easy to Love, *778;* Million Dollar Mermaid,
794; Neptune's Daughter, *795;* Pagan Love
Song, *797;* That's Entertainment, *807;* Ziegfeld Follies, *814*

Williams, Gary: Where the Green Ants
Dream, *632*

Williams, Grant: Incredible Shrinking Man,
The, *843;* PT 109, *569;* Texas John Slaughter:
Stampede at Bitter Creek, *937*

Williams, Guinn: American Empire, *879;* You
Only Live Once, *640;* You'll Never Get Rich,
814

Williams, Guy: Sign of Zorro, The, *204*

Williams, Hugh: Human Monster, The (Dark
Eyes of London), *702*

Williams, JoBeth: American Dreamer, *217;*
Day After, The, *828;* Desert Bloom, *449;* Endangered Species, *834;* Kramer vs. Kramer, *510;* Poltergeist II: The Otherside, *729;*
Poltergeist, *729;* Stir Crazy, *359;* Teachers,
364

Williams, John: Dial M for Murder, *675;* To
Catch a Thief, *756;* Witness for the Prosecution, *637;* Young Philadelphians, The, *640*

Williams, Jori: Faster Pussycat! Kill! Kill!, *52*

Williams, Kenneth: Carry On Cowboy, *238;*
Carry on Nurse, *239*

Williams, Michael: Educating Rita, *255*

Williams, Paul: Battle for the Planet of the
Apes, *819;* Muppet Movie, The, *193;* Phantom of the Paradise, *798;* Smokey and the
Bandit III, *355;* Smokey and the Bandit II,

355; Smokey and the Bandit, *354;* Stone Cold Dead, *141*

Williams, Peter: Robin Hood and the Sorcerer, *123*

Williams, Quinn: Silver Queen, *932*

Williams, Rhys: Raintree County, *574*

Williams, Robert B.: Unexpected Guest, *942*

Williams, Robin: Best of Times, The, *228;* Can I Do It 'Til I Need Glasses?, *237;* Club Paradise, *245;* Evening with Robin Williams, An, *256;* Moscow on the Hudson, *314;* Popeye, *199;* Survivors, The, *362;* Tale of the Frog Prince, *207;* World According to Garp, The, *639*

Williams, Rosalie: Adventures of Sherlock Holmes: A Scandal in Bohemia, *2;* Adventures of Sherlock Holmes: The Blue Carbuncle, *2;* Adventures of Sherlock Holmes: The Final Problem, *4;* Adventures of Sherlock Holmes: The Speckled Band, *6*

Williams, Samm-Art: Blood Simple, *19*

Williams, Simon: Blood on Satan's Claw, *653*

Williams, Spencer: Harlem Rides the Range, *900*

Williams, Steven: Missing in Action 2: The Beginning, *100*

Williams, Treat: 1941, *319;* Flashpoint, *57;* Hair, *785;* Little Mermaid, The, *189;* Once upon a Time in America (Long Version), *110;* Prince of the City, *568;* Pursuit of D. B. Cooper, *116;* Ritz, The, *342;* Smooth Talk, *596*

Willis, Bruce: Moonlighting, *102*

Willis, Hope Alexander: Pack, The, *726*

Willis, Matt: Return of the Vampire, The, *735;* So Dear to My Heart, *206*

Wills, Chill: Alamo, The, *878;* Allegheny Uprising, *878;* Mr. Billion, *100;* Ride the Man Down, *926;* Rio Grande, *927;* Steagle, The, *359;* Tulsa, *623;* Westerner, The, *944;* Yearling, The, *213*

Wills, Chill, voice of: Francis, the Talking Mule, *263*

Wilmer, Douglas: Golden Voyage of Sinbad, The, *839*

Wilroy, Channing: Pink Flamingos, *330*

Wilsey, Jay: 'Neath Arizona Skies, *917*

Wilshere, Barbara: Adventures of Sherlock Holmes: The Solitary Cyclist, *5*

Wilson, Dorothy: Craig's Wife, *439;* Last Days of Pompeii, The, *513*

Wilson, Elizabeth: Grace Quigley, *271;* Happy Hooker, The, *275;* Incredible Shrinking Woman, The, *286;* Prisoner of Second Avenue, The, *334*

Wilson, Flip: Fish That Saved Pittsburgh, The, *261;* Uptown Saturday Night, *376*

Wilson, Frank: Green Pastures, The, *479*

Wilson, George: Attack of the Killer Tomatoes, *221*

Wilson, Jim: Charlie, The Lonesome Cougar, *176*

Wilson, Kara: Reuben, Reuben, *339*

Wilson, Lambert: Five Days One Summer, *466;* Sahara, *126*

Wilson, Marie: Girl in Every Port, A, *268*

Wilson, Michael: Nutcase, *321*

Wilson, Nancy: Big Score, The, *16*

Wilson, Paul: Devonsville Terror, The, *674*

Wilson, Richard: Adventures of Sherlock Holmes: The Red-Headed League, *5*

Wilson, Rita: Volunteers, *377*

Wilson, Robert Brian: Silent Night, Deadly Night, *743*

Wilson, Roger: Porky's II: The Next Day, *333;* Porky's, *333*

Wilson, Scott: Aviator, The, *403;* Blue City, *20;* In Cold Blood, *493;* Ninth Configuration, The, *546;* Right Stuff, The, *580*

Wilson, Sheree: Fraternity Vacation, *263*

Wilson, Stuart: Highest Honor, The, *73*

Wilson, Thomas F.: Back to the Future, *819*

Winchester, Anna-Maria: Chain Reaction, *29*

Windom, William: Escape from the Planet of the Apes, *835;* Grandview, U.S.A., *477;* Now You See Him, Now You Don't, *196*

Windsor, Marie: Cat Women of the Moon, *823;* Force of Evil, *467;* Hellfire, *902*

Windsor, Mark: Fighting Kentuckian, The, *896*

Winfield, Gil: Fiend without a Face, *684*

Winfield, Paul: Blue City, *20;* Conrack, *438;* Damnation Alley, *827;* King, *507;* Sounder, *598;* Twilight's Last Gleaming, *156*

Winfrey, Oprah: Color Purple, The, *436*

Winger, Debra: Cannery Row, *237;* French Postcards, *263;* Legal Eagles, *88;* Mike's Murder, *534;* Officer and a Gentleman, An, *549;* Terms of Endearment, *613;* Thank God It's Friday, *806;* Urban Cowboy, *627*

Wingett, Mark: Quadrophenia, *799*

Winkler, Angela: Lost Honor of Katharina Blum, The, *522;* Tin Drum, The, *619*

Winkler, Henry: Heroes, *486;* Lords of Flatbush, The, *522;* Night Shift, *319;* One and Only, The, *551*

Winninger, Charles: Babes in Arms, *769;* Fighting Caravans, *896;* Nothing Sacred, *321;* Pot O' Gold, *566*

Winningham, Mare: St. Elmo's Fire, *586*

Winn, Kitty: Exorcist II: The Heretic, *681*

Winslow, George: Gentlemen Prefer Blondes, *266*

Winslow, Michael: Police Academy III: Back in Training, *332;* Alphabet City, *394;* Lovelines, *302;* Police Academy II: Their First Assignment, *332;* Police Academy, *332*

Winter, Edward: Act of Passion, *389;* Porky's II: The Next Day, *333*

Winter, Vincent: Gorgo, *694;* Three Lives Of Thomasina,The, *209*

Winters, Deborah: Blue Sunshine, *20;* Class of '44, *434;* Kotch, *394*

Winters, Grant: College, *246*

Winters, Jonathan: Fish That Saved Pittsburgh, The, 261; It's a Mad Mad Mad Mad World, 288; Oh Dad, Poor Dad—Mama's Hung You in the Closet and I'm Feeling So Sad, 322; Russians Are Coming, the Russians Are Coming, The, 344; Viva Max!, 377

Winters, Shelley: Alfie, 216; Bloody Mama, 20; Blume in Love, 416; Cleopatra Jones, 31; Deja Vu, 448; Delta Force, The, 41; Diary of Anne Frank, The, 451; Double Life, A, 453; Enter Laughing, 256; Greatest Story Ever Told, The, 478; Harper, 69; Initiation of Sarah, The, 705; Journey Into Fear, 503; Journey into Fear, 708; King of the Gypsies, 508; Knickerbocker Holiday, 791; Lolita, 520; Over the Brooklyn Bridge, 326; Place in the Sun, A, 563; Poseidon Adventure, The, 115; Revenge, 735; S.O.B., 355; Tenant, The, 751; Tentacles, 752; Treasure of Pancho Villa, The, 940; Who Slew Auntie Roo?, 764

Winwood, Estelle: Magic Sword, The, 191; Misfits, The, 535

Wirth, Billy: Seven Minutes In Heaven, 350

Wiseman, Joseph: Journey Into Fear, 503; Viva Zapata!, 629

Wise, Ray: Journey of Natty Gann, The, 187; Swamp Thing, 750

Witherspoon, Cora: Bank Dick, The, 224

Withers, Grant: Bells of Coronado, 881; Hellfire, 902; Mr. Wong, Detective, 101; Trigger, Jr., 940; Yellow Rose of Texas, 946

Witney, Michael: W, 763

Witt, William: Torment, 757

Wi: Hysterical, 284

Wolfe, Ian: Bedlam, 649; Brighton Strangler, The, 657; Homebodies, 698; Marauders, 913; Mutiny on the Bounty (Original), 105

Wolfe, Nancy: Helter Skelter, 486

Wolheim, Louis: All Quiet on the Western Front, 7; Danger Lights, 443

Wolk, Reiner: Christiane F., 433

Wonder, Martha the Armless: Freaks, 689

Wong, Anna May: Thief of Baghdad, The, 871

Wong, Carter: Big Trouble in Little China, 17

Wong, Janet: Bustin' Loose, 236

Wong, Victor: Big Trouble in Little China, 17; Dim Sum: A Little Bit Of Heart, 451; Son of Kong, The, 745

Wontner, Arthur: Silver Blaze, 136

Wood, Annabella: Bloodthirsty Butchers, 654

Wood, David: If . . . , 285

Wood, Gary: Hardbodies, 275

Wood, Harley: Border Phantom, 885

Wood, John: Ladyhawke, 86; Purple Rose of Cairo, The, 337; Wargames, 875

Wood, Lana: Searchers, The, 930

Wood, Natalie: Affair, The, 389; Bob & Carol & Ted & Alice, 231; Brainstorm, 821; Great Race, The, 273; Green Promise, The, 479; Gypsy, 785; Last Married Couple in America, The, 296; Meteor, 852; Miracle on 34th Street, 192; Rebel without a Cause, 576;

Searchers, The, 930; Splendor in the Grass, 599; This Property is Condemned, 617; West Side Story, 812

Wood, Ron: Let's Spend the Night Together, 792; Video Rewind: The Rolling Stones Great Video Hits, 811

Wood, Thomas: Blood Feast, 653

Wood, Wilson: Satan's Satellites, 128; Zombies of the Stratosphere (Satan's Satellites), 167

Woodard, Alfre: Extremities, 460; Puss in Boots, 200

Woodbury, Joan: King of the Zombies, 709; Sunset Serenade, 935

Woodell, Patricia: Commies Are Coming, the Commies Are Coming, The, 246

Woode, Margo: Bullfighters, The, 235

Woodnutt, John: Adventures of Sherlock Holmes: The Red-Headed League, 5

Woodruff, Largo: Bill, 411; Funhouse, The, 691

Woods, Aubrey: Willy Wonka and the Chocolate Factory, 213

Woods, Donald: 13 Ghosts, 755; Bridge of San Luis Rey, The, 420; Sea Devils, 129

Woods, Eddie: Public Enemy, The, 116

Woods, Edward: Tarzan the Fearless, 146

Woods, Harry: Dawn on the Great Divide, 891

Woods, James: Against All Odds, 390; Cat's Eye, 660; Eyewitness, 682; Fast-Walking, 464; Incredible Journey of Dr. Meg Laurel, The, 494; Joshua Then and Now, 290; Once upon a Time in America (Long Version), 110; Onion Field, The, 553; Salvador, 587; Split Image, 599; Videodrome, 762

Woods, Maurice: with, G. Gordon Liddy, 635

Woods, Nan: One More Saturday Night, 324

Woodward, Edward: Breaker Morant, 24; Champions, 430; King David, 507; Wicker Man, The, 765

Woodward, Frances: Riders of the Deadline, 926

Woodward, Joanne: Drowning Pool, The, 45; End, The, 255; Fine Madness, A (1987 release), 260; Harry and Son, 483; Paris Blues, 558; Rachel, Rachel, 573; Sybil, 610; They Might Be Giants, 616; Winning, 164

Woodward, Morgan: Final Chapter—Walking Tall, 54; Girls Just Want to Have Fun, 268; Small Town in Texas, A, 137; Which Way Is Up?, 381

Wooland, Norman: Hamlet, 481

Woolley, Monty: Night and Day, 544

Worlock, Frederic: Dressed to Kill, 45

Woronov, Mary: Angel of H.E.A.T., 8; Death Race 2000, 829; Eating Raoul, 254; Hollywood Boulevard, 282; Night of the Comet, 854; Nomads, 724

Worth, Irene: Deathtrap, 448; Forbidden, 467

Worth, Nicholas: Don't Answer the Phone,

677; Swamp Thing, 750

Wray, Fay: Hell on Frisco Bay, 70; King Kong (Original), 709; Most Dangerous Game, The, 718; Tammy and the Bachelor, 611

Wray, John: Death Kiss, The, 39

Wrey, Jeff: Wild Geese, The, 163

Wright, Amy: Inside Moves, 496; Wise Blood, 636

Wright, Howard: Last of the Pony Riders, 907

Wright, Jenny: Out of Bounds, 111; Wild Life, The, 382

Wright, Michael: Streamers, 605

Wright, Teresa: Best Years of Our Lives, The, 409; Flood!, 685; Men, The, 532; Pride of the Yankees, The, 568; Roseland, 584; Somewhere in time, 863

Wyatt, Jane: Buckskin Frontier, 886; Kansan, The, 906; None But the Lonely Heart, 546; Tom Sawyer, 210

Wycherly, Margaret: Call It Murder, 424; White Heat, 161

Wyman, Bill: Gimme Shelter, 783; Let's Spend the Night Together, 792; Sympathy for the Devil, 806; Video Rewind: The Rolling Stones Great Video Hits, 811

Wyman, Jane: Incredible Journey of Dr. Meg Laurel, The, 494; Johnny Belinda, 503; Lost Weekend, The, 523; Magic Town, 526; Magnificent Obsession, 527; Night and Day, 544; Pollyanna, 198; Stage Fright, 747; Yearling, The, 213

Wymark, Patrick: Blood on Satan's Claw, 653; Where Eagles Dare, 161

Wymore, Patrice: Big Trees, The, 16

Wyner, George: Bad News Bears Go to Japan, The, 223

Wyngarde, Peter: Prisoner, The (television series), 857

Wynn, Ed: Absent-Minded Professor, The, 169; Cinderfella, 774; Daydreamer, The, 179; Gnome-Mobile, The, 182; Greatest Story Ever Told, The, 478; Mary Poppins, 191; That Darn Cat, 208

Wynn, Keenan: Absent-Minded Professor, The, 169; Around the World Under the Sea, 10; Bikini Beach, 771; Call to Glory, 424; Dark, The, 669; Devil's Rain, The, 674; Dr. Strangelove or How I Learned to Stop Worrying and Love the Bomb, 252; Finian's Rainbow, 779; Great Race, The, 273; Herbie Rides Again, 185; Hysterical, 284; Internecine Project, The, 705; Just Tell Me What You Want, 292; Kiss Me Kate, 790; Laserblast, 847; Mechanic, The, 98; Mission to Glory, 536; Neptune's Daughter, 795; Orca, 726; Patsy, The, 328; Perfect Furlough, 329; Piano for Mrs. Cimino, A, 562; Piranha, 728; Prime Risk, 115; Return of the Man from U.N.C.L.E., The, 121; Royal Wedding, 800; Song of the Thin Man, 138; Son of Flubber, 206; Three Musketeers, The (1948), 150; Untouchables: Scarface Mob, The, 157; Viva

Max!, 377; War Wagon, The, 944; Wavelength, 876

Wynter, Dana: D-Day the Sixth of June, 442; Invasion of the Body Snatchers (Original), 844; List of Adrian Messenger, The, 90; Santee, 929; Something of Value, 138

Wyss, Amanda: Better Off Dead, 228

Yachigusa, Kaoru: Samurai Trilogy, The, 127

Yamada, Isuzu: Throne of Blood, 617

Yamamura, So: Tora! Tora! Tora!, 154

Yamanouchi, Al: Endgame, 834

Yamauchi, Takaya: MacArthur's Children, 525

Yamazaki, Tomako: Dodes 'Ka-Den, 452

Yamazaki, Tsutomu: Kagemusha, 81

Yanne, Jean: Hanna K., 481

Yates, Cassie: Of Mice and Men, 549; St. Helens, 587

Yawley, Yvonne: Among the Cinders, 397

Yesno, John: King of The Grizzlies, 188

Yi, Maria: Fists of Fury, 56

Yohn, Erica: Roadhouse 66, 122

Yokoshimaru, Hiroku: Legend of the Eight Samurai, 89

York, Dick: Inherit the Wind, 495

York, Eve: Bloody Trail, 884

York, Jeff: Davy Crockett and the River Pirates, 179; Great Locomotive Chase, The, 182; Savage Sam, 202; Westward Ho The Wagons, 212

York, Michael: Accident, 388; Cabaret, 773; Four Musketeers, The, 60; Island of Dr. Moreau, The, 845; Last Remake of Beau Geste, The, 297; Logan's Run, 849; Murder on the Orient Express, 104; Riddle of the Sands, 121; Romeo and Juliet, 584; Taming of the Shrew, The, 364; Three Musketeers, The (1973), 150

York, Sarah: Evil Dead, The, 681

York, Susannah: Awakening, The, 648; Falling in Love Again, 258; Man for All Seasons, A, 528; Shout, The, 743; Silent Partner, The, 743; Tom Jones, 369; Tunes of Glory, 624

Yothers, Tina: Shoot the Moon, 592

Youb, Sammy Den: Madame Rosa, 526

Youngs, Jim: Youngblood, 641

Young, Alan: Time Machine, The, 872; Tom Thumb, 210

Young, Artie: Harlem Rides the Range, 900

Young, Burt: All the Marbles, 217; Amityville II: The Possession, 645; Back To School, 222; Convoy, 34; Killer Elite, The, 83; Lookin' to Get Out, 300; Once upon a Time in America (Long Version), 110; Over the Brooklyn Bridge, 326; Rocky II, 582; Rocky IV, 582; Rocky, 582; Twilight's Last Gleaming, 156

Young, Calvin: Challenge, The, 29

Young, Carleton: Git Along, Little Dogies, 898; Pride of the Bowery, 567; Reefer Madness, 338; Smash-up: The Story of a Woman, 595

Young, Clifton: Bells of Coronado, 881; Trail

of Robin Hood, 939

Young, Desmond: Desert Fox, The, 42

Young, Dey: Doin' Time, 253; Rock 'n' Roll High School, 342

Young, Gig: Air Force, 7; Game of Death, 61; Killer Elite, The, 83; Teacher's Pet, 364; That Touch of Mink, 365; They Shoot Horses, Don't They?, 616; Three Musketeers, The (1948), 150; Wake of the Red Witch, 160

Young, Jessie Colin: No Nukes, 795

Young, Karen: 9 1/2 Weeks, 545; Almost You, 217

Young, Karen: Birdy, 412

Young, Loretta: Along Came Jones, 879; Bishop's Wife, The, 229; Farmer's Daughter, The, 258; Rachel and the Stranger, 923; Stranger, The, 748

Young, Nedrick: Dead Men Walk, 670; Devil's Playground, 893

Young, Ned: Unexpected Guest, 942

Young, Neil: Last Waltz, The, 791

Young, Otis: Blood Beach, 653; Last Detail, The, 513

Young, Paul: Another Time, Another Place, 400

Young, Polly Ann: Invisible Ghost, 705; Man from Utah, The, 912

Young, Richard: Friday the 13th, Part V—A New Beginning, 690

Young, Robert: Secret Agent, The, 131; Spitfire, 599

Young, Roland: And Then There Were None, 398; His Double Life, 281; Topper Returns, 370; Topper Takes a Trip, 370; Topper, 369

Young, Sean: Baby...Secret of the Lost Legend, 818; Blade Runner, 821; Dune, 832; Stripes, 360; Young Doctors in Love, 385

Young, Stephen: Between Friends, 409; Lifeguard, 518; Patton, 559; Spring Fever, 357

Young, Tammany: It's a Gift, 288

Youskevitch, Igor: Invitation to the Dance, 788

Yulin, Harris: End of the Road, 458

Yune, Johnny: They Call Me Bruce?, 365

Yung, Victor Sen: Valley of Fire, 942

Yurka, Blanche: At Sword's Point, 10; Bridge of San Luis Rey, The, 420

Zabka, William: Back To School, 222; Karate Kid, Part 2, The, 81

Zabriskie, Grace: Burning Bed, The, 421

Zacharias, Ann: Nea (A Young Emmanuelle), 542; Montenegro, 313

Zadora, Pia: Butterfly, 422; Lonely Lady, The, 520

Zagarino, Frank: Barbarian Queen, 819

Zal, Roxanna: Testament, 870

Zambelli, Zaira: Bye Bye Brazil, 422

Zanetti, Giancarlo: Warning, The, 160

Zanin, Bruno: Amarcord, 395

Zann, Lenore: Defcon 4, 829

Zanolli, Angelo: Morgan the Pirate, 103

Zappa, Frank: Boy Who Left Home to Find Out about the Shivers, The, 174

Zarini, Lucio: His Name Was King, 903

Zaslow, Michael: Seven Minutes In Heaven, 350; You Light Up My Life, 640

Zelewovic, Srdjan: Andy Warhol's Frankenstein, 646

Zenthe, Fereno: Revolt of Job, The, 579

Zerbe, Anthony: First Deadly Sin, The, 55; Laughing Policeman, The, 88; Omega Man, The, 854; Return of the Man from U.N.C.L.E., The, 121; Rooster Cogburn, 928; Who'll Stop the Rain, 162

Zerner, Larry: Friday the 13th, Part III, 690

Zien, Chip: Grace Quigley, 271; Howard the Duck, 842

Zimbalist Jr., Efrem: Family Upside Down, A, 462; Wait until Dark, 763

Zimbalist, Stephanie: Awakening, The, 648; Magic of Lassie, The, 191

Zimmer, Laurie: Assault on Precinct 13, 10

Zimmet, Marya: Rain People, The, 574

Zmed, Adrian: Bachelor Party, 222; Final Terror, The, 685; Grease 2, 785

Znamenak, Istvan: Time Stands Still, 619

Zola, Jean-Pierre: My Uncle (Mon Oncle), 317

Zorek, Michael: Hot Moves, 283; Private School, 335

Zorina, Vera: Goldwyn Follies, The, 784

Zucco, George: Adventures of Sherlock Holmes, The, 2; Dead Men Walk, 670

Zuniga, Daphne: Sure Thing, The, 361

Zushi, Yoshitaka: Dodes 'Ka-Den, 452

Zwerling, Darrell: Doc Savage...The Man of Bronze, 830

DIRECTOR INDEX

Aaron, Paul: Deadly Force, 39; Different Story, A. 451; Force of One, 59; Maxie, 308

Abbott, George: Damn Yankees, 776

Abrahams, Jim: Airplane!, 216; Police Squad!, 332; Ruthless People, 344; Top Secret, 369

Adamson, Al: Blood of Dracula's Castle, 653; Dracula vs. Frankenstein, 679

Adler, Lou: Up in Smoke, 375

Akkad, Moustapha: Lion of the Desert, 90; Message, The (Mohammad, Messenger of God), 533

Alda, Alan: Four Seasons, The, 469; M*A*S*H: Goodbye Farewell, Amen, 307; Sweet Liberty, 362

Aldrich, Adell: Kid from Left Field, The, 187

Aldrich, Robert: All the Marbles, 217; Apache, 879; Dirty Dozen, The, 43; Flight of the Phoenix, The, 58; Frisco Kid, The, 897; Hush...Hush, Sweet Charlotte, 703; Hustle, The, 76; Longest Yard, The, 92; Twilight's Last Gleaming, 156; Vera Cruz, 943; What Ever Happened to Baby Jane?, 764

Algar, James: Legend of Sleepy Hollow, The, 188

Allen, Corey: Avalanche, 10; Thunder and Lightning, 151

Allen, Irwin: Beyond the Poseidon Adventure, 14; Five Weeks in a Balloon, 56; Swarm, The, 751; Towering Inferno, The, 154; Voyage to the Bottom of the Sea, 874

Allen, Lewis: Another Time, Another Place, 400; At Sword's Point, 10; Suddenly, 606

Allen, Woody: Annie Hall, 219; Bananas, 224; Broadway Danny Rose, 235; Everything You Always Wanted to Know about Sex But Were Afraid to Ask, 257; Hannah and Her Sisters, 275; Interiors, 496; Love and Death, 302; Manhattan, 305; Midsummer Night's Sex Comedy, A, 309; Purple Rose of Cairo, The, 337; Sleeper, 354; Stardust Memories, 358; Take the Money and Run, 363; What's Up Tiger Lily?, 380; Zelig, 385

Allmendinger, Knute: House of the Dead, 700

Almo, John: RSVP, 343

Almo, Lem: RSVP, 343

Alonzo, John A.: Portrait of a Stripper, 565

Alston, Emmet: Nine Deaths of the Ninja, 107

Altman, Robert: Brewster McCloud, 234; Buffalo Bill and the Indians, 886; Come Back to the Five and Dime, Jimmy Dean, Jimmy Dean, 436; Countdown, 439; Fool For Love, 466; McCabe and Mrs. Miller, 914; M*A*S*H, 307; Nashville, 542; Popeye, 199; Quintet, 858; Streamers, 605; Wedding, A, 378

Alton, Robert: Pagan Love Song, 797

Alves, Joe: Jaws 3, 707

Amar, Denis: L'Addition, 510

Amateau, Rod: High School, USA, 280; Lovelines, 302

Amir, Gideon: P.O.W.: The Escape, 112

Anderson, Clyde: Monster Dog, 717

Anderson, Gerry: Invasion UFO, 845;

Anderson, John Murray: King of Jazz, The, 790

Anderson, Lindsay: Britannia Hospital, 235; If..., 285; O Lucky Man!, 548

Anderson, Michael: Around the World in 80 Days, 220; Dam Busters, The, 38; Doc

Savage... The Man of Bronze, *830;* Dominique Is Dead, *677;* Logan's Run, *849;* Murder by Phone, *719;* Orca, *726*

Andolino, Emile: Rumpelstiltskin, *202*

Andrei, Yannick: Beyond Fear, *409*

Angel, Mikel: Love Butcher, *713*

Annakin, Ken: Battle of the Bulge, *13;* Call of the Wild, *27;* Cheaper to Keep Her, *242;* Fifth Musketeer, The, *53;* Longest Day, The, *92;* Paper Tiger, *112;* Pirate Movie, The, *798;* Swiss Family Robinson, The, *207;* Sword and the Rose, The, *207;* Third Man on the Mountain, *208;* Those Magnificent Men in their Flying Machines, *367*

Annaud, Jean-Jacques: Quest for Fire, *858*

Annett, Paul: Adventures of Sherlock Holmes: A Scandal in Bohemia, *2;* Adventures of Sherlock Holmes: The Copper Beeches, *3;* Adventures of Sherlock Holmes: The Solitary Cyclist, *5;* Beast Must Die, The, *649*

Anthony, Joseph: Tomorrow, *620*

Antonelli, John: Kerouac, *506*

Antonioni, Michelangelo: Blow-Up, *654;* Passenger, The, *558;* Zabriskie Point, *641*

Antonio, Lou: Between Friends, *409*

Apted, Michael: Agatha, *390;* Bring on the Night, *772;* Coal Miner's Daughter, *775;* Continental Divide, *247;* First Born, *465;* Gorky Park, *64*

Arbuckle, Roscoe: Keystone Comedies, Vol. 1, *292;* Keystone Comedies, Vol. 2, *292;* Keystone Comedies, Vol. 3, *292;* Keystone Comedies, Vol. 4, *292;* Keystone Comedies: Vol. 5, *292*

Archainbaud, George: Blue Canadian Rockies, *884;* Borrowed Trouble, *885;* Dangerous Venture, *891;* Dead Don't Dream, The, *892;* Devil's Playground, *893;* False Colors, *895;* False Paradise, *896;* Hoppy's Holiday, *904;* Kansan, The, *906;* Last of the Pony Riders, *907;* Marauders, *913;* Night Stage to Galveston, *917;* On-Top of Old Smoky, *919;* Silent Conflict, *931;* Sinister Journey, *932;* Strange Gamble, *935;* Unexpected Guest, *942;* Winning of the West, *946*

Argento, Dario: Bird with the Crystal Plumage, The, *651;* Creepers, *665;* Deep Red, *672*

Arkush, Alan: DeathSport, *829;* Get Crazy, *266;* Heartbeeps, *184;* Hollywood Boulevard, *282;* Rock 'n' Roll High School, *342*

Arliss, Leslie: Man in Grey, The, *528*

Armstrong, Gillian: Mrs. Soffel, *536;* My Brilliant Career, *540;* Starstruck, *805*

Arnold, Jack: Creature from the Black Lagoon, *665;* High School Confidential!, *487;* Incredible Shrinking Man, The, *843;* It Came from Outer Space, *845;* Mouse That Roared, The, *314*

Arthur, Karen: My Sister, My Love, *720*

Arzner, Dorothy: Christopher Strong, *433;* Craig's Wife, *439*

Ashby, Hal: 8 Million Ways to Die, *47;* Being There, *226;* Bound For Glory, *418;* Coming Home, *437;* Harold and Maude, *276;* Last Detail, The, *513;* Let's Spend the Night Together, *792;* Lookin' to Get Out, *300;* Shampoo, *591;* Slugger's Wife, The, *354*

Asher, Robert: Make Mine Mink, *305*

Asher, William: Beach Blanket Bingo, *770;* Bikini Beach, *771;* How to Stuff a Wild Bikini, *788;* Movers and Shakers, *315;* Night Warning, *723*

Aslanian, Samson: Torment, *757*

Asquith, Anthony: Carrington, V. C., *427;* I Stand Condemned, *492;* Winslow Boy, The, *635*

Assonitis, Ovidio: Beyond the Door, *650;* Tentacles, *752*

Attenborough, Richard: Bridge Too Far, A, *25;* Chorus Line, A, *774;* Gandhi, *471;* Magic, *713;* Young Winston, *641*

Attias, Daniel: Silver Bullet, *743*

Auer, John H.: Wheel of Fortune, *944*

Auster, Sam: Screen Test, *346*

Austin, Ray: Return of the Man from U.N.C.L.E., The, *121*

Auzins, Igor: High Rolling, *72;* We of the Never Never, *161*

Avakian, Aram: 11 Harrowhouse, *48;* End of the Road, *458*

Avati, Pupi: Revenge of the Dead, *736*

Avedis, Howard: Fifth Floor, The, *684;* Mortuary, *718;* They're Playing with Fire, *616*

Averback, Hy: Chamber of Horrors, *661;* I Love You Alice B. Toklas!, *285;* Where the Boys Are '84, *380*

Avildsen, John G.: Formula, The, *467;* Karate Kid, Part 2, The, *81;* Karate Kid, The, *505;* Neighbors, *318;* Night in Heaven, A, *544;* Rocky, *582;* Save the Tiger, *588*

Avildsen, Tom: Things Are Tough All Over, *366*

Axelrod, George: Secret Life of an American Wife, The, *347*

Babenco, Hector: Kiss of the Spider Woman, *509;* Pixote, *563*

Bacon, Lloyd: 42nd Street, *781;* Footlight Parade, *780;* Fuller Brush Girl, The, *264;* Knute Rockne—All American, *510;* Oklahoma Kid, The, *918;* Silver Queen, *932*

Badham, John: American Flyers, *396;* Bingo Long Traveling All-Stars and Motor Kings, The, *229;* Blue Thunder, *21;* Dracula (Remake), *678;* Saturday Night Fever, *801;* Short Circuit, *862;* WarGames, *875;* Whose Life Is It, Anyway?, *633*

Badiyi, Reza: Police Squad!, *332;* Of Mice and Men, *549*

Baer, Max: Ode to Billy Joe, *548*

Bail, Chuck: Gumball Rally, The, *67*

Baker, Graham: Final Conflict, The, *684;* Impulse, *704*

Baker, Roy Ward: And Now the Screaming Starts, *645;* Asylum, *647;* Monster Club, The, *717;* Scars of Dracula, *740;* Vault of Horror, *761*

Bakshi, Ralph: Fire and Ice, *837;* Fritz the Cat, *263;* Heavy Traffic, *485;* Hey Good Lookin', *487;* Lord of the Rings, The, *850*

Balch, Anthony: Horror Hospital, *699*

Baldi, Ferdinando: Treasure of the Four Crowns, *155*

Ballard, Carroll: Black Stallion, The, *173;* Never Cry Wolf, *105*

Band, Albert: Tramplers, The, *940*

Band, Charles: Metalstorm: The Destruction of Jared-Syn, *852;* Parasite, *726;* Trancers, *873*

Banks, Monty: Great Guns, *272*

Bannert, Walter: Inheritors, The, *495*

Bannon, Fred: King of the Rocketmen, *846*

Barbera, Joseph: Hey There, It's Yogi Bear, *185*

Barreto, Bruno: Dona Flor and Her Two Husbands, *253;* Gabriela, *265*

Barron, Steve: Electric Dreams, *255*

Barry, Ian: Chain Reaction, *29*

Bartel, Paul: Cannonball, *27;* Death Race 2000, *829;* Eating Raoul, *254;* Lust in the Dust, *303;* Not for Publication, *320*

Bartlett, Hall: Children of Sanchez, The, *432*

Barton, Charles: Abbott and Costello Meet Frankenstein, *214;* Africa Screams, *215;* Shaggy Dog, The, *204;* Toby Tyler, *210*

Barton, Peter: Kill Castro, *82*

Barwood, Hal: Warning Sign, *763*

Bassoff, Lawrence: Weekend Pass, *378*

Bass, Jules: Daydreamer, The, *179;* Mad Monster Party, *191*

Bass, Saul: Phase IV, *856*

Batchelor, Joy: Animal Farm, *399*

Battiato, Giacomo: Hearts and Armour, *70*

Bava, Mario: Beyond the Door 2, *651;* Black Sabbath, *651;* Blood and Black Lace, *652;* Hatchet for the Honeymoon, *696;* House of Exorcism, The, *699;* Torture Chamber of Baron Blood, The, *758*

Beaird, David: My Chauffeur, *316*

Bearde, Chris: Hysterical, *284*

Beatty, Warren: Heaven Can Wait, *278;* Reds, *578*

Beaudine, William: Ape Man, The, *646;* Billy The Kid Vs. Dracula, *651;* Boys from Brooklyn, The, *656;* Ghosts on the Loose, *267;* Sparrows, *598;* Ten Who Dared, *208;* Westward Ho The Wagons, *212*

Beaumont, Gabrielle: Death of a Centerfold, *447*

Becker, Harold: Black Marble, The, *413;*

Onion Field, The, *553;* Taps, *611;* Vision Quest, *628*

Beck, Martin: Last Game, The, *513*

Beebe, Ford: Phantom Creeps, The, *727*

Beineix, Jean-Jacques: Diva, *675;* Moon in the Gutter, The, *538*

Bellamy, Earl: Against a Crooked Sky, *878;* Desperate Women, *893;* Fire!, *685;* Flood!, *685;* Sidewinder 1, *135;* Walking Tall Part II, *160*

Bellocchio, Marco: Eyes, The Mouth, The, *460*

Bemberg, Maria Luisa: Camila, *424*

Benedek, Laslo: Night Visitor, The, *723;* Wild One, The, *164*

Benjamin, Richard: City Heat, *243;* My Favorite Year, *316;* Racing with the Moon, *573*

Benner, Richard: Outrageous, *326*

Bennett, Compton: King Solomon's Mines, *84*

Bennett, Richard: Harper Valley P.T.A., *276*

Bennett, Spencer G.: Atomic Submarine, The, *818;* Gunman from Bodie, *900;* Manhunt in the African Jungle (Secret Service in Darkest Africa), *96;* Masked Marvel, The, *97*

Benson, Steven: Endgame, *834*

Bentley, Thomas: Silver Blaze, *136*

Benton, Robert: Bad Company, *880;* Kramer vs. Kramer, *510;* Late Show, The, *87;* Places in the Heart, *563;* Still of the Night, *748*

Beraud, Luc: Heat of Desire, *277*

Bercovici, Luca: Ghoulies, *693*

Beresford, Bruce: Breaker Morant, *24;* Don's Party, *253;* Getting of Wisdom, The, *471;* King David, *507;* Puberty Blues, *570;* Tender Mercies, *613*

Berger, Ludwig: Thief of Baghdad, The, *870*

Bergman, Andrew: So Fine, *355*

Bergman, Ingmar: After the Rehearsal, *390;* Autumn Sonata, *403;* Cries and Whispers, *440;* Devil's Eye, The, *250;* Fanny and Alexander, *463;* From the Lives of the Marionettes, *470;* Magician, The, *526;* Port of Call, *565;* Sawdust and Tinsel, *589;* Scenes from a Marriage, *589;* Secrets of Women (or Waiting Women), *348;* Serpent's Egg, The, *590;* Seventh Seal, The, *591;* Wild Strawberries, *635;* Winter Light, *636*

Berkeley, Busby: Babes in Arms, *769;* Hollywood Hotel, *787;* Strike Up the Band, *360;* They Made Me a Criminal, *616*

Berke, William: Dick Tracy, *42*

Bernds, Edward L.: Return of the Fly, The, *735*

Bernhardt, Curtis: Miss Sadie Thompson, *535;* Possessed, *565*

Bernstein, Armyan: Windy City, *635*

Bernstein, Walter: Little Miss Marker, *190*

Berri, Claude: One Wild Moment, *552;* Sex Shop, Le, *350*

Berry, John: Bad News Bears Go to Japan, The, *223*

Bertolucci, Bernardo: Conformist, The, *438;* Last Tango in Paris, *515*

Bertucelli, Jean-Louis: Ramparts of Clay, *575*

Beshears, James: Homework, *489*

Besson, Luc: Subway, *142*

Bettman, Gil: Never Too Young to Die, *106*

Betuel, Jonathan R.: My Science Project, *853*

Betwick, Wayne: Microwave Massacre, *716*

Bianchi, Bruno: Heathcliff—The Movie, *184*

Bianchi, Edward: Fan, The, *683*

Biberman, Herbert J.: Master Race, The, *531*

Bido, Anthony: Watch Me When I Kill, *763*

Bill, Tony: My Bodyguard, *540;* Princess and the Pea, The, *199;* Six Weeks, *594*

Bilson, Bruce: Chattanooga Choo Choo, *242;* North Avenue Irregulars, The, *196*

Binder, John: Uforia, *374*

Binder, Steve: Give 'Em Hell Harry!, *473;* That Was Rock, *808*

Birch, Patricia: Grease 2, *785*

Bischoff, Sam: Last Mile, The, *514*

Black, Noel: Man, a Woman and a Bank, A, *95;* Private School, *335*

Blakemore, Michael: Privates on Parade, *336*

Blanchard, John: Last Polka, The, *296*

Blatty, William Peter: Ninth Configuration, The, *546*

Blier, Bernard: Beau Pere, *225;* Get Out Your Handkerchiefs, *266;* Going Places, *270;* Les Comperes, *298*

Bloomfield, George: Nothing Personal, *321;* To Kill a Clown, *756*

Bloom, Jeffrey: Blood Beach, *653;* Dogpound Shuffle, *252*

Blum, Michael: Richard Pryor—Live and Smokin', *341*

Bluth, Don: Secret of Nimh, The, *203*

Blystone, John: Block-Heads, *230;* Great Guy, *478;* Swiss Miss, *363*

Boetticher, Budd: Bullfighter and the Lady, The, *26*

Bogart, Paul: Class of '44, *434;* Oh God, You Devil!, *323;* Skin Game, *933*

Bogdanovich, Peter: Daisy Miller, *442;* Last Picture Show, The, *514;* Mask, *530;* Paper Moon, *327;* Saint Jack, *587;* Targets, *751;* They All Laughed, *365;* What's Up Doc?, *380*

Boisset, Yves: Purple Taxi, The, *571*

Bolognini, Mauro: Grande Bourgeoise, La, *476*

Bonerz, Peter: When Things Were Rotten, *380*

Bonns, M. I.: Night of the Howling Beast, *723*

Books, Adam: Almost You, *217*

Boorman, John: Deliverance, *41;* Emerald

Forest, The, *48;* Excalibur, *835;* Exorcist II: The Heretic, *681;* Zardoz, *877*

Boris, Robert: Oxford Blues, *556*

Borris, Clay: Alligator Shoes, *394*

Borsos, Phillip: Grey Fox, The, *899;* Mean Season, The, *98;* One Magic Christmas, *552*

Borzage, Frank: Farewell to Arms, A, *463;* History Is Made at Night, *488;* Smilin' Through, *803;* Stage Door Canteen, *599*

Boulting, John: Heavens Above, *279;* I'm All Right Jack, *285*

Boulting, Roy: Heavens Above, *279;* There's a Girl in My Soup, *365*

Bowers, George: Body and Soul (Remake), *416;* Hearse, The, *697;* My Tutor, *317*

Boyer, Jean: Fernandel the Dressmaker, *259*

Bozzetto, Bruno: Allegro Non Troppo, *216*

Bradbury, Robert N.: Blue Steel, *885;* Dawn Rider, *892;* Desert Trail, *893;* Lawless Frontier, *908;* Lawless Range, *908;* Lucky Texan, *910;* Man from Utah, The, *912;* Riders of Destiny, *926;* Star Packer, The, *935;* Trail Beyond, The, *939;* West of the Divide, *944*

Bradley, Al: Captive Planet, *823*

Bradley, David: They Saved Hitler's Brain, *754*

Brando, Marlon: One-Eyed Jacks, *920*

Brannon, Fred: Radar Men from the Moon, *117;* Satan's Satellites, *128;* Zombies of the Stratosphere (Satan's Satellites), *167*

Brass, Tinto: Caligula, *434*

Brealey, Gil: Test of Love, A, *613*

Breen, Richard L.: Stopover Tokyo, *141*

Bresson, Robert: Diary of a Country Priest, *450*

Brest, Martin: Beverly Hills Cop, *228;* Going in Style, *269*

Bretherton, Howard: Dawn on the Great Divide, *891*

Brewers, Otto: Mystery Mountain, *916;* Phantom Empire, *114;* Radio Ranch (Men with Steel Faces, Phantom Empire), *923*

Brickman, Marshall: Lovesick, *303;* Manhattan Project, The, *714;* Simon, *352*

Brickman, Paul: Risky Business, *341*

Bridges, Alan: Return of the Soldier, The, *579;* Shooting Party, The, *592*

Bridges, James: China Syndrome, The, *432;* Mike's Murder, *534;* Paper Chase, The, *557;* Perfect, *561;* Urban Cowboy, *627*

Brinckerhoff, Burt: Can You Hear the Laughter? The Story of Freddie Prinze, *425*

Broderick, John: Warrior and the Sorceress, The, *875*

Broadbent, Wally: Little Match Girl, The, *189*

Brooks, Albert: Lost in America, *301;* Modern Romance, *312;* Real Life, *338*

Brooks, Bob: Tattoo, *611*

Brooks, James L.: Terms of Endearment, *613*

Brooks, Joseph: You Light Up My Life, *640*

Brooks, Mel: Audience with Mel Brooks, An, *221;* Blazing Saddles, *230;* High Anxiety, *280;* Mel Brooks' History of the World, Part I, *308;* Producers, The, *336;* Silent Movie, *351;* Twelve Chairs, The, *373;* Young Frankenstein, *385*

Brooks, Richard: Bite the Bullet, *884;* Brothers Karamazov, The, *420;* Cat on a Hot Tin Roof (Original), *428;* Deadline USA, *447;* $ (Dollars), *44;* Elmer Gantry, *457;* In Cold Blood, *493;* Looking for Mr. Goodbar, *521;* Lord Jim, *93;* Professionals, The, *116;* Something of Value, *138;* Wrong Is Right, *384*

Brook, Peter: Lord of the Flies, *521*

Brower, Otto: Fighting Caravans, *896*

Browning, Tod: Devil Doll, The, *674;* Dracula (Original), *678;* Freaks, *689*

Brown, Barry: Cloud Dancer, *32*

Brown, Bruce: Endless Summer, The, *48*

Brown, Clarence: Anna Christie, *399;* Anna Karenina, *400;* Idiot's Delight, *492;* National Velvet, *195;* Yearling, The, *213*

Brown, Edwin Scott: Prey, The, *730*

Brown, Harry: Knickerbocker Holiday, *791*

Brown, Jim: Wasn't That a Time!, *811*

Brown, Melville: Check and Double Check, *242*

Bruce, John: Adventures of Sherlock Holmes: The Dancing Men, *3;* Adventures of Sherlock Holmes: The Red-Headed League, *5;* Adventures of Sherlock Holmes: The Speckled Band, *6*

Bucksey, Colin: Blue Money, *231*

Bucquet, Harold S.: Dragon Seed, *454;* Dr. Kildare's Strange Case, *43*

Buechler, John: Troll, *873*

Buntzman, Mark: Exterminator 2, The, *51*

Buñuel, Luis: Discreet Charm of the Bourgeoisie, The, *251;* Exterminating Angel, The, *257;* Land Without Bread, *512;* Los Olvidados, *522;* Simon of the Desert, *352;* That Obscure Object of Desire, *615;* Viridiana, *628*

Burke, Martyn: Last Chase, The, *847*

Burns, Allan: Just Between Friends, *505*

Burrows, James: Partners, *328*

Burstall, Tim: Attack Force Z, *10*

Burtin, Tim: Aladdin and His Wonderful Lamp, *170*

Burton, David: Fighting Caravans, *896*

Burton, Tim: Pee-Wee's Big Adventure, *328*

Buschmann, Christel: Comeback, *775*

Bushnell Jr., William H.: Four Deuces, The, *59*

Butler, David: Princess and the Pirate, The, *334;* Thank Your Lucky Stars, *807;* They Got Me Covered, *366*

Butler, George: Pumping Iron II: The Women, *570;* Pumping Iron, *570*

Butler, Robert: Barefoot Executive, The, *172;*

Computer Wore Tennis Shoes, The, *178;* Moonlighting, *102;* Night of the Juggler, *107;* Now You See Him, Now You Don't, *196;* Scandalous John, *203;* Underground Aces, *374;* Up the Creek, *375*

Buzzell, Edward: At the Circus, *221;* Best Foot Forward, *770;* Go West, *269;* Neptune's Daughter, *795;* Song of the Thin Man, *138*

Byrum, John: Heart Beat, *483;* Inserts, *496;* Razor's Edge, The (Remake), *576*

Byrum, Rob: Scandalous, *345*

Caan, James: Hide in Plain Sight, *487*

Cacoyannis, Michael: Iphigenia, *497;* Trojan Women, The, *622;* Zorba the Greek, *642*

Cahn, Edward: Zombies of Mora Tau, *767*

Cain, Christopher: Stone Boy, The, *603;* That Was Then... This is Now, *615*

Calmanowicz, Max: Children, The, *662*

Cameron, James: Aliens, *816;* Piranha Part Two: The Spawning, *728;* Terminator, The, *870*

Cameron, Ray: Bloodbath at the House of Death, *230*

Cammell, Donald: Demon Seed, *830;* Performance, *561*

Campogalliani, Carlo: Goliath and the Barbarians, *63*

Camp, Joe: Benji, *172;* Hawmps!, *277;* Oh, Heavenly Dog!, *196*

Camus, Marcel: Black Orpheus, *414*

Capitani, Giorgio: Ruthless Four, The, *928*

Capra, Frank: Arsenic and Old Lace, *220;* It Happened One Night, *287;* It's a Wonderful Life, *499;* Meet John Doe, *532;* Mr. Smith Goes to Washington, *536;* Pocketful of Miracles, *564;* State of the Union, *602*

Cardenas, Hernan: Island Claws, *706*

Cardona, René: Rock 'n' Roll Wrestling Women vs. the Aztec Mummy, *342*

Cardos, John (Bud): Dark, The, *669;* Kingdom of the Spiders, *709;* Mutant, *720*

Card, Lamar: Clones, The, *824*

Carlino, Lewis John: Class, *244;* Great Santini, The, *478;* Sailor Who Fell from Grace with the Sea, The, *586*

Carné, Marcel: Children of Paradise, *432*

Carne, Marcel: Le Jour Se Leve (Daybreak), *516*

Carpenter, John: Assault on Precinct 13, *10;* Big Trouble in Little China, *17;* Christine, *662;* Dark Star, *828;* Escape from New York, *49;* Fog, The, *686;* Halloween, *695;* Starman, *867;* Thing, The, *871*

Carpenter, Stephen: Dorm That Dripped Blood, The, *678;* Power, The, *730*

Carradine, David: Americana, *396*

Carreras, Michael: Maniac, *714*

Carr, Adrian: Now and Forever, *547*

Carr, Thomas: Dino, *451*

Carson, David: Adventures of Sherlock

Holmes: The Blue Carbuncle, 2; Adventures of Sherlock Holmes: The Resident Patient, 5

Carter, Peter: High Point, 280; High-Ballin', 71; Intruder Within, The, 844

Carter, Thomas: Call to Glory, 424; Miami Vice, 98

Carver, Steve: Big Bad Mama, 14; Eye for an Eye, 51; Lone Wolf McQuade, 92

Cassavetes, John: Big Trouble, 228; Gloria, 62; Love Streams, 524

Castellari, Enzo G.: 1990: The Bronx Warriors, 854; High Crime, 72; Shark Hunter, The, 133

Castle, Nick: Boy Who Could Fly, The, 419; Last Starfighter, The, 848

Castle, William: 13 Ghosts, 755; Americano, The, 879; House on Haunted Hill, 700; Strait-Jacket, 748; Zotz!, 386

Cates, Gilbert: Affair, The, 389; Goldilocks and the Three Bears, 182; Last Married Couple in America, The, 296; Oh, God! Book II, 323; Rapunzel, 200

Cavalcanti, Alberto: Nicholas Nickleby, 544

Cavani, Liliana: Night Porter, The, 545

Chabrol, Claude: High Heels, 280

Chaffey, Don: Greyfriars Bobby, 183; Jason and the Argonauts, 846; Magic of Lassie, The, 191; Pete's Dragon, 197; Prisoner, The (television series), 857; Three Lives of Thomasina, The, 209

Chaplin, Charles: City Lights, 243; Gold Rush, The, 270; Great Dictator, The, 272; King in New York, A, 292; Limelight, 299; Modern Times, 312; Monsieur Verdoux, 313; Woman of Paris, A, 638; Charlie Chaplin—The Early Years, Vol. 1, 241; Charlie Chaplin—The Early Years, Vol. 2, 241; Charlie Chaplin—The Early Years, Vol. 3, 241; Charlie Chaplin—The Early Years, Vol. 4, 241

Chapman, Michael: All the Right Moves, 394; Clan of the Cave Bear, 824

Chase, Richard: Hell's Angels Forever, 486

Cheek, Douglas: C.H.U.D., 658

Chomsky, Marvin J.: Murph the Surf, 104; Tank, 145

Chong, Thomas: Cheech and Chong's Next Movie, 242; Corsican Brothers, The, 247; Nice Dreams, 318; Still Smokin, 359

Chopra, Joyce: Smooth Talk, 596

Christensen, Benjamin: Witchcraft Through the Ages (Haxon), 637

Christian, Roger: Sender, The, 742

Chudnow, Byron: Daring Dobermans, The, 38; Doberman Gang, The, 43

Chudnow, David and Byron: Amazing Dobermans, 171

Chukhrai, Grigori: Ballad of a Soldier, 404

Cimino, Michael: Deer Hunter, The, 448; Heaven's Gate, 902; Thunderbolt and Lightfoot, 152; Year of the Dragon, 166

Clair, Rene: A Nous la Liberte, 219; And Then There Were None, 398; Crazy Ray, The, 826; Ghost Goes West, The, 267; I Married a Witch, 842; Le Million, 298

Clarke, Robert: Hideous Sun Demon, The, 697

Clark, Benjamin (Bob): Children Shouldn't Play with Dead Things, 662

Clark, Bob: Christmas Story, A, 177; Murder by Decree, 103; Porky's II: The Next Day, 333; Porky's, 333; Rhinestone, 340; Tribute, 621; Turk 182, 624

Clark, B. D.: Galaxy of Terror, 839

Clark, Greydon: Final Justice, 54; Without Warning, 876

Clark, James B.: Dog of Flanders, A, 180

Clark, Lawrence Gordon: Belfast Assassin, 407

Clavell, James: To Sir with Love, 619

Clayton, Jack: Great Gatsby, The, 477; Something Wicked This Way Comes, 863

Clegg, Tom: Children of the Full Moon, 662; House That Bled to Death, The, 701; McVicar, 532

Clemens, Brian: Captain Kronos: Vampire Hunter, 659

Clement, Dick: Bullshot, 236; Catch Me a Spy, 28; Water, 377

Clement, René: Forbidden Games, 467; Rider on the Rain, 122

Clifford, Graeme: Boy Who Left Home to Find Out about the Shivers, The, 174; Frances, 469; Little Red Riding Hood, 190

Clifton, Elmer: Assassin of Youth (aka Marijuana), 402

Clifton, Peter: Song Remains the Same, The, 803

Climber, Matt: Butterfly, 422

Cline, Eddie: Bank Dick, The, 224

Cline, Edward F.: Villain Still Pursued Her, The, 159; Never Give a Sucker an Even Break, 318; Private Buckaroo, 799

Clouse, Robert: Amsterdam Kill, The, 7; Big Brawl, The, 15; Black Belt Jones, 18; Deadly Eyes, 671; Enter the Dragon, 49; Ultimate Warrior, The 874

Clouse, Robert: Game of Death, 61; Gymkata, 68; Pack, The, 726

Clouzot, Henri-Georges: Diabolique, 675; Wages of Fear, The, 763

Clucher, E. B.: They Call Me Trinity, 938; Trinity Is Still My Name, 941

Coates, Lewis: Adventures of Hercules, The, 815; Hercules, 841; Star Crash, 864

Cockliss, Harley: Warlords of the 21st Century, 875

Cocteau, Jean: Beauty and the Beast, 820

Coen, Joel: Blood Simple, 19

Coe, Fred: Thousand Clowns, A, 367

Cohen, Howard R.: Saturday the 14th, 739; Space Raiders, 864

Cohen, Larry: Demon (God Told Me To), 830; It Lives Again, 706; It's Alive!, 707; Q, 732; Special Effects, 746; Stuff, The, 750

Cokliss, Harley: Black Moon Rising, 18

Colla, Richard A.: Battlestar Galactica, 820; Fuzz, 265

Collinson, Peter: Earthling, The, 46; Ten Little Indians, 147

Colombo, Fernando: Skyline, 353

Comencini, Luigi: Till Marriage Do Us Part, 368

Compton, Richard: Angels Die Hard, 8; Macon County Line, 94; Ransom, 118; Return to Macon County, 121; Wild Times, 945

Connelly, Marc: Green Pastures, The, 479

Conner, Kevin: At the Earth's Core, 818; Land That Time Forgot, The, 847; Motel Hell, 718; People That Time Forgot, The, 855

Conrad, Robert: Crossfire, 890

Conway, Jack: Dragon Seed, 454; Libeled Lady, 298; Tale of Two Cities, A, 611

Conway, James L.: Hangar 18, 840

Coolidge, Martha: Real Genius, 338; Valley Girl, 376

Cooper, Jackie: Rodeo Girl, 583

Cooper, Merian C.: King Kong (Original), 709

Cooper, Stuart: Disappearance, The, 43

Coppola, Francis Ford: Apocalypse Now, 9; Conversation, The, 438; Cotton Club, The, 36; Dementia 13, 673; Finian's Rainbow, 779; Godfather Epic, The, 474; Godfather, The, Part II, 474; Godfather, The, 473; One from the Heart, 797; Outsiders, The, 555; Rain People, The, 574; Rip Van Winkle, 859; Rumble Fish, 585; You're a Big Boy Now, 385

Corbucci, Bruno: Cop in Blue Jeans, The, 35

Corbucci, Sergio: Super Fuzz, 868

Corman, Roger: Attack of the Crab Monsters, 647; Bloody Mama, 20; Little Shop of Horrors, The, 713; Masque of the Red Death, The, 716; Pit and the Pendulum, The, 728; Premature Burial, The, 730; Raven, The, 733; St. Valentine's Day Massacre, The, 126; Tales of Terror, 751; Terror, The, 752; Tomb of Ligeia, 757; Trip, The, 622; Wild Angels, The, 163; X (The Man with the X-Ray Eyes), 877

Corr, Eugene: Desert Bloom, 449

Cosby Jr., William H.: Bill Cosby—Himself, 229

Coscarelli, Don: Beastmaster, The, 820; Phantasm, 727

Cosmatos, George Pan: Cassandra Crossing, The, 428; Escape to Athena, 50; Of Unknown Origin, 725; Rambo: First Blood II, 118; Cobra, 32

Costa-Gavras, Constantin: Hanna K., 481; Missing, 535; State of Seige, 602; Z, 641

Cotter, John: Mountain Family Robinson, 193

Coughlan, Ian: Alison's Birthday, 644

Coward, Noel: In Which We Serve, 494

Cowen, William: Oliver Twist, 550

Cox, Alex: Repo Man, 338

Cox, Paul: Lonely Hearts, 520; Man of Flowers, 306; My First Wife, 541

Crabtree, Arthur: Fiend Without a Face, 684

Crain, William: Blacula, 652

Crane, Kenneth: Monster from Green Hell, 717

Craven, Wes: Deadly Blessing, 671; Hills Have Eyes, The, 697; Last House on the Left, 711; Nightmare on Elm Street, A, 722; Swamp Thing, 750

Crenna, Richard: Better Late than Never, 228

Crichton, Charles: Lavender Hill Mob, The, 297

Crichton, Michael: Coma, 664; Great Train Robbery, The, 66; Looker, 850; Runaway, 860; Westworld, 876

Crispino, Armando: Commandos, 33

Crombie, Donald: Caddie, 423

Cromwell, John: Abe Lincoln in Illinois, 387; Algiers, 392; Ann Vickers, 399; In Name Only, 493; Little Lord Fauntleroy, 519; Made for Each Other, 304; Of Human Bondage (Original), 549; Spitfire, 599

Cronenberg, David: Brood, The, 657; Dead Zone, The, 671; Fly, The (Remake), 686; Rabid, 732; Scanners, 740; Videodrome, 762

Cruze, James: Great Gabbo, The, 477; I Cover the Waterfront, 76

Cukor, George: Adam's Rib, 215; Born Yesterday, 232; Camille, 425; Corn Is Green, The, 439; David Copperfield, 445; Dinner at Eight, 251; Double Life, A, 453; Gaslight, 692; Heller in Pink Tights, 902; It Should Happen to You, 287; Les Girls, 792; Little Women, 519; My Fair Lady, 794; Philadelphia Story, The, 329; Rich and Famous, 579; Star Is Born, A (Remake), 601; Women, The, 383

Cullingham, Mark: Cinderella, 177; Princess Who Had Never Laughed, The, 199

Cunningham, Sean S.: Friday the 13th, 691; New Kids, The, 721; Spring Break, 357; Stranger Is Watching, A, 749

Curtis, Dan: Burnt Offerings, 658; Dead of Night, 671; Last Ride of the Dalton Boys, The, 908; Trilogy of Terror, 759

Curtiz, Michael: Adventures of Robin Hood, The, 2; Angels with Dirty Faces, 8; Breath of Scandal, A, 233; Captain Blood, 27; Casablanca, 427; Charge of the Light Brigade, The, 30; Comancheros, The, 889; Dodge City, 894; Kennel Murder Case, The, 82; King Creole, 790; Life with Father, 299; Mildred Pierce, 534; Night and Day, 544;

Passage to Marseilles, *113;* Private Lives of Elizabeth and Essex, The, *569;* Proud Rebel, The, *923;* Santa Fe Trail, *929;* Sea Hawk, The, *130;* This Is the Army, *808;* We're No Angels, *379;* Yankee Doodle Dandy, *813*

Czinner, Paul: Catherine the Great, *428*

Daalder, Renee: Massacre at Central High, *716*

Da Costa, Morton: Auntie Mame, *222;* Music Man, The, *794*

Dallamano, Massimo: Dorian Gray, *678*

Dalrymple, Ian: Storm in a Teacup, *360*

Dalva, Robert: Black Stallion Returns, The, *73*

Damiani, Damiano: Amityville II: The Possession, *645;* Confessions of a Police Captain, *437;* Warning, The, *160*

Damski, Mel: Mischief, *310;* Yellowbeard, *385*

Dane, Lawrence: Heavenly Bodies, *278*

Daniels, Marc: Star Trek (television series), *966;* Star Trek: The Menagerie, *865*

Daniel, Rod: Teen Wolf, *751*

Dante, Joe: Explorers, *836;* Gremlins, *840;* Hollywood Boulevard, *282;* Howling, The, *701;* Piranha, *728;* Police Squad!, *332;* Twilight Zone—The Movie, *759*

Dassin, Jules: Circle of Two, *434;* Never on Sunday, *543;* Rififi, *122;* Topkapi, *154*

Daugherty, Herschel: Light in the Forest, The, *189*

Davenport, Harry: Xtro, *766*

Daves, Delmar: Dark Passage, *38;* Drum Beat, *894;* Red House, The, *734;* 3:10 to Yuma, *939*

Davidson, Boaz: Last American Virgin, The, *296;* Private Popsicle, *335*

Davidson, Martin: Eddie and the Cruisers, *778;* Hero at Large, *279;* Lords of Flatbush, The, *522*

Davis, Andrew: Final Terror, The, *685;* Code of Silence, *33*

Davis, Desmond: Clash of the Titans, *824;* Ordeal by Innocence, *111*

Davis, Peter: Hearts and Minds, *484*

Dawn, Vincent: Night of the Zombies, *723*

Dawson, Anthony M.: Ark of the Sun God . . Temple of Hell, The, *9;* Stranger and the Gunfighter, The, *935;* Yor: The Hunter from the Future, *877*

Day, Ernest: Green Ice, *66*

Day, Robert: Grass Is Always Greener over the Septic Tank, The, *272;* Haunted Strangler, The, *696;* Initiation of Sarah, The, *705;* Man with Bogart's Face, The, *96*

Deardon, Basil: Man Who Haunted Himself, The, *714*

Dear, William: Timerider, *152*

Deconcini, Ennio: Hitler, the Last Ten Days, *488*

Deem, Miles: Jungle Master, The, *80*

DeFelitta, Frank: Two Worlds of Jennie Logan, The, *874*

Deitch, Donna: Desert Hearts, *449*

De Bello, John: Attack of the Killer Tomatoes, *221*

De Bosio, Gianfranco: Moses, *539*

de Broca, Philippe: Jupiter's Thigh, *291;* King of Hearts, *294;* Le Cavaleur, *297*

De Cordova, Frederick: Bedtime for Bonzo, *226*

De Luise, Dom: Hot Stuff, *283*

De Martino, Alberto: Holocaust 2000, *698*

De Mille, Cecil B.: Greatest Show on Earth, The, *478;* King of Kings, The, *508;* Samson and Delilah, *588;* Ten Commandments, The, *612*

de Mille, Wm. C.: His Double Life, *281*

De Palma, Brian: Blow Out, *654;* Body Double, *655;* Obsession, *725;* Phantom of the Paradise, *798;* Scarface (Remake), *129;* Carrie, *659;* Dressed to Kill, *679;* Fury, The, *692;* Home Movies, *282;* Sisters, *744;* Wise Guys, *382*

De Scola, Ettore: La Nuit de Varennes, *511*

De Sica, Vittorio: After the Fox, *216;* Bicycle Thief, The, *410;* Boccaccio 70, *231;* Garden of the Finzi-Continis, The, *471;* Indiscretion of an American Wife, *495;* Umberto D, *625*

De Toth, André: Dark Waters, *445;* House of Wax, *700;* Morgan the Pirate, *103*

Del Monte, Peter: Invitation au Voyage, *497*

Del Ruth, Roy: Broadway Melody of 1936, *772;* Broadway Melody of 1938, *773;* Du Barry Was a Lady, *777;* Topper Returns, *370*

DeLuca, Rudy: Transylvania 6-5000, *371*

DeMartino, Alberto: Puma-Man, The, *732*

Dembo, Richard: Dangerous Moves, *443*

Demme, Jonathan: Crazy Mama, *36;* Last Embrace, The, *87;* Melvin and Howard, *309;* Stop Making Sense, *805;* Swing Shift, *610*

DeMoro, Pierre: Savannah Smiles, *203*

Demy, Jacques: Umbrellas of Cherbourg, The, *625*

Derek, John: Bolero, *417;* Fantasies, *463;* Tarzan the Ape Man (Remake), *146*

Deschanel, Caleb: Escape Artist, The, *181*

Desimone, Tom: Hell Night, *697*

Deutch, Howard: Pretty in Pink, *567*

Deville, Michel: Peril, *561*

Deyries, Bernard: Rainbow Brite and the Star Stealer, *200*

Diegues, Carlos: Bye Bye Brazil, *422*

Dieterle, William: Hunchback of Notre Dame, The (Remake), *703;* Juarez, *504;* Life of Emile Zola, The, *518*

Di Leo, Fernando: Loaded Guns, *91*

Diling, Bert: Dead Easy, *447*

Dinner, Michael: Heaven Help Us, *278;* Off Beat, *322*

Disney, Walt: Pinocchio, *198;* Three Caballeros, The, *209*

Dixon, Ken: Best of Sex and Violence, *650*

Dmytryk, Edward: Alvarez Kelly, *879;* Back to Bataan, *11;* Behind the Rising Sun, *13;* Bluebeard, *655;* Caine Mutiny, The, *423;* Cornered, *35;* Hitler's Children, *73;* Left Hand of God, The, *88;* Murder My Sweet, *103;* Raintree County, *574;* Shalako, *930;* Till the End of Time, *618;* Warlock, *944*

Dobson, Kevin: Squizzy Taylor, *139*

Dohler, Don: Alien Factor, The, *816*

Dolman, Martin: After the Fall of New York, *815*

Donaldson, Roger: Bounty, The, *23;* Marie, *529;* Nutcase, *321;* Sleeping Dogs, *137;* Smash Palace, *595*

Donavan, Tom: Love Spell, *93*

Donehue, Vincent J.: Sunrise at Campobello, *609*

Donen, Stanley: Arabesque, *9;* Bedazzled, *225;* Blame It on Rio, *230;* Charade, *29;* Damn Yankees, *776;* Funny Face, *781;* Grass Is Greener, The, *272;* It's Always Fair Weather, *789;* Movie Movie, *315;* On the Town, *796;* Royal Wedding, *800;* Saturn 3, *861;* Seven Brides for Seven Brothers, *802;* Singin' in the Rain, *802*

Donnelly, Tom: Quicksilver, *572*

Donner, Clive: Charlie Chan and the Curse of the Dragon Queen, *240;* Luv, *304;* To Catch a King, *756;* What's New Pussycat?, *379*

Donner, Richard: Goonies, The, *63;* Inside Moves, *496;* Ladyhawke, *86;* Omen, The, *726;* Superman, *868;* Toy, The, *371*

Donovan, Paul: Defcon 4, *829*

Dornhelm, Robert: Echo Park, *455*

Douglas, Gordon: Black Arrow, The, *18;* First Yank into Tokyo, *55;* Harlow, *482;* Rio Conchos, *927;* Saps at Sea, *345;* Them!, *870;* They Call Me Mister Tibbs, *148;* Viva Knievel, *159*

Downey, Robert: Putney Swope, *337;* Up the Academy, *375*

Dragoti, Stan: Love at First Bite, *302;* Man with One Red Shoe, The, *306;* Mr. Mom, *311*

Drake, T. Y.: Keeper, The, *708*

Dreyer, Carl: Day of Wrath, *446;* Master of the House (Du Skal Aere Din Hustru), *308;* Passion of Joan of Arc, The, *559;* Vampyr, *761*

Dryhurst, Michael: Hard Way, The, *69*

Duffell, Peter John: House That Dripped Blood, The, *701;* Experience Preferred... But Not Essential, *257;* Far Pavilions, The, *463;* Inside Out, *77*

Duigan, John: Winter of Our Dreams, *636*

Duke, Daryl: I Heard the Owl Call My Name, *491;* Payday, *560;* Silent Partner, The, *743;* Thorn Birds, The, *617*

Dunne, Philip: Wild in the Country, *634*

Durabont, Frank: Stephen King's Night Shift Collection, *747*

Durand, Rudy: Tilt, *368*

Duvall, Robert: Angelo My Love, *399*

Duvivier, Julien: Black Jack, *18;* Pepe Le Moko, *560*

Dwan, Allan: Brewster's Millions (1945), *234;* Cattle Queen of Montana, *888;* Escape to Burma, *459;* Gorilla, The, *271;* Heidi, *184;* Pearl of the South Pacific, *560;* Sands of Iwo Jima, *128;* Slightly Scarlet, *595;* Tennessee's Partner, *937*

D'Almeida, Neville: Lady on the Bus, *296*

D'Antoni, Philip: Seven-Ups, The, *131*

Eason, B. Reeves "Breezy": Man of the Frontier, (Red River Valley), *912;* Mystery Mountain, *916;* Phantom Empire, *114;* Radio Ranch (Men with Steel Faces, Phantom Empire), *923*

Eastwood, Clint: Bronco Billy, *886;* Eiger Sanction, The, *47;* Firefox, *54;* Gauntlet, The, *62;* High Plains Drifter, *903;* HonkyTonk Man, *489;* Outlaw Josey Wales, The, *920;* Pale Rider, *921;* Play Misty for Me, *729;* Sudden Impact, *142*

Eberhardt, Thom: Night of the Comet, *854;* Sole Survivor, *744*

Edel, Ulrich: Christiane F., *433*

Edwards, Blake: 10, *364;* Breakfast at Tiffany's, *419;* Curse of the Pink Panther, The, *248;* Days of Wine and Roses, *447;* Experiment in Terror, *681;* Fine Mess, A, *260;* Great Race, The, *273;* Man Who Loved Women, The, *306;* Micki & Maude, *309;* Operation Petticoat, *325;* Perfect Furlough, *329;* Pink Panther Strikes Again, The, *330;* Pink Panther, The, *330;* Return of the Pink Panther, The, *339;* Revenge of the Pink Panther, The, *340;* Shot in the Dark, A, *351;* S.O.B., *355;* Tamarind Seed, The, *145;* 10, *364;* Trail of the Pink Panther, The, *371;* Victor/Victoria, *377*

Edwards, George: Attic, The, *648*

Eisenstein, Sergei: Alexander Nevsky, *392;* Battleship Potemkin, The, *406;* Ivan the Terrible—Part I & Part II, *499;* Strike, *605;* Ten Days That Shook the World (October), *613*

Elfman, Richard: Forbidden Zone, *838*

Elikann, Larry: Great Wallendas, The, *478*

Elliot, Michael: Fatal Games, *683*

Elliott, Lang: Private Eyes, The, *335*

Enders, Robert: Stevie, *603*

Endfield, Cy: Mysterious Island, *853;* Zulu, *167*

English, John: Adventures of Captain Marvel, The, *1;* Cow Town, *890;* Daredevils of the Red Circle, *38;* Hills of Utah, The, *903;* Valley of Fire, *942*

Enright, Ray: Dames, *776;* Gung Ho, *67;* Return of the Badmen, *925;* Spoilers, The, *934*

Epstein, Marcelo: Body Rock, *771*

Epstein, Robert: Times of Harvey Milk, The, *619*

Erman, John: My Old Man, *541*

Erskine, Chester: Call It Murder, *424;* Girl in Every Port, A, *268*

Essex, Harry: Octaman, *725*

Fairchild, Bill: Horsemasters, *185*

Fairfax, Ferdinand: Nate and Hayes, *105*

Fakasaku, Kinji: Tora! Tora! Tora!, *154*

Falk, Harry: Death Squad, The, *40*

Fanaka, Jamaa: Penitentiary I and II, *113*

Fancisci, Pietro: Hercules, *71*

Fargo, James: Enforcer, The, *49;* Every Which Way But Loose, *257;* Forced Vengeance, *59*

Farris, John: Dear Dead Delilah, *672*

Farrow, John: Botany Bay, *22;* Five Came Back, *465;* His Kind of Woman, *73;* Wake Island, *159*

Fassbinder, Rainer Werner: Berlin Alexanderplatz, *408;* Despair, *449;* Querelle, *572*

Feferman, Linda: Seven Minutes in Heaven, *350*

Feist, Felix: Big Trees, The, *16*

Feldman, Marty: Last Remake of Beau Geste, The, *297*

Feldman, Marty: When Things Were Rotten, *380*

Fellini, Federico: Amarcord, *395;* And the Ship Sails On, *398;* Boccaccio 70, *231;* Clowns, The, *244;* 8½, *455;* Juliet of the Spirits, *291;* La Dolce Vita, *511;* La Strada, *512*

Fenady, Georg: Arnold, *646;* Terror in the Wax Museum, *753*

Ferrara, Abel: Fear City, *52;* Ms. .45, *103*

Feyder, Jacques: Carnival in Flanders, *426*

Finkleman, Ken: Airplane II: The Sequel, *216*

Fiore, Robert: Pumping Iron, *570*

Firstenberg, Sam: American Ninja, *7;* Breakin' 2 Electric Boogaloo, *772;* Ninja III: The Domination, *108;* Revenge of the Ninja, *121*

Firth, Michael: Heart of the Stag, *484*

Fischer, Max: Killing 'Em Softly, *506*

Fisher, David: Liar's Moon, *517;* Toy Soldiers, *154*

Fisher, Terence: Curse of Frankenstein, The, *667;* Gorgon, The, *694;* Horror of Dracula, *699;* Hound of the Baskervilles, The (Remake), *75;* Mummy, The (Remake), *719*

Fisk, Jack: Raggedy Man, *733;* Violets Are Blue, *628*

Flaherty, Robert: Elephant Boy, *48*

Fleischer, Dave: Gulliver's Travels, *183*

Fleischer, Richard: 20,000 Leagues Under the Sea, *155;* Amin: The Rise and Fall, *397;* Amityville III: The Demon, *645;* Barabbas,

405; Boston Strangler, The, *656;* Conan the Destroyer, *826;* Doctor Dolittle, *180;* Don Is Dead, The, *44;* Fantastic Voyage, *836;* Jazz Singer, The, *789;* Mandingo, *528;* Mr. Majestyk, *101;* New Centurions, The, *543;* Prince and the Pauper, The (Remake), *198;* Red Sonja, *120;* See No Evil, *741;* Soylent Green, *863;* Tora! Tora! Tora!, *154;* Tough Enough, *154;* Vikings, The, *159*

Fleming, Edward: Topsy Turvy, *370*

Fleming, Victor: Captains Courageous, *425;* Dr. Jekyll and Mr. Hyde, *676;* Gone with the Wind, *475;* Red Dust, *577;* Treasure Island, *211;* Wizard of Oz, The, *812*

Flemyng, Gordon: Dr. Who and the Daleks, *831*

Flynn, John: Defiance, *41;* Rolling Thunder, *123*

Foleg, Peter: Unseen, The, *760*

Foley, James: Reckless, *577*

Forbes, Bryan: International Velvet, *186;* King Rat, *508;* Naked Face, The, *720;* Seance on a Wet Afternoon, *741;* Wrong Box, The, *384*

Ford, John: Arrowsmith, *401;* Cheyenne Autumn, *888;* Donovan's Reef, *44;* Fort Apache, *897;* Grapes of Wrath, The, *477;* Horse Soldiers, The, *904;* How the West Was Won, *904;* Hurricane, The, *490;* Informer, The, *495;* Judge Priest, *504;* Long Voyage Home, The, *520;* Lost Patrol, The, *93;* Man Who Shot Liberty Valance, The, *913;* Mary of Scotland, *530;* Mogambo, *102;* Mr. Roberts, *311;* My Darling Clementine, *916;* Quiet Man, The, *117;* Rio Grande, *927;* Searchers, The, *930;* She Wore a Yellow Ribbon, *930;* Stagecoach, *934;* They Were Expendable, *148;* Wagonmaster, *943;* What Price Glory, *379*

Forman, Milos: Amadeus, *769;* Hair, *785;* One Flew over the Cuckoo's Nest, *551;* Ragtime, *574*

Forsyth, Bill: Comfort and Joy, *246;* Gregory's Girl, *273;* Local Hero, *300;* That Sinking Feeling, *365*

Fosse, Bob: All That Jazz, *768;* Cabaret, *773;* Lenny, *516;* Star 80, *600*

Foster, Lewis R.: Dakota Incident, *891;* Sign of Zorro, The, *204;* Tonka, *211*

Foster, Norman: Davy Crockett and the River Pirates, *179;* Davy Crockett (King of the Wild Frontier), *179;* Mr. Moto's Last Warning, *101;* Rachel and the Stranger, *923;* Sign of Zorro, The, *204*

Fowler, Jr., Gene: I Married a Monster from Outer Space, *842*

Fox, Wallace: Corpse Vanishes, The, *664*

Frakas, Michael: Prime Risk, *115*

Fraker, William A.: Legend of the Lone Ranger, The, *908;* Monte Walsh, *915*

Francisci, Pietro: Hercules Unchained, *841*

Francis, Freddie: Creeping Flesh, The, *666;* Doctor and the Devils, The, *676;* Dr. Terror's

House of Horrors, 677; Ghoul, The, 693; Tales from the Crypt, 751; Torture Garden, 758

Franco, Jess (Jesus): Against All Odds (Kiss and Kill, Blood of Fu Manchu), 643; Count Dracula, 664; Deadly Sanctuary, 671; Jack the Ripper, 707

Franju, Georges: Judex, 79

Frankel, Cyril: Permission to Kill, 114

Frankenheimer, John: Birdman of Alcatraz, 412; Black Sunday, 19; Challenge, The, 29; French Connection II, The, 469; Holcroft Covenant, The, 74; 99 and 44/100 Percent Dead, 108; Prophecy, 730; Seven Days in May, 591; Train, The, 155

Franklin, Richard: Cloak and Dagger, 32; Patrick, 726; Psycho II, 731; Road Games, 736

Franklin, Sidney: Good Earth, The, 475

Franklin, Wendell J.: Bus Is Coming, The, 422

Frank, Melvin: Court Jester, The, 248; Duchess and the Dirtwater Fox, The, 894; Lost and Found, 301; Prisoner of Second Avenue, The, 334; Touch of Class, A, 370

Frank, T. C.: Born Losers, 22

Franzese, Michael: Mausoleum, 716

Fraser, Christopher: Summer City, 143

Frawley, James: Big Bus, The, 229; Fraternity Vacation, 263; Hansel and Gretel, 183; Muppet Movie, The, 193

Frazer, Henry: 'Neath Arizona Skies, 917; Randy Rides Alone, 936

Frears, Stephen: Gumshoe, 274; Hit, The, 73; My Beautiful Launderette, 540

Freed, Herb: Beyond Evil, 650; Graduation Day, 694; Tomboy, 153

Freedman, Jerrold: Borderline, 22

Freeland, Thornton: Flying Down to Rio, 780; Whoopee, 812

Freeman, Joan: Streetwalkin', 605

Freleng, Friz: 1001 Rabbit Tales, 196; Daffy Duck's Movie: Fantastic Island, 178

French, Harold: Rob Roy, the Highland Rogue, 201

Freund, Karl: Mummy, The (Original), 719

Friedenberg, Richard: Deerslayer, The, 893; Life and Times of Grizzly Adams, The, 189

Friedkin, William: Boys in the Band, The, 419; Brinks Job, The, 234; Cruising, 441; Deal of the Century, 249; Exorcist, The, 681; French Connection, The, 60; Night They Raided Minsky's, The, 319; To Live and Die in L.A., 153

Friedman, Ed: Secret of the Sword, The, 203

Fruet, William: Search and Destroy, 130; Spasms, 746

Fuest, Robert: Abominable Dr. Phibes, The, 643; Devil's Rain, The, 674; Dr. Phibes Rises Again, 676; Last Days of Man on Earth, The, 848

Fukuda, Jun: Son of Godzilla, 745

Fulci, Lucio: Zombie, 766

Fuller, Samuel: Big Red One, The, 15; Shark! (aka Maneaters!), 133

Funt, Allen: What Do You Say to a Naked Lady?, 379

Furie, Sidney J.: Boys in Company C, The, 23; Entity, The, 680; Iron Eagle, 78; Lady Sings the Blues, 791; Purple Hearts, 570

Gable, Martin: Lost Moment, The, 522

Gabor, Pal: Brady's Escape, 23

Gage, George: Fleshburn, 685

Gallu, Samuel: Theatre of Death, 754

Gance, Abel: Napoleon, 542

Garcia, Jerry: Grateful Dead Movie, The, 784

Gardner, Herb: Goodbye People, The, 475

Garnett, Tay: Bataan, 12; Cheers for Miss Bishop, 432; China Seas, 30; Postman Always Rings Twice, The, (Original), 565; Stand-In, 358

Gasnier, Louis J.: Reefer Madness, 338

Gast, Leon: Grateful Dead Movie, The, 784

Germi, Pietro: Seduced and Abandoned, 348

Geronimi, Clyde: Alice in Wonderland, 170; Legend of Sleepy Hollow, The, 188; Sleeping Beauty, 204

Gessner, Nicolas: It Rained All Night the Day I Left, 498; Little Girl Who Lives Down the Lane, The, 712

Gibbins, Duncan: Fire with Fire, 464

Gibson, Alan: Woman Called Golda, A, 638

Gibson, Brian: Breaking Glass, 772; Poltergeist II: The Other Side, 729

Gibson, Tom: Singing Buckaroo, 932

Gilbert, Lewis: Alfie, 216; Educating Rita, 255; Moonraker, 102; Sea Shall Not Have Them, The, 130; Spy Who Loved Me, The, 139; You Only Live Twice, 166

Giler, David: Black Bird, The, 230

Gillard, Stuart: Paradise, 113

Gilliam, Terry: Brazil, 233; Jabberwocky, 289; Monty Python and the Holy Grail, 313; Time Bandits, 872

Gilling, John: Gamma People, The, 839

Girard, Bernard: Mind Snatchers, The, 717

Girdler, William: Day of the Animals, 670; Grizzly, 695; Manitou, The, 714

Glaser, Paul Michael: Band of the Hand, 12; Miami Vice: "The Prodigal Son", 99

Glen, John: For Your Eyes Only, 58; Octopussy, 109; View to a Kill, A, 158

Glenville, Peter: Becket, 406

Glickenhaus, James: Exterminator, The, 50; Protector, The, 116; Soldier, The, 137

Glicker, Paul: Running Scared (1980), 126

Godard, Jean-Luc: Breathless (Original), 419; Contempt, 247; Hail Mary, 480; Sympathy for the Devil, 806

Golan, Menahem: Delta Force, The, *41;* Enter the Ninja, *49;* Escape to the Sun, *459;* Lepke, *89;* Operation Thunderbolt, *111;* Over the Brooklyn Bridge, *326*

Goldbeck, Willis: Love Laughs at Andy Hardy, *302*

Goldberg, Danny: No Nukes, *795*

Goldstein, Bruce: Hollywood Outtakes, *282*

Goldstone, James: Rita Hayworth: The Love Goddess, *581;* Rollercoaster, *737;* When Time Ran Out!, *764;* Winning, *164*

Gold, Jack: Catholics, *428;* Murrow, *539;* Sakharov, *587*

Goodkind, Saul A.: Phantom Creeps, The, *727*

Gordon, Bert I.: Cyclops, The, *668;* Empire of the Ants, *833;* Food of the Gods, *838;* Magic Sword, The, *191;* Village of the Giants, *762;* Witching, The (Necromancy), *765*

Gordon, Michael: Cyrano de Bergerac, *441;* Pillow Talk, *330*

Gordon, Robert: It Came from Beneath the Sea, *706*

Gordon, Steve: Arthur, *220*

Gordon, Stuart: Re-animator, *733*

Gordy, Berry: Mahogany, *527*

Goren, Serif: Yol, *639*

Gorris, Marleen: Question of Silence, A, *572*

Gothar, Peter: Time Stands Still, *619*

Gottlieb, Carl: Caveman, *240*

Gottlieb, Lisa: Just One of the Guys, *292*

Goulding, Alfred: Chump at Oxford, A, *243*

Goulding, Edmund: Dark Victory, *445;* Dawn Patrol, The, *39;* Grand Hotel, *476;* Razor's Edge, The (Original), *576;* Reaching for the Moon, *337*

Gowers, Bruce: Eddie Murphy—Delirious, *255*

Graef, Roger: Secret Policeman's Private Parts, The, *347;* Secret Policemen's Other Ball, The, *347*

Graham, Eddy: Sherlock Holmes and the Baskerville Curse, *204*

Graham, William A.: Amazing Howard Hughes, The, *395;* Birds of Prey, *17;* Change of Habit, *430;* Doomsday Flight, The, *453;* Harry Tracy, *901*

Grant, James Edward: Angel and the Badman, *879*

Grant, Lee: Tell Me a Riddle, *612*

Grauman, Walter: Force Five, *59;* Lady in a Cage, *710;* Pleasure Palace, *564*

Gray, Mike: Wavelength, *876*

Greene, David: Count of Monte Cristo, The (Remake), *36;* Hard Country, *68;* Rehearsal for Murder, *120*

Greenspan, Bud: 16 Days of Glory, *594;* Wilma, *635*

Greenwald, Robert: Burning Bed, The, *421;* Xanadu, *813*

Greenwalt, David: Secret Admirer, *346*

Green, Alfred E.: Copacabana, *247;* Fabulous Dorseys, The, *778;* Mr. Winkle Goes to War, *311;* South of Pago Pago, *138*

Green, David: Guardian, The, *480*

Green, Guy: Incredible Journey of Dr. Meg Laurel, The, *494*

Green, Joseph: Brain That Wouldn't Die, The, *821*

Green, Walon: Hellstrom Chronicle, The, *841*

Grefe, William: Stanley, *747*

Gries, Tom: 100 Rifles, *920;* Breakheart Pass, *886;* Breakout, *24;* Glass House, The, *473;* Greatest, The, *479;* Helter Skelter, *486;* QB VII, *571*

Grieve, Ken: Adventures of Sherlock Holmes: The Norwood Builder, *5*

Griffith, Charles: Eat My Dust, *47*

Griffith, D. W.: Abraham Lincoln, *388;* Birth of a Nation, The, *412;* Intolerance, *497;* True Heart Susie, *623;* Way Down East, *631*

Griffith, Edward H.: Sky's the Limit, The, *803;* Young and Willing, *640*

Griffith, Mark: Hardbodies, *275*

Griffiths, Mark: Running Hot, *586*

Griffi, Giuseppe Patroni: Divine Nymph, The, *452*

Grindé, Nick: Before I Hang, *649;* Man They Could Not Hang, The, *714*

Grint, Alan: Adventures of Sherlock Holmes: The Crooked Man, *3;* Adventures of Sherlock Holmes: The Final Problem, *4;* Adventures of Sherlock Holmes: The Naval Treaty, *4*

Grissmer, John: Scalpel, *740*

Grosbard, Ulu: Falling in Love, *462;* Straight Time, *603;* True Confessions, *623*

Guenette, Robert: Man Who Saw Tomorrow, The, *851*

Guerra, Ruy: Erendira, *459*

Guest, Val: Casino Royale, *239;* Day the Earth Caught Fire, The, *828*

Guillermin, John: Blue Max, The, *20;* Death on the Nile, *40;* King Kong (Remake), *710;* Never Let Go, *543;* Sheena, *134;* Towering Inferno, The, *154;* Waltz of the Toreadors, *377*

Guitry, Sacha: Napoleon, *542*

Gullenhaal, Stephen: Certain Fury, *29*

Gunn, Gilbert: Cosmic Monsters, The, *664*

Gyongyossy, Imre: Revolt of Job, The, *579*

Hackford, Taylor: Against All Odds, *390;* Idolmaker, The, *788;* Officer and a Gentleman, An, *549;* White Nights, *632*

Haedrick, Rolf: Among the Cinders, *397*

Haggard, Mark: First Nudie Musical, The, *779*

Haggard, Piers: Blood on Satan's Claw, *653;*

Fiendish Plot of Dr. Fu Manchu, The, *260;* Venom, *761;*

Hagman, Larry: Son of Blob (Beware! The Blob), *745*

Hagman, Stuart: Strawberry Statement, The, *604*

Halas, John: Animal Farm, *399*

Halecki, H. B.: Junkman, The, *80*

Haley Jr., Jack: That's Dancing, *807;* That's Entertainment, *807*

Hale, William: Murder in Texas, *719;* S.O.S. Titanic, *586*

Halicki, H. B.: Gone in 60 Seconds, *63*

Haller, Daniel: Buck Rogers in the 25th Century, *822;* Dunwich Horror, The, *680;* Follow That Car, *58;* Paddy, *326*

Hall, Alexander: Here Comes Mr. Jordan, *279;* Little Miss Marker, *190*

Hall, Ivan: Kill and Kill Again, *82;* Kill or Be Killed, *83*

Halperin, Victor: White Zombie, *764*

Hamer, Robert: Kind Hearts and Coronets, *292;* To Paris with Love, *369*

Hamilton, David: Bilitis, *411;* Tendres Cousines, *365*

Hamilton, Guy: Diamonds Are Forever, *42;* Evil Under the Sun, *50;* Force Ten from Navarone, *59;* Funeral in Berlin, *61;* Goldfinger, *63;* Live and Let Die, *91;* Man with the Golden Gun, The, *96;* Mirror Crack'd, The, *99;* Remo Williams: The Adventure Begins, *120*

Hammer, Robert: Don't Answer the Phone, *677*

Hancock, John: Bang the Drum Slowly, *405;* California Dreaming, *424;* Let's Scare Jessica to Death, *712*

Hannam, Ken: Sunday Too Far Away, *608*

Hanna, William: Hey There, It's Yogi Bear, *185*

Hanson, Curtis: Losin' It, *301*

Hanson, John: Wild Rose, *634*

Hardy, Joseph: Users, The, *627*

Hardy, Robin: Wicker Man, The, *765*

Harington, Curtis: Devil Dog: The Hound of Hell, *673*

Harris, Richard W.: Splatter University, *747*

Harmon, Robert: Hitcher, The, *698*

Harrington, Curtis: Ruby, *737;* Who Slew Auntie Roo?, *764*

Harrison, Paul: House of Seven Corpses, The, *700*

Harris, Denny: Silent Scream, *743*

Harris, Frank: Kill Point, *83*

Harris, James B.: Bedford Incident, The, *407;* Fast-Walking, *464;* Some Call It Loving, *597*

Hartman, Don: Every Girl Should Be Married, *256*

Hart, Harvey: East of Eden (Remake), *454;* Shoot, *135;* Party Animal, *328;* Utilities, *376*

Harvey, Anthony: Grace Quigley, *271;* Lion

in Winter, The, *519;* Players, *564;* They Might Be Giants, *616*

Harvey, Herk: Carnival of Souls, *659*

Hashimoto, Kohji: Godzilla 1985, *694*

Haskin, Byron: From the Earth to the Moon, *838;* Long John Silver, *92;* Treasure Island, *211;* War of the Worlds, The, *874*

Hathaway, Henry: 13 Rue Madeleine, *149;* Circus World, *889;* Desert Fox, The, *42;* How the West Was Won, *904;* Lives of a Bengal Lancer, The, *91;* Nevada Smith, *917;* North to Alaska, *919;* Raid on Rommel, *118;* Sons of Katie Elder, The, *934;* True Grit, *941*

Hawks, Howard: Air Force, *7;* Ball of Fire, *224;* Big Sky, The, *883;* Big Sleep, The (Original), *16;* Bringing Up Baby, *234;* Criminal Code, The, *440;* El Dorado, *895;* Gentlemen Prefer Blondes, *266;* Hatari!, *69;* His Girl Friday, *281;* Outlaw, The, *920;* Red River, *924;* Rio Bravo, *926;* Rio Lobo, *927;* Scarface (Original), *129;* Sergeant York, *131;* To Have and Have Not, *152;* Thing (From Another World), The, *871*

Haydn, Richard: Dear Wife, *249*

Hayers, Sidney: Circus of Horrors, *663;* King Arthur, the Young Warlord, *84*

Hayes, John: End of the World, *834;* Grave of the Vampire, *695*

Heckerling, Amy: European Vacation, *256;* Fast Times at Ridgemont High, *258*

Heerman, Victor: Animal Crackers, *218*

Heffron, Richard T.: Foolin' Around, *261;* Futureworld, *838;* I, the Jury, *77;* Newman's Law, *106;* Outlaw Blues, *325;* Rumor of War, A, *125*

Heisler, Stuart: Along Came Jones, *879;* Hitler, *488;* Lone Ranger, The, *910;* Smash-up: The Story of a Woman, *595;* Tulsa, *623*

Hellbom, Olle: Brothers Lionheart, The, *175*

Hellman, Jerome: Promises in the Dark, *569*

Hellman, Monte: Cockfighter, *32;* Ride in the Whirlwind, *925;* Shooting, The, *931*

Hellman, Oliver: Beyond the Door, *650;* Tentacles, *752*

Henenlotter, Frank: Basket Case, *648*

Henry, Buck: First Family, *261;* Heaven Can Wait, *278*

Henson, Jim: Dark Crystal, The, *827;* Great Muppet Caper, The, *183;* Labyrinth, *847*

Henzell, Perry: Harder They Come, The, *786*

Herbert, Henry: Emily, *457*

Hereck, Stephen: Critters, *666*

Herman, Jean: Honor Among Thieves, *74*

Heroux, Denis: Uncanny, The, *760*

Herzfeld, John: Two of a Kind, *373*

Herzog, Werner: Aguirre: Wrath of God, *6;* Every Man for Himself and God Against All, *460;* Fitzcarraldo, *465;* Where the Green Ants Dream, *632*

Hessler, Gordon: Golden Voyage of Sinbad, The, 839; Murders in the Rue Morgue, 720; Oblong Box, The, 725; Scream and Scream Again, 740

Hess, David: To All a Good Night, 756

Heston, Charlton: Antony and Cleopatra, 401; Mother Lode, 103

Hewitt, David: Bloodsuckers, The, 654

Hewitt, Jean: Blood of Dracula's Castle, 653

Heynemann, Laurent: Birgit Haas Must Be Killed, 18

Hibbs, Jesse: To Hell and Back, 152

Hibou, La Riviere du: Occurrence at Owl Creek Bridge, An, 548

Hickox, Douglas: Brannigan, 23; Theater of Blood, 754; Zulu Dawn, 168

Higgins, Colin: Best Little Whorehouse in Texas, The, 771; Foul Play, 262; Nine to Five, 319

Higgin, Howard: Hell's House, 71; Painted Desert, The, 921

Hiller, Arthur: Author! Author!, 222; Hospital, The, 283; In-Laws, The, 286; Lonely Guy, The, 300; Love Story, 524; Making Love, 527; Man of La Mancha, 793; Nightwing, 723; Out of Towners, The, 325; Plaza Suite, 331; Romantic Comedy, 343; Silver Streak, 352; Teachers, 364; Tobruk, 153

Hillman, David Michael: Strangeness, The, 748

Hillman, Wiliam Byron: Double Exposure, 678

Hills, David: Ator: The Fighting Eagle, 818

Hill, George: Min and Bill, 534

Hill, George Roy: Butch Cassidy and the Sundance Kid, 887; Great Waldo Pepper, The, 66; Hawaii, 483; Little Drummer Girl, The, 90; Little Romance, A, 300; Slap Shot, 353; Slaughterhouse Five, 862; Sting, The, 144; World According to Garp, The, 639; World of Henry Orient, The, 384

Hill, James: Born Free, 174; Corrupt Ones, The, 35

Hill, Robert: Tarzan the Fearless, 146

Hill, Walter: Brewster's Millions (1985), 235; Crossroads, 775; Driver, The, 45; Hard Times, 69; 48 Hrs., 262; Long Riders, The, 910; Southern Comfort, 138; Streets of Fire, 142; Warriors, The, 160

Hilton, Arthur: Cat Women of the Moon, 823

Hitchcock, Alfred: Birds, The, 651; Blackmail, 414; Dial M for Murder, 675; Family Plot, 683; Foreign Correspondent, 687; Frenzy, 689; I Confess, 703; Jamaica Inn, 500; Lady Vanishes, The (Original), 710; Lifeboat, 518; Man Who Knew Too Much, The (Original), 715; Man Who Knew Too Much, The (Remake), 715; Marnie, 715; Mr. and Mrs. Smith, 310; North by Northwest, 724; Notorious, 725; Psycho, 731; Rear Window, 734; Rebecca, 576; Rope, 737; Sabotage, 738; Saboteur, 738; Secret Agent, The,

131; Spellbound, 746; Stage Fright, 747; Strangers on a Train, 749; Suspicion, 750; Thirty-Nine Steps, The, 755; To Catch a Thief, 756; Topaz, 757; Torn Curtain, 758; Trouble with Harry, The, 372; Under Capricorn, 626; Vertigo, 762; Wrong Man, The, 766; Young and Innocent, 166

Hively, Jack B.: Adventures of Huckleberry Finn, The, 169

Hodges, Mike: Flash Gordon, 837; Morons from Outer Space, 314; Terminal Man, The, 752

Hoeger, Mark: Little Match Girl, The, 189

Hofsiss, Jack: Cat on a Hot Tin Roof (Remake), 428; I'm Dancing As Fast As I Can, 492

Holcomb, Rod: Red Light Sting, The, 577

Holland, Savage Steve: Better Off Dead, 228; One Crazy Summer, 324

Holland, Tom: Fright Night, 691

Holleb, Alan: School Spirit, 346

Holzman, Allan: Forbidden World, 686

Homsky, Marvin C.: Evel Knievel, 50

Honda, Inoshiro: Dagora, the Space Monster, 827; Ghidrah, the Three-Headed Monster, 692; Godzilla, King of the Monsters (Original), 693; Godzilla vs. Monster Zero, 694; Godzilla vs. Mothra, 693; Mothra, 853; Mysterians, The, 853; Rodan, 860; Varan, the Unbelievable, 761

Hong, Elliot: They Call Me Bruce?, 365

Hool, Lance: Missing in Action 2: The Beginning, 100

Hooper, Tobe: Eaten Alive, 680; Funhouse, The, 691; Invaders from Mars (Remake), 844; Lifeforce, 849; Poltergeist, 729; Salem's Lot, 739; Texas Chainsaw Massacre 2, The, 753; Texas Chainsaw Massacre, The, 753

Hopkins, Arthur: His Double Life, 281

Hopkins, John: Torment, 757

Hopper, Dennis: Easy Rider, 455

Hopper, Jerry: Pony Express, 922

Horne, James W.: Bohemian Girl, The, 232; College, 246; Way Out West, 378

Horn, Leonard: Hunter, 75

Houck Jr., Joy: Creature from Black Lake, 665

Hough, John: Brass Target, 24; Escape to Witch Mountain, 181; Incubus, The, 705; Legend of Hell House, The, 711; Return from Witch Mountain, 201; Triumphs of a Man Called Horse, 941; Twins of Evil, 760; Watcher in the Woods, The, 764

Hous, David Weisman and Robert: Shogun Assassin, 135

Howard, David: Daniel Boone, 891

Howard, Ron: Cocoon, 825; Grand Theft Auto, 64; Gung Ho, 274; Night Shift, 319; Splash, 357

Hoyt, Harry: Lost World, The, 850

Hua-Shan: Infra-Man, 844

Hudson, Gary: Thunder Run, *151*

Hudson, Hugh: Chariots of Fire, *431;* Greystoke: The Legend of Tarzan, Lord of the Apes, *67;* Revolution, *579*

Hugh, R. John: Naked in the Sun, *917*

Hughes, Howard: Outlaw, The, *920*

Hughes, John: Breakfast Club, The, *233;* Ferris Bueller's Day Off, *259;* Sixteen Candles, *353;* Weird Science, *379*

Hughes, Kenneth: Casino Royale, *239;* Chitty Chitty Bang Bang, *177;* Internecine Project, The, *705;* Of Human Bondage (Remake), *549;* Oh, Alfie, *549;* Sextette, *350*

Hughes, Terry: Monty Python Live at the Hollywood Bowl, *313*

Hulette, Don: Breaker! Breaker!, *24;* Tennessee Stallion, *147*

Humberstone, Bruce: Happy Go Lovely, *786*

Hunter, Tim: Sylvester, *610;* Tex, *614*

Hunt, Edward: Alien Warrior, *816*

Hunt, Paul: Clones, The, *824*

Hunt, Peter: 1776, *802;* Death Hunt, *39;* On Her Majesty's Secret Service, *110;* Shout at the Devil, *135;* Wild Geese II, *163*

Hurst, Brian Desmond: Christmas Carol, A, *177;* Malta Story, The, *527*

Hurwitz, Harry: Projectionist, The, *336;* Rosebud Beach Hotel, The, *343*

Hussein, Waris: Quackser Fortune Has a Cousin in the Bronx, *571*

Huston, Jimmy: Final Exam, *684*

Huston, John: African Queen, The, *389;* Annie, *769;* Beat the Devil, *225;* Bible, The, *410;* Casino Royale, *239;* Key Largo, *82;* Life and Times of Judge Roy Bean, The, *909;* List of Adrian Messenger, The, *90;* Mackintosh Man, The, *94;* Maltese Falcon, The, *95;* Man Who Would Be King, The, *96;* Misfits, The, *535;* Moby Dick, *102;* Night of the Iguana, The, *544;* Prizzi's Honor, *569;* Reflections in a Golden Eye, *578;* Treasure of the Sierra Madre, The, *155;* Under the Volcano, *626;* Victory, *158;* Wise Blood, *636*

Hutton, Brian G.: First Deadly Sin, The, *55;* High Road to China, *72;* Kelly's Heroes, *81;* Where Eagles Dare, *161*

Huyck, Willard: Best Defense, *227;* French Postcards, *263;* Howard the Duck, *842*

Hyams, Peter: 2010, *874;* Capricorn One, *822;* Hanover Street, *481;* Outland, *855;* Running Scared (1986), *125;* Star Chamber, The, *600*

Ichaso, Leon: Crossover Dreams, *775*

Idle, Eric: Tale of the Frog Prince, *207*

Imhoof, Markus: Boat Is Full, The, *416*

Inagaki, Hiroshi: Kojiro, *85;* Samurai Trilogy, The, *127*

Ingster, Boris: Stranger on the Third Floor, *141*

Irving, Richard: Cyborg: The Six Million Dollar Man, *827*

Irvin, John: Champions, *430;* Dogs of War, The, *44;* Ghost Story, *693;* Raw Deal, *119;* Turtle Diary, *373*

Isasi, Antonio: Summertime Killer, The, *143*

Iscove, Robert: Little Mermaid, The, *189;* Puss in Boots, *200*

Israel, Neal: Americathon, *218;* Bachelor Party, *222;* Moving Violations, *315;* Tunnelvision, *373*

Ivory, James: Bostonians, The, *417;* Heat and Dust, *485;* Quartet, *571;* Room with a View, A (1987 Release), *584;* Roseland, *584;* Wild Party, The, *634*

Jabor, Arnaldo: I Love You (Eu Te Amo), *491*

Jackson, Donald B.: Demon Lover, The, *673*

Jackson, Lewis: Christmas Evil, *663*

Jackson, Patrick: King Arthur, the Young Warlord, *84*

Jackson, Pat: Prisoner, The (television series), *857*

Jackson, Wilfred: Alice in Wonderland, *170*

Jacoby, Joseph: Great Bank Hoax, The, *272*

Jaeckin, Just: Emmanuelle, *457;* Lady Chatterley's Lover, *512;* Perils of Gwendoline, The, *114*

Jaffe, Stanley: Without a Trace, *637*

Jaglom, Henry: Can She Bake a Cherry Pie?, *238;* Tracks, *621*

Jameson, Jerry: Airport 77, *391;* High Noon, Part Two, *903;* Raise the Titanic, *118;* Starflight One, *867;* Terror on the 40th Floor, *753*

Jarmusch, Jim: Stranger than Paradise, *360*

Jarrott, Charles: Amateur, The, *395;* Anne of the Thousand Days, *400;* Boy in Blue, The, *418;* Condorman, *178;* Last Flight of Noah's Ark, *188;* Littlest Horse Thieves, The, *190;* Other Side of Midnight, The, *554*

Jason, Leigh: Lady for a Night, *512;* Mad Miss Manton, The, *304;* Out of the Blue, *325*

Jeffrey, Tom: Odd Angry Shot, The, *548*

Jeffries, Richard: Bloodtide, *654*

Jewison, Norman: Agnes of God, *390;* And Justice for All, *397;* Best Friends, *227;* Cincinnati Kid, The, *31;* Fiddler on the Roof, *779;* F.I.S.T., *461;* In the Heat of the Night, *494;* Rollerball, *860;* Russians Are Coming, the Russians Are Coming, The, *344;* Soldier's Story, A, *138;* Thomas Crown Affair, The, *150*

Joannon, Léo: Atoll K (Utopia), *221*

Joens, Michael: My Little Pony: The Movie, *194*

Joffe, Roland: Killing Fields, The, *506*

Johnson, Alan: To Be or Not to Be (Remake), *369*

Johnson, Jed: Andy Warhol's Bad, *398*

Johnson, Kenneth: Incredible Hulk, The, *843*

Johnson, Lamont: Jack and the Beanstalk, *186;* Last American Hero, The, *86;* Lipstick, *712;* One on One, *552;* Spacehunter: Adventures in the Forbidden Zone, *864*

Jones, Amy: Love Letters, *523*

Jones, Chuck: Bugs Bunny/Road Runner Movie, The, *175;* 1001 Rabbit Tales, *196*

Jones, David: Betrayal, *409*

Jones, Don: Forest, The, *687;* Love Butcher, *713;* Sweater Girls, *362*

Jones, F. Richard: Bulldog Drummond, *25*

Jones, Harmon: Bullwhip, *887*

Jones, L. Q.: Boy and His Dog, A, *821*

Jones, Terry: Life of Brian, *299;* Monty Python's The Meaning of Life, *313*

Jordan, Glenn: Buddy System, The, *421;* Frankenstein (Remake), *688;* Mass Appeal, *531;* Only When I Laugh, *553*

Jordan, Neil: Company of Wolves, The, *825;* Danny Boy, *444;* Mona Lisa, *537*

Julian, Rupert: Phantom of the Opera, The, *727*

Juran, Nathan: Attack of the 50-Foot Woman, *647;* Brain from Planet Arous, The, *821;* Hellcats of the Navy, *70;* 7th Voyage of Sinbad, The, *861;*

Jutra, Claude: Surfacing, *143*

Kachivas, Lou: Secret of the Sword, The, *203*

Kaczender, George: Agency, *390;* Chanel Solitaire, *430;* In Praise of Older Women, *493*

Kadár, Ján: Shop on Main Street, The, *593*

Kaduwara, Haruki: Legend of the Eight Samurai, *89*

Kagan, Jeremy Paul: Big Fix, The, *15;* Chosen, The, *433;* Heroes, *486;* Sting II, The, *140;* Sleeping Beauty, *205;* Journey of Natty Gann, The

Kahn, Richard: Harlem Rides the Range, *900*

Kanew, Jeff: Eddie Macon's Run, *47;* Gotcha!, *64;* Revenge of the Nerds, *340*

Kane, Joseph: Billy the Kid Returns, *883;* Boots and Saddles, *885;* Colorado, *889;* Dakota, *890;* Flame of the Barbary Coast, *56;* Frontier Pony Express, *898;* Git Along, Little Dogies, *898;* Heart of the Golden West, *901;* Man from Music Mountain, *912;* Maverick Queen, The, *914;* Melody Trail, *915;* Old Corral, The, *919;* Ride the Man Down, *926;* Rough Riders' Roundup, *928;* Saga of Death Valley, *929;* Shine On Harvest Moon, *931;* Song of Nevada, *933;* Song of Texas, *933;* Sunset Serenade, *935;* Yellow Rose of Texas, *946*

Kanievska, Mark: Another Country, *400*

Kanin, Garson: My Favorite Wife, *316;* They Knew What They Wanted, *616*

Kanter, Hal: Loving You, *793*

Kaplan, Jonathan: Heart Like a Wheel, *70;* Mr. Billion, *100;* Over the Edge, *555;* White Line Fever, *162*

Kaplan, Nelly: Nea (A Young Emmanuelle), *542*

Karlson, Phil: Ben, *650;* Big Cat, The, *15;* Framed, *60;* Hell to Eternity, *485;* Untouchables: Scarface Mob, The, *157;* Walking Tall, *160*

Karson, Eric: Octagon, The, *109*

Kasdan, Lawrence: Big Chill, The, *411;* Body Heat, *417;* Silverado, *932*

Katselas, Milton: Butterflies Are Free, *422;* Forty Carats, *262*

Katzin, Lee H.: Savages, *739*

Kaufer, Jonathon: Soup for One, *356*

Kaufman, George S.: Senator Was Indiscreet, The, *349*

Kaufman, Phil: Invasion of the Body Snatchers (Remake), *845;* Right Stuff, The, *580;* Wanderers, The, *629;* White Dawn, The, *161*

Kaylor, Robert: Carny, *426*

Kazan, Elia: Arrangement, The, *401;* Baby Doll, *403;* East of Eden (Original), *454;* Face in the Crowd, A, *461;* Last Tycoon, The, *515;* On the Waterfront, *551;* Splendor in the Grass, *599;* Streetcar Named Desire, A, *605;* Viva Zapata!, *629*

Keaton, Buster: General, The, *266*

Keeslar, Don: Bog, *655*

Keighley, William: Green Pastures, The, *479;* Prince and the Pauper, The (Original), *199*

Keller, Harry: Tammy and the Doctor, *611;* Texas John Slaughter: Stampede at Bitter Creek, *937;* Texas John Slaughter: Wild Times, *938*

Kelljan, Bob: Count Yorga, Vampire, *664*

Kellman, Barnet: Key Exchange, *506*

Kellogg, Ray: Green Berets, The, *66*

Kelly, Gene: Guide for the Married Man, A, *273;* Hello, Dolly!, *787;* Invitation to the Dance, *788;* It's Always Fair Weather, *789;* On the Town, *796;* Singin' in the Rain, *802;* That's Entertainment Part II, *807*

Kelly, James: Beast in the Cellar, The, *649*

Kelly, Patrick: Beer, *226*

Kelly, Ron: King of the Grizzlies, *188*

Kennedy, Burt: Support Your Local Sheriff, *936;* Train Robbers, The, *940;* War Wagon, The, *944*

Kennedy, Ken: Mission to Glory, *536*

Kennedy, Tom: Time Walker, *755*

Kernochan, Sarah: Marjoe, *529*

Kershner, Irvin: Empire Strikes Back, The, *833;* Eyes of Laura Mars, The, *682;* Fine Madness, A, *260;* Flim-Flam Man, The, *466;*

Never Say Never Again, *106;* Return of a Man Called Horse, The, *924;* Up the Sandbox, *375*

Kessler, Bruce: Cruise into Terror, *667*

Kiersch, Fritz: Children of the Corn, *662;* Tuff Turf, *623*

Kimmel, Bruce: Spaceship, *356*

King, Allan Winton: Silence of the North, *593*

King, Henry: Love Is a Many-Splendored Thing, *523;* Stanley and Livingstone, *600;* Twelve O'Clock High, *155*

King, Stephen: Maximum Overdrive, *716*

Kinney, Jack: Legend of Sleepy Hollow, The, *188*

Kirby, John Mason: Savage Weekend, *739*

Kizer, R. J.: Godzilla 1985, *694*

Klane, Robert: Thank God It's Friday, *806*

Klein, Dennis: One More Saturday Night, *324*

Kleiser, Randal: Blue Lagoon, The, *415;* Boy in the Plastic Bubble, The, *418;* Flight of the Navigator, *837;* Grandview, U.S.A., *477;* Grease, *784;* Summer Lovers, *607*

Kleven, Max: Ruckus, *124*

Kline, Edward: My Little Chickadee, *316*

Koch, Howard W.: Badge 373, *11;* Frankenstein—1970, *689*

Kollek, Amos: Goodbye New York, *271*

Komack, James: Porky's Revenge, *333*

Konchalovsky, Andrei: Maria's Lovers, *528;* Runaway Train, *125*

Kong, Jackie: Being, The, *650;* Night Patrol, *318*

Kopple, Barbara: Harlan County, U.S.A., *482*

Korda, Alexander: Fire over England, *54;* Marius, *529;* Private Life of Don Juan, The, *568;* Private Life of Henry the Eighth, The, *568;* Rembrandt, *578;* That Hamilton Woman, *614*

Korda, Zoltán: Drums, *46;* Elephant Boy, *48;* Sanders of the River, *127;* Four Feathers, The, *60;* Jungle Book, *187;* Sahara, *126*

Korty, John: Autobiography of Miss Jane Pittman, The, *402;* Haunting Passion, The, *840;* Oliver's Story, *551;* People, The, *855;* Who Are the Debolts and Where Did They Get 19 Kids?, *632*

Koster, Henry: Bishop's Wife, The, *229;* D-Day the Sixth of June, *442;* Flower Drum Song, *780;* Inspector General, The, *287;* Robe, The, *581*

Kotani, Tom: Bushido Blade, *26*

Kotcheff, Ted: Apprenticeship of Duddy Kravitz, The, *401;* First Blood, *55;* Fun with Dick and Jane, *265;* North Dallas Forty, *546;* Split Image, *599;* Uncommon Valor, *156*

Kowalski, Bernard: Stiletto, *140*

Kramer, Frank: Five for Hell, *56*

Kramer, Stanley: Bless the Beasts and the Children, *414;* Champion, *430;* Defiant Ones,

The, *448;* Domino Principle, The, *453;* Guess Who's Coming to Dinner, *273;* Inherit the Wind, *495;* It's a Mad Mad Mad Mad World, *288;* Judgment at Nuremberg, *504;* On the Beach, *854;* Pride and the Passion, The, *567;* Runner Stumbles, The, *585;* R.P.M. (Revolutions Per Minute), *572;* Ship of Fools, *592*

Krasny, Paul: Christina, *31*

Kronsbert, Jeremy: Going Ape!, *269*

Kubrick, Stanley: 2001: A Space Odyssey, *873;* Barry Lyndon, *405;* Clockwork Orange, A, *824;* Dr. Strangelove or How I Learned to Stop Worrying and Love the Bomb, *252;* Lolita, *520;* Paths of Glory, *559;* Shining, The, *742;* Spartacus, *559*

Kuehn, Andrew: Terror in the Aisles, *753*

Kulik, Buzz: Hidden Fortress, The, *71;* Shamus, *132;* Villa Rides, *943*

Kurosawa, Akira: Dersu Uzala, *448;* Dodes 'Ka-Den, *454;* Hidden Fortress, The, *71;* Ikiru, *493;* Kagemusha, *81;* Ran, *575;* Rashomon, *575;* Red Beard, *577;* Sanjuro, *128;* Seven Samurai, The, *131;* Throne of Blood, *617;* Yojimbo, *166*

Kurys, Diane: Entre Nous (Between Us), *458*

Kusturica, Emir: When Father Was Away on Business, *632*

Kwapis, Ken: (Sesame Street Presents) Follow That Bird, *204*

La Cava, Gregory: My Man Godfrey, *317;* Stage Door, *357*

Lachman, Harry: Our Relations, *325*

Laloggia, Frank: Fear No Evil, *683*

Laloux, René: Fantastic Planet, *836*

Lamont, Charles: Abbott and Costello Meet Captain Kidd, *214;* Abbott and Costello Meet Dr. Jekyll and Mr. Hyde, *214*

Lamore, Marsh: Secret of the Sword, The, *203*

Lamorisse, Albert: Red Balloon, The, *201*

Lancaster, Burt: Kentuckian, The, *906*

Landers, Lew: Enchanted Forest, The, *180;* Raven and the Black Cat, The, *733;* Ridin' on a Rainbow, *926;* Return of the Vampire, The, *735*

Landis, John: American Werewolf in London, An, *644;* Animal House, *218;* Blues Brothers, The, *231;* Into the Night, *496;* Kentucky Fried Movie, *292;* Schlock, *346;* Spies Like Us, *356;* Trading Places, *371;* Twilight Zone—The Movie, *759*

Landon, Michael: Sam's Son, *588*

Lane, Andrew: Jake Speed, *78*

Lane, Dave: Invasion UFO, *845*

Lanfield, Sidney: Hound of the Baskervilles, The (Original), *75;* You'll Never Get Rich, *814*

Lang, Fritz: Beyond a Reasonable Doubt, *409;* Big Heat, The, *15;* Clash by Night, *434;* Metropolis, *852;* Metropolis (musical version), *793;* M, *713;* Rancho Notorious, *923;* Return of Frank James, The, *925;* Scarlet Street, *589;* You Only Live Once, *640*

Lang, Michael: Gift, The, *268;* Holiday Hotel, *281*

Lang, Richard: Change of Seasons, A, *240;* Fantasy Island, *837;* Mountain Men, The, *915;* Vega$, *158;* Word, The, *638*

Lang, Walter: King and I, The, *790;* Little Princess, The, *190;* Snow White and the Three Stooges, *205;* There's No Business Like Show Business, *808*

Langton, Simon: Act of Passion, *389*

Lanzmann, Claude: Shoah, *592*

Larry, Sheldon: Terminal Choice, *752*

Larsen, Keith: Whitewater Sam, *162*

Lathan, Stan: Beat Street, *770*

Lattuada, Alberto: Stay As You Are, *602*

Laughlin, Michael: Strange Behavior, *748;* Strange Invaders, *867*

Laughlin, Tom: Billy Jack, *17*

Launder, Frank: Belles of St. Trinian's, The, *227*

Lautner, Georges: La Cage Aux Folles III, The Wedding, *295;* My Other Husband, *541*

Lauzier, Gerard: Petit Con, *329*

Lawrence, Quentin: Crawling Eye, The, *665*

Layton, Joe: Richard Pryor Live on the Sunset Strip, *341*

Leach, Wilford: Pirates of Penzance, The, *799*

Leacock, Philip: Curse of King Tut's Tomb, The, *667;* War Lover, The, *630*

Lean, David: Bridge on the River Kwai, The, *25;* Dr. Zhivago, *452;* Hobson's Choice, *281;* In Which We Serve, *494;* Lawrence of Arabia, *88;* Oliver Twist, *550;* Passage to India, A, *558;* Ryan's Daughter, *586;* Summertime, *608*

Leaver, Don: Witching Time, *765*

LeBorg, Reginald: Psycho Sisters, *732*

Lederer, Charles: Never Steal Anything Small, *795*

Lederman, Ross: Tarzan's Revenge, *146*

Leder, Paul: I Dismember Mama, *703*

Lee, Bruce: Return of the Dragon, *120*

Lee, Rowland V.: Bridge of San Luis Rey, The, *420;* Captain Kidd, *27;* Count of Monte Cristo, The (Original), *36*

Lehman, Ernest: Portnoy's Complaint, *565*

Leiberman, Robert: Fighting Back, *53;* Will, G. Gordon Liddy, *635*

Lelouch, Claude: And Now, My Love, *398;* Cat and Mouse, *28;* Edith and Marcel, *778;* Happy New Year (La Bonne Annee), *68;* Robert et Robert, *582*

Lemmon, Jack: Kotch, *294*

Lenzi, Umberto: Battle of the Commandos, *13*

Leonard, Robert Z.: In the Good Old Summertime, *788;* Maytime, *793;* Pride and Prejudice, *567*

Leone, John: Great Smokey Roadblock, The, *65*

Leone, Sergio: Fistful of Dollars, A, *896;* For a Few Dollars More, *897;* Good the Bad and the Ugly, The, *899;* Once upon a Time in America (long version), *110;* Once upon a Time in the West, *919*

Leo, Malcolm: Beach Boys: An American Band, The, *770;* It Came from Hollywood, *287;* This Is Elvis, *808*

Lerner, Carl: Black Like Me, *413*

Lerner, Irving: Cry of Battle, *37*

Lerner, Murray: From Mao to Mozart, *781*

LeRoy, Mervyn: Devil at 4 O'Clock, The, *450;* Gold Diggers of 1933, *783;* Gypsy, *785;* I Am a Fugitive from a Chain Gang, *490;* Little Caesar, *90;* Million Dollar Mermaid, *794;* Mr. Roberts, *311;* No Time for Sergeants, *320;* Thirty Seconds over Tokyo, *149;* Waterloo Bridge, *631;* Without Reservations, *382*

Lester, Mark L.: Armed and Dangerous, *220;* Bobbie Jo and the Outlaw, *21;* Class of 1984, *663;* Commando, *33;* Firestarter, *685*

Lester, Richard: Butch and Sundance: The Early Days, *887;* Cuba, *37;* Finders Keepers, *260;* Four Musketeers, The, *60;* Funny Thing Happened on the Way to the Forum, A, *265;* Hard Day's Night, *786;* Help!, *787;* How I Won the War, *284;* Juggernaut, *80;* Ritz, The, *342;* Robin and Marian, *123;* Superman III, *869;* Superman II, *869;* Three Musketeers, The (1973), *150*

Levey, William A.: Happy Hooker Goes to Washington, The, *275*

Levick, David: Gospel, *784*

Levinson, Barry: Diner, *251;* Natural, The, *542;* Young Sherlock Holmes, *167*

Levin, Henry: Lonely Man, The, *909;* Murderers' Row, *104;* Where the Boys Are, *380*

Levy, I. Robert: Can I Do It 'Til I Need Glasses?, *237*

Levy, William A.: Blackenstein, *652*

Lewicki, Stephen Jon: Certain Sacrifice, A, *429*

Lewin, Albert: Picture of Dorian Gray, The, *728*

Lewis, Christopher: Ripper, The, *736*

Lewis, Herschell Gordon: Blood Feast, *653;* Color Me Blood Red, *663;* Wizard of Gore, The, *766*

Lewis, Jerry: Bellboy, The, *226;* Cracking Up, *248;* Errand Boy, The, *256;* Hardly Working, *276;* Nutty Professor, The, *321;* Patsy, The, *328*

Lewis, Joseph H.: Big Combo, The, *15;* Invisible Ghost, *705;* Pride of the Bowery, *567*

Lewis, Robert: Fallen Angel, *462;* S.H.E., *134*

Lieberman, Jeff: Blue Sunshine, 20; Squirm, 747

Lieberman, Robert: Table for Five, 610

Liebman, Max: 10 from Your Show of Shows, 364

Lindsay-Hogg, Michael: Let It Be, 792; Nasty Habits, 317; Thumbelina, 209

Linson, Art: Where the Buffalo Roam, 381; Wild Life, The, 382

Lion, Mickey: House of Exorcism, The, 699

Lipstadt, Aaron: Android, 817; City Limits, 823

Lisberger, Steven: Tron, 873

Littman, Lynne: Testament, 870

Litvak, Anatole: Mayerling, 531; Night of the Generals, 107; Sorry, Wrong Number, 745

Lloyd, Frank: Blood on the Sun, 19; Last Command, The, 907; Mutiny on the Bounty (Original), 105

Loader, Jayne: Atomic Cafe, The, 402

Locke, Rick: Petronella, 197

Logan, Joshua: Bus Stop, 236; Camelot, 773; Ensign Pulver, 255; Fanny, 463; Paint Your Wagon, 797; Sayonara, 589; South Pacific, 805

Lo Bianco, Tony: Too Scared to Scream, 757

Lomas, Raoul: Minor Miracle, A, 192

Lommel, Ulli: Boogeyman, The, 655; Devonsville Terror, The, 674

Loncraine, Richard: Brimstone and Treacle, 657; Missionary, The, 310

London, Jerry: Chiefs, 432; Shogun (full-length version), 134; Shogun (short version), 134

Longon, Humphrey: Battle Force, 12

Lord, Jean Claude: Visiting Hours, 762

Losey, Joseph: Accident, 388; Boy with Green Hair, The, 419; Concrete Jungle, The (aka The Criminal), 437; Doll's House, A, 453; La Truite (The Trout), 512; Mr. Klein, 536; Romantic Englishwoman, The, 584; Servant, The, 590

Lourie, Eugene: Gorgo, 694

Lowry, Dick: Jayne Mansfield Story, The, 501; Smokey and the Bandit III, 355

Lubin, Arthur: Buck Privates, 235; Francis, the Talking Mule, 263; Hold That Ghost, 281

Lubitsch, Ernst: Ninotchka, 319; To Be or Not to Be (Original), 368

Luby, S. Roy: Border Phantom, 885

Lucas, George: American Graffiti, 218; Star Wars, 867; THX 1138, 872

Ludwig, Edward: Fighting Seabees, The, 53; Wake of the Red Witch, 160

Lumet, Sidney: 12 Angry Men, 624; Anderson Tapes, The, 8; Daniel, 444; Deathtrap, 448; Dog Day Afternoon, 452; Equus, 458; Failsafe, 461; Garbo Talks, 265; Group, The, 480; Just Tell Me What You Want, 292; Long

Day's Journey into Night, 520; Murder on the Orient Express, 104; Network, 543; Pawnbroker, The, 560; Power, 566; Prince of the City, 568; Serpico, 590; Verdict, The, 628; Wiz, The, 812

Lupino, Ida: Trouble with Angels, The, 372

Luske, Hamilton: Alice in Wonderland, 170

Lustig, William: Maniac, 714

Lynch, David: Dune, 832; Elephant Man, The, 456; Eraserhead, 680

Lynch, Paul: Cross Country, 440; Humongous, 702; Prom Night, 730

Lyne, Adrian: Flashdance, 780; 9 1/2 Weeks, 545; Foxes, 469

Lynn, Jonathan: Clue, 245

Lyon, Francis D.: Great Locomotive Chase, The, 182

Maas, Dick: Lift, The, 712

MacGregor, Sean: Gentle Savage, 898

Machaty, Gustav: Ecstasy, 455

Mackendrick, Alexander: Ladykillers, The, 295; Man in the White Suit, The, 306

MacKenzie, John: Beyond the Limit, 410; Long Good Friday, The, 92

Maetzig, Kurt: First Spaceship on Venus, 837

Magnoli, Albert: American Anthem, 395; Purple Rain, 799

Makavejev, Dusan: Coca Cola Kid, The, 246; Montenegro, 313

Makk, Karoly: Lily in Love, 299

Malick, Terence: Badlands, 404; Days of Heaven, 446

Malle, Louis: Alamo Bay, 391; Atlantic City, 402; Crackers, 248; My Dinner with Andre, 540; Pretty Baby, 566

Malmuth, Bruce: Man Who Wasn't There, The, 306; Nighthawks, 107

Malone, William: Creature, 826

Mamoulian, Rouben: Becky Sharp, 407; Blood and Sand, 414; Golden Boy, 475; Mark of Zorro, 97; Silk Stockings, 802

Mandel, Robert: F/X, 51; Independence Day, 494

Manfredi, Nino: Nudo di Donna (Portrait of a Woman, Nude), 321

Mankiewicz, Joseph L.: All About Eve, 393; Cleopatra, 435; Guys and Dolls, 785; Sleuth, 595; Suddenly, Last Summer, 607; There Was a Crooked Man, 938

Mankiewirk, Henry: Hell's Brigade, 71

Manning, Michelle: Blue City, 20

Mann, Abby: King, 507

Mann, Anthony: Bend of the River, 882; El Cid, 48; Fall of the Roman Empire, The, 462; Glenn Miller Story, The, 783; God's Little Acre, 473; Men in War, 98; Thunder Bay, 151

Mann, Daniel: Hot Spell, *489;* Matilda, *308;* Willard, *765*

Mann, Delbert: All Quiet on the Western Front, *393;* Desire Under the Elms, *449;* Lover Come Back, *303;* Marty, *529;* Night Crossing, *106;* That Touch of Mink, *365*

Mann, Edward: Cauldron of Blood, *661*

Mann, Michael: Keep, The, *708;* Manhunter, *97;* Thief, *148*

Manoogian, Peter: Eliminators, *832*

Manski, Mel: Legend of Walks Far Woman, The, *909*

Marcel, Terry: Hawk the Slayer, *69*

Margolin, Stuart: Glitter Dome, The, *62*

Margolis, Jeff: Richard Pryor—Live in Concert, *341*

Marin, Edwin L.: Abilene Town, *878;* Death Kiss, The, *39;* Mr. Ace, *100;* Tall in the Saddle, *936*

Markle, Fletcher: Incredible Journey, The, *186*

Markle, Peter: Hot Dog...The Movie, *283;* Youngblood, *641*

Markowitz, Robert: Belarus File, The, *13*

Marks, Arthur: Bonnie's Kids, *22*

Marlowe, Derek: Adventures of Sherlock Holmes: The Greek Interpreter, *4*

Marquand, Richard: Eye of the Needle, *51;* Jagged Edge, *500;* Legacy, The, *711;* Return of the Jedi, *859;* Until September, *627*

Marshall, Garry: Flamingo Kid, The, *261;* Nothing in Common, *547;* Young Doctors in Love, *385*

Marshall, George: Boy, Did I Get a Wrong Number!, *233;* Goldwyn Follies, The, *784;* How the West Was Won, *904;* Off Limits, *322;* Pack Up Your Troubles, *326;* Papa's Delicate Condition, *557;* Perils of Pauline, The, *329;* Pot o' Gold, *566;* Texas, *937*

Marshall, William: Adventures of Captain Fabian, *2*

Martino, Sergio: Screamers, *741;* Sex with a Smile, *350;* Slave of the Cannibal God, *136*

Martinson, Leslie: Batman, *172;* Kid with the 200 I.Q., The, *188;* PT 109, *569*

Martin, Andrew: King Solomon's Mines, *84*

Martin, Eugenio: Horror Express, *698;* Pancho Villa, *922*

Martin, Gene: Bad Man's River, *880*

Marton, Andrew: Africa—Texas Style!, *6;* Around the World Under the Sea, *10;* Longest Day, The, *92*

Marvin, Mike: Hamburger—The Motion Picture, *274*

Massot, Joe: Song Remains the Same, The, *803*

Masterson, Peter: Trip to Bountiful, The, *622*

Masters, Quentin: Dangerous Summer, A, *444;* Stud, The, *606*

Mastroianni, Armand: He Knows You're Alone, *696;* Killing Hour, The, *709*

Masuda, Toshio: Tora! Tora! Tora!, *154*

Masuni, Kenji: Shogun Assassin (Japan), *135*

Matalon, Eddy: Blackout, *19*

Maté, Rudolph: D.O.A., *442;* When Worlds Collide, *876;* Union Station, *760*

Matinson, Burney: Mickey's Christmas Carol, *192*

Maxwell, Peter: Highest Honor, The, *73;* Run, Rebecca, Run, *202*

Maxwell, Ronald F.: Little Darlings, *299;* Night the Lights Went Out in Georgia, The, *545*

Mayberry, Russ: Fer-de-Lance, *684;* Unidentified Flying Oddball, *212*

Mayer, Gerald: Man Inside, The, *95*

Maylam, Tony: Burning, The, *658;* Riddle of the Sands, *121*

Mayo, Archie: Angel on My Shoulder, *399;* House Across the Bay, The, *489;* Petrified Forest, The, *562;* Svengali, *750*

Maysles, Albert: Gimme Shelter, *783*

Maysles, David: Gimme Shelter, *783*

May, Elaine: Heartbreak Kid, The, *277;* Mikey and Nicky, *309*

Mazursky, Paul: Blume in Love, *416;* Bob & Carol & Ted & Alice, *231;* Down and Out in Beverly Hills, *254;* Harry and Tonto, *483;* Moscow on the Hudson, *314;* Tempest, *612;* Unmarried Woman, An, *626*

McBride, Jim: Breathless (Remake), *420*

McCarey, Leo: Bells of St. Mary's, The, *408;* Duck Soup, *254;* Going My Way, *474;* Good Sam, *271;* Indiscreet, *286;* Milky Way, The, *310;* Once upon a Honeymoon, *324*

McCowan, George: Frogs, *691*

McDonald, David: Devil Girl from Mars, *674*

McDonald, Frank: Big Sombrero, The, *883;* My Pal Trigger, *916;* Sioux City Sue, *933*

McEveety, Bernard: Brotherhood of Satan, *658*

McEveety, Vincent: Apple Dumpling Gang Rides Again, The, *171;* Castaway Cowboy, The, *176;* Charlie and the Angel, *176;* Gus, *183;* Herbie Goes Bananas, *184;* Herbie Goes to Monte Carlo, *185;* Million Dollar Duck, The, *192*

McGann, William: American Empire, *879;* In Old California, *905*

McGavin, Darren: Run Stranger Run, *738*

McGoohan, Patrick: Prisoner, The (television series), *857*

McGowan, J. P.: Hurricane Express, *76;* When a Man Rides Alone, *944*

McGowan, Stuart E.: They Went That-A-Way and That-A-Way, *208*

McGrath, Joe: Casino Royale, *239;* Magic Christian, The, *304*

McKeown, Douglas: Return of the Alien's Deadly Spawn, The, *734*

McLaglen, Andrew V.: Bandolero!, *881;* Breakthrough, *24;* Cahill—US Marshal, *887;* Chisum, *889;* ffolkes, *53;* Hellfighters, *70;* Rare Breed, The, *924;* Sahara, *126;* Sea Wolves, The, *130;* Shenandoah, *930;* Wild Geese, The, *163*

McLeod, Norman Z.: It's a Gift, *288;* Kid from Brooklyn, The, *292;* Little Men, *519;* Monkey Business, *312;* Secret Life of Walter Mitty, The, *347;* Topper, *369;* Topper Takes a Trip, *370*

McLeod, Norman: Paleface, The, *327*

McLoughlin, Tom: Friday the 13th Part VI: Jason Lives, *691;* One Dark Night, *726*

McNamara, Richard (aka Anton Giulio Masano): Atom Age Vampire, *647*

McNaughton, Ian: And Now for Something Completely Different, *218*

McTiernan, John: Nomads, *724*

Meahy, Francis: Carpathian Eagle, *659*

Medak, Peter: Changeling, The, *661;* Dancing Princesses, The, *178;* Emperor's New Clothes, The, *833;* Pinocchio, *198;* Ruling Class, The, *344;* Snow Queen, *205;* Snow White and the Seven Dwarfs, *205;* Zorro, the Gay Blade, *386*

Medford, Don: Organization, The, *111*

Medoway, Cary: Heavenly Kid, The, *278*

Megahy, Francis: Great Riviera Bank Robbery, The, *65*

Meins, Gus: March of the Wooden Soldiers, *307*

Meisel, Norbert: Adultress, The, *389*

Melchior, Ib: Angry Red Planet, The, *817*

Melendez, Bill: Bon Voyage, Charlie Brown, *174;* Boy Named Charlie Brown, A, *174;* It's an Adventure, Charlie Brown, *186;* Race for Your Life, Charlie Brown, *200;* Snoopy, Come Home, *205*

Melville, Jean-Pierre: Bob le Flambeur, *21*

Menduluk, George: Doin' Time, *253;* Kidnapping of the President, The, *709;* Stone Cold Dead, *141*

Menshov, Vladimir: Moscow Does Not Believe in Tears, *538*

Menzel, Jiří: Closely Watched Trains, *435*

Menzies, William Cameron: Invaders from Mars (Original), *844;* Things to Come, *871*

Merrill, Keith: Take Down, *363;* Windwalker, *946*

Metter, Alan: Back to School, *222;* Girls Just Want to Have Fun, *268*

Metzger, Radley: Cat and the Canary, The, *660*

Meyerson, Alan: Steelyard Blues, *359*

Meyer, Nicholas: Day After, The, *828;* Pied Piper of Hamelin, The, *198;* Star Trek II: The Wrath of Khan, *865;* Time After Time, *872;* Volunteers, *377*

Meyer, Russ: Beyond the Valley of the Dolls, *410;* Faster Pussycat! Kill! Kill!, *52*

Michaels, Richard: Blue Skies Again, *416*

Mihalka, George: My Bloody Valentine, *720*

Mikels, Ted V.: Astro-Zombies, *646*

Mikhalkov, Nikita: Slave of Love, A, *594*

Milestone, Lewis: All Quiet on the Western Front, *7;* Arch of Triumph, *401;* Front Page, The, *264;* Mutiny on the Bounty (Remake), *105;* North Star, The, *108;* Ocean's Eleven, *109;* Purple Heart, The, *570;* Rain, *574;* Red Pony, The, *201;* Strange Love of Martha Ivers, The, *604*

Miles, Christopher: Priest of Love, *568*

Milius, John: Big Wednesday, *411;* Conan the Barbarian, *825;* Red Dawn, *119;* Wind and the Lion, The; *164*

Milland, Ray: Man Alone, A, *911*

Millar, Gavin: Dreamchild, *831*

Millar, Stuart: Rooster Cogburn, *928;* When the Legends Die, *945*

Miller, Dan T.: Screamers, *741*

Miller, David: Back Street, *404;* Executive Action, *460;* Flying Tigers, The, *58;* Lonely Are the Brave, *909;* Love Happy, *302*

Miller, George: Aviator, The, *403;* Man from Snowy River, *95;* Chain Reaction, *29;* Mad Max Beyond Thunderdome, *850;* Mad Max, *850;* Road Warrior, The, *859;* Twilight Zone—The Movie, *759*

Miller, Harvey: Bad Medicine, *223*

Miller, Ira: Loose Shoes, *301*

Miller, Jason: That Championship Season, *614*

Miller, Michael: Class Reunion, *244;* Jackson County Jail, *78;* Silent Rage, *136*

Miller, Robert Ellis: Heart Is a Lonely Hunter, The, *483;* Reuben, Reuben, *339*

Miller, Sidney: 30 Foot Bride of Candy Rock, The, *366*

Milligan, Andy: Bloodthirsty Butchers, *654;* Rats Are Coming!, The Werewolves Are Here!, The, *733*

Miner, Steve: Friday the 13th, Part III, *690;* Friday the 13th, Part II, *690;* House, *699*

Minnelli, Vincente: American in Paris, An, *769;* Band Wagon, The, *769;* Brigadoon, *772;* Cabin in the Sky, *423;* Father's Little Dividend, *259;* Four Horsemen of the Apocalypse, *60;* Gigi, *782;* Madame Bovary, *526;* Matter of Time, A, *531;* Meet Me in St. Louis, *793;* On a Clear Day, You Can See Forever, *796;* Pirate, The, *798;* Sandpiper, The, *588;* Yolanda and the Thief, *640;* Ziegfeld Follies, *814*

Mischer, Don: Evening with Robin Williams, An, *256*

Mizoguchi, Kenji: Ugetsu, *625*

Mizrahi, Moshe: I Sent a Letter to My Love, *491;* Madame Rosa, *526*

Moberly, Luke: Little Laura and Big John, *90*

Molinaro, Edouard: Just the Way You Are,

505; La Cage aux Folles, *294;* Pain in the A——, A, *327;* Ravishing Idiot, The, *337;* La Cage aux Folles II, *294*

Monicelli, Mario: Lovers and Liars, *303*

Monroe, Phil: Bugs Bunny/Road Runner Movie, The, *175*

Montagne, Edward: They Went That-A-Way and That-A-Way, *208*

Montgomery, Patrick: Compleat Beatles, The, *775*

Moore, Michael: Paradise Hawaiian Style, *797*

Moore, Richard: Circle of Iron, *31*

Moore, Robert: Chapter Two, *431;* Murder by Death, *315;* Thursday's Game, *618*

Moore, Ronald W.: Future-Kill, *692*

Moranis, Rick: Strange Brew, *360*

Mora, Philippe: Beast Within, The, *649;* Howling II . . . Your Sister Is a Werewolf, *702;* Mad Dog Morgan, *94*

Morgan, William: Heart of the Rio Grande, *901*

Moroder, Giorgio: Metropolis (musical version), *793*

Morrison, Bruce: Shaker Run, *132*

Morrissey, Paul: Andy Warhol's Dracula, *645;* Andy Warhol's Frankenstein, *646;* Mixed Blood, *101*

Morris, Howard: Who's Minding the Mint?, *381;* With Six You Get Eggroll, *383*

Morse, Terry: Godzilla, King of the Monsters (U.S. version), *693*

Moses, Gilbert: Fish That Saved Pittsburgh, The, *261*

Moskowitz, Steward: Adventures of an American Rabbit, The, *169*

Mowbray, Malcolm: Private Function, A, *335*

Moxey, John Llewellyn: Night Stalker, The, *723*

Moyle, Alan: Times Square, *809*

Mulcahy, Russell: Highlander, *841;* Razorback, *733*

Mulligan, Robert: Baby the Rain Must Fall, *404;* Bloodbrothers, *415;* Kiss Me Goodbye, *294;* Same Time Next Year, *345;* Summer of '42, *608;* To Kill a Mockingbird, *619*

Mune, Ian: Came a Hot Friday, *27*

Munger, Chris: Kiss of the Tarantula, *710*

Murakami, Jimmy T.: Battle Beyond the Stars, *819*

Murch, Walter: Return to Oz, *201*

Murnau, F. W.: Last Laugh, The, *514;* Nosferatu, *724*

Murphy, Geoff: Quiet Earth, The, *858;* UTU, *157*

Murphy, Maurice: Fatty Finn, *181*

Murphy, Richard: Wackiest Ship in the Army, The, *377*

Mutrux, Floyd: Aloha, Bobby and Rose, *7*

Myerson, Alan: Private Lessons, *335*

Nankin, Michael: Midnight Madness, *309*

Narizzano, Silvio: Class of Miss Mac-Michael, The, *435;* Die! Die! My Darling!, *675;* Why Shoot the Teacher?, *633*

Nava, Gregory: El Norte, *456*

Nazarro, Ray: Kansas Pacific, *906*

Neame, Ronald: First Monday in October, *465;* Hopscotch, *74;* Meteor, *852;* Odessa File, The, *110;* Poseidon Adventure, The, *115;* Scrooge, *801;* Tunes of Glory, *624*

Needham, Hal: Cannonball Run II, *237;* Cannonball Run, *237;* Hooper, *283;* Megaforce, *851;* Rad, *117;* Smokey and the Bandit II, *355;* Smokey and the Bandit, *354;* Stroker Ace, *361*

Negrin, Alberto: Mussolini and I, *539*

Negulesco, Jean: How to Marry a Millionaire, *284*

Neill, Roy William: Black Room, The, *652;* Dressed to Kill, *45;* Dr. Syn, *45;* Frankenstein Meets the Wolf Man, *688;* Pursuit to Algiers, *117;* Sherlock Holmes and the Secret Weapon, *134;* Terror by Night, *148;* Woman in Green, The, *165*

Neilson, James: Mooncussers, *193;* Moon Pilot, *193;* Moonspinners, The, *193;* Texas John Slaughter: Geronimo's Revenge, *937*

Nelson, David: Last Plane Out, *87*

Nelson, Gary: Black Hole, The, *821;* Freaky Friday, *182;* Santee, *929*

Nelson, Gene: Harum Scarum, *787*

Nelson, Ralph: Charly, *823;* Embryo, *833;* Father Goose, *259;* Lady of the House, *512;* Lilies of the Field, *518;* Requiem for a Heavyweight, *578;* Soldier Blue, *933;* Soldier in the Rain, *596*

Nesher, Avi: She, *861*

Neumann, Kurt: Carnival Story, *426;* Fly, The (Original), *686;* Kronos, *846;* Rocketship X-M, *860;* Return of the Vampire, The, *735*

Newbrook, Peter: Spirit of the Dead, *746*

Newell, Michael: Awakening, The, *648;* Dance with a Stranger, *443;* Man in the Iron Mask, The, *95*

Newfield, Sam: Dead Men Walk, *670;* Lawman Is Born, A, *908;* Terror of Tiny Town, The, *937;* Traitor, The, *940*

Newland, John: Don't Be Afraid of the Dark, *677*

Newman, Joseph M.: Great Dan Patch, The, *477;* This Island Earth, *871*

Newman, Paul: Harry and Son, *483;* Rachel, Rachel, *573;* Sometimes a Great Notion, *597*

Nicholson, Jack: Goin' South, *898*

Nichols, Charles A.: Charlotte's Web, *176*

Nichols, Mike: Carnal Knowledge, *426;* Catch-22, *239;* Day of the Dolphin, The, *828;* Gilda Live, *268;* Graduate, The, *475;* Heartburn, *277;* Silkwood, *593;* Who's Afraid of Virginia Woolf?, *633*

Nicolas, Paul: Chained Heat, *29*

Nielson, James: Tom Sawyer, *210*

Nierenberg, George T.: Say Amen, Somebody, *801*

Nigh, William: Mr. Wong, Detective, *101*

Nimoy, Leonard: Star Trek III: The Search for Spock, *865*

Norton, Bill: Baby . . . Secret of the Lost Legend, *818*

Nossack, Noel: King of the Mountain, *508*

Nosseck, Max: Brighton Strangler, The, *657;* Dillinger, *42*

Noyce, Phillip: Heatwave, *485;* Newsfront, *543*

Nugent, Elliott: My Favorite Brunette, *316*

Nunez, Victor: Flash of Green, A, *466*

Nutter, David: Cease Fire, *429*

Nyby, Christian: Elfego Baca: Six Gun Law, *895;* Operation C.I.A., *110;* Thing (from Another World), The, *871*

O'Bannon, Dan: Return of the Living Dead, The, *735*

O'Connor, Kevin: House Where Evil Dwells, The, *701*

O'Connor, Pat: Cal, *423*

O'Hara, Gerry: Bitch, The, *412*

O'Herlihy, Michael: Cry of the Innocent, *37;* Fighting Prince of Donegal, The, *181*

O'Neil, Robert Vincent: Angel, *8;* Avenging Angel, *11*

O'Steen, Sam: Best Little Girl in the World, The, *408;* Queen of the Stardust Ballroom, *572;* Sparkle, *805*

Obrow, Jeffrey: Power, The, *730*

Odets, Clifford: None But the Lonely Heart, *546*

Ogilvie, George: Mad Max Beyond Thunderdome, *850*

Oliansky, Joel: Competition, The, *437*

Olivera, Hector: Funny Dirty Little War (No Habra Mas Pensas ni Olvido), *264*

Oliver, David: Cave Girl, *823*

Oliver, Hector: Barbarian Queen, *819*

Olivier, Laurence: Hamlet, *481;* Henry V, *486;* Prince and the Showgirl, The, *334;* Richard III, *580*

Ophuls, Max: Caught, *429;* La Ronde, *295*

Ophüls, Marcel: Sorrow and the Pity, The, *597*

Osbrow, Jeffrey: Dorm That Dripped Blood, The, *678*

Oshima, Nagisa: Merry Christmas, Mr. Lawrence, *533*

Oswald, Gerd: Star Trek (television series), *866*

Oz, Frank: Dark Crystal, The, *827;* Muppets Take Manhattan, The, *194*

Pabst, G. W.: Pandora's Box, *556;* Threepenny Opera, The, *809*

Padget, Calvin Jackson: Battle of El Alamein, The, *12*

Page, Anthony: Bill, *411;* Forbidden, *467;* I Never Promised You a Rose Garden, *491*

Pagnol, Marcel: Baker's Wife, The, *224*

Pakula, Alan J.: All the President's Men, *394;* Comes a Horseman, *889;* Dream Lover, *679;* Klute, *509;* Parallax View, The, *557;* Rollover, *583;* Sophie's Choice, *597;* Sterile Cuckoo, The, *603;* Starting Over, *358*

Palmer, John: Ciao! Manhattan, *433*

Palmer, Tony: Wagner, *811*

Paloy, Euzhan: Sugar Cane Alley, *607*

Paltrow, Bruce: Little Sex, A, *300*

Pal, George: 7 Faces of Dr. Lao, *861;* Time Machine, The, *872;* Tom Thumb, *210*

Panama, Norman: Court Jester, The, *248;* I Will, I Will . . . For Now, *285;* Trap, The, *759*

Paris, Jerry: Don't Raise the Bridge, Lower the River, *253;* How to Break Up a Happy Divorce, *284;* Never a Dull Moment, *195;* Police Academy III: Back in Training, *332;* Police Academy II: Their First Assignment, *332;* Viva Max!, *377*

Parker, Alan: Birdy, *412;* Bugsy Malone, *175;* Fame, *778;* Midnight Express, *533;* Pink Floyd the Wall, *798;* Shoot the Moon, *592*

Parks Jr., Gordon: Superfly, *143;* Three the Hard Way, *151;* Shaft, *132*

Parrish, Robert: Bobo, The, *231;* Casino Royale, *239;* Fire Down Below, *464*

Parrott, James: Pardon Us, *327*

Pascal, Gabriel: Caesar and Cleopatra, *423*

Passer, Ivan: Creator, *440;* Cutter's Way, *441;* Nightingale, The, *195;* Silver Bears, *351*

Patel, Raju: In the Shadow of Kilimanjaro, *704*

Pate, Michael: Tim, *618*

Paulsen, David: Schizoid, *740*

Paul, Byron: Lt. Robin Crusoe, U.S.N., *188*

Paul, Steven: Falling in Love Again, *258;* Slapstick of Another Kind, *354*

Pearce, Michael: James Joyce's Women, *500*

Pearce, Richard: Country, *439;* Heartland, *902;* Threshold, *872*

Peckinpah, Sam: Ballad of Cable Hogue, The, *880;* Convoy, *34;* Cross of Iron, *37;* Getaway, The, *62;* Junior Bonner, *906;* Killer Elite, The, *83;* Major Dundee, *911;* Osterman Weekend, The, *111;* Pat Garrett and Billy the Kid, *922;* Ride the High Country, *925;* Straw Dogs, *749;* Wild Bunch, The, *945*

Peerce, Larry: Bell Jar, The, *408;* Goodbye Columbus, *271;* Hard to Hold, *786;* Love Child, *523;* Other Side of the Mountain, Part II, The, *554;* Other Side of the Mountain, The, *554;* That Was Rock, *808*

Pennebaker, D. A.: Don't Look Back, *777;* Ziggy Stardust and the Spiders from Mars, *814*

Penn, Arthur: Alice's Restaurant, *393;* Bonnie and Clyde, *21;* Chase, The, *431;* Four Friends, *468;* Little Big Man, *909;* Miracle Worker, The, *535;* Missouri Breaks, The, *915;* Night Moves, *106;* Target, *145*

Penn, Leo: Dark Secret of Harvest Home, The, *669*

Perkins, Anthony: Psycho III, *731*

Perry, Frank: Compromising Positions, *247;* Diary of a Mad Housewife, *450;* Last Summer, *514;* Mommie Dearest, *537;* Monsignor, *538;* Skag, *594;* Swimmer, The, *609*

Persky, Bill: Serial, *349*

Petersen, Wolfgang: Das Boot (The Boat), *38;* Enemy Mine, *834;* NeverEnding Story, The, *853*

Peters, Barbara: Humanoids from the Deep, *702*

Petrie, Daniel: Bay Boy, The, *406;* Betsy, The, *409;* Buster and Billie, *422;* Fort Apache—The Bronx, *467;* Lifeguard, *518;* Moon of the Wolf, *718;* Raisin in the Sun, A, *575;* Resurrection, *858;* Six Pack, *353;* Sybil, *610*

Petri, Elio: Tenth Victim, The, *869*

Petroni, Giulio: Death Rides a Horse, *892*

Pett, John: World at War Vol. 1–26, *639*

Pevney, Joseph: Away All Boats, *11;* Night of the Grizzly, The, *918;* Star Trek (television series), *866;* Tammy and the Bachelor, *611*

Peyser, John: Four Rode Out, *897;* Kashmiri Run, The, *81;* Untouchables: Alcatraz Express, The, *157*

Philips, Lee: Hardhat and Legs, *482;* On the Right Track, *197*

Pialat, Maurice: A Nos Amours, *387*

Pichel, Irving: Colonel Effingham's Raid, *246;* Destination Moon, *830;* Miracle of the Bells, The, *534;* Most Dangerous Game, The, *718;* Mr. Peabody and the Mermaid, *311*

Pierce, Charles B.: Legend of Boggy Creek, *711;* Norseman, The, *108;* Sacred Ground, *929;* Town That Dreaded Sundown, The, *759*

Pierson, Carl: New Frontier, *917;* Paradise Canyon, *922*

Pierson, Frank: King of the Gypsies, *508;* Looking Glass War, The, *521;* Star Is Born, A (Remake), *601*

Pinoteau, Claude: La Boum, *511*

Pintoff, Ernest: St. Helens, *587*

Poe, Amos: Alphabet City, *394*

Poitier, Sidney: Buck and the Preacher, *886;* Fast Forward, *779;* Hanky Panky, *274;* Let's Do It Again, *298;* Piece of the Action, A, *329;* Stir Crazy, *359;* Uptown Saturday Night, *376*

Polanski, Roman: Chinatown, *30;* Knife in the Water, *509;* Macbeth, *525;* Pirates, *331;* Rosemary's Baby, *737;* Tess, *613*

Pollack, Sydney: Absence of Malice, *388;*

Bobby Deerfield, *416;* Electric Horseman, The, *456;* Out of Africa, *555;* They Shoot Horses, Don't They?, *616;* This Property Is Condemned, *617;* Three Days of the Condor, *150;* Tootsie, *369;* Way We Were, The, *631;* Yakuza, The, *165*

Pollexfen, Jack: Indestructible Man, *705*

Polonsky, Abraham: Force of Evil, *467;* Tell Them Willie Boy Is Here, *936*

Pommer, Erich: Beachcomber, The, *406*

Pontecorvo, Gillo: Battle of Algiers, *405;* Burn!, *421*

Post, Ted: Baby, The, *648;* Beneath the 12-Mile Reef, *13;* Beneath the Planet of the Apes, *820;* Go Tell the Spartans, *63;* Good Guys Wear Black, *63;* Hang 'Em High, *900;* Harrad Experiment, The, *482;* Magnum Force, *94;* Nightkill, *107*

Potenza, Anthony: No Nukes, *795*

Potter, H. C.: Farmer's Daughter, The, *258;* Mr. Blandings Builds His Dream House, *310;* Mr. Lucky, *101;* Second Chorus, *801;* Story of Vernon and Irene Castle, The, *806*

Powell, Dick: Conqueror, The, *34*

Powell, Michael: Black Narcissus, *413;* 49th Parallel, The, *468;* Ill Met by Moonlight, *493;* Life and Death of Colonel Blimp, The, *517;* Peeping Tom, *727;* Red Shoes, The, *800;* Thief of Baghdad, The, *870*

Preece, Michael: Prizefighter, The, *200*

Preminger, Otto: Anatomy of a Murder, *397;* Exodus, *460;* Laura, *88;* Moon Is Blue, The, *314*

Pressburger, Emeric: Life and Death of Colonel Blimp, The, *517*

Pressman, Michael: Bad News Bears in Breaking Training, The, *223;* Doctor Detroit, *252;* Great Texas Dynamite Chase, The, *66;* Some Kind of Hero, *355*

Previn, Steve: Almost Angels, *171;* Escapade in Florence, *180*

Price, Will: Rock, Rock, Rock, *800*

Prince, Harold: Little Night Music, A, *793*

Prince Under the Cherry Moon, *626*

Pryor, Richard: Richard Pryor—Here and Now, *340*

Pyun, Albert: Dangerously Close, *668;* Sword and the Sorcerer, The, *869*

Quine, Richard: Bell, Book and Candle, *226;* Oh Dad, Poor Dad—Mama's Hung You in the Closet and I'm Feeling So Sad, *322;* Prisoner of Zenda, The, *334;* W, *763*

Quinn, Anthony: Buccaneer, The, *25*

Quintero, Jose: Roman Spring of Mrs. Stone, The, *583*

Radford, Michael: Another Time, Another Place, *400*

Raeburn, Michael: Killing Heat, *507*

Rafelson, Bob: Postman Always Rings Twice, The (Remake), *566;* Stay Hungry, *602*

Rafferty, Kevin: Atomic Cafe, The, *402*

Rafferty, Pierce: Atomic Cafe, The, *402*

Raffill, Stewart: Across the Great Divide, *169;* Adventures of the Wilderness Family, *170;* "High Risk, *72;* Ice Pirates, *842;* Philadelphia Experiment, The, *856*

Raimi, Sam: Evil Dead, The, *681*

Rakoff, Alvin: Dirty Tricks, *251;* Mr. Halpern and Mr. Johnson, *536*

Ramis, Harold: Caddyshack, *236;* Club Paradise, *245;* Vacation, *376*

Rankin Jr., Arthur: Last Unicorn, The, *848*

Rappeneau, Jean-Paul: Swashbuckler, The, *144*

Rapper, Irving: Now, Voyager, *547;* Sextette, *350*

Rapp, Paul: Go for It, *62*

Rash, Steve: Under the Rainbow, *374*

Ratoff, Gregory: Adam Had Four Sons, *389;* Black Magic, *413;* Corsican Brothers, The, *35;* Intermezzo, *496*

Rawlins, John: Dick Tracy Meets Gruesome, *42*

Raye, Michael: Laserblast, *847*

Ray, Nicholas: 55 Days at Peking, *464;* Flying Leathernecks, The, *58;* Knock on Any Door, *509;* Lusty Men, The, *911;* Rebel Without a Cause, *576*

Rebane, Bill: Alpha Incident, The, *816;* Demons of Ludlow, The, *673*

Redford, Robert: Ordinary People, *554*

Reed, Bill: Secret of the Sword, The, *203*

Reed, Carol: Fallen Idol, The, *462;* Oliver, *796;* Stars Look Down, The, *601;* Third Man, The, *755*

Reggio, Godfrey: Koyaanisqatsi, *791*

Reichert, Mark: Union City, *626*

Reiner, Carl: All of Me, *217;* Comic, The, *437;* Dead Men Don't Wear Plaid, *249;* Enter Laughing, *256;* Man With Two Brains, The, *307;* Oh God!, *323;* One and Only, The, *551;* Summer Rental, *361;* Where's Poppa?, *381*

Reiner, Rob: Stand by Me, *600;* Sure Thing, The, *361;* This Is Spinal Tap, *367*

Reinhardt, Max: Midsummer Night's Dream, A, *852*

Reisz, Karel: French Lieutenant's Woman, The, *469;* Gambler, The, *470;* Morgan, *314;* Sweet Dreams, *806;* Who'll Stop the Rain, *162*

Reis, Irving: Bachelor and the Bobby-Soxer, The, *222;* Falcon Takes Over, The, *52;* Hitler's Children, *73*

Reitherman, Wolfgang: Robin Hood, *202;* Sword in the Stone, *207;* Wind in the Willows, The, *213*

Reitman, Ivan: Ghostbusters, *267;* Legal Eagles, *88;* Meatballs, *308;* Stripes, *360*

Renoir, Jean: Boudu Saved from Drowning, *232;* Elusive Corporal, The, *457;* Grand Illusion, *476;* La Bete Humaine, *510;* La Marseillaise, *511;* Rules of the Game, The, *344;* Southerner, The, *598;* This Land Is Mine, *617;* Toni, *620*

Resnais, Alain: Hiroshima, Mon Amour, *488;* Last Year at Marienbad, *516;* Providence, *569*

Reynolds, Burt: End, The, *255;* Gator, *61;* Sharky's Machine, *133;* Stick, *140*

Reynolds, Don: His Name Was King, *903*

Reynolds, Kevin: Fandango, *258*

Richardson, Tony: Border, The, *22;* Hotel New Hampshire, The, *489;* Look Back in Anger, *521;* Tom Jones, *369*

Richards, Dick: Death Valley, *672;* Farewell My Lovely, *52;* Man, Woman and Child, *528;* Rafferty and the Gold Dust Twins, *337*

Richert, William: Winter Kills, *636*

Richmond, Anthony: Deja Vu, *448*

Richter, Ota: Skullduggery, *744*

Richter, W. D.: Adventures of Buckaroo Banzai, The, *815*

Rich, David Lowell: Airport '79: The Concorde, *391;* Chu Chu and the Philly Flash, *243;* Enola Gay: The Men, the Mission, the Atomic Bomb, *458;* Family Upside Down, A, *462;* Madame X, *526;* Satan's School for Girls, *739*

Rich, John: Roustabout, *800*

Rickman, Tom: River Rat, The, *581*

Riefenstahl, Leni: Triumph of the Will, *622*

Riesner, Charles F.: Manhattan Merry-Go-Round, *913;* Steamboat Bill, Jr., *359*

Rilla, Wolf: Village of the Damned, *762*

Ritchie, Michael: Bad News Bears, The, *223;* Candidate, The, *425;* Divine Madness, *777;* Downhill Racer, *454;* Fletch, *57;* Island, The, *706;* Prime Cut, *115;* Semi-Tough, *349;* Survivors, The, *362;* Wildcats, *382*

Ritelis, Viktors: Crucible of Horror, *666*

Ritt, Martin: Back Roads, *404;* Casey's Shadow, *176;* Conrack, *438;* Cross Creek, *441;* Front, The, *470;* Hombre, *904;* Hud, *490;* Molly Maguires, The, *537;* Murphy's Romance, *539;* Norma Rae, *546;* Paris Blues, *558;* Sounder, *598*

Rivers, Joan: Rabbit Test, *337*

Rizenberg, Frederick A.: Gospel, *784*

Roach Jr., Hal: One Million B.C., *855*

Robbie, Seymour: C.C. & Company, *28*

Robbins, Jerome: West Side Story, *812*

Robbins, Matthew: Dragonslayer, *831;* Legend of Billy Jean, The, *89*

Robertson, Cliff: Pilot, The, *563*

Roberts, Matthew: Corvette Summer, *35*

Roberts, Stephen: Star of Midnight, *139*

Robert, Yves: Pardon Mon Affaire, *327;* Return of the Tall Blond Man with One Black

Shoe, The, *339;* Tall Blond Man with One Black Shoe, The, *363*

Robinson, John Mark: Roadhouse 66, *122*

Robinson, Richard: Bloody Trail, *884*

Robson, Mark: Bedlam, *649;* Earthquake, *46;* Harder They Fall, The, *482;* Home of the Brave, *488;* Inn of the Sixth Happiness, The, *495;* Isle of the Dead, *706;* Von Ryan's Express, *159*

Roddam, Franc: Bride, The, *656;* Lords of Discipline, The, *521;* Quadrophenia, *799*

Roeg, Nicolas: Don't Look Now, *677;* Eureka, *459;* Man Who Fell to Earth, The, *851;* Performance, *561*

Rogell, Albert S.: War of the Wildcats, *943*

Rogers, Charles R.: Bohemian Girl, The, *232*

Rogers, Maclean: Down Among the "Z" Men, *253*

Rohmer, Eric: Aviator's Wife, The, *403;* Claire's Knee, *243;* Full Moon in Paris, *264;* Le Beau Mariage, *297;* My Night at Maud's, *541;* Pauline at the Beach, *559*

Romero, Eddie: Beyond Atlantis, *14*

Romero, George A.: Dawn of the Dead, *670;* Knightriders, *84;* Martin, *715;* Night of the Living Dead, *723;* Creepshow, *666*

Rosenberg, Stuart: Amityville Horror, The, *645;* Brubaker, *421;* Cool Hand Luke, *35;* Drowning Pool, The, *45;* Laughing Policeman, The, *88;* Love and Bullets, *93;* Pope of Greenwich Village, The, *564;* Voyage of the Damned, *629*

Rosenthal, Rick: American Dreamer, *217;* Bad Boys, *404;* Halloween II, *695*

Rosenthal, Robert J.: Zapped!, *385*

Rosen, Martin: Plague Dogs, The, *856;* Watership Down, *876*

Rosen, Phil: Spooks Run Wild, *357*

Rosen, Robert L.: Raw Courage, *119*

Rose, Les: Gas, *265*

Rose, Mickey: Student Bodies, *749*

Rosi, Francesco: Bizet's Carmen, *771;* Lucky Luciano, *93*

Rosman, Mark: Blue Yonder, The, *173;* House on Sorority Row, *701*

Rossellini, Roberto: Open City, *553;* Paisan, *556;* Stromboli, *606*

Rossen, Robert: Alexander the Great, *392;* All the King's Men, *394;* Body and Soul (Original), *416;* Hustler, The, *490;* Lilith, *518;* They Came to Cordura, *615*

Ross, Herbert: California Suite, *237;* Footloose, *781;* Funny Lady, *782;* Goodbye Girl, The, *271;* I Ought to Be in Pictures, *287;* Last of Sheila, The, *87;* Max Dugan Returns, *531;* Owl and the Pussycat, The, *326;* Pennies from Heaven, *797;* Play It Again Sam, *331;* Protocol, *336;* Seven-Per-Cent Solution, The, *131;* Sunshine Boys, The, *361*

Roth, Bobby: Heartbreakers, *484*

Rouse, Russell: Oscar, The, *554*

Ruben, Joseph: Dreamscape, *832*

Rubie, Howard: Island Trader, *78*

Rudolph, Alan: Choose Me, *433;* Endangered Species, *834;* Songwriter, *804;* Trouble in Mind, *622;* Welcome to L.A., *631*

Ruggles, Wesley: No Man of Her Own, *320*

Rush, Richard: Freebie and the Bean, *263;* Getting Straight, *472;* Hell's Angels on Wheels, *71;* Stunt Man, The, *606*

Ruskin, Coby: When Things Were Rotten, *380*

Russell, Ken: Altered States, *817;* Crimes of Passion, *440;* Devils, The, *450;* Lisztomania, *792;* Mahler, *527;* Tommy, *810;* Women in Love, *638*

Russell, William D.: Green Promise, The, *479*

Rust, John: Smurfs and the Magic Flute, The, *205*

Rydell, Mark: Cowboys, The, *890;* Harry and Walter Go to New York, *276;* On Golden Pond, *551;* Reivers, The, *338;* River, The, *581;* Rose, The, *800*

Sachs, William: Galaxina, *839;* Incredible Melting Man, The, *843*

Safran, Henri: Wild Duck, The, *634;* Norman Loves Rose, *320*

Sagal, Boris: Masada, *530;* Night Gallery, *721;* Omega Man, The, *854*

St. Clair, Malcolm: Bullfighters, The, *235*

Saks, Gene: Barefoot in the Park, *224;* Last of the Red Hot Lovers, *296;* Mame, *793;* Odd Couple, The, *322*

Salkow, Sidney: Last Man on Earth, The, *848*

Samperi, Salvatore: Malicious, *305*

Sanders, Denis: Invasion of the Bee Girls, *844*

Sandrich, Jay: Seems Like Old Times, *349*

Sandrich, Mark: Carefree, *774;* Follow the Fleet, *780;* Gay Divorcee, The, *782;* Holiday Inn, *787;* Shall We Dance?, *802;* Top Hat, *810*

San Fernando, Manuel: Rock 'n Roll Wrestling Women vs. the Aztec Mummy, *342*

Sanger, Jonathan: Code Name: Emerald, *33*

Sangster, Jimmy: Fear in the Night (Dynasty of Fear), *683;* Horror of Frankenstein, *699;* Lust for a Vampire, *713*

Santell, Alfred: Jack London, *499;* Winterset, *636*

Santiago, Cirio: Stryker, *868;* Wheels of Fire, *161*

Santley, Joseph: Call of the Canyon, *887;* Melody Ranch, *914*

Santostefano, Damon: Scream Greats, Vol. 1, *741*

Santos, Steven J.: Carlin at Carnegie, *238*

Sarafian, Richard C.: Gangster Wars, 61; Man Who Loved Cat Dancing, The, 912; Sunburn, 143; Vanishing Point, 158

Sargent, Joseph: Coast to Coast, 245; Goldengirl, 840; Hustling, 490; MacArthur, 525; Nightmares, 722; Taking of Pelham One Two Three, The, 144; White Lightning, 162

Sasdy, Peter: Devil's Undead, The, 674; King Arthur, the Young Warlord, 84; Lonely Lady, The, 520; Rude Awakening, 738

Sautet, Claude: Simple Story, A, 594

Saville, Philip: Secrets, 590

Saville, Victor: Dark Journey, 445; Iron Duke, The, 498; Kim, 83; Storm in a Teacup, 360

Sayles, John: Brother from Another Planet, The, 822; Lianna, 517; Return of the Secaucus 7, 339

Scanlan, Joseph L.: Spring Fever, 357

Schaefer, Armand: Hurricane Express, 76; Sagebrush Trail, 929

Schaefer, George: Pendulum, 113; Piano for Mrs. Cimino, A, 562

Schaffner, Franklin J.: Boys from Brazil, The, 656; Islands in the Stream, 498; Nicholas and Alexandra, 543; Patton, 559; Papillon, 112; Planet of the Apes, 856; Sphinx, 746; Yes, Giorgio, 813

Schatzberg, Jerry: Honeysuckle Rose, 788; Misunderstood, 537; No Small Affair, 320; Scarecrow, 589; Seduction of Joe Tynan, The, 590

Scheerer, Robert: Hans Brinker, 183; How to Beat the High Co$t of Living, 284; World's Greatest Athlete, The, 213

Schellerup, Henning: Tom Edison—The Boy Who Lit Up the World, 210; Wilbur and Orville: The First to Fly, 212

Schepisi, Fred: Barbarosa, 881; Chant of Jimmie Blacksmith, The, 431; Iceman, 843; Plenty, 564

Schertzinger, Victor: Uptown New York, 627

Schertzinger, Walter: Something to Sing About, 803

Schiller, Lawrence: Executioner's Song, The, 460

Schiro, Jeffrey C.: Stephen King's Night Shift Collection, 747

Schlesinger, John: Billy Liar, 412; Darling, 445; Day of the Locust, The, 446; Falcon and the Snowman, The, 461; Honky Tonk Freeway, 282; Marathon Man, 97; Midnight Cowboy, 533; Separate Tables, 590; Sunday, Bloody Sunday, 608

Schlondorff, Volker: Lost Honor of Katharina Blum, The, 522; Swann in Love, 609; Tin Drum, The, 619

Schlossberg, Julian: No Nukes, 795

Schmoeller, David: Seduction, The, 741; Tourist Trap, 759

Schoedsack, Ernest B.: King Kong (Original), 709; Last Days of Pompeii, The, 513;

Mighty Joe Young, 852; Most Dangerous Game, The, 718; Son of Kong, The, 745

Schrader, Paul: American Gigolo, 396; Blue Collar, 415; Cat People (Remake), 660; Hardcore, 481; Mishima: A Life in Four Chapters, 535

Schreibman, Myrl A.: Angel of H.E.A.T., 8

Schultz, Carl: Careful He Might Hear You, 426

Schultz, Michael: Carbon Copy, 238; Car Wash, 239; Greased Lightning, 64; Last Dragon, The, 87; Scavenger Hunt, 346; Sgt. Pepper's Lonely Hearts Club Band, 802

Schulz, Bob: Robbers of the Sacred Mountain, 123

Schumacher, Joel: D.C. Cab, 249; Incredible Shrinking Woman, The, 286; St. Elmo's Fire, 586

Schuster, Harold: Dinner at the Ritz, 43; So Dear to My Heart, 206

Scola, Ettore: Le Bal, 791; Macaroni, 304; Passion of Love, 559; Special Day, A, 598

Scorsese, Martin: After Hours, 215; Alice Doesn't Live Here Anymore, 392; Boxcar Bertha, 23; King of Comedy, The, 507; Last Waltz, The, 791; Mean Streets, 532; New York, New York, 795; Raging Bull, 574; Taxi Driver, 612

Scott, Gene: Mystery Island, 194

Scott, George C.: Rage, 573; Savage Is Loose, The, 588

Scott, Oz: Bustin' Loose, 236

Scott, Ridley: Alien, 815; Blade Runner, 821; Duellists, The, 46; Legend, 849

Scott, Tony: Hunger, The, 703; Top Gun, 153

Sears, Fred F.: Earth vs. the Flying Saucers, 832

Seaton, George: Airport, 7; Country Girl, The, 439; Miracle on 34th Street, 192; Teacher's Pet, 364

Sebastian, Ferd: Flash and the Firecat, 56

Sedgwick, Edward: Riding on Air, 341

Seiter, William: Allegheny Uprising, 878; One Touch of Venus, 325; Allegheny Uprising, 878; Room Service, 343; Sons of the Desert, 356; You Were Never Lovelier, 814

Seitz, George B.: Danger Lights, 443; Kit Carson, 907; Last of the Mohicans, The, 907

Sekely, Steve: Day of the Triffids, The, 828; Revenge of the Zombies, 436

Selander, Lesley: Buckskin Frontier, 886; Flat Top, 57; Riders of the Deadline, 926; Robin Hood of Texas, 927

Sellier Jr., Charles E.: Silent Night, Deadly Night, 743

Seltzer, David: Lucas, 524

Selznick, Aran: Care Bears Movie, The, 175

Serreau, Coline: Three Men and a Cradle, 367

Sgarro, Nicholas: Happy Hooker, The, 275

Shaefer, George: Right of Way, 580

Shapiro, Alan: Tiger Town, 209

Shapiro, Ken: Groove Tube, The, 273; Modern Problems, 311

Sharman, Jim: Shock Treatment, 351

Sharpstein, Ben: Dumbo, 180

Sharp, Alan: Little Treasure, 91

Sharp, Don: Bear Island, 648; Dark Places, 669; Guardian of the Abyss, 695; Psychomania, 731; Thirty-Nine Steps, The (Second Remake), 149

Sharp, Ian: Final Option, The, 54; Robin Hood and the Sorcerer, 123

Shavelson, Melville: Cast a Giant Shadow, 28

Shear, Barry: Across 110th Street, 1; Night Gallery, 721

Shebib, Donald: Heartaches, 484; Running Brave, 585

Shelach, Riki: Last Winter, The, 515

Sherman, Gary A.: Dead and Buried, 670; Vice Squad, 158

Sherman, George: Big Jake, 882; Night Riders, The, 918; Pals of the Saddle, 921; Santa Fe Stampede, 929; South of the Border, 934; Treasure of Pancho Villa, The, 940

Sherman, Vincent: Bogie, 417; Lady of the House, 512; Young Philadelphians, The, 640

Shields, Frank: Savage Attraction, 739

Shinoda, Masahiro: MacArthur's Children, 525

Shin, Nelson: Transformers, the Movie, 211

Sholder, Jack: Alone in the Dark, 644; Nightmare on Elm Street Part 2: Freddy's Revenge, A, 722

Shultz, Michael: Which Way Is Up?, 381

Shumlin, Herman: Watch on the Rhine, 630

Shyer, Charles: Irreconcilable Differences, 498

Sidney, George: Bye Bye Birdie, 773; Kiss Me Kate, 790; Show Boat, 802; Thousands Cheer, 808; Three Musketeers, The (1948), 150; Viva Las Vegas, 811

Sidney, Scott: Tarzan of the Apes, 145

Siedelman, Susan: Desperately Seeking Susan, 250; Smithereens, 596

Siegel, Don: Beguiled, The, 407; Charley Varrick, 30; Coogan's Bluff, 34; Dirty Harry, 43; Escape from Alcatraz, 49; Flaming Star, 896; Invasion of the Body Snatchers (Original), 844; Madigan, 94; Riot in Cell Block 11, 581; Rough Cut, 124; Shootist, The, 931; Telefon, 147; Two Mules for Sister Sara, 942

Signorelli, James: Easy Money, 254

Silberg, Joel: Bad Guys, 11; Breakin', 771; Rappin', 799

Silverstein, Elliot: Cat Ballou, 888; Man Called Horse, A, 911

Silver, Joan Micklin: Chilly Scenes of Winter, 432; Hester Street, 487

Silver, Marisa: Old Enough, 550

Silvester, Dario: Between God, the Devil and a Winchester, 882

Simon, Francis: Chicken Chronicles, The, 243

Simon, Juan Piquer: Pieces, 728

Simon, S. Sylvan: Abbott and Costello in Hollywood, 214; Fuller Brush Man, The, 264

Simo, Sandor: Train Killer, The, 621

Singer, Alexander: Bunco, 26; Captain Apache, 888

Siodmak, Robert: Dark Mirror, The, 669; Killers, The, 83

Sirk, Douglas: Magnificent Obsession, 527

Sjoman, Vilgot: I Am Curious Yellow, 491

Skolimowski, Jerzy: Deep End, 672; Moonlighting, 538; Shout, The, 743

Slatzer, Robert: Big Foot, 651

Smight, Jack: Airport 1975, 391; Damnation Alley, 827; FastBreak, 258; Harper, 69; Loving Couples, 33; Midway, 99; No Way to Treat a Lady, 546; Rabbit Run, 573; Secret War of Harry Frigg, The, 348

Smith, Howard: Gizmo!, 268; Marjoe, 529

Sole, Alfred: Alice, Sweet Alice (Communion and Holy Terror), 643

Sollima, Sergio: Blood in the Streets, 19; Family, The, 52

Solt, Andrew: It Came from Hollywood, 287; This Is Elvis, 808

Sotos, Jim: Hot Moves, 283

Sparr, Robert: Swingin' Summer, A, 362

Spheeris, Penelope: Hollywood Vice Squad, 74; Suburbia, 606

Spielberg, Steven: 1941, 319; Close Encounters of the Third Kind, 825; Color Purple, The, 436; Duel, 679; E.T.—The Extraterrestrial, 832; Indiana Jones and the Temple of Doom, 843; Jaws, 707; Night Gallery, 721; Raiders of the Lost Ark, 858; Sugarland Express, The, 607; Twilight Zone—The Movie, 759

Spottiswoode, Roger: Best of Times, The, 228; Pursuit of D. B. Cooper, 116; Under Fire, 156

Springsteen, R. G.: Hellfire, 902

Stallone, Sylvester: Paradise Alley, 557; Rocky II, 582; Rocky III, 582; Rocky IV, 582; Staying Alive, 805

Stall, John M.: Letter of Introduction, 516

Starrett, Jack: Cleopatra Jones, 31; Final Chapter—Walking Tall, 54; Mr. Horn, 915; Race with the Devil, 732; Small Town in Texas, A, 137; Summer Heat, 607

Star, Bruce: Boogeyman 2, The, 656

Steensland, David: Escapes, 835

Steinberg, David: Going Berserk, 269; Paternity, 328

Steinmann, Danny: Friday the 13th, Part V—A New Beginning, 690; Savage Streets, 128

Stein, Jeff: Kids Are Alright, The, 790

Sterling, William: Alice's Adventures in Wonderland, 171

Stern, Steven Hillard: Devil and Max Devlin, The, *250;* Draw, *894;* Park Is Mine, The, *558;* Young Love, First Love, *640*

Stevenson, Robert: Absent-Minded Professor, The, *169;* Bedknobs and Broomsticks, *172;* Blackbeard's Ghost, *173;* Darby O'Gill and the Little People, *179;* Gnome-Mobile, The, *182;* Herbie Rides Again, *185;* In Search of the Castaways, *185;* Island at the Top of the World, The, *845;* Kidnapped, *82;* Love Bug, The, *190;* Mary Poppins, *191;* Misadventures of Merlin Jones, The, *192;* Monkey's Uncle, The, *192;* Old Yeller, *196;* One of Our Dinosaurs Is Missing, *196;* Shaggy D.A., The, *204;* Son of Flubber, *206;* That Darn Cat, *208;* Tom Brown's School Days, *620*

Stevens, Arnold: Attack of the Swamp Creature, *647*

Stevens, George: Alice Adams, *392;* Damsel in Distress, A, *776;* Diary of Anne Frank, The, *451;* Giant, *472;* Greatest Story Ever Told, The, *478;* Gunga Din, *67;* I Remember Mama, *491;* Penny Serenade, *560;* Place in the Sun, A, *563;* Shane, *930;* Swing Time, *806;* Woman of the Year, *383*

Stewart, Douglas Day: Thief of Hearts, *617*

Stoloff, Benjamin: Palooka, *556;* Sea Devils, *129*

Stoloff, Victor: Washington Affair, The, *630*

Stone, Andrew L.: Song of Norway, *803*

Stone, Oliver: Hand, The, *696;* Salvador, *587*

Storm, Howard: Once Bitten, *323;* Three Little Pigs, The, *209*

Straub, Ralph: Prairie Moon, *922*

Streisand, Barbra: Yentl, *813*

Strock, Herbert L.: Crawling Hand, The, *665*

Stromberg, William R.: Crater Lake Monster, The, *665*

Stryker, Jonathan: Curtains, *668*

Stuart, Brian: Sorceress, *863*

Stuart, Mel: I Love My Wife, *285;* Willy Wonka and the Chocolate Factory, *213*

Sturges, John: Chino, *888;* Eagle Has Landed, The, *46;* Great Escape, The, *65;* Gunfight at the O.K. Corral, *900;* Ice Station Zebra, *77;* Ice Station Zebra, *77;* Magnificent Seven, The, *911;* Marooned, *851;* McQ, *98*

Sturges, Preston: Lady Eve, The, *295;* Sin of Harold Diddlebock (aka Mad Wednesday), *352;* Unfaithfully Yours (Original), *374*

Sullivan, Fred G.: Cold River, *177*

Summers, Walter: Human Monster, The (Dark Eyes of London), *702*

Suso, Henry: DeathSport, *829*

Sutherland, Edward: Flying Deuces, *261;* Mr. Robinson Crusoe, *101*

Swackhamer, E. W.: Dain Curse, The, *37;* Death at Love House, *672*

Swaim, Bob: La Balance, *85*

Swarc, Jeannot: Supergirl, *868*

Swift, David: Good Neighbor Sam, *270;* Parent Trap, The, *197;* Pollyanna, *198*

Swimmer, Saul: Mrs. Brown You've Got a Lovely Daughter, *794*

Swirnoff, Brad: Tunnelvision, *373*

Sykes, Peter: To the Devil, a Daughter, *757*

Sylbert, Paul: Steagle, The, *359*

Szabo, Istvan: Colonel Redl, *435;* Mephisto, *532*

Szwarc, Jeannot: Bug, *658;* Enigma, *49;* Jaws 2, *707;* Santa Claus—The Movie, *202;* Somewhere in Time, *863*

Tacchella, Jean-Charles: Cousin, Cousine, *248*

Takabayashi, Yoichi: Irezumi (Spirit of Tattoo), *497*

Takamoto, Iwao: Charlotte's Web, *176*

Tallas, Gregg: Prehistoric Women, *857*

Tannen, William: Flashpoint, *57*

Tashlin, Frank: Cinderfella, *774*

Tati, Jacques: Mr. Hulot's Holiday, *311;* My Uncle (Mon Oncle), *317;* Playtime, *331*

Taurog, Norman: Adventures of Tom Sawyer, The, *170;* Blue Hawaii, *771;* Double Trouble, *777;* Girls! Girls! Girls!, *783;* G.I. Blues, *782;* It Happened at the World's Fair, *789;* Speedway, *805;* Tickle Me, *809*

Tavernier, Bertrand: Clean State (Coup de Torchon), *244;* Death Watch, *829*

Taviani, Vittorio and Paolo: Night of the Shooting Stars, *545*

Taylor, Don: Damien: Omen II, *668;* Escape from the Planet of the Apes, *835;* Final Countdown, The, *837;* Great Scout and Cathouse Thursday, The, *899;* Night Games, *544*

Taylor, Jud: Revenge, *735*

Taylor, Robert: Heidi's Song, *184*

Teague, Lewis: Alligator, *644;* Cat's Eye, *660;* Cujo, *667*

Temple, Julian: Absolute Beginners, *768;* Secret Policeman's Private Parts, The, *347;* Secret Policemen's Other Ball, The, *347;* Video Rewind: The Rolling Stones Great Video Hits, *811*

Tewkesbury, Joan: Old Boyfriends, *550*

Thau, Leon: Save the Lady, *203*

Thew, Harvey: Confessions of a Vice Baron, *438*

Thomason, Harry: Encounter with the Unknown, *833*

Thomas, Dave: Strange Brew, *360*

Thomas, Gerald: Carry on Cowboy, *238;* Carry on Nurse, *239*

Thomas, Ralph: Ticket to Heaven, *618;* Doctor at Large, *252;* Doctor at Sea, *252;* Doctor in Distress, *252*

Thompson, J. Lee: Ambassador, The, *395;* Battle for the Planet of the Apes, *819;* Cabo Blanco, *26;* Conquest of the Planet of the

Apes, 826; Evil That Men Do, The, 50; Greek Tycoon, The, 479; Guns of Navarone, The, 68; Happy Birthday to Me, 696; King Solomon's Mines (1984), 84; Mackenna's Gold, 911; Murphy's Law, 104; Reincarnation of Peter Proud, The, 734; St. Ives, 126; Ten to Midnight, 147

Thorpe, Jerry: All God's Children, 393; Kung Fu, 85

Thorpe, Richard: Fun in Acapulco, 781; Great Caruso, The, 785; Ivanhoe, 78; Jailhouse Rock, 789; Knights of the Round Table, 85; Prisoner of Zenda, The, 115; Thin Man Goes Home, The, 149

Till, Eric: Case of Libel, A, 427; If You Could See What I Hear, 492; Improper Channels, 286

Toback, James: Exposed, 681; Fingers, 464

Tokar, Norman: Apple Dumpling Gang, The, 171; Big Red, 173; Boatniks, The, 174; Candleshoe, 175; Cat from Outer Space, The, 176; Follow Me Boys!, 181; Happiest Millionaire, The, 184; No Deposit, No Return, 195; Savage Sam, 202; Those Calloways, 209; Ugly Dachshund, The, 211; Where the Red Fern Grows, 212

Tomblin, David: Invasion UFO, 845; Prisoner, The (television series), 857

Totten, Robert: Sacketts, The, 928

Tourneur, Jacques: Appointment in Honduras, 9; Cat People (Original), 660; Curse of the Demon, 667; I Walked with a Zombie, 704; Leopard Man, The, 712; Out of the Past, 112

Tourneur, Maurice: Volpone, 629

Towne, Robert: Personal Best, 562

Townsend, Bud: Nightmare in Wax (Crimes in the Wax Museum), 721

Townsend, Pat: Beach Girls, The, 225

Tramcount, Jean-Claude: All Night Long, 393

Traxler, Stephen: Slithis, 744

Trenchard-Smith, Brian: Escape 2000, 835

Trent, John: Best Revenge, 14

Trikonis, Gus: Jungle Heat, 80; Moonshine County Express, 103; Take This Job and Shove It, 363; Touched by Love, 621

Troell, Jan: Flight of the Eagle, 57; Hurricane, 76

Truffaut, Francois: Confidentially Yours, 34; Day for Night, 446; Fahrenheit 451, 836; Green Room, The, 479; Jules and Jim, 505; Last Metro, The, 514; Love on the Run, 524; Small Change, 595; Story of Adele H, The, 603; Woman Next Door, The, 638; 400 Blows, The, 468; Soft Skin, The, 596; Stolen Kisses, 360; Two English Girls, 625

Trumbull, Douglas: Brainstorm, 821; Silent Running, 862

Tsukerman, Slava: Liquid Sky, 849

Tuchner, Michael: Mr. Quilp, 794; Trenchcoat, 372

Tucker, Phil: Dance Hall Racket, 442; Robot Monster, 736

Tuggle, Richard: Out of Bounds, 111; Tightrope, 755

Tully, Montgomery: Battle Beneath the Earth, 12

Tuttle, Frank: Hell on Frisco Bay, 70; This Gun for Hire, 150

Ulmer, Edgar G.: Bluebeard, 654; Daughter of Dr. Jekyll, 670; Detour, 450; Raven and the Black Cat, The, 733

Ustinov, Peter: Billy Budd, 411; Lion and the Hawk, The, 89

Uys, Jamie: Gods Must Be Crazy, The, 269

Vadim, Roger: And God Created Woman, 397; Barbarella, 819; Beauty and the Beast, 172

Valerii, Tonino: Massacre at Fort Holman (Reason to Live... A Reason to Die, A), 914

Van Ackeren, Robert: Woman in Flames, A, 638

Van Dyke II, W. S.: After the Thin Man, 6; Shadow of the Thin Man, 132; Rose Marie, 800; San Francisco, 588; Tarzan the Ape Man (Original), 146; Thin Man, The, 149

Van Horn, Buddy: Any Which Way You Can, 219

Van Peebles, Melvin: Sweet Sweetback's Baadasssss Song, 144; Watermelon Man, 378

Varda, Agnes: One Sings, the Other Doesn't, 552; Vagabond, 627

Veber, Francis: Le Chevre (The Goat), 298

Verhoeven, Paul: Flesh and Blood, 57; Fourth Man, The, 687; Soldier of Orange, 137; Spetters, 598

Verona, Stephen F.: Lords of Flatbush, The, 522; Pipe Dreams, 563

Vicario, Marco: Wifemistress, 633

Vidor, Charles: Gilda, 472; Song to Remember, A, 804; Tuttles of Tahiti, The, 373

Vidor, King: Bird of Paradise, 17; Champ, The (Original), 429; Fountainhead, The, 468; Man Without a Star, 913; Our Daily Bread, 555; Ruby Gentry, 585; Solomon and Sheba, 597; Stella Dallas, 602; Street Scene, 605; War and Peace, 630

Vigne, Daniel: Return of Martin Guerre, The, 578

Vigo, Jean: Zero for Conduct, 642

Vincent, Chuck: Hollywood Hot Tubs, 282; Preppies, 333

Visconti, Luchino: Bellissima, 227; Boccaccio 70, 231; Conversation Piece, 438; Damned, The, 442; Death in Venice, 447; Innocent, The, 495; Wanton Contessa, The, 630

Vogel, Virgil W.: Streethawk, 142

Von Fristch, Gunther: Curse of the Cat People, The, 668

von Sternberg, Joseph: Blue Angel, The, *415*

Vorhaus, Bernard: Lady from Louisiana, *907;* Three Faces West, *939*

Wadleigh, Michael: Wolfen, *766;* Woodstock, *812*

Waggner, George: Commies Are Coming, the Commies Are Coming, The, *246;* Fighting Kentuckian, The, *896*

Wajda, Andrezej: Danton, *444;* Love in Germany, A, *523*

Walker, Dorian: Making the Grade, *305*

Walker, Hal: At War with the Army, *221;* Road to Bali, *342*

Walker, Nancy: Can't Stop the Music, *773*

Walker, Pete: Die Screaming, Marianne, *675;* House of the Long Shadows, *700*

Wallace, Richard: Bombardier, *21;* It's in the Bag, *289;* Little Minister, The, *519;* Sinbad the Sailor, *136;* Tycoon, *156*

Wallace, Tommy Lee: Halloween III: Season of the Witch, *695*

Walsh, Raoul: Battle Cry, *12;* Big Trail, The, *883;* Dark Command, *891;* Gentleman Jim, *471;* High Sierra, *72;* Naked and the Dead, The, *105;* Northern Pursuit, *108;* Roaring Twenties, The, *122;* Strawberry Blonde, The, *604;* They Died with their Boots On, *938;* They Drive by Night, *148;* Thief of Baghdad, The, *871;* White Heat, *161*

Walters, Charles: Easter Parade, *777;* Dangerous When Wet, *776;* Easy to Love, *778;* Good News, *784;* High Society, *787*

Walton, Fred: April Fool's Day, *646;* When a Stranger Calls, *764*

Wanamaker, Sam: Sinbad and the Eye of the Tiger, *862*

Wang, Wayne: Dim Sum: A Little Bit of Heart, *451*

Ward, David S.: Cannery Row, *237*

Ware, Clyde: Hatfields and the McCoys, The, *901*

Warren, Jerry: Frankenstein Island, *688*

Warren, Norman J.: Alien Prey, *644*

Wasson, James C.: Night of the Demon, *722*

Waters, Charles: Unsinkable Molly Brown, The, *810*

Waters, John: Desperate Living, *250;* Female Trouble, *259;* Mondo Trasho, *312;* Multiple Maniacs, *718;* Pink Flamingos, *330;* Polyester, *333*

Watson, John: Deathstalker, *829*

Wayne, John: Alamo, The, *878;* Green Berets, The, *66*

Webb, Jack: Dragnet, *45*

Webb, Peter: Give My Regards to Broad Street, *783*

Webb, Robert D.: Love Me Tender, *910*

Webster, Nicholas: Santa Claus Conquers the Martians, *860*

Wechter, David: Midnight Madness, *309*

Weeks, Stephen: Sword of the Valiant, *207*

Wegener, Paul: The Golem (How He Came into the World) (Der Golem, Wie er in die Welt Kam), *754*

Weiderhorn, Ken: Eyes of a Stranger, *682;* Meatballs Part II, *308*

Weill, Claudia: Girlfriends, *472;* It's My Turn, *499*

Weimer, Robert: Somewhere, Tomorrow, *206*

Weir, Peter: Cars That Eat People (The Cars That Ate Paris), *660;* Gallipoli, *470;* Last Wave, The, *711;* Plumber, The, *729;* Witness, *165;* Year of Living Dangerously, The, *165*

Weisman, David: Ciao! Manhattan, *433*

Weis, Gary: Wholly Moses!, *381*

Wei, Lo: Chinese Connection, The, *31;* Fists of Fury, *56*

Welles, Mel: Lady Frankenstein, *710*

Welles, Orson: Citizen Kane, *434;* Lady from Shanghai, *86;* Macbeth, *525;* Magnificent Ambersons, The, *526;* Stranger, The, *748;* Touch of Evil, *758*

Wellman, William A.: Public Enemy, The, *116;* Lady of Burlesque, *526;* Magic Town, *526;* Nothing Sacred, *321;* Ox-Bow Incident, The, *921;* Star Is Born, A (Original), *600;* Wings, *164*

Wenders, Wim: American Friend, The, *396;* Hammett, *68;* Paris, Texas, *558*

Wendkos, Paul: Cocaine: One Man's Seduction, *435;* Gidget Goes Hawaiian, *267;* Gidget, *267;* Ordeal of Dr. Mudd, The, *553*

Wenk, Richard: Vamp, *760*

Werker, Alfred: Adventures of Sherlock Holmes, The, *2;* He Walked by Night, *697*

Werner, Jeff: Die Laughing, *251*

Werner, Peter: Don't Cry, It's Only Thunder, *453*

Wertmuller, Lina: Love and Anarchy, *301;* Seduction of Mimi, The, *348;* Seven Beauties, *349;* Swept Away, *609*

Weston, Armand: Nesting, The, *721*

Weston, Eric: Evilspeak, *681;* Marvin and Tige, *530*

Wetzler, Gwen: Secret of the Sword, The, *203*

Wexler, Haskell: Medium Cool, *532*

Whale, James: Bride of Frankenstein, *657;* Frankenstein (Original), *687;* Frankenstein (restored version), *688*

Wharmby, Tony: Partners in Crime—The Secret Adversary, *113*

Whelan, Tim: Badman's Territory, *880;* Divorce of Lady X, The, *251;* Mill on the Floss, The, *534;* Sidewalks of London, *593;* Texas Lady, *938;* Thief of Baghdad, The, *870*

Whorf, Richard: Champagne for Caesar, *240;*

Love from a Stranger, *713;* Till the Clouds Roll By, *809*

Wiard, William: Tom Horn, *939*

Wicki, Bernhard: Longest Day, The, *92*

Widerberg, Bo: Elvira Madigan, *457*

Wiederhorn, Ken: Shock Waves (Death Corps), *742*

Wiemer, Robert: Anna to the Infinite Power, *817*

Wiene, Robert: Cabinet of Doctor Caligari, The, *659*

Wilcox, Fred McLeod: Forbidden Planet, *838*

Wilcox, Herbert: Nurse Edith Cavell, *548;* Trouble in the Glen, *372*

Wilder, Billy: Apartment, The, *219;* Buddy, Buddy, *235;* Fortune Cookie, The, *262;* Irma La Douce, *287;* Lost Weekend, The, *523;* One, Two, Three, *224;* Private Life of Sherlock Holmes, The, *115;* Seven Year Itch, The, *350;* Some Like It Hot, *356;* Spirit of St. Louis, The, *599;* Stalag 17, *139;* Sunset Blvd., *609;* Witness for the Prosecution, *637*

Wilder, Gene: Adventures of Sherlock Holmes' Smarter Brother, The, *215;* Haunted Honeymoon, *277;* Woman in Red, The, *383;* World's Greatest Lover, The, *384*

Wilde, Cornel: Naked Prey, The, *105;* Shark's Treasure, *133;* Sword of Lancelot, *144*

Wiles, Gordon: Ginger in the Morning, *472*

Williamson, Fred: Big Score, The, *16;* Mean Johnny Barrows, *98;* One Down, Two to Go, *110*

Williams, Scott: Man with Two Heads, *715*

Williams, Tony: Solo, *596*

Wilson, Hugh: Police Academy, *332;* Rustler's Rhapsody, *344*

Wilson, Richard: Invitation to a Gunfighter, *905*

Wincer, Simon: Dark Forces, *669;* D.A.R.Y.L., *827;* Phar Lap, *562*

Winer, Harry: Space Camp, *864*

Winner, Michael: Big Sleep, The, *16;* Death Wish III, *40;* Death Wish II, *40;* Death Wish, *40;* Firepower, *55;* Mechanic, The, *98;* Nightcomers, The, *721;* Sentinel, The, *742;* Stone Killer, The, *141;* Wicked Lady, The, *163*

Winters, David: Last Horror Film, The, *711*

Wise, Herbert: Gathering Storm, *471*

Wise, Robert: Andromeda Strain, The, *817;* Audrey Rose, *648;* Blood on the Moon, *884;* Body Snatcher, The, *655;* Curse of the Cat People, The, *668;* Day the Earth Stood Still, The, *828;* Hindenburg, The, *487;* Run Silent, Run Deep, *125;* Sand Pebbles, The, *127;* Set-Up, The, *591;* Sound of Music, The, *804;* Star Trek—The Motion Picture, *865;* West Side Story, *812*

Witney, William: Adventures of Captain Marvel, The, *1;* Bells of Coronado, *881;*

Daredevils of the Red Circle, *38;* Down Dakota Way, *894;* Golden Stallion, The, *898;* Grand Canyon Trail, *899;* Island of Dr. Moreau, The, *845;* Master of the World, *851;* North of the Great Divide, *918;* Nyoka and the Tiger Men (Perils of Nyoka), *109;* Outcast, The, *920;* Spy Smasher, *139;* Susanna Pass, *936;* Trail of Robin Hood, *939;* Trigger, Jr., *940;* Twilight in the Sierras, *941;* Under California Stars, *942*

Woodburn, Bob: Little Laura and Big John, *90*

Wood Jr., Edward D.: Bride of the Monster, *657;* Glen or Glenda, *473;* Night of the Ghouls, *722;* Plan 9 from Outer Space, *856*

Woods, Jack: Equinox (The Beast), *680*

Wood, Sam: Day at the Races, A, *249;* Devil and Miss Jones, The, *250;* Goodbye, Mr. Chips, *475;* King's Row, *508;* Kitty Foyle, *509;* Night at the Opera, A, *318;* Our Town, *555;* Pride of the Yankees, The, *568*

Worsley, Wallace: Hunchback of Notre Dame, The (Original), *702*

Wright, Mack V.: Rootin' Tootin' Rhythm, *928;* Winds of the Wasteland, *945*

Wright, Tom: Torchlight, *620*

Wrye, Donald: Ice Castles, *492*

Wyler, William: Ben-Hur, *14;* Best Years of Our Lives, The, *409;* Big Country, *882;* Collector, The, *663;* Dead End, *447;* Dodsworth, *452;* Funny Girl, *782;* Heiress, The, *485;* Letter, The, *516;* Liberation of L. B. Jones, The, *517;* Roman Holiday, *583;* These Three, *615;* Westerner, The, *944;* Wuthering Heights, *639*

Wynn, Bob: Resurrection of Zachary Wheeler, The, *859*

Wyre, Donald: Born Innocent, *417*

Yabuki, Kimio: Rainbow Brite and the Star Stealer, *200*

Yanagimachi, Mitsuo: Himatsuri, *487*

Yarbrough, Jean: Brute Man, The, *658;* Devil Bat, The, *673;* Hillbillys in a Haunted House, *280;* King of the Zombies, *709*

Yates, Peter: Breaking Away, *233;* Bullitt, *26;* Deep, The, *41;* Dresser, The, *454;* Eleni, *456;* Eyewitness, *682;* For Pete's Sake, *262;* Hot Rock, The, *75;* Krull, *847;* Murphy's War, *104*

Yeaworth Jr., Irvin S.: Blob, The, *652;* Dinosaurus!, *675;* 4D Man, *838*

Yen, Chang Hsin: Shaolin Temple, *132*

Yorkin, Bud: Start the Revolution Without Me, *358;* Thief Who Came to Dinner, The, *366;* Twice in a Lifetime, *624*

Youngson, Robert: Golden Age of Comedy, The, *270*

Young, Harold: Scarlet Pimpernel, The, *129*

Young, Robert M.: Ballad of Gregorio Cortez, The, *881;* Charlie Boy, *661;* Extremities,

460; One Trick Pony, *797;* Rich Kids, *580;* Romance with a Double Bass, *343;* Short Eyes, *593*

Young, Roger: Bitter Harvest, *413;* Gulag, *480;* Lassiter, *86*

Young, Terence: Bloodline, *415;* Dr. No, *44;* From Russia with Love, *61;* Red Sun, *924;* Thunderball, *151;* Wait Until Dark, *763;* When Wolves Cry, *632*

Yust, Larry: Homebodies, *698*

Zacharias, Alfredo: Bees, The, *649;* Crossfire, *890*

Zaphiratos, Fabrice A.: Bloodbeat, *653*

Zappa, Frank: 200 Motels, *810*

Zarchi, Meir: I Spit on Your Grave, *704*

Zeffirelli, Franco: Brother Sun Sister Moon, *420;* Champ, The (Remake), *430;* Endless Love, *458;* La Traviata, *791;* Romeo and Juliet, *584;* Taming of the Shrew, The, *364*

Zeglio, Primo: Morgan the Pirate, *103*

Zeisler, Alfred: Amazing Adventure, *217*

Zemeckis, Robert: Back to the Future, *819;*

Romancing the Stone, *124;* Used Cars, *376*

Zieff, Howard: House Calls, *283;* Main Event, The, *305;* Private Benjamin, *334;* Unfaithfully Yours (Remake), *375*

Zielinski, Rafal: Screwballs, *346*

Zimmerman, Jerry: Mausoleum, *716*

Zimmerman, Vernon: Fade to Black, *682*

Zinnemann, Fred: Behold a Pale Horse, *407;* Day of the Jackal, The, *39;* Five Days One Summer, *466;* High Noon, *903;* Julia, *505;* Man for All Seasons, A, *528;* Men, The, *532;* Oklahoma!, *796*

Zito, Joseph: Abduction, *387;* Friday the 13th—The Final Chapter, *690;* Invasion U.S.A., *77;* Missing in Action, *100*

Zucker, David: Airplane!, *216;* Police Squad!, *332;* Ruthless People, *344;* Top Secret, *369*

Zucker, Jerry: Airplane!, *216;* Police Squad!, *332;* Ruthless People, *344;* Top Secret, *369*

Zuniga, Frank: Golden Seal, The, *182;* Wilderness Family, Part 2, The, *212*

Zwerin, Charlotte: Gimme Shelter, *783*

Zwick, Edward: About Last Night, *388*

Family Viewing

Abbott and Costello in Hollywood, *214*
Abbott and Costello Meet Captain Kidd, *214*
Abbott and Costello Meet Dr. Jekyll and Mr. Hyde, *214*
Abbott and Costello Meet Frankenstein, *214*
Abe Lincoln in Illinois, *387*
Abilene Town, *878*
Absent-Minded Professor, The, *169*
Across the Great Divide, *169*
Adam Had Four Sons, *389*
Adam's Rib, *215*
Adventures of an American Rabbit, The, *169*
Adventures of Captain Marvel, The, *1*
Adventures of Huckleberry Finn, The, *169*
Adventures of the Wilderness Family, *170*
Adventures of Tom Sawyer, The, *170*
Adventures of Robin Hood, The, *2*
Adventures of Sherlock Holmes, The, *2*
Africa Screams, *215*
Africa—Texas Style!, *6*
African Queen, The, *6*
Aladdin and His Wonderful Lamp, *170*
Alamo, The, *878*
Alice in Wonderland, *170*
Alice's Adventures in Wonderland, *171*
All About Eve, *393*
Allegheny Uprising, *878*
All Quiet on the Western Front, *7*
Almost Angels, *171*
Along Came Jones, *879*
Amazing Dobermans, *171*
American Graffiti, *218*
American in Paris, An, *769*

And Then There Were None, *398*
Angel and the Badman, *879*
Animal Crackers, *218*
Anna Christie, *399*
Anna Karenina, *400*
Annie, *769*
Apple Dumpling Gang, The, *171*
Apple Dumpling Gang Rides Again, The, *171*
Around the World in 80 Days, *220*
Around the World Under the Sea, *10*
Arsenic and Old Lace, *220*
At the Earth's Core, *818*
Atoll K (Utopia), *221*
Attack of the Killer Tomatoes, *221*
At the Circus, *221*
At War with the Army, *221*
Auntie Mame, *222*
Autobiography of Miss Jane Pittman, The, *402*

Babes in Arms, *769*
Back to Bataan, *11*
Bad News Bears Go to Japan, The, *223*
Bad News Bears in Breaking Training, The, *223*
Ball of Fire, *224*
Band Wagon, The, *769*
Bank Dick, The, *224*
Barefoot Executive, The, *172*
Batman, *172*
Battleship Potemkin, The, *406*
Battlestar Galactica, *820*
Beauty and the Beast, *172*
Becket, *406*

Bedknobs and Broomsticks, *172*
Bedtime for Bonzo, *226*
Bell, Book and Candle, *226*
Bells of St. Mary's, The, *408*
Ben-Hur, *14*
Benji, *172*
Best Foot Forward, *770*
Bible, The, *410*
Big Red, *173*
Big Sky, The, *883*
Big Sleep, The (Original), *16*
Bill, *411*
Bill Cosby—Himself, *229*
Bishop's Wife, The, *229*
Black Hole, The, *821*
Blackbeard's Ghost, *173*
Black Stallion, The, *173*
Black Stallion Returns, The, *173*
Block-Heads, *230*
Blue Yonder, The, *173*
Blue Hawaii, *771*
Blue Steel, *885*
Boatniks, The, *174*
Bohemian Girl, The, *232*
Bon Voyage, Charlie Brown, *174*
Boots and Saddles, *885*
Border Phantom, *885*
Born Free, *174*
Born Yesterday, *232*
Boy in the Plastic Bubble, The, *418*
Boy, Did I Get a Wrong Number!, *233*
Boy Named Charlie Brown, A, *174*
Boy Who Left Home to Find Out about the
    Shivers, The, *174*
Breakfast at Tiffany's, *419*
Breaking Away, *233*
Brian's Song, *420*
Bridge on the River Kwai, The, *25*
Bridge Too Far, A, *25*
Brigadoon, *772*
Broadway Melody of 1936, *772*
Bronco Billy, *886*
Brothers Lionheart, The, *175*
Buck Privates, *235*
Buckskin Frontier, *886*
Bugs Bunny/Road Runner Movie, The, *175*
Bugsy Malone, *175*
Bullfighters, The, *235*
Bye Bye Birdie, *773*

Caine Mutiny, The, *423*
Camelot, *773*
Candleshoe, *175*
Captain Blood, *27*
Captains Courageous, *28*
Care Bears Movie, The, *175*
Casablanca, *427*
Casey's Shadow, *176*
Castaway Cowboy, The, *176*
Cat from Outer Space, The, *176*
Cattle Queen of Montana, *888*
Champ, The (Original), *429*

Champ, The (Remake), *430*
Change of Habit, *430*
Charge of the Light Brigade, The, *30*
Charlie and The Angel, *176*
Charlie, The Lonesome Cougar, *176*
Charlotte's Web, *176*
China Seas, *30*
Chitty Chitty Bang Bang, *177*
Christmas Carol, A, *177*
Christmas Story, A, *177*
Chump at Oxford, A, *243*
Cinderella, *177*
Cinderfella, *774*
Circus World, *889*
Citizen Kane, *434*
City Lights, *243*
City Limits, *823*
Clash of the Titans, *824*
Cloak and Dagger, *32*
Close Encounters of the Third Kind, *825*
Cold River, *177*
Computer Wore Tennis Shoes, The, *178*
Condorman, *178*
Conrack, *438*
Copacabana, *247*
Corn Is Green, The, *439*
Court Jester, The, *249*
Cyborg: The Six Million Dollar Man, *827*

D.A.R.Y.L., *827*
Daffy Duck's Movie: Fantastic Island, *178*
Dakota, *890*
Dames, *776*
Damn Yankees, *776*
Darby O'Gill and the Little People, *179*
Daredevils of the Red Circle, *38*
Dark Crystal, The, *827*
Dark Victory, *445*
Dark Command, *891*
Dark Passage, *38*
David Copperfield, *445*
Davy Crockett and the River Pirates, *17*
Davy Crockett (King of the Wild Frontie.
    179
Dawn Patrol, The, *39*
Dawn Rider, *892*
Day the Earth Stood Still, The, *828*
Day at the Races, A, *249*
Daydreamer, The, *179*
Deadline USA, *447*
Desert Trail, *893*
Destination Moon, *830*
Devil and Max Devlin, The, *250*
Dinner at Eight, *251*
Dinner at the Ritz, *43*
Doctor Dolittle, *180*
Dr. Who and the Daleks, *831*
Dr. Zhivago, *452*
Dodge City, *894*
Dog of Flanders, A, *180*
Donovan's Reef, *44*

Don't Raise the Bridge, Lower the River, 253
Double Life, A, 453
Duck Soup, 254
Duel, 679
Dumbo, 180

E.T.—The Extra-terrestrial, 832
Earthling, The, 46
Easter Parade, 777
Eat My Dust, 47
El Dorado, 895
Emperor's New Clothes, The, 833
Empire Strikes Back, The, 833
Enchanted Forest, The, 180
Errand Boy, The, 256
Escapade In Florence, 180
Escape Artist, The, 181
Escape to Witch Mountain, 181

Fabulous Dorseys, The, 778
Falcon Takes Over, The, 52
Fantastic Planet, 836
Fantastic Voyage, 836
Fantasy Island, 837
Father Goose, 259
Father's Little Dividend, 259
Fatty Finn, 181
Fiddler on the Roof, 779
Fighting Kentuckian, The, 896
Fighting Prince of Donegal, The, 181
Fighting Seabees, The, 53
Finian's Rainbow, 779
Five Came Back, 465
Flaming Star, 896
Flash Gordon, 837
Flying Deuces, 261
Flying Down to Rio, 780
Flying Leathernecks, The, 58
Flying Tigers, The, 58
Follow Me Boys!, 181
Follow the Fleet, 780
Footlight Parade, 780
Foreign Correspondent, 687
Fort Apache, 897
42nd Street, 781
Fountainhead, The, 468
Four Feathers, The, 60
Four Horsemen of the Apocalypse, 60
Freaky Friday, 182
From Mao to Mozart, 781
Front Page, The, 264
Fun in Acapulco, 781
Funny Girl, 782

Gandhi, 471
Gaslight, 692
Gay Divorcee, The, 782
General, The, 266
Gentlemen Prefer Blondes, 266
Giant, 472
G.I. Blues, 782

Gidget, 267
Gidget Goes Hawaiian, 267
Gigi, 782
Girls! Girls! Girls!, 783
Git Along, Little Dogies, 898
Gnome-Mobile, The, 182
Going My Way, 474
Gold Diggers of 1933, 783
Golden Boy, 475
Golden Voyage of Sinbad, The, 839
Golden Seal, The, 182
Goldilocks and the Three Bears, 182
Gold Rush, The, 270
Goldwyn Follies, The, 784
Gone with the Wind, 475
Good Earth, The, 475
Good Neighbor Sam, 270
Good News, 784
Good Sam, 271
Goodbye, Mr. Chips, 475
Gospel, 784
Grand Illusion, 476
Grapes of Wrath, The, 477
Grass Is Greener, The, 272
Grease, 784
Grease 2, 785
Great Gatsby, The, 477
Great Guy, 478
Great Caruso, The, 785
Great Chase, The, 65
Great Dictator, The, 272
Great Escape, The, 65
Greatest Show on Earth, The, 478
Greatest Story Ever Told, The, 478
Great Guns, 272
Great Locomotive Chase, The, 182
Great Muppet Caper, The, 183
Great Race, The, 273
Greyfriars Bobby, 183
Guess Who's Coming to Dinner, 480
Gulliver's Travels, 183
Gunga Din, 67
Guns of Navarone, The, 68
Gus, 183
Guys and Dolls, 785
Gypsy, 785

Hans Brinker, 183
Hansel and Gretel, 183
Happiest Millionaire, The, 184
Hard Day's Night, A, 786
Harder They Fall, The, 482
Hardly Working, 276
Hatari!, 69
Hawmps!, 277
Heartbeeps, 184
Heathcliff—The Movie, 184
Heaven Can Wait, 278
Heidi, 184
Heidi's Song, 184
Heiress, The, 485
Hellcats of the Navy, 70

Hellfire, 902
Herbie Goes Bananas, 184
Herbie Goes to Monte Carlo, 185
Herbie Rides Again, 185
Here Comes Mr. Jordan, 279
Hey There, It's Yogi Bear, 185
High Noon, 903
High Road to China, 72
High Sierra, 72
His Girl Friday, 281
Hobson's Choice, 281
Hold That Ghost, 281
Holiday Inn, 787
Hoppy's Holiday, 904
Horse Soldiers, The, 904
Horsemasters, 185
How to Marry a Millionaire, 284
Hunchback of Notre Dame, The (Remake), 703

I Am a Fugitive from a Chain Gang, 490
I Remember Mama, 491
Ice Castles, 492
In Search of the Castaways, 185
Incredible Journey, The, 186
Incredible Shrinking Man, The, 843
Inherit the Wind, 495
In Old California, 905
Inspector General, The, 287
International Velvet, 186
Island at the Top of the World, The, 845
It Happened One Night, 287
It Should Happen to You, 287
It's a Wonderful Life, 499
It's a Mad Mad Mad Mad World, 288
It's an Adventure, Charlie Brown, 186
Ivanhoe, 78

Jason and the Argonauts, 846
Jezebel, 501
Jimmy the Kid, 186
Johnny Belinda, 503
Johnny Tremain, 187
Journey Back to Oz, 187
Journey of Natty Gann, The, 187
Journey to the Center of the Earth, 846
Juarez, 504
Judge Priest, 504
Jungle Book, 187

Karate Kid, The, 505
Kennel Murder Case, The, 82
Key Largo, 82
Kid from Brooklyn, The, 292
Kid from Left Field, The, 187
Kid With the 200 I.Q., The, 188
Kidnapped, 82
Killers, The, 83
King and I, The, 790
King Creole, 790
King of The Grizzlies, 188
King of the Rocketmen, 846

King's Row, 508
King Kong (original), 709
King Kong (remake), 710
King Solomon's Mines, 84
Kitty Foyle, 509
Knock on Any Door, 509
Knute Rockne—All American, 510
Kotch, 294
Koyaanisqatsi, 791

Lady for a Night, 512
Lady Eve, The, 295
Lady from Louisiana, 907
Lady in a Cage, 710
Ladykillers, The, 295
Lady Vanishes, The (original), 710
Last Command, The, 907
Last Flight of Noah's Ark, 188
Last of the Mohicans, The, 907
Last of the Pony Riders, 907
Last Ride of the Dalton Boys, The, 908
Last Unicorn, The, 848
Laura, 88
Lavender Hill Mob, The, 297
Lawless Frontier, 908
Lawless Range, 908
Lawman Is Born, A, 908
Left Hand of God, The, 88
Legend of Sleepy Hollow, The, 188
Legend of the Lone Ranger, The, 908
Let's Do It Again, 298
Letter, The, 516
Lt. Robin Crusoe, U.S.N., 188
Life and Times of Grizzly Adams, The, 189
Life of Emile Zola, The, 518
Light In The Forest, The, 189
Lilies of the Field, 518
Little Caesar, 90
Little Lord Fauntleroy, 519
Little Match Girl, The, 189
Little Mermaid, The, 189
Little Miss Marker, 190
Little Miss Marker, 190
Little Princess, The, 190
Little Red Riding Hood, 190
Little Romance, A, 300
Little Women, 519
Littlest Horse Thieves, The, 190
Lives of a Bengal Lancer, The, 91
Lone Ranger, The, 910
Long John Silver, 92
Longest Day, The, 92
Love Happy, 302
Love Bug, The, 190
Love Me Tender, 910

Mad Monster Party, 191
Magic of Lassie, The, 191
Magic Sword, The, 191
Magic Town, 526
Magnificent Ambersons, The, 526
Magnificent Obsession, 527

Magnificent Seven, The, *911*
Maltese Falcon, The, *95*
Mame, *793*
Man for All Seasons, A, *528*
Man Who Shot Liberty Valance, The, *913*
Manhunt in the African Jungle (Secret Service in Darkest Africa), *96*
Man in the White Suit, The, *306*
Man of La Mancha, *793*
Man Who Knew Too Much, The (original), *715*
Man Who Knew Too Much, The (remake), *715*
March of the Wooden Soldiers, *307*
Mark of Zorro, *97*
Mary of Scotland, *530*
Mary Poppins, *191*
M*A*S*H: Goodbye Farewell, Amen, *307*
Masked Marvel, The, *97*
Meet John Doe, *532*
Meet Me in St. Louis, *793*
Melody Ranch, *914*
Melody Trail, *915*
Metropolis (musical version), *793*
Mickey's Christmas Carol, *192*
Midsummer Night's Dream, A, *852*
Million Dollar Duck, The, *192*
Minor Miracle, A, *192*
Miracle on 34th Street, *192*
Miracle Worker, The, *535*
Misadventures of Merlin Jones, The, *192*
Mr. and Mrs. Smith, *310*
Mr. Blandings Builds His Dream House, *310*
Mr. Hulot's Holiday, *311*
Mr. Lucky, *101*
Mr. Peabody and the Mermaid, *311*
Mr. Roberts, *311*
Mr. Robinson Crusoe, *101*
Mr. Smith Goes to Washington, *536*
Moby Dick, *102*
Modern Times, *312*
Mogambo, *102*
Monkey Business, *312*
Monkey's Uncle, The, *192*
Moon Pilot, *193*
Mooncussers, *193*
Moonspinners, The, *193*
Moses, *539*
Most Dangerous Game, The, *718*
Mountain Family Robinson, *193*
Mouse That Roared, The, *314*
Mrs. Brown You've Got a Lovely Daughter, *794*
Muppet Movie, The, *193*
Muppets Take Manhattan, The, *194*
My Bodyguard, *540*
My Dinner with Andre, *540*
My Fair Lady, *794*
My Favorite Brunette, *316*
My Favorite Wife, *316*
My Favorite Year, *316*
My Little Chickadee, *316*

My Little Pony: The Movie, *194*
My Man Godfrey, *317*
Mystery Island, *194*
Mystery Mountain, *916*

National Velvet, *195*
'Neath Arizona Skies, *917*
Never Cry Wolf, *105*
Never a Dull Moment, *195*
NeverEnding Story, The, *853*
New Frontier, *917*
Nicholas and Alexandra, *543*
Night Crossing, *106*
Night Stage to Galveston, *917*
Night at the Opera, A, *318*
Night Gallery, *721*
Night Riders, The, *918*
No Deposit, No Return, *195*
North Avenue Irregulars, The, *196*
North by Northwest, *724*
Northern Pursuit, *108*
Notorious, *725*
Now You See Him, Now You Don't, *196*
Now, Voyager, *547*
Nutty Professor, The, *321*
Nyoka and the Tiger Men (Perils of Nyoka), *109*

Oh God!, *323*
Oh, God! Book II, *323*
Oh God, You Devil!, *323*
Oh, Heavenly Dog!, *196*
Oklahoma!, *796*
Old Corral, The, *919*
Old Yeller, *196*
Oliver Twist, *550*
Oliver Twist, *550*
On Golden Pond, *551*
On the Town, *796*
One Million B.C., *855*
One Of Our Dinosaurs Is Missing, *196*
One on One, *552*
1001 Rabbit Tales, *196*
On the Right Track, *197*
Operation Petticoat, *325*
Orca, *726*
Ordeal of Dr. Mudd, The, *553*
Our Daily Bread, *555*
Our Relations, *325*
Our Town, *555*

Pack Up Your Troubles, *326*
Painted Desert, The, *921*
Paleface, The, *327*
Pals of the Saddle, *921*
Paper Moon, *327*
Paradise Canyon, *922*
Paradise Hawaiian Style, *797*
Pardon Us, *327*
Parent Trap, The, *197*
Passage to Marseilles, *113*
Penny Serenade, *560*

Perils of Pauline, the, *329*
Pete's Dragon, *197*
Petrified Forest, The, *562*
Petronella, *197*
Phantom Creeps, The, *727*
Phantom Empire, *114*
Philadelphia Story, The, *329*
Pillow Talk, *330*
Pinocchio, *198*
Pirate, The, *798*
Pirates of Penzance, The, *799*
Playtime, *331*
Police Squad!, *332*
Pollyanna, *198*
Pony Express, *922*
Popeye, *199*
Prairie Moon, *922*
Pride of the Yankees, The, *568*
Prince and the Pauper, The (Original), *199*
Prince and the Pauper, The (Remake), *198*
Princess and the Pea, The, *199*
Princess Who Had Never Laughed, The, *199*
Private Eyes, The, *335*
Private Life of Henry the Eighth, The, *568*
Private Lives of Elizabeth and Essex, The, *569*
Prizefighter, The, *200*
Puss in Boots, *200*

Queen of the Stardust Ballroom, *572*
Quiet Man, The, *117*

Race for Your Life, Charlie Brown, *200*
Radar Men from the Moon, *117*
Radio Ranch (Men With Steel Faces, Phantom Empire), *923*
Raiders of the Lost Ark, *858*
Rainbow Brite and the Star Stealer, *200*
Randy Rides Alone, *924*
Rear Window, *734*
Rebecca, *576*
Rebel without a Cause, *576*
Red Balloon, The, *201*
Red Pony, The, *201*
Red River, *924*
Return From Witch Mountain, *201*
Return of the Jedi, *859*
Riders of Destiny, *926*
Riders of the Deadline, *926*
Ridin' on a Rainbow, *926*
Right of Way, *580*
Right Stuff, The, *580*
Rio Bravo, *926*
Rio Grande, *927*
Rio Lobo, *927*
Rita Hayworth: The Love Goddess, *581*
River, The, *581*
Roaring Twenties, The, *122*
Rob Roy, The Highland Rogue, *201*
Robin Hood, *202*
Robin Hood of Texas, *927*

Roman Holiday, *583*
Room Service, *343*
Rooster Cogburn, *928*
Rootin' Tootin' Rhythm, *928*
Rope, *737*
Rose Marie, *800*
Rough Riders' Roundup, *928*
Roustabout, *800*
Royal Wedding, *800*
Rules of the Game, The, *344*
Run, Rebecca, Run, *202*
Running Brave, *585*

Sacketts, The, *928*
Sacred Ground, *929*
Saga of Death Valley, *929*
Sagebrush Trail, *929*
Sahara, *126*
Sahara, *126*
Sam's Son, *588*
Samson and Delilah, *588*
San Francisco, *588*
Sands of Iwo Jima, *128*
Santa Claus—The Movie, *202*
Santa Fe Stampede, *929*
Santa Fe Trail, *929*
Saps at Sea, *345*
Savage Sam, *202*
Savannah Smiles, *203*
Save The Lady, *203*
Say Amen, Somebody, *801*
Scandalous John, *203*
Scarlet Pimpernel, The, *129*
Scavenger Hunt, *346*
Sea Hawk, The, *130*
Searchers, The, *930*
Secret of Nimh, The, *203*
Secret of the Sword, The, *203*
Sgt. Pepper's Lonely Hearts Club Band, *802*
Sergeant York, *131*
(Sesame Street Presents) Follow That Bird, *204*
Seven Brides for Seven Brothers, *802*
1776, *802*
7TH Voyage of Sinbad, The, *861*
Shaggy D.A., The, *204*
Shaggy Dog, The, *204*
Shall We Dance?, *802*
Shane, *930*
Shenandoah, *930*
Sherlock Holmes and the Baskerville Curse, *204*
She Wore a Yellow Ribbon, *930*
Shine On Harvest Moon, *931*
Show Boat, *802*
Sign of Zorro, The, *204*
Silk Stockings, *802*
Sinbad the Sailor, *136*
Singin' in the Rain, *802*
Singing Buckaroo, *932*
Sioux City Sue, *933*
Sleeping Beauty, *204*

Smurfs and the Magic Flute, The, *205*
Snoopy, Come Home, *205*
Snow Queen, *205*
Snow White and the Seven Dwarfs, *205*
Snow White and the Three Stooges, *205*
So Dear to My Heart, *206*
Somewhere, Tomorrow, *206*
Song of Nevada, *933*
Song of Texas, *933*
Son of Flubber, *206*
Sons of the Desert, *356*
Sounder, *598*
Sound of Music, The, *804*
South Pacific, *805*
Spirit of St. Louis, The, *599*
Spy Smasher, *139*
Stagecoach, *934*
Stage Door, *357*
Stage Door Canteen, *599*
Star Trek: The Menagerie, *865*
Star Trek—The Motion Picture, *865*
Star Trek II: The Wrath of Khan, *865*
Star Trek III: The Search for Spock, *865*
Star Wars, *867*
Starman, *867*
Star Packer, The, *935*
State of the Union, *602*
Sting II, The, *140*
Story of Vernon and Irene Castle, The, *806*
Sunrise at Campobello, *609*
Sunset Blvd., *609*
Sunset Serenade, *935*
Supergirl, *868*
Superman, *868*
Superman II, *869*
Superman III, *869*
Support Your Local Sheriff!, *936*
Susanna Pass, *936*
Swing Time, *806*
Swiss Family Robinson, The, *207*
Swiss Miss, *363*
Sword and the Rose, The, *207*
Sword in the Stone, *207*
Sword of the Valiant, *207*

Tale of the Frog Prince, *207*
Tale of Two Cities, A, *611*
Tall in the Saddle, *936*
Tarzan the Ape Man (Original), *146*
Tarzan the Fearless, *146*
Ten Commandments, The, *612*
10 from Your Show of Shows, *364*
Ten Who Dared, *208*
Tennessee's Partner, *937*
Terror By Night, *148*
Texas John Slaughter: Geronimo's Revenge, *937*
Texas John Slaughter: Stampede at Bitter Creek, *937*
Texas John Slaughter: Wild Times, *938*
That Darn Cat, *208*
That's Dancing, *807*

That's Entertainment, *807*
That's Entertainment Part II, *807*
That Touch of Mink, *365*
They Died with their Boots On, *938*
They Drive by Night, *148*
They Went That-A-Way and That-A-Way, *208*
Thief of Baghdad, The, *870*
Thief of Baghdad, The, *871*
Things to Come, *871*
Third Man On The Mountain, *208*
Third Man, The, *755*
Thirty-nine Steps, The, *755*
This Gun for Hire, *150*
This Island Earth, *871*
Those Calloways, *209*
Three Caballeros, The, *209*
Three Faces West, *939*
Three Little Pigs, The, *209*
Three Lives Of Thomasina,The, *209*
Thumbelina, *209*
Tickle Me, *809*
Tiger Town, *209*
Time Bandits, *872*
Time Machine, The, *872*
To Be or Not to Be (Original), *368*
Toby Tyler, *210*
Tom EdisonmThe Boy Who Lit Up The World, *210*
Tom Sawyer, *210*
Tom Thumb, *210*
Tonka, *211*
Top Hat, *810*
Topper, *369*
Topper Returns, *370*
Touched by Love, *621*
Trail Beyond, The, *939*
Trail of Robin Hood, *939*
Transformers, The Movie, *211*
Treasure Island, *211*
Treasure Island, *211*
Treasure of the Sierra Madre, The, *155*
Trigger, Jr., *940*
Tron, *873*
Trouble With Angels, The, *372*
True Grit, *941*
12 Angry Men, *624*
Twelve O'Clock High, *155*
20,000 Leagues under the Sea, *155*
2001: A Space Odyssey, *873*
2010, *874*

Ugly Dachshund, The, *211*
Under California Stars, *942*
Unexpected Guest, *942*
Unidentified Flying Oddball, *212*
Uptown Saturday Night, *376*

Valley of Fire, *942*
Vega$, *158*
Viva Las Vegas, *811*

Wagonmaster, *943*
Wake of the Red Witch, *160*
War of the Wildcats, *943*
War of the Worlds, The, *874*
War Wagon, The, *944*
Wargames, *875*
Waterloo Bridge, *631*
Watership Down, *876*
Way Out West, *378*
We of the Never Never, *161*
West of the Divide, *944*
Westward Ho The Wagons, *212*
Wheel of Fortune, *944*
When Worlds Collide, *876*
Where the Boys Are, *380*
Where the Red Fern Grows, *212*
Whitewater Sam, *162*
Wilbur and Orville: The First To Fly, *212*
Wild in the Country, *634*
Wilderness Family, Part 2, The, *212*
Wild Times, *945*
Will, G. Gordon Liddy, *635*
Willy Wonka and the Chocolate Factory, *213*

Wilma, *635*
Wind in the Willows, The, *213*
Winds of the Wasteland, *945*
Windwalker, *946*
Wings, *164*
Winning of the West, *946*
Witness for the Prosecution, *637*
Wiz, The, *812*
Wizard of Oz, The, *812*
Woman Called Golda, A, *638*
Woman of Paris, A, *638*
Women, The, *383*
World of Abbott and Costello, The, *383*
World's Greatest Athlete, The, *213*

Yankee Doodle Dandy, *813*
Yearling, The, *213*
Yellow Rose of Texas, *946*
You Were Never Lovelier, *814*
You'll Never Get Rich, *814*

Ziegfeld Follies, *814*
Zombies of the Stratosphere (Satan's Satellites), *167*

Alphabetical Listing of Movies

A Nos Amours, *387*

Abbott and Costello in Hollywood, *214*

Abbott and Costello Meet Captain Kidd, *214*

Abbott and Costello Meet Dr. Jekyll and Mr. Hyde, *214*

Abbott and Costello Meet Frankenstein, *214*

Abduction, *387*

Abe Lincoln in Illinois, *387*

Abilene Town, *878*

Abominable Dr. Phibes, The, *643*

About Last Night, *388*

Abraham Lincoln, *388*

Absence of Malice, *388*

Absent-Minded Professor, The, *169*

Absolute Beginners, *768*

Accident, *388*

Across 110th Street, *1*

Across the Great Divide, *169*

Act of Passion, *389*

Adam Had Four Sons, *389*

Adam's Rib, *215*

Adultress, The, *389*

Adventures of Sherlock Holmes' Smarter Brother, The, *215*

Adventures of an American Rabbit, The, *169*

Adventures of Buckaroo Banzai, The, *815*

Adventures of Captain Marvel, The, *1*

Adventures of Captain Fabian, *2*

Adventures of Huckleberry Finn, The, *169*

Adventures of Hercules, The, *815*

Adventures of the Wilderness Family, *170*

Adventures of Tom Sawyer, The, *170*

Adventures of Robin Hood, The, *2*

Adventures of Sherlock Holmes, The, *2*

Adventures of Sherlock Holmes: A Scandal in Bohemia, *2*

Adventures of Sherlock Holmes: The Blue Carbuncle, *2*

Adventures of Sherlock Holmes: The Copper Beeches, *3*

Adventures of Sherlock Holmes: The Crooked Man, *3*

Adventures of Sherlock Holmes: The Dancing Men, *3*

Adventures of Sherlock Holmes: The Final Problem, *4*

Adventures of Sherlock Holmes: The Greek Interpreter, *4*

Adventures of Sherlock Holmes: The Naval Treaty, *4*

Adventures of Sherlock Holmes: The Norwood Builder, *5*

Adventures of Sherlock Holmes: The Red-Headed League, *5*

Adventures of Sherlock Holmes: The Resident Patient, *5*

Adventures of Sherlock Holmes: The Solitary Cyclist, *5*

Adventures of Sherlock Holmes: The Speckled Band, *6*

Affair, The, *389*

Africa Screams, *215*

Africa—Texas Style!, *6*

African Queen, The, *389*

After Hours, *215*

After the Fall of New York, *815*

After the Fox, *216*

After the Rehearsal, *390*

After the Thin Man, 6
Against a Crooked Sky, 878
Against All Odds, 390
Against All Odds (Kiss and Kill, Blood of Fu Manchu), 643
Agatha, 390
Agency, 390
Agnes of God, 390
Aguirre: Wrath of God, 6
Air Force, 7
Airplane!, 216
Airplane II: The Sequel, 216
Airport, 7
Airport 1975, 391
Airport 77, 391
Airport '79: The Concorde, 391
Aladdin and His Wonderful Lamp, 170
Alamo Bay, 391
Alamo, The, 878
Alexander Nevsky, 392
Alexander the Great, 392
Alfie, 216
Algiers, 392
Alice Adams, 392
Alice Doesn't Live Here Anymore, 392
Alice in Wonderland, 170
Alice's Adventures in Wonderland, 171
Alice's Restaurant, 393
Alice, Sweet Alice (Communion and Holy Terror), 643
Alien, 815
Alien Factor, The, 816
Alien Prey, 644
Alien Warrior, 816
Aliens, 816
Alison's Birthday, 644
All About Eve, 393
All God's Children, 393
All Night Long, 393
All Quiet on the Western Front, 393
All the King's Men, 394
All the President's Men, 394
All the Right Moves, 394
Allegheny Uprising, 878
Allegro Non Troppo, 216
Alligator, 644
Alligator Shoes, 394
All of Me, 217
All Quiet on the Western Front, 7
All That Jazz, 768
All the Marbles, 217
Almost Angels, 171
Almost You, 217
Aloha, Bobby and Rose, 7
Alone in the Dark, 644
Along Came Jones, 879
Alpha Incident, The, 816
Alphabet City, 394
Altered States, 817
Alvarez Kelly, 879
Amadeus, 769
Amarcord, 395

Amateur, The, 395
Amazing Adventure, 217
Amazing Dobermans, 171
Amazing Howard Hughes, The, 395
Ambassador, The, 395
American Anthem, 395
American Empire, 879
American Flyers, 396
American Friend, The, 396
American Gigolo, 396
American Dreamer, 217
American Graffiti, 218
American in Paris, An, 769
American Ninja, 7
American Werewolf in London, An, 644
Americana, 396
Americano, The, 879
Americathon, 218
Amin: The Rise and Fall, 397
Amityville Horror, The, 645
Amityville II: The Possession, 645
Amityville III: The Demon, 645
Among the Cinders, 397
Amsterdam Kill, The, 7
Anatomy of a Murder, 397
And God Created Woman, 397
And Justice for All, 397
And Now the Screaming Starts, 645
And Now, My Love, 398
And the Ship Sails On, 398
And Then There Were None, 398
Anderson Tapes, The, 8
And Now for Something Completely Different, 218
Android, 817
Andromeda Strain, The, 817
Andy Warhol's Bad, 398
Andy Warhol's Dracula, 645
Andy Warhol's Frankenstein, 646
Angel, 8
Angel and the Badman, 879
Angel of H.E.A.T., 8
Angel on My Shoulder, 399
Angelo My Love, 399
Angels Die Hard, 8
Angels with Dirty Faces, 8
Angry Red Planet, The, 817
Animal Crackers, 218
Animal Farm, 399
Animal House, 218
Ann Vickers, 399
Anna Christie, 399
Anna Karenina, 400
Anna to the Infinite Power, 817
Anne of the Thousand Days, 400
Annie, 769
Annie Hall, 219
Another Country, 400
Another Time, Another Place, 400
A Nous la Liberte, 219
Antony and Cleopatra, 401
Any Which Way You Can, 219

Apache, 879
Apartment, The, 219
Ape Man, The, 646
Apocalypse Now, 9
Apple Dumpling Gang, The, 171
Apple Dumpling Gang Rides Again, The, 171
Appointment in Honduras, 9
Apprenticeship of Duddy Kravitz, The, 401
April Fool's Day, 646
Arabesque, 9
Arch of Triumph, 401
Ark of the Sun God . . . Temple of Hell, The, 9
Armed and Dangerous, 220
Arnold, 646
Around the World in 80 Days, 220
Around the World Under the Sea, 10
Arrangement, The, 401
Arrowsmith, 401
Arsenic and Old Lace, 220
Arthur, 220
Assassin of Youth (aka Marijuana), 402
Assault on Precinct 13, 10
Astro-Zombies, 646
Asylum, 647
At Sword's Point, 10
At the Earth's Core, 818
Atlantic City, 402
Atoll K (Utopia), 221
Atom Age Vampire, 647
Atomic Cafe, The, 402
Atomic Submarine, The, 818
Ator: The Fighting Eagle, 818
Attack Force Z, 10
Attack of the Killer Tomatoes, 221
Attack of the Crab Monsters, 647
Attack of the 50-Foot Woman, 647
Attack of the Swamp Creature, 647
At the Circus, 221
Attic, The, 648
At War with the Army, 221
Audience with Mel Brooks, An, 221
Audrey Rose, 11
Auntie Mame, 222
Author! Author!, 222
Autobiography of Miss Jane Pittman, The, 402
Autumn Sonata, 403
Avalanche, 10
Avenging Angel, 11
Aviator, The, 403
Aviator's Wife, The, 222
Aviator's Wife, The, 403
Awakening, The, 648
Away All Boats, 11

Babes in Arms, 769
Baby Doll, 403
Baby the Rain Must Fall, 404
Baby, The, 648
Baby . . . Secret of the Lost Legend, 818

Bachelor and the Bobby-soxer, The, 222
Bachelor Party, 222
Back Roads, 404
Back Street, 404
Back to Bataan, 11
Back To School, 222
Back to the Future, 819
Bad Boys, 404
Bad Company, 880
Bad Guys, 11
Bad Medicine, 223
Badge 373, 11
Badlands, 404
Bad Man's River, 880
Badman's Territory, 880
Bad News Bears, The, 223
Bad News Bears Go to Japan, The, 223
Bad News Bears in Breaking Training, The, 223
Baker's Wife, The, 224
Ballad of a Soldier, 404
Ballad of Cable Hogue, The, 880
Ballad of Gregorio Cortez, The, 881
Ball of Fire, 224
Bananas, 224
Band of the Hand, 12
Band Wagon, The, 769
Bandolero!, 881
Bang the Drum Slowly, 405
Bank Dick, The, 224
Barabbas, 405
Barbarella, 819
Barbarian Queen, 819
Barbarosa, 881
Barefoot Executive, The, 172
Barefoot in the Park, 224
Barry Lyndon, 405
Basket Case, 648
Bataan, 12
Batman, 172
Battle beneath the Earth, 12
Battle beyond the Stars, 819
Battle Cry, 12
Battle for the Planet of the Apes, 819
Battle Force, 12
Battle of Algiers, 405
Battle of El Alamein, The, 12
Battle of the Bulge, 13
Battle of the Commandos, 13
Battleship Potemkin, The, 406
Battlestar Galactica, 820
Bay Boy, The, 406
Beach Blanket Bingo, 770
Beach Boys: An American Band, The, 770
Beachcomber, The, 406
Beach Girls, The, 225
Bear Island, 648
Beast in The Cellar, The, 649
Beast Must Die, The, 649
Beastmaster, The, 820
Beast Within, The, 649
Beat Street, 770

Beat the Devil, *225*
Beau Pere, *225*
Beauty and the Beast, *172*
Beauty and the Beast, *820*
Becket, *406*
Becky Sharp, *407*
Bedazzled, *225*
Bedford Incident, The, *407*
Bedknobs and Broomsticks, *172*
Bedlam, *649*
Bedtime for Bonzo, *226*
Beer, *226*
Bees, The, *649*
Before I Hang, *649*
Beguiled, The, *407*
Behind the Rising Sun, *13*
Behold a Pale Horse, *407*
Being, The, *650*
Being There, *226*
Belarus File, The, *13*
Belfast Assassin, *407*
Bell, Book and Candle, *226*
Bell Jar, The, *408*
Bellboy, The, *226*
Belles of St. Trinian's, The, *227*
Bellissima, *227*
Bells of Coronado, *881*
Bells of St. Mary's, The, *408*
Ben, *650*
Bend of the River, *882*
Beneath the Planet of the Apes, *820*
Beneath the 12-Mile Reef, *13*
Ben-Hur, *14*
Benji, *172*
Berlin Alexanderplatz, *408*
Best Defense, *227*
Best Foot Forward, *770*
Best Friends, *227*
Best Little Girl in the World, The, *408*
Best Little Whorehouse in Texas, The, *771*
Best of Sex and Violence, *650*
Best of Times, The, *228*
Best Revenge, *14*
Best Years of Our Lives, The, *409*
Betrayal, *409*
Betsy, The, *409*
Better Late than Never, *228*
Better Off Dead, *228*
Between Friends, *409*
Between God, The Devil and a Winchester, *882*
Beverly Hills Cop, *228*
Beyond A Reasonable Doubt, *409*
Beyond Atlantis, *14*
Beyond Evil, *650*
Beyond Fear, *409*
Beyond the Door, *650*
Beyond the Door 2, *651*
Beyond the Limit, *410*
Beyond the Poseidon Adventure, *14*
Beyond the Valley of the Dolls, *410*
Bible, The, *410*

Bicycle Thief, The, *410*
Big Bad Mama, *14*
Big Brawl, The, *15*
Big Cat, The, *15*
Big Chill, The, *411*
Big Combo, The, *15*
Big Country, *882*
Big Fix, The, *15*
Big Foot, *651*
Big Heat, The, *15*
Big Jake, *882*
Big Red, *173*
Big Red One, The, *15*
Big Score, The, *16*
Big Sky, The, *883*
Big Sleep, The (Original), *16*
Big Sleep, The, *16*
Big Sombrero, The, *883*
Big Trail, The, *883*
Big Trees, The, *16*
Big Trouble, *228*
Big Trouble in Little China, *17*
Big Wednesday, *411*
Big Bus, The, *229*
Bikini Beach, *771*
Bilitis, *411*
Bill, *411*
Bill Cosby—Himself, *229*
Billy Budd, *411*
Billy Jack, *17*
Billy Liar, *412*
Billy the Kid Returns, *883*
Billy The Kid Vs. Dracula, *651*
Bingo Long Traveling All-Stars and Motor Kings, The, *229*
Bird with the Crystal Plumage, The, *651*
Birdman of Alcatraz, *412*
Bird of Paradise, *17*
Birds, The, *651*
Birds of Prey, *17*
Birdy, *412*
Birgit Haas Must Be Killed, *18*
Birth of a Nation, The, *412*
Bishop's Wife, The, *229*
Bitch, The, *412*
Bite the Bullet, *884*
Bitter Harvest, *413*
Bizet's Carmen, *771*
Black Arrow, The, *18*
Black Belt Jones, *18*
Black Bird, The, *230*
Black Hole, The, *821*
Black Jack, *18*
Black Like Me, *413*
Black Magic, *413*
Black Marble, The, *413*
Black Moon Rising, *18*
Black Narcissus, *413*
Black Orpheus, *414*
Black Sabbath, *651*
Black Sunday, *19*
Blackbeard's Ghost, *173*

Black Room, The, 652
Black Stallion, The, 173
Black Stallion Returns, The, 173
Blackenstein, 652
Blackmail, 414
Blackout, 19
Blacula, 652
Blade Runner, 821
Blame It on Rio, 230
Blazing Saddles, 230
Bless the Beasts and the Children, 414
Blob, The, 652
Block-Heads, 230
Blood and Sand, 414
Blood and Black Lace, 652
Blood of Dracula's Castle, 653
Blood on Satan's Claw, 653
Blood Beach, 653
Blood Feast, 653
Bloodbath at the House of Death, 230
Bloodbeat, 653
Bloodbrothers, 415
Blood in the Streets, 19
Bloodline, 415
Blood on the Moon, 884
Blood on the Sun, 19
Blood Simple, 19
Bloodsuckers, The, 654
Bloodthirsty Butchers, 654
Bloodtide, 654
Bloody Mama, 20
Bloody Trail, 884
Blow Out, 654
Blow-Up, 654
Blue Angel, The, 415
Blue Canadian Rockies, 884
Blue City, 20
Blue Collar, 415
Blue Lagoon, The, 415
Blue Money, 231
Blue Skies Again, 416
Blue Yonder, The, 173
Bluebeard, 654
Bluebeard, 655
Blue Hawaii, 771
Blue Max, The, 20
Blues Brothers, The, 231
Blue Steel, 885
Blue Sunshine, 20
Blue Thunder, 21
Blume in Love, 416
Boat Is Full, The, 416
Boatniks, The, 174
Bob & Carol & Ted & Alice, 231
Bob le Flambeur, 21
Bobbie Jo and the Outlaw, 21
Bobby Deerfield, 416
Bobo, The, 231
Boccaccio 70, 231
Body and Soul (Original), 416
Body and Soul (Remake), 416
Body Double, 655

Body Heat, 417
Body Rock, 771
Body Snatcher, The, 655
Bog, 655
Bogie, 417
Bohemian Girl, The, 232
Bolero, 417
Bombardier, 21
Bonnie and Clyde, 21
Bonnie's Kids, 22
Bon Voyage, Charlie Brown, 174
Boogeyman, The, 655
Boogeyman 2, The, 656
Boots and Saddles, 885
Border Phantom, 885
Border, The, 22
Borderline, 22
Born Free, 174
Born Innocent, 417
Born Losers, 22
Born Yesterday, 232
Borrowed Trouble, 885
Bostonians, The, 417
Boston Strangler, The, 656
Botany Bay, 22
Boudu Saved From Drowning, 232
Bound For Glory, 418
Bounty, The, 23
Boxcar Bertha, 23
Boy and His Dog, A, 821
Boy in Blue, The, 418
Boy in the Plastic Bubble, The, 418
Boy Who Could Fly, The, 419
Boy With Green Hair, The, 419
Boy, Did I Get a Wrong Number!, 233
Boy Named Charlie Brown, A, 174
Boys in the Band, The, 419
Boys from Brazil, The, 656
Boys from Brooklyn, The, 656
Boys in Company C, The, 23
Boy Who Left Home to Find Out about the
   Shivers, The, 174
Brady's Escape, 23
Brain from Planet Arous, The, 821
Brain That Wouldn't Die, The, 821
Brainstorm, 821
Brannigan, 23
Brass Target, 24
Brazil, 233
Breaker! Breaker!, 24
Breaker Morant, 24
Breakfast at Tiffany's, 419
Breakfast Club, The, 233
Breakheart Pass, 886
Breakin', 771
Breakin' 2 Electric Boogaloo, 772
Breaking Away, 233
Breaking Glass, 772
Breakout, 24
Breakthrough, 24
Breath of Scandal, A, 233
Breathless (Original), 419

Breathless (Remake), 420
Brewster McCloud, 234
Brewster's Millions (1945), 234
Brewster's Millions (1985), 235
Brian's Song, 420
Bride, The, 656
Bride of the Monster, 657
Bride of Frankenstein, 657
Bridge of San Luis Rey, The, 420
Bridge on the River Kwai, The, 25
Bridge Too Far, A, 25
Brigadoon, 772
Brighton Strangler, The, 657
Brimstone and Treacle, 657
Bring on the Night, 772
Bringing up Baby, 234
Brinks Job, The, 234
Britannia Hospital, 235
Broadway Danny Rose, 235
Broadway Melody of 1936, 772
Broadway Melody of 1938, 773
Bronco Billy, 886
Brood, The, 657
Brother from Another Planet, The, 822
Brother Sun Sister Moon, 420
Brotherhood of Satan, 658
Brothers Karamazov, The, 420
Brothers Lionheart, The, 175
Brubaker, 421
Brute Man, The, 658
Buccaneer, The, 25
Buck and the Preacher, 886
Buck Privates, 235
Buck Rogers in the 25th Century, 822
Buckskin Frontier, 886
Buddy System, The, 421
Buddy, Buddy, 235
Buffalo Bill and the Indians, 886
Bug, 658
Bugs Bunny/Road Runner Movie, The, 175
Bugsy Malone, 175
Bulldog Drummond, 25
Bullfighter and the Lady, The, 26
Bullfighters, The, 235
Bullitt, 26
Bullshot, 236
Bullwhip, 887
Bunco, 26
Burn!, 421
Burning Bed, The, 421
Burning, The, 658
Burnt Offerings, 658
Bus Is Coming, The, 422
Bushido Blade, 26
Bus Stop, 236
Buster and Billie, 422
Bustin' Loose, 236
Butch Cassidy and the Sundance Kid, 887
Butch and Sundance: The Early Days, 887
Butterflies Are Free, 422
Butterfly, 422

Bye Bye Birdie, 773
Bye Bye Brazil, 422

C.H.U.D., 658
Cabaret, 773
Cabin in the Sky, 423
Cabinet of Doctor Caligari, The, 659
Cabo Blanco, 26
Caddie, 423
Caddyshack, 236
Caesar and Cleopatra, 423
Cahill—US Marshal, 887
Caine Mutiny, The, 423
Cal, 423
California Dreaming, 424
California Suite, 237
Caligula, 424
Call It Murder, 424
Call of the Canyon, 887
Call of the Wild, 27
Call to Glory, 424
Came a Hot Friday, 27
Camelot, 773
Camila, 424
Camille, 425
Can I Do It 'Til I Need Glasses?, 237
Can You Hear The Laughter? The Story of
Freddie Prinze, 425
Candidate, The, 425
Candleshoe, 175
Cannery Row, 237
Cannonball, 27
Cannonball Run, 237
Cannonball Run II, 237
Can She Bake a Cherry Pie?, 238
Can't Stop the Music, 773
Capricorn One, 822
Captain Apache, 888
Captain Blood, 27
Captain Kidd, 27
Captain Kronos: Vampire Hunter, 659
Captains Courageous, 28
Captains Courageous, 425
Captive Planet, 823
Carbon Copy, 238
Care Bears Movie, The, 175
Carefree, 774
Careful He Might Hear You, 426
Carlin at Carnegie, 238
Carnal Knowledge, 426
Carnival in Flanders, 426
Carnival of Souls, 659
Carnival Story, 426
Carny, 426
Carpathian Eagle, 659
Carrie, 659
Carrington, V. C., 427
Carry On Cowboy, 238
Carry on Nurse, 239
Cars That Ate Paris, The (The Cars That
Eat People), 823

Cars That Eat People, The (The Cars That Ate Paris), 660
Car Wash, 239
Casablanca, 427
Case of Libel, A, 427
Casey's Shadow, 176
Casino Royale, 239
Cassandra Crossing, The, 428
Castaway Cowboy, The, 176
Cast a Giant Shadow, 28
Cat on a Hot Tin Roof (Original), 428
Cat on a Hot Tin Roof (Remake), 428
Cat Women of the Moon, 823
Cat and The Canary, The, 660
Cat and Mouse, 28
Cat Ballou, 888
Catch Me a Spy, 28
Catch-22, 239
Cat from Outer Space, The, 176
Catherine the Great, 428
Catholics, 428
Cat People (Original), 660
Cat People (Remake), 660
Cat's Eye, 660
Cattle Queen of Montana, 888
Caught, 429
Cauldron of Blood, 661
Cave Girl, 823
Caveman, 240
C.C. & Company, 28
Cease Fire, 429
Certain Fury, 29
Certain Sacrifice, A, 429
Chain Reaction, 29
Chained Heat, 29
Challenge, The, 29
Chamber of Horrors, 661
Champ, The (Original), 429
Champ, The (Remake), 430
Champagne for Caesar, 240
Champion, 430
Champions, 430
Chanel Solitaire, 430
Change of Habit, 430
Changeling, The, 661
Change of Seasons, A, 240
Chant of Jimmie Blacksmith, The, 431
Chapter Two, 431
Charade, 29
Charge of the Light Brigade, The, 30
Chariots of Fire, 431
Charley Varrick, 30
Charlie and The Angel, 176
Charlie Boy, 661
Charlie Chan and the Curse of the Dragon Queen, 240
Charlie, The Lonesome Cougar, 176
Charlie Chaplin—The Early Years, Vol. 1, 241
Charlie Chaplin—The Early Years, Vol. 2, 241

Charlie Chaplin, The Early Years, Vol. 3, 241
Charlie Chaplin—The Early Years, Vol. 4, 241
Charlotte's Web, 176
Charly, 823
Chase, The, 431
Chattanooga Choo Choo, 242
Cheaper to Keep Her, 242
Check and Double Check, 242
Cheech and Chong's Next Movie, 242
Cheers for Miss Bishop, 432
Cheyenne Autumn, 888
Chicken Chronicles, The, 243
Chiefs, 432
Children of Paradise, 432
Children of Sanchez, The, 432
Children Of The Full Moon, 662
Children, The, 662
Children of the Corn, 662
Children Shouldn't Play with Dead Things, 662
Chilly Scenes of Winter, 432
China Seas, 30
China Syndrome, The, 432
Chinatown, 30
Chinese Connection, The, 31
Chino, 888
Chisum, 889
Chitty Chitty Bang Bang, 177
Choose Me, 433
Chorus Line, A, 774
Chosen, The, 433
Christiane F., 433
Christina, 31
Christine, 662
Christmas Carol, A, 177
Christmas Evil, 663
Christmas Story, A, 177
Christopher Strong, 433
Chu Chu and the Philly Flash, 243
Chump at Oxford, A, 243
Ciao! Manhattan, 433
Cincinnati Kid, The, 31
Cinderella, 177
Cinderfella, 774
Circle of Iron, 31
Circle of Two, 434
Circus Of Horrors, 663
Circus World, 889
Citizen Kane, 434
City Heat, 243
City Lights, 243
City Limits, 823
Claire's Knee, 243
Clan of the Cave Bear, 824
Clash by Night, 434
Clash of the Titans, 824
Class, 244
Class of '44, 434
Class of Miss MacMichael, The, 435

Class of 1984, *663*
Class Reunion, *244*
Clean State (Coup de Torchon), *244*
Cleopatra, *435*
Cleopatra Jones, *31*
Cloak and Dagger, *32*
Clockwork Orange, A, *824*
Clones, The, *824*
Close Encounters of the Third Kind, *825*
Closely Watched Trains, *435*
Cloud Dancer, *32*
Clowns, The, *244*
Club Paradise, *245*
Clue, *245*
Coal Miner's Daughter, *775*
Coast to Coast, *245*
Cobra, *32*
Coca Cola Kid, The, *246*
Cocaine: One Man's Seduction, *435*
Cockfighter, *32*
Cocoon, *825*
Code Name: Emerald, *33*
Code of Silence, *33*
Cold River, *177*
Collector, The, *663*
College, *246*
Colonel Effingham's Raid, *246*
Colonel Redl, *435*
Color Me Blood Red, *663*
Color Purple, The, *436*
Colorado, *889*
Coma, *664*
Comancheros, The, *889*
Come Back to the Five and Dime, Jimmy
    Dean, Jimmy Dean, *436*
Comeback, *775*
Comes a Horseman, *889*
Comfort and Joy, *246*
Comic, The, *437*
Coming Home, *437*
Commando, *33*
Commandos, *33*
Commies Are Coming, the Commies Are
    Coming, The, *246*
Company of Wolves, The, *825*
Competition, The, *437*
Compleat Beatles, The, *775*
Compromising Positions, *247*
Computer Wore Tennis Shoes, The, *178*
Conan the Barbarian, *825*
Conan the Destroyer, *826*
Concrete Jungle, The (aka The Criminal),
    437
Condorman, *178*
Confessions of a Police Captain, *437*
Confessions of a Vice Baron, *438*
Confidentially Yours, *34*
Conformist, The, *438*
Conqueror, The, *34*
Conquest of the Planet of the Apes, *826*
Conrack, *438*
Contempt, *247*

Continental Divide, *247*
Conversation, The, *438*
Conversation Piece, *438*
Convoy, *34*
Coogan's Bluff, *34*
Cool Hand Luke, *35*
Cop in Blue Jeans, The, *35*
Copacabana, *247*
Corn Is Green, The, *439*
Cornered, *35*
Corpse Vanishes, The, *664*
Corrupt Ones, The, *35*
Corsican Brothers, The, *35*
Corsican Brothers, The, *247*
Corvette Summer, *35*
Cosmic Monsters, The, *664*
Cotton Club, The, *36*
Count of Monte Cristo, The (Remake), *36*
Count of Monte Cristo, The (Original), *36*
Countdown, *439*
Count Dracula, *664*
Country, *439*
Country Girl, The, *439*
Count Yorga, Vampire, *664*
Court Jester, The, *248*
Cousin, Cousine, *248*
Cow Town, *890*
Cowboys, The, *890*
Crackers, *248*
Cracking Up, *248*
Craig's Wife, *439*
Crater Lake Monster, The, *665*
Crawling Eye, The, *665*
Crawling Hand, The, *665*
Crazy Mama, *36*
Crazy Ray, The, *826*
Creator, *440*
Creature, *826*
Creature from Black Lake, *665*
Creature from the Black Lagoon, *665*
Creepers, *665*
Creeping Flesh, The, *666*
Creepshow, *666*
Cries and Whispers, *440*
Crimes of Passion, *440*
Criminal Code, The, *440*
Critters, *666*
Cross Country, *440*
Cross Creek, *441*
Cross of Iron, *37*
Crossfire, *890*
Crossover Dreams, *775*
Crossroads, *775*
Crucible of Horror, *666*
Cruise into Terror, *667*
Cruising, *441*
Cry of Battle, *37*
Cry of the Innocent, *37*
Cuba, *37*
Cujo, *667*
Curse of the Demon, *667*
Curse of Frankenstein, The, *667*

Curse of King Tut's Tomb, The, 667
Curse of the Cat People, The, 668
Curse of the Pink Panther, The, 248
Curtains, 668
Cutter's Way, 441
Cyborg: The Six Million Dollar Man, 827
Cyclops, The, 668
Cyrano De Bergerac, 441

D-Day the Sixth of June, 442
D.A.R.Y.L., 827
D.O.A., 442
Daffy Duck's Movie: Fantastic Island, 178
Dagora, the Space Monster, 827
Dain Curse, The, 37
Daisy Miller, 442
Dakota, 890
Dakota Incident, 891
Dam Busters, The, 38
Dames, 776
Damien: Omen II, 668
Damnation Alley, 827
Damned, The, 442
Damn Yankees, 776
Damsel in Distress, A, 776
Dance Hall Racket, 442
Dance With a Stranger, 443
Dancing Princesses, The, 178
Danger Lights, 443
Dangerous Moves, 443
Dangerous Summer, A, 444
Dangerous Venture, 891
Dangerous When Wet, 776
Dangerously Close, 668
Daniel, 444
Daniel Boone, 891
Danny Boy, 444
Danton, 444
Darby O'Gill and the Little People, 179
Daredevils of the Red Circle, 38
Daring Dobermans, The, 38
Dark Crystal, The, 827
Dark Forces, 669
Dark Journey, 445
Dark Places, 669
Dark Secret of Harvest Home, The, 669
Dark Star, 828
Dark Victory, 445
Dark Waters, 445
Dark, The, 669
Dark Command, 891
Dark Mirror, The, 669
Dark Passage, 38
Darling, 445
Das Boot (The Boat), 38
Daughter of Dr. Jekyll, 670
David Copperfield, 445
Davy Crockett and the River Pirates, 179
Davy Crockett (King of the Wild Frontier), 179
Dawn of the Dead, 670
Dawn on the Great Divide, 891

Dawn Patrol, The, 39
Dawn Rider, 892
Day After, The, 828
Day for Night, 446
Day of the Dolphin, The, 828
Day of the Locust, The, 446
Day of the Triffids, The, 828
Day of Wrath, 446
Day the Earth Caught Fire, The, 828
Day the Earth Stood Still, The, 828
Day at the Races, A, 249
Daydreamer, The, 179
Day of the Animals, 670
Day of the Jackal, The, 39
Days of Heaven, 446
Days of Wine and Roses, 447
D.C. Cab, 249
Dead and Buried, 670
Dead Don't Dream, The, 892
Dead Easy, 447
Dead End, 447
Dead Men Walk, 670
Dead of Night, 671
Dead Zone, The, 671
Deadline USA, 447
Deadly Blessing, 671
Deadly Eyes, 671
Deadly Sanctuary, 671
Deadly Force, 39
Dead Men Don't Wear Plaid, 249
Deal of the Century, 249
Dear Dead Delilah, 672
Dear Wife, 249
Death Hunt, 39
Death in Venice, 447
Death Kiss, The, 39
Death of a Centerfold, 447
Death Race 2000, 829
Death Sport, 829
Death Watch, 829
Death at Love House, 672
Death on the Nile, 40
Death Rides a Horse, 892
Death Squad, The, 40
Deathstalker, 829
Deathtrap, 448
Death Valley, 672
Death Wish, 40
Death Wish II, 40
Death Wish III, 40
Deep, The, 41
Deep End, 672
Deep Red, 672
Deer Hunter, The, 448
Deerslayer, The, 893
Defcon 4, 829
Defiance, 41
Defiant Ones, The, 448
Deja Vu, 448
Deliverance, 41
Delta Force, The, 41
Dementia 13, 673

Demon (God Told Me To), *830*
Demon Lover, The, *673*
Demon Seed, *830*
Demons of Ludlow, The, *673*
Dersu Uzala, *448*
Desert Bloom, *449*
Desert Fox, The, *42*
Desert Hearts, *449*
Desert Trail, *893*
Desire Under the Elms, *449*
Despair, *449*
Desperate Living, *250*
Desperate Women, *893*
Desperately Seeking Susan, *250*
Destination Moon, *830*
Detour, *450*
Devil and Max Devlin, The, *250*
Devil and Miss Jones, The, *250*
Devil at 4 O'Clock, The, *450*
Devil Bat, The, *673*
Devil Dog: The Hound Of Hell, *673*
Devil Doll, The, *674*
Devil Girl from Mars, *674*
Devil's Playground, *893*
Devil's Rain, The, *674*
Devils, The, *450*
Devil's Eye, The, *250*
Devil's Undead, The, *674*
Devonsville Terror, The, *674*
Diabolique, *675*
Dial M for Murder, *675*
Diamonds Are Forever, *42*
Diary Of A Country Priest, *450*
Diary of a Mad Housewife, *450*
Diary of Anne Frank, The, *451*
Dick Tracy, *42*
Dick Tracy Meets Gruesome, *42*
Die! Die! My Darling!, *675*
Die Laughing, *251*
Die Screaming, Marianne, *675*
Different Story, A, *451*
Dillinger, *42*
Dim Sum: A Little Bit Of Heart, *451*
Diner, *251*
Dinner at Eight, *251*
Dinner at the Ritz, *43*
Dino, *451*
Dinosaurus!, *675*
Dirty Dozen, The, *43*
Dirty Harry, *43*
Dirty Tricks, *251*
Disappearance, The, *43*
Discreet Charm Of The Bourgeoisie, The, *251*
Diva, *675*
Divine Madness, *777*
Divine Nymph, The, *452*
Divorce of Lady X, The, *251*
Doberman Gang, The, *43*
Doc Savage ... The Man of Bronze, *830*
Doctor and the Devils, The, *676*
Doctor at Large, *252*

Doctor at Sea, *252*
Doctor Detroit, *252*
Doctor Dolittle, *180*
Doctor in Distress, *252*
Dr. Zhivago, *452*
Dr. Jekyll and Mr. Hyde, *676*
Dr. Kildare's Strange Case, *43*
Dr. No, *44*
Dr. Phibes Rises Again, *676*
Dr. Strangelove or How I Learned to Stop Worrying and Love the Bomb, *252*
Dr. Terror's House of Horrors, *677*
Dodes 'Ka-Den, *452*
Dodge City, *894*
Dodsworth, *452*
Dog Day Afternoon, *452*
Dog of Flanders, A, *180*
Dogpound Shuffle, *252*
Dogs of War, The, *44*
Doin' Time, *253*
Doll's House, A, *453*
Dominique Is Dead, *677*
Domino Principle, The, *453*
Don is Dead, The, *44*
Don't Cry, It's Only Thunder, *453*
Don't Look Back, *253*
Dona Flor and Her Two Husbands, *253*
Donovan's Reef, *44*
Don's Party, *253*
Don't Answer the Phone, *677*
Don't Be Afraid of the Dark, *677*
Don't Look Now, *677*
Don't Raise the Bridge, Lower the River, *253*
Doomsday Flight, The, *453*
Dorian Gray, *678*
Dorm That Dripped Blood, The, *678*
Double Exposure, *678*
Double Life, A, *453*
Double Trouble, *777*
Down Among the "Z" Men, *253*
Down and Out in Beverly Hills, *254*
Down Dakota Way, *894*
Downhill Racer, *454*
Dr. Syn, *45*
Dr. Who and the Daleks, *831*
Dracula (Original), *678*
Dracula (Remake), *678*
Dracula vs. Frankenstein, *679*
Dragnet, *45*
Dragon Seed, *454*
Dragonslayer, *831*
Draw, *894*
Dream Lover, *679*
Dreamchild, *831*
Dreamscape, *832*
Dressed to Kill, *45*
Dressed to Kill, *679*
Dresser, The, *454*
Driver, The, *45*
Drowning Pool, The, *45*

Drum Beat, 894
Drums, 46
Du Barry Was a Lady, 777
Duchess and the Dirtwater Fox, The, 894
Duck Soup, 254
Duel, 679
Duellists, The, 46
Dumbo, 180
Dune, 832
Dunwich Horror, The, 680

E.T.—The Extra-terrestrial (1986 Release),
832
Eagle Has Landed, The, 46
Earth vs. the Flying Saucers, 832
Earthling, The, 46
Earthquake, 46
East of Eden (Original), 454
East of Eden (Remake), 454
Easter Parade, 777
Easy Money, 254
Easy Rider, 455
Easy to Love, 778
Eaten Alive, 680
Eating Raoul, 254
Eat My Dust, 47
Echo Park, 455
Ecstasy, 455
Eddie and the Cruisers, 778
Eddie Macon's Run, 47
Eddie Murphy—Delirious, 255
Edith and Marcel, 778
Educating Rita, 255
Eiger Sanction, The, 47
8½, 455
8 Million Ways to Die, 47
El Cid, 48
El Dorado, 895
El Norte, 456
Electric Dreams, 255
Electric Horseman, The, 456
Eleni, 456
Elephant Boy, 48
Elephant Man, The, 456
11 Harrowhouse, 48
Elfego Baca: Six Gun Law, 895
Eliminators, 832
Elmer Gantry, 457
Elusive Corporal, The, 457
Elvira Madigan, 457
Embryo, 833
Emerald Forest, The, 48
Emily, 457
Emmanuelle, 457
Emperor's New Clothes, The, 833
Empire of the Ants, 833
Empire Strikes Back, The, 833
Enchanted Forest, The, 180
Encounter with the Unknown, 833
End, The, 255
End of the Road, 458
End of the World, 834

Endangered Species, 834
Endgame, 834
Endless Love, 458
Endless Summer, The, 48
Enemy Mine, 834
Enforcer, The, 49
Enigma, 49
Enola Gay: The Men, the Mission, the Atomic
Bomb, 458
Ensign Pulver, 255
Enter Laughing, 256
Enter the Dragon, 49
Enter the Ninja, 49
Entity, The, 680
Entre Nous (Between Us), 458
Equinox (The Beast), 680
Equus, 458
Eraserhead, 680
Erendira, 459
Errand Boy, The, 256
Escapade In Florence, 180
Escape Artist, The, 181
Escape from Alcatraz, 49
Escape from New York, 49
Escape from the Planet of the Apes, 835
Escape to Burma, 459
Escape to the Sun, 459
Escape 2000, 835
Escapes, 835
Escape to Athena, 50
Escape to Witch Mountain, 181
Eureka, 459
European Vacation, 256
Evel Knievel, 50
Evening with Robin Williams, An, 256
Every Girl Should Be Married, 256
Every Man for Himself and God Against
All, 460
Every Which Way but Loose, 257
Everything You Always Wanted to Know
about Sex But Were Afraid to Ask, 257
Evil Dead, The, 681
Evilspeak, 681
Evil That Men Do, The, 50
Evil Under the Sun, 50
Excalibur, 835
Executioner's Song, The, 460
Executive Action, 460
Exodus, 460
Exorcist, The, 681
Exorcist II: The Heretic, 681
Experience Preferred . . . But Not Essential,
257
Experiment in Terror, 681
Explorers, 836
Exposed, 681
Exterminating Angel, The, 257
Exterminator, The, 50
Exterminator 2, The, 51
Extremities, 460
Eye for an Eye, 51
Eye of the Needle, 51

Eyes of a Stranger, 682
Eyes of Laura Mars, The, 682
Eyes, The Mouth, The, 460
Eyewitness, 682

F.I.S.T., 461
F/X, 51
Fabulous Dorseys, The, 778
Face in the Crowd, A, 461
Fade to Black, 682
Fahrenheit 451, 836
Failsafe, 461
Falcon and the Snowman, The, 461
Falcon Takes Over, The, 52
Fall of the Roman Empire, The, 462
Fallen Angel, 462
Fallen Idol, The, 462
Falling in Love, 462
Falling in Love Again, 258
False Colors, 895
False Paradise, 896
Fame, 778
Family, The, 52
Family Plot, 683
Family Upside Down, A, 462
Fan, The, 683
Fandango, 258
Fanny, 463
Fanny and Alexander, 463
Fantasies, 463
Fantastic Planet, 836
Fantastic Voyage, 836
Fantasy Island, 837
Far Pavilions, The, 463
Farewell My Lovely, 52
Farewell to Arms, A, 463
Farmer's Daughter, The, 258
Fast-Walking, 464
Fastbreak, 258
Faster Pussycat! Kill! Kill!, 52
Fast Forward, 779
Fast Times at Ridgemont High, 258
Fatal Games, 683
Father Goose, 259
Father's Little Dividend, 259
Fatty Finn, 181
Fear City, 52
Fear in The Night (Dynasty of Fear), 683
Fear No Evil, 683
Female Trouble, 259
Fer-de-Lance, 684
Fernandel The Dressmaker, 259
Ferris Bueller's Day Off, 259
ffolkes, 53
Fiddler on the Roof, 779
Fiendish Plot of Dr. Fu Manchu, The, 260
Fiend without a Face, 684
Fifth Floor, The, 684
Fifth Musketeer, The, 53
55 Days at Peking, 464
Fighting Back, 53
Fighting Caravans, 896

Fighting Kentuckian, The, 896
Fighting Prince of Donegal, The, 181
Fighting Seabees, The, 53
Final Chapter—Walking Tall, 54
Final Conflict, The, 684
Final Countdown, The, 837
Final Exam, 684
Final Justice, 54
Final Option, The, 54
Final Terror, The, 685
Finders Keepers, 260
Fine Madness, A, 260
Fine Mess, A, 260 (1987 release)
Fingers, 464
Finian's Rainbow, 779
Fire and Ice, 837
Fire Down Below, 464
Fire With Fire, 464
Fire!, 685
Firefox, 54
Fire over England, 54
Firepower, 55
Firestarter, 685
First Blood, 55
First Born, 465
First Deadly Sin, The, 55
First Family, 261
First Monday in October, 465
First Nudie Musical, The, 779
First Spaceship on Venus, 837
First Yank into Tokyo, 55
Fish That Saved Pittsburgh, The, 261
Fistful of Dollars, A, 896
Fists of Fury, 56
Fitzcarraldo, 465
Five Came Back, 465
Five Days One Summer, 466
Five for Hell, 56
Five Weeks in a Balloon, 56
Flame of the Barbary Coast, 56
Flaming Star, 896
Flamingo Kid, The, 261
Flash and the Firecat, 56
Flash Gordon, 837
Flash of Green, A, 466
Flashdance, 780
Flashpoint, 57
Flat Top, 57
Flesh and Blood, 57
Fleshburn, 685
Fletch, 57
Flight of the Eagle, 57
Flight of the Navigator, 837
Flight of the Phoenix, The, 58
Flim-Flam Man, The, 466
Flood!, 685
Flower Drum Song, 780
Fly, The (original), 686
Fly, The (remake), 686
Flying Deuces, 261
Flying Down to Rio, 780
Flying Leathernecks, The, 58

Flying Tigers, The, *58*
Fog, The, *686*
Follow Me Boys!, *181*
Follow That Car, *58*
Follow the Fleet, *780*
Food of the Gods, *838*
Fool For Love, *466*
Foolin' Around, *261*
Footlight Parade, *780*
Footloose, *781*
For a Few Dollars More, *897*
For Your Eyes Only, *58*
Forbidden, *467*
Forbidden Games, *467*
Forbidden Planet, *838*
Forbidden World, *686*
Forbidden Zone, *838*
Force Five, *59*
Force of Evil, *467*
Force of One, *59*
Force Ten from Navarone, *59*
Forced Vengeance, *59*
Foreign Correspondent, *687*
Forest, The, *687*
Formula, The, *467*
For Pete's Sake, *262*
Fort Apache, *897*
Fort Apache—The Bronx, *467*
Fortune Cookie, The, *262*
Forty Carats, *262*
48 Hrs., *262*
49th Parallel, The, *468*
42nd Street, *781*
Foul Play, *262*
Fountainhead, The, *468*
4D Man, *838*
Four Deuces, The, *59*
Four Friends, *468*
400 Blows, The, *468*
Four Rode Out, *897*
Four Seasons, The, *469*
Four Feathers, The, *60*
Four Horsemen of the Apocalypse, *60*
Four Musketeers, The, *60*
Fourth Man, The, *687*
Foxes, *469*
Framed, *60*
Frances, *469*
Francis, the Talking Mule, *263*
Frankenstein (Original), *687*
Frankenstein (Restored Version), *688*
Frankenstein (Remake), *688*
Frankenstein Island, *688*
Frankenstein Meets the Wolf Man, *688*
Frankenstein—1970, *689*
Fraternity Vacation, *263*
Freaks, *689*
Freaky Friday, *182*
Freebie and the Bean, *263*
French Connection, The, *60*
French Connection II, The, *469*
French Lieutenant's Woman, The, *469*

French Postcards, *263*
Frenzy, *689*
Friday the 13th, Part V—A New Beginning, *690*
Friday the 13th, Part II, *690*
Friday the 13th, Part III, *690*
Friday the 13th—The Final Chapter, *690*
Friday the 13th, *691*
Friday the 13th Part VI: Jason Lives, *691*
Fright Night, *691*
Frisco Kid, The, *897*
Fritz the Cat, *263*
Frogs, *691*
From Mao to Mozart, *781*
From Russia with Love, *61*
From the Earth to the Moon, *838*
From the Lives of the Marionettes, *470*
Front, The, *470*
Frontier Pony Express, *898*
Front Page, The, *470*
Full Moon in Paris, *264*
Fuller Brush Girl, The, *264*
Fuller Brush Man, The, *264*
Funeral In Berlin, *61*
Funhouse, The, *691*
Fun in Acapulco, *264*
Funny Dirty Little War (No Habra Mas Pensas ni Olvido), *264*
Funny Face, *781*
Funny Girl, *782*
Funny Lady, *782*
Funny Thing Happened on the Way to the Forum, A, *265*
Fun with Dick and Jane, *265*
Fury, The, *692*
Future-Kill, *692*
Futureworld, *838*
Fuzz, *265*

Gabriela, *265*
Galaxina, *839*
Galaxy of Terror, *839*
Gallipoli, *470*
Gambler, The, *470*
Game of Death, *61*
Gamma People, The, *839*
Gandhi, *471*
Gangster Wars, *61*
Garbo Talks, *265*
Garden of the Finzi-Continis, The, *471*
Gas, *265*
Gaslight, *692*
Gathering Storm, *471*
Gator, *61*
Gauntlet, The, *62*
Gay Divorcee, The, *782*
General, The, *266*
Gentleman Jim, *471*
Gentlemen Prefer Blondes, *266*
Gentle Savage, *898*
Getaway, The, *62*
Get Crazy, *266*

Get Out Your Handkerchiefs, 266
Getting of Wisdom, The, 471
Getting Straight, 472
Ghidrah, the Three-Headed Monster, 692
Ghostbusters, 267
Ghost Goes West, The, 267
Ghosts on the Loose, 267
Ghost Story, 693
Ghoul, The, 693
Ghoulies, 693
Giant, 472
G.I. Blues, 782
Gidget, 267
Gidget Goes Hawaiian, 267
Gift, The, 268
Gigi, 782
Gilda, 472
Gilda Live, 268
Gimme Shelter, 783
Ginger In The Morning, 472
Girl in Every Port, A, 268
Girlfriends, 472
Girls! Girls! Girls!, 783
Girls Just Want to Have Fun, 268
Git Along, Little Dogies, 898
Give 'Em Hell Harry!, 473
Give My Regards to Broad Street, 783
Gizmo!, 268
Glass House, The, 473
Glen or Glenda, 473
Glenn Miller Story, The, 783
Glitter Dome, The, 62
Gloria, 62
Gnome-Mobile, The, 182
Go for It, 62
Go Tell the Spartans, 63
Go West, 269
God's Little Acre, 473
Godfather, The, 473
Godfather, The, Part II, 474
Godfather Epic, The, 474
Gods Must Be Crazy, The, 269
Godzilla, King of the Monsters, 693
Godzilla vs. Mothra, 693
Godzilla vs. Monster Zero, 694
Godzilla 1985, 694
Going My Way, 474
Going Ape!, 269
Going Berserk, 269
Going in Style, 269
Going Places, 270
Goin' South, 898
Gold Diggers of 1933, 783
Golden Age of Comedy, The, 270
Golden Boy, 475
Golden Stallion, The, 898
Golden Voyage of Sinbad, The, 839
Goldengirl, 840
Golden Seal, The, 182
Goldfinger, 63
Goldilocks and the Three Bears, 182
Gold Rush, The, 270

Goldwyn Follies, The, 784
Golem, The (How He Came Into The World)
(DER GOLEM, Wie er in die Welt Kam),
754
Goliath and the Barbarians, 63
Gone in 60 Seconds, 63
Gone with the Wind, 475
Good Earth, The, 475
Good Neighbor Sam, 270
Good News, 784
Good Sam, 271
Goodbye Columbus, 271
Goodbye Girl, The, 271
Goodbye, Mr. Chips, 475
Goodbye New York, 271
Goodbye People, The, 475
Good Guys Wear Black, 63
Good, the Bad and the Ugly, The, 899
Goonies, The, 63
Gorgo, 694
Gorgon, The, 694
Gorilla, The, 271
Gorky Park, 64
Gospel, 784
Gotcha!, 64
Grace Quigley, 271
Graduate, The, 475
Graduation Day, 694
Grand Canyon Trail, 899
Grand Hotel, 476
Grand Illusion, 476
Grand Theft Auto, 64
Grande Bourgeoise, La, 476
Grandview, U.S.A, 477
Grapes of Wrath, The, 477
Grass is Always Greener Over the Septic
Tank, The, 272
Grass Is Greener, The, 272
Grateful Dead Movie, The, 784
Grave Of The Vampire, 695
Grease, 784
Grease 2, 785
Greased Lightning, 64
Great Dan Patch, The, 477
Great Gabbo, The, 477
Great Gatsby, The, 477
Great Guy, 478
Great Riviera Bank Robbery, The, 65
Great Santini, The, 478
Great Wallendas, The, 478
Great Bank Hoax, The, 272
Great Caruso, The, 785
Great Chase, The, 65
Great Dictator, The, 272
Great Escape, The, 65
Greatest Show on Earth, The, 478
Greatest Story Ever Told, The, 478
Greatest, The, 479
Great Guns, 272
Great Locomotive Chase, The, 182
Great Muppet Caper, The, 183
Great Race, The, 273

Great Scout and Cathouse Thursday, The, 899
Great Smokey Roadblock, The, 65
Great Texas Dynamite Chase, The, 66
Great Train Robbery, The, 66
Great Waldo Pepper, The, 66
Greek Tycoon, The, 479
Green Berets, The, 66
Green Ice, 66
Green Pastures, The, 479
Green Promise, The, 479
Green Room, The, 479
Gregory's Girl, 273
Gremlins, 840
Grey Fox, The, 899
Greyfriars Bobby, 183
Greystoke: The Legend of Tarzan, Lord of the Apes, 67
Grizzly, 695
Groove Tube, The, 273
Group, The, 480
Guardian of the Abyss, 695
Guardian, The, 480
Guess Who's Coming to Dinner, 273
Guess Who's Coming to Dinner, 480
Guide For The Married Man, A, 273
Gulag, 480
Gulliver's Travels, 183
Gumball Rally, The, 67
Gumshoe, 274
Gunfight at the O.K. Corral, 900
Gung Ho, 67
Gung Ho, 274
Gunga Din, 67
Gunman from Bodie, 900
Guns of Navarone, The, 68
Gus, 183
Guys and Dolls, 785
Gymkata, 68
Gypsy, 785

Hail Mary, 480
Hair, 785
Halloween, 695
Halloween II, 695
Halloween III: Season of the Witch, 695
Hamburger—The Motion Picture, 274
Hamlet, 481
Hammett, 68
Hand, The, 696
Hangar 18, 840
Hang 'Em High, 900
Hanky Panky, 274
Hanna K., 481
Hannah and Her Sisters, 275
Hanover Street, 481
Hans Brinker, 183
Hansel and Gretel, 183
Happiest Millionaire, The, 184
Happy Birthday to Me, 696
Happy Go Lovely, 786
Happy Hooker, The, 275

Happy Hooker Goes to Washington, The, 275
Happy New Year (La Bonne Annee), 68
Hardbodies, 275
Hard Country, 68
Hard Day's Night, A, 786
Hard Times, 69
Hard to Hold, 786
Hard Way, The, 69
Hardcore, 481
Harder They Come, The, 786
Harder They Fall, The, 482
Hardhat and Legs, 482
Hardly Working, 276
Harlan County, U.S.A., 482
Harlem Rides the Range, 900
Harlow, 482
Harold and Maude, 276
Harper, 69
Harper Valley P.T.A., 276
Harrad Experiment, The, 482
Harry and Son, 483
Harry and Tonto, 483
Harry and Walter Go to New York, 276
Harry Tracy, 901
Harum Scarum, 787
Hatari!, 69
Hatchet for the Honeymoon, 696
Hatfields and the McCoys, The, 901
Haunted Honeymoon, 277
Haunted Strangler, The, 696
Haunting Passion, The, 840
Hawaii, 483
Hawk the Slayer, 69
Hawmps!, 277
He Knows You're Alone, 696
He Walked by Night, 697
Hearse, The, 697
Heart Beat, 483
Heart Is a Lonely Hunter, The, 483
Heart of the Golden West, 901
Heart of the Rio Grande, 901
Heart of the Stag, 484
Heartaches, 484
Heartbeeps, 184
Heartbreakers, 484
Heartbreak Kid, The, 277
Heartburn, 277
Heartland, 902
Heart Like a Wheel, 70
Hearts and Armour, 70
Hearts and Minds, 484
Heat and Dust, 485
Heat of Desire, 277
Heathcliff—The Movie, 184
Heatwave, 485
Heaven Can Wait, 278
Heaven Help Us, 278
Heavenly Bodies, 278
Heavenly Kid, The, 278
Heavenly Kid, The, 841
Heavens Above, 279

Heaven's Gate, 902
Heavy Traffic, 485
Heidi, 184
Heidi's Song, 184
Heiress, The, 485
Hell Night, 697
Hell on Frisco Bay, 70
Hell to Eternity, 485
Hell's Angels Forever, 486
Hellcats of the Navy, 70
Heller in Pink Tights, 902
Hellfighters, 70
Hellfire, 902
Hello, Dolly!, 787
Hell's Angels on Wheels, 71
Hell's Brigade, 71
Hell's House, 71
Hellstrom Chronicle, The, 841
Help!, 787
Helter Skelter, 486
Henry V, 486
Herbie Goes Bananas, 184
Herbie Goes to Monte Carlo, 185
Herbie Rides Again, 185
Hercules, 71
Hercules, 841
Hercules Unchained, 841
Here Comes Mr. Jordan, 279
Hero at Large, 279
Heroes, 486
Hester Street, 487
Hey Good Lookin', 487
Hey There, It's Yogi Bear, 185
Hidden Fortress, The, 71
Hide in Plain Sight, 487
Hideous Sun Demon, The, 697
High Anxiety, 280
High-Ballin', 71
High Crime, 72
High Heels, 280
High Noon, 903
High Noon, Part Two, 903
High Point, 280
High Risk, 72
High Road to China, 72
High Rolling, 72
High School Confidential!, 487
High School, USA, 280
High Sierra, 72
Highest Honor, The, 73
Highlander, 841
High Plains Drifter, 903
High Society, 787
Hillbillys in a Haunted House, 280
Hills Have Eyes, The, 697
Hills of Utah, The, 903
Himatsuri, 487
Hindenburg, The, 487
Hiroshima, Mon Amour, 488
His Double Life, 281
His Girl Friday, 281
His Kind of Woman, 73

His Name Was King, 903
History Is Made at Night, 488
Hit, The, 73
Hitcher, The, 698
Hitler, 488
Hitler's Children, 73
Hitler, the Last Ten Days, 488
Hobson's Choice, 281
Holcroft Covenant, The, 74
Hold That Ghost, 281
Holiday Hotel, 281
Holiday Inn, 787
Hollywood Boulevard, 282
Hollywood Hot Tubs, 282
Hollywood Outtakes, 282
Hollywood Vice Squad, 74
Hollywood Hotel, 787
Holocaust 2000, 698
Hombre, 904
Home Movies, 282
Home of the Brave, 488
Homebodies, 698
Homework, 489
Honeysuckle Rose, 788
Honky Tonk Freeway, 282
HonkyTonk Man, 489
Honor among Thieves, 74
Hooper, 283
Hoppy's Holiday, 904
Hopscotch, 74
Horror Express, 698
Horror Hospital, 699
Horror of Dracula, 699
Horror of Frankenstein, 699
Horse Soldiers, The, 904
Horsemasters, 185
Hospital, The, 283
Hot Rock, The, 75
Hot Spell, 489
Hot Dog...The Movie, 283
Hotel New Hampshire, The, 489
Hot Moves, 283
Hot Stuff, 283
Hound of the Baskervilles, The (Original), 75
Hound of the Baskervilles, The (Remake), 75
House, 699
House Across the Bay, The, 489
House Calls, 283
House of Exorcism, The, 699
House of Seven Corpses, The, 700
House of the Dead, 700
House of the Long Shadows, 700
House of Wax, 700
House on Haunted Hill, 700
House on Sorority Row, 701
House That Bled to Death, The, 701
House That Dripped Blood, The, 701
House Where Evil Dwells, The, 701
How the West Was Won, 904
Howard the Duck, 842

How I Won the War, 284
Howling, The, 701
Howling II . . . Your Sister is a Werewolf, 702
How to Beat the High Co$t of Living, 284
How to Break Up a Happy Divorce, 284
How to Marry a Millionaire, 284
How to Stuff a Wild Bikini, 788
Hud, 490
Human Monster, The (Dark Eyes of London), 702
Humanoids from the Deep, 702
Humongous, 702
Hunchback of Notre Dame, The (original), 702
Hunchback of Notre Dame, The (remake), 703
Hunger, The, 703
Hunter, 75
Hunter, The, 75
Hurricane, 76
Hurricane Express, 76
Hurricane, The, 490
Hush . . . Hush, Sweet Charlotte, 703
Hustle, The, 76
Hustler, The, 490
Hustling, 490
Hysterical, 284

I Am a Fugitive from a Chain Gang, 490
I Am Curious Yellow, 491
I Confess, 703
I Cover the Waterfront, 76
I Dismember Mama, 703
I Heard the Owl Call My Name, 491
I Love My Wife, 285
I Love You (Eu Te Amo), 491
I Love You Alice B. Toklas!, 285
I Married a Monster from Outer Space, 842
I Married a Witch, 842
I Never Promised You a Rose Garden, 491
I Remember Mama, 491
I Sent a Letter to My Love, 491
I Spit On Your Grave, 704
I Stand Condemned, 492
I, the Jury, 77
I Walked with a Zombie, 704
I Will, I Will . . . For Now, 285
I'm Dancing As Fast As I Can, 492
Ice Castles, 492
Ice Pirates, 842
Ice Station Zebra, 77
Iceman, 843
Idiot's Delight, 492
Idolmaker, The, 788
If . . . , 285
If You Could See What I Hear, 492
Ikiru, 493
Ill Met by Moonlight, 493
I'm All Right Jack, 285
Improper Channels, 286
Impulse, 704
In Cold Blood, 493

In Name Only, 493
In Praise of Older Women, 493
In Search of the Castaways, 185
In the Good Old Summertime, 788
In the Heat of the Night, 494
In the Shadow of Kilimanjaro, 704
In Which We Serve, 494
Incredible Hulk, The, 843
Incredible Journey, The, 186
Incredible Journey of Dr. Meg Laurel, The, 494
Incredible Melting Man, The, 843
Incredible Shrinking Man, The, 843
Incredible Shrinking Woman, The, 286
Incubus, The, 705
Independence Day, 494
Indestructible Man, 705
Indiana Jones and the Temple of Doom, 843
Indiscreet, 286
Indiscretion of an American Wife, 495
Informer, The, 495
Infra-Man, 844
Inherit the Wind, 495
Inheritors, The, 495
Initiation of Sarah, The, 705
In-Laws, The, 286
Inn of the Sixth Happiness, The, 495
Innocent, The, 495
In Old California, 905
Inserts, 496
Inside Moves, 496
Inside Out, 77
Inspector General, The, 287
Interiors, 496
Intermezzo, 496
International Velvet, 186
Internecine Project, The, 705
Into the Night, 496
Intolerance, 497
Intruder Within, The, 844
Invaders From Mars (Original), 844
Invaders from Mars (Remake), 844
Invasion of the Bee Girls, 844
Invasion of the Body Snatchers (Original), 844
Invasion of the Body Snatchers (Remake), 845
Invasion U.S.A., 77
Invasion UFO, 845
Invisible Ghost, 705
Invitation au Voyage, 497
Invitation to a Gunfighter, 905
Invitation to the Dance, 788
I Ought to Be in Pictures, 287
Iphigenia, 497
Irezumi (Spirit of Tattoo), 497
Irma La Douce, 287
Iron Duke, The, 498
Iron Eagle, 78
Irreconcilable Differences, 498
Island at the Top of the World, The, 845
Island of Dr. Moreau, The, 845

Island, The, 706
Island Claws, 706
Islands in the Stream, 498
Island Trader, 78
Isle of the Dead, 706
It Came from Outer Space, 845
It Came from Hollywood, 287
It Happened One Night, 287
It Happpened at the World's Fair, 789
It Rained All Night the Day I Left, 498
It Should Happen to You, 287
It's a Wonderful Life, 499
It's Always Fair Weather, 789
It's My Turn, 499
It Came from Beneath the Sea, 706
It Lives Again, 706
It's a Gift, 288
It's a Mad Mad Mad Mad World, 288
It's Alive!, 707
It's an Adventure, Charlie Brown, 186
It's in the Bag, 289
Ivan the Terrible—Part I & Part II, 499
Ivanhoe, 78

Jabberwocky, 289
Jack and the Beanstalk, 186
Jack London, 499
Jackson County Jail, 78
Jack the Ripper, 707
Jagged Edge, 500
Jailhouse Rock, 789
Jake Speed, 78
Jamaica Inn, 500
James Joyce's Women, 500
Jason and the Argonauts, 846
Jaws, 707
Jaws 2, 707
Jaws 3, 707
Jayne Mansfield Story, The, 501
Jazz Singer, The, 789
Je Vous Aime (I Love You All), 501
Jekyll & Hyde—Together Again, 289
Jeremiah Johnson, 905
Jericho Mile, The, 501
Jerk, The, 289
Jesse James, 905
Jesse James at Bay, 905
Jesse James Meets Frankenstein's Daughter, 708
Jessie Owens Story, The, 501
Jesus Christ Superstar, 789
Jewel of the Nile, The, 79
Jezebel, 501
Jigsaw Man, The, 708
Jimmy the Kid, 186
Jinxed, 289
Jo Jo Dancer, Your Life Is Calling, 502
Joan of Arc, 502
Joe, 502
Joe Kidd, 906
Johnny Angel, 79
Johnny Belinda, 503

Johnny Dangerously, 290
Johnny Got His Gun, 503
Johnny Guitar, 906
Johnny Tiger, 503
Johnny Tremain, 187
Joke of Destiny, 290
Jonathan Livingston Seagull, 503
Joseph Andrews, 290
Joshua Then and Now, 290
Journey Back to Oz, 187
Journey Into Fear, 503
Journey into Fear, 708
Journey of Natty Gann, The, 187
Journey to the Center of the Earth, 846
Journey to the Center of Time, 846
Joy House, 504
Joy of Sex, The, 291
Joy Sticks, 291
Joyride, 504
Juarez, 504
Judex, 79
Judge Priest, 504
Judgment at Nuremberg, 504
Juggernaut, 80
Jules and Jim, 505
Julia, 505
Juliet of the Spirits, 291
Jungle Book, 187
Jungle Heat, 80
Jungle Master, The, 80
Junior Bonner, 906
Junkman, The, 80
Jupiter's Thigh, 291
Just Between Friends, 505
Just One of the Guys, 292
Just Tell Me What You Want, 292
Just the Way You Are, 505

Kagemusha, 81
Kansan, The, 906
Kansas Pacific, 906
Karate Kid, Part 2, The, 81
Karate Kid, The, 505
Kashmiri Run, The, 81
Keep, The, 708
Keeper, The, 708
Kelly's Heroes, 81
Kennel Murder Case, The, 82
Kentuckian, The, 906
Kentucky Fried Movie, 292
Kerouac, 506
Key Exchange, 506
Key Largo, 82
Keystone Comedies, Vol. 1, 292
Keystone Comedies, Vol. 2, 292
Keystone Comedies, Vol. 3, 292
Keystone Comedies: Vol. 4, 292
Keystone Comedies: Vo. 5, 292
Kid from Brooklyn, The, 292
Kid from Left Field, The, 187
Kid With the 200 I.Q., The, 188
Kidnapped, 82

Kidnapping of the President, The, 709
Kids Are Alright, The, 790
Kill and Kill Again, 82
Kill Castro, 82
Kill or Be Killed, 83
Kill Point, 83
Killer Elite, The, 83
Killers, The, 83
Killing 'Em Softly, 506
Killing Fields, The, 506
Killing Heat, 507
Killing Hour, The, 709
Kim, 83
Kind Hearts and Coronets, 292
King, 507
King and I, The, 790
King Arthur, The Young Warlord, 84
King Creole, 790
King David, 507
King of Comedy, The, 507
King of Jazz, The, 790
King of Kings, The, 508
King of The Grizzlies, 188
King of the Gypsies, 508
King of the Mountain, 508
King of the Rocketmen, 846
King of the Zombies, 709
King Rat, 508
King's Row, 508
Kingdom of the Spiders, 709
King in New York, A, 292
King Kong (original), 709
King Kong (remake), 710
King of Hearts, 294
King Solomon's Mines, 84
King Solomon's Mines (1985), 84
Kiss Me Goodbye, 294
Kiss Me Kate, 790
Kiss of the Spider Woman, 509
Kiss of the Tarantula, 710
Kit Carson, 907
Kitty Foyle, 509
Klute, 509
Knickerbocker Holiday, 791
Knife in the Water, 509
Knightriders, 84
Knights of the Round Table, 85
Knock on Any Door, 509
Knute Rockne—All American, 510
Kojiro, 85
Kotch, 294
Koyaanisqatsi, 791
Kramer vs. Kramer, 510
Kronos, 846
Krull, 847
Kung Fu, 85

L'Addition, 510
La Balance, 85
La Bete Humaine, 510
La Boum, 511
La Cage aux Folles, 294

La Cage aux Folles II, 294
La Cage Aux Folles III, The Wedding, 295
La Dolce Vita, 511
La Marseillaise, 511
La Nuit de Varennes, 511
La Ronde, 295
La Strada, 512
La Traviata, 791
La Truite (The Trout), 512
Labyrinth, 847
Lady Chatterley's Lover, 512
Lady for a Night, 512
Lady from Shanghai, 86
Lady of Burlesque, 86
Lady of the House, 512
Lady Eve, The, 295
Lady Frankenstein, 710
Lady from Louisiana, 907
Ladyhawke, 86
Lady in a Cage, 710
Ladykillers, The, 295
Lady on the Bus, 296
Lady Sings the Blues, 791
Lady Vanishes, The (original), 710
Land That Time Forgot, The, 847
Land Without Bread, 512
Laserblast, 847
Lassiter, 86
Last American Hero, The, 86
Last American Virgin, The, 296
Last Chase, The, 847
Last Command, The, 907
Last Days of Man on Earth, The, 848
Last Days of Pompeii, The, 513
Last Detail, The, 513
Last Dragon, The, 87
Last Embrace, The, 87
Last Flight of Noah's Ark, 188
Last Game, The, 513
Last Horror Film, The, 711
Last House on the Left, 711
Last Laugh, The, 514
Last Man On Earth, The, 848
Last Married Couple in America, The, 296
Last Metro, The, 514
Last Mile, The, 514
Last of Sheila, The, 87
Last of the Mohicans, The, 907
Last of the Pony Riders, 907
Last of the Red Hot Lovers, 296
Last Picture Show, The, 514
Last Plane Out, 87
Last Polka, The, 296
Last Remake of Beau Geste, The, 297
Last Ride of the Dalton Boys, The, 908
Last Starfighter, The, 848
Last Summer, 514
Last Tango in Paris, 515
Last Tycoon, The, 515
Last Unicorn, The, 848
Last Waltz, The, 791
Last Wave, The, 711

Last Winter, The, *515*
Last Year At Marienbad, *516*
Late Show, The, *87*
Laughing Policeman, The, *88*
Laura, *88*
Lavender Hill Mob, The, *297*
Lawless Frontier, *908*
Lawless Range, *908*
Lawman Is Born, A, *908*
Lawrence of Arabia, *88*
Le Bal, *791*
Le Beau Mariage, *297*
Le Cavaleur, *297*
Le Chevre (The Goat), *298*
Le Jour Se Leve (Daybreak), *516*
Le Million, *298*
Left Hand of God, The, *88*
Legacy, The, *711*
Legal Eagles, *88*
Legend, *849*
Legend of Billy Jean, The, *89*
Legend of Boggy Creek, *711*
Legend of Hell House, The, *711*
Legend of Sleepy Hollow, The, *188*
Legend of the Eight Samurai, *89*
Legend of the Lone Ranger, The, *908*
Legend of Walks Far Woman, The, *909*
Lenny, *516*
Leopard Man, The, *712*
Lepke, *89*
Les Comperes, *298*
Les Girls, *792*
Let It Be, *792*
Let's Do It Again, *298*
Let's Scare Jessica to Death, *712*
Let's Spend the Night Together, *792*
Letter of Introduction, *516*
Letter, The, *516*
Lianna, *517*
Liar's Moon, *517*
Libeled Lady, *298*
Liberation of L. B. Jones, The, *517*
Lt. Robin Crusoe, U.S.N., *188*
Life and Death of Colonel Blimp, The, *517*
Life and Times of Grizzly Adams, The, *189*
Life of Brian, *299*
Life of Emile Zola, The, *518*
Life With Father, *299*
Life and Times of Judge Roy Bean, The, *909*
Lifeboat, *518*
Lifeforce, *849*
Lifeguard, *518*
Lift, The, *712*
Light In The Forest, The, *189*
Lilies of the Field, *518*
Lilith, *518*
Lily in Love, *299*
Limelight, *299*
Lion and the Hawk, The, *89*
Lion In Winter, The, *519*
Lion of the Desert, *90*
Lipstick, *712*

Liquid Sky, *849*
List of Adrian Messenger, The, *90*
Lisztomania, *792*
Little Big Man, *909*
Little Caesar, *90*
Little Darlings, *299*
Little Drummer Girl, The, *90*
Little Girl Who Lives Down the Lane, The, *712*
Little Laura and Big John, *90*
Little Lord Fauntleroy, *519*
Little Match Girl, The, *189*
Little Men, *519*
Little Mermaid, The, *189*
Little Minister, The, *519*
Little Miss Marker, *190*
Little Miss Marker, *190*
Little Night Music, A, *793*
Little Princess, The, *190*
Little Red Riding Hood, *190*
Little Romance, A, *300*
Little Sex, A, *300*
Little Shop of Horrors, The, *713*
Little Treasure, *91*
Little Women, *519*
Littlest Horse Thieves, The, *190*
Live and Let Die, *91*
Lives of a Bengal Lancer, The, *91*
Loaded Guns, *91*
Local Hero, *300*
Logan's Run, *849*
Lolita, *520*
Lonely Are the Brave, *909*
Lonely Guy, The, *300*
Lonely Hearts, *520*
Lonely Lady, The, *520*
Lonely Man, The, *909*
Lone Ranger, The, *910*
Lone Wolf McQuade, *92*
Long Day's Journey into Night, *520*
Long Good Friday, The, *92*
Long John Silver, *92*
Long Voyage Home, The, *520*
Longest Day, The, *92*
Longest Yard, The, *92*
Long Riders, The, *910*
Look Back in Anger, *521*
Looker, *850*
Looking for Mr. Goodbar, *521*
Looking Glass War, The, *521*
Lookin' to Get Out, *300*
Loose Shoes, *301*
Lord Jim, *93*
Lord of the Flies, *521*
Lord of the Rings, The, *850*
Lords of Discipline, The, *521*
Lords of Flatbush, The, *522*
Los Olvidados, *522*
Losin' It, *301*
Lost and Found, *301*
Lost Honor of Katharina Blum, The, *522*
Lost in America, *301*

Lost Moment, The, *522*
Lost Patrol, The, *93*
Lost Weekend, The, *523*
Lost World, The, *850*
Love and Anarchy, *301*
Love and Bullets, *93*
Love and Death, *302*
Love at First Bite, *302*
Love Child, *523*
Love from a Stranger, *713*
Love Happy, *302*
Love in Germany, A, *523*
Love is a Many-Splendored Thing, *523*
Love Laughs at Andy Hardy, *302*
Love Letters, *523*
Lovelines, *302*
Love on the Run, *524*
Love Spell, *93*
Love Story, *524*
Love Streams, *524*
Love Bug, The, *190*
Love Butcher, *713*
Love Me Tender, *910*
Lover Come Back, *303*
Lovers and Liars, *303*
Lovesick, *303*
Loving Couples, *33*
Loving You, *793*
Lucas, *524*
Lucky Luciano, *93*
Lucky Texan, *910*
Lust for a Vampire, *713*
Lust in the Dust, *303*
Lusty Men, The, *911*
Luv, *304*

M, *713*
Macaroni, *304*
MacArthur, *525*
MacArthur's Children, *525*
Macbeth, *525*
Macbeth, *525*
Mackenna's Gold, *911*
Mackintosh Man, The, *94*
Macon County Line, *94*
Mad Dog Morgan, *94*
Mad Max, *850*
Mad Max Beyond Thunderdome, *850*
Mad Miss Manton, The, *304*
Mad Monster Party, *191*
Madame Bovary, *526*
Madame Rosa, *526*
Madame X, *526*
Made for Each Other, *304*
Madigan, *94*
Magic, *713*
Magic Christian, The, *304*
Magic of Lassie, The, *191*
Magic Sword, The, *191*
Magic Town, *526*
Magician, The, *526*
Magnificent Ambersons, The, *526*

Magnificent Obsession, *527*
Magnificent Seven, The, *911*
Magnum Force, *94*
Mahler, *527*
Mahogany, *527*
Main Event, The, *305*
Major Dundee, *911*
Make Mine Mink, *305*
Making Love, *527*
Making the Grade, *305*
Malicious, *305*
Malta Story, The, *527*
Maltese Falcon, The, *95*
Mame, *793*
Man, A Woman and a Bank, A, *95*
Man Alone, A, *911*
Man Called Horse, A, *911*
Man for All Seasons, A, *528*
Man From Music Mountain, *912*
Man from Snowy River, *95*
Man from Utah, The, *912*
Man in Grey, The, *528*
Man in the Iron Mask, The, *95*
Man Inside, The, *95*
Man of the Frontier, (Red River Valley), *912*
Man Who Fell to Earth, The, *851*
Man Who Loved Cat Dancing, The, *912*
Man Who Shot Liberty Valance, The, *913*
Man Who Would Be King, The, *96*
Man with Bogart's Face, The, *96*
Man With the Golden Gun, The, *96*
Man without a Star, *913*
Man, Woman and Child, *528*
Mandingo, *528*
Manhattan, *305*
Manhattan Merry-Go-Round, *913*
Manhattan Project, The, *714*
Manhunt in the African Jungle (Secret Service in Darkest Africa), *96*
Manhunter, *97*
Maniac, *714*
Maniac, *714*
Man in the White Suit, The, *306*
Manitou, The, *714*
Man of Flowers, *306*
Man of La Mancha, *793*
Man They Could Not Hang, The, *714*
Man Who Haunted Himself, The, *714*
Man Who Knew Too Much, The (original), *715*
Man Who Knew Too Much, The (remake), *715*
Man Who Loved Women, The, *306*
Man Who Saw Tomorrow, The, *851*
Man Who Wasn't There, The, *306*
Man With One Red Shoe, The, *306*
Man With Two Brains, The, *307*
Man with Two Heads, *715*
Marathon Man, *97*
Marauders, *913*
March of the Wooden Soldiers, *307*
Maria's Lovers, *528*

Marie, 529
Marius, 529
Marjoe, 529
Mark of Zorro, 97
Marnie, 715
Marooned, 851
Martin, 715
Marty, 529
Marvin and Tige, 530
Mary of Scotland, 530
Mary Poppins, 191
Masada, 530
M*A*S*H, 307
M*A*S*H: Goodbye Farewell, Amen, 307
Mask, 530
Masked Marvel, The, 97
Masque of the Red Death, The, 716
Mass Appeal, 531
Massacre at Central High, 716
Massacre At Fort Holman (Reason to Live
   . . . A Reason to Die, A), 914
Master Of The House (Du Skal Aere Din
   Hustru), 308
Master of the World, 851
Master Race, The, 531
Matilda, 308
Matter of Time, A, 531
Mausoleum, 716
Maverick Queen, The, 914
Max Dugan Returns, 531
Maxie, 308
Maximum Overdrive, 716
Mayerling, 531
Maytime, 793
McCabe and Mrs. Miller, 914
McQ, 98
McVicar, 532
Mean Johnny Barrows, 98
Mean Season, The, 98
Mean Streets, 532
Meatballs, 308
Meatballs Part II, 308
Mechanic, The, 98
Medium Cool, 532
Meet John Doe, 532
Meet Me in St. Louis, 793
Megaforce, 851
Mel Brooks' History of the World, Part I,
   308
Melody Ranch, 914
Melody Trail, 915
Melvin and Howard, 309
Men, The, 532
Men in War, 98
Mephisto, 532
Merry Christmas, Mr. Lawrence, 533
Message, The (Mohammad, Messenger of
   God), 533
Metalstorm: The Destruction of Jared-Syn,
   852
Meteor, 852
Metropolis, 852

Metropolis (musical version), 793
Miami Vice, 98
Miami Vice: "The Prodigal Son", 99
Mickey's Christmas Carol, 192
Micki & Maude, 309
Microwave Massacre, 716
Midnight Cowboy, 533
Midnight Express, 533
Midnight Madness, 309
Midsummer Night's Dream, A, 852
Midsummer Night's Sex Comedy, A, 309
Midway, 99
Mighty Joe Young, 852
Mike's Murder, 534
Mikey and Nicky, 309
Mildred Pierce, 534
Milky Way, The, 310
Mill On the Floss, The, 534
Million Dollar Duck, The, 192
Million Dollar Mermaid, 794
Min and Bill, 534
Mind Snatchers, The, 717
Minor Miracle, A, 192
Miracle of the Bells, The, 534
Miracle on 34th Street, 192
Miracle Worker, The, 535
Mirror Crack'd, The, 99
Misadventures of Merlin Jones, The, 192
Mischief, 310
Misfits, The, 535
Mishima: A Life in Four Chapters, 535
Miss Sadie Thompson, 535
Missing, 535
Missing in Action, 100
Missing in Action 2: The Beginning, 100
Mission to Glory, 536
Missionary, The, 310
Missouri Breaks, The, 915
Mr. Ace, 100
Mr. and Mrs. Smith, 310
Mr. Billion, 100
Mr. Blandings Builds His Dream House, 310
Mr. Halpern and Mr. Johnson, 536
Mr. Hulot's Holiday, 311
Mr. Klein, 536
Mr. Lucky, 101
Mr. Majestyk, 101
Mr. Mom, 311
Mr. Moto's Last Warning, 101
Mr. Peabody and the Mermaid, 311
Mr. Roberts, 311
Mr. Robinson Crusoe, 101
Mr. Smith Goes to Washington, 536
Mr. Winkle Goes to War, 311
Mr. Wong, Detective, 101
Mrs. Soffel, 536
Misunderstood, 537
Mixed Blood, 101
Moby Dick, 102
Modern Problems, 311
Modern Romance, 312
Modern Times, 312

Mogambo, *102*
Molly Maguires, The, *537*
Mommie Dearest, *537*
Mona Lisa, *537*
Mondo Trasho, *312*
Monkey Business, *312*
Monkey's Uncle, The, *192*
Monsieur Verdoux, *313*
Monsignor, *538*
Monster Club, The, *717*
Monster Dog, *717*
Monster From Green Hell, *717*
Montenegro, *313*
Monte Walsh, *915*
Monty Python and the Holy Grail, *313*
Monty Python Live at the Hollywood Bowl, *313*
Monty Python's the Meaning of Life, *313*
Moon in the Gutter, The, *538*
Moon Is Blue, The, *314*
Moon Pilot, *193*
Mooncussers, *193*
Moonlighting, *102*
Moonlighting, *538*
Moon of the Wolf, *718*
Moonraker, *102*
Moonshine County Express, *103*
Moonspinners, The, *193*
Morgan, *314*
Morgan the Pirate, *103*
Morons from Outer Space, *314*
Mortuary, *718*
Moscow Does Not Believe in Tears, *538*
Moscow on the Hudson, *314*
Moses, *539*
Most Dangerous Game, The, *718*
Motel Hell, *718*
Mother Lode, *103*
Mothra, *853*
Mountain Family Robinson, *193*
Mountain Men, The, *915*
Mouse That Roared, The, *314*
Movers and Shakers, *315*
Movie Movie, *315*
Moving Violations, *315*
Mr. Horn, *915*
Mr. Quilp, *794*
Mrs. Brown You've Got a Lovely Daughter, *794*
Ms. .45, *103*
Multiple Maniacs, *718*
Mummy, The (original), *719*
Mummy, The (remake), *719*
Muppet Movie, The, *193*
Muppets Take Manhattan, The, *194*
Murder by Death, *315*
Murder By Decree, *103*
Murder by Phone, *719*
Murder My Sweet, *103*
Murder on the Orient Express, *104*
Murderers' Row, *104*
Murder in Texas, *719*

Murders In The Rue Morgue, *720*
Murph the Surf, *104*
Murphy's Law, *104*
Murphy's Romance, *539*
Murphy's War, *104*
Murrow, *539*
Music Man, The, *794*
Mussolini and I, *539*
Mutant, *720*
Mutiny on the Bounty (Original), *105*
Mutiny on the Bounty (Remake), *105*
My Beautiful Launderette, *540*
My Bloody Valentine, *720*
My Bodyguard, *540*
My Brilliant Career, *540*
My Chauffeur, *316*
My Darling Clementine, *916*
My Dinner with Andre, *540*
My Fair Lady, *794*
My Favorite Brunette, *316*
My Favorite Wife, *316*
My Favorite Year, *316*
My First Wife, *541*
My Little Chickadee, *316*
My Little Pony: The Movie, *194*
My Man Godfrey, *317*
My Night At Maud's, *541*
My Old Man, *541*
My Other Husband, *541*
My Pal Trigger, *916*
My Science Project, *853*
My Sister, My Love, *720*
Mysterians, The, *853*
Mysterious Island, *853*
Mystery Island, *194*
Mystery Mountain, *916*
My Tutor, *317*
My Uncle (Mon Oncle), *317*

Naked and the Dead, The, *105*
Naked Prey, The, *105*
Naked Face, The, *720*
Naked in the Sun, *917*
Napoleon, *542*
Napoleon, *542*
Nashville, *542*
Nasty Habits, *317*
Nate and Hayes, *105*
National Velvet, *195*
Natural, The, *542*
Nea (A Young Emmanuelle), *542*
'Neath Arizona Skies, *917*
Neighbors, *318*
Neptune's Daughter, *795*
Nesting, The, *721*
Network, *543*
Nevada Smith, *917*
Never Cry Wolf, *105*
Never Give a Sucker an Even Break, *318*
Never Let Go, *543*
Never on Sunday, *543*
Never Say Never Again, *106*

Never Steal Anything Small, 795
Never Too Young To Die, 106
Never a Dull Moment, 195
NeverEnding Story, The, 853
New Centurions, The, 543
New Frontier, 917
New Kids, The, 721
Newman's Law, 106
Newsfront, 543
New York, New York, 795
Nice Dreams, 318
Nicholas and Alexandra, 543
Nicholas Nickleby, 544
Night and Day, 544
Night Crossing, 106
Night Games, 544
Night in Heaven, A, 544
Night Moves, 106
Night of the Comet, 854
Night of the Generals, 107
Night of the Iguana, The, 544
Night of the Juggler, 107
Night of the Shooting Stars, 545
Night Porter, The, 545
Night Stage to Galveston, 917
Night the Lights Went Out in Georgia, The, 545
Night at the Opera, A, 318
Nightcomers, The, 721
Night Gallery, 721
Nighthawks, 107
Nightingale, The, 195
Nightkill, 107
Nightmare In Wax (Crimes In The Wax Museum), 721
Nightmare on Elm Street, A, 722
Nightmare on Elm Street Part 2: Freddy's Revenge, A, 722
Nightmares, 722
Night of the Demon, 722
Night of the Ghouls, 722
Night of the Grizzly, The, 918
Night of the Howling Beast, 723
Night of the Living Dead, 723
Night of the Zombies, 723
Night Patrol, 318
Night Riders, The, 918
Night Shift, 319
Night Stalker, The, 723
Night They Raided Minsky's, The, 319
Night Visitor, The, 723
Night Warning, 723
Nightwing, 723
9 1/2 Weeks, 545
Nine Deaths of the Ninja, 107
1941, 319
1990: The Bronx Warriors, 854
Nine to Five, 319
99 and 44/100 Percent Dead, 108
Ninja III: The Domination, 108
Ninotchka, 319
Ninth Configuration, The, 546

No Deposit, No Return, 195
No Man of Her Own, 320
No Nukes, 795
No Small Affair, 320
No Time for Sergeants, 320
No Way to Treat a Lady, 546
Nomads, 724
None But the Lonely Heart, 546
Norma Rae, 546
Norman Loves Rose, 320
Norseman, The, 108
North Avenue Irregulars, The, 196
North by Northwest, 724
North Dallas Forty, 546
North of the Great Divide, 918
North Star, The, 108
Northern Pursuit, 108
North to Alaska, 918
Nosferatu, 724
Not for Publication, 320
Nothing In Common, 547
Nothing Personal, 321
Nothing Sacred, 321
Notorious, 725
Now and Forever, 547
Now You See Him, Now You Don't, 196
Now, Voyager, 547
Nudo di Donna (Portrait of a Woman, Nude), 321
Nurse Edith Cavell, 548
Nutcase, 321
Nutty Professor, The, 321
Nyoka and the Tiger Men (Perils of Nyoka), 109

O Lucky Man!, 548
Oblong Box, The, 725
Obsession, 725
Occurrence at Owl Creek Bridge, An, 548
Ocean's Eleven, 109
Octagon, The, 109
Octaman, 725
Octopussy, 109
Odd Angry Shot, The, 548
Odd Couple, The, 322
Ode to Billy Joe, 548
Odessa File, The, 110
Of Human Bondage (Original), 549
Of Human Bondage (Remake), 549
Of Mice and Men, 549
Off Beat, 322
Off Limits, 322
Officer and a Gentleman, An, 549
Of Unknown Origin, 725
Oh, Alfie, 549
Oh Dad, Poor Dad—Mama's Hung You in the Closet and I'm Feeling So Sad, 322
Oh God!, 323
Oh, God! Book II, 323
Oh God, You Devil, 323
Oh, Heavenly Dog!, 196
Oklahoma Kid, The, 918

Oklahoma!, 796
Old Boyfriends, 550
Old Corral, The, 919
Old Enough, 550
Old Yeller, 196
Oliver, 796
Oliver Twist, 550
Oliver Twist, 550
Oliver's Story, 551
Omega Man, The, 854
Omen, The, 726
On a Clear Day, You Can See Forever, 796
On Golden Pond, 551
On Her Majesty's Secret Service, 110
On the Beach, 854
On the Town, 796
On the Waterfront, 551
On Top of Old Smoky, 919
Once Bitten, 323
Once Upon a Honeymoon, 324
Once Upon a Time in America (Long Version), 110
Once Upon a Time in the West, 919
One and Only, The, 551
One Crazy Summer, 324
One Dark Night, 726
One Down, Two to Go, 110
One-Eyed Jacks, 920
One Flew over the Cuckoo's Nest, 551
100 Rifles, 920
One Magic Christmas, 552
One Million B.C., 855
One More Saturday Night, 324
One Of Our Dinosaurs Is Missing, 196
One on One, 552
One Sings, The Other Doesn't, 552
1001 Rabbit Tales, 196
One Wild Moment, 552
One, Two, Three, 324
One from the Heart, 797
One Touch of Venus, 325
One Trick Pony, 797
Onion Field, The, 553
Only When I Laugh, 553
On the Right Track, 197
Open City, 553
Operation C.I.A., 110
Operation Petticoat, 325
Operation Thunderbolt, 111
Orca, 726
Ordeal By Innocence, 111
Ordeal of Dr. Mudd, The, 553
Ordinary People, 554
Organization, The, 111
Oscar, The, 554
Osterman Weekend, The, 111
Other Side of Midnight, The, 554
Other Side of the Mountain, The, 554
Other Side of the Mountain, Part II, The, 554
Our Daily Bread, 555
Our Relations, 325

Our Town, 555
Out of Africa, 555
Out of Bounds, 111
Out of the Blue, 325
Outcast, The, 920
Outland, 855
Outlaw, The, 920
Outlaw Blues, 325
Outlaw Josey Wales, The, 920
Out of the Past, 112
Out of Towners, The, 325
Outrageous, 326
Outsiders, The, 555
Over the Brooklyn Bridge, 326
Over the Edge, 555
Owl and the Pussycat, The, 326
Ox-Bow Incident, The, 921
Oxford Blues, 556

P.O.W.: The Escape, 112
Pack, The, 726
Pack Up Your Troubles, 326
Paddy, 326
Pagan Love Song, 797
Pain in the A———, A, 327
Paint Your Wagon, 797
Painted Desert, The, 921
Paisan, 556
Paleface, The, 327
Pale Rider, 921
Palooka, 556
Pals of the Saddle, 921
Pancho Villa, 922
Pandora's Box, 556
Papa's Delicate Condition, 557
Paper Chase, The, 557
Paper Moon, 327
Paper Tiger, 112
Papillon, 112
Paradise, 113
Paradise Alley, 557
Paradise Canyon, 922
Paradise Hawaiian Style, 797
Parallax View, The, 557
Parasite, 726
Pardon Mon Affaire, 327
Pardon Us, 327
Parent Trap, The, 197
Paris Blues, 558
Paris, Texas, 558
Park is Mine, The, 558
Partners, 328
Partners in Crime—The Secret Adversary, 113
Party Animal, 328
Passage to India, A, 558
Passage to Marseilles, 113
Passenger, The, 558
Passion of Joan of Arc, The, 559
Passion of Love, 559
Paternity, 328
Pat Garrett and Billy the Kid, 922

Paths of Glory, *559*
Patrick, *726*
Patsy, The, *328*
Patton, *559*
Pauline at the Beach, *559*
Pawnbroker, The, *560*
Payday, *560*
Pearl of the South Pacific, *560*
Peeping Tom, *727*
Pee-Wee's Big Adventure, *328*
Pendulum, *113*
Penitentiary I and II, *113*
Pennies from Heaven, *797*
Penny Serenade, *560*
People, The, *855*
People That Time Forgot, The, *855*
Pepe Le Moko, *560*
Perfect, *561*
Perfect Furlough, *329*
Performance, *561*
Peril, *561*
Perils of Gwendoline, The, *114*
Perils of Pauline, The, *329*
Permission to Kill, *114*
Personal Best, *562*
Pete's Dragon, *197*
Petit Con, *329*
Petrified Forest, The, *562*
Petronella, *197*
Phantasm, *727*
Phantom Creeps, The, *727*
Phantom Empire, *114*
Phantom of the Opera, *727*
Phantom of the Paradise, *798*
Phar Lap, *562*
Phase IV, *856*
Philadelphia Experiment, The, *856*
Philadelphia Story, The, *329*
Piano for Mrs. Cimino, A, *562*
Picture of Dorian Gray, The, *728*
Piece of the Action, A, *329*
Pieces, *728*
Pied Piper of Hamelin, The, *198*
Pillow Talk, *330*
Pilot, The, *563*
Pink Flamingos, *330*
Pink Floyd the Wall, *798*
Pink Panther, The, *330*
Pink Panther Strikes Again, The, *330*
Pinocchio, *198*
Pinocchio, *198*
Pipe Dreams, *563*
Piranha, *728*
Piranha Part Two: The Spawning, *728*
Pirate, The, *798*
Pirate Movie, The, *798*
Pirates, *331*
Pirates of Penzance, The, *799*
Pit and the Pendulum, The, *728*
Pixote, *563*
Place in the Sun, A, *563*
Places in the Heart, *563*

Plague Dogs, The, *856*
Plan 9 from Outer Space, *856*
Planet of the Apes, *856*
Play It Again Sam, *331*
Play Misty for Me, *729*
Players, *564*
Playtime, *331*
Plaza Suite, *331*
Pleasure Palace, *564*
Plenty, *564*
Plumber, The, *729*
Pocketful of Miracles, *564*
Police Academy, *332*
Police Academy II: Their First Assignment, *332*
Police Academy III: Back in Training, *332*
Police Squad!, *332*
Pollyanna, *198*
Poltergeist, *729*
Poltergeist II: The Other side, *729*
Polyester, *333*
Pony Express, *922*
Pope of Greenwich Village, The, *564*
Popeye, *199*
Porky's, *333*
Porky's II: The Next Day, *333*
Porky's Revenge, *333*
Port of Call, *565*
Portnoy's Complaint, *565*
Portrait of a Stripper, *565*
Poseidon Adventure, The, *115*
Possessed, *565*
Postman Always Rings Twice, The (Original), *565*
Postman Always Rings Twice, The (Remake), *566*
Pot O' Gold, *566*
Power, *566*
Power, The, *730*
Prairie Moon, *922*
Prehistoric Women, *857*
Premature Burial, The, *730*
Preppies, *333*
Pretty Baby, *566*
Pretty in Pink, *567*
Prey, The, *730*
Pride and Prejudice, *567*
Pride and the Passion, The, *567*
Pride of the Bowery, *567*
Pride of the Yankees, The, *568*
Priest of Love, *568*
Prime Cut, *115*
Prime Risk, *115*
Prince and the Pauper, The (Original), *199*
Prince and the Pauper, The (Remake), *198*
Prince and the Showgirl, The, *334*
Prince of the City, *568*
Princess and the Pea, The, *199*
Princess Who Had Never Laughed, The, *199*
Princess and the Pirate, The, *334*
Prisoner of Second Avenue, The, *334*

Prisoner of Zenda, The, 115
Prisoner of Zenda, The, 334
Prisoner, The (television series), 857
Private Benjamin, 334
Private Buckaroo, 799
Private Eyes, The, 335
Private Function, A, 335
Private Lessons, 335
Private Life of Don Juan, The, 568
Private Life of Sherlock Holmes, The, 115
Private Life of Henry the Eighth, The, 568
Private Lives of Elizabeth and Essex, The, 569
Private Popsicle, 335
Private School, 335
Privates on Parade, 336
Prizefighter, The, 200
Prizzi's Honor, 569
Producers, The, 336
Professionals, The, 116
Projectionist, The, 336
Promises in the Dark, 569
Prom Night, 730
Prophecy, 730
Protector, The, 116
Protocol, 336
Proud Rebel, The, 923
Providence, 569
Psycho, 731
Psycho II, 731
Psycho III, 731
Psychomania, 731
Psycho Sisters, 732
PT 109, 569
Puberty Blues, 570
Public Enemy, The, 116
Puma Man, The, 732
Pumping Iron, 570
Pumping Iron II: The Women, 570
Purple Heart, The, 570
Purple Hearts, 570
Purple Rain, 799
Purple Rose of Cairo, The, 337
Purple Taxi, The, 571
Pursuit of D. B. Cooper, 116
Pursuit to Algiers, 117
Puss in Boots, 200
Putney Swope, 337

Q, 732
QB VII, 571
Quackser Fortune Has a Cousin in the Bronx, 571
Quadrophenia, 799
Quartet, 571
Queen of the Stardust Ballroom, 572
Querelle, 572
Quest for Fire, 858
Question of Silence, A, 572
Quicksilver, 572
Quiet Earth, The, 858

Quiet Man, The, 117
Quintet, 858

R.P.M. (Revolutions Per Minute), 572
Rabbit Run, 573
Rabbit Test, 337
Rabid, 732
Race for Your Life, Charlie Brown, 200
Race with the Devil, 732
Rachel and the Stranger, 923
Rachel, Rachel, 573
Racing with the Moon, 573
Rad, 117
Radar Men from the Moon, 117
Radio Ranch (Men With Steel Faces, Phantom Empire), 923
Rafferty and the Gold Dust Twins, 337
Rage, 573
Raggedy Man, 733
Raging Bull, 574
Ragtime, 574
Raid on Rommel, 118
Raiders of the Lost Ark, 858
Rain, 574
Rain People, The, 574
Rainbow Brite and the Star Stealer, 200
Raintree County, 574
Raise the Titanic, 118
Raisin in the Sun, A, 575
Rambo: First Blood II, 118
Ramparts of Clay, 575
Ran, 575
Rancho Notorious, 923
Randy Rides Alone, 924
Ransom, 118
Rappin', 799
Rapunzel, 200
Rare Breed, The, 924
Rashomon, 575
Rats Are Coming!, The Werewolves Are Here!, The, 733
Raven, The, 733
Raven and the Black Cat, The, 733
Ravishing Idiot, The, 337
Raw Courage, 119
Raw Deal, 119
Razor's Edge, The (Original), 576
Razor's Edge, The (Remake), 576
Razorback, 733
Reaching for the Moon, 337
Real Genius, 338
Real Life, 338
Re-animator, 733
Rear Window, 734
Rebecca, 576
Rebel without a Cause, 576
Reckless, 577
Red Balloon, The, 201
Red Beard, 577
Red Dawn, 119
Red Dust, 119
Red Dust, 577

Red House, The, 734
Red Light Sting, The, 577
Red Pony, The, 201
Red River, 924
Red Shoes, The, 800
Red Sun, 924
Reds, 578
Red Sonja, 120
Reefer Madness, 338
Reflections in a Golden Eye, 578
Rehearsal for Murder, 120
Reincarnation of Peter Proud, The, 734
Reivers, The, 338
Rembrandt, 578
Remo Williams: The Adventure Begins, 120
Repo Man, 338
Requiem for a Heavyweight, 578
Resurrection, 858
Resurrection of Zachary Wheeler, The, 859
Return From Witch Mountain, 201
Return of a Man Called Horse, The, 924
Return of Frank James, The, 925
Return of Martin Guerre, The, 578
Return of the Badmen, 925
Return of the Dragon, 120
Return of the Jedi, 859
Return of the Man from U.N.C.L.E., The, 121
Return of the Soldier, The, 579
Return to Oz, 201
Return of the Alien's Deadly Spawn, The, 734
Return of the Fly, The, 735
Return of the Living Dead, The, 735
Return of the Pink Panther, The, 339
Return of the Secaucus 7, 339
Return of the Tall Blond Man with One Black Shoe, The, 339
Return of the Vampire, The, 735
Return to Macon County, 121
Reuben, Reuben, 339
Revenge, 735
Revenge of the Zombies, 736
Revenge of the Dead, 736
Revenge of the Nerds, 340
Revenge of the Ninja, 121
Revenge of the Pink Panther, The, 340
Revolt of Job, The, 579
Revolution, 579
Rhinestone, 340
Rich and Famous, 579
Rich Kids, 580
Richard III, 580
Richard Pryor—Here and Now, 340
Richard Pryor—Live and Smokin', 341
Richard Pryor—Live in Concert, 341
Richard Pryor Live on the Sunset Strip, 341
Riddle of the Sands, 121
Ride in the Whirlwind, 925
Ride the High Country, 925
Ride the Man Down, 926
Rider on the Rain, 122
Riders of Destiny, 926

Riders of the Deadline, 926
Ridin' on a Rainbow, 926
Riding on Air, 341
Rififi, 122
Right of Way, 580
Right Stuff, The, 580
Rio Bravo, 926
Rio Conchos, 927
Rio Grande, 927
Rio Lobo, 927
Riot in Cell Block Eleven, 122
Riot in Cell Block 11, 581
Rip Van Winkle, 859
Ripper, The, 736
Risky Business, 341
Rita Hayworth: The Love Goddess, 581
Ritz, The, 342
River, The, 581
River Rat, The, 581
Road Games, 736
Road to Bali, 342
Road Warrior, The, 859
Roadhouse 66, 122
Roaring Twenties, The, 122
Rob Roy, The Highland Rogue, 201
Robbers of the Sacred Mountain, 123
Robe, The, 581
Robert et Robert, 582
Robin and Marian, 123
Robin Hood, 202
Robin Hood and the Sorcerer, 123
Robin Hood of Texas, 927
Robot Monster, 736
Rock 'N Roll Wrestling Women Vs. The Aztec Mummy, 342
Rocketship X-M, 860
Rock 'n' Roll High School, 342
Rock, Rock, Rock, 800
Rocky, 582
Rocky II, 582
Rocky III, 582
Rocky IV, 582
Rodan, 860
Rodeo Girl, 583
Rollerball, 860
Rollercoaster, 737
Rolling Thunder, 123
Rollover, 583
Roman Holiday, 583
Roman Spring of Mrs. Stone, The, 583
Romance With A Double Bass, 343
Romancing the Stone, 124
Romantic Comedy, 343
Romantic Englishwoman, The, 584
Romeo and Juliet, 584
Room Service, 343
Room With a View, A (1987 Release), 584
Rooster Cogburn, 928
Rootin' Tootin' Rhythm, 928
Rope, 737
Rose, The, 800
Rose Marie, 800

Rosebud Beach Hotel, The, *343*
Roseland, *584*
Rosemary's Baby, *737*
Rough Cut, *124*
Rough Riders' Roundup, *928*
Roustabout, *800*
Royal Wedding, *800*
RSVP, *343*
Ruby, *737*
Ruby Gentry, *585*
Ruckus, *124*
Rude Awakening, *738*
Rules of the Game, The, *344*
Ruling Class, The, *344*
Rumble Fish, *585*
Rumor of War, A, *125*
Rumpelstiltskin, *202*
Run, Rebecca, Run, *202*
Run Silent, Run Deep, *125*
Runaway, *860*
Runaway Train, *125*
Runner Stumbles, The, *585*
Running Brave, *585*
Running Hot, *586*
Running Scared (1986), *125*
Running Scared (1980), *126*
Run Stranger Run, *738*
Russians Are Coming, the Russians Are Coming, The, *344*
Rustler's Rhapsody, *344*
Ruthless Four, The, *928*
Ruthless People, *344*
Ryan's Daughter, *586*

S.O.S. Titanic, *586*
Sabotage, *738*
Saboteur, *738*
Sacketts, The, *928*
Sacred Ground, *929*
Saga of Death Valley, *929*
Sagebrush Trail, *929*
Sahara, *126*
Sahara, *126*
Sailor Who Fell from Grace with the Sea, The, *586*
St. Elmo's Fire, *586*
St. Helens, *587*
St. Ives, *126*
Saint Jack, *587*
St. Valentine's Day Massacre, The, *126*
Sakharov, *587*
Salem's Lot, *739*
Salvador, *587*
Sam's Son, *588*
Same Time Next Year, *345*
Samson and Delilah, *588*
Samurai Trilogy, The, *127*
San Francisco, *588*
Sand Pebbles, The, *127*
Sanders of the River, *127*
Sandpiper, The, *588*
Sands of Iwo Jima, *128*

Sanjuro, *128*
Santa Claus Conquers the Martians, *860*
Santa Claus—The Movie, *202*
Santa Fe Stampede, *929*
Santa Fe Trail, *929*
Santee, *929*
Saps at Sea, *345*
Satan's Satellites, *128*
Satan's School for Girls, *739*
Saturday Night Fever, *801*
Saturday the 14th, *739*
Saturn 3, *861*
Savage Is Loose, The, *588*
Savage Sam, *202*
Savage Attraction, *739*
Savages, *739*
Savage Streets, *128*
Savage Weekend, *739*
Savannah Smiles, *203*
Save The Lady, *203*
Save the Tiger, *588*
Sawdust and Tinsel, *589*
Say Amen, Somebody, *801*
Sayonara, *589*
Scalpel, *740*
Scandalous, *345*
Scandalous John, *203*
Scanners, *740*
Scarecrow, *589*
Scarface (original), *129*
Scarface (Remake), *129*
Scarlet Pimpernel, The, *129*
Scarlet Street, *589*
Scars of Dracula, *740*
Scavenger Hunt, *346*
Scenes From A Marriage, *589*
Schizoid, *740*
Schlock, *346*
School Spirit, *346*
Scream and Scream Again, *740*
Scream Greats, Vol. 1, *741*
Screamers, *741*
Screen Test, *346*
Screwballs, *346*
Scrooge, *801*
Sea Devils, *129*
Sea Hawk, The, *130*
Sea Shall Not Have Them, The, *130*
Sea Wolves, The, *130*
Seance on a Wet Afternoon, *741*
Search and Destroy, *130*
Searchers, The, *930*
Second Chorus, *801*
Secret Admirer, *346*
Secret Agent, The, *131*
Secret Life of An American Wife, The, *347*
Secret Life of Walter Mitty, The, *347*
Secret of Nimh, The, *203*
Secret of the Sword, The, *203*
Secret Policeman's Private Parts, The, *347*
Secret Policemen's Other Ball, The, *347*
Secret War of Harry Frigg, The, *348*

Secrets, 590
Secrets of Women (or Waiting Women), 348
Seduced and Abandoned, 348
Seduction of Joe Tynan, The, 590
Seduction of Mimi, The, 348
Seduction, The, 741
See No Evil, 741
Seems Like Old Times, 349
Semi-Tough, 349
Senator Was Indiscreet, The, 349
Sender, The, 742
Sentinel, The, 742
Separate Tables, 590
Sgt. Pepper's Lonely Hearts Club Band, 802
Sergeant York, 131
Serial, 349
Serpent's Egg, The, 590
Serpico, 590
Servant, The, 590
(Sesame Street Presents) Follow That Bird, 204
Set-Up, The, 591
Seven Beauties, 349
Seven Days in May, 591
7 Faces of Dr. Lao, 861
Seven Minutes In Heaven, 350
Seven Brides for Seven Brothers, 802
Seven-Per-Cent Solution, The, 131
Seven Samurai, The, 131
1776, 802
Seventh Seal, The, 591
7TH Voyage of Sinbad, The, 861
Seven-Ups, The, 131
Seven Year Itch, The, 350
Severed Arm, The, 742
Sex Shop, Le, 350
Sex With a Smile, 350
Sextette, 350
Shadow of the Thin Man, 132
Shaft, 132
Shaggy D.A., The, 204
Shaggy Dog, The, 204
Shaker Run, 132
Shalako, 930
Shall We Dance?, 802
Shampoo, 591
Shamus, 132
Shane, 930
Shaolin Temple, 132
Shark! (aka Maneaters!), 133
Shark Hunter, The, 133
Shark's Treasure, 133
Sharky's Machine, 133
S.H.E., 134
She, 861
Sheena, 134
Shenandoah, 930
Sherlock Holmes and the Secret Weapon, 134
Sherlock Holmes and the Baskerville Curse, 204
She Wore a Yellow Ribbon, 930

Shine On Harvest Moon, 931
Shining, The, 742
Ship of Fools, 592
Shoah, 592
Shock Treatment, 351
Shock Waves (Death Corps), 742
Shogun (Short Version), 134
Shogun (Full-Length Version), 134
Shogun Assassin, 135
Shoot, 135
Shoot the Moon, 592
Shooting Party, The, 592
Shooting, The, 931
Shootist, The, 931
Shop on Main Street, The, 593
Short Circuit, 862
Short Eyes, 593
Shot in the Dark, A, 351
Shout, The, 743
Shout at the Devil, 135
Show Boat, 802
Sidewalks of London, 593
Sidewinder 1, 135
Sign of Zorro, The, 204
Silence of the North, 593
Silent Conflict, 931
Silent Movie, 351
Silent Night, Deadly Night, 743
Silent Partner, The, 743
Silent Rage, 136
Silent Running, 862
Silent Scream, 743
Silk Stockings, 802
Silkwood, 593
Silver Blaze, 136
Silver Bullet, 743
Silver Queen, 932
Silverado, 932
Silver Bears, 351
Silver Streak, 352
Simon, 352
Simon of the Desert, 352
Simple Story, A, 594
Sin of Harold Diddlebock (aka Mad Wednesday), 352
Sinbad and the Eye of the Tiger, 862
Sinbad the Sailor, 136
Singin' in the Rain, 802
Singing Buckaroo, 932
Sinister Journey, 932
Sioux City Sue, 933
Sisters, 744
Six Pack, 353
Six Weeks, 594
Sixteen Candles, 353
16 Days of Glory, 594
Skag, 594
Skin Game, 933
Skullduggery, 744
Sky's the Limit, The, 803
Skyline, 353
Slap Shot, 353

Slapstick of Another Kind, 354
Slaughterhouse Five, 862
Slave of Love, A, 594
Slave of the Cannibal God, 136
Sleeper, 354
Sleeping Beauty, 204
Sleeping Beauty, 205
Sleeping Dogs, 137
Sleuth, 595
Slightly Scarlet, 595
Slithis, 744
Slugger's Wife, The, 354
Small Change, 595
Small Town in Texas, A, 137
Smash Palace, 595
Smash-up: The Story of a Woman, 595
Smilin' Through, 803
Smithereens, 596
Smokey and the Bandit, 354
Smokey and the Bandit II, 355
Smokey and the Bandit III, 355
Smooth Talk, 596
Smurfs and the Magic Flute, The, 205
Snoopy, Come Home, 205
Snow Queen, 205
Snow White and the Seven Dwarfs, 205
Snow White and the Three Stooges, 205
So Dear to My Heart, 206
S.O.B., 355
So Fine, 355
Soft Skin, The, 596
Soldier, The, 137
Soldier Blue, 933
Soldier in the Rain, 596
Soldier of Orange, 137
Soldier's Story, A, 138
Sole Survivor, 744
Solo, 596
Solomon and Sheba, 597
Some Call It Loving, 597
Some Kind of Hero, 355
Some Like It Hot, 356
Something of Value, 138
Something to Sing About, 803
Something Wicked This Way Comes, 863
Sometimes a Great Notion, 597
Somewhere in time, 863
Somewhere, Tomorrow, 206
Son of Blob (Beware! The Blob), 745
Son of Godzilla, 745
Son of Kong, The, 745
Song of Nevada, 933
Song of Norway, 803
Song of Texas, 933
Song of the Thin Man, 138
Song Remains the Same, The, 803
Song to Remember, A, 804
Songwriter, 804
Son of Flubber, 206
Sons of Katie Elder, The, 934
Sons of the Desert, 356
Sophie's Choice, 597

Sorceress, 863
Sorrow and the Pity, The, 597
Sorry, Wrong Number, 745
Sounder, 598
Sound of Music, The, 804
Soup for One, 356
South of Pago Pago, 138
South of the Border, 934
Southern Comfort, 138
Southerner, The, 598
South Pacific, 805
Soylent Green, 863
Space Raiders, 864
SpaceCamp, 864
Spacehunter: Adventures in the Forbidden
  Zone, 864
Spaceship, 356
Sparkle, 805
Sparrows, 598
Spartacus, 138
Spasms, 746
Special Day, A, 598
Special Effects, 746
Speedway, 805
Spellbound, 746
Spetters, 598
Sphinx, 746
Spies Like Us, 356
Spirit of St. Louis, The, 599
Spirit of the Dead, 746
Spitfire, 599
Splash, 357
Splatter University, 747
Splendor in the Grass, 599
Split Image, 599
Spoilers, The, 934
Spooks Run Wild, 357
Spring Break, 357
Spring Fever, 357
Spy Smasher, 139
Spy Who Loved Me, The, 139
Squirm, 747
Squizzy Taylor, 139
Stagecoach, 934
Stage Door, 357
Stage Door Canteen, 599
Stage Fright, 747
Stalag 17, 139
Stand By Me, 600
Stand-In, 358
Stanley, 747
Stanley and Livingstone, 600
Star 80, 600
Star Chamber, The, 600
Star Crash, 864
Star Is Born, A (Original), 600
Star Is Born, A (Remake), 601
Star Is Born, A (Remake), 601
Star of Midnight, 139
Star Trek: The Menagerie, 865
Star Trek—The Motion Picture, 865
Star Trek II: The Wrath of Khan, 865

Star Trek III: The Search for Spock, 865
Star Trek (Television Series), 866
Star Wars, 867
Stardust Memories, 358
Stardust Memories, 601
Starflight One, 867
Starman, 867
Star Packer, The, 935
Stars Look Down, The, 601
Starstruck, 805
Starting Over, 358
Start the Revolution Without Me, 358
State of Seige, 602
State of the Union, 602
Stay As You Are, 602
Stay Hungry, 602
Staying Alive, 805
Steagle, The, 359
Steamboat Bill Jr., 359
Steelyard Blues, 359
Stella Dallas, 602
Stephen King's Night Shift Collection, 747
Sterile Cuckoo, The, 603
Stevie, 603
Stick, 140
Stiletto, 140
Still of the Night, 748
Still Smokin, 359
Sting, The, 144
Sting II, The, 140
Stir Crazy, 359
Stolen Kisses, 360
Stone Boy, The, 603
Stone Cold Dead, 141
Stone Killer, The, 141
Stop Making Sense, 805
Stopover Tokyo, 141
Storm in a Teacup, 360
Story of Adele H, The, 603
Story of Vernon and Irene Castle, The, 806
Straight Time, 603
Strait-Jacket, 748
Strange Brew, 360
Strange Gamble, 935
Strange Invaders, 867
Strange Love of Martha Ivers, The, 604
Strange Behavior, 748
Strangeness, The, 748
Stranger on the Third Floor, 141
Stranger than Paradise, 360
Stranger, The, 748
Stranger and the Gunfighter, The, 935
Stranger Is Watching, A, 749
Strangers on a Train, 749
Strawberry Blonde, The, 604
Strawberry Statement, The, 604
Straw Dogs, 749
Streamers, 605
Street Scene, 605
Streetcar Named Desire, A, 605
Streethawk, 142
Streets of Fire, 142

Streetwalkin', 605
Strike, 605
Strike Up the Band, 360
Stripes, 360
Stroker Ace, 361
Stromboli, 606
Stryker, 868
Stud, The, 606
Student Bodies, 749
Stuff, The, 750
Stunt Man, The, 606
Suburbia, 606
Subway, 142
Sudden Impact, 142
Suddenly, 606
Suddenly, Last Summer, 607
Sugar Cane Alley, 607
Sugarland Express, The, 607
Summer City, 143
Summer Heat, 607
Summer Lovers, 607
Summer of '42, 608
Summer Rental, 361
Summertime, 608
Summertime Killer, The, 143
Sunburn, 143
Sunday Too Far Away, 608
Sunday, Bloody Sunday, 608
Sunrise at Campobello, 609
Sunset Blvd., 609
Sunset Serenade, 935
Sunshine Boys, The, 361
Super Fuzz, 868
Superfly, 143
Supergirl, 868
Superman, 868
Superman II, 869
Superman III, 869
Support Your Local Sheriff!, 936
Sure Thing, The, 361
Surfacing, 143
Survivors, The, 362
Susanna Pass, 936
Suspicion, 750
Svengali, 750
Swamp Thing, 750
Swann In Love, 609
Swarm, The, 751
Swashbuckler, The, 144
Sweater Girls, 362
Sweet Dreams, 806
Sweet Liberty, 362
Sweet Sixteen, 144
Sweet Sweetback's Baadasssss Song, 144
Swept Away, 609
Swimmer, The, 609
Swing Shift, 610
Swing Time, 806
Swingin' Summer, A, 362
Swiss Family Robinson, The, 207
Swiss Miss, 363
Sword and the Rose, The, 207

Sword and the Sorcerer, The, 869
Sword in the Stone, 207
Sword of Lancelot, 144
Sword of the Valiant, 207
Sybil, 610
Sylvester, 610
Sympathy for the Devil, 806

Table for Five, 610
Take Down, 363
Take the Money and Run, 363
Take This Job and Shove It, 363
Taking of Pelham One Two Three, The, 144
Tale of the Frog Prince, 207
Tale of Two Cities, A, 611
Tales from the Crypt, 751
Tales of Terror, 751
Tall Blond Man With One Black Shoe, The, 363
Tall in the Saddle, 936
Tamarind Seed, The, 145
Taming of the Shrew, The, 364
Tammy and the Bachelor, 611
Tammy and the Doctor, 611
Tank, 145
Taps, 611
Target, 145
Targets, 751
Tarzan of the Apes, 145
Tarzan the Ape Man (Original), 146
Tarzan the Ape Man (Remake), 146
Tarzan the Fearless, 146
Tarzan's Revenge, 146
Tattoo, 611
Taxi Driver, 612
Teacher's Pet, 364
Teachers, 364
Teen Wolf, 751
Telefon, 147
Tell Me A Riddle, 612
Tell Them Willie Boy Is Here, 936
Tempest, 612
10, 364
Ten Commandments, The, 612
Ten Days That Shook The World (October), 613
10 from Your Show of Shows, 364
Ten Little Indians, 147
Ten to Midnight, 147
Ten Who Dared, 208
Tenant, The, 751
Tender Mercies, 613
Tendres Cousines, 365
Tennessee Stallion, 147
Tennessee's Partner, 937
Tentacles, 752
Tenth Victim, The, 869
Terminal Choice, 752
Terminal Man, The, 752
Terminator, The, 870
Terms of Endearment, 613
Terror By Night, 148

Terror, The, 752
Terror in the Aisles, 753
Terror in the Wax Museum, 753
Terror of Tiny Town, The, 937
Terror on the 40th Floor, 753
Tess, 613
Test of Love, A, 613
Testament, 870
Tex, 614
Texas, 937
Texas Chainsaw Massacre, The, 753
Texas Chainsaw Massacre 2, The, 753
Texas John Slaughter: Geronimo's Revenge, 937
Texas John Slaughter: Stampede at Bitter Creek, 937
Texas John Slaughter: Wild Times, 938
Texas Lady, 938
Thank God It's Friday, 806
Thank Your Lucky Stars, 807
That Championship Season, 614
That Hamilton Woman, 614
That Obscure Object of Desire, 615
That Was Then . . . This is Now, 615
That Darn Cat, 208
That's Dancing, 807
That's Entertainment, 807
That's Entertainment Part II, 807
That Sinking Feeling, 365
That Touch of Mink, 365
That Was Rock, 808
Theater of Blood, 754
Theatre of Death, 754
Them!, 870
There Was a Crooked Man, 938
There's a Girl in my Soup, 365
There's No Business Like Show Business, 808
These Three, 615
They All Laughed, 365
They Call Me Bruce?, 365
They Call Me Mister Tibbs, 148
They Call Me Trinity, 938
They Came to Cordura, 615
They Died with their Boots On, 938
They Drive by Night, 148
They Got Me Covered, 366
They Knew What They Wanted, 616
They Made Me a Criminal, 616
They Might Be Giants, 616
They Saved Hitler's Brain, 754
They Shoot Horses, Don't They?, 616
They Were Expendable, 148
They're Playing with Fire, 616
They Went That-A-Way and That-A-Way, 208
Thief, 148
Thief of Hearts, 617
Thief of Baghdad, The, 870
Thief of Baghdad, The, 871
Thief Who Came to Dinner, The, 366
Thin Man, The, 149

Thin Man Goes Home, The, *149*
Thing, The, *871*
Thing (From Another World), The, *871*
Things Are Tough All Over, *366*
Things to Come, *871*
Third Man On The Mountain, *208*
Third Man, The, *755*
13 Rue Madeleine, *149*
13 Ghosts, *755*
30 Foot Bride of Candy Rock, The, *366*
Thirty Seconds Over Tokyo, *149*
Thirty-Nine Steps, The (Second Remake), *149*
Thirty-nine Steps, The, *755*
This Gun for Hire, *150*
This Is Elvis, *808*
This is the Army, *808*
This Island Earth, *871*
This Is Spinal Tap, *367*
This Land Is Mine, *617*
This Property is Condemned, *617*
Thomas Crown Affair, The, *150*
Thorn Birds, The, *617*
Those Calloways, *209*
Those Magnificent Men in their Flying Machines, *367*
Thousand Clowns, A, *367*
Thousands Cheer, *808*
Three Caballeros, The, *209*
Three Days of the Condor, *150*
Three Faces West, *939*
Three Little Pigs, The, *209*
Three Lives Of Thomasina,The, *209*
Three Men and a Cradle, *367*
Three Musketeers, The (1973), *150*
Three Musketeers, The (1948), *150*
Threepenny Opera, The, *809*
Three Stooges, The (Volumes 1–10), *368*
3:10 to Yuma, *939*
Three the Hard Way, *151*
Threshold, *872*
Throne of Blood, *617*
Thumbelina, *209*
Thunder and Lightning, *151*
Thunder Bay, *151*
Thunder Run, *151*
Thunderball, *151*
Thunderbolt and Lightfoot, *152*
Thursday's Game, *618*
THX 1138, *872*
Ticket to Heaven, *618*
Tickle Me, *809*
Tiger Town, *209*
Tightrope, *755*
Till Marriage Do Us Part, *368*
Till the Clouds Roll By, *809*
Till the End of Time, *618*
Tilt, *368*
Tim, *618*
Time after Time, *872*
Time Bandits, *872*

Time Machine, The, *872*
Time Stands Still, *619*
Time Walker, *755*
Timerider, *152*
Times of Harvey Milk, The, *619*
Times Square, *809*
Tin Drum, The, *619*
To All a Good Night, *756*
To Catch a King, *756*
To Catch a Thief, *756*
To Have and Have Not, *152*
To Hell and Back, *152*
To Kill a Mockingbird, *619*
To Kill a Clown, *756*
To Live and Die in L.A., *153*
To Sir with Love, *619*
To the Devil, a Daughter, *757*
To Be or Not to Be (Original), *368*
To Be or Not to Be (Remake), *369*
Tobruk, *153*
Toby Tyler, *210*
Tom Brown's School Days, *620*
Tom Edison—The Boy Who Lit Up The World, *210*
Tom Jones, *369*
Tom Sawyer, *210*
Tom Thumb, *210*
Tomb of Ligeia, *757*
Tomboy, *153*
Tom Horn, *939*
Tommy, *810*
Tomorrow, *620*
Toni, *620*
Tonka, *211*
Too Scared to Scream, *757*
Tootsie, *369*
Top Gun, *153*
To Paris with Love, *369*
Topaz, *757*
Top Hat, *810*
Topkapi, *154*
Top Secret, *369*
Topper, *369*
Topper Returns, *370*
Topper Takes a Trip, *370*
Topsy Turvy, *370*
Tora! Tora! Tora!, *154*
Torchlight, *620*
Torment, *757*
Torn Curtain, *758*
Torture Chamber Of Baron Blood, The, *758*
Torture Garden, *758*
Touched by Love, *621*
Touch of Class, A, *370*
Touch of Evil, *758*
Tough Enough, *154*
Tourist Trap, *759*
Towering Inferno, The, *154*
Town That Dreaded Sundown, The, *759*
Toy, The, *371*
Toy Soldiers, *154*

Tracks, *621*
Trading Places, *371*
Trail Beyond, The, *939*
Trail of Robin Hood, *939*
Trail of the Pink Panther, The, *371*
Train Killer, The, *621*
Train Robbers, The, *940*
Train, The, *155*
Traitor, The, *940*
Tramplers, The, *940*
Trancers, *873*
Transformers, The Movie, *211*
Transylvania 6-5000, *371*
Trap, The, *759*
Trapeze, *621*
Treasure Island, *211*
Treasure Island, *211*
Treasure of Pancho Villa, The, *940*
Treasure of the Four Crowns, *155*
Treasure of the Sierra Madre, The, *155*
Trenchcoat, *372*
Tribute, *621*
Trigger, Jr., *940*
Trilogy of Terror, *759*
Trinity Is Still My Name, *941*
Trip, The, *622*
Trip to Bountiful, The, *622*
Triumph of the Will, *622*
Triumphs of a Man Called Horse, *941*
Trojan Women, The, *622*
Troll, *873*
Tron, *873*
Trouble in Mind, *622*
Trouble in the Glen, *372*
Trouble With Angels, The, *372*
Trouble With Harry, The, *372*
True Confessions, *623*
True Grit, *941*
True Heart Susie, *623*
Tuff Turf, *623*
Tulsa, *623*
Tunes of Glory, *624*
Tunnelvision, *373*
Turk 182, *624*
Turtle Diary, *373*
Tuttles of Tahiti, The, *373*
12 Angry Men, *624*
Twelve Chairs, The, *373*
Twelve O'Clock High, *155*
20,000 Leagues under the Sea, *155*
Twice in a Lifetime, *624*
Twilight in the Sierras, *941*
Twilight's Last Gleaming, *156*
Twilight Zone—The Movie, *759*
Twins of Evil, *760*
Two English Girls, *625*
200 Motels, *810*
Two Mules for Sister Sara, *942*
Two of a Kind, *373*
2001: A Space Odyssey, *873*
2010, *874*

Two Worlds of Jennie Logan, The, *874*
Tycoon, *156*

Uforia, *374*
Ugetsu, *625*
Ugly Dachshund, The, *211*
Ultimate Warrior, The, *874*
Umberto D, *625*
Umbrellas of Cherbourg, The, *625*
Uncanny, The, *760*
Uncommon Valor, *156*
Under California Stars, *942*
Under Capricorn, *626*
Under Fire, *156*
Under The Cherry Moon, *626*
Under the Rainbow, *374*
Under the Volcano, *626*
Underground Aces, *374*
Unexpected Guest, *942*
Unfaithfully Yours (Original), *374*
Unfaithfully Yours (Remake), *375*
Unidentified Flying Oddball, *212*
Union City, *626*
Union Station, *760*
Unmarried Woman, An, *626*
Unseen, The, *760*
Unsinkable Molly Brown, The, *810*
Until September, *627*
Untouchables: Alcatraz Express, The, *157*
Untouchables: Scarface Mob, The, *157*
Up in Smoke, *375*
Up the Academy, *375*
Up the Creek, *375*
Up the Sandbox, *375*
Uptown New York, *627*
Uptown Saturday Night, *376*
Urban Cowboy, *627*
Used Cars, *376*
Users, The, *627*
Utilities, *376*
Utu, *157*

Vacation, *376*
Vagabond, *627*
Valley Girl, *376*
Valley of Fire, *942*
Vamp, *760*
Vampyr, *761*
Vanishing Point, *158*
Varan, the Unbelievable, *761*
Vault of Horror, *761*
Vega$, *158*
Venom, *761*
Vera Cruz, *943*
Verdict, The, *628*
Vertigo, *762*
Vice Squad, *158*
Victor/Victoria, *377*
Victory, *158*
Videodrome, *762*
Video Rewind: The Rolling Stones Great

Video Hits, *811*
View to a Kill, A, *158*
Vikings, The, *159*
Villa Rides, *943*
Village of the Damned, *762*
Village of the Giants, *762*
Villain Still Pursued Her, The, *159*
Violets Are Blue, *628*
Viridiana, *628*
Vision Quest, *628*
Visiting Hours, *762*
Viva Knievel, *159*
Viva Las Vegas, *811*
Viva Maxl, *377*
Viva Zapata!, *629*
Volpone, *629*
Volunteers, *377*
Von Ryan's Express, *159*
Voyage of the Damned, *629*
Voyage to the Bottom of the Sea, *874*

W, *763*
Wackiest Ship in the Army, The, *377*
Wages of Fear, The, *763*
Wagner, *811*
Wagonmaster, *943*
Wait Until Dark, *763*
Wake Island, *159*
Wake of the Red Witch, *160*
Walking Tall, *160*
Walking Tall Part II, *160*
Waltz of the Toreadors, *377*
Wanderers, The, *629*
Wanton Contessa, The, *630*
War and Peace, *630*
War Lover, The, *630*
War of the Wildcats, *943*
War of the Worlds, The, *874*
War Wagon, The, *944*
Wargames, *875*
Warlock, *944*
Warlords of the 21st Century, *875*
Warning Sign, *763*
Warning, The, *160*
Warrior and the Sorceress, The, *875*
Warriors of the Wind, *875*
Warriors, The, *160*
Washington Affair, The, *630*
Wasn't That a Time!, *811*
Watch Me When I Kill, *763*
Watch on the Rhine, *630*
Watcher in the Woods, The, *764*
Water, *377*
Waterloo Bridge, *631*
Watermelon Man, *378*
Watership Down, *876*
Wavelength, *876*
Way Down East, *631*
Way Out West, *378*
Way We Were, The, *631*
Wedding, A, *378*
Weekend Pass, *378*

Weird Science, *379*
Welcome to L.A., *631*
We of the Never Never, *161*
We're No Angels, *379*
West of the Divide, *944*
West Side Story, *812*
Westerner, The, *944*
Westward Ho The Wagons, *212*
Westworld, *876*
What Price Glory, *379*
What Do You Say to a Naked Lady?, *379*
What Ever Happened to Baby Jane?, *764*
What's New Pussycat?, *379*
What's Up Doc?, *380*
What's Up Tiger Lily?, *380*
Wheel of Fortune, *944*
Wheels of Fire, *161*
When a Man Rides Alone, *944*
When a Stranger Calls, *764*
When Father Was Away On Business, *632*
When the Legends Die, *945*
When Things Were Rotten, *380*
When Time Ran Out!, *764*
When Wolves Cry, *632*
When Worlds Collide, *876*
Where Eagles Dare, *161*
Where the Boys Are, *380*
Where the Boys Are '84, *380*
Where the Buffalo Roam, *381*
Where the Green Ants Dream, *632*
Where's Poppa?, *381*
Where the Red Fern Grows, *212*
Which Way Is Up?, *381*
White Dawn, The, *161*
White Heat, *161*
White Lightning, *162*
White Line Fever, *162*
White Nights, *632*
Whitewater Sam, *162*
White Zombie, *764*
Who Are the Debolts and Where Did They Get 19 Kids?, *632*
Who's Afraid of Virginia Woolf?, *633*
Who'll Stop the Rain, *162*
Wholly Moses!, *381*
Whoopee, *812*
Whose Life Is It, Anyway?, *633*
Who Slew Auntie Roo?, *764*
Who's Minding the Mint?, *381*
Why Shoot the Teacher?, *633*
Wicked Lady, The, *163*
Wicker Man, The, *765*
Wifemistress, *633*
Wilbur and Orville: The First To Fly, *212*
Wild Angels, The, *163*
Wild Duck, The, *634*
Wild Geese, The, *163*
Wild Geese II, *163*
Wild in the Country, *634*
Wild One, The, *164*
Wild Party, The, *634*
Wild Rose, *634*

Wild Strawberries, 635
Wild Bunch, The, 945
Wildcats, 382
Wilderness Family, Part 2, The, 212
Wild Life, The, 382
Wild Times, 945
Will, G. Gordon Liddy, 635
Willard, 765
Willy Wonka and the Chocolate Factory, 213
Wilma, 635
Wind and the Lion, The, 164
Wind in the Willows, The, 213
Winds of the Wasteland, 945
Windwalker, 946
Windy City, 635
Wings, 164
Winning, 164
Winning of the West, 946
Winslow Boy, The, 635
Winter Kills, 636
Winter Light, 636
Winter of Our Dreams, 636
Winterset, 636
Wise Blood, 636
Wise Guys, 382
Witchcraft Through the Ages (Haxan), 637
Witching, The (Necromancy), 765
Witching Time, 765
Without a Trace, 637
Without Reservations, 382
Without Warning, 876
With Six You Get Eggroll, 383
Witness, 165
Witness for the Prosecution, 637
Wiz, The, 812
Wizard of Gore, The, 766
Wizard of Oz, The, 812
Wolfen, 766
Woman Called Golda, A, 638
Woman in Flames, A, 638
Woman In Green, The, 165
Woman Next Door, The, 638
Woman of Paris, A, 638
Woman in Red, The, 383
Woman of the Year, 383
Women in Love, 638
Women, The, 383
Woodstock, 812
Word, The, 638
World According to Garp, The, 639
World at War Vol. 1–26, 639
World of Abbott and Costello, The, 383
World of Henry Orient, The, 384
World's Greatest Athlete, The, 213
World's Greatest Lover, The, 384
Wrong Box, The, 384

Wrong Is Right, 384
Wrong Man, The, 766
Wuthering Heights, 639

X (The Man with the X-Ray Eyes), 877
Xanadu, 813
Xtro, 766

Yakuza, The, 165
Yankee Doodle Dandy, 813
Yearling, The, 213
Year of Living Dangerously, The, 165
Year of the Dragon, 166
Yellow Rose of Texas, 946
Yellowbeard, 385
Yellowbeard, 385
Yentl, 813
Yes, Giorgio, 813
Yojimbo, 166
Yol, 639
Yolanda and The Thief, 640
Yor: The Hunter from the Future, 877
You Light Up My Life, 640
You Only Live Once, 640
You Only Live Twice, 166
You Were Never Lovelier, 814
You'll Never Get Rich, 814
Young and Innocent, 166
Young and Willing, 640
Young Doctors in Love, 385
Young Frankenstein, 385
Young Love, First Love, 640
Young Philadelphians, The, 640
Young Sherlock Holmes, 167
Young Winston, 641
Youngblood, 641
You're a Big Boy Now, 385

Z, 641
Zabriskie Point, 641
Zapped!, 385
Zardoz, 877
Zelig, 385
Zero For Conduct, 642
Ziegfeld Follies, 814
Ziggy Stardust and the Spiders from Mars, 814
Zombie, 766
Zombies of Mora Tau, 767
Zombies of the Stratosphere (Satan's Satellites), 167
Zorba the Greek, 642
Zorro, the Gay Blade, 386
Zotz!, 386
Zulu, 167
Zulu Dawn, 168

ABOUT THE AUTHORS

Mick Martin is the film critic for the *Sacramento Union* newspaper, host/producer of "Mick Martin's Entertainment Showcase" on KTKL Channel 40 in Sacramento, film critic for KZAP radio, a contributing editor (on video) for Tower Records' *Pulse!* magazine, and a songwriter. His composition "Off the Chain Gang" is featured as part of the soundtrack for David Steensland's made-for-video release, "Escapes," starring Vincent Price, John Mitchum, Michael Patton-Hall, Ken Thorley, and Jerry Grisham.

Marsha Porter, author of several short stories and a teacher's handbook, holds a master's degree in educational administration. Currently, she does freelance editing and is an English instructor in Sacramento. Formerly, she was a newspaper advisor and collegiate actress.